# PRODUTTORI DI MANDURIA

D1446750

WWW.CPVINI.COM

*I am a lucky man, I have a beautiful family. The wine? An act of lov*

*Dr. Lorenzo Fonzone Caccese*

# ——TENUTA DI——
# LILLIANO

www.lilliano.it

# QUADRIGATO

### CANTINE

·

WE SAVE
## STORIES and TRADITIONS
## TROUBLES and PASSIONS
### TO PRESERVE THEM IN BOTTLES

*Aglianico*

*Falanghina*

*Malvasia*

*Greco*

*Fiano*

·

www.quadrigato.com

Soc. Agr. TerreNovae s.r.l. - C.da Taverna Vecchia, 82034 Guardia Sanframondi (BN)
Tel/fax: +39 0824 864296 - info@quadrigato.com - terrenovae@pec.it

**Gambero Rosso**

# 2019

# ITALIAN WINES

# VINI D'ITALIA 2019
## GAMBERO ROSSO®

**Senior Editors**
Gianni Fabrizio
Marco Sabellico

**Co-editor**
Giuseppe Carrus

**Technical Directors**
William Pregentelli

**Special Contributors**
Stefania Annese
Antonio Boco
Paolo De Cristofaro
Lorenzo Ruggeri
Paolo Zaccaria

**Regionali Coordinators**
Nino Aiello
Nicola Frasson
Massimo Lanza
Gianni Ottogalli
Nereo Pederzolli
Pierpaolo Rastelli

**Contributors**
Francesco Beghi
Sergio Bonanno
Michele Bressan
Pasquale Buffa
Dionisio Castello
Giacomo Mojoli
Elena Mozzini
Franco Pallini
Leonardo Romanelli
Giulia Sampognaro
Herbert Taschler
Cinzia Tosetti

**Other Contributors**
Giovanni Angelucci
Stefano Barone
Dagoberto Basilico
Enrico Battistella
Armando Biagioli
Francesca Carlini
Lucio Chiesa
Pietro Chirco
Francesca Ciancio
Palmiro Ciccarelli
Mario Demattè
Franco Fusco
Davide Giachino
Giovanni Lanzillo
Alessandro Mancuso
Michele Muraro
Alberto Parrinello
Dario Piccinelli
Nicola Piccinini
Massimo Ponzanelli
Mirko Rainer
Filippo Rapini
Riccardo Rossetti
Maurizio Rossi
Simona Silvestri
Sabrina Somigli
Andrea Vannelli
Liliana Zanellato
Monia Zanette
Danilo Zannella

**Editorial Secretary**
Giulia Sciortino

**Layout**
Marina Proietti

**Publisher**
Gambero Rosso S.p.A.
via Ottavio Gasparri, 13/17
00152 Roma
tel. 06/551121 -fax 06/55112260
www.gamberorosso.it
email: gambero@gamberorosso.it

**Managing Editor Books**
Laura Mantovano

**Graphics**
Chiara Buosi

**Commercial Director**
Francesco Dammicco

**Editorial product distribution
and sales manager**
Eugenia Durando

**Production**
Angelica Sorbara

**Translation**
Jordan De Maio

**Assistant translators**
Jane Upchurch
Paul Bullard

**Distribution**
USA and Canada
by ACC ART BOOKS LTD., 6 West 18th Street, 4B
New York, NY 10011
UK and Australia
by ACC ART BOOKS Sandy Lane, Old Martlesham,
Woodbridge, Suffolk IP12 4SD - United Kingdom

The final edit of Italian Wines was completed on
5 September 2018

ISBN 978-18-9014-216-2

Printed in Italy for
Gambero Rosso Holding S.p.A
in October 2018 by
FP Design Srl
Via Atto Tigri, 11
00197 Roma

# SUMMARY

# REGIONS

# INDEXES

# THE GUIDE

Italian Wines is now on its 32nd edition. The first was assembled by a handful of wine lovers over the course of one summer in 1987. It was a difficult moment for Italian wine, but it was also a decade rich in innovation, the period of the Italian wine renaissance. Since then we've gone from reviewing 500 wineries and 1500 wines to more than 2500 producers and more than 23,000 wines. More than 70 fantastic tasters make up the motivated, skilled team that we've built over the years and that help us evaluate more than 40,000 wines in every region of Italy (even Ticino). It's an increasingly rich panorama made up of thousands of different territories and thousands more grapes, where it's possible to find wines made according to the latest methods, as well as age-old materials, like stone or terra-cotta, whose use goes back 2500 years. How do we go about judging the wines? What are the parameters according to which we decide if a wine is good, very good or excellent (using our one, two or three 'Bicchieri' system). There's not a single answer or an easy way to sum up the complexity of our approach, considering Italy's fascinating panorama of wine and tremendous diversity (biodiversity, as it's commonly known today). Our criteria is probably at once hedonistic, humanistic and cultural. Our tastings are blind (bottles are covered), but we're not trying to identify a single score as much as relate to our readers how much we enjoyed a specific wine. It's a 'hedonistic' criteria inasmuch as there are moments when the maturity of a wine's tannins, or the freshness of its acidity are as important as a vintner's story. Don't forget that we are relating history here, the infinite history of Italian wine, which is the most complex, difficult and multi-layered on this splendid blue planet. But there are times when the palate wins out over technical skill, poetry over reason, because Italy holds a place for the artisan who makes 30,000 bottles a year, as well as the large producer who exports the world over.

Why do we award a wine from a certain vintage or vineyard with Tre Bicchieri when a neighboring producer can have the same vineyard position and grapes but only arrives in our finals? In our opinion scientific and technical explanations don't provide a complete picture of what happens in the vineyard and the cellar. The difference between a good wine and a great one at times (and often) depends on myriad variables that are difficult to quantify. And so, once again, what matters is our immediate perception, our emotions in that particular moment. It's useless to say that more than 30 years of experience represents a unique, non-replicable feat that allows us to intercept newsworthy events, trends, new terroir, and communicate this all to the world as it's happening. And we should add that we're not slaves of a single vision either. Indeed, we're fascinated by the complexity and range of approaches and styles that our multivariate terroir and grapes are able to express, thanks to the talent of our national vine growers. With this in mind, you can get a sense of how our tasters work.

Thirty-two editions of Italian Wines, now translated in English, German, Chinese and Japanese, testify to how well our commitment has been received in Italy and throughout the world. Being in the guide, and receiving Tre Bicchieri, is by now a universal 'benchmark', an obligatory achievement that continues to favor Italian wines across the globe. We'd add that every year we're part of more than 50 international events, in both established and emerging markets, telling the stories of Italian wines both big and small, as well as their artificers. We meet with consumers, the press, sommeliers, importers and distributers. Our team has managed to build an important instrument for a fundamental part of our economy, one that has earned undisputed international credibility and consensus, and of this we're truly proud.

Our special awards are a snapshot of our vision of Italian wine, as well as a summary of the work done over the course of a year.

Our 'Red of the Year' is Tenuta di Sesta's 2012 Brunello di Montalcino Duelecci Ovest Riserva, a wine of extraordinary elegance that caps off a fantastic year for Montalcino. Our 'White of the Year' is Silvio Jermann's extraordinarily elegant 2016 Capo Martino, which managed to beat out a particularly strong in-house competitor in their 2016 Vintage Tunina. Our 'Sparkler of the Year' is Guido Berlucchi's 2011 Franciacorta Nature 61, a fitting award for a producer that literally 'created' Franciacorta almost 60 years ago. Our 'Sweet of the Year' is Vite Colte's sumptuous 2016 Moscato Passito La Bella Estate. And this year we've got some big news: we've added a new special award dedicated to a wine that's taking off in Italy and throughout the world, 'Rosé of the Year'. The first ever goes to Costaripa's 2015 Valtènesi Chiaretto Molmenti, a wine that, thanks to the work of Mattia Vezzola (its artificer) opens up new stylistic prospects for our national rosés.

The Lunelli family's Ferrari is our 'Winery of the Year' for the excellent quality of its cuvées, but also for the strong results turned in by the group's other producers. Our 'Best Value for Money' award goes to Cantina di Caldaro's 2017 Lago di Caldaro Classico Superiore Quintessenz, a wine that's simply irresistible. Francesco Cambria, who gave up his suit so as to dedicate his heart and soul to a group of vineyards on Mt. Etna, is our 'Grower of the Year'. And our 'Up-and-Coming Winery' award goes to Serdiana's Antonella Corda. Thanks to an extraordinary 2016 Cannonau di Sardegna, a wine that literally enchants, they were chosen from a group of 54 producers who received Tre Bicchieri for the first time. Our 'Award for Sustainable Viticulture' goes to Torrevento, who have been working for years on behalf of a sector that's critical to our future, while our 'Solidarity Award' goes to San Patrignano, a choice that requires no further comment.

You'll also find our Tre Bicchieri Verdi in green, those wines made by certified organic or biodynamic producers (there are some 102 this year). Finally, we also make note of those wines awarded that can be bought for €15 or less (there are 92 in all, more than 20% of the wines awarded).

We would like to thank the Bolzano EOS Chamber of Commerce, the Oltrepò Pavese District of Quality Wine, the coordinators of the Umbria Olive Oil and Wine Road, the Arezzo Wine Road, the Marche Institute for Jesi Wine (IMT) and VINEA of Offida, ERSA Friuli Venezia Giulia, Brescia Wine Association, The Carcare Training Consortium (Savona), Committee for the Tuscan Coast's Great Cru, Assovini Sicilia, the E. del Giudice Viticultural Innovation Centre in Marsala. We'd also like to thank the following protection consortiums: Gavi, Barolo, Barbaresco, Alba, Langhe and Roero, Wines of the Colli Tortonesi, Nebbiolo dell'Alto Piemonte, Caluso, Carema and Canavese, Valtellina, Oltrepò Pavese, Franciacorta, Valcalepio, Mantova Wines, Lugana, Valtenesi, Conegliano Valdobbiadene, Soave, Valpolicella, the Trento Wine Consortium, the Lambrusci Modenesi Historic Wines Consortium, as well as Lambrusco di Modena, Bolgheri, Brunello di Montalcino, Chianti Classico, San Gimignano, Montepulciano, Chianti Colli Fiorentini, Chianti Rufina, Morellino di Scansano, Vini della Maremma Toscana, Montecucco,

Carmignano, Orvieto, Montefalco, the Piceno Wines Consortium and, finally, the DOC Sicilia Wines Consortium.

We'd also like to thank the Enoteca Regionale of Lombardy (Cassino Po), Roero and Nizza Monferrato, Canelli and Astesana, the Cantina Comunale I Söri in Diano d'Alba, the Bottega del Vino in Dogliani, Carpe Diem restaurant in Montaione, Calidario in Venturina, Tenuta Il Sassone in Massa Marittima, the City of Taste in Rome and Naples, the Enoteca Regionale of Basilicata in Venosa, Caneva in Mogliano Veneto, Da Nando restaurant in Mortegliano, Casa e Putia restaurant in Messina and, for Ticino, the Restaurant/winery Zoccolino in Bellinzona.

Finally, a sincere thanks to all our team, who showed true devotion in helping us realize Italian Wines, from local tastings to drafting the profiles, all the way to editing the volume itself, and to all those we've worked with down through the years. A special thanks to Danilo Zannella, director of all our tastings.

Gianni Fabrizio, Marco Sabellico

# I TRE BICCHIERI 2019

**VALLE D'AOSTA**

| | | |
|---|---|---|
| Sopraquota 900 | Rosset Terroir | 37 |
| Valle d'Aosta Chambave Muscat Flétri '16 | La Vrille | 37 |
| Valle d'Aosta Chardonnay Cuvée Bois '16 | Les Crêtes | 33 |
| Valle d'Aosta Chardonnay Main et Cœur '16 | Maison Anselmet | 32 |
| Valle d'Aosta Fumin '16 | Lo Triolet | 35 |
| Valle d'Aosta Petite Arvine '17 | Elio Ottin | 36 |

**PIEDMONT**

| | | |
|---|---|---|
| Alta Langa Zero Ris. '12 | Enrico Serafino | 170 |
| Barbaresco Albesani '14 | Cantina del Pino | 71 |
| Barbaresco Albesani Santo Stefano Ris. '13 | Castello di Neive | 81 |
| Barbaresco Asili '15 | Ca' del Baio | 67 |
| Barbaresco Asili '15 | Ceretto | 84 |
| Barbaresco Asili Ris. '13 | Produttori del Barbaresco | 150 |
| Barbaresco Asili V. Viti '13 | Roagna | 156 |
| Barbaresco Camp Gros Martinenga Ris. '13 | Tenute Cisa Asinari dei Marchesi di Grésy | 87 |
| Barbaresco Cottà '15 | Sottimano | 172 |
| Barbaresco Currà Ris. '12 | Bruno Rocca | 157 |
| Barbaresco Montaribaldi '14 | Fiorenzo Nada | 133 |
| Barbaresco Montefico '15 | Carlo Giacosa | 110 |
| Barbaresco Pajoré '15 | Bel Colle | 51 |
| Barbaresco Rabajà '15 | Giuseppe Cortese | 95 |
| Barbaresco Sorì Tildìn '15 | Gaja | 106 |
| Barbera d'Alba Vittoria '15 | Gianfranco Alessandria | 44 |
| Barbera d'Asti L'Avvocata '17 | Coppo | 93 |
| Barbera d'Asti Lavignone '17 | Pico Maccario | 145 |
| Barbera d'Asti Nuda '15 | Montalbera | 129 |
| Barbera d'Asti Sup. V. La Mandorla '16 | Luigi Spertino | 173 |
| Barbera del M.to '16 | F.lli Facchino | 100 |
| Barbera del M.to Sup. Bricco Battista '15 | Giulio Accornero e Figli | 42 |
| Barbera del M.to Sup. Le Cave '16 | Castello di Uviglie | 82 |
| Barolo Bricco Ambrogio '14 | Negretti | 134 |
| Barolo Bussia 90 Dì Ris. '12 | Giacomo Fenocchio | 101 |
| Barolo Bussia V. Mondoca Ris. '12 | Poderi e Cantine Oddero | 138 |
| Barolo Cannubi '14 | Marchesi di Barolo | 121 |
| Barolo Cerretta '14 | Giacomo Conterno | 91 |
| Barolo del Comune di La Morra '14 | Brandini | 61 |
| Barolo Falletto V. Le Rocche Ris. '12 | Bruno Giacosa | 109 |
| Barolo Ginestra Ris. '11 | Cascina Chicco | 75 |
| Barolo Ginestra Ris. '10 | Paolo Conterno | 91 |
| Barolo Lazzarito Ris. '12 | Ettore Germano | 108 |
| Barolo Monprivato '13 | Giuseppe Mascarello e Figlio | 125 |
| Barolo Monvigliero '14 | F.lli Alessandria | 44 |
| Barolo Novantesimo Ris. '11 | Paolo Scavino | 167 |
| Barolo Rapet '14 | Ca' Rome' | 68 |
| Barolo Ravera Bricco Pernice '13 | Elvio Cogno | 88 |

Riviera Ligure di Ponente

| | | |
|---|---|---|
| Pigato Via Maestra '16 | La Ginestraia | 211 |

## LOMBARDY

| | | |
|---|---|---|
| Bertone Pinot Nero '15 | Conte Vistarino | 240 |
| Botticino Gobbio '16 | Antica Tesa - Noventa | 223 |
| Brut M. Cl. '13 | Monsupello | 250 |
| Franciacorta Brut '13 | Lo Sparviere | 260 |
| Franciacorta Brut Teatro alla Scala '13 | Bellavista | 226 |
| Franciacorta Dosage Zéro Vintage Collection Noir '09 | Ca' del Bosco | 233 |
| Franciacorta Nature 61 '11 | Guido Berlucchi & C. | 227 |
| Franciacorta Nature Origines Ris. '12 | Lantieri de Paratico | 247 |
| Franciacorta Pas Dosé Ris. '08 | Mosnel | 252 |
| Franciacorta Pas Dosé Riserva 33 '11 | Ferghettina | 243 |
| Franciacorta Satèn | Ricci Curbastro | 257 |
| Franciacorta Zero '14 | Contadi Castaldi | 239 |
| Lugana Sel. Fabio Contato '16 | Cà Maiol | 232 |
| OP Pinot Nero Brut M. Cl. 1870 '14 | Giorgi | 246 |
| OP Pinot Nero Dosage Zéro M. Cl. Vergomberra '13 | Bruno Verdi | 263 |
| OP Pinot Nero Nature M. Cl Oltrenero '13 | Oltrenero | 253 |
| OP Pinot Nero Rile Nero '15 | Marchese Adorno | 222 |
| OP Riesling Oliva Ris. '16 | Ca' di Frara | 234 |
| Valtellina Sfursat 5 Stelle '15 | Nino Negri | 252 |
| Valtellina Sfursat Fruttaio Ca' Rizzieri '15 | Aldo Rainoldi | 256 |
| Valtellina Sup. Dirupi '16 | Dirupi | 242 |
| Valtellina Sup. Sassella San Lorenzo '16 | Mamete Prevostini | 248 |
| Valtellina Sup. Sassella V. Regina Ris. '09 | Ar.Pe.Pe. | 224 |
| Valtènesi Chiaretto Molmenti '15 | Costaripa | 241 |

## CANTON TICINO

| | | |
|---|---|---|
| Ticino Merlot Castanar '13 | Roberto e Andrea Ferrari | 284 |
| Ticino Merlot Vinattieri '15 | Vinattieri Ticinesi | 288 |

## TRENTINO

| | | |
|---|---|---|
| San Leonardo '14 | San Leonardo | 305 |
| Teroldego Rotaliano Luigi Ris. '13 | Dorigati | 297 |
| Trentino Müller Thurgau Viàch '17 | Corvée | 295 |
| Trentino Pinot Nero V. Cantanghel '15 | Maso Cantanghel | 301 |
| Trento Brut Rotari Flavio Ris. '10 | Mezzacorona | 302 |
| Trento Brut Madame Martis Ris. '08 | Maso Martis | 301 |
| Trento Brut Nature '12 | Moser | 303 |
| Trento Dosaggio Zero Ris. '11 | Letrari | 300 |
| Trento Extra Brut 1673 Ris. '11 | Cesarini Sforza | 295 |
| Trento Pas Dosé Balter Ris. '12 | Nicola Balter | 292 |
| Trento Perlé Zero Cuvée Zero '11 | Ferrari | 298 |

## ALTO ADIGE

| | | |
|---|---|---|
| A. A. Bianco Beyond the Clouds '16 | Elena Walch | 342 |
| A. A. Chardonnay Lafóa '16 | Cantina Colterenzio | 316 |
| A. A. Gewürztraminer Auratus '17 | Tenuta Ritterhof | 334 |
| A. A. Gewürztraminer Brenntal Ris. '16 | Cantina Kurtatsch | 326 |
| A. A. Gewürztraminer Nussbaumer '16 | Cantina Tramin | 339 |
| A. A. Lago di Caldaro Cl. Sup. Quintessenz '17 | Cantina di Caldaro | 315 |
| A. A. Lagrein Mirell Ris. '15 | Tenuta Waldgries | 342 |
| A. A. Lagrein Taber Ris. '16 | Cantina Bolzano | 313 |
| A. A. Müller Thurgau Feldmarschall von Fenner '16 | Tiefenbrunner | 339 |
| A. A. Pinot Bianco Klaser Ris. '15 | Niklaserhof - Josef Sölva | 332 |
| A. A. Pinot Bianco Praesulis '17 | Gumphof Markus Prackwieser | 322 |
| A. A. Pinot Bianco Sirmian '17 | Nals Margreid | 331 |
| A. A. Pinot Bianco Tyrol '16 | Cantina Meran | 330 |
| A. A. Pinot Nero Abtei Muri Ris. '15 | Cantina Convento Muri-Gries | 330 |
| A. A. Pinot Nero Ris. '15 | Stroblhof | 337 |
| A. A. Pinot Nero Sanct Valentin Ris. '15 | Cantina Produttori San Michele Appiano | 335 |
| A. A. Pinot Nero Trattmann Mazon Ris. '15 | Cantina Girlan | 320 |
| A. A. Santa Maddalena Cl. Hueb '16 | Untermoserhof Georg Ramoser | 340 |
| A. A. Spumante Extra Brut 1919 Ris. '12 | Kettmeir | 323 |
| A. A. Terlano Nova Domus Ris. '15 | Cantina Terlano | 338 |
| A. A. Terlano Pinot Bianco Eichhorn '16 | Manincor | 328 |
| A. A. Val Venosta Riesling Weingarten Windbichel '16 | Tenuta Unterortl Castel Juval | 340 |
| A. A. Valle Isarco Riesling '16 | Köfererhof Günther Kerschbaumer | 324 |
| A. A. Valle Isarco Sylvaner Alte Reben '16 | Pacherhof Andreas Huber | 332 |
| A. A. Valle Isarco Sylvaner Lahner '16 | Taschlerhof Peter Wachtler | 338 |

## VENETO

| | | |
|---|---|---|
| Amarone della Valpolicella '14 | Famiglia Cottini Monte Zovo | 378 |
| Amarone della Valpolicella Cl. '14 | Allegrini | 352 |
| Amarone della Valpolicella Cl. '10 | Cav. G. B. Bertani | 356 |
| Amarone della Valpolicella Cl. '09 | Giuseppe Quintarelli | 404 |
| Amarone della Valpolicella Cl. Albasini '11 | Villa Spinosa | 427 |
| Amarone della Valpolicella Cl. Casa dei Bepi '12 | Viviani | 428 |

| | | |
|---|---|---|
| Amarone della Valpolicella Cl. Costasera Ris. '13 | Masi | 390 |
| Amarone della Valpolicella Cl. De Buris Ris. '08 | Tommasi Viticoltori | 420 |
| Amarone della Valpolicella Cl. Monte Ca' Bianca '13 | Lorenzo Begali | 355 |
| Amarone della Valpolicella Cl. Vign. di Ravazzol '13 | Ca' La Bionda | 363 |
| Amarone della Valpolicella Cl. Villa Rizzardi '13 | Guerrieri Rizzardi | 386 |
| Amarone della Valpolicella Leone Zardini Ris. '11 | Pietro Zardini | 429 |
| Amarone della Valpolicella Pasqua Mai dire Mai '11 | Pasqua - Cecilia Beretta | 401 |
| Baon '15 | Conte Emo Capodilista La Montecchia | 380 |
| Bardolino Sup. Pràdicà '16 | Corte Gardoni | 376 |
| Campo Sella '15 | Sutto | 416 |
| Capitel Croce '17 | Roberto Anselmi | 353 |
| Cartizze Brut V. La Rivetta | Villa Sandi | 427 |
| Colli Berici Merlot Casara Roveri '15 | Dal Maso | 379 |
| Conegliano Valdobbiadene Rive di Ogliano Brut Nature '17 | BiancaVigna | 356 |
| Custoza Sanpietro '16 | Le Vigne di San Pietro | 426 |
| Custoza Sup. Amedeo '16 | Cavalchina | 371 |
| Custoza Sup. Ca' del Magro '16 | Monte del Frà | 393 |
| Lugana Molceo Ris. '16 | Ottella | 401 |
| Lugana Sergio Zenato Ris. '15 | Zenato | 430 |
| Madre '16 | Italo Cescon | 373 |
| Montello e Colli Asolani Il Rosso dell'Abazia '15 | Serafini & Vidotto | 414 |
| Riesling Renano Collezione di Famiglia '13 | Roeno | 406 |
| Soave Cl. Calvarino '16 | Leonildo Pieropan | 402 |
| Soave Cl. Monte Alto '16 | Ca' Rugate | 364 |
| Soave Cl. Monte Carbonare '16 | Suavia | 416 |
| Soave Cl. Monte Grande '16 | Graziano Prà | 403 |
| Valdobbiadene Brut Campofalco Vign. Monfalcon '17 | Canevel Spumanti | 366 |
| Valdobbiadene Brut Dirupo '17 | Andreola | 352 |
| Valdobbiadene Brut Nature Particella 232 | Sorelle Bronca | 361 |
| Valdobbiadene Brut Rive di Col San Martino Cuvée del Fondatore Graziano Merotto '17 | Merotto | 392 |
| Valdobbiadene Brut Rive San Pietro di Barbozza Grande Cuvée del Fondatore Motus Vitae '16 | Bortolomiol | 359 |
| Valdobbiadene Extra Dry Giustino B. '17 | Ruggeri & C. | 407 |
| Valpolicella Cl. Sup. Camporenzo '15 | Monte dall'Ora | 393 |
| Valpolicella Sup. Ripasso Campo Ciotoli '16 | I Campi | 365 |
| Valpolicella Sup. Tenuta Campocroce '16 | Tenute SalvaTerra | 408 |

## FRIULI VENEZIA GIULIA

| | | |
|---|---|---|
| Capo Martino '16 | Jermann | 468 |
| Collio Bianco Broy '17 | Eugenio Collavini | 455 |
| Collio Bianco Fosarin '16 | Ronco dei Tassi | 488 |
| Collio Bianco Giulio Locatelli Ris. '16 | Tenuta di Angoris | 444 |
| Collio Bianco Solarco '17 | Livon | 472 |
| Collio Chardonnay Gmajne '15 | Primosic | 483 |
| Collio Chardonnay Gräfin de La Tour '14 | Villa Russiz | 510 |
| Collio Friulano '17 | Schiopetto | 493 |
| Collio Pinot Bianco '17 | Doro Princic | 483 |
| Collio Pinot Bianco '17 | Franco Toros | 502 |
| Collio Pinot Grigio Mongris Ris. '16 | Marco Felluga | 464 |
| Collio Sauvignon '17 | Tiare - Roberto Snidarcig | 502 |
| Collio Sauvignon Ris. '13 | Russiz Superiore | 491 |
| Desiderium I Ferretti '16 | Tenuta Luisa | 500 |
| FCO BiancoSesto '16 | La Tunella | 503 |
| FCO Friulano Liende '17 | La Viarte | 505 |
| FCO Pinot Bianco '17 | Torre Rosazza | 503 |
| FCO Pinot Bianco Myò '17 | Zorzettig | 513 |
| FCO Sauvignon Zuc di Volpe '17 | Volpe Pasini | 511 |
| Friuli Chardonnay '17 | Vigneti Le Monde | 470 |
| Friuli Isonzo Pinot Bianco '16 | Masùt da Rive | 473 |
| Friuli Isonzo Sauvignon Piere '16 | Vie di Romans | 506 |
| Malvasia '15 | Il Carpino | 453 |
| Nekaj '14 | Damijan Podversic | 481 |
| Ograde '16 | Skerk | 496 |
| Rosazzo Terre Alte '16 | Livio Felluga | 463 |

## EMILIA ROMAGNA

| | | |
|---|---|---|
| Callas Malvasia '15 | Monte delle Vigne | 536 |
| Colli di Rimini Cabernet Sauvignon Montepirolo '15 | San Patrignano | 544 |
| Lambrusco di Sorbara del Fondatore '17 | Cleto Chiarli Tenute Agricole | 529 |
| Lambrusco di Sorbara Leclisse '17 | Alberto Paltrinieri | 538 |
| Lambrusco di Sorbara V. del Cristo '17 | Cavicchioli | 528 |
| Reggiano Lambrusco Brut Cadelvento Rosé '17 | Venturini Baldini | 547 |
| Reggiano Lambrusco Concerto '17 | Ermete Medici & Figli | 535 |
| Romagna Albana Secco I Croppi '17 | Celli | 529 |
| Romagna Sangiovese Modigliana I Probi di Papiano Ris. '15 | Villa Papiano | 549 |
| Romagna Sangiovese Predappio Godenza '16 | Noelia  Ricci | 541 |
| Romagna Sangiovese Sup. Bartimeo '16 | Stefano Berti | 525 |
| Romagna Sangiovese Sup. Biagio Antico '16 | Ancarani | 524 |
| Romagna Sangiovese Sup. Predappio di Predappio V. del Generale Ris. '15 | Fattoria Nicolucci | 537 |
| Romagna Sangiovese Sup. Sigismondo '17 | Le Rocche Malatestiane | 542 |

**TUSCANY**

| | | |
|---|---|---|
| Bolgheri Rosso Sup. Le Gonnare '15 | Fabio Motta | 641 |
| Bolgheri Rosso Sup. Millepassi '15 | Donna Olimpia 1898 | 607 |
| Bolgheri Rosso Sup. Sapaio '16 | Podere Sapaio | 673 |
| Bolgheri Rosso Sup. Sondraia '15 | Poggio al Tesoro | 656 |
| Bolgheri Sassicaia '15 | Tenuta San Guido | 671 |
| Bolgheri Sup. Grattamacco '15 | Grattamacco | 619 |
| Brunello di Montalcino '13 | Caprili | 580 |
| Brunello di Montalcino '13 | Corte dei Venti | 601 |
| Brunello di Montalcino '13 | Le Macioche | 630 |
| Brunello di Montalcino '13 | Piancornello | 650 |
| Brunello di Montalcino Duelecci Ovest Ris. '12 | Tenuta di Sesta | 681 |
| Brunello di Montalcino Giodo '13 | Giodo | 618 |
| Brunello di Montalcino Gualto Ris. '12 | Camigliano | 576 |
| Brunello di Montalcino Ris. '12 | Fattoi | 609 |
| Brunello di Montalcino Ris. '12 | Poggio di Sotto | 657 |
| Brunello di Montalcino Ris. '11 | Tenuta Le Potazzine | 661 |
| Brunello di Montalcino Tenuta Nuova '13 | Casanova di Neri | 583 |
| Brunello di Montalcino V. Loreto '13 | Mastrojanni | 631 |
| Brunello di Montalcino V. V. '13 | Le Ragnaie | 663 |
| Brunello di Montalcino Vallocchio '13 | Tenuta Fanti | 609 |
| Caburnio '14 | Tenuta Monteti | 637 |
| Carmignano Ris. '15 | Tenuta Le Farnete/Cantagallo | 625 |
| Carmignano Ris. '15 | Piaggia | 650 |
| Carmignano Santa Cristina in Pilli '15 | Fattoria Ambra | 559 |
| Cepparello '15 | Isole e Olena | 622 |
| Chianti Cl. '16 | Borgo Salcetino | 570 |
| Chianti Cl. '15 | Tenuta Carleone | 581 |
| Chianti Cl. '16 | Castello di Volpaia | 590 |
| Chianti Cl. '16 | Cinciano | 596 |
| Chianti Cl. '16 | Le Miccine | 634 |
| Chianti Cl. '16 | Rocca delle Macìe | 665 |
| Chianti Cl. Cultus Boni '15 | Badia a Coltibuono | 564 |
| Chianti Cl. Dofana '16 | Fattoria Carpineta Fontalpino | 582 |
| Chianti Cl. Gran Selezione Riserva Ducale Oro '14 | Ruffino | 668 |
| Chianti Cl. Gran Selezione V. Il Corno '14 | Castello di Radda | 589 |
| Chianti Cl. Il Campitello Ris. '15 | Monteraponi | 636 |
| Chianti Cl. Il Grigio Ris. '15 | San Felice | 670 |
| Chianti Cl. Il Poggio Ris. '13 | Castello di Monsanto | 589 |
| Chianti Cl. Lamole di Lamole Et. Blu '15 | Lamole di Lamole | 623 |
| Chianti Cl. Marchese Antinori Ris. '15 | Marchesi Antinori | 561 |
| Chianti Cl. Ris. '13 | Castellinuzza | 585 |
| Chianti Cl. Ris. '14 | Castello di Albola | 587 |
| Chianti Cl. Ris. '15 | Tenuta di Lilliano | 627 |
| Chianti Cl. Ris. '15 | Riecine | 665 |
| Chianti Cl. Riserva di Famiglia '15 | Famiglia Cecchi | 592 |

| | | |
|---|---|---|
| Chianti Cl. V. Cavarchione '16 | Istine | 622 |
| Chianti Colli Fiorentini Badia a Corte Ris. '15 | Torre a Cona | 685 |
| Chianti Colli Fiorentini La Torretta Ris. '15 | La Querce | 662 |
| Chianti Rufina Vign. Quona Ris. '15 | I Veroni | 691 |
| Colline Lucchesi Tenuta di Valgiano '15 | Tenuta di Valgiano | 690 |
| Cortona Syrah '15 | Stefano Amerighi | 560 |
| Costa dell'Argentario Ansonica '17 | Tenuta La Parrina | 647 |
| Duemani '15 | Duemani | 607 |
| I Sodi di San Niccolò '14 | Castellare di Castellina | 584 |
| Il Brecciolino '15 | Castelvecchio | 591 |
| Il Pareto '15 | Tenute Ambrogio e Giovanni Folonari | 611 |
| La Regola '15 | Podere La Regola | 663 |
| Le Pergole Torte '15 | Montevertine | 638 |
| Maremma Toscana Baffonero '16 | Rocca di Frassinello | 666 |
| Maremma Toscana Ciliegiolo V. Vallerana Alta '16 | Antonio Camillo | 576 |
| Maremma Toscana Grenache Oltreconfine '16 | Bruni | 573 |
| Mix36 '15 | Castello di Fonterutoli | 588 |
| Montecucco Sangiovese Ad Agio Ris. '14 | Basile | 567 |
| Montecucco Sangiovese Poggio Lombrone Ris. '14 | Colle Massari | 598 |
| Montesodi '15 | Frescobaldi | 616 |
| Morellino di Scansano Madrechiesa Ris. '15 | Terenzi | 682 |
| Morellino di Scansano Ris. '15 | Fattoria Le Pupille | 662 |
| Morellino di Scansano Rovente Ris. '15 | Col di Bacche | 597 |
| Nobile di Montepulciano '15 | Fattoria del Cerro | 610 |
| Nobile di Montepulciano '15 | Podere Le Bèrne | 655 |
| Nobile di Montepulciano Bossona Ris. '13 | Maria Caterina Dei | 605 |
| Nobile di Montepulciano Le Caggiole '15 | Poliziano | 660 |
| Nobile di Montepulciano Pagliareto '15 | Lunadoro | 628 |
| Oreno '16 | Tenuta Sette Ponti | 678 |
| Orma '16 | Orma | 643 |
| Paleo Rosso '15 | Le Macchiole | 629 |
| Petra Rosso '15 | Petra | 649 |
| Rosso di Montalcino '16 | Baricci | 566 |
| Rosso di Montalcino '16 | Sesti - Castello di Argiano | 678 |
| Rosso di Montalcino '16 | Uccelliera | 687 |
| Valadorna '13 | Tenuta di Arceno - Arcanum | 561 |
| Vernaccia di S. Gimignano Carato '13 | Montenidoli | 635 |
| Vernaccia di S. Gimignano Sanice Ris. '15 | Vincenzo Cesani | 593 |
| Vernaccia di S. Gimignano Selvabianca '17 | Il Colombaio di Santa Chiara | 601 |

**MARCHE**

| | | |
|---|---|---|
| Castelli di Jesi Verdicchio Cl. San Paolo Ris. '16 | Pievalta | 747 |
| Castelli di Jesi Verdicchio Cl. San Sisto Ris. '16 | Fazi Battaglia | 736 |
| Castelli di Jesi Verdicchio Cl. Tardivo ma non Tardo Ris. '16 | Santa Barbara | 749 |

| | | |
|---|---|---|
| Castelli di Jesi Verdicchio Cl. V. Il Cantico della Figura Ris. '15 | Andrea Felici | 737 |
| Conero Dorico Ris. '15 | Alessandro Moroder | 745 |
| Il Pollenza '15 | Il Pollenza | 747 |
| Lacrima di Morro d'Alba Sup. Orgiolo '16 | Marotti Campi | 743 |
| Offida Pecorino '17 | Tenuta Santori | 750 |
| Offida Pecorino Artemisia '17 | Tenuta Spinelli | 751 |
| Offida Pecorino Guido Cocci Grifoni '14 | Tenuta Cocci Grifoni | 730 |
| Piceno Sup. Morellone '13 | Le Caniette | 726 |
| Rosso Piceno Sup. Oro '15 | Tenuta De Angelis | 735 |
| Rosso Piceno Sup. Roggio del Filare '15 | Velenosi | 757 |
| Verdicchio dei Castelli di Jesi Cl. Sup. Grancasale '16 | CasalFarneto | 727 |
| Verdicchio dei Castelli di Jesi Cl. Sup. Il Priore '16 | Sparapani - Frati Bianchi | 751 |
| Verdicchio dei Castelli di Jesi Cl. Sup. Misco '17 | Tenuta di Tavignano | 752 |
| Verdicchio dei Castelli di Jesi Cl. Sup. Podium '16 | Gioacchino Garofoli | 739 |
| Verdicchio dei Castelli di Jesi Cl. Sup. V. V. '16 | Umani Ronchi | 755 |
| Verdicchio dei Castelli di Jesi Cl. Sup. Ylice '16 | Poderi Mattioli | 743 |
| Verdicchio di Matelica Mirum Ris. '16 | La Monacesca | 744 |
| Verdicchio di Matelica Vertis '16 | Borgo Paglianetto | 725 |

**UMBRIA**

| | | |
|---|---|---|
| Adarmando '16 | Giampaolo Tabarrini | 782 |
| Cervaro della Sala '16 | Castello della Sala | 770 |
| Fiorfiore '16 | Roccafiore | 780 |
| Montefalco Rosso Ziggurat '16 | Tenute Lunelli - Castelbuono | 775 |
| Montefalco Sagrantino 25 Anni '14 | Arnaldo Caprai | 769 |
| Montefalco Sagrantino Collenottolo '14 | Tenuta Bellafonte | 767 |
| Montefalco Sagrantino Sacrantino '14 | F.lli Pardi | 778 |
| Orvieto Cl. Sup. Il Bianco '17 | Decugnano dei Barbi | 773 |
| Orvieto Muffa Nobile Calcaia '15 | Barberani | 767 |
| Spoleto Trebbiano Spoletino Anteprima Tonda '16 | Antonelli - San Marco | 766 |
| Todi Grechetto I Rovi '16 | Cantina Peppucci | 779 |
| Torgiano Rosso Rubesco V. Monticchio Ris. '13 | Lungarotti | 776 |

**LAZIO**

| | | |
|---|---|---|
| Fieno di Ponza Bianco '17 | Antiche Cantine Migliaccio | 797 |
| Fiorano Bianco '16 | Tenuta di Fiorano | 800 |
| Frascati Sup. Eremo Tuscolano '17 | Valle Vermiglia | 801 |
| Habemus '16 | San Giovenale | 800 |
| Montiano '16 | Famiglia Cotarella | 795 |
| Poggio della Costa '17 | Sergio Mottura | 797 |
| Roma Rosso Ed. Limitata '15 | Poggio Le Volpi | 799 |

**ABRUZZO**

| | | |
|---|---|---|
| Abruzzo Pecorino Giocheremo con I Fiori '17 | Torre dei Beati | 821 |
| Cerasuolo d'Abruzzo Piè delle Vigne '16 | Luigi Cataldi Madonna | 810 |
| Montepulciano d'Abruzzo '13 | Valentini | 823 |
| Montepulciano d'Abruzzo | | |
| Colline Teramane Zanna Ris. '13 | Dino Illuminati | 816 |
| Montepulciano d'Abruzzo Mo' Ris. '14 | Cantina Tollo | 821 |
| Montepulciano d'Abruzzo | | |
| Podere Castorani Ris. '14 | Castorani | 810 |
| Montepulciano d'Abruzzo Spelt Ris. '15 | La Valentina | 822 |
| Montepulciano d'Abruzzo | | |
| Vign. di Sant'Eusanio '16 | Valle Reale | 823 |
| Pecorino '17 | Villa Medoro | 824 |
| Trebbiano d'Abruzzo Castello di Semivicoli '15 | Masciarelli | 816 |
| Trebbiano d'Abruzzo Sup. Mario's 44 '16 | Tenuta Terraviva | 820 |
| Tullum Pecorino Biologico '17 | Feudo Antico | 815 |

**MOLISE**

| | | |
|---|---|---|
| Molise Tintilia '16 | Di Majo Norante | 831 |

**CAMPANIA**

| | | |
|---|---|---|
| Aglianico '16 | Donnachiara | 843 |
| Caiatì Pallagrello Bianco '16 | Alois | 835 |
| Campi Flegrei Falanghina V. Astroni '15 | Cantine Astroni | 835 |
| Costa d'Amalfi Furore Bianco Fiorduva '17 | Marisa Cuomo | 841 |
| Costa d'Amalfi Ravello Bianco | | |
| Selva delle Monache '17 | Ettore Sammarco | 853 |
| Falanghina del Sannio Janare Senete '17 | La Guardiense | 847 |
| Falanghina del Sannio Svelato '17 | Terre Stregate | 858 |
| Fiano di Avellino '17 | Tenuta del Meriggio | 858 |
| Fiano di Avellino Pietramara '17 | I Favati | 844 |
| Fiano di Avellino Tognano '15 | Rocca del Principe | 852 |
| Fiano di Avellino Ventidue '16 | Villa Raiano | 861 |
| Greco di Tufo '17 | Pietracupa | 851 |
| Greco di Tufo Miniere '16 | Cantine dell'Angelo | 837 |
| Ischia Biancolella '17 | La Pietra di Tommasone | 851 |
| Montevetrano '16 | Montevetrano | 848 |
| Pashka' '17 | Casebianche | 838 |
| Pian di Stio '17 | San Salvatore 1988 | 854 |
| Sabbie di Sopra il Bosco '16 | Nanni Copè | 849 |
| Sannio Sant'Agata dei Goti Piedirosso Artus '16 | Mustilli | 849 |
| Sannio Taburno Falanghina Libero '07 | Fontanavecchia | 845 |
| Taurasi Piano di Montevergine Ris. '13 | Feudi di San Gregorio | 845 |
| Taurasi V. Macchia dei Goti '14 | Antonio Caggiano | 837 |
| Taurasi Vigne d'Alto '12 | Contrade di Taurasi | 841 |

**BASILICATA**

| | | |
|---|---|---|
| Aglianico del Vulture Don Anselmo '15 | Paternoster | 875 |

| | | |
|---|---|---|
| Faro '16 | Le Casematte | 926 |
| Faro Palari '14 | Palari | 936 |
| Malvasia delle Lipari Passito '17 | Caravaglio | 925 |
| Menfi Syrah Maroccoli '14 | Planeta | 939 |
| Mille e una Notte '14 | Donnafugata | 928 |
| Sicilia Mandrarossa Cartagho '16 | Cantine Settesoli | 942 |
| Sicilia Nero d'Avola Sàgana '16 | Cusumano | 928 |
| Sicilia Nero d'Avola Saia '16 | Feudo Maccari | 931 |
| Sicilia Nero d'Avola Deliella '16 | Feudo Priancipi di Butera | 940 |
| Sicilia Nero d'Avola Lorlando '17 | Assuli | 921 |
| Sicilia Syrah Kaid '16 | Alessandro di Camporeale | 920 |

**SARDINIA**

| | | |
|---|---|---|
| Alghero Torbato Catore '17 | Tenute Sella & Mosca | 972 |
| Bovale '16 | Su Entu | 973 |
| Cannonau di Sardegna '16 | Antonella Corda | 961 |
| Cannonau di Sardegna Cl. Dule '15 | Giuseppe Gabbas | 964 |
| Cannonau di Sardegna R Ris. '15 | Santa Maria La Palma | 970 |
| Carignano del Sulcis 6Mura Ris. '15 | Cantina Giba | 965 |
| Carignano del Sulcis Sup. Terre Brune '14 | Cantina di Santadi | 970 |
| Semidano di Mogoro Sup. Puistèris '16 | Cantina di Mogoro | |
| | Il Nuraghe | 967 |
| Vermentino di Gallura Sup. Sciala '17 | Surrau | 974 |
| Vermentino di Gallura Vigna'Ngena '17 | Capichera | 959 |
| Vermentino di Sardegna Azzesu | | |
|   Tenuta del Vulcano Pelao '17 | Andrea Ledda | 966 |
| Vermentino di Sardegna Die '17 | Tenute Delogu | 962 |
| Vermentino di Sardegna Stellato '17 | Pala | 968 |

# THE BEST

### RED OF THE YEAR

BRUNELLO DI MONTALCINO DUELECCI OVEST RIS. '12 - TENUTA DI SESTA

### WHITE OF THE YEAR

CAPO MARTINO '16 - JERMANN

### SPARKLER OF THE YEAR

FRANCIACORTA NATURE 61 '11 - GUIDO BERLUCCHI & C.

### SWEET OF THE YEAR

PIEMONTE MOSCATO PASSITO LA BELLA ESTATE '16 - VITE COLTE

### ROSÈ OF THE YEAR

VALTÈNESI CHIARETTO MOLMENTI '15 - COSTARIPA

# SPECIAL AWARDS

# WINERY OF THE YEAR

FERRARI

# BEST VALUE FOR MONEY

A. A. LAGO DI CALDARO CL. SUP. QUINTESSENZ '17 - CANTINA DI CALDARO

# GROWER OF THE YEAR

FRANCESCO CAMBRIA

# UP-AND-COMING WINERY

ANTONELLA CORDA

# AWARD FOR SUSTAINABLE VITICULTURE

TORREVENTO

# SOLIDARITY AWARD

SAN PATRIGNANO

# TRE BICCHIERI VERDI

With our Tre Bicchieri Verdi we make note of those wines made with certified organic or biodynamically cultivated grapes (here indicated in red). This year there were a record 102 in all, a figure that also represents a growing share of those wines awarded (23%). It's an important figure that testifies to the fact that an emphasis on ecology among Italy's best wineries is irreversible (it's a complex question, however, considering that many wineries work according to similar methods but never request certification). Finally, it's clear that sustainability is an increasingly widespread priority among winemakers. We use the label 'Sustainable Winery' to identify producers committed to such principles.

| | | |
|---|---|---|
| A. A. Terlano Pinot Bianco Eichhorn '16 | Manincor | Alto Adige |
| Abruzzo Pecorino Giocheremo con I Fiori '17 | Torre dei Beati | Abruzzo |
| Aglianico del Vulture Don Anselmo '15 | Paternoster | Basilicata |
| Aglianico del Vulture Titolo '16 | Elena Fucci | Basilicata |
| Alcamo Beleda '17 | Rallo | Sicilia |
| Amarone della Valpolicella Cl. Vign. di Ravazzol '13 | Ca' La Bionda | Veneto |
| Barbaresco Asili '15 | Ceretto | Piedmont |
| Barbaresco Cottà '15 | Sottimano | Piedmont |
| Barbaresco Currà Ris. '12 | Bruno Rocca | Piedmont |
| Barolo Bussia V. Mondoca Ris. '12 | Poderi e Cantine Oddero | Piedmont |
| Barolo del Comune di La Morra '14 | Brandini | Piedmont |
| Barolo Ravera Bricco Pernice '13 | Elvio Cogno | Piedmont |
| Bolgheri Sup. Grattamacco '15 | Grattamacco | Tuscany |
| Brunello di Montalcino Ris. '12 | Poggio di Sotto | Tuscany |
| Brunello di Montalcino V. V. '13 | Le Ragnaie | Tuscany |
| Campi Flegrei Falanghina V. Astroni '15 | Cantine Astroni | Campania |
| Carmignano Santa Cristina in Pilli '15 | Fattoria Ambra | Tuscany |
| Castelli di Jesi Verdicchio Cl. San Paolo Ris. '16 | Pievalta | Marche |
| Chianti Cl. '15 | Tenuta Carleone | Tuscany |
| Chianti Cl. '16 | Castello di Volpaia | Tuscany |
| Chianti Cl. '16 | Le Miccine | Tuscany |
| Chianti Cl. Cultus Boni '15 | Badia a Coltibuono | Tuscany |
| Chianti Cl. Dofana '16 | Fattoria Carpineta Fontalpino | Tuscany |
| Chianti Cl. Il Campitello Ris. '15 | Monteraponi | Tuscany |
| Chianti Cl. Ris. '15 | Tenuta di Lilliano | Tuscany |
| Chianti Cl. Ris. '15 | Riecine | Tuscany |
| Chianti Cl. V. Cavarchione '16 | Istine | Tuscany |
| Chianti Rufina Vign. Quona Ris. '15 | I Veroni | Tuscany |
| Colli di Rimini Cabernet Sauvignon Montepirolo '15 | San Patrignano | Emilia Romagna |
| Colline Lucchesi Tenuta di Valgiano '15 | Tenuta di Valgiano | Tuscany |
| Conero Dorico Ris. '15 | Alessandro Moroder | Marche |
| Cortona Syrah '15 | Stefano Amerighi | Tuscany |
| Duemani '15 | Duemani | Tuscany |
| Erbaluce di Caluso 13 Mesi '16 | Benito Favaro | Pieemont |
| Etna Bianco di Sei '17 | Palmento Costanzo | Sicily |
| Etna Rosso '16 | Graci | Sicily |
| Etna Rosso Cavanera Rovo delle Coturnie '14 | Firriato | Sicily |
| Etna Rosso Feudo di Mezzo '16 | Girolamo Russo | Sicily |
| Etna Rosso Vico Prephylloxera '15 | Tenute Bosco | Sicily |
| Etna Rosso Vign. Monte Gorna Ris. '12 | Cantine Nicosia | v |
| Faro '16 | Le Casematte | Sicily |
| Fiano di Avellino Ventidue '16 | Villa Raiano | Campania |
| Fiorano Bianco '16 | Tenuta di Fiorano | Lazio |
| Franciacorta Dosage Zéro Vintage Collection Noir '09 | Ca' del Bosco | Lombardy |
| Franciacorta Nature 61 '11 | Guido Berlucchi & C. | Lombardy |

| | | |
|---|---|---|
| Franciacorta Nature Origines Ris. '12 | Lantieri de Paratico | **Lombardy** |
| Franciacorta Pas Dosé Ris. '08 | Mosnel | **Lombardy** |
| Franciacorta Pas Dosé Riserva 33 '11 | Ferghettina | **Lombardy** |
| Gavi V. della Madonnina Ris. '16 | La Raia | **Piedmont** |
| Gioia del Colle Primitivo 16 Vign. San Benedetto '15 | Polvanera | **Puglia** |
| Gioia del Colle Primitivo Marpione Ris. '15 | Tenuta Viglione | **Puglia** |
| Gioia del Colle Primitivo Senatore '15 | Coppi | **Puglia** |
| Grisara '17 | Roberto Ceraudo | **Calabria** |
| Habemus '16 | San Giovenale | **Lazio** |
| Madre '16 | Italo Cescon | **Veneto** |
| Malvasia delle Lipari Passito '17 | Caravaglio | **Sicily** |
| Maremma Toscana Ciliegiolo V. Vallerana Alta '16 | Antonio Camillo | **Tuscany** |
| Molise Tintilia '16 | Di Majo Norante | **Molise** |
| Montecucco Sangiovese Ad Agio Ris. '14 | Basile | **Tuscany** |
| Montecucco Sangiovese Poggio Lombrone Ris. '14 | Colle Massari | **Tuscany** |
| Montefalco Rosso Ziggurat '16 | Tenuta Castelbuono | **Umbria** |
| Montepulciano d'Abruzzo Podere Castorani Ris. '14 | Castorani | **Abruzzo** |
| Montepulciano d'Abruzzo Spelt Ris. '15 | La Valentina | **Abruzzo** |
| Montepulciano d'Abruzzo Vign. di Sant'Eusanio '16 | Valle Reale | **Abruzzo** |
| Moscato Passito '17 | Luigi Viola | **Calabria** |
| Nekaj '14 | Damijan Podversic | **Friuli Venezia Giulia** |
| Nobile di Montepulciano Pagliareto '15 | Lunadoro | **Tuscany** |
| Offida Pecorino '17 | Tenuta Santori | **Marche** |
| Ograde '16 | Skerk | **Friuli Venezia Giulia** |
| Orvieto Muffa Nobile Calcaia '15 | Barberani | **Umbria** |
| Otto '16 | Carvinea | **Puglia** |
| Pashka' '17 | Casebianche | **Campania** |
| Pian di Stio '17 | San Salvatore 1988 | **Campania** |
| Piceno Sup. Morellone '13 | Le Caniette | **Marche** |
| Piemonte Moscato Passito La Bella Estate '16 | Vite Colte | **Piedmont** |
| Poggio della Costa '17 | Sergio Mottura | **Lazio** |
| Primitivo di Manduria Sessantanni '15 | Cantine San Marzano | **Puglia** |
| Primitivo di Manduria Zinfandel Sinfarosa Terra Nera '16 | Felline | **Puglia** |
| Reggiano Lambrusco Brut Cadelvento Rosé '17 | Venturini Baldini | **Emilia Romagna** |
| Riviera Ligure di Ponente Pigato Bon in da Bon '17 | BioVio | **Liguria** |
| Roero Valmaggiore V. Audinaggio '16 | Cascina Ca' Rossa | **Piedmont** |
| Romagna Sangiovese Modigliana I Probi di Papiano Ris. '15 | Villa Papiano | **Emilia Romagna** |
| Sabbie di Sopra il Bosco '16 | Nanni Copè | **Campania** |
| San Leonardo '14 | San Leonardo | **Trentino** |
| Sicilia Syrah Kaid '16 | Alessandro di Camporeale | **Sicily** |
| Soave Cl. Calvarino '16 | Leonildo Pieropan | **Veneto** |
| Soave Cl. Monte Grande '16 | Graziano Prà | **Veneto** |
| Spoleto Trebbiano Spoletino Anteprima Tonda '16 | Antonelli - San Marco | **Umbria** |
| Taurasi Piano di Montevergine Ris. '13 | Feudi di San Gregorio | **Campania** |
| Taurasi Vigne d'Alto '12 | Contrade di Taurasi | **Campania** |
| Torgiano Rosso Rubesco V. Monticchio Ris. '13 | Lungarotti | **Umbria** |
| Trebbiano d'Abruzzo Sup. Mario's 44 '16 | Tenuta Terraviva | **Abruzzo** |
| Trentino Pinot Nero V. Cantanghel '15 | Maso Cantanghel | **Trentino** |
| Trento Brut Madame Martis Ris. '08 | Maso Martis | **Trentino** |
| Tullum Pecorino Biologico '17 | Feudo Antico | **Abruzzo** |
| Valpolicella Cl. Sup. Camporenzo '15 | Monte dall'Ora | **Veneto** |
| Verdicchio dei Castelli di Jesi Cl. Sup. V. V. '16 | Umani Ronchi | **Marche** |
| Verdicchio dei Castelli di Jesi Cl. Sup. Ylice '16 | Poderi Mattioli | **Marche** |
| Verdicchio di Matelica Vertis '16 | Borgo Paglianetto | **Marche** |
| Vernaccia di S. Gimignano Carato '13 | Montenidoli | **Tuscany** |
| Vernaccia di S. Gimignano Sanice Ris. '15 | Vincenzo Cesani | **Tuscany** |
| Vernaccia di S. Gimignano Selvabianca '17 | Il Colombaio di Santa Chiara | **Tuscany** |

# TABLE OF VINTAGES
# FROM 1995 TO 2017

| | ALTO ADIGE BIANCO | LUGANA / SOAVE | FRIULI BIANCO |
|---|---|---|---|
| 2006 | 🍾🍾🍾 (3) | 🍾🍾🍾 (3) | 🍾🍾🍾🍾🍾 (5) |
| 2007 | 🍾🍾🍾 (3) | 🍾🍾🍾🍾 (4) | 🍾🍾🍾🍾🍾 (5) |
| 2008 | 🍾🍾🍾 (3) | 🍾🍾🍾🍾 (4) | 🍾🍾🍾 (3) |
| 2009 | 🍾🍾🍾🍾 (4) | 🍾🍾🍾🍾🍾 (5) | 🍾🍾🍾🍾 (4) |
| 2010 | 🍾🍾🍾🍾🍾 (5) | 🍾🍾🍾🍾 (4) | 🍾🍾 (2) |
| 2011 | 🍾🍾🍾 (3) | 🍾🍾🍾 (3) | 🍾🍾🍾 (3) |
| 2012 | 🍾🍾🍾🍾 (4) | 🍾🍾🍾 (3) | 🍾🍾🍾🍾 (4) |
| 2013 | 🍾🍾🍾🍾 (4) | 🍾🍾🍾🍾 (4) | 🍾🍾🍾🍾 (4) |
| 2014 | 🍾🍾 (2) | 🍾🍾🍾 (3) | 🍾🍾🍾 (3) |
| 2015 | 🍾🍾🍾🍾 (4) | 🍾🍾🍾🍾🍾 (5) | 🍾🍾🍾🍾🍾 (5) |
| 2016 | 🍾🍾🍾🍾🍾 (5) | 🍾🍾🍾🍾🍾 (5) | 🍾🍾🍾🍾🍾 (5) |
| 2017 | 🍾🍾🍾🍾 (4) | 🍾🍾🍾🍾 (4) | 🍾🍾🍾🍾 (4) |

| VERDICCHIO DEI CASTELLI DI JESI | FIANO DI AVELLINO | GRECO DI TUFO | FRANCIACORTA |
|---|---|---|---|
| 🍾🍾🍾🍾🍾 | 🍾🍾🍾🍾 | 🍾🍾🍾🍾🍾 | 🍾🍾🍾🍾 |
| 🍾🍾 | 🍾🍾🍾🍾 | 🍾🍾🍾🍾 | 🍾🍾🍾 |
| 🍾🍾🍾🍾 | 🍾🍾🍾🍾 | 🍾🍾🍾🍾 | 🍾🍾🍾🍾🍾 |
| 🍾🍾🍾🍾 | 🍾🍾🍾 | 🍾🍾🍾🍾 | 🍾🍾🍾 |
| 🍾🍾🍾🍾🍾 | 🍾🍾🍾🍾🍾 | 🍾🍾🍾🍾🍾 | 🍾🍾🍾 |
| 🍾 | 🍾🍾🍾 | 🍾🍾 | 🍾🍾🍾🍾🍾 |
| 🍾🍾🍾🍾 | 🍾🍾🍾🍾 | 🍾🍾🍾🍾 | 🍾🍾🍾🍾 |
| 🍾🍾🍾🍾🍾 | 🍾🍾🍾🍾🍾 | 🍾🍾🍾 | 🍾🍾🍾🍾🍾 |
| 🍾🍾🍾 | 🍾🍾🍾🍾 | 🍾🍾🍾🍾 | 🍾🍾🍾 |
| 🍾🍾🍾🍾 | 🍾🍾🍾🍾 | 🍾🍾🍾 | |
| 🍾🍾🍾🍾🍾 | 🍾🍾🍾🍾🍾 | 🍾🍾🍾🍾 | |
| 🍾🍾🍾🍾 | 🍾🍾🍾 | 🍾🍾🍾 | |

| | BARBARESCO | BAROLO | AMARONE | CHIANTI CLASSICO |
|---|---|---|---|---|
| | 🍾🍾🍾 | 🍾🍾🍾 | 🍾🍾🍾🍾🍾 | 🍾🍾🍾🍾 |
| | 🍾🍾🍾🍾🍾 | 🍾🍾🍾🍾🍾 | 🍾🍾 | 🍾🍾🍾 |
| 1997 | 🍾🍾🍾 | 🍾🍾🍾 | 🍾🍾🍾🍾 | 🍾🍾🍾 |
| 1998 | 🍾🍾🍾 | 🍾🍾🍾🍾 | 🍾🍾🍾 | 🍾🍾🍾 |
| 1999 | 🍾🍾🍾🍾 | 🍾🍾🍾🍾🍾 | 🍾🍾🍾🍾 | 🍾🍾🍾🍾 |
| 2000 | 🍾🍾🍾 | 🍾🍾🍾🍾 | 🍾🍾🍾🍾 | 🍾🍾🍾🍾 |
| 2001 | 🍾🍾🍾🍾🍾 | 🍾🍾🍾🍾🍾 | 🍾🍾🍾🍾🍾 | 🍾🍾🍾🍾🍾 |
| 2002 | 🍾🍾 | 🍾 | 🍾🍾🍾 | 🍾🍾 |
| 2003 | 🍾🍾🍾 | 🍾🍾 | 🍾🍾🍾 | 🍾🍾 |
| 2004 | 🍾🍾🍾🍾🍾 | 🍾🍾🍾🍾🍾 | 🍾🍾🍾🍾 | 🍾🍾🍾🍾 |
| 2005 | 🍾🍾🍾🍾 | 🍾🍾🍾 | 🍾🍾🍾🍾 | 🍾🍾🍾 |
| 2006 | 🍾🍾🍾 | 🍾🍾🍾🍾 | 🍾🍾🍾 | 🍾🍾🍾 |
| 2007 | 🍾🍾🍾 | 🍾🍾🍾 | 🍾🍾🍾🍾🍾 | 🍾🍾🍾🍾🍾 |
| 2008 | 🍾🍾🍾🍾 | 🍾🍾🍾🍾🍾 | 🍾🍾🍾🍾 | 🍾🍾🍾🍾 |
| 2009 | 🍾 | 🍾🍾🍾 | 🍾🍾🍾 | 🍾🍾🍾 |
| 2010 | 🍾🍾🍾🍾🍾 | 🍾🍾🍾🍾🍾 | 🍾🍾🍾🍾 | 🍾🍾🍾🍾🍾 |
| 2011 | 🍾🍾🍾🍾 | 🍾🍾🍾🍾 | 🍾🍾🍾🍾 | 🍾🍾🍾🍾 |
| 2012 | 🍾🍾🍾 | 🍾🍾🍾🍾 | 🍾🍾🍾 | 🍾🍾🍾 |
| 2013 | 🍾🍾🍾🍾 | 🍾🍾🍾🍾 | 🍾🍾🍾🍾 | 🍾🍾🍾🍾 |
| 2014 | 🍾🍾🍾🍾 | 🍾🍾 | 🍾🍾 | 🍾🍾🍾 |
| 2015 | 🍾🍾🍾🍾 | | | 🍾🍾🍾🍾 |
| 2016 | | | | 🍾🍾🍾🍾🍾 |

| BRUNELLO DI MONTALCINO | BOLGHERI | TAURASI | MONTEPULCIANO D'ABRUZZO | ETNA ROSSO |
|---|---|---|---|---|
| 5 | 3 | 3 | 5 | 3 |
| 2 | 3 | 3 | 4 | 2 |
| 4 | 4 | 4 | 4 | 3 |
| 3 | 4 | 2 | 4 | 3 |
| 5 | 5 | 5 | 1 | 4 |
| 1 | 3 | 2 | 4 | 3 |
| 5 | 5 | 4 | 5 | 4 |
| 2 | 2 | 3 | 2 | 1 |
| 3 | 2 | 4 | 3 | 3 |
| 4 | 3 | 4 | 4 | 3 |
| 1 | 3 | 4 | 4 | 4 |
| 4 | 4 | 3 | 3 | 4 |
| 4 | 5 | 4 | 5 | 5 |
| 2 | 4 | 5 | 2 | 5 |
| 1 | 5 | 3 | 2 | 3 |
| 5 | 3 | 4 | 2 | 4 |
| 3 | 4 | 2 | 4 | 5 |
| 3 | 4 | 3 | 3 | 4 |
| 5 | 5 | 4 | 4 | 3 |
| | 2 | 2 | 2 | 5 |
| | 4 | | 4 | 3 |
| | 4 | | | 5 |

# STARS

★★★★★
**56**
Gaja (Piedmont)

★★★★
**43**
Ca' del Bosco (Lombardy)

★★★
**38**
La Spinetta (Piedmont)
**37**
Elio Altare (Piedmont)
**34**
Allegrini (Veneto)
Castello di Fonterutoli (Tuscany)
Valentini (Abruzzo)
**30**
Bellavista (Lombardy)
Giacomo Conterno (Piedmont)
Jermann (Friuli Venezia Giulia)
Tenuta San Guido (Tuscany)
Cantina Produttori San Michele
  Appiano (Alto Adige)

★★
**29**
Castello della Sala (Umbria)
Ferrari (Trentino)
Masciarelli (Abruzzo)
Planeta (Sicilia)

**28**
Fèlsina (Tuscany)

**27**
Poliziano (Tuscany)
Tasca d'Almerita (Sicilia)
Cantina Tramin (Alto Adige)
Vie di Romans
  (Friuli Venezia Giulia)

**26**
Marchesi Antinori (Tuscany)
Feudi di San Gregorio
  (Campania)
Bruno Giacosa (Piedmont)
Leonildo Pieropan (Veneto)

**25**
Castello di Ama (Tuscany)
Livio Felluga
  (Friuli Venezia Giulia)
Ornellaia (Tuscany)
Paolo Scavino (Piedmont)

**24**
Argiolas (Sardinia)
Cantina Bolzano (Alto Adige)

Arnaldo Caprai (Umbria)
Gravner (Friuli Venezia Giulia)
Nino Negri (Lombardy)
Schioppetto (Friuli Venezia Giulia)
Villa Russiz (Friuli Venezia Giulia)

**23**
Famiglia Cotarella (Lazio)
Fontodi (Tuscany)
Tenute Sella & Mosca (Sardinia)
Cantina Terlano (Alto Adige)

**22**
Ca' Viola (Piedmont)
Michele Chiarlo (Piedmont)
Domenico Clerico (Piedmont)
Cantina Colterenzio (Alto Adige)
Isole e Olena (Tuscany)
Barone Ricasoli (Tuscany)
San Leonardo (Trentino)
Vietti (Piedmont)

**21**
Cantina di Caldaro (Alto Adige)
Cascina La Barbatella (Piedmont)
Castello del Terriccio (Tuscany)
Les Crêtes (Valle d'Aosta)
Montevetrano (Campania)
Volpe Pasini (Friuli Venezia Giulia)
Elena Walch (Alto Adige)

**20**
Ca' Rugate (Veneto)
Castellare di Castellina (Tuscany)
Dorigo (Friuli Venezia Giulia)
Gioacchino Garofoli (Marche)
Le Macchiole (Tuscany)
Montevertine (Tuscany)
Serafini & Vidotto (Veneto)
Venica & Venica
  (Friuli Venezia Giulia)

★
**19**
Luigi Cataldi Madonna (Abruzzo)
Matteo Correggia (Piedmont)
Cusumano (Sicilia)
Donnafugata (Sicilia)
Elio Grasso (Piedmont)
Lis Neris (Friuli Venezia Giulia)
Palari (Sicilia)
Ruffino (Tuscany)
Cantina di Santadi (Sardinia)
Sottimano (Piedmont)
Franco Toros
  (Friuli Venezia Giulia)
Le Vigne di Zamò
  (Friuli Venezia Giulia)

**18**
Abbazia di Novacella (Alto Adige)
Antoniolo (Piedmont)
Brancaia (Tuscany)
Casanova di Neri (Tuscany)
Castello Banfi (Tuscany)
Conterno Fantino (Piedmont)
Firriato (Sicilia)
Livon (Friuli Venezia Giulia)
Masi (Veneto)
Massolino (Piedmont)
Mastroberardino (Campania)
Monsupello (Lombardy)
Cantina Convento Muri-Gries
  (Trentino Alto Adige)
Fiorenzo Nada (Piedmont)
Giuseppe Quintarelli (Veneto)
Bruno Rocca (Piedmont)
Ronco dei Tassi
  (Friuli Venezia Giulia)
San Patrignano (Emilia Romagna)
Luciano Sandrone (Piedmont)
Umani Ronchi (Marche)
Fattoria Zerbina
  (Emilia Romagna)

**17**
Roberto Anselmi (Veneto)
Lorenzo Begali (Veneto)
Coppo (Piedmont)
Kuenhof - Peter Pliger
  (Alto Adige)
Fattoria Petrolo (Tuscany)
Doro Princic
  (Friuli Venezia Giulia)
Querciabella (Tuscany)
Velenosi (Marche)

**16**
Cav. G. B. Bertani (Veneto)
Bucci (Marche)
Aldo Conterno (Piedmont)
Romano Dal Forno (Veneto)
Miani (Friuli Venezia Giulia)
La Monacesca (Marche)
Pietracupa (Campania)
Albino Rocca (Piedmont)
Suavia (Veneto)
Tenuta Unterortl - Castel Juval
  (Alto Adige)

**15**
Abbona (Piedmont)
Biondi - Santi Tenuta Greppo
  (Tuscany)
Cavit (Trentino)
Di Majo Norante (Molise)
Tenuta di Ghizzano (Tuscany)
Grattamacco (Tuscany)
Librandi (Calabria)

Lungarotti (Umbria)
Bartolo Mascarello (Piedmont)
Graziano Prà (Veneto)
Produttori del Barbaresco
 (Piedmont)
Rocca di Frassinello (Tuscany)
San Felice (Tuscany)
Tenuta Sant'Antonio (Veneto)
Speri (Veneto)
Vignalta (Veneto)
Viviani (Veneto)
Roberto Voerzio (Piedmont)

**14**

F.lli Alessandria (Piedmont)
Avignonesi (Tuscany)
Bricco Rocche - Bricco Asili
 (Piedmont)
Tenute Cisa Asinari dei Marchesi
 di Grésy (Piedmont)
Elvio Cogno (Piedmont)
Falkenstein Franz Pratzner
 (Alto Adige)
Ferghettina (Lombardy)
Dino Illuminati (Abruzzo)
Leone de Castris (Puglia)
Malvirà (Piedmont)
Franco M. Martinetti (Piedmont)
Sergio Mottura (Lazio)
Oasi degli Angeli (Marche)
Piaggia (Tuscany)
Fattoria Le Pupille (Tuscany)
Aldo Rainoldi (Lombardy)
Ronco del Gelso
 (Friuli Venezia Giulia)
Russiz Superiore
 (Friuli Venezia Giulia)
Uberti (Lombardy)
Valle Reale (Abruzzo)

**13**

Giulio Accornero e Figli (Piedmont)
Poderi Boscarelli (Tuscany)
Braida (Piedmont)
Pierguido Carlo Busso (Piedmont)
Ca' del Baio (Piedmont)
Cavalchina (Veneto)
Cavalleri (Lombardy)
Tenuta Col d'Orcia (Tuscany)
Eugenio Collavini
 (Friuli Venezia Giulia)
Le Due Terre
 (Friuli Venezia Giulia)
Poderi Luigi Einaudi (Piedmont)
Tenute Ambrogio e Giovanni
Folonari (Tuscany)
Foradori (Trentino)
Frescobaldi (Tuscany)
Elena Fucci (Basilicata)
Ettore Germano (Piedmont)
Gini (Veneto)
Edi Keber (Friuli Venezia Giulia)

Köfererhof - Günther Kerschbaumer
 (Alto Adige)
Cantina Kurtatsch (Alto Adige)
Maculan (Veneto)
Mamete Prevostini (Lombardy)
Marchesi di Barolo (Piedmont)
Vigneti Massa (Piedmont)
Monchiero Carbone (Piedmont)
Nals Margreid (Alto Adige)
Pecchenino (Piedmont)
Tormaresca (Puglia)
Tua Rita (Tuscany)
Tenuta di Valgiano (Tuscany)
Villa Medoro (Abruzzo)
Villa Sparina (Piedmont)
Zenato (Veneto)

**12**

Gianfranco Alessandria (Piedmont)
Azelia (Piedmont)
Brovia (Piedmont)
Cascina Ca' Rossa (Piedmont)
Castello dei Rampolla (Tuscany)
Castello di Albola (Tuscany)
Castello di Volpaia (Tuscany)
Còlpetrone (Umbria)
Dorigati (Trentino Alto Adige)
Cantine Due Palme (Puglia)
Galardi (Campania)
Cantina Girlan (Alto Adige)
Dario Raccaro
 (Friuli Venezia Giulia)
Rocche dei Manzoni (Piedmont)
Salvioni (Tuscany)
Torraccia del Piantavigna
 (Piedmont)
Torrevento (Puglia)

**11**

Abate Nero (Trentino)
Maison Anselmet (Valle d'Aosta)
Benanti (Sicilia)
Borgo San Daniele
 (Friuli Venezia Giulia)
Brigaldara (Veneto)
Cà Maiol (Lombardy)
F.lli Cigliuti (Piedmont)
Colle Massari (Tuscany)
Marisa Cuomo (Campania)
Fattoria del Cerro (Tuscany)
Guerrieri Rizzardi (Veneto)
Franz Haas (Alto Adige)
La Massa (Tuscany)
Mastrojanni (Tuscany)
Poderi e Cantine Oddero
 (Piedmont)
Pio Cesare (Piedmont)
Poggio di Sotto (Tuscany)
Prunotto (Piedmont)
Tenute Rubino (Puglia)
Giampaolo Tabarrini (Umbria)
G. D. Vajra (Piedmont)

**10**

Badia a Coltibuono (Tuscany)
Guido Berlucchi & C. (Lombardy)
Enzo Boglietti (Piedmont)
Bruna (Liguria)
I Campi (Veneto)
Tenuta di Capezzana (Tuscany)
Fattoria Carpineta Fontalpino
 (Tuscany)
Castello di Monsanto (Tuscany)
Cavallotto - Tenuta Bricco Boschis
 (Piedmont)
Tenute Chiaromonte (Puglia)
Cleto Chiarli Tenute Agricole
 (Emilia Romagna)
Colli di Lapio (Campania)
Corte Sant'Alda (Veneto)
Cottanera (Sicilia)
Fazi Battaglia (Marche)
Feudi del Pisciotto (Sicilia)
Feudo Maccari (Sicilia)
Fontanafredda (Piedmont)
Giuseppe Gabbas (Sardinia)
Giorgi (Lombardy)
Hilberg - Pasquero (Piedmont)
Tenuta J. Hofstätter (Alto Adige)
Alois Lageder (Alto Adige)
Lo Triolet (Valle d'Aosta)
Cantine Lunae Bosoni (Liguria)
Giuseppe Mascarello e Figlio
 (Piedmont)
Ermete Medici & Figli
 (Emilia Romagna)
Cantina Meran (Alto Adige)
Monte Rossa (Lombardy)
Orma (Tuscany)
Ottella (Veneto)
Poggio Antico (Tuscany)
Ruggeri & C. (Veneto)
Podere Sapaio (Tuscany)
Luigi Spertino (Piedmont)
Tenimenti Luigi d'Alessandro
 (Tuscany)
Tenuta delle Terre Nere (Sicilia)
Tiefenbrunner (Alto Adige)
Villa Matilde (Campania)
Tenuta Waldgries (Alto Adige)
Conti Zecca (Puglia)

# HOW TO USE THE GUIDE

## WINERY INFORMATION

ANNUAL PRODUCTION
HECTARES UNDER VINE
VITICULTURE METHOD

*N.B. The figures related here are provided annually by the producers.
The publisher is not responsible for eventual errors or inconsistencies.*

## SYMBOLS

○ WHITE WINE
⊙ ROSÈ
● RED WINE

## RATINGS

Ÿ MODERATELY GOOD TO GOOD WINES IN THEIR RESPECTIVE CATEGORIES
ŸŸ VERY GOOD TO EXCELLENT WINES IN THEIR RESPECTIVE CATEGORIES
ŸŸ VERY GOOD TO EXCELLENT WINES THAT WENT FORWARD TO THE FINAL TASTINGS
ŸŸŸ EXCELLENT WINES IN THEIR RESPECTIVE CATEGORIES

WINES RATED IN PREVIOUS EDITIONS OF THE GUIDE ARE INDICATED BY WHITE GLASSES (Ÿ, ŸŸ, ŸŸŸ),
PROVIDED THEY ARE STILL DRINKING AT THE LEVEL FOR WHICH THE ORIGINAL AWARD WAS MADE.

## STAR ★

INDICATES WINERIES THAT HAVE WON TEN TRE BICCHIERI AWARDS FOR EACH STAR

## PRICE RANGES

| | |
|---|---|
| 1 up to 5 euro | 2 from € 5.01 to € 10.00 |
| 3 from € 10.01 to € 15.00 | 4 from € 15.01 to € 20.00 |
| 5 from € 20.01 to € 30.00 | 6 from € 30.01 to € 40.00 |
| 7 from € 40.01 to € 50.00 | 8 more than € 50.01 |

PRICES INDICATED REFER TO AVERAGE PRICES IN WINE STORES

## ASTERISK *

INDICATES ESPECIALLY GOOD VALUE WINES

## ABBREVIATIONS

| | | | |
|---|---|---|---|
| A. A. | Alto Adige | P.R. | Peduncolo Rosso |
| C. | Colli | | (red bunchstem) |
| Cl. | Classico | P. | Prosecco |
| C.S. | Cantina Sociale | Rif. Agr. | Riforma Agraria |
| | (co-operative winery) | | (agrarian reform) |
| CEV | Colli Etruschi Viterbesi | Ris. | Riserva |
| Cons. | Consorzio | Sel. | Selezione |
| Coop.Agr. | Cooperativa Agricola | Sup. | Superiore |
| | (farming co-operative) | TdF | Terre di Franciacorta |
| C. B. | Colli Bolognesi | V. | Vigna (vineyard) |
| C. P. | Colli Piacentini | Vign. | Vigneto (vineyard) |
| Et. | Etichetta (label) | V. T. | Vendemmia Tardiva |
| FCO | Friuli Colli Orientali | | (late harvest) |
| M. | Metodo (method) | V. V. | Vecchia Vigna/Vecchie Vigne |
| M.to | Monferrato | | (old vine /old vines) |
| OP | Oltrepò Pavese | | |

# VALLE D'AOSTA

Aosta Valley remains a somewhat marginal wine producing region in Italy, with an average production volume of about two million liters. That is, if everything were to get bottled, it would amount to just over two and a half million bottles, significantly less than the largest national producers. What makes Aosta Valley truly unique is its geography. From Donnas to Courmayeur, it's impossible to find two territories that are alike. More than anything, the region offers a wide variety of cultivar, with native grapes and non-native varieties perfectly complementing one another. Among the reds, their succulent and powerful Syrahs and Fumins alternate with more multifaceted and delicate Pinot Noirs and Petit Rouges. Among the whites we see fresh Prié Blancs and Petite Arvines (a grape that's on the rise) serving as a counterpoint to more buttery Chardonnays and Malvoisies (Pinot Grigio). Its great variety comes from the enormous variability of its microclimates, brought about by the position of its vineyards (Envers is situated on the right bank of the Dora Baltea, with northeastern exposure, while Adret is the hotter and more well-suited area situated on the left bank, with southern or western exposure), their terrain and especially their elevation, with vineyards planted anywhere from 300 to over 1100 meters above sea level. This richness and variability represents the small region's true distinctive quality. After 2017, which was disastrous from a climatic point of view, the valley's vigneron are slowly recovering. After 2016 registered 2.1 million liters, 2017 saw just 1 million - that's a loss of 53%. We send out our encouragement to Blanc di Morgex et de La Salle, which saw an entire season of work go up in smoke. Some producers registered losses of 98%. In the 2019 edition of Italian Wines no new wineries from the region received awards but our tastings did see Anselmet back on top with their splendid selection of Chardonnay. The final count? Two Chardonnays, two Petite Arvines, a Fumin and a Moscato Passito. The nice surprise this year lies in the slow revival of Bassa Valle and Donnas, two areas we'll be sure to hear more from soon.

# VALLE D'AOSTA

## ★Maison Anselmet

FRAZ. VEREYTAZ, 30
11018 VILLENEUVE [AO]
TEL. +39 0165904851
www.maisonanselmet.it

CELLAR SALES
PRE-BOOKED VISITS
ANNUAL PRODUCTION 75,000 bottles
HECTARES UNDER VINE 11.00

Giorgio Anselmet's winery is situated in the prized winemaking territory of Torette, along the road leading to Monte Bianco. Here the Aosta Valley's traditional red wine is made according to tradition. Giorgio is a great interpreter of both the area's native cultivar and international varieties, such that Chardonnay serves the producer's cornerstone. His wines keep getting better, thanks to a recipe that brings together modern techniques and technology with the tradition that Renato, his father, was able to pass down. Their latest Chardonnay earns a Tre Bicchieri, with its aromas of vanilla and acacia blossom, aromatic herbs and apricot. It's a wine of great structure and balance, intense and truly long. Their Semel Pater is also noteworthy. A wine of impenetrable color, the nose is spicy and fruity, while the palate is potent. Their traditional Pinot Nero offers up fruity notes of wild strawberries and spices, with a truly full palate. Their Fumin also deserves mentioning.

| | |
|---|---|
| ○ Valle d'Aosta Chardonnay Main et Cœur '16 | ♟♟♟ 6 |
| ● Valle d'Aosta Pinot Noir Semel Pater '16 | ♟♟ 7 |
| ● Valle d'Aosta Pinot Noir Tradition '16 | ♟♟ 5 |
| ● Valle d'Aosta Fumin Élevé en Fût de Chêne '16 | ♟♟ 5 |
| ○ Valle d'Aosta Chardonnay Élevé en Fût de Chêne '15 | ♟♟♟ 5 |
| ○ Valle d'Aosta Chardonnay Élevé en Fût de Chêne '11 | ♟♟♟ 5 |
| ○ Valle d'Aosta Chardonnay Élevé en Fût de Chêne '10 | ♟♟♟ 5 |
| ○ Valle d'Aosta Chardonnay Élevé en Fût de Chêne '09 | ♟♟♟ 5 |
| ● Valle d'Aosta Pinot Noir Semel Pater '13 | ♟♟♟ 8 |

## Château Feuillet

LOC. CHÂTEAU FEUILLET, 12
11010 SAINT PIERRE
TEL. +39 3287673880
www.chateaufeuillet.vievini.it

CELLAR SALES
ACCOMMODATION AND RESTAURANT SERVICE
ANNUAL PRODUCTION 30,000 bottles
HECTARES UNDER VINE 5.00

Maurizio Fiorano doesn't need much introduction. Among the Aosta Valley's major wine producers he's one who's made his mark. Year after he year, he keeps improving the quality of his wines, which are made in one the region's best areas, northern Asta. Here the slopes have southern exposure, perfect both for white and red grapes. Most of his vineyards host native cultivar, but there have been successful experiments with international varieties as well. Once again, Maurizio didn't disappoint our expectations, with wines that delight the senses. Their Torrette Supérieur is a wine that exhibits typicity. Ruby red in color, it's redolent of dried prunes, while the palate is rich and pulpy, with slightly rough tannins, but it's long as well. Their Syrah delights the nose with its flowery aromas that call up violet, then fruit, giving way to a slightly vegetal finish. It shows good length on the palate. Their Fumin, a vibrant ruby garnet wine, offers up intense notes of raspberry, while the palate still needs some aging. Their Cornalin is a characteristic wine.

| | |
|---|---|
| ● Valle d'Aosta Torrette Sup. '16 | ♟♟ 3* |
| ● Valle d'Aosta Fumin '17 | ♟♟ 4 |
| ● Valle d'Aosta Syrah '17 | ♟♟ 3 |
| ● Valle d'Aosta Cornalin '17 | ♟ 4 |
| ○ Valle d'Aosta Petite Arvine '12 | ♟♟♟ 3* |
| ○ Valle d'Aosta Petite Arvine '11 | ♟♟♟ 3* |
| ○ Valle d'Aosta Petite Arvine '10 | ♟♟♟ 3* |
| ○ Valle d'Aosta Chardonnay '15 | ♟♟ 3 |
| ● Valle d'Aosta Cornalin '16 | ♟♟ 4 |
| ● Valle d'Aosta Fumin '16 | ♟♟ 4 |
| ○ Valle d'Aosta Petite Arvine '16 | ♟♟ 3 |
| ○ Valle d'Aosta Petite Arvine '15 | ♟♟ 3* |
| ● Valle d'Aosta Torrette Sup. '15 | ♟♟ 3 |
| ● Valle d'Aosta Torrette Sup. '14 | ♟♟ 3 |

# ★★Les Crêtes

LOC. VILLETOS, 50
11010 AYMAVILLES [AO]
TEL. +39 0165902274
www.lescretes.it

CELLAR SALES
PRE-BOOKED VISITS
ANNUAL PRODUCTION 180,000 bottles
HECTARES UNDER VINE 20.00
SUSTAINABLE WINERY

Costantino Charrère is one of the Aosta Valley's vine growing patriarchs. In his new cellar in Aymavilles, accompanied by his wife, Eleonora, and his collaborator in enology, Rafaela Crotta, he manages this solid winery of both national and international renown. His vineyards, which were hit by a brutal frost in 2017, host an array of grapes ranging from native cultivar like Petite Arvine, Petit Rouge and Fumin, and international varieties like Pinot Nero and Chardonnay (the last of which serves as the winery's flagship). They've also had excellent results with Nebbiolo, which is getting increasing attention of late. Once again their Chardonnay Cuvée Bois earns a Tre Bicchieri by virtue of its wide range of aromas. Vibrant notes of fruit close with a delicately spicy nuance, while in the mouth it's long and balanced. Their Nebbiolo Sommet also did very well, with its aromas of pleasant floral complexity giving way to notes of raspberry, harmonized by quinine and licorice. It's a fine, long wine. Their Syrah, Neige d'Or and Fumin also proved excellent.

| | |
|---|---|
| ○ Valle d'Aosta Chardonnay Cuvée Bois '16 | ♥♥♥ 6 |
| ● Valle d'Aosta Nebbiolo Sommet '16 | ♥♥ 6 |
| ● Valle d'Aosta Syrah '16 | ♥♥ 4 |
| ● Valle d'Aosta Fumin '16 | ♥♥ 4 |
| ○ Valle d'Aosta Neige D'Or '16 | ♥♥ 8 |
| ○ Valle d'Aosta Chardonnay Cuvée Bois '13 | ♡♡♡ 6 |
| ○ Valle d'Aosta Chardonnay Cuvée Bois '10 | ♡♡♡ 6 |
| ○ Valle d'Aosta Chardonnay Cuvée Bois '09 | ♡♡♡ 6 |
| ○ Valle d'Aosta Chardonnay Cuvée Bois '08 | ♡♡♡ 6 |
| ○ Valle d'Aosta Chardonnay Cuvée Bois '07 | ♡♡♡ 6 |
| ○ Valle d'Aosta Chardonnay Cuvée Bois '06 | ♡♡♡ 6 |
| ○ Valle d'Aosta Chardonnay Cuvée Frissonnière Les Crêtes Cuvée Bois '05 | ♡♡♡ 6 |
| ● Valle d'Aosta Nebbiolo Sommet '15 | ♡♡♡ 6 |
| ○ Valle d'Aosta Petite Arvine '13 | ♡♡♡ 3* |
| ● Valle d'Aosta Syrah Côteau La Tour '14 | ♡♡♡ 4* |

# La Crotta di Vegneron

P.ZZA RONCAS, 2
11023 CHAMBAVE [AO]
TEL. +39 016646670
www.lacrotta.it

CELLAR SALES
PRE-BOOKED VISITS
RESTAURANT SERVICE
ANNUAL PRODUCTION 350,000 bottles
HECTARES UNDER VINE 42.00

Chambave is a village just outside Aosta and its cooperative winery, Crotta di Vegneron, is one of the territory's most important. Some 120 grower members cover just over 40 hectares of small plots, all cultivated with passion and respect for tradition, but also under the agronomic guidance of the winery. Founded in 1980 (with the first bottles coming in 1985), from the beginning they've made wines with native grape varieties, Fumin, Cornalin, Vien de Nus and Petit Rouge, and local Moscato (a cultivar already appreciated at the time of the Savoias). Their Chambave passito is an appealing, straw-yellow and gold wine with pleasant aromas of yellow flowers and dried grapes. In the mouth it proves balanced and long. Their ruby garnet Syrah offers up vibrant aromas of black fruit, while its faint, vegetal sensations harmonize with spicy and delicate notes of wood. Their Moscato di Chambave leaves you with classic sensations, fruit with pleasant, tropical aromas that hover around varietal fragrances. of musk, which carry through fresh and elegant on the palate.

| | |
|---|---|
| ○ Valle d'Aosta Chambave Moscato Passito Prieuré '16 | ♥♥ 5 |
| ● Valle d'Aosta Syrah Crème '16 | ♥♥ 5 |
| ○ Valle d'Aosta Chambave Muscat '17 | ♥♥ 3 |
| ○ Valle d'Aosta Chambave Muscat Attente '14 | ♥♥ 4 |
| ○ Valle d'Aosta Chambave Moscato Passito Prieuré '15 | ♡♡♡ 5 |
| ○ Valle d'Aosta Chambave Moscato Passito Prieuré '13 | ♡♡♡ 5 |
| ○ Valle d'Aosta Chambave Moscato Passito Prieuré '12 | ♡♡♡ 5 |
| ○ Valle d'Aosta Chambave Moscato Passito Prieuré '11 | ♡♡♡ 5 |
| ○ Valle d'Aosta Chambave Moscato Passito Prieuré '08 | ♡♡♡ 5 |
| ● Valle d'Aosta Fumin Esprit Follet '09 | ♡♡♡ 3 |

## Caves Cooperatives de Donnas

VIA ROMA, 97
11020 DONNAS [AO]
TEL. +39 0125807096
www.donnasvini.it

CELLAR SALES
PRE-BOOKED VISITS
ANNUAL PRODUCTION 150,000 bottles
HECTARES UNDER VINE 26.00

Cave Cooperative's vineyards are some of the first you'll see upon entering Aosta Valley. Here vine growing traditions are deeply tied to those of nearby Piedmont. Indeed, the primary grape cultivated is Nebbiolo (locally known as Picotendro or Picutener). The cooperative is masterfully managed by Mario Dalbar who, in recent years, has managed to maintain their wines' quality and character. Indeed, in 1971 Donnas was named Aosta Valley's first appellation (now it's a subzone of the regional DOC zone). The quality of Donnas' wine is a constant over time. Their 2014 Vieilles Vignes is pleasant on the nose, with spicy hints of new wood and aromas of red fruit, as well as a strong accent of raspberry. It's also unusually fresh in the mouth. In short, it's a modern wine. Their Donnas, which features a lovely, ruby garnet color, is pleasant on the nose, with notes of tobacco and rhubarb standing out. In the mouth it's marked by a long, fine finish. Their Napoléon is also worth nothing, with its hints of medicinal herbs and red fruit, as well as its crisp, long palate.

| | |
|---|---|
| ● Valle d'Aosta Donnas Sup. Vieilles Vignes '14 | ▼▼ 5 |
| ● Valle d'Aosta Donnas '15 | ▼▼ 4 |
| ● Valle d'Aosta Donnas Napoléon '15 | ▼▼ 5 |
| ● Valle d'Aosta Donnas '14 | ♀♀ 4 |
| ● Valle d'Aosta Donnas '13 | ♀♀ 4 |
| ● Valle d'Aosta Donnas '11 | ♀♀ 2* |
| ● Valle d'Aosta Donnas Napoléon '14 | ♀♀ 5 |
| ● Valle d'Aosta Donnas Napoléon '13 | ♀♀ 5 |
| ● Valle d'Aosta Donnas Napoléon '11 | ♀♀ 3 |
| ● Valle d'Aosta Donnas Napoléon '10 | ♀♀ 3 |
| ● Valle d'Aosta Donnas Sup. V. V. '13 | ♀♀ 5 |
| ● Valle d'Aosta Donnas Sup. V. V. '12 | ♀♀ 5 |
| ● Valle d'Aosta Donnas Sup. V. V. '07 | ♀♀ 4 |
| ● Valle d'Aosta Donnas V. V. '09 | ♀♀ 4 |

## Cave Gargantua

FRAZ. CLOS CHATEL, 1
11020 GRESSAN [AO]
TEL. +39 3299271999
www.cavegargantua.it

ANNUAL PRODUCTION 20,000 bottles
HECTARES UNDER VINE 4.00

Gressan is a small municipality just outside Aosta. Over the town stands a mountain that, as legend has it, is the pinky finger of the giant Gargantua. It was here, along these slopes, that the Cuneaz brothers' passion for wine was kindled. To quote Laurent, 'Here my grandfather passed down his love of the land, showing me how important time dedicated to the vineyard is.' The Cuneaz family is strongly attached to (and respectful of) the territory, its tradition, as well as the Aosta Valley's culture and customs. Through this lens this small producer gives rise to their entire selection. Their Torrette Supérieur is a truly interesting wine with aromas of red berries and tobacco. On the palate it proves extraordinarily elegant and balanced. Their Impasse is a notable blend in which fruity notes harmonize with spices and a final hint of licorice. Their Daphne exhibits pleasant complexity, with aromas of vanilla and white fruit. Their Spillo d'Oro is a new botrytised wine. It's good but still not balanced.

| | |
|---|---|
| ● Valle d'Aosta Rosso Impasse '15 | ▼▼ 5 |
| ● Valle d'Aosta Torrette Sup. Labiè '16 | ▼▼ 4 |
| ○ Valle d'Aosta Chardonnay Daphne '16 | ▼▼ 5 |
| ○ Spillo d'Oro | ▼ 5 |
| ● Daphne '15 | ♀♀ 5 |
| ○ Gargantua Blanc | ♀♀ 4 |
| ● Valle d'Aosta Pinot Noir '16 | ♀♀ 3* |
| ● Vin de la Fée '16 | ♀♀ 5 |

# ★Lo Triolet

LOC. JUNOD, 7
11010 INTROD [AO]
TEL. +39 016595437
www.lotriolet.vievini.it

CELLAR SALES
PRE-BOOKED VISITS
ANNUAL PRODUCTION 42,000 bottles
HECTARES UNDER VINE 5.00

Introd is a small town just outside Aosta, on the road that takes you to the region's great mountains. Marco Martin's vineyards are situated right here, with Pinot Grigio taking center stage. Attentive to local customs and traditions, he's managed to make wines using the Aosta Valley's celebrated local cultivar in a modern way, even if international varieties also find a place in his selection (especially Syrah). In recent years the estate has seen major renovations, first the vineyards and then the cellar, and Marco has just finished work on his reception space and gorgeous tasting area. Their vibrantly colored Fumin is rich on the notes with aromas of red and black fruit and spicy hints. Cocoa and tobacco confer complexity, giving way to a rich, pulpy palate. Their Pinot Gris is truly delicious, vibrant and elegant in its fragrances of white fruit, with pineapple and pear standing out. The palate is balanced and well-structured. Their Petite Arvine is interesting, with its notes of fresh fruit and citrus, as well as its balanced palate. Their Pinot Grigio, which is matured in barriques, is also a quality wine.

| | | |
|---|---|---|
| ● Valle d'Aosta Fumin '16 | ♀♀♀ | 5 |
| ○ Valle d'Aosta Petite Arvine '17 | ♀♀ | 5 |
| ○ Valle d'Aosta Pinot Gris '17 | ♀♀ | 5 |
| ○ Valle d'Aosta Pinot Gris Élevé en Barriques '16 | ♀♀ | 6 |
| ○ Valle d'Aosta Pinot Gris '16 | ♀♀♀ | 5 |
| ○ Valle d'Aosta Pinot Gris '15 | ♀♀♀ | 5 |
| ○ Valle d'Aosta Pinot Gris '14 | ♀♀♀ | 3* |
| ○ Valle d'Aosta Pinot Gris '13 | ♀♀♀ | 3* |
| ○ Valle d'Aosta Pinot Gris '12 | ♀♀♀ | 3* |
| ○ Valle d'Aosta Pinot Gris '09 | ♀♀♀ | 3 |
| ○ Valle d'Aosta Pinot Gris '08 | ♀♀♀ | 3* |
| ○ Valle d'Aosta Pinot Gris Élevé en Barriques '10 | ♀♀♀ | 5 |

# Cave Mont Blanc de Morgex et La Salle

FRAZ. LA RUINE
CHEMIN DES ÎLES, 31
11017 MORGEX [AO]
TEL. +39 0165800331
www.caveduvinblanc.com

CELLAR SALES
PRE-BOOKED VISITS
ANNUAL PRODUCTION 140,000 bottles
HECTARES UNDER VINE 19.00

Blanc de Morgex is a regional cultural patrimony. Here Prie Blanc (still ungrafted) takes center stage across Europe's highest appellation, with the grapes clinging onto the slopes of Monte Bianco. It was Don Bougeat who began work in 1989, and today the producer continues to bring renown to all of Valdigne; vintages alternate, but their quality persists. A particularly complex season lowered yields, allowing for a limited selection, but in their quaint Morgex winery, made with wood and stone, the work continues with rugged tenacity. Cave's sparkling wines were tasted, all Metodo Classicos. Their Cuvée Prince features fine perlage and vibrant fragrances redolent of bread crust. It's a fruity wine with hints of damson that proves elegant and long on the palate. Their Extra Brut offers up a rich nose that's pleasant in its hints of yeast, biscuits and sensations of honey. In the mouth it's fresh and savory. Their Blanc du Blanc is a taut, vibrant wine with hints of white fruit. Their Glacier features long perlage, aromas of yeast and ripe white fruit, and a close-focused, fresh palate.

| | | |
|---|---|---|
| ○ Valle d'Aosta Blanc de Morgex et de La Salle Brut Blanc du Blanc M. Cl. '15 | ♀♀ | 4 |
| ○ Valle d'Aosta Blanc de Morgex et de La Salle Brut Nature Cuvée du Prince M. Cl. '11 | ♀♀ | 2* |
| ○ Valle d'Aosta Blanc de Morgex et de La Salle Extra Brut X.T. M.Cl. '15 | ♀♀ | 6 |
| ○ Valle d'Aosta Blanc de Morgex et de La Salle Extra Brut Glacier M. Cl. '16 | ♀ | 5 |
| ○ Valle d'Aosta Blanc de Morgex et de La Salle Extra Brut M. Cl. Glacier '14 | ♀♀ | 5 |
| ○ Valle d'Aosta Blanc de Morgex et de La Salle Vini Estremi '16 | ♀♀ | 3 |

# Elio Ottin

Fraz. Porossan Neyves, 209
11100 Aosta
Tel. +39 3474071331
www.ottinvini.it

**CELLAR SALES**
**PRE-BOOKED VISITS**
**ANNUAL PRODUCTION** 30,000 bottles
**HECTARES UNDER VINE** 4.50
**SUSTAINABLE WINERY**

It took Elio Ottin just over ten years to vault his winery into the higher echelons of Italy's winemakers. Since 2007, Elio has cultivated his vineyards just outside of Aosta, on the road sloping up towards Roisan and Gran San Bernardo. Most of their selection is dedicated to local cultivar, Petit Rouge, Fumin and Petite Arvine (this last is a bonafide flagship), with some space made for international varieties, especially Pinot Nero. They're all interpreted according to tradition, though with sensitivity and intelligence so as to avoid needless excess. For some years now Elio's son, Nicolas, has been following in his footsteps. Once again their Petite Arvine earns a Tre Bicchieri. It's a wine with vibrant aromas of citrus and mountain herbs with a delicate, mineral finish. In the mouth it proves fine, with pleasant savoriness. Their Torrette Supérieur exhibits great typicity. It's an intense wine with a fruity nose and elegant palate. The Fumin is an impenetrably colored wine with aromas of pepper and vegetal notes harmonized by a faint hint of mulberry. Their Pinot Nero also proved excellent.

| | |
|---|---|
| ○ Valle d'Aosta Petite Arvine '17 | ▼▼▼ 4* |
| ● Valle d'Aosta Fumin '16 | ▼▼ 5 |
| ● Valle d'Aosta Pinot Noir '16 | ▼▼ 4 |
| ● Valle d'Aosta Torrette Sup. '16 | ▼▼ 5 |
| ● Valle d'Aosta Fumin '12 | ♀♀♀ 3* |
| ○ Valle d'Aosta Petite Arvine '16 | ♀♀♀ 5 |
| ○ Valle d'Aosta Petite Arvine '15 | ♀♀♀ 5 |
| ○ Valle d'Aosta Petite Arvine '14 | ♀♀♀ 4* |
| ○ Valle d'Aosta Petite Arvine '12 | ♀♀♀ 3* |
| ○ Valle d'Aosta Petite Arvine '11 | ♀♀♀ 3* |
| ○ Valle d'Aosta Petite Arvine '10 | ♀♀♀ 3* |
| ● Valle d'Aosta Fumin '15 | ♀♀ 5 |
| ● Valle d'Aosta Pinot Noir '15 | ♀♀ 4 |

# Ermes Pavese

s.da Pineta, 26
11017 Morgex [AO]
Tel. +39 0165800053
www.ermespavese.it

**CELLAR SALES**
**PRE-BOOKED VISITS**
**ANNUAL PRODUCTION** 35,000 bottles
**HECTARES UNDER VINE** 5.00

In Morgex they will surely remember 2017 as a terrible year that destroyed practically an entire harvest. This year Ermes Pavese didn't present his Blanc de Morgex Classico. And so we will wait patiently in the hopes that next year will be more merciful to Morgex's vine growers. Naturally, the producer remains a sparkling winemaker, putting forward some bonafide pearls of Metodo Classico. Pavese is a truly gifted winemaker. Their Metodo Classico aged on the lees for 36 months is a delicious wine with extremely fine and long perlage. On the nose it offers up vibrant, mineral fragrances and notes of mountain herbs. In the mouth it's savory, fresh and long. We also point out their Ninive, a wine made with overripe grapes that's delicately sweet and balanced, and their vibrant, fine Sette Scalinate, which features aromas redolent of mountain flowers and a delicate minerality.

| | |
|---|---|
| ○ Valle d'Aoste Blanc de Morgex et de La Salle Pavese XXXVI Pas Dosé M. Cl. '13 | ▼▼ 5 |
| ○ Ninive | ▼▼ 6 |
| ○ Valle d'Aosta Vin Blanc de Morgex et La Salle Le Sette Scalinate Carlo Pavese '14 | ▼▼ 4 |
| ○ Valle d'Aosta Vin Blanc de Morgex et La Salle Nathan '16 | ▼▼ 5 |
| ○ Valle d'Aosta Vin Blanc de Morgex et La Salle '16 | ♀♀ 4 |
| ○ Valle d'Aosta Vin Blanc de Morgex et La Salle '15 | ♀♀ 4 |
| ○ Valle d'Aosta Vin Blanc de Morgex et La Salle Nathan '15 | ♀♀ 5 |
| ○ Valle d'Aosta Vin Blanc de Morgex et La Salle Pavese Pas Dosé M.Cl. XVIII '14 | ♀♀ 5 |

# Rosset Terroir

LOC. TORRENT DE MAILLOD, 4
11020 QUART [AO]
TEL. +39 0165774111
www.rosseterroir.it

**CELLAR SALES**
**PRE-BOOKED VISITS**
**ANNUAL PRODUCTION** 30,000 bottles
**HECTARES UNDER VINE** 3.00

Since 2001 the Rosset family have cultivated their private vineyards, three small plots in various parts of the region. Their terrain in Sant Cristophe hosts Chardonnay, Cornalin and Petit Rouge. In Chambave we find Moscato, while at their most recent acquisition in Villeneuve they cultivate Petite Arvine and Pinot Grigio. Nicola Rosset oversees one of the region's most modern and innovative wineries, a perfect testament to how a bond with the territory serves as the basis for a producer's success. Their Sopraquota debuts splendidly. It's a Petit Arvine cultivated at 900 meters above sea level, an elevation not considered by DOC protocols. It offers up elegant aromas of fruit and vegetal hints. In the mouth it's extremely balanced, fresh and long. Their Cornalin is a pleasant, fruity and floral wine with nice typicity that's balanced on the palate. Their Pinot Gris, a brilliantly colored wine with copper highlights, is also quite interesting, with a nose redolent of pears and damson, and a fresh, clean mouth. Their Chardonnay is also worth noting.

| | |
|---|---|
| ○ Sopraquota 900 | ♛♛♛ 4* |
| ● Valle d'Aosta Cornalin '17 | ♛♛ 4 |
| ○ Vallée d'Aoste Pinot Gris '17 | ♛♛ 5 |
| ○ Valle d'Aosta Chardonnay '17 | ♛♛ 4 |
| ● Valle d'Aosta Cornalin '16 | ♛♛♛ 4* |
| ● Valle d'Aosta Cornalin '15 | ♛♛♛ 4* |
| ● Valle d'Aosta Syrah '13 | ♛♛♛ 4* |
| ○ Valle d'Aosta Chambave Muscat '16 | ♛♛ 4 |
| ○ Valle d'Aosta Chardonnay '16 | ♛♛ 4 |
| ○ Valle d'Aosta Chardonnay '14 | ♛♛ 4 |
| ● Valle d'Aosta Cornalin '14 | ♛♛ 4 |
| ● Valle d'Aosta Syrah '15 | ♛♛ 4 |
| ● Valle d'Aosta Syrah '14 | ♛♛ 4 |

# La Vrille

LOC. GRANGEON, 1
11020 VERRAYES [AO]
TEL. +39 0166543018
www.lavrille-agritourisme.com

**CELLAR SALES**
**PRE-BOOKED VISITS**
**ACCOMMODATION AND RESTAURANT SERVICE**
**ANNUAL PRODUCTION** 16,000 bottles
**HECTARES UNDER VINE** 2.40
**SUSTAINABLE WINERY**

Despite the difficult year, Hervè Deguillame hasn't lost spirit. Production volumes may have decreased but not the quality we've grown used to. Hervè moved to the Aosta Valley in 1990 after eight years as a sailor. His family roots go back to the area, and he found his calling working the land and vineyards here. During the 1990s he planted his first plots and since then he's proved to be a splendid interpreter of the territory's traditional grape, Moscato Bianco. Flétri's great quality is by now a certainty. It's a lovely, gold-colored wine that features aromas of dried raisin and fruit, great harmony and finesse, and an extraordinarily well-balanced palate. Their Cornalin, a vibrant ruby wine, features great character and personality, elegant fragrances ranging from wild berries, a captivating hint of bark and flowers. In the mouth it comes through balanced and fine. Their Muscat offers up aromatic, fine fragrances of musk, fresh grape and fruit. In the mouth it's very elegant, balanced and long.

| | |
|---|---|
| ○ Valle d'Aosta Chambave Muscat Flétri '16 | ♛♛♛ 7 |
| ○ Valle d'Aosta Chambave Muscat '16 | ♛♛ 5 |
| ● Valle d'Aosta Cornalin '16 | ♛♛ 4 |
| ● Valle d'Aosta Fumin '14 | ♛♛ 6 |
| ○ Valle d'Aosta Chambave Muscat '12 | ♛♛♛ 4* |
| ○ Valle d'Aosta Chambave Muscat Flétri '15 | ♛♛♛ 7 |
| ○ Valle d'Aosta Chambave Muscat Flétri '14 | ♛♛♛ 7 |
| ○ Valle d'Aosta Chambave Muscat Flétri '11 | ♛♛♛ 6 |
| ○ Valle d'Aosta Chambave Muscat Flétri '10 | ♛♛♛ 5 |
| ○ Valle d'Aosta Chambave Muscat Flétri '07 | ♛♛♛ 4* |

## Di Barrò

LOC. CHÂTEAU FEUILLET, 8
11010 SAINT PIERRE
TEL. +39 0165903671
www.dibarro.vievini.it

CELLAR SALES
PRE-BOOKED VISITS
ANNUAL PRODUCTION 20,000 bottles
HECTARES UNDER VINE 2.50

| | |
|---|---|
| ● Valle d'Aosta Mayolet '16 | ♟♟ 3 |
| ○ Valle d'Aosta Pinot Gris '16 | ♟♟ 4 |
| ● Valle d'Aosta Torrette Sup. '15 | ♟♟ 5 |
| ○ Lo Flapì | ♟ 5 |

## Feudo di San Maurizio

FRAZ. MAILLOD, 44
11010 SARRE [AO]
TEL. +39 3383186831
www.vinievino.com

CELLAR SALES
PRE-BOOKED VISITS
ANNUAL PRODUCTION 40,000 bottles
HECTARES UNDER VINE 7.00

| | |
|---|---|
| ● Pierrots | ♟♟ 5 |
| ○ Valle d'Aosta Chardonnay '16 | ♟♟ 3 |
| ● Valle d'Aosta Cornalin '17 | ♟♟ 4 |
| ○ XXII Settembre | ♟ 6 |

## Grosjean

FRAZ. OLLIGNAN, 2
11020 QUART [AO]
TEL. +39 0165775791
www.grosjeanvins.it

CELLAR SALES
PRE-BOOKED VISITS
ANNUAL PRODUCTION 120,000 bottles
HECTARES UNDER VINE 12.00
VITICULTURE METHOD Certified Organic

| | |
|---|---|
| ● Valle d'Aosta Cornalin V. Rovettaz '16 | ♟♟ 5 |
| ● Valle d'Aosta Fumin V. Rovettaz '14 | ♟♟ 5 |
| ⊙ Montmarye Extra Brut Rosé M. Cl. | ♟ 6 |
| ○ Valle d'Aosta Petite Arvine V. Rovettaz '17 | ♟ 4 |

## Institut Agricole Régional

LOC. RÉGION LA ROCHÈRE, 1A
11100 AOSTA
TEL. +39 0165215811
www.iaraosta.it

CELLAR SALES
PRE-BOOKED VISITS
ANNUAL PRODUCTION 50,000 bottles
HECTARES UNDER VINE 7.30

| | |
|---|---|
| ● Valle d'Aosta Fumin '15 | ♟♟ 4 |
| ○ Valle d'Aosta Pinot Gris '17 | ♟♟ 3 |
| ○ Valle d'Aosta Petite Arvine '17 | ♟ 4 |

## Pianta Grossa

VIA ROMA, 123
11020 DONNAS [AO]
TEL. +39 3480077404
www.piantagrossadonnas.it

ANNUAL PRODUCTION 10,000 bottles
HECTARES UNDER VINE 2.00

| | |
|---|---|
| ● Valle d'Aosta Donnas Georgos '15 | ♟♟ 6 |
| ● Valle d'Aosta Nebbiolo 396 '16 | ♟♟ 5 |
| ● Valle d'Aosta Nebbiolo Dessus '16 | ♟♟ 5 |

## La Source

LOC. BUSSAN DESSOUS, 1
11010 SAINT PIERRE
TEL. +39 0165904038
www.lasource.it

CELLAR SALES
PRE-BOOKED VISITS
ANNUAL PRODUCTION 40,000 bottles
HECTARES UNDER VINE 7.00

| | |
|---|---|
| ● Valle d'Aosta Torrette Sup. '14 | ♟♟ 3 |
| ○ Valle d'Aosta Petite Arvine '16 | ♟ 3 |
| ● Valle d'Aosta Torrette '15 | ♟ 3 |

# PIEDMONT

After 51 Nebbiolos were awarded Tre Bicchieri in the 2018 edition of Italian Wines (just over 66% of the wines recognized that year), 2019 saw a slight dip. This year 43 Nebbiolos (58%) earned our highest honors, a good number considering that 2014 was a tough year for Barolo. Rather than being indicative of Nebbiolo's waning importance, however, it's a sign of Piedmont's overall vitality, foremost when it comes to Langhe, an area that's enjoying international attention. But one thing is for sure, both in terms of wine-growing and tourism, Piedmont is on the march. There are a number of points worth considering here. For example, it's interesting how the region is reasserting its role as Metodo Classico's birthland. For too long the name 'Alta Langa' hasn't received enough visibility, but today, finally, the work of promotion has begun, bringing together under a single brand the best of southern Piedmont's classic sparkling wines. For the first time some four cuvées took home Tre Bicchieri (only one displays 'Alta Langa' on the label, but the others will soon too). It's also worth noting the lovely overall performance put in by northern Piedmont, with a Canavese white (Erbaluce di Caluso) and six Nebbiolos (two Gattinaras, two Ghemmes, a Fara and a Coste della Sesia Nebbiolo) all earning top marks. Among the reds awarded, we see more readily enjoyable wines consolidating their presence, like Antoniotti's 2015 Nebbiolo, which stole the crown from the producer's more well-known 2014 Bramaterra. Another consideration is the splendid performance of the region's most planted cultivar, Barbera. Thanks to a trio of good years (with 2015 and 2017 proving particularly hot and dry) the grape served as the basis for 12 Tre Bicchieri, from Albese to Casalese and the subzone of Nizza Monferrato. And two 2017 Barberas stand out, Coppo's Avvocata and Pico Maccario's Lavignone, which beat out their respective producers' more well-known offerings. Finally, hats off to the eight neophytes that earned our highest honors for the first time: Negretti, Facchino, Roberto Ferraris, Isolabella della Croce, ColomboCascina Pastori, Boniperti, Ioppa and La Raia. And Piedmont also earned our award for the 'Sweet of the Year' thanks to La Bella Estate di Vite Colte's Moscato Passito.

## 460 Casina Bric

LOC. CASCINA BRICCO
FRAZ. VERGNE
VIA SORELLO, 1A
12060 BAROLO [CN]
TEL. +39 335283468
www.casinabric-barolo.it

CELLAR SALES
PRE-BOOKED VISITS
ANNUAL PRODUCTION 45,000 bottles
HECTARES UNDER VINE 10.00

Even if 460 Casina Bric is a young winery, Gianluca Viberti manages to produce something newsworthy every year. First off, it's important to note that as of the 2018 vintage their new cellar in Serralunga d'Alba will be operational. As a result, next year we'll have the chance to taste a new Barolo. Also, they've just released a Metodo Classico sparkling wine made exclusively with Nebbiolo and sold only in magnum bottles. Their two Barolos cultivated in Vergne prove rich in personality and luster while their Bricco delle Viole is once again at the top of its game. Delicate and subtle notes of oak come together with ripe but not overly ripe fruit in their 2014 Barolo Bricco delle Viole. Their enjoyable 2014 Barolo from Serralunga d'Alba exhibits commendable balance, without too much force. They continue to pursue sparkling wines made with Nebbiolo and the results are undoubtedly interesting, with a 2014 Rosé Brut Nature that's sold only in magnums.

| | | |
|---|---|---|
| ● Barolo Bricco delle Viole '14 | ♙♙ | 7 |
| ● Barolo del Comune di Serralunga d'Alba '14 | ♙♙ | 6 |
| ⊙ Nebbiolo d'Alba Brut M. Cl. Rosé '14 | ♙♙ | 5 |
| ● Langhe Rosso Ansj '16 | ♙ | 4 |
| ⊙ Nebbiolo d'Alba Brut Rosè Prêt-à-Porter Collezione N°8 | ♙ | 4 |
| ● Ansì '14 | ♘♘ | 4 |
| ● Ansj '11 | ♘♘ | 4 |
| ● Barolo '13 | ♘♘ | 6 |
| ● Barolo '12 | ♘♘ | 6 |
| ● Barolo '11 | ♘♘ | 6 |
| ● Barolo '10 | ♘♘ | 6 |
| ● Barolo Bricco delle Viole '13 | ♘♘ | 7 |
| ● Barolo Bricco delle Viole '11 | ♘♘ | 7 |
| ● Barolo Bricco delle Viole '10 | ♘♘ | 7 |

## ★Abbona

B.GO SAN LUIGI, 40
12063 DOGLIANI [CN]
TEL. +39 0173721317
www.abbona.com

CELLAR SALES
PRE-BOOKED VISITS
ANNUAL PRODUCTION 350,000 bottles
HECTARES UNDER VINE 50.00

Marziano Abbona is famous for his Dogliani Papà Celso, in addition to being known as one of Viognier's great interpreters thanks to his Cinerino. And he continues to show the same level of commitment with his Barolos, which keep getting better, to the point where his Ravera, Cerviano and Pressendas have earned well-deserved praise, even abroad. The cellar is particularly charming and we strongly suggest that wine lovers pay it a visit, both for its lovely architecture and for its barrels, which are spectacular in and of themselves. The best version yet (that we can remember) of their Nebbiolo d'Alba Bricco Barone shouldn't be missed. It's a pleasantly plush 2016 with great structure and excellent, silky mouthfeel. There's good news from their 2013 Extra Brut Rosé as well. Made primarily with Pinot Nero, it's a close-focused wine in its delicate hints of red fruit and yeast. Their exquisite, tight and almondy 2017 Papà Celso is a wine worthy of Tre Bicchieri. 2014 also saw a small selection of Barolos, but these weren't submitted for tasting.

| | | |
|---|---|---|
| ● Dogliani Papà Celso '17 | ♙♙♙ | 4* |
| ● Nebbiolo d'Alba Bricco Barone '16 | ♙♙ | 4 |
| ● Barbera d'Alba Rinaldi '16 | ♙♙ | 4 |
| ○ Langhe Bianco Cinerino '17 | ♙♙ | 5 |
| ⊙ Marziano Abbona Extra Brut Rosé '13 | ♙♙ | 5 |
| ● Barolo Cerviano '10 | ♘♘♘ | 7 |
| ● Barolo Terlo Ravera '08 | ♘♘♘ | 6 |
| ● Barolo Terlo Ravera '06 | ♘♘♘ | 6 |
| ● Dogliani Papà Celso '16 | ♘♘♘ | 4* |
| ● Dogliani Papà Celso '15 | ♘♘♘ | 4* |
| ● Dogliani Papà Celso '13 | ♘♘♘ | 4* |
| ● Dogliani Papà Celso '11 | ♘♘♘ | 3* |
| ● Dogliani Papà Celso '09 | ♘♘♘ | 3 |
| ● Dogliani Papà Celso '07 | ♘♘♘ | 3 |
| ● Dogliani Papà Celso '06 | ♘♘♘ | 3 |
| ● Dogliani Papà Celso '05 | ♘♘♘ | 3* |

# Anna Maria Abbona

FRAZ. MONCUCCO, 21
12060 FARIGLIANO [CN]
TEL. +39 0173797228
www.annamariaabbona.it

**CELLAR SALES**
**PRE-BOOKED VISITS**
**ANNUAL PRODUCTION** 75,000 bottles
**HECTARES UNDER VINE** 20.00

Maria Abbona, a passionate vine grower, isn't that worried about climate change. Her vineyards are situated at elevations that often surpass 500 meters. These give rise to her consistently fresh, aromatically selection of wines made primarily with Dolcetto. The winery is family-run, with her husband, Franco Schellino, active in the vineyards and in the cellar and her son Federico also involved in production. Their Dogliani are on center stage, once again proving valid and faithful to each vintage, but their Barolo di Monforte also put in a good performance. And their 2014 Bricco San Pietro demonstrates this well. It's a particularly close-focused wine that's generous in its classic notes of licorice and golden-leaf tobacco. In the mouth it's big with pronounced tannic presence. Their linear 2014 Barolo is just a bit simpler. In a selection in which all their Dolcettos are quite valid, their 2015 Dogliani Superiore San Bernardo stands out. It's endowed with splendid fruit while on the nose it elegantly brings together quinine and sweet spices.

| | | |
|---|---|---|
| ● Barolo Bricco San Pietro '14 | 🍷🍷 | 6 |
| ● Dogliani Sup. San Bernardo '15 | 🍷🍷 | 4 |
| ● Barbera d'Alba '17 | 🍷🍷 | 2* |
| ● Barolo '14 | 🍷🍷 | 6 |
| ● Dogliani Sorì Dij But '17 | 🍷🍷 | 2* |
| ● Dogliani Sup. Maioli '16 | 🍷🍷 | 3 |
| ● Langhe Dolcetto '17 | 🍷🍷 | 2* |
| ○ Langhe Nascetta Netta '16 | 🍷🍷 | 3 |
| ○ Langhe Riesling L'Alman '16 | 🍷 | 3 |
| ● Dogliani Sup. San Bernardo '12 | 🍷🍷🍷 | 4* |
| ● Dogliani Sup. San Bernardo '11 | 🍷🍷🍷 | 4* |
| ● Barbera d'Alba '16 | 🍷🍷 | 2* |
| ● Barolo '13 | 🍷🍷 | 6 |
| ● Dogliani Sorì dij But '16 | 🍷🍷 | 2* |
| ● Dogliani Sup. Maioli '15 | 🍷🍷 | 3 |
| ● Langhe Nebbiolo '14 | 🍷🍷 | 3 |
| ● Langhe Rosso Cadò '13 | 🍷🍷 | 5 |

# F.lli Abrigo

LOC. BERFI
VIA MOGLIA GERLOTTO, 2
12055 DIANO D'ALBA [CN]
TEL. +39 017369104
www.abrigofratelli.com

**CELLAR SALES**
**PRE-BOOKED VISITS**
**ANNUAL PRODUCTION** 100,000 bottles
**HECTARES UNDER VINE** 27.00

The Abrigo family's bond with the territory is deep, and so their production center is situated in Dolcetto di Diano d'Alba. But their size also allows them to offer a varied and interesting selection of wines. These range from Langhe Arneis to Barbera d'Alba and Alta Langa Sivà, a pleasant Brut made with Chardonnay. Their Sorì dei Berfi continues to prove fresh and highly drinkable, while their Pietrin is rounder and richer, availing itself of a subtle stay in wood barrels. Since 2013 their new vineyard in Novello has had a part in their selection, giving rise to a Barolo Ravera that's aged in large wood barrels. The 2014 of this Barolo features aromas of herbs in the sun, while on the palate it's characterized by delicate, close-woven tannins that boost its overall presence. Their 2016 Diano d'Alba Superiore is a wine that we strongly recommend to those who still aren't familiar with the potential of Dolcetto. It's an elegant, rich, fresh wine that's also highly enjoyable.

| | | |
|---|---|---|
| ● Barolo Ravera '14 | 🍷🍷 | 7 |
| ● Diano d'Alba Sup. '16 | 🍷🍷 | 3* |
| ● Barbera d'Alba Sup. '16 | 🍷🍷 | 3 |
| ● Dolcetto di Diano d'Alba '17 | 🍷🍷 | 2* |
| ● Nebbiolo d'Alba '16 | 🍷🍷 | 3 |
| ○ Alta Langa Brut Sivà '13 | 🍷🍷 | 4 |
| ● Barolo Ravera '13 | 🍷🍷 | 6 |
| ● Diano d'Alba Sorì dei Berfi '16 | 🍷🍷 | 3 |
| ● Diano d'Alba Sorì dei Berfi '15 | 🍷🍷 | 3* |
| ● Diano d'Alba Sörì dei Berfi '14 | 🍷🍷 | 2* |
| ● Diano d'Alba Sup. Pietrin '13 | 🍷🍷 | 3 |
| ● Diano d'Alba Sup. Pietrin '12 | 🍷🍷 | 3 |
| ● Dolcetto di Diano d'Alba Sup. Pietrin '15 | 🍷🍷 | 3 |
| ● Nebbiolo d'Alba Tardiss '15 | 🍷🍷 | 3 |
| ● Nebbiolo d'Alba Tardiss '14 | 🍷🍷 | 3 |
| ● Nebbiolo d'Alba Tardiss '13 | 🍷🍷 | 3 |
| ● Nebbiolo d'Alba Tardiss '12 | 🍷🍷 | 3 |

# Orlando Abrigo

VIA CAPPELLETTO, 5
12050 TREISO [CN]
TEL. +39 0173630533
www.orlandoabrigo.it

**CELLAR SALES**
**PRE-BOOKED VISITS**
**ACCOMMODATION**
**ANNUAL PRODUCTION** 90,000 bottles
**HECTARES UNDER VINE** 22.00
**SUSTAINABLE WINERY**

The Abrigo family winery has just turned 30. Today it's being guided by Giovanni who shows inexhaustible passion in performing his work. Their new, largely underground cellar is splendid, while the vineyards enjoy excellent positions. These are cultivated only when perfectly ripe, producing rich, concentrated grapes, especially Nebbiolo. Their Barbaresco Riserva Rongalio comes from the heart of their Meruzzano cru and proves to be a wine consistently endowed with sweet pulp, fine, caressing alcohol and delectable drinkability. Their agritourism, Settevie, is a sight to be enjoyed by wine lovers. Their 2013 Barbaresco Ronaglio Riserva is still rather unbridled. It's a bit rough in the mouth, with pronounced oak, but extremely elegant on the nose. Their valid 2015 Barbaresco Meruzzano is rich in spices and accents of oak. On the palate it proves slightly tannic and well-made. Their Très Plus, a white made primarily with Chardonnay, also did well.

| | |
|---|---|
| ● Barbaresco Meruzzano '15 | ♟♟ 5 |
| ● Barbaresco Montersino '15 | ♟♟ 7 |
| ● Barbaresco Rongaglio Ris. '13 | ♟♟ 8 |
| ○ Langhe Très Plus '16 | ♟♟ 3 |
| ● Barbaresco Meruzzano '14 | ♟♟ 5 |
| ● Barbaresco Meruzzano '13 | ♟♟ 5 |
| ● Barbaresco Montersino '14 | ♟♟ 7 |
| ● Barbaresco Montersino '13 | ♟♟ 7 |
| ● Barbaresco Rongaglio Ris. '12 | ♟♟ 8 |
| ● Barbaresco Rongaglio Ris. '11 | ♟♟ 8 |
| ● Barbera d'Alba Mervisano '15 | ♟♟ 4 |
| ● Barbera d'Alba Roreto '14 | ♟♟ 3 |
| ● Langhe Rosso Livraie '13 | ♟♟ 4 |
| ○ Langhe Très Plus '14 | ♟♟ 3 |

# ★Giulio Accornero e Figli

CASCINA CA' CIMA, 1
15049 VIGNALE MONFERRATO [AL]
TEL. +39 0142933317
www.accornerovini.it

**CELLAR SALES**
**PRE-BOOKED VISITS**
**ACCOMMODATION**
**ANNUAL PRODUCTION** 100,000 bottles
**HECTARES UNDER VINE** 22.00
**SUSTAINABLE WINERY**

Over the years the Accornero family has earned praise both in Italy and abroad. Their Bricco Battista and Giulin are masterful interpretations of Barbera. But among their vineyards, their powerful Bricco del Bosco Vigne Vecchie, made with Grignolino, is starting to emerge. It's a wine that has the peculiar capacity to emphasize tertiary aromas that are characteristic of the cultivar. And they're qualities that develop only after lengthy aging and, in this case, make it a wine that's comparable to Burgundy Pinot Nero. Their selection includes a bold Bricco Battista. It's an opaque ruby-colored wine that opens with delicate, complex aromas of black cherry, tobacco and camphor. In the mouth it exhibits extraordinary density and force, making for a palate of rare elegance. Their 2013 Vigne Vecchie is also quite young, with great aromatic complexity and a classy, though still evolving palate. Their 2012 Cima proved delicate and complex at every stage of tasting.

| | |
|---|---|
| ● Barbera del M.to Sup.<br>Bricco Battista '15 | ♟♟♟ 5 |
| ● Barbera del M.to Sup. Cima '12 | ♟♟ 7 |
| ● Grignolino del M.to Casalese<br>Bricco del Bosco V. Vecchie '13 | ♟♟ 6 |
| ● Casorzo Brigantino '17 | ♟♟ 2* |
| ● Grignolino del M.to Casalese<br>Bricco del Bosco '17 | ♟♟ 4 |
| ● M.to Girotondo '15 | ♟♟ 4 |
| ● Barbera del M.to Giulin '15 | ♟♟♟ 3* |
| ● Barbera del M.to Sup.<br>Bricco Battista '13 | ♟♟♟ 5 |
| ● Barbera del M.to Sup.<br>Bricco Battista '12 | ♟♟♟ 5 |
| ● Barbera del M.to Sup.<br>Bricco Battista '11 | ♟♟♟ 5 |
| ● Grignolino del M.to Casalese<br>Bricco del Bosco '16 | ♟♟ 3* |

## Marco e Vittorio Adriano

FRAZ. SAN ROCCO SENO D'ELVIO, 13A
12051 ALBA [CN]
TEL. +39 0173362294
www.adrianovini.it

**CELLAR SALES**
**PRE-BOOKED VISITS**
**ANNUAL PRODUCTION** 160,000 bottles
**HECTARES UNDER VINE** 27.00
**SUSTAINABLE WINERY**

It's here in San Rocco Seno d'Elvio, in one of Barbaresco's loveliest artisanal wineries, that brothers Marco and Vittorio cultivate vineyards with a strong territorial bond. Here we find Dolcetto, Barbera, Freisa and, of course, Nebbiolo. The crus of Basarin (Neive), Bicco and Fatti (Sanadaive) give rise to their Barbarescos, which age in 3000 or 5000 liter Slavonian oak barrels. For years their selection as been a benchmark in terms of stylistic precision, coherence and territorial identity. Moreover, their prices are excellent, considering the consistently strong quality of their wines. Their 2015 Barbaresco Sanadaive is a pure, natural wine in its aromatic development, with fragrances of thyme and rosemary, ripe and caressing fruit. These give way to a lengthy and savory finish that leaves behind a sensation of lightness. Their creamy and elegant 2013 Barbaresco Basarin Riserva features well-calibrated tannic extraction, and proves balanced in its aromas of tar and rich, fragrant fruit.

| | |
|---|---|
| ● Barbaresco Basarin Ris. '13 | ♀♀ 6 |
| ● Barbaresco Sanadaive '15 | ♀♀ 5 |
| ● Barbaresco Basarin '15 | ♀♀ 5 |
| ● Barbaresco Basarin '14 | ♀♀ 5 |
| ● Barbaresco Basarin '13 | ♀♀ 5 |
| ● Barbaresco Basarin '12 | ♀♀ 4 |
| ● Barbaresco Basarin '11 | ♀♀ 4 |
| ● Barbaresco Basarin Ris. '12 | ♀♀ 6 |
| ● Barbaresco Basarin Ris. '11 | ♀♀ 6 |
| ● Barbaresco Sanadaive '14 | ♀♀ 5 |
| ● Barbaresco Sanadaive '13 | ♀♀ 4 |
| ● Barbaresco Sanadaive '12 | ♀♀ 4 |
| ● Barbaresco Sanadaive '11 | ♀♀ 4 |
| ● Barbera d'Alba '15 | ♀♀ 2* |
| ● Dolcetto d'Alba '15 | ♀♀ 2* |
| ○ Langhe Sauvignon Basarico '15 | ♀♀ 3 |

## Claudio Alario

VIA SANTA CROCE, 23
12055 DIANO D'ALBA [CN]
TEL. +39 0173231808
www.alarioclaudio.it

**CELLAR SALES**
**PRE-BOOKED VISITS**
**ANNUAL PRODUCTION** 46,000 bottles
**HECTARES UNDER VINE** 10.00

Claudio Alario's hands are marked by the hoe and vine trimmers, and he's proud of it. Today he's helped by his motivated son Matteo, who's fresh off his studies but still active both in the vineyards and in their renovated and enlarged cellar. It's a winery that's deservedly well-known, both at home and abroad, for its Dolcetto di Diano d'Alba. The Pradurent is a powerful and vibrant wine that's aged in wood barrels. The Costa Fiora, made with very old vines, is fruitier and denser, while the close-focused Montagrilli is more fragrant and approachable. Their two Barolos also proved noteworthy. Their Sorano is a prime example and their 2014 manages to express a sophisticated tough of raspberry across a slightly oaky background. On the palate it proves endowed with a commendable and enjoyable fruity pulp. Their 2014 Riva Rocca features nice structure and oak. The rest of their selection weren't bottled in time for tastings, so we'll have to wait for next year.

| | |
|---|---|
| ● Barolo Sorano '14 | ♀♀ 6 |
| ● Barolo Riva Rocca '14 | ♀♀ 5 |
| ● Barolo Sorano '05 | ♀♀♀ 7 |
| ● Barolo Riva Rocca '13 | ♀♀ 5 |
| ● Barolo Riva Rocca '12 | ♀♀ 5 |
| ● Barolo Riva Rocca '11 | ♀♀ 5 |
| ● Barolo Sorano '13 | ♀♀ 6 |
| ● Barolo Sorano '12 | ♀♀ 6 |
| ● Dolcetto di Diano d'Alba Costa Fiore '15 | ♀♀ 2* |
| ● Dolcetto di Diano d'Alba Sorì Montagrillo '16 | ♀♀ 2* |
| ● Dolcetto di Diano d'Alba Sorì Montagrillo '15 | ♀♀ 2* |
| ● Dolcetto di Diano d'Alba Sup. Sorì Pradurent '15 | ♀♀ 3 |
| ● Nebbiolo d'Alba Cascinotto '15 | ♀♀ 4 |

# ★F.lli Alessandria

VIA B. VALFRÉ, 59
12060 VERDUNO [CN]
TEL. +39 0172470113
www.fratellialessandria.it

**CELLAR SALES**
**PRE-BOOKED VISITS**
**ANNUAL PRODUCTION** 90,000 bottles
**HECTARES UNDER VINE** 15.00

Vittore Alessandria is a young producer who's extremely attentive to the health of his vineyards and to the environment, in addition to being a curious and capable student when it comes to experimenting in pursuit of finesse and elegant. His Barolo Monvigliero testify to the fact. It's a cru that's proving to be one of Barolo's best. The San Lorenzo is a bit more supple and less dense. Their flagship Barolo, Gramolere, comes from higher up in Monforte. Their Verduno Pelaverga Speziale once again proves enchanting in its aromas of pink peppercorn and small wild berries. Hats off to their vintage 2014s, with a Barolo Monvigliero that brings home Tre Bicchieri thanks to its tantalizing spices, richness of fruit and a mouth that's full and balanced. Their Gramolere, a remarkably classical wine made with grapes cultivated in Monforte d'Alba, is darker with more pronounced shades of licorice.

| | | |
|---|---|---|
| ● Barolo Monvigliero '14 | ♟♟♟ | 6 |
| ● Barolo Gramolere '14 | ♟♟ | 6 |
| ● Barolo '14 | ♟ | 5 |
| ● Barolo Gramolere '11 | ♟♟♟ | 6 |
| ● Barolo Gramolere '10 | ♟♟♟ | 6 |
| ● Barolo Gramolere '05 | ♟♟♟ | 6 |
| ● Barolo Monvigliero '13 | ♟♟♟ | 6 |
| ● Barolo Monvigliero '12 | ♟♟♟ | 6 |
| ● Barolo Monvigliero '09 | ♟♟♟ | 6 |
| ● Barolo Monvigliero '06 | ♟♟♟ | 6 |
| ● Barolo Monvigliero '00 | ♟♟♟ | 6 |
| ● Barolo S. Lorenzo '08 | ♟♟♟ | 6 |
| ● Barolo S. Lorenzo '04 | ♟♟♟ | 6 |
| ● Barolo S. Lorenzo '01 | ♟♟♟ | 6 |

# ★Gianfranco Alessandria

LOC. MANZONI, 13
12065 MONFORTE D'ALBA [CN]
TEL. +39 017378576
www.gianfrancoalessandria.com

**CELLAR SALES**
**PRE-BOOKED VISITS**
**ANNUAL PRODUCTION** 50,000 bottles
**HECTARES UNDER VINE** 7.00

Gianfranco Alessandria began vine growing in the mid-1980s and was quickly caught up in the new Langhe craze, making his bottles known to the world starting in 1994. His wines were appreciated immediately, having been made with grapes cultivated in the great San Giovanni di Monforte cru and with a focus on elegance and precision (small wood casks are a friend and not an enemy). His most well-known wines are, obviously, his rich Barolo San Giovanni and the perennially exquisite Barbera d'Alba Vittoria. But the entire selection is excellent, starting with one of the best and most affordable base-level Barolos. Their full-bodied 2015 Barbera d'Alba Vittoria features splendid fruit. It's a great wine worthy of Tre Bicchieri. Their linear, well-balanced 2014 Barolo San Giovanni is a vibrant and lively wine, not rough, with delicate oak and lovely red fruit that's just ripe enough. Their 2014 Barolo does a nice job bringing together red fruit and oak.

| | | |
|---|---|---|
| ● Barbera d'Alba Vittoria '15 | ♟♟♟ | 5 |
| ● Barolo San Giovanni '14 | ♟♟ | 8 |
| ● Barolo '14 | ♟♟ | 6 |
| ● Barbera d'Alba Vittoria '11 | ♟♟♟ | 5 |
| ● Barbera d'Alba Vittoria '98 | ♟♟♟ | 5 |
| ● Barbera d'Alba Vittoria '97 | ♟♟♟ | 4* |
| ● Barbera d'Alba Vittoria '96 | ♟♟♟ | 6 |
| ● Barolo '93 | ♟♟♟ | 6 |
| ● Barolo S. Giovanni '04 | ♟♟♟ | 7 |
| ● Barolo S. Giovanni '01 | ♟♟♟ | 7 |
| ● Barolo S. Giovanni '00 | ♟♟♟ | 7 |
| ● Barolo S. Giovanni '99 | ♟♟♟ | 8 |
| ● Barolo S. Giovanni '98 | ♟♟♟ | 7 |
| ● Barolo S. Giovanni '97 | ♟♟♟ | 7 |

# Giovanni Almondo

VIA SAN ROCCO, 26
12046 MONTÀ [CN]
TEL. +39 0173975256
www.giovannialmondo.com

**PRE-BOOKED VISITS**
**ANNUAL PRODUCTION** 130,000 bottles
**HECTARES UNDER VINE** 18.00
**SUSTAINABLE WINERY**

Domenico Almondo, along with his sons Federico and Stefano, has made the family winery a leader in Roero. His Arneis is cultivated in Montà d'Alba, in the northernmost part of the winemaking district, where the acidic soil is sandy with layers of clay. Their Nebbiolo is cultivated in the southern part of the municipality, on sandy, calcareous soil. Additionally, Barbera, Brachetto, Freisa and Riesling are all also grown. Their wines are marked by elegance and richness of flavor. Roero Arneis Le Rive del Bricco delle Ciliegie affirmed its exceptional quality during our tastings. It's a fresh, taut wine, with flowery and mineral notes, an almost delicately salty touch, and a long, fruity finish. Their excellent 2015 Roero Bric Valdiana offers up aromas of red fruit while on the palate it proves savory, juicy, long and pervasive. Their close-focused and pleasant 2017 Roero Arneis Bricco delle Ciligie is a well-made wine with fragrances of citrus and spicy nuances, while their 2016 Barbera d'Alba Valbianchèra shows nice mouthfeel but it's a bit too marked by oak.

| | |
|---|---|
| ○ Roero Arneis Le Rive del Bricco delle Ciliegie '17 | ♀♀ 4 |
| ● Roero Bric Valdiana '15 | ♀♀ 5 |
| ● Barbera d'Alba Valbianchèra '16 | ♀♀ 3 |
| ○ Roero Arneis Bricco delle Ciliegie '17 | ♀♀ 3 |
| ○ Langhe Riesling Sassi e Sabbia '17 | ♀ 4 |
| ○ Roero Arneis Le Rive del Bricco delle Ciliegie '16 | ♀♀♀ 4* |
| ● Roero Giovanni Almondo Ris. '13 | ♀♀♀ 5 |
| ○ Roero Arneis Bricco delle Ciliegie '16 | ♀♀ 3 |
| ● Roero Bric Valdiana '14 | ♀♀ 5 |

# ★★★Elio Altare

FRAZ. ANNUNZIATA, 51
12064 LA MORRA [CN]
TEL. +39 017350835
www.elioaltare.com

**CELLAR SALES**
**PRE-BOOKED VISITS**
**ANNUAL PRODUCTION** 70,000 bottles
**HECTARES UNDER VINE** 11.00

Elio Altare became a wine celebrity because he managed to create exquisite, long-lived wines with innovative production techniques. It starts with extremely short maceration in which contact between must and skins is counted in terms of hours, not weeks (as tradition holds). French barriques are used instead of the classic, large Slavonian oak barrels. In the vineyard, as well, he's been an innovator, abandoning pesticides 40 years ago. His Barolos continue to prove splendid, and his Langhes are of rare elegance, starting with his Larigi, a bona fide Barbera archetype. 2016 gave rise to a Langhe Giàrborina that shouldn't be missed. Made primarily with Nebbiolo, it's rich and multifaceted, as can happen in great years. On the nose it moves elegantly from incense to licorice, while on the palate it exhibits exceptional fruit that's already extremely well-balanced. Their 2015 base line Barolo and exquisite 2016 Larigi also proved superb.

| | |
|---|---|
| ● Langhe Rosso Giàrborina '16 | ♀♀♀ 8 |
| ● Barolo '14 | ♀♀ 8 |
| ● Barolo Cerretta V. Bricco Ris. '12 | ♀♀ 8 |
| ● Langhe Rosso Larigi '16 | ♀♀ 8 |
| ● Barolo Arborina '14 | ♀♀ 8 |
| ● Langhe Rosso La Villa '16 | ♀♀ 8 |
| ● Barolo Arborina '09 | ♀♀♀ 8 |
| ● Barolo Cerretta V. Bricco '11 | ♀♀♀ 8 |
| ● Barolo Cerretta V. Bricco '10 | ♀♀♀ 8 |
| ● Barolo Cerretta V. Bricco '06 | ♀♀♀ 8 |
| ● Barolo Cerretta V. Bricco '05 | ♀♀♀ 8 |
| ● Langhe Arborina '08 | ♀♀♀ 8 |
| ● Langhe La Villa '06 | ♀♀♀ 8 |
| ● Langhe La Villa '05 | ♀♀♀ 8 |
| ● Langhe Larigi '13 | ♀♀♀ 8 |
| ● Langhe Larigi '12 | ♀♀♀ 8 |
| ● Langhe Larigi '07 | ♀♀♀ 7 |

# Amalia Cascina in Langa

LOC. SANT'ANNA, 85
12065 CUNEO
TEL. +39 0173789013
www.cascinaamalia.it

**CELLAR SALES**
**PRE-BOOKED VISITS**
**ACCOMMODATION**
**ANNUAL PRODUCTION** 60,000 bottles
**HECTARES UNDER VINE** 14.00
**SUSTAINABLE WINERY**

The Boffa family began working quietly, aware as they were that in Barolo you have to take small steps and that purchasing vineyards is a complex thing. They also realized that creating a new winery requires investment and skill. But the results achieved between 2003 and the present have been noteworthy. Their entire selection, which is led by their Barolo Le Coste di Monforte and their Barolo Bussia, is commendable, thanks in part to the presence of expert agronomists and enologists. And it's all further enriched by a comfortable and scenic bed & breakfast. Considering the difficult year, only one 2014 Barolo was submitted. It proves sound, robust and linear, clear and without the frills in its fresh, fruity and slightly herbaceous aromas. Their enjoyable 2016 Barbera d'Alba Superiore is a small, elegant wine, while their 2016 Langhe Rossese Bianco is an approachable, clean wine with sensations of wood resin.

| | | |
|---|---|---|
| ● Barbera d'Alba Sup. '16 | ♥♥ | 4 |
| ● Barolo '14 | ♥♥ | 6 |
| ● Dolcetto d'Alba '14 | ♥ | 3 |
| ● Langhe Nebbiolo '17 | ♥ | 4 |
| ○ Langhe Rossese Bianco '16 | ♥ | 4 |
| ● Barbera d'Alba '15 | ♥♥ | 4 |
| ● Barbera d'Alba Sup. '15 | ♥♥ | 4 |
| ● Barbera d'Alba Sup. '13 | ♥♥ | 4 |
| ● Barolo '13 | ♥♥ | 6 |
| ● Barolo '11 | ♥♥ | 6 |
| ● Barolo Bussia '13 | ♥♥ | 6 |
| ● Barolo Le Coste di Monforte '13 | ♥♥ | 6 |
| ● Barolo Le Coste di Monforte '11 | ♥♥ | 6 |
| ● Barolo Le Coste di Monforte '10 | ♥♥ | 5 |
| ○ Langhe Rossese Bianco '15 | ♥♥ | 4 |
| ○ Langhe Rossese Bianco '14 | ♥♥ | 4 |

# Antichi Vigneti di Cantalupo

VIA MICHELANGELO BUONARROTI, 5
28074 GHEMME [NO]
TEL. +39 0163840041
www.cantalupo.net

**CELLAR SALES**
**PRE-BOOKED VISITS**
**ANNUAL PRODUCTION** 180,000 bottles
**HECTARES UNDER VINE** 35.00

When it comes to the style that Alberto Arlunno wanted to confer on his winery, there's a lot to be said. It all starts with his vineyards, which are cultivated without any chemicals. Then there are the cultivar, with Nebbiolo holding the lion's share. The result is a range of Ghemme wines that exhibit a precise, classic style, led by their celebrated Collis Carellae and Collis Breclemae lines. Finally, there's the cellar, which is so lovely and charming that it surely deserves a visit. Their Colline Novaresi Il Mimo continue to have success on the market. It's a fresh, lively rosé that's also made with Nebbiolo. Their selection is quite commendable overall, with each of their wines doing well, thus affirming the producer's commitment to quality and skill. Their territorial and classic 2011 Ghemme Anno Primo is still slightly tannic, while their highly enjoyable 2016 Vespolina Villa Horta proves to be a particularly elegant and well-balanced wine. Their 2017 Mimo impresses with its fruity freshness.

| | | |
|---|---|---|
| ● Ghemme Cantalupo Anno Primo '11 | ♥♥ | 5 |
| ☉ Colline Novaresi Nebbiolo Il Mimo '17 | ♥♥ | 2* |
| ● Colline Novaresi Rosso Primigenia '17 | ♥♥ | 2* |
| ● Colline Novaresi Vespolina Villa Horta '16 | ♥♥ | 2* |
| ● Ghemme Collis Breclemae '11 | ♥♥ | 7 |
| ● Ghemme '05 | ♥♥♥ | 4 |
| ● Ghemme Collis Breclemae '00 | ♥♥♥ | 6 |
| ● Ghemme Cantalupo Anno Primo '10 | ♥♥ | 5 |
| ● Ghemme Cantalupo Anno Primo '09 | ♥♥ | 5 |
| ● Ghemme Collis Breclemae '10 | ♥♥ | 6 |
| ● Ghemme Collis Carellae '10 | ♥♥ | 6 |
| ● Ghemme Collis Carellae '09 | ♥♥ | 6 |
| ● Ghemme Signore di Bayard '08 | ♥♥ | 6 |

# ★Antoniolo

c.so Valsesia, 277
13045 Gattinara [VC]
Tel. +39 0163833612
antoniolovini@bmm.it

CELLAR SALES
PRE-BOOKED VISITS
ANNUAL PRODUCTION 60,000 bottles
HECTARES UNDER VINE 12.00

Lorella Zoppis Antoniolo is as much of an expert at managing her winery as she is at leading the Alto Piemonte Nebbiolo Consortium in an area that year after year gains in international visibility and market share. The winery, which celebrated its 70-year anniversary in 2018, features the prevalence of Nebbiolo, which plays a key role in their selection, especially their Gattinara line, with elegant wines that call up rhubarb and refreshing notes of pine and mint. Their Osso San Grato cru shines still, but their older San Francesco vineyard is often just as good. Their 2014 Gattinara Osso San Grato put in an absolutely first-rate performance, despite a difficult year. On the nose it proves complex in its aromas of rhubarb and tanned leather, along with small red berries. On the palate it proves steady and elegant, exhibiting excellent overall harmony and unexpected weight. Tre Bicchieri. Their 2014 Gattinara, wine that opts for greener, fresher sensations and a richly enticing palate, is at the top of its game.

| | |
|---|---|
| ● Gattinara Osso San Grato '14 | ♛♛♛ 8 |
| ● Gattinara '14 | ♛♛ 6 |
| ● Coste della Sesia Nebbiolo Juvenia '16 | ♛♛ 4 |
| ⊙ Bricco Lorella '17 | ♛ 3 |
| ● Gattinara Osso S. Grato '11 | ♛♛♛ 8 |
| ● Gattinara Osso S. Grato '10 | ♛♛♛ 8 |
| ● Gattinara Osso S. Grato '09 | ♛♛♛ 8 |
| ● Gattinara Osso San Grato '13 | ♛♛♛ 8 |
| ● Gattinara Osso San Grato '12 | ♛♛♛ 8 |
| ● Gattinara S. Francesco '08 | ♛♛♛ 7 |
| ● Gattinara S. Francesco '07 | ♛♛♛ 5 |
| ● Gattinara Vign. Osso S. Grato '06 | ♛♛♛ 6 |
| ● Gattinara Vign. Osso S. Grato '05 | ♛♛♛ 6 |
| ● Gattinara Vign. Osso S. Grato '04 | ♛♛♛ 6 |
| ● Gattinara Vign. S. Francesco '06 | ♛♛♛ 5 |
| ● Gattinara Vign. S. Francesco '05 | ♛♛♛ 6 |

# Odilio Antoniotti

fraz. Casa del Bosco
v.lo Antoniotti, 5
13868 Sostegno [BI]
Tel. +39 0163860309
antoniottiodilio@libero.it

CELLAR SALES
PRE-BOOKED VISITS
ANNUAL PRODUCTION 13,000 bottles
HECTARES UNDER VINE 4.50

20 years ago Odilio Antoniotti took up the activity that his family had begun in 1861, keeping alive a few hectares of vineyards in Bramaterra, a DOC appellation that's as small as it is commendable. In his small, private vineyards Nebbiolo dominates. It's accompanied by smaller amounts of Croatina, Vespolina and Uva Rara. Odilio's son Mattia has come on board, thus consolidating the winery's internal staff. Indeed, a new release has just been announced. Their Bramaterra is being sold four years after vintage, offering up complex aromas and notable mouthfeel. And this year their 2015 Coste della Sesia Nebbiolo takes center stage, proving to be one of the best of its kind. Finesse and elegance accompany an aromatic profile that moves from gentian to small red berries, while the palate brings together energy, pulp and freshness. Their fruity 2014 Bramaterra, a wine rich in notes of quinine and tobacco with a highly pleasant palate, also did extremely well.

| | |
|---|---|
| ● Coste della Sesia Nebbiolo '15 | ♛♛♛ 3* |
| ● Bramaterra '14 | ♛♛ 5 |
| ● Bramaterra '10 | ♛♛♛ 3* |
| ● Bramaterra '13 | ♛♛ 4 |
| ● Bramaterra '12 | ♛♛ 4 |
| ● Bramaterra '11 | ♛♛ 3* |
| ● Bramaterra '09 | ♛♛ 3* |
| ● Bramaterra '08 | ♛♛ 3* |
| ● Bramaterra '07 | ♛♛ 3* |

## L'Armangia

Fraz. San Giovanni, 122
14053 Canelli [AT]
Tel. +39 0141824947
www.armangia.it

CELLAR SALES
PRE-BOOKED VISITS
ACCOMMODATION
ANNUAL PRODUCTION 95,000 bottles
HECTARES UNDER VINE 11.00
SUSTAINABLE WINERY

Ignazio Giovine's winery is turning 25. Armangia's family plots in Canelli go back to 1850, and today they're dedicated almost exclusively to white grapes. Their vineyards in Moasca, San Marzano Oliveto and Castel Boglione host primarily red grapes, with Barbera in the lead. Their wines are modern, well-crafted, and seek to highlight the attributes of the territory as well as the cultivar used. Ignazio Giovine's selection confirms its continued high quality standards. This year their 2015 Nizza Vignali Riserva proved to be the most interesting wine, with its notes of fruit and forest undergrowth, and its juicy, determined palate (though it's still a bit too marked by oak). But their 2015 Nizza Titon also stood out, opting for tones of wet earth and Mediterranean scrubland, as did their 2017 Moscato d'Asti Canelli, a highly enjoyable wine in its notes of gingerbread and sage.

| | |
|---|---|
| ● Nizza Vignali Ris. '15 | ▼▼ 5 |
| ○ LorenzoMariaSole Pas Dosé M. Cl. | ▼▼ 4 |
| ○ Mesicaseu | ▼▼ 4 |
| ○ Moscato d'Asti Canelli '17 | ▼▼ 2* |
| ● Nizza Titon '15 | ▼▼ 4 |
| ○ Piemonte Chardonnay Pratorotondo '17 | ▼ 2 |
| ● Barbera d'Asti Sup. Nizza Titon '13 | ♀♀ 3* |
| ● Barbera d'Asti Sup. Nizza Titon '12 | ♀♀ 3* |
| ● Barbera d'Asti Sup. Nizza Vignali '11 | ♀♀ 5 |
| ○ M.to Bianco Enneenne '14 | ♀♀ 2* |
| ○ Moscato d'Asti Canelli '16 | ♀♀ 2* |
| ● Nizza Titon '14 | ♀♀ 3* |
| ○ Piemonte Chardonnay Pratorotondo '14 | ♀♀ 2* |
| ○ Piemonte Chardonnay Robi & Robi '15 | ♀♀ 4 |

## Paolo Avezza

Reg. Monforte, 62
14053 Canelli [AT]
Tel. +39 0141822296
www.paoloavezza.com

CELLAR SALES
PRE-BOOKED VISITS
ANNUAL PRODUCTION 25,000 bottles
HECTARES UNDER VINE 7.00

Founded in 1956, the Avezza family winery has undergone many changes since 2001. Under the guidance of Paolo, they've renovated their cellar and expanded their vineyards. Today their private plots are situated in Canelli and Nizza Monferrato. The former are comprised of three hectares of marly, calcareous terain, with Nebbiolo, Dolcetto, Pinot Nero, Chardonnay and Moscato being cultivated. The latter are constituted of four hectares of clay-silty terrain dedicated to Barbera. Their range of wines sees Nizza and their sparkling wines playing lead roles. Their 2015 Nizza delivered during our finals. On the nose it offers up aromas of black olives and forest undergrowth while on the palate it proves fruit-driven, dynamic, savory and highly pleasant. Their 2016 Barbera d'Asti is also extremely well-made, with its aromas of wild berries. In the mouth it proves rich in fruit, supple and fresh, well-supported by acidity, with a plucky finish. Their fresh and taut 2014 Alta Langa Brut features citrusy aromas with notes of bread crust.

| | |
|---|---|
| ● Nizza '15 | ▼▼ 4 |
| ○ Alta Langa Brut '14 | ▼▼ 4 |
| ● Barbera d'Asti '16 | ▼▼ 2* |
| ⊙ Brut Rosé M. Cl. | ▼▼ 3 |
| ○ Moscato d'Asti Canelli La Commenda '17 | ▼ 2 |
| ● Barbera d'Asti Sup. Nizza Sotto la Muda '10 | ♀♀♀ 4* |
| ● Barbera d'Asti Sup. Nizza Sotto la Muda '07 | ♀♀♀ 3* |
| ● Barbera d'Asti Sup. Nizza Sotto la Muda '13 | ♀♀ 4 |
| ● Barbera d'Asti Sup. Nizza Sotto la Muda '12 | ♀♀ 4 |
| ● Barbera d'Asti Sup. Nizza Sotto la Muda '11 | ♀♀ 4 |
| ○ Moscato d'Asti La Commenda '14 | ♀♀ 2* |
| ● Nizza Sotto la Muda '14 | ♀♀ 4 |

# A GUIDE TO THE LEADING 1200 COMPANIES PRODUCING FOODSTUFFS IN ITALY

An indispensable tool for foodies
but even more so for industry insiders
promoting the best of Made-in-Italy worldwide

## ★Azelia

via Alba Barolo, 143
12060 Castiglione Falletto [CN]
Tel. +39 017362859
www.azelia.it

CELLAR SALES
PRE-BOOKED VISITS
ANNUAL PRODUCTION 80,000 bottles
HECTARES UNDER VINE 16.00
SUSTAINABLE WINERY

Luigi Scavino is increasingly helped by his passionate son Lorenzo. Their property spans various municipalities in Langhe, but their Nebbiolo cru in Castiglione Falletto is still a cornerstone of their production, giving rise to their celebrated Bricco Fiasco. Their Serralunga d'Alba cru is also key, providing the grapes for their San Rocco ad Margheria. The powerful structure of such wines is softened by elegant aging in small wood barrels (and rarely new ones). The care shown for the rest of their selection is also commendable, from their fruity Dolcetto d'Alba Oriolo to their stylish Barbera d'Alba Punta. Their entire selection exhibits the producer's trademark elegance. Their 2014 Barolo San Rocco proved particularly noteworthy. It's a firmly structured wine that's endowed with bold aromas of red flowers and spices. Their leaner Margheria opts for lovely herbaceous notes, while their subtle Bricco Fiasco features pronounced tannins. Hats off to their highly enjoyable 2016 Langhe Nebbiolo as well.

| | |
|---|---|
| ● Barolo San Rocco '14 | 🍷🍷 8 |
| ● Barolo Bricco Fiasco '14 | 🍷🍷 8 |
| ● Barolo Margheria '14 | 🍷🍷 8 |
| ● Langhe Nebbiolo '16 | 🍷🍷 4 |
| ● Barolo Bricco Fiasco '12 | 🍷🍷🍷 8 |
| ● Barolo Bricco Fiasco '09 | 🍷🍷🍷 8 |
| ● Barolo Bricco Fiasco '01 | 🍷🍷🍷 7 |
| ● Barolo Margheria '06 | 🍷🍷🍷 7 |
| ● Barolo S. Rocco '11 | 🍷🍷🍷 8 |
| ● Barolo S. Rocco '08 | 🍷🍷🍷 8 |
| ● Barolo Voghera Brea Ris. '01 | 🍷🍷🍷 8 |
| ● Barolo '13 | 🍷🍷 6 |
| ● Barolo Bricco Fiasco '13 | 🍷🍷 8 |
| ● Barolo Bricco Fiasco '11 | 🍷🍷 8 |
| ● Barolo Margheria '13 | 🍷🍷 8 |
| ● Barolo Margheria '12 | 🍷🍷 8 |
| ● Barolo S. Rocco '12 | 🍷🍷 8 |

## Barbaglia

via Dante, 54
28010 Cavallirio [NO]
Tel. +39 016380115
www.vinibarbaglia.it

CELLAR SALES
PRE-BOOKED VISITS
ANNUAL PRODUCTION 25,000 bottles
HECTARES UNDER VINE 4.50

Today Silvia Barbaglia and her father, Sergio, are managing the family winery, founded just after World War II. Thanks to their production, which is so small that it borders on amateur, they've helped spread the name Boca throughout the world. Nebbiolo is the cornerstone, with smaller quantities of Vespolina and Uva Rara bringing freshness and spicy notes to their wines. Their small plots are separated by woods, and the terrain is particularly red, thanks to the presence of iron. The result is vibrant, almost sanguine wine of great personality that caresses the mouth but also offers good acidity and pervasive tannins. Their new Boca still wasn't ready in time for our tasting but wine lovers can delight in at least two superb offerings. Their subtle and lively 2015 Colline Novaresi Nebbiolo Il Silente offers up aromas of raspberry and licorice, which give way to a potent, long, tight-knit palate. Their complex 2017 Colline Novaresi Bianco Lucino is one of northern Piedmont's best whites.

| | |
|---|---|
| ○ Colline Novaresi Bianco Lucino '17 | 🍷🍷 3* |
| ● Colline Novaresi Nebbiolo Il Silente '15 | 🍷🍷 3* |
| ● Colline Novaresi Vespolina Ledi '17 | 🍷🍷 3 |
| ○ Curticella Dosaggio Zero M. Cl. | 🍷 8 |
| ● Boca '13 | 🍷🍷 5 |
| ● Boca '12 | 🍷🍷 5 |
| ● Boca '11 | 🍷🍷 5 |
| ● Boca '10 | 🍷🍷 5 |
| ○ Colline Novaresi Bianco Biancaluce '14 | 🍷🍷 3 |
| ○ Colline Novaresi Bianco Lucino '15 | 🍷🍷 3 |
| ● Colline Novaresi Croatina '13 | 🍷🍷 2* |
| ● Colline Novaresi Nebbiolo Il Silente '11 | 🍷🍷 3 |
| ● Colline Novaresi Vespolina Ledi '15 | 🍷🍷 3 |

# Osvaldo Barberis

B.TA VALDIBÀ, 42
12063 DOGLIANI [CN]
TEL. +39 017370054
www.osvaldobarberis.com

**CELLAR SALES**
**PRE-BOOKED VISITS**
**ANNUAL PRODUCTION** 20,000 bottles
**HECTARES UNDER VINE** 8.00
**VITICULTURE METHOD** Certified Organic

The Dolcetto cultivated on the hills of Dogliani is particularly lucky, especially because there's very little competition with Langhe's other traditional grapes (primarily Nebbiolo and Barbera). As a result, on Osvaldo Barberis's small estate the best slopes give rise to Dogliani, starting with the renamed Valdibà. Here organic agriculture and natural cycles are at the foundation of every agronomic and production choice, such that there's still a small barn with a dozen cattle. But that doesn't mean they're stuck in the past, as their Pinot Nero and white Langhe Nascetta prove. Not all of their wines were ready in time for our tastings, so only five were submitted. Their 2017 Dogliani Puncin is a firmly structured wine that's a bit thick at the moment. It should improve with time. Their Valdibà also features a tannin-rich palate and decidedly youthful aromas. Their potent 2016 Barbera d'Alba Cesca proves enriched by oak.

| | |
|---|---|
| ● Barbera d'Alba Cesca '16 | ♟♟ 3 |
| ● Dogliani Puncin '17 | ♟♟ 3 |
| ● Dogliani Valdibà '17 | ♟♟ 2* |
| ● Langhe Nebbiolo Muntajà '16 | ♟♟ 3 |
| ○ Langhe Nascetta Anì '17 | ♟ 3 |
| ● Barbera d'Alba Cesca '15 | ♟♟ 3 |
| ● Barbera d'Alba Cesca '13 | ♟♟ 3 |
| ● Dogliani Sup. Puncin '16 | ♟♟ 3 |
| ● Dogliani Sup. Puncin '13 | ♟♟ 3* |
| ● Dogliani Valdibà '16 | ♟♟ 2* |
| ● Dogliani Valdibà '15 | ♟♟ 2* |
| ● Dogliani Valdibà '14 | ♟♟ 2* |
| ● Langhe Barbera Brichat '16 | ♟♟ 2* |
| ○ Langhe Nascetta Anì '16 | ♟♟ 3 |
| ● Langhe Pinot Nero Ciabot Maifrin '15 | ♟♟ 3 |
| ● Nebbiolo d'Alba Muntajà '13 | ♟♟ 3 |

# Batasiolo

FRAZ. ANNUNZIATA, 87
12064 LA MORRA [CN]
TEL. +39 017350130
www.batasiolo.com

**CELLAR SALES**
**PRE-BOOKED VISITS**
**ANNUAL PRODUCTION** 2,500,000 bottles
**HECTARES UNDER VINE** 107.00

Brunate, Cerequio, Briccolina, Bussia Bofani, Boscareto… and the list of crus could go on. One of these, the one that constitutes the nucleus of the Dogliani family's winery, inspired its name. More than 100 hectares of vineyards give rise to a number of different Barolos - there's a base version, a reserve and give crus - making for a a a multifaceted selection. In addition to Nebbiolo, Cortese, Arneis, Sauvignon, Pinot Bianco, Moscato, Brachetto, Barbera and Dolcetto are all cultivated. Their style is defined by clear fruit and the use of small wood barrels, making for soft, juicy wines. Their 2014 Brunate is at the top of its game, proving to be one of the best of the year thanks to classic notes of sweet tobacco and fragrant fruit, with a slightly herbaceous notes. On the palate it's dynamic, subtle, with excellent acidity and a well-balanced finish. Their 2016 Barolo Briccolina and Barbera Sovrana also did well, with the former proving rich and potent, and the latter spirited. Their 2015 Barbaresco, a close-focused wine in its notes of flowers and juniper, features nice texture.

| | |
|---|---|
| ● Barbera d'Alba Sovrana '16 | ♟♟ 4 |
| ● Barolo Briccolina '14 | ♟♟ 8 |
| ● Barolo Brunate '14 | ♟♟ 7 |
| ● Barbaresco '15 | ♟♟ 6 |
| ● Barolo Boscareto '14 | ♟♟ 7 |
| ● Batasiolo Brut Millesimé M. Cl. '12 | ♟♟ 5 |
| ● Barolo '14 | ♟ 6 |
| ● Barolo Bussia Vign. Bofani '14 | ♟ 7 |
| ● Barolo Cerequio '14 | ♟ 7 |
| ○ Gavi del Comune di Gravi Granée '17 | ♟ 3 |
| ● Barolo Boscareto '05 | ♟♟♟ 7 |
| ● Barolo Corda della Briccolina '90 | ♟♟♟ 7 |
| ● Barolo Corda della Briccolina '89 | ♟♟♟ 7 |
| ● Barolo Corda della Briccolina '88 | ♟♟♟ 7 |

# Bava

s.da Monferrato, 2
14023 Cocconato [AT]
Tel. +39 0141907083
www.bava.com

**CELLAR SALES**
**PRE-BOOKED VISITS**
**ACCOMMODATION**
**ANNUAL PRODUCTION** 490,000 bottles
**HECTARES UNDER VINE** 55.00

The Bava family's winery has surpassed the
100-year mark (it was founded in 1911),
and over time it has become a steady
benchmark for many wine lovers. For 40
years it has owned the Cocchi brand, and
today it offers a selection of wines that
spans many of the Piedmont's most
important and traditional DOC appellations,
from Nizza to Barolo, Alta Langa and
Malvasia di Castelnuovo Don Bosco, all
made with grapes from their own private
plots. In the vineyards they are particularly
sensitive to environmental sustainability,
while their wines are of a modern style
but still deeply tied to the territory. Their
2015 Nizza Pianoalto made it into our finals
with its aromas of quinine and wet earth, On
the palate it has nice structure, fullness and
volume. But a number of well-made wines
were submitted. Their 2013 Alta Langa Brut
Bianc'd Bianc Giulio Cocchi proves taut and
creamy all at once, while their 2013 Barolo
Scarrone is a plush and pervasive wine.
Their 2017 Malvasia di Castelnuovo Don
Bosco Rosetta is highly pleasant in its sweet
and fruity tones.

| | |
|---|---|
| ● Nizza PianoAlto '15 | 🍷🍷 4 |
| ○ Alta Langa Brut Bianc 'd Bianc Giulio Cocchi '13 | 🍷🍷 6 |
| ● Barolo Scarrone '13 | 🍷🍷 7 |
| ● Malvasia di Castelnuovo Don Bosco Rosetta '17 | 🍷🍷 3 |
| ○ Alta Langa Brut Toto Corde Giulio Cocchi '13 | 🍷 5 |
| ● Barbera d'Asti Libera '16 | 🍷 3 |
| ○ Piemonte Chardonnay Thou Bianc '17 | 🍷 3 |
| ○ Alta Langa Brut Bianc 'd Bianc Giulio Cocchi '12 | 🍷🍷 6 |
| ○ Alta Langa Brut Bianc 'd Bianc Giulio Cocchi '10 | 🍷🍷 6 |
| ● Barbera d'Asti Libera '15 | 🍷🍷 3 |
| ● Barbera d'Asti Libera '14 | 🍷🍷 3 |
| ● Barolo Scarrone '11 | 🍷🍷 7 |
| ○ Piemonte Chardonnay Thou Bianc '16 | 🍷🍷 3 |

# Bel Colle

fraz. Castagni, 56
12060 Verduno [CN]
Tel. +39 0172470196
www.belcolle.eu

**CELLAR SALES**
**PRE-BOOKED VISITS**
**ANNUAL PRODUCTION** 180,000 bottles
**HECTARES UNDER VINE** 14.00

After almost 40 years leading in the winery,
in 2015 brothers Carlo Franco and Giuseppe
Priola Pontiglione accepted an offer from
Boise Family Estates. Entering the group,
whose 350-hectare viticultural patrimony
spans Langhe, Roero, Astigiano and
Mongerrato, hasn't changed the winery
though. Their headquarters are the same, in
Verduno, while their vineyards are situated in
La Morra, Treiso and Barbaresco. Leading
their selection are their great Nebbiolos and
the slightly spicy Pelaverga. Their selection
put in a solid and impressive performance,
led by their superb Barbaresco Pajoré, a
wine that handily brought home Tre Bicchieri.
On the nose it offers up close-focused,
fragrant aromas of fruit, raspberry and
strawberry, then tobacco and licorice. On the
palate it reveals a weight that's perfectly
calibrated between carefully measured
tannins and lively acidity, with a long, light
finish. Their 2014 Barolo Monvigliero is a
juicy, complex wine with a subtle but deep
tannic weave. It has energy and pace but it
still hasn't peaked. Their 2016 Barbera Le
Masche exhibits great personality.

| | |
|---|---|
| ● Barbaresco Pajoré '15 | 🍷🍷🍷 5 |
| ● Barolo Monvigliero '14 | 🍷🍷 6 |
| ● Barbera d'Alba Sup. Le Masche '16 | 🍷🍷 3 |
| ● Barbera d'Asti Sup. Nuwanda '16 | 🍷🍷 3 |
| ● Nebbiolo d'Alba La Reala '16 | 🍷🍷 3 |
| ● Verduno Pelaverga '17 | 🍷🍷 3 |
| ● Barolo Simposio '14 | 🍷 6 |
| ● Dolcetto d'Alba '17 | 🍷 2 |
| ○ Langhe Nasc-Cetta '17 | 🍷 3 |
| ○ Roero Arneis '17 | 🍷 3 |
| ● Barbaresco Roncaglie Ris. '08 | 🍷🍷🍷 5 |
| ● Barolo Monvigliero '09 | 🍷🍷🍷 5 |
| ● Barolo Monvigliero '07 | 🍷🍷🍷 5 |
| ● Barbera d'Alba Sup. Le Masche '15 | 🍷🍷 3* |
| ● Barolo Monvigliero '13 | 🍷🍷 6 |
| ● Barolo Monvigliero '12 | 🍷🍷 6 |

# Bera

loc. Cascina Palazzo
via Castellero, 12
12050 Neviglie [CN]
Tel. +39 0173630500
www.bera.it

**CELLAR SALES**
**PRE-BOOKED VISITS**
**RESTAURANT SERVICE**
**ANNUAL PRODUCTION** 140,000 bottles
**HECTARES UNDER VINE** 26.00

For more than 40 years the Bera family's
winery has served as a benchmark for
Moscato winemaking. Their vineyards are
situated primarily near the cellar itself, and
grow at 380 meters of elevation in
tufaceous-clay soil that's rich in limestone.
The growth in quality of their Barbarescos is
worth noting, made possible in part by their
private vineyards in the crus of Rabajà and
Basarin. Their wines are traditionally styled,
with great attention shown for aromatic
precision and pleasantness on the palate.
Their 2017 Moscato d'Asti Su Reimond
earned a place in our finals by virtue of its
aromas of white peach and sage, and its
fresh, taut palate. Their 2012 Barbaresco
Rabajà Riserva also delivered with its notes
of licorice, its fullness, length and
complexity. Their 2017 Moscato d'Asti is a
well-made wine, varietal in its flowery notes
and hints of aromatic herbs, as is their
fresh, assertive, pulpy 2015 Barbaresco.
Their linear and pervasive 2011 Barbaresco
Basarin Riserva offers up aromas of green
tea leaves, while their 2017 Barbera d'Alba
proves pervasive and rich in fruit.

| | |
|---|---|
| ● Barbaresco Rabajà Ris. '12 | ♟♟ 5 |
| ○ Moscato d'Asti Su Reimond '17 | ♟♟ 3* |
| ● Barbaresco '15 | ♟♟ 5 |
| ● Barbaresco Basarin Ris. '11 | ♟♟ 7 |
| ● Barbera d'Alba '17 | ♟♟ 2* |
| ○ Moscato d'Asti '17 | ♟♟ 2* |
| ● Barbera d'Alba Sup. La Lena '15 | ♟ 3 |
| ● Barbera d'Asti Sup. '16 | ♟ 2 |
| ○ Alta Langa Bera Brut '10 | ♙♙ 3 |
| ○ Asti '16 | ♙♙ 3 |
| ● Barbaresco '13 | ♙♙ 5 |
| ● Barbaresco '12 | ♙♙ 5 |
| ● Barbaresco Rabajà Ris. '11 | ♙♙ 5 |
| ○ Dell'Um.be '15 | ♙♙ 3 |
| ● Langhe Nebbiolo Alladio '15 | ♙♙ 3 |
| ○ Moscato d'Asti '16 | ♙♙ 2* |
| ○ Moscato d'Asti Su Reimond '16 | ♙♙ 3* |

# Cinzia Bergaglio

via Gavi, 29
15060 Tassarolo [AL]
Tel. +39 0143342203
www.vinicinziabergaglio.it

**CELLAR SALES**
**PRE-BOOKED VISITS**
**ANNUAL PRODUCTION** 30,000 bottles
**HECTARES UNDER VINE** 9.00

Cinzia and Massimo represent two families
with historic ties to the estate's vineyards.
It's a family-run winery that's getting a
boost from the new generation in the form
of Mattia. He's already got clear ideas about
the future, having shown a gift for vine
growing. Their vineyards are located in
Rovereto and Tassarolo, two different terrain
types that give rise to two wines with
different characteristics. The winery's
signature style is probably linked to their
minimally invasive approach in the cellar,
which amplifies the expressivity of their
grapes. Considering the somewhat
scattershot year, caused by extreme
climate conditions, Cinzia Bergaglio's La
Fornace stands out among their selection. It
offers up aromas of tropical fruit and
herbaceous notes. These give way to a
fresh, savory palate with excellent
persistence. Their Grifone delle Roveri
features nice overall aromatic complexity,
with flowery notes on a mineral
background, and a soft, fresh palate.

| | |
|---|---|
| ○ Gavi La Fornace '17 | ♟♟ 2* |
| ○ Gavi del Comune di Gavi Grifone delle Roveri '17 | ♟ 2 |
| ○ Gavi del Comune di Gavi Grifone delle Roveri '16 | ♙♙ 2* |
| ○ Gavi del Comune di Gavi Grifone delle Roveri '14 | ♙♙ 2* |
| ○ Gavi del Comune di Gavi Grifone delle Roveri '12 | ♙♙ 2* |
| ○ Gavi del Comune di Gavi Grifone delle Roveri '11 | ♙♙ 2* |
| ○ Gavi La Fornace '16 | ♙♙ 2* |
| ○ Gavi La Fornace '15 | ♙♙ 2* |
| ○ Gavi La Fornace '13 | ♙♙ 2* |

# Nicola Bergaglio

FRAZ. ROVERETO
LOC. PEDAGGERI, 59
15066 GAVI [AL]
TEL. +39 0143682195
nicolabergaglio@alice.it

**CELLAR SALES**
**PRE-BOOKED VISITS**
**ANNUAL PRODUCTION** 140,000 bottles
**HECTARES UNDER VINE** 17.00
**SUSTAINABLE WINERY**

Gianluigi Bergaglio can be proud of what he's built in Rovereto over almost 50 years. His wines are known everywhere and are a testament to an appellation that can only recently call itself 'long-lived'. Gavi was always considered early-drinking white wine country because people didn't know or underestimated the hidden potential of bottle aging, and the tertiary aromas that develop. That was the case until they put their nose in a glass of Minaia, aged for five or six years. And in a heartbeat everything changed. Even during difficult years, Bergaglio's Gavis manage to tantalize the palate. Two complex and elegant versions were submitted. Their Minaia offers up aromas of chlorophyll and flint, while their base level version opens across subtle notes of white flowers and ferns. On the palate both exhibit structure and freshness, which support a long and persistent finish.

# Bersano

P.ZZA DANTE, 21
14049 NIZZA MONFERRATO [AT]
TEL. +39 0141720211
www.bersano.it

**CELLAR SALES**
**PRE-BOOKED VISITS**
**ANNUAL PRODUCTION** 1,500,000 bottles
**HECTARES UNDER VINE** 230.00

With its 230 hectares of vineyards subdivided into various plots between Monferrato and Langhe, La Bersano proposes a wide range of wines, some 25 in all. Their selection includes some of the most important appellations in the region, from Nizza to Barolo, Barbaresco, Alta Langa and Gavi. Their wines stand out for their balance and classic style, yet they're also reassuring and territorially correct. Their 2015 Nizza Generala Riserva put in an excellent performance. It's the flagship wine of Bersano's Asti vineyards. On the nose it proves classic in its aromas of cherry and wet earth, with spicy nuances. On the palate it holds up well, with freshness and a long, elegant finish that features sensations of crisp fruit. Their 2016 Barbera d'Asti Superiore La Cremosina is a juicy, pervasive, highly quaffable wine. Their 2017 Moscato d'Asti is fresh and highly pleasant, as is their 2017 Ruché di Castagnole Monferrato San Pietro.

| | |
|---|---|
| ○ Gavi del Comune di Gavi Minaia '17 | ♟♟♟ 4* |
| ○ Gavi del Comune di Gavi '17 | ♟♟ 2* |
| ○ Gavi del Comune di Gavi Minaia '15 | ♟♟♟ 4* |
| ○ Gavi del Comune di Gavi Minaia '14 | ♟♟♟ 4* |
| ○ Gavi del Comune di Gavi Minaia '11 | ♟♟♟ 4* |
| ○ Gavi del Comune di Gavi Minaia '10 | ♟♟♟ 4 |
| ○ Gavi del Comune di Gavi '16 | ♟♟ 2* |
| ○ Gavi del Comune di Gavi '15 | ♟♟ 2* |
| ○ Gavi del Comune di Gavi Et. Bianca '14 | ♟♟ 3* |
| ○ Gavi del comune di Gavi' Minaia' '16 | ♟♟ 4 |

| | |
|---|---|
| ● Barbera d'Asti Sup. Cremosina '16 | ♟♟ 3* |
| ● Nizza Generala Ris. '15 | ♟♟ 5 |
| ○ Moscato d'Asti Monteolivo '17 | ♟♟ 3 |
| ● Ruché di Castagnole M.to San Pietro Realto '17 | ♟♟ 3 |
| ○ Arturo Bersano Pas Dosé M. Cl. | ♟ 5 |
| ○ Gavi del Comune di Gavi '17 | ♟ 3 |
| ● Barbaresco Mantico '14 | ♟♟ 6 |
| ● Barbera d'Asti Sup. Cremosina '12 | ♟♟ 3* |
| ● Barbera d'Asti Sup. Nizza Generala '13 | ♟♟ 5 |
| ● Barbera d'Asti Sup. Nizza Generala '12 | ♟♟ 5 |
| ● Barolo Ris. '08 | ♟♟ 7 |
| ● Nizza La Generala Ris. '14 | ♟♟ 5 |
| ● Ruché di Castagnole Monferrato S. Pietro '12 | ♟♟ 3* |

## Guido Berta

loc. Saline, 53
14050 San Marzano Oliveto [AT]
Tel. +39 0141856193
www.guidoberta.com

**CELLAR SALES**
**PRE-BOOKED VISITS**
**ANNUAL PRODUCTION** 50,000 bottles
**HECTARES UNDER VINE** 20.00

Guido Berta founded his winery in 1997 on his family's estate in San Marzano Oliveto, one of the best districts for making Barbera. Most of their private vineyards, which were planted between 1960 and 1988, are situated here, and grow in the area's calcareous-clay soil. The rest are in Calamandrana and Agliano Terme. Of course Barbera takes center stage here, accompanied by Chardonnay, Moscato and Nebbiolo. Their wines are modern but they still represent an authentic expression of the territory. Their Nizza Canto di Luna affirms its status as the star of their selection, with the 2015 also reaching our finals. Aromas of dark fruit and Mediterranean scrubland are accompanied by slightly spicy notes. These give way to a fresh, juicy, assertive palate. Their 2017 Moscato d'Asti is another well-made wine, offering up characteristic notes of candied citrus peels, with a rich, full palate that's well-supported by acidity, as is their supple, approachable 2016 Barbera d'Asti Le Rondini.

| | | |
|---|---|---|
| ● Nizza Canto di Luna '15 | ♟♟ | 5 |
| ● Barbera d'Asti Le Rondini '16 | ♟♟ | 3 |
| ○ Moscato d'Asti '17 | ♟♟ | 3 |
| ● Barbera d'Asti Sup. '15 | ♟ | 3 |
| ● Barbera d'Asti Le Rondini '15 | ♀♀ | 3 |
| ● Barbera d'Asti Sup. Nizza Canto di Luna '13 | ♀♀ | 5 |
| ● Barbera d'Asti Sup. Nizza Canto di Luna '12 | ♀♀ | 5 |
| ● Barbera d'Asti Sup. Nizza Canto di Luna '10 | ♀♀ | 5 |
| ○ Moscato d'Asti '16 | ♀♀ | 3 |
| ● Nizza Canto di Luna '14 | ♀♀ | 5 |

## La Bìòca

via Alba, 13a
12050 Serralunga d'Alba [CN]
Tel. +39 0173613022
www.labioca.it

**CELLAR SALES**
**PRE-BOOKED VISITS**
**ACCOMMODATION**
**ANNUAL PRODUCTION** 50,000 bottles
**HECTARES UNDER VINE** 9.00

La Bìòca, owned by the August group, is taking huge steps towards rapidly enlarging their estate and the selection of wines available (they already offer some 20 of them). The quality of their wines is overseen by a skilled staff that avails itself of international technicians and local viticultural experts. The cellar is situated in Serralunga, Fontanafredda, while most of their grapes are cultivated in Monforte d'Alba, La Morra, Novello and Barbaresco. Their style is somewhat modern, with the use of wood barrels in various sizes and a focus on bringing out the fruitiness of each cultivar. And during our tastings we tried a Barolo Aculei that, despite the small structured that 2014 conferred, proves to be well-orchestrated, with aromas of ripe red berries accompanied by an oaky nuance. Their enjoyable 2014 Ravera is just a bit more narrow and thick by virtue of its tannins.

| | | |
|---|---|---|
| ● Barolo Aculei '14 | ♟♟ | 6 |
| ● Barbera d'Alba Sup. Adae '16 | ♟♟ | 3 |
| ● Barolo Ravera '14 | ♟♟ | 6 |
| ○ Langhe Chardonnay V. Bussia '16 | ♟♟ | 3 |
| ● Nebbiolo d'Alba Sup. Stërmà '16 | ♟♟ | 4 |
| ● Barbera d'Alba Sup. Adae '15 | ♀♀ | 3 |
| ● Barolo Aculei '13 | ♀♀ | 6 |
| ● Barolo Bussia '13 | ♀♀ | 6 |

# ★Enzo Boglietti

VIA FONTANE, 18A
12064 LA MORRA [CN]
TEL. +39 017350330
www.enzoboglietti.com

**CELLAR SALES**
**PRE-BOOKED VISITS**
**ANNUAL PRODUCTION** 100,000 bottles
**HECTARES UNDER VINE** 22.50
**VITICULTURE METHOD** Certified Organic
**SUSTAINABLE WINERY**

All the Barolo experts agree that cru Brunate, which slopes down La Morra towards Barolo, is one of the best in the area. And it's here that the Boglietti brothers have built their well-deserved fame. Since 2003 they've also owned a part of the prestigious Serralunga vineyard, Arione, which has gained a lot of attention, as will Roberto Conterno's purchase of Gigi Rosso's part of the cru. In addition to these important holdings they have a number of other plots, which give rise to a rest range of wines that feature other Barolos and Barbera d'Alba. Theirs is an elegant and delectably drinkable enological style. The force of their Serralunga vineyard translates into the balsamic elegance of their 2014 Arione, a wine with a palate of rare balance. Their spicy and elegant 2014 Barolo Fossati is endowed with silky tannins and features commendable suppleness. Despite its smaller structure, their balsamic 2014 Case Nere behaves quite well. Their 2015 Barbera d'Alba Vigna dei Romani proves bold and austere.

| | |
|---|---|
| ● Barolo Arione '14 | ♥♥ 8 |
| ● Barolo Brunate '14 | ♥♥ 8 |
| ● Barolo Fossati '14 | ♥♥ 8 |
| ● Barbera d'Alba V. dei Romani '15 | ♥♥ 6 |
| ● Barolo Boiolo '14 | ♥♥ 6 |
| ● Barolo Case Nere '14 | ♥♥ 8 |
| ● Barolo Arione '06 | ♥♥♥ 8 |
| ● Barolo Arione '05 | ♥♥♥ 8 |
| ● Barolo Brunate '13 | ♥♥♥ 8 |
| ● Barolo Brunate '01 | ♥♥♥ 8 |
| ● Barolo Case Nere '04 | ♥♥♥ 8 |
| ● Barolo V. Arione '07 | ♥♥♥ 8 |

# Bondi

S.DA CAPPELLETTE, 73
15076 OVADA [AL]
TEL. +39 0131299186
www.bondivini.it

**CELLAR SALES**
**PRE-BOOKED VISITS**
**ANNUAL PRODUCTION** 20,000 bottles
**HECTARES UNDER VINE** 5.00

The Bondi family successfully manages two initiatives: a winery and a restaurant. Their winery was founded almost 20 years ago in one of Ovada's best areas, and each year they give us authentic gems of artisanal winemaking. Six wines are produced in total, with Dolcetto di Ovada and Barbera serving as the basis for most (Merlot is used for their Ansensò). Their Locanda dell'Olmo is situated in Bosco Marengo (Alessandria). Their style of cooking reflects their position on the border between lower Piedmont and Liguria, as well as the seasonal availability of the ingredients used. Their Ovada D'Uien earned a place in our finals with its dark, opaque color, and its aromas of blackcurrant and fruit preserves. On the palate it proves potent and rich, with a nice acidity to contrast its thickness and tannins, making for a highly persistent finish. Ansensò is a highly youthful wine with fruity aromas that give way to tobacco, licorice and sweet spices. Their 2016 Nani proves intriguing, with nice, buoyant fruit and a rich, vibrant palate whose tannins are still evolving.

| | |
|---|---|
| ● Ovada D'Uien '15 | ♥♥ 3* |
| ● Dolcetto di Ovada Nani '16 | ♥♥ 2* |
| ● M.to Rosso Ansensò '15 | ♥♥ 4 |
| ● Barbera del M.to Banaiotta '16 | ♥ 4 |
| ● Barbera del M.to Banaiotta '10 | ♀♀ 2* |
| ● Barbera del M.to Ruvrin '10 | ♀♀ 4 |
| ● Barbera del M.to Sup. Ruvrin '15 | ♀♀ 4 |
| ● Dolcetto di Ovada Nani '15 | ♀♀ 2* |
| ● Dolcetto di Ovada Nani '11 | ♀♀ 2* |
| ● Dolcetto di Ovada Nani '09 | ♀♀ 2* |
| ● M.to Barbera Banaiotta '09 | ♀♀ 4 |
| ● M.to Rosso Ansensò '11 | ♀♀ 4 |
| ● Nani | ♀♀ 2* |
| ● Nani | ♀♀ 3* |
| ● Ovada D'Uien '13 | ♀♀ 3 |
| ● Ovada D'Uien '11 | ♀♀ 4 |

# Marco Bonfante

S.DA VAGLIO SERRA, 72
14049 NIZZA MONFERRATO [AT]
TEL. +39 0141725012
www.marcobonfante.com

CELLAR SALES
PRE-BOOKED VISITS
ANNUAL PRODUCTION 250,000 bottles
HECTARES UNDER VINE 13.00
SUSTAINABLE WINERY

The Bonfante family have been making
wine in Nizza Monferrato for eight
generations, but it was only in 2000 that
Marco and his sister Micaela decided to
join together to found Marco Bonfante. In
addition to a selection that avails itself of
20 hectares of vineyards, all personally
overseen, they work as 'négociant', which
allows them to propose a vast range of
wines from a number of regional DOC
appellations. Their wines are technically
exemplary, with particular attention shown
to the characteristic of the grapes and the
territory. Their entire selection proves
well-made, foremost their 2013 Barolo
Bussia, with its aromas of tobacco, licorice
and red berries, and its complex, tannic
palate. Their 2014 Nizza Bricco Bonfante
Riserva is a fruit-forward wine with notable
supporting acidity. Their 2016 Barbera
d'Asti Superiore Stella Rossa is balsamic
and pervasive, their 2015 Barbera d'Asti
Superiore Menego rich in fruit, and their
2017 Moscato d'Asti redolent of sage,
candied orange peels and dried figs.

| | |
|---|---|
| ● Barbera d'Asti Sup. Menego '15 | ▼▼ 4 |
| ● Barbera d'Asti Sup. Stella Rossa '16 | ▼▼ 2* |
| ● Barolo Bussia '13 | ▼▼ 6 |
| ○ Moscato d'Asti '17 | ▼▼ 2* |
| ● Nizza Bricco Bonfante Ris. '14 | ▼▼ 5 |
| ● Barbera d'Asti Sup. Bricco Bonfante '12 | ♀♀ 5 |
| ● Barbera d'Asti Sup. Menego '14 | ♀♀ 4 |
| ● Barbera d'Asti Sup. Stella Rossa '15 | ♀♀ 2* |
| ● Barbera d'Asti Sup. Stella Rossa '14 | ♀♀ 2* |
| ● Barbera d'Asti Sup. Stella Rossa '12 | ♀♀ 2* |
| ● Barolo Bussia '11 | ♀♀ 6 |
| ● Barolo Bussia '10 | ♀♀ 6 |
| ● Nizza Bricco Bonfante '14 | ♀♀ 5 |
| ● Piemonte Rosso Albarone '13 | ♀♀ 5 |

# Gilberto Boniperti

VIA VITTORIO EMANUELE, 43/45
28010 BARENGO [NO]
TEL. +39 0321997123
www.bonipertivignaioli.com

CELLAR SALES
ANNUAL PRODUCTION 12,000 bottles
HECTARES UNDER VINE 3.50

Enologist Gilberto Boniperti began
wine-growing some 20 years ago,
eventually revitalizing an area in the Fara
appellation that's lesser known but still
capable of great Nebbiolo. The other local
variety cultivated is Vespolina, which brings
freshness and spicy intensity. The winery's
motto is 'Sun, Land, Tradition', but this
they've also adopted a sensible approach
that's up-to-date with modern techniques.
In their cellar French oak barrels of
different sizes are used. Their 2015 Fara
Bartön enchants. It's a wine of great
character and complexity with flowery
sensations accompanied by hints of
tobacco and quinine. In the mouth it proves
rich and full-bodied, with elegant tannins
and a delicious, delicately salty sensation
that confers personality. Tre Bicchieri. Their
2016 Barbera Barblin is a captivating wine,
one of the year's best. On the nose it offers
up notes of dark fruit, olives and pepper,
while in the mouth it proves succulent and
fresh. Their elegant 2016 Nebbiolo Carlin is
another noteworthy wine.

| | |
|---|---|
| ● Fara Bartön '15 | ▼▼▼ 5 |
| ● Colline Novaresi Barbera Barblin '16 | ▼▼ 4 |
| ● Colline Novaresi Nebbiolo Carlin '16 | ▼▼ 4 |
| ● Colline Novaresi Nebbiolo Carlin '15 | ♀♀ 4 |
| ● Colline Novaresi Nebbiolo Carlin '14 | ♀♀ 4 |
| ● Colline Novaresi Nebbiolo Carlin '13 | ♀♀ 4 |
| ● Colline Novaresi Nebbiolo Carlin '12 | ♀♀ 4 |
| ● Colline Novaresi Vespolina Favolalunga '15 | ♀♀ 2* |
| ● Colline Novaresi Vespolina Favolalunga '12 | ♀♀ 3 |
| ● Fara Bartön '14 | ♀♀ 4 |
| ● Fara Bartön '13 | ♀♀ 4 |
| ● Fara Bartön '12 | ♀♀ 4 |

# Borgo Maragliano

VIA SAN SEBASTIANO, 2
14051 LOAZZOLO [AT]
TEL. +39 014487132
www.borgomaragliano.com

**CELLAR SALES**
**PRE-BOOKED VISITS**
**ANNUAL PRODUCTION** 292,000 bottles
**HECTARES UNDER VINE** 39.00
**SUSTAINABLE WINERY**

As of late, Carlo and Silvia Galliano's Borgo Maragliano has managed to build a solid reputation for sparkling winemaking. Situated in Loazzolo, at 450 meters above sea level, their estate features Moscato, Chardonnay and Pino Nero, cultivated across 12 different plots of sandy, tufaceous and calcareous terrain lacking in clay and mineral substances. Their wines, particularly their sparklers, exhibit depth and aromatic richness. Borgo Maragliano's Metodo Classicos once again prove to be of excellent quality. Their 2014 Dogma Blanc de Noirs opens with flowery hints and aromas of bread crust, while on the palate it exhibits nice mouthfeel, but it's also fresh, assertive and pleasant. Their 2013 Giuseppe Galliano Brut Nature opts for citrusy notes and custard followed by a palate that's full of character and vibrant supporting acidity. It takes home Tre Bicchieri. Their well-made and varietal 2017 Moscato d'Asti La Caliera exhibits nice typicity while also proving approachable and extremely fresh.

| | |
|---|---|
| ○ Giuseppe Galliano Brut Nature M. Cl. '13 | ▼▼▼ 5 |
| ○ Dogma Blanc de Noirs Brut Nature M. Cl. '14 | ▼▼ 5 |
| ○ Moscato d'Asti La Caliera '17 | ▼▼ 3 |
| ○ Chardonnay Brut | ▼ 2 |
| ○ El Calié '17 | ▼ 2 |
| ○ Federico Galliano Brut Nature M. Cl. '15 | ▼ 5 |
| ○ Francesco Galliano Blanc de Blancs Brut M. Cl. | ▼ 4 |
| ⊙ Giovanni Galliano Brut Rosé M. Cl. '14 | ▼ 5 |
| ○ Loazzolo V. T. '13 | ▼ 5 |
| ○ Giuseppe Galliano Ris. Brut M. Cl. '01 | ▼▼▼ 4* |

# Giacomo Borgogno & Figli

VIA GIOBERTI, 1
12060 BAROLO [CN]
TEL. +39 017356108
www.borgogno.com

**CELLAR SALES**
**PRE-BOOKED VISITS**
**ANNUAL PRODUCTION** 250,000 bottles
**HECTARES UNDER VINE** 16.00
**SUSTAINABLE WINERY**

In the eternal debate over which cellar best represents the area of Barolo, in terms of history and quality, Giacomo Borgogno has a pretty strong hand to play. A lot of that has to do with the winery's age. It was founded in 1761, making it one of the area's oldest. But it's also about the fact that his wines are once again shining stars in this jigsaw puzzle of an appellation. In part it's thanks to the Farinetti's family purchase of the winery in 2008, with young Andrea now managing things. Among their numerous valid wines, their Barolo Riserva, Cannubi and Liste are consistent standouts. Their sumptuous 2011 Barolo Riserva is extremely enjoyable on the nose, and endowed with exquisite vitality on the palate, finishing on tones of rose. Their 2013 Barolo Fossati stands out for its lovely, close-woven palate and for its pleasant aromas of cherries in liquor. Their 2014 Barolo offers up elegant fruity notes, maybe a bit austere on the palate. Their innovative Barbera d'Asti Cascina Valle Asinari offerings also debuted, while their extremely well-made 2014 No Name exhibits surprising vigor and elegance.

| | |
|---|---|
| ● Barolo Ris. '11 | ▼▼▼ 8 |
| ● Barolo Fossati '13 | ▼▼ 8 |
| ● Barolo Liste '13 | ▼▼ 8 |
| ● Langhe Nebbiolo No Name '14 | ▼▼ 7 |
| ● Barbera d'Asti Cascina Valle Asinari '16 | ▼▼ 6 |
| ● Barolo '14 | ▼▼ 8 |
| ● Barolo Cannubi '13 | ▼▼ 8 |
| ○ Langhe Riesling Era Ora '16 | ▼▼ 6 |
| ● Barbera d'Alba Sup. '16 | ▼ 6 |
| ● Barbera d'Asti Sup. Cascina Valle Asinari '16 | ▼ 6 |
| ○ Colli Tortonesi Timorasso Derthona '16 | ▼ 7 |
| ● Barolo Liste '11 | ▼▼▼ 8 |
| ● Barolo Liste '10 | ▼▼▼ 8 |
| ● Barolo Ris. '10 | ▼▼▼ 8 |

## Boroli

VIA PUGNANE, 4
12060 CASTIGLIONE FALLETTO [CN]
TEL. +39 017362927
www.boroli.it

CELLAR SALES
PRE-BOOKED VISITS
ACCOMMODATION AND RESTAURANT SERVICE
ANNUAL PRODUCTION 200,000 bottles
HECTARES UNDER VINE 32.00
SUSTAINABLE WINERY

The farm manor of La Brunella is situated in
the cru of the same name in Castiglione
Falletto. It's the heart of production for the
Boroli family, who own various estates in the
municipalities of Barolo and La Morra. Their
estate comprises prized crus like Cerequio,
Villero and Serradenari, with vineyards going
back anywhere from 15 to 40 years. Almost
all are dedicated to Nebbiolo, with the
exception of Chardonnay (used for the
winery's only white). Their style is
characterized by the use of medium-small
wood barrels and a focus on vibrant fruit.
Their 2014 Barolo Cerequio landed in our
finals, proving one of the best of the year. It's
a close-focused, airy wine aromatically, with
delicate, penetrating fragrances ranging
from small red berries to mint. On the palate
it proves pure and creamy, with a long, fresh
finish. Their 2014 Barolo opts for more
vibrant spiciness, finding balance and energy
on the palate. Their 2014 Barolo Brunella
offers up a flowery whiff and notes of sweet
red fruit while their 2014 Barolo Villero
comes through tight.

| | |
|---|---|
| ● Barolo Cerequio '14 | ♟♟ 8 |
| ● Barolo '14 | ♟♟ 6 |
| ● Barolo Brunella '14 | ♟♟ 8 |
| ● Barolo Villero '14 | ♟ 8 |
| ● Barolo Villero '01 | ♟♟♟ 6 |
| ● Barolo '12 | ♟♟ 6 |
| ● Barolo Brunella '13 | ♟♟ 8 |
| ● Barolo Cerequio '13 | ♟♟ 8 |
| ● Barolo Cerequio '12 | ♟♟ 7 |
| ● Barolo Cerequio '09 | ♟♟ 7 |
| ● Barolo Villero '13 | ♟♟ 8 |
| ● Barolo Villero '12 | ♟♟ 7 |
| ● Barolo Villero '11 | ♟♟ 7 |
| ● Barolo Villero '09 | ♟♟ 7 |
| ● Barolo Villero Ris. '09 | ♟♟ 8 |

## Chiara Boschis
## E. Pira & Figli

VIA VITTORIO VENETO, 1
12060 BAROLO [CN]
TEL. +39 017356247
www.pira-chiaraboschis.com

CELLAR SALES
PRE-BOOKED VISITS
ANNUAL PRODUCTION 35,000 bottles
HECTARES UNDER VINE 8.50
VITICULTURE METHOD Certified Organic

The winery was founded some 130 years
ago but Chiara Boschis isn't afraid of not
living up to the legacy. Indeed, through
humility as much as tenacity, the producer
has become a brilliant example of how to
interpret Barolo through a modern lens. The
small cellar immediately adopted small
French wood barrels and in the fields they've
gradually abolished the use of chemicals. As
a result Cannubi, one of the area's most
celebrated crus, is giving rise to lively,
elegant, sophisticated and fresh wine. Their
whole selection turns on this model, which
sees the use of only Langhe's traditional red
grapes. In a year that was rather up and
down for Barolo, their 2014 Cannubi stands
out for the enchanting way it balances its
various parts. Freshness is pronounced,
tannins not too much, oak just emerges from
the background, spices are close-focused
and tantalizing. Their Via Nuova is more
youthful, immature even. Their 2016 Barbera
d'Alba Superiore is particularly lively and
bold, offering a rare pleasantness.

| | |
|---|---|
| ● Barbera d'Alba Sup. '16 | ♟♟ 4 |
| ● Barolo Cannubi '14 | ♟♟ 8 |
| ● Barolo Via Nuova '14 | ♟♟ 8 |
| ● Langhe Nebbiolo '16 | ♟♟ 4 |
| ● Barolo Mosconi '14 | ♟ 8 |
| ● Barolo Cannubi '11 | ♟♟♟ 8 |
| ● Barolo Cannubi '10 | ♟♟♟ 8 |
| ● Barolo Cannubi '06 | ♟♟♟ 8 |
| ● Barolo Cannubi '05 | ♟♟♟ 8 |
| ● Barolo Cannubi '00 | ♟♟♟ 8 |
| ● Barolo Cannubi '13 | ♟♟ 8 |
| ● Barolo Cannubi '12 | ♟♟ 8 |
| ● Barolo Mosconi '13 | ♟♟ 8 |
| ● Barolo Mosconi '12 | ♟♟ 8 |
| ● Barolo Mosconi '11 | ♟♟ 8 |
| ● Barolo Via Nuova '13 | ♟♟ 8 |

# Agostino Bosco

VIA FONTANE, 24
12064 LA MORRA [CN]
TEL. +39 0173509466
www.barolobosco.com

**CELLAR SALES**
**PRE-BOOKED VISITS**
**ANNUAL PRODUCTION** 28,000 bottles
**HECTARES UNDER VINE** 5.50
**SUSTAINABLE WINERY**

Andrea Bosco, an expert winemaker, continues to refine and consolidate his winery's signature style. In the vineyards he's chosen to pursue respect for the environment, eliminating weedkillers and invasive chemicals. Both his Barolo La Serra and Neirane see a short stay in small French casks and then a longer period in large Slavonian oak barrels. The recent renovation of an old vineyard has allowed for a vast production of Langhe Nebbiolo, another of their strong points, along with Barbera d'Alba Volupta. Their 2014 Barolo La Serra offers up medium-ripe fruit and the occasional herbaceous note. It's a wine endowed with enough structure that it's guaranteed to age well. Their valid 2014 Barolo Neirane is a tight and firm wine in its youth, offering up clean notes of quinine and alcohol. Their enjoyable 2016 Barbera d'Alba Superiore Volupta is anything but simple, proving rich in ripe red berries and herbs in the sun.

| | |
|---|---|
| ● Barbera d'Alba Sup. Volupta '16 | ♛♛ 3* |
| ● Barolo La Serra '14 | ♛♛ 6 |
| ● Barolo Neirane '14 | ♛♛ 5 |
| ● Dolcetto d'Alba Vantrin '17 | ♛ 2 |
| ● Langhe Nebbiolo Rurem '16 | ♛ 3 |
| ● Barbera d'Alba Sup. Volupta '15 | ♙♙ 3 |
| ● Barbera d'Alba Sup. Volupta '14 | ♙♙ 3 |
| ● Barbera d'Alba Sup. Volupta '13 | ♙♙ 3 |
| ● Barolo La Serra '13 | ♙♙ 6 |
| ● Barolo La Serra '12 | ♙♙ 6 |
| ● Barolo La Serra '11 | ♙♙ 6 |
| ● Barolo Neirane '13 | ♙♙ 5 |
| ● Barolo Neirane '11 | ♙♙ 5 |
| ● Barolo Neirane '10 | ♙♙ 5 |
| ● Dolcetto d'Alba Vantrin '15 | ♙♙ 2* |
| ● Dolcetto d'Alba Vantrin '14 | ♙♙ 2* |
| ● Langhe Nebbiolo Rurem '15 | ♙♙ 3 |

# Luigi Boveri

LOC. MONTALE CELLI
VIA XX SETTEMBRE, 6
15050 COSTA VESCOVATO [AL]
TEL. +39 0131838165
www.boveriluigi.com

**CELLAR SALES**
**PRE-BOOKED VISITS**
**ANNUAL PRODUCTION** 80,000 bottles
**HECTARES UNDER VINE** 15.00

In a territory like Tortona that's experiencing a rise in wine production, Luigi Boveri is certainly a benchmark. His wines never fall short of expectations. His Timorasso comes in two versions: Filari di Timorasso and Derthona offer up buoyant sensations. But there's more than that (we're talking about his reds, specifically those made with Barbera). There's his base level Boccanera, the more structured Poggio delle Amarene, and a version aged in barriques, Vignalunga. It's a selection that's deeply tied to the territory and that's rounded out with commendable versions of Croatina and Cortese. Their Timorasso di Luigi once again lands in our finals thanks to two decidedly intriguing versions. Their Filari di Timorasso features vibrant, complex aromas of benzine and camphor accompanied by notes of flint. On the palate it proves potent with the acidity of a very young wine. It has excellent aging prospects. Their 2016 Derthona is already closer to being ready, proving subtle and elegant on the nose. On the palate it's potent and rich, with lovely persistence.

| | |
|---|---|
| ○ Colli Tortonesi Timorasso Derthona '16 | ♛♛ 4 |
| ○ Colli Tortonesi Timorasso Derthona Filari di Timorasso '16 | ♛♛ 5 |
| ● Colli Tortonesi Barbera Boccanera '17 | ♛♛ 2* |
| ○ Colli Tortonesi Cortese Terre del Prete '17 | ♛ 2 |
| ○ Colli Tortonesi Timorasso Derthona '11 | ♙♙♙ 4* |
| ○ Colli Tortonesi Timorasso Filari di Timorasso '12 | ♙♙♙ 5 |
| ○ Colli Tortonesi Timorasso Filari di Timorasso '07 | ♙♙♙ 3 |
| ● Colli Tortonesi Barbera Boccanera '15 | ♙♙ 2* |
| ● Colli Tortonesi Barbera Vignalunga '13 | ♙♙ 5 |
| ● Colli Tortonesi Croatina Sensazioni '15 | ♙♙ 4 |
| ○ Colli Tortonesi Timorasso Derthona '15 | ♙♙ 4 |
| ○ Colli Tortonesi Timorasso Derthona Filari di Timorasso '15 | ♙♙ 5 |

## Gianfranco Bovio

FRAZ. ANNUNZIATA
B.TA CIOTTO, 63
12064 LA MORRA [CN]
TEL. +39 017350667
www.boviogianfranco.com

**CELLAR SALES**
**PRE-BOOKED VISITS**
**ANNUAL PRODUCTION** 55,000 bottles
**HECTARES UNDER VINE** 8.50

Alessandra Bovio has put together a
first-rate team and given them the
responsibility of overseeing every aspect of
the winery founded by his father, Gianfranco,
a famous restaurant owner. Their general
direction is clear: go back to large wood
barrels, either French or Slavonian, to allow
the most authentic and direct expression of
Nebbiolo. Here the grape is endowed with
particularly floral and spicy aromas. At the
center of their selection are the Arborina and
Gattera crus, which continue to prove candid
and elegant, never aggressive. All their
wines can be tasted by directly at the cellar,
or else at a nice family restaurant. Their
subtle and rather complex 2014 Barolo
opens on the nose with lovely, close-focused
fruit, raspberries and strawberries, then
tobacco and quinine, as well as nicely
controlled greener notes. On the palate
it proves well-balanced, with notable
structure and close-woven tannins. Their
2016 Barbera d'Alba Superiore Regiaveja
is a potent, alcohol-dominated wine, while
their lovely 2016 Langhe Nebbiolo Firagnetti
proves delicate and flowery.

| | |
|---|---|
| ● Barolo '14 | ♟♟ 6 |
| ● Barbera d'Alba Il Ciotto '17 | ♟♟ 2* |
| ● Barbera d'Alba Sup. Regiaveja '16 | ♟♟ 4 |
| ● Langhe Nebbiolo Firagnetti '16 | ♟♟ 3 |
| ● Barolo Bricco Parussi Ris. '01 | ♟♟♟ 6 |
| ● Barolo Gattera '11 | ♟♟♟ 6 |
| ● Barolo Rocchettevino '06 | ♟♟♟ 5* |
| ● Barbera d'Alba Regiaveja '15 | ♟♟ 4 |
| ● Barbera d'Alba Sup. Regiaveja '13 | ♟♟ 4 |
| ● Barolo '13 | ♟♟ 6 |
| ● Barolo '12 | ♟♟ 6 |
| ● Barolo Arborina '13 | ♟♟ 6 |
| ● Barolo Arborina '12 | ♟♟ 6 |
| ● Barolo Gattera '13 | ♟♟ 6 |
| ● Barolo Gattera '12 | ♟♟ 6 |
| ● Dolcetto d'Alba Dabbene '15 | ♟♟ 2* |

## ★Braida

LOC. CIAPPELLETTE
S.DA PROVINCIALE 27, 9
14030 ROCCHETTA TANARO [AT]
TEL. +39 0141644113
www.braida.it

**CELLAR SALES**
**PRE-BOOKED VISITS**
**ACCOMMODATION**
**ANNUAL PRODUCTION** 700,000 bottles
**HECTARES UNDER VINE** 70.00
**SUSTAINABLE WINERY**

The Bologna family's La Braida has been a
benchmark among Piedmont's winemakers
for more than 50 years. Their estate is
divided into various plots spread throughout
five different districts. Rocchetta Tanaro
gives rise to their most important Barberas,
while Costigliole d'Asti and Castelnuovo
Calcea are devoted to the red grapes used
in their fresher, more approachable wines.
Trezzo Tinella hosts the white grapes used in
their Serra dei Fiori line while Mango sees
the cultivation of Moscato. Their historic
Barbera d'Asti Bricco dell'Uccellone proved
excellent during our tastings. The 2016 is in
perfect keeping with previous years,
exhibiting great structure and fullness with
notes of still-pronounced notes of oak
accompanying black cherry, pencil lead and
tar. It's a true classic. Their 2016 Barbera
d'Asti Bricco della Bigotta runs along the
same lines, opting for more pronounced
tones of wet earth. It's a bit simpler but
succulent and rich in fruit. As always the rest
of their selection proved well-made.

| | |
|---|---|
| ● Barbera d'Asti Bricco dell'Uccellone '16 | ♟♟ 7 |
| ● Barbera d'Asti Bricco della Bigotta '16 | ♟♟ 7 |
| ● Barbera d'Asti Ai Suma '15 | ♟♟ 7 |
| ● Barbera d'Asti Montebruna '16 | ♟♟ 3 |
| ● Grignolino d'Asti Limonte '17 | ♟♟ 3 |
| ○ Langhe Chardonnay Asso di Fiori '16 | ♟♟ 5 |
| ○ Moscato d'Asti V. Senza Nome '17 | ♟♟ 3 |
| ● Barbera del M.to La Monella '17 | ♟ 3 |
| ○ Langhe Bianco Il Fiore '17 | ♟ 3 |
| ○ Langhe Nascetta La Regina '17 | ♟ 3 |
| ● Barbera d'Asti Bricco dell'Uccellone '15 | ♟♟♟ 7 |
| ● Barbera d'Asti Bricco dell'Uccellone '12 | ♟♟♟ 7 |
| ● Barbera d'Asti Bricco dell'Uccellone '09 | ♟♟♟ 6 |
| ● Barbera d'Asti Bricco della Bigotta '07 | ♟♟♟ 6 |
| ● Barbera d'Asti Montebruna '11 | ♟♟♟ 3* |

# Brandini

FRAZ. BRANDINI, 16
12064 LA MORRA [CN]
TEL. +39 017350266
www.agricolabrandini.com

**CELLAR SALES**
**PRE-BOOKED VISITS**
**ACCOMMODATION AND RESTAURANT SERVICE**
**ANNUAL PRODUCTION** 80,000 bottles
**HECTARES UNDER VINE** 15.00
**VITICULTURE METHOD** Certified Organic
**SUSTAINABLE WINERY**

The Brandini brand has been around since 1985. Today it's managed by the Bagnasco family, who continue to pursue organic management with conviction. The cellar is decidedly dynamic. After the release of their Barolo Resa 56, which was immediately well-received by critics and the market, their most recent purchases are being put to use. The winery has bet on Serralunga's strong Nebbiolo with a Barolo from the Meriame cru and soon with Cerretta. The entire selection is classically styled and elegant, though their Barbera d'Alba Rocche del Santo and two Alta Langas are standouts. Their 2014 Barolo, made with grapes from La Morra, features harmony, subtleness and a fresh palate while striking a perfect balance between acidity and tannins. It takes home Tre Bicchieri. Their 2014 Meriame, a limited edition Barolo from Serralunga, is among the year's best. Their Barolo R56 proves a bit bridled. It should benefit, along with their Annunziata, from more time in the bottle. Their Rebelle, a blend made primarily with Viognier, proved interesting.

| | |
|---|---|
| ● Barolo del Comune di La Morra '14 | 🍷🍷🍷 8 |
| ● Barolo Meriame '14 | 🍷🍷 8 |
| ● Barolo Annunziata '14 | 🍷🍷 8 |
| ● Barolo R56 '14 | 🍷🍷 8 |
| ○ Langhe Bianco Rebelle '17 | 🍷🍷 7 |
| ● Barolo Resa 56 '13 | 🍷🍷🍷 8 |
| ● Barolo Resa 56 '12 | 🍷🍷🍷 8 |
| ● Barolo Resa 56 '11 | 🍷🍷🍷 7 |
| ● Barolo Resa 56 '10 | 🍷🍷🍷 7 |
| ○ Alta Langa Brut '10 | 🍷🍷 8 |
| ☉ Alta Langa Brut Rosé '11 | 🍷🍷 6 |
| ● Barolo '12 | 🍷🍷 7 |
| ● Barolo del Comune di La Morra '14 | 🍷🍷 8 |
| ● Barolo del Comune di La Morra '13 | 🍷🍷 8 |
| ● Barolo Resa 56 Ris. '10 | 🍷🍷 8 |
| ● Langhe Nebbiolo Filari Corti '15 | 🍷🍷 5 |
| ● Langhe Nebbiolo Filari Corti '14 | 🍷🍷 5 |

# Brangero

VIA PROVINCIALE, 26
12055 DIANO D'ALBA [CN]
TEL. +39 017369423
www.brangero.com

**PRE-BOOKED VISITS**
**ANNUAL PRODUCTION** 50,000 bottles
**HECTARES UNDER VINE** 9.00

Since 1999 Marco Brangero has been leading his winery, situated on the highest point of the hill that looks out at Diano d'Alba. Piedmont's classic grape varieties are cultivated in the vineyard around his cellar, with Dolcetto accompanied by Barbera, Nebbiolo and Arneis, as well as a few plots dedicated to international cultivar. In addition to a small parcel of land in Verduno (Monvigliero cru), Marco produces two Barolos. But Marco's efforts go beyond Piedmont, and for some years now he's been managing La Ginestraia, a Ligurian producer in the province of Imperia. A pale but brightly colored 2014 Barolo Monvigliero proved ethery and vibrant in its aromas, with accents of pencil lead and wild strawberries. On the palate it's still a bit clenched but its structure is there, with close-woven tannins that will need a bit more time in the bottle. Their 2016 Barbera d'Alba Superiore La Soprana offers up fragrances of spices and small red fruit, while on the palate it comes through with a fresh, minty finish.

| | |
|---|---|
| ● Barolo Monvigliero '14 | 🍷🍷 6 |
| ● Langhe Nebbiolo Quattro Cloni '16 | 🍷🍷 4 |
| ● Barbera d'Alba Sup. La Soprana '16 | 🍷 3 |
| ● Barbera d'Alba La Soprana '13 | 🍷🍷 3 |
| ● Barolo Monvigliero '12 | 🍷🍷 6 |
| ● Barolo Monvigliero '11 | 🍷🍷 6 |
| ● Barolo Monvigliero '09 | 🍷🍷 6 |
| ● Dolcetto di Diano d'Alba Sörì Cascina Rabino '16 | 🍷🍷 2* |
| ● Dolcetto di Diano d'Alba Sörì Rabino Soprano '15 | 🍷🍷 2* |
| ● Dolcetto di Diano d'Alba Sörì Rabino Soprano '11 | 🍷🍷 2* |
| ○ Langhe Chardonnay Centofile '13 | 🍷🍷 3 |
| ● Langhe Nebbiolo Quattro Cloni '15 | 🍷🍷 4 |
| ● Langhe Rosso Tremarzo '15 | 🍷🍷 4 |
| ● Nebbiolo d'Alba Bricco Bertone '12 | 🍷🍷 4 |

## Brema

VIA POZZOMAGNA, 9
14045 INCISA SCAPACCINO [AT]
TEL. +39 014174019
www.vinibrema.com

CELLAR SALES
PRE-BOOKED VISITS
ANNUAL PRODUCTION 150,000 bottles
HECTARES UNDER VINE 25.00
SUSTAINABLE WINERY

The Brema family winery boasts more than
130 years of history and has at its disposal
a series of vineyards situated in various
districts through Asti: Nizza Monferrato,
Fontanile d'Asti, San Marzano Oliveto,
Incisa Scapaccino and Sessame d'Asti.
Barbera is their principal cultivar, obviously,
and gives rise to most of their wines. Their
style is modern while also exhibiting a
strong territorial identity and typicity. Once
again the Brema family's Barbera proves
that it's one of the best of its kind, earning
a place in our finals. Their more aristocratic
2015 Nizza A Luigi Veronelli is balsamic on
the nose, with notes of cherry, aniseed and
juniper, while on the palate it proves rich in
pulp, fresh and juicy, with nice structure.
Their 2015 Barbera d'Asti Superiore La
Volpettona features notes of red fruit,
proving highly approachable, supple and
quaffable. The other wines submitted were
all also sound.

| | |
|---|---|
| ● Barbera d'Asti Sup. Volpettona '15 | ♟♟ 5 |
| ● Nizza A Luigi Veronelli '15 | ♟♟ 6 |
| ● Barbera d'Asti Ai Cruss '16 | ♟♟ 2* |
| ● Barbera del M.to Vivace Castagni '17 | ♟♟ 2* |
| ● M.to Rosso Umberto '15 | ♟ 4 |
| ● Barbera d'Asti Sup. Nizza A Luigi Veronelli '12 | ♟♟♟ 6 |
| ● Barbera d'Asti Sup. Nizza A Luigi Veronelli '06 | ♟♟♟ 6 |
| ● Barbera d'Asti Ai Cruss '15 | ♟♟ 2* |
| ● Barbera d'Asti Sup. Nizza A Luigi Veronelli '13 | ♟♟ 6 |
| ● Barbera d'Asti Sup. Nizza A Luigi Veronelli '11 | ♟♟ 6 |
| ● Barbera d'Asti Sup. Volpettona '13 | ♟♟ 5 |
| ● M.to Rosso Umberto '13 | ♟♟ 4 |

## Giacomo Brezza & Figli

VIA LOMONDO, 4
12060 BAROLO [CN]
TEL. +39 0173560921
www.brezza.it

CELLAR SALES
PRE-BOOKED VISITS
ACCOMMODATION AND RESTAURANT SERVICE
ANNUAL PRODUCTION 100,000 bottles
HECTARES UNDER VINE 17.50
VITICULTURE METHOD Certified Organic
SUSTAINABLE WINERY

Brezza is a name that evokes tradition, a
bond with the land, sharing. Their symbol is
an osteria-winery where you can enjoy
hospitality while surrounded by a range of
wines whose brilliant color invites drinking.
Their wines are matured slowly in medium
and large Slavonian oak barrels, while their
vineyards are situated in Barolo (Castellero,
Cannubi, Sarmassa and Sarmassa Vigna
Bricco, available as a reserve wine), with
plots in Monforte d'Alba, Novello, Diano
d'Alba and Alba as well. Their style is
extremely classic, with wines rich in acidic
and savory contrasts, and designed for the
long haul. Their 2014 Barolo Sarmassa
offers up hints of wood resin and tobacco.
It's a spicy, lean wine, delicately salty, rich
in counterpoint. The finish comes through
long, it's only a bit lacking in the energy
we've grown used. Their valid 2014 Barolo
opts more for tones of herbs in the sun
than for fruit, while their 2014 Barolo
Cannubi is more light-bodied. Their
2016 Barbera d'Alba Superiore is a rustic,
delectable wine that hits the mark.

| | |
|---|---|
| ● Barolo Sarmassa '14 | ♟♟ 7 |
| ● Barbera d'Alba Sup. '16 | ♟♟ 4 |
| ● Barolo '14 | ♟♟ 5 |
| ● Barolo Cannubi '14 | ♟ 6 |
| ● Nebbiolo d'Alba V. Santa Rosalia '16 | ♟ 3 |
| ● Barolo Bricco Sarmassa '08 | ♟♟♟ 7 |
| ● Barolo Bricco Sarmassa '07 | ♟♟♟ 7 |
| ● Barolo Sarmassa '11 | ♟♟♟ 6 |
| ● Barolo Sarmassa '05 | ♟♟♟ 6 |
| ● Barolo Sarmassa '04 | ♟♟♟ 6 |
| ● Barolo Sarmassa V. Bricco Ris. '11 | ♟♟♟ 7 |
| ● Barolo Cannubi '12 | ♟♟ 6 |
| ● Barolo Sarmassa '13 | ♟♟ 7 |
| ● Barolo Sarmassa '12 | ♟♟ 7 |

# Gallino Domenico
# Bric Castelvej

Madonna Loreto, 70
12043 Canale [CN]
Tel. +39 017398108
www.briccastelvej.com

**CELLAR SALES**
**PRE-BOOKED VISITS**
**ANNUAL PRODUCTION** 100,000 bottles
**HECTARES UNDER VINE** 12.40

Mario and Cristiano Repellino manage the winery founded by Domenico Gallino in 1956. Bric Castelvej offers a wide range of wines, all traditionally styled and attentive both to structure and drinkability. Their vineyards, which host Roero's traditional grape varieties (foremost Arneis, Barbera and Nebbiolo), are situated in Canale. The terrain here is rich in sand with pockets of loam and calcareous clay. Their 2015 Roero Panera Alta earned a place in our finals thanks to its aromas of blackberry and forest undergrowth, an a juicy, long palate with nice fruit and structure. Among the rest of their selection we most appreciated two of their 'base-level' wines rather than their respective crus. We were most impressed with their 2017 Barbera d'Alba, a pleasant and drinkable wine with nice acidity and rich fruit, and their savory, citrusy and approachable 2017 Roero Arneis, a wine with nice tension. The rest of their selection proved sound and consistent.

| | |
|---|---|
| ● Roero Panera Alta '15 | ♟♟ 6 |
| ● Barbera d'Alba '17 | ♟♟ 2* |
| ○ Roero Arneis '17 | ♟♟ 2* |
| ● Barbera d'Alba V. Mompissano '17 | ♟ 2 |
| ○ Langhe Favorita '17 | ♟ 2 |
| ● Langhe Nebbiolo '17 | ♟ 3 |
| ● Roero '15 | ♟ 4 |
| ○ Roero Arneis Bricco Novara '17 | ♟ 3 |
| ● Barbera d'Alba '16 | ♟♟ 2* |
| ● Barbera d'Alba Sup. Mompissano '16 | ♟♟ 2* |
| ● Roero '13 | ♟♟ 4 |
| ○ Roero Arneis '16 | ♟♟ 2* |
| ○ Roero Arneis '15 | ♟♟ 2* |
| ○ Roero Arneis V. Bricco Novara '15 | ♟♟ 3* |
| ● Roero Panera Alta Ris. '14 | ♟♟ 6 |
| ● Roero Panera Alta Ris. '13 | ♟♟ 6 |

# Bric Cenciurio

via Roma, 24
12060 Barolo [CN]
Tel. +39 017356317
www.briccenciurio.com

**CELLAR SALES**
**PRE-BOOKED VISITS**
**ANNUAL PRODUCTION** 50,000 bottles
**HECTARES UNDER VINE** 15.00

Fiorella Sacchetto, originally from Castellinaldo, moved to Barolo for love. Today, along with her brother Carlo and her children Alberto and Alessandro Pittatore, she manages this small winery. The estate's vineyards are situated in both Langhe and nearby Roero. Their Barolo is quite classic in style with fruit at the forefront. Their Barbera d'Alba Naunda expresses aromas closer to oak. Those who want to deepen their understanding of the grapes used, on this side of the Tanaro and beyond, Carlo Arnulfo's 'Langhe and Roero, from the Soil to the Glass ' (published by ArabAFenice) is a succinct guide. Their 2014 Barolo Coste di Rose offers up close-focused, complex aromas, moving from red fruit to quinine to licorice. On the palate it's a bit marked by tannins. Their more austere and herbaceous Monrobiolo di Bussia (same year) is a fresh wine, while their 2015 Barbera d'Alba Naunda is simple and rather plush. Their 2016 Langhe Nebbiolo is quite spicy and approachable, while their Langhe Riesling proves rich and elegant.

| | |
|---|---|
| ● Barolo Coste di Rose '14 | ♟♟ 6 |
| ● Barolo Monrobiolo di Bussia '14 | ♟♟ 6 |
| ● Langhe Nebbiolo '16 | ♟♟ 4 |
| ○ Langhe Riesling '16 | ♟♟ 2* |
| ● Barbera d'Alba Sup. Naunda '15 | ♟ 4 |
| ● Barolo '14 | ♟ 5 |
| ○ Langhe Arneis Sito dei Fossili '17 | ♟ 2 |
| ● Barbera d'Alba Sup. Naunda '13 | ♟♟ 4 |
| ● Barolo '13 | ♟♟ 5 |
| ● Barolo '12 | ♟♟ 5 |
| ● Barolo Coste di Rose Ris. '11 | ♟♟ 7 |
| ● Barolo Coste di Rose Ris. '10 | ♟♟ 7 |
| ● Barolo Monrobiolo di Bussia '13 | ♟♟ 6 |
| ● Langhe Nebbiolo '15 | ♟♟ 4 |
| ● Langhe Nebbiolo '14 | ♟♟ 4 |
| ○ Langhe Riesling '15 | ♟♟ 3 |

## Bricco Maiolica

FRAZ. RICCA
VIA BOLANGINO, 7
12055 DIANO D'ALBA [CN]
TEL. +39 0173612049
www.briccomaiolica.it

**CELLAR SALES**
**PRE-BOOKED VISITS**
**ACCOMMODATION**
**ANNUAL PRODUCTION** 110,000 bottles
**HECTARES UNDER VINE** 24.00
**SUSTAINABLE WINERY**

Beppe Accomo has been recognized both in Italy and abroad thanks to the three cultivar that he interprets best: Dolcetto, Nebbiolo and Barbera. The first gives rise to a benchmark wine in the appellation, Dolcetto di Diano d'Alba. In the case of the second, after years of positive results with his Nebbiolo d'Alba Cumot, he's recently bet on a Barolo called Contadin. And finally, with his Barbera d'Alba Cigna Vigia he's delivered a charming wine, vibrant and intense. His opulent Chardonnay Pensiero Infinito features a nice, exotic touch. Their 2014 Barolo, from Diano d'Alba Contadin, features nice, fresh red fruit and a pleasant background of licorice and spices. On the palate it comes through rich and potent, with abundant pulp and well-behaved acidity. Their elegant 2015 Barbera d'Alba Superiore Vigna Vigia is a plush wine, still slightly marked by oak, while their Nebbiolo d'Alba Cumot is always a sure bet. Their Langhe Rosso Tris is a modern, pleasantly herbaceous wine.

## Francesco Brigatti

VIA OLMI, 31
28019 SUNO [NO]
TEL. +39 032285037
www.vinibrigatti.it

**CELLAR SALES**
**PRE-BOOKED VISITS**
**ANNUAL PRODUCTION** 25,000 bottles
**HECTARES UNDER VINE** 6.50

A century ago this part of Alto Piemonte was a chain of vineyards as far as the eye can see. Phylloxera, the two world wars and an exodus of farmers towards to factories deeply changed the landscape here, with woods replacing the fields. Expert Francesco Brigatti is among the numerous small producers who are reviving the vineyards here. Francesco is primarily cultivating Nebbiolo, along with historic varieties like Croatina, Uva Rara, Barbera, and a touch of Greco Bianco. In addition to their Ghemme Oltre il Bosco, standouts include their Nebbiolo Möt Ziflon and Möt Frei Their selection put in an excellent overall performance, with some six wines earning at least Due Bicchieri. Their 2013 Ghemme Oltre Il Bosco leads the group, with its aromas of lovely, fresh red fruit, quinine and gentian. On the palate it proves elegant, with excellent development, medium-weight and a commendably elegant finish. Their exceptionally pleasant Vespolina Maria and bold Bianco Mottobello are also both notable.

| | |
|---|---|
| ● Barbera d'Alba Sup. V. Vigia '15 | ♟♟ 5 |
| ● Barolo del Comune di Diano d'Alba Contadin '14 | ♟♟ 8 |
| ● Nebbiolo d'Alba Sup. Cumot '15 | ♟♟ 5 |
| ● Dolcetto di Diano d'Alba '17 | ♟♟ 3 |
| ○ Langhe Chardonnay Pensiero Infinito '14 | ♟♟ 6 |
| ● Langhe Rosso Tris '16 | ♟♟ 3 |
| ● Barbera d'Alba Sup. '16 | ♟ 3 |
| ● Langhe Nebbiolo '16 | ♟ 3 |
| ● Langhe Pinot Nero '15 | ♟ 5 |
| ● Diano d'Alba Sup. Sörì Bricco Maiolica '07 | ♟♟♟ 3* |
| ● Nebbiolo d'Alba Cumot '11 | ♟♟♟ 5 |
| ● Nebbiolo d'Alba Cumot '10 | ♟♟♟ 4* |
| ● Nebbiolo d'Alba Cumot '09 | ♟♟♟ 4* |
| ● Nebbiolo d'Alba Sup. Cumot '13 | ♟♟♟ 5 |

| | |
|---|---|
| ● Ghemme Oltre il Bosco '13 | ♟♟ 4 |
| ● Colline Novaresi Barbera Campazzi '17 | ♟♟ 3 |
| ○ Colline Novaresi Bianco Mottobello '17 | ♟♟ 3 |
| ● Colline Novaresi Nebbiolo Mötfrei '15 | ♟♟ 3 |
| ● Colline Novaresi Nebbiolo MötZiflon '15 | ♟♟ 3 |
| ● Colline Novaresi Vespolina Maria '17 | ♟♟ 3 |
| ● Colline Novaresi Uva Rara Selvalunga '17 | ♟ 2 |
| ● Ghemme Oltre il Bosco '14 | ♟ 4 |
| ● Colline Novaresi Barbera Campazzi '16 | ♙♙ 3 |
| ● Colline Novaresi Nebbiolo Mötfrei '13 | ♙♙ 3 |
| ● Colline Novaresi Nebbiolo MötZiflon '14 | ♙♙ 3 |
| ● Colline Novaresi Nebbiolo MötZiflon '13 | ♙♙ 3 |
| ● Colline Novaresi Vespolina Maria '16 | ♙♙ 3* |
| ● Colline Novaresi Vespolina Maria '15 | ♙♙ 3 |
| ● Ghemme Oltre il Bosco '12 | ♙♙ 4 |
| ● Ghemme Oltre il Bosco '11 | ♙♙ 4 |

# ★Brovia

VIA ALBA-BAROLO, 145
12060 CASTIGLIONE FALLETTO [CN]
TEL. +39 017362852
www.brovia.net

**CELLAR SALES**
**PRE-BOOKED VISITS**
**ANNUAL PRODUCTION** 60,000 bottles
**HECTARES UNDER VINE** 17.00
**VITICULTURE METHOD** Certified Organic

Elena and Cristina Brovia are leading one of Barolo's most celebrated and appreciated wineries. It's all thanks to the work that started more than 60 years ago with their skilled father, Giacinto, and to their ability to make wines that go beyond fashion and debates over local tradition. Indeed, their wines represent the purest of classic Barolo. Their grapes, which come from Castiglione Falletto and Serralunga d'Alba, are selected carefully, making the yield per hectare quite low and guaranteeing splendid results year after year. A selection of grapes from their private vineyards wasn't enough to confer their newborn 2014 Barolo Unio with Brovia's trademark complexity and aromatic appeal. The palate it is nice, nevertheless, with good weight and balance. Their 2016 Barbera d'Alba Sorì del Drago is a complete, pure wine endowed elegant hints of licorice. Their 2016 Vignavillej is exemplary of what Dolcetto d'Alba can do in terms of pleasantness, complexity and freshness.

| | |
|---|---|
| ● Barolo Unio '14 | ♟♟ 8 |
| ● Dolcetto d'Alba Vignavillej '16 | ♟♟ 3* |
| ● Barbera d'Alba Sorì del Drago '16 | ♟♟ 4 |
| ● Barolo Brea V. Ca' Mia '10 | ♟♟♟ 8 |
| ● Barolo Ca' Mia '09 | ♟♟♟ 8 |
| ● Barolo Ca' Mia '00 | ♟♟♟ 8 |
| ● Barolo Rocche dei Brovia '06 | ♟♟♟ 7 |
| ● Barolo Rocche di Castiglione '12 | ♟♟♟ 8 |
| ● Barolo Villero '13 | ♟♟♟ 8 |
| ● Barolo Villero '11 | ♟♟♟ 8 |
| ● Barolo Villero '10 | ♟♟♟ 8 |
| ● Barolo Villero '08 | ♟♟♟ 7 |
| ● Barolo Villero '06 | ♟♟♟ 7 |

# G. B. Burlotto

VIA VITTORIO EMANUELE, 28
12060 VERDUNO [CN]
TEL. +39 0172470122
www.burlotto.com

**CELLAR SALES**
**PRE-BOOKED VISITS**
**ACCOMMODATION**
**ANNUAL PRODUCTION** 60,000 bottles
**HECTARES UNDER VINE** 15.00

It all began in the second half of the 19th century when commander Giovanni Battista Burlotto founded his winery in Verduno. Today, under Favio Alessandria, the estate is carving out an important place for itself among Langhe's producers. Half of its 15 hectares of vineyards are dedicated to Nebbiolo, with plots in Verduno (Monvigliero, Neirane, Breri, Rocche dell'Olmo) and Barolo (Cannubi). The other half features Piedmont's other principal varieties: Barbera, Dolcetto, Freisa and the unmistakable Pelaverga. Their approach to winemaking could be called traditional, with their classically styled Barolos matured in 3500 and 5000 liter barrels. Their 2014 Barolo Cannubi just fell short of Tre Bicchieri. It's a crisp wine in its fruity aromas enriched by sensations of quinine and licorice. On the palate it proves steady and persistent, with an average weight for the year and a long, sustained finish. Their 2014 Barolo Monvigliero is also excellent, with a deep, complex palate and a commendable tannic extraction, considering the year.

| | |
|---|---|
| ● Barolo Cannubi '14 | ♟♟ 7 |
| ● Barolo Monvigliero '14 | ♟♟ 7 |
| ● Barbera d'Alba Aves '16 | ♟♟ 4 |
| ● Barolo '14 | ♟♟ 6 |
| ○ Langhe Sauvignon Dives '16 | ♟♟ 3 |
| ○ Langhe Sauvignon Viridis '17 | ♟♟ 3 |
| ● Verduno Pelaverga '17 | ♟♟ 3 |
| ● Barolo Acclivi '11 | ♟♟♟ 6 |
| ● Barolo Acclivi '07 | ♟♟♟ 6 |
| ● Barolo Cannubi '12 | ♟♟♟ 7 |
| ● Barolo Monvigliero '10 | ♟♟♟ 7 |
| ● Barolo '13 | ♟♟ 6 |
| ● Barolo Acclivi '13 | ♟♟ 6 |
| ● Barolo Cannubi '13 | ♟♟ 7 |
| ● Barolo Monvigliero '12 | ♟♟ 7 |
| ● Verduno Pelaverga '16 | ♟♟ 3 |

## ★Pierguido Carlo Busso

VIA ALBESANI
12052 NEIVE [CN]
TEL. +39 017367156
www.bussopiero.com

CELLAR SALES
PRE-BOOKED VISITS
ACCOMMODATION
ANNUAL PRODUCTION 45,000 bottles
HECTARES UNDER VINE 11.50
SUSTAINABLE WINERY

For 30 years the name Piero Busso has brought admiration and amazement in lieu of the stylistic precision the producer manages to confer on its wines year after year. Their four Barbarescos represent a rare purity of fruit and a personality that reflects both the vintage and the vineyard. Aging in oak barrels is needed only to harmonize and round out the tannins in their Nebbiolo. The contribution of Piero's wife, Lucia, has always been fundamental, while young Emanuela and Pierguido are now on board full time. Their work in the cellar is aimed at further perfecting the classic style that's already expressed so well. Their three Barbarescos all delivered during our tastings, particularly their elegant San Stunet, a wine that stands out for its delicate tannins. Their Vigna Borgese is a bit firmer and more pronounced in the mouth, while their Gallina proves complex and robust. Their 2016 Barbera d'Alba S. Stefanetto is a warm, mouthfilling wine, while their Majano comes through a bit more assertive. Their 2016 Langhe Nebbiolo is particularly enjoyable.

| | | |
|---|---|---|
| ● Barbaresco Albesani V. Borgese '14 | ▼▼ | 7 |
| ● Barbaresco S. Stunet '14 | ▼▼ | 7 |
| ● Barbaresco Gallina '14 | ▼▼ | 8 |
| ● Barbera d'Alba S. Stefanetto '16 | ▼▼ | 5 |
| ● Langhe Nebbiolo '16 | ▼▼ | 4 |
| ● Barbera d'Alba Majano '16 | ▼ | 3 |
| ● Barbaresco Borgese '09 | ♀♀♀ | 6 |
| ● Barbaresco Borgese '08 | ♀♀♀ | 6 |
| ● Barbaresco Gallina '12 | ♀♀♀ | 8 |
| ● Barbaresco Gallina '11 | ♀♀♀ | 8 |
| ● Barbaresco Gallina '09 | ♀♀♀ | 8 |
| ● Barbaresco Gallina '05 | ♀♀♀ | 7 |
| ● Barbaresco S. Stefanetto '07 | ♀♀♀ | 7 |
| ● Barbaresco S. Stefanetto '04 | ♀♀♀ | 7 |
| ● Barbaresco S. Stefanetto '03 | ♀♀♀ | 7 |
| ● Barbaresco S. Stunet '11 | ♀♀♀ | 7 |

## Ca' Bianca

REG. SPAGNA, 58
15010 ALICE BEL COLLE [AL]
TEL. +39 0144745420
www.cantinacabianca.it

CELLAR SALES
PRE-BOOKED VISITS
ANNUAL PRODUCTION 500,000 bottles
HECTARES UNDER VINE 24.00

Owned by Gruppo Italiano Vini, Piedmont's Ca' Bianco is situated in Alice Bel Colle, within the hills that separate Acqui Terme and Nizza Monferrato. It's a picturesque and scenic position, with the winery and its surrounding vineyards perched on the hilltop. Their selection features a modern style centered around the typicity of the wines and the vineyards cultivated. But quality remains a top priority. For example, they work to maintain the stability and persistence of their Moscato and Brachetto's primary aromas. Their splendid Barbera d'Asti Superiore leads their sizable selection. It's a subtle, elegant wine at every stage of tasting, opening with aromas of fresh red fruit and slightly toasty notes. In the mouth it brings together pulp, acidity and tannins with great harmony, making for a succulent, persistent palate. It's followed by a number of extremely well-made wines, from Barbera and Dolcetto d'Acqui, as well as an excellent Gavi, possibly their best ever.

| | | |
|---|---|---|
| ● Barbera d'Asti Sup. Chersì '15 | ▼▼ | 5 |
| ● Barbera d'Asti Sup. Antè '16 | ▼▼ | 3 |
| ● Barbera d'Asti Teis '17 | ▼▼ | 3 |
| ● Dolcetto d'Acqui '17 | ▼▼ | 3 |
| ○ Gavi '17 | ▼▼ | 3 |
| ○ Moscato d'Asti '17 | ▼ | 3 |
| ○ Roero Arneis '17 | ▼ | 3 |
| ● Barbera d'Asti Sup. Antè '15 | ♀♀ | 3 |
| ● Barbera d'Asti Sup. Chersì '14 | ♀♀ | 5 |
| ● Barbera d'Asti Sup. Chersì '13 | ♀♀ | 5 |
| ● Barbera d'Asti Teis '16 | ♀♀ | 3 |
| ● Dolcetto d'Acqui '15 | ♀♀ | 3 |
| ○ Gavi '16 | ♀♀ | 3 |
| ○ Roero Arneis '15 | ♀♀ | 3 |

# Ca' d' Gal

FRAZ. VALDIVILLA
S.DA VECCHIA DI VALDIVILLA, 1
12058 SANTO STEFANO BELBO [CN]
TEL. +39 0141847103
www.cadgal.it

**CELLAR SALES**
**PRE-BOOKED VISITS**
**ACCOMMODATION AND RESTAURANT SERVICE**
**ANNUAL PRODUCTION** 95,000 bottles
**HECTARES UNDER VINE** 12.00

For some years now, Alessandro Boido has been a benchmark for Moscato winemaking. The reason has to do with the consistently high quality of his wines, but also for a style that's bound to the idea of a Moscato d'Asti that's easy-drinking but also capable of taking on a unique charm and a distinct character over time. His vineyards are situated primarily on the hills of Santo Stefano Belbo, with some going back more than 60 years. In addition to Moscato, the estate cultivates Chardonnay, Sauvignon, Pinot Nero and Freisa. During our tastings, their Moscato d'Asti Canelli Sant'Ilario affirmed its status as one of the best in the appellation. 2017 gave rise to aromas of honey, aromatic herbs and candied citrus peel. On the palate it's generous, complex and rich, yet also fresh, assertive and highly drinkable. Their 2015 Moscato d'Asti Vite Vecchia is the only wine to be released three years after vintage, and it too proves to be one of a kind with its notes of dried fruit and nuts, and sweet spices.

| | | |
|---|---|---|
| ○ Moscato d'Asti Canelli Sant'Ilario '17 | ♈♈ | 4 |
| ○ Moscato d'Asti Vite Vecchia '15 | ♈♈ | 7 |
| ○ Asti | ♈♈ | 3 |
| ○ Moscato d'Asti Lumine '17 | ♈♈ | 3 |
| ○ Moscato d'Asti Canelli Sant'Ilario '16 | ♈♈♈ | 4* |
| ○ Moscato d'Asti Canelli Sant'Ilario '15 | ♈♈♈ | 3* |
| ○ Moscato d'Asti V. V. '11 | ♈♈♈ | 3* |
| ○ Moscato d"Asti Vite Vecchia '14 | ♈♈ | 7 |
| ○ Moscato d'Asti Lumine '15 | ♈♈ | 3* |
| ○ Moscato d'Asti Sant'Ilario '14 | ♈♈ | 3* |
| ○ Moscato d'Asti V. Vecchia '10 | ♈♈ | 7 |

# ★Ca' del Baio

VIA FERRERE SOTTANO, 33
12050 TREISO [CN]
TEL. +39 0173638219
www.cadelbaio.com

**CELLAR SALES**
**PRE-BOOKED VISITS**
**ANNUAL PRODUCTION** 130,000 bottles
**HECTARES UNDER VINE** 25.00

Ca' del Baio is close to its 100-year anniversary, but the watershed moment came about 20 years ago, when Giulio Grasso opted for a new emphasis on quality. And so it was that he built a first-rate team and created one of Barbaresco's best producers (his 3 children are also contributing). And their investment in their vineyards continues, such that today they're offering 5 Barbarescos and an award-winning Langhe Riesling. Their Moscato d'Asti also continues to impress. Their 2015 Barbersco Asili is an intense, classically styled wine with notes of tobacco and licorice on a fruity background. In the mouth it exhibits great force and vitality, as well as close-woven but never dry tannins. A lengthy, well-balanced finish tops off an elegant and complex wine worthy of Tre Bicchieri. Their 2015 Vallegrande is well-defined and enticing thanks to its delicate personality, while their 2013 Asili Riserva, a wine endowed with extraordinary texture, will still need a bit more time before its great expressivity can peak.

| | | |
|---|---|---|
| ● Barbaresco Asili '15 | ♈♈♈ | 6 |
| ● Barbaresco Asili Ris. '13 | ♈♈ | 8 |
| ● Barbaresco Vallegrande '15 | ♈♈ | 5 |
| ● Barbaresco Autinbej '15 | ♈♈ | 5 |
| ○ Langhe Riesling '16 | ♈♈ | 3 |
| ● Barbaresco Asili '12 | ♈♈♈ | 6 |
| ● Barbaresco Asili '10 | ♈♈♈ | 6 |
| ● Barbaresco Asili '09 | ♈♈♈ | 5 |
| ● Barbaresco Asili '06 | ♈♈♈ | 5 |
| ● Barbaresco Asili Ris. '11 | ♈♈♈ | 8 |
| ● Barbaresco Pora '10 | ♈♈♈ | 6 |
| ● Barbaresco Pora '06 | ♈♈♈ | 6 |
| ● Barbaresco Pora '04 | ♈♈♈ | 6 |
| ● Barbaresco Valgrande '08 | ♈♈♈ | 5 |
| ● Barbaresco Valgrande '04 | ♈♈♈ | 5 |
| ● Barbaresco Vallegrande '14 | ♈♈♈ | 5 |

# Ca' Nova

VIA SAN ISIDORO, 1
28010 BOGOGNO [NO]
TEL. +39 0322863406
www.cascinacanova.it

CELLAR SALES
PRE-BOOKED VISITS
ACCOMMODATION
ANNUAL PRODUCTION 45,000 bottles
HECTARES UNDER VINE 10.00

The winery may be small but their project is clear: create outstanding wines, develop and get the best out of their cru, and offer visitors a lovely cellar as well as an elegant relais. It was all accomplished in less than 20 years and the results are brilliant, with wines that are receiving awards and accolades both at home and abroad. Ghemme stands firm at the top of their range, made in large barrels with a commendable respect for the peculiarities of each vintage. But their entire selection of still and sparkling wines deserves to be recognized and tasted. Their 2017 Vespolina is exemplary for the typology. Its elegant spices and herbaceous notes anticipate a rich, complex palate that features excellent pulp and a pervasive weight. Licorice and rhubarb form part of their 2013 Ghemme's broad aromatic profile while on the palate it demonstrates excellent balance and personality. Their 2017 Rosato Aurora is commendably soft on the palate, pleasantly fresh on the nose.

| | | |
|---|---|---|
| ● Colline Novaresi Vespolina '17 | ♟♟ | 2* |
| ● Ghemme '13 | ♟♟ | 5 |
| ● Colline Novaresi Nebbiolo Melchior '11 | ♟♟ | 3 |
| ⊙ Colline Novaresi Nebbiolo Rosato Aurora '17 | ♟♟ | 2* |
| ○ Jad'or Brut M. Cl. | ♟♟ | 4 |
| ○ Colline Novaresi Bianco Rugiada '17 | ♟ | 2 |
| ● Colline Novaresi Nebbiolo Bocciòlo '17 | ♟ | 2 |
| ● Colline Novaresi Nebbiolo Bocciòlo '16 | ♟♟ | 2* |
| ● Colline Novaresi Nebbiolo Melchiòr '09 | ♟♟ | 3* |
| ● Colline Novaresi Nebbiolo San Quirico '10 | ♟♟ | 4 |
| ● Colline Novaresi Nebbiolo V. San Quirico '09 | ♟♟ | 4 |
| ○ Colline Novaresi Vespolina '15 | ♟♟ | 2* |
| ● Ghemme '12 | ♟♟ | 5 |
| ● Ghemme '11 | ♟♟ | 5 |

# Ca' Rome'

S.DA RABAJA, 86
12050 BARBARESCO [CN]
TEL. +39 0173635126
www.carome.com

CELLAR SALES
PRE-BOOKED VISITS
ANNUAL PRODUCTION 30,000 bottles
HECTARES UNDER VINE 5.00

Some thirty years ago, Romano Marengo's first visitors were amazed by the elegance that went into each detail of the winery: the barrel staves glittered and the floor shone, all testifying to the attention paid to every aspect of the process. His skilled son Giuseppe wanted equal care shown in the vineyards and has adopted a biodynamic cultivation approach. Only two varieties are grown in their lovely Barbaresco and Serralunga d'Alba crus: Nebbiolo, which makes up the lion's share, and Barbera. Their wines exhibit rare finesse. Both their Barolos prove to be splendid interpretations of 2014, with their Rapet handily earning Tre Bicchieri thanks to its impressive aromas of quinine and licorice followed by a delectably fresh and savory palate with lovely texture. Their complex Cerretta is quite similar, just a bit fruitier and slightly more tannic, while their 2015 Barbaresco Chiaramanti impresses for its charm and balance.

| | | |
|---|---|---|
| ● Barolo Rapet '14 | ♟♟♟ | 7 |
| ● Barbaresco Chiaramanti '15 | ♟♟ | 7 |
| ● Barolo Cerretta '14 | ♟♟ | 7 |
| ● Barbaresco Rio Sordo '15 | ♟♟ | 7 |
| ● Barbaresco Maria di Brün '13 | ♟♟♟ | 8 |
| ● Barbaresco Sorì Rio Sordo '06 | ♟♟♟ | 6 |
| ● Barolo Rapet '11 | ♟♟♟ | 7 |
| ● Barolo Rapet '08 | ♟♟♟ | 7 |
| ● Barolo V. Cerretta '09 | ♟♟♟ | 7 |
| ● Barbaresco Chiaramanti '14 | ♟♟ | 7 |
| ● Barbaresco Chiaramanti Ris. '12 | ♟♟ | 6 |
| ● Barbaresco Rio Sordo '13 | ♟♟ | 7 |
| ● Barbaresco Sorì Rio Sordo '14 | ♟♟ | 6 |
| ● Barolo Cerretta '13 | ♟♟ | 7 |
| ● Barolo del Comune di Serralunga d'Alba Rapet '13 | ♟♟ | 7 |
| ● Barolo Rapet '12 | ♟♟ | 7 |

# ★★Ca' Viola

B.TA SAN LUIGI, 11
12063 DOGLIANI [CN]
TEL. +39 017370547
www.caviola.com

**CELLAR SALES**
**PRE-BOOKED VISITS**
**ACCOMMODATION AND RESTAURANT SERVICE**
**ANNUAL PRODUCTION** 70,000 bottles
**HECTARES UNDER VINE** 10.00

Beppe Caviola is an esteemed enologist who has relationships with prestigious wineries from Veneto to Marche. In 25 years he has gone from taking a casual interest in his private cellar to managing a well-equipped producer. It all starts in the vineyards, with his original Barolo plots in Montelupo Albese now accompanied by the lovely Sottocastello (in Novello) and a vineyard in Cissone for his Langhe Riesling. No artificial products are used. The entire selection is commendable, from the approachable and flavorsome Dolcetto Vilot and Barbera Brichet to the wines that made him world-famous. Their robust and commendably vigorous 2016 Dolcetto d'Alba Barturot proves chocolaty and fruity. Their 2013 Barolo Sottocastello di Novello, a wine endowed with aromas of spices, oak and small black berries, is still quite youthful. Their 2016 Riesling offers up close-focused aromas of incense, while the palate comes through crisp and sharp, even with its notable structure. Their Barolo Caviot is a tasty, linear wine, fruity and firm on the palate.

| | | |
|---|---|---|
| ● Barolo Sottocastello di Novello '13 | ♥♥♥ | 8 |
| ● Barbera d'Alba Bric du Luv '16 | ♥♥ | 5 |
| ● Dolcetto d'Alba Barturot '16 | ♥♥ | 4 |
| ● Langhe Nebbiolo '16 | ♥♥ | 5 |
| ● Barbera d'Alba Brichet '16 | ♥♥ | 4 |
| ● Barolo Caviot '14 | ♥♥ | 8 |
| ● Dolcetto d'Alba Vilot '17 | ♥♥ | 3 |
| ○ Langhe Riesling '16 | ♥♥ | 5 |
| ● Barbera d'Alba Bric du Luv '12 | ♀♀♀ | 5 |
| ● Barbera d'Alba Bric du Luv '10 | ♀♀♀ | 5 |
| ● Barolo Sottocastello '06 | ♀♀♀ | 7 |
| ● Barolo Sottocastello di Novello '12 | ♀♀♀ | 8 |
| ● Barolo Sottocastello di Novello '11 | ♀♀♀ | 8 |
| ● Barolo Sottocastello di Novello '10 | ♀♀♀ | 7 |
| ● Barolo Sottocastello di Novello '08 | ♀♀♀ | 7 |

# Fabrizia Caldera

FRAZ. PORTACOMARO STAZIONE, 53

14100 ASTI
TEL. +39 0141296154
www.vinicaldera.it

**CELLAR SALES**
**PRE-BOOKED VISITS**
**ACCOMMODATION**
**ANNUAL PRODUCTION** 90,000 bottles
**HECTARES UNDER VINE** 22.00
**SUSTAINABLE WINERY**

Founded in the early 20th century, the Caldera family's winery is today being led by the fourth generation, Fabrizia Caldera (accompanied by her husband, Roberto Rossi, and son Fabio). The grapes cultivated are all local varieties (with the exception of Chardonnay), from Barbera to Ruché. Grignolino, Dolcetto and Moscatto, with some vineyards going back 50 years. Their wines are all monovarietal, with an emphasis on the pursuit of balance, drinkability and pleasantness. Their 2017 Ruché di Castegnole Monferrato Prevost is an excellent wine with aromas of red fruit and a slightly spice notes. On the palate it's juicy, exhibiting nice aromatic precision and drinkability. Their full-bodied 2015 Barbera d'Asti is another well-made wine. It offers up aromas of black fruit, roots and forest undergrowth and has nice mouthfeel to it. And their 2017 Grignolino d'Asti Leserre also delivers, exhibiting typicity in its flowery and spicy aromas, which give way to a tannic, buoyant palate. Their 2015 Barbera d'Asti Superiore Balmèt is a bit too marked by oak.

| | | |
|---|---|---|
| ● Barbera d'Asti '15 | ♥♥ | 3 |
| ● Grignolino d'Asti Leserre '17 | ♥♥ | 2* |
| ● Ruché di Castegnole Monferrato Prevost '17 | ♥♥ | 3 |
| ● Barbera d'Asti Superiore Balmèt '15 | ♥ | 4 |

# Cantina del Glicine

VIA GIULIO CESARE, 1
12052 NEIVE [CN]
TEL. +39 017367215
www.cantinadelglicine.it

**CELLAR SALES**
**PRE-BOOKED VISITS**
**ANNUAL PRODUCTION** 37,000 bottles
**HECTARES UNDER VINE** 6.00

It was 1980 when young Adriana Marzi and Roberto Bruno decided to abandon the city and move in the historic and charming Cantina del Glicine. Since then they've personally overseen every major stage of production, deservedly earning praise and accolades. Roberto has left but Adriana is firm in her resolve to not abandon the activity or the warm relationship they've established with friends and customers, who are visiting the winery in ever greater numbers. Barbaresco is still a key wine, in particular their Marcorino and Currà, as is Barbera d'Alba. This year we didn't get a chance to taste all their wines because Adriana decided to postpone bottling. But her elegant and fresh 2016 Barbera d'Alba La Sconsolata has never been quite so seductive and enjoyable (it's made with just a small share of Nebbiolo). Her youthful 2015 Barbaresco Currà is a penetrating, decisive wine that deserves a bit more time in the bottle.

| | |
|---|---|
| ● Barbera d'Alba La Sconsolata '16 | ♟♟ 3* |
| ● Barbaresco Currà '15 | ♟♟ 5 |
| ○ Roero Arneis Il Mandolo '17 | ♟ 3 |
| ● Barbaresco Currà '10 | ♟♟♟ 4* |
| ● Barbaresco Marcorino '12 | ♟♟♟ 5 |
| ● Barbaresco Currà '14 | ♟♟ 5 |
| ● Barbaresco Currà '13 | ♟♟ 5 |
| ● Barbaresco Marcorino '14 | ♟♟ 5 |
| ● Barbaresco Marcorino '13 | ♟♟ 5 |
| ● Barbaresco Vigne Sparse '13 | ♟♟ 5 |
| ● Barbaresco Vignesparse '14 | ♟♟ 5 |
| ● Barbera d'Alba La Dormiosa '15 | ♟♟ 3 |
| ● Barbera d'Alba Sup. La Dormiosa '14 | ♟♟ 3 |
| ○ Dolcetto d'Alba Olmiolo '15 | ♟♟ 2* |
| ● Nebbiolo d'Alba Calcabrume '15 | ♟♟ 3 |
| ● Nebbiolo d'Alba Calcabrume '14 | ♟♟ 3 |

# Cantina del Nebbiolo

VIA TORINO, 17
12050 VEZZA D'ALBA [CN]
TEL. +39 017365040
www.cantinadelnebbiolo.com

**CELLAR SALES**
**PRE-BOOKED VISITS**
**ANNUAL PRODUCTION** 300,000 bottles
**HECTARES UNDER VINE** 300.00
**VITICULTURE METHOD** Certified Organic

From the ashes of the Cantina Sociale Parrocchiale di Vezza d'Alba, Cantina del Nebbiolo was founded in 1959 by 23 partners. Today the winery is comprised of 170 vine growers working in 18 different municipalities throughout Langhe and Roero. In addition to Nebbiolo, which gives rise to most of their 23 wines, they make wines with Arneis, Barbera, Bonarda, Favorita, Moscato, Nascetta and Neretta Cuneese, making for a selection of traditionally styled wines. As always Cantina del Nebbiolo's entire selection proved to be of notable quality. Their 2015 Barbaresco is an elegant wine, rich and charming, while their 2014 Barolo and 2014 Barolo Perno features a nice tannic weave and a plucky, spicy finish. Their 2015 Barbera d'Alba Superiore is quite in the same vein, proving pleasant with balsamic and fruity aromas, while their 2016 Nebbiolo d'Alba Vigna Valmaggiore offers up fragrances of forest undergrowth and pepper (it's a bit dried by oak, but the finish comes through savory and taut). Their 2016 Nebbiolo d'Alba is a flowery, supple wine.

| | |
|---|---|
| ● Barbaresco '15 | ♟♟ 4 |
| ● Barbera d'Alba Sup. '15 | ♟♟ 2* |
| ● Barolo '14 | ♟♟ 5 |
| ● Barolo Perno '14 | ♟♟ 5 |
| ● Nebbiolo d'Alba '16 | ♟♟ 2* |
| ● Nebbiolo d'Alba V. Valmaggiore '16 | ♟♟ 3 |
| ● Barbera d'Alba '16 | ♟ 2 |
| ⊙ Langhe Rosato '17 | ♟ 2 |
| ○ Moscato d'Asti '17 | ♟ 2 |
| ○ Roero Arneis '17 | ♟ 2 |
| ○ Roero Arneis Arenarium '17 | ♟ 2 |
| ● Barbaresco Meruzzano '10 | ♟♟ 4* |
| ● Barolo del Comune di Serralunga d'Alba '13 | ♟♟ 6 |

# Cantina del Pino

S.DA OVELLO, 31
12050 BARBARESCO [CN]
TEL. +39 0173635147
www.cantinadelpino.com

**ANNUAL PRODUCTION** 35,000 bottles
**HECTARES UNDER VINE** 7.00

Renato Vacca has Langhe in his DNA. He
trained as a technical manager at
Produttori di Barbaresco, and started his
work with Cantina del Pino in 1997. Today
he's continuing to build his fame, producing
smooth, modern Barbarescos made with
low yields, long maceration and high
quality, small wood barrels. It's an approach
that highlights the attributes of crus as
elegant and unique as Ovello and Albesani.
His ability to maintain consistently high
quality, as our tastings have revealed for
some time now, is truly impressive. Their
2014 Barbersco Albesani took home Tre
Bicchieri this year. It's a wine of rare finesse
and complexity, vibrant and delicate, with
fragrant fruit and a light background of
sweet tobacco. ON the palate its tannic
weave proves rich, steadily unfolding, with
a long, well-balanced finish. Their delicate
2014 Barbersco, a wine of medium-weight
but nice complexity, proves endowed with
perfectly ripe fruit, despite the year, while
their 2014 Barbersco Ovello is more ethery
and ripe in its aromas, with nice balance
and a persistent, linear finish.

| | |
|---|---|
| ● Barbaresco Albesani '14 | ▼▼▼ 7 |
| ● Barbaresco '14 | ▼▼ 5 |
| ● Barbaresco Ovello '14 | ▼▼ 7 |
| ● Barbera d'Alba '16 | ▼ 4 |
| ● Langhe Nebbiolo '17 | ▼ 4 |
| ● Barbaresco '04 | ♀♀♀ 5* |
| ● Barbaresco '03 | ♀♀♀ 4* |
| ● Barbaresco Albesani '05 | ♀♀♀ 6 |
| ● Barbaresco Ovello '13 | ♀♀♀ 7 |
| ● Barbaresco Ovello '07 | ♀♀♀ 6 |
| ● Barbaresco '13 | ♀♀ 5 |
| ● Barbaresco Albesani '13 | ♀♀ 7 |
| ● Barbaresco Albesani '12 | ♀♀ 6 |
| ● Barbaresco Ovello '12 | ♀♀ 6 |
| ● Barbaresco Ovello '10 | ♀♀ 6 |
| ● Langhe Nebbiolo '16 | ♀♀ 4 |

# La Caplana

VIA CIRCONVALLAZIONE, 4
15060 BOSIO [AL]
TEL. +39 0143684182
www.lacaplana.com

**CELLAR SALES**
**PRE-BOOKED VISITS**
**ANNUAL PRODUCTION** 120,000 bottles
**HECTARES UNDER VINE** 5.00

In Bosio, the district of Gavi meets the
Dolcetto di Ovada appellation. It's in this
crossing of local vineyards that we find La
Caplana's strongpoint. Guido Natalino is an
excellent interpreter of both varieties,
managing to revive and carry out an almost
100-year family winemaking tradition. Nine
wines are made. In addition to those
already mentioned he offers Barbera d'Asti
and Chardonnay. There's also a Charmat
method sparkling wine made with
Chardonnay, Cortese and Moscato. La
Caplana submitted a well-balance selection
of wines for tasting, with their Narcys
proving to be the best in show. It's an
elegant Dolcetto di Ovada with aromas of
black berries and cocoa. These re-emerge
on a vibrant palate with steady tannins
supporting a nice, long finish. Their Gavi
exhibits great nose-palate symmetry, with
complex aromas and a balanced palate
making for a highly drinkable wine. Their
Barbera d'Asti Rubis and Dolcetto di Ovada
also put in nice performances.

| | |
|---|---|
| ● Dolcetto di Ovada Narcys '15 | ▼▼ 3* |
| ○ Gavi del Comune di Gavi '17 | ▼▼ 2* |
| ● Barbera d'Asti Rubis '15 | ▼▼ 3 |
| ● Dolcetto di Ovada '17 | ▼▼ 2* |
| ● Barbera d'Asti '16 | ▼ 3 |
| ○ Caplana Brut | ▼ 3 |
| ○ Gavi '17 | ▼ 2 |
| ○ Gavi Villavecchia '17 | ▼ 2 |
| ● Dolcetto di Ovada Narcys '13 | ♀♀ 3* |
| ● Dolcetto di Ovada Narcys '12 | ♀♀ 3* |
| ○ Gavi del Comune di Gavi '16 | ♀♀ 2* |
| ○ Gavi del Comune di Gavi '14 | ♀♀ 2* |
| ○ Gavi Villa Vecchia '15 | ♀♀ 2* |

## Tenuta Carretta

LOC. CARRETTA, 2
12040 PIOBESI D'ALBA [CN]
TEL. +39 0173619119
www.tenutacarretta.it

CELLAR SALES
PRE-BOOKED VISITS
ACCOMMODATION AND RESTAURANT SERVICE
ANNUAL PRODUCTION 480,000 bottles
HECTARES UNDER VINE 70.00

Over the years the Miroglio family has
managed to enlarge its property, comprised
by a number of estates situated in some of
Piedmont's most prestigious appellations.
They have vineyards near their main
production facility in Roero, in Langhe, in
Barolo and Treiso, as well as San Rocco
Seno d'Elvio and Madonna di Como, all the
way to Malgrà (in Asti). Their wines are
impeccable in technical terms, and aim to
best express the various territories of
origin. The two Barolos submitted did
extremely well during our tastings. Their
2012 Barolo Cannubi offers up flowery
hints while on the palate it exhibits nice
mouthfeel and a delicate tannic weave. The
finish comes through long and elegant.
Their 2012 Barolo Cannubi Riserva is quite
tight-knit, well-structured and assertive, but
less approachable and pleasant than the
first. Their 2015 Nizza Mora di Sassi landed
in our finals with its characteristic hints of
black fruit and notes of wet earth. On the
palate it comes through savory,
well-supported by acidity. The rest of their
selection also proved well-made.

| | |
|---|---|
| ● Barolo Cannubi '12 | ♟♟ 8 |
| ● Barolo Cannubi Ris. '12 | ♟♟ 8 |
| ● Nizza Mora di Sassi '15 | ♟♟ 6 |
| ● Barbera d'Asti Sup. Gaiana '15 | ♟♟ 3 |
| ● Barolo Cannubi Collezione Rag. Franco Miroglio Ris. '12 | ♟♟ 8 |
| ○ Roero Arneis Cayega '17 | ♟♟ 3 |
| ○ Asti '17 | ♟ 3 |
| ● Barbera d'Asti Bevicisù '16 | ♟ 3 |
| ● Roero Bric Paradiso Ris. '13 | ♟ 5 |
| ● Barbera d'Asti Sup. Nizza Mora dei Sassi '12 | ♟♟ 5 |
| ● Roero Bric Paradiso '10 | ♟♟ 4 |

## La Casaccia

VIA D. BARBANO, 10
15034 CELLA MONTE [AL]
TEL. +39 0142489986
www.lacasaccia.biz

CELLAR SALES
PRE-BOOKED VISITS
ANNUAL PRODUCTION 25,000 bottles
HECTARES UNDER VINE 6.70
VITICULTURE METHOD Certified Organic

We should thank the Rava family for their
commitment during their winemaking
journey. It's a journey that's involved all the
difficulties of maintaining a business in
complicated times, but with the style and
simplicity of days gone by, when life had a
human dimension linked to tradition and
territory. The winery, certified organic,
offers a selection grounded in native grape
varieties: Barbera, Freisa and Grignolino.
These are transformed into forthright,
long-lived wines full of character. During
our tastings, their selection opened with a
2013, their Grignolino Ernesto. On the nose
it offers up evolved aromas of spices and
balsamic notes, while on the palate it
comes through vibrant, with a tannic
presence. Poggeto has a nice aromatic
profile, with notes of pepper and saffron.
The palate features rustic tannins and a
flavorful finish. Claichè opts for tertiary
aromas: plums in liquor and tobacco, with
notes of coffee. Their Bricco dei Boschi is
more youthful, with vibrant aromas of ripe
fruit and a delicate note of quinine.

| | |
|---|---|
| ● Barbera del M.to Bricco dei Boschi '15 | ♟♟ 3 |
| ● Barbera del M.to Calichè '15 | ♟♟ 3 |
| ● Grignolino del M.to Casalese Ernesto '13 | ♟♟ 3 |
| ● Grignolino del M.to Casalese Poggeto '16 | ♟♟ 2* |
| ● M.to Freisa Monfiorenza '16 | ♟♟ 3 |
| ○ Piemonte Chardonnay Charnò '17 | ♟ 3 |
| ● Barbera del M.to Calichè '14 | ♟♟ 3 |
| ● Barbera del M.to Giuanìn '15 | ♟♟ 2* |
| ● Grignolino del M.to Casalese Ernesto '12 | ♟♟ 3* |
| ● Grignolino del M.to Casalese Poggeto '15 | ♟♟ 2* |
| ● M.to Freisa Monfiorenza '15 | ♟♟ 3 |

## Casalone

VIA MARCONI, 100
15040 LU [AL]
TEL. +39 0131741280
www.casalone.it

**CELLAR SALES**
**PRE-BOOKED VISITS**
**ANNUAL PRODUCTION** 50,000 bottles
**HECTARES UNDER VINE** 10.00

Almost 100 years of winemaking tradition continued at this family-run winery when Paolo received the torch from his rock-hard father, Ernesto. It's a solidly artisanal winery, with quality wines that find their strongpoint in Malvasia Greca. The Casalone family brought out the aromatic qualities of this cultivar in a still white wine, a passito dried-grape wine and a Metodo Classico sparkler. This last spends 36 months on the lees, and surprises for the elegance and finesse of its bouquet. It's also worth noting the recent minimalist redesign of their labels. Casalone's selection is a solid one, with their Bricco Morlantino standing out during our tastings. It's an opaque ruby-red wine with lovely aromas of cherry accompanied by notes of cocoa and cinnamon. On the palate it features great structure and a lovely, well-balanced finish. Their Pinot Nero Fandamat is a well-made wine. Its accompanied by some lovely offerings made with Malvasia Greca whose names have changed this year from Monemvasia to Monvasia.

| | |
|---|---|
| ● Barbera del M.to Sup. Bricco Morlantino '15 | 🍷🍷 2* |
| ● Monferrato Rosso Fandamat '14 | 🍷🍷 2* |
| ○ Monvasia | 🍷🍷 2* |
| ○ Monvasia Brut M. Cl. | 🍷🍷 4 |
| ○ Monvasia Passito | 🍷🍷 3 |
| ● Barbera d'Asti Rubermillo '11 | 🍷🍷 3* |
| ● Barbera del M.to Sup. Bricco Morlantino '13 | 🍷🍷 2* |
| ○ Monemvasia | 🍷🍷 2 |
| ○ Monemvasia Affinato Barrique | 🍷🍷 4 |
| ○ Monemvasia Brut M. Cl. | 🍷🍷 4 |
| ● Piemonte Grignolino La Caplëtta '15 | 🍷🍷 3* |

## Cascina Adelaide

VIA AIE SOTTANE, 14
12060 BAROLO [CN]
TEL. +39 0173560503
www.cascinaadelaide.com

**CELLAR SALES**
**PRE-BOOKED VISITS**
**ANNUAL PRODUCTION** 50,000 bottles
**HECTARES UNDER VINE** 9.50

The lovely winery founded by Amabile Drocco receives grapes from some 11 different crus around Barolo, including the historic Cannubi cru. The modern structure, designed by architect Paolo Dellapiana, was built 15 years ago and is exemplary in terms of its low environmental impact. A visit is strongly suggested, both for wine lovers and those who simply appreciate beauty. Barolo takes center stage in a selection that's quite classic, with an attentive use of oak that guarantees it will never dominate. Their 2014 Barolo Baudana is a marvel of aromatic and structural richness, with Serralunga's unique soil conferring a robust austerity. Their 2014 Pernanno proves exquisite in its enchanting aromas of barely ripe fruit and its buoyantly fresh palate. Their highly elegant Fossati is more approachable, while their 2012 Riserva Per Elen is nicely evolved with pronounced notes of tar and licorice. Their 2016 Nascetta is a delicately aromatic and pleasant wine.

| | |
|---|---|
| ● Barolo Baudana '14 | 🍷🍷 7 |
| ● Barolo Fossati '14 | 🍷🍷 8 |
| ● Barolo Pernanno '14 | 🍷🍷 8 |
| ● Barolo 4 Vigne '14 | 🍷🍷 6 |
| ● Barolo Per Elen Ris. '12 | 🍷🍷 8 |
| ○ Langhe Nascetta del Comune di Novello '16 | 🍷🍷 3 |
| ● Barbera d'Alba Sup. V. Preda '16 | 🍷 4 |
| ● Barolo Baudana '13 | 🍷🍷 7 |
| ● Barolo Baudana '11 | 🍷🍷 7 |
| ● Barolo Cannubi '13 | 🍷🍷 8 |
| ● Barolo Cannubi '11 | 🍷🍷 8 |
| ● Barolo Cannubi '10 | 🍷🍷 8 |
| ● Barolo Fossati '13 | 🍷🍷 8 |
| ● Barolo Pernanno '10 | 🍷🍷 8 |

# Cascina Barisél

REG. SAN GIOVANNI, 30
14053 CANELLI [AT]
TEL. +39 0141824848
www.barisel.it

**CELLAR SALES**
**PRE-BOOKED VISITS**
**ANNUAL PRODUCTION** 35,000 bottles
**HECTARES UNDER VINE** 4.50

For more than 30 years the Penna family's small winery has served as a benchmark for quality Asti wines. Apart from a small plot in San Marzano Oliveto where Favorita is cultivated, their property is situated entirely in Canelli, on the calcareous terrain around the farm manor, and gives rise primarily to Barbera and Moscato, with vineyards going back anywhere from 40 to more than 60 years. Their modern wines seek to express both the characteristics of the cultivar and the territory. Their 2013 Barbera d'Asti Superiore Nizza Vigna dei Pilati earned a place in our finals with its notable fullness, richness of fruit and a fresh, taut finish. It was accompanied by their 2016 Barbera d'Asti Superiore Listoria, a wine redolent of small red berries, with spicy nuances, and a soft, pervasive palate. Their 2017 Moscato d'Asti Canelli, with its aromas of sage and gingerbread, proved to be well-made, as did their simple, pleasant and approachable 2017 Barbera d'Asti.

| | |
|---|---|
| ● Barbera d'Asti Sup. Listoria '16 | ♟♟2* |
| ● Barbera d'Asti Sup. Nizza V. dei Pilati '13 | ♟♟6 |
| ● Barbera d'Asti '17 | ♟♟2* |
| ● Barbera d'Asti Canelli '17 | ♟♟2* |
| ○ L'Avija | ♟4 |
| ● Barbera d'Asti Sup. La Cappelletta '15 | ♟♟4 |
| ● Barbera d'Asti Sup. La Cappelletta '13 | ♟♟4 |
| ● Barbera d'Asti Sup. La Cappelletta '12 | ♟♟4 |
| ● Barbera d'Asti Sup. La Cappelletta '11 | ♟♟4 |
| ● Barbera d'Asti Sup. La Cappelletta '10 | ♟♟4 |
| ○ Moscato d'Asti Canelli '11 | ♟♟2* |

# Cascina Bongiovanni

LOC. UCCELLACCIO
VIA ALBA BAROLO, 3
12060 CASTIGLIONE FALLETTO [CN]
TEL. +39 0173262184
www.cascinabongiovanni.com

**CELLAR SALES**
**PRE-BOOKED VISITS**
**ACCOMMODATION**
**ANNUAL PRODUCTION** 50,000 bottles
**HECTARES UNDER VINE** 7.20
**SUSTAINABLE WINERY**

It was 1950 when Giovanni Bongiovanni founded his estate. Initially their grapes were simply sold, but then, sometime in the 1960s, Giovanni began making wine with a part of the harvest, gradually creating a bonafide cellar. Today Davide Mozzone leads this historic Langhe producer, cultivating just under eight hectares of vineyards spread throughout Castiglione Falletto, Serralunga d'Alba, Monforte d'Alba, Diano d'Alba and San Pietro in Govone. Two Barolos and a delectable Dolcetto lead their wide and multifaceted selection of wines. Their 2014 Barolo Pernanno is a classically styled wine with aromas of red fruit and herbs in the sun presented on a background of tobacco and licorice. On the palate it exhibits finesse and complexity, in commendable combination of acidity, pulp and tannic extraction. Their 2014 Barolo is spicier, though it doesn't match the aromatic persistence of their Pernanno. Their 2016 Barbera is a well-crafted, juicy wine, while their 2017 Dolcetto proves fresh and close-focused.

| | |
|---|---|
| ● Barolo Pernanno '14 | ♟♟7 |
| ● Barbera d'Alba '16 | ♟♟4 |
| ● Barolo '14 | ♟♟6 |
| ● Dolcetto d'Alba '17 | ♟♟3 |
| ● Langhe Nebbiolo '16 | ♟♟4 |
| ● Langhe Rosso Faletto '16 | ♟4 |
| ● Barolo Pernanno '01 | ♟♟♟6 |
| ● Barolo '13 | ♟♟6 |
| ● Barolo '07 | ♟♟5 |
| ● Barolo Pernanno '13 | ♟♟7 |
| ● Barolo Pernanno '12 | ♟♟7 |
| ● Barolo Pernanno '11 | ♟♟6 |
| ● Dolcetto di Diano d'Alba '15 | ♟♟3* |

# ★Cascina Ca' Rossa

LOC. CASCINA CA' ROSSA, 56
12043 CANALE [CN]
TEL. +39 017398348
www.cascinacarossa.com

**CELLAR SALES**
**PRE-BOOKED VISITS**
**ANNUAL PRODUCTION** 90,000 bottles
**HECTARES UNDER VINE** 16.00
**VITICULTURE METHOD** Certified Organic

The Ferrio family's winery, managed by
Angelo and his son Stefano, offers some of
the most characteristic and expressive
wines of Roero. They cultivate all the
territory's classic grapes, from Arneis to
Barbera and Nebbiolo, while their vineyards
are situated in some of the most prestigious
MGAs (geographic mentions) of the area.
These include Valmaggiore, where the
grapes for their stylish and elegant
Audinaggio are cultivated, Mompissano, and
their recently acquired Le Coste, all situated
within the municipalities of Canale, Santo
Stefano Roero and Vezza d'Alba. Their
Roero Valmaggiore Vigna Audinaggio proves
that its one of Italy's best reds. Their 2016
is elegant and flowery, with notes of red fruit
and Mediterranean scrubland. It's a long,
savory, fine wine: a Tre Bicchieri hands
down. Their 2015 Roero Le Coste also
delivered, proving rich in fruit with
well-integrated tannins, while for the first
time their 2017 Roero Arneis Merica leads
the appellation. On the nose it offers up
citrusy aromas, while on the palate it comes
through fresh, with a lovely, long, taut finish.

| | | |
|---|---|---|
| ● Roero Valmaggiore V. Audinaggio '16 | 🍷🍷🍷 | 5 |
| ○ Roero Arneis Merica '17 | 🍷🍷 | 3* |
| ● Roero Le Coste '15 | 🍷🍷 | 5 |
| ● Barbera d'Alba Ansem '15 | 🍷🍷 | 3 |
| ● Langhe Nebbiolo Funsu '17 | 🍷🍷 | 3 |
| ● Roero Mompissano Ris. '15 | 🍷🍷 | 5 |
| ● Barbera d'Alba Mulassa '04 | 🏆🏆🏆 | 4* |
| ● Roero Audinaggio '07 | 🏆🏆🏆 | 5 |
| ● Roero Audinaggio '06 | 🏆🏆🏆 | 5 |
| ● Roero Audinaggio '01 | 🏆🏆🏆 | 5 |
| ● Roero Mompissano Ris. '13 | 🏆🏆🏆 | 5 |
| ● Roero Mompissano Ris. '12 | 🏆🏆🏆 | 5 |
| ● Roero Mompissano Ris. '10 | 🏆🏆🏆 | 5 |
| ● Roero Mompissano Ris. '07 | 🏆🏆🏆 | 6 |
| ● Roero Valmaggiore V. Audinaggio '15 | 🏆🏆🏆 | 5 |

# Cascina Chicco

VIA VALENTINO, 14
12043 CANALE [CN]
TEL. +39 0173979411
www.cascinachicco.com

**CELLAR SALES**
**PRE-BOOKED VISITS**
**ANNUAL PRODUCTION** 435,000 bottles
**HECTARES UNDER VINE** 50.00
**SUSTAINABLE WINERY**

For three generations the Faccenda family
have been leaders among Roero's
winemakers. Today Cascina Chicco has
various vineyards throughout the area, in
the municipalities of Canale, Castellinaldo,
Castagnito and Vezza d'Alba, as well as five
hectares in Monforte d'Alba, between the
MGAs (geographic mentions) of Castelletto
and Ginestra. The latter give rise to two
Barolos, their Rocche di Castelletto and their
Ginestra Riserva. Chicco's selection are
traditionally styled, exhibiting good texture
and rich in fruit. Cascina Chicco once again
takes home Tre Bicchieri, and they do it for
the first time with their Barolo Ginestra
Riserva. Their 2011 enchants. It's a subtle,
elegant wine with flowery fragrances and
notes of orange peel. ON the palate it
proves caressing, long and pervasive. Their
balsamic 2015 Roero Valmaggiore Riserva
is a truly delicious wine with nice structure,
it's just missing a bit of pluck. Finally their
pleasant and fresh 2017 Barbera d'Alba
Granera Alta proves well-made with its hints
of red fruit, as does their 2017 Roero Arneis
Anterisio, a savory, fruit-driven, supple wine.

| | | |
|---|---|---|
| ● Barolo Ginestra Ris. '11 | 🍷🍷🍷 | 8 |
| ● Roero Valmaggiore Ris. '15 | 🍷🍷 | 4 |
| ● Barbera d'Alba Granera Alta '17 | 🍷🍷 | 3 |
| ● Barolo Rocche di Castelletto '14 | 🍷🍷 | 5 |
| ○ Roero Arneis Anterisio '17 | 🍷🍷 | 3 |
| ○ Arcass | 🍷 | 4 |
| ● Barbera d'Alba Bric Loira '16 | 🍷 | 4 |
| ○ Cuvée Zero Extra Brut M. Cl. '14 | 🍷 | 4 |
| ○ Cuvée Zero Extra Brut M. Cl. Rosé '14 | 🍷 | 4 |
| ● Nebbiolo d'Alba Monpissano '16 | 🍷 | 4 |
| ● Roero Montespinato '16 | 🍷 | 3 |
| ○ Arcàss Passito '04 | 🏆🏆🏆 | 4 |
| ● Roero Valmaggiore Ris. '12 | 🏆🏆🏆 | 4* |

# Cascina Corte

FRAZ. SAN LUIGI
B.TA VALDIBERTI, 33
12063 DOGLIANI [CN]
TEL. +39 0173743539
www.cascinacorte.it

**CELLAR SALES**
**PRE-BOOKED VISITS**
**ACCOMMODATION**
**ANNUAL PRODUCTION** 30,000 bottles
**HECTARES UNDER VINE** 5.00
**VITICULTURE METHOD** Certified Organic
**SUSTAINABLE WINERY**

For many, Sandro Barosi is considered a benchmark, a figure who's capable of pointing out the direction that artisanal winemaking is taking, and not only in Langhe. But he prefers to continue to experiment in his small winery, doing his best each year to bring out the highest possible natural expression of his wines. Primarily Dolcetto is cultivated in his vineyards, giving rise to a quite approachable Dogliani and a complex Superore Pirochetta Vecchie Vigne. Hospitality at his bed & breakfast is so warm that a stay is highly recommended to wine tourists. Their offerings made in amphoras are certainly interesting. Their 2017 Dogliani Superiore Pirochetta Vecchie Vigna maintains its youthful, particularly fresh and grapey aromas while on the palate it already proves pleasantly balanced. The rest of their increasingly popular selection faithfully follow the producer's established style, with rustic, somewhat evolved aromas on the nose, and firm, full-bodied wines on the palate.

| | | |
|---|---|---|
| ● Dogliani Sup. Pirochetta V. V. Anfora '17 | ❦❦ | 3 |
| ● Langhe Nebbiolo Anfora '17 | ❦❦ | 4 |
| ● Dogliani '17 | ❦ | 3 |
| ● Dogliani Sup. Pirochetta V. V. '16 | ❦ | 3 |
| ● Langhe Barbera '16 | ❦ | 3 |
| ● Langhe Barbera Anfora '17 | ❦ | 3 |
| ● Dogliani Vecchie V. Pirochetta '08 | ❦❦❦ | 3* |
| ● Dogliani '15 | ♈♈ | 3* |
| ● Dogliani '14 | ♈♈ | 3 |
| ● Dogliani '13 | ♈♈ | 3 |
| ● Dogliani Sup. Pirochetta V. V. '15 | ♈♈ | 3 |
| ● Dogliani Sup. Pirochetta V. V. '13 | ♈♈ | 3 |
| ● Langhe Nebbiolo '14 | ♈♈ | 4 |
| ● Langhe Nebbiolo '13 | ♈♈ | 4 |

# Cascina delle Rose

VIA RIOSORDO, 58
12050 BARBARESCO [CN]
TEL. +39 0173638292
www.cascinadellerose.it

**CELLAR SALES**
**PRE-BOOKED VISITS**
**ANNUAL PRODUCTION** 20,000 bottles
**HECTARES UNDER VINE** 4.00
**VITICULTURE METHOD** Certified Organic

Giovanna Rizzolio's story is a lovely and long one. While still extremely young she decided to live in her grandparents' scenic home, dedicating herself to the vineyard, to wine and to hospitality. And that's how her wines come to be, the product of a deep and close bond with nature, through methods that respect the environment, the grapes, and the characteristics of each individual season. Their vineyards are dedicated primarily Nebbiolo, followed by a hefty share of Barbera and touch of Dolcetto. On the nose their 2015 Barbaresco Rio Sordo offers up notably spicy aromas and lovely fruit, primarily raspberry. On the palate it proves rich in soft pulp but still endowed with a tannic backbone that renders it pleasantly austere. It's a decidedly classic style that corresponds perfectly to the year. Their 2015 Barbaresco Tre Stelle is fresher and even citrusy, with a palate that's more docile and supple. Their 2016 Nebbiolo is a crisp, highly pleasant wine, while their minty Barbera Donna Elena proves particularly fine. Theirs is a highly drinkable and enjoyable selection overall.

| | | |
|---|---|---|
| ● Barbaresco Rio Sordo '15 | ❦❦ | 5 |
| ● Barbaresco Tre Stelle '15 | ❦❦ | 5 |
| ● Langhe Nebbiolo '16 | ❦❦ | 4 |
| ● Barbera d'Alba '16 | ❦❦ | 4 |
| ● Barbera d'Alba Sup. Donna Elena '15 | ❦❦ | 4 |
| ● Barbaresco Rio Sordo '09 | ♈♈ | 5 |
| ● Barbaresco Tre Stelle '09 | ♈♈ | 5 |
| ● Barbera d'Alba Donna Elena '08 | ♈♈ | 4 |

# Cascina Fontana

LOC. PERNO
V.LO DELLA CHIESA, 2
12065 MONFORTE D'ALBA [CN]
TEL. +39 0173789005
www.cascinafontana.com

**CELLAR SALES**
**PRE-BOOKED VISITS**
**ANNUAL PRODUCTION** 26,000 bottles
**HECTARES UNDER VINE** 5.00
**SUSTAINABLE WINERY**

Mario Fontana is proud of his artisanal approach, but he isn't resting on his laurels and he's making structural changes as well as putting forward new wines. This year the winery avails itself of a small facility dedicated to aging and bottling wines. Among the selection's new wines is their Vino Rosso, a Nebbiolo that's been included in the Triple A catalogue. The keystone of their production remains Barolo, in particular a new wine made with grapes cultivated in Castiglione Falletto, in addition to their Barbera, Dolcetto d'Alba, and a Langhe Nebbiolo. 2014 wasn't an easy year for Barolo but Mario Fontana's interpretation proves well-balanced and harmonious, despite somewhat underripe fruit and a small, lean body. Their elegant, rich and highly drinkable 2016 Langhe Nebbiolo delivered, as did their herbaceous 2016 Barbera d'Alba.

| | |
|---|---|
| ● Barbera d'Alba '16 | 🍷🍷 3 |
| ● Barolo '14 | 🍷🍷 6 |
| ● Langhe Nebbiolo '16 | 🍷🍷 4 |
| ● Vino Rosso '16 | 🍷 3 |
| ● Barolo '12 | 🍷🍷🍷 6 |
| ● Barolo '10 | 🍷🍷🍷 7 |
| ● Barbera d'Alba '15 | 🍷🍷 3 |
| ● Barbera d'Alba '14 | 🍷🍷 3 |
| ● Barbera d'Alba '13 | 🍷🍷 3 |
| ● Barolo '13 | 🍷🍷 6 |
| ● Barolo '11 | 🍷🍷 6 |
| ● Barolo '09 | 🍷🍷 7 |
| ● Barolo del Comune di Castiglione Falletto V. V. '13 | 🍷🍷 7 |
| ● Langhe Nebbiolo '15 | 🍷🍷 4 |
| ● Langhe Nebbiolo '14 | 🍷🍷 4 |
| ● Langhe Nebbiolo '13 | 🍷🍷 4 |

# Cascina Gilli

VIA NEVISSANO, 36
14022 CASTELNUOVO DON BOSCO [AT]
TEL. +39 0119876984
www.cascinagilli.it

**CELLAR SALES**
**PRE-BOOKED VISITS**
**ACCOMMODATION**
**ANNUAL PRODUCTION** 100,000 bottles
**HECTARES UNDER VINE** 15.00

Gianni Vergnano's winery is the standard bearer of a series of local grapes and winemaking districts that may be lesser known but worth watching. Freisa is cultivated in their Castelnuovo Don Bosco vineyards, which surround the farmhouse there, and on the slopes of Cornareto where the terrain is blue-gray marly clay. Their Malvasia, Bonarda and Barbera are cultivated on Schierano hill, in Passerano Marmorito. From their Freisa d'Asti to their Malvasia di Castelnuovo Don Bosco and Barbera d'Asti, their wines are exemplary for pleasantness and aromatic precision. Their 2016 Freisa d'Asti Il Forno is a long, juicy and highly enjoyable wine with aromas of red fruit, aromatic herbs and chili pepper. Their 2016 Piemonte Bonarda Sernù also did well, standing out for its fruit and well-integrated tannic weave, as did their 2017 Malvasia di Castelnuovo Don Bosco, an approachable wine that does a nice job balancing acidity and sweet fruit.

| | |
|---|---|
| ● Freisa d'Asti Il Forno '16 | 🍷🍷 2* |
| ● Malvasia di Castelnuovo Don Bosco '17 | 🍷🍷 2* |
| ● Piemonte Bonarda Sernù '16 | 🍷🍷 2* |
| ● Barbera d'Asti Sup. Dèdica '15 | 🍷 3 |
| ● Freisa d'Asti Sup. Arvelé '15 | 🍷 3 |
| ● Barbera d'Asti Le More '16 | 🍷🍷 2* |
| ● Barbera d'Asti Le More '15 | 🍷🍷 2* |
| ● Dlicà | 🍷🍷 3 |
| ● Freisa d'Asti Arvelé '13 | 🍷🍷 3 |
| ● Freisa d'Asti Il Forno '15 | 🍷🍷 2* |
| ● Freisa d'Asti Il Forno '14 | 🍷🍷 2* |
| ● Malvasia di Castelnuovo Don Bosco '16 | 🍷🍷 2* |
| ● Malvasia di Castelnuovo Don Bosco '14 | 🍷🍷 2* |
| ● Malvasia di Castelnuovo Don Bosco Spumante Dolce | 🍷🍷 2* |
| ○ Piemonte Chardonnay Rafé '15 | 🍷🍷 2* |

## ★★Cascina La Barbatella

S.DA ANNUNZIATA, 55
14049 NIZZA MONFERRATO [AT]
TEL. +39 0141701434
www.labarbatella.com

**CELLAR SALES**
**PRE-BOOKED VISITS**
**ANNUAL PRODUCTION** 25,000 bottles
**HECTARES UNDER VINE** 4.00

Since 2010, Lorenzo and Cinzia Perego have run this prestigious winery, founded in 1981 by Angelo Sonvico. The vineyards are situated within a single, contiguous tract around the farmhouse and hill over Nizza Monferrato. The terrain here is calcareous and sandy. Barbera, obviously, plays a leading role, also considering the presence of vineyards that go back 70 years. Their wines are unabashedly modern, emphasizing complexity and a welcome territorial identity. Their Nizza La VIgna dell'Angelo just fell short of Tre Bicchieri. Despite a marked presence of oak, the 2015 impressed for its flowery and fruity hints, and its palate which, while weighty, features subtle, elegant tannins and a fresh finish. Their 2013 Monferrato Rosso Sonvico, a half-and-half blend of Barbera and Cabernet Sauvignon, proved well-made, rich in dark fruit and spices, as did their 2016 Barbera d'Asti la Barbatella, a softer, more approachable wine.

## Cascina Montagnola

S.DA MONTAGNOLA, 1
15058 VIGUZZOLO [AL]
TEL. +39 3480742701
www.cascinamontagnola.com

**CELLAR SALES**
**PRE-BOOKED VISITS**
**ANNUAL PRODUCTION** 30,000 bottles
**HECTARES UNDER VINE** 10.00

Donatella Giannotti is certainly among those entrepreneurs who got involved in winemaking out of passion. You can feel it when she talks about her products, and her life in the vineyards and the cellar. Her bond with the territory, as evidenced by her use of native grape varieties, has been further strengthened by her relatively recent use of Timorasso. It's the cultivar that gives rise to Morasso, a wine that in just a few vintages has carved out a space among the best in the appellation. Their 2016 Morasso exhibited character and personality during our tastings. Aromas of fresh herbs and white peach emerge across a mineral background. On the palate it proves extraordinary for fullness and structure, with a lovely, fresh and persistent finish. Their Rodeo fought off a difficult year with a 2014 that offers up plenty of flavor, while their Amaranto features vibrant aromas and a deep palate. Their intense and buoyant Donaldo is a rustic Croatina with some character.

| | |
|---|---|
| ● Nizza La V. dell'Angelo '15 | ♥♥ 5 |
| ● Barbera d'Asti La Barbatella '16 | ♥♥ 3 |
| ● M.to Rosso Sonvico '13 | ♥♥ 6 |
| ○ M.to Bianco Noè '16 | ♥ 3 |
| ○ M.to Bianco Non È '15 | ♥ 3 |
| ● M.to Rosso Ruanera '16 | ♥ 2 |
| ● Barbera d'Asti Sup. Nizza V. dell'Angelo '11 | ♥♥♥ 5 |
| ● Barbera d'Asti Sup. Nizza V. dell'Angelo '07 | ♥♥♥ 5 |
| ● M.to Rosso Sonvico '09 | ♥♥♥ 6 |
| ● M.to Rosso Sonvico '06 | ♥♥♥ 5 |
| ● M.to Rosso Sonvico '04 | ♥♥♥ 5 |
| ● M.to Rosso Sonvico '03 | ♥♥♥ 5 |
| ● Nizza La V. dell'Angelo '14 | ♥♥♥ 5 |

| | |
|---|---|
| ○ Colli Tortonesi Timorasso Morasso '16 | ♥♥ 4 |
| ● Colli Tortonesi Barbera Amaranto '15 | ♥♥ 2* |
| ● Colli Tortonesi Barbera Rodeo '14 | ♥♥ 5 |
| ● Colli Tortonesi Croatina Donaldo '16 | ♥♥ 3 |
| ● Margherita | ♥ 3 |
| ● Colli Tortonesi Barbera Amaranto '13 | ♀♀ 2* |
| ● Colli Tortonesi Barbera Amaranto '11 | ♀♀ 2* |
| ○ Colli Tortonesi Cortese Dunin '15 | ♀♀ 2* |
| ● Colli Tortonesi Croatina Donaldo '15 | ♀♀ 3 |
| ○ Colli Tortonesi Timorasso Morasso '15 | ♀♀ 4 |
| ○ Colli Tortonesi Timorasso Morasso '14 | ♀♀ 4 |
| ○ Colli Tortonesi Timorasso Morasso '13 | ♀♀ 4 |

## Cascina Morassino

s.da Bernino, 10
12050 Barbaresco [CN]
Tel. +39 3471210223
morassino@gmail.com

**CELLAR SALES**
**PRE-BOOKED VISITS**
**ANNUAL PRODUCTION** 20,000 bottles
**HECTARES UNDER VINE** 4.50
**SUSTAINABLE WINERY**

For 35 years Roberto Bianco has managed her winery with a consistence in quality that is certainly commendable. That doesn't mean that there aren't slow but continuous adjustments in cultivation and in the cellar. For example, there are frequent changes in the use of wood barrels. Today 2500 liter French oak is used for their Barbaresco. Their most important vineyard can be in the upper part of the largest cru in Barbaresco, Ovello. Almost 80 hectares overall, it's deservedly famous, rich in aromas, freshness and good tannins. Both their 2015 Barbarescos shone with their austere Ovello (just 4,000 bottles produced) just falling short of Tre Bicchieri for its perfect nose-palate symmetry. Dark notes of roots and tobacco are followed by a long, pronounced weight on the palate. Their elegant Morassino (6,000 bottles) is just a bit less firm, proving fresh and appealing.

| | |
|---|---|
| ● Barbaresco Morassino '15 | ▼▼ 5 |
| ● Barbaresco Ovello '15 | ▼▼ 6 |
| ● Barbaresco Morassino '09 | YYY 5 |
| ● Barbaresco Ovello '14 | YYY 6 |
| ● Barbaresco Morassino '14 | YY 5 |
| ● Barbaresco Morassino '13 | YY 5 |
| ● Barbaresco Morassino '12 | YY 5 |
| ● Barbaresco Morassino '11 | YY 5 |
| ● Barbaresco Morassino '10 | YY 5 |
| ● Barbaresco Morassino '08 | YY 5 |
| ● Barbaresco Ovello '13 | YY 6 |
| ● Barbaresco Ovello '12 | YY 6 |
| ● Barbaresco Ovello '11 | YY 6 |
| ● Barbaresco Ovello '10 | YY 6 |
| ● Barbaresco Ovello '09 | YY 6 |
| ● Barbaresco Ovello '08 | YY 6 |
| ● Barbera d'Alba Vignot '09 | YY 4 |

## Cascina Salicetti

via Cascina Salicetti, 2
15050 Montegioco [AL]
Tel. +39 0131875192
www.cascinasalicetti.it

**CELLAR SALES**
**PRE-BOOKED VISITS**
**ANNUAL PRODUCTION** 25,000 bottles
**HECTARES UNDER VINE** 16.00

The Tre Bicchieri that went to Anselmo Franzosi's Timorasso in the last edition of the guide was a further confirmation of the winery's direction. It's a virtuous cycle that's rewarding the young enologist, both for his vineyard management style and for his approach in the cellar. Their selection features an interesting level of quality, with structured, vibrant wines that have proven aging potential. There are eight wines in all, primarily made with native grape varieties. Their whites are made with Timorasso and Cortese while their reds we inevitably find Barbera, along with Croatina, Dolcetto and Bonarda Piemontese. Their Ombra di Luna is back in our finals with a version that's full of character. On the nose it proves vibrant, multifaceted, with lovely notes of white fruit and medicinal herbs on a mineral background. On the palate it's fresh, well-balanced, with a persistent finish. Their Montarlino enjoys an aromatic profile of discrete finesse and a fresh, highly drinkable palate. Their Mont'Effe has a fruity ring to it, with a succulently pulpy palate made steady by somewhat rustic tannins.

| | |
|---|---|
| ○ Colli Tortonesi Timorasso Ombra di Luna '16 | ▼▼ 4 |
| ○ Colli Tortonesi Cortese Montarlino '17 | ▼▼ 4 |
| ● Colli Tortonesi Dolcetto Mont'Effe '17 | ▼ 2 |
| ○ Colli Tortonesi Timorasso Ombra di Luna '15 | YYY 4* |
| ● Colli Tortonesi Barbera Morganti '13 | YY 4 |
| ○ Colli Tortonesi Cortese Montarlino '14 | YY 4 |
| ● Colli Tortonesi Croatina Risulò '12 | YY 4 |
| ● Colli Tortonesi Dolcetto Di Marzi '12 | YY 2* |
| ● Colli Tortonesi Dolcetto Mont'Effe '16 | YY 2* |
| ● Colli Tortonesi Rosso Il Seguito '15 | YY 2* |
| ● Colli Tortonesi Rosso Il Seguito '12 | YY 2* |
| ○ Colli Tortonesi Timorasso Ombra di Luna '13 | YY 4 |

# PIEDMONT

## Francesca Castaldi

VIA NOVEMBRE, 6
28072 BRIONA [NO]
TEL. +39 0321826045
www.cantinacastaldi.it

**CELLAR SALES**
**PRE-BOOKED VISITS**
**ANNUAL PRODUCTION** 20,000 bottles
**HECTARES UNDER VINE** 6.30
**SUSTAINABLE WINERY**

Fara became a DOC (controlled appellation) in 1969 when Pierino Castaldi had almost 30 vintages under his belt. 20 years later his daughter Francesca has taken over the reins here at Castaldi, renovating the cellar, enlarging the vineyards and, above all, making his wines famous among those who love Alto Piemonte's Nebbiolo. 20 more years have passed and now her son Marco has begun training in the vineyard and in the cellar. Castaldi's Fara are always elegant, well-structured and, thanks to a splash of Vespolina, intensely fruity and fresh. Their Fara did well despite a difficult 2014. It's subtle yet complex, with refreshing hints of gentian and a note of rhubarb that enriches its trademark aromas of licorice, both on the nose and the palate. Surprisingly, their Rosato Rosa Alba turns out to be one of the best in the region, thanks to a crisp, fresh palate that follows delicate, pure aromas of red and white fruit.

| | | |
|---|---|---|
| ● Fara '14 | ♟♟ | 5 |
| ○ Colline Novaresi Bianco Lucia '17 | ♟♟ | 3 |
| ◉ Colline Novaresi Rosato Rosa Alba '17 | ♟♟ | 3 |
| ● Colline Novaresi Uva Rara Valceresole '17 | ♟ | 3 |
| ● Colline Novaresi Vespolina Nina '17 | ♟ | 3 |
| ○ Colline Novaresi Bianco Lucia '16 | ♙♙ | 3 |
| ○ Colline Novaresi Bianco Lucia '15 | ♙♙ | 3 |
| ● Colline Novaresi Nebbiolo Bigin '15 | ♙♙ | 3 |
| ● Colline Novaresi Nebbiolo Bigin '12 | ♙♙ | 3 |
| ◉ Colline Novaresi Rosato Rosa Alba '15 | ♙♙ | 3 |
| ● Colline Novaresi Vespolina Nina '16 | ♙♙ | 3 |
| ● Colline Novaresi Vespolina Nina '15 | ♙♙ | 3 |
| ● Fara '13 | ♙♙ | 5 |
| ● Fara '12 | ♙♙ | 5 |
| ● Fara '11 | ♙♙ | 5 |

## Castellari Bergaglio

FRAZ. ROVERETO, 136R
15066 GAVI [AL]
TEL. +39 0143644000
www.castellaribergaglio.it

**CELLAR SALES**
**PRE-BOOKED VISITS**
**ANNUAL PRODUCTION** 90,000 bottles
**HECTARES UNDER VINE** 11.00

Relating Marco Bergaglio's work isn't easy at all. This is because various generations of vine growers are part of the family history, and they've passed down culture and traditions. Then there's the passion and the strength of those who have the ideas and the strength to make them a reality, developing and getting the best out of their grapes. That's how Castellari Bergaglio's selection of wines brings out the attributes of Cortese di Gavi. Their wines are made according to the position of their vineyards, rather than the age of the vineyards themselves. They can be enjoyed early or allowed to develop their full potential in a cellar. This their their Rolona does the honors, with a version that's highly elegant and complex. On the nose, flowery aromas are accompanied by notes of citrus and a mineral background. On the palate it proves extraordinary for finesse and balance. Their Fornaci features characters and personality, with distinct spicy notes and a well-balanced palate.

| | | |
|---|---|---|
| ○ Gavi del Comune di Gavi Rolona '17 | ♟♟ | 3* |
| ○ Gavi del Comune di Tassarolo Fornaci '17 | ♟♟ | 2* |
| ○ Gavi del Comune di Gavi Rovereto Vignavecchia '15 | ♟ | 3 |
| ○ Gavi Brut Ardé M. Cl. '11 | ♙♙ | 4 |
| ○ Gavi del Comune di Gavi Rovereto Vignavecchia '14 | ♙♙ | 3 |
| ○ Gavi del Comune di Gavi Rovereto Vignavecchia '12 | ♙♙ | 3* |
| ○ Gavi del Comune di Tassarolo Fornaci '16 | ♙♙ | 2* |
| ○ Gavi del Comune di Tassarolo Fornaci '15 | ♙♙ | 2* |
| ○ Gavi del Comune di Tassarolo Fornaci '14 | ♙♙ | 2* |
| ○ Gavi Pilin '13 | ♙♙ | 5 |
| ○ Gavi Salluvii '14 | ♙♙ | 2* |

## Castello di Gabiano

VIA SAN DEFENDENTE, 2
15020 GABIANO [AL]
TEL. +39 0142945004
www.castellodigabiano.com

CELLAR SALES
PRE-BOOKED VISITS
ACCOMMODATION AND RESTAURANT SERVICE
ANNUAL PRODUCTION 130,000 bottles
HECTARES UNDER VINE 24.00

Castello di Gabiano, led by marquis Cattaneo Adorno Giustiniani, is a symbol of the area's wine tourism renaissance. Their facilities are situated in a charming position, adjacent to the cellars that are perpetuating the lineage's wine-growing tradition. Their production center, which has been updated with equipment for modern winemaking, has been overseen by enologist Mario Ronco since 2007. Their selection features wines made with Monferrato's traditional cultivar as well as international varieties. Pinot Nero converges with Barbera in their Gavius, Chardonnay is used in their Castello and Sauvignon Blanc in their Corte. Their selection of wines exhibits extremely high quality, starting with their Grignolino Il Ruvo. Delicate fruity aromas and notes of pepper give way to a potent palate, with soft tannins and a lengthy finish. Their La Braja also proved excellent, with its fruity aromas accompanied by notes of coffee. On the palate it's splendid for force and balance. Their Gabiano Riserva, an ageworthy, classy wine, also gets a special mention.

| | |
|---|---|
| ● Barbera d'Asti La Braja '16 | 🍷🍷 2* |
| ● Grignolino del M.to Casalese Il Ruvo '17 | 🍷🍷 2* |
| ● Gabiano A Matilde Giustiniani Ris. '11 | 🍷🍷 6 |
| ○ M. to Bianco Corte '17 | 🍷🍷 3 |
| ⊙ M.to Chiaretto Castelvere '17 | 🍷🍷 2* |
| ● M.to Rosso Gavius '15 | 🍷🍷 3 |
| ● Malvasia di Casorzo d'Asti Il Giardino di Flora '17 | 🍷🍷 3 |
| ● Gabiano A Matilde Giustiniani Ris. '10 | 🍷🍷 6 |
| ● Grignolino del M.to Casalese Il Ruvo '16 | 🍷🍷 2* |
| ● M.to Rosso Gavius '12 | 🍷🍷 3* |
| ● Malvasia di Casorzo Il Giardino di Flora '16 | 🍷🍷 3 |
| ○ Piemonte Chardonnay Castello '15 | 🍷🍷 6 |

## Castello di Neive

C.SO ROMANO SCAGLIOLA, 205
12052 NEIVE [CN]
TEL. +39 017367171
www.castellodineive.it

CELLAR SALES
PRE-BOOKED VISITS
ACCOMMODATION
ANNUAL PRODUCTION 170,000 bottles
HECTARES UNDER VINE 26.00
SUSTAINABLE WINERY

La Casetta del Castello di Neive is the name of their hospitality center, which is hosting increasing numbers of visitors. Italo Stupino's choice to organize production into a modern building in the lower part of the district was a forward-thinking one, thus reserving the splendid castle for guided visits and tastings. Their selection, which has grown over the years, now includes their Barbera d'Alba, Langhe Arnei, a Riesling and a Pinot Nero (both still and sparkling). But the heart of the winery is still their Barbaresco, thanks to their splendid crus in Santo Stefano and Gallina. Their potent, well-orchestrated Barbaresco Santo Stefano Riserva is outstanding, with a 2013 that offers up aromas of ripe, red fruit and fine tannins. Their 2015 Barbaresco Santo Stefano is a linear, fruit-driven and fresh wine that's highly drinkable. Their 2016 Barbera d'Alba Vigna Santo Stefano is exceptionally soft, and a bit oaky. In addition to their classics, their tasty Albarossa and Riesling shouldn't be missed.

| | |
|---|---|
| ● Barbaresco Albesani Santo Stefano Ris. '13 | 🍷🍷🍷 8 |
| ● Barbaresco Albesani Santo Stefano '15 | 🍷🍷 8 |
| ● Barbaresco '15 | 🍷🍷 7 |
| ● Barbaresco Gallina '15 | 🍷🍷 7 |
| ● Barbera d'Alba V. Santo Stefano '16 | 🍷🍷 5 |
| ○ Langhe Riesling '16 | 🍷🍷 5 |
| ● Piemonte Albarossa '16 | 🍷🍷 5 |
| ● Barbera d'Alba Sup. '15 | 🍷 5 |
| ○ Langhe Arneis Montebertotto '17 | 🍷 4 |
| ● Barbaresco Albesani S. Stefano '12 | 🍷🍷🍷 6 |
| ● Barbaresco Albesani S. Stefano Ris. '12 | 🍷🍷🍷 8 |
| ● Barbaresco Albesani S. Stefano Ris. '11 | 🍷🍷🍷 8 |
| ● Barbaresco S. Stefano Ris. '01 | 🍷🍷🍷 7 |
| ● Barbaresco S. Stefano Ris. '99 | 🍷🍷🍷 7 |

## Castello di Tassarolo

LOC. ALBORINA, 1
15060 TASSAROLO [AL]
TEL. +39 0143342248
www.castelloditassarolo.it

CELLAR SALES
PRE-BOOKED VISITS
ANNUAL PRODUCTION 130,000 bottles
HECTARES UNDER VINE 20.00
VITICULTURE METHOD Certified Organic
SUSTAINABLE WINERY

The Spinolas have a deep, centuries-old history of wine-growing. It's a legacy that the Spinola siblings transformed into a dynamic and diverse producer. The cellar is equipped with modern technology, with a biodynamic approach adopted in the vineyard; it's not just a production style, it's a lifestyle as well. Nine wines are produced overall, six of which are made with Cortese di Gavi, one Piemonte Barbera, a Monferrato Chiaretto and a Monferrato Rosso made with Barbera and Cabernet Sauvignon. Our tastings revealed a uniform selection of wines with one standout, a lovely version of their 2016 Alborina. It's a wine that offers up sweet, spicy aromas accompanied by caramel on a fruity background. On the palate it proves rich and firm, with a body and structure that lengthen across a vibrant, persistent finish. Their Gavi Spinola and Monferrato Rosso Cuvée also put in nice performances.

| | |
|---|---|
| ○ Gavi del Comune di Tassarolo Alborina '16 | 🍷🍷 3* |
| ○ Gavi del Comune di Tassarolo Spinola '17 | 🍷🍷 2* |
| ● M.to Rosso Cuvée '17 | 🍷🍷 3 |
| ○ Gavi del Comune di Tassarolo Il Castello '17 | 🍷 3 |
| ● Piemonte Barbera Titouan '17 | 🍷 3 |
| ○ Gavi del Comune di Tassarolo Alborina '15 | 🍷🍷 3 |
| ○ Gavi del Comune di Tassarolo Alborina '13 | 🍷🍷 3* |
| ○ Gavi del Comune di Tassarolo Il Castello '16 | 🍷🍷 3* |
| ○ Gavi del Comune di Tassarolo Spinola '15 | 🍷🍷 2* |
| ○ Gavi del Comune di Tassarolo Titouan '16 | 🍷🍷 3 |

## Castello di Uviglie

VIA CASTELLO DI UVIGLIE, 73
15030 ROSIGNANO MONFERRATO [AL]
TEL. +39 0142488132
www.castellodiuviglie.com

CELLAR SALES
PRE-BOOKED VISITS
ANNUAL PRODUCTION 90,000 bottles
HECTARES UNDER VINE 25.00

A splendid location and great wines are what make Monferrato Casalese a territory that can stand shoulder-to-shoulder with Italy's best. Simone Lupano is most certainly one of Monferrato Casalese's principal supporters when it comes to wine tourism, thanks to his Castello di Uviglie, his production center. Lupano's wines are vibrant and full of body, in addition to being long-lived. It's the result of a modern style and the careful use of wood. Lined concrete is also used. It's a return to traditions that were never completely abandoned. During our tastings we found their selection exceptional. It speaks for itself. Their Le Cave is a complex wine on the nose, with aromas of fresh fruit, notes of cocoa, sweet spices and pencil lead. On the palate it exhibits great structure and freshness, with an extraordinarily long finish. Their two Grignolinos also greatly impressed, with their Terre Bianche showing great finesse and complexity and the latter a more classic profile. Their Bricco del Conte is simply succulent.

| | |
|---|---|
| ● Barbera del M.to Sup. Le Cave '16 | 🍷🍷🍷 3* |
| ● Barbera del M.to Bricco del Conte '17 | 🍷🍷 2* |
| ● Grignolino del M.to Casalese San Bastiano '17 | 🍷🍷 2* |
| ● Grignolino del M.to Casalese San Bastiano Terre Bianche '13 | 🍷🍷 5 |
| ● Barbera del M.to Sup. Pico Gonzaga '15 | 🍷🍷 5 |
| ○ Le Cave Extra Brut M. Cl. '14 | 🍷🍷 5 |
| ● M.to Rosso 1491 '15 | 🍷🍷 5 |
| ○ Piemonte Chardonnay Ninfea '17 | 🍷🍷 2* |
| ● Barbera del M.to Sup. Le Cave '13 | 🍷🍷🍷 3* |
| ● Barbera del M.to Sup. Le Cave '09 | 🍷🍷🍷 3* |
| ● Barbera del M.to Sup. Pico Gonzaga '13 | 🍷🍷🍷 5 |
| ● Barbera del M.to Sup. Pico Gonzaga '07 | 🍷🍷🍷 4* |

# Castello di Verduno

VIA UMBERTO I, 9
12060 VERDUNO [CN]
TEL. +39 0172470284
www.cantinecastellodiverduno.it

CELLAR SALES
PRE-BOOKED VISITS
ACCOMMODATION AND RESTAURANT SERVICE
ANNUAL PRODUCTION 68,000 bottles
HECTARES UNDER VINE 10.00
SUSTAINABLE WINERY

Already at the time of King Charles Albert of Sardinia, Castello di Verduno was a winery-castle. Today it's one of Piedmont's most solid and inspired wineries, thanks to Gabriella Burlotto and Franco Bianco, who are perfectly supported by young Marcella and Giovanna. Together they painstakingly look after ten hectares of vineyards in Barbaresco (Faset and Rabajà) and Barolo (Massara and Monvigliero). Matured in large wood barrels, their wines are extremely classic, rich in nuances and rhythm, perfect companions at the dinner table, from Nebbiolo to their delectable Pelaverga (interpreted in some three versions, including a sparkler) The selection submitted this year proved sound and of high quality. Their 2015 Barbaresco Rabajà-Bas, an unusually light and expressive red, is luminous in its airy fragrances of flowers and small wild berries. On the palate it feature a relaxed, long finish. Their 2012 Barolo Monvigliero Riserva is subtle in its riper, delicately spicy notes, while their 2017 Verduno Basadone is to be enjoyed fresh, without hesitations.

| | |
|---|---|
| ● Barbaresco '15 | ♈♈ 5 |
| ● Barbaresco Rabajà-Bas '15 | ♈♈ 6 |
| ● Verduno Basadone '17 | ♈♈ 3* |
| ● Barolo '14 | ♈♈ 5 |
| ● Barolo Monvigliero Ris. '12 | ♈♈ 7 |
| ● Barolo Massara '08 | ♈♈♈ 6 |
| ● Barolo Monvigliero Ris. '08 | ♈♈♈ 7 |
| ● Barolo Monvigliero Ris. '04 | ♈♈♈ 7 |
| ● Barbaresco '14 | ♈♈ 5 |
| ● Barbaresco Rabajà '13 | ♈♈ 6 |
| ● Barbaresco Rabajà Ris. '11 | ♈♈ 7 |
| ● Barbera d'Alba Bricco del Cuculo '14 | ♈♈ 4 |
| ● Barolo '13 | ♈♈ 5 |
| ● Barolo Massara '13 | ♈♈ 6 |
| ● Barolo Monvigliero Ris. '11 | ♈♈ 7 |
| ● Barolo Monvigliero Ris. '10 | ♈♈ 7 |
| ● Verduno Pelaverga Basadone '16 | ♈♈ 3 |

# ★Cavallotto
# Tenuta Bricco Boschis

LOC. BRICCO BOSCHIS
VIA ALBA-MONFORTE
12060 CASTIGLIONE FALLETTO [CN]
TEL. +39 017362814
www.cavallotto.com

CELLAR SALES
PRE-BOOKED VISITS
ANNUAL PRODUCTION 110,000 bottles
HECTARES UNDER VINE 25.00
VITICULTURE METHOD Certified Organic

90 years of a prized cru. It was 1928 when Giacomo Cavallotto purchased the entire hill of Bricco Boschis. But it was only with Olivio, right after the war (in 1948) that they began bottling the fruit of that gorgeous vineyard. Alfio, Giuseppe and Laura, his children, have carried on their father's legacy and today, along this contiguous tract of 25 hectares, they cultivate Barbera, Dolcetto, Freisa, Grignolino, Pinot Nero and Chardonnay, all with the utmost respect for the environment. The best plots are dedicated to Nebbiolo, their star, which serves as the basis for a selection rich in energy and vitality. Their 2012 Vignolo Riserva exhibits all the complexity that a great Barolo has to offer: aromas of dried flowers, tobacco, licorice. On the palate it's full and succulent, well-supported by tannins and lively acidity, with a long finish that's full of character. Their 2012 Bricco Boschis Vigna San Giuseppe Riserva is more ethery, subtle, just a bit more marked by alcohol. Their highly enjoyable 2016 Barbera d'Alba Vigna del Cuculo exhibits a meaty profile with a delectable, herbaceous pluck to it.

| | |
|---|---|
| ● Barbera d'Alba Sup. V. del Cuculo '16 | ♈♈ 5 |
| ● Barolo Bricco Boschis<br>V. S. Giuseppe Ris. '12 | ♈♈ 8 |
| ● Barolo Vignolo Ris. '12 | ♈♈ 8 |
| ● Langhe Freisa '16 | ♈♈ 4 |
| ● Langhe Nebbiolo '16 | ♈ 5 |
| ● Barolo Bricco Boschis '12 | ♈♈♈ 8 |
| ● Barolo Bricco Boschis '05 | ♈♈♈ 6 |
| ● Barolo Bricco Boschis '04 | ♈♈♈ 7 |
| ● Barolo Bricco Boschis<br>V. S. Giuseppe Ris. '05 | ♈♈♈ 8 |
| ● Barolo Bricco Boschis<br>V. S. Giuseppe Ris. '01 | ♈♈♈ 7 |
| ● Barolo Vignolo Ris. '06 | ♈♈♈ 8 |
| ● Barolo Vignolo Ris. '04 | ♈♈♈ 8 |
| ● Barolo Bricco Boschis '13 | ♈♈ 8 |

# Ceretto

loc. San Cassiano, 34
12051 Alba [CN]
Tel. +39 0173282582
www.ceretto.com

**CELLAR SALES**
**PRE-BOOKED VISITS**
**RESTAURANT SERVICE**
**ANNUAL PRODUCTION** 900,000 bottles
**HECTARES UNDER VINE** 130.00
**VITICULTURE METHOD** Certified Organic
**SUSTAINABLE WINERY**

As demonstrated by our regional tastings, Ceretto's wines continue to prove more well-defined, airier, more flavorful and vital. It's the result of a recent recalibration of style in favor of purer, more contemporary wines. Initially Federico, Lisa, Alessandro and Roberta Ceretto, the third generation of producers, focused on organic cultivation, then moving to biodynamic. This has been accompanied by a series of projects aimed at highlighting the territory's extraordinary biodiversity. Their selection might even been considered too wide, with more than 20 wines offered, though their average quality is decidedly high. Their selection shines, featuring two Barbarescos that get lighter and more expressive by the year. Their 2015 Asili takes home Tre Bicchieri with its delicate, pure aromas of fruit enriched by roots and licorice. On the palate it comes through creamy and steady, with excellent length. Their enchanting 2015 Barbaresco offers up notes of green tea and extremely subtle, elegant aromas. It's a close-focused wine, sublime on the palate. Their 2014 Barolo proves richer and riper.

| | |
|---|---|
| ● Barbaresco Asili '15 | ♟♟♟ 8 |
| ● Barbaresco '15 | ♟♟ 6 |
| ● Barbaresco Bernardot '15 | ♟♟ 8 |
| ● Barolo '14 | ♟♟ 7 |
| ● Barolo Prapò '14 | ♟♟ 8 |
| ● Nebbiolo d'Alba Bernardina '16 | ♟♟ 5 |
| ○ Langhe Arneis Blangé '17 | ♟ 4 |
| ● Langhe Rosso Monsordo '16 | ♟ 6 |
| ● Barbaresco Asili '13 | ♟♟♟ 8 |
| ● Barolo Bricco Rocche '13 | ♟♟♟ 8 |
| ● Barolo Bricco Rocche '11 | ♟♟♟ 8 |
| ● Barolo Bricco Rocche '09 | ♟♟♟ 8 |
| ● Barbaresco Asili '14 | ♟♟ 8 |
| ● Barbaresco Asili '12 | ♟♟ 8 |
| ● Barbaresco Bernardot '13 | ♟♟ 8 |
| ● Barbaresco Bernardot '12 | ♟♟ 8 |
| ● Barolo Prapò '13 | ♟♟ 8 |

# ★★Michele Chiarlo

s.da Nizza-Canelli, 99
14042 Calamandrana [AT]
Tel. +39 0141769030
www.michelechiarlo.it

**CELLAR SALES**
**PRE-BOOKED VISITS**
**ACCOMMODATION**
**ANNUAL PRODUCTION** 1,100,000 bottles
**HECTARES UNDER VINE** 120.00
**SUSTAINABLE WINERY**

The winery founded by Michele Chiarlo in 1956 remains a benchmark for Piedmont's vine growing and winemaking culture. There are 3 facilities and 11 vineyards situated throughout Monferrato, Langhe and Alessandrino, which give rise to some 24 wines from the Barolo, Barbaresco, Nizza, Barbera d'Asti, Gavi and Moscato d'Asti appellations, as well as others. Their wines are decidedly modern, attentive to aromatic precision, and highlight the best attributes of each territory of origin. Chiarlo once again earned Tre Bicchieri, this time with their 2015 La Court Riserva, a fruit-forward wine with notes of aromatic herbs. On the palate it proves supple yet assertive, with a long, savory, fresh, well-structured finish that features brilliant tones of Mediterranean scrubland. Their 2015 Barbaresco Faset proves delicate and flowery, with an elegant tannic weave. Other well-made standouts include their 2016 Nizza Cipressi with its simplicity and suppleness, their balsamic and austere 2010 Barolo Cerequio Riserva and their soft, varietal 2017 Moscato d'Asti Nivole.

| | |
|---|---|
| ● Nizza La Court Ris. '15 | ♟♟♟ 6 |
| ● Barbaresco Faset '15 | ♟♟ 8 |
| ● Barolo Cerequio Ris. '10 | ♟♟ 8 |
| ● Barbaresco Asili '15 | ♟♟ 8 |
| ● Barolo Tortoniano '14 | ♟♟ 7 |
| ○ Moscato d'Asti Nivole '17 | ♟♟ 3 |
| ● Nizza Cipressi '16 | ♟♟ 4 |
| ○ Gavi di Gavi Rovereto '17 | ♟ 3 |
| ● Barbera d'Asti Sup. Nizza La Court '13 | ♟♟♟ 5 |
| ● Barbera d'Asti Sup. Nizza La Court '12 | ♟♟♟ 5 |
| ● Barbera d'Asti Sup. Nizza La Court '09 | ♟♟♟ 5 |
| ● Barolo Cannubi '06 | ♟♟♟ 7 |
| ● Barolo Cerequio '10 | ♟♟♟ 7 |
| ● Barolo Cerequio '09 | ♟♟♟ 7 |

# Chionetti

Fraz. Fraz. San Luigi
b.ta Valdiberti, 44
12063 Dogliani [CN]
Tel. +39 017371179
www.chionettiquinto.com

**CELLAR SALES**
**PRE-BOOKED VISITS**
**ANNUAL PRODUCTION** 83,000 bottles
**HECTARES UNDER VINE** 15.00
**VITICULTURE METHOD** Certified Organic
**SUSTAINABLE WINERY**

Even if he's inherited a tradition of winemaking from his father, Quinto, Nicola Chionetti is proving up to the difficult task of managing the family winery. He's helped by an excellent staff, both in the vineyards and in the cellar, maintaining the same classical approach that has always defined the winery. One such example is the use of concrete vats for aging their Dolcetto. Their most praised wines, Dogliani Biccolero and San Luigi, are now accompanied by La Costa and a Langhe Nebbiolo. And their newest additions are on the way: a Barolo and a Langhe Riesling. Their 2017 Dogliani San Luigi features distinctly enticing and pronounced aromas of ripe blackberry and almond across a pleasant background of cocoa. On the palate it exhibits a lovely pervasiveness of pulp and tannins, as well as length. Their Briccolero, a wine that has deservedly become a flagship for the area, is even weightier and fruitier, while their Nebbiolo La Chiusa is a pleasantly evolved wine.

| | |
|---|---|
| ● Dogliani Briccolero '17 | ♟♟ 3* |
| ● Dogliani San Luigi '17 | ♟♟ 3* |
| ● Langhe Nebbiolo La Chiusa '16 | ♟♟ 4 |
| ● Dogliani La Costa '16 | ♟ 4 |
| ● Dolcetto di Dogliani Briccolero '07 | ♟♟♟ 3* |
| ● Dolcetto di Dogliani Briccolero '04 | ♟♟♟ 3* |
| ● Dogliani Briccolero '16 | ♟♟ 3 |
| ● Dogliani Briccolero '15 | ♟♟ 3* |
| ● Dogliani Briccolero '14 | ♟♟ 3 |
| ● Dogliani Briccolero '13 | ♟♟ 3 |
| ● Dogliani Briccolero '12 | ♟♟ 3* |
| ● Dogliani La Costa '13 | ♟♟ 4 |
| ● Dogliani San Luigi '16 | ♟♟ 3 |
| ● Dogliani San Luigi '15 | ♟♟ 3* |
| ● Langhe Nebbiolo La Chiusa '14 | ♟♟ 4 |
| ● Langhe Nebbiolo La Chiusa '13 | ♟♟ 4 |

# Ciabot Berton

Fraz. Santa Maria, 1
12064 La Morra [CN]
Tel. +39 017350217
www.ciabotberton.it

**CELLAR SALES**
**PRE-BOOKED VISITS**
**ANNUAL PRODUCTION** 65,000 bottles
**HECTARES UNDER VINE** 14.00

The Oberto family's bond with the hills of La Morra goes back as far as anyone can remember. It's sure that in the 19th century they were already involved in wine-growing, though the turning point came in the 1960s, when they began producing wines under their own brand. Today Marco is leading the estate, which comprises plots in historic crus like Roggeri, Bricco San Biagio, Rive, Cappallotti, Pira and Rocchettevino. Naturally their selection centers on Nebbiolo, though other regional grapes are represented as well, Dolcetto, Barbera and Favorita. Their 2013 Barolo Rocchettevino put in an excellent performance with a harmonious, delicate spiciness that ties in perfectly with notes of red fruit. On the palate it's well-balanced, soft, endowed with close-knit tannins and a long, elegant finish. Their 2013 Barolo Roggeri offers up notes of tar and licorice. Their 2016 Barbera Vigna Bricco San Biagio is a highly drinkable wine that proves close-focused and succulent, with a notable tannic grip.

| | |
|---|---|
| ● Barbera d'Alba V. Bricco S. Biagio '16 | ♟♟ 4 |
| ● Barolo Rocchettevino '13 | ♟♟ 6 |
| ● Barolo Roggeri '13 | ♟♟ 6 |
| ● Langhe Nebbiolo 3 Utin '16 | ♟♟ 3 |
| ● Barolo '13 | ♟ 5 |
| ● Barolo '12 | ♟♟ 5 |
| ● Barolo del Comune di La Morra '13 | ♟♟ 5 |
| ● Barolo del Comune di La Morra '11 | ♟♟ 5 |
| ● Barolo Rocchettevino '12 | ♟♟ 6 |
| ● Barolo Roggeri '10 | ♟♟ 6 |
| ● Langhe Nebbiolo 3 Utin '15 | ♟♟ 3 |

# PIEDMONT

## Cieck

Cascina Castagnola, 2
10090 San Giorgio Canavese [TO]
Tel. +39 0124330522
www.cieck.it

CELLAR SALES
PRE-BOOKED VISITS
ANNUAL PRODUCTION 85,000 bottles
HECTARES UNDER VINE 12.00

Founder Remo Falconieri is surrounded by a number of expert collaborators who guarantee awards and recognition both at home and abroad. The versatility of Erbaluce is on display both in their still wines, foremost the cru Misobolo, and their sparkling wines, which are gaining in importance and best represented by their Nature Pas Dosé. The cultivar's good acidity has continued to the continued success of their Erbaluce di Caluso Passito Alladium, made from grapes that are hung out for six months in well-ventilated spaces. Lengthy aging in the cellar allows their 2016 Erbaluce di Caluso T to offer up its best, with elegant hints of mint and bon-bons giving way to a rich, gratifying, well-balanced palate that exhibits just the right amount of freshness. Their 2017 Misobolo yields delicate notes of wild herbs and proves pleasant on the palate. Their sweet Passito Alladium is redolent of walnuts and dried figs, and endowed with a vivifying acidity.

| | |
|---|---|
| ○ Caluso Passito Alladium Ris. '05 | ♟♟ 5 |
| ○ Erbaluce di Caluso T '16 | ♟♟ 3* |
| ○ Erbaluce di Caluso Brut San Giorgio '15 | ♟♟ 4 |
| ○ Erbaluce di Caluso Misobolo '17 | ♟♟ 3 |
| ● Canavese Nebbiolo '16 | ♟ 3 |
| ○ Erbaluce di Caluso '17 | ♟ 2 |
| ○ Erbaluce di Caluso Passito Alladium '06 | ♟♟♟ 5 |
| ● Canavese Nebbiolo '15 | ♟♟ 3 |
| ● Canavese Nebbiolo '14 | ♟♟ 3 |
| ○ Erbaluce di Caluso Cieck Nature '13 | ♟♟ 5 |
| ○ Erbaluce di Caluso Misobolo '16 | ♟♟ 3 |
| ○ Erbaluce di Caluso Misobolo '15 | ♟♟ 3 |
| ○ Erbaluce di Caluso Passito Alladium '09 | ♟♟ 5 |

## ★F.lli Cigliuti

via Serraboella, 17
12052 Neive [CN]
Tel. +39 0173677185
www.cigliuti.it

CELLAR SALES
PRE-BOOKED VISITS
ANNUAL PRODUCTION 30,000 bottles
HECTARES UNDER VINE 7.50

Renato Cigliuti began making his Barbaresco Serraboella in 1964 and quickly managed to gain attention, thanks to a robust, pure style based heavily on his work in the vineyards. When it comes to vine growing, he's always been a true master, though less so when it comes to the technical side of winemaking. After a period in which small French casks were preferred, today larger barrels are used, giving rise to a precise structural and aromatic expression of Nebbiolo. Daughters Claudia and Silvia gladly welcome visitors in their scenic farm manor immersed in the vineyards. Their 2014 Barbaresco Serraboella possesses a textbook palate. Its tannic weave and fruity pulp are perfectly balanced, forming together the basis for a long, close-focused finish of rare pleasantness. Its nose is up to the task, with enticingly fresh notes that range from balsamic to blackcurrant. Their Vie Erte did well, though it's a bit oaky and hard.

| | |
|---|---|
| ● Barbaresco Serraboella '14 | ♟♟ 8 |
| ● Barbaresco Vie Erte '14 | ♟♟ 6 |
| ● Barbera d'Alba Campass '15 | ♟♟ 5 |
| ● Barbera d'Alba V. Serraboella '15 | ♟ 4 |
| ● Barbaresco '83 | ♟♟♟ 6 |
| ● Barbaresco Serraboella '13 | ♟♟♟ 8 |
| ● Barbaresco Serraboella '11 | ♟♟♟ 7 |
| ● Barbaresco Serraboella '10 | ♟♟♟ 7 |
| ● Barbaresco Serraboella '09 | ♟♟♟ 7 |
| ● Barbaresco Serraboella '01 | ♟♟♟ 6 |
| ● Barbaresco Serraboella '00 | ♟♟♟ 6 |
| ● Barbaresco V. Erte '04 | ♟♟♟ 6 |

# ★Tenute Cisa Asinari dei Marchesi di Grésy

LOC. MARTINENGA
S.DA DELLA STAZIONE, 21
12050 BARBARESCO [CN]
TEL. +39 0173635222
www.marchesidigresy.com

CELLAR SALES
PRE-BOOKED VISITS
ANNUAL PRODUCTION 200,000 bottles
HECTARES UNDER VINE 35.00
SUSTAINABLE WINERY

Dolcetto, Chardonnay and Sauvignon are cultivated on Monte Aribaldo in Treiso; Moscato, Barbera and Merlot are grown in La Serra and Montecolombo di Cassine. And we mustn't forget their gem, Tenute Cisa Asinari, more than 10 hectares on Martinenga hill. This last gives rise to their highly prized reds, their Camp Gros and Gaiun, wines that shine for finesse and stylistic precision. They're just a bit surly in the first months, but for those who can wait (and know a good wine when they taste one), over time they'll offer up a marvelous array of sensations. Their 2013 Barbaresco Camp Gros brought home Tre Bicchieri, a wine redolent of fresh aromas of red fruit. It's delicate and pure, a cut above the rest. Their 2015 Barbaresco Martinenga also proved excellent. It's an approachable wine in its profile of meaty fruit, with a truly an elegant spicy touch. The finish comes through minty, with nice presence. Their 2014 Gaiun is more intense in its smoky weave, with shades of camphor and tobacco. On the palate it exhibits nice pulp, and a long finish.

| | | |
|---|---|---|
| ● Barbaresco Camp Gros Martinenga Ris. '13 | ▼▼▼ | 8 |
| ● Barbaresco Martinenga '15 | ▼▼ | 8 |
| ○ Langhe Chardonnay Gresy '16 | ▼▼ | 5 |
| ● Barbaresco Gaiun '14 | ▼▼ | 8 |
| ● Barbera d'Asti Monte Colombo '13 | ▼▼ | 5 |
| ● Langhe Nebbiolo '17 | ▼▼ | 4 |
| ● M.to Rosso MerlotdaSolo '10 | ▼ | 5 |
| ● Barbaresco Camp Gros '06 | ♀♀♀ | 8 |
| ● Barbaresco Camp Gros Martinenga '09 | ♀♀♀ | 8 |
| ● Barbaresco Camp Gros Martinenga '08 | ♀♀♀ | 8 |
| ● Barbaresco Martinenga Camp Gros Ris. '12 | ♀♀♀ | 8 |

# ★★Domenico Clerico

LOC. MANZONI, 67
12065 MONFORTE D'ALBA [CN]
TEL. +39 017378171
www.domenicoclerico.com

PRE-BOOKED VISITS
ANNUAL PRODUCTION 110,000 bottles
HECTARES UNDER VINE 21.00

Domenico Clerico, a loved and esteemed producer and man, an explosive interpreter of Barolo and central figure in Langhe's 'New Wave', left us, but for those who knew him his smiling expression and curious eyes will remain forever etched in our memories. For 40 years his wife, Giuliana Viberti, has helped oversee every detail, and she's forging ahead in Domenico's footsteps, well-supported by a young squad coordinated by Oscar Arrivabene and Gianmatteo Raineri (for enology) and Francesco Salinitro (on the commercial end of things). Their 2014 Barolos impressed, with their Pajana standing out for the elegant subtlety of its aromas of mint and licorice, and the plush harmony of its palate. We found their base-level Barolo noteworthy and highly drinkable, just a bit marked by oak and already endowed with a precise, enjoyable balance of flavor. Their savory Barbera d'Alba Trevigne once again proved commendable.

| | | |
|---|---|---|
| ● Barolo '14 | ▼▼ | 6 |
| ● Barolo Pajana '14 | ▼▼ | 8 |
| ● Barbera d'Alba Trevigne '16 | ▼▼ | 6 |
| ● Barolo Aeroplanservaj '14 | ▼▼ | 7 |
| ● Barolo Ciabot Mentin '14 | ▼▼ | 8 |
| ● Langhe Nebbiolo Capismee '17 | ▼▼ | 5 |
| ● Barolo Ciabot Mentin '08 | ♀♀♀ | 8 |
| ● Barolo Ciabot Mentin Ginestra '05 | ♀♀♀ | 8 |
| ● Barolo Ciabot Mentin Ginestra '04 | ♀♀♀ | 8 |
| ● Barolo Ciabot Mentin Ginestra '01 | ♀♀♀ | 7 |
| ● Barolo Ciabot Mentin Ginestra '92 | ♀♀♀ | 8 |
| ● Barolo Ciabot Mentin Ginestra '86 | ♀♀♀ | 8 |
| ● Barolo Percristina '01 | ♀♀♀ | 8 |

## ★Elvio Cogno

VIA RAVERA, 2
12060 NOVELLO [CN]
TEL. +39 0173744006
www.elviocogno.com

CELLAR SALES
PRE-BOOKED VISITS
ACCOMMODATION
ANNUAL PRODUCTION 90,000 bottles
HECTARES UNDER VINE 15.00
VITICULTURE METHOD Certified Organic
SUSTAINABLE WINERY

Elvio Cogno was a first-rate winemaker and
transmitted his enological sensibility to his
daughter Nadia, as well as her husband,
Valter Cogno. Together they've had
outstanding results, bolstered by an estate
whose heart resides in the magnificent
Ravera cru (little known when they began
some 20 years ago, it has since gained
international attention). Their Barolo is aged
according to the characteristics of each cru:
three years for their Cascina Nuova and
Ravera, four for their Bricco Pernice and five
for their Riserva Vigna Elena. Their decidedly
youthful and complex 2013 Barolo Bricco
Bernice features aromas of raspberry,
quinine and licorice. On the palate its tannic
presence is still pronounced. Their deep and
rhythmic 2012 Riserva Vigna Elena did well
in terms of maturity and evolution. Their
2014 Barolo Ravera does a a nice job
bringing together red fruit, golden-leaf
tobacco, oak and vegetal notes, while their
austere and clean 2015 Barbaresco Bordini
is noteworthy for its tight structure.

| | |
|---|---|
| ● Barolo Ravera Bricco Pernice '13 | ♼♼♼ 8 |
| ● Barolo Ravera '14 | ♼♼ 8 |
| ● Barolo Ravera V. Elena Ris. '12 | ♼♼ 8 |
| ● Barbaresco Bordini '15 | ♼♼ 5 |
| ● Barbera d'Alba Bricco dei Merli '16 | ♼♼ 4 |
| ○ Langhe Nascetta del Comune di Novello Anas-Cëtta '17 | ♼♼ 4 |
| ● Langhe Nebbiolo Montegrilli '17 | ♼ 4 |
| ● Barolo Bricco Pernice '11 | ♼♼♼ 8 |
| ● Barolo Bricco Pernice '09 | ♼♼♼ 8 |
| ● Barolo Bricco Pernice '08 | ♼♼♼ 8 |
| ● Barolo Bricco Pernice '05 | ♼♼♼ 8 |
| ● Barolo Ravera '11 | ♼♼♼ 7 |
| ● Barolo Ravera '07 | ♼♼♼ 7 |
| ● Barolo Ravera Bricco Pernice '12 | ♼♼♼ 8 |
| ● Barolo V. Elena '04 | ♼♼♼ 8 |
| ● Barolo V. Elena Ris. '06 | ♼♼♼ 8 |

## Poderi Colla

FRAZ. SAN ROCCO SENO D'ELVIO, 82
12051 ALBA [CN]
TEL. +39 0173290148
www.podericolla.it

CELLAR SALES
PRE-BOOKED VISITS
ANNUAL PRODUCTION 150,000 bottles
HECTARES UNDER VINE 26.00

The Colla family is deeply bound to
Piedmont's wine-growing tradition, steeped
in 300 years of history that saw them
prefigure what are today considered
fundamental principles of winemaking.
They were among the first to vinify their
grapes separately, and contributed to
developing several typologies, including
Rosatello, Moscatello, Vino Negro,
Vermouth and Asti's sparkling wines. And of
course we shouldn't forget their prestigious
Barolos (Bussia Dardi Le Rose) and
Barbarescos (Roncaglie), aged at length in
Slavonian oak. 'Enchanting' is the right
word for their 2015 Barbaresco Roncaglie.
On the nose it opens with notes of licorice
and herbs in the sun, only to give way to
extraordinary aromas of red fruit. On the
palate it joins power and harmony, with
creamy tannins and a buoyant, persistent
finish. Their 2014 Barolo Bussia Dardi Le
Rose exhibits a flowery character, with
delicate aromas of violets and small red
fruit. The rest of their selection proved
exceptionally consistent and sound.

| | |
|---|---|
| ● Barbaresco Roncaglie '15 | ♼♼ 6 |
| ● Barolo Bussia Dardi Le Rose '14 | ♼♼ 6 |
| ● Barbera d'Alba Costa Bruna '16 | ♼♼ 3 |
| ● Dolcetto d'Alba Pian Balbo '17 | ♼♼ 2* |
| ● Langhe Bricco del Drago '15 | ♼♼ 4 |
| ○ Langhe Riesling '16 | ♼♼ 3 |
| ● Nebbiolo d'Alba Drago '16 | ♼♼ 3 |
| ● Barbaresco Roncaglie '14 | ♼♼♼ 6 |
| ● Barolo Bussia Dardi Le Rose '09 | ♼♼♼ 6 |
| ● Barbaresco Roncaglie '13 | ♼♼ 6 |
| ● Barbaresco Roncaglie '12 | ♼♼ 6 |
| ● Barbaresco Roncaglie '11 | ♼♼ 6 |
| ● Barolo Bussia Dardi Le Rose '12 | ♼♼ 6 |
| ● Langhe Bricco del Drago '13 | ♼♼ 4 |
| ● Langhe Bricco del Drago '10 | ♼♼ 4 |
| ● Nebbiolo d'Alba Drago '15 | ♼♼ 3 |

## Colle Manora

S.DA BOZZOLA, 5
15044 QUARGNENTO [AL]
TEL. +39 0131219252
www.collemanora.it

**CELLAR SALES**
**PRE-BOOKED VISITS**
**ACCOMMODATION**
**ANNUAL PRODUCTION** 90,000 bottles
**HECTARES UNDER VINE** 21.00

Colle Manora is quite a large estate, totaling 75 hectares in all. 21 of these are vineyards, the rest are woods and farmland. They're situated in the lower hills that rise up out of the Alessandrino plains. Their cellar is managed by Valter Piccinino and the consultant Piero Ballario, who's been working with the winery since 2013. The new team's results weren't a long time coming and last year we were able to taste their wines, which proved to have consistent quality overall. A recent addition is their Piangalardo, a Barolo made with grapes for a vineyard in Monforte called 'Lontano'. Their wide selection demonstrates the level of quality achieved, with their Barolo Piagalardo leading the way. It's a wine that stands out for its nice array of aromas and flavors, and a long, determined finish. Their Albarossa Ray exhibits nice aromatic complexity while in the mouth it comes through full-bodied and quaffable. Their Rosso Barchetta put in a nice performance, while both their Barbera Pais and their Sauvignon Mimosa proved sound.

| | | |
|---|---|---|
| ● Barbera del M.to Pais '17 | ♟♟ 2* |
| ● Barolo Piangalardo '13 | ♟♟ 6 |
| ○ M.to Bianco Mimosa '17 | ♟♟ 2* |
| ● M.to Rosso Barchetta '15 | ♟♟ 3 |
| ● Piemonte Albarossa Ray '15 | ♟♟ 3 |
| ● Barbera d'Asti Sup. Manora '15 | ♟♟ 3* |
| ● Barbera d'Asti Sup. Manora '14 | ♟♟ 3 |
| ● Barbera del M.to Pais '16 | ♟♟ 2* |
| ○ M.to Bianco Mimosa '16 | ♟♟ 2* |
| ● Piemonte Albarossa Ray '14 | ♟♟ 3 |

## La Colombera

LOC. VHO
S.DA COMUNALE PER VHO, 7
15057 TORTONA [AL]
TEL. +39 0131867795
www.lacolomberavini.it

**CELLAR SALES**
**PRE-BOOKED VISITS**
**ANNUAL PRODUCTION** 80,000 bottles
**HECTARES UNDER VINE** 24.00
**SUSTAINABLE WINERY**

La Colombera has seen consistent growth over the years. Today the winery is sound, dynamic and well-represented on national and international markets. They offer a number of wines with an overall quality that's quite notable, starting with their base-line offering. Their selection doesn't stop at their renamed Tomasso, one of the area's regular strongpoints. It encompasses a number of wines made with native grape varieties: Barbera, Croatina and Nibiò (a Dolcetto clone) for their reds and Cortese (along with the already mentioned Timorasso) for their whites. 2016 gave rise to two Timorassos that made it into our finals. Their Montino is subtle and complex on the nose, with aromas of ripe citrus accompanied by notes of medicinal herbs. These give way to a palate of great structure and freshness, with a well-balanced, persistent finish. Derthona offers up vibrant, elegant aromas of camphor and flint across a background of orange peel. On the palate it's unhesitating, with a big body that's well-balanced by acidity, and a long finish.

| | | |
|---|---|---|
| ○ Colli Tortonesi Timorasso Il Montino '16 | ♟♟♟ 5 |
| ○ Colli Tortonesi Timorasso Derthona '16 | ♟♟ 4 |
| ● Colli Tortonesi Barbera Elisa '15 | ♟♟ 4 |
| ● Colli Tortonesi Rosso Vegia Rampana '17 | ♟♟ 3 |
| ⚜ Colli Tortonesi Cortese Bricco Bartolomeo '17 | ♟ 2 |
| ● Colli Tortonesi Croatina Arché '16 | ♟ 4 |
| ● Colli Tortonesi Croatina La Romba '17 | ♟ 3 |
| ● Colli Tortonesi Rosso Suciaja '16 | ♟ 4 |
| ● Colli Tortonesi Barbera Elisa '11 | ♟♟♟ 3* |
| ○ Colli Tortonesi Timorasso Il Montino '13 | ♟♟♟ 5 |
| ○ Colli Tortonesi Timorasso Il Montino '09 | ♟♟♟ 5 |
| ● Colli Tortonesi Rosso Suciaja '15 | ♟♟ 4 |
| ○ Colli Tortonesi Timorasso Derthona '15 | ♟♟ 4 |
| ○ Colli Tortonesi Timorasso Il Montino '15 | ♟♟ 5 |

## Colombo - Cascina Pastori

REG. CAFRA, 172B
14051 BUBBIO [AT]
TEL. +39 0144852807
www.colombovino.it

**CELLAR SALES**
**PRE-BOOKED VISITS**
**ANNUAL PRODUCTION** 40,000 bottles
**HECTARES UNDER VINE** 10.00
**SUSTAINABLE WINERY**

It was 2004 when Antonio Colombo purchased Cascina Pastori and the ten hectares of vineyards that surround it. Two years later he'd build a new cellar, showing great care for its environmental impact. Their vineyards are situated on primarily marl and calcareous terrain of marine origin, with Pinot Nero occupying more than half the estate (followed by Chardonnay and Moscato). The producer aims primarily at highlighting the attributes of Pinot Nero, with a traditional approach adopted in the vineyard and a modern approach in the cellar. Their 2015 Piemonte Pinot Nero Apertura takes home Tre Bicchieri, with its characteristic aromas of wild berries and a light note of Mediterranean scrubland on the nose. On the palate it proves coherent, fresh, elegant, pleasant and long. Their 2012 Piemonte Pinot Nero Apertura Maxima is richer, but lacking in the freshness and sweeter notes, opting for aromas of ripe, dark fruit instead.

| | |
|---|---|
| ● Piemonte Pinot Nero Apertura '15 | ▼▼▼ 3* |
| ● Piemonte Pinot Nero Apertura Maxima '12 | ▼▼ 8 |
| ⊙ Alta Langa Brut Rosé Silvì Ris. '12 | ♀♀ 5 |
| ○ Piemonte Chardonnay Spumante Blanc de Blancs Andrè M. Cl. '13 | ♀♀ 5 |
| ○ Piemonte Chardonnay Spumante Blanc de Blancs Andrè M. Cl. '12 | ♀♀ 5 |
| ○ Piemonte Moscato Passito Pastù Tardi | ♀♀ 5 |
| ● Piemonte Pinot Nero Apertura '14 | ♀♀ 3* |
| ● Piemonte Pinot Nero Apertura '13 | ♀♀ 3 |
| ● Piemonte Pinot Nero Apertura Maxima '11 | ♀♀ 8 |
| ● Piemonte Pinot Nero Apertura Maxima Ris. '11 | ♀♀ 8 |

## Diego Conterno

VIA MONTÀ, 27
12065 MONFORTE D'ALBA [CN]
TEL. +39 0173789265
www.diegoconterno.it

**CELLAR SALES**
**PRE-BOOKED VISITS**
**ANNUAL PRODUCTION** 40,000 bottles
**HECTARES UNDER VINE** 7.50

It's 18 candles for Diego Conterno's winery. It was 2000 when Diego decided to leave a collaboration with his cousins at Conterno-Fantino and found his own brand. Today his son Stefano is chipping in, helping to oversee their seven hectares of property. Barbera, Dolcetto, Nascetta and Nebbiolo are cultivated, the last of which in two prized Monforte crus, Le Coste and Ginestra. In the cellar they have different approaches and methods, from the use of new, small wood barrels, to larger ones, making for a solid selection of rigorously well-made wines. Their excellent 2014 Barolo Ginestra is rich in balsamic whiffs and vibrant notes of roots and licorice. On the palate it exhibits excellent grip and creaminess, with smooth tannins and a long, earthy, minty finish. It's a wine with some character. Their 2014 Barolo features notes of rhubarb and quinine. It's well-made, though still a bit clenched and closed. Their 2016 Barbera Ferrione also did well, featuring nice acidity.

| | |
|---|---|
| ● Barolo Ginestra '14 | ▼▼ 7 |
| ● Barbera d'Alba Ferrione '16 | ▼▼ 3 |
| ● Barolo '14 | ▼▼ 6 |
| ○ Langhe Nascetta '17 | ▼▼ 3 |
| ● Nebbiolo d'Alba '16 | ▼ 3 |
| ● Barolo Le Coste '09 | ♀♀♀ 6 |
| ● Barolo '09 | ♀♀ 6 |
| ● Barolo Ginestra '13 | ♀♀ 7 |
| ● Barolo Ginestra '12 | ♀♀ 7 |
| ● Barolo Ginestra '11 | ♀♀ 6 |
| ● Barolo Ginestra '10 | ♀♀ 6 |

## ★★★Giacomo Conterno

LOC. ORNATI, 2
12065 MONFORTE D'ALBA [CN]
TEL. +39 017378221
www.conterno.it

**PRE-BOOKED VISITS**
**ANNUAL PRODUCTION** 60,000 bottles
**HECTARES UNDER VINE** 23.00

Monfortino's 100-year anniversary is getting close. The brand was presented for the first time in 1924 by forward-thinking Giacomo Conterno. Their Barolo gained its reputation for excellent starting in 1974, when Giacomo's son Giovanni purchased the splendid Francia vineyard, their only source for grapes in the years that followed. The winery grew further when, 12 years ago, his son Roberto purchased a part of the prized Cerretta cru, and three years after that with the addition of Arione, also in Serralunga d'Alba. It's a story that continued in 2018 with the purchase of the winery Nervi di Gattinara. Roberto Conterno told us that 'his' 2014 was better than even the best expectations. And he proves it, for one, with his superb Barolo Cerretta, a fresh wine in its aromas of balsamic and a palate that's not only fresh and lively, but also extremely well-textured. Their Vigna Francia wins out the battle for the best Barbera d'Alba, proving just a bit more elegant and complex than the youthful Vigna Cerretta.

| | |
|---|---|
| ● Barolo Cerretta '14 | ♥♥♥ 8 |
| ● Barbera d'Alba V. Francia '16 | ♥♥ 5 |
| ● Barbera d'Alba V. Cerretta '16 | ♥♥ 5 |
| ● Barolo Cascina Francia '06 | ♀♀♀ 8 |
| ● Barolo Cascina Francia '05 | ♀♀♀ 8 |
| ● Barolo Cascina Francia '04 | ♀♀♀ 8 |
| ● Barolo Francia '12 | ♀♀♀ 8 |
| ● Barolo Francia '10 | ♀♀♀ 8 |
| ● Barolo Monfortino Ris. '10 | ♀♀♀ 8 |
| ● Barolo Monfortino Ris. '08 | ♀♀♀ 8 |
| ● Barolo Monfortino Ris. '06 | ♀♀♀ 8 |
| ● Barolo Monfortino Ris. '05 | ♀♀♀ 8 |
| ● Barolo Monfortino Ris. '04 | ♀♀♀ 8 |
| ● Barolo Monfortino Ris. '02 | ♀♀♀ 8 |
| ● Barolo Monfortino Ris. '01 | ♀♀♀ 8 |
| ● Barolo Monfortino Ris. '00 | ♀♀♀ 8 |
| ● Barolo Monfortino Ris. '74 | ♀♀♀ 8 |

## Paolo Conterno

LOC. GINESTRA, 34
12065 MONFORTE D'ALBA [CN]
TEL. +39 017378415
www.paoloconterno.com

**CELLAR SALES**
**PRE-BOOKED VISITS**
**ACCOMMODATION**
**ANNUAL PRODUCTION** 180,000 bottles
**HECTARES UNDER VINE** 37.00
**SUSTAINABLE WINERY**

It was 1886 when Paolo Conterno founded his winery. Today we find the fourth generation at the helm, represented by Giorgio Conterno. In addition to looking after an important vineyard situated on the steeped slopes of Ginestra cru (in Monforte d'Alba), he's enlarged the estate beyond Barolo with his Antico Podere del Sant'Uffizio, in Astigiano and Monferrato. We shouldn't forget his purchase of Tenuta Ortaglia in Pratolino, on the hills north of Florence, either. Their 2010 Barolo Ginestra Riserva is a sumptuous wine that yields distinctive balsamic force, unleashing richness, tension and exceptional tannic presence on the palate. Their 2014 Barolo Riva del Bric offers up aromas of black pepper and forest undergrowth. It's a dense and full-bodied wine, though it's also endowed with a deep savoriness. Their 2014 Ginestra is fresh and minty, and finishes on notes of citrus and cloves. Their fresh 2016 Barbera d'Asti Bricco is highly enjoyable while their 2016 Chardonnay Divers exhibits a skillful use of oak.

| | |
|---|---|
| ● Barolo Ginestra Ris. '10 | ♥♥♥ 8 |
| ● Barbera d'Alba La Ginestra '16 | ♥♥ 3* |
| ● Barolo Riva del Bric '14 | ♥♥ 6 |
| ● Barbera d'Asti Bricco '16 | ♥♥ 3 |
| ● Barolo Ginestra '14 | ♥♥ 8 |
| ● Langhe Nebbiolo A Mont '16 | ♥♥ 4 |
| ● Langhe Nebbiolo Bric Ginestra '16 | ♥♥ 5 |
| ○ Piemonte Chardonnay Divers '16 | ♥♥ 5 |
| ● Barolo Ginestra '10 | ♀♀♀ 8 |
| ● Barolo Ginestra Ris. '09 | ♀♀♀ 8 |
| ● Barolo Ginestra Ris. '08 | ♀♀♀ 8 |
| ● Barolo Ginestra Ris. '06 | ♀♀♀ 8 |
| ● Barbera d'Alba La Ginestra '15 | ♀♀ 3 |
| ● Barolo Ginestra '13 | ♀♀ 8 |

# Contratto

VIA G. B. GIULIANI, 56
14053 CANELLI [AT]
TEL. +39 0141823349
www.contratto.it

**CELLAR SALES**
**PRE-BOOKED VISITS**
**ANNUAL PRODUCTION** 140,000 bottles
**HECTARES UNDER VINE** 21.00

It was 2011 when the historic winery of Contratto was purchased by Giorgio Rivetti and his La Spinetta. It was his clear intention to maintain a separate structure, and to bring the winery back to its roots, focusing entirely on Metodo Classico sparkling wines. Their current selection is bound to grow significantly, and concentrate on Piedmont's cultivar (considering that in addition to their 40 hectares of Pinot Nero and Chardonnay in Bossolasco, the total size of the property has practically tripled). Their selection put in an excellent overall performance, demonstrating the path of quality undertaken, in particular their charming 2013 Millesimato Pas Dosé. It's a vibrant and creamy sparkler that features aromas of aniseed and lemon twist, and extremely fine mousse. It finishes nice, clean and long. Their 2013 Alta Langa Blanc de Blancs Pas Dosé also delivered, proving richer and more potent, complex and full of character. It's difficult to find a sweet sparkling wine that's as good as their 2012 Demiranda.

| | | |
|---|---|---|
| ○ Millesimato Pas Dosé M. Cl. '13 | ♟♟♟ 5 | |
| ○ Alta Langa Pas Dosé | | |
| Blanc de Blancs '13 | ♟♟ 6 | |
| ○ Asti De Miranda M. Cl. '12 | ♟♟♟ 5 | |
| ○ Alta Langa Pas Dosé | | |
| For England Blanc de Noir '14 | ♟♟ 6 | |
| ○ Special Cuvée Pas Dosé '10 | ♟♟ 5 | |
| ○ Bacco d'Oro Brut '12 | ♟ 4 | |
| ○ Alta Langa Pas Dosé | | |
| For England Blanc de Noir '13 | ♟♟ 6 | |
| ○ Asti De Miranda M. Cl. '11 | ♟♟ 5 | |
| ○ Blanc de Blancs Pas Dosé '12 | ♟♟ 5 | |
| ⊙ For England Pas Dosé Rosé M. Cl. '12 | ♟♟ 6 | |
| ○ Millesimato Pas Dosé M. Cl. '12 | ♟♟ 5 | |
| ○ Special Cuvée Pas Dosé '09 | ♟♟ 5 | |

# Vigne Marina Coppi

VIA SANT'ANDREA, 5
15051 CASTELLANIA [AL]
TEL. +39 0131837089
www.vignemarinacoppi.com

**CELLAR SALES**
**PRE-BOOKED VISITS**
**ANNUAL PRODUCTION** 25,000 bottles
**HECTARES UNDER VINE** 4.50

Castellania is a small municipality situated at about 400 meters above sea level and about 15 kilometers from Tortona. It's here that we find Vigne Marina Coppi, a small but great artisanal producer. The territory is inextricably linked with the history of the family itself. Indeed, Francesco Bellocchio realized they're not just a business, but rather a life philosophy centered on age-old ethical and cultural principles. But they're looking forward as well. Their wines are made only with the region's traditional cultivar: Timorasso, Favorita, Barbera, Nebbiolo, Croatina, making for a selection that's of noteworthy quality. Their Fausto, a wine used to being in our finals, offers up vibrant, complex aromas of dried herbs accompanied by citrus peel on a mineral background. These converge on a highly persistent palate of great structure and notable alcohol. Francesco is a rich, firm Timorasso with great aging potential. Marine is vibrant and quite drinkable, while their I Grop features lovely fruit and nice structure. Their 2017 Sant'Andrea has plenty of zip.

| | | |
|---|---|---|
| ● Colli Tortonesi Barbera | | |
| Sant'Andrea '17 | ♟♟ 3* | |
| ○ Colli Tortonesi Timorasso Fausto '16 | ♟♟ 6 | |
| ● Colli Tortonesi Barbera Sup. | | |
| I Grop '14 | ♟♟ 5 | |
| ○ Colli Tortonesi Favorita Marine '16 | ♟♟ 5 | |
| ○ Colli Tortonesi Timorasso | | |
| Francesca '17 | ♟♟ 3 | |
| ● Colli Tortonesi Rosso Lindin '15 | ♟ 5 | |
| ○ Colli Tortonesi Timorasso Fausto '15 | ♟♟♟ 6 | |
| ○ Colli Tortonesi Timorasso Fausto '12 | ♟♟♟ 6 | |
| ○ Colli Tortonesi Timorasso Fausto '11 | ♟♟♟ 6 | |
| ○ Colli Tortonesi Timorasso Fausto '10 | ♟♟♟ 6 | |
| ○ Colli Tortonesi Timorasso Fausto '09 | ♟♟♟ 6 | |
| ● Colli Tortonesi Barbera | | |
| Sant'Andrea '15 | ♟♟ 3* | |
| ● Colli Tortonesi Barbera Sup. I Grop '13 | ♟♟ 5 | |

# ★Coppo

VIA ALBA, 68
14053 CANELLI [AT]
TEL. +39 0141823146
www.coppo.it

**CELLAR SALES**
**PRE-BOOKED VISITS**
**ANNUAL PRODUCTION** 400,000 bottles
**HECTARES UNDER VINE** 52.00

Having surpassed its first 125 years, the Coppo family's winery remains a leader among Asti's producers. Their vineyards span Canelli, Castelnuovo Calcea and Agliano Terme, and give rise to 15 wines, from Barbera to Chardonnay, Metodo Classico sparkling wines, and appellations like Moscato d'Asti, Barolo and Gavi. The result is a selection that sees close-focused aromas and in many cases excellent aging potential as its defining characteristics. Hats off to their 2017 Barbera d'Asti L'Avvocata, a splendid example of a vintage Barbera, fresh and savory, gutsy in its peppery tones, with a long, juicy, delectable finish. Tre Bicchieri. But their entire selection shines, as their 2015 Barbera d'Asti Pomorosso demonstrates with its notes of spices and cherry, its nice body, its fruity richness and subtle tannins. Their 2015 Piemonte Chardonnay Monteriolo is another example, exhibiting great richness and depth, as is their 2007 Piero Coppo Riserva del Fondatore, a mature and complex Metodo Classico sparkler.

| | | |
|---|---|---|
| ● Barbera d'Asti L'Avvocata '17 | ♟♟♟ | 3* |
| ● Barbera d'Asti Pomorosso '15 | ♟♟ | 7 |
| ○ Piemonte Chardonnay Monteriolo '15 | ♟♟ | 6 |
| ○ Piero Coppo Ris. del Fondatore M. Cl. '07 | ♟♟ | 5 |
| ● Barbera d'Asti Camp du Rouss '16 | ♟♟ | 3 |
| ● Barolo '12 | ♟♟ | 8 |
| ☉ Clelia Coppo Brut Rosé '12 | ♟♟ | 6 |
| ○ Extra Brut Ris. M. Cl. '10 | ♟♟ | 5 |
| ○ Luigi Coppo Brut M. Cl. | ♟♟ | 5 |
| ○ Gavi La Rocca '17 | ♟ | 3 |
| ○ Moscato d'Asti Moncalvina '17 | ♟ | 3 |
| ● Barbera d'Asti Pomorosso '13 | ♟♟♟ | 7 |
| ● Barbera d'Asti Pomorosso '12 | ♟♟♟ | 7 |
| ● Barbera d'Asti Pomorosso '11 | ♟♟♟ | 7 |
| ● Barbera d'Asti Sup. Nizza Riserva della Famiglia '09 | ♟♟♟ | 8 |

# Giovanni Corino

FRAZ. ANNUNZIATA, 25B
12064 LA MORRA [CN]
TEL. +39 0173509452
www.corino.it

**CELLAR SALES**
**PRE-BOOKED VISITS**
**ANNUAL PRODUCTION** 50,000 bottles
**HECTARES UNDER VINE** 9.50

Giuliano Corino began cultivating the land when his father, Giovanni, was managing a classic agricultural producer in Langhe. At the time grapes were only one of the fruits grown and put to market in Alba. Now that they've divided their production, and with the help of his family, his brother Renato has been personally overseeing every aspect of wine production for 13 years now. Their small cellar avails itself of small French casks. These are often new, both in the case of their Barolos (Arborina, Giachini and La Morra) and in their prized Riserva. Their Barbera d'Alba Ciabot du Re once again proves highly enjoyable. Their enchanting 2014 Barolo Arborina is already offering up enticing, lively aromas of rose, licorice and tobacco. The palate isn't too potent, proving balanced and deliciously pervasive. Their Giachini is just a bit more austere on the nose, with dark notes of quinine and rhubarb emerging, while on the palate it demonstrates body and pleasantness. Their version from La Morra is also more than valid, proving rich in pulp while still slightly marked by oak.

| | | |
|---|---|---|
| ● Barolo Arborina '14 | ♟♟ | 8 |
| ● Barolo del Comune di La Morra '14 | ♟♟ | 6 |
| ● Barolo Giachini '14 | ♟♟ | 8 |
| ● Barbera d'Alba Ciabot du Re '16 | ♟♟ | 5 |
| ● Dolcetto d'Alba '17 | ♟ | 2 |
| ● Barbera d'Alba V. Pozzo '97 | ♟♟♟ | 5 |
| ● Barbera d'Alba V. Pozzo '96 | ♟♟♟ | 5 |
| ● Barolo Giachini '12 | ♟♟♟ | 7 |
| ● Barolo Giachini '11 | ♟♟♟ | 7 |
| ● Barolo Rocche '01 | ♟♟♟ | 7 |
| ● Barolo Rocche '90 | ♟♟♟ | 7 |
| ● Barolo V. V. '99 | ♟♟♟ | 8 |
| ● Barolo V. V. '98 | ♟♟♟ | 8 |
| ● Barolo Arborina '13 | ♟♟ | 7 |
| ● Barolo Arborina '12 | ♟♟ | 7 |
| ● Barolo del Comune di La Morra '13 | ♟♟ | 6 |
| ● Barolo Giachini '13 | ♟♟ | 7 |

## Renato Corino

FRAZ. ANNUNZIATA
B.TA POZZO, 49A
12064 LA MORRA [CN]
TEL. +39 0173500349
www.renatocorino.it

CELLAR SALES
PRE-BOOKED VISITS
ANNUAL PRODUCTION 50,000 bottles
HECTARES UNDER VINE 7.00

The style of Renato Corino's wines aims for elegance, which is brought out in their Barolos through aging in small, mostly new French oak casks. But you shouldn't think for a moment that wood dominates, because the grapes used come from extremely old vines that endow their wines with structure and force. This is accompanied by polished aromas that, especially in the case of their Rocche dell'Annunziata, feature an irresistibly fresh, balsamic note. Renato's children Chiara and Stefano recently began working in the lovely cellar they built 15 years ago in the notable Arborina di La Morra cru. Their youthful and fresh 2014 Barolo Rocche dell'Annunziata is a highly elegant wine on the nose and even more commendable on the palate, with a finish of crisp, ripe fruit that confers persistent sensations. Their La Morra has a bit less weight to it but exhibits rare balance and distinctly soft, juicy tannins. Their robust, spicy Arborina is still a bit marked by oak.

| | | |
|---|---|---|
| ● Barolo Rocche dell'Annunziata '14 | 🍷🍷🍷 | 8 |
| ● Barolo del Comune di La Morra '14 | 🍷🍷 | 5 |
| ● Barbera d'Alba '17 | 🍷🍷 | 3 |
| ● Barbera d'Alba Pozzo '16 | 🍷🍷 | 5 |
| ● Barolo Arborina '14 | 🍷🍷 | 7 |
| ● Dolcetto d'Alba '17 | 🍷🍷 | 3 |
| ● Barolo Rocche dell'Annunziata '11 | 🍷🍷🍷 | 8 |
| ● Barolo Rocche dell'Annunziata '10 | 🍷🍷🍷 | 7 |
| ● Barolo Rocche dell'Annunziata '09 | 🍷🍷🍷 | 7 |
| ● Barolo Vign. Rocche '06 | 🍷🍷🍷 | 7 |
| ● Barolo Vign. Rocche '04 | 🍷🍷🍷 | 8 |
| ● Barolo Vign. Rocche '03 | 🍷🍷🍷 | 8 |
| ● Barolo Arborina '12 | 🍷🍷 | 7 |
| ● Barolo Arborina '11 | 🍷🍷 | 7 |
| ● Barolo Rocche dell'Annunziata '13 | 🍷🍷 | 8 |
| ● Barolo Rocche dell'Annunziata '12 | 🍷🍷 | 8 |

## Cornarea

VIA VALENTINO, 150
12043 CANALE [CN]
TEL. +39 017365636
www.cornarea.com

CELLAR SALES
PRE-BOOKED VISITS
ACCOMMODATION
ANNUAL PRODUCTION 90,000 bottles
HECTARES UNDER VINE 14.00

Just outside Canale, on Cornarea hill, the Bovone family works its calcareous-clay and magnesium-rich terrain. Its a single tract of contiguous land whose vineyards were planted between 1975 and 1978. The area's two major grapes are grown, with Arneis making up two-thirds and Nebbiolo providing the rest. Their wines seek to point up the attributes of the territory, with a particular attention to freshness and close-focused aromas. Both their 2015 Roero and their 2017 Roero Arneis made it to our finals. The former features notes of Mediterranean scrubland and spicy nuances on the nose, with a fresh, juicy palate that exhibits nice mouthfeel. The latter sees hints of melon and pineapple. It's pleasant and approachable wine rich in fruit. Their 2014 Tarasco Passito, a historic sweet wine, also did well, proving redolent of dried fruit, nuts and figs. On the palate it's long, fresh and well-supported by acidity.

| | | |
|---|---|---|
| ● Roero '15 | 🍷🍷 | 4 |
| ○ Roero Arneis '17 | 🍷🍷 | 3* |
| ○ Enritard '14 | 🍷🍷 | 3 |
| ● Nebbiolo d'Alba '16 | 🍷🍷 | 3 |
| ○ Tarasco Passito '14 | 🍷🍷 | 5 |
| ● Roero '12 | 🍷🍷 | 4 |
| ● Roero '11 | 🍷🍷 | 4 |
| ○ Roero Arneis '16 | 🍷🍷 | 3* |
| ○ Roero Arneis '15 | 🍷🍷 | 3* |
| ○ Roero Arneis '14 | 🍷🍷 | 3* |
| ○ Roero Arneis '13 | 🍷🍷 | 3 |
| ○ Tarasco Passito '12 | 🍷🍷 | 5 |
| ○ Tarasco Passito '11 | 🍷🍷 | 5 |
| ○ Tarasco Passito '10 | 🍷🍷 | 5 |

# ★Matteo Correggia

LOC. GARBINETTO
VIA SANTO STEFANO ROERO, 124
12043 CANALE [CN]
TEL. +39 0173978009
www.matteocorreggia.com

**CELLAR SALES**
**PRE-BOOKED VISITS**
**ANNUAL PRODUCTION** 150,000 bottles
**HECTARES UNDER VINE** 20.00

Ornella Costa Correggia, along with her children Brigitta and Giovanni manage the winery founded by Matteo in 1985. In recent years they have been making changes, while still maintaining continuity with the past. They've adopted an organic approach to cultivation and have been experimenting with winemaking, as well as the use of screw caps. Their vineyards are situated throughout Canale and Santo Stefano Roero, primarily on the sandy terrain that's characteristic of the Tanaro river's left bank. Their historic Roero Ròche d'Ampsèj Riserva is back with Tre Bicchieri. On the nose it offers up notes of Mediterranean scrubland, tea leaves, spices and dark fruit, while on the palate it exhibits length, savoriness and notable structure, with pronounced but elegant tannins. Their long and juicy 2015 Roero La Val dei Preti is rich in fruit and well-supported by acidity. The rest of their selection also proved well-made.

| | | |
|---|---|---|
| ● Roero Ròche d'Ampsèj Ris. '14 | ♟♟♟ | 6 |
| ● Roero La Val dei Preti '15 | ♟♟ | 5 |
| ● Barbera d'Alba Marun '15 | ♟♟ | 5 |
| ○ Roero Arneis '17 | ♟♟ | 3 |
| ● Barbera d'Alba Bricco Marun '94 | ♟♟♟ | 5 |
| ● Barbera d'Alba Marun '04 | ♟♟♟ | 5 |
| ● Roero Ròche d'Ampsèj '04 | ♟♟♟ | 6 |
| ● Roero Ròche d'Ampsèj '01 | ♟♟♟ | 6 |
| ● Roero Ròche d'Ampsèj '00 | ♟♟♟ | 6 |
| ● Roero Ròche d'Ampsèj Ris. '09 | ♟♟♟ | 6 |
| ● Roero Ròche d'Ampsèj Ris. '07 | ♟♟♟ | 6 |
| ● Roero Ròche d'Ampsèj Ris. '06 | ♟♟♟ | 6 |

# Giuseppe Cortese

S.DA RABAJÀ, 80
12050 BARBARESCO [CN]
TEL. +39 0173635131
www.cortesegiuseppe.it

**CELLAR SALES**
**PRE-BOOKED VISITS**
**ACCOMMODATION**
**ANNUAL PRODUCTION** 50,000 bottles
**HECTARES UNDER VINE** 8.00

The Cortese siblings, Pier Carlo and Tiziana (along with her husband, Gabriele) are carrying on the legacy left to them by their parents, Giuseppe and Rossella. It was they who began making wines with grapes form their private vineyards in the early 1970s. The heart of production is situated on the hill of Rabajà, a cru that gives rise to two Barbarescos, one a vintage and the other a reserve. Winemaking is extremely traditional, with various sizes and kinds of oak barrels used, making for wines that combine force and tannic rigor, characteristics common to the terroir, with extraordinary expressive grace. Their 2015 Barbaresco Rabajà is an exquisite, classically styled wine with aromas of flowers and red fruit on an elegant background of forest undergrowth. On the palate it proves rich in acidic counterpoint, with a firm, austere tannic weave and a penetrating finish that's full of personality. Their 2011 Riserva exhibits great maturity of fruit and force, with a long, warm finish. Their 2016 Langhe Nebbiolo, with its memorable balsamic whiffs, is a truly great buy.

| | | |
|---|---|---|
| ● Barbaresco Rabajà '15 | ♟♟♟ | 6 |
| ● Barbaresco Rabajà Ris. '11 | ♟♟ | 8 |
| ● Langhe Nebbiolo '16 | ♟♟ | 3* |
| ● Barbera d'Alba Morassina '15 | ♟♟ | 3 |
| ● Barbaresco Rabajà '11 | ♟♟♟ | 5 |
| ● Barbaresco Rabajà '10 | ♟♟♟ | 5 |
| ● Barbaresco Rabajà '08 | ♟♟♟ | 5 |
| ● Barbaresco Rabajà '14 | ♟♟ | 6 |
| ● Barbaresco Rabajà '13 | ♟♟ | 5 |
| ● Barbaresco Rabajà '12 | ♟♟ | 5 |
| ● Barbaresco Rabajà Ris. '08 | ♟♟ | 8 |
| ● Barbera d'Alba '16 | ♟♟ | 3 |
| ● Barbera d'Alba '15 | ♟♟ | 3 |
| ● Barbera d'Alba Morassina '14 | ♟♟ | 3 |
| ● Langhe Nebbiolo '15 | ♟♟ | 3 |
| ● Langhe Nebbiolo '14 | ♟♟ | 3* |

## Clemente Cossetti

VIA GUARDIE, 1
14043 CASTELNUOVO BELBO [AT]
TEL. +39 0141799803
www.cossetti.it

CELLAR SALES
PRE-BOOKED VISITS
ACCOMMODATION AND RESTAURANT SERVICE
ANNUAL PRODUCTION 500,000 bottles
HECTARES UNDER VINE 28.00

Since 1891 the Cossetti family has been making wines on the hills of Monferrato. The estate's vineyards are in Castelnuovo Belbo, situated on medium-bodied clay soil that's rich in minerals. Primarily Barbera is cultivated, with smaller shares of Cortese, Dolcetto and Chardonnay. IN addition to the wines made with grapes from their private vineyards, Cossetti operates as a négociant, representing some of the region's most important DOC appellations. Their wines are decidedly modern. Their 2016 Nizza proves that it's one of the best in the appellation. On the nose it offers up aromas of wild berries, while in the mouth it proves gutsy, with a long finish that's well-supported by acidity. Their 2015 Barbera d'Asti Superiore La Vigna Vecchia, 2017 Ruché di Castagnole Monferrato and 2017 Grignolino d'Asti are all also well-made wines. The first is full and rich, with notes of ripe red fruit. The second is supple and juicy, with aromas of Mediterranean scrubland and aromatic herbs. The third is flowery and citrusy.

| | |
|---|---|
| ● Nizza '16 | ❸❸ 4 |
| ● Barbera d'Asti La Vigna Vecchia '15 | ❸❸ 2* |
| ● Grignolino d'Asti '17 | ❸❸ 2* |
| ● Ruché di Castagnole M.to '17 | ❸❸ 3 |
| ● Barbera d'Asti Sup. Nizza '13 | ❷❷ 4 |
| ● Barbera d'Asti Sup. Nizza '10 | ❷❷ 4 |
| ○ Moscato d'Asti La Vita '15 | ❷❷ 2* |
| ● Nizza '15 | ❷❷ 4 |
| ● Ruché di Castagnole M.to '16 | ❷❷ 3 |
| ● Ruché di Castagnole Monferrato '15 | ❷❷ 3 |

## Stefanino Costa

B.TA BENNA, 5
12046 MONTÀ [CN]
TEL. +39 0173976336
ninocostawine@gmail.com

CELLAR SALES
PRE-BOOKED VISITS
ANNUAL PRODUCTION 50,000 bottles
HECTARES UNDER VINE 9.50

Nino Costa, along with his son Alessandro, manage this classic family-run winery in Roero. Their wines pursue a synthesis between structure and finesse, so as to best express the unique characteristics of this territory. Their vineyards, which are situated on mostly sandy soil in the municipalities of Canale, Montà and Santo Stefano Roero, grow at between 350 and 400 meters above sea level. Roero's major grape varieties are cultivated: Arneis, Barbera, Brachetto and Nebbiolo. Nino and Alessandro Costa are most well-known for the quality of their Roeros, and this year their Roero Arneis delivered. Tre Bicchieri for their 2017 Sarun, a fresh and citrusy wine with nuances of Mediterranean herbs, and a long, energetic finish. Their savory and pleasant 2017 Seminari also impressed, with its notes of bitter orange and cedar. Their supple and drinkable 2014 Roero Gepin proves supported more by acidity than richness of fruit. It was a bit affected by the difficult year, but it's still of high quality.

| | |
|---|---|
| ○ Roero Arneis Sarun '17 | ❸❸❸ 3* |
| ○ Roero Arneis Seminari '17 | ❸❸ 3* |
| ● Roero Gepin '14 | ❸❸ 4 |
| ● Barbera d'Alba Cichin '16 | ❸❸ 3 |
| ● Roero Gepin '13 | ❷❷❷ 4* |
| ● Roero Gepin '12 | ❷❷❷ 4* |
| ● Roero Gepin '11 | ❷❷❷ 4* |
| ● Roero Gepin '10 | ❷❷❷ 4* |
| ● Barbera d'Alba Sup. Genna '13 | ❷❷ 2* |
| ○ Langhe Bianco Ricordi '16 | ❷❷ 3 |
| ● Nebbiolo d'Alba Cabora '15 | ❷❷ 4 |
| ○ Roero Arneis Sarun '16 | ❷❷ 3 |
| ○ Roero Arneis Sarun '15 | ❷❷ 3* |
| ○ Roero Arneis Sarun '13 | ❷❷ 3* |
| ● Roero Medic '12 | ❷❷ 3 |

OUR PASSION FOR WINE
BELONGS TO THIS LAND.

BiancaVigna S.S. Soc. Agr.
Conegliano (TV) - Italy    tel. 0039.0438.788403
info@biancavigna.it    www.biancavigna.it

SISTEMA DI QUALITÀ NAZIONALE
PRODUZIONE INTEGRATA

CAMPAGNA FINANZIATA AI SENSI DEL REG. UE N. 1308/2013

CAMPAIGN FINANCED ACCORDING TO UE REGULATION NO. 1308/2013

MONTEFUSCO

ITALY

**TERREDORA DI PAOLO**

via Serra – 83030 – Montefusco – AV – Italy
export@terredora.com – info@terredora.com
www.terredora.com

# Tenuta Cucco

via Mazzini, 10
12050 Serralunga d'Alba [CN]
Tel. +39 0173613003
www.tenutacucco.it

**CELLAR SALES**
**PRE-BOOKED VISITS**
**ACCOMMODATION**
**ANNUAL PRODUCTION 70,000 bottles**
**HECTARES UNDER VINE 13.00**

Piero Rossi Cairo is looking after this small winery for his family. It's a lovely and environmentally sustainable estate, thanks to their adoption of organic management principles. When the winery was purchased four years ago, the choice was made to avail themselves of a first-rate team, experts of the territory, both in the case of their vineyards (Gran Piero Romana) and winemaking (Piero Ballario). And so it is that a selection of wines characterized by consistency and typicity came to be. It's led by three elegant Barolos, whose tannins prove non-invasive even in their first few years in the bottle. Their 2012 Barolo Cerrati Vigna Cucco Riserva is particularly pleasant on the palate, velvety, soft and well-balanced. Its preceded by elegant aromas of licorice and herbs in the sun. Their juicy, fresh and lively 2014 Barolo from Serralunga d'Alba offers up fragrances of red fruit and tobacco on a background of tobacco. Their Barolo Cerrati is quite rich in acidity, while their more international 2016 Langhe Rosso is an elegant and minty wine.

| | |
|---|---|
| ● Barolo Cerrati V. Cucco Ris. '12 | 🍷🍷 8 |
| ● Barolo del Comune di Serralunga d'Alba '14 | 🍷🍷 6 |
| ● Barolo Cerrati '14 | 🍷🍷 7 |
| ○ Langhe Chardonnay '16 | 🍷🍷 3 |
| ● Langhe Rosso '16 | 🍷🍷 4 |
| ● Langhe Nebbiolo '17 | 🍷 4 |
| ● Barbera d'Alba Sup. '15 | 🍷🍷 4 |
| ● Barolo Cerrati '13 | 🍷🍷 7 |
| ● Barolo Cerrati V. Cucco Ris. '11 | 🍷🍷 8 |
| ● Barolo Cerrati V. Cucco Ris. '10 | 🍷🍷 8 |
| ● Barolo del Comune di Serralunga d'Alba '13 | 🍷🍷 6 |
| ● Barolo del Comune di Serralunga d'Alba '12 | 🍷🍷 6 |
| ● Langhe Nebbiolo '16 | 🍷🍷 4 |
| ● Langhe Rosso '15 | 🍷🍷 4 |

# Giovanni Daglio

via Montale Celli, 10
15050 Costa Vescovato [AL]
Tel. +39 0131838262
www.vignetidaglio.com

**CELLAR SALES**
**ANNUAL PRODUCTION 15,000 bottles**
**HECTARES UNDER VINE 10.00**

Giovanni's family have always been vine growers and even if he studied pharmacy in his youth, Giovanni has always maintained a bond with the territory. His age hasn't changed his determination and passion for making special wines that have often reached our finals. Why are they special? We're convinced that Giovanni's wines are among the finest and most elegant in the district. They're long-lived wines that even in difficult years (like 2014) demonstrate how age can confer extraordinary qualities. A masterful version of their Cantico landed in our finals with its elegant aromas of flint and benzine accompanied by citrusy notes. On the palate plenty of pulp and acidity lengthen across a deep, classy finish. Their Basinas is an intense Barbera on the nose, with aromas of ripe red fruit and notes of cocoa anticipating a well-balanced palate and long finish. Their Dolcetto features lovely fruity notes and a vibrant, balanced palate.

| | |
|---|---|
| ● Colli Tortonesi Barbera Basinas '16 | 🍷🍷 4 |
| ○ Colli Tortonesi Timorasso Cantico '16 | 🍷🍷 4 |
| ● Colli Tortonesi Dolcetto Nibiö '16 | 🍷🍷 3 |
| ● Negher | 🍷🍷 3 |
| ● Colli Tortonesi Barbera Basinas '13 | 🍷🍷 4 |
| ● Colli Tortonesi Barbera Pias '14 | 🍷🍷 2* |
| ○ Colli Tortonesi Timorasso Cantico '15 | 🍷🍷 4 |
| ○ Colli Tortonesi Timorasso Cantico '13 | 🍷🍷 4 |
| ○ Colli Tortonesi Timorasso Cantico '12 | 🍷🍷 4 |
| ○ Colli Tortonesi Timorasso Derthona '15 | 🍷🍷 4 |
| ○ Colli Tortonesi Timorasso Derthona Cantico '14 | 🍷🍷 4 |

# Deltetto

c.so Alba, 43
12043 Canale [CN]
Tel. +39 0173979383
www.deltetto.com

**CELLAR SALES**
**PRE-BOOKED VISITS**
**ANNUAL PRODUCTION** 170,000 bottles
**HECTARES UNDER VINE** 21.00
**VITICULTURE METHOD** Certified Organic
**SUSTAINABLE WINERY**

More than 40 years have passed since
young Antonio Deltetto decided to bottle his
first Arneis. Today the winery offers a series
of wines that are among the most
interesting in the territory, from their Roeros
to their Roero Arneis, Barberas and
sparkling wines (not to mention wines from
other appellations, like Barolo and Gavi).
Their wines are modern, exhibiting balance
and character. During our tastings, their
long and plucky 2013 Barolo Parussi did
particularly well, with nice texture and
well-integrated tannins. Their 2015 Roero
Braja Riserva also delivered, proving
flowery and deep. Oak is still evident here
but the finish comes through juicy, with
nice aromatic clarity. Their Metodo
Classicos continue to prove well-made, in
particular their Rosé, an original, fresh and
fruity blend of Pinot Nero and Nebbiolo, and
their taut and assertive 2012 Extra Brut, a
more classic blend of Pinot Nero and
Chardonnay. But in general their entire
selection proved sound.

| | |
|---|---|
| ● Barolo Parussi '13 | ♟♟6 |
| ● Roero Braja Ris. '15 | ♟♟5 |
| ○ Deltetto Brut M. Cl. '13 | ♟♟4 |
| ○ Deltetto Extra Brut M. Cl. '12 | ♟♟5 |
| ☉ Deltetto Rosé Brut M. Cl. | ♟♟5 |
| ● Nebbiolo d'Alba I Lioni '16 | ♟♟3 |
| ● Roero '15 | ♟♟3 |
| ● Barbera d'Alba Sup. Bramé '16 | ♟3 |
| ○ Langhe Favorita Servaj '17 | ♟2 |
| ○ Roero Arneis Daivej '17 | ♟3 |
| ○ Roero Arneis San Michele '17 | ♟3 |
| ● Barbera d'Alba Sup. Rocca delle Marasche '04 | ♟♟♟5 |
| ● Roero Braja Ris. '09 | ♟♟♟4* |
| ● Roero Braja Ris. '08 | ♟♟♟4 |
| ● Roero Braja Ris. '07 | ♟♟♟4 |

# Gianni Doglia

via Annunziata, 56
14054 Castagnole delle Lanze [AT]
Tel. +39 0141878359
www.giannidoglia.it

**CELLAR SALES**
**PRE-BOOKED VISITS**
**ANNUAL PRODUCTION** 100,000 bottles
**HECTARES UNDER VINE** 12.00
**SUSTAINABLE WINERY**

Gianni Doglia maintains that the personality
of his wines comes from the great attention
shown to detail in the cellar and the
vineyards themselves. These are somewhat
elevated, with older vines that produce very
sweet grapes. That's how his Moscato
Casa di Bianca comes to be. It's a marvel
of substance in the mouth and citrus on the
nose. His Barberas are another example,
with the Superiore Genio now challenged
by the newbie Nizza Docg. Great attention
is shown for the environment, so no
chemicals or weedkillers. Once again
Doglia's Moscato Casa di Bianca proved a
beacon for the category, bringing home top
marks during our tastings. It's a vibrant,
savory wine, striking the right tension
between freshness and sweetness. Their
Moscato d'Asti is also an excellent version,
well-defined and endowed with a
superlative palate. In terms of their reds
their 2016 Nizza, undoubtedly one of the
best in the appellation, stood out, as did
their 2016 Barbera Genio, a wine whose
character shows plenty of potential.

| | |
|---|---|
| ○ Moscato d'Asti Casa di Bianca '17 | ♟♟♟5 |
| ○ Moscato d'Asti '17 | ♟♟4 |
| ● Nizza '16 | ♟♟6 |
| ● Barbera d'Asti Sup. Genio '16 | ♟♟6 |
| ● Grignolino d'Asti '17 | ♟♟4 |
| ● Barbera d'Asti Sup. Genio '12 | ♟♟♟4* |
| ○ Moscato d'Asti Casa di Bianca '16 | ♟♟♟3* |
| ○ Moscato d'Asti Casa di Bianca '15 | ♟♟♟3* |
| ● Barbera d'Asti Sup. Genio '15 | ♟♟4 |
| ○ Moscato d'Asti '16 | ♟♟2* |

# Dosio

REG. SERRADENARI, 6
12064 LA MORRA [CN]
TEL. +39 017350677
www.dosiovigneti.com

**CELLAR SALES**
**PRE-BOOKED VISITS**
**ACCOMMODATION**
**ANNUAL PRODUCTION** 65,000 bottles
**HECTARES UNDER VINE** 11.00

Marco Dotta's abilities as an agronomist and winemaker are particularly evident when you drink his wines. His Barolos are commendable for the sensations they offer, with well-integrated tannins that never overreach. It's not an easy feat to pull off, especially if you think that the Serradenari cru is situated in the highest, coolest part of La Morra. Their Fossati vineyard in Barolo provides the grapes for an important Riserva. They use almost exclusively traditional cultivar: Nebbiolo, Barbera and Dolcetto, with a small amount of delectable Merlot Eventi. Their 2012 Barolo Fossati Riserva is a supple wine on the palate, richly fragrant and just inflected by oak. Their youthful 2013 Barolo Fossati exhibits buoyant fruit, and is extremely pleasant on the palate. Their Nebbiolo Barilà represents a highly elegant combination of fruit and oak, while their 2014 Barolo Serradenari is more marked by oak and lacking body. Their modern 2015 Langhe Momenti is an enjoyable wine made with Nebbiolo and Barbera.

| | |
|---|---|
| ● Barolo Fossati '13 | ♟♟ 7 |
| ● Barolo Fossati Ris. '12 | ♟♟ 8 |
| ● Langhe Nebbiolo Barilà '15 | ♟♟ 5 |
| ● Barbera d'Alba Sup. '16 | ♟♟ 4 |
| ● Barolo Serradenari '14 | ♟♟ 6 |
| ● Dolcetto d'Alba Sup. Nassone '16 | ♟♟ 3 |
| ● Langhe Rosso Momenti '15 | ♟♟ 5 |
| ● Barolo '14 | ♟ 5 |
| ● Dolcetto d'Alba '17 | ♟ 3 |
| ● Barolo '13 | ♟♟ 5 |
| ● Barolo '12 | ♟♟ 5 |
| ● Barolo Fossati Ris. '11 | ♟♟ 8 |
| ● Barolo Serradenari '13 | ♟♟ 6 |
| ● Barolo Serradenari '12 | ♟♟ 6 |
| ● Langhe Momenti '13 | ♟♟ 4 |
| ● Langhe Nebbiolo Barilà '14 | ♟♟ 5 |

# ★Poderi Luigi Einaudi

LOC. CASCINA TECC
B.TA GOMBE, 31/32
12063 DOGLIANI [CN]
TEL. +39 017370191
www.poderieinaudi.com

**CELLAR SALES**
**PRE-BOOKED VISITS**
**ACCOMMODATION**
**ANNUAL PRODUCTION** 350,000 bottles
**HECTARES UNDER VINE** 60.00
**SUSTAINABLE WINERY**

Back in 1961 the great critic Luigi Veronelli wrote that if Dolcetto comes from Dogliani it's suitable for 'longer aging'. Since 2005 the exquisite Dogliani Superiore Vigna Tecc, a wine that guarantees charm and structure, has been proving just that. Owner Matteo Sardagna is showing a similar commitment towards his Barolo, with his Cannubi and Terlo doing battle for a top place in their selection. It's a past that began with Italian president Luigi Einaudi and continues to pursue high quality. A fine herbaceous note emerges in their elegant Terlo Vigna Costa Grimaldi, a wine of sound structure. Their Cannubi delights with its aromas of not overly-ripe fruit and a palate that's highly pleasant, just marked by the warmth of alcohol. Their new Barolo Ludo, made with grapes from their Cannubi, Terlo and Bussia vineyards, is a pleasantly balanced wine endowed with enjoyable notes of spices. Their Dolcettos are also valid, starting with their elegant 2017 Dogliani.

| | |
|---|---|
| ● Barolo Ludo '14 | ♟♟ 6 |
| ● Barolo Terlo V. Costa Grimaldi '14 | ♟♟ 7 |
| ● Barolo Cannubi '14 | ♟♟ 8 |
| ● Dogliani '17 | ♟♟ 3 |
| ● Langhe Luigi Einaudi '15 | ♟♟ 6 |
| ● Barolo Cannubi '11 | ♟♟♟ 8 |
| ● Barolo Cannubi '10 | ♟♟♟ 8 |
| ● Barolo Costa Grimaldi '05 | ♟♟♟ 8 |
| ● Barolo Costa Grimaldi '01 | ♟♟♟ 7 |
| ● Barolo nei Cannubi '00 | ♟♟♟ 8 |
| ● Dogliani Sup. V. Tecc '10 | ♟♟♟ 3* |
| ● Dogliani V. Tecc '06 | ♟♟♟ 4 |
| ● Langhe Rosso Luigi Einaudi '04 | ♟♟♟ 5 |

# F.lli Facchino

LOC. VAL DEL PRATO, 210
15078 ROCCA GRIMALDA [AL]
TEL. +39 014385401
www.vinifacchino.it

CELLAR SALES
PRE-BOOKED VISITS
ANNUAL PRODUCTION 80,000 bottles
HECTARES UNDER VINE 30.00

Giorgio and Diego have demonstrated over time that they aren't happy with good quality. Indeed, they'd like to raise the bar a bit, aiming for excellence. They have the space to move, both in terms of winemaking and grape quality. Their Dolcetto di Ovada possesses extraordinary potential, while their Albarossa, already a proven winner, can count exuberance among its qualities. Here the challenge lies in pursuing finesse and elegance. And here they aren't afraid of challenges. The producer is the fastest growing in the area in terms of quality, and submitted a pair of wines that exhibit plenty of character (both of which landed in our finals). Their Dolcetto surprises with its elegant aromas of blackberries and cherries, enriching an extraordinary nose-palate balance and long aromatic persistence. Their 2016 Barbera is masterful with its fruity aromas accompanied by spicy notes. These lengthen across a rich and potent palate of rare elegance, earning the wine Tre Bicchieri.

| | |
|---|---|
| ● Barbera del M.to '16 | ▼▼▼ 2* |
| ● Dolcetto di Ovada '16 | ▼▼ 2* |
| ● Barbera del M.to Terre del Re '15 | ▼▼ 2* |
| ○ Cortese dell'Alto M.to Pacialan '17 | ▼ 2 |
| ● Barbera del M.to '15 | ♀♀ 2* |
| ○ Cortese dell'Alto M.to Pacialan '16 | ♀♀ 2* |
| ● Dolcetto di Ovada Poggiobello '15 | ♀♀ 2* |
| ● Dolcetto di Ovada Poggiobello '14 | ♀♀ 2* |
| ● Dolcetto di Ovada Poggiobello '12 | ♀♀ 2* |
| ● M.to Rosso Note d'Autunno '11 | ♀♀ 3 |
| ● Ovada Carasöi '15 | ♀♀ 3 |
| ● Ovada Carasöi '13 | ♀♀ 3 |
| ● Piemonte Albarossa Note d'Autunno '12 | ♀♀ 3 |

# Tenuta Il Falchetto

FRAZ. CIOMBI
VIA VALLE TINELLA, 16
12058 SANTO STEFANO BELBO [CN]
TEL. +39 0141840344
www.ilfalchetto.com

CELLAR SALES
PRE-BOOKED VISITS
ANNUAL PRODUCTION 280,000 bottles
HECTARES UNDER VINE 47.00

The Forno family's winery is a historic producer when it comes to Moscato, and not only. Their vineyards are situated in Santo Stefano Belbo (Il Falchetto and Marini), Agliano Terme (Bricco Paradiso, Lovetta Lurei, Pian Scorrone, Vigna del Ciabot) and Calosso (Vigneto del Fant). Primarily Moscato and Barbera are cultivated, accounting for 80% of their crop. Cabernet Sauvignon, Chardonnay, Dolcetto, Merlot and Pinot Nero provide the rest. Their wines, whose style is in keeping with a great, classic tradition, are geared towards pleasantness. Their 2017 Moscato d'Asti Canelli Ciombo is back with Tre Bicchieri. It's an elegant and vibrant wine in its aromas of gingerbread and aromatic herbs, and a highly pleasant palate that's fresh while also offering up sweet tones. Their other 2017 Moscato d'Asti, Tenuta del Fant, also proved excellent, as did their 2015 Barbera d'Asti Superiore Bricco Paradiso. The former is a more full-flavored wine that features notes of candied fruit, the latter is fruit-driven and well-supported by acidity.

| | |
|---|---|
| ○ Moscato d'Asti Canelli Ciombo '17 | ▼▼▼ 2* |
| ● Barbera d'Asti Sup. Bricco Paradiso '15 | ▼▼ 4 |
| ○ Moscato d'Asti Canelli Tenuta del Fant '17 | ▼▼ 2* |
| ● Barbera d'Asti Lurei '15 | ▼▼ 3 |
| ● Barbera d'Asti Pian Scorrone '17 | ▼▼ 2* |
| ● M.to Rosso La Mora '15 | ▼▼ 3 |
| ○ Piemonte Chardonnay Incompreso '16 | ▼▼ 4 |
| ● Piemonte Pinot Nero Solo '15 | ▼ 3 |
| ○ Moscato d'Asti Ciombo '15 | ♀♀♀ 2* |
| ○ Moscato d'Asti Tenuta del Fant '11 | ♀♀♀ 2* |
| ○ Moscato d'Asti Tenuta del Fant '09 | ♀♀♀ 2* |
| ● Barbera d'Asti Sup. Bricco Paradiso '14 | ♀♀ 3* |

# Benito Favaro

.DA CHIUSURE, 1BIS
10010 PIVERONE [TO]
TEL. +39 012572606
www.cantinafavaro.it

CELLAR SALES
PRE-BOOKED VISITS
ANNUAL PRODUCTION 20,000 bottles
HECTARES UNDER VINE 3.50
VITICULTURE METHOD Certified Organic

Camillo Favaro manages to find time to write
books, foremost about his beloved Burgundy,
and collaborate with other wineries. But his
first commitment remains to his lovely,
small family winery. His most important
wines are two bona fide benchmarks in the
Erbaluce di Caluso appellation. Le Chiusure
(whose release has been delayed a year) is
fresher and more direct in its aromas of
sage and wild herbs. Their 13 Mesi is
enriched by notes of hazelnut with a
rounded palate made possible by delicate
maturation, partially in small wooden casks.
Additionally, they offer a small selection
made with Nebbiolo, Freisa and Syrah. Their
2016 Erbaluce di Caluso 13 Mesi proves it's
one of the appellation's best, delicate as it is
and elegant, with a thousand sensations that
never overwhelm, a feat that only great
wines can manage. Its superior quality is
made most evident on the palate, where
acidity is brushed away at the end by a soft,
honeyed note that lingers in the mouth, and
our memories. Tre Bicchieri.

| | |
|---|---|
| ○ Erbaluce di Caluso 13 Mesi '16 | ♟♟♟ 3* |
| ● F2 '16 | ♟♟ 2* |
| ● Rossomeraviglia '16 | ♟♟ 5 |
| ● Ros '16 | ♟ 4 |
| ○ Erbaluce di Caluso Le Chiusure '16 | ♟♟♟ 2* |
| ○ Erbaluce di Caluso Le Chiusure '13 | ♟♟♟ 2* |
| ○ Erbaluce di Caluso Le Chiusure '12 | ♟♟♟ 2* |
| ○ Erbaluce di Caluso Le Chiusure '11 | ♟♟♟ 2* |
| ○ Erbaluce di Caluso Le Chiusure '10 | ♟♟♟ 2* |
| ○ Erbaluce di Caluso 13 Mesi '15 | ♟♟ 3* |
| ○ Erbaluce di Caluso 13 Mesi '14 | ♟♟ 3 |
| ○ Erbaluce di Caluso 13 Mesi '13 | ♟♟ 3 |
| ○ Erbaluce di Caluso Le Chiusure '15 | ♟♟ 2* |
| ○ Erbaluce di Caluso Le Chiusure '14 | ♟♟ 2* |
| ⊙ Rosacherosanonsei '16 | ♟♟ 3 |
| ● Rossomeraviglia '15 | ♟♟ 5 |
| ○ Sole d'Inverno '13 | ♟♟ 5 |

# Giacomo Fenocchio

LOC. BUSSIA, 72
12065 MONFORTE D'ALBA [CN]
TEL. +39 017378675
www.giacomofenocchio.com

CELLAR SALES
PRE-BOOKED VISITS
ANNUAL PRODUCTION 90,000 bottles
HECTARES UNDER VINE 15.00
SUSTAINABLE WINERY

Good today and good tomorrow. That's our
slogan for the Fenocchio family's incredible
abilities when it comes to winemaking. Their
selection can be appreciated while young,
with their exquisite freshness and
approachability, yet at the same time they're
remarkably ageworthy. Their Barolos are
made with grapes from prized crus like
Cannubi and Castellero di Barolo, Villero di
Castiglione Falletto, and Bussia di Monforte
(available in a 90 Dì Riserva as well). Their
approach calls for long maceration and the
use of large barrels, giving rise to wines with
plenty of energy. The selection submitted for
tasting proved one of the best yet, a handful
of Barolos to remember. We start with an
excellent 2014 Brunate, it's an airy, balsamic
wine aromatically, whose palate unfolds with
steady acidity and savoriness, finishing on
dark fruit and mint. Their 2012 Barolo
Bussia 90 Dì Riserva offers up aromas of
Mediterranean scrubland. On the palate it's
supple, complex and very deep, with a long,
lingering finish. Their 2014 Barolo Bussia is a
vibrant, vigorous wine. Their 2014 Castellero
and Villero also proved sound.

| | |
|---|---|
| ● Barolo Bussia 90 Dì Ris. '12 | ♟♟♟ 8 |
| ● Barolo Brunate '14 | ♟♟ 5 |
| ● Barolo Bussia '14 | ♟♟ 6 |
| ● Barolo Castellero '14 | ♟♟ 6 |
| ● Barolo Villero '14 | ♟♟ 7 |
| ● Barolo Bussia '11 | ♟♟♟ 6 |
| ● Barolo Bussia '09 | ♟♟♟ 6 |
| ● Barolo Bussia 90 Dì Ris. '10 | ♟♟♟ 8 |
| ● Barolo Bussia '13 | ♟♟ 6 |
| ● Barolo Bussia 90 Dì Ris. '11 | ♟♟ 8 |
| ● Barolo Cannubi '13 | ♟♟ 6 |
| ● Barolo Cannubi '11 | ♟♟ 6 |
| ● Barolo Castellero '13 | ♟♟ 6 |
| ● Barolo Villero '13 | ♟♟ 6 |
| ● Barolo Villero '12 | ♟♟ 6 |

# Ferrando

VIA TORINO, 599
10015 IVREA [TO]
TEL. +39 0125633550
www.ferrandovini.it

CELLAR SALES
PRE-BOOKED VISITS
ANNUAL PRODUCTION 50,000 bottles
HECTARES UNDER VINE 5.00

Luigi Ferrando began breathing in aromas of mountain Nebbiolo when he was young, in the cellar built by his father Giuseppe in 1964, in Carema. Over the following years he managed to make two wines known to the world. The Carema Etichetta Bianca is a leaner wine while the Etichetta Nera is more structured. Today his sons Roberto and Andrea are leading the winery and receiving well-deserved praise in part for their Erbaluce di Caluso line of wines, which is led by the rich Cariola. When the vintage permits, they also offer the exquisite Passito Solativo, made with Erbaluce harvested in December. Ferrando deserves its reputation for quality. Their exquisite 2017 Erbaluce di Caluso La Torrazza is styled around elegant hints of mint and ripe white fruit. On the palate they proves soft and enticing. Their prized Cariola opts for pleasantness, freshness and close-focused vegetal notes on the nose. These give way to a slightly austere palate in terms of acidity and savoriness. Their 2012 Caluso Passito exhibits excellent balance between sweetness and acidity.

| | | |
|---|---|---|
| ○ Caluso Passito '12 | ♆♆ 5 | |
| ○ Erbaluce di Caluso La Torrazza '17 | ♆♆ 3* | |
| ○ Erbaluce di Caluso Cariola '17 | ♆♆ 3 | |
| ● Carema Et. Bianca '14 | ♆ 5 | |
| ● Carema Et. Bianca '12 | ♆♆♆ 5 | |
| ● Carema Et. Nera '11 | ♆♆♆ 7 | |
| ● Carema Et. Nera '09 | ♆♆♆ 6 | |
| ● Carema Et. Nera '08 | ♆♆♆ 6 | |
| ● Carema Et. Nera '07 | ♆♆♆ 6 | |
| ● Carema Et. Nera '06 | ♆♆♆ 6 | |
| ● Carema Et. Nera '05 | ♆♆♆ 6 | |
| ● Carema Et. Nera '01 | ♆♆♆ 5 | |

# Luca Ferraris

LOC. RIVI, 7
S.DA PROV.LE 14
14030 CASTAGNOLE MONFERRATO [AT]
TEL. +39 0141292202
www.ferrarisagricola.it

CELLAR SALES
PRE-BOOKED VISITS
ANNUAL PRODUCTION 220,000 bottles
HECTARES UNDER VINE 21.00
SUSTAINABLE WINERY

Luca Ferraris's family winery was founded in 1921 by his great-grandmother Teresa. After a long period in which they supplied a cooperative, in 1999 Luca transformed and revived the winery. The producer was among the first to believe in the potential of Ruché di Castagnole Monferrato, privileging the wine and focusing on high quality. And that's why, thanks in part to a completely renovated cellar and the support of Californian Randall Grahm, today it is a benchmark for the entire appellation. Aromas of spices, rose and wild berries tie together the Ruché di Castagnole Monferratos submitted. Their fresh and juicy 2017 Sant'Eufemia features notable aromaticity, while their 2016 Opera Prima per il Fondatore is a bit less aromatic, but exhibits length and nice tension. Their 2017 Classic is a supple wine, rich in fruit. Their excellent 2016 Barbera d'Asti Superiore La Regina also stood out, with its assertive, dynamic and fruit-forward palate.

| | | |
|---|---|---|
| ● Barbera d'Asti Sup La Regina '16 | ♆♆ 3 | |
| ● Ruché di Castagnole M.to Clàsic '17 | ♆♆ 2* | |
| ● Ruché di Castagnole M.to Opera Prima per il Fondatore '16 | ♆♆ 6 | |
| ● Ruché di Castagnole M.to Sant'Eufemia '17 | ♆♆ 3 | |
| ● Barbera d'Asti del Martin '17 | ♆ 2 | |

# Roberto Ferraris

FRAZ. DOGLIANO
REG. DOGLIANO, 33
14041 AGLIANO TERME [AT]
TEL. +39 0141954234
www.robertoferraris.com

**CELLAR SALES**
**PRE-BOOKED VISITS**
**ANNUAL PRODUCTION** 60,000 bottles
**HECTARES UNDER VINE** 12.00
**SUSTAINABLE WINERY**

For over a century the Ferraris family's
winery, today managed by Roberto, has
been a leader in the production of Barbera
d'Asti. Their vineyards are situated primarily
around the cellar, on white, calcareous soil,
with high percentages of loam and little
clay. Barbera is cultivated almost
exclusively, though there are small
quantities of Nebbiolo, making for a
selection that features only red wines. Their
style is traditional and careful to express
typicity and territorial character. For the first
time their 2015 Nizza Liberta takes home
Tre Bicchieri. It's a highly elegant, fresh and
plucky Barbera rich in fruit, with classic
aromas of dark fruit and forest undergrowth,
and a long, juicy finish. Their 2016 Barbera
d'Asti Nobbio also delivered. It's a full,
tight-knit wine though also pleasant and
dynamic. Their two 2016 Barbera d'Asti
Superiores also impressed. Their Bisavolo
stands out for its aromas of blackcurrant
and cherry, while La Cricca features
aromas of damp earth and a notable
tannic presence.

| | |
|---|---|
| ● Nizza Liberta '15 | 🍷🍷🍷 5 |
| ● Barbera d'Asti Nobbio '16 | 🍷🍷 3* |
| ● Barbera d'Asti Sup. Bisavolo '16 | 🍷🍷 3 |
| ● Barbera d'Asti Sup. La Cricca '16 | 🍷🍷 4 |
| ● Barbera d'Asti Nobbio '15 | 🍷🍷 3 |
| ● Barbera d'Asti Nobbio '14 | 🍷🍷 2* |
| ● Barbera d'Asti Nobbio '13 | 🍷🍷 2* |
| ● Barbera d'Asti Suôri '15 | 🍷🍷 2* |
| ● Barbera d'Asti Sup. Bisavolo '15 | 🍷🍷 4 |
| ● Barbera d'Asti Sup. Bisavolo '13 | 🍷🍷 3 |
| ● Barbera d'Asti Sup. Bisavolo '12 | 🍷🍷 3 |
| ● Barbera d'Asti Sup. Bisavolo '11 | 🍷🍷 3* |
| ● Barbera d'Asti Sup. La Cricca '15 | 🍷🍷 5 |
| ● Barbera d'Asti Sup. La Cricca '13 | 🍷🍷 3* |
| ● Barbera d'Asti Sup. La Cricca '12 | 🍷🍷 3* |
| ● Barbera d'Asti Sup. La Cricca '11 | 🍷🍷 3* |
| ● M.to Rosso Grixa '12 | 🍷🍷 3 |

# Carlo Ferro

FRAZ. SALERE, 41
14041 AGLIANO TERME [AT]
TEL. +39 0141954000
www.ferrovini.com

**CELLAR SALES**
**PRE-BOOKED VISITS**
**ANNUAL PRODUCTION** 15,000 bottles
**HECTARES UNDER VINE** 12.00

The Ferro family have been active in
Barbera d'Asti since 1900, even if they only
decided to create their own wines some 25
years ago. Their private vineyards host red
grapes, primarily native varieties, foremost
Barbera (though there's also Dolcetto,
Grignolino, Nebbiolo and Cabernet
Sauvignon). Their wines are traditionally
styled and great attention is shown to
aromatic precision and richness of fruit.
This year their 2015 Barbera d'Asti
Superiore Notturno reached our finals
thanks to its notable aromas of dark fruit,
and a generous, open, fruit-forward, highly
pleasing palate. Their 2016 Barbera d'Asti
Giulia continues to prove excellent, with its
characteristic fragrances of cherry and wet
earth, and its tight-knit, weighty palate.
Their 2015 Nizza La Corazziera features
aromas of spices and a palate that's
well-supported by acidity, though still a bit
too oaky.

| | |
|---|---|
| ● Barbera d'Asti Sup. Notturno '15 | 🍷🍷 3* |
| ● Barbera d'Asti Giulia '16 | 🍷🍷 2* |
| ● Nizza La Corazziera '15 | 🍷🍷 4 |
| ● Barbera d'Asti Sup. Roche '15 | 🍷 3 |
| ● Barbera d'Asti '14 | 🍷🍷 2* |
| ● Barbera d'Asti Giulia '15 | 🍷🍷 2* |
| ● Barbera d'Asti Giulia '14 | 🍷🍷 2* |
| ● Barbera d'Asti Giulia '13 | 🍷🍷 2* |
| ● Barbera d'Asti Sup. Notturno '15 | 🍷🍷 2* |
| ● Barbera d'Asti Sup. Notturno '14 | 🍷🍷 3 |
| ● Barbera d'Asti Sup. Notturno '12 | 🍷🍷 2* |
| ● Barbera d'Asti Sup. Roche '13 | 🍷🍷 3 |
| ● M.to Rosso Paolo '13 | 🍷🍷 4 |

## ★Fontanafredda

LOC. FONTANAFREDDA
VIA ALBA, 15
12050 SERRALUNGA D'ALBA [CN]
TEL. +39 0173626111
www.fontanafredda.it

**CELLAR SALES**
**PRE-BOOKED VISITS**
**ACCOMMODATION AND RESTAURANT SERVICE**
**ANNUAL PRODUCTION** 8,500,000 bottles
**HECTARES UNDER VINE** 100.00
**SUSTAINABLE WINERY**

Casa E. di Mirafiore continues to take on its own proper identity at Fontanafredda. But that doesn't mean that there's a different approach in terms of quality, with both production approaches increasingly intent on achieving excellence. The proof lies in their numerous Barolos, which are always noteworthy, but also in the rest of their selection. It's overseen with great professional care, starting with their two Alta Langas. Fontanafredda was purchased by the Farinetti group in 2008, one year before the Casa E. di Mirafiore brand was taken back up. Their least-expensive Barolo put in a performance that was more than commendable.'Silver', as it's known (for the color of its label), proves balanced and well-orchestrated on palate, with a nose that features aromas of quinine and licorice. Their Paiagallo is even fresher and more elegant, but the real winner this year is their 2010 Barolo Centosessanta Anni Riserva, an extremely long, multifaceted, potent wine that's got plenty of personality.

| | | |
|---|---|---|
| ● Barolo Centosessanta Anni Ris. '10 | ▼▼ | 8 |
| ● Barolo Fontanafredda V. La Rosa '14 | ▼▼ | 7 |
| ● Barolo Paiagallo Casa E. di Mirafiore '14 | ▼▼ | 8 |
| ● Barolo Silver '14 | ▼▼ | 6 |
| ○ Alta Langa Brut Blanc de Noir '14 | ▼▼ | 5 |
| ⊙ Alta Langa Brut Contessa Rosa Rosé '12 | ▼▼ | 6 |
| ● Barbaresco Coste Rubin '15 | ▼▼ | 7 |
| ● Barolo Casa E. di Mirafiore '14 | ▼▼ | 8 |
| ● Barolo del Comune di Serralunga d'Alba '14 | ▼▼ | 8 |
| ● Langhe Nebbiolo '16 | ▼▼ | 6 |
| ● Barbera d'Alba Sup. '16 | ▼ | 5 |
| ● Barolo '14 | ▼ | 8 |
| ● Barolo Paiagallo Casa E. di Mirafiore '13 | ♀♀♀ | 7 |
| ● Barolo Paiagallo Casa E. di Mirafiore '12 | ♀♀♀ | 7 |

## Fortemasso

LOC. CASTELLETTO, 21
12065 MONFORTE D'ALBA [CN]
TEL. +39 0306527218
www.fortemasso.it

**CELLAR SALES**
**ANNUAL PRODUCTION** 27,000 bottles
**HECTARES UNDER VINE** 5.20

In addition to important producers in Tuscany (Castello di Radda), Abruzzo (Orlandi Contucci Ponno) and Lombardy (Lo Sparviere), Agricole Gussalli Beretta recently added a new estate in the heart of Langhe: ForteMasso (Monforte d'Alba) in the prestigious district of Castelletto. The wines offered are based on the area's traditional cultivar, and they feature a precise personality. Indeed, their Barolo ages for 30 months in sizable oak barrels, while their Langhe Nebbiolo is released only after a few months in stainless steel. Their Barbera d'Alba, on the other hand, is a more modern wine and ages in French barriques. Their 2014 Barolo Castelletto is already rather open and evolved, exhibiting nice complexity. It was a difficult year and as a result it's slightly lacking in the classic red fruit that young Barolo is known for. Their 2016 Barbera d'Alba and 2017 Langhe Nebbiolo are both textbook interpretations. The former is a close-focused, fruity and well-structured wine with a light acidity that's pleasantly invigorating, while the second proves highly drinkable and approachable.

| | | |
|---|---|---|
| ● Barolo Castelletto '14 | ▼▼ | 6 |
| ● Barbera d'Alba '16 | ▼▼ | 3 |
| ● Langhe Nebbiolo '17 | ▼▼ | 3 |
| ● Barbera d'Alba '15 | ♀♀ | 3 |
| ● Barolo Castelletto '13 | ♀♀ | 6 |
| ● Langhe Nebbiolo '16 | ♀♀ | 3 |

# Gabutti - Franco Boasso

B.TA GABUTTI, 3A
12050 SERRALUNGA D'ALBA [CN]
TEL. +39 0173613165
www.gabuttiboasso.com

CELLAR SALES
PRE-BOOKED VISITS
ACCOMMODATION
ANNUAL PRODUCTION 25,000 bottles
HECTARES UNDER VINE 7.00

Active since 1970, today Gabutti is managed with skill by Franco Boasso, who's increasingly helped by his two sons Ezio and Claudio. Their strongpoint lies in their two first-rate vineyards, Gabutti and Margheria, and in their classic approach to winemaking, which sees their Barolos matured in mid-sized Slavonian oak barrels. Hospitality for visitors is enriched by the precious of a bona fide agritourism, I Grappoli. For those who love Barolo's aromas, or just wines in general, we can confidently recommend Luigi Moio's 'Il Respiro del Vino' ('The Breath of Wine'), published by Mondadori. Their 2014 Barolo Gabutti features a generous, persistent palate of rare balance, while on the nose it's still slightly marked by oak. Their 2014 Barolo from Serralungna opts for more pronounced vegetal hints. It's an enjoyable wine in its fruity simplicity,

| | | |
|---|---|---|
| ● Barolo Gabutti '14 | ♈♈ 6 | |
| ● Barolo del Comune di Serralunga d'Alba '14 | ♈♈ 5 | |
| ● Langhe Nebbiolo '16 | ♈♈ 3 | |
| ● Barbera d'Alba Sup. '16 | ♈ 2 | |
| ● Dolcetto d'Alba '17 | ♈ 2 | |
| ● Barolo Gabutti '13 | ♈♈♈ 6 | |
| ● Barolo Margheria '05 | ♈♈♈ 5* | |
| ● Barbera d'Alba '12 | ♈♈ 2* | |
| ● Barbera d'Alba Sup. '13 | ♈♈ 2* | |
| ● Barolo del Comune di Serralunga d'Alba '13 | ♈♈ 5 | |
| ● Barolo Gabutti '12 | ♈♈ 6 | |
| ● Barolo Gabutti '11 | ♈♈ 6 | |
| ● Barolo Margheria '13 | ♈♈ 6 | |
| ● Barolo Margheria '12 | ♈♈ 6 | |
| ● Barolo Margheria '11 | ♈♈ 6 | |

# Gaggino

S.DA SANT'EVASIO, 29
15076 OVADA [AL]
TEL. +39 0143822345
www.gaggino.it

CELLAR SALES
PRE-BOOKED VISITS
ANNUAL PRODUCTION 150,000 bottles
HECTARES UNDER VINE 20.00

Gaggino's roots go back nearly 100 years. The winery has undergone a change in production and quality, thanks to the insistence of Gabriele, a forthright, dynamic figure. His selection is characterized by excellent overall quality. And it's not a coincidence that his Dolcetto di Ovada wines are recognized for their good value for the money. Some 15 wines are offered in total, and this year sees the addition of a Gavi made with grapes cultivated in Aureliana, Capriata d'Orba. Roberto Olivieri, an expert enologist with extensive experience, oversees production. Their selection's flagship wine is a superb Ovada Convivio. It's a true classic that offers up lovely, fruity aromas accompanied by notes of bitter almond. These follow through elegantly on a rich, balanced palate with an extremely persistent finish. Their excellent 2017 Dolcetto features red fruit, notes of quinine and licorice, while both their Lazzarina, a Barbera, and their new Gavi La Sverva also proved well-made.

| | | |
|---|---|---|
| ● Ovada Convivio '16 | ♈♈♈ 3* | |
| ● Barbera del M.to La Lazzarina '16 | ♈♈ 2* | |
| ● Dolcetto di Ovada '17 | ♈♈ 2* | |
| ○ Gavi La Sverza '17 | ♈♈ 3 | |
| ○ Courtesia Brut | ♈ 2 | |
| ○ Piemonte Bianco Pagliuzza '17 | ♈ 2 | |
| ● Ovada Convivio '13 | ♈♈♈ 2* | |
| ● Barbera del M.to La Lazzarina '15 | ♈♈ 2* | |
| ● Barbera del M.to Lazzarina '14 | ♈♈ 3 | |
| ● Dolcetto di Ovada '16 | ♈♈ 2* | |
| ● Ovada Convivio '15 | ♈♈ 3* | |
| ● Ovada Convivio '14 | ♈♈ 3* | |
| ● Ovada Sant'Evasio '13 | ♈♈ 4 | |
| ● Ovada Sant'Evasio '12 | ♈♈ 4 | |
| ○ Piemonte Cortese Courteisa Brut | ♈♈ 2* | |

## ★★★★★Gaja

VIA TORINO, 18
12050 BARBARESCO [CN]
TEL. +39 0173635158
info@gaja.com

**ANNUAL PRODUCTION** 350,000 bottles
**HECTARES UNDER VINE** 92.00

A generational changing of the guard has seen Gaia, Rosanna and Giovanni increasingly involved in their family's winery, and they're guiding this prestigious Langhe producer towards bright prospects. Gaja continues to be a bonafide benchmark in Italy and the world for its wines. In addition to their high-quality, they're known for their ageworthiness, complexity and strong territorial identity. Their products now fall within the DOCG geographic and quality controlled regimes, and we aren't concealing our pleasure at reading names like Barolo and Barbaresco, names that represent enological excellence, on their labels. And their Barbaresco Sorì Tildin is the offering that most impressed during our tastings. 2015 gave rise to a wine of incredible elegance, silky, long, endowed with great complexity, yet enjoyable on the palate right from the outset. Their other Barbaresco, a 2015 Sorì San Lorenzo, also proved top-notch, as did their 2014 Barolo Sperss (despite its youth). As always, the rest of their selection proved to be of high quality.

| | |
|---|---|
| ● Barbaresco Sorì Tildin '15 | ♟♟♟ 8 |
| ● Barbaresco Sorì San Lorenzo '15 | ♟♟ 8 |
| ● Barolo Sperss '14 | ♟♟ 8 |
| ● Barbaresco '15 | ♟♟ 8 |
| ● Barbaresco Costa Russi '15 | ♟♟ 8 |
| ● Barolo Conteisa '14 | ♟♟ 8 |
| ● Barbaresco '09 | ♟♟♟ 8 |
| ● Barbaresco '08 | ♟♟♟ 8 |
| ● Barbaresco Costa Russi '13 | ♟♟♟ 8 |
| ● Barbaresco Sorì Tildin '14 | ♟♟♟ 8 |
| ● Langhe Nebbiolo Costa Russi '10 | ♟♟♟ 8 |
| ● Langhe Nebbiolo Costa Russi '08 | ♟♟♟ 8 |
| ● Langhe Nebbiolo Sorì Tildin '11 | ♟♟♟ 8 |
| ● Langhe Nebbiolo Sperss '11 | ♟♟♟ 8 |
| ● Barbaresco '14 | ♟♟ 8 |
| ● Barbaresco Costa Russi '14 | ♟♟ 8 |

## Filippo Gallino

FRAZ. VALLE DEL POZZO, 63
12043 CANALE [CN]
TEL. +39 017398112
www.filippogallino.com

**CELLAR SALES**
**PRE-BOOKED VISITS**
**ACCOMMODATION**
**ANNUAL PRODUCTION** 100,000 bottles
**HECTARES UNDER VINE** 14.00
**SUSTAINABLE WINERY**

The Gallino family winery is one of Roero's historic producers. They avail themselves of a number of vineyards situated throughout Canale, primarily on the area's trademark clay-sandy soil and within some of Roero's best crus, from Briccola to Renesio and Mompissano. These give rise to the territory's classic grapes, Arneis, Barbera and Nebbiolo, making for a selection that brings together tradition (especially when it comes to vineyard management) and a modern approach (foremost in the cellar). This year the Gallino family's selection proved tight and consistent. Their fresh 2016 Barbera d'Alba is rich in fruit and highly pleasing. Their 2017 Roero Arneis is a classic in its savoriness, its notes of white fruit, and its supple, easy palate, while their 2016 Langhe Nebbiolo features fruit and well-integrated tannins. Their Seventy Brut is a pleasant, sparkling Arneis with nice tension.

| | |
|---|---|
| ● Barbera d'Alba '16 | ♟♟ 2* |
| ● Langhe Nebbiolo '16 | ♟♟ 2* |
| ○ Roero Arneis '17 | ♟♟ 2* |
| ○ Seventy Brut M. Cl. | ♟♟ 3 |
| ● Barbera d'Alba Sup. '05 | ♟♟♟ 4* |
| ● Roero '06 | ♟♟♟ 4* |
| ● Barbera d'Alba '15 | ♟♟ 2* |
| ● Barbera d'Alba Sup. '12 | ♟♟ 4 |
| ● Barbera d'Alba Sup. Bonora '13 | ♟♟ 4 |
| ○ Roero Arneis '15 | ♟♟ 2* |
| ○ Roero Arneis '14 | ♟♟ 2* |

## Garesio

LOC. SORDO, 1
12050 SERRALUNGA D'ALBA [CN]
TEL. +39 3667076775
www.garesiovini.it

CELLAR SALES
PRE-BOOKED VISITS
ANNUAL PRODUCTION 35,000 bottles
HECTARES UNDER VINE 5.80
VITICULTURE METHOD Certified Organic

The Garesio family only got their start in winemaking back in 2010, but the results are definitely worth noting thanks both to their lovely estate and to a team of experts who contribute both in the cellar and in the vineyards. Their wines come from two places, Nizza (a DOC controlled appellation since 2014) where the focus is on Barbera, and Serralunga d'Alba, where they make their two Barolos, most notably the celebrated Cerretta cru. Their winemaking style focuses on a classic style (rather long maceration and medium-large wood barrels) and elegance (French and Austrian oak). Their 2014 Barolo del Comune di Serralunga d'Alba features fresh, vegetal notes both on the nose and on the palate, with tannins and acidity well-balanced by a fruity pulp that allows for a nice overall equilibrium. Their clean and appealing 2015 Nizza exhibits robust body, while their 2016 Langhe Nebbiolo proves minty and delicate on the nose, crisp and austere on the palate.

| | |
|---|---|
| ● Barolo del Comune di Serralunga d'Alba '14 | ▼▼ 5 |
| ● Nizza '15 | ▼▼ 4 |
| ● Langhe Nebbiolo '16 | ▼▼ 3 |
| ● Barbera d'Asti Superiore Nizza '13 | ♀♀ 4 |
| ● Barbera d'Asti Superiore Nizza '12 | ♀♀ 4 |
| ● Barbera d'Asti Superiore Nizza '11 | ♀♀ 5 |
| ● Barolo Cerretta '13 | ♀♀ 7 |
| ● Barolo del Comune di Serralunga d'Alba '13 | ♀♀ 5 |
| ○ Geresio Pas Dosé M. Cl. | ♀♀ 4 |
| ● Langhe Nebbiolo '15 | ♀♀ 3 |
| ● Nizza '14 | ♀♀ 4 |

## Gaudio - Bricco Mondalino

C.NE REG. MONDALINO, 5
15049 VIGNALE MONFERRATO [AL]
TEL. +39 0142933204
www.gaudiovini.it

CELLAR SALES
PRE-BOOKED VISITS
ANNUAL PRODUCTION 100,000 bottles
HECTARES UNDER VINE 19.50
SUSTAINABLE WINERY

Their production center is in Mondalino, Vignale Monferrato, situated on a hilltop from which you get a lovely, panoramic view of the surrounding area. Gaudio - Bricco Mondalino is one of Monferrato Casalese's historic wineries, though it's evolved over time. This is true both for winemaking, with the use of modern equipment and methods, as well as their image and in terms of communication. In the meantime a kind of generational shift is underway in the Gaudio family, with Mauro's daughter Beatrice graduating in enology and viticulture in Alba. Their 2016 Barbera del Monferrato was the first wine tasted. It's complex on the nose, with fruity notes and the spiciness of oak merging well. On the palate it exhibits nice structure, with acidity lengthening a persistent finish. Their Bergantino opens with aromas of plum preserves and spices. On the palate it proves intense, with a finish that's rich in alcohol. Their 2017 Grignolino offers up flowery aromas accompanied by notes of tobacco and pepper. These re-emerge on the palate, which also features close-woven tannins and a persistent finish.

| | |
|---|---|
| ● Barbera del M.to Sup. '16 | ▼▼ 2* |
| ● Barbera d'Asti Il Bergantino '15 | ▼▼ 4 |
| ● Grignolino del M.to Casalese '17 | ▼▼ 3 |
| ● Grignolino del M.to Casalese Bricco Mondalino '16 | ▼ 3 |
| ● Barbera d'Asti Zerolegno '13 | ♀♀ 4 |
| ● Barbera del M.to Sup. '15 | ♀♀ 2* |
| ● Grignolino del M.to Casalese '16 | ♀♀ 3 |
| ● Grignolino del M.to Casalese Bricco Mondalino '13 | ♀♀ 2* |
| ● Grignolino del M.to Casalese Monte della Sala '13 | ♀♀ 4 |
| ● Malvasia di Casorzo Dolce Stil Novo '16 | ♀♀ 2* |
| ● Malvasia di Casorzo Dolce Stil Novo '13 | ♀♀ 2* |

# Generaj

B.TA TUCCI, 4
12046 MONTÀ [CN]
TEL. +39 0173976142
www.generaj.it

CELLAR SALES
PRE-BOOKED VISITS
ANNUAL PRODUCTION 50,000 bottles
HECTARES UNDER VINE 12.00
SUSTAINABLE WINERY

Founded in 1947 by Giuseppe, the current owner's grandfather, the Viglione family winery avails itself of vineyards situated in Montà, in a particularly cool area, on sandy, calcareous and pebbly terrain. The grapes grown are those common to the left bank of the Tanaro river: Arneis, Barbera and Nebbiolo, making for a selection of decidedly modern wines, while also attentive to express the territory of origin. Indeed, all their wines carry the name of the vineyard where their grapes are cultivated. Even with the difficult year, their 2014 Roero Bric Aût Riserva showed why it's one of the best in the appellation. Aromas of dark fruit are accompanied by light spices; an elegant, pleasant palate with nice tension follows. Their 2015 Roero Bric Aût also delivered, proving full-bodied and rich in fruit, with a nice tannic weave, as did their 2017 Roero Arneis Bric Varomaldo, a fresh and citrusy wine. The rest of their selection also proved sound.

| | | |
|---|---|---|
| ● Roero Bric Aût Ris. '14 | ♟♟ | 5 |
| ○ Roero Arneis Bric Varomaldo '17 | ♟♟ | 2* |
| ● Roero Bric Aût '15 | ♟♟ | 4 |
| ● Barbera d'Alba Sup. Ca' d' Pistola '15 | ♟ | 3 |
| ○ Quindicilune '16 | ♟ | 3 |
| ● Barbera d'Alba Sup. Ca' d' Pistola '14 | ♟♟ | 3 |
| ● Barbera d'Alba Sup. Ca' d' Pistola '13 | ♟♟ | 3* |
| ○ Roero Arneis Quindicilune '12 | ♟♟ | 3* |
| ● Roero Bric Aût '14 | ♟♟ | 4 |
| ● Roero Bric Aût '12 | ♟♟ | 4 |
| ● Roero Bric Aût Ris. '13 | ♟♟ | 5 |
| ○ Roero Arneis Bric Varomaldo '16 | ♟ | 2 |

# ★Ettore Germano

LOC. CERRETTA, 1
12050 SERRALUNGA D'ALBA [CN]
TEL. +39 0173613528
www.germanoettore.com

CELLAR SALES
PRE-BOOKED VISITS
ACCOMMODATION
ANNUAL PRODUCTION 90,000 bottles
HECTARES UNDER VINE 16.00

Sergio Germano has made a name for himself primarily for his highly prized Riesling Hérzu. But we're still convinced that his abilities as a Barolo producer need to be adequately underlined and appreciated. His estate is shifting to organic management and comprises prestigious crus such as Cerretta, Lazzarito and Prapò, as well as the recently added Vigna Riondo, which for the moment is presented as their Langhe Nebbiolo. And apropos new additions, their Alta Langa Brut is already proving valid while their Nascetta, aged 30% in amphora, is also worth noting. Their 2012 Barolo Lazzarito does a nice job expressing the year, proving elegant and juicy, rich in iodine nuances and notes of Mediterranean scrubland. On the palate it finish long and energetic. Their 2014 Barolo Prapò is a tight, approachable wine. Their 2014 Barolo Cerretta doesn't exhibit particularly full structure, but it's a multifaceted and delicate wine. They also make a Barolo with grapes from various crus around Serralunga d'Alba, and as is often the case with this particular wine, it proves to be of rare balance and pleasantness.

| | | |
|---|---|---|
| ● Barolo Lazzarito Ris. '12 | ♟♟♟ | 8 |
| ● Barolo del Comune di Serralunga d'Alba '14 | ♟♟ | 6 |
| ● Barolo Prapò '14 | ♟♟ | 7 |
| ○ Langhe Riesling Hérzu '16 | ♟♟ | 4 |
| ○ Alta Langa Brut '14 | ♟♟ | 5 |
| ● Barolo Cerretta '14 | ♟♟ | 7 |
| ○ Langhe Bianco Binel '16 | ♟♟ | 3 |
| ● Langhe Nebbiolo '16 | ♟♟ | 3 |
| ● Barbera d'Alba Sup. della Madre '15 | ♟ | 5 |
| ○ Langhe Nascetta '17 | ♟ | 3 |
| ○ Rosanna Brut Rosé M. Cl. '15 | ♟ | 4 |
| ● Barolo Lazzarito Ris. '11 | ♟♟♟ | 8 |
| ● Barolo Lazzarito Ris. '10 | ♟♟♟ | 8 |
| ● Barolo Lazzarito Ris. '08 | ♟♟♟ | 8 |
| ● Barolo Prapò '11 | ♟♟♟ | 7 |

# La Ghibellina

FRAZ. MONTEROTONDO, 61
15066 GAVI [AL]
TEL. +39 0143686257
www.laghibellina.it

CELLAR SALES
PRE-BOOKED VISITS
RESTAURANT SERVICE
ANNUAL PRODUCTION 60,000 bottles
HECTARES UNDER VINE 17.00

Marina Galli Ghibellini's winery has a good
number of vintages under its belt and it's
proving to be among the most interesting
producers in the area. Their Monterotondo
vineyards give rise to vibrant, full-bodied
wines with notable minerality. Two versions
of Gavi are offered: the Mainìn and Altrius,
while the same cultivar is used for their
Metodo Classico sparkler, including their
Cuvée Marina. It's a wine that stands out
thanks to a minimum of 48 months aging on
the lees. Let's not forget their Sandrino,
either, a rosé made with Barbera, the same
grape used for their Nero del Montone, as
well as their Pituj, a Merlot blend. For our
latest edition, Ghibellina's selection was
missing a few wines. But in return we tasted
two splendid Gavis. Altius opens with aromas
of white peach accompanied by notes of
saffron and tobacco. On the palate it proves
fresh and balanced, with nice acidity in the
foreground. Mainìn is a subtle though
complex wine on the nose, with a palate
that features character, firm structure and
vibrant finish.

| | |
|---|---|
| ○ Gavi del Comune di Gavi Altius '16 | 🍷🍷 5 |
| ○ Gavi del Comune di Gavi Mainìn '17 | 🍷🍷 3* |
| ● M.to Rosso Pituj '16 | 🍷 4 |
| ○ Gavi del Comune di Gavi Altius '14 | 🍷🍷 5 |
| ○ Gavi del Comune di Gavi Altius '13 | 🍷🍷 3* |
| ○ Gavi del Comune di Gavi Mainìn '16 | 🍷🍷 3* |
| ○ Gavi del Comune di Gavi Mainìn '15 | 🍷🍷 3* |
| ○ Gavi del Comune di Gavi Mainìn '14 | 🍷🍷 3* |

# ★★Bruno Giacosa

VIA XX SETTEMBRE, 52
12052 NEIVE [CN]
TEL. +39 017367027
www.brunogiacosa.it

ANNUAL PRODUCTION 300,000 bottles
HECTARES UNDER VINE 20.00
SUSTAINABLE WINERY

Bruno Giacosa left behind a legacy of
winemaking that's at the top of its class. It's
constituted of pure, vibrant wines, variegated
and fine, endowed with a complexity that
can be traced back to the grape only, and
never to gimmicks employed in the cellar.
His selection of Barolos and Barbarescos
dominated the international scene for 60
years, and they haven't stopped, thanks to a
continuity provided by his favorite pupil,
Dante Scaglione. For those who love Bruno
Giacosa and his reds, we've told his story in
our magazine and on www.gamberorosso.it
(available also in English). Grazie Bruno.
Their wines sum up all the classic style for
which Langhe's great reds are known, with
the extraordinary distinction of representing
the characteristics of each vintage as well.
Their 2012 Barolo Falletto Vigna Le Rocche
Riserva is exemplary in this respect,
standing out for its elegance more than
its freshness, and complexity more than
force. Their splendid 2014 Barbaresco
Rabajà is in the same vein, featuring
elegance and balance.

| | |
|---|---|
| ● Barolo Falletto V. Le Rocche Ris. '12 | 🍷🍷🍷 8 |
| ● Barbaresco Asili '15 | 🍷🍷 8 |
| ● Barbaresco Rabajà '14 | 🍷🍷 8 |
| ● Barolo Falletto '14 | 🍷🍷 8 |
| ● Nebbiolo d'Alba Valmaggiore '16 | 🍷🍷 6 |
| ○ Roero Arneis '17 | 🍷🍷 4 |
| ● Barbaresco Asili '12 | 🍷🍷🍷 8 |
| ● Barbaresco Asili '05 | 🍷🍷🍷 8 |
| ● Barbaresco Asili Ris. '11 | 🍷🍷🍷 8 |
| ● Barbaresco Asili Ris. '07 | 🍷🍷🍷 8 |
| ● Barolo Falletto '07 | 🍷🍷🍷 8 |
| ● Barolo Falletto V. Le Rocche Ris. '11 | 🍷🍷🍷 8 |
| ● Barolo Le Rocche del Falletto '05 | 🍷🍷🍷 8 |
| ● Barolo Le Rocche del Falletto '04 | 🍷🍷🍷 8 |
| ● Barolo Le Rocche del Falletto Ris. '08 | 🍷🍷🍷 8 |
| ● Barolo Le Rocche del Falletto Ris. '07 | 🍷🍷🍷 8 |

## Carlo Giacosa

S.DA OVELLO, 9
12050 BARBARESCO [CN]
TEL. +39 0173635116
www.carlogiacosa.it

CELLAR SALES
PRE-BOOKED VISITS
ANNUAL PRODUCTION 42,000 bottles
HECTARES UNDER VINE 5.50

Carlo Giacosa is a solid benchmark for those who love pure, direct wines that are capable of expressing the essence of the grape without enhancements or the invasive use of oak. This is the production philosophy that describes all the choices made at Carlo Giacosa's cellar (today managed by Maria Grazia Giacosa) over its 50 years of operations. That doesn't mean that major decisions aren't made, from fermentation to temperature control and the use of various sizes of French oak barrels. And their prices are commendably good, even their prized Barbarescos. Their 2015 Barbaresco Montefico is truly a masterpiece. Anise and licorice fade into an explosive background of red fruit, with delicate notes of sunny herbs for a nose of astounding complexity. The palate is harmonic, rich in tannins and pulp with a trace of acidity that refreshes its long finish. Their tempting 2016 Barbera d'Alba Superiore Lina proves velvety and expansive.

| | |
|---|---|
| ● Barbaresco Montefico '15 | ���� 6 |
| ● Barbaresco Narin '15 | ��� 5 |
| ● Barbera d'Alba Sup. Lina '16 | �� 4 |
| ● Langhe Nebbiolo Maria Grazia '16 | � 4 |
| ● Barbaresco Montefico '08 | ��� 5* |
| ● Barbaresco Luca Ris. '10 | �� 6 |
| ● Barbaresco Montefico '14 | �� 5 |
| ● Barbaresco Montefico '13 | �� 5 |
| ● Barbaresco Montefico '12 | �� 5 |
| ● Barbaresco Narin '14 | �� 5 |
| ● Barbaresco Narin '12 | �� 5 |
| ● Barbera d'Alba Mucin '16 | �� 3 |
| ● Barbera d'Alba Mucin '15 | �� 3 |
| ● Barbera d'Alba Sup. Lina '15 | �� 3 |
| ● Langhe Nebbiolo Maria Grazia '15 | �� 4 |
| ● Langhe Nebbiolo Maria Grazia '14 | �� 3 |

## F.lli Giacosa

VIA XX SETTEMBRE, 64
12052 NEIVE [CN]
TEL. +39 017367013
www.giacosa.it

CELLAR SALES
PRE-BOOKED VISITS
ANNUAL PRODUCTION 500,000 bottles
HECTARES UNDER VINE 50.00
VITICULTURE METHOD Certified Organic
SUSTAINABLE WINERY

Over its 120 years of history, this major Langhe producer (today managed by Maurizio and Paolo Giacosa) has gradually proceeded to purchase prized vineyards in a number of appellations. Among these the prestigious Bussia and Scarrone plots stand out, as well as Basarin. The formed are dedicated to Barolo and the latter to Barbaresco. Visiting the cellar you get a sense of how they're able to achieve high production volumes, especially considering the area, while maintaining an artisanal approach. Their selection comprises the area's traditional cultivar, with some variation near Roero and Monferrato. Red fruit and oak compete in their powerful and resolute 2015 Barbaresco Basarin Vigna Gianmaté. Nice, soft tannins and good pulp define their 2014 Barolo Bussia, while the rustic aromas of their 2013 Barolo Scarrone Vigna Mandorlo lead to rich body and a rather austere palate. Their supple 2015 Barbera d'Alba evinces its wood barrel aging.

| | |
|---|---|
| ● Barbaresco Basarin V. Gianmatè '15 | �� 7 |
| ● Barbera d'Alba Canavere '15 | �� 4 |
| ● Barolo Bussia '14 | �� 7 |
| ○ Langhe Chardonnay Ca' Lunga '16 | �� 5 |
| ● Barbera d'Alba Madonna Como '15 | � 4 |
| ● Barolo Scarrone V. Mandorlo '13 | � 8 |
| ○ Langhe Chardonnay Rorea '17 | � 4 |
| ● Barbaresco Basarin V. Gianmatè '14 | �� 7 |
| ● Barbera d'Alba Maria Gioana '14 | �� 5 |
| ● Barbera d'Alba Maria Gioana '13 | �� 5 |
| ● Barbera d'Alba Maria Gioana '12 | �� 5 |
| ● Barolo Bussia '13 | �� 7 |
| ● Barolo Bussia '12 | �� 7 |
| ● Barolo Scarrone V. Mandorlo '12 | �� 8 |
| ● Barolo Scarrone V. Mandorlo '11 | �� 8 |
| ○ Langhe Chardonnay Ca' Lunga '15 | �� 5 |

# Giovanni Battista Gillardi

Cascina Corsaletto, 69
12060 Farigliano [CN]
Tel. +39 017376306
www.gillardi.it

**CELLAR SALES**
**PRE-BOOKED VISITS**
**ANNUAL PRODUCTION** 35,000 bottles
**HECTARES UNDER VINE** 7.00

Some time ago we participated in a vertical tasting of Gillardi's Dolcetto di Doglianis. And so it was that we turned back the clock, discovering the integrity and pleasantness of bottles that were more than 10 years old. We mention this to remind wine lovers that Dogliani doesn't have to be imbibed as soon as it hits the market, indeed it's a wine that deserves time and attention. The winery also offers a small selection made with French grapes, with their Langhe Harys at the forefront. And since 2011 they've also produced two Barolos, which get more interesting every year. To know more about Giacolino, Pietro Stara's rich volume 'Il discorso del vino' ('The Discourse of Wine') is a useful read. Red fruit, quinine and rhubarb lead into their overall somewhat austere and fresh but highly agreeable 2014 Barolo. Their Dolcetto Dogliani Cursalet offers very pleasant hints of black berry and juniper on the nose and a palate rich in body and its suite of tannins. Their Maestra proves more down-to-earth.

| | |
|---|---|
| ● Barolo '14 | ♟♟6 |
| ● Dogliani Cursalet '17 | ♟♟3* |
| ● Dogliani Maestra '17 | ♟♟3 |
| ● Langhe Fiore di Harys '16 | ♟7 |
| ● Dogliani Cursalet '11 | ♟♟♟3* |
| ● Harys '00 | ♟♟♟6 |
| ● Barolo '12 | ♟♟6 |
| ● Barolo del Comune di Barolo '13 | ♟♟4 |
| ● Barolo Vignane '13 | ♟♟6 |
| ● Dogliani Cursalet '16 | ♟♟3* |
| ● Dogliani Cursalet '15 | ♟♟3* |
| ● Dogliani Maestra '16 | ♟♟3 |
| ● Dogliani Maestra '15 | ♟♟3 |
| ● Langhe Harys '15 | ♟♟7 |
| ● Langhe Harys '14 | ♟♟7 |
| ● Langhe Nebbiolo '14 | ♟♟4 |

# La Gironda

s.da Bricco, 12
14049 Nizza Monferrato [AT]
Tel. +39 0141701013
www.lagironda.com

**CELLAR SALES**
**PRE-BOOKED VISITS**
**ANNUAL PRODUCTION** 60,000 bottles
**HECTARES UNDER VINE** 9.00
**SUSTAINABLE WINERY**

Susanna Galandrino, along with her husband Alberto Adamo, manages with passion and skill the winery founded by her father, Agostino, in 2000. Situated on a hill overlooking Nizza Monferrato, her selection centers around Barbera, with some vineyards going back as far as 50 years. Brachetto, Moscato, Nebbiolo, Cabernet Sauvignon and Sauvignon are also cultivated. Their style is modern, careful to highlight their wines close-focused aromas and pleasantness. An overall fine showing for the winery, their well-structured 2015 Nizzi Le Nicchie standing out. With a floral background and notes of aromatic herbs and black fruit, it promises to age very well. Their 2016 Barbera d'Asti La Gena gambles on fruit, offering a savory and dynamic palate, while their pleasant 2017 Moscato d'Asti gives off citron and rosemary, if a bit sweet. Their 2015 Monteferrato Rosso Soul is equally good.

| | |
|---|---|
| ● Nizza Le Nicchie '15 | ♟♟5 |
| ● Barbera d'Asti La Gena '16 | ♟♟3 |
| ● M.to Rosso Soul '15 | ♟♟5 |
| ○ Moscato d'Asti '17 | ♟♟2* |
| ● Brachetto d'Acqui '17 | ♟3 |
| ● Barbera d'Asti Sup. Nizza Le Nicchie '11 | ♟♟♟5 |
| ● Barbera d'Asti La Gena '15 | ♟♟3* |
| ● Barbera d'Asti La Lippa '16 | ♟♟2* |
| ● Barbera d'Asti Sup. Nizza Le Nicchie '13 | ♟♟5 |
| ● M.to Rosso Soul '14 | ♟♟5 |
| ○ Moscato d'Asti '16 | ♟♟2* |
| ● Nizza La Gironda '14 | ♟♟5 |
| ○ Piemonte Sauvignon L'Aquilone '16 | ♟3 |

## Tenuta La Giustiniana

Fraz. Rovereto, 5
15066 Gavi [AL]
Tel. +39 0143682132
www.lagiustiniana.it

CELLAR SALES
PRE-BOOKED VISITS
ANNUAL PRODUCTION 200,000 bottles
HECTARES UNDER VINE 39.00

In February of 2016 a majority stake in Tenuta La Giustiniana was purchased by local entrepreneurs Magda Pedrini (owner of Cà da Meo) and Stefano Massone (owner of the winery Stefano Massone). In 2017 a renovation and vineyard reorganization project began. As far as their wines are concerned, the change in ownership sees enologist Cristian Pomo back in the cellar. Product standards remain extremely high, and a vertical tasting in Montessora reminded us just how ageworthy Rovereto's Gavi is. Their intensely straw-yellow Montessora Gavi del Comune di Gavi stands out from other interpretations. Strong notes of white fruit and almond lead to a fresh, lively and persistent palate. Lugarara releases aromas of wisteria and acacia with light mineral notes that converge on a fresh, savory and enduring palate.

| | |
|---|---|
| ○ Gavi del Comune di Gavi Montessora '17 | 🍷🍷 4 |
| ○ Gavi del Comune di Gavi Lugarara '17 | 🍷🍷 3 |
| ○ Gavi del Comune di Gavi Lugarara '16 | 🍷🍷 3* |
| ○ Gavi del Comune di Gavi Lugarara '15 | 🍷🍷 3 |
| ○ Gavi del Comune di Gavi Lugarara '14 | 🍷🍷 3 |
| ○ Gavi del Comune di Gavi Lugarara '13 | 🍷🍷 3* |
| ○ Gavi del Comune di Gavi Montessora '16 | 🍷🍷 4 |
| ○ Gavi del Comune di Gavi Montessora '14 | 🍷🍷 4 |
| ○ Gavi del Comune di Gavi Montessora '13 | 🍷🍷 4 |
| ○ Giustiniana Brut M. Cl. | 🍷🍷 4 |

## ★Elio Grasso

loc. Ginestra, 40
12065 Monforte d'Alba [CN]
Tel. +39 017378491
www.eliograsso.it

PRE-BOOKED VISITS
ANNUAL PRODUCTION 90,000 bottles
HECTARES UNDER VINE 18.00
SUSTAINABLE WINERY

At the end of the 1960s, Elio Grasso began bottling the wine he'd been making with grapes from his vineyards.18 hectares of land comprise some of the most interesting plots to be found in Monforte d'Alba, Ginestra Casa Matè, Gavarini Chiniera and Rüncot. Accompanied by his son Gianluca, Elio has established a well-defined style that features the use of 2500 liter Slavonian oak barrels, along with barriques made of French oak, conferring more pronounced toastiness to subtler wines. In addition to Nebbiolo, their vineyards give rise to Dolcetto, Barbera and Chardonnay. Their 2014 Barolo, the only one we tasted from them this year, is characterized by juniper and wood resin. It offers a playful contrast between its steady, supple palate of tenacious acidity and its touch of rustic flavor. Clean, crisp and pulpy, their 2015 Barbera d'Alba Vigna Martina possesses a lively, pleasant palate.

| | |
|---|---|
| ● Barbera d'Alba V. Martina '15 | 🍷🍷 5 |
| ● Barolo '14 | 🍷🍷 8 |
| ● Barolo Gavarini Chiniera '09 | 🍷🍷🍷 8 |
| ● Barolo Gavarini V. Chiniera '06 | 🍷🍷🍷 8 |
| ● Barolo Ginestra Casa Maté '12 | 🍷🍷🍷 8 |
| ● Barolo Ginestra Casa Maté '07 | 🍷🍷🍷 8 |
| ● Barolo Ginestra V. Casa Maté '05 | 🍷🍷🍷 8 |
| ● Barolo Ginestra V. Casa Maté '04 | 🍷🍷🍷 8 |
| ● Barolo Rüncot '01 | 🍷🍷🍷 8 |
| ● Barbera d'Alba V. Martina '13 | 🍷🍷 5 |
| ● Barolo Gavarini Chiniera '12 | 🍷🍷 8 |
| ● Barolo Gavarini Chiniera '11 | 🍷🍷 8 |
| ● Barolo Ginestra Casa Maté '13 | 🍷🍷 8 |
| ● Barolo Rüncot Ris. '11 | 🍷🍷 8 |

# Silvio Grasso

FRAZ. ANNUNZIATA, 112
12064 LA MORRA [CN]
TEL. +39 3355273168
www.silviograsso.com

**CELLAR SALES**
**PRE-BOOKED VISITS**
**ANNUAL PRODUCTION** 80,000 bottles
**HECTARES UNDER VINE** 14.00

The winery is getting close to its 100-year anniversary, even if international fame only began arriving some 30 years when Federico Grasso began bottling his own wines. Their selection features only red wines, with the modern and elegant Barolo Bricco Manzoni and Bricco Luciani leading the way. Their Turné is an interesting wine, characterized by long maceration on the skins and aging in untoasted Slavonian oak barrels. Those who are interested in knowing more about the origins of Barolo may want to read Anna Richard Candiani's essay 'Louis Oudart e i vini nobili del Piemonte: storia di un enologo francese' ('Louis Oudart and Piedmont's Noble Wines: A History of French Enology'). With the 2015 vintage, their dense, fruity Barbera d'Alba Fontanile, delicately expressing oak aging, again reaches the highest levels. On the other hand, wood dominates their nonetheless quite tasty 2014 Barolo. Kudos for their elegant, harmonic 2016 Langhe Nebbiolo, possessing smooth tannins and hints of licorice.

| | | |
|---|---|---|
| ● Barbera d'Alba Fontanile '15 | ♀♀ | 5 |
| ● Langhe Nebbiolo '16 | ♀♀ | 3 |
| ● Barolo '14 | ♀ | 5 |
| ● Barolo Bricco Luciani '04 | ♀♀♀ | 7 |
| ● Barolo Bricco Luciani '01 | ♀♀♀ | 6 |
| ● Barolo Bricco Manzoni '10 | ♀♀♀ | 7 |
| ● Barbera d'Alba '15 | ♀♀ | 3 |
| ● Barbera d'Alba Fontanile '13 | ♀♀ | 5 |
| ● Barolo '13 | ♀♀ | 5 |
| ● Barolo Annunziata V. Plicotti '13 | ♀♀ | 7 |
| ● Barolo Bricco Luciani '12 | ♀♀ | 7 |
| ● Barolo Bricco Luciani '11 | ♀♀ | 7 |
| ● Barolo Bricco Manzoni '13 | ♀♀ | 8 |
| ● Barolo Turné '13 | ♀♀ | 7 |
| ● Barolo Turne' '12 | ♀♀ | 7 |

# Bruna Grimaldi

VIA PAREA, 7
12060 GRINZANE CAVOUR [CN]
TEL. +39 0173262094
www.grimaldibruna.it

**CELLAR SALES**
**PRE-BOOKED VISITS**
**ANNUAL PRODUCTION** 70,000 bottles
**HECTARES UNDER VINE** 15.00

Bricco Ambrogio is a cru of 25 hectares situated in the municipality of Roddi. It's come into the limelight in recent years as a source of Barolo, thanks to a renewed commitment by certain producers, among whom we find Bruna Grimaldi. The results are already more than noteworthy, even if the winery's more structured and important wines continue to come from Badarina in Serralunga d'Alba, which also gives rise to a perennially valid Riserva. Their lovely and recently renovated cellar is situated in Grinzane Cavour, where their Barolo Camilla is produced. Their entire selection is well crafted, with their Barbera d'Alba Scassa an enjoyable standout. Their 2014 Barolo Bricco Ambrogio features stimulating spices and a velvety, flowing palate. Their 2014 Badarina Barolo, offers elegance and slightly under-ripe fruit on a long palate made a bit thin by tannins. Austere and mature, their 2012 Barolo Badarina Riserva lacks a little bit of freshness on the palate. Their brilliant 2016 Nebbiolo d'Alba is particularly distinguished.

| | | |
|---|---|---|
| ● Barolo Badarina '14 | ♀♀ | 6 |
| ● Barolo Bricco Ambrogio '14 | ♀♀ | 5 |
| ● Barbera d'Alba Sup. Scassa '15 | ♀♀ | 3 |
| ● Barolo Badarina Ris. '12 | ♀♀ | 7 |
| ● Nebbiolo d'Alba '16 | ♀♀ | 3 |
| ● Barolo Camilla '14 | ♀ | 5 |
| ● Barbera d'Alba Sup. Scassa '14 | ♀♀ | 3 |
| ● Barbera d'Alba Sup. Scassa '13 | ♀♀ | 3 |
| ● Barolo Badarina '13 | ♀♀ | 6 |
| ● Barolo Badarina '12 | ♀♀ | 6 |
| ● Barolo Badarina Ris. '11 | ♀♀ | 7 |
| ● Barolo Badarina Ris. '10 | ♀♀ | 7 |
| ● Barolo Bricco Ambrogio '13 | ♀♀ | 5 |
| ● Barolo Bricco Ambrogio '12 | ♀♀ | 5 |
| ● Barolo Camilla '13 | ♀♀ | 5 |
| ● Barolo Camilla '12 | ♀♀ | 5 |
| ● Nebbiolo d'Alba '15 | ♀♀ | 3 |

## Giacomo Grimaldi

VIA LUIGI EINAUDI, 8
12060 BAROLO [CN]
TEL. +39 0173560536
www.giacomogrimaldi.com

CELLAR SALES
PRE-BOOKED VISITS
ANNUAL PRODUCTION 50,000 bottles
HECTARES UNDER VINE 13.00

Ferruccio Grimaldi isn't one for attention, but he's become a benchmark for those who love Langhe's wines, thanks to a classical style that's both complex and charming. And as far as his Barolo is concerned, credit also goes to two of his most important vineyards, Le Coste, situated near the cellar, and Sotto Castello in Novello (both of whose names appear on the label). Their Nebbiolo d'Alba is cultivated in one of nearby Roero's most scenic and deservedly celebrated vineyards, Valmaggiore. The only space made for white grapes is a small selection of Langhe Sauvignon. Despite the difficulties that came with the vintage, both of their 2104 Barolo are wonderful. Their less ambitious version proves very soft and overall quite ripe, while their remarkably harmonious Sotto Castello di Novello, though not terribly powerful, offers a commendable balance between its suite of tannins and appealing, fruity pulp.

| | |
|---|---|
| ● Barolo Le Coste '14 | ▼▼7 |
| ● Barolo Sotto Castello di Novello '14 | ▼▼6 |
| ● Barolo Sotto Castello di Novello '05 | ▼▼▼6 |
| ● Barbera d'Alba Fornaci '12 | ♀♀4 |
| ● Barbera d'Alba Pistin '15 | ♀♀3 |
| ● Barbera d'Alba Pistin '14 | ♀♀3 |
| ● Barolo '13 | ♀♀6 |
| ● Barolo '12 | ♀♀6 |
| ● Barolo '11 | ♀♀6 |
| ● Barolo Le Coste '13 | ♀♀7 |
| ● Barolo Le Coste '12 | ♀♀7 |
| ● Barolo Le Coste '11 | ♀♀7 |
| ● Barolo Sotto Castello di Novello '13 | ♀♀6 |
| ● Barolo Sotto Castello di Novello '12 | ♀♀6 |
| ● Barolo Sotto Castello di Novello '11 | ♀♀6 |
| ● Dolcetto d'Alba '14 | ♀♀2* |

## Sergio Grimaldi Ca' du Sindic

LOC. SAN GRATO, 15
12058 SANTO STEFANO BELBO [CN]
TEL. +39 0141840341
www.cadusindic.it

CELLAR SALES
PRE-BOOKED VISITS
ANNUAL PRODUCTION 100,000 bottles
HECTARES UNDER VINE 17.00
SUSTAINABLE WINERY

Ca' du Sindic, the Grimaldi family's winery, was founded by Sergio in 1989. Their vineyards are entirely situated in Santo Stefano Belbo, in the districts of San Maurizio, Bauda and Moncucco, on the San Grato hills near to their main facility. Moscato makes up the lion's share, though Pinot Nero and Chardonnay are cultivated for their sparkling wines, along with Dolcetto, Barbera and Brachetto. The Moscato d'Astis they offer can now be considered model wines for the typology. Their proposals performed a bit less brilliantly than in the past, but one made the final. Their classic 2017 Moscato d'Asti Vigna Moncucco offers aromas of candied citron peel and brioche on a fresh, assertive palate with a tight, pleasant finish. Their well-crafted 2017 Barbera d'Asti San Grato delivers abundant roundness and structure though the suite of tannins is still a bit too noticeable.

| | |
|---|---|
| ○ Moscato d'Asti V. Moncucco '17 | ▼▼3* |
| ● Barbera d'Asti SanGrato '17 | ▼▼2* |
| ○ Moscato d'Asti Ca' du Sindic '17 | ▼▼3 |
| ○ Moscato d'Asti '17 | ▼2 |
| ○ Ventuno Brut '16 | ▼3 |
| ⊙ Ventuno Brut Rosè '16 | ▼3 |
| ● Barbera d'Asti San Grato '15 | ♀♀2* |
| ○ Moscato d'Asti Ca' du Sindic '15 | ♀♀3* |
| ○ Moscato d'Asti Ca' du Sindic Capsula Oro '16 | ♀♀3 |
| ○ Moscato d'Asti Capsula Argento '16 | ♀♀3 |
| ○ Moscato d'Asti V. Moncucco '16 | ♀♀3* |
| ○ Moscato d'Asti V. Moncucco '15 | ♀♀3* |
| ○ Ventuno Brut '14 | ♀♀3 |

# ★Hilberg - Pasquero

VIA BRICCO GATTI, 16
12040 PRIOCCA [CN]
TEL. +39 0173616197
www.hilberg-pasquero.com

**CELLAR SALES**
**PRE-BOOKED VISITS**
**ANNUAL PRODUCTION** 24,000 bottles
**HECTARES UNDER VINE** 6.50
**VITICULTURE METHOD** Certified Organic

Miclo Pasquero and Annette Hilberg's winery is by now one of Roero's historic producers. Their cellar is situated in Bricco Gatti, on a hill overlooking Priocca, surrounded by their private vineyards. These grow in white, silt and marl soils, and give rise to the territory's classic red grapes: Barbera, Brachetto and Nebbiolo. Their wines are highly original, proving traditional and personal at the same time, such that none of them adhere to the Roero DOC appellation. Their elegant, 2017 Barbera d'Alba Stella, balsamic and tannic, proves particularly pleasant and remarkably full. Their 2015 Nebbiolo d'Alba Superiore gives off rich notes of fruit while their 2017 Vareij (a 70 Brachetto/ 30 Barbera blend) delivers an intense, aromatic nose and beautifully balanced palate that is smooth without being sweet. Their full 2016 Nebbiolo d'Alba Sul Monte offers great body.

| | |
|---|---|
| ● Barbera d'Alba Stella '17 | ♏♏ 3* |
| ● Nebbiolo d'Alba Sul Monte '16 | ♏♏ 5 |
| ● Nebbiolo d'Alba Sup. '15 | ♏♏ 5 |
| ● Vareij '17 | ♏♏ 3 |
| ● Barbera d'Alba Sup. '15 | ♏ 5 |
| ● Barbera d'Alba '15 | ♎♎ 3* |
| ● Barbera d'Alba Sup. '14 | ♎♎ 5 |
| ● Barbera d'Alba Sup. '13 | ♎♎ 5 |
| ● Nebbiolo d'Alba Sul Monte '15 | ♎♎ 5 |
| ● Nebbiolo d'Alba Sup. '14 | ♎♎ 5 |
| ● Vareij '16 | ♎♎ 3 |
| ● Barbera d'Alba Stella '16 | ♎ 3 |
| ● Langhe Nebbiolo '14 | ♎ 4 |

# Ioppa

FRAZ. MAULETTA
VIA DELLE PALLOTTE, 10
28078 ROMAGNANO SESIA [NO]
TEL. +39 0163833079
www.viniioppa.it

**CELLAR SALES**
**PRE-BOOKED VISITS**
**ANNUAL PRODUCTION** 140,000 bottles
**HECTARES UNDER VINE** 20.50

Andrea, Luca and Marco represent the seventh generation of Ioppa family to work in viticulture, with Giorgio continuing to skillfully coordinate production. Their more than century-old winemaking tradition had a watershed moment in 2003, with the decision to build a new cellar and rethink the way wines were made. The change saw a focus on fermentation in steel at controlled temperatures and the attentive use of small wood casks and large barrels. For their prized Ghemme crus, Balsina and Santa Fè, they continue to prefer the more delicate Slavonian oak. Tre Bicchieri to their 2013 Ghemme Balsina, which richly expresses the full aromatic potential of North Piemonte Nebbiolo in quinine, gentian, licorice and iodine. The extraordinary palate is dense and offers exceptionally fine tannins. Their 2015 Coda Rossa raises the bar for how stimulating, refined and complex a Vespolina can be.

| | |
|---|---|
| ● Ghemme Balsina '13 | ♏♏♏ 6 |
| ● Colline Novaresi Nebbiolo '15 | ♏♏ 2* |
| ● Colline Novaresi Vespolina Coda Rossa '15 | ♏♏ 3* |
| ● Ghemme '13 | ♏♏ 4 |
| ⊙ Colline Novaresi Nebbiolo Rosato Rusin '17 | ♏ 2 |
| ● Colline Novaresi Vespolina Mauletta '13 | ♏ 3 |
| ○ San Grato Bianco | ♏ 2 |
| ● Colline Novaresi Vespolina Coda Rossa '13 | ♎♎ 3 |
| ● Ghemme '12 | ♎♎ 4 |
| ● Ghemme '11 | ♎♎ 4 |
| ● Ghemme Balsina '12 | ♎♎ 6 |
| ● Ghemme Santa Fé '12 | ♎♎ 6 |

## Isolabella della Croce

LOC. SARACCHI
REGIONE CAFFI, 3
14051 LOAZZOLO [AT]
TEL. +39 014487166
www.isolabelladellacroce.it

CELLAR SALES
PRE-BOOKED VISITS
ANNUAL PRODUCTION 90,000 bottles
HECTARES UNDER VINE 14.00

In 2001 the Isolabella della Croce family chose Italy's smallest appellation, Loazzolo, for their winery (it's just five hectares). Their vineyards are situated amidst the woods here at 500 meters above sea level, and grow in marly, calcareous soil. Various grapes are cultivated, both traditional and international, from Moscato to Chardonnay and Pinot Nero. They also have an estate in Calamandrana, in the area of Nizza, that's devoted primarily to Barbera. Some 15 decidedly modern wines are offered. Their 2017 Moscato d'Asti Canelli Valdiserre offers significant notes of aromatic herbs and tropical fruit with a pleasant and vibrant palate that balances acidity and sweetness. Tre Bicchieri for their 2014 Nizza Augusta, which delivers incredible freshness even in its notes of ripe red fruit. The 2014 Piemonte Pinot Nero Bricco del Falco shows quintessential hints of wild berries.

## Tenuta Langasco

FRAZ. MADONNA DI COMO, 10
12051 ALBA [CN]
TEL. +39 0173286972
www.tenutalangasco.it

CELLAR SALES
PRE-BOOKED VISITS
ANNUAL PRODUCTION 60,000 bottles
HECTARES UNDER VINE 22.00

Since 1979 the Sacco family have been looking after this truly picturesque estate. Their cellar is situated in an extraordinarily scenic area, on a hill facing the the towers of nearby Alba. Here they make wines with grapes from their private vineyards, from Langhe Arneis to Nebbiolo d'Alba, Moscato d'Asti. There's also an interesting Langhe Favorita, a Brachetto and Dolcetto Madonna di Como (which includes a 'cru', their Vigna Miclet). The repeated strength and consistency of their proposals attests to the winery's gravitas. Their austere red 2017 Dolcetto d'Alba Vigna Miclet opens with quinine and tar notes, moves to sublime dark fruit and ends with a spicy finish. The fine marriage of acidity, freshness and tannic extraction gives their 2015 Langhe Saccorosso a truly pleasant palate. Their 2016 Barbera d'Alba Vigna Madonna di Como proves ready to drink with creamy, satisfying red fruit.

| | |
|---|---|
| ● Nizza Augusta '14 | ♟♟♟ 4* |
| ○ Moscato d'Asti Canelli Valdiserre '17 | ♟♟ 3* |
| ● Piemonte Pinot Nero Bricco del Falco '14 | ♟♟ 5 |
| ● Barbera d'Asti Sup. Serena '15 | ♟♟ 4 |
| ○ Piemonte Sauvignon '17 | ♟ 3 |
| ● Barbera d'Asti Sup. Nizza Augusta '13 | ♟♟ 5 |
| ● Barbera d'Asti Sup. Serena '14 | ♟♟ 4 |
| ● Barbera d'Asti Sup. Serena '13 | ♟♟ 4 |
| ○ Piemonte Chardonnay Solum '15 | ♟♟ 4 |
| ● Piemonte Pinot Nero Bricco del Falco '13 | ♟♟ 5 |
| ● Piemonte Pinot Nero Bricco del Falco '12 | ♟♟ 5 |
| ○ Piemonte Sauvignon Blanc '16 | ♟♟ 3 |

| | |
|---|---|
| ● Barbera d'Alba V. Madonna di Como '16 | ♟♟ 2* |
| ● Dolcetto d'Alba V. Miclet '17 | ♟♟ 3 |
| ● Langhe Saccorosso '15 | ♟♟ 4 |
| ● Barbera d'Alba Sortì '16 | ♟ 3 |
| ● Nebbiolo d'Alba Sorì Coppa '16 | ♟ 4 |
| ● Dolcetto d'Alba Madonna di Como V. Miclet '16 | ♟♟ 3* |
| ● Dolcetto d'Alba Madonna di Como V. Miclet '15 | ♟♟ 3* |
| ● Dolcetto d'Alba Madonna di Como V. Miclet '11 | ♟♟ 2* |
| ● Dolcetto d'Alba V. Miclet '13 | ♟♟ 3* |
| ● Nebbiolo d'Alba Sorì Coppa '13 | ♟♟ 4 |
| ● Nebbiolo d'Alba Sorì Coppa '11 | ♟♟ 4 |
| ● Nebbiolo d'Alba Sorì Coppa '08 | ♟♟ 3 |

# Ugo Lequio

VIA DEL MOLINO, 10
12057 NEIVE [CN]
TEL. +39 0173677224
www.ugolequio.it

**CELLAR SALES**
**PRE-BOOKED VISITS**
**ANNUAL PRODUCTION** 30,000 bottles
**HECTARES UNDER VINE**

Ugo Lequio is one of Gallina cru's most reliable and consistent interpreters. For more than thirty years he's been working grapes cultivated in one of Neive's most prized and noble crus. Their cellar is situated in Molino di Neive, where painstaking care is shown for the grapes supplied by trusted, veteran vine growers. Their production style calls for medium-long maceration and maturation in mid-sized, French oak barrels. Their wines are lush and extremely potent in their youth - they need time to soften their unbridled temperament. In addition to Barbaresco Gallina, which is also offered as a reserve, their selection includes wines made with Barbera, Dolcetto and Arneis. Their meaty, elegant 2015 Barbera d'Alba proves delicious, offering notes of raspberry and blackberry along with hints of cocoa and pepper. Creamy and powerful on the palate, it lengthens into a well-nuanced and flavorful finish. Fully-developed fruit and pronounced tannins characterize their 2015 Barbaresco Gallina.

| | |
|---|---|
| ● Barbera d'Alba Sup. V. Gallina '15 | 🍷🍷 4 |
| ● Barbaresco Gallina '15 | 🍷🍷 6 |
| ● Barbaresco Gallina '14 | 🍷🍷 6 |
| ● Barbaresco Gallina '13 | 🍷🍷 5 |
| ● Barbaresco Gallina '12 | 🍷🍷 5 |
| ● Barbaresco Gallina '11 | 🍷🍷 5 |
| ● Barbaresco Gallina '10 | 🍷🍷 5 |
| ● Barbaresco Gallina '08 | 🍷🍷 5 |
| ● Barbaresco Gallina Ris. '10 | 🍷🍷 6 |
| ● Barbaresco Gallina Ris. '07 | 🍷🍷 6 |
| ● Barbera d'Alba Sup. Gallina '12 | 🍷🍷 4 |
| ● Barbera d'Alba Sup. V. Gallina '14 | 🍷🍷 4 |
| ● Langhe Nebbiolo '15 | 🍷🍷 4 |

# Podere Macellio

VIA ROMA, 18
10014 CALUSO [TO]
TEL. +39 0119833511
www.erbaluce-bianco.it

**CELLAR SALES**
**PRE-BOOKED VISITS**
**ANNUAL PRODUCTION** 25,000 bottles
**HECTARES UNDER VINE** 3.50

The controlled appellation of Erbaluce di Caluso was established in 1967, when Renato Bianco had just begun making wines. This white grape is characterized by a tonifying acidity that makes for drinkable, approachable and pleasant wines. But Erbaluce is capable of aging well in the bottle, and can deliver even many years after vintage. Young Davide has joined management, but their approach hasn't changed: only steel is used for their perennially valid Podere Macellio, and a minimum of 10 years aging for their sumptuous Caluso Passito. The 2017 vintage brought problems for the Bianco family, or so it seems from their Erbaluce di Caluso, which doesn't offer its usual freshness. Simple and formally well-done, it comes across a bit soft and lacks some of the features that justify its fame. Their Extra Brut proves crisp and flows across the palate.

| | |
|---|---|
| ○ Erbaluce di Caluso '17 | 🍷🍷 2* |
| ○ Erbaluce di Caluso Extra Brut | 🍷🍷 3 |
| ○ Erbaluce di Caluso '16 | 🍷🍷🍷 2* |
| ○ Caluso Passito '09 | 🍷🍷 5 |
| ○ Caluso Passito '08 | 🍷🍷 5 |
| ○ Caluso Passito Ris. '04 | 🍷🍷 5 |
| ○ Caluso Passito Ris. '03 | 🍷🍷 5 |
| ○ Erbaluce di Caluso '15 | 🍷🍷 2* |
| ○ Erbaluce di Caluso '13 | 🍷🍷 2* |
| ○ Erbaluce di Caluso '12 | 🍷🍷 2* |
| ○ Erbaluce di Caluso '11 | 🍷🍷 2* |
| ○ Erbaluce di Caluso '10 | 🍷🍷 2* |

## Malabaila di Canale

via Madonna dei Cavalli, 93
12043 Canale [CN]
Tel. +39 017398381
www.malabaila.com

CELLAR SALES
PRE-BOOKED VISITS
ANNUAL PRODUCTION 100,000 bottles
HECTARES UNDER VINE 22.00
SUSTAINABLE WINERY

Founded in 1986, Malabaila di Canale relaunched the name and role of the Malabaila lineage, who've been operating as wine producers since the 13th century. Their vineyards comprise a single, contiguous tract of land within a larger, 100-hectare estate. In some cases these go back more than 60 years and grow in a loose, marly-sandy soil. Their wines are of a modern style, but attentive to express the characteristics of the territory as well. Their fresh, juicy 2016 Barbera d'Alba Giardino makes our finals offering notes of black fruit and aromatic herbs with a long forceful finish. Their austere 2014 Roero Castelletto Riserva, offering notes of forest underbrush and tea leaves, with slightly over-firm tannins that lead to an enduring and assertive finish, and their full 2017 Roero Arneis Pradvaj, richly fruited and pleasantly savory, are both well-made.

| | |
|---|---|
| ● Barbera d'Alba Giardino '16 | TT 2* |
| ○ Roero Arneis Pradvaj '17 | TT 3 |
| ● Roero Castelletto Ris. '14 | TT 4 |
| ● Barbera d'Alba Sup. Mezzavilla '15 | T 3 |
| ○ Langhe Favorita Donna Costanza '17 | T 2 |
| ○ Roero Arneis Le Tre '17 | T 3 |
| ● Barbera d'Alba Sup. Mezzavilla '14 | YY 3 |
| ○ Roero Arneis Le Tre '16 | YY 3 |
| ○ Roero Arneis Pradvaj '16 | YY 3* |
| ○ Roero Arneis Pradvaj '14 | YY 3* |
| ● Roero Bric Volta '13 | YY 3* |
| ● Roero Castelletto Ris. '13 | YY 4 |
| ● Roero Castelletto Ris. '12 | YY 4 |

## ★Malvirà

loc. Canova
via Case Sparse, 144
12043 Canale [CN]
Tel. +39 0173978145
www.malvira.com

CELLAR SALES
PRE-BOOKED VISITS
ACCOMMODATION AND RESTAURANT SERVICE
ANNUAL PRODUCTION 300,000 bottles
HECTARES UNDER VINE 42.00

Brothers Massimo and Roberto Damonte manage La Malvirà, one of Roero's major wineries, both in terms of quality and in terms of its important role in the territory. Their 42 hectares of vineyards include prestigious MGAs (geographic mentions) like Mombeltramo, Renesio, San Michele or Trinità, not to mention La Morra, which is used for their Barolo. Their wines stand for their typicity and for their ability to age well. Wines from their Trinità vineyard stood out during this year's tastings. Their 2014 Roero Trinità Riserva offers notes of spices and black fruit with a hint of aromatic herbs and a generally fruity, supple palate ending in a long, fresh finish. Their 2017 Roero Arneis S.S. Trinità gives off notes of almonds and sweet grapefruit followed by a juicy, savory palate. As usual, all of their proposals were well-made.

| | |
|---|---|
| ○ Roero Arneis S. S. Trinità '17 | TT 3* |
| ● Roero Trinità Ris. '14 | TT 5 |
| ● Barbera d'Alba '16 | TT 3 |
| ○ Roero Arneis Renesio '17 | TT 3 |
| ○ Roero Arneis V. Saglietto '16 | TT 3 |
| ● Roero Mombeltramo Ris. '14 | TT 5 |
| ● Roero Renesio Ris. '14 | TT 5 |
| ○ Roero Arneis '17 | T 2 |
| ● Roero Mombeltramo Ris. '11 | YYY 5 |
| ● Roero Mombeltramo Ris. '10 | YYY 5 |
| ● Roero Mombeltramo Ris. '05 | YYY 5 |
| ● Roero Renesio Ris. '05 | YYY 5 |
| ● Roero Sup. Mombeltramo '04 | YYY 5 |
| ● Roero Sup. Trinità '03 | YYY 4 |
| ● Roero Trinità Ris. '07 | YYY 5 |
| ● Roero V. Mombeltramo Ris. '12 | YYY 5 |

# Giovanni Manzone

VIA CASTELLETTO, 9
12065 MONFORTE D'ALBA [CN]
TEL. +39 017378114
www.manzonegiovanni.com

**CELLAR SALES**
**PRE-BOOKED VISITS**
**ANNUAL PRODUCTION** 45,000 bottles
**HECTARES UNDER VINE** 7.50
**SUSTAINABLE WINERY**

Mauro Manzone is getting more and more comfortable in his large and well-renovated farm manor, along with his father, Giovanni, while carrying forward a tradition that began almost a century ago. The estate, which is well-known thanks to crus like Castelletto and Gramolere, is situated a good elevation and surrounded by a large wooded area. The result is wines with nice, fresh acidity. Their approach calls for the use of wood barrels, though never invasively, of various ages and sizes, making for wines that are enjoyable even a few years after vintage. Their lively and bold Barbera d'Alba Le Ciliegie once again proves valid. Refined red fruit and viola petals permeate their 2014 Barolo Bricat, which despite the challenging vintage offers a sublimely balanced palate. Their slightly more rugged 2014 Gramolere proves equally delicious. Their 2012 Riserva del Barolo Gramolere welcomes with open, evolved aromas and a pulpy, velvety palate, while their 2016 Langhe Nebbiolo Il Crutin is delectably drinkable.

| | | |
|---|---|---|
| ● Barolo Bricat '14 | ▼▼ | 6 |
| ● Barolo Gramolere '14 | ▼▼ | 6 |
| ● Barbera d'Alba Sup. La Marchesa '15 | ▼▼ | 5 |
| ● Barolo Castelletto '14 | ▼▼ | 6 |
| ● Barolo Gramolere Ris. '12 | ▼▼ | 8 |
| ● Langhe Nebbiolo Il Crutin '16 | ▼▼ | 3 |
| ○ Langhe Rossese Bianco Rosserto '16 | ▼▼ | 3 |
| ● Barolo Bricat '05 | ♀♀♀ | 6 |
| ● Barolo Castelletto '09 | ♀♀♀ | 5 |
| ● Barolo Gramolere Ris. '05 | ♀♀♀ | 7 |
| ● Barolo Le Gramolere '04 | ♀♀♀ | 6 |
| ● Barolo Le Gramolere Ris. '01 | ♀♀♀ | 7 |
| ● Barolo Le Gramolere Ris. '00 | ♀♀♀ | 7 |
| ● Barolo Bricat '13 | ♀♀ | 6 |
| ● Barolo Castelletto '13 | ♀♀ | 6 |
| ● Barolo Gramolere '13 | ♀♀ | 6 |
| ● Barolo Gramolere Ris. '11 | ♀♀ | 8 |

# Paolo Manzone

LOC. MERIAME, 1
12050 SERRALUNGA D'ALBA [CN]
TEL. +39 0173613113
www.barolomeriame.com

**CELLAR SALES**
**PRE-BOOKED VISITS**
**ACCOMMODATION**
**ANNUAL PRODUCTION** 85,000 bottles
**HECTARES UNDER VINE** 10.00
**SUSTAINABLE WINERY**

Paolo Manzone's winery has witnessed splendid growth in terms of quality over recent years, starting with their Barolo of course. Paolo puts it like this: 'I simply decided to bottle fantastic wines, not just good, but the best in the area'. In this respect he's favored by extensive experience in enology and a cru like Meriame, which still isn't particularly famous but is blessed with an excellent position ranging from southwest to west. The cellar deserves a visit, thanks to their comfortable and elegant agritourism. THeir Barolo is offered in three versions: Meriame, a Serralunga d'Alba and, at times, a Riserva. It's their Riserva, this year the 2012, that once again deserves the highest marks. Offering licorice, raspberry and a hint of anise on the nose, it proves velvety soft on its rich palate. Their 2014 Meriame is spicy and their rather vegetal Barolo del Comune di Serralunga d'Alba proves a bit small, but well-proportioned with clear, focused aromas. Their 2016 Barbera d'Alba Superiore Fiorenza shows many signs of wood aging.

| | | |
|---|---|---|
| ● Barolo Ris. '12 | ▼▼ | 7 |
| ● Barolo del Comune di Serralunga d'Alba '14 | ▼▼ | 6 |
| ● Barolo Meriame '14 | ▼▼ | 7 |
| ● Langhe Rosso Luvi '16 | ▼▼ | 3 |
| ● Barbera d'Alba Sup. Fiorenza '16 | ▼ | 3 |
| ● Nebbiolo d'Alba Mirinè '16 | ▼ | 3 |
| ● Barolo Ris. '11 | ♀♀♀ | 7 |
| ● Barbera d'Alba Sup. Fiorenza '15 | ♀♀ | 3 |
| ● Barbera d'Alba Sup. Fiorenza '14 | ♀♀ | 3 |
| ● Barolo del Comune di Serralunga d'Alba '13 | ♀♀ | 6 |
| ● Barolo del Comune di Serralunga d'Alba '12 | ♀♀ | 6 |
| ● Barolo Meriame '13 | ♀♀ | 7 |
| ● Barolo Meriame '12 | ♀♀ | 7 |
| ● Langhe Rosso Luvì '15 | ♀♀ | 3 |

# Marcalberto

VIA PORTA SOTTANA, 9
12058 SANTO STEFANO BELBO [CN]
TEL. +39 0141844022
www.marcalberto.it

CELLAR SALES
PRE-BOOKED VISITS
ANNUAL PRODUCTION 30,000 bottles
HECTARES UNDER VINE 5.00

The Cane family continues along the path of excellence, investing in their winery's present and future prospects. Their most recent acquisition concerns an extraordinary press that allows for delicate and precise extraction that's perfect for maintaining the core properties of the grape. All this attention is aimed, of course, at a small selection of regional Metodo Classicos that, year after year, has been winning over the palates of qualified national and international tasters. This year's proposals are rich in character and distinguished by dynamism and originality. Replicating the top scores of last year for their 2012, their 2013 Millesimato stands out, delivering a complex, harmonious wine playing on multiple expressive notes. Their Rosé proves very well defined, and their Blanc de Blancs, generally not an easy type to produce, is particularly precise. Their Nature Senza Solfiti is appealing with continually evolving dynamics.

| | |
|---|---|
| ○ Marcalberto Extra Brut Millesimo2Mila13 M. Cl. '13 | ♟♟♟ 5 |
| ⊙ Marcalberto Brut Rosé M. Cl. | ♟♟ 4 |
| ○ Marcalberto Pas Dosé Blanc de Blancs M. Cl. | ♟♟ 4 |
| ○ Marcalberto Brut Sansannée M. Cl. | ♟♟ 4 |
| ○ Marcalberto Nature M. Cl. Senza Aggiunta di Solfiti | ♟♟ 6 |
| ○ Marcalberto Extra Brut Millesimo2Mila12 M. Cl. '12 | ♟♟♟ 5 |
| ⊙ Marcalberto Brut Rosé M. Cl. | ♟♟ 4 |
| ○ Marcalberto Brut Sansannée M. Cl. | ♟♟ 4 |
| ○ Marcalberto Nature M. Cl. Senza Aggiunta di Solfiti | ♟♟ 6 |
| ○ Marcalberto Pas Dosé Blanc de Blancs M. Cl. | ♟♟ 4 |

# Poderi Marcarini

P.ZZA MARTIRI, 2
12064 LA MORRA [CN]
TEL. +39 017350222
www.marcarini.it

CELLAR SALES
PRE-BOOKED VISITS
ACCOMMODATION
ANNUAL PRODUCTION 125,000 bottles
HECTARES UNDER VINE 20.00

Operational since the mid-19th century, Podere Marcarini is among La Morra's historic producers. Today it's being led by the sixth generation of family, availing itself of noteworthy plots in what can be considered the area's 'great crus', Brunate and La Serra, two areas that are close in geographic terms, but quite different when it comes to expression. Their selection isn't limited to Barolo. Indeed, recent years saw the Marchetti family purchase Poderi Sargentin in Neviglie, and Muschiadivino in Montaldo Roero, where Dolcetto, Barbera, Moscato and Arneis are also produced. The two Barolo they submitted this year show signs of a complicated 2014. Their Barolo Brunate gives off notes of quinine and tar with a stiff, austere palate, close-knit but with and acidic and savory grip. Hints of leather and pepper mark their 2014 Barolo La Serra, which proves a bit immature in tannins Their extremely lively 2016 Barbera d'Alba Ciabot Camerano has juice to sell with the support of pencil lead and cocoa.

| | |
|---|---|
| ● Barbera d'Alba Ciabot Camerano '16 | ♟♟ 3 |
| ● Barolo Brunate '14 | ♟♟ 7 |
| ● Barolo La Serra '14 | ♟♟ 7 |
| ● Barolo Brunate '05 | ♟♟♟ 6 |
| ● Barolo Brunate '03 | ♟♟♟ 6 |
| ● Barolo Brunate '01 | ♟♟♟ 6 |
| ● Barbera d'Alba Ciabot Camerano '12 | ♟♟ 3* |
| ● Barolo Brunate '13 | ♟♟ 7 |
| ● Barolo Brunate '12 | ♟♟ 7 |
| ● Barolo Brunate '11 | ♟♟ 6 |
| ● Barolo La Serra '13 | ♟♟ 7 |
| ● Barolo La Serra '12 | ♟♟ 7 |
| ● Barolo La Serra '10 | ♟♟ 6 |
| ○ Moscato d'Asti '15 | ♟♟ 2* |

# Marchesi Alfieri

P.ZZA ALFIERI, 28
14010 SAN MARTINO ALFIERI [AT]
TEL. +39 0141976015
www.marchesialfieri.it

CELLAR SALES
PRE-BOOKED VISITS
ACCOMMODATION
ANNUAL PRODUCTION 100,000 bottles
HECTARES UNDER VINE 21.00

The San Martino di San Germano sisters
have been running Marchesi Alfieri since
1985. 16 of their 21 hectares of vineyards
host Barbera, with some going back 80
years. The rest are made up of Grignolino,
Pinot Nero and Nebbiolo. Their selection,
which is dedicated entirely to red wines
(with the exception of a Metodo Classico
Blanc de Noir sparkler made with Pinot
Nero) pursues territorial identity along with
elegance and complexity. Among the best of
its kind, their 2015 Barbera d'Asti Superiore
Alfiera has notes of wild berries, especially
blackberry, and Mediterranean scrub
leading to a fresh, crunchy palate with a
long, grippy finish. Their 2016 Barbera
d'Asti La Tota offers fruit notes and
pepper nuances on a direct, savory and
flavorful palate, much as their well-made
2016 Monferrato Rosso Sostegno, a 70
Barbera/30 Pinot Nero blend, delivers fruit
and fullness.

| | | |
|---|---|---|
| ● Barbera d'Asti Sup. Alfiera '15 | 🍷🍷 | 5 |
| ● Barbera d'Asti La Tota '16 | 🍷🍷 | 3 |
| ● M.to Rosso Sostegno '16 | 🍷🍷 | 2* |
| ○ Blanc de Noir Extra Brut M. Cl. '14 | 🍷 | 5 |
| ● Piemonte Grignolino Sansoero '17 | 🍷 | 3 |
| ● Terre Alfieri Nebbiolo Costaquaglia '15 | 🍷 | 4 |
| ● Barbera d'Asti Sup. Alfiera '07 | 🍷🍷🍷 | 5 |
| ● Barbera d'Asti Sup. Alfiera '05 | 🍷🍷🍷 | 5 |
| ● Barbera d'Asti Sup. Alfiera '01 | 🍷🍷🍷 | 5 |
| ● Barbera d'Asti Sup. Alfiera '00 | 🍷🍷🍷 | 5 |
| ● Barbera d'Asti La Tota '15 | 🍷🍷 | 3 |
| ● Barbera d'Asti La Tota '13 | 🍷🍷 | 3* |
| ● Barbera d'Asti Sup. Alfiera '14 | 🍷🍷 | 5 |
| ● Barbera d'Asti Sup. Alfiera '13 | 🍷🍷 | 5 |
| ● Piemonte Pinot Nero San Germano '15 | 🍷🍷 | 5 |
| ● Terre Alfieri Nebbiolo Costa Quaglia '13 | 🍷🍷 | 4 |

# ★Marchesi di Barolo

VIA ROMA, 1
12060 BAROLO [CN]
TEL. +39 0173564400
www.marchesibarolo.com

CELLAR SALES
PRE-BOOKED VISITS
RESTAURANT SERVICE
ANNUAL PRODUCTION 1,500,000 bottles
HECTARES UNDER VINE 201.00

A historical legacy of more than 150 years
and a continued desire to improve serve as
the foundation of this marvelous brand.
Today Marchesi di Barolo, who were among
the first to bottle the wine, is being led by
Anna and Ernesto Abbona (though they also
have the crucial support of their daughter
Valentina, an increasingly central figure in
promoting their wines the world over). Their
scenic cellars are situated within Castello
Falletti, a mecca for wine lovers, while their
vineyards span some 200 hectares of
terrain, including the gems Barolo Cannubi,
Costa di Rose and Sarmassa. Tre Bicchieri
for their 2014 Barolo Cannubi, winning with
its austere profile, airy aromas and
excellently pulpy palate for the vintage. It
presents exquisite tannins, intense yet
assertive and well-modulated, and an
enduring, energetic finish. Their other Barolo
also hit close to the bullseye, starting with
their peppery, savory 2014 Sarmassa. Their
meaty 2015 Barbaresco Serragrilli delivers
ripe red fruit and a long, warm finish.

| | | |
|---|---|---|
| ● Barolo Cannubi '14 | 🍷🍷🍷 | 8 |
| ● Barbaresco Serragrilli '15 | 🍷🍷 | 6 |
| ● Barbera d'Alba Peiragal '16 | 🍷🍷 | 5 |
| ● Barolo Coste di Rose '14 | 🍷🍷 | 8 |
| ● Barolo del Comune di Barolo '14 | 🍷🍷 | 8 |
| ● Barolo Sarmassa '14 | 🍷🍷 | 8 |
| ● Barolo Cannubi '12 | 🍷🍷🍷 | 8 |
| ● Barolo Cannubi '11 | 🍷🍷🍷 | 8 |
| ● Barolo Cannubi '10 | 🍷🍷🍷 | 8 |
| ● Barolo Sarmassa '09 | 🍷🍷🍷 | 8 |
| ● Barolo Sarmassa '08 | 🍷🍷🍷 | 7 |
| ● Barolo Sarmassa '07 | 🍷🍷🍷 | 7 |
| ● Barolo Cannubi '13 | 🍷🍷 | 8 |
| ● Barolo Coste di Rose '13 | 🍷🍷 | 8 |
| ● Barolo Sarmassa '13 | 🍷🍷 | 8 |

## Marchesi Incisa della Rocchetta

VIA ROMA, 66
14030 ROCCHETTA TANARO [AT]
TEL. +39 0141644647
www.marchesiincisawines.it

**CELLAR SALES**
**PRE-BOOKED VISITS**
**ACCOMMODATION AND RESTAURANT SERVICE**
**ANNUAL PRODUCTION** 80,000 bottles
**HECTARES UNDER VINE** 17.00

The Incisa della Rocchetta family's winery is one of Asti's historic producers. Their vineyards, situated on the hills that surround Rocchetta Tanaro and in the natural park, are characterized by sandy clay soil. Primarily Barbera is cultivated, along with Grignolino, Pinot Nero (cultivated here since the late 19th century) and Merlot. In addition to the wines made from these plots, their offer wines from other denominations, like Barolo, Roero Arneis and Moscato d'Asti, making for a selection of modern, well-crafted, close-focused wines. Their excellent 2016 Barbera d'Asti Superiore Sant'Emiliano offers fruity notes of blackberry and currant shaded by forest underbrush on a nice tight, enduring palate and a pleasant, juicy finish. Their fresh, supple 2017 Barbera d'Asti Valmorena plays on its fruit, while their 2017 Grignolino d'Asti gives off a nose of rose and aromatic herbs with spicy hints of curcuma and ginger, proving grippy and well-structured.

| | |
|---|---|
| ● Barbera d'Asti Sup. Sant' Emiliano '16 | 🍷🍷 5 |
| ● Barbera d'Asti Valmorena '17 | 🍷🍷 3 |
| ● Grignolino d'Asti '17 | 🍷🍷 3 |
| ● Piemonte Pinot Nero Marchese Leopoldo '15 | 🍷 5 |
| ● Barbera d'Asti Sup. Sant' Emiliano '15 | 🍷🍷🍷 5 |
| ● Barbera d'Asti Sup. Sant'Emiliano '14 | 🍷🍷 5 |
| ● Barbera d'Asti Valmorena '16 | 🍷🍷 3 |
| ● Barbera d'Asti Valmorena '14 | 🍷🍷 3* |
| ● Grignolino d'Asti '16 | 🍷🍷 3 |
| ● Grignolino d'Asti '15 | 🍷🍷 3 |
| ● Piemonte Pinot Nero Barbera Rollone '16 | 🍷🍷 3 |
| ● Piemonte Pinot Nero Marchese Leopoldo '14 | 🍷🍷 5 |

## Mario Marengo

LOC. SERRA DENARI, 2A
12064 LA MORRA [CN]
TEL. +39 017350115
marengo1964@libero.it

**CELLAR SALES**
**PRE-BOOKED VISITS**
**ANNUAL PRODUCTION** 38,000 bottles
**HECTARES UNDER VINE** 7.00
**SUSTAINABLE WINERY**

Marco Marengo leads the small but thriving Langhe winery that bears the name of his father, Mario. Already back in 1899 they were making the first bottles of Barolo. Their seven hectares of private vineyards in La Morra and Bricco delle Viole (in Barolo) are looked after with painstaking care. The style is deliberately modern. Short fermentation in vertical macerators, and intense but well-dosed extraction are aimed at bringing out the strong, decisive characters of the vineyards and terroir, making for wines of great character and personality. Their 2016 Barbera d'Alba Vigna Pugnane has a lovely personality that progresses steadily and enlivened by aromas of dark fruit. Its tenacious palate proves dry, well-sustained, ending incisively on orange peel and almond. Their 2014 Barolo Brunate also appears in the final. Despite being a bit tight-knit from the intense severity of tannins, it offers great overall energy and a good spicy profile.

| | |
|---|---|
| ● Barbera d'Alba V. Pugnane '16 | 🍷🍷 3* |
| ● Barolo Bricco delle Viole '14 | 🍷🍷 6 |
| ● Barolo Brunate '14 | 🍷🍷 7 |
| ● Barolo '14 | 🍷🍷 5 |
| ● Nebbiolo d'Alba Valmaggiore '16 | 🍷🍷 4 |
| ● Barolo Brunate '12 | 🍷🍷🍷 7 |
| ● Barolo Brunate '11 | 🍷🍷🍷 7 |
| ● Barolo Brunate '09 | 🍷🍷🍷 6 |
| ● Barolo Brunate '07 | 🍷🍷🍷 6 |
| ● Barolo Brunate '06 | 🍷🍷🍷 6 |
| ● Barolo '13 | 🍷🍷 5 |
| ● Barolo Bricco delle Viole '13 | 🍷🍷 6 |
| ● Barolo Bricco delle Viole '12 | 🍷🍷 6 |
| ● Barolo Brunate '13 | 🍷🍷 7 |

# Claudio Mariotto

S.DA PER SAREZZANO, 29
15057 TORTONA [AL]
TEL. +39 0131868500
www.claudiomariotto.it

CELLAR SALES
PRE-BOOKED VISITS
ANNUAL PRODUCTION 100,000 bottles
HECTARES UNDER VINE 32.00

Claudio Mariotto is part of that class of talented producers who are capable of presenting outstanding wines each year. But it's when a season proves difficult in terms of climate that his management skills in the vineyard and the cellar emerge. His wines are a guarantee, always exemplary and never standardized or homologated. Claudio's signature style can be described as elegant and long-lived. They are peculiar characteristics that we find year after year in masterly interpretations, of Timorasso and Babera and, years later, in precious vertical tastings. Their dream team opens with a great Pitasso, whose complex, subtle nose offers flint, citrus and a mineral vein on a rich, intense palate of vibrant acidity with an enduring finish. Their Cavallina and Derthona share an intense and elegant nose and while both prove rich and fresh on the palate, the Cavallina enters more smoothly. Their Poggio del Rosso has a splendid nose-palate balance.

| | | |
|---|---|---|
| ○ Colli Tortonesi Timorasso Cavallina '16 | 🍷🍷 | 5 |
| ○ Colli Tortonesi Timorasso Derthona '16 | 🍷🍷 | 5 |
| ○ Colli Tortonesi Timorasso Pitasso '16 | 🍷🍷 | 6 |
| ● Colli Tortonesi Barbera Territorio '16 | 🍷🍷 | 3 |
| ● Colli Tortonesi Barbera Vhò '15 | 🍷🍷 | 4 |
| ● Colli Tortonesi Croatina Montemirano '15 | 🍷🍷 | 4 |
| ● Colli Tortonesi Poggio del Rosso '15 | 🍷🍷 | 5 |
| ○ L'indagato | 🍷🍷 | 3 |
| ○ Colli Tortonesi Timorasso Pitasso '13 | 🍷🍷🍷 | 6 |
| ○ Colli Tortonesi Timorasso Pitasso '12 | 🍷🍷🍷 | 6 |
| ○ Colli Tortonesi Timorasso Pitasso '08 | 🍷🍷🍷 | 5 |
| ○ Colli Tortonesi Timorasso Derthona '15 | 🏆🍷 | 5 |
| ○ Colli Tortonesi Timorasso Derthona Cavallina '15 | 🏆🍷 | 5 |
| ○ Colli Tortonesi Timorasso Derthona Pitasso '15 | 🏆🍷 | 6 |

# Marsaglia

VIA MADAMA MUSSONE, 2
12050 CASTELLINALDO [CN]
TEL. +39 0173213048
www.cantinamarsaglia.it

CELLAR SALES
PRE-BOOKED VISITS
ANNUAL PRODUCTION 80,000 bottles
HECTARES UNDER VINE 15.00

Marina and Emilio Marsaglia, along with their children Enrico and Monica, manage this family-run winery (Est. 1900). Their vineyards are situated entirely in the municipality of Castellinaldo where the terrain varies from sandy (in the area near Canale, where their most famous cru are located) to compact (as you get closer to Castagnito). Arneis, Barbera, Brachetto, Dolcetto and Nebbiolo are all cultivated, giving rise to a selection centered on balance and pleasantness. Their juicy 2015 Barbera d'Alba Superiore Castellinaldo makes our finals. It offers expected notes of black fruit and wet earth, well-supported by taut, enduring acidity. Their 2014 Roero Brich d'America offers rich fruit and assertive, slightly over-developed tannins. Their 2105 Nebbiolo d'Alba San Pietro leans more on notes of Mediterranean scrub. Their fresh, tight 2017 Roero Arneis Serramiana, and rich, full, fruity 2016 Armonia round out their quality proposals.

| | | |
|---|---|---|
| ● Barbera d'Alba Sup. Castellinaldo '15 | 🍷🍷 | 4 |
| ● Nebbiolo d'Alba San Pietro '15 | 🍷🍷 | 3 |
| ○ Roero Arneis Armonia '16 | 🍷🍷 | 3 |
| ○ Roero Arneis Serramiana '17 | 🍷🍷 | 3 |
| ● Roero Brich d'America '14 | 🍷🍷 | 4 |
| ● Barbera d'Alba S. Cristoforo '17 | 🍷 | 3 |
| ● Barbera d'Alba Castellinaldo '11 | 🏆🏆 | 4 |
| ● Barbera d'Alba S. Cristoforo '16 | 🏆🏆 | 3 |
| ● Barbera d'Alba S. Cristoforo '15 | 🏆🏆 | 3 |
| ● Nebbiolo d'Alba '12 | 🏆🏆 | 3 |
| ● Nebbiolo d'Alba San Pietro '14 | 🏆🏆 | 3 |
| ○ Roero Arneis Serramiana '16 | 🏆🏆 | 3 |
| ○ Roero Arneis Serramiana '14 | 🏆🏆 | 3 |
| ● Roero Brich d'America '12 | 🏆🏆 | 4 |
| ● Roero Brich d'America '11 | 🏆🏆 | 4 |

## ★Franco M. Martinetti

c.so TURATI, 14
10128 TORINO
TEL. +39 0118395937
www.francomartinetti.it

**PRE-BOOKED VISITS**
**ANNUAL PRODUCTION** 140,000 bottles
**HECTARES UNDER VINE** 5.00

Fascinated by Piedmont's red grapes, 'wine-grower' Franco Martinetti has explored them in depth, from Nebbiolo to Freisa and Croatina, with a love for Barbera that's never wavered. But don't think that their whites take a back seat, considering wines as celebrated as his ageworthy Gavi Minaia and rich Colli Tortonesi Timorasso Martin. Their selection is consistently outstanding, without exception, even in their more approachable wines like the highly praised Barbera d'Asti Bric dei Banditi. Their grapes are primarily supplied by qualified and well-established vine growers. Their particularly full, balsamic 2016 Barbera d'Asti Bric dei Banditi, is not only a pure expression of the cultivar, it also serves as the prototype of pleasant drinkability for straight-forward, approachable wines. Their exhilaratingly drinkable 2016 Montruc offers notes of medicinal herbs while their Sul Bric, more wrapped in wood, proves intriguing.

| | |
|---|---|
| ● Barbera d'Asti Bric dei Banditi '16 | ♥♥ 4 |
| ● Barbera d'Asti Sup. Montruc '16 | ♥♥ 6 |
| ● Barolo Marasco Ris. '12 | ♥♥ 8 |
| ○ Colli Tortonesi Timorasso Martin '16 | ♥♥ 6 |
| ○ Gavi Minaia '17 | ♥♥ 5 |
| ● M.to Rosso Sul Bric '16 | ♥♥ 6 |
| ● Barolo Marasco '14 | ♥ 8 |
| ○ Gavi del Comune di Gavi '17 | ♥ 4 |
| ● Barbera d'Asti Sup. Montruc '06 | ♀♀♀ 5 |
| ● Barolo Marasco '01 | ♀♀♀ 7 |
| ○ Colli Tortonesi Timorasso Martin '12 | ♀♀♀ 6 |
| ○ Gavi Minaia '14 | ♀♀♀ 5 |
| ● M.to Rosso Sul Bric '10 | ♀♀♀ 6 |
| ● M.to Rosso Sul Bric '09 | ♀♀♀ 6 |

## ★Bartolo Mascarello

VIA ROMA, 15
12060 BAROLO [CN]
TEL. +39 017356125

**CELLAR SALES**
**PRE-BOOKED VISITS**
**ANNUAL PRODUCTION** 30,000 bottles
**HECTARES UNDER VINE** 5.00

Bartolo Mascarello has always pursued the purity of Nebbiolo and respect for Langhe's enological tradition. It's a mission that has brought them international fame, thanks to Bartolo, a bona fide wine intellectual endowed with a social sensibility and broad-mindedness that often brought illustrious guests, like Nuto Revelli, Giulio Einaudi, Giorgio Bocca and Primo Levi to his living room. His daughter Maria Teresa is forging ahead, with equal awareness and care, continually crafting a superior Barolo. To round out their selection they offer smaller quantities of Langhe Freisa, Nebbiolo, Barbera and Dolcetto d'Alba. The very elegant, traditional nose opens beautifully with clear, focused tobacco and licorice followed by classic notes of red fruit and just a bit of alcohol. The rich and powerful palate of their excellent 2014 Barolo offers tight-knit tannins and remarkable pulp.

| | |
|---|---|
| ● Barolo '14 | ♥♥ 8 |
| ● Barolo '13 | ♀♀♀ 8 |
| ● Barolo '12 | ♀♀♀ 8 |
| ● Barolo '11 | ♀♀♀ 8 |
| ● Barolo '10 | ♀♀♀ 8 |
| ● Barolo '09 | ♀♀♀ 8 |
| ● Barolo '07 | ♀♀♀ 8 |
| ● Barolo '06 | ♀♀♀ 8 |
| ● Barolo '05 | ♀♀♀ 8 |
| ● Barolo '01 | ♀♀♀ 8 |

# ★Giuseppe Mascarello e Figlio

VIA BORGONUOVO, 108
12060 MONCHIERO [CN]
TEL. +39 0173792126
www.mascarello1881.com

CELLAR SALES
PRE-BOOKED VISITS
ANNUAL PRODUCTION 60,000 bottles
HECTARES UNDER VINE 13.50

At the height of Langhe's classic style stands a winery founded in the late 19th century and that has since mastered the purest, most integrated form of Barolo. Their grapes are cultivated in splendid vineyards and then worked in large Slavonian oak barrels. Their most prized wine is Monprivato, which began being produced in 1970 in a six-hectare plot. In certain vintages, though rarely, the same plot gives rise to their superb Riserva Ca' d'Morissio. Mauro Mascarello's Barolo is enriched by lesser quantities of grapes cultivated in their scenic Santo Stefano di Perno vineyard and their prized Villero cru, both of which give rise to grapes of great typicity. Two of their 2013 interpretations are truly stellar. Their fruity Monprivato proves the more expansive and complex with a well-structured palate that progresses splendidly. Their slightly more spicy Villero offers less body, but instead delivers rare length and enveloping tannins. Their extremely classic Perno Vigna Santo Stefano, with very noticeable alcohol, is just slightly less fresh.

| | | |
|---|---|---|
| ● Barolo Monprivato '13 | ♟♟♟ | 8 |
| ● Barolo Perno V. Santo Stefano '13 | ♟♟ | 8 |
| ● Barolo Villero '13 | ♟♟ | 8 |
| ● Barolo Monprivato '12 | ♛♛♛ | 8 |
| ● Barolo Monprivato '11 | ♛♛♛ | 8 |
| ● Barolo Monprivato '10 | ♛♛♛ | 8 |
| ● Barolo Monprivato '09 | ♛♛♛ | 8 |
| ● Barolo Monprivato '08 | ♛♛♛ | 8 |
| ● Barolo Monprivato '01 | ♛♛♛ | 8 |
| ● Barolo Perno V. Santo Stefano '12 | ♛♛ | 8 |
| ● Barolo Perno V. Santo Stefano '11 | ♛♛ | 8 |
| ● Barolo Perno V. Santo Stefano '10 | ♛♛ | 8 |
| ● Barolo Villero '12 | ♛♛ | 8 |
| ● Barolo Villero '11 | ♛♛ | 8 |
| ● Barolo Villero '10 | ♛♛ | 8 |
| ● Barolo Villero '09 | ♛♛ | 8 |

# ★Vigneti Massa

P.ZZA G. CAPSONI, 10
15059 MONLEALE [AL]
TEL. +39 013180302
vignetimassa@libero.it

CELLAR SALES
PRE-BOOKED VISITS
ANNUAL PRODUCTION 120,000 bottles
HECTARES UNDER VINE 25.00
SUSTAINABLE WINERY

Walter Massa is a fundamental figure for the entire district, both in terms of his rediscovering and reevaluating Timorasso through modern winemaking techniques, and in terms of how the cultivar has been presented to the public, with Walter serving as its principal spokesperson. And he's managed this without neglecting his work in the countryside and in the cellar. His production approach gives rise to complex wines that are never easy to taste, nor approachable. They are extremely long-lived, though they offer their best after lengthy aging. Their intense, refined Sterpi opens in a dance of lovely anise, grapefruit and hints of hydrocarbons, while its mighty, full-bodied palate ends in an enduring finish. The intense nose of their Montecitorio offers dried herbs and tobacco with a mineral vein, while its complex palate ends in pronounced alcohol. Their Derthona gives off composite notes of medicinal herbs, citrus and mineral tones leading to an excellently structured, full-bodied palate that ends in a sophisticated finish.

| | | |
|---|---|---|
| ○ Derthona Sterpi '16 | ♟♟♟ | 6 |
| ○ Derthona '16 | ♟♟ | 5 |
| ○ Montecitorio '16 | ♟♟ | 6 |
| ● Colli Tortonesi Barbera Monleale '14 | ♟♟ | 6 |
| ● Pietra del Gallo '17 | ♟ | 3 |
| ● Sentieri '17 | ♟ | 4 |
| ○ Colli Tortonesi Bianco Costa del Vento '05 | ♛♛♛ | 7 |
| ○ Colli Tortonesi Timorasso Sterpi '08 | ♛♛♛ | 7 |
| ○ Costa del Vento '15 | ♛♛♛ | 6 |
| ○ Costa del Vento '12 | ♛♛♛ | 6 |
| ○ Derthona '09 | ♛♛♛ | 5 |
| ○ Montecitorio '11 | ♛♛♛ | 6 |
| ○ Montecitorio '10 | ♛♛♛ | 6 |
| ○ Sterpi '13 | ♛♛♛ | 6 |

## ★Massolino

P.ZZA CAPPELLANO, 8
12050 SERRALUNGA D'ALBA [CN]
TEL. +39 0173613138
www.massolino.it

CELLAR SALES
PRE-BOOKED VISITS
ANNUAL PRODUCTION 257,000 bottles
HECTARES UNDER VINE 36.00
SUSTAINABLE WINERY

Parafada, Margheria and Vigna Rionda are
situated on the western side of Serralunga
d'Alba. Parussi is in Castiglione Falletto.
These are the prized crus that give rise to
the Massolino family's grapes. They've
been active producers in the region since
1896, and today they make wines that
privilege texture and tannic presence,
qualities the lengthen their Barolos. They
also make wines with Barbera, Dolcetto,
Chardonnay and Moscato, making for a
solid and consistent selection that also has
vision and a future. Their 2012 Vigna
Rionda just misses Tre Bicchieri. Fruit steps
back slightly allowing fascinating notes of
sunny herbs, pepper and hints of
Mediterranean scrub to enliven it, but its
austere, refined palate but the tannins are
a bit too present at this stage. Their
excellent 2014 Barolo Margheria offers a
fragrant, dynamic profile bearing notes of
forest underbrush and just the amount
amount of spice, with a vital, savory finish.
Their weightier 2014 Barolo Parafada is
richer, while the relaxed 2015 Barbera
d'Alba Gisep proves delicious.

| | |
|---|---|
| ● Barolo Margheria '14 | ♟♟ 8 |
| ● Barolo Parafada '14 | ♟♟ 8 |
| ● Barolo Vigna Rionda Ris. '12 | ♟♟ 8 |
| ● Barbera d'Alba Gisep '15 | ♟♟ 5 |
| ● Barolo '14 | ♟♟ 5 |
| ● Dolcetto d'Alba '17 | ♟♟ 2* |
| ● Langhe Nebbiolo '16 | ♟♟ 3 |
| ○ Langhe Chardonnay '16 | ♟ 3 |
| ● Barolo Margheria '05 | ♟♟♟ 7 |
| ● Barolo Parafada '11 | ♟♟♟ 8 |
| ● Barolo Vigna Rionda Ris. '11 | ♟♟♟ 8 |
| ● Barolo Vigna Rionda Ris. '10 | ♟♟♟ 8 |
| ● Barolo Vigna Rionda Ris. '08 | ♟♟♟ 8 |
| ● Barolo Vigna Rionda Ris. '06 | ♟♟♟ 8 |
| ● Barolo Vigna Rionda Ris. '05 | ♟♟♟ 8 |

## Tiziano Mazzoni

VIA ROMA, 73
28010 CAVAGLIO D'AGOGNA [NO]
TEL. +39 3488200635
www.vinimazzoni.it

CELLAR SALES
PRE-BOOKED VISITS
ANNUAL PRODUCTION 20,000 bottles
HECTARES UNDER VINE 4.50
SUSTAINABLE WINERY

Tiziano Mazzoni's winery is turning 20,
with Tiziano and his family overseeing all
stages of production with an artisan's care.
In the countryside and in the cellar they
are supported by an expert staff. The
results are commendable, such that two of
their Ghemmes (Mazzoni and Livelli) and
their Colline Novaresi Nebbiolo del
Monteregio are among the best of their
kind. Their Vespolina Il Ricetto is also
highly enjoyable. Particular attention is
shown to protect the environment and so
neither pesticides nor weedkillers are
used. This year's tasting confirm it as a
strong, careful winery capable of
producing quality even with its most
economical wines. Their 2016 Nebbiolo del
Monteregio, characterized by notes of
rhubarb, tobacco and iodine, proves an
excellent example of balance and delicious
drinkability. Both of their Ghemme offer
great vitality and personality.

| | |
|---|---|
| ● Ghemme dei Mazzoni '14 | ♟♟ 5 |
| ● Colline Novaresi Nebbiolo del Monteregio '16 | ♟♟ 3 |
| ● Colline Novaresi Vespolina Il Ricetto '17 | ♟♟ 3 |
| ● Elia '15 | ♟♟ 3 |
| ● Ghemme Ai Livelli '13 | ♟♟ 6 |
| ○ Iris | ♟♟ 3 |
| ● Ghemme dei Mazzoni '12 | ♟♟♟ 5 |
| ● Colline Novaresi Nebbiolo del Monteregio '15 | ♟♟ 3 |
| ● Colline Novaresi Nebbiolo del Monteregio '13 | ♟♟ 3 |
| ● Ghemme ai Livelli '11 | ♟♟ 6 |
| ● Ghemme dei Mazzoni '13 | ♟♟ 5 |
| ● Ghemme dei Mazzoni '11 | ♟♟ 5 |

# La Mesma

FRAZ. MONTEROTONDO, 7
15066 GAVI [AL]
TEL. +39 0143342012
www.lamesma.it

**CELLAR SALES**
**PRE-BOOKED VISITS**
**ACCOMMODATION**
**ANNUAL PRODUCTION** 52,000 bottles
**HECTARES UNDER VINE** 25.00
**VITICULTURE METHOD** Certified Organic

La Mesma's vineyards are situated in Tassarolo and Monterotondo. Different terrain types confer peculiar characteristics to their grapes. In Tassarolo ferritization has made for red earth, which gives rise to fruity wines that are rich in flavor. Monterotondo's marl, sandstone soil bestows minerality. These qualities can be found across their seven wines made with Cortese, stills, semi-sparkling wines and Metodo Classico sparklers. There's also a red blend of Barbera, Cabernet Sauvignon and Merlot. They send an unquestionably appealing trio to the finals. Their complex and intense Indo offers floral aromas over notes of white peach and a mineral base. Their refined, elegant Etichetta Nera opens on more vegetal notes that evolve into citrus and exotic fruit over lovely hints of minerals. The classic style of their Vigna della Rovere Verde finds expression in its intense, elegant nose and palate.

| | |
|---|---|
| ○ Gavi del Comune di Gavi Et. Nera '17 | ♥♥ 3* |
| ○ Gavi del Comune di Gavi Indi '17 | ♥♥ 4 |
| ○ Gavi V. della Rovere Verde Ris. '16 | ♥♥ 5 |
| ○ Gavi del Comune di Gavi Et. Gialla '17 | ♥♥ 3 |
| ○ Gavi V. della Rovere Verde Ris. '15 | ♥♥♥ 5 |
| ○ Gavi Brut M. Cl. '11 | ♀♀ 5 |
| ○ Gavi Brut M. Cl. '09 | ♀♀ 4 |
| ○ Gavi del Comune di Gavi Et. Gialla '16 | ♀♀ 2* |
| ○ Gavi del Comune di Gavi Et. Gialla '15 | ♀♀ 2* |
| ○ Gavi del Comune di Gavi Et. Gialla '14 | ♀♀ 2* |
| ○ Gavi del Comune di Gavi Et. Nera '16 | ♀♀ 3* |
| ○ Gavi V. della Rovere Verde Ris. '14 | ♀♀ 5 |
| ○ Gavi V. della Rovere Verde Ris. '13 | ♀♀ 3 |

# Moccagatta

S.DA RABAJÀ, 46
12050 BARBARESCO [CN]
TEL. +39 0173635228
www.moccagatta.eu

**CELLAR SALES**
**PRE-BOOKED VISITS**
**ANNUAL PRODUCTION** 65,000 bottles
**HECTARES UNDER VINE** 12.00
**SUSTAINABLE WINERY**

Skillful work in the vineyards and the use of small French oak casks in their lovely underground cellar are the two elements that define the Minuto brothers' winery. The arrival of children Martina and Stefano isn't making waves yet, if you don't consider an even more rigorous adherence to environmentally-friendly principles through the adoption of organic cultivation. Their four Barbarescos are just as dense and concentrated as their white Chardonnay Buschet is pure. Langhe Nebbiolo, Dolcetto and Barbera d'Alba round out a noteworthy selection. We only tried 2015 Barbaresco this year. Their modern (but not too modern) Bric Balin gives off rich spices on a background of red fruit and great, fresh body on the palate that expresses wood nicely without being too tannic. Both their Basarin and Cole evince unambiguous oak and should be laid down for quite some time to achieve the ideal balance of flavors.

| | |
|---|---|
| ● Barbaresco Bric Balin '15 | ♥♥ 6 |
| ● Barbaresco Basarin '15 | ♥ 6 |
| ● Barbaresco Cole '15 | ♥ 7 |
| ● Barbaresco Bric Balin '05 | ♀♀♀ 6 |
| ● Barbaresco Bric Balin '04 | ♀♀♀ 6 |
| ● Barbaresco Bric Balin '01 | ♀♀♀ 6 |
| ● Barbaresco Basarin '14 | ♀♀ 6 |
| ● Barbaresco Basarin '11 | ♀♀ 6 |
| ● Barbaresco Bric Balin '14 | ♀♀ 6 |
| ● Barbaresco Bric Balin '13 | ♀♀ 6 |
| ● Barbaresco Bric Balin '12 | ♀♀ 6 |
| ● Barbaresco Bric Balin '11 | ♀♀ 6 |
| ● Barbaresco Bric Balin '10 | ♀♀ 6 |
| ● Barbaresco Cole '12 | ♀♀ 7 |
| ● Barbaresco Cole '11 | ♀♀ 6 |

## Mauro Molino

FRAZ. ANNUNZIATA GANCIA, 111A
12064 LA MORRA [CN]
TEL. +39 017350814
www.mauromolino.com

CELLAR SALES
PRE-BOOKED VISITS
ANNUAL PRODUCTION 95,000 bottles
HECTARES UNDER VINE 12.00
SUSTAINABLE WINERY

The project started by hard-working Mauro Molino in 1979 is close to reaching its goal. His children Martina and Matteo are well-integrated and the cellar has been renovated and enlarged for efficiency and elegance. To close the circle they've produced an homage to the family's past, a new Barbera d'Asti called 'Leradici', a wine made possible by a recent purchase in the land of the family's ancestors, Costigliole d'Asti. Their Barolo maintains its modern style, rich in aromas of red fruit and oak, the result of short maceration and aging in small French casks. 2014 Nebbiolo grapes often resulted in wines that generally lack structure and require careful attention in the cellar to obtain harmony and balance. Molino's Barolo are particularly marked by wood and offer very little or no fruity aromas. Their elegant Bricco Luciani slightly dries the palate and their Conca gives off some fresh vegetal nuances.

## ★Monchiero Carbone

VIA SANTO STEFANO ROERO, 2
12043 CANALE [CN]
TEL. +39 017395568
www.monchierocarbone.com

CELLAR SALES
PRE-BOOKED VISITS
ANNUAL PRODUCTION 180,000 bottles
HECTARES UNDER VINE 25.00
SUSTAINABLE WINERY

For some years now Francesco and Lucrezia Monchiero's winery has been a leader among Roero's top producers. They offer a selection of wines that bring together expression of the territory with close-focused aromas, complexity and exemplary elegance. Their vineyards are situated primarily in Canale, including prestigious MGAs (geographic mentions) like Mombirone, Renesio or Sru, though they also have plots in Vezza d'Alba, Monteu Roero e Priocca. Monchiero Carbone's wines once again prove among the best in the Roero area. Tre Bicchieri for their 2017 Roero Arneis Cecu d'la Biunda, which gives off almonds, anise, yellow fruit and aromatic herbs, while its simultaneously savory, rich and well-structured palate offers both length and good acidity. Their splendid 2014 Roero Printi Riserva, elegant with notes of red fruit, spices and incense, delivers highly refined tannins and great drinkability, serves as a reminder that in Roero the 2014 vintage produced some very intriguing wines.

| | |
|---|---|
| ● Barolo Bricco Luciani '14 | 🍷🍷 6 |
| ● Barolo Conca '14 | 🍷🍷 7 |
| ● Barolo La Serra '14 | 🍷 7 |
| ● Barbera d'Alba V. Gattere '00 | 🍷🍷🍷 6 |
| ● Barolo Gallinotto '11 | 🍷🍷🍷 6 |
| ● Barolo Gallinotto '03 | 🍷🍷🍷 6 |
| ● Barolo Gallinotto '01 | 🍷🍷🍷 6 |
| ● Barolo V. Conca '00 | 🍷🍷🍷 7 |
| ● Barolo Bricco Luciani '13 | 🍷🍷 6 |
| ● Barolo Bricco Luciani '12 | 🍷🍷 6 |
| ● Barolo Conca '13 | 🍷🍷 7 |
| ● Barolo Gallinotto '13 | 🍷🍷 6 |
| ● Barolo La Serra '13 | 🍷🍷 7 |
| ● Barolo La Serra '12 | 🍷🍷 7 |

| | |
|---|---|
| ○ Roero Arneis Cecu d'la Biunda '17 | 🍷🍷🍷 3* |
| ● Roero Printi Ris. '14 | 🍷🍷 5 |
| ● Roero Srü '15 | 🍷🍷 4 |
| ● Barbera d'Alba MonBirone '15 | 🍷🍷 5 |
| ● Barbera d'Alba Pelisa '16 | 🍷🍷 2* |
| ○ Roero Arneis Recit '17 | 🍷🍷 2* |
| ○ Tamardi '17 | 🍷🍷 2* |
| ● Barbera d'Alba MonBirone '10 | 🍷🍷🍷 4* |
| ○ Roero Arneis Cecu d'la Biunda '16 | 🍷🍷🍷 3* |
| ● Roero Printi Ris. '12 | 🍷🍷🍷 5 |
| ● Roero Printi Ris. '11 | 🍷🍷🍷 5 |
| ● Roero Printi Ris. '10 | 🍷🍷🍷 5 |
| ● Roero Printi Ris. '09 | 🍷🍷🍷 5 |
| ● Roero Printi Ris. '07 | 🍷🍷🍷 5 |
| ● Roero Printi Ris. '06 | 🍷🍷🍷 5 |
| ● Roero Srü '06 | 🍷🍷🍷 3 |

# La Montagnetta

FRAZ. BRICCO CAPPELLO, 4
14018 ROATTO [AT]
TEL. +39 0141938343
www.lamontagnetta.com

**CELLAR SALES**
**PRE-BOOKED VISITS**
**ANNUAL PRODUCTION** 50,000 bottles
**HECTARES UNDER VINE** 10.00

La Montagnetta, a winery managed by
Domenico Capello, has in recent years
stood out as being among the few producers
to focus seriously on Freisa, which is used
in practically every possible way, from still
wines to sparkling, semi-sparkling wines
and rosés. Their vineyards are situated at
more than 250 meters above sea level, in
the municipalities of Roatto, San Paolo
Solbrito and Piovà Massaia, along the Val
Triversa hills. In addition to Freisa, they
cultivate Barbera, Bonarda, and small
quantities of Chardonnay, Sauvignon and
Viognier. Their highly aromatic 2014 La
Freisa d'Asti Superiore Bugianen presents
the vintage at its best. Its nose highlights
classic notes of pepper and its lean,
supple palate has lovely tension. Their
beautiful 2015 Barbera d'Asti Superiore
Piovà offers fresh notes of blackberry and
Mediterranean scrub along with rich fruit
and noteworthy acidity. Their approachable,
full-bodied 2017 Pi-Cit smells of drenched
earth and their 2017 Piemonte Bonarda
Insolita proves varietal and pleasant.

| | |
|---|---|
| ● Barbera d'Asti Pi Cit '17 | 🍷🍷 2* |
| ● Barbera d'Asti Sup. Piova '15 | 🍷🍷 4 |
| ● Freisa d'Asti Sup. Bugianen '14 | 🍷🍷 4 |
| ● Piemonte Bonarda Frizzante Insolita '17 | 🍷🍷 2* |
| ● Freisa d'Asti Frizzante I Ronchi '17 | 🍷 2 |
| ● Barbera d'Asti Pi-Cit '16 | 🍷🍷 2* |
| ● Barbera d'Asti Sup. Piovà '14 | 🍷🍷 4 |
| ● Barbera d'Asti Sup. Piovà '13 | 🍷🍷 4 |
| ● Freisa d'Asti Bugianen '15 | 🍷🍷 2* |
| ● Freisa d'Asti Sup. Bugianen '13 | 🍷🍷 2* |
| ● Piemonte Bonarda Frizzante Insolita '15 | 🍷🍷 2* |

# Montalbera

VIA MONTALBERA, 1
14030 CASTAGNOLE MONFERRATO [AT]
TEL. +39 0119433311
www.montalbera.it

**CELLAR SALES**
**PRE-BOOKED VISITS**
**ANNUAL PRODUCTION** 650,000 bottles
**HECTARES UNDER VINE** 175.00
**SUSTAINABLE WINERY**

Founded in the early 20th century,
Montalbera was transformed during the
1980s, when the Morando family decided
to begin acquiring new vineyards and grow
the producer into the regional leader it is
today. 82 hectares of Ruché are cultivated
on their Castagnole Monferrato estate,
along with Grignolino, Barbera and Viognier.
Castagnole Mongerrato is accompanied
by their plots in Langhe: Castiglione Tinella,
La Morra, Barbaresco and Neive. Their
wines are decidedly modern and exhibit
superior stylistic focus. Their prposals
perform very admirably. Their fresh,
unhesitating 2017 Ruché di Castagnole
Monferrato Laccento, releases rose, fruit
and hints of aromatic herbs, while their
simpler 2017 Ruché La Tradizione, proves
pleasant and juicy. Their 2016 Grignolino
d'Asti Lanfora offers oriental spices, red
fruit and a well-directed suite of tannins.
And Tre Bicchieri for their richly fruited
2015 Barbera d'Asti Nuda, which is
complex, multifaceted and long.

| | |
|---|---|
| ● Barbera d'Asti Nuda '15 | 🍷🍷🍷 5 |
| ● Grignolino d'Asti Lanfora '16 | 🍷🍷 3* |
| ● Ruché di Castagnole M.to La Tradizione '17 | 🍷🍷 3* |
| ● Ruché di Castagnole M.to Laccento '17 | 🍷🍷 4 |
| ● Barbera d'Asti Sup. Lequilibrio '15 | 🍷🍷 3 |
| ● Barbera d'Asti Solo Acciaio '17 | 🍷 3 |
| ● Grignolino d'Asti Grigné '17 | 🍷 3 |
| ● Ruché di Castagnole M.to La Tradizione '15 | 🍷🍷🍷 3* |
| ● Ruché di Castagnole M.to Laccento '16 | 🍷🍷🍷 3* |
| ● Ruché di Castagnole M.to La Tradizione '16 | 🍷🍷 3* |

# Cecilia Monte

VIA SERRACAPELLI, 17
12052 NEIVE [CN]
TEL. +39 017367454
cecilia.monte@libero.it

CELLAR SALES
ANNUAL PRODUCTION 19,000 bottles
HECTARES UNDER VINE 3.50

Having finished her studies, Cecilia decided to dedicate herself to wine, creating a small winery that deserves a visit because of its artistic appeal. The main cultivar is Nebbiolo, which gives rise both to their Barbaresco Serracapelli and their Riserva Dedicata a Paolo, (for her father). But the winery offers solid interpretations of Barbera and Dolcetto d'Alba as well. Cecila, strong-willed in her pursuits, has for some time been associated with Treiso's Ciau del Tornavento and recently collaborated on the creation of Campamac di Barbaresco, a restaurant that describes itself as a 'high-level osteria'. Very expressive and intense, well-developed and with clear notes of tar and licorice, their elegant 2013 Barbaresco Serracapelli Dedicato a Paolo features harmony both on the nose and on the palate. Their slightly more straight-forward, approachable 2014 Serracapelli proves especially pleasant in its notes of quinine and black currant. Their highly refined 2016 Barbera d'Alba Maria Teresa showcases the variety, with a perfect union of fruit and vegetal notes.

| | |
|---|---|
| ● Barbaresco Serracapelli Dedicato a Paolo '13 | ▼▼ 6 |
| ● Barbaresco Serracapelli '14 | ▼▼ 5 |
| ● Barbera d'Alba Maria Teresa '16 | ▼▼ 3 |
| ● Barbaresco Serracapelli '13 | ♀♀ 5 |
| ● Barbaresco Serracapelli '11 | ♀♀ 5 |
| ● Barbaresco Serracapelli Dedicato a Paolo '11 | ♀♀ 6 |
| ● Barbaresco Vign. Serracapelli '12 | ♀♀ 5 |
| ● Barbaresco Vign. Serracapelli '09 | ♀♀ 5 |
| ● Barbera d'Alba Maria Teresa '15 | ♀♀ 3 |
| ● Dolcetto d'Alba Montubert '16 | ♀♀ 2* |
| ● Langhe Nebbiolo '12 | ♀♀ 3 |
| ● Langhe Nebbiolo '10 | ♀♀ 3 |

# Tenuta Montemagno

VIA CASCINA VALFOSSATO, 9
14030 MONTEMAGNO [AT]
TEL. +39 014163624
www.tenutamontemagno.it

CELLAR SALES
PRE-BOOKED VISITS
ACCOMMODATION AND RESTAURANT SERVICE
ANNUAL PRODUCTION 140,000 bottles
HECTARES UNDER VINE 15.00
SUSTAINABLE WINERY

For those who drive along the state road between Altavilla and Montemagno it's difficult not to notice the old looming farm manor perched on the edge of the hill. It's a luxurious complex dedicated to those who love wine and the territory, and whose owners invested heavily in it. Their wines demonstrate excellent overall quality. Their reds are solid, derived primarily from native grape varieties. Aroma and structure are conferred on their whites thanks to the use of Sauvignon Blanc and Timorasso. Their intriguing Metodo Classico, made with Barbera, also relies on a native cultivar. Their intense Grignolino d'Asti Ruber is a pleasant surprise among their overall excellent selections. Its spicy profile lengthens on a palate of tannic elegance and ends in a very persistent finish. Mysterium and Austerum each deliver a nice nose and palate, while their Brut TM24 offers fruity aromas, yeasty notes and a sophisticated, enduring palate. Their white Timorasso and Sauvignon Blanc are sure bets.

| | |
|---|---|
| ● Grignolino d'Asti Ruber '17 | ▼▼ 2* |
| ● Barbera d'Asti Austerum '16 | ▼▼ 3 |
| ● Barbera d'Asti Sup. Mysterium '15 | ▼▼ 4 |
| ○ M.to Bianco Musae '17 | ▼▼ 3 |
| ○ M.to Bianco Nymphae '17 | ▼▼ 2* |
| ○ M.to Bianco Solis Vis '16 | ▼▼ 3 |
| ○ TM24 Brut M. Cl. | ▼▼ 5 |
| ● M.to Rosso Violae '17 | ▼ 2 |
| ● Malvasia di Casorzo Dulcem '17 | ▼ 2 |
| ● Ruché di Castagnole M.to '17 | ▼ 3 |
| ● Barbera d'Asti Sup. Mysterium '13 | ♀♀ 4 |
| ● Barbera d'Asti Sup. Mysterium '12 | ♀♀ 4 |
| ○ M.to Bianco Musae '17 | ♀♀ 3 |

# Paolo Monti

Fraz. Camie
loc. San Sebastiano, 39
12065 Monforte d'Alba [CN]
Tel. +39 017378391
www.paolomonti.com

**CELLAR SALES**
**PRE-BOOKED VISITS**
**ANNUAL PRODUCTION 50,000 bottles**
**HECTARES UNDER VINE 16.00**

Paolo Monti puts expert care and attention into every detail of his wines, foremost Barolo and Barbera d'Alba, which are made with the area's historic red grape varieties. But the challenge doesn't finish there, because he's decided to prove that this prized wine country is capable of doing great things even with classic French cultivar, like Chardonnay, Merlot and Cabernet Sauvignon, as well as a touch Riesling, a choice made out of a passion for the grape. Their style centers on elegance and international tastes, with great respect shown for the personality of the vineyards and different vintages. Notes of oak on a background of quinine and black fruit, and a slightly tannin palate characterize their young 2014 Barolo Bussia. Their Barbera d'Alba commendably interprets the fruity 2015 vintage with notes of cherry united with spices, while their Superiore proves slightly more astringent.

| | | |
|---|---|---|
| ● Barolo Bussia '14 | ♟♟ 8 | |
| ● Barbera d'Alba '15 | ♟♟ 5 | |
| ● Barbera d'Alba Sup. '15 | ♟♟ 7 | |
| ● Nebbiolo d'Alba '15 | ♟ 4 | |
| ● Barbera d'Alba '14 | ♟♟ 5 | |
| ● Barbera d'Alba '13 | ♟♟ 5 | |
| ● Barbera d'Alba '12 | ♟♟ 5 | |
| ● Barbera d'Alba Sup. '13 | ♟♟ 7 | |
| ● Barolo Bussia Ris. '11 | ♟♟ 8 | |
| ● Barolo Bussia Ris. '10 | ♟♟ 8 | |
| ● Barolo del Comune di Monforte d'Alba '13 | ♟♟ 7 | |
| ● Barolo del Comune di Monforte d'Alba '12 | ♟♟ 7 | |
| ● Nebbiolo d'Alba '14 | ♟♟ 4 | |
| ● Nebbiolo d'Alba '12 | ♟♟ 4 | |

# Stefanino Morra

loc. San Pietro
via Castagnito, 50
12050 Castellinaldo [CN]
Tel. +39 0173213489
www.morravini.it

**CELLAR SALES**
**PRE-BOOKED VISITS**
**ANNUAL PRODUCTION 70,000 bottles**
**HECTARES UNDER VINE 11.00**
**SUSTAINABLE WINERY**

Stefanino Morra bottled his first Arneis in 1990, and the family are now on its third generation of producers in the area. Their vineyards are situated at notable elevations in Canale, Castellinaldo and Vezza d'Alba, where the soil is characteristically sandy with layers of marl and a touch of limestone. The territory's major grapes are grown, from Arneis to Barbera, Favorita, Nebbiolo and Brachetto for their sweet wines, making for traditionally styled wines with nice structure. With the 2015 vintage, their Roero Sräi Riserva returns to the top of their range, making the finals thanks to its rich fruit and lovely, structured palate, staying power and long, assertive finish. Their lovely, juicy 2015 Barbera d'Alba Castellinaldo offers black fruit and pepper along a lovely roundness. Their 2017 Roero Arneis delivers pronounced notes of white fruit and a very savory palate.

| | | |
|---|---|---|
| ● Roero Sräi Ris. '15 | ♟♟ 5 | |
| ● Barbera d'Alba Castellinaldo '15 | ♟♟ 4 | |
| ○ Roero Arneis '17 | ♟♟ 2* | |
| ● Roero '15 | ♟ 3 | |
| ○ Roero Arneis M. Cl. Elena | ♟ 4 | |
| ○ Roero Arneis Vign. San Pietro '16 | ♟ 3 | |
| ● Barbera d'Alba '15 | ♟♟ 3* | |
| ● Barbera d'Alba '14 | ♟♟ 3 | |
| ● Barbera d'Alba Castellinaldo '13 | ♟♟ 4 | |
| ● Roero '14 | ♟♟ 3 | |
| ● Roero '13 | ♟♟ 4 | |
| ○ Roero Arneis '16 | ♟♟ 2* | |
| ○ Roero Arneis '15 | ♟♟ 3* | |
| ○ Roero Arneis '14 | ♟♟ 3* | |
| ○ Roero Arneis Vign. San Pietro '15 | ♟♟ 3 | |
| ● Roero Sräi Ris. '12 | ♟♟ 5 | |

## F.lli Mossio

FRAZ. CASCINA CARAMELLI
VIA MONTÀ, 12
12050 RODELLO [CN]
TEL. +39 0173617149
www.mossio.com

CELLAR SALES
PRE-BOOKED VISITS
ACCOMMODATION
ANNUAL PRODUCTION 50,000 bottles
HECTARES UNDER VINE 10.00
SUSTAINABLE WINERY

Rodello has always been one of the most important municipalities for Dolcetto d'Alba, as a number of famous and decades-old wineries testify to. Remo and Valerio Mossio are expert interpreters of the wine, bolstered by splendid vineyard positions situated in a scenic landscape not far from the city of Alba. Their entire selection features fruit, but the crisp, caressing sensations their Dolcettos offer are incomparable, a line that proves chewy and extremely enjoyable. Their Barbera d'Alba and Langhe Nebbiolo are well-crafted and pleasant as well. As they had announced, their 2016 Dolcetto d'Alba selections, the always compelling Piano delli Perdoni and Bricco Caramelli, were left to age an extra year. However, we strongly recommend their 2016 Gamvs which proves well-rounded by one year in wood barrels. Nebbiolo and Barbera work together in their rich, elegant 2015 Lange Rosso.

| | |
|---|---|
| ● Barbera d'Alba '16 | ♟♟ 4 |
| ● Dolcetto d'Alba Piano delli Perdoni '16 | ♟♟ 2* |
| ● Dolcetto d'Alba Sup. Bricco Caramelli '16 | ♟♟ 3 |
| ● Dolcetto d'Alba Sup. Gamvs '16 | ♟♟ 4 |
| ● Langhe Rosso '15 | ♟♟ 4 |
| ● Langhe Nebbiolo Luen '14 | ♟ 4 |
| ● Dolcetto d'Alba Bricco Caramelli '00 | ♟♟♟ 3* |
| ● Barbera d'Alba '15 | ♟♟ 4 |
| ● Barbera d'Alba '14 | ♟♟ 4 |
| ● Dolcetto d'Alba Bricco Caramelli '15 | ♟♟ 3* |
| ● Dolcetto d'Alba Piano delli Perdoni '15 | ♟♟ 2* |
| ● Dolcetto d'Alba Piano delli Perdoni '14 | ♟♟ 2* |
| ● Langhe Nebbiolo '12 | ♟♟ 4 |
| ● Langhe Nebbiolo Luen '12 | ♟♟ 4 |

## Ada Nada

LOC. ROMBONE
VIA AUSARIO, 12
12050 TREISO [CN]
TEL. +39 0173638127
www.adanada.it

CELLAR SALES
PRE-BOOKED VISITS
ACCOMMODATION AND RESTAURANT SERVICE
ANNUAL PRODUCTION 45,000 bottles
HECTARES UNDER VINE 9.00

In addition to their cellar (managed by Giancarlo's son-in-law Elvio), the 18th-century farm manor also hosts a charming farm holiday managed by his daughter Anna Lisa. Their production style calls for the use of primarily native grape varieties, and a calibrated mix of large, untoasted oak barrels and barriques, making for classically styled wines, with their three Barbarescos on center stage. The crus of Valeirano and Rombone give rise to their Elisa and their Riserva Cichin, which also makes use of the oldest plots. Their classic 2013 Barbaresco Cichin Riserva plays on notes of dark berries and forest underbrush with a well-structured, palate that is still tannic and offers a long finish. The aromatic finesse and pleasant overall harmony of their 2015 Barbaresco Valeirano lead to a juicy, satisfying palate with a long, multifaceted fruity finish. Their final Barbaresco, the 2015 Rombone Elisa is ripe and well-focused with fruit, offering developed tannins and a fresh, persistent finish.

| | |
|---|---|
| ● Barbaresco Rombone Elisa '15 | ♟♟ 5 |
| ● Barbaresco Valeirano '15 | ♟♟ 5 |
| ● Barbaresco Cichin Ris. '13 | ♟♟ 6 |
| ● Barbera d'Alba Sup. Salgà '16 | ♟♟ 3 |
| ○ Langhe Sauvignon Neta '17 | ♟♟ 2* |
| ● Barbera d'Alba Pierin '17 | ♟ 3 |
| ● Barbera d'Alba Pierin '16 | ♟ 3 |
| ● Dolcetto d'Alba Autinot '17 | ♟ 2 |
| ● Barbaresco Cichin '11 | ♟♟ 6 |
| ● Barbaresco Cichin Ris. '12 | ♟♟ 6 |
| ● Barbaresco Valeirano '14 | ♟♟ 5 |
| ● Barbaresco Valeirano '11 | ♟♟ 5 |
| ● Barbera d'Alba Sup. Salgà '15 | ♟♟ 3 |
| ● Langhe Nebbiolo Serena '14 | ♟ 3 |

## ★Fiorenzo Nada

via Ausario, 12c
12050 Treiso [CN]
Tel. +39 0173638254
www.nada.it

**CELLAR SALES**
**PRE-BOOKED VISITS**
**ANNUAL PRODUCTION** 45,000 bottles
**HECTARES UNDER VINE** 10.00
**SUSTAINABLE WINERY**

Bruno Nada, one of Langhe's major producers, has made a name for itself abroad thanks to the freshness of its wines (a consequence of the elevation of their vineyards), the texture conferred by painstaking work in the field, a stylistic elegance bestowed by the use of French wood barrels, and an artisanal, family-run approach. Indeed, the winery has become a benchmark for wine lovers everywhere. And they've done it not only with their premium offers, their three Barbarescos and their Seifile, but also with Barbera and Dolcetto d'Alba, which accompany a high-range Langhe Nebbiolo. They are currently converting to organic. Their 2014 Barbaresco Montaribaldi unfolds with aromas of red fruit, tobacco and licorice adorned by sweet spices and a balsamic dash. The rich, powerful palate sees slightly austere tannins. Their Manzola is a bit lighter but full of elegant hints of wild berries. Their austere and well-defined Rombone lacks some of the fruity pulp, while their Barbera d'Alba and Langhe Nebbiolo prove as compelling and elegant as ever.

| | |
|---|---|
| ● Barbaresco Montaribaldi '14 | ▼▼▼ 7 |
| ● Barbaresco Manzola '14 | ▼▼ 6 |
| ● Barbaresco Rombone '14 | ▼▼ 7 |
| ● Barbera d'Alba '16 | ▼▼ 4 |
| ● Langhe Nebbiolo '16 | ▼▼ 3 |
| ● Barbaresco '01 | ▽▽▽ 6 |
| ● Barbaresco Manzola '08 | ▽▽▽ 6 |
| ● Barbaresco Manzola '06 | ▽▽▽ 6 |
| ● Barbaresco Montaribaldi '13 | ▽▽▽ 7 |
| ● Barbaresco Rombone '12 | ▽▽▽ 7 |
| ● Barbaresco Rombone '10 | ▽▽▽ 7 |
| ● Barbaresco Rombone '09 | ▽▽▽ 7 |
| ● Barbaresco Rombone '07 | ▽▽▽ 7 |
| ● Barbaresco Rombone '06 | ▽▽▽ 7 |
| ● Barbaresco Rombone '05 | ▽▽▽ 7 |
| ● Barbaresco Rombone '04 | ▽▽▽ 7 |
| ● Langhe Rosso Seifile '01 | ▽▽▽ 6 |

## Cantina dei Produttori Nebbiolo di Carema

via Nazionale, 32
10010 Carema [TO]
Tel. +39 0125811160
www.caremadoc.it

**CELLAR SALES**
**PRE-BOOKED VISITS**
**RESTAURANT SERVICE**
**ANNUAL PRODUCTION** 65,000 bottles
**HECTARES UNDER VINE** 20.00

Carema is a town that's so lovely that it deserves to be visited even by tourists who aren't primarily interested in wine. Here, along the border between Piedmont and Valle d'Aosta, near France, you can admire vineyards that are literally set in rocks, with the vines supported by stone pillars that release the heat accumulated during the day. Here 70 vine growers look after their Nebbiolo, most of which are delivered to this praiseworthy cooperative winery. Their Carema Doc is buoyant, fresh but not acidic, tannic but not aggressive, and always complex. The 2015 offers a pleasant and assured drinkability with strong aromas of ripe red fruit already hinting at tar and sweet spices. Its fresh, tempting palate is very light in tannins through to its correspondingly clean finish. More assertive and impetuous as a result of of its remarkable acidity, their 2016 Canavese Nebbiolo Paré still proves compelling.

| | |
|---|---|
| ● Carema Et. Nera '15 | ▼▼ 3 |
| ● Canavese Nebbiolo Parè '16 | ▼ 2 |
| ● Carema Et. Bianca '07 | ▽▽▽ 3* |
| ● Carema Et. Bianca Ris. '11 | ▽▽▽ 3* |
| ● Carema Et. Bianca Ris. '09 | ▽▽▽ 3* |
| ● Carema Et. Bianca Ris. '08 | ▽▽▽ 3* |
| ● Carema Et. Bianca Ris. '12 | ▽▽ 3 |
| ● Carema Et. Bianca Ris. '10 | ▽▽ 3* |
| ● Carema Et. Nera '14 | ▽▽ 3 |
| ● Carema Et. Nera '13 | ▽▽ 2* |
| ● Carema Et. Nera '12 | ▽▽ 2* |
| ● Carema Et. Nera '11 | ▽▽ 2* |
| ● Carema Et. Nera '10 | ▽▽ 2* |
| ● Carema Ris. '13 | ▽▽ 4 |

## Negretti

FRAZ. SANTA MARIA, 53
12064 LA MORRA [CN]
TEL. +39 0173509850
www.negrettivini.com

**CELLAR SALES**
**PRE-BOOKED VISITS**
**ANNUAL PRODUCTION 40,000 bottles**
**HECTARES UNDER VINE 13.00**

Brothers Ezio and Massimo Negretti, who took over the reins of their family's winery back in 2002, have brought new life to the producer. The estate comprises 13 hectares of vineyards along the hills of La Morra (crus Rive and Bettolotti) and Bricco Ambrogio (with a geographic mention for Roddi, an emerging and increasingly important part of Barolo). They've settled on a production style that avoids extremes of 'modern' and 'traditional'. In the cellar, in addition to mid-sized barrels, they also use barriques made of French oak. Their excellent interpretation of the 2014 vintage deserves Tre Bicchieri. Their Barolo Bricco Ambrogio shows a high level of spicy complexity with notes of quinine and tobacco supported by fresh, crisp fruit. The multifaceted palate proves rich in pulp, enlivened by creamy tannins and a long, continuous finish. Their Barolo Rive is earthy and savory, while their 'base-level' Barolo proves fresher and balsamic.

| | |
|---|---|
| ● Barolo Bricco Ambrogio '14 | 🍷🍷🍷 6 |
| ● Barolo '14 | 🍷🍷 6 |
| ● Barolo Rive '14 | 🍷🍷 6 |
| ● Barbera d'Alba Sup. '15 | 🍷🍷 3 |
| ○ Langhe Chardonnay Dadà '16 | 🍷🍷 3 |
| ● Nebbiolo d'Alba Minot '15 | 🍷🍷 3 |
| ● Barolo Mirau '14 | 🍷 6 |
| ● Barbera d'Alba Sup. '14 | 🍷🍷 3 |
| ● Barolo '13 | 🍷🍷 6 |
| ● Barolo Bricco Ambrogio '13 | 🍷🍷 6 |
| ● Barolo Bricco Ambrogio '09 | 🍷🍷 6 |
| ● Barolo Mirau '13 | 🍷🍷 6 |
| ● Barolo Rive '13 | 🍷🍷 6 |
| ○ Langhe Chardonnay Dadà '15 | 🍷🍷 3 |
| ● Nebbiolo d'Alba '14 | 🍷🍷 3 |

## Lorenzo Negro

FRAZ. SANT'ANNA, 55
12040 MONTEU ROERO [CN]
TEL. +39 017390645
www.negrolorenzo.com

**CELLAR SALES**
**PRE-BOOKED VISITS**
**ANNUAL PRODUCTION 35,000 bottles**
**HECTARES UNDER VINE 8.00**
**SUSTAINABLE WINERY**

Lorenzo Negro's cellar is situated on the hill of Serra Lupini, surrounded by their private vineyards. The sandy, silt and clay soil here gives rise to those grapes most commonly cultivated along the Tanaro's left bank: Arneis, Barbera and Nebbiolo (with small amounts of Albarossa, Bonarda and Dolcetto as well). Their wines are modern, bringing together the pursuit of territorial expression with exceptional aromatic precision. Lorenzo Negro's excellent 2015 Roero Prachiosso offers beautiful, driving red fruit with refined tannins and a juicy, highly pleasant final. Though the vintage can be felt in their 2014 Roero Riserva San Francesco, it delivers rich fruit with hints of orange zest on an assertive, lingering palate. Their fruity, spicy 2015 Barbera d'Alba and pleasant, approachable 2012 Roero Arneis Brut with notes of peach, are both well-crafted.

| | |
|---|---|
| ● Roero Prachiosso '15 | 🍷🍷 3* |
| ● Barbera d'Alba '15 | 🍷🍷 2* |
| ○ Roero Arneis Brut M. Cl. '12 | 🍷🍷 4 |
| ● Roero San Francesco Ris. '14 | 🍷🍷 3 |
| ○ Roero Arneis '17 | 🍷 2 |
| ● Barbera d'Alba '11 | 🍷🍷 2* |
| ● Barbera d'Alba Sup. La Nanda '13 | 🍷🍷 3 |
| ● Barbera d'Alba Sup. La Nanda '12 | 🍷🍷 3 |
| ○ Roero Arneis '16 | 🍷🍷 2* |
| ○ Roero Arneis '14 | 🍷🍷 2* |
| ○ Roero Arneis Brut M. Cl. '11 | 🍷🍷 4 |
| ● Roero Prachiosso '14 | 🍷🍷 3 |
| ● Roero Prachiosso '13 | 🍷🍷 3 |
| ● Roero San Francesco Ris. '13 | 🍷🍷 3* |
| ● Roero San Francesco Ris. '11 | 🍷🍷 3* |
| ● Roero San Francesco Ris. '08 | 🍷🍷 3* |

# Angelo Negro e Figli

FRAZ. SANT'ANNA, 1
12040 MONTEU ROERO [CN]
TEL. +39 017390252
www.negroangelo.it

**CELLAR SALES**
**PRE-BOOKED VISITS**
**ANNUAL PRODUCTION** 350,000 bottles
**HECTARES UNDER VINE** 60.00
**SUSTAINABLE WINERY**

The Negro family's historic winery is a benchmark for Roero, having in recent years enlarged its notable estate to include plots in the Basarin cru in Neive. They're also offering a Barolo made with grapes cultivated in Serralunga, where they've made recent acquisitions as well. Roero's wines are among the most important on the left bank of the Tanaro, classically styled, attentive to aromatic precision and superior expressivity. Three wines stand out among their, as always, excellent proposals. Their expansive 2105 Roero Sudisfà Riserva, with well-integrated tannins and notes of spices and black fruit, offers length and staying power. Their 2017 Roero Arneis Perdaudin gives off floral and citrus notes with hints of ginger on a full, rounded palate, both savory and fresh. And their 2015 Barbaresco Basarin proves beautifully complex though still a bit closed and with a bit too much tannic presence.

| | |
|---|---|
| ● Barbaresco Basarin '15 | ♟♟ 5 |
| ○ Roero Arneis Perdaudin '17 | ♟♟ 3* |
| ● Roero Sudisfà Ris. '15 | ♟♟ 6 |
| ● Barbera d'Alba Bertu '16 | ♟♟ 5 |
| ○ Roero Arneis 7 Anni '11 | ♟♟ 6 |
| ○ Roero Arneis Serra Lupini '17 | ♟♟ 3 |
| ● Roero Ciabot San Giorgio Ris. '15 | ♟♟ 5 |
| ● Roero Prachioso '15 | ♟♟ 4 |
| ● Roero Sudisfà '04 | ♟♟♟ 5 |
| ● Roero Sudisfà '03 | ♟♟♟ 5 |
| ● Roero Sudisfà Ris. '13 | ♟♟♟ 6 |
| ● Roero Sudisfà Ris. '12 | ♟♟♟ 6 |
| ● Roero Sudisfà Ris. '10 | ♟♟♟ 6 |
| ● Roero Sudisfà Ris. '09 | ♟♟♟ 5 |
| ● Roero Sudisfà Ris. '08 | ♟♟♟ 5 |

# Nervi

C.SO VERCELLI, 117
13045 GATTINARA [VC]
TEL. +39 0163833228
www.nervicantine.it

**CELLAR SALES**
**PRE-BOOKED VISITS**
**ANNUAL PRODUCTION** 120,000 bottles
**HECTARES UNDER VINE** 27.00

The slow, constant progress that Nervi has been making towards quality is about to receive a kick. Indeed, in early 2018 Monforte d'Alba's Giacomo Conterno purchased 90% of the winery. The results achieved by the former ownership, a Norwegian group well-represented by Erling Astrup, were certainly valid, as evidenced by the international success of their Gattinara Molsino. But that takes nothing away from the enthusiasm of wine lovers over seeing this historic north Piedmont winery in the hands of none other than the producers of Barolo Monfortino. Their 2103 Vigna Valferana offers the prototype for the harmony that Gattinara can achieve only a few years after its vintage. Its smooth, velvety palate follows a nose of licorice, tobacco and red fruit. Their even more approachable and evolved Vigna Molsina delivers loads of personality, while their 2107 Rosa is fresh and citrusy. The fabulous premiere of their 2015 Gattinara bodes very well for their new property.

| | |
|---|---|
| ● Gattinara '15 | ♟♟ 5 |
| ● Gattinara V. Valferana '13 | ♟♟ 6 |
| ● Gattinara V. Molsino '13 | ♟♟ 7 |
| ● Gattinara '14 | ♟ 4 |
| ⊙ Rosa '17 | ♟ 3 |
| ● Gattinara Podere dei Ginepri '01 | ♟♟♟ 5 |
| ● Gattinara Vign. Molsino '00 | ♟♟♟ 5 |
| ● Colline Novaresi Spanna '15 | ♟♟ 3 |
| ● Gattinara '13 | ♟♟ 4 |
| ● Gattinara '12 | ♟♟ 4 |
| ● Gattinara Molsino '11 | ♟♟ 5 |
| ● Gattinara V. Molsino '12 | ♟♟ 5 |
| ● Gattinara Valferana '11 | ♟♟ 5 |

## Cantina Sociale di Nizza

S.DA ALESSANDRIA, 57
14049 NIZZA MONFERRATO [AT]
TEL. +39 0141721348
www.nizza.it

CELLAR SALES
PRE-BOOKED VISITS
ANNUAL PRODUCTION 200,000 bottles
HECTARES UNDER VINE 560.00
VITICULTURE METHOD Certified
OrganicCertified Biodynamic
SUSTAINABLE WINERY

Founded in 1955, Cantina Sociale di Nizza
Monferrato works with 200 vine growers
who give rise to 18 wines. Barbera, which
is of course the cornerstone of their
selection, is accompanied by Brachetto,
Chardonnay, Cortese, Dolcetto, Freisa and
Moscato. Their wines exhibit a modern
style, fashioned so as to exhibit a marked
territorial identity, with increasing attention
to organic cultivation techniques in recent
years. Despite its rather noticeable
presence of wood, their fresh and fruit
2015 Nizza Riserva proves excellent,
providing notes of licorice and ash on a
fresh, well-structured palate. Their supple,
fresh 2016 Barbera d'Asti Le Pole is juicy
and pleasant, their 2016 Barbera d'Asti
Superiore Magister, closer-knit and more
full-bodied, and their 2015 Piedmont
Rosso Baccherosse, a 60 Barbera /40
Cabernet Sauvignon blend, offering fruity
tones with vegetal nuances, is assertive
with a pleasant, approachable finish. All
are quite good.

| | |
|---|---|
| ● Nizza Ris. '15 | 🏆🏆 5 |
| ● Barbera d'Asti Le Pole '16 | 🏆🏆 2* |
| ● Barbera d'Asti Sup. Magister '16 | 🏆🏆 3 |
| ● Piemonte Rosso Baccherosse '15 | 🏆🏆 2* |
| ● Barbera d'Asti Sup. 50 Vendemmie '15 | 🏆 3 |
| ● Nizza Ceppi Vecchi '16 | 🏆 5 |
| ● Piemonte Barbera In Origine '17 | 🏆 3 |
| ● Barbera d'Asti Sup. Magister '15 | 🏆🏆 2* |
| ● Barbera d'Asti Sup. Magister '14 | 🏆🏆 2* |
| ● Barbera d'Asti Sup. Nizza Ceppi Vecchi '14 | 🏆🏆 4 |
| ● Nizza Ceppi Vecchi '15 | 🏆🏆 4 |
| ● Piemonte Barbera In Origine '16 | 🏆🏆 2* |
| ● Piemonte Barbera Progetto in Origine '15 | 🏆🏆 2* |

## Silvano Nizza

FRAZ. BALLA LORA 29A
12040 SANTO STEFANO ROERO [CN]
TEL. +39 017390516
www.nizzasilvano.com

CELLAR SALES
PRE-BOOKED VISITS
ANNUAL PRODUCTION 65,000 bottles
HECTARES UNDER VINE 8.00

Founded in 2001, the Nizza family's winery
is situated in the Ca' Boscarone farm
manor, in one of Santo Stefano Roero's
best districts for wine making. Their
vineyards fall within the municipalities of
Canale and Montà, and give rise to the
territory's classic grapes: Arneis, Barbera,
Brachetto and Nebbiolo. Their wines are
decidedly modern, though while respecting
the characteristics both of the cultivar and
the territory of origin. Silvano Nozzo's
winery enters this section of the guide due
to the remarkable consistency shown in
recent years by a series of wines, like their
Roero Ca' Boscarone Riserva. The 2014
offers a nose of forest undergrowth,
aromatic herbs and black fruit while the
palate, with the smoothness characteristic
of the vintage, is long, savory and taut.
Other selections, like their well-structured
and saffron-noted 2017 Roero Arneis, or
pleasant and approachable 2015 Barbera
d'Alba, also prove quite well-made.

| | |
|---|---|
| ● Roero Ca' Boscarone Ris. '14 | 🏆🏆 6 |
| ● Barbera d'Alba '15 | 🏆🏆 4 |
| ● Roero '15 | 🏆🏆 5 |
| ○ Roero Arneis '17 | 🏆🏆 3 |
| ● Nebbiolo d'Alba '16 | 🏆 4 |
| ● Barbera d'Alba Sup. '14 | 🏆🏆 4 |
| ● Nebbiolo d'Alba '15 | 🏆🏆 4 |
| ● Roero '13 | 🏆🏆 5 |
| ○ Roero Arneis '16 | 🏆🏆 3 |
| ● Roero Ca' Boscarone Ris. '13 | 🏆🏆 6 |

## Noah

via Forte, 48
13862 Brusnengo [BI]
Tel. +39 3201510906
info@noah.wine

CELLAR SALES
PRE-BOOKED VISITS
ANNUAL PRODUCTION 10,000 bottles
HECTARES UNDER VINE 4.50
SUSTAINABLE WINERY

Theirs is a young and highly dynamic winery. In fact, they're about to begin works on what will be in just a few short months the new production center. And not only, for the first time since the 2014 vintage, their Lessona will see the light of day. Andrea Mosca and Giovanna Pepe Diaz are firm believers in Nebbiolo, which is the only cultivar used in their Lessona, and is 80% of their Bramaterra (with Croatina, Vespolina and Uva Rara making up the rest). A small line of Coste della Sesia Croatina makes up the rest of a selection that's managed with extreme care, with a different approach in terms of maceration and aging taken for each wine. Lovely notes of sun-soaked herbs energized by raspberry add to the precise elegance of their 2014 Bramaterra's nose, while its rather delicate palate proves balanced and persistent. Their refined 2014 Lessona releases licorice and sweet tobacco over an unhesitating if a bit austere palate.

| | | |
|---|---|---|
| ● Bramaterra '14 | 🍷🍷 | 5 |
| ● Lessona '14 | 🍷🍷 | 5 |
| ● Bramaterra '12 | 🍷🍷🍷 | 5 |
| ● Bramaterra '13 | 🍷🍷 | 5 |

## Figli Luigi Oddero

fraz. Santa Maria
loc. Tenuta Parà, 95
12604 La Morra [CN]
Tel. +39 0173500386
www.figliluigioddero.it

CELLAR SALES
PRE-BOOKED VISITS
ANNUAL PRODUCTION 110,000 bottles
HECTARES UNDER VINE 20.00
SUSTAINABLE WINERY

Luigi Oddero is rightfully considered one of Langhe's lodestars. In 2006, after managing Poderi e Cantine Oddero along with his brother Giacomo, he decided to go out on his own. Today he's joined by his wife, Lena, and children Maria and Giovanni, carrying on the family legacy with an estate that comprises important plots in Rive (Santa Maria, La Morra), Scarrone (Castiglione Falletto), Vignarionda (Serralunga d'Alba) and Rombone (Treiso). There's also their Moscato from Cascina Fiori (Trezzo Tinella). Their approach sees Piedmont's traditional grapes interpreted with a well-defined, classic style. Their proposals were phenomenal with a couple to really stock up on. Their 2012 Vigna Rionda enthralls with Mediterranean character expressed in aromas of rosemary and raspberry, offering exceptional dynamism and a long, salty, flavorful finish. Their 2013 Rocche Rivera, is a vibrant, juicy Barolo embellished by invigoratingly fresh red fruit and an breezy, menthol nose.

| | | |
|---|---|---|
| ● Barbaresco Rombone '15 | 🍷🍷 | 8 |
| ● Barolo Rocche Rivera '13 | 🍷🍷 | 6 |
| ● Barolo Vigna Rionda '12 | 🍷🍷 | 8 |
| ● Barolo '14 | 🍷🍷 | 8 |
| ● Dolcetto d'Alba '17 | 🍷 | 2 |
| ● Langhe Nebbiolo '15 | 🍷 | 6 |
| ● Barolo Vigna Rionda '10 | 🍷🍷🍷 | 8 |
| ● Barbaresco '10 | 🍷🍷 | 5 |
| ● Barbaresco Rombone '14 | 🍷🍷 | 8 |
| ● Barbaresco Rombone '13 | 🍷🍷 | 5 |
| ● Barolo '13 | 🍷🍷 | 8 |
| ● Barolo Rocche Ris. '11 | 🍷🍷 | 8 |
| ● Barolo Rocche Rivera '10 | 🍷🍷 | 6 |
| ● Barolo Rocche Rivera '09 | 🍷🍷 | 8 |
| ● Barolo Specola '11 | 🍷🍷 | 8 |

## ★Poderi e Cantine Oddero

FRAZ. SANTA MARIA
VIA TETTI, 28
12064 LA MORRA [CN]
TEL. +39 017350618
www.oddero.it

**CELLAR SALES**
**PRE-BOOKED VISITS**
**ANNUAL PRODUCTION** 150,000 bottles
**HECTARES UNDER VINE** 35.00
**VITICULTURE METHOD** Certified Organic
**SUSTAINABLE WINERY**

Mariacristina and Mariavittoria Oddero's precious portfolio of vineyards includes Villero and Rocche (Castiglione Falletto), Brunate (La Morra), Vigna Mondoca (Bussia Soprana, Monforte d'Alba), Vignarionda (Serralunga). And, if that weren't enough, there's also Gallina in Barbaresco. It's the legacy left behind by their father, Giacomo, who was among the artificers of Langhe's success. And their style continues to prove rigorous and sophisticated, interpreted with a masterful sensibility in terms of the length of maceration and the use of wood barrels. Two words: class and elegance. Their fantastic 2008 Barolo Vignarionda Riserva delivers power, maturity and incredible depth of flavor. It's complex and full-bodied with a spicy finish. Their extraordinary 2012 Barolo Bussia Vigna Mondoca Riserva proves energetic and vibrant. Though starting slowly, it ends deep and wide with a truly impressive grip. The high quality of their Langhe Nebbiolo and Barbera d'Alba confirm the gravitas of their range overall.

| | | |
|---|---:|---|
| ● Barolo Bussia V. Mondoca Ris. '12 | ▼▼▼ 8 | |
| ● Barolo Brunate '13 | ▼▼ 8 | |
| ● Barolo Vignarionda Ris. '08 | ▼▼ 8 | |
| ● Barbera d'Alba Sup. '15 | ▼▼ 4 | |
| ● Barolo Brunate '14 | ▼▼ 8 | |
| ● Barolo Rocche di Castiglione '14 | ▼▼ 8 | |
| ● Langhe Nebbiolo '16 | ▼▼ 4 | |
| ● Barbaresco Gallina '15 | ▼ 6 | |
| ● Barolo '14 | ▼ 6 | |
| ● Barolo Bussia V. Mondoca Ris. '10 | ♕♕♕ 8 | |
| ● Barolo Bussia V. Mondoca Ris. '08 | ♕♕♕ 8 | |
| ● Barolo Mondoca di Bussia Soprana '04 | ♕♕♕ 7 | |
| ● Barolo Rocche di Castiglione '09 | ♕♕♕ 7 | |
| ● Barolo Bussia V. Mondoca Ris. '11 | ♕♕ 8 | |
| ● Barolo Rocche di Castiglione '13 | ♕♕ 8 | |

## Tenuta Olim Bauda

VIA PRATA, 50
14045 INCISA SCAPACCINO [AT]
TEL. +39 0141702171
www.tenutaolimbauda.it

**CELLAR SALES**
**PRE-BOOKED VISITS**
**ANNUAL PRODUCTION** 200,000 bottles
**HECTARES UNDER VINE** 30.00
**SUSTAINABLE WINERY**

The Bertolino family founded Olim Bauda in 1961 and now have several estates at their disposal throughout Nizza Monferrato, Isola d'Asti, Fontanile, Castelnuovo Calcea and Gavi. The primary varieties grown are Barbera and Moscato, which are accompanied by Grignolino, Nebbiolo, Cortese, Chardonnay and a small quantity of Freisa. A dozen wines are offered, making for a modern selection of precisely styled wines that do a good job expressing the territory. Tre Bicchieri for their 2015 Nizza, with its nose of black fruit, drenched earth and hints of wood on a remarkably structured palate that remains juicy and fruity to its long, enveloping finish. Their exceptional 2016 Barbera d'Asti Superiore Le Rocchette offers notes of wild berries and forest undergrowth on a compact palate of significant, but well-managed tannins. Their fresh, aromatic 2017 Moscato d'Asti Centive stands out among the rest of their well-made selections.

| | | |
|---|---:|---|
| ● Nizza '15 | ▼▼▼ 5 | |
| ● Barbera d'Asti Sup. Le Rocchette '16 | ▼▼ 4 | |
| ● Barbera d'Asti La Villa '17 | ▼▼ 3 | |
| ● Grignolino d'Asti Isolavilla '17 | ▼▼ 3 | |
| ○ Moscato d'Asti Centive '17 | ▼▼ 3 | |
| ○ Gavi del Comune di Gavi '17 | ▼ 3 | |
| ● M.to Rosso Trigo '15 | ▼ 4 | |
| ○ Piemonte Chardonnay I Boschi '15 | ▼ 3 | |
| ● Barbera d'Asti Sup. Nizza '13 | ♕♕♕ 5 | |
| ● Barbera d'Asti Sup. Nizza '12 | ♕♕♕ 5 | |
| ● Barbera d'Asti Sup. Nizza '11 | ♕♕♕ 5 | |
| ● Barbera d'Asti Sup. Nizza '08 | ♕♕♕ 5 | |
| ● Barbera d'Asti Sup. Nizza '07 | ♕♕♕ 5 | |
| ● Barbera d'Asti Sup. Nizza '06 | ♕♕♕ 5 | |
| ● Nizza '14 | ♕♕ 5 | |

# Orsolani

VIA MICHELE CHIESA, 12
10090 SAN GIORGIO CANAVESE [TO]
TEL. +39 012432386
www.orsolani.it

**CELLAR SALES**
**PRE-BOOKED VISITS**
**ANNUAL PRODUCTION** 140,000 bottles
**HECTARES UNDER VINE** 19.00

Orsolani's sparkling wines, crafted by Gian Francesco and later developed by his son Gianluigi, are turning 40. Erbaluce is the most important cultivar here, a grape they use in a number of different ways, including still wines and their rich Caluso Passito Sulé, a wine whose sweetness convinces thanks to good acidity and caressing viscosity. Their warhorse is their Erbaluce di Caluso La Rustìa, a wine that's earned international praise. It's aged in steel only and is surprisingly ageworthy. It's a lovely depiction of the winery can be found in Electa's rich volume 'Grandi Cru d'Italia'. 2017's heat impacted the vitality and freshness of their La Rustìa, though those characteristics do find expression in their 2011 Brut Cuvée Tradizione 1968, with fresh notes including catmint. Their 2016 Canavese Rosso Acini Sparsi, a mainly Barbera and Nebbiolo blend, also proves commendable, proving smooth and enhanced by notes of wild strawberry.

| | |
|---|---|
| ○ Caluso Passito Sulé '10 | ♀♀ 5 |
| ○ Caluso Brut Cuvée Tradizione 1968 '11 | ♀♀ 5 |
| ● Canavese Rosso Acini Sparsi '16 | ♀♀ 3 |
| ○ Erbaluce di Caluso La Rustìa '17 | ♀♀ 3 |
| ○ Erbaluce di Caluso Vintage '15 | ♀♀ 4 |
| ○ Caluso Passito Sulé '04 | ♀♀♀ 5 |
| ○ Erbaluce di Caluso La Rustìa '15 | ♀♀♀ 3* |
| ○ Erbaluce di Caluso La Rustìa '13 | ♀♀♀ 3* |
| ○ Erbaluce di Caluso La Rustìa '12 | ♀♀♀ 3* |
| ○ Erbaluce di Caluso La Rustìa '11 | ♀♀♀ 3* |
| ○ Erbaluce di Caluso La Rustìa '10 | ♀♀♀ 2* |
| ○ Erbaluce di Caluso La Rustìa '09 | ♀♀♀ 2* |

# Paitin

FRAZ. BRICCO
VIA SERRABOELLA, 20
12052 NEIVE [CN]
TEL. +39 017367343
www.paitin.it

**CELLAR SALES**
**PRE-BOOKED VISITS**
**ACCOMMODATION**
**ANNUAL PRODUCTION** 80,000 bottles
**HECTARES UNDER VINE** 17.00

The adoption of a biodynamic approach and the use of large wood barrels in the cellar haven't caused Giovanni and Silvano Pasquero Elia to forget the importance of making elegant, close-focused wines. It's an objective that they've achieved across their entire selection, which also features a faithful expression of the various cultivar used. It starts with their Barbarescos: Sorì Paitin, Serraboella and occasionally their Sorì Paitin Vecchie Vigne. These are accompanied by Langhe's classics, Dolcetto, Barbera, Nebbiolo, along with a small but successful line of Langhe Arneis. Their excellent 2015 Barbaresco Serraboella Sorì Paitin proves intense, complex and classic in style, with delicate aromas of fresh raspberry and hints of licorice and tobacco. Its balanced, measured palate has well-gauged, continuous tannic development up to its long, character-filled finish. Their fresh, vegetal 2016 Langhe Nebbiolo Starda has a beautiful personality while their 2015 Ca Veja proves more subtle and slightly woody.

| | |
|---|---|
| ● Barbaresco Serraboella Sorì Paitin '15 | ♀♀ 6 |
| ● Barbaresco Serraboella '15 | ♀♀ 5 |
| ● Langhe Nebbiolo Ca Veja '15 | ♀♀ 4 |
| ● Langhe Nebbiolo Starda '16 | ♀♀ 3 |
| ● Barbera d'Alba Sup. Campolive '15 | ♀ 5 |
| ● Barbaresco Sorì Paitin '07 | ♀♀♀ 5 |
| ● Barbaresco Sorì Paitin '04 | ♀♀♀ 5 |
| ● Barbaresco Sorì Paitin V. V. '04 | ♀♀♀ 7 |
| ● Barbaresco Sorì Paitin V. V. '01 | ♀♀♀ 7 |
| ● Barbaresco Serraboella '14 | ♀♀ 5 |
| ● Barbaresco Serraboella '13 | ♀♀ 5 |
| ● Barbaresco Serraboella Sorì Paitin '14 | ♀♀ 6 |
| ● Barbaresco Sorì Paitin '13 | ♀♀ 6 |
| ● Barbaresco Sorì Paitin '12 | ♀♀ 6 |
| ● Barbera d'Alba Serra '15 | ♀♀ 4 |

# Palladino

P.ZZA CAPPELLANO, 9
12050 SERRALUNGA D'ALBA [CN]
TEL. +39 0173613108
www.palladinovini.com

**CELLAR SALES**
**ANNUAL PRODUCTION** 180,000 bottles
**HECTARES UNDER VINE** 11.00

The winery managed today by Maurilio Palladino is turning 35 and is celebrating by earning greater recognition both in Italy and abroad. The credit goes to a series of wines made with grapes cultivated in their private vineyards or provided by independent vine growers. These have the virtue of being rich in close-focused, variegated aromas bestowed by superior grapes and not oak, as well as notable structure without being flabby or overdone. Their Barolo are the result of an attentive, traditional style and splendid crus like Ornato and Parafada di Serralunga d'Alba. Complexity, finesse and harmony characterize their 2014 Barolo Parafada, which proves smooth on the palate and already offers hints of licorice. Their elegant 2012 San Bernardo Riserva evinces a bit more alcohol in addition to pleasing notes of catmint and forest undergrowth. Their 2014 Ornato remains enveloped in notes of oak. Their harmonic 2016 Nebbiolo d'Alba presents remarkably pleasant flavor.

| | |
|---|---|
| ● Barolo Parafada '14 | ▼▼ 6 |
| ● Barolo San Bernardo Ris. '12 | ▼▼ 6 |
| ● Barbera d'Alba Sup. Bricco delle Olive '15 | ▼▼ 3 |
| ● Barolo del Comune di Serralunga d'Alba '14 | ▼▼ 5 |
| ● Barolo Ornato '14 | ▼▼ 6 |
| ● Nebbiolo d'Alba '16 | ▼▼ 4 |
| ● Barolo San Bernardo Ris. '10 | ♈♈♈ 6 |
| ● Barolo Ornato '13 | ♈♈ 6 |
| ● Barolo Ornato '11 | ♈♈ 6 |
| ● Barolo Ornato '10 | ♈♈ 6 |
| ● Barolo Parafada '13 | ♈♈ 6 |
| ● Barolo Parafada '12 | ♈♈ 6 |
| ● Barolo Parafada '11 | ♈♈ 6 |
| ● Barolo Parafada '10 | ♈♈ 6 |

# Armando Parusso

LOC. BUSSIA, 55
12065 MONFORTE D'ALBA [CN]
TEL. +39 017378257
www.parusso.com

**CELLAR SALES**
**PRE-BOOKED VISITS**
**ANNUAL PRODUCTION** 125,000 bottles
**HECTARES UNDER VINE** 23.00
**SUSTAINABLE WINERY**

Not only has Marco Parusso opted for a biodynamic approach, but also for a winemaking style aimed at Barolos of great personality, driven by extremely ripe red fruit. Marco puts respect for nature at the center of production here in Bussia, with cru that have already been identified as excellent, along with the winery itself, in the commendable work 'Italy's Noble Red Wines' penned in the 1980s by Sheldon and Pauline Wasserman (and still of interest today). Their Langhe Sauvignon Bricco is a perennially valid wine. Generally characterized by the strong presence of ripe fruit, tannins and oak, their reds lack some of the freshness and vitality typically associated with Nebbiolo and Barbera. However, the deliberately decadent style of their 2009 Barolo Bussia Riserva fascinates with a nose of peach and white truffle. Their 2016 Langhe Sauvignon Rovella releases elegant notes of elderflower and delicate tomato leaves.

| | |
|---|---|
| ● Barolo Bussia Ris. '09 | ▼▼ 8 |
| ● Barolo '14 | ▼▼ 6 |
| ○ Langhe Sauvignon Rovella '16 | ▼▼ 5 |
| ● Barbera d'Alba Sup. '16 | ▼ 5 |
| ● Langhe Nebbiolo '16 | ▼ 4 |
| ● Barbera d'Alba Sup. '00 | ♈♈♈ 5 |
| ● Barolo Bussia V. Munie '99 | ♈♈♈ 8 |
| ● Barolo Bussia V. Munie '97 | ♈♈♈ 8 |
| ● Barolo Bussia V. Munie '96 | ♈♈♈ 8 |
| ● Barolo Le Coste Mosconi '03 | ♈♈♈ 7 |
| ● Barolo V. V. in Mariondino Ris. '99 | ♈♈♈ 8 |
| ● Langhe Rosso Bricco Rovella '96 | ♈♈♈ 8 |
| ● Barolo '13 | ♈♈ 6 |
| ● Barolo Bussia '13 | ♈♈ 8 |
| ● Barolo Bussia '12 | ♈♈ 8 |
| ● Barolo Mariondino '13 | ♈♈ 7 |

# ★Pecchenino

B.TA VALDIBERTI, 59
12063 DOGLIANI [CN]
TEL. +39 017370686
www.pecchenino.com

**CELLAR SALES**
**PRE-BOOKED VISITS**
**ACCOMMODATION**
**ANNUAL PRODUCTION** 130,000 bottles
**HECTARES UNDER VINE** 28.00
**SUSTAINABLE WINERY**

The legal circumstances that caused Orlando Pecchenino to resign as president of the Barolo Protection Consortium haven't made an impact on their wines. Dolcetto is still their primary cultivar and serves as the basis for a number of different wines, including their perennially valid Dogliani Superiore Sirì d'Jermu. Those who love more structured and complex wines aged at length in oak barrels will find a benchmark of sophisticated complexity in their Bricco Botti. Their cultivation approach is respectful towards the environment and their expertise in the cellar soften Dolcetto's trademark tannins. Their harmonic 2014 Barolo San Guiseppe offers a relatively closed nose and a plate of medium structure, while their dense 2013 Barolo Le Coste di Monforte proves complex and already releases hints of licorice. Their most interesting wines come from Dolcetto, particularly their 2016 Dogliani Superiore Sirì d'Jermu, which confidently presents the great wine's characteristic flavors.

| | |
|---|---|
| ● Dogliani Sup. Sirì d'Jermu '16 | ▼▼ 4 |
| ● Langhe Nebbiolo Bricco Ravera '15 | ▼▼ 3* |
| ● Barolo Bussia '13 | ▼▼ 7 |
| ● Barolo Le Coste di Monforte '13 | ▼▼ 7 |
| ● Barolo San Giuseppe '14 | ▼▼ 6 |
| ● Dogliani Luigi '17 | ▼▼ 3 |
| ● Langhe Nebbiolo Botti '17 | ▼▼ 3 |
| ○ Alta Langa Brut Zero Psea '14 | ▼ 5 |
| ● Barbera d'Alba Quass '16 | ▼ 4 |
| ○ Langhe Maestro '17 | ▼ 3 |
| ● Barolo Le Coste '05 | ▽▽▽ 8 |
| ● Dogliani Bricco Botti '07 | ▽▽▽ 4 |
| ● Dogliani Sirì d'Jermu '09 | ▽▽▽ 3* |
| ● Dogliani Sirì d'Jermu '06 | ▽▽▽ 4 |
| ● Dogliani Sup. Bricco Botti '10 | ▽▽▽ 4* |
| ● Dolcetto di Dogliani Sup. Bricco Botti '04 | ▽▽▽ 4 |

# Pelassa

B.GO TUCCI, 43
12046 MONTÀ [CN]
TEL. +39 0173971312
www.pelassa.com

**CELLAR SALES**
**ANNUAL PRODUCTION** 80,000 bottles
**HECTARES UNDER VINE** 14.00

For some years now Davide and Daniele Pelassa have made this Roero winery a leader in the area. Their estate comprises vineyards situated in the northernmost part of Montà d'Alba, in an area that's particularly fresh and wooded. Their wines are classically styled so as to best express the territory and cultivar used. We should also mention an estate in Verduno, which gives rise to their Barolos. One of the best of its type, their 2017 Roero Arneis San Vito makes the finals. Its nose offers citrus followed by light notes of aromatic herbs while the fresh, assertive plate is full-bodied, leading to a long pleasant finish. Their 2013 Barolo San Lorenzo di Verduno expresses itself in character with rich fruity notes. Not quite as brilliant as in other in vintages, their still very well-made 2015 Roero Antaniolo Riserva gives off notes of red fruit on a palate of medium complexity still quite marked with wood.

| | |
|---|---|
| ○ Roero Arneis San Vito '17 | ▼▼ 2* |
| ● Barolo San Lorenzo di Verduno '13 | ▼▼ 6 |
| ● Nebbiolo d'Alba Sot '12 | ▼▼ 3 |
| ● Roero Antaniolo Ris. '15 | ▼▼ 4 |
| ● Barbera d'Alba Sup. San Pancrazio '16 | ▼ 3 |
| ● Langhe Bricco Enrichetta '15 | ▼ 2 |
| ● Barbera d'Alba Sup. San Pancrazio '15 | ▽▽ 3 |
| ● Barolo '12 | ▽▽ 6 |
| ● Barolo Bussia '11 | ▽▽ 6 |
| ● Nebbiolo d'Alba Sot '14 | ▽▽ 3 |
| ● Roero Antaniolo Ris. '13 | ▽▽ 4 |
| ● Roero Antaniolo Ris. '12 | ▽▽ 4 |
| ○ Roero Arneis San Vito '16 | ▽▽ 2* |

## Pelissero

VIA FERRERE, 10
12050 TREISO [CN]
TEL. +39 0173638430
www.pelissero.com

CELLAR SALES
PRE-BOOKED VISITS
ANNUAL PRODUCTION 250,000 bottles
HECTARES UNDER VINE 43.00
SUSTAINABLE WINERY

Over the years Giorgio Pelissero managed to build a large and qualified team of collaborators capable of expertly managing his 50 hectares of vineyards. Their cellar, which has expanded notably over time, was designed to allow for the most attentive work possible in terms of vinification and aging. A visit to the winery is a truly educational experience for those working in the field. Barbaresco serves as the basis of their selection and is offered in three versions as well as some Riserva wines, but their range is truly complete when it comes to Langhe's enological potential. Sun-soaked herbs and tobacco unite with fresher red fruit in their 2015 Barbaresco Vanotu. Modern and traditional styles also synthesize on the palate, with oak embracing its notable structure. Their woody 2015 Barbaresco Nubiolo offers a spicy nose and rather monolithic palate, whereas their fresh, delicate 2015 Barbera d'Alba Tulin proves truly elegant.

| | |
|---|---|
| ● Barbaresco Vanotu '15 | ♟♟ 8 |
| ● Barbera d'Alba Tulin '15 | ♟♟ 5 |
| ● Barbaresco Nubiola '15 | ♟♟ 5 |
| ● Langhe Long Now '15 | ♟♟ 5 |
| ● Barbera d'Alba Piani '16 | ♟ 3 |
| ○ Langhe Riesling Rigadin '17 | ♟ 3 |
| ● Barbaresco Vanotu '08 | ♟♟♟ 8 |
| ● Barbaresco Vanotu '07 | ♟♟♟ 8 |
| ● Barbaresco Vanotu '06 | ♟♟♟ 8 |
| ● Barbaresco Vanotu '01 | ♟♟♟ 7 |
| ● Barbaresco Nubiola '14 | ♟♟ 5 |
| ● Barbaresco Tulin '13 | ♟♟ 7 |
| ● Barbaresco Vanotu '14 | ♟♟ 8 |
| ● Barbaresco Vanotu '13 | ♟♟ 8 |
| ● Barbera d'Alba Piani '15 | ♟♟ 3 |
| ● Dolcetto d'Alba Augenta '16 | ♟♟ 3 |
| ● Langhe Long Now '14 | ♟♟ 5 |

## Pasquale Pelissero

CASCINA CROSA, 2
12052 NEIVE [CN]
TEL. +39 017367376
www.pasqualepelissero.com

CELLAR SALES
PRE-BOOKED VISITS
ANNUAL PRODUCTION 35,000 bottles
HECTARES UNDER VINE 8.00

Ornella Pelissero began helping harvest Nebbiolo grapes when she was still a child. The early death of her father, Pasquale, a proud and tenacious vigneron, forced her to assume responsibility for the entire winery while still young. It's a role that she's performing with skill and enthusiasm. The small producer's approach centers on tradition. Their Barbaresco, especially, features personality, a forthrightness that at times borders on a welcome rusticity, without the frills that come with the use of wood or excessive displays of muscularity. This year they presented only Barbaresco and their Ciabot Riserva repeats last year's fine result. The 2013 releases aromas of fresh red fruit, licorice and tobacco over its well-structured, lively and balanced palate. Their slightly less-complicated and juicy 2015 Bricco, rich in raspberry, spices and licorice, delivers powerful flavor.

| | |
|---|---|
| ● Barbaresco Ciabot Ris. '13 | ♟♟ 5 |
| ● Barbaresco San Giuliano Bricco '15 | ♟♟ 5 |
| ● Barbaresco Bricco San Giuliano '14 | ♟♟ 5 |
| ● Barbaresco Bricco San Giuliano '12 | ♟♟ 5 |
| ● Barbaresco Bricco San Giuliano '11 | ♟♟ 5 |
| ● Barbaresco Bricco San Giuliano '10 | ♟♟ 5 |
| ● Barbaresco Bricco San Giuliano '09 | ♟♟ 5 |
| ● Barbaresco Cascina Crosa '14 | ♟♟ 4 |
| ● Barbaresco Cascina Crosa '13 | ♟♟ 4 |
| ● Barbaresco Ciabot Ris. '12 | ♟♟ 4 |
| ● Barbaresco Ciabot Ris. '10 | ♟♟ 4 |
| ● Barbaresco San Giuliano Bricco '13 | ♟♟ 5 |
| ● Dolcetto d'Alba '11 | ♟♟ 2* |
| ● Langhe Nebbiolo Pasqualin '11 | ♟♟ 2* |

# Pertinace

LOC. PERTINACE, 2/5
12050 TREISO [CN]
TEL. +39 0173442238
www.pertinace.com

**CELLAR SALES**
**PRE-BOOKED VISITS**
**ANNUAL PRODUCTION** 650,000 bottles
**HECTARES UNDER VINE** 90.00

The small cooperative winery of Pertinace, whose names comes from the Roman emperor and military leader born in the area, was founded in the early 1960s. Today it's composed of 17 partners who cultivate 90 hectares of vineyards in Treiso. Year-by-year they've been consolidating their high quality standards and maintaining their excellent prices while also follow a classic, traditional style that's winning over international customers as well. The combination of fruit and oak in their 2015 Barbaresco Nervo impressed, with harmonic toasted aromas and notes of cherry. Still quite young, it shows character and sophistication with a strong, energetic palate. Their 2015 Barbaresco Marcarini offers notes of quinine and black berries with a rich, weighty palate lightly marked by slightly tight tannins. Their 2015 Barbaresco still needs time as it proves a bit closed.

| | |
|---|---|
| ● Barbaresco Nervo '15 | ♟♟ 5 |
| ● Barbaresco '15 | ♟♟ 5 |
| ● Barbaresco Castellizzano '15 | ♟♟ 5 |
| ● Barbaresco Marcarini '15 | ♟♟ 5 |
| ● Dolcetto d'Alba '17 | ♟♟ 3 |
| ● Langhe Nebbiolo '16 | ♟ 3 |
| ● Barbaresco '14 | ♀♀ 5 |
| ● Barbaresco '13 | ♀♀ 5 |
| ● Barbaresco Castellizzano '14 | ♀♀ 5 |
| ● Barbaresco Castellizzano '13 | ♀♀ 5 |
| ● Barbaresco Marcarini '14 | ♀♀ 5 |
| ● Barbaresco Marcarini '13 | ♀♀ 5 |
| ● Barbaresco Nervo '13 | ♀♀ 5 |
| ● Barbera d'Alba '15 | ♀♀ 3 |
| ● Dolcetto d'Alba '16 | ♀♀ 3 |
| ● Dolcetto d'Alba '15 | ♀♀ 2* |

# Pescaja

VIA SAN MATTEO, 59
14010 CISTERNA D'ASTI [AT]
TEL. +39 0141979711
www.pescaja.com

**PRE-BOOKED VISITS**
**ANNUAL PRODUCTION** 200,000 bottles
**HECTARES UNDER VINE** 23.50

Giuseppe Guido's winery is among the few to propose wines from the Terre Alfieri appellation. Founded in 1990 and significantly enlarged in 1998 (with the purchase of most of Nizza's Pescaja Opera Pia), it avails itself of two principal estates. One of these is in Cisterna d'Asti, an area characterized by primarily sandy soil, and which hosts their cellar. The other is in Nizza Monferrato, where the soil is more calcareous. Their wines are modern, with particular attention shown to aromatic clarity and the richness of fruity. Despite offering a bit too much wood, their very compelling 2105 Nizza Solineri reaches the finals by virtue of its notes of black fruit, hints of cocoa and long, juicy palate of rich fruit. Their fresh, plucky and aromatic 2017 Terre Alfieri Arneis Sololuce, as well as their flavorful, well-structured 2017 Roero Arneis, with notes of aromatic herbs and annurca apple, are both well made.

| | |
|---|---|
| ● Nizza Solneri '15 | ♟♟ 4 |
| ● Barbera d'Asti Soliter '17 | ♟♟ 2* |
| ○ Roero Arneis '17 | ♟♟ 2* |
| ○ Terre Alfieri Arneis Sololuce '17 | ♟♟ 2* |
| ⊙ Piemonte Rosato Le Fleury '17 | ♟ 2 |
| ● Terre Alfieri Nebbiolo Tuké '16 | ♟ 3 |
| ● Barbera d'Asti Soliter '16 | ♀♀ 2* |
| ● Barbera d'Asti Soliter '15 | ♀♀ 2* |
| ○ M.to Solo Luna '14 | ♀♀ 5 |
| ● Nizza Solneri '14 | ♀♀ 4 |
| ○ Roero Arneis '16 | ♀♀ 2* |
| ○ Terre Alfieri Arneis '16 | ♀♀ 2* |
| ○ Terre Alfieri Arneis '15 | ♀♀ 2* |

## Le Piane

P.ZZA MATTEOTTI, 1
28010 BOCA [NO]
TEL. +39 3483354185
www.bocapiane.com

CELLAR SALES
PRE-BOOKED VISITS
ANNUAL PRODUCTION 45,000 bottles
HECTARES UNDER VINE 8.00
SUSTAINABLE WINERY

Christopf Künzli's story began some 20 years ago when he fell in love with a territory and its temperate climate, with its landscapes shaped by a centuries-old tradition of vine growing, and with a robust, elegant wine. And so it was that he took on the responsibility of managing a new winery, one that has revitalized an entire area and become a model for the many smaller producers that have popped up over recent years. This is the background behind Le Piane's Boca, a wine aged at length in Slavonian oak barrels and that sees Nebbiolo accompanied by a spicy touch of Vespolina. Their 2015 Boca will be ready for next year, but they're still waiting on the 2013, given its over-abundance of energy. 2014 only saw a version of their Maggiorina, testifying to their gravitas. However, there are things to report, including three newly acquired hectares in Boca and new Erbaluce in the pipeline. Retasting of their 2010, 2008 and 2004 Boca sees them all in good health.

| | |
|---|---|
| ● Boca '12 | ♟♟♟ 8 |
| ● Boca '11 | ♟♟♟ 8 |
| ● Boca '10 | ♟♟♟ 7 |
| ● Boca '08 | ♟♟♟ 7 |
| ● Boca '06 | ♟♟♟ 6 |
| ● Boca '05 | ♟♟♟ 6 |
| ● Boca '04 | ♟♟♟ 6 |
| ● Boca '03 | ♟♟♟ 6 |
| ● Maggiorina '12 | ♟♟ 3 |
| ● Mimmo '11 | ♟♟ 5 |
| ● Mimmo '10 | ♟♟ 4 |
| ● Piane '12 | ♟♟ 6 |
| ● Piane '11 | ♟♟ 5 |

## Le Pianelle

S.DA FORTE, 24
13862 BRUSNENGO [BI]
TEL. +39 3478772726
www.lepianelle.com

PRE-BOOKED VISITS
ANNUAL PRODUCTION 12,000 bottles
HECTARES UNDER VINE 3.00

Peter Dipoli is known in Alto Adige as the producer of the prized Sauvignon Voglar. His decision to try his hand at north Piedmont's Nebbiolo was made along with his friend Dieter Heuskel 15 years ago. It was followed by a busy period that saw the purchases of dozens of small plots and preparing the cellar for production. With the 2010 vintage operations began and today their selection centers on three wines: their Bramaterra (80% Nebbiolo with the rest made up of Croatina and Vespolina), their Croatina and a Rosato. This last belongs to the Coste della Sesia appellation. Their extraordinary 2105 Bramaterra reaches the finals thanks to fresh, crisp red fruit over licorice and iodine. The palate is sophisticated, creamy and tactile with a glove of tannin and fruit for a progression of flavors enlivened by remarkable freshness leading to a long, ample, multifaceted finish. Their Rosato Al Posto dei Fiori proves simple and linear.

| | |
|---|---|
| ● Bramaterra '15 | ♟♟ 8 |
| ☉ Coste della Sesia Rosato Al Posto dei Fiori '17 | ♟♟ 3 |
| ● Bramaterra '14 | ♟♟ 8 |
| ● Bramaterra '13 | ♟♟ 8 |
| ● Bramaterra '12 | ♟♟ 8 |
| ● Bramaterra '11 | ♟♟ 8 |
| ☉ Coste della Sesia Rosato Al Posto dei Fiori '16 | ♟♟ 3 |

# Pico Maccario

VIA CORDARA, 87
14046 MOMBARUZZO [AT]
TEL. +39 0141774522
www.picomaccario.com

CELLAR SALES
PRE-BOOKED VISITS
ANNUAL PRODUCTION 650,000 bottles
HECTARES UNDER VINE 70.00

Pico Maccario was founded by brothers
Pico and Vitaliano Maccario in 1997 on an
estate of 70 hectares of contiguous
vineyards in the Barbera d'Asti appellation.
The terrain cultivated here is clay, medium
textured and dominated by Barbera, which
constitutes 80% of the estate. Small
quantities of Cabernet Sauvignon,
Chardonnay, Merlot, Favorita, Freisa and
Sauvignon make up the rest. Their selection
features 11 wines and exhibits a decidedly
modern style aimed at richness of fruit and
texture. Their aromatic 2017 Barbera d'Asti
Lavignone, a lovely example of Barbera
from that vintage, proves approachable and
juicy with a pleasant, fresh finish. Their
2016 Barbera d'Asti Superiore Epico offers
aromas that reflect its wood aging and
notes of blackberry jam leading to a
rounded, enfolding palate. Their well-made
2016 Barbera d'Asti Superiore Tre Roveri
releases notes of rain-soaked earth.

| | |
|---|---|
| ● Barbera d'Asti Lavignone '17 | 🍷🍷🍷 3* |
| ● Barbera d'Asti Sup. Epico '16 | 🍷🍷 5 |
| ● Barbera d'Asti Sup. Tre Roveri '16 | 🍷🍷 4 |
| ● Barbera d'Asti Villa della Rosa '17 | 🍷🍷 2* |
| ○ M.to Bianco Vita '17 | 🍷 5 |
| ● Barbera d'Asti Sup. Epico '15 | 🍷🍷🍷 5 |
| ● Barbera d'Asti Lavignone '16 | 🍷🍷 3 |
| ● Barbera d'Asti Lavignone '15 | 🍷🍷 3 |
| ● Barbera d'Asti Lavignone '14 | 🍷🍷 3 |
| ● Barbera d'Asti Sup. Epico '14 | 🍷🍷 5 |
| ● Barbera d'Asti Sup. Tre Roveri '15 | 🍷🍷 4 |
| ● Barbera d'Asti Sup. Tre Roveri '14 | 🍷🍷 4 |
| ● Barbera d'Asti Sup. Tre Roveri '13 | 🍷🍷 4 |
| ● Barbera d'Asti Villa della Rosa '16 | 🍷🍷 2* |
| ○ M.to Bianco Vita '15 | 🍷🍷 4 |

# ★Pio Cesare

VIA CESARE BALBO, 6
12051 ALBA [CN]
TEL. +39 0173440386
www.piocesare.it

ANNUAL PRODUCTION 400,000 bottles
HECTARES UNDER VINE 70.00

It was 1881 when Cesare Pio founded what
would become one of Langhe's most
prestigious and important brands. Today the
winery is led by Pio Boffa, who's
accompanied by his cousin Augusto,
nephew Cesare and daughter Federica
Rosy. The team oversee an estate of some
70 hectares situated both in Barolo (Ornato,
Colombaro, Gustava, Roncaglie and Ravera)
and in Barbaresco (Il Bricco and Santo
Stefanetto). Their selection is wide and
exceptionally consistent. In addition to
Nebbiolos, they make wines with Barbera,
Dolcetto, Grignolino, Cortese, Arneis,
Moscato and Chardonnay. They presented a
high-quality selection for tasting and two
made our finals. Their 2014 Barbaresco Il
Bricco presents virtually impenetrable color,
a quinine and tobacco nose, and a powerful,
extractive palate with still-integrating wood.
Notes of roots and sweet tobacco from their
2014 Barolo Ornato hit the nose while the
palate offers structure and savory energy.
Their extremely pleasant 2016 Barbera
d'Alba Fides delivers balsamic notes along
with well-defined, crunchy fruit.

| | |
|---|---|
| ● Barbaresco Il Bricco '14 | 🍷🍷 8 |
| ● Barbera d'Alba Fides '16 | 🍷🍷 5 |
| ● Barolo Ornato '14 | 🍷🍷 8 |
| ● Barbaresco '14 | 🍷🍷 8 |
| ● Barolo '14 | 🍷🍷 8 |
| ● Barolo Ornato '13 | 🍷🍷🍷 8 |
| ● Barolo Ornato '12 | 🍷🍷🍷 8 |
| ● Barolo Ornato '11 | 🍷🍷🍷 8 |
| ● Barolo Ornato '10 | 🍷🍷🍷 8 |
| ● Barolo Ornato '09 | 🍷🍷🍷 8 |
| ● Barolo Ornato '08 | 🍷🍷🍷 8 |
| ● Barolo Ornato '06 | 🍷🍷🍷 8 |
| ● Barbaresco '13 | 🍷🍷 8 |
| ● Barbaresco Il Bricco '13 | 🍷🍷 8 |
| ● Barolo '13 | 🍷🍷 8 |

# Luigi Pira

VIA XX SETTEMBRE, 9
12050 SERRALUNGA D'ALBA [CN]
TEL. +39 0173613106
pira.luigi@alice.it

CELLAR SALES
PRE-BOOKED VISITS
ANNUAL PRODUCTION 50,000 bottles
HECTARES UNDER VINE 12.00

In the 1950s, Luigi Pira began selling grapes and bulk wine. The turning point came sometime around the 1960s, when he decided to start bottling wines under his own name. Today his sons Gianpaolo, Romolo and Claudio look after the family's 12 hectares of vineyards. Half of these, in Barolo, are dedicated to Nebbiolo, which gives rise to four wines: a 'base version' and three crus (Margheria, Marenca and Vignarionda). The other half host Barbera, Dolcetto and more Nebbiolo (for their Langhe selection). It's difficult to find such high quality through an entire range, a testament to the winery's gravitas. They merged all their crus into their only 2014 Barolo and it proves sophisticated, ripe and harmonious, embellished with pencil lead and watermelon tones. Don't miss the snappy mint and juniper hints of their 2016 Langhe Nebbiolo, offering red fruit of extraordinary fragrance and flavor. Their Dolcetto and Barbera are both more than compelling.

| | |
|---|---|
| ● Langhe Nebbiolo '16 | 🍷🍷 3* |
| ● Barbera d'Alba Sup. '16 | 🍷🍷 3 |
| ● Barolo del Comune di Serralunga d'Alba '14 | 🍷🍷 5 |
| ● Dolcetto d'Alba '17 | 🍷🍷 2* |
| ● Barolo Marenca '11 | 🍷🍷🍷 7 |
| ● Barolo Marenca '09 | 🍷🍷🍷 7 |
| ● Barolo Marenca '08 | 🍷🍷🍷 7 |
| ● Barolo V. Rionda '06 | 🍷🍷🍷 8 |
| ● Barolo V. Rionda '04 | 🍷🍷🍷 8 |
| ● Barolo Vignarionda '12 | 🍷🍷🍷 8 |
| ● Barolo Marenca '13 | 🍷🍷 7 |
| ● Barolo Marenca '10 | 🍷🍷 7 |
| ● Barolo Margheria '11 | 🍷🍷 6 |
| ● Barolo V. Rionda '11 | 🍷🍷 8 |
| ● Barolo Vignarionda '13 | 🍷🍷 8 |

# Guido Platinetti

VIA ROMA, 60
28074 GHEMME [NO]
TEL. +39 3389945783
www.platinettivini.com

CELLAR SALES
PRE-BOOKED VISITS
ANNUAL PRODUCTION 15,000 bottles
HECTARES UNDER VINE 5.50

Platinetti's roots go back more than a century, when Stefano and Andrea Fontana's grandparents began cultivating and selling grapes. Today the brothers are carrying on a 50-year legacy of wine production, managing both the cellar and their vineyards, and making an important contribution towards reviving the Ghemme appellation. At the center of everything is Nebbiolo, which is produced both as a monovarietal both in their Ghemme and their Colline Novaresi. Their production style is classic and traditional, with oak never dominating. Fleshy fruit and seductive harmony characterize their sumptuous 2014 Ghemme Vigne Ronco al Maso, which offers clear hints of rhubarb and captivating fresh red fruit on an enveloping palate with a long, very clean finish. Their deft and inviting 2017 Vespolina proves vegetal and spicy with hints of both peppercorn and pepper, while their tightly-knit 2016 Nebbiolo proves easy and linear with notes of raspberry and sweet tobacco.

| | |
|---|---|
| ● Ghemme V. Ronco al Maso '13 | 🍷🍷 4 |
| ● Colline Novaresi Nebbiolo '16 | 🍷🍷 3 |
| ● Colline Novaresi Vespolina '17 | 🍷🍷 3 |
| ● Colline Novaresi Barbera Pieleo '16 | 🍷 3 |
| ● Guido | 🍷 2 |
| ● Colline Novaresi Barbera Pieleo '11 | 🍷🍷 3 |
| ● Colline Novaresi Nebbiolo '11 | 🍷🍷 3 |
| ● Colline Novaresi Vespolina '16 | 🍷🍷 2* |
| ● Colline Novaresi Vespolina '14 | 🍷🍷 2* |
| ● Colline Novaresi Vespolina '12 | 🍷🍷 2* |
| ● Ghemme V. Ronco Maso '12 | 🍷🍷 4 |
| ● Ghemme V. Ronco Maso '10 | 🍷🍷 4 |

# Marco Porello

C.SO ALBA, 71
12043 CANALE [CN]
TEL. +39 0173979324
www.porellovini.it

**CELLAR SALES**
**PRE-BOOKED VISITS**
**ANNUAL PRODUCTION** 130,000 bottles
**HECTARES UNDER VINE** 15.00

Marco Porello has been leading this family-run winery since 1994. There are two facilities, in Canale the cellar for winemaking and bottling (as well as their administrative head office) and a cellar for aging that's directly adjacent to Castello di Guarene. They have vineyards in Vezza d'Alba, where the terrain is sandy and mineral rich, and in Canale, where the terrain is medium-dense calcareous clay. Some of the vineyards in the latter go back to the mid-20th century. Their selection features wines that pursue freshness and elegance. Whichever appellation they are from, Marco Porello's wines are always among the best and their 2017 Roero Arneis Camestrì proves no exception. It offers citrus aromas and notes of aromatic herbs on a long, savory palate with good staying power and grip. Their equally commendable 2105 Roero Rorretta, delivers noticeable red fruit, rich juicy pulp and a persistent finish. The rest of their proposed selections are also well made.

| | | |
|---|---|---|
| ○ Roero Arneis Camestrì '17 | ♟♟ 3* |
| ● Roero Torretta '15 | ♟♟ 4 |
| ● Barbera d'Alba Filatura '16 | ♟♟ 4 |
| ● Barbera d'Alba Mommiano '17 | ♟♟ 2* |
| ● Nebbiolo d'Alba '16 | ♟♟ 3 |
| ○ Roero Arneis '17 | ♟♟ 2* |
| ○ Langhe Favorita '17 | ♟ 2 |
| ● Roero Torretta '06 | ♟♟♟ 3* |
| ● Roero Torretta '04 | ♟♟♟ 3* |
| ● Barbera d'Alba Filatura '15 | ♟♟ 4 |
| ● Barbera d'Alba Filatura '14 | ♟♟ 3 |
| ● Barbera d'Alba Mommiano '15 | ♟♟ 2* |
| ○ Roero Arneis '16 | ♟♟ 2* |
| ○ Roero Arneis Camestrì '15 | ♟♟ 3 |
| ● Roero Torretta '14 | ♟♟ 4 |
| ● Roero Torretta '13 | ♟♟ 3* |

# Guido Porro

VIA ALBA, 1
12050 SERRALUNGA D'ALBA [CN]
TEL. +39 0173613306
www.guidoporro.com

**CELLAR SALES**
**PRE-BOOKED VISITS**
**ACCOMMODATION**
**ANNUAL PRODUCTION** 35,000 bottles
**HECTARES UNDER VINE** 8.00

The first bottles labeled Guido Porro (grandfather of the current owner, also named Guido) go back to the early 1980s. Their prized Lazzarito is the winery's historic cru and gives rise to two versions, their Lazzairasco, a full-bodied wine, and their Santa Canterina, which is more nuanced and graceful. In addition to these important plots, since 2011 they've also availed themselves of cru Gianetto, while in 2012 they added new vineyards on Vignarionda. Their approach is openly classic, with fermentation in steel and concrete vats, and aging in 2500 liter Slavonian oak barrels. The three Barolos they presented faithfully reflect 2014 and their pure, austere Barolo Vigna clearly belongs among the best of the vintage. Savory, and with clean, clear red fruit it delivers a far-reaching, long, balsamic finish. Their floral, delicate and truly classic Barolo Vigna Lazzairasco already proves focused, expressive and enjoyable.

| | | |
|---|---|---|
| ● Barolo V. Lazzairasco '14 | ♟♟ 5 |
| ● Barolo V. Rionda '14 | ♟♟ 8 |
| ● Barolo V. Santa Caterina '14 | ♟♟ 5 |
| ● Lange Nebbiolo Camilu '16 | ♟♟ 4 |
| ● Barolo Gianetto '14 | ♟ 5 |
| ● Dolcetto d'Alba V. Pari '17 | ♟ 3 |
| ● Barolo V. Lazzairasco '13 | ♟♟♟ 5 |
| ● Barolo V. Lazzairasco '12 | ♟♟♟ 5 |
| ● Barolo V. Lazzairasco '11 | ♟♟♟ 5 |
| ● Barolo V. Lazzairasco '09 | ♟♟♟ 5 |
| ● Barolo V. Lazzairasco '07 | ♟♟♟ 5 |
| ● Barolo Gianetto '13 | ♟♟ 5 |
| ● Barolo V. Santa Caterina '13 | ♟♟ 5 |

## Post dal Vin
## Terre del Barbera

FRAZ. POSSAVINA
VIA SALIE, 19
14030 ROCCHETTA TANARO [AT]
TEL. +39 0141644143
www.postdalvin.it

CELLAR SALES
PRE-BOOKED VISITS
ANNUAL PRODUCTION 80,000 bottles
HECTARES UNDER VINE 100.00

This cooperative winery, one of the most important in Asti, was founded in 1959 and today it's comprised of 100 grower members. Their vineyards, which are situated primarily in the municipalities of Rocchetta Tanaro, Cortiglione and Masio, give rise primarily to Barbera (in accordance with established local tradition), accompanied by other traditional grape varieties, like Grignolino, Dolcetto, Freisa and Moscato. Most of the wines produced are dedicated to various types of Barbera, all of them traditionally styled with a focus on pleasantness and richness of fruit. Post dal Vin's wines are always consistent, especially their vintage ones: the 2017 Barbera d'Asti proves floral, fresh and supple, while their richer and spicier 2017 Barbera d'Asti Maricca plays on approachable fruit. Their two 2016 Barbera d'Asti Superiore wines also appear excellent: the Castagnassa, with its notes of black wild berries, reveals good juice and structure while the Briccofiore offers up rich pulp and more structure.

| | |
|---|---|
| ● Barbera d'Asti '17 | ♟♟ 1* |
| ● Barbera d'Asti Maricca '17 | ♟♟ 2* |
| ● Barbera d'Asti Sup. Briccofiore '16 | ♟♟ 2* |
| ● Barbera d'Asti Sup. Castagnassa '16 | ♟♟ 3 |
| ● Barbera del M.to La Matutona '17 | ♟ 2 |
| ● Grignolino d'Asti '17 | ♟ 1* |
| ● Barbera d'Asti Maricca '16 | ♟♟ 2* |
| ● Barbera d'Asti Maricca '14 | ♟♟ 2* |
| ● Barbera d'Asti Sup. Bricco Fiore '13 | ♟♟ 2* |
| ● Barbera d'Asti Sup. Briccofiore '15 | ♟♟ 2* |
| ● Barbera d'Asti Sup. BriccoFiore '14 | ♟♟ 2* |
| ● Barbera d'Asti Sup. Castagnassa '14 | ♟♟ 2* |
| ● Barbera del M.to La Matutona '15 | ♟♟ 2* |
| ● Grignolino d'Asti '16 | ♟♟ 2* |

## Giovanni Prandi

FRAZ. CASCINA COLOMBÈ
VIA FARINETTI, 5
12055 DIANO D'ALBA [CN]
TEL. +39 017369248
www.prandigiovanni.it

CELLAR SALES
PRE-BOOKED VISITS
ANNUAL PRODUCTION 20,000 bottles
HECTARES UNDER VINE 5.00
SUSTAINABLE WINERY

The controlled appellation of Diano d'Alba is so small that it's unable to penetrate that markets it deserves. Here Dolcetto gives rise to particularly fruity, fresh, caressing and charming wines with a vibrant purple-red color and violet highlights. Alessandro Prandi is one of the wine's best interpreters, drawing on an approach centered on absolute purity, thus eschewing aging in wood barrels in favor of steel or concrete. His Sörì Cristina and Sörì Colombé are definitely worth trying, though the entire selection is of sure quality. Their 2017 Sörì Cristina wins the friendly Dolcetto di Diano competition. Its great richness on the nose adds a delicate note of peach stone to elegant and intense red fruit. The palate comes through juicy and balanced, without particularly evident tannins or acidity. Their sound and very enjoyable 2016 Nebbiolo d'Alba is well worth tasting.

| | |
|---|---|
| ● Dolcetto di Diano d'Alba Sörì Cristina '17 | ♟♟ 2* |
| ● Barbera d'Alba '17 | ♟♟ 2* |
| ● Dolcetto di Diano d'Alba Sörì Colombè '17 | ♟♟ 2* |
| ● Nebbiolo d'Alba '16 | ♟♟ 3 |
| ○ Langhe Arneis '17 | ♟ 2 |
| ● Barbera d'Alba '16 | ♟♟ 2* |
| ● Barbera d'Alba '15 | ♟♟ 2* |
| ● Dolcetto di Diano d'Alba Sörì Colombé '16 | ♟♟ 2* |
| ● Dolcetto di Diano d'Alba Sörì Cristina '16 | ♟♟ 2* |
| ● Dolcetto di Diano d'Alba Sörì Cristina '15 | ♟♟ 2* |
| ● Nebbiolo d'Alba '15 | ♟♟ 3 |

# La Prevostura

VIA CASCINA PREVOSTURA, 1
13853 LESSONA [BI]
TEL. +39 0158853188
www.laprevostura.it

**CELLAR SALES**
**PRE-BOOKED VISITS**
**RESTAURANT SERVICE**
**ANNUAL PRODUCTION** 15,000 bottles
**HECTARES UNDER VINE** 5.50

The winery's name comes from the historic Prevostura vineyard, a plot characterized by the presence of sand, which guarantees the development of broad aromas and tannins that are never too assertive. Another characteristic of Lessona, a municipality that gives rise to a number of northern Piedmont's Nebbiolos, is the high acidity, which confers a freshness of taste across every vintage. Marco and Davide Bellini began 15 years ago with a clear plan: their Lessona had to be made exclusively with Nebbiolo and maturation had to take place in small French wood barrels so as to bring out a sophisticated elegance. Their 2014 Lessona doesn't overdo power and structure but comes through rather elegant with exciting drinkability. It offers up hints of spice, quinine and licorice that follow through onto a lively, full-flavored and slightly tannic palate. Aromas of red fruit, tobacco and rhubarb are featured in the rich and savory 2015 Coste della Seisa Rosso Muntacc, a very successful blend of 85% Nebbiolo and Vespolina. Their tempting 2016 Garsun proves just a touch firmer.

| | | |
|---|---|---|
| ● Coste della Sesia Rosso Muntacc '15 | 🍷🍷 | 4 |
| ● Coste della Sesia Rosso Garsun '16 | 🍷🍷 | 3 |
| ● Lessona '14 | 🍷🍷 | 5 |
| ⊙ Piemonte Rosato Corinna '17 | 🍷 | 3 |
| ● Lessona '12 | 🍷🍷🍷 | 5 |
| ● Bramaterra '12 | 🍷🍷 | 5 |
| ● Bramaterra '11 | 🍷🍷 | 5 |
| ● Coste della Sesia Rosso Muntacc '13 | 🍷🍷 | 3* |
| ● Coste della Sesia Rosso Muntacc '12 | 🍷🍷 | 3* |
| ● Coste della Sesia Rosso Muntacc '11 | 🍷🍷 | 3 |
| ● Coste della Sesia Rosso Muntacc '10 | 🍷🍷 | 3 |
| ● Lessona '13 | 🍷🍷 | 5 |
| ● Lessona '11 | 🍷🍷 | 5 |
| ● Lessona '10 | 🍷🍷 | 5 |
| ● Lessona '09 | 🍷🍷 | 5 |
| ⊙ Piemonte Rosato Corinna '16 | 🍷🍷 | 3 |

# Prinsi

VIA GAIA, 5
12052 NEIVE [CN]
TEL. +39 017367192
www.prinsi.it

**CELLAR SALES**
**PRE-BOOKED VISITS**
**ANNUAL PRODUCTION** 60,000 bottles
**HECTARES UNDER VINE** 14.50

The winery's goal has always been to privilege the vineyard over the cellar, doing everything possible to preserve the purest qualities of the grape. Maximum respect is shown to the characteristics of each vintage, no invasive oak is used for aging, nothing is done to so as to force a wine to become more muscular. Daniele Lequio has absorbed this philosophy and is acting accordingly, supported by his entire family. The heart of the estate beats for Barbaresco, which comes in the form of their Fausoni, Gallina and Gaia Principe wines, but they also produce Langhe's classics and, for some years now, a Brut 'Metodo Classico' sparkler. Their 2015 Barbaresco Gaia Principe is already rather complex and elegant. It features a flavorsome, moderate body, good balance and very sweet tannins. Their 2015 Gallina proves spicy and reminiscent of raspberry aromas, while the palate comes through slightly alcoholic and firm. Of the Barbera Superiore wines from the 2016 vintage, their Bosco appeared more balanced and elegant, while the Much is still dealing with the impact of oak.

| | | |
|---|---|---|
| ● Barbaresco Gaia Principe '15 | 🍷🍷 | 5 |
| ● Barbaresco Gallina '15 | 🍷🍷 | 5 |
| ● Barbera d'Alba Sup. Il Bosco '16 | 🍷🍷 | 3 |
| ● Barbera d'Alba Sup. Much '16 | 🍷 | 3 |
| ○ Langhe Arneis Il Nespolo '17 | 🍷 | 3 |
| ● Barbaresco Fausoni Ris. '11 | 🍷🍷 | 5 |
| ● Barbaresco Fausoni Ris. '10 | 🍷🍷 | 5 |
| ● Barbaresco Gaia Principe '14 | 🍷🍷 | 5 |
| ● Barbaresco Gaia Principe '13 | 🍷🍷 | 5 |
| ● Barbaresco Gallina '14 | 🍷🍷 | 5 |
| ● Barbaresco Gallina '13 | 🍷🍷 | 5 |
| ● Barbaresco Gallina '12 | 🍷🍷 | 5 |
| ○ Camp'd Pietru '16 | 🍷🍷 | 4 |

## ★Produttori del Barbaresco

VIA TORINO, 54
12050 BARBARESCO [CN]
TEL. +39 0173635139
www.produttoridelbarbaresco.com

CELLAR SALES
PRE-BOOKED VISITS
ACCOMMODATION
ANNUAL PRODUCTION 500,000 bottles
HECTARES UNDER VINE 105.00

This praiseworthy cooperative winery, which just celebrated its 60-year anniversary, avails itself of the support of 50 vine growing members. Their forward-thinking and winning philosophy centers exclusively on Nebbiolo, with only three kinds produced: their Langhe Nebbiolo, their Barbaresco and their Riserva wines. These last are only produced when director Gianni Testa believes conditions are right. For example, they weren't produced even during the valid 2010 and 2012 vintages. Their crus do a good job of recounting Barbaresco's history: Asili, Montefico, Muncagota, Montestefano, Ovello, Pajé, Pora, Rabajà and Rio Sordo. Their basic Barbaresco from 2015 is one of the most pleasant vintages ever produced. It proves elegant, succulent and pleasantly drinkable. But it's their 2013 Asili Riserva that earns the Tre Bicchieri: its elegant aromas ranging from raspberries to spices lead into a sensationally juicy and lingering palate. Their whole range displays high quality, especially their Rio Sordo, Montestefano and Rabajà.

| | | |
|---|---|---|
| ● Barbaresco Asili Ris. '13 | ♟♟♟ | 6 |
| ● Barbaresco '15 | ♟♟ | 5 |
| ● Barbaresco Montestefano Ris. '13 | ♟♟ | 6 |
| ● Barbaresco Rabaja' Ris. '13 | ♟♟ | 6 |
| ● Barbaresco Rio Sordo Ris. '13 | ♟♟ | 6 |
| ● Barbaresco Montefico Ris. '13 | ♟♟ | 6 |
| ● Barbaresco Muncagota Ris. '13 | ♟♟ | 6 |
| ● Barbaresco Ovello Ris. '13 | ♟♟ | 6 |
| ● Barbaresco Paje' Ris. '13 | ♟♟ | 6 |
| ● Barbaresco Pora Ris. '13 | ♟♟ | 6 |
| ● Barbaresco Ovello Ris. '09 | ♟♟♟ | 6 |
| ● Barbaresco Vign. in Montestefano Ris. '05 | ♟♟♟ | 6 |
| ● Barbaresco Vign. in Ovello Ris. '08 | ♟♟♟ | 6 |
| ● Barbaresco Vign. in Pora Ris. '07 | ♟♟♟ | 6 |

## Cantina Produttori del Gavi

VIA CAVALIERI DI VITTORIO VENETO, 45
15066 GAVI [AL]
TEL. +39 0143642786
www.cantinaproduttoridelgavi.it

CELLAR SALES
PRE-BOOKED VISITS
ANNUAL PRODUCTION 300,000 bottles
HECTARES UNDER VINE 220.00

For some years now the staff at Cantina Produttori have been doing well and the arrival of a good vintage, 2015, highlighted the virtuous cycle. A dozen wines are produced, both stills and sparklers, with Cortese serving as the cornerstone of the entire selection. Their wines are modern, tight and aimed at highlighting the attributes of the cultivar. Maturation occurs on the fine lees in temperature-controlled inox tanks right up to the moment they're bottled. Winemaker Andrea Pancotti, who's collaborated with the winery since 2005, oversees production. We found two new wines in our tastings: their Mille951, which replaces the Etichetta Nera, and the Forte. The former offers up intense and stylish aromas of fresh herbs and fern, shifting towards notes of citrus and white peach. The palate comes through intense and elegant, with acidity lengthening into a very lingering finish. Their polished and intense Forte displays lovely floral and flinty notes, giving way to a rich and powerful palate, with lovely acidity and a long and savory finish.

| | | |
|---|---|---|
| ○ Gavi del Comune di Gavi Mille951 '17 | ♟♟ | 3* |
| ○ Gavi Il Forte '17 | ♟♟ | 2* |
| ○ Gavi G '16 | ♟ | 3 |
| ○ Gavi del Comune di Gavi GG '15 | ♟♟♟ | 3* |
| ○ Gavi del Comune di Gavi Et. Nera '15 | ♟♟ | 2* |
| ○ Gavi del Comune di Gavi Et. Nera '14 | ♟♟ | 2* |
| ○ Gavi del Comune di Gavi GG '13 | ♟♟ | 3* |
| ○ Gavi del Comune di Gavi La Maddalena '15 | ♟♟ | 3* |
| ○ Gavi G '15 | ♟♟ | 3* |
| ○ Gavi G '14 | ♟♟ | 3* |
| ○ Gavi Maddalena '16 | ♟♟ | 2* |
| ○ Gavi Primi Grappoli '15 | ♟♟ | 2* |

# ★Prunotto

c.so Barolo, 14
12051 Alba [CN]
Tel. +39 0173280017
www.prunotto.it

**CELLAR SALES**
**PRE-BOOKED VISITS**
**ACCOMMODATION**
**ANNUAL PRODUCTION** 850,000 bottles
**HECTARES UNDER VINE** 55.00

The winery was founded in the early 20th
century as a cooperative (back then it went
under the name Ai Vini delle Langhe). In the
1950s it was taken over by Alfredo
Prunotto, one of the original founders, and
then left to brothers Beppe and Tino Colla,
and Carlo Filiberti. The most recent chapter
of this long story saw the Antinori family
purchase the estate in the mid-1990s,
enlarging it (with vineyards in Bussia, Bric
Turot and Costamiole), modernizing its
facilities and recalibrating its selection
with a focus on solid, modern wines. Their
2014 Barolo Bussia exhibits intense minty
aromas and good ripe fruit, making for a
very pleasant palate. Their 2014 Barolo
follows along similar lines, featuring richer
juice and the same good tannic extraction.
Their 2012 Barolo Bussia Vigna Colonello
Riserva offers up overtones of leather and
pencil lead, combined with very ripe fruit
and an earthy palate. The 2015 Barbaresco
Bric Turot proves very elegant, close-
focused and creamy.

| | | |
|---|---|---|
| ● Barbaresco Bric Turot '15 | ♟♟ | 5 |
| ● Barbera d'Alba Pian Romualdo '16 | ♟♟ | 3 |
| ● Barbera d'Asti Fiulot '17 | ♟♟ | 2* |
| ● Barolo '14 | ♟♟ | 5 |
| ● Barolo Bussia '14 | ♟♟ | 6 |
| ● Barolo Bussia V. Colonello Ris. '12 | ♟♟ | 8 |
| ● M.to Mompertone '15 | ♟♟ | 2* |
| ● Nizza Costamiole Ris. '15 | ♟♟ | 4 |
| ● Dolcetto d'Alba '17 | ♟ | 2 |
| ● Langhe Nebbiolo Occhetti '16 | ♟ | 3 |
| ● Barbera d'Asti Costamiòle '99 | ♟♟♟ | 4* |
| ● Barolo Bussia '01 | ♟♟♟ | 8 |
| ● Barolo Bussia '99 | ♟♟♟ | 8 |
| ● Barolo Bussia '98 | ♟♟♟ | 8 |

# La Raia

s.da Monterotondo, 79
15067 Novi Ligure [AL]
Tel. +39 0143743685
www.la-raia.it

**CELLAR SALES**
**PRE-BOOKED VISITS**
**ACCOMMODATION**
**ANNUAL PRODUCTION** 150,000 bottles
**HECTARES UNDER VINE** 50.00
**VITICULTURE METHOD** Certified Biodynamic
**SUSTAINABLE WINERY**

On the road that runs from Novi Ligure to
Monterotondo the Rossi Cairo family
created a bona fide microcosm: vineyards,
pastures, farmland where various ancient
grains are cultivated, woods of chestnut and
acacia trees. There's also hospitality, thanks
to the renovation of Borgo Merlassino, and
much more. In short, it's a model of a vision
tied to the environment and ecosystem. The
winery has been certified biodynamic by
Demeter since 2007. Piero Ballario, their
valued winemaker, oversees their selection
of five wines: three Gavis and two Piemonte
Barberas. Their Gavi Riserva Vigna della
Madonnina and Pisè both performed quite
well and reached our finals. The first
exhibits remarkably elegant floral, white fruit
and flinty aromas, while the palate offers up
great body and a very lingering fresh finish
full of character. It earned the Tre Bicchieri.
Their Pisè features tertiary aromas of
tobacco and dried flowers leading into a
full-bodied, long and fresh palate.

| | | |
|---|---|---|
| ○ Gavi V. della Madonnina Ris. '16 | ♟♟♟ | 3* |
| ○ Gavi Pisè '15 | ♟♟ | 5 |
| ○ Gavi '17 | ♟♟ | 3 |
| ● Piemonte Barbera Largé '13 | ♟ | 4 |
| ○ Gavi '16 | ♟♟ | 3* |
| ○ Gavi '15 | ♟♟ | 3* |
| ○ Gavi Pisé '14 | ♟♟ | 4 |
| ○ Gavi Pisé '11 | ♟♟ | 3* |
| ○ Gavi Ris. '15 | ♟♟ | 3* |
| ○ Gavi Ris. '12 | ♟♟ | 3* |
| ○ Gavi V. della Madonnina Ris. '14 | ♟♟ | 3* |
| ○ Gavi V. della Madonnina Ris. '13 | ♟♟ | 3* |
| ● Piemonte Barbera '16 | ♟♟ | 3 |
| ● Piemonte Barbera '13 | ♟♟ | 3 |

# Renato Ratti

FRAZ. ANNUNZIATA, 7
12064 LA MORRA [CN]
TEL. +39 017350185
www.renatoratti.com

CELLAR SALES
PRE-BOOKED VISITS
ACCOMMODATION
ANNUAL PRODUCTION 350,000 bottles
HECTARES UNDER VINE 35.00

In addition to being an innovative producer, Renato Ratti deserves to be remembered for his writings on enology and his extremely useful map, 'Carta del Barolo'. For those who are passionate about the area, we should also note that his grandson Massimo Martinelli, for many years his close collaborator in the cellar, recently published a new and brilliant edition of the volume 'Il Barolo come lo sento io' ('Barolo as I See It'). Today Massimo's son Pietro Ratti is managing the winery, offering a vast array of lovely wines, with Barolo at the forefront, naturally, starting with their Rocche dell'Annunziata and Marcenasco crus. Good wood and remarkable spices feature in this fruity 2014 Barolo Conca, exhibiting a powerful palate, not too much tannin and good suppleness. Their 2014 Barolo Marcenasco displays clear toastiness and comes through rather firm, with no lack of exciting vegetal notes. Their caressing 2016 Langhe Nebbiolo Ochetti, from nearby Roero, offers up elegant rose aromas and a pleasantly plush palate.

# Réva

LOC. SAN SEBASTIANO, 68
12065 MONFORTE D'ALBA [CN]
TEL. +39 0173789269
www.revamonforte.it

CELLAR SALES
PRE-BOOKED VISITS
ACCOMMODATION AND RESTAURANT SERVICE
ANNUAL PRODUCTION 35,000 bottles
HECTARES UNDER VINE 8.00
SUSTAINABLE WINERY

Miroslav Lekes doesn't rest on his laurels and continues his policy of fine-tuning his winery. His strategy includes purchasing small but prized crus, creating a brilliant staff that he leaves plenty of room to work, developing and promoting his wines, and creating a space to receive visitors between Monforte and Doglianti. The young, passionate and experienced enologist Gian Luca Colombo oversees winemaking. A not overly-abundant vintage combined with careful winemaking choices have geared this 2014 Barolo towards elegance, freshness and supple drinkability, contrasted with slightly vegetal tannins. Their modern 2016 Nebbiolo d'Alba proves elegant and enjoyable, with good acidity and body. However, it doesn't display excessive power and is refreshed by pleasant tannins at the finish. Their delicate and fresh Bianco Grey, made with Sauvignon grapes, comes through charming.

| | |
|---|---|
| ● Barolo Conca '14 | ¶¶ 8 |
| ● Barolo Marcenasco '14 | ¶¶ 6 |
| ● Barolo Rocche dell'Annunziata '14 | ¶¶ 8 |
| ● Langhe Nebbiolo Ochetti '16 | ¶¶ 4 |
| ○ Langhe Chardonnay Brigata '17 | ¶ 3 |
| ● Langhe Dolcetto Colombè '17 | ¶ 3 |
| ● Barolo Rocche '06 | ¶¶¶ 8 |
| ● Barbera d'Alba Battaglione '15 | ¶¶ 3 |
| ● Barolo Conca '13 | ¶¶ 8 |
| ● Barolo Conca '12 | ¶¶ 8 |
| ● Barolo Marcenasco '13 | ¶¶ 6 |
| ● Barolo Rocche dell'Annunziata '13 | ¶¶ 8 |
| ● Barolo Rocche dell'Annunziata '12 | ¶¶ 8 |
| ● Dolcetto d'Alba Colombè '14 | ¶¶ 3 |
| ● M.to Rosso Villa Pattono '15 | ¶¶ 5 |
| ● Nebbiolo d'Alba Ochetti '14 | ¶¶ 4 |

| | |
|---|---|
| ● Barolo '14 | ¶¶ 5 |
| ● Nebbiolo d'Alba '16 | ¶¶ 3* |
| ○ Langhe Bianco Grey '17 | ¶¶ 3 |
| ● Barbera d'Alba Sup. '16 | ¶ 3 |
| ● Barbera d'Alba Sup. '15 | ¶¶ 3 |
| ● Barolo '13 | ¶¶ 5 |
| ● Barolo '12 | ¶¶ 5 |
| ● Barolo Ravera '13 | ¶¶ 7 |
| ● Barolo Ravera '12 | ¶¶ 7 |
| ● Nebbiolo d'Alba '15 | ¶¶ 3 |

# Carlo & Figli Revello

FRAZ. SANTA MARIA
12064 LA MORRA [CN]
TEL. +39 3356765021
www.carlorevello.com

PRE-BOOKED VISITS
ANNUAL PRODUCTION 25,000 bottles
HECTARES UNDER VINE 7.00

Carlo Revello's hands speak to his philosophy: a wine producer has to know each of his vines, pruning and attending to each personally, teaching his collaborators what the desired vitality and yield to be extracted from each plant is. And the same principle holds for the cellar, where Carlo continually follows the fermentation of each barrel. In the new facility, built after he and his brother parted ways, only large wood barrels are used, testifying to the choice to return to a past that doesn't only mean tradition, but also the pursuit of a new regional classic. Their 2014 Barolo features a restrained structure but great pleasantness. It balances hints of the maturation barrels with fruity and vegetal overtones. Their 2014 Barolo R.G. reveals a lot of red fruit on the nose, with a balsamic background and lovely pulp. When you consider the rather small vintage, its balance proves surprisingly pleasant. Their 2016 Barbera d'Alba appears interesting and noteworthy.

| | |
|---|---|
| ● Barolo R.G. '14 | ♟♟ 7 |
| ● Barbera d'Alba '16 | ♟♟ 3 |
| ● Barolo '14 | ♟♟ 5 |
| ● Langhe Nebbiolo '16 | ♟ 3 |
| ● Barolo '13 | ♟♟ 5 |
| ● Barolo R.G. '13 | ♟♟ 7 |

# F.lli Revello

FRAZ. ANNUNZIATA, 103
12064 LA MORRA [CN]
TEL. +39 017350276
www.revellofratelli.it

CELLAR SALES
PRE-BOOKED VISITS
ACCOMMODATION
ANNUAL PRODUCTION 45,000 bottles
HECTARES UNDER VINE 8.00
SUSTAINABLE WINERY

The cellar was founded in 1992 by the Revello brothers. Today it's managed only by Lorenzo, a strong, capable worker both in the field and in the cellar who avails himself of the important support of his wife and two children. In addition to the winery's four classic crus Rocche dell'Annunziata, Conca, Gattera and Giachini, all in the municipality of La Morra, they've just added a small plot in one of Serraluna d'Alba's prized crus, Cerretta. Their style is modern and always fruit-driven, with a background of elegant French oak in the serious and perennially well-crafted Barbera d'Alba Ciabot du Re. Their 2016 Ciabot du Re is a very high-quality expression of Barbera d'Alba: sweet flowers merge with aromas of plum and juniper in a delicate framework shaped by oak aging. Its very elegant palate is refreshed by vegetal overtones. Their 2014 Barolo Giachini offers up lovely balance, with still clearly evident wood.

| | |
|---|---|
| ● Barbera d'Alba Ciabot du Re '16 | ♟♟ 5 |
| ● Barolo Giachini '14 | ♟♟ 7 |
| ● Langhe Nebbiolo '16 | ♟♟ 3 |
| ● Barbera d'Alba Ciabot du Re '05 | ♟♟♟ 5 |
| ● Barbera d'Alba Ciabot du Re '00 | ♟♟♟ 5 |
| ● Barolo '93 | ♟♟♟ 5 |
| ● Barolo Rocche dell'Annunziata '01 | ♟♟♟ 8 |
| ● Barolo Rocche dell'Annunziata '00 | ♟♟♟ 8 |
| ● Barolo Rocche dell'Annunziata '97 | ♟♟♟ 8 |
| ● Barolo V. Conca '99 | ♟♟♟ 7 |
| ● Barolo '13 | ♟♟ 5 |
| ● Barolo Conca '13 | ♟♟ 7 |
| ● Barolo Gattera '13 | ♟♟ 6 |
| ● Barolo Gattera '12 | ♟♟ 6 |
| ● Barolo Giachini '13 | ♟♟ 7 |
| ● Barolo Rocche dell'Annunziata '12 | ♟♟ 8 |

## Michele Reverdito

FRAZ. RIVALTA
B.TA GARASSINI, 74B
12064 LA MORRA [CN]
TEL. +39 017350336
www.reverdito.it

CELLAR SALES
PRE-BOOKED VISITS
ANNUAL PRODUCTION 70,000 bottles
HECTARES UNDER VINE 16.00

Michele Reverdito avails himself of a
number of crus for the production of
Barolos. In La Morra there's Ascheri, Bricco
Cogni, Castagni and La Serra. In Monforte
d'Alba there's Bricco San Pietro. In
Serralunga there's the elevated and prized
Badarina, in Verduno there's Riva Rocca.
Today their winemaking style is the result of
a number of carefully followed experiments,
which led Michele to hold firm to the belief
that a classic approach is the best. In the
cellar their barrels are getting bigger so that
aging is restricted to its original purpose
without the aromatic enhancements. Both
their Bricco Cogni and 2014 Ascheri exhibit
marked and clean vegetal overtones. The
first maintains the notable structure typical
of Barolos, while the second plays more on
balance. Their Castagni comes through
small but well-orchestrated. Their
noteworthy 2016 Langhe Nebbiolo Simane
features lovely body and good wood.

| | |
|---|---|
| ● Barolo Ascheri '14 | ♥♥ 8 |
| ● Barolo Bricco Cogni '14 | ♥♥ 8 |
| ● Barolo Castagni '14 | ♥♥ 7 |
| ● Langhe Nebbiolo Simane '16 | ♥♥ 4 |
| ● Barolo Bricco Cogni '04 | ♥♥♥ 6 |
| ● Barolo 10 Anni Ris. '05 | ♥♥ 8 |
| ● Barolo Ascheri '13 | ♥♥ 5 |
| ● Barolo Ascheri '12 | ♥♥ 5 |
| ● Barolo Badarina '12 | ♥♥ 6 |
| ● Barolo Badarina '11 | ♥♥ 5 |
| ● Barolo Bricco Cogni '13 | ♥♥ 6 |
| ● Barolo Bricco Cogni '12 | ♥♥ 6 |
| ● Barolo Riva Rocca '12 | ♥♥ 5 |
| ● Barolo Riva Rocca '11 | ♥♥ 5 |
| ● Langhe Nebbiolo Simane '15 | ♥♥ 3 |

## Giuseppe Rinaldi

VIA MONFORTE, 5
12060 BAROLO [CN]
TEL. +39 017356156
rinaldimarta@libero.it

CELLAR SALES
PRE-BOOKED VISITS
ANNUAL PRODUCTION 35,000 bottles
HECTARES UNDER VINE 6.50

We will never forget the late Beppe Rinaldi.
Probably no other Italian producer has been
able to make wines that transmit such
thrilling, edge-of-your-seat energy in the
glass. And it's not a coincidence that Beppe
Rinaldi's wines have been among Italy's
most appreciated in recent years, bolstered
by strong domestic and international
demand. His legacy now passes on to his
daughters Marta and Carlotta, who've been
exceptionally skilled at handling both
production and communications. Their
approach calls for spontaneous
fermentation and aging in large wood
barrels. Their 2014 Brunate starts out softly
with raspberry and rosemary overtones and
a light whiff of alcohol, then accelerates
across a well-defined and savory palate. It
comes through citrusy and unbridled, with a
never-ending finish. Their 2014 Tre Tine
offers up a spicier profile, reminiscent of
earth and roots, while its powerful palate
closes with elegant herbaceous overtones.

| | |
|---|---|
| ● Barolo Brunate '14 | ♥♥ 7 |
| ● Barolo Tre Tine '14 | ♥♥ 7 |
| ● Barolo Brunate '13 | ♥♥♥ 7 |
| ● Barolo Brunate '11 | ♥♥♥ 7 |
| ● Barolo Brunate-Le Coste '07 | ♥♥♥ 7 |
| ● Barolo Brunate-Le Coste '06 | ♥♥♥ 7 |
| ● Barolo Brunate-Le Coste '01 | ♥♥♥ 6 |
| ● Barolo Cannubi S. Lorenzo-Ravera '04 | ♥♥♥ 6 |
| ● Barolo Brunate '12 | ♥♥ 7 |
| ● Barolo Tre Tine '13 | ♥♥ 7 |
| ● Barolo Tre Tine '12 | ♥♥ 7 |
| ● Barolo Tre Tine '11 | ♥♥ 7 |
| ● Barolo Tre Tine '10 | ♥♥ 7 |
| ● Langhe Nebbiolo '13 | ♥♥ 4 |

# Francesco Rinaldi & Figli

VIA CROSIA, 30
12060 BAROLO [CN]
TEL. +39 0173440484
www.rinaldifrancesco.it

CELLAR SALES
PRE-BOOKED VISITS
ACCOMMODATION
ANNUAL PRODUCTION 70,000 bottles
HECTARES UNDER VINE 11.00

Here they've only ever used old, large Slavonian oak barrels so as to capture the purity of the grapes cultivated on their family's highly prized crus, Cannubi and Brunate. Of course, today their barrels are replaced more frequently and their wines have gained in elegance and aromatic precision. But sisters Piera and Paolo Rinaldi are firm believers in classic Barolo. In their cellar you can find the enlightening historical portrait and philosophy of winemaking 'Barolo: personaggi e mito' ('Barolo: Figures and Myths'), edited by Omega Arte and adorned with Chris Meier's lovely images. The quality of their historic Cannubi vineyard has come out again in the 2014 vintage, producing a Barolo with a limited structure but admirable balance: its nose features lovely tobacco and licorice notes on a red fruit background, with slight green overtones. The palate reveals balanced and docile tannins and a long finish full of character. Their Brunate proves less mature and rather green, while the 2016 Nebbiolo d'Alba comes through delicate and spicy.

| | |
|---|---|
| ● Barolo Cannubi '14 | 🍷🍷 7 |
| ● Nebbiolo d'Alba '16 | 🍷🍷 3 |
| ● Barolo Brunate '14 | 🍷 7 |
| ● Barbaresco '14 | 🍷🍷 5 |
| ● Barbaresco '13 | 🍷🍷 5 |
| ● Barbera d'Alba '13 | 🍷🍷 3 |
| ● Barolo '10 | 🍷🍷 6 |
| ● Barolo Brunate '13 | 🍷🍷 7 |
| ● Barolo Brunate '12 | 🍷🍷 7 |
| ● Barolo Brunate '11 | 🍷🍷 6 |
| ● Barolo Brunate '10 | 🍷🍷 7 |
| ● Barolo Cannubi '13 | 🍷🍷 7 |
| ● Barolo Cannubi '12 | 🍷🍷 7 |
| ● Barolo Cannubi '11 | 🍷🍷 7 |
| ● Barolo Cannubi '10 | 🍷🍷 7 |
| ● Dolcetto d'Alba Roussot '15 | 🍷🍷 2* |

# Massimo Rivetti

VIA RIVETTI, 22
12052 NEIVE [CN]
TEL. +39 017367505
www.rivettimassimo.it

CELLAR SALES
PRE-BOOKED VISITS
ANNUAL PRODUCTION 70,000 bottles
HECTARES UNDER VINE 25.00

As highlighted on their labels, Massimo Rivetti's winery is a 'family farm'. They're able to look after their some 25 hectares of vineyards and a cozy tavern in Neive's historical center, the Porta San Rocco Wine Bar, thanks to a collective enthusiasm for their work. The scenic Froi farm manor houses their production center. It's been owned by the family for 60 years and serves as the heart of their vineyards, which are all organically managed. In many cases these are as old as the manor itself. Their Barbaresco is excellent, foremost their Serrabolella and Froi, but that's not all. They also offer a Barbera d'Alba and two Metodo Classico sparkling wines Lovely classic notes of licorice and tar in the 2015 Barbaresco Froi give way to overtones of meadow herbs on a fresh fruity background. Its palate comes through solid, balanced and pleasant with a long and slightly austere finish. The 2016 Barbera d'Alba Vigna Serraboella is very satisfying, elegant, not biting, with close-focused notes of black fruit. Their flavorsome, clean and pleasant 2015 Pinot Nero also impressed us.

| | |
|---|---|
| ● Barbaresco Froi '15 | 🍷🍷 6 |
| ● Barbera d'Alba Sup. V. Serraboella '16 | 🍷🍷 4 |
| ● Barbera d'Alba Sup. Froi '16 | 🍷🍷 2* |
| ● Langhe Pinot Nero '15 | 🍷🍷 3 |
| ● Langhe Nebbiolo Avene '16 | 🍷 3 |
| ● Barbaresco '14 | 🍷🍷 5 |
| ● Barbaresco '13 | 🍷🍷 5 |
| ● Barbaresco Froi '14 | 🍷🍷 6 |
| ● Barbaresco Froi '13 | 🍷🍷 5 |
| ● Barbaresco Froi '12 | 🍷🍷 5 |
| ● Barbaresco Froi '11 | 🍷🍷 5 |
| ● Barbaresco Serraboella '13 | 🍷🍷 7 |
| ● Barbera d'Alba Sup. V. Serraboella '12 | 🍷🍷 4 |
| ● Langhe Garasin '13 | 🍷🍷 3 |
| ● Langhe Nebbiolo Avene '15 | 🍷🍷 3 |

## Rizzi

VIA RIZZI, 15
12050 TREISO [CN]
TEL. +39 0173638161
www.cantinarizzi.it

CELLAR SALES
PRE-BOOKED VISITS
ACCOMMODATION
ANNUAL PRODUCTION 70,000 bottles
HECTARES UNDER VINE 38.00
SUSTAINABLE WINERY

Quality, professionalism and consistency. The Dellapiana family's winery, active since 1974, takes its name from the cru where their production center is situated (with crus Nervo and Pajoré providing the rest when it comes to Barbaresco, though they can also count on plots in the prized crus of Manzola, Bricco di Neive and Giacone). All their wines are offered at consumer-friendly prices, and If you consider the quality they've reached in recent decades, it's not a surprise that Rizzi's selection is increasingly popular among the most well-informed wine lovers. Their excellent 2013 Barbaresco Rizzi Boito Riserva stands out for its pure, fresh and close-focused aromas, steady savoriness and the flavor shock that confers complexity and length to a charming palate. Their fine and airy 2015 Barbaresco Pajorè goes along the same lines, while the 2015 Barbaresco Nervo proves more approachable, with a very pleasant creaminess.

| | |
|---|---|
| ● Barbaresco Nervo '15 | ♟♟ 6 |
| ● Barbaresco Pajorè '15 | ♟♟ 6 |
| ● Barbaresco Rizzi Boito Ris. '13 | ♟♟ 5 |
| ○ Alta Langa Pas Dosé '13 | ♟♟ 5 |
| ● Barbaresco Rizzi '15 | ♟♟ 5 |
| ● Barbera d'Alba '16 | ♟♟ 3 |
| ● Dolcetto d'Alba '17 | ♟♟ 3 |
| ○ Langhe Chardonnay '17 | ♟ 3 |
| ● Langhe Nebbiolo '16 | ♟ 3 |
| ● Barbaresco Boito Ris. '10 | ♟♟♟ 6 |
| ● Barbaresco Nervo '14 | ♟♟♟ 6 |
| ● Barbaresco Pajorè '14 | ♟♟ 6 |
| ● Barbaresco Pajorè '13 | ♟♟ 6 |
| ● Barbaresco Rizzi '14 | ♟♟ 5 |
| ● Barbaresco Rizzi '13 | ♟♟ 5 |
| ● Barbaresco Rizzi '12 | ♟♟ 5 |

## Roagna

LOC. PAJÉ
S.DA PAGLIERI, 7
12050 BARBARESCO [CN]
TEL. +39 0173635109
www.roagna.com

CELLAR SALES
PRE-BOOKED VISITS
ANNUAL PRODUCTION 50,000 bottles
HECTARES UNDER VINE 15.00

Alfredo Roagna began making wine in 1971 and in 1978 he created Crichët Pajé. The rest, as they say, is history. His winery's second life began in 1989 with the purchase of the Pira vineyard in Castiglione Falletto, where young Luca came into his own in the field and in the cellar. It's here that we find their new, spacious, modern cellar, surrounded by Nebbiolo vineyards cultivated without the use of pesticides. Their wines are among the most sought after in the world. In addition to their superb Crichët Pajé they offer three Barbarescos and a Barolo called Vecchie Vlti. But their entire Docg line is of outstanding quality. Their Crichët Pajé is an excellent interpretation of the 2010 vintage. It comes through rich in sun-drenched herbs and refreshing hints of raspberry, leading into a palate with magical balance. But our Tre Bicchieri went to their marvelous 2013 Barbaresco Asili Vecchie Viti, where blueberries, redcurrants, licorice and tobacco make for an overall excellent combination. Its palate combines the elegance of this famous variety with the craftsmanship of the greatest cellarman.

| | |
|---|---|
| ● Barbaresco Asili V. Viti '13 | ♟♟♟ 8 |
| ● Barbaresco Crichët Pajé '10 | ♟♟ 8 |
| ● Barbaresco Pajè V. Viti '13 | ♟♟ 8 |
| ● Barbaresco Asili V. Viti '07 | ♟♟♟ 8 |
| ● Barbaresco Crichët Pajé '08 | ♟♟♟ 8 |
| ● Barbaresco Crichët Pajé '06 | ♟♟♟ 8 |
| ● Barbaresco Crichët Pajé '05 | ♟♟♟ 8 |
| ● Barbaresco Crichët Pajé '04 | ♟♟♟ 8 |
| ● Barbaresco Pajé '11 | ♟♟♟ 8 |
| ● Barbaresco Asili V. Viti '12 | ♟♟ 8 |
| ● Barbaresco Pajé '12 | ♟♟ 8 |
| ● Barbaresco Pajè V. Viti '12 | ♟♟ 8 |
| ● Barolo Pira '12 | ♟♟ 8 |
| ● Barolo Pira V. Viti '12 | ♟♟ 8 |
| ● Langhe Rosso '12 | ♟♟ 3 |

# ★Albino Rocca

S.DA RONCHI, 18
12050 BARBARESCO [CN]
TEL. +39 0173635145
www.albinorocca.com

CELLAR SALES
PRE-BOOKED VISITS
ANNUAL PRODUCTION 100,000 bottles
HECTARES UNDER VINE 18.00
SUSTAINABLE WINERY

Albino Rocca made a name for itself under Angelo Rocca, but today its managed by his three daughters, with results that keep getting better. Indeed, their Barbaresco Ronchi, a symbol of exceptional quality, is included in Hugh Johnson and Jancis Robinson's 'World Atlas of Wines'. Their Barbaresco is another interesting wine, made with grapes cultivated in their Montersino cru, as is their new release, which is dedicated to Angelo. Their Cortese La Rocca, a wine made with grapes from San Rocco Seno d'Elvio in Alba and aged in wood barrels, is regularly counted among Piedmont's best whites. This year we only tasted their Barbarescos. Their 2015 Barbaresco Cottà proves elegant, with subtle aromas of tobacco, licorice and dried flowers. Its palate may not be powerful, but it comes through well-orchestrated, with nice tannins and a fresh, juicy finish. Sun-drenched herbs and tannins feature in their pleasant and long 2014 Barbaresco Ronchi, while the 2015 Angelo is bright, lively and graceful.

| | | |
|---|---|---|
| ● Barbaresco Angelo '15 | ♟♟ | 5 |
| ● Barbaresco Cottà '15 | ♟♟ | 5 |
| ● Barbaresco Ronchi '14 | ♟♟ | 6 |
| ● Barbaresco Montersino '15 | ♟♟ | 6 |
| ● Barbaresco Ovello V. Loreto '15 | ♟♟ | 6 |
| ● Barbaresco Angelo '13 | ♟♟♟ | 5 |
| ● Barbaresco Ovello V. Loreto '11 | ♟♟♟ | 6 |
| ● Barbaresco Ovello V. Loreto '09 | ♟♟♟ | 6 |
| ● Barbaresco Ovello V. Loreto '07 | ♟♟♟ | 6 |
| ● Barbaresco Ronchi '10 | ♟♟♟ | 6 |
| ● Barbaresco Vign. Brich Ronchi '05 | ♟♟♟ | 6 |
| ● Barbaresco Vign. Brich Ronchi '03 | ♟♟♟ | 6 |
| ● Barbaresco Vign. Brich Ronchi Ris. '06 | ♟♟♟ | 8 |
| ● Barbaresco Vign. Brich Ronchi Ris. '04 | ♟♟♟ | 8 |
| ● Barbaresco Vign. Loreto '04 | ♟♟♟ | 6 |

# ★Bruno Rocca

S.DA RABAJÀ, 60
12050 BARBARESCO [CN]
TEL. +39 0173635112
www.brunorocca.it

CELLAR SALES
PRE-BOOKED VISITS
ANNUAL PRODUCTION 70,000 bottles
HECTARES UNDER VINE 15.00
VITICULTURE METHOD Certified Organic

Over his 40 years of activity Bruno Rocca has never rested on his laurels, even if he's seen a lot them since his first bottles of Barbaresco Rabajà. He's purchased a number of new Nebbiolo vineyards, and when it comes to Barbera he's pushed all the way into Astigiano. The cellar, which is constantly being enlarged and enriched, is a structure of rare beauty. His son Francesco is no less explosive than he and is dedicating himself with an infectious passion to improving both cultivation and winemaking itself. His goal is to identify the purest possible yeasts and a method of working the grapes without oxygen. Their Barbaresco Rabajà is an excellent interpretation of the 2014 vintage, hingeing more on balance, freshness and elegance than power of taste, although it displays considerable fruity pulp. The open, close-focused and complex aromas of their 2012 Riserva Currà lead into a plush palate, thanks to the presence of very sweet tannins. Our acclaim also goes to their very balanced and flavorsome 2015 Barbaresco.

| | | |
|---|---|---|
| ● Barbaresco Currà Ris. '12 | ♟♟♟ | 8 |
| ● Barbaresco '15 | ♟♟ | 7 |
| ● Barbaresco Rabajà '14 | ♟♟ | 8 |
| ● Barbera d'Alba '16 | ♟♟ | 5 |
| ● Barbera d'Asti '16 | ♟♟ | 4 |
| ● Barbaresco Coparossa '04 | ♟♟♟ | 8 |
| ● Barbaresco Maria Adelaide '07 | ♟♟♟ | 8 |
| ● Barbaresco Maria Adelaide '04 | ♟♟♟ | 8 |
| ● Barbaresco Maria Adelaide '01 | ♟♟♟ | 8 |
| ● Barbaresco Rabajà '13 | ♟♟♟ | 8 |
| ● Barbaresco Rabajà '12 | ♟♟♟ | 8 |
| ● Barbaresco Rabajà '11 | ♟♟♟ | 8 |
| ● Barbaresco Rabajà '10 | ♟♟♟ | 8 |
| ● Barbaresco Rabajà '09 | ♟♟♟ | 8 |
| ● Barbaresco Rabajà '01 | ♟♟♟ | 8 |

# Rocche Costamagna

VIA VITTORIO EMANUELE, 8
12064 LA MORRA [CN]
TEL. +39 0173509225
www.rocchecostamagna.it

CELLAR SALES
PRE-BOOKED VISITS
ACCOMMODATION
ANNUAL PRODUCTION 95,000 bottles
HECTARES UNDER VINE 15.80

Rocche Costamagna is a historic winery that's been operational since the mid-19th century. Today the vast estate, which is situated in Rocche dell'Annunziata, is overseen by Alessandro Locatelli. This prized cru gives rise to a Barolo with particularly fresh aromas, with balsamic and minty hints, and a mouth that features delicate tannins. Their Barbera d'Alba Rocche delle Rocche is a perennially valid wine made with grapes cultivated in Verduno. Those who are interested in knowing more about Langhe's geological and viticultural features can read more in the 'Atlante dei territori del vino italiano' ('Atlas of Italian Territories and Wines'). Their 2014 Barolo Rocche dell'Annunziata merges wonderfully balanced wood and just-ripe red fruit with spices and tobacco. Its palate comes through rather powerful and rich, with tight-knit tannins inserted in an elegant and lively pulp. Their modern 2012 Riserva Bricco Francesco is still slightly tannic, while their 2015 Barbera d'Alba Superiore Rocche delle Rocche proves rich in fruit and rather plush. Their overall selection displays certain quality.

| | |
|---|---|
| ● Barolo Rocche dell'Annunziata '14 | 🍷🍷 6 |
| ● Barbera d'Alba '16 | 🍷🍷 3 |
| ● Barbera d'Alba Sup. Rocche delle Rocche '15 | 🍷🍷 4 |
| ● Barolo Rocche dell'Annunziata Bricco Francesco Ris. '12 | 🍷🍷 8 |
| ○ Langhe Arneis '17 | 🍷🍷 3 |
| ● Langhe Nebbiolo Roccardo '16 | 🍷🍷 3 |
| ● Dolcetto d'Alba '17 | 🍷 2 |
| ● Barolo Rocche dell'Annunziata '04 | 🍷🍷🍷 5 |
| ● Barbera d'Alba Sup. Rocche delle Rocche '14 | 🍷🍷 4 |
| ● Barbera d'Alba Sup. Rocche delle Rocche '13 | 🍷🍷 4 |
| ● Barolo '13 | 🍷🍷 5 |
| ● Barolo Rocche dell'Annunziata '13 | 🍷🍷 6 |
| ● Barolo Rocche dell'Annunziata Bricco Francesco Ris. '11 | 🍷🍷 8 |

# ★Rocche dei Manzoni

LOC. MANZONI SOPRANI, 3
12065 MONFORTE D'ALBA [CN]
TEL. +39 017378421
www.rocchedeimanzoni.it

CELLAR SALES
PRE-BOOKED VISITS
ANNUAL PRODUCTION 250,000 bottles
HECTARES UNDER VINE 40.00

Valentino Migliorini's arrival in Langhe, in the mid-1970s, was met with curiosity and even bewilderment by Barolo's rather static wine industry. But soon enough Podere Rocche dei Manzoni had established itself as a dynamic, valid producer, earning the trust both of local winemakers and the markets. In addition to their splendid production center, the estate comprises a number of important crus (primarily Nebbiolo). Their wines are modern and mature, a bit woody in their first years, soft. Both of their Metodo Classico sparkling wines are noteworthy. Their Chardonnay L'Angelica has never been so good. In 2015 they adopted a style where oak, hazelnut and a buttery background make an elegant combination. Their supple, clean and fresh 2015 Barbera d'Alba La Cresta exhibits lovely drinkability. Their two Barolos display the winery's trademark personality almost opulent fruit and lots of sweet oak. Their justly famous sparkling wines are excellent as always.

| | |
|---|---|
| ● Barbera d'Alba La Cresta '15 | 🍷🍷 6 |
| ○ Langhe Chardonnay L'Angelica '15 | 🍷🍷 8 |
| ⊙ Valentino Brut Zero M. Cl. Rosé '12 | 🍷🍷 8 |
| ● Barolo Bricco San Pietro V. d'la Roul '13 | 🍷🍷 8 |
| ● Barolo Perno V. Cappella di S. Stefano '13 | 🍷🍷 8 |
| ○ Valentino Brut Elena M. Cl. Ris. '13 | 🍷🍷 7 |
| ● Barbera d'Alba Sup. Sorito Mosconi '15 | 🍷 7 |
| ● Langhe Nebbiolo '16 | 🍷 6 |
| ● Barolo V. Big 'd Big '99 | 🍷🍷🍷 8 |
| ● Barolo V. Cappella di S. Stefano '01 | 🍷🍷🍷 8 |
| ● Barolo V. d'la Roul '07 | 🍷🍷🍷 8 |
| ○ Valentino Brut Zero Ris. '98 | 🍷🍷🍷 5 |
| ○ Valentino Brut Zero Ris. '93 | 🍷🍷🍷 5 |
| ○ Valentino Brut Zerò Ris. '92 | 🍷🍷🍷 5 |

# Il Rocchin

LOC. VALLEMME, 39
15066 GAVI [AL]
TEL. +39 0143642228
www.ilrocchin.it

**CELLAR SALES**
**PRE-BOOKED VISITS**
**ANNUAL PRODUCTION** 50,000 bottles
**HECTARES UNDER VINE** 20.00

Bruno Zerbo's story, as well as that of his children Francesca and Angelo (who today lead his winery) is written on the walls of the Rocchin farm manor. It's the building from which the winery takes its name, and it testifies to producer's evolution of the years, with the conversion from cattle raising to winemaking. It started with the extant vineyards, which grew over time. Then in 1992 the first bottles were made. Since then it's been a continued pattern of renovation and acquisition. Today they can be found on international markets with modern wines, both in terms of winemaking style and packaging. We started off with a lovely version of a Gavi del Comune di Gavi, Il Bosco. It exhibits an intense straw color and the nose opens intense, floral and fruity with an underlying mineral sensation. The palate comes through balanced and fresh, with a lingering finish. Their basic Gavi and Barbera del Monferrato Il Basacco also delivered.

| | |
|---|---|
| ○ Gavi del Comune di Gavi Il Bosco '17 | ♥♥ 3* |
| ● Barbera del M.to Il Basacco '16 | ♥♥ 3 |
| ○ Gavi del Comune di Gavi '17 | ♥♥ 2* |
| ● Dolcetto di Ovada '16 | ♀♀ 2* |
| ● Dolcetto di Ovada '15 | ♀♀ 2* |
| ○ Gavi del Comune di Gavi '16 | ♀♀ 2* |
| ○ Gavi del Comune di Gavi '15 | ♀♀ 2* |
| ○ Gavi del Comune di Gavi '14 | ♀♀ 2* |
| ○ Gavi del Comune di Gavi Il Bosco '16 | ♀♀ 3* |
| ○ Gavi del Comune di Gavi Il Bosco '15 | ♀♀ 3* |
| ● Barbera del M.to '15 | ♀ 3 |

# Flavio Roddolo

FRAZ. BRICCO APPIANI
LOC. SANT'ANNA, 5
12065 MONFORTE D'ALBA [CN]
TEL. +39 017378535
info@roddolo.it

**CELLAR SALES**
**PRE-BOOKED VISITS**
**ANNUAL PRODUCTION** 25,000 bottles
**HECTARES UNDER VINE** 6.00

Few words are need to describe Flavio Roddolo, an authentic, low-profile, soft-spoken vigneron based in Langhe. His small Monforte d'Alba winery gives rise to wines that benefit from the time Flavio dedicates to them, with no predetermined schemes followed, just the will and sensibility needed to embrace and interpret each moment. Nebbiolo is cultivated (with Ravera cru serving as the basis of a Barolo), along with Barbera, Dolcetto and even Cabernet (from Bricco Appiani). Together they make for a selection that's faithful to the territory. Their 2010 Barbera d'Alba Superiore Bricco Appiani features a really charming rustic and traditional style. Aromas of black olives and redcurrants follow through onto a palate marked by vibrant savoriness and good acid backbone. This makes for a firm, taut palate, playing on peppery overtones and light gamey sensations. Their 2011 Nebbiolo d'Alba comes through mature and charming, with its notes of quinine and coffee powder and a long, juicy finish.

| | |
|---|---|
| ● Barbera d'Alba Sup.<br>Bricco Appiani '10 | ♥♥ 4 |
| ● Barolo Ravera '11 | ♥♥ 5 |
| ● Nebbiolo d'Alba '11 | ♥♥ 4 |
| ● Barolo Ravera '08 | ♀♀♀ 5 |
| ● Barolo Ravera '07 | ♀♀♀ 5 |
| ● Barolo Ravera '04 | ♀♀♀ 5 |
| ● Barolo Ravera '10 | ♀♀ 5 |
| ● Dolcetto d'Alba '09 | ♀♀ 2* |
| ● Dolcetto d'Alba Sup. '13 | ♀♀ 3 |
| ● Dolcetto d'Alba Sup. '12 | ♀♀ 3 |
| ● Dolcetto d'Alba Sup. '11 | ♀♀ 3* |
| ● Dolcetto d'Alba Sup. '10 | ♀♀ 3* |
| ● Nebbiolo d'Alba '10 | ♀♀ 4 |
| ● Nebbiolo d'Alba '08 | ♀♀ 4 |
| ● Nebbiolo d'Alba '07 | ♀♀ 4 |

# Ronchi

S.DA RONCHI, 23
12050 BARBARESCO [CN]
TEL. +39 0173635156
www.aziendaagricolaronchi.it

CELLAR SALES
PRE-BOOKED VISITS
ANNUAL PRODUCTION 30,000 bottles
HECTARES UNDER VINE 7.00

It doesn't often happen that a winery can adopt the name of a cru, but that came to pass thanks to the centuries-old presence of the Rocca family's farm manor in the Ronchi vineyard. It's a 19-hectare plot of Nebbiolo that's used by other wineries as well, and that guarantees a constant, notable freshness with respect to its grapes thanks to its significant eastern exposure. Barbaresco is the cornerstone of their selection, in addition to smaller quantities of wines made with the area's traditional grapes, Barbera, Freisa and Dolcetto. Chardonnay and Arneis is used for their whites. Their particularly fine, delicate and complex 2014 Barbaresco displays good acidity and a restrained character. The Barbaresco Ronchi from the same vintage proves more assertive and generous, with pleasant balsamic hints, no frills and good balance of taste. Their Langhe Chardonnay proves sounds once again: soft, spicy and slightly marked by oak. Their new white aged 'in amphôris' is slightly tannic and oxidative.

| | | |
|---|---|---|
| ● Barbaresco Ronchi '14 | ♟♟ | 5 |
| ● Barbaresco '14 | ♟♟ | 5 |
| ○ Langhe Chardonnay '16 | ♟♟ | 3 |
| ○ Langhe In Amphôris '17 | ♟ | 3 |
| ● Barbaresco Ronchi '04 | ♟♟♟ | 6 |
| ● Barbaresco '13 | ♟♟ | 5 |
| ● Barbaresco '11 | ♟♟ | 5 |
| ● Barbaresco '10 | ♟♟ | 5 |
| ● Barbaresco Ronchi '13 | ♟♟ | 5 |
| ● Barbaresco Ronchi '12 | ♟♟ | 5 |
| ● Barbaresco Ronchi '11 | ♟♟ | 5 |
| ● Barbera d'Alba Terlé '15 | ♟♟ | 3 |
| ○ Langhe Arneis '15 | ♟♟ | 2* |
| ○ Langhe Chardonnay '15 | ♟♟ | 3 |
| ○ Langhe Chardonnay '13 | ♟♟ | 3 |
| ○ Langhe Chardonnay Ronchi '12 | ♟♟ | 3* |

# Giovanni Rosso

LOC. BAUDANA, 6
12050 SERRALUNGA D'ALBA [CN]
TEL. +39 0173613340
www.giovannirosso.com

CELLAR SALES
PRE-BOOKED VISITS
ANNUAL PRODUCTION 130,000 bottles
HECTARES UNDER VINE 18.00

Davide Rosso is forging ahead, both in producing delicious wines and enlarging the family's cellar. Today the latter is situated in a small farm manor, which also hosts their production headquarters. And the first batches are coming in from the slopes of Etna, where the winery recently purchased a lovely plot. Their superb Barolo Vigna Rionda Ester Canale Rosso is still their lead wine, but their Cerretta and Serra are also exceptional, as is their more accessible Serralunga d'Alba. Their classic production style features aging in medium-large wood barrels. Their famous Vigna Rionda never disappoints, with a fresh and lively 2014 whose charming vegetal notes combine with quinine and small black fruit to add complexity: Tre Bicchieri. Their 2014 Barolo Ceretta offers up sensations of fresh fruit, then licorice. Its strong and full-bodied palate features tight-knit and supple tannins combined with marked acidity. Their pleasant Barolo Serra from the same vintage proves less structured and a touch greener.

| | | |
|---|---|---|
| ● Barolo Vigna Rionda Ester Canale Rosso '14 | ♟♟♟ | 8 |
| ● Barolo Serra '14 | ♟♟ | 8 |
| ● Langhe Nebbiolo Ester Canale Rosso '14 | ♟♟ | 8 |
| ● Barbera d'Alba Donna Margherita '17 | ♟♟ | 3 |
| ● Barolo Cerretta '14 | ♟♟ | 8 |
| ● Barolo del Comune di Serralunga d'Alba '14 | ♟♟ | 5 |
| ● Langhe Nebbiolo '16 | ♟♟ | 5 |
| ● Barolo Cerretta '12 | ♟♟♟ | 8 |
| ● Barolo La Serra '09 | ♟♟♟ | 7 |
| ● Barolo La Serra '08 | ♟♟♟ | 7 |
| ● Barolo Serra '10 | ♟♟♟ | 7 |
| ● Barolo Vigna Rionda Ester Canale Rosso '13 | ♟♟♟ | 8 |

# Poderi Rosso Giovanni

P.zza Roma, 36/37
14041 Agliano Terme [AT]
Tel. +39 0141954006
www.poderirossogiovanni.it

CELLAR SALES
PRE-BOOKED VISITS
ANNUAL PRODUCTION 53,000 bottles
HECTARES UNDER VINE 12.00

The Rosso family winery avails itself of vineyards situated in Agliano Terme, around the farmsteads of Perno and San Sebastiano. Almost all the estate is dedicated to Barbera, with a small share of Cabernet Sauvignon. Obviously the winery specializes in Barbera d'Asti and all its various versions (in addition to a Monferrato Rosso). Their modern style of winemaking pursues fruit and pleasantness. Their excellent 2016 Barbera d'Asti Superiore Cascina Perno exhibits aromas of wild berries and herbs, leading into a fresh, juicy palate and a long and pleasant finish. Their 2017 Barbera d'Asti San Bastian appears well-made, supple and approachable. The 2015 Barbera d'Asti Superiore Gioco dell'Oca is still marked by wood, austere and full-bodied, with a lingering finish featuring notes of porcini mushrooms and Mediterranean scrub.

| | |
|---|---|
| ● Barbera d'Asti Sup. Cascina Perno '16 | 🍷🍷 3* |
| ● Barbera d'Asti San Bastian '17 | 🍷🍷 2* |
| ● Barbera d'Asti Sup. Gioco dell'Oca '15 | 🍷🍷 6 |
| ● Barbera d'Asti Podere San Bastian '14 | 🍷🍷 2* |
| ● Barbera d'Asti San Bastian '15 | 🍷🍷 2* |
| ● Barbera d'Asti San Bastian '13 | 🍷🍷 2* |
| ● Barbera d'Asti Sup. Carlinet '15 | 🍷🍷 4 |
| ● Barbera d'Asti Sup. Carlinet '13 | 🍷🍷 4 |
| ● Barbera d'Asti Sup. Cascina Perno '15 | 🍷🍷 3 |
| ● Barbera d'Asti Sup. Cascina Perno '14 | 🍷🍷 3 |
| ● Barbera d'Asti Sup. Cascina Perno '13 | 🍷🍷 3 |
| ● Barbera d'Asti Sup. Gioco dell'Oca '13 | 🍷🍷 6 |
| ● Barbera d'Asti Sup. Gioco dell'Oca '12 | 🍷🍷 6 |

# Podere Ruggeri Corsini

loc. Bussia Bovi 18
12065 Monforte d'Alba [CN]
Tel. +39 017378625
www.ruggericorsini.com

CELLAR SALES
PRE-BOOKED VISITS
ANNUAL PRODUCTION 75,000 bottles
HECTARES UNDER VINE 9.80
SUSTAINABLE WINERY

Ghemme's recipe is a medieval castle still endowed with great charm, where you can enjoy the quiet that pervades Antonio and Paolo Rovellotti's historic winery. Nebbiolo is the cornerstone of their selection, giving rise to their premium wines, their Ghemme Chioso dei Pomi and their Riserva Costa del Salmino, which both age for five years before going to market. The result can be found in their particularly vibrant and multi-faceted aromas, which are favored by a small presence of the spicy Vespolina grape. Moreover, their delicate, sandy tannins are never aggressive. But their entire selection is highly enjoyable. Their pleasant 2014 Barolo Bussia Corsini plays more on balance than richness and already displays charming hints of licorice. Their full-bodied 2015 Barbera d'Alba Superiore Armujan reveals a slightly rustic personality. The Albarossa variety (a cross between Nebbiolo and Barbera) has produced a delicate and pleasant 2015 Autenzio, while their youthful Dolcetto d'Alba proves rich and close-focused.

| | |
|---|---|
| ● Barbera d'Alba Sup. Armujan '15 | 🍷🍷 3 |
| ● Barolo Bussia Corsini '14 | 🍷🍷 5 |
| ● Dolcetto d'Alba '16 | 🍷🍷 2* |
| ● Piemonte Albarossa Autenzio '15 | 🍷🍷 4 |
| ○ Langhe Bianco '17 | 🍷 2 |
| ● Barbera d'Alba '13 | 🍷🍷 2* |
| ● Barbera d'Alba Sup. Armujan '13 | 🍷🍷 3 |
| ● Barbera d'Alba Sup. Armujan '12 | 🍷🍷 3* |
| ● Barolo Bricco San Pietro '13 | 🍷🍷 5 |
| ● Barolo Bussia Corsini '13 | 🍷🍷 5 |
| ● Langhe Nebbiolo '15 | 🍷🍷 3 |
| ● Langhe Nebbiolo '13 | 🍷🍷 3 |
| ● Langhe Pinot Nero Argamakow '14 | 🍷🍷 4 |
| ⊙ Langhe Rosato Rosin '16 | 🍷🍷 2* |

## Josetta Saffirio

LOC. CASTELLETTO, 39
12065 MONFORTE D'ALBA [CN]
TEL. +39 0173787278
www.josettasaffirio.com

**CELLAR SALES**
**PRE-BOOKED VISITS**
**ANNUAL PRODUCTION** 30,000 bottles
**HECTARES UNDER VINE** 5.00
**VITICULTURE METHOD** Certified Organic
**SUSTAINABLE WINERY**

Sara Vezza, having concluded a collaboration with her mother, Josetta, is personally managing the family's winery. Founded in the 1970s, Josetta Saffirio brilliantly came into the limelight 10 years later with a prized selection of Barolos and Barbera d'Alba Superiores. Their production is still firmly rooted in these wines, with the addition of a fresh Nebbiolo Metodo Classico sparkler and a mature Langhe Rossese Bianco. Among the Barolos offered, the best versions of their Riserva wines stand out. They're made with grapes from a some 60-year old vineyard. Their 2012 Barolo Millenovecento48 Riserva achieved an excellent result. It displays a fresh fruity background merging into overtones of quinine and licorice. Its powerful and rich palate features slightly mouth-drying tannins, combined with great pulp that leaves a long sweet finish. Their pleasant 2014 Persiera comes through plush and vegetal. Few producers have a go at making Rossese Bianco, but this 2016 vintage is well-orchestrated and a great success.

| | | |
|---|---|---|
| ● Barolo Millenovecento48 Ris. '12 | ♥♥ | 8 |
| ● Barolo Persiera '14 | ♥♥ | 8 |
| ● Langhe Nebbiolo '16 | ♥♥ | 3 |
| ○ Langhe Rossese Bianco '16 | ♥♥ | 3 |
| ● Barolo '89 | ♥♥♥ | 6 |
| ● Barolo '88 | ♥♥♥ | 6 |
| ● Barbera d'Alba Sup. '15 | ♥♥ | 3 |
| ● Barolo '13 | ♥♥ | 6 |
| ● Barolo '12 | ♥♥ | 5 |
| ● Barolo '11 | ♥♥ | 5 |
| ● Barolo Millenovecento48 Ris. '11 | ♥♥ | 8 |
| ● Barolo Millenovecento48 Ris. '10 | ♥♥ | 7 |
| ● Barolo Persiera '13 | ♥♥ | 8 |
| ● Barolo Persiera '12 | ♥♥ | 8 |
| ● Langhe Nebbiolo '15 | ♥♥ | 3 |
| ● Langhe Nebbiolo '14 | ♥♥ | 3 |
| ○ Langhe Rossese Bianco '15 | ♥♥ | 3 |

## San Bartolomeo

LOC. VALLEGGE
CASCINA SAN BARTOLOMEO, 26
15066 GAVI [AL]
TEL. +39 0143643180
www.sanbartolomeogavi.com

**CELLAR SALES**
**PRE-BOOKED VISITS**
**ANNUAL PRODUCTION** 50,000 bottles
**HECTARES UNDER VINE** 21.00
**SUSTAINABLE WINERY**

The winery can be found on state road 160, that runs from Gavi to Francavilla Bisio. It's the area to the right of the Lemme river, situated on its rocky bank, just ahead of a scenic gorge. Their 20 hectares of vineyards are dedicated entirely to Cortese di Gavi, vertical-trellised with Guyot pruning. Among the technical stages of vineyard managed is a berry thinning that's carried out according to the plant's potential. It's more effective than a predetermined berry thinning. Their cellar is well-equipped to transform the grapes in some of the area's most classic wines. San Bartolomeo's wines show great form once again and their Gavi del Comune di Gavi Pelöia just missed out on a place in the finals. Their 2017 vintage flaunts a characteristically intriguing nose and an vibrant, lingering palate. Their Quinto is less assertive, with a nice aromatic profile and length.

| | | |
|---|---|---|
| ○ Gavi del Comune di Gavi Pelöia '17 | ♥♥ | 3 |
| ○ Gavi Quinto '17 | ♥♥ | 2* |
| ○ Gavi del Comune di Gavi Pelöia '15 | ♥♥♥ | 3* |
| ○ Gavi del Comune di Gavi Pelöia '16 | ♥♥ | 3* |
| ○ Gavi del Comune di Gavi Pelöia '14 | ♥♥ | 3* |
| ○ Gavi del Comune di Gavi Pelöia '13 | ♥♥ | 3* |
| ○ Gavi Quinto '15 | ♥♥ | 2* |
| ○ Gavi Quinto '14 | ♥♥ | 2* |
| ○ Gavi Quinto '13 | ♥♥ | 3* |
| ○ Gavi Quinto '12 | ♥♥ | 2* |

# Tenuta San Sebastiano

CASCINA SAN SEBASTIANO, 41
15040 LU [AL]
TEL. +39 0131741353
www.dealessi.it

CELLAR SALES
PRE-BOOKED VISITS
ANNUAL PRODUCTION 70,000 bottles
HECTARES UNDER VINE 9.00

Three vintages brought historic results for
Roberto de Alessi's Grignolino, thus
pointing up the efficacy of the producer's
long-term vision. He's a passionate vine
grower who was among the few in
Monferrato to bet on aging Grignolino in
wood barrels. It was a way of returning to
the territory and its history so as to guide it
towards a future, though without
overwhelming its essence. The small path
taken a few years ago has become a
full-fledged road and considering the
recent results we hope it will go a long way.
Monfiorato reached our final once again. It
displays classic aromas of pepper, tobacco
and sweet spices, while the intense and
full-bodied palate leads into a very lingering
finish. Fruity aromas feature in their
Barbera Mepari, together with clear wood
and a full-bodied and balanced palate.
Their Barbera del Monferrato offers up an
intense and multi-faceted nose that gives
way to a powerful and structured taste.
Their Monferrato Rosso Dalera and
Nebbiolo Capolinea also did well.

| | |
|---|---|
| ● Piemonte Grignolino Monfiorato '13 | ♟♟ 4 |
| ● Barbera del M.to '16 | ♟♟ 2* |
| ● Barbera del M.to Sup. Mepari '16 | ♟♟ 4 |
| ● M.to Rosso Capolinea '16 | ♟♟ 2* |
| ● M.to Rosso Dalera '16 | ♟♟ 3 |
| ○ M.to Bianco Sperilium '17 | ♟ 2 |
| ● Piemonte Grignolino '17 | ♟ 2 |
| ● Barbera del M.to Sup. Mepari '15 | ♟♟ 4 |
| ● Barbera del M.to Sup. Mepari '11 | ♟♟ 4 |
| ○ LV Quinquagesimaquinta Mansio Passito '14 | ♟♟ 4 |
| ○ M.to Bianco Sperilium '16 | ♟♟ 2* |
| ● Piemonte Grignolino Monfiorato '12 | ♟♟ 4 |
| ● Piemonte Grignolino Monfiorato '11 | ♟♟ 4 |

# ★Luciano Sandrone

VIA PUGNANE, 4
12060 BAROLO [CN]
TEL. +39 0173560023
www.sandroneluciano.com

PRE-BOOKED VISITS
ANNUAL PRODUCTION 110,000 bottles
HECTARES UNDER VINE 27.00
SUSTAINABLE WINERY

At Luciano Sandrone's winery new
generations spring up in rapid succession.
That's how it came to pass that in addition
to his brother and wife, Luciano is also
supported by his daughter and
grandchildren Alessia and Stefano (who
inspired 'Aleste', a Barolo from Cannubi
Boschis that's earned Sandrone a
reputation as a top producer). Their
neoclassic style emerges in a range of
wines that includes Barolo 'Le Vigne' (Merli
(Novello) Baudana (Serralunga d'Alba),
Villero (Castiglione Falletto), Vignane
(Barolo) and Nebbiolo Valmaggiore (Vezza
d'Alba and Roero). Not to mention their
Barberas and Dolcettos. Their 2014 Barolo
Aleste features a dark profile of licorice and
redcurrants. Its spicy profile and lingering,
coffee finish is accompanied by freshness
and zip. Their 2014 Barolo Le Vigne
displays more pulp, with aromas of morello
and cherry. It comes through dense with
good supporting acidity and a peppery,
citrusy finish. Their 2016 Barbera d'Alba
exhibits elegant fruity aromas with nice
acidity, oak and pulp.

| | |
|---|---|
| ● Barbera d'Alba '16 | ♟♟ 5 |
| ● Barolo Aleste '14 | ♟♟ 8 |
| ● Barolo Le Vigne '14 | ♟♟ 8 |
| ● Nebbiolo d'Alba Valmaggiore '16 | ♟♟ 5 |
| ● Barolo Cannubi Boschis '11 | ♟♟♟ 8 |
| ● Barolo Cannubi Boschis '10 | ♟♟♟ 8 |
| ● Barolo Cannubi Boschis '08 | ♟♟♟ 8 |
| ● Barolo Cannubi Boschis '07 | ♟♟♟ 8 |
| ● Barolo Cannubi Boschis '06 | ♟♟♟ 8 |
| ● Barolo Cannubi Boschis '05 | ♟♟♟ 8 |
| ● Barolo Aleste '13 | ♟♟ 8 |
| ● Barolo Cannubi Boschis '12 | ♟♟ 8 |
| ● Barolo Le Vigne '12 | ♟♟ 8 |
| ● Barolo Le Vigne '11 | ♟♟ 8 |

# Tenuta Santa Caterina

VIA GUGLIELMO MARCONI, 17
14035 GRAZZANO BADOGLIO [AT]
TEL. +39 0141925108
www.tenuta-santa-caterina.it

CELLAR SALES
PRE-BOOKED VISITS
ACCOMMODATION
ANNUAL PRODUCTION 50,000 bottles
HECTARES UNDER VINE 23.00

The Alleva family purchased the estate in 2000, carefully renovating its antique structures. In terms of their vineyards, zoning allowed them to choose the most well-suited cultivar, rootstocks and clones, in consideration of the characteristics of the terrain, with Chardonnay, Sauvignon Blanc, Nebbiolo, Barbera, Freisa and Grignolino all cultivated for a total of seven wines. The winery is also part of the Monferace project, an association of producers from Monferrato Casalese and Asti that's dedicated to Grignolino. Of their high-quality selection submitted for tasting, two wines reached our final. Their M2012 Grignolino displays aromas of quinine, camphor and hints of pepper, while the perceptible wood doesn't diminish its complexity. Its powerful palate features vigorous tannins and a lingering finish. Vigna Lina brings out lovely intense fruit, spicy notes and a balanced and well-orchestrated palate. Their Grignolino Arlandino offers up overtones of tobacco and spices.

| | |
|---|---|
| ● Barbera d'Asti Sup. V. Lina '15 | ♥♥ 3* |
| ● Grignolino d'Asti M2012 '12 | ♥♥ 3* |
| ● Grignolino d'Asti Arlandino '16 | ♥♥ 3 |
| ● Freisa d'Asti Sorì di Giul '14 | ♥ 5 |
| ○ Monferrato Salidoro '16 | ♥ 3 |
| ● Barbera d'Asti Sup. Setecàpita '13 | ♀♀ 5 |
| ● Barbera d'Asti Sup. Setecàpita '12 | ♀♀ 3 |
| ● Barbera d'Asti Sup. V. Lina '14 | ♀♀ 3 |
| ● Barbera d'Asti Sup. V. Lina '13 | ♀♀ 3 |
| ● Freisa d'Asti Sorì di Giul '13 | ♀♀ 5 |
| ● Freisa d'Asti Sorì di Giul '12 | ♀♀ 3 |

# Santa Clelia

REG. ROSSANA, 7
10035 MAZZÈ [TO]
TEL. +39 0119835187
www.santaclelia.it

CELLAR SALES
PRE-BOOKED VISITS
ANNUAL PRODUCTION 70,000 bottles
HECTARES UNDER VINE 12.00
VITICULTURE METHOD Certified Organic
SUSTAINABLE WINERY

Gabriella and Sergio Dezzutto, whose winery just celebrated its 18th birthday, decided to adopt organic cultivation methods for their vineyards, which host primarily Erbaluce grapes. We strongly recommend a visit to their estate, which comprises vineyards, fruit orchards and centuries-old woodlands. Here wine lovers will get an appreciation for the sincere respect they show for the environment and the care taken in looking after their vineyards. Their 2017 Erbaluces delivered. Their Ypa proves particularly charming, thanks to its polished and balsamic freshness on the nose, which follows through onto the decidedly rich (but not fat) palate, with excellent balance. Rich aromas and pleasant notes of meadow herbs feature in their robust Essenthia, which is balanced by lovely supporting acidity. Their Passito Dus comes through pleasantly volatile.

| | |
|---|---|
| ○ Erbaluce di Caluso Ypa '17 | ♥♥ 3* |
| ○ Erbaluce di Caluso Essenthia '17 | ♥♥ 3 |
| ○ Caluso Passito Dus '08 | ♥ 5 |
| ○ Caluso Passito Dus '09 | ♀♀ 4 |
| ○ Erbaluce di Caluso Essenthia '16 | ♀♀ 3 |
| ○ Erbaluce di Caluso Ypa '16 | ♀♀ 3 |

# Paolo Saracco

VIA CIRCONVALLAZIONE, 6
12053 CASTIGLIONE TINELLA [CN]
TEL. +39 0141855113
www.paolosaracco.it

**CELLAR SALES**
**PRE-BOOKED VISITS**
**ANNUAL PRODUCTION** 600,000 bottles
**HECTARES UNDER VINE** 46.00

For some years now Paolo Saracco's estate has been considered a gem for the production of Moscato. Their vineyards span some 14 different tracts of land, situated on soil composed primarily of white sand, silt and limestone in the municipalities of Calosso, Castagnole Lanze, Castiglione Tinella and Santo Stefano Belbo, at elevations ranging from 300 to 500 meters above sea level (Pinot Nero, Chardonnay, Riesling and Barbera are also cultivated). Their personal style gives rise to wines that also express the grape varieties used and territory of origin. Their 2017 Moscato d'Asti and 2017 Piemonte Moscato d'Autunno are always among the best of their kind. The former proves floral, with hints of cinnamon and dried fruit on the nose and a fresh and pleasant palate. The latter plays on overtones of sage and rose, with great grip and length. This year the winery submitted a Barbera for the first time: their 2016 Barbera d'Alba is taut with good structure, overtones of black fruit and spices, making for a really successful debut.

| | |
|---|---|
| ○ Moscato d'Asti '17 | ♟♟ 3* |
| ○ Piemonte Moscato d'Autunno '17 | ♟♟ 3* |
| ● Barbera d'Alba '16 | ♟♟ 3 |
| ○ Langhe Chardonnay Prasué '17 | ♟ 3 |
| ● Piemonte Pinot Nero '16 | ♟ 5 |
| ○ Moscato d'Asti '16 | ♟♟♟ 3* |
| ○ Langhe Chardonnay Prasué '16 | ♟♟ 3 |
| ○ Langhe Riesling '14 | ♟♟ 3 |
| ○ Moscato d'Asti '15 | ♟♟ 3 |
| ○ Piemonte Moscato d'Autunno '16 | ♟♟ 3* |
| ○ Piemonte Moscato d'Autunno '15 | ♟♟ 3* |
| ○ Piemonte Moscato d'Autunno '14 | ♟♟ 3* |
| ● Piemonte Pinot Nero '13 | ♟♟ 5 |

# Roberto Sarotto

VIA RONCONUOVO, 13
12050 NEVIGLIE [CN]
TEL. +39 0173630228
www.robertosarotto.com

**CELLAR SALES**
**PRE-BOOKED VISITS**
**ANNUAL PRODUCTION** 700,000 bottles
**HECTARES UNDER VINE** 84.00
**SUSTAINABLE WINERY**

Roberto Sarotto is among the few producers in Piedmont intent on drawing on such a diverse and heterogenous mix of sources. In fact, he manages his private vineyards in Barolo, Barbaresco, Gavi and Moscato d'Asti without neglecting other traditional grapes like Barbera, Dolcetto and Arneis (and international varieties as well). It's a sizable selection (uncommon for the region) for a style that privileges richness and intensity, with fruit and oak at the fore. Consistent quality and consumer-friendly prices complete the package. Their 2017 Gavi del Comune di Gavi Tenuta Manenti Bric Sassi reached our finals with its biting notes of fresh grass and deep and assertive savoriness. Their 2014 Barolo Audace also proved sound, with intense ripe cherry and plum overtones and hints of cocoa and coffee. The powerful, dense, well-balanced flavor gives way to a fresher palate and balanced finish. Their 2013 Barolo Bricco Bergera comes through plush and juicy, reminiscent of wood resin and sweet tobacco.

| | |
|---|---|
| ● Barolo Audace '14 | ♟♟ 4 |
| ○ Gavi del Comune di Gavi Bric Sassi Tenuta Manenti '17 | ♟♟ 2* |
| ● Barbaresco Gaia Principe '15 | ♟♟ 6 |
| ● Barolo Briccobergera '13 | ♟♟ 4 |
| ○ Gavi Aurora '17 | ♟♟ 2* |
| ● Barbera d'Alba Elena la Luna '16 | ♟ 4 |
| ● Langhe Rosso Enrico I '17 | ♟ 7 |
| ● Barbaresco Currà Ris. '10 | ♟♟ 5 |
| ● Barbaresco Gaia Principe '14 | ♟♟ 6 |
| ● Barbaresco Gaia Principe '10 | ♟♟ 6 |
| ● Barolo Audace '13 | ♟♟ 6 |
| ○ Gavi Aurora '16 | ♟♟ 2* |
| ○ Gavi del Comune di Gavi Bric Sassi Tenuta Manenti '16 | ♟♟ 2* |

## Scagliola

VIA SAN SIRO, 42
14052 CALOSSO [AT]
TEL. +39 0141853183
www.scagliolavini.com

CELLAR SALES
PRE-BOOKED VISITS
ANNUAL PRODUCTION 200,000 bottles
HECTARES UNDER VINE 37.00

For four generations the Scagliola family
have devoted themselves to vine growing.
Primarily Barbera is cultivated in Calosso,
at 350-400 meters above sea level, on
medium textured calcareous clay terrain,
while primarily Moscato is grown in Canelli,
where the terrain is sandy-marl. Some 22
wines are made, all aimed at highlighting
the attributes of the territory and the
cultivar used. Their 2017 Moscato d'Asti
Volo di Farfalle displays classic overtones of
candied citrus peel and tropical fruit,
especially mango. It comes through soft,
but also fresh, with a good balance
between acidity and sweet fruit. Their
excellent 2015 Barbera d'Asti Superiore
Sansì Antologia exhibits great structure
with light toasty overtones, but is also rich
in fruit and juicy. Their other two Barbera
d'Asti wines also proved sound: the elegant
and compact 2016 Superiore SanSì and
the supple and approachable 2017 Frem.

| | |
|---|---|
| ● Barbera d'Asti Sup. SanSì Antologia '15 | ♥♥ 8 |
| ○ Moscato d'Asti Volo di Farfalle '17 | ♥♥ 3* |
| ● Barbera d'Asti Frem '17 | ♥♥ 4 |
| ● Barbera d'Asti Sup. SanSì '16 | ♥♥ 6 |
| ● M.to Rosso Azörd '16 | ♥ 5 |
| ○ Piemonte Chardonnay Casot Dan Vian '17 | ♥ 3 |
| ● Barbera d'Asti Frem '16 | ♀♀ 4 |
| ● Barbera d'Asti Sup. Nizza Foravia '13 | ♀♀ 5 |
| ● Barbera d'Asti Sup. SanSì '15 | ♀♀ 6 |
| ● Barbera d'Asti Sup. SanSì Antologia '13 | ♀♀ 8 |
| ○ Moscato d'Asti Volo di Farfalle '16 | ♀♀ 3 |
| ○ Moscato d'Asti Volo di Farfalle '15 | ♀♀ 3* |
| ● Nizza Foravia '14 | ♀♀ 5 |

## Simone Scaletta

LOC. MANZONI, 61
12065 MONFORTE D'ALBA [CN]
TEL. +39 3484912733
www.simonescaletta.it

CELLAR SALES
PRE-BOOKED VISITS
ACCOMMODATION
ANNUAL PRODUCTION 35,000 bottles
HECTARES UNDER VINE 5.50

Simone Scaletta's estate comprises five
hectares in Monforte d'Alba. In just 15
years this young producer has managed to
bring together a minimally-invasive
philosophy (in the vineyard and cellar) with
high quality production. His wines bear the
name of his vineyards, Viglioni, Sarsera,
Chirlet and Autin'd Madama, classic
regional offerings made with Dolcetto,
Barbera and Nebbiolo. All of these exhibit a
strong territorial identity, expressing the
grapes and territory while oak remains in
the background, making for a highly
drinkable selection of wines. The wines
submitted display a truly admirable stylistic
maturity and are headed by a Barbera for
real enthusiasts. This 2016 Superiore
Sarsera proves meaty, with very fresh
close-focused fruit, embellished with
overtones of orange rind and soot. It
displays a rustic kind of pluck, relaxed
palate, energy and long, minty finish. Both
of their Barolos proved sound, featuring
measured extraction and good balance.

| | |
|---|---|
| ● Barbera d'Alba Sup. Sarsera '16 | ♥♥ 5 |
| ● Barolo Bricco San Pietro Chirlet '14 | ♥♥ 8 |
| ● Barolo Bussia '14 | ♥♥ 8 |
| ● Langhe Nebbiolo Autin 'd Madama '16 | ♥♥ 5 |
| ● Barbera d'Alba Sup. Sarsera '15 | ♀♀ 4 |
| ● Barolo Bricco San Pietro Chirlet '12 | ♀♀ 6 |
| ● Barolo Chirlet '13 | ♀♀ 6 |
| ● Barolo Chirlet '11 | ♀♀ 6 |
| ● Barolo Chirlet '10 | ♀♀ 6 |
| ● Barolo Chirlet '04 | ♀♀ 6 |
| ● Barolo Ris. '11 | ♀♀ 7 |
| ● Dolcetto d'Alba Viglioni '13 | ♀♀ 2* |
| ● Langhe Nebbiolo Autin 'd Madama '13 | ♀♀ 3 |

## Giorgio Scarzello e Figli

VIA ALBA, 29
12060 BAROLO [CN]
TEL. +39 017356170
www.barolodibarolo.com

**CELLAR SALES**
**PRE-BOOKED VISITS**
**ANNUAL PRODUCTION** 25,000 bottles
**HECTARES UNDER VINE** 5.50

The Scarzello family's small winery has just turned 60 and today Federico is at the helm. Their selection centers on Barolo, which is accompanied by a small quantity of Barbera d'Alba. Their grapes are primarily cultivated in their magnificent Sarmassa cru, which manages to express richness and complexity of flavor as well as a rare and fresh aromatic finesse. Their Barolo is decidedly classically styled, and can age in the bottle for decades. Their passion for sparkling wines led the multi-talented Federico to found the Erpacrife brand along with three friends. Marked vegetal aromas pave the way to moderate raspberry and good licorice in their 2014 Barolo del Comune di Barolo. Its not overly-large palate starts out a bit hard, but then relaxes and offers up good length. Their 2012 Barolo Sarmassa Vigna Merenda proves rather evolved, with a balanced structure, but slightly lacking in freshness. Their tannic 2016 Langhe Nebbiolo comes through austere and close-focused.

| | | |
|---|---|---|
| ● Barolo del Comune di Barolo '14 | ♟♟ | 5 |
| ● Barolo Sarmassa V. Merenda '12 | ♟♟ | 6 |
| ● Langhe Nebbiolo '16 | ♟♟♟ | 3 |
| ● Barolo Sarmassa V. Merenda '10 | ♟♟♟ | 6 |
| ● Barolo V. Merenda '99 | ♟♟♟ | 5 |
| ● Barbera d'Alba Sup. '15 | ♟♟ | 4 |
| ● Barbera d'Alba Sup. '10 | ♟♟ | 4 |
| ● Barolo del Comune di Barolo '11 | ♟♟ | 5 |
| ● Barolo del Comune di Barolo '10 | ♟♟ | 5 |
| ● Barolo del Comune di Barolo '09 | ♟♟ | 5 |
| ● Barolo Sarmassa V. Merenda '11 | ♟♟ | 6 |
| ● Barolo Sarmassa V. Merenda '09 | ♟♟ | 6 |
| ● Langhe Nebbiolo '15 | ♟♟ | 3 |
| ● Langhe Nebbiolo '13 | ♟♟ | 3 |
| ● Langhe Nebbiolo '12 | ♟♟ | 3 |
| ● Langhe Nebbiolo '10 | ♟♟ | 3 |

## ★★Paolo Scavino

FRAZ. GARBELLETTO
VIA ALBA-BAROLO, 157
12060 CASTIGLIONE FALLETTO [CN]
TEL. +39 017362850
www.paoloscavino.com

**CELLAR SALES**
**PRE-BOOKED VISITS**
**ANNUAL PRODUCTION** 130,000 bottles
**HECTARES UNDER VINE** 29.00

Enrico Scavino's passion for Barolo is matched by his enological skill. It's a name that became internationally well-established starting in the 1980s. A visit to the cellar shows how much attention goes into each stage of production, from fermentation to the storage of bottles before being sent to market. Some eight Barolos are made, including their new Ravera and their highly prized Riserva Rocche dell'Annunziata. Those who want to know more about the area will find Alessandro Masnaghetti's essential 'Barolo MGA' to be helpful reading. The rich, plush style of their opulent and well-orchestrated 2011 Barolo Novantesimo Riserva is beyond compare: Tre Bicchieri. Aromas of tobacco and quinine give way to red fruit in their 2014 Barolo Bric dël Fiasc. The clear acidity on the palate isn't too biting and it shows great character at the finish. Roddi (Bricco Ambrogio) and Verduno (Monvigliero) also produced excellent interpretations of a not easy vintage. Black fruit and excellent pulp feature in their Carobric.

| | | |
|---|---|---|
| ● Barolo Novantesimo Ris. '11 | ♟♟♟ | 8 |
| ● Barolo Bric dël Fiasc '14 | ♟♟ | 8 |
| ● Barolo Bricco Ambrogio '14 | ♟♟ | 8 |
| ● Barolo Carobric '14 | ♟♟ | 8 |
| ● Barolo Monvigliero '14 | ♟♟ | 8 |
| ● Barbera d'Alba Affinato in Carati '16 | ♟♟ | 4 |
| ● Barolo Cannubi '14 | ♟♟ | 8 |
| ● Barolo Enrico Scavino '14 | ♟♟ | 7 |
| ● Langhe Nebbiolo '16 | ♟ | 4 |
| ● Barolo Bric dël Fiasc '12 | ♟♟♟ | 8 |
| ● Barolo Bric dël Fiasc '11 | ♟♟♟ | 8 |
| ● Barolo Bric dël Fiasc '09 | ♟♟♟ | 8 |
| ● Barolo Monvigliero '08 | ♟♟♟ | 8 |
| ● Barolo Rocche dell'Annunziata Ris. '11 | ♟♟♟ | 8 |
| ● Barolo Rocche dell'Annunziata Ris. '08 | ♟♟♟ | 8 |

## Schiavenza

VIA MAZZINI, 4
12050 SERRALUNGA D'ALBA [CN]
TEL. +39 0173613115
www.schiavenza.com

CELLAR SALES
PRE-BOOKED VISITS
RESTAURANT SERVICE
ANNUAL PRODUCTION 43,000 bottles
HECTARES UNDER VINE 10.00
SUSTAINABLE WINERY

This noteworthy family-run winery is today managed by Luciano Pira and Walter Anselma. Each year they propose eight wines made only with red grapes, four of which are Barolos. Maturation is carried out in large Slavonian oak barrels, which allows the producers to bring out the various nuances of taste and flavor that are peculiar to each cru. Their Cerretta is harmonic and slightly mintier while their Broglio is more vegetal and tannic. Their Prapò is a fresh wine and, in certain vintages, downright citrusy. Right beneath the looming castle of Serralunga, visitors can enjoy a meal in the traditional Trattoria Schiavenza. All their 2014 Barolos show good development and drinkability. Their already expressive Broglio is well-balanced, with fine aromas of licorice fruit; their Prapò exhibits elegant aromas and a rather contained palate; Cerretta features notes of cherry jam and a slightly taut, close-knit palate; their modern Serralunga d'Alba offers up aromas of dark berries and cocoa, with lots of pulp. Kudos to their Barbera and Nebbiolo.

| | | |
|---|---|---|
| ● Barolo Broglio '14 | ♟♟ | 6 |
| ● Barbera d'Alba '16 | ♟♟ | 3 |
| ● Barolo Cerretta '14 | ♟♟ | 6 |
| ● Barolo del Comune di Serralunga d'Alba '14 | ♟♟ | 5 |
| ● Barolo Prapò '14 | ♟♟ | 6 |
| ● Langhe Nebbiolo '16 | ♟♟ | 4 |
| ● Barolo Broglio '11 | ♟♟♟ | 5 |
| ● Barolo Broglio '05 | ♟♟♟ | 5 |
| ● Barolo Broglio '04 | ♟♟♟ | 5 |
| ● Barolo Broglio Ris. '08 | ♟♟♟ | 7 |
| ● Barolo Broglio Ris. '04 | ♟♟♟ | 5 |
| ● Barolo Prapò '08 | ♟♟♟ | 6 |

## Mauro Sebaste

FRAZ. GALLO D'ALBA
VIA GARIBALDI, 222BIS
12051 ALBA [CN]
TEL. +39 0173262148
www.maurosebaste.it

CELLAR SALES
PRE-BOOKED VISITS
ANNUAL PRODUCTION 150,000 bottles
HECTARES UNDER VINE 30.00

Having made it through more than 25 years on his own, Mauro can now avail himself of the help of his two daughters, Angelica and Sylla. Along with Mauro's wife, Maria Teresa, they have the duty of overseeing a winery that's in constant expansion. Here only Langhe's traditional grapes are used, with the recent addition of a vineyard in the Nizza DOC appellation, as well as a small plot in Rodano that gives rise to a Langhe Bianco made with Viogner. Barolo takes center stage, a wine that's offered in four versions. Among these their two Serralunga d'Alba crus, Cerretta and Prapò stand out for their force and elegance. Their 2012 Barolo Riserva Ghè offers up thrilling warm rich aromas, such as licorice, tar and ripe red fruit. It comes through just as pleasant in the mouth, where mellow tannins leave ample space to an enjoyable plushness. Their 2014 Barolo Cerretta proves sound, with oak slightly dominating both the nose and palate. Oak is also a strong feature of their wines made with Barbera grapes, with both the Superiore Centrobicchi and their new Nizza exhibiting well-orchestrated palates.

| | | |
|---|---|---|
| ● Barolo Ghè Ris. '12 | ♟♟ | 8 |
| ● Barbera d'Alba Sup. Centobricchi '16 | ♟♟ | 5 |
| ● Barolo Cerretta '14 | ♟♟ | 6 |
| ● Barolo Trèsùrì '14 | ♟♟ | 6 |
| ● Nizza Costemonghisio '15 | ♟♟ | 4 |
| ● Nebbiolo d'Alba Parigi '16 | ♟ | 4 |
| ● Barbera d'Alba S. Rosalia '15 | ♟♟ | 4 |
| ● Barbera d'Alba Sup. Centobricchi '15 | ♟♟ | 5 |
| ● Barolo Ghè Ris. '11 | ♟♟ | 8 |
| ● Barolo Ghé Ris. '10 | ♟♟ | 8 |
| ● Barolo Prapò '12 | ♟♟ | 8 |
| ● Barolo Trèsùrì '13 | ♟♟ | 6 |
| ● Barolo Trèsùrì '12 | ♟♟ | 6 |
| ○ Gavi '16 | ♟♟ | 3 |
| ○ Langhe Bianco Centobricchi '16 | ♟♟ | 5 |
| ● Nebbiolo d'Alba Parigi '15 | ♟♟ | 5 |

# F.lli Seghesio

LOC. CASTELLETTO, 19
12065 MONFORTE D'ALBA [CN]
TEL. +39 017378108
www.fratelliseghesio.com

**CELLAR SALES**
**PRE-BOOKED VISITS**
**ANNUAL PRODUCTION 55,000 bottles**
**HECTARES UNDER VINE 10.00**

The Seghesio family's winery just turned 30 with Riccardo increasingly supported by his grandchildren Marco, Michela and Sandro. The presence of the new generation has brought greater care to the vineyards, with a biodynamic approach taking hold. But they're wines were always delicious, consistently frank and close-focused in their flowery, fruity aromas. Their multi-award winning Barolo La Villa is still on center stage, a wine whose grapes are cultivated on the steep, scenic cru after which it was name. In its own way their Barbera d'Alba La Chiesa is just as enjoyable, proving rich in texture but also endowed with a vivid freshness. This year they only submitted two wines for tasting. Aromas of tobacco and wood, with underlying fruit, feature in their sound 2014 Barolo La Villa, which proves not very complex and simple on the palate. Their 2014 Barolo appears just as pleasant and already open, but displays a lack of tannin content.

| | | |
|---|---|---|
| ● Barolo '14 | ♟♟ | 7 |
| ● Barolo La Villa '14 | ♟♟ | 7 |
| ● Barbera d'Alba Vign. della Chiesa '00 | ♕♕ | 4* |
| ● Barbera d'Alba Vign. della Chiesa '97 | ♕♕ | 4* |
| ● Barolo La Villa '10 | ♕♕♕ | 7 |
| ● Barolo Vign. La Villa '04 | ♕♕♕ | 6 |
| ● Barolo Vign. La Villa '99 | ♕♕♕ | 7 |
| ● Barolo Vign. La Villa '91 | ♕♕♕ | 6 |
| ● Barbera d'Alba '16 | ♟♟ | 3 |
| ● Barbera d'Alba '15 | ♟♟ | 3 |
| ● Barolo '13 | ♟♟ | 7 |
| ● Barolo '12 | ♟♟ | 7 |
| ● Barolo La Villa '13 | ♟♟ | 7 |
| ● Barolo La Villa '12 | ♟♟ | 7 |
| ● Barolo La Villa '11 | ♟♟ | 7 |
| ● Dolcetto d'Alba '15 | ♟♟ | 2* |
| ● Langhe Rosso Bouquet '14 | ♟♟ | 4 |

# Tenute Sella

VIA IV NOVEMBRE, 130
13060 LESSONA [BI]
TEL. +39 01599455
www.tenutesella.it

**CELLAR SALES**
**PRE-BOOKED VISITS**
**ANNUAL PRODUCTION 70,000 bottles**
**HECTARES UNDER VINE 22.50**
**SUSTAINABLE WINERY**

This winery has been making history in the area for 350 years and continues to be an essential benchmark. Indeed, if it weren't for the dedication shown by the Sella family for wine-growing (in addition to textiles, finance and politics), it wouldn't be possible to talk about Lessona and Bramaterra. Both wines are splendid, capable of aging for decades in the bottle. The former is more robust, tannic, savory and meaty (85% Nebbiolo and 15% Vespolina) while the latter is perennially elegant, a charming wines that's just a bit richer and spicier (70% Nebbiolo with smaller quantities of Croatina and Vespolina). Their extremely classic 2012 Bramaterra is a pure and perfect expression of its kind. It already displays open elegant aromas of rhubarb and iodine, and proves austere but not aggressive on the well-balanced palate. Their 2012 Lessona displays a slightly more modern approach, thanks to the addition of wood. It features good tannins and alcohol. Their sound 2010 San Sebastiano allo Zoppo still proves close-knit and rigid, but will continue to improve with bottle maturation.

| | | |
|---|---|---|
| ● Bramaterra '12 | ♟♟ | 5 |
| ● Lessona S. Sebastiano allo Zoppo '10 | ♟♟ | 6 |
| ● Lessona '12 | ♟♟ | 5 |
| ○ Piemonte Bianco Piandoro '17 | ♟♟ | 3 |
| ⊙ Clementina Brut Rosé | ♟ | 3 |
| ⊙ Coste della Sesia Rosato Majoli '17 | ♟ | 3 |
| ● Coste della Sesia Rosso Orbello '16 | ♟ | 3 |
| ○ Insubrico Pas Dosé M. Cl. | ♟ | 5 |
| ● Bramaterra I Porfidi '07 | ♕♕♕ | 5 |
| ● Bramaterra I Porfidi '05 | ♕♕♕ | 5 |
| ● Bramaterra I Porfidi '03 | ♕♕♕ | 5 |
| ● Lessona Omaggio a Quintino Sella '06 | ♕♕♕ | 7 |
| ● Lessona Omaggio a Quintino Sella '05 | ♕♕♕ | 6 |
| ● Lessona S. Sebastiano allo Zoppo '04 | ♕♕♕ | 5 |
| ● Lessona S. Sebastiano allo Zoppo '01 | ♕♕♕ | 5 |

## Enrico Serafino

c.so Asti, 5
12043 Canale [CN]
Tel. +39 0173979485
www.enricoserafino.it

**CELLAR SALES**
**PRE-BOOKED VISITS**
**ANNUAL PRODUCTION 400,000 bottles**
**HECTARES UNDER VINE 60.00**
**SUSTAINABLE WINERY**

The Krause family's Roero winery is one of the area's historic producers and one of the first to make Metodo Classico sparkling wine. Today they offer a series of wines that span Roero and Alta Langa, from Langhe's most prestigious appellations to those of Alessandrino. Their red Roeros stand out among their selection for their modern style, close-focused and precise aromas. But it's their Alta Langas that really deliver, proving to be among Italy's top Metodo Classico sparklers. Serafino proves once again to be one of the best sparkling wine producers in the country. Their 2012 Alta Langa Zero Riserva offers up aromas of white fruit and pastry-shop sensations. It is creamy, complex and caressing, but also fresh and easy-drinking, with fruity notes following through onto the palate. It thoroughly deserves our Tre Bicchieri. Their 2014 Barolo also impressed, with its hints of quinine and tobacco and rich and juicy palate. So did their 2014 Nebbiolo d'Alba, with its floral and orange rind overtones, savoriness and good body.

| | | |
|---|---|---|
| ○ Alta Langa Zero Ris. '12 | ♥♥♥ | 7 |
| ● Barolo '14 | ♥♥ | 7 |
| ● Nebbiolo d'Alba '15 | ♥♥ | 5 |
| ○ Alta Langa Brut '13 | ♥♥ | 5 |
| ○ Alta Langa Brut Zero Nature Ris. '05 | ♥♥ | 4 |
| ⊙ Alta Langa Rosé '14 | ♥♥ | 5 |
| ● Barbera d'Alba '16 | ♥♥ | 5 |
| ○ Moscato d'Asti Black Edition '17 | ♥♥ | 5 |
| ○ Moscato d'Asti '17 | ♥ | 4 |
| ○ Roero Arneis '17 | ♥ | 4 |
| ○ Alta Langa Brut Zero Cantina Maestra '09 | ♀♀♀ | 6 |
| ○ Alta Langa Brut Zero Cantina Maestra '07 | ♀♀♀ | 6 |
| ○ Alta Langa Brut Zero Cantina Maestra '06 | ♀♀♀ | 6 |

## Giovanni Silva

Cascine Rogge, 1b
10011 Agliè [TO]
Tel. +39 3473075648
www.silvavini.com

**CELLAR SALES**
**PRE-BOOKED VISITS**
**ANNUAL PRODUCTION 50,000 bottles**
**HECTARES UNDER VINE 12.00**

Young Stefano is increasingly involved with his uncle Giovanni and in managing the producer's cellar. The estate is situated just outside the lovely park of castle Agliè. The style of their two Erbaluce di Calusos is different. The Dry Ice tends aromatically towards fresh wild herbs and pine needles while their Tre Ciochè is characterized by ripe white fruit. Their Spumante sparkling wine is made with the Martinotti method and lengthy aging on the lees, while their Passito Poetica avails itself of three years in wood barrels. It's a round, soft, caressing wine that's rich in aromas of honey. The 2005 vintage of their Caluso Passito submitted for tasting this year (thirteen years after the vintage) reveals once again the potential of Erbaluce as an eclectic and versatile variety. Notes of walnut, candied citrus fruit and honey go hand in hand with a complex and fresh palate, despite the underlying sweetness. Their 2017 Erbaluce Tre Cioché weaves between aromas of white flowers and sage, with a supple and inviting palate.

| | | |
|---|---|---|
| ○ Erbaluce di Caluso Passito Poetica '05 | ♥♥ | 5 |
| ○ Erbaluce di Caluso Tre Ciochè '17 | ♥♥ | 2* |
| ○ Erbaluce di Caluso Dry Ice '17 | ♥ | 2 |
| ○ Caluso Passito Poetica '03 | ♀♀ | 5 |
| ○ Erbaluce di Caluso Brut M. Cl. '09 | ♀♀ | 5 |
| ○ Erbaluce di Caluso Dry Ice '16 | ♀♀ | 2* |
| ○ Erbaluce di Caluso Dry Ice '15 | ♀♀ | 2* |
| ○ Erbaluce di Caluso Passito Poetica '04 | ♀♀ | 5 |
| ○ Erbaluce di Caluso Tre Ciochè '16 | ♀♀ | 2* |
| ○ Erbaluce di Caluso Tre Ciochè '15 | ♀♀ | 2* |
| ○ Erbaluce di Caluso Tre Ciochè '12 | ♀♀ | 2* |

# La Smilla

VIA GARIBALDI, 7
15060 BOSIO [AL]
TEL. +39 0143684245
www.lasmilla.it

**CELLAR SALES**
**ANNUAL PRODUCTION** 100,000 bottles
**HECTARES UNDER VINE** 5.00

Danilo Guido, one of Bosie's young producers, has over the years brought out the attributes of the local appellations near the coast. The terrain gets increasingly rugged, with Monte Tobbio standing at an elevation 1092 meters above sea level (which makes it popular with adventurers). This is reflected in the Cortese wines he produces. They're intense, full-bodied and very savory. Among Danilo's selection includes a Dolcetto di Ovada and a Barbera. His Metodo Classico Gavi shouldn't be missed. It's a sparkling wine that spends 18 months on the lees and is excellent value for the money. Their 2017 Gavi del Comune di Gavi heads the selection with an excellent performance. It offers up intense and generous aromas of ripe white fruit and candied citrus, which pave the way for a rich and intense palate with a balanced finish. Their 2017 Gavi and 2016 Monferrato Bianco Bergi prove well-crafted. The former displays aromas of dried flowers and white fruit, while the latter reveals exotic fruit and pear overtones.

| | |
|---|---|
| ○ Gavi del Comune di Gavi '17 | ▼▼ 2* |
| ○ Gavi '17 | ▼▼ 2* |
| ○ Gavi I Bergi '16 | ▼▼ 3 |
| ● Barbera del M.to '16 | ▼ 2 |
| ● Dolcetto di Ovada '16 | ▼ 2 |
| ● M.to Rosso Calicanto '14 | ▼ 3 |
| ● Dolcetto di Ovada '13 | ♉♉ 2* |
| ○ Gavi '15 | ♉♉ 2* |
| ○ Gavi Brut M. Cl. '14 | ♉♉ 3 |
| ○ Gavi del Comune di Gavi '15 | ♉♉ 2* |
| ○ Gavi I Bergi '15 | ♉♉ 3* |

# Socré

S.DA TERZOLO, 7
12050 BARBARESCO [CN]
TEL. +39 3487121685
www.socre.it

**CELLAR SALES**
**PRE-BOOKED VISITS**
**ANNUAL PRODUCTION** 30,000 bottles
**HECTARES UNDER VINE** 5.50

Marco Piacentino's full-time job as a vine grower only began about a decade or so ago. Since then, as Kerin O'Keefe's 'Barolo and Barbaresco' sums up well, 'This winery continues to improve wines that are already very good'. Their selection centers on two Barbarescos, though it comprises all the area's classics, from Barbera Superiore to Dolcetto d'Alba and a small, though often delectable selection of Langhe Freisa or Croatina. A piece of news is their sumptuous and highly aromatic Chardonnay. We're going to see some changes in their winemaking over the next few years, given the purchase of a new farmstead in Dogliani and the sale of part of their Roncaglie vineyard in Vietta di Castiglione Falletto. For the moment, however, we can enjoy a selection led by the balanced 2014 Barbaresco Roncaglie, alongside a fruity and spicy 2015 Barbaresco with a medium structure. Their extremely rich Chardonnay proves sensational.

| | |
|---|---|
| ● Barbaresco Roncaglie '14 | ▼▼ 6 |
| ○ Langhe Chardonnay Paint It Black '16 | ▼▼ 3* |
| ● Barbaresco '15 | ▼▼ 5 |
| ● Barbaresco '14 | ♉♉ 5 |
| ● Barbaresco '13 | ♉♉ 5 |
| ● Barbaresco '12 | ♉♉ 5 |
| ● Barbaresco '11 | ♉♉ 5 |
| ● Barbaresco Roncaglie '13 | ♉♉ 6 |
| ● Barbaresco Roncaglie '12 | ♉♉ 6 |
| ● Barbaresco Roncaglie '11 | ♉♉ 6 |
| ● Barbera d'Alba Sup. '15 | ♉♉ 3 |
| ● Barbera d'Alba Sup. '13 | ♉♉ 3 |
| ● Cisterna d'Asti De Scapin '13 | ♉♉ 2* |
| ● Cisterna d'Asti De Scapin '12 | ♉♉ 2* |
| ● Langhe Nebbiolo '15 | ♉♉ 3 |
| ● Langhe Nebbiolo '14 | ♉♉ 3 |

## Giovanni Sordo

FRAZ. GARBELLETTO
VIA ALBA BAROLO, 175
12060 CASTIGLIONE FALLETTO [CN]
TEL. +39 017362853
www.sordogiovanni.it

CELLAR SALES
PRE-BOOKED VISITS
ANNUAL PRODUCTION 350,000 bottles
HECTARES UNDER VINE 53.00

Giorgio Sordo hasn't rested on the laurels earned over more than a century of family winemaking tradition. Indeed, he's purchased new vineyards and has created a cellar of rare beauty. At the center of their selection is Nebbiolo, even if it ranges from Roero Arneis to Langhe Sauvignon, Alta Langa, and classics like Barbera and Dolcetto d'Alba. Their line of Barolos is splendid, thanks in part to vineyards situated in some of the area's best crus, from Gabutti in Serralunga to Perno in Monforte, Monvigliero in Verduno and Rocche in Castiglione Falletto. Their signature style is sophisticated, in keeping with the best of what tradition can offer. The 2014 vintage wasn't a simple one, but the Barolos they submitted achieved brilliant results. Their Monvigliero opens with an unexpected richness featuring notes of licorice and bottled cherries. Their Parussi displays exemplary balance between tannins, fruit and alcohol. Their Perno exhibits pleasant aromas of red fruit, contrasted with vegetal overtones and a touch of alcohol. Its palate comes through fresh and lingering.

| | | |
|---|---|---|
| ● Barolo Monvigliero '14 | 🍷🍷 | 7 |
| ● Barolo Parussi '14 | 🍷🍷 | 7 |
| ● Barolo '14 | 🍷🍷 | 5 |
| ● Barolo Gabutti '14 | 🍷🍷 | 7 |
| ● Barolo Monprivato '14 | 🍷🍷 | 8 |
| ● Barolo Perno '14 | 🍷🍷 | 7 |
| ● Barolo Rocche di Castiglione '14 | 🍷🍷 | 7 |
| ● Barolo Villero '14 | 🍷🍷 | 8 |
| ● Barolo Ravera '14 | 🍷 | 7 |
| ○ Roero Arneis Garblet Suè '17 | 🍷 | 3 |
| ● Barolo Monprivato '13 | 🍷🍷 | 8 |
| ● Barolo Monvigliero '13 | 🍷🍷 | 7 |
| ● Barolo Parussi '13 | 🍷🍷 | 7 |
| ● Barolo Perno '13 | 🍷🍷 | 7 |
| ● Barolo Perno Ris. '10 | 🍷🍷 | 7 |
| ● Barolo Ravera '13 | 🍷🍷 | 7 |
| ● Barolo Villero '13 | 🍷🍷 | 8 |

## ★Sottimano

LOC. COTTÀ, 21
12052 NEIVE [CN]
TEL. +39 0173635186
www.sottimano.it

CELLAR SALES
PRE-BOOKED VISITS
ANNUAL PRODUCTION 85,000 bottles
HECTARES UNDER VINE 18.00
VITICULTURE METHOD Certified Organic

On visiting the winery you realize immediately that the elegance and sophistication of Andrea and Reno Sottimano's wines aren't the result of specific enological techniques but rather of the tremendous care they show for their grapes. Their vineyards are managed organically and only the healthiest and ripest grapes are chosen for their five Barbarescos. Among these, the Pajoré is a regular standout for the grace of its aromas. The more forceful Currà always undergoes a year of aging before being put to market. Their wines shouldn't be missed. Their savory 2015 Barbaresco Cottà already features an exquisite and charming complexity. Its intense color leads into multifaceted aromas ranging from violets to licorice, while its palate comes through powerful with exquisite savoriness: Tre Bicchieri. Their 2015 Pajoré offers up an enchanting spiciness and savoriness, while their firmer Fausoni reveals a great palate. A splendid 2016 Langhe Nebbiolo also stands out from their excellent selection.

| | | |
|---|---|---|
| ● Barbaresco Cottà '15 | 🍷🍷🍷 | 7 |
| ● Barbaresco Fausoni '15 | 🍷🍷 | 7 |
| ● Barbaresco Pajoré '15 | 🍷🍷 | 7 |
| ● Barbaresco Basarin '15 | 🍷🍷 | 7 |
| ● Langhe Nebbiolo '16 | 🍷🍷 | 3 |
| ● Barbaresco Cottà '05 | 🍷🍷🍷 | 7 |
| ● Barbaresco Currà '12 | 🍷🍷🍷 | 8 |
| ● Barbaresco Currà '10 | 🍷🍷🍷 | 8 |
| ● Barbaresco Currà '08 | 🍷🍷🍷 | 7 |
| ● Barbaresco Currà '04 | 🍷🍷🍷 | 6 |
| ● Barbaresco Pajoré '14 | 🍷🍷🍷 | 7 |
| ● Barbaresco Pajoré '10 | 🍷🍷🍷 | 7 |
| ● Barbaresco Pajoré '08 | 🍷🍷🍷 | 7 |
| ● Barbaresco Ris. '10 | 🍷🍷🍷 | 8 |
| ● Barbaresco Ris. '05 | 🍷🍷🍷 | 8 |
| ● Barbaresco Ris. '04 | 🍷🍷🍷 | 8 |

# ★Luigi Spertino

VIA LEA, 505
14047 MOMBERCELLI [AT]
TEL. +39 0141959098
luigi.spertino@libero.it

**CELLAR SALES**
**PRE-BOOKED VISITS**
**ANNUAL PRODUCTION** 40,000 bottles
**HECTARES UNDER VINE** 9.00

The Spertino family's winery is famous when it comes to Grignolino, though for some years it's been a veritable benchmark for Barbera d'Asti as well. Their vineyards grow along the area's steep slopes with some of their Barbera vines going back 75 years. Cortese, Grignolino and Pinot Nero are also cultivated. Their wines exhibit superior character and originality, though without having lost their distinctiveness or territorial identity either. Once again our Tre Bicchieri go to their Barbera d'Asti Superiore Vigna La Mandorla. The 2016 vintage displays the right balance between notes of sweet fruit, close-knit body and acidity, which lengthens, refreshes and supports the finish. Their 2017 Grignolino d'Asti Margherita Barbero pleasantly surprised us, this is the first release of the version fermented and aged in amphorae. It exhibits no traces of oxidation whatsoever, in fact it comes through fresh, approachable, lingering and pleasant.

| | |
|---|---|
| ● Barbera d'Asti Sup. V. La Mandorla '16 | ♀♀♀ 8 |
| ● Grignolino d'Asti '17 | ♀♀ 3* |
| ● Grignolino d'Asti Margherita Barbero '17 | ♀♀ 3* |
| ● Barbera d'Asti La Grisa '16 | ♀♀ 4 |
| ● Barbera d'Asti Sup. La Mandorla '13 | ♀♀♀ 8 |
| ● Barbera d'Asti Sup. La Mandorla '10 | ♀♀♀ 8 |
| ● Barbera d'Asti Sup. La Mandorla '09 | ♀♀♀ 8 |
| ● Barbera d'Asti Sup. La Mandorla '07 | ♀♀♀ 7 |
| ● Barbera d'Asti Sup. V. La Mandorla '15 | ♀♀♀ 8 |
| ● Barbera d'Asti Sup. V. La Mandorla '12 | ♀♀♀ 8 |
| ● Barbera d'Asti Sup. V. La Mandorla Edizione La Grisa '14 | ♀♀♀ 8 |
| ● M.to Rosso La Mandorla '09 | ♀♀♀ 7 |
| ● M.to Rosso La Mandorla '07 | ♀♀♀ 5 |

# ★★★La Spinetta

VIA ANNUNZIATA, 17
14054 CASTAGNOLE DELLE LANZE [AT]
TEL. +39 0141877396
www.la-spinetta.com

**CELLAR SALES**
**PRE-BOOKED VISITS**
**ACCOMMODATION**
**ANNUAL PRODUCTION** 500,000 bottles
**HECTARES UNDER VINE** 100.00
**SUSTAINABLE WINERY**

The Rivetti family's vast estate comprises some of Barbaresco's most splendid cru, as one can appreciate by reading the highly useful 'MGA Barbaresco', a work published by Alessandro Masnaghetti. It's difficult to find a ranking, but it's sure that the Gallina vineyard, where their prized Barbera d'Alba is cultivated, is deservedly famous. The great success of the producer's reds, which include the vigorous Barolo Campé, shouldn't make us forget that La Spinetta also produce a charming, appealing selection of Moscato d'Astis. All their reds are characterized by a punchy component of ripe red fruit. Their magnificent 2015 Barbaresco Starderi offers up an excellent nose of sweet spices and raspberries, while the powerful palate comes through plush, thanks to sweet tannins. Their other wines, made with Nebbiolo, are rich and elegant, and more marked by oak. Among their Barberas, the elegant Gallina stands out for its complexity, richness, freshness and balance, while their Sauvignon, Langhe Bianco, proves splendid.

| | |
|---|---|
| ● Barbaresco Starderi '15 | ♀♀ 8 |
| ● Barbera d'Alba Gallina '15 | ♀♀ 6 |
| ○ Langhe Bianco '15 | ♀♀ 6 |
| ● Barbaresco Gallina '15 | ♀♀ 8 |
| ● Barbaresco Valeirano '15 | ♀♀ 8 |
| ● Barbaresco Vign. Bordini '15 | ♀♀ 7 |
| ● Barbera d'Asti Ca' di Pian '15 | ♀♀ 4 |
| ● Barolo Campè '14 | ♀♀ 8 |
| ● Langhe Nebbiolo '15 | ♀♀ 5 |
| ○ Moscato d'Asti Bricco Quaglia '17 | ♀♀ 3 |
| ○ Piemonte Chardonnay Lidia '15 | ♀♀ 6 |
| ● Barbera d'Asti Sup. Bionzo '15 | ♀ 6 |
| ● Barbaresco Gallina '11 | ♀♀♀ 8 |
| ● Barbaresco Vign. Starderi '07 | ♀♀♀ 8 |
| ● Barbera d'Asti Sup. Bionzo '09 | ♀♀♀ 6 |
| ● Barolo Campè '08 | ♀♀♀ 8 |

# Marchese Luca Spinola

FRAZ. ROVERETO DI GAVI
LOC. CASCINA MASSIMILIANA, 97
15066 GAVI [AL]
TEL. +39 0143682514
www.marcheselucaspinola.it

**CELLAR SALES**
**PRE-BOOKED VISITS**
**ANNUAL PRODUCTION** 30,000 bottles
**HECTARES UNDER VINE** 15.00
**VITICULTURE METHOD** Certified Organic

Halfway between Rovereto and Pessenti, at the top of the first slope, a flatland stretches out that's characterized by red earth. It's here that we find Luca Spinola. Their vineyards span 15 hectares between Rovereto and Tassarolo. They're certified organic after completing the final conversion stage in the cellar, in addition to their vineyards. They offer three wines, all made with Cortese: two stills and a semi-sparkling. Tenuta Massimiliana, their crown jewel, is fermented in wood barrels with an inoculation of native yeasts. TFor this edition of the Guide, we only tasted their 2017 Gavi del Comune di Gavi Carlo, which enthralls the nose and offers a sturdy, savory palate that leaves room for a long finish. We were unable to try their 2017 Tenuta Massimiliana, which is being aged for an additional year before being released.

| | |
|---|---|
| ○ Gavi del Comune di Gavi Carlo '17 | ♟♟ 2* |
| ○ Gavi del Comune di Gavi '16 | ♟♟ 2* |
| ○ Gavi del Comune di Gavi '15 | ♟♟ 2* |
| ○ Gavi del Comune di Gavi '11 | ♟♟ 2* |
| ○ Gavi del Comune di Gavi Et. Blu '14 | ♟♟ 2* |
| ○ Gavi del Comune di Gavi Tenuta Massimiliana '16 | ♟♟ 3* |
| ○ Gavi del Comune di Gavi Tenuta Massimiliana '13 | ♟♟ 3 |
| ○ Gavi del Comune di Gavi Tenuta Massimiliana '12 | ♟♟ 3 |
| ○ Gavi del Comune di Tassarolo '13 | ♟♟ 2* |

# Sulin

V.LE PININFARINA, 14
14035 GRAZZANO BADOGLIO [AT]
TEL. +39 0141925136
www.sulin.it

**CELLAR SALES**
**PRE-BOOKED VISITS**
**ANNUAL PRODUCTION** 220,000 bottles
**HECTARES UNDER VINE** 19.50

The new direction that Sulin undertook in the late 1990s has made sustainable agriculture a cardinal rule with an eye towards protecting the environment. It's a principle that they've been directly applying since joining VignEtico, a project aimed at maximizing quality while minimizing environmental impact. This virtuous cycle terminates every year with the publication of an analysis of grapes and wines so as to certify the absence of residual effects. Their excellent Ornella makes the finals with impenetrable, ruby color, a nose of intense red fruit and vegetal notes over sweet spices. Its consistent, intense and full-bodied palate ends in a long, pleasant, fruity finish. Their evolved 2016 Barbera offers powder and tobacco with an intense, vigorous palate and a finish that's very light in alcohol. Their intriguing Malvasia di Casorzo, like their Chardonnay, is well made.

| | |
|---|---|
| ● Barbera del M.to Sup. Ornella '15 | ♟♟ 5 |
| ● Barbera del M.to '16 | ♟♟ 2* |
| ● Casorzo '17 | ♟♟ 2* |
| ○ Piemonte Chardonnay '17 | ♟♟ 2* |
| ● Grignolino del M.to Casalese '17 | ♟ 2 |
| ● Barbera del M.to '15 | ♟♟ 2* |
| ● Casorzo '16 | ♟♟ 2* |
| ● Grignolino del M.to Casalese '16 | ♟♟ 2* |
| ● M.to Rosso Adriano '15 | ♟♟ 3 |
| ○ Piemonte Chardonnay '16 | ♟♟ 2* |

# Tacchino

VIA MARTIRI DELLA BENEDICTA, 26
15060 CASTELLETTO D'ORBA [AL]
TEL. +39 0143830115
www.luigitacchino.it

**CELLAR SALES**
**PRE-BOOKED VISITS**
**ANNUAL PRODUCTION** 120,000 bottles
**HECTARES UNDER VINE** 12.00

Tacchino is a benchmark for Ovada, both in terms of its consistent production volumes and the intrinsic quality of their wines. These are made entirely with native grape varieties, except for their Monferrato red, Di Fatto, which sees Cabernet Sauvignon blended with Barbera and Dolcetto. Their production style relies heavily on tradition, with a slightly modern touch brought about by the use of barriques for fermenting and maturing their Selezione line of wines. An impressive show by Tacchino, sending three wines to the final and underlining the inherent gravitas. Their Du Riva met the challenges of a difficult vintage with great elegance. Its complex nose develops with intensity and leads into a full-bodied, fresh palate of great persistence. Their stunning 2016 Dolcetto is well-deserving of Tre Bicchieri. It delivers notes of blackberry and chocolate, a powerful, intense palate, and a very long finish. Their truly appealing Barbera releases aromas of jam with hints of quinine and cocoa.

| | |
|---|---|
| ● Dolcetto di Ovada '16 | ♛♛♛ 2* |
| ● Barbera del M.to '16 | ♛♛ 2* |
| ● Dolcetto di Ovada Sup. Du Riva '14 | ♛♛ 4 |
| ○ Gavi del Comune di Gavi '17 | ♛♛ 3 |
| ● M.to Rosso Di Fatto '15 | ♛♛ 4 |
| ● Dolcetto di Ovada '15 | ♛♛♛ 2* |
| ● Dolcetto di Ovada Sup. Du Riva '13 | ♛♛♛ 4* |
| ● Dolcetto di Ovada Sup. Du Riva '12 | ♛♛♛ 5 |
| ● Dolcetto di Ovada Sup. Du Riva '11 | ♛♛♛ 5 |
| ● Dolcetto di Ovada Sup. Du Riva '10 | ♛♛♛ 4* |
| ● Dolcetto di Ovada Sup. Du Riva '09 | ♛♛♛ 4* |
| ● Dolcetto di Ovada Sup. Du Riva '08 | ♛♛♛ 4* |
| ● Barbera del M.to '15 | ♛♛ 2* |
| ● Barbera del M.to Albarola '14 | ♛♛ 5 |
| ○ Piemonte Cortese Marsenca '16 | ♛♛ 2* |

# Michele Taliano

C.SO A. MANZONI, 24
12046 MONTÀ [CN]
TEL. +39 0173975658
www.talianomichele.com

**CELLAR SALES**
**PRE-BOOKED VISITS**
**ANNUAL PRODUCTION** 60,000 bottles
**HECTARES UNDER VINE** 12.00

Alberto and Ezio Taliano have led the family winery since the mid-90s. Their Roero vineyards are situated in the municipality of Montà (in the districts of Bossola, Rolandi and Benna) while their Barbarescos are in the MGA (geographic mention) of Montersino (San Rocco Seno d'Elvio). The territory's classic grapes are cultivated: Arneis, Barbera, Favorita and Nebbiolo, making for wines that exhibit a modern style, with wood used attentively on behalf of pleasantness and aromatic precision. Their 2017 Roero Arnieis is among the appellation's best. Mulberry and peach precede its well-structured palate of rich fruit and long, pleasant finish. Their 2017 Roero Arneis U R Nice offers elegant citrus and tropical fruit, their 2104 Barbera d'Alba Superiore gambles on fruit and their sophisticated 2014 Roero proves easy on the palate. Their 2014 Ad Altiora, with notes of forest brush, and more austere 2011 Tera Mia Riserva, are both well-designed Barbaresco Montersino.

| | |
|---|---|
| ○ Roero Arneis '17 | ♛♛ 2* |
| ● Barbaresco Montersino Ad Altiora '14 | ♛♛ 5 |
| ● Barbaresco Montersino Tera Mia Ris. '11 | ♛♛ 5 |
| ● Barbera d'Alba Sup. '14 | ♛♛ 3 |
| ○ Roero '14 | ♛♛ 2* |
| ○ Roero Arneis U R Nice '17 | ♛♛ 2* |
| ● Barbera d'Alba A Bon Rendre '17 | ♛ 2 |
| ● Barbaresco Ad Altiora '10 | ♛♛ 5 |
| ● Barbera d'Alba A Bon Rendre '16 | ♛♛ 2* |
| ● Barbera d'Alba Laboriosa '09 | ♛♛ 3* |
| ● Nebbiolo d'Alba Blagheur '09 | ♛♛ 3* |
| ● Roero Ròche dra Bòssora Ris. '12 | ♛♛ 3* |
| ● Roero Ròche dra Bòssora Ris. '11 | ♛♛ 3* |

## Tenuta Tenaglia

s.da Santuario di Crea, 5
15020 Serralunga di Crea [AL]
Tel. +39 0142940252
www.tenutatenaglia.it

CELLAR SALES
PRE-BOOKED VISITS
ACCOMMODATION
ANNUAL PRODUCTION 100,000 bottles
HECTARES UNDER VINE 30.00
SUSTAINABLE WINERY

La Tenaglia is part of a complex overlooking
Santuario di Crea, surrounded by oaks
and ash trees, which serve to render the
site even more scenic (if that's possible).
As far as their wines are concerned,
these are made in a modern, well-equipped
cellar expertly overseen by enologist
Roberto Imarisio. They offer 13 wines
made with native grape varieties, except
for their whites where a Chardonnay leads
the way, and their Monferrato Rosso
Paradiso, a Syrah monovarietal. Their
fantastic 2017 Grignolino gets Tre Bicchieri.
Deep ruby and garnet-tinged, it opens with
beautiful notes of pepper and rose that
converge in a rich, intense palate with
tightly-knit tannins and an enduring finish.
Their Barbera really shine. Their Monferrato
Cappella III delivers generous fruit on the
nose and a rich, persistent palate, and
their less complex Asti Bricco, offers
excellent drinkability. Their Chardonnay is
also intriguing.

| | |
|---|---|
| ● Grignolino del M.to Casalese '17 | 🍷🍷🍷 2* |
| ● Barbera D'Asti Bricco '17 | 🍷🍷 3 |
| ● Barbera del M.to Cappella III '17 | 🍷🍷 2* |
| ○ Piemonte Chardonnay '17 | 🍷🍷 3 |
| ○ M.to Bianco '17 | 🍷 2 |
| ⊙ M.to Chiaretto Edenrose '17 | 🍷 2 |
| ● Barbera d'Asti Emozioni '10 | 🍷🍷 5 |
| ● Barbera d'Asti Giorgio Tenaglia '10 | 🍷🍷 3* |
| ● Barbera del M.to Sup. 1930 Una Buona Annata '13 | 🍷🍷 5 |
| ● Grignolino del M.to Casalese '16 | 🍷🍷 2* |
| ● Grignolino del M.to Casalese '13 | 🍷🍷 2* |

## Terre del Barolo

via Alba - Barolo, 8
12060 Castiglione Falletto [CN]
Tel. +39 0173262053
www.arnaldorivera.com

CELLAR SALES
PRE-BOOKED VISITS
ANNUAL PRODUCTION 3,000,000 bottles
HECTARES UNDER VINE 600.00
VITICULTURE METHOD Certified Organic
SUSTAINABLE WINERY

Founded in 1958, this important
cooperative winery has continually evolved
in pursuit of quality, such that they've
dedicated a premium line of excellent
wines to their founder, the loved master
and mayor Arnaldo Rivera. Despite the fact
that Barolo has spawned scores of new
producers over the past 30 years, Terre del
Barolo's vine growers cover some 650
hectares of terrain across each of Barolo's
municipalities, testifying to the trust and
faith they have in the winery. In return, they
receive agronomic assistance from expert
technicians. One of the vintage's best, their
Barolo Undicicomuni del 2014 offers rare
balance albeit without exaggerated flavor.
Their equally brilliant Castello evinces
slightly more austere tannins. Tar and red
fruit help define their resolute Bussia, while
their Vignarionda offers a complex
harmony. Their Rocche of Castiglione is
good, giving subtle signs of wood aging.
Their 2017 Diano proves very enjoyable.

| | |
|---|---|
| ● Barolo Bussia '14 | 🍷🍷 6 |
| ● Barolo Castello '14 | 🍷🍷 6 |
| ● Barolo Undicicomuni '14 | 🍷🍷 5 |
| ● Barolo Vignarionda '14 | 🍷🍷 7 |
| ● Barolo Boiolo '14 | 🍷🍷 6 |
| ● Barolo Rocche di Castiglione '14 | 🍷🍷 7 |
| ● Diano d'Alba Sorì del Cascinotto '17 | 🍷🍷 2* |
| ● Barbera d'Alba Valdisera '16 | 🍷 3 |
| ● Barolo Monvigliero '14 | 🍷 6 |
| ● Barolo Vignarionda Arnaldo Rivera '13 | 🍷🍷🍷 7 |
| ● Barolo Monvigliero '13 | 🍷🍷 6 |
| ● Barolo Ravera '13 | 🍷🍷 6 |
| ● Barolo Undicicomuni '13 | 🍷🍷 5 |

# ★Torraccia del Piantavigna

VIA ROMAGNANO, 20
28074 GHEMME [NO]
TEL. +39 0163840040
www.torracciadelpiantavigna.it

**CELLAR SALES**
**PRE-BOOKED VISITS**
**ANNUAL PRODUCTION** 150,000 bottles
**HECTARES UNDER VINE** 38.00
**SUSTAINABLE WINERY**

Expert Nigel Brown has come on board as technical director, as well as a partner to the Francoli and Ponti families. He's brought vitality to the winery, both in terms of commerce and planning. And so new plots are being purchased and, as of the 2010 vintage, they've added a true pearl to their selection, the Ghemme Vigna Pelizzane. Their Gattinara also continues to prove more than valid. Their enological style is both deferential to local tradition, as evidenced by the use of large barrels, and attentive to elegance, as pointed up by the use of French oak. Their entire selection, however, proves sound. Offering classic hints of tobacco, cacao and licorice, their characterful 2013 Ghemme earns Tre Bicchiere more for its complexity and enduring flavor than for its power. Their fruitier 2012 Riserva delivers a very harmonious palate and the promise of long-term improvement. Characteristic of the vintage, their 2014 Gattinare proves fresh and lively. Balanced and pleasant, their 2017 Bianco Erbavoglio is particularly successful.

| | | |
|---|---|---|
| ● Ghemme '13 | ▼▼▼ | 6 |
| ● Gattinara '14 | ▼▼ | 6 |
| ● Ghemme Ris. '12 | ▼▼ | 6 |
| ○ Colline Novaresi Bianco ErbaVoglio '17 | ▼▼ | 3 |
| ● Colline Novaresi Nebbiolo Ramale '15 | ▼▼ | 4 |
| ● Colline Novaresi Nebbiolo Tre Confini '16 | ▼▼ | 3 |
| ● Colline Novaresi Vespolina La Mostella '17 | ▼ | 3 |
| ● Gattinara '09 | ♀♀♀ | 5 |
| ● Gattinara '06 | ♀♀♀ | 5 |
| ● Ghemme '11 | ♀♀♀ | 5 |
| ● Ghemme '10 | ♀♀♀ | 5 |
| ● Ghemme '07 | ♀♀♀ | 5 |
| ● Ghemme V. Pelizzane '10 | ♀♀♀ | 6 |

# Giancarlo Travaglini

VIA DELLE VIGNE, 36
13045 GATTINARA [VC]
TEL. +39 0163833588
www.travaglinigattinara.it

**CELLAR SALES**
**PRE-BOOKED VISITS**
**ANNUAL PRODUCTION** 250,000 bottles
**HECTARES UNDER VINE** 52.00
**SUSTAINABLE WINERY**

Today the winery founded by Giancarlo Travaglini, which just turned 60, is managed by his daughter Cinzia and her husband, Massimo Collauto. Prized, time-honored vineyards and traditional winemaking in large barrels are at the foundation of their classically-styled Gattinaras. Indeed, theirs is a perfect interpretation of Alto Piemonte's Nebbiolo. At the top of their selection is a Riserva that's not to be missed. Travaglini wanted to be part of a recent regional trend towards the use of Nebbiolo for 'Metodo Classico' sparkling wines, a fact that's given rise to their Nebolé Extra Brut, a wine absolutely worth watching. Their seriously complex 2013 Gattinara Riserva begins to express its remarkable structure and refined balance in its mellow nose of rhubarb and gentian on a rusty background. Equally successful but a slightly different in character, their 2103 Gattinara Tre Vigne proves a little richer with its fresh red fruit and enlivening spices.

| | | |
|---|---|---|
| ● Gattinara Ris. '13 | ▼▼▼ | 7 |
| ● Gattinara Tre Vigne '13 | ▼▼ | 7 |
| ● Coste della Sesia Nebbiolo '17 | ▼▼ | 3 |
| ● Gattinara '14 | ▼▼ | 6 |
| ○ Nebolé Dosaggio Zero M. Cl. '13 | ▼ | 8 |
| ● Gattinara Ris. '12 | ♀♀♀ | 7 |
| ● Gattinara Ris. '06 | ♀♀♀ | 6 |
| ● Gattinara Ris. '04 | ♀♀♀ | 5 |
| ● Gattinara Ris. '01 | ♀♀♀ | 5 |
| ● Gattinara Tre Vigne '04 | ♀♀♀ | 5 |
| ● Coste della Sesia Nebbiolo '15 | ♀♀ | 3 |
| ● Gattinara '13 | ♀♀ | 6 |
| ● Gattinara '12 | ♀♀ | 6 |
| ● Gattinara Ris. '11 | ♀♀ | 7 |
| ● Gattinara Tre Vigne '12 | ♀♀ | 7 |
| ● Il Sogno '12 | ♀♀ | 8 |

## ★G. D. Vajra

FRAZ. VERGNE
VIA DELLE VIOLE, 25
12060 BAROLO [CN]
TEL. +39 017356257
www.gdvajra.it

PRE-BOOKED VISITS
ACCOMMODATION
ANNUAL PRODUCTION 350,000 bottles
HECTARES UNDER VINE 60.00

The Vaira family has managed to satisfy growing market demand with a highly-disciplined adeptness and constance, managing to achieve production volumes of 400,000 per year. It's all thanks to the continued purchase of prized vineyards throughout Langhe, including Barolo (Bricco delle Viole), Serralunga (Baudana), Novello (Ravera) and Sinio, which gives rise to their celebrated Riesling. In their charming cellar, which is adorned with splendid stained glass, medium-large wood barrels prevail. Their 2014 Barolo Baudena opens with notes of fresh strawberry on a blanket of delicate licorice and a well-balance palate that isn't terribly heavy but offers excellent vitality and progression. Still a bit too astringent with tannins, their wonderful 2014 Barolo Bricco delle Viole proves exceptionally well-made. Their rich 2015 Barbera d'Alba Superiore delivers fully ripe fruit, while their lovely 2015 Freisa is unified and clean.

| | |
|---|---|
| ● Barolo Baudana Luigi Baudana '14 | ♟♟ 6 |
| ● Barolo Bricco delle Viole '14 | ♟♟ 8 |
| ● Barolo Ravera '14 | ♟♟ 7 |
| ● Barbera d'Alba Sup. '15 | ♟♟ 5 |
| ● Dolcetto d'Alba Coste & Fossali '17 | ♟♟ 4 |
| ● Langhe Freisa '15 | ♟♟ 5 |
| ● Barolo Cerretta Luigi Baudana '14 | ♟ 6 |
| ○ Langhe Bianco Dragon Luigi Baudana '17 | ♟ 4 |
| ○ Langhe Riesling '17 | ♟ 5 |
| ● Barolo Baudana Luigi Baudana '09 | ♟♟♟ 6 |
| ● Barolo Bricco delle Viole '12 | ♟♟♟ 8 |
| ● Barolo Bricco delle Viole '10 | ♟♟♟ 8 |
| ● Barolo Bricco delle Viole '05 | ♟♟♟ 8 |
| ● Barolo Bricco delle Viole '01 | ♟♟♟ 8 |
| ● Barolo Bricco delle Viole '00 | ♟♟♟ 8 |
| ● Barolo Cerretta Luigi Baudana '08 | ♟♟♟ 6 |

## Mauro Veglio

FRAZ. ANNUNZIATA
LOC. CASCINA NUOVA, 50
12064 LA MORRA [CN]
TEL. +39 0173509212
www.mauroveglio.com

CELLAR SALES
PRE-BOOKED VISITS
ANNUAL PRODUCTION 80,000 bottles
HECTARES UNDER VINE 14.00
SUSTAINABLE WINERY

The news is good (and worth paying attention to). As of this year Mauro Veglio has a partner in his grandson Alessandro, born in 1982 and already well-prepared, thanks to a number of solid vintages as a producer himself. The two wineries are merging into one, and wine lovers everywhere are applauding the move. It's their intension to maintain the same consistence in quality, which is rooted in major Barolo crus (Rocche dell'Annunziata, Gattera, Arborina in La Morra and Castelletto in Monforte d'Alba). Their Barbera and Dolcetto d'Alba also continue to prove valid, as does their rich Langhe Nebbiolo. Their highly enjoyable 2014 Barolo Castelletto opens on a nose of red and black fruit with fresh currants and elegant hints of wood leading into a long, exceptionally well-balanced, fresh, almost savory, palate. The exquisite balance of their 2014 Barolo Rocche dell'Annunziata comes from the magnificently skillful inclusion of oak in its well-fruited structure. Kudos also for their elegant 2016 Barbera d'Alba Cascina Nuova, balsamic, harmonic and never excessive.

| | |
|---|---|
| ● Barbera d'Alba Cascina Nuova '16 | ♟♟ 5 |
| ● Barolo Castelletto '14 | ♟♟ 7 |
| ● Barolo Rocche dell'Annunziata '14 | ♟♟ 8 |
| ● Barolo Arborina '14 | ♟♟ 7 |
| ● Barolo Gattera '14 | ♟♟ 7 |
| ● Langhe Rosso L'Insieme '16 | ♟ 6 |
| ● Barolo Arborina '10 | ♟♟♟ 6 |
| ● Barolo Rocche dell'Annunziata '12 | ♟♟♟ 8 |
| ● Barolo Vign. Arborina '01 | ♟♟♟ 6 |
| ● Barolo Vign. Arborina '00 | ♟♟♟ 6 |
| ● Barolo Vign. Gattera '05 | ♟♟♟ 6 |
| ● Barbera d'Alba Cascina Nuova '15 | ♟♟ 5 |
| ● Barolo '13 | ♟♟ 5 |
| ● Barolo Arborina '13 | ♟♟ 7 |
| ● Barolo Castelletto '13 | ♟♟ 7 |
| ● Barolo Gattera '13 | ♟♟ 7 |
| ● Barolo Rocche dell'Annunziata '13 | ♟♟ 8 |

# Giovanni Viberti

FRAZ. VERGNE
VIA DELLE VIOLE, 30
12060 BAROLO [CN]
TEL. +39 017356192
www.viberti-barolo.com

CELLAR SALES
PRE-BOOKED VISITS
RESTAURANT SERVICE
ANNUAL PRODUCTION 100,000 bottles
HECTARES UNDER VINE 18.00
SUSTAINABLE WINERY

Here in upper Barolo, at elevations that range from 400 to 550 meters above sea level, Nebbiolo offers up good acidity, firm tannins and fresh fruit. Taking into account these qualities, Claudio Viberti is focusing on three Barolo Riservas (Bricco delle Viole, San Pietro and La Volta), which are capable of going to market already well-integrated thanks to 24 extra months of aging (on top of Barolo's already canonical three years of maturation). A nice side note is that their classically-styled Buon Padre restaurant has been offering house wines since 1923. Their 2014 Barolo Buon Padre presents lovely aromas of fresh red fruit and a lightweight palate with pleasant pulp that doesn't bite. Their highly drinkable 2016 Dolbà, paired Dolcetto and Barbera, proves fragrant, sound and spirited. Their equally pleasing 2016 Dolcetto d'Alba Superiore, gives off notes of almonds and plums, while their spicy, minty 2015 Barbera Bricco Airoli provides more of a challenge.

| | |
|---|---|
| ● Barbera d'Alba La Gemella '17 | 🍷🍷 3 |
| ● Barbera d'Alba Sup. Bricco Airoli '15 | 🍷🍷 4 |
| ● Barolo Buon Padre '14 | 🍷🍷 6 |
| ● Dolcetto d'Alba Sup. '16 | 🍷🍷 3 |
| ● Langhe Dolbà '16 | 🍷🍷 2* |
| ○ Piemonte Chardonnay '17 | 🍷 3 |
| ● Barbera d'Alba Sup. Airoli '13 | 🍷🍷 4 |
| ● Barolo Bricco delle Viole Ris. '10 | 🍷🍷 7 |
| ● Barolo Buon Padre '12 | 🍷🍷 6 |
| ● Barolo La Volta Ris. '11 | 🍷🍷 8 |
| ● Barolo San Pietro Ris. '11 | 🍷🍷 8 |
| ● Barolo San Pietro Ris. '10 | 🍷🍷 8 |
| ● Langhe Inisj '11 | 🍷🍷 5 |
| ● Langhe Nebbiolo '15 | 🍷🍷 3 |
| ○ Piemonte Chardonnay '16 | 🍷🍷 3 |

# Vicara

VIA MADONNA DELLE GRAZIE, 5
15030 ROSIGNANO MONFERRATO [AL]
TEL. +39 0142488054
www.vicara.it

CELLAR SALES
PRE-BOOKED VISITS
ANNUAL PRODUCTION 200,000 bottles
HECTARES UNDER VINE 37.00
VITICULTURE METHOD Certified Biodynamic

Vicara is a well-established winery in Monferrato Casalese, in addition to representing a territory rich in well-preserved agricultural history and traditions. The quality of their selection is excellent, starting with their base selection, with wines like Barbera Volpuva, a splendid example of a young Barbera. Their Grignolino, as well, has been showered with praise over the past two years. Their Uccelletta is another top wine, a historic Grignolino, while their Cantico della Crosia is a Monferrato Barbera Superiore. Impressive showing from Vicara with both their exceptional Grignolino and amazing 2017 Volpuva going to the finals. The former offers classic style with strong territoriality, while the latter gives off crunchy fruit, a dense, fresh palate and a long finish. Their Cantino della Crosia relies more on tertiary aromas of jam, sweet spices and balsamic notes, while the woody presence in their Cascina Rocca doesn't diminish its fruit. Their 2015 Sarni also deserves mention.

| | |
|---|---|
| ● Barbera del M.to Volpuva '17 | 🍷🍷 3* |
| ● Grignolino del M.to Casalese '17 | 🍷🍷 3* |
| ● Barbera del M.to '17 | 🍷🍷 2* |
| ● Barbera del M.to Cascina La Rocca 33 '16 | 🍷🍷 6 |
| ● Barbera del M.to Sup. Cantico della Crosia '15 | 🍷🍷 4 |
| ○ M.to Bianco Sarni '15 | 🍷🍷 5 |
| ○ M.to Airales '17 | 🍷 3 |
| ● M.to Rosso Rubello '15 | 🍷 4 |
| ● Grignolino del M.to Casalese '16 | 🍷🍷🍷 3* |
| ● Grignolino del M.to Casalese °G '15 | 🍷🍷🍷 4* |
| ● Barbera del M.to Cascina Rocca 33 '13 | 🍷🍷 3* |
| ● Barbera del M.to La Rocca '10 | 🍷🍷 3* |
| ● Barbera del M.to Sup. Vadmò '12 | 🍷🍷 4 |
| ● Barbera del M.to Sup. Vadmò '11 | 🍷🍷 4 |

## ★★Vietti

P.zza Vittorio Veneto, 5
12060 Castiglione Falletto [CN]
Tel. +39 017362825
www.vietti.com

**CELLAR SALES**
**PRE-BOOKED VISITS**
**ANNUAL PRODUCTION** 300,000 bottles
**HECTARES UNDER VINE** 40.00

The first bottles to display the Vietti name go back exactly one century ago, to 1919. Since then it's been non-stop international success, which continues today under Luca Currado (and the winery's new owners, the Krause family). The producer's success hinges on their ability to offer a selection of extremely valid wines across the board, from their Dolcetto d'Alba Tre Vigne to their Barolo Riserva Villero. For fans of labels, we point out that many of Vietti's were designed by Gianni Gallo, whose work can be found in Silvia Sala's catalog 'Dall'altra parte della natura' ('The Other Side of Nature'). Their Rocche di Castiglione proves why its at the head of the class even in a difficult vintage like 2014. It unleashes unparalleled power and harmony for Tre Bicchieri. Their 2010 Villero, a wine of uncommon personality, lives up to the high expectations it has set for itself. Their 2014 Barbaresco Masseria displays remarkable texture and refinement. Their Castiglione is pure and extremely pleasant. Their complex 2015 Barbera d'Asti La Crena offers fruity elegance.

| | |
|---|---|
| ● Barolo Rocche di Castiglione '14 | ♛♛♛ 8 |
| ● Barbaresco Masseria '14 | ♛♛ 8 |
| ● Barbera d'Asti La Crena '15 | ♛♛ 6 |
| ● Barolo Ravera '14 | ♛♛ 8 |
| ● Barolo Villero Ris. '10 | ♛♛ 8 |
| ● Barbera d'Alba Scarrone V. V. '16 | ♛♛ 6 |
| ● Barolo Castiglione '14 | ♛♛ 7 |
| ● Barolo Lazzarito '14 | ♛♛ 8 |
| ● Barbera d'Alba V. Scarrone '16 | ♛ 6 |
| ● Barbera d'Asti Sup. Nizza La Crena '09 | ♟♟♟ 5 |
| ● Barolo Ravera '12 | ♟♟♟ 8 |
| ● Barolo Rocche '08 | ♟♟♟ 8 |
| ● Barolo Rocche di Castiglione '11 | ♟♟♟ 8 |
| ● Barolo Villero Ris. '09 | ♟♟♟ 8 |
| ● Barolo Villero Ris. '07 | ♟♟♟ 8 |
| ● Barolo Villero Ris. '06 | ♟♟♟ 8 |

## I Vignaioli di Santo Stefano

loc. Marini, 26
12058 Santo Stefano Belbo [CN]
Tel. +39 0141840419
www.ivignaiolidisantostefano.it

**CELLAR SALES**
**PRE-BOOKED VISITS**
**ANNUAL PRODUCTION** 275,000 bottles
**HECTARES UNDER VINE** 32.00
**SUSTAINABLE WINERY**

In 1976 the Ceretto and Scavino families decided to create a winery that would become a model for the production of Moscato d'Asti and, later, Asti Spumante. Today Vignaioli di Santo Stefano has a series of vineyards throughout Santo Stefano Belbo, Calosso and Canelli, all at elevations of between 320 and 450 meters and all dedicated to Moscato Bianco. The soil here is loose and marly, composed of clay, sand and loam, and the vineyards go back anywhere from 8 to 40 years. As usual, the winery only presented two selections. Their 2017 Moscato d'Asti, proves very fresh both on its nose of sage and green apple and on its palate, long and grippy thanks to the balance of a lovely acidity and sweet notes of candied fruit. Also showing a good balance between sweet and acidic elements on the palate, their creamy Asti releases hints of citrus and jasmine, for a pleasant and approachable sparkling wine.

| | |
|---|---|
| ○ Asti '17 | ♛♛ 3 |
| ○ Moscato d'Asti '17 | ♛♛ 3 |
| ○ Asti '16 | ♟♟ 3 |
| ○ Asti '15 | ♟♟ 3 |
| ○ Asti '14 | ♟♟ 3 |
| ○ Asti '13 | ♟♟ 3 |
| ○ Asti '12 | ♟♟ 3 |
| ○ Asti '11 | ♟♟ 3 |
| ○ Moscato d'Asti '16 | ♟♟ 3 |
| ○ Moscato d'Asti '15 | ♟♟ 3* |
| ○ Moscato d'Asti '14 | ♟♟ 5 |
| ○ Moscato d'Asti '13 | ♟♟ 4 |
| ○ Moscato d'Asti '12 | ♟♟ 4 |
| ○ Moscato d'Asti '11 | ♟♟ 3 |

## Villa Giada

REG. CEIROLE, 10
14053 CANELLI [AT]
TEL. +39 0141831100
www.villagiada.wine

CELLAR SALES
PRE-BOOKED VISITS
ACCOMMODATION AND RESTAURANT SERVICE
ANNUAL PRODUCTION 180,000 bottles
HECTARES UNDER VINE 25.00
SUSTAINABLE WINERY

The Faccio family has three estates, each around a farmhouse. Moscato is cultivated at Cascina Ceirole, in the municipality of Canelli (where the original nucleus of the winery and cellar are located). Cascina del Parroco, in Calosso, is comprised of four hectares on a small plateau overlooking the valley of Rio Nizza. Casina Dani, which serves as the heart of their Barbera production, is constituted of 14 hectares in Agliano Terme. The vineyards are in excellent locations and grow in loose, medium-textured soil that's rich in minerals. Their 2016 Barbera d'Asti Superiore Quescia makes the finals with its notes of red fruit and hints of spices on the nose, while on its fresh, pleasant palate it offers grip and balance. Their range includes several selections worth noting. Perhaps a bit overly marked by wood, their 2105 Nizza Dedicato proves rich with fruit, and their approachable, easy-drinking 2017 Moscato d'Asti Canelli delivers hints of candied citron. And their 2017 Piemonte Chardonnay Cortese Manè delivers Mediterranean scrub and nice body.

| | |
|---|---|
| ● Barbera d'Asti Sup. La Quercia '16 | ▼▼ 3* |
| ○ Moscato d'Asti Canelli '17 | ▼▼ 2* |
| ● Nizza Dedicato '15 | ▼▼ 5 |
| ○ Piemonte Chardonnay Cortese Manè '17 | ▼▼ 2* |
| ● Barbera d'Asti Ajan '17 | ▼ 2 |
| ● Barbera d'Asti Surì '17 | ▼ 2 |
| ○ Moscato d'Asti Surì '17 | ▼ 2 |
| ● Barbera d'Asti Ajan '16 | ♀♀ 2* |
| ● Barbera d'Asti Sup. Nizza Dedicato a... '13 | ♀♀ 5 |
| ● Barbera d'Asti Surì '15 | ♀♀ 2* |
| ○ Moscato d'Asti Canelli '16 | ♀♀ 2* |
| ○ Moscato d'Asti Canelli '15 | ♀♀ 2* |
| ○ Moscato d'Asti Surì '15 | ♀♀ 2* |
| ● Nizza Bricco Dani '15 | ♀♀ 4 |

## ★Villa Sparina

FRAZ. MONTEROTONDO, 56
15066 GAVI [AL]
TEL. +39 0143633835
www.villasparina.it

PRE-BOOKED VISITS
ACCOMMODATION AND RESTAURANT SERVICE
ANNUAL PRODUCTION 550,000 bottles
HECTARES UNDER VINE 65.00

Villa Sparina and Monterotondo share an inextricable bond thanks to their prestigious resort, a hub of sophistication and elegance in the area. Then there's their Monterotondo Gavi, a emblem of the wine and the producer's signature style. The Moccagatta family's creation began here in 1970s and developed over time, eventually becoming one of Gavi's largest estates. Their eight wines are all extremely well-made, with their Rivalta, a Barbera del Monferrato Superiore, and their Villa Sparina, a brut 'Metodo Classico', both standing out. This year's proposals for the guide contain some pleasant surprises. Retasting their 2007 Monterotondo happily reconfirms the sensational longevity of the Gavi, expressed in aromas that continue to become more faceted and more complex. Their excellent 2017 Barbera also surprises as perhaps the best-ever Gavi del Comune di Gavi. And their Metodo Classico once again proves superb.

| | |
|---|---|
| ● Barbera del M.to '17 | ▼▼ 3* |
| ○ Gavi del Comune di Gavi '17 | ▼▼ 3* |
| ○ Villa Sparina Blanc de Blancs Brut M. Cl. '14 | ▼▼ 3 |
| ○ Gavi del Comune di Gavi Monterotondo '14 | ♀♀♀ 6 |
| ○ Gavi del Comune di Gavi Monterotondo '12 | ♀♀♀ 6 |
| ○ Gavi del Comune di Gavi Monterotondo '11 | ♀♀♀ 6 |
| ○ Gavi del Comune di Gavi Monterotondo '15 | ♀♀♀ 6 |
| ○ Gavi del Comune di Gavi Monterotondo '10 | ♀♀♀ 6 |
| ○ Gavi del Comune di Gavi '16 | ♀♀ 3* |
| ○ Gavi del Comune di Gavi Et. Gialla '15 | ♀♀ 3 |

## Viticoltori Associati di Vinchio Vaglio Serra

Fraz. Reg. San Pancrazio, 1
S.da prov.le 40 km. 3,75
14040 Vinchio [AT]
Tel. +39 0141950903
www.vinchio.com

CELLAR SALES
PRE-BOOKED VISITS
ANNUAL PRODUCTION 1,600,000 bottles
HECTARES UNDER VINE 472.00

Sometimes, to truly appreciate a winery's importance, you just have to let the numbers speak. Here are a few: the cooperative winery Vinchio Vaglio Serra, founded in 1959 by a group of 19 producers, works with 187 vine growers who operate on 472 hectares of land and give rise to 50 wines. In addition to Vinchio and Vaglio Serra, their vineyards are situated in the municipalities of Castelnuovo Belbo, Castelnuovo Calcea, Cortiglione, Incisa Scapaccino, Mombercelli and Nizza Monferrato. Primarily Barbera is cultivated, with some vineyards going back as far as 60 years. Their wonderful 2015 Barbera d'Asti Superiore Vigne Vecchie offers notes of red berries and hints of pencil lead on a fresh, dynamic, assertive palate. Marked by wood but also rich in fruit with good acidic support, their 2016 Barbera d'Asti Superiore I Tre Vescovi proves well made, as do their dense and austere 2016 Barbera d'Asti 50 Vecchie Vigne and their 2017 Grignolino d'Asti Le Nocche, which is pleasant and expresses great typicity in its spicy, floral notes.

| | |
|---|---|
| ● Barbera d'Asti Sup. Vigne Vecchie '15 | 🍷🍷 5 |
| ● Barbera d'Asti Sup. I Tre Vescovi '16 | 🍷🍷 2* |
| ● Barbera d'Asti Vigne Vecchie 50° '16 | 🍷🍷 3 |
| ● Grignolino d'Asti Le Nocche '17 | 🍷🍷 2* |
| ● Barbera d'Asti Sori dei Mori '17 | 🍷 2 |
| ● Barbera d'Asti Sup. Sei Vigne Insynthesis '11 | 🍷 6 |
| ☉ I Tre Vescovi Brut Rosé M. Cl. | 🍷 4 |
| ○ Moscato d'Asti Valamasca '17 | 🍷 2 |
| ● Piemonte Barbera Le Tane '17 | 🍷 1* |
| ● Barbera d'Asti Sup. Sei Vigne Insynthesis '01 | 🍷🍷🍷 6 |
| ● Barbera d'Asti Sup. Sei Vigne Insynthesis '09 | 🍷🍷 6 |
| ● Barbera d'Asti Vigne Vecchie 50° '15 | 🍷🍷 3* |

## Vite Colte

via Bergesia, 6
12060 Barolo [CN]
Tel. +39 0173564611
www.vitecolte.it

CELLAR SALES
PRE-BOOKED VISITS
ANNUAL PRODUCTION 1,200,000 bottles
HECTARES UNDER VINE 300.00
VITICULTURE METHOD Certified Organic
SUSTAINABLE WINERY

It's full steam ahead for Vite Colte, Terre da Vino's premium production line. Founded in 1980, it's comprised of 180 vine growers, all of whom follow meticulous agronomic protocols in cultivating 300 hectares of land, making for a high quality selection of wines that faithfully express the characteristics of Barolo. Some of their best vineyards are situated in Barolo and Serralunga d'Alba, and their grapes are then aged in large wood barrels. Their wide range also includes Barbaresco and Dolcetto, whites Gavi and Roero Arneis, and a Moscato Passito sweet wine. And this last earned Tre Bicchieri during our tastings, as well as our award for Sweet Wine of the Year. Intense with notes of walnuts, rose and pepper, it offers a long, soft and enduring palate. Classic notes of dried flowers and dark fruit contribute to their powerful 2013 Barolo del Comune di Serralunga d'Alba. The exceptional palate of their 2013 Barolo Comune di Monforte d'Alba offers cadence, length, depth and a radiant future. Their 2008 Barolo Riserva Essenze is at the top of its game and ready to drink.

| | |
|---|---|
| ○ Piemonte Moscato Passito La Bella Estate '16 | 🍷🍷🍷 5 |
| ● Barolo del Comune di Monforte d'Alba Essenze '13 | 🍷🍷 7 |
| ● Barolo del Comune di Serralunga d'Alba Essenze '13 | 🍷🍷 7 |
| ● Barbera d'Alba Sup. Croere '16 | 🍷🍷 4 |
| ● Barbaresco La Casa in Collina '15 | 🍷 5 |
| ● Barolo del Comune di Barolo Essenze '13 | 🍷🍷🍷 7 |
| ● Barolo del Comune di Barolo Essenze '12 | 🍷🍷🍷 6 |
| ● Barbaresco Spezie Ris. '08 | 🍷🍷 6 |
| ● Barbera d'Alba Sup. Croere '15 | 🍷🍷 4 |
| ● Nizza La Luna e i Falò '15 | 🍷🍷 5 |
| ○ Piemonte Moscato Passito La Bella Estate '15 | 🍷🍷 5 |

## 499

VIA ROMA, 3
12050 CAMO [CN]
TEL. +39 0141840155
www.499vino.it

| | |
|---|---|
| ● Langhe Freisa '16 | ♟♟ 3 |
| ● Langhe Freisa Coste dei Fre '15 | ♟♟ 3 |
| ○ Moscato d'Asti '17 | ♟♟ 3 |

## Giovanni Abrigo

VIA SANTA CROCE, 9
12055 DIANO D'ALBA [CN]
TEL. +39 017369345
www.abrigo.it

CELLAR SALES
PRE-BOOKED VISITS
ANNUAL PRODUCTION 40,000 bottles
HECTARES UNDER VINE 10.00

| | |
|---|---|
| ● Barolo Ravera '14 | ♟♟ 6 |
| ● Barbera d'Alba Marminela '16 | ♟♟ 2* |
| ● Dolcetto di Diano d'Alba '17 | ♟♟ 2* |
| ● Dolcetto di Diano d'Alba Sup. Garabei '16 | ♟♟ 2* |

## Annamaria Alemanni

FRAZ. CHERLI INFERIORE, 64
15070 TAGLIOLO MONFERRATO [AL]
TEL. +39 0143896229
doppiaa@libero.it

CELLAR SALES
ACCOMMODATION
ANNUAL PRODUCTION 6,000 bottles
HECTARES UNDER VINE 4.00
SUSTAINABLE WINERY

| | |
|---|---|
| ● Dolcetto di Ovada Anvud '16 | ♟♟ 2* |
| ● Dolcetto di Ovada Sup. Ansè '15 | ♟ 3 |

## Alice Bel Colle

REG. STAZIONE, 9
15010 ALICE BEL COLLE [AL]
TEL. +39 014474103
www.cantinaalicebc.it

CELLAR SALES
PRE-BOOKED VISITS
ANNUAL PRODUCTION 100,000 bottles
HECTARES UNDER VINE 370.00

| | |
|---|---|
| ● Barbera d'Asti '17 | ♟♟ 3 |
| ○ Moscato d'Asti Paiè '17 | ♟♟ 2* |
| ● Barbera d'Asti Al Casò '17 | ♟ 2 |
| ● Barbera d'Asti Sup. Alix '15 | ♟ 3 |

## Antica Cascina dei Conti di Roero

VIA VAL RUBIAGNO
12040 VEZZA D'ALBA [CN]
TEL. +39 017365459
www.oliveropietro.it

CELLAR SALES
PRE-BOOKED VISITS
ANNUAL PRODUCTION 100,000 bottles
HECTARES UNDER VINE 13.50
SUSTAINABLE WINERY

| | |
|---|---|
| ● Barbera d'Alba '16 | ♟♟ 2* |
| ● Nebbiolo d'Alba '16 | ♟♟ 3 |
| ○ Roero Arneis '17 | ♟♟ 2* |
| ○ Langhe Favorita '17 | ♟ 2 |

## F.lli Aresca

VIA PONTETTO, 8A
14047 MOMBERCELLI [AT]
TEL. +39 0141955128
www.arescavini.it

CELLAR SALES
PRE-BOOKED VISITS
ANNUAL PRODUCTION 120,000 bottles
HECTARES UNDER VINE 10.00
SUSTAINABLE WINERY

| | |
|---|---|
| ● Barbera d'Asti La Moretta '16 | ♟♟ 2* |
| ● Barbera d'Asti Superiore La Rossa '15 | ♟♟ 3 |
| ● Grignolino d'Asti '17 | ♟♟ 2* |
| ● Nizza San Luigi '15 | ♟♟ 5 |

## L'Astemia Pentita

VIA CROSIA, 40
12060 BAROLO [CN]
TEL. +39 0173560501
www.astemiapentita.it

CELLAR SALES
ANNUAL PRODUCTION 70,000 bottles
HECTARES UNDER VINE 15.00

| | |
|---|---|
| ● Barolo Cannubi '14 | 🍷🍷 8 |
| ● Barolo Terlo '14 | 🍷🍷 8 |
| ○ Langhe Nascetta '17 | 🍷🍷 3 |
| ● Barolo '14 | 🍷 8 |

## Cantina Sociale Barbera dei Sei Castelli

VIA OPESSINA, 41
14040 CASTELNUOVO CALCEA [AT]
TEL. +39 0141957137
www.barberaseicastelli.it

CELLAR SALES
PRE-BOOKED VISITS
ANNUAL PRODUCTION 80,000 bottles
HECTARES UNDER VINE 620.00

| | |
|---|---|
| ● Barbera d'Asti 50 Anni di Barbera '16 | 🍷🍷 2* |
| ● Barbera d'Asti Sup. Le Vignole '15 | 🍷🍷 3 |
| ● Nizza '15 | 🍷🍷 4 |
| ● Barbera d'Asti Venti Forti '17 | 🍷 2 |

## Fabrizio Battaglino

LOC. BORGONUOVO
VIA MONTALDO ROERO, 44
12040 VEZZA D'ALBA [CN]
TEL. +39 0173658156
www.battaglino.com

CELLAR SALES
PRE-BOOKED VISITS
ANNUAL PRODUCTION 25,000 bottles
HECTARES UNDER VINE 5.00

| | |
|---|---|
| ● Barbera d'Alba Munbèl '16 | 🍷🍷 3 |
| ● Nebbiolo d'Alba Colla '15 | 🍷🍷 4 |
| ○ Roero Arneis Bastia '17 | 🍷 2 |
| ● Roero Sergentin '15 | 🍷 4 |

## Bea - Merenda con Corvi

S.DA SANTA CATERINA, 8
10064 PINEROLO [TO]
TEL. +39 3356824880
www.merendaconcorvi.it

CELLAR SALES
PRE-BOOKED VISITS
ACCOMMODATION
ANNUAL PRODUCTION 5,500 bottles
HECTARES UNDER VINE 1.00

| | |
|---|---|
| ● Merenda con Corvi '16 | 🍷🍷 5 |
| ● Pinerolese Rosso '16 | 🍷🍷 4 |
| ● Pinerolese Barbera Foravia '17 | 🍷 4 |

## Antonio Bellicoso

FRAZ. MOLISSO, 5A
14048 MONTEGROSSO D'ASTI [AT]
TEL. +39 0141953233
antonio.bellicoso@alice.it

CELLAR SALES
PRE-BOOKED VISITS
ANNUAL PRODUCTION 15,000 bottles
HECTARES UNDER VINE 4.00
SUSTAINABLE WINERY

| | |
|---|---|
| ● Barbera d'Asti Amormio '17 | 🍷🍷 2* |
| ● Freisa d'Asti '17 | 🍷🍷 2* |
| ● Barbera d'Asti Merum '16 | 🍷 3 |

## Silvano Bolmida

LOC. BUSSIA 30
12065 MONFORTE D'ALBA [CN]
TEL. +39 0173789877
www.silvanobolmida.com

CELLAR SALES
PRE-BOOKED VISITS
ANNUAL PRODUCTION 30,000 bottles
HECTARES UNDER VINE 6.00

| | |
|---|---|
| ● Barolo Bussia V. dei Fantini '13 | 🍷🍷 5 |
| ● Barolo Bussia Ris. '12 | 🍷🍷 7 |
| ● Barolo Le Coste di Monforte '13 | 🍷🍷 5 |
| ● Barbera d'Alba Sup. Conca del Grillo '16 | 🍷 3 |

# F.lli Serio & Battista Borgogno

LOC. CANNUBI
VIA CROSIA, 12
12060 BAROLO [CN]
TEL. +39 017356107
www.borgognoseriobattista.it

CELLAR SALES
PRE-BOOKED VISITS
ANNUAL PRODUCTION 60,000 bottles
HECTARES UNDER VINE 7.50

| | |
|---|---|
| ● Barolo Cannubi Ris. '12 | ♟♟ 7 |
| ● Barbera d'Alba Sup. '14 | ♟♟ 3 |
| ● Barolo '14 | ♟♟ 5 |
| ● Barolo Cannubi '14 | ♟ 6 |

# F.lli Botto

S.DA PROV. S. STEFANO ROERO, 9
12046 MONTÀ [CN]
TEL. +39 0173976015
botto@hotmail.it

CELLAR SALES
PRE-BOOKED VISITS
ANNUAL PRODUCTION 10,000 bottles
HECTARES UNDER VINE 3.00

| | |
|---|---|
| ● Roero '15 | ♟♟ 4 |
| ○ Roero Arneis '17 | ♟♟ 2* |

# Bricco del Cucù

LOC. BRICCO, 10
12060 BASTIA MONDOVÌ [CN]
TEL. +39 017460153
www.briccocucu.com

CELLAR SALES
PRE-BOOKED VISITS
ANNUAL PRODUCTION 50,000 bottles
HECTARES UNDER VINE 10.00

| | |
|---|---|
| ● Dogliani La Chiesetta Barone Riccardi '17 | ♟♟ 2* |
| ● Langhe Rosso Superboum '16 | ♟♟ 2* |
| ● Dogliani '17 | ♟ 2 |
| ● Langhe Dolcetto L'impronta '17 | ♟ 2 |

# Francesco Boschis

B.TA PIANEZZO, 57
12063 DOGLIANI [CN]
TEL. +39 017370574
www.boschisfrancesco.it

CELLAR SALES
PRE-BOOKED VISITS
ANNUAL PRODUCTION 40,000 bottles
HECTARES UNDER VINE 11.00

| | |
|---|---|
| ● Dogliani Sup. V. dei Prey '16 | ♟♟ 2* |
| ● Dogliani Sup. V. Sorì San Martino '16 | ♟♟ 2* |
| ● Barbera d'Alba Sup. V. Le Masserie '14 | ♟ 3 |
| ● Dogliani V. in Pianezzo '17 | ♟ 2 |

# Giacomo Boveri

FRAZ. MONTALE CELLI
VIA COSTA VESCOVATO, 15
15050 COSTA VESCOVATO [AL]
TEL. +39 0131838223
www.vignetiboveri.it

CELLAR SALES
PRE-BOOKED VISITS
ANNUAL PRODUCTION 25,000 bottles
HECTARES UNDER VINE 9.00

| | |
|---|---|
| ○ Colli Tortonesi Timorasso Muntà L'è Ruma '15 | ♟♟ 4 |
| ○ Colli Tortonesi Timorasso Lacrime del Bricco '15 | ♟♟ 4 |

# La Briccolina

VIA RODDINO, 7
12050 SERRALUNGA D'ALBA [CN]
TEL. +39 3282217094
labriccolina@gmail.com

ANNUAL PRODUCTION 3,000 bottles
HECTARES UNDER VINE 5.50

| | |
|---|---|
| ● Barolo Briccolina '14 | ♟♟ 5 |
| ● Barolo Briccolina '13 | ♟♟ 5 |

## Broccardo

LOC. MANZONI, 22
12065 MONFORTE D'ALBA [CN]
TEL. +39 017378180
www.broccardo.it

CELLAR SALES
PRE-BOOKED VISITS
ANNUAL PRODUCTION 50,000 bottles
HECTARES UNDER VINE 8.00
SUSTAINABLE WINERY

| | |
|---|---|
| ● Barbera d'Alba La Martina '16 | ♛♛ 4 |
| ● Barolo Bricco San Pietro '14 | ♛♛ 7 |
| ● Langhe Nebbiolo '16 | ♛♛ 5 |

## Bussia Soprana

LOC. BUSSIA, 88A
12065 MONFORTE D'ALBA [CN]
TEL. +39 039305182
www.bussiasoprana.it

CELLAR SALES
PRE-BOOKED VISITS
ANNUAL PRODUCTION 60,000 bottles
HECTARES UNDER VINE 16.00

| | |
|---|---|
| ● Barbera d'Alba Mosconi '14 | ♛♛ 4 |
| ● Barolo Bussia V. Gabutti '13 | ♛♛ 8 |
| ● Barolo Bussia V. Colonnello '13 | ♛ 7 |

## Oreste Buzio

V. PIAVE, 13
15049 VIGNALE MONFERRATO [AL]
TEL. +39 0142933197
www.orestebuzio.altervista.org

CELLAR SALES
PRE-BOOKED VISITS
ANNUAL PRODUCTION 25,000 bottles
HECTARES UNDER VINE 6.00
VITICULTURE METHOD Certified Organic

| | |
|---|---|
| ● Grignolino del M.to Casalese '17 | ♛♛ 3* |
| ● Barbera del M.to '17 | ♛ 2 |
| ○ Piemonte Chardonnay '17 | ♛ 2 |

## Marco Canato

FRAZ. FONS SALERA
LOC. CA' BALDEA, 18/2
15049 VIGNALE MONFERRATO [AL]
TEL. +39 0142933653
www.canatovini.it

CELLAR SALES
PRE-BOOKED VISITS
ANNUAL PRODUCTION 30,000 bottles
HECTARES UNDER VINE 11.00

| | |
|---|---|
| ● Barbera del M.to Gambaloita '17 | ♛♛ 3 |
| ● Barbera del M.to La Baldea '15 | ♛♛ 2* |
| ● Barbera del M.to Sup. Rupes '10 | ♛♛ 4 |
| ● Grignolino del M.to Casalese Celio '17 | ♛♛ 3 |

## Pierangelo Careglio

LOC. APRATO, 15
12040 BALDISSERO D'ALBA [CN]
TEL. +39 017240436
www.cantinacareglio.com

CELLAR SALES
PRE-BOOKED VISITS
ANNUAL PRODUCTION 30,000 bottles
HECTARES UNDER VINE 8.00

| | |
|---|---|
| ○ Roero Arneis '17 | ♛♛ 2* |
| ● Barbera d'Alba '16 | ♛ 2 |
| ○ Langhe Favorita '17 | ♛ 2 |

## Casavecchia

VIA ROMA, 2
12055 DIANO D'ALBA [CN]
TEL. +39 017369321
www.cantinacasavecchia.com

CELLAR SALES
PRE-BOOKED VISITS
ANNUAL PRODUCTION 40,000 bottles
HECTARES UNDER VINE 8.00

| | |
|---|---|
| ● Barbera d'Alba Sup. '15 | ♛♛ 3 |
| ● Barolo del Comune di Castiglione Falletto '12 | ♛ 5 |
| ● Diano d'Alba Sörì Bruni '17 | ♛ 2 |

## Cascina Alberta

VIA ALBA, 5
12050 TREISO [CN]
TEL. +39 0173638047
www.calberta.it

CELLAR SALES
PRE-BOOKED VISITS
ACCOMMODATION
ANNUAL PRODUCTION 28,000 bottles
HECTARES UNDER VINE 9.00
VITICULTURE METHOD Certified Organic
SUSTAINABLE WINERY

| | |
|---|---|
| ● Barbaresco Giacone '15 | ♟♟ 5 |
| ● Langhe Nebbiolo '16 | ♟♟ 3 |
| ○ Langhe Riesling '17 | ♟♟ 3 |
| ⊙ Langhe Rosato '17 | ♟ 3 |

## Cascina Ballarin

FRAZ. ANNUNZIATA, 115
12064 LA MORRA [CN]
TEL. +39 017350365
www.cascinaballarin.it

CELLAR SALES
PRE-BOOKED VISITS
ACCOMMODATION
ANNUAL PRODUCTION 60,000 bottles
HECTARES UNDER VINE 9.00
VITICULTURE METHOD Certified Organic
SUSTAINABLE WINERY

| | |
|---|---|
| ● Barbera d'Alba Giuli '15 | ♟♟ 5 |
| ● Barolo Tre Ciabót '14 | ♟♟ 6 |
| ● Barolo Bricco Rocca Tistot Ris. '09 | ♟ 8 |

## Cascina del Monastero

LOC. LA MORRA
FRAZ. ANNUNZIATA, 112A
FRAZ. FRAZIONE ANNUNZIATA 112/A
12064 LA MORRA [CN]
TEL. +39 0173509245509245
www.cascinadelmonastero.it

CELLAR SALES
PRE-BOOKED VISITS
ACCOMMODATION
ANNUAL PRODUCTION 40,000 bottles
HECTARES UNDER VINE 12.00
VITICULTURE METHOD Certified Organic
SUSTAINABLE WINERY

| | |
|---|---|
| ● Barolo Bricco Rocca Riund Ris. '12 | ♟♟ 7 |
| ● Barolo Bricco Luciani '14 | ♟ 6 |
| ● Langhe Nebbiolo Monastero '14 | ♟ 3 |

## Cascina Faletta

MANDOLETTA 81
15033 CASALE MONFERRATO [AL]
TEL. +39 0142670068
www.faletta.it

ANNUAL PRODUCTION 25,000 bottles
HECTARES UNDER VINE 6.00

| | |
|---|---|
| ● Barbera del Monferrato Braja '16 | ♟♟ 3 |
| ● Rosso di Rosso | ♟♟ 3 |
| ● Piemonte Chardonnay Primo Bianco '17 | ♟ 3 |

## Cascina Galarin

VIA CAROSSI, 12
14054 CASTAGNOLE DELLE LANZE [AT]
TEL. +39 0141878586
www.galarin.it

CELLAR SALES
ANNUAL PRODUCTION 30,000 bottles
HECTARES UNDER VINE 6.00
VITICULTURE METHOD Certified Organic

| | |
|---|---|
| ● Barbera d'Asti Sup. Tinella '15 | ♟♟ 5 |
| ○ Moscato d'Asti Prá Dône '17 | ♟♟ 2* |
| ● Barbera d'Asti Le Querce '16 | ♟ 2 |

## Cascina Gentile

S.DA PROV.LE PER SAN CRISTOFORO. 11
15060 CAPRIATA D'ORBA [AL]
TEL. +39 0143468975
www.cascinagentile.tumblr.com

CELLAR SALES
PRE-BOOKED VISITS
ANNUAL PRODUCTION 30,000 bottles
HECTARES UNDER VINE 10.00
SUSTAINABLE WINERY

| | |
|---|---|
| ● Barbera del M.to Barberrique '14 | ♟♟ 3 |
| ○ Colli Tortonesi Timorasso Derthona '15 | ♟♟ 3 |
| ● Ovada Le Parole Servon Tanto '15 | ♟♟ 3 |
| ● Ovada Tre Passi Avanti '16 | ♟♟ 3 |

## Cascina Pellerino

LOC. SANT'ANNA, 93
12040 MONTEU ROERO [CN]
TEL. +39 3393370470
www.cascinapellerino.com

CELLAR SALES
PRE-BOOKED VISITS
ANNUAL PRODUCTION 50,000 bottles
HECTARES UNDER VINE 7.00
SUSTAINABLE WINERY

| | |
|---|---|
| ● Barbera d'Alba Eleonora '17 | ♟♟ 3 |
| ● Roero V. del Padre Ris. '15 | ♟♟ 6 |
| ● Roero Vicot '16 | ♟♟ 5 |
| ○ Poch ma Bon Passito | ♟ 5 |

## Cascina Val del Prete

S.DA SANTUARIO, 2
12040 PRIOCCA [CN]
TEL. +39 0173616534
www.valdelprete.com

CELLAR SALES
PRE-BOOKED VISITS
ANNUAL PRODUCTION 55,000 bottles
HECTARES UNDER VINE 11.00
VITICULTURE METHOD Certified Organic

| | |
|---|---|
| ● Barbera d'Alba Serra de' Gatti '17 | ♟♟ 3 |
| ○ Roero Arneis Luèt '17 | ♟♟ 2* |
| ● Roero Ris. '15 | ♟♟ 5 |
| ● Nebbiolo d'Alba '15 | ♟ 4 |

## Renzo Castella

VIA ALBA, 15
12055 DIANO D'ALBA [CN]
TEL. +39 017369203
renzocastella@virgilio.it

CELLAR SALES
PRE-BOOKED VISITS
ANNUAL PRODUCTION 20,000 bottles
HECTARES UNDER VINE 8.00

| | |
|---|---|
| ● Dolcetto di Diano d'Alba Sorì della Rivolia '17 | ♟♟ 2* |
| ● Langhe Nebbiolo Madonnina '16 | ♟ 2 |

## Tenuta Castello di Razzano

FRAZ. CASARELLO
VIA SAN CARLO, 2
15021 ALFIANO NATTA [AL]
TEL. +39 0141922124
www.castellodirazzano.it

CELLAR SALES
PRE-BOOKED VISITS
ACCOMMODATION
ANNUAL PRODUCTION 200,000 bottles
HECTARES UNDER VINE 30.00

| | |
|---|---|
| ○ Bellaria Rosé '17 | ♟♟ 2* |
| ● Grignolino del M.to Casalese Pianaccio '17 | ♟♟ 2* |
| ● M.to Ruchè di Castagnole '17 | ♟♟ 3 |
| ○ Piemonte Chardonnay Costa al Sole '17 | ♟♟ 2* |

## Cavalier Bartolomeo

VIA ALBA BAROLO, 55
12060 CASTIGLIONE FALLETTO [CN]
TEL. +39 017362866
www.cavalierbartolomeo.com

ANNUAL PRODUCTION 15,000 bottles
HECTARES UNDER VINE 3.50

| | |
|---|---|
| ● Barolo Altenasso '14 | ♟♟ 6 |
| ● Barolo San Lorenzo '14 | ♟ 6 |

## Davide Cavelli

VIA PROVINCIALE, 77
15010 PRASCO [AL]
TEL. +39 0144375706
www.cavellivini.com

ANNUAL PRODUCTION 60,000 bottles
HECTARES UNDER VINE 10.50

| | |
|---|---|
| ● Dolcetto di Ovada Bricco Le Zerbe '17 | ♟♟ 2* |
| ● Ovada Bricco Le Zerbe '15 | ♟♟ 3 |

# Le Cecche

VIA MOGLIA GERLOTTO, 10
12055 DIANO D'ALBA [CN]
TEL. +39 017369323
www.lececche.com

CELLAR SALES
PRE-BOOKED VISITS
ANNUAL PRODUCTION 35,000 bottles
HECTARES UNDER VINE 5.00

| | |
|---|---|
| ● Barbera d'Alba '16 | ♟♟ 3 |
| ● Barolo Sorano '14 | ♟♟ 5 |
| ● Diano d'Alba '17 | ♟♟ 2* |
| ● Nebbiolo d'Alba '15 | ♟♟ 3 |

# Centovigne

VIA CASTELLO, 31
13836 COSSATO [BI]
TEL. +39 3383543101
www.centovigne.it

ANNUAL PRODUCTION 30,000 bottles
HECTARES UNDER VINE 6.50

| | |
|---|---|
| ● Rosso della Motta '16 | ♟♟ 3 |
| ● Coste della Sesia Rosato Il Rosa '17 | ♟ 3 |

# Cerutti

VIA CANELLI, 205
14050 CASSINASCO [AT]
TEL. +39 0141851286
www.cascinacerutti.it

CELLAR SALES
PRE-BOOKED VISITS
ANNUAL PRODUCTION 20,000 bottles
HECTARES UNDER VINE 7.00
SUSTAINABLE WINERY

| | |
|---|---|
| ● Barbera d'Asti '17 | ♟♟ 2* |
| ● Barbera d'Asti Sup. Föje Rùsse '15 | ♟♟ 4 |
| ○ Moscato d'Asti Canelli Surì Sandrinet '17 | ♟ 2 |

# Erede di Armando Chiappone

S.DA SAN MICHELE, 51
14049 NIZZA MONFERRATO [AT]
TEL. +39 0141721424
www.erededichiappone.com

CELLAR SALES
PRE-BOOKED VISITS
RESTAURANT SERVICE
ANNUAL PRODUCTION 35,000 bottles
HECTARES UNDER VINE 10.00

| | |
|---|---|
| ● Nizza Ru '13 | ♟♟ 4 |
| ● Barbera d'Asti Brentura '15 | ♟♟ 2* |

# Paride Chiovini

VIA GIUSEPPE GARIBALDI, 20
28070 SIZZANO [NO]
TEL. +39 3394304954
www.paridechiovini.it

CELLAR SALES
PRE-BOOKED VISITS
ANNUAL PRODUCTION 10,000 bottles
HECTARES UNDER VINE 3.00

| | |
|---|---|
| ● Ghemme '14 | ♟♟ 4 |
| ● Sizzano '13 | ♟♟ 4 |

# Cantina Clavesana

FRAZ. MADONNA DELLA NEVE, 19
12060 CLAVESANA [CN]
TEL. +39 0173790451
www.inclavesana.it

CELLAR SALES
PRE-BOOKED VISITS
ANNUAL PRODUCTION 3,400,000 bottles
HECTARES UNDER VINE 520.00
SUSTAINABLE WINERY

| | |
|---|---|
| ● Dogliani '17 | ♟♟ 2* |
| ● Langhe Nebbiolo Lan '16 | ♟♟ 2* |

## Aldo Clerico

LOC. MANZONI, 69
12065 MONFORTE D'ALBA [CN]
TEL. +39 017378509
www.aldoclerico.it

CELLAR SALES
PRE-BOOKED VISITS
ANNUAL PRODUCTION 30,000 bottles
HECTARES UNDER VINE 8.00

| | |
|---|---|
| ● Barolo '14 | ♟♟ 6 |
| ● Barolo Ginestra '14 | ♟♟ 8 |
| ● Barolo del Comune di Serralunga d'Alba '14 | ♟ 7 |

## Col dei Venti

S.DA COMUNALE BALBI, 25
12053 CASTIGLIONE TINELLA [CN]
TEL. +39 0141793071
www.coldeiventi.com

PRE-BOOKED VISITS
ANNUAL PRODUCTION 30,000 bottles
HECTARES UNDER VINE 10.00

| | |
|---|---|
| ● Barbaresco Túfoblu '15 | ♟♟ 6 |
| ● Barolo Debútto '14 | ♟♟ 7 |
| ● Langhe Nebbiolo Lampio '16 | ♟ 4 |

## Colombera & Garella

VIA CASCINA COTTIGNANO, 2
13866 MASSERANO [BI]
TEL. +39 01596967
colomberaegarella@gmail.com

CELLAR SALES
PRE-BOOKED VISITS
ANNUAL PRODUCTION 20,000 bottles
HECTARES UNDER VINE 9.00

| | |
|---|---|
| ● Lessona Pizzaguerra '14 | ♟♟ 5 |
| ● Bramaterra Cascina Cottignano '14 | ♟ 5 |
| ● Costa della Sesia Rosso Cascina Cottignano '15 | ♟ 3 |

## Comero

VIA GIUSEPPE CORNA, 8
28070 SIZZANO [NO]
TEL. +39 3332575651
www.cantinacomero.it

CELLAR SALES
ANNUAL PRODUCTION 7,000 bottles
HECTARES UNDER VINE 6.00

| | |
|---|---|
| ● Colline Novaresi Vespolina '15 | ♟♟ 3 |
| ● Sizzano '13 | ♟♟ 4 |
| ○ Colline Novaresi Bianco La Grazia del Marchese '17 | ♟ 2 |

## Costa Catterina

VIA CASTELLINALDO, 14
12050 CASTAGNITO [CN]
TEL. +39 0173213403
www.costacatterina.com

CELLAR SALES
PRE-BOOKED VISITS
ANNUAL PRODUCTION 40,000 bottles
HECTARES UNDER VINE 14.00

| | |
|---|---|
| ● Barbera d'Alba Sup. '15 | ♟♟ 3 |
| ● Roero '15 | ♟♟ 3 |

## Crissante Alessandria

LOC. B.TA ROGGERI, 44
12064 LA MORRA [CN]
TEL. +39 3333671499
www.crissantewines.it

ANNUAL PRODUCTION 28,000 bottles
HECTARES UNDER VINE 6.00

| | |
|---|---|
| ● Barbera d'Alba Sup. Rugé '15 | ♟♟ 3 |
| ● Barolo del Comune di La Morra '14 | ♟♟ 5 |
| ● Barolo Galina '14 | ♟ 5 |
| ● Dolcetto d'Alba Pian delle Masche '16 | ♟ 3 |

# Cantine Crosio

VIA ROMA, 75
10010 CANDIA CANAVESE [TO]
TEL. +39 0119836048
www.cantinecrosio.it

CELLAR SALES
RESTAURANT SERVICE
ANNUAL PRODUCTION 35,000 bottles
HECTARES UNDER VINE 6.50

| | | |
|---|---|---|
| ● Canavese Nebbiolo Gemini '16 | ♟♟ | 3 |
| ○ Erbaluce di Caluso Brut Incanto '14 | ♟♟ | 5 |
| ○ Erbaluce di Caluso Primavigna '17 | ♟♟ | 3 |

# Cuvage

STRADALE ALESSANDRIA, 90
15011 ACQUI TERME [AL]
TEL. +39 0144371600
www.cuvage.com

ANNUAL PRODUCTION 80,000 bottles
HECTARES UNDER VINE 200.00

| | | |
|---|---|---|
| ○ Brut Blanc de Blancs M. Cl. | ♟♟ | 3 |
| ○ Asti Secco Acquesi | ♟ | 2 |
| ⊙ Nebbiolo d'Alba Brut Rosé M.Cl. | ♟ | 3 |
| ○ Pas Dosé Cuvage de Cuvage M. Cl. | ♟ | 3 |

# Dacapo

S.DA ASTI MARE, 4
14041 AGLIANO TERME [AT]
TEL. +39 0141964921
www.dacapo.it

CELLAR SALES
PRE-BOOKED VISITS
ANNUAL PRODUCTION 50,000 bottles
HECTARES UNDER VINE 8.50

| | | |
|---|---|---|
| ● Barbera d'Asti Sup. Valrionda '15 | ♟♟ | 3 |
| ○ Moscato d'Asti Ca' ed Balos '17 | ♟♟ | 2* |
| ● Piemonte Pinot Nero Cantacucco '15 | ♟ | 5 |
| ● Ruchè di Castagnole M.to Majoli '17 | ♟ | 3 |

# Duilio Dacasto

FRAZ. VIANOCE, 26
14041 AGLIANO TERME [AT]
TEL. +39 3339828612
www.dacastoduilio.com

ANNUAL PRODUCTION 24,000 bottles
HECTARES UNDER VINE 8.00

| | | |
|---|---|---|
| ● Nizza Moncucco '15 | ♟♟ | 4 |
| ● Barbera d'Asti La Maestra '16 | ♟♟ | 3 |
| ● Barbera d'Asti Sup. Camp Riond '16 | ♟♟ | 3 |
| ○ Piemonte Chardonnay '17 | ♟ | 3 |

# Fabio Fidanza

VIA RODOTIGLIA, 55
14052 CALOSSO [AT]
TEL. +39 0141826921
a.a.fidanza@gmail.com

CELLAR SALES
PRE-BOOKED VISITS
ANNUAL PRODUCTION 20,000 bottles
HECTARES UNDER VINE 10.00

| | | |
|---|---|---|
| ● Barbera d'Asti Sup. Sterlino '16 | ♟♟ | 4 |
| ○ Moscato d'Asti '17 | ♟♟ | 2* |
| ● Barbera d'Asti '16 | ♟ | 2 |

# Fontanabianca

VIA BORDINI, 15
12057 NEIVE [CN]
TEL. +39 017367195
www.fontanabianca.it

CELLAR SALES
PRE-BOOKED VISITS
ANNUAL PRODUCTION 70,000 bottles
HECTARES UNDER VINE 14.00

| | | |
|---|---|---|
| ● Barbaresco '15 | ♟♟ | 5 |
| ● Barbaresco Bordini '15 | ♟♟ | 6 |
| ● Barbera d'Alba Sup. '16 | ♟♟ | 3 |
| ○ Classe 91 Brut M. Cl. | ♟♟ | 4 |

## Forteto della Luja

REG. CANDELETTE, 4
14051 LOAZZOLO [AT]
TEL. +39 014487197
www.fortetodellaluja.it

CELLAR SALES
PRE-BOOKED VISITS
ANNUAL PRODUCTION 50,000 bottles
HECTARES UNDER VINE 11.00
VITICULTURE METHOD Certified Organic

| | |
|---|---|
| ○ Moscato d'Asti Piasa Sanmaurizio '17 | 🍷🍷 3 |
| ● Piemonte Brachetto Passito Pian dei Sogni '15 | 🍷🍷 5 |
| ● Barbera d'Asti Mon Ross '17 | 🍷 2 |

## La Fusina - Luigi Abbona

FRAZ. SANTA LUCIA, 33
12063 DOGLIANI [CN]
TEL. +39 017370488
www.lafusina.com

CELLAR SALES
PRE-BOOKED VISITS
ANNUAL PRODUCTION 80,000 bottles
HECTARES UNDER VINE 20.00
SUSTAINABLE WINERY

| | |
|---|---|
| ● Barolo '14 | 🍷🍷 5 |
| ● Barbera d'Alba '17 | 🍷🍷 3 |
| ● Dogliani Gombe '17 | 🍷🍷 2* |
| ● Dogliani Sup. Cavagnè '16 | 🍷🍷 3 |

## Gagliasso

BORGATA TORRIGLIONE, 7
12064 LA MORRA [CN]
TEL. +39 017350180
www.gagliassovini.it

CELLAR SALES
PRE-BOOKED VISITS
RESTAURANT SERVICE
ANNUAL PRODUCTION 50,000 bottles
HECTARES UNDER VINE 12.50

| | |
|---|---|
| ● Barolo Rocche dell'Annunziata '14 | 🍷🍷 6 |
| ● Barolo Torriglione '14 | 🍷🍷 6 |
| ● Barolo Tre Utin '14 | 🍷 5 |

## La Ganghija – Enzo Rapalino

VIA TORINO, 4
12050 TREISO [CN]
TEL. +39 3332878624
www.laganghija.com

ANNUAL PRODUCTION 35,000 bottles
HECTARES UNDER VINE 6.00

| | |
|---|---|
| ● Barbaresco '15 | 🍷🍷 4 |
| ● Barbaresco Giacosa '15 | 🍷🍷 5 |

## Cantine Garrone

VIA SCAPACCIANO, 36
28845 DOMODOSSOLA [VB]
TEL. +39 0324242990
www.cantinegarrone.it

CELLAR SALES
PRE-BOOKED VISITS
ANNUAL PRODUCTION 50,000 bottles
HECTARES UNDER VINE 10.00

| | |
|---|---|
| ● Valli Ossolane Nebbiolo Sup. Prünent '15 | 🍷🍷 4 |
| ● Valli Ossolane Rosso Tarlàp '16 | 🍷🍷 2* |
| ● Valli Ossane Rosso Cà d'Maté '15 | 🍷 3 |

## La Giribaldina

FRAZ. SAN VITO, 39
14042 CALAMANDRANA [AT]
TEL. +39 0141718043
www.giribaldina.com

CELLAR SALES
PRE-BOOKED VISITS
ACCOMMODATION
ANNUAL PRODUCTION 70,000 bottles
HECTARES UNDER VINE 11.00

| | |
|---|---|
| ● Barbera d'Asti Montedelmare '17 | 🍷🍷 2* |
| ● Nizza Cala delle Mandrie '15 | 🍷🍷 4 |
| ● Barbera d'Asti Sup. Valsarmassa '16 | 🍷 3 |
| ○ Moscato d'Asti '17 | 🍷 2 |

## Gozzelino

S.DA BRICCO IU, 7
14055 COSTIGLIOLE D'ASTI [AT]
TEL. +39 0141966134
www.gozzelinovini.com

ANNUAL PRODUCTION 100,000 bottles
HECTARES UNDER VINE 30.00

● Barbera d'Asti Sergio '11 ♀♀ 4
● Barbera d'Asti Sup.
  Ciabot d'la Mandorla '17 ♀♀ 2*
● Grignolino d'Asti Bric d'la Riva '17 ♀ 3

## La Guardia

POD. LA GUARDIA, 74
15010 MORSASCO [AL]
TEL. +39 014473076
www.laguardiavilladelfini.it

CELLAR SALES
PRE-BOOKED VISITS
ANNUAL PRODUCTION 100,000 bottles
HECTARES UNDER VINE 35.00

● Ovada Il Gamondino Ris. '15 ♀♀ 4
● Piemonte Albarossa L'Intrigante '15 ♀♀ 3
● Barbera del M.to Ornovo '15 ♀ 3

## Clemente Guasti

C.SO IV NOVEMBRE, 80
14049 NIZZA MONFERRATO [AT]
TEL. +39 0141721350
www,clemente.guasti.it

CELLAR SALES
PRE-BOOKED VISITS
ANNUAL PRODUCTION 120,000 bottles
HECTARES UNDER VINE 10.00

● Barbera d'Asti Severa '13 ♀♀ 3
● Nizza Barcarato '15 ♀♀ 5
● Barbera d'Asti Boschetto Vecchio '13 ♀ 4

## Paride Iaretti

VIA PIETRO MICCA, 23B
13045 GATTINARA [VC]
TEL. +39 0163826899
www.parideiaretti.it

CELLAR SALES
PRE-BOOKED VISITS
ANNUAL PRODUCTION 15,000 bottles
HECTARES UNDER VINE 5.00

● Coste della Sesia Nebbiolo Velut Luna '16 ♀ 3
● Uvenere ♀ 2

## Franco Ivaldi

S.DA CARANZANO, 211
15016 CASSINE [AL]
TEL. +39 348 7492231
www.francoivaldivini.com

ANNUAL PRODUCTION 40,000 bottles
HECTARES UNDER VINE 7.00

● Barbera d'Asti La Guerinotta '17 ♀♀ 2*
● Barbera d'Asti Sup. La Balzana '16 ♀♀ 3
● Dolcetto d'Acqui Sup. La Uèca '16 ♀♀ 3
● Piemonte Albarossa '15 ♀♀ 3

## Lagobava

FRAZ. CA' BERGANTINO, 5
15049 VIGNALE MONFERRATO [AL]
TEL. +39 3476900656
www.lagobava.it

CELLAR SALES
PRE-BOOKED VISITS
ANNUAL PRODUCTION 14,000 bottles
HECTARES UNDER VINE 5.40
VITICULTURE METHOD Certified Organic
SUSTAINABLE WINERY

● M.to Rosso '11 ♀♀ 6
● Piemonte Barbera '16 ♀♀ 3
● Solorosso '13 ♀♀ 3

## Gianluigi Lano

fraz. San Rocco Seno d'Elvio
s.da Basso, 38
12051 Alba [CN]
Tel. +39 0173286958
www.lanovini.it

CELLAR SALES
PRE-BOOKED VISITS
ANNUAL PRODUCTION 40,000 bottles
HECTARES UNDER VINE 6.00

| | |
|---|---|
| ● Barbera d'Alba Sup. V. Altavilla '15 | 🍷🍷 3* |
| ● Barbaresco Rocche Massalupo '15 | 🍷🍷 5 |

## Maccagno

via Bonora, 29
12043 Canale [CN]
Tel. +39 0173979438
www.cantinamaccagno.it

CELLAR SALES
PRE-BOOKED VISITS
ANNUAL PRODUCTION 50,000 bottles
HECTARES UNDER VINE 10.00

| | |
|---|---|
| ● Barbera d'Alba Sup. Arcalè '15 | 🍷🍷 3 |
| ○ Roero Arneis La Perla Bianca '16 | 🍷🍷 3 |
| ● Roero S. Michele '14 | 🍷🍷 3 |

## Tenuta La Marchesa

via Gavi, 87
15067 Novi Ligure [AL]
Tel. +39 0143743362
www.tenutalamarchesa.it

CELLAR SALES
PRE-BOOKED VISITS
ACCOMMODATION AND RESTAURANT SERVICE
ANNUAL PRODUCTION 250,000 bottles
HECTARES UNDER VINE 56.45

| | |
|---|---|
| ○ Gavi Golden Label '17 | 🍷🍷 3* |
| ● Piemonte Albarossa '16 | 🍷🍷 3 |

## Marenco

p.zza Vittorio Emanuele II, 10
15019 Strevi [AL]
Tel. +39 0144363133
www.marencovini.com

CELLAR SALES
PRE-BOOKED VISITS
ACCOMMODATION
ANNUAL PRODUCTION 250,000 bottles
HECTARES UNDER VINE 80.00
SUSTAINABLE WINERY

| | |
|---|---|
| ● Barbera d'Asti Bassina '16 | 🍷🍷 3 |
| ● Brachetto d'Acqui Pineto '17 | 🍷🍷 3 |
| ● Piemonte Albarossa Red Sunrise '15 | 🍷🍷 4 |
| ○ Strevi Passrì di Scrapona '17 | 🍷🍷 6 |

## Le Marie

via San Defendente, 6
12032 Barge [CN]
Tel. +39 0175345159
www.lemarievini.eu

CELLAR SALES
PRE-BOOKED VISITS
RESTAURANT SERVICE
ANNUAL PRODUCTION 24,000 bottles
HECTARES UNDER VINE 8.00

| | |
|---|---|
| ○ Blanc de Lissart '17 | 🍷🍷 2* |
| ○ Pas Dosé M. Cl. | 🍷🍷 4 |
| ● Pinerolese Barbera Colombe '15 | 🍷🍷 3 |
| ● Pinerolese Dolcetto '17 | 🍷 2 |

## La Masera

s.da San Pietro, 32
10010 Piverone [TO]
Tel. +39 0113164161
www.lamasera.it

CELLAR SALES
PRE-BOOKED VISITS
ANNUAL PRODUCTION 25,000 bottles
HECTARES UNDER VINE 5.00
SUSTAINABLE WINERY

| | |
|---|---|
| ○ Erbaluce di Caluso Anima '17 | 🍷🍷 3* |
| ● Canavese Rosso '16 | 🍷🍷 2* |
| ○ Erbaluce di Caluso Pas Dosé Masilé | 🍷 5 |

# Tenuta La Meridiana

FRAZ. TANA BASSA
VIA TANA BASSA, 5
14048 MONTEGROSSO D'ASTI [AT]
TEL. +39 0141956172
www.tenutalameridiana.com

CELLAR SALES
PRE-BOOKED VISITS
ANNUAL PRODUCTION 100,000 bottles
HECTARES UNDER VINE 10.00
SUSTAINABLE WINERY

| | |
|---|---|
| ● Barbera d'Asti Sup. Tra la Terra e il Cielo '16 | 🍷🍷 5 |
| ● Barbera d'Asti Le Quattro Terre '17 | 🍷🍷 2* |
| ● Barbera d'Asti Vitis '17 | 🍷🍷 2* |

# F.lli Molino

VIA AUSARIO, 5
12050 TREISO [CN]
TEL. +39 0173638384
www.molinovini.com

CELLAR SALES
PRE-BOOKED VISITS
ANNUAL PRODUCTION 70,000 bottles
HECTARES UNDER VINE 14.00

| | |
|---|---|
| ● Barbaresco Ausario Ris. '13 | 🍷🍷 7 |
| ● Piemonte Rosso Selvaggia '17 | 🍷🍷 2* |
| ● Barbaresco Teorema '15 | 🍷 6 |
| ○ Langhe Chardonnay Sofia '16 | 🍷 5 |

# F.lli Monchiero

VIA ALBA MONFORTE, 49
12060 CASTIGLIONE FALLETTO [CN]
TEL. +39 017362820
www.monchierovini.it

CELLAR SALES
PRE-BOOKED VISITS
ANNUAL PRODUCTION 40,000 bottles
HECTARES UNDER VINE 12.00
SUSTAINABLE WINERY

| | |
|---|---|
| ● Barolo Rocche di Castiglione Ris. '12 | 🍷🍷 7 |
| ● Barbera d'Alba Sup. '16 | 🍷🍷 3 |
| ● Barolo Montanello '14 | 🍷🍷 5 |
| ● Barolo Rocche di Castiglione '14 | 🍷 5 |

# Morgassi Superiore

CASE SPARSE SERMORIA, 7
15066 GAVI [AL]
TEL. +39 0143642007
www.morgassisuperiore.it

CELLAR SALES
PRE-BOOKED VISITS
ANNUAL PRODUCTION 130,000 bottles
HECTARES UNDER VINE 20.00

| | |
|---|---|
| ○ Gavi del Comune di Gavi Tuffo '17 | 🍷🍷 3 |
| ○ Gavi del Comune di Gavi Volo '16 | 🍷 4 |

# Diego Morra

VIA CASCINA MOSCA, 37
12060 VERDUNO [CN]
TEL. +39 3284623209
www.morrawines.com

CELLAR SALES
PRE-BOOKED VISITS
ANNUAL PRODUCTION 25,000 bottles
HECTARES UNDER VINE 32.00

| | |
|---|---|
| ● Barolo '14 | 🍷🍷 6 |
| ● Barolo Monvigliero '14 | 🍷🍷 6 |
| ● Langhe Nebbiolo '14 | 🍷🍷 3 |
| ● Verduno Pelaverga '17 | 🍷🍷 3 |

# Musso

VIA D. CAVAZZA, 5
12050 BARBARESCO [CN]
TEL. +39 0173635129
www.mussobarbaresco.it

CELLAR SALES
PRE-BOOKED VISITS
ANNUAL PRODUCTION 80,000 bottles
HECTARES UNDER VINE 10.00

| | |
|---|---|
| ● Barbaresco Rio Sordo '15 | 🍷🍷 5 |
| ● Barbaresco Pora '15 | 🍷🍷 4 |
| ● Barbera d'Alba '16 | 🍷🍷 3 |
| ○ Roero Arneis '17 | 🍷 3 |

## Giuseppe Negro

VIA GALLINA, 22
12052 NEIVE [CN]
TEL. +39 0173677468
www.negrogiuseppe.com

CELLAR SALES
PRE-BOOKED VISITS
ANNUAL PRODUCTION 52,000 bottles
HECTARES UNDER VINE 9.00

| | |
|---|---|
| ● Langhe Nebbiolo Monsù '15 | ♟♟ 4 |
| ● Barbaresco Gallina '15 | ♟ 6 |
| ● Barbaresco PianCavallo '15 | ♟ 6 |
| ● Barbera d'Alba Pulin '16 | ♟ 4 |

## Oltretorrente

VIA CINQUE MARTIRI
15050 PADERNA [AL]
TEL. +39 3398195360
www.oltretorrente.com

CELLAR SALES
PRE-BOOKED VISITS
ANNUAL PRODUCTION 20,000 bottles
HECTARES UNDER VINE 7.00
VITICULTURE METHOD Certified Organic
SUSTAINABLE WINERY

| | |
|---|---|
| ● Colli Tortonesi Barbera Sup. '15 | ♟♟ 6 |
| ○ Colli Tortonesi Timorasso Derthona '16 | ♟♟ 5 |
| ● Colli Tortonesi Bianco '17 | ♟ 3 |

## Pace

FRAZ. MADONNA DI LORETO
CASCINA PACE, 52
12043 CANALE [CN]
TEL. +39 0173979544
www.pacevini.it

CELLAR SALES
PRE-BOOKED VISITS
ANNUAL PRODUCTION 60,000 bottles
HECTARES UNDER VINE 22.00

| | |
|---|---|
| ○ Roero Arneis '17 | ♟♟ 3* |
| ○ Langhe Favorita '17 | ♟♟ 2* |
| ● Barbera d'Alba '16 | ♟ 2 |
| ● Roero '14 | ♟ 3 |

## Massimo Pastura
## Cascina La Ghersa

VIA CHIARINA, 2
14050 MOASCA [AT]
TEL. +39 0141856012
www.laghersa.it

CELLAR SALES
PRE-BOOKED VISITS
ACCOMMODATION
ANNUAL PRODUCTION 150,000 bottles
HECTARES UNDER VINE 23.00

| | |
|---|---|
| ● Barbera d'Asti Sup. Camparò '16 | ♟♟ 2* |
| ● Barbera d'Asti Sup. Le Cave '15 | ♟♟ 3 |
| ● Nizza Vignassa '15 | ♟♟ 5 |
| ● Nizza Muaschae Ris. '15 | ♟ 6 |

## Magda Pedrini

LOC. CA' D'MEO
VIA PRATOLUNGO, 163
15066 GAVI [AL]
TEL. +39 0143667923
www.magdapedrini.it

CELLAR SALES
PRE-BOOKED VISITS
ANNUAL PRODUCTION 90,000 bottles
HECTARES UNDER VINE 10.50
SUSTAINABLE WINERY

| | |
|---|---|
| ○ Gavi del Comune di Gavi La Piacentina '17 | ♟♟ 3* |
| ○ Gavi del Comune di Gavi E' '17 | ♟♟ 3 |

## Elio Perrone

S.DA SAN MARTINO, 3BIS
12053 CASTIGLIONE TINELLA [CN]
TEL. +39 0141855803
www.elioperrone.it

CELLAR SALES
PRE-BOOKED VISITS
ANNUAL PRODUCTION 200,000 bottles
HECTARES UNDER VINE 14.00
SUSTAINABLE WINERY

| | |
|---|---|
| ● Barbera d'Asti Tasmorcan '17 | ♟♟ 2* |
| ○ Moscato d'Asti Sourgal '17 | ♟♟ 2* |

# Fabrizio Pinsoglio

FRAZ. MADONNA DEI CAVALLI, 31BIS
12050 CANALE [CN]
TEL. +39 0173968401
fabriziopinsoglio@libero.it

PRE-BOOKED VISITS
ANNUAL PRODUCTION 40,000 bottles
HECTARES UNDER VINE 8.00

| | |
|---|---|
| ● Nebbiolo d'Alba '15 | ♟♟ 3 |
| ○ Roero Arneis Malinat '17 | ♟♟ 2* |
| ● Roero Ris. '13 | ♟♟ 4 |

# Poderi dei Bricchi Astigiani

FRAZ. REPERGO
VIA RITANE, 7
14057 ISOLA D'ASTI [AT]
TEL. +39 0141958974
www.bricchiastigiani.it

CELLAR SALES
PRE-BOOKED VISITS
ANNUAL PRODUCTION 40,000 bottles
HECTARES UNDER VINE 15.00

| | |
|---|---|
| ● Barbera d'Asti '16 | ♟♟ 2* |
| ● Barbera d'Asti Sup. Bricco del Perg '15 | ♟♟ 3 |
| ○ Blanc de Noir M. Cl. | ♟ 3 |
| ⊙ Piemonte Rosato Bricco San Giovanni '17 | ♟ 2 |

# Paolo Giuseppe Poggio

VIA ROMA, 67
15050 BRIGNANO FRASCATA [AL]
TEL. +39 0131784929
www.cantinapoggio.com

CELLAR SALES
PRE-BOOKED VISITS
ANNUAL PRODUCTION 18,000 bottles
HECTARES UNDER VINE 3.50

| | |
|---|---|
| ○ Colli Tortonesi Timorasso Ronchetto '16 | ♟♟ 2* |
| ● Colli Tortonesi Barbera Campo La Bà '16 | ♟ 2 |
| ● Colli Tortonesi Barbera Derio '15 | ♟ 3 |

# Pomodolce

VIA IV NOVEMBRE, 7
15050 MONTEMARZINO [AL]
TEL. +39 0131878135
www.pomodolce.it

CELLAR SALES
PRE-BOOKED VISITS
RESTAURANT SERVICE
ANNUAL PRODUCTION 14,000 bottles
HECTARES UNDER VINE 4.00
VITICULTURE METHOD Certified Organic

| | |
|---|---|
| ○ Colli Tortonesi Timorasso Diletto '16 | ♟♟ 3 |
| ○ Colli Tortonesi Timorasso Grue '16 | ♟♟ 5 |

# Maurizio Ponchione

VIA R. SACCO, 9/A
12040 GOVONE [CN]
TEL. +39 017358149
www.ponchionemaurizio.com

CELLAR SALES
PRE-BOOKED VISITS
ANNUAL PRODUCTION 35,000 bottles
HECTARES UNDER VINE 11.00

| | |
|---|---|
| ● Barbera d'Alba Monfrini '15 | ♟♟ 3 |
| ● Roero Arneis Monfrini '17 | ♟♟ 3 |
| ● Roero Monfrin '14 | ♟♟ 3 |

# Diego Pressenda
# La Torricella

LOC. SANT'ANNA, 98
12065 MONFORTE D'ALBA [CN]
TEL. +39 017378327
www.latorricella.eu

ANNUAL PRODUCTION 50,000 bottles
HECTARES UNDER VINE 13.00

| | |
|---|---|
| ○ Langhe Riesling '16 | ♟♟ 3 |
| ● Nebbiolo d'Alba Il Donato '15 | ♟♟ 4 |
| ● Barolo Barbadelchi '14 | ♟ 6 |
| ● Barolo Bricco San Pietro '14 | ♟ 6 |

## Raineri

Loc. Panerole, 24
12060 Novello [CN]
Tel. +39 3396009289
www.rainerivini.com

CELLAR SALES
PRE-BOOKED VISITS
ANNUAL PRODUCTION 20,000 bottles
HECTARES UNDER VINE 3.30
SUSTAINABLE WINERY

| | |
|---|---|
| ● Barolo Monserra '14 | ♥♥ 7 |
| ● Langhe Nebbiolo Snart '16 | ♥♥ 3 |
| ● Barolo '14 | ♥ 5 |
| ○ Langhe Bianco Elfobianco '17 | ♥ 3 |

## Ressia

via Canova, 28
12052 Neive [CN]
Tel. +39 0173677305
www.ressia.com

CELLAR SALES
PRE-BOOKED VISITS
ANNUAL PRODUCTION 3,000 bottles
HECTARES UNDER VINE 5.50
SUSTAINABLE WINERY

| | |
|---|---|
| ● Barbaresco Canova '15 | ♥♥ 5 |
| ○ Evien '17 | ♥♥ 2* |
| ● Barbaresco Canova Ris. Oro '13 | ♥ 6 |
| ● Barbera d'Alba Sup. V. Canova '16 | ♥ 3 |

## Pietro Rinaldi

fraz. Madonna di Como
12051 Alba [CN]
Tel. +39 0173360090
www.pietrorinaldi.com

CELLAR SALES
PRE-BOOKED VISITS
ACCOMMODATION
ANNUAL PRODUCTION 70,000 bottles
HECTARES UNDER VINE 10.00

| | |
|---|---|
| ● Barbaresco Massirano '15 | ♥♥ 5 |
| ● Barolo '14 | ♥♥ 6 |
| ● Barolo Monvigliero '14 | ♥♥ 6 |
| ○ Langhe Arneis Hortensia '17 | ♥♥ 2* |

## Rivetto

Loc. Lirano, 2
12050 Sinio [CN]
Tel. +39 0173613380
www.rivetto.it

CELLAR SALES
PRE-BOOKED VISITS
ACCOMMODATION
ANNUAL PRODUCTION 100,000 bottles
HECTARES UNDER VINE 20.00

| | |
|---|---|
| ● Barolo Briccolina '13 | ♥♥ 7 |
| ● Barolo del Comune di Serralunga D'Alba '14 | ♥♥ 6 |
| ● Barbaresco Marcarini '15 | ♥ 5 |

## Tenuta Rocca

Loc. Ornati, 19
12065 Monforte d'Alba [CN]
Tel. +39 017378412
www.tenutarocca.com

CELLAR SALES
PRE-BOOKED VISITS
ACCOMMODATION
ANNUAL PRODUCTION 90,000 bottles
HECTARES UNDER VINE 15.00

| | |
|---|---|
| ● Barolo '14 | ♥♥ 6 |
| ● Barolo Bussia '14 | ♥♥ 6 |
| ● Barolo del Comune di Serralunga d'Alba '14 | ♥ 8 |

## Emanuele Rolfo

b.go Valle Casette, 52
12046 Montà [CN]
Tel. +39 0173971263
www.emanuelerolfo.it

PRE-BOOKED VISITS
ANNUAL PRODUCTION 50,000 bottles
HECTARES UNDER VINE 3.50

| | |
|---|---|
| ○ Roero Arneis '17 | ♥♥ 2* |
| ○ Roero Arneis Menelic '15 | ♥♥ 2* |
| ● Roero Ris. '12 | ♥♥ 3 |

# Rossi Contini

S.DA SAN LORENZO, 20
15076 OVADA [AL]
TEL. +39 0143822530
www.rossicontini.com

CELLAR SALES
PRE-BOOKED VISITS
ANNUAL PRODUCTION 17,000 bottles
HECTARES UNDER VINE 4.50
SUSTAINABLE WINERY

| | | |
|---|---|---|
| ● Dolcetto di Ovada San Lorenzo '17 | ♟♟ | 3 |
| ● Ovada Viign. Ninan '16 | ♟♟ | 4 |

# San Cristoforo

VIA PASTURA, 10
12057 NEIVE [CN]
TEL. +39 0173677122
www.sassiwines.com

CELLAR SALES
PRE-BOOKED VISITS
ANNUAL PRODUCTION 10,000 bottles
HECTARES UNDER VINE 1.30

| | | |
|---|---|---|
| ● Barbaresco San Cristoforo '15 | ♟♟ | 6 |
| ● Langhe Nebbiolo '16 | ♟♟ | 3 |
| ● Barbaresco '15 | ♟ | 6 |

# Tenuta San Pietro

LOC. SAN PIETRO, 2
15060 TASSAROLO [AL]
TEL. +39 0143342422
www.tenutasanpietro.it

CELLAR SALES
PRE-BOOKED VISITS
ANNUAL PRODUCTION 250,000 bottles
HECTARES UNDER VINE 30.00
VITICULTURE METHOD Certified Organic
SUSTAINABLE WINERY

| | | |
|---|---|---|
| ○ Gavi del Comune di Tassarolo San Pietro '17 | ♟♟ | 3* |
| ● M.to Rosso Nero San Pietro '15 | ♟♟ | 3 |

# Cantine Sant'Agata

REG. MEZZENA, 19
14030 SCURZOLENGO [AT]
TEL. +39 0141203186
www.santagata.com

CELLAR SALES
PRE-BOOKED VISITS
RESTAURANT SERVICE
ANNUAL PRODUCTION 150,000 bottles
HECTARES UNDER VINE 12.00

| | | |
|---|---|---|
| ● Barbera d'Asti Sup. Cavalé '15 | ♟♟ | 4 |
| ● Ruché di Castagnole M.to 'Na Vota '17 | ♟♟ | 3 |
| ● Ruchè di Castagnole M.to Pro Nobis '15 | ♟ | 4 |

# Sant'Anna dei Bricchetti

FRAZ. SANT'ANNA
S.DA BRICCHETTI, 11
14055 COSTIGLIOLE D'ASTI [AT]
TEL. +39 01411851012
www.santanna-dei-bricchetti.it

PRE-BOOKED VISITS
ANNUAL PRODUCTION 20,000 bottles
HECTARES UNDER VINE 5.00

| | | |
|---|---|---|
| ● Barbera d'Asti Sup. V. dei Bricchetti '15 | ♟♟ | 3 |
| ○ Moscato d'Asti '17 | ♟♟ | 3 |
| ● Barbera d'Asti Ricordi '16 | ♟ | 3 |

# Giacomo Scagliola

REG. SANTA LIBERA, 20
14053 CANELLI [AT]
TEL. +39 0141831146
www.scagliola-canelli.it

CELLAR SALES
ANNUAL PRODUCTION 80,000 bottles
HECTARES UNDER VINE 15.00

| | | |
|---|---|---|
| ● Barbera d'Asti Sup. La Faia '16 | ♟♟ | 2* |
| ○ Moscato d'Asti Canelli Sifasol '17 | ♟♟ | 2* |
| ● Barbera d'Asti Camp d'la Bela '16 | ♟ | 2 |

## Segni di Langa

LOC. RAVINALI, 25
12060 RODDI [CN]
TEL. +39 3803945151
www.segnidilanga.it

CELLAR SALES
PRE-BOOKED VISITS
ACCOMMODATION
ANNUAL PRODUCTION 6,000 bottles
HECTARES UNDER VINE 0.90
SUSTAINABLE WINERY

| | |
|---|---|
| ● Nebbiolo d'Alba '16 | ♥♥ 4 |
| ● Barbera d'Alba Sup. '16 | ♥♥ 4 |
| ● Dogliani '17 | ♥♥ 3 |
| ● Langhe Pinot Nero '16 | ♥♥ 4 |

## Collina Serragrilli

FRAZ. SERRAGRILLI, 30
12052 NEIVE [CN]
TEL. +39 0173677010
www.serragrilli.it

CELLAR SALES
PRE-BOOKED VISITS
ANNUAL PRODUCTION 100,000 bottles
HECTARES UNDER VINE 15.00

| | |
|---|---|
| ● Barbaresco Serragrilli '15 | ♥♥ 6 |
| ● Langhe Nebbiolo Bailè '15 | ♥♥ 3 |
| ● Langhe Rosso Grillorosso '14 | ♥♥ 3 |
| ● Barbera d'Alba Serraia '16 | ♥ 2 |

## Francesco Sobrero

VIA PUGNANE, 5
12060 CASTIGLIONE FALLETTO [CN]
TEL. +39 017362864
www.sobrerofrancesco.it

CELLAR SALES
PRE-BOOKED VISITS
ACCOMMODATION
ANNUAL PRODUCTION 90,000 bottles
HECTARES UNDER VINE 16.00

| | |
|---|---|
| ● Barolo Ciabot Tanasio '14 | ♥♥ 6 |
| ● Barolo Pernanno Ris. '12 | ♥♥ 7 |
| ● Barolo Parussi '14 | ♥ 7 |

## Le Strette

VIA LE STRETTE, 1F
12060 NOVELLO [CN]
TEL. +39 0173744002
www.lestrette.com

CELLAR SALES
PRE-BOOKED VISITS

| | |
|---|---|
| ● Barbera d'Alba Sup. '16 | ♥♥ 3 |
| ● Barolo '14 | ♥♥ 5 |
| ● Barolo Bergeisa '14 | ♥♥ 6 |
| ● Barolo Bergera-Pezzole '14 | ♥♥ 6 |

## Cantina Stroppiana

FRAZ. RIVALTA SAN GIACOMO, 6
12064 LA MORRA [CN]
TEL. +39 0173509419
www.cantinastroppiana.com

CELLAR SALES
PRE-BOOKED VISITS
ANNUAL PRODUCTION 35,000 bottles
HECTARES UNDER VINE 5.00

| | |
|---|---|
| ● Barolo Bussia '13 | ♥♥ 6 |
| ● Barolo Leonardo '14 | ♥♥ 5 |
| ● Barolo San Giacomo '14 | ♥ 6 |

## Sylla Sebaste

VIA SAN PIETRO, 4
12060 BAROLO [CN]
TEL. +39 017356266
www.syllasebaste.com

CELLAR SALES
PRE-BOOKED VISITS
RESTAURANT SERVICE
ANNUAL PRODUCTION 120,000 bottles
HECTARES UNDER VINE 7.00

| | |
|---|---|
| ● Barolo Bussia '14 | ♥♥ 6 |
| ● Barolo '14 | ♥ 5 |

## Tenute Rade

FRAZ. SALINE 13/14
14050 SAN MARZANO OLIVETO [AT]
TEL. +39 0141769091
www.cusmano.it

CELLAR SALES
PRE-BOOKED VISITS
HECTARES UNDER VINE 50.00

| | | |
|---|---|---|
| ○ Alta Langa Extra Brut Pas Dosé '14 | ♟♟ | 4 |
| ○ Moscato d'Asti Preludio '17 | ♟♟ | 2* |
| ● Barbera d'Asti La Pruna '17 | ♟ | 4 |
| ● Barbera d'Asti Sup. La Grissa '16 | ♟ | 4 |

## Terre Astesane

VIA MARCONI, 42
14047 MOMBERCELLI [AT]
TEL. +39 0141959155
www.terreastesane.it

CELLAR SALES
PRE-BOOKED VISITS
ANNUAL PRODUCTION 100,000 bottles
HECTARES UNDER VINE 240.00

| | | |
|---|---|---|
| ● Barbera d'Asti Sup. Savej '15 | ♟♟ | 2* |
| ● Grignolino d'Asti Ganassa '17 | ♟♟ | 2* |
| ● Nizza Mumbersè '15 | ♟♟ | 4 |
| ● Barbera d'Asti Maniman '17 | ♟ | 1* |

## Tibaldi

S.DA SAN GIACOMO, 49
12060 POCAPAGLIA [CN]
TEL. +39 0172421221
www.cantinatibaldi.com

CELLAR SALES
ANNUAL PRODUCTION 35,000 bottles
HECTARES UNDER VINE 7.00

| | | |
|---|---|---|
| ○ Langhe Favorita '17 | ♟♟ | 3 |
| ○ Roero Arneis Bricco delle Passere '17 | ♟♟ | 3 |
| ○ Roero '15 | ♟ | 3 |

## La Toledana

LOC. SERMOIRA,5
15066 GAVI [AL]
TEL. +39 0141837211
www.latoledana.it

CELLAR SALES
PRE-BOOKED VISITS
ANNUAL PRODUCTION 160,000 bottles
HECTARES UNDER VINE 28.00

| | | |
|---|---|---|
| ○ Gavi del Comune di Gavi La Toledana '17 | ♟♟ | 5 |
| ● Barolo Ravera Lo Zoccolaio Ris. '12 | ♟♟ | 7 |
| ○ Gavi La Doria '17 | ♟♟ | 3 |

## Trediberri

B.TA TORRIGLIONE, 4
12064 LA MORRA [CN]
TEL. +39 3391605470
www.trediberri.com

CELLAR SALES
PRE-BOOKED VISITS
ANNUAL PRODUCTION 50,000 bottles
HECTARES UNDER VINE 8.00
VITICULTURE METHOD Certified Organic

| | | |
|---|---|---|
| ● Barbera d'Alba '17 | ♟♟ | 2* |
| ● Barolo Rocche dell'Annunziata '14 | ♟♟ | 7 |
| ● Barolo '14 | ♟ | 5 |
| ● Langhe Nebbiolo '17 | ♟ | 2 |

## Poderi Vaiot

BORGATA LAIONE, 43
12046 MONTÀ [CN]
TEL. +39 0173976283
www.poderivaiot.it

ANNUAL PRODUCTION 25,000 bottles
HECTARES UNDER VINE 4.00

| | | |
|---|---|---|
| ○ Roero Arneis Franco '17 | ♟♟ | 2* |
| ● Roero Pierin '15 | ♟♟ | 2* |
| ● Barbera d'Alba Lupestre '15 | ♟ | 2 |

## Valfaccenda

FRAZ. MADONNA LORETO
LOC. VAL FACCENDA, 43
12043 CANALE [CN]
TEL. +39 3397303837
www.valfaccenda.it

CELLAR SALES
PRE-BOOKED VISITS
ANNUAL PRODUCTION 16,000 bottles
HECTARES UNDER VINE 3.00
SUSTAINABLE WINERY

| | |
|---|---|
| ● Roero '16 | ♟♟ 4 |
| ● Roero V. Valmaggiore Ris. '14 | ♟♟ 4 |
| ○ Roero Arneis '17 | ♟ 3 |
| ○ Roero Arneis Loreto '17 | ♟ 3 |

## La Vecchia Posta

VIA MONTEBELLO, 2
15050 AVOLASCA [AL]
TEL. +39 0131876254
www.lavecchiaposta-avolasca.com

CELLAR SALES
PRE-BOOKED VISITS
ACCOMMODATION AND RESTAURANT SERVICE
ANNUAL PRODUCTION 10,000 bottles
HECTARES UNDER VINE 2.70
VITICULTURE METHOD Certified Organic

| | |
|---|---|
| ○ Colli Tortonesi Timorasso Il Selvaggio '16 | ♟ 3 |

## Vigneti Valle Roncati

VIA NAZIONALE, 10A
28072 BRIONA [NO]
TEL. +39 3355732548
www.vignetivalleroncati.it

CELLAR SALES
PRE-BOOKED VISITS
ANNUAL PRODUCTION 50,000 bottles
HECTARES UNDER VINE 13.00
SUSTAINABLE WINERY

| | |
|---|---|
| ○ Colline Novaresi Bianco Particella 40 '17 | ♟♟ 3 |
| ● Fara V. di Sopra Ris. '12 | ♟ 5 |
| ● Ghemme Leblanque '12 | ♟ 5 |

## Virna

VIA ALBA, 24
12060 BAROLO [CN]
TEL. +39 017356120
www.virnabarolo.it

CELLAR SALES
PRE-BOOKED VISITS
ANNUAL PRODUCTION 60,000 bottles
HECTARES UNDER VINE 12.00

| | |
|---|---|
| ● Barolo Cannubi Boschis '14 | ♟♟ 6 |
| ● Barolo del Comune di Barolo '14 | ♟♟ 6 |
| ● Barolo Sarmassa '14 | ♟♟ 6 |

## Alberto Voerzio

B.GO BRANDINI, 1A
12064 LA MORRA [CN]
TEL. +39 3333927654
www.albertovoerzio.com

CELLAR SALES
ANNUAL PRODUCTION 13,000 bottles
HECTARES UNDER VINE 6.00
SUSTAINABLE WINERY

| | |
|---|---|
| ● Barolo Castagni '14 | ♟♟ 6 |
| ● Barolo La Serra '14 | ♟♟ 7 |
| ● Barbera d'Alba '15 | ♟ 3 |

## Voerzio Martini

S.DA LORETO, 3
12064 LA MORRA [CN]
TEL. +39 0173509194
voerzio.gianni@tiscali.it

CELLAR SALES
PRE-BOOKED VISITS
ANNUAL PRODUCTION 54,000 bottles
HECTARES UNDER VINE 12.00

| | |
|---|---|
| ● Barbera d'Alba Ciabot della Luna '16 | ♟♟ 4 |
| ○ Langhe Arneis Bricco Cappellina '17 | ♟♟ 3 |
| ● Langhe Nebbiolo Ciabot della Luna '16 | ♟♟ 5 |

# LIGURIA

The image that our annual tastings gave us is of a Liguria that's in perfect health and great form. That's not an easy feat for a region whose vineyards are constituted of strips of mountainous land made cultivatable by sheer human force, and where only a few estates (apart from its cooperatives) can boast more than 10 hectares of land. Over the centuries, Liguria's vigneron have dug out ridge upon ridge, creating dry walls using the area's stones so as to delineate and support family-managed vineyards and olive groves. Today all the hard work is paying off and the region's coastal, terraced vineyards are proving more than just a scenic feature of landscape - they're giving rise to wines of unique character. In fact, in these Mediterranean wines you can literally taste the land, with its balsamic hints and shrubs, its delicately salty breeze, its sun-baked rocks, its aromatic herbs and citrus, all elements that have extraordinarily intense fragrance and flavor here. The definition of 'heroic winemaking' applies precisely to these small artisan producers, for whom every harvest is a miracle of commitment, sweat and good-fortune, especially today with its unpredictable and changing climate. But Liguria's vine growers have an innate tenacity, and they're used to facing challenges, against time, against fashion, against a global market that demands production volumes unthinkable for a region like this. This year seven of these artisans took home awards, six veterans and one new entry, thus providing a perfect picture of Liguria's wine industry. Colli di Luni spawned three extraordinary Vermentinos, Terenzuola's 2017 Losso di Corsano, Giacomelli's 2017 Boboli (with the producer debuting in the exclusive Tre Bicchieri club), and Lunae Bosoni's classic Etichetta Nera. Ponente gave us three excellent Pigatos: BioVio's 2017 Bon in da Bon, Bruna's 2016 U Baccan and La Ginestraia's Via Maestra. In closing we mention the only red awarded, Kà Manciné's highly elegant 2017 Dolceacqua Beragna, an ambassador of a territory and a style of red whose popularity is growing. But overall a number of wines made it to our finals, thus confirming the extraordinary vitality and talent of Liguria's vigneron.

## Massimo Alessandri

VIA COSTA PARROCCHIA, 42
18020 RANZO [IM]
TEL. +39 018253458
www.massimoalessandri.it

CELLAR SALES
PRE-BOOKED VISITS
RESTAURANT SERVICE
ANNUAL PRODUCTION 35,000 bottles
HECTARES UNDER VINE 7.00

Despite new plantings such as those at the edge of Ranzo, Massimo Alessandri continues to experience limited production volumes. This is particularly true because of climatic conditions that complicated the 2017 vintage. Nonetheless, this small winery remains a leader in inland Imperia, especially regarding the Pigato whites, cultivated among the area's traditional terraces from 280 to 400 meters above sea level. Vermentino, Syrah, Granaccia and other varieties complete a tempting range. Their 2016 Pigato Vigne Vegie is rich in vibrant, well-balanced aromas. The body is round, though still young, with warmth and savory emerging from an intensely mineral texture. Their 2016 Granaccia is also excellent. It's a bright ruby wine with a classic weave on the palate that's softened by pulp and nice freshness.

| | | |
|---|---|---|
| ● Ligustico '15 | ▼▼ | 6 |
| ● Riviera Ligure di Ponente Granaccia '16 | ▼▼ | 4 |
| ○ Riviera Ligure di Ponente Pigato Vigne Vèggie '16 | ▼▼ | 4 |
| ○ Riviera Ligure di Ponente Vermentino Costa de Vigne '17 | ▼▼ | 3 |
| ○ Riviera Ligure di Ponente Pigato Costa de Vigne '17 | ▼ | 3 |
| ● Riviera Ligure di Ponente Granaccia '15 | ♀♀ | 4 |
| ○ Riviera Ligure di Ponente Pigato Costa de Vigne '15 | ♀♀ | 3 |
| ○ Riviera Ligure di Ponente Pigato Vigne Vèggie '15 | ♀♀ | 4 |
| ● Riviera Ligure di Ponente Rossese Costa de Vigne '16 | ♀♀ | 4 |
| ○ Viorus Costa di Vigne '14 | ♀♀ | 5 |

## Tenuta Anfosso

C.SO VERBONE, 175
18036 SOLDANO [IM]
TEL. +39 0184289906
www.tenutaanfosso.it

CELLAR SALES
ACCOMMODATION
ANNUAL PRODUCTION 23,000 bottles
HECTARES UNDER VINE 4.50

This historic Dolceacqua-area winery has existed since the end of the 19th century, when Alessandro Anfosso's great-grandfather Giacomo laid its foundations by cultivating grapes at the Pini and Fulavin vineyards in Soldano. Though just over one hectare, the nucleus of the estate still produces eponymous wines and continues as its headquarters. The estate reached its current area of four and a half hectares of vineyards with the addition of the Luvaira vineyard in San Biagio della Cima. Alessandro is responsible for all aspects of winegrowing and winemaking; his wife Marisa handles commercial activities in Italy and abroad. Their 2016 Fulavin is an excellent wine, intense and sophisticated with notes of red berries, tobacco, licorice and an elegant peppery background. The body shows great structure and balance, with a lengthy finish. Their 2016 Luvaira, a brilliant, ruby garnet wine with aromas of quinine, tobacco and red berries, proves sophisticated and balanced, with a palate defined by its thrust and balance.

| | | |
|---|---|---|
| ● Dolceacqua Sup. Fulavin '16 | ▼▼ | 5 |
| ● Dolceacqua Sup. Luvaira '16 | ▼▼ | 5 |
| ● Dolceacqua Sup. '16 | ▼▼ | 4 |
| ● Dolceacqua Sup. Poggio Pini '16 | ▼▼ | 5 |
| ● Dolceacqua '15 | ♀♀ | 4 |
| ● Dolceacqua Sup. '13 | ♀♀ | 4 |
| ● Dolceacqua Sup. Fulavin '13 | ♀♀ | 4 |
| ● Dolceacqua Sup. Luvaira '13 | ♀♀ | 4 |
| ● Dolceacqua Sup. Poggio Pini '15 | ♀♀ | 4 |
| ● Dolceacqua Sup. Poggio Pini '12 | ♀♀ | 4 |
| ● Rossese di Dolceacqua Sup. '10 | ♀♀ | 3 |
| ● Rossese di Dolceacqua Sup. Poggio Pini '11 | ♀♀ | 4 |

# Laura Aschero

P.ZZA VITTORIO EMANUELE, 7
18027 PONTEDASSIO [IM]
TEL. +39 0183710307
www.lauraaschero.it

**CELLAR SALES**
**PRE-BOOKED VISITS**
**ANNUAL PRODUCTION** 60,000 bottles
**HECTARES UNDER VINE** 50.00

Carlo Rizzo and wife Carla, along with her daughter, Bianca, lead this lovely winery named after Carla's mother. In the mid-1970s, Laura Aschero dedicated family lands in Pontedassio, in western Liguria, to vineyards. In recent years, plots at Posai were added to the original parcels around Monti. Though the estate has expanded, it remains anchored strongly in the area's traditional varieties. Vermentino, Pigato, Rossese, form a knock-out trio that lets Laura Aschero offer a wide selection of vivacious and sun-filled wines. Their 2017 Pigato is their most captivating wine. It's a straw-yellow wine with green highlights. Vibrant aromas of tropical fruit and Mediterranean shrub are juxtaposed on saltier hints that add complexity. The palate is rich and lingering. Their 2017 Vermentino is intense and full of color. Round in its body, the wine unfolds with slow generosity.

| | |
|---|---|
| ○ Riviera Ligure di Ponente Pigato '17 | 🍷🍷 3 |
| ○ Riviera Ligure di Ponente Vermentino '17 | 🍷🍷 3 |
| ● Riviera Ligure di Ponente Rossese '17 | 🍷 3 |
| ○ Riviera Ligure di Ponente Vermentino '10 | 🍷🍷🍷 3* |
| ○ Riviera Ligure di Ponente Pigato '16 | 🍷🍷 3 |
| ○ Riviera Ligure di Ponente Pigato '15 | 🍷🍷 3* |
| ○ Riviera Ligure di Ponente Pigato '13 | 🍷🍷 3* |
| ○ Riviera Ligure di Ponente Vermentino '16 | 🍷🍷 3 |
| ○ Riviera Ligure di Ponente Vermentino '15 | 🍷🍷 3 |
| ○ Riviera Ligure di Ponente Vermentino '14 | 🍷🍷 3 |

# La Baia del Sole - Federici

FRAZ. LUNI ANTICA
VIA FORLINO, 3
19034 LUNI [SP]
TEL. +39 0187661821
www.cantinefederici.com

**CELLAR SALES**
**PRE-BOOKED VISITS**
**ANNUAL PRODUCTION** 180,000 bottles
**HECTARES UNDER VINE** 35.00

Baia del Sole, located on the border of Liguria and Tuscany in Luni di Ortonovo, was founded in 1985 by Isa and Giulio Federici. However, it can trace its roots back to the early 1900s. Luca and Andrea are the latest generation involved in the winery, whose production focuses primarily on Vermentino that is crafted in the cellar without added sulfites in the early stages and using gravity reliant racking. The vineyards are distributed in the Magra River hills and valley, including parcels cultivated by some seventy winemakers in the area. The 2017 vintage gave rise to excellent wines, starting with their Solaris, a wine with vibrant and pleasant notes of dried herbs and Mediterranean scrubland. In the mouth it proves rich and complex, with a warm intensity and long, lingering finish. Their Gladius, a wine with flavors of white fruit and an tropical note, ins't far off. Its velvety body expands with elegance.

| | |
|---|---|
| ○ Colli di Luni Bianco Gladius '17 | 🍷🍷 2* |
| ○ Colli di Luni Vermentino Solaris '17 | 🍷🍷 3* |
| ● Colli di Luni Rosso Eutichiano '17 | 🍷🍷 3 |
| ○ Colli di Luni Vermentino Oro d'Isée '17 | 🍷🍷 4 |
| ○ Colli di Luni Vermentino Sarticola '17 | 🍷🍷 5 |
| ○ Muri Grandi '17 | 🍷🍷 2* |
| ○ Colli di Luni Vermentino Sarticola '15 | 🍷🍷🍷 4* |
| ● Colli di Luni Eutichiano '16 | 🍷🍷 3 |
| ● Colli di Luni Eutichiano '15 | 🍷🍷 3 |
| ○ Colli di Luni Vermentino Gladius '16 | 🍷🍷 2* |
| ○ Colli di Luni Vermentino Oro d'Isée '16 | 🍷🍷 4 |
| ○ Colli di Luni Vermentino Oro d'Isée '15 | 🍷🍷 4 |
| ○ Colli di Luni Vermentino Sarticola '16 | 🍷🍷 4 |
| ○ Colli di Luni Vermentino Sarticola '14 | 🍷🍷 4 |

## Maria Donata Bianchi

VIA MEREA, 101
18013 DIANO ARENTINO [IM]
TEL. +39 0183498233
www.aziendaagricolabianchi.it

CELLAR SALES
PRE-BOOKED VISITS
ACCOMMODATION
ANNUAL PRODUCTION 30,000 bottles
HECTARES UNDER VINE 4.00

Young Marta now works full time at the winery, supporting her father, Emanuele, and mother, Maria Donata Bianchi, after whom their small estate in Diano Arentino is named. Marta's influence is beginning to show. In the vineyard the method of pruning has changed and a request for biological certification has been initiated, though the system itself has been in use for years. Changes in the cellar have been made as well. Nonetheless, it continues to focus on the classic white varieties of western Liguria, particularly Pigato and Vermentino. At the time of tasting, this lovely producer's wines were still young. Their 2017 Vermentino features fragrances of Mediterranean herbs and delicate sensations of fruit. Its body is somewhat green, but it still offers close-focused aromas and great savoriness. Their 2017 Pigato sees nice freshness with hints of rosemary and sage that open to vibrant fruit.

| | |
|---|---|
| ○ Riviera Ligure di Ponente Pigato '17 | ♟♟ 3 |
| ○ Riviera Ligure di Ponente Vermentino '17 | ♟♟ 3 |
| ○ Antico Sfizio '17 | ♟ 4 |
| ○ Riviera Ligure di Ponente Pigato '12 | ♟♟♟ 3* |
| ○ Riviera Ligure di Ponente Vermentino '09 | ♟♟♟ 3 |
| ○ Riviera Ligure di Ponente Vermentino '07 | ♟♟♟ 3* |
| ○ Riviera Ligure di Ponente Pigato '16 | ♟♟ 3 |
| ○ Riviera Ligure di Ponente Pigato '14 | ♟♟ 3* |
| ○ Riviera Ligure di Ponente Pigato '13 | ♟♟ 3* |
| ○ Riviera Ligure di Ponente Pigato '11 | ♟♟ 4 |
| ○ Riviera Ligure di Ponente Vermentino '16 | ♟♟ 3 |
| ○ Riviera Ligure di Ponente Vermentino '15 | ♟♟ 3 |

## BioVio

FRAZ. BASTIA
VIA CROCIATA, 24
17031 ALBENGA [SV]
TEL. +39 018220776
www.biovio.it

CELLAR SALES
PRE-BOOKED VISITS
ACCOMMODATION
ANNUAL PRODUCTION 60,000 bottles
HECTARES UNDER VINE 6.00
VITICULTURE METHOD Certified Organic

Young sisters of the Vio family, Camilla, Carolina, and Caterina now work full-time at the winery and they have helped bring about small but significant transformations. An example is the adoption of spontaneous fermentation across the entire Rossese and Vermentino, Pigato lines, including Bon in da Bon, undoubtedly the Albenga winery's most famous selection. The slightly over-ripe grapes are harvested in the second half of September, and according to the tradition of the area, part are macerated with the skins, bringing out power and long length. And with their 2017 Bonin da Bon the Pio family continues to offer extremely high and consistent quality. Round and well-balanced, with notes of Mediterranean scrubland and ripe white fruit, it exhibits extraordinary richness. Their 2017 Ma René isn't far off, with its lavish body and vibrant finish. Their 2017 Granaccia is rich in extract and demonstrates great character.

| | |
|---|---|
| ○ Riviera Ligure di Ponente Pigato Bon in da Bon '17 | ♟♟♟ 5 |
| ● Gigò Granaccia '17 | ♟♟ 4 |
| ○ Riviera Ligure di Ponente Pigato Ma René '17 | ♟♟ 3* |
| ○ Riviera Ligure di Ponente Vermentino Aimone '17 | ♟♟ 4 |
| ○ Riviera Ligure di Ponente Pigato Bon in da Bon '16 | ♟♟♟ 5 |
| ○ Riviera Ligure di Ponente Pigato Bon in da Bon '15 | ♟♟♟ 2* |
| ○ Riviera Ligure di Ponente Vermentino Aimone '11 | ♟♟♟ 2* |
| ○ Riviera Ligure di Ponente Pigato Ma René '16 | ♟♟ 3* |

# Samuele Heydi Bonanini

VIA SAN ANTONIO, 72
19017 RIOMAGGIORE [SP]
TEL. +39 0187920959
www.possa.it

CELLAR SALES
PRE-BOOKED VISITS
ANNUAL PRODUCTION 7,000 bottles
HECTARES UNDER VINE 1.50

Difficult to imagine, superb to live in, impossible to work. That is Cinque Terre in a nutshell. Passionate, biodynamic winemaker Samuele Heydi Bonanini cultivates small patches of land that cling to rock located entirely within the protected area of the National Park. Bosco, Rossese Bianco, Albarola, Piccabon, Frapelao, Cannaiolo, and Bonamico are just some of the traditional varieties used in this winery's range of wines. Both red and white are macerated and aged in wood barrels. Their 2016 Sciacchetrà, an amber wine, proved excellent. Its vibrant aromas open to notes of dried fruit and walnuts. In the mouth it expands in complexity with a sophisticated balance between sugars and acidity. Their 2017 Cinque Terre is quite pleasant. Intense and multifaceted, its aromas of dried fruit open to a powerful structure, which broadens across its long finish.

| | | |
|---|---|---|
| ○ Cinque Terre Sciacchetrà '16 | ▼▼ | 8 |
| ○ Cinque Terre '17 | ▼▼ | 5 |
| ○ Er Giancu '17 | ▼ | 4 |
| ○ Cinque Terre '13 | ♀♀♀ | 5 |
| ○ Cinque Terre '12 | ♀♀♀ | 5 |
| ○ Cinque Terre '16 | ♀♀ | 5 |
| ○ Cinque Terre '15 | ♀♀ | 5 |
| ○ Cinque Terre '14 | ♀♀ | 5 |
| ○ Cinque Terre Sciacchetrà '14 | ♀♀ | 8 |
| ○ Cinque Terre Sciacchetrà Fermentato in Terracotta '15 | ♀♀ | 8 |
| ○ Cinque Terre Sciacchetrà Ris. '12 | ♀♀ | 8 |
| ○ Cinque Terre Sciacchetrà Ris. '10 | ♀♀ | 8 |
| ○ Er Giancu '15 | ♀♀ | 4 |
| ● Rinascita Renfursà '16 | ♀♀ | 8 |

# Cantine Bregante

VIA UNITÀ D'ITALIA, 47
16039 SESTRI LEVANTE [GE]
TEL. +39 018541388
www.cantinebregante.it

CELLAR SALES
PRE-BOOKED VISITS
ANNUAL PRODUCTION 100,000 bottles
HECTARES UNDER VINE 1.00

Bregante has an interesting story. It started at the end of the 1800s when Bartolomeo and his small fleet of wine-laden commercial ships were active along the Mediterranean's most important routes. Today, his descendants, Sergio and Simona, are proud to cultivate various plots in Moneglia (on the Tigullio coast) and the innermost hills of Chiavari and Lavagna. The dominant varieties of Vermentino, Bianchetta Genovese, Moscato and Ciliegiolo are made into wine at facilities in the center of Sestri Levante. Their 2017 Moscato features a harmony of fragrances with a rich cordon. Pleasant, fresh aromas of musk are juxtaposed on elegant peach in what is a pleasing balance between sugars and freshness. Their Brut Baia delle Favole sees persistent colors and perlage, with complex notes of dried herbs and red fruit. Their 2017 Bianchetta Genovese is vibrant in its fragrances of Mediterranean scrubland.

| | | |
|---|---|---|
| ○ Golfo del Tigullio Baia delle Favole Brut M. Cl. | ▼▼ | 5 |
| ○ Golfo del Tigullio Portofino Bianchetta Genovese '17 | ▼▼ | 2* |
| ○ Golfo del Tigullio Portofino Bianco '17 | ▼▼ | 2* |
| ○ Golfo del Tigullio Portofino Moscato '17 | ▼▼ | 3 |
| ○ Sole della Costa Passito '16 | ▼▼ | 5 |
| ○ Golfo del Tigullio Portofino Vermentino '17 | ▼ | 2 |
| ○ Golfo del Tigullio Portofino Bianchetta Genovese '16 | ♀♀ | 2* |
| ○ Golfo del Tigullio Portofino Bianco '15 | ♀♀ | 2* |
| ● Golfo del Tigullio Portofino Ciliegiolo '16 | ♀♀ | 2* |
| ○ Golfo del Tigullio Portofino Moscato '15 | ♀♀ | 2* |
| ● Golfo del Tigullio Portofino Rosso Cà du Diau '16 | ♀♀ | 2* |
| ○ Golfo del Tigullio Portofino Vermentino '16 | ♀♀ | 2* |

## ★Bruna

FRAZ. BORGO
VIA UMBERTO I, 81
18020 RANZO [IM]
TEL. +39 0183318082
www.brunapigato.it

CELLAR SALES
PRE-BOOKED VISITS
ANNUAL PRODUCTION 40,000 bottles
HECTARES UNDER VINE 8.50

This winery, situated in the small village of Ranzo, was founded by Riccardo Bruna. It is now run by his daughter Francesca and her husband Roberto, who continue to grow the area's historical cultivars. Special attention is given to Pigato, which the winery interprets particulary well. Managed in line with natural viticulture methods, their main plots meander through the heights between Ranzo and Ortovero, with spaces dedicated also to Rossese, Granaccia and Syrah. It produces a small but distinctive range that is easily recognizable by its energetic and savory style. This small producer continues its tradition of high quality. Their wines are always well-made. One example is their 2016 U Baccan, a wine with slightly salty notes of Mediterranean scrubland and the sweet spiciness of wood, all of which weave across an imperious body with a long, balanced finish. Their 2017 Le Russeghine is vibrant in its notes of dried flowers, medicinal herbs and Mediterranean shrub.

| | |
|---|---|
| ○ Riviera Ligure di Ponente Pigato U Baccan '16 | ♙♙♙ 5 |
| ○ Riviera Ligure di Ponente Pigato Le Russeghine '17 | ♙♙ 4 |
| ● Bansigu '17 | ♙♙ 3 |
| ○ Riviera Ligure di Ponente Pigato Majé '17 | ♙♙ 3 |
| ● Pulin '16 | ♙ 5 |
| ○ Riviera Ligure di Ponente Pigato U Baccan '15 | ♛♛♛ 5 |
| ○ Riviera Ligure di Ponente Pigato U Baccan '13 | ♛♛♛ 5 |
| ○ Riviera Ligure di Ponente Pigato U Baccan '12 | ♛♛♛ 5 |

## Cantine Calleri

LOC. SALEA
REG. FRATTI, 2
17031 ALBENGA [SV]
TEL. +39 018220085
www.cantinecalleri.com

ANNUAL PRODUCTION 55,000 bottles
HECTARES UNDER VINE 6.00

Calleri is a long-standing family name in Albenga, indissolubly linked to both the small village of Salea and western Liguria's Pigato. The winery was started by Aldo in 1968 and today Marcello carries this heritage forward, adding new acreages dedicated to wine growing. The parcel taken under management in Arnasco municipality, for example, an area particularly well-suited for luscious and spicy wines, also gives rise to Vermentino, Rossese and Ormeasco (a rare traditional cultivar presumably related to Dolcetto). Their 2017 Saleasco is vibrant with lovely terpene notes of flowers and white fruit across broad fragrances of Mediterranean scrubland. It's an elegant, mineral wine that's full of personality. Their brilliantly colored 2017 Müzazzi, another wine of great character, offers up fruity notes on elegant minerality. It's a fine, complex wine that expands across the palate and proves highly enjoyable to drink.

| | |
|---|---|
| ○ Riviera Ligure di Ponente Pigato di Albenga Saleasco '17 | ♙♙ 3* |
| ○ Riviera Ligure di Ponente Vermentino I Müzazzi '17 | ♙♙ 3* |
| ● Ormeasco di Pornassio '16 | ♙♙ 3 |
| ○ Riviera Ligure di Ponente Pigato di Albenga '17 | ♙♙ 3 |
| ○ Riviera Ligure di Ponente Vermentino '17 | ♙♙ 3 |
| ○ Riviera Ligure di Ponente Pigato di Albenga '15 | ♛♛ 3 |
| ○ Riviera Ligure di Ponente Pigato di Albenga Saleasco '16 | ♛♛ 3* |
| ○ Riviera Ligure di Ponente Pigato di Albenga Saleasco '15 | ♛♛ 3* |
| ○ Riviera Ligure di Ponente Vermentino '16 | ♛♛ 3 |

# Cheo

VIA BRIGATE PARTIGIANE, 1
19018 VERNAZZA [SP]
TEL. +39 0187821189
www.cheo.it

CELLAR SALES
PRE-BOOKED VISITS
ANNUAL PRODUCTION 13,000 bottles
HECTARES UNDER VINE 2.00
SUSTAINABLE WINERY

Like many producers in Cinque Terre, Bartolomeo Lercari and Lise Bertram operate on the front line of a picturesque but challenging territory. The winery is recovering slowly from the heavy flooding a few years ago that destroyed part of their vineyards and flooded their cellar. They have come back in small steps with the addition of new plots. Their vineyards are composed of dozens of terraces ranging from 30 to 150 meters above sea level, connecting the coast with the interior and forming a jewelry box filled with Fossà, Croci, Lamma, Contra, Mavà, and Vernazzola. Their 2017 Perciò is an excellent wine with complex notes of medicinal herbs, slightly salty notes and Mediterranean scrubland across a background of white fruit. Its balanced structure finishes with a intensity. Their 2015 Sciacchetrà is fine, elegant and full of character. A bold body that's rich in sugars is balanced thanks to a pleasant bitterness in its finish.

| | |
|---|---|
| ○ Cinque Terre Perciò '17 | ♛♛ 4 |
| ○ Cinque Terre Sciacchetrà '15 | ♛♛ 8 |
| ○ Cinque Terre Cheo '17 | ♛♛♛ 3 |
| ○ Cinque Terre Cheo '16 | ♔♔ 3 |
| ○ Cinque Terre Cheo '15 | ♔♔ 3 |
| ○ Cinque Terre Cheo '14 | ♔♔ 3 |
| ○ Cinque Terre Cheo '13 | ♔♔ 3* |
| ○ Cinque Terre Perciò '16 | ♔♔ 4 |
| ○ Cinque Terre Perciò '15 | ♔♔ 4 |
| ○ Cinque Terre Perciò '14 | ♔♔ 4 |
| ○ Cinque Terre Perciò '13 | ♔♔ 4 |
| ○ Cinque Terre Perciò '12 | ♔♔ 4 |
| ○ Cinque Terre Sciacchetrà '14 | ♔♔ 8 |
| ○ Cinque Terre Sciacchetrà '13 | ♔♔ 8 |
| ○ Cinque Terre Sciacchetrà '12 | ♔♔ 8 |
| ○ Cinque Terre Sciacchetrà '11 | ♔♔ 8 |

# Cantina Cinque Terre

FRAZ. MANAROLA
LOC. GROPPO
19010 RIOMAGGIORE [SP]
TEL. +39 0187920435
www.cantinacinqueterre.com

PRE-BOOKED VISITS
ANNUAL PRODUCTION 200,000 bottles
HECTARES UNDER VINE 45.00

One can't fully understand Cinque Terre wines without visiting the area and admiring firsthand the sturdy vineyards on terraces preserved out of great passion for producing wine. From this perspective, the cooperative Riomaggiore, with its 200 grower-members and dozens of scattered parcels perched high above the sea, plays a key role. The traditional low pergola system that dominates helps protect the grapes from both the intense summer heat and the insidious salty breezes. Their 2012 Sciacchetrà Riserva is a clear, amber wine with classic aromas of walnut skin and dried fruit across a background of white chocolate. It's fine and complex, elegant and bold with a body that's imbued with acidity and a long finish that's rich in alcohol. Their 2017 Vigne Alte opens with flowery fragrances. It's an elegant and intensely savory wine with a lengthy finish.

| | |
|---|---|
| ○ Cinque Terre Sciacchetrà Ris. '12 | ♛♛ 6 |
| ○ Cinque Terre Vigne Alte '17 | ♛♛♛ 2* |
| ○ Cinque Terre '17 | ♛♛ 2* |
| ○ Cinque Terre Costa da' Posa '17 | ♛♛ 3 |
| ○ Cinque Terre Costa de Campu '17 | ♛♛ 3 |
| ○ Cinque Terre Pergole Sparse '17 | ♛♛ 3 |
| ○ Cinque Terre '16 | ♔♔ 2* |
| ○ Cinque Terre Costa da Posa '16 | ♔♔ 3* |
| ○ Cinque Terre Costa da' Posa '15 | ♔♔ 3 |
| ○ Cinque Terre Costa de Campu '16 | ♔♔ 3 |
| ○ Cinque Terre Costa de Sèra '14 | ♔♔ 3 |
| ○ Cinque Terre Pergole Sparse '16 | ♔♔ 3 |
| ○ Cinque Terre Sciacchetrà '15 | ♔♔ 6 |
| ○ Cinque Terre Sciacchetrà '13 | ♔♔ 6 |
| ○ Cinque Terre Sciacchetrà '12 | ♔♔ 6 |

## Fontanacota

FRAZ. PONTI
VIA PROVINCIALE, 137
18100 PORNASSIO [IM]
TEL. +39 3339807442
www.fontanacota.it

CELLAR SALES
PRE-BOOKED VISITS
ANNUAL PRODUCTION 40,000 bottles
HECTARES UNDER VINE 6.00

New forces are reviving the Berta family winery, Fontanacota. Marina, along with her son Andreas, manages the cellar and welcomes guests while brother Fabio is soon to be joined in the vineyard by his son Ludovico. They lead one of the Imperia area's most respected estates, with plots in Val Prino and Alta Valle Arroscia in Pornassio, where the winery has its headquarters. Small plots cultivated in Vermentino, Pigato, Rossese and Ormeasco, bring forth a diverse array of wines with a pure style. Fragrant, vibrant notes open their 2017 Pigato in a classic way with hints of fresh, aromatic herbs and white fruit. The body doesn't exhibit particular structure, but it's boosted by a fresh vein that runs through the wine's elegant, multi-faceted texture. Their 2017 Vermentino is more vibrant, with clear sensations of fruit and sweet spices and a structured (though young) body.

| | | |
|---|---|---|
| ○ Riviera Ligure di Ponente Pigato '17 | 🍷🍷 | 3 |
| ● Riviera Ligure di Ponente Rossese '17 | 🍷🍷 | 3 |
| ○ Riviera Ligure di Ponente Vermentino '17 | 🍷🍷 | 3 |
| ○ Riviera Ligure di Ponente Vermentino Sup. Barbazenà '16 | 🍷🍷 | 3 |
| ○ Riviera Ligure di Ponente Pigato '11 | 🍷🍷🍷 | 3* |
| ● Pornassio '15 | 🍷🍷 | 3 |
| ○ Riviera Ligure di Ponente Pigato '16 | 🍷🍷 | 3 |
| ○ Riviera Ligure di Ponente Pigato '15 | 🍷🍷 | 3 |
| ○ Riviera Ligure di Ponente Pigato '14 | 🍷🍷 | 3* |
| ○ Riviera Ligure di Ponente Vermentino '16 | 🍷🍷 | 3 |
| ○ Riviera Ligure di Ponente Vermentino '15 | 🍷🍷 | 3* |
| ○ Riviera Ligure di Ponente Vermentino '14 | 🍷🍷 | 3 |

## Giacomelli

VIA PALVOTRISIA, 134
19030 CASTELNUOVO MAGRA [SP]
TEL. +39 3496301516
www.azagricolagiacomelli.it

CELLAR SALES
PRE-BOOKED VISITS
ANNUAL PRODUCTION 85,000 bottles
HECTARES UNDER VINE 9.00
SUSTAINABLE WINERY

This winery founded by Roberto Petacchi at Castelnuovo Magra in 1993 continues to grow. The new Vermentino, Giardino dei Vescovi, which debuted with the 2016 vintage exemplifies its growth. The estate has expanded its wine-growing capacity through slow and steady acquisitions, the most recent being parcels within the prestigious Villa Baracchini. The winery offers true crus from Colli di Luni Boboli and Pianacce (da Caprignano), each clearly expressing its terroir, as well as selections based on Trebbiano, Albarola, Malvasia, Sangiovese, Canaiolo, and Merlot. Their 2017 Boboli is a great wine with vibrant notes of white fruit, Mediterranean scrubland and slightly salty aromas. It's a sublime wome, fine and complex, rich and full of power, balance and length. It's also just a bit plush with a savory finish. Their 2017 Giardino dei Vescovi also pleased for its white fruit, Mediterranean shrub and a slight hint of salt.

| | | |
|---|---|---|
| ○ Colli di Luni Vermentino Boboli '17 | 🍷🍷🍷 | 4* |
| ○ Colli di Luni Vermentino Giardino dei Vescovi '17 | 🍷🍷 | 5 |
| ○ Colli di Luni Vermentino Pianacce '17 | 🍷🍷 | 2* |
| ○ Colli di Luni Bianco Paduletti '16 | 🍷🍷 | 2* |
| ● Colli di Luni Rosso Canal di Bocco '11 | 🍷🍷 | 4 |
| ○ Colli di Luni Vermentino Boboli '15 | 🍷🍷 | 4 |
| ○ Colli di Luni Vermentino Boboli '13 | 🍷🍷 | 4 |
| ○ Colli di Luni Vermentino Boboli '11 | 🍷🍷 | 4 |
| ○ Colli di Luni Vermentino Pianacce '16 | 🍷🍷 | 2* |
| ○ Colli di Luni Vermentino Pianacce '15 | 🍷🍷 | 2* |
| ○ Colli di Luni Vermentino Pianacce '14 | 🍷🍷 | 2* |
| ○ Colli di Luni Vermentino Pianacce '12 | 🍷🍷 | 2* |
| ⊙ Gorgonia Rosato '16 | 🍷🍷 | 2* |

## La Ginestraia

via Steria
18100 Cervo [IM]
Tel. +39 3482613723
www.laginestraia.com

**ANNUAL PRODUCTION** 50,000 bottles
**HECTARES UNDER VINE** 7.00

Founded in 2007, La Ginestraia is immersed in green olive trees and grapevines on a small hill where the Ponente joins the Ligurian Riviera near Cervo. It's the headquarters of a significant agricultural complex that includes estates at Arnasco di Albenga and Ortovero and a new facility at San Bartolomeo. Marco Brangero e Mauro Leporieri, produce small quantities of wine based on Vermentino and Pigato, which are acclaimed for their traditional but never old-fashioned style. Their 2016 Via Maestra is a vibrant, well-balanced wine whose complexity expands. It opens with aromas of dried herbs and Mediterranean scrubland, apricot and mineral hints. On the palate it proves elegant, with noble, endless finish. Their 2017 Le Marige is extremely well-made, with good, varietal character. Its structure is supported by a delectable savoriness.

| | |
|---|---|
| ○ Riviera Ligure di Ponente Pigato Via Maestra '16 | ▼▼▼ 5 |
| ○ Riviera Ligure di Ponente Pigato Le Marige '17 | ▼▼ 3 |
| ○ Riviera Ligure di Ponente Vermentino '17 | ▼▼ 3 |
| ○ Riviera Ligure di Ponente Pigato '17 | ▼ 3 |
| ○ Riviera Ligure di Ponente Pigato Le Marige '15 | ▽▽▽ 3* |
| ○ Riviera Ligure di Ponente Pigato '16 | ▽▽ 3 |
| ○ Riviera Ligure di Ponente Pigato '15 | ▽▽ 3* |
| ○ Riviera Ligure di Ponente Pigato Le Marige '16 | ▽▽ 3 |
| ○ Riviera Ligure di Ponente Pigato Via Maestra '15 | ▽▽ 3* |
| ○ Riviera Ligure di Ponente Vermentino '16 | ▽▽ 3 |

## Ka' Manciné

fraz. San Martino
via Maciurina, 7
18036 Soldano [IM]
Tel. +39 339 3965477
www.kamancine.it

**CELLAR SALES**
**PRE-BOOKED VISITS**
**ANNUAL PRODUCTION** 20,000 bottles
**HECTARES UNDER VINE** 3.00

Fiery and enthusiastic, Mario Anfosso is one of the most skilled grape growers in the Ponente area of Liguria. Ka' Manciné's selections center around its two Soldano crus. Beragna is located with a northeast orientation 350 meters above sea level, and Galeae faces southeast with an elevations of between 300 and 390 meters. For many years, both have been dedicated to cultivating Rossese that is turned into wine using 20 to 30 percent whole grapes removed from the stem. The winery's decision to continue in this style further distinguishes this small but notable producer. All the wines presented put in good performances. Their 2017 Beragna offers up broad aromas of raspberry on a peppery, licorice background. On the palate elegant tannins give way to a long finish. Their dense, intense ruby 2017 Galeae features notes of tobacco on buoyant black fruit. Its palate is defined by great harmony and a long, classic finish. Their 2016 Angè is a complex, pleasantly lingering wine.

| | |
|---|---|
| ● Dolceacqua Beragna '17 | ▼▼▼ 3* |
| ● Dolceacqua Galeae '17 | ▼▼ 3* |
| ● Dolceacqua Galeae Angè Ris. '16 | ▼▼ 3* |
| ⊙ Sciakk '17 | ▼ 3 |
| ○ Tabaka '17 | ▼ 3 |
| ● Dolceacqua Beragna '16 | ▽▽▽ 3* |
| ● Dolceacqua Galeae '13 | ▽▽▽ 3* |
| ● Dolceacqua Beragna '15 | ▽▽ 3* |
| ● Dolceacqua Beragna '14 | ▽▽ 3* |
| ● Dolceacqua Galeae '16 | ▽▽ 3* |
| ● Dolceacqua Galeae '15 | ▽▽ 3 |
| ● Dolceacqua Galeae '14 | ▽▽ 3 |
| ● Dolceacqua Galeae Angè Ris. '15 | ▽▽ 3 |
| ● Dolceacqua Galeae Angè Ris. '14 | ▽▽ 3* |
| ● Dolceacqua Galeae Angè Ris. '13 | ▽▽ 3* |

## LIGURIA

# Ottaviano Lambruschi

VIA OLMARELLO, 28
19030 CASTELNUOVO MAGRA [SP]
TEL. +39 0187674261
www.ottavianolambruschi.com

CELLAR SALES
PRE-BOOKED VISITS
ANNUAL PRODUCTION 36,000 bottles
HECTARES UNDER VINE 10.00

With the help of son Fabio and granddaughter Ylenia, Ottaviano Lambruschi is one of the Lunigiana area's leaders in wine production, particularly when it comes to white Vermentino. Located in Castelnuovo, the winery provides a stylistic model of how best to maximize the freshness and tanginess characteristic of Tyrranean cultivars. These same characteristics also reflect the hillside position of the vineyards which catch the sea air. Sangiovese, Merlot and Canaiolo round out the varieties. Their wines are always at the top, starting with their 2017 Costa Marina with its notes of dried herbs, white fruit and pineapple. It's a bold wine with lovely, elegant balance and along, highly-pleasant finish. Their 2017 Ottaviano, straw-yellow in color, offers up aromas of elderflower and broom flower across Mediterranean scrubland. It's a complex wine with fresh acidity and lengthy aftertaste.

| | |
|---|---|
| ○ Colli di Luni Bianco Ottaviano '17 | 🍷🍷 3* |
| ○ Colli di Luni Vermentino Costa Marina '17 | 🍷🍷 4 |
| ○ Colli di Luni Vermentino Il Maggiore '17 | 🍷🍷 5 |
| ○ Colli di Luni Vermentino Costa Marina '16 | 🍷🍷🍷 4* |
| ○ Colli di Luni Vermentino Costa Marina '11 | 🍷🍷🍷 4* |
| ○ Colli di Luni Vermentino Costa Marina '09 | 🍷🍷🍷 3 |
| ○ Colli di Luni Vermentino Il Maggiore '15 | 🍷🍷🍷 5 |
| ○ Colli di Luni Vermentino Il Maggiore '14 | 🍷🍷🍷 5 |
| ○ Colli di Luni Vermentino Il Maggiore '13 | 🍷🍷🍷 5 |
| ○ Colli di Luni Vermentino Il Maggiore '12 | 🍷🍷🍷 4* |

# ★Cantine Lunae Bosoni

VIA PALVOTRISIA, 2
19030 CASTELNUOVO MAGRA [SP]
TEL. +39 0187669222
www.cantinelunae.com

CELLAR SALES
PRE-BOOKED VISITS
ANNUAL PRODUCTION 550,000 bottles
HECTARES UNDER VINE 80.00

The inauguration of a new cellar marks another step forward in Colli di Luni. Paolo Bosoni roughed in the framework of the winery in the 1970s, and today his children, Debora and Diego, continue to refine his work. The estate includes various plots on the plain around the ancient city of Luni and in the hills of Castelnuovo Magra and Ortonovo, but the winery also relies on supplies from the more than 100 wine growers they work with. The offerings revolve around a range of Vermentino wines notable for their contemporary style. Lunae's tradition of high quality continues with their 2017 Etichetta Nera. It's a sublime wine with aromas of sage, tropical fruit and a slight hint of aniseed. On the palate it proves fresh, with a long, multifaceted finish. Their 2017 Cavagino features aromas of orange and citrus peel. It's a vibrant, warm and well-balanced wine that's pleasant to drink and features complex structure.

| | |
|---|---|
| ○ Colli di Luni Vermentino Lunae Et. Nera '17 | 🍷🍷🍷 4* |
| ○ Colli di Luni Bianco Fior di Luna '17 | 🍷🍷 3* |
| ○ Colli di Luni Vermentino Cavagino '17 | 🍷🍷 5 |
| ● Colli di Luni Rosso Niccolò V '14 | 🍷🍷 4 |
| ○ Colli di Luni Vermentino Albarola '17 | 🍷🍷 4 |
| ○ Colli di Luni Vermentino Et. Grigia '17 | 🍷🍷 3 |
| ○ Colli di Luni Vermentino Et. Nera '15 | 🍷🍷🍷 4* |
| ○ Colli di Luni Vermentino Et. Nera '14 | 🍷🍷🍷 4* |
| ○ Colli di Luni Vermentino Et. Nera '13 | 🍷🍷🍷 4* |
| ○ Colli di Luni Vermentino Et. Nera '12 | 🍷🍷🍷 4* |
| ○ Colli di Luni Vermentino Et. Nera '11 | 🍷🍷🍷 4* |
| ○ Colli di Luni Vermentino Et. Nera '10 | 🍷🍷🍷 4 |
| ○ Colli di Luni Vermentino Lunae Et. Nera '16 | 🍷🍷🍷 4* |

# Maccario Dringenberg

VIA TORRE, 3
18036 SAN BIAGIO DELLA CIMA [IM]
TEL. +39 0184289947
maccariodringenberg@yahoo.it

CELLAR SALES
PRE-BOOKED VISITS
ANNUAL PRODUCTION 23,000 bottles
HECTARES UNDER VINE 4.00

Calleri is a long-standing family name in Albenga, indissolubly linked to both the small village of Salea and the traditional Pigato of western Liguria. The winery was started by Aldo in 1968 and today Marcello carries this heritage forward, adding new acreages dedicated to wine growing. For example, the parcel taken under management in Arnasco municipality, an area particularly well-suited for luscious and spicy wines, also supports Vermentino, Rossese and Ormeasco (a rare traditional cultivar presumably related to Dolcetto). Their wines are extremely well-made, such that it's difficult to choose the best. Their 2017 Dolceacqua entices with its notes of quinine, licorice, tobacco and black pepper on a background of red fruit, and a body that's full of character. Their 2016 Posaù Biamonti features mature aromas and a hint of quinine with nice, young, tight-knit tannins.

# Maixei

LOC. PORTO
18035 DOLCEACQUA [IM]
TEL. +39 0184205015
www.maixei.it

CELLAR SALES
PRE-BOOKED VISITS
ANNUAL PRODUCTION 45,000 bottles
HECTARES UNDER VINE 10.00

Cooperativa Agricola Riviera dei Fiori came into existance in 2007. In recent months, Gianfranco Croese has succeeded Giancarlo Cassini as president, but that has not changed the cooperative's production or agricultural structure, which is firmly tied to its member-growers. The cooperative's premium line is named Maixei, which is local dialect for the dry-stone walls used in terracing. Rossese dominates member vineyards, but Vermentina and Pigato are slowly gaining ground. Their 2016 Dolceacqua Superiore features hints of quinine and a vibrant note of forest undergrowth. In the mouth it proves bold with pliant tannins and a fresh, well-structured body. The lovely 2016 Barbadirame offers up red fruit, tobacco and pepper on a note of fruit preserves. The body proves complex, rich in pulp and warm with good acidity and a long, savory finish.

| | |
|---|---|
| ● Rossese di Dolceacqua '17 | ♟♟ 3* |
| ● Rossese di Dolceacqua Sup. Posaù Biamonti '16 | ♟♟ 5 |
| ○ L'Amiral '17 | ♟♟ 3 |
| ● Rossese di Dolceacqua Sup. Brae '17 | ♟♟ 3 |
| ● Rossese di Dolceacqua Sup. Luvaira '16 | ♟♟ 4 |
| ● Dolceacqua Sup. Vign. Posaù '13 | ♟♟♟ 3* |
| ● Rossese di Dolceacqua Sup. Vign. Luvaira '07 | ♟♟♟ 4* |
| ● Rossese di Dolceacqua Sup. Vign. Posaù '10 | ♟♟♟ 3* |
| ● Rossese di Dolceacqua Sup. Vign. Posaù '08 | ♟♟♟ 3 |
| ● Rossese di Dolceacqua Sup. '16 | ♟♟ 3* |
| ● Rossese di Dolceacqua Sup. Luvaira '15 | ♟♟ 4 |

| | |
|---|---|
| ● Dolceacqua Sup. '16 | ♟♟ 4 |
| ● Dolceacqua Sup. Barbadirame '16 | ♟♟ 4 |
| ○ Riviera Ligure di Ponente Riviera dei Fiori Vermentino '17 | ♟♟ 3 |
| ● Dolceacqua '15 | ♟♟ 3 |
| ● Dolceacqua '14 | ♟♟ 3* |
| ● Dolceacqua '12 | ♟♟ 3 |
| ● Dolceacqua Sup. '15 | ♟♟ 4 |
| ● Dolceacqua Sup. '14 | ♟♟ 4 |
| ● Dolceacqua Sup. '13 | ♟♟ 4 |
| ● Dolceacqua Sup. '12 | ♟♟ 4 |
| ● Dolceacqua Sup. Barbadirame '15 | ♟♟ 4 |
| ● Dolceacqua Sup. Barbadirame '12 | ♟♟ 4 |
| ● Mistral '15 | ♟♟ 4 |

# Il Monticello

VIA GROPPOLO, 7
19038 SARZANA [SP]
TEL. +39 0187621432
www.ilmonticello.it

CELLAR SALES
PRE-BOOKED VISITS
ACCOMMODATION
ANNUAL PRODUCTION 68,000 bottles
HECTARES UNDER VINE 10.00

This winery, founded by Pier Luigi Neri in 1982 and today run by sons Davide and Alessandro, continues its growth thanks to the acquisition of new plots like those at Monterosso di Sarzana. The clay and schist soil are planted with Vermentino, which dominates the eastern part of Liguria, and to a lesser extent, Sangiovese, Canaiolo, Ciliegiolo, Pollera Nera and Massaretta. Operated according to biodynamic methods, the diverse parcels contribute to a small selection of wines, recognizable for their clear expression of the territory's character. Their 2017 Groppolo opens with fresh, mineral hints of flint and medicinal herbs. In the mouth it proves delicate and savory, with a body driven by fruit and a nice, long finish. The 2017 Poggio Paterno, faintly colored with green highlights, opens with vibrant. Aromas. On the palate it's delicate and well-balanced.

| | | |
|---|---|---|
| ○ Colli di Luni Vermentino Groppolo '17 | | ♟♟ 3* |
| ○ Colli di Luni Vermentino Poggio Paterno '17 | | ♟♟ 3 |
| ● Colli di Luni Rosso Poggio dei Magni Ris. '15 | | ♟ 3 |
| ⊙ Colli di Luni Rosato Serasuolo '16 | | ♟♟ 2* |
| ● Colli di Luni Rosso Poggio dei Magni Ris. '11 | | ♟♟ 3 |
| ● Colli di Luni Rosso Rupestro '15 | | ♟♟ 2* |
| ○ Colli di Luni Vermentino '12 | | ♟♟ 3* |
| ○ Colli di Luni Vermentino Groppolo '15 | | ♟♟ 3 |
| ○ Colli di Luni Vermentino Groppolo '14 | | ♟♟ 3* |
| ○ Colli di Luni Vermentino Poggio Paterno '14 | | ♟♟ 3* |
| ○ Passito dei Neri '12 | | ♟♟ 4 |

# Conte Picedi Benettini

VIA MAZZINI, 57
19038 SARZANA [SP]
TEL. +39 0187625147
www.picedibenettini.it

CELLAR SALES
PRE-BOOKED VISITS
ACCOMMODATION
ANNUAL PRODUCTION 30,000 bottles
HECTARES UNDER VINE 7.00

Picedi is an historical family from eastern Liguria. The heart of this estate is Baccano di Arcola at Il Chioso, a walled post-Renaissance villa surrounded by a roughly 150-hectare hillside farm. Picedo is also the surname of viticultural engineer Nino Papirio (called 'il Conte'), quite rightly considered the father of winegrowing and winemaking in Lunigiana. Nowadays he is increasingly assisted by his son Eugenio, who brought innovation to a winery that guarantees high quality and traditional enological production. Their 2017 Vermentino Stemma is aromatically vibrant with notes of chlorophyll and flint on a background of fresh herbs and ferns. In the mouth it opts for elegance and freshness with a long, complex finish. Their 2017 Chioso features different aromas, with ginger and pear merging on a background of fresh Mediterranean herbs. In the mouth it proves close-knit and full of character.

| | | |
|---|---|---|
| ○ Colli di Luni Vermentino Stemma '17 | | ♟♟ 3* |
| ○ Colli di Luni Vermentino Il Chioso '17 | | ♟♟ 3 |
| ● Colli di Luni Rosso Villa Il Chioso '17 | | ♟ 3 |
| ○ Colli di Luni Vermentino Il Chioso '14 | | ♟♟♟ 2* |
| ● Colli di Luni Rosso Villa Il Chioso '15 | | ♟♟ 3 |
| ○ Colli di Luni Vermentino '16 | | ♟♟ 2* |
| ○ Colli di Luni Vermentino '15 | | ♟♟ 2* |
| ○ Colli di Luni Vermentino '13 | | ♟♟ 2* |
| ○ Colli di Luni Vermentino Il Chioso '16 | | ♟♟ 3 |
| ○ Colli di Luni Vermentino Il Chioso '15 | | ♟♟ 3* |
| ○ Colli di Luni Vermentino Il Chioso '13 | | ♟♟ 2* |
| ○ Colli di Luni Vermentino Stemma '16 | | ♟♟ 3 |
| ○ Colli di Luni Vermentino Stemma '15 | | ♟♟ 3 |
| ○ Colli di Luni Vermentino Stemma '14 | | ♟♟ 3 |
| ○ Passito del Chioso '14 | | ♟♟ 5 |

# La Pietra del Focolare

FRAZ. ISOLA DI LUNI
VIA ISOLA, 76
19034 LUNI [SP]
TEL. +39 0187662129
www.lapietradelfocolare.it

CELLAR SALES
PRE-BOOKED VISITS
ANNUAL PRODUCTION 30,000 bottles
HECTARES UNDER VINE 6.00
SUSTAINABLE WINERY

Stefano Salvetti and Laura Angelini continue the progression of wines from La Pietra del Focolare. The winery cultivates some 15 vineyards spread between Sarzana, Castelnuovo Magra and Ortonovo, where the cellar is located in the eastern part of Liguria at the Tuscan border. Vermentino, Albarola, Trebbiano, Malvasia, Ansonica, Sangiovese, Canaiolo and Massareta are assembled into a precise range of wines that take their names from people and historic estates, or from the imagination of the proprietors. Their 2017 Vigna delle Rose is a vibrant wine with lovely notes of flowers, white fruit and aniseed. In the mouth it offers nice freshness with a slight whiff of alcohol. It's a wine long in aftertaste and proves enjoyable with lovely, pleasant length. Their 2017 Villa Linda, a straw-yellow wine, offers up herbaceous notes and quinine. It's pervasive in the mouth, pleasantly savory and well-balanced.

| | |
|---|---|
| ○ Colli di Luni Vermentino Sup. Villa Linda '17 | ▼▼ 4 |
| ○ Vigna delle Rose '17 | ▼▼ 3* |
| ○ Colli di Luni Vermentino Augusto '17 | ▼▼ 3 |
| ○ Solarancio '17 | ▼▼ 5 |
| ○ Colli di Luni Vermentino Augusto '16 | ♀♀ 3 |
| ○ Colli di Luni Vermentino Augusto '15 | ♀♀ 3 |
| ○ Colli di Luni Vermentino L'Aura di Sarticola '16 | ♀♀ 6 |
| ○ Colli di Luni Vermentino Solarancio '15 | ♀♀ 4 |
| ○ Colli di Luni Vermentino Sup. Villa Linda '16 | ♀♀ 4 |
| ○ Colli di Luni Vermentino Sup. Villa Linda '15 | ♀♀ 4 |
| ○ Colli di Luni Vermentino Villa Linda '14 | ♀♀ 3* |

# Poggio dei Gorleri

FRAZ. DIANO GORLERI
VIA SAN LEONARDO
18013 DIANO MARINA [IM]
TEL. +39 0183495207
www.poggiodeigorleri.com

CELLAR SALES
PRE-BOOKED VISITS
ACCOMMODATION
ANNUAL PRODUCTION 80,000 bottles
HECTARES UNDER VINE 10.50

The Merano family continues to invest in the winery's reception activities, having recently expanded the capacity of their hotel with new rooms and a new restaurant offering an a la carte menu during the summer. After obtaining notable results with Pigato, Poggio dei Gorleri is focusing its attention on two Granaccia wines. Shalok is released after 24 months in mid-sized oak casks and one year in bottles, and Rebosso undergoes 12 months of wood aging. Their 2016 Albium is full of character, personality and elegance. It's a pervasive wine in all its structure, proving warm, with notes of broom flowers and ripe, tropical fruit. On the palate it's elegant, well-balanced and appealingly complex. Their 2017 Cycnus exhibits gratifying character, with aromas of white fruit and mineral hints. It's a pleasant wine thanks to its lovely, still somewhat green finesse.

| | |
|---|---|
| ○ Riviera Ligure di Ponente Pigato Albium '16 | ▼▼ 5 |
| ○ Riviera Ligure di Ponente Pigato Cycnus '17 | ▼▼ 3* |
| ● Riviera Ligure di Ponente Granaccia Shalok '15 | ▼▼ 5 |
| ○ Riviera Ligure di Ponente Vermentino Blu di Mare '17 | ▼▼ 3 |
| ○ Riviera Ligure di Ponente Vermentino V. Sorì '17 | ▼▼ 3 |
| ● Ormeasco di Pornassio Peinetti '17 | ▼ 3 |
| ○ Riviera Ligure di Ponente Pigato Albium '15 | ♀♀♀ 5 |
| ○ Riviera Ligure di Ponente Pigato Albium '13 | ♀♀♀ 5 |
| ○ Riviera Ligure di Ponente Pigato Cycnus '13 | ♀♀♀ 3* |

## Terenzuola

VIA VERCALDA, 14
54035 FOSDINOVO [MS]
TEL. +39 0187670387
www.terenzuola.it

PRE-BOOKED VISITS
ANNUAL PRODUCTION 180,000 bottles
HECTARES UNDER VINE 18.00

Ivan Giuliani works about 20 hectares of vineyards in a vast territory that stretches from Bonassola (Liguria) to Tuscany, near Carrara, where a historic vineyard of just four hectares give rise to Permano Rosso (not submitted for tasting this year). Even the elevations are varying, with plots that are just a few meters above sea level (in the Cinque Terre appellation) to about 450 meters, where the grapes for their Fosso di Corsano are cultivated. Already this year Ivan, who had already starting converting to organic, began working with spontaneous fermentation, which he uses with all his musts. Their 2017 Fosso di Corsano is spectacular, offering up elegant and assertive sulfurous notes on a bed of Mediterranean herbs and hay accompanied by notes of medicinal herbs and lime. On the palate it's delicate and complex, with a generous structure and notable length. Their Sciacchetrà Riserva, a brilliant, clear amber-colored 2016, features generous and harmonic notes of ripe apricots, honey and walnuts.

| | |
|---|---|
| ○ Colli di Luni Vermentino Sup. Fosso di Corsano '17 | ♔♔♔ 3* |
| ○ Cinque Terre Sciacchetrà Ris. '16 | ♔♔ 8 |
| ○ Cinque Terre '17 | ♔♔ 4 |
| ○ Colli di Luni Bianco Permano '16 | ♔♔ 5 |
| ● Merla della Miniera '15 | ♔♔ 4 |
| ○ Colli di Luni Vermentino Sup. Fosso di Corsano '16 | ♕♕♕ 3* |
| ○ Colli di Luni Vermentino Sup. Fosso di Corsano '11 | ♕♕♕ 3* |
| ○ Cinque Terre '16 | ♕♕ 4 |
| ○ Colli di Luni Vermentino Sup. Fosso di Corsano '15 | ♕♕ 3 |
| ○ Colli di Luni Vermentino V. Basse '16 | ♕♕ 3* |
| ○ Colli di Luni Vermentino V. Basse '15 | ♕♕ 3* |
| ● Merla della Miniera '14 | ♕♕ 4 |
| ● Permano Rosso '13 | ♕♕ 5 |

## Terre Bianche

LOC. ARCAGNA
18035 DOLCEACQUA [IM]
TEL. +39 018431426
www.terrebianche.com

CELLAR SALES
PRE-BOOKED VISITS
ACCOMMODATION
ANNUAL PRODUCTION 55,000 bottles
HECTARES UNDER VINE 8.50
SUSTAINABLE WINERY

In terms of history, size and purpose, Arcagna is the most highly-prized of the vineyards belonging to the winery of Filippo Rondelli and Franco Locani. Located in the Val Nerva at 300 to 400 meters above sea level, it holds an eastern exposure. And, cultivated following organic winemaking methods, it regularly delivers some of the most elegant and best-tasting Rossese of the appellation. But Terre Bianche's brilliance goes further. Vermentino and Pigato, serving more than as simple complements to the range, offer natural and faithful expressions of their varieties. Their 2016 Bricco Arcagna, a wine colored a brilliant and dense ruby garnet, is elegant with a lovely sensation of licorice and black pepper across a bed of ripe red fruit. The body is warm, with close-woven tannins and a long finish. Their 2016 Terrabianca is also vibrant, with a note of wood that evolves into tanned leather. Its body features bold structure and character.

| | |
|---|---|
| ● Rossese di Dolceacqua Bricco Arcagna '16 | ♔♔ 6 |
| ● Rossese di Dolceacqua Terrabianca '16 | ♔♔ 5 |
| ○ Riviera Ligure di Ponente Pigato '17 | ♔♔ 3 |
| ○ Riviera Ligure di Ponente Vermentino '17 | ♔♔ 3 |
| ● Rossese di Dolceacqua '17 | ♔ 3 |
| ● Dolceacqua Bricco Arcagna '12 | ♕♕♕ 5 |
| ● Rossese di Dolceacqua '12 | ♕♕♕ 3* |
| ● Rossese di Dolceacqua Bricco Arcagna '09 | ♕♕♕ 4 |
| ● Rossese di Dolceacqua Bricco Arcagna '08 | ♕♕♕ 5 |
| ○ Riviera Ligure di Ponente Pigato '16 | ♕♕ 3 |
| ● Rossese di Dolceacqua '16 | ♕♕ 3 |
| ● Rossese di Dolceacqua Bricco Arcagna '15 | ♕♕ 5 |

# Il Torchio

VIA DELLE COLLINE, 24
19033 CASTELNUOVO MAGRA [SP]
TEL. +39 3318585633
gildamusetti@gmail.com

**CELLAR SALES**
**PRE-BOOKED VISITS**
**ACCOMMODATION AND RESTAURANT SERVICE**
**ANNUAL PRODUCTION 60,000 bottles**
**HECTARES UNDER VINE 12.00**

Il Torchio, the result of intuition from Giorgio Tendola, a true pioneer in Lunigiana winemaking, is today in the hands of his grandchildren, Gilda and Edoardo. In an unusual manner for the area, the grapes are cultivated in one large vineyard, a south-facing ampitheater on the Castelnuovo hill that looks toward the sea at elevations of 20 to 80 meters. The lower, younger part has clay matrix soil characteristic of Colli di Luni, whereas the older, higher part is on rocky soil, and produces wines with greater vigor and freshness, primarily Vermentino. Two wines were submitted for tasting, their 2017 Bianco with aromas of white fruit across hints of grassy field. Its complexity expands across the palate, with tropical fragrances and a note of almond. The mouth is austere, rich in extract with a long finish. Their 2017 Nero gratifies, with its vibrant aromas of morello cherry and wild berry, and a long, velvety body.

| | |
|---|---|
| ○ Il Bianco '17 | 🍷🍷 3 |
| ● Il Nero '17 | 🍷🍷 4 |
| ● Colli di Luni Rosso Il Torchio '13 | 🍷🍷 4 |
| ○ Colli di Luni Vermentino '16 | 🍷🍷 3 |
| ○ Colli di Luni Vermentino '15 | 🍷🍷 3 |
| ○ Colli di Luni Vermentino '14 | 🍷🍷 3* |
| ○ Colli di Luni Vermentino Il Bianco '14 | 🍷🍷 3 |
| ○ Colli di Luni Vermentino Il Bianco '13 | 🍷🍷 3 |
| ○ Colli di Luni Vermentino Il Torchio '13 | 🍷🍷 3* |
| ● Il Nero '16 | 🍷🍷 4 |
| ○ Stralunato '15 | 🍷🍷 3 |

# Vis Amoris

LOC. CARAMAGNA
S.DA PER VASIA, 1
18100 IMPERIA
TEL. +39 3483959569
www.visamoris.it

**CELLAR SALES**
**PRE-BOOKED VISITS**
**ANNUAL PRODUCTION 24,000 bottles**
**HECTARES UNDER VINE 3.50**
**VITICULTURE METHOD Certified Organic**
**SUSTAINABLE WINERY**

Vis Amoris has been experiencing significant changes. Robert Tozzi is still in charge of the vineyards and cellar, but his son Simone has joined as administrator while finishing his studies in enology and viticulture at Alba. At the same time, Roberto's brother Danilo is getting help in the business and marketing side from his children, Francesca and Mattia, who are still students. Thus, the next generation is ready to take the reins of this lovely Imperia winery, which is well-known especially for its versatile Pigato-based range of wines. Their 2017 Verum, a brilliantly colored wine, offers up flavors of spices. The body exhibits lovely harmony and lingering aftertaste, making for a version that respects the qualities of the cultivar. Their 2016 Sogno features a young, vibrant color, flavors of chlorophyll, mint, apricot and melon. The wine finishes with a balanced aftertaste of aromatic herbs and rosemary.

| | |
|---|---|
| ○ Riviera Ligure di Ponente Pigato Verum '17 | 🍷🍷 3* |
| ○ Riviera Ligure di Ponente Pigato Sogno '16 | 🍷🍷 4 |
| ○ Vis Amoris Brut M.Cl. | 🍷🍷 5 |
| ○ Riviera Ligure di Ponente Pigato Domè '17 | 🍷 4 |
| ○ Riviera Ligure di Ponente Pigato Domè '13 | 🍷🍷 3* |
| ○ Riviera Ligure di Ponente Pigato Sogno '15 | 🍷🍷 4 |
| ○ Riviera Ligure di Ponente Pigato Sogno '14 | 🍷🍷 4 |
| ○ Riviera Ligure di Ponente Pigato Sogno '13 | 🍷🍷 4 |
| ○ Riviera Ligure di Ponente Pigato Verum '16 | 🍷🍷 3 |

## Michele Alessandri

VIA UMBERTO I, 15
18020 RANZO [IM]
TEL. +39 0183318114
az.alessandricarlo@libero.it

CELLAR SALES
PRE-BOOKED VISITS
ANNUAL PRODUCTION 23,000 bottles
HECTARES UNDER VINE 2.13

| | |
|---|---|
| ● Pornassio '17 | ♟♟ 3 |
| ○ Riviera Ligure di Ponente Vermentino '17 | ♟♟ 2* |
| ○ Riviera Ligure di Ponente Pigato '17 | ♟ 3 |

## aMaccia

FRAZ. BORGO
VIA UMBERTO I, 54
18020 RANZO [IM]
TEL. +39 0183318003
www.amaccia.it

CELLAR SALES
PRE-BOOKED VISITS
ACCOMMODATION
ANNUAL PRODUCTION 25,000 bottles
HECTARES UNDER VINE 3.80
SUSTAINABLE WINERY

| | |
|---|---|
| ○ Riviera Ligure di Ponente Pigato '17 | ♟♟ 3 |
| ○ Riviera Ligure di Ponente Pigato Collezione '16 | ♟♟ 3 |

## Riccardo Arrigoni

VIA SARZANA, 224
19126 LA SPEZIA
TEL. +39 0187504060
www.arrigoni1913.it

CELLAR SALES
PRE-BOOKED VISITS
ACCOMMODATION AND RESTAURANT SERVICE
ANNUAL PRODUCTION 150,000 bottles
HECTARES UNDER VINE 18.00
SUSTAINABLE WINERY

| | |
|---|---|
| ○ Cinque Terre Sciacchetrà Passito Rosa di Maggio '09 | ♟♟ 8 |
| ○ Cinque Terre Tramonti '17 | ♟♟ 3* |
| ○ Colli di Luni Vermentino V. del Prefetto '17 | ♟♟ 3 |

## Berry and Berry

VIA MATTEOTTI, 2
17020 BALESTRINO [SV]
TEL. +39 3332805368
www.berryandberry.it

CELLAR SALES
PRE-BOOKED VISITS
ANNUAL PRODUCTION 8,500 bottles
HECTARES UNDER VINE 2.00

| | |
|---|---|
| ○ Baitinin '17 | ♟♟ 4 |
| ○ Campulou '16 | ♟ 5 |
| ● Lappazucche | ♟ 4 |

## Cantine Bondonor

VIA ISOLA ALTA, 53
19034 LUNI [SP]
TEL. +39 3488713641
www.cantinebondonor.it

ANNUAL PRODUCTION 15,000 bottles
HECTARES UNDER VINE 3.00

| | |
|---|---|
| ○ Colli di Luni Vermentino Aegidius Vintage I '16 | ♟♟ 4 |
| ☉ RosaLuna '17 | ♟♟ 3 |
| ○ Colli di Luni Vermentino Lunaris '17 | ♟ 3 |

## Andrea Bruzzone

VIA BOLZANETO, 96R
16162 GENOVA
TEL. +39 0107455157
www.andreabruzzonevini.it

CELLAR SALES
PRE-BOOKED VISITS
ANNUAL PRODUCTION 10,000 bottles
HECTARES UNDER VINE 2.00
SUSTAINABLE WINERY

| | |
|---|---|
| ○ Val Polcèvera Bianchetta Genovese Bunassa '17 | ♟♟ 3 |
| ○ Val Polcèvera Coronata La Superba '17 | ♟♟ 3 |
| ○ Val Polcèvera Janua Brut '16 | ♟♟ 6 |

## Luca Calvini

VIA SOLARO, 76/78A
18038 SANREMO [IM]
TEL. +39 0184660242
www.luigicalvini.com

CELLAR SALES
PRE-BOOKED VISITS
ANNUAL PRODUCTION 50,000 bottles
HECTARES UNDER VINE 3.50
SUSTAINABLE WINERY

| | |
|---|---|
| ○ Riviera Ligure di Ponente Vermentino Gold Label '17 | ¶¶ 5 |
| ○ Riviera Ligure di Ponente Pigato '17 | ¶¶ 3 |

## La Cappelletta di Portofino

VIA DEL FONDACO, 30
16034 PORTOFINO [GE]
TEL. +39 3482551501
info@lacappellettadiportofino.it

ANNUAL PRODUCTION 3,700 bottles
HECTARES UNDER VINE 1.00
SUSTAINABLE WINERY

| | |
|---|---|
| ○ Portofino Vermentino '17 | ¶¶ 5 |

## I Cerri

VIA GARIBOTTI
19012 CARRO [SP]
TEL. +39 3485102780
www.icerrivaldivara.it

ANNUAL PRODUCTION 8,000 bottles
HECTARES UNDER VINE 1.00

| | |
|---|---|
| ○ Cian dei Seri '17 | ¶¶ 3* |
| ○ Campo Grande '17 | ¶ 3 |
| ● Fonte Dietro il Sole '17 | ¶ 3 |

## Gajaudo

LOC. BUNDA
S.DA PROV.LE 7
18035 ISOLABONA [IM]
TEL. +39 0184208095
www.gajaudo.it

CELLAR SALES
PRE-BOOKED VISITS
ANNUAL PRODUCTION 110,000 bottles
HECTARES UNDER VINE 10.00

| | |
|---|---|
| ● Dolceacqua '17 | ¶¶ 3* |
| ● Dolceacqua Sup. Vign. Pini '16 | ¶¶ 4 |
| ● Dolceacqua Arcagna '16 | ¶¶ 4 |

## Guglierame

VIA CASTELLO, 4
18024 PORNASSIO [IM]
TEL. +39 3475696718
www.ormeasco-guglierame.it

CELLAR SALES
ANNUAL PRODUCTION 15,000 bottles
HECTARES UNDER VINE 2.50

| | |
|---|---|
| ● Ormeasco di Pornassio Sup. '15 | ¶¶ 4 |
| ● Ormeasco di Pornassio '16 | ¶ 4 |

## Gino Pino

FRAZ. MISSANO
VIA PODESTÀ, 31
16030 CASTIGLIONE CHIAVARESE [GE]
TEL. +39 0185408036
pinogino.az.agricola@tin.it

ANNUAL PRODUCTION 25,000 bottles
HECTARES UNDER VINE 3.50

| | |
|---|---|
| ○ Golfo del Tigullio-Portofino Vermentino '17 | ¶¶ 3 |
| ○ Portofino Bianchetta Genovese '17 | ¶ 3 |
| ● Portofino Ciliegiolo '17 | ¶ 3 |

# Podere Grecale

LOC. BUSSANA
VIA CIOUSSE
18038 SANREMO [IM]
TEL. +39 01841955158
www.poderegrecale.it

CELLAR SALES
PRE-BOOKED VISITS
ANNUAL PRODUCTION 18,000 bottles
HECTARES UNDER VINE 3.00

| | | |
|---|---|---|
| ● Riviera Ligure di Ponente Sup. Granaccia Beusi '16 | | ♟♟ 4 |
| ○ Riviera Ligure di Ponente Vermentino '17 | ♟♟ 3 | |

# Podere Lavandaro

VIA CASTIGLIONE
54035 FOSDINOVO [MS]
TEL. +39 018768202
www.poderelavandaro.it

CELLAR SALES
PRE-BOOKED VISITS
ANNUAL PRODUCTION 25,000 bottles
HECTARES UNDER VINE 5.00

| | |
|---|---|
| ○ Colli di Luni Vermentino '17 | ♟♟ 3 |
| ● Vermentino Nero '17 | ♟♟ 3 |
| ● Vignanera '16 | ♟♟ 3 |
| ⊙ Merlarosa '17 | ♟ 3 |

# Rossana Ruffini

VIA TIROLO, 58
19020 BOLANO [SP]
TEL. +39 0187939988
g.brandani@libero.it

ANNUAL PRODUCTION 10,000 bottles
HECTARES UNDER VINE 3.00

| | |
|---|---|
| ○ Colli di Luni Vermentino Costa Tirolo '17 | ♟♟ 2* |
| ○ Colli di Luni Vermentino Portolano '17 | ♟♟ 2* |
| ● Portolano Rosso '17 | ♟ 3 |

# Natale Sassarini

LOC. PIAN DEL CORSO 1
19016 MONTEROSSO AL MARE [SP]
TEL. +39 0187818063
www.sassarini5terre.it

| | |
|---|---|
| ○ Cinque Terre Sciacchetrà '16 | ♟♟ 5 |
| ○ Cinque Terre '17 | ♟♟ 4 |
| ○ Cinque Terre Cian du Corsu '17 | ♟♟ 4 |

# Terre di Levanto

LOC. SAN GOTTARDO, 1
19015 LEVANTO [SP]
TEL. +39 3395432482
www.terredilevanto.com

CELLAR SALES
PRE-BOOKED VISITS
ANNUAL PRODUCTION 2,500 bottles
HECTARES UNDER VINE 2.50
SUSTAINABLE WINERY

| | |
|---|---|
| ○ Colline di Levanto Bianco Giaè '17 | ♟♟ 3 |
| ● Colline di Levanto Rosso di Mare '17 | ♟ 3 |
| ○ Gianco '17 | ♟ 2 |

# Zangani

LOC. PONZANO SUPERIORE
VIA GRAMSCI, 46
19037 SANTO STEFANO DI MAGRA [SP]
TEL. +39 0187632406
www.zangani.it

CELLAR SALES
PRE-BOOKED VISITS
ACCOMMODATION AND RESTAURANT SERVICE
ANNUAL PRODUCTION 40,000 bottles
HECTARES UNDER VINE 10.00

| | |
|---|---|
| ○ Colli di Luni Vermentino Sup. Boceda '17 | ♟♟ 4 |
| ○ Colli di Luni Vermentino Mortedo '17 | ♟♟ 3 |
| ● Colli di Luni Rosso Montale '17 | ♟ 3 |

# LOMBARDY

Even if it's not the first region that comes to mind when you think of Italian wine, this year's tastings gave us a sense of Veneto's extraordinary vitality. And yet year after year its viticulture and its wines prove to be on the rise, foremost when it comes to quality, but also on the market. We start by mentioning two cornerstones of classic Italian sparkling winemaking. Franciacorta leads the category with more than 17 million bottles produced in 2017. Its producers (more than 100) operate at the heights of excellence, and indeed nine of our Tre Bicchieri (24 in all, a record) go to the appellation. And there's big news among this veteran platoon of wineries: our Sparkler of the Year award goes to the Ziliani brothers' Guido Berlucchi & C., with their spectacular selection of cuvées. Even if Oltrepò hasn't launched definitively as a territory for sparkling winemaking, it has plenty of ammunition. In fact seven of its wines (of various typologies) received our highest honors. Four of these are cuvées made with that local classic, Pinot Nero, while two other producers, Conte Vistarino and Marchese Adorno (who are making their debut in the Tre Bicchieri club) took home golds for their two traditional Pinot Neros, thus confirming the territory's extraordinary gift for this difficult grape. Ca' di Frara were also awarded for the first time thanks to their Riesling Riserva, a feat that further highlights the district's unique ability to successfully host some of the world's most 'complicated' cultivar. It's worth mentioning that the five Valtellinas, Ar.Pe.Pe., Rainoldi, Dirupi, Mamete Prevostini and Nino Negri also offer superwines made with grapes cultivated in the shadow of the Alps. And once again, Ca' Maiol brings home its umpteenth Tre Bicchieri for its sumptuous Lugana (another first-rate terroir). Though we'd like to focus on two new releases. One is the Noventa family's 2016 Botticino Gobbio, a 'little-big' artisanal wine from an area that's still not particularly well-known. The other is a truly noteworthy feat, the double-debut of a winery, Mattia Vezzola's Costaripa, and an extremely promising appellation, Valtènesi, among our awards. In fact, Costaripa's Molmenti, a Chiaretto made with Groppello that's only now been released, is extraordinary proof of this Doc Garda's potential and the enological talent of Mattia Vezzola (whose name until today was automatically associated with Franciacorta). Il Molmenti is a wine of such extreme finesse that it convinced us to establish a new award: Rosé of the Year.

## Marchese Adorno

VIA GARLASSOLO, 30
27050 RETORBIDO [PV]
TEL. +39 0383374404
www.marcheseadorno-wines.it

CELLAR SALES
PRE-BOOKED VISITS
ANNUAL PRODUCTION 250,000 bottles
HECTARES UNDER VINE 85.00

For some years now the winery owned by the marquis Marcello Cattaneo Adorno family have been trying to develop their significant resources and potential. Their sizable investments included the building of a splendid cellar, renovation of the entire property and new management of their 60 hectares of vineyards. Riesling, Barbera and Pinot Nero are the principal cultivar used for their ambitious selection of wines, which is overseen by young Filippo Prè and Enrico Rovino, along with the expert technical support of Francesco Cervetti. Their best Rile Nero yet gets a gold. 2015 gave rise to an elegant, precise, balsamic wine with multivariate aromas of blackcurrant, dried flowers, cloves, coffee and cocoa. In the mouth it proves vibrant and racy towards the end. Their younger 2016 Brugherio also delivers. It's a balanced, linear wine that's redolent of forest undergrowth and mint. Their 2016 Riesling Arcolaio is a savory, mineral wine that's both vibrant and deep. Their 2015 Barbera exhibits typicity and fragrance.

| | |
|---|---|
| ● OP Pinot Nero Rile Nero '15 | ▼▼▼ 5 |
| ● OP Pinot Nero Brugherio '16 | ▼▼ 2* |
| ○ OP Riesling Arcolaio '16 | ▼▼ 3* |
| ● OP Barbera V. del Re '15 | ▼▼ 4 |
| ● OP Bonarda Costa del Sole '17 | ▼ 3 |
| ○ Pinot Grigio '17 | ▼ 3 |
| ● Cliviano '15 | ♀♀ 3 |
| ● Cliviano '14 | ♀♀ 3 |
| ● Cliviano '13 | ♀♀ 3 |
| ● OP Barbera V. del Re '14 | ♀♀ 4 |
| ● OP Barbera V. del Re '12 | ♀♀ 4 |
| ● OP Bonarda Vivace Costa del Sole '16 | ♀♀ 2* |
| ● OP Bonarda Vivace Costa del Sole '15 | ♀♀ 2* |
| ● OP Pinot Nero Brugherio '15 | ♀♀ 2* |
| ● OP Pinot Nero Brugherio '14 | ♀♀ 2* |
| ● OP Pinot Nero Rile Nero '13 | ♀♀ 5 |
| ○ OP Riesling Sup. Arcolaio '13 | ♀♀ 3* |

## F.lli Agnes

VIA CAMPO DEL MONTE, 1
27040 ROVESCALA [PV]
TEL. +39 038575206
www.fratelliagnes.it

CELLAR SALES
PRE-BOOKED VISITS
ANNUAL PRODUCTION 120,000 bottles
HECTARES UNDER VINE 21.00

Rovescala is the homeland of Bonarda, the cultivar that serves as the basis of Sergio and Cristiano Agnes's selection. Every possible variation is offered, with only native yeasts used, making for a range of wines with a marked territorial identity. The terrain, which is some of the best in the territory, was identified by the brothers' father, Luigi, and their uncle Alberto. It was chosen to host that particular variety of Croatina known as 'Pignola' because of the small, compact shape of the bunch on the vine (resembling a pine). The fact that they work with practically only variety, something that's rare in Oltrepò Pavese, allows them to hone their resources. Their notable and consistent results are proof that theirs is a winning approach. Fratelli Agnes always do a nice job during years that are difficult for Bonarda, as evidenced by their 2017 Campo del Monte. It's a fragrant wine in its fruit and delicate in its tannins. Their highly pleasant 2017 Cresta del Ghiffi, as usual, is a more sweetish wine. Their 2016 Loghetto exhibits strongly balsamic aromas.

| | |
|---|---|
| ● OP Bonarda Frizzante Campo del Monte '17 | ▼▼ 2* |
| ● OP Bonarda Frizzante Cresta del Ghiffi '17 | ▼▼ 2* |
| ● Loghetto '16 | ▼ 5 |
| ● OP Bonarda Vivace Campo del Monte '15 | ♀♀♀ 2* |
| ● OP Bonarda Millennium '13 | ♀♀ 4 |
| ● OP Bonarda Vivace Campo del Monte '16 | ♀♀ 2* |
| ● OP Bonarda Vivace Cresta del Ghiffi '16 | ♀♀ 2* |
| ● OP Bonarda Vivace Cresta del Ghiffi '15 | ♀♀ 2* |
| ● Possessione del Console '15 | ♀♀ 3 |

# Antica Fratta

VIA FONTANA, 11
25040 MONTICELLI BRUSATI [BS]
TEL. +39 030652068
www.anticafratta.it

**CELLAR SALES**
**PRE-BOOKED VISITS**
**ANNUAL PRODUCTION** 350,000 bottles
**HECTARES UNDER VINE** 35.00

Monticelli Brusati's Antica Cantina Fratta is owned by the Ziliani family but the producer has its own identity in terms of management and estate vineyards. It's situated in a lovely 19th century palazzo that the family renovated in the 1960s and that's known as 'il Cantinon' for its scenic underground vaults, which form a Greek cross. Indeed, the palazzo was once the residence of a rich wine merchant, and today it hosts events and receptions. Their Essence Brut is among the best wines to emerge from the 2014 vintage. It impressed for its straw-yellow color and fine perlage, its lovely flowery aromas and savory, taut, full palate that finishes on long notes of white peace. Their 2014 Nature, a wine made with Chardonnay and a small (10%) amount of Pinot Nero, ages for more than three years on the lees. It's a crisp, spirited, elegant wine. Their 2014 Rosé also did extremely well. It's a pale rose-colored wine that features aromas of raspberry and red currant.

| | | |
|---|---|---|
| ○ Franciacorta Brut Essence '14 | ♈♈ | 5 |
| ○ Franciacorta Nature Essence '14 | ♈♈ | 5 |
| ○ Franciacorta Rosé Essence '14 | ♈♈ | 5 |
| ○ Franciacorta Brut Essence '13 | ♈♈ | 5 |
| ○ Franciacorta Brut Essence '08 | ♈♈ | 5 |
| ○ Franciacorta Extra Brut Quintessence Ris. '07 | ♈♈ | 7 |
| ○ Franciacorta Extra Brut Quintessence Ris. '07 | ♈♈ | 7 |
| ○ Franciacorta Nature Essence '13 | ♈♈ | 5 |
| ○ Franciacorta Nature Essence '11 | ♈♈ | 5 |
| ○ Franciacorta Rosé Essence '11 | ♈♈ | 5 |
| ○ Franciacorta Rosé Essence '10 | ♈♈ | 5 |
| ○ Franciacorta Satèn Essence '11 | ♈♈ | 5 |
| ○ Franciacorta Satèn Essence '11 | ♈♈ | 5 |
| ○ Franciacorta Satèn Essence '10 | ♈♈ | 5 |

# Antica Tesa - Noventa

LOC. MATTINA
VIA MERANO, 28
25080 BOTTICINO [BS]
TEL. +39 0302691500
info@noventabotticino.it

**CELLAR SALES**
**PRE-BOOKED VISITS**
**ANNUAL PRODUCTION** 40,000 bottles
**HECTARES UNDER VINE** 10.00

Once again there's new life in this small but prestigious family-run winery that's helping promote the reputation of the Botticino appellation. For more than 40 years Pierangelo Noventa and his family have been working their vineyards here passionately. These are organically cultivated and situated in a scenic position as 450 meters of elevation with ideal exposure to the sun. Having eschewed more aggressive maturation and grape drying in recent years, their range of reds exhibits elegance and a remarkable finesse. 2016 gave rise to an achievement that Pierangelo and his daughter Alessandra have long sought after. Their first Tre Bicchieri is made with grapes from their Gobbio vineyards, planted more than 20 years ago at 400 meters above sea level on calcareous-clay terrain. It's a vibrant red with ruby garnet highlights, rich in fruity notes and spices with nuances of cocoa. It impressed for its balance, elegance and persistence on the palate. Hats off!

| | | |
|---|---|---|
| ● Botticino Gobbio '16 | ♈♈♈ | 5 |
| ● Botticino Colle degli Ulivi '16 | ♈♈ | 2* |
| ● Botticino Pià della Tesa '16 | ♈♈ | 3 |
| ● Botticino Gobbio '15 | ♈♈ | 5 |
| ● Botticino Pià de la Tesa '15 | ♈♈ | 3 |
| ● Botticino Pià de la Tesa '12 | ♈♈ | 3 |
| ● Botticino Pià de la Tesa '11 | ♈♈ | 3 |
| ● Botticino Pià de la Tesa '10 | ♈♈ | 3 |
| ● Botticino Pià de la Tesa '08 | ♈♈ | 3* |
| ● Botticino V. del Gobbio '11 | ♈♈ | 5 |
| ● Botticino V. del Gobbio '10 | ♈♈ | 5 |
| ● Botticino V. del Gobbio '09 | ♈♈ | 5 |
| ● Botticino V. del Gobbio 50 '12 | ♈♈ | 5 |

## Antinori - Tenuta Montenisa

Fraz. Calino
via Paolo VI, 62
25046 Cazzago San Martino [BS]
Tel. +39 0307750838
www.montenisa.it

PRE-BOOKED VISITS
ANNUAL PRODUCTION 300,000 bottles
HECTARES UNDER VINE 60.00

The Antinoris would have to own a winery dedicated entirely to sparkling wines in a territory as prestigious as Franciacorta. Indeed, in 1999 they purchased the count Maggi family's lovely estate of Calino. After renovating the vineyards and the cellar, Montenisa was born. Their selection is comprised of two lines, one dedicated to the single-vintages and Riservas produced only during the best years. This year, a Brut Rosé was the cuvée that most impressed among the Franciacortina wines submitted by this historic producer. It's an antique rose-colored wine, pale and brilliant, with fine perlage. On the nose it features aromas of small red fruit, fresh and lively, revived by a citrusy nuance. On the palate it's savory, energetic and fresh in its fruit. Their Cuvée Royale and Blanc de Blancs are both top wines, while we would have expected greater freshness and vitality from their 2012 Donna Cora.

| | | |
|---|---|---|
| ○ Franciacorta Brut Blanc de Blancs | ♈♈ | 5 |
| ○ Franciacorta Brut Cuvée Royale | ♈♈ | 5 |
| ⊙ Franciacorta Brut Rosé | ♈♈ | 5 |
| ○ Franciacorta Brut Satèn Donna Cora '12 | ♈ | 6 |
| ○ Franciacorta Brut Conte Aimo '07 | ♉♉ | 8 |
| ○ Franciacorta Brut Conte Aimo Ris. '09 | ♉♉ | 8 |
| ○ Franciacorta Brut Contessa Maggi '06 | ♉♉ | 7 |
| ○ Franciacorta Brut Contessa Maggi Ris. '07 | ♉♉ | 7 |
| ○ Franciacorta Brut Satèn Donna Cora '11 | ♉♉ | 6 |
| ○ Franciacorta Satèn '09 | ♉♉ | 6 |
| ○ Franciacorta Satèn '04 | ♉♉ | 6 |
| ○ Franciacorta Satèn '04 | ♉♉ | 6 |

## Ar.Pe.Pe.

via del Buon Consiglio, 4
23100 Sondrio
Tel. +39 0342214120
www.arpepe.com

CELLAR SALES
PRE-BOOKED VISITS
ANNUAL PRODUCTION 100,000 bottles
HECTARES UNDER VINE 13.00

The Pelizzati Perego family bolstered by a legacy of four generations of vine growers, have managed to develop an unmistakable style, one of the keys to their success. It's based on subtle, steady, airy wines that are only released after a lengthy stay in their bottles. There may be more wines, and crus, but the substance and consistently outstanding quality hasn't changed. They've decided to delay the release of their Sassella Rocce Rosse, which will be presented next year. Their 2009 Sassella Vigna Regina, a wine of rare finesse, is one of a kind. It's vibrant and etheric, with extraordinary sensations of raspberries, fresh notes of roots and delicate spices. On the palate its tannins are elegant and silky, to say the least. Pulp is harmoniously integrated and long in its balanced, embellished finish. Their 2009 Grumello Buon Consiglio also delivered. It's redolent of tobacco, licorice and rhubarb while in the mouth it proves close-knit and continuous, very charming, with a merry, harmonious finish. Their 2009 Grumello Sant'Antonio Riserva also made it into our finals.

| | | |
|---|---|---|
| ● Valtellina Sup. Sassella V. Regina Ris. '09 | ♈♈♈ | 8 |
| ● Valtellina Sup. Grumello Buon Consiglio Ris. '09 | ♈♈ | 8 |
| ● Valtellina Sup. Grumello Sant'Antonio Ris. '09 | ♈♈ | 8 |
| ● Rosso di Valtellina '16 | ♈♈ | 4 |
| ● Valtellina Sup. Il Pettirosso '15 | ♈♈ | 5 |
| ● Valtellina Sup. Inferno Sesto Canto Ris. '09 | ♈♈ | 8 |
| ● Valtellina Sup. Grumello Buon Consiglio Ris. '07 | ♉♉♉ | 6 |
| ● Valtellina Sup. Sassella Rocce Rosse Ris. '07 | ♉♉♉ | 8 |
| ● Valtellina Sup. Sassella Rocce Rosse Ris. '05 | ♉♉♉ | 7 |
| ● Valtellina Sup. Sassella Stella Retica Ris. '10 | ♉♉♉ | 5 |

# Giovanni Avanzi

VIA TREVISAGO, 19
25080 MANERBA DEL GARDA [BS]
TEL. +39 0365551013
www.avanzi.net

CELLAR SALES
PRE-BOOKED VISITS
RESTAURANT SERVICE
ANNUAL PRODUCTION 600,000 bottles
HECTARES UNDER VINE 63.00

The Avanzi family took their first steps in the world of wine almost 90 years ago, in 1931. Today the fifth generation of family are overseeing 70 hectares of vineyards and olive groves, divided into four different terroir in Garda. These give rise to their selection of high-quality wines (from various local appellations) and olive oils. In 2007 their facility was entirely renovated with the latest equipment and new vaulted underground cellars. For some years now the family have also been working in Franciacorta, where they created Romantica. Their 2017 Rosso Riviera is a truly interesting wine, a classic blend of Groppello, Barbera, Sangiovese and Marzemino aged in small, new, wood barrels. It's dark, ruby red in color, while on the nose it offers up vibrant aromas of red fruit and spices, with herbaceous and oaky nuances. On the palate it comes through plush, whole, rich in fruit and smooth tannins. Their 2017 Dorobianco is a savory, crisp wine with lovely notes of white fruit, chlorophyll and sap. Their 2014 Lugana Riserva Borghetta has aged well.

| | |
|---|---|
| ○ Garda Bresciano Bianco Dorobianco '17 | ▼▼ 3 |
| ⊙ Garda Brut M. Cl. Rosé | ▼▼ 2* |
| ○ Lugana Borghetta Ris. '14 | ▼▼ 4 |
| ● Riviera del Garda Bresciano Rosso Cl. Sup. '16 | ▼▼ 3 |
| ⊙ Valtènesi Riviera del Garda Cl. Chiaretto '17 | ▼▼ 3 |
| ● Garda Cabernet Sauvignon Bragagna '15 | ▼ 4 |
| ● Garda Cl. Groppello Predelli '17 | ▼ 3 |
| ○ Lugana Brut | ▼ 3 |
| ○ Lugana di Sirmione '17 | ▼ 2 |
| ● Montecorno '15 | ▼ 5 |
| ○ Dorobianco Avanzi '16 | ♈♈ 2* |
| ● Garda Cl. Groppello '14 | ♈♈ 3 |
| ⊙ Valtènesi Chiaretto Giovanni Avanzi '16 | ♈♈ 2* |

# Ballabio

VIA SAN BIAGIO, 32
27045 CASTEGGIO [PV]
TEL. +39 0383805728
www.ballabio.net

CELLAR SALES
PRE-BOOKED VISITS
ANNUAL PRODUCTION 100,000 bottles
HECTARES UNDER VINE 60.00

Angelo Ballabio was one of Oltrepò Pavese's viticultural pioneers. Today he's a legend for Filippo Nevelli, the winery's current manager, as well as his son Mattia, who's taking on a more active role. Their facility is everything a sparkling winemaker could hope for, considering the large, modern cellar that's perfectly equipped. In fact, Ballabio is now entirely dedicated to producing Metodo Classico sparklers, with a number of wines (and bottles) whose quality and quantity are bound to grow thanks in part to the skillful support of Carlo Casavecchia. This year their most recent addition is their Farfalla Zero Dosage, a wine of rare mineral clarity, the spirit of Pinot Nero with extremely fine sparkle, vigor, class and depth. Wild fruit and balsamic notes are even more pronounced in their Extra Brut, another exceptional wine. Their Rosé has made decided progress with its delicate, citrusy and flowery aromas and an elegance that distinguishes their entire selection.

| | |
|---|---|
| ⊙ Farfalla Brut M. Cl. Rosé | ▼▼ 4 |
| ○ Farfalla Brut Zero Dosage M. Cl. | ▼▼ 4 |
| ○ Farfalla Extra Brut M. Cl. | ▼▼ 4 |
| ● OP Bonarda V. delle Cento Pertiche '15 | ♈♈ 3 |
| ● OP Bonarda V. delle Cento Pertiche '13 | ♈♈ 3 |
| ● OP Bonarda V. delle Cento Pertiche '11 | ♈♈ 2* |
| ○ OP Pinot Grigio Clastidium '15 | ♈♈ 3 |
| ○ Pinot Grigio Clastidium '16 | ♈♈ 2* |

# Barone Pizzini

VIA SAN CARLO, 14
25050 PROVAGLIO D'ISEO [BS]
TEL. +39 0309848311
www.baronepizzini.it

CELLAR SALES
PRE-BOOKED VISITS
ACCOMMODATION
ANNUAL PRODUCTION 290,000 bottles
HECTARES UNDER VINE 55.00
VITICULTURE METHOD Certified Organic
SUSTAINABLE WINERY

Thanks to the commitment of the owners and the passionate management style of Silvano Bescianini, Barone Pizzini is one of Franciacorta's most noteworthy wineries. And that's not all. They're also at the vanguard in terms of organic and biodynamic cultivation, as well as environmental sustainability. All it takes is a visit to their modern cellar, a model of sustainable architecture and respect for the territory (in addition to tasting their excellent blends), to appreciate the depth of their commitment. And with wineries in Pievalta (Marche) and Ghiaccioforte (Tuscany), it's a commitment that goes beyond Franciacorta. As always, Barone Pizzini's selection is top quality. This year two wines made it into our finals. Their fresh and elegant 2014 Satèn is a truly balanced wine rich in succulent notes of white fruit. Their 2014 Naturae proves taut and pure. It's just missing a bit of depth, otherwise it would have received top marks. Their 2012 Riserva Bagnadore, a wine defined by its complexity and fragrances of vanilla, is also noteworthy.

| | |
|---|---|
| ○ Franciacorta Brut Satèn '14 | ♛♛ 5 |
| ○ Franciacorta Dosage Zero Nature '14 | ♛♛ 5 |
| ○ Franciacorta Dosaggio Zero Bagnadore Ris. '12 | ♛♛ 5 |
| ○ Franciacorta Extra Brut Animante | ♛♛ 5 |
| ○ Franciacorta Brut Golf 1927 | ♛ 5 |
| ○ Franciacorta Dosaggio Zero Animante LA | ♛ 5 |
| ⊙ Franciacorta Extra Brut Rosé | ♛ 5 |
| ○ Franciacorta Brut Naturae '13 | ♛♛♛ 5 |
| ○ Franciacorta Brut Naturae '11 | ♛♛♛ 5 |
| ○ Franciacorta Brut Nature '10 | ♛♛♛ 5 |
| ○ Franciacorta Brut Nature '09 | ♛♛♛ 5 |
| ○ Franciacorta Non Dosato Bagnadore Ris. '09 | ♛♛♛ 6 |

# ★★★Bellavista

VIA BELLAVISTA, 5
25030 ERBUSCO [BS]
TEL. +39 0307762000
www.bellavistawine.it

CELLAR SALES
PRE-BOOKED VISITS
ANNUAL PRODUCTION 1,400,000 bottles
HECTARES UNDER VINE 190.00
SUSTAINABLE WINERY

Everything started in the 1960s thanks to Vittorio Moretti's passion for great wine. But the producer's recent purchase of Sella & Mosca in Sardegna and Teruzzi in Tuscany, in addition to their estates in Tuscany (Petra and La Badiola) and Franciacorta (Contadi Castaldi), has sealed their status as one of Italy's most important players in the industry. Today Francesca Moretti, who was raised among the vineyards and cellar in Bellavista, is at the helm. And she's supported by a first-rate staff. As often occurs, Bellavista submitted a selection of top quality wines for tasting. Their 2013 Teatro alla Scala gets a gold with its aromas of cakes, aromatic herbs and chamomile. On the palate it proves savory, elegant and extraordinarily long, as well as rich in sensations of white peach. Their 2011 Vittorio Moretti Riserva is a complex, deep and balanced wine, while their 2012 Pas Operé is generous and creamy. Their multi-vintage wine Meraviglioso (available solo in magnum bottles) is enchanting but hors concours.

| | |
|---|---|
| ○ Franciacorta Brut Teatro alla Scala '13 | ♛♛♛ 7 |
| ○ Franciacorta Extra Brut Vittorio Moretti Ris. '11 | ♛♛ 8 |
| ○ Franciacorta Pas Operé '12 | ♛♛ 7 |
| ○ Franciacorta Brut Gran Cuvée Alma | ♛♛ 6 |
| ⊙ Franciacorta Brut Rosé '14 | ♛♛ 7 |
| ○ Franciacorta Satèn '14 | ♛♛ 7 |
| ○ Franciacorta Extra Brut Vittorio Moretti Ris. '08 | ♛♛♛ 8 |
| ○ Franciacorta Extra Brut Vittorio Moretti Ris. '06 | ♛♛♛ 8 |
| ○ Franciacorta Pas Operé '10 | ♛♛♛ 7 |
| ○ Franciacorta Pas Operé '09 | ♛♛♛ 7 |

# F.lli Berlucchi

FRAZ. BORGONATO
VIA BROLETTO, 2
25040 CORTE FRANCA [BS]
TEL. +39 030984451
www.fratelliberlucchi.it

**CELLAR SALES**
**PRE-BOOKED VISITS**
**ANNUAL PRODUCTION 400,000 bottles**
**HECTARES UNDER VINE 70.00**

Berlucchi is one of Franciacorta's historic producers. Their family villa in Borgonato, Casa delle Colonne, testifies to the fact. It's a 16th-century structure that also hosts the winery's cellars. The estate boasts 70 hectares of vineyards, managed with passion by Pia Donata and her daughter Tilli Rizzo. The selection is divided into two lines, Casa delle Colonne, dedicated to Franciacorta Riserva, and their single-vintage line, Freccia Nera. Their Brut 25, a wine that serves as their base offering, is without a vintage. Few wineries are able to put forward a selection that's as strong as theirs is across the board. Once again their 2011 Brut Casa delle Colonne stood out during our finals. It's a tight-knit, fine, creamy, savory and elegant wine with close-focused aromas of aniseed and saffron. Elegant notes of yeast and biscotti characterize their 2014 Freccianera Nature, while their 2014 Freccicanera Satèn offers up enticing fruity nuances. Their Brut 25 proves it's an excellent base-level wine.

| | |
|---|---|
| ○ Franciacorta Brut Casa delle Colonne Ris. '11 | ♟♟ 8 |
| ○ Franciacorta Brut 25 | ♟♟ 6 |
| ○ Franciacorta Casa delle Colonne Zero Ris. '11 | ♟♟ 8 |
| ○ Franciacorta Nature Freccianera '14 | ♟♟ 6 |
| ⊙ Franciacorta Rosé Freccianera Rosa '14 | ♟♟ 6 |
| ○ Franciacorta Satèn Freccianera '14 | ♟♟ 6 |
| ○ Franciacorta Brut Freccianera '13 | ♟ 5 |
| ○ Franciacorta Brut Casa delle Colonne Ris. '10 | ♟♟ 8 |
| ○ Franciacorta Brut Freccianera '12 | ♟♟ 6 |
| ○ Franciacorta Casa delle Colonne Zero Ris. '10 | ♟♟ 8 |
| ○ Franciacorta Nature Freccianera '13 | ♟♟ 7 |
| ○ Franciacorta Satèn Freccianera '13 | ♟♟ 7 |

# ★Guido Berlucchi & C.

LOC. BORGONATO
P.ZZA DURANTI, 4
25040 CORTE FRANCA [BS]
TEL. +39 030984381
www.berlucchi.it

**CELLAR SALES**
**PRE-BOOKED VISITS**
**ACCOMMODATION**
**ANNUAL PRODUCTION 4,400,000 bottles**
**HECTARES UNDER VINE 550.00**
**VITICULTURE METHOD Certified Organic**
**SUSTAINABLE WINERY**

It was Franco Ziliani who, in the early 1960s, made modern Franciacorta what it is today, an area that's considered a choice terroir for Metodo Classico blends. Currently Franco's children are steering the producer, having formed a tight and highly experienced team that's successfully facing the change in generations. Arturo serves as enologist while Cristina and Paolo manage marketing and sales (respectively). The winery is a leader among Franciacorta's producers, successfully exporting their products throughout the world. It's difficult to choose between the two cuvées submitted this year. It's really a question of splitting hairs. Their Nature 61 stands out for the third time. It's a rigorously styled 2011 Dosaggio Zero, though it also exhibits an appealing elegance and drinkability. It's creamy, fine, fresh and truly long, and it brings home our award for Sparkling Wine of the Year. Their Palazzo Lana Extra Brut Extrême is no less excellent, though it's more austere and delicate. It's a 2008 Blanc de Noirs with a sharpish profile and close-focused aromas of red fruit. The rest of their selection is also superb.

| | |
|---|---|
| ○ Franciacorta Nature 61 '11 | ♟♟♟ 7 |
| ○ Franciacorta Extra Brut Extreme Palazzo Lana Ris. '08 | ♟♟ 7 |
| ○ Franciacorta Brut '61 | ♟♟ 5 |
| ⊙ Franciacorta Nature Rosé 61 '11 | ♟♟ 8 |
| ○ Franciacorta Satèn 61 | ♟♟ 5 |
| ⊙ Franciacorta Rosé 61 | ♟ 5 |
| ○ Franciacorta Brut Cellarius '08 | ♟♟♟ 7 |
| ○ Franciacorta Nature '61 '10 | ♟♟♟ 7 |
| ○ Franciacorta Brut Cellarius '07 | ♟♟♟ 5 |
| ○ Franciacorta Brut Extrême Palazzo Lana Ris. '06 | ♟♟♟ 6 |
| ○ Franciacorta Extra Brut Extreme Palazzo Lana Ris. '07 | ♟♟♟ 7 |
| ○ Franciacorta Nature 61 '09 | ♟♟♟ 5 |
| ○ Franciacorta Satèn Palazzo Lana '06 | ♟♟♟ 6 |

## Cantina Bersi Serlini

VIA CERETO, 7
25050 PROVAGLIO D'ISEO [BS]
TEL. +39 0309823338
www.bersiserlini.it

**CELLAR SALES**
**PRE-BOOKED VISITS**
**ACCOMMODATION AND RESTAURANT SERVICE**
**ANNUAL PRODUCTION** 200,000 bottles
**HECTARES UNDER VINE** 30.00
**VITICULTURE METHOD** Certified Organic

In 1886 the Bersi Serlini family purchased this lovely estate in Provaglio, on the banks of Lake d'Iseo. The area was once a monastic grange owned by the nearby convent of San Pietro in Lamosa. Today the winery is surrounded by well-maintained vineyards that overlook the lake. It's an elegant combination of old and modern that offers a range of high-quality wines. Bersi Serlini is also an important location for conferences, events and wine tourism. Strangely, this year their non-vintage wines impressed the most, starting with their Brut Anniversario, one of the best Franciacortas in its category. This vibrant straw yellow-colored wine features an elegant aromatic profile with notes of medicinal herbs (foremost marjoram) and a crisp, round, soft and appealing palate with succulent notes of white peach. Their Brut Anteprima is also noteworthy with its fresh notes of herbs and white fruit. Their Nuvola is a delicious Demi Sec redolent of honey and damson plums.

| | |
|---|---|
| ○ Franciacorta Brut Anniversario | ♥♥ 5 |
| ○ Franciacorta Brut Anteprima | ♥♥ 5 |
| ○ Franciacorta Demi Sec Nuvola | ♥♥ 4 |
| ○ Franciacorta Extra Brut '14 | ♥♥ 6 |
| ○ Franciacorta Brut Cuvée n. 4 '14 | ♥ 6 |
| ○ Franciacorta Satèn | ♥ 5 |
| ○ Franciacorta Brut Cuvée n. 4 '12 | ♀♀ 5 |
| ○ Franciacorta Brut Rosé Rosa Rosae '10 | ♀♀ 5 |
| ○ Franciacorta Extra Brut '13 | ♀♀ 6 |
| ○ Franciacorta Extra Brut '12 | ♀♀ 6 |
| ○ Franciacorta Extra Brut '11 | ♀♀ 6 |
| ○ Franciacorta Non Dosato Mia Ris. '05 | ♀♀ 6 |

## Bertè & Cordini

VIA CAIROLI, 67
27043 BRONI [PV]
TEL. +39 038551028
www.bertecordini.it

**CELLAR SALES**
**PRE-BOOKED VISITS**
**ACCOMMODATION**
**ANNUAL PRODUCTION** 700,000 bottles
**HECTARES UNDER VINE** 18.00
**SUSTAINABLE WINERY**

For 40 years this historic winery (Est. 1895) has been in the hands of the Berté and Cordini families, who've kept the original name. The winery has evolved over time, and today Natale Berté has passed the torch to the new generation, represented by his enologist son, Matteo, and young Marzia and Luca Cordini (also both enologists). Many wines are offered, as is customary in Oltrepò Pavese, with an overall quality that keeps getting better. Matteo's passion for Metodo Classico sparkling wines has meant they get special attention, and it's reflected in the results. This year their Cuvée Nero d'Oro was our favorite. It's a full, balanced, savory and creamy monovarietal Pinot Nero. Their Cuvée della Casa opts more for aromas of tropical fruit. It features fine, persistent sparkle and a long finish. Their 2014 Cuvée Tradizione reflects the year. It has plenty of vigor but it's lacking a bit of substance on the mid-palate. Their 2010 Oblio Pas Dosé is a ripe, spicy wine while their Cruasé features clear, citrusy notes.

| | |
|---|---|
| ○ OP Pinot Nero Brut Cuvée Nero d'Oro M. Cl. | ♥♥ 5 |
| ○ OP Cuvée Tradizione Brut M. Cl. '14 | ♥♥ 5 |
| ○ OP Pinot Nero Brut Cuvée della Casa M. Cl. | ♥♥ 5 |
| ○ OP Pinot Nero Dosage Zéro Oblio M. Cl. '10 | ♥♥ 7 |
| ⊘ OP Cruasé '13 | ♥ 5 |
| ● OP Sangue di Giuda Frizzante '17 | ♥ 2 |
| ○ OP Pinot Nero Brut M. Cl. Cuvée della Casa | ♀♀♀ 5 |
| ● OP Bonarda Sabion '15 | ♀♀ 2* |
| ● OP Buttafuoco Bertè & Cordini '13 | ♀♀ 2* |
| ○ OP Pinot Nero Brut Cuvée Tradizione '12 | ♀♀ 4 |
| ○ OP Pinot Nero Brut Cuvée Tradizione '10 | ♀♀ 4 |
| ● OP Sangue di Giuda Bertè & Cordini '14 | ♀♀ 2* |

## F.lli Bettini

LOC. SAN GIACOMO
VIA NAZIONALE, 4A
23036 TEGLIO [SO]
TEL. +39 0342786068
www.vinibettini.it

**CELLAR SALES**
**PRE-BOOKED VISITS**
**ANNUAL PRODUCTION 200,000 bottles**
**HECTARES UNDER VINE 15.00**

It's full steam ahead for this historic cellar in Teglio, bolstered by its more than 130 years of history and its status as one of Valtellina's most noteworthy producers. They're situated in the heart of Valgella, the largest of Valtellina Superiore's subzones. Their 15-hectare estate, which enjoys a favorable position among the area's principal subzones, gives rise to a broad and diverse selection. Their approach calls for rich and expressive wines with pronounced fruit; new wood barrels are used for their premium line. Their elegant 2013 Sassella Reale impresses for its fruit with lovely notes of raspberry and nuances of rhubarb. Fine and complex, the palate proves firm, with a long and pleasant finish. Once again their 2013 Valgella Vigna La Cornella does well, proving vibrant and sophisticated in its aromas with notes of preserves and tobacco. In the mouth it's big, generous, with a long, juicy finish.

| | |
|---|---|
| ● Sforzato di Valtellina '13 | ♟♟ 6 |
| ● Valtellina Sup. Inferno Prodigio '13 | ♟♟ 5 |
| ● Valtellina Sup. Sassella Reale '13 | ♟♟ 5 |
| ● Valtellina Sup. Valgella V. La Cornella '13 | ♟♟ 5 |
| ● Sforzato di Valtellina Fruttaio di Spina '13 | ♟♟ 7 |
| ● Sforzato di Valtellina Vign. di Spina '11 | ♟♟ 7 |
| ● Sforzato di Valtellina Vign. di Spina '10 | ♟♟ 6 |
| ● Valtellina Sup. Inferno Prodigio '11 | ♟♟ 5 |
| ● Valtellina Sup. Inferno Prodigio '10 | ♟♟ 5 |
| ● Valtellina Sup. La Botte Ventitrè Ris. '07 | ♟♟ 3 |
| ● Valtellina Sup. Sant'Andrea '13 | ♟♟ 5 |
| ● Valtellina Sup. Sant'Andrea '11 | ♟♟ 5 |
| ● Valtellina Sup. Sassella Reale '11 | ♟♟ 5 |
| ● Valtellina Sup. Sassella Reale '10 | ♟♟ 4 |
| ● Valtellina Sup. Valgella V. La Cornella '11 | ♟♟ 5 |
| ● Valtellina Sup. Valgella V. La Cornella '10 | ♟♟ 4 |

## Bisi

LOC. CASCINA SAN MICHELE
FRAZ. VILLA MARONE, 70
27040 SAN DAMIANO AL COLLE [PV]
TEL. +39 038575037
www.aziendagricolabisi.it

**CELLAR SALES**
**PRE-BOOKED VISITS**
**ANNUAL PRODUCTION 90,000 bottles**
**HECTARES UNDER VINE 30.00**

Claudio Bisi's passion for his work is unspoken. Indeed, he doesn't like talking about his wines, preferring instead that they speak for themselves. And do they ever speak. These are wines of marked personality that are capable of expressing deeply the terroir and vineyards that Claudio attends to with painstaking care. He's not afraid to purchase additional plots when they become available, overseeing them all, the various soils, microclimates and cultivar, with a fundamental coherence and expertise that point up the emotional intensity he brings to his work. His wines are best enjoyed after a long stay in the bottle. For a producer like Bisi, who are heavily focused on reds, getting their highly fragrant 2017 Riesling LaGrà into the finals is proof that none of their wines should be considered 'second tier'. Their 2015 Ca' Long also delivered. It's a clear, open, deep Pinot Nero. For the vintage, their 2017 La Peccatrice, a dry and succulent Bonarda, is among their best, while their 2015 Barbera Roncolongo is a wine to be enjoyed in 10 years (or even 20).

| | |
|---|---|
| ● Ca' Longa Pinot Nero '15 | ♟♟ 5 |
| ○ LaGrà Riesling Renano '17 | ♟♟ 2* |
| ● OP Bonarda Vivace La Peccatrice '17 | ♟♟ 2* |
| ● Roncolongo Barbera '15 | ♟♟ 5 |
| ○ Villa Marone Malvasia Passita '15 | ♟♟ 5 |
| ● Barbera Pezzabianca '15 | ♟♟ 3 |
| ● Barbera Roncolongo '14 | ♟♟ 5 |
| ● Barbera Roncolongo '12 | ♟♟ 3 |
| ○ Bianco Passito Villa Marone '14 | ♟♟ 5 |
| ○ Bianco Passito Villa Marone '12 | ♟♟ 4 |
| ● OP Bonarda Vivace La Peccatrice '16 | ♟♟ 2* |
| ● OP Bonarda Vivace La Peccatrice '15 | ♟♟ 2* |
| ● OP Pinot Nero Calonga '13 | ♟♟ 3 |
| ○ OP Riesling LaGrà '15 | ♟♟ 2* |
| ○ Riesling LaGrà '16 | ♟♟ 2* |

## Castello Bonomi

VIA SAN PIETRO, 46
25030 COCCAGLIO [BS]
TEL. +39 0307721015
www.castellobonomi.it

CELLAR SALES
PRE-BOOKED VISITS
ANNUAL PRODUCTION 100,000 bottles
HECTARES UNDER VINE 24.00
SUSTAINABLE WINERY

Carlo, Lucia and Roberto Paladin have deep roots in Veneto, but in they also own Bosco del Merlo in Friuli, Castelvecchi in Radda in Chianti and, for some years now, Castello Bonomi in Coccaglio, at the foot of Monte Orfano. Castello Bonomi, whose name comes from the lovely art nouveau villa situated here, boasts 24 hectares of vineyards. The calcareous terrain here gives rise to Pinot Nero, in addition to Chardonnay, each of which expresses its character and fullness. Their Franciacorta Castello Bonomi once again prove to be top quality wines, with two making it into our finals. It's their Cuvée Lucrezia, a 2006 Riserva that does a good job expressing the vintage and distinctive qualities of Coccaglio. It's a brilliant straw-yellow color, with extremely fine and long perlage. On the nose it offers up complex aromas of healthy, crisp fruit and medicinal herbs with iodine nuances of forest undergrowth. On the palate it's slightly salty, taut, mineral and quite long. Their 2009 Cru Perdu Riserva is a charming, evolved wine, a product of an excellent vintage.

| | |
|---|---|
| ○ Franciacorta Brut CruPerdu Ris. '09 | ▼▼ 7 |
| ○ Franciacorta Extra Brut Cuvée Lucrezia '06 | ▼▼ 8 |
| ○ Franciacorta Brut Cru Perdü | ▼▼ 6 |
| ○ Franciacorta Brut Gran Cuvée | ▼▼ 7 |
| ○ Franciacorta Dosage Zéro '12 | ▼▼ 7 |
| ○ Franciacorta Dosage Zéro Gran Cuvée del Laureato '10 | ▼▼ 8 |
| ○ Franciacorta Satèn | ▼▼ 5 |
| ○ Franciacorta Brut Cru Perdu '04 | ♈♈♈ 7 |
| ○ Franciacorta Extra Brut Lucrezia Et. Nera '04 | ♈♈♈ 8 |
| ○ Franciacorta Brut Cru Perdu Ris. '08 | ♈♈ 7 |
| ○ Franciacorta Dosage Zero '10 | ♈♈ 8 |
| ○ Franciacorta Dosage Zero '09 | ♈♈ 8 |
| ○ Franciacorta Extra Brut Cuvée Lucrezia Et. Nera '06 | ♈♈ 8 |

## Bosco Longhino

FRAZ. MOLINO MARCONI
27047 SANTA MARIA DELLA VERSA [PV]
TEL. +39 0385798049
www.bosco-longhino.it

PRE-BOOKED VISITS
ACCOMMODATION AND RESTAURANT SERVICE
ANNUAL PRODUCTION 200,000 bottles
HECTARES UNDER VINE 29.00

Bosco Longhino's long history goes back to 1895 and its founder Edoardo Faravelli. Since then it's seen a succession of generations, all leading up to the present with brothers Marco and Antonio Faravelli. 10 years ago, in 2008, they parted ways, with Marco remaining at their historic facility of Molino Marconi (he's now helped by his children Massimiliano and Greta). It was he who gave the winery its name, inspired by an area that's particularly well-suited to the cultivation of red grapes. With their debut in our main section, they've submitted a truly valid selection of wines. Their 2015 Bonarda Prete Bertino is a still wine with some depth to it. Generous and airy, it's redolent of wild berries and mint. It's right on target. Their fine and pleasant 2016 Campo dei Graci is a Pinot Nero that offers up aromas of spices, chocolate, herbs and wild fruit. Their 2017 Pinot Grigio Campo dei Fitti is a highly fresh and varietal wine, while their 2017 Riesling calls up fragrances of flowers and white fruit, while on the palate it features pulp and balance.

| | |
|---|---|
| ○ Campo dei Fitti Pinot Grigio '17 | ▼▼ 3 |
| ● OP Bonarda Prete Bertino '15 | ▼▼ 3 |
| ● Pinot Nero Campo dei Graci '16 | ▼▼ 3 |
| ○ Riesling '17 | ▼▼ 3 |
| ○ Casto Extra Brrut M. Cl. | ▼ 5 |
| ● OP Buttafuoco '15 | ▼ 3 |
| ● OP Buttafuoco '11 | ♈♈ 2* |

# Bosio

FRAZ. TIMOLINE
VIA M. GATTI, 4
25040 CORTE FRANCA [BS]
TEL. +39 0309826224
www.bosiofranciacorta.it

CELLAR SALES
PRE-BOOKED VISITS
ANNUAL PRODUCTION 100,000 bottles
HECTARES UNDER VINE 30.00
SUSTAINABLE WINERY

As many in the area have, the close-knit team of Cesare Bosio and his sister Laura have transformed their family's small, almost amateur winery into a full-blown producer that's among the best in Franciacorta. Their estate now comprises 30 hectares of vineyards and they've built a new, modern cellar in Corte Franca. The level of their wines is excellent, thanks to the skill of Cesare, who serves as agronomist (and also provides consulting services throughout the area), and the management prowess of Laura. Their Girolamo Bosio stood out during our tastings and earned a place in our finals. It's a 2011 Riserva with a complex, linear character that features fruit, great balance and harmony. But as they teach you on the other side of the Alps, a maison shouldn't be judged by its Gran Cuvée but by its base level wines. In that case, in our opinion, Boise is one of the appellation's most important and consisted brands. Their Brut is a true delight: elegant, complex, mineral, smoky and fruity on the nose, it's redolent of aromatic herbs and bread crust ...

| | |
|---|---|
| ○ Franciacorta Pas Dosè Girolamo Bosio Ris. '11 | ♥♥ 8 |
| ○ Franciacorta Brut | ♥♥ 5 |
| ○ Franciacorta Dosaggio Zero B.C. Ris. '07 | ♥♥ 8 |
| ⊙ Franciacorta Extra Brut Rosé '14 | ♥♥ 5 |
| ○ Franciacorta Nature '13 | ♥♥ 5 |
| ○ Franciacorta Extra Brut Boschedòr '12 | ♥ 6 |
| ○ Franciacorta Pas Dosé Girolamo Bosio Ris. '09 | ♀♀♀ 5 |
| ⊙ Franciacorta Brut Rosé '13 | ♀♀ 5 |
| ⊙ Franciacorta Brut Rosé '12 | ♀♀ 5 |
| ○ Franciacorta Extra Brut Boschedòr '11 | ♀♀ 5 |
| ○ Franciacorta Nature '12 | ♀♀ 5 |
| ○ Franciacorta Nature '11 | ♀♀ 5 |

# Alessio Brandolini

FRAZ. BOFFALORA, 68
27040 SAN DAMIANO AL COLLE [PV]
TEL. +39 038575232
www.alessiobrandolini.com

CELLAR SALES
PRE-BOOKED VISITS
ANNUAL PRODUCTION 70,000 bottles
HECTARES UNDER VINE 11.00
SUSTAINABLE WINERY

Right after graduating in enology, Alessio Brandolini found himself having to face the early death of his father, Costante, whose absence on the estate was most felt in terms of vineyard management. The young man wasn't discouraged and worked to bring out all his terrain's potential. It's an area that's particularly well-suited to Oltrepò Pavese's traditional reds, but Alessio's passion is for sparkling wines, and so he began working in that direction with a focus on Pinot Nero, obviously. The results so far have been encouraging and his future prospects are looking good. Their 2014 Beneficio is a classic Oltrepò blend of Croatina and Barbera that's macerated at length and aged in oak barriques. In this case a poor year isn't particularly detectable - it has a bit less structure than usual but it's well-made, proving ripe in its fruit and tannins with a spicy, racy finish. Their 2017 Soffio features pulp and aromas of wild berries expertly managed. Among their two Metodo Classicos we prefer their Rosé, a fragrant and pleasantly citrusy wine.

| | |
|---|---|
| ● Il Beneficio '14 | ♥♥ 4 |
| ● Il Soffio Croatina '17 | ♥♥ 2* |
| ⊙ Note d'Agosto Brut M. Cl. Rosé | ♥♥ 5 |
| ● Il Pozzo Barbera '16 | ♥ 3 |
| ○ Luogo d'Agosto Brut Nature M. Cl. | ♥ 5 |
| ● OP Bonarda Vivace Il Cassino '17 | ♥ 2 |
| ⊙ Brut M. Cl. Rosé Note d'Agosto '13 | ♀♀ 5 |
| ○ Il Bardughino '16 | ♀♀ 2* |
| ○ Il Bardughino '15 | ♀♀ 2* |
| ○ Il Bardughino '14 | ♀♀ 2* |
| ● Il Beneficio '13 | ♀♀ 4 |
| ● Il Beneficio '12 | ♀♀ 2* |
| ● Il Beneficio '11 | ♀♀ 2* |
| ● OP Bonarda Vivace Il Cassino '15 | ♀♀ 2* |
| ● OP Bonarda Vivace Il Cassino '14 | ♀♀ 2* |

# ★Cà Maiol

VIA COLLI STORICI, 119
25015 DESENZANO DEL GARDA [BS]
TEL. +39 0309910006
www.camaiol.it

CELLAR SALES
PRE-BOOKED VISITS
ANNUAL PRODUCTION 1,500,000 bottles
HECTARES UNDER VINE 160.00
SUSTAINABLE WINERY

The lovely winery of Ca' Maiol (previously known as Provenza) was founded by the Contato family in Lugana. Over time they've earned a solid reputation for their elegant Luganas, and more. As of last year they've formed part of the Marzotto family's Santa Margherita group, a move that's further boosted the commercial side as well as the quality of their production. Fabio Contato continues to work with the winery, whose estate comprises 150 hectares of vineyards in Valtènesi and Lugana. Fabio Contato's selection of Luganas demonstrates the structure and longevity that Turbiana can achieve when cultivated along the lake's white clay banks. Aged for six months in small, new wood, his 2016 Fabio Contato is made with grapes from the estate's oldest vineyards. It's a vibrant straw-yellow gold wine with a complex and deep nose that sees aromas of fruit join with spicy nuances and notes of vanilla. In the mouth it proves deep, generous and tight-knit.

| | |
|---|---|
| ○ Lugana Sel. Fabio Contato '16 | ♟♟♟ 5 |
| ○ Lugana Molin '17 | ♟♟ 3* |
| ○ Lugana Brut M. Cl. | ♟♟ 4 |
| ○ Lugana Prestige '17 | ♟♟ 3 |
| ☉ Valtènesi Chiaretto Roseri '17 | ♟♟ 3 |
| ● Valtènesi Jöel '16 | ♟ 3 |
| ● Valtènesi Negresco '12 | ♟ 3 |
| ○ Lugana Molin '16 | ♟♟♟ 3* |
| ○ Lugana Molin '15 | ♟♟♟ 3* |
| ○ Lugana Molin '14 | ♟♟♟ 3* |
| ○ Lugana Molin '13 | ♟♟♟ 3* |
| ○ Lugana Molin '12 | ♟♟♟ 3* |
| ○ Lugana Sup. Sel. Fabio Contato '11 | ♟♟♟ 5 |
| ○ Lugana Sup. Sel. Fabio Contato '10 | ♟♟♟ 5 |

# Cà Tessitori

VIA MATTEOTTI, 15
27043 BRONI [PV]
TEL. +39 038551495
www.catessitori.it

CELLAR SALES
PRE-BOOKED VISITS
ANNUAL PRODUCTION 120,000 bottles
HECTARES UNDER VINE 40.00

Year after year, with patience and passion, the Giorgi family have managed to carve out a position among Oltrepò Pavese's principal viticulturists. Father Luigi is helped by his sons Giovanni and Francesco. Together they oversee an estate whose organization is reminiscent of a past age. Their cellar, situated in the Broni town center, features concrete tanks that double as a support for the house above it, while their vineyards lie two different municipalities, Montecalvo Versiggia and Finigeto. Ca' Tessitori produces wines with a strong character. The use of wood barrels is extremely limited and great attention is paid to tradition, with results that speak for themselves. Their 2015 Marona, a commendable Barbera (though young), is a spirited wine, forthright and vibrant in its unmistakable aromas of morello cherry. Their Metodo Classico LB9 has become an Extra Brut, benefiting in linearity and vigor. Their 2017 Bonarda is a tasty, balanced wine, while their fruity and generous 2017 Rosso Borghesa is an early-drinking blend of Barbera and Croatina with a small share of Pinot Nero.

| | |
|---|---|
| ● Marona Barbera '15 | ♟♟ 4 |
| ○ Agòlo '17 | ♟♟ 2* |
| ● Borghesa Rosso '17 | ♟♟ 3 |
| ● OP Bonarda Frizzante '17 | ♟♟ 2* |
| ○ OP Pinot Nero Extra Brut LB9 M. Cl. | ♟♟ 5 |
| ● Gnese '16 | ♟ 3 |
| ● OP Bonarda Avita '16 | ♟♟ 3 |
| ● OP Bonarda Avita '15 | ♟♟ 3 |
| ● OP Bonarda Vivace '16 | ♟♟ 2* |
| ● OP Bonarda Vivace '15 | ♟♟ 2* |
| ○ OP Pinot Nero Brut M. V. '12 | ♟♟ 4 |
| ○ OP Pinot Nero Brut M. V. '11 | ♟♟ 4 |
| ● OP Rosso Borghesa '16 | ♟♟ 2* |
| ● OP Rosso Borghesa '15 | ♟♟ 2* |

## ★★★★Ca' del Bosco

VIA ALBANO ZANELLA, 13
25030 ERBUSCO [BS]
TEL. +39 0307766111
www.cadelbosco.com

**CELLAR SALES**
**PRE-BOOKED VISITS**
**ANNUAL PRODUCTION** 1,470,000 bottles
**HECTARES UNDER VINE** 218.50
**VITICULTURE METHOD** Certified Organic
**SUSTAINABLE WINERY**

Ca' del Bosco was founded in 1968 by Maurizio Zanella and in just a short time it became one of Italy's most important wine producers. Today it's the crown jewel of the Marzotto family's Gruppo Santa Margherita. President Maurizio coordinates an expert team led by the highly talented cellarmaster Stefano Capelli. Their extremely modern production facility, which features sophisticated technology, fine hospitality and works of art, is tucked away amidst woods and vineyards, and it's definitely worth a visit. Their 2009 Dosage Zero Noir handily earned Tre Bicchieri. It's an extraordinary Blanc de Noirs that's aged for some eight years on the lees in a futuristic cave in Erbusco. It exhibits depth and extraordinary complexity, but at the same time it has a smooth elegance that renders it graceful and irresistible. Their Annamaria Clementi is at the same level. It's a reserve wine that with the 2008 vintage achieved the absolute excellence. But from their 2014 Chardonnay to their 'simple' Curtefranca Rosso, each of Ca' del Bosco's wines will move you.

| | | |
|---|---|---|
| ○ Franciacorta Dosage Zéro Vintage Collection Noir '09 | ♀♀♀ | 8 |
| ○ Curtefranca Chardonnay '14 | ♀♀ | 8 |
| ○ Franciacorta Extra Brut Cuvée Annamaria Clementi Ris. '08 | ♀♀ | 8 |
| ● Carmenero '11 | ♀♀ | 8 |
| ● Curtefranca Rosso '15 | ♀♀ | 5 |
| ○ Franciacorta Brut Cuvée Prestige | ♀♀ | 5 |
| ○ Franciacorta Dosage Zéro Vintage Collection '13 | ♀♀ | 8 |
| ☉ Franciacorta Extra Brut Cuvée Annamaria Clementi Rosé Ris. '08 | ♀♀ | 8 |
| ○ Franciacorta Satèn Vintage Collection '13 | ♀♀ | 8 |
| ● Maurizio Zanella '13 | ♀♀ | 8 |
| ☉ Franciacorta Rosé Cuvée Prestige | ♀ | 8 |
| ○ Franciacorta Dosage Zéro Vintage Collection '12 | ♀♀♀ | 8 |

## Ca' del Gè

FRAZ. CA' DEL GÉ, 3
27040 MONTALTO PAVESE [PV]
TEL. +39 0383870179
www.cadelge.com

**CELLAR SALES**
**PRE-BOOKED VISITS**
**ANNUAL PRODUCTION** 160,000 bottles
**HECTARES UNDER VINE** 45.00

The late Enzo Padroggi left his winery in truly capable hands. His children Carlo, Stefania and Sara are proving up to the task, leading the family winery with care and dedication. Their 36 hectare estate, which is divided between two districts, is cultivated with an approach that minimizes environmental impact. In Montalto Pavese, where the family residence and production facility are situated, the calcareous, limestone-rich terrain is perfect for Riesling and Pinot Nero, while their vineyards in Cigognola give rise to the area's traditional red grapes. The overall quality of their selection is high, and some of their Metodo Classico sparklers and Rieslings prove outstanding. Thanks to its greater body and substance, their 2017 Riesling Brinà, a monovarietal Italico with vibrant aromas of chamomile and tropical fruit, outdid its still valid 'twin', their 2017 Filagn Long. Their 2016 Marinoni is a Riesling Renano that's still evolving at this stage. On the nose flowers and citrus give way to the cultivar's characteristic tertiary aromas, but with time it will acquire greater depth and complexity.

| | | |
|---|---|---|
| ○ Brinà Riesling '17 | ♀♀ | 2* |
| ○ Brut M. Cl. '13 | ♀♀ | 5 |
| ● OP Bonarda Frizzante La Fidela '16 | ♀♀ | 4 |
| ○ Filagn Long Riesling '17 | ♀ | 3 |
| ○ Il Marinoni Riesling '16 | ♀ | 3 |
| ○ Il Marinoni '15 | ♀♀ | 3 |
| ○ OP Brut Cà del Gé '13 | ♀♀ | 5 |
| ○ OP Pinot Nero Brut M. Cl. '11 | ♀♀ | 3 |
| ○ OP Pinot Nero Brut M. Cl. '10 | ♀♀ | 3* |
| ○ OP Riesling Brinà '16 | ♀♀ | 2* |
| ○ OP Riesling Brinà '15 | ♀♀ | 2* |
| ○ OP Riesling Brinà '14 | ♀♀ | 2* |

## Ca' di Frara

via Casa Ferrari, 1
27040 Mornico Losana [PV]
Tel. +39 0383892299
www.cadifrara.com

**CELLAR SALES**
**PRE-BOOKED VISITS**
**ANNUAL PRODUCTION** 400,000 bottles
**HECTARES UNDER VINE** 46.00

20 years have past since Luca Bellani took over the reins of the family winery. He was certainly aided by the experience he gained under his father, Tullio, and mother, Daniela (even if there was surely the occasional generational difference of opinion). In just a few years the winery experienced a major boost in quality that allowed Ca' di Frara to establish itself as one of Oltrepò Pavese's most well-known and praised producers. The period was followed by the ambitious 'Oltre il Classico' project dedicated to sparkling wines, with excellent results in some cases. This year's tastings revealed further growth in quality. Since its creation, their Riesling Oliva (named after the municipality of Oliva Gessi where the vineyards are situated) has been under close watch. And now we've tasted the best version yet. It's austere, mineral, rich and firm, taut, full and long. Their 2015 Mornico, a Pinot Nero, is noteworthy for its balance of fruit, acidity and evolution. Their Extra Brut, a linear Metodo Classico with some personality, features hints of lime and an oxidative style.

| | |
|---|---|
| ○ OP Riesling Oliva Ris. '16 | ♟♟♟ 4* |
| ● Mornico Pinot Nero '15 | ♟♟ 5 |
| ○ Oltre il Classico Extra Brut M. Cl. | ♟♟ 4 |
| ○ Oltre il Classico Brut M. Cl. Rosé | ♟ 5 |
| ● Io Rosso '15 | ♟♟ 5 |
| ● OP Bonarda La Casetta '15 | ♟♟ 3 |
| ● OP Bonarda Vivace Monpezzato '15 | ♟♟ 2* |
| ○ OP Riesling '15 | ♟♟ 4 |
| ○ OP Riesling Sup. '16 | ♟♟ 2* |

## Ca' Lojera

loc. Rovizza
via 1866, 19
25019 Sirmione [BS]
Tel. +39 0457551901
www.calojera.com

**CELLAR SALES**
**PRE-BOOKED VISITS**
**RESTAURANT SERVICE**
**ANNUAL PRODUCTION** 120,000 bottles
**HECTARES UNDER VINE** 20.00

The Tiraboschi family are the owners of Ca' Lojera, 'the den of the wolves', an 18-hectare estate. Their vineyards are situated along the plains near the lake, in the area's classic white clay soil, choice terrain for local Trebbiano (now commonly known as Turbiana). Franco dedicates himself to the vineyards and the cellar, accompanied by his wife, Ambra, who oversees reception, and Alessandra, who deals primarily with sales and hospitality. Franco and Ambra have been working painstakingly to bring out Lugana's potential. Surely one of the gifts for which this wine is universally recognized is its longevity. For this reason an extraordinary wine going back to 1999 has been put on the market. It's called 'Annata Storica', and it impresses for its freshness, complexity, depth and elegance. Their 2017 Lugana also did well. It's a wine we enjoyed while waiting for their Riserva del Lupo and Superiore, which are still aging.

| | |
|---|---|
| ○ Lugana Annata Storica '99 | ♟♟ 4 |
| ○ Lugana '17 | ♟♟ 3 |
| ○ Lugana '16 | ♟♟ 3 |
| ○ Lugana '15 | ♟♟ 3 |
| ○ Lugana '14 | ♟♟ 3 |
| ○ Lugana Riserva del Lupo '15 | ♟♟ 5 |
| ○ Lugana Riserva del Lupo '14 | ♟♟ 5 |
| ○ Lugana Riserva del Lupo '13 | ♟♟ 5 |
| ○ Lugana Riserva del Lupo '12 | ♟♟ 5 |
| ○ Lugana Riserva del Lupo '11 | ♟♟ 4 |
| ○ Lugana Sup. '15 | ♟♟ 3 |
| ○ Lugana Sup. '14 | ♟♟ 3 |
| ○ Lugana Sup. '13 | ♟♟ 3 |
| ○ Lugana Sup. '12 | ♟♟ 3 |
| ○ Lugana Sup. '11 | ♟♟ 3 |

# Calatroni

LOC. CASA GRANDE, 7
27040 MONTECALVO VERSIGGIA [PV]
TEL. +39 038599013
www.calatronivini.it

**CELLAR SALES**
**PRE-BOOKED VISITS**
**RESTAURANT SERVICE**
**ANNUAL PRODUCTION** 70,000 bottles
**HECTARES UNDER VINE** 15.00
**SUSTAINABLE WINERY**

It's worth reminding readers of how Calatroni has managed to establish itself as one of Oltrepò Pavese's most interesting and dynamic wineries in such a short time. Founded in 1964 by Luigi Calatroni, today the winery is led by the fourth generation of family in brothers Cristian and Stefano. The two deserve credit for their commitment to their grapes and their ability to bring out the best of their terrain (with the instrumental help of their father, Fausto, especially in the vineyard), with particularly striking results when it comes to their sparkling wines. Primarily Montecalvo Versiggia's white grapes are cultivated, Riesling and Pinot Nero. For just a hair, their 2014 Pinot '64 didn't take home the Tre Bicchieri earned two years ago. It's a clear, fresh wine with fine sparkle, balsamic hints and a lavender finish. It's a well made, supple wine. Their 2015 Riesling delivers, proving mineral and mature, rich and savory. Their 2017 Bonarda Frizzante Vigiò is forthright and fruity, striking a nice balance between tannins and residual sweetness.

| | |
|---|---|
| ○ Pinot Nero Brut 64 M. Cl. '14 | ♟♟ 4 |
| ● OP Bonarda Frizzante Vigiò '17 | ♟♟ 2* |
| ○ Riesling '15 | ♟♟ 2* |
| ○ Campo del Dottore Riesling '17 | ♟ 3 |
| ○ NorEma Brut M. Cl. Ros '15 | ♟ 4 |
| ● OP Pinot Nero Fioravanti '16 | ♟ 3 |
| ⊙ OP Pinot Nero Rosé M. Cl. NorEma '13 | ♟♟♟ 4* |
| ○ Pinot Nero Brut 64 '11 | ♟♟♟ 5 |
| ● OP Bonarda Vivace Vigiò '15 | ♟♟ 2* |
| ○ OP Riesling '13 | ♟♟ 2* |
| ○ OP Riesling Viticoltori in Montecalvo '14 | ♟♟ 5 |
| ● OP Sangue di Giuda '16 | ♟♟ 2* |
| ○ Pinot Nero Brut 64 '13 | ♟♟ 4 |
| ○ Pinot Nero Brut 64 '12 | ♟♟ 5 |

# Il Calepino

VIA SURRIPE, 1
24060 CASTELLI CALEPIO [BG]
TEL. +39 035847178
www.ilcalepino.it

**CELLAR SALES**
**PRE-BOOKED VISITS**
**ANNUAL PRODUCTION** 230,000 bottles
**HECTARES UNDER VINE** 15.00

We'll never stop eulogizing the work that Franco and Marco Plebani have been doing along the left bank of Lake Iseo over these past 40 years. Their sparkling wines, in particular, stand shoulder-to-shoulder with the right bank's more well-known producers. Their Metodo Classicos undergo long aging on the lees, while their premium reds age in wood barrels. The result is wines of great personality, with a highly recognizable style that's robust, though without compromising elegance. Unfortunately the latest vintages of their two premium sparkling wines (Fra' Ambrogio Riserva and Non Dosato) aren't available. Nevertheless they submitted wines that proved plenty interesting: their Blanc de Blancs, a blend of Chardonnay, Pinot Bianco and Pinot Grigio, is rich and graceful, flowery, fragrant and persistent. Their 2011 Brut Il Calepino is savory, dry, spirited and racy, as well as generous in its aromas. Their 2013 Kalos, a Cabernet that's anything but banal, receives an honorable mention thanks to its aromas of fruit, hay and spices.

| | |
|---|---|
| ○ Terre del Colleoni B.D.B. Brut M. Cl. | ♟♟ 4 |
| ○ Brut Cl. Il Calepino '11 | ♟♟ 3 |
| ● Kalòs Cabernet '13 | ♟♟ 5 |
| ● Merlot M.A.S '13 | ♟ 5 |
| ● Valcalepio Rosso '15 | ♟ 2 |
| ○ Brut M. Cl. Fra' Ambrogio Ris. '09 | ♟♟ 4 |
| ⊙ Brut M. Cl. Rosé '11 | ♟♟ 3 |
| ● Kalòs '11 | ♟♟ 5 |

# Camossi

VIA METELLI, 5
25030 ERBUSCO [BS]
TEL. +39 0307268022
www.camossi.it

CELLAR SALES
PRE-BOOKED VISITS
ANNUAL PRODUCTION 60,000 bottles
HECTARES UNDER VINE 30.00

The winery was founded by Pietro Camossi, but today it's in the hands of his grandchildren Dario and Claudio, passionate vine growers. In 1996 they began making their own wine, but recent years have seen them carrying out bottle fermentation with the must of the same grapes used, without added sucrose. The Camossi make wines only with the grapes cultivated in their 24 hectares of vineyards. These are situated in Erbusco, where their cellar is also located, Paratico, which gives rise to their Pinot Nero, and Proaglio d'Iseo, especially in the district of Provezze. Our tastings this year find Camossi in excellent health, proceeding along the path of quality. For proof, it's enough to taste their 2010 Riserva, a savory, succulent and fresh Extra Brut that's rich in vigor and fruit on the palate. Their Satèn is another example, a lean and fresh wine that proves lively in its notes of fruit and aromatic herbs. Their Rosé Extra Brut is also a top wine, thanks to the clarity of its aromas of small fruit, the finesse of its sparkle and its freshness on the palate.

| | |
|---|---|
| ○ Franciacorta Extra Brut | ♟♟ 6 |
| ○ Franciacorta Extra Brut Ris. '10 | ♟♟ 6 |
| ⊙ Franciacorta Extra Brut Rosé | ♟♟ 6 |
| ○ Franciacorta Satèn | ♟♟ 6 |
| ○ Franciacorta Dosaggio Zero | ♟ 5 |
| ○ Franciacorta Extra Brut '13 | ♟ 6 |
| ○ Franciacorta Brut Satèn '11 | ♟♟ 6 |
| ○ Franciacorta Extra Brut '12 | ♟♟ 6 |
| ○ Franciacorta Extra Brut '11 | ♟♟ 6 |
| ○ Franciacorta Extra Brut '09 | ♟♟ 6 |
| ○ Franciacorta Extra Brut '08 | ♟♟ 6 |
| ○ Franciacorta Extra Brut '08 | ♟♟ 6 |
| ○ Franciacorta Extra Brut Ris. '09 | ♟♟ 6 |
| ○ Franciacorta Extra Brut Ris. '08 | ♟♟ 6 |

# CastelFaglia - Monogram

FRAZ. CALINO
LOC. BOSCHI, 3
25046 CAZZAGO SAN MARTINO [BS]
TEL. +39 0307751042
www.cavicchioli.it

CELLAR SALES
PRE-BOOKED VISITS
ANNUAL PRODUCTION 350,000 bottles
HECTARES UNDER VINE 22.00

The Cavicchioli family, a historic name in Modena's winemaking industry, produce Metodo Classico both in their Modena winery, Bellei di Bomporto, and at Castelfaglia, in Franciacorta. Here in their cellar, which is carved in the hillside, Sandro Cavicchioli fashions elegant blends that are offered in two lines, CastelFaglia and Monogram (the latter is dedicated to single-vintages and speciality wines). Their 22 hectares of vineyards, mostly terraced, are situated at the foot of the historic Faglia di Calino castel. Their Monogram Blanc de Blancs proves to be the cuvée that stood out this year in our finals. It's a Franciacorta that opts for freshness and the clarity of its fruity, flowery aromas, which reemerge on the palate. In the mouth it exhibits a creamy effervescence and notable overall harmony. They're qualities it shares with their Monogram Satèn, a close-focused, lean wine, as well as their Castelfaglia Brut, with its enticing notes of vanilla.

| | |
|---|---|
| ○ Franciacorta Brut Blanc de Blancs Monogram | ♟♟ 5 |
| ○ Franciacorta Brut | ♟♟ 4 |
| ○ Franciacorta Brut Monogram '11 | ♟♟ 5 |
| ○ Franciacorta Dosage Zéro | ♟♟ 5 |
| ○ Franciacorta Extra Brut | ♟♟ 4 |
| ○ Franciacorta Satèn Monogram | ♟♟ 5 |
| ○ Franciacorta Satèn Monogram Zero '14 | ♟♟ 5 |
| ⊙ Franciacorta Rosé | ♟ 5 |
| ○ Franciacorta Brut Monogram '10 | ♟♟ 5 |
| ○ Franciacorta Brut Monogram '09 | ♟♟ 5 |
| ○ Franciacorta Dosage Zero Monogram '13 | ♟♟ 5 |
| ○ Franciacorta Dosage Zero Monogram '12 | ♟♟ 5 |
| ○ Franciacorta Satèn Monogram '12 | ♟♟ 5 |
| ○ Franciacorta Satèn Monogram '11 | ♟♟ 5 |

# Castello di Cigognola

P.ZZA CASTELLO, 1
27040 CIGOGNOLA [PV]
TEL. +39 0385284828
www.castellodicigognola.com

CELLAR SALES
PRE-BOOKED VISITS
ANNUAL PRODUCTION 75,000 bottles
HECTARES UNDER VINE 30.00

Situated in a splendid position overlooking the Padania plains and the Scuropasso valley, Castello di Cigognola has historic roots. Founded in 1212, it was a court during the renaissance. In the early 19th century it was put to use for wine-growing. Today, thanks to Letizia and Gianmarco Moratti (who passed away last February), not only is it a quality wine producer, it's also partnered with the University of Milan as a research center for studying ancient local cultivar and newer, disease-resistant varieties. We shouldn't forget the contribution of local enologist Emilio Defilippi and consultant Riccardo Cotarella as well. Their 2015 Barbera La Maga features nice, succulent fruit, highly characteristic aromas of cherry and black cherry, nice oak, vigor and length. Their 2014 'More Brut is a Metodo Classico with lovely finesse, as well as clear fragrances of apricot and aniseed. Their balanced and pleasant 2015 Rosé opts for greater presence of wild berries. Their 2016 Barbera Dodicidodici, a wine redolent of black fruit, exhibits a bit less substance than usual.

| | |
|---|---|
| ● La Maga Barbera '15 | ▼▼ 4 |
| ○ 'More Brut M. Cl. '14 | ▼▼ 4 |
| ⊙ 'More Brut M. Cl. Rosé '15 | ▼▼ 4 |
| ○ Bianca '17 | ▼ 3 |
| ● Dodicidodici Barbera '16 | ▼ 3 |
| ● Nebbiolo per Papà '13 | ▼ 5 |
| ○ Brut 'More '11 | ▽▽▽ 4* |
| ○ Brut 'More '10 | ▽▽▽ 4* |
| ● OP Barbera Castello di Cigognola '07 | ▽▽▽ 6 |
| ● OP Barbera Castello di Cigognola '06 | ▽▽▽ 6 |
| ● OP Barbera Dodicidodici '11 | ▽▽▽ 3* |
| ○ OP Brut 'More '12 | ▽▽▽ 4* |
| ○ OP Brut Pinot Nero 'More '13 | ▽▽▽ 4* |
| ○ OP Brut Pinot Nero 'More '08 | ▽▽▽ 4* |

# Castello di Gussago La Santissima

VIA MANICA, 9
25064 GUSSAGO [BS]
TEL. +39 0302525267
www.castellodigussago.it

CELLAR SALES
PRE-BOOKED VISITS
ANNUAL PRODUCTION 120,000 bottles
HECTARES UNDER VINE 15.00
SUSTAINABLE WINERY

In the early years of the new millennium, the Gozio family renovated an old Dominican convent on the Colle della Santissima, in Gussago, and brought a modern winery to life. Their grapes are cultivated in its 20 hectares of vineyards in various positions throughout the municipality. Some of these are situated just by the abbey, at 450 meters above sea level. The producer, which is also involved in the business of environmental sustainability, has impressed in recent years, with our tastings testifying to their commitment and continued growth in terms of quality. A medley of tastings this year sees an elegant Blanc de Blancs leading their selection. Its green highlights reemerge on the nose, with herbaceous notes and fruit merging. On the palate it finishes long and creamy. Their Franciacorta Brut offers up elegant, fruity notes while on the palate it exhibits cohesion, savoriness and persistence. Their 2014 Satèn Club Cuvée delivered for its lean structure, freshness and elegance. Finally, their 2013 Brut Selezione Gozio features lovely citrus notes and drinkability.

| | |
|---|---|
| ○ Curtefranca Bianco Malandrino '15 | ▼▼ 5 |
| ● Curtefranca Rosso Pomaro '15 | ▼▼ 4 |
| ⊙ Franciacorta Brut | ▼▼ 5 |
| ○ Franciacorta Brut Blanc de Blancs | ▼▼ 5 |
| ○ Franciacorta Brut Sel. Gozio '13 | ▼▼ 6 |
| ○ Franciacorta Club Cuvée Satèn | ▼▼ 5 |
| ○ Franciacorta Pas Dosé 800 '14 | ▼▼ 5 |
| ● Curtefranca Rosso Sanrocco '16 | ▼ 4 |
| ⊙ Franciacorta Extra Brut Rosé '13 | ▼ 5 |
| ⊙ Franciacorta Pas Dosé '13 | ▼ 5 |
| ○ Curtefranca Bianco Malandrino '14 | ▽▽ 5 |
| ● Curtefranca Rosso Pomaro '13 | ▽▽ 4 |
| ⊙ Franciacorta Extra Brut Rosé '12 | ▽▽ 5 |
| ⊙ Franciacorta Pas Dosé '12 | ▽▽ 5 |
| ○ Franciacorta Satèn '12 | ▽▽ 5 |

## ★Cavalleri

VIA PROVINCIALE, 96
25030 ERBUSCO [BS]
TEL. +39 0307760217
www.cavalleri.it

PRE-BOOKED VISITS
ANNUAL PRODUCTION 200,000 bottles
HECTARES UNDER VINE 42.00
VITICULTURE METHOD Certified Organic

Not only are the Cavalleri among the founders of modern Franciacorta, they are a historic family whose roots in the territory go as far back as 1450. In 1968 Gian Paolo and his son Giovanni began producing wine and, later, Franciacorta. After some 50 years at the helm, we find Giovanni's daughters Maria and Giulia and grandchildren Francesco and Diletta accompanied by a staff of well-skilled collaborators. The winery boasts 42 hectares of vineyards in Erbusco, all managed with natural methods. Their Riserva Giovanni Cavalleri is dedicated to one of the figures who was an important part of the territory's recent past. It's made with Chardonnay from Erbusco, cultivated in their private vineyards, then aged for nine years on the lees before disgorgement. It's a brilliant, straw-yellow gold color and features fine perlage. On the nose it proves complex and deep, with close-focused aromas of fruit giving way to elegant, flowery notes of yeast and bitter honey. On the palate it proves creamy, succulent and savory, endowed with vigor and minerality.

| | |
|---|---|
| ○ Franciacorta Brut Giovanni Cavalleri Ris. '07 | ♈♈ 8 |
| ○ Curtefranca Bianco Rampaneto '16 | ♈♈ 4 |
| ● Curtefranca Rosso Tajardino '15 | ♈♈ 5 |
| ○ Franciacorta Brut Blanc de Blancs | ♈♈ 5 |
| ⊙ Franciacorta Brut Rosé '13 | ♈♈ 6 |
| ○ Franciacorta Pas Dosé '13 | ♈♈ 6 |
| ○ Franciacorta Satèn '14 | ♈♈ 6 |
| ○ Franciacorta Brut Collezione '05 | ♈♈♈ 6 |
| ○ Franciacorta Brut Collezione Esclusiva Giovanni Cavalleri '05 | ♈♈♈ 8 |
| ○ Franciacorta Brut Collezione Esclusiva Giovanni Cavalleri '04 | ♈♈♈ 7 |
| ○ Franciacorta Brut Collezione Esclusiva Giovanni Cavalleri '01 | ♈♈♈ 7 |
| ○ Franciacorta Collezione Grandi Cru '08 | ♈♈♈ 6 |
| ○ Franciacorta Pas Dosé '07 | ♈♈♈ 5 |
| ○ Franciacorta Pas Dosé R. D. '06 | ♈♈♈ 6 |

## Citari

FRAZ. SAN MARTINO DELLA BATTAGLIA
LOC. CITARI, 2
25015 DESENZANO DEL GARDA [BS]
TEL. +39 0309910310
www.citari.it

CELLAR SALES
PRE-BOOKED VISITS
ANNUAL PRODUCTION 150,000 bottles
HECTARES UNDER VINE 21.00
SUSTAINABLE WINERY

Francesco Mascini is at the helm of this winery founded in 1975 by his grandfather, Francesco Gettuli. It's a 25-hectare estate (21 of which are vineyards) situated at the foot of a historic, commemorative tower between the Lugana and San Martino della Battaglia appellations. The marly, mineral-rich calcareous-clay soil here gives rise to wines characterized by savoriness and aromatic finesse, while the more calcareous soils make for elegant, ageworthy wines. Their approach to cultivation is low-impact, while manual harvests and a modern cellar complete the picture. We very much appreciated their 2017 Lugana Sorgente, a lovely wine in its freshness and vitality, with a nice fruity thrust and elegant nuances of citron and aromatic herbs. Their 2017 Conchiglia features a softer, brighter style. It too is well-balanced, though it privileges roundness. The same qualities can be found in their 2017 Chiaretto, a savory, succulent wine that features lovely aromas of red fruit. Their 2017 San Marino della Battaglia also proved to be a sound wine.

| | |
|---|---|
| ○ Lugana Conchiglia '17 | ♈♈ 4 |
| ○ Lugana Sorgente '17 | ♈♈ 3 |
| ⊙ Garda Cl. Chiaretto 18 e Quarantacinque '17 | ♈ 3 |
| ○ San Martino della Battaglia '17 | ♈ 2 |
| ○ Eretico '16 | ♉♉ 2* |
| ○ Lugana Conchiglia '15 | ♉♉ 4 |
| ○ Lugana Sorgente '16 | ♉♉ 3 |
| ○ Lugana Sorgente '14 | ♉♉ 3 |
| ○ Lugana Terre Bianche '16 | ♉♉ 3 |
| ○ Lugana Torre '15 | ♉♉ 2* |
| ○ Lugana Vign. La Sorgente '13 | ♉♉ 2* |
| ○ Mimi' '14 | ♉♉ 2* |
| ○ San Martino della Battaglia Il Vecchio Vigneto '13 | ♉♉ 3 |

# Battista Cola

VIA INDIPENDENZA, 3
25030 ADRO [BS]
TEL. +39 0307356195
www.colabattista.it

CELLAR SALES
PRE-BOOKED VISITS
ANNUAL PRODUCTION 70,000 bottles
HECTARES UNDER VINE 10.00
SUSTAINABLE WINERY

Battista Cola began producing wine in 1985, but with the arrival of his son Stefano the winery grew and took on a new commercial dimension (even if their some 10 hectares of vineyards on Monte Alto di Adro were already cultivated by Stefano's grandfather Giovanni). Their selection hovers around 70,000 bottles per year, but their Franciacorta and Cola wines have maintained the authentic 'récoltant' character, with a proudly artisanal approach adopted both in the vineyard and in the cellar. Stefano Cola's 2013 Non Dosato is one of the best expressions of the year, standing out during our finals. A brilliant straw-yellow color, it features fine perlage and complex nose with nuances of white fruit (damson plum in particular). These reemerge on the palate, which proves savory, taut, fresh and vibrant. If their 2012 Brut entices with its flowery hints, we can't help but recommend their non-vintage Brut, a close-focused, soft and fresh wine that finishes on a lovely note of vanilla.

| | | |
|---|---|---|
| ○ Franciacorta Non Dosato '13 | ♟♟ | 5 |
| ○ Franciacorta Brut '12 | ♟♟ | 5 |
| ○ Franciacorta Brut | ♟♟ | 5 |
| ○ Franciacorta Extra Brut | ♟♟ | 4 |
| ○ Franciacorta Satèn '14 | ♟♟ | 5 |
| ⊙ Franciacorta Brut Rosé Athena '14 | ♟ | 5 |
| ○ Franciacorta Brut '11 | ♟♟ | 5 |
| ○ Franciacorta Non Dosato '12 | ♟♟ | 5 |
| ○ Franciacorta Non Dosato '11 | ♟♟ | 5 |
| ⊙ Franciacorta Rosé Athena '12 | ♟♟ | 5 |
| ○ Franciacorta Satèn '11 | ♟♟ | 5 |

# Contadi Castaldi

LOC. FORNACE BIASCA
VIA COLZANO, 32
25030 ADRO [BS]
TEL. +39 0307450126
www.contadicastaldi.it

CELLAR SALES
PRE-BOOKED VISITS
ANNUAL PRODUCTION 1,000,000 bottles
HECTARES UNDER VINE 150.00
SUSTAINABLE WINERY

In the 1990s Vittorio Moretti renovated his historic furnaces in Adro, transforming the buildings into a modern cellar for the production of Franciacorta. The idea was to create an innovative winery to receive and transform grapes from the area's various terroir. That's how they've reached their elevated production volumes, with over 90 different vineyards covering more than 130 hectares (some of which are private plots and some of which are cultivated by independent vine growers). The brand's style is based on freshness and pleasantness. All this comes through when tasting their non-vintage Brut, which impressed for its vibrance and freshness and put in a strong performance during our finals. It's a blend of primarily Chardonnay with 10% Pinot Bianco and 10% Pinot Nero that ages for two years on the lees before disgorgement. It's a taut, fresh and racy wine that will win you over with its close-focused, fruity notes, its nuances of jasmine and aromatic herbs, its finesse and fruity pulp. Tre Bicchieri.

| | | |
|---|---|---|
| ○ Franciacorta Zero '14 | ♟♟♟ | 5 |
| ○ Franciacorta Brut | ♟♟ | 5 |
| ⊙ Franciacorta Brut Rosé | ♟♟ | 5 |
| ○ Franciacorta Satèn '14 | ♟♟ | 6 |
| ⊙ Franciacorta Brut Rosé Mariella Ris. '11 | ♟ | 6 |
| ○ Franciacorta Brut Satèn Soul '11 | ♟♟♟ | 6 |
| ○ Franciacorta Satèn Soul '06 | ♟♟♟ | 6 |
| ○ Franciacorta Satèn Soul '05 | ♟♟♟ | 6 |
| ○ Franciacorta Zero '12 | ♟♟♟ | 5 |
| ○ Franciacorta Zero '09 | ♟♟♟ | 5 |

## Conte Vistarino

FRAZ. SCORZOLETTA, 82/84
27040 PIETRA DE' GIORGI [PV]
TEL. +39 038585117
www.contevistarino.it

CELLAR SALES
PRE-BOOKED VISITS
ANNUAL PRODUCTION 400,000 bottles
HECTARES UNDER VINE 200.00

In 1865 count Giorgi di Vistarino and count Garcia (who had studied in Champagne and fell in love with its sparkling wine) identified the Scuropasso valley as the perfect area for French clones of Pinot Nero and for sparkling wine production. Today Ottavia Vistarino oversees the estate (more than 800 hectares, 120 of which are vineyards), aiming for excellence, both in terms of Metodo Classico sparkling wines and their Pinot Nero, which is fermented on the skins. The same holds for a number of crus that are now considered among the most expressive in the country. Their selection of 2015 Pinot Neros dazzles. Every cru has different characteristics, from Bertone's generous and elegant aromas of flower and fruit to Pernice's notes of coffee and forest undergrowth and Tavernetto's fragrances of aromatic herbs. They're all close-focused, precise, complete, exemplary, balanced and destined to improve over time. Their 2016 Buttafuoco is a tight-knit and crisp wine, while their 2016 Ries, a Renano, proves sharp and savory.

| | |
|---|---|
| ● Bertone Pinot Nero '15 | ▼▼▼ 6 |
| ● Pernice Pinot Nero '15 | ▼▼ 5 |
| ● Tavernetto Pinot Nero '15 | ▼▼ 3* |
| ○ Cépage Brut M. Cl. | ▼▼ 4 |
| ● OP Bonarda L'Alcova '17 | ▼▼ 3 |
| ● OP Buttafuoco '16 | ▼▼ 3 |
| ○ Ries Riesling '16 | ▼▼ 3 |
| ● Costa del Nero Pinot Nero '16 | ▼ 4 |
| ● Bertone Pinot Nero '13 | ♈♈♈ 5 |
| ○ OP Pinot Nero Brut Conte Vistarino 1865 '08 | ♈♈♈ 4* |
| ● OP Pinot Nero Pernice '06 | ♈♈♈ 4* |
| ● OP Bonarda L'Alcova '16 | ♈♈ 3 |
| ● OP Buttafuoco '15 | ♈♈ 3 |
| ○ OP Pinot Nero Brut Conte Vistarino 1865 '12 | ♈♈ 5 |
| ● Pernice Pinot Nero '13 | ♈♈ 5 |

## La Costa

FRAZ. COSTA
VIA GALBUSERA NERA, 2
23888 PEREGO [LC]
TEL. +39 0395312218
www.la-costa.it

CELLAR SALES
PRE-BOOKED VISITS
RESTAURANT SERVICE
ANNUAL PRODUCTION 30,000 bottles
HECTARES UNDER VINE 12.00
VITICULTURE METHOD Certified Organic

The Crippa family's lovely estate, situated within the Montevecchia Regional Park and Curone Valley (in Monticello Brianza) definitely deserves a visit. It's an intact natural landscape made up of woods and vineyards, 12 hectares of them cultivated organically. And their energy is supplied by solar panels. Riesling Renano and Pinot Nero do particularly well in the calcareous, stony terrain hair, making for a style that draws on the excellent freshness and fragrance of the grapes. Their 2016 San Giobbe, a Pinot Nero, is truly exemplary, especially when it comes to finesse. On the nose it features lovely notes of raspberry, with spicy and flowery nuances. On the palate it's rich and balanced with a long, elegant finish. Their 2015 Solesta, a wine full of character, is a classic by now. Made with Riesling Renano, it expresses notes of petrol, medicinal herbs and flint. On the palate it proves mouthfilling, with a nice, fresh acidity and a long, balanced finish.

| | |
|---|---|
| ● San Giobbe '16 | ▼▼ 5 |
| ○ Solesta '15 | ▼▼ 4 |
| ○ Brigante Bianco '17 | ▼▼ 3 |
| ● Brigante Rosso '16 | ▼▼ 3 |
| ○ Brigante Bianco '15 | ♈♈ 3 |
| ● Brigante Rosso '15 | ♈♈ 3 |
| ○ Càlido '15 | ♈♈ 5 |
| ● San Giobbe '15 | ♈♈ 4 |
| ● San Giobbe '13 | ♈♈ 4 |
| ● San Giobbe '12 | ♈♈ 4 |
| ● Seriz '12 | ♈♈ 3 |
| ● Seriz '11 | ♈♈ 3 |
| ○ Solesta '14 | ♈♈ 4 |
| ○ Solesta '13 | ♈♈ 4 |
| ○ Solesta '12 | ♈♈ 3* |
| ● Vino del Quattordici '14 | ♈♈ 3 |

# La Costaiola

FRAZ. COSTAIOLA
VIA COSTAIOLA, 25
27054 MONTEBELLO DELLA BATTAGLIA [PV]
TEL. +39 038383169
www.lacostaiola.it

CELLAR SALES
ACCOMMODATION
ANNUAL PRODUCTION 80,000 bottles
HECTARES UNDER VINE 13.00

Costaiola is situated in a splendid position in the district of the same name, on the lower hills between Montebello della Battaglia and Casteggio. For some years now the Rossetti and Scrivani families have been producing the brand that bears their name, entirely dedicated to Metodo Classico sparklers made with Pinot Nero. The results are proving increasingly convincing, a good sign that they're on the right track. Their Nature just missed earning Tre Bicchieri. It features vigor, determination, savoriness, fine sparkle, fragrances of yellow citrus, consistent and subtle tension, and notable personality. Their Brut also delivered, proving supple, linear, lean, persistent and redolent of lime and mandarin orange. Their Rosé offers up aromas of small wild berries while also exhibiting a quality common to their entire selection: elegance and finesse of sparkle. Onward.

| | |
|---|---|
| ○ Brut Nature M. Cl. | ▼▼ 4 |
| ○ Blanc de Noirs Brut M. Cl. | ▼▼ 4 |
| ⊙ Rosé de Noir Brut M. Cl. | ▼▼ 4 |
| ● OP Barbera Giada '12 | ♀♀ 2* |
| ● OP Bonarda Vivace Giada '13 | ♀♀ 2* |
| ● Pinot Nero Bricca '15 | ♀♀ 3 |

# Costaripa

VIA COSTA, 1A
25080 MONIGA DEL GARDA [BS]
TEL. +39 0365502010
www.costaripa.it

CELLAR SALES
PRE-BOOKED VISITS
ANNUAL PRODUCTION 400,000 bottles
HECTARES UNDER VINE 40.00

Mattia Vezzola, a famous enologist who divides his time between his winery and a number of other commitments, is on a mission. His purpose is to develop and promote the attributes of Valtènesi's traditional grape varieties (foremost Groppello). It's his homeland and the area where his family's winery is based, and here Mattia (a passionate sparkling winemaker) makes his prized Metodo Classico cuvées as well as various elegant Chiarettos, some of which prove surprisingly ageworthy. He's accompanied by his children Nicole and Gherardo. For years Mattia has been making some of Italy's best rosés, and he's been working to create a great rosé that can stand the test of time. Following the directions of Pompeo Molmenti who had indicated Groppello and Valtènesi as the perfect cultivar and terroir for the wine. After an excellent 2013 Pompeo Molmenti, this year they submitted a 2015 of refined elegance. It too is a wine that's bound to evolve gracefully over the years. Rich, deep, elegant and savory, it takes home Tre Bicchieri and our award for Rosé of the Year.

| | |
|---|---|
| ⊙ Valtènesi Chiaretto Molmenti '15 | ▼▼▼ 2* |
| ⊙ Brut Grande Annata '13 | ▼▼ 5 |
| ○ Mattia Vezzola Brut | ▼▼ 5 |
| ⊙ Mattia Vezzola Brut Rosé | ▼▼ 5 |
| ⊙ Valtènesi Chiaretto RosaMara '17 | ▼▼ 2* |
| ○ Garda Brut Crémant Mattia Vezzola | ♀♀ 4 |
| ○ Lugana Pievecroce '15 | ♀♀ 2* |
| ○ Mattia Vezzola Brut '11 | ♀♀ 5 |
| ⊙ Mattia Vezzola Rosé '11 | ♀♀ 5 |
| ⊙ Valtènesi Chiaretto Molmenti '13 | ♀♀ 2* |
| ⊙ Valtènesi Chiaretto Molmenti '12 | ♀♀ 2* |
| ⊙ Valtènesi Chiaretto RosaMara '16 | ♀♀ 2* |
| ⊙ Valtènesi Chiaretto RosaMara '15 | ♀♀ 2* |

## Derbusco Cives

VIA PROVINCIALE, 83
25030 ERBUSCO [BS]
TEL. +39 0307731164
www.derbuscocives.com

CELLAR SALES
PRE-BOOKED VISITS
RESTAURANT SERVICE
ANNUAL PRODUCTION 90,000 bottles
HECTARES UNDER VINE 12.00

In 2004, a group of five friends, Dario and Giuseppe Vezzoli, Luigi Dotti, Paolo Brescianini and Vanni Bordiga founded this lovely winery called simply 'Cittadini di Erbusco' ('Citizens of Erbusco'). The name was chosen so as to underline the importance and unique qualities of the terroir of Erbusco, the capital of Franciacorta. The winery boasts some 12 hectares of vineyards and draws on an approach that's somewhat unconventional, like refermentation with Franciacorta must and late disgorgement. Their commitment to environmental sustainability is noteworthy. Giuseppe Vezzoli and his partners are tireless experimenters. They referment with unfermented must, prefer lengthy stays on the lees and late disgorgement when it comes to their cuvées (thus the name Doppio RD). With honors, their Doppio Erre DV made it into our finals this year, thanks to its lovely notes of ripe fruit, and an evolved, complex character of great class. Their 2012 Brut is fruity and pleasant while their 2012 Crisalis, a blanc de noirs, is complex, deep and well-balanced.

| | | |
|---|---|---|
| ○ Franciacorta Brut Doppio Erre DV | 🍷🍷 | 5 |
| ○ Franciacorta Brut '12 | 🍷🍷 | 6 |
| ○ Franciacorta Brut Crisalis '12 | 🍷🍷 | 6 |
| ○ Franciacorta Extra Brut '12 | 🍷🍷 | 8 |
| ○ Franciacorta Brut Doppio Erre Di | 🍷 | 5 |
| ○ Franciacorta Brut '11 | 🍷🍷 | 6 |
| ○ Franciacorta Brut '10 | 🍷🍷 | 6 |
| ○ Franciacorta Brut '09 | 🍷🍷 | 6 |
| ○ Franciacorta Brut Crisalis '11 | 🍷🍷 | 6 |
| ○ Franciacorta Extra Brut '11 | 🍷🍷 | 8 |
| ○ Franciacorta Extra Brut '10 | 🍷🍷 | 8 |

## Dirupi

LOC. MADONNA DI CAMPAGNA
VIA GRUMELLO, 1
23020 MONTAGNA IN VALTELLINA [SO]
TEL. +39 3472909779
www.dirupi.com

CELLAR SALES
PRE-BOOKED VISITS
ANNUAL PRODUCTION 15,000 bottles
HECTARES UNDER VINE 4.50

Founded in 2003, Birba and Faso's vivacious winery is proving ever more complete. It's growing, in fact, in terms of wines offered and variety, all of which are interpreted according to an exquisitely contemporary style that puts details first, fragrance, energy of flavor and excellent supporting acidity. The result, often, is wines of uncommon drinkability. This year they've added their Inferno and Grumello, limited edition wines that will surely prove valuable. Their 2016 Valtellina Superiore exhibits great personality and elegance. On the nose it offers up all its aromatic endowment: red fruit, tobacco and dried flowers. On the palate it proves complex, with freshness and a very lengthy finish. It brings home Tre Bicchieri. Their 2015 Inferno Guast surprises with its strong territorial identity. Its web of aromas is perfect: dried herbs, spices, gentian and raspberry. On the palate it proves velvety but taut. Their 2015 Grumello Gess is vibrant, multifaceted and very complex. It's a truly ageworthy wine

| | | |
|---|---|---|
| ● Valtellina Sup. Dirupi '16 | 🍷🍷🍷 | 4* |
| ● Valtellina Sup. Grumello Gess '15 | 🍷🍷 | 5 |
| ● Valtellina Sup. Inferno Guast '15 | 🍷🍷 | 6 |
| ● Sforzato di Valtellina Vino Sbagliato '16 | 🍷🍷 | 6 |
| ● Valtellina Sup. Grumello Dirupi Ris. '15 | 🍷🍷 | 6 |
| ● Rosso di Valtellina Olè '17 | 🍷 | 3 |
| ● Valtellina Sup. Dirupi Ris. '14 | 🍷🍷🍷 | 6 |
| ● Valtellina Sup. Dirupi Ris. '12 | 🍷🍷🍷 | 6 |
| ● Valtellina Sup. Dirupi Ris. '11 | 🍷🍷🍷 | 6 |
| ● Valtellina Sup. Dirupi Ris. '09 | 🍷🍷🍷 | 6 |
| ● Rosso di Valtellina Olè '16 | 🍷🍷 | 3 |
| ● Sforzato di Valtellina Vino Sbagliato '15 | 🍷🍷 | 6 |
| ● Sforzato di Valtellina Vino Sbagliato '14 | 🍷🍷 | 6 |
| ● Valtellina Sup. Dirupi '15 | 🍷🍷 | 4 |
| ● Valtellina Sup. Dirupi '14 | 🍷🍷 | 4 |
| ● Valtellina Sup. Dirupi Ris. '13 | 🍷🍷 | 6 |

# Sandro Fay

LOC. SAN GIACOMO DI TEGLIO
VIA PILA CASELLI, 1
23030 TEGLIO [SO]
TEL. +39 0342786071
www.vinifay.it

CELLAR SALES
PRE-BOOKED VISITS
ANNUAL PRODUCTION 38,000 bottles
HECTARES UNDER VINE 13.00

'Aim high' has always been the mission of the winery founded by Sandro Fay in the heart of Valgella, in Valtellina. He proved well ahead of his time when, with the help of his son Marco, he was researching the impact of altitude on viticulture, gradually moving his plots higher so as to take full advantage of the positions and characteristics of a territory whose strength lies in its elevation. And his foreword-thinking agronomic intuitions have favored the entire area. All the wines presented exhibit noteworthy personality, including their magnificent 2014 Carterìa Riserva, a wine redolent of fresh red fruit crossed by spicy notes. In the mouth it proves subtle, complex, savory and consistent, with a long finish. Their 2014 Sforzato Ronco del Picchio is a rock. It's a vibrant wine with nuances of dried herbs, tobacco and quinine - truly classy. On the palate it's austere, fresh even, but never opulent, and features a very long finish.

| | |
|---|---|
| ● Sforzato di Valtellina Ronco del Picchio '14 | ♥♥ 6 |
| ● Valtellina Sup. Valgella Carterìa Ris. '14 | ♥♥ 6 |
| ● Valtellina Sup. Costa Bassa '15 | ♥♥ 4 |
| ● Valtellina Sup. Sassella Il Glicine '15 | ♥♥ 5 |
| ● Valtellina Sup. Valgella Ca' Morèi '15 | ♥♥ 5 |
| ● Valtellina Sforzato Ronco del Picchio '02 | ♥♥♥ 6 |
| ● Valtellina Sup. Valgella Cà Morèi '13 | ♥♥♥ 5 |
| ● La Faya '13 | ♥♥ 5 |
| ● Sforzato di Valtellina Ronco del Picchio '13 | ♥♥ 6 |
| ● Valtellina Sup. Costa Bassa '14 | ♥♥ 4 |
| ● Valtellina Sup. Sassella Il Glicine '15 | ♥♥ 5 |
| ● Valtellina Sup. Sassella Il Glicine '13 | ♥♥ 4 |
| ● Valtellina Sup. Valgella Cà Morèi '14 | ♥♥ 5 |
| ● Valtellina Sup. Valgella Carterìa Ris. '13 | ♥♥ 5 |

# ★Ferghettina

VIA SALINE, 11
25030 ADRO [BS]
TEL. +39 0307451212
www.ferghettina.it

CELLAR SALES
PRE-BOOKED VISITS
ANNUAL PRODUCTION 400,000 bottles
HECTARES UNDER VINE 160.00
VITICULTURE METHOD Certified Organic
SUSTAINABLE WINERY

They only began in 1991 with a few thousand bottles but today Roberto Gatti and family's Ferghettina is one of Franciacorta's crown jewels. If Roberto and Andreina, his wife, had the intuition, their enologist children Laura and Matteo are to thank for the fact that the estate controls 160 hectares of vineyards and produces top blends in their spacious and modern cellar (6000 square meters). Their cuvées are among the best representatives of the terroir. Their Riserva 33 is a cuvèe made with their best Chardonnay grapes vinified in steel and blended the following spring. The second fermentation lasts for more than 80 months, and this explains the wine's charm and complexity. By now it's a house classic. Their 2011 wins you over from the outset, with its brilliant straw-yellow and light green color. Its complex nose calls up ripe fruit, acacia honey and white flowers, with subtle strokes of chamomile and herbs. These reemerge close-focused on its subtle palate and persist right up through its long finish.

| | |
|---|---|
| ○ Franciacorta Pas Dosé Riserva 33 '11 | ♥♥♥ 6 |
| ○ Franciacorta Brut Milledì '14 | ♥♥ 5 |
| ● Baladello Merlot '13 | ♥♥ 5 |
| ○ Curtefranca Bianco '17 | ♥♥ 2* |
| ○ Franciacorta Brut | ♥♥ 4 |
| ⊙ Franciacorta Brut Rosé '14 | ♥♥ 5 |
| ○ Franciacorta Extra Brut '12 | ♥♥ 6 |
| ○ Franciacorta Saten '14 | ♥♥ 5 |
| ● Curtefranca Rosso '16 | ♥ 2 |
| ○ Franciacorta Extra Brut '09 | ♥♥♥ 5 |
| ○ Franciacorta Extra Brut '05 | ♥♥♥ 5 |
| ○ Franciacorta Pas Dosé 33 Ris. '10 | ♥♥♥ 6 |
| ○ Franciacorta Pas Dosé 33 Ris. '09 | ♥♥♥ 6 |
| ○ Franciacorta Pas Dosé 33 Ris. '07 | ♥♥♥ 6 |
| ○ Franciacorta Pas Dosé 33 Ris. '06 | ♥♥♥ 6 |

# Fiamberti

VIA CHIESA, 17
27044 CANNETO PAVESE [PV]
TEL. +39 038588019
www.fiambertivini.it

**CELLAR SALES**
**PRE-BOOKED VISITS**
**ANNUAL PRODUCTION** 140,000 bottles
**HECTARES UNDER VINE** 18.00

The Fiamberti family winery sees father
Ambrogio dedicating himself to the area's
traditional classics while his son Giulio
focuses on Metodo Classico and
Buttafuoco Storico. They posses some of
Canneto Pavese's best vineyards in a
district famous for its red wines. As per
local tradition, the winery produces various
typologies: whites, reds, still, semi-
sparkling and sparkling, with a noteworthy
overall quality and detectable improvement
in recent years. They still haven't produced
a crown jewel, but it's a goal that's well
within their grasp if they continue with the
same uncompromising perseverance. Their
2013 Vigna Sacca del Prete is a
Buttafuoco Storico of notable depth,
exhibiting savoriness and vigor, with
abundant aromas of wild fruit, mint and a
long finish. Their Brut Metodo Classico is
an opulent Pinot Nero with notes of
aromatic herbs and citrus, while their
fragrant 2015 Cacciatore, a Buttafuoco
redolent of ripe fruit, features well-
managed tannins and excellent drinkability.

| | |
|---|---:|
| ● OP Buttafuoco Storico V. Sacca del Prete '13 | 🍷🍷 4 |
| ● OP Buttafuoco Cacciatore '15 | 🍷🍷 3 |
| ○ OP Pinot Nero Brut M. Cl. | 🍷🍷 3 |
| ○ Ida Riesling '17 | 🍷 2 |
| ⊙ OP Cruasé | 🍷 4 |
| ● OP Bonarda La Briccona '17 | 🍷 2 |
| ● OP Bonarda Vivace La Briccona '15 | 🍷🍷 2* |
| ● OP Buttafuoco Storico V. Sacca del Prete '12 | 🍷🍷 4 |
| ● OP Buttafuoco Storico V. Sacca del Prete '11 | 🍷🍷 4 |
| ● OP Pinot Nero Nero '13 | 🍷🍷 2* |
| ● OP Sangue di Giuda Lella '16 | 🍷🍷 2* |
| ● OP Sangue di Giuda Lella '15 | 🍷🍷 2* |

# Frecciarossa

VIA VIGORELLI, 141
27045 CASTEGGIO [PV]
TEL. +39 0383804465
www.frecciarossa.com

**CELLAR SALES**
**PRE-BOOKED VISITS**
**ANNUAL PRODUCTION** 80,000 bottles
**HECTARES UNDER VINE** 34.00

The beautiful estate purchased by Mario
Odero in 1919, and later renovated by his
granddaughter Margherita, features a 19th
century villa, a rustic courtyard, cellar and
vineyards managed by Pierluigi Donna.
Here in upper Casteggio, along the road
that goes to Montalto, the soil various
greatly from plot to plot. For some years
now the winery has been overseen by
Valeria Radici, Margherita's daughter, with
the critical of Gianluca Scaglione and
Cristiano Garella. Together they've made it
a benchmark for high-quality wines in
Oltrepò. Their Pinot Nero and Riesling are
the cultivar that have had the most
success. Valeria Radici wanted us to know
that this year she preferred not to send us
samples. Considering the situation, we
decided to purchase three of her top wines
and found them, as always, of a high
quality standard, with a special mention for
her extremely pleasant, elegant and brilliant
Carillo. Her 2016 Riesling Gli Orti is a
fragrant, austere and elegant wine, while
her 2015 Giorgio Odero still needs more
time in the bottle.

| | |
|---|---:|
| ○ Gli Orti Riesling '16 | 🍷🍷 2* |
| ● OP Pinot Nero Carillo '16 | 🍷🍷 3* |
| ● OP Pinot Nero Giorgio Odero '15 | 🍷🍷 5 |
| ● OP Pinot Nero Giorgio Odero '12 | 🍷🍷🍷 5 |
| ● OP Pinot Nero Giorgio Odero '11 | 🍷🍷🍷 5 |
| ● OP Pinot Nero Giorgio Odero '10 | 🍷🍷🍷 5 |
| ● OP Pinot Nero Giorgio Odero '08 | 🍷🍷🍷 5 |
| ● OP Pinot Nero Giorgio Odero '07 | 🍷🍷🍷 5 |
| ● OP Pinot Nero Giorgio Odero '05 | 🍷🍷🍷 5 |
| ● OP Pinot Nero Carillo '15 | 🍷🍷 2* |
| ● OP Pinot Nero Carillo '14 | 🍷🍷 2* |
| ● OP Pinot Nero Giorgio Odero '14 | 🍷🍷 5 |
| ● OP Pinot Nero Giorgio Odero '13 | 🍷🍷 5 |
| ○ OP Riesling Gli Orti '15 | 🍷🍷 2* |
| ○ OP Riesling Gli Orti '14 | 🍷🍷 2* |

# Enrico Gatti

VIA METELLI, 9
25030 ERBUSCO [BS]
TEL. +39 0307267999
www.enricogatti.it

CELLAR SALES
PRE-BOOKED VISITS
ANNUAL PRODUCTION 120,000 bottles
HECTARES UNDER VINE 17.00

In 1975 Enrico Gatti founded this lovely Franciacorta winery, which has established itself as one of the appellation's best. Brothers Lorenzo and Paola Gatti form a close-knit family team, along with Paola's husband, Enzo Balzarini. The Gatti family bring artisanal attention to their work and only use grapes from the family's private vineyards. There are 17 hectares of them, all in Erbusco, a territory that confers structure, fullness and a nice mineral streak to all their cuvées. Their Nature represents the essence of their style. The proof lies in the brilliant performance put in during our finals by their non-vintage. It's a brilliant and pale, straw-yellow and light green colored wine with extremely fine perlage. On the nose it proves fresh and enticing in its aromas of white fruit and citrusy nuances. These come through perfectly on its savory, crisp, lean and highly drinkable palate. Their 2014 Satèn features style and freshness. It's a soft wine, though without being too round, making for one of the best representations of the style.

| | |
|---|---|
| ○ Franciacorta Nature | ▼▼ 5 |
| ○ Franciacorta Brut | ▼▼ 5 |
| ○ Franciacorta Brut Satèn '14 | ▼▼ 5 |
| ◉ Franciacorta Brut Rosé | ▼ 5 |
| ○ Franciacorta Brut '05 | ▼▼▼ 6 |
| ○ Franciacorta Nature '07 | ▼▼▼ 5 |
| ○ Franciacorta Satèn '05 | ▼▼▼ 5 |
| ○ Franciacorta Satèn '03 | ▼▼▼ 5 |
| ○ Franciacorta Satèn '02 | ▼▼▼ 4 |
| ○ Franciacorta Satèn '01 | ▼▼▼ 4 |
| ○ Franciacorta Satèn '00 | ▼▼▼ 5 |
| ○ Franciacorta Brut Satèn '13 | ▼▼ 5 |
| ○ Franciacorta Nature '11 | ▼▼ 6 |

# I Gessi

FRAZ. CASCINA FOSSA, 8
27050 OLIVA GESSI [PV]
TEL. +39 0383896606
www.cantineigessi.it

CELLAR SALES
PRE-BOOKED VISITS
ACCOMMODATION
ANNUAL PRODUCTION 160,000 bottles
HECTARES UNDER VINE 41.00

Fabbio Defilippi is leading this lovely, organically managed winery and farm stay with noteworthy results. The estate is comprised of 27 hectares, primarily cultivated in calcareous, limestone rich terrain (as the name of the winery and district suggest, 'Gessi' being the Italian word for 'chalk'). Fabbio's brother Emilio, an expert enologist, oversees production of their wines, which offer the best when it comes to Riesling, and a line of sparkling wines that keep getting better each year. Their chewy 2012 Maria Cristina Pas Dosé, a wine with firmly rooted acidity, features fruity pulp, aromas of pineapple and citrus. Their non-vintage Maria Cristina Brut opts for greater simplicity, with its delicious tropical notes. Their well-balanced 2017 Bonarda, a wine redolent of plums and ripe wild berries, proves extremely well-made. Their pleasant and varietal 2015 Pinot Nero is enriched by nuances of coffee and chocolate, while their 2017 Riesling features freshness and aromas of wild flowers.

| | |
|---|---|
| ○ OP Pinot Nero Pas Dosé M. Cl. Maria Cristina '12 | ▼▼ 8 |
| ○ Maria Cristina Brut M. Cl. | ▼▼ 3 |
| ● OP Bonarda Frizzante '17 | ▼▼ 2* |
| ● Pinot Nero 1907 '15 | ▼▼ 6 |
| ○ Riesling di Oliva '17 | ▼ 3 |
| ● OP Barbera '13 | ▽▽ 2* |
| ● OP Bonarda I Gessi '15 | ▽▽ 2* |
| ○ OP Pinot Grigio Crocetta '15 | ▽▽ 2* |
| ○ OP Pinot Nero Pas Dosé Maria Cristina '11 | ▽▽ 5 |
| ○ OP Pinot Nero Pas Dosé Maria Cristina '10 | ▽▽ 5 |
| ○ OP Riesling '13 | ▽▽ 1* |
| ○ OP Riesling I Gessi '16 | ▽▽ 1* |

## ★Giorgi

FRAZ. CAMPONOCE, 39A
27044 CANNETO PAVESE [PV]
TEL. +39 0385262151
www.giorgi-wines.it

CELLAR SALES
PRE-BOOKED VISITS
ANNUAL PRODUCTION 1,600,000 bottles
HECTARES UNDER VINE 60.00

The Giorgi family's winery is one of the largest private producers in Oltrepò. Since the beginning it's focused on bottled wine, rather than bulk. The explosive Fabiano (Antonio's son), his sister Eleonora and his wife, Ileana, are giving the winery a boost, aiming for high-quality wines (as our tastings have confirmed), with the best results achieved when it comes to Metodo Classico sparklers. There are some 20 of them, all of them well-made (and some even outstanding), with production volumes on the rise. And their 2014 '1870' takes home the winery's 10th Tre Bicchieri. It offers up aromas of peach, apricot, aniseed and aromatic herbs. On the palate it proves extremely fine in its sparkle and well-orchestrated, yielding a masterful, savory weave. Their 2015 Gianfranco Giorgi opts for more marked residual sweetness and more evolved aromas, while their Gerry Scotti, an Extra Brut, does better. Their 2016 Monteroso, a red Pinot Nero, is the best ever, though their entire selection proves sound and consistent.

| | | |
|---|---|---|
| ○ OP Pinot Nero Brut M. Cl. 1870 '14 | ♥♥♥ | 5 |
| ○ OP Pinot Nero Brut M. Cl. Gianfranco Giorgi '15 | ♥♥ | 5 |
| ○ Top Zero Pas Dosé M. Cl. | ♥♥ | 4 |
| ○ Gerry Scotti Extra Brut M. Cl. | ♥♥ | 4 |
| ● OP Bonarda Vivace La Brughera '17 | ♥♥ | 2* |
| ● OP Pinot Nero Monteroso '16 | ♥♥ | 3 |
| ○ OP Riesling Il Bandito '17 | ♥♥ | 4 |
| ○ Lady Ginevra '16 | ♥ | 4 |
| ☉ OP Cruasé | ♥ | 4 |
| ● Vigalòn '17 | ♥ | 2 |
| ○ OP Pinot Nero Brut 1870 '12 | ♡♡♡ | 5 |
| ○ OP Pinot Nero Brut 1870 '11 | ♡♡♡ | 5 |
| ○ OP Pinot Nero Brut 1870 '10 | ♡♡♡ | 5 |
| ○ OP Pinot Nero Brut 1870 '09 | ♡♡♡ | 5 |
| ○ OP Pinot Nero Brut 1870 '08 | ♡♡♡ | 5 |

## Isimbarda

FRAZ. CASTELLO
CASCINA ISIMBARDA
27046 SANTA GIULETTA [PV]
TEL. +39 0383899256
www.isimbarda.com

CELLAR SALES
PRE-BOOKED VISITS
ANNUAL PRODUCTION 130,000 bottles
HECTARES UNDER VINE 40.00

Isimbarda is situated in the innermost part of Santa Giuletta, near Pietra de' Giorgi. It's one of Oltrepò Pavese's most charming districts. Here, in the 17th century, stood the feudal estate of the marquis Isimbarda family, and as early as the 19th century quality wine was made. Luigi Meroni is its current owner, presiding over 40 hectares of vineyards with the support of Venetian enologist Daniele Zangelmi. Wines with a territorial identity, Riesling Renano and Pinot Nero, are cultivated on various types of soil, from marly, calcareous terrain to clay. Their 2017 Vigna Martina confirmed its status as one of the most interesting Rieslings in the territory, with its abundant fragrances of herbs and wild flowers (though it will still need a few more years before peaking). Their 2016 Pinot Nero Vigna del Cardinale is a pleasant and varietal wine with ripe aromas. Their 2014 Première Cuvée, a Metodo Classico sparkler made with Pinot Nero and 20% Chardonnay, features close-focused fragrances of peach. Their Cruasé offers up characteristic notes of red wild berries.

| | | |
|---|---|---|
| ○ OP Riesling Renano V. Martina '17 | ♥♥ | 3* |
| ● OP Pinot Nero V. del Cardinale '16 | ♥♥ | 4 |
| ● OP Bonarda '17 | ♥ | 2 |
| ☉ OP Cruasé | ♥ | 4 |
| ○ Première Cuvée Brut M. Cl. '14 | ♥ | 4 |
| ● OP Bonarda Vivace V. delle More '13 | ♡♡ | 2* |
| ● OP Bonarda Vivace V. delle More '15 | ♡♡ | 2* |
| ● OP Pinot Nero V. dei Giganti '16 | ♡♡ | 3 |
| ● OP Pinot Nero V. del Cardinale '11 | ♡♡ | 4 |
| ○ OP Riesling Renano V. Martina '16 | ♡♡ | 2* |
| ○ OP Riesling Renano V. Martina '14 | ♡♡ | 2* |
| ○ OP Riesling Renano V. Martina '13 | ♡♡ | 2* |
| ○ OP Riesling V. Martina '15 | ♡♡ | 3 |
| ● OP Rosso Monplò '13 | ♡♡ | 3 |

# Lantieri de Paratico

LOC. COLZANO
VIA VIDETTI (INGRESSO DA VIA 2 AGOSTO)
25031 CAPRIOLO [BS]
TEL. +39 030736151
www.lantierideparatico.it

CELLAR SALES
PRE-BOOKED VISITS
ACCOMMODATION AND RESTAURANT SERVICE
ANNUAL PRODUCTION 140,000 bottles
HECTARES UNDER VINE 18.00
VITICULTURE METHOD Certified Organic

Fabio Lantieri inherited a centuries-old legacy of viticulture. Indeed, the Lantieri de Paratico family have been in the territory since 930 CE. In 1500 they settled in Capriolo and since then their wine has been known and appreciated in Italy and throughout Europe. Fabio transformed the family's historic villa into a modern cellar where outstanding Franciacorta is made from grapes cultivated in their 20 hectares of organically managed vineyards. Their 2012 Riserva Origines brought home the producer's second Tre Bicchieri. It's an elegant cuvée made with Chardonnay (75%) and Pinot Nero, vinified partially in wood barrels and partially in steel and then matured on the lees for more than five years. It features a complex and highly elegant bouquet that spans white fruit, citrus and flowery notes with hints of vanilla. On the palate it proves savory, linear, deep and pulp, long and extremely elegant. Their 2014 Arcadia Brut did extremely well, though their entire selection proved exceptionally sound.

| | | |
|---|---|---|
| ○ Franciacorta Nature Origines Ris. '12 | ♔♔♔ | 7 |
| ○ Franciacorta Brut | ♔♔ | 4 |
| ○ Franciacorta Brut Arcadia '14 | ♔♔ | 5 |
| ○ Franciacorta Satèn | ♔♔ | 5 |
| ⊙ Franciacorta Brut Rosé | ♔ | 5 |
| ○ Franciacorta Extra Brut | ♔ | 4 |
| ● L'Enio '15 | ♔ | 5 |
| ○ Franciacorta Brut Arcadia '13 | ♔♔♔ | 5 |
| ○ Franciacorta Brut Arcadia '12 | ♔♔ | 5 |
| ○ Franciacorta Brut Arcadia '11 | ♔♔ | 5 |
| ○ Franciacorta Extra Brut Origines Ris. '10 | ♔♔ | 7 |
| ○ Franciacorta Extra Brut Origines Ris. '09 | ♔♔ | 7 |
| ○ Franciacorta Nature Origines Ris. '11 | ♔♔ | 7 |

# Lazzari

VIA MELLA, 49
25020 CAPRIANO DEL COLLE [BS]
TEL. +39 0309747387
www.lazzarivini.it

CELLAR SALES
PRE-BOOKED VISITS
ANNUAL PRODUCTION 40,000 bottles
HECTARES UNDER VINE 9.50
VITICULTURE METHOD Certified Organic
SUSTAINABLE WINERY

After years on the sidelines, this winery is making its well-deserved debut in our main section. Originally built in the late 19th century by Pasquale Lazzari, forefather of four generations of vigneron, it's now led by Davide Lazzari. Davide is in love with Monte Netto, a small hill situated at 133 meters elevation, and he's serving as an ambassador for the small appellation of Capriano del Colle. He's brought new life to the winery, moving it off the grid and obtaining organic certification. Their 2015 Riserva degli Angeli is a clear, focused wine with bold fruit, much like the hill itself. Pleasantly over-ripe aromas and hints of fruit preserves emerge, along with spices. On the palate it proves assertive and racy towards the finish; it's a red that can be enjoyed now, but will still age well. Their 2012 Adamah is an Extra Brut made with 100% Chardonnay that offers up rich and buoyant aromas of flowers and tropical fruit. Their 2016 Fausta is a blend of Trebbiano and Chardonnay that features nuances of pineapple and lime, as well as a clear mineral component.

| | | |
|---|---|---|
| ○ Adamah Extra Brut '12 | ♔♔ | 4 |
| ○ Capriano del Colle Bianco Fausto '16 | ♔♔ | 2* |
| ● Capriano del Colle Rosso Riserva degli Angeli '15 | ♔♔ | 4 |
| ● Capriano del Colle Adagio '15 | ♔ | 3 |
| ○ Capriano del Colle Bianco Sup. Bastian Contrario '15 | ♔ | 5 |
| ● Capriano del Colle Marzemino Berzami '16 | ♔ | 2 |

# Majolini

LOC. VALLE
VIA A. MANZONI, 3
25050 OME [BS]
TEL. +39 0306527378
www.majolini.it

CELLAR SALES
PRE-BOOKED VISITS
ANNUAL PRODUCTION 150,000 bottles
HECTARES UNDER VINE 24.00
VITICULTURE METHOD Certified Organic
SUSTAINABLE WINERY

The Maiolini are one of Ome's historic families, successfully entrepreneurs with deep agricultural roots that go back to the 15th century in Franciacorta. And so it was that in 1981 their lovely winery specializing in Franciacorta wine came to be. Their estate comprises 34 hectares of terrain, situated in lovely positions and in part terraced, in the municipality of Ome. Today it's being guided with passion and skill by Simone Majolini, with enology entrusted to the French consultant Jean Pierre Valade. Majolini worked hard this year and submitted an exceptionally sound selection. In particular, we point out their 2014 Brut Vintage, with its soft, fruity tones. It's a wine rich in vigor, freshness and minerality. Their Blanc de Noirs, straw-yellow colored wine with copper highlights, is also noteworthy. Elegant and linear, it calls up aromas of red fruit on the nose, while the palate comes through creamy, savory and elegant. Their non-vintage Brut is among the best in its category.

| | |
|---|---|
| ○ Franciacorta Brut | ♟♟ 5 |
| ○ Franciacorta Brut Blanc de Noir | ♟♟ 5 |
| ○ Franciacorta Brut Vintage '14 | ♟♟ 5 |
| ○ Franciacorta Pas Dosé Aligi Sassu '14 | ♟♟ 5 |
| ○ Franciacorta Satèn '14 | ♟♟ 5 |
| ⊙ Franciacorta Rosé Altera | ♟ 5 |
| ○ Franciacorta Brut Electo '00 | ♟♟♟ 6 |
| ○ Franciacorta Brut Electo '99 | ♟♟♟ 5 |
| ○ Franciacorta Brut Electo '97 | ♟♟♟ 5 |
| ○ Franciacorta Brut Satèn '13 | ♟♟ 5 |
| ○ Franciacorta Brut Vintage '09 | ♟♟ 6 |
| ○ Franciacorta Pas Dosé Aligi Sassu '08 | ♟♟ 5 |
| ○ Franciacorta Pas Dosé Aligi Sassu '07 | ♟♟ 5 |
| ○ Franciacorta Satèn '11 | ♟♟ 5 |

# ★Mamete Prevostini

LOC. SAN VITTORE
VIA DON PRIMO LUCCHINETTI, 63
23020 SONDRIO
TEL. +39 034341522
www.mameteprevostini.com

CELLAR SALES
PRE-BOOKED VISITS
RESTAURANT SERVICE
ANNUAL PRODUCTION 180,000 bottles
HECTARES UNDER VINE 20.00
SUSTAINABLE WINERY

The good work carried out by this lovely winery is bearing fruit. Managed by Mamete Prevostini, a long time leading figure of the Valtellina Wine Consortium, they're an exemplary producer when it comes to sustainability, and on the front lines in many respects. Their solid, complete selection includes racy, airy wines, as well as reserves, and wines rich in concentration and depth of flavor. Their 2016 Sassella San Lorenzo handily brings home Tre Bicchieri with its notes of tobacco and licorice, and its nuances of raspberry. In the mouth it impresses for its masterful, well-honed palate, as well as its endless, extremely fresh finish. Their 2016 Sommarovina is also excellent with its aromas of dried herbs and fruit. On the palate it goes all in on pulp, harmony and fresh acidity. Their excellent 2016 Sforzato Albareda offers up aromas of medicinal herbs and tobacco, with fresh notes of fruit preserves. In the mouth it proves extraordinary for fullness and balance, with fresh acidity and extremely fine tannins.

| | |
|---|---|
| ● Valtellina Sup. Sassella San Lorenzo '16 | ♟♟♟ 6 |
| ● Valtellina Sforzato Albareda '16 | ♟♟ 6 |
| ● Valtellina Sup. Sassella Sommarovina '16 | ♟♟ 5 |
| ● Valtellina Sforzato Corte di Cama '16 | ♟♟ 6 |
| ● Valtellina Sup. Inferno La Cruus '16 | ♟♟ 5 |
| ● Valtellina Sforzato Albareda '15 | ♟♟♟ 6 |
| ● Valtellina Sforzato Albareda '13 | ♟♟♟ 6 |
| ● Valtellina Sforzato Albareda '09 | ♟♟♟ 6 |
| ● Valtellina Sforzato Albareda '08 | ♟♟♟ 6 |
| ● Valtellina Sforzato Albareda '06 | ♟♟♟ 6 |
| ● Valtellina Sup. Ris. '09 | ♟♟♟ 5 |
| ● Valtellina Sup. Sassella San Lorenzo '10 | ♟♟♟ 5 |
| ● Valtellina Sup. Sassella Sommarovina '13 | ♟♟♟ 5 |

# Le Marchesine

VIA VALLOSA, 31
25050 PASSIRANO [BS]
TEL. +39 030657005
www.lemarchesine.it

**CELLAR SALES**
**PRE-BOOKED VISITS**
**ANNUAL PRODUCTION** 450,000 bottles
**HECTARES UNDER VINE** 47.00
**SUSTAINABLE WINERY**

Loris Biatta, along with his children Alice and Andrea, is forging ahead with passion and skill, carrying on the legacy begun by his father, Giovanni. It was he who founded Le Marchesine in the 1980s, a winery that immediately pursued top-quality wines. The estate is comprised of 47 lovely vineyards, and production volumes that approach half a million bottles. Enology is entrusted to the French consultant Jean Pierre Valade, a winemaker with international experience in the production of Metodo Classico sparkling wines. Biatta's high-quality selection features a 2011 Brut Blanc de Blancs that impressed during our finals. It exhibits a complex, appealing bouquet with notes of white and yellow fruit elegantly giving way to vanilla. These emerge punctually on the palate, where it proves creamy in its fresh sparkle and nice vigor. Their 2014 Satèn is just as worthy. It's characterized by a lovely fulness, plushness and balance with aromas of ripe white fruit and cake.

| | |
|---|---|
| ○ Franciacorta Brut Blanc de Blancs '11 | ♟♟ 8 |
| ○ Franciacorta Brut | ♟♟ 4 |
| ⊙ Franciacorta Brut Rosé '13 | ♟♟ 6 |
| ○ Franciacorta Extra Brut | ♟♟ 5 |
| ○ Franciacorta Satèn '14 | ♟♟ 6 |
| ○ Franciacorta Brut '04 | ♟♟♟ 5 |
| ○ Franciacorta Brut Blanc de Noir '09 | ♟♟♟ 5 |
| ○ Franciacorta Brut Secolo Novo '05 | ♟♟♟ 7 |
| ○ Franciacorta Dosage Zero Secolo Novo Ris. '08 | ♟♟♟ 8 |
| ⊙ Franciacorta Brut Rosé '12 | ♟♟ 6 |
| ○ Franciacorta Brut Satèn '13 | ♟♟ 6 |
| ○ Franciacorta Brut Secolo Novo '10 | ♟♟ 8 |
| ○ Franciacorta Dosage Zero Secolo Novo Ris. '09 | ♟♟ 8 |

# Tenuta Mazzolino

VIA MAZZOLINO, 34
27050 CORVINO SAN QUIRICO [PV]
TEL. +39 0383876122
www.tenuta-mazzolino.com

**CELLAR SALES**
**PRE-BOOKED VISITS**
**ANNUAL PRODUCTION** 100,000 bottles
**HECTARES UNDER VINE** 20.00

Mazzolino is a winery that should be visited when passing through Oltrepò Pavese. Their 19th century farm manor, owned by the Braggiotti family since 1980, is a bona fide rural complex complete with a villa and a lovely Italian garden. Here you breathe Burgundy, considering that almost all their estate is dedicated to Pinot Nero and Chardonnay. And that's precisely where their consultant, Kyriakos Kynigopoulos, comes from, while management is in the hands of young Francesca Seralvo Braggiotti and direction has been entrusted to the young enologist Stefano Malchiodi, from Piacenza. Their 2015 Noir is a monovarietal Pinot Nero, generous in its aromas and rich in the mouth with notes of chocolate and wild berries enriched by spicy wood. Their Cruasé is a well-made, balanced and highly drinkable wine that's also precise and fragrant in its aromas of red fruit and mint. Their 2016 Blanc is a Chardonnay whose aromas of tropical fruit and vanilla still need some time to integrate. It may be young, but it's definitely ageworthy.

| | |
|---|---|
| ● OP Pinot Nero Noir '15 | ♟♟ 5 |
| ○ OP Chardonnay Blanc '16 | ♟♟ 3 |
| ⊙ OP Cruasé Mazzolino | ♟♟ 4 |
| ○ Camarà Chardonnay '17 | ♟ 2 |
| ○ Mazzolino Blanc de Blancs Brut M. Cl. | ♟ 4 |
| ● Terrazze Pinot Nero '17 | ♟ 3 |
| ● OP Pinot Nero Noir '12 | ♟♟♟ 5 |
| ● OP Pinot Nero Noir '10 | ♟♟♟ 5 |
| ● OP Pinot Nero Noir '09 | ♟♟♟ 5 |
| ● OP Pinot Nero Noir '08 | ♟♟♟ 5 |
| ● OP Pinot Nero Noir '07 | ♟♟♟ 5 |
| ● OP Pinot Nero Noir '06 | ♟♟♟ 5 |
| ● OP Pinot Nero Noir '14 | ♟♟ 5 |
| ● OP Pinot Nero Noir '13 | ♟♟ 5 |
| ● OP Pinot Nero Noir '11 | ♟♟ 5 |

# Mirabella

VIA CANTARANE, 2
25050 RODENGO SAIANO [BS]
TEL. +39 030611197
www.mirabellafranciacorta.it

CELLAR SALES
PRE-BOOKED VISITS
ACCOMMODATION
ANNUAL PRODUCTION 450,000 bottles
HECTARES UNDER VINE 56.00
SUSTAINABLE WINERY

It was 1979 when Teresio Schiavi, an enologist, and a group of vigneron friends created a brand for their grapes. Thanks to the commitment of administrator Francesco Bracchì, and Teresio's sons Alessandro (enologist) and Alberto (commercial director), today we could say that they've proved their mettle. Bolstered by lovely headquarters, 50 hectares of vineyards and a well-equipped, modern cellar, it's full steam ahead for Mirabella with a quality selection (almost half a million bottles annually) that also demonstrates a notable sensitivity to sustainable development. We very much appreciated their Satèn and it earned a place in our finals. It's a truly lovely representation of the style, a soft, creamy, pleasing wine in its aromas of glycerine, broom and mint. On the palate it's round, though without being too rich, impressing for its creamy sparkle and freshness. Their 2009 Riserva Dom is rich, deep, savory and gratifying with lovely aromas of vanilla.

| | |
|---|---|
| ○ Franciacorta Satèn | 🍷🍷 5 |
| ◉ Franciacorta Brut Rosé | 🍷🍷 5 |
| ○ Franciacorta Dosaggio Zero Dom Ris. '09 | 🍷🍷 6 |
| ○ Franciacorta Exra Brut Demetra '12 | 🍷🍷 5 |
| ○ Franciacorta Brut Edea | 🍷 5 |
| ○ Franciacorta Extra Brut Elite | 🍷 7 |
| ○ Franciacorta Dosaggio Zero Dom '06 | 🍷🍷 6 |
| ○ Franciacorta Dosaggio Zero Dom '04 | 🍷🍷 6 |
| ○ Franciacorta Extra Brut '09 | 🍷🍷 5 |
| ● Nero d'Ombra '04 | 🍷🍷 5 |
| ○ Passito Incanto '05 | 🍷 5 |

# ★Monsupello

VIA SAN LAZZARO, 5
27050 TORRICELLA VERZATE [PV]
TEL. +39 0383896043
www.monsupello.it

CELLAR SALES
PRE-BOOKED VISITS
ANNUAL PRODUCTION 260,000 bottles
HECTARES UNDER VINE 50.00

Monsupello is managed by Pierangelo and Laura, descendants of legend Carlo Boatti. He was one of the first to believe in the quality of Oltrepò Pavese's wines and his winery continues to be a benchmark for the territory and beyond. The cellar, which is skilfully overseen by Marco Bertelegni, is particularly successful when it comes to sparkling wine, as testified to by the awards received over the years. Despite being a family-run winery, Monsupello has managed to produce a selection of very high overall quality. Among an excellent selection of Metodo Classico sparklers, their 2013 Millesimato stands out in particular. It's a wine that's complex and intriguing on the nose, with aromas ranging from flowers to bread crust and candied fruit. In the mouth it features fine sparkle, with a generous, savory, long palate. Their multi-award winning Nature proves spirited, supple and racy. Their Ca' del Tava is more complex, while their 'base line' Brut surprises (and not for the first time) for its plucky substance.

| | |
|---|---|
| ○ Brut M. Cl. '13 | 🍷🍷🍷 5 |
| ○ Brut M. Cl. | 🍷🍷 5 |
| ○ Brut M. Cl. Rosé | 🍷🍷 4 |
| ○ Brut Nature M. Cl. | 🍷🍷 4 |
| ○ Ca' del Tava Brut M. Cl. | 🍷🍷 6 |
| ● OP Bonarda Vivace Vaiolet '17 | 🍷🍷 2* |
| ○ Riesling '16 | 🍷🍷 2* |
| ● Pinot Nero Junior '17 | 🍷 3 |
| ● Podere La Borla '13 | 🍷 3 |
| ○ Brut '11 | 🍷🍷🍷 5 |
| ○ Brut '08 | 🍷🍷 5 |
| ○ OP Brut Classese '06 | 🍷🍷🍷 5 |
| ○ OP Brut Classese '04 | 🍷🍷🍷 5 |
| ● Barbera I Gelsi '13 | 🍷🍷 3 |
| ○ Brut '11 | 🍷🍷 5 |
| ○ Chardonnay '15 | 🍷🍷 2* |
| ● OP Bonarda Vivace Vaiolet '16 | 🍷🍷 2* |

# ★Monte Rossa

FRAZ. BORNATO
VIA MONTE ROSSA, 1
25040 CAZZAGO SAN MARTINO [BS]
TEL. +39 030725066
www.monterossa.com

CELLAR SALES
PRE-BOOKED VISITS
ANNUAL PRODUCTION 500,000 bottles
HECTARES UNDER VINE 70.00

Monte Rossa was founded in 1972 thanks to the efforts of the husband and wife team of Paolo and Paola Rabotti. Today their son Emanuele, who's partnered with Oscar Farinetti, is carrying forward the family winery with attention and creativity, maintaining its status as one Franciacorta's most historic and representative wineries. The estate boasts 70 hectares of vineyards in various positions, which give rise to about 500,000 bottles of excellent wine each year. Their cuvée Riserva, which is matured at length on the yeasts, has had success throughout the world. Their 2012 Cabochon Doppiozero was the wine that most impressed during our tastings. It's the younger, crisper version of Rabotti's historic and prized cuvée, a wine with a subtle and fresh charm whose close-focused aromas call up apricot, white fruit and citrus peel. On the palate it exhibits fine sparkle and a subtle vein of aromatic herbs. Their Satèn Sansevè and undosed Coupé also did well.

| | |
|---|---|
| ○ Franciacorta Cabochon Doppiozero '12 | ▼▼ 8 |
| ○ Franciacorta Brut Sansevé | ▼▼ 5 |
| ○ Franciacorta Non Dosato Coupé | ▼▼ 5 |
| ○ Franciacorta Brut P. R. | ▼ 5 |
| ○ Franciacorta Brut Prima Cuvée | ▼ 4 |
| ○ Franciacorta Brut Rosé Flamingo | ▼ 6 |
| ○ Franciacorta Brut Cabochon '05 | ▼▼▼ 6 |
| ○ Franciacorta Brut Cabochon '04 | ▼▼▼ 6 |
| ○ Franciacorta Brut Cabochon '03 | ▼▼▼ 6 |
| ○ Franciacorta Brut Cabochon '01 | ▼▼▼ 6 |
| ○ Franciacorta Brut Cabochon '99 | ▼▼▼ 7 |
| ○ Franciacorta Brut Cabochon '98 | ▼▼▼ 6 |
| ○ Franciacorta Brut Cabochon '97 | ▼▼▼ 6 |

# Monzio Compagnoni

VIA NIGOLINE, 98
25030 ADRO [BS]
TEL. +39 0307457803
www.monziocompagnoni.com

CELLAR SALES
PRE-BOOKED VISITS
ANNUAL PRODUCTION 170,000 bottles
HECTARES UNDER VINE 17.00

In 1995 Marcello Monzio Compagnoni moved from his homeland of Valcalepio to Franciacorta, where he now boasts a modern, well-equipped cellar and a sizable estate (around 30 hectares). Their cuvées, which are made in their Adro cellar, are accompanied by wines from their Scanzorosciate estate in Bergamo, with the quality of their selection reaching notable levels (despite the occasional setback). After a year off Marcello is back in our main section, and thanks to their noteworthy 2013 Satèn they also made it into our finals. It's a brilliant straw-yellow and light green colored wine with extremely fine, close-woven perlage. On the nose it offers up an array of plush and compelling, fruity aromas, calling up apricot and white peach. These reemerge on the palate, where it proves soft and tempting, but supported by a nice, lively acidity. Their 2013 Brut is assertive, fresh and determined with lovely notes of aromatic herbs.

| | |
|---|---|
| ○ Franciacorta Satèn '13 | ▼▼ 6 |
| ○ Franciacorta Brut '13 | ▼▼ 6 |
| ○ Franciacorta Brut Cuvée alla Moda | ▼▼ 5 |
| ● Colle della Luna Bergamasca '15 | ▼ 3 |
| ○ Colle della Luna Bianco '17 | ▼ 2 |
| ○ Curtefranca Bianco Ronco della Seta '17 | ▼ 3 |
| ○ Tenuta delle Farfalle Brut | ▼ 3 |
| ○ Franciacorta Extra Brut '04 | ▼▼▼ 5 |
| ○ Franciacorta Extra Brut '03 | ▼▼▼ 5 |
| ○ Curtefranca Bianco della Seta '15 | ▼▼ 4 |
| ○ Franciacorta Brut '12 | ▼▼ 5 |
| ○ Franciacorta Satèn '12 | ▼▼ 5 |
| ● Moscato di Scanzo Don Quijote '09 | ▼▼ 6 |
| ● Valcalepio Rosso di Luna '10 | ▼▼ 5 |

# Mosnel

FRAZ. CAMIGNONE
C.DA BARBOGLIO, 14
25050 PASSIRANO [BS]
TEL. +39 030653117
www.mosnel.com

CELLAR SALES
PRE-BOOKED VISITS
RESTAURANT SERVICE
ANNUAL PRODUCTION 250,000 bottles
HECTARES UNDER VINE 39.50
VITICULTURE METHOD Certified Organic

Giulio and Lucia Barzanò are the fifth generation of family to manage this historic winery in Camignone. It's a perfectly renovated 16th century farm manor and villa that can be visited or used for events. This rural complex, which also hosts their cellar, is at the center of 40 contiguous hectares of organically managed vineyards. Giulio and Lucia are honoring the passion and commitment of their mother, Emanuela Barboglio, one of Franciacorta's pioneers, by producing a range of excellent cuvées. The stylistic maturity achieved by Mosnel is made evident by the excellent performance put in by their 2008 Pas Dosé Riserva, which handily brought home Tre Bicchieri. It's a brilliant gold cuvée made primarily with Chardonnay (and smaller parts Pinot Bianco and Pinot Nero) that spends more than 100 months on the lees before disgorgement. On the nose it proves complex, with aromas of white fruit giving way to citrus and then sweeter, spicier notes. On the palate it's firm, deep and assertive. It's lengthy finish closes on delicately salty notes and iodine.

| | | |
|---|---|---|
| ○ Franciacorta Pas Dosé Ris. '08 | ♥♥♥ | 8 |
| ○ Franciacorta Extra Brut EBB '13 | ♥♥ | 7 |
| ○ Curtefranca Bianco Campolarga '17 | ♥♥ | 3 |
| ○ Franciacorta Brut | ♥♥ | 4 |
| ○ Franciacorta Nature Bio | ♥♥ | 4 |
| ○ Franciacorta Pas Dosé | ♥♥ | 4 |
| ☉ Franciacorta Pas Dosè Parosé '12 | ♥♥ | 7 |
| ○ Franciacorta Satèn '14 | ♥♥ | 5 |
| ● Curtefranca Rosso Fontecolo '16 | ♥ | 3 |
| ☉ Franciacorta Brut Rosé | ♥ | 5 |
| ○ Franciacorta Extra Brut EBB '09 | ♥♥♥ | 5 |
| ○ Franciacorta Pas Dosé QdE Ris. '04 | ♥♥♥ | 6 |
| ○ Franciacorta Satèn '05 | ♥♥♥ | 5 |
| ○ Franciacorta Extra Brut EBB '12 | ♥♥ | 5 |
| ○ Franciacorta Satèn '13 | ♥♥ | 5 |

# ★★Nino Negri

VIA GHIBELLINI
23030 CHIURO [SO]
TEL. +39 0342485211
www.ninonegri.it

CELLAR SALES
PRE-BOOKED VISITS
RESTAURANT SERVICE
ANNUAL PRODUCTION 800,000 bottles
HECTARES UNDER VINE 155.00
SUSTAINABLE WINERY

For more than 120 years Nino Negri has brought the unique character of his Valtellina wines to Italy and the world. All it takes is a few minutes to their cellar in Chiuro to understand what a historic winery this is (now owned by Gruppo Italiano Vini), and how it's contributing with its many projects to such a rich and varied territory. Over time their wide selection of wines, which easily covers the appellation's best subzones, has been taking on a more fragrant and etheric quality. Their 2015 Sforzato 5 Stelle brought home Tre Bicchieri. It's a wine that's unmistakable for its elegance, vibrant and complex with notes of quinine and tobacco, then hints of dried herbs and blackberry preserves. In the mouth it impresses for its depth, while its body proves multifaceted, with a long finish. Their extremely fine 2015 Grumello Sasso Rosso exhibits great personality. Delicate fragrances of raspberry alternate with tobacco and licorice. On the palate it proves well-orchestrated, with close-woven tannins, rich and balanced pulp and nice length. It should age well.

| | | |
|---|---|---|
| ● Valtellina Sfursat 5 Stelle '15 | ♥♥♥ | 8 |
| ● Valtellina Sup. Grumello Sassorosso '15 | ♥♥ | 5 |
| ● Valtellina Sup. Sassella Le Tense '15 | ♥♥ | 5 |
| ○ Ca' Brione '17 | ♥♥ | 5 |
| ● Valtellina Sup. Castel Chiuro Ris. '09 | ♥♥ | 8 |
| ● Valtellina Sup. Inferno Carlo Negri '15 | ♥♥ | 5 |
| ● Valtellina Sup. Mazer '15 | ♥♥ | 5 |
| ● Valtellina Sup. Vign. Fracia '15 | ♥♥ | 6 |
| ● Valtellina Sfursat 5 Stelle '13 | ♥♥♥ | 8 |
| ● Valtellina Sfursat 5 Stelle '11 | ♥♥♥ | 8 |
| ● Valtellina Sfursat 5 Stelle '10 | ♥♥♥ | 7 |
| ● Valtellina Sfursat 5 Stelle '09 | ♥♥♥ | 7 |
| ● Valtellina Sfursat 5 Stelle '07 | ♥♥♥ | 7 |
| ● Valtellina Sfursat 5 Stelle '06 | ♥♥♥ | 7 |
| ● Valtellina Sfursat Carlo Negri '15 | ♥♥♥ | 6 |
| ● Valtellina Sfursat Carlo Negri '11 | ♥♥♥ | 8 |
| ● Valtellina Sup. Vign. Fracia '08 | ♥♥♥ | 6 |

# Oltrenero

LOC. BOSCO
27049 ZENEVREDO [PV]
TEL. +39 0385245326
www.ilbosco.com

**CELLAR SALES**
**PRE-BOOKED VISITS**
**ANNUAL PRODUCTION** 1,000,000 bottles
**HECTARES UNDER VINE** 152.00

More than 30 years have passed since the Zonin family founded this lovely estate in Oltrepò Pavese on a piece of land that once hosted a monastery. Today Barbera, Croatina and Pinot Nero are cultivated on an estate that's grown from 30 to 150 hectares. In addition to being fermented on the skins, Pinot Nero, especially, figures centrally to their selection of sparkling wines. These are skillfully overseen by director Piernicola Olmo, who's turned in excellent results and made a name for Oltrenero when it comes to Metodo Classico. Their 2013 Brut Nature has reached the heights of excellence. Aromas of flowers, small fruit and lime emerge while on the palate it proves full, lively, close-focused and taut, with extremely fine sparkle and a deep, long finish. Their non-vintage Brut is just as good, with its generous nose and a determined, mineral, persistent and racy palate. Their Cruasé also delivered, opting for fruitier notes with accents of straw and aromatic herbs. It's a highly enjoyable, technically impeccable wine that also exhibits fine sparkle.

| | |
|---|---|
| ○ OP Pinot Nero Nature M. Cl Oltrenero '13 | ▼▼▼ 6 |
| ○ OP Pinot Nero Brut M. Cl. Oltrenero | ▼▼ 5 |
| ⊙ OP Cruasé Oltrenero | ▼▼ 5 |
| ● OP Bonarda '13 | ♀♀ 2* |
| ● OP Bonarda Vivace '15 | ♀♀ 2* |
| ● OP Bonarda Vivace '14 | ♀♀ 2* |
| ○ OP Pinot Nero Nature Oltrenero '10 | ♀♀ 6 |

# Pasini San Giovanni

FRAZ. RAFFA
VIA VIDELLE, 2
25080 PUEGNAGO SUL GARDA [BS]
TEL. +39 0365651419
www.pasinisangiovanni.it

**CELLAR SALES**
**PRE-BOOKED VISITS**
**RESTAURANT SERVICE**
**ANNUAL PRODUCTION** 300,000 bottles
**HECTARES UNDER VINE** 36.00
**SUSTAINABLE WINERY**

For more than 20 years cousins Luca, Sara, Laura and Paolo Pasini have been managing the family's winery and estate, which comprises more than 30 hectares along the western bank of Garda, and dividing their attention between the wines of Lugana and Valtènesi. For years the third generation of Pasini vigneron have been committed to protecting the environment and to sustainability. Their wines were among the area's first to be certified organic and their modern cellar is off the grid. This year our tastings gave us the idea of a producer that's in a period of growth in pursuit of greater stylistic definition. Their 2016 Valtènesi, a wine made with Groppello, features freshness, cleanness and character. By virtue of its fruit, it also exhibits notable drinkability. Their 2017 Chiaretto Rosagreen is a savory, fruity, crisp and mineral wine. Their two 2017 Luganas prove exceptionally sound, with a special mention for their succulent and savory Buso Caldo, a lightly macerated wine that's fermented with native yeasts.

| | |
|---|---|
| ○ Lugana '17 | ▼▼ 2* |
| ○ Lugana Buso Caldo '17 | ▼▼ 3 |
| ● Valtènesi '16 | ▼▼ 2* |
| ● Valtènesi Arzane '14 | ▼▼ 3 |
| ⊙ Valtènesi Riviera del Garda Cl. Chiaretto Rosagreen '17 | ▼▼ 3 |
| ○ 100% Extra Brut M. Cl. | ▼ 4 |
| ○ Brut Rosé M. Cl. | ▼ 4 |
| ○ Lugana Brut M. Cl. | ▼ 3 |
| ⊙ Valtènesi Riviera del Garda Cl. Chiaretto '17 | ▼ 2 |
| ○ Lugana '16 | ♀♀ 2* |
| ○ Lugana Il Lugana '16 | ♀♀ 3 |
| ○ Lugana Il Lugana Bio '15 | ♀♀ 2* |
| ⊙ Valtènesi Chiaretto '16 | ♀♀ 2* |
| ⊙ Valtènesi Il Chiaretto '16 | ♀♀ 3 |
| ⊙ Valtènesi Il Chiaretto '15 | ♀♀ 2* |

## Andrea Picchioni

FRAZ. CAMPONOCE, 4
27044 CANNETO PAVESE [PV]
TEL. +39 0385262139
www.picchioniandrea.it

CELLAR SALES
PRE-BOOKED VISITS
ACCOMMODATION
ANNUAL PRODUCTION 70,000 bottles
HECTARES UNDER VINE 10.00
VITICULTURE METHOD Certified Organic
SUSTAINABLE WINERY

For some years now Andrea Picchioni and family have managed to transform their small winery in Canneto Pavese into a top producer. Their wines are proudly territorial, made with grapes cultivated across 11 hectares of steep ridges. They'd been abandoned for years before Andrea revived them, and today he's celebrating his 30th year as a vigneron. His wines, made primarily with Croatina, Barbera and Ughetta di Canneto (and recently also Pinot Nero), exhibit character and personality in spades. Picchioni's was already a selection 'par excellence', but they've managed to do it again, with the debut of a delectable offering called Da Cima a Fondo (70% Croatina, 30% Uva Rara), which undergoes second fermentation in the bottle. The 2016 is a great, lively wine, intriguing, fragrant, appetizing, as focused and full of contrast as a poetic photo. Their 2017 Bonarda Ipazia proves tasty by virtue of its expressive fruit, while their vin de garde are aged for some ten years so as to reach their full potential.

| | |
|---|---|
| ● Da Cima a Fondo '16 | ♛♛ 3* |
| ● OP Bonarda Vivace Ipazia '17 | ♛♛ 2* |
| ● Arfena Pinot Nero '16 | ♛♛ 4 |
| ● OP Buttafuoco Bricco Riva Bianca '15 | ♛♛ 4 |
| ● OP Buttafuoco Cerasa '17 | ♛♛ 3 |
| ● Rosso d'Asia '15 | ♛♛ 4 |
| ● Arfena Pinot Nero '15 | ♛♛♛ 4* |
| ● OP Bonarda Vivace '15 | ♛♛ 2* |
| ● OP Buttafuoco Bricco Riva Bianca '13 | ♛♛ 4 |
| ● OP Buttafuoco Bricco Riva Bianca '12 | ♛♛ 4 |
| ● OP Buttafuoco Bricco Riva Bianca '11 | ♛♛ 4 |
| ● OP Buttafuoco Cerasa '14 | ♛♛ 2* |
| ● OP Sangue di Giuda Fior del Vento '16 | ♛♛ 2* |
| ● Rosso d'Asia '13 | ♛♛ 4 |

## Plozza

VIA CAPPUCCINI, 26
23037 TIRANO [SO]
TEL. +39 0342701297
www.plozza.com

CELLAR SALES
PRE-BOOKED VISITS
ANNUAL PRODUCTION 450,000 bottles
HECTARES UNDER VINE 28.00

Andrea Zanolari, whose wines can be found throughout the world, is leading this historic winery, one that's on the verge of celebrating its 100-year anniversary. Pietro Plozza founded the project that today avails itself of 28 hectares of vineyards (some private, some rented) situated at between 400 and 700 meters elevation. Their style is characterized by wines rich in intensity and fruit, dosed ever more carefully over the years, with toastiness conferred by the use of large and small wood barrels. Their 2014 Inferno Rededition, a reserve, is vibrant in its aromas, with nice sensations of spices, coffee cream and fruit preserves. The palate proves structured and this finish is long enough. Their 2014 Sforzato Blackedition offers up aromas of dried fruit, with notes of tobacco and quinine. On the palate it's mouthfilling, rich and very warm.

| | |
|---|---|
| ● Sforzato di Valtellina Blackedition '14 | ♛♛ 5 |
| ● Valtellina Sup. Inferno Rededition Ris. '14 | ♛♛ 5 |
| ● Valtellina Sup. Sassella Rededition Ris. '14 | ♛♛ 5 |
| ● Valtellina Numero Uno '01 | ♛♛♛ 7 |
| ● Numero 1 '14 | ♛♛ 8 |
| ● Numero 1 '13 | ♛♛ 7 |
| ● Sforzato di Valtellina Blackedition '13 | ♛♛ 5 |
| ● Sforzato di Valtellina Blackedition '12 | ♛♛ 5 |
| ● Valtellina Sup. Inferno Rededition '12 | ♛♛ 4 |
| ● Valtellina Sup. Inferno Rededition Ris. '13 | ♛♛ 5 |
| ● Valtellina Sup. Sassella Rededition '12 | ♛♛ 3 |
| ● Valtellina Sup. Sassella Rededition Ris. '13 | ♛♛ 5 |

# Pratello

VIA PRATELLO, 26
25080 PADENGHE SUL GARDA [BS]
TEL. +39 0309907005
www.pratello.com

CELLAR SALES
ACCOMMODATION AND RESTAURANT SERVICE
ANNUAL PRODUCTION 600,000 bottles
HECTARES UNDER VINE 70.00
VITICULTURE METHOD Certified Organic

To consider Pratello, Vincenzo Bertola's lovely winery in Garda, 'organic' would be reductive. In every thing he does, Vincenzo adopts a 'holistic' approach that goes beyond certifications (he calls it the Pratello method)! It's evident in his intensive approach to viticulture, in the non-use of copper and in a million other ways, whether it's wine, oil or produce, bioarchitecture or rural hospitality. His 70 hectares of vineyards give rise to a well-crafted selection of wines that are exported the world over. We very much appreciated their 2017 Chiaretto Sant'Emiliano, a modern, fresh rosé. It's a lovely, faint blush-colored wine with close-focused aromas of red fruit and aromatic herbs, both on the nose and on the palate. In the mouth it has a nice, fresh and sharp profile, proving crisp, savory and supple. Their 2017 Lugana 90+10 has depth, balance and presence. Their 2016 Lieti Conversari, a late-harvest wine made with Manzoni Bianco, is an evocative wine that brings together freshness, opulence, fruit and minerality.

| | | |
|---|---|---|
| ○ Lieti Conversari '16 | ♟♟ | 4 |
| ○ Lugana 90+10 '17 | ♟♟ | 3 |
| ⊙ Valtènesi Riviera del Garda Cl. Chiaretto Sant'Emiliano '17 | ♟♟ | 3 |
| ○ Benaco Bresciano '17 | ♟ | 3 |
| ○ Lugana Catulliano '17 | ♟ | 4 |
| ○ Lieti Conversari '15 | ♟♟ | 4 |
| ○ Lieti Conversari '15 | ♟♟ | 4 |
| ○ Lugana Catulliano '16 | ♟♟ | 4 |
| ○ Lugana Catulliano '15 | ♟♟ | 4 |
| ○ Lugana Il Rivale '16 | ♟♟ | 5 |
| ● Mille 1 '15 | ♟♟ | 3 |
| ● Nero per Sempre '15 | ♟♟ | 5 |
| ● Nero per Sempre '15 | ♟♟ | 5 |
| ○ Riesling '16 | ♟♟ | 3* |
| ⊙ Valtènesi Chiaretto Sant'Emiliano '16 | ♟♟ | 3 |
| ⊙ Valtènesi Torrazzo '15 | ♟♟ | 3 |

# Quadra

VIA SANT'EUSEBIO, 1
25033 COLOGNE [BS]
TEL. +39 0307157314
www.quadrafranciacorta.it

CELLAR SALES
PRE-BOOKED VISITS
RESTAURANT SERVICE
ANNUAL PRODUCTION 150,000 bottles
HECTARES UNDER VINE 32.00

In 2003 Ugo Ghezzi and his children Cristina and Marco decided to purchase a small winery and surrounding vineyards. In 2008 enologist and researcher Marco Falcetti joined the team and took over winemaking. Today they boast some 32 hectares of organically cultivated vineyards. Pinot Bianco figures centrally to their Quadra cuvée, so the grape is cultivated in three areas that complement each other well. Pinot Nero is also important to their selection and grown in a group of hill plots that are well-suited to the cultivar. Don't let yourself be prejudiced by the name or numbers, their 2011 Quvée 58 is truly delicious! It's a blend of Chardonnay (65%) and Pinot Nero from four different vineyards, vinified in part in steel and then in wood, and then aged for 66 months on the lees before disgorgement (and with minimum dosage). Fresh, elegant, deep and rich, it features nuances of ripe fruit, mint, citrus and aromatic herbs, which give way to a close-focused, mineral finish. They're definitely on the right track.

| | | |
|---|---|---|
| ○ Franciacorta Extra Brut Quvée 58 Ris. '11 | ♟♟ | 5 |
| ○ Franciacorta Satèn QSatèn '13 | ♟♟ | 5 |
| ○ Franciacorta Brut QBlack | ♟ | 5 |
| ○ Franciacorta Brut Q39 '08 | ♟♟ | 5 |
| ○ Franciacorta Dosaggio Zero EretiQ '11 | ♟♟ | 6 |
| ○ Franciacorta Dosaggio Zero EretiQ '10 | ♟♟ | 6 |
| ○ Franciacorta Dosaggio Zero EretiQ '10 | ♟♟ | 6 |
| ○ Franciacorta Dosaggio Zero QZero '11 | ♟♟ | 5 |
| ○ Franciacorta Dosaggio Zero QZero '10 | ♟♟ | 5 |
| ○ Franciacorta Extra Brut Cuvée 55 '10 | ♟♟ | 5 |
| ○ Franciacorta Extra Brut QZero '09 | ♟♟ | 5 |
| ○ Franciacorta QSatèn '12 | ♟♟ | 5 |
| ○ Franciacorta QSatèn '11 | ♟♟ | 5 |
| ○ Franciacorta QSatèn '10 | ♟♟ | 5 |
| ○ Franciacorta Quvée 46 '09 | ♟♟ | 5 |

# Francesco Quaquarini

LOC. MONTEVENEROSO
VIA CASA ZAMBIANCHI, 26
27044 CANNETO PAVESE [PV]
TEL. +39 038560152
www.quaquarinifrancesco.it

**CELLAR SALES**
**PRE-BOOKED VISITS**
**ANNUAL PRODUCTION** 650,000 bottles
**HECTARES UNDER VINE** 60.00
**VITICULTURE METHOD** Certified Organic

The Quaquarini family winery, Francesco and his children (enologist Umberto and Maria Teresa), is a sound operation that has always managed to maintain a medium-high level of quality while producing wines that are good value for the money. And there's never a gap in their selection when it comes to wines that stand out, whatever the vintage may be. Numerous wines are produced, as one would expect from an area with such a diversity of appellations and typologies, with a focus on semi-sparklers. In some cases you get the sense that Quaquarini could aim even higher. Their 2017 Bonarda Riva di Sass, a wine with truly lovely texture, offers up characteristic aromas of violet and small wild berries. On the palate residual sweetness and tannins are well-balanced. Their 2017 Sangue di Giuda features similar characteristics, with fragrances of fruit and a sweetness that's never cloying. Their 2013 Buttafuoco Storico Vigna Pregana is ripe, full-bodied, redolent of preserves, a classic wine to be enjoyed in winter together with a nice piece of braised meat.

| | |
|---|---|
| ● OP Bonarda Riva di Sass '17 | ♛♛ 3 |
| ● OP Buttafuoco Storico V. Pregana '13 | ♛♛ 6 |
| ● OP Sangue di Giuda '17 | ♛♛ 2* |
| ● OP Pinot Nero Blau '15 | ♛ 3 |
| ○ Riesling '17 | ♛ 2 |
| ● OP Barbera Poggio Anna '12 | ♕♕ 2* |
| ● OP Bonarda Vivace '15 | ♕♕ 2* |
| ● OP Bonarda Vivace '13 | ♕♕ 2* |
| ● OP Pinot Nero Blau '14 | ♕♕ 3 |
| ● OP Pinot Nero Blau '13 | ♕♕ 3 |
| ○ OP Riesling '16 | ♕♕ 2* |
| ● OP Sangue di Giuda '16 | ♕♕ 2* |
| ● OP Sangue di Giuda '15 | ♕♕ 2* |
| ● OP Sangue di Giuda '13 | ♕♕ 2* |
| ● OP Sangue di Giuda V. Acqua Calda '13 | ♕♕ 3 |

# ★Aldo Rainoldi

FRAZ. CASACCE
VIA STELVIO, 128
23030 CHIURO [SO]
TEL. +39 0342482225
www.rainoldi.com

**CELLAR SALES**
**PRE-BOOKED VISITS**
**ANNUAL PRODUCTION** 180,000 bottles
**HECTARES UNDER VINE** 9.60

Casacce is reaching out to the world, thanks in part to Aldo Rainoldi and the increasingly international scope of this solid winery situated just outside Chiuro. They're bolstered by a group of historic vineyards and well-targeted acquisitions, making for a selection that has for years proved to be of excellent quality. Their gift for Sforzato is especially evident, bringing together force and raciness, richness and nuance, for a style that's become a model. Their 2015 Sforzato Ca' Rizzieri, a supreme expression of the territory, may well be one of the best interpretations yet. Great attention is shown to the freshness of its fruit, with notes of incense and tobacco contributing to a truly impressive aromatic complexity. In the mouth it proves rich and austere, while managing to balance its multiple layers exceptionally well. Their 2015 Sfursat also shines with its notes of tobacco and spices, nuances of cherry, fruit preserved in alcohol and pencil lead. On the palate tannins are abundant though perfectly integrated, while its finish comes through long and subtle.

| | |
|---|---|
| ● Valtellina Sfursat Fruttaio Ca' Rizzieri '15 | ♛♛♛ 6 |
| ● Valtellina Sfursat '15 | ♛♛ 5 |
| ○ Cuvée Maria Vittoria Brut Rosé '12 | ♛♛ 4 |
| ● Valtellina Sup. Prugnolo '15 | ♛♛ 3 |
| ● Valtellina Sfursat '08 | ♕♕♕ 5 |
| ● Valtellina Sfursat Fruttaio Ca' Rizzieri '11 | ♕♕♕ 6 |
| ● Valtellina Sfursat Fruttaio Ca' Rizzieri '10 | ♕♕♕ 6 |
| ● Valtellina Sfursat Fruttaio Ca' Rizzieri '09 | ♕♕♕ 6 |
| ● Valtellina Sfursat Fruttaio Ca' Rizzieri '06 | ♕♕♕ 6 |
| ● Valtellina Sfursat Fruttaio Ca' Rizzieri '02 | ♕♕♕ 6 |
| ● Valtellina Sup. Sassella Ris. '13 | ♕♕♕ 5 |
| ● Valtellina Sup. Sassella Ris. '12 | ♕♕♕ 5 |

# Ricci Curbastro

VIA ADRO, 37
25031 CAPRIOLO [BS]
TEL. +39 030736094
www.riccicurbastro.it

CELLAR SALES
PRE-BOOKED VISITS
ACCOMMODATION
ANNUAL PRODUCTION 200,000 bottles
HECTARES UNDER VINE 27.00
SUSTAINABLE WINERY

Thanks to more than 25 years of patient work, Riccardo Ricci Curbastro has made the family winery one of the best in Franciacorta. In addition to his related institutional work in the field (he was president of the Franciacorta Wine Consortium and has led other associations), he managed to grow the size of his estate's vineyards to almost 30 hectares. He also wisely accompanied the stylistic evolution of the territory's wines in light of new climatic challenges, cultivating his vineyards in a way that respects environmental sustainability while also producing elegant wines. This year it wasn't an older vintage that brought home top marks but a fragrant and charming 2014 Satèn, an achievement that affirms the maturity of the producer's style. It's a straw-yellow colored wine with green highlights that offers up an array of aromas - notes of fruit and Mediterranean scrubland, bay leaf, helichrysum and mint. On the palate it's plush and creamy, in keeping with the wine's style, though it's also supported by a fresh acidity that accompanies its long, gratifying finish.

| | |
|---|---|
| ○ Franciacorta Satèn '14 | ▼▼▼ 5 |
| ○ Franciacorta Dosaggio Zero Gualberto '09 | ▼▼ 6 |
| ○ Franciacorta Brut | ▼▼ 4 |
| ○ Franciacorta Extra Brut '14 | ▼▼ 5 |
| ⊙ Franciacorta Rosé | ▼▼ 5 |
| ● Pinot Nero '10 | ▼▼ 4 |
| ○ Curtefranca Bianco '17 | ▼ 2 |
| ● Curtefranca Rosso '15 | ▼ 2 |
| ○ Franciacorta Demi Sec | ▼ 4 |
| ● Sebino Rosso '16 | ▼ 2 |
| ○ Franciacorta Brut Museum Release '07 | ♀♀♀ 6 |
| ○ Franciacorta Dosaggio Zero Gualberto '06 | ♀♀♀ 6 |
| ○ Franciacorta Extra Brut '12 | ♀♀♀ 5 |
| ○ Franciacorta Extra Brut '07 | ♀♀♀ 5 |

# Ronco Calino

LOC. QUATTRO CAMINI
FRAZ. TORBIATO
VIA FENICE, 45
25030 ADRO [BS]
TEL. +39 0307451073
www.roncocalino.it

CELLAR SALES
PRE-BOOKED VISITS
ANNUAL PRODUCTION 70,000 bottles
HECTARES UNDER VINE 13.00
VITICULTURE METHOD Certified Organic
SUSTAINABLE WINERY

Ronco Calino was founded just over 20 years ago when Paolo Radici decided to purchase the estate previously owned by pianist Arturo Benedetti Michelangeli and entrust it to his passionate wife, Laura. Today it's a recognized producer with 13 hectares of vineyards in the spectacular morainic amphitheater and supported by Leonardo Valenti (enologist) as well as Pierluigi Donna (agronomist). In their modern winery they make a range of Franciacortas and superb, local wines. Our tastings revealed a selection that knows no weak points and features a number of top wines. Their 2011 Brut impressed greatly during our finals. The product of an excellent year, it exhibits a less concentrated character, more elegant and expansive than in the past. It offers up notes of grilled bread, cakes and oak on the nose. These introduce a lean and fresh palate that's lively in its fruit and concludes with a lovely finish of flowers and orange blossom.

| | |
|---|---|
| ○ Franciacorta Brut '11 | ▼▼ 5 |
| ○ Curtefranca Bianco Lèant '17 | ▼▼ 3 |
| ● Curtefranca Rosso Ponènt '15 | ▼▼ 4 |
| ○ Franciacorta Brut | ▼▼ 4 |
| ○ Franciacorta Brut Nature '12 | ▼▼ 5 |
| ○ Franciacorta Extra Brut Centoventi Ris. '07 | ▼▼ 8 |
| ⊙ Franciacorta Rosé Radijan | ▼▼ 5 |
| ○ Franciacorta Satèn | ▼▼ 5 |
| ● L'Arturo Pinot Nero '15 | ▼▼ 5 |
| ○ Curtefranca Bianco Lèant '16 | ♀♀ 3 |
| ● Curtefranca Rosso Ponènt '12 | ♀♀ 4 |
| ○ Franciacorta Brut '10 | ♀♀ 5 |
| ○ Franciacorta Brut Nature '11 | ♀♀ 5 |
| ○ Franciacorta Brut Nature '10 | ♀♀ 5 |

# Tenuta Roveglia

LOC. ROVEGLIA, 1
25010 POZZOLENGO [BS]
TEL. +39 030918663
www.tenutaroveglia.it

CELLAR SALES
PRE-BOOKED VISITS
ANNUAL PRODUCTION 650,000 bottles
HECTARES UNDER VINE 86.00

As far back as the late 19th century, the Zweifel family, Swiss industrialists, had chosen to move to the southern bank of Garda so as to make wine. Over the years the small 15th-century farm manor was rebuilt and today the vineyards give rise to a well-crafted selection of Luganas and local wines. The third and fourth generation of Zweifel Azzone family are accompanied by Paolo Fabiani, who was also president of the Lugana Conservation Consortium. Filo di Arianna is undoubtedly the producer's most intriguing Lugana. Its grapes are harvested late and then vinified in large wood barrels. Their 2016 expresses truly noted depth and character. It's a brilliant, straw-yellow colored wine with a complex bouquet of super-ripe fruit revived by notes of candied citrus, saffron and spices. In the mouth it proves pervasive, gratifying and soft. It finishes with notes of fresh almonds and hazelnuts, and it's never cloying. The rest of their selection is also exceptionally sound.

| | | |
|---|---|---|
| ○ Lugana V. T. Filo di Arianna '16 | ♥♥ | 3* |
| ○ Lugana Limne '17 | ♥♥ | 2* |
| ○ Lugana Vigne di Catullo Ris. '15 | ♥♥ | 4 |
| ○ Lugana Brut | ♥ | 3 |
| ⊙ Riviera delGrda Bresciano Chiaretto '17 | ♥ | 2 |
| ● Garda Merlot '11 | ♀♀ | 2* |
| ○ Lugana Limne '14 | ♀♀ | 2* |
| ○ Lugana Limne '13 | ♀♀ | 2* |
| ○ Lugana Limne '10 | ♀♀ | 2 |
| ○ Lugana Sup. Vigne di Catullo Ris. '11 | ♀♀ | 3 |
| ○ Lugana V. T. Filo di Arianna '12 | ♀♀ | 3* |
| ○ Lugana V. T. Filo di Arianna '11 | ♀♀ | 3* |

# San Cristoforo

FRAZ. VILLA D'ERBUSCO
VIA VILLANUOVA, 2
25030 ERBUSCO [BS]
TEL. +39 0307760482
www.sancristoforo.eu

CELLAR SALES
PRE-BOOKED VISITS
ANNUAL PRODUCTION 80,000 bottles
HECTARES UNDER VINE 10.00
SUSTAINABLE WINERY

Bruno and Claudia Dotti perfectly embody the philosophy of the récoltant-manipulant. In 1997 they took over this small winery, which was already known for its quality selection. In just over 20 years of passionate work they grew their estate to its current size of about 10 hectares, and renovated the cellar, equipping it with the latest technology. Their selection may be 'intimate' but the quality of their San Cristoforo cuvées is excellent, thanks in part to their daughter Celeste, who's now a full-fledged member of the staff. The Dotti submitted an excellent selection of wines this year. Their Franciacorta made it back to our finals, this time with a 'Non Dosato' (and non-vintage) called simply 'ND'. It impressed with its stylistic precision, the cleanness of its fruity aromas and the nice acid thrust that assures excellent drinkability. Additionally they submitted one of the best Bruts we tasted this year, a savory, taut and crisp wine in its fruit. The rest of their selection also proved excellent.

| | | |
|---|---|---|
| ○ Franciacorta ND | ♥♥ | 6 |
| ○ Franciacorta Brut '13 | ♥♥ | 6 |
| ○ Franciacorta Brut | ♥♥ | 5 |
| ○ Franciacorta Pas Dosé '13 | ♥♥ | 6 |
| ○ Franciacorta Pas Dosé Celeste '10 | ♥♥ | 8 |
| ○ Franciacorta Brut '11 | ♀♀ | 6 |
| ○ Franciacorta Dosaggio Zero '11 | ♀♀ | 6 |
| ○ Franciacorta Dosaggio Zero Celeste '08 | ♀♀ | 8 |
| ○ Franciacorta Pas Dosé '12 | ♀♀ | 6 |
| ○ Franciacorta Pas Dosé '10 | ♀♀ | 6 |
| ○ Franciacorta Pas Dosé Celeste '09 | ♀♀ | 8 |

## Scuropasso

Fraz. Scorzoletta, 40/42
27043 Pietra de' Giorgi [PV]
Tel. +39 038585143
www.scuropasso.it

CELLAR SALES
PRE-BOOKED VISITS
ANNUAL PRODUCTION 200,000 bottles
HECTARES UNDER VINE 15.00

Fabio Marazzi and his young daughter
Flavia focus primarily on two types of wine:
Sparkling wine (which has always been one
of Fabio's strong suits, considering his
passion for Champagne and Metodo
Classico in general) and Buttafuoco, the
area's traditional red. Currently Cantina
Scuropasso has 15 hectares of vineyards
at their disposal, all currently being
converted to organic, and they've invested
in renewable energy to the point that
they're now off the grid. This year it was
their Pas Dosé Roccapietra that stood out
during our finals, with its hints of yellow
fruit and aniseed, and its long, sharp vigor.
Their 2012 Cruasé Roccapietra once again
proves that it's a top-level wine, rich in pulp
and fragrance. It features aromas of ripe
fruit, citrus and small red fruit, as well as
nice sparkle. Their 2013 Buttafuoco
Lunapiena is rich, spicy and complete wine
that does a nice job managing wood and
tannins. Their 2011 Brut Roccapietra is
highly evolved, going in on notes of dried
fruit and nuts.

| | |
|---|---|
| ⊙ OP Cruasé Roccapietra '12 | ♟♟ 4 |
| ○ Roccapietra Pas Dosé M. Cl. '12 | ♟♟ 4 |
| ● OP Buttafuoco Lunapiena '13 | ♟♟ 3 |
| ○ Roccapietra Brut M. Cl. '11 | ♟♟ 4 |
| ● OP Buttafuoco Scuropasso '15 | ♟ 3 |
| ○ Brut Roccapietra Zero '10 | ♟♟ 3 |
| ○ Moscato '16 | ♟♟ 2* |
| ● OP Buttafuoco '15 | ♟♟ 4 |
| ⊙ OP Cruasé '11 | ♟♟ 4 |
| ○ OP Pinot Nero Brut Roccapietra '10 | ♟♟ 4 |

## Selva Capuzza

Fraz. San Martino della Battaglia
Loc. Selva Capuzza
25010 Desenzano del Garda [BS]
Tel. +39 0309910381
www.selvacapuzza.it

CELLAR SALES
PRE-BOOKED VISITS
ACCOMMODATION AND RESTAURANT SERVICE
ANNUAL PRODUCTION 300,000 bottles
HECTARES UNDER VINE 25.00
SUSTAINABLE WINERY

Selva Capuzza is a flourishing estate that
spans 50 hectares of woods, vineyards and
olive groves, situated in the morainic
amphitheater to the south of Garda, an area
that falls within the Lugana, San Martino
della Battaglia and Garda appellations. Luca
Formentini serves as manager of the winery,
which also features an excellent restaurant
and a farmstay. Great attention is shown
for the environment and sustainability,
while their selection is specialized in
traditional wines made only with grapes
from their private vineyards. Among Garda's
complex geography of DOC appellations,
Selva Capuzza has managed to stay out of
the fray while also producing some nice
wines. Their 2017 Groppello San Biagio
exhibits freshness, pulp and character. Their
2015 Rosso Dunant, a wine that features
fruit and smooth tannins, is gratifying and
soft, with firm structure. Their 2013 Mader
is aging gracefully. Their two Luganas are
also excellent, with their 2017 Selva proving
fresh and racy while their 2017 San Vigilio
opts for greater body. But their entire
selection is high-quality.

| | |
|---|---|
| ● Garda Cl. Dunant '15 | ♟♟ 2* |
| ● Garda Cl. Groppello San Biagio '17 | ♟♟ 3 |
| ● Garda Cl. Sup. Rosso Madèr '13 | ♟♟ 3 |
| ○ Lugana San Vigilio '17 | ♟♟ 3 |
| ○ Lugana Selva '17 | ♟♟ 4 |
| ○ Passito Lume | ♟♟ 5 |
| ○ San Martino della Battaglia Campo del Soglio '17 | ♟♟ 4 |
| ⊙ Valtènesi Riviera del Garda Cl. Chiaretto San Donino '17 | ♟ 2 |
| ● Garda Cl. Groppello San Biagio '16 | ♟♟ 3 |
| ○ San Martino della Battaglia Campo del Soglio '16 | ♟♟ 4 |

## Lo Sparviere

VIA COSTA
25040 MONTICELLI BRUSATI [BS]
TEL. +39 030652382
www.losparviere.com

CELLAR SALES
PRE-BOOKED VISITS
ANNUAL PRODUCTION 120,000 bottles
HECTARES UNDER VINE 30.00

Ugo Gussalli Beretta, who leads one of Italy's oldest industrial dynasties (documented as far back as 1526), shares his passion for the land and wine with his wife, Monique, and son Piero. And the Aziende Agricole group continues to grow. In addition to Castello di Radda in Chianti Classico and Orlando Contucci Ponno in Abruzzo they've taken on ForteMasso in Monforte d'Alba and, most recently, Steinhauserhof in Alto Adige, Pochi di Salorno. Sparviere spans 150 hectares, 30 of which are vineyards. Their 2013 Brut is a subtle, elegant, savory and succulent wine that's supported by extremely fresh acidity and a creamy effervescence. Its complex bouquet calls up crisp white fruit, like apple and white peach, with citrusy nuances and aromatic herbs. It handily brought home Tre Bicchieri, thus affirming the value of the work being done by the producer and its staff. It's accompanied by a noteworthy 2012 Extra Brut, with a fragrant Rosé Monique and a valid Extra Brut completing the selection.

| | |
|---|---|
| ○ Franciacorta Brut '13 | ▼▼▼ 5 |
| ○ Franciacorta Extra Brut '12 | ▼▼ 6 |
| ○ Franciacorta Extra Brut | ▼▼ 5 |
| ⊙ Franciacorta Rosé Monique | ▼▼ 5 |
| ○ Franciacorta Brut '12 | ♈♈♈ 5 |
| ○ Franciacorta Dosaggio Zero Ris. '08 | ♈♈♈ 6 |
| ○ Franciacorta Extra Brut '09 | ♈♈♈ 5 |
| ○ Franciacorta Extra Brut '08 | ♈♈♈ 5 |
| ○ Franciacorta Extra Brut '07 | ♈♈♈ 5 |
| ○ Franciacorta Brut '11 | ♈♈ 5 |
| ○ Franciacorta Dosaggio Zero Ris. '09 | ♈♈ 6 |

## Torrevilla

VIA EMILIA, 4
27050 TORRAZZA COSTE [PV]
TEL. +39 038377003
www.torrevilla.it

CELLAR SALES
PRE-BOOKED VISITS
ANNUAL PRODUCTION 3,000,000 bottles
HECTARES UNDER VINE 650.00

Cantina Sociale di Torrazza Coste was founded in 1907 while in 1970 it merged with Cantina di Codevilla, thus forming a single producer, Torrevilla, an Oltrepò cooperative with more than 300 members. In 2008 a substantial investment was made to upgrade their equipment and set in motion a process aimed at putting their best grapes to use. This was made possible, in part, thanks to a collaboration with the University of Milan and the Riccagioia Research Center (which whom they're also working on a zoning project that includes four weather stations). Genisia is the name of their premium line of wines. Among these a 2013 Brut Nature stands out. It's a wine redolent of mint, aromatic herbs and custard. In the mouth it delivers, proving well-supported and lively, with fine sparkle and a nice, clear finish. Their 2017 Riesling Superiore offers up floral notes that merge with a marked mineral vein.

| | |
|---|---|
| ○ OP Pinot Nero Brut Nature M. Cl. La Genisia '13 | ▼▼ 5 |
| ○ OP Riesling Sup. La Genisia '17 | ▼▼ 3 |
| ● OP Barbera La Genisia '16 | ▼ 2 |
| ● OP Bonarda Bio '16 | ▼ 2 |
| ⊙ OP Cruasè La Genisia | ▼ 4 |
| ● OP Barbera La Genisia '15 | ♈♈ 2* |
| ● OP Bonarda Vivace La Genisia '16 | ♈♈ 2* |
| ⊙ OP Cruasé La Genisia '12 | ♈♈ 4 |
| ⊙ OP Cruasé La Genisia '10 | ♈♈ 4 |
| ○ OP Pinot Grigio La Genisia '14 | ♈♈ 2* |

# Pietro Torti

FRAZ. CASTELROTTO, 9
27047 MONTECALVO VERSIGGIA [PV]
TEL. +39 038599763
www.pietrotorti.it

CELLAR SALES
PRE-BOOKED VISITS
ACCOMMODATION
ANNUAL PRODUCTION 40,000 bottles
HECTARES UNDER VINE 18.00
VITICULTURE METHOD Certified Organic

For some years now, Sandro Torti (son of Pietro, after whom the winery is named) has had the help of his young daughter Chiara, an agriculturalist in the true sense of the word. For years he's been practically alone in carrying forward this small but important producer situated in the Versa Valley, looking after its vineyards, cellar and the commercial side. When it comes to their wines, there's always the inevitable swings but, nevertheless, something interesting always emerges. Their 2015 Barbera Campo Rivera reached levels seen with their 2012 (two similar years, all told). Nice fruit gives rise to a highly characteristic Barbera that's intriguingly expressed more on notes of small black berries than on the classic aromas of cherry-black cherry. Spices and pulp make for a highly delectable wine. THeir 2012 Cruasé is among the best of its kind, with its aromas of small red fruits and pomegranate. It's a fruity, plucky wine. As usual, their 2017 Bonarda is at the top of its game, proving chewy, fragrant and rich, with nice fizziness and well-managed tannins.

| | | |
|---|---|---|
| ● OP Barbera Campo Rivera '15 | ♙♙ 4 | |
| ● OP Bonarda Frizzante '17 | ♙♙ 2* | |
| ☉ OP Cruasé '12 | ♙♙ 4 | |
| ○ Dosaggio Zero M. Cl. '14 | ♙ 4 | |
| ○ Fagù '17 | ♙ 2 | |
| ○ Fagù '16 | ♟♟ 2* | |
| ● OP Barbera Campo Rivera '12 | ♟♟ 4 | |
| ● OP Bonarda '13 | ♟♟ 2* | |
| ● OP Bonarda Vivace '16 | ♟♟ 2* | |
| ● OP Bonarda Vivace '15 | ♟♟ 2* | |
| ○ OP Pinot Nero Brut M. Cl. Torti '13 | ♟♟ 4 | |
| ○ OP Pinot Nero Brut M. Cl. Torti '12 | ♟♟ 3 | |
| ● Uva Rara '15 | ♟♟ 3 | |

# Travaglino

LOC. TRAVAGLINO, 6A
27040 CALVIGNANO [PV]
TEL. +39 0383872222
www.travaglino.it

CELLAR SALES
PRE-BOOKED VISITS
ACCOMMODATION AND RESTAURANT SERVICE
ANNUAL PRODUCTION 200,000 bottles
HECTARES UNDER VINE 80.00

For 150 years the Comi family has owned this historic producer in central Oltrepò Pavese, which comprises some of the area's best terrain and vineyards, especially when it comes to Riesling Renano and Pinot Nero. In the 1960s Vincenzo Comi laid the foundation for researching and identifying the crus. For some years now his granddaughter Cristina Cerri, who's supported by winemaker Achille Bergami, has taken over the reins. Their Riesling Campo della Fojada returns to its former glory. We slightly preferred the 2017, a fresh and savory wine, redolent of chamomile, wild flowers and sage. Their 2015 Rlserva is elegant full, standing out for its savoriness and mineral vein. We also welcome back their 2015 Poggio della Buttinera, a well-balanced, deep Pinot Nero with vibrant fruit. Their 2014 Brut Gran Cuvée is a highly pleasant wine, fresh and redolent of aromatic herbs.

| | | |
|---|---|---|
| ○ OP Riesling Campo della Fojada '17 | ♙♙ 3* | |
| ○ OP Brut M. Cl. Gran Cuvée | ♙♙ 4 | |
| ● OP Pinot Nero Poggio della Buttinera '15 | ♙♙ 5 | |
| ○ OP Riesling Campo della Fojada Ris. '15 | ♙♙ 3 | |
| ○ OP Pinot Nero Brut M. Cl. Cuvée 59 '14 | ♙ 4 | |
| ● OP Pinot Nero Pernero '17 | ♙ 3 | |
| ○ Brut Cuvée 59 '13 | ♟♟ 4 | |
| ○ OP Pinot Grigio Ramato '15 | ♟♟ 4 | |
| ○ OP Pinot Nero Brut Cuvée 59 '12 | ♟♟ 3 | |
| ● OP Pinot Nero Pernero '15 | ♟♟ 2* | |
| ○ OP Riesling Campo della Fojada '15 | ♟♟ 3 | |
| ○ OP Riesling Campo della Fojada '14 | ♟♟ 3 | |
| ○ OP Riesling Campo della Fojada Ris. '14 | ♟♟ 3* | |
| ● Pinot Nero Poggio della Buttinera '14 | ♟♟ 5 | |

## ★Uberti

LOC. SALEM
VIA E. FERMI, 2
25030 ERBUSCO [BS]
TEL. +39 0307267476
www.ubertivini.it

PRE-BOOKED VISITS
ANNUAL PRODUCTION 180,000 bottles
HECTARES UNDER VINE 25.00
VITICULTURE METHOD Certified Organic
SUSTAINABLE WINERY

On the brink of its 40-year anniversary, Uberti is in excellent health. Agostino and Eleonora are carrying on their legacy of viticulture and, from the beginning, they've been garnering praise for the quality of their wines, such that names like Comarì del Salem have become classics of the territory. Their secret lies in an estate par excellence, 25 hectares in Erbusco, but also in the dedication shown by their daughters Silvia (enologist) and Francesca, who oversees administration. Their Dequinque is a truly unique Franciacorta made with Chardonnay from five different years. The grapes are fermented in large wood barrels and then kept in the same vats. Every year the same amount that's removed for refermentation is re-added, allowing them to have a constant reserve. The magnum that we tasted during our finals was atypical but exhibited strong personality. It's a rich, close-woven wine with elegant notes of aromatic herbs. Their other Franciacortas are excellent, as are their Curtefrancas.

| | |
|---|---|
| ○ Franciacorta Extra Brut Dequinque Magnum | ♀♀ 8 |
| ○ Curtefranca Bianco Maria Medici '14 | ♀♀ 4 |
| ○ Franciacorta Dosaggio Zero Sublimis Ris. '10 | ♀♀ 7 |
| ○ Franciacorta Extra Brut Francesco I | ♀♀ 5 |
| ○ Franciacorta Satèn Magnificentia '14 | ♀♀ 6 |
| ● Rosso dei Frati Priori '14 | ♀♀ 5 |
| ○ Franciacorta Brut Francesco I | ♀ 5 |
| ○ Franciacorta Extra Brut Quinque | ♀ 8 |
| ⊙ Franciacorta Rosé Francesco I | ♀ 5 |
| ○ Franciacorta Extra Brut Comari del Salem '03 | ♀♀♀ 6 |
| ○ Franciacorta Extra Brut Comari del Salem '02 | ♀♀♀ 6 |
| ○ Franciacorta Extra Brut Comari del Salem '01 | ♀♀♀ 6 |

## Vanzini

FRAZ. BARBALEONE, 7
27040 SAN DAMIANO AL COLLE [PV]
TEL. +39 038575019
www.vanzini-wine.com

CELLAR SALES
PRE-BOOKED VISITS
ANNUAL PRODUCTION 600,000 bottles
HECTARES UNDER VINE 27.00

The winery being led by siblings Michela, Antonio and Pierpaolo Vanzini has proved to be steady as a rock, especially when it comes to semi-sparkling and sparkling Metodo Martinottis made with the area's classic grapes. Their wines have evolved over time, gaining in cleanness, fragrance, fruit and balance. Sangue di Giuda and Moscato are both offered as standard cork semi-sparklers and mushroom cork sparklers. Their Metodo Martinotti whites and rosés, which are made entirely with Pinot Nero from their private vineyards, once again demonstrated their high quality. Martinotti confers intensity and complexity, with greater aromatic presence of small wild berries in their Rosé and a more flowery bouquet in their white. Their standard cork 2017 Sangue di Giuda also did very well, proving buoyant in its fruit. Their 2017 Barbera La Desiderata is still, fragrant, varietal, intact, well-balanced and highly drinkable. Their Moscato Spumante is a pleasantly citrus wine.

| | |
|---|---|
| ○ Moscato Spumante Dolce | ♀♀ 3 |
| ● OP Barbera La Desiderata '17 | ♀♀ 2* |
| ● OP Sangue di Giuda '17 | ♀♀ 3 |
| ● Pinot Nero Extra Dry | ♀♀ 3 |
| ⊙ Pinot Nero Extra Dry Rosé | ♀♀ 3 |
| ● OP Bonarda Frizzante '17 | ♀ 2 |
| ○ Pinot Grigio '17 | ♀ 3 |
| ○ Riesling '17 | ♀ 2 |
| ○ Moscato Spumante '14 | ♀♀ 3 |
| ● OP Bonarda '16 | ♀♀ 2* |
| ● OP Bonarda Vivace '15 | ♀♀ 2* |
| ● OP Bonarda Vivace '14 | ♀♀ 2* |
| ● OP Sangue di Giuda '16 | ♀♀ 3 |
| ● OP Sangue di Giuda '15 | ♀♀ 3 |
| ● OP Sangue di Giuda '14 | ♀♀ 3 |

# Bruno Verdi

VIA VERGOMBERRA, 5
27044 CANNETO PAVESE [PV]
TEL. +39 038588023
www.brunoverdi.it

CELLAR SALES
PRE-BOOKED VISITS
ANNUAL PRODUCTION 90,000 bottles
HECTARES UNDER VINE 12.00

For years now we have highlighted Paolo Verdi's gifts. It's not easy to find yourself managing a winery at 20, after the early death of your father. But Paolo has moved on, with tenacity and patience, and managed to make Bruno Verdi one of the best producers in all of Oltrepò Pavese. They offer a wide range of medium-high quality wines, from absolutely valid local reds to ageworthy Metodo Classico sparklers that exhibit notable personality. The fact that Paolo's son Jacopo is on board full-time is reason to hope that the tradition will continue. By now their Vergomberra has taken on a well-defined personality, setting itself up for the heights of excellence. This brilliant straw yellow-colored 2013 offers up aromas of lime, basil and mint, while in the mouth it expresses force and generosity, with extremely fine sparkle that tantalizes the palate and generates an electric tension. Among the rest of their excellent selection, we point out their chewy, succulent fruit of their 2016 Barbera Campo del Marrone.

| | | |
|---|---|---|
| ○ OP Pinot Nero Dosage Zéro M. Cl. Vergomberra '13 | ♛♛♛ | 5 |
| ● OP Barbera Campo del Marrone '16 | ♛♛ | 4 |
| ● OP Bonarda Frizzante Possessione di Vergombera '17 | ♛♛ | 2* |
| ● OP Buttafuoco '17 | ♛♛ | 2* |
| ○ OP Riesling V. Costa '16 | ♛♛ | 3 |
| ● OP Sangue di Giuda Paradiso '17 | ♛ | 2 |
| ○ OP Dosage Zero Vergomberra '12 | ♛♛♛ | 5 |
| ● OP Rosso Cavariola Ris. '10 | ♛♛♛ | 5 |
| ● OP Rosso Cavariola Ris. '07 | ♛♛♛ | 4 |
| ● OP Barbera Campo del Marrone '15 | ♛♛ | 3 |
| ● OP Bonarda Vivace Possessione di Vergomberra '16 | ♛♛ | 2* |
| ● OP Buttafuoco '16 | ♛♛ | 2* |
| ○ OP Riesling V. Costa '15 | ♛♛ | 2* |
| ● OP Rosso Cavariola Ris. '13 | ♛♛ | 5 |

# Villa Crespia

VIA VALLI, 31
25030 ADRO [BS]
TEL. +39 0307451051
www.villacrespia.it

PRE-BOOKED VISITS
ANNUAL PRODUCTION 360,000 bottles
HECTARES UNDER VINE 55.00
VITICULTURE METHOD Certified Organic
SUSTAINABLE WINERY

Villa Crespia is the Muratori family's ambitious project. They've built a modern and efficient cellar that goes 12 meters underground so as to bring out the best of their 60 hectares of private vineyards situated across the territory's six tracts of wine-growing land. Their sound selection of wines expresses Franciacorta's various facets, while their style focuses on frequently non-dosed cuvées, with each vineyard vinified separately, and the complexity wrought by long maturation. Their Novalia, which is among the best non-vintage Bruts in the territory, performed exceptionally well during our finals. It's a lovely straw-yellow and light green colored wine made with grapes from five different Chardonnay crus. It has fine perlage and on the nose it offers up close-focused, enticing notes of white fruit. These give way to riper, flowery aromas only to finish with vanilla. On the palate it proves crisp and soft, rich in fruit and fragrances of aromatic herbs. The rest of their selection also did well.

| | | |
|---|---|---|
| ○ Franciacorta Brut Novalia | ♛♛ | 4 |
| ○ Franciacorta Brut Millé '10 | ♛♛ | 5 |
| ○ Franciacorta Brut Miolo | ♛♛ | 5 |
| ○ Franciacorta Dosaggio Zero Francesco Iacono Ris. '11 | ♛♛ | 7 |
| ○ Franciacorta Satèn Cesonato | ♛♛ | 5 |
| ○ Franciacorta Brut Simbiotico | ♛ | 5 |
| ○ Franciacorta Dosaggio Zero Cisiolo | ♛ | 5 |
| ○ Franciacorta Dosaggio Zero Numerozero | ♛ | 5 |
| ⊙ Franciacorta Extra Brut Rosé Brolese | ♛ | 5 |
| ○ Franciacorta Dosaggio Zero Francesco Iacono Ris. '04 | ♛♛♛ | 7 |

# Villa Franciacorta

FRAZ. VILLA
VIA VILLA, 12
25040 MONTICELLI BRUSATI [BS]
TEL. +39 030652329
www.villafranciacorta.it

PRE-BOOKED VISITS
ACCOMMODATION AND RESTAURANT SERVICE
ANNUAL PRODUCTION 300,000 bottles
HECTARES UNDER VINE 37.00

Alessandra Bianchi and her husband, Paolo
Piziol, passionately manage the winery
founded by Alessandro Bianchi. He was the
one who brought the 16th century manor of
Villa, in Monticelli Brusati, to its former glory
and transformed it into a luxurious relais
and restaurant. The same holds for the
surrounding vineyards, with the replanting
of the terraced plots on Monte della
Madonna della Rosa. Today the estate
comprises 100 hectares, 40 of which are
vineyards, and features an entirely
underground modern cellar where a million
bottles await remuage. Their Extra Brut
Extra Blu is a skillful blend of various crus
of Chardonnay (90%) with an added part
Pinot Nero, all from their private vineyards
in Monticelli Brusati. After fermentation in
steel tanks, it ages for some months in
small wood barrels before lengthy, five-year
refermentation. Their 2013 delivered during
our finals, thanks to the producer's taut,
close-focused and mineral-rich style. We
can also recommend their 2014 Brut
Emozione and their subtle Mon Satèn.

| | |
|---|---|
| ○ Franciacorta Extra Brut Extra Blu '13 | 🍷🍷 6 |
| ○ Franciacorta Brut Emozione '14 | 🍷🍷 5 |
| ○ Franciacorta Mon Satèn '14 | 🍷🍷 5 |
| ● Curtefranca Rosso Gradoni '13 | 🍷 5 |
| ⊙ Franciacorta Brut Rosé Bokè Noir '14 | 🍷 5 |
| ⊙ Franciacorta Demi Sec Rosé Briolette | 🍷 5 |
| ○ Franciacorta Pas Dosé Diamant '12 | 🍷 6 |
| ○ Franciacorta Brut Emozione '09 | 🍷🍷🍷 5 |
| ○ Franciacorta Brut Rosé Bokè '12 | 🍷🍷🍷 5 |
| ○ Franciacorta Brut Cuvette '10 | 🍷🍷 5 |
| ○ Franciacorta Brut Emozione '13 | 🍷🍷 5 |
| ⊙ Franciacorta Brut Rosé Bokè '13 | 🍷🍷 5 |
| ⊙ Franciacorta Brut Rosé Bokè Noir '13 | 🍷🍷 7 |
| ○ Franciacorta Pas Dosé Diamant '11 | 🍷🍷 5 |

# Chiara Ziliani

VIA FRANCIACORTA, 7
25050 PROVAGLIO D'ISEO [BS]
TEL. +39 030981661
www.cantinachiaraziliani.it

PRE-BOOKED VISITS
ANNUAL PRODUCTION 40,000 bottles
HECTARES UNDER VINE 22.00
SUSTAINABLE WINERY

Chiara Ziliani founded this lovely winery
atop a hill in Provaglio. It's a position that
enjoys a scenic view of the estate's 21
hectares, 17 of which provide the quality
grapes that Chiara transforms into a large
number of Franciacortas and local wines.
Their vineyards are cultivated so as to have
a low environmental impact, with elevated
planting density (more than 7000 plants
per hectare). Thanks to the their position, at
250 meters elevation and highly attentive
winemaking, Chiara is able to offer an
excellent selection. We tasted a number of
cuvées, which confirm the hard work. Their
Satèn Ziliani C stood out for its fresh notes
of apples, their Satèn Conte di Provaglio for
its savoriness and creaminess. In terms of
their rosés, we appreciated their Conte di
Provaglio, with its lovely notes of aromatic
herbs and their Ziliani C, a wine redolent of
red fruit and sweet spices. Their Brut, from
the same line, features tension, freshness
and fruit, while their Duca d'Iseo Brut opts
for greater softness and roundness.

| | |
|---|---|
| ○ Franciacorta Satèn Ziliani C '13 | 🍷🍷 4 |
| ○ Franciacorta Brut Conte di Provaglio | 🍷🍷 3 |
| ○ Franciacorta Brut Duca d'Iseo | 🍷🍷 5 |
| ○ Franciacorta Brut Gran Cuvée<br>Italo Ziliani Ris. '12 | 🍷🍷 5 |
| ⊙ Franciacorta Brut Rosé<br>Conte di Provaglio | 🍷🍷 3 |
| ⊙ Franciacorta Brut Rosé Ziliani C | 🍷🍷 4 |
| ○ Franciacorta Brut Ziliani C '13 | 🍷🍷 4 |
| ○ Franciacorta Brut Ziliani C | 🍷🍷 3 |
| ○ Franciacorta Pas Dosé Ziliani C '13 | 🍷🍷 4 |
| ○ Franciacorta Satèn Conte di Provaglio | 🍷🍷 3 |
| ○ Franciacorta Satèn Duca d'Iseo | 🍷🍷 3 |
| ○ Franciacorta Satèn<br>Maria Maddalena Cavalieri Ris. '12 | 🍷🍷 5 |
| ○ Franciacorta Satèn Ziliani C | 🍷🍷 3 |

# 1701

P.ZZA MARCONI, 6
25046 CAZZAGO SAN MARTINO [BS]
TEL. +39 0307750875
www.1701franciacorta.it

CELLAR SALES
PRE-BOOKED VISITS
ANNUAL PRODUCTION 60,000 bottles
HECTARES UNDER VINE 10.50
VITICULTURE METHOD Certified
OrganicCertified Biodynamic

| | |
|---|---|
| ○ Franciacorta Dosaggio Zero '11 | ♟♟ 7 |
| ○ Surnat '17 | ♟♟ 4 |
| ○ Franciacorta Brut | ♟ 5 |
| ○ Franciacorta Satèn | ♟ 5 |

# Al Rocol

VIA PROVINCIALE, 79
25050 OME [BS]
TEL. +39 0306852542
www.alrocol.com

CELLAR SALES
PRE-BOOKED VISITS
ACCOMMODATION AND RESTAURANT SERVICE
ANNUAL PRODUCTION 60,000 bottles
HECTARES UNDER VINE 13.00

| | |
|---|---|
| ○ Franciacorta Brut Ca' del Luf '14 | ♟♟ 3 |
| ○ Franciacorta Brut Rosé Le Rive '14 | ♟ 5 |
| ○ Franciacorta Satèn Martignac '14 | ♟ 5 |

# Barbacarlo - Lino Maga

S.DA BRONESE, 3
27043 BRONI [PV]
TEL. +39 038551212
barbacarlodimaga@libero.it

CELLAR SALES
PRE-BOOKED VISITS
ANNUAL PRODUCTION 20,000 bottles
HECTARES UNDER VINE 12.00

| | |
|---|---|
| ● Barbacarlo '16 | ♟♟ 5 |

# Elisabetta Abrami

VIA VICINALE DELLE FOSCHE
25050 PROVAGLIO D'ISEO [BS]
TEL. +39 0306857185
www.vinielisabettaabrami.it

CELLAR SALES
ACCOMMODATION
ANNUAL PRODUCTION 60,000 bottles
HECTARES UNDER VINE 15.00
VITICULTURE METHOD Certified Organic

| | |
|---|---|
| ○ Franciacorta Brut | ♟♟ 5 |
| ○ Franciacorta Satèn | ♟♟ 5 |
| ○ Franciacorta Pas Dosé | ♟ 6 |

# Annibale Alziati

LOC. SCAZZOLINO, 55
27040 ROVESCALA [PV]
TEL. +39 038575261
www.gaggiarone.it

CELLAR SALES
PRE-BOOKED VISITS
ANNUAL PRODUCTION 100,000 bottles
HECTARES UNDER VINE 19.00
VITICULTURE METHOD Certified Organic
SUSTAINABLE WINERY

| | |
|---|---|
| ● OP Bonarda '16 | ♟♟ 2* |
| ● OP Bonarda Gaggiarone Ris. '07 | ♟♟ 4 |

# Barboglio De Gaioncelli

FRAZ. COLOMBARO
VIA NAZARIO SAURO
25040 CORTE FRANCA [BS]
TEL. +39 0309826831
www.barbogliodegaioncelli.it

CELLAR SALES
PRE-BOOKED VISITS
RESTAURANT SERVICE
ANNUAL PRODUCTION 90,000 bottles
HECTARES UNDER VINE 60.00

| | |
|---|---|
| ○ Franciacorta Brut | ♟♟ 4 |
| ○ Franciacorta Brut Satèn '14 | ♟♟ 5 |
| ○ Franciacorta Extra Brut '14 | ♟♟ 5 |
| ○ Franciacorta Extra Dry 1875 | ♟♟ 4 |

## Cantina Sociale Bergamasca

VIA BERGAMO, 10
24060 SAN PAOLO D'ARGON [BG]
TEL. +39 035951098
www.cantinabergamasca.it

CELLAR SALES
PRE-BOOKED VISITS
ANNUAL PRODUCTION 650,000 bottles
HECTARES UNDER VINE 90.00

| | |
|---|---|
| ○ Sottosopra Brut Cl. | 🏆🏆 |
| ● Valcalepio Moscato Passito Perseo '12 | 🏆🏆 4 |
| ○ Terre del Colleoni Incrocio Manzoni 6013 '17 | 🏆 5 |

## Bonfadini

FRAZ. CLUSANE
VIA L. DI BERNARDO, 85
25049 ISEO [BS]
TEL. +39 0309826721
www.bonfadini.it

CELLAR SALES
PRE-BOOKED VISITS
ANNUAL PRODUCTION 120,000 bottles
HECTARES UNDER VINE 12.00

| | |
|---|---|
| ○ Franciacorta Brut Nobilium '15 | 🏆🏆 5 |
| ○ Franciacorta Satèn Carpe Diem '14 | 🏆🏆 5 |
| ⊙ Franciacorta Rosé Opera '15 | 🏆 5 |
| ○ Franciacorta Veritas Nature '13 | 🏆 5 |

## La Boscaiola Vigneti Cenci

VIA RICCAFANA
25033 COLOGNE [BS]
TEL. +39 0307156386
www.vigneticenci.com

CELLAR SALES
PRE-BOOKED VISITS
ANNUAL PRODUCTION 50,000 bottles
HECTARES UNDER VINE 6.00

| | |
|---|---|
| ○ Franciacorta Brut La Capinera | 🏆🏆 4 |
| ○ Franciacorta Pas Dosé Zero | 🏆🏆 4 |
| ○ Franciacorta Satèn La Via della Seta | 🏆🏆 5 |
| ⊙ Franciacorta Brut Rosé La Capinera | 🏆 4 |

## Bulgarini

LOC. VAIBÒ, 1
25010 POZZOLENGO [BS]
TEL. +39 030918224
www.vini-bulgarini.com

CELLAR SALES
ANNUAL PRODUCTION 750,000 bottles
HECTARES UNDER VINE 40.00

| | |
|---|---|
| ○ Lugana 010 '17 | 🏆🏆 3 |
| ○ Lugana '17 | 🏆 2 |
| ⊙ Riviera del Garda Cl. Chiaretto '17 | 🏆 2 |

## Ca' del Santo

LOC. CAMPOLUNGO, 4
27040 MONTALTO PAVESE [PV]
TEL. +39 0383870545
www.cadelsanto.it

CELLAR SALES
PRE-BOOKED VISITS
ANNUAL PRODUCTION 25,000 bottles
HECTARES UNDER VINE 6.00

| | |
|---|---|
| ○ Mon Amie Brut Nature M. Cl. | 🏆🏆 4 |
| ● Il Nero Pinot Nero '15 | 🏆 3 |
| ⊙ OP Cruasé Brut '12 | 🏆 4 |

## Andrea Calvi

FRAZ. VIGALONE, 13
27044 CANNETO PAVESE [PV]
TEL. +39 038560034
www.andreacalvi.it

CELLAR SALES
PRE-BOOKED VISITS
ANNUAL PRODUCTION 100,000 bottles
HECTARES UNDER VINE 26.00

| | |
|---|---|
| ● Fiume di Luna '17 | 🏆🏆 2* |
| ● OP Bonarda Frizzante '17 | 🏆 2 |

## Davide Calvi

FRAZ. PALAZZINA, 24
27040 CASTANA [PV]
TEL. +39 038582136
www.vinicalvi.it

CELLAR SALES
PRE-BOOKED VISITS
ANNUAL PRODUCTION 45,000 bottles
HECTARES UNDER VINE 8.00

| | |
|---|---|
| ● OP Bonarda di Calvi '16 | ♟2 |
| ● OP Buttafuoco V. Montarzolo '13 | ♟4 |

## Camillucci

C.SO BONOMELLI,41
25038 ROVATO [BS]
TEL. +39 0307702739
www.camilucci.it

PRE-BOOKED VISITS
ANNUAL PRODUCTION 50,000 bottles
HECTARES UNDER VINE 6.00

| | |
|---|---|
| ○ Franciacorta Brut | ♟♟5 |
| ○ Franciacorta Satèn '12 | ♟♟5 |
| ○ Franciacorta Extra Brut Anthologie Noir '14 | ♟6 |

## Le Cantorìe

FRAZ. CASAGLIO
VIA CASTELLO DI CASAGLIO, 24/25
25064 GUSSAGO [BS]
TEL. +39 0302523723
www.lecantorie.it

ANNUAL PRODUCTION 75,000 bottles
HECTARES UNDER VINE 12.00

| | |
|---|---|
| ○ Franciacorta Brut Armonia | ♟♟4 |
| ○ Franciacorta Pas Dosé Armonia Ris. '11 | ♟♟4 |
| ○ Franciacorta Rosé Rosi delle Margherite | ♟♟4 |
| ○ Franciacorta Satèn Armonia | ♟♟5 |

## Cantrina

VIA COLOMBERA, 7
25081 BEDIZZOLE [BS]
TEL. +39 3356362137
www.cantrina.it

CELLAR SALES
ANNUAL PRODUCTION 42,000 bottles
HECTARES UNDER VINE 7.90

| | |
|---|---|
| ● Nepomuceno '13 | ♟♟5 |
| ○ Riné '16 | ♟♟3 |
| ○ Sole di Dario Passito '12 | ♟♟5 |
| ⊙ Chiaretto '17 | ♟2 |

## Tenuta Casa Virginia

LOC. GAGGIO
VIA CASCINA VIOLO, 1
24018 VILLA D'ALMÉ [BG]
TEL. +39 035571223
cantina.tenutacasavirginia.it

CELLAR SALES
PRE-BOOKED VISITS
ANNUAL PRODUCTION 10,000 bottles
HECTARES UNDER VINE 4.00

| | |
|---|---|
| ○ Il Lupo e La Volpe '17 | ♟♟2* |
| ○ L'Oro del Diavolo '17 | ♟♟2* |
| ● Il Violino Essenza '15 | ♟5 |

## Cascina Gnocco

FRAZ. LOSANA, 20
27040 MORNICO LOSANA [PV]
TEL. +39 0383892280
www.cascinagnocco.it

CELLAR SALES
PRE-BOOKED VISITS
ANNUAL PRODUCTION 60,000 bottles
HECTARES UNDER VINE 13.00

| | |
|---|---|
| ● Orione '11 | ♟♟4 |
| ⊙ Brut Rosé | ♟5 |

## Cascina Maddalena

FRAZ. LUGANA DI SIRMIONE
VIA MADDALENA, 21
25019 SIRMIONE [BS]
TEL. +39 030 9905139
www.cascinamaddalena.com

ANNUAL PRODUCTION 10,000 bottles
HECTARES UNDER VINE 3.50

| | | |
|---|---|---|
| ○ Lugana Capotesta '17 | ♟♟ | 3 |

## Cascina Piano

LOC. ANGERA
VIA VALCASTELLANA, 33
21021 ANGERA [VA]
TEL. +39 0331930928
www.cascinapiano.it

CELLAR SALES
PRE-BOOKED VISITS
ANNUAL PRODUCTION 23,000 bottles
HECTARES UNDER VINE 3.00

| | | |
|---|---|---|
| ○ San Quirico '17 | ♟♟ | 3 |
| ● Angliano '14 | ♟ | 4 |

## Castello di Grumello

VIA FOSSE, 11
24064 GRUMELLO DEL MONTE [BG]
TEL. +39 0354420817
www.castellodigrumello.it

CELLAR SALES
PRE-BOOKED VISITS
ACCOMMODATION
ANNUAL PRODUCTION 100,000 bottles
HECTARES UNDER VINE 18.00
SUSTAINABLE WINERY

| | | |
|---|---|---|
| ● Valcalepio Rosso Colle del Calvario Ris. '10 | ♟♟ | 5 |
| ○ Valcalepio Bianco '17 | ♟ | 2 |
| ● Valcalepio Rosso Il Castello Ris. '15 | ♟ | 3 |

## Castello di Luzzano

LOC. LUZZANO, 5
27040 ROVESCALA [PV]
TEL. +39 0523863277
www.castelloluzzano.com

CELLAR SALES
PRE-BOOKED VISITS
ACCOMMODATION AND RESTAURANT SERVICE
ANNUAL PRODUCTION 120,000 bottles
HECTARES UNDER VINE 76.00

| | | |
|---|---|---|
| ● OP Bonarda Frizzante Sommossa '17 | ♟♟ | 2* |
| ● OP Pinot Nero Umore Nero '17 | ♟♟ | 3 |
| ○ OP Pinot Nero Brut Magot '17 | ♟ | 3 |

## Castelveder

VIA BELVEDERE, 4
25040 MONTICELLI BRUSATI [BS]
TEL. +39 030652308
www.castelveder.it

CELLAR SALES
PRE-BOOKED VISITS
ANNUAL PRODUCTION 70,000 bottles
HECTARES UNDER VINE 11.00

| | | |
|---|---|---|
| ○ Franciacorta Brut '12 | ♟♟ | 6 |
| ○ Franciacorta Extra Brut | ♟♟ | 5 |
| ○ Franciacorta Pas Dosé | ♟ | 5 |
| ○ Franciacorta Satèn | ♟ | 5 |

## Catturich Ducco

FRAZ. CAMIGNONE
VIA DEGLI EROI, 70
25050 PASSIRANO [BS]
TEL. +39 0306850566
www.catturichducco.it

| | | |
|---|---|---|
| ○ Franciacorta Extra Brut | ♟♟ | 5 |
| ○ Curtefranca Bianco Blanc '1 | ♟ | 3 |
| ○ Franciacorta Brut '14 | ♟ | 5 |

## Le Chiusure

FRAZ. PORTESE
VIA BOSCHETTE, 2
25010 SAN FELICE DEL BENACO [BS]
TEL. +39 0365626243
www.lechiusure.net

CELLAR SALES
PRE-BOOKED VISITS
ACCOMMODATION
ANNUAL PRODUCTION 22,000 bottles
HECTARES UNDER VINE 4.00

| | |
|---|---|
| ● Malborghetto '15 | ♟♟ 5 |
| ⊙ Valtenesi Riviera del Garda Cl. | |
|   Chiaretto '17 | ♟♟ 2* |
| ● Valtènesi Portese '16 | ♟ 2 |

## Il Cipresso

FRAZ. TRIBULINA
VIA CERRI, 2
24020 SCANZOROSCIATE [BG]
TEL. +39 0354597005
www.ilcipresso.info

CELLAR SALES
PRE-BOOKED VISITS
ANNUAL PRODUCTION 20,000 bottles
HECTARES UNDER VINE 4.00

| | |
|---|---|
| ● Moscato di Scanzo Serafino '14 | ♟♟ 6 |
| ● Valcalepio Rosso Dionisio '15 | ♟♟ 3 |
| ○ Valcalepio Bianco Melardo '17 | ♟ 2 |

## Girolamo Conforti

VIA ISEO, 108
25030 ERBUSCO [BS]
TEL. +39 0307750405
www.girolamoconforti.it

CELLAR SALES
ANNUAL PRODUCTION 30,000 bottles
HECTARES UNDER VINE 15.00

| | |
|---|---|
| ○ Franciacorta Brut | ♟♟ 3 |
| ○ Franciacorta Brut Satèn | ♟ 4 |

## Corte Aura

VIA COLZANO, 13
25030 ADRO [BS]
TEL. +39 030 7357281
www.corteaura.it

CELLAR SALES
PRE-BOOKED VISITS
ANNUAL PRODUCTION 170,000 bottles
HECTARES UNDER VINE 6.00

| | |
|---|---|
| ○ Franciacorta Pas Dosé Insè '12 | ♟♟ 7 |
| ○ Franciacorta Satèn | ♟♟ 5 |
| ⊙ Franciacorta Brut Rosé | ♟ 5 |
| ○ Franciacorta Pas Dosé | ♟ 5 |

## Delai

VIA MORO, 1
25080 PUEGNAGO SUL GARDA [BS]
TEL. +39 0365555527

ANNUAL PRODUCTION 80,000 bottles
HECTARES UNDER VINE 8.00

| | |
|---|---|
| ● Garda Bresciano Groppello Mogrì '17 | ♟♟ 2* |
| ● Marzemino Sovenigo '15 | ♟♟ 3 |
| ⊙ Valtenesi Riviera del Garda Cl. | |
|   Chiaretto Notte Rosa '17 | ♟ 3 |

## Due Pini

LOC. PICEDO
VIA NOVAGLIO, 16
25080 POLPENAZZE DEL GARDA [BS]
TEL. +39 0365675123
www.viniduepini.it

ANNUAL PRODUCTION 35,000 bottles
HECTARES UNDER VINE 6.00

| | |
|---|---|
| ● Garda Cl. Groppello Sara '16 | ♟♟ 3 |
| ● Garda Cl. Sup. Samantha '15 | ♟♟ 4 |
| ○ Garda Riesling Emanuela '17 | ♟♟ 2* |

## Luca Faccinelli

VIA MEDICI, 3A
23030 CHIURO [SO]
TEL. +39 3470807011
www.lucafaccinelli.it

CELLAR SALES
PRE-BOOKED VISITS
ANNUAL PRODUCTION 17,000 bottles
HECTARES UNDER VINE 3.00
SUSTAINABLE WINERY

| | |
|---|---|
| ● Rosso di Valtellina Matteo Bandello '16 | ♟♟ 4 |
| ● Valtellina Sup. Grumello Ortensio Lando '15 | ♟♟ 5 |

## Feliciana

LOC. FELICIANA
25010 POZZOLENGO [BS]
TEL. +39 030918228
www.feliciana.it

ANNUAL PRODUCTION 220,000 bottles
HECTARES UNDER VINE 20.00

| | |
|---|---|
| ○ Lugana Felugan '17 | ♟♟ 3 |
| ○ Lugana Sercè Ris. '15 | ♟♟ 4 |

## Il Feudo Nico

VIA SAN ROCCO, 63
27040 MORNICO LOSANA [PV]
TEL. +39 0383892452

ANNUAL PRODUCTION 40,000 bottles
HECTARES UNDER VINE 16.00

| | |
|---|---|
| ○ Maria Antonietta Blanc de Blanc Extra Brut M. Cl. '14 | ♟♟ 4 |
| ● OP Pinot Nero V. Spiaggi '15 | ♟ 4 |

## Finigeto

LOC. CELLA, 27
27040 MONTALTO PAVESE [PV]
TEL. +39 328 7095347
www.finigeto.com

CELLAR SALES
PRE-BOOKED VISITS
ACCOMMODATION
ANNUAL PRODUCTION 80,000 bottles
HECTARES UNDER VINE 42.00

| | |
|---|---|
| ● OP Bonarda Frizzante Il Baldo '17 | ♟♟ 3 |
| ● OP Pinot Nero Il Nirò '15 | ♟♟ 5 |
| ⊙ Pinot Nero Extrà Rosé '16 | ♟ 3 |

## La Fiòca

FRAZ. NIGOLINE
VIA VILLA, 13B
25040 CORTE FRANCA [BS]
TEL. +39 0309826313
www.lafioca.com

CELLAR SALES
PRE-BOOKED VISITS
ACCOMMODATION AND RESTAURANT SERVICE
ANNUAL PRODUCTION 40,000 bottles
HECTARES UNDER VINE 5.00
VITICULTURE METHOD Certified Organic

| | |
|---|---|
| ○ Franciacorta Brut | ♟♟ 5 |
| ○ Franciacorta Brut Nature Nudo | ♟♟ 7 |
| ○ Franciacorta DZ Orazio Ris. '11 | ♟♟ 8 |
| ● Rosso del Diavolo Allegro '16 | ♟♟ 5 |

## La Fiorita

VIA MAGLIO, 10
25020 OME [BS]
TEL. +39 030652279
www.lafioritafranciacorta.com

CELLAR SALES
PRE-BOOKED VISITS
ACCOMMODATION AND RESTAURANT SERVICE
ANNUAL PRODUCTION 94,000 bottles
HECTARES UNDER VINE 10.00

| | |
|---|---|
| ○ Franciacorta Brut | ♟♟ 4 |
| ○ Franciacorta Dosaggio Zero | ♟♟ 4 |
| ○ Franciacorta Extra Brut Eurosia Ris. '09 | ♟♟ 6 |

## Le Fracce

FRAZ. MAIRANO
VIA CASTEL DEL LUPO, 5
27045 CASTEGGIO [PV]
TEL. +39 038382526
www.lefracce.com

CELLAR SALES
PRE-BOOKED VISITS
ANNUAL PRODUCTION 180,000 bottles
HECTARES UNDER VINE 40.00

| | | |
|---|---|---|
| ● OP Bonarda Vivace Rubiosa '17 | ♟♟ | 3 |
| ○ OP Pinot Nero Extra Brut M. Cl. Special Cuvée Bussolera '15 | ♟♟ | 4 |
| ○ OP Riesling Landò '17 | ♟ | 3 |

## Franca Contea

VIA VALLI, 130
25030 ADRO [BS]
TEL. +39 0307451217
www.francacontea.it

CELLAR SALES
PRE-BOOKED VISITS
ANNUAL PRODUCTION 70,000 bottles
HECTARES UNDER VINE 12.00

| | | |
|---|---|---|
| ● Bolesna '04 | ♟♟ | 8 |
| ○ Franciacorta Brut Primus Cuvée | ♟♟ | 5 |
| ○ Franciacorta Satèn '13 | ♟ | 5 |

## Tenuta La Vigna

CASCINA LA VIGNA
25020 CAPRIANO DEL COLLE [BS]
TEL. +39 0309748061
www.tenutalavigna.it

CELLAR SALES
PRE-BOOKED VISITS
ANNUAL PRODUCTION 35,000 bottles
HECTARES UNDER VINE 6.00

| | | |
|---|---|---|
| ○ Capriano del Colle Bianco Torrazza '17 | ♟♟ | 3 |
| ● Capriano del Colle Rosso Rubinera '16 | ♟♟ | 3 |
| ○ Brut M. Cl. Anna Botti | ♟ | 4 |

## Cantine Lebovitz

FRAZ. GOVERNOLO
V.LE RIMEMBRANZE, 4
46037 RONCOFERRARO [MN]
TEL. +39 0376668115
www.cantinelebovitz.it

CELLAR SALES
PRE-BOOKED VISITS
ANNUAL PRODUCTION 500,000 bottles
HECTARES UNDER VINE

| | | |
|---|---|---|
| ● Al Scagarun '17 | ♟♟ | 1* |
| ● Sedamat '17 | ♟♟ | 1* |

## Francesco Maggi

FRAZ. COSTIOLO, 87

27044 CANNETO PAVESE [PV]
TEL. +39 038560233
www.maggifrancesco.it

| | | |
|---|---|---|
| ● OP Buttafuoco Storico V. Costera '13 | ♟♟ | 3* |
| ● OP Bonarda Frizzante Fatum '17 | ♟♟ | 2* |
| ● OP Buttafuoco Abbondanza '16 | ♟ | 2 |

## Manuelina

FRAZ. RUINELLO DI SOTTO, 3A
27047 SANTA MARIA DELLA VERSA [PV]
TEL. +39 0385278247
Fraz. Ruinello di Sotto 3/a

CELLAR SALES
PRE-BOOKED VISITS
ANNUAL PRODUCTION 230,000 bottles
HECTARES UNDER VINE 22.00

| | | |
|---|---|---|
| ○ OP Pinot Nero Brut M. Cl. 137 '13 | ♟♟ | 4 |
| ● OP Pinot Nero Solo Nero '16 | ♟♟ | 3 |
| ● OP Sangue di Giuda Il Traditore '17 | ♟♟ | 2* |

## Marangona

LOC. MARANGONA 1
25010 POZZOLENGO [BS]
TEL. +39 030919379
www.marangona.com

CELLAR SALES
PRE-BOOKED VISITS
ANNUAL PRODUCTION 30,000 bottles
HECTARES UNDER VINE 27.00

| | |
|---|---|
| ○ Lugana Rabbiosa '15 | ♀♀ 3 |
| ○ Lugana Tre Campane '16 | ♀♀ 2* |
| ○ Lugana Cemento '16 | ♀ 4 |

## Marsadri

LOC. RAFFA DI PUEGNAGO
VIA NAZIONALE, 26
25080 PUEGNAGO SUL GARDA [BS]
TEL. +39 0365651005
www.cantinamarsadri.it

PRE-BOOKED VISITS
ANNUAL PRODUCTION 200,000 bottles
HECTARES UNDER VINE 15.00
SUSTAINABLE WINERY

| | |
|---|---|
| ● Garda Marzemino '17 | ♀♀ 2* |
| ○ Lugana Brolo '17 | ♀♀ 3 |
| ● Riviera del Garda Groppello Brolo '17 | ♀♀ 3 |

## Alberto Marsetti

VIA SCARPATETTI, 15
23100 SONDRIO
TEL. +39 0342216329
www.marsetti.it

ANNUAL PRODUCTION 20,000 bottles
HECTARES UNDER VINE 5.00

| | |
|---|---|
| ● Sforzato di Valtellina '13 | ♀♀ 6 |
| ● Valtellina Sup. Grumello '14 | ♀♀ 5 |
| ● Valtellina Sup. Le Prudenze '14 | ♀♀ 5 |

## Medolago Albani

VIA REDONA, 12
24069 TRESCORE BALNEARIO [BG]
TEL. +39 035942022
www.medolagoalbani.it

CELLAR SALES
PRE-BOOKED VISITS
ANNUAL PRODUCTION 200,000 bottles
HECTARES UNDER VINE 23.00

| | |
|---|---|
| ● Valcalepio Rosso I Due Lauri Ris. '13 | ♀♀ 4 |
| ● Villa Redona Cabernet '15 | ♀♀ 3 |
| ⊙ Brut Rosè M. Cl. | ♀ 4 |

## Montelio

VIA D. MAZZA, 1
27050 CODEVILLA [PV]
TEL. +39 0383373090
montelio.gio@alice.it

CELLAR SALES
PRE-BOOKED VISITS
ACCOMMODATION AND RESTAURANT SERVICE
ANNUAL PRODUCTION 130,000 bottles
HECTARES UNDER VINE 27.00

| | |
|---|---|
| ○ La Stroppa Brut | ♀♀ 3 |
| ● OP Bonarda '17 | ♀♀ 2* |
| ○ OP Riesling Il Nadòt '17 | ♀♀ 2* |

## Monterucco

VALLE CIMA, 38
27040 CIGOGNOLA [PV]
TEL. +39 038585151
www.monterucco.it

CELLAR SALES
PRE-BOOKED VISITS
ANNUAL PRODUCTION 100,000 bottles
HECTARES UNDER VINE 20.00

| | |
|---|---|
| ● OP Buttafuoco Sanluigi '16 | ♀♀ 3 |
| ○ OP Pinot Nero Brut Nature M. Cl. '11 | ♀♀ 3 |
| ● OP Bonarda Frizzante V. Il Modello '17 | ♀ 2 |

## La Montina

FRAZ. BAIANA, 17
25040 MONTICELLI BRUSATI [BS]
TEL. +39 030653278
www.lamontina.it

CELLAR SALES
PRE-BOOKED VISITS
RESTAURANT SERVICE
ANNUAL PRODUCTION 450,000 bottles
HECTARES UNDER VINE 70.00

| | |
|---|---|
| ○ Franciacorta Brut '11 | ♟♟ 5 |
| ○ Franciacorta Extra Brut | ♟♟ 5 |
| ○ Franciacorta Brut | ♟ 5 |
| ○ Franciacorta Satèn | ♟ 5 |

## Montonale

LOC. CONTA, 7
25015 DESENZANO DEL GARDA [BS]
TEL. +39 0309103358
www.montonale.com

ANNUAL PRODUCTION 100,000 bottles
HECTARES UNDER VINE 25.00

| | |
|---|---|
| ○ Lugana Orestilla '16 | ♟♟ 4 |
| ○ Lugana Montunal '17 | ♟ 3 |

## Nettare dei Santi

VIA CAPRA, 17
20078 SAN COLOMBANO AL LAMBRO [MI]
TEL. +39 0371200523
www.nettaredeisanti.it

CELLAR SALES
PRE-BOOKED VISITS
ANNUAL PRODUCTION 600,000 bottles
HECTARES UNDER VINE 40.00

| | |
|---|---|
| ○ Brut M. Cl. Domm '15 | ♟♟ 4 |
| ● Franco Riccardi '13 | ♟♟ 4 |
| ● San Colombano Rosso Ris. '15 | ♟ 3 |

## Oselara

S.DA VICINALE DELLA BAZZOLA 1
25010 POZZOLENGO [BS]
TEL. +39 347 229 5623
www.oselara.it

CELLAR SALES
PRE-BOOKED VISITS
ANNUAL PRODUCTION 50,000 bottles
HECTARES UNDER VINE 14.00

| | |
|---|---|
| ○ Lugana '17 | ♟♟ 2* |
| ○ Lugana Terra Dorata '17 | ♟♟ 3 |

## Panigada - Banino

VIA DELLA VITTORIA, 13
20078 SAN COLOMBANO AL LAMBRO [MI]
TEL. +39 037189103
www.banino.it

CELLAR SALES
PRE-BOOKED VISITS
ANNUAL PRODUCTION 30,000 bottles
HECTARES UNDER VINE 5.00

| | |
|---|---|
| ○ Aureum '15 | ♟♟ 4 |
| ● San Colombano Rosso V. La Merla Ris. '13 | ♟♟ 3 |
| ● San Colombano Vivace '17 | ♟ 2 |

## Peri Bigogno

VIA GARIBALDI, 64
25014 CASTENEDOLO [BS]
TEL. +39 0302731572
www.peribigogno.com

CELLAR SALES
PRE-BOOKED VISITS
ANNUAL PRODUCTION 50,000 bottles
HECTARES UNDER VINE 9.00

| | |
|---|---|
| ⊙ Talento Brut Rosé '14 '14 | ♟♟ 4 |
| ○ Talento Pas Dosé MB '13 | ♟♟ 4 |
| ○ Talento Brut Peri 46 '14 | ♟ 4 |

## La Perla

LOC. TRESENDA
VIA VALGELLA, 29B
23036 TEGLIO [SO]
TEL. +39 3462878894
www.vini-laperla.com

CELLAR SALES
PRE-BOOKED VISITS
ANNUAL PRODUCTION 20,000 bottles
HECTARES UNDER VINE 3.30

| | |
|---|---|
| ● Sforzato di Valtellina Quattro Soli '13 | ♈♈ 7 |
| ● Valtellina Sup. La Mossa '13 | ♈♈ 4 |

## Perla del Garda

VIA FENIL VECCHIO, 9
25017 LONATO [BS]
TEL. +39 0309103109
www.perladelgarda.it

CELLAR SALES
PRE-BOOKED VISITS
ANNUAL PRODUCTION 120,000 bottles
HECTARES UNDER VINE 30.00
VITICULTURE METHOD Certified Organic
SUSTAINABLE WINERY

| | |
|---|---|
| ○ Lugana Perla '17 | ♈♈ 3 |
| ○ Lugana Perla Bio '17 | ♈ 2 |

## Pian del Maggio

VIA ISEO, 108
25030 ERBUSCO [BS]
TEL. +39 3355638610
www.piandelmaggio.it

CELLAR SALES
PRE-BOOKED VISITS
ANNUAL PRODUCTION 25,000 bottles
HECTARES UNDER VINE 1.80

| | |
|---|---|
| ○ Franciacorta Brut Proscenio | ♈♈ 4 |
| ○ Franciacorta Brut Millumino '12 | ♈ 5 |
| ○ Franciacorta Satèn Capriccio | ♈ 5 |

## Piccolo Bacco dei Quaroni

FRAZ. COSTAMONTEFEDELE
27040 MONTÙ BECCARIA [PV]
TEL. +39 038560521
www.piccolobaccodeiquaroni.it

CELLAR SALES
PRE-BOOKED VISITS
RESTAURANT SERVICE
ANNUAL PRODUCTION 35,000 bottles
HECTARES UNDER VINE 10.00
VITICULTURE METHOD Certified Organic

| | |
|---|---|
| ● OP Pinot Nero Vign. La Fiocca '16 | ♈♈ 3 |
| ⊙ OP Cruasé PBQ | ♈♈ 3 |
| ● OP Buttafuoco Vign. Ca' Padroni '15 | ♈ 3 |

## Pietta

FRAZ. CASTREZZONE
P.ZZA ZANARDELLI
25080 MUSCOLINE [BS]
TEL. +39 0365 32143
www.cantinepietta.it

CELLAR SALES
PRE-BOOKED VISITS
ACCOMMODATION AND RESTAURANT SERVICE
ANNUAL PRODUCTION 20,000 bottles
HECTARES UNDER VINE 30.00
VITICULTURE METHOD Certified Organic

| | |
|---|---|
| ○ Riviera del Garda Cl. '17 | ♈♈ 2* |
| ● Valtènesi '15 | ♈♈ 2* |
| ● Riviera del Garda Cl. Groppello Piazzole '16 | ♈ 2 |

## Pilandro

FRAZ. SAN MARTINO DELLA BATTAGLIA
LOC. PILANDRO, 1
25015 DESENZANO DEL GARDA [BS]
TEL. +39 0309910363
www.pilandro.it

CELLAR SALES
PRE-BOOKED VISITS
ANNUAL PRODUCTION 300,000 bottles
HECTARES UNDER VINE 33.00

| | |
|---|---|
| ○ Lugana Sup. Arilica '16 | ♈♈ 2* |
| ○ Lugana Terecrea '17 | ♈♈ 3 |

## La Piotta

LOC. PIOTTA, 2
27040 MONTALTO PAVESE [PV]
TEL. +39 0383870178
www.padroggilapiotta.it

CELLAR SALES
PRE-BOOKED VISITS
ANNUAL PRODUCTION 90,000 bottles
HECTARES UNDER VINE 20.00
VITICULTURE METHOD Certified Organic

| | |
|---|---|
| ○ OP Pinot Nero Extra Brut M. Cl. Talento '14 | ▼▼ 4 |
| ● 89/90 Rosso '15 | ▼▼ 4 |
| ○ OP Pinot Nero Pas Dosé M. Cl. C3 '14 | ▼▼ 4 |
| ○ OP Riesling Piota '16 | ▼ 2 |

## Prime Alture

VIA MADONNA, 109
27045 CASTEGGIO [PV]
TEL. +39 038383214
www.primealture.it

CELLAR SALES
PRE-BOOKED VISITS
ACCOMMODATION AND RESTAURANT SERVICE
ANNUAL PRODUCTION 40,000 bottles
HECTARES UNDER VINE 8.00

| | |
|---|---|
| ○ Il Bianco 60&40 '17 | ▼▼ 4 |
| ○ OP Pinot Nero Brut M. Cl. Io per Te | ▼▼ 6 |
| ● L'Altra Metà del Cuore '15 | ▼ 5 |

## Le Quattro Terre

FRAZ. BORGONATO
VIA RISORGIMENTO, 11
25040 CORTE FRANCA [BS]
TEL. +39 030984312
www.quattroterre.it

CELLAR SALES
PRE-BOOKED VISITS
ACCOMMODATION AND RESTAURANT SERVICE
ANNUAL PRODUCTION 50,000 bottles
HECTARES UNDER VINE 10.00

| | |
|---|---|
| ○ Franciacorta Brut Grano Salis | ▼▼ 5 |
| ○ Franciacorta Dosaggio Zero Genius Loci '13 | ▼▼ 6 |
| ○ Franciacorta Extra Brut Sinequal | ▼▼ 5 |

## Cantina Sociale Cooperativa di Quistello

VIA ROMA, 46
46026 QUISTELLO [MN]
TEL. +39 0376618118
www.cantinasocialequistello.it

CELLAR SALES
PRE-BOOKED VISITS
ANNUAL PRODUCTION 1,000,000 bottles
HECTARES UNDER VINE 330.00

| | |
|---|---|
| ☉ 80 Vendemmie Rosato '17 | ▼▼ 2* |
| ● Gran Rosso del Vicariato di Quistello '17 | ▼▼ 2* |
| ● 80 Vendemmie Rosso '16 | ▼ 2 |

## Tenuta Quvestra

LOC. CASE NUOVE 9
27047 SANTA MARIA DELLA VERSA [PV]
TEL. +39 3476014109
www.quvestra.it

CELLAR SALES
PRE-BOOKED VISITS
ACCOMMODATION
ANNUAL PRODUCTION 35,000 bottles
HECTARES UNDER VINE 12.00

| | |
|---|---|
| ● OP Bonarda Frizzante '16 | ▼▼ 2* |
| ● Sinfonia in Rosso '15 | ▼▼ 3 |

## Rebollini

LOC. SBERCIA
27040 BORGORATTO MORMOROLO [PV]
TEL. +39 0383872295
www.rebollini.it

CELLAR SALES
PRE-BOOKED VISITS
ANNUAL PRODUCTION 100,000 bottles
HECTARES UNDER VINE 35.00
SUSTAINABLE WINERY

| | |
|---|---|
| ○ Cuvée Brut M. Cl. | ▼▼ 4 |
| ● OP Bonarda Frizzante Sel. '16 | ▼▼ 3 |
| ○ OP Riesling '17 | ▼▼ 2* |
| ○ Brut Nature M. Cl. '13 | ▼ 5 |

## La Riccafana

VIA F.LLI FACCHETTI, 91
25033 COLOGNE [BS]
TEL. +39 0307156797
www.riccafana.com

CELLAR SALES
ANNUAL PRODUCTION 100,000 bottles
HECTARES UNDER VINE 12.00
VITICULTURE METHOD Certified Organic

| | |
|---|---|
| ○ Franciacorta Brut | ♟♟ 5 |
| ⊙ Franciacorta Rosé Linea Territori '13 | ♟♟ 6 |
| ○ Franciacorta Satèn Zero Linea Territori '11 | ♟ 6 |

## Ricchi

FRAZ. RICCHI
VIA FESTONI, 13D
46040 MONZAMBANO [MN]
TEL. +39 0376800238
www.cantinaricchi.it

CELLAR SALES
PRE-BOOKED VISITS
ANNUAL PRODUCTION 300,000 bottles
HECTARES UNDER VINE 40.00

| | |
|---|---|
| ○ Brut M. Cl. Pas Dosé Essenza 0 '13 | ♟♟ 4 |
| ● Rosso Cornalino 50/50 '15 | ♟ 2 |

## La Rifra

LOC. PILANDRO, 2
25010 DESENZANO DEL GARDA [BS]
TEL. +39 0309108023
claudiofraccaroli@virgilio.it

ANNUAL PRODUCTION 90,000 bottles
HECTARES UNDER VINE 14.00

| | |
|---|---|
| ○ Lugana Il Bepi Ris. '15 | ♟♟ 3 |
| ○ Lugana Libiam '17 | ♟♟ 2* |
| ○ Lugana Brut | ♟ 3 |

## Romantica

VIA VALLOSA, 29
25050 PASSIRANO [BS]
TEL. +39 030657362
www.romanticafranciacorta.com

CELLAR SALES
PRE-BOOKED VISITS
ACCOMMODATION AND RESTAURANT SERVICE
ANNUAL PRODUCTION 60,000 bottles
HECTARES UNDER VINE 10.00

| | |
|---|---|
| ○ Franciacorta Brut '14 | ♟♟ 5 |
| ○ Franciacorta Brut | ♟♟ 4 |
| ○ Franciacorta Satèn | ♟ 5 |

## La Rotonda

LOC. CALINO
FRAZ. 25046
VIA BOSCHI,1
25046 CAZZAGO SAN MARTINO [BS]
TEL. +39 0307750909
www.larotondafranciacorta.it

PRE-BOOKED VISITS
ANNUAL PRODUCTION 80,000 bottles
HECTARES UNDER VINE 12.72

| | |
|---|---|
| ⊙ Franciacorta Rosé | ♟♟ 5 |
| ○ Franciacorta Brut EsseA | ♟♟ 5 |
| ○ Franciacorta Saten '14 | ♟♟ 3 |

## Ruinello

FRAZ. RUINELLO DI SOPRA, 15
27047 SANTA MARIA DELLA VERSA [PV]
TEL. +39 0385278057
www.ruinello.it

ANNUAL PRODUCTION 500,000 bottles
HECTARES UNDER VINE 20.00

| | |
|---|---|
| ○ OP Pinot Nero Brut M. Cl Gran Cuvée | ♟♟ 5 |
| ● OP Bonarda Frizzante '17 | ♟ 2 |
| ○ OP Brut M. Cl. | ♟ 5 |

# San Michele

VIA PARROCCHIA, 57
25020 CAPRIANO DEL COLLE [BS]
TEL. +39 0309444091
www.sanmichelevini.it

CELLAR SALES
PRE-BOOKED VISITS
ANNUAL PRODUCTION 70,000 bottles
HECTARES UNDER VINE 16.00
VITICULTURE METHOD Certified Organic

| | |
|---|---|
| ○ Capriano del Colle Bianco Netto '17 | ♙♙ 2* |
| ● Capriano del Colle Rosso 1884 Ris. '15 | ♙♙ 4 |
| ● Capriano del Colle Marzemino '17 | ♙ 2 |

# Santa Lucia

VIA VERDI, 6
25030 ERBUSCO [BS]
TEL. +39 0307769814
www.santaluciafranciacorta.it

CELLAR SALES
PRE-BOOKED VISITS
ANNUAL PRODUCTION 100,000 bottles
HECTARES UNDER VINE 28.00
VITICULTURE METHOD Certified Organic

| | |
|---|---|
| ○ Franciacorta Brut | ♙♙ 5 |
| ⊙ Franciacorta Brut Rosé | ♙ 5 |
| ○ Franciacorta Brut Satèn | ♙ 5 |

# Santus

VIA BADIA, 68
25060 CELLATICA [BS]
TEL. +39 0308367074
www.santus.it

CELLAR SALES
PRE-BOOKED VISITS
ANNUAL PRODUCTION 50,000 bottles
HECTARES UNDER VINE 9.50
VITICULTURE METHOD Certified Organic

| | |
|---|---|
| ○ Franciacorta Satèn '13 | ♙♙ 5 |
| ○ Franciacorta Extra Brut | ♙ 5 |
| ⊙ Franciacorta Extra Brut Rosé | ♙ 5 |

# Tenuta Scerscé

VIA STELVIO, 18
23037 TIRANO [SO]
TEL. +39 3461542970
www.tenutascersce.it

CELLAR SALES
PRE-BOOKED VISITS
ANNUAL PRODUCTION 22,000 bottles
HECTARES UNDER VINE 2.50
SUSTAINABLE WINERY

| | |
|---|---|
| ● Valtellina Sforzato Infinito '13 | ♙♙ 6 |
| ● Valtellina Sup. Essenza '15 | ♙♙ 5 |
| ● Rosso di Valtellina Nettare '16 | ♙ 3 |

# La Spia

LOC. SASSELLA
23012 CASTIONE ANDEVENNO [SO]
TEL. +39 3356407139
www.laspia.wine

ANNUAL PRODUCTION 15,000 bottles
HECTARES UNDER VINE 4.00

| | |
|---|---|
| ● Valtellina Sup. La Spia '13 | ♙♙ 5 |
| ● Valtellina Sup. Sassella PG40 '12 | ♙♙ 5 |

# Sullali

VIA COSTA DI SOPRA, 22
25030 ERBUSCO [BS]
TEL. +39 3930206080
info@sullali.com

ANNUAL PRODUCTION 10,000 bottles
HECTARES UNDER VINE 3.50

| | |
|---|---|
| ○ Franciacorta Extra Brut Blanc de Noir | ♙♙ 5 |
| ○ Franciacorta Extra Brut | ♙ 4 |

## Terre d'Oltrepò

VIA TORINO, 96
27045 CASTEGGIO [PV]
TEL. +39 038551505
www.bronis.it

CELLAR SALES
PRE-BOOKED VISITS
ANNUAL PRODUCTION 4,000,000 bottles
HECTARES UNDER VINE 4500.00

| | |
|---|---|
| ● OP Bonarda Frizzante Dolium '17 | ♟♟ 2* |
| ⊙ OP Cruasé Svic | ♟♟ 2 |
| ○ OP Brut M. Cl. Svic 1907 | ♟ 3 |

## Benedetto Tognazzi

FRAZ. CAIONVICO
VIA SANT'ORSOLA, 161
25135 BRESCIA
TEL. +39 0302692695
www.tognazzivini.it

CELLAR SALES
PRE-BOOKED VISITS
ANNUAL PRODUCTION 80,000 bottles
HECTARES UNDER VINE 12.00
SUSTAINABLE WINERY

| | |
|---|---|
| ○ Lugana Cascina Ardea '17 | ♟♟ 2* |
| ○ Lugana Et. Oro '17 | ♟♟ 3 |

## Tenute Tonalini 1865

VIA MARCONI, 10
27040 MONTÙ BECCARIA [PV]
TEL. +39 0385262252
www.tenutetonalini1865.com

| | |
|---|---|
| ○ Blanc de Noir Brut M. Cl. | ♟♟ 3 |
| ⊙ OP Cruasé '13 | ♟♟ 4 |
| ○ Pinot Nero Brut | ♟ 3 |

## La Tordela

VIA TORRICELLA, 1
24060 TORRE DE' ROVERI [BG]
TEL. +39 035580172
www.latordela.it

CELLAR SALES
PRE-BOOKED VISITS
ACCOMMODATION AND RESTAURANT SERVICE
ANNUAL PRODUCTION 25,000 bottles
HECTARES UNDER VINE 25.00

| | |
|---|---|
| ● Valcalepio Rosso Campo Roccoli Vecchi Ris. '11 | ♟♟ 5 |
| ○ Valcalepio Bianco '17 | ♟ 2 |
| ● Valcalepio Rosso '15 | ♟ 2 |

## Torre degli Alberi

LOC. TORRE DEGLI ALBERI
27040 RUINO [PV]
TEL. +39 0385955905
www.torredeglialberi.it

ANNUAL PRODUCTION 20,000 bottles
HECTARES UNDER VINE 4.00
VITICULTURE METHOD Certified Organic

| | |
|---|---|
| ⊙ OP Cruasé '15 | ♟♟ 3 |
| ○ OP Pinot Nero Brut Pas Dosé M. Cl. '14 | ♟ 3 |

## Tosi

VIA PIANAZZA, 45
27040 MONTESCANO [PV]
TEL. +39 3384781752
www.vinitosi.com

ANNUAL PRODUCTION 50,000 bottles
HECTARES UNDER VINE 12.00

| | |
|---|---|
| ● Thermin Pinot Nero '16 | ♟♟ 3 |

# La Travaglina

FRAZ. CASTELLO
VIA TRAVAGLINA, 1
27046 SANTA GIULETTA [PV]
TEL. +39 0383899195
www.latravaglina.it

CELLAR SALES
PRE-BOOKED VISITS
ANNUAL PRODUCTION 230,000 bottles
HECTARES UNDER VINE 30.50

| | |
|---|---|
| ● OP Bonarda Frizzante Zavola '17 | ♟♟ 2* |
| ● OP Pinot Nero Casaia '15 | ♟♟ 3 |

# Triacca

VIA NAZIONALE, 121
23030 VILLA DI TIRANO [SO]
TEL. +39 0342701352
www.triacca.eu

CELLAR SALES
PRE-BOOKED VISITS
RESTAURANT SERVICE
ANNUAL PRODUCTION 450,000 bottles
HECTARES UNDER VINE 40.00

| | |
|---|---|
| ● Valtellina Sforzato San Domenico '13 | ♟♟ 6 |
| ● Valtellina Sup. Casa La Gatta '15 | ♟♟ 5 |
| ● Valtellina Sup. Prestigio '14 | ♟♟ 6 |
| ● Valtellina Sup. Sassella Ris. '13 | ♟♟ 5 |

# F.lli Turina

VIA PERGOLA, 68
25080 MONIGA DEL GARDA [BS]
TEL. +39 0365502103
www.turinavini.it

CELLAR SALES
PRE-BOOKED VISITS
ANNUAL PRODUCTION 300,000 bottles
HECTARES UNDER VINE 20.00

| | |
|---|---|
| ○ Lugana '17 | ♟♟ 2* |
| ⊙ Valtènesi Riviera del Garda Cl. Chiaretto Fontanamora '17 | ♟♟ 2* |
| ○ Lugana Brut | ♟ 2 |

# Valdamonte

FRAZ. VALDAMONTE, 47
27047 SANTA MARIA DELLA VERSA [PV]
TEL. +39 038579665
www.valdamonte.it

ANNUAL PRODUCTION 17,000 bottles
HECTARES UNDER VINE 16.00
VITICULTURE METHOD Certified Organic
SUSTAINABLE WINERY

| | |
|---|---|
| ● 347 M.S.L.M '17 | ♟♟ 2* |
| ● OP Bonarda Frizzante Novecento '17 | ♟ 2 |

# Agricola Vallecamonica

VIA XXV APRILE, 11
25040 ARTOGNE [BS]
TEL. +39 3355828410
www.vinivallecamonica.com

CELLAR SALES
PRE-BOOKED VISITS
ANNUAL PRODUCTION 20,000 bottles
HECTARES UNDER VINE 4.50

| | |
|---|---|
| ○ Bianco delle Colture '15 | ♟♟ 3 |
| ○ Bianco dell'Annunciata '16 | ♟ 3 |

# Giuseppe Vezzoli

VIA COSTA SOPRA, 22
25030 ERBUSCO [BS]
TEL. +39 0307267579
www.vezzolivini.it

CELLAR SALES
PRE-BOOKED VISITS
ANNUAL PRODUCTION 200,000 bottles
HECTARES UNDER VINE 63.00

| | |
|---|---|
| ○ Franciacorta Satén | ♟♟ 5 |
| ○ Franciacorta Brut | ♟♟ 4 |
| ○ Franciacorta Extra Brut | ♟♟ 5 |
| ○ Franciacorta Pas Dosé Vendemmia Zero | ♟ 6 |

## Vi Bù

VIA NAZIONALE 132C
25040 MALONNO [BS]
TEL. +39 3341417064
info@vi-bu.it

ANNUAL PRODUCTION 5,000 bottles
HECTARES UNDER VINE 1.00
SUSTAINABLE WINERY

| | |
|---|---|
| ○ Sellero Primo Vino '16 | 🍷🍷 3 |

## Vigna Dorata

FRAZ. CALINO
VIA SALA, 80
25046 CAZZAGO SAN MARTINO [BS]
TEL. +39 0307254275
www.vignadorata.it

CELLAR SALES
PRE-BOOKED VISITS
ANNUAL PRODUCTION 70,000 bottles
HECTARES UNDER VINE 6.00

| | |
|---|---|
| ○ Franciacorta Brut Nature | 🍷🍷 5 |
| ⊙ Franciacorta Rosé | 🍷🍷 6 |
| ○ Franciacorta Satèn '12 | 🍷🍷 6 |
| ○ Franciacorta Brut | 🍷 5 |

## Vigne Olcru

VIA BUCA, 26
27047 SANTA MARIA DELLA VERSA [PV]
TEL. +39 0385799958
www.vigneolcru.com

PRE-BOOKED VISITS
ANNUAL PRODUCTION 190,000 bottles
HECTARES UNDER VINE 29.00
SUSTAINABLE WINERY

| | |
|---|---|
| ● Enigma Nero Pinot Nero '17 | 🍷🍷 3 |
| ● OP Bonarda Buccia Rossa '16 | 🍷🍷 4 |
| ○ Virtus Brut M. Cl. '13 | 🍷🍷 4 |

## Cantine Virgili Luigi

VIA M. DONATI, 2
46100 MANTOVA
TEL. +39 0376322560
www.cantinevirgili.it

CELLAR SALES
PRE-BOOKED VISITS
ANNUAL PRODUCTION 300,000 bottles
HECTARES UNDER VINE 10.00

| | |
|---|---|
| ● Inciostar '17 | 🍷🍷 2* |
| ● Lambrusco Mantovano Loghino Dante '17 | 🍷🍷 1* |
| ● Pjafoc '17 | 🍷 2 |

## Visconti

FRAZ. SAN MARTINO DELLA BATTAGLIA
VIA SELVA CAPUZZA, 1
25010 DESENZANO DEL GARDA [BS]
TEL. +39 0309910381
www.viscontiwines.it

CELLAR SALES
PRE-BOOKED VISITS
ANNUAL PRODUCTION 250,000 bottles
HECTARES UNDER VINE 20.00

| | |
|---|---|
| ○ Lugana Antica Casa '17 | 🍷🍷 3 |
| ○ Lugana Franco Visconti '17 | 🍷🍷 3 |
| ○ Lugana Collo Lungo '17 | 🍷 2 |

## Zatti

VIA LANFRANCHI, 10
25080 CALVAGESE DELLA RIVIERA [BS]
TEL. +39 3464273907
www.cantinazatti.it

ANNUAL PRODUCTION 10,000 bottles
HECTARES UNDER VINE 2.00

| | |
|---|---|
| ⊙ Brut Rosé Sandriolè M. Cl. | 🍷🍷 5 |
| ○ Garda Riesling Gep '13 | 🍷🍷 3 |
| ● Garda Marzemino '15 | 🍷 3 |

# CANTON TICINO

A year after Ticino's 'return' to Italian Wines, the region is making its way in the world of wine-growing. Over the past decade this corner of the globe situated in the shadow of the Alps is truly consolidating the quality of its production, with Merlot, the region's crown prince, seeming to have found a second homeland. Its vine growers know it well, and they've learned how to play on all its expressions, even fermenting it without the skins, and with excellent results. But Ticino is also a land of many other grapes, among these Bondola, a native red grape that's slowly making a comeback, even if it's through small selections. Even if the territory isn't particularly large and the predominant grape is Merlot, the differences between its northern and southern parts translates into a varied and interesting array of wines. A feature of Cantone that can't be neglected is its having rediscovered a 'young' culture of winemaking. Indeed, the number of youth graduating in enology and going back to the vineyards to follow in their family's footsteps is bringing new life to the region, as well as new, modern winemaking techniques. And such techniques aren't uprooting the territory's natural makeup either, if anything it's doing the opposite, by exploring and working with its characteristics. Despite the fact that Ticino isn't particularly well-suited to white wine production, this year we tasted some excellent ones. Fratelli Corti's 2016 Sileno stood out most, proving fresh, savory and delicately aromatic - in short, irresistible. But it was a 2015 Vinattieri that performed at the highest levels. The other Tre Bicchieri turned out to be a real surprise: Andrea Ferrari's 2013 Castanar, an unforgettable drink. Ticino is a small territory that manages to amaze. And we'd be willing to bet that it won't finish here.

# CANTON TICINO

## Agriloro

VIA PRELLA, 14
6852 GENESTRERIO
TEL. +41916405454
www.agriloro.ch

CELLAR SALES
PRE-BOOKED VISITS
ANNUAL PRODUCTION 200,000 bottles
HECTARES UNDER VINE 23.00

Agriloro is comprised of two branches: Tenuta dell'Ör, in Arzo, and Tenuta La Prella, in Genestrerio. Meinrad Perler is the winery's founder and owner, overseeing both the estate and winemaking. His passion led him to create a vineyard, whose ampelography is unique in Ticino. Agriloro's selection is vast, ranging from Gewürztraminer to Moscato and Viognier for their whites, Carmenère, Tannat and Arinarnoa for their reds. Their Merlot Riserva La Prella exhibits great depth and highlights the grape's attributes, showing lovely structure, soft fruit and good body, great balance and elegance. Their Granito, a white made with Chardonnay, Sauvignon, Pinot Bianco and Grigio, proves remarkably pleasant and fresh.

| | |
|---|---|
| ○ Ticino Bianco Granito '16 | ♛♛ 5 |
| ● Ticino Merlot La Prella Ris. '16 | ♛♛ 6 |
| ● Casimiro '14 | ♛ 6 |
| ● Syrah '14 | ♛ 6 |
| ● Ticino Merlot La Prella Ris. '15 | ♛♛ 6 |
| ● Ticino Rosso Sottobosco '15 | ♛♛ 6 |

## Castello Luigi

VIA BELVEDERE, 1
6863 BESAZIO
TEL. +41916300808
www.zanini.ch

CELLAR SALES
PRE-BOOKED VISITS
ANNUAL PRODUCTION 12,000 bottles
HECTARES UNDER VINE 12.50

In 1988 Luigi Zanini bought a property in Besazio called 'Belvadere'. In 1997 the old building was torn down so as to build 'Luigi Castle', a structure with a spiral, 20-meter-deep underground cellar. Its vertical space allows for gravity-flow winemaking, which doesn't damage their wines' molecular structure in the way that pumps and mechanical equipment do. Although they also produce a white version, we tasted their Castello Luigi Rosso. This 2015 vintage is a serious, weighty wine, based on the Bordeaux model. It may be young, but the palate proves exciting. It needs time to open up in the glass, gradually revealing aromas of red and black fruit, spices, with hints of earth and undergrowth. It gives its best in the mouth, with a very charming finish that isn't too invasive.

| | |
|---|---|
| ● Ticino Rosso Castello Luigi '15 | ♛♛ 8 |

# F.lli Corti

VIA SOTTOBISIO, 13A
6828 BALERNA
TEL. +41916833702
www.fratellicorti.ch

CELLAR SALES
PRE-BOOKED VISITS
ANNUAL PRODUCTION 60,000 bottles
HECTARES UNDER VINE 2.00

The Corti family's winery has a long history behind it. For years they only made wines with Mendrisiotto's grapes, producing local reds and whites, before moving on to Merlot. After finishing his studies, Nicola Corti accepted the challenge of rethinking and enlarging the selection being forged in the family's historic cellar. From the beginning his philosophy was that of bringing out the elegance and structure of Merlot, a cultivar that is thriving in Ticino. Their 2016 Sileno proved to be one of the best whites we tasted this year. Chardonnay grapes express lovely rich aromas, making for a sumptuous, deep palate, supported by crisp acidity. It's a white that exhibits great structure and pleasantness. Their 2015 Léneo, with its plushness and exuberant fruit, reflects the vintage and proves ready for drinking. But Nicola's wines certainly evolve well over time.

| | |
|---|---|
| ○ Ticino Chardonnay Sileno Ris. '16 | 🍷🍷 7 |
| ● Ticino Merlot Lenéo '15 | 🍷🍷 8 |
| ● Ticino Rosso Sileno '15 | 🍷 5 |
| ○ Ticino Stria Bianca '17 | 🍷 5 |
| ○ Ticino Chardonnay Sileno '15 | 🍷🍷 7 |
| ● Ticino Merlot Lenéo '14 | 🍷🍷 8 |
| ○ Ticino Stria Bianca '16 | 🍷🍷 5 |

# Vini Angelo Delea

VIA ZANDONE
6616 LOSONE
TEL. +41917910817
www.delea.ch

CELLAR SALES
PRE-BOOKED VISITS
ANNUAL PRODUCTION 550,000 bottles
HECTARES UNDER VINE 24.00

There's no doubt that it was a love for his work that led Angelo Delea to join the world of winemaking in 1983. He's managed to evolve year after year, giving rise to modern wines that exhibit great depth. For some years now, his passion has rubbed off on his sons David and Cesare. A wine range of wines are made from their private vineyards and select vine growers. Each one has its own identity, the result of careful study and great respect for the environment. Their whites showed impressive elegance and intensity this year. Their 2017 Sauvignon turned out to be a great discovery, with its well-orchestrated nose of peach and passion fruit, leading into a pleasant, close-focused palate and a lingering and fruity finish. Their Carato Bianco is a blend of Merlot and Pinot Nero (fermented off the skins) with Chardonnay and Sauvignon, fermented and matured in barriques. The 2017 vintage comes through fresh with lovely oaky notes on the nose, youthful and tangy in the mouth, with a racy finish.

| | |
|---|---|
| ○ Ticino Carato Bianco '17 | 🍷🍷 4 |
| ○ Ticino Il Sauvignon '17 | 🍷🍷 3 |
| ● Ticino Merlot San Carlo '16 | 🍷 4 |
| ● Ticino Tiziano '16 | 🍷 4 |
| ○ Ticino Carato Bianco '15 | 🍷🍷 4 |
| ● Ticino Diamante '13 | 🍷🍷 8 |
| ○ Ticino Il Sauvignon '16 | 🍷🍷 3 |
| ● Ticino Merlot Carato Ris. '15 | 🍷🍷 6 |

# Fawino Vini & Distillati

VIA BORROMINI, 20
6850 MENDRISIO
TEL. +4912258664
www.fawino.ch

CELLAR SALES
PRE-BOOKED VISITS
ANNUAL PRODUCTION 40,000 bottles
HECTARES UNDER VINE 6.00

Young enologists Simone Favini and
Claudio Widmer are moving full speed
ahead along the road to quality. With
passion they cultivate their three hectares
of vineyards along the slopes of Monte
Generoso and Monte San Giorgio, at
elevations ranging from 500 to 600 meters,
in a landscape that's truly unique in the
world. Their approach centers on respect
for the environment, with winemaking that's
faithful to the grape and terroir. We
particularly appreciated the character,
coherent style and consistency of their
2015 Musa. The nose immediately exhibits
elegant fruity aromas, followed by good
body and structure. The palate is perfectly
expressed, powerful but well-orchestrated,
with mature tannins and good acidity. It's
easy to predict how well it will evolve over
the years. Their 2017 Meride proves
fresher, racier and more approachable.

| | |
|---|---|
| ● Ticino Merlot Musa '15 | ♟♟ 5 |
| ● Ticino Merlot Meride '17 | ♟ 5 |
| ● Ticino Merlot Musa '14 | ♟♟♟ 5 |

# Roberto e Andrea Ferrari

LOC. CAPOLAGO
VIA BELLA CIMA, 2
6855 STABIO
TEL. +41765662255
www.viniferrari.ch

ANNUAL PRODUCTION 50,000 bottles
HECTARES UNDER VINE 9.00

Ferrari was founded in 1977, when
Roberto Ferrari, an agronomist, decided to
plant his first hectare of vineyards. Over
the years the winery grew both in terms of
quality and quantity, and today they boast
over eight hectares in lovely positions in
Stabio and Ligornetto. Andrea Ferrari
discovered he had the same passion for
wine as his father and is following in his
footsteps, having studied enology before
joining the family business. Although most
of their vineyards are planted with Merlot,
they also grow other grapes such as
Syrah and Viognier. Their 2013 Castanar
is a complex blend of two Cabernets, with
added parts Petit Verdot, Carminoir and
Merlot. It impresses not only for its elegant
and balanced fruity aromas, but also for
its serious body and never-ending spicy
finish: it thoroughly deserves Tre Bicchieri.
This is definitely a wine that will be difficult
to forget.

| | |
|---|---|
| ● Ticino Merlot Castanar '13 | ♟♟♟ 7 |
| ○ Ticino Bianco Zagara '16 | ♟ 4 |
| ○ Ticino Chardonnay Ibisco '17 | ♟ 4 |
| ● Ticino Castanar Ris. '10 | ♟♟ 7 |

# Gialdi Vini - Brivio

VIA VIGNOO, 3
6850 MENDRISIO
TEL. +41916403030
www.gialdi.ch

CELLAR SALES
PRE-BOOKED VISITS
ANNUAL PRODUCTION 1,000,000 bottles
HECTARES UNDER VINE 120.00

Gialdi began in 1953 as a bottling and
commercial center. It was only in 1985
that they decided to focus on making their
own wines, resulting in their becoming one
of Ticino's leading producers. Since 2001
enologist Alfred Demartin has been
availing himself of the grapes of 300
different vine growers, situated primarily in
the Three Valleys (mostly Giornico, Biasca
and Malvaglia). The selection, which
focuses on Merlot, is rich and complete,
offering wines of varying character, some
of which show notable depth. The Gialdi
group comes under the Brivio Vino brand.
We tasted their 2015 Riflessi d'Epoca,
which exhibits close-focused aromas of
red fruit and a generous structure, rich
fruit, spices and velvety tannins on the
palate. It displays finesse as well as great
depth. Their 2013 Trentasei undergoes
long aging, which confers complexity,
balsamic and multifaceted overtones. Their
Sassi Grossi, with its hints of fruit and
licorice, keeps up the name of the winery
with its power, character and verve.

| | |
|---|---|
| ● Ticino Brivio Merlot Riflessi d'Epoca '15 | ♟♟ 5 |
| ● Ticino Merlot Trentasei '13 | ♟♟ 7 |
| ● Ticino Merlot Arzo '15 | ♟♟ 5 |
| ● Ticino Merlot Sassi Grossi '15 | ♟♟ 6 |
| ● Ticino Merlot Arzo '13 | ♟♟ 5 |
| ● Ticino Merlot Sassi Grossi '13 | ♟♟ 6 |
| ● Ticino Merlot Trentasei '10 | ♟♟ 7 |
| ● Estro '13 | ♟ 5 |

# Moncucchetto

VIA MARIETTA CRIVELLI TORRICELLI, 27
6900 LUGANO
TEL. +41919677060
www.moncucchetto.ch

CELLAR SALES
PRE-BOOKED VISITS
RESTAURANT SERVICE
ANNUAL PRODUCTION 30,000 bottles
HECTARES UNDER VINE 6.50

In the heart of Lugano, in an innovative
cellar (designed by archistar Mario Botta)
that integrates perfectly with the landscape
and historic property, the Lucchini family
continues to produce wines full of
character and finesse, fully expressing
what the terroir has to offer. Their main
facility is surrounded by terraced vineyards
and enjoys a splendid view of lakes
Lugano and Muzzano. The passion and
skill of enologist Cristina Monico has
brought out the best qualities of their
selection. Their 2016 Moncucchetto
proves elegantly pleasant. Lovely aromas
of generous fruit, ranging from cherries to
blackberries, follow through onto the
palate, where the wine comes through
round, with good verve and balance. Their
2017 Sauvignon also turned out to be
excellent, possibly one of the best we
tasted. Delicate citrusy aromas lead into a
lovely fresh palate, with a tangy and
delicately aromatic finish. Their other
wines appeared sound.

| | |
|---|---|
| ● Ticino Merlot Moncucchetto '16 | ♟♟ 6 |
| ○ Ticino Sauvignon '17 | ♟♟ 5 |
| ○ Il Murchì '17 | ♟ 5 |
| ● Ticino Collina d'Oro Agra '16 | ♟ 6 |

# Pelossi

VIA CARONA, 8
6912 PAZZALLO
TEL. +41919945677
s.pelossi@gmail.com

CELLAR SALES
PRE-BOOKED VISITS
ANNUAL PRODUCTION 35,000 bottles
HECTARES UNDER VINE 6.00

Pelossi was founded in 1987 in the municipality of Agra. In 1993 Sacha Pelossi earned a diploma in enology at Changin-Nyon. In 1995 he began working in a 'temporary cellar' in his paternal home, in Pazzallo, and produced his first 500 bottles. Today he works with his brother Christian, and their success has led them to enlarge their vineyards in Agra, as well as purchasing more plots. In 2013 they also took over Cantina San Matteo in Cagiallo. A blend of Merlot, Carminoir and Cabernet Sauvignon matures for two years in barriques to produce their Riserva del Ronco. This elegant, well-structured and fruit-rich red evolves with elegance over time. Their Bianco della Piana, made with Chardonnay, Sémillon and Sauvignon matured in new wood, features lovely floral notes, juicy freshness and elegant oaky overtones. Their well-made range of wines includes the high level Merlot Lamone.

| | |
|---|---|
| ○ Ticino Bianco della Piana '16 | 🍷🍷 5 |
| ● Ticino Merlot Lamone '15 | 🍷🍷 6 |
| ● Ticino Rosso Riserva del Ronco '15 | 🍷🍷 6 |
| ○ Ticino Bianco V. dell'Aspide '17 | 🍷 4 |
| ● Ticino Merlot Agra Ris. '15 | 🍷 6 |
| ● Ticino Merlot Sassarei '16 | 🍷 4 |
| ● Ticino Rosso Riva del Tasso '15 | 🍷 6 |
| ○ Ticino Bianco della Piana '15 | 🍷🍷 5 |
| ● Ticino Merlot Agra Ris. '14 | 🍷🍷 6 |
| ● Ticino Merlot Lamone '14 | 🍷🍷 6 |
| ● Ticino Rosso Riserva del Ronco '14 | 🍷🍷 6 |
| ● Ticino Rosso Riva del Tasso '14 | 🍷🍷 6 |

# Tamborini Vini

VIA SERTA, 18
6814 LAMONE
TEL. +4191935747
www.tamborinivini.ch

CELLAR SALES
PRE-BOOKED VISITS
ANNUAL PRODUCTION 60,000 bottles
HECTARES UNDER VINE 30.00

At the end of the 1960s Claudio Tamborini gave a boost to the family winery, which had been active since the 1940s, by leading them to produce their own wines. Since then their estate has grown continuously, expanding along the Lugano hills, Malcantone and Bellinzona. Today they avail themselves of some 30 hectares. Their best wines are made with Merlot, which delivers concentrated, elegant wines that speak to their vineyards of origin. Their San Domenico and Vigna Vecchia wines stood out from the rest of their range. They display character and structure and are great expressions of Merlot from the Ticino area. Their daughter Valentina's new line, including her Cabernet Franc Credi and Vivi, a blend of Johanniter and Viognier, also achieved excellent results during tasting. The latter particularly impressed us with its rich fruity aromas and lovely acid backbone.

| | |
|---|---|
| ● Ticino Credi '15 | 🍷🍷 7 |
| ● Ticino Merlot San Domenico '15 | 🍷🍷 7 |
| ● Ticino Merlot V. V. '15 | 🍷🍷 4 |
| ○ Ticino Vivi '17 | 🍷🍷 5 |
| ○ Ticino Bianco Mosaico '16 | 🍷 5 |
| ○ Ticino Merlot Bianco Terre di Gudo '17 | 🍷 5 |
| ● Ticino Merlot Castelrotto '15 | 🍷 7 |
| ● Ticino Merlot Comano '15 | 🍷🍷 7 |

## Tenuta Vitivinicola Trapletti

VIA P. F. MOLA, 34
6877 COLDRERIO
TEL. +41916460361
www.avvt.ch

CELLAR SALES
PRE-BOOKED VISITS
ANNUAL PRODUCTION 50,000 bottles
HECTARES UNDER VINE 13.60

Enrico Trapletti has always been enchanted by the land. It was a passion that led him to start growing in vines in 1992. He left his job in the rail industry and began managing the family vineyards that had produced grapes for the local cooperative winery. And so he began a path of success, based on commitment and the desire to experience the territory. Merlot is a major cultivar, but it's not the only one. In fact, his vineyards host a number of varieties, from Nebbiolo to international grapes and interspecies hybrids. The Culdrée, made with grapes grown in their first Merlot vineyard in Colderio, is a great example of the artisan character of their wines. It features rich notes of cherry, morello and black fruit, elegant overtones of oak, spice and cocoa and a very elegant body. Their Merlot Terra Creda and their white wine Avigia, a tangy mix of Chardonnay, Kerner and Sauvignon Blanc, prove high-level but simpler and more supple.

| | | |
|---|---|---|
| ● Ticino Merlot Culdrée '15 | 🍷🍷 | 7 |
| ● Ticino Bianco Avigia '17 | 🍷 | 5 |
| ● Ticino Merlot Terra Creda '16 | 🍷 | 5 |
| ● Ticino Merlot Culdrée '13 | 🍷🍷 | 7 |
| ● Trapletti Rosso '13 | 🍷🍷 | 5 |

## Valsangiacomo Vini

V.LE ALLE CANTINE, 6
6850 MENDRISIO
TEL. +41916836053
www.valswine.ch

CELLAR SALES
PRE-BOOKED VISITS
ANNUAL PRODUCTION 250,000 bottles
HECTARES UNDER VINE 20.00

Uberto Valsangiacomo represents the sixth generation of family to work in the world of wine. Today, in his modern cellar in Chiasso, a well-crafted selection of wines are produced. Merlot takes center staging, forming the basis for a number of wines, from whites to rosés, sparkling wines and reds matured in new wood that are well-suited to lengthy aging. But Cabernet Franc, Chardonnay and Syrah are also cultivated here, enriching the range of wines offered. Founded in 1831, they're one of Ticino's historic brands. Chardonnay grapes grown in a single vineyard in Pedrinate are used to make their Gran Segreto Bianco Fondo del Bosco. It then matures in second-use oak for over a year in Forte Airolo, near San Gottardo, at over 1300 meters above sea level. It proves charming, complex and quite gratifying, rich in fruit, backbone and minerals. Harmonious notes of red and black fruit feature in their 2015 Piccolo Ronco.

| | | |
|---|---|---|
| ○ Ticino Gransegreto Fondo del Bosco '16 | 🍷🍷 | 5 |
| ● Ticino Merlot Piccolo Ronco '13 | 🍷🍷 | 5 |
| ● Ticino Gransegreto Merlot '15 | 🍷 | 5 |
| ● Ticino Rubro '15 | 🍷 | 8 |

# Vinattieri Ticinesi

VIA COMI, 4
6853 LIGORNETTO
TEL. +41916472332
www.zanini.ch

**CELLAR SALES**
**PRE-BOOKED VISITS**
**ANNUAL PRODUCTION** 500,000 bottles
**HECTARES UNDER VINE** 100.00

The Zanini family's two wines brands are among the most important in Ticino. Vinattieri Ticinesi was founded in 1985, and comprises some 100 hectares of vineyards in Mendrisiotto. Their wines are made primarily with Merlot. Castello Luigi produces two prestigious wines. One is a characteristically Bordeaux blend of Merlot, Cabernet Sauvignon and Franc. The other is a white made with Chardonnay. Their 2015 Merlot Vinattieri gave us a great thrill during tasting and earned Tre Bicchieri once again. This thoroughbred red opens on the nose with delicate nuances of wild berries, tobacco and vanilla, which give way to a rising palate that's generous, deep and round, with perfectly distributed tannins, juicy fruit and a long finish. Their 2015 Roncaia Riserva also performed well, exhibiting texture, lovely complexity and character.

| | |
|---|---|
| ● Ticino Merlot Vinattieri '15 | 🍷🍷🍷 8 |
| ● Ticino Merlot Ligornetto '15 | 🍷🍷 6 |
| ● Ticino Merlot Roncaia Ris. '15 | 🍷🍷 5 |
| ● Ticino Merlot Vinattieri '13 | 🍷🍷🍷 8 |
| ● Ticino Merlot Ligornetto '13 | 🍷🍷 6 |

# Vini Rovio Ronco Gianfranco Chiesa

VIA IN BASSO, 21
6921 ROVIO
TEL. +41916495831
www.vinirovio.ch

**CELLAR SALES**
**PRE-BOOKED VISITS**
**ANNUAL PRODUCTION** 35,000 bottles
**HECTARES UNDER VINE** 6.00

In Gianfranco Chiesa's modern cellar in Rovio it's easy to be enchanted by the picturesque panorama overlooking the lake of Lugano, and by the wonderful, impeccably maintained vineyards. It's here in this magical place that Gianfranco's wines take form. These exhibit great elegance, the result of painstaking care with respect to each stage of production, starting with their grapes. And this is, in part, the secret to his success: bring out the unique characteristics of each vintage. We rediscover their San Vigilio every year. This blend of Gamaret and Syrah proves a spot-on combination, with Gamaret grapes in the majority. It matures in new wood barrels and comes out concentrated, round and spicy. Gianfranco Chiesa has always maintained a high level for all his wines, as his thoroughbred Merlot Rovio Riserva shows: each sip strikes you with its pleasantness, richness of fruit and overtones of sweet spices.

| | |
|---|---|
| ● San Vigilio '15 | 🍷🍷 5 |
| ● Ticino Merlot Rovio Ris. '16 | 🍷🍷 5 |
| ● San Vigilio 75.25 '13 | 🍷🍷 5 |
| ● Ticino Merlot Rovio Ris. '15 | 🍷🍷 5 |

# Bianchi

S.DA DA RÖV, 24
6822 AROGNO
TEL. +4176 2732050
www.bianchi.bio

CELLAR SALES
PRE-BOOKED VISITS
ANNUAL PRODUCTION 12,000 bottles
HECTARES UNDER VINE 6.00

| | | |
|---|---|---|
| ○ Ticino Bianco None Bio '17 | ▼▼ | 5 |
| ○ Bio Alma '17 | ▼ | 5 |
| ● Ticino Merlot Piaz Bio '16 | ▼ | 6 |

# Cantina Cagi

VIA LINOLEUM, 11
6512 GIUBIASCO
TEL. +41918572531
www.cagivini.ch

PRE-BOOKED VISITS
ANNUAL PRODUCTION 600,000 bottles
SUSTAINABLE WINERY

| | | |
|---|---|---|
| ● Ticino Merlot Camorino '15 | ▼▼ | 6 |
| ○ Ticino Merlot Bianco del Centenario '17 | ▼ | 5 |
| ● Ticino Merlot del Locarnese '16 | ▼ | 5 |
| ● Ticino Merlot Montecarasso '15 | ▼ | 6 |

# I Fracc

I FRACC, 26A
6513 MONTE CARASSO
TEL. +4179 7723735
www.ifracc.ch

ANNUAL PRODUCTION 30,000 bottles
HECTARES UNDER VINE 2.50

| | | |
|---|---|---|
| ● Ido '16 | ▼▼ | 5 |
| ● Duetto '16 | ▼ | 3 |

# Cantine Ghidossi

VIA RONCO REGINA, 2
6988 CROGLIO
TEL. +4179 6193133
www.cantine-ghidossi.ch

ANNUAL PRODUCTION 10,000 bottles
HECTARES UNDER VINE 5.00

| | | |
|---|---|---|
| ● Ticino Merlot Saetta '15 | ▼▼ | 7 |
| ○ Ticino Bianco Dialogo '16 | ▼ | 6 |
| ● Ticino Merlot Terra del Sole '16 | ▼ | 4 |
| ● Ticino Rosso Triade '14 | ▼ | 5 |

# Hubervini

6998 MONTEGGIO
TEL. +4191 6081754
www.hubervini.ch

| | | |
|---|---|---|
| ● Ticino Rosso Costera Ris. '14 | ▼▼ | 5 |
| ● Ticino Merlot Vigneti di Castello '15 | ▼ | 5 |

# Luigina

VIA BRUCIATA, 2
8655 STABIO
TEL. +41916821543
www.tenutaluigina.ch

| | | |
|---|---|---|
| ● Ronco dei Profeti '16 | ▼▼ | 7 |
| ○ Centoquindici '17 | ▼ | 8 |
| ○ Millepetali '17 | ▼ | 7 |
| ● Ticino Gemma dell' Est '15 | ▼ | 8 |

## F.lli Matasci

VIA VERBANO
6598 TENERO
TEL. +41917356011
www.matasci.com

CELLAR SALES
PRE-BOOKED VISITS
ANNUAL PRODUCTION 80,000 bottles
SUSTAINABLE WINERY

| | | |
|---|---|---|
| ● Ticino Merlot Sirio '16 | | ♥♥ 6 |
| ○ Ticino Bianco Cherubino '17 | | ♥ 4 |
| ● Ticino Merlot Tendro '16 | | ♥ 5 |

## Mondò

VIA AL MONDÒ
6514 SEMENTINA
TEL. +41918574558
www.aziendamondo.ch

ANNUAL PRODUCTION 40,000 bottles
HECTARES UNDER VINE 6.30

| | | |
|---|---|---|
| ● Ticino Mondò '15 | | ♥♥ 7 |
| ● Ticino Ronco dei Ciliegi '15 | | ♥♥ 6 |
| ● Ticino Scintilla '15 | | ♥ 4 |

## Tenuta Pian Marnino

AL GAGGIOLETTO, 2
6515 GUDO
TEL. +41918590960
pianmarnino@bluewin.ch

PRE-BOOKED VISITS
ANNUAL PRODUCTION 20,000 bottles
HECTARES UNDER VINE 5.00

| | | |
|---|---|---|
| ● Ticino Merlot Oro di Gudo '15 | | ♥♥ 5 |
| ○ Ticino Bianco Vignabianca '17 | | ♥ 5 |
| ● Ticino Merlot Tenuta Pian Marnino '16 | | ♥ 6 |

## Ronchi Biaggi

VIA INDUSTRIE, 18
6593 CADENAZZO
TEL. +41919106353
www.ronchibiaggi.ch

PRE-BOOKED VISITS
ANNUAL PRODUCTION 20,000 bottles
HECTARES UNDER VINE 4.00
SUSTAINABLE WINERY

| | | |
|---|---|---|
| ● Ticino Merlot '16 | | ♥♥ 5 |
| ● Ticino Merlot Torlem Ris. '15 | | ♥♥ 8 |
| ○ Ticino Bianco Verdabbio '17 | | ♥ 5 |
| ● Ticino Merlot Torlem '16 | | ♥ 7 |

## Tenuta San Giorgio

VIA AL BOSCO, 40
6990 CASSINA D'AGNO
TEL. +41916055868
www.tenutasangiorgio.ch

PRE-BOOKED VISITS
ANNUAL PRODUCTION 30,000 bottles
HECTARES UNDER VINE 7.00
SUSTAINABLE WINERY

| | | |
|---|---|---|
| ● Ticino Rosso Crescendo '16 | | ♥ 7 |
| ● Ticino Rosso Sottoroccia '15 | | ♥ 5 |

## Tenuta Sasso Chierico

VIA CANTONALE, 3
6515 GUDO
TEL. +41918592928
www.sassochierico.ch

| | | |
|---|---|---|
| ● Ticino Sasso Chierico Ris. '15 | | ♥♥ 6 |
| ○ Ticino Bianco A Due '16 | | ♥ 5 |

# TRENTINO

Once again it's a TrentoDoc that leads Trentino's wines. It's an appellation that's served as an ambassador of the territory throughout Italy and the world. It's constituted of a consolidated platoon of wines that this year, for the first time, sees a sparkler earn Tre Bicchieri. It's Francesco Moser's Trento Nature, a wine made possible thanks to the work done by the cycling champion and his family on their private estate. There were seven other true standouts that crossed the finish line, just beating out a number of equally lively sparklers, wines that proved anything but mediocre. This photo-finish saw Balter, Letrari, Rotari, Cesarini Sforza, Ferrari and Maso Martis all taking home golds along with Moser. But a number of other Trentos also obtained top scores, Cavit, Pisoni, Bellaveder, Revì, Casata Monfort and Mas dei Chini's Rosé Inkino, one of the loveliest new wines we tasted. There were other newsworthy offerings, the 2017 Müller Thurgau Viàch by the young producer Corvée (a splendid winery in the Cembra Valley) accompanied by Maso Cantanghel's exquisite 2015 Pinot Nero. It's a truly great wine, as is Guerrieri Gonazaga's San Leonardo, a carefully made, elegant and ageworthy red of international stature that's always at the peaks of excellence. Then there's Dorigati's 2013 Riserva Teroldego Rotaliano (dedicated to the Luigi, the winery's founder), which just beat out Giulio De Vescovi's and that produced by the emerging winery Martinelli. Ferrari brought the Winery of the Year award to Trentino for the impressive quality of its entire selection, and the incessant work it does in promoting the 'Made in Italy' brand. Finally, in this edition you won't find awards for certain historic brands, like Zeni, who decided to let their premium wines rest a bit longer in the cellar. A region's development depends on choices like these as well.

# ★Abate Nero

FRAZ. GARDOLO
S.DA TRENTINA, 45
38121 TRENTO
TEL. +39 0461246566
www.abatenero.it

CELLAR SALES
PRE-BOOKED VISITS
ANNUAL PRODUCTION 65,000 bottles
HECTARES UNDER VINE 65.00

Here at Abate Nero they only produce
Metodo Classico sparkling wines, all of
which are proudly Trento Doc. The winery's
reputation is founded on the careful
selection of its grapes, cultivated in the
vineyards around their cellar. These are
situated on the slopes by Paganella, in
Lavis and upper Trento. Luciano Lunelli, an
enologist and leader of the Teroldego
Rotaliano renaissance (he was director of a
renowned cooperative winery in
Mezzolombardo) is also an expert in
sparkling winemaking and the winery's
founder. His Trentodoc are unmistakable for
their aromatic force and tempting palate.
The winery's most highly-regarded cuvée
were still on the lees, so we tried their
Trento Extra Brut, instead. It offers a
well-calibrated, gentle touch that gives
good acidity and abundant juiciness. Their
Rosé (Pinot Noir), proves a 'must' of its type
and their reliable Brut is always enjoyable,
well-suited to relaxed consumption.

| | | |
|---|---|---|
| ○ Trento Brut | ♙♙ | 4 |
| ⊙ Trento Brut Rosé | ♙♙ | 4 |
| ○ Trento Extra Brut | ♙♙ | 5 |
| ○ Trento Brut Cuvée dell'Abate Ris. '04 | ♙♙♙ | 6 |
| ○ Trento Brut Cuvée dell'Abate Ris. '03 | ♙♙♙ | 5 |
| ○ Trento Brut Cuvée dell'Abate Ris. '02 | ♙♙♙ | 5 |
| ○ Trento Brut Cuvée dell'Abate Ris. '01 | ♙♙♙ | 5 |
| ○ Trento Brut Domini '10 | ♙♙♙ | 5 |
| ○ Trento Brut Domini '07 | ♙♙♙ | 5 |
| ○ Trento Brut Domini '05 | ♙♙♙ | 5 |
| ○ Trento Brut Domini Nero '10 | ♙♙♙ | 5 |
| ○ Trento Brut Domini Nero '08 | ♙♙♙ | 5 |
| ○ Trento Domini Nero '09 | ♙♙♙ | 5 |
| ○ Trento Brut Domini '11 | ♙♙ | 5 |
| ○ Trento Brut Domini Nero '11 | ♙♙ | 5 |

# Nicola Balter

VIA VALLUNGA II, 24
38068 ROVERETO [TN]
TEL. +39 0464430101
www.balter.it

CELLAR SALES
PRE-BOOKED VISITS
ANNUAL PRODUCTION 80,000 bottles
HECTARES UNDER VINE 10.00

The Balter family's beautiful estate is
situated among the woods overlooking
Rovereto. It's a highly relaxing rural
enclave. Here the seasons dictate the work
rhythms of farmers who straddle both city
and country life. Originally they just made
wine for themselves, but then Nicola Balter
transformed the producer into a model,
involving his two children, Clementina and
Giacomo. Only a few wines are made, but
great determination is shown. An extremely
well-deserved Tre Bicchieri for their Trento
Pas Dosé Riserva, which unites vigor and
delicacy with unique floral notes and
savoriness in one exceptional sparkling
wine. Kudos also for some of their wines
ranging from the basic Trento Brut to the
brand new Traminer. Each offers vibrant
spicy notes that are as unusual as they are
satisfying, rare in Vallagarina wine. Their
Sauvignon proves safe and reliable with
notes of elderberry and flint.

| | | |
|---|---|---|
| ○ Trento Pas Dosé Balter Ris. '12 | ♙♙♙ | 6 |
| ○ Trento Brut | ♙♙ | 4 |
| ○ Vallagarina Traminer Aromatico '17 | ♙♙ | 5 |
| ○ Sauvignon '17 | ♙ | 4 |
| ○ Barbanico '97 | ♙♙♙ | 4* |
| ○ Trento Balter Ris. '06 | ♙♙♙ | 5 |
| ○ Trento Balter Ris. '05 | ♙♙♙ | 5 |
| ○ Trento Balter Ris. '04 | ♙♙♙ | 5 |
| ○ Trento Balter Ris. '01 | ♙♙♙ | 5 |
| ○ Trento Dosaggio Zero Ris. '10 | ♙♙♙ | 7 |
| ○ Trento Pas Dosé Balter Ris. '11 | ♙♙♙ | 5 |
| ○ Trento Pas Dosé Balter Ris. '09 | ♙♙♙ | 5 |
| ○ Trento Brut | ♙♙ | 4 |
| ⊙ Trento Brut Rosé | ♙♙ | 5 |
| ● Vallegarina Cabernet Sauvignon '14 | ♙♙ | 3 |

# Bellaveder

Loc. Maso Belvedere
38010 Faedo [TN]
Tel. +39 0461650171
www.bellaveder.it

CELLAR SALES
PRE-BOOKED VISITS
ANNUAL PRODUCTION 70,000 bottles
HECTARES UNDER VINE 12.00
SUSTAINABLE WINERY

Bellaveder continues to grow in terms of quality. It's owned by Tranquillo Lucchetta, whose name is in perfect harmony with the their production philosophy. Indeed, he doesn't like to amaze with his wines, preferring instead to privilege balance. The landscape that his vineyards enjoy is stunning, as is the entire area for that matter. Here in Faeda, over San Michele all'Adige, the hills divide the Cavedine valley from the fertile Sarca plains, heading towards Lake Garda. Their vineyards are organically cultivated and the wines themselves are just as 'sustainable', independent of any certification. Virtually all of the wines from this gorgeous estate deserve top marks. Their Trento, a complex Riserva Nature, presents persistent beading and hints of wild herbs that lean into notes of fruit. Their Pinot Nero, with its unmistakable imprint of strawberry and maraschino is delicious. Their Müeller Thurgau San Lorenz, as aromatic as ever, offers a precise linear palate and clearly deserves inclusion among their best. And last but not least, their Mansum, proves juicy with bombastic Lagrein.

| | | |
|---|---|---|
| ○ Trento Brut Nature Ris. '12 | ♜♜ | 6 |
| ● Trentino Lagrein Mansum '15 | ♜♜ | 5 |
| ○ Trentino Müller Thurgau San Lorenz '17 | ♜♜ | 4 |
| ● Trentino Pinot Nero Faedi '15 | ♜♜ | 6 |
| ● Trentino Lagrein Mansum '13 | ♟♟ | 4 |
| ○ Trentino Müller Thurgau San Lorenz '16 | ♟♟ | 3 |
| ● Trentino Pinot Nero '15 | ♟♟ | 5 |
| ● Trentino Pinot Nero Faedi '13 | ♟♟ | 5 |
| ○ Trentino Sauvignon '16 | ♟♟ | 2* |
| ○ Trentino Traminer '16 | ♟♟ | 3 |
| ○ Trento Brut Nature Ris. '12 | ♟♟ | 5 |
| ○ Trento Brut Nature Ris. '11 | ♟♟ | 5 |

# Borgo dei Posseri

Loc. Pozzo Basso, 1
38061 Ala [TN]
Tel. +39 0464671899
www.borgodeiposseri.com

CELLAR SALES
PRE-BOOKED VISITS
ANNUAL PRODUCTION 60,000 bottles
HECTARES UNDER VINE 21.00
VITICULTURE METHOD Certified Organic
SUSTAINABLE WINERY

The Dolomites, those situated to the south of its largest peaks, serve as the background for this mountain estate, situated among rock-climbing gyms and routes for mountain bikes. These dynamic, well-tread paths proceed through their rows of Pinot Nero, Chardonnay and Mueller Thurgau. Indeed, the map that you'll find in their cellar, traces out a relaxing wine tour, with stops for tasting wines made with grapes from the various vineyards crossed. Martin Mainenti oversees agriculture, and there's news on the way in terms of sparkling wine production. Their Tananai, a true mountain Trento, immediately hits you with its aromas, both sober and crystalline in brightness. It delivers well-calibrated length that plays between comforting citric acidity and the goodness of bread. Their Malusel, a white blend from which Traminer stands out, surprises with its gentle silkiness. Their always dependable Quaron proves even more aromatic than usual. They have an enjoyable Sauvignon, called Furiel.

| | | |
|---|---|---|
| ○ Cuvée Malusel '15 | ♜♜ | 4 |
| ○ Trento Brut Tananai '14 | ♜♜ | 5 |
| ○ Müller Thurgau Quaron '17 | ♜ | 4 |
| ○ Sauvignon Furiel '17 | ♜ | 4 |
| ○ Cuvée Malusel '14 | ♟♟ | 3 |
| ● Merlot Rocol '14 | ♟♟ | 3 |
| ○ Müller Thurgau Quaron '16 | ♟♟ | 3 |
| ○ Müller Thurgau Quaron '15 | ♟♟ | 3 |
| ○ Müller Thurgau Quaron '14 | ♟♟ | 3 |
| ● Pinot Nero Paradis '15 | ♟♟ | 3 |
| ○ Sauvignon Furiel '16 | ♟♟ | 3 |
| ○ Traminer Arliz '15 | ♟♟ | 3 |
| ○ Trento Brut Tananai '13 | ♟♟ | 5 |
| ○ Trento Brut Tananai '12 | ♟♟ | 5 |
| ○ Trento Brut Tananai '11 | ♟♟ | 5 |

# TRENTINO

## Bossi Fedrigotti

VIA UNIONE, 43
38068 ROVERETO [TN]
TEL. +39 0456832511
www.masi.it

CELLAR SALES
PRE-BOOKED VISITS
ANNUAL PRODUCTION 120,000 bottles
HECTARES UNDER VINE 40.00
SUSTAINABLE WINERY

Bossi Fedrigotti's estate is one of Trentino's most scenic, bolstered by a historic cultural patrimony situated largely in Vallagarina. With pride and dedication, the family continue their work in the countryside. And they've done it by developing their historic Maso Fojaneghe, a name we associate with the first Italian 'Bordeauxs', and by cultivating Teroldego (as well as Marzemino, obviously) here on Isera's classic volcanic terrain. For some years now they've been partnered with Gruppo Masi, who've pushed notably for grapes used for the production of Metodo Classico sparkling wines. Their classic sparkler 2013 Conte Federico Il Conte Federico stands out in the Trento appellation less for its noble emblem than for an aromatic floral range mixing damson plum and wholegrain bread and offering just as much succulent flavor. Among still wines, their Vign'Asmara, a Chardonnay and Traminer blend, stands out equally for its full-bodied structure and unique, pleasant aroma. Their Mas'Est, a Teroldego also deserves attention.

| | | |
|---|---|---|
| ○ Trento Brut Conte Federico Ris. '13 | ♔♔ | 5 |
| ○ Trentino Bianco Vign'Asmara '16 | ♔♔ | 4 |
| ● Trentino Teroldego Mas'Est '16 | ♔♔ | 3 |
| ● Fojaneghe Rosso '12 | ♔♔♔ | 5 |
| ○ Trento Brut Conte Federico Ris. '12 | ♔♔♔ | 5 |
| ● Fojaneghe Rosso '13 | ♔♔ | 5 |
| ● Fojaneghe Rosso '11 | ♔♔ | 5 |
| ● Fojaneghe Rosso '10 | ♔♔ | 5 |
| ● Mas'est '13 | ♔♔ | 3 |
| ● Mas'est '12 | ♔♔ | 3 |
| ○ Trento Brut Conte Federico '11 | ♔♔ | 5 |
| ○ Trento Conte Federico Brut | ♔♔ | 5 |
| ○ Vign'Asmara '15 | ♔♔ | 4 |
| ○ Vign'Asmara '14 | ♔♔ | 4 |
| ○ Vign'Asmara '13 | ♔♔ | 4 |

## ★Cavit

VIA DEL PONTE, 31
38040 TRENTO
TEL. +39 0461381711
www.cavit.it

CELLAR SALES
PRE-BOOKED VISITS
ANNUAL PRODUCTION 70,000,000 bottles
HECTARES UNDER VINE 5500.00

Enologist Anselmo Martini coordinates a technical staff that are as numerous as they are talented, constantly evolving in terms of agronomic innovation and production techniques. It's all overseen by Enrico Zanoni, the manager leading this bona fide wine giant, a group that encompasses many of Trentino's cooperative wineries while also controlling producers in Oltrepò Pavese and even Germany. Millions of bottles are produced for international markets, but they offer more targeted wines as well, from Riesling to Pinot Nero and their Trentodocs, which are always at the top of the appellation. Once again their Altemasi Graal proves to be among Trento's top wines, earning a place in our finals. There were also some surprises from the other wines submitted, including their impressive Pinot Nero Brusafer with its elegance and aromatic depth, their Maso Toresella, a white Riesling blend, and their Quattro Vicariati, a Bordeaux blend.

| | | |
|---|---|---|
| ● Trentino Rosso Quattro Vicariati '14 | ♔♔ | 4 |
| ● Trentino Sup. Pinot Nero Brusafer '15 | ♔♔ | 5 |
| ○ Trento Brut Altemasi Graal Ris. '11 | ♔♔ | 6 |
| ○ Trentino Chardonnay Maso Toresella '16 | ♔♔ | 4 |
| ○ Trento Altemasi Pas Dosé '12 | ♔♔ | 5 |
| ○ Trentino Pinot Grigio Rulendis '16 | ♔ | 3 |
| ● Teroldego Rotaliano Maso Cervara '07 | ♔♔♔ | 4 |
| ○ Trento Altemasi Graal Brut Ris. '03 | ♔♔♔ | 6 |
| ○ Trento Brut Altemasi Graal Ris. '10 | ♔♔♔ | 6 |
| ○ Trento Brut Altemasi Graal Ris. '09 | ♔♔♔ | 6 |
| ○ Trento Brut Altemasi Graal Ris. '08 | ♔♔♔ | 6 |
| ○ Trento Brut Altemasi Graal Ris. '06 | ♔♔♔ | 6 |
| ○ Trento Brut Altemasi Graal Ris. '05 | ♔♔♔ | 7 |
| ○ Trento Brut Altemasi Graal Ris. '04 | ♔♔♔ | 7 |

# Cesarini Sforza

FRAZ. RAVINA
VIA STELLA, 9
38123 TRENTO
TEL. +39 0461382200
www.cesarinisforza.com

**CELLAR SALES**
**PRE-BOOKED VISITS**
**ANNUAL PRODUCTION** 1,300,000 bottles
**HECTARES UNDER VINE** 800.00

1673, a year belonging to the past but that's helping to face the future - and therein lies the strategy undertaken by this historic Trentino sparkling winemaker. The date represents the marriage between the noble Cesarini and Sforza families, two names etched onto every bottle of Trento Riserva they make today. Simultaneously they've finalized a relationship with Cantina Lavis to increase their production of sparkling wine and enlarge their distribution network. It's a restyling that goes beyond their labels, and a commitment to continue improving the quality of all their products. The three in the date on their Trento Riserva bottle reflects the Tre Bicchieri it deserves. This golden-hued Chardonnay sparkler offers an intense nose of dried herbs, flowers and damson plums. The balance is excellent due to the unmistakable aromas of Trento with a long finish that is atypically savory and quite satisfying. Their two other classic sparkling wines deliver outstanding results.

| | | |
|---|---|---|
| ○ Trento Extra Brut 1673 Ris. '11 | ♟♟♟ | 5 |
| ○ Trento 1673 | ♟♟ | 4 |
| ○ Trento Brut Nature Noir 1673 '12 | ♟♟ | 5 |
| ○ Trento Aquila Reale Ris. '05 | ♟♟♟ | 7 |
| ○ Trento Aquila Reale Ris. '02 | ♟♟♟ | 7 |
| ○ Trento Extra Brut Tridentum '09 | ♟♟♟ | 4* |
| ○ Trento Aquila Reale Ris. '08 | ♟♟ | 6 |
| ☉ Trento Brut Rosé Ris. '11 | ♟♟ | 4 |
| ○ Trento Brut Tridentum '12 | ♟♟ | 4 |
| ○ Trento Dosaggio Zero Tridentum '12 | ♟♟ | 5 |
| ○ Trento Extra Brut 1673 Ris. '10 | ♟♟ | 5 |
| ☉ Trento Tridentum Rosé '10 | ♟♟ | 4 |

# Corvée

LOC. BEDIN, 1
38034 LISIGNAGO [TN]
TEL. +39 3440260170
www.corvee.wine

**CELLAR SALES**
**PRE-BOOKED VISITS**
**ANNUAL PRODUCTION** 50,000 bottles
**HECTARES UNDER VINE** 13.60

Corvée may have just a couple vintages under their belt, but they're already one of Trentino's top producers, with a series of wines that are truly 'high range' (here in the Cembra Valley the vineyards seem to reach up into the sky). Corvée, a name dedicated to the agricultural practice used by the most well-prepared vigneron, features a staff coordinated by enologists Beppe Caviola and Moreno Nardin. They put forward a selection of excellent regional interpretations made both with white grapes, and with Pinot Nero and Lagrein.Their 2017 Müller Thurgau Viàch proved to be the most surprising wine during our tastings. It's made with grapes cultivated at 700 meters. It offers up aromas of white fruit and citrus, while on the palate it shows tension and excellent depth. It's a truly lovely wine. Their reds didn't disappoint either. Both their Agole (Pinot Nero) and their Passo della Croce (Lagrein) clearly express their varietal characteristics (strawberry in their Pinot Nero, blackberry in their Lagrein), and are set to do well over time.

| | | |
|---|---|---|
| ○ Trentino Müller Thurgau Viàch '17 | ♟♟♟ | 4* |
| ○ Trentino Pinot Bianco Cor '17 | ♟♟ | 5 |
| ● Trentino Pinot Nero Agole '16 | ♟♟ | 6 |
| ○ Trentino Chardonnay Quaràs '17 | ♟♟ | 5 |
| ● Trentino Lagrein Passo della Croce '16 | ♟♟ | 5 |
| ○ Trentino Sauvignon Salesà '17 | ♟♟ | 5 |
| ○ Trentino Pinot Grigio O'm '17 | ♟ | 5 |
| ○ Trentino Traminer Clongiàn '17 | ♟ | 5 |
| ○ Trentino Chardonnay Rorè '16 | ♟♟ | 4 |
| ○ Trentino Müller Thurgau Portegnàc '16 | ♟♟ | 4 |
| ○ Trentino Müller Thurgau Viach '16 | ♟♟ | 4 |
| ○ Trentino Pinot Bianco Cor '16 | ♟♟ | 4 |
| ○ Trentino Pinot Grigio Corvaia '16 | ♟♟ | 4 |

## De Vescovi Ulzbach

P.ZZA GARIBALDI, 12
38016 MEZZOCORONA [TN]
TEL. +39 04611740050
www.devescoviulzbach.it

CELLAR SALES
PRE-BOOKED VISITS
ANNUAL PRODUCTION 20,000 bottles
HECTARES UNDER VINE 3.50

Giulio De Vescovi doesn't have many vintages under his belt, but he knows what he wants: to diversify while developing the intrinsic peculiarities of the grapes planted in his private vineyards. He's young but he belongs to a dynasty that boasts centuries of experience in the field, especially when it comes to Teroldego Rotaliano. He interprets the grape well, eclectically, though he's also been showing attention to the white grapes he rears in the highlands, and to an exquisite sparkling wine. Surely we'll be talking about it more soon. This year we only tasted their 2016 Teroldego Rotaliano (last year we gave Tre Bicchieri to their 2015 Vigilius, truly a great Trentino red) and it also proves exemplary. Truly regal, its velvety color and highlights deliver silky smoothness on the palate, as well as a finish that is steady in its vigorous elegance.

| | |
|---|---|
| ● Teroldego Rotaliano '16 | **YY** 3* |
| ● Teroldego Rotaliano '15 | YYY 3* |
| ● Teroldego Rotaliano Vigilius '12 | YYY 5 |
| ○ Empeiria '16 | YY 5 |
| ○ Empeiria '15 | YY 5 |
| ● Kino Nero '15 | YY 4 |
| ○ Sauvignon '16 | YY 4 |
| ○ Sauvignon '15 | YY 4 |
| ● Teroldego Rotaliano '14 | YY 3* |
| ● Teroldego Rotaliano '13 | YY 3 |
| ● Teroldego Rotaliano '12 | YY 3* |
| ● Teroldego Rotaliano '11 | YY 3 |
| ● Teroldego Rotaliano Vigilius '15 | YY 5 |
| ● Teroldego Rotaliano Vigilius '13 | YY 5 |
| ● Teroldego Rotaliano Vigilius '11 | YY 5 |

## Marco Donati

VIA CESARE BATTISTI, 41
38016 MEZZOCORONA [TN]
TEL. +39 0461604141
www.cantinadonatimarco.it

CELLAR SALES
PRE-BOOKED VISITS
ANNUAL PRODUCTION 100,000 bottles
HECTARES UNDER VINE 20.00
SUSTAINABLE WINERY

Donati is a vigneron of old, with many harvests under his belt, but he still wants to amaze those who love Teroldego. Today the veteran is accompanied by his daughter Elisabetta and wife, Emanuela, who represent the sixth generation to work among the vineyards here in the Rotaliana plains. Moreover, Elisabetta is among those promoting a new fashion when it comes to Teroldghista, forming part of a group of those working between the Adige and Noce rivers. The results thus far have been more than positive. Donati's symbolic wine, Sangue di Drago, clearly articulates the recent evolution of Teroldego. The red is once again dominated by an unmistakable flavor of jam but without losing vivaciousness. Among their other extremely complete range of wines, Solo Alto (Nosiola in pure form) deserves mention, as do two other whites, Albeggio (Müeller Thurgau) and Tramonti (Traminer).

| | |
|---|---|
| ● Teroldego Rotaliano Sangue di Drago '15 | **YY** 6 |
| ○ Trentino Müller Thurgau Albeggio '17 | **YY** 4 |
| ○ Trentino Nosiola Sole Alto '17 | **YY** 4 |
| ○ Trentino Traminer Aromatico Tramonti '17 | **Y** 4 |
| ● Teroldego Rotaliano Sangue del Drago '98 | YYY 5 |
| ● Teroldego Rotaliano Bagolari '15 | YY 4 |
| ● Teroldego Rotaliano Bagolari '13 | YY 4 |
| ● Teroldego Rotaliano Sangue del Drago '12 | YY 5 |
| ● Teroldego Rotaliano Sangue del Drago '11 | YY 5 |
| ● Teroldego Rotaliano Sangue di Drago '14 | YY 5 |
| ● Teroldego Rotaliano Sangue di Drago '13 | YY 5 |
| ● Trentino Marzemino Orme '14 | YY 3 |
| ○ Trentino Traminer '13 | YY 4 |
| ○ Vendemmia Tardiva Traminer '12 | YY 5 |

# ★Dorigati

via Dante, 5
38016 Mezzocorona [TN]
Tel. +39 0461605313
www.dorigati.it

CELLAR SALES
PRE-BOOKED VISITS
ANNUAL PRODUCTION 100,000 bottles
HECTARES UNDER VINE 10.00
SUSTAINABLE WINERY

Dorigati is defined by the farm laborer's perseverance, specialized knowledge in agronomy and the personality of the vigneron who've carried forward a commitment to quality that began some 170 years ago. Cousins Michele and Paolo manage to perfectly interpret the style set by their fathers. They do it with dedication, attention to detail when it comes to their multi-award winning Trentos and to their painstakingly produced Riserva di Teroldego. And the results have been excellent. Their wines made with white grapes, Trentos included, will debut in a few years so as to fully develop and promote their Teroldego reds. Their special Riserva di Teroldego, dedicated to founder Luigi, hits a bullseye, thanks to its impenetrable ruby color, as vibrant in its appearance as in its notes of quinine and red berries, crossing the senses with graceful versatility. Very long and impressive on the palate, its good structure has excellent aging prospects. Their other two Teroldegos also ehxibit perfect execution.

| | | |
|---|---|---|
| ● Teroldego Rotaliano Luigi Ris. '13 | ♙♙♙ | 6 |
| ● Teroldego Rotaliano Cl. '16 | ♙♙ | 4 |
| ● Teroldego Rotaliano Diedri Ris. '15 | ♙♙ | 5 |
| ○ Trento Brut Methius Ris. '09 | ♙♙♙ | 6 |
| ○ Trento Brut Methius Ris. '08 | ♙♙♙ | 6 |
| ○ Trento Brut Methius Ris. '06 | ♙♙♙ | 6 |
| ○ Trento Brut Methius Ris. '05 | ♙♙♙ | 6 |
| ○ Trento Brut Methius Ris. '04 | ♙♙♙ | 6 |
| ○ Trento Brut Methius Ris. '03 | ♙♙♙ | 6 |
| ○ Trento Brut Methius Ris. '02 | ♙♙♙ | 6 |
| ○ Trento Brut Methius Ris. '00 | ♙♙♙ | 6 |
| ○ Trento Brut Methius Ris. '98 | ♙♙♙ | 6 |
| ○ Trento Methius Ris. '95 | ♙♙♙ | 4 |
| ○ Trento Methius Ris. '92 | ♙♙♙ | 4* |

# Endrizzi

loc. Masetto, 2
38010 San Michele all'Adige [TN]
Tel. +39 0461650129
www.endrizzi.it

CELLAR SALES
PRE-BOOKED VISITS
ANNUAL PRODUCTION 600,000 bottles
HECTARES UNDER VINE 55.00
SUSTAINABLE WINERY

Siblings Lisa and Daniele Endrici are accompanying their parents, Christine and Paolo, in the continued growth of the family winery. Theirs is a historic winery with almost two centuries under their belt and a feel for innovation. And their approach reflects the utmost respect for nature, with organic cultivation and a waste reduced to a minimum. Their vineyards are perfect, veritable gardens in which you find works of art and abodes for the various animals who visit them. These are situated in Castel Monreale and Faedo, looking towards the Rotaliana plains. Two particularly fine wines were presented this year. Their Trento Masetto Privé sparkling wine, offering both strength and graciousness, deserves to be tasted with full attention due to its significant gustatory versatility. Somewhat unusual for the Dolomite area, their unforgettable Gran Masetto is a powerful Teroldego made of intentionally overripe grapes that result in a dense, strong and full-bodied wine.

| | | |
|---|---|---|
| ● Gran Masetto '13 | ♙♙ | 8 |
| ○ Trento Masetto Privè '08 | ♙♙ | 6 |
| ● Teroldego Rotaliano Leoncorno Ris. '15 | ♙♙ | 5 |
| ○ Trento Piancastello '13 | ♙♙ | 5 |
| ● Masetto Nero '15 | ♙ | 4 |
| ● Gran Masetto '12 | ♙♙ | 8 |
| ○ Masetto Bianco '15 | ♙♙ | 3 |
| ○ Masetto Dorè '15 | ♙♙ | 5 |
| ● Masetto Due '14 | ♙♙ | 5 |
| ● Masetto Nero '14 | ♙♙ | 4 |
| ● Masetto Nero '13 | ♙♙ | 3 |
| ● Teroldego Rotaliano Sup. '13 | ♙♙ | 3 |
| ○ Trento Brut Pian Castello Ris. '12 | ♙♙ | 4 |
| ○ Trento Brut Pian di Castello '11 | ♙♙ | 4 |

## ★★Ferrari

VIA PONTE DI RAVINA, 15
38123 TRENTO
TEL. +39 0461972311
www.ferraritrento.it

CELLAR SALES
PRE-BOOKED VISITS
RESTAURANT SERVICE
ANNUAL PRODUCTION 4,450,000 bottles
HECTARES UNDER VINE 120.00
SUSTAINABLE WINERY

Constant growth both in terms of production volumes and quality. At Ferrari there's vision. They're planning new wines (even a new rosé aimed at replicating their Giulio Ferrari brand) and developing an image that's able to evolve without breaking with the past. The Lunelli dynasty has established their brand's fame, starting with an approach that's increasingly attentive to sustainability and organic agriculture. They offer a number of Metodo Classico sparklers, all of which are incredibly authoritative and versatile, thanks in part to their historic lead winemaker, Ruben Larentis. A number of wines put in excellent performances. Tre Bicchieri, however, go to their innovative 2011 Perlè Zero, a true star, whose elegant aromas and mighty palate give way to a long finish. Their incredibly powerful and simply named Giulio Ferrari continues to be an absolute standout, while their other wines also offer great drinkability, including their Perlé Nero and Perlé Bianco. And so it is that we've chosen Ferrari as our Winery of the Year.

| | |
|---|---|
| ○ Trento Perlé Zero Cuvée Zero '11 | ▼▼▼ 8 |
| ○ Trento Brut Perlé Bianco '09 | ▼▼ 6 |
| ○ Trento Brut Perlé Nero '10 | ▼▼ 6 |
| ○ Trento Giulio Ferrari '07 | ▼▼ 8 |
| ○ Trentino Chardonnay Villa Margon '16 | ▼▼ 4 |
| ○ Trento Brut Giulio Ferrari Riserva del Fondatore '06 | ♀♀♀ 8 |
| ○ Trento Brut Giulio Ferrari Riserva del Fondatore '05 | ♀♀♀ 8 |
| ○ Trento Brut Giulio Ferrari Riserva del Fondatore '04 | ♀♀♀ 8 |
| ○ Trento Extra Brut Lunelli Ris. '07 | ♀♀♀ 7 |
| ○ Trento Extra Brut Perlé Nero '07 | ♀♀♀ 8 |
| ○ Trento Extra Brut Perlé Nero '06 | ♀♀♀ 8 |

## Fondazione Mach

VIA EDMONDO MACH, 1
38010 SAN MICHELE ALL'ADIGE [TN]
TEL. +39 0461615252
www.fem.it

CELLAR SALES
PRE-BOOKED VISITS
ANNUAL PRODUCTION 250,000 bottles
HECTARES UNDER VINE 60.00
VITICULTURE METHOD Certified Organic

From Austro-Hungarian school of agriculture to enological institute to the bonafide University of Wine that it is today. Founded back in 1874 by Edmund Mach, the Mach Foundation has contributed to the education of a number of modern professionals working in the field, and not just from the Dolomites. Projects, research, innovation are all made possible thanks to the support of ecologists and biologists studying genomic issues in the field of viticulture. But we shouldn't forget their work as a producer either, which is carried out in a cellar situated in a millennium-old monastery. We only tasted a few wines this year as their most-respected reds undergo further aging. Thus the standard bearer for the winery is a very serious Trento that fully respects the typology of the wine, austere but approachable. Equally powerful is their Pinot Bianco, one of the, if not the, best in Trentino. The other wines we sampled also guarantee quality with their Sauvignon in particular proving truly impressive.

| | |
|---|---|
| ○ Trento Pinot Bianco Monastero '16 | ▼▼ 3* |
| ○ Trento Mach Riserva del Fondatore '13 | ▼▼ 5 |
| ○ Trentino Sauvignon Monastero '17 | ▼▼ 3 |
| ○ Trentino Nosiola '17 | ▼ 3 |
| ○ Trentino Traminer Aromatico '17 | ▼ 3 |
| ○ Trento Mach Riserva del Fondatore '09 | ♀♀♀ 5 |
| ○ Trento Mach Riserva del Fondatore '07 | ♀♀♀ 5 |
| ○ Trento Mach Riserva del Fondatore '04 | ♀♀♀ 5 |
| ● Cabernet Franc Monastero '15 | ♀♀ 3 |
| ○ Manzoni Bianco '16 | ♀♀ 4 |
| ● Trentino Marzemino '15 | ♀♀ 3 |
| ○ Trentino Riesling Monastero '15 | ♀♀ 5 |
| ○ Trentino Traminer Aromatico Monastero '16 | ♀♀ 3 |
| ○ Trento Mach Riserva del Fondatore '12 | ♀♀ 5 |

# Grigoletti

via Garibaldi, 12
38060 Nomi [TN]
Tel. +39 0464834215
www.grigoletti.com

CELLAR SALES
PRE-BOOKED VISITS
ANNUAL PRODUCTION 60,000 bottles
HECTARES UNDER VINE 6.00

Authenticity and drinkability are the two essential characteristics that define this agricultural family's wines. For generations they've worked to steward their viticultural enclave on the right bank of the Adige, across Trento and Rovereto. Here wine is made exclusively with the grapes cultivated around their scenic cellar, a small temple to wine that's also a museum of local rural culture. In the vineyards the area's traditional cultivar are preferred, foremost Marzemino, though they can also boast excellent wines made with international grapes, like Merlot. With very few exceptions, every step of production is overseen by the family themselves. 2017 brought out the best of their selection. Their Marzemino remains a benchmark of the category, rich in flavor and highly enjoyable. The same holds true for their Chardonnay, a savory wine with trademark hints of golden apple. Other compelling wines ranged from their grape San Martim, to their Retiko, a blend of Chardonnay, Sauvignon and Manzoni.

| | | |
|---|---|---|
| ○ Retiko '15 | ♟♟ | 3 |
| ○ San Martim V. T. '16 | ♟♟ | 4 |
| ○ Trentino Chardonnay L'Opera '17 | ♟♟ | 3 |
| ● Trentino Marzemino '17 | ♟♟ | 3 |
| ● Gonzalier '14 | ♟♟ | 5 |
| ● Gonzalier '13 | ♟♟ | 5 |
| ● Gonzalier '12 | ♟♟ | 5 |
| ○ Trentino Chardonnay L'Opera '14 | ♟♟ | 3 |
| ● Trentino Marzemino '16 | ♟♟ | 2* |
| ● Trentino Marzemino '15 | ♟♟ | 2* |
| ● Trentino Merlot Antica Vigna '13 | ♟♟ | 4 |
| ● Trentino Merlot Antica Vigna '12 | ♟♟ | 4 |

# La Vis - Valle di Cembra

via Carmine, 7
38015 Lavis [TN]
Tel. +39 0461440111
www.la-vis.com

CELLAR SALES
PRE-BOOKED VISITS
ACCOMMODATION AND RESTAURANT SERVICE
ANNUAL PRODUCTION 1,000,000 bottles
HECTARES UNDER VINE 850.00
SUSTAINABLE WINERY

Their strength lies not only in the legacy of their name, but also in their determination to move beyond all the issues of the past. That's how the La Vis team has become not only more resolute but once again successful, from president Pietro Patton to director Massimo Benetello, enologist Ezio Dallagiacoma, brand ambassador Luciano Rappo and the thousands of members who work their mountain vineyards. Partnered with Cantina Valle di Cembra and Cesarini Sforza, La Vis serves as a crown jewel of local sparkling winemaking, with excellent results. First things first. Their Chardonnay Diaol is powerful in a way that rarely happens in Trentino wines. Also coming out swinging, their Ritratto, a blend of Teroldego, Merlot and Lagrein, proves big and muscular. The Müller Thurgau Vigna delle Forche shows itself as one of their best ever, as does the Pinot Noir Vigna Saosent, from the upper reaches of Valle di Cembra. Expect unquestionable quality from these and many, many other wines.

| | | |
|---|---|---|
| ○ Trentino Chardonnay Diaol '16 | ♟♟ | 3* |
| ○ Trentino Müller Thurgau '17 | ♟♟ | 3 |
| ● Trentino Pinot Nero V. di Saosent '15 | ♟♟ | 5 |
| ○ Trentino Chardonnay '17 | ♟ | 3 |
| ● Trentino Lagrein '17 | ♟ | 5 |
| ○ Trentino Nosiola '17 | ♟ | 5 |
| ○ Ritratto Bianco '07 | ♟♟♟ | 4 |
| ● Ritratto Rosso '13 | ♟♟♟ | 4* |
| ● Ritratto Rosso '03 | ♟♟♟ | 4 |
| ● Ritratto Rosso '91 | ♟♟♟ | |
| ○ Trentino Müller Thurgau V. delle Forche '14 | ♟♟♟ | 3* |
| ○ Trentino Müller Thurgau V. delle Forche '13 | ♟♟♟ | 3* |
| ○ Trentino Müller Thurgau V. delle Forche '12 | ♟♟♟ | 3* |
| ○ Trentino Pinot Grigio Ritratti '95 | ♟♟♟ | |

## Letrari

VIA MONTE BALDO, 13/15
38068 ROVERETO [TN]
TEL. +39 0464480200
www.letrari.it

CELLAR SALES
PRE-BOOKED VISITS
ANNUAL PRODUCTION 160,000 bottles
HECTARES UNDER VINE 23.00

The patriarch is no more: Leonello 'Nello' Letrari left us after some 60 vintages, but his daughter Lucia and the entire family are forging ahead in accordance with his teachings. Indeed, Letrari is one of Trentino's most important and reputable brands, committed to making wines solely with grapes cultivated in their private vineyards in the heart of Vallagarina. Their Metodo Classico sparklers takes center stage, thanks to a selection of diverse, complex and evocative wines. Nello would be pleased. We'll gladly raise our glasses with their Trento Letrari Dosaggio Zero, which proves not only impeccable in its lively texture but also as engaging in its keen body as in its aromatic allure – all this despite perfect dryness and a sharp edge. However, it does not end here based on the extremely high evaluations given to both their Riserva del Fondatore and Quore. We did not try their Rosé, but their other Trentos deserve praise, starting with the Cuvée Blance, a sparkling wine that is playful in its simplicity.

| | | |
|---|---|---|
| ○ Trento Dosaggio Zero Ris. '11 | ♀♀♀ 6 |
| ○ Trento Brut Riserva del Fondatore 976 '08 | ♀♀ 8 |
| ○ Trento Brut Ris. '11 | ♀♀ 5 |
| ○ Trento Quore '11 | ♀♀ 5 |
| ○ Trento Cuvée Blanche | ♀ 4 |
| ○ Trento Brut 976 Riserva del Fondatore '05 | ♀♀♀ 8 |
| ○ Trento Brut Letrari Ris. '09 | ♀♀♀ 5 |
| ○ Trento Brut Letrari Ris. '08 | ♀♀♀ 5 |
| ○ Trento Brut Letrari Ris. '07 | ♀♀♀ 5 |
| ○ Trento Brut Letrari Ris. '05 | ♀♀♀ 5 |
| ○ Trento Brut Ris. '10 | ♀♀♀ 5 |
| ○ Trento Brut Ris. '06 | ♀♀♀ 5 |
| ☉ Trento Brut Rosé +4 '09 | ♀♀♀ 6 |

## Mas dei Chini

FRAZ. MARTIGNANO
VIA BASSANO, 3
38121 TRENTO
TEL. +39 0461821513
www.cantinamasdeichini.it

CELLAR SALES
HECTARES UNDER VINE 5.00

Graziano Chini is an entrepreneur who manages a series of industrial vehicle and imported car dealerships, but he's always cultivated a passion for great wine. And so it was that he decided to take advantage of a generational shift among a Venetian dynasty to purchase a splendid estate on the sunny slopes of Trento, renovating it entirely, reinforcing its cellar and vineyards, and reviving the farm manor, which is now used as a modern agritourism. Supported by a team of agronomists and expert enologists, the entrepreneur/vine grower has immediately brought out the potential of his vineyards and their grapes. Their Pinot Noir-based Trento Rosé Nature could quite possibly be the best rosé we tasted all year. The Riserva dedicated to Charles V has taken a great step forward and the same can be said for their classic Brut Riserva. The concentration of Traminer is perfect, providing a beautiful backdrop for the Lagrein. Their Theodor, a unique Incrocio Manzoni, is also quite intriguing.

| | |
|---|---|
| ○ Trento Inkino Rosè Nature | ♀♀ 6 |
| ○ Inkino Brut Riserva '10 | ♀♀ 5 |
| ○ Trento Inkino Carlo V '08 | ♀♀ 6 |
| ○ Theodor '17 | ♀ 4 |
| ● Trentino Lagrein '16 | ♀ 4 |
| ○ Trentino Traminer '17 | ♀ 4 |

# Maso Cantanghel

VIA CARLO SETTE, 21
38015 LAVIS [TN]
TEL. +39 0461246353
www.masocantanghel.eu

CELLAR SALES
PRE-BOOKED VISITS
ANNUAL PRODUCTION 20,000 bottles
HECTARES UNDER VINE 8.50
VITICULTURE METHOD Certified Organic
SUSTAINABLE WINERY

Federico Simoni, a young vine grower, is carrying forward his family's solid winery with entrepreneurial determination. They're one of the area's historic producers, and oversee an estate of private vineyards scattered throughout the hills of Adige and Avisio, as well as an area situated along the Valsugana promontory. Maso Cantanghel's red rocks are perfect for giving rise to aromatic wines and conferring character to certain selections of Trento. They intend to increase production of their Metodo Classico sparklers (sold under the name Monfort) though without neglecting the work they do with native cultivar such as Nosiola. Federico Simoni earns his first Tre Bicchieri with an outstanding Pinot Noir. Intense in its characteristic, fruity notes and aromas calling up the Dolomites, this garnet-colored beauty shows fine development, proving both harmonious and well-structured. Their intense Chardonnay Trento Riserva also delivers a good performance, offering vibrant purity and noteworthy power on the palate.

| | |
|---|---|
| ● Trentino Pinot Nero V. Cantanghel '15 | ♥♥♥ 5 |
| ○ Trento Brut Ris. Monfort '12 | ♥♥ 6 |
| ○ Blanc de Sers '16 | ♥♥ 4 |
| ○ Trentino Nosiola Corylus '16 | ♥♥ 4 |
| ○ Trentino Sauvignon Maso Cantanghel '17 | ♥♥ 4 |
| ○ Sot Sàs Cuvée '12 | ♀♀ 3 |
| ● Trentino Pinot Nero V. Cantanghel '11 | ♀♀ 5 |

# Maso Martis

LOC. MARTIGNANO
VIA DELL'ALBERA, 52
38121 TRENTO
TEL. +39 0461821057
www.masomartis.it

CELLAR SALES
PRE-BOOKED VISITS
ANNUAL PRODUCTION 65,000 bottles
HECTARES UNDER VINE 12.00
VITICULTURE METHOD Certified Organic

The winds of change are blowing at Maso Martis. Alessandra and Maddalena are now officially an integral part of this small winery, situated atop the city's sunniest hill, joining their parents, Roberta and Antonio Stelzer. They'll help continue to maintain the prestige of a brand that's managed to stand out among Trentodoc's almost 50 producers. Maso Martis focuses primarily on Metodo Classico sparkling wines. To improve production, the Stelzer family have enlarged their cellar, though without losing their wines' historic style and character. Their 2008 Trento Madame Martis sparkling wine stands out in every sense and is very deserving of Tre Bicchieri, offering great harmony with a blend that includes Pinot Meunier. It presents just the right amount of honey and releases captivating aromas and scents, with an invigorating, full, supple palate. Two other admirable Trentos also admirably demostrate the Stelzers' skill – their Brut Riserva and a crunchy Dosaggio Zero. Last but certainly not least comes their delicious chardonnay.

| | |
|---|---|
| ○ Trento Brut Madame Martis Ris. '08 | ♥♥♥ 8 |
| ○ Trento Brut Maso Martis Ris. '13 | ♥♥ 6 |
| ○ Trento Dosaggio Zero '13 | ♥♥ 5 |
| ○ Trentino Chardonnay L'Incanto '15 | ♥♥ 3 |
| ○ Trento Dosaggio Zero Ris. '12 | ♀♀♀ 6 |
| ○ Trento Dosaggio Zero Ris. '11 | ♀♀♀ 5 |
| ○ Trento Brut Ris. '11 | ♀♀ 5 |
| ○ Trento Brut Ris. '08 | ♀♀ 5 |
| ⊙ Trento Brut Rosé '11 | ♀♀ 5 |
| ⊙ Trento Dosaggio Zero Ris. '10 | ♀♀ 5 |
| ⊙ Trento Extra Brut Rosé Bio Ris. '13 | ♀♀ 5 |
| ○ Trento Madame Martis '06 | ♀♀ 6 |
| ○ Trento Madame Martis Ris. '05 | ♀♀ 6 |
| ⊙ Trento Rosé Ris. '11 | ♀♀ 5 |

# Maso Poli

Loc. Masi di Pressano, 33
38015 Lavis [TN]
Tel. +39 0461871519
www.masopoli.it

CELLAR SALES
PRE-BOOKED VISITS
ANNUAL PRODUCTION 75,000 bottles
HECTARES UNDER VINE 13.00

The Togn family's winery is supported by an entirely female cast. Luigi's three daughters (Martina, Romina and Valentina) oversee every stage of production, communication and sales, availing themselves of the help of their father and Goffredo Pasolli, president of Trentino's enology association (as well as Valentina's husband). And they're the ones who cultivate their hill estate, Maso Poli, as well as Gaierhof in Roveré della Luna. Their vast selection of wines is as varied as it is consistent and of excellent quality. Their truly intriguing Traminer falls among the most curious of the range of wines tasted: it has star quality and just as much versatility, offering more flavor than aroma, it provides good balance and promises to age well. Their Marmoran's blend of Teroldego and Lagrein come together in a complex wine with vital and engaging balsamic tones. Finally, the Riesling gives off youthful traits and suggestions of exotic fruit, guaranteeing fullness and aging potential.

| | | |
|---|---|---|
| ○ Trentino Gewürztraminer '17 | ♟♟ | 4 |
| ● Trentino Marmoram '15 | ♟♟ | 5 |
| ○ Trentino Riesling '17 | ♟♟ | 4 |
| ○ Trento Maso Poli | ♟♟ | 5 |
| ○ Trentino Nosiola '16 | ♀♀ | 3 |
| ○ Trentino Nosiola '15 | ♀♀ | 3 |
| ○ Trentino Pinot Grigio '16 | ♀♀ | 3 |
| ● Trentino Pinot Nero '12 | ♀♀ | 3 |
| ● Trentino Pinot Nero Sup. '14 | ♀♀ | 3 |
| ● Trentino Sorni Rosso Marmoram '13 | ♀♀ | 3* |
| ● Trentino Sorni Rosso Marmoram '12 | ♀♀ | 3 |
| ● Trentino Sorni Rosso Marmoram '11 | ♀♀ | 3 |
| ● Trentino Sup. Pinot Nero '13 | ♀♀ | 3 |
| ○ Trentino Traminer '15 | ♀♀ | 3 |
| ○ Trento Brut Ris. '10 | ♀♀ | 5 |

# Mezzacorona

Via del Teroldego, 1e
38016 Mezzocorona [TN]
Tel. +39 0461616399
www.mezzacorona.it

CELLAR SALES
PRE-BOOKED VISITS
ACCOMMODATION
ANNUAL PRODUCTION 48,000,000 bottles
HECTARES UNDER VINE 2800.00

Force, elegance and versatility. The Mezzacorona Group encompasses all these ideas, presenting itself as a forward-thinking winery (just think of the agreement they made with Chinese magnate Jack Ma) but without betraying their origins and roots in the territory. And they do it with wines geared towards approachability, wines that can satisfy a number of different tastes thanks to balance and precision. Indeed, they are among Italy's most representative wine giants, and they aren't afraid of more targeted selections either, as evidenced by their Brioso and successful Trentodocs. A highly-deserved Tre Bicchieri goes once again to their precise and austere Flavio, a sparkling wine whose every nuance engages. Their Nòs, an amazing interpretation of Teroldego, demonstrates the great quality of Trentino still wines. The Pinot Grigio also deserves mention, given that the winery is one of the world's leading producers of it.

| | | |
|---|---|---|
| ○ Trento Brut Rotari Flavio Ris. '10 | ♟♟♟ | 8 |
| ● Teroldego Rotaliano Nos '11 | ♟♟ | 5 |
| ● Teroldego Rotaliano Castel Firmian '14 | ♟♟ | 3 |
| ⊙ Trentino Moscato Rosa Dabèn '16 | ♟♟ | 5 |
| ○ Trento Pas Dosé Rotari AlpeRegis '12 | ♟♟ | 6 |
| ○ Trento Talento Cuvée 28° | ♟♟ | 4 |
| ● Trentino Marzemino Castel Firmian '16 | ♟ | 4 |
| ○ Trentino Pinot Grigio Castel Firmian Ris. '17 | ♟ | 5 |
| ○ Trento Brut Rotari Flavio Ris. '09 | ♀♀♀ | 8 |
| ○ Trento Brut Rotari Flavio Ris. '08 | ♀♀♀ | 5 |
| ○ Trento Brut Rotari Flavio Ris. '07 | ♀♀♀ | 5 |

# Moser

FRAZ. GARDOLO DI MEZZO
VIA CASTEL DI GARDOLO, 5
38121 TRENTO
TEL. +39 0461990786
www.cantinemoser.com

CELLAR SALES
PRE-BOOKED VISITS
ACCOMMODATION
ANNUAL PRODUCTION 120,000 bottles
HECTARES UNDER VINE 17.00

It's off to the races for the Mosers, never ones to rest, even if Francesco is spending more time in the vineyard than on his bike. Accompanied by his children Carlo, Francesca and Ignazio, the 'World Champion' and record-breaker astutely oversees his splendid estate situated across Trento and Val di Cembra. It's a landscape that seems created by mother nature for vine growing, thanks to its perfect position, elevation and the terrain itself, which is volcanic in origin. Their wines are also full of flavor, tasty, cellarable (including their Trentos) and capable of withstanding the test of time, obviously. Their lively and intense Trento Brut Nature offers the nose nuances from Alpine grasses to hints of tobacco turning powerful, fresh and honed on the palate – a truly great wine. Their 51.151, named for the bicycling duration record set by Francesco Moser, has the supple elegance of an endurance cyclist, while their other wines also prove more than compelling, gregarious and persuasive.

| | | |
|---|---|---|
| ○ Trento Brut Nature '12 | ♔♔♔ | 5 |
| ○ Trentino Chardonnay '17 | ♔♔ | 2* |
| ○ Trento Brut 51,151 | ♔♔ | 5 |
| ○ Moscato Giallo '17 | ♔ | 3 |
| ○ Trentino Riesling Renano '17 | ♔ | 3 |
| ○ Moscato Giallo '14 | ♕♕ | 3 |
| ○ Riesling '15 | ♕♕ | 3 |
| ● Teroldego '13 | ♕♕ | 3 |
| ○ Trento Brut Nature '11 | ♕♕ | 5 |
| ⊙ Trento Rosé '12 | ♕♕ | 5 |

# Pojer & Sandri

LOC. MOLINI, 4
38010 FAEDO [TN]
TEL. +39 0461650342
www.pojeresandri.it

CELLAR SALES
PRE-BOOKED VISITS
ACCOMMODATION
ANNUAL PRODUCTION 200,000 bottles
HECTARES UNDER VINE 26.00
VITICULTURE METHOD Certified Organic

Theatrical Mario Pojer matches perfectly with sly Fiorentino Sandri, thus forming a duo that as far back as 1975 began formulating a new fashion among the Dolomites' wine producers. They deserve credit for a number of things: reviving cultivar considered banal (Schiava and Nosiola foremost) and choosing other grapes for still wines, aromatic whites and Metodo Classico sparklers (including varieties resistant to certain parasites). Through research and experimentation, by involving their respective children and encouraging young producers to challenge old practices, they've been writing a new chapter in the area's enological history. Pojer and Sandri proves once again the unquestionable reliability of its wines with a sparker that is completely outside the norms for Trentino. The same thing can be said of their Faye, a white in which the grace of Chardonnay mixes with the power of Pinot Bianco to satisfy all the senses. A true 'feel-good' wine. These are followed by the traditional Faye Rosso, Palai (Müller Thurgau) and a Riesling that should stand up well over time.

| | | |
|---|---|---|
| ○ Cuveé Extra Brut 13/14 | ♔♔ | 6 |
| ○ Faye Bianco '15 | ♔♔ | 5 |
| ● Faye Rosso '13 | ♔♔ | 6 |
| ○ Palai '17 | ♔♔ | 3 |
| ○ Trentino Riesling '17 | ♔♔ | 4 |
| ○ Trentino Traminer Aromatico '17 | ♔♔ | 4 |
| ○ Bianco Faye '08 | ♕♕♕ | 5 |
| ○ Bianco Faye '01 | ♕♕♕ | 5 |
| ● Pinot Nero Rodel Pianezzi '09 | ♕♕♕ | 5 |
| ● Rosso Faye '05 | ♕♕♕ | 5 |
| ● Rosso Faye '00 | ♕♕♕ | 5 |
| ● Rosso Faye '94 | ♕♕♕ | 5 |
| ● Rosso Faye '93 | ♕♕♕ | 5 |
| ○ Müller Thurgau Palai '16 | ♕♕ | 3 |

# Pravis

LOC. LE BIOLCHE, 1
38076 LASINO [TN]
TEL. +39 0461564305
www.pravis.it

CELLAR SALES
PRE-BOOKED VISITS
ANNUAL PRODUCTION 200,000 bottles
HECTARES UNDER VINE 32.00

Zero impact: two words sum up the effort that this winery is making. It starts with the cultivation of 'interspecies' grapes, natural cross-breeds that are capable of resisting the most common diseases and therefore don't require the use of chemicals. An approach centered on protecting the ecosystem and respecting the environment goes perfectly with the gorgeous scenery here, where vineyards are accompanied by medieval castles, rocky routes leading to the Dolomites and blue lakes. The area is ideal for wines made from overly-ripe grapes. Thanks to the Goltraminer variety in particular (harvested in December 2012), the golden Soliva, offers outstanding aromas of ripe fruit and a truly long, delicious palate. Their Syrae, from Shiraz grapes presents a well-structured palate, inviting and very balanced with underlying fruit that remains present in the nose. Their Ora, from Nosiola grapes and Sauvignon Teramara, is also very enjoyable.

| | |
|---|---|
| ○ Soliva '12 | ♛♛ 6 |
| ● Syrae '15 | ♛♛ 5 |
| ○ l'Ora '14 | ♛♛ 5 |
| ○ Kerner '17 | ♛ 4 |
| ○ Sauvignon Teramara '17 | ♛ 4 |
| ● Fratagranda '10 | ♛♛♛ 4* |
| ● Fratagranda '09 | ♛♛♛ 4* |
| ● Fratagranda '07 | ♛♛♛ 4 |
| ○ Stravino di Stravino '99 | ♛♛♛ 4* |
| ○ Vino Santo Arèle '06 | ♛♛♛ 6 |
| ● Fratagranda '13 | ♛♛ 4 |
| ○ l'Ora '13 | ♛♛ 4 |
| ● Madruzzo '15 | ♛♛ 3 |
| ○ Nosiola Le Frate '16 | ♛♛ 2* |
| ○ Stravino di Stravino '13 | ♛♛ 4 |

# Agraria Riva del Garda

LOC. SAN NAZZARO, 4
38066 RIVA DEL GARDA [TN]
TEL. +39 0464552133
www.agririva.it

CELLAR SALES
PRE-BOOKED VISITS
ANNUAL PRODUCTION 250,000 bottles
HECTARES UNDER VINE 280.00

Agririva takes advantage of the breeze that blows across the lake to undertake truly innovative viticulture. And they do it without ever neglecting the respect they have for Garda. The Trentino bank of the lake is a mild, typical waterside area that's perfect for cultivating vines and olives. In fact both are grown here, drawing on a modern, sustainable agricultural approach that includes the use of satellites and geolocation. It all guarantees maximum efficiency in the field and perfect work in the cellar. Their Bordeaux-style Maso Lizzone immediately captivates with its impenetrable ruby color and balsamic-scented nose, as powerful on the palate as it is graceful in its harmony. Loré, from Chardonnay grapes, also delivers on the palate, though nuance laden in every other sense as well. Their La Prea, a Traminer and Pinot Grigio mix, is a veritable olfactory symphony and their organic Trento Brezza, proves a classic sparkling wine.

| | |
|---|---|
| ● Maso Lizzone '16 | ♛♛ 4 |
| ○ Trentino Chardonnay Loré '16 | ♛♛ 3 |
| ○ Trentino Traminer Aromatico La Prea '16 | ♛♛ 3 |
| ○ Trento Brut Brezza Bio | ♛♛ 4 |
| ● Maso Lizzone '15 | ♛♛ 3 |
| ● Maso Lizzone '14 | ♛♛ 3 |
| ● Rosso Gère '13 | ♛♛ 3 |
| ● Teroldego Rivaldego '15 | ♛♛ 2* |
| ● Trentino Lagrein Sasera '15 | ♛♛ 4 |
| ● Trentino Merlot Crèa '11 | ♛♛ 4 |
| ● Trentino Sup. Pinot Nero Elesi '15 | ♛♛ 4 |
| ○ Trentino Sup. Rena V. T. '12 | ♛♛ 5 |
| ○ Trento Brut Brezza Riva | ♛♛ 3 |
| ○ Trento Brut BrezzaRiva | ♛♛ 3 |

# ★★San Leonardo

LOC. SAN LEONARDO, 1
38063 AVIO [TN]
TEL. +39 0464689004
www.sanleonardo.it

CELLAR SALES
PRE-BOOKED VISITS
ANNUAL PRODUCTION 270,000 bottles
HECTARES UNDER VINE 40.00
VITICULTURE METHOD Certified Organic
SUSTAINABLE WINERY

San Leonardo is a model winery in all
respects, defined by its deep roots and
historic reputation, but also by a
management approach that's looking to the
future. And they're starting from the
principle of sustainability, from organic
certification, to Friends of Biodiversity,
water quality, microclimate and agronomic
practices. Being immersed in a lovely,
scenic landscape means that ethics and
aesthetics go hand in hand, and give rise to
a fantastic selection, whatever the cultivar
used. Their 2014 San Leonardo is one of
Geurrieri Gonzaga's most successful
interpretations. Juicy, satisfying, almost
overwhelming, it delivers complete sensory
intensity and an unbridled freshness that
promises to age well. Their equally
engaging Villa Gresti proves softer,
combining power and delicacy. Their Terre
dances with the same versatility that helps
maintain the exclusivity of the wines of this
wonderful winery.

| | |
|---|---|
| ● San Leonardo '14 | ▼▼▼ 8 |
| ● Villa Gresti di San Leonardo '14 | ▼▼ 5 |
| ● Terre di San Leonardo '15 | ▼▼ 3 |
| ● Carmenère '07 | ♀♀♀ 8 |
| ● San Leonardo '13 | ♀♀♀ 8 |
| ● San Leonardo '11 | ♀♀♀ 8 |
| ● San Leonardo '10 | ♀♀♀ 7 |
| ● San Leonardo '08 | ♀♀♀ 7 |
| ● San Leonardo '07 | ♀♀♀ 7 |
| ● San Leonardo '06 | ♀♀♀ 7 |
| ● San Leonardo '05 | ♀♀♀ 7 |
| ● San Leonardo '04 | ♀♀♀ 7 |
| ● San Leonardo '03 | ♀♀♀ 7 |
| ● San Leonardo '01 | ♀♀♀ 7 |
| ● Villa Gresti '03 | ♀♀♀ 6 |

# Toblino

FRAZ. SARCHE
VIA LONGA, 1
38076 MADRUZZO
TEL. +39 0461564168
www.toblino.it

PRE-BOOKED VISITS
RESTAURANT SERVICE
ANNUAL PRODUCTION 400,000 bottles
HECTARES UNDER VINE 700.00
VITICULTURE METHOD Certified Organic
SUSTAINABLE WINERY

Toblino's work centers on the versatility and
revival of a romantic wine: il Vino Santo. It's
a nectar that springs forth from the
favorable climate of the territory and the
care taken by the members of this
cooperative winery, artificers of a renewed
commitment to the wine, and thanks to the
involvement of a large number of Valle dei
Laghi's vine growers. They're the ones who
tend to the vineyards spread throughout
Garda and the Dolomites, with specialized
methods and attentive harvesting. Their
work ranges from the drying of grapes, like
Nosiola (a decidedly local cultivar) to
sparkling winemaking, not to mention the
cultivation of varieties destined for their
forthright, approachable wines, like Schiava
and Mueller Turgau. While not their
speciality, their Pinot Nero performed well,
offering up hints of delicate violets and red
currants. The palate is supple and sure to
age well. Their traditional Nosiola is
vigorous, juicy and ready to drink. Their
Manzoni Bianco, one of the cooperative's
organic offerings, also delivered.

| | |
|---|---|
| ○ Goldtraminer '16 | ▼▼ 3 |
| ○ Trentino Manzoni Bianco Bio '17 | ▼▼ 5 |
| ○ Trentino Nosiola '17 | ▼▼ 2* |
| ● Trentino Pinot Nero '16 | ▼▼ 2* |
| ○ Trentino Vino Santo '03 | ▼▼ 6 |
| ● eLimarò '13 | ♀♀ 3 |
| ○ Trentino Chardonnay Bio '15 | ♀♀ 2* |
| ○ Trentino Nosiola '16 | ♀♀ 2* |
| ● Trentino Pinot Nero '15 | ♀♀ 2* |
| ○ Trentino Traminer Aromatico Bio '15 | ♀♀ 2* |
| ○ Trentino Vino Santo '02 | ♀♀ 6 |
| ○ Trento Brut Antares '12 | ♀♀ 3 |
| ○ Trento Brut Antares '11 | ♀♀ 3 |
| ○ Trento Brut Antares '10 | ♀♀ 3 |

# Vallarom

LOC. VO' SINISTRO
FRAZ. MASI, 21
38063 AVIO [TN]
TEL. +39 0464684297
www.vallarom.it

CELLAR SALES
PRE-BOOKED VISITS
ACCOMMODATION AND RESTAURANT SERVICE
ANNUAL PRODUCTION 35,000 bottles
HECTARES UNDER VINE 7.00
VITICULTURE METHOD Certified Organic
SUSTAINABLE WINERY

They transformed the family estate into a kind of garden devoted to biodiversity. Their rows of vineyards are situated along the left bank of the Adige, marking the clay sediment left centuries ago by the river. It's well-suited terrain that was being cultivated even before the turn of the first millennium. Here a number of plants are grown, buckwheat included, rendering the estate/winery a picturesque area for an agritour. And with the utmost respect for environmental sustainability, here they also make a series of Trento wines, including a captivating Pinot Nero. Their Vadum Caesaris blend of Pinot Bianco, Chardonnay, Sauvignon and Riesling helps explain why Scienza's wines have achieved such prestige. This white bursts with juice and great agility on the palate. Their classic sparkling versions of Vò prove highly satisfying, this vintage even better than usual. Their Trentatrè is simple and intentionally drinkable, and the same goes for both their drier Moscato Giallo and juicy Cabernet Sauvignon.

| | |
|---|---|
| ○ Vadum Caesaris '17 | 🍷🍷 3* |
| ○ Vo' '14 | 🍷🍷 4 |
| ● Cabernet Sauvignon '16 | 🍷 3 |
| ○ Trentatrè '17 | 🍷 3 |
| ○ Vallagarina Moscato Giallo '17 | 🍷 3 |
| ● Cabernet Sauvignon Bio '13 | 🏆 3 |
| ● Fuflus '12 | 🏆 4 |
| ○ Trentatrè '16 | 🏆 3 |
| ○ Trentino Marzemino Bio '15 | 🏆 3 |
| ○ Vadum Caesaris '16 | 🏆 3 |
| ● Vallagarina Pinot Nero '15 | 🏆 4 |
| ○ Vo' '13 | 🏆 4 |
| ○ Vo' | 🏆 4 |

# Villa Corniole

FRAZ. VERLA
VIA AL GREC', 23
38030 GIOVO [TN]
TEL. +39 0461695067
www.villacorniole.com

CELLAR SALES
PRE-BOOKED VISITS
ANNUAL PRODUCTION 60,000 bottles
HECTARES UNDER VINE 4.00
SUSTAINABLE WINERY

Villa Corniole is absolutely a producer operating 'at a high level'. They're so rooted to the Cembra Valley that they keep their winemaking equipment in a picturesque cave carved out of a block of porphyry, the volcanic mineral that characterizes the banks of the Avisio river. Their vineyards are situated along the valley's steep slopes, and the terrain is supported by spectacular stone walls. It's easy to lose yourself amidst the vineyards, the woods, the rural features here and the dolomitic sky. And it's here that the Pellegrini family, constituted of three young daughters, manages a winery that's clearly evolving under the enological guidance of Mattia Clementi. Their Teroldego Rotaliano 7 Pergole stands out for its graceful drinkability and indomitable majesty. Their Kròz, a Chardonnay and Müeller Thurgau blend, also proves successful, as does their Petramontis of the same blend, which gets more and more interesting and complex every year. Their classic sparkling Salisa deserves recognition for its prowess and optimal drinkability.

| | |
|---|---|
| ● Teroldego Rotaliano 7 Pergole '13 | 🍷🍷 6 |
| ○ Kròz '16 | 🍷🍷 5 |
| ○ Trentino Müller Thurgau Petramontis '17 | 🍷🍷 4 |
| ○ Trento Dosaggio Zero Salísa '14 | 🍷🍷 6 |
| ○ Trento Brut Salísa | 🍷 5 |
| ○ Kroz '15 | 🏆 4 |
| ● Teroldego Rotaliano 7 Pergole '11 | 🏆 5 |
| ○ Trentino Müller Thurgau Petramontis '15 | 🏆 3 |
| ○ Trento Brut Salísa '13 | 🏆 5 |
| ○ Trento Brut Salísa '12 | 🏆 5 |
| ○ Trento Dosaggio Zero Salísa '12 | 🏆 5 |

## Cantina Aldeno

via Roma, 76
38060 Aldeno [TN]
Tel. +39 0461842511
www.cantinaaldeno.com

CELLAR SALES
PRE-BOOKED VISITS
ANNUAL PRODUCTION 240,000 bottles
HECTARES UNDER VINE 340.00

| | |
|---|---|
| ○ San Zeno Bianco '15 | 🍷🍷 5 |
| ○ Trento Pas Dosé Altinum '14 | 🍷🍷 5 |
| ○ Trentino Moscato Giallo Enopere '17 | 🍷 4 |

## Bolognani

via Stazione, 19
38015 Lavis [TN]
Tel. +39 0461246354
www.bolognani.com

CELLAR SALES
PRE-BOOKED VISITS
ANNUAL PRODUCTION 60,000 bottles
HECTARES UNDER VINE 4.40

| | |
|---|---|
| ○ Nosiola '17 | 🍷🍷 2* |
| ○ Trentino Traminer Aromatico Sanròc '17 | 🍷🍷 3 |
| ○ Trento Extra Brut PerNilo '13 | 🍷🍷 6 |
| ○ Moscato Giallo '17 | 🍷 2 |

## Cantina Sociale di Trento

via dei Viticoltori, 2/4
38123 Trento
Tel. +39 0461920186
www.cantinasocialetrento.it

CELLAR SALES
PRE-BOOKED VISITS
ANNUAL PRODUCTION 250,000 bottles
HECTARES UNDER VINE 50.00
SUSTAINABLE WINERY

| | |
|---|---|
| ○ Trento Brut Zell | 🍷🍷 5 |
| ○ Santacolomba '17 | 🍷 3 |
| ● Trentino Marzemino Heredia Ziresi '16 | 🍷 3 |
| ○ Trentino Riesling 1339 '13 | 🍷 3 |

## Concilio

Zona Ind. 2
38060 Volano [TN]
Tel. +39 0464411000
www.concilio.it

CELLAR SALES
PRE-BOOKED VISITS
ANNUAL PRODUCTION 200,000 bottles
HECTARES UNDER VINE 600.00
SUSTAINABLE WINERY

| | |
|---|---|
| ○ Trentino Chardonnay Amsela d'Oro '17 | 🍷🍷 3 |
| ○ Trento Dosaggio Zero 600Uno | 🍷🍷 5 |
| ○ Il Miliare '15 | 🍷 4 |

## Etyssa

loc. Moià, 4
38121 Trento
Tel. +39 3938922784
www.etyssaspumanti.it

ANNUAL PRODUCTION 3,500 bottles
HECTARES UNDER VINE 14.00

| | |
|---|---|
| ○ Trento Extra Brut Cuvée N. 2 '14 | 🍷🍷 5 |

## Gaierhof

via IV Novembre, 51
38030 Roverè della Luna [TN]
Tel. +39 0461658514
www.gaierhof.com

CELLAR SALES
PRE-BOOKED VISITS
ANNUAL PRODUCTION 500,000 bottles
HECTARES UNDER VINE 150.00
SUSTAINABLE WINERY

| | |
|---|---|
| ○ Trentino Müller Thurgau dei '700 '17 | 🍷🍷 3 |
| ● Trentino Teroldego Rotoliano '16 | 🍷🍷 2* |
| ○ Trento Siris | 🍷🍷 4 |
| ○ Trentino Nosiola '17 | 🍷 2 |

## Bruno Grigolli

VIA SAN BERNARDINO, 10
38065 MORI [TN]
TEL. +39 0464917368
www.grigollibruno.it

CELLAR SALES
ANNUAL PRODUCTION 13,000 bottles
HECTARES UNDER VINE 5.00

| | |
|---|---|
| ● Trentino Cabernet Sauvignon Germano '09 | ♟♟ 4 |
| ● Trentino Rosso Trilogia '11 | ♟♟ 6 |
| ○ Traminer '16 | ♟ 5 |

## Cantina d' Isera

VIA AL PONTE, 1
38060 ISERA [TN]
TEL. +39 0464433795
www.cantinaisera.it

CELLAR SALES
PRE-BOOKED VISITS
ANNUAL PRODUCTION 500,000 bottles
HECTARES UNDER VINE 246.00
VITICULTURE METHOD Certified Organic

| | |
|---|---|
| ● Trentino Marzemino Corè '15 | ♟♟ 4 |
| ○ Trento Brut Ris. '12 | ♟♟ 5 |
| ● Trentino Marzemino '16 | ♟ 2 |
| ● Trentino Marzemino Etichetta Verde '16 | ♟ 3 |

## Madonna delle Vittorie

VIA LINFANO, 81
38062 ARCO [TN]
TEL. +39 0464505432
www.madonnadellevittorie.it

PRE-BOOKED VISITS
ANNUAL PRODUCTION 170,000 bottles
HECTARES UNDER VINE 38.00

| | |
|---|---|
| ○ Trentino Traminer Capolago '17 | ♟♟ 4 |
| ○ Trento Madonna delle Vittorie Brut '13 | ♟♟ 5 |
| ○ Nosiola '17 | ♟ 4 |

## Martinelli

VIA CASTELLO, 10
38016 MEZZOCORONA [TN]
TEL. +39 3388288686
www.cantinamartinelli.com

ANNUAL PRODUCTION 12,000 bottles
HECTARES UNDER VINE 3.00

| | |
|---|---|
| ● Teroldego Rotaliano Maso Chini '15 | ♟♟ 5 |
| ● Trentino Lagrein '15 | ♟♟ 5 |

## Tenuta Maso Corno

LOC. VALBONA
38061 ALA [TN]
TEL. +39 0464421130
www.tenutamasocorno.it

PRE-BOOKED VISITS
ANNUAL PRODUCTION 10,000 bottles
HECTARES UNDER VINE 5.00

| | |
|---|---|
| ○ Trento Giulio Larcher Clou '13 | ♟♟ 6 |
| ○ Trento Giulio Larcher '14 | ♟♟ 5 |

## Maso Grener

LOC. MASI DI PRESSANO
38015 LAVIS [TN]
TEL. +39 0461871514
www.masogrener.it

CELLAR SALES
PRE-BOOKED VISITS
ANNUAL PRODUCTION 18,000 bottles
HECTARES UNDER VINE 3.00

| | |
|---|---|
| ○ Maso Grener '17 | ♟♟ 4 |
| ○ Nosiola '17 | ♟ 4 |

# Pedrotti Spumanti

VIA ROMA, 2A
38060 NOMI [TN]
TEL. +39 0464835111
www.predottispumanti.it

CELLAR SALES
ANNUAL PRODUCTION 30,000 bottles
HECTARES UNDER VINE 3.00
SUSTAINABLE WINERY

| | | |
|---|---|---|
| ○ Trento Nature Bouquet | ♥♥ | 4 |
| ○ Trento Pas Dosé Ris. 111 '11 | ♥♥ | 6 |
| ○ Trento Brut Bouquet | ♥ | 4 |

# Pisoni

LOC. SARCHE
FRAZ. PERGOLESE DI LASINO
VIA SAN SIRO, 7A
38076 MADRUZZO
TEL. +39 0461564106
www.pisoni.net

CELLAR SALES
PRE-BOOKED VISITS
ANNUAL PRODUCTION 23,500 bottles
HECTARES UNDER VINE 16.00

| | | |
|---|---|---|
| ○ Trentino Vino Santo '03 | ♥♥ | 7 |
| ○ Trento Brut Nature '14 | ♥♥ | 4 |
| ○ Trento Extra Brut Erminia Segalla '09 | ♥♥ | 6 |
| ○ Trentino Nosiola '17 | ♥ | 4 |

# Revì

VIA FLORIDA, 10
38060 ALDENO [TN]
TEL. +39 0461843155
www.revispumanti.com

CELLAR SALES
PRE-BOOKED VISITS
ANNUAL PRODUCTION 20,000 bottles
HECTARES UNDER VINE 1.70
VITICULTURE METHOD Certified Organic

| | | |
|---|---|---|
| ○ Trento Extra Brut Bio Paladino '12 | ♥♥ | 7 |
| ○ Trento Dosaggio Zero '14 | ♥♥ | 5 |

# Cantina Rotaliana

VIA TRENTO, 65B
38017 MEZZOLOMBARDO [TN]
TEL. +39 0461601010
www.cantinarotaliana.it

CELLAR SALES
PRE-BOOKED VISITS
ANNUAL PRODUCTION 1,000,000 bottles
HECTARES UNDER VINE 330.00
SUSTAINABLE WINERY

| | | |
|---|---|---|
| ● Trentino Lagrein Cortuta '15 | ♥♥ | 4 |
| ● Teroldego Rotaliano Clesurae '15 | ♥♥ | 6 |
| ○ Trento Brut Ris. '10 | ♥♥ | 6 |
| ● Teroldego Rotaliano Et. Rossa '17 | ♥ | 3 |

# Armando Simoncelli

VIA NAVICELLO, 7
38068 ROVERETO [TN]
TEL. +39 0464432373
www.simoncelli.it

CELLAR SALES
PRE-BOOKED VISITS
ANNUAL PRODUCTION 90,000 bottles
HECTARES UNDER VINE 10.50

| | | |
|---|---|---|
| ● Trentino Marzemino '17 | ♥♥ | 4 |
| ● Trentino Navesèl '15 | ♥♥ | 5 |
| ○ Trento Simoncelli Brut '14 | ♥♥ | 4 |
| ● Trentino Lagrein '17 | ♥ | 4 |

# Enrico Spagnolli

VIA G. B. ROSINA, 4A
38060 ISERA [TN]
TEL. +39 0464409054
www.vinispagnolli.it

CELLAR SALES
PRE-BOOKED VISITS
ANNUAL PRODUCTION 85,000 bottles
HECTARES UNDER VINE 18.00

| | | |
|---|---|---|
| ● Pinot Nero '13 | ♥♥ | 4 |
| ● Trentino Marzemino '16 | ♥♥ | 4 |
| ○ Trentino Chardonnay '17 | ♥ | 4 |
| ● Vallagarina Lagrein '16 | ♥ | 2 |

## Marco Tonini

LOC. FOLASO
VIA ROSMINI, 8
38060 ISERA [TN]
TEL. +39 3404991043

CELLAR SALES
PRE-BOOKED VISITS
ANNUAL PRODUCTION 8,000 bottles
HECTARES UNDER VINE 4.00

| | | |
|---|---|---|
| ● Trentino Marzemino '16 | ♥♥ 4 |
| ○ Trento Brut Nature Ris. '14 | ♥♥ 5 |

## Vin de la Neu

FRAZ. COREDO
VIA SAN REMEDIO, 8
38012 PREDAIA
TEL. +39 3474116854
www.vindelaneu.it

ANNUAL PRODUCTION 508 bottles
HECTARES UNDER VINE 0.35

| | |
|---|---|
| ○ Vin de la Neu '15 | ♥♥ 8 |

## Vivallis

VIA PER BRANCOLINO, 4
38068 NOGAREDO [TN]
TEL. +39 0464834113
www.vivallis.it

CELLAR SALES
PRE-BOOKED VISITS
ANNUAL PRODUCTION 1,000,000 bottles
HECTARES UNDER VINE 730.00
VITICULTURE METHOD Certified Organic

| | |
|---|---|
| ● Trentino Marzemino dei Ziresi Sup. '16 | ♥♥ 4 |
| ○ Trentino Moscato Giallo Castel Beseno '17 | ♥♥ 4 |
| ● Trentino Pinot Nero '15 | ♥ 4 |
| ○ Trento Brut Valentini di Weinfeld '14 | ♥ 5 |

## Luigi Zanini

VIA DE GASPERI, 42
38017 MEZZOLOMBARDO [TN]
TEL. +39 0461601496
www.zaniniluigi.com

CELLAR SALES
PRE-BOOKED VISITS
ANNUAL PRODUCTION 90,000 bottles
HECTARES UNDER VINE 8.50

| | |
|---|---|
| ● Teroldego Rotaliano '17 | ♥♥ 2* |
| ● Teroldego Rotaliano Le Cervare '16 | ♥♥ 4 |

## Zanotelli

V.LE 4 NOVEMBRE, 52
38034 CEMBRA [TN]
TEL. +39 0461683131
www.zanotelliwines.com

CELLAR SALES
PRE-BOOKED VISITS
ANNUAL PRODUCTION 40,000 bottles
HECTARES UNDER VINE 11.00

| | |
|---|---|
| ○ Trentino Chardonnay Le Strope '17 | ♥♥ 3 |
| ○ Trentino Traminer Le Strope '11 | ♥♥ 4 |
| ○ Trento Brut Forneri Ris. '12 | ♥♥ 5 |
| ○ Trentino Müller Thurgau '17 | ♥ 4 |

## Roberto Zeni

FRAZ. GRUMO
VIA STRETTA, 2
38010 SAN MICHELE ALL'ADIGE [TN]
TEL. +39 0461650456
www.zeni.tn.it

CELLAR SALES
PRE-BOOKED VISITS
ANNUAL PRODUCTION 150,000 bottles
HECTARES UNDER VINE 14.00
VITICULTURE METHOD Certified Organic

| | |
|---|---|
| ○ Nosiola Schwarzhof '17 | ♥♥ 3 |

# ALTO ADIGE

A series of extremely varied seasons put Alto Adige's many vine growers to the test. Despite the fact that a notorious 2014 has virtually disappeared from our tastings, the differences are easily detected in the glass. 2015 saw excellent maturation and wines of great richness, while 2016 gave rise to a more elegant, spirited profile. Finally, 2017 was a controversial year that began with a terrible freeze that affected all of northern Italy, and while it eventually gave way to a hot, dry summer, it concluded with a bit too much hail, especially in the Eisack Valley. But the final results were still excellent. Pinot Bianco, the region's crown prince, lived up to expectations and took home a number of awards, with wines that explore the territory's various personalities, from the aromatic freshness and tension of Nals' Sirmian to the elegance of Merano's Tyrol, to the complexity of Manincor's Eichhorn. Nor should we forget Prackwieser's Praesulis or Niklaserhof's Riserva Klaser or the numerous wines that earned a place in our finals. Pinot Nero also put in a great performance, with wines that are increasingly showing an ability to highlight the attributes of the territory, from the richness and solidity of Mazzon to the finesse and tension that characterize the wines of Appiano Monte. Bolzano continues to serve as a laboratory for churning out wines whose distinctive traits are aromatic fullness of fruit and power, as is the case with Cantina di Bolzano's and Christian Plattner's Lagreins. In the same way the Eisack and Vinschgau valleys are able to continually bring out the finesse of their best whites. The trio of Brenntal, Auratus, Nussbaumer is by a now a kind of playlist for those who love Gewürztraminer, while those who prefer less explosive offerings will enjoy three top-notch whites: Elena Walch's Beyond the Clouds, Terlano's Nova Domus and Colterenzio's Lafòa Chardonnay, a wine that's difficult to forget. We also want to mention a sector that still hasn't blossomed but is showing great promise, sparkling winemaking, as evidenced by Kettmeir's Riserva 1919 '12. Among the other wines awarded we wanted to mention Tiefenbrunner's 2016 Feldmarschall and two Schiavas, Untermoserhof's 2016 Santa Maddalena Classico Hueb and Cantina di Caldaro's delicious 2017 Lago di Caldaro Quintessenz, a wine that also took home our award for Best Value for Money.

# ★Abbazia di Novacella

FRAZ. NOVACELLA
VIA DELL'ABBAZIA, 1
39040 VARNA/VAHRN [BZ]
TEL. +39 0472836189
www.abbazianovacella.it

CELLAR SALES
PRE-BOOKED VISITS
RESTAURANT SERVICE
ANNUAL PRODUCTION 650,000 bottles
HECTARES UNDER VINE 20.00

This winery belonging to the Novacella
Abbey is one of the most important in
Eisack Valley and indeed the entire Alto
Adige region. Their vineyards in the Bolzano
and Cornaiano hills host red grape varieties
while their plots in the Bressanone enclave
are mainly dedicated to whites. They enjoy
a decidedly 'Alpine' climate with elevations
skimming 900 meters above sea level.
These conditions demand strict vineyard
management, along with making use of the
best exposures. Their most interesting
wines, a Riesling and a Grüner Veltliner
from their Paepositus line, are both made
with grapes cultivated in the Eisack Valley
and are both vintage 2016. The former
sees sophisticated aromas of flowers and
white fruit, an acidic tension that fuses
perfectly with savoriness, and elegant
length. The second expresses a riper, more
caressing character, impressing for its
harmony and fullness in the mouth and its
juicy, lingering palate.

| | | |
|---|---|---|
| ○ A. A. Valle Isarco Grüner Veltliner Praepositus '17 | 🍷🍷 3* |
| ○ A. A. Valle Isarco Riesling Praepositus '16 | 🍷🍷 4 |
| ● A. A. Lagrein Praepositus Ris. '14 | 🍷🍷 5 |
| ● A. A. Moscato Rosa Praepositus '16 | 🍷🍷 5 |
| ○ A. A. Valle Isarco Gewürztraminer '17 | 🍷🍷 3 |
| ○ A. A. Valle Isarco Grüner Veltliner '17 | 🍷🍷 3 |
| ○ A. A. Valle Isarco Kerner '17 | 🍷🍷 3 |
| ○ A. A. Valle Isarco Kerner Praepositus '17 | 🍷🍷 4 |
| ○ A. A. Valle Isarco Müller Thurgau '17 | 🍷🍷 3 |
| ○ A. A. Valle Isarco Sylvaner '17 | 🍷🍷 3 |
| ○ A. A. Valle Isarco Sylvaner Praepositus '17 | 🍷🍷 4 |
| ○ A. A. Valle Isarco Riesling Praepositus '13 | 🍷🍷🍷 4* |
| ○ A. A. Valle Isarco Sylvaner Praepositus '15 | 🍷🍷🍷 4* |

# Tenuta Baron Di Pauli

VIA CANTINE, 12
39052 CALDARO/KALTERN [BZ]
TEL. +39 0471963696
www.barondipauli.com

CELLAR SALES
PRE-BOOKED VISITS
ANNUAL PRODUCTION 46,000 bottles
HECTARES UNDER VINE 15.00

Baron di Pauli's consistently solid range of
wines is made with grapes grown in two
distinct vineyard plots, situated in some of
the most interesting areas of Bolzano
province. Mainly Bordeaux varieties and
Schiava are grown in Arzenhof in Caldaro,
whereas white cultivars are grown in
Termeno (Höfl unterm Stein estate), with
Gewürztraminer taking the lion's share.
There has been a conscious decision to
cultivate grape varieties which thrive in
distinctly different weather conditions,
making for a range of wines that are
strong on expressivity. Their best wines are
made with grapes cultivate in the area
more well-suited to reds, starting with their
fragrant 2017 Lago di Caldaro Classico
Superiore Kalkofen, a wine aged for seven
months in barrels before offering up its
sensations of small red fruit and spices,
which follow through onto a fine, savory
palate. The other in-house champion is
their 2015 Arzio Riserva, a Bordeaux
blend that proves generous in fruit, as
well as harmonic and pleasant in its
smooth tannins.

| | | |
|---|---|---|
| ● A. A. Lago di Caldaro Cl. Sup. Kalkofen '17 | 🍷🍷 3* |
| ● A. A. Merlot Cabernet Arzio Ris. '15 | 🍷🍷 6 |
| ○ A. A. Gewürztraminer Elix '17 | 🍷🍷 6 |
| ○ A. A. Sauvignon Kinesis '17 | 🍷🍷 4 |
| ○ Dynamis '17 | 🍷🍷 4 |
| ○ Enosi '17 | 🍷🍷 3 |
| ● A. A. Lagrein Carano Ris. '15 | 🍷 5 |
| ○ A. A. Gewürztraminer Elix '16 | 🍷🍷 4 |
| ○ A. A. Gewürztraminer Exilissi '13 | 🍷🍷 6 |
| ● A. A. Lago di Caldaro Cl. Sup. Kalkofen '16 | 🍷🍷 3* |
| ● A. A. Merlot Cabernet Arzio Ris. '13 | 🍷🍷 6 |
| ○ A. A. Sauvignon Kinesis '16 | 🍷🍷 4 |
| ○ Enosi '16 | 🍷🍷 3 |

# Bessererhof - Otmar Mair

LOC. NOVALE DI PRESULE, 10
39050 FIÈ ALLO SCILIAR/VÖLS AM SCHLERN [BZ]
TEL. +39 0471601011
www.bessererhof.it

CELLAR SALES
PRE-BOOKED VISITS
ANNUAL PRODUCTION 40,000 bottles
HECTARES UNDER VINE 4.50

Although Eisack Valley has a lot of talent, vine growing has never been as widespread in this territory as in other parts of the province. But producers in the area are now taking on a larger role, managing vineyards that are situated on impervious high ground and dominated by extreme temperature swings. The Mair family winery is based here and covers just a few hectares, as is common in these parts. They produce a wide range of wines with a distinctive close-focused tension of aromas and flavor. One such example is their 2015 Chardonnay Riserva, which is aged at length in their cellar before being put to market. The nose comes through closed, needing some time before offering up its fragrances. Ripe fruit dominates, though it leaves some space for flowers and mineral notes. The palate is crisp and well supported by a fresh, acidic vein. Their 2017 Pinot Bianco, which opens with faint, young aromas, proves even edgier.

| | | |
|---|---|---|
| ○ A. A. Chardonnay Ris. '15 | ♥♥ | 3 |
| ○ A. A. Pinot Bianco '17 | ♥♥ | 3 |
| ○ A. A. Valle Isarco Kerner '17 | ♥♥ | 4 |
| ○ A. A. Sauvignon '17 | ♥ | 4 |
| ○ A. A. Chardonnay Ris. '13 | ♀♀ | 3 |
| ○ A. A. Chardonnay Ris. '11 | ♀♀ | 3 |
| ○ A. A. Chardonnay Ris. '14 | ♀♀ | 3 |
| ○ A. A. Gewürztraminer '15 | ♀♀ | 4 |
| ○ A. A. Pinot Bianco '16 | ♀♀ | 3* |
| ○ A. A. Sauvignon '16 | ♀♀ | 4 |
| ○ A. A. Valle Isarco Kerner '16 | ♀♀ | 4 |
| ○ A. A. Valle Isarco Kerner '15 | ♀♀ | 4 |
| ○ A. A. Valle Isarco Kerner '14 | ♀♀ | 4 |

# ★★Cantina Bolzano

P.ZZA GRIES, 2
39100 BOLZANO/BOZEN
TEL. +39 0471270909
www.cantinabolzano.com

CELLAR SALES
PRE-BOOKED VISITS
ANNUAL PRODUCTION 3,000,000 bottles
HECTARES UNDER VINE 350.00
SUSTAINABLE WINERY

After working many vintages in the center of Gries, this year Cantina Bolzano will be using their new premises in Via San Maurizio, a modern structure set perfectly among the vineyards. It is just one of the several sites used by the grower-members, ranging from the Anreiter and Taber plateaus to the Santa Maddalena hill, along the slopes of Kleinstein, Mock and Mumelter and overlooking the regional capital. Stephan Filippi and his staff skillfully transform grapes grown in the various vineyards into a faultless range of wines with trademark drinkability. And the dedication that the cooperative shows to its emblematic wines hasn't changed. Their 2015 Taber Riserva is at the top of its game. It's a Lagrein with a deep, spicy aromatic profile that sees ripe fruit following through onto a close-knit palate that's well-supported by acidity. Their 2017 Santa Maddalena Huck am Bach is a supple, savory wine that's charming on the palate. Their 2016 Sauvignon Riserva also put in a good performance.

| | | |
|---|---|---|
| ● A. A. Lagrein Taber Ris. '16 | ♥♥♥ | 6 |
| ● A. A. Santa Maddalena Cl. Huck am Bach '17 | ♥♥ | 2* |
| ○ A. A. Sauvignon Ris. '16 | ♥♥ | 4 |
| ● A. A. Cabernet Mumelter Ris. '16 | ♥♥ | 6 |
| ○ A. A. Chardonnay Ris. '16 | ♥♥ | 5 |
| ○ A. A. Gewürztraminer Kleinstein '17 | ♥♥ | 5 |
| ● A. A. Lagrein Prestige Line Ris. '16 | ♥♥ | 4 |
| ● A. A. Merlot Siebeneich '16 | ♥♥ | 5 |
| ○ A. A. Moscato Giallo Passito Vinalia '16 | ♥♥ | 3 |
| ○ A. A. Pinot Bianco Dellago '17 | ♥♥ | 4 |
| ● A. A. Pinot Nero Ris. '16 | ♥♥ | 5 |
| ○ A. A. Sauvignon Mock '17 | ♥♥ | 4 |
| ● A. A. Lagrein Taber Ris. '15 | ♀♀♀ | 6 |
| ● A. A. Lagrein Taber Ris. '14 | ♀♀♀ | 6 |
| ● A. A. Lagrein Taber Ris. '13 | ♀♀♀ | 6 |

## Josef Brigl

LOC. SAN MICHELE APPIANO
VIA MADONNA DEL RIPOSO, 3
39057 APPIANO/EPPAN [BZ]
TEL. +39 0471662419
www.brigl.com

**CELLAR SALES**
**PRE-BOOKED VISITS**
**ACCOMMODATION**
**ANNUAL PRODUCTION** 1,000,000 bottles
**HECTARES UNDER VINE** 50.00
**SUSTAINABLE WINERY**

Alto Adige's vine growing structure is based on the productive synergy of cooperatives, small vine growers and historic dynasties. The Brigl family belongs to this last group. They have been working for centuries in the Appiano district and are famous well beyond regional boundaries. Their complete range of wines is made with classic local grape varieties interpreted to perfection. Their vineyards are concentrated in the best vine growing areas, such as Kaltenburg, Windegg, Haselhof and Reilerhof. Additionally, other plots are cultivated with the invaluable collaboration of numerous local growers. The hot 2017 vintage brought out the best of their Gewürztraminer Windegg's generous aromatic profile. It's a white with strong fragrances of candied citrus and rose, spices and licorice. In the mouth it impresses for its full palate and great depth, which are sustained by a rich savoriness. Their 2017 Schiava Haselhof delivers just what we'd expect from a wine of its kind. It's an approachable, fragrant wine that's charming to drink, to say the least.

| | | |
|---|---|---|
| ○ A. A. Gewürztraminer V. Windegg '17 | 🏆🏆 | 3* |
| ● A. A. Lago di Caldaro Cl. Sup. V. Kaltenburg '17 | 🏆🏆 | 2* |
| ● A. A. Lagrein Anno 1309 Ris. '15 | 🏆🏆 | 3 |
| ● A. A. Lagrein Ris. '15 | 🏆🏆 | 5 |
| ○ A. A. Pinot Bianco V. Haselhof '17 | 🏆🏆 | 3 |
| ○ A. A. Pinot Grigio V. Windegg '17 | 🏆🏆 | 3 |
| ● A. A. Pinot Nero Ris. '15 | 🏆🏆 | 2* |
| ● A. A. Santa Maddalena V. Rielerhof '17 | 🏆🏆 | 3 |
| ● A. A. Schiava V. Haselhof '17 | 🏆🏆 | 2* |
| ○ A. A. Sauvignon '17 | 🏆 | 3 |
| ○ A. A. Pinot Grigio Windegg '11 | 🏆🏆🏆 | 3* |
| ○ A. A. Gewürztraminer V. Windegg '16 | 🏆🏆 | 3 |
| ● A. A. Lagrein Kaltenburg Ris. '14 | 🏆🏆 | 5 |

## Brunnenhof - Kurt Rottensteiner

LOC. MAZZON
VIA DEGLI ALPINI, 5
39044 EGNA/NEUMARKT [BZ]
TEL. +39 0471820687
www.brunnenhof-mazzon.it

**CELLAR SALES**
**PRE-BOOKED VISITS**
**ANNUAL PRODUCTION** 35,000 bottles
**HECTARES UNDER VINE** 5.50
**VITICULTURE METHOD** Certified Organic

Kurt Rottensteiner runs his family's winery in the Mazzon district. It comprises a handful of hectares cultivated with just a few varieties which have found their ideal habitat on the eastern slope of the Adige valley. They focus on Pinot Nero, which benefits from limited morning sunlight, compensated by warmth lasting until sunset in the best vineyard plots. Lagrein, on the other hand, is grown on the valley floor. This very old vineyard expresses qualities of unusual freshness and savoriness. Only a Pinot Nero could turn out to be the most impressive wine during this round of tastings. Indeed, their 2015 Zis Riserva offers up vibrant aromas of wild berries and aromatic herbs enriched by smoky nuances. These give way to a minerality that today is just emerging. It's a wine that brings together force and elegance. Their 2015 Pinot Nero Mazzon Riserva opts for richness and exuberance, which is expressed across a generous palate. Their 2016 Lagrein Vecchie Vigne is also excellent.

| | | |
|---|---|---|
| ● A. A. Lagrein V. V. '16 | 🏆🏆 | 3 |
| ● A. A. Pinot Nero Mazzon Ris. '15 | 🏆🏆 | 5 |
| ● A. A. Pinot Nero Mazzon V. Zis Ris. '15 | 🏆🏆 | 5 |
| ○ Eva '17 | 🏆🏆 | 4 |
| ○ A. A. Moscato Giallo V. T. Tilda '17 | 🏆 | 5 |
| ○ A. A. Gewürztraminer '14 | 🏆🏆 | 4 |
| ● A. A. Lagrein V. V. '15 | 🏆🏆 | 3 |
| ● A. A. Lagrein V. V. '12 | 🏆🏆 | 5 |
| ● A. A. Pinot Nero Ris. '14 | 🏆🏆 | 5 |
| ● A. A. Pinot Nero Ris. '13 | 🏆🏆 | 5 |
| ● A. A. Pinot Nero Ris. '12 | 🏆🏆 | 5 |
| ● A. A. Pinot Nero Ris. '11 | 🏆🏆 | 5 |
| ● A.A. Lagrein '13 | 🏆🏆 | 5 |
| ○ Eva '16 | 🏆🏆 | 4 |
| ○ Eva '15 | 🏆🏆 | 4 |
| ○ Eva '14 | 🏆🏆 | 4 |

## ★★Cantina di Caldaro

VIA CANTINE, 12
39052 CALDARO/KALTERN [BZ]
TEL. +39 0471963149
www.kellereikaltern.com

CELLAR SALES
PRE-BOOKED VISITS
ANNUAL PRODUCTION 3,400,000 bottles
HECTARES UNDER VINE 480.00

It's not easy trace out the history of this large cooperative in Caldaro. It came into being after many mergers between the various cooperatives that were formed in the town going back to the early 1900s. Today, it is the largest winery in the province of Bolzano, based on the strength of its top-level vineyards cultivated by over 800 members, and which give rise to Überetsch's classic grape varieties. Red wines made with Lagrein and Schiava head a range which includes dozens of wines and various themed selections. This year their Quintessenz line stood out. These wines are made with grapes cultivated on plots with southern exposure, at elevations ranging from 200 to 500 meters. Their 2017 Lago di Caldaro Classico Superiore features vibrant, fruity aromas, which follow through perfectly on a sound, fragrant palate. It brings home Tre Bicchieri and our prize for the Best Value for the Money. The 2016 vintage gave rise to an exotic and sulfurous Sauvignon, a wine supported by notable savoriness. Their Pinot Bianco of the same year, a wine that opts for finesse, is still quite young.

| | |
|---|---|
| ● A. A. Lago di Caldaro Cl. Sup. Quintessenz '17 | ♟♟♟ 3* |
| ○ A. A. Pinot Bianco Quintessenz '16 | ♟♟ 5 |
| ○ A. A. Sauvignon Quintessenz '16 | ♟♟ 5 |
| ● A. A. Cabernet Sauvignon Campaner Ris. '15 | ♟♟ 4 |
| ● A. A. Cabernet Sauvignon Quintessenz Ris. '15 | ♟♟ 5 |
| ○ A. A. Chardonnay Saleit '17 | ♟♟ 2* |
| ○ A. A. Gewürztraminer Campaner '17 | ♟♟ 3 |
| ● A. A. Lago di Caldaro Cl. Sup. Leuchtenberg '17 | ♟♟ 2* |
| ○ A. A. Pinot Bianco Vial '17 | ♟♟ 3 |
| ● A. A. Pinot Nero Saltner '16 | ♟♟ 4 |
| ○ A. A. Sauvignon Stern '17 | ♟♟ 3 |
| ○ A. A. Pinot Grigio Söll '17 | ♟ 3 |
| ● A. A. Lago di Caldaro Cl. Sup. Pfarrhof '16 | ♟♟♟ 3* |

## Castel Sallegg

V.LO DI SOTTO, 15
39052 CALDARO/KALTERN [BZ]
TEL. +39 0471963132
www.castelsallegg.it

CELLAR SALES
PRE-BOOKED VISITS
ANNUAL PRODUCTION 170,000 bottles
HECTARES UNDER VINE 30.00

Castel Sallegg is owned by the Kuenburg Counts and occupies an advantageous position on the western side of Caldaro, on the slope rising towards Mendola. Inside their historic cellars, they work grapes grown in the winery's numerous vineyards, which stretch from the hilly area surrounding the lake, right up to Appiano. The grape varieties give rise to wines with a distinct style due to their clean aromas and respect for cultivars. The wines are crisp and full-flavored and manage an effortless finish. Their 2015 Pinot Bianco Pratum is made with grapes cultivated on their oldest vineyard, Prehof, at more than 500 meters above sea level. It's a wine redolent of ripe, yellow fruit and flowers, with oak just peeping out in the background. In the mouth it proves full, juicy and long. Their 2017 Bischofsleiten is an entirely different wine. It expresses all the fragrance and elegance that the Schiava cultivated around Caldaro low can bestow.

| | |
|---|---|
| ● A. A. Lago di Caldaro Cl. Sup. Bischofsleiten '17 | ♟♟ 3* |
| ○ A. A. Terlano Pinot Bianco Pratum '15 | ♟♟ 5 |
| ● A. A. Cabernet Sauvignon Ris. '15 | ♟♟ 5 |
| ○ A. A. Gewürztraminer '17 | ♟♟ 3 |
| ● A. A. Lagrein Ris. '15 | ♟♟ 5 |
| ● A. A. Merlot Ris. '15 | ♟♟ 4 |
| ● A. A. Moscato Rosa V. T. '15 | ♟♟ 7 |
| ○ A. A. Pinot Bianco '17 | ♟♟ 3 |
| ○ A. A. Pinot Grigio '17 | ♟♟ 3 |
| ● A. A. Pinot Nero '16 | ♟♟ 3 |
| ○ A. A. Sauvignon '17 | ♟ 3 |
| ● A. A. Lago di Caldaro Scelto Sup. Bischofsleiten '15 | ♟♟♟ 2* |

# Castelfeder

VIA PORTICI, 11
39040 EGNA/NEUMARKT [BZ]
TEL. +39 0471820420
www.castelfeder.it

CELLAR SALES
PRE-BOOKED VISITS
ANNUAL PRODUCTION 400,000 bottles
HECTARES UNDER VINE 20.00

Ivan and Ines Giovannett run the family winery together with their father Günther. It was founded by Alfons almost half a century ago and is now one of the most important wineries in the South Tyrolean Unterland. The cellar is situated on the Egna plain. However, their vineyards and those cultivated by local grape growers stretch across the whole Cortaccia valley and up to the high Glen hills, where Pinot Nero grapes are grown. Classic regional grapes give rise to a multi-faceted and close-focused range of wines aspiring to elegance and tension. The hot 2015 vintage brought out their Burgum Novum Riserva's close-focused richness of ripe fruit. It's a Chardonnay that expresses superior firmness of taste. Their 2015 Pinot Nero is more multifaceted and complex on the nose, with acidity and tannins that preside over a juicy and lengthy palate. Finally, we point out their well-crafted 2017 Schiava Alte Reben, a fragrant wine endowed with a supple, racy palate.

| | |
|---|---|
| ○ A. A. Chardonnay Burgum Novum Ris. '15 | ♀♀ 4 |
| ● A. A. Pinot Nero Burgum Novum Ris. '15 | ♀♀ 5 |
| ○ A. A. Gewürztraminer '17 | ♀♀ 3 |
| ● A. A. Lagrein Burgum Novum Ris. '15 | ♀♀ 4 |
| ○ A. A. Pinot Bianco Tecum '16 | ♀♀ 3 |
| ○ A. A. Pinot Bianco Vom Stein '17 | ♀♀ 2* |
| ○ A. A. Pinot Grigio 15 '17 | ♀♀ 2* |
| ○ A. A. Sauvignon Burgum Novum Ris. '15 | ♀♀ 2* |
| ● A. A. Schiava Alte Reben '17 | ♀♀ 2* |
| ○ Sauvignon Raif '17 | ♀♀ 3 |
| ○ A. A. Chardonnay Doss '17 | ♀ 2 |
| ● A. A. Pinot Nero Glener '16 | ♀ 3 |
| ○ A. A. Gewürztraminer Vom Lehm '15 | ♀♀♀ 3* |
| ○ A. A. Pinot Bianco Tecum '10 | ♀♀♀ 3* |

# ★★Cantina Colterenzio

LOC. CORNAIANO/GIRLAN
S.DA DEL VINO, 8
39057 APPIANO/EPPAN [BZ]
TEL. +39 0471664246
www.colterenzio.it

CELLAR SALES
PRE-BOOKED VISITS
ANNUAL PRODUCTION 1,600,000 bottles
HECTARES UNDER VINE 300.00
SUSTAINABLE WINERY

Cornaiano is an undulating territory where vineyards appear to stretch as far as the eye can see. It's here that Cantina Colterenzio and their main vineyards are situated. They are cultivated by about 300 grower-members -- small family-run wineries often owning less than a single hectare each. Then it becomes the task of winemaker Martin Leymar to draw out the best of each individual batch of grapes. He interprets the different varieties to produce finesse and distinctiveness in both their reds and whites. It's difficult to choose the best wine from their Lafòa line, with some three wines making it into our finals. Their 2016 Chardonnay offers up multi-layered aromas, with fruit gradually giving way to mineral and flowery notes across a rich, lengthy palate. Their 2016 Sauvignon is more exotic and supple, while their 2015 Cabernet Sauvignon proves firm and potent, endowed with great length.

| | |
|---|---|
| ○ A. A. Chardonnay Lafóa '16 | ♀♀♀ 5 |
| ● A. A. Cabernet Sauvignon Lafóa '15 | ♀♀ 7 |
| ○ A. A. Sauvignon Lafóa '16 | ♀♀ 5 |
| ○ A. A. Chardonnay Altkirch '17 | ♀♀ 2* |
| ○ A. A. Gewürztraminer Lafóa '16 | ♀♀ 5 |
| ○ A. A. Gewürztraminer Perelise '17 | ♀♀ 3 |
| ● A. A. Merlot Siebeneich Ris. '15 | ♀♀ 4 |
| ○ A. A. Pinot Bianco Cora '17 | ♀♀ 3 |
| ○ A. A. Sauvignon Prail '17 | ♀♀ 3 |
| ● A. A. Cabernet Sauvignon Lafóa '10 | ♀♀♀ 7 |
| ● A. A. Cabernet Sauvignon Lafóa '12 | ♀♀♀ 7 |
| ● A. A. Cabernet Sauvignon Lafóa '11 | ♀♀♀ 7 |
| ● A. A. Cabernet Sauvignon Lafóa '09 | ♀♀♀ 7 |
| ○ A. A. Chardonnay Lafóa '15 | ♀♀♀ 5 |
| ○ A. A. Sauvignon Lafóa '14 | ♀♀♀ 5 |

# Hartmann Donà

VIA RAFFEIN, 8
39010 CERMES/TSCHERMS [BZ]
TEL. +39 3292610628
hartmann.dona@rolmail.net

**ANNUAL PRODUCTION** 35,000 bottles
**HECTARES UNDER VINE** 4.65

Hartmann Donà has assumed different roles in the wine world, both as an employee and consultant at a large winery, then as a producer of rare sensibility himself. His vineyards comprise a handful of hectares in different areas, allocating each variety to its best habitat. Work in the cellar focuses on the type of wine: simplicity and aromas are enhanced in vintage wines, while elegance and territorial expression are highlighted in their more ambitious ones. We didn't get to taste their best Riservas, which are still aging, but it was a chance to appreciate the depth of Donà's most recent creation. It's their 2010 Dona D'Or, a monovarietal Chardonnay that offers up complex, multi-layered aromas in which fruit is initially hidden by mineral, spicy notes, but gradually opens up on a palate of great firmness and tension. Savoriness plays an important role here, and the wine closes with notable elegance.

# Tenuta Donà

FRAZ. RIVA DI SOTTO
39057 APPIANO/EPPAN [BZ]
TEL. +39 0473221866
www.weingut-dona.com

**CELLAR SALES**
**PRE-BOOKED VISITS**
**ACCOMMODATION**
**ANNUAL PRODUCTION** 30,000 bottles
**HECTARES UNDER VINE** 6.00

Despite relatively recent inclusion in Italian Wines, Tenuta Donà is now a benchmark for South Tyrolean winemaking. Credit for success is due to Hansjörg, who runs the winery with his wife Martina and sons Josef and Martin. He grows the varieties most well-suited to the area between Bolzano and Merano, passing through Riva di Sotto (a district of Appiano), where the house and winery are situated. They grow Pinot Bianco, Chardonnay, Gewürztraminer, Sauvignon, Lagrein and Pinot Nero, which are enhanced with minimally invasive and precise winemaking. Among the few wines presented, a 2016 blend of Merlot and Lagrein stands out. On the nose it displays vibrant aromas of plums and spices, with a palate that impresses for its glyceric fullness. The wine offers up all the sunniness of the territory along a double track of tension and savoriness. Their 2017 Sauvignon also impressed. It's a white that doesn't pursue aromatic fireworks for their sake, focusing instead on the firmness and harmony of the palate.

| | |
|---|---|
| ○ A. A. Chardonnay Donà D'Or '10 | 🍷🍷 5 |
| ○ A. A. Chardonnay '17 | 🍷🍷 3 |
| ○ A. A. Gewürztraminer '17 | 🍷🍷 3 |
| ○ A. A. Pinot Bianco '17 | 🍷🍷 3 |
| ○ Blanc de Rouge Extra Brut M. Cl. | 🍷🍷 3 |
| ● A. A. Pinot Nero '16 | 🍷 3 |
| ○ A. A. Sauvignon '17 | 🍷 3 |
| ○ A. A. Chardonnay '16 | 🍷🍷 3 |
| ○ A. A. Gewürztraminer '16 | 🍷🍷 3 |
| ● A. A. Lagrein '15 | 🍷🍷 3 |
| ○ A. A. Sauvignon '16 | 🍷🍷 3 |
| ○ Donà Blanc '12 | 🍷🍷 3* |
| ● Donà Noir '12 | 🍷🍷 3 |
| ● Donà Rouge '11 | 🍷🍷 3 |

| | |
|---|---|
| ○ A. A. Sauvignon '17 | 🍷🍷 5 |
| ● A. A. Schiava '17 | 🍷🍷 3 |
| ● Merlot - Lagrein '16 | 🍷🍷 4 |
| ○ A. A. Terlano Chardonnay '17 | 🍷 4 |
| ● A. A. Lagrein '15 | 🍷🍷 5 |
| ● A. A. Lagrein '14 | 🍷🍷 4 |
| ○ A. A. Sauvignon '16 | 🍷🍷 5 |
| ○ A. A. Sauvignon '15 | 🍷🍷 3 |
| ● A. A. Schiava '16 | 🍷🍷 3 |
| ● A. A. Schiava '14 | 🍷🍷 2* |
| ○ A. A. Terlano Chardonnay '16 | 🍷🍷 4 |
| ○ A. A. Terlano Chardonnay '15 | 🍷🍷 3 |
| ○ A. A. Terlano Chardonnay '14 | 🍷🍷 3 |

## Tenuta Ebner
## Florian Unterthiner

FRAZ. CAMPODAZZO, 18
39054 RENON/RITTEN [BZ]
TEL. +39 0471353386
www.weingutebner.it

CELLAR SALES
PRE-BOOKED VISITS
RESTAURANT SERVICE
ANNUAL PRODUCTION 20,000 bottles
HECTARES UNDER VINE 4.50

The Eisack river's long passage starts in Brennero and suddenly widens at the Bolzano plain. Here it abandons the Alpine landscape to embrace a gentler one around the regional capital. The last part of its route is dominated in the west by the Renon plateau, covered with vineyards alternating with woods and pastures. And it's here, in the eastern district of Campodazzo, at elevations ranging from 300 to over 2000 meters, that the Unterthiner family work their handful of hectares. Their 2017 Pinot Bianco is one of the best of the DOC appellation. In the glass it's redolent of apple and wild flowers, and offers up a faint mineral nuance. The palate is pure, yet rich and taut, giving way little by little, and impressing for sophistication and length. Their 2017 Gewürztraminer is also interesting, opting instead for a more naturally pervasive aromatic profile, and an energetic, crisp palate.

## Erbhof Unterganzner
## Josephus Mayr

FRAZ. CARDANO
VIA CAMPIGLIO, 15
39053 BOLZANO/BOZEN
TEL. +39 0471365582
www.mayr-unterganzner.it

CELLAR SALES
PRE-BOOKED VISITS
ANNUAL PRODUCTION 65,000 bottles
HECTARES UNDER VINE 9.00

Josephus Mayr and his wife Barbara have reinvented the role of South Tyrolean vine grower by facing the complex challenges of modern agriculture. They run the Erbhof Unterganzner farm's vineyards with meticulous care, following a farming tradition that has always been important in this region. However, their production of traditional crops such as walnuts and figs, as well as completely new crops for this territory such as olives, is equally commendable. The producer's heart, however, lies in winemaking, with a range of wines that perfectly express the spirit of the territory. Their 2015 Lagrein Riserva is in its usual top form. It's a rich, yet supple wine that points up the attributes of this Bolzano cultivar with sophistication and depth. Their 2015 Lamarein is even thicker and more potent, while their 2015 Composition Reif exhibits freshness on the nose and tension on the palate.

| | |
|---|---|
| ○ A. A. Pinot Bianco '17 | 🍷🍷 3* |
| ● A. A. Pinot Nero '16 | 🍷🍷 3 |
| ○ A. A. Sauvignon '17 | 🍷🍷 3 |
| ● A. A. Schiava '17 | 🍷🍷 2* |
| ○ A. A. Valle Isarco Gewürztraminer '17 | 🍷🍷 4 |
| ○ A. A. Valle Isarco Grüner Veltliner '17 | 🍷🍷 3 |
| ○ A. A. Pinot Bianco '16 | 🍷🍷 3 |
| ○ A. A. Pinot Bianco '15 | 🍷🍷 3 |
| ● A. A. Pinot Nero '16 | 🍷🍷 3 |
| ○ A. A. Sauvignon '16 | 🍷🍷 3 |
| ○ A. A. Sauvignon '15 | 🍷🍷 3* |
| ○ A. A. Valle Isarco Gewürztraminer '16 | 🍷🍷 4 |
| ○ A. A. Valle Isarco Gewürztraminer '15 | 🍷🍷 4 |
| ○ A. A. Valle Isarco Grüner Veltliner '15 | 🍷🍷 3* |

| | |
|---|---|
| ● A. A. Lagrein Ris. '15 | 🍷🍷 5 |
| ● Composition Reif '15 | 🍷🍷 6 |
| ● Lamarein '15 | 🍷🍷 6 |
| ● A. A. Cabernet Ris. '15 | 🍷🍷 5 |
| ○ A. A. Chardonnay Platt & Pignat '17 | 🍷🍷 3 |
| ● A. A. Santa Maddalena Cl. '17 | 🍷🍷 3 |
| ● A. A. Santa Maddalena Cl. Heilman '16 | 🍷🍷 3 |
| ○ Marie Josephine Passito '16 | 🍷🍷 6 |
| ○ Sauvignon Platt & Pignat '17 | 🍷🍷 3 |
| ● A. A. Lagrein Ris. '13 | 🍷🍷🍷 5 |
| ● A. A. Lagrein Ris. '11 | 🍷🍷🍷 5 |
| ● A. A. Lagrein Scuro Ris. '05 | 🍷🍷🍷 4 |
| ● A. A. Lagrein Scuro Ris. '01 | 🍷🍷🍷 4 |
| ● Lamarein '05 | 🍷🍷🍷 6 |

# ★Falkenstein Franz Pratzner

VIA CASTELLO, 19
39025 NATURNO/NATURNS [BZ]
TEL. +39 0473666054
www.falkenstein.bz

**CELLAR SALES**
**PRE-BOOKED VISITS**
**ANNUAL PRODUCTION** 90,000 bottles
**HECTARES UNDER VINE** 12.00

This marvelous territory enjoys a distinctive climate, consisting of low rainfall and extreme day-night temperature swings. It forms the bedrock of a small but unique winemaking jewel in Alto Adige. This is Vinschgau Valley, an area that Franz Pratzner interprets with skill. About thirty years ago, he and his wife Bernadette abandoned fruit farming to concentrate exclusively on vineyards. He produces a range of wines with a coherent style: whites are made with Riesling, Pinot Bianco and Sauvignon, and reds are made with Pinot Nero. Once again their Riesling is at the top of their selection with a 2016 that expresses its Middle-European character through aromas of benzine, chamomile and flint, offering up its various nuances little-by-little. The warmth of the Vinschgau Valley, however, is more evident on the palate, which proves generous, potent and lengthy. We appreciated the rest of their selection for its commendable balance of concentration and richness of flavor.

| | | |
|---|---|---|
| ○ A. A. Val Venosta Riesling '16 | ♈♈ | 5 |
| ○ A. A. Val Venosta Pinot Bianco '16 | ♈♈ | 4 |
| ● A. A. Val Venosta Pinot Nero '15 | ♈♈ | 5 |
| ○ A. A. Val Venosta Sauvignon '16 | ♈♈ | 4 |
| ○ A. A. Val Venosta Riesling '15 | ♈♈♈ | 5 |
| ○ A. A. Val Venosta Riesling '14 | ♈♈♈ | 5 |
| ○ A. A. Val Venosta Riesling '13 | ♈♈♈ | 5 |
| ○ A. A. Val Venosta Riesling '12 | ♈♈♈ | 5 |
| ○ A. A. Val Venosta Riesling '11 | ♈♈♈ | 5 |
| ○ A. A. Val Venosta Riesling '10 | ♈♈♈ | 5 |
| ○ A. A. Val Venosta Riesling '09 | ♈♈♈ | 5 |
| ○ A. A. Val Venosta Riesling '08 | ♈♈♈ | 5 |

# Garlider
# Christian Kerschbaumer

VIA UNTRUM, 20
39040 VELTURNO/FELDTHURNS [BZ]
TEL. +39 0472847296
www.garlider.it

**CELLAR SALES**
**PRE-BOOKED VISITS**
**ANNUAL PRODUCTION** 26,000 bottles
**HECTARES UNDER VINE** 4.20
**VITICULTURE METHOD** Certified Organic

Unlike South Tyrolean areas with higher production due to a wide range of varieties, Eisack Valley's vine growing is based on a limited number of grape varieties. The selection here expresses the area well, but is marginal with respect to other districts. Christian Kerschbaumer and his wife are among the top producers when it comes to getting the best from Sylvaner, Grüner Veltliner and Riesling grapes at their small estate in Velturno. The organic vineyards are situated on the right bank of the Eisack river between 500 and 800 meters above sea level. Once again their Sylvaner puts in a great performance thanks to a surprising vintage 2016. There are no fireworks on the nose, its aromas unfold little-by-little with yellow fruit giving way to sulphur and dried flowers. The potent, rigorous palate emerges immediately, proving savory and taut, yet highly enjoyable. Their 2016 Grüner Veltliner is just as complex, multi-layered and well-integrated.

| | | |
|---|---|---|
| ○ Grüner Veltliner '16 | ♈♈ | 4 |
| ○ Sylvaner '16 | ♈♈ | 3* |
| ○ Müller Thurgau '16 | ♈♈ | 3 |
| ○ Pinot Grigio '16 | ♈♈ | 3 |
| ● A. A. Pinot Nero '15 | ♈ | 4 |
| ○ A. A. Valle Isarco Sylvaner '15 | ♈♈♈ | 3* |
| ○ A. A. Valle Isarco Sylvaner '14 | ♈♈♈ | 3* |
| ○ A. A. Valle Isarco Sylvaner '13 | ♈♈♈ | 3* |
| ○ A. A. Valle Isarco Sylvaner '09 | ♈♈♈ | 3* |
| ○ A. A. Valle Isarco Veltliner '08 | ♈♈♈ | 3* |
| ○ A. A. Valle Isarco Veltliner '07 | ♈♈♈ | 3 |
| ○ A. A. Valle Isarco Veltliner '05 | ♈♈♈ | 3* |

# ★Cantina Girlan

LOC. CORNAIANO
VIA SAN MARTINO, 24
39057 APPIANO/EPPAN [BZ]
TEL. +39 0471662403
www.girlan.it

CELLAR SALES
PRE-BOOKED VISITS
ANNUAL PRODUCTION 1,500,000 bottles
HECTARES UNDER VINE 220.00

During the last decade Cantina Cornaiano has quietly carried out an overhaul of its production. The focus now is on cultivating their vineyards and selecting the best grapes from the large number of members in the area. More importantly, however, is bringing out the finest expression of historic Überetsch varieties, with a modern sensibility. The result is a dynamic winery on the threshold of its first century of history. It owes its key role in South Tyrolean winemaking to the hard work of Gerhald Kofler. From the great Italian cru of Mazzon we get a sumptuous 2015 Pinot Nero Trattman Riserva, drawing on the rich vintage to offer up clear notes of red fruit, aromatic herbs and spices. It's a wine that will give up its best to those who can wait. Their 2016 Bianco Flora Riserva, a blend of Chardonnay, Pinot Bianco and Sauvignon, also delivered, bringing together richness and elegance. Their 2016 Schiava Gschleier proved racy and juicy.

| | |
|---|---|
| ● A. A. Pinot Nero Trattman Mazon Ris. '15 | 🍷🍷🍷 5 |
| ○ A. A. Bianco Flora Ris. '16 | 🍷🍷 4 |
| ● A. A. Moscato Rosa V. T. Pasithea Rosa '16 | 🍷🍷 5 |
| ● A. A. Schiava Gschleier Alte Reben '16 | 🍷🍷 3* |
| ○ A. A. Bianco Flora Ris. '16 | 🍷🍷 4 |
| ○ A. A. Chardonnay Flora '16 | 🍷🍷 5 |
| ○ A. A. Gewürztraminer Flora '17 | 🍷🍷 6 |
| ○ A. A. Gewürztraminer V. T. Pasithea Oro '16 | 🍷🍷 6 |
| ● A. A. Lagrein Sandbichler H. Lun Ris. '15 | 🍷🍷 5 |
| ○ A. A. Pinot Bianco Plattenriegl '17 | 🍷🍷 3 |
| ○ A. A. Pinot Bianco Sanbichler H. Lun. '17 | 🍷🍷 3 |
| ● A. A. Pinot Nero Patricia '16 | 🍷🍷 3 |
| ● A. A. Pinot Nero Sanbichler H. Lun Ris. '15 | 🍷🍷 3 |
| ○ A. A. Sauvignon Flora '16 | 🍷🍷 4 |

# Glögglhof - Franz Gojer

FRAZ. SANTA MADDALENA
VIA RIVELLONE, 1
39100 BOLZANO/BOZEN
TEL. +39 0471978775
www.gojer.it

CELLAR SALES
PRE-BOOKED VISITS
ACCOMMODATION
ANNUAL PRODUCTION 55,000 bottles
HECTARES UNDER VINE 7.40

Franz Gojer's small winery is located in the heart of Santa Maddalena. The house-cum-winery is surrounded by vineyards at the foot of the hill of the same name. Historic vines are rigorously trained in the traditional pergola system and they supply Schiava grapes used to make wines which fully express their varietal character. Younger vineyard plots in Cornedo all'Isarco are mainly cultivated with Kerner, Pinot Bianco and Sauvignon grapes for producing white wines. The outskirts of Bolzano gave rise to the most interesting wines, with their 2017 Santa Maddalena Rondell once again leading the way. It's a wine that's anything but approachable, opening with a rapid succession of red fruit, sweet spices and aromatic herbs. A savory palate is sustained by juiciness and extraordinary pleasantness. Their dense 2015 Lagrein Riserva features aromas of bramble and pepper, as well as an intriguing smoky note that emerges on its full, harmonic palate.

| | |
|---|---|
| ● A. A. Lagrein Ris. '15 | 🍷🍷 4 |
| ● A. A. Santa Maddalena Cl. Rondell '17 | 🍷🍷 3* |
| ○ A. A. Kerner Karneid '17 | 🍷🍷 3 |
| ● A. A. Santa Maddalena Cl. '17 | 🍷🍷 2* |
| ● A. A. Sauvignon Karneid '17 | 🍷🍷 2* |
| ● A. A. Schiava Alte Reben '17 | 🍷🍷 2* |
| ○ A.A. Pinot Bianco Karneid '17 | 🍷 4 |
| ● A. A. Santa Maddalena Cl. Rondell '16 | 🍷🍷🍷 3* |
| ● A. A. Santa Maddalena Cl. Rondell '15 | 🍷🍷🍷 3* |
| ○ A. A. Kerner Karneid '16 | 🍷🍷 3 |
| ● A. A. Lagrein '14 | 🍷🍷 3* |
| ● A. A. Santa Maddalena Cl. '16 | 🍷🍷 2* |
| ● A. A. Schiava Alte Reben '16 | 🍷🍷 2* |
| ○ A.A. Pinot Bianco Karneid '16 | 🍷🍷 3 |

# Griesbauerhof
# Georg Mumelter

VIA RENCIO, 66
39100 BOLZANO/BOZEN
TEL. +39 0471973090
www.griesbauerhof.it

**CELLAR SALES**
**PRE-BOOKED VISITS**
**ANNUAL PRODUCTION** 30,000 bottles
**HECTARES UNDER VINE** 3.80

Situated in the Santa Maddalena district, the Griesbauerhof farm has belonged to the Mumelter family for over two centuries. The origins of this winery are deep-rooted in the area and they have increased their vineyards over time with purchases in other parts of the province of Bolzano. The core of their production is faithfully linked to Schiava and Lagrein, which make up the very history of this territory. The winery's style enhances the surprisingly hot and sunny climate, with reds exhibiting a generous and caressing character, with great aging potential. The excellent 2015 vintage gave rise to two reserve wines, a Lagrein and Cabernet Sauvignon, that both pursue the same aromatic profile featuring fragrances of ripe red fruit, spices and forest undergrowth. In the mouth the wines part ways, with the former opting for force and vigor, sustained by a close-knit tannic weave, and the latter proving more elegant and harmonious. Their 2015 Merlot Spitz, a wine that's ripe in its aromas and supple on the palate, also delivered.

| | |
|---|---|
| ● A. A. Cabernet Sauvignon Ris. '15 | 🍷🍷 3 |
| ● A. A. Lagrein Ris. '15 | 🍷🍷 5 |
| ● A. A. Merlot Spitz '16 | 🍷🍷 3 |
| ○ A. A. Pinot Grigio '17 | 🍷🍷 3 |
| ● A. A. Schiava Isarcus '16 | 🍷🍷 3 |
| ● A. A. Lagrein '17 | 🍷 3 |
| ● A. A. Santa Maddalena Cl. '17 | 🍷 2 |
| ● A. A. Lagrein Ris. '09 | 🍷🍷🍷 5 |
| ● A. A. Lagrein Scuro Ris. '99 | 🍷🍷🍷 5 |
| ● A. A. Cabernet Sauvignon Ris. '14 | 🍷🍷 3 |
| ● A. A. Lagrein '16 | 🍷🍷 3 |
| ● A. A. Lagrein Ris. '14 | 🍷🍷 5 |
| ○ A. A. Pinot Grigio '16 | 🍷🍷 3 |
| ● Schiava Isarcus '15 | 🍷🍷 3 |

# Gummerhof - Malojer

VIA WEGGESTEIN, 36
39100 BOLZANO/BOZEN
TEL. +39 0471972885
www.malojer.it

**CELLAR SALES**
**PRE-BOOKED VISITS**
**ANNUAL PRODUCTION** 100,000 bottles
**HECTARES UNDER VINE** 18.00

The Malojer family winery is located at the entrance of the impassable Val Sarentino, just to the north of Bolzano city center. There it bears witness to the city's flourishing trade and local industry. The Gummerhof estate is their vine-growing headquarters, where they have been producing classic local wines for over 500 years. Lagrein and Santa Maddalena, which are made according to local tradition, aim for an effective combination of power and tension. Almost all the area's major cultivar are represented in the selection put forward by the Malojer family, but it's their Lagrein Riserva to lead the way. A vintage 2015, rather than opting exclusively for aromatic richness and strength of taste, it discretely expresses its aromas of fruit and bouquet garni, moving lightly between spices and smoky notes. On the palate it proves solid, but it maintains a nice acidic tension that confers suppleness and length.

| | |
|---|---|
| ● A. A. Lagrein Ris. '15 | 🍷🍷 4 |
| ○ A. A. Bianco Cuvée Bautzanum '17 | 🍷🍷 4 |
| ● A. A. Cabernet Lagrein Bautzanum Cuvée Ris. '15 | 🍷🍷 4 |
| ● A. A. Cabernet Ris. '15 | 🍷🍷 4 |
| ● A. A. Lagrein Gummerhof zu Gries '16 | 🍷🍷 4 |
| ○ A. A. Pinot Bianco Kreiter '17 | 🍷🍷 3 |
| ○ A. A. Pinot Grigio Gur zu Sand '17 | 🍷🍷 3 |
| ● A. A. Pinot Nero Ris. '15 | 🍷🍷 4 |
| ● A. A. Santa Maddalena Cl. Loamer '17 | 🍷🍷 2* |
| ○ A. A. Sauvignon Gur zur Sand '17 | 🍷🍷 3 |
| ○ A. A. Valle Isarco Sylvaner Kreiter '17 | 🍷🍷 2* |
| ○ A. A. Gewürztraminer Kui '17 | 🍷 3 |
| ● A. A. Lagrein Gries '09 | 🍷🍷🍷 2* |
| ● A. A. Lagrein Ris. '14 | 🍷🍷 4 |

# Gumphof
## Markus Prackwieser

LOC. STRADA DI FIÈ, 11
FRAZ. NOVALE DI PRESULE
39050 FIÈ ALLO SCILIAR/VÖLS AM SCHLERN [BZ]
TEL. +39 0471601190
www.gumphof.it

**CELLAR SALES**
**PRE-BOOKED VISITS**
**ANNUAL PRODUCTION** 45,000 bottles
**HECTARES UNDER VINE** 5.00

Markus Prackwieser runs his family winery based in Novale di Presule, at the entrance of Eisack Valley where the river winds westwards before merging with the Adige. The steep vineyard plots are located at around 500 meters above sea level, where calcareous soils alternate with the area's Bolzano porphyry. A splendid southwestern exposure, combined with constant breezes and a remarkable temperature range, favor complete ripening of white and red grapes, packing them with aromatic richness and freshness. Some three Gumphof wines were chosen for our finals. Their 2015 Pinot Bianco Renaissance Riserva proves delicate and slight on the nose, with fruity notes fusing with oak and spices. It's a profile that follows through on the wine's elegant, lingering palate. Their 2017 Pinot Bianco Praesulis is more approachable, opting for vibrant aromas of white fruit and a supple palate. Their Sauvignon Praesulis proves fresh and juicy, offering superior tension on the palate.

# ★Franz Haas

VIA VILLA, 6
39040 MONTAGNA/MONTAN [BZ]
TEL. +39 0471812280
www.franz-haas.it

**CELLAR SALES**
**PRE-BOOKED VISITS**
**ANNUAL PRODUCTION** 350,000 bottles
**HECTARES UNDER VINE** 55.00
**SUSTAINABLE WINERY**

Franziskus Haas -- or Franz to his friends -- is the dynamic producer heading his family winery in Montagna. The vineyards (either owned, rented or ones supplying him with grapes) are all situated on the left bank of the Adige, between 240 and 1150 meters above sea level. These varying soil and climate features allow each variety to grow in its most optimal conditions, and enrich the wines with the character of each plot. Their selection of wines ranges from classic monovarietals to ones with a more original South Tyrolean stylistic inflection. All the wines presented put in excellent performances, with their Sauvignon, Moscato Rosa and Pinot Nero Schweizer proving to be our favorites. The first, a vintage 2016, alternates green, vegetable notes with tropical fruit only to explode onto an elegant, lengthy palate. Their 2016 Moscato Rosa opts for greater roundness on the palate while their 2014 Schweizer expresses superior aromatic freshness and a supple, taut palate.

| | |
|---|---|
| ○ A. A. Pinot Bianco Praesulis '17 | ♛♛♛ 4* |
| ○ A. A. Pinot Bianco Renaissance Ris. '15 | ♛♛ 6 |
| ○ A. A. Sauvignon Praesulis '17 | ♛♛ 5 |
| ○ A. A. Gewürztraminer Praesulis '17 | ♛♛ 5 |
| ○ A. A. Pinot Bianco Mediaevum '17 | ♛♛ 4 |
| ● A. A. Pinot Nero Praesulis '16 | ♛♛ 5 |
| ● A. A. Schiava Mediaevum '17 | ♛♛ 4 |
| ○ A. A. Pinot Bianco Praesulis '15 | ♛♛♛ 3* |
| ○ A. A. Pinot Bianco Praesulis '14 | ♛♛♛ 3* |
| ○ A. A. Pinot Bianco Praesulis '06 | ♛♛♛ 3* |
| ○ A. A. Sauvignon Praesulis '13 | ♛♛♛ 4* |
| ○ A. A. Sauvignon Praesulis '09 | ♛♛♛ 3 |
| ○ A. A. Sauvignon Praesulis '07 | ♛♛♛ 3* |
| ○ A. A. Sauvignon Praesulis '04 | ♛♛♛ 3* |
| ○ A. A. Sauvignon Renaissance '14 | ♛♛♛ 4* |

| | |
|---|---|
| ● A. A. Moscato Rosa '16 | ♛♛ 5 |
| ● A. A. Pinot Nero Schweizer '14 | ♛♛ 6 |
| ○ A. A. Sauvignon '16 | ♛♛ 5 |
| ○ A. A. Gewürztraminer '17 | ♛♛ 4 |
| ○ A. A. Pinot Bianco Lepus '17 | ♛♛ 3 |
| ● A. A. Pinot Nero '16 | ♛♛ 5 |
| ○ Manna '16 | ♛♛ 5 |
| ○ Moscato Giallo '17 | ♛♛ 5 |
| ● A. A. Moscato Rosa '12 | ♛♛♛ 5 |
| ● A. A. Moscato Rosa '11 | ♛♛♛ 5 |
| ● A. A. Pinot Nero Schweizer '13 | ♛♛♛ 5 |
| ○ A. A. Sauvignon '13 | ♛♛♛ 5 |
| ○ Manna '07 | ♛♛♛ 4 |
| ○ Manna '05 | ♛♛♛ 4 |
| ○ Manna '04 | ♛♛♛ 4 |

# Haderburg

FRAZ. BUCHOLZ
LOC. POCHI, 30
39040 SALORNO/SALURN [BZ]
TEL. +39 0471889097
www.haderburg.it

**CELLAR SALES**
**PRE-BOOKED VISITS**
**ANNUAL PRODUCTION** 100,000 bottles
**HECTARES UNDER VINE** 12.00
**VITICULTURE METHOD** Certified Biodynamic

Arriving in Alto Adige from the south,
Salorno is the first village you'll encounter.
It is a flat territory stretching alongside the
river which leads to Pochi, a kind of plateau
situated between 400 and 500 meters
above sea level. Alois Ochsenreiter's wines,
produced under the Haderburg brand
name, are strongly influenced by the local
soil and climate. This is especially true of
his famous sparkling wines. He also makes
more local, traditional wines at the
recently-purchased Obermairlhof estate,
drawing on the same style: vigorous, dry
and racy. Their 2008 Hausmannhof
Riserva, a sparkling wine, exhibits great
expressive depth. Aromas of yellow fruit
and croissant emerge little-by-little, while
the palate proves rich yet well-controlled by
an acidic, savory push. It's a complex wine
that deserves to be tried. Their Pas Dosé
and Brut opt for greater freshness, both
aromatically and in the mouth, clearly
expressing the vibrance and fragrance of
their typologies.

| | |
|---|---|
| ○ A. A. Spumante Hausmannhof Brut Ris. '08 | ♟♟ 5 |
| ○ A. A. Gewürztraminer Hausmannhof '17 | ♟♟ 4 |
| ● A. A. Merlot Cabernet Erah '14 | ♟♟ 5 |
| ○ A. A. Pinot Grigio Salurn Pfatten '17 | ♟♟ 5 |
| ● A. A. Pinot Nero Hausmannhof '16 | ♟♟ 5 |
| ○ A. A. Spumante Brut | ♟♟ 5 |
| ○ A. A. Spumante Pas Dosé | ♟♟ 4 |
| ○ A. A. Chardonnay Hausmannhof '17 | ♟ 3 |
| ○ A. A. Sauvignon Hausmannhof '17 | ♟ 4 |
| ○ A. A. Spumante Hausmannhof Ris. '97 | ♟♟♟ 6 |
| ○ A. A. Valle Isarco Sylvaner Obermairlhof '05 | ♟♟♟ 3* |
| ○ A. A. Spumante Pas Dosé '13 | ♟♟ 4 |
| ○ A. A. Spumante Hausmannhof Brut Ris. '07 | ♟♟ 5 |

# Kettmeir

VIA DELLE CANTINE, 4
39052 CALDARO/KALTERN [BZ]
TEL. +39 0471963135
www.kettmeir.com

**CELLAR SALES**
**PRE-BOOKED VISITS**
**ANNUAL PRODUCTION** 330,000 bottles
**HECTARES UNDER VINE** 41.00

This historic Caldaro winery, one of
Bolzano's most consistent producers
(especially for sparkling wines), is
approaching its 100-year anniversary.
About sixty vine growers supply Josef
Romen with grapes, which he turns into a
range of wines with a clear-cut and distinct
character. He has shown great insight in
his choice of plots for his premium
offerings.  They are inextricably linked to
the nature of such great winemaking areas
as Pochi di Salorno or Soprabolzano di
Renon. With each passing year, we're
more impressed with Kettmeir's selection,
starting with their 2012 Extra Brut 1919
Riserva, which proves intensely fragrant on
the nose with aromas of white fruit and
dried flowers. It's a wine that deliver for
tension and depth. Their truly surprising
2016 Chardonnay Maso Reiner has never
been so good. White fruit, citrus and
smoky notes give way to a palate marked
by savory density. Their 2016 Pinot Bianco
Athesis is in its usual top form thanks to
the wine's sophistication and length.

| | |
|---|---|
| ○ A. A. Spumante Extra Brut 1919 Ris. '12 | ♟♟♟ 6 |
| ○ A. A. Chardonnay V. Maso Reiner '16 | ♟♟ 4 |
| ○ A. A. Pinot Bianco Athesis '16 | ♟♟ 4 |
| ○ A. A. Chardonnay '17 | ♟♟ 3 |
| ○ A. A. Müller Thurgau Athesis '16 | ♟♟ 4 |
| ○ A. A. Pinot Bianco '17 | ♟♟ 3 |
| ● A. A. Pinot Nero V. Maso Reiner '15 | ♟♟ 4 |
| ○ A. A. Sauvignon '17 | ♟♟ 3 |
| ○ A. A. Spumante Brut Athesis '15 | ♟♟ 4 |
| ⊙ A. A. Spumante Brut Athesis Rosé '15 | ♟♟ 5 |
| ○ A. A. Gewürztraminer '17 | ♟ 3 |
| ○ A. A. Müller Thurgau '17 | ♟ 3 |
| ○ A. A. Spumante Brut 1919 M. Cl. Ris. '11 | ♟♟♟ 6 |
| ○ A. A. Chardonnay Maso Reiner '15 | ♟♟ 4 |

## Tenuta Klosterhof
## Oskar Andergassen

LOC. CLAVENZ, 40
39052 CALDARO/KALTERN [BZ]
TEL. +39 0471961046
www.garni-klosterhof.com

**CELLAR SALES**
**PRE-BOOKED VISITS**
**ACCOMMODATION AND RESTAURANT SERVICE**
**ANNUAL PRODUCTION** 38,000 bottles
**HECTARES UNDER VINE** 5.00

Like many producers in this area, the
Andergassen family have divided their work
between managing the farm and hotel
accommodation. But don't be deceived by
this duality. Their relatively small vineyard
area, extending over Trifall, Panigl and
Plantaditsch, produces select quantities of
very high-quality wine. Varying exposures
and climates favor perfect ripening of Pinot
Bianco, Schiava and Pinot Nero grapes, but
produce a limited quantity of Merlot and
Moscato Giallo as well. Their 2015 Pinot
Bianco put in a fantastic performance.
Closed fragrances need oxygen to open,
and then comes the smoky aromas, ripe,
white fruit and spices. In the mouth it
impresses for its austerity. It's an energetic
wine with great prospects. Their 2015 Pinot
Nero also delivers, proving complex in its
aromas of forest undergrowth and wild
fruit, which carry over well into a full,
potent palate.

| | |
|---|---|
| ○ A. A. Pinot Bianco Ris. '15 | ♥♥ 3* |
| ● A. A. Pinot Nero Schwarze Madonna '15 | ♥♥ 5 |
| ● A. A. Lago di Caldaro Cl. Sup. Plantaditsch '17 | ♥♥ 2* |
| ● A. A. Merlot Ris. '15 | ♥♥ 4 |
| ○ A. A. Moscato Giallo Birnbaum '17 | ♥♥ 3 |
| ○ A. A. Pinot Bianco Acapella '17 | ♥♥ 3 |
| ● A. A. Lago di Caldaro Cl. Sup. Plantaditsch '16 | ♀♀ 2* |
| ○ A. A. Pinot Bianco Acapella '16 | ♀♀ 3 |
| ○ A. A. Pinot Bianco Trifall '15 | ♀♀ 3 |
| ● A. A. Pinot Nero Panigl '14 | ♀♀ 5 |
| ● A. A. Pinot Nero Panigl '13 | ♀♀ 5 |
| ● A. A. Pinot Nero Ris. '14 | ♀♀ 4 |
| ● A. A. Pinot Nero Ris. '13 | ♀♀ 4 |

## ★Köfererhof
## Günther Kerschbaumer

FRAZ. NOVACELLA
VIA PUSTERIA, 3
39040 VARNA/VAHRN [BZ]
TEL. +39 3474778009
www.koefererhof.it

**CELLAR SALES**
**PRE-BOOKED VISITS**
**RESTAURANT SERVICE**
**ANNUAL PRODUCTION** 80,000 bottles
**HECTARES UNDER VINE** 10.00

Few areas have managed to express such
a strong and distinctive identity as Eisack
Valley, a long gorge stretching
northeastwards from Bolzano all the way to
Brennero. One of the key players in this
mountain viticulture is the Kerschbaumer
family, which faithfully interprets the
territory, focusing on the cultivation of
historic varieties such as Sylvaner, Veltliner
and Kerner. These grapes are superb at
capturing the freshness and considerable
temperature swings linked to these high
elevations. It's difficult to choose the best of
a selection of wines marked by their
typicity. Their 2016 Sylvaner Riserva offers
up vibrant, smoky notes and aromas of
dried flowers. Ripe, white fruit dictates the
rhythm of its decisive palate, which
lengthens with tension and personality.
Their juicy and satisfying 2016 Veltliner
also delivers, while their 2016 Riesling
reveals sophisticated aromas and a more
linear palate.

| | |
|---|---|
| ○ A. A. Valle Isarco Riesling '16 | ♥♥♥ 5 |
| ○ A. A. Valle Isarco Sylvaner Ris. '16 | ♥♥ 5 |
| ○ A. A. Valle Isarco Veltliner '16 | ♥♥ 4 |
| ○ A. A. Valle Isarco Gewürztraminer '17 | ♥♥ 4 |
| ○ A. A. Valle Isarco Kerner '17 | ♥♥ 3 |
| ○ A. A. Valle Isarco Müller Thurgau '17 | ♥♥ 3 |
| ○ A. A. Valle Isarco Pinot Grigio '17 | ♥♥ 3 |
| ○ A. A. Valle Isarco Sylvaner '17 | ♥♥ 3 |
| ○ A. A. Valle Isarco Pinot Grigio '15 | ♀♀♀ 3* |
| ○ A. A. Valle Isarco Pinot Grigio '13 | ♀♀♀ 3* |
| ○ A. A. Valle Isarco Pinot Grigio '12 | ♀♀♀ 3* |
| ○ A. A. Valle Isarco Pinot Grigio '11 | ♀♀♀ 3* |
| ○ A. A. Valle Isarco Riesling '10 | ♀♀♀ 4 |
| ○ A. A. Valle Isarco Sylvaner '16 | ♀♀♀ 3* |
| ○ A. A. Valle Isarco Sylvaner R '13 | ♀♀♀ 5 |

# Tenuta Kornell

FRAZ. SETTEQUERCE
VIA COSMA E DAMIANO, 6
39018 TERLANO/TERLAN [BZ]
TEL. +39 0471917507
www.kornell.it

**CELLAR SALES**
**PRE-BOOKED VISITS**
**ANNUAL PRODUCTION** 120,000 bottles
**HECTARES UNDER VINE** 15.00

As you leave the center of Bolzano, going westwards, you come across a quaint little village called Settequerce, near Terlano. The area is intensely cultivated, with vines and apple trees contending for the best plots. Flat land rises rapidly just before the mountain, and cool breezes sweep through this stretch of Valdadige enabling local grapes to reach perfect ripeness. The Brigl family headquarters are based here, where Florian produces remarkable wines with a solid and dynamic style. With each passing year, we're more impressed by Brigl's wines, with at least three of them leading the pack. Their 2013 Merlot Kressfeld Riserva features vibrant aromas of red fruit and an energetic palate. The wine's balsamic streak is even more pronounced in their 2015 Lagrein Staves Riserva, a supple, close-knit wine. Then there's their 2016 Sauvignon Olberberg, with its hints of white fruit and citrus on the nose and a palate that features commendable tension as well as a pleasantly crisp finish.

# ★Kuenhof - Peter Pliger

LOC. LA MARA, 110
39042 BRESSANONE/BRIXEN [BZ]
TEL. +39 0472850546
pliger.kuenhof@rolmail.net

**CELLAR SALES**
**PRE-BOOKED VISITS**
**ANNUAL PRODUCTION** 38,000 bottles
**HECTARES UNDER VINE** 6.00
**SUSTAINABLE WINERY**

Peter Pliger has aided in the success of Eisack Valley, a territory where South Tyrolean traits are pushed to the extreme. Mountain viticulture, constant breezes, and wide temperature swings result in wines with sharp acidity and a lustrous character. As often occurs in an area fragmented into small plots, this winery cultivates just a few hectares. Dedicated to white grapes exhibiting unmistakable expressiveness, Riesling, Veltliner and Sylvaner lead the way. Despite the difficult 2017 vintage, their Kaiton is in usual form, debuting with fresh aromas of white fruit and subtle, savory length on the palate. Their Sylvaner is more approachable. Mountain country aromas of fruit and flowers follow through onto a flavorful, engaging palate that features a commendable fusion of force and balance. Their citrusy and vigorous Veltliner is also well ahead of the pack.

| | |
|---|---|
| ● A. A. Lagrein Staves Ris. '15 | ♟♟ 5 |
| ● A. A. Merlot Kressfeld Ris. '13 | ♟♟ 5 |
| ● A. A. Merlot Staves Ris. '15 | ♟♟ 5 |
| ○ A. A. Sauvignon Oberberg '16 | ♟♟ 6 |
| ○ A. A. Bianco Aichberg '16 | ♟♟ 4 |
| ● A. A. Cabernet Sauvignon Staves Ris. '15 | ♟♟ 5 |
| ○ A. A. Gewürztraminer Damian '17 | ♟♟ 4 |
| ○ A. A. Pinot Grigio Gris '17 | ♟♟ 4 |
| ○ A. A. Sauvignon Cosmas '17 | ♟♟ 3 |
| ● A. A. Lagrein Greif '17 | ♟ 3 |
| ○ A. A. Pinot Bianco Eich '17 | ♟ 4 |
| ● A. A. Pinot Nero Marith '17 | ♟ 6 |
| ● A. A. Lagrein Staves Ris. '14 | ♛♛♛ 5 |
| ● A. A. Lagrein Staves Ris. '12 | ♛♛♛ 5 |

| | |
|---|---|
| ○ A. A. Valle Isarco Riesling Kaiton '17 | ♟♟ 3* |
| ○ A. A. Valle Isarco Sylvaner '17 | ♟♟ 3* |
| ○ A. A. Valle Isarco Veltliner '17 | ♟♟ 3 |
| ○ A. A. Valle Isarco Grüner Veltliner '15 | ♛♛♛ 3* |
| ○ A. A. Valle Isarco Riesling Kaiton '16 | ♛♛♛ 3* |
| ○ A. A. Valle Isarco Riesling Kaiton '12 | ♛♛♛ 4* |
| ○ A. A. Valle Isarco Riesling Kaiton '11 | ♛♛♛ 4* |
| ○ A. A. Valle Isarco Riesling Kaiton '10 | ♛♛♛ 4 |
| ○ A. A. Valle Isarco Riesling Kaiton '07 | ♛♛♛ 3* |
| ○ A. A. Valle Isarco Sylvaner '14 | ♛♛♛ 3* |
| ○ A. A. Valle Isarco Sylvaner '13 | ♛♛♛ 3* |
| ○ A. A. Valle Isarco Sylvaner '08 | ♛♛♛ 3 |
| ○ A. A. Valle Isarco Sylvaner '06 | ♛♛♛ 3* |
| ○ A. A. Valle Isarco Veltliner '09 | ♛♛♛ 3* |

## ★Cantina Kurtatsch

LOC. BREITBACH
S.DA DEL VINO, 23
39040 CORTACCIA/KURTATSCH [BZ]
TEL. +39 0471880115
www.cantina-cortaccia.it

CELLAR SALES
PRE-BOOKED VISITS
ANNUAL PRODUCTION 1,300,000 bottles
HECTARES UNDER VINE 190.00
SUSTAINABLE WINERY

Brenntal, Penon and Graun are just some of the famous crus that have given Cantina di Cortaccia its distinguished vine-growing heritage. The winery is deeply rooted in the South Tyrolean Unterland and has just under 200 members who work almost exclusively within the municipality. The vineyards stretch from the low hills, where Merlot, Cabernet and Pinot Grigio are planted, right up to 900 meters above sea level, where plots are dedicated to Müller Thurgau. Not to be forgotten is Gewürztraminer, which in many ways is the flagship wine of a lustrous and sunny range. Their 2016 Gewürztraminer Brenntal Riserva leads a great overall performance by their selection. One of the region's warmest vineyards gives rise to this wine, which features vibrant and multi-faceted aromas on the nose, and a potent palate that's well-sustained by savoriness. Then there's their 2015 Amos, an elegant blend of Kerner, Sauvignon and Müller Thurgau. Their 2016 Penóner proves to be a solid, harmonious Pinot Grigio. Finally, we point out their fragrant 2017 Schiava Grigia Sonntaler.

| | | |
|---|---|---|
| ○ A. A. Gewürztraminer Brenntal Ris. '16 | ♆♆♆ | 5 |
| ○ A. A. Bianco Amos '16 | ♆♆ | 5 |
| ○ A. A. Chardonnay Pichl '16 | ♆♆ | 4 |
| ○ A. A. Pinot Grigio Penóner '16 | ♆♆ | 4 |
| ● A. A. Schiava Grigia Sonntaler '17 | ♆♆ | 3* |
| ● A. A. Cabernet Kirchhügel Ris. '15 | ♆♆ | 4 |
| ● A. A. Lagrein Frauriegl Ris. '15 | ♆♆ | 5 |
| ● A. A. Merlot Brenntal Ris. '15 | ♆♆ | 6 |
| ○ A. A. Müller Thurgau Graun '17 | ♆♆ | 3 |
| ○ A. A. Pinot Bianco Hofstatt '17 | ♆♆ | 3 |
| ○ A. A. Sauvignon Kofl '16 | ♆♆ | 4 |
| ○ Aruna V. T. '16 | ♆♆ | 4 |
| ○ A. A. Gewürztraminer Brenntal Ris. '15 | ♆♆♆ | 5 |
| ○ A. A. Gewürztraminer Brenntal Ris. '14 | ♆♆♆ | 5 |
| ○ A. A. Gewürztraminer Brenntal Ris. '12 | ♆♆♆ | 5 |

## ★Alois Lageder

LOC. TÒR LÖWENGANG
V.LO DEI CONTI, 9
39040 MAGRÈ/MARGREID [BZ]
TEL. +39 0471809500
www.aloislageder.eu

CELLAR SALES
PRE-BOOKED VISITS
RESTAURANT SERVICE
ANNUAL PRODUCTION 1,200,000 bottles
HECTARES UNDER VINE 150.00
VITICULTURE METHOD Certified Biodynamic
SUSTAINABLE WINERY

Few people have made such a powerful impact on Alto Adige's vine growing and winemaking as Alois Lageder. His family winery has expanded thanks to their close collaboration with a network of growers. Increasingly, many of the suppliers are producing grapes cultivated in vineyards that use biodynamic methods. Added value is derived from the unique locations around Magré, where the cellar is situated. The range of wines, made with the main local varieties (primarily Chardonnay and Cabernet), exhibits an unmistakable style. Only four wines were presented this year by Tòr Löwengang, with their 2015 Cor Römigberg standing out among them. It's a Cabernet Sauvignon made with grapes cultivated on the historic vineyard situated over Caldaro Lake (once the cradle of Lageder's Schiava). It's a deep wine in its aromas of red fruit and spices, with a generous, chamois-soft, pervasive palate that's refreshed at the end by savory acidity and tannic presence.

| | | |
|---|---|---|
| ● A. A. Cabernet Sauvignon Cor Römigberg '15 | ♆♆ | 8 |
| ○ A. A. Gewürztraminer '16 | ♆♆ | 3 |
| ● A. A. Pinot Nero Krafuss '15 | ♆♆ | 6 |
| ○ Fòrra Manzoni Bianco '16 | ♆♆ | 5 |
| ● A. A. Cabernet Löwengang '10 | ♆♆♆ | 7 |
| ● A. A. Cabernet Löwengang '07 | ♆♆♆ | 6 |
| ● A. A. Cabernet Sauvignon Cor Römigberg '11 | ♆♆♆ | 7 |
| ● A. A. Cabernet Sauvignon Cor Römigberg '08 | ♆♆♆ | 7 |
| ○ A. A. Chardonnay Löwengang '13 | ♆♆♆ | 6 |
| ● A. A. Cabernet Löwengang '13 | ♆♆ | 7 |
| ○ A. A. Casòn '14 | ♆♆ | 6 |
| ○ A. A. Chardonnay Gaun '15 | ♆♆ | 4 |
| ○ A. A. Gewürztraminer Am Sand '15 | ♆♆ | 5 |

# Laimburg

LOC. LAIMBURG, 6
39040 VADENA/PFATTEN [BZ]
TEL. +39 0471969590
www.laimburg.bz.it

CELLAR SALES
PRE-BOOKED VISITS
ANNUAL PRODUCTION 100,000 bottles
HECTARES UNDER VINE 20.00
SUSTAINABLE WINERY

Laimburg deserves a special place among the many important wineries in the province of Bolzano. It is owned by an agricultural research center and is named after a district in Vadena. The vineyards are spread over several areas, including some with quite extreme weather and soil conditions, such as Val Pusteria. They produce wines with a close-focused and solid character, divided into two selections. Vini del Podere is dedicated to simple, monovarietal wines, while Selezione del Maniero is for their more ambitious and ageworthy ones. Their 2017 Pinot Bianco put in an excellent performance, with a nose that feature's the grape's trademark fruity and flowery profile. It's a wine that surprises for its ability to bring together fullness and length, unfolding unhesitatingly and impressing for its crisp, dynamic palate. Their 2015 Barbagòl Riserva, an entirely different wine, is a Lagrein that opts for generosity and fruity sensations, which are perfectly expressed in a close-knit palate that's well-sustained by its tannic weave.

| | | |
|---|---|---|
| ● A. A. Lagrein Barbagòl Ris. '15 | | ♟♟ 5 |
| ○ A. A. Pinot Bianco '17 | | ♟♟ 2* |
| ● A. A. Cabernet Sauvignon Sass Roà Ris. '15 | | ♟♟ 5 |
| ● A. A. Lago di Caldaro Vernacius Solemnis '17 | | ♟♟ 3 |
| ● A. A. Merlot Ris. '16 | | ♟♟ 4 |
| ○ A. A. Sauvignon Passito Saphir '16 | | ♟♟ 6 |
| ● Col de Réy '14 | | ♟♟ 6 |
| ● A. A. Gewürztraminer '94 | | ♟♟♟ 5 |
| ● A. A. Lagrein Scuro Barbagòl Ris. '00 | | ♟♟♟ 5 |
| ● A. A. Lago di Caldaro Cl. Sup. Vernacius Solemnis '16 | | ♟♟ 3* |
| ● A. A. Merlot Ris. '15 | | ♟♟ 4 |
| ○ A. A. Sauvignon Passito Saphir '15 | | ♟♟ 6 |

# Klaus Lentsch

S.DA REINSPERG, 18A
39057 APPIANO/EPPAN [BZ]
TEL. +39 0471967263
www.klauslentsch.eu

CELLAR SALES
PRE-BOOKED VISITS
ANNUAL PRODUCTION 50,000 bottles
HECTARES UNDER VINE 6.00

Klaus Lentsch's winery is rapidly growing, increasing both the amount of grapes worked and the number of bottles produced. The vineyards are divided into two main areas: Eisack Valley, where it began, and the Überetsch, location of their most recently purchased plots. Their wines range from fresh whites produced in the northern district to classic reds from the province. Lagrein and Pinot Nero lead the group and the latter is offered in both a ready-to-drink version and a Riserva. Not all their wines were presented during this round of tasting, but the quality of their selection proves to be excellent, as demonstrated by their 2016 Grüner Veltliner Eichberg. Aromatically complex and multi-layered, it's a wine with vibrant mineral notes that gradually give way to hints of licorice and Mediterranean scrubland. In the mouth it proves rich, solid, lengthening gracefully towards a crisp finish. Their super-ripe 2017 Pinot Grigio is a full, potent wine that finishes with a curious aromatic note.

| | |
|---|---|
| ○ A. A. Gewürztraminer Fuchslahn '16 | ♟♟ 2* |
| ○ A. A. Grüner Veltliner Eichberg '16 | ♟♟ 3 |
| ○ A. A. Pinot Grigio '17 | ♟♟ 2* |
| ● A. A. Pinot Nero Bachgart '15 | ♟♟ 4 |
| ● A. A. Pinot Nero Bachgart Ris. '14 | ♟♟ 3 |
| ○ A. A. Gewürztraminer Amperg '17 | ♟ 2 |
| ○ A. A. Moscato Giallo Amperg '17 | ♟ 2 |
| ○ A. A. Sauvignon Amperg '17 | ♟ 3 |
| ● A. A. Pinot Nero Bachgart '13 | ♟♟♟ 4* |
| ○ A. A. Bianco Cuvée Syvi '16 | ♟♟ 3 |
| ● A. A. Lagrein Amperg Ris. '15 | ♟♟ 4 |
| ● A. A. Pinot Nero Bachgart Ris. '13 | ♟♟ 3 |
| ○ A. A. Sauvignon Amperg '16 | ♟♟ 3 |
| ○ A. A. Valle Isarco Grüner Veltliner Eichberg '15 | ♟♟ 3 |

## Loacker Schwarhof

Loc. Sankt Justina, 3
39100 Bolzano/Bozen
Tel. +39 0471365125
www.loacker.bio

**CELLAR SALES**
**PRE-BOOKED VISITS**
**ANNUAL PRODUCTION** 60,000 bottles
**HECTARES UNDER VINE** 7.00
**VITICULTURE METHOD** Certified Organic
**SUSTAINABLE WINERY**

The Loacker family winery is situated in the extreme northeastern part of the city of Bolzano, at the entrance to Eisack Valley. Houses give way to vineyards, which rise up slowly towards the Santa Maddalena hill. Their headquarters are based in the Sankt Justina district and the estate stretches over a handful of hectares cultivated under biodynamic management. They grow the region's best-known varieties, including Lagrein and Gewürztraminer, as well as producing interesting interpretations of Merlot and Cabernet. Loacker's gift for Lagrein was confirmed by our latest tastings, with their 2015 Gran Lareyn Riserva bursting its way into our finals. Close-focused, ripe fruit is accompanied by spicy notes and fine herbs. These unfold on a rich, appealing palate that's lengthened by savoriness in a general context of harmony and personality. Their 2016 'base' Lagrein of the same name features a similar profile, though with greater approachability and ease.

| | | |
|---|---|---|
| ● A. A. Lagrein Gran Lareyn Ris. '15 | ♟♟ | 4 |
| ● A. A. Santa Maddalena Cl. Morit '17 | ♟♟ | 3 |
| ○ Chardonnay Ateyon '16 | ♟♟ | 4 |
| ● Lagrein Gran Lareyn '16 | ♟♟ | 4 |
| ○ Sauvignon Blanc Tasnim '17 | ♟ | 4 |
| ● A. A. Merlot Ywain '04 | ♟♟♟ | 4* |
| ● A. A. Lagrein Gran Lareyn Ris. '13 | ♟♟ | 4 |
| ● A. A. Santa Maddalena Cl. Morit '16 | ♟♟ | 3 |
| ○ Chardonnay Ateyon '15 | ♟♟ | 4 |
| ● Kastlet '14 | ♟♟ | 5 |
| ● Lagrein Gran Lareyn '15 | ♟♟ | 4 |
| ● Merlot Ywain '14 | ♟♟ | 4 |
| ● Merlot Ywain '13 | ♟♟ | 4 |
| ○ Sauvignon Blanc Tasnim '16 | ♟♟ | 4 |

## Manincor

Loc. San Giuseppe al Lago, 4
39052 Caldaro/Kaltern [BZ]
Tel. +39 0471960230
www.manincor.com

**CELLAR SALES**
**PRE-BOOKED VISITS**
**ANNUAL PRODUCTION** 330,000 bottles
**HECTARES UNDER VINE** 50.00
**VITICULTURE METHOD** Certified Biodynamic
**SUSTAINABLE WINERY**

The Göess-Enzenberg Counts' winery is one of the most charming in the whole of South Tyrol. Their estate, with its deep-rooted vine growing traditions, is managed according to biodynamic methods and comprises three main vineyard plots. The Manincor area surrounds the cellar, in Mason; an area on a kind of large terrace overlooks Caldaro; and lastly, there is an area behind Terlano in the Lieben Aich district. As well as their main estates, they also own Campan in Caldaro, and Panholzer and Keil near the lake. Their Pinot Nero Mason di Mason performed excellently, drawing on the freshness of this prized vineyard so as to bring out the aromatic grace and tension that the 2015 vintage could have withheld. Terlano gave rise to their extraordinary 2016 Sauvignon Lieben Aich, a wine with a flowery, citrusy profile that delivers for the liveliness and firmness of its palate. Finally, their 2016 Eichhorn opts for warmer, riper shades, but it's just as supple and long.

| | | |
|---|---|---|
| ○ A. A. Terlano Pinot Bianco Eichhorn '16 | ♟♟♟ | 5 |
| ● A. A. Pinot Nero Mason di Mason '15 | ♟♟ | 8 |
| ○ A. A. Terlano Sauvignon Lieben Aich '16 | ♟♟ | 7 |
| ○ A. A. Terlano Chardonnay Sophie '16 | ♟♟ | 5 |
| ○ A. A. Terlano Réserve della Contessa '17 | ♟♟ | 4 |
| ○ A. A. Terlano Sauvignon Tannenberg '16 | ♟♟ | 5 |
| ● A.A. Pinot Nero Mason '16 | ♟♟ | 8 |
| ○ Le Petit '16 | ♟♟ | 8 |
| ○ A. A. Terlano Pinot Bianco Eichhorn '15 | ♟♟♟ | 5 |
| ○ A. A. Terlano Pinot Bianco Eichhorn '13 | ♟♟♟ | 5 |
| ○ A. A. Terlano Pinot Bianco Eichhorn '12 | ♟♟♟ | 5 |
| ○ A. A. Terlano Sauvignon Tannenberg '13 | ♟♟♟ | 5 |

## Lorenz Martini

loc. Cornaiano/Girlan
via Pranzol, 2d
39057 Appiano/Eppan [BZ]
Tel. +39 0471664136
www.lorenz-martini.it

CELLAR SALES
PRE-BOOKED VISITS
ANNUAL PRODUCTION 15,000 bottles
HECTARES UNDER VINE 2.00

Although the South Tyrolean territory provides excellent conditions for growing grapes for Metodo Classico sparkling wines, not much attention has been paid to the typology. Instead, preference has been given to producing the extraordinary quality that still whites express year after year. Yet, Lorenz Martini believes strongly in sparklers, so much so that he has created a cellar dedicated entirely to their production. He exploits different elevations, temperature ranges and soils to create wines that enhance qualities of finesse after the second fermentation. When an exceptional vintage allows for it, their Comitissa Pas Dosé, the only wine produced, is accompanied by their Comitissa Gold. 2013 gave rise to a fragrant, elegant version made with equal parts Chardonnay and Pinot Bianco and a small share of Pinot Nero. The nose features flowery notes and white fruit. These are perfectly supported by an energetic, linear, crisp palate that expresses the region's best attributes in terms of vivacity and freshness.

| | |
|---|---|
| ○ A. A. Spumante Pas Dosé Comitissa Ris. '13 | ▼▼ 5 |
| ○ A. A. Brut Comitissa Ris. '10 | ▽▽ 5 |
| ○ A. A. Brut Comitissa Ris. '09 | ▽▽ 5 |
| ○ A. A. Spumante Brut Comitissa Gold Gran Riserva '06 | ▽▽ 5 |
| ○ A. A. Spumante Brut Comitissa Ris. '12 | ▽▽ 5 |
| ○ A. A. Spumante Brut Comitissa Ris. '11 | ▽▽ 5 |
| ○ A. A. Spumante Comitissa Brut Ris. '08 | ▽▽ 5 |
| ○ A. A. Spumante Comitissa Brut Ris. '07 | ▽▽ 5 |
| ○ A. A. Spumante Comitissa Brut Ris. '06 | ▽▽ 5 |
| ○ A. A. Spumante Comitissa Brut Ris. '01 | ▽▽ 5 |
| ○ A. A. Spumante Comitissa Brut Ris. '00 | ▽▽ 5 |
| ○ A. A. Spumante Pas Dosé Comitissa Ris. '13 | ▽▽ 5 |

## K. Martini & Sohn

loc. Cornaiano
via Lamm, 28
39057 Appiano/Eppan [BZ]
Tel. +39 0471663156
www.martini-sohn.it

CELLAR SALES
PRE-BOOKED VISITS
ANNUAL PRODUCTION 230,000 bottles
HECTARES UNDER VINE 30.00

The small town of Cornaiano is situated on a sort of plateau enclosed by the Adige valley to the east, the Bolzano plain to the north and Caldaro and San Michele to the southwest. The Martini family winery stands out from among the dense network of vineyards and cellars that we find at the center. Their extensive vineyards grow grapes used to make a range of wines with consistent quality and a precise style. They focus on the most significant regional varieties and produce several selections. Their 2016 Chardonnay Maturum, made with grapes cultivated in Cornaiano and Appiano Monte, put in an excellent performance. After six months aging in new oak it offers up vibrant aromas of fresh flowers and white fruit, with toasty notes serving as an elegant background. In the mouth its impact is solid, with a delicate expansion of flavor that's perfectly sustained by acidity. Their 2015 Lagrein Riserva from the same line came in just short of our finals.

| | |
|---|---|
| ○ A. A. Chardonnay Maturum '16 | ▼▼ 4 |
| ○ A. A. Gewürztraminer Palladium '17 | ▼▼ 4 |
| ● A. A. Lagrein Maturum Ris. '15 | ▼▼ 5 |
| ○ A. A. Moscato Giallo '17 | ▼▼ 4 |
| ● A. A. Pinot Nero Palladium '16 | ▼▼ 3 |
| ○ A. A. Sauvignon Palladium '17 | ▼▼ 3 |
| ● Coldirus Palladium '16 | ▼▼ 3 |
| ○ A. A. Chardonnay Palladium '17 | ▼ 3 |
| ○ A. A. Kerner Palladium '17 | ▼ 2 |
| ● A. A. Lagrein Ruesl Gurnzan '17 | ▼ 2 |
| ○ A. A. Müller Thurgau Palladium '17 | ▼ 3 |
| ○ A. A. Pinot Bianco Palladium '17 | ▼ 2 |
| ○ A. A. Sauvignon Palladium '04 | ▽▽▽ 2* |
| ○ A. A. Pinot Bianco Palladium '16 | ▽▽ 2* |
| ● A. A. Pinot Nero Palladium '15 | ▽▽ 3 |
| ○ A. A. Sauvignon Palladium '16 | ▽▽ 3* |

# ★Cantina Meran

VIA CANTINA, 9
39020 MARLENGO/MARLING [BZ]
TEL. +39 0473447137
www.cantinamerano.it

**CELLAR SALES**
**PRE-BOOKED VISITS**
**ANNUAL PRODUCTION** 1,600,000 bottles
**HECTARES UNDER VINE** 265.00

This cooperative in Merano counts on the work of almost three hundred members. They cultivate a similar number of hectares of vineyards in the hills surrounding the town, between Lagundo, Marlengo and Tirolo. Additional growers supply grapes cultivated in nearby Vinschgau. The vine growing area is sheltered from the cold northerly winds by the Tessa mountains, while warm breezes flow along the wide Adige valley, enabling the grapes to ripen and retain their rich fruit and fresh acidity. Their 2016 Pinot Bianco is cultivated at about 500 meters above sea level in Tyrol (from which it's taken its name). The nose features white fruit, hints of flowers and a subtle mineral vein. The palate proves crisp, elegant and quite long. Their rich and succulent 2015 Lagrein Segen Riserva comes from Bolzano in what is one of their few vineyards outside of Merano.

| | |
|---|---|
| ○ A. A. Pinot Bianco Tyrol '16 | ♟♟♟ 4* |
| ● A. A. Lagrein Segen Ris. '15 | ♟♟ 4 |
| ● A. A. Cabernet Graf Ris. '15 | ♟♟ 4 |
| ○ A. A. Chardonnay Goldegg '16 | ♟♟ 4 |
| ● A. A. Meranese Fürst '17 | ♟♟ 5 |
| ● A. A. Meranese Schickenburg Graf '17 | ♟♟ 3 |
| ● A. A. Merlot Freiherr Ris. '15 | ♟♟ 5 |
| ● A. A. Pinot Nero Zeno Ris. '15 | ♟♟ 4 |
| ○ A. A. Sauvignon Mervin '16 | ♟♟ 4 |
| ○ A. A. Val Venosta Pinot Bianco Sonnenberg '17 | ♟♟ 3 |
| ○ A. A. Val Venosta Kerner Sonnenberg '17 | ♟ 4 |
| ○ A. A. Pinot Bianco Tyrol '15 | ♟♟♟ 4* |
| ○ A. A. Pinot Bianco Tyrol '13 | ♟♟♟ 4* |
| ○ A. A. Sauvignon Mervin '14 | ♟♟♟ 4* |

# ★Cantina Convento Muri-Gries

P.ZZA GRIES, 21
39100 BOLZANO/BOZEN
TEL. +39 0471282287
www.muri-gries.com

**CELLAR SALES**
**ANNUAL PRODUCTION** 700,000 bottles
**HECTARES UNDER VINE** 55.00
**SUSTAINABLE WINERY**

The cellar connected to the Muri-Gries monastery is possibly the most iconic of those that developed inside the city of Bolzano centuries ago. Today it consists of only a few meagre plots, and from this point of view, Klosteranger is an icon. Basically it is a clos, a walled vineyard, which embodies the meatier and more dynamic essence of Lagrein. Kellermeister Christian Werth uses white grapes cultivated in vineyards concentrated in the nearby Appiano area to produce white wines featuring the same juicy and racy style. Once again their Lagrein Abtei Muri Riserva takes center stage. The hot and sunny 2015 vintage brought out the wine's aromatic intensity, with fragrances ranging from smoky notes to black fruit, aromatic herbs and spices. The palate exhibits its trademark potency, though this is managed with elegance and tension. Their 2015 Pinot Bianco Riserva and 2016 Pinot Nero Riserva also proved delicious. The former opts for elegance while the second is full-bodied and progressive.

| | |
|---|---|
| ● A. A. Pinot Nero Abtei Muri Ris. '15 | ♟♟♟ 5 |
| ● A. A. Lagrein Abtei Muri Ris. '15 | ♟♟ 5 |
| ○ A. A. Terlano Pinot Bianco Abtei Muri Ris. '15 | ♟♟ 5 |
| ● A. A. Lagrein '17 | ♟♟ 3 |
| ● A. A. Moscato Rosa V. T. Abtei Muri '16 | ♟♟ 5 |
| ○ A. A. Pinot Grigio '17 | ♟♟ 3 |
| ○ A. A. Terlano Pinot Bianco '17 | ♟♟ 3 |
| ⊙ A. A. Lagrein Rosato '17 | ♟ 3 |
| ● A. A. Lagrein Abtei Muri Ris. '14 | ♟♟♟ 5 |
| ● A. A. Lagrein Abtei Muri Ris. '12 | ♟♟♟ 5 |
| ● A. A. Lagrein Abtei Muri Ris. '11 | ♟♟♟ 5 |
| ● A. A. Lagrein Abtei Muri Ris. '10 | ♟♟♟ 5 |
| ● A. A. Lagrein Abtei Muri Ris. '09 | ♟♟♟ 5 |
| ● A. A. Lagrein Abtei Ris. '07 | ♟♟♟ 5 |

# ★Nals Margreid

VIA HEILIGENBERG, 2
39010 NALLES/NALS [BZ]
TEL. +39 0471678626
www.kellerei.it

CELLAR SALES
PRE-BOOKED VISITS
ANNUAL PRODUCTION 980,000 bottles
HECTARES UNDER VINE 165.00
SUSTAINABLE WINERY

Nals Margreid is one of the smallest cooperatives in the province of Bolzano, and comprises about 150 members who cultivate vineyards scattered throughout the territory. This vineyard fragmentation enables Harald Schraffl to exploit the best exposures and elevations for each cultivar, allowing the grapes to ripen in the most suitable location. All winemaking is done in the cellar in Nalles, which has been renovated recently in keeping with the historic buildings in the town center. Both 2017s, their Sirmian and Punggi affirm their status as benchmark wines. The former is a Pinot Bianco that delivers for the freshness of its aromas and for its crisp, dynamic palate. The second highlights power, but also the elegance of Pinot Grigio, with fragrances of pear, dried flowers and medicinal herbs supported by a full-flavored and gutsy palate. Their 2015 Chardonnay Baron Salvadori is a sophisticated, deep, multi-layered wine.

# Ignaz Niedrist

LOC. CORNAIANO/GIRLAN
VIA RONCO, 5
39057 APPIANO/EPPAN [BZ]
TEL. +39 0471664494
www.ignazniedrist.com

CELLAR SALES
PRE-BOOKED VISITS
ANNUAL PRODUCTION 45,000 bottles
HECTARES UNDER VINE 10.00
SUSTAINABLE WINERY

The Ignaz Niedrist winery is situated in the heart of Cornaiano, within a dense network of vineyards surrounding the small town. The plots are concentrated in this warm, breezy area, with shallow soils and elevations skimming 500 meters. Others are located in Appiano Monte, where the climate is decidedly cooler with marked day-night temperature swings. And lastly there is the small Gries estate, where Lagrein is cultivated on porphyry soils. And the biggest news happens to come out of Gries, with a sumptuous 2015 Lagrein Berger Gei Riserva. Despite the unwieldy and rustic character of the grape, Niedrist crafts a deep red in its expression of fruit and aromatic herbs. The palate proves elegant in its savory and acidic tension, which confers grace and energy. Their 2016 Sauvignon Limes is also quite good. The nose is still a bit clenched and young, while the palate delivers for its vivacity and length.

| | |
|---|---|
| ○ A. A. Pinot Bianco Sirmian '17 | ♈♈♈ 5 |
| ○ A. A. Chardonnay Baron Salvadori Ris. '15 | ♈♈ 6 |
| ● A. A. Merlot - Cabernet Anticus Baron Salvadori Ris. '15 | ♈♈ 5 |
| ○ A. A. Pinot Grigio Punggl '17 | ♈♈ 5 |
| ○ A. A. Gewürztraminer Lyra '17 | ♈♈ 4 |
| ● A. A. Lagrein Gries Ris. '15 | ♈♈ 5 |
| ○ A. A. Moscato Giallo Passito Baronesse Baron Salvadori '15 | ♈♈ 6 |
| ○ A. A. Pinot Bianco Penon '17 | ♈♈ 3 |
| ● A. A. Pinot Nero Jura Ris. '15 | ♈♈ 5 |
| ○ A. A. Sauvignon Gennen '17 | ♈♈ 3 |
| ○ A. A. Sauvignon Mantele '17 | ♈♈ 5 |
| ● A. A. Schiava Galea '17 | ♈♈ 3 |
| ○ A. A. Pinot Bianco Sirmian '16 | ♈♈♈ 5 |

| | |
|---|---|
| ● A. A. Lagrein Berger Gei Ris. '15 | ♈♈ 4 |
| ○ A. A. Sauvignon Limes '16 | ♈♈ 4 |
| ○ A. A. Pinot Bianco Limes '16 | ♈♈ 4 |
| ● A. A. Pinot Nero Ris. '15 | ♈♈ 5 |
| ○ A. A. Riesling Berg '17 | ♈ 4 |
| ○ A. A. Riesling Berg '11 | ♈♈♈ 4* |
| ○ A. A. Terlano Pinot Bianco '12 | ♈♈♈ 3* |
| ○ A. A. Terlano Sauvignon '10 | ♈♈♈ 3 |
| ○ A. A. Terlano Sauvignon '00 | ♈♈♈ 3* |
| ○ Trias '14 | ♈♈♈ 4* |
| ● A. A. Lagrein Berger Gei Ris. '14 | ♈♈ 4 |
| ● A. A. Pinot Nero Vom Kalk '13 | ♈♈ 6 |
| ○ A. A. Riesling Berg '16 | ♈♈ 4 |
| ○ Trias '16 | ♈♈ 4 |

# Niklaserhof - Josef Sölva

LOC. SAN NICOLÒ
VIA DELLE FONTANE, 31A
39052 CALDARO/KALTERN [BZ]
TEL. +39 0471963434
www.niklaserhof.it

**CELLAR SALES**
**PRE-BOOKED VISITS**
**ANNUAL PRODUCTION** 50,000 bottles
**HECTARES UNDER VINE** 6.00

Many South Tyrolean wineries cultivate small areas to produce high profile wines, limiting the grape varieties to those best suited to varying soil conditions, elevations and vineyard exposures. The Sölva family is one such producer. Their plots are situated mostly around Lake Caldaro, where we find varieties needing a warmer climate. Whereas higher areas of the municipality -- Vial and Kardatsch -- are traditionally cultivated with Pinot Bianco and Sauvignon. And so Schiava takes center stage, as demonstrated by a splendid 2017 Lago di Caldaro Klaser, a red that's redolent of small fruit and spices, with a curious nuance of fines herbes in the background. In the mouth the wine proves firm, though without losing tension and drinkability. Their 2015 Pinot Bianco Riserva, on the other hand, is a wine that opts for substance. The nose offers up hints of sulphur and citrus, which open onto a full, juicy palate that has plenty of personality.

| | |
|---|---|
| ○ A. A. Pinot Bianco Klaser Ris. '15 | ▼▼▼ 4* |
| ● A. A. Lago di Caldaro Cl. Sup. Klaser '17 | ▼▼ 2* |
| ○ A. A. Kerner Luxs '17 | ▼▼ 3 |
| ○ A. A. Kerner Mondevinum Ris. '15 | ▼▼ 4 |
| ● A. A. Lagrein Mondevinum Ris. '15 | ▼▼ 4 |
| ● A. A. Lagrein-Cabernet Klaser Ris. '15 | ▼▼ 4 |
| ● A. A. Merlot DJJ Ris. '15 | ▼▼ 4 |
| ○ A. A. Pinot Bianco Hos '17 | ▼▼ 3 |
| ○ A. A. Sauvignon Doxs '17 | ▼▼ 3 |
| ○ Kerner Without SO2 '16 | ▼ 2 |
| ○ A. A. Kerner Mondevinum Ris. '14 | ♀♀ 4 |
| ● A. A. Lagrein Cabernet Klaser Ris. '14 | ♀♀ 4 |
| ○ A. A. Pinot Bianco Klaser Ris. '14 | ♀♀ 3* |
| ○ A. A. Sauvignon '16 | ♀♀ 3 |

# Pacherhof - Andreas Huber

FRAZ. NOVACELLA
V.LO PACHER, 1
39040 VARNA/VAHRN [BZ]
TEL. +39 0472835717
www.pacherhof.com

**CELLAR SALES**
**PRE-BOOKED VISITS**
**ACCOMMODATION AND RESTAURANT SERVICE**
**ANNUAL PRODUCTION** 90,000 bottles
**HECTARES UNDER VINE** 8.50

Andreas Huber is a meticulous vine grower who interprets the territory of Eisack Valley with precision and character. He runs a small estate overlooking the city of Bressanone, at elevations ranging from 600 to 900 meters. His vineyards exhibit the distinctive features of the territory: brightness, wide temperature ranges, and mountain climate. These aspects are perfectly expressed by the wines whose aromatic fragrance and acid tension are faithfully brought out in the cellar. And tasting their 2016 Sylvaner Alte Reben is emblematic in that sense, with its aromatic profile that alternates between hints of ripe yellow fruit, Mediterranean scrubland, smoky notes and flint. In the mouth, great depth is accompanied by energy and pluck, all perfectly sustained by acidity, making for a charming wine that's a joy to drink. Their 2017 Grüner Veltliner, on the other hand, opens with sulphur, which gradually gives way to flowery nuances that follow through on its lean, supple palate.

| | |
|---|---|
| ○ A. A. Valle Isarco Sylvaner Alte Reben '16 | ▼▼▼ 5 |
| ○ A. A. Valle Isarco Grüner Veltliner '17 | ▼▼ 4 |
| ○ A. A. Valle Isarco Kerner '17 | ▼▼ 4 |
| ○ A. A. Valle Isarco Müller Thurgau '17 | ▼▼ 3 |
| ○ A. A. Valle Isarco Pinot Grigio '17 | ▼▼ 4 |
| ○ A. A. Valle Isarco Sylvaner '17 | ▼▼ 4 |
| ○ Private Cuvée Andreas Huber '16 | ▼▼ 6 |
| ○ A. A. Valle Isarco Grüner Veltliner '16 | ♀♀♀ 4* |
| ○ A. A. Valle Isarco Riesling '04 | ♀♀♀ 3 |
| ○ A. A. Valle Isarco Sylvaner '13 | ♀♀♀ 3* |
| ○ A. A. Valle Isarco Sylvaner Alte Reben '05 | ♀♀♀ 4 |
| ○ A. A. Valle Isarco Kerner '16 | ♀♀ 4 |
| ○ A. A. Valle Isarco Pinot Grigio '16 | ♀♀ 4 |
| ○ A. A. Valle Isarco Sylvaner '16 | ♀♀ 4 |

## Pfannenstielhof Johannes Pfeifer

VIA PFANNESTIEL, 9
39100 BOLZANO/BOZEN
TEL. +39 0471970884
www.pfannenstielhof.it

CELLAR SALES
PRE-BOOKED VISITS
ANNUAL PRODUCTION 43,000 bottles
HECTARES UNDER VINE 4.00

The winery run by Hannes Pfeifer and his wife Margareth is situated a few hundred meters from the center of Bolzano, at the foot of the Santa Maddalena hill and a stone's throw from the Eisack river. Their handful of hectares are planted exclusively with the traditional varieties from this corner of Alto Adige. Schiava and Lagrein are cultivated so as to enhance their authentic and unrestrained character. And skillful interpretation of these two regional red grapes 'par excellence' gives rise to a limited but high-level range of wines. Their 2017 Santa Maddalena is at its best. It's a red that enchants with its aromas of cherry and pepper, fresh flowers and aromatic herbs. Approachable and easy-going, its luscious savoriness drives a juicy palate - it's a highly pleasurable wine to drink. Their Lagreins also proved delicious, with their palish 2017 Rosé and its energetic, gratifying palate standing out for their originality. Their 2017 Vom Boden and their 2015 Riserva are both more intense wines.

| | | |
|---|---|---|
| ● A. A. Santa Maddalena Cl. '17 | ♟♟ | 3* |
| ● A. A. Lagrein Ris. '15 | ♟♟ | 5 |
| ⊙ A. A. Lagrein Rosé '17 | ♟♟ | 3 |
| ● A. A. Lagrein vom Boden '17 | ♟♟ | 3 |
| ● A. A. Santa Maddalena Cl. '14 | ♟♟♟ | 3* |
| ● A. A. Santa Maddalena Cl. '09 | ♟♟♟ | 2* |
| ● A. A. Lagrein Ris. '14 | ♟♟ | 5 |
| ● A. A. Lagrein Ris. '13 | ♟♟ | 5 |
| ● A. A. Lagrein vom Boden '16 | ♟♟ | 3 |
| ● A. A. Lagrein vom Boden '15 | ♟♟ | 3 |
| ● A. A. Santa Maddalena Cl. '16 | ♟♟ | 3* |
| ● A. A. Santa Maddalena Cl. '15 | ♟♟ | 3* |
| ⊙ Lagrein Rosé '16 | ♟♟ | 2* |

## Tenuta Pfitscher

VIA DOLOMITI, 17
39040 MONTAGNA/MONTAN [BZ]
TEL. +39 04711681317
www.pfitscher.it

CELLAR SALES
PRE-BOOKED VISITS
ANNUAL PRODUCTION 60,000 bottles
HECTARES UNDER VINE 7.00

The Pfitscher family cellar is located in the heart of their vineyards in Montagna, recognized as one of the best areas for cultivating Pinot Nero. Many of their plots are concentrated here, but they also own smaller parcels in Fié allo Sciliar and Cortaccia. Such variety in climate, soils and exposures offers Klaus and his family the opportunity to work their grapes in optimal conditions and to produce wines that fully respect the specific attributes of the variety. The selection put forward this year proved generous and well-appreciated. Their 2015 Lagrein Riserva, especially, impressed. It's a wine made with grapes cultivated in Egna, which give rise to aromas of red fruit and medicinal herbs. In the mouth it expresses a union of tension and suppleness that's characteristic of the Lagrein grown in this enclave, making for a long, juicy wine. Their 2017 Pinot Bianco Langefeld also proved delicious. It's a wine that ops for ripeness of fruit and a full palate.

| | | |
|---|---|---|
| ○ A. A. Chardonnay Arvum '17 | ♟♟ | 3 |
| ○ A. A. Gewürztraminer Rutter '16 | ♟♟ | 4 |
| ○ A. A. Gewürztraminer Stoass '17 | ♟♟ | 4 |
| ○ A. A. Lagrein Ris. '15 | ♟♟ | 5 |
| ○ A. A. Pinot Bianco Langefeld '17 | ♟♟ | 3 |
| ● A. A. Pinot Nero Matan '15 | ♟♟ | 5 |
| ○ A. A. Sauvignon Saxum '17 | ♟♟ | 4 |
| ○ A. A. Sauvignon Mathias '16 | ♟ | 4 |
| ○ A. A. Valle Isarco Müller Thurgau Dola '17 | ♟ | 4 |
| ○ A. A. Gewürztraminer Stoass '16 | ♟♟ | 4 |
| ● A. A. Merlot Kotznloater '15 | ♟♟ | 4 |
| ○ A. A. Pinot Bianco Langefeld '16 | ♟♟ | 3* |
| ● A. A. Pinot Nero Matan '14 | ♟♟ | 5 |
| ○ A. A. Sauvignon Saxum '16 | ♟♟ | 4 |

# Tenuta Ritterhof

S.DA DEL VINO, 1
39052 CALDARO/KALTERN [BZ]
TEL. +39 0471963298
www.ritterhof.it

CELLAR SALES
PRE-BOOKED VISITS
RESTAURANT SERVICE
ANNUAL PRODUCTION 300,000 bottles
HECTARES UNDER VINE 7.50

In just a few years the Roner family winery has moved up the regional hit parade to become a winemaking benchmark in the province of Bolzano. The recognition comes in particular from Gewürztraminer enthusiasts. Credit is due to Ludwig Kaneppele and his staff for their skill in interpreting the territory and grape variety with precision and personality. And we shouldn't overlook the work of trusted growers who supply grapes to their Caldaro site situated along the 'Strada di Vino' ('Wine Route'). Their 2017 Gewürztraminer Auratus brings out the cultivar's aromatic attributes, conferring exuberance and elegance at the same time, charming the palate with its roundness though without losing savoriness or acidity. Their 2015 Lagrein Manus Riserva also delivered. Only made on occasion of excellent vintages, here it offers up deep aromas and an energetic, close-knit palate. Their 2017 Pinot Bianco Verus is a fresh, savory, racy wine.

# Tenuta Hans Rottensteiner

FRAZ. GRIES
VIA SARENTINO, 1A
39100 BOLZANO/BOZEN
TEL. +39 0471282015
www.rottensteiner-weine.com

CELLAR SALES
PRE-BOOKED VISITS
ANNUAL PRODUCTION 450,000 bottles
HECTARES UNDER VINE 90.00

The Rottensteiner family's winemaking venture began about fifty years ago, when their sole aim was to produce simple wines in large quantities (their impressive cellar is a testament to their commitment to that priority). However, today what Hannes says and does underlines a difference. Wine quality is now their main priority, thanks to vineyards located in various scenic farms, which are particularly well-suited to vine growing, and which supply grapes for their more ambitious wines. And Rottensteiner's selection put in a great performance, starting with their 2015 Lagrein Grieser Select Riserva, a wine whose grapes are cultivated in Gries, the cradle of the local cultivar. Its dense color anticipates multi-layered fragrances in which red fruit fuses with smoky, spicy notes, which then give way to medicinal herbs. In the mouth its weight is notable, but acidity and tannins manage the difficult task of conferring tension and suppleness.

| | |
|---|---|
| ○ A. A. Gewürztraminer Auratus '17 | ♟♟♟ 4* |
| ● A. A. Lagrein Manus Ris. '15 | ♟♟ 5 |
| ○ A. A. Pinot Bianco Verus '17 | ♟♟ 3* |
| ● A. A. Cabernet Merlot Ramus '14 | ♟♟ 4 |
| ○ A. A. Gewürztraminer '17 | ♟♟ 3 |
| ● A. A. Lago di Caldaro Cl. Sup. Novis '17 | ♟♟ 3 |
| ○ A. A. Pinot Bianco '17 | ♟♟ 2* |
| ● A. A. Pinot Nero Dignus '14 | ♟♟ 5 |
| ○ A. A. Sauvignon '17 | ♟♟ 2* |
| ○ A. A. Sauvignon Paratus '17 | ♟♟ 2* |
| ● A. A. Lagrein '17 | ♟ 3 |
| ● A. A. Santa Maddalena Perlhof '17 | ♟ 2 |
| ○ A. A. Gewürztraminer Auratus '16 | ♟♟♟ 4* |
| ○ A. A. Gewürztraminer Auratus Crescendo '15 | ♟♟♟ 4* |
| ○ A. A. Gewürztraminer Auratus Crescendo '13 | ♟♟♟ 4* |

| | |
|---|---|
| ● A. A. Lagrein Grieser Select Ris. '15 | ♟♟ 5 |
| ● A. A. Cabernet Select Ris. '15 | ♟♟ 5 |
| ○ A. A. Gewürztraminer Cancenai '17 | ♟♟ 4 |
| ○ A. A. Gewürztraminer Passito Cresta '16 | ♟♟ 6 |
| ○ A. A. Pinot Bianco Carnol '17 | ♟♟ 3 |
| ● A. A. Pinot Nero Select Ris. '15 | ♟♟ 5 |
| ● A. A. Santa Maddalena Cl. V. Premstallerhof '17 | ♟♟ 3 |
| ○ A. A. Valle Isarco Sylvaner '17 | ♟♟ 2* |
| ○ A. A. Lagrein Rosé '17 | ♟ 5 |
| ○ A. A. Müller Thurgau '17 | ♟ 3 |
| ○ A. A. Sauvignon '17 | ♟ 3 |
| ● A. A. Lagrein Ris. '02 | ♟♟♟ 2* |
| ○ A. A. Gewürztraminer Cancenai '16 | ♟♟ 4 |
| ○ A. A. Müller Thurgau '16 | ♟♟ 3 |

# ★★★Cantina Produttori San Michele Appiano

VIA CIRCONVALLAZIONE, 17/19
39057 APPIANO/EPPAN [BZ]
TEL. +39 0471664466
www.stmichael.it

CELLAR SALES
PRE-BOOKED VISITS
ANNUAL PRODUCTION 2,200,000 bottles
HECTARES UNDER VINE 380.00

The great South Tyrolean wine renaissance in the 1980s owes much to the work of the Produttori San Michele Appiano winery and its kellermeister, Hans Terzer. He has never tired of exploring the region's vine growing potential and is back at the head of the cooperative's more than 300 families. Mostly, the vineyards are situated in municipalities right around Appiano. The cellar, set out on different floors, gives rise to a range of wines that are noteworthy both for their quantity and quality. San Michele Appiano's selection bowled us over during our tastings. And we're not just talking about their 2013 Appius, an extraordinary, limited-edition white that we don't rank. Their 2016 Pinot Grigio and their 2016 Chardonnay, from their Sanct Valentin line, both delivered in spades, but it was their 2015 Pinot Nero Riserva that most impressed (a project that Hanz has been working on passionately for years). It's an outstanding red for its stylistic precision and the richness of its varietal aromas. Tre Bicchieri.

| | |
|---|---|
| ● A. A. Pinot Nero Sanct Valentin Ris. '15 | 🍷🍷🍷 5 |
| ○ A. A. Chardonnay Sanct Valentin '16 | 🍷🍷 5 |
| ○ A. A. Pinot Grigio Sanct Valentin '16 | 🍷🍷 5 |
| ● A. A. Cabernet Merlot Sanct Valentin Ris. '15 | 🍷🍷 5 |
| ○ A. A. Gewürztraminer Passito Comtess Sanct Valentin '16 | 🍷🍷 7 |
| ○ A. A. Gewürztraminer Sanct Valentin '16 | 🍷🍷 5 |
| ○ A. A. Pinot Bianco Sanct Valentin '16 | 🍷🍷 5 |
| ○ A. A. Pinot Bianco Schulthauser '17 | 🍷🍷 3 |
| ○ A. A. Pinot Grigio Anger '17 | 🍷🍷 4 |
| ○ A. A. Sauvignon Sanct Valentin '16 | 🍷🍷 5 |
| ○ A. A. Pinot Bianco Sanct Valentin '15 | 🍷🍷🍷 5 |
| ○ A. A. Pinot Grigio Sanct Valentin '14 | 🍷🍷🍷 5 |

# Cantina Produttori San Paolo

LOC. SAN PAOLO
VIA CASTEL GUARDIA, 21
39057 APPIANO/EPPAN [BZ]
TEL. +39 0471662183
www.stpauls.wine

CELLAR SALES
PRE-BOOKED VISITS
ANNUAL PRODUCTION 1,200,000 bottles
HECTARES UNDER VINE 175.00
SUSTAINABLE WINERY

Important renovation work is currently under way at Cantina Produttori San Paolo, with an aim to improve work flow, especially during the hot harvest period. With this in place, kellermeister Wolfgang Tratter expects to fully exploit the distinctive quality of the grapes supplied by over 200 members. His passion and attention to the various vineyard plots remains unchanged. The vineyards are concentrated in the northern district of the Überetsch (where slopes rise steeply before the Bolzano plain) and they are what make up the real heritage of this Appiano cooperative. The 2015 Sanctissimus, a wine cultivated in one of San Paolo's loveliest vineyards, is a Pinot Bianco Riserva tied to the steep slopes that host century-old vines. The nose is endowed with great sophistication and depth, while the mouth proves firm, tapered, very elegant. Their 2015 Gewürztraminer Passito Passion is more buoyant aromatically, offering balanced sweetness that's well-sustained by savoriness.

| | |
|---|---|
| ○ A. A. Gewürztraminer Passito Passion '15 | 🍷🍷 6 |
| ○ A. A. Pinot Bianco Sanctissimus Ris. '15 | 🍷🍷 8 |
| ○ A. A. Gewürztraminer Justina '17 | 🍷🍷 3 |
| ● A. A. Merlot Passion Ris. '15 | 🍷🍷 7 |
| ○ A. A. Pinot Bianco Kössler '17 | 🍷🍷 2* |
| ○ A. A. Pinot Bianco Passion Ris. '16 | 🍷🍷 5 |
| ○ A. A. Pinot Bianco Plötzner '17 | 🍷🍷 3 |
| ○ A. A. Pinot Grigio Kössler '17 | 🍷🍷 3 |
| ○ A. A. Sauvignon Gfill '17 | 🍷🍷 3 |
| ● A. A. Schiava Missianer '17 | 🍷🍷 2* |
| ○ A. A. Spumante Praeclarus Brut | 🍷🍷 5 |
| ○ Petit Manseng Passion '17 | 🍷🍷 5 |
| ○ A. A. Pinot Bianco Passion '09 | 🍷🍷🍷 4 |
| ○ A. A. Pinot Bianco Passion Ris. '11 | 🍷🍷🍷 4* |
| ○ A. A. Pinot Bianco Passion Ris. '15 | 🍷🍷 5 |

## Peter Sölva & Söhne

VIA DELL'ORO, 33
39052 CALDARO/KALTERN [BZ]
TEL. +39 0471964650
www.soelva.com

CELLAR SALES
PRE-BOOKED VISITS
ANNUAL PRODUCTION 75,000 bottles
HECTARES UNDER VINE 12.00

The Sölva family winery enjoys a long history, but it was the regional wine renaissance in the 1980s that brought a change in pace to production. Today it is one of the most interesting wineries in the area around Lake Caldaro, with large and varied vineyards stretching from the Überetsch to the South Tyrolean Unterland. They produce three lines of wines with differing styles and prices, but always focusing on the varieties best-suited to the temperate climate in this corner of Alto Adige. These are the perfect conditions for bringing their Cabernet Franc to its full ripeness, and a sunny 2015 vintage gave rise to a commendable version of their Amistar. The nose features vibrant notes of wild fruit and spices, with well-integrated oak, while the palate reveals a power that's never for its own sake, as the wine lengthens with elegance, supported by pliant, smooth tannins. Their 2016 Amistar Bianco, a blend of Chardonnay, Pinot Grigio and Sauvignon, opts for greater plush.

| | |
|---|---|
| ● A. A. Cabernet Franc Amistar '15 | ♟♟ 5 |
| ● A. A. Lagrein '16 | ♟♟ 3 |
| ○ Amistar Bianco '16 | ♟♟ 6 |
| ● Amistar Rosso '15 | ♟♟ 5 |
| ○ A. A. Gewürztraminer '17 | ♟ 5 |
| ● A. A. Lago di Caldaro Cl. Sup. Peterleiten DeSilva '17 | ♟ 2 |
| ○ A. A. Pinot Bianco DeSilva '17 | ♟ 4 |
| ○ A. A. Terlano Pinot Bianco DeSilva '10 | ♟♟♟ 3 |
| ○ A. A. Terlano Pinot Bianco DeSilva '09 | ♟♟♟ 3 |
| ○ A. A. Pinot Bianco DeSilva '16 | ♟♟ 4 |
| ○ Amistar Bianco '15 | ♟♟ 6 |
| ● Amistar Edizione Rossa Serie A6 '13 | ♟♟ 6 |
| ● Amistar Rosso '14 | ♟♟ 5 |

## Stachlburg
## Baron von Kripp

VIA MITTERHOFER, 2
39020 PARCINES/PARTSCHINS [BZ]
TEL. +39 0473968014
www.stachlburg.com

CELLAR SALES
PRE-BOOKED VISITS
ANNUAL PRODUCTION 30,000 bottles
HECTARES UNDER VINE 7.00
VITICULTURE METHOD Certified Organic

Situated at the entrance of Vinschgau Valley, the Kripp family's farming business is divided between wine grape and apple production. The vineyards cover just a few hectares of a much larger estate in various areas of Bolzano's northern district. They range from 300 to 650 meters above sea level and extend to Andriano. Traditional South Tyrolean varieties are cultivated under organic management and are sited according to their agronomical traits. The result is a range of wines that play on elegance rather than power. At Kripp, great attention is paid to Pinot Nero, as demonstrated by a convincing vintage 2015. Aromas of wild fruit gradually give way to smoky and spicy notes, which finally open to clear hints of medicinal herbs. On the palate the wine proves graceful and broad, sustained by acidity and savoriness, not to mention sweet, ripe tannins, all of which prepares the way for a very clean finish.

| | |
|---|---|
| ● A. A. Merlot Wolfsthurn R '15 | ♟♟ 4 |
| ○ A. A. Pinot Grigio Wolfsthurn R '17 | ♟♟ 2* |
| ○ A. A. Terlano Sauvignon Wolfsthurn '17 | ♟♟ 4 |
| ● A. A. Val Venosta Pinot Nero '15 | ♟♟ 5 |
| ○ Dulcitudo Eustachius '16 | ♟♟ 5 |
| ○ A. A. Pinot Grigio Wolfsthurn '17 | ♟ 2 |
| ○ A. A. Valle Venosta Pinot Bianco '13 | ♟♟♟ 3* |
| ○ A. A. Valle Venosta Pinot Bianco '10 | ♟♟♟ 3* |
| ● A. A. Merlot '13 | ♟♟ 4 |
| ● A. A. Merlot Ris. '14 | ♟♟ 5 |
| ○ A. A. Pinot Bianco '16 | ♟♟ 4 |
| ● A. A. Pinot Nero '13 | ♟♟ 3* |
| ○ A. A. Val Venosta Chardonnay Ris. '14 | ♟♟ 5 |
| ● A. A. Val Venosta Pinot Nero '14 | ♟♟ 5 |

# Strasserhof
# Hannes Baumgartner

FRAZ. NOVACELLA
LOC. UNTERRAIN, 8
39040 VARNA/VAHRN [BZ]
TEL. +39 0472830804
www.strasserhof.info

**CELLAR SALES**
**PRE-BOOKED VISITS**
**ACCOMMODATION**
**ANNUAL PRODUCTION** 45,000 bottles
**HECTARES UNDER VINE** 5.50

Hannes Baumgartner has been running his family's winery for about fifteen years. This beautiful estate extending over a few hectares on the high Varna hill, with vineyards overlooking Eisack Valley and the city of Bressanone, forms part of Italy's most northerly viticulture. Great attention is paid to the territory's local white grapes, particularly Sylvaner, Riesling and Veltliner, which are fermented in steel. At the same time, selections made with grapes grown in their historic vineyards are matured in large barrels in order to enhance their finesse and tension. Thanks to an excellent vintage (2016) and lengthy aging in their cellar, today their Sylvaner Anjo offers up great surprises. The nose features vibrant aromas of ripe, yellow fruit, enriched by smoky notes and Mediterranean scrub. The palate proves racy, savory and highly enjoyable. Their 2017 Riesling is another wine entirely, expressing lovely, citrusy and flowery freshness with a spirited, almost sharp palate.

| | | |
|---|---|---|
| ○ A. A. Valle Isarco Riesling '17 | ♟♟ | 4 |
| ○ A. A. Valle Isarco Sylvaner Anjo '16 | ♟♟ | 4 |
| ○ A. A. Valle Isarco Grüner Veltliner '17 | ♟♟ | 3 |
| ○ A. A. Valle Isarco Kerner '17 | ♟♟ | 3 |
| ○ A. A. Valle Isarco Müller Thurgau '17 | ♟♟ | 3 |
| ○ A. A. Valle Isarco Sylvaner '17 | ♟♟ | 3 |
| ○ A. A. Valle Isarco Riesling '12 | ♟♟♟ | 3* |
| ○ A. A. Valle Isarco Riesling '11 | ♟♟♟ | 3* |
| ○ A. A. Valle Isarco Veltliner '10 | ♟♟♟ | 3* |
| ○ A. A. Valle Isarco Veltliner '09 | ♟♟♟ | 3* |
| ○ A. A. Valle Isarco Grüner Veltliner '16 | ♟♟ | 3* |
| ○ A. A. Valle Isarco Kerner '16 | ♟♟ | 3 |
| ○ A. A. Valle Isarco Riesling '16 | ♟♟ | 4 |
| ○ A. A. Valle Isarco Sylvaner '16 | ♟♟ | 3 |

# Stroblhof

LOC. SAN MICHELE
VIA PIGANÒ, 25
39057 APPIANO/EPPAN [BZ]
TEL. +39 0471662250
www.stroblhof.it

**CELLAR SALES**
**PRE-BOOKED VISITS**
**ANNUAL PRODUCTION** 40,000 bottles
**HECTARES UNDER VINE** 5.20

For more than three centuries Stroblhof has existed here in Appiano Monte. It is a splendid estate surrounded by lush green vineyards, located at around 500 meters above sea level, and a stone's throw from Costiera della Mendola. This mountain range channels the cool evening breezes and softens the surprisingly hot and sunny summer weather typical of this area. All winemaking is done in the small, functional cellar, and aims to enhance the finesse and personality intrinsic to the DNA of this territory's well-established white and red cultivars. In many ways their 2015 Pinot Nero Riserva is an unusual expression of Mazzon Hill, a bona fide cru for the cultivar. Its dense color already gives you an idea of its aromatic profile, which features small forest fruits, aromatic herbs and mineral notes pushing up from the background. In the mouth the wine is supported primarily by acidity. It unfolds crisply and elegantly. Their 2017 Pinot Bianco Strahler is a similar wine, though it opts for greater richness of fruit.

| | | |
|---|---|---|
| ● A. A. Pinot Nero Ris. '15 | ♟♟♟ | 6 |
| ○ A. A. Pinot Bianco Strahler '17 | ♟♟ | 4 |
| ○ A. A. Chardonnay Schwarzhaus '17 | ♟♟ | 4 |
| ● A. A. Pinot Nero Pigeno '15 | ♟♟ | 5 |
| ○ A. A. Sauvignon Nico '17 | ♟♟ | 4 |
| ○ A. A. Pinot Bianco Strahler '09 | ♟♟♟ | 3* |
| ● A. A. Pinot Nero Ris. '05 | ♟♟♟ | 5 |
| ○ A. A. Chardonnay Schwarzhaus '16 | ♟♟ | 4 |
| ○ A. A. Pinot Bianco Strahler '15 | ♟♟ | 3 |
| ● A. A. Pinot Nero Pigeno '14 | ♟♟ | 5 |
| ● A. A. Pinot Nero Pigeno '13 | ♟♟ | 5 |
| ● A. A. Pinot Nero Ris. '13 | ♟♟ | 6 |
| ○ A. A. Sauvignon Nico '16 | ♟♟ | 4 |
| ○ A. A. Sauvignon Nico '15 | ♟♟ | 4 |

# Taschlerhof - Peter Wachtler

Loc. Mara, 107
39042 Bressanone/Brixen [BZ]
Tel. +39 0472851091
www.taschlerhof.com

CELLAR SALES
PRE-BOOKED VISITS
ANNUAL PRODUCTION 30,000 bottles
HECTARES UNDER VINE 4.20

The Taschlerhof brand began in the early 1990s by supplying grapes to other cellars before moving to bottling their own wines. They went from an almost pedantic application of winemaking procedures to an equally rigorous interpretation of the wines, albeit with their own stylistic personality. Peter Wachtler is a most attentive grape grower who has demonstrated his in-depth knowledge of Eisack Valley's potential, and expressed it by way of his solid and charming range of wines. Sylvaner di Taschlerhof put in an excellent performance during our tastings, especially their 2016 Lahner. Made with grapes harvested late, it's a wine aged half in barrels and half in steel. The nose offers up fragrances of pear and flowers, which unfold on a crisp, long palate. Their 2017 'base wine' is more approachable and fresher, with aromas of fresh fruit and straw followed by a dynamic, savory palate. Their 2017 Riseling and Kerner also did well.

| | |
|---|---|
| ○ A. A. Valle Isarco Sylvaner Lahner '16 | ♟♟♟ 5 |
| ○ A. A. Valle Isarco Sylvaner '17 | ♟♟ 3* |
| ○ A. A. Riesling V. T. '15 | ♟♟ 4 |
| ○ A. A. Valle Isarco Kerner '17 | ♟♟ 4 |
| ○ A. A. Valle Isarco Riesling '17 | ♟♟ 4 |
| ○ A. A. Valle Isarco Riesling '14 | ♟♟♟ 4* |
| ○ A. A. Valle Isarco Sylvaner '15 | ♟♟♟ 3* |
| ○ A. A. Valle Isarco Kerner '16 | ♟♟ 4 |
| ○ A. A. Valle Isarco Kerner '15 | ♟♟ 4 |
| ○ A. A. Valle Isarco Riesling '16 | ♟♟ 4 |
| ○ A. A. Valle Isarco Riesling '15 | ♟♟ 4 |
| ○ A. A. Valle Isarco Sylvaner '16 | ♟♟ 3* |
| ○ A. A. Valle Isarco Sylvaner Lahner '15 | ♟♟ 4 |

# ★★Cantina Terlano

Via Silberleiten, 7
39018 Terlano/Terlan [BZ]
Tel. +39 0471257135
www.cantina-terlano.com

CELLAR SALES
PRE-BOOKED VISITS
ANNUAL PRODUCTION 1,000,000 bottles
HECTARES UNDER VINE 165.00

To understand why South Tyrol enjoys fame and the respect of professionals and enthusiasts alike, look no further than number 7 Via Silberleiten in Terlano. Over the decades, this estate has produced ageworthy wines with a rare and precise style that enhances the special bond between variety, vineyard and grower. Now more than a century after it was founded, it remains the most important interpreter of this unique enclave, dominated by rocks and minerals, on slopes that are challenging to cultivate (to say the least). Several of their wines delivered, starting with their Terlano Not Domus. The excellent 2015 vintage gave rise to vibrant aromas of yellow fruit, with mineral and spicy hints front and center on the wine's energetic, elegant palate. More than 10 years after vintage, it's as if time has stopped for their 2005 Pinot Bianco Rarità, while their 2016 Quarz and 2015 Vorberg feature their trademark power and precision.

| | |
|---|---|
| ○ A. A. Terlano Nova Domus Ris. '15 | ♟♟♟ 6 |
| ○ A. A. Terlano Pinot Bianco Rarità '05 | ♟♟ 8 |
| ○ A. A. Terlano Pinot Bianco Vorberg Ris. '15 | ♟♟ 5 |
| ○ A. A. Terlano Sauvignon Quarz '16 | ♟♟ 6 |
| ○ A. A. Gewürztraminer Lunare '16 | ♟♟ 6 |
| ○ A. A. Gewürztraminer Movado Andriano '16 | ♟♟ 5 |
| ○ A. A. Gewürztraminer Passito Juvelo Andriano '16 | ♟♟ 5 |
| ● A. A. Lagrein Porphyr Ris. '15 | ♟♟ 6 |
| ○ A. A. Pinot Grigio Andriano '17 | ♟♟ 2* |
| ● A. A. Pinot Nero Anrar Andriano Ris. '15 | ♟♟ 5 |
| ● A. A. Pinot Nero Montigl Ris. '15 | ♟♟ 5 |
| ○ A. A. Terlano Chardonnay Kreuth '16 | ♟♟ 4 |
| ○ A. A. Terlano Cl. '17 | ♟♟ 2* |
| ○ A. A. Terlano Sauvignon Winkl '17 | ♟♟ 3 |

# ★Tiefenbrunner

FRAZ. NICLARA
VIA CASTELLO, 4
39040 CORTACCIA/KURTATSCH [BZ]
TEL. +39 0471880122
www.tiefenbrunner.com

**CELLAR SALES**
**PRE-BOOKED VISITS**
**RESTAURANT SERVICE**
**ANNUAL PRODUCTION** 650,000 bottles
**HECTARES UNDER VINE** 78.00

Situated in the southernmost tip of the province of Bolzano, the Tiefenbrunner family winery is an historic estate now in its fifth generation. Today, the task of running the business falls to Cristof and his wife Sabine. They can count on a wide range of grape varieties, some grown on their own plots, which are concentrated between Niclara, Cortaccia and Magré, and others supplied by a consolidated network of grape growers. The winery produces four selections, all of which enhance the varietal and territorial nature of their wines. If we expected a great performance from their 2016 Feldmarschall, which hit the mark in terms of aromatic elegance and tension on the palate, it was difficult to image such a good showing from their 2015 Chardonnay Au Rls. A fresh deep wine in which fruit is enveloped by mineral and toasty notes, its palate is noble (to say the least) and taut. Their 2015 Sauvignon Rachtl is sulfurous and exotic, with a firm, savory palate.

| | |
|---|---|
| ○ A. A. Müller Thurgau Feldmarschall von Fenner '16 | ♛♛♛ 5 |
| ○ A. A. Chardonnay V. Au Ris. '15 | ♛♛ 3* |
| ○ A. A. Sauvignon Rachtl Ris. '15 | ♛♛ 4 |
| ● A. A. Cabernet Sauvignon Merlot Linticlarus Ris. '15 | ♛♛ 6 |
| ○ A. A. Gewürztraminer Turmhof '16 | ♛♛ 5 |
| ● A. A. Lagrein Linticlarus Ris. '15 | ♛♛ 5 |
| ○ A. A. Lagrein Turmhof '16 | ♛♛ 3 |
| ○ A. A. Pinot Bianco Anna '16 | ♛♛ 3 |
| ● A. A. Pinot Nero Linticlarus Ris. '15 | ♛♛ 6 |
| ● A. A. Pinot Nero Turmhof '16 | ♛♛ 3 |
| ○ A. A. Sauvignon Turmhof '16 | ♛♛ 4 |
| ○ A. A. Müller Thurgau Feldmarschall von Fenner '15 | ♛♛♛ 5 |
| ○ A. A. Müller Thurgau Feldmarschall von Fenner zu Fennberg '13 | ♛♛♛ 5 |

# ★★Cantina Tramin

S.DA DEL VINO, 144
39040 TERMENO/TRAMIN [BZ]
TEL. +39 0471096633
www.cantinatramin.it

**CELLAR SALES**
**PRE-BOOKED VISITS**
**ANNUAL PRODUCTION** 1,500,000 bottles
**HECTARES UNDER VINE** 250.00

Cantina Tramin is a cooperative of about 300 members located between the South Tyrolean Unterland and the Überetsch, in the southern part of Bolzano. A clear-cut vision from Willy Stürz and his staff has ensured the production of high-profile wines for several years now. Paying the utmost attention to the territorial suitability of different grape varieties, their results are astonishing. This holds true for both their basic level wines, as well as for their more ambitious ones. The latter feature a lustrous style that marries complexity and freshness. Knowledge and the age of their vines have gradually given rise to a rereading of their Gewürztraminer Nussbaumer, which is a bit less explosive than in the past but more elegant and taut. Its aromas are still intoxicating, while the 2016 features a more defined, supple palate. Their 2015 Terminum Vendemmia Tardiva features an exotic aromatic profile with candied aromas and a palate in which sweetness and savoriness proceed together. Their 2016 Pinot Grigio Unterebner is also worth noting.

| | |
|---|---|
| ○ A. A. Gewürztraminer Nussbaumer '16 | ♛♛♛ 5 |
| ○ A. A. Gewürztraminer Passito Terminum V. T. '15 | ♛♛ 7 |
| ○ A. A. Pinot Grigio Unterebner '16 | ♛♛ 5 |
| ○ A. A. Bianco Stoan '16 | ♛♛ 4 |
| ○ A. A. Gewürztraminer Roen V. T. '16 | ♛♛ 5 |
| ○ A. A. Gewürztraminer Selida '17 | ♛♛ 3 |
| ● A. A. Lagrein Urban Ris. '16 | ♛♛ 5 |
| ○ A. A. Pinot Bianco Moriz '17 | ♛♛ 2* |
| ● A. A. Pinot Nero Maglen '15 | ♛♛ 5 |
| ○ A. A. Sauvignon Pepi '17 | ♛♛ 3 |
| ● A. A. Schiava Freisinger '17 | ♛♛ 3 |
| ○ A. A. Gewürztraminer Nussbaumer '15 | ♛♛♛ 5 |
| ○ A. A. Gewürztraminer Nussbaumer '14 | ♛♛♛ 5 |
| ○ A. A. Gewürztraminer Nussbaumer '13 | ♛♛♛ 5 |
| ○ A. A. Gewürztraminer Nussbaumer '12 | ♛♛♛ 5 |

## Untermoserhof Georg Ramoser

VIA SANTA MADDALENA, 36
39100 BOLZANO/BOZEN
TEL. +39 0471975481
untermoserhof@rolmail.net

CELLAR SALES
PRE-BOOKED VISITS
ACCOMMODATION
ANNUAL PRODUCTION 30,000 bottles
HECTARES UNDER VINE 3.70

The Santa Maddalena hill is an enchanting place. A small ridge just outside the city of Bolzano, it is planted densely with vines, dotted with a few farms, and overlooked by a small church at the top. This unique setting is home to the Untermoserhof estate, consisting of a handful of hectares planted with Schiava and Lagrein, varieties that have been cultivated on these slopes for centuries. Georg Ramoser and his family produce fruity, close-focused wines with a distinctive style that are characterized by a lively palate. And only a Santa Maddalena could have turned out to be the most impressive wine in their selection. It's their 2016 Hueb, a wine that opens with aromas ranging from morello cherry to fines herbes, with a lovely hint of spices. It's a wine of medium structure that proves extraordinarily pleasant in the mouth, endowed as it is with juiciness and flavor. Their 2017 Santa Maddalena Classico, a more approachable and aromatic wine, also did quite well.

## ★Tenuta Unterortl Castel Juval

LOC. JUVAL, 1B
39020 CASTELBELLO CIARDES/KASTELBELL TSCHARS [BZ]
TEL. +39 0473667580
www.unterortl.it

CELLAR SALES
PRE-BOOKED VISITS
ANNUAL PRODUCTION 33,000 bottles
HECTARES UNDER VINE 4.00

Vinschgau Valley is a wide strip of land heading westward at the foot of the mountains near Merano. It is famed for its apple production and heroic viticulture, which is limited to just a few south-facing hectares on dizzyingly steep slopes. Martin and Gisela Aurich are two grape growers who love this land and its wines. They run the Unterortl estate, which comprises small plots ranging between 600 and 850 meters above sea level. The grapes cultivated are used to produce their Castel Juval range of wines, with Riesling as their forte. Right away, their 2016 Windbichel transmits all the freshness and vibrance of the territory. On the nose it features intense fragrances of tropical fruit and flowers, with a subtle, timid note of benzene that takes center stage on the wine's taut, electric palate. A long finish follows. Their 2017 Pinot Bianco is also quite good, opting for fragrance of fruit and savoriness on the palate. But their entire selection shined.

| | |
|---|---|
| ● A. A. Santa Maddalena Cl. Hueb '16 | ♔♔♔ 3* |
| ○ A. A. Chardonnay '16 | ♔♔ 3 |
| ● A. A. Santa Maddalena Cl. '17 | ♔♔ 3 |
| ● A. A. Lagrein '17 | ♔ 3 |
| ● A. A. Lagrein Scuro Ris. '03 | ♔♔♔ 4* |
| ● A. A. Lagrein Scuro Ris. '97 | ♔♔♔ 4* |
| ○ A. A. Chardonnay '15 | ♔♔ 3 |
| ● A. A. Lagrein Ris. '15 | ♔♔ 4 |
| ● A. A. Lagrein Ris. '13 | ♔♔ 5 |
| ● A. A. Lagrein Ris. '12 | ♔♔ 5 |
| ● A. A. Merlot Ris. '15 | ♔♔ 4 |
| ● A. A. Merlot Ris. '13 | ♔♔ 5 |
| ● A. A. Merlot Untermoserhof Ris. '11 | ♔♔ 4 |
| ● A. A. Santa Maddalena Cl. '14 | ♔♔ 3 |
| ● A. A. Santa Maddalena Cl. '13 | ♔♔ 2* |

| | |
|---|---|
| ○ A. A. Val Venosta Riesling Weingarten Windbichel '16 | ♔♔♔ 5 |
| ○ A. A. Val Venosta Pinot Bianco '17 | ♔♔ 2* |
| ○ A. A. Val Venosta Müller Thurgau '17 | ♔♔ 3 |
| ● A. A. Val Venosta Pinot Nero '15 | ♔♔ 5 |
| ○ A. A. Val Venosta Riesling '17 | ♔♔ 4 |
| ○ A. A. Val Venosta Riesling Gletscherschliff '17 | ♔♔ 4 |
| ○ A. A. Val Venosta Pinot Bianco Castel Juval '13 | ♔♔♔ 3* |
| ○ A. A. Val Venosta Pinot Bianco Castel Juval '12 | ♔♔♔ 3* |
| ○ A. A. Val Venosta Riesling '14 | ♔♔♔ 4* |
| ○ A. A. Val Venosta Riesling Castel Juval '11 | ♔♔♔ 4* |
| ○ A. A. Val Venosta Riesling Unterortl '15 | ♔♔♔ 4* |
| ○ A. A. Val Venosta Riesling Windbichel '15 | ♔♔♔ 5 |

# Cantina Produttori Valle Isarco

VIA COSTE, 50
39043 CHIUSA/KLAUSEN [BZ]
TEL. +39 0472847553
www.cantinavalleisarco.it

**CELLAR SALES**
**PRE-BOOKED VISITS**
**ANNUAL PRODUCTION** 900,000 bottles
**HECTARES UNDER VINE** 150.00
**SUSTAINABLE WINERY**

Cantina della Valle Isarco is the smallest cooperative in the region, which underlines the difficulties created by forced fragmentation of vineyard plots in this corner of Alto Adige. Elevations are high and the vineyards lie on slopes that become steeper and steeper, requiring Herculean effort from grower-members. The other side of the coin, however, is that these soils give rise to wines with great character. And thanks to the careful selection of such distinctive grapes, the reward is significantly added value for the area. Two wines from their Aristos line stood out during our most recent tastings. Their 2017 Grüner Veltliner expresses rich aromas with yellow fruit crossing notes of dried flowers and straw. In the mouth the wine proves firm and savory, endowed with a lovely, smoky length. Their 2016 Riesling is more complex with deep aromas and an energetic palate that features great tension and length.

# Von Blumen

FRAZ. POCHI, 18
39040 SALORNO/SALURN [BZ]
TEL. +39 0457230110
www.vonblumenwine.com

**CELLAR SALES**
**PRE-BOOKED VISITS**
**ANNUAL PRODUCTION** 38,000 bottles
**HECTARES UNDER VINE** 11.00
**SUSTAINABLE WINERY**

The Fugatti family winery is situated in Pochi di Salorno, a kind of large terrace overlooking Valdadige between 400 and 600 meters above sea level. They focus on cultivating classic the South Tyrolean varieties that have best adapted to soil conditions and climate here. This explains why their production is limited to just a handful of grape varieties. These are interpreted into a basic line styled on aromatic delicacy and depth of taste, in addition to their Flowers selections of core wines. Their 2016 Pinot Bianco, part of the second line, unleashes aromas of rennet apple and flowers, delicately lined by toasty and spicy notes. The palate privileges finesse and tension, making for one of the region's most convincing versions. Their Sauvignon also did quite well. It's a wine that opts for a mix of tropical and balsamic aromas, with an expansive, long palate. Among their newest wines, we most appreciated their fragrant and juicy 2017 Pinot Bianco.

| | |
|---|---|
| ○ A. A. Valle Isarco Grüner Veltliner Aristos '17 | ♟♟ 4 |
| ○ A. A. Valle Isarco Riesling Aristos '16 | ♟♟ 4 |
| ○ A. A. Valle Isarco Pinot Bianco Aristos '17 | ♟♟ 4 |
| ○ A. A. Valle Isarco Gewürztraminer Passito Nectaris '16 | ♟♟ 6 |
| ○ A. A. Valle Isarco Kerner Aristos '17 | ♟♟ 4 |
| ○ A. A. Valle Isarco Kerner Passito Nectaris '16 | ♟♟ 6 |
| ○ A. A. Valle Isarco Müller Thurgau Aristos '17 | ♟♟ 4 |
| ○ A. A. Valle Isarco Pinot Grigio Aristos '17 | ♟♟ 4 |
| ○ A. A. Valle Isarco Sauvignon Aristos '17 | ♟♟ 4 |
| ○ A. A. Valle Isarco Sylvaner Aristos '17 | ♟♟ 4 |
| ○ A. A. Valle Isarco Gewürztraminer Aristos '17 | ♟ 4 |
| ○ A. A. Valle Isarco Sylvaner Aristos '16 | ♟♟♟ 4* |
| ○ A. A. Valle Isarco Sylvaner Aristos '15 | ♟♟♟ 4* |

| | |
|---|---|
| ○ A. A. Pinot Bianco Flowers '16 | ♟♟ 5 |
| ○ A. A. Gewürztraminer '17 | ♟♟ 4 |
| ● A. A. Lagrein '16 | ♟♟ 4 |
| ○ A. A. Pinot Bianco '17 | ♟♟ 3 |
| ● A. A. Pinot Nero '17 | ♟♟ 3 |
| ○ A. A. Sauvignon '17 | ♟♟ 3 |
| ○ A. A. Sauvignon Flowers '16 | ♟♟ 5 |
| ○ A. A. Gewürztraminer '16 | ♟♟ 4 |
| ● A. A. Lagrein '15 | ♟♟ 4 |
| ○ A. A. Pinot Bianco '17 | ♟♟ 3 |
| ○ A. A. Pinot Bianco Flowers Selection '15 | ♟♟ 4 |
| ● A. A. Pinot Nero '16 | ♟♟ 4 |
| ○ A. A. Sauvignon Flowers Selection '15 | ♟♟ 5 |
| ○ A.A. Sauvignon '16 | ♟♟ 3 |

# ALTO ADIGE

## ★★Elena Walch

VIA A. HOFER, 1
39040 TERMENO/TRAMIN [BZ]
TEL. +39 0471860172
www.elenawalch.com

CELLAR SALES
PRE-BOOKED VISITS
RESTAURANT SERVICE
ANNUAL PRODUCTION 500,000 bottles
HECTARES UNDER VINE 33.00

In order to fully understand the work carried out at this historic Termeno winery by Elena Walch and her daughters, Julia and Karolina, you have to visit their new cellar. Here you can get a clear idea of their desire to leave nothing to chance, and at the same time bring out the best of what nature has to offer. It's also worth walking down to their vineyards to see how meticulously they are cultivated and to breathe in the air that caresses the hilly slopes in Kastelaz or Castel Ringberg. And Walch's two great crus gave rise to their most impressive wines. Their 2017 Gewürztraminer Kastelaz offers up vibrant aromas of candied citrus and tropical fruit. In the mouth it delivers for savoriness and harmony. Their 2015 Lagrein Castel Ringberg opts for power and precision, but we were most surprised by their 2016 Beyond the Clouds. It's a white made with Chardonnay that stands out for its aromas of medicinal herbs and spices.

| | | |
|---|---|---|
| ○ A. A. Bianco Beyond the Clouds '16 | ♟♟♟ | 6 |
| ○ A. A. Gewürztraminer V. Kastelaz '17 | ♟♟ | 5 |
| ● A. A. Lagrein V. Castel Ringberg Ris. '15 | ♟♟ | 5 |
| ○ A. A. Chardonnay Cardellino '17 | ♟♟ | 3 |
| ● A. A. Merlot V. Kastelaz Ris. '15 | ♟♟ | 6 |
| ● A. A. Pinot Nero Ludwig '15 | ♟♟ | 5 |
| ○ A. A. Sauvignon V. Castel Ringberg '17 | ♟♟ | 4 |
| ● Kermesse '15 | ♟♟ | 6 |
| ○ A. A. Gewürztraminer Kastelaz '13 | ♟♟♟ | 5 |
| ○ A. A. Gewürztraminer Kastelaz '12 | ♟♟♟ | 5 |
| ○ A. A. Gewürztraminer Kastelaz '11 | ♟♟♟ | 5 |
| ○ A. A. Gewürztraminer Kastelaz '10 | ♟♟♟ | 3* |
| ○ A. A. Gewürztraminer Kastelaz '09 | ♟♟♟ | 5 |
| ○ A. A. Gewürztraminer Kastelaz '08 | ♟♟♟ | 5 |
| ● A. A. Lagrein Castel Ringberg Ris. '11 | ♟♟♟ | 5 |

## ★Tenuta Waldgries

LOC. SANTA GIUSTINA, 2
39100 BOLZANO/BOZEN
TEL. +39 0471323603
www.waldgries.it

CELLAR SALES
PRE-BOOKED VISITS
ANNUAL PRODUCTION 65,000 bottles
HECTARES UNDER VINE 8.20

The Santa Maddalena hill to the northeast of Bolzano is a farming area of extraordinary beauty, literally a stone's throw from the city center. Christian Plattner's Waldgries winery is based here, comprising three estates with different vine growing qualities. The first, Santa Giustina, hosts Lagrein and Schiava Lagrein also plays a key role in the Ora vineyards, while the plots in Appiano are dedicated mostly to white grapes. Our last round of tastings saw a selection of precision, with some three wines delivering for their well-defined personality and adherence to the territory. Their 2015 Lagrein Mirell Riserva opts for power and elegance, thanks to careful work in the cellar which brings out the sophistication of a cultivar famous for being unwieldy. Their 2016 Pinot Bianco Isos shines for its vibrance and tension, while the 2017 Santa Maddalena Antheos is deliciously juicy.

| | | |
|---|---|---|
| ● A. A. Lagrein Mirell Ris. '15 | ♟♟♟ | 6 |
| ○ A. A. Pinot Bianco Isos '16 | ♟♟ | 4 |
| ● A. A. Santa Maddalena Cl. Antheos '17 | ♟♟ | 5 |
| ● A. A. Lagrein Ris. '15 | ♟♟ | 5 |
| ● A. A. Lagrein Roblinus de Waldgries '15 | ♟♟ | 8 |
| ● A. A. Moscato Rosa '15 | ♟♟ | 5 |
| ● A. A. Santa Maddalena Cl. '17 | ♟♟ | 3 |
| ○ A. A. Sauvignon Myra '17 | ♟♟ | 4 |
| ● A. A. Lagrein Mirell '09 | ♟♟♟ | 6 |
| ● A. A. Lagrein Scuro Mirell '08 | ♟♟♟ | 6 |
| ● A. A. Santa Maddalena Cl. Antheos '16 | ♟♟♟ | 5 |
| ● A. A. Santa Maddalena Cl. Antheos '13 | ♟♟♟ | 4* |
| ● A. A. Santa Maddalena Cl. Antheos '12 | ♟♟♟ | 4* |
| ● A. A. Santa Maddalena Cl. Antheos '11 | ♟♟♟ | 4* |

# Josef Weger

LOC. CORNAIANO
VIA CASA DEL GESÙ, 17
39050 APPIANO/EPPAN [BZ]
TEL. +39 0471662416
www.wegerhof.it

CELLAR SALES
PRE-BOOKED VISITS
ACCOMMODATION AND RESTAURANT SERVICE
ANNUAL PRODUCTION 80,000 bottles
HECTARES UNDER VINE 8.00

The history of the Weger family winery merges with that of Cornaiano and its vineyards. Over the centuries it has been at the forefront of activity, while remaining up-to-date on the production and business side of things. Today they remain firmly linked to this small town in the Überetsch, where gentle hills are densely planted with vines. The winery's cellar is located in rooms below street level, allowing the wines to rest for long periods before their release onto the market. The entire selection proved strong though there wasn't a single stand out. Our favorites come from their Maso delle Rose line, in particular their 2015 Merlot and 2016 Sauvignon. The former sees an interesting fusion of aromas of ripe fruit and medicinal herbs, while the mouth proves rich, crisp and juicy. The second impresses more for its harmony and dense savoriness on the palate than for its aromatic intensity.

| | |
|---|---|
| ○ A. A. Gewürztraminer Maso delle Rose '16 | 🍷🍷 3 |
| ● A. A. Merlot Maso delle Rose '15 | 🍷🍷 5 |
| ○ A. A. Pinot Bianco Maso delle Rose '16 | 🍷🍷 4 |
| ○ A. A. Sauvignon Maso delle Rose '16 | 🍷🍷 4 |
| ○ A. A. Sauvignon Myron '17 | 🍷🍷 2* |
| ● Joanni Maso delle Rose '16 | 🍷🍷 4 |
| ○ A. A. Müller Thurgau Pursgla '17 | 🍷 3 |
| ○ A. A. Gewürztraminer Artyo '16 | 🏆🏆 2* |
| ● A. A. Lagrein Stoa '15 | 🏆🏆 3 |
| ● A. A. Merlot Maso delle Rose '13 | 🏆🏆 5 |
| ○ A. A. Pinot Bianco Lithos '16 | 🏆🏆 3 |
| ○ A. A. Pinot Grigio Ried '16 | 🏆🏆 3 |
| ● A. A. Pinot Nero Johann '15 | 🏆🏆 3 |
| ○ A. A. Sauvignon Myron '16 | 🏆🏆 2* |

# Peter Zemmer

S.DA DEL VINO, 24
39040 CORTINA SULLA STRADA DEL VINO/KURTINIG [BZ]
TEL. +39 0471817143
www.peterzemmer.com

CELLAR SALES
PRE-BOOKED VISITS
ANNUAL PRODUCTION 500,000 bottles
HECTARES UNDER VINE 65.00

Peter Zemmer's winery is situated on the plain which follows the course of the Adige river, between Trento and Bolzano. The vineyards, however, extend across the area nearest the river, as well as on the eastern and western slopes of the mountains, reaching up to 800 meters above sea level. They cultivate a large number of hectares and produce two main lines. One is dedicated to monovarietals while the other is comprised of territorial wines, which are enhanced by the unique character of the soils and microclimates they are grown in. Kudos to their 2016 Pinot Grigio Giatl Riserva, which did an excellent job expressing the warmth of South Tyrolean Unterland, without a doubt one of the cultivar's territory's of reference. It's a wine that's vibrant in its aromas of pear and smoky nuances while the mouth delivers for its ability to balance power and suppleness. Their 2016 Chardonnay Crivelli Riserva is sunnier and more pervasive, representing a perfect fusion between the cultivar's trademark qualities and toastiness, with a juicy, charming palate.

| | |
|---|---|
| ○ A. A. Chardonnay Crivelli Ris. '16 | 🍷🍷 4 |
| ○ A. A. Pinot Grigio Giatl Ris. '16 | 🍷🍷 3* |
| ○ A. A. Gewürztraminer Frauenrigl '17 | 🍷🍷 3 |
| ● A. A. Lagrein Fruggl Ris. '16 | 🍷🍷 4 |
| ○ A. A. Müller Thurgau Caprile '17 | 🍷🍷 3 |
| ○ A. A. Pinot Bianco '17 | 🍷🍷 3 |
| ○ A. A. Pinot Grigio '17 | 🍷🍷 3 |
| ● A. A. Pinot Nero Rollhüt '17 | 🍷🍷 4 |
| ○ A. A. Riesling '17 | 🍷🍷 2* |
| ○ A. A. Sauvignon '17 | 🍷🍷 3 |
| ● Cortinie Rosso '17 | 🍷🍷 3 |
| ○ A. A. Chardonnay '17 | 🍷 2 |
| ○ A. A. Pinot Grigio Giatl Ris. '15 | 🏆🏆🏆 3* |
| ○ A. A. Chardonnay Crivelli Ris. '15 | 🏆🏆 4 |

## Weingut Martin Abraham

VIA MADERNETO, 29
39057 APPIANO/EPPAN [BZ]
TEL. +39 0471664192
www.weingutabraham.it

ANNUAL PRODUCTION 20,000 bottles
HECTARES UNDER VINE 3.00

| | | |
|---|---|---|
| ○ Gewürztraminer Upupa Orange '16 | ♥♥ | 4 |
| ○ Pinot Bianco In der Lamm '16 | ♥♥ | 3 |
| ○ Pinot Bianco Vom Muschelkalk '16 | ♥♥ | 3 |
| ● Pinot Nero '15 | ♥♥ | 3 |

## Baron Longo

VIA VAL DI FIEMME 30
39044 EGNA/NEUMARKT [BZ]
TEL. +39 0471 820007
www.baronlongo.com

ANNUAL PRODUCTION 30,000 bottles
HECTARES UNDER VINE 17.00

| | | |
|---|---|---|
| ● A. A. Cabernet Sauvignon Merlot Wellenburg '16 | ♥♥ | 4 |
| ● A. A. Lagrein Friedberg '16 | ♥♥ | 3 |
| ○ Solaris '17 | ♥♥ | 3 |

## Baron Widmann

ENDERGASSE, 3
39040 CORTACCIA/KURTATSCH [BZ]
TEL. +39 0471880092
www.baron-widmann.it

CELLAR SALES
PRE-BOOKED VISITS
ANNUAL PRODUCTION 35,000 bottles
HECTARES UNDER VINE 15.00

| | | |
|---|---|---|
| ● A. A. Cabernet Merlot Auhof '15 | ♥♥ | 4 |
| ○ A. A. Gewürztraminer '16 | ♥♥ | 3 |
| ○ A. A. Pinot Bianco '17 | ♥♥ | 3 |
| ○ A. A. Sauvignon '17 | ♥♥ | 3 |

## Befehlhof

VIA VEZZANO, 14
39028 SILANDRO/SCHLANDERS [BZ]
TEL. +39 0473742197
www.befehlhof.it

CELLAR SALES
PRE-BOOKED VISITS
ANNUAL PRODUCTION 7,000 bottles
HECTARES UNDER VINE 1.20

| | | |
|---|---|---|
| ○ Riesling '16 | ♥♥ | 3 |
| ● Zweigelt '15 | ♥♥ | 4 |
| ○ Jera '17 | ♥ | 3 |
| ● Pinot Nero '15 | ♥ | 2 |

## Bergmannhof

LOC. SAN PAOLO
RIVA DI SOTTO, 46
39050 APPIANO/EPPAN [BZ]
TEL. +39 0471637082
www.bergmannhof.it

CELLAR SALES
PRE-BOOKED VISITS
ANNUAL PRODUCTION 13,000 bottles
HECTARES UNDER VINE 2.20

| | | |
|---|---|---|
| ● A.A. Lagrein Der Bergmann Ris. '15 | ♥♥ | 4 |
| ○ A. A. Chardonnay Der Bergmann Ris. '16 | ♥♥ | 4 |
| ● A.A. Lagrein '17 | ♥♥ | 4 |
| ○ A. A. Chardonnay '17 | ♥ | 2 |

## Tenuta Ceo

VIA ASILO, 9
39040 SALORNO/SALURN [BZ]
TEL. +39 329 9377504
www.ceo-wine.i

ANNUAL PRODUCTION 20,000 bottles
HECTARES UNDER VINE 2.00

| | | |
|---|---|---|
| ○ A. A. Chardonnay '16 | ♥♥ | 5 |
| ● A. A. Merlot '16 | ♥♥ | 5 |
| ○ A. A. Pinot Grigio '16 | ♥♥ | 5 |
| ● A. A. Lagrein '16 | ♥ | 5 |

## Egger-Ramer

VIA GUNCINA, 5
39100 BOLZANO/BOZEN
TEL. +39 0471280541
www.egger-ramer.com

CELLAR SALES
PRE-BOOKED VISITS
ANNUAL PRODUCTION 120,000 bottles
HECTARES UNDER VINE 14.00

| | |
|---|---|
| ● A. A. Lagrein Kristan '16 | ♙♙ 3 |
| ● A. A. Lagrein Kristan Ris. '15 | ♙♙ 3 |
| ● A. A. Pinot Nero '17 | ♙♙ 2* |
| ○ A. A. Sauvignon '17 | ♙ 2 |

## Eichenstein

KATZENSTEINSTRASSE, 34
39012 MERANO/MERAN [BZ]
TEL. +39 3442820179
www.eichenstein.it

ANNUAL PRODUCTION 25,000 bottles
HECTARES UNDER VINE 4.50
SUSTAINABLE WINERY

| | |
|---|---|
| ○ A. A. Riesling Eichenstein '16 | ♙♙ 3 |
| ⊙ A. A. Schiava Rosé Carina '17 | ♙ 3 |

## Fliederhof - Stefan Ramoser

LOC. SANTA MADDALENA DI SOTTO, 33
39100 BOLZANO/BOZEN
TEL. +39 0471979048
www.fliederhof.it

CELLAR SALES
PRE-BOOKED VISITS
ANNUAL PRODUCTION 25,000 bottles
HECTARES UNDER VINE 2.40

| | |
|---|---|
| ● A. A. Lagrein Ris. '15 | ♙♙ 5 |
| ● A. A. Santa Maddalena Cl. '17 | ♙♙ 3 |
| ● A. A. Santa Maddalena Cl. Gran Marie '16 | ♙♙ 4 |
| ○ Peperum '17 | ♙ 3 |

## Haidenhof

VIA MONTELEONE, 17
39010 CERMES/TSCHERMS [BZ]
TEL. +39 0473562392
www.haidenhof.it

CELLAR SALES
PRE-BOOKED VISITS
RESTAURANT SERVICE
ANNUAL PRODUCTION 30,000 bottles
HECTARES UNDER VINE 3.50

| | |
|---|---|
| ○ A. A. Gewurztraminer '17 | ♙♙ 3 |
| ○ A. A. Kerner '16 | ♙♙ 3 |
| ○ A. A. Pinot Bianco '17 | ♙♙ 3 |
| ○ A. A. Sauvignon '17 | ♙♙ 3 |

## Himmelreichhof

LOC. CIARDEF
VIA CONVENTO, 15A
39020 CASTELBELLO CIARDES/KASTELBELL TSCHARS [BZ]
TEL. +39 0473624417
www.himmelreich-hof.info

ANNUAL PRODUCTION 20,000 bottles
HECTARES UNDER VINE 3.50

| | |
|---|---|
| ○ A .A. Val Venosta Pinot Bianco '17 | ♙♙ 4 |
| ● A. A. Val Venosta Pinot Nero '16 | ♙♙ 5 |
| ○ A. A. Val Venosta Riesling Geieregg '17 | ♙♙ 4 |
| ○ A .A. Val Venosta Riesling '16 | ♙ 4 |

## Hof Gandberg
## Thomas Niedermayr

S.DA CASTEL PALÙ, 1
39057 APPIANO/EPPAN [BZ]
TEL. +39 0471664152
www.thomas-niedermayr.com

CELLAR SALES
PRE-BOOKED VISITS
ANNUAL PRODUCTION 10,000 bottles
HECTARES UNDER VINE 1.50
VITICULTURE METHOD Certified Organic

| | |
|---|---|
| ○ Abendrot T. N. 06 '15 | ♙♙ 4 |
| ○ Bronner T. N. 04 '16 | ♙♙ 3 |
| ○ Solaris T. N. 14 '16 | ♙♙ 5 |

## Kandlerhof

VIA SANTA MADDALENA DI SOTTO, 30
39100 BOLZANO/BOZEN
TEL. +39 0471973033
www.kandlerhof.it

ANNUAL PRODUCTION 20,000 bottles
HECTARES UNDER VINE 2.00

| | |
|---|---|
| ● A. A. Santa Maddalena Cl. '17 | ♟♟ 3 |
| ● A. A. Lagrein '17 | ♟♟ 3 |
| ● A. A. Santa Maddalena Cl. Schloterpöck '16 | ♟♟ 4 |

## Larcherhof - Spögler

VIA RENCIO, 82
39100 BOLZANO/BOZEN
TEL. +39 0471365034
larcherhof@yahoo.de

CELLAR SALES
PRE-BOOKED VISITS
ANNUAL PRODUCTION 30,000 bottles
HECTARES UNDER VINE 5.00

| | |
|---|---|
| ● A. A. Lagrein '16 | ♟♟ 3 |
| ● A. A. Lagrein Rivelaun Ris. '15 | ♟♟ 4 |
| ● A. A. Merlot '16 | ♟♟ 3 |
| ○ A. A. Pinot Grigio '17 | ♟ 3 |

## Lehengut

VIA DELLE FONTI, 2
39020 COLSANO
TEL. +39 3487562676
www.lehengut.it

ANNUAL PRODUCTION 10,000 bottles
HECTARES UNDER VINE 3.00
VITICULTURE METHOD Certified Organic

| | |
|---|---|
| ● A .A. Val Venosta Pinot Nero Ris. '16 | ♟♟ 3 |
| ○ A. A. Val Venosta Pinot Bianco '17 | ♟♟ 3 |
| ○ A. A. Val Venosta Riesling '17 | ♟♟ 3 |

## Lieselehof
## Werner Morandell

VIA KARDATSCH, 6
39052 CALDARO/KALTERN [BZ]
TEL. +39 3299011593
www.lieselehof.com

CELLAR SALES
PRE-BOOKED VISITS
ACCOMMODATION
ANNUAL PRODUCTION 20,000 bottles
HECTARES UNDER VINE 3.00
VITICULTURE METHOD Certified Organic

| | |
|---|---|
| ○ Julian '17 | ♟♟ 3 |
| ○ Pinot Bianco '17 | ♟♟ 3 |
| ○ Sweet Claire '17 | ♟♟ 6 |
| ○ Vino del Passo '17 | ♟♟ 6 |

## Thomas Pichler

FRAZ. VILLA DI MEZZO
VIA DELLE VIGNE, 4A
39052 CALDARO/KALTERN [BZ]
TEL. +39 0471963094
www.thomas-pichler.it

CELLAR SALES
PRE-BOOKED VISITS
ANNUAL PRODUCTION 15,000 bottles
HECTARES UNDER VINE 2.00

| | |
|---|---|
| ○ A. A. Chardonnay Furioso '16 | ♟♟ 5 |
| ● A. A. Lago di Caldaro Cl. Sup. Olte Reben '17 | ♟♟ 3 |
| ● A. A. Lagrein Sond Ris. '16 | ♟♟ 5 |

## Pitzner

VIA CORNEDO, 15
39053 CORNEDO ALL'ISARCO/KARNEID [BZ]
TEL. +39 3384521694
www.pitzner.it

ANNUAL PRODUCTION 16,000 bottles
HECTARES UNDER VINE 3.00

| | |
|---|---|
| ○ A. A. Pinot Grigio Finell '17 | ♟♟ 4 |
| ○ Cuvée Marthò '17 | ♟♟ 3 |
| ● A. A. Lagrein Scharfegg '17 | ♟ 5 |
| ● Hexagon HX15 '15 | ♟ 7 |

## Plonerhof - Erhard Tutzer

VIA TRAMONTANA, 29
39020 MARLENGO/MARLING [BZ]
TEL. +39 0471975559
www.weingut-plonerhof.it

ANNUAL PRODUCTION 5,000 bottles
HECTARES UNDER VINE 1.30

| | |
|---|---|
| ● A. A. Pinot Nero '17 | ♙♙ 3 |
| ● A. A. Pinot Nero Exclusiv Ris. '15 | ♙♙ 3 |
| ○ Nörder Cuvée Blanc '16 | ♙♙ 4 |
| ○ A. A. Sauvignon '17 | ♙ 4 |

## Röckhof - Konrad Augschöll

VIA SAN VALENTINO, 22
39040 VILLANDRO/VILLANDERS [BZ]
TEL. +39 0472847130
roeck@rolmail.net

CELLAR SALES
PRE-BOOKED VISITS
RESTAURANT SERVICE
ANNUAL PRODUCTION 20,000 bottles
HECTARES UNDER VINE 3.50

| | |
|---|---|
| ○ A. A. Valle Isarco Veltliner Gail Fuass '17 | ♙♙ 3 |
| ○ Riesling Viel Anders '16 | ♙♙ 3 |
| ○ A. A. Valle Isarco Müller Thurgau '17 | ♙ 3 |

## Schloss Englar

LOC. PIGENO, 42
39057 APPIANO/EPPAN [BZ]
TEL. +39 0471662628
www.weingut-englar.com

ANNUAL PRODUCTION 15,000 bottles
HECTARES UNDER VINE 7.00

| | |
|---|---|
| ○ A. A. Pinot Bianco '17 | ♙♙ 3 |
| ● A. A. Pinot Nero '15 | ♙♙ 3 |
| ○ A. A. Riesling '17 | ♙♙ 4 |
| ○ A. A. Sauvignon '16 | ♙ 4 |

## Schloss Plars

FRAZ. PLARS DI MEZZO, 25
39022 LAGUNDO/ALGUND [BZ]
TEL. +39 0473448472
www.schlossplars.com

CELLAR SALES
PRE-BOOKED VISITS
ACCOMMODATION
ANNUAL PRODUCTION 12,000 bottles
HECTARES UNDER VINE 2.00

| | |
|---|---|
| ○ A. A. Pinot Bianco Pataun '17 | ♙♙ 3 |
| ○ A. A. Sauvignon Marzan '16 | ♙♙ 3 |
| ● A. A. Lagrein Merlot Yhrn '16 | ♙ 3 |
| ● A. A. Meranese Wenger '16 | ♙ 3 |

## Tenuta Seeperle

LOC. SAN GIUSEPPE AL LAGO, 28
39052 CALDARO/KALTERN [BZ]
TEL. +39 0471960158
www.seeperle.it

ANNUAL PRODUCTION 15,000 bottles
HECTARES UNDER VINE 2.00

| | |
|---|---|
| ○ A. A. Lago di Caldaro Cl. Sup. Scheinheilig '17 | ♙♙ 4 |
| ○ A. A. Lago di Caldaro Cl. Sup. Waschecht '17 | ♙♙ 4 |

## St. Quirinus - Robert Sinn

VIA PIANIZZA DI SOPRA, 4B
39052 CALDARO/KALTERN [BZ]
TEL. +39 3298085003
www.st-quirinus.it

CELLAR SALES
PRE-BOOKED VISITS
ACCOMMODATION
ANNUAL PRODUCTION 12,000 bottles
HECTARES UNDER VINE 2.50
VITICULTURE METHOD Certified Organic

| | |
|---|---|
| ○ A. A. Chardonnay Bergwerk '16 | ♙♙ 3 |
| ● A. A. Merlot Quirinus '16 | ♙♙ 3 |
| ○ Planties Weiss '17 | ♙♙ 3 |
| ● A. A. Lagrein '17 | ♙ 3 |

## Thurnhof - Andreas Berger

LOC. ASLAGO
VIA CASTEL FLAVON, 7
39100 BOLZANO/BOZEN
TEL. +39 0471288460
www.thurnhof.com

CELLAR SALES
PRE-BOOKED VISITS
ANNUAL PRODUCTION 25,000 bottles
HECTARES UNDER VINE 3.50

| | |
|---|---|
| ● A. A. Cabernet Sauvignon Weinegg Ris. '15 | ♟♟ 5 |
| ● A. A. Lagrein Ris. '15 | ♟♟ 4 |
| ○ A. A. Sauvignon 800 '17 | ♟♟ 3 |
| ● A. A. Lagrein '17 | ♟ 3 |

## Thomas Unterhofer

LOC. PIANIZZA DI SOPRA, 5
39052 CALDARO/KALTERN [BZ]
TEL. +39 0471669133
www.weingut-unterhofer.com

CELLAR SALES
PRE-BOOKED VISITS
ANNUAL PRODUCTION 12,000 bottles
HECTARES UNDER VINE 3.00

| | |
|---|---|
| ○ A. A. Pinot Bianco '17 | ♟♟ 2* |
| ● A. A. Santa Maddalena '17 | ♟♟ 3 |
| ○ A. A. Sauvignon '17 | ♟♟ 2* |
| ○ Reitl Weiss '17 | ♟ 3 |

## Vivaldi - Arunda

VIA JOSEF-SCHWARZ, 18
39010 MELTINA/MÖLTEN [BZ]
TEL. +39 0471668033
www.arundavivaldi.it

CELLAR SALES
PRE-BOOKED VISITS
ANNUAL PRODUCTION 90,000 bottles
HECTARES UNDER VINE 12.00

| | |
|---|---|
| ○ A. A. Spumante Extra Brut<br>   Arunda Ris. '12 | ♟♟ 7 |
| ○ A. A. Spumante Extra Brut Cuvée<br>   Marianna Arunda | ♟♟ 5 |

## Wilhelm Walch

VIA A. HOFER, 1
39040 TERMENO/TRAMIN [BZ]
TEL. +39 0471860172
www.walch.it

CELLAR SALES
PRE-BOOKED VISITS
ANNUAL PRODUCTION 600,000 bottles
HECTARES UNDER VINE 73.00

| | |
|---|---|
| ○ A. A. Pinot Bianco '17 | ♟♟ 3* |
| ● A. A. Cabernet Sauvignon Prestige '16 | ♟♟ 4 |
| ○ A. A. Chardonnay Pilat '17 | ♟ 2 |
| ○ A. A. Müller Thurgau '17 | ♟ 2 |

## Wassererhof

LOC. NOVALE DI FIÉ, 21
39050 FIÉ ALLO SCILIAR/VÖLS AM SCHLERN [BZ]
TEL. +39 0471724114
www.wassererhof.com

CELLAR SALES
PRE-BOOKED VISITS
RESTAURANT SERVICE
ANNUAL PRODUCTION 35,000 bottles
HECTARES UNDER VINE 4.00

| | |
|---|---|
| ● A. A. Cabernet Ris. '15 | ♟♟ 3 |
| ● A. A. Santa Maddalena Cl. '17 | ♟♟ 3 |
| ○ A. A. Sauvignon '17 | ♟♟ 3 |

## Weinberghof Christian Bellutti

IN DER AU, 4A
39040 TERMENO/TRAMIN [BZ]
TEL. +39 0471863224
www.weinberg-hof.com

ANNUAL PRODUCTION 20,000 bottles
HECTARES UNDER VINE 2.80

| | |
|---|---|
| ○ A. A. Gewürztraminer '17 | ♟♟ 3 |
| ○ A. A. Gewürztraminer Plon '17 | ♟♟ 3 |
| ○ A. A. Pinot Grigio '17 | ♟♟ 3 |
| ● A. A. Lagrein '17 | ♟ 3 |

# VENETO

Veneto's terroir vary greatly, but viticulture has always been a prominent form of agriculture in the region. Apart from its southernmost corner, Veneto's appellations comprise both plains and hills, from gravelly soil to terrain rich in clay and volcanic material, and grapes ranging from international cultivar to the various native grapes with which it's been identified for centuries. Over the course of history, various areas within it have known their peaks and valleys, but today two are undoubtedly the most noteworthy, representing Italian wine the world over: Valpolicella, with its Superiore and Amarone, and Conegliano Valdobbiadene, which has made Prosecco and Italian sparkling wine in general its flagship products. As Veneto's most active DOC appellations, they've seen an accelerated pace of development, both in terms of quality and when it comes to the commercial side of things. A number of Valpolicellas earned Tre Bicchieri in this edition, and we're pleased to observe how the style of their Superiore is finding a more authentic identity, limiting the process of partial grape drying and giving rise to wines defined by their tension and aromatic finesse. It's a similar story with Amarone, where drying hasn't been entirely renounced, but a more complete, less soft profile is pursued. Conegliano Valdobbiadene's Prosecco Bruts are increasingly convincing, testifying to their commitment to the savoriness and delicacy of the grape, without relying too much on sugar. The Colli Euganei hills continue to serve as a bastion of vigorous, elegant reds, as evidenced perfectly by Giordano Emo Capodilista's Baon, while in the nearby Colli Berici it's Dal Maso who once again shines with a sumptuous Merlot Casara Roveri. In the eastern part of the region, an increasing number of producers are eschewing pre-set models, choosing instead to develop and promote their territory with originality. The Sutto and Cescon families are accompanied by Serafini and Vidotto in speaking for an area that does more than just Prosecco, showing great potential for still wines as well. Finally, Soave, Custoza and Bardolina are defined by their adherence to a clear notion of elegance, eschewing over-concentration or cultivar from outside local tradition.

# A Mi Manera

Fraz. Lison
via Caduti per la Patria, 29
30026 Portogruaro [VE]
Tel. +39 336592660
www.vinicolamimanera.com

CELLAR SALES
PRE-BOOKED VISITS
ANNUAL PRODUCTION 42,000 bottles
HECTARES UNDER VINE 7.00

For some years now Toni Bigai has been working in Lison Pramaggiore, a strip of land that perfectly joins the Adriatic coast with the Venetian Pre-Alps. It's an area rich in clay that's often characterized by hot summers and cold winters. Here history has brought together various international grapes, but many vine growers find that the area's traditional cultivar deliver the best results. And so it is that Tai and Malvasia are cultivated for the whites, Refosco for their reds, in addition Merlot in those cases where it adapted well to the territory. Only a Malvasia and Tai, both 2017s, could have led their selection during our last round of tastings. The former, which we preferred, offers up aromas ranging from fresh fruit to Mediterranean shrub, with good follow through to a savory palate and nice tension. The second is a bit simpler on the nose, characterized by a rich and properly assertive palate. Among their reds, their excellent 2017 Merlot proved noteworthy.

| | | |
|---|---|---|
| ● Cabernet '17 | ▼▼ 3 | |
| ○ Malvasia '17 | ▼▼ 3 | |
| ○ Malvasia Anfora '17 | ▼▼ 4 | |
| ● Merlot '17 | ▼▼ 2* | |
| ○ Tai '17 | ▼▼ 3 | |
| ○ A Mi Manera Bianco Decimo Tercero | ▼ 3 | |
| ● A Mi Manera Rosso Anfora '17 | ▼ 3 | |
| ● A Mi Manera Rosso Rls. '15 | ▼ 3 | |
| ● A Mi Manera Rosso Undecimo | ▼ 3 | |
| ○ Chardonnay '17 | ▼ 3 | |
| ○ Tai Anfora '17 | ▼ 4 | |
| ○ Malvasia '16 | ♀♀ 3 | |
| ○ Malvasia '15 | ♀♀ 3 | |
| ● Merlot '15 | ♀♀ 2* | |
| ○ Tai '16 | ♀♀ 3 | |
| ○ Tai '15 | ♀♀ 3 | |

# Stefano Accordini

Fraz. Cavalo
loc. Camparol, 10
37022 Fumane [VR]
Tel. +39 0457760138
www.accordinistefano.it

CELLAR SALES
PRE-BOOKED VISITS
ANNUAL PRODUCTION 120,000 bottles
HECTARES UNDER VINE 13.00

Tiziano and Daniele Accordini began their adventure into winemaking many years ago when the two acted on Stefano's desire to purchase five hectares of terrain at Cà Bessole (Negrar). More terrain followed, with an area on the Fumane hills (in the district of Cavalo) and Sant'Ambrogio (Monte). Their vineyards are situated primarily in Alta Valpolicella, along with their new, lovely cellar. Their style of winemaking, however, has never veered off course, focusing on the richness of fruit and generous taste. Their 2016 Recioto Classico Acinatico put in an excellent performance, offering up vibrant notes of ripe cherry, pepper and aromatic herbs. In the mouth the wines proves sweet, but it surprises for its compactness and tension, which are supported by a close-knit, spirited, tannic weave. Despite the difficult year, their 2014 Amarone Classico Acinatico manages to bring out the richness of ripe fruit on an energetic, potent palate characterized by notable savoriness.

| | | |
|---|---|---|
| ● Recioto della Valpolicella Cl. Acinatico '16 | ▼▼ 5 | |
| ● Amarone della Valpolicella Cl. Acinatico '14 | ▼▼ 7 | |
| ● Paxxo '16 | ▼▼ 4 | |
| ● Valpolicella Cl. Sup. Ripasso Acinatico '16 | ▼▼ 3 | |
| ● Valpolicella Cl. '17 | ▼ 2 | |
| ● Amarone della Valpolicella Cl. Acinatico '95 | ♀♀♀ 5 | |
| ● Amarone della Valpolicella Cl. Vign. Il Fornetto '95 | ♀♀♀ 5 | |
| ● Recioto della Valpolicella Cl. Acinatico '04 | ♀♀♀ 6 | |
| ● Recioto della Valpolicella Cl. Acinatico '00 | ♀♀♀ 8 | |

# Adami

FRAZ. COLBERTALDO
VIA ROVEDE, 27
31020 VIDOR [TV]
TEL. +39 0423982110
www.adamispumanti.it

**CELLAR SALES**
**PRE-BOOKED VISITS**
**ANNUAL PRODUCTION** 700,000 bottles
**HECTARES UNDER VINE** 12.00

The winery being led by brothers Armando and Franco Adami is firmly rooted in the agricultural values and traditions of Alta Marca Trevigiana. It's not a coincidence that the area was among the first to propose a proper cru: Riva Giardino Asciutto, a veritable amphitheatre purchased by grandpa Abele almost a century ago. It's the crown jewel of a selection that has grown over time, thanks in part to the family's vineyards in Credazzo, an area characterized by its clay-rich soil and steep slopes. And these two vineyards give rise to their most interesting wines. Their 2017 Col Credas features a fresh aromatic profile dominated by sensations of white fruit and enriched by a subtle, herbaceous note. In the mouth it proves decisive and gutsy, endowed with a taut and almost sharp palate. Their 2017 Giardino is sunnier and ripe, an amenable wine. It's redolent of fresh fruit and citrus, with a delicately plush palate that disappears across its long and crisp finish.

# Ida Agnoletti

LOC. SELVA DEL MONTELLO
VIA SACCARDO, 55
31040 VOLPAGO DEL MONTELLO [TV]
TEL. +39 0423621555
www.agnoletti.it

**CELLAR SALES**
**PRE-BOOKED VISITS**
**ANNUAL PRODUCTION** 50,000 bottles
**HECTARES UNDER VINE** 7.00

Even if Ida Agnoletti has only been working twenty years in Valpago del Montello, she's deeply bonded to the territory and its agricultural traditions. Her small estate has resisted the monovarietal temptations brought about by the Prosecco boom, leaving space for a varied range of cultivar. Her ability to bring out the best of the iron-rich soil here continues to grow, in particular when it comes to Bordeaux varieties, which she interprets through a style that privileges finesse and tension. Their 2015 Seneca, for example, is a blend made primarily with Merlot from a plot that goes back to World War II. The nose features aromas of plums enriched by the presence of medicinal herbs and spices. These follow through on a firm but never overreaching palate that's supported by fresh acidity and tannins that are as smooth as they are forward. Their 2015 Vita Life Is Red is a Bordeaux made with Malbec, Syrah and Petit Verdot that exhibits more vivid fruit and an energetic, generous palate.

| | |
|---|---|
| ○ Valdobbiadene Rive di Colbertaldo Asciutto Vign. Giardino '17 | ♥♥ 3* |
| ○ Valdobbiadene Rive di Farra di Soligo Brut Col Credas '17 | ♥♥ 3* |
| ○ Cartizze | ♥♥ 5 |
| ○ Valdobbiadene Brut Bosco di Gica | ♥♥ 3 |
| ○ Valdobbiadene Extra Dry Dei Casel | ♥♥ 3 |
| ○ Prosecco di Treviso Extra Dry Garbel | ♥ 2 |
| ○ Prosecco Frizzante sul Lievito | ♥ 2 |
| ○ Valdobbiadene Rive di Colbertaldo Asciutto Vign. Giardino '16 | ♥♥♥ 3* |
| ○ Valdobbiadene Rive di Farra di Soligo Brut Col Credas '13 | ♥♥♥ 3* |
| ○ Valdobbiadene Rive di Farra di Soligo Brut Col Credas '12 | ♥♥♥ 3* |
| ○ Valdobbiadene Rive di Farra di Soligo Brut Col Credas '16 | ♀♀ 3* |

| | |
|---|---|
| ● Montello e Colli Asolani Merlot La Ida '16 | ♥♥ 2* |
| ● Montello e Colli Asolani Recantina '16 | ♥♥ 2* |
| ● Montello e Colli Asolani Rosso Seneca '15 | ♥♥ 3 |
| ● Vita Life is Red '15 | ♥♥ 3 |
| ● Montello e Colli Asolani Cabernet Sauvignon Love Is... '16 | ♥ 2 |
| ○ PSL Always Frizzante | ♥ 2 |
| ● Montello e Colli Asolani Cabernet Sauvignon Love Is... '15 | ♀♀ 2* |
| ● Montello e Colli Asolani Merlot '14 | ♀♀ 2* |
| ● Montello e Colli Asolani Merlot '13 | ♀♀ 2* |
| ● Montello e Colli Asolani Merlot La Ida '14 | ♀♀ 2* |
| ● Montello e Colli Asolani Merlot La Ida '15 | ♀♀ 2* |
| ● Montello e Colli Asolani Recantina '15 | ♀♀ 2* |
| ● Seneca '13 | ♀♀ 3 |
| ● Vita Life is Red '13 | ♀♀ 3 |

## ★★★Allegrini

VIA Via Giare, 5
37022 Fumane [VR]
Tel. +39 0456832011
www.allegrini.it

CELLAR SALES
PRE-BOOKED VISITS
ACCOMMODATION AND RESTAURANT SERVICE
ANNUAL PRODUCTION 1,000,000 bottles
HECTARES UNDER VINE 150.00
SUSTAINABLE WINERY

The Allegrini family have been central players in Valpolicella winemaking for at least five centuries, and have built, over time, a formidable cluster of wineries with roots in various important national territories. Their 'casa madre' stills serves as a fulcrum, producing a complete range of traditional and international wines thanks to prestigious estates like Palazzo della Torre, La Grola, La Poja, Villa Cavarena, Fieramonte and Monte dei Galli. Franco and Marilisa's well-known viticultural patrimony pursues clearness of expression and fruity vigor. Today their are joined by young Francesco, Caterina and Silvia. The 2014 vintage is a difficult puzzle to figure out, but at Allegrini the result was a year to remember, starting with their Amarone Classico, which features its trademark fragrance and fruit, spices and aromatic herbs. In the mouth it shows greater tension and pluck than usual, pointing up the year's fresh climate. Their 2013 Poja is an elegant and potent wine, while their 2015 Recioto Giovanni Allegrini proves buoyant and balanced.

| | | |
|---|---|---|
| ● Amarone della Valpolicella Cl. '14 | ♛♛♛ | 8 |
| ● La Poja '13 | ♛♛ | 8 |
| ● Recioto della Valpolicella Cl. Giovanni Allegrini '15 | ♛♛ | 7 |
| ● La Grola '15 | ♛♛ | 5 |
| ● Palazzo della Torre '15 | ♛♛ | 3 |
| ○ Soave '17 | ♛♛ | 3 |
| ● Valpolicella Cl. '17 | ♛♛ | 3 |
| ● Amarone della Valpolicella Cl. '13 | ♛♛♛ | 8 |
| ● Amarone della Valpolicella Cl. '12 | ♛♛♛ | 8 |
| ● Amarone della Valpolicella Cl. '11 | ♛♛♛ | 8 |
| ● Amarone della Valpolicella Cl. '10 | ♛♛♛ | 8 |
| ● Amarone della Valpolicella Cl. '09 | ♛♛♛ | 8 |
| ● Amarone della Valpolicella Cl. '08 | ♛♛♛ | 8 |
| ● Amarone della Valpolicella Cl. '07 | ♛♛♛ | 8 |
| ● Amarone della Valpolicella Cl. '06 | ♛♛♛ | 8 |
| ● Amarone della Valpolicella Cl. '05 | ♛♛♛ | 7 |

## Andreola

FRAZ. Col San Martino
VIA Cavre,19
31010 Farra di Soligo [TV]
Tel. +39 0438989379
www.andreola.eu

CELLAR SALES
PRE-BOOKED VISITS
ANNUAL PRODUCTION 900,000 bottles
HECTARES UNDER VINE 77.00
SUSTAINABLE WINERY

Stefano Pola has managed to steer the family winery (founded by his father, Nazzareno, in the mid-1980s) in a new direction, revolutionizing it in just a few short seasons. What was once a small-time winery has grown into a large, forward-thinking agricultural producer that today is dedicated almost entirely to the Valdobbiadene Prosecco Superiore. It's a wine that's interpreted with a style that points up aromatic expression, joining it with surprisingly easy drinkability. Their new Rive line features four high-quality offerings, including their 2017 Rive di Refrontolo Col del Forno Brut, a wine that stands out for an aromatic profile dominated by apple and pear. Their Cartizze is a buoyant wine in its expression of fruit, and characterized by a pervasive, creamy palate. But it's their classic Brut Dirupo, the house speciality, that most impressed. Made with select grapes cultivated on the steep hilltops, it has fruit, savory elegance and class. Tre Bicchieri.

| | | |
|---|---|---|
| ○ Valdobbiadene Brut Dirupo '17 | ♛♛♛ | 3* |
| ○ Valdobbiadene Rive Di Refrontolo Brut Col Del Forno '17 | ♛♛ | 3* |
| ○ Cartizze | ♛♛ | 5 |
| ○ Valdobbiadene Extra Dry Dirupo | ♛♛ | 3 |
| ○ Valdobbiadene Rive di Col San Martino Extra Dry 26° Primo '17 | ♛♛ | 3 |
| ○ Valdobbiadene Rive di Rolle Dry Vigne del Piai '17 | ♛♛ | 3 |
| ○ Valdobbiadene Rive di Soligo Extra Dry Mas de Fer '17 | ♛♛ | 3 |
| ○ Valdobbiadene Dry Sesto Senso | ♛ | 3 |
| ○ Valdobbiadene Prosecco Frizzante Casilir | ♛ | 3 |
| ○ Valdobbiadene Prosecco Tranquillo Romit '17 | ♛ | 3 |
| ○ Valdobbiadene Rive Di Refrontolo Brut Col Del Forno '16 | ♛♛ | 3 |

## ★Roberto Anselmi

VIA SAN CARLO, 46
37032 MONTEFORTE D'ALPONE [VR]
TEL. +39 0457611488
www.anselmi.eu

CELLAR SALES
PRE-BOOKED VISITS
RESTAURANT SERVICE
ANNUAL PRODUCTION 700,000 bottles
HECTARES UNDER VINE 70.00

Much of the peak of Mount Foscarino, an area of Soave that has long been associated with grand crus, belongs to the Anselmi family. After a long path forward, Roberto (helped by his children Lisa and Tommaso) decided to give life to new vineyards on this splendid, volcanic hill at 300 meters above sea level. At their lovely cellar in San Carlo (Monteforte d'Alpone), nothing is left to chance, resulting in a style that is rich and unmistakable, and focused primarily on Garganega. Their 2017 Capitel Croce is a wine that delivers in all respects, a white with fine, flowery fragrances and aromas of white fruit. These follow through on a firm palate that goes all in on elegance, brought out by savoriness and a fresh, acidic tension. Their 2017 Capitel Foscarino opts for greater aromatic presence accompanied by hints of tropical fruit, notes of elderflower and jasmine. Their 2017 San Vincenzo is a fresh, dynamic and highly drinkable wine.

| | | |
|---|---|---|
| ○ Capitel Croce '17 | ♔♔♔ | 3* |
| ○ Capitel Foscarino '17 | ♔♔ | 3 |
| ● Realda '15 | ♔♔ | 3 |
| ○ San Vincenzo '17 | ♔♔ | 2* |
| ○ Capitel Croce '15 | ♕♕♕ | 3* |
| ○ Capitel Croce '09 | ♕♕♕ | 3* |
| ○ Capitel Croce '06 | ♕♕♕ | 3 |
| ○ Capitel Croce '05 | ♕♕♕ | 3 |
| ○ Capitel Croce '04 | ♕♕♕ | 3 |
| ○ Capitel Croce '03 | ♕♕♕ | 3 |
| ○ Capitel Croce '02 | ♕♕♕ | 3* |
| ○ Capitel Croce '01 | ♕♕♕ | 3 |
| ○ Capitel Croce '00 | ♕♕♕ | 3 |
| ○ Capitel Croce '99 | ♕♕♕ | 3* |
| ○ Recioto dei Capitelli '85 | ♕♕♕ | 8 |
| ○ Recioto di Soave I Capitelli '96 | ♕♕♕ | 5 |

## Antolini

VIA PROGNOL, 22
37020 MARANO DI VALPOLICELLA [VR]
TEL. +39 0457755351
www.antolinivini.it

CELLAR SALES
PRE-BOOKED VISITS
ACCOMMODATION
ANNUAL PRODUCTION 60,000 bottles
HECTARES UNDER VINE 9.00
SUSTAINABLE WINERY

Pier Paolo and Stefano Antolini's lovely winery was founded just a few years ago. It's operating in one of Valpolicella's most interesting territories: the Marano Valley. Among the areas that branch throughout the 'classic zone' it's one that usually gives rise to reds with greater aromatic freshness and dynamism of the palate. Here these are interpreted with great personality, in a small selection that's dedicated almost entirely to the area's traditional wines with an eye towards their acidic profile and development on the palate. Their Valpolicella Sup. Persegà made a sparkling debut with a 2016 that just missed out on a gold. It's an elegant yet gutsy wine in its aromatic expression of wild fruit and pepper. On the palate it proves energetic and taut, well supported by a savory, linear backbone. In terms of their Amarone we point out their excellent 2014 Moròpio, a wine that exhibits ripe, complex fruit with a full palate that unfolds nicely.

| | | |
|---|---|---|
| ● Valpolicella Cl. Sup. Persegà '16 | ♔♔ | 3* |
| ● Amarone della Valpolicella Cl. Moròpio '14 | ♔♔ | 8 |
| ● Corvina '15 | ♔♔ | 4 |
| ● Valpolicella Cl. Sup. Ripasso '15 | ♔♔ | 5 |
| ● Valpolicella Cl. '17 | ♔ | 3 |
| ● Amarone della Valpolicella Cl. Ca' Coato '12 | ♕♕ | 8 |
| ● Amarone della Valpolicella Cl. Moròpio '13 | ♕♕ | 8 |
| ● Amarone della Valpolicella Cl. Moròpio '12 | ♕♕ | 8 |
| ● Corvina '13 | ♕♕ | 4 |
| ● Recioto della Valpolicella Cl. '15 | ♕♕ | 6 |
| ● Recioto della Valpolicella Cl. '13 | ♕♕ | 6 |
| ● Recioto della Valpolicella Cl. '11 | ♕♕ | 5 |

# Albino Armani

VIA CERADELLO, 401
37020 DOLCÈ [VR]
TEL. +39 0457290033
www.albinoarmani.com

**CELLAR SALES**
**PRE-BOOKED VISITS**
**ANNUAL PRODUCTION** 900,000 bottles
**HECTARES UNDER VINE** 220.00
**SUSTAINABLE WINERY**

Albino Armani's historic winery is situated in Dolcé, on the border between the province of Verona and Trento. In addition to vineyards in Val d'Adige the winery has estates in Valpolicella and Marca Trevigiana, not to mention Vallagarina (southern Trentino) and Grave. Tradition, dedication and eclectic skill come together to give life to a wide range of classic northeastern wines (made with both local and international varieties), still and sparkling whites, as well as great red wines for aging. Albino Armani hasn't been active in Valpolicella for long, but the results achieved get more notable by the year. Their 2013 Amarone is a red with ripe, spicy aromas dominated by fruit preserves. Its potent palate is well-managed and its finish proves warm and pervasive. In terms of Valdadige, we once again appreciated their Foja Tonda, a red that features aromas of fruit and spices, and a palate that proves firm and long.

| | | |
|---|---|---|
| ● Amarone della Valpolicella Cl. Cuslanus '13 | | ♟♟ 6 |
| ○ Campo Napoleone Sauvignon '17 | | ♟♟ 2* |
| ● Valdadige Terra dei Forti Foja Tonda '14 | | ♟♟ 3 |
| ○ Valdadige Pinot Grigio Corvara '17 | | ♟ 2 |
| ○ Valdadige Terra dei Forti Pinot Grigio Colle Ara '17 | | ♟ 2 |
| ● Amarone della Valpolicella Cl. '12 | | ♟♟ 5 |
| ● Amarone della Valpolicella Cl. Cuslanus '12 | | ♟♟ 6 |
| ● Valdadige Terra dei Forti Foja Tonda Casetta '13 | | ♟♟ 3 |
| ○ Valdadige Terra dei Forti Pinot Grigio Colle Ara '16 | | ♟♟ 2* |
| ● Valpolicella Cl. Sup. Egle '14 | | ♟♟ 2* |
| ● Valpolicella Cl. Sup. Ripasso '15 | | ♟♟ 3 |

# Barollo

VIA RIO SERVA, 4B
31022 PREGANZIOL [TV]
TEL. +39 0422633014
www.barollo.com

**CELLAR SALES**
**PRE-BOOKED VISITS**
**ANNUAL PRODUCTION** 88,000 bottles
**HECTARES UNDER VINE** 45.00
**SUSTAINABLE WINERY**

Even if it was founded fewer than twenty years ago, the winery led by brothers Marco and Nicola Barollo has quickly become an important benchmark in the district of Preganzol. Their primary goal is to provide a snapshot of this unique territory and so their production remains limited, despite their 50 hectares of terrain. It's an area situated halfway between the Alto Adriatico and the eastern Dolomites, and it's captured in the winery's 'genius loci': its variegated ampelography, elegant style and eschewal of false trends. Their 2016 Frank! is a perfect example of their vision. It's a red made with Cabernet Franc that draws on the cultivar's trademark vibrant, spicy nuances and aromas of black fruit, while leaving a faint herbaceous note on the background, conferring freshness and lightness. On the palate the wine comes through full but gradually slims down as it moves towards its long and slender finish, perfectly supported by smooth, sweet tannins. Their 2016 Chardonnay also did well.

| | | |
|---|---|---|
| ● Frank! '16 | | ♟♟ 4 |
| ○ Alfredo Barollo M. Cl. Brut Ris. '12 | | ♟♟ 5 |
| ○ Chardonnay '16 | | ♟♟ 4 |
| ● Venezia Merlot Frater '17 | | ♟♟ 3 |
| ○ Pinot Bianco '17 | | ♟ 3 |
| ○ Prosecco di Treviso Extra Dry '17 | | ♟ 2 |
| ○ Sauvignon '17 | | ♟ 3 |
| ○ Venezia Chardonnay Frater '17 | | ♟ 3 |
| ○ Alfredo Barollo M. Cl. Brut Ris. '11 | | ♟♟ 5 |
| ● Frank! '15 | | ♟♟ 4 |
| ● Frank! '14 | | ♟♟ 4 |
| ● Frank! '13 | | ♟♟ 4 |
| ○ Manzoni Bianco '16 | | ♟♟ 3 |
| ○ Manzoni Bianco '15 | | ♟♟ 3 |
| ○ Piave Chardonnay '15 | | ♟♟ 4 |
| ○ Piave Chardonnay '14 | | ♟♟ 4 |

# Le Battistelle

FRAZ. BROGNOLIGO
VIA SAMBUCO, 110
37032 MONTEFORTE D'ALPONE [VR]
TEL. +39 0456175621
www.lebattistelle.it

**CELLAR SALES**
**PRE-BOOKED VISITS**
**ANNUAL PRODUCTION** 22,000 bottles
**HECTARES UNDER VINE** 9.00
**SUSTAINABLE WINERY**

Gelmino and Cristina del Bosco's lovely winery has developed in the heart of classic Soave, immersed in the black hills that evoke long past volcanic eruptions. Theirs is an artisanal winery that draws on a series of very old vineyards spread out across a series plots, like pieces of a puzzle laid out across this historic appellation. Naturally, Garganega takes center stage in a selection that's certainly worth following thanks to its richness, typicity and character. Their 2016 Roccolo del Durlo put in a notable performance. This Soave offered a year after vintage just missed out on a gold. On the nose it offers up vibrant notes of yellow fruit, dried flowers and Mediterranean shrub. The palate is crisp and assertive, expressing all the character of Garganega cultivated on the high hills. Their Soave Battistelle of the same year opts for fresher, more approachable aromas, while in the mouth it delivers for fragrance and savoriness.

# ★Lorenzo Begali

VIA CENGIA, 10
37020 SAN PIETRO IN CARIANO [VR]
TEL. +39 0457725148
www.begaliwine.it

**CELLAR SALES**
**PRE-BOOKED VISITS**
**ANNUAL PRODUCTION** 90,000 bottles
**HECTARES UNDER VINE** 12.00

Situated on the slopes of Castelrotto, in the heart of Valpolicella Classica, the district of Cengia hosts the Begali family's cellar, as well as some of their vineyards (they also have elevated plots in Monte Ca' Bianca and Masua, both of which are also in San Pietro in Cariano). Year in, year out, Lorenzo manages to transform this viticultural patrimony into veritable gems characterized by power and rigor. In addition to his wife, Adriana, Lorenzo is helped by his children, Tiliana and Giordano, an agricultural family that brings nobility to their work thanks to their high-quality selection. Their 2013 Amarone Monte Ca' Bianca offers up deep fragrances that unfold little by little. First comes red fruit, then spicy notes and finally fresh nuances of medicinal herbs. These confer lightness to a close-woven, assertive palate supported by a nice acidic push. The difficult 2014 vintage marked their Amarone Classico with flowery and balsamic aromas followed by a crisp, slender palate.

| | |
|---|---|
| ○ Soave Cl. Roccolo del Durlo '16 | ♟♟ 3* |
| ○ Soave Cl. Le Battistelle '16 | ♟♟ 3 |
| ○ Soave Cl. Montesei '17 | ♟♟ 2* |
| ○ Soave Cl. Battistelle '14 | ♟♟ 3 |
| ○ Soave Cl. Le Battistelle '15 | ♟♟ 3 |
| ○ Soave Cl. Montesei '16 | ♟♟ 2* |
| ○ Soave Cl. Montesei '10 | ♟♟ 2* |
| ○ Soave Cl. Roccolo del Durlo '15 | ♟♟ 3* |
| ○ Soave Cl. Roccolo del Durlo '14 | ♟♟ 3 |

| | |
|---|---|
| ● Amarone della Valpolicella Cl. Monte Ca' Bianca '13 | ♟♟♟ 8 |
| ● Amarone della Valpolicella Cl. '14 | ♟♟ 6 |
| ● Tigiolo '14 | ♟♟ 5 |
| ● Valpolicella Cl. '17 | ♟ 2 |
| ● Amarone della Valpolicella Cl. Monte Ca' Bianca '12 | ♟♟♟ 8 |
| ● Amarone della Valpolicella Cl. Monte Ca' Bianca '11 | ♟♟♟ 8 |
| ● Amarone della Valpolicella Cl. Monte Ca' Bianca '10 | ♟♟♟ 8 |
| ● Amarone della Valpolicella Cl. Vign. Monte Ca' Bianca '09 | ♟♟♟ 8 |
| ● Amarone della Valpolicella Cl. Vign. Monte Ca' Bianca '08 | ♟♟♟ 8 |

## ★Cav. G. B. Bertani

VIA ASIAGO, 1
37023 GREZZANA [VR]
TEL. +39 0458658444
www.bertani.net

CELLAR SALES
PRE-BOOKED VISITS
ANNUAL PRODUCTION 2,100,000 bottles
HECTARES UNDER VINE 200.00
SUSTAINABLE WINERY

There's no doubt that the image of this large Grezzana winery, founded in 1857 by brothers Giovan Battista and Gaetano Bertani, has been bound up with Amarone Classico. Nevertheless, as of late we see increasing attention to the other wines produced on their large, sprawling estates (Novare, Valpantena, Soave, Garda), especially their vintage Valpolicella, made from only select vineyards so as to bring out the originality, acidity and tension of the territory's historic grape varieties. Their 2017 is a worthy example, a version that points up the attributes of a flowery, racy Valpolicella. Their 2010 Amarone, however, is still champion, a wine that amazes for the delicacy of its aromas, smooth yet potent, supported by acidity and almost salty vein that confers expansion without weighing down the palate. Their enticing 2015 Secco Vintage proves spicy and wild on the nose, assertive on the palate.

| | | |
|---|---|---|
| ● Amarone della Valpolicella Cl. '10 | ♟♟♟ | 8 |
| ● Secco Bertani Vintage '15 | ♟♟ | 4 |
| ● Amarone della Valpolicella Valpantena '15 | ♟♟ | 7 |
| ○ Soave Sereole '17 | ♟♟ | 3 |
| ○ Soave Vintage '16 | ♟♟ | 4 |
| ● Valpolicella '17 | ♟♟ | 3 |
| ● Valpolicella Cl. Sup. Ognisanti '16 | ♟♟ | 5 |
| ● Amarone della Valpolicella Cl. '09 | ♟♟♟ | 8 |
| ● Amarone della Valpolicella Cl. '08 | ♟♟♟ | 8 |
| ● Amarone della Valpolicella Cl. '07 | ♟♟♟ | 8 |
| ● Amarone della Valpolicella Cl. '06 | ♟♟♟ | 8 |
| ● Amarone della Valpolicella Cl. '05 | ♟♟♟ | 8 |
| ● Amarone della Valpolicella Cl. '04 | ♟♟♟ | 8 |
| ● Amarone della Valpolicella Cl. '03 | ♟♟♟ | 8 |
| ● Amarone della Valpolicella Cl. '01 | ♟♟♟ | 8 |
| ● Valpolicella Cl. Sup. Vign. Ognisanti '06 | ♟♟♟ | 4* |

## BiancaVigna

LOC. OGLIANO
VIA MONTE NERO, 8
31015 CONEGLIANO [TV]
TEL. +39 0438788403
www.biancavigna.it

CELLAR SALES
PRE-BOOKED VISITS
ANNUAL PRODUCTION 600,000 bottles
HECTARES UNDER VINE 30.20
SUSTAINABLE WINERY

In the dense hills that rise up north of Conegliano we find Elena and Enrico Mochetta's lovely cellar. It's a young winery that sprang up in the early 1900s, when grandfather Genesio purchased the first vineyards in San Gallo. The estate was further developed by father Luigi, with plots throughout the area, including veritable pearls like the vineyards in Rive di Collalto, Soligo and Ogliano. Theirs is a prestigious selection founded on a style that brings together the fragrant lightness of Prosecco with solidity and rigor. Once again their 2017 Rive di Ogliano leads the way. It's a Prosecco with fine, flowery aromas and fragrances of white fruit that lengthen along a taut, energetic palate. Its prickle is perfectly integrated, caressing with precision and delicacy. Their 2017 Rive di Soligo is more timid on the nose. It's a wine characterized by a crisp, assertive palate that renders it well-suited to gastronomic purposes.

| | | |
|---|---|---|
| ○ Conegliano Valdobbiadene Rive di Ogliano Brut Nature '17 | ♟♟♟ | 3* |
| ○ Conegliano Valdobbiadene Rive di Soligo Dosaggio Zero '17 | ♟♟ | 3* |
| ○ Conegliano Valdobbiadene Brut '17 | ♟♟ | 3 |
| ○ Conegliano Valdobbiadene Brut Bio | ♟♟ | 3 |
| ○ Conegliano Valdobbiadene Extra Dry '17 | ♟♟ | 3 |
| ○ Brut Nature Sui Lieviti | ♟ | 3 |
| ○ Prosecco Frizzante | ♟ | 2 |
| ○ Prosecco Tranquillo '17 | ♟ | 2 |
| ○ Conegliano Valdobbiadene Rive di Ogliano Brut Nature '16 | ♟♟♟ | 3* |
| ○ Conegliano Valdobbiadene Brut Rive di Soligo '15 | ♟♟ | 3* |
| ○ Conegliano Valdobbiadene Rive di Soligo Brut Dosaggio Zero '16 | ♟♟ | 3 |

# Bisol

FRAZ. SANTO STEFANO
VIA FOLLO, 33
31049 VALDOBBIADENE [TV]
TEL. +39 0423900138
www.bisol.it

**CELLAR SALES**
**PRE-BOOKED VISITS**
**ANNUAL PRODUCTION** 1,800,000 bottles
**HECTARES UNDER VINE** 126.00

For some years now this historic Valdobbiadene winery has been part of the Lunelli family's operations, and it continues to be a bedrock for Prosecco Superiore, thanks to the precious support of the Bisol family and a large estate that spans Cartizze, Rive di Guia and Campea. They focus on a somewhat limited number of wines, despite large production volumes, with a selection that is extremely faithful to the varieties used and that highlights their attributes through an emphasis on pleasant, balanced taste. They've reworked the packaging of their entire selection, stopped production of certain wines and introduced new offerings that correspond to individual vineyards. In light of these changes, their 2017 Rive di Campea Extra Dry stands out. It's a sparkling wine that highlights the flowery and fruity subtleness of Glera, making for a savory, light and extraordinarily pleasant palate. Their 2017 Rive di Guida Relio Brut is fresher on the nose and resolute in the mouth, but their entire selection shines.

| | |
|---|---|
| ○ Valdobbiadene Extra Dry Rive di Campea '17 | ♟♟ 4 |
| ○ Cartizze '17 | ♟♟ 4 |
| ○ Valdobbiadene Brut Crede '17 | ♟♟ 4 |
| ○ Valdobbiadene Brut Rive di Guia Relio '17 | ♟♟ 4 |
| ○ Valdobbiadene Brut Jeio | ♟ 2 |
| ○ Valdobbiadene Extra Dry Molera '17 | ♟ 3 |
| ○ Cartizze '15 | ♔♔ 5 |
| ○ Cartizze Brut Private '13 | ♔♔ 5 |
| ○ Cartizze Brut Private Fermentato in Bottiglia '14 | ♔♔ 5 |
| ○ Relio Extra Brut M. Cl. Private '10 | ♔♔ 6 |
| ○ Valdobbiadene Brut Crede '16 | ♔♔ 4 |
| ○ Valdobbiadene Extra Dry Molera '16 | ♔♔ 3 |
| ○ Valdobbiadene Extra Dry Vign. del Fol '16 | ♔♔ 4 |

# Bolla

FRAZ. PEDEMONTE
VIA A. BOLLA, 3
37029 SAN PIETRO IN CARIANO [VR]
TEL. +39 0456836555
www.bolla.it

**CELLAR SALES**
**PRE-BOOKED VISITS**
**ANNUAL PRODUCTION** 9,000,000 bottles
**HECTARES UNDER VINE** 185.00

Founded by Abela Bolla in the late 1800s, this large Pedemonte winery is one of Gruppo Italiano Vini's crown jewels. Indeed, the producer has been integral for the success of Veneto's wines throughout the world, with a style that's always well-calibrated to each typology. Both in their lighter, racier interpretations and their classic, sought-after wines, they've stayed faithful to the territory of origin (Valpolicella, Soave, Custoza, Bardolino, Valdadige, Lugana, Conegliano-Valdobbiadene). Once again their Amarone Le Origini, a 2012 reserve wine, leads the way. It's a wine that manages to balance young integrity of fruit and the evolved complexity of more traditional wines. It's a dual track that follows through on a potent but never showy palate that features harmony and depth. Their elegant and full 2015 Soave Classico Superiore Tufaie also proves quite interesting.

| | |
|---|---|
| ● Amarone della Valpolicella Cl. Le Origini Ris. '12 | ♟♟ 7 |
| ● Amarone della Valpolicella Cl. '13 | ♟♟ 5 |
| ● Bardolino Cl. La Doria '17 | ♟♟ 2* |
| ○ Soave Cl. Retrò '17 | ♟♟ 2* |
| ○ Soave Cl. Sup. Tufaie '16 | ♟♟ 2* |
| ⊙ Bardolino Chiaretto Cl. La Canestraia '17 | ♟ 2 |
| ● Creso '15 | ♟ 4 |
| ● Valpolicella Cl. Il Calice '17 | ♟ 2 |
| ● Amarone della Valpolicella Cl. Le Origini Ris. '11 | ♔♔ 6 |
| ● Creso '13 | ♔♔ 4 |
| ● Valpolicella Cl. Sup. Ripasso Le Poiane '14 | ♔♔ 4 |
| ● Valpolicella Cl. Sup. Ripasso Le Poiane '13 | ♔♔ 4 |

# Borgo Stajnbech

VIA BELFIORE, 109
30020 PRAMAGGIORE [VE]
TEL. +39 0421799929
www.borgostajnbech.com

CELLAR SALES
PRE-BOOKED VISITS
ANNUAL PRODUCTION 90,000 bottles
HECTARES UNDER VINE 15.00

Immersed in the stretch of land that separates the Adriatic from the Pre-Alps of Trevigiano, the Valent family's winery is an attentive interpreter of the area's classic wines. Stajnbeck means 'stonebrook', though it was baptized with the name Belfiore, an area of Pramaggiore that's well-known for its calcareous clay soil. Giuliano and Adriana's vineyards are concentrated here, with the couple using environmentally-friendly methods to cultivate a variety of native and international grape varieties, giving life to wines rich in personality. Their 2016 Bianco Stajnbech is a Chardonnay made with grapes from their Belfiore vineyard in Pizzo. The nose features vibrant notes of ripe fruit perfectly accompanied by spices. An oaky background and a full palate are well-supported by rich savoriness and a fresh, acidic thrust. Their 2016 Merlot, another intriguing wine, features balsamic and spicy sensations, and a juicy, supple palate.

| | |
|---|---|
| ● Merlot '16 | ▼▼ 3 |
| ○ Pinot Grigio '17 | ▼▼ 2* |
| ● Refosco P. R. '16 | ▼▼ 2* |
| ○ Stajnbech Bianco '16 | ▼▼ 3 |
| ○ Bosco della Donna Sauvignon '17 | ▼ 3 |
| ● Stajnbech Rosso '15 | ▼ 3 |
| ○ Bianco Stajnbech '13 | ♔♔ 3 |
| ○ Lison Cl. 150 '15 | ♔♔ 3 |
| ○ Lison Cl. 150 '14 | ♔♔ 3 |
| ○ Lison-Pramaggiore Cl. 150 '13 | ♔♔ 3 |
| ● Malbech '16 | ♔♔ 2* |
| ● Refosco P. R. '14 | ♔♔ 2* |
| ● Rosso Stajnbech '13 | ♔♔ 3 |
| ○ Sauvignon Bosco della Donna '15 | ♔♔ 3 |
| ○ Stajnbech Bianco '15 | ♔♔ 3 |

# Borgoluce

LOC. MUSILE, 2
31058 SUSEGANA [TV]
TEL. +39 0438435287
www.borgoluce.it

CELLAR SALES
PRE-BOOKED VISITS
ACCOMMODATION AND RESTAURANT SERVICE
ANNUAL PRODUCTION 250,000 bottles
HECTARES UNDER VINE 70.00

Looking at the entrance to Susegana, if it weren't for the small building near their head office and sales point, it would seem that nothing has changed here in recent years. In reality, however, this is just the tip of the iceberg for the new cellar built by the Collalto and Giustiniani families. Indeed, the structure is entirely below ground level so as to manage all phases of production with an eye towards energy savings and minimal environmental impact. Prosecco, interpreted with precision and character, continues to occupy the lion's share of their production efforts. Their 2017 Rive di Collalto Brut had an excellent day during our tastings. It's a Vadobbiadene that manages to express the territory while maintaining an enticing, approachable profile, as one would expect from a Treviso sparkler. On the nose it's dominated by white fruit, a precious note of medicinal herbs and herbaceous aromas. In the mouth it's firm enough to support its crisp, dry palate, making it perfect for gastronomic purposes.

| | |
|---|---|
| ○ Valdobbiadene Rive di Collalto Brut '17 | ▼▼ 3* |
| ○ Valdobbiadene Brut | ▼▼ 3 |
| ○ Valdobbiadene Extra Dry | ▼▼ 3 |
| ○ Valdobbiadene Rive di Collalto Extra Dry '17 | ▼▼ 3 |
| ○ Valdobbiadene Rive di Collalto Brut '16 | ♔♔ 2* |
| ○ Valdobbiadene Rive di Collalto Brut '15 | ♔♔ 2* |
| ○ Valdobbiadene Rive di Collalto Brut '14 | ♔♔ 2* |
| ○ Valdobbiadene Rive di Collalto Brut '13 | ♔♔ 2* |
| ○ Valdobbiadene Rive di Collalto Extra Dry '16 | ♔♔ 2* |
| ○ Valdobbiadene Rive di Collalto Extra Dry '14 | ♔♔ 2* |
| ○ Valdobbiadene Rive di Collalto Extra Dry '13 | ♔♔ 2* |

# Borin Vini & Vigne

Fraz. Monticelli
via dei Colli, 5
35043 Monselice [PD]
Tel. +39 042974384
www.viniborin.it

**CELLAR SALES**
**PRE-BOOKED VISITS**
**ANNUAL PRODUCTION** 105,000 bottles
**HECTARES UNDER VINE** 28.00

Over the years the Borin family has pushed for increased growth, enlarging their vineyards towards the hills and adding new production phases. Today Gianni and Teresa are accompanied by Francesco and Giampaolo; together they are an enthusiastic and close-knit team attending to a varied selection of wines made with grapes from Arquà Petrarca and Monticelli di Monselice. Such prestigious crus from the Colli Euganei come through in an unmistakable style that's capable of bringing together richness and harmony. Their Cabernet Sauvignon Mons Silicis is a 2015 reserve wine that offers up a vibrant note of ripe red fruit, proving full and enticing. Its aromatic richness carries over to a robust palate, supported by nice acidity and smooth tannins. In terms of their whites, we appreciated their 2016 Corte Borin most of all. It's a Manzoni Bianco with a tropical aromatic profile and a generous, long palate.

| | | |
|---|---|---|
| ● Colli Euganei Cabernet Sauvignon Mons Silicis Ris. '15 | ♟♟ 4 | |
| ○ Colli Euganei Manzoni Bianco Corte Borin '16 | ♟♟ 3* | |
| ○ Colli Euganei Chardonnay V. Bianca '16 | ♟♟ 3 | |
| ○ Colli Euganei Fior d'Arancio Fiore di Gaia '17 | ♟♟ 2* | |
| ● Colli Euganei Merlot Rocca Chiara Ris. '15 | ♟♟ 4 | |
| ● Syrah Coldivalle '15 | ♟♟ 3 | |
| ○ Colli Euganei Fior d'Arancio Spumante | ♟ 3 | |
| ○ Colli Euganei Pinot Bianco Monte Archino '17 | ♟ 2 | |
| ○ Sauvignon '17 | ♟ 3 | |
| ● Colli Euganei Cabernet Sauvignon Mons Silicis Ris. '12 | ♟♟ 4 | |
| ● Colli Euganei Rosso Zuan '15 | ♟♟ 3* | |

# Bortolomiol

via Garibaldi, 142
31049 Valdobbiadene [TV]
Tel. +39 04239749
www.bortolomiol.com

**CELLAR SALES**
**PRE-BOOKED VISITS**
**RESTAURANT SERVICE**
**ANNUAL PRODUCTION** 1,800,000 bottles
**HECTARES UNDER VINE** 5.00
**SUSTAINABLE WINERY**

The historic brand founded by Giuliano Bortolomiol after World War II has made decisive changes over the last decade, thanks in part to the work of daughters Maria, Elena, Elvira, Luisa and Gluliana. Together they have transformed a winery dedicated to Prosecco into a producer that brings out this sparkling wine's originality while also exploring its potential. As is often the case in Conegliano Valdobbiadene, the winery only owns and cultivates a small part of its vineyards, with the remaining quantities of grapes entrusted to a close-knit group of local vine growers. The grapes used in their 2016 Motus Vitae are cultivated in San Pietro di Barbozza. It's a Valdobbiadene with a ripe, complex profile in which fruit crosses notes of dried flowers and Mediterranean scrubland. In the mouth it lengthens thanks gracefully and decisively, finishing with tension and pluck. Their 2017 Brut Prior also delivered. It's a more outgoing wine on the nose, with a palate that manages to confer fullness while maintaining lightness and fragrance.

| | |
|---|---|
| ○ Valdobbiadene Brut Rive San Pietro di Barbozza Grande Cuvée del Fondatore Motus Vitae '16 | ♟♟♟ 5 |
| ○ Cartizze '17 | ♟♟ 5 |
| ○ Valdobbiadene Brut Audax 3.0 '17 | ♟♟ 3 |
| ○ Valdobbiadene Brut Prior '17 | ♟♟ 3 |
| ○ Valdobbiadene Extra Dry Banda Rossa Special Reserve '17 | ♟♟ 3 |
| ⊙ Filanda Brut Rosé Ris. '17 | ♟ 3 |
| ○ Riserva del Governatore Extra Brut '16 | ♟ 3 |
| ○ Valdobbiadene Demi Sec Suavis '17 | ♟ 3 |
| ○ Valdobbiadene Dry Maior '17 | ♟ 3 |
| ○ Valdobbiadene Rive San Pietro di Barbozza Motus Vitae '15 | ♟♟♟ 5 |

# Carlo Boscaini

VIA SENGIA, 15
37015 SANT'AMBROGIO DI VALPOLICELLA [VR]
TEL. +39 0457731412
www.boscainicarlo.it

CELLAR SALES
PRE-BOOKED VISITS
ACCOMMODATION
ANNUAL PRODUCTION 60,000 bottles
HECTARES UNDER VINE 14.00

Carlo and Mario Boscaini manage the
family estate on the highlands of
Sant'Ambrogio, the area of Valpolicella
Classica that's most heavily influenced by
Lake Garda. At a certain point the hills
disappear, giving way to the Etschtal Valley
and the low, gentle slopes that signal the
start of the Garda basin. Their vineyards are
situated on the southern slope of the hill
that leads to San Giorgio, and hosts only
traditional cultivar. These give rise to a
selection of wines that's characteristically
rich and captivating. During our tastings,
their 2013 S. Giorgio delivered. It's an
Amarone Classico that offers up all the
warmth of dried fruit. It's sweet and
pervasive, in the mouth it exhibits a certain
dense mouthfeel that's well contrasted by
acidity and pleasantly rough tannins. Their
2017 Valpolicella Ca' Bussin opts for
greater expressive lightness and fragrance,
which follow through well to a peppery,
savory, racy palate.

| | |
|---|---|
| ● Amarone della Valpolicella Cl. San Giorgio '13 | ▼▼ 6 |
| ● Valpolicella Cl. Ca' Bussin '17 | ▼ 2 |
| ● Amarone della Valpolicella Cl. San Giorgio '12 | ♀♀ 6 |
| ● Amarone della Valpolicella Cl. San Giorgio '11 | ♀♀ 5 |
| ● Amarone della Valpolicella Cl. San Giorgio '10 | ♀♀ 5 |
| ● Recioto della Valpolicella Cl. La Sengia '14 | ♀♀ 4 |
| ● Recioto della Valpolicella Cl. La Sengia '12 | ♀♀ 4 |
| ● Valpolicella Cl. Ca' Bussin '16 | ♀♀ 2* |
| ● Valpolicella Cl. Ca' Bussin '12 | ♀♀ 2* |
| ● Valpolicella Cl. Sup. La Preosa '14 | ♀♀ 3 |
| ● Valpolicella Cl. Sup. La Preosa '12 | ♀♀ 3 |
| ● Valpolicella Cl. Sup. Ripasso Zane '15 | ♀♀ 4 |

# Bosco del Merlo

VIA POSTUMIA, 12
30020 ANNONE VENETO [VE]
TEL. +39 0422768167
www.boscodelmerlo.it

CELLAR SALES
PRE-BOOKED VISITS
ANNUAL PRODUCTION 950,000 bottles
HECTARES UNDER VINE 90.00

The estates managed by Lucia, Carlo and
Roberto Paladin spans a large area across
the Venetian plains, between the Adriatic
sea and the nearby Pre-Alps, which protect
the vineyards from the northern winds. Their
selection focuses on the territory's historic
grapes, Refosco dal Penduncolo foremost,
leading to a range of wines interpreted with
precision while also highlighting the
attributes of the varieties used. The team
leave it up to their most ambitious wines,
however, to point up the connection
between grape, territory and the human
hand. Their emblematic 2015 Vineargenti
Riserva is a blend of Merlot and a smaller,
but important part Refosco. On the nose it
features primary aromas of ripe fruit
alternating with spices, and secondary
notes of wild rose and medicinal herbs. The
palate is firm but never overreaching,
moving with decisiveness and lightness, a
combination that makes for supple
drinkability. In terms of their whites, we
appreciated the aromatic drive of their
2017 Sauvignon Turranio, which confers
tension and length to the palate.

| | |
|---|---|
| ● Lison-Pramaggiore Rosso Vineargenti Ris. '15 | ▼▼ 6 |
| ● Lison-Pramaggiore Refosco P. R. Roggio dei Roveri Ris. '15 | ▼▼ 5 |
| ○ Lison-Pramaggiore Sauvignon Turranio '17 | ▼▼ 4 |
| ○ Tudajo Pinot Grigio '17 | ▼▼ 3 |
| ○ Prosecco Brut '17 | ▼ 3 |
| ○ Prosecco Extra Dry '17 | ▼ 3 |
| ● Lison-Pramaggiore Refosco P. R. Roggio dei Roveri Ris. '14 | ♀♀ 5 |
| ● Lison-Pramaggiore Rosso Vineargenti Ris. '14 | ♀♀ 6 |
| ● Lison-Pramaggiore Rosso Vineargenti Ris. '13 | ♀♀ 6 |
| ○ Lison-Pramaggiore Sauvignon Turranio '16 | ♀♀ 4 |

## ★Brigaldara

FRAZ. SAN FLORIANO
VIA BRIGALDARA, 20
37029 SAN PIETRO IN CARIANO [VR]
TEL. +39 0457701055
www.brigaldara.it

**CELLAR SALES**
**PRE-BOOKED VISITS**
**ANNUAL PRODUCTION** 300,000 bottles
**HECTARES UNDER VINE** 50.00

Over the years, Stefano Cesari has managed to grow the family winery, enlarging the vineyards towards eastern Valpolicella and gradually increasing the size of their cellar. Today they boast various estates in San Floriano (San Pietro in Cariano), Marano, Grezzana and Marcellise, all dedicated exclusively to the area's historic grape varieties. The producer is proving increasingly consistent and constant, with wines that range from well-structured and juicy to elegant and grippy. 2014 was a complicated year and as a result a number of wines weren't produced. But we were compensated by an excellent 2011 Amarone Riserva. It's a highly fruit-driven wine that features cherry, plums and damson. In the mouth it proves full and potent, with a vigorous alcoholic embrace that comes through on its soft, pervasive palate. Their 2016 Valpolicella Case Vecie is a fresher, more dynamic, racier wine that delivers for its vibrant tension on the palate.

| | | |
|---|---|---|
| ● Amarone della Valpolicella Ris. '11 | ♥♥ | 8 |
| ● Valpolicella Sup. Case Vecie '16 | ♥♥ | 3* |
| ● Amarone della Valpolicella Cavolo '12 | ♥♥ | 6 |
| ● Recioto della Valpolicella '16 | ♥♥ | 6 |
| ○ Soave '17 | ♥♥ | 3 |
| ● Valpolicella '17 | ♥ | 3 |
| ● Valpolicella Sup. Ripasso Il Vegro '16 | ♥ | 4 |
| ● Amarone della Valpolicella Case Vecie '07 | ♥♥♥ | 7 |
| ● Amarone della Valpolicella Case Vecie '03 | ♥♥♥ | 7 |
| ● Amarone della Valpolicella Cl. '13 | ♥♥♥ | 6 |
| ● Amarone della Valpolicella Cl. '10 | ♥♥♥ | 7 |
| ● Amarone della Valpolicella Cl. '06 | ♥♥♥ | 6 |
| ● Amarone della Valpolicella Cl. '05 | ♥♥♥ | 6 |
| ● Amarone della Valpolicella Ris. '07 | ♥♥♥ | 8 |

## Sorelle Bronca

FRAZ. COLBERTALDO
VIA MARTIRI, 20
31020 VIDOR [TV]
TEL. +39 0423987201
www.sorellebronca.com

**CELLAR SALES**
**PRE-BOOKED VISITS**
**ACCOMMODATION**
**ANNUAL PRODUCTION** 350,000 bottles
**HECTARES UNDER VINE** 24.00

We often imagine Prosecco as an industry in which technology reigns supreme, with little space for poetry. But all it takes is a trip to Bronca to realize that this isn't necessarily the case. Sisters Ersiliana and Antonella attend to the family vineyards with a lucid, well-reasoned approach that draws on the past. It's an approach that has always characterized the area of Conegliano Valdobbiadene. The same holds true for the cellar, where their methods are never planned ahead, but rather adapt in step with the needs of each individual vintage. Their new Valdobbiadene delle Sorelle Bronca put in a sparkling debut. It's a Brut Nature whose name comes from the plots where its grapes are cultivated: 232. On the nose it offers up vibrant notes of ripe and crisp fruit. These flow through onto a palate whose main quality is savoriness. It's an unforgettable wine. Their more approachable and juicy Particella 68 also did quite well. We also want to point out the rich expression of their 2015 Rosso Ser Bele.

| | | |
|---|---|---|
| ○ Valdobbiadene Brut Nature Particella 232 | ♥♥♥ | 5 |
| ● Colli di Conegliano Rosso Ser Bele '15 | ♥♥ | 5 |
| ○ Valdobbiadene Brut Particella 68 | ♥♥ | 4 |
| ○ Colli di Conegliano Bianco Delico '17 | ♥♥ | 3 |
| ○ Valdobbiadene Brut | ♥♥ | 3 |
| ○ Valdobbiadene Extra Dry | ♥♥ | 3 |
| ● Colli di Conegliano Rosso Ser Bele '09 | ♥♥♥ | 5 |
| ● Colli di Conegliano Rosso Ser Bele '05 | ♥♥♥ | 5 |
| ○ Valdobbiadene Brut Particella 68 '15 | ♥♥♥ | 4* |
| ○ Valdobbiadene Brut Particella 68 '13 | ♥♥♥ | 4* |
| ○ Colli di Conegliano Bianco Delico '15 | ♥♥ | 3 |
| ● Colli di Conegliano Rosso Ser Bele '13 | ♥♥ | 5 |
| ● Colli di Conegliano Rosso Ser Bele '12 | ♥♥ | 5 |
| ○ Valdobbiadene Brut Particella 68 '16 | ♥♥ | 4 |
| ○ Valdobbiadene Brut Particella 68 '14 | ♥♥ | 4 |

## Luigi Brunelli

VIA CARIANO, 10
37029 SAN PIETRO IN CARIANO [VR]
TEL. +39 0457701118
www.brunelliwine.com

CELLAR SALES
PRE-BOOKED VISITS
ACCOMMODATION
ANNUAL PRODUCTION 120,000 bottles
HECTARES UNDER VINE 14.00

Situated a bit outside the heart of Valpolicella Classica, the Brunelli family's winery interprets traditional wines with precision and character. Theirs is a lovely story that continues with Alberto, the fourth generation to work in the cellar, along with his father, Luigi, and mother, Luciana. Together they attend to their prized vineyards, which encompass the hillside crus of Campo Inferi and Campo del Titari. These are, no doubt, the crown jewels of a selection that consistently holds together firm structure and taste, and not just their Amarone. Their 2013 Amarone Capo del Titari Riserva put in a fantastic performance. On the nose it features a multivariate array of aromas, with overripe fruit merging with notes of fines herbes and spices, lending the wine its freshness and lightness. In the mouth the wine is supported by its force, with close-woven tannins promising it will age well. Their 2015 Valpolicella Classico Superiore impressed with its great vitality of fruit and its juicy, supple palate.

## Buglioni

FRAZ. CORRUBBIO
VIA CAMPAGNOLE, 55
37029 SAN PIETRO IN CARIANO [VR]
TEL. +39 0456760681
www.buglioni.it

CELLAR SALES
PRE-BOOKED VISITS
ACCOMMODATION
ANNUAL PRODUCTION 170,000 bottles
HECTARES UNDER VINE 48.00

Founded 25 years ago, the Buglioni family's winery has made important changes as of late, emphasizing their bond with the territory and its development. It's all thanks to Mariano, who's enlarged the estate with plots in Sant'Ambrogio and San Pietro in Cariano, both dedicated to Valpolicella's primary cultivar. He's also responsible for putting forth a versatile range of wines that are distinct for their rich yet agile style, as well as the choice to use colorful adjectives on each label. Their 2013 Amarone Lussurioso delivered, expressing vibrant notes of ripe cherries enriched by medicinal herbs and a subtle mineral vein. In the mouth it opens with fullness and force, only to be refreshed and lengthened as it unfolds. Their 2015 Valpolicella Superiore L'Imperfetto, a very interesting wine, opts for greater freshness and fragrance in its aromas, but it's just as juicy and long on the palate.

| | |
|---|---|
| ● Amarone della Valpolicella Cl. Campo del Titari Ris. '13 | ▼▼ 8 |
| ● Amarone della Valpolicella Cl. '14 | ▼▼ 8 |
| ● Recioto della Valpolicella Cl. '17 | ▼▼ 5 |
| ● Valpolicella Cl. Sup. '15 | ▼▼ 2* |
| ● Corte Cariano '15 | ▼ 2 |
| ● Valpolicella Cl. Sup. Ripasso Pa' Riondo '16 | ▼ 4 |
| ● Amarone della Valpolicella Cl. Campo del Titari '97 | ♔♔♔ 8 |
| ● Amarone della Valpolicella Cl. Campo del Titari '96 | ♔♔♔ 8 |
| ● Amarone della Valpolicella Cl. Campo Inferi Ris. '12 | ♔♔ 8 |
| ● Amarone della Valpolicella Cl. Campo Inferi Ris. '11 | ♔♔ 8 |

| | |
|---|---|
| ● Amarone della Valpolicella Cl. Il Lussurioso '13 | ▼▼ 7 |
| ● Valpolicella Cl. Sup. L'Imperfetto '15 | ▼▼ 4 |
| ● Amarone della Valpolicella Cl. Teste Dure Ris. '10 | ▼▼ 8 |
| ● Valpolicella Cl. Sup. Ripasso Il Bugiardo '15 | ▼▼ 5 |
| ● Amarone della Valpolicella Cl. Il Lussurioso Ris. '12 | ♔♔ 7 |
| ● Amarone della Valpolicella Cl. Il Lussurioso Ris. '11 | ♔♔ 7 |
| ● Valpolicella Cl. Sup. L'Imperfetto '14 | ♔♔ 5 |
| ● Valpolicella Cl. Sup. L'Imperfetto '13 | ♔♔ 5 |
| ● Valpolicella Cl. Sup. Ripasso Il Bugiardo '14 | ♔♔ 5 |
| ● Valpolicella Cl. Sup. Ripasso Il Bugiardo '13 | ♔♔ 5 |

# Ca' La Bionda

FRAZ. VALGATARA
VIA BIONDA, 4
37020 MARANO DI VALPOLICELLA [VR]
TEL. +39 0456801198
www.calabionda.it

CELLAR SALES
PRE-BOOKED VISITS
ACCOMMODATION
ANNUAL PRODUCTION 150,000 bottles
HECTARES UNDER VINE 29.00
VITICULTURE METHOD Certified Organic

Alessandro and Nicola Castellani are among Valpolicella's most attentive and aware producers, having proven that they can manage the success that has overwhelmed the area's most celebrated appellations. In many ways their journey has gone in the opposite direction, away from market demand. Their first priority is establishing relationships with vine growers who respect the environment (even when that conflicts with production numbers). Their second is a style that brings out the finesse and character of the wines, rather than the force that comes with drying the grapes. It's a profile that's perfectly reflected by their 2013 Amarone Vigneti di Ravazzol, with fruit that's almost concealed on its primary notes and a minimalist though definitely not meagre palate. It's supported by a frothy, spirited, flavorful backbone. Their 2016 Valpolicella Campo Casal Vegri is an elegant red with great personality We also point out their classy 2016 Bianco del Casal. Made with Trebbiano grapes from historic vineyards, it's a wine that exhibits substance and depth.

| | |
|---|---|
| ● Amarone della Valpolicella Cl. Vign. di Ravazzol '13 | ♟♟♟ 8 |
| ● Valpolicella Cl. Sup. Campo Casal Vegri '16 | ♟♟ 6 |
| ○ Bianco del Casal '16 | ♟♟ 3 |
| ● Corvina '13 | ♟♟ 7 |
| ● Valpolicella Cl. '17 | ♟♟ 5 |
| ● Amarone della Valpolicella Cl. Vign. di Ravazzol '11 | ♟♟♟ 8 |
| ● Amarone della Valpolicella Cl. Vign. di Ravazzol '07 | ♟♟♟ 6 |
| ● Valpolicella Cl. Sup. Campo Casal Vegri '15 | ♟♟♟ 6 |
| ● Valpolicella Cl. Sup. Campo Casal Vegri '11 | ♟♟♟ 5 |

# Ca' Lustra - Zanovello

LOC. FAEDO
VIA SAN PIETRO, 50
35030 CINTO EUGANEO [PD]
TEL. +39 042994128
www.calustra.it

CELLAR SALES
PRE-BOOKED VISITS
ANNUAL PRODUCTION 160,000 bottles
HECTARES UNDER VINE 25.50
VITICULTURE METHOD Certified Organic
SUSTAINABLE WINERY

Ca' Lustra has been operational for more than 40 years and remains an absolute benchmark for Colli Euganei wine enthusiasts. Managed by Franco Zanovello, along with his son, Marco, over the past decade their approach to vine growing and winemaking has been completely rethought with a focus on minimal environmental impact and restraining their wines less during early production phases. The result is a selection that stands out for firmness and character. Their 2013 Merlot Sassonero opens rather closed on the nose, but gradually offers up notes of ripe red fruit, amplified by aromatic herbs and the territory's trademark, slightly salty touch. In the mouth it proves approachable and enjoyable, with nice richness and acidic tension. Their 2016 Fior d'Arancio Passito is an exotic, mineral wine that features hints of candied peels and Mediterranean scrubland. It manages to balance sweetness and a notable savoriness.

| | |
|---|---|
| ● Colli Euganei Merlot Sassonero '13 | ♟♟ 3* |
| ○ Colli Euganei Bianco Olivetani '16 | ♟♟ 2* |
| ● Colli Euganei Cabernet Girapoggio '13 | ♟♟ 3 |
| ○ Colli Euganei Fior d'Arancio Passito '16 | ♟♟ 4 |
| ○ Colli Euganei Moscato Secco 'A Cengia '16 | ♟♟ 2* |
| ● Colli Euganei Rosso Natio '13 | ♟♟ 5 |
| ○ Colli Euganei Manzoni Bianco Pedevenda '16 | ♟ 3 |
| ● Colli Euganei Cabernet Girapoggio '05 | ♟♟♟ 3 |
| ○ Colli Euganei Fior d'Arancio Passito '07 | ♟♟♟ 4 |
| ● Colli Euganei Merlot Sassonero Villa Alessi '05 | ♟♟♟ 3 |
| ● Colli Euganei Cabernet Girapoggio '12 | ♟♟ 3* |
| ● Colli Euganei Moro Polo '14 | ♟♟ 2* |
| ○ Colli Euganei Moscato Secco 'A Cengia '15 | ♟♟ 2* |

# Ca' Orologio

VIA CA' OROLOGIO, 7A
35030 BAONE [PD]
TEL. +39 042950099
www.caorologio.com

**CELLAR SALES**
**PRE-BOOKED VISITS**
**ACCOMMODATION**
**ANNUAL PRODUCTION** 30,000 bottles
**HECTARES UNDER VINE** 10.00
**VITICULTURE METHOD** Certified Organic
**SUSTAINABLE WINERY**

Maria Gioia Rosellini's winery operates in one of the Colli Euganei's most productive areas for vine growing. Here, in Barone, in the southern part of the Regional Park, the climate is almost Mediterranean, thanks to its protection from northern winds and elevations ranging between 50 and 150 meters. Another factor that characterizes the territory is its naturally calcareous and volcanic soil, which, in combination with organic vineyard management, gives life to rich, juicy wines, made primarily with Merlot, Cabernet, Carmenère, Barbera and Raboso. An excellent 2016 gave rise to a sumptuous version of their Relògio, a blend of Carmenère rounded out with Cabernet Franc that features vibrant aromas of ripe red fruit and spices. On the palate is changes pace. The initial impact is full and pervasive, but then it unfolds gracefully, perfectly sustained by acidity and tannins. Their Calaòne, a Bordeaux blend made primarily with Merlot, delivers for the balance and generosity of its palate.

| | | |
|---|---|---|
| ● Relógio '16 | ♟♟ | 5 |
| ● Colli Euganei Rosso Calaóne '16 | ♟♟ | 4 |
| ● Lunisóle '16 | ♟♟ | 4 |
| ○ Salaróla '17 | ♟♟ | 3 |
| ● Colli Euganei Rosso Calaóne '05 | ♟♟♟ | 3* |
| ● Relógio '09 | ♟♟♟ | 4* |
| ● Relógio '07 | ♟♟♟ | 4 |
| ● Relógio '06 | ♟♟♟ | 4 |
| ● Relógio '04 | ♟♟♟ | 4* |
| ● Caò '15 | ♟♟ | 3 |
| ● Colli Euganei Rosso Calaóne '15 | ♟♟ | 4 |
| ● Colli Euganei Rosso Calaóne '13 | ♟♟ | 4 |
| ● Lunisóle '15 | ♟♟ | 4 |
| ● Relógio '15 | ♟♟ | 5 |
| ● Relógio '13 | ♟♟ | 5 |
| ○ Salaróla '16 | ♟♟ | 3 |
| ○ Salaróla '15 | ♟♟ | 3 |

# ★★Ca' Rugate

VIA PERGOLA, 36
37030 MONTECCHIA DI CROSARA [VR]
TEL. +39 0456176328
www.carugate.it

**CELLAR SALES**
**PRE-BOOKED VISITS**
**ACCOMMODATION**
**ANNUAL PRODUCTION** 650,000 bottles
**HECTARES UNDER VINE** 72.00
**SUSTAINABLE WINERY**

Few wineries have the ability to interpret territories and wines as different as those common to Valpolicella and Soave. Michele Tessari, however, certainly is managing one of them. Their estate is among the largest of the district, though they still maintain a decidedly 'artisanal' approach, both in terms of agriculture and enology. In their Montecchia di Crosara cellar, their steel tanks are of limited size so as to best highlight the attributes of each single plot, making for a style that has elegance and tension as its distinctive traits. As their Monte Fiorentine has been left to age another year in their cellar, our attention turned to their 2016 Soave Monte Alto, a wine of great aromatic depth in its fragrances of summer fruit, flowers and toasty hints, fused into a highly elegant profile. These give way to a savory, elegant and long palate. Their 2014 Amarone Punta Tolotti also put in a noteworthy performance, offering up fresh aromas and significant acidic vigor on its taut, supple palate.

| | | |
|---|---|---|
| ○ Soave Cl. Monte Alto '16 | ♟♟♟ | 3* |
| ● Amarone della Valpolicella Punta Tolotti '14 | ♟♟ | 7 |
| ○ Lessini Durello Pas Dosé M. Cl. Amedeo '13 | ♟♟ | 5 |
| ○ Recioto di Soave La Perlara '15 | ♟♟ | 5 |
| ○ Studio '16 | ♟♟ | 4 |
| ● Recioto della Valpolicella L'Eremita '15 | ♟♟ | 5 |
| ○ Soave Cl. San Michele '17 | ♟♟ | 2* |
| ● Valpolicella Rio Albo '17 | ♟♟ | 2* |
| ● Valpolicella Sup. Campo Lavei '16 | ♟♟ | 4 |
| ● Amarone della Valpolicella Punta Tolotti '12 | ♟♟♟ | 7 |
| ○ Soave Cl. Monte Alto '13 | ♟♟♟ | 3* |
| ○ Soave Cl. Monte Alto '11 | ♟♟♟ | 3* |
| ○ Soave Cl. Monte Fiorentine '13 | ♟♟♟ | 3* |
| ○ Studio '15 | ♟♟♟ | 4* |

## Giuseppe Campagnola

FRAZ. VALGATARA
VIA AGNELLA, 9
37020 MARANO DI VALPOLICELLA [VR]
TEL. +39 0457703900
www.campagnola.com

**CELLAR SALES**
**PRE-BOOKED VISITS**
**ANNUAL PRODUCTION** 5,000,000 bottles
**HECTARES UNDER VINE** 155.00

The Campagnola family's large winery operates in the heart of Valpolicella Classica, with a particularly strong presence in the sunny valley of Marano where vineyards alternate with small wooded groves. While their basic line of wines are made with grapes cultivated across the area, the grapes used in their more ambitious wines come exclusively from the Caterina Zardini estate, which lends its name to the product line and feature a combination of richness and balance. Wines from Roccolo del Lago (Garda) and Arnaces (Mortegliano in Friuli) complete the selection. Their 2013 Amarone Caterina Zardini Riserva put in an excellent performance. On the nose it features vibrant notes of sweet, ripe red fruit, while on the palate it delivers power and a close-woven tannic weave. Their 2016 Valpolicella Superiore Giuseppe Campagnola opts for a fresher, more flowery expression before unfolding decisively on the palate, well-supported by acidity. Their 2015 Amarone Vallata di Marano is a deliciously harmonious wine.

| | |
|---|---|
| ● Amarone della Valpolicella Cl. Caterina Zardini Ris. '13 | ⚏⚏ 6 |
| ● Valpolicella Cl. Sup. Caterina Zardini '16 | ⚏⚏ 4 |
| ● Amarone della Valpolicella Cl. Vign. Vallata di Marano '15 | ⚏⚏ 6 |
| ● Recioto della Valpolicella Cl. Casotto del Merlo '15 | ⚏⚏ 5 |
| ● Valpolicella Cl. Sup. Ripasso '16 | ⚏⚏ 3 |
| ⊙ Bardolino Chiaretto Cl. Roccolo del Lago Bio '17 | ⚏ 2 |
| ● Bardolino Cl. Roccolo del Lago '17 | ⚏ 2 |
| ○ Pinot Grigio delle Venezie Vign. Campo dei Gelsi Arnaces '17 | ⚏ 2 |
| ○ Prosecco Brut Arnaces | ⚏ 3 |
| ● Roccolo del Lago Corvina Veronese V. T. '16 | ⚏ 3 |
| ○ Soave Cl. Vign. Monte Foscarino Le Bine '17 | ⚏ 3 |

## ★ I Campi

LOC. ALLODOLA
FRAZ. CELLORE D'ILLASI
VIA DELLE PEZZOLE, 3
37032 ILLASI [VR]
TEL. +39 0456175915
www.icampi.it

**CELLAR SALES**
**PRE-BOOKED VISITS**
**ANNUAL PRODUCTION** 80,000 bottles
**HECTARES UNDER VINE** 12.00

Every year, Flavio Prà's project finds more of a foothold in the territory. If the building of a cellar in Cellore di Illasi has guaranteed further clarity on the technical and logistical side, it's mostly in the vineyard that we're seeing things reach a new level. It's all thanks to the fruition of the younger vines and an approach to viticulture that's increasingly in line with modern principles. And the winery's journey is equally reflected in their selection, where decisive, juicy reds exist alongside more elegant, slim whites. When it comes to their 2016 Ripasso Campo Ciotoli and their 2017 Soave Campo Vulcano, choosing the better performance was more difficult than usual. The former opens with vibrant aromas of wild fruit and pepper, with a subtle mineral note on the background. In the mouth it's full and juicy, supported by a savory acidity. The latter opts for a finer profile, with flowers and white fruit in the foreground of its crisp, long palate.

| | |
|---|---|
| ● Valpolicella Sup. Ripasso Campo Ciotoli '16 | ⚏⚏⚏ 3* |
| ○ Soave Cl. Campo Vulcano '17 | ⚏⚏ 3* |
| ● Amarone della Valpolicella Campi Lunghi '15 | ⚏⚏ 6 |
| ○ Soave Campo Base '17 | ⚏⚏ 2* |
| ● Valpolicella Campo Base '16 | ⚏⚏ 3 |
| ⊙ Lugana Campo Argilla '17 | ⚏ 2 |
| ○ Soave Cl. Campo Vulcano '15 | ♛♛♛ 3* |
| ○ Soave Cl. Campo Vulcano '13 | ♛♛♛ 3* |
| ○ Soave Cl. Campo Vulcano '12 | ♛♛♛ 3* |
| ○ Soave Cl. Campo Vulcano '11 | ♛♛♛ 5 |
| ○ Soave Cl. Campo Vulcano '10 | ♛♛♛ 3* |
| ● Valpolicella Sup. Ripasso Campo Ciotoli '15 | ♛♛♛ 3* |
| ● Valpolicella Sup. Ripasso Campo Ciotoli '13 | ♛♛♛ 3* |

## Canevel Spumanti

Loc. Saccol
via Roccat e Ferrari, 17
31049 Valdobbiadene [TV]
Tel. +39 0423975940
www.canevel.it

**PRE-BOOKED VISITS**
**ANNUAL PRODUCTION** 700,000 bottles
**HECTARES UNDER VINE** 12.00

Canevel has seen many changes over the past two years. This veteran of Valdobbiadene, whose name comes from a local word meaning 'small cellar', has passed into the hands of the Masi group, but they're still just as committed to promoting and developing the territory as they are to their prestigious sparkling wines. The vine growers who supply their grapes are even more involved now, while the wines themselves continue to pursue the most luxurious and pervasive qualities of of each typology. In short, there's something for everyone in this rich selection. Canevel's latest creation is their Campofalco, a Prosecco Brut made with organically cultivated grapes from their Monfalcon vineyard in Refrontolo. On the nose it features fresh flowery hints, with notes of white fruit emerging later. It's creamy and caressing, with a prickle that confers lightness and elegance on the palate. Their 2017 Valdobbiadene Vigneto del Faè Dosaggio Zero, a more spirited, racy wine, also delivered

| | |
|---|---|
| ○ Valdobbiadene Brut Campofalco Vign. Monfalcon '17 | 🍷🍷🍷 5 |
| ○ Cartizze '17 | 🍷🍷 4 |
| ○ Valdobbiadene Dosaggio Zero Vign. del Faè '17 | 🍷🍷 4 |
| ○ Valdobbiadene Extra Dry Il Millesimato '17 | 🍷🍷 5 |
| ○ Cartizze '16 | 🍷🍷 5 |
| ○ Valdobbiadene Brut '15 | 🍷🍷 4 |
| ○ Valdobbiadene Dosaggio Zero Vign. del Faè '16 | 🍷🍷 4 |
| ○ Valdobbiadene Dosaggio Zero Vign. del Faè '15 | 🍷🍷 4 |
| ○ Valdobbiadene Extra Dry '16 | 🍷🍷 4 |
| ○ Valdobbiadene Extra Dry '15 | 🍷🍷 4 |
| ○ Valdobbiadene Extra Dry Il Millesimato '16 | 🍷🍷 5 |

## Canoso

Loc. Monteforte d'Alpone
via Roma, 97
37032 Verona
Tel. +39 0456101981
www.canoso.it

**CELLAR SALES**
**PRE-BOOKED VISITS**
**ANNUAL PRODUCTION** 40,000 bottles
**HECTARES UNDER VINE** 15.00

We can think of only a handful of producers in Soave that have managed to interpret this historic Verona wine with originality and achieved the status of territorial leaders. The Canoso family is without a doubt among them. Massimo, Primo, Giovanni Giuseppe and Micheal seek to bring out the most forceful and energetic temperament of the DOC appellation, starting with their own private vineyards, certified crus like Boschetti and Ca' del Vento (where primarily Garganega is cultivated), which give rise to their most ambitious wines. The vibrant straw-yellow color of their 2017 Soave Vento anticipates its remarkable expressive density, with ripe yellow fruit enriched by nuances of dried flowers, spices and aromatic herbs. In the mouth it follows the same line, proving full and potent, but also well-contrasted by its linear palate. Their 2016 Soave Sup. Verso opts for even greater complexity, with notable minerality. It's a wine that features a richly-textured mid-palate and a pleasant, almond finish.

| | |
|---|---|
| ○ Soave Cl. Fonte '17 | 🍷🍷 2* |
| ○ Soave Cl. Sup. Verso '16 | 🍷🍷 3 |
| ○ Soave Cl. Vento '16 | 🍷🍷 3 |
| ○ Oltre '15 | 🍷🍷 4 |
| ○ Recioto di Soave Passo '09 | 🍷🍷 5 |
| ○ Soave Cl. Fonte '16 | 🍷🍷 2* |
| ○ Soave Cl. Sup. Verso '15 | 🍷🍷 3 |

# Cantina del Castello

V.LO CORTE PITTORA, 5
37038 SOAVE [VR]
TEL. +39 0457680093
www.cantinacastello.it

**CELLAR SALES**
**PRE-BOOKED VISITS**
**ANNUAL PRODUCTION** 120,000 bottles
**HECTARES UNDER VINE** 13.00

For Corte Pittora there's only one possible interpretation of Soave: one that centers on the finesse and grace of style for which this celebrated white wine of Verona has become famous. Their clear idea of expression is explored by Arturo Stocchetti and family by drawing on a highly reputable estate that extends entirely across the classic heart of the appellation. Limited volume, a tight range, non-invasive winemaking: the connection with tradition is reinforced throughout every stage of production. Their 2017 Soave Pressoni, a wine named after the eastern exposed vineyard where its grapes are cultivated, opens with flowery notes and aromas of white fruit that gradually give way to deeper, more personal fragrances of dried fruit, apple seeds and scrubland. In the mouth it proves savory, with a slender profile, a gentle and long palate. Their fresher and more approachable 2017 Castello is characterized by a natural drinkability made possible by a union of savoriness and softness.

| | |
|---|---|
| ○ Soave Cl. Pressoni '17 | 🍷🍷 3 |
| ○ Brut | 🍷 2 |
| ○ Soave Cl. Castello '17 | 🍷 2 |
| ○ Soave Cl. Sup. Monte Pressoni '01 | 🍷🍷🍷 3 |
| ○ Soave Cl. Carniga '14 | 🍷🍷 3 |
| ○ Soave Cl. Carniga '13 | 🍷🍷 3* |
| ○ Soave Cl. Carniga '11 | 🍷🍷 3* |
| ○ Soave Cl. Carniga '10 | 🍷🍷 3 |
| ○ Soave Cl. Castello '16 | 🍷🍷 2* |
| ○ Soave Cl. Castello '15 | 🍷🍷 2* |
| ○ Soave Cl. Castello '12 | 🍷🍷 2* |
| ○ Soave Cl. Pressoni '15 | 🍷🍷 3* |
| ○ Soave Cl. Pressoni '14 | 🍷🍷 3 |
| ○ Soave Cl. Pressoni '13 | 🍷🍷 3 |

# La Cappuccina

FRAZ. COSTALUNGA
VIA SAN BRIZIO, 125
37032 MONTEFORTE D'ALPONE [VR]
TEL. +39 0456175036
www.lacappuccina.it

**CELLAR SALES**
**PRE-BOOKED VISITS**
**RESTAURANT SERVICE**
**ANNUAL PRODUCTION** 310,000 bottles
**HECTARES UNDER VINE** 42.00
**VITICULTURE METHOD** Certified Organic

Even if their headquarters are outside the classic heart of the appellation, the Tessari family winery has long been a faithful interpreter of Soave. Their vineyards, which have been managed using organic methods for more than 30 years, are situated both on the hillside and on flatter terrain. For the most part Garganega is cultivated, though other prestigious varieties (native and non-native) are also grown. Today Elena, Pietro and Sisto manage the house style, which calls for elegance and tension, though they've also made space for more energetic, forceful interpretations, especially among their reds. Two classic wines, their 2015 Recioto Arzimo and their 2016 Soave San Brizio took center stage during our tastings. The former enchants with its tropical aromas and hints of dried flowers, while in the mouth sweetness, savoriness and acidity come together perfectly. The latter features fainter, finer aromas, with a delicate mineral note that follows through onto its supple, yet potent palate, making for a highly enjoyable drink.

| | |
|---|---|
| ○ Recioto di Soave Arzimo '15 | 🍷🍷 5 |
| ○ Soave San Brizio '16 | 🍷🍷 3* |
| ○ Basaltik Sauvignon '17 | 🍷🍷 2* |
| ● Campo Buri '13 | 🍷🍷 4 |
| ○ Soave Fontégo '17 | 🍷🍷 3 |
| ○ Soave Cl. Monte Stelle '17 | 🍷🍷 3 |
| ● Madégo '16 | 🍷 2 |
| ○ Soave '17 | 🍷 2 |
| ● Camp Buri Cabernet Sauvignon '95 | 🍷🍷🍷 5 |
| ○ Recioto di Soave Arzimo '14 | 🍷🍷 5 |
| ○ Recioto di Soave Arzimo '13 | 🍷🍷 5 |
| ○ Recioto di Soave Arzimo '12 | 🍷🍷 5 |
| ○ Soave Fontégo '16 | 🍷🍷 3 |
| ○ Soave Cl. Monte Stelle '15 | 🍷🍷 3 |
| ○ Soave Cl. Monte Stelle '14 | 🍷🍷 3 |
| ○ Soave San Brizio '15 | 🍷🍷 3* |
| ○ Soave San Brizio '14 | 🍷🍷 3* |

# Le Carline

VIA CARLINE, 24
30020 PRAMAGGIORE [VE]
TEL. +39 0421799741
www.lecarline.com

**CELLAR SALES**
**PRE-BOOKED VISITS**
**ANNUAL PRODUCTION** 400,000 bottles
**HECTARES UNDER VINE** 18.00
**VITICULTURE METHOD** Certified Organic

In a territory like Lison-Pramaggiore, which can often appear limited to the production of simple wines without particular ambitions, Daniele Riccinin has managed to carve out a name for himself. It started by adopting organic methods, and from there he focused on producing wines capable of standing shoulder-to-shoulder with the best. Finally, he chose to explore new approaches, like the resistant cultivar used today. Vintage after vintage, he's been sculpting a range of wines with a well-structured style that's faithful to the varieties cultivated. And these new cultivar, which are starting to take on a prominent role in all of Italy, have given rise to their most interesting recent additions. Their Resiliens Bianco is one example. It's a blend of various cultivar resistant to fungal diseases that's allowed for a further step forward in terms of sustainable agriculture. On the nose it features vibrant notes of white, tropical fruit, which follow through on a rich and extraordinarily fresh palate that sees acidity and savoriness come together perfectly.

| | | |
|---|---|---|
| ○ Diana Brut M. Cl. '16 | ♟♟ | 4 |
| ○ Dogale Passito | ♟♟ | 3 |
| ○ Resiliens | ♟♟ | 2* |
| ● Lison-Pramaggiore Cabernet '17 | ♟ | 2 |
| ○ Venezia Pinot Grigio '17 | ♟ | 2 |
| ● Carline Rosso '12 | ♙♙ | 3 |
| ● Carline Rosso '11 | ♙♙ | 3 |
| ○ Diana Brut M. Cl. '15 | ♙♙ | 4 |
| ○ Diana Brut M. Cl. '15 | ♙♙ | 4 |
| ○ Lison Cl. '12 | ♙♙ | 2* |
| ● Lison-Pramaggiore Merlot '16 | ♙♙ | 2* |
| ● Lison-Pramaggiore Refosco P. R. senza solfiti aggiunti '13 | ♙♙ | 2* |

# Carpenè Malvolti

VIA ANTONIO CARPENÈ, 1
31015 CONEGLIANO [TV]
TEL. +39 0438364611
www.carpene-malvolti.com

**PRE-BOOKED VISITS**
**ANNUAL PRODUCTION** 5,300,000 bottles
**HECTARES UNDER VINE** 26.00

It wouldn't be much of a stretch to say that Carpenè Malvolti is to Prosecco what Ferrari is to automobiles. In fact, the historic Conegliano winery has not only contributed decisively to the success of this regional sparkling wine in the world, it has also influenced it stylistically, in terms of production techniques and territorial identity. Today, as in the past, they draw on partnerships with a host of vine growers, giving rise to a complete and consistent selection of wines that ranges from Cartizze to Superiore, Rosé and Metodo Classico sparklers. Their best grapes are used for their PVXINVM, a Prosecco Extra Dry that offers up vibrant notes of ripe yellow fruit enriched by flowers and a subtle, herbaceous note. In the mouth a slight sweetness is well-contrasted by a juicy acidity, while its bubbles do the work of accompanying the palate towards a long finish. Their Cartizze 1868 is a pervasive, creamy sparkling wine.

| | | |
|---|---|---|
| ○ Conegliano Valdobbiadene Extra Dry PVXINVM | ♟♟ | 5 |
| ○ Cartizze 1868 | ♟♟ | 5 |
| ○ Conegliano Valdobbiadene Extra Dry 1868 | ♟♟ | 3 |
| ○ Conegliano Valdobbiadene Brut 1868 | ♟ | 3 |
| ○ Conegliano Valdobbiadene Extra Dry PVXINVM '14 | ♙♙ | 5 |

# Casa Cecchin

VIA AGUGLIANA, 11
36054 MONTEBELLO VICENTINO [VI]
TEL. +39 0444649610
www.casacecchin.it

**CELLAR SALES**
**PRE-BOOKED VISITS**
**ANNUAL PRODUCTION** 30,000 bottles
**HECTARES UNDER VINE** 7.00

When talking about Veneto's volcanic terrain, most of the time we think of the Colli Euganei hills or Soave, forgetting that the district of Gambellara is situated on volcanic basalt. It's a primitive land that the most attentive producers manage to transform into wines with personality and finesse. The Cecchin family, who've made Durello the grape of choice of their noteworthy selection, are one such example, thanks in part to their more than 30 years of experience in Metodo Classico sparkling wines. Their 2017 Pietralava represents a high expression of the grape, cultivated when super-ripe. On the nose sunny notes of yellow fruit are enriched by the presence of tropical aromas and a background of dried flowers and flint. This array of aromas takes center stage on a rich, well-structure palate with limited alcohol content and a strong acidic thrust. Their 2013 Metodo Classico Nostrum Brut is a deep, spirited highly drinkable wine.

| | | |
|---|---|---|
| ○ Durello Passito Montebello '15 | ♥♥ | 5 |
| ○ Lessini Durello Brut M. Cl. Nostrum '13 | ♥♥ | 4 |
| ○ Pietralava '17 | ♥♥ | 3 |
| ○ Mandégolo Frizzante sui lieviti '17 | ♥ | 3 |
| ○ Gambellara San Nicolò '15 | ♀♀ | 2* |
| ○ Il Durello '16 | ♀♀ | 2* |
| ○ Lessini Durello Dosaggio Zero M. Cl. '11 | ♀♀ | 5 |
| ○ Lessini Durello Extra Brut M. Cl. Nostrum '12 | ♀♀ | 4 |
| ○ Lessini Durello Extra Brut M. Cl. Nostrum '10 | ♀♀ | 4 |
| ○ Lessini Durello Il Durello '14 | ♀♀ | 2* |
| ○ Lessini Durello Pietralava '14 | ♀♀ | 2* |
| ○ Lessini Durello San Nicolò '14 | ♀♀ | 2* |
| ○ Pietralava '15 | ♀♀ | 3 |
| ○ San Nicolò '16 | ♀♀ | 2* |

# Casa Roma

VIA ORMELLE, 19
31020 SAN POLO DI PIAVE [TV]
TEL. +39 0422855339
www.casaroma.com

**CELLAR SALES**
**PRE-BOOKED VISITS**
**ANNUAL PRODUCTION** 200,000 bottles
**HECTARES UNDER VINE** 15.00

Year after year, Luigi 'Gigi' Peruzzetto has managed to inject new life into the family winery, ultimately finding himself at the head of one of the most important producers in the Piave appellation. Their vineyards, which feature both international grape varieties (present in the territory for at least a century) and more traditional cultivar extend across the gravelly terrain of San Polo. Marzemina Bianca and the more representative Raboso are just two of the varieties that are interpreted here in a style that alternates between a more 'natural' approach and a more ambitious, complex one. Considering the lengthy maturation the wine undergoes in large barrels, and the fact that we're tasting it 10 years after vintage, their 2007 Raboso Indigeno offers up an extraordinarily fresh aromatic profile. Sunny fruit and spices embrace mineral notes and aromas of medicinal herbs. Time has smoothed its tannins and the wine lengthens with elegance and decisiveness in a truly charming finish. Their 2012 Raboso is vibrant on the nose and gutsier on the palate. It shows personality and tension.

| | | |
|---|---|---|
| ● Piave Raboso Indigeno '07 | ♥♥ | 6 |
| ○ Peruzzet Marzemina Bianca '17 | ♥♥ | 2* |
| ● Piave Carmenère Peruzzet '17 | ♥♥ | 2* |
| ● Piave Raboso '12 | ♥♥ | 4 |
| ● Sestier Raboso '17 | ♥♥ | 2* |
| ○ Venezia Pinot Grigio Peruzzet '17 | ♥♥ | 2* |
| ○ Piave Manzoni Bianco Peruzzet '17 | ♥ | 2 |
| ● Venezia Cabernet Sauvignon Peruzzet '17 | ♥ | 2 |
| ○ Venezia Chardonnay Peruzzet '17 | ♥ | 2 |
| ● Venezia Merlot Peruzzet '17 | ♥ | 2 |
| ○ Marzemina Bianca '16 | ♀♀ | 2* |
| ● Piave Carmenère '16 | ♀♀ | 2* |
| ● Piave Malanotte '11 | ♀♀ | 6 |
| ○ Piave Manzoni Bianco '16 | ♀♀ | 2* |
| ● Piave Raboso '10 | ♀♀ | 4 |

# VENETO

## Case Paolin

VIA MADONNA MERCEDE, 55
31040 VOLPAGO DEL MONTELLO [TV]
TEL. +39 0423871433
www.casepaolin.it

CELLAR SALES
PRE-BOOKED VISITS
ANNUAL PRODUCTION 130,000 bottles
HECTARES UNDER VINE 15.00
VITICULTURE METHOD Certified Organic
SUSTAINABLE WINERY

Situated on the slopes of Montello, the winery managed by brothers Diego, Adelino and Mirco Pozzobon is one of the most active in the district. Their vineyards are in close proximity to one another but they differ in terms of pedoclimate. The Belvedere plain is characterized by stony, alluvial soil, while moving up the hill red, iron-rich earth dominates. Such factors determine where Glera, Manzoni Bianco, Merlot, Cabernet and Carmenère are grown, making for a stylistically versatile ampelography. In the absence of their San Carlo, which spending a while longer in their cellar, our attention was captured by their 2015 Costa deli Angeli. It's a Manzoni Bianco whose aromatic profile features citrus and dried flowers, with gradually emerging white fruit. In the mouth an opening savory thrust gives way to a long, elegant palate. Their Rosso del Milio, a Bordeaux, also delivered thanks to fruity richness and a supple palate.

| | | |
|---|---|---|
| ○ Costa degli Angeli Manzoni '16 | ♟♟ | 3* |
| ○ Asolo Brut | ♟♟ | 3 |
| ● Cabernet '17 | ♟♟ | 2* |
| ● Rosso del Milio '16 | ♟♟ | 3 |
| ● Rosso del Milio '15 | ♟♟ | 3 |
| ○ Asolo Prosecco Col Fondo | ♟ | 3 |
| ○ Prosecco Extra Dry | ♟ | 2 |
| ○ Manzoni Bianco Costa degli Angeli '15 | ♟♟ | 3 |
| ○ Manzoni Bianco Costa degli Angeli '14 | ♟♟ | 3 |
| ○ Manzoni Bianco Costa degli Angeli '13 | ♟♟ | 3 |
| ● Montello e Colli Asolani Rosso San Carlo '13 | ♟♟ | 4 |
| ● Montello e Colli Asolani Rosso San Carlo '12 | ♟♟ | 4 |
| ● Rosso del Milio '14 | ♟♟ | 3 |
| ● Rosso del Milio '13 | ♟♟ | 3 |

## Michele Castellani

FRAZ. VALGATARA
VIA GRANDA, 1
37020 MARANO DI VALPOLICELLA [VR]
TEL. +39 0457701253
www.castellanimichele.it

CELLAR SALES
PRE-BOOKED VISITS
ANNUAL PRODUCTION 300,000 bottles
HECTARES UNDER VINE 50.00

Moving up Route 34 we find the winery founded by Michele Castellani in 1945 and today led by Sergio, his wife Maria and their three children. It's nestled in an artisanal district surrounded by vineyards. A bit further north the buildings thin out and the viticulture of Marano valley comes into full force. In addition to vineyards in Ca' del Pipa and Castei, which provide the grapes for their selections of the same name, they've recently added plots in Maso di Negrar. In all cases, only the best grapes are chosen, contributing to a rich and dynamic style. We were most impressed with their 2016 Recioto Monte Fasenara, a wine that's undoubtedly in the Castellani family's wheelhouse. The nose is redolent of vibrant ripe cheery, crossed by timbres of Valpolicella's aromatic herbs, which explode on the palate, where extraordinary sweetness is supported by a tight backbone of acidity. Their 2015 Amarone Campo Casalin, a fresh, dynamic and juicy wine, also delivered.

| | | |
|---|---|---|
| ● Recioto della Valpolicella Cl. Monte Fasenara I Castei '16 | ♟♟ | 5 |
| ● Amarone della Valpolicella Cl. Campo Casalin I Castei '15 | ♟♟ | 6 |
| ● Valpolicella Cl. Sup. Ripasso Costamaran I Castei '16 | ♟♟ | 3 |
| ● Valpolicella Cl. Campo del Biotto I Castei '17 | ♟ | 2 |
| ● Recioto della Valpolicella Cl. Le Vigne Ca' del Pipa '99 | ♟♟♟ | 6 |
| ● Amarone della Valpolicella Cl. Campo Casalin I Castei '13 | ♟♟ | 6 |
| ● Amarone della Valpolicella Cl. Cinquestelle Collezione Ca' del Pipa '13 | ♟♟ | 7 |
| ● Amarone della Valpolicella Cl. Cinquestelle Collezione Ca' del Pipa '12 | ♟♟ | 7 |
| ● Recioto della Valpolicella Cl. Monte Fasenara I Castei '15 | ♟♟ | 5 |

# ★Cavalchina

LOC. CAVALCHINA
FRAZ. CUSTOZA
VIA SOMMACAMPAGNA, 7
37066 SOMMACAMPAGNA [VR]
TEL. +39 045516002
www.cavalchina.com

**CELLAR SALES**
**PRE-BOOKED VISITS**
**ANNUAL PRODUCTION 445,000 bottles**
**HECTARES UNDER VINE 50.00**

Over the years, Franco and Luciano Piona have managed to transform their family's winery, strengthening their relationship with their vine growers and respecting tradition while also exploring cultivar unusual for Garda (such as, for example, Riesling). They've also enlarged their estate in Mantovano (with the La Prendina) and in nearby Valpolicella (Torre d'Orti, in San Martino Buon Albergo). They adapt their production style according to the conditions of the territory, starting with the fragrant lightness of their Garda whites. Their 2016 Custoza Amedeo put in its trademark, one-of-a-kind performance, with its delicate and gradual aromas of white fruit, Mediterranean scrubland and smoky accents that follow through onto an elegant, lengthy palate. In terms of their reds, we point out their excellent 2016 Bardolino Santa Lucia, a wine redolent in its aromas, savory and juicy in the mouth. When it comes to Valpolicella, their 2015 Superiore stands out for its fruity richness.

| | |
|---|---|
| ○ Custoza Sup. Amedeo '16 | ▼▼▼ 3* |
| ● Amarone della Valpolicella Torre d'Orti '14 | ▼▼ 6 |
| ● Bardolino Sup. Santa Lucia '16 | ▼▼ 3 |
| ○ Custoza '17 | ▼▼ 2* |
| ● Garda Cabernet Sauvignon Falcone '15 | ▼▼ 4 |
| ● Garda Merlot Faial '15 | ▼▼ 5 |
| ○ Garda Riesling '17 | ▼▼ 3 |
| ● Valpolicella Sup. Morari Torre d'Orti '15 | ▼▼ 4 |
| ● Valpolicella Sup. Ripasso Torre d'Orti '15 | ▼▼ 3 |
| ⊙ Bardolino Chiaretto '17 | ▼ 2 |
| ○ Garda Pinot Grigio Prendina '17 | ▼ 2 |
| ○ Custoza Sup. Amedeo '15 | ▽▽▽ 2* |
| ○ Custoza Sup. Amedeo '14 | ▽▽▽ 3* |

# Cavazza

C.DA SELVA, 22
36054 MONTEBELLO VICENTINO [VI]
TEL. +39 0444649166
www.cavazzawine.com

**CELLAR SALES**
**PRE-BOOKED VISITS**
**ACCOMMODATION**
**ANNUAL PRODUCTION 860,000 bottles**
**HECTARES UNDER VINE 150.00**
**SUSTAINABLE WINERY**

The generational change at Cavazza has set off decisive transformations in Selva (a district of Montebello Vicentino). Their viticultural heart remains divided between the historic areas of Gambellara (Bocara, Creari, Capitel, Selva, with the best plots reserved for Garganega) and the nearby Colli Berici (Tenuta Cicogna, where mostly red grape varieties are cultivated). Their work in the cellar features great attention to preserving the quality attained in the vineyards, making for a selection that offers firmness and harmony with every bottle. Their Gambellara Bocara gets more impressive by the year for its richness and clarity. 2017 gave rise to a version redolent in fresh flowers and citrus, with a subtle note of white fruit pushing out from the background. In the mouth it delivers for its energy and perfect balance between softness and savory vigor. Their 2015 Cabernet Cicogna also performed quite well, bringing together toasty and spicy notes with the generosity of ripe fruit.

| | |
|---|---|
| ○ Gambellara Cl. Bocara '17 | ▼▼ 2* |
| ● Cicogna Syrah '15 | ▼▼ 5 |
| ● Colli Berici Cabernet Cicogna '15 | ▼▼ 4 |
| ● Colli Berici Tai Rosso Corallo '16 | ▼▼ 3 |
| ● Fornetto '16 | ▼▼ 3 |
| ● Colli Berici Cabernet Cicogna '13 | ▽▽ 4 |
| ● Colli Berici Cabernet Cicogna '12 | ▽▽ 4 |
| ● Colli Berici Cabernet Cicogna '11 | ▽▽ 4 |
| ● Colli Berici Merlot Cicogna '13 | ▽▽ 5 |
| ● Colli Berici Merlot Cicogna '12 | ▽▽ 4 |
| ● Colli Berici Merlot Cicogna '11 | ▽▽ 4 |
| ● Colli Berici Tai Rosso Corallo '13 | ▽▽ 3 |
| ○ Gambellara Cl. La Bocara '16 | ▽▽ 2* |
| ○ Gambellara Cl. La Bocara '15 | ▽▽ 2* |
| ○ Recioto di Gambellara Cl. Capitel '15 | ▽▽ 4 |
| ○ Recioto di Gambellara Cl. Capitel S. Libera '10 | ▽▽ 4 |

# VENETO

## Giorgio Cecchetto

FRAZ. TEZZE DI PIAVE
VIA PIAVE, 67
31028 VAZZOLA [TV]
TEL. +39 043828598
www.rabosopiave.com

**CELLAR SALES**
**PRE-BOOKED VISITS**
**ANNUAL PRODUCTION** 200,000 bottles
**HECTARES UNDER VINE** 73.00
**SUSTAINABLE WINERY**

For thirty years now Giorgio Cecchetto has been at the helm of the family winery and today the producer is one of the loveliest operations in this corner of Veneto (Tezze di Piave, Vazzola). Their notable estate extends across three distinct areas, characterized by different elevations, positions and terrain types, which naturally lend themselves to local grape varieties. And so it is that their red grapes are cultivated primarily on the gravelly soil around the cellar, whites are grown on the calcareous clay of Lorenza, and Glera is cultivated in Cornuda. Kudos to their 2015 Raboso. It takes advantage of an excellent year to offer up vibrant notes of red fruit, plums and cherries, which unfold on a rich palate governed by the cultivar's trademark precision and acidity. It's a wine that features tension and length. Their Rosa Bruna Cuvée 21 is also made with Raboso. It's a Metodo Classico rosé sparkler that's redolent of wild berries and delivers for its supple palate.

| | |
|---|---|
| ● Piave Raboso '15 | 🍷🍷 3 |
| ⊙ Rosa Bruna Cuvée 21 Brut M. Cl. '12 | 🍷🍷 3 |
| ● Sante Rosso '16 | 🍷🍷 4 |
| ● Carmenère '17 | 🍷 2 |
| ○ Manzoni Bianco '17 | 🍷 2 |
| ● Malanotte Gelsaia '13 | 🍷🍷 5 |
| ● Malanotte Gelsaia '11 | 🍷🍷 5 |
| ○ Manzoni Bianco '15 | 🍷🍷 2* |
| ● Merlot Sante Rosso '11 | 🍷🍷 3 |
| ● Merlot Sante Rosso '10 | 🍷🍷 3 |
| ● Piave Raboso '13 | 🍷🍷 3 |
| ● Piave Raboso '12 | 🍷🍷 3 |
| ● Piave Raboso '11 | 🍷🍷 3 |
| ⊙ Rosa Bruna Cuvée 21 Brut M.Cl. '11 | 🍷🍷 3 |
| ● Sante Rosso '12 | 🍷🍷 3 |

## Gerardo Cesari

LOC. SORSEI, 3
37010 CAVAION VERONESE [VR]
TEL. +39 0456260928
www.cesariverona.it

**CELLAR SALES**
**PRE-BOOKED VISITS**
**ANNUAL PRODUCTION** 1,500,000 bottles
**HECTARES UNDER VINE** 120.00
**SUSTAINABLE WINERY**

Michele Farruggio manages this large winery founded by the Cesari family in 1936 (and reporting today to the Gruppo Caviro). They move along two tracks. On the one hand there are the historic wines of Garda, made in their cellars in Cavaion using grapes cultivated on the estate of Cento Filari (between Peschiera and Pozzolengo). Then there are their Valpolicellas, made in San Pietro in Cariano using grapes from their Bosan, Bosco and Jèma vineyards. With their simpler wines, the producer's style seeks to highlight each variety's natural attributes, while their more ambitious wines pursue complexity and power. Their 2012 Amarone Il Bosco succeeds in the difficult task of bringing together two distinct tracks. On the one hand there's the force and aromatic depth of the dried grapes, on the other there's the fragrance and lightness of traditional grapes. The result is a juicy wine that's exquisitely drinkable. Their 2017 Lugano Cento Filari also performed well, with its taut, energetic, and lengthy palate.

| | |
|---|---|
| ● Amarone della Valpolicella Cl. Il Bosco '12 | 🍷🍷 6 |
| ● Amarone della Valpolicella Cl. '14 | 🍷🍷 5 |
| ● Amarone della Valpolicella Cl. Bosan Ris. '09 | 🍷🍷 8 |
| ○ Lugana Cento Filari '17 | 🍷🍷 3 |
| ● Valpolicella Sup. Ripasso Bosan '15 | 🍷🍷 4 |
| ● Jèma Corvina '13 | 🍷 4 |
| ● Valpolicella Sup. Ripasso Mara '16 | 🍷 3 |
| ● Amarone della Valpolicella Cl. Bosan Ris. '08 | 🍷🍷 8 |
| ● Amarone della Valpolicella Cl. '13 | 🍷🍷 6 |
| ● Amarone della Valpolicella Cl. '12 | 🍷🍷 6 |
| ● Amarone della Valpolicella Cl. Il Bosco '11 | 🍷🍷 7 |
| ● Amarone della Valpolicella Cl. Il Bosco '10 | 🍷🍷 7 |
| ● Valpolicella Sup. Ripasso Bosan '14 | 🍷🍷 5 |

# Italo Cescon

FRAZ. RONCADELLE
P.ZZA DEI CADUTI, 3
31024 ORMELLE [TV]
TEL. +39 0422851033
www.cesconitalo.it

**CELLAR SALES**
**PRE-BOOKED VISITS**
**ANNUAL PRODUCTION** 800,000 bottles
**HECTARES UNDER VINE** 115.00
**VITICULTURE METHOD** Certified Organic
**SUSTAINABLE WINERY**

Roncadelle goes back more than 60 years, but as of late, especially, Gabriella, Graziella and Domenico Cescon have honed their efforts, attentively and decisively managing the winery founded by their father, Italo. In addition to the continued pursuit of quality, they are focusing on a management approach that respects the environment. If their simpler wines are all about being true to eastern Veneto's traditional cultivar, their more ambitious wines bring together harmony and personality. Their Madre is a splendid wine, made with Manzoni Bianco, that drew on an excellent 2016 for depth and character. Its citrusy notes come through forcefully, only to give way to an aromatic sequence of flint, dried flowers and tropical fruit. These follow through on a palate of great tension and personality, enriched by freshness and flavor, and not lacking in density. Their 2016 Pinot Grigio Choku Res opts for riper aromas, and delivers for its firm, flavorful palate.

| | | |
|---|---|---|
| ○ Madre '16 | 🏆🏆🏆 | 5 |
| ● Chieto '15 | 🏆🏆 | 5 |
| ○ Choku Rei Pinot Grigio '16 | 🏆🏆 | 4 |
| ● Piave Raboso Rabià Ris. '11 | 🏆 | 7 |
| ○ Madre '14 | 🏆🏆🏆 | 4* |
| ● Amaranto 72 '12 | 🏆🏆 | 5 |
| ● Chieto '13 | 🏆🏆 | 4 |
| ● Chieto '12 | 🏆🏆 | 4 |
| ○ Choku Rei Pinot Grigio '15 | 🏆🏆 | 4 |
| ○ Madre '15 | 🏆🏆 | 5 |
| ○ Manzoni Bianco Non Filtrato '13 | 🏆🏆 | 5 |
| ○ Mejo Sauvignon '16 | 🏆🏆 | 3 |
| ○ Mejo Sauvignon '15 | 🏆🏆 | 3 |
| ○ Svejo Manzoni Bianco '16 | 🏆🏆 | 3 |
| ○ Svejo Manzoni Bianco '15 | 🏆🏆 | 3 |
| ○ Svejo Manzoni Bianco '14 | 🏆🏆 | 3 |

# Coffele

VIA ROMA, 5
37038 SOAVE [VR]
TEL. +39 0457680007
www.coffele.it

**CELLAR SALES**
**PRE-BOOKED VISITS**
**ANNUAL PRODUCTION** 120,000 bottles
**HECTARES UNDER VINE** 25.00
**VITICULTURE METHOD** Certified Organic

Chiara and Alberto Coffele manage their family winery in the heart of classic Soave, bolstered by a viticultural patrimony that goes back generations. Their property is concentrated on the southeastern side of Castelcerino hill. It's practically a contiguous plot that extends across composite soils in which calcareous and basaltic terrain alternate in turns. Garganega makes up the lion's share of the cultivar (though Trebbiano, Chardonnay, Merlot and Cabernet are also grown), giving rise to a selection that features harmony and elegance. Their 2016 Soave Alzari expresses precisely these characteristics, a wine who's aromatic profile is crossed by flowery fragrances and ripe, white fruit, with supporting note of oak in the background. A part of the grapes used are left in their drying loft, which explains the delicacy and roundness that guides its palate. Their 2016 Recioto Le Sponde, an exotic and racy passito, is more buoyant in its aromatic expressiveness.

| | | |
|---|---|---|
| ○ Recioto di Soave Cl. Le Sponde '16 | 🏆🏆 | 5 |
| ○ Soave Cl. Alzari '16 | 🏆🏆 | 3* |
| ○ Soave Cl. Ca' Visco '17 | 🏆🏆 | 3 |
| ○ Soave Cl. Castel Cerino '17 | 🏆🏆 | 3 |
| ○ Recioto di Soave Cl. Le Sponde '09 | 🏆🏆🏆 | 5 |
| ○ Soave Cl. Ca' Visco '14 | 🏆🏆🏆 | 3* |
| ○ Soave Cl. Ca' Visco '05 | 🏆🏆🏆 | 3* |
| ○ Soave Cl. Ca' Visco '04 | 🏆🏆🏆 | 2 |
| ○ Soave Cl. Ca' Visco '03 | 🏆🏆🏆 | 2 |
| ○ Recioto di Soave Cl. Le Sponde '15 | 🏆🏆 | 5 |
| ○ Recioto di Soave Cl. Le Sponde '14 | 🏆🏆 | 5 |
| ○ Soave Cl. Alzari '15 | 🏆🏆 | 3 |
| ○ Soave Cl. Alzari '14 | 🏆🏆 | 3 |
| ○ Soave Cl. Ca' Visco '16 | 🏆🏆 | 3* |
| ○ Soave Cl. Ca' Visco '15 | 🏆🏆 | 3* |
| ○ Soave Cl. Castel Cerino '16 | 🏆🏆 | 3 |

# Col Vetoraz

FRAZ. SANTO STEFANO
S.DA DELLE TRESIESE, 1
31040 VALDOBBIADENE [TV]
TEL. +39 0423975291
www.colvetoraz.it

**CELLAR SALES**
**PRE-BOOKED VISITS**
**ANNUAL PRODUCTION** 1,200,000 bottles
**HECTARES UNDER VINE** 130.00

Col Vetoraz is among the most renowned producers of Valdobbiadene. The winery is situated in Santo Stefano, and has a thriving estate at its disposal, which includes both their own vineyards and those managed by their trusted suppliers. The three partners, Loris Dall'Acqua, Francesco Miotto and Paolo De Bortoli, have chosen to use only the best grapes for their selection. Today all phases of production are carried out in their new facility, situated in an artisanal area not far from their historic cellar, making for the perfect logistical situation. Recent years have seen a drier style that eschews sugar in favor of a more spirited, versatile palate. Their Dosaggio Zero is a good example, with a 2017 that delivered (to say the least). Aromatically faint and delicate, fragrances of white fruit meet flowers nuances and herbaceous accents, while the palate points up the wine's savoriness, lengthening with elegance and rigor.

| | | |
|---|---|---|
| ○ Valdobbiadene Dosaggio Zero '17 | ♔♔ | 3* |
| ○ Cartizze '17 | ♔♔ | 4 |
| ○ Valdobbiadene Brut '17 | ♔♔ | 3 |
| ○ Valdobbiadene Dry '17 | ♔♔ | 3 |
| ○ Valdobbiadene Extra Dry '17 | ♔♔ | 3 |
| ○ Cartizze '16 | ♕♕ | 4 |
| ○ Cartizze '14 | ♕♕ | 4 |
| ○ Valdobbiadene Brut '16 | ♕♕ | 3 |
| ○ Valdobbiadene Brut Zero '15 | ♕♕ | 3* |
| ○ Valdobbiadene Brut Zero '14 | ♕♕ | 3 |
| ○ Valdobbiadene Dosaggio Zero '16 | ♕♕ | 3* |
| ○ Valdobbiadene Dry '16 | ♕♕ | 3 |
| ○ Valdobbiadene Dry Mill. '15 | ♕♕ | 3 |
| ○ Valdobbiadene Dry Mill. '14 | ♕♕ | 3 |
| ○ Valdobbiadene Extra Dry '16 | ♕♕ | 3 |

# Le Colture

LOC. SANTO STEFANO
VIA FOLLO, 5
31049 VALDOBBIADENE [TV]
TEL. +39 0423900192
www.lecolture.com

**CELLAR SALES**
**PRE-BOOKED VISITS**
**ACCOMMODATION**
**ANNUAL PRODUCTION** 750,000 bottles
**HECTARES UNDER VINE** 40.00

Founded by Cesare Ruggeri in the early 1980s, today Le Colture is a quality leader in the area of Conegliano Valdobbiadene. This is thanks in part to a deep knowledge of the territory and its traditional grapes, though it's also thanks to the forward-thinking acquisition of vineyards, which have allowed the family to directly manage a large portion of their wine production. Today Cesare is accompanied by his children, Silvia, Alberto and Veronica, who are increasingly involved in managing the winery and the style of its wines (made mostly with Glera). Their 2016 Gerardo is made with grapes cultivated on their lovely Santo Stefano vineyards. It's a Valdobbiadene Brut that comes out the same year and that offers up fresh aromas of fruit that gradually unfold, rather than exploding all at once. These are crossed by herbaceous notes and hints of dried flowers, while the palate proves crisp and slender. Their Fagher Brut opts for more exuberance and freshness. It's a wine that features approachable aromas and a juicy, dynamic palate.

| | | |
|---|---|---|
| ○ Cartizze | ♔♔ | 5 |
| ○ Valdobbiadene Brut Fagher | ♔♔ | 3 |
| ○ Valdobbiadene Brut Rive di Santo Stefano Gerardo '16 | ♔♔ | 3 |
| ○ Valdobbiadene Extra Dry Pianer | ♔♔ | 3 |
| ○ Prosecco di Treviso Brut Sylvoz | ♔ | 2 |
| ○ Valdobbiadene Dry Cruner | ♔ | 3 |
| ○ Valdobbiadene Prosecco Frizzante Mas | ♔ | 3 |
| ○ Valdobbiadene Rive di Santo Stefano Brut Gerardo '15 | ♕♕ | 3 |
| ○ Valdobbiadene Sup. Rive di Santo Stefano Brut Gerardo '14 | ♕♕ | 3 |

# Conte Collalto

VIA XXIV MAGGIO, 1
31058 SUSEGANA [TV]
TEL. +39 0438435811
www.cantine-collalto.it

CELLAR SALES
PRE-BOOKED VISITS
ANNUAL PRODUCTION 850,000 bottles
HECTARES UNDER VINE 164.00
SUSTAINABLE WINERY

Isabella Collalto De Croÿ's winery is one of Veneto's largest. It's a sizable estate situated just by the Pre-Alps of Treviso where vineyards and pastures alternate with farmland and woods across an endless chain of hills. In the historic cellars situated along Via XXIV Maggio all stages of production are carried out, giving rise to a range of wines of which Prosecco is the undisputed star. Still wines made with international varieties are made, as are wines made with Professor Manzoni's celebrated crossbred grapes. Their 2013 Torrai Riserva is made with grapes from their plots on the southwestern side of Castello di San Salvatore. It's a blend of Cabernet Sauvignon, Franc and Carmenère that's redolent of ripe fruit and spices. The palate delivers for its harmony and silky tannins. Among their sparklers, we appreciate Collato's most recent creation, their 2017 Ponte Rosso, a Prosecco Nature with sophisticated aromas and a crisp, assertive palate. Their 2017 Extra Dry Gaio also did well.

| | |
|---|---|
| ● Piave Cabernet Torrai Ris. '13 | ▼▼ 5 |
| ○ Conegliano Valdobbiadene Brut Nature Ponte Rosso '17 | ▼▼ 3 |
| ○ Conegliano Valdobbiadene Extra Dry Gaio '17 | ▼▼ 3 |
| ● Incrocio Manzoni 2.15 '15 | ▼▼ 2* |
| ● Colli di Conegliano Rosso Vinciguerra '12 | ▼ 5 |
| ○ Conegliano Valdobbiadene Brut San Salvatore '17 | ▼ 3 |
| ○ Conegliano Valdobbiadene Dry Dame '17 | ▼ 3 |
| ○ Manzoni Bianco '17 | ▼ 2 |
| ○ Rosabianco '17 | ▼ 2 |
| ☉ Sogno Rossorosa '17 | ▼ 2 |
| ☉ Violette Rosé Extra Dry '17 | ▼ 2 |
| ● Wildbacher '13 | ▼ 2 |
| ● Piave Cabernet Torrai Ris. '11 | ▽▽ 5 |

# Corte Adami

VIA CIRCONVALLAZIONE ALDO MORO, 32
37038 SOAVE [VR]
TEL. +39 0456190218
www.corteadami.it

CELLAR SALES
PRE-BOOKED VISITS
ANNUAL PRODUCTION 100,000 bottles
HECTARES UNDER VINE 38.00
SUSTAINABLE WINERY

Corte Adami, founded just over a decade ago, is led by a family that has deep roots in the territory's viticultural traditions. The estate is situated in the plains that lay to the west of residential Soave, in an area where vineyards dominate, and the hills are just a stone's throw away. The property extends across various plots comprising the area's principal appellations, giving rise to whites made primarily with Garganega and Valpolicella reds. Theirs is a consistent selection (to say the least), stylistically distinct for its fruity opulence and pleasant taste. Their 2016 Soave Vigna della Corte comes from Castelcerino, where basalt gives way to tufa. The nose features aromas of ripe yellow fruit, amplified by tropical notes and dried fruit, while on the palate the wine impresses for the way it balances savoriness and richness of flavor. In terms of their reds, we appreciated their Amarone, which overcame a difficult 2014 season. It's a wine that unfolds with aromatic vivacity, accompanied by a firm, crisp palate.

| | |
|---|---|
| ● Amarone della Valpolicella '14 | ▼▼ 6 |
| ○ Soave '17 | ▼▼ 2* |
| ○ Soave Cl. Cimalta '17 | ▼▼ 2* |
| ○ Soave Sup. V. della Corte '16 | ▼▼ 3 |
| ● Valpolicella Sup. '16 | ▼ 3 |
| ● Valpolicella Sup. Ripasso '15 | ▼ 4 |
| ● Amarone della Valpolicella '12 | ▽▽ 6 |
| ○ Soave '16 | ▽▽ 2* |
| ○ Soave Cl. Cimalta '16 | ▽▽ 2* |
| ○ Soave Decennale '15 | ▽▽ 3 |
| ○ Soave V. della Corte '15 | ▽▽ 3* |
| ○ Soave V. della Corte '14 | ▽▽ 3 |
| ○ Soave V. della Corte '13 | ▽▽ 3 |
| ● Valpolicella Sup. '14 | ▽▽ 3 |
| ● Valpolicella Sup. '13 | ▽▽ 3 |
| ● Valpolicella Sup. Ripasso '14 | ▽▽ 3 |

# Corte Gardoni

LOC. GARDONI, 5
37067 VALEGGIO SUL MINCIO [VR]
TEL. +39 0457950382
www.cortegardoni.it

**CELLAR SALES**
**PRE-BOOKED VISITS**
**ANNUAL PRODUCTION** 180,000 bottles
**HECTARES UNDER VINE** 25.00

The Piccoli family's winery is undoubtedly a benchmark for those who love the pure fragrance of those wines born on the banks of Lake Garda. Situated in the southeastern most point of the Custoza appellation, the estate is dedicated primarily to the territory's traditional grape varieties. Their painstaking work began many years ago and has since developed gradually without falling prey to fashionable trends. Indeed their work has always focused on the bond between terroir and cultivar, a bond whose potential can be brought out by the human hand. Their 2016 Bardolino Pràdicà is a perfect example of this synergy, with the delicacy of Corvina meeting the morainic soil that surrounds the Garda basin. Its aromas range from wild fruit to wild rose and black pepper. In the mouth it impresses for its savory, light palate, which also manages to exhibit substances. It's an wine that lingers in your memory. Hats off to their 2016 Custoza Mael as well, a wine that's complex on the nose and juicy on the palate.

| | | |
|---|---|---|
| ● Bardolino Sup. Pràdicà '16 | ♟♟♟ | 3* |
| ○ Custoza Mael '16 | ♟♟ | 3* |
| ● Bardolino Le Fontane '17 | ♟♟ | 2* |
| ● Becco Rosso '16 | ♟♟ | 3 |
| ○ Custoza '17 | ♟♟ | 2* |
| ☉ Bardolino Chiaretto '17 | ♟ | 2 |
| ○ Bianco di Custoza Mael '09 | ♟♟♟ | 2* |
| ○ Bianco di Custoza Mael '08 | ♟♟♟ | 2* |
| ○ Custoza Mael '13 | ♟♟♟ | 3* |
| ○ Custoza Mael '11 | ♟♟♟ | 3* |
| ● Bardolino Le Fontane '16 | ♟♟ | 2* |
| ● Bardolino Sup. Pradicà '15 | ♟♟ | 3* |
| ● Bardolino Sup. Pradicà '13 | ♟♟ | 3* |
| ● Bardolino Sup. Pradicà '12 | ♟♟ | 3* |
| ○ Custoza Mael '15 | ♟♟ | 3* |
| ○ Custoza Mael '14 | ♟♟ | 3* |

# Corte Moschina

VIA MOSCHINA, 1
37030 RONCÀ [VR]
TEL. +39 0457460788
www.cortemoschina.it

**CELLAR SALES**
**PRE-BOOKED VISITS**
**ANNUAL PRODUCTION** 95,000 bottles
**HECTARES UNDER VINE** 35.00
**SUSTAINABLE WINERY**

The Niero family's estate extends across the eastern part of Soave, on the border with the Gambellara DOC appellation and just in front of Monte Calvarina, a large volcano that's still leaving its mark on the territory. All it takes is a glance at the black, basaltic terrain, which alternates with the limestone pushing up the ridge of the Lessini highlands, to appreciate the puzzle of soils and climate types here. These are interpreted by Patrizia, with the help of her sons Alessandro and Giacomo, giving rise to a lovely selection of Soave and Durello wines defined by their exuberant, racy style. Their 2016 Soave I Tarai, a wine from the hills of Roncà, offers up aromas of ripe yellow fruit and dried flowers, which follow through well on a rich, large palate that unfolds generously. Kudos to their 2011 Durello Riserva as well. It's a sparkling wine that lets the assertive character of the cultivar emerge across a crisp, slender and very lengthy palate. Their 2013 Durello Brut and 2015 Recite di Soave Incanto mustn't be forgotten either.

| | | |
|---|---|---|
| ○ Soave Sup. I Tarai '16 | ♟♟ | 3* |
| ○ Lessini Durello Brut M. Cl. '13 | ♟♟ | 4 |
| ○ Lessini Durello Brut Nature M. Cl. Ris. '11 | ♟♟ | 5 |
| ○ Recioto di Soave Incanto '15 | ♟♟ | 4 |
| ○ Soave Roncathe '17 | ♟♟ | 2* |
| ○ Lessini Durello Brut M. Cl. '12 | ♟♟ | 4 |
| ○ Lessini Durello Brut M. Cl. 60 Mesi Ris. '10 | ♟♟ | 5 |
| ○ Ràise '13 | ♟♟ | 5 |
| ○ Recioto di Soave Incanto '14 | ♟♟ | 4 |
| ○ Soave Evaos '16 | ♟♟ | 3 |
| ○ Soave Evaos '15 | ♟♟ | 3* |
| ○ Soave I Tarai '12 | ♟♟ | 3* |
| ○ Soave Roncathe '16 | ♟♟ | 2* |
| ○ Soave Sup. I Tarai '15 | ♟♟ | 3* |

# Corte Rugolin

FRAZ. VALGATARA
VIA RUGOLIN, 1
37020 MARANO DI VALPOLICELLA [VR]
TEL. +39 0457702153
www.corterugolin.it

**CELLAR SALES**
**PRE-BOOKED VISITS**
**ANNUAL PRODUCTION** 80,000 bottles
**HECTARES UNDER VINE** 12.00
**SUSTAINABLE WINERY**

Twins Elena and Federico Coati have fully embraced the family business, using the Corte Rugolin brand to give further shape to the activity begun by their great-grandfather Fortunato, and pursued by their grandfather Giuseppe as well as their father, Bruno. The estate is situated in Valgatara, at the mouth of the Marano valley, a part of Valpolicella Classica that has deep agricultural roots. The winery's vineyards are almost exclusively dedicated to the territory's traditional grape varieties and contribute to a limited range of wines that feature an authentic, juicy style. Their Amarone Monte Danieli, a wine that's aged at length in their cellar, is made with grapes cultivated on the hill of Castelrotto. Their 2012 comes through harmonious and deep, with fruity notes fused perfectly with spices and medicinal herbs. It's the prelude to a rich, full palate that unfolds towards a penetrating, warm finish. Their fresher and suppler 2013 Amarone Corsara de le Strie opts for greater savoriness and tension.

| | |
|---|---|
| ● Amarone della Valpolicella Cl. Monte Danieli Ris. '12 | 🍷🍷 8 |
| ● Amarone della Valpolicella Cl. Crosara de le Strie '13 | 🍷🍷 7 |
| ● Valpolicella Cl. Rugolin '17 | 🍷🍷 3 |
| ● Valpolicella Cl. Sup. Ripasso '15 | 🍷🍷 5 |
| ● Valpolicella Cl. Sup. San Giorgio '15 | 🍷🍷 5 |
| ● Amarone della Valpolicella Cl. Crosara de le Strie '12 | 🍷🍷 7 |
| ● Amarone della Valpolicella Cl. Crosara de le Strie '11 | 🍷🍷 7 |
| ● Recioto della Valpolicella Cl. '15 | 🍷🍷 5 |
| ● Valpolicella Cl. Rugolin '16 | 🍷🍷 3 |
| ● Valpolicella Cl. Sup. Ripasso '14 | 🍷🍷 5 |
| ● Valpolicella Cl. Sup. San Giorgio '14 | 🍷🍷 5 |
| ● Valpolicella Cl. Sup. San Giorgio '13 | 🍷🍷 5 |

# ★Corte Sant'Alda

LOC. FIOI
VIA CAPOVILLA, 28
37030 MEZZANE DI SOTTO [VR]
TEL. +39 0458880006
www.cortesantalda.it

**CELLAR SALES**
**PRE-BOOKED VISITS**
**ACCOMMODATION**
**ANNUAL PRODUCTION** 90,000 bottles
**HECTARES UNDER VINE** 19.00
**VITICULTURE METHOD** Certified Biodynamic

Marinella Camerani has been managing Corte Sant'Alda in the heart of eastern Valpolicella for more than three decades. Considering the area's somewhat unexpected success, a lot has changed over the years, especially in terms of environment and traditions. And yet Marinella's winery has managed to protect a special bond with the territory that developed before the boom, starting with the decision to use biodynamic management and with an ability to express each vineyard (including those dedicated to Soave). The result is a complete, noteworthy selection. Their 2015 Ripasso Campi Magri proves assertive and proud, rich in aromas of wild fruit, spices and balsamic nuances, which give way to an energetic, juicy and very charming palate. Their 2012 Amarone Mithas opens with more complex and tertiary aromas sustained by a full, pervasive palate. Their Adalia wines are interesting. They're part of a new viticultural effort on the other side of the valley that's dedicated to simpler, more approachable wines.

| | |
|---|---|
| ● Amarone della Valpolicella Mithas '12 | 🍷🍷 8 |
| ● Valpolicella Sup. Ripasso Campi Magri '15 | 🍷🍷 5 |
| ○ Agathe '17 | 🍷🍷 4 |
| ● Valpolicella Ca' Fiui '17 | 🍷🍷 3 |
| ● Valpolicella Laute Adalia '17 | 🍷🍷 3 |
| ● Valpolicella Sup. Ripasso Balt Adalia '16 | 🍷🍷 4 |
| ○ Soave '17 | 🍷 3 |
| ○ Soave Singan Adalia '17 | 🍷 3 |
| ● Amarone della Valpolicella '10 | 🍷🍷🍷 8 |
| ● Amarone della Valpolicella '06 | 🍷🍷🍷 7 |
| ● Amarone della Valpolicella '00 | 🍷🍷🍷 7 |
| ● Amarone della Valpolicella '98 | 🍷🍷🍷 7 |
| ● Amarone della Valpolicella Mithas '95 | 🍷🍷🍷 7 |
| ● Valpolicella Sup. Mithas '12 | 🍷🍷🍷 8 |
| ● Valpolicella Sup. Mithas '04 | 🍷🍷🍷 6 |

## Famiglia Cottini
## Monte Zovo

LOC. ZOVO, 23A
37013 CAPRINO VERONESE [VR]
TEL. +39 0457281301
www.montezovo.com

**CELLAR SALES**
**PRE-BOOKED VISITS**
**ACCOMMODATION AND RESTAURANT SERVICE**
**ANNUAL PRODUCTION** 1,000,000 bottles
**HECTARES UNDER VINE** 140.00
**SUSTAINABLE WINERY**

The Cottini family winery can be found in Caprino Veronese, in the westernmost part of Valpolicella, on the border with Valdadige. It's an imposing structure, equipped for a selection of high quality wines that manage to respect the peculiar character of each harvest. Their vineyards span out across the eastern part of the appellation, primarily. It's an area less influenced by the climate of Lake Garda, thus conferring fullness and rigor to their more ambitious wines. Having such a large estate at their disposal allowed the Cottini family to manage a year as difficult as 2014. It gave rise to an intensely aromatic Amarone with fragrances of fruit, chocolate and ground coffee. These follow through to a potent palate that exhibits surprising extractive force. Their interesting 2017 Sauvignon, made with grapes cultivated on the high hills, features flowery aromas and an energetic palate. Their 2016 Ripasso also proved excellent.

## Dal Cero
## Tenuta Corte Giacobbe

VIA MOSCHINA, 11
37030 RONCÀ [VR]
TEL. +39 0457460110
www.dalcerofamily.it

**CELLAR SALES**
**PRE-BOOKED VISITS**
**ANNUAL PRODUCTION** 300,000 bottles
**HECTARES UNDER VINE** 40.00

Few producers have managed to achieve such rapid critical and market success as the Dal Cero family. It's all thanks to a bond with Soave's viticulture that goes back to the first half of the 20th century and that's been reinforced by the most recent generation through a dynamic, modern outlook. Their vineyards run along the slopes of the Crocetta and Calvarina mountain ridges and include both the Soave appellation and that of Monti Lessini Durello. The grapes for their Valpolicella reds are supplied by a solid network of local vine growers. Their Runcata vineyard, situated at 450 meters of elevation with southwestern exposure, gives rise to their 2016 Soave. It's a highly characteristic wine (to say the least) in its aromas of citrus and flowers, crossed by a mineral vein. The palate features fullness and drive thanks to an extraordinary acidic backbone, which also lends the wine it's concomitant drinkability. Their 2013 Amarone also impressed, with its pure fruit anticipating a crisp, pleasantly austere palate.

| | |
|---|---|
| ● Amarone della Valpolicella '14 | ♟♟♟ 8 |
| ● Ca' Linverno '14 | ♟♟ 4 |
| ● La Sogara Comis '13 | ♟♟ 3 |
| ○ Sauvignon '17 | ♟♟ 4 |
| ● Valpolicella Sup. Ripasso '16 | ♟♟ 5 |
| ● Valpolicella Sup. '16 | ♟ 4 |
| ● Amarone della Valpolicella '13 | ♀♀ 7 |
| ● Amarone della Valpolicella '12 | ♀♀ 6 |
| ● Amarone della Valpolicella '11 | ♀♀ 6 |
| ● Amarone della Valpolicella Ris. '09 | ♀♀ 8 |
| ● Amarone della Valpolicella Ris. '08 | ♀♀ 8 |
| ○ Sauvignon '16 | ♀♀ 4 |
| ○ Sauvignon '15 | ♀♀ 4 |
| ● Valpolicella Sup. '15 | ♀♀ 4 |
| ● Valpolicella Sup. Ripasso '15 | ♀♀ 4 |
| ● Valpolicella Sup. Ripasso '14 | ♀♀ 4 |
| ● Valpolicella Sup. Ripasso '12 | ♀♀ 4 |

| | |
|---|---|
| ○ Soave Sup. Vign. Runcata '16 | ♟♟ 5 |
| ● Amarone della Valpolicella '13 | ♟♟ 7 |
| ○ Pino Grigio delle Venezie Ramato '17 | ♟♟ 2* |
| ○ Soave '17 | ♟♟ 2* |
| ● Valpolicella Sup. Ripasso '15 | ♟♟ 4 |
| ○ Soave Sup. Vign. Runcata '14 | ♀♀♀ 2* |
| ● Amarone della Valpolicella '12 | ♀♀ 7 |
| ● Amarone della Valpolicella '11 | ♀♀ 7 |
| ○ Lessini Durello Dosaggio Zero M. Cl. Augusto '12 | ♀♀ 5 |
| ○ Soave '15 | ♀♀ 2* |
| ○ Soave Corte Giacobbe '16 | ♀♀ 2* |
| ○ Soave Sup. Runcata '12 | ♀♀ 2* |
| ○ Soave Sup. Vign. Runcata '15 | ♀♀ 4 |
| ○ Soave Sup. Vign. Runcata '15 | ♀♀ 4 |
| ○ Soave Sup. Vign. Runcata '13 | ♀♀ 2* |
| ● Valpolicella Sup. Ripasso '14 | ♀♀ 5 |

# Dal Maso

c.da Selva, 62
36054 Montebello Vicentino [VI]
Tel. +39 0444649104
www.dalmasovini.com

**CELLAR SALES**
**PRE-BOOKED VISITS**
**ACCOMMODATION AND RESTAURANT SERVICE**
**ANNUAL PRODUCTION** 350,000 bottles
**HECTARES UNDER VINE** 30.00
**SUSTAINABLE WINERY**

The Dal Maso family's historic estate, today firmly in the hands of Nicola, Anna and Silvia, is slowly moving the heart of production away from Gambellara and towards its complementary neighbor, Colli Berici. On the one hand, Garganega continues to take center stage, with a style focused on finesse and tension (aspects that should be considered in relation to the volcanic character of the territory). On the other hand, there's increased attention to Bordeaux varieties and Tai Rosso, thus balancing with accuracy and clarity the natural prowess of the area's traditional wines. The release of their Riva del Molino has been postponed, so this year their Merlot Casara Roveri took on the role of leader. A favorable 2015 gave rise to a complete, fruit-driven wine with balsamic finesse and foresty aromatic atmospheres. It's all held together by a close-knit and balanced palate, made possible by the right amount of acidity and tannic presence. Their 2015 Tai Rosso Colpizzarda also put in a good performance, proving tauter and crisp.

| | |
|---|---|
| ● Colli Berici Merlot Casara Roveri '15 | ▼▼▼ 5 |
| ● Colli Berici Tai Rosso Colpizzarda '15 | ▼▼ 5 |
| ● Colli Berici Rosso Terra dei Rovi '15 | ▼▼ 6 |
| ● Colli Berici Tai Rosso Montemitorio '16 | ▼▼ 3 |
| ○ Gambellara Ca' Fischele '17 | ▼▼ 3 |
| ● Montebelvedere Cabernet '16 | ▼▼ 3 |
| ○ Gambellara '17 | ▼ 2 |
| ○ Lessini Durello Brut | ▼ 3 |
| ○ Gambellara Cl. Riva del Molino '07 | ▼▼▼ 2* |
| ● Cabernet Casara Roveri '15 | ♈♈ 4 |
| ● Cabernet Montebelvedere '15 | ♈♈ 3 |
| ● Colli Berici Tai Rosso Montemitorio '15 | ♈♈ 2* |
| ● Colli Berici Tai Rosso Montemitorio '14 | ♈♈ 2* |
| ○ Gambellara Ca' Fischele '16 | ♈♈ 2* |
| ○ Gambellara Riva del Molino '16 | ♈♈ 3* |
| ○ Recioto di Gambellara Cl. Riva dei Perari '15 | ♈♈ 5 |

# De Stefani

via Cadorna, 92
30020 Fossalta di Piave [VE]
Tel. +39 042167502
www.de-stefani.it

**CELLAR SALES**
**PRE-BOOKED VISITS**
**ANNUAL PRODUCTION** 500,000 bottles
**HECTARES UNDER VINE** 60.00
**SUSTAINABLE WINERY**

The area of Piave slopes down from the northern Vittorio Veneto hills all the way to the Adriatic coast and nearby Jesolo. It's a vast and varied territory that ranges from steep peaks to gravelly plains, giving way, finally, to clay and sand. This is the background against which Alessando De Stefani's work unfolds. Spread out along Refrontolo, Monastier and Fossalta di Piave, his large estate is carefully managed so as to make possible a range of wines that are recognizable for their richness and elegance. Thanks to a particularly successful 2016 vintage, their Olmera, a blend, once again proves to be the symbol of the De Stefani family's work. Their Tai Bianco is harvested slightly dried and then it's matured in barrels, while their Sauvignon is vinified in steel vats. The two are blended only after. The result is a vibrant expression of tropical fruit and citrus supported by a full, taut palate that's long and juicy.

| | |
|---|---|
| ○ Olmera '16 | ▼▼ 5 |
| ● Kreda '15 | ▼▼ 5 |
| ● Piave Merlot Plavis '15 | ▼▼ 4 |
| ● Solèr '15 | ▼▼ 4 |
| ● Stefen 1624 '13 | ▼▼ 8 |
| ○ Conegliano Valdobbiadene Brut '17 | ▼ 3 |
| ● Cabernet Sauvignon '14 | ♈♈ 3 |
| ● Colli di Conegliano Rosso Stefan 1624 '11 | ♈♈ 8 |
| ● Kreda '14 | ♈♈ 5 |
| ● Kreda Refosco '13 | ♈♈ 5 |
| ○ Olmera '15 | ♈♈ 5 |
| ● Piave Malanotte '12 | ♈♈ 3 |
| ● Piave Raboso Vign. Terre Nobili '11 | ♈♈ 4 |
| ● Soler '14 | ♈♈ 4 |
| ● Stefen 1624 '12 | ♈♈ 8 |
| ○ Tombola di Pin Brut M. Cl. '08 | ♈♈ 7 |

## Conte Emo Capodilista
## La Montecchia

VIA MONTECCHIA, 16
35030 SELVAZZANO DENTRO [PD]
TEL. +39 049637294
www.lamontecchia.it

**CELLAR SALES**
**PRE-BOOKED VISITS**
**ACCOMMODATION**
**ANNUAL PRODUCTION** 144,000 bottles
**HECTARES UNDER VINE** 30.00
**SUSTAINABLE WINERY**

The Euganei hills are a system of volcanic slopes that rise up in the heart of the Po Valley. It's a feature that would make you think of a certain type of climate, especially in terms of summer temperatures and rainfall. These qualities have been fundamental for the viticultural decisions made by the Emo Capodilista family. At the estate situated in Selvazzano Dentro they focus on white grape varieties, Merlot and Carmenère while in Baone, in the southernmost part of the territory, they work to bring out the sunny character of Sabernet Sauvignon. Their 2015 Baon is a blend of the best Cabernet Sauvignon and Merlot grapes. Aromatically it's an extremely deep wine with fragrances of ripe fruit giving way to hints of pencil led, fines herbes and spices. The palate is potent, gradually gaining in tension and guts, and closing with a crisp, fine finish. Their 2015 Ireneo, an energetic, substantive Cabernet Sauvignon, proves rich in fruit and mineral sensations.

| | |
|---|---|
| ● Baon '15 | 🍷🍷🍷 7 |
| ● Colli Euganei Cabernet Sauvignon Ireneo '15 | 🍷🍷 4 |
| ○ Colli Euganei Fiori d'Arancio Spumante | 🍷🍷 2* |
| ● Colli Euganei Rosso Ca' Emo '16 | 🍷🍷 3 |
| ● Colli Euganei Rosso Villa Capodilista '13 | 🍷🍷 5 |
| ● Progetto Recupero Carmenere '15 | 🍷🍷 3 |
| ○ Colli Euganei Pinot Bianco '17 | 🍷 2 |
| ● Forzaté Raboso '14 | 🍷 2 |
| ○ Piuchebello '17 | 🍷 2 |
| ● Colli Euganei Cabernet Sauvignon Ireneo '12 | 🍷🍷🍷 4* |
| ○ Colli Euganei Fior d'Arancio Passito Donna Daria '06 | 🍷🍷🍷 5 |

## Farina

LOC. PEDEMONTE
VIA BOLLA, 11
37029 SAN PIETRO IN CARIANO [VR]
TEL. +39 0457701349
www.farinawines.com

**CELLAR SALES**
**PRE-BOOKED VISITS**
**ANNUAL PRODUCTION** 800,000 bottles
**HECTARES UNDER VINE** 45.00

Claudio, Elena and Fabio have taken the reins of the family winery and in just a short time they have revolutionized production. In addition to their private vineyards, they have reached out to a large group of Valpolicella vine growers who supply grapes to the family's lovely cellar in Pedemonte, a district of San Pietro in Cariano. If their fresher wines aim for stylistic lightness and varietal expression, their more ambitious wines pursue complexity and elegance. Their 2012 Amarone Montefante Riserva put in an excellent performance. It's a wine made with grapes from Castelrotto and that features a vibrant color. On the nose it offers up classic aromas of ripe cherry, hints of aromatic herbs and spices, and a deep note of forest undergrowth. In the mouth it proves full and potent, sustained by a lively acidity and smooth tannins. Their 2016 Recioto unfolds sweet and juicy on the palate.

| | |
|---|---|
| ● Amarone della Valpolicella Cl. Montefante Ris. '12 | 🍷🍷 8 |
| ● Amarone della Valpolicella Cl. '15 | 🍷🍷 5 |
| ● Recioto della Valpolicella Cl. '16 | 🍷🍷 5 |
| ● Valpolicella Cl. Sup. Ripasso Montecorna '16 | 🍷🍷 3 |
| ● Valpolicella Cl. Sup. Ripasso Remo Farina '16 | 🍷🍷 2* |
| ● Corte Cavalli '16 | 🍷 4 |
| ● Nodo d'Amore '16 | 🍷 3 |
| ● Amarone della Valpolicella Cl. '13 | 🍷🍷 5 |
| ● Amarone della Valpolicella Cl. Montefante Ris. '11 | 🍷🍷 8 |
| ● Valpolicella Cl. Sup. '15 | 🍷🍷 2* |
| ● Valpolicella Cl. Sup. Ripasso '15 | 🍷🍷 2* |
| ● Valpolicella Cl. Sup. Ripasso Montecorna '15 | 🍷🍷 3 |

# Fattori

FRAZ. TERROSSA
VIA OLMO, 6
37030 RONCÀ [VR]
TEL. +39 0457460041
www.fattoriwines.com

**CELLAR SALES**
**PRE-BOOKED VISITS**
**ANNUAL PRODUCTION** 280,000 bottles
**HECTARES UNDER VINE** 72.00
**SUSTAINABLE WINERY**

In recent years the center of Antonio Fattori's operations have shifted from the hills of Soave towards Valpolicella where in addition to their new vineyards they've built a cellar designed to carry out the various stages of production. Today they avail themselves of a sizable estate, concentrating on three types of wines: Verona's great reds, mineral whites made with Garganega and Lessini Durello, a sparkler common along the hill area that borders with Vicenza. Their multifaceted 2013 Amarone and 2014 Col de La Bastia both feature tertiary fragrances that can be traced back to the dried grapes used in production. The former comes through savory and balanced, while the second proves softer and more pervasive on the palate, refreshed by a taut acidity. Their 2017 Soave Runcaris is an interesting wine made with grapes cultivated in the 'classic' heart of the appellation, at elevations ranging from 150 to 250 meters. Aromatically it sees fresh, varietal fragrances while its energetic palate exhibits nice tension.

| | |
|---|---|
| ● Amarone della Valpolicella '13 | ♥♥ 8 |
| ● Amarone della Valpolicella Col de La Bastia '14 | ♥♥ 6 |
| ○ Lessini Durello Brut Roncà M. Cl. 36 Mesi | ♥♥ 4 |
| ○ Soave Cl. Runcaris '17 | ♥♥ 2* |
| ○ Soave Danieli '17 | ♥ 2 |
| ○ Soave Motto Piane '16 | ♥ 4 |
| ● Valpolicella Col della Bastia '17 | ♥ 3 |
| ● Valpolicella Ripasso Col de la Bastia '16 | ♥ 5 |
| ● Amarone della Valpolicella Col de la Bastia '13 | ♡♡ 6 |
| ○ Lessini Durello Brut M. Cl. 60 Mesi Roncà '11 | ♡♡ 6 |
| ○ Recioto di Soave Motto Piane '15 | ♡♡ 5 |
| ○ Soave Danieli '16 | ♡♡ 2* |
| ○ Soave Motto Piane '15 | ♡♡ 4 |

# Il Filò delle Vigne

VIA TERRALBA, 14
35030 BAONE [PD]
TEL. +39 042956243
www.ilfilodellevigne.it

**CELLAR SALES**
**PRE-BOOKED VISITS**
**ANNUAL PRODUCTION** 50,000 bottles
**HECTARES UNDER VINE** 22.00

Entrepreneur Carlo Giordani is deeply connected to the territory of Euganeo and in love with the wines made here. The family's winery is situated in the southernmost part of the district, sprawling out along the Baone hills that slope down towards the Padana plains. It's an area characterized by a hot, dry climate, which, along with soil conditions, gives rise to an authoritative selection. Their Bordeaux wines are offered in limited numbers and feature a style that makes flavor and the expression of fruit its guiding principles. This year the only thing missing from Giordani's strong and flawless selection is a standout. Their 2015 Borgo delle Casette Riserva once again proves to be a quintessential Cabernet, deep in its expression of red fruit and spices. These are complemented by a rich, firm palate that's well-sustained by tannins. Their 2015 Casa del Merlo (made with Merlot) is more mature and approachable in its aromas, characterized by a caressing palate with nice length. Their 2015 Cecilia di Barone also proved excellent.

| | |
|---|---|
| ● Colli Euganei Cabernet Borgo delle Casette Ris. '15 | ♥♥ 5 |
| ● Colli Euganei Merlot Casa del Merlo '15 | ♥♥ 5 |
| ○ Calto delle Fate '15 | ♥♥ 4 |
| ● Colli Euganei Cabernet Cecilia di Baone Ris. '15 | ♥♥ 4 |
| ○ Terralba di Baone '17 | ♥♥ 3 |
| ● Volo '16 | ♥♥ 3 |
| ● Colli Euganei Cabernet Borgo delle Casette Ris. '12 | ♡♡♡ 5 |
| ● Colli Euganei Cabernet Borgo delle Casette Ris. '10 | ♡♡♡ 5 |
| ● Colli Euganei Cabernet Borgo delle Casette Ris. '06 | ♡♡♡ 5 |
| ● Colli Euganei Cabernet Borgo delle Casette Ris. '13 | ♡♡ 5 |
| ● Colli Euganei Merlot Casa del Merlo '13 | ♡♡ 5 |

## Silvano Follador

LOC. FOLLO
FRAZ. SANTO STEFANO
VIA CALLONGA, 11
31040 VALDOBBIADENE [TV]
TEL. +39 0423900295
www.silvanofollador.it

**CELLAR SALES**
**PRE-BOOKED VISITS**
**ANNUAL PRODUCTION** 20,000 bottles
**HECTARES UNDER VINE** 3.50

Alberta and Silvano Follador manage the family winery in the heart of the historic DOC appellation of Conegliano Valdobbiadene, the 'capital' of Prosecco winemaking. You'd be off the mark, however, if you thought of the classic winery that purchases its grapes and works them into sparkling wine every day. Theirs is a small operation that makes you think of a garage winemaker (or just a bit more). Part of that has to do with their steep and difficult vineyards, cultivated according to the principles of sustainable agriculture and worked into wines that explore Glera's hidden soul, constituted of faint aromas, acidity and tension. On the palate, their 2017 Brut Nature proves their stylistic choices are right on track. It's a Prosecco that eschews tropical tones and citrus in favor of wild flowers, apple and a slightly herbaceous touch. The palate is absent of redundant sugars, unfolding with vigor and savoriness. Their 2017 Bianco Fermo is also very interesting. It's a wine that brings out the best of Glera's varietal qualities, with a palate that's natural and rigorous at the same time.

| | |
|---|---|
| ○ Valdobbiadene Brut Nature '17 | ▼▼ 5 |
| ○ Bianco Fermo '17 | ▼▼ 3 |
| ○ Cartizze Brut Nature M. Cl. '16 | ▼▼ 4 |
| ○ Cartizze Brut '08 | ▼▼▼ 4 |
| ○ Valdobbiadene Brut Nature '16 | ▼▼▼ 5 |
| ○ Bianco Fermo '16 | ♈♈ 3 |
| ○ Cartizze Brut Nature '13 | ♈♈ 4 |
| ○ Cartizze Brut Nature '11 | ♈♈ 4 |
| ○ Cartizze Nature '12 | ♈♈ 4 |
| ○ Valdobbiadene Brut Nature '15 | ♈♈ 4 |
| ○ Valdobbiadene Brut Nature '14 | ♈♈ 4 |
| ○ Valdobbiadene Brut Nature '13 | ♈♈ 4 |
| ○ Valdobbiadene Brut Nature '12 | ♈♈ 3* |
| ○ Valdobbiadene Brut Nature '11 | ♈♈ 3* |
| ○ Valdobbiadene Sup. Brut Dosaggio Zero M. Cl. '12 | ♈♈ 3 |

## Le Fraghe

LOC. COLOMBARA, 3
37010 CAVAION VERONESE [VR]
TEL. +39 0457236832
www.fraghe.it

**CELLAR SALES**
**PRE-BOOKED VISITS**
**ACCOMMODATION**
**ANNUAL PRODUCTION** 120,000 bottles
**HECTARES UNDER VINE** 28.00
**VITICULTURE METHOD** Certified Organic

The low valley of Adige is a gravelly plain closed in between Monte Baldo and the Lessinia highlands, an area that's well-ventilated and characterized by its lean soil, which rises between 150 and 200 meters above sea level. It's here, in Cavaion Veronese, that Matilde Poggi manages the family winery, an estate dedicated almost exclusively to the traditional varieties used for making Bardolino. Their wines point up the rigorous character of the territory while simultaneously highlighting its spirit of elegance and grace. Made with grapes cultivate in the appellation's 'classic' heart, their 2016 Bardolino Brol Grande reveals a multifaceted aromatic complexity with primary notes of fruit, then gradual hints of spices, forest undergrowth and medicinal herbs. It's a profile reflected even more clearly in the mouth, with smoky and mineral notes pointing up an extremely juicy and sapid palate. Aromatically, their 2017 Bardolino follows in its footsteps, though with greater approachability and suppleness.

| | |
|---|---|
| ● Bardolino '17 | ▼▼ 2* |
| ● Bardolino Cl. Brol Grande '16 | ▼▼ 3* |
| ○ Camporengo Garganega '17 | ▼▼ 2* |
| ● Quaiare Cabernet '16 | ▼▼ 4 |
| ⊙ Bardolino Chiaretto Ròdon '17 | ▼ 2 |
| ● Chelidon Rondinella '16 | ▼ 2 |
| ● Bardolino Cl. Brol Grande '15 | ♈♈♈ 3* |
| ● Bardolino Cl. Brol Grande '12 | ♈♈♈ 3* |
| ● Bardolino Cl. Brol Grande '11 | ♈♈♈ 3* |
| ● Bardolino '16 | ♈♈ 2* |
| ● Bardolino '15 | ♈♈ 2* |
| ⊙ Bardolino Chiaretto Rodon '16 | ♈♈ 2* |
| ⊙ Bardolino Chiaretto Ròdon '15 | ♈♈ 2* |
| ● Bardolino Cl. Brol Grande '13 | ♈♈ 3* |
| ○ Camporengo Garganega '16 | ♈♈ 2* |
| ○ Camporengo Garganega '15 | ♈♈ 2* |
| ● Quaiare Cabernet '15 | ♈♈ 4 |

# Marchesi Fumanelli

FRAZ. SAN FLORIANO
VIA SQUARANO, 1
37029 SAN PIETRO IN CARIANO [VR]
TEL. +39 0457704875
www.squarano.com

CELLAR SALES
PRE-BOOKED VISITS
RESTAURANT SERVICE
ANNUAL PRODUCTION 50,000 bottles
HECTARES UNDER VINE 23.00

The Marquis Fumanelli's headquarters in San Pietro in Cariano is a lovely villa situated atop a hill, surrounded by cypress trees and vineyards that go back to the Roman era. The varieties cultivated here are primarily those common to Valpolicella, though more plots are scattered throughout the classic heart of the appellation. Only the best grapes are used for their selection, whose style is characterized by finesse and depth of taste. We have an excellent example in their 2015 Valpolicella Superiore, which doesn't draw on grape drying for richness of flavor or fragrance, but for fresher notes of wild fruit and fines herbes, enriched by a suffuse mineral presence. It's one of the most elegant wines of its kind, proving long and penetrating on the palate. It's an expressive trajectory that's replicated by their 2013 Amarone, which is naturally sweeter and riper on the nose, but just as supple and taut on the palate.

| | |
|---|---|
| ● Valpolicella Cl. Sup. '15 | ▼▼ 3* |
| ● Amarone della Valpolicella Cl. '13 | ▼▼ 5 |
| ○ Terso '15 | ▼ 3 |
| ● Amarone della Valpolicella Cl. '11 | ♀♀ 5 |
| ● Amarone della Valpolicella Cl. Octavius Ris. '10 | ♀♀ 8 |
| ● Amarone della Valpolicella Cl. Octavius Ris. '07 | ♀♀ 8 |
| ● Valpolicella Cl. Sup. '14 | ♀♀ 3 |
| ● Valpolicella Cl. Sup. '11 | ♀♀ 3 |
| ● Valpolicella Cl. Sup. Squarano '14 | ♀♀ 3 |
| ● Valpolicella Cl. Sup. Squarano '10 | ♀♀ 3 |

# Gamba

VIA GNIREGA, 19
37020 MARANO DI VALPOLICELLA [VR]
TEL. +39 0456801714
www.vinigamba.it

CELLAR SALES
PRE-BOOKED VISITS
ANNUAL PRODUCTION 70,000 bottles
HECTARES UNDER VINE 15.00

The Aldrighetti brothers cultivate their family vineyards in the valley of Marano, a territory that has resisted urbanization. It's a territory that still today contributes to Valpolicella's rural image, kept green by its substantially sized viticultural patrimony. Giovanni, Giuseppe and Martino attend to all phases of production, from the fields to bottling, refining a selection of wines dedicated almost exclusively to the DOC appellation's classic wines. Theirs is a deep tie with tradition that's highlighted in their stylistic approach, which sees power and vigor at the center. Their Campedel wines, which are made with grapes cultivated on Gnirega hill, represent their premium line. Their 2015 Ripasso is among them, a wine that's distinct for its aromas of very ripe red fruit, enriched by nuances of forest undergrowth and aromatic herbs. In the mouth it surprises for its suppleness, proving savory and gutsy. Their 2014 Amarone Le Quare opts for greater aromatic complexity and pervasiveness, though it's also more tannic and austere.

| | |
|---|---|
| ● Amarone della Valpolicella Cl. Campedel Ris. '11 | ▼▼ 8 |
| ● Amarone della Valpolicella Cl. Le Quare '14 | ▼▼ 6 |
| ● Valpolicella Cl. Sup. Ripasso Campedel '15 | ▼▼ 5 |
| ● Campedel '15 | ▼ 4 |
| ● Valpolicella Cl. Le Quare '17 | ▼ 2 |
| ● Valpolicella Cl. Sup. Ripasso Le Quare '15 | ▼ 3 |
| ● Amarone della Valpolicella Cl. Campedel '13 | ♀♀ 8 |
| ● Amarone della Valpolicella Cl. Campedel '12 | ♀♀ 8 |
| ● Amarone della Valpolicella Cl. Campedel Ris. '10 | ♀♀ 8 |
| ● Amarone della Valpolicella Le Quare Cl. '13 | ♀♀ 5 |

## ★Gini

VIA MATTEOTTI, 42
37032 MONTEFORTE D'ALPONE [VR]
TEL. +39 0457611908
www.ginivini.com

CELLAR SALES
PRE-BOOKED VISITS
ANNUAL PRODUCTION 200,000 bottles
HECTARES UNDER VINE 58.00
VITICULTURE METHOD Certified Organic

There's important news at Monteforte d'Alpone: in addition to their classic Soaves, this year they're offering their first Valpolicellas. This wasn't just some offhand choice, but rather the result of a forward-thinking viticultural project that began more than a decade ago and is just now coming into fruition. Sandro and Claudio Gini have faced the challenge with the grit of true vigneron, leaving nothing up to chance and offering their most ambitious wines only in the moment they felt they were ready. Nonetheless, the heart of their selection rests with Soave, as our recent tastings demonstrated with three wines that tell different stories and express different territories. Their 2015 Salvarenza is made with grapes cultivated in historic, ungrafted vineyards. It exhibits great aromatic depth and a full, potent palate that's supported by a savory acidity. Their 2016 La Frosca, on the other hand, goes all in on elegance, with flowery aromas and white fruit following through to a racy palate that's highly drinkable in its juiciness.

| | |
|---|---|
| ○ Soave Cl. Contrada Salvarenza V. V. '15 | 🍷🍷 5 |
| ○ Soave Cl. La Froscà '16 | 🍷🍷 4 |
| ○ Soave Cl. '17 | 🍷🍷 3 |
| ○ Soave Cl. Contrada Salvarenza V. V. '14 | 🍷🍷🍷 5 |
| ○ Soave Cl. Contrada Salvarenza V. V. '09 | 🍷🍷🍷 5 |
| ○ Soave Cl. Contrada Salvarenza V. V. '08 | 🍷🍷🍷 5 |
| ○ Soave Cl. Contrada Salvarenza V. V. '07 | 🍷🍷🍷 5 |
| ○ Soave Cl. La Froscà '11 | 🍷🍷🍷 4* |
| ○ Soave Cl. La Froscà '06 | 🍷🍷🍷 4* |
| ○ Soave Cl. La Froscà '05 | 🍷🍷🍷 4* |
| ○ Soave Cl. Sup. Contrada Salvarenza V. V. '00 | 🍷🍷🍷 5 |

## Giusti Wine

VIA DEL VOLANTE, 4
31040 NERVESA DELLA BATTAGLIA [TV]
TEL. +39 0422720198
www.giustiwine.com

CELLAR SALES
PRE-BOOKED VISITS
ACCOMMODATION
ANNUAL PRODUCTION 200,000 bottles
HECTARES UNDER VINE 75.00
SUSTAINABLE WINERY

Ermenegildo Giusti's winery may have only been founded a few years ago, but it has gradually developed to encompass already active vineyards situated primarily along the slopes of Montello, near Nervesa della Battaglia. In the plains that lay below the Treviso hill a new cellar is taking shape, one that will serve all phases of production and whose construction is designed to have a minimum environmental impact. Their selection is divided between sparkling and still wines, and comprises various typologies. Their versatile style is the result of adapting methods for winemaking and maturation. Their 2016 Recantina Augusto put in a solid performance during our tastings. It's a red that only partially tames the cultivar's more rustic qualities, leaving room for fragrances of wild berries and wild herbs, with oak guiding the background. On the palate, aromatic richness is well-contrasted by a healthy, spirited acidity. Their Asolo Brut also delivered. It's a Prosecco that features varietal sensations before unfolding on a crisp, savory palate with fine prickle.

| | |
|---|---|
| ● Amarone della Valpolicella Cl. '14 | 🍷🍷 8 |
| ● Antonio '15 | 🍷🍷 5 |
| ○ Asolo Brut | 🍷🍷 2 |
| ○ Longheri Pinot Grigio '17 | 🍷🍷 3 |
| ● Montello e Colli Asolani Recantina Augusto '16 | 🍷🍷 5 |
| ● Valpolicella Cl. Sup. '16 | 🍷🍷 5 |
| ○ Asolo Extra Dry | 🍷 2 |
| ○ Chardonnay Dei Carni '17 | 🍷 3 |
| ○ Prosecco Extra Dry Rosalia | 🍷 3 |
| ● Amarone della Valpolicella Cl. '13 | 🍷🍷 8 |
| ○ Chardonnay Dei Carni '16 | 🍷🍷 3 |
| ○ Chardonnay Dei Carni '15 | 🍷🍷 3 |
| ● Montello e Colli Asolani Recantina '15 | 🍷🍷 5 |
| ○ Pinot Grigio Longheri '16 | 🍷🍷 3 |
| ● Valpolicella Ripasso Sup. '13 | 🍷🍷 5 |

# La Giuva

VIA TREZZOLANO, 20C
37141 VERONA
TEL. +39 3421117089
www.lagiuva.com

CELLAR SALES
PRE-BOOKED VISITS
ANNUAL PRODUCTION 20,000 bottles
HECTARES UNDER VINE 9.50
VITICULTURE METHOD Certified Organic

Alberti Malesani, along with his daughters Giulia and Valentina, have given life to a lovely winery in Val Squaranto, one of the few corners of Valpolicella in which vine growing is a less prevalent activity. Today, a small estate managed organically is coming into its own, providing grapes for a limited selection of wines, but one that's endowed with an original profile. At the center of it all are Verona's classic reds, which manage to preserve freshness and dynamism even when expressing power. Without a shadow of a doubt, their most representative wine is their Valpo, a wine made exclusively with the area's traditional grapes, harvested and left to rest for two weeks before crushing. A brilliantly colored and lovely 2017 features aromas of cherry crossed by notes of pepper and wild rose. In the mouth, the vineyards' elevation is on display, with a juicy acidity that lengthens the palate.

# Gorgo

FRAZ. CUSTOZA
LOC. GORGO
37066 SOMMACAMPAGNA [VR]
TEL. +39 045516063
www.cantinagorgo.com

ANNUAL PRODUCTION 350,000 bottles
HECTARES UNDER VINE 50.00

There's no doubt that this is a good moment for wines like Bardolino, a red that can even be enjoyed cool. It's a wine that offers up intense aromas of rose and pepper, endowed with the juicy, sapid, highly pleasing flavor. The Gorgo family are authoritative interpreters, bolstered by almost 50 years of winemaking and an estate that extends across the southeast part of the Garda basin. Here they also cultivate varieties used for making Custoza. And it's a Custoza that leads their selection, their 2017 San Michelin, an aromatic wine in its fragrances of fresh flowers and white fruit. It's an energetic and crisp profile that lengthens the palate gracefully, highlighting tension and suppleness. Their 2016 Summa is of an entirely different style. Its grapes are harvested late, and the wine is worked more slowly, making for a wine of notable aromatic depth, with a potent and flavorful palate.

| | |
|---|---|
| ● Recioto della Valpolicella '16 | ♔♔ 6 |
| ● Valpolicella Il Valpo '17 | ♔♔ 3 |
| ● Valpolicella Sup. Il Rientro '15 | ♔♔ 5 |
| ● Amarone della Valpolicella '13 | ♕♕ 7 |
| ● Amarone della Valpolicella '12 | ♕♕ 7 |
| ● Recioto della Valpolicella '15 | ♕♕ 6 |
| ● Recioto della Valpolicella '13 | ♕♕ 3 |
| ● Recioto della Valpolicella '12 | ♕♕ 3 |
| ● Valpolicella '13 | ♕♕ 2* |
| ● Valpolicella Il Valpo '16 | ♕♕ 3 |
| ● Valpolicella Il Valpo '15 | ♕♕ 3 |
| ● Valpolicella Sup. Il Rientro '14 | ♕♕ 5 |
| ● Valpolicella Sup. Il Rientro '13 | ♕♕ 5 |
| ● Valpolicella Sup. Il Rientro '12 | ♕♕ 3 |
| ● Valpolicella Sup. Il Rientro '11 | ♕♕ 3 |

| | |
|---|---|
| ○ Custoza San Michelin '17 | ♔♔ 2* |
| ● Ca' Nova '15 | ♔♔ 3 |
| ○ Custoza '17 | ♔♔ 2* |
| ○ Custoza Sup. Summa '16 | ♔♔ 2* |
| ● Bardolino '17 | ♔ 2 |
| ⊘ Bardolino Chiaretto '17 | ♔ 2 |
| ⊘ Custoza Brut Perlato | ♔ 3 |
| ⊘ Bardolino Chiaretto '16 | ♕♕ 2* |
| ● Bardolino Sup. Monte Maggiore '15 | ♕♕ 3 |
| ○ Custoza San Michelin '16 | ♕♕ 2* |
| ○ Custoza San Michelin '15 | ♕♕ 2* |
| ○ Custoza San Michelin '14 | ♕♕ 2* |
| ○ Custoza San Michelin '13 | ♕♕ 2* |
| ○ Custoza Sup. Summa '15 | ♕♕ 2* |
| ○ Custoza Sup. Summa '14 | ♕♕ 2* |
| ○ Custoza Sup. Summa '13 | ♕♕ 2* |

# Gregoletto

FRAZ. PREMAOR
VIA SAN MARTINO, 83
31050 MIANE [TV]
TEL. +39 0438970463
www.gregoletto.com

**CELLAR SALES**
**PRE-BOOKED VISITS**
**ANNUAL PRODUCTION** 200,000 bottles
**HECTARES UNDER VINE** 18.00

The Gregoletto family's estate is concentrated in a small patch of flatlands amid the hills famously used for growing Glera, the white grape that gives rise to Prosecco. Luigi is at the helm, and he's the one who deserves credit for having reinforced the identity of winery's selection without being thrown off by the sparkling wine's incredible success. He's also managed to stay true to their still wines, which are interpreted with authenticity and simplicity. Their 2017 Manzoni Bianco isn't designed to amaze. Its aromas are fresh and fragrant, dominated by sensations of ripe and juicy apple enriched by flowery and delicately citrusy nuances. In the mouth it proves crisp and firm, with a long, taut finish. In terms of Prosecco, their Tranquillo once again leads. The 2017 is a wine that's simple but never banal in its aromatic expression and endowed with a natural, savory and highly enjoyable palate.

| | |
|---|---|
| ● Cabernet '16 | ♟♟ 3 |
| ○ Colli di Conegliano Bianco Albio '17 | ♟♟ 3 |
| ○ Conegliano Valdobbiadene Prosecco Tranquillo '17 | ♟♟ 2* |
| ○ Manzoni Bianco '17 | ♟♟ 3 |
| ● Merlot '16 | ♟♟ 3 |
| ○ Verdiso '17 | ♟♟ 3 |
| ○ Verdiso Frizzante Sui Lieviti '17 | ♟♟ 3 |
| ○ Conegliano Valdobbiadene Extra Dry | ♟ 3 |
| ○ Pinot Bianco '17 | ♟ 3 |
| ○ Prosecco di Treviso Frizzante sui Lieviti '17 | ♟ 3 |
| ○ Zophai Chardonnay '17 | ♟ 2 |
| ○ Conegliano Valdobbiadene Prosecco Tranquillo '16 | ♛♛ 2* |
| ● Merlot '15 | ♛♛ 3 |

# ★Guerrieri Rizzardi

S.DA CAMPAZZI, 2
37011 BARDOLINO [VR]
TEL. +39 0457210028
www.guerrieri-rizzardi.it

**CELLAR SALES**
**PRE-BOOKED VISITS**
**ANNUAL PRODUCTION** 700,000 bottles
**HECTARES UNDER VINE** 100.00
**SUSTAINABLE WINERY**

Giuseppe and Agostino Rizzardi are leading one of Veneto's most important wineries, a producer that has deep ties with Verona's viticulture and can boast vineyards in some of the province's most important appellations. Their notable estate is concentrated primarily in Valpolicella, Bardolino and Soave, though they also have vineyards along the Valdadige valley. Their selection, which features tremendous stylistic precision, pursues elegance and tension rather than body at all costs. 2013 was a sunny year that wasn't too hot either, conditions that brought out aromatic finesse in the grapes. It's a quality that's perfectly expressed in Rizzardi's Amarone Villa Rizzardi, a wine redolent of sweet fruit and spices, with a refreshing balsamic note. In the mouth its trademark firmness and power emerge, balanced by a vigorous acidic thrust. Their 2016 Ripasso Pojega exhibits a richer character than usual, though it's still governed by the characteristic vigor of the traditional grapes used.

| | |
|---|---|
| ● Amarone della Valpolicella Cl. Villa Rizzardi '13 | ♟♟♟ 7 |
| ● Valpolicella Cl. Sup. Ripasso Pojega '16 | ♟♟ 3* |
| ⊙ Bardolino Chiaretto Cl. '17 | ♟♟ 2* |
| ● Bardolino Cl. '17 | ♟♟ 2* |
| ● Bardolino Cl. Tacchetto '17 | ♟♟ 2* |
| ● Clos Roareti Merlot '15 | ♟♟ 5 |
| ● Munus '16 | ♟♟ 3 |
| ○ Soave Cl. Costeggiola '17 | ♟♟ 2* |
| ○ Soave Cl. Ferra '15 | ♟♟ 3 |
| ● Valpolicella Cl. '17 | ♟♟ 2* |
| ○ Soave Cl. '17 | ♟ 2 |
| ○ Vignaunica '16 | ♟ 2 |
| ● Amarone della Valpolicella Cl. Calcarole '13 | ♛♛♛ 8 |
| ● Amarone della Valpolicella Cl. Calcarole '11 | ♛♛♛ 8 |

# ILatium Morini

VIA FIENILE, 2
37030 MEZZANE DI SOTTO [VR]
TEL. +39 0457834648
www.latiummorini.it

**CELLAR SALES**
**PRE-BOOKED VISITS**
**ANNUAL PRODUCTION** 150,000 bottles
**HECTARES UNDER VINE** 40.00
**SUSTAINABLE WINERY**

The Morini family's estate spans several hectares in eastern Valpolicella, in Valpanetna, the Illasi Valley and especially the Mezzane Valley. It's a large, gravelly terrace situated at 100 meters of elevation that straddles both Valpolicella and Soave. The cellar's style sees various interpretations. Power and exuberance are the focus of their reds, aromatic freshness and tension when it comes to their whites. Their 2013 Amarone Campo Leon comes from vineyards situated both around the cellar and in the nearby Illasi Valley. It's a thick wine (to the eye) rich in aromas of sweet and dried fruit, spices and chocolate. In the mouth it proves warm and pervasive, supported by a close-knit tannic weave. Their 2017 Soave Campo Le Calle is a monovarietal Garganega whose grapes are left in a drying loft for 12 days before crushing. Its vibrant, multifaceted aromas call up tropical fruit and dried flowers, while the palate comes through savory and potent.

| | |
|---|---:|
| ● Amarone della Valpolicella | |
| Campo Leon '13 | 🍷🍷 6 |
| ○ Soave '17 | 🍷🍷 2* |
| ○ Soave Campo Le Calle '17 | 🍷🍷 2* |
| ● Valpolicella Sup. Campo Prognai '14 | 🍷 4 |
| ● Valpolicella Sup. Ripasso | |
| Campo dei Ciliegi '15 | 🍷 3 |
| ● Amarone della Valpolicella | |
| Campo Leon '12 | 🍷🍷 6 |
| ○ Soave '16 | 🍷🍷 2* |
| ○ Soave '10 | 🍷🍷 2* |
| ● Valpolicella Sup. Campo Prognai '13 | 🍷🍷 4 |
| ● Valpolicella Sup. Campo Prognai '11 | 🍷🍷 4 |
| ● Valpolicella Sup. Ripasso | |
| Campo dei Ciliegi '13 | 🍷🍷 3 |

# Conte Loredan Gasparini

FRAZ. VENEGAZZÙ
VIA MARTIGNAGO ALTO, 23
31040 VOLPAGO DEL MONTELLO [TV]
TEL. +39 0423870024
www.loredangasparini.it

**CELLAR SALES**
**ACCOMMODATION**
**ANNUAL PRODUCTION** 450,000 bottles
**HECTARES UNDER VINE** 60.00

The southern side of the Montello hill has been used for viticulture as far back as anyone can remember, and for at least half a century it has been the choice territory for the so-called 'Bordeaux blends'. Loredan Gasparini's Capo di Stato is one of its symbols. It's a wine with a long history that made the name Venegazzù known throughout the world (the district of Volpago where the cellar managed by the Palla family is located). The Giavera estate came later, with plots primarily dedicated to Prosecco's Glera grape variety, making for a complete selection of wines that brings together elegance and pleasantness. Only a few wines were submitted this year, but these were led by their 2013 Capo di Stato, obviously. It's made with grapes from their best plots, in particular their '100 piante' vineyard, which goes back more than 60 years. On the nose it unfolds slowly, with notes of ripe fruit giving way to aromatic herbs. Finally, a charming mineral stroke emerges, a feature that follows through to a rigorous palate, supported by a close-knit tannic weave.

| | |
|---|---:|
| ● Montello e Colli Asolani Rosso | |
| Capo di Stato '13 | 🍷🍷 7 |
| ● Montello e Colli Asolani | |
| Cabernet Sauvignon '15 | 🍷🍷 3 |
| ● Montello e Colli Asolani Rosso | |
| Venegazzù della Casa '13 | 🍷🍷 4 |
| ● Falconera Merlot '12 | 🍷🍷 3 |
| ● Montello e Colli Asolani | |
| Cabernet Sauvignon '14 | 🍷🍷 3 |
| ● Montello e Colli Asolani Rosso | |
| Capo di Stato '12 | 🍷🍷 7 |
| ● Montello e Colli Asolani Rosso | |
| Venegazzù della Casa '12 | 🍷🍷 4 |
| ● Montello e Colli Asolani | |
| Venegazzù della Casa '11 | 🍷🍷 4 |
| ● Montello e Colli Asolani | |
| Venegazzù Sup. Capo di Stato '11 | 🍷🍷 6 |

# ★Maculan

VIA CASTELLETTO, 3
36042 BREGANZE [VI]
TEL. +39 0445873733
www.maculan.net

CELLAR SALES
PRE-BOOKED VISITS
ANNUAL PRODUCTION 650,000 bottles
HECTARES UNDER VINE 50.00

Few wineries have had as much a part in turning around Italian winemaking as Fausto Maculan's, especially during the complicated years that followed the methanol scandal. Today he's joined by daughters Angela and Maria Vittoria, and continues attending to the family vineyards, which are concentrated in the area of Breganze. Here gentle hills with mostly southern exposure, cooled by the fresh winds that descend off the high Asiago plateau, give rise to a multifaceted range of wines. Force and complexity emerge as the selection's distinctive traits, which holds true both for their reds and their celebrated passito wines. The rich 2015 harvest gave rise to a one-of-a-kind Fratta. The Cabernet Sauvignon used comes from their Ferrata vineyard, Merlot from Villa Elettra. Both plots are situated on terrain of volcanic origin. On the nose aromas of ripe red fruit are enriched by a fresh balsamic and spicy presence. The palate is full and decisive. It lengthens will elegance towards a crisp finish, supported by grippy tannins.

| | |
|---|---|
| ○ Acininobili '12 | ♟♟ 8 |
| ● Fratta '15 | ♟♟ 8 |
| ● Breganze Cabernet Sauvignon Palazzotto '15 | ♟♟ 4 |
| ○ Breganze Torcolato '13 | ♟♟ 6 |
| ● Brentino '16 | ♟♟ 3 |
| ○ Dindarello '17 | ♟♟ 4 |
| ○ Ferrata Chardonnay '16 | ♟♟ 4 |
| ○ Bidibi '17 | ♟ 2 |
| ● Breganze Pinot Nero '16 | ♟ 3 |
| ○ Breganze Vespaiolo '17 | ♟ 2 |
| ● Cabernet '16 | ♟ 2 |
| ○ Pino & Toi '17 | ♟ 2 |
| ○ Tre Volti Brut M. Cl. | ♟ 3 |
| ● Breganze Cabernet Sauvignon Palazzotto '05 | ♟♟♟ 4 |

# Manara

LOC. SAN FLORIANO
VIA DON CESARE BIASI, 53
37029 SAN PIETRO IN CARIANO [VR]
TEL. +39 0457701086
www.manaravini.it

CELLAR SALES
PRE-BOOKED VISITS
ANNUAL PRODUCTION 150,000 bottles
HECTARES UNDER VINE 11.00
SUSTAINABLE WINERY

The critical and market success that overwhelmed Valpolicella's winemaking industry has certainly brought benefits, but it's also taken something away from its most celebrated wines. Brothers Lorenzo, Fabio and Giovanni Manara, however, have stayed true to tradition, continuing to privilege complexity and subtlety over power for power's sake. Today they're helped in part by their children, and together their important work unfolds in their private vineyards, which occupy some of the best positions in San Pietro in Cariano. Their 2013 Amarone Corte Manara stands out among their lovely selection, with its generous and ripe aromas of sweet fruit and fines herbes on a subtle, mineral vein. In the mouth it impresses for its savoriness, which a palate that comes through long and juicy. Their 2012 Amarone Postera is more compact on the nose, with spicy hints accompanying the wine's usual aromatic profile. On the palate it proves energetic, supported by a pleasantly rough tannic weave.

| | |
|---|---|
| ● Amarone della Valpolicella Cl. Corte Manara '13 | ♟♟ 5 |
| ● Amarone della Valpolicella Cl. Postera '12 | ♟♟ 6 |
| ● Recioto della Valpolicella Cl. El Rocolo '15 | ♟♟ 5 |
| ● Guido Manara '12 | ♟ 6 |
| ● Valpolicella Cl Sup. Ripasso Le Morete '16 | ♟ 3 |
| ● Valpolicella Cl. Sup. Vecio Belo '16 | ♟ 2 |
| ● Amarone della Valpolicella Cl. '00 | ♟♟♟ 5 |
| ● Amarone della Valpolicella Cl. Postera '11 | ♟♟ 6 |
| ● Recioto della Valpolicella Cl. Moronalto '14 | ♟♟ 5 |
| ● Valpolicella Cl. Sup. Ripasso Le Morete '15 | ♟♟ 3 |
| ● Valpolicella Cl. Sup. Vecio Belo '14 | ♟♟ 2* |

## Le Mandolare

Loc. Brognoligo
via Sambuco, 180
37032 Monteforte d'Alpone [VR]
Tel. +39 0456175083
www.cantinalemandolare.com

**CELLAR SALES**
**PRE-BOOKED VISITS**
**ANNUAL PRODUCTION** 65,000 bottles
**HECTARES UNDER VINE** 20.00

Brognoligo is a small village that's literally immersed in vineyards, where the land is redolent of Garganega and Pergola, Fruttai and Trebbiano di Soave. It's one of this historic appellation's 'capitals', with all its wines. And it's here that Le Mandolare operates, a lovely producer that boasts an extremely well-suited estate situated on a mix of terrain types: volcanic basalt and limestone, for a selection that alternates fresh and approachable wines with richer and more structured ones. Their 2015 Soave Monte Sella refers more to the second profile, with its vibrant aromas of yellow fruit and flowers, and a hint of oak that just emerges from the background. In the mouth it proves full and meaty, but manages to lengthen decisively by virtue of energetic acidity. Their 2016 Recioto di Soave Le Schiavette also delivered. It's a passito that calls up notes of tropical fruit and citrus. On the palate it brings sweetness to the forefront, though this is well-contrasted by a slightly salty streak and acidity.

| | |
|---|---|
| ○ 3B Trebbiano | ▼▼ 2* |
| ○ Il Vignale Passito '15 | ▼▼ 4 |
| ○ Recioto di Soave Cl. Le Schiavette '16 | ▼▼ 5 |
| ○ Soave Cl. Sup. Monte Sella '15 | ▼▼ 3 |
| ○ Soave Cl. Corte Menini '17 | ▼ 2 |
| ○ Soave Cl. Il Roccolo '17 | ▼ 2 |
| ○ Il Vignale Passito '11 | ▽▽ 4 |
| ○ Recioto di Soave Le Schiavette '15 | ▽▽ 5 |
| ○ Soave Cl. Il Roccolo '15 | ▽▽ 2* |
| ○ Soave Cl. Il Roccolo '13 | ▽▽ 2* |
| ○ Soave Cl. Monte Sella '13 | ▽▽ 3 |
| ○ Soave Cl. Monte Sella '12 | ▽▽ 3 |
| ○ Soave Cl. Monte Sella '11 | ▽▽ 3 |
| ○ Soave Il Roccolo '16 | ▽▽ 2* |
| ○ Soave Monte Sella '14 | ▽▽ 3 |

## Masari

loc. Maglio di Sopra
c.da Bevilacqua, 2a
36078 Valdagno [VI]
Tel. +39 0445410780
www.masari.it

**CELLAR SALES**
**PRE-BOOKED VISITS**
**ANNUAL PRODUCTION** 30,000 bottles
**HECTARES UNDER VINE** 4.00

With a calm that's unique to the world of agriculture, Massimo Dal Lago and Arianna Tessari's winery continues to take on a more definite shape. In addition to the original vineyards spread out on the two sides of the Agno valley, they have added new plots along the Cornedo Vicentino hills, where mostly white grapes are cultivated. Even before stylistic or production considerations are taken into account, they work to protect a landscape in which biodiversity is essential, and viticulture is anything but dominant. Their Masari, a Bordeaux blend made primarily with Cabernet cultivated at 500 meters above sea level, affirms its status as their selection's leading wine. The 2015 expresses vibrant notes of red fruit, aromatic herbs and spices that unfold on a rich, decisive palate anchored to a rigorous tannic weave. It will offer up its best to those who can wait. Their 2017 Agnobianco is a fragrant, citrusy and flowery wine, an original blend of Riesling, Durella and Garganega with an energetic, vibrant palate.

| | |
|---|---|
| ● Masari '15 | ▼▼ 6 |
| ○ Agnobianco '17 | ▼▼ 3 |
| ○ Doro Passito '15 | ▼▼ 5 |
| ○ Leon Durello Dosaggio Zero M. Cl. | ▼▼ 5 |
| ● Vicenza Rosso San Martino '15 | ▼▼ 3 |
| ○ AgnoBianco '15 | ▽▽ 2* |
| ○ AgnoBianco '14 | ▽▽ 2* |
| ○ Antico Pasquale Passito Bianco '08 | ▽▽ 8 |
| ○ Antico Pasquale Passito Bianco '07 | ▽▽ 8 |
| ○ Doro Passito Bianco 10 Anni '07 | ▽▽ 5 |
| ● Masari '13 | ▽▽ 5 |
| ● Masari '12 | ▽▽ 5 |
| ● Monte Pulgo '11 | ▽▽ 8 |
| ● Monte Pulgo '09 | ▽▽ 8 |
| ● Vicenza Rosso San Martino '14 | ▽▽ 3 |
| ● Vicenza Rosso San Martino '13 | ▽▽ 3* |

## ★Masi

FRAZ. GARGAGNAGO
VIA MONTELEONE, 26
37015 SANT'AMBROGIO DI VALPOLICELLA [VR]
TEL. +39 0456832511
www.masi.it

CELLAR SALES
PRE-BOOKED VISITS
ACCOMMODATION
ANNUAL PRODUCTION 4,300,000 bottles
HECTARES UNDER VINE 670.00

If Masi has been one of the most famous Italian brands in the world for some time, it's thanks to the Boscaini family. Their headquarters are in Gargagnago (Sant'Ambrogio di Valpolicella), but their incredible estate extends throughout some of Veneto's most important appellations. It's also thanks to the collaboration of local vine growers, who their trusted and skilled staff manage step by step. If the quality of their more ambitious wines is evident to all (Amarone foremost), it's worth underlining their renewed commitment to wines that are theoretically simpler and suppler. Their 2017 Colbaraca returned with a bang. It's a meaty Soave that features aromas of ripe yellow fruit and a rich, pervasive palate. Their 2013 Amarone Costasera Riserva, however, continues to lead their selection. On the nose it offers up aromas of wild fruit and spices, with an intriguing flowery nuance emerging in the background. In the mouth it proves close-knit, potent, endowed with tightly-woven tannins but commendable sweetness as well. Their 2011 Amarone Mazzano also delivered.

| | |
|---|---|
| ● Amarone della Valpolicella Cl. Costasera Ris. '13 | ♟♟♟ 8 |
| ● Amarone della Valpolicella Cl. Mazzano '11 | ♟♟ 8 |
| ● Osar '11 | ♟♟ 8 |
| ○ Soave Cl. Sup. Colbaraca '17 | ♟♟ 3 |
| ● Valpolicella Cl. Sup. Monte Piazzo Serego Alighieri '15 | ♟♟ 5 |
| ● Recioto della Valpolicella Cl. Casal dei Ronchi Serego Alighieri '13 | ♟ 7 |
| ● Amarone della Valpolicella Cl. Campolongo di Torbe '11 | ♟♟♟ 8 |
| ● Amarone della Valpolicella Cl. Campolongo di Torbe '09 | ♟♟♟ 8 |
| ● Amarone della Valpolicella Cl. Costasera Ris. '09 | ♟♟♟ 8 |
| ● Amarone della Valpolicella Cl. Vaio Armaron Serègo Alighieri '11 | ♟♟♟ 8 |

## Masottina

LOC. CASTELLO ROGANZUOLO
VIA BRADOLINI, 54
31020 SAN FIOR [TV]
TEL. +39 0438400775
www.masottina.it

CELLAR SALES
PRE-BOOKED VISITS
ANNUAL PRODUCTION 1,000,000 bottles
HECTARES UNDER VINE 230.00

The Dal Bianco family has managed to carve out a role as leaders in the competitive district of Conegliano Valdobbiadene, moving forward with an activity that began after the Second World War. Their cellar is in San Fior, in the easternmost part of the DOC appellation, with vineyards that extend into Ogliano and the Treviso plains as well (where grapes for their still wines are cultivated). A complete and consistent selection are offered, featuring a distinctive style that pursues lightness and balance. And Rive di Ogliano has given rise to Massottina's two best performing wines, both 2017s. Their Extra Dry offers up fine aromas of ripe fruit and flowers, while a balance of sweetness, acidity and sparkle makes for a juicy and highly enjoyable palate. Their Contrada Granda Brut opts for fresher aromas, crossed by a subtle, herbaceous note. These anticipate a pure, crisp palate that lengthens with elegance.

| | |
|---|---|
| ○ Conegliano Valdobbiadene Brut | ♟♟ 4 |
| ○ Conegliano Valdobbiadene Rive di Ogliano Brut Contrada Granda '17 | ♟♟ 5 |
| ○ Conegliano Valdobbiadene Rive di Ogliano Extra Dry '17 | ♟♟ 5 |
| ○ Conegliano Valdobbiadene Brut Costabella | ♟ 4 |
| ○ Dorsoduro Pinot Grigio Ai Palazzi '17 | ♟ 4 |
| ○ Venezia Pinot Grigio Ai Palazzi '17 | ♟ 4 |
| ● Colli di Conegliano Rosso Montesco '10 | ♟♟ 6 |
| ○ Conegliano Valdobbiadene Rive di Ogliano Brut Contrada Granda '16 | ♟♟ 5 |
| ○ Conegliano Valdobbiadene Rive di Ogliano Extra Dry '16 | ♟♟ 5 |
| ○ Conegliano Valdobbiadene Rive di Ogliano Extra Dry '15 | ♟♟ 4 |
| ● Piave Merlot Ai Palazzi Ris. '10 | ♟♟ 3 |

# Roberto Mazzi e Figli

LOC. SAN PERETTO
VIA CROSETTA, 8
37024 NEGRAR [VR]
TEL. +39 0457502072
www.robertomazzi.it

**CELLAR SALES**
**PRE-BOOKED VISITS**
**ACCOMMODATION AND RESTAURANT SERVICE**
**ANNUAL PRODUCTION** 50,000 bottles
**HECTARES UNDER VINE** 8.00

It's always a pleasure to find yourself in a winery like the one founded by Roberto Mazzi in Negrar (today managed by sons Antonio and Stefano). Theirs is a small operation that's managed to resist the temptation to pursue unfettered growth amidst the extraordinary success that Valpolicella is enjoying. Rather, they've focused on bringing out the best of their private, family vineyards, and their wines. These are worked in a cellar connected to what was once a watermill, giving rise to a 'classic' selection (in the best sense of the word), interpreted with precision and elegance. Their 2013 Amarone Punta di Villa is without a doubt one of the Mazzi family's best performing wines. On the nose it calls up raspberry preserves, gradually refreshed by notes of pepper and aromatic herbs. It's the prelude to a plush and generous palate, lengthened gracefully by vigorous acidity. Their 2013 Recioto Le Calcarole features greater aromatic exuberance and a potent, juicy palate.

| | |
|---|---|
| ● Amarone della Valpolicella Cl. Punta di Villa '13 | 🍷🍷 7 |
| ● Recioto della Valpolicella Cl. Le Calcarole '13 | 🍷🍷 5 |
| ● Amarone della Valpolicella Cl. Castel '13 | 🍷🍷 7 |
| ● Valpolicella Cl. '17 | 🍷🍷 2* |
| ● Valpolicella Cl. Sup. Poiega '14 | 🍷🍷 4 |
| ● Amarone della Valpolicella Cl. Punta di Villa '11 | 🍷🍷🍷 7 |
| ● Valpolicella Cl. Sup. Sanperetto '11 | 🍷🍷🍷 3* |
| ● Amarone della Valpolicella Cl. Punta di Villa '12 | 🍷🍷 7 |
| ● Amarone della Valpolicella Cl. Vign. Castel '10 | 🍷🍷 7 |
| ● Valpolicella Cl. Sup. Sanperetto '15 | 🍷🍷 3* |
| ● Valpolicella Cl. Sup. Sanperetto '14 | 🍷🍷 3* |
| ● Valpolicella Cl. Sup. Vign. Poiega '14 | 🍷🍷 4 |

# Menegotti

LOC. ACQUAROLI, 7
37069 VILLAFRANCA DI VERONA [VR]
TEL. +39 0457902611
www.menegotticantina.com

**CELLAR SALES**
**PRE-BOOKED VISITS**
**ACCOMMODATION**
**ANNUAL PRODUCTION** 250,000 bottles
**HECTARES UNDER VINE** 30.00
**SUSTAINABLE WINERY**

The area to the southeast of Lake Garda has historically been dedicated to Custoza and Bardolino. Shifting ice patterns have resulted in a veritable territorial jigsaw puzzle spread out across the morainic hills, which bring out the natural elegance and richness of flavor of the area's most important wines (not to mention the varieties that serve as their backbone). If the white appellation has remained central to the Menegotti's selection, their reds have been partially rethought in favor of their interesting sparkling wines. In any case, their most interesting offering is their 2016 Custoza Elianto, a wine made with Cortese and Garganega and a splash of Trebbiano. The nose offers up ripe, yellow fruit, which follows through on a rich and balanced palate. Their 2014 Brut is another interesting wine. It's an original blend of equal parts Chardonnay and Corvina fermented without the skins. The result is a Metodo Classico redolent of delicately flowery aromas and a crisp, slender palate.

| | |
|---|---|
| ○ Custoza Sup. Elianto '16 | 🍷🍷 3* |
| ○ Brut M. Cl. '14 | 🍷🍷 4 |
| ● Mezzacosta '15 | 🍷🍷 3 |
| ● Bardolino '17 | 🍷 2 |
| ○ Biancospino Frizzante | 🍷 2 |
| ○ Custoza '17 | 🍷 2 |
| ○ Extra Dry M. Cl | 🍷 3 |
| ○ Lugana '17 | 🍷 3 |
| ○ Brut M. Cl. '13 | 🍷🍷 4 |
| ○ Brut M. Cl. '12 | 🍷🍷 4 |
| ○ Custoza '16 | 🍷🍷 2* |
| ○ Custoza '15 | 🍷🍷 2* |
| ○ Custoza Sup. Elianto '15 | 🍷🍷 3 |
| ○ Custoza Sup. Elianto '14 | 🍷🍷 3 |
| ○ Custoza Sup. Elianto '13 | 🍷🍷 2* |
| ● Mezzacosta '14 | 🍷🍷 3 |

# Merotto

LOC. COL SAN MARTINO
VIA SCANDOLERA, 21
31010 FARRA DI SOLIGO [TV]
TEL. +39 0438989000
www.merotto.it

**CELLAR SALES**
**PRE-BOOKED VISITS**
**ANNUAL PRODUCTION** 610,000 bottles
**HECTARES UNDER VINE** 28.00

For more than 40 years, the winery managed by Graziano Merotto has continued to develop in the heart of Conegliano Valdobbiadene, along a tract of land that connects Treviso's two sparkling wine capitals. These are steep, impervious hills that local farmworkers have cultivated for centuries with passion in pursuit of the perfect fusion between soil, grape and sky. In their Farra di Soligo cellar, their work is aimed at bringing out the best of this special relationship, which is highlighted across their selection. It's a selection that has Glera as its cornerstone and sees creamy bubbles as a true stylistic trademark. Their 2017 Graziano Merotto Brut delivers. Anything but simple, it exhibits all of Prosecco's attributes as a great sparkler for mealtime, and not only for casual drinking. On the nose, flowery aromas and hints of white fruit anticipate a highly sophisticated palate in which vigor and creamy prickle fuse harmoniously. Their 2017 Castèl Extra Dry also performed well. It's a wine that opts for riper expression of fruit and a gentle, racy palate.

| | | |
|---|---|---|
| ○ Valdobbiadene Brut Rive di Col San Martino Cuvée del Fondatore Graziano Merotto '17 | ♟♟♟ 4* | |
| ○ Cartizze | ♟♟ 5 | |
| ○ Le Fare Extra Brut | ♟♟ 3 | |
| ○ Valdobbiadene Brut Bareta | ♟♟ 3 | |
| ○ Valdobbiadene Dry La Primavera di Barbara '17 | ♟♟ 3 | |
| ○ Valdobbiadene Extra Dry Castèl '17 | ♟♟ 4 | |
| ○ Valdobbiadene Extra Dry Colbelo | ♟♟ 3 | |
| ⊙ Grani Rosa Di Nero Brut | ♟ 3 | |
| ○ Valdobbiadene Brut Rive di Col San Martino Cuvée del Fondatore Graziano Merotto '16 | ♟♟♟ 4* | |
| ○ Valdobbiadene Brut Rive di Col San Martino Cuvée del Fondatore Graziano Merotto '15 | ♟♟♟ 4* | |

# Ornella Molon

FRAZ. CAMPO DI PIETRA
VIA RISORGIMENTO, 40
31040 SALGAREDA [TV]
TEL. +39 0422804807
www.ornellamolon.it

**CELLAR SALES**
**PRE-BOOKED VISITS**
**RESTAURANT SERVICE**
**ANNUAL PRODUCTION** 500,000 bottles
**HECTARES UNDER VINE** 42.00
**SUSTAINABLE WINERY**

The strip of flatlands that extends between the provinces of Venice and Treviso, bordered by the Adriatic to the south and protected by hills to the north, has seen its vineyards overwhelmed of late by a boom in Glera. Ornella Molon and Giancarlo Traverso chose a personal path, however, never losing sight of what have been Basso Piave's leading varietals for more than a century and a half. And so they've maintained continuity for a selection of still wines that are consistently among the area's most interesting. Their 2014 Bianco di Ornella performed exceptionally well. It's a wine made with super-ripe Verduzzo, dried Sauvignon and dried Traminer. On the nose it proves explosive, rich in tropical aromas, citrus and flowery, while on the palate its overwhelming sweetness is kept at bay by a fresh and taut acidity. Their elegant 2013 Rosso di Villa, a Merlot with commendable savoriness, features a deep, ripe, complex aromatic profile.

| | | |
|---|---|---|
| ○ Bianco di Ornella '14 | ♟♟ 5 | |
| ○ Traminer '17 | ♟♟ 3 | |
| ● Venezia Merlot Rosso di Villa '13 | ♟♟ 6 | |
| ○ Piave Raboso '12 | ♟ 5 | |
| ○ Prosecco di Treviso Brut | ♟ 2 | |
| ○ Prosecco di Treviso Extra Dry | ♟ 3 | |
| ● Vite Rossa '14 | ♟ 5 | |
| ○ Bianco di Ornella '13 | ♟♟ 4 | |
| ● Piave Merlot Rosso di Villa '12 | ♟♟ 5 | |
| ● Piave Merlot Rosso di Villa '11 | ♟♟ 5 | |
| ● Vite Rossa '13 | ♟♟ 4 | |
| ● Vite Rossa '11 | ♟♟ 4 | |

# Monte dall'Ora

LOC. CASTELROTTO
VIA MONTE DALL'ORA, 5
37029 SAN PIETRO IN CARIANO [VR]
TEL. +39 0457704462
www.montedallora.com

**CELLAR SALES**
**PRE-BOOKED VISITS**
**ANNUAL PRODUCTION** 35,000 bottles
**HECTARES UNDER VINE** 6.00
**VITICULTURE METHOD** Certified Organic

Situated in Castelrotto (San Pietro in Cariano), Monte dall'Ora is led by Carlo Venturini and his wife, Alessandra. Theirs is a small winery that has managed to forge ahead, bringing out the best of the bond that's upheld by many of Valpolicella's agricultural leaders. Indeed, here cultivar, soil, climate and the human hand also come together for a selection that focuses on the territory's classic wines. Their stylistic choices are never pre-determined, but adapt to the wine, from the richly flavored forthrightness of the Saseti to their rich Amarone. Their 2015 Camporenzo represents the meeting point between these two interpretations. It's a Valpolicella that transmits all the fragrance of the traditional cultivar used with its aromas of wild fruit, spices and flowers. On the palate it brings together depth and structure while maintaining a strong personality without sugary lapses. Their 2010 Amarone Stropa also eschews richer, more concentrated expressions in favor of elegance and tension.

| | |
|---|---|
| ● Valpolicella Cl. Sup. Camporenzo '15 | ▼▼▼ 4* |
| ● Amarone della Valpolicella Cl. Stropa '10 | ▼▼ 8 |
| ● Valpolicella Cl. Saseti '17 | ▼▼ 2* |
| ● Valpolicella Cl. Sup. Ripasso Saustò '15 | ▼▼ 5 |
| ● Valpolicella Cl. Sup. Camporenzo '13 | ♈♈♈ 4* |
| ● Valpolicella Cl. Sup. Camporenzo '11 | ♈♈♈ 4* |
| ● Valpolicella Cl. Sup. Camporenzo '10 | ♈♈♈ 4* |
| ● Valpolicella Cl. Sup. Ripasso Saustò '07 | ♈♈♈ 5 |
| ● Amarone della Valpolicella Cl. Stropa '09 | ♈♈ 8 |
| ● Amarone della Valpolicella Cl. Stropa '08 | ♈♈ 8 |
| ● Valpolicella Cl. Saseti '16 | ♈♈ 2* |
| ● Valpolicella Cl. Saseti '15 | ♈♈ 2* |
| ● Valpolicella Cl. Sup. Camporenzo '14 | ♈♈ 4 |
| ● Valpolicella Cl. Sup. Camporenzo '12 | ♈♈ 4 |
| ● Valpolicella Cl. Sup. Ripasso Saustò '12 | ♈♈ 5 |
| ● Valpolicella Cl. Sup. Saustò '13 | ♈♈ 5 |

# Monte del Frà

S.DA PER CUSTOZA, 35
37066 SOMMACAMPAGNA [VR]
TEL. +39 045510490
www.montedelfra.it

**CELLAR SALES**
**PRE-BOOKED VISITS**
**ANNUAL PRODUCTION** 1,000,000 bottles
**HECTARES UNDER VINE** 197.00

There are at least two territorial poles that give rise to the lovely selection marked Monte del Frà. On the one hand there are the vineyards rolling along the morainic hills that dominate the southern bank of Garda. On the other, there are the plots spread throughout the classic heart of nearby Valpolicella. It's a dichotomy that comes together in the enological sensibility of Marica and Massimo Bonomo, two cousins who have brilliantly upheld the work begun by fathers Eligio and Claudio (still key players in managing both the vineyards and the cellar). Their 2016 Custoza Ca' del Magro explores the appellation's great potential. With its hill vineyards and great variety of cultivar, it's a territory that's capable of giving rise to wines of quality and character. Here the wine's aromas feature ripe white fruit crossed by spicy notes of saffron and dried flowers. On the palate it proves rich and firm, refreshed by a racy acidity. Their 2015 Colombara, a gutsy though charming monovarietal Garganega, is even more complex aromatically and potent in the mouth.

| | |
|---|---|
| ○ Custoza Sup. Ca' del Magro '16 | ▼▼▼ 3* |
| ○ Colombara '15 | ▼▼ 3* |
| ● Bardolino '17 | ▼▼ 2* |
| ○ Custoza '17 | ▼▼ 2* |
| ● Valpolicella Cl. Lena di Mezzo '17 | ▼▼ 3 |
| ● Valpolicella Cl. Sup. Lena di Mezzo '16 | ▼▼ 3 |
| ⊙ Bardolino Chiaretto '17 | ▼ 2 |
| ○ Custoza Sup. Ca' del Magro '15 | ♈♈♈ 3* |
| ○ Custoza Sup. Ca' del Magro '14 | ♈♈♈ 3* |
| ○ Custoza Sup. Ca' del Magro '13 | ♈♈♈ 3* |
| ○ Custoza Sup. Ca' del Magro '12 | ♈♈♈ 2* |
| ○ Custoza Sup. Ca' del Magro '11 | ♈♈♈ 2* |
| ○ Custoza Sup. Ca' del Magro '10 | ♈♈♈ 2* |
| ○ Custoza Sup. Ca' del Magro '09 | ♈♈♈ 2* |
| ○ Custoza Sup. Ca' del Magro '08 | ♈♈♈ 2* |

## Monte Santoccio

loc. Santoccio, 6
37022 Fumane [VR]
Tel. +39 3496461223
www.montesantoccio.it

CELLAR SALES
ANNUAL PRODUCTION 40,000 bottles
HECTARES UNDER VINE 6.00

Nicola and Laura Ferrari are young
Valpolicella vigneron with notable
experience. They're situated in Santoccio,
a ridge that separates the Fumane and
Marano valleys. It's an area almost entirely
dedicated to the classic varietals and
wines of the territory, which are interpreted
according to tradition and with an
enological style that continually pursues a
balance between opulence and
suppleness. Their entire selection is
encompassed by just a few wines, each of
which faithfully reflects the DOC
appellation. Their 2013 Amarone put in an
excellent performance. From the outset, its
color suggests a character that's anything
but showy. On the nose it offers up
fragrances of sweet, ripe fruit, adorned by
vibrant notes of aromatic herbs and spices.
These gradually broaden, giving way to a
more nuanced, relaxed aromatic profile. In
the mouth it proves firm, refreshed by
acidity, making for a juicy palate of great
tension. Their Valpolicellas form a nice
threesome: 2017 Classico, 2016 Superiore
and 2016 Ripasso.

| | | |
|---|---|---|
| ● Amarone della Valpolicella Cl. '13 | ♟♟ 7 | |
| ● Valpolicella Cl. '17 | ♟ 2 | |
| ● Valpolicella Cl. Sup. '16 | ♟ 2 | |
| ● Valpolicella Cl. Sup. Ripasso '16 | ♟ 4 | |
| ● Amarone della Valpolicella Cl. '12 | ♟♟ 7 | |
| ● Amarone della Valpolicella Cl. '11 | ♟♟ 7 | |
| ● Amarone della Valpolicella Cl. '10 | ♟♟ 7 | |
| ● Recioto della Valpolicella Cl. Amandorlarto '14 | ♟♟ 5 | |
| ● Valpolicella Cl. Sup. '15 | ♟♟ 2* | |
| ● Valpolicella Cl. Sup. '14 | ♟♟ 2* | |
| ● Valpolicella Cl. Sup. Ripasso '15 | ♟♟ 4 | |
| ● Valpolicella Cl. Sup. Ripasso '13 | ♟♟ 4 | |
| ● Valpolicella Cl. Sup. Ripasso '12 | ♟♟ 4 | |
| ● Valpolicella Cl. Sup. Ripasso '11 | ♟♟ 4 | |

## Monte Tondo

loc. Monte Tondo
via San Lorenzo, 89
37038 Soave [VR]
Tel. +39 0457680347
www.montetondo.it

CELLAR SALES
PRE-BOOKED VISITS
ACCOMMODATION
ANNUAL PRODUCTION 200,000 bottles
HECTARES UNDER VINE 32.00

Headquartered in Soave (where their cellar
is situated), the winery run by Gino
Magnabosco and sons is now universally
considered one of the most notable in the
province. Their vineyards are concentrated
in the heart of the historic appellation,
though these are accompanied by a
handful of 'fields' in the area of
Valpolicella. It's a double track that is
harmonized into a solid selection of wines,
made up of intense but racy whites and
reds that go more for cohesion and aging
potential. Their 2016 Soave Casette
Foscarin, a Garganega with a splash of
local Trebbiano, leads a sound selection.
On the nose it offers up notes of ripe white
fruit, enriched by flowery nuances and a
subtle mineral vein that should grow with
age. In the mouth it proves juicy and
savory, with a supple palate and a crisp
finish. Their 2016 Foscarin Slavinus is
even richer and warmer, opting for
softness and roundness.

| | |
|---|---|
| ○ Soave Cl. Casette Foscarin '16 | ♟♟ 3* |
| ● Amarone della Valpolicella '14 | ♟♟ 6 |
| ○ Recioto di Soave Nettare di Bacco '16 | ♟♟ 4 |
| ○ Soave Cl. Monte Tondo '17 | ♟♟ 2* |
| ○ Soave Cl. Sup. Foscarin Slavinus '16 | ♟♟ 4 |
| ● Valpolicella Ripasso Campo Grande '16 | ♟ 4 |
| ● Valpolicella Sup. San Pietro '16 | ♟ 2 |
| ○ Soave Cl. Monte Tondo '06 | ♟♟♟ 2* |
| ● Amarone della Valpolicella '12 | ♟♟ 6 |
| ○ Soave Cl. '15 | ♟♟ 2* |
| ○ Soave Cl. Casette Foscarin '15 | ♟♟ 3 |
| ○ Soave Cl. Casette Foscarin '14 | ♟♟ 3 |
| ○ Soave Cl. Casette Foscarin '14 | ♟♟ 3 |
| ○ Soave Cl. Monte Tondo '16 | ♟♟ 2* |
| ○ Soave Cl. Sup. Foscarin Slavinus '15 | ♟♟ 4 |
| ○ Soave Cl. Sup. Foscarin Slavinus '14 | ♟♟ 4 |
| ○ Soave Cl. Sup. Foscarin Slavinus '14 | ♟♟ 4 |

# Cantina Sociale di Monteforte d'Alpone

VIA XX SETTEMBRE, 24
37032 MONTEFORTE D'ALPONE [VR]
TEL. +39 0457610110
www.cantinadimonteforte.it

CELLAR SALES
PRE-BOOKED VISITS
ANNUAL PRODUCTION 3,000,000 bottles
HECTARES UNDER VINE 1300.00

The district of Soave Classico extends to the north of the residential zones of Soave and Monteforte d'Alpone. It's a chain of steep, volcanic hills that seem to overlap one another down towards the plains. It's here, in this area of rare beauty, that Cantina Sociale operates. They're a cooperative with more than 50 years of history behind them, and today they're guided by the sure hand of Gaetano Tobin. Of the enormous quantities of grapes supplied, only the best are used for a selection that's focused on sparkling wines, whites and reds, all an excellent value (to say the least). This year two wines landed in our finals, both just missing out on a gold. Their 2016 Soave Foscarino had a smashing debut, highlighting the finesse and generosity for which the celebrated cru is famous. Their 2016 Castellaro exhibited greater depth and richness, in part by virtue of the time spent in oak barrels, which is particularly evident in its pervasive palate.

| | |
|---|---|
| ○ Soave Cl. Foscarino '16 | 🏆🏆 3* |
| ○ Soave Cl. Sup. Castellaro '16 | 🏆🏆 2* |
| ○ Recioto di Soave Cl. Sigillo '15 | 🏆🏆 3 |
| ○ Soave Cl. Clivus '17 | 🏆🏆 2* |
| ○ Soave Cl. Vicario '17 | 🏆🏆 2* |
| ○ Lessini Durello Brut | 🏆 2 |
| ● Valpolicella Ripasso '16 | 🏆 2 |
| ○ Soave Cl. Sup. Vign. di Castellaro '15 | 🏆🏆🏆 2* |
| ○ Recioto di Soave Cl. Il Sigillo '15 | 🏆🏆 3 |
| ○ Soave Cl. Clivus '16 | 🏆🏆 2* |
| ○ Soave Cl. Il Vicario '16 | 🏆🏆 2* |
| ○ Soave Cl. Sup. Vign. di Castellaro '14 | 🏆🏆 2* |
| ○ Soave Cl. Sup. Vign. di Castellaro '13 | 🏆🏆 2* |
| ○ Soave Cl. Sup. Vign. di Castellaro '12 | 🏆🏆 2* |
| ● Valpolicella Ripasso '14 | 🏆🏆 2* |

# Montegrande

VIA TORRE, 2
35030 ROVOLON [PD]
TEL. +39 0495226276
www.vinimontegrande.it

CELLAR SALES
PRE-BOOKED VISITS
ANNUAL PRODUCTION 250,000 bottles
HECTARES UNDER VINE 30.00

For years it seemed like the Cristofanon family limited themselves to making sound wines, without venturing to explore the potential of that fantastic treasure trove of a territory, the Colli Euganei hills. Today something's changed, and their selection has taken an unexpected step forward across the board. Their sizable estate spans various vineyards, primarily situated in the northwestern part of the DOC appellation. These are dedicated primarily to Bordeaux varieties as well as the area's traditional Moscato. There's also news from their cellar. Among their new wines their impressive 2015 Ottomano Ris. stands out. It's a classic, ruby-colored blend (primarily Merlot) that offers up aromas of red fruit and spices, which follow through exceptionally well on the palate. In the mouth it features a firm body and excellent length. Their 2015 Vigna delle Roche Ris. also delivered. It's a more generous, structured wine with respect to previous versions, though it hasn't lost the suppleness that's always defined its palate.

| | |
|---|---|
| ● Colli Euganei Cabernet Borgomoro '16 | 🏆🏆 3 |
| ● Colli Euganei Cabernet Sereo Ris. '15 | 🏆🏆 3 |
| ○ Colli Euganei Moscato Spumante Dolce '17 | 🏆🏆 2* |
| ● Colli Euganei Rosso Momi '16 | 🏆🏆 3 |
| ● Colli Euganei Rosso Ottomano Ris. '15 | 🏆🏆 4 |
| ● Colli Euganei Rosso V. delle Roche Ris. '15 | 🏆🏆 3 |
| ○ Castearo | 🏆 2 |
| ○ Colli Euganei Chardonnay S. Giorgio '16 | 🏆 2 |
| ● Colli Euganei Merlot Corterocco '16 | 🏆 3 |
| ○ Colli Euganei Pinot Bianco Marani '17 | 🏆 2 |
| ○ Colli Euganei Seprino Extra Dry | 🏆 2 |
| ● Colli Euganei Cabernet Sereo '13 | 🏆🏆 3 |
| ● Colli Euganei Rosso '16 | 🏆🏆 2* |
| ● Colli Euganei Rosso V. delle Roche '13 | 🏆🏆 3 |

## Monteversa

via Monte Versa, 1024
35030 Vò [PD]
Tel. +39 0499941092
www.monteversa.it

**CELLAR SALES**
**PRE-BOOKED VISITS**
**ANNUAL PRODUCTION** 23,000 bottles
**HECTARES UNDER VINE** 17.00
**VITICULTURE METHOD** Certified Organic

Even if it's called Monte, Versa is a small slope that doesn't even reach 150 meters above sea level on the western side of the Collli Euganei hills. And yet the grapes cultivated here are always highly sought after for the regularity with which they ripen and their perfect mix of concentration, savoriness and acidity. And it's here that we find the Voltazza family's estate, the most representative in the area, bolstered by first-rate, organically managed vineyards. In our last round of tastings, their Animaversa affirmed its status as leader of their selection. It's a Bordeaux made primarily with Merlot and the 2015 features great ripeness of fruit, enriched by nuances of spices and medicinal herbs. In the mouth it comes through rich and savory, supported by a close-knit tannic weave. Their 2017 Versavò also delivered. It's an original blend of Garganega, Manzoni Bianco, Chardonnay and Moscato Giallo with a delicate aromatic profile, and a juicy, pleasantly crisp palate.

| | |
|---|---|
| ● Colli Euganei Rosso Animaversa '15 | 🍷🍷 4 |
| ○ Versavò '17 | 🍷🍷 2* |
| ● Biodiversa '17 | 🍷 3 |
| ● Colli Euganei Rosso Versacinto '17 | 🍷 3 |
| ○ Colli Euganei Bianco Animaversa '12 | YY 3 |
| ○ Colli Euganei Bianco Versavò '13 | YY 2* |
| ● Colli Euganei Cabernet Animaversa '12 | YY 4 |
| ○ Colli Euganei Fior d'Arancio Spumante '16 | YY 4 |
| ● Colli Euganei Rosso Animaversa '13 | YY 4 |
| ● Colli Euganei Rosso Animaversa '11 | YY 4 |
| ● Colli Euganei Rosso Versacinto '16 | YY 3 |
| ● Colli Euganei Rosso Versacinto '15 | YY 3 |
| ● Colli Euganei Rosso Versacinto '13 | YY 3 |
| ● Colli Euganei Rosso Versacinto '12 | YY 2* |
| ○ Versavò '15 | YY 2* |
| ○ Versavò '14 | YY 2* |

## Le Morette

fraz. San Benedetto di Lugana
v.le Indipendenza, 19d
37019 Peschiera del Garda [VR]
Tel. +39 0457552724
www.lemorette.it

**CELLAR SALES**
**PRE-BOOKED VISITS**
**ANNUAL PRODUCTION** 380,000 bottles
**HECTARES UNDER VINE** 32.00
**SUSTAINABLE WINERY**

Brothers Fabio and Paolo Zenato's estate extends to the south of Garda, in the heart of the Lugana DOC appellation around Peschiera. Close proximity to the lake basin means that the terrain exhibits a strong presence of clay, which tapers gradually as you move up the morainic slopes. This pedoclimate contributes to the character of Le Morette's wines, which are increasingly distinct (and consistent), thanks in part to their prestigious estate and deep knowledge of Turbiana. A one-of-a-kind 2015 Lugana Riserva led their selection. It's made with choice grapes from vineyards with higher concentrations of clay. Its fruity impact is accompanied by smoky timbres. These gradually give way to a subtle minerality on its decisive, potent palate, with a greater acidic tension emerging as the wine unfolds. Their 2016 Lugana Benedictus, a wine that opts for greater approachability in its fruity expression, also delivered.

| | |
|---|---|
| ○ Lugana Ris. '15 | 🍷🍷 4 |
| ⊙ Bardolino Chiaretto Cl. '17 | 🍷🍷 2* |
| ○ Lugana Benedictus '16 | 🍷🍷 3 |
| ○ Lugana Mandolara '17 | 🍷🍷 3 |
| ⊙ Bardolino Chiaretto Brut Cépage | 🍷 2 |
| ● Perseo '15 | 🍷 5 |
| ○ Accordo Passito Bianco '12 | YY 4 |
| ⊙ Bardolino Chiaretto Cl. '16 | YY 2* |
| ● Bardolino Cl. '15 | YY 2* |
| ○ Lugana Benedictus '15 | YY 3 |
| ○ Lugana Benedictus '14 | YY 3 |
| ○ Lugana Mandolara '16 | YY 3 |
| ○ Lugana Mandolara '15 | YY 3 |
| ○ Lugana Mandolara '14 | YY 2* |
| ○ Lugana Ris. '13 | YY 4 |
| ○ Lugana Ris. '12 | YY 5 |
| ● Perseo '12 | YY 5 |

# Marco Mosconi

VIA PARADISO, 5
37031 ILLASI [VR]
TEL. +39 0456529109
www.marcomosconi.it

**CELLAR SALES**
**PRE-BOOKED VISITS**
**ANNUAL PRODUCTION** 25,000 bottles
**HECTARES UNDER VINE** 10.00

The valley of Illasi is universally recognized as a reference point for those in search of powerful, concentrated Valpolicella and Amarones that can bowl you over with their fullness of body. Marco Mosconi has managed to find a personal touch, however. While his wines express all their richness, they also give you an idea of elegance and tension that are truly rare for this area. It's all thanks to the care with which the vineyards are managed and the choice to follow methods aimed at bringing out finesse and drinkability. Their 2013 Amarone put in an excellent performance. It offers up rich aromas of ripe fruit that let through fresher notes of medicinal herbs and pepper. In the mouth it changes pace, and with great precision it makes glycerine power, lengthening with elegance towards a crisp, assertive finish. Their 2014 Valpolicella Superiore exhibits a multifaceted aromatic profile in which herbaceous notes take center stage along with fruit. On the palate it comes through crisp and dynamic with nice tension.

| | |
|---|---|
| ● Amarone della Valpolicella '13 | ♥♥ 8 |
| ● Valpolicella Sup. '14 | ♥♥ 5 |
| ○ Soave Corte Paradiso '17 | ♥♥ 2* |
| ● Valpolicella Sup. '13 | ♥♥♥ 5 |
| ● Valpolicella Sup. '12 | ♥♥♥ 5 |
| ● Amarone della Valpolicella '12 | ♀♀ 8 |
| ● Amarone della Valpolicella '11 | ♀♀ 8 |
| ● Recioto della Valpolicella '11 | ♀♀ 6 |
| ○ Recioto di Soave '13 | ♀♀ 5 |
| ○ Soave Corte Paradiso '16 | ♀♀ 2* |
| ○ Soave Corte Paradiso '15 | ♀♀ 2* |
| ○ Soave Rosetta '15 | ♀♀ 3 |
| ○ Soave Sup. Corte Paradiso '13 | ♀♀ 2* |
| ● Turan '13 | ♀♀ 3 |
| ● Valpolicella Montecurto '16 | ♀♀ 3 |
| ● Valpolicella Montecurto '15 | ♀♀ 3 |
| ● Valpolicella Sup. '11 | ♀♀ 5 |

# Mosole

LOC. CORBOLONE
VIA ANNONE VENETO, 60
30029 SANTO STINO DI LIVENZA [VE]
TEL. +39 0421310404
www.mosole.com

**CELLAR SALES**
**PRE-BOOKED VISITS**
**ANNUAL PRODUCTION** 230,000 bottles
**HECTARES UNDER VINE** 30.00

All it takes is a glance at the new packaging used for Mosole's simpler wines to get a sense of where their selection is going. Each typology is associated with an image that represents human history in the territory, our collective endeavors and past, thus expressing an important and noteworthy bond. A highly specialized approach to viticulture provides what are by now considered the 'classic' grapes of the Venetian territory (Merlot and Tai foremost), giving rise to a forthright though charming selection of wines. Even if no wine got a gold, Mosole's selection proved extremely sound. Their 2016 Hora Prima is a blend of Chardonnay, Tai and a smaller part Sauvignon that delivers for its aromatic sophistication and its savory, balanced, enticing palate. Their 2015 Merlot Ad Nonam is an entirely different wine. It features aromas of ripe fruit and spices that are brought out on its rich, potent palate. Their 2017 Eleo, a Lison made with Tai, also impressed for its freshness and personality.

| | |
|---|---|
| ○ Hora Prima '16 | ♥♥ 4 |
| ○ Lison Eleo '17 | ♥♥ 3* |
| ● Lison-Pramaggiore Merlot Ad Nonam '15 | ♥♥ 5 |
| ● Lison-Pramaggiore Cabernet Hora Sexta '15 | ♥♥ 4 |
| ● Lison-Pramaggiore Refosco P. R. '17 | ♥♥ 2* |
| ○ Tai '17 | ♥♥ 2* |
| ● Venezia Cabernet Franc '17 | ♥♥ 2* |
| ● Venezia Chardonnay '17 | ♥♥ 2* |
| ○ Venezia Pinot Grigio '17 | ♥♥ 2* |
| ○ Sauvignon '17 | ♥ 2 |
| ● Venezia Merlot '17 | ♥ 2 |
| ○ Ad Nonam Passito '15 | ♀♀ 4 |
| ○ Hora Prima '15 | ♀♀ 4 |
| ○ Lison Eleo '16 | ♀♀ 2* |
| ○ Venezia Chardonnay '16 | ♀♀ 2* |

## Il Mottolo

loc. Le Contarine
via Comezzara, 13
35030 Baone [PD]
Tel. +39 3479456155
www.ilmottolo.it

**CELLAR SALES**
**PRE-BOOKED VISITS**
**ANNUAL PRODUCTION** 27,000 bottles
**HECTARES UNDER VINE** 7.00

In just a few years, Sergio Fortin has managed to create a producer that has earned itself a primary position in the viticultural panorama of the Colli Euganei. The estate extends along the southernmost slopes of the regional park, an area where limited rainfall, along with a warm and sunny climate, allow the grapes to reach the perfect ripeness with virtually every vintage. In their small cellar, every action is aimed at making wines that faithfully express the character of this splendid area. Their Serro is a blend of Merlot and Cabernet Sauvignon that, thanks to an excellent year in 2015, offers up vibrant aromas of ripe red fruit, crossed by spices and a stroke of forest undergrowth. In the mouth it delivers fullness and power, well-governed by tannins and an acidic backbone, making for a long, elegant wine. Their 2015 Vignànima is a buoyant Carmenère that features the cultivar's trademark balsamic and peppery sensations, and delivers on the palate for harmony and savoriness.

| | |
|---|---|
| ● Serro '15 | 🍷🍷 4 |
| ○ Le Contarine '17 | 🍷🍷 2* |
| ● V. Marè Cabernet '16 | 🍷🍷 2* |
| ● Vignànima '15 | 🍷🍷 4 |
| ● Comezzara Merlot '16 | 🍷 2 |
| ● Colli Euganei Rosso Serro '11 | 🍷🍷🍷 3* |
| ● Colli Euganei Rosso Serro '10 | 🍷🍷🍷 3* |
| ● Colli Euganei Rosso Serro '09 | 🍷🍷🍷 3* |
| ○ Colli Euganei Fior d'Arancio Passito V. del Pozzo '15 | 🍷🍷 3 |
| ● Colli Euganei Rosso Serro '14 | 🍷🍷 4 |
| ● Colli Euganei Rosso Serro '13 | 🍷🍷 4 |
| ● Colli Euganei Rosso Serro '12 | 🍷🍷 3* |
| ○ Le Contarine '16 | 🍷🍷 2* |
| ● Merlot Comezzara '15 | 🍷🍷 2* |
| ● Vingnànima '13 | 🍷🍷 3* |
| ● Vingnànima '12 | 🍷🍷 3* |

## Mulin di Mezzo

via Molin Di Mezzo,16
30020 Annone Veneto [VE]
Tel. +39 0422 769398
www.mulindimezzo.com

**PRE-BOOKED VISITS**
**ANNUAL PRODUCTION** 40,000 bottles
**HECTARES UNDER VINE** 6.00

The Venetian plains extend primarily along the Adriatic coast, with soil that alternates between deep layers of clay and decidedly more gravelly terrain, in accordance to their proximity to the area's principal rivers: the Piave, Livenza and Tagliamento to the east. It's here that Paolo Lazzarini operates. He's a vine grower that takes pains to follow each stage of production with passion and skill, both when it comes to native cultivar and international varieties, making for a selection of defined by their stylistic firmness. Our tastings proved Mulin di Mezzo's gift for Lison Classico, a white made with Tai. Their 2017 features vibrant fragrances of ripe yellow fruit brought out by charming almondy sensations and herbaceous hints. In the mouth it proves rich, potent and chewy, governed by an assertive acidity that never lets down its guard. Their 2017 Chardonnay is broader in its aromas of yellow fruit and yet delicate on the palate. It features softness and consistency in its sensations.

| | |
|---|---|
| ○ Lison Cl. '17 | 🍷🍷 2* |
| ○ Lison Pramaggiore Chardonnay '17 | 🍷🍷 2* |
| ● Il Priore '11 | 🍷 4 |
| ● Lison Pramaggiore Merlot '12 | 🍷 2 |
| ● Il Priore '10 | 🍷🍷 4 |
| ○ Lison Cl. '16 | 🍷🍷 2* |
| ● Rosso Molino '15 | 🍷🍷 2* |

# Musella

LOC. FERRAZZE
VIA FERRAZZETTE, 2
37036 SAN MARTINO BUON ALBERGO [VR]
TEL. +39 045973385
www.musella.it

**CELLAR SALES**
**PRE-BOOKED VISITS**
**ACCOMMODATION**
**ANNUAL PRODUCTION** 260,000 bottles
**HECTARES UNDER VINE** 50.00
**VITICULTURE METHOD** Certified Biodynamic

Maddalena Pasqua's journey has, over the past twenty years, raised her awareness of the importance of territory and the respect that we must show it. Her winery is situated in San Marino Buonalbergo, in an area of rare beauty and integrity just outside Verona. Her selection focuses on the district's historic wines, with curious digressions among her whites and rosés. These are wines full of character, and that manage to point up Valpolicella's elegant, airy side with decisiveness and pluck. Their 2016 Valpolicella Superiore features great finesse, bringing together notes of cherry with hits of white pepper and flowers. The palate comes through crisp and slender, making for a clear interpretation of the wine, one that opts for tension and vigor over opulence. Their 2008 Amarone Senza Titolo is similarly styled, though even smoother thanks to lengthy aging in the cellar and bottle. Their 2016 Drago Bianco, a wine made with Garganega, also put in excellent performance.

| | | |
|---|---|---|
| ● Valpolicella Sup. '16 | ▼▼ | 3* |
| ○ Drago Bianco '16 | ▼▼ | 3 |
| ○ Pinot Bianco Fibio '16 | ▼ | 2 |
| ● Amarone della Valpolicella Ris. '07 | ▼▼▼ | 6 |
| ● Valpolicella Sup. '13 | ▼▼▼ | 3* |
| ● Valpolicella Sup. '12 | ▼▼▼ | 2* |
| ● Amarone della Valpolicella '12 | ▼▼ | 6 |
| ● Amarone della Valpolicella Senza Titolo '08 | ▼▼ | 8 |
| ○ Drago Bianco '15 | ▼▼ | 3 |
| ● Recioto della Valpolicella '12 | ▼▼ | 5 |
| ● Valpolicella Sup. '15 | ▼▼ | 3* |
| ● Valpolicella Sup. '14 | ▼▼ | 3* |
| ● Valpolicella Sup. Ripasso '11 | ▼▼ | 4 |

# Daniele Nardello

VIA IV NOVEMBRE, 56
37032 MONTEFORTE D'ALPONE [VR]
TEL. +39 0457612116
www.nardellovini.it

**CELLAR SALES**
**PRE-BOOKED VISITS**
**ANNUAL PRODUCTION** 75,000 bottles
**HECTARES UNDER VINE** 16.00
**SUSTAINABLE WINERY**

Daniele and Federica Nardello manage a lovely estate that extends across the southern part of Soave Classico, along the slopes of Monte Zoppega. The most important cultivar here is Garganega, of course, though local Trebbiano also gets plenty of attention, making for a selection based almost exclusively on the appellation's historic wines. In recent years, they've moved away from a softer, more caressing style, opting instead for an approach that focuses on vigor and citrus. Its a determination that we find in their 2017 Vigna Turbian, a Soave in all respects with its aromas of flowers and citrus anticipating a slender, crisp palate regulated by a flavorful savoriness. Their 2016 Monte Zoppega opts for sweeter and riper fruit, with a plush, harmonious palate. Their 2014 Suavissimus also delivered. It proves to be an exotic Recioto on the nose and highly supple in the mouth. We shouldn't forget their 2017 Soave Meridies either.

| | | |
|---|---|---|
| ○ Soave Cl. Monte Zoppega '16 | ▼▼ | 4 |
| ○ Soave Cl. V. Turbian '17 | ▼▼ | 3* |
| ○ Recioto di Soave Suavissimus '14 | ▼▼ | 4 |
| ○ Soave Cl. Meridies '17 | ▼▼ | 2* |
| ○ Aetas Brut | ▼ | 4 |
| ○ Blanc de Fe' '17 | ▼ | 3 |
| ○ Recioto di Soave Suavissimus '11 | ▼▼ | 4 |
| ○ Soave Cl. Meridies '15 | ▼▼ | 2* |
| ○ Soave Cl. Monte Zoppega '15 | ▼▼ | 3* |
| ○ Soave Cl. Monte Zoppega '14 | ▼▼ | 3* |
| ○ Soave Cl. V. Turbian '16 | ▼▼ | 2* |

## Nicolis

VIA VILLA GIRARDI, 29
37029 SAN PIETRO IN CARIANO [VR]
TEL. +39 0457701261
www.vininicolis.com

CELLAR SALES
PRE-BOOKED VISITS
ANNUAL PRODUCTION 220,000 bottles
HECTARES UNDER VINE 42.00

The Nicolis family winery is a consistent benchmark for those who love Valpolicella. Their vineyards extend primarily across the classic heart of the appellation, and five rise to a selection that's for the most part dedicated to the territory's traditional wines. Their cellar, which is large and well-equipped, serves as the base from which Giuseppe attentively and patiently transforms each harvest into wine. His selection is marked by a classic style that emphasizes elegance over power. Their Amarone Ambrosan is only released during the best years, like 2009, after lengthy aging in the cellar. Almost 10 years after vintage it yields deep aromas with fruit merging perfectly with spices and aromatic herbs. In the mouth softness, vigor and tannic weave come together for a balanced, charming palate. Their 2012 Amarone is fresher on the nose and racy on the palate.

| | |
|---|---|
| ● Amarone della Valpolicella Cl. Ambrosan '09 | ♟♟ 7 |
| ● Amarone della Valpolicella Cl. '12 | ♟♟ 6 |
| ● Testal '15 | ♟♟ 4 |
| ● Valpolicella Cl. '17 | ♟ 2 |
| ● Amarone della Valpolicella Cl. Ambrosan '06 | ♟♟♟ 7 |
| ● Amarone della Valpolicella Cl. '11 | ♟♟ 6 |
| ● Amarone della Valpolicella Cl. '10 | ♟♟ 6 |
| ● Amarone della Valpolicella Cl. '09 | ♟♟ 6 |
| ● Amarone della Valpolicella Cl. Ambrosan '08 | ♟♟ 7 |
| ● Recioto della Valpolicella Cl. '13 | ♟♟ 5 |
| ● Recioto della Valpolicella Cl. '11 | ♟♟ 5 |
| ● Testal '12 | ♟♟ 4 |
| ● Valpolicella Cl. Sup. Ripasso Seccal '13 | ♟♟ 3 |
| ● Valpolicella Cl. Sup. Ripasso Seccal '12 | ♟♟ 3 |

## Novaia

VIA NOVAIA, 1
37020 MARANO DI VALPOLICELLA [VR]
TEL. +39 0457755129
www.novaia.it

CELLAR SALES
PRE-BOOKED VISITS
ANNUAL PRODUCTION 50,000 bottles
HECTARES UNDER VINE 7.00
VITICULTURE METHOD Certified Organic
SUSTAINABLE WINERY

The Vaona family seems to have Valpolicella's history tucked away in its family trunk, with a selection that's strongly influenced by tradition and that eschews easier, market-friendly interpretations. The high valley of Marano hosts their vineyards, which are cultivated with both modern, vertical-trellised systems and pergolas (in the case of their oldest plots). It's an area that allows the grapes to offer up their best in terms of elegance and finesse, rather than over-concentration. Despite the fact that five years have passed, their 2013 Amarone comes across as decidedly young, even a bit unruly in its aromas, with fruit almost hidden amidst sulfurous notes, medicinal herbs and woodlands. After a few moments it opens to finer sensations, which follow through onto an energetic, taut and extremely long palate. Their 2016 Recioto le Novaje is more explosive in its expression of fruit. It's a wine characterized by a buoyant, pleasant palate.

| | |
|---|---|
| ● Amarone della Valpolicella Cl. Corte Vaona '13 | ♟♟ 6 |
| ● Recioto della Valpolicella Cl. Le Novaje '16 | ♟♟ 4 |
| ● Valpolicella Cl. '17 | ♟♟ 3 |
| ● Valpolicella Cl. Sup. I Cantoni '15 | ♟ 4 |
| ● Valpolicella Cl. Sup. Ripasso '15 | ♟ 4 |
| ● Amarone della Valpolicella Cl. Corte Vaona '12 | ♟♟ 6 |
| ● Amarone della Valpolicella Cl. Le Balze '11 | ♟♟ 8 |
| ● Recioto della Valpolicella Cl. Le Novaje '15 | ♟♟ 4 |
| ● Valpolicella Cl. '16 | ♟♟ 2* |
| ● Valpolicella Cl. Sup. I Cantoni '12 | ♟♟ 4 |
| ● Valpolicella Cl. Sup. Ripasso '14 | ♟♟ 3 |
| ● Valpolicella Cl. Sup. Ripasso '13 | ♟♟ 3 |
| ● Valpolicella Cl. Sup. Ripasso '12 | ♟♟ 3 |

# ★Ottella

FRAZ. SAN BENEDETTO DI LUGANA
LOC. OTTELLA
37019 PESCHIERA DEL GARDA [VR]
TEL. +39 0457551950
www.ottella.it

**CELLAR SALES**
**PRE-BOOKED VISITS**
**ANNUAL PRODUCTION** 350,000 bottles
**HECTARES UNDER VINE** 40.00

Brothers Francesco and Michele Montresor have the family winery firmly in hand. Over the past twenty years they have transformed their estate, situated to the south of Lake Garda, into one of the most interesting producers in the area. Their vineyards are divided into two primary sections: the plains that line the lake basin are dedicated mostly to Lugana, while the gentle hills around it are used to cultivate red grapes. To complement their selection, they have a small but interesting line focused on Valpolicella's classic wines. Thanks to an excellent year in 2016, their Lugana Molceo Riserva put in an unforgettable performance. It's made with grapes harvested late, from vineyards with a particularly high clay content. On the nose the wine offers up tropical fruit crossed with citrus, while the palate unfolds elegantly by virtue of its strong acidic backbone. Their 2017 Le Creete also did well. It's a Lugana that features aromas of flowers and fresh fruit, and a slender, juicy palate.

# Pasqua - Cecilia Beretta

LOC. SAN FELICE EXTRA
VIA BELVEDERE, 135
37131 VERONA
TEL. +39 0458432111
www.pasqua.it

**CELLAR SALES**
**PRE-BOOKED VISITS**
**ANNUAL PRODUCTION** 13,000,000 bottles
**HECTARES UNDER VINE** 300.00

A lot has changed at Pasqua in recent years, and today the celebrated Verona winery is in great form, bolstered by wines of excellent quality but also heralding new, courageous and charming interpretations of the appellation's traditional wines. No doubt, it's thanks to the visionary management style of Riccardo Pasqua and a group of technicians who've managed bring out the expressive qualities of areas as prestigious as Castello di Montorio, Mizzole and Montevegro, which give rise to their most ambitious wines. One result of this new effort is their Mai Dire Mai line. It features Amarone and Valpolicella from a vineyard in the Illasi Valley, interpreted in a contemporary way. A 2011 version of the former brings home Tre Bicchieri thanks to deep, multilayered aromas that accompany a potent, assertive palate. Their Amarone 'classici' continue to prove charming as well. Their 2010 Famiglia Pasqua Riserva is a complex and balanced wine while their 2013 Cecilia Beretta proves crisper and juicier.

| | |
|---|---|
| ○ Lugana Molceo Ris. '16 | ♟♟♟ 4* |
| ○ Lugana Le Creete '17 | ♟♟ 3* |
| ○ Blanc de Blancs Brut M. Cl. | ♟♟ 4 |
| ● Campo Sireso '15 | ♟♟ 4 |
| ○ Lugana '17 | ♟♟ 2* |
| ○ Lugana Back to Silence '17 | ♟♟ 2* |
| ○ Nasomatto '17 | ♟♟ 2* |
| ○ Prima Luce Passito '11 | ♟♟ 5 |
| ● Valpolicella Ripasso Ripa della Volta '15 | ♟♟ 4 |
| ● Gemei '17 | ♟ 2 |
| ☉ RosesRoses '17 | ♟ 2 |
| ☉ RosesRoses Brut M. Cl. | ♟ 4 |
| ○ Lugana Molceo Ris. '15 | ♟♟♟ 4* |
| ○ Lugana Molceo Ris. '14 | ♟♟♟ 4* |
| ○ Lugana Molceo Ris. '13 | ♟♟♟ 4* |
| ○ Lugana Sup. Molceo '11 | ♟♟♟ 4* |

| | |
|---|---|
| ● Amarone della Valpolicella Pasqua Mai dire Mai '11 | ♟♟♟ 8 |
| ● Amarone della Valpolicella Cl. Terre di Cariano Cecilia Beretta Ris. '13 | ♟♟ 8 |
| ● Amarone della Valpolicella Famiglia Pasqua Ris. '10 | ♟♟ 8 |
| ○ Soave Cl. Cecilia Beretta Brognoligo '17 | ♟♟ 5 |
| ● Valpolicella Sup. Pasqua Mai dire Mai '13 | ♟♟ 8 |
| ● Amarone della Valpolicella Cl. Terre di Cariano '04 | ♟♟♟ 8 |
| ● Amarone della Valpolicella Famiglia Pasqua '13 | ♟♟♟ 6 |
| ● Amarone della Valpolicella Cl. Terre di Cariano Cecilia Beretta '12 | ♟♟ 8 |
| ● Amarone della Valpolicella Cl. Terre di Cariano Cecilia Beretta Ris. '11 | ♟♟ 8 |

## ★★Leonildo Pieropan

VIA CAMUZZONI, 3
37038 SOAVE [VR]
TEL. +39 0456190171
www.pieropan.it

CELLAR SALES
PRE-BOOKED VISITS
ANNUAL PRODUCTION 550,000 bottles
HECTARES UNDER VINE 70.00
VITICULTURE METHOD Certified Organic

Just a few short months have passed since Nino Pieropan left us and it seems like nothing has changed at the winery. Teresita surely deserves credit, along with her children Dario and Andrea, who are passionately carrying forward the work begun so long ago by one of Italy's wine giants. Thanks to his teachings, they're overseeing the estate he grew over time, spanning primarily Soave but also nearby Valpolicella. Their vineyards give rise to a selection that's simply one-of-a-kind for elegance and ageworthiness. Their 2016 Calvarino is a bona fide symbol of this Soave winery and put in an unforgettable performance during our tastings. It's a fresh wine in its aromas of white fruit and flowers, complex in its mineral notes. It proves vigorous and yet supple and elegant. A splendid version will deliver for years to come. Their Rocca opts for warmer, riper atmospheres, letting through a smoky note and fragrances of yellow fruit that follow through on a rich, taut, flavorful palate.

| | |
|---|---|
| ○ Soave Cl. Calvarino '16 | ♔♔♔ 4* |
| ○ Soave Cl. La Rocca '16 | ♔♔ 5 |
| ● Amarone della Valpolicella V. Garzon '14 | ♔♔ 7 |
| ○ Recioto di Soave Cl. Le Colombare '15 | ♔♔ 5 |
| ○ Soave Cl. '17 | ♔♔ 3 |
| ● Valpolicella Sup. Ruberpan '15 | ♔♔ 4 |
| ○ Soave Cl. Calvarino '15 | ♔♔♔ 4* |
| ○ Soave Cl. Calvarino '13 | ♔♔♔ 4* |
| ○ Soave Cl. Calvarino '09 | ♔♔♔ 4* |
| ○ Soave Cl. Calvarino '08 | ♔♔♔ 4 |
| ○ Soave Cl. Calvarino '07 | ♔♔♔ 4 |
| ○ Soave Cl. Calvarino '06 | ♔♔♔ 4 |
| ○ Soave Cl. La Rocca '14 | ♔♔♔ 5 |
| ○ Soave Cl. La Rocca '12 | ♔♔♔ 5 |
| ○ Soave Cl. La Rocca '11 | ♔♔♔ 5 |
| ○ Soave Cl. La Rocca '10 | ♔♔♔ 5 |

## Albino Piona

FRAZ. CUSTOZA
VIA BELLAVISTA, 48
37060 SOMMACAMPAGNA [VR]
TEL. +39 045516055
www.albinopiona.it

CELLAR SALES
PRE-BOOKED VISITS
ANNUAL PRODUCTION 350,000 bottles
HECTARES UNDER VINE 77.00

The Piona brothers, Silvio, Monica, Alessandro and Massimo, are among the most interesting interpreters of those appellations situated around the Lake Garda basin, Bardolino and Custoza. Their strength derives from an estate that extends for many hectares and that is almost exclusively dedicated to those cultivar that are the foundation of Verona's historic wines. In the cellar, oak is used sparingly while great attention is paid to aging, giving rise to wines endowed with elegance and longevity. The two most interesting wines tasted this year bear the letters SP on their label. One is a Custoza, the other a Bardolino, both 2015s. Lengthy aging conferred vibrant flowery notes to the former. These give way to citrusy nuances and hints of saffron. The palate is slender, supported by a racy acidity and an extremely charming savory stroke. The latter is fresher on the nose, while on the palate fullness of fruit is supported by pleasantly rough tannins. Their Custoza Campo del Selese and Corvina Campo Massimo, also 2015s, both impressed as well.

| | |
|---|---|
| ● Bardolino SP '15 | ♔♔ 2* |
| ○ Custoza SP '15 | ♔♔ 2* |
| ● Bardolino '17 | ♔♔ 2* |
| ⊙ Bardolino Chiaretto '17 | ♔♔ 2* |
| ● Campo Massimo Corvina Veronese '15 | ♔♔ 2* |
| ○ Custoza '17 | ♔♔ 2* |
| ○ Custoza Sup. Campo del Selese '15 | ♔♔ 2* |
| ○ Estro di Piona Blanc Brut | ♔ 4 |
| ⊙ Estro di Piona Rosé Brut | ♔ 4 |
| ○ Verde Piona Frizzante | ♔ 2 |
| ● Bardolino SP '13 | ♔♔♔ 2* |
| ● Bardolino SP '12 | ♔♔ 2* |
| ○ Custoza '16 | ♔♔ 2* |
| ○ Custoza '14 | ♔♔ 2* |
| ○ Custoza SP '12 | ♔♔ 2* |
| ○ Custoza Sup. Campo del Selese '13 | ♔♔ 2* |

# Piovene Porto Godi

FRAZ. TOARA DI VILLAGA
VIA VILLA, 14
36021 VILLAGA [VI]
TEL. +39 0444885142
www.piovene.com

CELLAR SALES
PRE-BOOKED VISITS
ACCOMMODATION
ANNUAL PRODUCTION 120,000 bottles
HECTARES UNDER VINE 40.00
SUSTAINABLE WINERY

The Colli Berici constitute one of the most interesting areas for red winemaking in Veneto. Gentle slopes situated at lower elevations stretch up in the heart of the Po Valley. Here the climate is decidedly warm and dry, conditions that allow Bordeaux varieties to reach maturity with consistency and balance. Tai Rosso, which Tomaso Piovene interprets with great skill, is also an important cultivar here, thus pointing up the sunny qualities of the plots around Toara. Their Thovara once again proves to be a quintessential Tai Rosso, drawing on an excellent 2015 for its approachable, fragrant profile dominated by sensations of ripe fruit and spices, well-integrated with varietal aromas of wild rose. On the palate it comes through full, contrasted by a close-knit tannic weave. Their 2015 Cabernet Pozzare also delivered, offering up notably fruit-driven aromas on the nose, while in the mouth it exhibits great extractive force, with a rigor made possible by acidity and tannins.

| | |
|---|---|
| ● Colli Berici Cabernet Vign. Pozzare '15 | 🍷🍷 4 |
| ● Colli Berici Tai Rosso Thovara '15 | 🍷🍷 5 |
| ○ Colli Berici Garganega Vign. Riveselle '17 | 🍷🍷 2* |
| ○ Colli Berici Pinot Bianco Vign. Polveriera '17 | 🍷🍷 2* |
| ○ Colli Berici Sauvignon Vign. Fostine '17 | 🍷🍷 2* |
| ● Colli Berici Tai Rosso Vign. Riveselle '17 | 🍷🍷 2* |
| ○ Sauvignon Campigie '16 | 🍷🍷 3 |
| ● Colli Berici Cabernet Vign. Pozzare '12 | 🍷🍷🍷 4* |
| ● Colli Berici Cabernet Vign. Pozzare '07 | 🍷🍷🍷 3 |
| ○ Colli Berici Garganega Vign. Riveselle '16 | 🍷🍷 2* |
| ● Colli Berici Merlot Fra i Broli '15 | 🍷🍷 4 |
| ○ Colli Berici Pinot Bianco Polveriera '16 | 🍷🍷 4 |
| ● Colli Berici Tai Rosso Thovara '13 | 🍷🍷 5 |
| ● Polveriera Rosso '16 | 🍷🍷 2* |

# ★Graziano Prà

VIA DELLA FONTANA, 31
37032 MONTEFORTE D'ALPONE [VR]
TEL. +39 0457612125
www.vinipra.it

CELLAR SALES
PRE-BOOKED VISITS
ACCOMMODATION
ANNUAL PRODUCTION 350,000 bottles
HECTARES UNDER VINE 35.00
VITICULTURE METHOD Certified Organic
SUSTAINABLE WINERY

After having dedicated some years to developing his estate in Valpolicella, Graziano Prà has gone back to devoting great attention to the territory of Soave, where his winemaking journey began. Presumably, the acquisition of a notable property on Monte Bisson will allow further improvements in terms of quality, though a natural, low-impact approach to vine growing remains a top priority. The red-white dichotomy continues to coalesce in a selection of wines that's rich in racy, flavorful interpretations. Once again, it's hard to choose the best of Prà's selection, with a range of wines that's as good as any. Their 2016 Soave Monte Grande, which enjoys lengthy aging, stood out for its aromas of ripe white fruit enriched by notes of almond and Mediterranean scrubland. On the palate it proves savory, balanced, generous and very long. It's absolutely one of their top wines. Their 2016 Soave Staforte is just as good in terms of expressive brilliance and energy of flavor.

| | |
|---|---|
| ○ Soave Cl. Monte Grande '16 | 🍷🍷🍷 4* |
| ○ Soave Cl. Staforte '16 | 🍷🍷 3* |
| ● Amarone della Valpolicella '12 | 🍷🍷 7 |
| ○ Soave Cl. Colle Sant'Antonio '15 | 🍷🍷 5 |
| ○ Soave Cl. Otto '17 | 🍷🍷 3 |
| ● Valpolicella Morandina '17 | 🍷🍷 3 |
| ● Valpolicella Sup. Ripasso Morandina '16 | 🍷🍷 4 |
| ○ Soave Cl. Monte Grande '11 | 🍷🍷🍷 4* |
| ○ Soave Cl. Staforte '15 | 🍷🍷🍷 3* |
| ○ Soave Cl. Staforte '14 | 🍷🍷🍷 4* |
| ○ Soave Cl. Staforte '13 | 🍷🍷🍷 4* |
| ● Amarone della Valpolicella '10 | 🍷🍷 6 |
| ○ Soave Cl. Colle S. Antonio '12 | 🍷🍷 4 |
| ○ Soave Cl. Monte Grande '14 | 🍷🍷 4 |
| ● Valpolicella Sup. Ripasso Morandina '15 | 🍷🍷 4 |

## ★Giuseppe Quintarelli

VIA CERÉ, 1
37024 NEGRAR [VR]
TEL. +39 0457500016
vini@giuseppequintarelli.it

CELLAR SALES
PRE-BOOKED VISITS
ANNUAL PRODUCTION 60,000 bottles
HECTARES UNDER VINE 10.00

With the help of their parents, Francesco and Lorenzo Quintarelli manage the winery that was once owned by their grandfather, Giuseppe Quintarelli, a figure important for Valpolicella's winemaking history and for Italian wine throughout the world. The two brothers are having success in the difficult work of carrying on their family legacy without abandoning tradition, and that includes the patient aging of wines in oak or in the bottle. At the same time they are perfecting a style in which complexity and charm coexist with clarity and vitality. Quintarelli submitted only one wine for tasting this year, but it was an unforgettable performance (to say the least). Their 2009 Amarone is an almost transparent ruby garnet wine with an elegant aromatic profile. It unfolds slowly, with super-ripe fruit followed by spices and crushed flowers. Finally a delicate and unwavering minerality emerges. In the mouth it proves big, but it's refreshed by a vivacious acidity that lightens and lengthens the palate, only to close with vital tannins. It's easy to imagine a bright future ahead for the wine.

| | | |
|---|---|---|
| ● Amarone della Valpolicella Cl. '09 | ♥♥♥ | 8 |
| ● Amarone della Valpolicella Cl. '06 | ♀♀♀ | 8 |
| ● Amarone della Valpolicella Cl. '03 | ♀♀♀ | 8 |
| ● Amarone della Valpolicella Cl. Ris. '07 | ♀♀♀ | 8 |

## Le Ragose

FRAZ. ARBIZZANO
VIA LE RAGOSE, 1
37024 NEGRAR [VR]
TEL. +39 0457513241
www.leragose.com

CELLAR SALES
PRE-BOOKED VISITS
ANNUAL PRODUCTION 120,000 bottles
HECTARES UNDER VINE 18.00

Today more than ever, Alta Valpolicella is a district in which vine growers fight for the best locations, seeking out those areas that made the territory world-famous. Marco and Paolo Galli never abandoned these hills, staying true to the family plots concentrated in Negrar, between 250 and 400 meters above sea level. At the same time they've stuck to a clear idea of wine making, one that's able to express its ties to gastronomy and authentic rural traditions. Their Amarone Caloetto is made with grapes from their highest vineyards, which thrive at 400 meters above sea level. It's only put on the market after a long stay in the cellar, and today we're tasting their 2008. On the nose it unfolds slowly, gradually offering up aromas of dried fruit, then spices and finally a fresh note of medicinal herbs. In the mouth it exhibits fullness and a firm body, progressively revealing savoriness and tension.

| | | |
|---|---|---|
| ● Amarone della Valpolicella Cl. Caloetto '08 | ♥♥ | 7 |
| ● Valpolicella Cl. Sup. Marta Galli '14 | ♥♥ | 5 |
| ● Valpolicella Cl. Sup. Ripasso Le Sassine '14 | ♥♥ | 4 |
| ● Amarone della Valpolicella Cl. Caloetto '06 | ♀♀♀ | 7 |
| ● Amarone della Valpolicella Cl. Marta Galli '05 | ♀♀♀ | 8 |
| ● Amarone della Valpolicella Cl. '08 | ♀♀ | 7 |
| ● Amarone della Valpolicella Cl. Caloetto '07 | ♀♀ | 7 |
| ● Recioto della Valpolicella Cl. '14 | ♀♀ | 5 |
| ● Recioto della Valpolicella Cl. '13 | ♀♀ | 5 |
| ● Rhagos Ammandorlato '07 | ♀♀ | 8 |
| ● Valpolicella Cl. '15 | ♀♀ | 2* |

# F.lli Recchia

LOC. JAGO
VIA CA' BERTOLDI, 30
37024 NEGRAR [VR]
TEL. +39 0457500584
www.recchiavini.it

**CELLAR SALES**
**PRE-BOOKED VISITS**
**ANNUAL PRODUCTION** 250,000 bottles
**HECTARES UNDER VINE** 100.00

The Recchia family's past is strongly tied to viticulture, but in recent years especially it seems that they've turned a corner. Thanks to their sizable estate they've rapidly increased their production volumes. In the past they were primarily cultivators only, and even today they're actually growing more than what they use, which allows the family to choose only the best batches for their selection. Their 2015 Recioto La Guardia put in an excellent performance. It's a wine intensely redolent of morello cherry and crushed flowers, with an important, peppery vein in the background. In the mouth it reveals its youth, bringing together a highly generous palate with rigorous acidity and tannins. Their more traditional wines are represented by their Masua di Jago line, and among these we appreciated their 2016 Valpolicella Superiore, which offers up notes of wild fruit spices. These follow through well onto a crisp, racy palate.

| | |
|---|---|
| ● Amarone della Valpolicella Cl. Masua di Jago '14 | ▼▼ 5 |
| ● Recioto della Valpolicella Cl. Masua di Jago '16 | ▼▼ 4 |
| ● Recioto della Valpolicella Cl. La Guardia '15 | ▼▼ 4 |
| ● Valpolicella Cl. Sup. Masua di Jago '16 | ▼▼ 2* |
| ☉ Bardolino Chiaretto Poderi del Roccolo '17 | ▼ 2 |
| ○ Custoza Brut | ▼ 2 |
| ○ Custoza Poderi del Roccolo '17 | ▼ 2 |
| ● Korvilot '16 | ▼ 5 |
| ● Valpolicella Cl. Masua di Jago '17 | ▼ 2 |
| ● Valpolicella Cl. Sup. Ripasso Masua di Jag '16 | ▼ 2 |
| ● Amarone della Valpolicella Cl. Ca' Bertoldi '11 | ▼▼ 5 |

# Roccolo Grassi

VIA SAN GIOVANNI DI DIO, 19
37030 MEZZANE DI SOTTO [VR]
TEL. +39 0458880089
www.roccolograssi.it

**PRE-BOOKED VISITS**
**ANNUAL PRODUCTION** 49,000 bottles
**HECTARES UNDER VINE** 14.00
**SUSTAINABLE WINERY**

Immersed in the heart of the Mezzane valley, Francesca and Marco Sartori's estate is a shining example of how this territory has reacted to the unexpected success it began receiving more than 20 years ago. Rather than increasing production and attacking the markets, the brothers have preferred to develop their estate. They've focused on quality and stayed true to a limited range of sound wines imbued with character, which holds true both for their classic Soave whites and their interpretations of Valpolicella's celebrated reds. We often appreciate Di Roccolo Grassi, especially their Valpolicella reds, which manage the wines' great richness with elegance and tension. This year it's their 2016 Soave La Broia that most impressed. It's made with grapes cultivated at about 100 meters above sea level on calcareous terrain. On the nose it proves generous and complex with notes of white fruit, spices and flint, while exhibiting energy and great finesse on the palate.

| | |
|---|---|
| ○ Soave La Broia '16 | ▼▼ 3* |
| ● Valpolicella Sup. '14 | ▼▼ 5 |
| ● Amarone della Valpolicella '13 | ▼▼ 8 |
| ● Amarone della Valpolicella Roccolo Grassi '07 | ▼▼▼ 8 |
| ● Amarone della Valpolicella Roccolo Grassi '00 | ▼▼▼ 7 |
| ● Amarone della Valpolicella Roccolo Grassi '99 | ▼▼▼ 7 |
| ● Valpolicella Sup. '13 | ▼▼▼ 5 |
| ● Valpolicella Sup. '11 | ▼▼▼ 5 |
| ● Valpolicella Sup. Roccolo Grassi '09 | ▼▼▼ 5 |
| ● Valpolicella Sup. Roccolo Grassi '07 | ▼▼▼ 5 |
| ● Valpolicella Sup. Roccolo Grassi '04 | ▼▼▼ 5 |
| ● Amarone della Valpolicella '12 | ▼▼ 8 |
| ○ Soave Sup. La Broia '15 | ▼▼ 3* |
| ○ Soave Sup. La Broia '14 | ▼▼ 3* |

# Roeno

via Mama, 5
37020 Brentino Belluno [VR]
Tel. +39 0457230110
www.cantinaroeno.com

CELLAR SALES
PRE-BOOKED VISITS
ACCOMMODATION AND RESTAURANT SERVICE
ANNUAL PRODUCTION 350,000 bottles
HECTARES UNDER VINE 80.00
SUSTAINABLE WINERY

There aren't many wineries that have been able to revolutionize their production in little time, expanding and achieving exceptional results. Roeno has managed just that, thanks to the work of siblings Roberta, Cristina and Giuseppe Fugatti, who took over some 15 years ago and transformed the winery into a benchmark, not only for Valdadige, but for the entire area of Verona. Their vineyards run from the lower valley to the high hills, giving rise to an elegant selection designed to evolve over time. Their 2013 Riesling Collezione di Famiglia is the result of a careful selection of their best grapes. These are matured in large barrels and only released five years after vintage. On the nose vibrant aromas call up chamomile and tropical fruit, with a faint note of benzine on the background. These follow through onto its crisp, linear palate. Their 2015 Cristina is a classic late-harvest wine, complex on the nose, elegant and sweet on the palate.

| | |
|---|---|
| ○ Riesling Renano Collezione di Famiglia '13 | ♟♟♟ 6 |
| ○ Praecipuus Riesling Renano '16 | ♟♟ 4 |
| ● Terra dei Forti Enantio '15 | ♟♟ 4 |
| ● Valdadige Marzemino La Rua '17 | ♟♟ 2* |
| ○ Valdadige Pinot Grigio Rivoli '15 | ♟♟ 5 |
| ○ Valdadige Pinot Grigio Tera Alta '17 | ♟♟ 2* |
| ○ Cristina V. T. '13 | ♟♟♟ 5 |
| ○ Cristina V. T. '12 | ♟♟♟ 5 |
| ○ Cristina V. T. '11 | ♟♟♟ 5 |
| ○ Cristina V. T. '08 | ♟♟♟ 5 |
| ○ Riesling Renano Collezione di Famiglia '12 | ♟♟♟ 6 |
| ○ Cristina V. T. '15 | ♟♟ 5 |
| ○ Cristina V. T. '14 | ♟♟ 5 |
| ● La Rua Marzemino '16 | ♟♟ 2* |
| ○ Praecipuus Riesling Renano '15 | ♟♟ 4 |

# Ronca

via Val di Sona, 7
37066 Sommacampagna [VR]
Tel. +39 0458961641
www.cantinaronca.it

CELLAR SALES
PRE-BOOKED VISITS
ANNUAL PRODUCTION 60,000 bottles
HECTARES UNDER VINE 20.00

Going west along the Po Valley, shortly after Verona, you start to see the gentle slopes that extend some 30 kilometers before disappearing back into the flatlands. In the middle of these ridges, created by Garda's moraines, we find the Ronca family's winery, a producer that avails itself of a sizable estate dedicated primarily to the grapes historically cultivated along Lake Garda's southern bank. Their 2016 Custoza Sup. Ulderico is partially matured in oak. On the nose it calls up white fruit and flowers, which give way to vibrant balsamic notes. On the palate it exhibits commendable richness sustained by a pronounced and almost electric acidic vein. Their 2017 Custoza also delivered. It's a wine that opts for greater expression of fruit and a more approachable palate that's both juicy and highly drinkable. Their aromatic and carefree 2017 Bardolino also put in an excellent performance.

| | |
|---|---|
| ○ Custoza Sup. Ulderico '16 | ♟♟ 3* |
| ● Bardolino '17 | ♟♟ 2* |
| ○ Custoza '17 | ♟♟ 2* |
| ◐ Bardolino Chiaretto '17 | ♟ 2 |
| ○ Venezia Pinot Grigio '17 | ♟ 2 |
| ● Bardolino '16 | ♟♟ 2* |
| ● Bardolino '15 | ♟♟ 2* |
| ● Corvina '16 | ♟♟ 2* |
| ● Corvina '15 | ♟♟ 2* |
| ○ Custoza '16 | ♟♟ 2* |
| ○ Custoza '15 | ♟♟ 2* |
| ○ Custoza Sup. Ulderico '15 | ♟♟ 3 |

# Rubinelli Vajol

FRAZ. SAN FLORIANO
VIA PALADON, 31
37029 SAN PIETRO IN CARIANO [VR]
TEL. +39 0456839277
www.rubinellivajol.it

**CELLAR SALES**
**PRE-BOOKED VISITS**
**ACCOMMODATION**
**ANNUAL PRODUCTION** 50,000 bottles
**HECTARES UNDER VINE** 10.00

The Rubinelli brothers' estate is situated in the heart of a small viticultural amphitheater facing south, with vineyards that grow along the slopes of the hills that divide the Fumane and Marano valleys, at elevations ranging between 150 and 200 meters above sea level. This is where they cultivate the grapes for their interpretations of Valpolicella's classic wines, which pursue complexity and elegance, rather than power. It's a stylistic choice that wasn't particularly fashionable during the boom years, but that's surely appreciated today. Their 2012 Amarone proves emblematic from this point of view. It's a wine that offers up aromas of ripe cherry, crushed flowers and medicinal herbs. On the mouth it unfolds gracefully, eschewing extractive concentration and glycerine in favor of slowness, supported by a vigorous acidic and tannic backbone across its long, crisp finish. Their 2014 Valpolicella Superiore also delivered, despite the difficult year. It's a wine that features tension and integrity.

| | | |
|---|---|---|
| ● Amarone della Valpolicella Cl. '12 | ♟♟ 7 | |
| ● Valpolicella Cl. Sup. '14 | ♟♟ 4 | |
| ● Valpolicella Cl. '17 | ♟ 2 | |
| ● Amarone della Valpolicella Cl. '11 | ♟♟ 7 | |
| ● Amarone della Valpolicella Cl. '10 | ♟♟ 6 | |
| ● Recioto della Valpolicella Cl. '13 | ♟♟ 6 | |
| ● Recioto della Valpolicella Cl. '12 | ♟♟ 6 | |
| ● Recioto della Valpolicella Cl. '11 | ♟♟ 6 | |
| ● Valpolicella Cl. '13 | ♟♟ 2* | |
| ● Valpolicella Cl. Sup. '12 | ♟♟ 4 | |
| ● Valpolicella Cl. Sup. '11 | ♟♟ 4 | |
| ● Valpolicella Cl. Sup. '10 | ♟♟ 4 | |
| ● Valpolicella Cl. Sup. Ripasso '14 | ♟♟ 5 | |
| ● Valpolicella Cl. Sup. Ripasso '12 | ♟♟ 5 | |
| ● Valpolicella Cl. Sup. Ripasso '11 | ♟♟ 4 | |

# ★Ruggeri & C.

FRAZ. ZECCHEI
VIA PRÀ FONTANA, 4
31049 VALDOBBIADENE [TV]
TEL. +39 04239092
www.ruggeri.it

**CELLAR SALES**
**PRE-BOOKED VISITS**
**ANNUAL PRODUCTION** 1,500,000 bottles
**HECTARES UNDER VINE** 28.00
**SUSTAINABLE WINERY**

Valdobbiadene is peppered with small vine growers that supply grapes to larger producers. Considering that there is practically one cultivar, each vintage can become frenetic and involve large quantities delivered for crushing on a daily basis. Paolo Bisol has managed to optimize the family business over the decades so as to manage each plot's harvest with the necessary calm and precision, even in the most hectic moments. The result is one of the most consistent selections in the area in terms of verve and pulp. Ruggeri's selection starts with theoretically simpler wines. Yet these are capable of exhibiting the peculiar character of Treviso's sparklers, like their Giall'Oro or Quartese. The head of the class, however, once again proves to be their Giustino B. Extra Dry, a wine that's an icon by now for its category, with its aromas of fresh fruit and flowers. The 2017 brings out the essence of Prosecco on the palate, with its softness, savoriness and acidic tension.

| | | |
|---|---|---|
| ○ Valdobbiadene Extra Dry Giustino B. '17 | ♟♟♟ 5 | |
| ○ Valdobbiadene Brut V. V. '17 | ♟♟ 5 | |
| ○ Cartizze | ♟♟ 5 | |
| ○ Cartizze Brut | ♟♟ 5 | |
| ○ Valdobbiadene Brut Quartese | ♟♟ 4 | |
| ○ Valdobbiadene Extra Dry Giall'Oro | ♟♟ 4 | |
| ○ Valdobbiadene Dry S. Stefano | ♟ 4 | |
| ○ Valdobbiadene Brut V. V. '14 | ♟♟♟ 4* | |
| ○ Valdobbiadene Brut Vecchie Viti '13 | ♟♟♟ 4* | |
| ○ Valdobbiadene Extra Dry Giustino B. '16 | ♟♟♟ 4* | |
| ○ Valdobbiadene Extra Dry Giustino B. '15 | ♟♟♟ 4* | |
| ○ Valdobbiadene Extra Dry Giustino B. '12 | ♟♟♟ 3* | |
| ○ Valdobbiadene Extra Dry Giustino B. '11 | ♟♟♟ 3* | |
| ○ Valdobbiadene Extra Dry Giustino B. '10 | ♟♟♟ 3 | |
| ○ Valdobbiadene Extra Dry Giustino B. '09 | ♟♟♟ 3 | |

## Le Salette

VIA PIO BRUGNOLI, 11c
37022 FUMANE [VR]
TEL. +39 0457701027
www.lesalette.it

CELLAR SALES
PRE-BOOKED VISITS
ANNUAL PRODUCTION 130,000 bottles
HECTARES UNDER VINE 20.00

Franco Scamperle's estate comprises some of the best positions in Valpolicella: Ca' Carnocchio and Santuario delle Salette in the Fumane Valley, Masua in San Pietro in Cariano and Conca d'Ora in Sant'Ambrogio. Varying conditions allow them to choose the best grapes for a selection that manages to bring together force and richness of fruit with elegance and suppleness. Their premium reds weren't produced during the complicated 2014 season, as they weren't judged sufficiently up to their usual quality standards. And so we content ourselves, so to speak, with their 2015 Recioto Le Traversagne. Its multifaceted aromatic profile alternates notes of cherry with pepper, crushed flowers and aromatic herbs. On the palate it follows through with a certain weight, thanks to a pronounced sweetness well-contrasted by acidity. Their 2016 Ripasso I Progni offers up fresher, crisper fruit that comes together with a juicy, very long palate. The rest of their selection also proved sound.

| | |
|---|---|
| ● Recioto della Valpolicella Cl. Le Traversagne '15 | ♟♟ 5 |
| ● Valpolicella Cl. Sup. Ripasso I Progni '16 | ♟♟ 3 |
| ● Amarone della Valpolicella Cl. La Marega '14 | ♟ 6 |
| ● Ca' Carnocchio '15 | ♟ 4 |
| ● Valpolicella Cl. '17 | ♟ 2 |
| ● Amarone della Valpolicella Cl. Pergole Vece '05 | ♟♟♟ 8 |
| ● Amarone della Valpolicella Cl. Pergole Vece '95 | ♟♟♟ 8 |
| ● Amarone della Valpolicella Cl. La Marega '13 | ♟♟ 6 |
| ● Amarone della Valpolicella Cl. Pergole Vece '13 | ♟♟ 8 |
| ● Recioto della Valpolicella Cl. Le Traversagne '14 | ♟♟ 5 |

## Tenute SalvaTerra

LOC. CENGIA
VIA CENGIA, 8
37029 SAN PIETRO IN CARIANO [VR]
TEL. +39 0456859025
www.tenutesalvaterra.it

CELLAR SALES
PRE-BOOKED VISITS
ANNUAL PRODUCTION 80,000 bottles
HECTARES UNDER VINE 16.00

SalvaTerra is certainly one of the most interesting producers to have sprung up in Valpolicella in recent decades. It's all thanks to a large estate and staff with clear ideas about the best way forward, both in the classic heart of the appellation in the to the east. Their cellar is housed in a lovely building next to Villa Giona, in Cengia (San Pietro in Cariano), and gives rise to elegant, complex wines. It's the result of a flexible, adaptive approach when it comes to fermentation, maturation and aging. Their 2016 Valpolicella Superiore Tenuta Campocroce debuts with a bang. It's part of their new line, made with grapes from vineyards in the Mezzane valley. No grape drying was necessary for the wine's vibrant aromas of wild fruit, medicinal herbs and pepper. The palate walks a razor thin line as it unfolds splendidly, tautly and with determination. Their 2011 Amarone also delivered with its still-fresh and intact aromas, which give way to a rich, balanced palate.

| | |
|---|---|
| ● Valpolicella Sup. Tenuta Campocroce '16 | ♟♟♟ 4* |
| ● Amarone della Valpolicella Cl. '11 | ♟♟ 8 |
| ● Amarone della Valpolicella Cl. Cave di Prun Ris. '09 | ♟♟ 8 |
| ● Valpolicella Tenuta Campocroce '17 | ♟♟ 3 |
| ● Valpolicella Cl. Sup. Ripasso '14 | ♟ 5 |
| ● Amarone della Valpolicella Cl. '10 | ♟♟ 8 |
| ● Amarone della Valpolicella Cl. '09 | ♟♟ 8 |
| ● Amarone della Valpolicella Cl. Cave di Prun Ris. '08 | ♟♟ 8 |
| ● Amarone della Valpolicella Cl. Cave di Prun Ris. '07 | ♟♟ 8 |
| ● Valpolicella Cl. '15 | ♟♟ 3 |
| ● Valpolicella Cl. Sup. '14 | ♟♟ 3 |
| ● Valpolicella Cl. Sup. Ripasso '13 | ♟♟ 5 |
| ● Valpolicella Cl. Sup. Ripasso '12 | ♟♟ 5 |

# Marco Sambin

LOC. VALNOGAREDO
VIA FATTORELLE, 20A
35030 CINTO EUGANEO [PD]
TEL. +39 3456812050
www.vinimarcus.com

**CELLAR SALES**
**PRE-BOOKED VISITS**
**RESTAURANT SERVICE**
**ANNUAL PRODUCTION** 20,000 bottles
**HECTARES UNDER VINE** 3.00
**VITICULTURE METHOD** Certified Organic
**SUSTAINABLE WINERY**

Marco Sambin is a university professor dedicated to agriculture who created a small but culturally important winery in the westernmost part of the Colli Euganei hills, practically at the foot of Monte Lozzo. The estate comprises just a few hectares of organically cultivated, highly calcareous terrain that naturally limits the yield per plant. The extraordinarily concentrated grapes that result give rise to a selection of sunny wines that are full of character. Their 2015 Marcus leads their selection. It's a densely ruby-colored Bordeaux blend with a splash of Syrah to round things out. Its aromas are dominated by ripe red fruit that are gradually amplified by spicy notes, pencil lead and forest undergrowth. These follow through perfectly to a palate that delivers for power and tension, proving long and charming. Their 2017 Le Femminelle, a blend of Cabernet Sauvignon, Merlot and Roboso, is a fresher, suppler wine on the palate. Their 2015 Helena Passito also did well.

# San Cassiano

VIA SAN CASSIANO, 17
37030 MEZZANE DI SOTTO [VR]
TEL. +39 0458880665
www.cantinasancassiano.it

**CELLAR SALES**
**PRE-BOOKED VISITS**
**ANNUAL PRODUCTION** 50,000 bottles
**HECTARES UNDER VINE** 11.00
**SUSTAINABLE WINERY**

Despite having experienced an unfettered viticultural explosion, the valley of Mezzane still offers glimpses of environmental harmony, with vineyards surrounded by woods, olives and the occasional cherry tree. It's in one of these areas that Mirko Sella works. He's a committed cultivator who divides his time between wine and olive oil, with excellent results in both cases. The house style privileges rich, well-structured reds sustained by a characteristic acidic vigor deriving from the high elevations here and the genetic makeup of the traditional cultivar used. Their 2014 Amarone put in an excellent performance. Despite the difficult year, it proves to be an intact, vivid wine. On the nose fruit comes through ripe and fleshy, crossed by notes of dried flowers and medicinal herbs, while its generous palate is well-contrasted by acidity. Their most recent creation, a 2017 Soave, also proved interesting, with its fresh and reassuring aromas of fruit and flowers. On the palate it delivers for tension and pleasantness.

| | |
|---|---|
| ○ Helena Passito '15 | 🍷🍷 5 |
| ● Le Femminelle '17 | 🍷🍷 3 |
| ● Marcus '15 | 🍷🍷 5 |
| ○ Sarah '17 | 🍷🍷 3 |
| ● Francisca XII Passito '12 | 🍷 5 |
| ○ Martha Sur Lie Frizzante '16 | 🍷 3 |
| ● Alter '15 | 🍷🍷 4 |
| ● Alter '14 | 🍷🍷 4 |
| ● Alter '13 | 🍷🍷 4 |
| ● Marcus '13 | 🍷🍷 5 |
| ● Marcus '12 | 🍷🍷 5 |
| ● Marcus '11 | 🍷🍷 5 |
| ● Marcus '10 | 🍷🍷 5 |
| ● Marcus al Quadrato '13 | 🍷🍷 6 |
| ○ Martha Frizzante '14 | 🍷🍷 4 |
| ○ Martha.due '14 | 🍷🍷 3 |

| | |
|---|---|
| ● Amarone della Valpolicella '14 | 🍷🍷 6 |
| ● Recioto della Valpolicella '15 | 🍷🍷 5 |
| ○ Soave '17 | 🍷🍷 3 |
| ● Valpolicella '16 | 🍷🍷 2* |
| ● Amarone della Valpolicella '13 | 🍷🍷 6 |
| ● Amarone della Valpolicella '11 | 🍷🍷 6 |
| ● Valpolicella '15 | 🍷🍷 2* |
| ● Valpolicella '10 | 🍷🍷 2* |
| ● Valpolicella Sup. Ripasso '14 | 🍷🍷 3 |
| ● Valpolicella Sup. Ripasso '12 | 🍷🍷 2* |

## La Sansonina

LOC. SANSONINA
37019 PESCHIERA DEL GARDA [VR]
TEL. +39 0457551905
www.sansonina.it

**CELLAR SALES**
**ANNUAL PRODUCTION** 35,000 bottles
**HECTARES UNDER VINE** 13.00

Carla Prospero has managed to capture the essence of a territory that today appears to be going towards a kind of monoculture dominated by Turbiana. Her estate, which is situated in the heart of Lugana winemaking country (in Sansonina di Peschiera), is dedicated to the historic white grape of Lake Garda and Bordeaux varieties. Her wines, which are forged in a lovely cellar built in an 18th century farmhouse, are inspired by principles of natural viticulture and bring together pleasantness with decisive character and identity. As the name suggestions, Fermentazione Spontanea is the result of spontaneous fermentation, which transforms the best grapes from their historic Lugana vineyard into a wine of great personality. The 2016 enchants with its aromas of golden delicious apples, refreshed by subtle, herbaceous nuances and aromatic herbs. These provide the pace for its deliciously crisp palate, which manages to lengthen with savoriness and tension. Among their reds we preferred their 2016 Sansonina, a sunny and weighty Merlot.

| | | |
|---|---|---|
| ○ Lugana Fermentazione Spontanea '16 | ♟♟ | 3* |
| ● Garda Cabernet Evaluna '16 | ♟♟ | 4 |
| ● Sansonina '16 | ♟♟ | 6 |
| ● Garda Cabernet Evaluna '15 | ♟♟ | 4 |
| ● Garda Evaluna '14 | ♟♟ | 4 |
| ○ Lugana Sansonina '13 | ♟♟ | 3 |
| ○ Lugana Sansonina '12 | ♟♟ | 3 |
| ○ Lugana Sansonina '11 | ♟♟ | 3 |
| ○ Lugana Sansonina '10 | ♟♟ | 6 |
| ○ Lugana Sansonina '09 | ♟♟ | 3* |
| ○ Lugana V. del Morano Verde '15 | ♟♟ | 4 |
| ○ Lugana V. del Morano Verde '14 | ♟♟ | 3 |
| ● Sansonina '14 | ♟♟ | 6 |
| ● Sansonina '13 | ♟♟ | 6 |
| ● Sansonina '12 | ♟♟ | 6 |
| ● Sansonina '10 | ♟♟ | 6 |
| ● Sansonina '09 | ♟♟ | 6 |

## Tenuta Sant'Anna

FRAZ. LONCON
VIA MONSIGNOR P. L. ZOVATTO, 71
30020 ANNONE VENETO [VE]
TEL. +39 0422864511
www.tenutasantanna.it

**CELLAR SALES**
**PRE-BOOKED VISITS**
**ANNUAL PRODUCTION** 2,800,000 bottles
**HECTARES UNDER VINE** 140.00

Tenuta Sant'Anna, a large winery that's part of the Genagricola group, has managed to meet the challenges faced daily by wine producers and position itself as one of the most representative producers in Venice, especially with respect to the strip of plains that extends towards Friuli. They have a large estate at their disposal, which gives rise to a selection of wines oriented around close-focused monovarietals, Merlot and Tai foremost. Also, their sparkling winemaking production is increasingly strategic, with Prosecco at the center of it all. With a selection this rich, only a Prosecco could most impressed this year. By virtue of its precision, it's their Cartizze, a wine that features aromas of golden delicious apples and jasmine flowers. In the mouth it reveals commendable symmetry, with an elegant sparkle to accompany the palate. Among their still wines we point out a nice performance by their 2017 Cabernet Sauvignon, from their Poderi line. It's a red with forthright and fruity aromas that highlight a juicy, supply palate.

| | | |
|---|---|---|
| ○ Cartizze | ♟♟ | 5 |
| ○ Valdobbiadene Extra Dry | ♟♟ | 3 |
| ● Venezia Cabernet Sauvignon Poderi '17 | ♟♟ | 2* |
| ○ Cuvée Blanche Extra Dry | ♟ | 2 |
| ○ Cuvée Rosé Brut | ♟ | 2 |
| ○ Lison Cl. Goccia '17 | ♟ | 2 |
| ○ Lison-Pramaggiore Chardonnay Goccia '17 | ♟ | 2 |
| ● Lison-Pramaggiore Merlot Poderi '17 | ♟ | 2 |
| ● Lison-Pramaggiore Refosco P. R. Poderi '17 | ♟ | 2 |
| ○ Lison-Pramaggiore Savignon Goccia '17 | ♟ | 2 |
| ○ Traminer '17 | ♟ | 2 |
| ○ Venezia Pinot Grigio Goccia '17 | ♟ | 2 |
| ● Lison-Pramaggiore Merlot Poderi '16 | ♟♟ | 2* |
| ○ Venezia Pinot Grigio '16 | ♟♟ | 2* |

# ★Tenuta Sant'Antonio

LOC. SAN ZENO
VIA CERIANI, 23
37030 COLOGNOLA AI COLLI [VR]
TEL. +39 0457650383
www.tenutasantantonio.it

**CELLAR SALES**
**PRE-BOOKED VISITS**
**ANNUAL PRODUCTION** 700,000 bottles
**HECTARES UNDER VINE** 100.00

Brothers Armando, TIziano, Paolo and Massimo Castagnedi began growing vines in the mid 1990s. Today they are managed by one of Valpolicella's most representative wineries. Their vineyards include the hills around their Colognola cellar and areas situated primarily in the lower valley. Painstaking care goes into cultivating their vineyards, which host primarily Verona's classic grapes (and not only red). Their selection focuses on volume and the fullness of fruit, characteristics that emerge especially over time and in their most important Riserva wines. This year we tasted a reduced number of wines, though there were some surprises. The wine that most impressed was their 2016 Soave Vecchie Vigne, a monovarietal Garganega from a historic vineyard on Monte Ceriani. On the nose it offers up aromas of ripe white fruit, while the palate features well-integrated oak and fullness supported by a juicy, acidic thrust. Their 2015 Valpolicella La Bandina is redolent of opulent fruit, which follows through well on a generous palate.

| | |
|---|---|
| ○ Soave V. V. '16 | ♟♟ 3* |
| ● Valpolicella Sup. La Bandina '15 | ♟♟ 5 |
| ○ Soave Monte Ceriani '17 | ♟♟ 3 |
| ● Valpolicella Sup. Ripasso Monti Garbi '16 | ♟♟ 3 |
| ○ Telos Il Bianco '17 | ♟ 3 |
| ● Amarone della Valpolicella Campo dei Gigli '13 | ♟♟♟ 8 |
| ● Amarone della Valpolicella Campo dei Gigli '12 | ♟♟♟ 8 |
| ● Amarone della Valpolicella Campo dei Gigli '11 | ♟♟♟ 8 |
| ○ Soave Monte Ceriani '15 | ♟♟ 3* |
| ● Valpolicella Sup. La Bandina '13 | ♟♟ 5 |

# Santa Margherita

VIA ITA MARZOTTO, 8
30025 FOSSALTA DI PORTOGRUARO [VE]
TEL. +39 0421246111
www.santamargherita.com

**CELLAR SALES**
**PRE-BOOKED VISITS**
**ANNUAL PRODUCTION** 13,500,000 bottles
**HECTARES UNDER VINE** 50.00

If Fossalta di Portogruaro has become a central node for Italian vine growing and winemaking, it's almost entirely thanks to the Marzotto family. With great, forward-thinking vision, they have faced production challenges, overcoming the difficulties of producing high volumes of wine while maintaining high quality standards. Bolstered by close ties with a number of vine growers as well as an exceptional estate, Santa Margherita has raised the bar for their entire selection, from Pinot Grigio to Prosecco, while also making investments outside the region. A shining example in that sense is their 2017 Pinot Grigio Impronta del Fondatore, a wine made with grapes cultivated throughout Alto Adige. On the nose smoky notes and aromas of pear take center stage, while in the mouth its body proves firm, with a crisp, well-balanced palate. It's also worth pointing out the continued growth, in terms of quality, of their Proseccos, led by their 2017 Rive di Refrontolo Brut, a plucky wine with commendable finesse.

| | |
|---|---|
| ○ A. A. Pinot Grigio Impronta del Fondatore '17 | ♟♟ 3* |
| ○ A. A. Bianco Luna dei Feldi '16 | ♟♟ 3 |
| ○ Cartizze | ♟♟ 5 |
| ○ Valdobbiadene Brut | ♟♟ 3 |
| ○ Valdobbiadene Brut Rive di Refrontolo '17 | ♟♟ 3 |
| ○ Valdobbiadene Extra Dry | ♟♟ 3 |
| ● Lison-Pramaggiore Malbech Impronta del Fondatore '16 | ♟ 3 |
| ○ Valdadige Pinot Grigio '17 | ♟ 3 |
| ○ A. A. Bianco Luna dei Feldi '15 | ♟♟ 3 |
| ○ A. A. Pinot Grigio Impronta del Fondatore '16 | ♟♟ 3 |
| ○ A. A. Pinot Grigio Impronta del Fondatore '15 | ♟♟ 2* |

# VENETO

## Santa Sofia

Fraz. Pedemonte di Valpolicella
via Ca' Dedé, 61
37029 San Pietro in Cariano [VR]
Tel. +39 0457701074
www.santasofia.com

**CELLAR SALES**
**PRE-BOOKED VISITS**
**ANNUAL PRODUCTION** 550,000 bottles
**HECTARES UNDER VINE** 53.00

This historic winery situated in Pedemonte, a district of San Pietro in Cariano, has begun an extensive renovation project, both in terms of production and vineyard management. And the effort is bearing its first fruit. Their selection, which touches on all of Verona's appellations, is focusing more on clarity and precision, pursuing a style centered on finesse and elegance. This change in expression is particularly detectable in their Valpolicellas. Their 2012 Amarone, a wine that's released only after lengthy aging in the cellar, delivered clear results. On the nose it's a bit closed at first, needing time to open. But then aromas of ripe cherry, spices and forest undergrowth emerge. In the mouth it comes through full, plush and marked by smooth tannins. Their 2015 Valpolicella also put in an excellent performance, with Montegradella proving fresh in its notes of pepper, and a supple, spicy palate. Their Ripasso is a richer wine.

| | |
|---|---|
| ● Amarone della Valpolicella Cl. '12 | ♟♟ 7 |
| ● Valpolicella Cl. Sup. Montegradella '15 | ♟♟ 4 |
| ● Valpolicella Cl. '16 | ♟♟ 3 |
| ● Valpolicella Sup. Ripasso '15 | ♟♟ 4 |
| ○ Lugana '17 | ♟ 3 |
| ● Amarone della Valpolicella Cl. '12 | ♟♟ 7 |
| ● Amarone della Valpolicella Cl. '11 | ♟♟ 7 |
| ● Amarone della Valpolicella Cl. '09 | ♟♟ 7 |
| ● Amarone della Valpolicella Cl. '08 | ♟♟ 6 |
| ● Amarone della Valpolicella Cl. Gioé '07 | ♟♟ 7 |
| ● Recioto della Valpolicella Cl. '11 | ♟♟ 5 |
| ● Valpolicella Cl. '14 | ♟♟ 2* |
| ● Valpolicella Cl. Sup. Montegradella '14 | ♟♟ 4 |
| ● Valpolicella Cl. Sup. Montegradella '11 | ♟♟ 4 |
| ● Valpolicella Sup. Ripasso '14 | ♟♟ 4 |
| ● Valpolicella Sup. Ripasso '13 | ♟♟ 4 |
| ● Valpolicella Sup. Ripasso '12 | ♟♟ 4 |

## Santi

via Ungheria, 33
37031 Illasi [VR]
Tel. +39 0456529068
www.cantinasanti.it

**CELLAR SALES**
**PRE-BOOKED VISITS**
**ANNUAL PRODUCTION** 1,400,000 bottles
**HECTARES UNDER VINE** 53.00

After many years that saw Illasi's cellars move to Gruppo Italiano Vini's other facilities, not only has Santi found new life, but today it's one of eastern Valpolicella's most dynamic wineries. Under the technical guidance of Cristian Ridolfi, their selection has taken on a well-defined style aimed at highlighting the classic qualities of Verona's appellations, with elegance and tension at the forefront, while eschewing easy shortcuts that opt for power and aroma. Last year we already pointed the notable recent edition of their Valpolicella Superiore Venatel, and this year we can only confirm our excellent impression of the wine. 2016 gave rise to elegant aromas that feature spices alternating with wild fruit and aromatic herbs. Its decisive, slender palate is supported by fresh and racy acidity. Their 2012 Amarone Proemio, a serious red that brings together power and rigor, also performed well, as did their 2013 Amarone and their 2017 Lugana Melibeo.

| | |
|---|---|
| ● Amarone della Valpolicella Cl. Proemio '12 | ♟♟ 7 |
| ● Valpolicella Sup. Ventale '16 | ♟♟ 3* |
| ● Amarone della Valpolicella Cl. '13 | ♟♟ 6 |
| ○ Lugana Melibeo '17 | ♟♟ 3 |
| ● Valpolicella Cl. Le Caselle '17 | ♟ 2 |
| ● Amarone della Valpolicella Proemio '05 | ♟♟♟ 6 |
| ● Amarone della Valpolicella Proemio '03 | ♟♟♟ 6 |
| ● Amarone della Valpolicella Proemio '00 | ♟♟♟ 5 |
| ● Valpolicella Cl. Sup. Ripasso Solane '09 | ♟♟♟ 3* |
| ● Amarone della Valpolicella Cl. '12 | ♟♟ 6 |
| ● Amarone della Valpolicella Cl. '11 | ♟♟ 6 |
| ● Amarone della Valpolicella Cl. Proemio '11 | ♟♟ 6 |
| ○ Soave Cl. Vign. Monteforte '16 | ♟♟ 2* |
| ● Valpolicella Cl. Sup. Ripasso Solane '15 | ♟♟ 4 |
| ● Valpolicella Cl. Sup. Ripasso Solane '14 | ♟♟ 4 |

# Sartori

FRAZ. SANTA MARIA
VIA CASETTE, 4
37024 NEGRAR [VR]
TEL. +39 0456028011
www.sartorinet.com

**CELLAR SALES**
**PRE-BOOKED VISITS**
**ANNUAL PRODUCTION** 16,000,000 bottles
**HECTARES UNDER VINE** 120.00
**SUSTAINABLE WINERY**

The Sartori family's winery is one of the most important in Verona, bolstered by a range of wines that spans all of western Veneto's appellations, and isn't afraid to venture further either. Their selection centers on close collaborations with important partners and local suppliers throughout the territory. Their private vineyards are dedicated to their crown jewel, Saltari, a line that comprises a Valpolicella Superiore and a premium Amarone. This year their most impressive offering proves to be their 2015 Recioto Rerum, a wine made with grapes that dry until the start of the new year. On the nose it offers up a rich array of aromas, morello cherry and pepper refreshed by a subtle balsamic vein. On the palate its pronounced sweetness delicately caresses the palate while acidity lengthens its finish. Their 2011 Amarone I Saltari opts for greater aromatic depth and density of the palate. Their 2011 Amarone Corte Brà and 2013 Valpolicella I Saltari round out their selection.

| | |
|---|---|
| ● Amarone della Valpolicella Cl. Corte Brà '11 | 🍷🍷 7 |
| ● Amarone della Valpolicella I Saltari '11 | 🍷🍷 8 |
| ● Recioto della Valpolicella Cl. Rerum '15 | 🍷🍷 5 |
| ● Valpolicella Sup. I Saltari '13 | 🍷🍷 5 |
| ● Valpolicella Sup. Ripasso Regolo '15 | 🍷 3 |
| ● Amarone della Valpolicella Cl. Corte Brà '09 | 🍷🍷 7 |
| ● Amarone della Valpolicella Cl. Reius '11 | 🍷🍷 7 |
| ● Amarone della Valpolicella I Saltari '10 | 🍷🍷 8 |
| ● Cent'Anni '13 | 🍷🍷 4 |
| ● Valpolicella Cl. Sup. Montegradella '13 | 🍷🍷 3 |
| ● Valpolicella Sup. I Saltari '12 | 🍷🍷 4 |
| ● Valpolicella Sup. I Saltari '11 | 🍷🍷 4 |
| ● Valpolicella Sup. Ripasso Regolo '14 | 🍷🍷 4 |
| ● Valpolicella Sup. Ripasso Regolo '13 | 🍷🍷 4 |

# Secondo Marco

VIA CAMPOLONGO, 9
37022 FUMANE [VR]
TEL. +39 0456800954
www.secondomarco.it

**CELLAR SALES**
**PRE-BOOKED VISITS**
**ACCOMMODATION**
**ANNUAL PRODUCTION** 75,000 bottles
**HECTARES UNDER VINE** 15.00

In just a short time Benedetto and Marco Speri's winery has become a benchmark for Valpolicella's slender, more elegant wines. Their vineyards are situated in the heart of the area and are dedicated entirely to local cultivar. In the cellar large wood barrels are used, along with steel and concrete, making for a selection that shows its best over time. Their wines (including their dried-grape wines) focus on the finesse that only the area's best reds can offer. The wait endowed their 2012 Amarone with an expression of ripe, meaty fruit, enriched by the presence of medicinal herbs, a veritable trademark of their reds. In the mouth the wine's power is managed prudently and the palate lengthens elegantly towards a crisp finish. Their simpler Valpolicella is another wine that requires patience. Their 2016 proves fresh in its hints of wild fruit and thyme, while the palate proves slender and notably savory.

| | |
|---|---|
| ● Amarone della Valpolicella Cl. '12 | 🍷🍷 8 |
| ● Solo per un Amico '12 | 🍷🍷 8 |
| ● Valpolicella Cl. '16 | 🍷🍷 3 |
| ● Amarone della Valpolicella Cl. '11 | 🍷🍷🍷 8 |
| ● Amarone della Valpolicella Cl. '10 | 🍷🍷 7 |
| ● Amarone della Valpolicella Cl. '09 | 🍷🍷 7 |
| ● Recioto della Valpolicella Cl. '13 | 🍷🍷 6 |
| ● Recioto della Valpolicella Cl. '12 | 🍷🍷 6 |
| ● Recioto della Valpolicella Cl. '10 | 🍷🍷 6 |
| ● Valpolicella Cl. '15 | 🍷🍷 3 |
| ● Valpolicella Cl. '14 | 🍷🍷 3 |
| ● Valpolicella Cl. '13 | 🍷🍷 3 |
| ● Valpolicella Cl. '12 | 🍷🍷 2* |
| ● Valpolicella Cl. Sup. Ripasso '14 | 🍷🍷 5 |
| ● Valpolicella Cl. Sup. Ripasso '13 | 🍷🍷 5 |
| ● Valpolicella Cl. Sup. Ripasso '12 | 🍷🍷 5 |
| ● Valpolicella Cl. Sup. Ripasso '11 | 🍷🍷 4 |

## ★★Serafini & Vidotto

VIA LUIGI CARRER, 8
31040 NERVESA DELLA BATTAGLIA [TV]
TEL. +39 0422773281
www.serafinividotto.it

**CELLAR SALES**
**PRE-BOOKED VISITS**
**ANNUAL PRODUCTION** 250,000 bottles
**HECTARES UNDER VINE** 23.00
**SUSTAINABLE WINERY**

Without getting too grandiose, this Nervesa della Battaglia winery has taken important steps towards developing a low-impact approach to viticulture while keeping up with lofty production ambitions. Their project in the cellar is moving forward, with Francesco Serafini and Antonello Vidotto making every effort to bring out the best of each batch. The producers are among the most important interpreters of Italian Bordeaux blends, with wines of unmistakable elegance and character, deeply bound to the Montello hills where their prestigious estate is cultivated. Their 2015 Rosso dell'Abazia put in an excellent performance. It's a classic blend, primarily Cabernet Sauvignon, that offers up vibrant notes of wild berries with nuances of medicinal herbs and spices. On the palate it features richness, supported by Montello's trademark acidity and tannins of rare precision. Their two Phigaias also delivered. Their 2015 Rosso is fresh in its aromas, dynamic in the mouth. Their 2016 El Blanco is a delicately aromatic wine that's savory on the palate.

| | |
|---|---|
| ● Montello e Colli Asolani Il Rosso dell'Abazia '15 | ▼▼▼ 6 |
| ○ Asolo Extra Dry Bollicine di Prosecco | ▼▼ 3 |
| ○ Montello e Colli Asolani Manzoni Bianco '17 | ▼▼ 3 |
| ● Montello e Colli Asolani Phigaia '15 | ▼▼ 4 |
| ● Montello e Colli Asolani Recantina '17 | ▼▼ 3 |
| ○ Phigaja El Blanco '16 | ▼▼ 4 |
| ● Pinot Nero '15 | ▼▼ 7 |
| ○ Prosecco di Treviso Extra Dry Bollicine di Prosecco | ▼ 3 |
| ● Montello e Colli Asolani Il Rosso dell'Abazia '13 | ♀♀♀ 6 |
| ● Montello e Colli Asolani Il Rosso dell'Abazia '12 | ♀♀♀ 5 |
| ● Montello e Colli Asolani Il Rosso dell'Abazia '11 | ♀♀♀ 6 |

## ★Speri

LOC. PEDEMONTE
VIA FONTANA, 14
37029 SAN PIETRO IN CARIANO [VR]
TEL. +39 0457701154
www.speri.com

**CELLAR SALES**
**PRE-BOOKED VISITS**
**ANNUAL PRODUCTION** 350,000 bottles
**HECTARES UNDER VINE** 60.00
**VITICULTURE METHOD** Certified Organic
**SUSTAINABLE WINERY**

The transition towards natural agriculture that the Speri family have undertaken over recent years at their historic Pedemonte winery has resulted in their entire selection being certified organic, an accomplishment made possible in part by the absence of their 2014 Amarone (not produced because of a poor season). Another fact worth noting is expansion of their vineyards on Sant'Urbano, which reach 300 meters above sea level facing north. But their selection still exhibits the same overall soundness and ties to tradition, making for elegant, long-lived wines. Considering the bad year, the Speri family decided not to produce a 2014 Amarone Monte Sant'Urbano, a true symbol of a selection worthy of its fame. So this year they were led by a 2015 Valpolicella Sant'Urbano, an outgoing, sunny wine in its aromas of ripe cherry and pepper, refreshed by nuances of bouquet garni. It's a profile that confers an almost unexpected lightness on the palate, which certainly isn't lacking in force and length.

| | |
|---|---|
| ● Recioto della Valpolicella Cl. La Roggia '15 | ▼▼ 6 |
| ● Valpolicella Cl. Sup. Sant'Urbano '15 | ▼▼ 4 |
| ● Valpolicella Cl. '17 | ▼▼ 3 |
| ● Valpolicella Cl. Sup. Ripasso '16 | ▼▼ 4 |
| ● Amarone della Valpolicella Cl. Vign. Monte Sant'Urbano '12 | ♀♀♀ 7 |
| ● Amarone della Valpolicella Cl. Vign. Monte Sant'Urbano '09 | ♀♀♀ 7 |
| ● Amarone della Valpolicella Cl. Vign. Monte Sant'Urbano '08 | ♀♀♀ 7 |
| ● Amarone della Valpolicella Cl. Vign. Monte Sant'Urbano '07 | ♀♀♀ 7 |
| ● Amarone della Valpolicella Cl. Vign. Sant'Urbano '11 | ♀♀♀ 7 |
| ● Amarone della Valpolicella Vign. Monte Sant'Urbano '13 | ♀♀♀ 7 |

# I Stefanini

VIA CROSARA, 21
37032 MONTEFORTE D'ALPONE [VR]
TEL. +39 0456175249
www.istefanini.it

**CELLAR SALES**
**PRE-BOOKED VISITS**
**ANNUAL PRODUCTION** 100,000 bottles
**HECTARES UNDER VINE** 17.00

Not even 20 years have passed since the first wines labeled 'I Stefanini' were released. And yet this small winery in Monteforte d'Alpone has managed to earn an important role among Soave's wine producers. They have at least a couple things going for them: a few hectares of vineyards on Tenda hill, three ledges of Garganega cultivated according to the traditional pergola system, and, especially, the skill of Francesco Tessari. By limiting production he's managed to create rich, gutsy wines. Their simplest wine on paper is their 2017 Soave Il Selese. It's enough to taste it to get a sense of the house style: intensely fruit-driven, with a firm profile and nice tension. We were most impressed, however, by their 2017 Soave monte de Toni, a white with notable aromatic ripeness and a flowery character. On the palate it proves decisive, coming through crisp and consistent.

# David Sterza

VIA CASTERNA, 37
37022 FUMANE [VR]
TEL. +39 3471343121
www.davidsterza.it

**CELLAR SALES**
**PRE-BOOKED VISITS**
**ANNUAL PRODUCTION** 40,000 bottles
**HECTARES UNDER VINE** 4.50

David Sterza and his cousin Paolo Mascanzoni manage this small Casterna winery. It's a tiny village in the heart of classic Valpolicella. Their vineyards span a few hectares around their production center, and are dedicated primarily to Corvina, Corvinone and Rondinella, the historic cultivar that constitute the backbone of the area's traditional wines. In the cellar they show great attention to maintaining the dignity of their wines, as well as the vibrance of fruit. It's a contemporary style that often features tension and pluck. Their recognized skill in vineyard management allowed the winery to produce a splendid Amarone, even during a season as difficult as 2014. It's a wine that yields aromas of wild fruit and forest undergrowth. On the palate it highlights a firm and crisp body supported by acidity, lengthening decisively. Their 2016 Ripasso also delivered, opting for greater freshness and fragrance, amplified by a crisp, dynamic palate.

| | |
|---|---|
| ○ Soave Cl. Monte de Toni '17 | 🏆🏆 2* |
| ○ Soave Cl. Sup. Monte di Fice '17 | 🏆🏆 3 |
| ○ Soave Il Selese '17 | 🏆🏆 1* |
| ○ Soave Cl. Monte de Toni '12 | 🏆🏆🏆 2* |
| ○ Soave Cl. Sup. Monte di Fice '07 | 🏆🏆🏆 2* |
| ○ Soave Cl. Monte de Toni '16 | 🏆🏆 2* |
| ○ Soave Cl. Monte de Toni '15 | 🏆🏆 2* |
| ○ Soave Cl. Monte de Toni '14 | 🏆🏆 2* |
| ○ Soave Cl. Monte de Toni '13 | 🏆🏆 2* |
| ○ Soave Cl. Monte de Toni '11 | 🏆🏆 2* |
| ○ Soave Cl. Monte di Fice '14 | 🏆🏆 3 |
| ○ Soave Cl. Sup. Monte di Fice '16 | 🏆🏆 3* |
| ○ Soave Cl. Sup. Monte di Fice '15 | 🏆🏆 3 |
| ○ Soave Cl. Sup. Monte di Fice '13 | 🏆🏆 3* |
| ○ Soave Cl. Sup. Monte di Fice '12 | 🏆🏆 3* |
| ○ Soave Il Selese '16 | 🏆🏆 1* |
| ○ Soave Il Selese '14 | 🏆🏆 1* |

| | |
|---|---|
| ● Amarone della Valpolicella Cl. '14 | 🏆🏆 6 |
| ● Valpolicella Cl. '17 | 🏆🏆 2* |
| ● Valpolicella Cl. Sup. Ripasso '16 | 🏆🏆 3 |
| ● Amarone della Valpolicella Cl. '13 | 🏆🏆🏆 6 |
| ● Amarone della Valpolicella Cl. '12 | 🏆🏆🏆 6 |
| ● Amarone della Valpolicella Cl. '11 | 🏆🏆 6 |
| ● Amarone della Valpolicella Cl. '10 | 🏆🏆 6 |
| ● Recioto della Valpolicella Cl. '15 | 🏆🏆 5 |
| ● Recioto della Valpolicella Cl. '14 | 🏆🏆 5 |
| ● Recioto della Valpolicella Cl. '13 | 🏆🏆 5 |
| ● Recioto della Valpolicella Cl. '12 | 🏆🏆 5 |
| ● Valpolicella Cl. '14 | 🏆🏆 2* |
| ● Valpolicella Cl. '13 | 🏆🏆 2* |
| ● Valpolicella Cl. Sup. Ripasso '15 | 🏆🏆 3 |
| ● Valpolicella Cl. Sup. Ripasso '14 | 🏆🏆 3 |
| ● Valpolicella Cl. Sup. Ripasso '13 | 🏆🏆 3* |
| ● Valpolicella Cl. Sup. Ripasso '12 | 🏆🏆 3 |

## ★Suavia

FRAZ. FITTÀ DI SOAVE
VIA CENTRO, 14
37038 SOAVE [VR]
TEL. +39 0457675089
www.suavia.it

**CELLAR SALES**
**PRE-BOOKED VISITS**
**ANNUAL PRODUCTION** 100,000 bottles
**HECTARES UNDER VINE** 12.00

Meri, Valentina and Alessandra Tessari are leading the family winery and in two decades they have transformed it into one of Soave's crown jewels. Their estate is situated entirely in hill areas and only traditional grapes are cultivated, especially Garganega and a small part local Trebbiano. These grow in the black, volcanic terrain that characterizes the area, giving rise to a selection with character and depth. Over the years the estate has grown, thanks to purchases around the prestigious district of upper Fittà. A stunning selection of wines were submitted by the Tessari sisters, with their Soave Monte Carbonare once again leading the way. 2016 conferred an aromatic quality that's sunnier than usual, with fruit emerging generous and crisp, and then giving way to flowery notes. On the palate it proves crisp, taut and endlessly long. Their 2015 Massifitti also did extremely well. It's a monovarietal Trebbiano that delivers for aromatic complexity and savoriness on the palate.

| | |
|---|---|
| ○ Soave Cl. Monte Carbonare '16 | ♀♀♀ 3* |
| ○ Massifitti '15 | ♀♀ 3* |
| ○ Le Rive '15 | ♀♀ 4 |
| ○ Recioto di Soave Acinatium '13 | ♀♀ 5 |
| ○ Soave Cl. '17 | ♀♀ 2* |
| ○ Soave Cl. Le Rive '02 | ♀♀♀ 4 |
| ○ Soave Cl. Monte Carbonare '15 | ♀♀♀ 3* |
| ○ Soave Cl. Monte Carbonare '14 | ♀♀♀ 3* |
| ○ Soave Cl. Monte Carbonare '12 | ♀♀♀ 3* |
| ○ Soave Cl. Monte Carbonare '11 | ♀♀♀ 3* |
| ○ Soave Cl. Monte Carbonare '10 | ♀♀♀ 3* |
| ○ Soave Cl. Monte Carbonare '09 | ♀♀♀ 3* |
| ○ Soave Cl. Monte Carbonare '08 | ♀♀♀ 3* |
| ○ Soave Cl. Monte Carbonare '07 | ♀♀♀ 3* |
| ○ Soave Cl. Monte Carbonare '06 | ♀♀♀ 3* |
| ○ Soave Cl. Monte Carbonare '05 | ♀♀♀ 3* |
| ○ Soave Cl. Monte Carbonare '04 | ♀♀♀ 3 |

## Sutto

LOC. CAMPO DI PIETRA
VIA ARZERI, 34/1
31040 SALGAREDA [TV]
TEL. +39 0422744063
www.sutto.it

**CELLAR SALES**
**PRE-BOOKED VISITS**
**ACCOMMODATION AND RESTAURANT SERVICE**
**ANNUAL PRODUCTION** 400,000 bottles
**HECTARES UNDER VINE** 75.00

Brother Stefano and Luigi Sutto work in the territory that joins the Venetian plains with Friuli, an area characterized by clay soil alternating with deep pockets of gravel. In addition to their vast property here, we need to consider their estate in Valdobbiadene, which supports a complete selection, from Prosecco to still wines. In their Campodipietra cellar two stylistic paths are pusued. One is focused on more approachable and varietal wines, while the other aims for more ambitious wines that bring together fullness and elegance. Work in the vineyards allowed their Campo Sella to progress further in terms of quality. The 2015 version of this monovarietal Merlot offers up vibrant aromas of red fruit and spices, with a fresh vein of aromatic herbs lending lightness and fragrance. In the mouth its body proves full, supported by pronounced savory acidity. Their Valdobbiadenes are also commendable, while among their simpler wines we appreciated the fruity freshness of their 2017 Merlot and Cabernet.

| | |
|---|---|
| ● Campo Sella '15 | ♀♀♀ 5 |
| ○ Bianco di Sutto '17 | ♀♀ 2* |
| ● Cabernet '17 | ♀♀ 2* |
| ● Merlot '17 | ♀♀ 2* |
| ○ Valdobbiadene Brut | ♀♀ 3 |
| ○ Valdobbiadene Extra Dry Batiso | ♀♀ 3 |
| ○ Venezia Pinot Grigio '17 | ♀♀ 2* |
| ○ Chardonnay '17 | ♀ 2 |
| ○ Prosecco Extra Dry | ♀ 3 |
| ○ Bianco di Sutto '16 | ♀♀ 2* |
| ● Cabernet '16 | ♀♀ 2* |
| ○ Chardonnay '16 | ♀♀ 2* |
| ● Dogma Rosso '15 | ♀♀ 4 |
| ● Merlot Campo Sella '14 | ♀♀ 5 |
| ○ Pinot Grigio '16 | ♀♀ 2* |
| ○ Ultimo Passito '15 | ♀♀ 4 |
| ○ Valdobbiadene Extra Dry Batiso '16 | ♀♀ 3 |

# Tamellini

FRAZ. COSTEGGIOLA
VIA TAMELLINI, 4
37038 SOAVE [VR]
TEL. +39 0457675328
piofrancesco.tamellini@tin.it

**CELLAR SALES**
**PRE-BOOKED VISITS**
**ANNUAL PRODUCTION** 250,000 bottles
**HECTARES UNDER VINE** 27.00

The Tamellini brothers' winery is situated in
the western part of classic Soave, where
black basalt gradually gives where to tracts
of calcareous terrain and the vineyards
stretch along the hills for as far as the eye
can see. Their selection is dedicated
entirely to Garganega, which is interpreted
according to local tradition. They have a
fresh, racy 'base offering' that can be
enjoyed right away and a premium
selection that's intended to ago. A Metodo
Classico sparkler is also offered on
occasion. Their most representative wine is
a Soave made in Costeggiola, which
inspired the name Bine de Costiola. The
2016 version of this monovarietal
Garganega features notes of ripe yellow
fruit crossed by dried flowers and mineral
nuances. In the mouth it proves crisp,
characterized by a nice acidic thrust that
lengthens the palate. Their 2017 Soave
also delivered, with its fresher more
approachable aromas and a palate that
stands out for its dynamism.

| | | |
|---|---|---|
| ○ Soave Cl. Le Bine de Costiola '16 | ▼▼ | 3* |
| ○ Extra Brut M. Cl. '10 | ▼▼ | 5 |
| ○ Soave '17 | ▼▼ | 2* |
| ○ Soave Cl. Le Bine '04 | ♟♟♟ | 3* |
| ○ Soave Cl. Le Bine de Costiola '14 | ♟♟♟ | 3* |
| ○ Soave Cl. Le Bine de Costiola '13 | ♟♟♟ | 3* |
| ○ Soave Cl. Le Bine de Costiola '11 | ♟♟♟ | 3* |
| ○ Soave Cl. Le Bine de Costiola '06 | ♟♟♟ | 3* |
| ○ Soave Cl. Le Bine de Costiola '05 | ♟♟♟ | 3* |
| ○ Soave '15 | ♟♟ | 2* |
| ○ Soave '14 | ♟♟ | 2* |
| ○ Soave '11 | ♟♟ | 2* |
| ○ Soave Cl. '16 | ♟♟ | 2* |
| ○ Soave Cl. '13 | ♟♟ | 2* |
| ○ Soave Cl. '12 | ♟♟ | 2* |
| ○ Soave Cl. Le Bine de Costiola '15 | ♟♟ | 3* |
| ○ Soave Cl. Le Bine de Costiola '12 | ♟♟ | 3* |

# Giovanna Tantini

FRAZ. OLIOSI
LOC. I MISCHI
37014 CASTELNUOVO DEL GARDA [VR]
TEL. +39 3488717577
www.giovannatantini.it

**CELLAR SALES**
**PRE-BOOKED VISITS**
**ACCOMMODATION**
**ANNUAL PRODUCTION** 30,000 bottles
**HECTARES UNDER VINE** 11.50

Giovanna Tantini works in the area that
stretches to the south of Lake Garda, within
the municipalities of Sona and Castelnuovo.
It's an area whose terrain is morainic and
has a historic link with Bardolino grapes.
From the first vintages, the utmost care has
been shown for Garda's unmistakable wine,
all in pursuit of the perfect balance
between personality, lightness, fragrance
and structure. Lengthy aging is employed
even for their theoretically 'simpler' wines.
For some years now their Custoza has been
part of their roster of whites, a wine that's
interpreted with the same expressive
sensitivity. The Tantini family prove
particularly gifted when it comes to fresher
wines. One example is their 2017 Corvina
Ma.Gi.Co., a wine whose aromas of wild
fruit, pepper and herbaceous notes give
way to a juicy, crisp and highly pleasant
palate. Their 2017 Custoza opts for more
pronounced fruity sensations revived by
flowery hints. In the mouth it changes pace,
featuring a balanced palate that finds depth
in its overt savoriness.

| | | |
|---|---|---|
| ○ Custoza '17 | ▼▼ | 2* |
| ● Ettore '12 | ▼▼ | 4 |
| ● Garda Corvina Ma.Gi.Co. '17 | ▼▼ | 2* |
| ● Bardolino '16 | ▼ | 2 |
| ⊙ Bardolino Chiaretto '17 | ▼ | 2 |
| ● Bardolino '15 | ♟♟ | 2* |
| ● Bardolino '14 | ♟♟ | 2* |
| ● Bardolino '12 | ♟♟ | 2* |
| ● Bardolino '11 | ♟♟ | 2* |
| ● Bardolino '10 | ♟♟ | 2* |
| ⊙ Bardolino Chiaretto '16 | ♟♟ | 2* |
| ⊙ Bardolino Chiaretto '15 | ♟♟ | 2* |
| ● Ettore '11 | ♟♟ | 4 |

# F.lli Tedeschi

FRAZ. PEDEMONTE
VIA G. VERDI, 4
37029 SAN PIETRO IN CARIANO [VR]
TEL. +39 0457701487
www.tedeschiwines.com

CELLAR SALES
PRE-BOOKED VISITS
ANNUAL PRODUCTION 500,000 bottles
HECTARES UNDER VINE 46.00
SUSTAINABLE WINERY

Pedemonte's Tedeschi is one of Valpolicella's historic wineries. Bolstered by a deeply-rooted presence in the territory, the past decade has seen their center of production shift eastward. Their vineyards pan many hectares, at elevations and in positions that are extremely varied, leading to different maturation periods. Antonietta, Sabrina and Riccardo Tedeschi carefully manage every parcel of grapes cultivated in Monte Olmi, Fabriseria and Maternigo, giving rise to a sound but spirited selection of wines. Their 2012 Amarone Capital Monte Olmi, a reserve wine, put in a notable performance. It starts slow on the nose, with notes ripe, sweet fruit gradually emerging along with spices and balsams. In the mouth it proves to be a trademark red in its grip. It's close-knit yet potent and assertive with vigorous tannins that stroke the palate. Their 2015 Valpolicella Maternigo opts for fresher, fruitier notes while in the mouth it proves firm and slender.

| | |
|---|---|
| ● Amarone della Valpolicella Cl. Capitel Monte Olmi Ris. '12 | ▼▼ 8 |
| ● Valpolicella Sup. Maternigo '15 | ▼▼ 5 |
| ● Amarone della Valpolicella '14 | ▼▼ 6 |
| ● Valpolicella Cl. Lucchine '17 | ▼▼ 2* |
| ● Valpolicella Cl. Sup. La Fabriseria '15 | ▼▼ 5 |
| ● Valpolicella Ripasso Sup. Capitel San Rocco '16 | ▼▼ 4 |
| ● Valpolicella Sup. Capitel Nicalò '16 | ▼▼ 3 |
| ● Corasco '16 | ▼ 3 |
| ● Amarone della Valpolicella Cl. Capitel Monte Olmi '11 | ♈♈♈ 8 |
| ● Valpolicella Sup. Maternigo '11 | ♈♈♈ 4* |
| ● Amarone della Valpolicella Cl. '11 | ♈♈ 6 |
| ● Valpolicella Cl. Sup. La Fabriseria '13 | ♈♈ 5 |

# Le Tende

VIA TENDE, 35
37017 LAZISE [VR]
TEL. +39 0457590748
www.letende.it

CELLAR SALES
PRE-BOOKED VISITS
ANNUAL PRODUCTION 100,000 bottles
HECTARES UNDER VINE 12.50
VITICULTURE METHOD Certified Organic

The Fortuna and Lucillini families' estate spans a dozen hectares in inner Garda, just a few hundred meters from the lake's southeastern shore. Here great attention is shown to the area's traditional grapes, which give rise to a selection of wines that, at their best, feature notable lightness and savoriness. Their private, organically managed vineyards supply all the grapes they need and the results are significant, a fact that holds true both for their red and white wines. Their 2016 Bardolino Sup. put in an excellent performance with its complex, dynamic fragrances. Ripe red fruit and pepper meet a fresh, flowery note while the palate proves taut and elegant, supported by acidity and characteristic savoriness. Their 2017 Bardolino also delivered. It pursues a similar aromatic profile, focusing on crisper fruit and a more natural palate. It's among the appellation's most notable.

| | |
|---|---|
| ⊙ Bardolino Chiaretto Cl. '17 | ▼▼ 2* |
| ● Bardolino Cl. '17 | ▼▼ 2* |
| ● Bardolino Cl. Sup. '16 | ▼▼ 3 |
| ○ Sabia '16 | ▼▼ 2* |
| ⊙ Bardolino Chiaretto Brut Voluttà | ▼ 3 |
| ● Cicisbeo '16 | ▼ 4 |
| ○ Custoza '17 | ▼ 2 |
| ● Bardolino Cl. '14 | ♈♈ 2* |
| ● Bardolino Cl. '13 | ♈♈ 2* |
| ● Bardolino Cl. Sup. '15 | ♈♈ 3 |
| ● Bardolino Cl. Sup. '14 | ♈♈ 3 |
| ● Cicisbeo '13 | ♈♈ 4 |
| ● Corvina '16 | ♈♈ 3 |
| ● Corvina '15 | ♈♈ 3 |
| ○ Custoza '15 | ♈♈ 2* |
| ○ Custoza '14 | ♈♈ 2* |

# Gianni Tessari

VIA PRANDI, 10
37030 RONCÀ [VR]
TEL. +39 0457460070
www.giannitessari.wine

CELLAR SALES
PRE-BOOKED VISITS
ANNUAL PRODUCTION 450,000 bottles
HECTARES UNDER VINE 55.00

After a long period spent working for the family winery, Gianni Tessari founded his own, taking over a sizable estate in the area with vineyards across three appellations: Soave, Lessini and Colli Berici. Each represents a very different terroir and cultivation approach, which is then explored with great sensitivity and awareness at their headquarters in Ronca. It's here that their style has been developing, bringing together sparkling wines, whites and reds, all of which pursue varietal coherence and clarity of taste. Their 2016 Pigno, a wine made with grapes from a vineyard situated by Soave Castle, stood out among their selection. It's a white with great aromatic depth that ranges from ripe yellow fruit to dried flowers, only to close on a subtle mineral vein. In the mouth it comes through full and juicy, endowed with a long, crisp finish. When it comes to their sparkling wines, their plucky and charmingly complex 2006 Durello Extra Brut 120 Mesi delivered, as did their 2010 60 Mesi.

| | | |
|---|---|---|
| ○ Soave Cl. Pigno '16 | 🍷🍷 | 3* |
| ● Colli Berici Tocai Rosso '16 | 🍷🍷 | 2* |
| ○ Lessini Durello Brut 36 Mesi | 🍷🍷 | 3 |
| ○ Lessini Durello Extra Brut M. Cl. 120 Mesi '06 | 🍷🍷 | 5 |
| ○ Lessini Durello Extra Brut M. Cl. 60 Mesi '10 | 🍷🍷 | 5 |
| ○ Soave '17 | 🍷🍷 | 1* |
| ● Colli Berici Rosso Pianalto '14 | 🍷 | 5 |
| ● Due '15 | 🍷 | 2 |
| ○ Rebellis '17 | 🍷 | 3 |
| ○ Soave Cl. Monte Tenda '17 | 🍷 | 3 |
| ○ Soave Cl. Pigno Gianni Tessari '13 | 🍷🍷🍷 | 3* |
| ○ Soave Cl. Pigno '15 | 🍷🍷 | 3* |
| ○ Soave Cl. Pigno Gianni Tessari '14 | 🍷🍷 | 3* |

# Tezza

FRAZ. POIANO DI VALPANTENA
VIA STRADELLA MAIOLI, 4
37142 VERONA
TEL. +39 045550267
www.tezzawines.it

CELLAR SALES
PRE-BOOKED VISITS
ANNUAL PRODUCTION 200,000 bottles
HECTARES UNDER VINE 28.00

Valpantena is a large valley that, to its south (the area situated between Grezzana and Verona), features gravelly soil and a climate that's influenced by the northern winds. Here the Tezza cousins operate, overseeing their sizable, organically managed estate, which hosts almost exclusively Valpolicella's traditional grape varieties. These give rise to a selection of rich, plush wines centered primarily on the region's great, ageworthy reds. The wine that most impressed this year was their 2015 Recioto della Valpolicella. It's a wine that exhibits all the fruity drive that Corvina and Rondinella can offer, with notes of morello cherry alternating with spices and balsamic aromas. On the palate it explodes with a pronounced sweetness that's well-balanced by acidity. Their 2012 Amarone proves more complex and evolved, with herbaceous strokes accompanying fruit and anticipating a firm, savory palate that finishes with an intriguing mineral vein.

| | | |
|---|---|---|
| ● Amarone della Valpolicella Valpantena '12 | 🍷🍷 | 6 |
| ● Recioto della Valpolicella Valpantena '15 | 🍷🍷 | 5 |
| ● Amarone della Valpolicella Valpantena Brolo delle Giare Ris. '11 | 🍷 | 7 |
| ● Valpolicella Valpantena Sup. Ripasso '15 | 🍷 | 3 |
| ● Valpolicella Valpantena Sup. Ripasso Brolo delle Giare '14 | 🍷 | 5 |
| ● Amarone della Valpolicella Valpantena Brolo delle Giare Ris. '09 | 🍷🍷 | 7 |
| ● Amarone della Valpolicella Valpantena Brolo delle Giare Ris. '06 | 🍷🍷 | 7 |
| ● Recioto della Valpolicella Valpantena '09 | 🍷🍷 | 5 |
| ● Valpolicella Valpantena Sup. Ripasso '14 | 🍷🍷 | 3 |
| ● Valpolicella Valpantena Sup. Ripasso Brolo delle Giare '13 | 🍷🍷 | 5 |
| ● Valpolicella Valpantena Sup. Ripasso Brolo delle Giare '11 | 🍷🍷 | 4 |

# Tommasi Viticoltori

LOC. PEDEMONTE
VIA RONCHETTO, 4
37029 SAN PIETRO IN CARIANO [VR]
TEL. +39 0457701266
www.tommasi.com

**CELLAR SALES**
**PRE-BOOKED VISITS**
**ACCOMMODATION AND RESTAURANT SERVICE**
**ANNUAL PRODUCTION** 1,500,000 bottles
**HECTARES UNDER VINE** 205.00
**SUSTAINABLE WINERY**

The Tommasi family left Pedemonte (San Pietro in Cariano) more than a century ago. Today they own a number of estates that comprise some of Italy's most important districts for wine production. The heart of the estate remains faithfully anchored to their original home, Valpolicella, where they manage an extensive number of vineyards, either directly or through third party vine growers. Today Giancarlo is at the helm, personally overseeing each stage of production and shaping a selection that's increasingly distinctive for its tension and suppleness. Their 2008 Amarone De Buris, their new house reserve wine, is debuting 10 years after vintage. After lengthy aging it offers up deep aromas, still intact in terms of fruit, amplified by notes of finest herbes and spices. In the mouth it exhibits great extractive force. This is channeled along a dual track of precision and elegance, guided by a lively acidic and tannic backbone. Their 2011 Amarone Ca' Florian Ris. is more approachable and vivacious with its aromas of cherry and forest undergrowth.

| | |
|---|---|
| ● Amarone della Valpolicella Cl. De Buris Ris. '08 | ♛♛♛ 7 |
| ● Amarone della Valpolicella Cl. Ca' Florian Ris. '11 | ♛♛ 7 |
| ● Crearo della Conca d'Oro '15 | ♛♛ 4 |
| ● Valpolicella Cl. Sup. Ripasso '16 | ♛♛ 4 |
| ○ Lugana Le Fornaci '17 | ♛ 3 |
| ● Valpolicella '17 | ♛ 3 |
| ● Valpolicella Cl. Sup. Rafael '16 | ♛ 3 |
| ● Amarone della Valpolicella Cl. '13 | ♙♙ 7 |
| ● Amarone della Valpolicella Cl. '10 | ♙♙ 7 |
| ● Amarone della Valpolicella Cl. Ca' Florian Ris. '09 | ♙♙ 7 |
| ● Amarone della Valpolicella Cl. Ca' Florian Ris. '08 | ♙♙ 7 |
| ● Valpolicella Cl. Sup. Ripasso '15 | ♙♙ 4 |

# La Tordera

VIA ALNÉ BOSCO, 23
31020 VIDOR [TV]
TEL. +39 0423985362
www.latordera.it

**CELLAR SALES**
**PRE-BOOKED VISITS**
**ANNUAL PRODUCTION** 450,000 bottles
**HECTARES UNDER VINE** 33.00
**VITICULTURE METHOD** Certified Organic
**SUSTAINABLE WINERY**

Valdobbiadene is rich with enchanting views, with its dense hills making their way headlong down to the valley bellow. Guia is one such district, and it's here that the Vettoretti family (Renato, Gabriella and Paolo) operate, with various roles that cover every stage of production, from cultivation to production and managing the market. Their sizable estate is situated within the historic appellation, and the winery works only with grapes that they oversee directly. Their 2017 Otreval Brut, made with grapes from Rive di Guia's loveliest vineyards, performed quite well. It's a sparkling wine redolent of apple, pear and flowers, while in the mouth it delivers for its rather dry impact, compensated for by a fullness of fruit and a creamy sparkle that accompanies the palate to its crisp, pleasantly bitter finish. Their 2017 Brunei, which can be traced back to their Cobertaldo vineyard, proves generous in its aromas, balanced on the balanced. Their trio of Valdobbiadenes are rounded out by an excellent 2017 Rive di Vidor Tittoni Dry.

| | |
|---|---|
| ○ Valdobbiadene Brut Brunei '17 | ♛♛ 3 |
| ○ Valdobbiadene Rive di Guia Brut Otreval '17 | ♛♛ 3 |
| ○ Valdobbiadene Rive di Vidor Dry Tittoni '17 | ♛♛ 3 |
| ○ Cartizze '17 | ♛ 4 |
| ⊙ Gabry Brut Rosé | ♛ 2 |
| ○ Valdobbiadene Extra Dry Serrai '17 | ♛ 3 |
| ○ Valdobbiadene Extra Dry Serrai '16 | ♙♙ 3 |
| ○ Valdobbiadene Rive di Guida Brut Otreval '16 | ♙♙ 3 |

# Trabucchi d'Illasi

LOC. MONTE TENDA
37031 ILLASI [VR]
TEL. +39 0457833233
www.trabucchidillasi.it

**CELLAR SALES**
**PRE-BOOKED VISITS**
**ANNUAL PRODUCTION** 120,000 bottles
**HECTARES UNDER VINE** 25.00
**VITICULTURE METHOD** Certified Organic

The Trabucchi family's winery is constituted of a lovely estate situated in Monte Tenda, a district that divides the Illasi and Valtramigna valleys. For years now they have been organic, with vineyards olive groves that give rise to a selection of products that are dedicated almost exclusively to the area's traditional cultivar. These form the basis of a varied selection that features aromatic mobility and solidity on the palate, especially when it comes to their great, ageworthy reds. Only a few wines were submitted this year, but their 2010 Amarone more than makes up for the fact. On the nose it offers up vibrant aromas dominated by stewed cherry, revived by a fresh balsamic vein and forest undergrowth. In the mouth it proves forceful, close-knit in its tannins and balanced on the palate. Their 2012 Valpolicella Terre di San Colombano is fresher in its aromas, featuring notes of red fruit and dried flowers, while in the mouth it opens with softness only to close with a pleasantly rough weave.

| | |
|---|---|
| ● Amarone della Valpolicella '10 | ♟♟ 8 |
| ● Valpolicella Sup. Terre di San Colombano '12 | ♟♟ 3 |
| ● Valpolicella Un Anno '17 | ♟ 2 |
| ● Amarone della Valpolicella '06 | ♟♟♟ 8 |
| ● Amarone della Valpolicella '04 | ♟♟♟ 8 |
| ● Recioto della Valpolicella Cereolo '05 | ♟♟♟ 8 |
| ● Valpolicella Sup. Terre di S. Colombano '03 | ♟♟♟ 4* |
| ● Amarone della Valpolicella '09 | ♟♟ 8 |
| ● Amarone della Valpolicella '08 | ♟♟ 8 |
| ● Amarone della Valpolicella Alberto Trabucchi Ris. '08 | ♟♟ 8 |
| ● Recioto della Valpolicella '07 | ♟♟ 7 |
| ● Valpolicella Sup. Terre del Cereolo '09 | ♟♟ 5 |
| ● Valpolicella Sup. Terre del Cereolo '08 | ♟♟ 5 |

# Spumanti Valdo

VIA FORO BOARIO, 20
31049 VALDOBBIADENE [TV]
TEL. +39 04239090
www.valdo.com

**CELLAR SALES**
**PRE-BOOKED VISITS**
**ANNUAL PRODUCTION** 9,000,000 bottles
**HECTARES UNDER VINE** 155.00

The agricultural landscape of Conegliano Valdobbiadene is populated by a tight network of vine growers who cultivate small patches of land that are so steep that they seem suspended in air. It's the job of large sparkling wine producers to transform this territorial puzzle into famous wines that are winning favor the world over. This is how the historic brand Valdo works, dedicating maximum attention to the production of Prosecco, which is interpreted with an eye towards its more sensual, fruit forward qualities. Their 2017 Nature is made with grapes from their lovelies vineyards in San Pietro di Barbozza, in the heart of Valdobbiadene wine country. It's a new, limited-edition Prosecco that features of an aromatic profile of great elegance, with white fruit caressing flowery and citrusy notes. On the palate it proves crisp and slender, particularly impressive for its overall balance. Their 2017 Cuvée del Fondatore is more buoyant on the nose and dynamic in the mouth.

| | |
|---|---|
| ○ Valdobbiadene Brut Cuvée del Fondatore '17 | ♟♟ 3* |
| ○ Cartizze Cuvée Viviana | ♟♟ 5 |
| ○ Valdobbiadene Brut M. Cl. Numero 10 '15 | ♟♟ 4 |
| ○ Valdobbiadene Rive di San Pietro di Barbozza Brut Nature '17 | ♟♟ 3 |
| ○ Prosecco Brut Bio | ♟ 2 |
| ○ Valdobbiadene Brut Cuvée di Boj | ♟ 2 |
| ○ Valdobbiadene Extra Dry Cuvée 1926 | ♟ 2 |
| ○ Numero 10 Brut M. Cl. '10 | ♟♟ 4 |
| ○ Valdobbiadene Brut Cuvée del Fondatore '14 | ♟♟ 3 |
| ○ Valdobbiadene Brut M. Cl. Numero 10 '14 | ♟♟ 4 |
| ○ Valdobbiadene Cuvée del Fondatore | ♟♟ 3 |

# VENETO

## Cantina Valpantena Verona

LOC. QUINTO
VIA COLONIA ORFANI DI GUERRA, 5B
37142 VERONA
TEL. +39 045550032
www.cantinavalpantena.it

**CELLAR SALES**
**PRE-BOOKED VISITS**
**ANNUAL PRODUCTION** 9,000,000 bottles
**HECTARES UNDER VINE** 750.00

Quinto is an important leader among Verona's wine producers. It's a cooperative winery that's been active since the 1950s, bringing together more than 250 vine growers. The vineyards are situated primarily in the eastern part of the district, stretching from the capital towards Monti Lessini, though there are also members with plots in Valpolicella classica. Their wines focus on the pleasantness of fruit and are interpreted with precision and tension. Their 2015 Tesauro is a splendid Recioto della Valpolicella with a vibrant aromatic profile. On the nose oak quickly gives way to notes of dried cherries, aromatic herbs and cocoa powder. In the mouth sweetness is pronounced, but it manages to lengthen thanks to a lively acidic and savory thrust, thus recovering some lightness on the palate. Their 2014 Amarone Torre del Falasco also did well. It's a wine that opts for less explosive fruit and a dynamic palate that manages to bring together force and tension.

| | |
|---|---|
| ● Recioto della Valpolicella Tesauro '15 | ♟♟ 5 |
| ● Amarone della Valpolicella '15 | ♟♟ 6 |
| ● Amarone della Valpolicella Torre del Falasco '14 | ♟♟ 7 |
| ● Valpolicella Sup. Ripasso Torre del Falasco '16 | ♟♟ 4 |
| ○ Chardonnay Baroncino '17 | ♟ 2 |
| ● Corvina Torre del Falasco '17 | ♟ 1* |
| ○ Garganega Torre del Falasco '17 | ♟ 1* |
| ○ Lugana Torre del Falasco '17 | ♟ 3 |
| ● Valpolicella Valpantena Ripasso Ritocco '16 | ♟ 4 |
| ● Amarone della Valpolicella '14 | ♟♟ 5 |
| ● Amarone della Valpolicella Torre del Falasco '13 | ♟♟ 6 |
| ● Valpolicella Sup. Ripasso Torre del Falasco '15 | ♟♟ 3 |

## Cantina Valpolicella Negrar

VIA CA' SALGARI, 2
37024 NEGRAR [VR]
TEL. +39 0456014300
www.cantinanegrar.it

**CELLAR SALES**
**PRE-BOOKED VISITS**
**RESTAURANT SERVICE**
**ANNUAL PRODUCTION** 7,000,000 bottles
**HECTARES UNDER VINE** 700.00

The territory of Valpolicella is teeming with vine growers who merely cultivate grapes and supply them to third party producers. More than 200 such businesses got together to form the heart and entrepreneurial force behind the cooperative of Valpolicella Negrar. Under the technical guidance of Daniele Accordini, they produce some of the area's most representative wines. Their style focuses on all the power and richness that tradition can offer, especially with their Domini Veneti, their premium line of wines. Their Pruviniano line of wines highlights the characteristics of the Marano Valley, its lightness and elegance. Their 2013 Amarone Pruviniano expresses fragrances of super-ripe ripe, which give way to notes of aromatic herbs and crushed flowers. These follow through on a crisp and commendably long palate. Their 2014 Recioto Vigneti di Moron also delivered, with its aromas of ripe and buoyant fruit, and a palate in which pronounced sweetness is well-managed by acidity.

| | |
|---|---|
| ● Amarone della Valpolicella Cl. Pruviniano Domini Veneti '13 | ♟♟ 5 |
| ● Amarone della Valpolicella Cl. Biologico Domini Veneti '15 | ♟♟ 6 |
| ● Recioto della Valpolicella Cl. Vign. di Moron Domini Veneti '14 | ♟♟ 4 |
| ● Valpolicella Cl. Sup. Domini Veneti '15 | ♟♟ 2* |
| ● Valpolicella Cl. Sup. Pruviniano Domini Veneti '14 | ♟♟ 2* |
| ● Valpolicella Cl. Sup. Ripasso Pruviniano Domini Veneti '15 | ♟♟ 3 |
| ● Valpolicella Cl. Biologico Domini Veneti '17 | ♟ 2 |
| ● Valpolicella Cl. Domini Veneti '17 | ♟ 2 |
| ● Valpolicella Cl. Sup. Verjago Domini Veneti '15 | ♟ 4 |
| ● Amarone della Valpolicella Cl. S. Rocco Domini Veneti '08 | ♟♟♟ 8 |

## Odino Vaona

LOC. VALGATARA
VIA PAVERNO, 41
37020 MARANO DI VALPOLICELLA [VR]
TEL. +39 0457703710
www.vaona.it

**CELLAR SALES**
**PRE-BOOKED VISITS**
**ANNUAL PRODUCTION** 70,000 bottles
**HECTARES UNDER VINE** 10.00
**SUSTAINABLE WINERY**

The Marano Valley proceeds northward from Pieve di San Floriano and, after passing through the center of Valgatara, it begins a rapid upward ascent, surrounded by vineyards that sprawl in every direction. Here property development has been carefully regulated and the landscape maintains its charming, rural qualities. And it's here that Alberto Vaona operates, a soft-spoken producer who lets his wines 'do the talking' when it comes to expressing his passion for his work. His selection, which includes all of Valpolicella's main wines, pursues a balance between tradition and elegance. Their 2016 Superiore starts out timid in its aromatic impact, but after just a few moments in the glass its trademark timbres of wild fruit, thyme and pepper emerge. In the mouth it doesn't pursue softness, but moves supply and tautly by virtue of its pronounced acidity. Their 2013 Amarone Pegrandi opts for warmer, riper fruit, which follows through in a big, pervasive, relaxed palate.

| | |
|---|---|
| ● Amarone della Valpolicella Cl. Pegrandi '13 | ▼▼ 6 |
| ● Recioto della Valpolicella Cl. Le Peagnè '15 | ▼▼ 4 |
| ● Valpolicella Sup. '16 | ▼▼ 3 |
| ● Amarone della Valpolicella Cl. Paverno '14 | ▼ 5 |
| ● Castaroto '15 | ▼ 4 |
| ● Valpolicella Cl. '17 | ▼ 2 |
| ● Amarone della Valpolicella Cl. Pegrandi '09 | ▽▽▽ 5 |
| ● Amarone della Valpolicella Cl. Pegrandi '12 | ▽▽ 6 |
| ● Amarone della Valpolicella Cl. Pegrandi Ris. '11 | ▽▽ 8 |
| ● Valpolicella Cl. '16 | ▽▽ 2* |

## Venturini

FRAZ. SAN FLORIANO
VIA SEMONTE, 20
37029 SAN PIETRO IN CARIANO [VR]
TEL. +39 0457701331
www.viniventurini.com

**CELLAR SALES**
**PRE-BOOKED VISITS**
**ANNUAL PRODUCTION** 130,000 bottles
**HECTARES UNDER VINE** 15.00
**SUSTAINABLE WINERY**

Siblings Giuseppina, Daniele and Mirco Venturini manage the estate founded by their father just over 50 years ago, and the spirit hasn't changed. It's a family deeply bound to their agricultural roots and passionate about Valpolicella's tradition of winemaking. Their production center is situated in at the foot of the mountain that divides the Negrar and Marano valleys. Their vineyards comprise some of the best positions in the area, starting with their plots in San Floriano, a celebrated district in San Pietro in Cariano. Masua is certainly a good example, a vineyard that gives rise to the grapes used in a deep, traditional Amarone. Their 2012 calls up aromas of dried morello cherries, refreshed by fines herbes and crushed flowers. These anticipate a juicy, energetic palate. Their 2007 Amarone Riserva opts for more tertiary notes. Its savory and harmonious palate maintains a balance between vitality and complexity. It's a truly charming wine.

| | |
|---|---|
| ● Amarone della Valpolicella Cl. Campomasua '12 | ▼▼ 6 |
| ● Amarone della Valpolicella Cl. Ris. '07 | ▼▼ 8 |
| ● Recioto della Valpolicella Cl. Le Brugnine '13 | ▼▼ 6 |
| ● Valpolicella Cl. Sup. Ripasso Semonte Alto '14 | ▼▼ 4 |
| ● Valpolicella Cl. '17 | ▼ 2 |
| ● Valpolicella Cl. Sup. Campomasua '15 | ▼ 2 |
| ● Amarone della Valpolicella Cl. Campomasua '07 | ▽▽▽ 6 |
| ● Amarone della Valpolicella Cl. '12 | ▽▽ 6 |
| ● Amarone della Valpolicella Cl. '11 | ▽▽ 5 |
| ● Amarone della Valpolicella Cl. Campo Masua '11 | ▽▽ 7 |
| ● Amarone della Valpolicella Cl. Campomasua '10 | ▽▽ 6 |

# Agostino Vicentini

FRAZ. SAN ZENO
VIA C. BATTISTI, 62c
37030 COLOGNOLA AI COLLI [VR]
TEL. +39 0457650539
www.vinivicentini.com

**CELLAR SALES**
**PRE-BOOKED VISITS**
**ANNUAL PRODUCTION** 100,000 bottles
**HECTARES UNDER VINE** 20.00

Agostino Vicentini is a determined vine grower with a past that's inextricably linked to Colognola ai Colli. He began by cultivating fruit, but today only a few cherry and olive trees remain as a testament to that part of his past. Most of the estate is now comprised of vineyards, with particular attention paid to the area's traditional grapes. Agostini is supported by his wife, Teresa, and his children Manuele and Francesca. Together they're putting forward a selection of red wines that pursue elegance and tension, and whites that show character and pluck (thanks in part to yields that are often very low). Bottling of their Soave Il Casale was put off this year, and so their 2017 Vigneto Terrelunghe took on the role of leading the Vicentini family's lovely selection. Ripe yellow fruit, chamomile and almond emerge on the nose, while in the mouth Garganega's trademark character is confirmed with determination and tension. The result is one of the appellation's most interesting wines. Their 2015 Recioto di Soave goes all in on balance and subtleness.

| | | |
|---|---|---|
| ○ Recioto di Soave '15 | ♟♟ | 5 |
| ○ Soave Vign. Terre Lunghe '17 | ♟♟ | 2* |
| ● Valpolicella Sup. '15 | ♟♟ | 3 |
| ● Valpolicella Boccascaluce '16 | ♟ | 3 |
| ○ Soave Sup. Il Casale '16 | ♟♟♟ | 3* |
| ○ Soave Sup. Il Casale '15 | ♟♟♟ | 3* |
| ○ Soave Sup. Il Casale '14 | ♟♟♟ | 3* |
| ○ Soave Sup. Il Casale '13 | ♟♟♟ | 3* |
| ○ Soave Sup. Il Casale '12 | ♟♟♟ | 3* |
| ○ Soave Vign. Terre Lunghe '16 | ♟♟ | 2* |
| ● Valpolicella Boccascaluce '15 | ♟♟ | 3 |
| ● Valpolicella Sup. Idea Bacco '13 | ♟♟ | 5 |
| ● Valpolicella Sup. Palazzo di Campiano '12 | ♟♟ | 5 |
| ● Valpolicella Sup. '14 | ♟ | 3 |

# Vigna Roda

LOC. CORTELÀ
VIA MONTE VERSA, 1569
35030 VÒ [PD]
TEL. +39 0499940228
www.vignaroda.com

**CELLAR SALES**
**PRE-BOOKED VISITS**
**ANNUAL PRODUCTION** 52,000 bottles
**HECTARES UNDER VINE** 17.00

Together with his wife, Elena, Gianni Strazzacappa manages one of Padova's most interesting new wineries. His impressive estate stretches along the gentle slopes of the southwestern Colli Euganei hills. The terrain here is tenacious, rich in minerals, endowing the grapes cultivated with spirit and flavor (primarily red Bordeaux varieties). Their fresher wines are buoyant and fruity while their Riserva wines are more elegant and balanced. Thanks in part to an excellent 2015, their Scarlatto Rosso put in an unforgettable performance. IT's a blend of Merlot and Cabernet Sauvignon that features a whirlwind of aromas: red fruit, aromatic herbs and spices. It's a ripe wine, though fresh and enticing, with a palate that exhibits further elegance thanks to a long finish supported by juicy tannins. Their 2012 Petali d'Ambra is an interesting Fior d'Arancio Passito that impresses for its balance and sensations on the palate.

| | | |
|---|---|---|
| ● Colli Euganei Rosso Scarlatto '15 | ♟♟ | 3* |
| ○ Colli Euganei Fior d'Arancio Passito Petali d'Ambra '12 | ♟♟ | 4 |
| ● Colli Euganei Rosso '17 | ♟♟ | 2* |
| ● Merlot Il Damerino '17 | ♟♟ | 2* |
| ○ Aroma 2.0 '17 | ♟ | 2 |
| ○ Colli Euganei Bianco '17 | ♟ | 2 |
| ● Colli Euganei Cabernet Espero '16 | ♟♟ | 2* |
| ○ Colli Euganei Fior d'Arancio Passito Petali d'Ambra '11 | ♟♟ | 4 |
| ○ Colli Euganei Fior d'Arancio Spumante | ♟♟ | 2* |
| ● Colli Euganei Rosso '16 | ♟♟ | 2* |
| ● Colli Euganei Rosso Scarlatto '14 | ♟♟ | 3 |
| ● Colli Euganei Rosso Scarlatto '13 | ♟♟ | 3 |
| ● Colli Euganei Rosso Scarlatto '12 | ♟♟ | 3* |
| ● Merlot Il Damerino '16 | ♟♟ | 2* |

# Vignale di Cecilia

LOC. FORNACI
VIA CROCI, 14
35030 BAONE [PD]
TEL. +39 042951420
www.vignaledicecilia.it

**PRE-BOOKED VISITS**
**ANNUAL PRODUCTION** 20,000 bottles
**HECTARES UNDER VINE** 8.00
**VITICULTURE METHOD** Certified Organic

Paolo Brunello is an eclectic producer who loves his work and his homeland. Here, in the Colli Euganei, one of Veneto's most intriguing areas for wine production, the conic shape of the land betrays the its volcanic origins. Paolo's estate is managed with the utmost respect for the environment, without predetermined cultivation regimes. The same holds true for the cellar. Their wines are never held back, but treated like a father might treat his children: protected from their most serious errors, but also left free to find their own way. There's no doubt that character is Vignale di Cecilia's wines principal strongpoint. Their 2016 Cocai is a good example. It's a monovarietal Tai with warm and ripe notes, aromas of yellow fruit and dried flowers that are follow through well onto a big, chewy, pervasive palate. Their 2015 Passacaglia, however, once again proves to be a cut above the rest. It's a Bordeaux blend made primarily with Merlot. On the nose it features deep aromas of fruit accompanied by herbaceous notes that revive a firm, crisp palate.

| | | |
|---|---|---|
| ● Colli Euganei Rosso Passacaglia '15 | ♟♟ | 4 |
| ○ Benavides '16 | ♟♟ | 2* |
| ○ Cocài '16 | ♟♟ | 3 |
| ● El Moro Cabernet '15 | ♟♟ | 3 |
| ○ Benavides '15 | ♟♟ | 2* |
| ○ Cocài '12 | ♟♟ | 3 |
| ● Colli Euganei Rosso Covolo '15 | ♟♟ | 3 |
| ● Colli Euganei Rosso Covolo '14 | ♟♟ | 3 |
| ● Colli Euganei Rosso Covolo '13 | ♟♟ | 3 |
| ● Colli Euganei Rosso Passacaglia '13 | ♟♟ | 4 |
| ● Colli Euganei Rosso Passacaglia '12 | ♟♟ | 4 |
| ● Colli Euganei Rosso Passacaglia '11 | ♟♟ | 4 |

# ★Vignalta

VIA SCALETTE, 23
35032 ARQUÀ PETRARCA [PD]
TEL. +39 0429777305
www.vignalta.it

**CELLAR SALES**
**PRE-BOOKED VISITS**
**ANNUAL PRODUCTION** 230,000 bottles
**HECTARES UNDER VINE** 35.00
**SUSTAINABLE WINERY**

Vignalta is one Euganeo's most representative wineries, bolstered by a presence that's deeply rooted to the area in space and time (to say the least). But it's their vineyards, especially, that stand out. Their sizable estate has given rise to a selection capable of quality from the first vintage, as well as expressing the Colli's sunny, powerful character. A number of cultivar can be found in their plots, but red Bordeaux varieties make up the lion's share, delivering a selection that will satisfy even the shrewdest palates. This year we didn't taste their most important reserve wines, which are still aging, but their 2015 Alpianae more than compensated. It's a Fior d'Arancio Passito that's explosive in its aromas of citrus, tropical fruit and flowers, surrounded by sweeter notes of candied peels and botrytis. On the palate it immediately exhibits great sweetness, which is harmoniously contrasted by a backbone of acidity and savoriness. Their 2011 Agno Tinto is a very interesting monovarietal Syrah with character and determination.

| | | |
|---|---|---|
| ○ Colli Euganei Fiori d'Arancio Passito Alpianae '15 | ♟♟ | 5 |
| ● Agno Tinto '11 | ♟♟ | 5 |
| ○ Brut Nature M. Cl. | ♟♟ | 4 |
| ○ Colli Euganei Chardonnay '16 | ♟♟ | 4 |
| ○ Colli Euganei Pinot Bianco '17 | ♟♟ | 3 |
| ● Colli Euganei Rosso Ris. '13 | ♟♟ | 3 |
| ● Pinot Nero '15 | ♟♟ | 5 |
| ○ Colli Euganei Fior d'Arancio Passito Alpianae '12 | ♟♟♟ | 5 |
| ● Colli Euganei Rosso Gemola '13 | ♟♟♟ | 6 |
| ● Colli Euganei Rosso Gemola '08 | ♟♟♟ | 5 |
| ● Colli Euganei Cabernet Ris. '07 | ♟♟ | 8 |
| ○ Colli Euganei Fior d'Arancio Passito Alpianae '14 | ♟♟ | 6 |
| ● Colli Euganei Rosso Arquà '11 | ♟♟ | 6 |
| ⊙ Extra Brut Rosé | ♟♟ | 4 |

## Le Vigne di San Pietro

VIA SAN PIETRO, 23
37066 SOMMACAMPAGNA [VR]
TEL. +39 045510016
www.levignedisanpietro.it

**CELLAR SALES**
**PRE-BOOKED VISITS**
**ANNUAL PRODUCTION** 70,000 bottles
**HECTARES UNDER VINE** 10.00

Despite limited production volumes by regional standards, Carlo Nerozzi's winery is one southeastern Garda's most notable producers. The morainic hills seem to expand endlessly from the lake, and have hosted fertile vineyards for as long as anyone can remember. These give rise to the area's historic wines, Bardolino and Custoza foremost, which are then interpreted with elegance and tension, and an overriding ability to get better with age. Their 2016 Custoza Sanpietro is a marvelous white aged in oak for about six months and still some in the bottle. On the nose it features an elegant, generous aromatic profile with flowers and white fruit merging with sweeter nuances that can be traced back to the use of wood barrels. In the mouth it's not a showy wine, but delivers for its unfolding of flavor and elegance. Their 2016 Bardolino Sup. also did well. It's a deep wine in its aromas and long on the palate by virtue of its lively energy.

## Vigneto Due Santi

V.LE ASIAGO, 174
36061 BASSANO DEL GRAPPA [VI]
TEL. +39 0424502074
www.vignetoduesanti.it

**CELLAR SALES**
**PRE-BOOKED VISITS**
**ANNUAL PRODUCTION** 100,000 bottles
**HECTARES UNDER VINE** 18.00
**SUSTAINABLE WINERY**

Adriano and Stefano Zonta manage the family winery situated in the outskirts of Bassano del Grappa. It stretches for some 20 hectares along the lower hills, at elevations just over 100 meters. They also represent far more land than what's needed. This allows the family to effectively intervene at any stage of production and whenever needed with the awareness of being able to draw on the best grapes of any vintage. The result is opulent wines that go all in on the clarity of fruit. Their 2015 Cabernet Due Santi is emblematic in that sense. It's a thickly-colored ruby red wine whose color anticipates vibrant, fruity aromas of cherry and plum well-fused with balsamic notes and forest undergrowth. In the mouth it opens with generosity and fullness, refreshed by a taut acidity that highlights its savoriness. Their 2015 Cavallare on the other hand is a Bordeaux made primarily with Merlot that proves generous in its aromas and commendably balanced on the palate.

| | | |
|---|---|---|
| ○ Custoza Sanpietro '16 | ♟♟♟ 4* |
| ● Bardolino Sup. '16 | ♟♟ 3* |
| ● Bardolino '17 | ♟♟ 2* |
| ⊙ Bardolino Chiaretto CorDeRosa '17 | ♟♟ 2* |
| ○ Custoza '17 | ♟ 2 |
| ● Bardolino '14 | ♟♟♟ 2* |
| ● Bardolino '11 | ♟♟♟ 2* |
| ● Bardolino '15 | ♟♟ 2* |
| ● Bardolino '15 | ♟♟ 2* |
| ⊙ Bardolino Chiaretto CorDeRosa '16 | ♟♟ 2* |
| ⊙ Bardolino Chiaretto CorDeRosa '15 | ♟♟ 2* |
| ● Bardolino Sup. '15 | ♟♟ 3* |
| ○ Custoza '16 | ♟♟ 2* |
| ○ Custoza Sup. Sanpietro '15 | ♟♟ 3* |
| ○ Custoza Sup. Sanpietro '13 | ♟♟ 3* |

| | | |
|---|---|---|
| ● Breganze Cabernet Due Santi '15 | ♟♟ 4 |
| ● Breganze Cabernet '15 | ♟♟ 2* |
| ● Breganze Merlot '16 | ♟♟ 2* |
| ● Breganze Rosso Cavallare '15 | ♟♟ 4 |
| ○ Breganze Sauvignon '17 | ♟♟ 3 |
| ○ Breganze Torcolato '15 | ♟♟ 5 |
| ○ Breganze Bianco Rivana '17 | ♟ 2 |
| ○ Malvasia Campo di Fiori '17 | ♟ 2 |
| ○ Prosecco Extra Dry | ♟ 2 |
| ● Breganze Cabernet Due Santi '14 | ♟♟♟ 4* |
| ● Breganze Cabernet Vign. Due Santi '12 | ♟♟♟ 4* |
| ● Breganze Cabernet Vign. Due Santi '08 | ♟♟♟ 4* |
| ○ Breganze Bianco Rivana '16 | ♟♟ 2* |
| ● Breganze Cabernet '13 | ♟♟ 2* |
| ○ Malvasia Campo di Fiori '16 | ♟♟ 2* |

# Villa Sandi

VIA ERIZZO, 113/A
31035 CROCETTA DEL MONTELLO [TV]
TEL. +39 04238607
www.villasandi.it

**CELLAR SALES**
**PRE-BOOKED VISITS**
**ACCOMMODATION AND RESTAURANT SERVICE**
**ANNUAL PRODUCTION** 5,500,000 bottles
**HECTARES UNDER VINE** 560.00
**SUSTAINABLE WINERY**

The Moretti Polegato family is strongly tied to Alta Marca Trevigiana and has made Villa Sandi a benchmark for lovers of the region's sparkling wines. Their estate is sizable, to the say the least, encompassing the hills of the Prosecco DOCG appellation as well as nearby DOC zones. Here both international and classic local varieties are cultivated. Their Metodo Classico sparklers, which age at length in their underground cellar, are also interesting. And their Amalia Moretti Brut Riserva comes precisely from those vaults. It's a highly elegant and deep sparkling wine. The grapes used in their Vigna La Rivetta, on the other hand, is from one of Valdobbiadene's loveliest areas. It's a Cartizze adapted into a Brut that delivers for the subtleness of its flowery aromas and notes of white fruit. In the mouth it comes through with lightness and savoriness, which are perfectly accompanied by its creamy sparkle - it's a great version.

| | |
|---|---|
| ○ Cartizze Brut V. La Rivetta | ♙♙♙ 6 |
| ○ Amalia Moretti Brut M. Cl. Opere Trevigiane Ris. | ♙♙ 8 |
| ● Còrpore '15 | ♙♙ 5 |
| ● Montello Colli Asolani Cabernet Filio '15 | ♙♙ 4 |
| ○ Serenissima Brut Opere M. Cl. | ♙♙ 5 |
| ○ Valdobbiadene Dry Rive di San Pietro di Barbozza '17 | ♙♙ 4 |
| ○ Asolo Brut | ♙ 3 |
| ○ Ribolla Gialla Brut '16 | ♙ 4 |
| ○ Cartizze V. La Rivetta | ♔♔♔ 6 |
| ● Còrpore '13 | ♔♔ 5 |
| ○ Serenissima Opere Trevigiane Brut | ♔♔ 5 |
| ○ Valdobbiadene Dry Cuvée Oris | ♔♔ 3 |
| ○ Valdobbiadene Extra Dry | ♔♔ 3 |

# Villa Spinosa

LOC. JAGO
VIA JAGO DALL'ORA, 14
37024 NEGRAR [VR]
TEL. +39 0457500093
www.villaspinosa.it

**CELLAR SALES**
**PRE-BOOKED VISITS**
**ACCOMMODATION**
**ANNUAL PRODUCTION** 45,000 bottles
**HECTARES UNDER VINE** 20.00
**SUSTAINABLE WINERY**

Enrico Casella's winery has been active for many years, but it's really been over the past two decades that it's made a name for itself, initially through a collaboration with Roberto Ferrarini and today with his students. Their vineyards span Negrar and Marano di Valpolicella and give rise to a selection that's strongly tied to tradition. The utmost care is taken in the cellar and great patience is shown before wines go to market. These are the keys that allow their wines to perfectly represent the classical style of Valpolicella. Their 2011 Amarone Albasani seems to move along two tracks. On the one hand there's the wine's trademark aromatic profile, rich in fruity notes, minerals and medicinal herbs. On the other hand, in the mouth, it doesn't opt for force, but rather unfolds savory and slender across an elegant, charming palate. Their 2015 Ripasso Jago also delivered, once again interpreting its typology with an eye towards depth and tension.

| | |
|---|---|
| ● Amarone della Valpolicella Cl. Albasini '11 | ♙♙♙ 7 |
| ● Valpolicella Cl. Sup. Ripasso Jago '15 | ♙♙ 3* |
| ● Amarone della Valpolicella Cl. '14 | ♙♙ 6 |
| ● Amarone della Valpolicella Cl. Guglielmi di Jago 20 anni '08 | ♙♙ 8 |
| ● Recioto della Valpolicella Cl. Francesca Finato Spinosa '13 | ♙♙ 5 |
| ● Valpolicella Cl. Sup. Figari '15 | ♙♙ 3 |
| ● Valpolicella Cl. '16 | ♙ 2 |
| ● Amarone della Valpolicella Cl. '08 | ♔♔♔ 7 |
| ● Amarone della Valpolicella Cl. Albasini '10 | ♔♔♔ 7 |
| ● Valpolicella Cl. Sup. Ripasso Jago '11 | ♔♔♔ 3* |
| ● Amarone della Valpolicella Cl. Guglielmi di Jago 10 Anni '07 | ♔♔ 8 |
| ● Valpolicella Cl. Sup. Ripasso Jago '12 | ♔♔ 3 |

# Vigneti Villabella

Fraz. Calmasino di Bardolino
Loc. Canova, 2
37011 Bardolino [VR]
Tel. +39 0457236448
www.vignetivillabella.com

**CELLAR SALES**
**PRE-BOOKED VISITS**
**ACCOMMODATION**
**ANNUAL PRODUCTION** 500,000 bottles
**HECTARES UNDER VINE** 220.00

The Delibori and Cristoforetti families founded this lovely producer many years ago. The winery's strength centers around their extremely large estate. While the bulk of their vineyards are concentrated primarily in the area of Bardolino, they're gradually moving into Custoza, Lugana and Valpolicella as well. Their house wines are made with grapes cultivated on the best plots, and only the best batches are used, making for a high-profile selection whose signature style features finesse and tension. And their most interesting wines are made with grapes cultivated around Garda. They're two 2016 Bardolinos that express very different characters, though while both maintaining the same lightness and drinkability. Their Vigna Morlongo focuses on ripe, sweet, approachable fruit while in the mouth it proves juicy and commendably balanced. Their Villa Cordevigo opts for aromas of wild fruit enriched with peppery notes and wild rose. These reemerge on a dynamic, savory, racy palate. But their entire selection shines for its balance.

| | |
|---|---|
| ● Bardolino Cl. V. Morlongo '16 | ♟♟ 2* |
| ● Bardolino Cl. Villa Cordevigo '16 | ♟♟ 2* |
| ● Amarone della Valpolicella Cl. '11 | ♟♟ 5 |
| ● Amarone della Valpolicella Cl. Fracastoro Ris. '09 | ♟♟ 7 |
| ● Montemazzano '15 | ♟♟ 3 |
| ○ Villa Cordevigo Bianco '15 | ♟♟ 4 |
| ⊙ Bardolino Chiaretto Cl. '17 | ♟ 2 |
| ⊙ Bardolino Chiaretto Cl. Villa Cordevigo '17 | ♟ 2 |
| ○ Garda Pinot Grigio '17 | ♟ 2 |
| ○ Lugana '17 | ♟ 3 |
| ● Valpolicella Cl. Sup. Ripasso '16 | ♟ 3 |
| ● Villa Cordevigo Rosso '11 | ♟ 5 |
| ● Bardolino Cl. V. Morlongo '14 | ♟♟♟ 2* |
| ⊙ Bardolino Chiaretto Cl. '15 | ♟♟ 2* |
| ● Bardolino Villa Cordevigo '15 | ♟♟ 5 |

# ★Viviani

via Mazzano, 8
37020 Negrar [VR]
Tel. +39 0457500286
www.cantinaviviani.com

**CELLAR SALES**
**PRE-BOOKED VISITS**
**ANNUAL PRODUCTION** 80,000 bottles
**HECTARES UNDER VINE** 10.00
**SUSTAINABLE WINERY**

Claudio Viviani is a restless producer and in constant movement. He's a kind of explorer who's never content with what he knows, and studies continually. His vineyards are situated primarily in the upper valley of Negrar. The oldest are cultivated with the pergola system, the most recent guyot. They provide the grapes for a selection that is deeply tied to tradition, though reinterpreted by bringing together the richness of fruit, tension and suppleness that comes with being cultivated at higher elevations. Their 2012 Amarone Casa dei Bepi is a quintessential red whose aromas range from ripe morello cherry to pepper, from thyme to mineral notes, which continuously arise and retreat. In the mouth it proves rich and pervasive, but acidity and tannins confer tension and determination. Their 2013 Amarone is fresher aromatically and endowed with an energetic, commendably free and easy palate. Finally, their 2015 Valpolicella Campo Morar is crisp and intact.

| | |
|---|---|
| ● Amarone della Valpolicella Cl. Casa dei Bepi '12 | ♟♟♟ 8 |
| ● Amarone della Valpolicella Cl. '13 | ♟♟ 6 |
| ● Valpolicella Cl. Sup. Campo Morar '15 | ♟♟ 5 |
| ● Valpolicella Cl. '17 | ♟♟ 2* |
| ● Amarone della Valpolicella Cl. Casa dei Bepi '11 | ♟♟♟ 8 |
| ● Amarone della Valpolicella Cl. Casa dei Bepi '10 | ♟♟♟ 8 |
| ● Amarone della Valpolicella Cl. '12 | ♟♟ 6 |
| ● Amarone della Valpolicella Cl. '11 | ♟♟ 6 |
| ● Recioto della Valpolicella Cl. '11 | ♟♟ 6 |
| ● Recioto della Valpolicella Cl. '10 | ♟♟ 6 |
| ● Valpolicella Cl. Sup. Campo Morar '13 | ♟♟ 5 |
| ● Valpolicella Cl. Sup. Campo Morar '12 | ♟♟ 5 |
| ● Valpolicella Cl. Sup. Campo Morar '11 | ♟♟ 5 |

# Pietro Zanoni

FRAZ. QUINZANO
VIA ARE ZOVO, 16D
37125 VERONA
TEL. +39 0458343977
www.pietrozanoni.it

CELLAR SALES
PRE-BOOKED VISITS
ANNUAL PRODUCTION 25,000 bottles
HECTARES UNDER VINE 7.50

There are parts of Valpolicella that weren't as affected by the explosion in vine growing, the flourishing of hospitality services and artisanal craft seen over recent decades, and that still quietly express a strong tie with the world of agriculture. The valley of Quinzano is surely one of these. It's a district with enormous unexplored potential, and Pietro Zanoni is one of its most intriguing interpreters. This young producer has managed to re-read the celebrated appellation's wines by bringing together richness and fragrance. The care shown in their vineyards is intended to give rise to wines of extraordinary quality, which becomes clear when tasting their 2015 Campo Denari. It's a Valpolicella Superiore that exhibits a vibrant array of aromas dominated by fruity sensations and spices. In the mouth it proves firm, fragrant, well-supported by tannins. Their 2013 Amarone Zovo opts for sweeter, riper fruit, almost preserves, while its potent palate features tight-knit tannins.

# Pietro Zardini

VIA DON P. FANTONI, 3
37029 SAN PIETRO IN CARIANO [VR]
TEL. +39 0456800989
www.pietrozardini.it

CELLAR SALES
PRE-BOOKED VISITS
ANNUAL PRODUCTION 60,000 bottles
HECTARES UNDER VINE 10.00

The Zardini family estate is situated in classic Valpolicella, a handful of hectares dedicated primarily to the area's traditional grapes, which are interpreted according to the wine being produced. Their extensive experience comes after many years of working with other wineries in the area, making for a classic selection that exhibit complexity, subtlety, exuberance and finesse. And then there are those cases in which Pietro feels free to follow his own whims. Two Amarones are produced. Their 2013 Pietro Junior represents a more modern version of the wine, opting for pronounced fruit, crispness and juiciness across a full, dynamic palate. Their 2011 Leone Zardini Ris., a wine dedicated to their grandfather, explores the more reserved, complex side of the wine, with fruit hiding behind mineral notes and hints of medicinal herbs. On the palate it proves as potent as it is taut, savory and elegant. Their 2016 Recioto is an approachable, fragrant wine of great harmony.

| | |
|---|---|
| ● Valpolicella Sup. Campo Denari '15 | ♟♟ 4 |
| ● Amarone della Valpolicella Zovo '13 | ♟♟ 7 |
| ● Valpolicella Sup. '16 | ♟♟ 3 |
| ● Amarone della Valpolicella Zovo '12 | ♟♟ 7 |
| ● Amarone della Valpolicella Zovo '11 | ♟♟ 7 |
| ● Amarone della Valpolicella Zovo '10 | ♟♟ 6 |
| ● Recioto della Valpolicella '11 | ♟♟ 5 |
| ● Valpolicella Sup. '15 | ♟♟ 2* |
| ● Valpolicella Sup. '14 | ♟♟ 2* |
| ● Valpolicella Sup. '13 | ♟♟ 2* |
| ● Valpolicella Sup. Campo Denari '11 | ♟♟ 4 |
| ● Valpolicella Sup. Campo Denari '10 | ♟♟ 4 |
| ● Valpolicella Sup. Ripasso '15 | ♟♟ 4 |
| ● Valpolicella Sup. Ripasso '13 | ♟♟ 4 |

| | |
|---|---|
| ● Amarone della Valpolicella Leone Zardini Ris. '11 | ♟♟♟ 8 |
| ● Amarone della Valpolicella Pietro Junior '13 | ♟♟ 6 |
| ● Recioto della Valpolicella Pietro Junior '16 | ♟♟ 4 |
| ● Valpolicella Sup. Ripasso Pietro Junior '15 | ♟♟ 3 |
| ● Rosignol '13 | ♟ 4 |
| ⊙ Rosignol Rosato Brut | ♟ 3 |
| ● Amarone della Valpolicella Cl. '12 | ♟♟ 6 |
| ● Amarone della Valpolicella Cl. Leone Zardini Ris. '10 | ♟♟ 6 |
| ● Amarone della Valpolicella Cl. Leone Zardini Ris. '09 | ♟♟ 6 |
| ● Recioto della Valpolicella Cl. '15 | ♟♟ 4 |
| ● Valpolicella Cl. Sup. Ripasso '13 | ♟♟ 3 |

# ★Zenato

FRAZ. SAN BENEDETTO DI LUGANA
VIA SAN BENEDETTO, 8
37019 PESCHIERA DEL GARDA [VR]
TEL. +39 0457550300
www.zenato.it

**CELLAR SALES**
**PRE-BOOKED VISITS**
**ANNUAL PRODUCTION** 2,000,000 bottles
**HECTARES UNDER VINE** 95.00

The Zenato family winery has managed to carve out a role as a leader in all respects among Verona's wine producers. It was the case in the past with Sergio, and still is today with his children Nadia and Alberto. And it's as true of Lugana as it is Valpolicella. Indeed, their sizable estate spans two appellations, giving rise to a selection that can be found in virtually every corner of the planet. The winery's style privileges richness of fruit and concentration in the reds, clarity and varietal identity in the whites. The grapes for their 2015 Sergio Zenato Ris. are cultivated in Lugana. In this latest round of tasting it proved to be their most complete wine, delivering for the generosity of its aromas. Fragrances of yellow fruit alternate with notes of dried flowers and Mediterranean shrub, refreshed by a citrusy nuances. In the mouth it proves full and ripe, supported by a savory acidity that lengthens its lovely, crisp finish. Their 2013 Amarone features an elegant, sophisticated aromatic profile while on the palate it exhibits body and decisiveness.

| | |
|---|---|
| ○ Lugana Sergio Zenato Ris. '15 | ♥♥♥ 5 |
| ● Amarone della Valpolicella Cl. '13 | ♥♥ 7 |
| ● Cresasso '12 | ♥♥ 5 |
| ● Recioto della Valpolicella Cl. '12 | ♥♥ 6 |
| ○ Lugana Vign. Massoni S. Cristina '17 | ♥ 3 |
| ● Amarone della Valpolicella Cl. Sergio Zenato Ris. '11 | ♀♀♀ 8 |
| ● Amarone della Valpolicella Cl. Sergio Zenato Ris. '10 | ♀♀♀ 8 |
| ● Amarone della Valpolicella Cl. Sergio Zenato Ris. '09 | ♀♀♀ 8 |
| ● Amarone della Valpolicella Cl. '12 | ♀♀ 7 |
| ● Cresasso '11 | ♀♀ 5 |
| ○ Lugana Massoni S. Cristina '16 | ♀♀ 3 |
| ○ Lugana Sergio Zenato Ris. '14 | ♀♀ 5 |
| ○ Lugana Sergio Zenato Ris. '13 | ♀♀ 5 |
| ● Recioto della Valpolicella Cl. '14 | ♀♀ 6 |

# Zeni 1870

VIA COSTABELLA, 9
37011 BARDOLINO [VR]
TEL. +39 0457210022
www.zeni.it

**CELLAR SALES**
**PRE-BOOKED VISITS**
**ANNUAL PRODUCTION** 1,000,000 bottles
**HECTARES UNDER VINE** 25.00

The winery founded by Nino Zeni and today managed by his children Fausto, Elena and Federica is a benchmark for those who love Lake Garda's wines. The producer's strength resides in its close relationship with a number of vine growers in the area, who deliver their grapes to Zeni's production center in Bardolino. Their selection is constituted of many wines, but the style is singular: the pursuit of varietal expressivity, character and tension. This is especially true when it comes to their rosés and reds, some of which come from nearby Valpolicella. Their Amarone, dedicated to their founder, drew on an excellent 2013 for its multilayered aromas. Fragrances of fruit take center stage before giving way to spices, forest undergrowth and notes that can be traced back to the use of oak. These gradually take over on a close-knit palate that features great extractive force. Their 2017 Bardolino Vigne Alte also did well. It's a distinctive wine for its buoyant fruit and for a structured palate that never loses its suppleness and tension.

| | |
|---|---|
| ● Amarone della Valpolicella Cl. Nino Zeni '13 | ♥♥ 8 |
| ● Amarone della Valpolicella Barrique '13 | ♥♥ 7 |
| ● Amarone della Valpolicella Cl. '15 | ♥♥ 6 |
| ● Bardolino Cl. Vigne Alte '17 | ♥♥ 2* |
| ● Costalago '16 | ♥♥ 2* |
| ○ Lugana Vigne Alte '17 | ♥♥ 2* |
| ● Valpolicella Sup. Vigne Alte '16 | ♥♥ 2* |
| ⊙ Bardolino Chiaretto Brut | ♥ 2 |
| ⊙ Bardolino Chiaretto Cl. Vigne Alte '17 | ♥ 2 |
| ● Bardolino Cl. Filari del Nino '17 | ♥ 5 |
| ● Bardolino Cl. Sup. '16 | ♥ 3 |
| ● Cruino '13 | ♥ 6 |
| ● Valpolicella Sup. Ripasso Marogne '16 | ♥ 3 |
| ● Amarone della Valpolicella Cl. Barrique '11 | ♀♀ 7 |

# Zonin 1821

VIA BORGOLECCO, 9
36053 GAMBELLARA [VI]
TEL. +39 0444640111
www.zonin.it

**CELLAR SALES**
**PRE-BOOKED VISITS**
**ANNUAL PRODUCTION** 38,000,000 bottles
**HECTARES UNDER VINE** 2000.00

Zonin is more than a brand. It's one of Italy's largest producers, bolstered by vineyards that stretch for thousands of hectares across the peninsula, and beyond, including Virginia and Chile. But their selection of wines from Veneto (which started it all) is still central to their business, from their Gambellara, which is literally produced 'around the block' to their Valpolicella reds, and their strategically important Procesccos. These are just a few of the 'musts' that this European juggernaut has to offer. Their 2017 Gambellara, a wine made with grapes from Il Giangio, led their selection this year. In recent years it's taken on more and more personality and depth, offering up flowery fragrances and aromas of white fruit. These follow through on a crisp, highly savory and well-balanced palate. Their 2014 Amarone is more exuberant in its expression of fruit and, despite the difficult year, in the mouth it exhibits intensity and clarity across a juicy and potent palate.

| | |
|---|---|
| ● Amarone della Valpolicella '14 | ♟♟ 6 |
| ○ Gambellara Cl. Il Giangio '17 | ♟♟ 2* |
| ● Valpolicella Sup. Ripasso '16 | ♟♟ 3 |
| ○ Lugana '17 | ♟ 2 |
| ○ Prosecco Brut Cuvée 1821 | ♟ 3 |
| ○ Soave Cl. '17 | ♟ 2 |
| ● Valpolicella Cl. '17 | ♟ 2 |
| ● Amarone della Valpolicella '13 | ♟♟ 6 |
| ● Amarone della Valpolicella '12 | ♟♟ 5 |
| ● Amarone della Valpolicella '11 | ♟♟ 6 |
| ○ Gambellara Cl. Il Giangio '16 | ♟♟ 2* |
| ○ Recioto di Gambellara Il Giangio '11 | ♟♟ 5 |
| ● Valpolicella Sup. Ripasso '15 | ♟♟ 3 |
| ● Valpolicella Sup. Ripasso '13 | ♟♟ 3 |

# Zymè

LOC. SAN FLORIANO
VIA CA' DEL PIPA, 1
37029 SAN PIETRO IN CARIANO [VR]
TEL. +39 0457701108
www.zyme.it

**CELLAR SALES**
**PRE-BOOKED VISITS**
**ANNUAL PRODUCTION** 80,000 bottles
**HECTARES UNDER VINE** 30.00
**SUSTAINABLE WINERY**

Celestino Gaspari's career has allowed him to gain an in-depth knowledge of the territory and the world of wine production in a number of ways. He was a cellar hand in one of Valpolicella's most iconic wineries, and a consultant for various other important producers throughout the area (in some cases contributing to their founding). It was a journey that brought him to found his own operation in the district of San Floriano in Cariano. From the outset he's managed to make a name for himself for the potent yet multivariate style of his selection, in particular his top reds. Their 2011 Amarone is one of the appellation's most interesting wines. It opens slowly, still dominated by notes of super-ripe fruit with flowery timbres and almost hidden aromas of medicinal herbs. On the palate it proves splendid, with superior body, though certainly not lacking in suppleness and tension. Their 2009 Harlequin is another noteworthy wine. It's an original blend made with various local cultivar that features a complex nose and pronounced force on the palate, thanks to lengthy aging.

| | |
|---|---|
| ● Amarone della Valpolicella Cl. '11 | ♟♟ 8 |
| ● Harlequin '09 | ♟♟ 8 |
| ○ Il Bianco From Black to White '17 | ♟♟ 3 |
| ● Kairos '15 | ♟♟ 8 |
| ● Valpolicella Cl. Sup. '15 | ♟♟ 5 |
| ● Valpolicella Reverie '17 | ♟ 3 |
| ● Amarone della Valpolicella Cl. '06 | ♟♟♟ 8 |
| ● Amarone della Valpolicella Cl. La Mattonara Ris. '03 | ♟♟♟ 8 |
| ● Amarone della Valpolicella Cl. La Mattonara Ris. '01 | ♟♟♟ 8 |
| ● Amarone della Valpolicella Cl. '09 | ♟♟ 8 |
| ● Amarone della Valpolicella Cl. La Mattonara Ris. '06 | ♟♟ 8 |
| ● Amarone della Valpolicella Cl. La Mattonara Ris. '04 | ♟♟ 8 |

## Ai Galli

via Loredan, 28
30020 Pramaggiore [VE]
Tel. +39 0421799314
www.aigalli.it

CELLAR SALES
PRE-BOOKED VISITS
ACCOMMODATION AND RESTAURANT SERVICE
ANNUAL PRODUCTION 600,000 bottles
HECTARES UNDER VINE 60.00

| | |
|---|---|
| ○ Lison-Pramaggiore Chardonnay '16 | ♟♟ 3 |
| ○ Lison Cl. '17 | ♟ 3 |
| ● Lison-Pramaggiore Cabernet Franc '16 | ♟ 3 |
| ● Lison-Pramaggiore Rosso Probus '14 | ♟ 4 |

## Luciano Arduini

loc. Corrubbio
via Belvedere, 3
37029 San Pietro in Cariano [VR]
Tel. +39 0457725880
www.arduinivini.it

CELLAR SALES
PRE-BOOKED VISITS
ANNUAL PRODUCTION 45,000 bottles
HECTARES UNDER VINE 8.00

| | |
|---|---|
| ● Amarone della Valpolicella Cl. '15 | ♟♟ 5 |
| ● Recioto della Valpolicella Cl. '13 | ♟♟ 4 |
| ● Valpolicella Cl. Fontana del Fongo '17 | ♟ 2 |
| ● Valpolicella Cl. Sup. Ripasso '16 | ♟ 3 |

## Astoria Vini

via Crevada
31020 Refrontolo [TV]
Tel. +39 04236699
www.astoria.it

CELLAR SALES
PRE-BOOKED VISITS
ANNUAL PRODUCTION 15,000,000 bottles
HECTARES UNDER VINE 40.00
SUSTAINABLE WINERY

| | |
|---|---|
| ○ Cartizze Arzanà | ♟♟ 4 |
| ○ Valdobbiadene Extra Dry Tenute Val de Brun '17 | ♟♟ 4 |
| ● El Ruden '16 | ♟ 3 |

## Bacio della Luna

via Rovede, 36
31020 Vidor [TV]
Tel. +39 0423983111
www.baciodellaluna.it

ANNUAL PRODUCTION 12,000,000 bottles
HECTARES UNDER VINE 25.00
VITICULTURE METHOD Certified Organic

| | |
|---|---|
| ○ Valdobbiadene Brut | ♟♟ 3* |
| ○ Cartizze | ♟♟ 3 |

## Balestri Valda

via Monti, 44
37038 Soave [VR]
Tel. +39 0457675393
www.vinibalestrivalda.com

CELLAR SALES
PRE-BOOKED VISITS
ACCOMMODATION
ANNUAL PRODUCTION 65,000 bottles
HECTARES UNDER VINE 15.00
VITICULTURE METHOD Certified Organic
SUSTAINABLE WINERY

| | |
|---|---|
| ○ Soave Cl. '17 | ♟♟ 2* |
| ○ Soave Cl. Vign. Sengialta '15 | ♟♟ 3 |

## Beato Bartolomeo da Breganze

via Roma, 100
36042 Breganze [VI]
Tel. +39 0445873112
www.cantinabreganze.it

CELLAR SALES
ANNUAL PRODUCTION 2,500,000 bottles
HECTARES UNDER VINE 700.00

| | |
|---|---|
| ● Breganze Cabernet Kilò Ris. '14 | ♟♟ 4 |
| ● Breganze Cabernet Bosco Grande Ris. '14 | ♟ 3 |
| ● Breganze Cabernet Sup. Savardo '16 | ♟ 2 |

## Bellussi Spumanti

via Erizzo, 215
31049 Valdobbiadene [TV]
Tel. +39 0423983411
www.bellussi.com

CELLAR SALES
PRE-BOOKED VISITS
ANNUAL PRODUCTION 1,300,000 bottles
HECTARES UNDER VINE

| | |
|---|---|
| ○ Valdobbiadene Brut Belcanto | 🍷🍷 3 |
| ○ Valdobbiadene Extra Dry Belcanto | 🍷🍷 3 |
| ○ Valdobbiadene Brut | 🍷 3 |
| ○ Valdobbiadene Extra Dry | 🍷 3 |

## Bergamini

loc. Colà
via Cà Nova, 3
37017 Lazise [VR]
Tel. +39 0456490407
www.bergaminivini.it

CELLAR SALES
PRE-BOOKED VISITS
ANNUAL PRODUCTION 65,000 bottles
HECTARES UNDER VINE 13.00

| | |
|---|---|
| ● Bardolino Colline di Colà '17 | 🍷🍷 2* |
| ● Bardolino Sup. '16 | 🍷🍷 2* |
| ○ Custoza '17 | 🍷 2 |
| ○ Custoza Sup. '17 | 🍷 2 |

## Bonotto delle Tezze

fraz. Tezze di Piave
via Duca d'Aosta, 36
31028 Vazzola [TV]
Tel. +39 0438488323
www.bonottodelletezze.it

CELLAR SALES
PRE-BOOKED VISITS
ANNUAL PRODUCTION 150,000 bottles
HECTARES UNDER VINE 48.00

| | |
|---|---|
| ● Piave Malanotte '14 | 🍷🍷 6 |
| ● Piave Raboso Potestà '15 | 🍷🍷 3 |
| ○ Novalis Manzoni Bianco '17 | 🍷 2 |

## Angelo Bortolin

loc. Guia
s.da di Guia, 107
31040 Valdobbiadene [TV]
Tel. +39 0423900125
www.spumantibortolin.com

CELLAR SALES
PRE-BOOKED VISITS
ANNUAL PRODUCTION 230,000 bottles
HECTARES UNDER VINE 7.00

| | |
|---|---|
| ○ Valdobbiadene Brut '17 | 🍷🍷 2* |
| ○ Valdobbiadene Dry Desiderio '17 | 🍷🍷 2* |
| ○ Valdobbiadene Extra Dry '17 | 🍷🍷 2* |

## F.lli Bortolin

fraz. Santo Stefano
via Menegazzi, 5
31049 Valdobbiadene [TV]
Tel. +39 0423900135
www.bortolin.com

CELLAR SALES
PRE-BOOKED VISITS
ANNUAL PRODUCTION 300,000 bottles
HECTARES UNDER VINE 20.00

| | |
|---|---|
| ○ Cartizze | 🍷🍷 4 |
| ○ Valdobbiadene Brut Rù '17 | 🍷🍷 3 |
| ○ Valdobbiadene Brut | 🍷 2 |
| ○ Valdobbiadene Extra Dry | 🍷 2 |

## Cà Rovere

via Bocara
36045 Alonte [VI]
Tel. +39 0444436234
www.carovere.it

CELLAR SALES
PRE-BOOKED VISITS
ANNUAL PRODUCTION 50,000 bottles
HECTARES UNDER VINE 30.00
SUSTAINABLE WINERY

| | |
|---|---|
| ○ Brut M. Cl. '13 | 🍷🍷 4 |
| ○ Brut Cuvée M. Cl. '13 | 🍷 4 |
| ○ Brut Nature M. Cl. '14 | 🍷 4 |
| ○ Demi Sec Cuvée M. Cl. '14 | 🍷 4 |

## Calalta

VIA GIARETTA, 10
36065 MUSSOLENTE [VI]
TEL. +39 042487565
www.calalta.it

ANNUAL PRODUCTION 15,000 bottles
HECTARES UNDER VINE 5.00

| | |
|---|---|
| ● Grijer '15 | ♛♛ 4 |
| ○ Mentelibera '16 | ♛♛ 4 |
| ○ Riesling Davvero '16 | ♛ 4 |

## Castello di Roncade

VIA ROMA, 141
31056 RONCADE [TV]
TEL. +39 0422708736
www.castellodironcade.com

CELLAR SALES
PRE-BOOKED VISITS
ANNUAL PRODUCTION 200,000 bottles
HECTARES UNDER VINE 45.00

| | |
|---|---|
| ● Baronessa Ilaria Raboso Passito '13 | ♛♛ 5 |
| ● Piave Raboso dell'Arnasa '14 | ♛♛ 2* |
| ● Piave Merlot Rosso dell'Arnasa '15 | ♛ 2 |
| ● Villa Giustinian '15 | ♛ 3 |

## Colvendrà

VIA LIBERAZIONE, 39
31020 REFRONTOLO [TV]
TEL. +39 0438894265
www.colvendra.it

CELLAR SALES
PRE-BOOKED VISITS
ANNUAL PRODUCTION 180,000 bottles
HECTARES UNDER VINE 27.00

| | |
|---|---|
| ○ Conegliano Valdobbiadene Rive di Refontolo Bepi Dry '17 | ♛♛ 4 |
| ○ Conegliano Valdobbiadene Rive di Refontolo Extra Dry Bepi Sec '17 | ♛♛ 4 |

## Vignaioli Contrà Soarda

S.DA SOARDA, 26
36061 BASSANO DEL GRAPPA [VI]
TEL. +39 0424505562
www.contrasoarda.it

CELLAR SALES
PRE-BOOKED VISITS
RESTAURANT SERVICE
ANNUAL PRODUCTION 80,000 bottles
HECTARES UNDER VINE 20.00
VITICULTURE METHOD Certified Organic
SUSTAINABLE WINERY

| | |
|---|---|
| ○ Breganze Torcolato Sarson Ris. '15 | ♛♛ 5 |
| ○ Breganze Vespaiolo Vignasilan '15 | ♛♛ 5 |
| ○ Breganze Vespaiolo Soarda '17 | ♛ 3 |
| ● Ettaro Musso '14 | ♛ 3 |

## Corte Figaretto

FRAZ. POIANO
VIA CLOCEGO, 48A
37142 VERONA
TEL. +39 0458700753
www.cortefigaretto.it

CELLAR SALES
PRE-BOOKED VISITS
ANNUAL PRODUCTION 49,500 bottles
HECTARES UNDER VINE 7.50

| | |
|---|---|
| ● Amarone della Valpolicella Valpantena Brolo del Figaretto '14 | ♛♛ 5 |
| ● Valpolicella Valpantena Sup. Ripasso '16 | ♛♛ 3 |

## Corte Mainente

V.LE DELLA VITTORIA, 45
37038 SOAVE [VR]
TEL. +39 0457680303
www.cantinamainente.com

CELLAR SALES
PRE-BOOKED VISITS
ANNUAL PRODUCTION 20,000 bottles
HECTARES UNDER VINE 12.00
SUSTAINABLE WINERY

| | |
|---|---|
| ○ Soave Cengelle '17 | ♛♛ 2* |
| ○ Soave Netrroir '16 | ♛♛ 3 |
| ○ Recioto di Soave Luna Nova '16 | ♛ 3 |
| ○ Soave Cl. Tovo al Pigno '17 | ♛ 2 |

## Costa Arente

LOC. COSTA, 86
37023 GREZZANA [VR]
TEL. +39 0422864511
www.arente.it

PRE-BOOKED VISITS
ANNUAL PRODUCTION 50,000 bottles
HECTARES UNDER VINE 17.00
SUSTAINABLE WINERY

| | | |
|---|---|---|
| ● Amarone della Valpolicella '15 | 🍷🍷 | 7 |
| ● Valpolicella Valpantena '17 | 🍷🍷 | 3 |
| ● Valpolicella Valpantena Ripasso '16 | 🍷 | 4 |

## Paolo Cottini

FRAZ. CASTELROTTO
VIA BELVEDERE, 29
37029 VERONA
TEL. +39 0456837293
www.paolocottini.it

CELLAR SALES
PRE-BOOKED VISITS
ANNUAL PRODUCTION 40,000 bottles
HECTARES UNDER VINE 3.50

| | | |
|---|---|---|
| ● Amarone della Valpolicella Cl. '14 | 🍷🍷 | 6 |
| ● Scriba Passito '15 | 🍷🍷 | 5 |
| ● Valpolicella Cl. '17 | 🍷 | 2 |
| ● Valpolicella Cl. Sup. Ripasso '15 | 🍷 | 4 |

## Cantina di Custoza

LOC. CUSTOZA
VIA STAFFALO, 1
37066 SOMMACAMPAGNA [VR]
TEL. +39 045516200
www.cantinadicustoza.it

CELLAR SALES
PRE-BOOKED VISITS
ANNUAL PRODUCTION 4,000,000 bottles
HECTARES UNDER VINE 1000.00
VITICULTURE METHOD Certified Organic

| | | |
|---|---|---|
| ○ Custoza Sup. Custodia '16 | 🍷🍷 | 3* |
| ● Amarone della Valpolicella Cl. '13 | 🍷🍷 | 5 |
| ● Bardolino Val dei Molini '17 | 🍷 | 3 |
| ○ Custoza Val dei Molini '17 | 🍷 | 2 |

## Dal Din

VIA MONTEGRAPPA, 29
31020 VIDOR [TV]
TEL. +39 0423987295
www.daldin.it

CELLAR SALES
PRE-BOOKED VISITS
ANNUAL PRODUCTION 350,000 bottles
HECTARES UNDER VINE 12.00
SUSTAINABLE WINERY

| | | |
|---|---|---|
| ○ Valdobbiadene Brut Tre Dame '17 | 🍷🍷 | 3 |
| ○ Valdobbiadene Dry Vidoro '17 | 🍷🍷 | 3 |
| ○ Valdobbiadene Brut | 🍷 | 3 |
| ○ Valdobbiadene Extra Dry | 🍷 | 3 |

## La Dama

FRAZ. SAN VITO
VIA GIOVANNI QUINTARELLI, 39
37024 NEGRAR [VR]
TEL. +39 0456000728
www.ladamavini.com

ANNUAL PRODUCTION 50,000 bottles
HECTARES UNDER VINE 10.00
VITICULTURE METHOD Certified Organic

| | | |
|---|---|---|
| ● Amarone della Valpolicella Cl. '13 | 🍷🍷 | 7 |
| ● Recioto della Valpolicella Cl. '15 | 🍷🍷 | 6 |
| ● Valpolicella Cl. Sup. Ca' Besi '15 | 🍷🍷 | 5 |
| ● Valpolicella Cl. '17 | 🍷 | 3 |

## Sandro De Bruno

VIA SANTA MARGHERITA, 26
37030 MONTECCHIA DI CROSARA [VR]
TEL. +39 0456540465
www.sandrodebruno.it

ANNUAL PRODUCTION 80,000 bottles
HECTARES UNDER VINE 22.00

| | | |
|---|---|---|
| ○ Lessini Durello Dosaggio Zero M. Cl. Ris. '10 | 🍷🍷 | 5 |
| ○ Lessini Durello Extra Brut M. Cl. Ris. '10 | 🍷🍷 | 5 |
| ○ Soave '17 | 🍷🍷 | 2* |

## Francesco Drusian

FRAZ. BIGOLINO
VIA ANCHE, 1
31030 VALDOBBIADENE [TV]
TEL. +39 0423982151
www.drusian.it

CELLAR SALES
PRE-BOOKED VISITS
ANNUAL PRODUCTION 1,200,000 bottles
HECTARES UNDER VINE 80.00
SUSTAINABLE WINERY

| | |
|---|---|
| ○ Valdobbiadene Dosaggio Zero 30 Raccolti | 🍷🍷 3 |
| ○ Valdobbiadene Dry '17 | 🍷🍷 3 |
| ○ Valdobbiadene Brut | 🍷 3 |

## Fongaro

VIA MOTTO PIANE, 12
37030 RONCÀ [VR]
TEL. +39 0457460240
www.fongarospumanti.it

CELLAR SALES
PRE-BOOKED VISITS
ANNUAL PRODUCTION 68,000 bottles
HECTARES UNDER VINE 7.00
VITICULTURE METHOD Certified Organic

| | |
|---|---|
| ○ Lessini Durello Brut M. Cl. Ris. '10 | 🍷🍷 5 |

## Fraccaroli

FRAZ. SAN BENEDETTO
LOC. BERRA VECCHIA, 1
37019 PESCHIERA DEL GARDA [VR]
TEL. +39 0457550949
www.fraccarolivini.it

CELLAR SALES
PRE-BOOKED VISITS
ANNUAL PRODUCTION 280,000 bottles
HECTARES UNDER VINE 50.00

| | |
|---|---|
| ○ Lugana Pansere '17 | 🍷🍷 2* |
| ● Garda Cabernet Sauvignon '16 | 🍷 2 |
| ⊙ Garda Colli Mantovani Chiaretto '17 | 🍷 2 |
| ○ Lugana Sup. Campo Serà '16 | 🍷 2 |

## Frozza

VIA MARTIRI, 31
31020 VIDOR [TV]
TEL. +39 0423987069
prosecco.frozza@tiscali.it

CELLAR SALES
PRE-BOOKED VISITS
ANNUAL PRODUCTION 80,000 bottles
HECTARES UNDER VINE 7.50

| | |
|---|---|
| ○ Valdobbiadene Brut Rive di Colbertaldo '17 | 🍷🍷 3 |
| ○ Valdobbiadene Extra Dry | 🍷🍷 3 |

## Fattoria Garbole

LOC. GARBOLE
VIA FRACANZANA, 6
37039 TREGNAGO [VR]
TEL. +39 0457809020
www.fattoriagarbole.it

CELLAR SALES
PRE-BOOKED VISITS
ANNUAL PRODUCTION 15,000 bottles
HECTARES UNDER VINE 6.00

| | |
|---|---|
| ● Amarone della Valpolicella Hatteso '10 | 🍷🍷 8 |
| ● Heletto '11 | 🍷🍷 6 |
| ● Recioto della Valpolicella Hestremo '11 | 🍷🍷 5 |

## Tenuta La Presa

LOC. ZUANE 12
37013 CAPRINO VERONESE [VR]
TEL. +39 045 7242314
www.tenutalapresa.it

CELLAR SALES
PRE-BOOKED VISITS
ACCOMMODATION AND RESTAURANT SERVICE
ANNUAL PRODUCTION 10,000 bottles
HECTARES UNDER VINE 95.00
SUSTAINABLE WINERY

| | |
|---|---|
| ○ Qveé Serena Brut M. Cl. | 🍷🍷 3 |
| ● Bardolino Baldovino '17 | 🍷 2 |
| ○ Garda Pinot Grigio '17 | 🍷 2 |
| ○ Qveé Assoluta Brut M. Cl. | 🍷 5 |

# Maeli

VIA DIETRO CERO, 1C
35031 BAONE [PD]
TEL. +39 0429538144
www.maeliwine.it

ANNUAL PRODUCTION 55,000 bottles
HECTARES UNDER VINE 13.50

| | |
|---|---|
| ○ Brut Nature Dilà M. Cl. '15 | ♟♟ 5 |
| ● Colli Euganei Rosso Infinito '16 | ♟♟ 5 |
| ● Colli Euganei D+ Even More '15 | ♟ 5 |
| ○ Moscato Giallo Frizzante Dalì '16 | ♟ 4 |

# Le Manzane

LOC. BAGNOLO
VIA MASET, 47B
31020 SAN PIETRO DI FELETTO [TV]
TEL. +39 0438486606
www.lemanzane.com

CELLAR SALES
PRE-BOOKED VISITS
ANNUAL PRODUCTION 1,000,000 bottles
HECTARES UNDER VINE 72.00

| | |
|---|---|
| ○ Conegliano Sup. Rive di Manzana Dry Springo '17 | ♟♟ 4 |
| ○ Conegliano Valdobbiadene Extra Dry 20.10 '17 | ♟♟ 3 |

# Le Marognole

LOC. VALGATARA
VIA MAROGNOLE, 7
37020 MARANO DI VALPOLICELLA [VR]
TEL. +39 0457755114
www.lemarognole.it

CELLAR SALES
PRE-BOOKED VISITS
ANNUAL PRODUCTION 15,000 bottles
HECTARES UNDER VINE 5.50

| | |
|---|---|
| ● Amarone della Valpolicella Cl. Campo Rocco '13 | ♟♟ 5 |
| ● Valpolicella Cl. Sup. Ripasso '14 | ♟♟ 3 |

# Marsuret

LOC. GUIA DI VALDOBBIADENE
VIA BARCH, 17
31049 VALDOBBIADENE [TV]
TEL. +39 0423900139
www.marsuret.it

CELLAR SALES
PRE-BOOKED VISITS
ANNUAL PRODUCTION 600,000 bottles
HECTARES UNDER VINE 50.00

| | |
|---|---|
| ○ Cartizze '17 | ♟♟ 4 |
| ○ Valdobbiadene Brut Rive di Guia '17 | ♟♟ 3 |
| ○ Valdobbiadene Brut San Boldo | ♟♟ 3 |
| ○ Valdobbiadene Extra Dry Il Soller | ♟ 3 |

# Firmino Miotti

VIA BROGLIATI CONTRO, 53
36042 BREGANZE [VI]
TEL. +39 0445873006
www.firminomiotti.it

CELLAR SALES
PRE-BOOKED VISITS
ANNUAL PRODUCTION 25,000 bottles
HECTARES UNDER VINE 5.00

| | |
|---|---|
| ○ Breganze Torcolato '10 | ♟♟ 5 |
| ● Breganze Rosso '15 | ♟ 3 |
| ○ Pedevendo Frizzante | ♟ 2 |
| ○ Sampagna Frizzante | ♟ 2 |

# Monte Cillario

FRAZ. PARONA DI VALPOLICELLA
VIA SANTA CRISTINA, 1B
37124 VERONA
TEL. +39 045941387
www.montecillariovini.com

CELLAR SALES
PRE-BOOKED VISITS
ANNUAL PRODUCTION 22,000 bottles
HECTARES UNDER VINE 30.00
SUSTAINABLE WINERY

| | |
|---|---|
| ● Amarone della Valpolicella Casa Erbisti '14 | ♟♟ 6 |
| ● Valpolicella Marchesini '17 | ♟♟ 3 |
| ● Valpolicella Sup. Borgo Antico '15 | ♟♟ 3 |
| ● Valpolicella Sup. Ripasso I Berari '15 | ♟ 4 |

## Monteci

VIA SAN MICHELE, 34
37026 PESCANTINA [VR]
TEL. +39 0457151188
www.monteci.it

CELLAR SALES
PRE-BOOKED VISITS
ANNUAL PRODUCTION 500,000 bottles
HECTARES UNDER VINE 190.00
VITICULTURE METHOD Certified Organic
SUSTAINABLE WINERY

| | |
|---|---|
| ● Amarone della Valpolicella Cl. | |
| Costa delle Corone '09 | 🍷🍷 6 |
| ● Valpolicella Cl. '17 | 🍷 2 |
| ● Valpolicella Cl. Sup. Ripasso '14 | 🍷 3 |

## Montelvini

FRAZ. VENEGAZZÙ
VIA CAL TREVIGIANA, 51
31040 VOLPAGO DEL MONTELLO [TV]
TEL. +39 042387778777
www.montelvini.it

CELLAR SALES
ANNUAL PRODUCTION 4,800,000 bottles
HECTARES UNDER VINE 35.00

| | |
|---|---|
| ○ Asolo Extra Brut '17 | 🍷🍷 2* |
| ○ Asolo Dry '17 | 🍷 2 |
| ○ Luna Storta Passito | 🍷 4 |
| ● Venezia Cabernet Franc S.Osvaldo '17 | 🍷 2 |

## Walter Nardin

LOC. RONCADELLE
VIA FONTANE, 5
31024 ORMELLE [TV]
TEL. +39 0422851622
www.vinwalternardin.it

PRE-BOOKED VISITS
ANNUAL PRODUCTION 350,000 bottles
HECTARES UNDER VINE 30.00

| | |
|---|---|
| ● Piave Raboso La Zerbaia '13 | 🍷🍷 3 |
| ● Rosso del Nane La Zerbaia '16 | 🍷🍷 2* |
| ○ Tai La Zerbaia '16 | 🍷🍷 2* |
| ● Rosso della Ghiaia La Zerbaia '14 | 🍷 4 |

## Pegoraro

VIA CALBIN, 24
36024 MOSSANO [VI]
TEL. +39 0444886461
www.cantinapegoraro.it

CELLAR SALES
PRE-BOOKED VISITS
ANNUAL PRODUCTION 45,000 bottles
HECTARES UNDER VINE 7.00

| | |
|---|---|
| ● Colli Berici Tai Rosso '17 | 🍷🍷 3 |
| ● Syrah '16 | 🍷🍷 3 |
| ● Colli Berici Tai Rosso Rovea '15 | 🍷 4 |

## Perlage

LOC. FARRA DI SOLIGO
VIA CAL DEL MUNER, 16
31020 FARRA DI SOLIGO [TV]
TEL. +39 0438900203
www.perlagewines.com

CELLAR SALES
PRE-BOOKED VISITS
ANNUAL PRODUCTION 2,300,000 bottles
HECTARES UNDER VINE 100.00
VITICULTURE METHOD Certified
OrganicCertified Biodynamic
SUSTAINABLE WINERY

| | |
|---|---|
| ○ Valdobbiadene Brut Canah | 🍷🍷 3 |
| ○ Valdobbiadene Extra Dry | |
| Col di Manza '17 | 🍷🍷 5 |
| ○ Valdobbiadene Extra Dry Quorum | 🍷 3 |

## Tenuta Polvaro

VIA POLVARO, 35
30020 ANNONE VENETO [VE]
TEL. +39 0421281023
www.tenutapolvaro.it

CELLAR SALES
PRE-BOOKED VISITS
ANNUAL PRODUCTION 300,000 bottles
HECTARES UNDER VINE 60.00

| | |
|---|---|
| ○ Lison Cl. '16 | 🍷 2 |
| ○ Polvaro Oro '17 | 🍷 2 |
| ● Venezia Cabernet Sauvignon '16 | 🍷 2 |
| ● Venezia Rosso Polvaro Nero '16 | 🍷 2 |

# Viticoltori Ponte

VIA VERDI, 50
31047 PONTE DI PIAVE [TV]
TEL. +39 0422858211
www.viticoltoriponte.it

CELLAR SALES
ANNUAL PRODUCTION 15,000,000 bottles
HECTARES UNDER VINE 2000.00

| | |
|---|---|
| ● Venezia Merlot Campe Dhei '15 | ♟♟ 3 |
| ○ Conegliano Valdobbiadene Brut | ♟ 3 |

# Umberto Portinari

LOC. BROGNOLIGO
VIA SANTO STEFANO, 2
37032 MONTEFORTE D'ALPONE [VR]
TEL. +39 0456175087
portinarivini@libero.it

CELLAR SALES
PRE-BOOKED VISITS
ANNUAL PRODUCTION 30,000 bottles
HECTARES UNDER VINE 4.00

| | |
|---|---|
| ○ Anna Giulia Passito '00 | ♟♟ 6 |
| ○ Soave Albare '16 | ♟♟ 2* |
| ○ Soave Cl. Ronchetto '16 | ♟♟ 2* |
| ○ Soave Santo Stefano '15 | ♟ 3 |

# PuntoZero

VIA MONTE PALÙ, 1
36045 LONIGO [VI]
TEL. +39 049659881
www.puntozerowine.it

CELLAR SALES
PRE-BOOKED VISITS
ANNUAL PRODUCTION 16,000 bottles
HECTARES UNDER VINE 11.00

| | |
|---|---|
| ● Carmenère '16 | ♟♟ 5 |
| ● Tai '16 | ♟ 5 |

# Quota 101

VIA MALTERRENO, 12
35038 TORREGLIA [PD]
TEL. +39 0425410922
www.quota101.com

PRE-BOOKED VISITS
ACCOMMODATION
ANNUAL PRODUCTION 45,000 bottles
HECTARES UNDER VINE 18.00
VITICULTURE METHOD Certified Organic
SUSTAINABLE WINERY

| | |
|---|---|
| ○ Colli Euganei Fior d'Arancio Passito Il Gelso di Lapo '15 | ♟♟ 5 |
| ○ Colli Euganei Manzoni Bianco '16 | ♟♟ 3 |
| ● Colli Euganei Rosso Ortone '15 | ♟♟ 4 |

# Poderi Salvarolo

VIA STRADATTA, 30
30020 PRAMAGGIORE [VE]
TEL. +39 0421200162
www.salvarolo.com

ANNUAL PRODUCTION 150,000 bottles
HECTARES UNDER VINE 65.00
SUSTAINABLE WINERY

| | |
|---|---|
| ● Lison-Pramaggiore Cabernet Franc '16 | ♟♟ 2* |
| ○ Lison '17 | ♟ 2 |
| ● Lison-Pramaggiore Merlot '16 | ♟ 2 |
| ● Lison-Pramaggiore Refosco P.R. '16 | ♟ 2 |

# San Nazario

LOC. CORTELÀ
VIA MONTE VERSA, 1519
35030 VÒ [PD]
TEL. +39 0499940194
www.vinisannazario.it

CELLAR SALES
PRE-BOOKED VISITS
ANNUAL PRODUCTION 50,000 bottles
HECTARES UNDER VINE 10.00
VITICULTURE METHOD Certified Organic

| | |
|---|---|
| ● Colli Euganei Rosso Brolo delle Femmine '16 | ♟♟ 2* |
| ● Prà dei Mistri '16 | ♟♟ 3 |
| ○ Colli Euganei Bianco Dulcamara '17 | ♟ 2 |

## San Rustico

FRAZ. VALGATARA DI VALPOLICELLA
VIA POZZO, 2
37020 MARANO DI VALPOLICELLA [VR]
TEL. +39 0457703348
www.sanrustico.it

CELLAR SALES
PRE-BOOKED VISITS
ANNUAL PRODUCTION 250,000 bottles
HECTARES UNDER VINE 22.00

| | |
|---|---|
| ● Valpolicella Cl. Sup. '16 | 🍷🍷 2* |
| ● Amarone della Valpolicella Cl. '13 | 🍷 6 |
| ● Valpolicella Cl. '17 | 🍷 2 |
| ● Valpolicella Cl. Sup. Ripasso Gaso '15 | 🍷 4 |

## Sandre

FRAZ. CAMPODIPIETRA
VIA RISORGIMENTO, 16
31040 SALGAREDA [TV]
TEL. +39 0422804135
www.sandre.it

CELLAR SALES
PRE-BOOKED VISITS
ANNUAL PRODUCTION 100,000 bottles
HECTARES UNDER VINE 33.00

| | |
|---|---|
| ○ Acini Bianchi '16 | 🍷🍷 2* |
| ○ Passito aMora '14 | 🍷🍷 5 |
| ○ Manzoni '17 | 🍷 2 |
| ● Piave Merlot '16 | 🍷 2 |

## Savian

V.LE VITTORIA, 22
30020 ANNONE VENETO [VE]
TEL. +39 0422864068
www.savianvini.it

ANNUAL PRODUCTION 500,000 bottles
HECTARES UNDER VINE 42.00
VITICULTURE METHOD Certified Organic
SUSTAINABLE WINERY

| | |
|---|---|
| ● Venezia Cabernet Franc '17 | 🍷🍷 2* |
| ○ Venezia Pinot Grigio '17 | 🍷🍷 2* |
| ○ Lison Cl. '17 | 🍷 2 |
| ○ Venezia Chardonnay '17 | 🍷 2 |

## Spagnol - Col del Sas

VIA SCANDOLERA, 51
31020 VIDOR [TV]
TEL. +39 0423987177
www.coldelsas.it

CELLAR SALES
PRE-BOOKED VISITS
ANNUAL PRODUCTION 450,000 bottles
HECTARES UNDER VINE 32.00

| | |
|---|---|
| ○ Valdobbiadene Brut Col del Sas '17 | 🍷🍷 3 |
| ○ Valdobbiadene Dosaggio Zero Quindici16 | 🍷🍷 4 |
| ○ Valdobbiadene Extra Dry Col del Sas | 🍷🍷 2 |

## Terra Felice

VIA MARLUNGHE, 19
35032 ARQUÀ PETRARCA [PD]
TEL. +39 3477025928
agri.terrafelice@gmail.com

CELLAR SALES
PRE-BOOKED VISITS
ANNUAL PRODUCTION 45,000 bottles
HECTARES UNDER VINE 10.00

| | |
|---|---|
| ● AltaVia Rosso '15 | 🍷🍷 5 |
| ○ Chardonnay '16 | 🍷🍷 4 |
| ● Pinot Nero '15 | 🍷 7 |

## Terre di Leone

LOC. PORTA
37020 MARANO DI VALPOLICELLA [VR]
TEL. +39 0456895040
www.terredileone.it

CELLAR SALES
PRE-BOOKED VISITS
ANNUAL PRODUCTION 36,000 bottles
HECTARES UNDER VINE 10.00

| | |
|---|---|
| ● Amarone della Valpolicella Cl. '10 | 🍷🍷 4 |
| ● Valpolicella Cl. Sup. '14 | 🍷🍷 3 |
| ● Valpolicella Cl. Sup. Ripasso '14 | 🍷🍷 4 |
| ● Dedicatum '12 | 🍷 4 |

## Terre di San Venanzio Fortunato

Via Capitello Ferrari, 1
31049 Valdobbiadene [TV]
Tel. +39 0423974083
Via Capitello Ferrari, 1

ANNUAL PRODUCTION 300,000 bottles

| | |
|---|---|
| ○ Cartizze Brut | 🍷🍷 4 |
| ○ Valdobbiadene Brut Demi Long | 🍷🍷 3 |
| ○ Valdobbiadene Extra Dry | 🍷🍷 2 |
| ○ Valdobbiadene Dry '17 | 🍷 2 |

## Cantina Produttori di Valdobbiadene - Val d'Oca

Via San Giovanni, 45
31030 Valdobbiadene [TV]
Tel. +39 0423982070
www.valdoca.com

CELLAR SALES
PRE-BOOKED VISITS
ANNUAL PRODUCTION 13,000,000 bottles
HECTARES UNDER VINE 950.00
VITICULTURE METHOD Certified Organic

| | |
|---|---|
| ○ Valdobbiadene Rive di Colbertaldo Extra Dry '17 | 🍷🍷 4 |
| ○ Valdobbiadene Rive di Santo Stefano Brut '17 | 🍷🍷 4 |

## Vigneti di Ettore

Via Casetta di Montecchio, 2
37024 Negrar [VR]
Tel. +39 0457540158
www.vignetidiettore.it

ACCOMMODATION
ANNUAL PRODUCTION 60,000 bottles
HECTARES UNDER VINE 15.00
VITICULTURE METHOD Certified Organic
SUSTAINABLE WINERY

| | |
|---|---|
| ● Amarone della Valpolicella Cl. '14 | 🍷🍷 7 |
| ● Recioto della Valpolicella Cl. '15 | 🍷🍷 5 |
| ● Valpolicella Cl. '17 | 🍷 3 |
| ● Valpolicella Cl. Sup. '16 | 🍷 3 |

## Tenute Ugolini

S.da di Bonamico, 11
37029 San Pietro in Cariano [VR]
Tel. +39 0457703830
www.tenuteugolini.it

ANNUAL PRODUCTION 50,000 bottles
HECTARES UNDER VINE 22.00

| | |
|---|---|
| ● Valpolicella Cl. Sup. Ripasso Monte Solane '15 | 🍷🍷 5 |
| ● Valpolicella Cl. Sup. San Michele '14 | 🍷🍷 4 |

## Virgilio Vignato

Via Guizza, 8
36053 Gambellara [VI]
Tel. +39 0444444262
www.virgiliovignato.it

CELLAR SALES
PRE-BOOKED VISITS
ACCOMMODATION
ANNUAL PRODUCTION 50,000 bottles
HECTARES UNDER VINE 15.00
SUSTAINABLE WINERY

| | |
|---|---|
| ○ Gambellara Cl. Vin Santo '11 | 🍷🍷 7 |
| ○ Gambellara Cl. Capitel Vicenzi '16 | 🍷🍷 3 |
| ○ Gambellara Spumante M. Cl. '16 | 🍷🍷 3 |
| ○ Caliverna '16 | 🍷 3 |

## Villa Angarano

Fraz. Sant'Eusebio
Via Contrà Corte S.Eusebio, 15
36061 Bassano del Grappa [VI]
Tel. +39 0424503086
www.villaangarano.com

CELLAR SALES
PRE-BOOKED VISITS
ANNUAL PRODUCTION 30,000 bottles
HECTARES UNDER VINE 8.00
VITICULTURE METHOD Certified Organic

| | |
|---|---|
| ○ Breganze Torcolato San Biagio Ris. '15 | 🍷🍷 5 |
| ○ Ca' Michiel '15 | 🍷🍷 4 |
| ● Breganze Rosso Angarano '15 | 🍷 3 |
| ○ Breganze Vesapaiola Angarano Bianco '17 | 🍷 3 |

## Villa Calicantus

Via Concordia, 13
37011 Bardolino [VR]
Tel. +39 3403666740
www.villacalicantus.it

ACCOMMODATION AND RESTAURANT SERVICE
ANNUAL PRODUCTION 18,000 bottles
HECTARES UNDER VINE 5.00
VITICULTURE METHOD Certified Organic
SUSTAINABLE WINERY

| | |
|---|---|
| ● Bardolino Cl. Sup. '15 | ♟♟ 5 |
| ● Bardolino Cl. Sup. Avresir '14 | ♟♟ 6 |

## Villa Canestrari

Via Dante Broglio, 2
37030 Colognola ai Colli [VR]
Tel. +39 0457650074
www.villacanestrari.com

CELLAR SALES
PRE-BOOKED VISITS
ANNUAL PRODUCTION 150,000 bottles
HECTARES UNDER VINE 15.00

| | |
|---|---|
| ● Amarone della Valpolicella Plenum Ris. '11 | ♟♟ 7 |
| ○ Soave Sup. Ris. '15 | ♟♟ 3 |
| ● Amarone della Valpolicella '13 | ♟ 5 |
| ● Valpolicella Terre di Lanoli '17 | ♟ 2 |

## Villa Medici

Via Campagnol, 11
37066 Sommacampagna [VR]
Tel. +39 045515147
www.cantinavillamedici.it

ANNUAL PRODUCTION 220,000 bottles
HECTARES UNDER VINE 32.00

| | |
|---|---|
| ○ Custoza Sup. '17 | ♟♟ 2* |
| ● Bardolino '17 | ♟ 2 |
| ⊙ Bardolino Chiaretto '17 | ♟ 2 |
| ● Bardolino Sup. '15 | ♟ 3 |

## Villa Minelli

Via Postioma, 66
31020 Villorba [TV]
Tel. +39 0422912355
www.villaminelli.it

CELLAR SALES
PRE-BOOKED VISITS
ANNUAL PRODUCTION 65,000 bottles
HECTARES UNDER VINE 9.50
SUSTAINABLE WINERY

| | |
|---|---|
| ○ Brut M. Cl. | ♟♟ 4 |
| ● Merlot '16 | ♟♟ 3 |
| ● Merlot V.V. '15 | ♟♟ 4 |

## Viticoltori Riuniti dei Colli Euganei

Via G. Marconi, 314
35030 Vo [PD]
Tel. +39 0499940011
www.cantinacollieuganei.it

CELLAR SALES
PRE-BOOKED VISITS
ANNUAL PRODUCTION 1,500,000 bottles

| | |
|---|---|
| ● Colli Euganei Rosso Notte di Galileo Ris. '15 | ♟♟ 3 |
| ○ Colli Euganei Chardonnay Rialto '17 | ♟ 2 |
| ● Colli Euganei Merlot Rialto '17 | ♟ 2 |

## Zardetto

Via Martiri delle Foibe, 18
31015 Conegliano [TV]
Tel. +39 0438394969
www.zardettoprosecco.com

CELLAR SALES
ANNUAL PRODUCTION 2,000,000 bottles
HECTARES UNDER VINE 40.00
VITICULTURE METHOD Certified Organic

| | |
|---|---|
| ○ Conegliano Valdobbiadene Rive di Cozzuolo Viti di San Mor '16 | ♟♟ 5 |
| ○ Conegliano Valdobbiadene Refosso Brut '17 | ♟ 3 |

# FRIULI
# VENEZIA GIULIA

Once again some 16 wines broke through the threshold of excellence and received Tre Bicchieri. They're all whites, and all made both with native grapes and international varieties, thus confirming Friuli Venezia Giulia's propensity for the typology. It's commonly thought that white wines are already ready in the spring, that they aren't particularly ageworthy and that they should be drunk within a year of vintage. But a quick consultation of the wines awarded proves otherwise: indeed, less than half of these were 2017s. It's a significant statistic that points up the sensibility of the producers here, who understand the territory's potential for white grapes well-enough to renounce immediate sales in favor of lengthier aging in the bottle. Russiz Superiore's 2013 Sauvignon Riserva is a perfect example, as is Villa Russiz's 2014 Chardonnay Grafin del la Tour, and Primosic's 2015 Chardonnay Gmajne. They represent 3 of the 12 Tre Bicchieri attributed to Collio Goriziano, a list that also includes Angoris's 2016 Collio Bianco Riserva, Ronco dei Tassi's 2016 Fosari, Collavini's 2017 Broy and Livon's 2017 Solarco. Capping off the roster is Schiopetto's legendary 2017 Friulano, Marco Felluga's 2016 Pinot Grigio Mongris Riserva, Tiare's Sauvignon and two fantastic Pinot Biancos, one by Door Prinic, the other by Toros. Indeed, this year Pinot Bianco took home the most number of awards. In addition to Collio's, there's Zorzettig's 2017 Pinot Bianco Myò and Torre Rosazza's 2017 Pinot Bianco, as well as a new entry, Masut da Rive's 2016 Pinot Bianco. The last of these is from the Friuli Isonzo appellation, where the stars Vie di Romans and Tenuta Luisa continue to shine thanks to their 2016 Sauvignon Piere and 2016 Desiderium i Ferretti (respectively). Tunella took him a gold with their 2016 BiancoSesto, a mix of native grapes. Volpe Pasini once again delivers with their 2017 Sauvignon Zuc di Volpe, as did La Viarte with their 2017 Friulano Liende and Livio Felluga with their 2016 Rosazzo Bianco Terre Alte. Jermann's sumptuous 2016 Capo Martino managed to beat out their Vintage Tunina, and for us it's the White of the Year. Grave's Le Monde also earned top honors thanks to their 2017 Chardonnay. And certain regional macerated whites also found their peak expression: Skerk's 2016 Ograde, Carpino's 2015 Malvasia and Podversic's Nekaj.

## Tenuta di Angoris

LOC. ANGORIS, 7
34071 CORMÒNS [GO]
TEL. +39 048160923
www.angoris.it

**CELLAR SALES**
**PRE-BOOKED VISITS**
**RESTAURANT SERVICE**
**ANNUAL PRODUCTION** 650,000 bottles
**HECTARES UNDER VINE** 85.00
**SUSTAINABLE WINERY**

Tenuta di Angoris boasts properties that span some of the region's best-suited areas for viticulture. Founded in 1648, the winery has always been a benchmark for the territory, bringing together notable production volumes and high quality. Since 1968 the winery has been in the hands of the Locatelli family, who've managed to further develop its potential, steering it to the heights of regional excellence. Marta's entrepreneurial skills and the support of her staff (coordinated by Alessandro Dal Zovo) deserve credit for the producer's achievements in terms of elevated quality standards. Their well-rounded selection of wines offers a good idea of the producer's potential. At the head of the rankings we find the same two wines that made it into the last edition's finals. It's an encouraging and gratifying sign of continuity. Their splendid 2016 Collio Bianco Giulio Locatelli Riserva earns a Tre Bicchieri for the second year in a row and makes a case for itself as their flagship wine.

| | |
|---|---|
| ○ Collio Bianco Giulio Locatelli Ris. '16 | 🍷🍷🍷 4* |
| ○ FCO Chardonnay Spìule Giulio Locatelli Ris. '16 | 🍷🍷 4 |
| ○ Collio Pinot Grigio '17 | 🍷🍷 3 |
| ○ FCO Friulano '17 | 🍷🍷 3 |
| ● FCO Merlot Ravost Giulio Locatelli Ris. '15 | 🍷🍷 4 |
| ● FCO Pignolo Giulio Locatelli Ris. '13 | 🍷🍷 5 |
| ● FCO Refosco P. R. '15 | 🍷🍷 3 |
| ● Friuli Isonzo Pinot Nero Albertina '16 | 🍷🍷 4 |
| ○ Friuli Isonzo Friulano Villa Locatelli '17 | 🍷 2 |
| ○ Friuli Isonzo Pinot Bianco Villa Locatelli '17 | 🍷 2 |
| ○ Collio Bianco Giulio Locatelli Ris. '15 | 🍷🍷🍷 4* |
| ○ FCO Chardonnay Spìule '13 | 🍷🍷🍷 4* |
| ○ FCO Friulano '15 | 🍷🍷🍷 3* |

## Antonutti

FRAZ. COLLOREDO DI PRATO
VIA D'ANTONI, 21
33037 PASIAN DI PRATO [UD]
TEL. +39 0432662001
www.antonuttivini.it

**CELLAR SALES**
**PRE-BOOKED VISITS**
**ANNUAL PRODUCTION** 780,000 bottles
**HECTARES UNDER VINE** 51.00
**SUSTAINABLE WINERY**

In 1921, Ignazio Antonutti founded his winery in Colloredo di Prato. Today the producer is managed by Adriana, her husband Lino and their children, Caterina and Nicola. It's a close-knit group, tied to tradition but open to innovation. The union of the two families has led to a notable increase in production, with their Barbeano vineyards (in Spilimbergo) aiding the winery's reputation as one of the region's most interesting. Both estates are situated on middle-Friuli's lean, stony terrain, an area that's long been considered ideal for vine growing. Their varied selection offers a wide range of choice. Among their reds, their 2015 Ròs di Murì stands out for its vigorous palate, with potent but smooth tannins. Their 2017 Traminer Aromatico delights the nose with a mix of flowers, tropical fruit and aromatic herbs. Their sparkling 2013 Ant Brut Metodo Classico excels for its fragrance and savoriness, while their 2015 Lindul leaves the palate imbued with sweet sensations.

| | |
|---|---|
| ○ Ant Brut M. Cl. '13 | 🍷🍷 5 |
| ○ Friuli Grave Traminer Aromatico '17 | 🍷🍷 3 |
| ○ Lindul '15 | 🍷🍷 6 |
| ● Ros di Murì '15 | 🍷🍷 5 |
| ● Friuli Grave Cabernet Franc '16 | 🍷 3 |
| ○ Friuli Grave Friulano '17 | 🍷 3 |
| ○ Friuli Grave Pinot Grigio Ramato '17 | 🍷 3 |
| ● Poppone '15 | 🍷 5 |
| ○ Ant Brut M. Cl. '12 | 🍷🍷 5 |
| ○ Friuli Grave Friulano '16 | 🍷🍷 3 |
| ○ Friuli Grave Pinot Grigio Ramato '16 | 🍷🍷 3 |
| ● Ros di Murì '14 | 🍷🍷 5 |

# Ascevi - Luwa

LOC. UCLANZI, 24
34070 SAN FLORIANO DEL COLLIO [GO]
TEL. +39 0481884140
www.asceviluwa.it

**CELLAR SALES**
**PRE-BOOKED VISITS**
**ANNUAL PRODUCTION** 200,000 bottles
**HECTARES UNDER VINE** 30.00

San Floriano del Collio is situated just by
the Slovenian border in a magnificent
landscape of gentle hills amidst cherry and
acacia orchards. In 1972 it was here that
Mariano Pintar planted his first small
vineyard, in Asci, which inspired the name
'Ascevi'. Over time Mariano has been
joined by his children Walter and Luana,
and the vineyards have grown to 30
hectares spread throughout Collio and the
Friuli Isonzo appellation. The two first letters
of their name forms the brand name
('LuWa'), though it also calls up the Italian
word for 'grape' ('l'uva'). Their selection
includes primarily white wines made
according to traditional methods, though
with modern equipment. In order to
maintain the freshness and aromatic
attributes of their wines, vinification and
maturation are carried out exclusively in
steel vats. Their 2017 Chardonnay Rupis,
2017 Ribolla Gialla and 2017 Sauvignon
Ronco dei Sassi all exhibit their own clear
varietal characters, but they have one thing
in common: creaminess.

| | |
|---|---|
| ○ Collio Chardonnay Rupis '17 | 🍷🍷 4 |
| ○ Collio Sauvignon Ronco dei Sassi '17 | 🍷🍷 3 |
| ○ Ribolla Gialla '17 | 🍷🍷 4 |
| ○ Collio Pinot Grigio Grappoli '17 | 🍷 4 |
| ○ Friuli Isonzo Friulano '17 | 🍷 2 |
| ○ Collio Sauvignon Ronco dei Sassi '11 | 🍷🍷 3 |
| ○ Ribolla Gialla Ronco de Vigna Veci '10 | 🍷🍷 3 |
| ○ Collio Pinot Grigio Grappoli '11 | 🍷 2 |

# Bastianich

LOC. GAGLIANO
VIA DARNAZZACCO, 44/2
33043 CIVIDALE DEL FRIULI [UD]
TEL. +39 0432700943
www.bastianich.com

**CELLAR SALES**
**PRE-BOOKED VISITS**
**ACCOMMODATION AND RESTAURANT SERVICE**
**ANNUAL PRODUCTION** 270,000 bottles
**HECTARES UNDER VINE** 35.00

The Bastianich brand is one of Italy's wine
and food ambassadors to the world. In
1997, after his success in the restaurant
business, Joe decided to go back to his
family roots, taking over Premariacco and
an estate on the Buttrio hills. In 2006 he
completed his investment with the
purchase of another estate and cellar in
Gagliano, Cividale del Friuli, where his
winery is currently headquartered. Today
his selection's excellence is upheld by
renowned winemaker Emilio Del Medico,
who also has the support of Maurizio
Castelli. Their 2015 Plus is made with Tocai
Friulano cultivated on a vineyard that goes
back more than 60 years. A part of the
grapes are dried and then it's vinified in
steel for 16 months, 8 of which are on the
lees. It's a rich wine that emanates
fragrances of ripe tropical fruit, crème
anglaise, sweet spices and marzipan, while
in the mouth it's plush and caressing.

| | |
|---|---|
| ○ Plus '15 | 🍷🍷 6 |
| ● Calabrone '13 | 🍷🍷 8 |
| ○ FCO Friulano '17 | 🍷🍷 3 |
| ○ FCO Pinot Grigio '17 | 🍷🍷 3 |
| ○ FCO Ribolla Gialla '17 | 🍷🍷 3 |
| ○ FCO Sauvignon '17 | 🍷🍷 3 |
| ● Vespa Rosso '14 | 🍷🍷 5 |
| ○ FCO Friulano '16 | 🍷🍷 3 |
| ○ FCO Pinot Grigio '16 | 🍷🍷 3 |
| ○ FCO Sauvignon '16 | 🍷🍷 3* |

# Borgo delle Oche

VIA BORGO ALPI, 5
33098 VALVASONE ARZENE [PN]
TEL. +39 0434840640
www.borgodelleoche.it

CELLAR SALES
PRE-BOOKED VISITS
ACCOMMODATION
ANNUAL PRODUCTION 35,000 bottles
HECTARES UNDER VINE 7.00
SUSTAINABLE WINERY

Borgo delle Oche, officially founded in
2004, got its name from the small village
that hosts its estate in the splendid
medieval district of Valvasone Arzene
(province of Pordenone). It belongs to Luisa
Menini, the latest in a long line of vine
growers, who works in perfect tandem with
her husband, Nicola Pittini (she in the field
and he in the cellar). They've adopted an
approach to viticulture centered on low
yields and aimed at highlighting the
territorial potential of Grave Friulane, as
well as the unique characteristics of each
cultivar. Among their 2017s, their Friulano
and Pinot Grigio stood out, both proving
highly fragrant wines characterized by
notes of ripe fruit and honey, and both with
excellent nose-palate symmetry. Their
2016 Malvasia, a lovely gold colored wine,
offers up vibrant aromas, enriched by
whiffs of sage and wood resin. Their
2014 Terra & Cielo Extra Brut proves to
be at the top of its game.

| | |
|---|---|
| ○ Friuli Friulano '17 | ♥♥ 2* |
| ○ Friuli Pinot Grigio '17 | ♥♥ 2* |
| ○ Malvasia '16 | ♥♥ 2* |
| ● Merlot '15 | ♥♥ 2* |
| ● Svual Rosso '12 | ♥♥ 4 |
| ○ Terra e Cielo Extra Brut '14 | ♥♥ 5 |
| ● Refosco P. R. '14 | ♥ 3 |
| ○ Traminer Aromatico '17 | ♥ 2 |
| ○ Friuli Friulano '16 | ♀♀ 2* |
| ○ Malvasia '15 | ♀♀ 2* |
| ○ Pinot Grigio '16 | ♀♀ 2* |
| ○ Traminer Passito Alba '15 | ♀♀ 5 |

# ★Borgo San Daniele

VIA SAN DANIELE, 28
34071 CORMÒNS [GO]
TEL. +39 048160552
www.borgosandaniele.it

CELLAR SALES
PRE-BOOKED VISITS
ACCOMMODATION
ANNUAL PRODUCTION 60,000 bottles
HECTARES UNDER VINE 19.00
VITICULTURE METHOD Certified Organic
SUSTAINABLE WINERY

Mauro and Alessandra Mauri are siblings
of rare sensibility and enviable culture.
In 1990, while still very young, they
inherited from their grandfather a group
of vineyards. Showing great initiative,
they decided to manage them themselves.
It was a courageous decision that
immediately paid off. The few wines that
make up their selection fully express the
territory's potential. Their blends go by
the name Arbis, so as to remind the public
that grass is allowed to grow in their
vineyards. It's a choice designed to
mitigate the strength of the vines and the
negative effects of monoculture. For some
years now, their Arbis Res has been a
monovarietal Pignolo. It's a potent wine
that features a commendable mix of
balsamic and spicy aromas and a
pervasive palate with a gutsy tannic
weave. Their 2016 Arbis Blanc, a blend of
Sauvignon, Chardonnay, Pinot Bianco and
Friulano, distinguishes itself for its aromas
and linearity, while their 2016 Malvasia
offers up pleasant, fruity notes with whiffs
of rosemary.

| | |
|---|---|
| ● Friuli Isonzo Pignolo Arbis Ròs '13 | ♥♥ 5 |
| ○ Arbis Blanc '16 | ♥♥ 5 |
| ○ Friuli Isonzo Friulano '16 | ♥♥ 4 |
| ○ Friuli Isonzo Malvasia '16 | ♥♥ 4 |
| ○ Friuli Isonzo Pinot Grigio '16 | ♥♥ 4 |
| ○ Arbis Blanc '10 | ♀♀♀ 4* |
| ○ Arbis Blanc '15 | ♀♀ 5 |
| ○ Friuli Isonzo Friulano '15 | ♀♀ 4 |
| ○ Friuli Isonzo Malvasia '15 | ♀♀ 4 |
| ○ Friuli Isonzo Pinot Grigio '15 | ♀♀ 4 |

## Borgo Savaian

via Savaian, 36
34071 Cormòns [GO]
Tel. +39 048160725
stefanobastiani@libero.it

CELLAR SALES
PRE-BOOKED VISITS
ANNUAL PRODUCTION 100,000 bottles
HECTARES UNDER VINE 18.00

In 2001, Stefano Bastiani, along with his sister Rosanna, took over their father's winery, thus beginning a path that would see their enological studies and experience in the field put to use. It's an old story, but always current. With every new generation a family of farmworkers finds new life, energy and enthusiasm. Stefano is proving that he knows how to bring out the best of Collio Goriziano's extraordinary potential, achieving results that are getting people's attention (to say the least). This holds true for their vineyards in the Friuli Isonzo appellation as well. Their 2017 Friulano highlights the grapes varietal qualities, both on the nose and in the mouth, and distinguishes itself for a highly pleasant, slightly bitter note at the end. Their 2017 Malvasia is redolent of ripe fruit, custard and malaga liquor, and enjoys perfect balance in the mouth. The plushness of their 2017 Pinot Grigio was highly appreciated, as was the fragrance of their 2017 Ribolla Gialla and 2017 Sauvignon.

| | |
|---|---|
| ○ Collio Friulano '17 | 🍷🍷 3 |
| ○ Collio Pinot Grigio '17 | 🍷🍷 3 |
| ○ Collio Ribolla Gialla '17 | 🍷🍷 3 |
| ○ Friuli Isonzo Malvasia '17 | 🍷🍷 3 |
| ○ Friuli Isonzo Sauvignon '17 | 🍷🍷 3 |
| ○ Friuli Isonzo Traminer Aromatico '17 | 🍷 3 |
| ○ Collio Friulano '16 | 🍸🍸 3 |
| ○ Collio Friulano '15 | 🍸🍸 3* |
| ○ Collio Pinot Grigio '16 | 🍸🍸 3 |
| ○ Collio Pinot Grigio '15 | 🍸🍸 3 |
| ○ Collio Sauvignon '16 | 🍸🍸 3* |
| ● Friuli Isonzo Merlot '15 | 🍸🍸 3 |

## Cav. Emiro Bortolusso

via Oltregorgo, 10
33050 Carlino [UD]
Tel. +39 043167596
www.bortolusso.it

CELLAR SALES
PRE-BOOKED VISITS
ACCOMMODATION
ANNUAL PRODUCTION 120,000 bottles
HECTARES UNDER VINE 40.00

In 1975, Emiro Bortolusso, a major supporter of the Friuli Annia appellation, founded the producer now managed by his children, Sergio and Clara. Situated in Carlino, in an area that faces the Adriatic just outside the green oasis of Marano Lagunare, it's a flourishing operation that's in continued expansion. Pedoclimate conditions have a strong influence on their entire range of wines, which are universally recognized for their richness of flavor, consistence in quality terms, and prices that are affordable to say the least. In recent editions of Italian Wines we pointed out how every year, with enviable regularity, all their wines are unanimously praised. They enjoy exemplary suppleness while preserving each wine's distinct varietal characteristics. Their 2017 Friulano excels for fragrance and coherence, their 2017 Malvasia for elegance and creaminess, their 2017 Pinot Grigio for its simplicity and pleasantness.

| | |
|---|---|
| ○ Friuli Annia Friulano '17 | 🍷🍷 2* |
| ○ Friuli Annia Pinot Grigio '17 | 🍷🍷 2* |
| ○ Malvasia '17 | 🍷🍷 2* |
| ○ Sauvignon '17 | 🍷🍷 2* |
| ○ Chardonnay '17 | 🍷 2 |
| ○ Traminer Aromatico '17 | 🍷 2 |
| ○ Chardonnay '16 | 🍸🍸 2* |
| ○ Malvasia '16 | 🍸🍸 2* |
| ○ Pinot Grigio '16 | 🍸🍸 2* |
| ○ Sauvignon '16 | 🍸🍸 2* |

# Branko

LOC. ZEGLA, 20
34071 CORMÒNS [GO]
TEL. +39 0481639826
www.brankowines.com

CELLAR SALES
PRE-BOOKED VISITS
ANNUAL PRODUCTION 45,000 bottles
HECTARES UNDER VINE 9.00

Zegla di Cormòns, a district on the border with Slovenia, hosts a number of family-run wineries. Among these is Branko, a small producer that Igor Erzetic has transformed into a veritable benchmark for those who appreciate Collio's white wines. It bears the name of his father, who deserves credit for the foresight he had in identifying these splendid hills' potential. It's an area protected by the Alps but exposed to the breeze that comes in off the nearby Adriatic. Their modern main facility is surrounded by the area's characteristic calcareous terrain, which give rise to some of their vineyards. Their 2017 Chardonnay repeated the stellar performance put in last year and landed in our finals. Even if it doesn't get a gold, it received significant praise for its elegance and creaminess on the palate. Their 2017 Capo Branko, made primarily with Malvasia Istriana accompanied by Tocai Friulano and a touch of Sauvignon, proved to be a sound, pleasant representative of the winery's brand.

| | |
|---|---|
| ○ Collio Chardonnay '17 | ♟♟ 4 |
| ○ Capo Branko '17 | ♟♟ 4 |
| ○ Collio Friulano '17 | ♟♟ 4 |
| ○ Collio Pinot Grigio '17 | ♟♟ 4 |
| ● Red Branko '15 | ♟♟ 4 |
| ○ Collio Pinot Grigio '14 | ♟♟♟ 4* |
| ○ Collio Chardonnay '16 | ♟♟ 4 |
| ○ Collio Friulano '16 | ♟♟ 4 |
| ○ Collio Pinot Grigio '16 | ♟♟ 4 |
| ○ Collio Pinot Grigio '15 | ♟♟ 4 |
| ○ Collio Sauvignon '16 | ♟♟ 4 |
| ● Red Branko '14 | ♟♟ 4 |

# Livio e Claudio Buiatti

VIA LIPPE, 25
33042 BUTTRIO [UD]
TEL. +39 0432674317
www.buiattivini.it

CELLAR SALES
PRE-BOOKED VISITS
ANNUAL PRODUCTION 35,000 bottles
HECTARES UNDER VINE 8.00

The Buiatti family can boast more than a century of vine growing experience on the Buttrio hills, a history that has allowed them to realize the potential of these gentle slopes as few others have. When Livio passed on the torch to Claudio, the latter began a gradual process of modernizing the estate, making the vineyards denser and pruning so as to limit production. His minimally invasive approach had the desired effect, endowing their entire selection with an absolute quality that's held up over time. Now, along with his son Matteo, their setting their sights on the heights of regional excellence. Once again one of their wines made it into our finals. It's their 2017 Friulano, a wine that brings together vibrant, elegant, penetrating aromas and a pleasant palate. Their 2017 Pinot Grigio also distinguished itself for its fragrance and crispness, both on the nose and in the mouth, while their 2017 Sauvignon proves particularly varietal. Their reds also earned praise.

| | |
|---|---|
| ○ FCO Friulano '17 | ♟♟ 3* |
| ● FCO Merlot '15 | ♟♟ 3 |
| ○ FCO Pinot Grigio '17 | ♟♟ 3 |
| ● FCO Refosco P. R. '15 | ♟♟ 3 |
| ○ FCO Sauvignon '17 | ♟♟ 3 |
| ○ FCO Malvasia '17 | ♟ 3 |
| ○ FCO Friulano '16 | ♟♟ 3 |
| ○ FCO Malvasia '15 | ♟♟ 3 |
| ● FCO Merlot '13 | ♟♟ 3 |
| ○ FCO Pinot Grigio '16 | ♟♟ 3 |
| ○ FCO Sauvignon '16 | ♟♟ 3* |
| ○ FCO Sauvignon '15 | ♟♟ 3 |
| ○ FCO Malvasia '16 | ♟ 3 |

## La Buse dal Lôf

VIA RONCHI, 90
33040 PREPOTTO [UD]
TEL. +39 0432701523
www.labusedallof.com

CELLAR SALES
PRE-BOOKED VISITS
ANNUAL PRODUCTION 100,000 bottles
HECTARES UNDER VINE 25.00

La Buse dal Lôf is a lovely Prepotto winery founded in 1972 by Giuseppe Pavan and today managed by his son Michele. It's oriented around respect for regional traditions, both in terms of cultivation and winemaking, and aims to highlight the varietal attributes of each cultivar. Their vineyards span 25 hectares, a sizable estate in these parts, situated on terrain whose roots go back to the Eocene. The primarily marl and sandstone soil here is protected by the Julian Alps, and slopes gradually towards the lowlands. Their 2015 Schioppettino di Prepotto is the district's most representative wine, and the fact that it's leading their selection indicates the particular care taken for its production. It offers up aromas of forest undergrowth, quinine, dark spices and cooked prunes. It features nice freshness and poised tannins. Their rest of their selection also did well, with their 2016 Chardonnay, a particularly plush and savory wine, standing out.

| | | |
|---|---|---|
| ○ FCO Chardonnay '16 | ♟♟ 3 | |
| ● FCO Merlot '16 | ♟♟ 3 | |
| ● FCO Schioppettino di Prepotto '15 | ♟♟ 4 | |
| ○ FCO Friulano '17 | ♟ 3 | |
| ○ FCO Sauvignon '17 | ♟ 3 | |
| ● Giardo Rosso '13 | ♟ 3 | |
| ○ FCO Friulano '15 | ♟♟ 3 | |
| ○ FCO Pinot Bianco In Bocca al Lupo '15 | ♟♟ 3 | |
| ● FCO Refosco P. R. '15 | ♟♟ 3 | |
| ○ FCO Ribolla Gialla '16 | ♟♟ 3 | |
| ○ FCO Sauvignon '15 | ♟♟ 3 | |
| ● FCO Schioppettino di Prepotto '13 | ♟♟ 4 | |

## Valentino Butussi

VIA PRÀ DI CORTE, 1
33040 CORNO DI ROSAZZO [UD]
TEL. +39 0432759194
www.butussi.it

CELLAR SALES
PRE-BOOKED VISITS
ACCOMMODATION
ANNUAL PRODUCTION 120,000 bottles
HECTARES UNDER VINE 18.00
VITICULTURE METHOD Certified Organic
SUSTAINABLE WINERY

It was 1910 when Valentino Butussi kick-started the project later developed by his son Angelo, an effort that allowed Corno di Rosazzo to establish itself as among the most region's most praised producers. Tobia, Filippo, Mattia and Erika represent the latest generation to lead a high-level family-run winery founded on the principles of maintaining their agricultural roots, and the importance of teamwork and collectivity. Converting their vineyards to organic was the logical consequence of their desire to respect the environment and make wholesome wines. Their entire selection put in an excellent performance, thus confirming their well-established quality. Some of their did particularly well, approaching excellence, with their 2017 Chardonnay leading the way thanks to its elegance and fragrance but especially for its balanced palate. Their entire selection shines for its excellent value for the money.

| | | |
|---|---|---|
| ○ FCO Chardonnay '17 | ♟♟ | 2* |
| ○ COF Picolit '11 | ♟♟ | 6 |
| ○ FCO Bianco di Corte '16 | ♟♟ | 3 |
| ● FCO Cabernet Sauvignon '16 | ♟♟ | 3 |
| ● FCO Merlot '16 | ♟♟ | 3 |
| ○ FCO Pinot Grigio '17 | ♟♟ | 2* |
| ○ FCO Pinot Grigio Et. Storica '14 | ♟♟ | 5 |
| ○ Ribolla Gialla Brut | ♟♟ | 5 |
| ○ FCO Friulano '17 | ♟ | 2 |
| ● FCO Refosco P. R. '16 | ♟ | 3 |
| ○ FCO Ribolla Gialla '17 | ♟ | 2 |
| ● FCO Rosso di Corte '12 | ♟ | 4 |
| ○ FCO Verduzzo Friulano '15 | ♟ | 2 |
| ○ FCO Chardonnay '16 | ♟♟ | 2* |
| ○ FCO Friulano '16 | ♟♟ | 2* |
| ○ FCO Friulano '16 | ♟♟ | 2* |
| ○ FCO Sauvignon '16 | ♟♟ | 2* |

## Maurizio Buzzinelli

LOC. PRADIS, 20
34071 CORMÒNS [GO]
TEL. +39 048160902
www.buzzinelli.it

CELLAR SALES
PRE-BOOKED VISITS
ACCOMMODATION
ANNUAL PRODUCTION 120,000 bottles
HECTARES UNDER VINE 35.00

Maurizio Buzzinelli is the third generation of
a family to have dedicated itself to
viticulture since at least as far back as
1937. It was then that his grandfather Luigi
decided to establish himself on the Pradis
hills, in Cormòns, attracted by the natural
beauty of the landscape but also driven by
a necessity for subsistence. Having
gradually abandoned general agriculture in
favor of specialized production, today the
producer dedicates great attention to the
grapes that have traditionally grown along
the Collio hills and Isonzo's flat terrain. The
high (and almost uniform) scores earned
during our tastings confirm the high quality
standard they've achieved and maintained
over time. Both their 2017 Friulano and
their 2017 Sauvignon distinguished
themselves for the complexity of their
aromas and the fragrant palates. Their
2017 Pinot and 2017 Traminer Aromatico
both proved excellent, especially for the
way they finish on the palate.

| | |
|---|---|
| ○ Collio Friulano '17 | ♟♟ 3 |
| ○ Collio Pinot Grigio '17 | ♟♟ 3 |
| ○ Collio Sauvignon '17 | ♟♟ 3 |
| ○ Collio Traminer Aromatico '17 | ♟♟ 3 |
| ○ Collio Malvasia '17 | ♟ 2 |
| ○ Collio Chardonnay '15 | ♟♟ 3 |
| ○ Collio Friulano '16 | ♟♟ 3* |
| ○ Collio Friulano '15 | ♟♟ 3 |
| ○ Collio Malvasia '16 | ♟♟ 2* |
| ○ Collio Ribolla Gialla '15 | ♟♟ 3 |
| ○ Collio Sauvignon '16 | ♟♟ 3 |
| ○ Collio Sauvignon '15 | ♟♟ 3 |

## Ca' Bolani

VIA CA' BOLANI, 2
33052 CERVIGNANO DEL FRIULI [UD]
TEL. +39 043132670
www.cabolani.it

CELLAR SALES
PRE-BOOKED VISITS
ANNUAL PRODUCTION 2,700,000 bottles
HECTARES UNDER VINE 550.00

Tenuta Cà Bolani is situated in the heart of
the Friuli Aquileia appellation and
comprises the Molin del Ponte vineyards
as well as Cà Vescovo. Once owned by the
count Bolani family, it was purchased in
1970 by the Zonins, who brought it back
to its former glory by renovating the main
facility and building a cellar equipped with
the latest technology. It's one of northern
Italy's largest estates, but high production
volumes, which are unusual in the region,
are accompanied by high quality
standards. The enological experience of
Marco Rabino is also as an important part
of their success. A truly excellent
performance was put in by their entire
selection, with points of excellence
achieved by their 2016 Sauvignon Aquilis,
which earned a place in our finals. The
nose delivers for the elegance and
incisiveness of its aromas, while freshness
and fragrances invigorate the palate with
citrus notes of rare pleasantness. Among
their 2017s, their highly fruity Pinot Grigio
proved gratifying on the palate.

| | |
|---|---|
| ○ Friuli Aquileia Sauvignon Aquilis '16 | ♟♟ 5 |
| ○ Friuli Aquileia Pinot Bianco Opimio '16 | ♟♟ 5 |
| ○ Friuli Aquileia Pinot Grigio '17 | ♟♟ 3 |
| ● Friuli Aquileia Refosco P. R. '16 | ♟♟ 3 |
| ● Friuli Aquileia Refosco P. R. Alturio '15 | ♟♟ 4 |
| ○ Friuli Aquileia Sauvignon '17 | ♟♟ 3 |
| ○ Friuli Aquileia Traminer Aromatico '17 | ♟♟ 3 |
| ○ Friuli Aquileia Friulano '17 | ♟ 3 |
| ○ Friuli Aquileia Pinot Bianco '17 | ♟ 3 |
| ○ Prosecco Brut | ♟ 3 |
| ○ Friuli Aquileia Pinot Bianco '09 | ♟♟♟ 2* |
| ○ Friuli Aquileia Pinot Bianco '16 | ♟♟ 4 |
| ○ Friuli Aquileia Pinot Bianco Opimio '15 | ♟♟ 6 |
| ○ Friuli Aquileia Pinot Grigio '16 | ♟♟ 4 |

## Ca' Tullio

VIA BELIGNA, 41
33051 AQUILEIA [UD]
TEL. +39 0431919700
www.catullio.it

CELLAR SALES
PRE-BOOKED VISITS
ANNUAL PRODUCTION 200,000 bottles
HECTARES UNDER VINE 100.00

In the well-known archeological zone of Aquieleia stands a large brick building built in the early 20th century and once used to dry tobacco. In 1994 it was purchased by Paolo Calligaris and transformed into a modern, efficient winery. Half of the estate's vineyards are situated here, while the rest extend along the Manzano hills, an area in the Friuli Colli Orientali appellation. The various subsoils and microclimates here distinguish the two areas of production, offering an exhaustive picture of the identity of each vineyard. It's natural that wines cultivated along the hills, both whites and reds, should demonstrate greater aromatic depth and complexity, but their 2017 Traminer Viola and 2017 Müller Thurgau also proved intriguing aromatically, as well as light but pleasant on the palate. Excellent scores across the board point up the winery's production choices, aimed at a constant improvement in quality.

| | | |
|---|---|---|
| ○ FCO Chardonnay '17 | 🍷🍷 | 2* |
| ○ FCO Friulano '17 | 🍷🍷 | 2* |
| ● FCO Pignolo '14 | 🍷🍷 | 3 |
| ○ FCO Pinot Grigio '17 | 🍷🍷 | 2* |
| ● FCO Schioppettino '15 | 🍷🍷 | 3 |
| ○ FCO Ribolla Gialla '17 | 🍷 | 3 |
| ○ FCO Sauvignon '17 | 🍷 | 2 |
| ○ Friuli Aquileia Müller Thurgau '17 | 🍷 | 2 |
| ○ Friuli Aquileia Traminer Viola '17 | 🍷 | 2 |
| ○ Prosecco Extra Dry | 🍷 | 2 |
| ○ FCO Chardonnay '16 | 🍷🍷 | 2* |
| ● FCO Merlot '16 | 🍷🍷 | 2* |
| ○ FCO Pinot Grigio '16 | 🍷🍷 | 2* |

## Cadibon

LOC. CASALI GALLO, 1
33040 CORNO DI ROSAZZO [UD]
TEL. +39 04327593163398752013
www.cadibon.com

CELLAR SALES
PRE-BOOKED VISITS
ACCOMMODATION
ANNUAL PRODUCTION 55,000 bottles
HECTARES UNDER VINE 13.00
VITICULTURE METHOD Certified Organic

In local dialect Cadibon means 'Here at the Bon's house'. It's an open invitation to visit the winery founded in 1997 by Gianni and led today with skill and enthusiasm by his children Luca and Francesca. Their organically managed vineyards span various areas throughout the region. The largest concentration is in Colli Orientali del Friuli, though they have plots in Grave and others on the Collio hills. This diverse estate is supported by an original approach in the cellar. Spontaneous fermentation is among the techniques used to give rise to a selection of wines distinct for their freshness and drinkability. The unanimous consensus from our entire selection earned confirms Luca's approach. Once again their 2017 Sauvignon was presented in two versions: one traditional and highly varietal, the other (called Lavoron) features intriguing and unusual nuances of alchermes liquor and rosemary. But it delivers primarily for its originality and for its fragrant, pleasant palate.

| | | |
|---|---|---|
| ○ Collio Chardonnay '17 | 🍷🍷 | 3 |
| ○ Collio Pinot Grigio '17 | 🍷🍷 | 3 |
| ○ Collio Sauvignon '17 | 🍷🍷 | 3 |
| ○ Collio Sauvignon Lavoron '17 | 🍷🍷 | 3 |
| ● Epoca '16 | 🍷🍷 | 5 |
| ● FCO Merlot '16 | 🍷🍷 | 3 |
| ● FCO Refosco P. R. '16 | 🍷🍷 | 3 |
| ○ FCO Ribolla Gialla '17 | 🍷🍷 | 3 |
| ○ Friuli Bianco Ronco del Nonno '17 | 🍷 | 3 |
| ○ Verduzzo Friulano '16 | 🍷 | 3 |
| ○ Collio Pinot Grigio '16 | 🍷🍷 | 3 |
| ○ Collio Sauvignon '16 | 🍷🍷 | 3* |
| ○ Collio Sauvignon Lavoron '16 | 🍷🍷 | 3 |
| ○ FCO Friulano Bontaj '16 | 🍷🍷 | 3 |
| ○ Friuli Bianco Ronco del Nonno '16 | 🍷🍷 | 3 |

# Canus

LOC. CASALI GALLO
VIA GRAMOGLIANO, 21
33040 CORNO DI ROSAZZO [UD]
TEL. +39 0432759427
www.canus.it

CELLAR SALES
PRE-BOOKED VISITS
ANNUAL PRODUCTION 55,000 bottles
HECTARES UNDER VINE 11.00

Since 2015 Ottorino Casonato ('Otto' to his friends) has been Canus's new owner. The winery, whose origins go a long way back, gets its name from a Latin term that reminds us of the wisdom and benefits of aging. To experience the estate is to experience a return to the family's agricultural roots in an 'exciting area that's rich in potential' (to use his words). Otto's well-experienced and recognized staff attends to a sizable estate situated around Casali Gallo di Corno di Rosazzo. Their plots are favored by their excellent position and the area's enviable microclimate. The last edition saw the debut of this lovely producer in Italian Wines, confirming its auspicious beginnings. Evidently our instinct was right, as this year saw their entire selection lauded, with their 2016 Chardonnay standing out and earning a well-deserved place in our finals.

| | |
|---|---|
| ○ FCO Chardonnay '16 | ♥♥ 4 |
| ○ FCO Bianco Gramogliano '16 | ♥♥ 4 |
| ● FCO Merlot '12 | ♥♥ 5 |
| ● FCO Pignolo '11 | ♥♥ 6 |
| ○ FCO Pinot Grigio '16 | ♥♥ 4 |
| ● FCO Refosco P. R. '12 | ♥ 5 |
| ○ FCO Ribolla Gialla '16 | ♥ 4 |
| ○ COF Pinot Grigio '15 | ♀♀ 3 |
| ○ FCO Bianco Gramogliano '15 | ♀♀ 4 |
| ○ FCO Friulano '15 | ♀♀ 3 |
| ○ FCO Ribolla Gialla '15 | ♀♀ 3 |

# Fernanda Cappello

S.DA DI SEQUALS, 15
33090 SEQUALS [PN]
TEL. +39 042793291
www.fernandacappello.it

CELLAR SALES
PRE-BOOKED VISITS
RESTAURANT SERVICE
ANNUAL PRODUCTION 100,000 bottles
HECTARES UNDER VINE 126.00
SUSTAINABLE WINERY

The Cappello family's winery has one of the largest estates in western Friuli, an area characterized by lean, stony soil formed by calcareous-dolomitic alluvial sediment that's perfect for viticulture. Since 1988 the winery has been managed by Fernanda, whose father purchased it in the late 60s. She's the one who deserves credit for having begun the modernization process that's allowed the producer to attract so much attention. It's also thanks to a first-rate staff that avails itself of winemaker Fabio Coser's precious guidance. The vast selection of wines presented allowed us to get a nice sense of the winery's overall production potential. We saw how each cultivar is treated with equal dignity, maintaining their individual varietal qualities. Their wines are lean, modern and easy to drink, though they also exhibit marked fragrance and crispiness. It's a selection that's excellent value for the money.

| | |
|---|---|
| ● Friuli Grave Cabernet Franc '16 | ♥♥ 2* |
| ● Friuli Grave Cabernet Sauvignon '15 | ♥♥ 2* |
| ○ Friuli Grave Pinot Grigio '17 | ♥♥ 2* |
| ○ Friuli Grave Sauvignon '17 | ♥♥ 2* |
| ○ Ribolla Gialla '17 | ♥♥ 2* |
| ○ Friuli Grave Chardonnay '17 | ♥ 2 |
| ○ Friuli Grave Friulano '17 | ♥ 2 |
| ● Friuli Grave Refosco P. R. '15 | ♥ 2 |
| ○ Friuli Grave Traminer Aromatico '17 | ♥ 2 |
| ○ Prosecco Extra Dry | ♥ 2 |
| ○ Ribolla Gialla Brut | ♥ 2 |
| ○ Friuli Grave Chardonnay '16 | ♀♀ 2* |
| ○ Friuli Grave Pinot Grigio '16 | ♀♀ 2* |
| ○ Friuli Grave Ribolla Gialla '16 | ♀♀ 2* |

# Il Carpino

LOC. SOVENZA, 14A
34070 SAN FLORIANO DEL COLLIO [GO]
TEL. +39 0481884097
www.ilcarpino.com

**CELLAR SALES**
**PRE-BOOKED VISITS**
**ANNUAL PRODUCTION** 70,000 bottles
**HECTARES UNDER VINE** 16.00

It was 1987 when Anna and Franco Sasol decided to join forces and jump back into agriculture, reclaiming their rural roots and founding Carpino. To this day they are leading this splendid winery, accompanied by their children Naike and Manuel. The family management style has allowed them to oversee every stage of production, starting with their vineyards in Sovenza, a district in San Floriano del Collio. Their premium wines are the result of slow maceration and time-honored techniques, while their Vigna Runc wines are crafted in steel. This year the wines from this last line weren't presented, so we tasted only the whites that undergo long maceration. They are all quite good, but two made it into our finals and one, their 2015 Malvasia, earned Tre Bicchieri. It's a wine that intrigues the nose with its hints of ripe tropical fruit and creme caramel. Its long and constant palate unfolds vividly.

| | |
|---|---|
| ○ Malvasia '15 | ♟♟♟ 5 |
| ○ Exordium '15 | ♟♟ 5 |
| ○ Sauvignon '15 | ♟♟ 4 |
| ○ Vis Uvae '15 | ♟♟ 5 |
| ○ Collio Bianco V. Runc '10 | ♟♟♟ 2* |
| ○ Collio Malvasia V. Runc '11 | ♟♟♟ 3* |
| ○ Malvasia '11 | ♟♟♟ 5 |
| ● Rubrum '99 | ♟♟♟ 3* |
| ○ Chardonnay '12 | ♟♟ 5 |
| ○ Collio Chardonnay V. Runc '15 | ♟♟ 3 |
| ○ Collio Malvasia V. Runc '15 | ♟♟ 3 |
| ○ Collio Malvasia V. Runc '14 | ♟♟ 3* |
| ○ Exordium '13 | ♟♟ 5 |
| ○ Exordium '12 | ♟♟ 5 |
| ○ Malvasia '12 | ♟♟ 5 |
| ● Rubrum Carpino '07 | ♟♟ 8 |
| ○ Vis Uvae '13 | ♟♟ 5 |

# Castello di Buttrio

VIA DEL POZZO, 5
33042 BUTTRIO [UD]
TEL. +39 0432673015
www.castellodibuttrio.it

**CELLAR SALES**
**PRE-BOOKED VISITS**
**ACCOMMODATION AND RESTAURANT SERVICE**
**ANNUAL PRODUCTION** 60,000 bottles
**HECTARES UNDER VINE** 25.00

The Buttrio hills are the first to overlook Friuli Colli Orientali's splendid natural amphitheater. These are the nearest slopes to the sea and loom over large plains. Here your gaze is lost in the infinite expanse of space, so it's no coincidence that a castle was once built here. It's a structure that today serves as the base for Alessandra Felluga's winery, a producer that has managed to get the attention of the last decade's best palates. Their success is thanks in part to a stylistic recalibration that coincided with the decision to collaborate with Trento winemaker Harmann Donà. This year their selection's best wine turns out to be a red: their 2013 Merlot Uve Carate Riserva, which landed a well-deserved place in our finals. On the nose it offers up aromas of sliced morello cherries, coffee beans and liquorice with balsamic and minty nuances. On the palate it proves plush and creamy, with potent but well-calibrated tannins. Their 2016 Mon Blanc and 2014 Mon Rouge, both skillful blends, are also excellent.

| | |
|---|---|
| ● FCO Merlot Uve Carate Ris. '13 | ♟♟ 3* |
| ○ FCO Bianco Mon Blanc '16 | ♟♟ 3 |
| ○ FCO Ribolla Gialla '16 | ♟♟ 4 |
| ● FCO Rosso Mon Rouge '14 | ♟♟ 3 |
| ○ FCO Sauvignon '16 | ♟♟ 3 |
| ○ FCO Traminer Aromatico La Ruggine '14 | ♟ 5 |
| ○ FCO Bianco Mon Blanc '15 | ♟♟ 3 |
| ○ FCO Bianco Mon Blanc '14 | ♟♟ 3 |
| ○ FCO Bianco Torre Butria Ris. '13 | ♟♟ 5 |
| ○ FCO Friulano '15 | ♟♟ 4 |
| ○ FCO Sauvignon '15 | ♟♟ 3 |

# FRIULI VENEZIA GIULIA

## Castello di Spessa

VIA SPESSA, 1
34070 CAPRIVA DEL FRIULI [GO]
TEL. +39 048160445
www.castellodispessa.it

CELLAR SALES
PRE-BOOKED VISITS
ACCOMMODATION AND RESTAURANT SERVICE
ANNUAL PRODUCTION 300,000 bottles
HECTARES UNDER VINE 83.00

Castello di Spessa, an estate whose history goes back almost a thousand years, rises up elegantly in the heart of Collio Goriziano. In 1987 its current owner, Loretto Pali, transformed it into the winery that it is today, reconverting the nearby vineyards and beginning a path that would in a short time allow the producer to achieve exceptional results. Pali is convinced of the territory's potential for the production of the three Pinots (Bianco, Grigio and Nero) and for some years he's been working to bring out further elegance and verve in his wines, thanks in part to the guidance of expert winemaker Enrico Paternoster. Once again their 2017 Pinot Bianco Santarosa earned the greatest praise and landed a place in our finals. Even if it didn't get a gold, it proved to be a pureblood in its category, winning appreciation for its aromatic elegance as well as its fragrance and poise on the palate, from beginning to end.

## Castello Sant'Anna

LOC. SPESSA
VIA SANT'ANNA, 9
33043 CIVIDALE DEL FRIULI [UD]
TEL. +39 0432716289
www.castellosantanna.it

CELLAR SALES
PRE-BOOKED VISITS
ANNUAL PRODUCTION 25,000 bottles
HECTARES UNDER VINE 7.00
VITICULTURE METHOD Certified Organic

Castello Sant'Anna, in Spessa di Cividale, was founded in 1966 by the Andrea Giaiotti's grandfather Giuseppe. Giuseppe had abandoned his work in industry to return to his agricultural roots. Today Andrea is leading this small winery, whose limited size allows each stage of production to be followed closely, from agronomy to enology. Over time the vineyards that surround the estate's historic manor have been patiently revived and reorganized, while a new underground cellar has proved perfect for maturing their wines, thanks to its natural humidity and constant temperature. In the last edition of Italian Wines no whites were proposed inasmuch as they still had to be bottled. This time we had the chance to taste and appreciate them. Lengthy aging in the bottle worked in their favor, so Andrea's choice proved to be the right one. Naturally their reds didn't disappoint while their sparkling Metodo Classico Afroso Brut represents their latest edition.

| | |
|---|---|
| ○ Collio Pinot Bianco Santarosa '17 | ♙♙ 3* |
| ○ Collio Friulano '17 | ♙♙ 3 |
| ● Collio Merlot Torriani '15 | ♙♙ 5 |
| ○ Collio Pinot Grigio Joy '17 | ♙♙ 4 |
| ● Collio Pinot Nero Casanova '15 | ♙♙ 5 |
| ○ Collio Ribolla Gialla '17 | ♙♙ 3 |
| ○ Collio Sauvignon Segrè '17 | ♙♙ 5 |
| ○ Collio Pinot Bianco '14 | ♙♙♙ 3* |
| ○ Collio Pinot Bianco '13 | ♙♙♙ 3* |
| ○ Collio Pinot Bianco '11 | ♙♙♙ 3* |
| ○ Collio Friulano '16 | ♙♙ 3 |
| ○ Collio Pinot Bianco '15 | ♙♙ 3* |
| ○ Collio Pinot Bianco Santarosa '16 | ♙♙ 3* |
| ○ Collio Pinot Grigio '16 | ♙♙ 3 |
| ○ Collio Sauvignon '16 | ♙♙ 3 |
| ○ Collio Sauvignon Segrè '15 | ♙♙ 5 |

| | |
|---|---|
| ○ Afroso Brut M. Cl. | ♙♙ 5 |
| ● FCO Cabernet Franc '16 | ♙♙ 4 |
| ○ FCO Friulano '16 | ♙♙ 3 |
| ● FCO Merlot '15 | ♙♙ 4 |
| ● FCO Merlot Ris. '13 | ♙♙ 4 |
| ○ FCO Pinot Grigio '16 | ♙♙ 3 |
| ○ FCO Ribolla Gialla '16 | ♙♙ 3 |
| ○ FCO Sauvignon '16 | ♙♙ 3 |
| ○ FCO Friulano '15 | ♙♙ 3 |
| ○ FCO Pinot Grigio '15 | ♙♙ 3* |
| ● FCO Refosco P. R. '13 | ♙♙ 4 |
| ○ FCO Sauvignon '15 | ♙♙ 3 |

# Castelvecchio

VIA CASTELNUOVO, 2
34078 SAGRADO [GO]
TEL. +39 048199742
www.castelvecchio.com

CELLAR SALES
PRE-BOOKED VISITS
ACCOMMODATION AND RESTAURANT SERVICE
ANNUAL PRODUCTION 140,000 bottles
HECTARES UNDER VINE 35.00
SUSTAINABLE WINERY

Castelvecchio, a winery owned by the
Terraneo family, is one of Carso Goriziano's
loveliest producers. The landscape of the
area fuses with the estate's noble, ancient
roots, still visible today in its renaissance
villa and a scenic park punctuated by
age-old cypresses and oaks. The terrain is
primarily rocky and rich in iron and
limestone, while its microclimate and
exposure to the sea breeze make for
healthy, ripe grapes. The precious
guidance of Gianni Menotti shouldn't be
overlooked either. For the third year in a
row their 2017 Malvasia Dileo landed in
our finals, affirming its status as the
producer's flagship wine. By now it's a
benchmark for the potential of this
splendid vineyard of native grapes and,
along with their 2017 Vitovska, it
represents en of Karst's crown jewel. Their
reds also proved to live up to the
performances put in over previous years.

# ★Eugenio Collavini

LOC. GRAMOGLIANO
VIA DELLA RIBOLLA GIALLA, 2
33040 CORNO DI ROSAZZO [UD]
TEL. +39 0432753222
www.collavini.it

CELLAR SALES
PRE-BOOKED VISITS
RESTAURANT SERVICE
ANNUAL PRODUCTION 1,200,000 bottles
HECTARES UNDER VINE 140.00
SUSTAINABLE WINERY

The Collavini family's winery is deeply
rooted in Friuli, with more than a century of
history behind it and a brand that pays
homage to the name of its founder. Since
the 1970s Manlio has been at the helm, a
man universally recognized as one of the
region's modern pioneers when it comes to
wine-growing. He was one of the first to
ferment Pinot Grigio without the skins and
to use Ribolla Gialla in a sparkling wine.
Over time, he gradually and notably
enlarged the estate; with the help of his
esteemed staff, he integrated Collavini's
private vineyards with those managed by
independent growers. Their 2017 Collio
Bianco Broy took back the scepter it had
handed over for a year to their Ribolla Gialla
Brut, earning Tre Bicchieri and confirming
its place at the top of their selection. It's
half Tocai Friulano (their local cultivar par
excellence), with Chardonnay and
Sauvignon making up the other half. You'd
think that it's a classic mix, but the
extraordinary result is a work of art.

| | | |
|---|---|---|
| ○ Carso Malvasia Dileo '17 | ♙♙ 4 |
| ● Carso Cabernet Franc '15 | ♙♙ 3 |
| ● Carso Cabernet Sauvignon '15 | ♙♙ 3 |
| ○ Carso Malvasia '17 | ♙♙ 3 |
| ○ Carso Pinot Grigio '17 | ♙♙ 3 |
| ● Carso Refosco P. R. '15 | ♙♙ 3 |
| ○ Carso Traminer Aromatico '17 | ♙♙ 3 |
| ○ Carso Vitovska '17 | ♙♙ 3 |
| ○ Carso Sauvignon '17 | ♙ 3 |
| ● Carso Terrano '16 | ♙ 3 |
| ○ Carso Malvasia Dileo '15 | ♟♟♟ 4* |
| ○ Carso Malvasia '16 | ♟♟ 3 |
| ○ Carso Malvasia Dileo '16 | ♟♟ 4 |
| ○ Carso Pinot Grigio '16 | ♟♟ 3 |
| ○ Carso Sauvignon '16 | ♟♟ 3 |
| ○ Carso Vitovska '16 | ♟♟ 3 |

| | | |
|---|---|---|
| ○ Collio Bianco Broy '17 | ♙♙♙ 6 |
| ○ Ribolla Gialla Brut '14 | ♙♙ 5 |
| ○ Collio Friulano '17 | ♙♙ 3 |
| ● Collio Merlot dal Pic '13 | ♙♙ 5 |
| ● FCO Pignolo '11 | ♙♙ 8 |
| ○ FCO Ribolla Gialla Turian '17 | ♙♙ 5 |
| ○ Collio Bianco Broy '15 | ♟♟♟ 5 |
| ○ Collio Bianco Broy '14 | ♟♟♟ 5 |
| ○ Collio Bianco Broy '13 | ♟♟♟ 5 |
| ○ Collio Bianco Broy '11 | ♟♟♟ 4* |
| ○ Collio Bianco Broy '10 | ♟♟♟ 4 |
| ○ Collio Bianco Broy '09 | ♟♟♟ 4* |
| ○ Collio Bianco Broy '08 | ♟♟♟ 4* |
| ○ Collio Bianco Broy '07 | ♟♟♟ 4 |
| ○ Ribolla Gialla Brut '13 | ♟♟♟ 5 |

## Colle Duga

LOC. ZEGLA, 10
34071 CORMÒNS [GO]
TEL. +39 048161177
www.colleduga.com

CELLAR SALES
PRE-BOOKED VISITS
ANNUAL PRODUCTION 50,000 bottles
HECTARES UNDER VINE 9.00

Damijan Princic rightfully holds a place among Collio Goriziano's leading producers. In 1991, while still young, he took on the responsibility of leading the family winery. Today he's proving to be in his prime, bringing out the best of what the Colle Duga hills (in Cormòns, in the district of Zegla) have to offer.. Here a number of the area's traditional grape varieties are cultivated and interpreted with an eye towards their typicity and mineral energy. It's an established style that the new generation, Karin and Patrik, will soon inherit. An  excellent performance by their entire selection is capped off by their 2017 Collio Bianco, which repeated last year's success and landed in our finals. Damijan makes it with equal parts Chardonnay, Malvasia Istriana, Sauvignon and Tocai Friulano, bringing together elegance, fragrance and structure for a well-balanced, enticing wine.

| | | |
|---|---|---|
| ○ Collio Bianco '17 | ♀♀ | 4 |
| ○ Collio Chardonnay '17 | ♀♀ | 3 |
| ○ Collio Friulano '17 | ♀♀ | 3 |
| ● Collio Merlot '16 | ♀♀ | 4 |
| ○ Collio Pinot Grigio '17 | ♀♀ | 3 |
| ○ Collio Sauvignon '17 | ♀♀ | 3 |
| ○ Collio Bianco '16 | ♀♀♀ | 4* |
| ○ Collio Bianco '11 | ♀♀♀ | 4* |
| ○ Collio Bianco '08 | ♀♀♀ | 3* |
| ○ Collio Bianco '07 | ♀♀♀ | 3 |
| ○ Collio Friulano '09 | ♀♀♀ | 3* |
| ○ Collio Tocai Friulano '06 | ♀♀♀ | 3* |
| ○ Collio Tocai Friulano '05 | ♀♀♀ | 3* |

## Colli di Poianis

VIA POIANIS, 23
33040 PREPOTTO [UD]
TEL. +39 0432713185
www.collidipoianis.it

CELLAR SALES
PRE-BOOKED VISITS
ACCOMMODATION
ANNUAL PRODUCTION 65,000 bottles
HECTARES UNDER VINE 11.00
SUSTAINABLE WINERY

This Prepotto producer, whose name was inspired by the buzzards ('poiane' in Italian) known to hover in and around the estate vineyards, continues to push the bar in terms of raising quality standards. It all started with a dream that was stubbornly pursued over 60 years by Paolino Marinig, and that took shape over time thanks in part to the work of his son, Gabriele. They deserve credit for having adopted as their primary goal the protection of the area's biodiversity and then reconverting their vineyards without ever disturbing the landscape's distinct features. Last year we praised the performance of their 2016 whites inasmuch as no reds were proposed. This year not only did their whites perform smashingly, but our kudos to their excellent 2015 Schioppettino di Prepotto and their 2015 Ronco della Poiana as well. They are two wines of excellent structure that call up aromas of tobacco and smoky notes of coffee beans, with palates that prove velvety and pervasive.

| | | |
|---|---|---|
| ○ FCO Chardonnay '17 | ♀♀ | 4 |
| ○ FCO Friulano '17 | ♀♀ | 4 |
| ○ FCO Malvasia '17 | ♀♀ | 4 |
| ○ FCO Ribolla Gialla '17 | ♀♀ | 4 |
| ● FCO Rosso Ronco della Poiana '15 | ♀♀ | 4 |
| ● FCO Schioppettino di Prepotto '15 | ♀♀ | 5 |
| ○ FCO Sauvignon '17 | ♀ | 4 |
| ○ FCO Chardonnay '16 | ♀♀ | 4 |
| ○ FCO Friulano '16 | ♀♀ | 4 |
| ○ FCO Friulano '15 | ♀♀ | 3 |
| ○ FCO Malvasia '16 | ♀♀ | 4 |
| ○ FCO Malvasia '15 | ♀♀ | 3 |
| ○ FCO Ribolla Gialla '16 | ♀♀ | 4 |
| ○ FCO Sauvignon '16 | ♀♀ | 4 |

# Gianpaolo Colutta

VIA ORSARIA, 32A
33044 MANZANO [UD]
TEL. +39 0432510654
www.coluttagianpaolo.com

CELLAR SALES
PRE-BOOKED VISITS
ANNUAL PRODUCTION 150,000 bottles
HECTARES UNDER VINE 30.00

In 1999 the Colutta brothers decided to subdivide the family winery founded in the early 20th century. It was Gianpaolo who gave life to the producer today managed by his daughter Elisabetta. She's inherited an agricultural tradition going back more than a millennium (in part through the family of her mother, the Countess Anna di Prampero). The estate is situated entirely in the Friuli Colli Orientali appellation, and many of the area's traditional grapes are cultivated. It's a decision that's paid off, thanks in part to a solid selection of classically styled wines. A surprising 2017 Ribolla Gialla stood out for its elegant, flowery notes that delight the nose, but especially for its freshness on the palate. Well-deserved kudos for their 2016 Cabernet as well, a wine with penetrating aromas of ripe cherries and sweet spices - it's soft and fragrant at the same time. Their 2017 Pinot Grigio and 2017 Sauvignon, both pleasantly varietal, also proved notably well-made.

| | | |
|---|---|---|
| ● FCO Cabernet '16 | ♟♟ | 3 |
| ○ FCO Pinot Grigio '17 | ♟♟ | 3 |
| ○ FCO Ribolla Gialla '17 | ♟♟ | 4 |
| ○ FCO Sauvignon '17 | ♟♟ | 3 |
| ○ FCO Friulano '17 | ♟ | 3 |
| ● FCO Schioppettino '16 | ♟ | 5 |
| ○ FCO Bianco Prariòn '16 | ♟♟ | 4 |
| ○ FCO Chardonnay '15 | ♟♟ | 3 |
| ○ FCO Friulano '16 | ♟♟ | 3 |
| ○ FCO Pinot Grigio '16 | ♟♟ | 3 |
| ○ FCO Pinot Grigio '15 | ♟♟ | 3 |
| ○ FCO Verduzzo Friulano '14 | ♟♟ | 4 |
| ○ FCO Verduzzo Friulano '14 | ♟♟ | 4 |

# Giorgio Colutta

VIA ORSARIA, 32
33044 MANZANO [UD]
TEL. +39 0432740315
www.colutta.it

CELLAR SALES
PRE-BOOKED VISITS
ACCOMMODATION
ANNUAL PRODUCTION 140,000 bottles
HECTARES UNDER VINE 21.00

For some time now, tradition and innovation have found the perfect union here at Giorgio Colutta's winery. It's a quality that can be found across their entire selection, thanks in part to their environmentally-friendly approach. Their vineyards span the prestigious 'Park of Vines and Wines' in the southernmost part of the natural amphitheater formed by the gentle slopes of Colli Orientali. It's an area that's protected by the Julian Alps and that faces the Adriatic sea, a postion that's universally recognized as ideal for high-quality wine-growing, both for white and red grape varities. Once again wine that's fruit-driven on the nose and creamy in the mouth, stood out, earning a well-deserved place in our finals. His 2015 Merlot also did well, it's still a bit spirited but very promising. His 2017 Pinot Grigio and 2017 Ribolla Gialla both proved to be excellently made, enjoyable wines.

| | | |
|---|---|---|
| ○ FCO Friulano '17 | ♟♟ | 3* |
| ● FCO Cabernet '15 | ♟♟ | 3 |
| ● FCO Merlot '15 | ♟♟ | 3 |
| ○ FCO Pinot Grigio '17 | ♟♟ | 3 |
| ○ FCO Ribolla Gialla '17 | ♟♟ | 3 |
| ● FCO Cabernet Sauvignon '15 | ♟ | 3 |
| ○ FCO Sauvignon '17 | ♟ | 3 |
| ○ Friuli Pinot Grigio Kosher '17 | ♟ | 3 |
| ○ Prosecco Brut | ♟ | 2 |
| ○ FCO Friulano '16 | ♟♟ | 3 |
| ○ FCO Pinot Grigio '16 | ♟♟ | 3 |
| ○ FCO Sauvignon '16 | ♟♟ | 3 |
| ● FCO Schioppettino '13 | ♟♟ | 5 |

# Paolino Comelli

B.GO CASE COLLOREDO, 8
33040 FAEDIS [UD]
TEL. +39 0432711226
www.comelli.it

CELLAR SALES
PRE-BOOKED VISITS
ACCOMMODATION
ANNUAL PRODUCTION 60,000 bottles
HECTARES UNDER VINE 12.50
SUSTAINABLE WINERY

Pierluigi Comelli ('Pigi' to his friends)
manages one of the area's most notable
wineries, a real crown jewel of the Friuli
Colli Orientali appellation. Here in Colloredo
di Soffumbergo, a territory of rare beauty,
vineyards and olive trees thrive and peace
reigns just a few minutes from more
heavily trafficked areas. Nicola and Filippo
are the new generation, having inherited a
project set in motion by their grandfather
Paolino, who, showing foresight,
purchased an old abandoned hamlet and
transformed it into a agricultural producer
all the way back in 1946. It's a truly
unusual coincidence that some eight
wines, tasted on different days by different
panels, all obtained the same score, and a
high score at that, thus affirming the
excellent quality of their entire selection.
Among it their 2016 Bianco Soffumbergo
(a blend of Tocai Friulano and Malvasia
with smaller parts Chardonnay and Picolit)
stood out just a slight bit above the rest.
It's a highly fragrant, glycerine, tasty wine.

| | |
|---|---|
| ○ COF Picolit '15 | ♟♟ 5 |
| ○ FCO Bianco Soffumbergo '16 | ♟♟ 3 |
| ○ FCO Friulano '17 | ♟♟ 3 |
| ○ FCO Malvasia '16 | ♟♟ 3 |
| ● FCO Merlot Jacò '16 | ♟♟ 3 |
| ● FCO Pignolo '11 | ♟♟ 5 |
| ○ FCO Pinot Grigio Amplius '17 | ♟♟ 3 |
| ○ FCO Sauvignon '17 | ♟♟ 3 |
| ○ Amplius Pinot Grigio '16 | ♟♟ 2* |
| ○ COF Picolit '14 | ♟♟ 5 |
| ○ FCO Malvasia '15 | ♟♟ 3 |
| ○ FCO Sauvignon '16 | ♟♟ 3* |
| ● Soffumbergo '15 | ♟♟ 4 |

# Dario Coos

LOC. RAMANDOLO, 5
33045 NIMIS [UD]
TEL. +39 0432790320
www.dariocoos.it

CELLAR SALES
PRE-BOOKED VISITS
ANNUAL PRODUCTION 80 bottles
HECTARES UNDER VINE 12.00

The name Coos makes you think
immediately of Ramandolo, the sweet
nectar of the Verduzzo Giallo grape, a
cultivar known for its small clusters and
tough skins. It's perfect for drying, and rich
in sugars and tannins as well, which is
virtually unheard of for a white grape.
Nevertheless, over time Coos's selection
has come to include still wines, which
have further established this Nimis winery
within the heights of regional excellence.
Dario, a fifth generation wine-grower and
the brand's founder, is still at the helm.
Today that brand is also managed by a
small group of passionate partners. Their
2017s exhibit great potential, but still
aren't at their best, a bit more time in
the bottle will work in their favor. Their
2014 Pignolo is a wine of great structure,
vibrant and complex on the nose, plush
and tasty on the palate with potent but
smooth tannins. Both their excellent
sweet wines, their 2016 Ramandolo
Vendemmia Tardiva and their 2016 Picolit,
do a good job representing the brand's
high quality standard.

| | |
|---|---|
| ○ COF Picolit '16 | ♟♟ 6 |
| ● Pignolo '14 | ♟♟ 4 |
| ○ Ramandolo V.T. '16 | ♟♟ 4 |
| ○ Ribolla Gialla Brut | ♟♟ 3 |
| ○ FCO Friulano '17 | ♟ 3 |
| ○ Friuli Chardonnay '17 | ♟ 4 |
| ○ Friuli Sauvignon '17 | ♟ 3 |
| ○ Ribolla Gialla '17 | ♟ 3 |
| ○ COF Picolit '15 | ♟♟ 6 |
| ○ Friuli Chardonnay '16 | ♟♟ 4 |
| ○ Friuli Friulano '16 | ♟♟ 3 |
| ○ Friuli Malvasia '16 | ♟♟ 3 |
| ○ Friuli Pinot Grigio '15 | ♟♟ 3 |
| ○ Friuli Sauvignon '16 | ♟♟ 3 |
| ● Pignolo '12 | ♟♟ 4 |
| ○ Ramandolo V.T. '15 | ♟♟ 4 |

# Cantina Produttori Cormòns

VIA VINO DELLA PACE, 31
34071 CORMÒNS [GO]
TEL. +39 048162471
www.cormons.com

CELLAR SALES
PRE-BOOKED VISITS
ACCOMMODATION AND RESTAURANT SERVICE
ANNUAL PRODUCTION 2,250,000 bottles
HECTARES UNDER VINE 400.00
SUSTAINABLE WINERY

In 1968 a large group of Comòns' vine growers decided to join forces to make quality wines that they'd otherwise be unable to sell. Experience and agronomic organization have since allowed Cantina to grow into one of the most solid cooperatives in Italy's northeast. The producer is famous for its 'Vino della Pace', an emblem of its production and communication capabilities, made possible in part thanks to general director Andrea Russo. Young enologist Luca Belluzzo, on the other hand, is responsible for developing their various production lines, with their Riserve Cosmos speaking to the aging-potential of Friuli's wines. Not many wines were submitted for tasting, even if the producer has a vast selection for each typology. We still appreciated two new offerings, their 2016 Chardonnay n.108 and their 2016 Malvasia n.68, both the result of careful grape selection, thus testifying to the winery's desire to stand out and aim at the heights of excellent. The foundation is there.

| | |
|---|---|
| ○ Collio Bianco Collio & Collio '17 | ▼▼ 3 |
| ○ Collio Chardonnay n.108 '16 | ▼▼ 2* |
| ○ Friuli Isonzo Malvasia n.68 '16 | ▼▼ 2* |
| ○ Collio Pinot Grigio '17 | ▼ 3 |
| ○ Collio Sauvignon '17 | ▼ 3 |
| ○ Collio Bianco Collio & Collio '15 | ♥♥ 3 |
| ○ Collio Chardonnay '16 | ♥♥ 2* |
| ○ Collio Friulano '16 | ♥♥ 3 |
| ○ Friuli Isonzo Malvasia '16 | ♥♥ 2* |
| ○ Friuli Isonzo Malvasia '15 | ♥♥ 2* |
| ○ Collio Bianco Collio & Collio '16 | ♥ 3 |
| ● Friuli Isonzo Cabernet Sauvignon '15 | ♥ 2 |

# Crastin

LOC. RUTTARS, 33
34070 DOLEGNA DEL COLLIO [GO]
TEL. +39 0481630310
www.vinicrastin.it

CELLAR SALES
PRE-BOOKED VISITS
ANNUAL PRODUCTION 35,000 bottles
HECTARES UNDER VINE 6.00

The name Crastin comes from the splendid district that faces Slovenia from the Ruttars hills. In the 1980s it was here that Sergio Collarig, a passionate artisan who decided to abandon large-scale agriculture in favor of specialized viticulture, founded his winery. It's a small producer that's capable of getting attention vintage after vintage, thanks to wines that are increasingly enticing and respectful of varietal character. It's one of Collio Goriziano's true pearls, another feather in the cap of a territory that's famously well-suited to wine-growing. The level of quality that Sergio puts forward encompasses his entire range of wines. His 2017s, especially, enjoy a fragrance and exemplary linearity, without excesses or flaws. His 2017 Ribolla Gialla is the highest expression possible for this cultivar, though the entire selection highlights the territory's potential, as well as each grape's varietal qualities.

| | |
|---|---|
| ○ Collio Friulano '17 | ▼▼ 3 |
| ● Collio Merlot '15 | ▼▼ 4 |
| ○ Collio Pinot Grigio '17 | ▼▼ 3 |
| ○ Collio Ribolla Gialla '17 | ▼▼ 3 |
| ○ Collio Sauvignon '17 | ▼▼ 3 |
| ○ Verduzzo Friulano '15 | ▼▼ 3 |
| ● Collio Cabernet Franc '15 | ♥♥ 3 |
| ○ Collio Friulano '16 | ♥♥ 3 |
| ○ Collio Friulano '15 | ♥♥ 3* |
| ○ Collio Pinot Grigio '16 | ♥♥ 3 |
| ○ Collio Pinot Grigio '15 | ♥♥ 3 |
| ○ Collio Ribolla Gialla '15 | ♥♥ 3 |
| ○ Collio Sauvignon '16 | ♥♥ 3 |

## di Lenardo

LOC. ONTAGNANO
P.ZZA BATTISTI, 1
33050 GONARS [UD]
TEL. +39 0432928633
www.dilenardo.it

CELLAR SALES
PRE-BOOKED VISITS
ANNUAL PRODUCTION 750,000 bottles
HECTARES UNDER VINE 60.00
SUSTAINABLE WINERY

Lenardo Vineyards' plots are situated in the sunny plains of Friuli, while their cellar is located in the town center of Ontagnano, a district of Godars. Massimo, the man at the helm, has managed to grow his winery into of the region's most important, having demonstrated that it's possible to have a wide selection and large production volumes without compromising quality. For some time now his son Vittorio has been part of the team and is gaining experience with the knowledge that a few years from now the torch will be passed to him. In its second year of production, their 2017 Thanks (made with Chardonnay, Sauvignon, Tocai Friulano, Malvasia and Verduzzo Friulano) affirms its status as a top-of-the-range wine, joining that group of offerings chosen to participate in our finals. The quality of their two Chardonnays was also affirmed, followed by a number of impeccably well-made and highly enjoyable wines.

| | |
|---|---|
| ○ Thanks '17 | 🏆🏆 4 |
| ● Cabernet '17 | 🏆🏆 2* |
| ○ Chardonnay '17 | 🏆🏆 2* |
| ○ Chardonnay Father's Eyes '17 | 🏆🏆 3 |
| ○ Friuli Friulano Toh! '17 | 🏆🏆 2* |
| ● Merlot '17 | 🏆🏆 2* |
| ● Merlot Just Me '15 | 🏆🏆 4 |
| ○ Pinot Grigio Ramato Gossip '17 | 🏆🏆 2* |
| ○ Friuli Pinot Grigio '17 | 🏆 2 |
| ○ Ribolla Gialla Brut M. Cl. '16 | 🏆 3 |
| ○ Ribolla Gialla Comemivuoi '17 | 🏆 2 |
| ● Ronco Nolè | 🏆 2 |
| ○ Sarà Brut M. Cl. | 🏆 3 |
| ○ Sauvignon '17 | 🏆 2 |
| ○ Chardonnay '15 | 🏆🏆🏆 2* |
| ○ Thanks '16 | 🏆🏆 4 |

## ★★Dorigo

S.DA PROV.LE 79
33040 PREMARIACCO [UD]
TEL. +39 0432634161
www.dorigowines.com

CELLAR SALES
PRE-BOOKED VISITS
ANNUAL PRODUCTION 120,000 bottles
HECTARES UNDER VINE 20.00
SUSTAINABLE WINERY

Since 2012 Alessio Dorigo has been leading the winery founded in the 1960s by his father, Girolamo, a man remembered by many as one of Friuli's great wine innovators. Having drawn inspiration from French enology, Girolamo was among the first to focus on high density vineyards and maturation in barriques. He also contributed to promoting native grape varieties during a time when few were. Ribolla Gialla, in particular, benefited from his efforts and today the grape is getting international attention. We shouldn't forget their line of sparkling wines either, another of the Colli Orientali's great treasures. Once again, some two wines make it into our finals. It should be a satisfying result, even if the fact of not earning a gold might leave a somewhat bitter taste in the producer's mouth. In any case, their entire selection did extremely well, including their 2017s, their Metodo Classico sparklers and their reds, while their Ronc di Juri reserve wines proved to be a the winery's crown jewels. Hats off.

| | |
|---|---|
| ○ FCO Chardonnay Ronc di Juri '16 | 🏆🏆 5* |
| ○ FCO Sauvignon Ronc di Juri '16 | 🏆🏆 5* |
| ○ Blanc de Noir Dosage Zéro | 🏆🏆 5 |
| ○ Dorigo Brut Cuvée | 🏆🏆 5 |
| ● Dorigo Rosso | 🏆🏆 4 |
| ○ FCO Friulano '17 | 🏆🏆 3 |
| ○ FCO Pinot Grigio '17 | 🏆🏆 3 |
| ○ FCO Ribolla Gialla '17 | 🏆🏆 3 |
| ● Friuli Cabernet Franc '16 | 🏆🏆 3 |
| ○ Verduzzo Friulano '15 | 🏆🏆 3 |
| ○ Blanc de Blancs Pas Dosé | 🏆🏆 5 |
| ○ COF Picolit '15 | 🏆🏆 8 |
| ○ FCO Chardonnay Ronc di Juri '15 | 🏆🏆 5 |
| ○ FCO Friulano '16 | 🏆🏆 3* |
| ○ FCO Ribolla Gialla '16 | 🏆🏆 3* |

# Draga - Miklus

LOC. SCEDINA, 8
34070 SAN FLORIANO DEL COLLIO [GO]
TEL. +39 0481884182
www.draga-miklus.com

CELLAR SALES
PRE-BOOKED VISITS
ANNUAL PRODUCTION 50,000 bottles
HECTARES UNDER VINE 14.00
SUSTAINABLE WINERY

Milan Miklus represents the third generation of vine growers to have put roots in San Floriano del Collio since the late 19th century. His vineyards, which are situated entirely on the hills, are divided into two principal sections. Draga is a sunny, well-ventilated area that generally gives rise to subtle, pleasant wines. At Breg the winds are stronger and, unsurprisingly, the grapes are tougher. Their approach in the cellar avails itself of long maceration on the skins and time-honored extraction methods. The same is true for their white grapes. All their macerated wines form part of the Miklus line, and one of these, their 2016 Pinot Grigio Miklus, stood out as the best of the selection and earned a place in our finals. Its a vibrant wine, both in color and aromas, which is unusual for a white, though intriguing nonetheless. Walnut skin, alchermes liquor and quinine emerge on the nose while the palate impresses for its tight-knit, linear quality.

| | | |
|---|---|---|
| ○ Collio Pinot Grigio Miklus '16 | ♟♟ | 6 |
| ○ Collio Friulano '17 | ♟♟ | 3 |
| ○ Collio Malvasia Miklus '15 | ♟♟ | 5 |
| ○ Collio Sauvignon Miklus '15 | ♟♟ | 5 |
| ○ Collio Ribolla Gialla '17 | ♟ | 3 |
| ○ Collio Malvasia Miklus '10 | ♟♟♟ | 7 |
| ○ Collio Friulano '16 | ♟♟ | 3 |
| ○ Collio Friulano '15 | ♟♟ | 3 |
| ○ Collio Malvasia Miklus '14 | ♟♟ | 4 |
| ○ Ribolla Gialla Miklus '12 | ♟♟ | 6 |

# Drius

VIA FILANDA, 100
34071 CORMÒNS [GO]
TEL. +39 048160998
www.drius.it

CELLAR SALES
PRE-BOOKED VISITS
ANNUAL PRODUCTION 50,000 bottles
HECTARES UNDER VINE 15.00
SUSTAINABLE WINERY

Mario Drius comes from a long line of farmers and cattle raisers. Today he's a full time vine grower, energetic and meticulous. He's a proud farmer, with calloused hands, large boots and a love for the land that's allowed him to bring out the best of his vineyards. These extend throughout both Friuli Isonzo and the slopes of Quarin hill, in the heart of Collio. For some years now he's trusted his young son Denis to oversee the cellar and soon the torch will be passed definitively. Their 2016 Vignis di Siris, half Tocai Friulano and half an international blend of Pinot Bianco and Sauvignon, represents one of the region's best wines. It's just ahead of two others, their 2017 Sauvignon and 2017 Friulano, and the rest of a selection that's second to none for its forthrightness and linearity, thus confirming the producer's well-established standard of quality.

| | | |
|---|---|---|
| ○ Friuli Isonzo Bianco Vignis di Siris '16 | ♟♟ | 3* |
| ○ Collio Friulano '17 | ♟♟ | 3 |
| ○ Collio Sauvignon '17 | ♟♟ | 3 |
| ● Friuli Isonzo Cabernet Sauvignon '16 | ♟♟ | 4 |
| ○ Friuli Isonzo Chardonnay '17 | ♟♟ | 3 |
| ○ Friuli Isonzo Friulano '17 | ♟♟ | 3 |
| ○ Friuli Isonzo Pinot Bianco '17 | ♟♟ | 3 |
| ○ Friuli Isonzo Pinot Grigio '17 | ♟♟ | 3 |
| ○ Friuli Isonzo Malvasia '17 | ♟ | 3 |
| ● Friuli Isonzo Merlot '16 | ♟ | 4 |
| ○ Collio Friulano '16 | ♟♟ | 3 |
| ○ Collio Sauvignon '16 | ♟♟ | 3 |
| ○ Friuli Isonzo Bianco Vignis di Siris '13 | ♟♟ | 3* |
| ○ Friuli Isonzo Pinot Bianco '16 | ♟♟ | 3 |
| ○ Friuli Isonzo Pinot Grigio '16 | ♟♟ | 3 |

# ★Le Due Terre

VIA ROMA, 68B
33040 PREPOTTO [UD]
TEL. +39 0432713189
fortesilvana@libero.it

**CELLAR SALES**
**PRE-BOOKED VISITS**
**ANNUAL PRODUCTION** 18,000 bottles
**HECTARES UNDER VINE** 5.00

Flavio Basilicata and Silvana Forte's vineyards and selection may be small (just four wines), but their passion and unquestionable gifts for production have allowed them to establish their winery as among the region's best. The estate is situated on a hill in the renamed district of Prepotto, whose terrain is composed of marl and sandstone on the one side and iron-rich soil on the other. This is how the name 'Le Due Terre' came about. Only native grape varieties are cultivated, Tocai Friulano, Ribolla Gialla, Schioppettino and Refosco dal Peduncolo Rosso. Their house blends are made exclusively with native grape varieties. Their Sacrisassi Rosso is a mix of equal parts Schioppettino and Refosco dal Peduncolo Rosso, while Tocai Friulano prevails in their Sacrisassi Bianco, a wine that also features a large share of Ribolla Gialla. As with the last edition of Italian Wines, this year their 2016 Sacrisassi Bianco proved to be our favorite, positioning itself at the head of their selection.

| | | |
|---|---|---|
| ○ FCO Bianco Sacrisassi '16 | ♥♥ | 5 |
| ● FCO Pinot Nero '16 | ♥♥ | 5 |
| ● FCO Merlot '16 | ♥♥ | 5 |
| ● FCO Rosso Sacrisassi '16 | ♥♥ | 5 |
| ○ COF Bianco Sacrisassi '05 | ♥♥♥ | 5 |
| ● COF Merlot '03 | ♥♥♥ | 5 |
| ● COF Merlot '02 | ♥♥♥ | 5 |
| ● COF Merlot '00 | ♥♥♥ | 5 |
| ● COF Rosso Sacrisassi '12 | ♥♥♥ | 5 |
| ● COF Rosso Sacrisassi '11 | ♥♥♥ | 5 |
| ● COF Rosso Sacrisassi '10 | ♥♥♥ | 5 |
| ● COF Rosso Sacrisassi '09 | ♥♥♥ | 5 |
| ● COF Rosso Sacrisassi '08 | ♥♥♥ | 5 |
| ● COF Rosso Sacrisassi '07 | ♥♥♥ | 5 |
| ● FCO Rosso Sacrisassi '13 | ♥♥♥ | 5 |

# Ermacora

FRAZ. IPPLIS
VIA SOLZAREDO, 9
33040 PREMARIACCO [UD]
TEL. +39 0432716250
www.ermacora.it

**CELLAR SALES**
**PRE-BOOKED VISITS**
**ANNUAL PRODUCTION** 180,000 bottles
**HECTARES UNDER VINE** 47.00
**SUSTAINABLE WINERY**

Dario and Luciano Ermacora successfully manage a winery that's at the vanguard, driven by a philosophy based on natural timing and minimally invasive techniques. It's an approach that has allowed them to put forward wines of superior varietal coherence that are also forthright and rich in personality. It all revolves around their base in Ipplis, a district of Premaracco that their grandfather Antonio chose as his agricultural headquarters almost a century ago. The property was successively enlarged with purchases in Bostonat di Buttrio and Montsclapade di Orsaria. To say that their selection put in a great performance this year would be an understatement. It was fantastic. Hats off to their entire range of wines, with their 2017 Pinot Bianco at the head of the class and earning a place in our finals. Both their whites and their reds enjoy impeccable cleanness, proving fragrant and respectful of their varietal characteristics.

| | | |
|---|---|---|
| ○ FCO Pinot Bianco '17 | ♥♥ | 3* |
| ○ FCO Friulano '17 | ♥♥ | 3 |
| ● FCO Pignolo '12 | ♥♥ | 5 |
| ● FCO Refosco P. R. '16 | ♥♥ | 3 |
| ○ FCO Ribolla Gialla '17 | ♥♥ | 3 |
| ● FCO Rosso Rîul '14 | ♥♥ | 4 |
| ○ FCO Sauvignon '17 | ♥♥ | 3 |
| ● FCO Schioppettino '16 | ♥♥ | 3 |
| ○ FCO Pinot Grigio '17 | ♥ | 3 |
| ● COF Pignolo '00 | ♥♥♥ | 5 |
| ○ COF Picolit '14 | ♥♥ | 6 |
| ○ FCO Friulano '16 | ♥♥ | 3 |
| ○ FCO Ribolla Gialla '16 | ♥♥ | 3 |
| ○ FCO Sauvignon '16 | ♥♥ | 3 |
| ● FCO Schioppettino '15 | ♥♥ | 3 |

# Fantinel

FRAZ. TAURIANO
VIA TESIS, 8
33097 SPILIMBERGO [PN]
TEL. +39 0427591511
www.fantinel.com

**CELLAR SALES**
**PRE-BOOKED VISITS**
**RESTAURANT SERVICE**
**ANNUAL PRODUCTION** 5,000,000 bottles
**HECTARES UNDER VINE** 300.00
**SUSTAINABLE WINERY**

Marco, Stefano and Mariaelena Fantinel represent the third generation to lead the winery founded by Mario in 1969, the year in which he purchased his first vineyards. The idea was to make wine for the clients of his hotel and restaurant in Carnia. Today it is one of the region's most important producers. Their Sant'Elena estate gives rise to a selection in which Collio's principal wines are represented. They also offer a line of sparkling wines made with grapes culture on flatter terrain. Freshness and drinkability are key features of their signature style. Their 2016 Bianco Frontiere Sant'Helena (made of Tocai Friulano, Pinot Bianco and Chardonnay) is redolent of candied citrus, bottled peaches and summer hay, while the palate comes through flavorful and pervasive. Their 2017 Ribolla Gialla Sant'Helena proves particularly intriguing on the nose, with flowery notes and fruity aromas. The palate features freshness that's well-supported by an enticing, mineral savoriness.

| | | |
|---|---|---|
| ○ Collio Bianco Frontiere Sant'Helena '16 | 🍷🍷 | 4 |
| ○ Collio Friulano Sant'Helena '17 | 🍷🍷 | 3 |
| ○ Collio Pinot Grigio Tenuta Sant'Helena '17 | 🍷🍷 | 3 |
| ○ Prosecco Brut One&Only '17 | 🍷🍷 | 3 |
| ○ Ribolla Gialla Tenuta Sant'Helena '17 | 🍷🍷 | 3 |
| ○ Collio Sauvignon Tenuta Sant'Helena '17 | 🍷 | 3 |
| ○ Ribolla Gialla Brut | 🍷 | 3 |
| ○ Collio Bianco Frontiere Sant'Helena '15 | 🍾🍾 | 4 |
| ○ Collio Friulano Sant'Helena '16 | 🍾🍾 | 3 |
| ○ Collio Pinot Grigio Sant'Helena '16 | 🍾🍾 | 3 |
| ○ Collio Pinot Grigio Sant'Helena '15 | 🍾🍾 | 3 |
| ○ Collio Sauvignon Sant'Helena '16 | 🍾🍾 | 3 |
| ○ Collio Sauvignon Sant'Helena '15 | 🍾🍾 | 3 |
| ○ Prosecco Brut One&Only '16 | 🍾🍾 | 3 |

# ★★Livio Felluga

FRAZ. BRAZZANO
VIA RISORGIMENTO, 1
34071 CORMÒNS [GO]
TEL. +39 048160203
www.liviofelluga.it

**PRE-BOOKED VISITS**
**ANNUAL PRODUCTION** 800,000 bottles
**HECTARES UNDER VINE** 170.00
**SUSTAINABLE WINERY**

Livio Felluga is known as 'The Patriarch' of Friuli's wine and enology culture. In the 1950s he founded his winery in Brazzano (Cormòns), purchasing the first plots in Rosazzo. Together with a handful of motivated vine growers he began promoting a project that was in many ways unthinkable in Italy at the time: make great white wines. Today his four children are at the helm, with an estate that comprises important hills in Collio and Collio Orientali in general. These are complemented by additional plots and a cellar in Abbazia di Rosazzo. Some three wines made it into our finals. The first is their extremely sweet 2013 Picolit, with its aromas of alchermes liquor, malt candy and almond bars. Their 2015 Rosazzo Abbazia di Rosazzo (made with Malvasia Istriana, Pinot Bianco, Ribolla Gialla, Sauvignon and Tocai Friulano) is a plush, tasty wine, while their 2016 Rosazzo Terre Alte (Sauvignon, Pinot Bianco and Tocai Friulano) proves fragrant and balanced.

| | | |
|---|---|---|
| ○ Rosazzo Terre Alte '16 | 🍷🍷🍷 | 7 |
| ○ COF Picolit '13 | 🍷🍷 | 8 |
| ○ Rosazzo Abbazia di Rosazzo '15 | 🍷🍷 | 7 |
| ○ FCO Friulano '17 | 🍷🍷 | 4 |
| ○ FCO Pinot Grigio '17 | 🍷🍷 | 4 |
| ● FCO Rosso Sossò Ris. '13 | 🍷🍷 | 7 |
| ○ FCO Sauvignon '17 | 🍷🍷 | 4 |
| ○ COF Bianco Illivio '10 | 🍾🍾🍾 | 5 |
| ○ COF Rosazzo Bianco Terre Alte '09 | 🍾🍾🍾 | 7 |
| ○ COF Rosazzo Bianco Terre Alte '08 | 🍾🍾🍾 | 7 |
| ○ COF Rosazzo Bianco Terre Alte '07 | 🍾🍾🍾 | 7 |
| ○ COF Rosazzo Bianco Terre Alte '06 | 🍾🍾🍾 | 6 |
| ○ FCO Bianco Illivio '14 | 🍾🍾🍾 | 5 |
| ○ Rosazzo Terre Alte '12 | 🍾🍾🍾 | 7 |
| ○ Rosazzo Terre Alte '11 | 🍾🍾🍾 | 7 |
| ○ Terre Alte '87 | 🍾🍾🍾 | 7 |

# Marco Felluga

VIA GORIZIA, 121
34072 GRADISCA D'ISONZO [GO]
TEL. +39 048199164
www.marcofelluga.it

**CELLAR SALES**
**PRE-BOOKED VISITS**
**RESTAURANT SERVICE**
**ANNUAL PRODUCTION** 600,000 bottles
**HECTARES UNDER VINE** 100.00
**SUSTAINABLE WINERY**

Quasi-centenarian Marco Felluga deserves credit for having set in motion a major acceleration in regional production, transforming his own winery into a benchmark for the whole territory. For Collio he was a great innovator, a gift that his son Roberto has also demonstrated. With foresight and persistence he has been working to develop the aging potential of white wines, selecting certain reserves dedicated to Friuli's principal cultivar and putting them on the market years after vintage. This year only white wines were presented. Their 2017s earned unanimous praise while their 2016 Pinot Grigio Mongris Riserva not only landed in our finals (as in the past), it took home its first Tre Bicchieri. It delights the nose with whiffs of orange, mandarin, dried fruit and vanilla while gratifying the palate with fragrant mineral notes.

# Feudi di Romans

FRAZ. PIERIS
VIA CÀ DEL BOSCO, 16
34075 SAN CANZIAN D'ISONZO [GO]
TEL. +39 048176445
www.ifeudidiromans.it

**CELLAR SALES**
**ANNUAL PRODUCTION** 500,000 bottles
**HECTARES UNDER VINE** 70.00

The Feudi di Romans stand out in the heart of Friuli Isonzo, having established itself as one of the appellation's most important producers. The farming business was founded in the 1970s by Enzo Lorenzon, who still manages it along with his children Davide and Nicola. Their philosophy is based on environmental sustainability and energy conservation. Thanks in part to the support of Fabio Coser in the cellar, they're able to offer a selection of classically styled wines in which all the area's traditional typologies are represented. In addition to their already rich selection of wines, this year they've added their 2016 Bianco Sontium (a blend of Pinot Bianco, Friulano and Malvasia with a touch of aromatic Traminer). On occasion of its debut, the wine distinguishes itself for its elegant and complex aromas, but primarily for its pervasive palate and long finish. Their 2015 Merlot Alfiere Rosso is also excellent, with its balsamic, spicy background.

| | |
|---|---|
| ○ Collio Pinot Grigio Mongris Ris. '16 | ♟♟♟ 5 |
| ○ Collio Chardonnay '17 | ♟♟ 5 |
| ○ Collio Friulano '17 | ♟♟ 3 |
| ○ Collio Pinot Grigio Mongris '17 | ♟♟ 5 |
| ○ Collio Ribolla Gialla '17 | ♟♟ 3 |
| ○ Collio Chardonnay '16 | ♟♟ 5 |
| ○ Collio Chardonnay '15 | ♟♟ 5 |
| ○ Collio Friulano '16 | ♟♟ 3* |
| ○ Collio Friulano '15 | ♟♟ 3 |
| ○ Collio Pinot Grigio '14 | ♟♟ 5 |
| ○ Collio Pinot Grigio Mongris '16 | ♟♟ 5 |
| ○ Collio Pinot Grigio Mongris Ris. '15 | ♟♟ 5 |
| ○ Collio Pinot Grigio Mongris Ris. '13 | ♟♟ 5 |
| ● Collio Rosso Carantan '10 | ♟♟ 7 |
| ○ Collio Sauvignon '15 | ♟♟ 3 |
| ● Refosco P.R. Ronco dei Moreri '13 | ♟♟ 3 |

| | |
|---|---|
| ○ Friuli Isonzo Bianco Sontium '16 | ♟♟ 5 |
| ○ Friuli Isonzo Chardonnay '17 | ♟♟ 3 |
| ○ Friuli Isonzo Malvasia '17 | ♟♟ 3 |
| ● Friuli Isonzo Merlot Alfiere Rosso '15 | ♟♟ 3 |
| ○ Friuli Isonzo Pinot Bianco '17 | ♟♟ 3 |
| ● Friuli Isonzo Pinot Nero '16 | ♟♟ 3 |
| ● Friuli Isonzo Cabernet Franc '16 | ♟ 3 |
| ○ Friuli Isonzo Pinot Grigio '17 | ♟ 3 |
| ○ Ribolla Gialla '17 | ♟ 3 |
| ○ Ribolla Gialla Brut Lorenzon | ♟ 3 |
| ○ Friuli Isonzo Friulano '16 | ♟♟ 3 |
| ○ Friuli Isonzo Malvasia '16 | ♟♟ 3 |
| ● Friuli Isonzo Merlot '15 | ♟♟ 3 |
| ○ Friuli Isonzo Pinot Bianco '16 | ♟♟ 3 |
| ● Friuli Isonzo Pinot Nero '15 | ♟♟ 3 |
| ○ Ribolla Gialla '16 | ♟♟ 3 |

# Fiegl

FRAZ. OSLAVIA
LOC. LENZUOLO BIANCO, 1
34170 GORIZIA
TEL. +39 0481547103
www.fieglvini.com

**CELLAR SALES**
**PRE-BOOKED VISITS**
**ANNUAL PRODUCTION** 160,000 bottles
**HECTARES UNDER VINE** 30.00
**SUSTAINABLE WINERY**

The picturesque district of Lenzuolo Bianco
hosts a number of Collio Goriziano's most
prestigious producers. It's a borderland
that has created entire armies of proud
farmworkers. It's here that for more than
two centuries the Fiegl family have worked
and lived. Originally from nearby Austria,
they make up a compact, hard-working
group that has managed to pass down
their agricultural know-how from one
generation to the next. The winery's current
owners are the three brothers Alessio,
Giuseppe and Rinaldo, but management is
entrusted to the energy and enthusiasm of
young Martin, Robert and Matej. Year after
year, with extraordinary consistency, Fiegl's
wines earn flattering praise from our
tasting panel, and often they make an
appearance in our finals. This year it's their
2017 Chardonnay's turn. Even if it was just
by a hair, the wine managed to beat out
the rest of the selection for its elegant
aromas and pleasing palate.

| | |
|---|---|
| ○ Collio Chardonnay '17 | ♟♟ 3* |
| ○ Collio Friulano '17 | ♟♟ 3 |
| ○ Collio Malvasia '17 | ♟♟ 3 |
| ● Collio Merlot Leopold '11 | ♟♟ 5 |
| ○ Collio Pinot Bianco '17 | ♟♟ 3 |
| ○ Collio Ribolla Gialla '17 | ♟♟ 3 |
| ○ Collio Sauvignon '17 | ♟♟ 3 |
| ○ Collio Pinot Grigio '17 | ♟ 3 |
| ● Collio Rosso Leopold Cuvée Rouge '11 | ♟ 5 |
| ○ Collio Bianco Leopold Cuvée Blanc '15 | ♟♟ 4 |
| ○ Collio Chardonnay '16 | ♟♟ 3 |
| ○ Collio Friulano '16 | ♟♟ 3* |
| ○ Collio Malvasia '16 | ♟♟ 3 |
| ○ Collio Pinot Grigio '16 | ♟♟ 3 |
| ● Collio Rosso Leopold Cuvée Rouge '10 | ♟♟ 5 |
| ☉ Fiegl Rosé Brut M. Cl. | ♟♟ 4 |

# Gigante

VIA ROCCA BERNARDA, 3
33040 CORNO DI ROSAZZO [UD]
TEL. +39 0432755835
www.adrianogigante.it

**CELLAR SALES**
**PRE-BOOKED VISITS**
**ACCOMMODATION**
**ANNUAL PRODUCTION** 100,000 bottles
**HECTARES UNDER VINE** 25.00

Adriano Gigante's is a well-established
winery that pays homage to the territorial
peculiarities of the Friuli Colli Orientali
appellation. This is particularly true of
Storico, a vineyard dedicated to Tocai
Friulano that, in 1957, served as a starting
point for the estate (and still represents its
crown jewel today). Now their plots extend
across the slopes of Rocca Bernarda,
and Adriano is joined by his wife, Giuliano,
and cousin Ariedo in managing both his
vineyards and winemaking. Thus it is
that the family tradition continues, with
wines of extremely high quality. Every
year Adriano submits a number of wines
to be tasted, and the fact of their earning
recognition is no news, nor is an
appearance in our final round of tastings.
Usually we see a couple, but this year
only one made it, his 2017 Friulano Vigneto
Storico, which proves to be one of the best
in its category.

| | |
|---|---|
| ○ FCO Friulano Vign. Storico '17 | ♟♟ 4 |
| ○ FCO Friulano '17 | ♟♟ 3 |
| ● FCO Merlot Ris. '12 | ♟♟ 5 |
| ○ FCO Pinot Grigio '17 | ♟♟ 3 |
| ○ FCO Sauvignon '17 | ♟♟ 3 |
| ● FCO Schioppettino '13 | ♟♟ 3 |
| ○ FCO Verduzzo Friulano '12 | ♟♟ 3 |
| ○ Friuli Malvasia '17 | ♟♟ 3 |
| ○ FCO Ribolla Gialla '17 | ♟ 3 |
| ☉ Prima Nera Brut Rosé | ♟ 3 |
| ○ Ribolla Gialla Brut | ♟ 3 |
| ○ COF Tocai Friulano Vign. Storico '06 | ♟♟♟ 4 |
| ○ COF Tocai Friulano Vign. Storico '05 | ♟♟♟ 4 |
| ○ FCO Picolit '08 | ♟♟♟ 6 |

# Gori Wines

VIA G.B. GORI, 14
33045 NIMIS [UD]
TEL. +39 0432878475
www.goriagricola.it

PRE-BOOKED VISITS
ANNUAL PRODUCTION 50,000 bottles
HECTARES UNDER VINE 18.00

Situated in Nimis, in the northern part of the Colli Orientali, Gianpiero Gori's head facility stands on a hilltop that overlooks the town below. The manor and cellar are integrated with the latter constituted of three underground stories that allow gravity to be harnassed during the various stages of winemaking. But the starting point for their selection remains care for their vineyards, mostly their own (though they rent others as well). Giovanni Bigot is responsible for looking after these while Natale Favretto oversees winemaking itself. Once again their entire selection ranked well (all similar scores, and quite high), thus confirming the excellent quality they've achieved and maintained with enviable consistency. Their 2016 Friulano Bonblanc put in a repeat performance and even if it just missed our finals, it distinguished itself for its fragrance and crispness. Their 2016 Sauvignon Busseben is also an excellent wine, proving extremely fresh and citrusy.

| | |
|---|---|
| ○ FCO Chardonnay Giùgiù '16 | ♟♟ 3 |
| ○ FCO Friulano Bonblanc '16 | ♟♟ 3 |
| ● FCO Merlot Toni Vasut '15 | ♟♟ 3 |
| ● FCO Pinot Nero Nemas I° '15 | ♟♟ 3 |
| ○ FCO Sauvignon Busseben '16 | ♟♟ 3 |
| ○ Ramandolo OrodiNemas '15 | ♟♟ 4 |
| ● Refosco P. R. Redelbosco '15 | ♟ 3 |
| ○ FCO Chardonnay Giugiù '15 | ♔♔ 3 |
| ○ FCO Friulano Bonblanc '15 | ♔♔ 3* |
| ● FCO Merlot Toni Vasùt '14 | ♔♔ 3 |
| ○ FCO Sauvignon Busseben '15 | ♔♔ 3 |
| ● FCO Schioppettino TitaG '15 | ♔♔ 3 |
| ● Refosco P. R. Redelbosco '13 | ♔♔ 3* |

# Gradis'ciutta

LOC. GIASBANA, 10
34070 SAN FLORIANO DEL COLLIO [GO]
TEL. +39 0481390237
www.gradisciutta.eu

CELLAR SALES
PRE-BOOKED VISITS
ANNUAL PRODUCTION 100,000 bottles
HECTARES UNDER VINE 20.00

After graduating in enology in 1997, Robert Princic was fully qualified to begin working with his father at Gradis'ciutta. Thus it was that he brought new life to the family tradition, which began in Kosana (in nearby in Slovenia) in the late 18th century. Today their base is in San Floriano del Collio, but their vineyards are spread throughout various districts and at varying elevations. The range of pedoclimates allow each cultivar to find its perfect habitat. Giabbana continues to host their most prestigious plots, with vineyards that go back almost 100 years. It's a unique patrimony that's vigorously safeguarded. Their entire selection achieved an excellent score, thus rewarding the work done by Robert in a year to remember. His 2017 Malvasia emerges on top, just by a hair, beating out their other wines and earning a place in our finals. It delights the nose with vibrant notes of wild flowers and ripe fruit, with aromatic whiffs of rare pleasantness that lengthen in the mouth, and endure well after.

| | |
|---|---|
| ○ Collio Malvasia '17 | ♟♟ 3* |
| ○ Collio Chardonnay '17 | ♟♟ 3 |
| ○ Collio Friulano '17 | ♟♟ 3 |
| ○ Collio Pinot Grigio '17 | ♟♟ 3 |
| ○ Collio Ribolla Gialla '17 | ♟♟ 3 |
| ○ Collio Sauvignon '17 | ♟♟ 3 |
| ○ Collio Bianco Bratinis '15 | ♔♔ 3* |
| ○ Collio Chardonnay '16 | ♔♔ 3 |
| ○ Collio Friulano '16 | ♔♔ 3* |
| ○ Collio Friulano '15 | ♔♔ 3* |
| ○ Collio Malvasia '15 | ♔♔ 3 |
| ○ Collio Pinot Grigio '16 | ♔♔ 3 |
| ○ Collio Pinot Grigio '15 | ♔♔ 3 |
| ○ Collio Ribolla Gialla '16 | ♔♔ 3 |
| ○ Collio Sauvignon '16 | ♔♔ 3* |

# Anna Grillo

VIA ALBANA, 60
33040 PREPOTTO [UD]
TEL. +39 0432713201
www.vinigrillo.it

CELLAR SALES
PRE-BOOKED VISITS
ACCOMMODATION
ANNUAL PRODUCTION 40,000 bottles
HECTARES UNDER VINE 9.00

Grillo was founded in the 1970s by Sergio Muzzolini and dedicated to his wife, Iole Grillo. For some time now the winery has been managed by his daughter, Anna, an energetic entrepreneur and wine woman. Born into a tradition of Schioppettino, the area's principle cultivar, she has since assumed her own identity, one that's open to innovation. Her Rosso Duedonne is the proof, a wine made with Schioppetttino and Sangiovese. It's the result of a friendship with Tuscan producer Susanna Grassi (from Lamole in Chianti). Anna oversees every stage of production with the support of her capable staff. Their 2015 Schioppettino di Prepotto earned the highest praise for the complexity of its aromas that bring together dark spices, coffee beans, forest undergrowth, rhubarb and tobacco in a close-knit but supple palate that exhibits poised tannins. Their 2016 Sauvignon is a highly elegant wine that opts for freshness of taste. Their 2016 Cabernet Franc proves excellent, both during and after tasting.

| | |
|---|---|
| ● FCO Cabernet Franc '16 | ♟♟ 3 |
| ○ FCO Friulano '17 | ♟♟ 3 |
| ○ FCO Il Sauvignon '16 | ♟♟ 4 |
| ○ FCO Sauvignon '17 | ♟♟ 3 |
| ● FCO Schioppettino di Prepotto '15 | ♟♟ 3 |
| ● Rosso Duedonne | ♟♟ 3 |
| ● FCO Refosco P. R. '15 | ♟ 3 |
| ○ FCO Ribolla Gialla '17 | ♟ 3 |
| ● FCO Merlot Ris. '13 | ♟♟ 3 |
| ● FCO Refosco P. R. '13 | ♟♟ 3 |
| ○ FCO Ribolla Gialla '16 | ♟♟ 3 |
| ○ FCO Sauvignon '16 | ♟♟ 3 |
| ○ FCO Sauvignon '15 | ♟♟ 3 |
| ○ FCO Sauvignon Blanc '15 | ♟♟ 3* |
| ● FCO Schioppettino di Prepotto '14 | ♟♟ 3 |
| ○ FCO Friulano '16 | ♟ 3 |

# Albano Guerra

LOC. MONTINA
V.LE KENNEDY, 39A
33040 TORREANO [UD]
TEL. +39 0432715479
www.guerraalbano.it

CELLAR SALES
PRE-BOOKED VISITS
ANNUAL PRODUCTION 60,000 bottles
HECTARES UNDER VINE 10.00

The Guerra family have cultivated the hills of Montana di Torreano practically forever, though it was in 1931 that Albano officially founded the winery bearing his name. Today Dario is at the helm. He's a true wine artisan that has fully embraced the tradition he inherited, one that's rooted in the sunny slopes that stretch along the northern strip of the Friuli Colli Orientali appellation. Protected by the Alps and exposed to the sea breeze, these vineyards give rise to an authoritative range of wines dedicated to the area's principal cultivar. All their wines earned praise, in particular their most recent releases. Their 2017 Malvasia enjoys aromas of bread crust and slightly unripe fruit. On the palate it proves soft and lean. Their 2017 Pinot Grigio offers up fragrances of flowers and fruit, as well as a touch of honey. It comes through long on the palate. Their 2017 Friulano opens well and finishes with lovely citrus notes.

| | |
|---|---|
| ○ FCO Friulano '17 | ♟♟ 2* |
| ○ FCO Malvasia '17 | ♟♟ 2* |
| ○ FCO Pinot Grigio '17 | ♟♟ 2* |
| ○ Ribolla Gialla Brut Giuliet M. Cl. '15 | ♟♟ 3 |
| ● FCO Refosco P. R. Ris '15 | ♟ 3 |
| ○ FCO Friulano '15 | ♟♟ 2* |
| ○ FCO Malvasia '16 | ♟♟ 2* |
| ○ FCO Malvasia '15 | ♟♟ 2* |
| ○ FCO Malvasia Istriana '14 | ♟♟ 2* |
| ○ FCO Pinot Grigio '16 | ♟♟ 2* |
| ○ FCO Sauvignon '16 | ♟♟ 2* |
| ○ FCO Sauvignon '15 | ♟♟ 2* |
| ○ Ribolla Gialla Brut Giuliet '14 | ♟♟ 3 |

## Jacùss

FRAZ. MONTINA
V.LE KENNEDY, 35A
33040 TORREANO [UD]
TEL. +39 0432715147
www.jacuss.it

**CELLAR SALES**
**PRE-BOOKED VISITS**
**ANNUAL PRODUCTION** 50,000 bottles
**HECTARES UNDER VINE** 11.00

It was 1990 when siblings Sandro and
Andrea Iacuzzi decided to transform their
agricultural business into a producer
specializing in wine-growing. And so it
was that Jacùss was founded (their
surname in local dialect). Starting with a
major upgrade to their vineyards, in a
short time they were able to distinguish
themselves among Cividale's many
wine producers. They remain firmly
anchored to tradition and have managed to
harmonize the famous patience of the
farmhand with the challenges of today. The
result is a selection that reflects their
personality: simple and forthright. In the
last edition of Italian Wines we previewed
their 2015 Forment, finding it of such high
quality that it earned a place in our finals.
And their 2016 Friulano Forment is also at
the head of its class, proving fruity and
fragrant, both on the nose and in the
mouth. Their 2014 Merlot is also excellent
for its plushness and the vivacity of its
tannins. Among their 2017s, we most
appreciated their Sauvignon.

| | |
|---|---|
| ○ Bianco Forment '16 | ♟♟ 3 |
| ○ COF Picolit '12 | ♟♟ 6 |
| ● FCO Merlot '14 | ♟♟ 3 |
| ○ FCO Sauvignon '17 | ♟♟ 3 |
| ○ FCO Verduzzo Friulano '16 | ♟♟ 3 |
| ○ FCO Friulano '17 | ♟ 3 |
| ○ FCO Pinot Bianco '17 | ♟ 3 |
| ○ Bianco Forment '15 | ♟♟ 3* |
| ○ FCO Friulano '15 | ♟♟ 3 |
| ● FCO Merlot '13 | ♟♟ 3 |
| ○ FCO Pinot Bianco '16 | ♟♟ 3 |
| ○ FCO Sauvignon '15 | ♟♟ 3 |
| ● FCO Schioppettino Fucs e Flamis '15 | ♟♟ 3 |
| ○ FCO Verduzzo Friulano '15 | ♟♟ 3 |

## ★★★Jermann

FRAZ. RUTTARS
LOC. TRUSSIO, 11
34072 DOLEGNA DEL COLLIO [GO]
TEL. +39 0481888080
www.jermann.it

**CELLAR SALES**
**PRE-BOOKED VISITS**
**ANNUAL PRODUCTION** 900,000 bottles
**HECTARES UNDER VINE** 160.00

Back in the 1970s a young Silvio Jermann
took over the reins of the family winery and
with formidable determination, transformed
it into an internationally recognized
producer. Their success is thanks in large
part their Vintage Tunia, a bona fide
flagship of Friuli's wine. This was later
accompanied by other prestigious
offerings, all worked in their splendid
Ruttars cellar (their traditional wines are
still made at their main facility in Villanova
di Farra). It's a multifaceted selection that
expresses the family's Germanic roots and
their propensity for the area's common
cultivar. In addition to an extraordinary
performance by their 2016 Vintage Tunina,
whose aromas and crispness awaken all
the senses, kudos to their 2016 W…
Dreams … and a fabulous 2016 Capo
Martino. What to say? It's a trio that points
up the region's potential for white wines.
And which of them gets Tre Bicchieri?
That's a big responsibility. This time it's
their 2016 Capo Martino, which also took
home our prize for White Wine of the Year.
Hats off.

| | |
|---|---|
| ○ Capo Martino '16 | ♟♟♟ 7 |
| ○ Vintage Tunina '16 | ♟♟ 7 |
| ○ W.... Dreams.... '16 | ♟♟ 8 |
| ○ Chardonnay '17 | ♟♟ 4 |
| ○ Pinot Grigio '17 | ♟♟ 4 |
| ○ Sauvignon '17 | ♟♟ 4 |
| ○ Vinnae Ribolla Gialla '16 | ♟♟ 4 |
| ○ Capo Martino '10 | ♟♟♟ 8 |
| ○ Pinot Grigio '15 | ♟♟♟ 4* |
| ○ Vintage Tunina '15 | ♟♟♟ 7 |
| ○ Vintage Tunina '13 | ♟♟♟ 6 |
| ○ Vintage Tunina '12 | ♟♟♟ 6 |
| ○ Vintage Tunina '11 | ♟♟♟ 6 |
| ○ W... Dreams... ... ... '12 | ♟♟♟ 8 |
| ○ W... Dreams... ... ... '09 | ♟♟♟ 6 |

# Kante

FRAZ. SAN PELAGIO
LOC. PREPOTTO, 1A
34011 DUINO AURISINA [TS]
TEL. +39 040200255
www.kante.it

**ANNUAL PRODUCTION** 45,000 bottles
**HECTARES UNDER VINE** 13.00

Edi Kante is the precursor to the heroic viticulture practiced today in Karst, where rocks and sinkholes coexist. These fertile basins host vineyards that enjoy a favorable position and sea breeze, though they're not easy to tend to. Kante is a stubborn and curious man, a volcano of ideas, his wines challenge the cold and drought, offering up a forthright genuineness that's in perfect keeping with the territory's identity. His wines age at length in his picturesque cellar, carved in rock, breathing the salty air that emerges from mysterious underground coves. In previous editions of Italian Wines we often pointed out how Edi's wines are children of his personality, his character. They are generous, audacious wines, vigorous, tenacious and at times buoyant. He managed to surprise us, nonetheless, presenting a 2010 Vitovska that for all these years he'd been keeping who knows where. It's an extremely fresh wine, a must try.

| | |
|---|---|
| ○ Vitovska Sel. '10 | ⚇⚇ 5 |
| ○ Chardonnay '15 | ⚇⚇ 4 |
| ○ Malvasia '15 | ⚇⚇ 4 |
| ○ Sauvignon '15 | ⚇⚇ 5 |
| ○ Vitovska '15 | ⚇⚇ 4 |
| ○ Carso Malvasia '07 | ⚇⚇⚇ 5 |
| ○ Carso Malvasia '06 | ⚇⚇⚇ 5 |
| ○ Carso Malvasia '05 | ⚇⚇⚇ 5 |
| ○ Carso Malvasia '98 | ⚇⚇⚇ 5 |
| ○ Carso Sauvignon '92 | ⚇⚇⚇ 5 |
| ○ Carso Sauvignon '91 | ⚇⚇⚇ 5 |
| ○ Chardonnay '94 | ⚇⚇⚇ 5 |
| ○ Chardonnay '90 | ⚇⚇⚇ 5 |
| ○ Malvasia '12 | ⚇⚇⚇ 4* |

# Alessio Komjanc

LOC. GIASBANA, 35
34070 SAN FLORIANO DEL COLLIO [GO]
TEL. +39 0481391228
www.komjancalessio.com

**CELLAR SALES**
**PRE-BOOKED VISITS**
**ANNUAL PRODUCTION** 80,000 bottles
**HECTARES UNDER VINE** 24.00
**SUSTAINABLE WINERY**

The Komjanc family's agricultural history in San Floriano del Collio goes back further than anyone can remember, though it can be traced at least to the late 19th century. The first wine to bear the brand name goes back to 1973, though the real turning point came in 2000, when Alessio's four children, Benjamin, Roberto, Patrik and Ivani, were welcomed into the fold. The quality demonstrated in recent vintages solidifies their position as a benchmark in the area, thanks in part to the precious guidance of Gianni Menotti. It's a selection that sees traditional but never tired interpretations of the territory's principal cultivar. By now it's almost a tradition for at least one of Komjanc's wines to make it into our finals, and this year the honor goes to their 2017 Pinot Grigio. The common thread running through the rest of their selection is elegance, both on the nose and the palate, while still pointing up each wine's varietal qualities.

| | |
|---|---|
| ○ Collio Pinot Grigio '17 | ⚇⚇ 2* |
| ○ Collio Chardonnay '17 | ⚇⚇ 3 |
| ○ Collio Friulano '17 | ⚇⚇ 3 |
| ○ Collio Ribolla Gialla '17 | ⚇⚇ 3 |
| ○ Collio Sauvignon '17 | ⚇⚇ 3 |
| ○ Malvasia '17 | ⚇⚇ 2* |
| ○ Collio Chardonnay '16 | ⚇⚇ 3 |
| ○ Collio Friulano '16 | ⚇⚇ 3* |
| ○ Collio Picolit '15 | ⚇⚇ 6 |
| ○ Collio Pinot Grigio '16 | ⚇⚇ 3 |
| ○ Collio Sauvignon '16 | ⚇⚇ 3 |
| ○ Malvasia '16 | ⚇⚇ 3 |
| ○ Malvasia Istriana '15 | ⚇⚇ 3* |

## Anita Vogric Kurtin

LOC. NOVALI, 9
34071 CORMÒNS [GO]
TEL. +39 048160685
www.winekurtin.it

**CELLAR SALES**
**PRE-BOOKED VISITS**
**ANNUAL PRODUCTION** 60,000 bottles
**HECTARES UNDER VINE** 10.00

The Kurtin family settled in Cormòns in the early 20th century and planted their first vineyards, aware of the territory's great potential. The family's third generation representative, Albino, formalized the winery and began bottling, thus affirming a virtuous compromise between tradition and innovation. Because of his early death, today the brand is in the hands of his wife, Anita Vogric. Management, however, is entrusted to their young son, Alessio, who has rapidly shown that he is up to the task. Their 2017 Friulano offers up fruity notes of pear, golden apple and banana. In the mouth it's creamy, linear and supple. Their 2017 Pinot Grigio is redolent of summer hay, dried flowers and clear honey, while the palate proves plush and juicy. Their 2017 Sauvignon is an extremely fresh wine, both on the nose and in the mouth. Their 2017 Chardonnay stands out for its complexity and appeal, while their 2017 Ribolla Gialla calls up citrus.

| | |
|---|---|
| ○ Collio Chardonnay '17 | ♟♟ 3 |
| ○ Collio Friulano '17 | ♟♟ 3 |
| ○ Collio Pinot Grigio '17 | ♟♟ 3 |
| ○ Collio Ribolla Gialla '17 | ♟♟ 3 |
| ○ Collio Sauvignon '17 | ♟♟ 3 |
| ○ Ribolla Gialla Brut | ♟ 3 |
| ○ Collio Chardonnay '15 | ♟♟ 3 |
| ○ Collio Friulano '16 | ♟♟ 3 |
| ○ Collio Friulano '15 | ♟♟ 3 |
| ○ Collio Pinot Grigio '16 | ♟♟ 3 |
| ○ Collio Ribolla Gialla '16 | ♟♟ 3 |
| ○ Collio Sauvignon '16 | ♟♟ 3 |
| ○ Collio Sauvignon '14 | ♟♟ 3 |
| ○ Opera Prima Bianco '15 | ♟♟ 3 |
| ○ Opera Prima Bianco '14 | ♟♟ 3 |

## Vigneti Le Monde

LOC. LE MONDE
VIA GARIBALDI, 2
33080 PRATA DI PORDENONE [PN]
TEL. +39 0434622087
www.lemondewine.com

**CELLAR SALES**
**PRE-BOOKED VISITS**
**ANNUAL PRODUCTION** 400,000 bottles
**HECTARES UNDER VINE** 80.00
**SUSTAINABLE WINERY**

Alex Maccan is the owner of Vigneti Le Monde, a brand founded in 1970 whose name comes from a flourishing district situated between the rivers Livenza and Meduna. It's a bona fide cru in terms of its low yields, something rare for plains cultivation, as is the average age of their vineyards, which are easily older than 30, and the calcareous-clay terrain, which is different from the gravelly soil that usually characterizes the lowlands. These unique qualities have brought this Prata di Pordenone winery to the heights of regional excellence. Every year it seems natural to remark on the price of their entire selection, whose value is truly excellent (considering the quality). For five years now their Pinot Bianco has led the way, earning Tre Bicchieri. This year it ran head to head with more than one other wine, and finally we chose an excellent 2017 Chardonnay. There's a first time for everything.

| | |
|---|---|
| ○ Friuli Chardonnay '17 | ♟♟♟ 2* |
| ● Friuli Cabernet Sauvignon '16 | ♟♟ 2* |
| ○ Friuli Friulano '17 | ♟♟ 2* |
| ● Friuli Grave Cabernet Franc '16 | ♟♟ 2* |
| ● Friuli Grave Merlot '16 | ♟♟ 2* |
| ○ Friuli Pinot Bianco '17 | ♟♟ 2* |
| ○ Friuli Pinot Grigio '17 | ♟♟ 2* |
| ⊙ Pinot Nero Rosé Brut | ♟♟ 2 |
| ○ Pratum Ris. '15 | ♟♟ 4 |
| ○ Ribolla Gialla '17 | ♟♟ 3 |
| ○ Ribolla Gialla Brut | ♟♟ 3 |
| ○ Friuli Grave Pinot Bianco '15 | ♟♟♟ 2* |
| ○ Friuli Grave Pinot Bianco '14 | ♟♟♟ 2* |
| ○ Friuli Grave Pinot Bianco '13 | ♟♟♟ 2* |
| ○ Friuli Grave Pinot Bianco '12 | ♟♟♟ 2* |
| ○ Friuli Pinot Bianco '16 | ♟♟♟ 2* |

## Lis Fadis

FRAZ. SPESSA
S.DA SANT'ANNA 66
33043 CIVIDALE DEL FRIULI [UD]
TEL. +39 0432719510
www.vinilisafadis.it

CELLAR SALES
PRE-BOOKED VISITS
ANNUAL PRODUCTION 11,000 bottles
HECTARES UNDER VINE 10.00

In local dialect 'Lis Fadis' means 'The Fairies'. It was the name chosen by Alessandro Marcorin and Vanilla Plozner when they founded their winery in 2005. He's an antiquarian and she's an entrepreneur, but they're both highly cultured figures of distinguished taste, and they took advantage of the chance to purchase an estate and an old farm manor. In just a short time they transformed it in to a model winery equipped with a cellar that's at the technological vanguard. Availing themselves of time-honored techniques, they immediately dedicated themselves to producing deep wines with personality, winning praise from wine lovers and connoisseurs. Lis Fadis' wines are anything but commonplace. They're wines that call for very long periods on the lees, at times years (according to the wine type) in concrete vats, like they used to do. After bottling they're left to age further, and are ready only four-five years after vintage.

| | |
|---|---|
| ○ FCO Sbilf '13 | 🍷🍷 5 |
| ● FCO Bergul '12 | 🍷🍷 6 |
| ● FCO Refosco P. R. Pavar '12 | 🍷 5 |
| ● Bergul '08 | 🍸🍸 5 |
| ● COF Merlot Gjan '09 | 🍸🍸 5 |
| ○ Friulano Sbilf '10 | 🍸🍸 5 |
| ○ Sbilf '09 | 🍸🍸 4 |

## ★Lis Neris

VIA GAVINANA, 5
34070 SAN LORENZO ISONTINO [GO]
TEL. +39 048180105
www.lisneris.it

CELLAR SALES
PRE-BOOKED VISITS
ACCOMMODATION
ANNUAL PRODUCTION 400,000 bottles
HECTARES UNDER VINE 74.00
SUSTAINABLE WINERY

Fourth generation winemaker Alvaro Pecorari took over management of the family winery in 1981 and has since presided over an exponential growth in production, fashioning a signature 'Stile Lis Neris' characterized by softness, fragrance and complexity. Their vineyards, which are as meticulously managed as a garden, sprawl along the deep, gravelly plateau between the Slovenian border and the right back of the Isonzo. Gris, Picol, Jurosa and Neris are four distinct sites bound together by notable day-night temperature swings and the winery's ability to bring out the unique attributes of each territory. With three wines in our finals, Lis Neris affirms its status as one of the best representatives of the region's potential, proving that even without the advantages of hill vineyards, it's possible to make exceptional wines. Their 2016 Pinot Grigio Gris, in particular, has for some years represented the truest expression of the cultivar, impeccably bringing together fragrance and structure.

| | |
|---|---|
| ○ Friuli Isonzo Chardonnay Jurosa '16 | 🍷🍷 5 |
| ○ Friuli Isonzo Friulano La Vila '16 | 🍷🍷 5 |
| ○ Friuli Isonzo Pinot Grigio Gris '16 | 🍷🍷 5 |
| ○ Friuli Isonzo Sauvignon Picòl '16 | 🍷🍷 5 |
| ● Lis Neris '15 | 🍷🍷 6 |
| ○ Friuli Isonzo Pinot Grigio Gris '13 | 🍸🍸🍸 4* |
| ○ Lis '15 | 🍸🍸🍸 5 |
| ○ Fiore di Campo '16 | 🍸🍸 3 |
| ○ Friuli Isonzo Pinot Grigio Gris '15 | 🍸🍸 5 |
| ○ Friuli Isonzo Sauvignon Picòl '15 | 🍸🍸 5 |

# ★Livon

FRAZ. DOLEGNANO
VIA MONTAREZZA, 33
33048 SAN GIOVANNI AL NATISONE [UD]
TEL. +39 0432757173
www.livon.it

**CELLAR SALES**
**PRE-BOOKED VISITS**
**ACCOMMODATION**
**ANNUAL PRODUCTION** 850,000 bottles
**HECTARES UNDER VINE** 180.00

Founded in 1964 by Dorino, the Livon brand has become a synonym for quality throughout the world, thanks mostly to the work of Dorino's sons, Valneo and Tonino. In addition to the famous winged woman who designates their main estate, they've added the lines RoncAlto (hailing from Collio Goriziano), Villa Chiopris (the Friuli lowlands), Borgo Salcetino (Tuscany) and Colsanto (Umbria), thus establishing a wide and varied selection. Today their respective children, Matteo and Francesca, are involved full-time, bringing enthusiasm and freshness to the winery, as well as interesting and innovative new ideas. The region's most representative white grapes are undoubtedly Tocai Friulano and Ribolla Gialla. They have diametrically opposed qualities and maybe it's for this reason that they're often used together, to take advantage of their potential. That's the case with this producer's 2017 Collio Bianco Solarco, a wine that masterfully brings together freshness, fragrance, structure and savoriness, earning itself Tre Bicchieri.

| | | |
|---|---|---|
| ○ Collio Bianco Solarco '17 | 🍷🍷🍷 | 3* |
| ○ Braide Alte '16 | 🍷🍷 | 6 |
| ○ Collio Friulano Manditocai '16 | 🍷🍷 | 5 |
| ○ Collio Malvasia Soluna '17 | 🍷🍷 | 3 |
| ● Collio Merlot TiareMate '15 | 🍷🍷 | 5 |
| ○ Collio Pinot Bianco Cavezzo '17 | 🍷🍷 | 2* |
| ○ Collio Ribolla Gialla RoncAlto '17 | 🍷🍷 | 3 |
| ● TiareBlù '15 | 🍷🍷 | 5 |
| ○ Braide Alte '13 | 🍷🍷🍷 | 5 |
| ○ COF Picolit '12 | 🍷🍷🍷 | 6 |
| ○ Collio Bianco Solarco '15 | 🍷🍷🍷 | 3* |
| ○ Collio Friulano Manditocai '12 | 🍷🍷🍷 | 5 |

# Magnàs

LOC. BOATINA
VIA CORONA, 47
34071 CORMÒNS [GO]
TEL. +39 048160991
www.magnas.it

**CELLAR SALES**
**PRE-BOOKED VISITS**
**ACCOMMODATION AND RESTAURANT SERVICE**
**ANNUAL PRODUCTION** 25,000 bottles
**HECTARES UNDER VINE** 10.00

Magnàs is undoubtedly one of the many small artisanal wineries that has made Cormòns famous. Magnàs is the surname of a branch of the Visintin family that goes back several generations, though the winery was only officially established in the late 60s by Luciano. He was able to grow the producer quickly and eventually pass the torch to his son Andrea, who has been personally overseeing each stage of production for some time now. Loyalty, pride and the spirit of sacrifice continue to be their principal values. They come through in the winery's pure, forthright style. Even if each grape variety is granted equal attention and dignity (independent of its territory of origin), it's their two Collios that stand out among their selection, even if it's just by a small amount. Their 2017 Friulano is particularly enjoyable, linear and clean, both on the nose and the palate, while their 2016 Collio Bianco offers up tropical notes and enjoys exemplary balance of taste.

| | | |
|---|---|---|
| ○ Chardonnay '17 | 🍷🍷 | 3 |
| ○ Collio Bianco '16 | 🍷🍷 | 3 |
| ○ Collio Friulano '17 | 🍷🍷 | 3 |
| ○ Friuli Isonzo Pinot Grigio '17 | 🍷🍷 | 3 |
| ● Merlot Neri dal Murzùl '15 | 🍷🍷 | 3 |
| ○ Malvasia '17 | 🍷 | 3 |
| ○ Sauvignon '17 | 🍷 | 3 |
| ● Cabernet Franc '15 | 🍷🍷 | 3 |
| ○ Chardonnay '16 | 🍷🍷 | 3* |
| ○ Friuli Isonzo Friulano '15 | 🍷🍷 | 3 |
| ○ Malvasia '16 | 🍷🍷 | 3 |
| ○ Malvasia '15 | 🍷🍷 | 3 |
| ○ Pinot Grigio '16 | 🍷🍷 | 3 |
| ○ Pinot Grigio '15 | 🍷🍷 | 3* |
| ○ Sauvignon '16 | 🍷🍷 | 3 |
| ○ Collio Friulano '16 | 🍷 | 3 |

# Marinig

VIA BROLO, 41
33040 PREPOTTO [UD]
TEL. +39 0432713012
www.marinig.it

CELLAR SALES
PRE-BOOKED VISITS
ANNUAL PRODUCTION 25,000 bottles
HECTARES UNDER VINE 9.00
SUSTAINABLE WINERY

In small family-run wineries there's almost always a man Friday who looks after all the little things. Here that role is played by Valerio Marinig. His vineyards grow along the hills of Prepotto, homeland to the Schioppettino grape, where geography and climate have always allowed for quality vine growing. These are the two slopes of the valley created by the river Judrio, which serves as a border between the Collio and Friuli Colli Orientali appellations. The fact that their 2017s and their previous vintage reds received almost equal scores points up the care and attention that's taken towards each grape. Their 2015 Schioppettino di Prepotto is one of the best interpretations by far. It's redolent of dark chocolate, black pepper and quinine, while the mouth proves plush and enticing. Their 2015 Biel Cûr is also excellent, even if it's tannins are still a bit too lively.

| | | |
|---|---|---|
| ○ FCO Friulano '17 | ♟♟ | 2* |
| ○ FCO Pinot Bianco '17 | ♟♟ | 2* |
| ● FCO Rosso Biel Cûr '15 | ♟♟ | 4 |
| ○ FCO Sauvignon '17 | ♟♟ | 3 |
| ● FCO Schioppettino di Prepotto '15 | ♟♟ | 4 |
| ○ FCO Friulano '16 | ♟♟ | 2* |
| ● FCO Refosco P. R. '15 | ♟♟ | 3 |
| ● FCO Refosco P. R. '14 | ♟♟ | 3 |
| ● FCO Refosco P. R. '12 | ♟♟ | 3* |
| ○ FCO Sauvignon '16 | ♟♟ | 3 |
| ○ FCO Sauvignon '15 | ♟♟ | 3 |

# Masùt da Rive

VIA MANZONI, 82
34070 MARIANO DEL FRIULI [GO]
TEL. +39 048169200
www.masutdarive.com

CELLAR SALES
PRE-BOOKED VISITS
ANNUAL PRODUCTION 120,000 bottles
HECTARES UNDER VINE 25.00
SUSTAINABLE WINERY

The Gallo family has been rooted in Mariano del Friuli since the early 20th century, working as wine-growers along the right bank of the Isonzo. The branching out of the family tree and the necessity of approaching the North American market led to different wineries, so as to avoid legal problems with the Californian giant Gallo of Sonoma. Silvano chose to call his 'Masùt da Rive', a local word for his lineage. He always believed in the potential of Pinot Nero and his sons Fabrizio and Marco have made it the winery's flagship cultivar. Amidst an excellent overall performance by their selection, their two Pinot Neros stood out, but it was their excellent 2017 Pinot Bianco that most impressed, with an elegance that earned it Tre Bicchieri. Its aromas deliver for their enticing floral notes of lily of the valley and hawthorn. In the mouth it proves plush and savory, with a finish redolent of minty talcum.

| | | |
|---|---|---|
| ○ Friuli Isonzo Pinot Bianco '16 | ♟♟♟ | 5 |
| ○ Friuli Isonzo Chardonnay Maurus '16 | ♟♟ | 5 |
| ○ Friuli Isonzo Pinot Grigio '17 | ♟♟ | 3 |
| ○ Friuli Isonzo Pinot Grigio Jesimis '16 | ♟♟ | 5 |
| ● Friuli Isonzo Pinot Nero '16 | ♟♟ | 5 |
| ● Friuli Isonzo Pinot Nero Maurus '15 | ♟♟ | 6 |
| ● Friuli Isonzo Sassirossi '16 | ♟♟ | 3 |
| ○ Friuli Isonzo Chardonnay '17 | ♟ | 3 |
| ○ Friuli Isonzo Sauvignon '17 | ♟ | 3 |
| ○ Friuli Isonzo Chardonnay Maurus '15 | ♟♟ | 3 |
| ○ Friuli Isonzo Friulano '16 | ♟♟ | 3 |
| ○ Friuli Isonzo Pinot Grigio '16 | ♟♟ | 3* |
| ● Friuli Isonzo Rosso Sassi Rossi '15 | ♟♟ | 5 |
| ○ Friuli Isonzo Sauvignon '16 | ♟♟ | 3 |

## Davino Meroi

VIA STRETTA, 7B
33042 BUTTRIO [UD]
TEL. +39 0432673369
www.meroi.wine

**CELLAR SALES**
**PRE-BOOKED VISITS**
**RESTAURANT SERVICE**
**ANNUAL PRODUCTION** 45,000 bottles
**HECTARES UNDER VINE** 19.00
**SUSTAINABLE WINERY**

Meroi bears the name of its founder, Davino, but for many years now management has been entrusted to Paolo, who's supported in sales by his son Damiano. The family's vineyards extend across the sunny slopes of the Buttrio hills, the nearest to the Adriatic, which are considered historic in as much as they were planted with the old wisdom of his grandfather Domenico. These give rise to wines characterized by a personal style, thanks in part to the skillful use of wood for maturation and the precious support of winemaker and agronomist Mirko Degan. They produce few wines but they're of excellent quality, affirming their status as one of the region's best wineries. Two of their offerings earned a place in our finals. Their 2016 Chardonnay was defined 'old style', but it garnered unanimous high praise. The same holds for they 2016 Sauvignon, which repeated last year's stunning performance. Both offer up magic, exotic sensations featuring whiffs of vanilla, and a palate that's velvety and creamy.

| | |
|---|---|
| ○ FCO Chardonnay '16 | ♈♈ 5 |
| ○ FCO Sauvignon '16 | ♈♈ 4 |
| ○ FCO Ribolla Gialla '16 | ♈♈ 5 |
| ● FCO Rosso Nèstri '16 | ♈♈ 3 |
| ○ COF Friulano '11 | ♈♈♈ 5 |
| ○ COF Friulano '10 | ♈♈♈ 5 |
| ○ COF Verduzzo Friulano '08 | ♈♈♈ 5 |
| ● FCO Refosco P. R. V. Dominin '13 | ♈♈ 8 |
| ○ FCO Chardonnay '15 | ♈♈ 5 |
| ○ FCO Chardonnay '14 | ♈♈ 5 |
| ○ FCO Friulano '15 | ♈♈ 5 |
| ○ FCO Malvasia Zitelle Durì '13 | ♈♈ 6 |
| ● FCO Merlot Ros di Buri '13 | ♈♈ 5 |
| ● FCO Merlot V. Dominin '13 | ♈♈ 8 |
| ○ FCO Sauvignon '15 | ♈♈ 4 |
| ○ FCO Verduzzo Friulano '13 | ♈♈ 5 |

## Modeano

FRAZ. MODEANO
VIA CASALI MODEANO, 1
33056 PALAZZOLO DELLO STELLA [UD]
TEL. +39 043158244
www.modeano.it

**CELLAR SALES**
**PRE-BOOKED VISITS**
**ANNUAL PRODUCTION** 40,000 bottles
**HECTARES UNDER VINE** 31.00
**SUSTAINABLE WINERY**

Some 37 years have passed since Emanuela and Gabriele Vialetto, then recently married, decided to look after the estate of Modeano and its winery, carrying forward a tradition that goes back to the early 20th century. Over time the vineyards and equipment were upgraded, but with the utmost respect for the environment. Their vineyards are cultivated on hard but well-drained terrain while the climate here, which is among the driest in Friuli, is mitigated by the nearby Adriatic. Their agricultural approach follows certified integrated principles, eschewing the use of chemicals or artificial pesticides. This year a number of wines were proposed. The unanimous praise they garnered affirms the value of this very reasonably priced selection. Their 2017 Friulano is a highly varietal wine whose palate is sustained by freshness. Their 2017 Chardonnay stands out for its creaminess, as does their 2015 Rosso Peng, a wine made with Merlot and Refosco.

| | |
|---|---|
| ● Friuli Cabernet Sauvignon '16 | ♈♈ 2* |
| ○ Friuli Chardonnay '17 | ♈♈ 2* |
| ○ Friuli Friulano '17 | ♈♈ 2* |
| ○ Friuli Pinot Grigio '17 | ♈♈ 2* |
| ○ Ribolla Gialla '17 | ♈♈ 2* |
| ● Rosso Peng '15 | ♈♈ 3 |
| ● Friuli Cabernet Franc '16 | ♈ 2 |
| ● Friuli Merlot '16 | ♈ 2 |
| ○ Friuli Sauvignon '17 | ♈ 2 |
| ○ Verduzzo Friulano Uepasse '15 | ♈ 3 |
| ● Friuli Latisana Cabernet Sauvignon '15 | ♈♈ 2* |
| ● Friuli Latisana Cabernet Sauvignon '13 | ♈♈ 2* |
| ● Friuli Latisana Refosco P. R. '13 | ♈♈ 2* |
| ○ Friuli Malvasia '16 | ♈♈ 2* |

# Murva - Renata Pizzulin

VIA CELSO MACOR, 1
34070 MORARO [GO]
TEL. +39 0432713027
www.murva.it

**CELLAR SALES**
**PRE-BOOKED VISITS**
**ANNUAL PRODUCTION** 15,000 bottles
**HECTARES UNDER VINE** 4.00
**SUSTAINABLE WINERY**

Murva is a tiny, recently established winery belonging to the young couple, Pelos and Renata Pizzulin. Their vineyards spans four different sites, spread out in the municipalities of Moraro and Mariano del Friuli and therefore part of the Friuli Isonzo appellation. Each vineyard is chosen for its suitability to a specific cultivar, with the resulting wines named after the vineyards' ancient place name. Right off the bat, their selection has managed to stand out for its consistent quality and authentic style. This year's performance testifies to the consistently high quality they've achieved. All their wines enjoy an impeccable adherence to the territory. But our highest accolades go to their 2016 Sauvignon Teolis for the pleasantest of of its aromas, which bring together lemon cream and elegant, tropical fruit salad. The mouth delivers for its fragrance and savoriness.

# Muzic

LOC. BIVIO, 4
34070 SAN FLORIANO DEL COLLIO [GO]
TEL. +39 0481884201
www.cantinamuzic.it

**CELLAR SALES**
**PRE-BOOKED VISITS**
**ANNUAL PRODUCTION** 90,000 bottles
**HECTARES UNDER VINE** 21.00
**SUSTAINABLE WINERY**

The Muzic family's winery can be reached by the 'Wine and Cherry Road' that runs from Gorizia up towards San Floriano del Collio. The producer, one of Friuli's true pearls, belongs to Giovanni (known as Ivan to the locals), a free spirit, lover of wine and passionate artisan. Elija and Fabijan represent the latest generation to work at the winery and are already well-integrated, while mother Orieta is the cherry on top. The group's cohesion is part of what's earned them a place among the region's élite producers. Once again their Friulano Vigna Valeris stands out for its fragrance and pleasantness, though it was surpassed by two wines that made it to our finals. Their 2016 Stare Brajde is made of native cultivar only (Tocai Friulano, Malvasia Istriana and Ribolla Gialla). It's a fruit-driven, long and creamy wine, both on the nose and in the mouth. It's on par with their 2017 Chardonnay, a wine that features a pleasant touch of vanilla.

| | |
|---|---|
| ○ Friuli Isonzo Sauvignon Teolis '16 | ♟♟ 4 |
| ○ Friuli Isonzo Chardonnay Monuments '16 | ♟♟ 3 |
| ○ Friuli Isonzo Chardonnay Paladis '16 | ♟♟ 4 |
| ○ Friuli Isonzo Sauvignon Corvatis '16 | ♟♟ 3 |
| ● Refosco P. R. Murellis '15 | ♟♟ 4 |
| ○ Friuli Isonzo Malvasia Melaris '16 | ♟ 4 |
| ○ Friuli Isonzo Bianco Teolis '15 | ♟♟ 4 |
| ○ Friuli Isonzo Bianco Teolis '14 | ♟♟ 4 |
| ○ Friuli Isonzo Chardonnay Monuments '15 | ♟♟ 3 |
| ○ Friuli Isonzo Chardonnay Paladis '15 | ♟♟ 4 |
| ○ Friuli Isonzo Malvasia Melaris '15 | ♟♟ 4 |
| ● Refosco P. R. Murellis '13 | ♟♟ 4 |

| | |
|---|---|
| ○ Collio Bianco Stare Brajde '16 | ♟♟ 3* |
| ○ Collio Chardonnay '17 | ♟♟ 3* |
| ○ Collio Friulano V. Valeris '17 | ♟♟ 3 |
| ○ Collio Malvasia '17 | ♟♟ 3 |
| ○ Collio Pinot Grigio '17 | ♟♟ 3 |
| ○ Collio Ribolla Gialla '17 | ♟♟ 3 |
| ○ Collio Sauvignon V. Pàjze '17 | ♟♟ 3 |
| ● Friuli Isonzo Merlot '16 | ♟♟ 3 |
| ○ Collio Chardonnay '16 | ♟♟ 3 |
| ○ Collio Friulano V. Valeris '16 | ♟♟ 3* |
| ○ Collio Friulano V. Valeris '15 | ♟♟ 3* |
| ○ Collio Malvasia '16 | ♟♟ 3 |
| ○ Collio Malvasia '15 | ♟♟ 3* |
| ○ Collio Ribolla Gialla '16 | ♟♟ 3 |
| ○ Collio Sauvignon V. Pàjze '16 | ♟♟ 3 |

## Alessandro Pascolo

LOC. RUTTARS, 1
34070 DOLEGNA DEL COLLIO [GO]
TEL. +39 048161144
www.vinipascolo.com

CELLAR SALES
PRE-BOOKED VISITS
ANNUAL PRODUCTION 25,000 bottles
HECTARES UNDER VINE 7.00
SUSTAINABLE WINERY

Alessandro Pascolo's winery is a classic small-time winery, which has allowed the owners to personally follow each stage of production and pay particular attention to their vineyards. Here in Dolegna del Collio, on the particularly productive Ruttàrs hill, their vineyards enjoy excellent positions, making for wines with a decidedly varietal character. Their whites are matured in steel, while their reds are exclusively aged in fine-grain mid-size casks. Their wines, which get better with each passing year, are bound together by their full-body and flavor. All of Alessandro's wines are elegant, respectful of the territory and cultivar, but his best wine this year is a house blend, their 2016 Bianco Agnul (made primarily with Tocai Friulano and Pinot Bianco, with a smaller part Sauvignon). It's a wine that brings together elegant aromas and a linear, progressive palate. Their 2015 Merlot Selezione, a potent and balanced wine, is also excellent.

| | |
|---|---|
| ○ Collio Bianco Agnul '16 | ♟♟ 4 |
| ● Collio Merlot Sel. '15 | ♟♟ 5 |
| ○ Collio Sauvignon '17 | ♟♟ 3 |
| ● Pascal '16 | ♟♟ 4 |
| ○ Collio Malvasia '17 | ♟ 3 |
| ○ Collio Pinot Bianco '17 | ♟ 3 |
| ○ Collio Friulano '16 | ♟♟ 3 |
| ○ Collio Malvasia '16 | ♟♟ 3 |
| ○ Collio Malvasia '15 | ♟♟ 3* |
| ● Collio Merlot Sel. '14 | ♟♟ 5 |
| ○ Collio Sauvignon '16 | ♟♟ 3 |
| ○ Collio Sauvignon '15 | ♟♟ 3 |

## Pierpaolo Pecorari

VIA TOMMASEO, 56
34070 SAN LORENZO ISONTINO [GO]
TEL. +39 0481808775
www.pierpaolopecorari.it

CELLAR SALES
PRE-BOOKED VISITS
ANNUAL PRODUCTION 150,000 bottles
HECTARES UNDER VINE 30.00

The Pecorari family are vine growers by tradition, having written an important chapter in the region's wine-growing history. In 1970 a young Pierpaolo founded his own winery and began a path that would in a short time earn him a place among Friuli Isonzo's most authoritative interpreters. Fashioned according to a minimally invasive agricultural and enological philosophy, without any of the frills, his wines show a decidedly mineral character and commendable varietal adherence. His products are rigorously monovarietal, made according to each territory's distinct attributes This year their Olivers, Kolaus and Soris weren't presented (from they're premium vineyards) as they'll need further aging in wood barrels, nor were any of their Altis line, which comprises those wines aged in steel, on the lees. We hope to find them in the next edition of Italian Wines.

| | |
|---|---|
| ○ Friuli Isonzo Friulano '17 | ♟ 3 |
| ○ Malvasia '17 | ♟ 3 |
| ○ Pinot Grigio '17 | ♟ 3 |
| ● Refosco P. R. '15 | ♟ 3 |
| ⊙ Rosato Ros'Alba '17 | ♟ 3 |
| ○ Sauvignon '17 | ♟ 3 |
| ○ Chardonnay '16 | ♟♟ 3 |
| ○ Chardonnay Sorjs '15 | ♟♟ 5 |
| ○ Malvasia '15 | ♟♟ 3* |
| ● Merlot Baolar '13 | ♟♟ 5 |
| ○ Traminer Aromatico '16 | ♟♟ 4 |

# Perusini

LOC. GRAMOGLIANO
VIA DEL TORRIONE, 13
33040 CORNO DI ROSAZZO [UD]
TEL. +39 0432759151
www.perusini.com

**CELLAR SALES**
**PRE-BOOKED VISITS**
**ACCOMMODATION AND RESTAURANT SERVICE**
**ANNUAL PRODUCTION** 100,000 bottles
**HECTARES UNDER VINE** 15.00
**VITICULTURE METHOD** Certified Organic
**SUSTAINABLE WINERY**

Teresa Perusini is the current owner of this historic winery founded in the 18th century. Some centuries later his grandfather Giacomo made himself famous for contributing to the cultivation of Picolit. It's an exceptional cultivar that is without a doubt a primary feature of his selection. Teresa, an art lover, continues the work of her ancestors, bringing out the best of the splendid vineyards that sprawl along the slopes of Friuli Colli Orientali. Her enthusiasm has proved contagious with the new generation, represented by Carlo, Tommaso and Michele, who've already been active with the winery for some time. With respect to last year's edition of Italian Wines, their selection earned the same scores, but garnered even further praise. One in particular, their 2017 Ribolla Gialla, is attracting greater interest and having market success by virtue of its moderate alcohol content and intrinsic freshness. It's a wine redolent of citrus and mint that refreshes the palate.

| | |
|---|---|
| ○ COF Picolit '15 | 🍷🍷 8 |
| ○ FCO Chardonnay '16 | 🍷🍷 3 |
| ○ FCO Friulano '17 | 🍷🍷 3 |
| ● FCO Merlot '15 | 🍷🍷 3 |
| ○ FCO Ribolla Gialla '17 | 🍷🍷 3 |
| ● FCO Rosso del Postiglione '15 | 🍷🍷 3 |
| ● FCO Cabernet Sauvignon '15 | 🍷 3 |
| ○ FCO Chardonnay '17 | 🍷 3 |
| ● FCO Refosco P.R. '15 | 🍷 3 |
| ○ COF Picolit '14 | 🍷🍷 8 |
| ○ FCO Friulano '16 | 🍷🍷 3 |
| ○ FCO Pinot Grigio '15 | 🍷🍷 3* |
| ○ FCO Sauvignon '16 | 🍷🍷 3 |

# Petrucco

VIA MORPURGO, 12
33042 BUTTRIO [UD]
TEL. +39 0432674387
www.vinipetrucco.it

**CELLAR SALES**
**PRE-BOOKED VISITS**
**ANNUAL PRODUCTION** 80,000 bottles
**HECTARES UNDER VINE** 25.00

Italo Balbo's war stories could fill many pages of 20th century history. Few know, however, that before leaving for Libya where his plane was shot down in 1940, he planted some vineyards on Buttrio di Monte, where Friuli Colli Orientali's marvelous natural amphitheater rises up out of the earth. These plots are the crown jewel of the estate taken over in 1981 by Paolo Petrucco and his wife, Lina. Flavio Cabas has been entrusted with tending to the estate, which hosts the quality grapes used for their reserve wine Ronco del Balbo. For a couple of years now their 2016 Bianco Cabas has enriched their already prestigious Ronco del Balbo line. It continues to impress, though without overshadowing the rest of the selection. It's a wine that points up the potential of the cultivar used (Chardonnay, Sauvignon, Tocai Friulano and Malvasia), fusing their qualities into a harmonic whole that emerges on the palate.

| | |
|---|---|
| ○ FCO Bianco Cabas Ronco del Balbo '16 | 🍷🍷 4 |
| ○ FCO Friulano '17 | 🍷🍷 3 |
| ○ FCO Malvasia '17 | 🍷🍷 3 |
| ○ FCO Pinot Bianco '17 | 🍷🍷 3 |
| ● FCO Refosco P. R. Ronco del Balbo '15 | 🍷🍷 4 |
| ○ FCO Ribolla Gialla '17 | 🍷🍷 3 |
| ● FCO Merlot Ronco del Balbo '15 | 🍷 4 |
| ○ FCO Sauvignon '17 | 🍷 3 |
| ○ COF Picolit '13 | 🍷🍷 6 |
| ○ FCO Friulano '16 | 🍷🍷 3 |
| ○ FCO Malvasia '15 | 🍷🍷 3 |
| ○ FCO Pinot Bianco '16 | 🍷🍷 3 |
| ○ FCO Pinot Grigio '16 | 🍷🍷 3 |
| ○ FCO Sauvignon '16 | 🍷🍷 3 |
| ○ FCO Sauvignon '15 | 🍷🍷 3 |

# Petrussa

VIA ALBANA, 49
33040 PREPOTTO [UD]
TEL. +39 0432713192
www.petrussa.it

CELLAR SALES
PRE-BOOKED VISITS
ACCOMMODATION
ANNUAL PRODUCTION 45,000 bottles
HECTARES UNDER VINE 10.00

The call of the land convinced brothers Gianni and Paolo Petrussa to take their parents' place in 1986 as managers of the family winery. Convinced proponents of Prepotto's potential, they put their centuries-old agricultural roots to use, bringing to life wines that reflect the forthright personalities of their ancestors. Their vineyards are divided into small plots located throughout the northern part of the Colli Orientali hills, just by the Julian Pre-Alps. The valley is protected from the strong eastern winds and enjoys a uniquely mild microclimate. Tracing out the classification of the wines submitted this year, we affirmed last year's result. More than a coincidence, it seems a clear testament to the producer's ability to interpret the peculiar qualities of each vintage and cultivar. Once again their 2015 Schioppettino di Prepotto led the way, earning a place for itself in our finals.

# Norina Pez

VIA ZORUTTI, 4
34070 DOLEGNA DEL COLLIO [GO]
TEL. +39 0481639951
www.norinapez.it

CELLAR SALES
PRE-BOOKED VISITS
ANNUAL PRODUCTION 40,000 bottles
HECTARES UNDER VINE 7.00

For some time now the winery owned by Norina Pez has been managed by her son Stefano Bernardis, who inherited a long family legacy of vine growing on the Dolegna hills, in the northernmost part of Gorizia. Their seven hectares of vineyards stretch along the gentle hills of Collio, the ridges that span the Isonzo and Judrio rivers. It's an area protected by the Julian Alps and well-exposed to the sea breeze coming in off the nearby Adriatic. The area's microclimate and particular subsoil (constituted of marl and sandstone from the Eocene epoch) create the conditions for producing high quality wines. The entire selection submitted earned high praise, affirming Stefano's work and pointing up his wines' value for the money. Their 2017 Sauvignon is a pleasant wine on the nose, incisive but poised, while in the mouth it excels for fragrances and crispness. Their 2017 Pinot Grigio is just as good, and does a good expressing the grape. Their 2015 Schioppettino is excellent for its plushness and character.

| | |
|---|---|
| ● FCO Schioppettino di Prepotto '15 | ♥♥ 5 |
| ○ FCO Chardonnay S. Elena '16 | ♥♥ 4 |
| ○ FCO Friulano '17 | ♥♥ 3 |
| ○ FCO Pinot Bianco '17 | ♥♥ 3 |
| ○ FCO Ribolla Gialla '17 | ♥♥ 3 |
| ● FCO Rosso Petrussa '15 | ♥♥ 5 |
| ○ FCO Sauvignon '17 | ♥♥ 3 |
| ○ Pensiero '15 | ♥♥ 5 |
| ○ FCO Chardonnay S. Elena '15 | ♀♀ 4 |
| ○ FCO Friulano '16 | ♀♀ 3 |
| ○ FCO Friulano '15 | ♀♀ 3 |
| ○ FCO Pinot Bianco '16 | ♀♀ 3 |
| ○ FCO Sauvignon '16 | ♀♀ 3 |
| ● FCO Schioppettino di Prepotto '14 | ♀♀ 5 |
| ○ Pensiero '14 | ♀♀ 5 |
| ○ FCO Ribolla Gialla '16 | ♀ 3 |

| | |
|---|---|
| ○ Collio Chardonnay '17 | ♥♥ 2* |
| ○ Collio Pinot Grigio '17 | ♥♥ 2* |
| ○ Collio Sauvignon '17 | ♥♥ 2* |
| ● Schioppettino '15 | ♥♥ 3 |
| ○ Collio Friulano '17 | ♥ 2 |
| ○ Collio Ribolla Gialla '17 | ♥ 3 |
| ○ Collio Chardonnay '16 | ♀♀ 2* |
| ○ Collio Friulano '15 | ♀♀ 2* |
| ● Collio Merlot '13 | ♀♀ 2* |
| ○ Collio Pinot Grigio '16 | ♀♀ 2* |
| ○ Collio Sauvignon '16 | ♀♀ 2* |
| ● El Neri di Norina '12 | ♀♀ 5 |
| ● Schioppettino '14 | ♀♀ 3 |
| ● Schioppettino '13 | ♀♀ 3 |

# Roberto Picéch

LOC. PRADIS, 11
34071 CORMÒNS [GO]
TEL. +39 048160347
www.picech.com

CELLAR SALES
PRE-BOOKED VISITS
ACCOMMODATION
ANNUAL PRODUCTION 30,000 bottles
HECTARES UNDER VINE 8.00
VITICULTURE METHOD Certified Organic

Roberto Picéch's winery sits atop a hill in Pradis, in Cormòns, surrounded by the precious vineyards he inherited from his father, Egidio. Egidio was something of a legend in the area. Known as 'the rebel' to the locals, he's remembered for his tenacity, generosity and availability, gifts that he passed on to the new generation. And they are showing the same resistance to enological fashion, a quality that helps us understand the stylistic character of their wines, which aren't always so easily approached. It's a personal style, intimately bound up with the authentic purity upheld by its authors. The wines that Roberto dedicated to his two children, Athena and Ruben, always elicit loving sentiments, but his 2017s are just as good. Their 2017 Friulano is redolent of yellow flowers, while its creamy palate closes with a characteristic, slightly bitter note. Their 2017 Malvasia is a very fruit-driven wine and lightly aromatic, but their 2017 Pinot Bianco, a wine that's fragrant on the nose and crisp on the palate, takes the cake.

| | |
|---|---|
| ○ Collio Pinot Bianco '17 | ♥♥ 3* |
| ○ Collio Bianco Athena Magnum '16 | ♥♥ 7 |
| ○ Collio Friulano '17 | ♥♥ 3 |
| ○ Collio Malvasia '17 | ♥♥ 3 |
| ● Collio Rosso Ruben Ris. '15 | ♥♥ 6 |
| ○ Collio Pinot Bianco '13 | ♥♥♥ 3* |
| ○ Collio Bianco Athena Magnum '15 | ♥♥ 7 |
| ○ Collio Friulano '16 | ♥♥ 3 |
| ○ Collio Malvasia '16 | ♥♥ 3* |
| ○ Collio Pinot Bianco '16 | ♥♥ 3* |

# Pitars

VIA TONELLO, 10
33098 SAN MARTINO AL TAGLIAMENTO [PN]
TEL. +39 043488078
www.pitars.it

CELLAR SALES
PRE-BOOKED VISITS
ANNUAL PRODUCTION 800,000 bottles
HECTARES UNDER VINE 150.00
SUSTAINABLE WINERY

I Pitars is a local word for the Pittaros, a historic family with long-standing ties to regional wine production. Stefano, Nicola, Jessica and Judy constitute the fourth generation to represent this well-established brand. They work in a splendid facility, a first-rate example of sustainable architecture that was built entirely according to principles of bio-construction and energy conservation (it's entirely self-sufficient). They avail themselves of some 150 hectares of terrain, which gives rise to an average of 800,000 bottles a year. In recent years they've focused on the quality of their sparkling wines, which are produced and bottled on site. In particular, their Ribolla Gialla sees about six months in their autoclave. Their vast range of wines manages to satisfy every market need, and their prices are decidedly competitive. Half of their production is distributed in Italy with the rest going to some 25 countries around the world.

| | |
|---|---|
| ○ Friuli Friulano '17 | ♥♥ 2* |
| ● Friuli Grave Cabernet Franc '16 | ♥♥ 2* |
| ● Friuli Grave Merlot '16 | ♥♥ 2* |
| ○ Friuli Grave Traminer Aromatico '17 | ♥♥ 2* |
| ○ Friuli Pinot Grigio '17 | ♥♥ 2* |
| ○ Friuli Sauvignon '17 | ♥♥ 2* |
| ○ Malvasia '17 | ♥ 2 |
| ○ Prosecco Brut Mill. '17 | ♥ 5 |
| ○ Prosecco Extra Dry Gold '17 | ♥ 5 |
| ○ Ribolla Gialla Brut | ♥ 2 |
| ● Friuli Grave Cabernet Franc '14 | ♥♥ 2* |
| ○ Friuli Grave Pinot Grigio '16 | ♥♥ 2* |
| ● Friuli Grave Rosso Brumal '15 | ♥♥ 3 |
| ○ Malvasia '16 | ♥♥ 2* |
| ○ Malvasia '15 | ♥♥ 2* |
| ○ Tureis '13 | ♥♥ 5 |

# Vigneti Pittaro

VIA UDINE, 67
33033 CODROIPO [UD]
TEL. +39 0432904726
www.vignetipittaro.com

CELLAR SALES
PRE-BOOKED VISITS
ACCOMMODATION
ANNUAL PRODUCTION 300,000 bottles
HECTARES UNDER VINE 90.00
SUSTAINABLE WINERY

Piero Pittaro's cellar is surrounded by vineyards and integrates perfectly with the natural environment, the result of bringing together architecture, technology and practical considerations. Here in Codroipo the terrain is characterized by Friuli Grave's dry, stony soil, though the estate also comprises plots on the Ramandolo hills, in the Friuli Colli Orientali appellation. It's at the latter that the grapes for their Ronco Vieri wines are cultivated. Their director Stefano Trinco also has proven experience in making Metodo Classico sparkling wine, which serves as their selection's crown jewel. Their selection offers an enormous range of choice and manages to satisfy every need. Year after year, we see different wines and the results are always extremely positive. Naturally there are plenty of sparkling wines, all strictly Metodo Classicos. And their 2011 Pittaro Brut Ettichetta affirms its status as their selection's top wine, as well as a regional flagship.

| | |
|---|---|
| ○ Pittaro Et. Oro Brut M. Cl. '11 | ▼▼ 5 |
| ○ Pittaro Brut Et. Argento | ▼▼ 4 |
| ⊙ Pittaro Brut Rosé Pink | ▼▼ 5 |
| ○ Ramandolo Ronco Vieri '15 | ▼▼ 3 |
| ○ Ribolla Gialla Brut | ▼▼ 5 |
| ⊙ Moscato Rosa Valzer in Rosa '17 | ▼ 3 |
| ○ Passito Apicio | ▼ 3 |
| ○ FCO Friulano Ronco Vieri '16 | ♀♀ 3 |
| ○ FCO Friulano Ronco Vieri '15 | ♀♀ 3 |
| ● FCO Refosco P. R. Ronco Vieri '15 | ♀♀ 3 |
| ○ Friuli Grave Chardonnay Mousquè '15 | ♀♀ 3 |
| ○ Manzoni Bianco '16 | ♀♀ 3 |

# Denis Pizzulin

VIA BROLO, 43
33040 PREPOTTO [UD]
TEL. +39 0432713425
www.pizzulin.com

CELLAR SALES
PRE-BOOKED VISITS
ANNUAL PRODUCTION 30,000 bottles
HECTARES UNDER VINE 11.00
SUSTAINABLE WINERY

Denis Pizzulin's small winery is further divided into various plots along the Prepotto hills. It's a narrow valley that borders Slovenia and Collio and that's teeming with artisanal, family-run producers. The area, whose long-cultivated terrain is characterized by a mix of marl and sandstone, serves as the homeland for Ribolla Nera. It's the cultivar used to make their Schioppettino, the cornerstone of a selection that proves sound and complete. Almost equal scores across the board and unanimous praise testifies to the soundness of their selection, both whites and reds, all perfectly in line with previous vintages. Their enticing and gratifying 2015 Schioppettino di Prepotto is always front and center, while their excellent 2015 Merlot Scaglia Rossa Riserva proves fragrant and balsamic. Among their whites we make note of their 2017 Friulano for its elegance, fragrance and drinkability.

| | |
|---|---|
| ○ FCO Friulano '17 | ▼▼ 3 |
| ● FCO Merlot Scaglia Rossa Ris. '15 | ▼▼ 5 |
| ○ FCO Pinot Bianco '17 | ▼▼ 3 |
| ● FCO Pinot Nero '15 | ▼▼ 5 |
| ● FCO Refosco P. R. Ris '15 | ▼▼ 5 |
| ○ FCO Sauvignon '17 | ▼▼ 3 |
| ● FCO Schioppettino di Prepotto '15 | ▼▼ 5 |
| ○ FCO Pinot Grigio '17 | ▼ 3 |
| ○ FCO Bianco Rarisolchi '15 | ♀♀ 3 |
| ○ FCO Friulano '16 | ♀♀ 3 |
| ○ FCO Friulano '15 | ♀♀ 3 |
| ● FCO Merlot Scaglia Rossa Ris. '13 | ♀♀ 4 |
| ○ FCO Pinot Grigio '16 | ♀♀ 3 |
| ○ FCO Pinot Grigio '15 | ♀♀ 3 |
| ● FCO Schioppettino di Prepotto '13 | ♀♀ 4 |

# Damijan Podversic

VIA BRIGATA PAVIA, 61
34170 GORIZIA
TEL. +39 048178217
www.damijanpodversic.com

CELLAR SALES
PRE-BOOKED VISITS
ANNUAL PRODUCTION 28,200 bottles
HECTARES UNDER VINE 10.00
VITICULTURE METHOD Certified Organic
SUSTAINABLE WINERY

From Monte Calvario, one of the highest peaks in Collio, you get a view of the waves of hills that stretch out along the immense lowlands down to the sea. It's a breathtaking panorama that Damijan Podversic has the fortune of enjoying every day while attending to his vineyards. Proud of his farming DNA, he's adopted time-honored practices so as to respect nature's rhythms, even when it means accepting adversity. This means long maceration on the skins, both for his reds and whites, and no action that might interfere with the slow, gradual process of transformation. For three of Damijan's wines to be in the finals certainly isn't a surprise, though there is one piece of news: for the first time their Nekaj earns Tre Bicchieri. The wine's name calls up the cultivar with which it's made, Tocai Friulano, but its sensory characteristics are quite different from what we're used to. Their 2014 offers up aromas of orange peel, cedar and toasted hazelnuts, while the palate proves fragrant and deep.

| | |
|---|---|
| ○ Nekaj '14 | 🍷🍷🍷 6 |
| ○ Malvasia '14 | 🍷🍷 8 |
| ○ Ribolla Gialla '14 | 🍷🍷 8 |
| ○ Kaplja '14 | 🍷🍷 6 |
| ● Prelit '14 | 🍷🍷 6 |
| ○ Malvasia '13 | 🍷🍷🍷 8 |
| ○ Ribolla Gialla '12 | 🍷🍷🍷 8 |
| ○ Nekaj '13 | 🍷🍷 6 |
| ○ Ribolla Gialla '13 | 🍷🍷 8 |

# Isidoro Polencic

LOC. PLESSIVA, 12
34071 CORMÒNS [GO]
TEL. +39 048160655
www.polencic.com

CELLAR SALES
PRE-BOOKED VISITS
ACCOMMODATION
ANNUAL PRODUCTION 120,000 bottles
HECTARES UNDER VINE 28.00

The Polenicic family's roots in Collio go back to the latter half of the 19th century. They're a stubborn clan that have maintained a love for the land and traditional values. Elisabetta, Michele and Alex manage the winery founded in 1968 by their father, Isidoro, fully embracing their vine growing heritage. A large part of their vineyards surround the winery's headquarters in Cormòns, in Plessiva, while others are spread out in neighboring districts. This allows for a diversification of their selection, drawing on the environmental characteristics best suited to each cultivar. Every year only white wines are submitted, as they're far more representative of Collio, and almost always at least one of them makes it into our finals. This year the honor goes to their 2016 Friulano Fisc, a wine that features an elegant, balsamic aromatic profile enriched by whiffs of tropical fruit. In the mouth it proves soft and velvety, though fresh and fragrant as well.

| | |
|---|---|
| ○ Collio Friulano Fisc '16 | 🍷🍷 4 |
| ○ Collio Chardonnay '17 | 🍷🍷 3 |
| ○ Collio Friulano '17 | 🍷🍷 3 |
| ○ Collio Pinot Grigio '17 | 🍷🍷 3 |
| ○ Oblin Blanc '16 | 🍷🍷 4 |
| ○ Collio Pinot Bianco '17 | 🍷 3 |
| ○ Collio Chardonnay '16 | 🍷🍷 3 |
| ○ Collio Friulano '16 | 🍷🍷 3 |
| ○ Collio Friulano '15 | 🍷🍷 3 |
| ○ Collio Friulano Fisc '15 | 🍷🍷 4 |
| ○ Collio Pinot Grigio '16 | 🍷🍷 3 |
| ○ Collio Pinot Grigio '15 | 🍷🍷 3 |
| ○ Collio Sauvignon '15 | 🍷🍷 3 |
| ○ Oblin Blanc '13 | 🍷🍷 4 |

## Polje

LOC. NOVALI, 11
34071 CORMÒNS [GO]
TEL. +39 047160660
www.polje.com

**CELLAR SALES**
**PRE-BOOKED VISITS**
**ANNUAL PRODUCTION** 45,000 bottles
**HECTARES UNDER VINE** 12.00

Polje was founded in 1926 in Novali
(Cormòns), a district known for its sizable
tracts of land with southern exposure. It's
an area particularly well-suited to
viticulture thanks in part to its sinkholes
(called 'polje'), formed by erosion. In the
early part of the century, brothers Luigi and
Stefano Sutto (Venetian entrepreneurs who
already owned the Sutto e Batiso brand)
had the chance to visit the territory. They
fell in love and decided to leave a mark
here. In 2015 Polje vaulted forward when
it became part of the Sutto Wine group.
Polje is specialized in whites and on the
market its high-profile production
philosophy is represented by only four
wines. Already last year we pointed out
the excellence of their selection, and this
year some two wines earned well-
deserved places in our finals: a superb
2017 Sauvignon and 2017 Pinot Grigio,
which are among the best in the region.

| | |
|---|---|
| ○ Collio Pinot Grigio '17 | ▼▼ 3* |
| ○ Collio Sauvignon '17 | ▼▼ 3* |
| ○ Collio Friulano '17 | ▼▼ 3 |
| ○ Collio Ribolla Gialla '17 | ▼▼ 3 |
| ○ Collio Friulano '16 | ♀♀ 3 |
| ○ Collio Pinot Grigio '16 | ♀♀ 3 |
| ○ Collio Ribolla Gialla '16 | ♀♀ 3 |
| ○ Collio Sauvignon '16 | ♀♀ 3* |
| ○ Collio Sauvignon '14 | ♀♀ 3 |
| ○ Malvasia '13 | ♀♀ 3 |

## Pradio

FRAZ. FELETTIS
VIA UDINE, 17
33050 BICINICCO [UD]
TEL. +39 0432990123
www.pradio.it

**CELLAR SALES**
**PRE-BOOKED VISITS**
**ANNUAL PRODUCTION** 300,000 bottles
**HECTARES UNDER VINE** 33.00

Pradio was founded in 1974, however the
Cielo family's experience in wine-growing
goes back more than a century. For more
than a decade now, the producer has been
managed by the fourth generation of family,
cousins Luca and Pierpaolo, who are driven
by the same passion for the land and wine
as their ancestors. Their vineyards are
concentrated along the stony, sunny slopes
that characterized Friuli Grave. Vineyard
management is entrusted to Enrico Della
Mora, who's supported in the cellar by
Gianni Menotti. It's a precious collaboration
that has resulted in a sound selection of
wines and increasing interest by the public.
This year no Starz blends were submitted,
neither their white nor their red, which
represent the winery's crown jewels
(evidently they needed more time to age).
We still appreciated the soundness of their
base line, in particular their 2017 Pinot
Grigio Priara and their 2016 Refosco Tuaro,
both which proved enjoyable on the nose
and on the palate.

| | |
|---|---|
| ● Friuli Grave Cabernet Sauvignon Crearo '16 | ▼▼ 3 |
| ○ Friuli Grave Pinot Grigio Priara '17 | ▼▼ 3 |
| ● Friuli Grave Refosco P.R. Tuaro '16 | ▼▼ 3 |
| ○ Friuli Grave Chardonnay Teraje '17 | ▼ 3 |
| ○ Friuli Grave Sauvignon Sobaja '17 | ▼ 3 |
| ○ Prosecco Brut | ▼ 2 |
| ○ Friuli Grave Friulano Gaiare '16 | ♀♀ 2* |
| ● Friuli Grave Merlot Roncomoro '16 | ♀♀ 2* |
| ○ Friuli Grave Pinot Grigio Priara '16 | ♀♀ 2* |
| ○ Friuli Grave Pinot Grigio Priara '15 | ♀♀ 2* |
| ● Friuli Grave Refosco P. R. Tuaro '15 | ♀♀ 2* |
| ○ Friuli Grave Sauvignon Sobaja '15 | ♀♀ 2* |
| ○ Friuli Grave Starz Bianco '16 | ♀♀ 2* |
| ● Friuli Grave Starz Rosso '13 | ♀♀ 2* |

# Primosic

FRAZ. OSLAVIA
LOC. MADONNINA DI OSLAVIA, 3
34070 GORIZIA
TEL. +39 0481535153
www.primosic.com

CELLAR SALES
PRE-BOOKED VISITS
ANNUAL PRODUCTION 210,000 bottles
HECTARES UNDER VINE 32.00

Marko and Boris Primosic are managing the winery founded by their father, Silvestro, in 1956. Oslavia is celebrated for its considerable number of family-run wineries and its reliance on age-old methods (some of which go back to ancient borderlands traditions). Long maceration on the skins, for both reds and whites (and especially Ribolla Gialla), is one of them. Modern technology is used to enrich their selection with more approachable wines as well. It's a two-track approach that allows Primosic to stand out among Collio's producers. With three wines in the finals, there's always a solid possibility of getting a gold. For some three years in a row, their Ribolla Gialla di Oslavia Riserva has led the way, but this year our highest praise was reserved for their 2015 Chardonnay Gmajne, which brought home Tre Bricchieri. Their 2013 Klin, made with Chardonnay, Sauvignon, Tocai Friulano and Ribolla Gialla, also gets an honorable mention.

| | | |
|---|---|---|
| ○ Collio Chardonnay Gmajne '15 | ▼▼▼ | 5 |
| ○ Collio Bianco Klin '13 | ▼▼ | 6 |
| ○ Collio Ribolla Gialla di Oslavia Ris. '15 | ▼▼ | 6 |
| ● Collio Rosso Metamorfosis '12 | ▼▼ | 6 |
| ○ Collio Sauvignon Gmajne '16 | ▼▼ | 5 |
| ○ Ribolla Gialla '17 | ▼▼ | 3 |
| ○ Collio Chardonnay Gmajne '11 | ♀♀♀ | 4* |
| ○ Collio Ribolla Gialla di Oslavia Ris. '13 | ♀♀♀ | 5 |
| ○ Collio Ribolla Gialla di Oslavia Ris. '12 | ♀♀♀ | 5 |
| ○ Collio Bianco Klin '12 | ♀♀ | 5 |
| ○ Collio Friulano '16 | ♀♀ | 3 |
| ○ Collio Pinot Grigio '15 | ♀♀ | 5 |
| ○ Ribolla Gialla '16 | ♀♀ | 3 |

# ★Doro Princic

LOC. PRADIS, 5
34071 CORMÒNS [GO]
TEL. +39 048160723
doroprincic@virgilio.it

CELLAR SALES
PRE-BOOKED VISITS
ANNUAL PRODUCTION 60,000 bottles
HECTARES UNDER VINE 10.00

The name Princic is a guarantee of absolute quality as far as Collio wines are concerned, and much of the credit goes to Alessandro. He's a tried-and-true vine grower that inherited a special combination of skills from his father, the ability to talk straight and to listen. He's a convinced supporter of monovarietal wines, and manages to get the best out of each cultivar by respecting nature's rhythms. A sly smile emerges from beneath his Austro-Hungarian mustache, and he and his wife make a likable, elegant couple. They also have the help of young Carlo both in the vineyard and in the cellar. Sandro's enological skills are well-known by now, and our scoring table underlines the fact. It's practically a photocopy of last year's result, at least in terms of the three wines that made it to our finals. And once again, their 2017 Pinot Bianco stands out, earning Tre Bicchieri. It's worth noting, however, the excellent performance put in by their 2017 Malvasia and 2017 Friulano, a highly drinkable wine.

| | | |
|---|---|---|
| ○ Collio Pinot Bianco '17 | ▼▼▼ | 5 |
| ○ Collio Friulano '17 | ▼▼ | 5 |
| ○ Collio Malvasia '17 | ▼▼ | 5 |
| ○ Collio Pinot Grigio '17 | ▼▼ | 5 |
| ○ Collio Ribolla Gialla '17 | ▼▼ | 5 |
| ○ Collio Sauvignon '17 | ▼▼ | 5 |
| ○ Collio Friulano '15 | ♀♀♀ | 5 |
| ○ Collio Malvasia '14 | ♀♀♀ | 5 |
| ○ Collio Malvasia '13 | ♀♀♀ | 5 |
| ○ Collio Malvasia '12 | ♀♀♀ | 5 |
| ○ Collio Malvasia '11 | ♀♀♀ | 5 |
| ○ Collio Malvasia '10 | ♀♀♀ | 4 |
| ○ Collio Malvasia '09 | ♀♀♀ | 4* |
| ○ Collio Malvasia '08 | ♀♀♀ | 4 |
| ○ Collio Pinot Bianco '16 | ♀♀♀ | 5 |

## Puiatti

LOC. ZUCCOLE, 4
34076 ROMANS D'ISONZO [GO]
TEL. +39 0481909608
www.puiatti.com

CELLAR SALES
PRE-BOOKED VISITS
ANNUAL PRODUCTION 450,000 bottles
HECTARES UNDER VINE 50.00
SUSTAINABLE WINERY

Founded by legend Vittorio Puiatti in 1967, the cellar that bears his name has since become a leader among Friuli's multitude of wineries. Over time he's managed to evolve, embracing and even anticipating developments in international markets. The brand has become synonymous with rigor, vision and creativity, with a signature style that aims to bring out the original character of each cultivar. Since joining Bertani Domains, enology has been entrusted to Andrea Giuriato, with particular attention reserved for their Ribolla Gialla whites, which come in various versions. During our tastings, the highest praise went to the two wines from their Archetipi line. In addition to their 2016 Ribolla Gialla Archetipi, whose originality we had the chance to describe and applaud in our last edition, we tasted their 2016 Sauvignon Archetipi, which distinguished itself for its broad-ranging and extremely varietal aromas, and for the savoriness of its palate.

| | |
|---|---|
| ○ Friuli Pinot Grigio '17 | ♀♀ 3 |
| ○ Fun Sauvignon '17 | ♀♀ 3 |
| ○ Ribolla Extra Brut M. Cl. | ♀♀ 4 |
| ○ Ribolla Gialla Archetipi '16 | ♀♀ 5 |
| ○ Sauvignon Archetipi '16 | ♀♀ 3 |
| ○ Ribolla Gialla '17 | ♀ 3 |
| ○ Collio Sauvignon Archetipi '88 | ♀♀♀ 5 |
| ○ Friuli Isonzo Friulano Vuj '16 | ♀♀ 3 |
| ○ Friuli Isonzo Friulano Vuj '15 | ♀♀ 3 |
| ○ Ribolla Gialla Archetipi '15 | ♀♀ 5 |
| ○ Ribolla Gialla Archetipi '14 | ♀♀ 5 |
| ○ Ribolla Gialla Extra Brut M. Cl. | ♀♀ 4 |
| ○ Sauvignon Fun '15 | ♀♀ 3 |

## La Rajade

LOC. PETRUS, 2
34070 DOLEGNA DEL COLLIO [GO]
TEL. +39 0481639273
www.larajade.it

CELLAR SALES
PRE-BOOKED VISITS
ANNUAL PRODUCTION 50,000 bottles
HECTARES UNDER VINE 6.50

La Rajade was founded in 1999 with the purchase of an estate that had already been active for some time (both the vineyards and cellar). Their vineyards are situated in the northernmost part of Collio, descending from Ronco Petrus down towards the valley. They follow the morphology of the hills, which naturally offer the ideal amount of sun. The winery is owned by Sergio Campeotto, but management is entrusted to Diego Zanin, a real jack-of-all-trades who has extensive experience in winemaking. Consultant Andrea Romano Rossi offers helpful guidance as well. And once again their 2015 Bianco Caprizi Riserva stood out in our tastings by virtue of its commendable aromatic and balsamic nuances, calling up dried medicinal herbs, tropical dried and candied fruit, clear honey and sweet biscuits. In the mouth it proves soft, balanced and especially long. Their 2016 Collio Rosso and 2015 Cabernet Sauvignon Riserva, both glycerin, flavorful wines, also proved excellent.

| | |
|---|---|
| ○ Collio Bianco Caprizi Ris. '15 | ♀♀ 5 |
| ● Collio Cabernet Sauvignon Ris. '15 | ♀♀ 5 |
| ● Collio Rosso '16 | ♀♀ 3 |
| ○ Collio Sauvignon '17 | ♀♀ 3 |
| ○ Collio Friulano '17 | ♀ 3 |
| ○ Collio Ribolla Gialla '17 | ♀ 3 |
| ○ Collio Bianco Caprizi Ris. '14 | ♀♀ 3* |
| ● Collio Cabernet Sauvignon Ris. '14 | ♀♀ 5 |
| ○ Collio Friulano '16 | ♀♀ 3 |
| ● Collio Merlot Ris. '14 | ♀♀ 5 |
| ○ Collio Pinot Grigio '15 | ♀♀ 3 |
| ○ Collio Sauvignon '16 | ♀♀ 3 |
| ○ Collio Sauvignon '15 | ♀♀ 3 |
| ● Schioppettino '15 | ♀♀ 3 |

## Rocca Bernarda

FRAZ. IPPLIS
VIA ROCCA BERNARDA, 27
33040 PREMARIACCO [UD]
TEL. +39 0432716914
www.sagrivit.it

CELLAR SALES
PRE-BOOKED VISITS
ANNUAL PRODUCTION 100,000 bottles
HECTARES UNDER VINE 38.50

Rocca Bernarda is headquartered in an ancient manor that features four picturesque cylindrical towers. It's a building that goes back to the 1500s, but was utilized for centuries as the summer home of the Cividalese family. It's here that count Acquini's Picolit found new life after it was bought by the count Perusini family. It was also they who handed the property over to the Sovereign Military Order of Malta in 1977. As of 2006 the winery has been managed by the Società Agricola Vitivinicola Italiana (SAGRIVIT), who have entrusted winemaking to Maurilio Chioccia. It's his responsibility to safeguard the quality of this historic brand. Their 2017 whites are decidedly well-made, balanced, with nice nose-mouth symmetry and varietal adherence. But their reds, especially, proved a cut above the rest. Their 2016 Refosco is redolent of cherries, quinine, tobacco and coffee, while the mouth is lean and pleasant. Their 2015 Merlot Centis is opulent, both on the nose and the palate, with potent but restrained tannins.

| | |
|---|---|
| ● FCO Merlot '16 | ♟♟ 3 |
| ● FCO Merlot Centis '15 | ♟♟ 6 |
| ● FCO Refosco P. R. '16 | ♟♟ 3 |
| ○ FCO Chardonnay '17 | ♟ 3 |
| ○ FCO Ribolla Gialla '17 | ♟ 3 |
| ○ FCO Sauvignon '17 | ♟ 3 |
| ● COF Merlot Centis '99 | ♟♟♟ 7 |
| ○ COF Picolit '03 | ♟♟♟ 7 |
| ○ COF Picolit '98 | ♟♟♟ 7 |
| ○ COF Picolit '97 | ♟♟♟ 7 |
| ○ FCO Friulano '16 | ♟♟ 3 |
| ● FCO Pignolo Novecento 1113-2013 '11 | ♟♟ 5 |
| ● FCO Refosco P. R. '15 | ♟♟ 3 |
| ○ FCO Sauvignon '15 | ♟♟ 3 |
| ○ Novecento 1113-2013 '16 | ♟♟ 4 |

## Paolo Rodaro

LOC. SPESSA
VIA CORMONS, 60
33043 CIVIDALE DEL FRIULI [UD]
TEL. +39 0432716066
www.rodaropaolo.it

CELLAR SALES
PRE-BOOKED VISITS
ANNUAL PRODUCTION 250,000 bottles
HECTARES UNDER VINE 57.00
SUSTAINABLE WINERY

The Rodaro family were producing wine as far back as 1846, and today it's the sixth generation's turn to lead the winery. Paolo, who shares his name with the winery's founder, is continuing on the path tread by his father, Luigi, and his uncle Edo during the 60s and 70s. It was during this time that the producer was transformed into one of the region's major wineries, starting with their vineyards in Spessa, a productive district in Cividale del Friuli. The vine grower's spirit, in its most noble sense, is expressed throughout their entire selection. This includes their Romain line of wines: reds of notable structure, made with late-harvest grapes. An excellent performance by their entire selection is pointed up by two wines that both did well in our finals last year, and this year repeated the exploit. Their 2017 Pinot Grigio excelled for its natural drinkability while the 2017 Malvasia proved extremely elegant and territorial. Their Metodo Classico sparklers are also excellent, both Nature Pas Dosès that feature exquisitely fine perlage.

| | |
|---|---|
| ○ FCO Malvasia '17 | ♟♟ 3* |
| ○ FCO Pinot Grigio '17 | ♟♟ 3* |
| ○ Brut Nature | ♟♟ 4 |
| ● FCO Cabernet Sauvignon Romain '12 | ♟♟ 5 |
| ○ FCO Friulano '17 | ♟♟ 3 |
| ● FCO Pignolo Romain '10 | ♟♟ 6 |
| ● FCO Refosco P. R. Romain '12 | ♟♟ 6 |
| ○ FCO Sauvignon '17 | ♟♟ 3* |
| ⊙ Rosé Nature '14 | ♟♟ 5 |
| ○ FCO Ribolla Gialla '17 | ♟ 3 |
| ○ FCO Malvasia '16 | ♟♟♟ 4* |
| ○ FCO Friulano '16 | ♟♟ 4 |
| ○ FCO Pinot Grigio '16 | ♟♟ 3* |
| ● FCO Schioppettino Romain '12 | ♟♟ 5 |

## La Roncaia

FRAZ. CERGNEU
VIA VERDI, 26
33045 NIMIS [UD]
TEL. +39 0432790280
www.laroncaia.it

CELLAR SALES
PRE-BOOKED VISITS
ANNUAL PRODUCTION 60,000 bottles
HECTARES UNDER VINE 25.00

In 1998 the Fantinel group, three generations of vine growers, decided to purchase a winery in Cergneu, Nimis, the cradle of Ramandolo that lies in the northernmost part of the Friuli Colli Orientali appellation. La Roncaia was founded with the goal of enlarging the group's already considerable selection of wines. This includes whites made at their Tenuta Sant'Helena in Collio and their more approachable wines produced at Borgo Tesis, in the Friuli lowlands. It's a modern combination of wines that's overseen by the young but motivated enologist Gabriele Tami. This year only a few wines were submitted and so we didn't get a complex picture of their range. However their 2016 Friulano and 2016 Bianco Eclisse once again delivered, leading the way and confirming the excellent quality that the producer has maintained with enviable consistency. They're both fruit-driven, fragrant wines on the nose, energetic and long on the palate.

## Il Roncal

FRAZ. COLLE MONTEBELLO
VIA FORNALIS, 148
33043 CIVIDALE DEL FRIULI [UD]
TEL. +39 0432730138
www.ilroncal.it

CELLAR SALES
PRE-BOOKED VISITS
ACCOMMODATION AND RESTAURANT SERVICE
ANNUAL PRODUCTION 130,000 bottles
HECTARES UNDER VINE 20.00

Roncal is a flourishing winery that's managed entirely by women, with Martina Moreale at the helm. She's the owner and a bona fide jack-of-all-trades. With personality, unquestionable entrepreneurial skill, courage and determination she has carried forward the project begun by her late husband, Roberto Zorzettig. She's also finishing work on the new cellar that stands atop the Montebello hills. It's an area rich in vegetation, with woods and vineyards that follow the shape of the slopes, as well as an amazing panoramic view. When a number of wines alternate in terms of making it into our finals, it's a good sign that the entire selection is in a position to compete, and that the principal variable is a year's climate. This year their 2017 Friulano, the region's most representative wine, leads the way, proving pleasantly flowery but also fruity on the nose, energetic and savory on the palate.

| | | |
|---|---|---|
| ○ Bianco Eclisse '16 | ♛♛ | 5 |
| ○ FCO Friulano '16 | ♛♛ | 4 |
| ○ FCO Pinot Grigio '16 | ♛ | 5 |
| ○ FCO Ribolla Gialla '16 | ♛ | 4 |
| ○ Eclisse '12 | ♛♛♛ | 4* |
| ○ Bianco Eclisse '15 | ♛♛ | 5 |
| ○ Bianco Eclisse '14 | ♛♛ | 5 |
| ○ COF Picolit '13 | ♛♛ | 5 |
| ● FCO Cabernet Franc '15 | ♛♛ | 4 |
| ○ FCO Friulano '15 | ♛♛ | 4 |
| ● FCO Merlot Fusco '13 | ♛♛ | 5 |
| ● FCO Refosco P.R. '12 | ♛♛ | 5 |
| ○ Ramandolo '13 | ♛♛ | 5 |

| | | |
|---|---|---|
| ○ FCO Friulano '17 | ♛♛ | 3* |
| ○ FCO Bianco Ploe di Stelis '16 | ♛♛ | 4 |
| ● FCO Merlot '15 | ♛♛ | 3 |
| ● FCO Pignolo '11 | ♛♛ | 5 |
| ○ FCO Pinot Grigio '17 | ♛♛ | 3 |
| ○ FCO Ribolla Gialla '17 | ♛♛ | 3 |
| ● FCO Schioppettino '15 | ♛♛ | 4 |
| ● FCO Refosco P.R. '15 | ♛ | 4 |
| ○ FCO Bianco Ploe di Stelis '15 | ♛♛ | 4 |
| ○ FCO Friulano '16 | ♛♛ | 3 |
| ○ FCO Pinot Grigio '16 | ♛♛ | 3* |
| ○ FCO Ribolla Gialla '16 | ♛♛ | 3 |
| ● FCO Rosso Civon '11 | ♛♛ | 5 |
| ○ FCO Sauvignon '16 | ♛♛ | 3 |
| ● FCO Schioppettino '13 | ♛♛ | 4 |

# Il Roncat - Giovanni Dri

FRAZ. RAMANDOLO
VIA PESCIA, 7
33045 NIMIS [UD]
TEL. +39 0432790260
www.drironcat.com

**CELLAR SALES**
**PRE-BOOKED VISITS**
**ANNUAL PRODUCTION** 40,000 bottles
**HECTARES UNDER VINE** 10.00

Giovanni Dri proudly calls himself a 'rocky' man. This might be because he was born among the bluffs of Ramandolo, an area just below Monte Bernadia, where the slopes are steep and, at times, almost impassible. He decided to build the cellar that he himself designed right here, thus realizing a dream cultivated for years. He calls it 'the shack'. It's a simple structure but one that integrates perfectly with the environment. It's cozy and efficient, made entirely with old, natural materials. In a family-run winery everyone does everything, but in their cellar it's Giovanni's daughter Stefania, a graduate in enology, who's primarily in charge. In a clear case of bucking regional tendencies, the producer focuses on sweet wines and reds. But it's a choice that's in perfect keeping with Piedmont's territorial identity. Their Verduzzo Giallo is made in Ramandolo and around here it's the principal cultivar. The wine was submitted in three different versions, which feature intriguing, enduring sweetness and fragrance. Their reds and exquisite 2014 Picolit also proved excellent.

| | | |
|---|---|---|
| ○ COF Picolit '14 | ♟♟ | 7 |
| ● FCO Cabernet '14 | ♟♟ | 3 |
| ● FCO Pignolo Monte dei Carpini '13 | ♟♟ | 5 |
| ● FCO Schioppettino Monte dei Carpin '15 | ♟♟ | 4 |
| ○ Ramandolo Il Roncat '12 | ♟♟ | 5 |
| ○ Ramandolo Uve Decembrine '12 | ♟♟ | 5 |
| ● FCO Rosso Il Roncat '12 | ♟ | 4 |
| ○ Ramandolo '14 | ♟ | 4 |
| ● FCO Refosco P. R. '13 | ♟♟ | 3 |
| ● FCO Refosco P.R. '12 | ♟♟ | 3 |
| ● FCO Rosso Il Roncat '11 | ♟♟ | 5 |
| ● FCO Schioppettino Monte dei Carpin '13 | ♟♟ | 4 |
| ○ Picolit Il Roncat '13 | ♟♟ | 7 |
| ○ Ramandolo Uve Decembrine '11 | ♟♟ | 5 |

# Ronchi di Manzano

VIA ORSARIA, 42
33044 MANZANO [UD]
TEL. +39 0432740718
www.ronchidimanzano.com

**CELLAR SALES**
**PRE-BOOKED VISITS**
**ANNUAL PRODUCTION** 200,000 bottles
**HECTARES UNDER VINE** 60.00

Ronchi di Manzano is one of the most representative producers in Friuli Colli Orientali, and a lot of the credit goes to Roberta Borghese. She's an entrepreneur with an artisanal heart, and a lover of beauty, who's job it is to oversee all stages of production, from the vineyard to the cellar. Today she's joined by her daughters Lisa and Nicole, making for an entirely female staff. The result is a selection of wines that are elegant and graceful. Most of the vineyards can be found around their underground cellar in Manzano, others on the hills of Rosazzo, an enchanting district that has earned classification as a subzone. In last year's edition of Italian Wines we pointed out the interesting way that each a year a different wine makes it into our finals, a clear sign that high quality pervades their entire selection. This year was no different, and the honor goes to their 2017 Chardonnay, which proved just a cut above a series of extraordinarily elegant and worthy wines.

| | | |
|---|---|---|
| ○ FCO Chardonnay '17 | ♟♟ | 3* |
| ○ Bianco Ellègri '17 | ♟♟ | 3 |
| ○ FCO Friulano '17 | ♟♟ | 3 |
| ● FCO Merlot '16 | ♟♟ | 3 |
| ○ FCO Pinot Grigio '17 | ♟♟ | 3 |
| ● FCO Refosco P. R. '16 | ♟♟ | 3 |
| ○ FCO Ribolla Gialla di Rosazzo '17 | ♟♟ | 3 |
| ○ FCO Sauvignon '17 | ♟♟ | 3 |
| ○ COF Ellegri '13 | ♟♟♟ | 3* |
| ○ COF Friulano '10 | ♟♟♟ | 3* |
| ○ COF Friulano '09 | ♟♟♟ | 3* |
| ● COF Merlot Ronc di Subule '99 | ♟♟♟ | 3* |
| ● COF Merlot Ronc di Subule '96 | ♟♟♟ | 3* |
| ○ COF Rosazzo Bianco Ellègri '11 | ♟♟♟ | 3* |
| ○ Rosazzo Bianco '13 | ♟♟♟ | 3* |

## Ronco Blanchis

VIA BLANCHIS, 70
34070 MOSSA [GO]
TEL. +39 048180519
www.roncoblanchis.it

PRE-BOOKED VISITS
ANNUAL PRODUCTION 60,000 bottles
HECTARES UNDER VINE 14.00
SUSTAINABLE WINERY

The Palla family's lovely winery is led by
Lorenzo Blanchis, along with the precious
support of Gianni Menotti. The estate is
situated on the hills behind the rural village
of Mossa, just outside Gorizia. Along the
valley floor the morning fog facilitates the
formation of botrytis cinerea, thus
whitening the grapes. It's a natural
phenomenon that's responsible for the
hills' name and, in certain years, endows
the grapes with original aromas. Only four
wines are made, all whites. Their oldest
vineyards come together in a single wine,
Collio, which represents a maximum
expression of the territory. All their wines
do an excellent job expressing the
territory's potential, highlighting the varietal
qualities of each individual cultivar. Their
2017 Friulano stood out for its superb,
fruity and flowery aromas, and especially
for its suppleness and appeal on the
palate. Their 2016 Collio Bianco Riserva a
wine that proves intriguing and complex on
the nose, while excelling in pleasantness
and balance, brought home Tre Bicchieri.

| | |
|---|---|
| ○ Collio Bianco Ris. '16 | ♟♟ 4 |
| ○ Collio Friulano '17 | ♟♟ 4 |
| ○ Collio Chardonnay '16 | ♟♟ 3 |
| ○ Collio Malvasia '17 | ♟♟ 3 |
| ○ Collio Pinot Grigio '17 | ♟♟ 4 |
| ○ Collio Sauvignon '17 | ♟♟ 4 |
| ○ Collio '13 | ♟♟♟ 3* |
| ○ Collio '12 | ♟♟♟ 3* |
| ○ Collio '15 | ♟♟ 5 |
| ○ Collio Blanc de Blanchis '16 | ♟♟ 3* |
| ○ Collio Blanc de Blanchis '15 | ♟♟ 3* |
| ○ Collio Chardonnay Particella 3 '16 | ♟♟ 3 |
| ○ Collio Friulano '16 | ♟♟ 4 |
| ○ Collio Sauvignon '16 | ♟♟ 4 |
| ○ Collio Sauvignon '15 | ♟♟ 4 |

## ★Ronco dei Tassi

LOC. MONTONA, 19
34071 CORMÒNS [GO]
TEL. +39 048160155
www.roncodeitassi.it

CELLAR SALES
PRE-BOOKED VISITS
ANNUAL PRODUCTION 110,000 bottles
HECTARES UNDER VINE 18.00

Ronco dei Tassi is among Friuli's most
flourishing wineries. Founded in 1989 by
Favio Coser and his wife, Daniela, it's
situated in Montona, Cormòns, on the
Collio Goriziano hills. Sons Matteo and
Enrico are an integral part of the team and
have taken on various responsibilities, like
all family-run wineries. Fabio also owns
Vigna del Lauro, a brand created with the
goal of producing simple wines that offer
drinkability while also being true to
territorial identity, and that bring together
quality and value. It was another year to
remember for the producer,
which saw three wines making it into our
finals (the same as last year), with their
2016 Bianco Fosarin once again earning
Tre Bicchieri. Pinot Bianco, Tocai Friulano
and Malvasia Istriana make up this
splendid blend, a true ambassador of the
region's white wines. Their 2017 Malvasia
also proved splendid by virtue of its
softness, savoriness and balance.

| | |
|---|---|
| ○ Collio Bianco Fosarin '16 | ♟♟♟ 3* |
| ○ Collio Malvasia '17 | ♟♟ 3* |
| ○ Collio Pinot Grigio '17 | ♟♟ 3* |
| ○ Collio Friulano '17 | ♟♟ 3 |
| ○ Collio Picolit '13 | ♟♟ 6 |
| ○ Collio Ribolla Gialla '17 | ♟♟ 3 |
| ○ Collio Sauvignon '17 | ♟♟ 3 |
| ○ Collio Bianco Fosarin '15 | ♟♟♟ 3* |
| ○ Collio Bianco Fosarin '10 | ♟♟♟ 3 |
| ○ Collio Malvasia '15 | ♟♟♟ 3* |
| ○ Collio Malvasia '14 | ♟♟♟ 3* |
| ○ Collio Malvasia '13 | ♟♟♟ 3* |
| ○ Collio Malvasia '12 | ♟♟♟ 3* |
| ○ Collio Malvasia '11 | ♟♟♟ 3* |

# Ronco delle Betulle

LOC. ROSAZZO
VIA ABATE COLONNA, 24
33044 MANZANO [UD]
TEL. +39 0432740547
www.roncodellebetulle.it

**CELLAR SALES**
**PRE-BOOKED VISITS**
**ANNUAL PRODUCTION** 60,000 bottles
**HECTARES UNDER VINE** 12.00
**SUSTAINABLE WINERY**

The vineyards of the Rosazzo hills surround a famous abbey. It was Giovanbattista Adami who sensed the potential of the area back in 1967, an idea well before its time. In 1990 he passed the torch to his daughter Ivana. With great care and dedication she took on the responsibility of managing the winery, personally overseeing every stage of production and transforming Ronco delle Betulle into one of the region's most prestigious brands. Today Ivana is accompanied her her son Simone, with whom she's carrying forward the work of bringing out the qualities of the area's cultivar. An excellent, extremely varietal 2017 Sauvignon earned the highest score of the group and landed a place in our finals. It tantalizes the nose with its aromas of citrus and elderflower syrup, but its especially gratifying on the palate, with a noteworthy finish. The rest of their selection garnered the same praise as in previous years, proving forthright and supple, without frills or flaws.

| | | |
|---|---|---|
| ○ FCO Sauvignon '17 | ♟♟♟ | 3* |
| ○ FCO Friulano '17 | ♟♟ | 3 |
| ● FCO Merlot '15 | ♟♟ | 3 |
| ○ FCO Pinot Grigio '17 | ♟♟ | 3 |
| ● FCO Refosco P. R. '15 | ♟♟ | 3 |
| ● FCO Rosso Narciso '15 | ♟♟ | 5 |
| ○ Rosazzo '16 | ♟♟ | 5 |
| ● FCO Cabernet Franc '15 | ♟ | 3 |
| ○ FCO Ribolla Gialla '17 | ♟ | 3 |
| ● Narciso Rosso '94 | ♟♟♟ | 4* |
| ○ FCO Friulano '16 | ♟♟ | 3 |
| ● FCO Pignolo Rosazzo '10 | ♟♟ | 6 |
| ○ FCO Pinot Grigio '16 | ♟♟ | 3 |
| ○ FCO Sauvignon '16 | ♟♟ | 3 |
| ○ Rosazzo Bianco '15 | ♟♟ | 5 |

# Ronco Scagnet

LOC. CIME DI DOLEGNA, 7
34070 DOLEGNA DEL COLLIO [GO]
TEL. +39 0481639870
www.roncoscagnet.it

**CELLAR SALES**
**PRE-BOOKED VISITS**
**ANNUAL PRODUCTION** 80,000 bottles
**HECTARES UNDER VINE** 12.50

Dolegna del Collio is a tiny town in the province of Gorizia that earned notoriety for hosting a sizable number of prestigious, primarily family-run producers. One of these is Ronco Scagnet, largely unknown until recently, but now one of the area's leading wineries thanks to a selection of excellent and impeccable wines that has been getting a lot of attention as of late. It's managed by Valter Cozzarolo and his son Dimitri, true wine artisans who oversee their vineyards along the gentle Lonzano hills with painstaking care. The vast range of wines submitted allowed us to get a sense of their entire selection and the consistent praise they received points up their strong overall quality. There weren't the standouts that we saw last year, but it's worth pointing out the excellent value for the money that each wine represents.

| | | |
|---|---|---|
| ● Collio Cabernet Franc '15 | ♟♟ | 2* |
| ○ Collio Chardonnay '16 | ♟♟ | 2* |
| ○ Collio Friulano '17 | ♟♟ | 2* |
| ○ Collio Malvasia Istriana '17 | ♟♟ | 2* |
| ● Collio Merlot '16 | ♟♟ | 2* |
| ○ Collio Pinot Grigio '17 | ♟♟ | 2* |
| ○ Collio Ribolla Gialla '17 | ♟♟ | 2* |
| ○ Collio Sauvignon '17 | ♟♟ | 2* |
| ● Schioppettino '16 | ♟♟ | 2* |
| ○ Collio Bianco Folie Blanc '13 | ♟♟ | 2* |
| ○ Collio Friulano '16 | ♟♟ | 2* |
| ○ Collio Pinot Grigio '16 | ♟♟ | 2* |
| ○ Collio Pinot Grigio '15 | ♟♟ | 2* |
| ○ Collio Ribolla Gialla '16 | ♟♟ | 2* |
| ○ Collio Sauvignon '16 | ♟♟ | 2* |
| ○ Raggio di Sole '16 | ♟♟ | 2* |

## Ronco Severo

via Ronchi, 93
33040 Prepotto [UD]
Tel. +39 04337133440
www.roncosevero.it

**CELLAR SALES**
**PRE-BOOKED VISITS**
**ANNUAL PRODUCTION** 22,000 bottles
**HECTARES UNDER VINE** 8.00
**VITICULTURE METHOD** Certified Organic

In 1968 Severo Novello had the chance to purchase a tract of land and farm manor, which he renovated and transformed into a cellar and residence. Today the winery is managed by his son Stefano, a firm believer in organic and biodynamic viticulture, which has led him to adopt an approach to winemaking rooted in ancestral traditions. For example, both their red and white wines undergo spontaneous fermentation and maceration with skin contact, in some cases for months. And their wines are bottled during a waning moon, without filtration or clarification. Long maceration makes for an unusual color. At times it's a bit disconcerting, but it's a logical consequence of the choice and should just be accepted. In any case they're successful wines with aromas of rare pleasantness and gratifying palates that offer up an explosion of flavor. This year their 2016 Ribolla Gialla and 2016 Friulano Riserva made it to our finals, proving juicy, tasty and moving.

| | | |
|---|---|---|
| ○ FCO Friulano Ris. '16 | 🍷🍷 | 4 |
| ○ Ribolla Gialla '16 | 🍷🍷 | 4 |
| ● FCO Merlot Ris. '15 | 🍷🍷 | 5 |
| ○ Pinot Grigio '16 | 🍷🍷 | 4 |
| ○ Severo Bianco '16 | 🍷🍷 | 4 |
| ○ Severo Bianco '12 | YYY | 4* |
| ○ FCO Friulano Ris. '15 | YY | 4 |
| ● FCO Merlot Artiûl Ris. '13 | YY | 5 |
| ● FCO Refosco P. R. '15 | YY | 4 |
| ● FCO Schioppettino di Prepotto '15 | YY | 4 |
| ○ Pinot Grigio '15 | YY | 4 |
| ○ Ribolla Gialla '15 | YY | 4 |
| ○ Ribolla Gialla '14 | YY | 4 |

## Roncùs

via Mazzini, 26
34076 Capriva del Friuli [GO]
Tel. +39 0481809349
www.roncus.it

**CELLAR SALES**
**PRE-BOOKED VISITS**
**ACCOMMODATION**
**ANNUAL PRODUCTION** 40,000 bottles
**HECTARES UNDER VINE** 10.00

In 1985 the Roncus brand was transformed by Marco Perco, when he decided to convert the family business into an estate specializing exclusively in wine production. His vineyards are made of up of various plots, spread out throughout Capriva del Friuli, in the heart of Collio, many of which go back more than a century. The wines they give life to, made strictly with native grape varities, exhibit a personal style. In many ways they resemble Alsatian wines in terms of concentration and aging potential. In last year's edition we pointed out the splendid performance put in by their entire selection, and this year they did it again. Not that this should come as a surprise, considering Marco's well-known enology skills, but it's always a pleasure to repeat the complement. Their 2016 Pinot Bianco stands out for its pleasing aromas of blooming hay and Mediterranean scrubland, but especially for its pleasantness in the mouth.

| | | |
|---|---|---|
| ○ Collio Bianco V. V. '14 | 🍷🍷 | 5 |
| ○ Pinot Bianco '16 | 🍷🍷 | 4 |
| ○ Collio Bianco '16 | 🍷🍷 | 3 |
| ○ Collio Friulano '16 | 🍷🍷 | 4 |
| ○ Malvasia '17 | 🍷🍷 | 3 |
| ● Val di Miez '15 | 🍷🍷 | 5 |
| ○ Ribolla Gialla '17 | 🍷 | 3 |
| ○ Collio Bianco V. V. '08 | YYY | 5 |
| ○ Roncùs Bianco V. V. '01 | YYY | 5 |
| ○ Collio Bianco '15 | YY | 3* |
| ○ Collio Bianco V. V. '13 | YY | 5 |
| ○ Collio Bianco V. V. '12 | YY | 5 |
| ○ Pinot Bianco '15 | YY | 4 |
| ● Val di Miez '14 | YY | 5 |

# ★Russiz Superiore

VIA RUSSIZ, 7
34070 CAPRIVA DEL FRIULI [GO]
TEL. +39 048180328
www.marcofelluga.it

CELLAR SALES
PRE-BOOKED VISITS
ACCOMMODATION
ANNUAL PRODUCTION 180,000 bottles
HECTARES UNDER VINE 50.00
SUSTAINABLE WINERY

Russiz Superiore's vineyards are situated on the Collio Goriziano hills and surround a centuries-old farm manor that hosted the patriarch Raimondo della Torre almost a millennium ago. The winery was founded in 1966 by Marco Felluga, now in his nineties. From the beginning they sought to be a model, a benchmark for the area. The basements of the manor house are used for the cellar, while the old building was transformed into a cozy relais that enjoys a marvelous view of the surrounding area. Today the winery is managed by Roberto with the same passion as his father. For three years in a row their 2017 Friulano earned a gold, and once again it stands out, earning a place in our finals along with a splendid 2013 Sauvignon Riserva that beat the competition and took home Tre Bicchieri. It's a crowning success for a winery that's taken it upon itself to get consumers used to ageworthy whites.

# Sant'Elena

VIA GASPARINI, 1
34072 GRADISCA D'ISONZO [GO]
TEL. +39 048192388
www.sant-elena.com

CELLAR SALES
PRE-BOOKED VISITS
ANNUAL PRODUCTION 130,000 bottles
HECTARES UNDER VINE 30.00

Founded in 1893 by the Kloldic family, Sant'Elena was purchased in 1997 by Dominic Nocerino, a noted wine importer based in the US. Their stated goal is to bring out the best of the Friuli Isonzo appellation. The terrain here is characterized by a lack of organic material and a top layer of red, alluvial earth, not to mention the wind caused by a convergence of the cold continental currents and the sea breeze. Enology is entrusted to the experience of Maurizio Drascek, whose proven capable of achieving consistent results. Their 2017 Pinot Grigio Altre stood out in our tastings for its sweet aromas of caramelized sugar and notes of freshly-harvested wheat. In the mouth it proves soft, but also fragrant. Their two reds, their 2013 Pignolo Quantum and their 2013 Tato, are also excellent, offering up aromas of licorice, dark chocolate and cloves. In the mouth they come through pervasive and flavorful.

| | |
|---|---|
| ○ Collio Sauvignon Ris. '13 | ♟♟♟ 5 |
| ○ Collio Friulano '17 | ♟♟ 4* |
| ● Collio Cabernet Franc '15 | ♟♟ 4 |
| ● Collio Merlot '14 | ♟♟ 4 |
| ○ Collio Pinot Bianco '17 | ♟♟ 4 |
| ○ Collio Pinot Bianco Ris. '15 | ♟♟ 5 |
| ○ Collio Pinot Grigio '17 | ♟♟ 4 |
| ○ Collio Sauvignon '17 | ♟♟ 4 |
| ○ Collio Friulano '16 | ♟♟♟ 4* |
| ○ Collio Friulano '15 | ♟♟♟ 4* |
| ○ Collio Friulano '14 | ♟♟♟ 4* |
| ○ Collio Bianco Col Disôre '15 | ♟♟ 5 |
| ○ Collio Bianco Col Disôre '13 | ♟♟ 5 |
| ○ Collio Pinot Bianco '16 | ♟♟ 4 |
| ○ Collio Pinot Grigio '16 | ♟♟ 4 |
| ○ Collio Sauvignon '16 | ♟♟ 4 |
| ○ Collio Sauvignon Ris. '12 | ♟♟ 5 |

| | |
|---|---|
| ● Friuli Isonzo Pignolo Quantum '13 | ♟♟ 7 |
| ○ Friuli Isonzo Pinot Grigio Rive Alte '17 | ♟♟ 3 |
| ● Tato '13 | ♟♟ 5 |
| ○ Friuli Isonzo Friulano Rive Alte '17 | ♟ 3 |
| ○ Friuli Isonzo Sauvignon Rive Alte '17 | ♟ 4 |
| ● Cabernet Franc '11 | ♟♟ 3 |
| ○ Friuli Isonzo Chardonnay Rive Alte '16 | ♟♟ 3 |
| ○ Friuli Isonzo Friulano Rive Alte '16 | ♟♟ 3 |
| ○ Friuli Isonzo Friulano Rive Alte '15 | ♟♟ 3 |
| ○ Friuli Isonzo Pinot Grigio Rive Alte '16 | ♟♟ 3 |
| ○ Friuli Isonzo Pinot Grigio Rive Alte '15 | ♟♟ 3 |
| ● Merlot '11 | ♟♟ 4 |

# Marco Sara

FRAZ. SAVORGNANO DEL TORRE
VIA DEI MONTI, 3A
33040 POVOLETTO [UD]
TEL. +39 0432666066
www.marcosara.com

**CELLAR SALES**
**PRE-BOOKED VISITS**
**ANNUAL PRODUCTION** 25,000 bottles
**HECTARES UNDER VINE** 8.00
**VITICULTURE METHOD** Certified Organic

Despite his young age, Marco Sara has managed the family winery for some years now. He's adopted a natural approach to viticulture in cultivating his vineyards in the hills of Pavoletto, an area historically populated by small agricultural producers. This fragmentation is reflected in the pedoclimatic conditions of the various plots. Riu Falcon hosts the oldest vineyards, with clay terrain that's well-suited to white grapes (as well as botrytis), while the higher areas of Roncus enjoy strong day-night temperature swings that give life to more aromatic wines. Marco's 2015 Picolit dei Colli Orientali del Friuli has become an icon and for the fourth year in a row we find it competing in our finals. Their 2016 Refosco el Rè offers up dark notes of black pepper and cloves, while the mouth proves potent and balanced. Their 2016 Verduzzo Friulano is a curious wine. We expected sweetness but it's actually a dry wine.

| | |
|---|---|
| ○ COF Picolit '16 | ♟♟6 |
| ○ FCO Bianco Erba Alta '16 | ♟♟4 |
| ● FCO Refosco P. R. el Rè '16 | ♟♟4 |
| ● FCO Schioppettino '16 | ♟♟4 |
| ○ FCO Verduzzo Friulano '16 | ♟♟4 |
| ○ FCO Friulano '16 | ♟3 |
| ○ COF Picolit '15 | ♟♟6 |
| ○ FCO Bianco Erba Alta '15 | ♟♟5 |
| ○ FCO Friulano '15 | ♟♟3 |
| ○ FCO Friulano '14 | ♟♟3 |
| ○ FCO Picolit '14 | ♟♟5 |
| ● FCO Schioppettino '15 | ♟♟4 |
| ○ FCO Verduzzo '14 | ♟♟3 |
| ○ FCO Verduzzo Friulano '15 | ♟♟4 |

# Sara & Sara

FRAZ. SAVORGNANO DEL TORRE
VIA DEI MONTI, 5
33040 POVOLETTO [UD]
TEL. +39 3393859042
www.saraesara.com

**CELLAR SALES**
**PRE-BOOKED VISITS**
**ANNUAL PRODUCTION** 25,000 bottles
**HECTARES UNDER VINE** 7.50
**SUSTAINABLE WINERY**

Young Alessandro Sara and his brother Manuele are wine artisans who have affirmed their ability to produce pleasant, modern wines using age-old techniques. Here in Savorgnano del Torre, a small rural area situated in the easternmost part of Friuli Colli Orientali, the terrain features streams, woods and marly, sandstone soil interwoven with clay. The particular microclimatic conditions of the area favor the natural formation of botrytis on their Verduzzo and Picolit grapes. Their Verduzzo Friulano Crei is the winery's flagship and for this reason it's given special attention. While we were conducting our tastings it still hadn't been bottled, and so it will be submitted for next year's edition. We can, however, confirm the quality of their 2013 Picolit, and for the first time we tried their white SaraGialla, a monovarietal Ribolla Gialla.

| | |
|---|---|
| ○ COF Picolit '13 | ♟♟6 |
| ○ SaraGialla '17 | ♟♟3 |
| ○ COF Verduzzo Friulano Crei '10 | ♟♟♟5 |
| ○ COF Friulano '12 | ♟♟3 |
| ○ COF Friulano '10 | ♟♟3 |
| ○ COF Picolit '12 | ♟♟6 |
| ○ COF Picolit '10 | ♟♟5 |
| ○ COF Picolit '09 | ♟♟5 |
| ○ COF Verduzzo Friulano Crei '11 | ♟♟5 |
| ○ FCO Friulano '16 | ♟♟6 |
| ○ FCO Picolit '11 | ♟♟6 |
| ○ FCO Verduzzo Friulano Crei '13 | ♟♟5 |
| ○ FCO Verduzzo Friulano Crei '12 | ♟♟5 |
| ○ Sauvignon '12 | ♟♟2* |

## ★★Schiopetto

VIA PALAZZO ARCIVESCOVILE, 1
34070 CAPRIVA DEL FRIULI [GO]
TEL. +39 048180332
www.schiopetto.it

**CELLAR SALES**
**PRE-BOOKED VISITS**
**ANNUAL PRODUCTION** 190,000 bottles
**HECTARES UNDER VINE** 30.00
**SUSTAINABLE WINERY**

Schiopetto's garden-like vineyards give rise to fresh, pleasant, extremely ageworthy wines of great structure. And it's all done with the utmost respect for sustainability, with technology that uses physical forces (not chemicals) for winemaking. This is just one of the missions that Mario Schiopetto, an authentic and undisputed founding father of Friuli's wine culture, set out to accomplish. Five years ago, Mario's legacy passed into the Rotolo family's hands, who've profoundly respected (and broadened) his approach and principles. In the near term they're planning wine tourism routes within the estate. Schiopetto's group of 2017s (a Pinot Bianco, Sauvignon, Malvasia and Pinot Grigio) are all extraordinary wines, but there's one piece of bad luck: the existence of their 2017 Friuliano. The wine's undisputed dominance continues and for years now it has proved to be the best in its category. It's a true pearl, a source of pride for Collio and the entire region. It's an honor to confer a very well-deserved Tre Bicchieri.

| | | |
|---|---|---|
| ○ Collio Friulano '17 | ♟♟♟ | 4* |
| ○ Collio Malvasia '17 | ♟♟ | 4 |
| ○ Collio Pinot Bianco '17 | ♟♟ | 4 |
| ○ Collio Sauvignon '17 | ♟♟ | 4 |
| ○ Blanc des Rosis '17 | ♟♟ | 4 |
| ○ Collio Pinot Grigio '17 | ♟♟ | 4 |
| ● Podere dei Blumeri Rosso '16 | ♟♟ | 5 |
| ○ Ribolla Gialla des Rosis '17 | ♟♟ | 3 |
| ● Rivarossa '16 | ♟♟ | 4 |
| ○ Blanc des Rosis '07 | ♟♟♟ | 4 |
| ○ Collio Friulano '16 | ♟♟♟ | 4* |
| ○ Collio Friulano '15 | ♟♟♟ | 4* |
| ○ Collio Friulano '14 | ♟♟♟ | 4* |
| ○ Collio Friulano '13 | ♟♟♟ | 4* |
| ○ Mario Schiopetto Bianco '08 | ♟♟♟ | 5 |
| ○ Mario Schiopetto Bianco '07 | ♟♟♟ | 5 |

## La Sclusa

LOC. SPESSA
VIA STRADA DI SANT'ANNA, 7/2
33043 CIVIDALE DEL FRIULI [UD]
TEL. +39 0432716259
www.lasclusa.it

**CELLAR SALES**
**PRE-BOOKED VISITS**
**ACCOMMODATION**
**ANNUAL PRODUCTION** 160,000 bottles
**HECTARES UNDER VINE** 30.00

Giobatta Zorzettig was the forefather of a generation of vine growers that have been active in Spessa di Cividale (Friuli Colli Orientali) since 1963. He spawned various family lineages dedicated to wine production. One of the most important is Gino. He's managed his own winery for more than 40 years. Today Germano, Maurizio and Luciano are at the helm, though they've renamed it as La Sclusa, drawing inspiration from a tract of the Corno river that passes through their vineyards. The fact that their selection received such consistently strong scores testifies to its quality. Their 2017 whites stand out for their fragrance and drinkability, while their 2016 Friulano 12 Viti delivers for its aromatic complexity and elegance. In the mouth it proves broad, long and satisfying. Their excellent 2014 Picolit also gratifies thanks to its sweet and juicy palate.

| | | |
|---|---|---|
| ○ COF Picolit '14 | ♟♟ | 6 |
| ○ FCO Chardonnay '17 | ♟♟ | 3 |
| ○ FCO Friulano '17 | ♟♟ | 3 |
| ○ FCO Friulano 12 Viti '16 | ♟♟ | 4 |
| ○ FCO Pinot Grigio '17 | ♟♟ | 3 |
| ○ FCO Ribolla Gialla '17 | ♟♟ | 3 |
| ● FCO Refosco P. R. '16 | ♟ | 3 |
| ○ FCO Chardonnay '16 | ♟♟ | 3 |
| ○ FCO Chardonnay '15 | ♟♟ | 3 |
| ○ FCO Friulano '16 | ♟♟ | 3* |
| ○ FCO Friulano '15 | ♟♟ | 3 |
| ○ FCO Pinot Grigio '16 | ♟♟ | 3 |
| ○ FCO Sauvignon '16 | ♟♟ | 3 |
| ○ FCO Sauvignon '15 | ♟♟ | 3 |

# Marco Scolaris

VIA BOSCHETTO, 4
34070 SAN LORENZO ISONTINO [GO]
TEL. +39 0481809920
www.scolaris.it

**CELLAR SALES**
**PRE-BOOKED VISITS**
**ANNUAL PRODUCTION 600,000 bottles**
**HECTARES UNDER VINE 20.00**
**SUSTAINABLE WINERY**

The winery founded in 1924 by Giovanni is today managed by his grandson Marco Scolaris, along with Marco's son Gianmarco (the fourth generation of family to be part of the winery). Production is overseen by Nevio Fedel, who brings expertise and passion to the work of capturing the family's philosophy in the bottle, with a number of internal and external collaborators completing the puzzle. Indeed, Marco Scolaris is made up of people, faith and ideas. It's an innovative winery with a human dimension that's committed to balancing humankind and nature. Marco Scolaris's wines are territorial, clean, simple but not banal, varietal, approachable. We could call them democratic inasmuch as they're high in quality, yet available to everyone. Their 2017 Chardonnay delights the nose with fine, exotic nuances. Their 2016 Malvasia offers up fresh apricot and proves very savory. Their 2017 Ribolla Gialla is delicate on the nose and fragrant on the palate. Their 2016 Merlot is a very spicy wine.

| | |
|---|---|
| ○ Collio Chardonnay '17 | 🏆🏆 3 |
| ○ Collio Friulano '17 | 🏆🏆 3 |
| ○ Collio Malvasia '16 | 🏆🏆 3 |
| ● Collio Merlot '16 | 🏆🏆 3 |
| ○ Collio Ribolla Gialla '17 | 🏆🏆 3 |
| ○ Traminer Aromatico '17 | 🏆🏆 3 |
| ● Collio Cabernet Franc '17 | 🏆 3 |
| ○ Collio Pinot Grigio '17 | 🏆 3 |
| ○ Collio Chardonnay '14 | 🏆🏆 3 |
| ○ Collio Friulano '15 | 🏆🏆 3 |
| ○ Collio Malvasia '15 | 🏆🏆 3 |
| ○ Collio Malvasia '14 | 🏆🏆 3 |
| ○ Collio Pinot Grigio '16 | 🏆🏆 3 |
| ○ Collio Pinot Grigio '14 | 🏆🏆 3 |
| ○ Collio Sauvignon '16 | 🏆🏆 3 |

# Roberto Scubla

FRAZ. IPPLIS
VIA ROCCA BERNARDA, 22
33040 PREMARIACCO [UD]
TEL. +39 0432716258
www.scubla.com

**CELLAR SALES**
**PRE-BOOKED VISITS**
**ANNUAL PRODUCTION 50,000 bottles**
**HECTARES UNDER VINE 11.00**

In 1991 Roberto Scubla decided to give up his job in a bank so as to purchase an estate of vineyards and a manor house on the slopes of the Rocca Bernarda. Today that building is an architectural achievement surrounded by a truly bucolic atmosphere, not to mention the particular geography of the surrounding hills, which facilitate the northern winds and the natural raisining of their Verduzzo grapes (put on on rush mats beneath a canopy). Their selection is also made possible by the support of Gianni Menotti. The number of wines that made it to our finals affirms the winery's status in the region. Their 2016 Pomèdes and 2017 Pinot Bianco stand out, but all their wines garnered praise. Their 2015 Verduzzo Friulano Passito Cràtis impressed most of all for its sweetness contrasted by a racy acidity.

| | |
|---|---|
| ○ FCO Bianco Pomèdes '16 | 🏆🏆 5 |
| ○ FCO Pinot Bianco '17 | 🏆🏆 3* |
| ○ FCO Verduzzo Friulano Cràtis '15 | 🏆🏆 6 |
| ● FCO Cabernet Sauvignon '16 | 🏆🏆 4 |
| ○ FCO Friulano '17 | 🏆🏆 3 |
| ○ FCO Malvasia Lo Speziale '17 | 🏆🏆 3 |
| ● FCO Merlot '16 | 🏆🏆 4 |
| ● FCO Refosco P. R. '16 | 🏆🏆 4 |
| ● FCO Rosso Scuro '15 | 🏆🏆 5 |
| ○ FCO Sauvignon '17 | 🏆🏆 3 |
| ○ COF Verduzzo Friulano Cràtis '09 | 🏆🏆🏆 5 |
| ○ FCO Friulano '16 | 🏆🏆 3* |
| ○ FCO Malvasia Lo Speziale '16 | 🏆🏆 3 |
| ○ FCO Pinot Bianco '16 | 🏆🏆 3* |
| ○ FCO Sauvignon '16 | 🏆🏆 3 |

# Renzo Sgubin

VIA FAET, 15
34071 CORMÒNS [GO]
TEL. +39 0481630297
www.renzosgubin.it

**CELLAR SALES**
**PRE-BOOKED VISITS**
**ANNUAL PRODUCTION** 28,000 bottles
**HECTARES UNDER VINE** 15.00
**SUSTAINABLE WINERY**

Renzo Sgubin is a proud vine grower who shares a deep love for the land with his ancestors. His father was a sharecropper who bought his own plots in the 1970s. These served as the basis for the family's own winery, founded in 1997, while the first bottles came in 2003. He's since earned a reputation as being among the region's leading enological artisans. The estate is situated in Cormòns, between the Collio and Friuli Isonzo appellations. Today, as in the past, the estate's smaller size allows him to personally oversee every stage of production, with results that are there for all to see. Their 2017 Malvasia did excellently, especially for its rich and complex aromatic profile, which features fragrances of fresh and dried herbs, citrus peel, yellow flowers and myrtle. In the mouth glycerine notes and fresh balsamic hints are perfectly balanced. Their 2017 Sauvignon and 2017 Chardonnay also distinguished themselves for their pure varietal qualities

| | |
|---|---|
| ○ 3, 4, 3 '16 | ♟♟ 3 |
| ○ Friuli Isonzo Chardonnay '17 | ♟♟ 3 |
| ○ Friuli Isonzo Malvasia '17 | ♟♟ 3 |
| ○ Friuli Isonzo Sauvignon '17 | ♟♟ 3 |
| ● Collio Merlot '15 | ♟ 3 |
| ○ Friuli Isonzo Friulano '17 | ♟ 3 |
| ○ Friuli Isonzo Pinot Grigio '17 | ♟ 3 |
| ○ 3, 4, 3 '15 | ♟♟ 3 |
| ○ Friuli Isonzo Chardonnay '16 | ♟♟ 3 |
| ○ Friuli Isonzo Friulano '16 | ♟♟ 3 |
| ○ Friuli Isonzo Malvasia '16 | ♟♟ 3 |
| ○ Friuli Isonzo Pinot Grigio '16 | ♟♟ 3 |
| ○ Friuli Isonzo Pinot Grigio '15 | ♟♟ 3 |
| ○ Friuli Isonzo Sauvignon '16 | ♟♟ 3 |

# Simon di Brazzan

FRAZ. BRAZZANO
VIA SAN ROCCO, 17
34070 CORMÒNS [GO]
TEL. +39 048161182
www.simondibrazzan.com

**CELLAR SALES**
**PRE-BOOKED VISITS**
**ANNUAL PRODUCTION** 70,000 bottles
**HECTARES UNDER VINE** 13.00
**VITICULTURE METHOD** Certified Organic

Four generations, one passion. This is the motto that has inspired Simon di Brazzan, a splendid winery situated in the famous district of Cormòns. Today it's managed by Daniele Drius, a firm supporter of biodynamic viticulture. Vine leaves are sprayed with a mixture of puzzlegrass and nettle, while soil is worked with ground cover, a mix of herbs in alternating rows, cut and buried after flowering. In the cellar they also avail themselves of traditional methods that are simple, effective and capable of interpreting modern market demands. Their 2016 Ri.nè Blanc (a blend) and 2017 Friulano Blanc di Simon repeated the extraordinary performance put in last year and once again found themselves leading a series of commendably well-made wines, as well as landing a place in our finals. Both are sunny, sophisticated, creamy, extremely fragrant and tasty wines. The palate is lean but exhibits extremely long aftertaste.

| | |
|---|---|
| ○ Friuli Friulano Blanc di Simon '17 | ♟♟ 3* |
| ○ Ri.nè Blanc '16 | ♟♟ 3* |
| ○ Friuli Pinot Grigio '17 | ♟♟ 3 |
| ○ Malvasia '17 | ♟♟ 3 |
| ● Merlot '15 | ♟♟ 4 |
| ○ Sauvignon '17 | ♟♟ 3 |
| ● Cabernet Franc '17 | ♟ 3 |
| ● Cabernet Franc '15 | ♟♟ 3 |
| ○ Friuli Friulano Blanc di Simon '16 | ♟♟ 3* |
| ○ Malvasia '16 | ♟♟ 3 |
| ○ Pinot Grigio '16 | ♟♟ 3 |
| ○ Ri.nè Blanc '15 | ♟♟ 3* |
| ○ Sauvignon '16 | ♟♟ 3 |
| ○ Tradizion '11 | ♟♟ 5 |

# FRIULI VENEZIA GIULIA

## Sirch

VIA FORNALIS, 277/1
33043 CIVIDALE DEL FRIULI [UD]
TEL. +39 0432709835
www.sirchwine.com

CELLAR SALES
PRE-BOOKED VISITS
ANNUAL PRODUCTION 150,000 bottles
HECTARES UNDER VINE 25.00

For some time we've known of the bond between the Sirch family winery and Feudi di San Gregorio, a large producer from Campania who handles distribution. In many ways the watershed vintage came in 2002, when Luca chose to focus on making expressive, approachable wines that didn't adhere to fashion or market trends. It's a philosophy that conceals their desire to achieve a subtle stylistic complexity, making for elegant whites that are rich in nuance. Their vineyards are divided into small plots that have allowed them to find the right position for each cultivar. This year we tasted a group of wines that we already evaluated for last year's edition. While they didn't make into Italian Wines, the results demonstrated that they'd aged well over the past 12 moths. Their 2017s are still exemplary in their precision, often proving intriguing on the nose for the originality of their fragrances and enjoyable on the palate.

| | | |
|---|---|---|
| ○ FCO Friulano '17 | 🍷🍷 | 3 |
| ○ FCO Pinot Grigio '17 | 🍷🍷 | 3 |
| ○ FCO Ribolla Gialla '17 | 🍷🍷 | 3 |
| ○ FCO Sauvignon '17 | 🍷🍷 | 3 |
| ○ FCO Chardonnay '17 | 🍷 | 3 |
| ○ FCO Traminer Aromatico '17 | 🍷 | 3 |
| ○ COF Friulano '07 | 🍷🍷🍷 | 2* |
| ○ FCO Bianco Cladrecis '15 | 🍷🍷 | 3* |
| ○ FCO Chardonnay '16 | 🍷🍷 | 3 |
| ○ FCO Friulano '16 | 🍷🍷 | 3 |
| ● FCO Refosco P. R. '15 | 🍷🍷 | 3 |
| ○ FCO Ribolla Gialla '16 | 🍷🍷 | 3 |

## Skerk

FRAZ. SAN PELAGIO
LOC. PREPOTTO, 20
34011 DUINO AURISINA [TS]
TEL. +39 040200156
www.skerk.com

CELLAR SALES
PRE-BOOKED VISITS
RESTAURANT SERVICE
ANNUAL PRODUCTION 22,000 bottles
HECTARES UNDER VINE 7.00
VITICULTURE METHOD Certified Organic

Sandi Skerk is one of Karst's best interpreters. It's an area that evokes the often overused word 'heroic agriculture', with its perennial conflict between farmer and rock. Here all activities are conducted by hand, and in the sunny coves that overlook the sea vineyards are treated with the same care as gardens. The grapes are then taken to a splendid underground cellar, a testament to human ingenuity. Here their wines are macerated at length on the skins, see little racking and undergo no filtration. These are the perfect conditions, thanks to cool temperatures and constant humidity throughout the year. Vitovska, Malvasia Istriana, Sauvignon and Pinot Grigio are the cultivar used to make their 2016 Ograde, a wine that expresses the best of Karst. By virtue of the unanimous praise it garnered, it also earned Tre Bicchieri. It's a wine that's vibrant in its color and aromas, with iodine notes of Mediterranean scrubland, candied citrus and ginger. It's rich on the palate, creamy and pervasive.

| | | |
|---|---|---|
| ○ Ograde '16 | 🍷🍷🍷 | 5 |
| ○ Malvasia '16 | 🍷🍷 | 5 |
| ○ Vitovska '16 | 🍷🍷 | 5 |
| ● Terrano '16 | 🍷🍷 | 5 |
| ○ Carso Malvasia '08 | 🍷🍷🍷 | 4 |
| ○ Malvasia '13 | 🍷🍷🍷 | 5 |
| ○ Ograde '15 | 🍷🍷🍷 | 5 |
| ○ Ograde '12 | 🍷🍷🍷 | 5 |
| ○ Ograde '11 | 🍷🍷🍷 | 5 |
| ○ Ograde '10 | 🍷🍷🍷 | 4 |
| ○ Ograde '09 | 🍷🍷🍷 | 4* |

# Edi Skok

LOC. GIASBANA, 15
34070 SAN FLORIANO DEL COLLIO [GO]
TEL. +39 3408034045
www.skok.it

CELLAR SALES
PRE-BOOKED VISITS
ANNUAL PRODUCTION 38,000 bottles
HECTARES UNDER VINE 11.00

The Skok family has deep agricultural roots and are deeply linked to Collio. In the 16th century they settled in a farm manor, wedged in between the slopes of Giasbana near San Floriano and just by the Slovenian border. It's an environment that's universally recognized as perfect for wine-growing, especially white grapes. Today it's managed by Edi and Orietta, two siblings who are respectful of tradition but also open to innovation. They've gradually moved away from long maceration in favor of more fragrant wines. All their monovarietals do an excellent job expressing the qualities of cultivar used, brought out by the undisputed territorial attributes of Collio. But sometimes it's through a well-fashioned blend that you manage to obtain a wine that's even more balanced and enticing. That's the case with their 2016 Bianco Pe Ar (made with Chardonnay, Pinot Grigio and Sauvignon), a wine that for the second year in a row lands a place in our finals.

| | | |
|---|---|---|
| ○ Collio Bianco Pe Ar '16 | ♛♛ | 3* |
| ○ Collio Chardonnay '17 | ♛♛ | 2* |
| ○ Collio Friulano Zabura '17 | ♛♛ | 3 |
| ● Collio Merlot '16 | ♛♛ | 3 |
| ● Collio Merlot Villa Jasbinae '13 | ♛♛ | 3 |
| ○ Collio Sauvignon '17 | ♛♛ | 3 |
| ○ Collio Pinot Grigio '17 | ♛ | 3 |
| ○ Collio Bianco Pe Ar '15 | ♟♟ | 3* |
| ○ Collio Chardonnay '16 | ♟♟ | 2* |
| ○ Collio Friulano Zabura '15 | ♟♟ | 3 |
| ● Collio Merlot '15 | ♟♟ | 3 |
| ● Collio Merlot Villa Jasbinae '11 | ♟♟ | 3 |
| ○ Collio Pinot Grigio '16 | ♟♟ | 3 |
| ○ Collio Sauvignon '16 | ♟♟ | 3 |

# Specogna

VIA ROCCA BERNARDA, 4
33040 CORNO DI ROSAZZO [UD]
TEL. +39 0432755840
www.specogna.it

CELLAR SALES
PRE-BOOKED VISITS
ACCOMMODATION
ANNUAL PRODUCTION 120,000 bottles
HECTARES UNDER VINE 24.00
SUSTAINABLE WINERY

The Friuli brand founded by Leonardo Specogna in 1963 has come to be synonymous with excellence. Most of the credit goes to his young grandchildren Michele and Cristian who, with the help of the rest of the family, brought the winery to regional prominence. It's thanks primarily to their wide and consistent range of wines, which are made with grapes cultivated on the slopes of Rocca Bernarda. Knowingly terraced by generations of vine growers, the vineyards enjoy expositional positions and ideal microclimates. In addition to the satisfaction that came with earning a Tre Bicchieri last year, this year the producer can feel good about the splendid performance put in by their entire selection, with some four wines making it into our finals. Their 2016 Bianco Identità, in particular, came close to repeating last year's exploit, while we we encountered two lovely surprises in their 2015 Malvasia Res. and their Pinot Grigio Ramato, a wine made of various vintages of the same wine.

| | | |
|---|---|---|
| ○ FCO Bianco Identità '16 | ♛♛ | 7 |
| ○ FCO Malvasia Ris. '15 | ♛♛ | 4 |
| ○ FCO Sauvignon Blanc Duality '16 | ♛♛ | 3* |
| ○ Pinot Grigio Ramato | ♛♛ | 6 |
| ● FCO Cabernet Sauvignon '16 | ♛♛ | 4 |
| ○ FCO Chardonnay '17 | ♛♛ | 3 |
| ○ FCO Friulano '17 | ♛♛ | 3 |
| ○ FCO Friulano Ris. '16 | ♛♛ | 3 |
| ● FCO Pignolo '13 | ♛♛ | 6 |
| ● FCO Rosso Oltre '15 | ♛♛ | 6 |
| ○ FCO Sauvignon '17 | ♛♛ | 3 |
| ○ FCO Bianco Identità '15 | ♟♟♟ | 7 |
| ● FCO Rosso Oltre '13 | ♟♟ | 6 |
| ○ FCO Sauvignon '16 | ♟♟ | 3 |
| ○ FCO Sauvignon Blanc Duality '15 | ♟♟ | 3* |

# Stanig

via Albana, 44
33040 Prepotto [UD]
Tel. +39 0432713234
www.stanig.it

**CELLAR SALES**
**ACCOMMODATION AND RESTAURANT SERVICE**
**ANNUAL PRODUCTION** 45,000 bottles
**HECTARES UNDER VINE** 9.00

Prepotto is a small district in the Friuli Colli Orientali DOC appellation, situated in the extreme northeast. It gets its notoriety from the wine named Schioppettino di Prepotto. Among the numerous family-run producers here we find brothers Federico and Francesco Stanig. They represent the third generation of family to lead this distinguished winery founded almost a century ago by their grandfather Giuseppe. Their estate comprises nine hectares of vineyards, a size that allows them to personally oversee every stage of production. Their limited range of wines shows the right attention to each typology. Their 2017 whites are very linear wines, respectful of each cultivar's varietal characteristics, enjoyable and highly drinkable. But their most intriguing and representative wine proved to be their 2015 Schioppettino di Prepotto. It delivers on the nose with unmistakable aromas of wild berries, dried aromatic herbs, rhubarb and green pepper, while on the palate it unfolds harmoniously.

| | |
|---|---|
| ○ FCO Friulano '17 | ♥♥ 3 |
| ○ FCO Malvasia '17 | ♥♥ 3 |
| ○ FCO Ribolla Gialla '17 | ♥♥ 3 |
| ○ FCO Sauvignon '17 | ♥♥ 3 |
| ● FCO Schioppettino di Prepotto '15 | ♥♥ 3 |
| ● FCO Cabernet '16 | ♥ 3 |
| ● FCO Rosso del Gelso '12 | ♥ 4 |
| ○ FCO Friulano '15 | ♀♀ 3 |
| ○ FCO Malvasia '16 | ♀♀ 3 |
| ○ FCO Malvasia '14 | ♀♀ 3 |
| ● FCO Merlot '15 | ♀♀ 3 |
| ● FCO Schioppettino di Prepotto '13 | ♀♀ 3* |

# Tenuta Stella

loc. Scriò
via Sdencina, 1
34070 Dolegna del Collio [GO]
Tel. +39 0481639895
www.tenutastellacollio.it

**CELLAR SALES**
**PRE-BOOKED VISITS**
**ANNUAL PRODUCTION** 35,000 bottles
**HECTARES UNDER VINE** 12.00
**VITICULTURE METHOD** Certified Organic
**SUSTAINABLE WINERY**

Erika Barbieri and Alberto Faggiani look after Tenuta Stella. The winery was founded in 2010 by Sergio Stevanato, who chose to cultivate only native white grapes. Tocai, Friulano, Ribolla Gialla and Malvasia Istriana can all be found here in Scriò, a terroir that brings out the best of each cultivar. The plots are situated in the district of Dolegna, in the highest part of Collio, where the steep hills prove as difficult as they are well-suited to cultivation. The rows of vineyards follow the shape of the slopes, and require For the region Ribolla Gialla is the wine of the moment. In recent years we witnessed a period of growth that brought the wine international markets. It's an interest that's seen the wine improve in quality terms, especially at higher elevations, with truly excellent results. And Tenuta Stella's 2016 Ribolla Gialla is among the first to break through into our finals.

| | |
|---|---|
| ○ Collio Ribolla Gialla '16 | ♥♥ 4 |
| ○ Collio Friulano '16 | ♥♥ 4 |
| ○ Collio Malvasia '16 | ♥♥ 4 |
| ○ Cuvée Tanni Brut | ♥♥ 5 |
| ○ Ribolla Gialla Brut | ♥♥ 5 |
| ○ Collio Friulano '15 | ♀♀ 3* |
| ○ Collio Friulano Scriò '14 | ♀♀ 3 |
| ○ Collio Friulano Scriò '13 | ♀♀ 3 |
| ○ Collio Malvasia '15 | ♀♀ 4 |
| ○ Collio Malvasia '14 | ♀♀ 4 |
| ○ Collio Malvasia '13 | ♀♀ 4 |
| ○ Collio Malvasia '12 | ♀♀ 4 |
| ○ Collio Ribolla Gialla '15 | ♀♀ 4 |
| ○ Collio Ribolla Gialla '14 | ♀♀ 4 |
| ○ Collio Ribolla Gialla '13 | ♀♀ 4 |

# Stocco

VIA CASALI STOCCO, 12
33050 BICINICCO [UD]
TEL. +39 0432934906
www.vinistocco.it

CELLAR SALES
PRE-BOOKED VISITS
RESTAURANT SERVICE
ANNUAL PRODUCTION 250,000 bottles
HECTARES UNDER VINE 49.00

The Stocco family's lovely estate was founded in the early 20th century here in Bicinicco, on Friuli's vast plains. For a time it was dedicated to agriculture in what would later be called 'Casali Stocco', but a turning point came in the 1960s and the estate was transformed into vineyards. It was Francesco who set about transforming the producer, but today its the fourth generation's turn (in the form of Andrea, Daniela and Paola) to carry forward the family's reputable brand. Together they're working to demonstrate that even in the flat lowlands, with its gravel and red earth, excellent wines can be made. For some time now we've known about Andrea's winemaking skills and the fact that he shows the same attention for each wine, thus guaranteeing them equal dignity. Both his whites and reds are made both in steel vats and wood barrels. It's a diversity that allows him to meet every market demand, with sparkling wines offered as well. His selection's value for the money makes it truly tempting for consumers.

| | |
|---|---|
| ○ Chardonnay '17 | ♟♟ 5 |
| ○ Friuli Grave Friulano Doghis '16 | ♟♟ 2* |
| ○ Friuli Grave Sauvignon '17 | ♟♟ 2* |
| ● Merlot '16 | ♟♟ 4 |
| ○ Sericus '16 | ♟♟ 3 |
| ● Cabernet Franc '17 | ♟ 2 |
| ○ Friuli Pinot Grigio '17 | ♟ 2 |
| ○ Malvasia '17 | ♟ 2 |
| ○ Ribolla Gialla Brut | ♟ 3 |
| ● Cabernet Franc '15 | ♟♟ 2* |
| ○ Friuli Grave Friulano '16 | ♟♟ 2* |
| ● Merlot Roos dai Lens '13 | ♟♟ 4 |
| ○ Pinot Grigio '16 | ♟♟ 2* |
| ○ Pinot Grigio Ramato '16 | ♟♟ 2* |
| ○ Sericus '15 | ♟♟ 3 |

# Subida di Monte

LOC. SUBIDA
VIA SUBIDA, 6
34071 CORMÒNS [GO]
TEL. +39 048161011
www.subidadimonte.it

CELLAR SALES
PRE-BOOKED VISITS
ACCOMMODATION
ANNUAL PRODUCTION 45,000 bottles
HECTARES UNDER VINE 9.00

Subida di Monte was conceived as a modern winery with ample space for both a cellar and hospitality. The producer, situated in a strategic position in the district of the same name (in Cormòns, Collio Goriziano), was founded by Luigi Antonutti. In 1972 this regional pioneer in quality winemaking managed to realize his dream of working as a full-time vine grower. Today his children Cristian and Andrea are looking after their vineyards, which are protected by the Julian Alps that rise up over the valley below, and are caressed by the nearby Adriatic's sea breeze. Their reds need more time for aging, and so only 2017s were submitted, with their Malvasia leading the way. We like to remind our readers that for some years now we've chosen it as the best wine in their selection. It once again earned a place in our finals for its lovely fragrances of fresh melon and apricot, but especially for its notable savoriness.

| | |
|---|---|
| ○ Collio Malvasia '17 | ♟♟ 3* |
| ○ Collio Friulano '17 | ♟♟ 3 |
| ○ Collio Pinot Grigio '17 | ♟♟ 3 |
| ○ Collio Sauvignon '17 | ♟♟ 3 |
| ● Collio Cabernet Franc '15 | ♟♟ 3 |
| ● Collio Cabernet Franc '14 | ♟♟ 3 |
| ○ Collio Friulano '16 | ♟♟ 3 |
| ○ Collio Friulano '15 | ♟♟ 3 |
| ○ Collio Malvasia '16 | ♟♟ 3 |
| ○ Collio Malvasia '15 | ♟♟ 3 |
| ● Collio Merlot '15 | ♟♟ 3 |
| ○ Collio Pinot Grigio '16 | ♟♟ 3 |
| ● Collio Rosso Poncaia '13 | ♟♟ 4 |
| ○ Collio Sauvignon '15 | ♟♟ 3 |

## Tenimenti Civa

FRAZ. BELLAZOIA POVOLETTO
VIA SUBIDA 16
33040 UDINE
TEL. +39 04321770380
www.tenimenticiva.com

ANNUAL PRODUCTION 280,000 bottles
HECTARES UNDER VINE 40.00

Valerio Civa has deep knowledge of the wine market, which she's been operating in for decades now. Attracted by the sudden attention around Ribolla Gialla, in February of 2016 she decided to create a new producer in the Friuli Colli Orientali DOC appellation, thus founding Tenimenti Civa. She immediately set in motion ambitious works dedicated to native grape varieties and, in an extremely short time, she completely renovated the cellar she'd taken over from Bellazoia di Povoletto. Even before the first harvest, it was equipped with cutting-edge systems and equipment. Last year we welcomed this new producer into Italian Wines, having truly appreciated the three wines that were submitted. This year we had the chance to taste a few reds, but the highest accolades go to their 2017 Ribolla Gialla, Valerio's workhorse, which stood out for its citrus fragrances, its nice body and natural drinkability.

| | |
|---|---|
| ○ FCO Ribolla Gialla '17 | 🍷🍷 3* |
| ○ FCO Friulano '17 | 🍷🍷 3 |
| ● FCO Merlot '16 | 🍷🍷 3 |
| ● FCO Refosco P. R. '17 | 🍷🍷 3 |
| ○ FCO Sauvignon '17 | 🍷🍷 3 |
| ○ Ribolla Gialla Extra Brut '17 | 🍷 2 |
| ○ FCO Friulano '16 | 🍷🍷 3 |
| ○ FCO Ribolla Gialla '16 | 🍷🍷 3 |
| ○ FCO Sauvignon '16 | 🍷🍷 3* |

## Tenuta Luisa

FRAZ. CORONA
VIA CAMPO SPORTIVO, 13
34070 MARIANO DEL FRIULI [GO]
TEL. +39 048169680
www.tenutaluisa.it

CELLAR SALES
PRE-BOOKED VISITS
ACCOMMODATION
ANNUAL PRODUCTION 350,000 bottles
HECTARES UNDER VINE 100.00
SUSTAINABLE WINERY

Eddi Luisa works with his wife Nella and his sons Michele and Davide in a splendid winery in Corona, Mariano del Friuli, in the Isonzo subzone. Two generations work in perfect synchronicity, with enthusiasm and foresight, contributing to the continued growth of Tenuta Luisa. Their vineyards stretch out across the sunny lowlands characterized by mineral-rich soil, especially iron. The unique red earth inspired the name of their Ferretti line of wines. It's just one example of the painstaking care that goes into every detail of cultivation and production. All their 2017s put in an excellent performance, but their Ferretti line, a group of wines that make regular appearances in our finals, once again stood out. Their 2016 Desiderium I Ferretti, a wine that proved elegant on the nose and tasty on the palate, garnered the highest accolades and took home Tre Bicchieri. Their 2016 Friulano I Ferretti excelled for its varietal characteristics, fragrance and lovely palate.

| | |
|---|---|
| ○ Desiderium I Ferretti '16 | 🍷🍷🍷 4* |
| ○ Friuli Isonzo Friulano I Ferretti '16 | 🍷🍷 4 |
| ○ Friuli Isonzo Chardonnay '17 | 🍷🍷 3 |
| ○ Friuli Isonzo Friulano '17 | 🍷🍷 3 |
| ○ Friuli Isonzo Pinot Bianco '17 | 🍷🍷 3 |
| ● Friuli Isonzo Refosco P. R. I Ferretti '13 | 🍷🍷 4 |
| ○ Friuli Isonzo Sauvignon '17 | 🍷🍷 3 |
| ○ Ribolla Gialla '17 | 🍷 3 |
| ○ Traminer Aromatico '17 | 🍷 3 |
| ○ Desiderium I Ferretti '13 | 🍷🍷🍷 4* |
| ○ Friuli Isonzo Friulano I Ferretti '15 | 🍷🍷🍷 3* |
| ○ Friuli Isonzo Friulano '16 | 🍷🍷 3 |
| ○ Friuli Isonzo Friulano I Ferretti '13 | 🍷🍷 3* |

# Matijaž Terčič

LOC. BUCUIE, 4A
34070 SAN FLORIANO DEL COLLIO [GO]
TEL. +39 0481884920
www.tercic.com

**CELLAR SALES**
**PRE-BOOKED VISITS**
**ANNUAL PRODUCTION** 30,000 bottles
**HECTARES UNDER VINE** 9.50

Matijaž Terčič family have a long tradition of wine-growing on the hills of San Floriano del Collio, one of eastern Friuli's most charming areas in terms of natural beauty. On the steep slopes here the vineyards and long rows of cherries form ordered geometric intervals all the way down to the splendid valley below. The first bottles go back to 1994 and since then the winery has earned renown, affirming its place at the heights of regional excellence Matijaz doesn't always submit wines for tasting with the same regularity, but we've already confirmed their quality. Leading the way this year is his 2016 Sauvignon, which once again earned a place in our finals. An excellent 2016 Vino degli Orti stood out for its perfect nose-mouth symmetry, while his 2016 Pinot Grigio impressed for its particular fragrance.

| | |
|---|---|
| ○ Collio Sauvignon '16 | ♥♥ 3* |
| ○ Collio Pinot Grigio '16 | ♥♥ 3 |
| ○ Vino degli Orti '16 | ♥♥ 3 |
| ○ Friuli Isonzo Friulano '16 | ♥ 3 |
| ○ Collio Pinot Grigio '07 | ♥♥♥ 3* |
| ○ Collio Bianco Planta '12 | ♥♥ 4 |
| ● Collio Merlot Seme '11 | ♥♥ 5 |
| ○ Collio Pinot Grigio '15 | ♥♥ 3 |
| ○ Collio Pinot Grigio '13 | ♥♥ 3 |
| ○ Collio Pinot Grigio Dar '12 | ♥♥ 4 |
| ○ Collio Ribolla Gialla '15 | ♥♥ 4 |
| ○ Collio Sauvignon '15 | ♥♥ 3* |
| ○ Collio Sauvignon '14 | ♥♥ 3 |
| ○ Friuli Isonzo Friulano '14 | ♥♥ 3 |
| ○ Vino degli Orti '13 | ♥♥ 3* |

# Terre di Ger

LOC. FRATTINA
S.DA DELLA MEDUNA, 17
33076 PRAVISDOMINI [PN]
TEL. +39 0434644452
www.terrediger.it

**CELLAR SALES**
**PRE-BOOKED VISITS**
**ANNUAL PRODUCTION** 100,000 bottles
**HECTARES UNDER VINE** 70.00

Terre di Ger is one of Friuli Occidentale's flourishing producers. In 1975 Gianluigi Spinazzè planted his first vineyard and in 1986 he renovated an old farm manor in Frattina di Pravisdomini, thus creating a cellar and starting to make his wines. Today he's joined by his son Robert and thanks to their initiative, in 2016 they started a new enological and agronomic project aimed at producing natural wines with new, highly resistant vineyards managed both organically and biodynamically. Additionally, great attention is shown towards protecting the environment. Limine and El Masut's wines, their house blends, are among the first to be produced using the latest generation of resistant cultivar. Their 23017 Limine is made with Fleurtai and a small share of Sauvignon Kretos. It's a wine redolent of citrus, tropical fruit, lime blossom and bitter orange. Their 2016 El Masut is made with Merlot Khantus and Merlot Khorus, and offers up aromas of red rose and cherries. But are enjoyable, intriguing wines.

| | |
|---|---|
| ● El Masut '16 | ♥♥ 3 |
| ● Friuli Grave Merlot '16 | ♥♥ 2* |
| ○ Limine '17 | ♥♥ 5 |
| ○ Friuli Friulano '17 | ♥ 2 |
| ● Friuli Grave Refosco P. R. '16 | ♥ 2 |
| ● Friuli Grave Cabernet Franc '13 | ♥♥ 2* |
| ○ Friuli Grave Chardonnay '16 | ♥♥ 2* |
| ○ Friuli Grave Chardonnay '15 | ♥♥ 2* |
| ○ Limine '16 | ♥♥ 3 |
| ○ Limine '13 | ♥♥ 3* |
| ○ Sauvignon Blanc '14 | ♥♥ 3* |

## Tiare - Roberto Snidarcig

Fraz. Vencò
Loc. Sant'Elena, 3a
34070 Dolegna del Collio [GO]
Tel. +39 048162491
www.tiaredoc.com

CELLAR SALES
PRE-BOOKED VISITS
RESTAURANT SERVICE
ANNUAL PRODUCTION 90,000 bottles
HECTARES UNDER VINE 10.00
SUSTAINABLE WINERY

For Friuli's inhabitants 'Tiare' means land, and it was Roberto Snidarcig's intimate bond with the countryside that inspired him to found a winery along the slopes of Quarin, in Cormòns, in 1991. It started as a small producer, not much more than a casual activity, and gradually grew in both numbers and quality, eventually earning a place among the region's top wineries. Today they are based out of Dolegna del Collio, and have a spacious and well-functioning cellar where Roberto continues to expand, helped on by his wife, Sandra. Once again this year two of Roberto's wines made it into our finals, one a new entry and one an old acquaintance. For the first time his 2017 Malvasia earned accolades for its fragrance and pleasant aromas, while his 2017 Sauvignon once again takes home Tre Bicchieri. It's truly their flagship wine thanks to the consistency with which varietal qualities are highlighted.

| | | |
|---|---|---|
| ○ Collio Sauvignon '17 | ▼▼▼ | 5 |
| ○ Collio Malvasia '17 | ▼▼ | 3* |
| ○ Collio Friulano '17 | ▼▼ | 4 |
| ○ Collio Pinot Grigio '17 | ▼▼ | 4 |
| ○ Collio Ribolla Gialla '17 | ▼▼ | 4 |
| ○ Il Tiare '17 | ▼▼ | 3 |
| ○ Collio Sauvignon '16 | ♀♀♀ | 5 |
| ○ Collio Sauvignon '15 | ♀♀♀ | 5 |
| ○ Collio Sauvignon '14 | ♀♀♀ | 5 |
| ○ Collio Sauvignon '13 | ♀♀♀ | 3* |
| ○ Collio Bianco Rosemblanc '15 | ♀♀ | 5 |
| ○ Collio Malvasia '16 | ♀♀ | 3 |
| ○ Collio Malvasia '14 | ♀♀ | 3* |
| ○ Collio Sauvignon Empire '15 | ♀♀ | 3 |
| ● Pinot Nero Pinòir '15 | ♀♀ | 5 |

## ★Franco Toros

Loc. Novali, 12
34071 Cormòns [GO]
Tel. +39 048161327
www.vinitoros.com

CELLAR SALES
PRE-BOOKED VISITS
ANNUAL PRODUCTION 60,000 bottles
HECTARES UNDER VINE 11.00

Franco Toros comes from a line of farmworkers who settled in Cormòns at the beginning of the 20th century. He's an authentic wine artisan, a shy man who prefers the silence of the vineyards to the din of the media, crediting mother nature for the quality of his wines. His selection consistently stands out for its linearity, forthrightness, varietal adherence and especially for its pleasantness. His interpretations are impeccable, territorial, among the Collio's best ambassadors and a source of pride for the entire region. Their 2017 Pinot Bianco is a concentration of elegance and force. It emanates amazing, intriguing, sophisticated fragrances while the palate comes through pervasive and extremely long. It takes home Tre Bicchieri. Their 2017 Pinot Grigio is redolent of recently baked bread and ripe yellow peach, while in the mouth it's soft and crisp. Their 2017 Friulano is a highly varietal wine, both on the nose and the palate, proving to be a real standout in its category.

| | | |
|---|---|---|
| ○ Collio Pinot Bianco '17 | ▼▼▼ | 4* |
| ○ Collio Friulano '17 | ▼▼ | 4 |
| ○ Collio Pinot Grigio '17 | ▼▼ | 4 |
| ○ Collio Chardonnay '17 | ▼▼ | 4 |
| ○ Collio Sauvignon '17 | ▼▼ | 4 |
| ○ Collio Pinot Bianco '14 | ♀♀♀ | 4* |
| ○ Collio Pinot Bianco '13 | ♀♀♀ | 4* |
| ○ Collio Friulano '16 | ♀♀ | 4 |
| ○ Collio Friulano '15 | ♀♀ | 4 |
| ○ Collio Pinot Bianco '16 | ♀♀ | 4 |
| ○ Collio Pinot Bianco '15 | ♀♀ | 4 |

# Torre Rosazza

FRAZ. OLEIS
LOC. POGGIOBELLO, 12
33044 MANZANO [UD]
TEL. +39 0422864511
www.torrerosazza.com

**CELLAR SALES**
**PRE-BOOKED VISITS**
**ANNUAL PRODUCTION** 200,000 bottles
**HECTARES UNDER VINE** 90.00
**SUSTAINABLE WINERY**

Torre Rosazza is of the Genagricola group's flagship brands. Genagricola owns businesses in Veneto, Piedmont, Romagna and Lazio, with their Friuli estates comprising Poggiobello, Borgo Magredo and Tenuta Sant'Anna. Torre Rosazza is based in the 18th century Palazzo De Marchi, which stands on a hill in Manzano, surrounded by vineyards. These extend across two splendid naturally terraced amphitheaters that are perennially sunny. Credit for their success goes to an expert and efficient staff, masterfully orchestrated by Enrico Raddi. This year we witnessed another great performance by this historic winery that, in addition to maintaining an extremely high level of quality, always manages to propose one or two extraordinary wines. Leading the way is their 2017 Pinot Bianco, which shines for its elegance and fragrance, but especially for the freshness and crispness of its palate. Tre Bicchieri.

# La Tunella

FRAZ. IPPLIS
VIA DEL COLLIO, 14
33040 PREMARIACCO [UD]
TEL. +39 0432716030
www.latunella.it

**CELLAR SALES**
**PRE-BOOKED VISITS**
**ANNUAL PRODUCTION** 390,000 bottles
**HECTARES UNDER VINE** 70.00
**SUSTAINABLE WINERY**

Descendants of a centuries-old tradition of quality winemaking, Massimo and Marco Zorzettig, along with their mother, Gabriella, lead this splendid winery in the Friuli Colli Orientali appellation. Three generations of vine growers have accumulated experience and traced out a path that the brothers are enthusiastically pursuing. La Tunella is a modern and dynamic producer with a young, tight staff. Luigino Zamparo oversees winemaking in a spacious cellar that avails itself of the latest technology and commendable architectural solutions. They've chosen to produce their two white blends, which usually lead their selection, exclusively with native grape varieties. Their BiancoSesto is made with equal parts Tocai Friulano and Ribolla Gialla while their LaLinda relies on the same two cultivar as well as Malvasia Istriana. Their 2016 BiancoSesto is a perfect wine for its balance and harmony. It brings home Tre Bicchieri.

| | |
|---|---|
| ○ FCO Pinot Bianco '17 | ▼▼▼ 3* |
| ○ Blanc di Neri Brut | ▼▼ 5 |
| ○ FCO Friulano '17 | ▼▼ 3 |
| ● FCO Merlot Altromerlot '14 | ▼▼ 5 |
| ○ FCO Pinot Grigio '17 | ▼▼ 3 |
| ● FCO Refosco P. R. '16 | ▼▼ 3 |
| ○ FCO Ribolla Gialla '17 | ▼▼ 3 |
| ○ FCO Sauvignon '17 | ▼▼ 3 |
| ● FCO Cabernet Sauvignon '15 | ▼ 3 |
| ○ FCO Pinot Bianco '14 | ♀♀♀ 3* |
| ○ FCO Pinot Grigio '16 | ♀♀♀ 3* |
| ○ FCO Pinot Grigio '15 | ♀♀♀ 3* |
| ○ FCO Friulano '16 | ♀♀ 3* |
| ● FCO Pignolo '13 | ♀♀ 5 |
| ○ FCO Pinot Bianco '16 | ♀♀ 3 |

| | |
|---|---|
| ○ FCO BiancoSesto '16 | ▼▼▼ 4* |
| ○ FCO Bianco LaLinda '16 | ▼▼ 4 |
| ○ FCO Sauvignon Col Matiss '16 | ▼▼ 4 |
| ○ FCO Dolce Noans '16 | ▼▼ 5 |
| ○ FCO Malvasia Valmasia '17 | ▼▼ 3 |
| ○ FCO Pinot Grigio Col Bajè '16 | ▼▼ 4 |
| ○ FCO Ribolla Gialla Col de Bliss '16 | ▼▼ 4 |
| ○ FCO Ribolla Gialla Rjgialla '17 | ▼▼ 3 |
| ● Pignolo '12 | ▼▼ 5 |
| ● Schioppettino '15 | ▼▼ 4 |
| ○ FCO Friulano '17 | ▼ 3 |
| ○ FCO Pinot Grigio '17 | ▼ 3 |
| ○ FCO Bianco LaLinda '14 | ♀♀♀ 4* |
| ○ Noans '12 | ♀♀♀ 5 |
| ○ FCO Sauvignon Col Matiss '15 | ♀♀ 4 |

# Valchiarò

FRAZ. TOGLIANO
VIA DEI LAGHI, 4C
33040 TORREANO [UD]
TEL. +39 0432715502
www.valchiaro.it

CELLAR SALES
PRE-BOOKED VISITS
ANNUAL PRODUCTION 45,000 bottles
HECTARES UNDER VINE 14.00
SUSTAINABLE WINERY

Valchiarò's story is one of passion and friendship. In 1991 six small producers with different backgrounds decided to form a partnership and bring their grapes together for a single purpose, thus founding a winery in Torreano di Cividale. What seemed like a mere bet turned out to be a strongly rooted project, capable of earning a place among the region's top producers. Their modern cellar is immersed in a beautiful landscape, with enologist Gianni Menotti entrusted to oversee winemaking. Their 2017 Friulano Nexus repeated last year's exploit, earning a place in our finals. It's a wine of superior elegance that offers up aromas of tropical fruit and citrus while caressing the palate thanks to a combination of softness and freshness. Their 2015 Merlot Riserva is also excellent for its aromatic complexity, which enchants the nose, and for the juicy pervasiveness of its palate.

| | |
|---|---|
| ○ FCO Friulano Nexus '17 | 🍷🍷 3* |
| ● FCO Merlot Ris. '15 | 🍷🍷 3 |
| ○ FCO Pinot Grigio '17 | 🍷🍷 3 |
| ● FCO Rosso Torre Qual Ris. '15 | 🍷🍷 3 |
| ○ FCO Friulano '17 | 🍷 3 |
| ○ FCO Sauvignon '17 | 🍷 3 |
| ○ FCO Friulano Nexus '16 | 🍷🍷 3* |
| ● FCO Merlot '13 | 🍷🍷 3 |
| ○ FCO Picolit '11 | 🍷🍷 6 |
| ○ FCO Pinot Grigio '16 | 🍷🍷 3 |
| ● FCO Refosco P. R. Ris. '13 | 🍷🍷 3 |
| ● FCO Rosso Torre Qual Ris. '13 | 🍷🍷 3 |
| ○ FCO Sauvignon '16 | 🍷🍷 3 |
| ○ FCO Verduzzo Friulano '15 | 🍷🍷 4 |

# Valpanera

VIA TRIESTE, 5A
33059 VILLA VICENTINA [UD]
TEL. +39 0431970395
www.valpanera.it

CELLAR SALES
PRE-BOOKED VISITS
ANNUAL PRODUCTION 450,000 bottles
HECTARES UNDER VINE 55.00

Studies and research have shown that Friuli Aquileia has been used for wine-growing for a millennium. The clay soil, the cool northern winds and the sea breeze blowing in off the nearby Adriatic guarantee quality grapes. It's here that Valpanera was founded in 1972 by Giampietro Dal Vecchio, who manages things today along with his son Giovanni. Their goal is to cultivate and promote Refosco dal Peduncolo Rosso, the region's most representative red grape variety. In recent years we've witnessed major changes and greater attention to market demand. In addition to their ubiquitous Refosco we find two new blends. Their 2017 Album is a white made with Malvasia Istriana, Chardonnay and Riesling Renano while their 2015 Atrum is a red made with Refosco, Cabernet Sauvignon and Merlot. Among their fresh 2017s, a Cabernet Sauvignon made in steel stands out.

| | |
|---|---|
| ○ Album '17 | 🍷🍷 2* |
| ● Atrum '15 | 🍷🍷 2* |
| ○ Friuli Aquileia Chardonnay '17 | 🍷🍷 3 |
| ● Friuli Aquileia Refosco P. R. Sup. '14 | 🍷🍷 3 |
| ○ Friuli Aquileia Sauvignon '17 | 🍷🍷 3 |
| ● Friuli Aquileia Cabernet Sauvignon '17 | 🍷 2 |
| ● Friuli Aquileia Refosco P. R. '16 | 🍷 2 |
| ● Friuli Aquileia Refosco P. R. '14 | 🍷🍷 2* |
| ● Friuli Aquileia Refosco P. R. '13 | 🍷🍷 2* |
| ● Friuli Aquileia Refosco P. R. Ris. '12 | 🍷🍷 5 |
| ● Friuli Aquileia Refosco P. R. Ris. '11 | 🍷🍷 5 |
| ● Friuli Aquileia Refosco P. R. Sup. '13 | 🍷🍷 3 |
| ● Friuli Aquileia Refosco P. R. Sup. '12 | 🍷🍷 3 |
| ● Friuli Aquileia Rosso Alma '13 | 🍷🍷 5 |
| ● Friuli Aquileia Rosso Alma '11 | 🍷🍷 5 |
| ○ Friuli Aquileia Verduzzo Friulano '13 | 🍷🍷 4 |

## ★★Venica & Venica

LOC. CERÒ, 8
34070 DOLEGNA DEL COLLIO [GO]
TEL. +39 048161264
www.venica.it

**CELLAR SALES**
**PRE-BOOKED VISITS**
**ACCOMMODATION**
**ANNUAL PRODUCTION 310,000 bottles**
**HECTARES UNDER VINE 40.00**
**SUSTAINABLE WINERY**

Gianni and Giorgio are the Venica & Venica that have managed to transform a small agricultural producer into a dynamic, well-organized business that's appreciated the world over. And they did it with the farmworker's spirit of cooperation and great entrepreneurial skill. Ornella and Giampaolo oversee public relations, with Serena and Marta by their sides. They are Gianni and Giorgio's daughters (respectively) and have officially joined the staff, helping to continue to promote the prestigious brand. Every single cultivar is vinified individually and separately and their consistently excellent scores testifies to the care and attention shown to each one. This year their 2017 Friulano Ronco delle Cime has the honor of leading the group by virtue of its impressive bouquet and surprisingly pleasant fragrance.

## La Viarte

VIA NOVACUZZO, 51
33040 PREPOTTO [UD]
TEL. +39 0432759458
www.laviarte.it

**CELLAR SALES**
**PRE-BOOKED VISITS**
**ACCOMMODATION**
**ANNUAL PRODUCTION 100,000 bottles**
**HECTARES UNDER VINE 27.00**
**SUSTAINABLE WINERY**

It's a particularly good period at La Viarte. The lovely Prepotto winery is earning universal consensus and praise, and has gained attention even from the most demanding figures in the sector. Credit has to go to the winery's current owner, Alberto Piovan. With the change in management he took on the work of further developing the territory's unique attributes, thanks in part to the estate's now mature vineyards. With the same vision, he's availed himself of the support of Gianni Menotti in the cellar. The fact that their wines earned such strong overall consensus testifies to soundness of their selection and the attention shown to each cultivar. Their 2017 Friulano Liende leads the way, proving it's a cut above the rest. Last year it earned Tre Bicchieri, but this year it's outdone itself in terms of elegance and style. It's a wine that delights the nose and caresses the palate with exemplary harmony.

| | | |
|---|---|---|
| ○ Collio Friulano Ronco delle Cime '17 | ♟♟ 5 | |
| ○ Collio Chardonnay Ronco Bernizza '17 | ♟♟ 4 | |
| ○ Collio Malvasia Pètris '17 | ♟♟ 4 | |
| ○ Collio Pinot Bianco Tàlis '17 | ♟♟ 4 | |
| ○ Collio Pinot Grigio Jesera '17 | ♟♟ 4 | |
| ○ Collio Ribolla Gialla L'Adelchi '17 | ♟♟ 4 | |
| ○ Collio Sauvignon Ronco del Cerò '17 | ♟♟ 5 | |
| ○ Collio Sauvignon Ronco delle Mele '17 | ♟♟ 6 | |
| ○ Collio Traminer Aromatico '17 | ♟♟ 4 | |
| ○ Collio Sauvignon Ronco delle Mele '16 | ♟♟♟ 6 | |
| ○ Collio Sauvignon Ronco delle Mele '13 | ♟♟♟ 6 | |
| ○ Collio Sauvignon Ronco delle Mele '12 | ♟♟♟ 6 | |
| ○ Collio Sauvignon Ronco delle Mele '11 | ♟♟♟ 6 | |
| ○ Collio Friulano Ronco delle Cime '16 | ♟♟ 5 | |
| ○ Collio Pinot Grigio Jesera '16 | ♟♟ 4 | |
| ○ Collio Sauvignon Ronco delle Mele '15 | ♟♟ 6 | |

| | | |
|---|---|---|
| ○ FCO Friulano Liende '17 | ♟♟♟ 5 | |
| ○ FCO Chardonnay '17 | ♟♟ 4 | |
| ○ FCO Friulano '17 | ♟♟ 4 | |
| ○ FCO Pinot Bianco '17 | ♟♟ 4 | |
| ○ FCO Pinot Grigio '17 | ♟♟ 4 | |
| ○ FCO Riesling '17 | ♟♟ 4 | |
| ○ FCO Sauvignon '17 | ♟♟ 4 | |
| ● FCO Schioppettino di Prepotto '11 | ♟♟ 5 | |
| ○ FCO Friulano Liende '16 | ♟♟♟ 5 | |
| ○ FCO Sauvignon Liende '15 | ♟♟♟ 5 | |
| ○ Arteus '16 | ♟♟ 4 | |
| ○ FCO Friulano '16 | ♟♟ 4 | |
| ● FCO Pignolo '07 | ♟♟ 8 | |
| ○ FCO Pinot Bianco '16 | ♟♟ 4 | |
| ○ FCO Sauvignon Liende '16 | ♟♟ 5 | |
| ● FCO Tazzelenghe '11 | ♟♟ 5 | |

# FRIULI VENEZIA GIULIA

## Vidussi

VIA SPESSA, 18
34071 CAPRIVA DEL FRIULI [GO]
TEL. +39 048180072
www.vinimontresor.it

**CELLAR SALES**
**PRE-BOOKED VISITS**
**ANNUAL PRODUCTION** 500,000 bottles
**HECTARES UNDER VINE** 30.00

Since 2000 the Vidussi family's winery has been rented by Verona's Montresor group. Their vineyards are situated primarily along the pleasant hills that run from Capriva del Friuli towards Cormòns, in the heart of Collio. Their other plots can be found in Friuli Colli Orientali and Friuli Isonzo. Naturally, mostly white grapes are cultivated, with particular attention paid to Ribolla Gialla. For some time now winemaking has been entrusted to the expert enologist Luigino De Giuseppe. Last year we pointed out the high level of quality demonstrated by their entire selection, which is particularly remarkable when considering their prices. This year their 2017 Ribolla Nera o Schioppettino put in a noteworthy performance. Even if it's a red, it's always submitted along with their most recent whites and consistently delivers for its harmony and pleasantness on the palate.

## ★★Vie di Romans

LOC. VIE DI ROMANS, 1
34070 MARIANO DEL FRIULI [GO]
TEL. +39 048169600
www.viediromans.it

**CELLAR SALES**
**PRE-BOOKED VISITS**
**ANNUAL PRODUCTION** 280,000 bottles
**HECTARES UNDER VINE** 60.00
**SUSTAINABLE WINERY**

Vie di Romans is one of Friuli Isonzo's most prestigious brands. The Gallo family has a history of winemaking that goes back more than a century, but it was Gianfranco who took things to a whole new level. In 1978 he founded the winery that continues to astonish for the quality of its entire selection. Whites dominate, and they are often characterized by bold structure. It doesn't matter if they're aged in steel or barriques, they manage to highlight the territory's identity, thanks in part to the estate's proximity to the sea, which endows their wines with a decidedly Mediterranean character. As has been the case for some time now, almost all Gianfranco's wines earn a place in our finals. It's even more difficult to choose which wine should be considered best when their scores are so consistently high. Their 2016 Sauvignon Piere proves to be just a cut above the rest, repeating last year's exploit and taking home Tre Bicchieri.

| | |
|---|---|
| ○ Collio Chardonnay '17 | ♈♈ 2* |
| ○ Collio Friulano '17 | ♈♈ 3 |
| ○ Collio Malvasia '17 | ♈♈ 2* |
| ○ Collio Pinot Grigio '17 | ♈♈ 2* |
| ○ Collio Ribolla Gialla '17 | ♈♈ 2* |
| ● Ribolla Nera o Schioppettino '17 | ♈♈ 3 |
| ○ Collio Sauvignon '17 | ♈ 2 |
| ○ Collio Traminer Aromatico '17 | ♈ 2 |
| ○ Collio Chardonnay '16 | ♉♉ 2* |
| ○ Collio Chardonnay '15 | ♉♉ 2* |
| ○ Collio Malvasia '16 | ♉♉ 2* |
| ○ Collio Pinot Grigio '15 | ♉♉ 2* |
| ○ Collio Ribolla Gialla '16 | ♉♉ 2* |
| ○ Collio Sauvignon '16 | ♉♉ 2* |
| ○ Collio Sauvignon '15 | ♉♉ 2* |
| ● Ribolla Nera o Schioppettino '16 | ♉♉ 3 |

| | |
|---|---|
| ○ Friuli Isonzo Sauvignon Piere '16 | ♈♈♈ 5 |
| ○ Friuli Isonzo Chardonnay '16 | ♈♈ 5 |
| ○ Friuli Isonzo Chardonnay Ciampagnis '16 | ♈♈ 5 |
| ○ Friuli Isonzo Sauvignon Vieris '16 | ♈♈ 5 |
| ○ Dut'Un '15 | ♈♈ 6 |
| ○ Friuli Isonzo Bianco Flors di Uis '16 | ♈♈ 5 |
| ○ Friuli Isonzo Pinot Grigio Dessimis '16 | ♈♈ 5 |
| ○ Friuli Isonzo Bianco Flors di Uis '09 | ♉♉♉ 4* |
| ○ Friuli Isonzo Chardonnay Ciampagnis Vieris '13 | ♉♉♉ 4* |
| ○ Friuli Isonzo Friulano Dolée '12 | ♉♉♉ 5 |
| ○ Friuli Isonzo Friulano Dolée '11 | ♉♉♉ 4* |
| ○ Friuli Isonzo Rive Alte Sauvignon Piere '07 | ♉♉♉ 4* |
| ○ Friuli Isonzo Sauvignon Piere '15 | ♉♉♉ 5 |
| ○ Friuli Isonzo Sauvignon Piere '10 | ♉♉♉ 4* |
| ○ Friuli Isonzo Sauvignon Piere '08 | ♉♉♉ 4* |

# Vigna del Lauro

Loc. Montona, 19
34071 Cormòns [GO]
Tel. +39 0481629549
www.vignadellauro.it

CELLAR SALES
PRE-BOOKED VISITS
ANNUAL PRODUCTION 60,000 bottles
HECTARES UNDER VINE 10.00

Vigna del Lauro was founded in 1994 by
Fabio Coser, who already owned the
well-known producer Ronco dei Tassi. His
goal was to diversify his selection by adding
more approachable, yet characteristic wines
that were also good value for the money.
And so it was that he identified the first
vineyard, one surrounded by laurel oaks
(hence the winery's name). More plots came
later, some private and others rented. All are
concentrated around Cormòns, some in the
Collio appellation and others in Friuli Isonzo.
And once again this year their Collio wines
prove to be just a cut above the rest and
lead the rankings. Their excellent prices are
even more impressive considering the high
level we've grown used to. They're wines
of exemplary precision, and while there
may not be standouts, theirs is an
approachable, enticing, gratifying selection
without any flaws.

| | |
|---|---|
| ○ Collio Friulano '17 | ▼▼ 3 |
| ○ Collio Pinot Grigio '17 | ▼▼ 3 |
| ○ Collio Sauvignon '17 | ▼▼ 3 |
| ● Friuli Isonzo Cabernet Franc '17 | ▼▼ 2* |
| ● Friuli Isonzo Merlot '16 | ▼▼ 2* |
| ○ Friuli Isonzo Traminer Aromatico '17 | ▼▼ 2* |
| ● Pinot Nero Novaj '15 | ▼▼ 3 |
| ○ Ribolla Gialla '17 | ▼▼ 3 |
| ○ Friuli Isonzo Friuliano '17 | ▼ 2 |
| ○ Collio Friulano '16 | ♀♀ 3 |
| ○ Collio Pinot Grigio '16 | ♀♀ 3 |
| ○ Collio Sauvignon '16 | ♀♀ 3 |
| ● Friuli Isonzo Merlot '15 | ♀♀ 2* |
| ○ Friuli Isonzo Traminer Aromatico '16 | ♀♀ 2* |
| ● Pinot Nero Novaj '13 | ♀♀ 3 |
| ○ Ribolla Gialla '16 | ♀♀ 3 |

# Vigna Petrussa

via Albana, 47
33040 Prepotto [UD]
Tel. +39 0432713021
www.vignapetrussa.it

CELLAR SALES
PRE-BOOKED VISITS
ANNUAL PRODUCTION 30,000 bottles
HECTARES UNDER VINE 7.00

Vigna Petrussa's roots go back to the late
19th century, but the winery found renewed
vigor after a difficult period in the mid-90s.
It was then that Hilde Petrussa decided to
settle in Albana di Prepotto and revive the
family estate, along with her husband
Renato. It's situated in a splendid valley
where the Judrio river forms a border
between the Collio and Friuli Colli Orientali
appellations. It's an area that's often subject
to strong winds, which dry the grapes but
also lead to notable day-night temperature
swings that give rise to aromatic complexity.
This year we had the chance to taste
various typologies, and the unanimity of the
praise they elicited works to the benefit of
their entire selection. Leading the way is
their very sweet 2015 Picolit, which proves
to be one of the best in its category and
landed a place in our finals. It's a wine that
gratifies the nose with notes of beeswax,
dates, sweet almond candy bars and
candied orange peel. On the palate it proves
pervasive and long.

| | |
|---|---|
| ○ COF Picolit '15 | ▼▼ 6 |
| ○ FCO Friulano '17 | ▼▼ 3 |
| ○ FCO Ribolla Gialla '17 | ▼▼ 3 |
| ● FCO Schioppettino di Prepotto '15 | ▼▼ 5 |
| ● FCO Schippettino RiNera '16 | ▼▼ 3 |
| ● Refosco P. R. '16 | ▼▼ 4 |
| ○ Richenza '16 | ▼▼ 4 |
| ● FCO Cabernet Franc '15 | ▼ 3 |
| ○ COF Picolit '13 | ♀♀ 6 |
| ● COF Schioppettino di Prepotto '10 | ♀♀ 4 |
| ○ FCO Friulano '16 | ♀♀ 3 |
| ○ FCO Friulano '15 | ♀♀ 3* |
| ○ Richenza '15 | ♀♀ 4 |

# Vigna Traverso

VIA RONCHI, 73
33040 PREPOTTO [UD]
TEL. +39 0422804807
www.vignatraverso.it

CELLAR SALES
PRE-BOOKED VISITS
RESTAURANT SERVICE
ANNUAL PRODUCTION 100,000 bottles
HECTARES UNDER VINE 22.00
SUSTAINABLE WINERY

In 1998 Vigna Traverso, once known as Ronco di Castagneto, was purchased and renamed by the Molon Traverso family, who already owned a winery near Veneto. Stefano Traverso is at the helm, managing both winemaking and vine growing. Particular care is shown for the old vineyards of native cultivar situated in Prepotto. Their new cellar is equipped with the latest technology, but avails itself of concrete vats, a classic example of innovation and respect for tradition. The strong overall performance of their entire selection is worth noting, though this year their 2015 Bianco Sottocastello proved to be the best of the lot. It's a wine made primarily with Chardonnay and a smaller share of Sauvignon. It's a perfect combination that gives rise to intriguing aromas of tropical fruit, candied citrus, lemon verbena and vanilla. In the mouth it comes through dense and closes with a freshness that's as unexpected as it is enjoyable.

| | |
|---|---|
| ○ FCO Bianco Sottocastello '15 | ♟♟ 5 |
| ○ FCO Friulano '17 | ♟♟ 3 |
| ● FCO Refosco P. R. '14 | ♟♟ 4 |
| ○ FCO Ribolla Gialla '17 | ♟♟ 3 |
| ● FCO Rosso Sottocastello '13 | ♟♟ 5 |
| ● FCO Rosso Troj '14 | ♟♟ 4 |
| ○ FCO Sauvignon '17 | ♟♟ 3 |
| ● FCO Schioppettino di Prepotto '14 | ♟♟ 5 |
| ● FCO Cabernet Franc '14 | ♟ 4 |
| ○ FCO Pinot Grigio '17 | ♟ 3 |
| ○ FCO Bianco Sottocastello '14 | ♟♟ 4 |
| ● FCO Cabernet Franc '13 | ♟♟ 3 |
| ● FCO Refosco P. R. '13 | ♟♟ 3* |
| ○ FCO Ribolla Gialla '16 | ♟♟ 3 |
| ○ FCO Sauvignon '16 | ♟♟ 3* |
| ● FCO Schioppettino di Prepotto '13 | ♟♟ 4 |

# Vigne del Malina

FRAZ. ORZANO
VIA PASINI VIANELLI, 9
33047 REMANZACCO [UD]
TEL. +39 0432649258
www.vignedelmalina.com

CELLAR SALES
PRE-BOOKED VISITS
ANNUAL PRODUCTION 45,000 bottles
HECTARES UNDER VINE 10.00
VITICULTURE METHOD Certified Organic

In 1967 the Bacchetti family purchased an estate in Orzano di Remanzacco, in the Friuli Grave appellation. Only in 2007 did Roberto Bacchetti and Maria Luisa Trevisan decided to start bottling their own wines, entrusting management to Omar Pantarotto, a jack-of-all-trades who oversees both the vineyards and cellar, along with the help of Natale Favretto. The brilliant results prove that you can produce personal and long-lived wines, even in the lowlands, thanks to low-yields and painstaking care. Their wines are only put on the market when they're ready, and never fewer than three years after vintage. As has already been the case in the past, this year only two macerated whites were submitted, so we'll have to wait another year to taste the rest of their offering. Both wines are 2011s, but they're only now being put on the market. Their 2011 Sauvignon Aur is redolent of ripe apricot and maple syrup. It's a soft and tasty wine. Their 2011 Pinot Grigio Ram proves pervasive, juicy and lingering.

| | |
|---|---|
| ○ Aur Sauvignon '11 | ♟♟ 5 |
| ○ Ram Pinot Grigio '11 | ♟♟ 5 |
| ● Cabernet Franc '11 | ♟♟ 3 |
| ○ Chardonnay '13 | ♟♟ 3 |
| ○ Chardonnay '12 | ♟♟ 3 |
| ○ Pinot Grigio '13 | ♟♟ 3* |
| ○ Pinot Grigio '12 | ♟♟ 3 |
| ○ Pinot Grigio '11 | ♟♟ 3 |
| ○ Sauvignon '13 | ♟♟ 3 |
| ○ Sauvignon '12 | ♟♟ 3 |
| ○ Sauvignon Aur '09 | ♟♟ 5 |

## ★Le Vigne di Zamò

LOC. ROSAZZO
VIA ABATE CORRADO, 4
33044 MANZANO [UD]
TEL. +39 0432759693
www.levignedizamo.com

CELLAR SALES
PRE-BOOKED VISITS
ANNUAL PRODUCTION 280,000 bottles
HECTARES UNDER VINE 42.00
SUSTAINABLE WINERY

The fame of this prestigious brand is derived primarily from its connection to legendary entrepreneur Tullio Zamò. His journey began with Vigne dal Leon, and proceeded with the foundation of Abbazia di Rosazzo and Le Vigne di Zamò in 1996 (together with his sons Pierluigi and Silvano). Today the estate, which overlooks the famous abbey, is in the hands of Farinetti group, a fact that has raised its visibility on global markets. The staff haven't changed, however, and their selection has maintained the same high quality standards. Once again two of their wines made it into our finals: their 2017 Friulano No Name and their 2017 Ribolla Gialla. Both are proudly made with native grape varieties. They're just the tip of the iceberg of a truly remarkable selection (despite some small exceptions) that goes back three vintages.

| | | |
|---|---|---|
| ○ FCO Friulano No Name '17 | ♈♈ | 5 |
| ○ FCO Ribolla Gialla '17 | ♈♈ | 5 |
| ○ FCO Chardonnay Ronco delle Acacie '15 | ♈♈ | 6 |
| ○ FCO Friuliano V. Cinquant'Anni '16 | ♈♈ | 6 |
| ● FCO Merlot V. Cinquant'Anni '15 | ♈♈ | 6 |
| ○ FCO Pinot Bianco Tullio Zamò '15 | ♈♈ | 5 |
| ○ FCO Pinot Grigio '17 | ♈♈ | 5 |
| ○ COF Friulano V. Cinquant'Anni '09 | ♈♈♈ | 5 |
| ○ COF Friulano V. Cinquant'Anni '08 | ♈♈♈ | 5 |
| ● COF Merlot V. Cinquant'Anni '09 | ♈♈♈ | 5 |
| ○ FCO Friulano No Name '15 | ♈♈♈ | 5 |
| ○ Friuli Friulano No Name '16 | ♈♈♈ | 4* |

## Villa de Puppi

VIA ROMA, 5
33040 MOIMACCO [UD]
TEL. +39 0432722461
www.depuppi.it

CELLAR SALES
PRE-BOOKED VISITS
ANNUAL PRODUCTION 70,000 bottles
HECTARES UNDER VINE 25.00
SUSTAINABLE WINERY

Credit for Villa de Puppi's success should go to count Luigi. Sensing the potential of a group of old vineyards in the late 1990s, he reorganized them and left them in the care of his young children Caterina and Valfredo. They represent the latest generation of a patrician family that have for centuries cultivated the private estate around their splendid manor. It's an effort that has found its footing definitively with the purchase of plots on the Rosazzo hills, and with the decision to take in the precious Rosa Bosco brand. Their 2015 Sauvignon Blanc from this last line gratifies the nose with its exotic notes of tropical fruit, juniper berries, medicinal herbs and candied citrus. They're fragrances that penetrate the palate, expand and endure along with balsamic whiffs. It's a delight. Their 2016 Sauvignon, a citrusy and mineral wine, is also excellent, as is their 2012 Merlot Il Boscorosso di Rosa Bosco, a pervasive and creamy wine that's in line with the best vintages.

| | | |
|---|---|---|
| ○ Sauvignon Blanc di Rosa Bosco '15 | ♈♈ | 5 |
| ● Merlot Il Boscorosso di Rosa Bosco '12 | ♈♈ | 6 |
| ○ Pinot Grigio '16 | ♈♈ | 3 |
| ● Refosco P.R. Cate '13 | ♈♈ | 5 |
| ○ Sauvignon '16 | ♈♈ | 3 |
| ○ Chardonnay '16 | ♈ | 3 |
| ○ Ribolla Gialla '16 | ♈ | 3 |
| ○ Chardonnay '15 | ♈♈ | 3 |
| ○ Chardonnay '14 | ♈♈ | 3 |
| ○ Ribolla Gialla di Rosa Bosco '15 | ♈♈ | 4 |
| ○ Sauvignon Blanc di Rosa Bosco '14 | ♈♈ | 5 |
| ○ Sauvignon Blanc di Rosa Bosco '13 | ♈♈ | 5 |
| ○ Taj Blanc '15 | ♈♈ | 3 |
| ○ Taj Blanc '14 | ♈♈ | 3 |

# ★★Villa Russiz

LOC. ITALIA
VIA RUSSIZ, 4/6
34070 CAPRIVA DEL FRIULI [GO]
TEL. +39 048180047
www.villarussiz.it

**CELLAR SALES**
**PRE-BOOKED VISITS**
**ANNUAL PRODUCTION** 220,000 bottles
**HECTARES UNDER VINE** 45.00
**SUSTAINABLE WINERY**

Villa Russiz's past is a story of foresight
and generosity. It was Teodoro de La Tour
who, in 1869, realized that the sunny hills
of Collio were the perfect place to live with
his wife, Elvine Ritter, and to cultivate wine
grapes. They deserve credit for having
introduced the French varieties that are
now established in the region, and for
adopting techniques that were unknown at
the time. As they had no children, they
decided to leave the winery in the hands of
an institute that works with children in
difficulty. And so it was that Fondazione
came to exist, and has continued operating
down to the present day. Their selection
includes wines from the most recent
vintage as well as those (sometimes more
highly prized) that are age for longer. And
so it is that we discovered a surprising
2014 Chardonnay Gräfin de La Tour, the
child of season that we remember as
particularly problematic. But with a few
years under its belt, the wine delivers and
earns a well-deserved Tre Bicchieri.

| | |
|---|---|
| ○ Collio Chardonnay Gräfin de La Tour '14 | ▼▼▼ 7 |
| ○ Collio Pinot Bianco '17 | ▼▼ 4 |
| ○ Collio Sauvignon de La Tour '17 | ▼▼ 6 |
| ○ Collio Friulano '17 | ▼▼ 4 |
| ○ Collio Malvasia '17 | ▼▼ 4 |
| ● Collio Merlot Gräf de La Tour '13 | ▼▼ 6 |
| ○ Collio Pinot Grigio '17 | ▼▼ 4 |
| ○ Collio Friulano '09 | ♀♀♀ 4* |
| ○ Collio Pinot Bianco '16 | ♀♀♀ 4* |
| ○ Collio Malvasia '15 | ♀♀ 4 |
| ○ Collio Pinot Bianco '14 | ♀♀ 4 |
| ○ Collio Sauvignon de La Tour '16 | ♀♀ 6 |

# Tenuta Villanova

LOC. VILLANOVA DI FARRA
VIA CONTESSA BERETTA, 29
34072 FARRA D'ISONZO [GO]
TEL. +39 0481889311
www.tenutavillanova.com

**CELLAR SALES**
**PRE-BOOKED VISITS**
**ANNUAL PRODUCTION** 600,000 bottles
**HECTARES UNDER VINE** 105.00

Tenuta Villanova, the oldest estate in the
region, embodies more than five centuries
of history. In 1932 it was purchased by the
entrepreneur Arnaldo Bennati, and his wife
continues to manage the winery today.
She's joined by their grandson Alberto
Grossi and a young technical staff. Their
vineyards are situated along the so-called
'Collio Island', a small hill area that's
surrounded by plains throughout which
Collio Goriziano's soil magically emerges.
Some of their selection (especially those
from their Ronco Cucco line) weren't
bottled in time to be submitted. As a result
we didn't get a complete sense of their
entire range of wines, though our tastings
pointed up the fact that their wines
cultivated on the plains can stand
shoulder-to-shoulder with those from the
hills. Indeed, their 2017 Pinot Grigio Ronco
Cucco and 2017 Friulano both stood out
and lead the rankings.

| | |
|---|---|
| ○ Collio Friulano Ronco Cucco '17 | ▼▼ 4 |
| ○ Collio Pinot Grigio Ronco Cucco '17 | ▼▼ 3 |
| ○ Friuli Isonzo Friulano '17 | ▼▼ 3 |
| ● Friuli Isonzo Refosco P. R. '16 | ▼▼ 2* |
| ○ Friuli Isonzo Chardonnay '17 | ▼ 2 |
| ○ Friuli Isonzo Malvasia '17 | ▼ 2 |
| ○ Collio Chardonnay Monte Cucco '97 | ♀♀♀ 3* |
| ○ Collio Chardonnay Ronco Cucco '16 | ♀♀ 4 |
| ○ Collio Friulano Ronco Cucco '16 | ♀♀ 4 |
| ○ Collio Friulano Ronco Cucco '15 | ♀♀ 4 |
| ○ Collio Picolit Ronco Cucco '15 | ♀♀ 5 |
| ○ Collio Sauvignon Ronco Cucco '16 | ♀♀ 4 |
| ● Friuli Isonzo Refosco P. R. '13 | ♀♀ 2* |

## ★★Volpe Pasini

FRAZ. TOGLIANO
VIA CIVIDALE, 16
33040 TORREANO [UD]
TEL. +39 0432715151
www.volpepasini.it

**CELLAR SALES**
**PRE-BOOKED VISITS**
**ACCOMMODATION**
**ANNUAL PRODUCTION** 400,000 bottles
**HECTARES UNDER VINE** 52.00
**SUSTAINABLE WINERY**

Volpe Pasini always charms with its magnificent plots, foremost the amphitheater-shaped Zuc vineyard, their crown jewel. Then there's their communication center, Villa Rosa, a rare, entirely renovated Venetian villa. And let's not forget their magnificent headquarters at Villa Volpe Pasini, with its historic cellars and 20,000 square meters of historic park, or their 18th century villa, which played an important cultural role in the early 20th century. But above all, it's their wines that impress for their freshness and structure, as well as the aloof, aristocratic charm bestowed by these vineyards situated along northern Friuli's hills. Their Zuc di Volpe wines are clearly a cut above the rest and all four earned a place in our finals (without taking anything away from their Volpe Pasini line, which are excellent value for the money). Their 2017 Zuc di Volpe is a constant by now, standing out for freshness and fragrance, and pointing up the cultivar's attributes through a modern lens.

## Francesco Vosca

FRAZ. BRAZZANO
VIA SOTTOMONTE, 19
34071 CORMÒNS [GO]
TEL. +39 048162135
www.voscavini.it

**CELLAR SALES**
**PRE-BOOKED VISITS**
**ANNUAL PRODUCTION** 60,000 bottles
**HECTARES UNDER VINE** 10.00
**SUSTAINABLE WINERY**

The Vosca family's small winery in Brazzano, a district of Cormòns, is proud of its agricultural roots. In the early 1990s Francesco decided to shift gears and focus exclusively on his vineyards, which are spread out across the Collio hills in the Friuli Isonzo appellation. The slopes aren't well-suited to mechanized work and require continual manual labor. Everyone gives a hand, with Francesco's wife, Anita, helping in the fields, while his son Gabriele has taken on responsibility for overseeing the winemaking. Both those wines made with grapes cultivated on the plains and the hills earned consistently strong scores pretty much across the board, thus testifying to the fact that each territory and cultivar is shown equal attention. Their 2017 whites all have fragrance and good nose-mouth symmetry in common, while their 2015 Merlot stood out for its copious aromas and pervasiveness on the palate.

| | |
|---|---|
| ○ FCO Sauvignon Zuc di Volpe '17 | 🍷🍷🍷 5 |
| ○ FCO Pinot Bianco Zuc di Volpe '17 | 🍷🍷 5 |
| ○ FCO Pinot Grigio Zuc di Volpe '17 | 🍷🍷 4 |
| ○ FCO Ribolla Gialla Zuc di Volpe '17 | 🍷🍷 4 |
| ○ FCO Chardonnay Volpe Pasini '17 | 🍷🍷 3 |
| ○ FCO Friulano Volpe Pasini '17 | 🍷🍷 3 |
| ○ FCO Pinot Grigio Grivò Volpe Pasini '17 | 🍷🍷 3 |
| ● FCO Refosco P.R. Volpe Pasini '15 | 🍷🍷 3 |
| ○ COF Pinot Bianco Zuc di Volpe '12 | 🍷🍷🍷 4* |
| ○ COF Sauvignon Zuc di Volpe '13 | 🍷🍷🍷 4* |
| ○ COF Sauvignon Zuc di Volpe '12 | 🍷🍷🍷 4* |
| ○ COF Sauvignon Zuc di Volpe '11 | 🍷🍷🍷 4* |
| ○ COF Sauvignon Zuc di Volpe '10 | 🍷🍷🍷 3* |
| ○ FCO Sauvignon Zuc di Volpe '16 | 🍷🍷🍷 5 |
| ○ FCO Sauvignon Zuc di Volpe '15 | 🍷🍷🍷 5 |
| ○ FCO Sauvignon Zuc di Volpe '14 | 🍷🍷🍷 5 |

| | |
|---|---|
| ○ Collio Friulano '17 | 🍷🍷 3 |
| ○ Collio Malvasia '17 | 🍷🍷 3 |
| ● Collio Merlot '15 | 🍷🍷 4 |
| ○ Collio Ribolla Gialla '17 | 🍷🍷 3 |
| ○ Friuli Isonzo Chardonnay '17 | 🍷🍷 3 |
| ○ Friuli Isonzo Sauvignon '17 | 🍷🍷 3 |
| ○ Collio Friulano '16 | 🍷🍷 3 |
| ○ Collio Friulano '15 | 🍷🍷 3 |
| ○ Collio Malvasia '16 | 🍷🍷 3 |
| ○ Collio Malvasia '15 | 🍷🍷 3 |
| ○ Collio Ribolla Gialla '16 | 🍷🍷 3 |
| ○ Collio Ribolla Gialla '15 | 🍷🍷 3 |
| ○ Friuli Isonzo Chardonnay '16 | 🍷🍷 3 |
| ○ Friuli Isonzo Chardonnay '15 | 🍷🍷 3 |
| ○ Friuli Isonzo Pinot Grigio '16 | 🍷🍷 3 |
| ○ Friuli Isonzo Pinot Grigio '15 | 🍷🍷 3 |

# Zaglia

LOC. FRASSINUTTI
VIA CRESCENZIA, 10
33050 PRECENICCO [UD]
TEL. +39 0431510320
www.zaglia.com

CELLAR SALES
PRE-BOOKED VISITS
ANNUAL PRODUCTION 100,000 bottles
HECTARES UNDER VINE 15.00

Giorgio Zaglia's winery is one of Friuli
Latisana's most notable. Situated in a
territory with an undisputed tradition of
wine-growing, his estate spans 30
hectares between the Stella and
Tagliamento rivers, in an area whose terrain
is characterized by mineral-rich clay that's
well-ventilated by the nearby Adriatic sea.
These conditions make for a particularly
favorable microclimate when it comes to
viticulture. The approach taken in the
vineyards aims for minimum environmental
impact, with strictly manual harvesting and
winemaking processes that draw on
physical force rather than artificial
techniques. Both their whites and reds are
well-balanced, authentic wines that respect
each cultivar's varietal qualities. Their
2015 Cabernet Franc Amanti Ris. opens
with intriguing aromas of medicinal herbs,
raspberry, cherry jam tart and cigar tobacco
while on the palate is unfolds gracefully.
Their 2017 Friulano and 2017 Merlot,
even if they're quite different, stood out for
their sophisticated simplicity and natural
drinkability.

| | | |
|---|---|---|
| ● FCO Cabernet Franc Amanti Ris. '15 | ♟♟ | 2* |
| ○ Friuli Friulano '17 | ♟♟ | 2* |
| ● Friuli Merlot '17 | ♟♟ | 2* |
| ○ Friuli Chardonnay '17 | ♟ | 2 |
| ● Friuli Latisana Cabernet Franc '17 | ♟ | 2 |
| ● Friuli Latisana Refosco P.R. '17 | ♟ | 2 |
| ○ Friuli Pinot Grigio '17 | ♟ | 2 |
| ● FCO Cabernet Franc Amanti Ris. '14 | ♟♟ | 2* |
| ○ Friuli Chardonnay '16 | ♟♟ | 2* |
| ○ Friuli Friulano '16 | ♟♟ | 2* |
| ● Friuli Latisana Cabernet Franc V. degli Amanti Ris. '10 | ♟♟ | 2* |
| ○ Friuli Latisana Pinot Grigio '15 | ♟♟ | 2* |
| ● Friuli Latisana Refosco P. R. '14 | ♟♟ | 2* |
| ● Friuli Merlot '16 | ♟♟ | 2* |

# Zidarich

LOC. PREPOTTO, 23
34011 DUINO AURISINA [TS]
TEL. +39 040201223
www.zidarich.it

CELLAR SALES
PRE-BOOKED VISITS
ANNUAL PRODUCTION 28,000 bottles
HECTARES UNDER VINE 8.00

Only those who have explored the Karst
Plateau can understand what 'heroic
viticulture' means. The climate here is
characterized by winds coming in off the
nearby Adriatic and the cold northern air
that can turn into violent gusts, thus limiting
the variety of grapes that can be cultivated.
These are the conditions under which
Beniamino Zidarich works. In 1988 he
revolutionized his father's winery, which at
the time comprised only a half hectare of
vineyards. In the tunnels carved out of hard
rock, their wines are aged in wood barrels
and at cool underground temperatures.
This year we only tasted three wines, all of
which were recently bottled. Though they're
the three wines that most represent Karst,
made with grapes that resist the cold,
northern winds. They're all macerated and
fermented on the skins, so as to bring out
the highest possible aromatic extraction,
and their 2016 Vitovska Kamen is made in
vats of Karst stone.

| | | |
|---|---|---|
| ○ Malvasia '16 | ♟♟ | 5 |
| ○ Vitovska '16 | ♟♟ | 5 |
| ○ Vitovska Kamen '16 | ♟♟ | 7 |
| ○ Carso Vitovska V. Collezione '09 | ♟♟♟ | 8 |
| ○ Prulke '10 | ♟♟♟ | 5 |
| ○ Malvasia '15 | ♟♟ | 5 |
| ○ Malvasia '13 | ♟♟ | 5 |
| ○ Prulke '15 | ♟♟ | 5 |
| ● Terrano '15 | ♟♟ | 5 |
| ○ Vitovska '15 | ♟♟ | 5 |
| ○ Vitovska Kamen '14 | ♟♟ | 7 |

# Zorzettig

FRAZ. SPESSA
S.DA SANT'ANNA, 37
33043 CIVIDALE DEL FRIULI [UD]
TEL. +39 0432716156
www.zorzettigvini.it

**CELLAR SALES**
**PRE-BOOKED VISITS**
**ACCOMMODATION AND RESTAURANT SERVICE**
**ANNUAL PRODUCTION** 800,000 bottles
**HECTARES UNDER VINE** 115.00
**SUSTAINABLE WINERY**

In Spessa di Cividale the name Zorzettig means wine producer. Several wineries have derived from the same lineage, but only Giuseppe, a decorated citizen, proudly kept the brand. Today the producer is managed by his children. Annalisa is an innovative and dynamic entrepreneur (not to mention a volcano of ideas), while her brother Alessandro prefers the quiet of the outdoors, overseeing vineyard management. Winemaking has been entrusted to the expert care of Fabio Coser. With his help they've produced a selection that stands out for its soundness and affordability, with their Myò line representing their more ambitious wines. It's always difficult to earn an award, and holding on to it is even more so. It's a special honor, then, for their 2017 Pinot Bianco Myò to earn Tre Bicchieri for the fourth year running. On the nose it delivers with its elegant aromas of flowers, delicate whiffs of talcum and hints of lemon wafer, while in the mouth it caresses the palate, alternating between velvety softness and citrus drive.

| | | |
|---|---|---|
| ○ FCO Pinot Bianco Myò '17 | ♟♟♟ 4* |
| ○ FCO Chardonnay '17 | ♟♟ 3 |
| ○ FCO Friulano Myò '17 | ♟♟ 4 |
| ○ FCO Malvasia Myò '17 | ♟♟ 4 |
| ● FCO Refosco P. R. Myò '15 | ♟♟ 5 |
| ○ FCO Ribolla Gialla Myò '17 | ♟♟ 4 |
| ● FCO Schioppettino Myò '15 | ♟♟ 5 |
| ○ Optimum Ribolla Gialla Brut Oz '17 | ♟♟ 3 |
| ○ FCO Friulano '17 | ♟ 3 |
| ○ FCO Pinot Grigio '17 | ♟ 3 |
| ○ FCO Sauvignon Myò '17 | ♟ 4 |
| ○ FCO Pinot Bianco Myò '16 | ♟♟♟ 4* |
| ○ FCO Pinot Bianco Myò '15 | ♟♟♟ 4* |
| ○ FCO Pinot Bianco Myò '14 | ♟♟♟ 4* |
| ● FCO Refosco P. R. Myò' '14 | ♟♟ 5 |

# Zuani

LOC. GIASBANA, 12
34070 SAN FLORIANO DEL COLLIO [GO]
TEL. +39 0481391432
www.zuanivini.it

**CELLAR SALES**
**PRE-BOOKED VISITS**
**ACCOMMODATION**
**ANNUAL PRODUCTION** 75,000 bottles
**HECTARES UNDER VINE** 15.00

Patrizia Felluga's winery is called Zuani, the result of an entrepreneurial philosophy that evolved over years of experience. She's deeply tied to the ancestral traditions of Collio, and helped by her children Antonio and Caterina. Together they've decided to utilize various cultivar to produce a single wine, as was once custom. And that's how their Collio Bianco Zuani came to be. It's made with grapes from their plots in Giasbana, on the beautiful slopes of San Floriano and comes in two versions: 'Vigne' (made using stainless steel) and 'Riserva' (matured in wood). This year the news is that their selection has been enriched with two new wines: their 2017 Pinot Grigio and 2017 Ribolla Gialla, which both stood out for their fragrance and pleasantness on the palate. But the top position in their selection is solidly in the hands of their 2017 Zuani Vigne, which has earned a place in our finals virtually every year since the turn of the new millennium thanks to its subtle and fine elegance.

| | | |
|---|---|---|
| ○ Collio Bianco Zuani Vigne '17 | ♟♟ 4 |
| ○ Collio Bianco Zuani Ris. '15 | ♟♟ 5 |
| ○ Collio Ribolla Gialla '17 | ♟♟ 3 |
| ○ Friuli Pinot Grigio '17 | ♟♟ 3 |
| ○ Collio Bianco Zuani Vigne '10 | ♟♟♟ 3 |
| ○ Collio Bianco Zuani Vigne '07 | ♟♟♟ 3 |
| ○ Collio Bianco Zuani Ris. '14 | ♟♟ 5 |
| ○ Collio Bianco Zuani Ris. '13 | ♟♟ 5 |
| ○ Collio Bianco Zuani Ris. '12 | ♟♟ 5 |
| ○ Collio Bianco Zuani Ris. '11 | ♟♟ 5 |
| ○ Collio Bianco Zuani Ris. '09 | ♟♟ 5 |
| ○ Collio Bianco Zuani Vigne '16 | ♟♟ 4 |
| ○ Collio Bianco Zuani Vigne '15 | ♟♟ 4 |
| ○ Collio Bianco Zuani Vigne '14 | ♟♟ 4 |
| ○ Collio Bianco Zuani Vigne '13 | ♟♟ 4 |
| ○ Collio Bianco Zuani Vigne '12 | ♟♟ 3* |

## Amandum

VIA F. PETRARCA, 40
34070 MORARO [GO]
TEL. +39 335242566
www.amandum.it

ANNUAL PRODUCTION 27,000 bottles
HECTARES UNDER VINE 2.00

| | |
|---|---|
| ● Friuli Isonzo Merlot '15 | ♟♟ 5 |
| ○ Friuli Isonzo Chardonnay Adonay '16 | ♟♟ 4 |
| ○ Friuli Isonzo Friulano '16 | ♟♟ 4 |
| ○ Friuli Isonzo Sauvignon Mysa '16 | ♟♟ 4 |

## Anzelin

VIA PLESSIVA, 4
34071 CORMÒNS [GO]
TEL. +39 0481639821
www.anzelin.it

CELLAR SALES
PRE-BOOKED VISITS
ANNUAL PRODUCTION 24,000 bottles
HECTARES UNDER VINE 9.00

| | |
|---|---|
| ○ Collio Friulano '17 | ♟♟ 3 |
| ○ Collio Pinot Bianco '17 | ♟♟ 3 |
| ○ Collio Pinot Grigio '17 | ♟♟ 3 |
| ○ Collio Sauvignon '17 | ♟♟ 3 |

## Aquila del Torre

FRAZ. SAVORGNANO DEL TORRE
VIA ATTIMIS, 25
33040 POVOLETTO [UD]
TEL. +39 0432666428
www.aquiladeltorre.it

CELLAR SALES
PRE-BOOKED VISITS
ACCOMMODATION
ANNUAL PRODUCTION 50,000 bottles
HECTARES UNDER VINE 18.00
VITICULTURE METHOD Certified Organic

| | |
|---|---|
| ○ FCO At Friulano '17 | ♟♟ 3 |
| ● FCO At Refosco P. R. '15 | ♟♟ 3 |
| ○ FCO At Riesling '15 | ♟♟ 3 |
| ● FCO Refosco P. R. Ris. '12 | ♟ 3 |

## Maurizio Arzenton

FRAZ. SPESSA
VIA CORMONS, 221
33043 CIVIDALE DEL FRIULI [UD]
TEL. +39 0432716139
www.arzentonvini.it

CELLAR SALES
PRE-BOOKED VISITS
ANNUAL PRODUCTION 30,000 bottles
HECTARES UNDER VINE 10.00

| | |
|---|---|
| ● FCO Cabernet Sauvignon '15 | ♟♟ 2* |
| ○ FCO Friulano '17 | ♟♟ 2* |
| ● FCO Merlot '16 | ♟♟ 2* |
| ● FCO Pinot Nero '16 | ♟♟ 2* |

## Attems

FRAZ. CAPRIVA DEL FRIULI
VIA AQUILEIA, 30
34070 GORIZIA
TEL. +39 0481806098
www.attems.it

CELLAR SALES
PRE-BOOKED VISITS
ANNUAL PRODUCTION 420,000 bottles
HECTARES UNDER VINE 44.00

| | |
|---|---|
| ○ Chardonnay '17 | ♟♟ 3 |
| ○ Collio Ribolla Gialla Trebes '16 | ♟♟ 4 |
| ○ Collio Sauvignon Blanc Cicinis '16 | ♟♟ 5 |
| ○ Sauvignon Blanc '17 | ♟♟ 3 |

## Bajta - Fattoria Carsica

VIA SALES, 108
34010 SGONICO [TS]
TEL. +39 0402296090
www.bajta.it

CELLAR SALES
PRE-BOOKED VISITS
ACCOMMODATION AND RESTAURANT SERVICE
ANNUAL PRODUCTION 30,000 bottles
HECTARES UNDER VINE 4.00

| | |
|---|---|
| ○ Malvasia '17 | ♟♟ 3 |
| ⊙ Rosato Brut M. Cl. | ♟♟ 3 |
| ○ Vitovska '17 | ♟♟ 3 |

## Tenute Barzan - dal 1961

VIA MENEGHINI, 3
33077 SACILE [PN]
TEL. +39 0434786850
www.tenutebarzan.wine

CELLAR SALES
PRE-BOOKED VISITS
ACCOMMODATION AND RESTAURANT SERVICE
ANNUAL PRODUCTION 700,000 bottles
HECTARES UNDER VINE 15.00
VITICULTURE METHOD Certified Organic

| | |
|---|---|
| ○ Collio Chardonnay '17 | ♟♟ 3 |
| ○ Collio Chardonnay '14 | ♟♟ 3 |
| ○ Collio Malvasia '17 | ♟♟ 3 |
| ○ Collio Sauvignon '17 | ♟♟ 3 |

## La Bellanotte

S.DA DELLA BELLANOTTE, 3
34072 FARRA D'ISONZO [GO]
TEL. +39 0481888020
www.labellanotte.it

CELLAR SALES
PRE-BOOKED VISITS
ANNUAL PRODUCTION 100,000 bottles
HECTARES UNDER VINE 14.00

| | |
|---|---|
| ○ Collio Friulano '17 | ♟♟ 3 |
| ○ Collio Pinot Grigio '17 | ♟♟ 3 |
| ○ Friuli Pinot Grigio '17 | ♟♟ 2* |
| ○ Friuli Isonzo Sauvignon '17 | ♟ 3 |

## Tenuta Beltrame

FRAZ. PRIVANO
LOC. ANTONINI, 4
33050 BAGNARIA ARSA [UD]
TEL. +39 0432923670
www.tenutabeltrame.it

CELLAR SALES
PRE-BOOKED VISITS
ANNUAL PRODUCTION 80,000 bottles
HECTARES UNDER VINE 25.00

| | |
|---|---|
| ○ Friuli Friulano '17 | ♟♟ 3 |
| ○ Friuli Chardonnay '17 | ♟ 3 |
| ● Friuli Refosco P.R. '16 | ♟ 3 |
| ● Pinot Nero '16 | ♟ 3 |

## Bidoli

FRAZ. ARCANO SUPERIORE
VIA FORNACE, 19
33030 RIVE D'ARCANO [UD]
TEL. +39 0432810796
www.bidolivini.com

CELLAR SALES
PRE-BOOKED VISITS
ANNUAL PRODUCTION 1,000,000 bottles
HECTARES UNDER VINE

| | |
|---|---|
| ● Friuli Grave Merlot Briccolo Ris. '15 | ♟♟ 3 |
| ○ Friuli Grave Friulano '17 | ♟ 2 |
| ○ Friuli Grave Pinot Grigio '17 | ♟ 2 |
| ○ Ribolla Gialla Brut Le Alte | ♟ 3 |

## Tenuta di Blasig

VIA ROMA, 63
34077 RONCHI DEI LEGIONARI [GO]
TEL. +39 0481475480
www.tenutadiblasig.it

CELLAR SALES
PRE-BOOKED VISITS
RESTAURANT SERVICE
ANNUAL PRODUCTION 80,000 bottles
HECTARES UNDER VINE 12.00

| | |
|---|---|
| ○ Friuli Isonzo Friulano '17 | ♟♟ 2* |
| ○ Friuli Isonzo Pinot Grigio Pink '16 | ♟♟ 2* |
| ● Friuli Isonzo Refosco P. R. '15 | ♟♟ 3 |
| ○ Elisabetta Brut | ♟ 3 |

## Blason

LOC. BRUMA
VIA ROMA, 32
34072 GRADISCA D'ISONZO [GO]
TEL. +39 048192414
www.blasonwines.com

CELLAR SALES
PRE-BOOKED VISITS
ANNUAL PRODUCTION 60,000 bottles
HECTARES UNDER VINE 18.00

| | |
|---|---|
| ○ Friuli Isonzo Bruma Bianco '16 | ♟♟ 3 |
| ● Friuli Isonzo Bruma Rosso '15 | ♟♟ 4 |
| ○ Friuli Isonzo Friulano '17 | ♟♟ 2* |
| ○ Malvasia '17 | ♟♟ 3 |

## Blazic

LOC. ZEGLA, 16
34071 CORMÒNS [GO]
TEL. +39 048161720
www.blazic.it

CELLAR SALES
PRE-BOOKED VISITS
ANNUAL PRODUCTION 20,000 bottles
HECTARES UNDER VINE 6.50

| | |
|---|---|
| ○ Collio Friulano '17 | ♟♟ 3 |
| ○ Collio Malvasia '17 | ♟♟ 3 |

## Tenuta Borgo Conventi

S.DA DELLA COLOMBARA, 13
34072 FARRA D'ISONZO [GO]
TEL. +39 0481888004
www.borgoconventi.it

CELLAR SALES
PRE-BOOKED VISITS
ANNUAL PRODUCTION 350,000 bottles
HECTARES UNDER VINE 40.00

| | |
|---|---|
| ○ Collio Friulano '17 | ♟♟ 3 |
| ● Collio Merlot '15 | ♟♟ 3 |
| ○ Collio Ribolla Gialla '17 | ♟♟ 3 |
| ○ Friuli Isonzo Sauvignon '17 | ♟♟ 3 |

## Borgo Magredo

FRAZ. TAURIANO
VIA BASALDELLA, 5
33090 SPILIMBERGO [PN]
TEL. +39 0422864511
www.borgomagredo.it

CELLAR SALES
PRE-BOOKED VISITS
ANNUAL PRODUCTION 450,000 bottles
HECTARES UNDER VINE 105.00
SUSTAINABLE WINERY

| | |
|---|---|
| ● Friuli Grave Cabernet Sauvignon '17 | ♟ 2 |
| ○ Friuli Grave Friulano '17 | ♟ 2 |
| ○ Friuli Grave Pinot Grigio '17 | ♟ 2 |
| ○ Friuli Grave Traminer Aromatico '17 | ♟ 2 |

## Braidot

LOC. VERSA
VIA PALMANOVA, 20 B
34076 ROMANS D'ISONZO [GO]
TEL. +39 0481908970
www.braidotwines.it

CELLAR SALES
PRE-BOOKED VISITS
ANNUAL PRODUCTION 400,000 bottles
HECTARES UNDER VINE 60.00

| | |
|---|---|
| ○ Friuli Friulano '17 | ♟♟ 3 |
| ○ Friuli Pinot Grigio '17 | ♟♟ 3 |
| ○ Friuli Sauvignon Blanc 1870 '17 | ♟♟ 3 |
| ○ Sauvignon Blanc '17 | ♟♟ 2* |

## Ca' Selva

VIA TREVISO
33083 CHIONS [PN]
TEL. +39 0434630216
www.caselva.it

ANNUAL PRODUCTION 1,300,000 bottles
HECTARES UNDER VINE 30.00
VITICULTURE METHOD Certified Organic

| | |
|---|---|
| ○ Friuli Pinot Grigio Bio '17 | ♟♟ 3 |
| ○ Friuli Sauvignon Bio '17 | ♟♟ 3 |
| ● Rosso 55 '15 | ♟♟ 3 |
| ○ Prosecco Extra Dry Bio '17 | ♟ 3 |

## Paolo Caccese

LOC. PRADIS, 6
34071 CORMÒNS [GO]
TEL. +39 048161062
www.paolocaccese.com

CELLAR SALES
PRE-BOOKED VISITS
ANNUAL PRODUCTION 38,000 bottles
HECTARES UNDER VINE 6.00

| | |
|---|---|
| ● Collio Cabernet Franc '16 | ♟♟ 3 |
| ○ Collio Friulano '16 | ♟♟ 3 |
| ○ Collio Sauvignon '17 | ♟♟ 3 |
| ○ Collio Pinot Bianco '17 | ♟ 3 |

# I Clivi

LOC. GRAMOGLIANO, 20
33040 CORNO DI ROSAZZO [UD]
TEL. +39 3287269979
www.clivi.it

CELLAR SALES
PRE-BOOKED VISITS
ANNUAL PRODUCTION 50,000 bottles
HECTARES UNDER VINE 12.00
VITICULTURE METHOD Certified Organic

| | | |
|---|---|---|
| ○ Collio Friulano Brazan '16 | | ♟♟ 5 |
| ○ FCO Bianco Galea '16 | | ♟♟ 4 |
| ○ Collio Malvasia '17 | | ♟ 5 |
| ○ FCO Verduzzo Friulano '16 | | ♟ 4 |

# Tenuta Conte Romano

VIA DELLE PRIMULE, 12
33044 MANZANO [UD]
TEL. +39 0432755339
www.tenutaconteromano.it

CELLAR SALES
PRE-BOOKED VISITS
ACCOMMODATION AND RESTAURANT SERVICE
ANNUAL PRODUCTION 40,000 bottles
HECTARES UNDER VINE 17.00

| | | |
|---|---|---|
| ○ FCO Friulano '17 | | ♟♟ 3 |
| ○ FCO Sauvignon '17 | | ♟♟ 2* |
| ○ FCO Malvasia '17 | | ♟ 3 |
| ● FCO Rosso '16 | | ♟ 3 |

# Viticoltori Friulani La Delizia

VIA UDINE, 24
33072 CASARSA DELLA DELIZIA [PN]
TEL. +39 0434869564
www.ladelizia.com

CELLAR SALES
PRE-BOOKED VISITS
ANNUAL PRODUCTION 16,000,000 bottles
HECTARES UNDER VINE 1950.00

| | | |
|---|---|---|
| ○ Jadèr Cuvée Brut | | ♟♟ 2* |
| ○ Ribolla Gialla Brut Naonis | | ♟♟ 2* |
| ○ Friuli Pinot Grigio Sass Ter' '17 | | ♟ 2 |

# Do Ville

VIA MITRAGLIERI, 2
34077 RONCHI DEI LEGIONARI [GO]
TEL. +39 0481775561
www.doville.it

CELLAR SALES
ANNUAL PRODUCTION 120,000 bottles
HECTARES UNDER VINE 15.00

| | | |
|---|---|---|
| ● Cabernet Ars Vivendi '16 | | ♟♟ 2* |
| ○ Friuli Isonzo Pinot Grigio Ars Vivendi '17 | | ♟♟ 2* |
| ○ Malvasia Ars Vivendi '17 | | ♟♟ 2* |
| ⊙ Rosé Ars Vivendi | | ♟ 3 |

# Le Due Torri

LOC. VICINALE DEL JUDRIO
VIA SAN MARTINO, 19
33040 CORNO DI ROSAZZO [UD]
TEL. +39 0432759150
www.le2torri.com

CELLAR SALES
PRE-BOOKED VISITS
ANNUAL PRODUCTION 36,000 bottles
HECTARES UNDER VINE 7.60

| | | |
|---|---|---|
| ○ Friuli Friulano '16 | | ♟♟ 2* |
| ○ Friuli Pinot Grigio '17 | | ♟♟ 2* |
| ○ Ribolla Gialla '16 | | ♟♟ 2* |
| ● Tazzelenghe '12 | | ♟♟ 3 |

# Fantin Nodar

LOC. ORSARIA
VIA CASALI OTTELIO, 4
33040 PREMARIACCO [UD]
TEL. +39 043428735
www.fantinnodar.it

CELLAR SALES
PRE-BOOKED VISITS
ANNUAL PRODUCTION 40,000 bottles
HECTARES UNDER VINE 22.00

| | | |
|---|---|---|
| ● FCO Cabernet '16 | | ♟♟ 2* |
| ○ FCO Friulano '16 | | ♟♟ 2* |
| ● FCO Merlot '16 | | ♟♟ 3 |
| ○ FCO Sauvignon '17 | | ♟♟ 2* |

## Le Favole

LOC. TERRA ROSSA
VIA DIETRO CASTELLO, 7
33070 CANEVA [PN]
TEL. +39 0434735604
www.lefavole-wines.com

CELLAR SALES
PRE-BOOKED VISITS
ACCOMMODATION
ANNUAL PRODUCTION 70,000 bottles
HECTARES UNDER VINE 20.00

| | | |
|---|---|---|
| ● Friuli Annia Merlot Noglar '15 | ♟♟ 3 | |
| ● Friuli Annia Refosco P. R. '15 | ♟♟ 2* | |
| ○ Friuli Bianco Picavèlt '17 | ♟♟ 2* | |
| ○ Friuli Malvasia '17 | ♟♟ 2* | |

## Foffani

FRAZ. CLAUIANO
P.ZZA GIULIA, 13
33050 TRIVIGNANO UDINESE [UD]
TEL. +39 0432999584
www.foffani.com

CELLAR SALES
PRE-BOOKED VISITS
ACCOMMODATION AND RESTAURANT SERVICE
ANNUAL PRODUCTION 80,000 bottles
HECTARES UNDER VINE 10.00
SUSTAINABLE WINERY

| | | |
|---|---|---|
| ● Friuli Merlot '15 | ♟♟ 3 | |
| ○ Friuli Friulano '17 | ♟ 3 | |
| ○ Friuli Pinot Grigio Sup. '17 | ♟ 3 | |
| ○ Friuli Sauvignon Sup. '17 | ♟ 3 | |

## Forchir

LOC. CASALI BIANCHINI
33030 CAMINO AL TAGLIAMENTO [UD]
TEL. +39 0432821525
www.forchir.it

CELLAR SALES
PRE-BOOKED VISITS
ANNUAL PRODUCTION 1,200,000 bottles
HECTARES UNDER VINE 240.00
VITICULTURE METHOD Certified Organic
SUSTAINABLE WINERY

| | | |
|---|---|---|
| ○ Friuli Grave Sauvignon Soresere '17 | ♟♟ 2* | |
| ● Refoscone Refosco P. R. '17 | ♟♟ 3 | |
| ○ Ribolla Gialla '17 | ♟♟ 3 | |
| ○ Joy Extra Brut | ♟ 3 | |

## Fossa Mala

VIA BASSI, 81
33080 FIUME VENETO [PN]
TEL. +39 0434957997
www.fossamala.it

CELLAR SALES
PRE-BOOKED VISITS
ACCOMMODATION AND RESTAURANT SERVICE
ANNUAL PRODUCTION 130,000 bottles
HECTARES UNDER VINE 37.00

| | | |
|---|---|---|
| ○ Friuli Grave Chardonnay '17 | ♟♟ 2* | |
| ● Friuli Grave Merlot '15 | ♟♟ 2* | |
| ● Friuli Grave Refosco P.R. '15 | ♟♟ 2* | |
| ○ Friuli Grave Friulano '17 | ♟ 2 | |

## Humar

LOC. VALERISCE, 20
34070 SAN FLORIANO DEL COLLIO [GO]
TEL. +39 0481884197
www.humar.it

CELLAR SALES
PRE-BOOKED VISITS
ANNUAL PRODUCTION 60,000 bottles
HECTARES UNDER VINE 12.00

| | | |
|---|---|---|
| ○ Collio Friulano '17 | ♟♟ 3 | |
| ○ Collio Pinot Grigio '17 | ♟♟ 3 | |
| ○ Collio Ribolla Gialla '17 | ♟♟ 3 | |
| ○ Collio Chardonnay '17 | ♟ 3 | |

## Isola Augusta

VIA CASALI ISOLA AUGUSTA, 4
33056 PALAZZOLO DELLO STELLA [UD]
TEL. +39 043158046
www.isolaaugusta.com

CELLAR SALES
PRE-BOOKED VISITS
ACCOMMODATION AND RESTAURANT SERVICE
ANNUAL PRODUCTION 270,000 bottles
HECTARES UNDER VINE 65.00
SUSTAINABLE WINERY

| | | |
|---|---|---|
| ○ Friuli Friulano '17 | ♟♟ 2* | |
| ○ Friuli Chardonnay '17 | ♟ 2 | |
| ○ Friuli Malvasia '17 | ♟ 2 | |
| ● Schioppettino '17 | ♟ 2 | |

## Rado Kocjancic

FRAZ. DOLINA
VIA DOLINA, 528
34018 SAN DORLIGO DELLA VALLE [TS]
TEL. +39 3483063298
www.radokocjancic.eu

CELLAR SALES
PRE-BOOKED VISITS
ANNUAL PRODUCTION 15,000 bottles
HECTARES UNDER VINE 5.00

| | |
|---|---|
| ○ Carso Malvasia '16 | ♆♆ 2* |
| ● Carso Rosso Krogle '15 | ♆♆ 3 |
| ○ Carso Vitovska '16 | ♆♆ 3 |

## Mulino delle Tolle

FRAZ. SEVEGLIANO
VIA MULINO DELLE TOLLE, 15
33050 BAGNARIA ARSA [UD]
TEL. +39 0432924723
www.mulinodelletolle.it

CELLAR SALES
PRE-BOOKED VISITS
ACCOMMODATION AND RESTAURANT SERVICE
ANNUAL PRODUCTION 100,000 bottles
HECTARES UNDER VINE 22.00

| | |
|---|---|
| ○ Friuli Aquileia Friulano '17 | ♆♆ 3 |
| ○ Friuli Aquileia Malvasia '17 | ♆♆ 3 |
| ○ Friuli Aquileia Bianco Palmade '17 | ♆ 3 |

## Obiz

B.GO GORTANI, 2
33052 CERVIGNANO DEL FRIULI [UD]
TEL. +39 043131900
www.obiz.it

CELLAR SALES
PRE-BOOKED VISITS
ANNUAL PRODUCTION 100,000 bottles
HECTARES UNDER VINE 40.00

| | |
|---|---|
| ○ Friuli Aquileia Friulano Tampia '17 | ♆♆ 2* |
| ● Friuli Aquileia Refosco P.R. Teodoro '16 | ♆♆ 2* |
| ● Friuli Aquileia Rosso Natissa '16 | ♆♆ 3 |
| ○ Friuli Aquileia Traminer Aromatico '17 | ♆ 2 |

## Cantina Odoni

FRAZ. LONGERA
34100 TRIESTE
TEL. +39 3409317794
www.cantinaodoni.com

CELLAR SALES
RESTAURANT SERVICE
ANNUAL PRODUCTION 50,000 bottles
HECTARES UNDER VINE 6.00

| | |
|---|---|
| ○ Chardonnay '16 | ♆♆ 3 |
| ○ Malvasia '15 | ♆♆ 3 |
| ○ Vitovska '17 | ♆♆ 3 |
| ○ Vitovska Dosaggio Zero | ♆♆ 3 |

## Ostrouska

LOC. SAGRADO, 1
34010 SGONICO [TS]
TEL. +39 0402296672
www.ostrouska.it

ANNUAL PRODUCTION 5,000 bottles
HECTARES UNDER VINE 1.50

| | |
|---|---|
| ○ Malvasia '16 | ♆♆ 5 |
| ○ Vitovska '16 | ♆♆ 5 |
| ● Terrano '16 | ♆ 5 |

## Parovel

LOC. CARESANA, 81
34018 SAN DORLIGO DELLA VALLE [TS]
TEL. +39 040227050
www.parovel.com

ANNUAL PRODUCTION 35,000 bottles
HECTARES UNDER VINE 11.00
SUSTAINABLE WINERY

| | |
|---|---|
| ○ Carso Malvasia Poje '16 | ♆♆ 5 |
| ○ Carso Vitovska Onavè '15 | ♆♆ 5 |
| ○ Matos Nonet '13 | ♆♆ 6 |
| ● Terrano Hodi '16 | ♆♆ 4 |

## Piè di Mont

LOC. PIEDIMONTE DEL CALVARIO
VIA MONTE CALVARIO, 30
34170 GORIZIA
TEL. +39 0481391338
www.piedimont.it

CELLAR SALES
PRE-BOOKED VISITS
ANNUAL PRODUCTION 10,000 bottles
HECTARES UNDER VINE 1.20

| | | |
|---|---|---|
| ○ Brut Cuvèe Mill. '12 | ♥♥ | 6 |
| ○ Brut Cuvée Mill. '14 | ♥♥ | 6 |

## Pighin

FRAZ. RISANO
V.LE GRADO, 11/1
33050 PAVIA DI UDINE [UD]
TEL. +39 0432675444
www.pighin.com

CELLAR SALES
PRE-BOOKED VISITS
ANNUAL PRODUCTION 1,000,000 bottles
HECTARES UNDER VINE 180.00

| | | |
|---|---|---|
| ○ Collio Chardonnay '17 | ♥♥ | 5 |
| ○ Collio Malvasia '17 | ♥♥ | 5 |
| ○ Collio Ribolla Gialla '17 | ♥♥ | 5 |
| ○ Friuli Grave Chardonnay '17 | ♥♥ | 4 |

## Tenuta Pinni

VIA SANT'OSVALDO, 3
33098 SAN MARTINO AL TAGLIAMENTO [PN]
TEL. +39 0434899464
www.tenutapinni.com

CELLAR SALES
PRE-BOOKED VISITS
ANNUAL PRODUCTION 30,000 bottles
HECTARES UNDER VINE 26.00
SUSTAINABLE WINERY

| | | |
|---|---|---|
| ○ Bianco della Tenuta '12 | ♥♥ | 3 |
| ○ Pinot Grigio '17 | ♥♥ | 2* |
| ● Refosco P. R. della Tenuta '11 | ♥♥ | 4 |
| ● Refosco P.R. '16 | ♥♥ | 2* |

## Flavio Pontoni

VIA PERUZZI, 8
33042 BUTTRIO [UD]
TEL. +39 0432674352
www.pontoni.it

CELLAR SALES
PRE-BOOKED VISITS
ACCOMMODATION
ANNUAL PRODUCTION 30,000 bottles
HECTARES UNDER VINE 4.50

| | | |
|---|---|---|
| ● Cabernet Sauvignon '16 | ♥♥ | 2* |
| ● FCO Merlot '16 | ♥♥ | 2* |
| ○ FCO Sauvignon '17 | ♥♥ | 2* |
| ○ FCO Friulano '17 | ♥ | 2 |

## Cantina di Rauscedo

VIA DEL SILE, 16
33095 RAUSCEDO
TEL. +39 042794020
www.cantinarauscedo.com

CELLAR SALES
ANNUAL PRODUCTION 700,000 bottles
HECTARES UNDER VINE 1500.00

| | | |
|---|---|---|
| ○ Friuli Grave Friulano '17 | ♥♥ | 2* |
| ○ Friuli Grave Friulano '16 | ♥♥ | 2* |
| ○ Friuli Grave Sauvignon '17 | ♥♥ | 2* |
| ○ Friuli Grave Traminer '16 | ♥ | 2 |

## Reguta

VIA BASSI, 16
33050 POCENIA [UD]
TEL. +39 0432779157
www.giuseppeeluigivini.it

CELLAR SALES
PRE-BOOKED VISITS
ANNUAL PRODUCTION 2,000,000 bottles
HECTARES UNDER VINE 240.00

| | | |
|---|---|---|
| ○ Collio Ribolla Gialla '17 | ♥♥ | 3 |
| ○ Sauvignon '17 | ♥♥ | 2* |
| ● Altropasso '16 | ♥ | 3 |
| ○ Traminer Aromatico '17 | ♥ | 2 |

## Ronco dei Pini

VIA RONCHI, 93
33040 PREPOTTO [UD]
TEL. +39 0432713239
www.roncodeipini.it

CELLAR SALES
PRE-BOOKED VISITS
ANNUAL PRODUCTION 90,000 bottles
HECTARES UNDER VINE 15.00

| | | |
|---|---|---|
| ● FCO Cabernet Sauvignon '16 | ♟♟ | 3 |
| ○ FCO Friulano '17 | ♟♟ | 3 |
| ● FCO Schiopettino di Prepotto '15 | ♟♟ | 5 |
| ○ Ribolla Gialla Brut Tre Lune | ♟ | 3 |

## Ronco Margherita

VIA XX SETTEMBRE, 106A
33094 PINZANO AL TAGLIAMENTO [PN]
TEL. +39 0432950845
www.roncomargherita.it

CELLAR SALES
PRE-BOOKED VISITS
ANNUAL PRODUCTION 100,000 bottles
HECTARES UNDER VINE 50.00
SUSTAINABLE WINERY

| | | |
|---|---|---|
| ○ Arzino Pas Dosé M. Cl. | ♟♟ | 5 |
| ○ Friuli Friulano '16 | ♟♟ | 3 |
| ○ Tiliae '15 | ♟♟ | 4 |
| ○ Pinot Grigio '17 | ♟ | 3 |

## Russolo

VIA SAN ROCCO, 58A
33080 SAN QUIRINO [PN]
TEL. +39 0434919577
www.russolo.it

CELLAR SALES
PRE-BOOKED VISITS
ANNUAL PRODUCTION 165,000 bottles
HECTARES UNDER VINE 16.00
SUSTAINABLE WINERY

| | | |
|---|---|---|
| ● Borgo di Peuma '15 | ♟♟ | 5 |
| ○ Doi Raps '17 | ♟♟ | 4 |
| ● Pinot Nero '15 | ♟♟ | 5 |
| ○ Ribolla Gialla '17 | ♟♟ | 3 |

## San Giorgio

VIA STAZIONE, 29
33095 SAN GIORGIO DELLA RICHINVELDA [PN]
TEL. +39 042796017
www.vinisangiorgio.com

ANNUAL PRODUCTION 50,000 bottles
HECTARES UNDER VINE 300.00

| | | |
|---|---|---|
| ○ Beato Bianco | ♟♟ | 3 |
| ○ Friuli Pinot Grigio '17 | ♟♟ | 3 |
| ● Pinot Nero '16 | ♟♟ | 3 |
| ● Rosso Pieve della Rosa | ♟ | 3 |

## San Simone

LOC. RONDOVER
VIA PRATA, 30
33080 PORCIA [PN]
TEL. +39 0434578633
www.sansimone.it

CELLAR SALES
PRE-BOOKED VISITS
ANNUAL PRODUCTION 900,000 bottles
HECTARES UNDER VINE 85.00
SUSTAINABLE WINERY

| | | |
|---|---|---|
| ● Friuli Grave Cabernet Franc Sugano '16 | ♟♟ | 3 |
| ● Friuli Grave Cabernet Sauvignon Nexus Ris. '12 | ♟♟ | 3 |
| ● Friuli Grave Merlot Evante Ris. '15 | ♟♟ | 3 |

## Scarbolo

FRAZ. LAUZACCO
V.LE GRADO, 4
33050 PAVIA DI UDINE [UD]
TEL. +39 0432675612
www.scarbolo.com

CELLAR SALES
PRE-BOOKED VISITS
RESTAURANT SERVICE
ANNUAL PRODUCTION 200,000 bottles
HECTARES UNDER VINE 28.00
SUSTAINABLE WINERY

| | | |
|---|---|---|
| ○ Friuli Pinot Grigio Ramato '17 | ♟♟ | 3 |
| ○ Friuli Pinot Grigio Ramato XL '14 | ♟♟ | 3 |
| ○ My Time '13 | ♟♟ | 5 |
| ● Friuli Grave Merlot '15 | ♟ | 3 |

## Ferruccio Sgubin

VIA MERNICO, 8
34070 DOLEGNA DEL COLLIO [GO]
TEL. +39 048160452
www.ferrucciosgubin.it

CELLAR SALES
PRE-BOOKED VISITS
ANNUAL PRODUCTION 100,000 bottles
HECTARES UNDER VINE 20.00

| | |
|---|---|
| ○ Collio Friulano '17 | 🍷🍷 3 |
| ○ Collio Friulano Petrusa '16 | 🍷🍷 3 |
| ○ Collio Ribolla Gialla '17 | 🍷🍷 3 |
| ○ Collio Sauvignon '17 | 🍷🍷 3 |

## Skerlj

VIA SALES, 44
34010 SGONICO [TS]
TEL. +39 040229253
www.skerlj.it

CELLAR SALES
PRE-BOOKED VISITS
ACCOMMODATION AND RESTAURANT SERVICE
ANNUAL PRODUCTION 5,000 bottles
HECTARES UNDER VINE 2.00
VITICULTURE METHOD Certified Organic

| | |
|---|---|
| ○ Malvasia '15 | 🍷🍷 5 |
| ● Terrano '15 | 🍷🍷 5 |
| ○ Vitovska '15 | 🍷🍷 5 |

## Tarlao

VIA SAN ZILI, 41
33051 AQUILEIA [UD]
TEL. +39 043191417
www.tarlao.eu

CELLAR SALES
PRE-BOOKED VISITS
ANNUAL PRODUCTION 18,000 bottles
HECTARES UNDER VINE 5.00

| | |
|---|---|
| ○ Friuli Aquileia Pinot Bianco Poc ma Bon '17 | 🍷🍷 3* |
| ● Friuli Aquileia Refosco P. R. Mosaic Ros '16 | 🍷🍷 3 |
| ● Friuli Aquileia Merlot '16 | 🍷 3 |

## Terre del Faet

LOC. CORMÒNS
FRAZ. FAET
V.LE ROMA, 82
34071 CORMÒNS [GO]
TEL. +39 3470103325
www.terredelfaet.it

CELLAR SALES
PRE-BOOKED VISITS
ANNUAL PRODUCTION 24,000 bottles
HECTARES UNDER VINE 4.50

| | |
|---|---|
| ○ Collio Bianco del Faet '16 | 🍷🍷 3 |
| ○ Collio Friulano '17 | 🍷🍷 3 |
| ○ Collio Malvasia '17 | 🍷🍷 3 |
| ○ Collio Pinot Bianco '17 | 🍷🍷 3 |

## Vicentini Orgnani

LOC. VALERIANO
VIA SOTTOPLOVIA, 4A
33094 PINZANO AL TAGLIAMENTO [PN]
TEL. +39 0432950107
www.vicentiniorgnani.it

CELLAR SALES
PRE-BOOKED VISITS
ANNUAL PRODUCTION 50,000 bottles
HECTARES UNDER VINE 18.00
SUSTAINABLE WINERY

| | |
|---|---|
| ● Cabernet Sauvignon '13 | 🍷🍷 2* |
| ○ Friuli Sauvignon '17 | 🍷🍷 2* |
| ○ Ucelut '12 | 🍷🍷 5 |
| ○ Friuli Pinot Grigio '17 | 🍷 2 |

## Villa Parens

VIA DANTE, 69
34072 FARRA D'ISONZO [GO]
TEL. +39 0481888198
www.villaparens.com

CELLAR SALES
PRE-BOOKED VISITS
ANNUAL PRODUCTION 50,000 bottles
HECTARES UNDER VINE 6.00

| | |
|---|---|
| ○ Blanc de Blancs Extra Brut M. Cl. | 🍷🍷 5 |
| ○ Chardonnay '13 | 🍷🍷 5 |
| ○ Ribolla Gialla Extra Brut M. Cl. | 🍷🍷 4 |
| ○ Rosé de Noirs Dosage Zero M. Cl. '14 | 🍷🍷 6 |

# EMILIA ROMAGNA

Something is stirring in the easternmost corner of
Emilia. After a few years of calm, both the hills of
Parma and, especially, of Piacenza, are showing
encouraging signs. The most representative
cultivar of this local renaissance is the Malvasia
di Candia, which serves as the basis of primarily dry and
still offerings, making for a wine that can be enjoyed young but shows surprising
evolutive potential. We have yet to see what Gutturnio will do when it's 'all grown
up'. The coexistence of young wines, aged wines, still and semi-sparkling wines
in the appellation runs the risk of creating confusion. On the hills of Bologna the
Pignoletto phenomenon is overshadowing the area's other traditional wines. And
then, in the middle, there's the vast lands of Lambrusco. Considering that 2017
was a better year for the lowlands than it was for the hills (which experienced the
drought to a greater degree), it's Sorbara, with its obvious attributes (especially
near Reggio Emilia) that most stood out during our tastings. The increasingly
popular return of the 'Metodo Ancestrale' and the growth of Metodo Classico in
terms of both quality and quality promise interesting developments in the future. In
Romagna they're working in a number of subzones. When it comes to Sangiovese,
the process has set out a well-defined map of Doc Romagna, where 'Additional
Geographic Mentions' are often included. And it needs to be mentioned that many
vine growers are working in this direction, redefining their style in pursuit of a clear
territorial identity. It's not an easy tast, considering the number of areas and the
incredible heterogeneity of the producers operating, from large cooperatives to
small artisans. And yet this long journey will be worth it. More than ever, we tasted
diverse wines, a mix of production ideas and varying territorial characters. Our Tre
Bicchieri are a recognition of this, of course, though it's important to note how this
emerging network of producers is giving rise to a 'New Romagna' of wine. In terms
of whites, the Albana phenomenon is showing no signs of slowing down. A number
of interpretations of this classic variety were submitted, some of them more pure
and minimalist, some of them richer and more full-bodied, and then there are the
versions macerated on the skins. It's an interesting phenomenon but there's a high
risk of confusion, and the cases of true excellence are still few. Having said that,
we're pleased to conclude our introduction with our special 'Solidarity Award'. This
year it goes to none other than San Patrignano.

## Ancarani

FRAZ. ORIOLO
VIA SAN BIAGIO ANTICO, 14
48018 FAENZA [RA]
TEL. +39 3338314188
www.viniancarani.it

**CELLAR SALES**
**PRE-BOOKED VISITS**
**RESTAURANT SERVICE**
**ANNUAL PRODUCTION** 30,000 bottles
**HECTARES UNDER VINE** 14.00

Year by year, Claudia Ancarani and his wife Rita Babini are building a truly noteworthy producer in Torre di Oriolo, Faenza. It's an area that's increasingly recognized for its quality wines, especially those made with Albana and Centesimino, two of the area's traditional grapes. In the cellar they bring an artisanal sensibility to their work, aiming to bring out the best of what nature has to offer. The results are intriguing, to say the least, making Ancarani a winery worth paying close attention to. Their whites may be the talk of the town, but we were more impressed by their 2016 Sangiovese Biagio Antico. It proves elegant, delectable, fresh and reminiscent of ripe blood oranges, coming through fruity, juicy and more pervasive than most. Their other wines include the excellent 2016 Sangiovese Oriolo, the delicious 2017 Centesimino, playing on fine aromas of wild berries, and the citrusy and well-made 2017 Famoso Signore.

| | |
|---|---|
| ● Romagna Sangiovese Sup. Biagio Antico '16 | ▼▼▼ 2* |
| ● Centesimino '17 | ▼▼ 3 |
| ○ Famoso Signore '17 | ▼▼ 2* |
| ● Sangiovese di Romagna Oriolo '16 | ▼▼ 2* |
| ○ Albana di Romagna Santa Lusa '12 | ♀♀ 3* |
| ○ Romagna Albana Secco Santa Lusa '15 | ♀♀ 3 |
| ○ Romagna Albana Secco Santa Lusa '14 | ♀♀ 3 |
| ● Romagna Sangiovese Sup. Biagio Antico '15 | ♀♀ 2* |
| ● Sangiovese di Romagna Oriolo '15 | ♀♀ 2* |

## Francesco Bellei & C.

FRAZ. CRISTO DI SORBARA
VIA NAZIONALE, 132
41030 BOMPORTO [MO]
TEL. +39 059902009
www.francescobellei.it

**CELLAR SALES**
**PRE-BOOKED VISITS**
**ANNUAL PRODUCTION** 70,000 bottles
**HECTARES UNDER VINE** 103.00

It was Beppe Bellei, a passionate enthusiast and cultivator of Champagne, who opted for second fermentation in the bottle and planted Chardonnay and Pinot Nero for his Metodo Classico sparkling wines. As of 2000, local, traditional grapes like Sorbara and Pignoletto were used for their Metodo Ancestrale sparklers (second fermentation in the bottle though without dégorgement). For some years now the winery, which is now situated in the heart of Cristo di Sorbara, has been owned by the Cavicchioli family, with Sandro Cavicchioli at the helm. A 100% Sorbara Metodo Classico impressed during our finals, their 2014 Cuvée Brut Rosso. On the nose it offers up lovely aromas of red fruit, citrus, spices, herbs and hay, while the palate holds well together, proving well-paced and drinkable, with balance, substance and backbone. Their very elegant 2016 Ancestrale sees a return of hay, herbs, saffron and orange. The whole range shows a high-level, especially the Cuvée Extra Brut (70% Pinot Nero and 30% Chardonnay), with its generously fruity aromas.

| | |
|---|---|
| ● Cuvée Brut Rosso M. Cl. '14 | ▼▼ 3* |
| ● Modena Lambrusco Rifermentazione Ancestrale '16 | ▼▼ 3* |
| ⊙ Cuvée Brut M. Cl. Rosé '14 | ▼▼ 5 |
| ○ Cuvè Extra Brut M. Cl. | ▼▼ 5 |
| ○ Cuvée Speciale Brut M. Cl. '10 | ▼ 6 |
| ● Cuvée Brut Rosso M.Cl. '13 | ♀♀ 3 |
| ⊙ Cuvée Brut Rosé M.Cl. '12 | ♀♀ 5 |
| ⊙ Cuvée Brut Rosé M.Cl. '11 | ♀♀ 5 |
| ● Lambrusco di Modena Rifermentazione Ancestrale '15 | ♀♀ 3* |
| ● Lambrusco di Modena Rifermentazione Ancestrale '14 | ♀♀ 3* |
| ● Modena Pignoletto Rifermentazione Ancestrale '15 | ♀♀ 3 |
| ● Modena Pignoletto Rifermentazione Ancestrale '14 | ♀♀ 3 |

# Stefano Berti

LOC. RAVALDINO IN MONTE
VIA LA SCAGNA, 18
47121 FORLÌ
TEL. +39 0543488074
www.stefanoberti.it

**CELLAR SALES**
**PRE-BOOKED VISITS**
**ANNUAL PRODUCTION** 40,000 bottles
**HECTARES UNDER VINE** 7.00

The Berti family's estate is situated in Ravaldino in Monte, on the hills near Forì. It was planted in the early 1960s, thanks to the purchase and merging of the two main plots. Stefano, after whom the winery is now named, entered the scene some 20 years later, with the title of expert agrarian and a desire to keep investing. The puzzle was completed at the turn of the new millennium when quality wine production became their principal activity. Their selection is characterized by precision, richness of flavor, balance and finesse, the result of well-calibrated winemaking and painstaking care both in the vineyard and the cellar. The 2016 Sangiovese Superiore Bartimeo is outstanding. It is a marvelous wine, by virtue of its intensity and finesse, which opens on nuances of fresh flowers, especially violets, and wild berries. A clear toastiness remains, but proves well-crafted and integrated. Its delicate body shows surprising extraction. The 2016 Nonà displays a similar aromatic framework, while their Ravaldo conveys too much wood.

| | |
|---|---|
| ● Romagna Sangiovese Sup. Bartimeo '16 | ♀♀♀ 2* |
| ● Romagna Sangiovese Sup. Nonà '16 | ♀♀ 2* |
| ○ Cipria Rosato '17 | ♀ 2 |
| ● Romagna Sangiovese Predappio Ravaldo '16 | ♀ 3 |
| ● Romagna Sangiovese Bartimeo '15 | ♀♀ 2* |
| ● Romagna Sangiovese Predappio Ravaldo '15 | ♀♀ 2* |
| ● Romagna Sangiovese Sup. Nonà '15 | ♀♀ 2* |

# Ca' di Sopra

LOC. MARZENO
VIA FELIGARA, 15
48013 BRISIGHELLA [RA]
TEL. +39 3284927073
www.cadisopra.com

**CELLAR SALES**
**PRE-BOOKED VISITS**
**ANNUAL PRODUCTION** 30,000 bottles
**HECTARES UNDER VINE** 28.00
**SUSTAINABLE WINERY**

Here in Marzeno, on the hills of Faenza, you're never far from Brisighella and Modigliana, names that have become famous among lovers of Romagna's wines. Ca' di Sopra was founded in the late 1960s, on an estate situated at 240 meters above sea level, on calcareous-clay terrain. In 2000 the Montanari family (founders and still owners) set out to significantly upgrade the winery. Another turning point came in 2006, which saw them earn a place among the area's most important producers. Its features a relaxed development on the nose and depth of flavor in the mouth. The 2017 Crepe is a Sangiovese that delivers on all levels, but just proves a little restrained by tannins throughout the palate, with some bitterish notes. Of the whites, we appreciated the fine and delicate 2017 Albana Secco Sandrona, despite the not particularly long finish.

| | |
|---|---|
| ○ Romagna Albana Secco Sandrona '17 | ♀♀ 3 |
| ● Romagna Sangiovese Marzeno Cà del Rosso '15 | ♀♀ 3 |
| ● Romagna Sangiovese Sup. Crepe '17 | ♀♀ 2* |
| ● Sangiovese di Romagna Marzeno Cadisopra '16 | ♀ 4 |
| ○ Romagna Albana Secco '15 | ♀♀ 3 |
| ● Romagna Sangiovese Marzeno '15 | ♀♀ 3 |
| ● Romagna Sangiovese Sup. Crepe '15 | ♀♀ 2* |

# Calonga

LOC. CASTIGLIONE
VIA CASTEL LEONE, 8
47121 FORLÌ
TEL. +39 0543753044
www.calonga.it

**CELLAR SALES**
**PRE-BOOKED VISITS**
**ANNUAL PRODUCTION** 30,000 bottles
**HECTARES UNDER VINE** 8.00

Calonga was founded by Maurizio Baravelli in the late 1960s. Today this family—run winery continues to dedicate itself to the cultivation of grapes and quality wine production. It's situated in Castiglione, on the lower hills of Forlì and Faenza, on terrain characterized by the area's proverbial 'molasses sand'. Traditional, local grapes are cultivated: Albana, Pagadebit and, of course, Sangiovese, giving rise to an artisanal selection, with all its charm and small imperfections. Two impressive Sangioveses are as temperamental as they are bright and original. The 2013 Riserva Michelangelo starts with reductive notes that leave positive developments in the bottle to your imagination. Humus and damp soil give way to plums and red fruit, while the palate holds well together, proving anything but docile, but rich in juice. Their Leggiolo appears more approachable but the tannic weight makes its presence felt in the mouth. The 2017 Pagadebit comes through acidulous, just as it should.

| | |
|---|---|
| ● Romagna Sangiovese Sup. Leggiolo '16 | 🍷🍷 3 |
| ● Romagna Sangiovese Sup. Michelangiolo Ris. '13 | 🍷🍷 5 |
| ○ Romagna Pagadebit '17 | 🍷 2 |
| ● Sangiovese di Romagna Sup. Michelangiolo Ris. '07 | 🍷🍷🍷 4* |
| ● Ordelaffo '15 | 🍷🍷 2* |
| ● Ordelaffo '14 | 🍷🍷 2* |
| ● Ordelaffo '13 | 🍷🍷 2* |
| ● Romagna Sangiovese Sup. Leggiolo '15 | 🍷🍷 3 |
| ● Romagna Sangiovese Sup. Michelangiolo Ris. '12 | 🍷🍷 4 |

# Cantina della Volta

VIA PER MODENA, 82
41030 BOMPORTO [MO]
TEL. +39 0597473312
www.cantinadellavolta.com

**CELLAR SALES**
**PRE-BOOKED VISITS**
**ANNUAL PRODUCTION** 120,000 bottles
**HECTARES UNDER VINE** 15.00
**VITICULTURE METHOD** Certified Organic

Four generations back, in 1920, Christian Bellei's family began making and selling Lambrusco di Sorbara. In 2010, thanks in part to the preparation he had working at his family's winery, Christian and a group of partners founded Cantina della Volta. Their primary aim is to produce high-quality Lambrusco Metodo Classico sparklers that exhibit some personality. You could say that they've hit the mark, considering the average level of their wines. Today Cantina della Volta is among the most notable of Emilia's sparkling wine producers. The outstanding 2014 Trentasei spends 36 months on the lees, as its name suggests. This Sorbara Metodo Classico sparkling wine features intact fruit and comes through close-knit with well-defined notes of blood orange. The palate holds well together, with a long, racy finish. We thought their non-vintage Mattaglio Brut was the best of the sparkling wines. This Chardonnay with sharp acidity exhibits aromas of dried herbs and a lively sparkle. Their 2014 Sorbara Rosé yields abundant fruit and proves very spirited in the mouth.

| | |
|---|---|
| ● Lambrusco di Sorbara Brut Trentasei M. Cl. '14 | 🍷🍷 4 |
| ○ Il Mattaglio Brut M. Cl. | 🍷🍷 5 |
| ⊙ Lambrusco di Sorbara Brut Rosé M. Cl. '14 | 🍷🍷 5 |
| ● Brutrosso M. Cl. '16 | 🍷 2 |
| ○ Il Mattaglio Blanc de Noir Brut M. Cl. '12 | 🍷 6 |
| ⊙ Lambrusco di Modena Brut Rosé M. Cl. '13 | 🍷🍷🍷 5 |
| ⊙ Lambrusco di Modena Brut Rosé M. Cl. '12 | 🍷🍷🍷 5 |
| ● Lambrusco di Sorbara Rimosso '13 | 🍷🍷🍷 3* |
| ● Lambrusco di Sorbara Rimosso '12 | 🍷🍷🍷 3* |
| ● Lambrusco di Modena Brut M. Cl. Trentasei '13 | 🍷🍷 4 |
| ● Lambrusco di Modena Brut M. Cl. Trentasei '12 | 🍷🍷 4 |

# Cantina di Santa Croce

FRAZ. SANTA CROCE
S.DA ST.LE 468 DI CORREGGIO, 35
41012 CARPI [MO]
TEL. +39 059664007
www.cantinasantacroce.it

CELLAR SALES
ANNUAL PRODUCTION 400,000 bottles
HECTARES UNDER VINE 600.00

Cantina di Santa Croce's story is one that goes back to the early 20th century, 1907 to be exact. 250 grower members cultivate primarily Lambrusco Salamino, a variety whose name comes right from Santa Croce di Carpi, though we shouldn't forget the other varieties grown, including Lancellotta. The terrain is primarily clay, and here Salamino gives up its best, even in dry years like 2017. Maurizio Boni is an enologist who knows well the qualities of the grape, which serves as the basis for a number of wines, including sparklers. Their 2017 Sorbara has earned the top score thanks to elegance and close-knit fruit. Its aromas range from sour cherries to citrus fruit, with bitter orange peel enriching a well-balanced picture. Of the Salamino wines, we preferred the dry one, with its aromas of violets and wild berries, and scented, savory and supple palate. Their 2017 Castello Rosso offers up pulp and aromas of small red fruit.

| | |
|---|---|
| ● Lambrusco di Sorbara '17 | ♟♟ 1* |
| ● Il Castello Lambrusco Semisecco '17 | ♟♟ 1* |
| ● Lambrusco Salamino di Santa Croce Secco Tradizione '17 | ♟♟ 1* |
| ☉ 100 Vendemmie Rosé Brut '17 | ♟ 2 |
| ● Lambrusco Grasparossa di Castelvetro '17 | ♟ 1* |
| ● Lambrusco Salamino di Santa Croce Amabile '17 | ♟ 1* |
| ● Lancellotta Filtrato Dolce '17 | ♟ 1* |
| ● Il Castello Lambrusco Secco '16 | ♟♟ 1* |
| ● Lambrusco Salamino di S. Croce Secco Linea '15 | ♟♟ 1* |
| ● Lambrusco Salamino di S. Croce Tradizione '15 | ♟♟ 1* |
| ● Lambrusco Salamino di Santa Croce Secco '16 | ♟♟ 1* |

# Cantina Sociale di Carpi e Sorbara

VIA CAVATA
41012 CARPI [MO]
TEL. +39 059 643071
www.cantinadicarpiesorbara.it

ANNUAL PRODUCTION 2,300,000 bottles
HECTARES UNDER VINE 2300.00

This cooperative winery was founded six years ago, in 2012, with the merger of two historic wineries; Cantine di Carpi (Est. 1903) and Sorbara (Est. 1923). Some 1200 members and some 6 production facilities give rise to 45 million liters of wine per year. The quality of their selection is good, especially when it comes to Sorbara (naturally). Their two wines dedicated to lawyer Gino Friedmann, a pioneer of Modena's cooperative producers, are particularly convincing. For us, their most impressive wine this year was the 2017 Omaggio a Gino Friedmann, fermented in bottle. It displays lovely citrusy aromas, especially tangerine, small red fruit and hints of freshly-cut hay. It holds well together in the mouth, with nice acidity. The version fermented in pressure tanks exhibits a nose dominated by wild strawberries, forthright fruit and a lovely finish. The winery also makes a pleasant, savory and very drinkable Lambrusco Mantovano with 100% Grappello Ruberti grapes.

| | |
|---|---|
| ● Lambrusco di Sorbara Secco Omaggio a Gino Friedmann FB '17 | ♟♟ 3* |
| ● Lambrusco di Sorbara Secco Omaggio a Gino Friedmann '17 | ♟♟ 3 |
| ● Lambrusco Mantovano 1946 '17 | ♟♟ 2* |
| ● Lambrusco di Sorbara Amabile Emma '17 | ♟ 2 |
| ● Lambrusco di Sorbara Secco Omaggio a Gino Friedmann '16 | ♟♟♟ 3* |
| ● Lambrusco di Sorbara Secco Omaggio a Gino Friedmann '13 | ♟♟♟ 3* |
| ● Lambrusco di Sorbara Secco Omaggio a Gino Friedmann FB '14 | ♟♟♟ 3* |
| ● Lambrusco di Sorbara Secco Omaggio a Gino Friedmann '15 | ♟♟ 3* |
| ● Lambrusco di Sorbara Secco Omaggio a Gino Friedmann FB '15 | ♟♟ 3* |

# EMILIA ROMAGNA

## Cavicchioli

VIA CANALETTO, 52
41030 SAN PROSPERO [MO]
TEL. +39 059812412
www.cavicchioli.it

CELLAR SALES
PRE-BOOKED VISITS
ANNUAL PRODUCTION 10,000,000 bottles
HECTARES UNDER VINE 90.00

Sandro and Claudio Cavicchioli represent the third generation of family to skillfully manage this giant of Modena's Lambrusco industry. And that's not all. They've covered a lot of ground in 90 years, since that April in 1928 when Umberto founded his winery in San Prospero. Their bottling facility is still there, while winemaking is carried out a few kilometers away in the municipality of Bomporto, the cradle of Lambrusco di Sorbara. And Sorbara is the cultivar that, year after year, delivers the best results, also when it comes to their Metodo Classico. Once again the 2017 Vigna del Cristo is in a class of its own. It comes through rich and savory, with strawberry and raspberry aromas, while the mouth holds well together, fragrant, close-focused, flavorsome and elegant: what more could you ask from a Sorbara? Their 2014 Brut Metodo Classico makes a lovely creamy impact, with backbone and a pleasant huskiness. The 2017 Tre Medaglie is taut, savory and drinkable.

## Caviro

VIA CONVERTITE, 12
48018 FAENZA [RA]
TEL. +39 0546629111
www.caviro.it

CELLAR SALES
ANNUAL PRODUCTION 25,000,000 bottles
HECTARES UNDER VINE 31.00

Caviro, a large group that's among Italy's major producers, brings together 32 smaller cooperatives and 12,000 vine growers spread out in 8 distinct regions. Obviously they have many projects, offer many selections and wines, and are represented on many markets. It's enough to think that their production facilities are responsible for Tavernello, just to provide a name that most will be familiar with. But they also offer more specialized wines whose scope is decidedly more limited, especially those made with grapes cultivated in Romagna. The young but promising 2017 Albana Secco Romio is a white displaying nice personality, depth, freshness and flavor. At the tasting, its aromas were still evolving, but it already proves vigorous and juicy on the palate. Their 2017 Sono Famoso moves at two speeds: it attacks with hints of ripe fruit and closes on an acidulous note.

| | | |
|---|---|---|
| ● Lambrusco di Sorbara V. del Cristo '17 | ▼▼▼ | 3* |
| ⊙ Lambrusco di Sorbara Brut Rosé del Cristo M. Cl. '14 | ▼▼ | 5 |
| ● Lambrusco di Sorbara Tre Medaglie '17 | ▼▼ | 2* |
| ● Lambrusco di Modena Tre Medaglie '17 | ▼ | 1* |
| ● Lambrusco di Sorbara Millenovecentoventotto '17 | ▼ | 2 |
| ● Lambrusco di Sorbara V. del Cristo '16 | ♀♀♀ | 2* |
| ● Lambrusco di Sorbara V. del Cristo '15 | ♀♀♀ | 2* |
| ● Lambrusco di Sorbara V. del Cristo '14 | ♀♀♀ | 2* |
| ● Lambrusco di Sorbara V. del Cristo '13 | ♀♀♀ | 2* |
| ● Lambrusco di Sorbara V. del Cristo '12 | ♀♀♀ | 2* |
| ● Lambrusco di Sorbara V. del Cristo '11 | ♀♀♀ | 2* |
| ⊙ Lambrusco di Sorbara Brut Rosé del Cristo M. Cl. '13 | ♀♀ | 4 |
| ⊙ Lambrusco di Sorbara Brut Rosé del Cristo M. Cl. '12 | ♀♀ | 4 |

| | | |
|---|---|---|
| ○ Romagna Albana Secco Romio '17 | ▼▼ | 2* |
| ○ Sono Famoso '17 | ▼▼ | 1* |
| ○ Pignoletto Frizzante Romio '15 | ♀♀ | 2* |
| ○ Romagna Albana Secco Romio '16 | ♀♀ | 2* |
| ○ Romagna Albana Secco Romio '15 | ♀♀ | 2* |
| ○ Romagna Trebbiano Terre Forti '15 | ♀♀ | 1* |

# Celli

v.le Carducci, 5
47032 Bertinoro [FC]
Tel. +39 0543445183
www.celli-vini.com

CELLAR SALES
PRE-BOOKED VISITS
ANNUAL PRODUCTION 300,000 bottles
HECTARES UNDER VINE 35.00
SUSTAINABLE WINERY

Celli, a winery belonging to the Sirri and Casadei families, cultivate a sizable estate in the area of Bertinoro that comprises both their private vineyards and rented property. The terrain is characterized by its calcareous soil that's rich in 'seabed tufa' and is distributed across various blocks: Tenuta Maestrina, Tenuta La Massa and Campi di Bracciano. The combination of land, vineyard management and winemaking allows them to produce high-quality wines, but especially wines with a clearly defined style and varietal identity. Celli's Albana di Romagna Secco I Croppi is in a class of its own. The 2017 vintage proves a monumental white for idea, style and execution. The suite of aromas is rich, but without superfluous frills. Sensations of grape skins alternate with notes of ripe yellow fruit, fading into delicate vegetal overtones reminiscent of meadow herbs. The wine holds well together perfectly on the palate, coming through mouthfilling and dynamic at the same time.

| | | |
|---|---|---|
| ○ Romagna Albana Secco I Croppi '17 | ♟♟♟ | 2* |
| ● Romagna Sangiovese Bertinoro Bron & Ruseval Ris. '15 | ♟ | 3 |
| ● Romagna Sangiovese Sup. Le Grillaie '17 | ♟ | 2 |
| ○ Romagna Albana Secco I Croppi '16 | ♟♟♟ | 2* |
| ○ Romagna Albana Secco I Croppi '15 | ♟♟♟ | 2* |
| ○ Romagna Albana Passito Solara '15 | ♟♟ | 4 |
| ○ Romagna Albana Secco I Croppi '14 | ♟♟ | 2* |
| ● Romagna Sangiovese Sup. Le Grillaie Ris. '14 | ♟♟ | 2* |

# ★Cleto Chiarli Tenute Agricole

via Belvedere, 8
41014 Castelvetro di Modena [MO]
Tel. +39 0593163311
www.chiarli.it

CELLAR SALES
PRE-BOOKED VISITS
ANNUAL PRODUCTION 900,000 bottles
HECTARES UNDER VINE 100.00

The history of Modena's Lambrusco would have been different if in 1860 Cleto Chiarli hadn't decided to dedicate himself exclusively to wine production (after spending 10 years managing the Osteria dell'Artigliere in Modena's city center). It was he who founded the business and began bottling his own wines, availing himself of second fermentation in the bottle and the so-called 'Metodo Ancestrale'. With time, the producer enlarged production and reached extremely high quality standards. The 2017 Lambrusco del Fondatore is juicy, with marked and charming fruity aromas. Close-focused strawberries and raspberries on the palate are enriched with notes of red citrus fruit, exhibiting savoriness and a sound acid structure. The 2017 Vecchia Modena Premium features a different, more elegant and streamlined style, with exemplary backbone and an intact finish. Their well-made 2017 Vigneto Cialdini comes through subtle and consistent, with flavors of wild black berries.

| | | |
|---|---|---|
| ● Lambrusco di Sorbara del Fondatore '17 | ♟♟♟ | 3* |
| ● Lambrusco di Sorbara Vecchia Modena Premium '17 | ♟♟ | 2* |
| ● Lambrusco Grasparossa di Castelvetro Vign. Cialdini '17 | ♟ | 2 |
| ⊙ Rosé de Noir Cuvée Brut | ♟ | 2 |
| ● Lambrusco di Sorbara del Fondatore '16 | ♟♟♟ | 3* |
| ● Lambrusco di Sorbara del Fondatore '15 | ♟♟♟ | 3* |
| ● Lambrusco di Sorbara del Fondatore '14 | ♟♟♟ | 3* |
| ● Lambrusco di Sorbara del Fondatore '12 | ♟♟♟ | 3* |
| ● Lambrusco di Sorbara del Fondatore '11 | ♟♟♟ | 2* |
| ● Lambrusco di Sorbara del Fondatore '09 | ♟♟♟ | 2* |
| ● Lambrusco di Sorbara Vecchia Modena Premium '13 | ♟♟♟ | 2* |
| ● Lambrusco di Sorbara Vecchia Modena Premium '10 | ♟♟♟ | 2* |

# Costa Archi

LOC. SERRA
VIA RINFOSCO, 1690
48014 CASTEL BOLOGNESE [RA]
TEL. +39 3384818346
costaarchi.wordpress.com

**CELLAR SALES**
**PRE-BOOKED VISITS**
**ANNUAL PRODUCTION** 15,000 bottles
**HECTARES UNDER VINE** 13.00

Founded in the 1960s in Castel Bolognese, today Costa Archi is led by Gabriele Succi, one of Romagna's most inspired and motivated vine growers. Two distinct plots are cultivated: Podere il Beneficio and Monte Brullo. They're both situated at more than 160 meters above sea level and feature red and yellow clay soil that's rich in limestone. Vineyard management eschews extreme choices in favor of prudence and awareness. The same holds for their winemaking, aging and general approach in the cellar. The result is a selection of balanced, elegant wines with a marked territorial identity. Our favorite wine is once again the Assiolo. This 2016 Sangiovese displays charm, territoriality and the intention of its creator. It is fermented exclusively with native yeasts, matures in barrels and offers up aromas of wild berries, violets and licorice. Iron-like notes add a charm which is not clouded by its toasty hints. The palate proves juicy and slightly restrained by marked tannins.

| | |
|---|---|
| ● Romagna Sangiovese Serra Assiolo '16 | ♟♟ 3* |
| ● GS Sangiovese '14 | ♟♟ 5 |
| ● Romagna Sangiovese Sup. Assiolo '13 | ♟♟♟ 4* |
| ● GS Sangiovese '12 | ♟♟ 5 |
| ● Romagna Sangiovese Serra Assiolo '15 | ♟♟ 2* |
| ● Romagna Sangiovese Sup. Assiolo '14 | ♟♟ 2* |
| ● Sangiovese di Romagna Sup. Monte Brullo Ris. '10 | ♟♟ 2* |

# Divina Lux

VIA CADUTI DI CRIVELLARI, 50
48025 RIOLO TERME [RA]
TEL. +39 3286084425
www.divinaluxwinery.com

**CELLAR SALES**
**PRE-BOOKED VISITS**
**ACCOMMODATION AND RESTAURANT SERVICE**
**ANNUAL PRODUCTION** 25,000 bottles
**HECTARES UNDER VINE** 7.00

The family of Divina Lux's current owner were originally from the Caucasus region and are well-acquainted with winemaking. They've been having success as of late, thanks to a commitment to quality and their splendid, seven-hectare estate, situated in the heart of Emilia Romagna's Regional Park. It's an area that faces Tuscany, situated at notable elevations spanning 250 to 500 meters above sea level. Their selection comprises the area's classic wines, Trebbiano and Albana for their whites, Sangiovese for their reds. Their excellent 2016 Albana Secco Dar exhibits grape skins and body, like all the best interpretations of this wine type. Another of their whites is the 2016 Hilla, a Trebbiano reminiscent of white peach, with nice pulp and vibrant acidity. Their 2016 Romagna Sangiovese Superiore Victores proves less impressive and rather mouth-drying.

| | |
|---|---|
| ○ Romagna Albana Secco Dar '16 | ♟♟ 4 |
| ○ Hilla Trebbiano '16 | ♟♟ 4 |
| ● Romagna Sangiovese Sup. Victores '16 | ♟ 4 |
| ○ Hilla Trebbiano '14 | ♟♟ 6 |
| ○ Romagna Albana Secco Dar '15 | ♟♟ 4 |
| ○ Romagna Albana Secco Dar '14 | ♟♟ 6 |

# Drei Donà Tenuta La Palazza

LOC. MASSA DI VECCHIAZZANO
VIA DEL TESORO, 23
47121 FORLÌ
TEL. +39 0543769371
www.dreidona.it

**CELLAR SALES**
**PRE-BOOKED VISITS**
**ANNUAL PRODUCTION** 130,000 bottles
**HECTARES UNDER VINE** 27.00
**SUSTAINABLE WINERY**

Drei Donà Tenuta La Palazza is among Romagna's noteworthy producers, a winery that's been both a pioneer and a steady source of quality. The turning point came in the 1980s, when Claudio Drei Donà decided to develop his family's land. From then it's been an upward path of success and continued attention from international markets. Today their wines are modern, well-presented, though we wouldn't mind a further step towards highlighting their territorial identity. The 2015 Sangiovese Superiore Pruno is a bit clouded by toasty notes, but underneath the fruit is chomping at the bit and it generally works. Their 2015 Riserva Palazza goes along similar lines, proving intense but featuring more mouth-drying tannins and undefined aromas. Their 2013 Magnificat, made with Cabernet grapes, offers up nice sensations, while the 2016 Notturno comes through a bit 'woody'.

# Emilia Wine

VIA 11 SETTEMBRE 2001, 3
42019 SCANDIANO [RE]
TEL. +39 0522989107
www.emiliawine.eu

**ANNUAL PRODUCTION** 300,000 bottles
**HECTARES UNDER VINE** 1900.00

Cooperation has always been one of Emilia's strongpoints, especially when it comes to agriculture, food and, of most interest to us, viticulture. That's how it came to pass that in 2014 three wineries from Arceto, Prato di Correggio and Correggio merged to form Emilia Wine, adding another name to the region's historic cooperative wineries. More than 700 grower members cultivate Lambrusco on the plains while primarily white grapes for sparkling wines are harvested on the lowers hills of Reggio Emilia, between the Enza and Secchia rivers. The 2017 Correggio is a juicy Reggiano, featuring raspberries and strawberries with fresh balsamic nuances. The palate proves rich, with a well-supported and balanced structure. Their 2017 Rosaspino displays a rather dark color and aromas of medicinal herbs, rosemary and wild berries, but doesn't lack vigor. The red version exhibits more marked vegetal overtones and a lovely fruity background.

| | | |
|---|---|---|
| ● Magnificat '13 | | ♟♟ 5 |
| ● Romagna Sangiovese Sup. Pruno Ris. '15 | | ♟♟ 7 |
| ● Romagna Sangiovese Predappio Notturno '16 | | ♟ 3 |
| ● Romagna Sangiovese Sup. Palazza Ris. '15 | | ♟ 5 |
| ○ Il Tornese '14 | | ♟♟ 3 |
| ● Magnificat Cabernet Sauvignon '12 | | ♟♟ 5 |
| ● Notturno Sangiovese '14 | | ♟♟ 3 |
| ● Notturno Sangiovese '13 | | ♟♟ 2* |
| ● Romagna Sangiovese Sup. Palazza Ris. '13 | | ♟♟ 5 |
| ● Romagna Sangiovese Sup. Pruno Ris. '13 | | ♟♟ 5 |
| ● Romagna Sangiovese Sup. Pruno Ris. '12 | | ♟♟ 5 |

| | | |
|---|---|---|
| ⊙ Colli di Scandiano e di Canossa Lambrusco Rosaspino Cantina di Arceto '17 | | ♟♟ 2* |
| ● Reggiano Lambrusco Il Correggio '17 | | ♟♟ 2* |
| ● 1077 Rosso Brut | | ♟ 2 |
| ● Colli di Scandiano e di Canossa Lambrusco Rossospino Cantina di Arceto '17 | | ♟ 2 |
| ● Migliolungo Lambrusco Cantina di Arceto '17 | | ♟ 2 |
| ● Colli di Scandiano e di Canossa Lambrusco Rossospino Cantina di Arceto '16 | | ♟♟ 2* |
| ● Colli di Scandiano e di Canossa Lambrusco Rossospino Cantina di Arceto '15 | | ♟♟ 2* |
| ● Reggiano Lambrusco Secco Niveo Cantina di Arceto '15 | | ♟♟ 2* |

## Paolo Francesconi

LOC. SARNA
VIA TULIERO, 154
48018 FAENZA [RA]
TEL. +39 054643213
www.francesconipaolo.it

CELLAR SALES
PRE-BOOKED VISITS
ANNUAL PRODUCTION 20,000 bottles
HECTARES UNDER VINE 8.00
VITICULTURE METHOD Certified Biodynamic
SUSTAINABLE WINERY

Francesconi is a winery with a clear style, as clear as the ideas that guided their production choices over time. Founded in the early 1990s, their approach was characterized first by organic cultivation techniques and then biodynamic. They're a sure bet for those who seek authentic wines, without the frills, both when it comes to their reds and their whites (as well as their 'orange' selection). The estate is situated on Faenza's lower hills, where the terrain is made up of clay and silt. The town of Faenza is a stone's throw away, just five kilometers. The land where the winery is situated is called Limbecca. It has appeared in old land registers since 1780 and gives its name to the 2016 Romagna Sangiovese Superiore (mistakenly reviewed in a past edition of the guide). This impressive red shows great aging potential, tight and firm aromas and flavor. It may not be very alluring right now, but it's certainly vigorous, with an assertive, well-extracted and lip-smacking tannic texture.

| | |
|---|---|
| ● Romagna Sangiovese Sup. Limbecca '16 | ♟♟ 3* |
| ○ Arcaica '17 | ♟ 3 |
| ○ Luna Nuova '16 | ♟ 2 |
| ● Romagna Sangiovese Sup. Le Iadi Ris. '15 | ♟ 5 |
| ● Vite in Fiore '17 | ♟ 3 |
| ● Romagna Sangiovese Sup. Limbecca '14 | ♟♟♟ 3* |
| ● Sangiovese di Romagna Sup. Limbecca '11 | ♟♟♟ 3* |
| ○ Arcaica '13 | ♟♟ 3* |
| ● Romagna Sangiovese Sup. Le Iadi Ris. '12 | ♟♟ 5 |
| ● Vite in Fiore '15 | ♟♟ 3 |

## Maria Galassi

FRAZ. PADERNO
VIA CASETTA, 688
47522 CESENA [FC]
TEL. +39 054721177
www.galassimaria.it

CELLAR SALES
PRE-BOOKED VISITS
ANNUAL PRODUCTION 18,000 bottles
HECTARES UNDER VINE 18.00
VITICULTURE METHOD Certified Organic

Maria Galassi has always had clear ideas concerning how to go about her work in the vineyards and the type of wine she wanted to make, such that her approach was a precursor to organic agriculture. Here the terrain is calcareous-clay with veins of gypsum and yellow sand rich in marine tufa, giving rise to elegant, aromatic wines. Their vineyards are surrounded by woods, guaranteeing an ecosystem that's perfectly balanced and protected in every possible way. The 2016 Romagna Sangiovese Superiore Smembar is an excellent example of this category, interpreted with an impressive style. This elegant red offers up nice balance between pulp and flavor, still proving rigid at the end palate, but with a certain future. The 2017 Smembar Bianco features a bright amber color, oxidative and salty notes (which are very seductive but never excessive), both for aroma and taste.

| | |
|---|---|
| ● Romagna Sangiovese Sup. Smembar '16 | ♟♟ 2* |
| ○ Smembar Bianco '17 | ♟♟ 2* |
| ● Sangiovese di Romagna Sup. natoRe '10 | ♟♟♟ 2* |
| ● Romagna Sangiovese Sup. Smembar '14 | ♟♟ 5 |
| ● Romagna Sangiovese Bertinoro natoRe Ris. '12 | ♟♟ 2* |
| ● Romagna Sangiovese Sup. Paternus '15 | ♟♟ 3 |
| ● Romagna Sangiovese Sup. Paternus '14 | ♟♟ 2* |
| ● Romagna Sangiovese Sup. Paternus '13 | ♟♟ 2* |
| ● Sangiovese di Romagna Sup. natoRe Ris. '11 | ♟♟ 2* |
| ● Sangiovese di Romagna Sup. Paternus '11 | ♟♟ 2* |
| ● Sangiovese di Romagna Sup. Smembar '13 | ♟♟ 5 |

## Gallegati

via Lugo, 182
48018 Faenza [RA]
Tel. +39 0546621149
www.aziendaagricolagallegati.it

CELLAR SALES
PRE-BOOKED VISITS
ACCOMMODATION
ANNUAL PRODUCTION 15,000 bottles
HECTARES UNDER VINE 6.00

Gallegati is a well-known name among those who love the region's wines. Brothers Antonio and Cesare are the principal managers of this producer situated in Faenza, where the vineyards grow in the area's classic clay-silt and calcareous terrain (part of the estate is also dedicated to cultivating fruit). The utmost respect is shown for the environment, and for terroir when it comes to wine production. Their style is authentic, with all its charm and small imperfections. Their Corallo Rosso Sangiovese di Brisighella performed quite well; it's a bit too toasty but shows great personality and depth. It features luxuriant fruit, but cumbersome wood prevents it from expressing more personality. The 2017 Corallo Giallo is an Albana that conveys the expressive richness of this variety and reveals oxidative and open tendencies.

| | |
|---|---|
| ● Romagna Sangiovese Brisighella Corallo Rosso '16 | 🍷🍷 2* |
| ○ Romagna Albana Secco Corallo Giallo '17 | 🍷🍷 3 |
| ○ Albana di Romagna Passito Regina di Cuori Ris. '10 | 🍷🍷🍷 4* |
| ○ Albana di Romagna Passito Regina di Cuori Ris. '09 | 🍷🍷🍷 4* |
| ○ Romagna Albana Passito Regina di Cuori Ris. '12 | 🍷🍷🍷 4* |
| ● Romagna Sangiovese Brisighella Corallo Nero Ris. '13 | 🍷🍷 4 |
| ● Romagna Sangiovese Sup. Brisighella Corallo Nero Ris. '11 | 🍷🍷 4 |
| ● Sangiovese di Romagna Sup. Corallo Nero Ris. '10 | 🍷🍷 4 |

## Lombardini

via Cavour, 15
42017 Novellara [RE]
Tel. +39 0522654224
www.lombardinivini.it

CELLAR SALES
PRE-BOOKED VISITS
ANNUAL PRODUCTION 800,000 bottles
HECTARES UNDER VINE

Cantine Lombardini was founded in 1925 by Angelo Lombardini, who was already the owner of Bar Roma (situated in the town center of Novellara, where the producer is still headquartered). Four generations of family have since passed through, and today Marco Lombardini is supported by his three daughters Chiara, Cecilia and Virginia. The 2017 Lambrusco di Sorbara C'era una Volta exhibits forthright notes of rose and strawberry, enriched with citrusy hints of cedar and tangerine. The palate comes through fragrant and meaty, with good supporting backbone. Their 2017 Campanone Secco, a blend of Lambrusco Salamino and Marani, offers up a generous, fruity nose and palate. The 2017 Signor Campanone, made with Salamino and Sorbara, proves dark and deep, quite rustic, fresh and savory. Their 2017 Rosato del Campanone, a blend of the same grapes, conveys overtones of citrus fruit and rennet apple.

| | |
|---|---|
| ● Lambrusco di Sorbara C'era Una Volta '17 | 🍷🍷 2* |
| ● Reggiano Lambrusco Il Campanone '17 | 🍷🍷 2* |
| ● Lambrusco di Sorbara Brut 1925 | 🍷 2 |
| ⊙ Reggian Lambrusco Rosato del Campanone '17 | 🍷 2 |
| ● Reggiano Lambrusco Il Signor Campanone '17 | 🍷 2 |
| ● Lambrusco della Dama '16 | 🍷🍷 1* |
| ● Reggiano Lambrusco Il Signor Campanone '16 | 🍷🍷 2* |

# EMILIA ROMAGNA

## Luretta

LOC. CASTELLO DI MOMELIANO
29010 GAZZOLA [PC]
TEL. +39 0523971070
www.luretta.com

CELLAR SALES
PRE-BOOKED VISITS
ANNUAL PRODUCTION 300,000 bottles
HECTARES UNDER VINE 50.00
VITICULTURE METHOD Certified Organic

The name was inspired by the Luretta river, a tributary of the Tidone. It was Felice Salamini, a rancher, world-traveler and lover of French wines, who fell in love with the territory and purchased an old abandoned vineyard in 1988, thus setting in motion a family adventure into winemaking. It was an adventure that eventually led him to take over 50 hectares of terrain, and plant international varieties. In the meantime his son Lucio joined him and in 2002 they made the definitive move to Castello di Momeliano. Their Pantera draws its claws: this is the founder's wine, a blend of Croatina, Barbera and Cabernet Sauvignon. The 2015 vintage expresses ripe fruit, body, graceful tannins, citrus fruit, hay and red fruit, making for a charming and multi-faceted wine. Their 2015 Carabas is a Barbera partly aged in new barriques, which add spice and sweet tannins to the variety's morello cherry notes. Their 2015 Gutturnio Superiore exhibits garden vegetables, while the 2017 Malvasia Boccadirosa proves very floral.

## Tenuta Mara

VIA CA' BACCHINO, 1665
47832 SAN CLEMENTE [RN]
TEL. +39 0541988870
www.tenutamara.com

CELLAR SALES
PRE-BOOKED VISITS
ANNUAL PRODUCTION 20,000 bottles
HECTARES UNDER VINE 6.50
VITICULTURE METHOD Certified Biodynamic

Giordano Emendatori's passion for wine is at the foundation of this extraordinary project, dedicated to his wife, Mara. It has all been made possible thanks to painstaking care and an attentive eye towards sustainability, both in the vineyard and in the cellar, where biodynamic principals prevail. And both their architectural approach and facility demonstrate great sensitivity to the environment and aesthetic principals. Their original wines consistently prove personal and intriguing, full of flavor. While awaiting their most serious wine, which is still undergoing aging, we enjoyed another 100% Sangiovese, a splendid 2016 Guiry. It offers up delectable, mature aromas, with no lack of fresher and more floral notes, hints of spices and medicinal herbs. The palate comes through supple and full-flavored with good supporting acidity.

| | |
|---|---|
| ● C. P. Barbera Carabas '15 | ♟♟ 3 |
| ● Pantera '15 | ♟♟ 4 |
| ○ C. P. Malvasia Boccadirosa '17 | ♟ 3 |
| ● Gutturnio Sup. '15 | ♟ 3 |
| ● C. P. Cabernet Sauvignon Corbeau '00 | ♟♟♟ 4* |
| ☉ C. P. Brut Rosé On Attend les Invités '11 | ♟♟ 4 |
| ○ C. P. Chardonnay Selín dl'Armari '15 | ♟♟ 4 |
| ○ C. P. Chardonnay Selín dl'Armari '11 | ♟♟ 4 |
| ○ C. P. Sauvignon I Nani e le Ballerine '16 | ♟♟ 3 |
| ● Gutturnio Sup. '12 | ♟♟ 3 |
| ○ Principessa Pas Dosé M. Cl. '10 | ♟♟ 4 |

| | |
|---|---|
| ● Guiry '16 | ♟♟ 5 |
| ● Maramia Sangiovese '15 | ♟♟ 7 |
| ● Maramia Sangiovese '13 | ♟♟ 7 |
| ● Maramia Sangiovese '12 | ♟♟ 4 |

# ★Ermete Medici & Figli

ʟᴏᴄ. Gᴀɪᴅᴀ
ᴠɪᴀ I. Nᴇᴡᴛᴏɴ, 13ᴀ
42124 Rᴇɢɢɪᴏ Eᴍɪʟɪᴀ
Tᴇʟ. +39 0522942135
www.medici.it

**CELLAR SALES**
**PRE-BOOKED VISITS**
**ANNUAL PRODUCTION** 800,000 bottles
**HECTARES UNDER VINE** 75.00
**SUSTAINABLE WINERY**

The Medici family's winery is a fundamental one in terms of the history of Reggiano Lambrusco. It was founded by Remigio Medici in the late 19th century and expanded by his son Ermete (after whom it is named), who was responsible for setting it on its course towards quality Lambrusco wine production. His kin pushed forward so that today Alberto represents the fourth generation of family to manage the winery. Recent years have seen a major effort to identify the best clones and sites for their premium offerings. Their 2017 Concerto lives up to expectations: lovely right from its color and mousse, with aromas of blackberry and redcurrant, generous fruit, it is lively, mature and scented. The 2017 I Quercioli, a savory and juicy Sorbara, offers up strawberry and raspberry notes with nice supporting acidity. But new this year is the 2016 Phermento: an Ancestral Method second fermentation, featuring a transparent bottle, crown cap and, most of all, complex aromas ranging from gentian to medicinal herbs, undergrowth and orange peel.

| | | |
|---|---|---|
| ● Reggiano Lambrusco Concerto '17 | ♟♟♟ | 2* |
| ● Lambrusco di Sorbara I Quercioli '17 | ♟♟ | 2* |
| ● Modena Lambrusco Phermento Metodo Ancestrale '16 | ♟♟ | 3* |
| ● Reggiano Lambrusco Dolce I Quercioli '17 | ♟♟ | 2* |
| ○ Nebbie d'Autunno Malvasia Dolce '17 | ♟ | 2 |
| ● Reggiano Lambrusco Assolo '17 | ♟ | 2 |
| ● Reggiano Lambrusco Concerto '16 | ♟♟♟ | 2* |
| ● Reggiano Lambrusco Concerto '15 | ♟♟♟ | 2* |
| ● Reggiano Lambrusco Concerto '14 | ♟♟♟ | 2* |
| ● Reggiano Lambrusco Concerto '13 | ♟♟♟ | 2* |
| ● Reggiano Lambrusco Concerto '12 | ♟♟♟ | 2* |
| ● Reggiano Lambrusco Concerto '11 | ♟♟♟ | 2* |
| ● Reggiano Lambrusco Concerto '10 | ♟♟♟ | 2* |
| ● Reggiano Lambrusco Concerto '09 | ♟♟♟ | 2* |
| ● Reggiano Lambrusco Concerto '08 | ♟♟♟ | 2* |

# Monte delle Vigne

ʟᴏᴄ. Oᴢᴢᴀɴᴏ Tᴀʀᴏ
ᴠɪᴀ Mᴏɴᴛɪᴄᴇʟʟᴏ, 22
43046 Cᴏʟʟᴇᴄᴄʜɪᴏ [PR]
Tᴇʟ. +39 0521309704
www.montedellevigne.it

**CELLAR SALES**
**PRE-BOOKED VISITS**
**ACCOMMODATION**
**ANNUAL PRODUCTION** 350,000 bottles
**HECTARES UNDER VINE** 60.00

The winery's history goes back to 1983 when Andrea Ferrari began his winemaking adventure with an estate of 15 hectares, seven of which were vineyards, situated on the Colli di Parma hills at 300 meters above sea level. In 2000 the estate grew to 20 hectares, but the real transformation came between 2003 and 2004 when the contractor Paolo Pizzarotti, who already owned 100 hectares adjacent to the estate, became a majority partner. By late 2006 a new, gorgeous hypogeum cellar powered by solar panels had been built. In the meantime new wines are springing up while the vineyards are being converted to organic. Their 2016 Nabucco is a blend of 70% Barbera and Merlot undergoing long maceration and aged for a year in oak barriques. Its varied nose ranges from morello cherry to freshly-cut hay, while the palate proves juicy, fruity and still young. Barbera also prevails in their 2017 Rosso and adds scented fruit and backbone. Their complex and intriguing white, the 2015 Malvasia Callas, features wild flowers, yellow fruit and tropical grass.

| | | |
|---|---|---|
| ○ Callas Malvasia '15 | ♟♟♟ | 4* |
| ● Nabucco '16 | ♟♟ | 5 |
| ● Colli di Parma Rosso MDV '17 | ♟♟ | 3 |
| ● Cabernet Franc '12 | ♟♟ | 5 |
| ● Colli di Parma Rosso MDV '16 | ♟♟♟ | 3* |
| ● Colli di Parma Rosso MDV '14 | ♟♟♟ | 2* |
| ○ Callas Malvasia '14 | ♟♟ | 4 |
| ○ Colli di Parma Malvasia Frizzante '15 | ♟♟ | 2* |
| ○ Colli di Parma Malvasia Frizzante '14 | ♟♟ | 2* |
| ○ Colli di Parma Malvasia Poem '14 | ♟♟ | 2* |
| ● Colli di Parma Malvasia Poem '12 | ♟♟ | 2* |
| ● Lambrusco Emilia '14 | ♟♟ | 2* |
| ○ Malvasia Frizzante Dolce '12 | ♟♟ | 2* |
| ● Nabucco '15 | ♟♟ | 5 |
| ⊙ Rubina Brut Rosé '13 | ♟♟ | 4 |

## Fattoria Monticino Rosso

VIA MONTECATONE, 7
40026 IMOLA [BO]
TEL. +39 054240577
www.fattoriadelmonticinorosso.it

CELLAR SALES
PRE-BOOKED VISITS
ANNUAL PRODUCTION 70,000 bottles
HECTARES UNDER VINE 18.00

This family-run winery was founded in 1965 thanks to Antonio Zeoli. In 1985 the Monticino Rosso farm, which lay adjacent to the original property, was puchased, thus giving the winery its current name. The Imola hills, near the municipality of Dozza (and therefore Emilia), is a borderland both geographically and in terms of enology. Today Luciano and Gianni are pushing forward with particular attention paid to Albana, a white grape that's enjoying greater popularity. The 2015 Sangiovese Superiore Riserva Le Morine impressed us, coming through juicy, taut, citrusy and well-extracted, with tannins that make their presence felt without being invasive. Their 2017 Albana Secco A is no less impressive, with truly masterful notes of ripe tropical fruit balanced by fresher, citrusy sensations and crisp acidity. The 2016 Passito offers up notes of apricot jam and spice.

| | | |
|---|---|---|
| ○ Albana di Romagna Passito '16 | ♟♟ | 4 |
| ○ Romagna Albana Secco A '17 | ♟♟ | 2* |
| ● Romagna Sangiovese Sup. Le Morine Ris. '15 | ♟♟ | 3 |
| ○ Romagna Albana Passito '11 | ♟♟ | 4 |
| ○ Romagna Albana Secco A '16 | ♟♟ | 2* |
| ○ Romagna Albana Secco Codronchio '15 | ♟♟ | 3 |
| ○ Romagna Albana Secco Codronchio '14 | ♟♟ | 3 |
| ● Romagna Sangiovese Sup. S '16 | ♟♟ | 2* |
| ● Romagna Sangiovese Sup. S '15 | ♟♟ | 2* |

## Fattoria Nicolucci

VIA UMBERTO I, 21
47016 PREDAPPIO [FC]
TEL. +39 0543922361
www.vininicolucci.com

CELLAR SALES
PRE-BOOKED VISITS
ANNUAL PRODUCTION 70,000 bottles
HECTARES UNDER VINE 10.00
SUSTAINABLE WINERY

The district of Predappio Alta itself is among Romagna's most renowned when it comes to making prized wines, especially Sangiovese. It's here that Fattoria Nicolucci was founded way back in 1885. Theirs is a classic family-run winery, focused on their work in the vineyards and keen on promoting an idea of wine that is decidedly territorial. The lean, calcareous and pebbly soil along with maturation in concrete and large wood barrels allows them to create classic wines, vibrant and flavorful, that are never excessive in their extraction. The whole selection they presented this year impressed: spot-on wines, with an unmistakable and personal style. The Vigna del Generale stands out, intense and full-bodied, with a heady mix of fruit and wood. It proves dense, focused, deep and complex and will continue to grow in the bottle until it reaches its peak. We found their 2017 Tre Rocche more pervasive and the Predappio di Predappio excellent.

| | | |
|---|---|---|
| ● Romagna Sangiovese Sup. Predappio di Predappio V. del Generale Ris. '15 | ♟♟♟ | 5 |
| ● Predappio di Predappio '16 | ♟♟ | 5 |
| ● Romagna Sangiovese Sup. Tre Rocche '17 | ♟♟ | 3 |
| ● Romagna Sangiovese Sup. V. del Generale Ris. '13 | ♟♟♟ | 5 |
| ● Romagna Sangiovese Sup. V. del Generale Ris. '12 | ♟♟♟ | 5 |
| ● Sangiovese di Romagna Predappio di Predappio V. del Generale '11 | ♟♟♟ | 5 |
| ● Sangiovese di Romagna Sup. V. del Generale Ris. '10 | ♟♟♟ | 5 |
| ● Romagna Sangiovese Sup. Predappio di Predappio V. del Generale Ris. '14 | ♟♟ | 5 |

# Enio Ottaviani

LOC. SANT'ANDREA IN CASALE
VIA PIAN DI VAGLIA, 17
47832 SAN CLEMENTE [RN]
TEL. +39 0541952608
www.enioottaviani.it

**CELLAR SALES**
**PRE-BOOKED VISITS**
**ANNUAL PRODUCTION** 130,000 bottles
**HECTARES UNDER VINE** 12.00

Enio Ottaviani is a historic winery today managed by the founder's grandsons Davide and Massimo Lorenzi, along with cousins Marco and Milena Tonelli. After a past that saw the brand solely concerned with commerce, today it is a full-fledged producer in all respects. Their estate is situated in San Clemente di Rimini, on the gentle hills that overlook the sea and enjoy the area's aromas and breezes. The terrain tends towards clay loam and gives rise to wines that are as sound as they are defined and balanced. Their 2015 Sangiovese Superiore Riserva Sole Rosso exhibits an interesting style did quite well. It immediately reveals a pale color and is subtractive, giving up a touch of body without losing flavor or aromatic intensity. Hints of leather and spices enrich the fruit, while the palate comes through a little closed by assertive and slightly bitterish tannins. Their 2017 Bio Primalba proves clearer and simpler.

| | |
|---|---|
| ● Romagna Sangiovese Sup. Sole Rosso Ris. '15 | ♛♛ 4 |
| ○ Romagna Pagadebit Strati '17 | ♛♛ 2* |
| ● Romagna Sangiovese Primalba Bio '17 | ♛♛ 2* |
| ● Romagna Sangiovese Sup. Caciara '17 | ♛♛ 3 |
| ○ Clemente Primo '15 | ♛♛ 2* |
| ● Romagna Sangiovese Caciara '15 | ♛♛ 3 |
| ● Romagna Sangiovese Primalba '14 | ♛♛ 2* |
| ● Romagna Sangiovese Sup. Caciara '16 | ♛♛ 3 |
| ● Romagna Sangiovese Sup. Caciara '14 | ♛♛ 2* |
| ● Romagna Sangiovese Sup. Sole Rosso Ris. '13 | ♛♛ 4 |

# Alberto Paltrinieri

FRAZ. SORBARA
VIA CRISTO, 49
41030 BOMPORTO [MO]
TEL. +39 059902047
www.cantinapaltrinieri.it

**CELLAR SALES**
**PRE-BOOKED VISITS**
**ANNUAL PRODUCTION** 90,000 bottles
**HECTARES UNDER VINE** 17.00

Alberto Paltrinieri is carrying on the legacy of his father, Gianfranco, and grandfather Achille, a chemist and pharmacist who built the cellar. He's also helped fundamentally by the support of his wife, Barbara, and together they've made their winery one of Modena's most noteworthy. Here in Cristo di Sorbara, between the Secchia and Panaro rivers, the terrain is alluvial, giving rise to a Lambrusco that manages to offer up its best in terms of savoriness and elegance. In addition to the traditional use of autoclaves, for some years now their Sorbara also undergoes secondary fermentation in the bottle. The 2017 Leclisse is an elegant, pink-hued Sorbara with floral aromas, close-focused fruit, savory, clear, scented and sharpish, making for an impeccable interpretation. The 2017 Piria plays more on intact wild berries supported by lovely vigor. Their 2017 Radice is a rather rustic Ancestral Method sparkling wine, where fruit merges with vegetal notes.

| | |
|---|---|
| ● Lambrusco di Sorbara Leclisse '17 | ♛♛♛ 3* |
| ● Lambrusco di Sorbara Piria '17 | ♛♛ 2* |
| ● Lambrusco di Sorbara Radice '17 | ♛ 3 |
| ● Lambrusco di Sorbara Sant'Agata '17 | ♛ 2 |
| ● Solco Lambrusco '17 | ♛ 2 |
| ● Lambrusco di Sorbara Leclisse '16 | ♛♛♛ 2* |
| ● Lambrusco di Sorbara Leclisse '10 | ♛♛♛ 3* |
| ● Lambrusco di Sorbara Radice '13 | ♛♛♛ 2* |
| ● Brut Grosso M. Cl. '13 | ♛♛ 2* |
| ● Lambrusco di Sorbara Leclisse '15 | ♛♛ 2* |
| ● Lambrusco di Sorbara Leclisse '14 | ♛♛ 2* |
| ● Lambrusco di Sorbara Piria '16 | ♛♛ 2* |
| ● Lambrusco di Sorbara Radice '15 | ♛♛ 2* |
| ● Lambrusco di Sorbara Radice '14 | ♛♛ 2* |
| ● Lambrusco di Sorbara Sant'Agata '16 | ♛♛ 2* |
| ● Lambrusco di Sorbara Sant'Agata '15 | ♛♛ 2* |
| ● Radice Tappo a Corona '15 | ♛♛ 2* |

# Pandolfa

FRAZ. FIUMANA
VIA PANDOLFA, 35
47016 PREDAPPIO [FC]
TEL. +39 0543940073
www.pandolfa.it

**CELLAR SALES**
**ANNUAL PRODUCTION** 120,000 bottles
**HECTARES UNDER VINE** 30.00
**SUSTAINABLE WINERY**

The name Pandolfa was inspired by Sigismondo Pandolfo Malatesta, a celebrated figure and patron of the arts during medieval times. Situated in Fiumana di Predappio, for more than three centuries the winery was owned by the Marquis Albicini family before falling into the hands of knight commander Giuseppe Ricci and later his daughter Noelia. More recently the estate was purchased by Paola Piscopo and today it's managed by her son Marco Cirese, who's responsible for transforming the winery into one of Romagna's brightest stars. Their 2015 Sangiovese Superiore Riserva Pandolfo is truly scintillating: its delightful nose is enhanced with delicate small red fruit and spices, spirited in the mouth, linear though embracing, playing on flavor rather than power. Its savory finish comes through iron-like, captivating and caressing. Their 2017 Sangiovese doesn't quite hit the bull's eye, at least that's how it seemed when we tasted it. The Ginevra rosé appears simpler.

| | |
|---|---:|
| ● Romagna Sangiovese Sup. Pandolfo Ris. '15 | ♥♥ 3* |
| ☉ Ginevra '17 | ♥ 2 |
| ● Romagna Sangiovese Sup. Pandolfo '17 | ♥ 2 |
| ● Romagna Sangiovese Sup. Federico '16 | ♈♈ 2* |
| ● Romagna Sangiovese Sup. Pandolfo '16 | ♈♈ 2* |

# Fattoria Paradiso

FRAZ. CAPOCOLLE
VIA PALMEGGIANA, 285
47032 BERTINORO [FC]
TEL. +39 0543445044
www.fattoriaparadiso.com

**CELLAR SALES**
**PRE-BOOKED VISITS**
**ANNUAL PRODUCTION** 130,000 bottles
**HECTARES UNDER VINE** 50.00

The Pezzi family's historic winery is situated in Bertinoro, on the lower Apennine hills, at medium elevations and in a position that's favored by an excellent microclimate. It's a producer with many merits. It's still family-run, cultivating and transforming grapes exclusively from their private vineyards. Their historic plots, which are divided into distinct parcels of land, feature emblematic crus, giving rise to a selection that highlights the attributes of the area's traditional grapes though while leaving space for innovation, without entirely eschewing experimentation. The first monovarietal Sangiovese Riserva, the Vigna delle Lepri cru, excelled at our tastings. The 2015 vintage shows pluck, classic aromas and juice, led by a dynamic and linear palate that makes it pleasant without losing complexity. Their 2017 Barbarossa appears aromatic with a rustic palate. It is certainly a good wine for pairing.

| | |
|---|---:|
| ● Romagna Sangiovese Bertinoro V. delle Lepri Ris. '15 | ♥♥ 4 |
| ● Barbarossa Cuvée Mario Pezzi V. dello Spungone '17 | ♥ 3 |
| ○ Romagna Albana Secco '17 | ♥ 2 |
| ○ Albana V.T. '15 | ♈♈ 2* |
| ● Il Dosso '14 | ♈♈ 4 |
| ● Mito '13 | ♈♈ 6 |
| ● Romagna Sangiovese Sup. V. del Molino Maestri di Vigna '16 | ♈♈ 2* |
| ● Romagna Sangiovese Sup. V. del Molino Maestri di Vigna '15 | ♈♈ 2* |
| ● Romagna Sangiovese Sup. V. delle Lepri Ris. '13 | ♈♈ 3 |

# Pertinello

VIA ARPINETO PERTINELLO, 2
47010 GALEATA [FC]
TEL. +39 0543983156
www.tenutapertinello.it

CELLAR SALES
PRE-BOOKED VISITS
ANNUAL PRODUCTION 70,000 bottles
HECTARES UNDER VINE 14.00
VITICULTURE METHOD Certified Organic

The estate is situated on the hills of the Bidente Valley, a choice and historic territory for regional wine production. Despite the area's heritage, it took the Mancini family's winery (founded in 2006) to give new life its enological tradition. Their artisanal, quality selection was based on reviving old vineyards of Sangiovese, which were needed for the new vine stocks. After finding their feet, the grapes from the various plots have all been separately harvested, vinified, aged and bottled. Of many wines tasted, the 2017 Il Bosco di Pertinello made an excellent impression. This young wine aged exclusively in steel, stands out from the rest of the vintage. It features a dark color, rich fruit and a balanced palate, slightly penalized by mouth-drying tannins. The 2016 Modigliana Gemme exhibits elegant tertiary notes ranging from leather to tobacco, while the Pinot Nero from the same vintage comes through juicy.

# Poderi dal Nespoli 1929

LOC. NESPOLI
VILLA ROSSI, 50
47012 CIVITELLA DI ROMAGNA [FC]
TEL. +39 0543989911
www.poderidalnespoli.com

CELLAR SALES
PRE-BOOKED VISITS
ACCOMMODATION
ANNUAL PRODUCTION 1,000,000 bottles
HECTARES UNDER VINE 180.00
SUSTAINABLE WINERY

This lovely winery is situated in the Bidente valley, on the Forlì hills at about 180 meters above sea level. It's a splendid area, where the Apennines of Romagna and Tuscany feel the sea breeze, a climate that's perfect for the cultivation of grapes and wine production. Poderi dal Nespoli was a dream come true for the Ravaioli family, which formed a partnership with Mondodelvino in 2009. Naturally, it was a turning point that's seen the start of new projects and a consolidation of their production facility. Their wines prove rich and impressive, especially those aged in wood. This is why we preferred the 2017 Prugneto, maybe simpler than others but more supple, balanced with lovely drive and flavor. The 2015 Superiore Riserva proves rather dark, it may need time to find more graceful wood. The future looks good.

| | |
|---|---|
| ● Romagna Sangiovese Il Bosco di Pertinello '17 | ▼▼ 2* |
| ● Pinot Nero '16 | ▼▼ 4 |
| ● Romagna Sangiovese Modigliana Gemme '16 | ▼▼ 3 |
| ○ Extra Brut M. Cl. | ▼ 5 |
| ● Colli Romagna Centrale Sangiovese Il Bosco '14 | ♀♀ 2* |
| ● Colli Romagna Centrale Sangiovese Il Sasso Ris. '11 | ♀♀ 5 |
| ● Colli Romagna Centrale Sangiovese Il Sasso Ris. '10 | ♀♀ 5 |
| ● Colli Romagna Centrale Sangiovese Pertinello '13 | ♀♀ 3* |
| ● Colli Romagna Centrale Sangiovese Pertinello '12 | ♀♀ 3 |
| ● Pinot Nero '15 | ♀♀ 4 |

| | |
|---|---|
| ● Romagna Sangiovese Sup. Il Nespoli Ris. '15 | ▼▼ 4 |
| ● Romagna Sangiovese Sup. Prugneto '17 | ▼▼ 3 |
| ● Borgo dei Guidi '16 | ▼ 5 |
| ○ Dogheria '17 | ▼ 2 |
| ● Borgo dei Guidi '13 | ♀♀ 5 |
| ● Borgo dei Guidi '12 | ♀♀ 5 |
| ○ Romagna Albana Campodora '15 | ♀♀ 4 |
| ● Romagna Sangiovese Sup. Il Nespoli Ris. '13 | ♀♀ 4 |
| ● Romagna Sangiovese Sup. Il Prugneto '15 | ♀♀ 2* |
| ● Sangiovese di Romagna Sup. Il Nespoli Ris. '12 | ♀♀ 4 |
| ● Sangiovese di Romagna Sup. Il Prugneto '14 | ♀♀ 2* |

## Il Poggiarello

LOC. SCRIVELLANO DI STATTO
29020 TRAVO [PC]
TEL. +39 0523957241
www.ilpoggiarellovini.it

CELLAR SALES
PRE-BOOKED VISITS
ANNUAL PRODUCTION 100,000 bottles
HECTARES UNDER VINE 18.00

Poggiarello is a lovely example of a historic winery that's experienced a revival. Founded in the mid-19th century, it had fallen into a period of total abandonment before being taken over by its current owner in 1980. It's situated in a beautiful area with a panoramic view looking out on Trebbia Valley, the Statto plains and city of Piacenza. Careful renovation and respect for tradition have allowed the winery to reach high levels of quality. They have presented a rather interesting selection of wines, including their 2017 Perticato Beatrice Quadri, a floral Malvasia scented with wild rose and medicinal herbs, taut and mineral in the mouth, with a slight residual sugar to balance it. Their 2017 Gutturnio and Ortrugo Frizzante, sealed with the traditional cord on the cork, are very territorial wines featuring red and yellow fruit aromas respectively. Their 2017 'L Piston deserves a mention: this Barbera exhibiting well-rounded cherries is only bottled in magnums, hence the name (and the Brotherhood dedicated to it).

| | |
|---|---|
| ○ Perticato Beatrice Quadri Malvasia '17 | ♀♀ 3* |
| ● 'l Piston Barbera '17 | ♀♀ 5 |
| ● Gutturnio Frizzante Spago '17 | ♀♀ 2* |
| ○ Colli Piacentini Ortrugo Frizzante Spago '17 | ♀ 2 |
| ● Gutturnio Sup. La Barbona '14 | ♀ 3 |

## Quarticello

VIA MATILDE DI CANOSSA, 1A
42027 MONTECCHIO EMILIA [RE]
TEL. +39 0522866220
www.quarticello.it

CELLAR SALES
PRE-BOOKED VISITS
ANNUAL PRODUCTION 45,000 bottles
HECTARES UNDER VINE 5.00
VITICULTURE METHOD Certified Organic

In the heart of Canossa, in 2001 the Maestri family purchased a vineyard in Quarticello along the bank of the Enza river. In the meantime Roberto Maestri graduated in enology and, in 2006, he began transforming the grapes cultivated on his small estate into wine: Lambrusco Maestri, Grasparossa, Salamino, Malbo Gentile and Malvasia di Candia. Organic vineyard management, careful selection and second fermentation in the bottle are the cornerstones of their approach. Stradora is a passito dried-grape wine made with Malvasia di Candia Aromatica. Long maceration confers an amber color and aromas of dried figs, dates, hazelnuts and candied citrus, while the palate features juicy pulp. Their 2015 Fiordiligi Bruscnature proves a difficult Metodo Classico, made exclusively with Salamino grapes, 24 months on the lees and no filtration. It needs to reveal its nature if it wants to be appreciated for its fruit and dried flowers. Their 2016 Ferrando, a Salamino fermented in the bottle, offers up aromas of wild rose and ripe black berries.

| | |
|---|---|
| ⊙ Fiordiligi Bruscnature Pas Dosé M. Cl. '15 | ♀♀ 4 |
| ○ Stradora Malvasia Passito | ♀♀ 5 |
| ⊙ Ferrando Lambrusco '16 | ♀ 3 |
| ● Neromaestri '17 | ♀ 3 |
| ○ Despina '14 | ♀♀ 2* |
| ○ Despina '13 | ♀♀ 2* |
| ○ Despina '12 | ♀♀ 2* |
| ○ Despina Rifermentato in Bottiglia '15 | ♀♀ 2* |
| ⊙ Ferrando '14 | ♀♀ 2* |
| ⊙ Ferrando '13 | ♀♀ 2* |
| ⊙ Ferrando '11 | ♀♀ 2* |
| ⊙ Ferrando '11 | ♀♀ 2* |
| ⊙ Ferrando Rifermentato in Bottiglia '15 | ♀♀ 2* |
| ○ Stradora '15 | ♀♀ 3 |
| ○ Stradora '13 | ♀♀ 3* |

# Noelia Ricci

Fraz. Fiumana
via Pandolfa, 35
47016 Predappio [FC]
Tel. +39 0543940073
www.noeliaricci.it

CELLAR SALES
PRE-BOOKED VISITS
ACCOMMODATION
ANNUAL PRODUCTION 58,000 bottles
HECTARES UNDER VINE 9.00
SUSTAINABLE WINERY

Noelia Ricci's wines aren't just good and personal, they've also contributed to Romagna's new, contemporary image, starting with Sangiovese, of course. It's all thanks to Marco Cirese and his staff, who've managed to build a project associated with a specific part of the family's estate (Tenuta Pandolfa, which has it's own profile in the guide). The entire range is characterized by an unmistakable style, constituted of lightness, extreme drinkability and flavor. It's an interpretation that could be called 'faux-simple', but whose worth is clear to the most attentive tasters. Their 2016 Godenza, a first-rate Sangiovese with a modern and charming style, manages to enhance flavor rather than texture. It is one of their best and most complete vintages yet, with perfect aromas and great balance of all the components. Delectable. Their 2017 Sangiovese comes through simpler but lip-smacking and elegant.

| | |
|---|---|
| ● Romagna Sangiovese Predappio Godenza '16 | ♟♟♟ 4* |
| ● Romagna Sangiovese Predappio '17 | ♟♟ 2* |
| ○ Brò '17 | ♟ 3 |
| ● Romagna Sangiovese Sup. Godenza '14 | ♟♟♟ 3* |
| ● Romagna Sangiovese Sup. Il Sangiovese '16 | ♟♟♟ 3* |
| ● Romagna Sangiovese Sup. Il Sangiovese '14 | ♟♟♟ 2* |
| ○ Bro '15 | ♟♟ 3 |
| ○ Brò '14 | ♟♟ 3 |
| ● Romagna Sangiovese Sup. Godenza '15 | ♟♟ 4 |
| ● Romagna Sangiovese Sup. Il Sangiovese '15 | ♟♟ 2* |

# Cantine Riunite & Civ

via G. Brodolini, 24
42040 Campegine [RE]
Tel. +39 0522905711
www.riuniteciv.com

CELLAR SALES
ANNUAL PRODUCTION 130,000,000 bottles
HECTARES UNDER VINE 3500.00

2500 grower members, 3500 hectares of vineyards and partnerships with 16 wineries: these are the numbers that define Italy's largest group in terms of revenue and bottles produced. It's a veritable giant that doesn't squeeze smaller producers, and not just because of its various market positions. Indeed, in recent years Cantine Riunite & Civ have managed to select the best grapes available and thus give rise to wines of excellent quality, from Lambrusco to Pignoletto, not to mention their stills. Some of their selection avails itself of organic viticulture. The 2017 Albinea Canali, a sparkling Pignoletto, exhibits nice backbone, hints of tropical fruit, white peach and herbs, with a supple and lively palate. Their 2017 Fojonico is a sweet, succulent and easy-drinking Grasparossa featuring intact fruit. Their 2015 Cabernet Albinea Canali comes through well-crafted, very varietal and fruity with good supporting acidity. Their Righi Rosato sparkling wine is ready to uncork, while their demi-sec wines prove interesting, especially the Righi Biologico, packed with dark wild berries.

| | |
|---|---|
| ● Colli di Scandiano e di Canossa Cabernet Sauvignon Monteleone Albinea Canali '15 | ♟♟ 2* |
| ● Lambrusco Grasparossa di Castelvetro Amabile Il Fojonco '17 | ♟♟ 2* |
| ⊙ Modena Lambrusco Extra Dry Rosé Righi | ♟♟ 1* |
| ● Modena Lambrusco Semisecco Righi '17 | ♟♟ 1* |
| ○ Pignoletto Extra Dry Stellato Albinea Canali '17 | ♟♟ 2* |
| ● Lambrusco di Sorbara Semisecco '17 | ♟ 2 |
| ● Lambrusco di Sorbara Gaetano Righi '16 | ♟♟ 2* |
| ● Lambrusco di Sorbara Semisecco '16 | ♟♟ 1* |
| ● Lambrusco Grasparossa di Castelvetro Secco Gaetano Righi '16 | ♟♟ 1* |
| ● Lambrusco Salamino di Santa Croce Secco '16 | ♟♟ 1* |

# EMILIA ROMAGNA

## Le Rocche Malatestiane

VIA EMILIA, 104
47900 RIMINI
TEL. +39 0541743079
www.lerocchemalatestiane.it

**CELLAR SALES**
**PRE-BOOKED VISITS**
**ANNUAL PRODUCTION** 700,000 bottles
**HECTARES UNDER VINE** 800.00

The winery is situated in Rimini but avails itself of grapes supplied by 500 different vine growers who cover a total of 800 hectares across High Marecchia Valley and Cattolica, not far from the border between Romagna and Marche. The brand embraces and highlights its relationship with the territory. The Malatesta family, in particular Sigismondo Pandolfo, were great patrons who managed to create works of art and architecture throughout the area, including still-visible fortresses and citadels. Today the results are part of a renovation project that began back in 2011, starting with the prince of the area's cultivar, Sangiovese. Once again, their wines delivered great results in the glass, including one achieving top marks. The Sangiovese Superiore Sigismondo makes a great first impact thanks to an excellently-crafted range of floral and fruity aromas, with hints of fresh plums and ripe cherries. It exhibits a lovely mouthfeel, supported by well-extracted tannins. A touch of leather and spice emerges at the finish.

| | |
|---|---|
| ● Romagna Sangiovese Sup. Sigismondo '17 | ♟♟♟ 2* |
| ● Romagna Sangiovese Sup. I Diavoli '17 | ♟♟ 2* |
| ● Romagna Sangiovese Sup. Tre Miracoli '17 | ♟ 2 |
| ● Romagna Sangiovese Il Mastino Ris. '15 | ♟ 3 |
| ● Romagna Sangiovese Sup. Sigismondo '16 | ♟♟♟ 2* |
| ● Romagna Sangiovese Sup. I Diavoli '14 | ♟♟ 2* |
| ● Romagna Sangiovese Sup. I Diavoli '13 | ♟♟ 2* |
| ● Romagna Sangiovese Sup. Tre Miracoli '15 | ♟♟ 2* |
| ● Colli di Rimini Sangiovese Mons Iovis '15 | ♟♟ 3 |
| ● Romagna Sangiovese Sup. I Diavoli '15 | ♟♟ 2* |
| ● Romagna Sangiovese Sup. Sigismondo '15 | ♟♟ 2* |

## Cantine Romagnoli

LOC. VILLÒ
VIA GENOVA, 20
29020 VIGOLZONE [PC]
TEL. +39 0523870904
www.cantineromagnoli.it

**CELLAR SALES**
**PRE-BOOKED VISITS**
**ANNUAL PRODUCTION** 300,000 bottles
**HECTARES UNDER VINE** 45.00
**SUSTAINABLE WINERY**

This lovely winery (established in 1857 and named after the Romagnoli family, who became its owners in 1926) was founded as a self-sufficient agricultural business, producing livestock, produce, poultry, silos and, naturally, grapes. Over time their other activities were gradually abandoned (though traces can be seen in their renovated cellar). As of 1978, with the addition of winemaker Franco Restani, they've dedicated themselves exclusively to wine and were the first in Piacenza to produce Metodo Classico sparklers. We appreciated their 2016 Colto Vitato della Filanda: this blend of partly late-harvest Malvasia and Ortrugo grapes displays generous and varied aromas, from peach and lemon to more organic and vegetal overtones. The palate comes through full, flavorsome and well-orchestrated. Their 2017 Gutturnio della Bellaria is true to type and fruity, with the right amount of tannins. Of the two Metodo Classico wines, the 2015 Brut impressed us with its depth in the mouth, while the Dosaggio Zero proves sharpish and linear.

| | |
|---|---|
| ○ Colto Vitato della Filanda n. 3 '16 | ♟♟ 3* |
| ○ Cuvée Il Pigro Brut M. Cl. Cuvée Il Pigro '15 | ♟♟ 4 |
| ● Gutturnio Sup. Colto Vitato della Bellaria n. 15 '17 | ♟♟ 2* |
| ● Caravaggio '16 | ♟ 5 |
| ● Colto Vitato del Cicotto Barbera n. 21 '17 | ♟ 2 |
| ○ Il Pigro M. Cl. '14 | ♟ 4 |
| ● C. P. Gutturnio Sup. Colto Vitato della Bellaria '16 | ♟♟ 2* |
| ● Caravaggio '12 | ♟♟ 5 |
| ● Colto Vitato del Cicotto '16 | ♟♟ 2* |
| ● Colto Vitato del Cicotto '15 | ♟♟ 2* |
| ● Colto Vitato del Cicotto '14 | ♟♟ 2* |
| ● Gutturnio Sup. Colto Vitato della Bellaria '15 | ♟♟ 2* |
| ○ Sasso Nero del Nure Bianco '14 | ♟♟ 2* |

# I Sabbioni

VIA BOLOGNA, 286
47122 FORLÌ
TEL. +39 0543755711
www.isabbioni.it

**CELLAR SALES**
**ANNUAL PRODUCTION** 70,000 bottles
**HECTARES UNDER VINE** 18.00

Sabbioni is situated between the provinces of Forlì and Faenza. Their vineyards are cultivated along hills at mid-range altitudes, on terrain characterized by red clay and yellow sand ('molasses', as it's known in the area). It's easy to understand, therefore, how the area got it's name, which the winery adopted as well ('Sabbioni', from the Italian word for sand). Great attention is paid to Sangiovese, which serves as the basis for a number of wines and is used throughout their selection. The results confirm that when cultivated in the area of Oriolo tower, the grape gives rise to elegant, flavorful wines that are a pleasure to drink. Their 2017 Oriolo proves to be one of the best examples of a wine combining complexity and drinkability. This is anything but a simple wine, in fact it's the quintessence of purity, flavor and faultless interpretation of the territory. The nose comes through clean, elegantly floral and fruity, with a sprinkling of spice. Don't be fooled by the palate's apparent docility, in reality it's dynamic, forthright and spacious.

| | |
|---|---|
| ● Romagna Sangiovese Sup. Oriolo '17 | 🍷🍷 5 |
| ● Romagna Sangiovese Sup. I Voli dei Gruccioni '17 | 🍷🍷 3 |
| ● Romagna Sangiovese I Rifugi Ris. '16 | 🍷 5 |
| ● Romagna Sangiovese Sup. Le Liti '17 | 🍷 4 |
| ● Romagna Sangiovese Sup. Oriolo '16 | 🍷🍷🍷 5 |
| ● Romagna Sangiovese Rubrarosa Oriolo Sisto '14 | 🍷🍷 2* |
| ● Romagna Sangiovese Sup. I Rifugi Ris. '14 | 🍷🍷 5 |
| ● Romagna Sangiovese Sup. I Voli dei Gruccioni '16 | 🍷🍷 3 |
| ● Romagna Sangiovese Sup. Rubrarosa Bonadea '15 | 🍷🍷 2* |
| ● Romagna Sangiovese Sup. Rubrarosa Bonadea '14 | 🍷🍷 2* |
| ● Romagna Sangiovese Sup. Rubrarosa Elaide Ris. '13 | 🍷🍷 4 |

# ★San Patrignano

VIA SAN PATRIGNANO, 53
47853 CORIANO [RN]
TEL. +39 0541362111
www.spaziosanpa.com

**PRE-BOOKED VISITS**
**RESTAURANT SERVICE**
**ANNUAL PRODUCTION** 500,000 bottles
**HECTARES UNDER VINE** 110.00
**VITICULTURE METHOD** Certified Organic

San Patrignano is among the most recognized and established wine brands in Romagna. Situated on the Colli di Rimini hills, it gets its name from the support community founded by Vincenzo Muccioli in 1978, and still active today, the reason why we've chosen it for our 'Solidarity Award'. A sizable estate is cultivated with extreme care, with Bordeaux varieties finding the perfect climate and Sangiovese whose acidity is less sharp, thus highlighting the grape's softer, more caressing attributes. Their winemaking approach gives rise to modern, impeccably-crafted wines that are difficult to mistake. Once again the Montepirolo came out on top at our tastings. The 2015 vintage gives us a Cabernet Sauvignon rich in toasty notes and dark spices, with hints of mint embracing ripe and intense fruit. The extractive palate features full-bodied and close-knit tannins which need further maturation in bottle. The '1978' Cabernet Franc from the 2017 vintage comes through pleasant and succulent, with nice pulp.

| | |
|---|---|
| ● Colli di Rimini Cabernet Sauvignon Montepirolo '15 | 🍷🍷🍷 4* |
| ● 1978 Cabernet Franc '17 | 🍷🍷 3 |
| ○ Aulente Bianco '17 | 🍷🍷 2* |
| ● Romagna Sangiovese Sup. Avi Ris. '15 | 🍷🍷 4 |
| ○ Avenir | 🍷 4 |
| ○ Vie '17 | 🍷 3 |
| ● Colli di Rimini Cabernet Sauvignon Montepirolo '13 | 🍷🍷🍷 4* |
| ● Colli di Rimini Cabernet Sauvignon Montepirolo '12 | 🍷🍷🍷 4* |
| ● Romagna Sangiovese Sup. Avi Ris. '11 | 🍷🍷🍷 5 |
| ○ Aulente Bianco '16 | 🍷🍷 2* |
| ○ Aulente Bianco '15 | 🍷🍷 2* |
| ● Noi '15 | 🍷🍷 3 |
| ● Romagna Sangiovese Sup. Ora '14 | 🍷🍷 3 |
| ● Romagna Sangiovese Sup. Ris. Avi '12 | 🍷🍷 4 |

## Tenuta Santini

FRAZ. PASSANO
VIA CAMPO, 33
47853 CORIANO [RN]
TEL. +39 0541656527
www.tenutasantini.com

**CELLAR SALES**
**PRE-BOOKED VISITS**
**ANNUAL PRODUCTION** 40,000 bottles
**HECTARES UNDER VINE** 22.00

Tenuta Santini was founded in the 1960s by brothers Giuseppe and Primo. It's situated on the sunny hills of Coriano, with its back to Rimini and Riccione, between San Marino and the Marecchia valley. The area is characterized by calcareous-clay soil and a rather mild climate, conditions that have favored the cultivation of Bordeaux varieties. But that doesn't mean that attention isn't shown to Romagna's cultivar par excellence, Sangiovese, for which they reserve the best plots. Indeed, Santini were among the first to believe in the area's potential for growing the grape. The 2015 Sangiovese Superiore Riserva Cornelianum is precise, well-made, polished, succulent and, in our opinion, the best wine in the selection presented this year. Aromas of red flowers, wild berries and black cherries lead into a palate with a weighty texture and excellent mouthfeel. A lack of verve just stops it achieving absolute excellence. Their Orione from the same vintage proves pleasant, while the 2016 Battarreo (a blend of Sangiovese, Cabernet and Merlot) is rather rugged.

| | |
|---|---|
| ● Romagna Sangiovese Sup. Cornelianum Ris. '15 | ♟♟ 4 |
| ● Romagna Sangiovese Sup. Orione '15 | ♟♟ 4 |
| ● Colli di Rimini Battarreo '16 | ♟ 3 |
| ● Battarreo '15 | ♟♟ 3 |
| ● Battarreo '14 | ♟♟ 3* |
| ● Romagna Sangiovese Sup. Beato Enrico '16 | ♟♟ 2* |
| ● Romagna Sangiovese Sup. Beato Enrico '15 | ♟♟ 2* |
| ● Romagna Sangiovese Sup. Cornelianum Ris. '13 | ♟♟ 4 |

## Terre Cevico

VIA FIUMAZZO, 72
48022 LUGO [RA]
TEL. +39 0545284711
www.gruppocevico.com

**CELLAR SALES**
**PRE-BOOKED VISITS**
**ANNUAL PRODUCTION** 50,000,000 bottles
**HECTARES UNDER VINE** 7000.00

Cevico is a true juggernaut, both in terms of economics and social importance. The terrain covered spans the whole of Romagna, with almost 4500 vine growers cultivating 7000 hectares of vineyards. Their most well-known and yet characteristic wines are those offered in the Terre Cevico, Vigneti Galassi, Sancrispino, Ronco, Romandiola and Bernardi lines. They may be more specific in terms of identity but they contribute to promoting the overall brand, with a style that in many cases hits the mark, proving perfectly calibrated to their consumers. Their 2017 Sangiovese Vigneti Galassi delivers once again. This dense and scented red proves intense and mature but also quite fresh, with a pleasant aftertaste and very lingering finish. Their 2017 Sangiovese Superiore Terre Cevico comes through pleasant but a bit evanescent, as does the Albana Secco from the same selection.

| | |
|---|---|
| ● Romagna Sangiovese Sup. Vign. Galassi '17 | ♟♟ 2* |
| ○ Romagna Albana Secco Terre Cevico '17 | ♟ 3 |
| ● Romagna Sangiovese B.io '16 | ♟ 2 |
| ● Romagna Sangiovese Sup. Terre Cevico '17 | ♟ 2 |
| ○ Albana di Romagna Secco Romandiola '15 | ♟♟ 3 |
| ○ Colli di Imola Pignoletto Frizzante Romandiola '15 | ♟♟ 2* |
| ● Romagna Sangiovese Sup. Romandiola Novilunio '14 | ♟♟ 2* |
| ● Romagna Sangiovese Sup. Vign. Galassi '16 | ♟♟ 2* |
| ● Romagna Sangiovese Sup. Vign. Galassi '15 | ♟♟ 2* |
| ● Romagna Sangiovese Sup. Vign. Galassi '14 | ♟♟ 2* |

# Torre San Martino

VIA SAN MARTINO IN MONTE
47015 MODIGLIANA [FC]
TEL. +39 0546940102
www.torre1922.it

CELLAR SALES
PRE-BOOKED VISITS
ANNUAL PRODUCTION 45,000 bottles
HECTARES UNDER VINE 10.00

Torre San Martino's historical value is pointed up by their patrimony of old vineyards still cultivated today (some of which go back to the 1920s). Even the area where they're situated is impressive for the fact that it's one of Romagna's most notable territories for fine, ageworthy wines. Modigliana, especially the Acerreta valley (one of the three that rises towards the Apennines) is characterized by the presence of clay, which guarantees the right mix of texture and elegance. Their 2015 Sangiovese Modigliana 'Vigna 1922' shines (it's named after the year the vineyard was planted). This red exhibits rare purity, proving focused, forthright and subtly embellished with elegant fruity and spicy sensations. It put in an excellent performance during our finals.

# La Tosa

LOC. LA TOSA
29020 VIGOLZONE [PC]
TEL. +39 0523870727
www.latosa.it

CELLAR SALES
PRE-BOOKED VISITS
RESTAURANT SERVICE
ANNUAL PRODUCTION 110,000 bottles
HECTARES UNDER VINE 19.00

Brothers Stefano and Ferruccio Pizzamiglio were born in Milan but adopted by Piacenza through their mother, who's from Vigolzone. They first became acquainted with the hills of the Nure Valley through holidays, but a passion for wine took over and, after abandoning medicine, the two purchased terrain in 1980, with Stefano later enrolling in the agriculture program at the University of Piacenza. In 1985 the first 1000 bottles of Gutturnio were produced. The 2017 Malvasia Secca Sorriso di Cielo proves scented and varietal: lemon, wild flowers and acacia honey give way to a generous, juicy and linear palate thanks to pleasant acidity. Their 2016 Vignamorello Gutturnio Superiore struggles to open up, but goes on to reveal intense black wild berries and an uncommonly deep palate. Their young and scented 2017 TerredellaTosa Gutturnio proves more fruity and approachable, while the varietal and well-mannered 2017 Sauvignon Blanc displays marked aromas of passion fruit.

| | |
|---|---|
| ● Romagna Sangiovese Modigliana V. 1922 '15 | 🍷🍷 5 |
| ● Romagna Sangiovese Modigliana Gemme '16 | 🍷🍷 3 |
| ● Romagna Sangiovese Modigliana Sup. V. 1922 Ris. '13 | 🍷🍷🍷 6 |
| ● Romagna Sangiovese Sup. Gemme '14 | 🍷🍷🍷 3* |
| ● Sangiovese di Romagna V. 1922 Ris. '11 | 🍷🍷🍷 6 |
| ● Colli di Faenza V. Claudia Ris. '13 | 🍷🍷 3 |
| ● Colli di Faenza V. Claudia Ris. '12 | 🍷🍷 3 |
| ● Romagna Sangiovese Sup. V. 1922 Ris. '12 | 🍷🍷 6 |
| ● Romagna Sangiovese Modigliana Sup. Gemme '15 | 🍷🍷 3* |
| ● Romagna Sangiovese Sup. V. 1922 Ris. '14 | 🍷🍷 5 |

| | |
|---|---|
| ○ C. P. Malvasia Sorriso di Cielo '17 | 🍷🍷 3 |
| ● Gutturnio Sup. Vignamorello '16 | 🍷🍷 4 |
| ○ C. P. Sauvignon '17 | 🍷 3 |
| ● Gutturnio Sup. TerredellaTosa '17 | 🍷 2 |
| ● C. P. Cabernet Sauvignon Luna Selvatica '06 | 🍷🍷🍷 5 |
| ● C. P. Cabernet Sauvignon Luna Selvatica '04 | 🍷🍷🍷 5 |
| ● C. P. Cabernet Sauvignon Luna Selvatica '97 | 🍷🍷🍷 5 |
| ● C. P. Gutturnio Sup. TerredellaTosa '16 | 🍷🍷 2* |
| ● C. P. Gutturnio Sup. TerredellaTosa '12 | 🍷🍷 2* |
| ● C. P. Gutturnio Sup. Vignamorello '15 | 🍷🍷 4 |
| ● C. P. Gutturnio Sup. Vignamorello '11 | 🍷🍷 4 |
| ○ C. P. Malvasia Passito L'Ora Felice '11 | 🍷🍷 5 |
| ○ C. P. Malvasia Sorriso di Cielo '12 | 🍷🍷 3 |
| ○ C. P. Valnure Riodeltordo '16 | 🍷🍷 2* |

## Tre Monti

LOC. BERGULLO
VIA LOLA, 3
40026 IMOLA [BO]
TEL. +39 0542657116
www.tremonti.it

**CELLAR SALES**
**PRE-BOOKED VISITS**
**ANNUAL PRODUCTION** 180,000 bottles
**HECTARES UNDER VINE** 40.00
**VITICULTURE METHOD** Certified Organic

Tre Monti's beginnings go back to the 1970s when Thea and Sergio Navacchia founded the winery, later inherited and upgraded by their sons David and Vittorio, in 1989. Their path forward has been significant, with wines that have stood out at regional, national and international levels. Today they avail themselves of two estates, one on the hills of Imola (Bergullo), and one on the hills of Forlì (Petrignone). A range of wines are offered, and with a selection this varied it's usually easy to find what you're looking for. Their 2015 Sangiovese Superiore Thea turned out quite well and features a dense framework of aromas. The palate comes through solid, clean and long, while the fruity and spicy notes that emerge over time prove just a bit too sweet. Their excellent 2017 Albana Secco Vigna Rocca displays the unmistakable grape skins, with an intriguing background of crusty bread and light tannins on the palate.

| | | |
|---|---|---|
| ● Romagna Sangiovese Sup. Thea Ris. '15 | ♀♀ 4 |
| ○ Romagna Albana V. Rocca '17 | ♀♀ 2* |
| ● Romagna Sangiovese Sup. Campo di Mezzo '17 | ♀♀ 2* |
| ○ Thea Bianco '16 | ♀♀ 4 |
| ○ Pignoletto Frizzante Doppio | ♀ 3 |
| ○ Romagna Albana Secco Vitalba '16 | ♀ 4 |
| ● Romagna Sangiovese Sup. Petrignone Ris. '15 | ♀ 3 |
| ● Sangiovese di Romagna Sup. Petrignone Ris. '08 | ♀♀♀ 3* |
| ● Sangiovese di Romagna Sup. Petrignone Ris. '07 | ♀♀♀ 4 |
| ● Romagna Sangiovese Sup. Campo di Mezzo '16 | ♀♀ 2* |
| ● Romagna Sangiovese Sup. Sono '16 | ♀♀ 2* |

## Trerè

LOC. MONTICORALLI
VIA CASALE, 19
48018 FAENZA [RA]
TEL. +39 054647034
www.trere.com

**CELLAR SALES**
**PRE-BOOKED VISITS**
**ACCOMMODATION AND RESTAURANT SERVICE**
**ANNUAL PRODUCTION** 150,000 bottles
**HECTARES UNDER VINE** 30.00

Situated on the hills of Faenza, this winery was founded in the 1960s by Valeriano Trerè when he purchased his first 14 hectares in Podere Saccona. In the late 1970s his daughter came on board full-time, and later his grandson as well. Together they've created a broad and varied selection (thanks in part to the purchase of Podere Ca' Lunga and three more hectares at Podere Saccona) that centers on premium wines. They've got their eyes on tradition so as to best face the future. Elegant, salty, fresh and mineral, with very clean and close-focused aromas, the 2017 Albana Secco Arlus is an excellently-crafted and balanced white. The best of the reds proved to be the 2015 Sangiovese Superiore Riserva Amarcord d'un Ross, which manages to offer up a multi-faceted and sensual nose, backed by hints of rain-soaked earth and dried leaves. However, it is slightly restrained by dusty tannins and lacking precision. Delectable black fruit emerges in the 2017 Sangiovese Lona Bona.

| | | |
|---|---|---|
| ○ Romagna Albana Secco Arlùs '17 | ♀♀ 2* |
| ○ Albana di Romagna Passito Mrosa '15 | ♀♀ 4 |
| ● Romagna Sangiovese Lôna Bôna '17 | ♀♀ 2* |
| ● Romagna Sangiovese Sup. Amarcord d'un Ross Ris. '15 | ♀♀ 3 |
| ○ Colli di Faenza Bianco Rebianco '17 | ♀ 2 |
| ○ Refamoso '17 | ♀ 2 |
| ○ Colli di Faenza Rebianco '13 | ♀♀ 2* |
| ● Colli di Faenza Rosso Montecorallo Ris. '12 | ♀♀ 3 |
| ● Sangiovese di Romagna Sup. Sperone '15 | ♀♀ 2* |
| ● Sangiovese di Romagna Sup. Sperone '13 | ♀♀ 2* |

# Marta Valpiani

LOC. CASTROCARO TERME
VIA BAGNOLO, 158
47011 CASTROCARO TERME E TERRA DEL SOLE
TEL. +39 0543769598
www.vinimartavalpiani.it

**CELLAR SALES**
**PRE-BOOKED VISITS**
**ANNUAL PRODUCTION** 19,000 bottles
**HECTARES UNDER VINE** 11.50

It may not necessarily be breaking news, but we can still identify Marta Valpiani as one of Romagna's great revelations in terms of wine producers, thanks to their achievements in recent years. This family-run winery was founded in 1999 in Castrocaro Terme by Marta, who's helped today by her daughter Elisa Mazzavillani. Quality comes before production volumes, with a style and expressive purity that's allowed them to keep getting better with each vintage. Their efforts are focused on traditional grape varieties like Albana and especially Sangiovese. No Crete Azzurre. The new vintage of the wine we awarded last year requires further bottle maturation, so we will have to wait to taste it. But we can console ourselves with an excellent 2016 Sangiovese Superiore exhibiting a bright ruby color, aromas of pomegranate and rain-soaked earth, and a succulent and linear palate. And it doesn't stop there: their 2016 La Farfalla and 2017 Bianco astonished us with their flavor and drinkability.

| | |
|---|---|
| ● LaFarfalla '16 | ♟♟ 2* |
| ○ Marta Valpiani Bianco '17 | ♟♟ 3 |
| ● Romagna Sangiovese Sup. '16 | ♟♟ 2* |
| ● Romagna Sangiovese Castrocaro e Terra del Sole Crete Azzurre '15 | ♟♟♟ 3* |
| ● Castrum Castrocari Et. Bianca '11 | ♟♟ 2* |
| ● Marta Valpiani '12 | ♟♟ 2* |
| ● Romagna Sangiovese Sup. '15 | ♟♟ 2* |
| ● Romagna Sangiovese Sup. '14 | ♟♟ 2* |

# Venturini Baldini

FRAZ. RONCOLO
VIA TURATI, 42
42020 QUATTRO CASTELLA [RE]
TEL. +39 0522249011
www.venturinibaldini.it

**CELLAR SALES**
**PRE-BOOKED VISITS**
**RESTAURANT SERVICE**
**ANNUAL PRODUCTION** 90,000 bottles
**HECTARES UNDER VINE** 35.00
**VITICULTURE METHOD** Certified Organic
**SUSTAINABLE WINERY**

The Venturini Baldini brand was founded in 1975, but the building that houses their facility goes back well before that - in fact, it was built in 1670. For some time now the estate has been in the hands of Iverna Holdings, a Luxembourg fund that decided to invest in Italian wines, starting with Lambrusco and the potential it represents. Its 150 hectares include woods, grasslands and, of course, vineyards. 35 hectares of are cultivated organically in Roncolo, in the territory of Quattro Castella, and give rise to Emilia's native grape varieties. Cadelvento is a blend of Sorbara and Grasparossa made into a pale-colored rosé. Its aromas of flowers, herbs and red berries make for a graceful, elegant, very fine and sharpish wine. Their 2017 Marchese Manodori proves more rustic, with its earthy notes of undergrowth. The Rubino del Cerro comes through as a vigorous, crisp and dry red sparkling wine.

| | |
|---|---|
| ⊙ Reggiano Lambrusco Brut Cadelvento Rosé '17 | ♟♟♟ 3* |
| ● Reggiano Lambrusco Marchese Manodori '17 | ♟♟ 3* |
| ● Reggiano Lambrusco Brut Rubino del Cerro '17 | ♟♟ 3 |
| ● Reggiano Manodori '16 | ♟♟♟ 3* |
| ○ Colli di Scandiano e di Canossa Malvasia Frizzante Secco Graniers '15 | ♟♟ 2* |
| ● Reggiano Lambrusco Marchese Manodori '15 | ♟♟ 3* |
| ⊙ Reggiano Lambrusco Rosato Spumante Secco Cadelvento '15 | ♟♟ 3 |
| ● Reggiano Lambrusco Secco Spumante Rubino del Cerro '15 | ♟♟ 3 |

## Francesco Vezzelli

FRAZ. SAN MATTEO
VIA CANALETTO NORD, 878A
41122 MODENA
TEL. +39 059318695
aavezzelli@gmail.com

CELLAR SALES
PRE-BOOKED VISITS
ANNUAL PRODUCTION 120,000 bottles
HECTARES UNDER VINE 15.00

Now on their third generation of family management, Francesco Vezzelli have managed to carve out a name for themselves in the world of Lambrusco di Sorbara. Founded in 1958, the estate is situated along the left bank of the Secchia, in Soliera, on the opposite side of the river with respect to Bomporto and Cristo di Sorbara. The terrain is the same, loose, sandy, fertile soil that allows Sorbara to offer its best in terms of elegance and minerality. The sparkling versions of the grape are proving to be the most intriguing. The Morosa Rosé, a remarkably elegant Sorbara Metodo Classico, displays aromas ranging from small red fruit to hay, with notes of herbs and citrus. The palate comes through plucky, savory and consistent. Their 2017 Selezione exhibits more marked red fruit, especially wild strawberries, with a touch of tangerine and a lovely taut finish. The 2017 Soldino is a demi-sec featuring fruit, undergrowth and vegetal overtones.

| | | |
|---|---|---|
| ● Lambrusco di Sorbara Brut II Selezione '17 | | ♛♛ 2* |
| ☉ Lambrusco di Sorbara Brut MoRosa M. Cl. | | ♛♛ 3 |
| ● Lambrusco di Sorbara Semisecco Soldino '17 | | ♛ 2 |
| ● Lambrusco di Sorbara II Selezione '15 | | ♛♛ 2* |
| ● Lambrusco di Sorbara II Selezione '14 | | ♛♛ 2* |
| ● Lambrusco di Sorbara Rifermentazione Ancestrale '14 | | ♛♛ 2* |
| ☉ Lambrusco di Sorbara Rosé MoRosa '14 | | ♛♛ 2* |
| ● Lambrusco di Sorbara Secco Soldino '15 | | ♛♛ 2* |
| ● Lambrusco di Sorbara Soldino '16 | | ♛♛ 2* |
| ☉ Lambrusco di Sorbara Spumante Brut MoRosa Rosé '15 | | ♛♛ 2* |
| ● Lambrusco Grasparossa di Castelvetro Rive dei Ciliegi '14 | | ♛♛ 2* |

## Villa di Corlo

LOC. BAGGIOVARA
S.DA CAVEZZO, 200
41126 MODENA
TEL. +39 059510736
www.villadicorlo.com

CELLAR SALES
PRE-BOOKED VISITS
ANNUAL PRODUCTION 85,000 bottles
HECTARES UNDER VINE 26.50

Maria Antonietta Munari manages this lovely winery in the southwest of Modena, in an area where primarily Lambrusco Grasparossa di Castelverto is cultivated. In the hills, at 320 meters above sea level and southern exposure, international grapes like Cabernet Sauvignon, Merlot and Chardonnay are grown. This last serves as the basis for their Metodo Classico sparkling wine. Their villa's loft houses their vinegar making facility, which gives rise to two versions of their Aceto Balsamico Tradizionale. As of 2012 the entire production center has been powered by solar panels. Elettra Rosé is a particularly tangy and citrusy Brut Metodo Classico, with sharp acidity and an energetic and electrifying palate. Their 2017 Grasparossa Corleto stays true to its vintage: lots of ripe fruit and marked abundant tannins, without being bitter. It's more suited to mealtimes than tastings. Their 2017 Grasparossa Amabile offers up balanced tannins with a sweetness deriving from bottled black cherries.

| | | |
|---|---|---|
| ☉ Lambrusco di Sorbara Brut Elettra Rosé | | ♛♛ 3* |
| ● Lambrusco Grasparossa di Castelvetro Corleto '17 | | ♛♛ 2* |
| ● Lambrusco Grasparossa di Castelvetro Amabile '17 | | ♛ 2 |
| ○ Fraeli Brut Blanc de Blancs '11 | | ♛♛ 3 |
| ● Lambrusco di Sorbara Primevo '14 | | ♛♛ 2* |
| ● Lambrusco Grasparossa di Castelvetro '16 | | ♛♛ 2* |
| ● Lambrusco Grasparossa di Castelvetro Corleto '16 | | ♛♛ 2* |
| ● Lambrusco Grasparossa di Castelvetro Corleto '15 | | ♛♛ 2* |

# Villa Papiano

VIA IBOLA, 24
47015 MODIGLIANA [FC]
TEL. +39 3381041271
www.villapapiano.it

CELLAR SALES
PRE-BOOKED VISITS
ANNUAL PRODUCTION 50,000 bottles
HECTARES UNDER VINE 10.00
VITICULTURE METHOD Certified Organic
SUSTAINABLE WINERY

With its noteworthy elevation, lean soils and landscapes that feature vineyards and woods, Modigliana is without a doubt one of Romagna's most fashionable terroir at the moment. It's here that we find Villa Papiano, a winery whose roots go back to the 15th century when this productive area was governed by Papiano, home to the Medici family. Its modern history began in 2001, with the renovation of old vineyards and an approach to winemaking that aims for elegant, linear, ageworthy wines that are more flavorful than they are full-bodied. Let's not beat about the bush, the 2015 Sangiovese Modigliana I Probi di Papiano is one of the best wines tasted in Romagna this year, if not the absolute best. Red citrus, fresh ripe cherries, raspberries and very delicate spices on the nose give way to juice, pulp and perfectly-managed tannins in the mouth. Overwhelmingly drinkable. Their 2017 Le Papesse proves delicious and floral, while their Terra! from the same vintage features grape skins and sea salt.

| | |
|---|---|
| ● Romagna Sangiovese Modigliana I Probi di Papiano Ris. '15 | ♀♀♀ 4* |
| ● Romagna Sangiovese Sup. Le Papesse di Papiano '17 | ♀♀ 3 |
| ○ Terra! '17 | ♀♀ 4 |
| ● Romagna Sangiovese I Probi di Papiano Ris. '12 | ♀♀♀ 3* |
| ● Romagna Sangiovese Modigliana I Probi di Papiano Ris. '14 | ♀♀♀ 4* |
| ● Romagna Sangiovese Modigliana I Probi di Papiano Ris. '13 | ♀♀♀ 3* |
| ● Sangiovese di Romagna I Probi di Papiano Ris. '11 | ♀♀♀ 3* |
| ● Sangiovese di Romagna I Probi di Papiano Ris. '10 | ♀♀♀ 3* |
| ● Romagna Sangiovese Sup. Le Papesse di Papiano '16 | ♀♀ 3 |

# Villa Venti

LOC. VILLAVENTI DI RONCOFREDDO
VIA DOCCIA, 1442
47020 FORLÌ
TEL. +39 0541949532
www.villaventi.it

CELLAR SALES
PRE-BOOKED VISITS
ACCOMMODATION
ANNUAL PRODUCTION 27,500 bottles
HECTARES UNDER VINE 7.00
VITICULTURE METHOD Certified Organic

Beyond the Rubicone river, in Roncofreddo and the 'perfect village' of Longiano lies the estate of Villa Venti. Mauro Giardini and Davide Castellucci have been as important to the winery as the area that hosts their vineyards. Tradition and respect for nature, family experience and organic cultivation are the cornerstones of their approach. But our primary interest is their wines, which exhibit authentic flavor and great drinkability as well as expressing the values of their creators and territory. Only native grape varieties are used, such as Sangiovese, Famoso and Centesimino. Their Primo Segno proves much more than just an excellent wine: it's an idea, a style and an intriguing way of making Sangiovese di Romagna. It comes through essential, savory and docile, with joyous red fruit, but salty and linear without seeming lean or punitive. In short, it is delicious, no need to add anything else. Their white wine, Serenano, made with the famous Cesena grape, appears approachable and floral.

| | |
|---|---|
| ● Sangiovese di Romagna Sup. Primo Segno '16 | ♀♀ 3* |
| ○ Serenaro '17 | ♀ 3 |
| ● Sangiovese di Romagna Longiano Primo Segno '11 | ♀♀♀ 3* |
| ● Centesimo A '16 | ♀♀ 4 |
| ● Sangiovese di Romagna Longiano Ris '11 | ♀♀ 4 |
| ● Sangiovese di Romagna Sup. Maggese '10 | ♀♀ 3* |
| ● Sangiovese di Romagna Sup. Primo Segno '15 | ♀♀ 3 |
| ● Sangiovese di Romagna Sup. Primo Segno '13 | ♀♀ 3* |

## ★Fattoria Zerbina

FRAZ. MARZENO
VIA VICCHIO, 11
48018 FAENZA [RA]
TEL. +39 054640022
www.zerbina.com

CELLAR SALES
PRE-BOOKED VISITS
ANNUAL PRODUCTION 220,000 bottles
HECTARES UNDER VINE 33.00

Romagna is experiencing a dynamic period that sees many small wineries renewing the area's stylistic approach. It's an increasingly detailed and diverse picture, though we shouldn't forget those producers who were the first to invest here, shining a light on the territory's innate attributes. Among these we find Cristiana Geminiani's Fattoria Zerbina, an estate situated in Marzeno where the terrain is of the red clay variety and where the vineyards are head-trained. Here Sangiovese and Albana are skillfully transformed in balance, flavorful wines that are faithful to their well-established style. Their 2014 Torre di Ceparano is a thoroughbred Sangiovese: beneath slightly toasty initial sensations we find intense and vibrant fruit, which manages to embellish the complex and evolving ensemble. Their 2015 Pietramora focuses more on flowers and small red fruit, while the 2017 Ceregio Rosso features a spicy, peppery nose and solid palate. Their 2014 Albana Passito AR displays jam on the nose, with a slightly overly-sweet palate.

| | |
|---|---|
| ● Albana di Romagna Passito AR '14 | ♟♟ 4 |
| ● Romagna Sangiovese Marzeno Pietramora '15 | ♟♟ 5 |
| ● Romagna Sangiovese Sup. Ceregio Rosso '17 | ♟♟ 2* |
| ● Romagna Sangiovese Sup. Torre di Ceparano Ris. '14 | ♟♟ 3 |
| ○ Romagna Albana Passito Scacco Matto '13 | ♟♟♟ 6 |
| ● Sangiovese di Romagna Sup. Pietramora Ris. '11 | ♟♟♟ 5 |
| ● Sangiovese di Romagna Sup. Pietramora Ris. '08 | ♟♟♟ 6 |
| ○ Albana di Romagna Passito Arrocco '13 | ♟♟ 5 |
| ○ Albana di Romagna Secco Ceparano '15 | ♟♟ 2* |
| ○ Romagna Albana Passito Arrocco '15 | ♟♟ 5 |
| ● Romagna Sangiovese Sup. Pietramora Ris. '12 | ♟♟ 5 |

## Cantina Zucchi

LOC. SAN LORENZO
VIA VIAZZA, 64
41030 SAN PROSPERO [MO]
TEL. +39 059908934
www.vinizucchi.it

CELLAR SALES
PRE-BOOKED VISITS
ANNUAL PRODUCTION 130,000 bottles
HECTARES UNDER VINE 10.00
SUSTAINABLE WINERY

Cantina Zucchi is situated in San Prospero, one of the best wine-growing districts for Lambrusco di Sorbara. It was Bruno who, in the 1950s, began making wines with grapes cultivated in his private vineyards. He was followed by his son Davide and Davide's wife, Maura. Silvia Zucchi, their daughter and a graduate in enology, represents the third generation. She's managed to keep improving the quality of their wines, interpreting Sorbara in as many ways as possible and bestowing a territorial identity to their wines. The dry, fresh, taut and savory 2017 Sorbara comes through very elegant and floral, with juicy red fruit. It shows great overall balance and pleasant drinkability. Their monovarietal Salamino, the 2017 Marascone, displays a darker color, with cherry and strawberry tart aromas, while the palate comes through dry, complex and supported by backbone and vigor. As its name suggests, the 2016 Fermentato in Questa Bottiglia is a rather rustic ancestral method, featuring aromas of ripe fruit. Their 2017 Brut Rito offers up notes of roses and violets.

| | |
|---|---|
| ● Lambrusco di Sorbara Et. Bianca '17 | ♟♟ 2* |
| ● Modena Lambrusco Marascone '17 | ♟♟ 2* |
| ● Lambrusco di Sorbara Brut Rito '17 | ♟ 3 |
| ● Lambrusco di Sorbara Fermentato in Questa Bottiglia '16 | ♟ 3 |
| ● Lambrusco di Sorbara Rito '14 | ♟♟♟ 2* |
| ● Lambrusco di Sorbara Secco Rito '15 | ♟♟♟ 2* |
| ● Lambrusco di Modena Marascone '16 | ♟♟ 2* |
| ● Lambrusco di Sorbara Dosaggio Zero M. Cl. '13 | ♟♟ 2* |
| ● Lambrusco di Sorbara Rito '16 | ♟♟ 3 |
| ● Lambrusco di Sorbara Secco '15 | ♟♟ 2* |
| ● Lambrusco di Sorbara Secco '14 | ♟♟ 2* |
| ● Lambrusco di Sorbara Secco '13 | ♟♟ 2* |
| ● Lambrusco di Sorbara Secco Rifermentazione in Bottiglia '14 | ♟♟ 2* |

## Agrintesa

VIA G. GALILEI, 15
48018 FAENZA [RA]
TEL. +39 0546941195
www.cantineintesa.it

CELLAR SALES
PRE-BOOKED VISITS
ANNUAL PRODUCTION 350,000 bottles
HECTARES UNDER VINE 44.00

● Romagna Sangiovese
  Poderi delle Rose '17                    ♟♟ 2*
○ Romagna Albana Secco
  Poderi delle Rose '17                    ♟ 2

## Riccardo Ballardini

VIA PIDEURA, 50
48013 BRISIGHELLA [RA]
TEL. +39 0543 700925
www.ballardinivini.it

CELLAR SALES
PRE-BOOKED VISITS
ANNUAL PRODUCTION 100,000 bottles
HECTARES UNDER VINE 30.00

○ Romagna Albana Secco Leggiadro '17    ♟♟ 3
● Romagna Sangiovese Sup.
  V. Le Case '17                          ♟♟ 3

## Braschi

VIA ROMA, 37
47025 MERCATO SARACENO [FC]
TEL. +39 054791061
www.cantinabraschi.com

CELLAR SALES
PRE-BOOKED VISITS
RESTAURANT SERVICE
ANNUAL PRODUCTION 100,000 bottles
HECTARES UNDER VINE 34.50
VITICULTURE METHOD Certified Organic

● Romagna Sangiovese
  San Vicinio Monte Sasso '16             ♟♟ 3
○ Romagna Albana Campo Mamante '16       ♟ 2
● Romagna Sangiovese Il Gelso '15        ♟ 3

## Balìa di Zola

VIA CASALE, 11
47015 MODIGLIANA [FC]
TEL. +39 0546940577
www.baliadizola.com

CELLAR SALES
PRE-BOOKED VISITS
ANNUAL PRODUCTION 30,000 bottles
HECTARES UNDER VINE 5.00

● Romagna Sangiovese Sup. Balitore '17   ♟♟ 2*
● Romagna Sangiovese
  Modigliana Redinoce Ris. '15            ♟ 4

## Conte Otto Barattieri
## di San Pietro

VIA DEI TIGLI, 100
29020 VIGOLZONE [PC]
TEL. +39 0523875111
ottobarattieri@libero.it

CELLAR SALES
PRE-BOOKED VISITS
ANNUAL PRODUCTION 120,000 bottles
HECTARES UNDER VINE 34.00

○ C. P. Vin Santo Albarola '07           ♟♟ 6
● Gutturnio Sup. '16                      ♟♟ 2*
● Gutturnio Frizzant '17                  ♟ 2

## Cantina di Soliera

VIA CARPI RAVARINO, 529
41011 SOLIERA [MO]
TEL. +39 0522942135
www.cantinadisoliera.it

ANNUAL PRODUCTION 20,000 bottles
HECTARES UNDER VINE 5.00
SUSTAINABLE WINERY

● Lambrusco di Sorbara '17                ♟♟ 2*

## Tenuta Carbognano

VIA CARBOGNANO, 3
47855 GEMMANO [RN]
TEL. +39 0541984507
www.tenutacarbognano.com

CELLAR SALES
PRE-BOOKED VISITS
ACCOMMODATION
ANNUAL PRODUCTION 10,000 bottles
HECTARES UNDER VINE 3.00
VITICULTURE METHOD Certified Organic
SUSTAINABLE WINERY

| | |
|---|---|
| ● Romagna Sangiovese Sup. '16 | ♟♟ 3 |

## Tenuta Casali

VIA DELLA LIBERAZIONE, 32
47025 MERCATO SARACENO [FC]
TEL. +39 0547690334
www.tenutacasali.it

PRE-BOOKED VISITS
ANNUAL PRODUCTION 95,000 bottles
HECTARES UNDER VINE 18.00

| | |
|---|---|
| ● Romagna Sangiovese San Vicinio Baruccia '16 | ♟♟ 3 |
| ● Romagna Sangiovese Quartosole Ris. '15 | ♟ 3 |
| ● Romagna Sangiovese Sup. Palazzina '16 | ♟ 2 |

## Castelluccio

LOC. POGGIOLO DI SOTTO
VIA TRAMONTO, 15
47015 MODIGLIANA [FC]
TEL. +39 0546942486
www.ronchidicastelluccio.it

CELLAR SALES
PRE-BOOKED VISITS
ACCOMMODATION
ANNUAL PRODUCTION 85,000 bottles
HECTARES UNDER VINE 16.00

| | |
|---|---|
| ● Romagna Sangiovese Sup. Le More '17 | ♟♟ 3 |
| ● Ronco delle Ginestre '12 | ♟ 5 |

## Cantine Ceci

VIA PROVINCIALE, 99
43030 TORRILE [PR]
TEL. +39 0521810252
www.lambrusco.it

CELLAR SALES
PRE-BOOKED VISITS
ANNUAL PRODUCTION 1,500,000 bottles
HECTARES UNDER VINE 12.00

| | |
|---|---|
| ● Bruno Lambrusco Brut | ♟♟ 4 |
| ● Otello Nero di Lambrusco '17 | ♟♟ 2* |
| ● Terre Verdiane 1813 Lambrusco '17 | ♟ 2 |

## Condé

LOC. FIUMANA DI PREDAPPIO
VIA LUCCHINA, 27
47016 PREDAPPIO [FC]
TEL. +39 0543940860
www.conde.it

CELLAR SALES
PRE-BOOKED VISITS
ACCOMMODATION AND RESTAURANT SERVICE
ANNUAL PRODUCTION 150,000 bottles
HECTARES UNDER VINE 77.00
SUSTAINABLE WINERY

| | |
|---|---|
| ● Romagna Sangiovese Predappio '15 | ♟ 4 |
| ● Romagna Sangiovese Predappio Raggio Brusa Ris. '15 | ♟ 8 |
| ● Romagna Sangiovese Sup. '15 | ♟ 3 |

## Donelli

VIA CARLO SIGONIO, 54
41124 MODENA
TEL. +39 0522908715
www.donellivini.it

CELLAR SALES
PRE-BOOKED VISITS
ACCOMMODATION
ANNUAL PRODUCTION 30,000,000 bottles
HECTARES UNDER VINE 120.00
VITICULTURE METHOD Certified Organic

| | |
|---|---|
| ● Lambrusco di Sorbara Brut Sergio Scaglietti '17 | ♟♟ 2* |
| ● Reggiano Lambrusco Brut Sergio Scaglietti | ♟ 2 |

## La Ferraia - Manara

LOC. VICOMARINO, 140
29010 ZIANO PIACENTINO [PC]
TEL. +39 0523860209
www.robertomanara.it

CELLAR SALES
PRE-BOOKED VISITS
ANNUAL PRODUCTION 150,000 bottles
HECTARES UNDER VINE 40.00

| | |
|---|---|
| ● Boujardò Brut | ♟♟ 3 |
| ● Gutturnio Cl. Sup Le Staffe '17 | ♟♟ 2* |
| ● Gutturnio Frizzante R '17 | ♟ 2 |

## Stefano Ferrucci

VIA CASOLANA, 3045
48014 CASTEL BOLOGNESE [RA]
TEL. +39 0546651068
www.stefanoferrucci.it

CELLAR SALES
PRE-BOOKED VISITS
ANNUAL PRODUCTION 130,000 bottles
HECTARES UNDER VINE 16.00

| | |
|---|---|
| ● Romagna Sangiovese Sup. Centurione '17 | ♟♟ 2* |
| ● Romagna Sangiovese Auriga '17 | ♟ 2 |

## Maria Letizia Gaggioli

VIA F. RAIBOLINI IL FRANCIA, 55
40069 ZOLA PREDOSA [BO]
TEL. +39 051753489
www.gaggiolivini.it

CELLAR SALES
PRE-BOOKED VISITS
ACCOMMODATION AND RESTAURANT SERVICE
ANNUAL PRODUCTION 160,000 bottles
HECTARES UNDER VINE 21.00
SUSTAINABLE WINERY

| | |
|---|---|
| ● C.B. Merlot M '16 | ♟♟ 3 |
| ○ C. B. Pignoletto Il Francia Brut '16 | ♟ 3 |

## Garuti

FRAZ. SORBARA
VIA PER SOLARA, 6
41030 BOMPORTO [MO]
TEL. +39 059902021
www.garutivini.it

ANNUAL PRODUCTION 130,000 bottles
HECTARES UNDER VINE 30.00

| | |
|---|---|
| ● Lambrusco di Sorbara Fermentazione Naturale '17 | ♟♟ 2* |
| ● Lambrusco di Sorbara Podere Ca' Bianca '17 | ♟♟ 2* |

## Gavioli

VIA PROVINCIALE OVEST
41015 NONANTOLA [MO]
TEL. +39 059545462
www.gaviolivini.com

CELLAR SALES
PRE-BOOKED VISITS
ANNUAL PRODUCTION 250,000 bottles
HECTARES UNDER VINE 60.00

| | |
|---|---|
| ● Lambrusco di Sorbara '17 | ♟♟ 2* |
| ● Lambrusco Brut M. Cl. '13 | ♟ 4 |
| ● Modena Lambrusco Rifermentazione Ancestrale '17 | ♟ 3 |

## Gualdora

FRAZ. MONTALBO
LOC. CASE GUALDORA, 196
29010 ZIANO PIACENTINO [PC]
TEL. +39 3923902160
www.gualdora.it

CELLAR SALES
PRE-BOOKED VISITS
ACCOMMODATION
ANNUAL PRODUCTION 12,000 bottles
HECTARES UNDER VINE 3.00
VITICULTURE METHOD Certified Organic
SUSTAINABLE WINERY

| | |
|---|---|
| ● Gutturnio Sup. Otto '16 | ♟♟ 2* |
| ○ C. P. Malvasia Frizzante Blanca '16 | ♟ 2 |
| ○ Dal Tramonto All'Alba Brut '14 | ♟ 3 |

## Tenuta La Viola

VIA COLOMBARONE, 888
47032 BERTINORO [FC]
TEL. +39 0543445496
www.tenutalaviola.it

CELLAR SALES
PRE-BOOKED VISITS
ANNUAL PRODUCTION 44,000 bottles
HECTARES UNDER VINE 11.00
VITICULTURE METHOD Certified Organic
SUSTAINABLE WINERY

| | |
|---|---|
| ● Romagna Sangiovese Bertinoro P. Honorii Ris. '14 | 🍷🍷 4 |
| ● Romagna Sangiovese Sup. Il Colombarone '16 | 🍷🍷 3 |

## Lini 910

FRAZ. CANOLO
VIA VECCHIA CANOLO, 7
42015 CORREGGIO [RE]
TEL. +39 0522690162
www.lini910.it

CELLAR SALES
PRE-BOOKED VISITS
ANNUAL PRODUCTION 400,000 bottles
HECTARES UNDER VINE 25.00

| | |
|---|---|
| ○ In Correggio Brut M. Cl. '14 | 🍷🍷 4 |
| ○ In Correggio Pas Dosé M. Cl | 🍷🍷 4 |

## Lusenti

LOC. CASA PICCIONI, 57
29010 ZIANO PIACENTINO [PC]
TEL. +39 0523868479
www.lusentivini.it

CELLAR SALES
PRE-BOOKED VISITS
ANNUAL PRODUCTION 100,000 bottles
HECTARES UNDER VINE 17.00
VITICULTURE METHOD Certified Organic

| | |
|---|---|
| ○ Pinot Nero Dosaggio Zero M. Cl. '12 | 🍷🍷 5 |
| ● Gutturnio Frizzante '17 | 🍷 2 |

## Giovanna Madonia

LOC. VILLA MADONIA
VIA DE' CAPPUCCINI, 130
47032 BERTINORO [FC]
TEL. +39 0543444361
www.giovannamadonia.it

CELLAR SALES
PRE-BOOKED VISITS
RESTAURANT SERVICE
ANNUAL PRODUCTION 60,000 bottles
HECTARES UNDER VINE 13.00

| | |
|---|---|
| ● Romagna Sangiovese Sup. Fermavento '16 | 🍷🍷 3 |

## Marengoni

LOC. PONTE DELL'OLIO
FRAZ. CASA BIANCA
29028 PONTE DELL'OLIO [PC]
TEL. +39 0523877229
www.vinimarengoni.com

CELLAR SALES
ANNUAL PRODUCTION 50,000 bottles
HECTARES UNDER VINE 11.00

| | |
|---|---|
| ● Gutturnio Frizzante Casa Bianca '17 | 🍷🍷 2* |
| ○ C. P. Valnure Frizzante '17 | 🍷 2 |
| ● Gutturnio Sup. Casa Bianca Migliorina '16 | 🍷 3 |

## Tenuta Masselina

LOC. SERRÀ
VIA POZZE, 1030
48014 CASTEL BOLOGNESE [RA]
TEL. +39 0545284711
www.masselina.it

ACCOMMODATION
ANNUAL PRODUCTION 50,000 bottles
HECTARES UNDER VINE 16.00

| | |
|---|---|
| ○ Romagna Albana Secco '17 | 🍷🍷 2* |
| ● 138 slm '17 | 🍷 2 |
| ○ Romagna Albana Secco '17 | 🍷🍷 2* |

## Poderi Morini

LOC. ORIOLO DEI FICHI
VIA GESUITA
48018 FAENZA [RA]
TEL. +39 0546634257
www.poderimorini.com

ANNUAL PRODUCTION 100,000 bottles
HECTARES UNDER VINE 26.00
SUSTAINABLE WINERY

| | |
|---|---|
| ● Savignone Centesimo '16 | 🏆🏆 2* |
| ○ Pignoletto Brivido '17 | 🏆 2 |

## Mossi

LOC. ALBARETO, 80
29010 ZIANO PIACENTINO [PC]
TEL. +39 0523860201
www.mossi1558.com

CELLAR SALES
PRE-BOOKED VISITS
ANNUAL PRODUCTION 600,000 bottles
HECTARES UNDER VINE 50.00
SUSTAINABLE WINERY

| | |
|---|---|
| ● C. P. Bonarda Sfacciato '16 | 🏆🏆 2* |
| ○ C. P. Ortrugo Brut Contro Tempo '17 | 🏆🏆 2* |
| ● Gutturnio Frizzante San Lupo '17 | 🏆 2 |

## Opera 02 di Ca' Montanari

FRAZ. LEVIZZANO RANGONE
VIA MEDUSIA, 32
41014 CASTELVETRO DI MODENA [MO]
TEL. +39 059741019
www.opera02.it

CELLAR SALES
PRE-BOOKED VISITS
ACCOMMODATION AND RESTAURANT SERVICE
ANNUAL PRODUCTION 75,000 bottles
HECTARES UNDER VINE 20.00
VITICULTURE METHOD Certified Organic
SUSTAINABLE WINERY

| | |
|---|---|
| ● Lambrusco di Modena Opera 02 Secco '17 | 🏆🏆 2* |
| ● Lambrusco Grasparossa di Castelvetro Brut Operapura | 🏆🏆 3 |

## Quinto Passo

LOC. SOZZIGALLI DI SOLIERA
VIA CANALE, 267
41019 SOLIERA [MO]
TEL. +39 0593163311
www.quintopasso.it

CELLAR SALES
ANNUAL PRODUCTION 40,000 bottles
HECTARES UNDER VINE 12.00

| | |
|---|---|
| ○ Cuvée Paradiso Brut M. Cl. '15 | 🏆🏆 5 |
| ⊙ Modena Brut M. Cl. Rosé '15 | 🏆 5 |

## Podere il Saliceto

VIA ALBONE, 10
41011 CAMPOGALLIANO [MO]
TEL. +39 3491459612
www.podereilsaliceto.com

ANNUAL PRODUCTION 13,000 bottles
HECTARES UNDER VINE 4.00

| | |
|---|---|
| ● Lambrusco di Sorbare Brut Nature M. Cl. Ring Adora '15 | 🏆🏆 3 |
| ● Modena Lambrusco Albone '17 | 🏆🏆 2* |
| ● Lambrusco di Sorbare Falistra '17 | 🏆 2 |

## Tenuta Santa Lucia

VIA GIARDINO, 1400
47025 MERCATO SARACENO [FC]
TEL. +39 054790441
www.santaluciavinery.it

CELLAR SALES
PRE-BOOKED VISITS
ACCOMMODATION
ANNUAL PRODUCTION 90,000 bottles
HECTARES UNDER VINE 17.00
VITICULTURE METHOD Certified Biodynamic
SUSTAINABLE WINERY

| | |
|---|---|
| ○ Occhio di Starna Passito | 🏆🏆 4 |
| ○ Romagna Albana Secco Alba Rara '17 | 🏆🏆 3 |
| ○ Famous Famoso '17 | 🏆 3 |
| ● Romagna Sangiovese Sup. Tàibo '16 | 🏆 2 |

## Matteo Serraglio - De Pietri

FRAZ. SALICETO BUZZALINO
VIA VECCHIA, 28
41100 CAMPOGALLIANO [MO]
TEL. +39 3356534069
www.lambruscoilserraglio.it

CELLAR SALES
PRE-BOOKED VISITS
ANNUAL PRODUCTION 16,500 bottles
HECTARES UNDER VINE 10.00

| | |
|---|---|
| ● Lambrusco di Sorbara Il Serraglio '17 | ♟♟ 3* |
| ● Lambrusco di Sorbara De Pietri '17 | ♟ 3 |

## Spalletti Colonna di Paliano

VIA SOGLIANO, 104
47039 SAVIGNANO SUL RUBICONE [FC]
TEL. +39 0541945111
www.spalletticolonnadipaliano.com

CELLAR SALES
PRE-BOOKED VISITS
ANNUAL PRODUCTION 350,000 bottles
HECTARES UNDER VINE 75.00
VITICULTURE METHOD Certified Organic

| | |
|---|---|
| ○ Romagna Albana Duchessa di Montemar '17 | ♟♟ 2* |
| ● Romagna Sangiovese Sup. Principe di Ribano '17 | ♟♟ 2* |

## Tenuta de' Stefenelli

FRAZ. FRATTA TERME
VIA FRATTA, KM 1,800
47032 BERTINORO [FC]
TEL. +39 3332182466
www.destefenelli.it

CELLAR SALES
PRE-BOOKED VISITS
ACCOMMODATION
ANNUAL PRODUCTION 16,000 bottles
HECTARES UNDER VINE 10.00

| | |
|---|---|
| ● Romagna Sangiovese Sup. Preludio '15 | ♟♟ 3 |
| ○ Swing '17 | ♟ 2 |

## Cantina Valtidone

VIA MORETTA, 58
29011 BORGONOVO VAL TIDONE [PC]
TEL. +39 0523846411
www.cantinavaltidone.it

CELLAR SALES
PRE-BOOKED VISITS
ANNUAL PRODUCTION 6,500,000 bottles
HECTARES UNDER VINE 1100.00
VITICULTURE METHOD Certified Organic
SUSTAINABLE WINERY

| | |
|---|---|
| ○ C. P. Malvasia 50 Vendemmie '17 | ♟♟ 2* |
| ● Gutturnio Frizzante 50 Vendemmie '17 | ♟♟ 2* |
| ○ Perlage Brut M. Cl. | ♟ 4 |

## Villa Liverzano

FRAZ. RONTANA
VIA VALLONI, 47
48013 BRISIGHELLA [RA]
TEL. +39 054680461
www.liverzano.it

CELLAR SALES
PRE-BOOKED VISITS
ACCOMMODATION
ANNUAL PRODUCTION 15,000 bottles
HECTARES UNDER VINE 3.20
VITICULTURE METHOD Certified Organic

| | |
|---|---|
| ● Don '14 | ♟♟ 5 |
| ● Rebello '15 | ♟♟ 5 |

## Consorzio Vini Tipici di San Marino

LOC. BORGO MAGGIORE - FRAZ. VALDRAGONE
S.DA SERRABOLINO, 89
47893 SAN MARINO
TEL. +39 0549903124
www.consorziovini.sm

CELLAR SALES
PRE-BOOKED VISITS
ANNUAL PRODUCTION 700,000 bottles
HECTARES UNDER VINE 120.00
SUSTAINABLE WINERY

| | |
|---|---|
| ○ Biancale di San Marino '17 | ♟♟ 2* |
| ● Sterpeto Ris. '13 | ♟♟ 5 |
| ○ Caldese di San Marino '16 | ♟ 4 |
| ○ Roncale di San Marino '17 | ♟ 2 |

# TUSCANY

In this edition of Italian Wines, Tuscany is the uncontested champion, with the region receiving a whopping 84 Tre Bicchieri, a record. Of course it was helped along by a few excellent years, like 2013 in Montalcino and 2015, which was a great year everywhere. But we also can't help but point out that the region's success in Italy and on global markets is well-deserved. In no other region (with the exception of Piedmont, possibly) do producers so consistently reinvest their profits in their vineyards, cellars and professional resources. Tuscany is a battleground in which the country's top enological talent competes, but it's also more than that. The magic hills of Chianti Classico, Montalcino, Bolgheri and Maremma are an irresistible magnet for those who believe themselves capable of making great wine. During our tastings we evaluated almost 350 of them, and we can assure our readers that there's not a lot of difference between the Tre Bicchieri awarded and the 250 offerings that received Due Bicchieri. Having said that, let's turn to Chianti Classico with its 22 gold medals (plus 6 supertuscans from the area), a feat that affirms the area's status as the region's beating heart, along with Montalcino, which saw 14 Brunellos and 2 Rosso di Montalcinos take home our highest honors (its best result ever). But all of Tuscany's prized districts delivered: Bolgheri with 6, Carmignano with 3, Rufina with 2, San Gimignano with 3, not to mention the rest of the region, from Maremma to Montecucco, Morellino, Scansano, Vino Nobile, Cortona and Parrina, and a hearty presence of IGT designated offerings. This year the entire region gave us wines of excellent quality, progressively more focused on expressing terroir by way of traditional grapes (a real challenge today, considering changes in climate). And as is custom we mention those wineries that received Tre Bicchieri for the first time (11 in all, representing 13% of the total, thus confirming the region's enological vitality): Fattoria Ambra, Tenuta di Arceno-Arcanum, Camigliano, Tenuta Carleone, Castellinuzza, Cinciano, Lunadoro, Tenuta Monteti, Tenuta La Parrina, Podere la Regola, and Veroni. We close by highlighting an extremely important achievement, this edition's Red of the Year award. It's Tenuta di Sesta's 2012 Brunello di Montalcino Duelecci Ovest Riserva, a wine of great finesse, depth and poignant elegance.

# Abbadia Ardenga

FRAZ. TORRENIERI
VIA ROMANA, 139
53028 MONTALCINO [SI]
TEL. +39 0577834150
www.abbadiardengapoggio.it

**CELLAR SALES**
**PRE-BOOKED VISITS**
**ANNUAL PRODUCTION** 40,000 bottles
**HECTARES UNDER VINE** 10.00

Abbadia Ardegna is situated in Torrenieri, a major winemaking district in Montalcino's northeast quarter. It was once a Benedictine monastery and a stop along the famed Via Francigena. Today it's in the hands of Siena's Society of Executors of a Pious Disposition, and hosts a bona fide museum. Here you'll also find their ten hectares of vineyards, mostly Sangiovese, which give rise to a traditionally styled Brunello. Three weeks of maceration and three months in 5000-liter Slavonian oak are the keys for both their 'basic' line of wines and their Vigna Piaggia cru. It's their most important wine on paper that heads the group: the 2013 is a magnificent version of their Brunello Vigna Piaggia, with its intertwining aromas of wild berries and spices. This mix of sunniness and vigor accompanies the palate right through to the finish. Their 2012 Brunello Riserva also features an expressive framework, proving meaty and caressing at entry, and a touch dry at the finish.

# Acquabona

LOC. ACQUABONA, 1
57037 PORTOFERRAIO [LI]
TEL. +39 0565933013
www.acquabonaelba.it

**CELLAR SALES**
**PRE-BOOKED VISITS**
**ANNUAL PRODUCTION** 90,000 bottles
**HECTARES UNDER VINE** 18.00

It might seem strange for a producer whose name comes from a freshwater spring to be making great wine, but for more than 30 years three agronomists have been doing just that. The estate, which is situated in Portoferraio and Porto Azzuro, is managed using the most natural methods possible, respectful of the predominantly native grape varieties grown here. Great attention is also shown to their Aleatico Passito dell'Elba, a dessert wine, and Ansonica, a traditional white grape that has always been cultivated in Tuscany but that risked disappearing from Elba altogether. Their pleasant 2013 Voltraio, a blend of Syrah and Merlot, features mature overtones of plum and cherry, hints of tobacco and mineral notes. Its caressing palate displays integrated tannins and proves long and enjoyable right to the end. Their 2012 Aleatico Passito exhibits aromas of cinnamon and cloves on a fruity background, with a sweet and caressing palate.

| | |
|---|---|
| ● Brunello di Montalcino V. Piaggia '13 | ♟♟ 5 |
| ● Brunello di Montalcino Ris. '12 | ♟♟ 6 |
| ● Brunello di Montalcino '13 | ♟ 5 |
| ● Brunello di Montalcino '08 | ♟♟ 5 |
| ● Brunello di Montalcino '07 | ♟♟ 5 |
| ● Brunello di Montalcino '06 | ♟♟ 5 |
| ● Brunello di Montalcino '05 | ♟♟ 5 |
| ● Brunello di Montalcino '05 | ♟♟ 5 |
| ● Brunello di Montalcino V. Piaggia '12 | ♟♟ 5 |
| ● Brunello di Montalcino V. Piaggia '10 | ♟♟ 5 |
| ● Brunello di Montalcino V. Piaggia '09 | ♟♟ 5 |
| ● Brunello di Montalcino V. Piaggia '08 | ♟♟ 5 |
| ● Brunello di Montalcino V. Piaggia '07 | ♟♟ 5 |
| ● Brunello di Montalcino V. Piaggia '04 | ♟♟ 5 |
| ● Rosso di Montalcino '10 | ♟♟ 3 |

| | |
|---|---|
| ● Elba Aleatico Passito '12 | ♟♟ 3 |
| ● Elba Rosso '16 | ♟♟ 2* |
| ○ Elba Vermentino '17 | ♟♟ 3 |
| ● Voltraio '13 | ♟♟ 4 |
| ● Benvenuto '16 | ♟ 2 |
| ○ Elba Ansonica '17 | ♟ 3 |
| ○ Elba Bianco '17 | ♟ 2 |
| ⊙ Elba Rosato '17 | ♟ 2 |
| ● Aleatico dell'Elba '11 | ♟♟ 5 |
| ● Elba Aleatico Passito '11 | ♟♟ 3* |
| ● Elba Rosso Ris. '13 | ♟♟ 4 |
| ○ Elba Vermentino '16 | ♟♟ 3 |

# Altesino

LOC. ALTESINO, 54
53024 MONTALCINO [SI]
TEL. +39 0577806208
www.altesino.it

**CELLAR SALES**
**PRE-BOOKED VISITS**
**ACCOMMODATION**
**ANNUAL PRODUCTION** 250,000 bottles
**HECTARES UNDER VINE** 49.00

It was 2002 when Elisabetta Gnudi
Angelini decided to take over the brand
founded by the Consonni family in the
1970s. Their Montosoli vineyards, in the
heart of northern Montalcino, were soon
accompanied by Castelnuovo dell'Abate
and Pianezzine. Sangiovese, as well as
Merlot, Cabernet, Chardonnay, Vlognier,
Trebbiano and Malvasia are all cultivated.
The cornerstone of their selection is made
up of three Brunellos ('vintages', select and
Riserva). These are distinct for their mix of
power and austerity. At Altesino traditional
and modern come together in one word:
contemporary. Once again their whole
selection proves outstanding, starting with
their 2016 Rosso, with its solid and juicy
taste profile, or their 2013 Brunello which
impressed us with its buoyant fruit, floral
grace and smoky and resinous contrasts.
Their 2013 Montosoli offers up power and
finer details: it may lack tension, but its
abundant tannic weight is well-integrated
in a great classic.

| | | |
|---|---|---|
| ● Brunello di Montalcino Montosoli '13 | ▼▼ | 8 |
| ● Brunello di Montalcino '13 | ▼▼ | 6 |
| ● Rosso di Montalcino '16 | ▼▼ | 3 |
| ● Brunello di Montalcino '11 | ♀♀ | 6 |
| ● Brunello di Montalcino '10 | ♀♀ | 6 |
| ● Brunello di Montalcino '00 | ♀♀ | 6 |
| ● Brunello di Montalcino '96 | ♀♀ | 8 |
| ● Brunello di Montalcino Montosoli '12 | ♀♀ | 8 |
| ● Brunello di Montalcino Montosoli '11 | ♀♀ | 8 |
| ● Brunello di Montalcino Montosoli '10 | ♀♀ | 8 |
| ● Brunello di Montalcino Montosoli '97 | ♀♀ | 8 |
| ● Brunello di Montalcino Our 40th Harvest '12 | ♀♀ | 7 |
| ● Brunello di Montalcino Ris. '10 | ♀♀ | 8 |
| ● Toscana Rosso '14 | ♀♀ | 3 |

# Fattoria Ambra

VIA LOMBARDA, 85
59015 CARMIGNANO [PO]
TEL. +39 3358282552
www.fattoriaambra.it

**CELLAR SALES**
**PRE-BOOKED VISITS**
**ANNUAL PRODUCTION** 80,000 bottles
**HECTARES UNDER VINE** 20.00
**VITICULTURE METHOD** Certified Organic

Cabernet Sauvignon was introduced to
Tuscany by the Medici family and since 1700
it's been cultivated in Carmignano and the
surrounding area. It's here viticultural
microcosm full of history, that we find
Fattoria Ambra, a producer owned by the
Romei Rigoli family since the mid-19th
century. Beppe and his wife oversee all the
winery's activities. In the vineyard Sangiovese
dominates, with Cabernet Sauvignon,
Canaiolo, Trebbiano and Vermentino getting
less and less attention. The winery is
converting to organic and their wines will be
certified as of 2018. Their 2015 Carmignano
Santa Cristina in Pilli earns our Tre Bicchieri.
It features a fresh nose with prominent
redcurrants and blackberries followed by
minty overtones. Its palate comes through
fresh and delicate, smooth and inviting,
with a juicy and flavorsome crescendo
finish. Their 2015 Carmignano Montefortini
Podere Lombarda offers up clean aromas
of close-focused cherry notes and vegetal
overtones. Its palate proves subtle,
well-defined and round, with a full and
clear finish.

| | | |
|---|---|---|
| ● Carmignano Santa Cristina in Pilli '15 | ▼▼▼ | 3* |
| ● Carmignano Montefortini Podere Lombarda '15 | ▼▼ | 3 |
| ● Barco Reale Vin Ruspo '17 | ▼ | 2 |
| ○ Trebbiano '17 | ▼ | 2 |
| ● Carmignano Elzana Ris. '13 | ♀♀ | 5 |
| ● Carmignano Montalbiolo Ris. '13 | ♀♀ | 5 |
| ● Carmignano Montalbiolo Ris. '12 | ♀♀ | 5 |
| ● Carmignano Santa Cristina in Pilli '13 | ♀♀ | 3 |
| ○ Trebbiano '15 | ♀♀ | 2* |
| ○ Vin Santo di Carmignano '09 | ♀♀ | 5 |

# Stefano Amerighi

LOC. POGGIOBELLO DI FARNETA
52044 CORTONA [AR]
TEL. +39 0575648340
www.stefanoamerighi.it

CELLAR SALES
PRE-BOOKED VISITS
ANNUAL PRODUCTION 35,000 bottles
HECTARES UNDER VINE 8.50
VITICULTURE METHOD Certified Biodynamic
SUSTAINABLE WINERY

Amerighi is a model producer, an excellent example of environmental and agricultural sustainability that has adopted biodynamic principles for the cultivation of cereals, vegetables and fruit and is attentive to their livestock. When it comes to viticulture their philosophy is the same. It's all aimed at making sure their Syrah finds a happy home on the hills of Cortona. Stefano Amerighi has managed to reach his goals thanks to his innovative approach, which is rooted in the belief that work should be done carefully and passionately. Their 2015 Syrah earns our Tre Bicchieri once again. Animal, fur and leather aromas give way to nuances of undergrowth and lively cherries and blueberries, with elegant peppery hints. The attack is assertive and inviting, with well-crafted tannins, freshness and a juicy dynamic finish. Their 2014 Syrah Apice, made with grapes grown in a single vineyard, features a complex bouquet and a minty, meaty and lingering flavor.

| | |
|---|---|
| ● Cortona Syrah '15 | ▼▼▼ 5 |
| ● Cortona Syrah Apice '14 | ▼▼ 6 |
| ● Cortona Syrah '14 | ♀♀♀ 5 |
| ● Cortona Syrah '11 | ♀♀♀ 5 |
| ● Cortona Syrah '10 | ♀♀♀ 5 |
| ● Cortona Syrah '09 | ♀♀♀ 5 |
| ● Cortona Syrah '13 | ♀♀ 5 |
| ● Cortona Syrah '12 | ♀♀ 5 |
| ● Cortona Syrah '08 | ♀♀ 5 |
| ● Cortona Syrah '07 | ♀♀ 5 |
| ● Cortona Syrah Apice '13 | ♀♀ 6 |
| ● Cortona Syrah Apice '11 | ♀♀ 6 |
| ● Cortona Syrah Apice '10 | ♀♀ 6 |
| ● Cortona Syrah Apice '09 | ♀♀ 5 |

# Antico Colle

VIA PROVINCIALE, 9
53040 MONTEPULCIANO [SI]
TEL. +39 0578707828
www.anticocolle.it

CELLAR SALES
PRE-BOOKED VISITS
ANNUAL PRODUCTION 150,000 bottles
HECTARES UNDER VINE 30.00

Antico Colle, owned by Andrea Fangiosa, is situated in the eastern part of the Nobile appellation, but their vineyards are spread out in various parts of the municipality. Their stylistic approach tends towards tradition, bringing together a mix of old practices in the vineyard and cellar with a touch of technology. Their wines are aged in barriques and mid-sized casks, as well as large barrels, with just enough oak present to deliver dynamic wines that aren't lacking in character and personality. Their 2013 Nobile di Montepulciano Riserva proves well-crafted. Floral and fruity aromas on a spicy background pave the way for a steady progression and well-sustained, savory palate. Their 2015 Nobile appears just as well-made, exhibiting aromas of red fruit and light smoky overtones leading into a juicy, full and relaxed palate. Their 2016 Rosso di Monte comes through easy to drink and fresh, with scented and approachable aromas.

| | |
|---|---|
| ● Nobile di Montepulciano Il Saggio Ris. '13 | ▼▼ 5 |
| ● Nobile di Montepulciano '15 | ▼▼ 3 |
| ● Rosso di Montepulciano '16 | ▼▼ 2* |
| ● Nobile di Montepulciano '10 | ♀♀ 3 |
| ● Nobile di Montepulciano '09 | ♀♀ 3 |
| ● Nobile di Montepulciano Il Saggio Ris. '07 | ♀♀ 5 |

## ★★Marchesi Antinori

P.ZZA DEGLI ANTINORI, 3
50123 FIRENZE
TEL. +39 05523595
www.antinori.it

CELLAR SALES
PRE-BOOKED VISITS
ACCOMMODATION AND RESTAURANT SERVICE
ANNUAL PRODUCTION 2,000,000 bottles
HECTARES UNDER VINE 2350.00

This Florence winery is the only producer to
possess plots in every Tuscan appellation
(except for San Gimignano). From Chianti
Classico, with Tignanello, Badia a
Passignano, Pèppoli, Castello di San Sano
and Capraia, to Montepulciano, with La
Baccesca in the Cortona appellation. From
Montalcino, with Pain delle Vigne, to
Bolgheri, with Guado al Tasso. From
Florence, with Monteloro, to Sovana, with
Fattoria Aldobrandesca, all the way to Le
Mortelle di Castiglione della Pescaia (which
is smack in the Maremma appellation). But
their heart beats for Chianti Classico, where
Antinori has focused his efforts. The range
of Chianti Classicos submitted by Antinori
reveals great depth. Their 2015 Chianti
Classico Marchese Antinori Riserva steals
the show with its close-focused style and
overall balance. Its nose features lush fruit
and hints of flint, supported by fine spices.
The wine's balanced impact in the mouth
progresses slim-bodied and lively, with
major integrated oak.

## Tenuta di Arceno - Arcanum

LOC. ARCENO
FRAZ. SAN GUSMÉ
53010 CASTELNUOVO BERARDENGA [SI]
TEL. +39 0577359346
www.tenutadiarceno.com

CELLAR SALES
PRE-BOOKED VISITS
ANNUAL PRODUCTION 250,000 bottles
HECTARES UNDER VINE 92.00

Arceno is American giant Kendall-Jackson's
Chianti satellite and operates out of
Castelnuovo Berardenga, a district in the
southern part of the Chianti Classico
appellation. Their production style can be
traced back to the area's climate, and a
more modern sensibility that's draws on
California's best wines. Their wines exhibit
mature aromas and bold structure, with oak
in the foreground. There are times,
however, that they prove capable of
revealing a more elegant, subtly complex
side. After a few uncertain vintages as
regards clarity of style, this year Arcanum's
wines really came back to impress. An
excellent vintage of their Valadorna, the
2013, earned its first Tre Bicchieri. This
Merlot-based red wine proves rich,
balanced and close-knit. Its very lingering
finish features fruity and spicy overtones,
where you can appreciate the elegant
tannins and perfectly integrated oaky notes.
We found their other wines excellent.

| | |
|---|---|
| ● Chianti Cl. Marchese Antinori Ris. '15 | 🍷🍷🍷 5 |
| ● Chianti Cl. Villa Antinori Ris. '15 | 🍷🍷 4 |
| ● Tignanello '15 | 🍷🍷 8 |
| ● Chianti Cl. Gran Selezione Badia a Passignano '15 | 🍷🍷 6 |
| ● Chianti Cl. Pèppoli '16 | 🍷 3 |
| ● Cortona Achelo La Braccesca '16 | 🍷 5 |
| ● Maremma Toscana Botrosecco Le Mortelle '16 | 🍷 3 |
| ○ Maremma Toscana Vivaia Tenuta Le Mortelle '17 | 🍷 4 |
| ● Nobile di Montepulciano La Braccesca '15 | 🍷 4 |
| ● Solaia '07 | 🍷🍷🍷 8 |
| ● Solaia '06 | 🍷🍷🍷 8 |
| ● Tignanello '13 | 🍷🍷🍷 8 |
| ● Tignanello '09 | 🍷🍷🍷 8 |
| ● Tignanello '08 | 🍷🍷🍷 8 |

| | |
|---|---|
| ● Valadorna '13 | 🍷🍷🍷 8 |
| ● Arcanum '13 | 🍷🍷 8 |
| ● Chianti Cl. Gran Selezione Strada al Sasso '15 | 🍷🍷 6 |
| ● Chianti Cl. '16 | 🍷🍷 4 |
| ● Chianti Cl. Ris. '15 | 🍷🍷 5 |
| ● Il Fauno di Arcanum '14 | 🍷🍷 6 |
| ● Chianti Cl. '15 | 🍷🍷 3 |
| ● Chianti Cl. '13 | 🍷🍷 3 |
| ● Chianti Cl. '12 | 🍷🍷 3 |
| ● Chianti Cl. Ris. '14 | 🍷🍷 5 |
| ● Chianti Cl. Ris. '12 | 🍷🍷 5 |
| ● Chianti Cl. Strada al Sasso Ris. '10 | 🍷🍷 5 |
| ● Valadorna '11 | 🍷🍷 7 |

# Tenuta Argentiera

LOC. I PIANALI
FRAZ. DONORATICO
VIA AURELIA, 412A
57022 CASTAGNETO CARDUCCI [LI]
TEL. +39 0565773176
www.argentiera.eu

**CELLAR SALES**
**PRE-BOOKED VISITS**
**ANNUAL PRODUCTION** 450,000 bottles
**HECTARES UNDER VINE** 75.00

Tenuta Argentiera is among Bolgheri's top producers, a true benchmark for the appellation in terms of organization, vineyards and production style. The estate, which includes exceptional plots and a cellar that was entirely renovated in 2008 (with particular attention paid to its environmental impact), is owned by Corrado and Marcello Fratini. Their vineyards are cultivated in clay, stony terrain and surrounded by the area's trademark Mediterranean scrub. These are cared for attentively and respectively, giving rise to a formidable selection of complex, personal wines with an unmistakable style. We have to say that the latest tastings have given us a rather unclear picture, with several wines appearing to gone a bit off track. Their 2015 Bolgheri Superiore features particularly dark aromas and a full-bodied palate, which is dense but still too marked by harsh tannins. This wine struggles to relax and may need more bottle maturation.

| | | |
|---|---|---|
| ● Bolgheri Sup. Argentiera '15 | ♟♟ | 8 |
| ○ Poggio ai Ginepri Bianco '17 | ♟♟ | 3 |
| ⊙ Bolgheri Rosato Poggio ai Ginepri '17 | ♟ | 2 |
| ● Bolgheri Rosso Poggio ai Ginepri '16 | ♟ | 3 |
| ● Bolgheri Rosso Villa Donoratico '16 | ♟ | 5 |
| ● Bolgheri Sup. '11 | ♟♟♟ | 8 |
| ● Bolgheri Sup. Argentiera '10 | ♟♟♟ | 7 |
| ● Bolgheri Sup. Argentiera '06 | ♟♟♟ | 7 |
| ● Bolgheri Rosso Sup. '14 | ♟♟ | 8 |
| ● Bolgheri Rosso Villa Donoratico '15 | ♟♟ | 8 |
| ● Giorgio Bartholomaus '12 | ♟♟ | 8 |

# Artimino

FRAZ. ARTIMINO
V.LE PAPA GIOVANNI XXIII, 1
59015 CARMIGNANO [PO]
TEL. +39 0558751423
www.artimino.com

**CELLAR SALES**
**PRE-BOOKED VISITS**
**ACCOMMODATION AND RESTAURANT SERVICE**
**ANNUAL PRODUCTION** 420,000 bottles
**HECTARES UNDER VINE** 88.00

The estate, which is owned by the Olmo group is comprised of 700 hectares. Amidst them stands the property's main feature, a villa that boasts 100 fireplaces. Since the new ownership took over they've been upgrading their vineyards, and a new approach to maturation has been adopted in the cellar. The transformation has allowed the winery to bring out the full potential of their products and more precisely express a territory such as Carmignano. Their 2013 Carmignano Grumarello Riserva features pleasant fruity overtones of cherries, wild berries and spices leading to soft notes in the mouth. Here we find lovely lingering fruit and a slim-bodied and drinkable palate. Their 2015 Carmignano Poggilarca exhibits elegant aromas of red and black fruit, a fresh and taut palate, supple body, balance, elegance, tension and moderate pulp. Their 2011 Vin Santo Occhio di Pernice offers up aromas of nuts (hazelnuts and almonds) and proves elegant and long.

| | | |
|---|---|---|
| ● Carmignano Poggilarca '15 | ♟♟ | 3 |
| ● Carmignano V. Grumarello Ris. '13 | ♟♟ | 4 |
| ● Vin Santo di Carmignano Occhio di Pernice '11 | ♟♟ | 5 |
| ● Barco Reale Ser Biagio '17 | ♟ | 2 |
| ⊙ Barco Reale Vin Ruspo '17 | ♟ | 2 |
| ● Chianti Montalbano '16 | ♟ | 2 |
| ● Carmignano '13 | ♟♟ | 3 |
| ● Carmignano Poggilarca '14 | ♟♟ | 3 |
| ● Carmignano V. Grumarello Ris. '12 | ♟♟ | 4 |
| ● Vin Santo di Carmignano Occhio di Pernice '10 | ♟♟ | 5 |
| ● Vin Santo di Carmignano Occhio di Pernice '09 | ♟♟ | 5 |

# Assolati

Fraz. Montenero
Pod. Assolati, 47
58040 Castel del Piano [GR]
Tel. +39 0564954146
www.assolati.it

**CELLAR SALES**
**PRE-BOOKED VISITS**
**ACCOMMODATION**
**ANNUAL PRODUCTION** 18,000 bottles
**HECTARES UNDER VINE** 5.00

Even if their standard of quality still hasn't reached its maximum potential, Floriano Giannetti's Montecucco winery (situated in Montenero d'Orcia) is capable of producing intriguing, original reds. This is made possible especially when the earthy quality of the local Sangiovese grapes, which can be too bold at times, finds the right contrast, giving way to balanced, fresh taste. It's difficult to consistently get the right conditions, in an area that often sees temperatures higher than the average. But the winery is right to pursue a style that emphasizes personality. Their 2015 Montecucco Sangiovese Riserva features a lovely spicy and fruity profile, with nuanced aromas of flowers and herbs. Its gratifying, elegant palate exhibits a steady progression, which is slightly reined in at the finish by exuberant oak. Their flavorsome and juicy 2015 Montecucco Sangiovese offers up close-focused and approachable fruity aromas that follow through onto the palate, where it really delivers.

| | |
|---|---|
| ● Montecucco Sangiovese Ris. '15 | ♥♥ 4 |
| ● Montecucco Sangiovese '15 | ♥♥ 3 |
| ○ Dionysos '16 | ♀♀ 2* |
| ● Montecucco Rosso '15 | ♀♀ 2* |
| ● Montecucco Rosso '14 | ♀♀ 2* |
| ● Montecucco Sangiovese '14 | ♀♀ 3 |
| ● Montecucco Sangiovese Ris. '13 | ♀♀ 4 |

# ★Avignonesi

Fraz. Valiano di Montepulciano
Via Colonica, 1
53045 Montepulciano [SI]
Tel. +39 0578724304
www.avignonesi.it

**CELLAR SALES**
**PRE-BOOKED VISITS**
**ACCOMMODATION AND RESTAURANT SERVICE**
**ANNUAL PRODUCTION** 500,000 bottles
**HECTARES UNDER VINE** 169.00
**VITICULTURE METHOD** Certified Organic

Avignonesi is the historic name of the Nobile di Montepulciano wine that contributed to the appellation's success. Today the estate is in the hands of the Belgian Virginie Saverys, who also purchased the winery Lodola Nuova da Ruffino. Avignonesi remains a benchmark for Tuscan enology and beyond. Their vineyards are managed according to biodynamic principles and in the cellar their approach is minimally invasive. Wines are aged in both small and large oak barrels. Their wines are gradually finding a clear style based on balance between aroma and taste, with quality standards increasingly on the rise. A new and complicated organization of their wines hasn't prevented their 2015 Nobile di Montepulciano Caprile from expressing its superior characteristics. Its intense aromas range from floral hints to light overtones of fresh fruit and flint. Its palate comes through generous and balanced with a crescendo finish. Their 2015 Nobile Progetto Alleanza proves spot-on, though slightly unpolished at the finish.

| | |
|---|---|
| ● Nobile di Montepulciano Caprile '15 | ♥♥ 5 |
| ● Nobile di Montepulciano Progetto Alleanza '15 | ♥♥ 5 |
| ● Nobile di Montepulciano '15 | ♥♥ 5 |
| ● Nobile di Montepulciano Ventisei '15 | ♥♥ 5 |
| ● Nobile di Montepulciano Oceano '15 | ♥ 5 |
| ● Rosso di Montepulciano '16 | ♥ 3 |
| ● Nobile di Montepulciano '12 | ♀♀♀ 4* |
| ● Nobile di Montepulciano '14 | ♀♀ 5 |
| ● Nobile di Montepulciano '13 | ♀♀ 5 |
| ● Nobile di Montepulciano Grandi Annate '13 | ♀♀ 7 |
| ● Rosso di Montepulciano '15 | ♀♀ 3* |
| ○ Vin Santo di Montepulciano '01 | ♀♀ 8 |

## ★Badia a Coltibuono

LOC. BADIA A COLTIBUONO
53013 GAIOLE IN CHIANTI [SI]
TEL. +39 0577746110
www.coltibuono.com

CELLAR SALES
PRE-BOOKED VISITS
ACCOMMODATION AND RESTAURANT SERVICE
ANNUAL PRODUCTION 240,000 bottles
HECTARES UNDER VINE 62.00
VITICULTURE METHOD Certified Organic
SUSTAINABLE WINERY

Badia a Coltibuono, owned by the Stucchi
Prinetti family, is one of the oldest wineries
in Chianti Classico. The producer has
managed to endow their wide range of
wines with a well-defined style that's
distinct, highly territorial and marked by
finesse and balance. The winery has
undergone major changes, starting with
vineyard management (now entirely
organic) and today the unmistakable
style of their wines, which are classy and
full of personality, has reinforced their
role as a leader in the appellation. Their
2015 Chianti Classico Cultus Boni
underlines Badia a Coltibuono's elegant
style, highlighting whispered aromas of
small red fruit, floral hints and flinty
overtones. Balance is the prominent
component on the palate, but the assertive
contrast makes for a truly charming palate.
Their 2015 Chianti Classico comes
through simpler, staking everything on
pleasant drinkability, with savoriness and a
supple palate at the forefront.

| | |
|---|---|
| ● Chianti Cl. Cultus Boni '15 | ♟♟♟ 4* |
| ● Chianti Cl. '16 | ♟♟ 4 |
| ● Chianti Cetamura '17 | ♟♟ 2* |
| ● Chianti Cl. RS '16 | ♟ 3 |
| ● Chianti Cl. '15 | ♀♀♀ 4* |
| ● Chianti Cl. '13 | ♀♀♀ 3* |
| ● Chianti Cl. '12 | ♀♀♀ 3* |
| ● Chianti Cl. '06 | ♀♀♀ 3* |
| ● Chianti Cl. Cultus Boni '09 | ♀♀♀ 4* |
| ● Chianti Cl. Ris. '09 | ♀♀♀ 5 |
| ● Chianti Cl. Ris. '07 | ♀♀♀ 5 |
| ● Chianti Cl. Ris. '04 | ♀♀♀ 5 |
| ● Sangioveto '95 | ♀♀♀ 6 |

## Badia di Morrona

VIA DEL CHIANTI, 6
56030 TERRICCIOLA [PI]
TEL. +39 0587658505
www.gaslinialberti.it

CELLAR SALES
PRE-BOOKED VISITS
ACCOMMODATION AND RESTAURANT SERVICE
ANNUAL PRODUCTION 350,000 bottles
HECTARES UNDER VINE 110.00

Badia di Morrona is situated in Terricciola,
within Pisa and Volterra, and has belonged
to the Gaslini Alberti family since 1939.
Their leap in quality, in terms of agriculture,
came in the 1970s, and has continued
steadily ever since. Recent vintages,
especially, have delivered a selection
whose style is on the rise. It's clear that the
territory's value is being respected. Their
vast property goes back to the turn of the
first millennium and has maintained a bond
with the Benedictine convent it hosted. We
were impressed by the overall performance
of their range. Their high-level and varied
product portfolio features different styles of
brilliant wines. Their star performer is
undoubtedly the 2015 Taneto, a blend of
Syrah, Sangiovese and Merlot with an
intense, fresh nose and a palate revealing
surprising consistency. Their 2015 Vigna
Alta proves very sound, with its aromas of
plum, earth and topsoil, and serious but
precise tannins.

| | |
|---|---|
| ● Taneto '15 | ♟♟ 3* |
| ● Chianti I Sodi del Paretaio '17 | ♟♟ 2* |
| ● N'antia '15 | ♟♟ 5 |
| ● VignaAlta '15 | ♟♟ 5 |
| ● Chianti I Sodi del Paretaio '16 | ♀♀ 2* |
| ● Taneto '11 | ♀♀ 3* |
| ● VignaAlta '13 | ♀♀ 5 |
| ○ Vin Santo del Chianti '11 | ♀♀ 4 |

# Fattoria di Bagnolo

LOC. BAGNOLO
VIA IMPRUNETANA PER TAVARNUZZE, 36
50023 IMPRUNETA [FI]
TEL. +39 0552313403
www.bartolinibaldelli.it

CELLAR SALES
PRE-BOOKED VISITS
ANNUAL PRODUCTION 25,000 bottles
HECTARES UNDER VINE 10.00

Villa di Bagnolo was built in 1500 by the Strozzi family. In 1965 it was inherited by Cristina Morrocchi, wife of Vittorio Pancrazi. A few years later came the event that would make the estate famous. In 1970, when the volcanic terrain at the foot of Monteferrato was replanted with new vineyards, the nurseryman at the time accidentally used Pinot Nero instead of the area's traditional Sangiovese. They only realized the mistake after a few years, but a well-suited climate meant that the vineyards flourished. And so began the history of Pinot Nero in Bagnolo. Their 2015 Riserva dei Colli Fiorentini got to our final: animal, fur and leather overtones give way to fresh fruity notes of blackberry and plum, finishing off with herbs such as thyme and bay. Its palate comes through juicy, with good weight, integrated tannins, fresh acid backbone and a complex and pleasant finish. Their 2015 Caprorosso, a blend of Sangiovese, Colorino and Cabernet Sauvignon, exhibits spicy and toasty aromas, a rich and caressing body and good length.

| | |
|---|---|
| ● Chianti Colli Fiorentini Ris. '15 | ♟♟ 4 |
| ● Capro Rosso '15 | ♟♟ 7 |
| ○ Vin Santo del Chianti Ris. '09 | ♟♟ 6 |
| ● Chianti Colli Fiorentini '16 | ♟ 2 |
| ● Chianti Colli Fiorentini Ris. '14 | ♟♟ 4 |
| ● Chianti Colli Fiorentini Ris. '13 | ♟♟ 4 |
| ● Chianti Colli Fiorentini Ris. '12 | ♟♟ 4 |

# Baracchi

LOC. CEGLIOLO, 21
52044 CORTONA [AR]
TEL. +39 0575612679
www.baracchiwinery.com

CELLAR SALES
PRE-BOOKED VISITS
ACCOMMODATION AND RESTAURANT SERVICE
ANNUAL PRODUCTION 140,000 bottles
HECTARES UNDER VINE 32.00
SUSTAINABLE WINERY

This Valdichiana winery has been producing wines on the hills around Cortona since 1860. Following in the footsteps of five generations of family, Riccardo Baracchi and his son Benedetto are now at the helm. Syrah has always been front and center, having found the perfect habitat in the area. Trebbiano and Sangiovese are also cultivated and used in different ways, for example in sparkling winemaking, which is carried out entirely on site. No challenge is off limits, as demonstrated by a plot of Pinot Nero as well. Their 2015 Syrah Smeriglio makes a pleasant impact on the nose, which comes through concentrated and fruity, with redcurrants and raspberries, spices such as pepper and ginger, as well as herbs. It features a pleasant juicy attack in the mouth, with well-embedded tannins and a tidy finish. We also enjoyed their 2015 Cabernet Riserva, with its bouquet of balsamic overtones, lightly roasted coffee, black fruit and cherries. Its flavor proves rich and generous, with subtle tannins. The rising finish gives way to an inviting, fruity aftertaste.

| | |
|---|---|
| ● Cortona Cabernet Ris. '15 | ♟♟ 6 |
| ● Cortona Syrah Ris. '15 | ♟♟ 6 |
| ● Cortona Syrah Smeriglio '15 | ♟♟ 4 |
| ☉ Sangiovese Brut Rosé '15 | ♟ 5 |
| ○ Trebbiano Brut '15 | ♟ 5 |
| ● Cortona Cabernet Ris. '13 | ♟♟ 6 |
| ● Cortona Pinot Nero '14 | ♟♟ 4 |
| ● Cortona Smeriglio Syrah '13 | ♟♟ 4 |
| ● Cortona Syrah Ris. '13 | ♟♟ 6 |
| ● Cortona Syrah Ris. '12 | ♟♟ 6 |
| ● Cortona Syrah Smeriglio '14 | ♟♟ 4 |
| ● Pinot Nero '13 | ♟♟ 6 |
| ● Pinot Nero '12 | ♟♟ 6 |

## Fattoria dei Barbi

LOC. PODERNOVI, 170
53024 MONTALCINO [SI]
TEL. +39 0577841111
www.fattoriadeibarbi.it

CELLAR SALES
PRE-BOOKED VISITS
ACCOMMODATION AND RESTAURANT SERVICE
ANNUAL PRODUCTION 600,000 bottles
HECTARES UNDER VINE 66.00

It's worth once again emphasizing the pioneering work carried out by this winery, universally recognized as one of Montalcino's great, classic producers. Fattoria dei Barbi, who were among the first to export Brunello in Europe and abroad, are an absolute benchmark, both for the style of their proudly rigorous Sangiovese reds, and for the awareness with which Stefano Cinelli Colombini balances historical memory and contemporary vision. They're more than just a cellar-museum. They're a winemaking headquarters capable of bringing out the character of Podernovi's vineyards. Recent tests have given us one of the best wines ever produced by Barbi, headed by a compact and multifaceted 2013 Brunello. Sour cherry, balsamic and root overtones lead into a full and assertive palate. Its flavorsome progression appears slightly held back by the alcohol. Their Vigna del Fiore from the same vintage is not far behind, but its aromatic framework proves more tertiary and the tannins a bit sharper.

|  |  |
|---|---|
| ● Brunello di Montalcino '13 | ♥♥ 5 |
| ● Brunello di Montalcino Ris. '12 | ♥♥ 7 |
| ● Brunello di Montalcino V. del Fiore '13 | ♥♥ 7 |
| ● Rosso di Montalcino '16 | ♥♥ 3 |
| ● Brunello di Montalcino '11 | ♡♡ 5 |
| ● Brunello di Montalcino '10 | ♡♡ 5 |
| ● Brunello di Montalcino Ris. '11 | ♡♡ 7 |
| ● Brunello di Montalcino Ris. '10 | ♡♡ 7 |
| ● Brunello di Montalcino Ris. '08 | ♡♡ 7 |
| ● Brunello di Montalcino V. del Fiore '12 | ♡♡ 7 |
| ● Brunello di Montalcino V. del Fiore '11 | ♡♡ 7 |
| ● Brunello di Montalcino V. del Fiore '10 | ♡♡ 7 |
| ● Morellino di Scansano '15 | ♡♡ 3 |
| ● Rosso di Montalcino '15 | ♡♡ 3 |
| ● Rosso di Montalcino '14 | ♡♡ 3 |

## Baricci

LOC. COLOMBAIO DI MONTOSOLI, 13
53024 MONTALCINO [SI]
TEL. +39 0577848109
www.baricci.it

CELLAR SALES
PRE-BOOKED VISITS
ANNUAL PRODUCTION 30,000 bottles
HECTARES UNDER VINE 5.00

Baricci's six plots are side-by-side, but worked separately, with long maceration and maturation in 2000 and 4000 liter Slavonian oak barrels. Federico and Francesco Buffi, along with their father, Piero, attend to Podere Colombaio's five hectares of vineyards on the eastern side of Montosoli hill. Forever linked to the name Nello Baricci, even after his death, it's one of northern Montalcino's most celebrated wine-growing areas. The winery's Sangioveses are unmistakable for their citrusy character, buoyant spiciness and vigor. They offer up their best over time, but they can be appreciated early as well. As usual, we are spoilt for choice with Baricci's selection. If you are looking for the complexity and balance of the most statuesque Brunellos, you'll be bewitched by their 2012 Nello Riserva, with its riot of pomegranate, balsamic herbs and hot spices. But the wine that everybody will agree on is once again their Rosso. Their fantastic 2016 vintage proves delectable, due to its combination of power and lightness.

|  |  |
|---|---|
| ● Rosso di Montalcino '16 | ♥♥♥ 4* |
| ● Brunello di Montalcino Nello Ris. '12 | ♥♥ 6 |
| ● Brunello di Montalcino '13 | ♥♥ 6 |
| ● Brunello di Montalcino '10 | ♡♡♡ 6 |
| ● Brunello di Montalcino '09 | ♡♡♡ 5 |
| ● Brunello di Montalcino '07 | ♡♡♡ 5 |
| ● Brunello di Montalcino '83 | ♡♡♡ 5 |
| ● Brunello di Montalcino Nello Ris. '10 | ♡♡♡ 6 |
| ● Rosso di Montalcino '15 | ♡♡♡ 4* |
| ● Brunello di Montalcino '12 | ♡♡ 6 |
| ● Brunello di Montalcino '11 | ♡♡ 6 |
| ● Brunello di Montalcino '08 | ♡♡ 5 |
| ● Rosso di Montalcino '14 | ♡♡ 4 |
| ● Rosso di Montalcino '13 | ♡♡ 4 |
| ● Rosso di Montalcino '11 | ♡♡ 3* |

# Fattoria di Basciano

V.LE DUCA DELLA VITTORIA, 159
50068 RUFINA [FI]
TEL. +39 0558397034
www.renzomasibasciano.it

**CELLAR SALES**
**PRE-BOOKED VISITS**
**ANNUAL PRODUCTION** 200,000 bottles
**HECTARES UNDER VINE** 35.00

The Masi family's business is less developed in Italy than it is in other countries, like France. It's the work of the 'négociant', a job that the family have been doing for three generations, and that today is in the hands of Paolo Masi, the agronomist who personally oversees the activities of the various growers (thus guaranteeing consistent quality of the wines produced). Their selection is wide ranging and varied, with particular attention paid to the territory of origin, Rufina. Their 2011 Vin Santo del Chianti Rufina displays an orange color, hints of moss, leather, dried fruit (figs) and spice. The mouth starts out docile, then becomes full-bodied, generous and caressing. Their 2016 Erta e China, an equal blend of Sangiovese and Cabernet Sauvignon, exhibits assertive notes of pepper and good elegance, leading into fruity overtones of redcurrants and blueberries. Its palate comes through firm, juicy and confident, with a long, fresh and pleasant finish.

| | |
|---|---|
| ● Erta e China '16 | ♟♟ 2* |
| ● Vigna Il Corto '16 | ♟♟ 3 |
| ○ Vin Santo del Chianti Rufina '11 | ♟♟ 3 |
| ● Chianti Ris. '15 | ♟ 2 |
| ● Chianti Rufina '16 | ♟ 2 |
| ● I Pini '16 | ♟ 4 |
| ● Chianti Ris. '13 | ♟♟ 2* |
| ● Chianti Rufina '13 | ♟♟ 2* |
| ● I Pini '15 | ♟♟ 4 |

# Basile

POD. MONTE MARIO
58044 CINIGIANO [GR]
TEL. +39 0564993227
www.basilessa.it

**CELLAR SALES**
**PRE-BOOKED VISITS**
**ANNUAL PRODUCTION** 50,000 bottles
**HECTARES UNDER VINE** 8.00
**VITICULTURE METHOD** Certified Organic
**SUSTAINABLE WINERY**

Giovanbattista Basile, originally from Naples, arrived on the Cinigiano hills in 1999 and bet unflinchingly on the young appellation of Montecucco. The winery's vineyards have been organically managed from the beginning, while a minimally invasive approach is taken in the cellar. Their wines tend to be well-defined, modern, capable of highlighting the qualities of the area's Sangiovese and the non-native grapes cultivated. The varieties used come through in a distinctive way, offering up aromas with a clear personality. Their 2014 Montecucco Sangiovese Adagio Riserva proves a constant; even in a complicated vintage it comes through as a consistent and well-made interpretation. Focused aromas of flowers and spices pave the way for a slim-bodied and punchy palate, with a savory finish. Their 2015 Montecucco Sangiovese Cartacanta appears well-crafted, with its intense aromas and juicy palate that's full of character.

| | |
|---|---|
| ● Montecucco Sangiovese Ad Agio Ris. '14 | ♟♟♟ 5 |
| ● Montecucco Sangiovese Cartacanta '15 | ♟♟ 3 |
| ● Maremma Toscana Rosso Comandante '15 | ♟ 4 |
| ● Montecucco Sangiovese Ad Agio Ris. '12 | ♟♟♟ 5 |
| ● Maremma Comandante '12 | ♟♟ 3 |
| ● Montecucco Sangiovese Ad Agio Ris. '13 | ♟♟ 5 |
| ● Montecucco Sangiovese Ad Agio Ris. '11 | ♟♟ 5 |
| ● Montecucco Sangiovese Cartacanta '13 | ♟♟ 3 |
| ● Montecucco Sangiovese Cartacanta '12 | ♟♟ 3 |

# Pietro Beconcini

FRAZ. LA SCALA
VIA MONTORZO, 13A
56028 SAN MINIATO [PI]
TEL. +39 0571464785
www.pietrobeconcini.com

**CELLAR SALES**
**PRE-BOOKED VISITS**
**ANNUAL PRODUCTION** 95,000 bottles
**HECTARES UNDER VINE** 12.00

In the 1990s, Leonardo Beconcini definitively took over his father's place at the family winery. He began working to promote a territory that was little known in terms of wine-growing, and to support (along with others) the creation of the San Miniato Vine Growers Consortium. He carried out major changes in terms of terrain cultivation, giving rise to truly distinctive wines, thanks in part to the rediscovery of Tempranillo, a variety that might have been brought to San Miniato by Spanish pilgrims. Their Maurleo, an equal blend of Sangiovese and Malvasia Nera, impressed. Intense aromas of ink and licorice merge with plums, blackberries and fresh grassy overtones. It comes through pleasantly caressing on the palate, exhibiting tannins and alcohol nicely in step. Their 2016 Ixe, a monovarietal Tempranillo, reveals a complex bouquet of mixed herbs, undergrowth, blood-rich meat and cherry jam. Its balanced body is well supported by lovely tannins and a savory finish.

| | | |
|---|---|---|
| ● Ixe Tempranillo '16 | ♀♀ 3 | |
| ● Maurleo '16 | ♀♀ 3 | |
| ● Vin Santo del Chianti Occhio di Pernice Aria '08 | ♀♀ 7 | |
| ● Chianti Ris. '15 | ♀ 3 | |
| ● Chianti Ris. '13 | ♀♀ 2* | |
| ● IXE '15 | ♀♀ 3 | |
| ● IXE '14 | ♀♀ 3 | |
| ● IXE '13 | ♀♀ 3 | |
| ● Maurleo '15 | ♀♀ 2* | |
| ● Maurleo '13 | ♀♀ 2* | |
| ● Reciso '13 | ♀♀ 5 | |
| ● Vigna alle Nicchie '12 | ♀♀ 6 | |
| ● Vigna alle Nicchie '11 | ♀♀ 6 | |
| ○ Vin Santo del Chianti Caratello '08 | ♀♀ 5 | |

# Bibbiano

VIA BIBBIANO, 76
53011 CASTELLINA IN CHIANTI [SI]
TEL. +39 0577743065
www.bibbiano.com

**CELLAR SALES**
**PRE-BOOKED VISITS**
**ACCOMMODATION**
**ANNUAL PRODUCTION** 125,000 bottles
**HECTARES UNDER VINE** 27.00
**VITICULTURE METHOD** Certified Organic
**SUSTAINABLE WINERY**

During the Second World War Tenuta di Bibbiano had been severely damaged. In its aftermath, Pier Tommaso Marzi and his son-in-law Alfredo Marocceshi performed major reconstruction works. Thanks to the precious support of Giulio Gambelli, the cellar was rebuilt and their vineyards in Chianti Classico once again thrived. Today the winery is managed by Tommaso and Federico Marrocchesi Marzi, with the same spirit and classic production style that, especially in recent years, is once again distinguishing the best of Chianti Classico's wines. Their well-made 2016 Chianti Classico features fruity and floral aromas, with hints of earth and spice leading into a full, steady and savory taste progression. Their 2015 Chianti Classico Gran Selezione Vigna del Capannino proved just as tasty, displaying intense lush fruit and a complex palate with good density. Their 2015 Chianti Classico Riserva also appears well-made, though the aromas aren't so well-defined and the palate not so steady.

| | | |
|---|---|---|
| ● Chianti Cl. '16 | ♀♀ 3* | |
| ● Chianti Cl. Gran Selezione V. del Capannino '15 | ♀♀ 5 | |
| ● Chianti Cl. Ris. '15 | ♀♀ 4 | |
| ● Chianti Cl. '15 | ♀♀ 3 | |
| ● Chianti Cl. '14 | ♀♀ 3 | |
| ● Chianti Cl. '13 | ♀♀ 3* | |
| ● Chianti Cl. '11 | ♀♀ 3* | |
| ● Chianti Cl. Montornello '11 | ♀♀ 3 | |
| ● Chianti Cl. Montornello Ris. '13 | ♀♀ 4 | |
| ● Chianti Cl. Montornello Ris. '12 | ♀♀ 4 | |
| ● Chianti Cl. V. del Capannino Gran Sel. '10 | ♀♀ 5 | |

# Bindella

FRAZ. ACQUAVIVA
VIA DELLE TRE BERTE, 10A
53045 MONTEPULCIANO [SI]
TEL. +39 0578767777
www.bindella.it

CELLAR SALES
PRE-BOOKED VISITS
ANNUAL PRODUCTION 160,000 bottles
HECTARES UNDER VINE 36.50

For more than 30 years, Rudolf Bindella's winery has been offering wines of superior stylistic coherence. Indeed, their wines have been less influenced by the recent influx of enological trends, with the producer maintaining its emphasis on the Nobile di Montepulciano appellation and their wines belonging to it. Their vineyards span various terrains and districts: Vallocaia, Santa Maira and Fossolupaio, some of the area's most notable crus. Large and small wood barrels are used to mature their principal wines, which show substance, depth and an exceptional capacity to evolve over time. Their 2015 Nobile di Montepulciano I Quadri is quite possibly their best version in recent years. Its complex aromas range from fruity overtones to floral and flinty notes, with a spicy finish. The palate displays a precise structure and pleasant flavorsome, crunchy tannins. It continues to develop with great savoriness and finishes on a lovely iron-like note.

| | |
|---|---|
| ● Nobile di Montepulciano I Quadri '15 | ▼▼ 5 |
| ● Nobile di Montepulciano '15 | ▼▼ 4 |
| ● Rosso di Montepulciano Fossolupaio '16 | ▼ 3 |
| ● Nobile di Montepulciano I Quadri '13 | ♀♀♀ 5 |
| ● Nobile di Montepulciano '14 | ♀♀ 4 |
| ● Nobile di Montepulciano Vallocaia Ris. '13 | ♀♀ 6 |
| ● Vin Santo di Montepulciano Occhio di Pernice Dolce Sinfonia '07 | ♀♀ 7 |
| ● Rosso di Montepulciano Fosso Lupaio '14 | ♀ 2 |

# ★Biondi Santi Tenuta Greppo

LOC. VILLA GREPPO, 183
53024 MONTALCINO [SI]
TEL. +39 0577848023
www.biondisanti.it

HECTARES UNDER VINE 26.00

There's great curiosity in the air over if and how things will change with Biondi Santi now that the they've partnered with the Epi Group. It's one of France's most important luxury holding firms, already a leader in the world of wine with producers like Piper and Charles Heidseck in Champagne and the Château la Verrerie in Rhone. Jacopo Biondi Santi and Christopher Descours form a decisive team whose job it will be to further the international reputation of Brunello and the winery that in a way brought the wine to the attention of consumers, having produced a countless series of immortal reserves. They have made significant change regarding the release dates of their wines, which they have put back a year with respect to recent decades. Therefore we'll have to wait for next year's edition of the guide to taste their 2015 Rosso di Montalcino and Brunellos (2013 and Riserva 2012 vintages).

| | |
|---|---|
| ● Brunello di Montalcino '12 | ♀♀♀ 8 |
| ● Brunello di Montalcino '10 | ♀♀♀ 8 |
| ● Brunello di Montalcino '09 | ♀♀♀ 8 |
| ● Brunello di Montalcino '06 | ♀♀♀ 7 |
| ● Brunello di Montalcino '04 | ♀♀♀ 8 |
| ● Brunello di Montalcino '03 | ♀♀♀ 8 |
| ● Brunello di Montalcino '01 | ♀♀♀ 8 |
| ● Brunello di Montalcino '83 | ♀♀♀ 8 |
| ● Brunello di Montalcino Ris. '10 | ♀♀♀ 8 |
| ● Brunello di Montalcino Ris. '07 | ♀♀♀ 8 |
| ● Brunello di Montalcino Ris. '06 | ♀♀♀ 8 |
| ● Brunello di Montalcino Ris. '04 | ♀♀♀ 8 |
| ● Brunello di Montalcino Ris. '01 | ♀♀♀ 8 |
| ● Brunello di Montalcino Ris. '99 | ♀♀♀ 8 |
| ● Brunello di Montalcino Ris. '95 | ♀♀♀ 8 |

## Tenuta di Biserno

LOC. PALAZZO GARDINI
P.ZZA GRAMSCI, 9
57020 BIBBONA [LI]
TEL. +39 0586671099
www.biserno.it

**ANNUAL PRODUCTION** 160,000 bottles
**HECTARES UNDER VINE** 99.00

The lovely winery of Biserno belongs to
Lodovico Antinori, his brother Piero and
Umberto Mannoni. Their desire is to repeat
in Bibbona what was achieved in Bolgheri.
It's true that the vineyards are situated in a
stunning area and the grapes cultivated
show similarities with Bolgheri's.
Winemaking is entrusted to their
super-consultant, Michel Rolland, an
enologist with a clear and precise stylistic
philosophy. The result is a modern selection
of wines, intense and well-calibrated by
maturation in wood. Their 2014 Pino di
Biserno displays a ruby color with purple
highlights, a nose reminiscent of roasted
coffee beans and notes of tobacco and
chocolate. Its creamy, well-structured
palate never forgoes a dynamic, juice-rich
texture. Their sound 2016 Insoglio del
Cinghiale proves in keeping with their
style: aromas of black fruit and mixed spice
lead into a warm, plush palate with good
tannic precision.

| | |
|---|---|
| ● Biserno '13 | 🍷🍷 8 |
| ● Il Pino di Biserno '14 | 🍷🍷 6 |
| ● Insoglio del Cinghiale '16 | 🍷🍷 4 |
| ☉ Sof '17 | 🍷 3 |
| ● Biserno '10 | 🍷🍷🍷 8 |
| ● Biserno '08 | 🍷🍷🍷 6 |
| ● Il Pino di Biserno '09 | 🍷🍷🍷 6 |
| ● Biserno '12 | 🍷🍷 8 |
| ● Biserno '11 | 🍷🍷 8 |
| ● Il Pino di Biserno '11 | 🍷🍷 6 |
| ● Il Pino di Biserno '10 | 🍷🍷 6 |
| ● Insoglio del Cinghiale '15 | 🍷🍷 4 |
| ● Insoglio del Cinghiale Campo del Sasso '11 | 🍷🍷 4 |

## Borgo Salcetino

LOC. LUCARELLI
53017 RADDA IN CHIANTI [SI]
TEL. +39 0577733541
www.livon.it

**PRE-BOOKED VISITS**
**ANNUAL PRODUCTION** 95,000 bottles
**HECTARES UNDER VINE** 15.00
**SUSTAINABLE WINERY**

Radda in Chianti's Borgo Salcetino is
owned by the Friuli-based Livon family. The
total estate spans 30 hectares, 15 of which
are vineyards. Here the area's traditional
grapes are cultivated, Sangiovese and
Canaiolo, as well as Merlot and Cabernet
Sauvignon. They've made a precise
enological choice to age their reds in
medium-large barrels. The result is a
well-defined style that's in keeping with the
territory and capable of delivering sound
and excellent wines, consistently among
the area's best. Their 2016 Chianti
Classico once again shows its aptitude
for excellence. It always manages to offer
up maximum enjoyability, as well as a
certain propensity for complexity, especially
on the nose, which displays all its
trademark elements. Red fruit, flowers,
stony overtones and light hints of
undergrowth pave the way for a vigorous
and delectable palate.

| | |
|---|---|
| ● Chianti Cl. '16 | 🍷🍷🍷 3* |
| ● Chianti Cl. Gran Selezione I Salci '15 | 🍷🍷 6 |
| ● Chianti Cl. '15 | 🍷🍷🍷 3* |
| ● Chianti Cl. '14 | 🍷🍷🍷 3* |
| ● Chianti Cl. '13 | 🍷🍷🍷 3* |
| ● Chianti Cl. '11 | 🍷🍷🍷 3* |
| ● Rossole '12 | 🍷🍷🍷 3* |
| ● Chianti Cl. Lucarello Ris. '13 | 🍷🍷 4 |
| ● Chianti Cl. Lucarello Ris. '12 | 🍷🍷 4 |
| ● Chianti Cl. Lucarello Ris. '11 | 🍷🍷 4 |

# Il Borro

Fraz. San Giustino Valdarno
Loc. Il Borro, 1
52020 Loro Ciuffenna [AR]
Tel. +39 055977053
www.ilborro.it

**CELLAR SALES**
**PRE-BOOKED VISITS**
**ACCOMMODATION AND RESTAURANT SERVICE**
**ANNUAL PRODUCTION** 160,000 bottles
**HECTARES UNDER VINE** 45.00
**VITICULTURE METHOD** Certified Organic
**SUSTAINABLE WINERY**

The earliest record of Borro goes back to 1254, when it was purchased by the marquis Borro Borria, a nobleman from Milan. In the centuries that followed, the castle would be owned by some of Europe's most important families. This continued until 1993, when Ferruccio Ferragamo purchased the estate and began renovating, protecting and reviving the terrain, along with its houses and villas. Local cultivar like Sangiovese are cultivated, but Merlot, Cabernet Sauvignon and Petit Verdot can also be found on an estate that has for some years now been managed organically, with biodynamic on the way. Two wines reached our finals. Their 2015 Borro, a Merlot-heavy blend impressed with its fresh bouquet of herbs, hints of juniper and cloves on a fruity background. Their 2015 Polissena is a monovarietal Sangiovese that features focused aromas of cherries and hints of Mediterranean scrub, reminiscent of bay leaves. It proves lively with good definition on the palate and calibrated tannins.

| | |
|---|---|
| ● Il Borro '15 | ♟♟ 7 |
| ● Polissena '15 | ♟♟ 5 |
| ● Petruna Sangiovese in Anfora '16 | ♟♟ 6 |
| ● Pian di Nova '15 | ♟♟ 3 |
| ⊙ Brut Bolle di Borro '12 | ♟ 8 |
| ● Valdarno di Sopra Borrigiano '16 | ♟ 3 |
| ⊙ Brut Bolle di Borro '11 | ♟♟ 8 |
| ● Il Borro '13 | ♟♟ 7 |
| ● Il Borro '12 | ♟♟ 7 |
| ● Petruna '14 | ♟♟ 7 |
| ● Pian di Nova '13 | ♟♟ 3 |
| ● Polissena '11 | ♟♟ 5 |
| ● Vin Santo del Chianti Occhio di Pernice '09 | ♟♟ 7 |

# ★Poderi Boscarelli

Loc. Cervognano
Via di Montenero, 28
53045 Montepulciano [SI]
Tel. +39 0578767277
www.poderiboscarelli.com

**CELLAR SALES**
**PRE-BOOKED VISITS**
**ANNUAL PRODUCTION** 100,000 bottles
**HECTARES UNDER VINE** 14.00

The De Ferrari Corradi family arrived in Tuscany from Genova in the early 1960s. At the moment they are making some of Nobile di Montepulciano's most well-defined and consistent wines. Situated in one of the appellation's best areas, Cervognano, the winery avails itself of the terrain's peculiar qualities, characterized by alluvial soil and deep red earth. It's a mix that gives rise to elegant, well-structured wines with a lovely character and pronounced acidity. In short, it's a veritable paradise for Sagiovese's expressive potential. Their Nobile di Montepulciano Il Nocio proves a reference point once again. The 2015 vintage features prominent fruit and slightly earthy and spicy overtones. Its juicy and savory mouth displays bitter-sweet contrasts that revive the palate. Their 2015 Nobile also appears well-made. It exhibits more approachable and intense aromas, with a juicy and scented palate. Their 2013 Riserva comes through sound, smoky and austere.

| | |
|---|---|
| ● Nobile di Montepulciano '15 | ♟♟ 5 |
| ● Nobile di Montepulciano Il Nocio '15 | ♟♟ 8 |
| ● Nobile di Montepulciano Ris. '13 | ♟♟ 5 |
| ● Nobile di Montepulciano Costa Grande '15 | ♟♟ 5 |
| ● Rosso di Montepulciano Prugnolo '17 | ♟♟ 3 |
| ● Nobile di Montepulciano Il Nocio '13 | ♟♟♟ 8 |
| ● Nobile di Montepulciano Il Nocio '12 | ♟♟♟ 8 |
| ● Nobile di Montepulciano Il Nocio '11 | ♟♟♟ 8 |
| ● Nobile di Montepulciano Nocio dei Boscarelli '10 | ♟♟♟ 8 |
| ● Cortona Merlot '14 | ♟♟ 4 |
| ● Nobile di Montepulciano '14 | ♟♟ 5 |
| ● Nobile di Montepulciano Sottocasa Ris. '12 | ♟♟ 6 |
| ● Rosso di Montepulciano Prugnolo '16 | ♟♟ 3* |

# ★Brancaia

loc. Poppi, 42
53017 Radda in Chianti [SI]
Tel. +39 0577742007
www.brancaia.it

CELLAR SALES
PRE-BOOKED VISITS
ACCOMMODATION
ANNUAL PRODUCTION 725,000 bottles
HECTARES UNDER VINE 80.00
SUSTAINABLE WINERY

Founded in 1981, the winery owned by the Swiss family Widmer avails itself of three production areas: 'Poppi' (in Radda in Chianti), 'Brancaia' (in Castellina in Chianti), and 'Poggio al Sasso' (in Maremma). In addition to painstaking care of their vineyards, Brancaia's production philosophy is characterized by absolute technical precision. The result is a selection of wines that privileges ripeness of fruit accompanied by the presence of oak, and a bold structure that's never lacking in the necessary freshness. Their Chianti Classico Riserva Brancaia's signature is its elegance, which is highlighted by aromas of wild berries, spices, chocolate and tobacco in the 2015 vintage. Its soft, non-excessive progression on the palate makes some concessions to oak maturation, however. Their 2016 Chianti Classico proves well-made and consistent. Their 2015 Ilatraia, a blend of Cabernet Franc, Petit Verdot and Cabernet Sauvignon, comes through juicy and well-structured.

| | | |
|---|---|---|
| ● Chianti Cl. Ris. '15 | ♟♟ | 5 |
| ● Chianti Cl. '16 | ♟♟ | 4 |
| ● Ilatraia '15 | ♟♟ | 6 |
| ● Brancaia Il Blu '08 | ♟♟♟ | 8 |
| ● Brancaia Il Blu '07 | ♟♟♟ | 7 |
| ● Brancaia Il Blu '06 | ♟♟♟ | 6 |
| ● Brancaia Il Blu '05 | ♟♟♟ | 6 |
| ● Brancaia Il Blu '04 | ♟♟♟ | 6 |
| ● Brancaia Il Blu '03 | ♟♟♟ | 6 |
| ● Chianti Cl. Brancaia '13 | ♟♟♟ | 4* |
| ● Chianti Cl. Ris. '13 | ♟♟♟ | 5 |
| ● Chianti Cl. Ris. '11 | ♟♟♟ | 5 |
| ● Chianti Cl. Ris. '10 | ♟♟♟ | 4* |
| ● Chianti Cl. Ris. '09 | ♟♟♟ | 7 |

# Brunelli - Le Chiuse di Sotto

loc. Podernovone, 157
53024 Montalcino [SI]
Tel. +39 0577849337
www.giannibrunelli.it

CELLAR SALES
PRE-BOOKED VISITS
ACCOMMODATION AND RESTAURANT SERVICE
ANNUAL PRODUCTION 30,000 bottles
HECTARES UNDER VINE 6.50
SUSTAINABLE WINERY

Since his passing, the historic winery once owned by Gianni Brunelli has been managed by his wife, Maria Laura. The estate comprises two different territories in Montalcino. In the northeast, not far from Canalicchi, lie the plots called 'Le Chiuse di Sotto'. Towards the south lie their Podernovone vineyards. Both make positive contributions to their Brunello, a wines that matures in 2000 and 3000 liter oak barrels, but that's difficult to pinpoint stylistically. Its best versions bring out the twin qualities of elegance and austerity, as well as exhibiting strong aging potential. The cool 2013 vintage produced a surprising Brunello compared to its usual style. Openly sunny on the nose, it is enriched in the glass with airier nuances, then unwinds significantly onto a delectable palate, with prominent but fine-grained tannins and controlled warmth. Their 2016 Rosso features an original expressive framework, but proves slightly closed at the finish.

| | | |
|---|---|---|
| ● Brunello di Montalcino '13 | ♟♟ | 6 |
| ● Rosso di Montalcino '16 | ♟♟ | 4 |
| ● Brunello di Montalcino Ris. '12 | ♟ | 8 |
| ● Amor Costante '05 | ♟♟♟ | 5 |
| ● Brunello di Montalcino '12 | ♟♟♟ | 6 |
| ● Brunello di Montalcino '10 | ♟♟♟ | 6 |
| ● Amor Costante '10 | ♟♟ | 5 |
| ● Brunello di Montalcino '11 | ♟♟ | 6 |
| ● Brunello di Montalcino '09 | ♟♟ | 6 |
| ● Brunello di Montalcino '08 | ♟♟ | 6 |
| ● Brunello di Montalcino '07 | ♟♟ | 6 |
| ● Brunello di Montalcino Ris. '10 | ♟♟ | 8 |
| ● Brunello di Montalcino Ris. '07 | ♟♟ | 8 |
| ● Rosso di Montalcino '13 | ♟♟ | 4 |
| ● Rosso di Montalcino '12 | ♟♟ | 4 |

# Bruni

FRAZ. FONTEBLANDA
S.DA VIC.LE MIGLIORINA, 6
58015 ORBETELLO [GR]
TEL. +39 0564885445
www.aziendabruni.it

**CELLAR SALES**
**ANNUAL PRODUCTION** 500,000 bottles
**HECTARES UNDER VINE** 48.00

This Maremma producer have been at the forefront since 1960. They began by selling grapes and bulk wine, but gradually became a winery in their own right. Today the winery is managed by Moreno and Marco Bruni, who've intelligently interpreted the principle characteristics of the area's generous terrain, with an eye towards quality. In the vineyard, much is left up to mother nature herself, thanks in part to a Mediterranean climate that helps the vines fight off potential diseases. In the cellar, which was renovated just this year, stainless steel vessels and barriques are used, along with large wood barrels. The 2016 vintage of Oltreconfine, a monovarietal Grenache, is probably Fonteblanda's best wine. Its elegant aromas range from delicate rose overtones to hints of small red fruits, giving way to notes of gunpowder and spices. The gentle attack in the mouth continues steadily with freshness and depth. The rest of their wines proved consistent.

| | | |
|---|---|---|
| ● Maremma Toscana Grenache Oltreconfine '16 | ♟♟♟ | 6 |
| ● Morellino di Scansano Laire Ris. '15 | ♟♟ | 4 |
| ○ Vermentino Perlaia '17 | ♟♟ | 3 |
| ○ Maremma Toscana Vermentino Plinio '17 | ♟ | 2 |
| ● Morellino di Scansano Marteto '17 | ♟ | 3 |
| ● Grenache Oltreconfine '13 | ♟♟♟ | 2* |
| ● Maremma Toscana Alicante Oltreconfine '15 | ♟♟♟ | 6 |
| ○ Dolce Muffato Perlaia '13 | ♟♟ | 5 |
| ● Maremma Toscana Grenache Oltreconfine '14 | ♟♟ | 5 |
| ○ Maremma Toscana Vermentino Plinio '16 | ♟♟ | 2* |
| ● Morellino di Scansano Laire Ris. '13 | ♟♟ | 4 |
| ● Morellino di Scansano Laire Ris. '12 | ♟♟ | 4 |
| ● Morellino di Scansano Marteto '16 | ♟♟ | 2* |

# Alejandro Bulgheroni Family Vineyards

FRAZ. VAGLIAGLI
LOC. DIEVOLE, 6
53019 CASTELNUOVO BERARDENGA [SI]
TEL. +39 0577322613
www.dievole.it

**CELLAR SALES**
**PRE-BOOKED VISITS**
**ACCOMMODATION AND RESTAURANT SERVICE**
**ANNUAL PRODUCTION** 350,000 bottles
**HECTARES UNDER VINE** 80.00

The project begun by Argentine magnate Bulgheroni may still be settling in, but it's availing itself of extremely valid territories: Montalcino, Bolgheri and Chianti Classico. The last of these has proven to be the producer's area of choice. Indeed, at Dievole, everything seems to be coming into focus. Painstaking care in the vineyards, winemaking in concrete and aging in large wood barrels are already giving rise to high-quality wines. These exhibit character and personality, as well as a solid link to the territory. The Chianti territory remains the one that Bulgheroni Estates interprets best, as demonstrated once again by their 2015 Vigna di Sessina. It is possessed of very complexed aromas ranging from clear and well-expressed fruity notes to earthy and spicy overtones. On the palate it's just as good: highly dynamic, with contrasts and sudden bursts of speed on the palate. Wines produced on their other estates weren't bad either.

| | | |
|---|---|---|
| ● Chianti Cl. Gran Selezione V. di Sessina Dievole '15 | ♟♟ | 7 |
| ● Bolgheri Rosso Sup. Tenuta Le Colonne '15 | ♟♟ | 6 |
| ● Bolgheri Rosso Tenuta Meraviglia '16 | ♟♟ | 4 |
| ● Chianti Cl. Novecento Ris. '14 | ♟♟♟ | 5 |
| ● Broccato '08 | ♟♟ | 5 |
| ● Chianti Cl. '15 | ♟♟ | 4 |
| ● Chianti Cl. '13 | ♟♟ | 4 |
| ● Chianti Cl. Dieulele Ris. '09 | ♟♟ | 7 |
| ● Chianti Cl. La Vendemmia '12 | ♟♟ | 3 |
| ● Chianti Cl. Novecento Ris. '10 | ♟♟ | 5 |
| ● Chianti Cl. Ris. '13 | ♟♟ | 5 |

## Tenuta del Buonamico

LOC. CERCATOIA
VIA PROVINCIALE DI MONTECARLO, 43
55015 MONTECARLO [LU]
TEL. +39 058322038
www.buonamico.it

CELLAR SALES
PRE-BOOKED VISITS
ACCOMMODATION AND RESTAURANT SERVICE
ANNUAL PRODUCTION 350,000 bottles
HECTARES UNDER VINE 43.00
SUSTAINABLE WINERY

Tenuta del Buonamico is one of Lucchesia's historic wineries, and certainly the crown jewel of Montecarlo. Having said this, many things have changed in recent years, starting with the ownership. Management is now in the hands of the Fontana family, who've made a decide push towards renovating the estate. It's a work-in-progress that's seen a lot of changes in terms of the business's organization and their wines. Their style remains modern, both in their classic wines and their most recent offerings. Their well-crafted 2016 Montecarlo Rosso Etichetta Blu is a broad-based grape blend of Sangiovese, Canaiolo, Syrah, Merlot and Cabernet Sauvignon. Fermentation and maceration are carried out in steel, followed by 7 months in barriques. Intense floral aromas lead into a medium-structured palate, with good freshness and a few unpolished overtones at the finish, which highlight well-extracted but slightly stiff tannins. Their Particolare Brut features notes of yeast and mixed citrus fruit.

| | |
|---|---|
| ● Montecarlo Rosso Et. Blu '16 | ♟♟ 3 |
| ○ Particolare Brut | ♟♟ 3 |
| ⊙ Particolare Brut Inedito Rosé | ♟ 5 |
| ● Cercatoja '15 | ♟♟ 5 |
| ● Cercatoja Rosso '11 | ♟♟ 5 |
| ● Il Fortino '12 | ♟♟ 6 |
| ○ Montecarlo Bianco '15 | ♟♟ 2* |

## Buondonno Casavecchia alla Piazza

LOC. LA PIAZZA, 37
53011 CASTELLINA IN CHIANTI [SI]
TEL. +39 0577749754
www.buondonno.com

CELLAR SALES
PRE-BOOKED VISITS
ACCOMMODATION
ANNUAL PRODUCTION 40,000 bottles
HECTARES UNDER VINE 11.00
VITICULTURE METHOD Certified Organic
SUSTAINABLE WINERY

Casavecchia alla Piazza is an area with a long history of agriculture. In 1988, agronomists (and couple) Gabriele Buondonno and Valeria Sodano became owners of the estate and founded their winemaking project. The decision to adopt organic vineyard management came almost immediately, during a period that was groundbreaking (to say the least). In the cellar, as well, they try to be as minimally invasive as possible, with aging carried out in large wood barrels. The result is a wide range of wines with a strong territorial identity, simultaneously pleasant and complex. The 2016 vintage of their Chianti Classico Casavecchia alla Piazza proves top-notch once again. Aromas of small red fruits merge with wild flowers and citrus. The wine flows across the palate with great pleasantness, by virtue of its continuous savoriness and very fresh fruity encore. Their 2015 Chianti Classico Riserva comes through more concentrated and mature, with its intense aromas and generous, though slightly unpolished, palate.

| | |
|---|---|
| ● Chianti Cl. Casavecchia alla Piazza '16 | ♟♟ 3* |
| ● Chianti Cl. Casavecchia alla Piazza Ris. '15 | ♟♟ 3 |
| ● Chianti Cl. Casavecchia alla Piazza '15 | ♟♟♟ 3* |
| ● Campo ai Ciliegi '07 | ♟♟ 5 |
| ● Campo ai Ciliegi '03 | ♟♟ 5 |
| ● Chianti Cl. '09 | ♟♟ 3 |
| ● Chianti Cl. '08 | ♟♟ 3 |
| ● Chianti Cl. Ris. '13 | ♟♟ 5 |
| ● Chianti Cl. Ris. '08 | ♟♟ 5 |
| ● Chianti Cl. Ris. '07 | ♟♟ 5 |

# Cacciagrande

FRAZ. TIRLI
LOC. AMPIO
58043 CASTIGLIONE DELLA PESCAIA [GR]
TEL. +39 0564944168
www.cacciagrande.com

**CELLAR SALES**
**PRE-BOOKED VISITS**
**ANNUAL PRODUCTION** 100,000 bottles
**HECTARES UNDER VINE** 20.00
**SUSTAINABLE WINERY**

Founded in 1997, Cacciagrande is a family-run producer that embodies Maremma's winemaking culture. The vineyards are situated particularly near to the sea, with merely 10 kilometers separating the estate from the coastal town of Castiglione della Pescaia. Their style is decidedly modern, with the use of small oak barrels (sometimes a bit excessively), notable extraction and an extreme pursuit of ripeness, making for a soft, appealing taste that periodically couples with nice drinkability. Their generous but not banal red, the 2016 Castiglione, is a blend of Petit Verdot and Syrah. Its aromas alternate between lush, clean fruit and overtones of pencil lead and black pepper. It becomes generous and soft on the palate, but never loses its acid verve and firm tannins. Their 2017 Cortigliano is slightly more marked by oak maturation. This blend of Petit Verdot, Syrah and Sangiovese proves well-made.

| | | |
|---|---|---|
| ● Castiglione '16 | ♟♟ | 4 |
| ● Cortigliano '17 | ♟♟ | 3 |
| ○ Maremma Toscana Vermentino '17 | ♟ | 3 |
| ● Castiglione '11 | ♟♟ | 4 |
| ● Cortigliano '15 | ♟♟ | 3 |
| ● Maremma Toscana Rosso Cacciagrande '16 | ♟♟ | 2* |
| ○ Maremma Toscana Vermentino '16 | ♟♟ | 3 |
| ○ Maremma Toscana Vermentino '15 | ♟♟ | 3 |
| ○ Maremma Toscana Viognier '16 | ♟♟ | 2* |
| ● Maremma Tosscana Castiglione '13 | ♟♟ | 4 |
| ○ Viognier '14 | ♟♟ | 3 |

# Tenuta Le Calcinaie

LOC. SANTA LUCIA, 36
53037 SAN GIMIGNANO [SI]
TEL. +39 0577943007
www.tenutalecalcinaie.it

**CELLAR SALES**
**PRE-BOOKED VISITS**
**ANNUAL PRODUCTION** 60,000 bottles
**HECTARES UNDER VINE** 9.50
**VITICULTURE METHOD** Certified Organic

It was a passion for vine growing that inspired Simone Santini, and for more than thirty years he's been living his dream. It all started when he planted his first vineyard back in 1986, with his first wine bottled in 1993. The choice to adopt organic cultivation techniques came almost immediately, and since then he's been bringing his expertise and his studies in enology (done in Siena) to his work. It's a path that saw him experiment with new approaches, like the recent choice to offer a selection of wines without added sulfites. Their 2015 Vernaccia Vigna I Sassi Riserva gave a good performance. Its varied aromas range from ripe fruit, such as apples and peaches, to vegetal overtones and herbs, through to almonds. Its caressing and meaty attack in the mouth reveals a distinctive but balanced crispness, while it finishes juicy and inviting. Their 2017 Vernaccia also proved interesting, with its fresher aromas of vegetal and catmint notes and delicate fruity texture, somewhere between damsons and whitecurrants. It features a supple structure and tangy finish.

| | | |
|---|---|---|
| ○ Vernaccia di S. Gimignano '17 | ♟♟ | 2* |
| ○ Vernaccia di S. Gimignano V. ai Sassi Ris. '15 | ♟♟ | 3 |
| ● Chianti '16 | ♟ | 2 |
| ● Chianti CS Santa Maria '12 | ♟ | 4 |
| ● Ingeredienti: Uva '17 | ♟ | 3 |
| ● Teodoro '13 | ♟♟ | 4 |
| ○ Vernaccia di S. Gimignano '15 | ♟♟ | 2* |
| ○ Vernaccia di S. Gimignano Benedetta di San Donato Ris. '14 | ♟♟ | 3 |
| ○ Vernaccia di S. Gimignano V. ai Sassi Ris. '14 | ♟♟ | 3 |
| ○ Vernaccia di S. Gimignano V. ai Sassi Ris. '13 | ♟♟ | 3* |
| ○ Vernaccia di S. Gimignano '16 | ♟ | 2 |

# Camigliano

LOC. CAMIGLIANO
VIA D'INGRESSO, 2
53024 MONTALCINO [SI]
TEL. +39 0577844068
www.camigliano.it

CELLAR SALES
PRE-BOOKED VISITS
ANNUAL PRODUCTION 350,000 bottles
HECTARES UNDER VINE 92.00
SUSTAINABLE WINERY

Camigliano, a village with a long history behind it, can be found in the westernmost limits of Montalcino, immersed in nature and with a splendid view over Upper Maremma and the Colline Metallifere hills. The Ghezzi family took over the estate in the late 1950s, making a decisive contribution towards preserving it as the headquarters of their production (which centers on Sangiovese Brunello). The selection features three Brunellos, all aged in 250 and 600 liter French oak barrels, and which regularly exhibit the wine's characteristically broad flavors. Their commendable work to protect the environment in Camigliano has been rounded up by the magnificent performance of their 2012 Brunello Gualto Riserva. Juniper berries, bay leaves, crushed herbs and a marked Mediterranean identity all follow through onto the caressing and savory palate, with its elegant palate. Their excellent 2013 Brunello offers up an appetizing balance, bearing witness to the good moment the whole selection is enjoying right now.

| | |
|---|---|
| ● Brunello di Montalcino Gualto Ris. '12 | ♟♟♟ 8 |
| ● Brunello di Montalcino '13 | ♟♟ 6 |
| ● Rosso di Montalcino '16 | ♟ 3 |
| ● Brunello di Montalcino '12 | ♟♟ 6 |
| ● Brunello di Montalcino '11 | ♟♟ 6 |
| ● Brunello di Montalcino '10 | ♟♟ 6 |
| ● Brunello di Montalcino '09 | ♟♟ 6 |
| ● Brunello di Montalcino Gualto Ris. '10 | ♟♟ 7 |
| ● Brunello di Montalcino Gualto Ris. '09 | ♟♟ 7 |
| ● Brunello di Montalcino Gualto Ris. '07 | ♟♟ 7 |
| ● Brunello di Montalcino Paesaggio Inatteso '12 | ♟♟ 7 |
| ● Brunello di Montalcino Ris. '11 | ♟♟ 6 |
| ● Rosso di Montalcino '15 | ♟♟ 3 |
| ● Rosso di Montalcino '13 | ♟♟ 3 |

# Antonio Camillo

LOC. PIANETTI DI MONTEMERANO
58014 MANCIANO [GR]
TEL. +39 3391525224
info@antoniocamillo.com

CELLAR SALES
PRE-BOOKED VISITS
ANNUAL PRODUCTION 65,000 bottles
HECTARES UNDER VINE 10.00
VITICULTURE METHOD Certified Organic

In terms of his winemaking and vine growing experience, Antonio Camillo has few equals. His sensibility was such that he decided to champion the virtues of an ancient cultivar, Ciliegiolo, and reintroduce it into the territory. His wines made with the grape are still his best, proving original and forthright, eschewing rustic character in favor of pleasantness and a rediscovered subtle complexity. Sangiovese is also cultivated and used, as well as the area's common white grapes. The 2016 is another sensational vintage of their Vallerana Alta, a red that has become a benchmark for its kind. Its extremely fresh aromas convey clean sensations of small red fruit, grass and earth. The wine proves steady on the palate, marked by continual contrasts and great savoriness. Their 2017 Ciliegiolo proves a slightly lower level, but certainly comes through delicious, fruity and pleasantly juicy.

| | |
|---|---|
| ● Maremma Toscana Ciliegiolo V. Vallerana Alta '16 | ♟♟♟ 5 |
| ● Maremma Toscana Ciliegiolo '17 | ♟♟ 3 |
| ● Maremma Toscana Ciliegiolo V. Vallerana Alta '15 | ♟♟♟ 6 |
| ● Maremma Toscana Ciliegiolo V. Vallerana Alta '14 | ♟♟♟ 3* |
| ● Maremma Toscana Ciliegiolo V. Vallerana Alta '13 | ♟♟ 3* |
| ● Maremma Toscana Ciliegiolo V. Vallerana Alta '12 | ♟♟ 3* |
| ● Maremma Toscana Ciliegiolo V. Vallerana Alta '11 | ♟♟ 3* |
| ● Morellino di Scansano Cotozzino '15 | ♟♟ 3 |

# Campo alla Sughera

LOC. CACCIA AL PIANO
S.DA PROV.LE BOLGHERESE, 280
57020 BOLGHERI [LI]
TEL. +39 0565766936
www.campoallasughera.com

CELLAR SALES
PRE-BOOKED VISITS
ACCOMMODATION
ANNUAL PRODUCTION 110,000 bottles
HECTARES UNDER VINE 16.50

Campo alla Sughera is a winery that's
well-managed down to the very last detail,
and enjoying increasing popularity. It's all
thanks to the Knauf family, who are shaping
its approach and positioning it among
Bolgheri's most well-organized producers.
Their cellar is modern, technologically
up-to-date and led by a technical staff
that's increasingly qualified and prestigious.
Their lovely main facility is surrounded by
their private vineyards, thus guaranteeing
quality work and the right space to make it
happen. Their 2015 Bolgheri Superiore
Arnione proves less impressive than the
previous year. This still-evolving wine needs
to find the right combination between the
components in the bottle. Its toasty notes
appear slightly unfocused, with rather
marked general spicy sensations. Time will
tell. Their 2016 Adeo comes through more
enjoyable, open on the nose but fresh and
linear in the mouth; their 2017 Achenio is a
pleasant white wine.

| | |
|---|---|
| ● Bolgheri Rosso Adeo '16 | ♟♟ 5 |
| ● Bolgheri Rosso Sup. Arnione '15 | ♟♟ 6 |
| ○ Bolgheri Bianco Achenio '17 | ♟ 5 |
| ● Bolgheri Sup. Arnione '06 | ♟♟♟ 6 |
| ○ Bolgheri Bianco Achenio '16 | ♟♟ 5 |
| ○ Bolgheri Bianco Achenio '14 | ♟♟ 5 |
| ○ Bolgheri Bianco Achenio '13 | ♟♟ 5 |
| ● Bolgheri Rosso Adeo '14 | ♟♟ 4 |
| ● Bolgheri Sup. Arnione '13 | ♟♟ 6 |
| ● Bolgheri Sup. Arnione '12 | ♟♟ 6 |

# Campo alle Comete

LOC. SUGHERICCIO
VIA FORNACELLE 249
57022 CASTAGNETO CARDUCCI [LI]
TEL. +39 0565766056
www.campoallecomete.it

CELLAR SALES
ANNUAL PRODUCTION 120,000 bottles
HECTARES UNDER VINE 15.00
VITICULTURE METHOD Certified Organic

Campo alle Comete is the Bolgheri offshoot
of Campania's Feudi di San Gregorio, a
producer headquartered in Sorbo Serpico,
Irpinia, and owned by the Capaldo family.
The project is still at the beginning, though
it's rooted in a solid foundation, a lovely
estate and an existing production facility
that's currently being renovated. Their 15
hectares of vineyards are planted at
high-densities, and give rise to the area's
most established cultivar: Merlot, Cabernet
Sauvignon, Cabernet Franc and Petit Verdot.
Their first wines are convincing, as intense
as they are balanced. Their 2015 Bolgheri
Superiore embodies this new winery's style.
It is a skillful blend of black grapes
combined with maturation in new and
second-year barriques. It features dark
colors and aromas, while the palate proves
silky, lingering and slightly alcoholic at the
finish. Their 2016 Bolgheri Rosso Stupore
comes through more delicate, with hints of
pomegranate and black pepper.

| | |
|---|---|
| ● Bolgheri Rosso Stupore '16 | ♟♟ 4 |
| ● Bolgheri Rosso Sup. '15 | ♟♟ 4 |
| ○ Vermentino '17 | ♟♟ 5 |
| ● Cabernet Sauvignon '16 | ♟ 4 |
| ● Cabernet Sauvignon '15 | ♟♟ 4 |

## Canalicchio di Sopra

LOC. CASACCIA, 73
53024 MONTALCINO [SI]
TEL. +39 0577848316
www.canalicchiodisopra.com

CELLAR SALES
PRE-BOOKED VISITS
ACCOMMODATION
ANNUAL PRODUCTION 55,000 bottles
HECTARES UNDER VINE 15.00

Siblings Simonetta, Marco and Francesco Ripaccioli are the third generation to manage Canalicchio di Sopra, the winery founded by their grandfather Primo Pacenti in 1961, and long managed by their father, Pier Luigi. The estate is situated on the slopes of Canalicchi and Montosoli, in the north of Montalcino, an area that's indirectly associated with caressing, solemn Brunellos. Here they're explored through calibrated fermentation and maturation primarily in 300 liter oak barrels. Their Sangioveses always do well over the long haul but can be enjoyed even in the mid-term. Canalicchio di Sopra's packed selection never shows any weakness. Their 2016 Rosso is a guarantee, due to its clean aromas and drinkability, while their 2012 Brunello Riserva reveals a classic profile playing on dried herbs and spices, with a creamy but austere development. However, we preferred their 2013 Brunello: wild berries, licorice and humus, but just lacking a bit of savory body on a fresh palate.

| | |
|---|---|
| ● Brunello di Montalcino '13 | ♟♟ 6 |
| ● Brunello di Montalcino Ris. '12 | ♟♟ 8 |
| ● Rosso di Montalcino '16 | ♟♟ 3 |
| ● Brunello di Montalcino '10 | ♟♟♟ 6 |
| ● Brunello di Montalcino '07 | ♟♟♟ 6 |
| ● Brunello di Montalcino '06 | ♟♟♟ 6 |
| ● Brunello di Montalcino '04 | ♟♟♟ 6 |
| ● Brunello di Montalcino Ris. '10 | ♟♟♟ 8 |
| ● Brunello di Montalcino Ris. '07 | ♟♟♟ 8 |
| ● Brunello di Montalcino Ris. '04 | ♟♟♟ 7 |
| ● Brunello di Montalcino Ris. '01 | ♟♟♟ 7 |
| ● Brunello di Montalcino '12 | ♟♟ 6 |
| ● Brunello di Montalcino '11 | ♟♟ 6 |
| ● Rosso di Montalcino '15 | ♟♟ 3* |
| ● Rosso di Montalcino '14 | ♟♟ 3 |

## Cantalici

FRAZ. CASTAGNOLI
VIA DELLA CROCE, 17-19
53013 GAIOLE IN CHIANTI [SI]
TEL. +39 0577731038
www.cantalici.it

CELLAR SALES
PRE-BOOKED VISITS
ANNUAL PRODUCTION 46,000 bottles
HECTARES UNDER VINE 30.00

The Cantalici brothers got their start some 20 years ago. After years of providing services to Chianti producers, they decided to open their own winery, investing in an old property that their father, Loris, had purchased in 1972, and transforming it into an estate. Since then their vineyards have grown and the cellar has been equipped with modern technology. Their wines are taking on a precise character. Their excellent 2013 Chianti Classico Gran Selezione Baruffo exhibits a generous and focused bouquet of cherries and blackberries, with refreshing notes of herbs, bay leaves and rosemary. Its palate nicely balances tannins and alcohol, with enjoyable acidity and an appetizing finish. Their 2013 Tangano also proves sound. This equal blend of Sangiovese, Merlot and Cabernet features spicy hints of cloves, sweet overtones of chocolate, good structure and smooth tannins.

| | |
|---|---|
| ● Chianti Cl. Gran Sel. Baruffo '13 | ♟♟ 3* |
| ○ Cantavento '16 | ♟♟ 4 |
| ● Chianti Cl. Baruffo '15 | ♟♟ 3 |
| ● Chianti Cl. Baruffo Ris. '15 | ♟♟ 3 |
| ● Petali Rosso '17 | ♟♟ 3 |
| ● Tangano '13 | ♟♟ 4 |
| ○ Vin Santo del Chianti Cl. Baruffo '11 | ♟♟ 6 |
| ● Chianti Cl. '14 | ♟ 3 |
| ⊙ Petali Rosato '17 | ♟ 3 |
| ● Chianti Cl. '08 | ♟♟ 3 |
| ● Chianti Cl. '03 | ♟♟ 2* |
| ● Chianti Cl. Baruffo Ris. '11 | ♟♟ 3 |
| ● Chianti Cl. Messer Ridolfo '04 | ♟♟ 3 |
| ● Chianti Cl. Messer Ridolfo Ris. '08 | ♟♟ 3 |

# Capanna

LOC. CAPANNA, 333
53024 MONTALCINO [SI]
TEL. +39 0577848298
www.capannamontalcino.com

**CELLAR SALES**
**PRE-BOOKED VISITS**
**ANNUAL PRODUCTION** 70,000 bottles
**HECTARES UNDER VINE** 21.00

Podere Capanna is a splendid estate situated at 300 meters above sea level on Montosoli hill (in the north of Montalcino), an area that features marly soil. The winey has been in the hands of the Cencioni family for more than 60 years. Today it's led by Patrizio, artificer of a Brunello strongly characterized by a sanguine heartiness. In the cellar a minimally invasive approach is adopted, with long maturation in 1000 and 3000 liter oak barrels. While still young, their wines can be at times a bit clenched aromatically but with time they prove decidedly broader and more open. Our latest round of tastings highlighted an overall strong performance by their entire selection, but as usual it's their Brunello Riserva that heads the group. Their 2012 offers up an irresistible floral character, enhanced by hints of roots and loose earth. A few notes of confit point to a warm maturity, which reins in its length, together with austere tannins. This makes for an ancient style that's sure to make an impression.

| | |
|---|---|
| ● Brunello di Montalcino Ris. '12 | ♟♟ 8 |
| ● Brunello di Montalcino '13 | ♟♟ 6 |
| ○ Moscadello di Montalcino V. T. '15 | ♟♟ 4 |
| ● Rosso di Montalcino '16 | ♟♟ 3 |
| ● Brunello di Montalcino Ris. '10 | ♟♟♟ 8 |
| ● Brunello di Montalcino Ris. '06 | ♟♟♟ 7 |
| ● Brunello di Montalcino Ris. '04 | ♟♟♟ 7 |
| ● Brunello di Montalcino Ris. '90 | ♟♟♟ 6 |
| ● Rosso di Montalcino '15 | ♟♟♟ 3* |
| ● Brunello di Montalcino '12 | ♟♟ 6 |
| ● Brunello di Montalcino '11 | ♟♟ 6 |
| ● Brunello di Montalcino '10 | ♟♟ 6 |
| ● Brunello di Montalcino '09 | ♟♟ 6 |
| ○ Moscadello di Montalcino V. T. '12 | ♟♟ 4 |
| ● Rosso di Montalcino '14 | ♟♟ 3 |

# Tenuta Caparzo

LOC. CAPARZO
S.DA PROV.LE DEL BRUNELLO KM 1,700
53024 MONTALCINO [SI]
TEL. +39 0577848390
www.caparzo.com

**CELLAR SALES**
**PRE-BOOKED VISITS**
**ACCOMMODATION**
**ANNUAL PRODUCTION** 900,000 bottles
**HECTARES UNDER VINE** 90.00

Elisabetta Gnudi's estate is one of Montalcino's major wineries, with plots on practically every slope and a variety of grapes cultivated (in addition to Sangiovese, a number of local and international cultivar). This mosaic of varieties matches well with their winemaking approach. Their three Brunellos ('Vintage', Riserva, and their Vigna La Casa cru) are aged in barriques and large barrels, without ever adopting a single predetermined regime. This is the Caparzo signature style, one that's widely appreciated for its ability to adapt to each season's temperament. Yet another superb performance by all their Sangiovese reds, especially the 2013 Brunello Vigna La Casa. Black cherries, mulberries and woodland overtones make for an assertive and dynamic nose from start to end. Its classic medium-weight on the palate exhibits savory dynamism and extractive quality rather than a show of strength. Their 2012 Riserva also proved sound, not particularly sharp, but solid and lively.

| | |
|---|---|
| ● Brunello di Montalcino V. La Casa '13 | ♟♟ 8 |
| ● Brunello di Montalcino '13 | ♟♟ 6 |
| ● Brunello di Montalcino Ris. '12 | ♟♟ 7 |
| ● Rosso di Montalcino (duplicato) '14 | ♟♟ 3 |
| ● Brunello di Montalcino La Casa '93 | ♟♟♟ 6 |
| ● Brunello di Montalcino La Casa '88 | ♟♟♟ 6 |
| ● Brunello di Montalcino '12 | ♟♟ 6 |
| ● Brunello di Montalcino '10 | ♟♟ 6 |
| ● Brunello di Montalcino Ris. '09 | ♟♟ 7 |
| ● Brunello di Montalcino V. La Casa '12 | ♟♟ 8 |
| ● Brunello di Montalcino V. La Casa '10 | ♟♟ 8 |
| ● Morellino di Scansano '13 | ♟♟ 3 |
| ● Rosso di Montalcino '14 | ♟♟ 3 |
| ● Rosso di Montalcino '13 | ♟♟ 3 |
| ● Rosso di Montalcino La Caduta '14 | ♟♟ 4 |

## ★Tenuta di Capezzana

LOC. SEANO
VIA CAPEZZANA, 100
59015 CARMIGNANO [PO]
TEL. +39 0558706005
www.capezzana.it

CELLAR SALES
PRE-BOOKED VISITS
ACCOMMODATION AND RESTAURANT SERVICE
ANNUAL PRODUCTION 450,000 bottles
HECTARES UNDER VINE 90.00
VITICULTURE METHOD Certified Organic

Some 90 years ago, Alessandro Contini
Bonacossi purchased the estate of
Capezzana. It was later enlarged to include
two neighboring tracts of land: Poggetto and
Trefiano. And so it was that the modern
winery was born. Today it's divided into
three main farms and more than 120 plots,
which give rise to a production of wine and
olive oil that goes back to 804 C.E. After
Vittorio's important efforts, his children
Beatrice, Filippo and Benedetto are moving
ahead. In 2009 they began working towards
a more environmentally-friendly approach
that eventually led to organic certification.
Their 2015 Carmignano Riserva Trefiano
reached our finals. Its explosive, clean and
precise fruity notes of cherries, blackberries
and redcurrants lead into a fresh attack in
the mouth, a solid structure and smooth
tannins. Their 2015 Carmignano Riserva
displays complex inky and delicate vegetal
aromas, with a well-structured, warm,
fresh, tannic palate and good pulp. Their
2015 Ugo Contini Bonacossi, a monovarietal
Sangiovese, offers up a bouquet of black
fruit, with a spirited and lingering palate.

| | | |
|---|---|---|
| ● Carmignano Trefiano Ris. '15 | ▼▼ | 6 |
| ● Carmignano Villa Capezzana '15 | ▼▼ | 5 |
| ● Ugo Contini Bonacossi '15 | ▼▼ | 3 |
| ● Barco Reale '16 | ▼ | 3 |
| ● Ghiaie della Furba '15 | ▼ | 6 |
| ○ Trebbiano '16 | ▼ | 4 |
| ○ Vin Santo di Carmignano Ris. '10 | ♀♀♀ | 6 |
| ○ Vin Santo di Carmignano Ris. '09 | ♀♀♀ | 6 |
| ● Carmignano Villa di Capezzana '13 | ♀♀ | 5 |
| ○ Chardonnay '15 | ♀♀ | 3 |
| ● Ghiaie della Furba '13 | ♀♀ | 6 |
| ○ Trebbiano '15 | ♀♀ | 4 |

## Caprili

FRAZ. TAVERNELLE
LOC. CAPRILI, 268
53024 MONTALCINO [SI]
TEL. +39 0577848566
www.caprili.it

CELLAR SALES
PRE-BOOKED VISITS
ACCOMMODATION
ANNUAL PRODUCTION 75,000 bottles
HECTARES UNDER VINE 21.00
SUSTAINABLE WINERY

Vigna Madre, Ceppo Nero, Testucchiaia,
Quadrucci, del Pino, Palazzetto: these are
the plots that the Bartolommei family rely on
for their Brunello wines. Caprili, considered
one of southeastern Montalcino's cru par
excellence was taken over by the
Castelli-Martinozzi family (owners of Villa
Santa Restituita) in the 1960s. The winery's
reputation continues to grow thanks to a
masterly series of authoritative wines
(including their Riserva and Rosso). Their
selection of Sangioveses is pulpy and
energetic, helped in part by long maturation
in large wooden barrels. Recent tastings
fully confirmed our initial impressions,
especially regarding their 2013 Brunello.
After a hesitant start, its aromas quickly
transform into a luxuriant sequence of
berries, Mediterranean herbs and sea
breezes. Then the best part proves its
deliciously sweet and delicately salty palate,
with velvety tannins. Their 2016 Rosso
displays an even more quintessentially
southern character, well-supported by a
powerful savory structure.

| | | |
|---|---|---|
| ● Brunello di Montalcino '13 | ▼▼▼ | 6 |
| ● Rosso di Montalcino '16 | ▼▼ | 3* |
| ● Brunello di Montalcino AdAlberto Ris. '12 | ▼▼ | 8 |
| ● Brunello di Montalcino '10 | ♀♀♀ | 6 |
| ● Brunello di Montalcino '06 | ♀♀♀ | 7 |
| ● Brunello di Montalcino AdAlberto Ris. '10 | ♀♀♀ | 8 |
| ● Brunello di Montalcino Ris. '08 | ♀♀♀ | 7 |
| ● Brunello di Montalcino Ris. '06 | ♀♀♀ | 7 |
| ● Brunello di Montalcino Ris. '04 | ♀♀♀ | 5 |
| ● Brunello di Montalcino '12 | ♀♀ | 6 |
| ● Brunello di Montalcino '11 | ♀♀ | 6 |
| ● Rosso di Montalcino '15 | ♀♀ | 3 |
| ● Rosso di Montalcino '14 | ♀♀ | 3 |

# Tenuta Carleone

LOC. CASTIGLIONI

53017 RADDA IN CHIANTI [SI]
TEL. +39 0577735613
www.carleone.it

**CELLAR SALES**
**PRE-BOOKED VISITS**
**ANNUAL PRODUCTION** 35,000 bottles
**HECTARES UNDER VINE** 15.00
**VITICULTURE METHOD** Certified Organic

After 25 years leading Riecine, Sean
O'Callaghan has gone in a new direction
with consulting and gone into producing his
own wines in Carleone di Castiglioni. In fact,
his wine is a personal, parallel project that's
channeled into his work in Chianti, in the
prized subzone of Radda in Chianti. Open air
fermentation, aging in concrete, and long
maceration (up to 60 days) give rise to their
'O'Callaghan' style of Sangiovese, clean
and natural. Their 2015 Chianti Classico is
simply delicious, one of the best ever for
finesse, flavor and depth. This wine reveals
a rare, just 'hinted at' elegance and
matchless charm. Very delicate subtraction
is featured in their 2016 Il Guercio, which
certainly proves intriguing but just lacks
specific weight and pulp. Their delectable
and scented 2015 Due comes through
very drinkable.

| | | |
|---|---|---|
| ● Chianti Cl. '15 | ♟♟♟ | 5 |
| ● Il Guercio '16 | ♟♟ | 7 |
| ● Il Due '15 | ♟♟ | 6 |
| ● Il Guercio '15 | ♟♟ | 7 |

# Podere Il Carnasciale

LOC. SAN LEOLINO, 82
52020 MERCATALE VALDARNO [AR]
TEL. +39 0559911142
www.caberlot.eu

**PRE-BOOKED VISITS**
**ANNUAL PRODUCTION** 10,000 bottles
**HECTARES UNDER VINE** 4.50
**SUSTAINABLE WINERY**

Caberlot was discovered in the early 1960s
in an old vineyard near Padova by the
agronomist Remigio Bordini. It was a
spontaneous hybrid that today is cultivated
exclusively at Podere Il Carnasciale. It was
here, on the hills of the Tuscan Apennines
and Chianti Classico, on a landscape
cultivated by humans since antiquity, that
Wolf Rogosky got his start in 1986. Today
Podere Carnasciale is managed by Bettina
and Mortiz Rogosky, who continue to make
this unique wine available to the world.
Their 2015 Caberlot, made with the
homonymous grapes, put in an excellent
performance. Its lovely floral notes of
geraniums merge with mixed fruit and the
vegetal freshness of rosemary and bay
leaves. Its striking attack in the mouth
proves dynamic and caressing. It features
fresh acidity, tannins and alcohol nicely in
step and a very long savory finish.

| | | |
|---|---|---|
| ● Il Caberlot '15 | ♟♟ | 8 |
| ● Caberlot '10 | ♟♟♟ | 8 |
| ● Caberlot '08 | ♟♟♟ | 8 |
| ● Caberlot '05 | ♟♟♟ | 8 |
| ● Caberlot '04 | ♟♟♟ | 8 |
| ● Caberlot '00 | ♟♟♟ | 8 |
| ● Caberlot '14 | ♟♟ | 8 |
| ● Caberlot '13 | ♟♟ | 8 |
| ● Caberlot '12 | ♟♟ | 8 |
| ● Caberlot '11 | ♟♟ | 8 |

## ★Fattoria Carpineta Fontalpino

FRAZ. MONTAPERTI
LOC. CARPINETA
53019 CASTELNUOVO BERARDENGA [SI]
TEL. +39 0577369219
www.carpinetafontalpino.it

**CELLAR SALES**
**PRE-BOOKED VISITS**
**ACCOMMODATION**
**ANNUAL PRODUCTION** 100,000 bottles
**HECTARES UNDER VINE** 23.00
**VITICULTURE METHOD** Certified Organic

Carpineta Fontalpino has taken significant steps recently to improve quality. Paying off in particular is their scrupulous work in the vineyard and an approach in the cellar that's as precise as it is delicate. The result is a range of modern wines never lacking in personality or character. These are generous, full-bodied and exhibit notable structure, as well as a tension and freshness that comes with fresh fruit, the result of aging in small wood barrels for limited periods. Gioia Cresti has submitted a trio with lovely energy and strong personality. Their 2016 Chianti Classico Dofana stands out for its generous aromas of red fruit and spices, combined with a sound, persistent and juicy palate. The other two wines are their flavorsome and lively 2015 Do Ut Des, a blend of Sangiovese, Merlot and Cabernet Sauvignon, and their delectable 2016 Chianti Classico Montaperto.

## Casa Emma

LOC. SAN DONATO IN POGGIO
S.DA PROV.LE DI CASTELLINA IN CHIANTI, 3
50021 BARBERINO VAL D'ELSA [FI]
TEL. +39 0558072239
www.casaemma.com

**CELLAR SALES**
**PRE-BOOKED VISITS**
**RESTAURANT SERVICE**
**ANNUAL PRODUCTION** 90,000 bottles
**HECTARES UNDER VINE** 31.00
**VITICULTURE METHOD** Certified Organic
**SUSTAINABLE WINERY**

The Bucalossi family winery, located between Siena and Florence, is divided into two main estates, near Castellina in Chianti and Barberino Val d' Elsa. These distinct zones express themselves throughout the winery's range, but at the same time often mixing in a complementary way. The style is defined by mature fruit, developed structure and clear expression of terroir. The result is well-defined wine presented with balance and personality. Aging occurs mostly in small wood barrels. Their 2016 Chianti Classico stands out for its lovely aromas of wild flowers, freshly-cut grass and smoky overtones at the finish. Its mouth offers up lively, assertive tannins that enhance a dynamic, scented palate. Their 2015 Chianti Classico Vigna al Parco favors more fruity aromas and flavors, a soft and juicy palate, though with a touch of exuberant wood. Their plush and charming monovarietal Merlot 2015 Soloio, however, shows no lack of savoriness or freshness.

| | |
|---|---|
| ● Chianti Cl. Dofana '16 | ♟♟♟ 4* |
| ● Do ut des '15 | ♟♟ 5 |
| ● Chianti Cl. Montaperto '16 | ♟♟ 4 |
| ● Chianti Cl. Montaperto '15 | ♟♟♟ 4* |
| ● Do ut des '13 | ♟♟♟ 5 |
| ● Do ut des '12 | ♟♟♟ 5 |
| ● Do ut des '11 | ♟♟♟ 5 |
| ● Do ut des '10 | ♟♟♟ 5 |
| ● Do ut des '09 | ♟♟♟ 5 |
| ● Do ut des '07 | ♟♟♟ 5 |
| ● Dofana '10 | ♟♟♟ 7 |
| ● Dofana '07 | ♟♟♟ 8 |

| | |
|---|---|
| ● Chianti Cl. '16 | ♟♟ 3* |
| ● Chianti Cl. Vigna al Parco '15 | ♟♟ 3 |
| ● Soloio '15 | ♟♟ 6 |
| ● Chianti Cl. Ris. '95 | ♟♟♟ 4* |
| ● Chianti Cl. Ris. '93 | ♟♟♟ 5 |
| ● Soloio '94 | ♟♟♟ 4* |
| ● Chianti Cl. '15 | ♟♟ 3* |
| ● Chianti Cl. '14 | ♟♟ 3 |
| ● Chianti Cl. Gran Sel. '12 | ♟♟ 5 |
| ● Chianti Cl. Ris. '13 | ♟♟ 5 |
| ● Chianti Cl. Ris. '13 | ♟♟ 5 |
| ● Soloio '12 | ♟♟ 6 |

# ★Casanova di Neri

POD. FIESOLE
53024 MONTALCINO [SI]
TEL. +39 0577834455
www.casanovadineri.com

PRE-BOOKED VISITS
ACCOMMODATION
ANNUAL PRODUCTION 225,000 bottles
HECTARES UNDER VINE 63.00

Run by Giacomo, Gianlorenzo and Giovanni Neri, this international star is experiencing a resurgence, thanks in part to the younger generation of the family. Success has also come from the expansive and varied vineyards of Cetine, Sesta, Cava dell'Onice, Podernuovo, Cerratalto, Sperata, Fiesole, Podderuccio, whose patchwork parcels provide a diversity of soil. They find synthesis in a proudly modern style, in continuous remodulation, linked to aging in small and new wood for the range of Brunello. This is undoubtedly one of the most exciting performances in recent years by the duo submitted by Casanova di Neri. Their 2013 Tenuta Nuova proves a true modern-style Brunello, playing on notes of dark overripe fruit, sweet spices and roots. It is possessed of an innovative round touch and classic tannic contrasts. Their Etichetta Bianca from the same vintage appears less close-knit, but carefree and supple.

| | | |
|---|---|---|
| ● Brunello di Montalcino Tenuta Nuova '13 | ♟♟♟ | 8 |
| ● Brunello di Montalcino '13 | ♟♟ | 6 |
| ● Brunello di Montalcino '09 | ♟♟♟ | 6 |
| ● Brunello di Montalcino '06 | ♟♟♟ | 5 |
| ● Brunello di Montalcino Cerretalto '07 | ♟♟♟ | 8 |
| ● Brunello di Montalcino Cerretalto '06 | ♟♟♟ | 8 |
| ● Brunello di Montalcino Cerretalto '04 | ♟♟♟ | 8 |
| ● Brunello di Montalcino Cerretalto '01 | ♟♟♟ | 8 |
| ● Brunello di Montalcino Cerretalto '99 | ♟♟♟ | 8 |
| ● Brunello di Montalcino Tenuta Nuova '06 | ♟♟♟ | 8 |
| ● Brunello di Montalcino Tenuta Nuova '05 | ♟♟♟ | 7 |
| ● Brunello di Montalcino Tenuta Nuova '01 | ♟♟♟ | 6 |
| ● Brunello di Montalcino Tenuta Nuova '99 | ♟♟♟ | 6 |
| ● Pietradonice '05 | ♟♟♟ | 8 |
| ● Sant'Antimo Pietradonice '01 | ♟♟♟ | 8 |

# Tenuta Casteani

LOC. CASTEANI
POD. FABBRI
58023 GAVORRANO [GR]
TEL. +39 0566871050
www.casteani.it

CELLAR SALES
PRE-BOOKED VISITS
ACCOMMODATION AND RESTAURANT SERVICE
ANNUAL PRODUCTION 80,000 bottles
HECTARES UNDER VINE 14.00
SUSTAINABLE WINERY

Mario Pelosi's estate is comprised of some 14 hectares of vineyards divided into two sections. The first was planted in 2004 and the second in 2012. Cordon-trained and spur-pruned plots, as well as Guyot-trained, give rise to Sangiovese, Alicante, Vermentino, Aleatico, Syrah, Merlot and Viognier. Their wines are of a clear, modern style that relies primarily on high-quality grapes. Maturation takes place in small wood barrels (new, second-fill and third-fill), large barrels and terra-cotta. Their juicy and drinkable 2013 Terra di Casteani is a blend of Sangiovese and Merlot featuring clean and complex aromas. Their 2014 Sessanta, a blend of Sangiovese and Alicante Bouchet aged in large wood, proves more approachable but just as pleasant. Their scented and flavorsome Vermentino, 2017 Spirito Libero, contains no added sulfites, while their very mature 2015 Marujo monovarietal Syrah wine matures in terracotta.

| | | |
|---|---|---|
| ● Maremma Toscana Rosso Terra di Casteani '13 | ♟♟ | 5 |
| ● Maremma Toscana Sessanta '14 | ♟♟ | 3 |
| ○ Maremma Toscana Vermentino Spirito Libero '17 | ♟♟ | 2* |
| ● Maremma Toscana Syrah Marujo '15 | ♟ | 5 |

## Castell'in Villa

LOC. CASTELL'IN VILLA
53019 CASTELNUOVO BERARDENGA [SI]
TEL. +39 0577359074
www.castellinvilla.com

CELLAR SALES
PRE-BOOKED VISITS
ANNUAL PRODUCTION 100,000 bottles
HECTARES UNDER VINE 54.00

It has taken a little time for the ultramodern paradigm of winemaking to merge with a return to more authentic style, but it means that Castell'In Villa has regained its place among the stars of Chianti Classico. Located near Castelnuovo Berardegna, where Riccardo Pignatelli della Leonessa arrived in 1967, the winery is now run by Coralia Ghertsos, better known as "la Principessa." The vintage wines of the estate are often exciting, but there are also younger wines that can really "wow," exemplifying the classic, powerful style of the past while adding the immediate drinkability of more contemporary winemaking. We retasted their 2010 Chianti Classico Poggio alle Rose: aromas of ripe cherries and roses merge with hints of flint, tobacco and light notes of aging, which add to its charm. Its mouth features assertive tannins, a savory development and a punchy, vigorous finish. Their 2014 Chianti Classico proves more subtle and delicate, with whispered aromas and a continuous and relaxed palate.

| | | |
|---|---|---|
| ● Chianti Cl. '14 | ♟♟ 5 | |
| ● Chianti Cl. '11 | ♟♟♟ 5 | |
| ● Chianti Cl. '09 | ♟♟♟ 5 | |
| ● Chianti Cl. '08 | ♟♟♟ 5 | |
| ● Chianti Cl. Ris. '85 | ♟♟♟ 6 | |
| ● Chianti Cl. '13 | ♟♟ 5 | |
| ● Chianti Cl. '12 | ♟♟ 5 | |
| ● Chianti Cl. Poggio delle Rose Ris. '10 | ♟♟ 8 | |
| ● Chianti Cl. Ris. '11 | ♟♟ 6 | |
| ● Chianti Cl. Ris. '10 | ♟♟ 6 | |

## ★★Castellare di Castellina

LOC. CASTELLARE
53011 CASTELLINA IN CHIANTI [SI]
TEL. +39 0577742903
www.castellare.it

CELLAR SALES
PRE-BOOKED VISITS
ACCOMMODATION
ANNUAL PRODUCTION 200,000 bottles
HECTARES UNDER VINE 28.00

*The owner of this producer is also a shareholder of Gambero Rosso spa. To avoid any conflict of interest, Paolo Panerai has subordinated the possible awarding of Tre Bicchieri (which, in any case, only occurs through a blind tasting) to the attainment of the same rating of excellence (upwards of 90/100) by an independent, international panel. This was the case here.*

Castellina in Chianti makes great, ageworthy wines. Their style focuses on technical rigor and draws on the principal character of the appellation's wines. A great 2014 I Sodi di San Niccolò features complex and multifaceted aromas, making for a truly top-of-the-class wine. But it's in the mouth that the wine gives its best, with a steady, savory and very juicy palate. Their 2015 Chianti Classico Riserva offers up nuanced aromas with lovely freshness and a flavorsome palate.

| | | |
|---|---|---|
| ● I Sodi di San Niccolò '14 | ♟♟♟ 8 | |
| ● Chianti Cl. '16 | ♟♟ 4 | |
| ● Chianti Cl. Ris. '15 | ♟♟ 5 | |
| ● Chianti Cl. Il Poggiale Ris. '15 | ♟♟ 6 | |
| ● I Sodi di S. Niccolò '13 | ♟♟♟ 8 | |
| ● I Sodi di S. Niccolò '12 | ♟♟♟ 8 | |
| ● I Sodi di S. Niccolò '11 | ♟♟♟ 8 | |
| ● I Sodi di S. Niccolò '10 | ♟♟♟ 8 | |
| ● I Sodi di S. Niccolò '09 | ♟♟♟ 8 | |
| ● I Sodi di S. Niccolò '08 | ♟♟♟ 7 | |
| ● I Sodi di S. Niccolò '07 | ♟♟♟ 7 | |
| ● I Sodi di S. Niccolò '06 | ♟♟♟ 7 | |
| ● I Sodi di S. Niccolò '05 | ♟♟♟ 7 | |
| ● I Sodi di S. Niccolò '04 | ♟♟♟ 7 | |

## Castellinuzza

VIA PETRIOLO, 14
50022 GREVE IN CHIANTI [FI]
TEL. 0558549033
www.chianticlassicocastellinuzza.it

CELLAR SALES
PRE-BOOKED VISITS
ACCOMMODATION
ANNUAL PRODUCTION 7,000 bottles
HECTARES UNDER VINE 2.00

The Cinuzzi family's winery is situated in the subzone of Greve in Chianti, along the road that leads to Lamole. It represents one of the many examples of artisan enology that it's possible to find in Gallo Nero. Just two hectares of vineyards give rise to the area's time-honored grapes: Sangiovese, Malvasia Bianca and Nera, Canaiolo, and Trebbiano. The style of their wines is decidedly traditional, starting with maturation in large wood barrels. Their 2013 Chianti Classico Riserva is not just extraordinary for its youthful fragrance, but also for its exquisite Chianti character. Notes of earth, undergrowth and flint emerge from beneath fruity and floral aromas. Its development in the mouth is assertive, almost rocky, while the palate comes through well-supported by great savoriness. Their 2014 Chianti Classico proves simpler and quite rustic. It's an accurate reflection of a difficult year.

| | |
|---|---|
| ● Chianti Cl. Ris. '13 | ♟♟♟ 5 |
| ● Chianti Cl. '14 | ♟ 2 |

## ★Castello Banfi

FRAZ. SANT'ANGELO SCALO
B.GO CASTELLO DI POGGIO ALLE MURA
53024 MONTALCINO [SI]
TEL. +39 0577840111
www.castellobanfi.com

CELLAR SALES
PRE-BOOKED VISITS
ACCOMMODATION AND RESTAURANT SERVICE
ANNUAL PRODUCTION 10,000,000 bottles
HECTARES UNDER VINE 850.00
SUSTAINABLE WINERY

The loss of Rudy Buratti still stings within the winemaking community. Born in Trento, he arrived at a tender age in Montalcino where he worked alongside Ezio Rivella for more than 15 years before becoming production head at Castello Banfi in 1999. He played a central role in the extraordinary story that lies behind the transformation of Poggio alle Mura into a true international symbol of Tuscan wine. The winery has parcels in Piemonte, Chianti Classico and Bolgheri, but their wines remain firmly anchored in the multiple vineyards cultivated with Sangiovese da Brunello. Recent tastings have highlighted the group's amazing performance, especially regarding their 2013 Brunellos. The version labelled Castello Banfi proves pleasant and juicy, with good tannic support. Their Poggio alle Mura exhibits a more generous suite of aromas, including some chocolatey notes from the oak. It reveals more fruity pulp and savory substance as it progresses.

| | |
|---|---|
| ● Brunello di Montalcino Poggio alle Mura '13 | ♟♟ 8 |
| ● Brunello di Montalcino Castello Banfi '13 | ♟♟ 8 |
| ● Brunello di Montalcino Poggio alle Mura Ris. '12 | ♟♟ 8 |
| ● Rosso di Montalcino Poggio alle Mura '16 | ♟♟ 5 |
| ● Rosso di Montalcino Castello Banfi '16 | ♟ 5 |
| ● Brunello di Montalcino Poggio all'Oro Ris. '04 | ♟♟♟ 8 |
| ● Sant'Antimo Mandrielle '04 | ♟♟♟ 3 |
| ● Summus '88 | ♟♟♟ 7 |

## ★★Castello del Terriccio

LOC. TERRICCIO
VIA BAGNOLI, 16
56040 CASTELLINA MARITTIMA [PI]
TEL. +39 050699709
www.terriccio.com

**CELLAR SALES**
**PRE-BOOKED VISITS**
**ANNUAL PRODUCTION** 150,000 bottles
**HECTARES UNDER VINE** 60.00

Spelt, wheat and fodder are cultivated on this organic winery's 1800 hectares, an estate that reaches nearly to the sea, and which also sees the presence of horses and livestock. As part of a general modernization some 40 years ago, Gian Annibale Rossi di Medelana extended the area dedicated to grapes to move more strenuously toward the production of high-quality wines. The new varieties he planted started with Chardonnay and Sauvignon Blanc, were followed by Cabernet Franc, Cabernet Sauvignon and Merlot, and most recently added Syrah and Petit Verdot. Their 2014 Lupicaia, a blend of Cabernet Sauvignon, Merlot and Petit Verdot, displays a fresh bouquet of herbs and minty notes on a redcurrant and blueberry background. Its palate exhibits balance, lively freshness and integrated tannins and finishes in a crescendo. They submitted two vintages of their Tassinaia, made with Cabernet Sauvignon and Merlot. Their 2014 stands out for its floral notes of geraniums, dynamic body and light taste, while their 2015 offers up toasty overtones, balance and roundness.

| | |
|---|---|
| ● Lupicaia '14 | ▼▼ 8 |
| ● Tassinaia '15 | ▼▼ 6 |
| ● Tassinaia '14 | ▼▼ 6 |
| ● Castello del Terriccio '11 | ♀♀♀ 8 |
| ● Castello del Terriccio '07 | ♀♀♀ 8 |
| ● Castello del Terriccio '04 | ♀♀♀ 8 |
| ● Lupicaia '13 | ♀♀♀ 8 |
| ● Lupicaia '11 | ♀♀♀ 8 |
| ● Lupicaia '10 | ♀♀♀ 8 |
| ● Lupicaia '07 | ♀♀♀ 8 |
| ● Lupicaia '06 | ♀♀♀ 8 |
| ● Lupicaia '05 | ♀♀♀ 8 |

## Castello del Trebbio

VIA SANTA BRIGIDA, 9
50065 PONTASSIEVE [FI]
TEL. +39 0558304900
www.castellodeltrebbio.it

**CELLAR SALES**
**PRE-BOOKED VISITS**
**ACCOMMODATION AND RESTAURANT SERVICE**
**ANNUAL PRODUCTION** 300,000 bottles
**HECTARES UNDER VINE** 60.00
**SUSTAINABLE WINERY**

Castello del Trebbio is known for its famous castle surrounded by forests, olive groves and vineyards. Here the Pazzi family conspired in a failed attempt to assassinate Lorenzo de' Medici and wrench control of Florence from the de' Medici family. Acquired in 1968 by Baj Macario, the winery is now part of a small wine empire owned by Anna Baj Maracio and her husband Stefano Casadei, who also own Tenuta Casa Dei e Olianas in Val di Cornia and Sardinia, respectively. They also have a line of cosmetics made from ingredients that are unused during the production of wine and olive oil. Their 2014 Lastricato truly delivered. Varied vegetal aromas of black pepper on the nose veer towards overtones of herbs, such as bay and sage. It reveals good nose-palate symmetry, a pleasant structure and a warm, savory and long finish. Their 2015 De' Pazzi is an equal blend of Sangiovese, Syrah and Merlot. Sensations of vanilla and cloves emerge on a background of blueberry jam. Its generous, warm and plush palate features fine-grained tannins and delectable drinkability.

| | |
|---|---|
| ● Chianti Rufina Lastricato Ris. '14 | ▼▼ 5 |
| ● De' Pazzi '15 | ▼▼ 4 |
| ○ Vin Santo del Chianti '11 | ▼▼ 5 |
| ● Chianti Sup. '16 | ▼ 2 |
| ● Chianti Rufina Lastricato Ris. '11 | ♀♀♀ 4* |
| ● Chianti Rufina Lastricato Ris. '12 | ♀♀ 5 |
| ● Chianti Sup. '15 | ♀♀ 3* |
| ● De' Pazzi '14 | ♀♀ 4 |
| ● Pazzesco '11 | ♀♀ 5 |

# ★Castello di Albola

LOC. PIAN D'ALBOLA, 31
53017 RADDA IN CHIANTI [SI]
TEL. +39 0577738019
www.albola.it

**CELLAR SALES**
**PRE-BOOKED VISITS**
**ANNUAL PRODUCTION** 800,000 bottles
**HECTARES UNDER VINE** 140.00

A part of Gruppo Zonin1821 since the 1980s, Castello d'Albola stands out among this Veneto giant's mosaic of wineries, due to its quality and stylistic consistency. Situated in Radda, one the areas closely associated with Chianti Classico, the winery produces wines that perfectly express the area's soil, climate and terroir. The combination of varied pedoclimates and the quality of the plots in Selvole, Ellere, Acciaiolo and Solatio, all more than 400 meters above sea level, combine to make this winery one of the true gems of the appellation. Their Chianti Classico Riserva di Castello d'Albola is a great interpretation of the 2014 vintage. Its very clean nose combines notes of flowers and spices with citrusy overtones. The palate proves taut and dynamic with a light but complex structure and an impressive finish. Their 2015 Chianti Classico Gran Selezione Santa Caterina offers up prominent fruity notes and a more compact structure, which still needs to develop thoroughly.

| | |
|---|---|
| ● Chianti Cl. Ris. '14 | ♟♟♟ 4* |
| ● Chianti Cl. Gran Selezione Santa Caterina '15 | ♟♟ 5 |
| ● Chianti Cl. '15 | ♟♟ 2* |
| ● Acciaiolo '06 | ♟♟♟ 6 |
| ● Acciaiolo '04 | ♟♟♟ 6 |
| ● Acciaiolo '01 | ♟♟♟ 6 |
| ● Chianti Cl. '14 | ♟♟♟ 3* |
| ● Chianti Cl. Gran Sel. '13 | ♟♟♟ 5 |
| ● Chianti Cl. Il Solatio Gran Sel. '11 | ♟♟♟ 5 |
| ● Chianti Cl. Il Solatio Gran Sel. '10 | ♟♟♟ 5 |
| ● Chianti Cl. Le Ellere '08 | ♟♟♟ 3 |
| ● Chianti Cl. Ris. '09 | ♟♟♟ 4* |
| ● Chianti Cl. Ris. '08 | ♟♟♟ 4* |

# ★★Castello di Ama

LOC. AMA
53013 GAIOLE IN CHIANTI [SI]
TEL. +39 0577746031
www.castellodiama.com

**CELLAR SALES**
**PRE-BOOKED VISITS**
**ANNUAL PRODUCTION** 300,000 bottles
**HECTARES UNDER VINE** 90.00

Ama, truly one of the jewels of Chianti Classico, derives its name from the small hilltop town where Lorenza Sebasti and Marco Pallanti built their winemaking masterpiece. Their estate comprises four main vineyards: Bellavista, San Lorenzo, La Casuccia and Montebuoni, and it's no accident that some of world's best single-vineyard Chianti comes from here. The vineyard is defined by a traditional style benefiting from targeted use of technology, employing both small and large barrels, and by meticulous attention in the vineyards. Their 2016 Chianti Classico Ama features a striking, focused and complex aromatic profile. Luxuriant fruit and notes of wild flowers give way to spicy and smoky hints at the finish. Great dynamism and freshness keep the palate docile and savory. Their well-made 2015 Chianti Classico Gran Selezione San Lorenzo exhibits fragrant and generous aromas with a soft and contrasting palate.

| | |
|---|---|
| ● Chianti Cl. Ama '16 | ♟♟ 4 |
| ● Chianti Cl. Gran Selezione San Lorenzo '15 | ♟♟ 6 |
| ● Chianti Cl. Gran Selezione Vign. La Casuccia '15 | ♟♟ 8 |
| ● Chianti Cl. Ama '11 | ♟♟♟ 4* |
| ● Chianti Cl. Bellavista '01 | ♟♟♟ 8 |
| ● Chianti Cl. Castello di Ama '05 | ♟♟♟ 5 |
| ● Chianti Cl. Castello di Ama '03 | ♟♟♟ 5 |
| ● Chianti Cl. Gran Sel. San Lorenzo '13 | ♟♟♟ 6 |
| ● Chianti Cl. La Casuccia '04 | ♟♟♟ 8 |
| ● Chianti Cl. La Casuccia '01 | ♟♟♟ 8 |
| ● Chianti Cl. San Lorenzo '83 | ♟♟♟ 8 |
| ● L'Apparita '01 | ♟♟♟ 8 |

# TUSCANY

## Castello di Bolgheri

LOC. BOLGHERI
S.DA LAURETTA, 7
57020 CASTAGNETO CARDUCCI [LI]
TEL. +39 0565762110
www.castellodibolgheri.eu

CELLAR SALES
PRE-BOOKED VISITS
ACCOMMODATION
ANNUAL PRODUCTION 80,000 bottles
HECTARES UNDER VINE 50.00

Historical documents going back to 1500 say the Castello di Bolgheri belonged to the enormous property of the count Gherardesca family. Today, the story revolves around a deeply-rooted winery in a modern skin, led with experience and professionality by the Zileri Dal Verme family. Slightly less than half of the property is dedicated to cultivating grapes, which are planted in sandy-clay soil that is rock and calcium rich. The resulting wines are impressive for their precise execution, balanced complexity and perfect extraction. Their 2015 Bolgheri Rosso Superiore faithfully reflects both the winery's style and the vintage. Very intense and complex aromas enhance lovely wild berries swathed in vegetal overtones and elegant notes of cocoa and toastiness. A hint of gunpowder leads into a generous, noble palate, which is slightly held back by alcohol and to the detriment of depth.

## ★★★Castello di Fonterutoli

LOC. FONTERUTOLI
VIA OTTONE III DI SASSONIA, 5
53011 CASTELLINA IN CHIANTI [SI]
TEL. +39 057773571
www.mazzei.it

CELLAR SALES
PRE-BOOKED VISITS
ACCOMMODATION AND RESTAURANT SERVICE
ANNUAL PRODUCTION 800,000 bottles
HECTARES UNDER VINE 117.00
SUSTAINABLE WINERY

The story of Mazzei is inexorably bound with Chianti. First led by Lapo and now his sons Filippo and Francesco, the winery today continues to be a flagship for the area, starting with a Chianto Classico that is the result of uncompromising choices. In addition to the vineyards of Castello di Fonterutoli (divided into Fonterutoli, Siepi, Badiola, Belvedere and Caggio), the family also maintains the Belguardo and Zisola estates in Maremma and southeast Sicily, respectively. Collectively, these make the winery one of the most notable in the world of Italian winemaking. Their 2015 monovarietal Sangiovese, Mix 36, is made with 36 different biotypes of the noble Tuscan variety, and this vintage proves the best ever. Its fresh and fragrant aromas pave the way for a steady and lively palate, finishing with a crescendo. Their 2016 Siepi, a blend of Sangiovese and Merlot, is close on its heels, with a great flavor-aroma impact and elegance.

| | |
|---|---|
| ● Bolgheri Rosso Sup. '15 | ♟♟♟ 7 |
| ● Bolgheri Varvàra '16 | ♟♟ 4 |
| ● Bolgheri Sup. Castello di Bolgheri '12 | ♟♟♟ 6 |
| ● Bolgheri Sup. Castello di Bolgheri '10 | ♟♟♟ 6 |
| ● Bolgheri Sup. Castello di Bolgheri '09 | ♟♟♟ 6 |
| ● Bolgheri Rosso Sup. '13 | ♟♟ 7 |
| ● Bolgheri Varvàra '12 | ♟♟ 4 |

| | |
|---|---|
| ● Mix36 '15 | ♟♟♟ 8 |
| ● Siepi '16 | ♟♟ 8 |
| ● Chianti Cl. Castello di Fonterutoli '16 | ♟♟ 8 |
| ● Chianti Cl. Gran Selezione Castello di Fonterutoli '16 | ♟♟ 7 |
| ● Morellino di Scansano Bronzone Tenuta di Belguardo Ris. '15 | ♟♟ 4 |
| ● Serrata di Belguardo Tenuta di Belguardo '16 | ♟♟ 4 |
| ● Chianti Cl. Ser Lapo Ris. '15 | ♟ 5 |
| ● Concerto '15 | ♟ 8 |
| ● Mix36 '11 | ♟♟♟ 8 |
| ● Mix36 '08 | ♟♟♟ 8 |
| ● Siepi '15 | ♟♟♟ 8 |
| ● Siepi '13 | ♟♟♟ 8 |
| ● Siepi '11 | ♟♟♟ 8 |
| ● Siepi '10 | ♟♟♟ 8 |

# ★Castello di Monsanto

VIA MONSANTO, 8
50021 BARBERINO VAL D'ELSA [FI]
TEL. +39 0558059000
www.castellodimonsanto.it

**CELLAR SALES**
**PRE-BOOKED VISITS**
**ANNUAL PRODUCTION** 450,000 bottles
**HECTARES UNDER VINE** 72.00

One of Chianti Classico's most beautiful wineries, Monsanto has combined its love of innovation with something that is both traditional and classic. The endeavor began with the idea of realizing a true cru from the Poggio vineyard, an idea that was almost unimaginable in 1962. The removal of all white grapes from the blend followed in 1968. Fabrizio Bianchi was behind these radical decisions, as well as pioneering the introduction of cooled steel vats and the replacement of chestnut barrels with oak. Their 2013 Chianti Classico Il Poggio Riserva honors a lovely vintage and proves top of the class. Its aromas of slightly wilted flowers and freshly-cut grass merge with smoky overtones and hints of tobacco and pencil lead. Its palate features tight-knit tannins but relaxes pleasantly savory alongside penetrating and fresh acidity. Their 2012 Sangioveto maintains great fruity fragrance and a contrasting palate.

| | | |
|---|---|---|
| ● Chianti Cl. Il Poggio Ris. '13 | ▼▼▼ | 7 |
| ● Sangioveto '12 | ▼▼ | 7 |
| ● Chianti Cl. '16 | ▼▼ | 3 |
| ● Chianti Cl. Ris. '15 | ▼▼ | 3 |
| ● Chianti Cl. '15 | ♀♀♀ | 3* |
| ● Chianti Cl. '11 | ♀♀♀ | 3* |
| ● Chianti Cl. Cinquantenario Ris. '08 | ♀♀♀ | 6 |
| ● Chianti Cl. Il Poggio Ris. '10 | ♀♀♀ | 8 |
| ● Chianti Cl. Il Poggio Ris. '06 | ♀♀♀ | 6 |
| ● Chianti Cl. Ris. '11 | ♀♀♀ | 5 |
| ● Nemo '01 | ♀♀♀ | 6 |
| ● Sangioveto '10 | ♀♀♀ | 7 |

# Castello di Radda

LOC. IL BECCO, 101A
53017 RADDA IN CHIANTI [SI]
TEL. +39 0577738992
www.castellodiradda.it

**CELLAR SALES**
**PRE-BOOKED VISITS**
**ANNUAL PRODUCTION** 100,000 bottles
**HECTARES UNDER VINE** 33.00

Gussalli Beretta, the agricultural group of the Beretta family, is doing impressive work at Castello di Radda, having found a way to consistently bring out the unique quality of the terroir without over-handling the grapes in either the vineyards or the cellar. The grapes are harvested from vines of different ages and then aged alternatively in large or small wood barrels to create a well-balanced selection. The winery produces elegant and enjoyable wines that exhibit complexity, character and connection to the area. Their 2014 Chianti Classico Gran Selezione Vigna Il Corno features an almost iron-like nose, where notes of flowers merge with small red fruit, making for a complex and fragrant suite of aromas. Its docile but not banal palate and continuous savoriness lead into a finish with a fruity encore. Their 2016 Chianti Classico comes through immediately pleasant, with floral aromas and a juicy mouth.

| | | |
|---|---|---|
| ● Chianti Cl. Gran Selezione V. Il Corno '14 | ▼▼▼ | 3* |
| ● Chianti Cl. '16 | ▼▼ | 3 |
| ● Chianti Cl. Ris. '15 | ▼ | 5 |
| ● Chianti Cl. '15 | ♀♀♀ | 3* |
| ● Chianti Cl. Ris. '13 | ♀♀♀ | 5 |
| ● Chianti Cl. Ris. '12 | ♀♀♀ | 5 |
| ● Chianti Cl. Ris. '11 | ♀♀♀ | 6 |
| ● Chianti Cl. Ris. '07 | ♀♀♀ | 5 |
| ● Chianti Cl. '14 | ♀♀ | 3 |
| ● Chianti Cl. Gran Sel. '13 | ♀♀ | 3 |
| ● Chianti Cl. Ris. '14 | ♀♀ | 5 |

## ★Castello di Volpaia

LOC. VOLPAIA
P.ZZA DELLA CISTERNA, 1
53017 RADDA IN CHIANTI [SI]
TEL. +39 0577738066
www.volpaia.com

**CELLAR SALES**
**PRE-BOOKED VISITS**
**ACCOMMODATION AND RESTAURANT SERVICE**
**ANNUAL PRODUCTION** 200,000 bottles
**HECTARES UNDER VINE** 46.00
**VITICULTURE METHOD** Certified Organic
**SUSTAINABLE WINERY**

The Mascheroni Stianti family combines organic methods with solid enological execution. The resulting wines are elegant, having impeccable style with a modern edge that comes largely from the personality brought out during small-barrel aging. This well-established balance is why Castello di Volpaia's wines are among the benchmarks of lower Radda in Chianti. Their 2015 Chianti Classico Gran Selezione Coltassala offers dense, incisive structure with dynamism and fresh acidity. Its complex aromas pass from wild flowers to pencil lead and hints of smoke. Their equally impressive 2016 Chianti Classico proves savory, captivating and closely-focused. The nose gives off red fruit and spices, while the palate delivers an exceptionally enjoyable, elegant, articulated structure.

| | |
|---|---|
| ● Chianti Cl. '16 | ▼▼▼ 4* |
| ● Chianti Cl. Gran Selezione Coltassala '15 | ▼▼ 7 |
| ● Chianti Cl. Ris. '15 | ▼▼ 5 |
| ● Balifico '15 | ▼ 7 |
| ● Chianti Cl. '15 | ♀♀♀ 4* |
| ● Chianti Cl. '13 | ♀♀♀ 3* |
| ● Chianti Cl. Coltassala Ris. '04 | ♀♀♀ 6 |
| ● Chianti Cl. Il Puro Vign. Casanova Ris. '08 | ♀♀♀ 8 |
| ● Chianti Cl. Il Puro Vign. Casanova Ris. '06 | ♀♀♀ 8 |
| ● Chianti Cl. Ris. '13 | ♀♀♀ 5 |
| ● Chianti Cl. Ris. '10 | ♀♀♀ 5 |
| ● Chianti Cl. Ris. '08 | ♀♀♀ 5 |
| ● Chianti Cl. Ris. '07 | ♀♀♀ 5 |

## Castello Romitorio

LOC. ROMITORIO, 279
53024 MONTALCINO [SI]
TEL. +39 0577847212
www.castelloromitorio.com

**CELLAR SALES**
**PRE-BOOKED VISITS**
**ACCOMMODATION**
**ANNUAL PRODUCTION** 150,000 bottles
**HECTARES UNDER VINE** 30.00

Year after year Castello Romitorio's reputation has grown due to its agricultural and productive merit (not to mention the intriguing story of its owner, internationally known artist Sandro Chia). The Romitorio and Poggio di Sopra estates are in Montalcino, and the Ghiaccio Forte estate is in Scansano. Additional parcels are situated in Chianti Senesi, an area that's particularly well-suited to the Mediterranean nature of Sangiovese reds. At one time we would have called their style 'innovative', but fortunately we've moved passed such dichotomies. Their proposed wines all once again achieve their usual excellent level starting with their 2013 Brunello, easily recognizable for its unusual hints of black olive and its soft, stealthy movement. Their 2013 Filo di Seta proves warmer and more mature but also with more tannic presence. And their lovely 2012 Riserva, develops juicily after a slow start.

| | |
|---|---|
| ● Brunello di Montalcino '13 | ▼▼ 8 |
| ● Brunello di Montalcino Filo di Seta '13 | ▼▼ 8 |
| ● Brunello di Montalcino Ris. '12 | ▼▼ 8 |
| ● Rosso di Montalcino '16 | ▼▼ 5 |
| ● Brunello di Montalcino '10 | ♀♀♀ 8 |
| ● Brunello di Montalcino '05 | ♀♀♀ 8 |
| ● Brunello di Montalcino Ris. '97 | ♀♀♀ 8 |
| ● Brunello di Montalcino '12 | ♀♀ 8 |
| ● Brunello di Montalcino '11 | ♀♀ 8 |
| ● Brunello di Montalcino '09 | ♀♀ 8 |
| ● Brunello di Montalcino Filo di Seta '12 | ♀♀ 8 |
| ● Brunello di Montalcino Filo di Seta '11 | ♀♀ 8 |
| ● Brunello di Montalcino Filo di Seta '10 | ♀♀ 8 |
| ● Brunello di Montalcino Ris. '10 | ♀♀ 8 |
| ● Rosso di Montalcino '15 | ♀♀ 5 |

# Castello Vicchiomaggio

LOC. LE BOLLE
VIA VICCHIOMAGGIO, 4
50022 GREVE IN CHIANTI [FI]
TEL. +39 055854079
www.vicchiomaggio.it

CELLAR SALES
PRE-BOOKED VISITS
ACCOMMODATION AND RESTAURANT SERVICE
ANNUAL PRODUCTION 300,000 bottles
HECTARES UNDER VINE 38.00
SUSTAINABLE WINERY

The wine of Castello Vicchiomaggio is second to none in Chianti Classico. The vineyards, on the Florentine side of the appellation, at Greve in Chianti, produce top-quality material for the cellar, where a minimally invasive approach has been adopted. The result is of reliable quality presented in a dependable range, which tends to be modern in style but still expressing the character and consistency of the area. The winery also produces Tenuta Vallemaggiore in Maremma. Their very fragrant 2015 Chianti Classico Agostino Petri Riserva proves smooth and juicy. Their impressive 2015 Ripa delle More, a blend of Sangiovese, Cabernet Sauvignon and Merlot, delivers balance with dynamism. From Tenuta Vallemaggiore in the Maremma, their 2016 Colle Alto offers immediate enjoyment with aromas of fresh cherry and a delectable, savory, palate.

# Castelvecchio

LOC. SAN PANCRAZIO
VIA CERTALDESE, 30
50026 SAN CASCIANO IN VAL DI PESA [FI]
TEL. +39 0558248032
www.castelvecchio.it

CELLAR SALES
PRE-BOOKED VISITS
ACCOMMODATION
ANNUAL PRODUCTION 100,000 bottles
HECTARES UNDER VINE 23.00
SUSTAINABLE WINERY

In 1960 Renzo Pocchi bought a tract of land that once hosted the Knights of Florence's castle. He then built a cellar and planted the vineyards. Today, his grandchildren Filippo and Stefania oversee the estate and cellar with renewed passion. The 30 hectares are planted with international cultivars Merlot, Cabernet Sauvignon and Petit Verdot. An old farmhouse has been converted to a hospitality structure with a pool and a picturesque chapel. Their 2105 Brecciolino makes our finals. The blend of Merlot, Petit Verdot and Sangiovese unites into a clean, fruity nose with pleasing aromatic sage and rosemary. It lands gently, juicily on the palate, with smooth, enveloping and persistent tannins. A Sangiovese dominated blend of the above varieties, their 2105 Orme in Rosso offers citrus notes, spices and candied fruit. Its pleasant palate is linear, elegant, without excesses and with some fresh acidity.

| | |
|---|---|
| ● Chianti Cl. Agostino Petri Ris. '15 | ♟♟ 5 |
| ● Maremma Toscana Colle Alto Tenuta Vallemaggiore '16 | ♟♟ 3 |
| ● Ripa delle More '15 | ♟♟ 6 |
| ● Chianti Cl. Gran Selezione La Prima '14 | ♟ 7 |
| ● Chianti Cl. Gran Sel. Vigna La Prima '10 | ♟♟♟ 7 |
| ● FSM '07 | ♟♟♟ 8 |
| ● FSM '04 | ♟♟♟ 5 |
| ● Ripa delle More '97 | ♟♟♟ 6 |
| ● Ripa delle More '94 | ♟♟♟ 7 |
| ● Chianti Cl. Gran Sel. Vign. La Prima '13 | ♟♟ 7 |
| ● Chianti Cl. San Jacopo da Vicchiomaggio '15 | ♟♟ 3 |

| | |
|---|---|
| ● Il Brecciolino '15 | ♟♟♟ 5 |
| ● Orme in Rosso '15 | ♟♟ 4 |
| ● Solo Uno '15 | ♟♟ 6 |
| ● Chianti Colli Fiorentini Il Castelvecchio '16 | ♟ 2 |
| ● Chianti Colli Fiorentini V. La Quercia Ris. '15 | ♟ 4 |
| ● Chianti Santa Caterina '16 | ♟ 2 |
| ○ San Lorenzo '17 | ♟ 2 |
| ● Il Brecciolino '11 | ♟♟♟ 5 |
| ● Chianti Colli Fiorentini V. La Quercia Ris. '13 | ♟♟ 4 |
| ● Chianti S. Caterina '15 | ♟♟ 2* |
| ● Il Brecciolino '13 | ♟♟ 5 |
| ● Il Brecciolino '12 | ♟♟ 5 |
| ● Numero Otto '13 | ♟♟ 3 |

## Castiglion del Bosco

LOC. CASTIGLION DEL BOSCO
53024 MONTALCINO [SI]
TEL. +39 05771913750
www.castigliondelbosco.com

**CELLAR SALES**
**PRE-BOOKED VISITS**
**ACCOMMODATION AND RESTAURANT SERVICE**
**ANNUAL PRODUCTION** 250,000 bottles
**HECTARES UNDER VINE** 62.00
**VITICULTURE METHOD** Certified Organic

Rebuilt in 2003 by the Ferragamo family, the walled-town of Castignion de Bosco is one of the most enchanting places in all of Tuscany. Home to restaurants, spas, golf clubs, popular resorts and a hub for the historic winery, it retains authenticity in this lush northeast section of Montalcino. Mostly Sangiovese is cultivated on the parcels that are divided among the vineyards of Gauggiole and Capanna, giving form to cool, yet lustrous Brunello. The range continues to become more interesting on an interpretative level. With each vintage, Castiglion del Bosco's Brunello improves. You have to taste their 2012 1100 Riserva to believe it. Vaguely reminiscent of dried flowers, forest essences and tangerine peel, it unwinds with gracefulness that preserves its effective tannic cohesion. Their tasty, robust 2013 Campo del Drago seems less brilliant aromatically, but only on its initial impact.

## Famiglia Cecchi

LOC. CASINA DEI PONTI, 56
53011 CASTELLINA IN CHIANTI [SI]
TEL. +39 057754311
www.cecchi.net

**CELLAR SALES**
**PRE-BOOKED VISITS**
**RESTAURANT SERVICE**
**ANNUAL PRODUCTION** 8,500,000 bottles
**HECTARES UNDER VINE** 385.00
**SUSTAINABLE WINERY**

Cecchi is one of the most noteworthy wineries in the Chianto Classico appellation; as of late, this has gone beyond mere production volumes. With increased attention on style, Cecchi has already made a significant qualitative leap forward. The move stems from rigorous choices and a decision to emphasize more distinguishable and personalized wine. The decision was recently re-enforced by the acquisition of the historical Villa Rosa winery. Their 2015 Chianti Classico Riserva di Famiglia releases a nose of viola, cherry and spices, while on the palate it proves expansive and sweet while simultaneously expressing a contrasting firm acidic verve that makes it savory and delectable. Their 2016 Classico Storia di Familia is equally good though clearly less complex. It offers fresh, defined aromas with a sustained, juicy savory palate.

| | |
|---|---|
| ● Brunello di Montalcino 1100 Ris. '12 | ♟♟ 6 |
| ● Brunello di Montalcino Campo del Drago '13 | ♟♟ 8 |
| ● Brunello di Montalcino '13 | ♟ 6 |
| ● Brunello di Montalcino '12 | ♟♟ 6 |
| ● Brunello di Montalcino '11 | ♟♟ 6 |
| ● Brunello di Montalcino 1100 Ris. '11 | ♟♟ 6 |
| ● Brunello di Montalcino Campo del Drago '12 | ♟♟ 8 |
| ● Brunello di Montalcino Campo del Drago '11 | ♟♟ 8 |
| ● Brunello di Montalcino Campo del Drago '10 | ♟♟ 8 |
| ● Brunello di Montalcino Ris. 1100 '10 | ♟♟ 6 |
| ● Rosso di Montalcino '15 | ♟♟ 3 |

| | |
|---|---|
| ● Chianti Cl. Riserva di Famiglia '15 | ♟♟♟ 5 |
| ● Chianti Cl. Storia di Famiglia '16 | ♟♟ 3* |
| ● Chianti Cl. Gran Selezione Valore di Famiglia '15 | ♟♟ 6 |
| ● Chianti Cl. Gran Selezione Villa Rosa '15 | ♟♟ 6 |
| ○ Maremma Toscana Vermentino Litorale Val delle Rose '17 | ♟♟ 3 |
| ● Chianti Cl. Villa Cerna Ris. '15 | ♟ 5 |
| ● Morellino di Scansano Poggio al Leone Ris. Val delle Rose '15 | ♟ 5 |
| ● Chianti Cl. Riserva di Famiglia '07 | ♟♟♟ 5 |
| ● Chianti Cl. Villa Cerna Ris. '13 | ♟♟♟ 5 |
| ● Chianti Cl. Villa Cerna Ris. '12 | ♟♟♟ 5 |
| ● Chianti Cl. Villa Cerna Ris. '08 | ♟♟♟ 5 |
| ● Coevo '11 | ♟♟♟ 8 |
| ● Coevo '10 | ♟♟♟ 7 |
| ● Coevo '06 | ♟♟♟ 7 |

# Centolani

LOC. FRIGGIALI
S.DA MAREMMANA
53024 MONTALCINO [SI]
TEL. +39 0577849454
www.tenutafriggialiepietranera.it

CELLAR SALES
PRE-BOOKED VISITS
ACCOMMODATION
ANNUAL PRODUCTION 260,000 bottles
HECTARES UNDER VINE 70.00

The Peluso Centolani family's selection of wines draws on two blocks of vineyards that quietly complement one another. Tenuta Friggiali is located in the western part of Montalcino about 400 meters above sea level. The Mediterranean climate becomes more accentuated at Pietranera in the south of the Abbazia di Sant'Antimo valley. The wines there are richer because of their lower elevation and largely clay soil. Variations in soil conditions are harmonized by a versatile, interpretive style, with Brunello aged in medium and large barrels. Recent tastings have shown why Centolani has one of the Montalcino area's most complete ranges. This time their 2013 Brunello Pietranera grabbed our attention. Offering a full nose with clear notes of red fruits, roots and balsams, its authoritative earthy background arrives most clearly on the palate, perhaps a bit leaner than one expected but without extractive flaws.

# Vincenzo Cesani

LOC. PANCOLE, 82D
53037 SAN GIMIGNANO [SI]
TEL. +39 0577955084
www.cesani.it

CELLAR SALES
PRE-BOOKED VISITS
ACCOMMODATION
ANNUAL PRODUCTION 100,000 bottles
HECTARES UNDER VINE 21.00
VITICULTURE METHOD Certified Organic

This family-run organic winery has secured a solid place for itself in the area's agricultural and tourism sectors. Just over 60 years ago the Cesani family left Marche and came to the countryside near San Gimignano. The winery's offerings are among the most unique and identifiable in the area. They stand out in terms of quality, reliability and clear expression of this subarea in Pancole. The whites in particular are salty, and full of character and depth. Their splendid, golden 2015 Riserva Sanice offers an intense, intriguing nose dominated by floral notes, potpourri and ripe yellow fruit. Delicious on the palate, it proves as savory and full-bodied as elegant, with good structure and an easy, tasty, drinkability. Their amber 2016 Clamys delivers citrus aromas and a full, enveloping palate with a clean finish. Their intriguing 2017 Vernaccia releases hints of chamomile, wildflowers and peach.

| | |
|---|---|
| ● Brunello di Montalcino Pietranera '13 | ♟♟ 5 |
| ● Brunello di Montalcino Pietranera Ris. '12 | ♟♟ 6 |
| ● Rosso di Montalcino Pietranera '16 | ♟♟ 3 |
| ● Rosso di Montalcino Tenuta Friggiali '16 | ♟♟ 3 |
| ● Brunello di Montalcino Tenuta Friggiali '13 | ♟ 6 |
| ● Brunello di Montalcino Tenuta Friggiali '04 | ♟♟♟ 5 |
| ● Brunello di Montalcino Tenuta Friggiali Ris. '99 | ♟♟♟ 7 |
| ● Brunello di Montalcino Pietranera '12 | ♟♟ 5 |
| ● Brunello di Montalcino Tenuta Friggiali '12 | ♟♟ 6 |

| | |
|---|---|
| ○ Vernaccia di S. Gimignano Sanice Ris. '15 | ♟♟♟ 3* |
| ○ Vernaccia di S. Gimignano '17 | ♟♟ 2* |
| ○ Vernaccia di S. Gimignano Clamys '16 | ♟♟ 2* |
| ● Chianti Colli Senesi '17 | ♟ 2 |
| ○ Vernaccia di S. Gimignano Sanice Ris. '14 | ♟♟♟ 3* |
| ● Chianti Colli Senesi '15 | ♟♟ 2* |
| ● Luenzo '12 | ♟♟ 4 |
| ● Luenzo '11 | ♟♟ 4 |
| ● San Gimignano Rosso Cellori '09 | ♟♟ 4 |
| ● Serisè '12 | ♟♟ 3 |
| ○ Vernaccia di S. Gimignano Clamys '15 | ♟♟ 2* |
| ○ Vernaccia di S. Gimignano Sanice '11 | ♟♟ 2* |

## Giovanni Chiappini

LOC. FELCIAINO
VIA BOLGHERESE, 189C
57020 BOLGHERI [LI]
TEL. +39 0565765201
www.giovannichiappini.it

CELLAR SALES
PRE-BOOKED VISITS
ANNUAL PRODUCTION 70,000 bottles
HECTARES UNDER VINE 23.00
VITICULTURE METHOD Certified Organic
SUSTAINABLE WINERY

The Chiappini family moved from Marche to Bolgheri in the 1950s and started an agricultural life filled with surprises, eventually leading to considerable success. The turning point was the arrival of wine that would become a standard-bearer for the area, and which brought the winery international recognition. Today, the winery remains a family-run business, embracing organic methods of cultivation with the utmost respect for nature. Their wines are luxurious, often intense and of welcome density. Their 2015 Lienà Cabernet Franc impresses with great body enhanced by intense, complex oak and refined by pleasing peppery, spicy notes. Their 2015 Bolgheri Rosso Superiore Guado de' Gemoli proves excellent, and their delicious 2016 Felciaino is fresh, delectable, juicy.

| | |
|---|---|
| ● Lienà Cabernet Franc '15 | ♟♟ 8 |
| ● Bolgheri Rosso Felciaino '16 | ♟♟ 4 |
| ● Bolgheri Rosso Sup. Guado de' Gemoli '15 | ♟♟ 8 |
| ● Lienà Cabernet Sauvignon '15 | ♟♟ 7 |
| ● Bolgheri Rosso Felciaino '15 | ♀♀ 3 |
| ● Bolgheri Sup. Guado de' Gemoli '13 | ♀♀ 8 |
| ● Bolgheri Sup. Guado de' Gemoli '12 | ♀♀ 8 |
| ● Lienà Cabernet Franc '13 | ♀♀ 8 |
| ● Lienà Cabernet Sauvignon '11 | ♀♀ 7 |

## Le Chiuse

LOC. PULLERA, 228
53024 MONTALCINO [SI]
TEL. +39 055597052
www.lechiuse.com

CELLAR SALES
PRE-BOOKED VISITS
ACCOMMODATION
ANNUAL PRODUCTION 30,000 bottles
HECTARES UNDER VINE 8.00
VITICULTURE METHOD Certified Organic

Simonetta Valiani, with the help of husband Nicolò Magnelli and son Lorenzo, manages an estate that is, to say the least, prestigious. The vineyards form a virtually contiguous body in the most famous part of Montalcino's north section. The lands were inherited from Fiorella Biondi Santi, a family closely connected to Sanviogese da Brunello. Made using organic methods and with spontaneous fermentation, aged in medium and large oak barrels, but above all with 'electric' wines, their offerings soar with energy and grace. Le Chiuse's most recent pair deliver on their promises in spades. Their 2016 Rosso is already a veritable compendium of Sangiovese Montalcinese's best qualities, offering an enchanting play of pomegranate, iris and bay leaf prior to a salty follow-through. This expressive character comes out even more prominently in their 2013 Brunello which adds citrus and sylvan facets for an almost spicy palate of satisfying depth.

| | |
|---|---|
| ● Brunello di Montalcino '13 | ♟♟ 7 |
| ● Rosso di Montalcino '16 | ♟♟ 4 |
| ● Brunello di Montalcino '12 | ♀♀♀ 7 |
| ● Brunello di Montalcino '11 | ♀♀♀ 7 |
| ● Brunello di Montalcino '10 | ♀♀♀ 7 |
| ● Brunello di Montalcino '07 | ♀♀♀ 7 |
| ● Brunello di Montalcino Ris. '07 | ♀♀♀ 8 |
| ● Brunello di Montalcino '09 | ♀♀ 7 |
| ● Brunello di Montalcino '08 | ♀♀ 7 |
| ● Brunello di Montalcino Ris. '09 | ♀♀ 8 |
| ● Rosso di Montalcino '15 | ♀♀ 4 |
| ● Rosso di Montalcino '14 | ♀♀ 4 |
| ● Rosso di Montalcino '13 | ♀♀ 4 |
| ● Rosso di Montalcino '12 | ♀♀ 4 |
| ● Rosso di Montalcino '11 | ♀♀ 4 |

## Ciacci Piccolomini D'Aragona

FRAZ. CASTELNUOVO DELL'ABATE
LOC. MOLINELLO
53024 MONTALCINO [SI]
TEL. +39 0577835616
www.ciaccipiccolomini.com

**CELLAR SALES**
**PRE-BOOKED VISITS**
**ACCOMMODATION**
**ANNUAL PRODUCTION** 200,000 bottles
**HECTARES UNDER VINE** 40.00

Paolo and Lucia Bianchini's lovely winery is situated on the southeastern side of Montalcino, near Castelnuovo dell'Abate, where you can still find the picturesque cellar housed within the 18th-century palazzo of Ciacci Piccolomini. The estate, which has been documented as far back as the 17th century, spans more than 200 hectares, more than half of which are vineyards and olive groves. In 1985, under Giuseppe Bianchini, it took on its current form. It was he who intuited the potential of the territory, enlarging the vineyards and creating a modern, entirely underground cellar. We are delighted, to say the least, to welcome this authoritative producer back in the Guide. This Montalcino area classic expresses their well-established style with their 2015 Rossofonte, which emphasizes its red fruit, but even more so with their dense, intense, deep and very elegant 2013 Brunello.

## Cigliano

VIA CIGLIANO, 17
50026 SAN CASCIANO IN VAL DI PESA [FI]
TEL. +39 055820033
www.villadelcigliano.it

**CELLAR SALES**
**PRE-BOOKED VISITS**
**ANNUAL PRODUCTION** 40,000 bottles
**HECTARES UNDER VINE** 25.00

We consider Cigliano to be one of Chianti Classico's most notable producers, with wine that intimately reflects the characteristics of the area it's cultivated in. The ends justify the means at this winery located in San Casciano Val di Pesa, on the side of the appellation closest to Florence. The well-balanced and elegant range is made possible in large part by its approach to aging, a traditional mixture in concrete and large barrels. The winery's adherence to minute details is a blessing that could become a curse in years with challenging conditions. Without a doubt, their 2015 is one of best of all Chianti Classicos. It opens with floral and slightly citrus aromas with hints of smoke and finishing touches of flint. The palate develops in a to say the least lively way, with continuous contrasts and a savoriness that remains present throughout. Their 2015 Chianti Classico Riserva, though less-expressive, is well-made and pleasant.

| | |
|---|---|
| ● Brunello di Montalcino '13 | ▼▼ 5 |
| ● Rosso di Montalcino Rossofonte '15 | ▼▼ |
| ● Rosso di Montalcino '16 | ▼ 4 |
| ● Brunello di Montalcino V. di Pianrosso '98 | ♈♈♈ 6 |
| ● Brunello di Montalcino V. di Pianrosso '90 | ♈♈♈ |
| ● Brunello di Montalcino V. di Pianrosso '88 | ♈♈♈ |
| ● Brunello di Montalcino V. di Pianrosso Ris. '01 | ♈♈♈ 8 |
| ● Brunello di Montalcino V. di Pianrosso Ris. '99 | ♈♈♈ |
| ● Brunello di Montalcino V. di Pianrosso Ris. '95 | ♈♈♈ |

| | |
|---|---|
| ● Chianti Cl. '15 | ▼▼ 3* |
| ● Chianti Cl. Ris. '15 | ▼▼ 4 |
| ● Chianti Cl. Cigliano '13 | ♈♈♈ 3* |
| ● Chianti Cl. '14 | ♈♈ 3 |
| ● Chianti Cl. '10 | ♈♈ 2* |
| ● Chianti Cl. Cigliano '12 | ♈♈ 3* |
| ● Chianti Cl. Cigliano '11 | ♈♈ 3 |
| ● Chianti Cl. Villa Cigliano Ris. '13 | ♈♈ 4 |
| ● Chianti Cl. Villa Cigliano Ris. '11 | ♈♈ 4 |
| ● Chianti Cl. Villa Cigliano Ris. '09 | ♈♈ 4 |

## Cinciano

LOC. CINCIANO, 2
53036 POGGIBONSI [SI]
TEL. +39 0577936588
www.cinciano.it

CELLAR SALES
PRE-BOOKED VISITS
ACCOMMODATION AND RESTAURANT SERVICE
ANNUAL PRODUCTION 140,000 bottles
HECTARES UNDER VINE 24.00

Fattoria di Cinciano, owned by the Garrè family, is situated on the border between Florence and Sienna. The 130-hectare estate extends across the crest of a knoll between Barberino Val d'Elsa and Poggibonsi, where the vineyards sit on calcareous Alberese soil characterized by low amounts of clay. Their offerings are presented in the 'old style', with fermentation in concrete or steel and aging in large wood barrels. The resulting wine has good personality and character that truly expresses its territory. Their intense 2016 Chianti Classico offers well-defined floral notes supported by notes of stone, tobacco and light smoke. Rich and complex on the palate, it combines a lovely savoriness with acidic freshness that crescendo in its character-filled finish. Their 2015 Chianti Classico Riserva provides aromas of fragrant fruit and spicy notes, capable of measured development though a bit too oaky.

| | |
|---|---|
| ● Chianti Cl. '16 | 🍷🍷🍷 4* |
| ● Chianti Cl. Gran Selezione '14 | 🍷🍷 6 |
| ● Chianti Cl. Ris. '15 | 🍷🍷 5 |
| ● Chianti Cl. '15 | 🍷🍷 3 |
| ● Chianti Cl. '12 | 🍷🍷 3 |
| ● Chianti Cl. '11 | 🍷🍷 3 |
| ● Chianti Cl. Gran Sel. '12 | 🍷🍷 5 |
| ● Chianti Cl. Gran Sel. '11 | 🍷🍷 5 |
| ● Chianti Cl. Ris. '14 | 🍷🍷 3 |
| ● Chianti Cl. Ris. '13 | 🍷🍷 3* |
| ● Chianti Cl. Ris. '12 | 🍷🍷 3* |
| ● Chianti Cl. Ris. '11 | 🍷🍷 3 |
| ● Chianti Cl. Ris. '10 | 🍷🍷 3* |

## Le Cinciole

VIA CASE SPARSE, 83
50020 PANZANO [FI]
TEL. +39 055852636
www.lecinciole.it

CELLAR SALES
PRE-BOOKED VISITS
ANNUAL PRODUCTION 45,000 bottles
HECTARES UNDER VINE 11.00
VITICULTURE METHOD Certified Organic
SUSTAINABLE WINERY

Luca and Valeria Orsini have been running this small winery in the lower area of Panzano since the 1990s. Their methodology is clear and uncompromising – an organic system in the vineyards with minimal handling in the cellar and aging in small, then large barrels. Overall their style emphasizes freshness, drinkability and balance, but selected wines can be allowed to enhance their character, often achieving true excellence. Their warm, juicy 2015 Chianti Classico offers largely fruity notes with hints of spices and licorice. The rhythm of its generous, substantial palate suffers a bit from the exuberance of wood at the finish. Their well-made 2016 Cinciorosso, of Sauvignon, Sangiovese and Syrah, offers savoriness and lovely, clearly-profiled aromas.

| | |
|---|---|
| ● Chianti Cl. '15 | 🍷🍷 3* |
| ● Cinciorosso '16 | 🍷🍷 3 |
| ● Camalaione '04 | 🍷🍷🍷 7 |
| ● Chianti Cl. '14 | 🍷🍷🍷 3* |
| ● Chianti Cl. '12 | 🍷🍷🍷 3* |
| ● Chianti Cl. Petresco Ris. '01 | 🍷🍷🍷 5 |
| ● Petresco '12 | 🍷🍷🍷 5 |
| ● Chianti Cl. '13 | 🍷🍷 3 |
| ● Chianti Cl. A Luigi Ris. '12 | 🍷🍷 3 |
| ● Cinciorosso '13 | 🍷🍷 3 |
| ● Petresco '13 | 🍷🍷 5 |

# ★Tenuta Col d'Orcia

VIA GIUNCHETI
53024 MONTALCINO [SI]
TEL. +39 057780891
www.coldorcia.it

CELLAR SALES
PRE-BOOKED VISITS
ANNUAL PRODUCTION 800,000 bottles
HECTARES UNDER VINE 142.00
VITICULTURE METHOD Certified Organic
SUSTAINABLE WINERY

Purchased by Count Marone Cinzano and family in the 1970s, this estate is situated between Sant'Angelo in Colle and the Orcia River, at the southern limit of the Brunello di Montalcino area. The history of Col d'Orcia goes back hundreds of years during which it has become one of the world's most recognized wineries. The range (not just Sangiovese) is appealing and muscular, offering up structure and storyline honed by the cool air descending from nearby Mount Amiata. This paradigm is exemplified by the Poggio Al Vento Cru, which is matured for almost four years in oak barrels of 2500 and 7500 liters. The rest of the winery's proposals always provide points of interest, starting with their 2015 Nearco, which is absolutely one of the best Sant'Antimo Rossos. The admirably natural expressiveness of their 2013 Brunello Biologico gambles on its notes of summer fruit and its progression on the palate, thin only in appearance. Their 2012 Nastagio proves richer and sunnier.

| | |
|---|---|
| ● Brunello di Montalcino Biologico '13 | ♟♟ 7 |
| ● Brunello di Montalcino Nastagio '12 | ♟♟ 8 |
| ● Sant'Antimo Nearco '15 | ♟♟ 5 |
| ● Rosso di Montalcino '16 | ♟ 5 |
| ● Rosso di Montalcino Banditella '15 | ♟ 5 |
| ● Brunello di Montalcino Poggio al Vento Ris. '10 | ♟♟♟ 8 |
| ● Brunello di Montalcino Poggio al Vento Ris. '06 | ♟♟♟ 8 |
| ● Brunello di Montalcino Poggio al Vento Ris. '04 | ♟♟♟ 8 |
| ● Brunello di Montalcino Poggio al Vento Ris. '83 | ♟♟♟ 7 |
| ● Olmaia '00 | ♟♟♟ 7 |

# Col di Bacche

FRAZ. MONTIANO
S.DA DI CUPI
58051 MAGLIANO IN TOSCANA [GR]
TEL. +39 0564589538
www.coldibacche.com

CELLAR SALES
PRE-BOOKED VISITS
ANNUAL PRODUCTION 80,000 bottles
HECTARES UNDER VINE 13.50

Alberto Carnasciali apparently made the right decision when he chose to make wine in Maremma instead of his home area of Radda in Chianti. Founded in 1998, Col di Bacche is a small winery with the potential to be a real standout in the Maremma wine scene. Their offerings rely on the perfectly mature fruit the area is known for, which make for flavorfully complex and enjoyable wines. The vineyards are located at Cupi, on hills near the sea, characterized by a sizable slope and favored by thermal breezes. The palate of their soft, rhythmic and fresh 2015 Morellino di Scansano Rovente Riserva offers power and character in addition to targeted, complex aromas. In short, all the marks of a great wine. Their 2017 Morellino di Scansano proves immediately pleasant and responsive while their well-made 2015 Cupinero is pure Merlot a decidedly not banal. Their 2017 Vermentino is fresh and savory.

| | |
|---|---|
| ● Morellino di Scansano Rovente Ris. '15 | ♟♟♟ 5 |
| ● Cupinero '15 | ♟♟ 5 |
| ● Morellino di Scansano '17 | ♟♟ 3 |
| ○ Vermentino '17 | ♟♟ 3 |
| ● Cupinero '09 | ♟♟♟ 5 |
| ● Morellino di Scansano Rovente '05 | ♟♟♟ 4 |
| ● Cupinero '12 | ♟♟ 5 |
| ● Morellino di Scansano '15 | ♟♟ 3* |
| ● Morellino di Scansano Rovente Ris. '13 | ♟♟ 5 |
| ● Morellino di Scansano Rovente Ris. '12 | ♟♟ 5 |
| ● Poggio alle Viole '14 | ♟♟ 5 |

## Fattoria Collazzi

LOC. TAVARNUZZE
VIA COLLERAMOLE, 101
50023 IMPRUNETA [FI]
TEL. +39 0552374902
www.collazzi.it

**CELLAR SALES**
**PRE-BOOKED VISITS**
**ANNUAL PRODUCTION** 80,000 bottles
**HECTARES UNDER VINE** 32.00

Collazzi's estate is situated around a lovely villa designed by Santi di Tito, a celebrated 16th-century architect. Since 1933 the estate has been in the hands of the Marchi family, with a greater importance shown for their wines over the past 30 years. 32 hectares of vineyards were revived and and new cultivar were planted along with their traditional Sangiovese: Cabernet Sauvignon and Franc, Merlot, Petit Verdot, Syrah, Malvasia Nera and Fiano (for their whites). Their 2015 Ferro, of pure Petit Verdot, reaches our finals with its incredibly clean aromas of black fruit followed by fresh notes of ginger and pepper, potpourri flowers and currants. On the palate it proves delicate, harmonic, with a soft, light, tasty structure and a long, appetizing finish. Their 2015 Collazzi, a Cabernet Franc, Sauvignon, Merlot and Petit Verdot blend offers complex aromas spiced with clove and cinnamon and a soft, broad, creamy tannin structure that ends in a persistent finish.

| | |
|---|---|
| ● Ferro '15 | ♟♟ 5 |
| ● Collazzi '15 | ♟♟ 6 |
| ● Libertà '16 | ♟♟ 3 |
| ○ Otto Muri '17 | ♟♟ 3 |
| ● Chianti Cl. I Bastioni '16 | ♟ 3 |
| ● Collazzi '13 | ♟♟ 6 |
| ● Collazzi '11 | ♟♟ 6 |
| ● Collazzi '10 | ♟♟ 6 |
| ● Ferro '13 | ♟♟ 5 |
| ● Ferro '12 | ♟♟ 5 |
| ● Libertà '13 | ♟♟ 3 |
| ● Libertà '12 | ♟♟ 2* |
| ○ Otto Muri '15 | ♟♟ 3 |
| ○ Otto Muri '14 | ♟♟ 3 |

## ★Colle Massari

LOC. POGGI DEL SASSO
58044 CINIGIANO [GR]
TEL. +39 0564990496
www.collemassari.it

**CELLAR SALES**
**PRE-BOOKED VISITS**
**ACCOMMODATION**
**ANNUAL PRODUCTION** 500,000 bottles
**HECTARES UNDER VINE** 110.00
**VITICULTURE METHOD** Certified Organic
**SUSTAINABLE WINERY**

Collemassari's winemaking project was founded in 1999 when the entrepreneur Claudio Tipa identified a little known area of Maremma as the perfect place to realize an old dream. In just over 15 years Collemassari has become a leader, and not just for Montecucco but for all of Italy, thanks to a decidedly well-made selection that's full of personality and almost always at the heights of excellence. Their vineyards are cultivated organically while their style is clearly modern, with aging carried out in small and large wood barrels. Their Montecucco Sangiovese Poggio Lombrone Riserva once again shows the gravitas of its character, even during a very complicated vintage. Their 2014 proves a floral red with notes of flint followed by a deep, savory palate that is continuous and well-modulated. The rest of their range also hits very close to the bullseye.

| | |
|---|---|
| ● Montecucco Sangiovese Poggio Lombrone Ris. '14 | ♟♟♟ 6 |
| ● Canaiolo Tenuta di Montecucco '17 | ♟♟ 2* |
| ● Montecucco Rosso Ris. '15 | ♟♟ 4 |
| ○ Montecucco Vermentino Irisse '16 | ♟ 4 |
| ○ Montecucco Vermentino Melacce '17 | ♟ 3 |
| ● Montecucco Rosso Ris. '13 | ♟♟♟ 3* |
| ● Montecucco Sangiovese Lombrone Ris. '11 | ♟♟♟ 6 |
| ● Montecucco Sangiovese Lombrone Ris. '10 | ♟♟♟ 6 |
| ● Montecucco Sangiovese Poggio Lombrone Ris. '13 | ♟♟♟ 6 |
| ● Montecucco Rosso Rigoleto '15 | ♟♟ 3 |
| ● Montecucco Rosso Ris. '14 | ♟♟ 4 |
| ● Montecucco Vin Santo Occhio di Pernice Scosciamonaca '11 | ♟♟ 7 |

# Colle Santa Mustiola

VIA DELLE TORRI, 86A
53043 CHIUSI [SI]
TEL. +39 057820525
www.poggioaichiari.it

CELLAR SALES
PRE-BOOKED VISITS
ANNUAL PRODUCTION 18,000 bottles
HECTARES UNDER VINE 5.00
SUSTAINABLE WINERY

Fabio Cenni is one of Tuscany's most passionate winemakers. He manages his small winery with a maniacal precision that has never wavered, despite the fads and trends recently infiltrating Italian winemaking. Poggio ai Chianti is one of the most successful examples of Sangiovese produced outside of its classic Tuscan range. Elegant, long-lived and stylistically defined, the wine constitutes a benchmark for its ability to reach balanced maturity, even in years when vintages are relatively poor. Their 2011 Poggio ai Chiari, a Sangiovese, can hold its own against Tuscany's best. Earthy, floral and spicy notes are veiled a bit too deeply by the smoky hints coming from its long oak aging. It expresses its real strength as it develops vigorously on the vital and continuous palate that ends in a lovely, savory finish.

| | | |
|---|---|---|
| ● Poggio ai Chiari '11 | 🏆🏆 | 6 |
| ● Poggio ai Chiari '07 | 🏆🏆🏆 | 6 |
| ● Poggio ai Chiari '06 | 🏆🏆🏆 | 6 |
| ⊙ Kernos '15 | 🏆🏆 | 4 |
| ● Poggio ai Chiari '10 | 🏆🏆 | 6 |
| ● Poggio ai Chiari '09 | 🏆🏆 | 6 |
| ● Poggio ai Chiari '08 | 🏆🏆 | 6 |
| ● Vigna Flavia '12 | 🏆🏆 | 5 |

# Fattoria Colle Verde

FRAZ. MATRAIA
LOC. CASTELLO
55010 LUCCA
TEL. +39 0583402310
www.colleverde.it

CELLAR SALES
PRE-BOOKED VISITS
ANNUAL PRODUCTION 30,000 bottles
HECTARES UNDER VINE 7.00

Piero Tartagni and Francesca Pardini made the life decision to move to the countryside, and shortly thereafter to build a dream life owning a winery. In hindsight, it seems to have been a good move, and Colleverde is now one of the most intriguing wineries in the Lucca area. Located in the hills of Matraia, the owners have embraced biodynamic agricultural methods, producing rigorous wines that are technically impeccable but with well-defined expressivity. It is also possible to stay on the estate, thanks to its amenities as a 'wine resort'. As refined as it is intense, their excellent 2015, Brania delle Ghiandaie, a Sangiovese with some Syrah, offers intriguing breezy fruit undiminished by toasted notes which find support on the palate of savory, supple body with juicy stamina. With a very different cadence and drinkability, their young but delicious 2017 Terra di Matraja Rosso proves punctuated by plum, pomegranate and red citrus.

| | | |
|---|---|---|
| ● Brania delle Ghiandaie '15 | 🏆🏆 | 5 |
| ● Terre di Matraja Rosso '17 | 🏆🏆 | 3 |
| ○ Brania del Cancello '16 | 🏆 | 4 |
| ● Nero della Spinosa '15 | 🏆 | 5 |
| ● Brania delle Ghiandaie '14 | 🏆🏆 | 5 |
| ● Colline Lucchesi Rosso Terre di Matraja '11 | 🏆🏆 | 2* |
| ● Nero della Spinosa '14 | 🏆🏆 | 5 |
| ● Terre di Matraja Rosso '16 | 🏆🏆 | 3 |

# Colline San Biagio

LOC. BACCHERETO
VIA SAN BIAGIO 6/8
59015 CARMIGNANO [PO]
TEL. +39 0558717143
www.collinesanbiagio.it

CELLAR SALES
PRE-BOOKED VISITS
ACCOMMODATION
ANNUAL PRODUCTION 35,000 bottles
HECTARES UNDER VINE 7.00
SUSTAINABLE WINERY

Colline San Biagio is a small winery whose management approach centers on love and respect for the territory, an old tradition that's made evident by the names of their wines (inspired by historic, local personages - it's said that Leonardo da Vinci lived here as a child, in the house of his paternal grandparents). In addition to their vineyards, which are cultivated according to the prescriptions set out by Carmignano, they rent out rooms from the main villa as a hospitality service. They also produce grappa and extra-virgin olive oil. Their 2016 Vigna Toia, a mix of Sangiovese, Merlot and Cabernet Sauvignon, offers a nose of wild berries, elegant balsamic notes and hints of Mediterranean scrub. It proves fresh, supple and clean on the palate with a pleasantly savory, pulpy finish. Their pure Merlot Quattrodicisei delivers a spicy nose, first of vanilla and cinnamon, then currant and and cherry. It enters warm, enbracing, soft on the palate followed by an enduring, enjoyable finish.

| | | |
|---|---|---|
| ● Quattordicisei Merlot '14 | 🍷🍷 | 3 |
| ● Vigna Toia '16 | 🍷🍷 | 4 |
| ☉ Balè Rosato '17 | 🍷 | 3 |
| ● Carmignano Sancti Blasii '12 | 🍷 | 4 |
| ● Donna Mingarda '14 | 🍷 | 4 |
| ● Carmignano Sancti Blasii '10 | 🍷🍷 | 4 |
| ● Donna Mingarda '10 | 🍷🍷 | 4 |
| ● Donna Mingarda Sangiovese '12 | 🍷🍷 | 4 |
| ● Quattordicisei Merlot '13 | 🍷🍷 | 3 |

# Colognole

LOC. COLOGNOLE
VIA DEL PALAGIO, 15
50065 PONTASSIEVE [FI]
TEL. +39 0558319870
www.colognole.it

CELLAR SALES
PRE-BOOKED VISITS
ACCOMMODATION AND RESTAURANT SERVICE
ANNUAL PRODUCTION 90,000 bottles
HECTARES UNDER VINE 27.00

Over 600 hectares along the banks of the Sieve River constitute Colognole, the Spalletti Trivelli family's winery for 130 years. Management of the vineyards and the harvest is in the hands of the Coda Nunziante brothers, sons of Gabriella, the last descendent of the Trivelli family. Sangiovese grapes dominate, and they provide the characteristics essential for the longevity of their wines. Three estate villas and two farm manors, all beautiful expressions of Tuscan architecture, are used for hosting agriturismo guests. Their excellent 2015 Riserva del Don delivers a lively nose rich in fruit (cherry), citrus (orange) and Medicinal herbs (thyme). On the warm, broad palate it offers clean, polished, silky tannins and a balanced finish. Fresh notes of rosemary and mint emerge from their equally excellent 2015 Chianti Rufina, which proves pleasant, fruity and drinkable. The mint aromas returns on the palate with well-blended tannins and a light, savory, balanced finish.

| | | |
|---|---|---|
| ● Chianti Rufina Riserva del Don '15 | 🍷🍷 | 5 |
| ● Chianti Rufina '15 | 🍷🍷 | 3 |
| ○ Quattro Chiacchiere a Oltrepoggio '15 | 🍷🍷 | 4 |
| ● Chianti Sinopie '17 | 🍷 | 2 |
| ○ Sinopie Bianco '17 | 🍷 | 2 |
| ● Chianti Rufina '12 | 🍷🍷 | 2* |
| ● Chianti Rufina Ris. del Don '09 | 🍷🍷 | 5 |
| ● Chianti Rufina Ris. del Don '04 | 🍷🍷 | 4 |
| ● Chianti Rufina Riserva del Don '12 | 🍷🍷 | 5 |
| ● Chianti Rufina Riserva del Don '11 | 🍷🍷 | 5 |
| ● Chianti Sinopie '15 | 🍷🍷 | 2* |
| ● Le Lastre '15 | 🍷🍷 | 4 |

## Il Colombaio di Santa Chiara

LOC. RACCIANO
VIA SAN DONATO, 1
53037 SAN GIMIGNANO [SI]
TEL. +39 0577942004
www.colombaiosantachiara.it

CELLAR SALES
PRE-BOOKED VISITS
ACCOMMODATION
ANNUAL PRODUCTION 90,000 bottles
HECTARES UNDER VINE 12.00
VITICULTURE METHOD Certified Organic

San Gimignano is so close you can walk to it. The history of the winery can be seen in the charming 12th-century Pieve di San Donato church and the 19th-century farm building (with its cellar carved out of local tufaceous stone) that has been converted into guest accommodations. The rest of the estate is defined by its current ownership, including the extremely intimate connections it maintains with the area. This attachment shows in the winery's close attention to the environment, in its refusal to use insecticides, its careful harvesting of grapes, and winemaking that is as natural and thoughtful as possible. Their Vernaccia Selvabianca is truly amazing, even more so given that 2017 was not an easy vintage. Its extremely pleasant, refined nose moves from apple to white peach to endless floral notes. The palate offers characteristic weight, juice, elegance and incredible balance with a fantastically savory, continuous finish. Their intriguing 2016 Campo della Pieve delivers fresh citrus (lemon peel) and a slender, dynamic body.

| | | |
|---|---|---|
| ○ Vernaccia di S. Gimignano Selvabianca '17 | ♟♟♟ | 3* |
| ● S. Gimignano Rosso Colombaio Ris. '14 | ♟♟ | 5 |
| ○ Vernaccia di S. Gimignano Campo della Pieve '16 | ♟♟ | 4 |
| ○ Vernaccia di S. Gimignano l'Alberta Ris. '15 | ♟♟ | 3 |
| ● Chianti Colli Senesi Il Priore Ris. '14 | ♟ | 4 |
| ○ Vernaccia di S. Gimignano Alberta Ris. '13 | ♟♟♟ | 3* |
| ○ Vernaccia di S. Gimignano Alberta Ris. '12 | ♟♟♟ | 5 |
| ○ Vernaccia di S. Gimignano Selvabianca '16 | ♟♟ | 3 |
| ○ Vernaccia di S. Gimignano Selvabianca '15 | ♟♟ | 3 |

## Corte dei Venti

LOC. PIANCORNELLO, 35
53024 MONTALCINO [SI]
TEL. +39 3473653718
www.lacortedeiventi.it

CELLAR SALES
PRE-BOOKED VISITS
ANNUAL PRODUCTION 20,000 bottles
HECTARES UNDER VINE 5.00

Without doubt, credit goes to Clara Monaci and Maurizio Machetti for recent improvements in the quality of Corte dei Venti, an estate situated in the heart of Piancornello, to the south of Montalcino. The area is characterized by its iron-rich soil, Mediterranean climate with steady breezes, and elevation at between 100 and 300 meters. Surprisingly light and fragrant Sangiovese are aged in 2500-liter barrels for the estate's Brunello, and mid-sized barrels or barriques are used for its Rosso and Sant'Antimo, respectively. These recent changes in the Corte dei Venti's wines are anything but random or isolated. Their 2013 Brunello, among the best of a particularly fortunate vintage for the category, delivers light fruit, notes of hot springs as well as a touch of leather and cigar. It reveals its full sophistication and complexity on a palate that proves as gentle as it is dense in its long, saline finish. Tre Bicchieri.

| | | |
|---|---|---|
| ● Brunello di Montalcino '13 | ♟♟♟ | 8 |
| ● Brunello di Montalcino Ris. '12 | ♟♟ | 8 |
| ● Rosso di Montalcino '16 | ♟♟ | 5 |
| ● Brunello di Montalcino '12 | ♟♟♟ | 8 |
| ● Brunello di Montalcino '11 | ♟♟ | 8 |
| ● Brunello di Montalcino Donna Elena Ris. '10 | ♟♟ | 8 |
| ● Rosso di Montalcino '15 | ♟♟ | 5 |
| ● Sant'Antimo Poggio dei Lecci '14 | ♟♟ | 3 |

## Villa Le Corti

LOC. LE CORTI
VIA SAN PIERO DI SOTTO, 1
50026 SAN CASCIANO IN VAL DI PESA [FI]
TEL. +39 055829301
www.principecorsini.com

CELLAR SALES
PRE-BOOKED VISITS
ACCOMMODATION
ANNUAL PRODUCTION 150,000 bottles
HECTARES UNDER VINE 50.00
VITICULTURE METHOD Certified Organic

In the past, the Corsini left their mark as great patrons of the arts. Today, they are making a name for themselves as winemakers. Duccio Corsini owns and manages Villa Le Corti, in Chianti Classico and Tenuta Marsiliana in Maremma. The winery, based near San Casciano Val di Pesa, has become known for a style that has much in common with traditional Chianti, but is distinguished by its character and balance. Grapes cultivated using organic methods and a good mix of concrete vats and different sizes of barrels highlight this winery's classic approach. Their polite 2015 Chianti Classico Corte Vecchia Riserva develops smoothly and steadily with fresh acidity and savory tannins. Its nose, though clean and defined, proves more monotone, primarily highlighting lush, mature fruit with some hints of spices. Their 2015 Chianti Classico Gran Selezione Don Tommaso is more concentrated and also more supported by its oak aging.

| | |
|---|---|
| ● Chianti Cl. Corte Vecchia Ris. '15 | ♟♟ 4 |
| ● Birillo Tenuta Marsiliana '15 | ♟♟ 3 |
| ● Chianti Cl.Gran Selezione Don Tommaso '15 | ♟♟ 5 |
| ● Chianti Cl. '12 | ♟♟♟ 3* |
| ● Chianti Cl. Cortevecchia Ris. '05 | ♟♟♟ 4 |
| ● Chianti Cl. Don Tommaso '99 | ♟♟♟ 4* |
| ● Chianti Cl. Le Corti '10 | ♟♟♟ 3* |
| ● Birillo Tenuta Marsiliana '13 | ♟♟ 3 |
| ● Chianti Cl. '14 | ♟♟ 3 |
| ● Chianti Cl. '13 | ♟♟ 3* |
| ● Chianti Cl. Cortevecchia Ris. '14 | ♟♟ 4 |
| ● Chianti Cl. Cortevecchia Ris. '13 | ♟♟ 4 |
| ● Chianti Cl. Don Tommaso Gran Sel. '11 | ♟♟ 5 |
| ● Marsiliana '12 | ♟♟ 5 |

## Cortonesi

LOC. LA MANNELLA, 322
53024 MONTALCINO [SI]
TEL. +39 0577848268
www.lamannella.it

PRE-BOOKED VISITS
ANNUAL PRODUCTION 35,000 bottles
HECTARES UNDER VINE 8.00

Also known as La Mannella, the Cortonesi family winery is currently run by young Tommaso and his father, Marco. Despite a long history connected with Montalcino, recent changes are just beginning to show and they will become more apparent in the near future. The estate's strongest wines are two Brunellos: La Mannella (reflecting more northernly vineyards and aging in 3000-liter Slovanian barrels), and I Poggiarelli (from the estate of Castelnuovo dell'Abate to the south-east and aged in small, 500-liter barrels). Their most recent proposals reveal a nice crescendo that starts with their agile, juicy 2016 Rosso. Intensity increases with their 2013 Brunello I Poggiarelli, which gambles on black fruit and spices, proving enveloping and continuous in its development. Even fuller, their 2013 La Mannella offers raspberry, marjoram, cinnamon. This sweetness is balanced by a generous but targeted, austere palate with a slightly too lean finish.

| | |
|---|---|
| ● Brunello di Montalcino La Mannella '13 | ♟♟ 5 |
| ● Brunello di Montalcino I Poggiarelli '13 | ♟♟ 5 |
| ● Rosso di Montalcino '16 | ♟ 3 |
| ● Brunello di Montalcino '10 | ♟♟ 5 |
| ● Brunello di Montalcino '09 | ♟♟ 5 |
| ● Brunello di Montalcino Ris. '10 | ♟♟ 6 |
| ● Brunello di Montalcino I Poggiarelli '12 | ♟♟ 5 |
| ● Brunello di Montalcino I Poggiarelli '11 | ♟♟ 5 |
| ● Brunello di Montalcino I Poggiarelli '10 | ♟♟ 5 |
| ● Brunello di Montalcino I Poggiarelli '09 | ♟♟ 5 |
| ● Brunello di Montalcino I Poggiarelli '08 | ♟♟ 5 |
| ● Brunello di Montalcino La Mannella '12 | ♟♟ 5 |
| ● Rosso di Montalcino '15 | ♟♟ 3* |
| ● Rosso di Montalcino '14 | ♟♟ 3 |
| ● Rosso di Montalcino '13 | ♟♟ 3 |

# Fattoria Corzano e Paterno

LOC. CORZANO
FRAZ. SAN PANCRAZIO
VIA SAN VITO DI SOPRA
50020 SAN CASCIANO IN VAL DI PESA [FI]
TEL. +39 0558248179
www.corzanoepaterno.com

**CELLAR SALES**
**PRE-BOOKED VISITS**
**ACCOMMODATION**
**ANNUAL PRODUCTION** 85,000 bottles
**HECTARES UNDER VINE** 19.00
**VITICULTURE METHOD** Certified Organic

In 1969, Wendel Gelpke acquired first the Corzano plot, then Paterno. Together they have become the nucleus of this modern organically-run winery. Today, the vineyards and cellar are managed by Aljoscha Goldschmidt and Arianna Gelpke, Wendel's niece and daughter, respectively. In addition to wine, they produce oil, high-quality cheese, and the fodder to feed their dairy cattle. The entire family is involved in all aspects of production, all of which remain faithful to Wendel's original values. Their 2015 Corzano, an equal blend of Cabernet Sauvignon, Sangiovese and Merlot, makes our finals. Its well-defined aromatic herbs and spices (predominantly bay leaf, sage and juniper) lead into wild berries like currants. Its balanced, juicy body with sophisticated tannins ends in a crescendo. Their intriguing 2013 Passito offers notes of dried fig, toasted hazelnuts and bitter herbs. On the palate it proves gentle, voluminous and very persistent, leaving a spicy aftertaste.

| | |
|---|---|
| ● Il Corzano '15 | 🍷🍷 5 |
| ● I Tre Borri '15 | 🍷🍷 5 |
| ○ Il Passito di Corzano '13 | 🍷🍷 6 |
| ☉ Rosato Corzanello '17 | 🍷 2 |
| ● Chianti I Tre Borri Ris. '07 | 🍷🍷🍷 5 |
| ● Il Corzano '05 | 🍷🍷🍷 5 |
| ● Il Corzano '97 | 🍷🍷🍷 6 |
| ● Chianti I Tre Borri Ris. '14 | 🍷🍷 5 |
| ● Chianti I Tre Borri Ris. '13 | 🍷🍷 5 |
| ● Chianti I Tre Borri Ris. '12 | 🍷🍷 5 |
| ● Chianti Terre di Corzano '14 | 🍷🍷 2* |
| ● Il Corzano '13 | 🍷🍷 5 |
| ○ Passito di Corzano '02 | 🍷🍷 6 |

# Andrea Costanti

LOC. COLLE AL MATRICHESE
53024 MONTALCINO [SI]
TEL. +39 0577848195
www.costanti.it

**CELLAR SALES**
**PRE-BOOKED VISITS**
**ANNUAL PRODUCTION** 60,000 bottles
**HECTARES UNDER VINE** 12.00

Characterized by the steeply inclined, marly slopes of a range reaching as high as 450 meters above sea level, the parcels of Colle al Matrichese are located on the eastern side of Montalcino. The vineyards are subdivided into Casottino and Calbello, where since 1983 they have been in the care of Andrea Costanti (who, with good reason, is recognized as one of the best interpreters of Brunello). Aging is in small and 3000-liter oak barrels. Because of the raw tannin fibers, for both the Annata and the Riserva, careful attention and patience are required throughout the process to draw out results that are sweet and flavorful. Their 2013 is everything a Brunello should be and one of the longest, most fascinating that they have produced. The cherry, paprika and Mediterranean herbs of its sunny, spicy nose return with almost surgical precision on a savory, vibrant palate that delivers a far from docile finish. Their 2012 Brunello Riserva is also outstanding.

| | |
|---|---|
| ● Brunello di Montalcino '13 | 🍷🍷 6 |
| ● Brunello di Montalcino Ris. '12 | 🍷🍷 8 |
| ● Brunello di Montalcino '06 | 🍷🍷🍷 6 |
| ● Brunello di Montalcino '88 | 🍷🍷🍷 6 |
| ● Brunello di Montalcino '12 | 🍷🍷 6 |
| ● Brunello di Montalcino '11 | 🍷🍷 6 |
| ● Brunello di Montalcino '10 | 🍷🍷 6 |
| ● Brunello di Montalcino '09 | 🍷🍷 6 |
| ● Brunello di Montalcino '08 | 🍷🍷 6 |
| ● Brunello di Montalcino Ris. '10 | 🍷🍷 8 |
| ● Brunello di Montalcino Ris. '07 | 🍷🍷 8 |
| ● Brunello di Montalcino Ris. '06 | 🍷🍷 8 |
| ● Rosso di Montalcino '15 | 🍷🍷 4 |
| ● Rosso di Montalcino '11 | 🍷🍷 4 |
| ● Rosso di Montalcino Vermiglio '14 | 🍷🍷 5 |

## La Cura

LOC. CURA NUOVA, 12
58024 MASSA MARITTIMA [GR]
TEL. +39 0566918094
www.cantinalacura.it

CELLAR SALES
PRE-BOOKED VISITS
ANNUAL PRODUCTION 30,000 bottles
HECTARES UNDER VINE 15.00
SUSTAINABLE WINERY

A small winery in the Monteregio di Massa Marittima appellation, La Cura is emblematic of the true potential for the 'Bel Paese's' artisanal winemaking (as Italians often refer to their 'beautiful country'). It is a classic family venture whose vineyards and cellar are overseen with passion and care by Enrico Corsi. Their wines have a well-defined structure that is modern yet intensely Mediterranean. Year after year, consistent and high-quality, these results have confirmed La Cura as one of the most noteworthy wineries in Maremma. Their 2016 Merlot gambles on its sweet palate and the aromatic finesse coming from lightly spiced notes of cherry and blueberry freshened by delicate hints of grasses. Their more forceful 2016 Vedetta blend of Cabernet Sauvignon and Cabernet Franc gives off notes of pencil lead and ripe red fruit, followed a progression of flavors made a tad heavy with oak.

| | |
|---|---|
| ● Merlot '16 | ▼▼ 5 |
| ● Predicatore '17 | ▼▼ 3 |
| ○ Valdemàr Vermentino '17 | ▼▼ 2* |
| ● Vedetta '16 | ▼▼ 4 |
| ● Maremma Toscana Cabernet Sauvignon Cabernets '15 | ♀♀ 5 |
| ● Maremma Toscana Merlot '15 | ♀♀ 5 |
| ● Maremma Toscana Sangiovese Cavaliere d'Italia '16 | ♀♀ 2* |
| ● Monteregio di Massa Marittima Rosso Valdemàr '16 | ♀♀ 2* |
| ○ Trinus '15 | ♀♀ 2* |

## De' Ricci

FRAZ. S.ALBINO
FRAZ. VIA FONTECORNINO, 15
53045 MONTEPULCIANO [SI]
TEL. +39 0578798152
www.dericci.it

CELLAR SALES
PRE-BOOKED VISITS
RESTAURANT SERVICE
ANNUAL PRODUCTION 90,000 bottles
HECTARES UNDER VINE 32.00
SUSTAINABLE WINERY

The cellar situated within Palazzo Poliziano is the symbolic center of the Trabalzini family winery. In a nod to history, in 2012 its owners changed the name of the winery to De' Ricci, from Cantina del Redi, which it had been called since 1959. Today there's a new, modern cellar, and a large number of hectares are cultivated so as to make sure the best Sangiovese reaches the cellar. The winery's range exhibits balance and finesse. Fermentation occurs in both steel and oak, with aging in large barrels. Their 2015 Nobile di Montepulciano SorAldo offers elegant aromas of fresh cherry mixed with traces of viola, flint and subtle spices. It lands on the palate gently until the fruit takes over to deliver lovely acidic energy, making it savory, fragrant and long. Their 2105 Nobile offers round and crunchy tannins, underscoring its clearly defined, close-knit structure.

| | |
|---|---|
| ● Nobile di Montepulciano '15 | ▼▼ 5 |
| ● Nobile di Montepulciano SorAldo '15 | ▼▼ 6 |
| ● Rosso di Montepulciano '16 | ▼ 3 |

# Maria Caterina Dei

VIA DI MARTIENA, 35
53045 MONTEPULCIANO [SI]
TEL. +39 0578716878
www.cantinedei.com

**CELLAR SALES**
**PRE-BOOKED VISITS**
**ACCOMMODATION**
**ANNUAL PRODUCTION** 230,000 bottles
**HECTARES UNDER VINE** 60.00
**SUSTAINABLE WINERY**

Caterina Dei is one of the most unique personalities in Italian wine. A talented singer in the past, she now runs one of Montepulciano's best wineries, producing sumptuous Nobile capable of defying time as few others can. The vineyards are located in lower Martiena, Bossona, La Ciarliana and La Piaggia, which at an average elevation of 300 meters is one of the most evocative areas of the appellation. In the new cellar grapes are transformed into well-focused and structured wines that reveal character and tannic finesse. Their 2013 Nobile di Montepulciano Bossona Riserva wows with intense aromas of fruit and spices that end in smoky notes. It becomes wide and encompassing on the palate with gentle, close-knit tannins and a finish that proves a bit too woody. Their solid, well-made 2015 Nobile offers a nuanced nose and immediate enjoyment. Their uncomplicated 2017 Rosso di Montepulciano does down easily.

| | |
|---|---|
| ● Nobile di Montepulciano Bossona Ris. '13 | 🍷🍷🍷 6 |
| ● Nobile di Montepulciano '15 | 🍷🍷 4 |
| ● Rosso di Montepulciano '17 | 🍷 3 |
| ● Nobile di Montepulciano '14 | 🍷🍷🍷 4* |
| ● Nobile di Montepulciano '13 | 🍷🍷🍷 4* |
| ● Nobile di Montepulciano Bossona Ris. '12 | 🍷🍷 6 |
| ● Nobile di Montepulciano Bossona Ris. '10 | 🍷🍷 6 |

# Dianella

VIA DIANELLA, 48
50059 VINCI [FI]
TEL. +39 0571508166
www.dianella.wine

**CELLAR SALES**
**PRE-BOOKED VISITS**
**ACCOMMODATION**
**ANNUAL PRODUCTION** 130,000 bottles
**HECTARES UNDER VINE** 25.00
**VITICULTURE METHOD** Certified Organic
**SUSTAINABLE WINERY**

On the hills of Vinci stands a Medicean villa that was once used by the Florentine noble family as their hunting headquarters. Today it hosts Francesco and Veronica Passerin d'Entrèves' winery, and is the heart of a 90-hectare estate (25 of which are vineyards, situated at 200 meters of elevation and cultivated organically). Sangiovese takes center stage, and is accompanied by Colorino, Cabernet Sauvignon, Malvasia Lunga del Chianti and Vermentino. Francesco and Veronica also oversee a museum of winemaking situated inside their historic cellards. Their lovely, pure Sangiovese 2015 Matto delle Giuncaie offers sophisticated mineral aromas with black fruit softened by bay leaf. Vertical and balanced on the palate it delivers well-integrated tannins and a lengthy finish. Their 2016 Veglie di Neri, a Sangiovese with some Cabernet Sauvignon, gives off slightly menthol aromas with notes of blackberry and blueberry. Flavors expand beautifully on the palate with vigor and supleness to its juicy finish. Their tempting 2017 Sereno e Nuvole proves floral and delicate.

| | |
|---|---|
| ● Il Matto delle Giuncaie '15 | 🍷🍷 5 |
| ● Le Veglie di Neri '16 | 🍷🍷 3 |
| ○ Sereno e Nuvole '17 | 🍷🍷 3 |
| ⊙ All'Aria Aperta '17 | 🍷 3 |
| ○ Dolci Ricordi '09 | 🍷🍷 5 |
| ● Il Matto delle Giuncaie '13 | 🍷🍷 2* |
| ● Il Matto delle Giuncaie '12 | 🍷🍷 4 |
| ● Le Veglie di Neri '11 | 🍷🍷 3 |

## Fabrizio Dionisio

LOC. IL CASTAGNO
FRAZ. OSSAIA, 87
52044 CORTONA [AR]
TEL. +39 063223391
www.fabriziodionisio.it

CELLAR SALES
PRE-BOOKED VISITS
ANNUAL PRODUCTION 45,000 bottles
HECTARES UNDER VINE 15.00
SUSTAINABLE WINERY

The story of this winery began in the 1970s, when Sergio Dionisio bought a country house in the hills near Cortona with seven hectares of grape vines and olive trees. With additional acquisitions, the property reached its current size some 20 years ago. Son and wife, Fabrizio and Alessandra, made the decision to remove the existing older Sangiovese and Trebbiano, and in 2000 they began to replace them on both estates with Syrah, which does particularly well in this locale. Their lovely 2015 Syrah Castagno offers a aromas of cleanly focused red fruit (cherry and raspberry) embellished with spicy hints of pepper and juniper. Its well-balanced body starts out thin, becomes more defined and leading to a flavorful, prolonged, notable acidic finish. Their pleasant 2017 Castagnino, also Syrah, delivers fruity aromas wrapped in floral notes, pepper and marjoram. It proves supple, fresh and relaxed on the palate.

| | |
|---|---|
| ● Cortona Syrah Il Castagno '15 | ▼▼ 5 |
| ● Cortona Syrah Castagnino '17 | ▼▼ 3 |
| ⊙ Rosa del Castagno '17 | ▼ 3 |
| ● Cortona Syrah Il Castagno '12 | ▼▼▼ 5 |
| ● Cortona Syrah Il Castagno '11 | ▼▼▼ 5 |
| ● Cortona Syrah Il Castagno '10 | ▼▼▼ 5 |
| ● Cortona Syrah Castagnino '16 | ▼▼ 3 |
| ● Cortona Syrah Castagnino '15 | ▼▼ 3* |
| ● Cortona Syrah Cuculaia '13 | ▼▼ 7 |
| ● Cortona Syrah Il Castagno '14 | ▼▼ 5 |
| ● Cortona Syrah Il Castagno '13 | ▼▼ 5 |

## Donna Olga

LOC. FRIGGIALI
S.DA MAREMMANA
53024 MONTALCINO [SI]
TEL. +39 0577849454
www.tenutedonnaolga.it

CELLAR SALES
PRE-BOOKED VISITS
ACCOMMODATION
ANNUAL PRODUCTION 25,000 bottles
HECTARES UNDER VINE 11.00

The lands on which Olga Peluso Centolani cultivates Sangiovese are divided into two sectors. The area to the southwest of Montalcino has volcanic soil and is influenced by the nearby sea climate. The southeast section ranges between 270 and 400 meters above sea level and features marly soil. These sections produce fruit that cooperates beautifully in Donna Olga's Brunello, which is aged in medium-large Slavonian oak barrels and mid-size casks. The most successful versions find the ideal blend of 'tradition' and 'modernity' filled with fruity richness and tannic rigor. It only took trying one wine to reconfirm our appreciation for the quality and character of Donna Olga. Their 2013 Brunello, recognizable by its cheerful nose with balsam, spices and roots, corresponds to its full, vital palate. It unravels with progression and flavor, revealing only a bit of youthful rawness at the end.

| | |
|---|---|
| ● Brunello di Montalcino '13 | ▼▼ 7 |
| ● Brunello di Montalcino '09 | ▼▼▼ 7 |
| ● Brunello di Montalcino '06 | ▼▼▼ 7 |
| ● Brunello di Montalcino '01 | ▼▼▼ 6 |
| ● Brunello di Montalcino Collezione Arte '06 | ▼▼▼ 7 |
| ● Brunello di Montalcino Ris. '01 | ▼▼▼ 6 |
| ● Brunello di Montalcino '12 | ▼▼ 7 |
| ● Brunello di Montalcino '11 | ▼▼ 7 |
| ● Brunello di Montalcino '10 | ▼▼ 7 |
| ● Brunello di Montalcino Favorito '12 | ▼▼ 7 |
| ● Brunello di Montalcino Favorito Collezione Arte '09 | ▼▼ 7 |
| ● Brunello di Montalcino Ris. '10 | ▼▼ 6 |
| ● Brunello di Montalcino Ris. '07 | ▼▼ 6 |

# Donna Olimpia 1898

FRAZ. BOLGHERI
LOC. MIGLIARINI, 142
57020 CASTAGNETO CARDUCCI [LI]
TEL. +39 0302279601
www.donnaolimpia1898.it

**CELLAR SALES**
**ACCOMMODATION AND RESTAURANT SERVICE**
**ANNUAL PRODUCTION** 250,000 bottles
**HECTARES UNDER VINE** 45.00
**SUSTAINABLE WINERY**

Signora Olimpia Alliata di Biserno, wife of
the famous Gherardo della Gherardesca,
had her name given to the estate in 1898.
Brainchild of Guido Folonari of the
well-known Tuscan wine family, the
vineyard is the offspring of his collaboration
in cloning varieties with Professor Scienza
of the University of Milan. On the relatively
level land Cabernet Sauvignon, Cabernet
Franc, Merlot, Syrah and Petit Verdot are
cultivated, as well as Vermentino, Viognier
and Petit Manseng. Its modern cellar is
dominated by a beautiful barrel hall. The
toasted woody notes still prove a bit too
evident in their sophisticated, substantial
2015 Bolgheri Superiore Millepassi, but its
incredibly rich and multifaceted body
guarantees it a radiant future. It delivers a
wide and silky palate with a delicious
herbaceous background just slightly
affected by the alcoholic balance of the
finish. Their pulpy, citrusy and balsamic
2017 Vermentino Obizzo, truly shines.

| | |
|---|---|
| ● Bolgheri Rosso Sup. Millepassi '15 | ▼▼▼ 7 |
| ○ Obizzo Vermentino '17 | ▼▼ 2* |
| ● Tageto '16 | ▼▼ 2* |
| ● Bolgheri Rosso Sup. Millepassi '13 | ♀♀♀ 6 |
| ● Bolgheri Rosso Sup. Millepassi '11 | ♀♀♀ 8 |
| ● Bolgheri Rosso '15 | ♀♀ 5 |
| ● Bolgheri Rosso Campo alla Giostra '15 | ♀♀ 5 |

# Duemani

LOC. ORTACAVOLI
56046 RIPARBELLA [PI]
TEL. +39 0583975048
www.duemani.eu

**ANNUAL PRODUCTION** 40,000 bottles
**HECTARES UNDER VINE** 10.00
**VITICULTURE METHOD** Certified Biodynamic
**SUSTAINABLE WINERY**

Duemani came about after Elena Celli, who
studied marketing and worked in fashion,
met Luca D'Attoma, an enologist who
collaborates with wineries all over Italy. On
the sea-facing hills of Riparbella, they are
realizing their dream of producing original
and purely biodynamic wines. For less than
20 years they have been cultivating their
favorite varieties like Cabernet Franc, Syrah
and Merlot, on land that is in their own
words: extreme, grumpy, wild and magnetic.
Tre Bicchieri for their 2015 Duemani, a pure
Cabernet Franc that expresses itself in fresh
notes of pepper and berries, like currant
and blueberry, before wafting menthol and
hints of ginger. It enters temptingly on the
palate with a dynamic body and a nice suite
of tannins. It proves juicy, vital and
continuous with a finish enhanced by its
persistence. Their 2105 Suisassi, a pure
Syrah leaning more toward tobacco and
licorice, is firm and juicy, with well-defined,
lingering flavors.

| | |
|---|---|
| ● Duemani '15 | ▼▼▼ 8 |
| ● Cifra '16 | ▼▼ 5 |
| ● Suisassi '15 | ▼▼ 8 |
| ○ Rosato Sì '17 | ▼ 5 |
| ● Altrovino '15 | ♀♀♀ 6 |
| ● Duemani '13 | ♀♀♀ 8 |
| ● Duemani '12 | ♀♀♀ 8 |
| ● Duemani '09 | ♀♀♀ 8 |
| ● Suisassi '10 | ♀♀♀ 8 |
| ● Cifra '15 | ♀♀ 5 |
| ● Cifra '14 | ♀♀ 5 |
| ● Cifra '13 | ♀♀ 5 |
| ● Duemani '14 | ♀♀ 8 |
| ● Suisassi '13 | ♀♀ 8 |

# I Fabbri

LOC. LAMOLE
VIA CASOLE, 52
50022 GREVE IN CHIANTI [FI]
TEL. +39 339412622
www.ifabbrichianticlassico.it

CELLAR SALES
PRE-BOOKED VISITS
ANNUAL PRODUCTION 35,000 bottles
HECTARES UNDER VINE 11.00
VITICULTURE METHOD Certified Organic

Lamole is one of the most intriguing and difficult of the subareas of Chianti Classico, but thanks to the Grassi sisters, I Fabbri has become one of the purist and most faithful interpreters of this unusual terroir. The sisters began the winery in 2000 with twin goals of respecting the environment and the character of the wines. The winery is named in memory of the blacksmith workshop in the old village overlooking the vineyards. The well-structured, original wines are decidedly 'Lamole', while a style not easy to decipher, nonetheless is consistent and possessing great charm. Their 2105 Chianti Classico Gran Selezione greets with somewhat indistinct aromas that slowly become increasingly defined by floral notes, flint and gunpowder. It also enters on the palate almost stealthily, developing in rhythm and incisiveness. Their 2016 Chianti Classico proves delectable and their 2015 Chianti Classico Terre di Lamole is fragrant, savory and intriguing with some rustic elements.

| | |
|---|---|
| ● Chianti Cl. '16 | ♥♥ 4 |
| ● Chianti Cl. Gran Selezione '15 | ♥♥ 6 |
| ● Chianti Cl. Terra di Lamole '15 | ♥♥ 3 |
| ● Chianti Cl. '13 | ♈ 4 |
| ● Chianti Cl. '12 | ♈ 4 |
| ● Chianti Cl. Gran Sel. '11 | ♈ 6 |
| ● Chianti Cl. Olinto '15 | ♈ 4 |
| ● Chianti Cl. Olinto '14 | ♈ 4 |
| ● Chianti Cl. Olinto '12 | ♈ 4 |
| ● Chianti Cl. Ris. '13 | ♈ 4 |
| ● Chianti Cl. Ris. '11 | ♈ 4 |
| ● Chianti Cl. Terra di Lamole '13 | ♈ 3* |

# Fabbrica Pienza

LOC. BORGHETTO
53026 PIENZA [SI]
TEL. +39 0578810030
info@fabbricapienza.com

CELLAR SALES
PRE-BOOKED VISITS
ANNUAL PRODUCTION 20,000 bottles
HECTARES UNDER VINE 35.00
VITICULTURE METHOD Certified Organic
SUSTAINABLE WINERY

The winemaking venture of Tonie and Philippe Bertherat, a couple from Luxembourg and Switzerland, respectively, has gotten off on the right foot. Pienza is not particularly well-known for wine production, but Fabbrica, rising to the challenge, has been able to find a balanced interpretation in this unusual territory planted with Sangiovese. At the moment, the limited range features wines of other eras and areas. The range continues to expand as the winery gains experience. Their 2015 470-3 is the prototype for a modern Sangiovese that remains faithful to the character of Tuscany's most important variety. It presents a fruity, floral nose with hints of fresh grass and a spicy finish. It develops rhythmically on the palate with contrasting notes and a decidedly savory finish. Their intriguing 2016 Bianco di Fabbrica results from a well-structured blend of Viognier, Marsanne, Roussanne and Vermentino.

| | |
|---|---|
| ○ Bianco di Fabbrica '16 | ♥♥ 6 |
| ● Prototipo 470.3 Sangiovese '15 | ♥♥ 8 |
| ● Prototipo 470.1 '13 | ♈ 5 |
| ● Prototipo 470.2 '14 | ♈ 5 |

# Tenuta Fanti

FRAZ. CASTELNUOVO DELL'ABATE
PODERE PALAZZO, 14
53020 MONTALCINO [SI]
TEL. +39 0577835795
www.tenutafanti.it

**CELLAR SALES**
**PRE-BOOKED VISITS**
**ANNUAL PRODUCTION** 200,000 bottles
**HECTARES UNDER VINE** 50.00

Upbeat, youthful, and always ready with a joke, Filippo Fanti is a living memory of Brunello and its early period of collective boom. Now with his daughter Elisa firmly installed beside him, Filippo oversees a sizable estate just outside of Castelnuovo dell'Abate, in the heart of southeastern Montalcino. The warmth of the area is mitigated by the play of air currents and thermal inversions from nearby Monte Amiata, giving form to enveloping, tannin-filled reds with an expressive style emphasized by modern-leaning technical inspiration. It wasn't difficult to predict that the Fanti family's most prestigious wines would reconfirm their exceptionally high levels. Their excellent 2103 Brunello Vallocchio delivers remarkably powerful fruit given extra dimension by notes of oriental spices, cocoa and tilled earth. Its double nature, both approachable and unyielding, manifests itself in a truly sophisticated, caressing and infiltrating progression on the palate.

| | |
|---|---|
| ● Brunello di Montalcino Vallocchio '13 | ▼▼▼ 7 |
| ● Brunello di Montalcino '13 | ▼▼ 6 |
| ● Rosso di Montalcino '16 | ▼▼ 3 |
| ● Brunello di Montalcino V. Le Macchiarelle Ris. '12 | ▼ 6 |
| ● Brunello di Montalcino '07 | ♀♀♀ 5 |
| ● Brunello di Montalcino '00 | ♀♀♀ 6 |
| ● Brunello di Montalcino '97 | ♀♀♀ 5 |
| ● Brunello di Montalcino Ris. '95 | ♀♀♀ 5 |
| ● Brunello di Montalcino '12 | ♀♀ 6 |
| ● Brunello di Montalcino '11 | ♀♀ 6 |
| ● Brunello di Montalcino V. Le Macchiarelle Ris. '11 | ♀♀ 6 |
| ● Brunello di Montalcino Vallocchio '11 | ♀♀ 6 |
| ● Rosso di Montalcino '15 | ♀♀ 3* |

# Fattoi

LOC. SANTA RESTITUTA
POD. CAPANNA, 101
53024 MONTALCINO [SI]
TEL. +39 0577848613
www.fattoi.it

**CELLAR SALES**
**PRE-BOOKED VISITS**
**ANNUAL PRODUCTION** 50,000 bottles
**HECTARES UNDER VINE** 9.00

Leonardo and Lamberto Fattoi support their father Ofelio in what is one of the most beautiful contemporary Montalcino wineries. They're not a new name, but Fattoi's prestigious vineyards, such as Santa Restituta to the southwest near Tavernelle, continue to reveal their power and originality. This is particularly true in the last ten years with their fiercely artisanal Brunello and Rosso aged in Slovenian oak barrels from 3300 to 4500 liters. Their wines give their best at the table, offering an easy, natural sip that is savory with some formal tones. Fattoi truly spoils with an embarrassment of choice. Their 2016 Rosso, already complete, offers energy and character, just as their 2103 Brunello conquers with its expressive spontaneity and ease of drink. Their 2012 Brunello completes their selection with its rustic sensations and vivid fruit. Its savoriness and tannic quality seal the deal.

| | |
|---|---|
| ● Brunello di Montalcino Ris. '12 | ▼▼▼ 7 |
| ● Brunello di Montalcino '13 | ▼▼ 5 |
| ● Rosso di Montalcino '16 | ▼▼ 3 |
| ● Brunello di Montalcino '10 | ♀♀♀ 5 |
| ● Brunello di Montalcino '12 | ♀♀ 5 |
| ● Brunello di Montalcino '11 | ♀♀ 5 |
| ● Brunello di Montalcino '09 | ♀♀ 5 |
| ● Brunello di Montalcino Ris. '10 | ♀♀ 7 |
| ● Brunello di Montalcino Ris. '08 | ♀♀ 7 |
| ● Brunello di Montalcino Ris. '07 | ♀♀ 7 |
| ● Brunello di Montalcino Ris. '06 | ♀♀ 4 |
| ● Rosso di Montalcino '15 | ♀♀ 3 |
| ● Rosso di Montalcino '14 | ♀♀ 3 |
| ● Rosso di Montalcino '13 | ♀♀ 3 |
| ● Rosso di Montalcino '12 | ♀♀ 3 |

## ★Fattoria del Cerro

Fraz. Acquaviva
via Grazianella, 5
53045 Montepulciano [SI]
Tel. +39 0578767722
www.fattoriadelcerro.it

**CELLAR SALES**
**PRE-BOOKED VISITS**
**ACCOMMODATION AND RESTAURANT SERVICE**
**ANNUAL PRODUCTION** 1,300,000 bottles
**HECTARES UNDER VINE** 181.00

The truly splendid landscape among rolling hills of grapes for as far as the eye can see is overlooked by the beautiful architecture of the Relais Villa Grazianella. The winery has 576 hectares, of which 150 are dedicated to grapes on soil of Pliocene origins. Tenute dell Cerro is a noteworthy Montepulciano winery owned by the Unipol Group. The winery's style tends to be modern, with the use of predominantly small barrels, and the decisive maturity of the fruit imprinting the wine with notable intensity and structure. Cerro's proposals are rich and well-structured this year as well. Their dark ruby 2015 Nobile presents black fruit and spice that veer into woody. Its balanced structure, finesse and persistence on the palate again deserve Tre Bicchieri. Their still developing 2014 Antica Chiusina proves more closed. Among other compelling offerings, their fresh, supple 2016 Rosso deserves special mention.

| | |
|---|---|
| ● Nobile di Montepulciano '15 | ♟♟♟ 4* |
| ● Nobile di Montepulciano Antica Chiusina '14 | ♟♟ 6 |
| ● Nobile di Montepulciano Ris. '14 | ♟♟ 5 |
| ● Rosso di Montepulciano '16 | ♟♟ 2* |
| ● Manero Rosso '16 | ♟ 2 |
| ● Nobile di Montepulciano '14 | ♟♟♟ 3* |
| ● Nobile di Montepulciano '11 | ♟♟♟ 3* |
| ● Nobile di Montepulciano '10 | ♟♟♟ 3* |
| ● Nobile di Montepulciano Ris. '12 | ♟♟♟ 4* |
| ● Nobile di Montepulciano Ris. '11 | ♟♟♟ 4* |
| ● Nobile di Montepulciano Ris. '06 | ♟♟♟ 4 |
| ● Nobile di Montepulciano Vign. Antica Chiusina '00 | ♟♟♟ 6 |

## Fattoria San Michele a Torri

via San Michele, 36
50018 Scandicci [FI]
Tel. +39 055769111
www.fattoriasanmichele.it

**CELLAR SALES**
**PRE-BOOKED VISITS**
**ANNUAL PRODUCTION** 200,000 bottles
**HECTARES UNDER VINE** 55.00
**VITICULTURE METHOD** Certified Organic

Paolo Nocentini, owner of Fattoria San Michele a Torri, has a unique story. He's an old-school, self-made man who started working at 16 as a telephone operator and today owns a logistics group made up of 4000 employees the world over. The 'Fattoria' is a nice example of modern agricultural management, with wine and oil at the center of it all. Their principal site is located in Colli Fiorentini, though they also have vineyards in Chianti Classico. Their Chianto Classico della Tenuta La Gabbiola goes to our finals by virtue of its lively, fruity, classic nose of cherry and wild berries with subtle aromatic herbs. Pleasant on the palate without being too powerful, with well-integrated tannins and a supple body that lead into a savory and enjoyable finish. Their 2015 Murtas, a Sangiovese and Cabernet Sauvignon blend with a bit of Colorino, offers aromas of green pepper, tomato leaves and black fruit. On the palate it proves warm, soft, juicy and rich, delivering a finish of flavor in crescendo.

| | |
|---|---|
| ● Chianti Cl. Tenuta La Gabbiola '16 | ♟♟ 3* |
| ● Chianti Cl. Tenuta La Gabbiola Ris. '14 | ♟♟ 4 |
| ● Murtas '15 | ♟♟ 5 |
| ● Chianti Cl. I Casali '15 | ♟ 3 |
| ● Chianti Colli Fiorentini S. Giovanni Novantasette Ris. '15 | ♟ 4 |
| ● Chianti Colli Fiorentini San Michele a Torri '16 | ♟ 2 |
| ○ Colli dell'Etruria Centrale Vin Santo '02 | ♟ 6 |
| ● Chianti Colli Fiorentini '14 | ♟♟ 2* |
| ● Chianti Colli Fiorentini '13 | ♟♟ 2* |
| ● Chianti Colli Fiorentini S. Giovanni Novantasette Ris. '13 | ♟♟ 4 |
| ● Chicchirossi '16 | ♟♟ 3 |

# Fattoria Fibbiano

VIA FIBBIANO, 2
56030 TERRICCIOLA [PI]
TEL. +39 0587635677
www.fattoria-fibbiano.it

CELLAR SALES
PRE-BOOKED VISITS
ACCOMMODATION AND RESTAURANT SERVICE
ANNUAL PRODUCTION 185,000 bottles
HECTARES UNDER VINE 17.00

The estate and its guest hosting facilities
are located among the hills between Pisa
and Volterra. The origins of the winery go
back to the 12th century, but Giuseppe
Cantoni purchased it just over 20 years
ago, after he returned from his industrial
work abroad. Giuseppe is joined by his
children, Matteo and Nicola, in running this
certified organic winery, the soils of which
are treated exclusively with organic
substances. From an energy consumption
point of view, Fattoria Fibbiano's
agriturismo is totally self-sufficient. Their
compelling 2016, a Sangiovese paired with
Colorino, offers a big, fruity nose of currant
and blueberry mixed with cherry. Its fresh,
harmonic structure proves quite pleasing
on the palate. Their 2015 Aspetto, of equal
parts Sangiovese and Canaiolo, delivers an
intense nose of black fruit and aromatic
herbs as well as a nice kick of acidity that
enlivens its well-structured body.

| | |
|---|---|
| ● Ciliegiolo '16 | ♟♟ 4 |
| ● L'Aspetto '15 | ♟♟ 5 |
| ● Le Pianette '16 | ♟♟ 2* |
| ● Sanforte '14 | ♟♟ 5 |
| ○ Fonte delle Donne '17 | ♟ 3 |
| ● Chianti Sup. Casalini '15 | ♟♟ 2* |
| ● Ciliegiolo '15 | ♟♟ 3 |
| ○ Fonte Delle Donne '15 | ♟♟ 3 |
| ○ Fonte delle Donne '14 | ♟♟ 2* |
| ● L'Aspetto '13 | ♟♟ 4 |
| ● Le Pianette '15 | ♟♟ 2* |
| ● Terre di Pisa Ceppatella '13 | ♟♟ 6 |
| ● Terre di Pisa Ceppatella '12 | ♟♟ 6 |

# ★Tenute Ambrogio e Giovanni Folonari

LOC. PASSO DEI PECORAI
VIA DI NOZZOLE, 12
50022 GREVE IN CHIANTI [FI]
TEL. +39 055859811
www.tenutefolonari.com

CELLAR SALES
PRE-BOOKED VISITS
ACCOMMODATION
ANNUAL PRODUCTION 1,400,000 bottles
HECTARES UNDER VINE 200.00

Folonari is one of the great historical
families of Italian wine. Since 2000, the
branch of the family led by Ambrogio and
Giovanni has been managing the five
historical Tuscan wineries of Cabreo and
Nozzole near Greve in Chianti, Campo al
Mare in Bolgheri, La Fuga at Montalcino,
Torcalvano at Montepulciano and Porrona
in Montecucco. Their wines have a modern
style, with aging done mainly in smaller
barrels. Recently they have benefited from
a lighter structure making them even more
enjoyable. Their well-made 2015 Chianti
Classico Gran Selezione delivers
multifaceted aromas of red fruit, spices
and hints of smoke. It offers acidic
freshness and balance on its well-
sustained palate. Their pure Cabernet
Sauvignon 2015 Pareto proves deeper,
more complex with concentrated aromas
and prominent oak that reach an elegant,
harmonic resolution on the palate.

| | |
|---|---|
| ● Il Pareto '15 | ♟♟♟ 8 |
| ● Chianti Cl. Gran Selezione '15 | ♟♟ 5 |
| ● Chianti Cl. '16 | ♟ 2 |
| ● Cabreo Il Borgo '06 | ♟♟♟ 5 |
| ● Chianti Cl. La Forra Ris. '90 | ♟♟♟ 4* |
| ● Il Pareto '09 | ♟♟♟ 7 |
| ● Il Pareto '07 | ♟♟♟ 7 |
| ● Il Pareto '04 | ♟♟♟ 7 |
| ● Il Pareto '01 | ♟♟♟ 7 |
| ● Il Pareto '00 | ♟♟♟ 7 |
| ● Il Pareto '98 | ♟♟♟ 7 |
| ● Il Pareto '97 | ♟♟♟ 7 |
| ● Il Pareto '93 | ♟♟♟ 7 |

# ★★Fontodi

FRAZ. PANZANO IN CHIANTI
VIA SAN LEOLINO, 89
50020 GREVE IN CHIANTI [FI]
TEL. +39 055852005
www.fontodi.com

**CELLAR SALES**
**PRE-BOOKED VISITS**
**ACCOMMODATION**
**ANNUAL PRODUCTION** 300,000 bottles
**HECTARES UNDER VINE** 80.00
**VITICULTURE METHOD** Certified Organic

Fontodi, property of the Manetti family since 1968, is a standard bearer of Chianti Classico. Possessing a clear style that is easily recognizable in its rich, robust reds, it has longevity that is always expressed in a controlled way. Their organic winegrowing provides top-quality material that respects the character of Chianti's Panzano subarea. Aged largely in small barrels, their wines offer an aromatic range fully expressed over time. The winery is a leading producer from the Conca d'Oro area of Panzano and their impressive 2015 Chianti Classico begins with aromas of fresh cherry and flint, turning spicy at the finish on a juicy, tasty and energetic palate. A bit more concentrated and with darker aromatic tones, their 2015 Gran Selezione Vigna del Sorbo offers a rich, smooth palate with a full, intense fruity finish.

# Fontuccia

VIA PROVINCIALE, 54
58012 ISOLA DEL GIGLIO [GR]
TEL. +39 0564809576
www.fontuccia.it

**ANNUAL PRODUCTION** 6,500 bottles
**HECTARES UNDER VINE** 3.00

After you've taken in your share of the beauty of the Island of Giglio, you're struck by the viticulture practiced here. It's truly heroic, with head-trained vines sprouting up out of the rocks and still propped up with canes found near the sea. Simone and Giovanni Rossi's Fontuccia is comprised of entirely terraced vineyards situated by the sea, conditions that require constant care and strong legs. The producer has been bottling since 2009, and from the beginning they've conferred their wines with lovely personality and purity. The pure Ansonica and steel aging of their complex white 2016 Carerrosso Senti Oh! result in iodated aromas and salty hints on the palate. The back of the bottle says all ones needs to know about their 2016 Saracio, which they describe as 'a red made from unidentified grapes of unknown origin that form a terrifying mix of resolute and intriguing character'. Their 2017 Senti Oh! and their sweet 2016 Ansonica 'Nantropo' both offer lovely aromas.

| | |
|---|---|
| ● Chianti Cl. '15 | ♟♟ 4 |
| ● Chianti Cl. Gran Sel. V. del Sorbo '15 | ♟♟ 6 |
| ● Flaccianello della Pieve '15 | ♟♟ 8 |
| ● Casevia '15 | ♟ 5 |
| ● Chianti Cl. '10 | ♟♟♟ 4* |
| ● Chianti Cl. Gran Sel. V. del Sorbo '14 | ♟♟♟ 6 |
| ● Chianti Cl. V. del Sorbo Ris. '01 | ♟♟♟ 6 |
| ● Flaccianello della Pieve '12 | ♟♟♟ 8 |
| ● Flaccianello della Pieve '09 | ♟♟♟ 8 |
| ● Flaccianello della Pieve '08 | ♟♟♟ 8 |
| ● Flaccianello della Pieve '07 | ♟♟♟ 6 |
| ● Flaccianello della Pieve '05 | ♟♟♟ 6 |
| ● Flaccianello della Pieve '03 | ♟♟♟ 6 |
| ● Flaccianello della Pieve '85 | ♟♟♟ 8 |
| ● Flaccianello della Pieve '83 | ♟♟♟ 8 |

| | |
|---|---|
| ○ Capperorosso Senti Oh! '16 | ♟♟ 4 |
| ● Saracio '16 | ♟♟ 6 |
| ○ Senti Oh! '17 | ♟♟ 4 |
| ○ 'Nantropo' '16 | ♟ 6 |
| ○ Capperorosso Senti Oh! '15 | ♟♟ 4 |
| ○ N'antro Po '11 | ♟♟ 3 |
| ○ N'antro Po' '13 | ♟♟ 6 |
| ○ Senti Oh! '16 | ♟♟ 4 |

# Fornacelle

LOC. FORNACELLE, 232A
57022 CASTAGNETO CARDUCCI [LI]
TEL. +39 0565775575
www.fornacelle.it

**CELLAR SALES**
**PRE-BOOKED VISITS**
**ANNUAL PRODUCTION** 35,000 bottles
**HECTARES UNDER VINE** 9.00

The estate's name and the ruins beneath it testify to the history of an area once filled with forges. Belonging to the Billi-Batistoni family for four generations, a turning point came in the early 1990s with a decisive renovation of both the vineyard and the cellar. This rebirth gave the winery the energy it needed to leap forward. The vineyards are located on variegated soils on the plains of medium density, which are mixed with differing amounts of small stones, silt, loamy sand and gravel. Their Bolgheri Superiore Guardaboschi offers spectacular finesse and makes our finals by virtue of its intensely fresh, balsamic profile that proves very focused and detailed yet mutable in the glass. On the palate it's silky and harmonic, with lively pulp refreshed by delicate acidic energy under notes of field herbs, fresh flowers and berries.

| | |
|---|---|
| ● Bolgheri Rosso Sup. Guarda Boschi '15 | ▼▼ 6 |
| ● Bolgheri Rosso Zizzolo '16 | ▼▼ 3 |
| ○ Bolgheri Vermentino Zizzolo '17 | ▼ 3 |
| ● Erminia Merlot '15 | ▼ 7 |
| ● Bolgheri Sup. Foglio 38 '14 | ♀♀ 7 |
| ● Bolgheri Sup. Guarda Boschi '13 | ♀♀ 6 |
| ● Bolgheri Sup. Guarda Boschi '11 | ♀♀ 6 |
| ● Foglio 38 '11 | ♀♀ 6 |

# Podere Forte

LOC. PETRUCCI, 13
53023 CASTIGLIONE D'ORCIA [SI]
TEL. +39 05778885100
www.podereforte.it

**CELLAR SALES**
**PRE-BOOKED VISITS**
**ANNUAL PRODUCTION** 12,000 bottles
**HECTARES UNDER VINE** 15.00
**VITICULTURE METHOD** Certified Biodynamic
**SUSTAINABLE WINERY**

Pasquale Forte has managed to realize his dream: make the land the principal element of his life, through grapes grown in the most natural way possible. Calabrese by birth, Lombard by adoption, he now finds himself in Tuscany, where he's making his ideas a reality, with biodynamic principles at the center of it all. The result is a modern, creative winery that also has a social commitment and an atypical vision of agriculture. The Merlot and Petit Verdot in their 2014 Guardiavia, offer intriguing fruity aromas of blueberry and currant with notes of mint and aromatic herbs like thyme and bay leaf. It hits the palate lightly and juicily gaining power and strength until its long, pleasantly persistent finish. Their 2015 Petruccino, of Sangiovese and Merlot, highlights its clearly-defined aroma of cherry and Mediterranean scrub. On the palate it proves linear and smooth, with a fresh vein of acidity and a clean finish.

| | |
|---|---|
| ● Guardiavigna '14 | ▼▼ 8 |
| ● Orcia Petruccino '15 | ▼▼ 6 |
| ● Orcia Guardiavigna '01 | ♀♀♀ 8 |
| ● Guardiavigna '13 | ♀♀ 8 |
| ● Guardiavigna '12 | ♀♀ 8 |
| ● Guardiavigna '11 | ♀♀ 8 |
| ● Guardiavigna '10 | ♀♀ 8 |
| ● Orcia Petrucci '10 | ♀♀ 8 |
| ● Orcia Petruccino '13 | ♀♀ 8 |
| ● Orcia Petruccino '11 | ♀♀ 8 |
| ● Orcia Rosso Petrucci '11 | ♀♀ 8 |
| ● Orcia Rosso Petruccino '12 | ♀♀ 8 |

## Fortulla - Agrilandia

LOC. CASTIGLIONCELLO
S.DA VICINALE DELLE SPIANATE
57016 ROSIGNANO MARITTIMO [LI]
TEL. +39 3404524453
www.fortulla.it

CELLAR SALES
PRE-BOOKED VISITS
ACCOMMODATION AND RESTAURANT SERVICE
ANNUAL PRODUCTION 50,000 bottles
HECTARES UNDER VINE 7.00
VITICULTURE METHOD Certified Organic
SUSTAINABLE WINERY

In the mid-1990s, Fulvio Martini moved to a mostly abandoned location in an enchanting position on the high plains of Castiglioncello, on the coast of Tuscany. It is the same countryside that inspired the Macchiaioli movement at the end of the 1800s. The land is covered by olive groves, vineyards and Mediterranean vegetation, while the restored farm manor now welcomes guests. Their wines have been certified organic since 2014, and all recyclable estate water is purified and reused for irrigation while electricity and thermal energy are powered by the sun. Their excellent 2103 Sorpesso features equal parts Cabernet Sauvignon and Cabernet Franc with a bit of Merlot. Clear coffee and toasty notes emerge on the nose before blackberry jam and hints of cinnamon. It envelops, well-structured and full bodied on the palate, reaching a lovely, long crescendo in the finish. Their 2017 Serpentino offers fruity notes of peach, then aromatic herbs and notes of menthol, proving light and juicy with a pleasing finish.

| | | |
|---|---|---|
| ● Sorpasso '13 | ♟♟ | 6 |
| ○ Terratico di Bibbona Serpentino '17 | ♟♟ | 4 |
| ● Fortulla '15 | ♟ | 4 |
| ○ Pelagico '16 | ♟ | 5 |
| ⊙ Rosato Epatta '17 | ♟ | 3 |
| ○ Bianco Fortulla '14 | ♟♟ | 4 |
| ● Fortulla Rosso '13 | ♟♟ | 4 |
| ● Fortulla Rosso '12 | ♟♟ | 4 |
| ○ Pelagico '15 | ♟♟ | 5 |
| ○ Serpentino '16 | ♟♟ | 4 |
| ● Sorpasso '12 | ♟♟ | 6 |
| ● Sorpasso '11 | ♟♟ | 5 |
| ● Sorpasso '10 | ♟♟ | 5 |

## Tenuta La Fortuna

LOC. LA FORTUNA, 83
53024 MONTALCINO [SI]
TEL. +39 0577848308
www.tenutalafortuna.it

CELLAR SALES
PRE-BOOKED VISITS
ANNUAL PRODUCTION 60,000 bottles
HECTARES UNDER VINE 18.00

For some time now siblings Angelo and Romina Zannoni have been working alongside their parents Gioberto and Felicetta, making them the sixth generation to run this winery. The estate is divided into two main parcels. The original tract is in the northeast quadrant of Montalcino, while a subsequently acquired plot is in the southeast area of Castelnuovo dell'Abate. The two terroir synthesize a multifaceted Sangiovese da Brunello, at times lofty and powerful. Aging occurs mostly in medium barrels. These tastings summarize La Fortuna's stylistic versatility. Their eager, multifaceted 2016 Rosso jumps between mandarin orange peel, pink pepper, ginseng, and a salty background that moves on its lithe palate. Their 2013 Brunello, on the other hand, proves rather tertiary and substantial, dominated by plum and dried fruit on both its nose and its decidedly horizontal palate.

| | | |
|---|---|---|
| ● Brunello di Montalcino '13 | ♟♟ | 6 |
| ● Rosso di Montalcino '16 | ♟♟ | 3 |
| ● Brunello di Montalcino '06 | ♟♟♟ | 6 |
| ● Brunello di Montalcino '04 | ♟♟♟ | 6 |
| ● Brunello di Montalcino '01 | ♟♟♟ | 5 |
| ● Brunello di Montalcino '12 | ♟♟ | 6 |
| ● Brunello di Montalcino '10 | ♟♟ | 6 |
| ● Brunello di Montalcino '08 | ♟♟ | 6 |
| ● Brunello di Montalcino '07 | ♟♟ | 6 |
| ● Brunello di Montalcino Giobi '12 | ♟♟ | 6 |
| ● Brunello di Montalcino Giobi '10 | ♟♟ | 6 |
| ● Brunello di Montalcino Ris. '07 | ♟♟ | 7 |
| ● Brunello di Montalcino Ris. '06 | ♟♟ | 6 |
| ● Brunello di Montalcino Ris. '04 | ♟♟ | 6 |
| ● Rosso di Montalcino '11 | ♟♟ | 3 |

# La Fralluca

LOC. BARBICONI, 153
57028 SUVERETO [LI]
TEL. +39 0565829076
www.lafralluca.com

**CELLAR SALES**
**PRE-BOOKED VISITS**
**ANNUAL PRODUCTION** 45,000 bottles
**HECTARES UNDER VINE** 10.00
**SUSTAINABLE WINERY**

One could say the story of Fralluca began 10 years ago with the planting of the vineyards, then took a leap forward a year later with the completion of an almost entirely underground cellar located amidst the rows of grapes. But in reality the story began more than 20 years ago when Francesca and Luca met each other while working in fashion. They formed a family and had two children. Their dream was to move to Tuscany to make wine, which they did when they found this spot with an abandoned farm manor at the top of a hill in Suvereto and a commanding view over the forest. Their 2105 Cabernet Franc proves interesting and inviting in its meaty tones of tomato leaves and aromatic herbs with hints of oregano and sage. It offers well-placed acidity and well-blended tannins on the vital, energetic palate. Even its alcohol is well-balanced and its finish, long and flavorful. Their 2015 Fillide, combines Sangiovese, Syrah and Alicante for a nose of tobacco, leather and blackberry. It enters well on the palate, enveloping with a supple, balanced body of great drinkability.

| | |
|---|---|
| ● Cabernet Franc '15 | ♟♟ 6 |
| ● Fillide '15 | ♟♟ 3 |
| ● Pitis '14 | ♟♟ 5 |
| ○ Bauci '16 | ♟ 4 |
| ○ Filemone '17 | ♟ 3 |
| ● Suvereto Sangiovese Ciparisso '14 | ♟ 5 |
| ● Suvereto Sangiovese Ciparisso '12 | ♟♟ 5 |
| ○ Bauci '15 | ♟♟ 3 |
| ○ Bauci '14 | ♟♟ 3 |
| ● Cabernet Franc '14 | ♟♟ 5 |
| ● Cabernet Franc '13 | ♟♟ 5 |
| ● Cabernet Franc '12 | ♟♟ 5 |
| ● Fillide '14 | ♟♟ 3 |
| ● Fillide '12 | ♟♟ 3 |

# Frascole

LOC. FRASCOLE, 27A
50062 DICOMANO [FI]
TEL. +39 0558386340
www.frascole.it

**CELLAR SALES**
**PRE-BOOKED VISITS**
**ACCOMMODATION**
**ANNUAL PRODUCTION** 65,000 bottles
**HECTARES UNDER VINE** 16.00
**VITICULTURE METHOD** Certified Organic

At the border of Mugello and Val Sieve sits the little medieval-walled town of Frascola, which itself rests on pre-existing Estruscan and Roman construction. From these same eras traces of the area's vibrant traditions in viticulture can be found. Enrico and Elisa Lippi bought and brought back to life a small estate at 400 meters above sea level, the upper limit of the Chianti Rufina producing area. Not surprisingly, some years ago work in the vineyards brought to light the ruins of an ancient Roman house. Their lovely 2105 Chianti Rufina Riserva begins with a mineral, floral nose before taking a sharp balsamic turn. Assorted fruit accompanies notes of forest and blood. Pleasing on the palate it proves elegant, with a silky suite of tannins. Their 2016 Bitorno, a varied blend of Sangiovese, Malvasia, Colorino del Valdarno, Trebbiano and Canaiolo, offers aromas of clove, grilling meat and aromatic herbs. It reveals itself with freshness on the spacious palate, offering great drinkability with a chocolaty finish.

| | |
|---|---|
| ● Chianti Rufina Ris. '15 | ♟♟ 3* |
| ● Bitornino '16 | ♟♟ 2* |
| ● Chianti Rufina '16 | ♟♟ 2* |
| ○ In Albis sulle bucce '15 | ♟♟ 5 |
| ○ In Albis '15 | ♟ 2 |
| ● Bitornino '15 | ♟♟ 2* |
| ● Chianti Rufina '14 | ♟♟ 2* |
| ● Chianti Rufina '13 | ♟♟ 2* |
| ● Chianti Rufina Ris. '14 | ♟♟ 3 |
| ● Chianti Rufina Ris. '12 | ♟♟ 3* |
| ○ In Albis '13 | ♟♟ 2* |
| ● Limine '10 | ♟♟ 2* |
| ● Rosso Limine '09 | ♟♟ 2* |

# ★Frescobaldi

VIA SANTO SPIRITO, 11
50125 FIRENZE
TEL. +39 05527141
www.frescobaldi.it

**CELLAR SALES**
**PRE-BOOKED VISITS**
**ANNUAL PRODUCTION** 7,500,000 bottles
**HECTARES UNDER VINE** 923.00

Frescobaldi is a historic yet incredible modern producer that's managed to understand how to interpret the territories in which it operates while eschewing standardized, soulless production approaches. The proof lies in their most recent purchase in Chianti Classico, a historic event that confirmed their desire to 'read' the grapes in the best way possible. It's all thanks to Lamberto Frescobaldi, who's leading the winery with talent and plenty of entrepreneurial curiosity. Their pure Sangiovese 2015 Montesodi reaches the nose with well-defined vegetal notes followed by bell pepper, lightly toasted with hints of geranium on a fruity background. It offers good body on the palate that remains fresh and a long, appetizing finish. Their 2015 Pinot Nero strikes the nose with intense aromas of black fruit and aromatic herbs, proving dynamic, elegant and enduring on the palate. Their 2015 Mormoreto delivers a powerful, toasted bouquet with a long, supple, lively palate.

| | |
|---|---|
| ● Montesodi '15 | ♟♟♟ 6 |
| ● Mormoreto '15 | ♟♟ 8 |
| ● Pomino Pinot Nero '15 | ♟♟ 4 |
| ● Castiglioni '15 | ♟♟ 8 |
| ● Chianti Cl. Tenuta Perano '15 | ♟♟ 4 |
| ● Chianti Rufina Nipozzano Ris. '14 | ♟♟ 4 |
| ● Lamaione '13 | ♟♟ 8 |
| ● Maremma Toscana Cabernet Sauvignon Terre More '16 | ♟♟ 3 |
| ○ Pomino Bianco Benefizio Ris. '16 | ♟♟ 5 |
| ○ Pomino Brut Leonia '14 | ♟♟ 6 |
| ⊙ Pomino Brut Rosé '15 | ♟♟ 7 |
| ○ Pomino Vin Santo '09 | ♟♟ 6 |
| ● Chianti Rufina V. V. Ris. '15 | ♟ 5 |
| ● Chianti Rufina Nipozzano V. V. Ris. '13 | ♟♟♟ 5 |
| ● Chianti Rufina V. V. Ris. '11 | ♟♟♟ 6 |

# Fuligni

VIA SALONI, 33
53024 MONTALCINO [SI]
TEL. +39 0577848710
www.fuligni.it

**CELLAR SALES**
**PRE-BOOKED VISITS**
**ANNUAL PRODUCTION** 52,000 bottles
**HECTARES UNDER VINE** 12.00

The Fuligni family winery is a standard-bearer of the Cottimelli, the eastern limit of the hill on which the walled town of Montalcino sits. The vineyards, at elevations reaching 450 meters, are characterized by rocky and marly terrain, as well as by a microclimate that results from humid westerly breezes. Worked separately, the St. John, Piano, Ginestreto and La Bandita parcels contribute to Sangiovese reds that are robust but approachable even in the early stages. Brunello is aged in mid-sized and 3000-liter barrels. Their latest releases also prove excellent expressions of Fuligni's juicy style. Wild berries, medicinal herbs and nuances of iodine of their 2013 reflect the lightness of the classic vintage. Their 2012 Brunello Riserva, on the other hand, offers greater aromatic maturity and extractive buttressing, with notes of sour black cherry jam and hints of herbs before its pleasantly dry finish.

| | |
|---|---|
| ● Brunello di Montalcino '13 | ♟♟ 6 |
| ● Brunello di Montalcino Ris. '12 | ♟♟ 8 |
| ● Brunello di Montalcino '10 | ♟♟♟ 6 |
| ● Brunello di Montalcino Ris. '01 | ♟♟♟ 8 |
| ● Brunello di Montalcino Ris. '97 | ♟♟♟ 8 |
| ● Brunello di Montalcino '12 | ♟♟ 6 |
| ● Brunello di Montalcino '11 | ♟♟ 6 |
| ● Brunello di Montalcino '09 | ♟♟ 6 |
| ● Brunello di Montalcino '08 | ♟♟ 6 |
| ● Brunello di Montalcino '07 | ♟♟ 6 |
| ● Brunello di Montalcino Ris. '07 | ♟♟ 8 |
| ● Rosso di Montalcino Ginestreto '15 | ♟♟ 4 |
| ● Rosso di Montalcino Ginestreto '13 | ♟♟ 4 |
| ● Rosso di Montalcino Ginestreto '10 | ♟♟ 3 |
| ● S. J. '12 | ♟♟ 3 |

# ★Tenuta di Ghizzano

FRAZ. GHIZZANO
VIA DELLA CHIESA, 4
56037 PECCIOLI [PI]
TEL. +39 0587630096
www.tenutadighizzano.com

CELLAR SALES
PRE-BOOKED VISITS
ACCOMMODATION
ANNUAL PRODUCTION 80,000 bottles
HECTARES UNDER VINE 20.00
VITICULTURE METHOD Certified Organic

Ginevra Venerosi Pesciolini runs an extraordinary operation no matter how you look at it. The location itself is seductively beautiful, embracing a vast estate among vineyards, olive groves, grains, woodlands and poplars. The grapes are planted in sandy, clayey fossil-rich soils of marine origin. Certified organic, the winery has for several years been looking to move fully to biodynamic methods. Their wines are punctual and expressive, strongly Mediterranean and showing a positive evolution in style. The winery's historical Ghizzano contains Sangiovese with a small percentage of Cabernet Franc and their perfectly made 2016 proves absolutely delicious. It offers grace, flavor and juice with a linear but never rough palate, achieved with and hightlighted by an inviting fruity array of blackberry, blueberry and myrtle. Mediterranean herbs and balsamic hints well-buttressed by pleasant tannins wrap up this lovely package.

| | |
|---|---|
| ● Il Ghizzano Rosso '16 | ♟♟ 3* |
| ● Terre di Pisa Nambrot '16 | ♟♟ 6 |
| ● Terre di Pisa Veneroso '15 | ♟ 5 |
| ● Nambrot '09 | ♟♟♟ 6 |
| ● Nambrot '08 | ♟♟♟ 6 |
| ● Terre di Pisa Nambrot '15 | ♟♟♟ 6 |
| ● Terre di Pisa Nambrot '13 | ♟♟♟ 6 |
| ● Terre di Pisa Nambrot '12 | ♟♟♟ 6 |
| ● Veneroso '10 | ♟♟♟ 5 |
| ● Veneroso '07 | ♟♟♟ 5 |
| ● Terre di Pisa Veneroso '14 | ♟♟ 5 |
| ● Terre di Pisa Veneroso '13 | ♟♟ 5 |

# Marchesi Ginori Lisci

FRAZ. PONTEGINORI
LOC. QUERCETO
56040 MONTECATINI VAL DI CECINA [PI]
TEL. +39 058837443
www.marchesiginorilisci.it

CELLAR SALES
ACCOMMODATION AND RESTAURANT SERVICE
ANNUAL PRODUCTION 35,000 bottles
HECTARES UNDER VINE 17.00
VITICULTURE METHOD Certified Organic

Perched atop a hill to the southwest of Volterra there is a medieval-walled village with guest apartments. This is the heart of the 2000-hectare estate that has been owned by the Ginori Lisci family for time immemorial. However, only in the last 20-something years have Leonardo Ginori and his grandson Luigi Malenchini made noteworthy changes by planting new vineyards and building a new cellar. Merlot, Cabernet Sauvignon, Sangiovese, Voignier and Vermentino are cultivated, some of which are used for their Montescudaio offerings. Their 2015 Merlot Castello Ginori presents fruity, vegetal notes lightly supported with subtle cinnamon and clove. Its smooth, well-balanced body offers good weight with blended tannins and a pleasantly long, juicy finish. Their 2016 Macchion del Lupo makes a lovely impression with fruity notes of currant, cherry and blackberry united with light hints of aromatic herbs. The pulpy red delivers tannins on the palate that support a powerful but limber structure and a long, enjoyable finish.

| | |
|---|---|
| ● Montescudaio Merlot Castello Ginori '15 | ♟♟ 2* |
| ● Montescudaio Cabernet Macchion del Lupo '16 | ♟♟ 3 |
| ● Montescudaio Merlot Campordigno '16 | ♟♟ 2* |
| ○ Vermentino Virgola '17 | ♟ 2 |
| ● Montescudaio Cabernet Macchion del Lupo '14 | ♟♟ 3* |
| ● Montescudaio Cabernet Macchion del Lupo '13 | ♟♟ 3 |
| ● Montescudaio Cabernet Macchion del Lupo '11 | ♟♟ 3* |
| ● Montescudaio Merlot Campordigno '12 | ♟♟ 2* |
| ● Montescudaio Merlot Castello Ginori '14 | ♟♟ 2* |
| ● Montescudaio Merlot Castello Ginori '12 | ♟♟ 2* |
| ● Montescudaio Merlot Castello Ginori '11 | ♟♟ 2* |
| ● Montescudaio Rosso Campordigno '15 | ♟♟ 2* |

# Giodo

loc. Piazzini
53011 Montalcino [SI]
Tel. +39
carlo.ferrini27@gmail.com

**ANNUAL PRODUCTION** 8,000 bottles
**HECTARES UNDER VINE** 2.50
**SUSTAINABLE WINERY**

It took only a few harvests for the Ferrini family to establish itself among the top tier of winemakers in the Montalcino district. Everything begins in a small vineyard in the heart of the southern sector on a hill between Castelnuovo Dell'Abate and Sant'Angelo in Colle. Their Brunello and Rosso vineyards give rise to contemporary styled wines: communicative but with depth, expressing strict adhesion to a finely-tailored paradigm. Here is an example of where enological protocols and barrel dimensions are secondary to the winemaker's skill. Giodo's thrilling ride gets new energy with its homonymous 2013 Brunello. Jovial in nature, its summer red fruit and menthol notes take on additional thermal and sylvan nuances after breathing in the glass. Taut, flavorful and supported by a silky suite of tannins, only the slight alcoholic tug on reins at the end slows down the finish.

| | |
|---|---|
| ● Brunello di Montalcino Giodo '13 | ▼▼▼ 8 |
| ● Giodo '16 | ▼▼ 6 |
| ● Brunello di Montalcino Giodo '12 | ♀♀♀ 8 |
| ● Brunello di Montalcino Giodo '11 | ♀♀♀ 8 |
| ● Giodo '15 | ♀♀ 6 |
| ● Giodo '13 | ♀♀ 6 |

# I Giusti & Zanza Vigneti

via dei Puntoni, 9
56043 Fauglia [PI]
Tel. +39 058544354
www.igiustiezanza.it

**CELLAR SALES**
**PRE-BOOKED VISITS**
**ACCOMMODATION**
**ANNUAL PRODUCTION** 100,000 bottles
**HECTARES UNDER VINE** 17.00
**VITICULTURE METHOD** Certified Organic

Giusti & Zanza Vigneti is definitely one of the Tuscan coast's most important wineries. Situated in Fauglia, it was founded by the Giusti family in the 1990s on the highlands between Pisa and Livorno. By now they're an established producer, though certainly not static. If anything they've shown increased attention to recent trends, while painting a clear stylistic identity. Their vineyards grow in sandy-clay soil, with a notable presence of gravel. Their wines show personality and definition, rigor and pluck. Their compelling 2015 Dulcamara, prevalently Cabernet Sauvignon but with some Cabernet Franc when the vintage permits, features black fruit like blackberry and blueberry, a dense, toasted, intense texture still in the process of uniting, and sturdy tannic support. Their similarly dark and intense 2016 Syrah Perbruno proves pulpy but overall quite dynamic on the palate.

| | |
|---|---|
| ● Dulcamara '15 | ▼▼ 5 |
| ● Nemorino Rosso '16 | ▼▼ 2* |
| ● Perbruno '16 | ▼▼ 4 |
| ● Belcore '16 | ▼ 3 |
| ● Belcore '15 | ♀♀ 3 |
| ● Dulcamara '12 | ♀♀ 5 |
| ● Dulcamara '11 | ♀♀ 5 |
| ● Nemorino Rosso '15 | ♀♀ 2* |
| ● Perbruno '15 | ♀♀ 4 |

# Bibi Graetz

VIA DI VINCIGLIATA, 19
50014 FIESOLE [FI]
TEL. +39 055597289
www.bibigraetz.com

PRE-BOOKED VISITS
**ANNUAL PRODUCTION** 500,000 bottles
**HECTARES UNDER VINE** 10.00

One wouldn't expect anything but the eccentric and unusual from a winery led by part artist, part visionary, Bibi Graetz. His character is immediately discernible by the names of his wines and the bottles' labels, which derive from his paintings. His family bought the land on the hillside around Castello di Vincigliata in Fiesole about 60 years ago and for the last 20 years he has immersed himself totally in the world of wine. Their unusual, always intriguing Colore, a mix of Sangiovese, Colorino and Canaiolo expresses the 2015 vintage with notes of thyme and marjoram followed by balsamic, black fruit hints of currant and blueberry. It hits the palate with significant but balanced freshness, poised tannins and a relaxed finish. Their 2017 Bugia, made of Ansonica from the Isola of Giglio, offers peach notes and mineral hints. Full-bodied on the palate it proves wonderfully fresh, enfolding and invitingly savory.

| | |
|---|---|
| ○ Bugia '17 | ♟♟ 7 |
| ● Colore '15 | ♟♟ 8 |
| ○ Scopeto '17 | ♟♟ 4 |
| ● Testamatta '16 | ♟♟ 8 |
| ○ Casamatta Bianco '17 | ♟ 2 |
| ● Casamatta Rosso '17 | ♟ 2 |
| ○ Testamatta Bianco '17 | ♟ 8 |
| ○ Bugia '16 | ♟♟ 6 |
| ● Colore '12 | ♟♟ 8 |
| ○ Scopeto '16 | ♟♟ 3 |
| ● Soffocone di Vincigliata '15 | ♟♟ 5 |
| ● Testamatta '15 | ♟♟ 8 |
| ● Testamatta '13 | ♟♟ 8 |
| ○ Testamatta Bianco '15 | ♟♟ 5 |

# ★Grattamacco

LOC. LUNGAGNANO
57022 CASTAGNETO CARDUCCI [LI]
TEL. +39 0565765069
www.collemassari.it

CELLAR SALES
PRE-BOOKED VISITS
**ANNUAL PRODUCTION** 120,000 bottles
**HECTARES UNDER VINE** 16.00
**VITICULTURE METHOD** Certified Organic
SUSTAINABLE WINERY

Grattamacco is a prestigious name and at the same time a pioneer among great Bolgheri wines. Founded in the 1970s, the winery is now in the hands of the Tipa brothers who are contributing to both its value and reputation. Thanks to more recent acquisitions, they have expanded the acreage of the vineyards. The estate's style continues to evolve in a manner consistent with its past. Their approach in the cellar brings out the best of their terroir, which features of predominantly sandy and calcareous-marly soils. Their impressive selection this year simply reconfirm their place at the top of Italian wine production. Their 2015 Bolgheri Superiore Grattamacco offers extraordinary elegance, articulation and complexity. It boasts a splendid nose and a superlative palate, as sinuous and elegant as it is juicy and pulpy, perfectly integrated in every component and of endless length. Virtually the same things can be said of their 2015 L'Alberello, which runs neck and neck.

| | |
|---|---|
| ● Bolgheri Sup. Grattamacco '15 | ♟♟♟ 8 |
| ● Bolgheri Sup. L'Alberello '15 | ♟♟ 8 |
| ● Bolgheri Rosso '16 | ♟♟ 4 |
| ○ Bolgheri Bianco '17 | ♟ 5 |
| ● Bolgheri Sup. Grattamacco '14 | ♟♟♟ 8 |
| ● Bolgheri Sup. Grattamacco '13 | ♟♟♟ 8 |
| ● Bolgheri Sup. L'Alberello '11 | ♟♟♟ 6 |

## Guado al Melo

LOC. MURROTTO, 130A
57022 CASTAGNETO CARDUCCI [LI]
TEL. +39 0565763238
www.guadoalmelo.it

CELLAR SALES
PRE-BOOKED VISITS
ANNUAL PRODUCTION 120,000 bottles
HECTARES UNDER VINE 15.00
SUSTAINABLE WINERY

Despite being a relatively young winery, perseverance and experimentation have allowed Guado al Melo to emerge quickly. Michele Scienza is at the helm, overseeing a sizable estate. A number of different grape varieties from the Mediterranean and Caucus regions are cultivated, with the area's classics all represented, of course. The estate's principal vineyards are situated in a valley of the Bolgheri hills while the rest are further west. In all cases, these are surrounded by Mediterranean scrub and olive trees. Their wines are well-crafted, impeccable and precise. Their truly original 2016 Criseo results from a mix of white varieties harvested and fermented together. After fermentation, the blend of predominantly Vermentino, followed by Fiano, Incrocio Manzoni and Petit Mansang ages for a year in steel tanks and for another year in bottles. It offers very fruity aromas combining tropical and citrus hints with a broad supported palate.

| | |
|---|---|
| ○ Bolgheri Bianco Criseo '16 | ♟♟ 5 |
| ● Jassarte '15 | ♟♟ 5 |
| ● Bolgheri Rosso Rute '16 | ♟ 4 |
| ● Bolgheri Rosso Sup. Atis '15 | ♟ 6 |
| ● Bolgheri Rosso Sup. Atis '12 | ♟♟♟ 6 |
| ● Bolgheri Rosso Rute '13 | ♟♟ 5 |
| ● Bolgheri Rosso Sup. Atis '13 | ♟♟ 6 |

## Tenuta Guado al Tasso

LOC. BOLGHERI
S.DA BOLGHERESE KM 3,9
57020 CASTAGNETO CARDUCCI [LI]
TEL. +39 0565749735
www.guadoaltasso.it

CELLAR SALES
ANNUAL PRODUCTION 1,500,000 bottles
HECTARES UNDER VINE 300.00

Guado al Tasso is one of the Antinori family's properties. Antinori is one of the most important and oldest names in Italian wine-making. Their estate is sizable, almost 1000 hectares of vineyards, woods and Mediterranean scrub. The varieties cultivated are the area's classics, though there are exceptions as well. Red grapes include Merlot, Cabernet Sauvignon, Petit Verdot and Sangiovese, while Vermentino dominates among the whites. Their wines are modern, well-crafted and well-presented, in line with the group's style. We preferred their 2016 Bolgheri Rosso Il Bruciato to their 2015 Superiore Guado al Tasso, which delivers very intense fruit, warmth and quite rich toasted notes. The first is more balanced, tasty and not in the least banal. Their 2017 Vermentino proves pleasant and their Rosato, simple but well made.

| | |
|---|---|
| ● Bolgheri Rosso Il Bruciato '16 | ♟♟ 5 |
| ● Bolgheri Rosso Sup. Guado al Tasso '15 | ♟♟ 8 |
| ⊙ Bolgheri Rosato '17 | ♟ 3 |
| ○ Bolgheri Vermentino '17 | ♟ 3 |
| ● Bolgheri Sup. Guado al Tasso '01 | ♟♟♟ 8 |
| ⊙ Bolgheri Rosato Scalabrone '16 | ♟♟ 3 |
| ● Bolgheri Rosso Il Bruciato '15 | ♟♟ 5 |
| ● Bolgheri Rosso Il Bruciato '14 | ♟♟ 5 |
| ● Bolgheri Rosso Il Bruciato '13 | ♟♟ 5 |
| ● Bolgheri Rosso Il Bruciato '12 | ♟♟ 4 |
| ● Bolgheri Sup. Guado al Tasso '13 | ♟♟ 8 |
| ● Bolgheri Sup. Guado al Tasso '12 | ♟♟ 8 |
| ○ Bolgheri Vermentino '14 | ♟♟ 3 |
| ○ Bolgheri Vermentino '13 | ♟♟ 3 |

# Gualdo del Re

LOC. NOTRI, 77
57028 SUVERETO [LI]
TEL. +39 0565829888
www.gualdodelre.it

**CELLAR SALES**
**PRE-BOOKED VISITS**
**ACCOMMODATION AND RESTAURANT SERVICE**
**ANNUAL PRODUCTION** 100,000 bottles
**HECTARES UNDER VINE** 20.00
**VITICULTURE METHOD** Certified Organic

Gualdo del Re (the name derives from the German 'wald', which means 'delightful place') has been in the Rossi family for generations, though it took on a new sophistication and visibility in the 1990s when Nico, an industrial expert working at Magona, left his job and realized his dream: live and work on the land. Thanks in part to the support of his wife, Teresa, he's been a true pioneer, reviving the area's (and his winery's) prospects in the field of winemaking, and gradually growing their importance. Their lovely 2015 Guardo del Re offers a nose of coffee, cocoa and leather that infiltrates a background of fruit and herbs (grilled sweet peppers, aromatic herbs, bay leaves). Warm and pleasant on the palate, it proves flavorful, relaxed and well-balanced through its agreeable finish. Their 2015 Rennero delivers a fruity composite nose with cherry and currant enlivened by fresh vegetal notes. Perfectly ripe, juicy and lively on the palate, it possesses a long, enjoyable finish. Their 2015 Eliseo releases intense fruity aromas with its balanced body.

| | |
|---|---|
| ○ Eliseo Bianco '15 | ▼▼ 2* |
| ● Suvereto Merlot l'Rennero '15 | ▼▼ |
| ● Suvereto Sangiovese Gualdo del Re '15 | ▼▼ 5 |
| ● Cabraia '15 | ▼ 6 |
| ⊙ Shiny Rosato '17 | ▼ 3 |
| ○ Valentina Vermentino '17 | ▼ 3 |
| ● Val di Cornia Rosso l'Rennero '05 | ▼▼▼ 6 |
| ● Val di Cornia Rosso l'Rennero '01 | ▼▼▼ 7 |
| ● Cabraia '12 | ♀♀ 6 |
| ● Federico Primo '11 | ♀♀ 5 |

# Guicciardini Strozzi

LOC. CUSONA, 5
53037 SAN GIMIGNANO [SI]
TEL. +39 0577950028
www.guicciardinistrozzi.it

**CELLAR SALES**
**PRE-BOOKED VISITS**
**ANNUAL PRODUCTION** 800,000 bottles
**HECTARES UNDER VINE** 100.00

Tenuta di Cusona, an estate situated on the hills around San Gimignano, represents a family history that goes back more than a thousand years. In the early 20th century Francesco Guicciardini, a Minister of Agriculture and mayor of Florence, gave a boost to the winery in terms of production. In 1933 the first bottling took place in Vernaccia, and in the 1970s Girolamo Strozzi began a push for growth, eventually earning success on national and international markets. Their classically styled 2015 Vernaccia Riserva offers a nose of almond, traces of apple and light vegetal notes with a sturdy, enveloping and measured body of good weight. The well-calibrated and never overwhelming palate leads to an extended, enjoyable finish. Their straw-colored, pure Vermentino 2017 Arabesque gives off fresh, very citrusy aromas. Its savory, flavorful, and full palate resolves in a long finish. Their reds all prove very drinkable with tannins well-blended to alcohol.

| | |
|---|---|
| ○ Arabesque '17 | ▼▼ 2* |
| ● Millanni '12 | ▼▼ 6 |
| ○ Vernaccia di S. Gimignano Ris. '15 | ▼▼ 3 |
| ● Chianti Colli Senesi Titolato Strozzi '17 | ▼ 2 |
| ● Sodole '13 | ▼ 5 |
| ○ Vernaccia di S. Gimignano Titolato Strozzi '17 | ▼ 2 |
| ○ Vernaccia di S. Gimignano '16 | ♀♀ 2* |
| ○ Vernaccia di S. Gimignano Ris. '14 | ♀♀ 3 |
| ○ Vernaccia di S. Gimignano Ris. '13 | ♀♀ 3* |
| ○ Vernaccia di S. Gimignano Ris. '12 | ♀♀ 3 |
| ○ Vernaccia di S. Gimignano Titolato Strozzi '16 | ♀♀ 2* |

## ★★Isole e Olena

LOC. ISOLE, 1
50021 BARBERINO VAL D'ELSA [FI]
TEL. +39 0558072763
www.isoleolena.it

CELLAR SALES
PRE-BOOKED VISITS
ANNUAL PRODUCTION 250,000 bottles
HECTARES UNDER VINE 56.00

Paolo De Marchi's winery is an established benchmark in Chianti Classico. Some of the region's most intriguing wines have been produced (and continued to be produced) here, establishing the area's position as one of Italy's most well-suited terroir. Their excellence is grounded in the exceptional subzone of Barberino d'Elsa, but credit also goes to agricultural skill, which has managed to express the area's qualities. Their wines demonstrate balance and clarity, thanks to the proper ripeness of the grapes used and the careful use of oak. Their truly sophisticated 2015 Cepparello presents clear, limpid aromas, revealing a fruitiness refined by evident but well-controlled spicy notes of oak. On the palate it follows a wide, contrast-filled progression leading to a long and incisive finish. Their fragrant, delicious 2015 Chianti Classico also proves very good and their 2015 Collezione Private Syrah is well-made.

| | |
|---|---|
| ● Cepparello '15 | ▼▼▼ 8 |
| ● Chianti Cl. '15 | ▼▼ 5 |
| ● Collezione Privata Syrah '15 | ▼▼ 8 |
| ● Cabernet Sauvignon Collezione Privata '14 | ▼ 8 |
| ● Cepparello '13 | ♀♀♀ 8 |
| ● Cepparello '12 | ♀♀♀ 8 |
| ● Cepparello '09 | ♀♀♀ 8 |
| ● Cepparello '07 | ♀♀♀ 8 |
| ● Cepparello '06 | ♀♀♀ 8 |
| ● Cepparello '05 | ♀♀♀ 8 |
| ● Cepparello '03 | ♀♀♀ 7 |
| ● Cepparello '01 | ♀♀♀ 6 |
| ● Cepparello '00 | ♀♀♀ 6 |

## Istine

LOC. ISTINE
53017 RADDA IN CHIANTI [SI]
TEL. +39 0577733684
www.istine.it

CELLAR SALES
PRE-BOOKED VISITS
ANNUAL PRODUCTION 45,000 bottles
HECTARES UNDER VINE 26.00
VITICULTURE METHOD Certified Organic

Three distinct vineyards in terms of elevation, position and soil spread throughout the municipalities of Radda in Chianti (Casanuova and Istine) and Gaiole (Cavarchione), organic management and a traditional approach to winemaking. This is the winning recipe proposed by Angela Fronti. And so it is that we can talk about a winery that is stylistically focused, even if young, considering that their first bottles came in 2012. Istine is already capable of producing highly drinkable wines that exhibit finesse and flavor, as well as adherence to the territory. Their 2016 Chianti Classico Vigna Cavarchione expresses balance and finesse. Its aromas are close-focused and fragrant, while on the palate it proves steady and savory, with well-integrated oak. Their fruitier and more approachable 2015 Chianti Classico Le Vigne Riserva features suppleness and balance on the palate.

| | |
|---|---|
| ● Chianti Cl. V. Cavarchione '16 | ▼▼▼ 5 |
| ● Chianti Cl. Le Vigne Ris. '15 | ▼▼ 3* |
| ● Chianti Cl. '16 | ▼▼ 3 |
| ● Chianti Cl. V. Istine '16 | ▼▼ 3 |
| ● Chianti Cl. LeVigne Ris. '13 | ♀♀♀ 3* |
| ● Chianti Cl. V. Istine '15 | ♀♀♀ 3* |
| ● Chianti Cl. '15 | ♀♀ 3 |
| ● Chianti Cl. '14 | ♀♀ 3* |
| ● Chianti Cl. LeVigne Ris. '14 | ♀♀ 3 |
| ● Chianti Cl. V. Casanova '14 | ♀♀ 3 |
| ● Chianti Cl. V. Cavarchione '15 | ♀♀ 3* |
| ● Chianti Cl. V. Istine '14 | ♀♀ 3 |

# Lamole di Lamole

LOC. LAMOLE
50022 GREVE IN CHIANTI [FI]
TEL. +39 0559331256
www.lamole.com

**CELLAR SALES**
**PRE-BOOKED VISITS**
**RESTAURANT SERVICE**
**ANNUAL PRODUCTION** 294,000 bottles
**HECTARES UNDER VINE** 57.00
**SUSTAINABLE WINERY**

Lamole is an estate in the district of Gallo
Nero. It's an area that features terraced
vineyards at 650 meters above sea level,
late harvests, notable day-night
temperature swings, and almost extinct
agricultural techniques. The Santa
Margherita group arrived in 1993 and has
done its best to maintain the original
character of the estate. Indeed, in Lamole it
has found one of its gems, giving them a
top place in their selection and great
visibility, independent of the amount of
Chianti Classico it produces and markets
(along with Vistarenni). Despite notable
production volumes, for some time now
their Chianti Classico Etichetta Blu has
been at the top of their selection. The
2015 offers up nuances of red fruit and
wild flowers, which anticipate a dynamic,
enjoyable and highly savory palate. Their
2015 Chianti Classico Etichetta Bianca
also did well, though its less-defined,
somewhat veiled aromas are something
of a weakness.

| | |
|---|---|
| ● Chianti Cl. Lamole di Lamole Et. Blu '15 | ▼▼▼ 3* |
| ● Chianti Cl. Lamole di Lamole Et. Bianca '15 | ▼▼ 3 |
| ● Chianti Cl. Ris. '14 | ▼▼ 5 |
| ● Maremma Toscana Sangiovese Sassoregale '16 | ▼▼ 2* |
| ● Maremma Toscana Tenuta Sassoregale '15 | ▼▼ 2* |
| ● Chianti Cl. Gran Sel. Vign. di Campolungo '10 | ♀♀♀ 5 |
| ● Chianti Cl. Lamole di Lamole Et. Bianca '13 | ♀♀♀ 3* |
| ● Chianti Cl. Lamole di Lamole Et. Blu '14 | ♀♀♀ 3* |
| ● Chianti Cl. Lamole di Lamole Et. Blu '12 | ♀♀♀ 3* |
| ● Chianti Cl. Vign. di Campolungo Ris. '09 | ♀♀♀ 5 |
| ● Chianti Cl. Vign. di Campolungo Ris. '08 | ♀♀♀ 5 |

# Lanciola

FRAZ. POZZOLATICO
VIA IMPRUNETANA, 210
50023 IMPRUNETA [FI]
TEL. +39 055208324
www.lanciola.it

**CELLAR SALES**
**PRE-BOOKED VISITS**
**ANNUAL PRODUCTION** 250,000 bottles
**HECTARES UNDER VINE** 40.00

The winery is owned by the Guarnieri
family, who also work in tourism and show
their love for the land through viticulture
and olive growing, as well as 'agritourism'
services that allow guests to see and touch
their products with their own hands. Their
vineyards are situated in the Colli Fiorentini,
but also Greve in Chianti (where their
Chianti Classico is produced). They've also
demonstrated an ability to go beyond
tradition, successfully cultivating varieties
like Pinot Nerot as well. Their 2015 Chianti
Colli Fiorentini delivered, proving austere on
the nose with fruit-forward aromas of
cherry and plum giving way to juniper and
aromatic herbs. On the palate it's
enjoyable, enticing and fresh, with a
relaxed finish. Their 2015 Chianti Classico
Le Masse di Greve opens with etheric notes
of cherry in liquor, then cloves and hints of
forest undergrowth. In the mouth it's warm,
docile, with well-integrated tannins and a
persistent, relaxed finish.

| | |
|---|---|
| ● Chianti Cl. Le Masse di Greve '15 | ▼▼ 4 |
| ● Chianti Colli Fiorentini Lanciola '15 | ▼▼ 3 |
| ● Terricci '15 | ▼▼ 5 |
| ● Vin Santo del Chianti Cl. Occhio di Pernice '09 | ▼▼ 6 |
| ○ Vin Santo del Chianti Colli Fiorentini '09 | ▼▼ 6 |
| ● Chianti Cl. Le Masse di Greve Ris. '15 | ▼ 4 |
| ○ Ricciobianco Chardonnay '17 | ▼ 4 |
| ● Chianti Cl. Le Masse di Greve Gran Sel. '11 | ♀♀ 5 |
| ● Chianti Cl. Le Masse di Greve Ris. '12 | ♀♀ 4 |
| ● Riccionero '12 | ♀♀ 3 |
| ● Ricciotto '13 | ♀♀ 4 |
| ● Terricci '11 | ♀♀ 5 |

# La Lastra

FRAZ. SANTA LUCIA
VIA R. DE GRADA, 9
53037 SAN GIMIGNANO [SI]
TEL. +39 0577941781
www.lalastra.it

CELLAR SALES
PRE-BOOKED VISITS
ANNUAL PRODUCTION 58,000 bottles
HECTARES UNDER VINE 7.00
SUSTAINABLE WINERY

Nadia Betti and her husband, Renato Spanu, began their adventure almost 40 years ago. Today they are helped by the personal and professional support of her brother Christian and friends Enrico Paternoster and Valerio Zorzi. Today Lastra comprises 23 hectares, 7 of which are vineyards and 7 more olive groves situated just outside of Siena. Their red grapes are fermented in an old cellar in Marciano, where a farm holiday can also be found, while their Vernaccia is made in San Gimignano. Their 2016 Vernaccia di San Gimignano Riserva is a high quality wine. Straw-yellow in color, it opens with delicate, enticing aromas of white peach and flowers supported by vanilla and black pepper. A sumptuous finish caps off a splendid palate, calibrated in its structure, without excessive acidity. Their 2017 Vernaccia is also interesting, with its herbaceous tones of aromatic herbs (sage and mint), fruit (apple), its firm body, delicately salty and refreshing. Their two reds also proved enjoyable.

| | | |
|---|---|---|
| ○ Vernaccia di S. Gimignano Ris. '16 | ♟♟ ● |
| ○ Vernaccia di S. Gimignano Ris. '17 | ♟♟ 2* |
| ● Canaiolo '16 | ♟ 3 |
| ● Chianti Colli Senesi '16 | ♟ 2 |
| ○ Vernaccia di S. Gimignano Ris. '09 | ♟♟♟ 3* |
| ● Chianti Colli Senesi '15 | ♟♟ 2* |
| ○ Vernaccia di S. Gimignano '11 | ♟♟ 2* |
| ○ Vernaccia di S. Gimignano Ris. '15 | ♟♟ 3* |
| ○ Vernaccia di S. Gimignano Ris. '14 | ♟♟ 3* |
| ○ Vernaccia di S. Gimignano Ris. '12 | ♟♟ 3* |
| ○ Vernaccia di S. Gimignano Ris. '11 | ♟♟ 3* |
| ○ Vernaccia di S. Gimignano Ris. '10 | ♟♟ 3* |

# Fattoria Lavacchio

LOC. LAVACCHIO
VIA DI MONTEFIESOLE, 55
50065 PONTASSIEVE [FI]
TEL. +39 0558317472
www.fattorialavacchio.com

CELLAR SALES
PRE-BOOKED VISITS
ACCOMMODATION AND RESTAURANT SERVICE
ANNUAL PRODUCTION 120,000 bottles
HECTARES UNDER VINE 25.00
VITICULTURE METHOD Certified Organic
SUSTAINABLE WINERY

The historic estate of Lavacchio, situated on Montefiesole hill, was purchased by the Lottero family in 1978. Among Chianti Rufina's producers, Lavacchio was the first to subscribe to an organic management regime. All their grapes, olives, wheat and vegetables are cultivated with the utmost respect for nature. No added sulfites, yeasts or tannins are used in their winemaking. Sulphur dioxide as an antioxidant and antibacterial agent is substituted with physical means, not chemical. Their 2015 Chianti Rufina Riserva Cedro offers up decisive, enticing aromas of blackberry and blackcurrant, then tertiary notes emerge, tobacco and tanned leather, capped off by etheric hints. The palate is warm, potent. Tannins are present but well-integrated, and the finish comes through chocolatey. Their 2016 Chianti Rufina Cedro features a clean, elegant nose, redolent of Mediterranean scrubland and forest undergrowth. The palate is balanced, docile, with tannic presence and a savory, relaxed finish. Their 2011 Ludiè features riper notes, while the palate is relaxed and soft.

| | | |
|---|---|---|
| ● Chianti Rufina Cedro '16 | ♟♟ 2* |
| ● Chianti Rufina Cedro Ris. '15 | ♟♟ 3 |
| ● Chianti Rufina Ludiè Bio '11 | ♟♟ 7 |
| ○ Vin Santo del Chianti Rufina '11 | ♟♟ 4 |
| ● Chianti Puro Ris. '15 | ♟ 4 |
| ● Chianti Rufina Cedro '15 | ♟♟ 2* |
| ● Chianti Rufina Cedro '14 | ♟♟ 2* |
| ● Chianti Rufina Cedro '12 | ♟♟ 2* |
| ● Chianti Rufina Cedro Ris. '13 | ♟♟ 3 |
| ● Chianti Rufina Cedro Ris. '10 | ♟♟ 4 |
| ● Chianti Rufina Ludié Ris. '10 | ♟♟ 5 |
| ● Fontegalli '11 | ♟♟ 4 |

# Tenuta Le Farnete/Cantagallo

FRAZ. COMEANA
VIA MACIA
59100 CARMIGNANO [PO]
TEL. +39 0571910078
www.tenutacantagallo.it

CELLAR SALES
PRE-BOOKED VISITS
ACCOMMODATION AND RESTAURANT SERVICE
ANNUAL PRODUCTION 65,000 bottles
HECTARES UNDER VINE 40.00
SUSTAINABLE WINERY

The Pierazzuoli family's farming property
is divided into two distinct portions. The
first, in terms of age and size, is Tenuta
Cantagallo, purchased in 1970. Here
primarily Sangiovese is cultivated along
with Merlot, Syrah, Trebbiano, Malvasia
and Colorino. Since 1990, the family
have owned Farnete, an estate situated
in the heart of Camignano wine-country
that hosts Sangiovese and Cabernet
Sauvignon, as well as one hectare of
Aleatico. Their Carmignano Riserva brought
home Tre Bicchieri during our tastings, this
time with the 2015. On the nose it stands
out for its balsamic, minty notes, then
cherry and blackberry accompanied by
herbaceous hints. The mouth opens
weighty, creamy and soft, endowed with
pulp and freshness. It finishes long and
generous. Their 2015 Gioveto, a blend of
Sangiovese, Merlot and Cabernet, offers up
mixed aromas with spices prevailing, then
lively notes of wild berries. The body is
weighty, firm and potent, and exhibits
excellent persistence.

| | |
|---|---|
| ● Carmignano Ris. '15 | ▼▼▼ 4* |
| ● Gioveto Tenuta Cantagallo '15 | ▼▼ 4 |
| ● Carmignano '16 | ▼▼ 3 |
| ● Chianti Montalbano Tenuta Cantagallo '17 | ▼▼ 2* |
| ● Chianti Montalbano Tenuta Cantagallo Il Fondatore Ris. '15 | ▼▼ 2* |
| ● Chianti Montalbano Tenuta Cantagallo Ris. '15 | ▼▼ 3 |
| ● Barco Reale Le Farnese '17 | ▼ 2 |
| ● Carmignano Ris. '14 | ♈♈♈ 4* |
| ● Chianti Montalbano Tenuta Cantagallo '16 | ♈♈ 2* |
| ● Chianti Montalbano Tenuta Cantagallo Ris. '14 | ♈♈ 3* |
| ● Gioveto '14 | ♈♈ 4 |

# Tenuta Lenzini

FRAZ. GRAGNANO
VIA DELLA CHIESA, 44
55012 CAPANNORI [LU]
TEL. +39 0583974037
www.tenutalenzini.it

CELLAR SALES
PRE-BOOKED VISITS
ACCOMMODATION
ANNUAL PRODUCTION 60,000 bottles
HECTARES UNDER VINE 14.00
VITICULTURE METHOD Certified Organic

Tenuta Lenzini is situated in Gragnano, an
area well-known for its extra-virgin olive oil
and wines. In addition to being a natural
wonder, the estate is also one of Colline
Lucche's mainstays. Merlot, Cabernet
Sauvignon, Syrah and Alicante Bouchet are
all cultivated in their vineyards, which
constitute only a part of the overall
property. An organic approach has given
way to biodynamic principles. In the cellar
they avail themselves of spontaneous
fermentation, minimum use of sulfites, and
maturation that's respectful of fruit (thanks
to steel, concrete and old wood vats). Their
2015 La Syrah was a pleasant surprise,
defying stereotypes with its relaxed, natural
character, both on the nose and in the
mouth. Black cherry, Mediterranean herbs
and pepper accompany a flavorful palate
that's not particularly dynamic but certainly
charming. Their 2017 Vermignon
possesses intriguing notes of ripe yellow
fruit (peach in particular), and a mid-sized
but highly drinkable palate. Their Colline
Lucchesi Casa and Chiesa also did well.

| | |
|---|---|
| ● La Syrah '15 | ▼▼ 5 |
| ○ Vermignon '17 | ▼▼ 3 |
| ● Colline Lucchesi Merlot Casa e Chiesa '16 | ▼ 3 |
| ● La Syrah '13 | ♈♈ 5 |
| ● Poggio de' Paoli '13 | ♈♈ 4 |
| ○ Vermignon '15 | ♈♈ 3 |

## Cantine Leonardo da Vinci

Loc. Vinci
via Provinciale Mercatale, 291
50059 Vinci [FI]
Tel. +39 0571902444
www.cantineleonardo.it

**CELLAR SALES**
**PRE-BOOKED VISITS**
**ACCOMMODATION AND RESTAURANT SERVICE**
**ANNUAL PRODUCTION** 4,500,000 bottles
**HECTARES UNDER VINE** 750.00

It's a story that's concentrated into fewer than 60 years. It started when 30 small wine producers (who owned 60 hectares of land between them) founded a cooperative. From there a growth in quality and quantity included the building of a single cellar. In 1988 they purchased the old Fattoria Montalbano and in 1990 Cantina di Montalcino, which has allowed them to further increase production. As of 2012 the winery is part of the Caviro group, Italy's leading wine producer. Their Sant'Ippolito, a blend of Merlot and Syrah, with a small amount of Sangiovese, features enticing aromas of spices with clear nuances of pepper, cloves and cinnamon supported by cherry and blackcurrant. On the palate it proves soft, with well-integrated tannins and a finish that's as steady as it is long. Their 2013 Brunello di Montalcino opens with austere tones, aromas of tobacco, licorice and blackberry preserves. On the palate it proves linear and lively, subtle but persistent.

| | |
|---|---|
| ● Brunello di Montalcino Cantina di Montalcino '13 | 🍷🍷 5 |
| ● Leonardo '16 | 🍷🍷 2* |
| ● Sant'Ippolito '16 | 🍷🍷 5 |
| ○ Streda '17 | 🍷🍷 3 |
| ● Chianti dalle Vigne Ris. '15 | 🍷 2 |
| ● Chianti Leonardo '17 | 🍷 2 |
| ● Linarius Villa Vinci '16 | 🍷 8 |
| ○ Bianco dell'Empolese Vin Santo Da Vinci '10 | 🍷🍷 5 |
| ● Brunello di Montalcino Cantina di Montalcino '12 | 🍷🍷 5 |
| ● Chianti Da Vinci Ris. '14 | 🍷🍷 3 |
| ● Chianti Da Vinci Ris. '13 | 🍷🍷 3* |

## Leuta

via Pietraia, 21
52044 Cortona [AR]
Tel. +39 3385033560
www.leuta.it

**CELLAR SALES**
**PRE-BOOKED VISITS**
**ANNUAL PRODUCTION** 25,000 bottles
**HECTARES UNDER VINE** 12.60

Enzo Berlanda and Denis Zeni founded their winery In Tuscany in 2000. They'd decided to change lifestyles, leave their jobs in finance and go back to their origins, the work done by their parents, the land. Their first choice was Trentino, the region they're from, but the few hectares left by their parents weren't enough to make a living, and so they went elsewhere. Today Denis is leading the winery with a modern and dynamic vision of viticulture. Their 2015 2,618 earned a place in our finals (the name refers to the plot of Cabernet Franc in which it's cultivated). A complex bouquet features mineral hints accompanied by earth, then notes of bay leaf, tarragon and ginger, all supported by fruit. On the palate it's warm and firm, elegant, with a sparkling finish. Their 2015 0,618, a Syrah, also proved excellent, with hints of blackcurrant and cherry dominating, then tanned leather and fur. On the palate it opens chewy, with well-distributed pulp and balanced tannins giving way to a long, crisp finish.

| | |
|---|---|
| ● Cortona Cabernet Franc 2,618 '15 | 🍷🍷 6 |
| ● Cortona Merlot 1.618 '14 | 🍷🍷 5 |
| ● Cortona Sangiovese Solitario di Leuta '14 | 🍷🍷 6 |
| ● Cortona Syrah 0,618 '15 | 🍷🍷 5 |
| ○ Cortona Vin Santo '06 | 🍷🍷 8 |
| ● Nautilus '15 | 🍷🍷 8 |
| ● Tau '13 | 🍷 4 |
| ● Cortona Cabernet Franc 2,618 '13 | 🍷🍷 5 |
| ● Cortona Merlot 1,618 '13 | 🍷🍷 5 |
| ● Cortona Sangiovese Solitario '13 | 🍷🍷 6 |
| ● Cortona Sangiovese Solitario '12 | 🍷🍷 6 |
| ○ Cortona Vin Santo '05 | 🍷🍷 8 |
| ● Tau '12 | 🍷🍷 4 |

# Tenuta di Lilliano

loc. Lilliano, 8
53011 Castellina in Chianti [SI]
Tel. +39 0577743070
www.lilliano.com

**CELLAR SALES**
**PRE-BOOKED VISITS**
**ACCOMMODATION**
**ANNUAL PRODUCTION** 150,000 bottles
**HECTARES UNDER VINE** 36.00
**VITICULTURE METHOD** Certified Organic

Lilliano has been bottling and selling wine since 1958, thanks in part to the commitment of princess Eleonora Ruspoli Berlingieri, whose family purchased the estate in 1920. Today Giulio and Pietro Ruspoli own the estate, and their wines have changed notably, with a somewhat more modern approach that includes the use of barriques accompanied by large wood barrels. And so their wines are contemporary but endowed with class and personality, shining a light on the Castellina in Chianti subzone and raising the bar for the area's wines. Their 2015 Chianti Classico Riserva features aromas of lush fruit and spices, then a soft and sweet palate that's well-contrasted by vigorous acidity. The result is delectable and savory. Their 2016 Chianti Classico is along the same lines, though less complex. Oak is detectable in their 2015 Chianti Classico Gran Selezione, a wine with a richer, more concentrated style.

| | |
|---|---|
| ● Chianti Cl. Ris. '15 | ♟♟♟ 5 |
| ● Chianti Cl. Gran Selezione '15 | ♟♟ 5 |
| ● Chianti Cl. '16 | ♟♟ 3 |
| ● Anagallis '14 | ♟ 5 |
| ● Chianti Cl. '10 | ♟♟♟ 3* |
| ● Chianti Cl. '09 | ♟♟♟ 3 |
| ● Chianti Cl. E. Ruspoli Berlingieri Ris. '85 | ♟♟♟ 8 |
| ● Chianti Cl. Gran Sel. '14 | ♟♟♟ 6 |
| ● Chianti Cl. Gran Sel. '11 | ♟♟♟ 5 |
| ● Chianti Cl. Gran Sel. Ris. '10 | ♟♟♟ 6 |
| ● Chianti Cl. Ris. '13 | ♟♟♟ 5 |

# Lisini

fraz. Sant'Angelo in Colle
pod. Casanova
53024 Montalcino [SI]
Tel. +39 0577844040
www.lisini.com

**CELLAR SALES**
**PRE-BOOKED VISITS**
**ANNUAL PRODUCTION** 90,000 bottles
**HECTARES UNDER VINE** 21.00

Lisini is often mentioned when talking about classic, long-lived Brunellos that can express the Mediterranean atmosphere of southern Montalcino. Most of their vineyards are situated near the cellar, in the productive zone that spans Sesta and Sant'Angelo in Colle, an area characterized by cool terrain that's rich in minerals. The site that gives rise to their cru Ugolaia features red and tufaceous soil, making it quite different. Carlo, Lorenzo and Ludovica are at the helm, carrying on the work begun by the legendary Signora Ellina. The stylistic personality of their Brunello di Lisini is well-expressed by their most recent releases, foremost their 2013. Mulberry blossoms, mint and a hint of rust reveal a slender silhouette and a pleasantly almondy finish. But once again their Ugolaia proves to be a cut above the rest. A hot 2012 season conferred aromas of cherries in liquor while shaping the wine's firm, chewy palate.

| | |
|---|---|
| ● Brunello di Montalcino Ugolaia '12 | ♟♟ 8 |
| ● Brunello di Montalcino '13 | ♟♟ 6 |
| ● Brunello di Montalcino Ris. '12 | ♟♟ 7 |
| ● Rosso di Montalcino '16 | ♟ 4 |
| ● Brunello di Montalcino '90 | ♟♟♟ 5 |
| ● Brunello di Montalcino '88 | ♟♟♟ 5 |
| ● Brunello di Montalcino Ugolaia '06 | ♟♟♟ 8 |
| ● Brunello di Montalcino Ugolaia '04 | ♟♟♟ 8 |
| ● Brunello di Montalcino Ugolaia '01 | ♟♟♟ 8 |
| ● Brunello di Montalcino Ugolaia '00 | ♟♟♟ 7 |
| ● Brunello di Montalcino Ugolaia '91 | ♟♟♟ 7 |
| ● Brunello di Montalcino '12 | ♟♟ 6 |
| ● Brunello di Montalcino Ris. '10 | ♟♟ 7 |
| ● Brunello di Montalcino Ugolaia '11 | ♟♟ 8 |
| ● Brunello di Montalcino Ugolaia '10 | ♟♟ 8 |

## Lunadoro

FRAZ. VALIANO
VIA TERRA ROSSA
53045 MONTEPULCIANO [SI]
TEL. +39 348 2215188
www.nobilelunadoro.it

CELLAR SALES
PRE-BOOKED VISITS
ACCOMMODATION
ANNUAL PRODUCTION 60,000 bottles
HECTARES UNDER VINE 12.00
VITICULTURE METHOD Certified Organic
SUSTAINABLE WINERY

The subzone of Valiano is one of Nobile di Montepulciano's most important, featuring clay, stony terrain. Some of the vineyards are older than 40 years, guaranteeing complex flavors. Their approach to winemaking is careful but minimally invasive, with aging in large wood barrels and mid-size casks. This is a snapshot of Lunadoro, owned by the Schenk Italia group who have judiciously let the winery proceed as before. In short, it's a small-medium sized producer that's committed to quality and to the territory that makes their wines possible. Their 2015 Nobile di Montepulciano Pagliareto features a juicy, well-contrasted palate as well as a lovely aromatic weave of flowery hints and fruity notes adorned by spices and balsamic fragrances. Their 2014 Nobile di Montepulciano Quercione is a highly elegant wine, especially when it comes to its flowery, citrusy aromas. On the palate it has freshness and a delicate structure.

| | | |
|---|---|---|
| ● Nobile di Montepulciano Pagliareto '15 | ▼▼▼ | 3* |
| ● Nobile di Montepulciano Quercione Ris. '14 | ▼▼ | 4 |
| ● Rosso di Montepulciano Prugnanello '16 | ▼▼ | 3 |
| ● Nobile di Montepulciano Pagliareto '14 | ♀♀ | 3* |
| ● Nobile di Montepulciano Pagliareto '12 | ♀♀ | 4 |
| ● Nobile di Montepulciano Quercione '11 | ♀♀ | 4 |
| ● Nobile di Montepulciano Quercione Ris. '12 | ♀♀ | 4 |
| ● Rosso di Montepulciano Prugnanello '15 | ♀♀ | 2* |
| ● Rosso di Montepulciano Prugnanello '14 | ♀♀ | 2* |

## I Luoghi

LOC. CAMPO AL CAPRIOLO, 201
57022 CASTAGNETO CARDUCCI [LI]
TEL. +39 0565777379
www.iluoghi.it

CELLAR SALES
ANNUAL PRODUCTION 15,000 bottles
HECTARES UNDER VINE 3.80
VITICULTURE METHOD Certified Organic

A producer that's as artisanal as it is original, I Luoghi represents a splash of color in Bolgheri. It's a style that Stefano Granata deeply desired and shaped, along with his wife, starting in 2000. It all starts with their vineyards, which are the cornerstone of the winery's philosophy. These are divided into two plots and attended to with painstaking care, respectful of the ecosystem (pesticides and chemicals are prohibited, the use of fertilizer is kept to a minimum). Their selection refuses comprises, and bristles with personal wines that may not always be 'domesticated' but are fascinating interpretations nonetheless. The right bottle of their 2015 Bolgheri Superiore Campo al Fico makes up for the occasional issue when it comes to consistence. It's an elegant wine that doesn't opt for clear parameters, but rather aims to amaze, bewitching with its aromas of humus, wild berries and Mediterranean scrubland, accompanied by mineral and slightly foxy notes. On the palate it's extremely delicate, long and flavorful, a truly lovely wine.

| | | |
|---|---|---|
| ● Bolgheri Sup. Campo al Fico '15 | ▼▼ | 7 |
| ● Bolgheri Sup. Podere Ritorti '15 | ▼▼ | 5 |
| ● Bolgheri Sup. Campo al Fico '10 | ♀♀♀ | 7 |
| ● Bolgheri Sup. Campo al Fico '09 | ♀♀♀ | 7 |
| ● Bolgheri Sup. Campo al Fico '08 | ♀♀♀ | 7 |
| ● Bolgheri Sup. Podere Ritorti '13 | ♀♀♀ | 5 |
| ● Bolgheri Sup. Podere Ritorti '14 | ♀♀ | 5 |
| ● Bolgheri Sup. Podere Ritorti '12 | ♀♀ | 5 |

## ★★Le Macchiole

LOC. BOLGHERI
VIA BOLGHERESE, 189A
57022 CASTAGNETO CARDUCCI [LI]
TEL. +39 0565766092
www.lemacchiole.it

**PRE-BOOKED VISITS**
**ANNUAL PRODUCTION** 165,000 bottles
**HECTARES UNDER VINE** 27.00

Le Macchiole was founded by Eugenio Compolmi and Cinzia Merli in Bolgheri, in 1983, a period in which the area certainly wasn't what it is today. The winery has been an absolute leader in building this territory's well-deserved reputation. Today it's a major international brand that has, over time, also preserved its family dimension. The decision to adopt organic management, as well as their elegant stylistic evolution, have made them a current, dynamic producer. In short, they are an fundamental benchmark. Their 2015 Paleo is a wonder, incarnating the ideas of their new project and the character of the year. On the nose there's still just a dash of oak in the foreground, but its fruit is extraordinary and it will all come together soon. Balsamic notes emerge both on the nose and on its juicy, linear palate, whose texture proves perfectly extracted. Their 2015 Scrio is a lovely wine, as is their delicious 2016 Bolgheri Rosso.

## Podere Il Macchione

FRAZ. GRACCIANO
VIA PROVINCIALE, 18
53045 MONTEPULCIANO [SI]
TEL. +39 0578 758595
www.podereilmacchione.it

**CELLAR SALES**
**PRE-BOOKED VISITS**
**ANNUAL PRODUCTION** 20,000 bottles
**HECTARES UNDER VINE** 6.00

Trento's Leonardo and Simone Abram have owned this winery in Montepulciano since 2005. They were already active in the sector, with notable results, and now they're offering wines that are distinctive for their verve and uncommon style, as well as their relationship to the appellation's productive roots. Undoubtedly the winery has potential in terms of quality, but it's still suffering from a lack of consistence. This is also a consequence, however, of their wine's tendency to offer up their best only after a lengthy stay in the bottle. Their 2013 Nobile di Montepulciano Riserva is an austere wine with flowery aromas and less pronounced notes of wild herbs and chocolate. In the mouth its structure tends towards force, with pronounced, close-woven tannins, making for a decisive palate that's not lacking in character, and a long, fragrant finish. For obvious reasons (associated with the year), their 2014 Nobile is a subtler wine with fresh, nuanced aromas.

| | |
|---|---|
| ● Paleo Rosso '15 | ♟♟♟ 8 |
| ● Scrio '15 | ♟♟ 8 |
| ● Bolgheri Rosso '16 | ♟♟ 4 |
| ● Messorio '15 | ♟♟ 8 |
| ● Bolgheri Sup. Paleo '14 | ♟♟♟ 8 |
| ● Messorio '07 | ♟♟♟ 8 |
| ● Messorio '06 | ♟♟♟ 8 |
| ● Paleo Rosso '13 | ♟♟♟ 8 |
| ● Paleo Rosso '12 | ♟♟♟ 8 |
| ● Paleo Rosso '11 | ♟♟♟ 8 |
| ● Scrio '08 | ♟♟♟ 8 |
| ● Bolgheri Rosso '15 | ♟♟ 4 |
| ● Messorio '12 | ♟♟ 8 |
| ● Scrio '11 | ♟♟ 8 |

| | |
|---|---|
| ● Nobile di Montepulciano Ris. '13 | ♟♟ 5 |
| ● Nobile di Montepulciano '14 | ♟♟ 5 |
| ● Rosso di Montepulciano '16 | ♟ 4 |
| ● Nobile di Montepulciano '13 | ♟♟ 5 |
| ● Rosso di Montepulciano '15 | ♟♟ 4 |

## Le Macioche

s.da prov.le 55 di Sant'Antimo km 4,850
53024 Montalcino [SI]
Tel. +39 0577849168
www.lemacioche.it

**CELLAR SALES**
**PRE-BOOKED VISITS**
**ACCOMMODATION**
**ANNUAL PRODUCTION** 18,000 bottles
**HECTARES UNDER VINE** 3.00

There's been yet another change in ownership for the winery founded by Matilde Zecca and Achille Mazzocchi in 1985. The name comes from a local word for the root of the strawberry tree (a Mediterranean shrub that thrives in the woods around the estate). The Cotarella family's decision to purchase Macioche has signaled yet a new phase in the winery's evolution, though the vineyards remain the same: four plots situated at 450 meters above sea level in Sant'Antimo, in the south of Montalcino, where the terrain is rich in stony material and marl. It's a Mediterranean environment but until now their Brunellos are 'minimalist', going all in on fruit and lightness. Our most recent tastings demonstrate stylistic continuity. Their 2013 Brunello is a good example, with its clear, almost tart fruit, flowery and balsamic nuances, and a delicacy that guides the palate as well. In the mouth it proves more supported by a pronounced, linear vigor than extractive volume. Their 2012 Brunello Riserva is more mature and austere, with touches of confit and a clenched palate.

| | |
|---|---|
| ● Brunello di Montalcino '13 | ♛♛♛ 7 |
| ● Brunello di Montalcino Ris. '12 | ♛♛ 8 |
| ● Brunello di Montalcino Ris. '11 | ♛♛♛ 8 |
| ● Brunello di Montalcino '11 | ♛♛ 7 |
| ● Brunello di Montalcino '10 | ♛♛ 7 |
| ● Brunello di Montalcino '09 | ♛♛ 7 |
| ● Brunello di Montalcino '08 | ♛♛ 7 |
| ● Brunello di Montalcino '07 | ♛♛ 7 |
| ● Brunello di Montalcino '06 | ♛♛ 6 |
| ● Brunello di Montalcino '04 | ♛♛ 6 |
| ● Brunello di Montalcino Ris. '06 | ♛♛ 8 |
| ● Rosso di Montalcino '13 | ♛♛ 4 |
| ● Rosso di Montalcino '11 | ♛♛ 4 |
| ● Rosso di Montalcino '10 | ♛♛ 4 |
| ● Rosso di Montalcino '09 | ♛♛ 4 |

## Il Marroneto

loc. Madonna delle Grazie, 307
53024 Montalcino [SI]
Tel. +39 0577849382
www.ilmarroneto.it

**CELLAR SALES**
**PRE-BOOKED VISITS**
**ANNUAL PRODUCTION** 30,000 bottles
**HECTARES UNDER VINE** 6.00
**SUSTAINABLE WINERY**

The Mori family's 'den' can be found on Madonna delle Grazie, just outside the walls of Montalcino facing north. It's situated in what was until the 1970s a drying space for chestnuts. Giuseppe converted it, setting in motion a journey in wine production that has been, in many ways, unique, and that continues today with his son Alessandro. Recent years have seen particular success, with their Brunello de Il Marroneto regularly at the top of its class. Their fearless, crepuscular character are finally appreciated, especially by those who can approach the wine with care and patience. And their two 2013 Brunellos are perfect examples. The vintage version is anything but a 'base level' wine, exhibiting commendable layers of raspberry, peach, pine resin and spices, unfolding on a naturally succulent palate. Their Madonna delle Grazie opts for greater weight and density. Time should smooth out the wrinkles.

| | |
|---|---|
| ● Brunello di Montalcino '13 | ♛♛ 7 |
| ● Brunello di Montalcino Madonna delle Grazie '13 | ♛♛ 8 |
| ● Brunello di Montalcino Madonna delle Grazie '11 | ♛♛♛ 8 |
| ● Brunello di Montalcino Madonna delle Grazie '10 | ♛♛♛ 8 |
| ● Brunello di Montalcino Madonna delle Grazie '08 | ♛♛♛ 8 |
| ● Brunello di Montalcino '12 | ♛♛ 7 |
| ● Brunello di Montalcino '11 | ♛♛ 7 |
| ● Brunello di Montalcino '10 | ♛♛ 7 |
| ● Brunello di Montalcino Madonna delle Grazie '12 | ♛♛ 8 |
| ● Rosso di Montalcino Ignaccio '15 | ♛♛ 5 |

# Cosimo Maria Masini

VIA POGGIO A PINO, 16
56028 SAN MINIATO [PI]
TEL. +39 0571465032
www.cosimomariamasini.it

**CELLAR SALES**
**PRE-BOOKED VISITS**
**ANNUAL PRODUCTION** 50,000 bottles
**HECTARES UNDER VINE** 14.00
**VITICULTURE METHOD** Certified Biodynamic
**SUSTAINABLE WINERY**

At the heart of San Minato's Cosimo Maria Masini (an estate owned by the Masini family since 2000) lies an old residence purchased by the marquis Cosimo Ridolfi in the mid-1800s. He was also the one to begin applying innovative cultivation techniques and to build the cellar that's still used today. Tuscany's classic grapes are grown according to biodynamic principles, as well as lesser-known varieties like Buonamico, San Colombano and Sanforte. Their most recent vineyards also host international cultivar. Their 2017 Daphné put in a nice performance. It's a blend of mostly Trebbiano with close-focused aromas of apple and aromatic herbs. It's a full-bodied, fresh wine with well-calibrated savoriness and a flavorful finish. Their 2017 Nicole is a monovarietal Sangiovese with a clean bouquet redolent of cherry and wild berries. On the palate it's lean, well-defined, with crisp tannins and a clear, precise finish. Their 2017 Sincere opts for fresh, balsamic aromas, while on the palate it proves supple and dynamic.

| | | |
|---|---|---|
| ○ Daphné '17 | ♥♥ 4 | |
| ● Nicole '17 | ♥♥ 3 | |
| ● Sincero '17 | ♥♥ 2* | |
| ○ Annick '17 | ♥ 2 | |
| ○ Matilde '17 | ♥ 2 | |
| ○ Annick '16 | ♀♀ 2* | |
| ● Cosimo '15 | ♀♀ 5 | |
| ○ Daphné '16 | ♀♀ 4 | |
| ○ Daphné '15 | ♀♀ 4 | |
| ● Nicole '15 | ♀♀ 3 | |
| ● Nicole '12 | ♀♀ 3 | |
| ● San Forte Rosso '16 | ♀♀ 2* | |
| ○ Vin Santo del Chianti Fedardo '09 | ♀♀ 4 | |
| ○ Vin Santo del Chianti Fedardo '08 | ♀♀ 4 | |

# ★Mastrojanni

FRAZ. CASTELNUOVO DELL'ABATE
POD. LORETO E SAN PIO
53024 MONTALCINO [SI]
TEL. +39 0577835681
www.mastrojanni.com

**CELLAR SALES**
**PRE-BOOKED VISITS**
**ACCOMMODATION**
**ANNUAL PRODUCTION** 110,000 bottles
**HECTARES UNDER VINE** 33.00

Since 2008 the Illy family has managed the not easy job of reinforcing the authority and fame of the brand launched by Gabriele Mastrojanni in the 1970s. It's all thanks to Andrea Machetti and the stylistic continuity expressed by the Sangiovese cultivated in Castelnuovo dell'Abate, a major vine growing junction in southeast Montalcino. They've had particular success with the cru of Vigna Loreto (tufaceous terrain, large wood barrels) and Vigna Schiena d'Asino (sandy soil, 1600 liter oak), making for intense Brunellos that are best enjoyed after lengthy aging but also ready from the outset. An apparently classic year, 2013, served as the ideal foundation for Mastrojanni's unmistakable style. Their 'base level' Barolo and Vigneto Loreto make up a truly sensational couple. The former proves vivid and racy, with a palate crossed by a supporting, smoky vein. The latter offers up aromas of fresh red fruit, medicinal herbs and humus, while the palate proves vigorous yet relaxed in its essential tannic weave.

| | | |
|---|---|---|
| ● Brunello di Montalcino V. Loreto '13 | ♥♥♥ 7 | |
| ● Brunello di Montalcino '13 | ♥♥ 5 | |
| ● Rosso di Montalcino '16 | ♥ 4 | |
| ● Brunello di Montalcino '97 | ♀♀♀ 7 | |
| ● Brunello di Montalcino Ris. '88 | ♀♀♀ 6 | |
| ● Brunello di Montalcino Schiena d'Asino '08 | ♀♀♀ 8 | |
| ● Brunello di Montalcino Schiena d'Asino '93 | ♀♀♀ 7 | |
| ● Brunello di Montalcino Schiena d'Asino '90 | ♀♀♀ 7 | |
| ● Brunello di Montalcino V. Loreto '10 | ♀♀♀ 7 | |
| ● Brunello di Montalcino V. Loreto '09 | ♀♀♀ 7 | |
| ● Brunello di Montalcino V. Schiena d'Asino '12 | ♀♀♀ 8 | |
| ● Brunello di Montalcino V. Schiena d'Asino '10 | ♀♀♀ 8 | |

# Máté

LOC. SANTA RESTITUTA
53024 MONTALCINO [SI]
TEL. +39 0577847215
www.matewine.com

CELLAR SALES
PRE-BOOKED VISITS
ACCOMMODATION
ANNUAL PRODUCTION 25,000 bottles
HECTARES UNDER VINE 6.50
VITICULTURE METHOD Certified Organic

The decision had been in the air for a while for the Canadian couple of Ferenc and Candace Máté. He a writer and she a painter decided to leave New York in the early 90s so as to move to the estate they bought in Santa Restituta, a bona fide cru in the southeast of Montalcino. Merlot, Cabernet Sauvignon and Syrah are cultivated, along with Sangiovese. Wines are matured in barriques, mid-size casks or 4000 liter Allier oak, making for pulpy, multifaceted Brunellos that have impressed in recent vintages for their balance and precision. From this point of view there couldn't be a better calling card than their 2012 Riserva. It's a classic wine with its aromas of red fruit, pipe tobacco and ginger. It's crossed by a delicate yet gratifying spiciness that's supported by a clear, flavorful mid-palate, with tannins just emerging. Their 2013 Brunello is just as aromatically fresh and supple on the palate.

| | | |
|---|---|---|
| ● Brunello di Montalcino Ris. '12 | ▼▼ | 7 |
| ● Brunello di Montalcino '13 | ▼▼ | 6 |
| ● Rosso di Montalcino '16 | ▼ | 3 |
| ● Brunello di Montalcino '11 | ♈♈ | 6 |
| ● Brunello di Montalcino '10 | ♈♈ | 6 |
| ● Brunello di Montalcino '04 | ♈♈ | 6 |
| ● Brunello di Montalcino Ris. '10 | ♈♈ | 7 |
| ● Rosso di Montalcino '15 | ♈♈ | 3 |
| ● Rosso di Montalcino '14 | ♈♈ | 3 |

# Giorgio Meletti Cavallari

VIA CASONE UGOLINO,12
57022 CASTAGNETO CARDUCCI [LI]
TEL. +39 0565775620
www.giorgiomeletticavallari.it

CELLAR SALES
PRE-BOOKED VISITS
ACCOMMODATION
ANNUAL PRODUCTION 40,000 bottles
HECTARES UNDER VINE 10.00

The Meletti Cavalleri are certainly not the most recent arrivals in Bolgheri, but they're part of a generation of pioneers that have shaped the appellation. Their cellar gets its name from Giorgio, who represents the latest generation of family vine growers (he was born in the early 2000s, making him quite young). Their major vineyards are divided into two main blocks, Piastraia (situated on Castagneto hill) and Vallone, which is lower and nearer to the hospitality facilities. The terrain here is characterized by marl and stone, making for wines that come across as stylish and flavorful. We prefer their 2016 Bolgheri Rosso Borgeri to their 2015 Bolgheri Superiore Impronte. The former may exhibit a bit less body but it's also more well-defined, clear and close-focused in its style and execution. On the nose it's well-orchestrated, bringing together small red fruit, delicate herbaceous whiffs and fine spices, while the palate proves gratifying and tasty. The second is more muddled, at least at the time of our tasting.

| | | |
|---|---|---|
| ☉ Bolgheri Rosato Borgeri '17 | ▼▼ | 3 |
| ● Bolgheri Rosso Borgeri '16 | ▼▼ | 3 |
| ○ Bolgheri Vermentino Borgeri '17 | ▼▼ | 3 |
| ● Bolgheri Rosso Sup. Impronte '15 | ▼ | 5 |
| ● Bolgheri Rosso Borgeri '13 | ♈♈ | 3 |
| ● Bolgheri Rosso Borgeri '12 | ♈♈ | 3 |
| ● Bolgheri Sup. Impronte '13 | ♈♈ | 5 |
| ● Bolgheri Sup. Impronte '12 | ♈♈ | 5 |
| ● Bolgheri Sup. Impronte '11 | ♈♈ | 5 |

# Melini

LOC. GAGGIANO
53036 POGGIBONSI [SI]
TEL. +39 0577998511
www.cantinemelini.it

**CELLAR SALES**
**PRE-BOOKED VISITS**
**ANNUAL PRODUCTION** 3,000,000 bottles
**HECTARES UNDER VINE** 136.00

The wineries of Melini di Poggibonsi and Macchiavelli di San Casciano Val di Pesa are both part of Gruppo Italiano Vini. Situated in Chianti Classico, they represent an important part of the appellation. They are probably the most well-known Chianti brands in the world, and their selection offers a consistence in quality terms that's by now well-established. Aged primarily in large wood barrels, their wines feature commendable precision. They don't lack in personality, and at times they are even outstanding. This Poggibonsi winery's Chianti Classicos are solid and well-made. Their 2016 goes all in on pleasantness and enjoyability, with fresh aromas and a supple palate. Their 2014 Chianti Classico Vigneti La Selvanella Riserva is a nice interpretation of a difficult year, with defined aromas and a persistent, flavorful palate that's well-supported by the right amount of oak.

| | | |
|---|---|---|
| ● Chianti Cl. Granaio '16 | ♛♛ | 3 |
| ● Chianti Cl. Vign. La Selvanella Ris. '14 | ♛♛ | 4 |
| ● I Coltri '17 | ♛ | 2 |
| ● Chianti Cl. La Selvanella Ris. '06 | ♛♛♛ | 5 |
| ● Chianti Cl. La Selvanella Ris. '03 | ♛♛♛ | 4 |
| ● Chianti Cl. La Selvanella Ris. '01 | ♛♛♛ | 4 |
| ● Chianti Cl. La Selvanella Ris. '00 | ♛♛♛ | 4 |
| ● Chianti Cl. La Selvanella Ris. '99 | ♛♛♛ | 5 |
| ● Chianti Cl. La Selvanella Ris. '90 | ♛♛♛ | 3* |
| ● Chianti Cl. La Selvanella Ris. '86 | ♛♛♛ | 4* |
| ● Chianti Cl. Granaio '15 | ♛♛ | 4 |
| ● Chianti Cl. La Selvanella Ris. '13 | ♛♛ | 4 |
| ● I Coltri '16 | ♛♛ | 2* |

# Stefania Mezzetti

LOC. VERNAZZANO BASSO
06069 TUORO SUL TRASIMENO [PG]
TEL. 0758254060
www.vinimezzetti.it

**CELLAR SALES**
**PRE-BOOKED VISITS**
**ACCOMMODATION AND RESTAURANT SERVICE**
**ANNUAL PRODUCTION** 40,000 bottles
**HECTARES UNDER VINE** 10.00
**VITICULTURE METHOD** Certified Organic

Sometimes it takes a generational shift to appreciate the foundation laid by one's ancestors. And that's what happened to Stefania Mezzetti, whose winery operates in Cortona and Trasimeno Lake, straddling two appellations and two regions. Over time Stefania grew to love the winemaking work done by her grandfather Pietro, later involving her father, Giuliano, and brother Stefano. In addition to their work as agricultural producers, in Umbria Stefania manages a farmstay. Their 2016 Principe Syrah features fresh aromas of ginger, juniper and pepper, with red fruit in the foreground. On the palate it has a nice impact, coming through full, with balanced structure, fine-grained tannins and a long, complex finish. Their 2016 Annibale, a blend of Sangiovese, Merlot and Cabernet Sauvignon, exhibits a nice aromatic harmony between fruit and spices. It has a balanced body, proving soft, with lively acidity and a relaxed finish. Their 2016 Lucumone, a monovarietal Cabernet Sauvignon, is a fresh, balsamic wine.

| | | |
|---|---|---|
| ● Annibale '16 | ♛♛ | 2* |
| ● Cortona Cabernet Sauvignon Lucumone '16 | ♛♛ | 4 |
| ● Cortona Syrah Principe '16 | ♛♛ | 4 |
| ● Cortona Merlot Selvans '16 | ♛ | 4 |
| ● Cortona Cabernet Sauvignon Lucumone '15 | ♛♛ | 4 |
| ● Cortona Merlot Selvans '15 | ♛♛ | 4 |
| ● Cortona Sangiovese Dardano '14 | ♛♛ | 4 |
| ● Cortona Syrah Principe '10 | ♛♛ | 6 |
| ○ Cortona Vin Santo Luce di Vino '07 | ♛♛ | 5 |

# Le Miccine

s.s. Traversa Chiantigiana, 44
53013 Gaiole in Chianti [SI]
Tel. +39 0577749526
www.lemiccine.com

**CELLAR SALES**
**PRE-BOOKED VISITS**
**ACCOMMODATION**
**ANNUAL PRODUCTION** 25,000 bottles
**HECTARES UNDER VINE** 7.00
**VITICULTURE METHOD** Certified Organic

At Le Miccine the vineyards are cultivated
organically, in the cellar their approach is
minimally invasive with aging that calls for
mid-size casks or large wood barrels.
These are simple but definitive choices that
guarantee that the winery managed by
Paula Papini Cook offers a well-focused
selection of wines. Stylistically, they pursue
the identity of the territory where they are
cultivated, in the subzone of Gaiole in
Chianti. The result is a well-defined,
forthright and drinkable selection of wines.
At times their subtle profile can make for
less complexity overall. Their 2016 Chianti
Classico is hands down the best of their
selection. It stands out aromatically for its
flowery hints, which become extremely
fresh citrusy notes. On the palate it's
extremely steady, with a persistent
savoriness and decisive fragrance. Their
2015 Chianti Classico Riserva is more
oriented around sweetness of fruit, with
clean but less complex aromas and a more
concentrated palate.

| | |
|---|---|
| ● Chianti Cl. '16 | ▼▼▼ 4* |
| ● Chianti Cl. Ris. '15 | ▼▼ 5 |
| ● Chianti Cl. Gran Selezione '14 | ▼ 4 |
| ● Chianti Cl. '15 | ♈♈♈ 4* |
| ● Chianti Cl. Ris. '10 | ♈♈♈ 5 |
| ● Carduus '10 | ♈♈ 5 |
| ● Chianti Cl. '11 | ♈♈ 2* |
| ● Chianti Cl. '09 | ♈♈ 2* |
| ● Chianti Cl. '07 | ♈♈ 2 |
| ● Chianti Cl. Don Alberto Ris. '07 | ♈♈ 4 |
| ● Chianti Cl. Ris. '13 | ♈♈ 5 |
| ● Chianti Cl. Ris. '12 | ♈♈ 5 |
| ● Chianti Cl. Ris. '09 | ♈♈ 2* |

# Fattoria Montellori

via Pistoiese, 1
50054 Fucecchio [FI]
Tel. +39 0571260641
www.fattoriamontellori.it

**CELLAR SALES**
**PRE-BOOKED VISITS**
**ACCOMMODATION AND RESTAURANT SERVICE**
**ANNUAL PRODUCTION** 250,000 bottles
**HECTARES UNDER VINE** 51.00
**VITICULTURE METHOD** Certified Organic
**SUSTAINABLE WINERY**

Montellori was founded in the late 19th
century when Giuseppe Nieri decided to
invest a part of the profits he earned from
the fur industry in a villa and some land. His
grandson enlarged the vineyards to what
they are today. For some 30 years now, in
correspondence with Alessandro's arrival as
manager, the winery has moved towards
more current tendencies in the world of
wine production. Their selection shows
personality and expresses the character of
the territory. For the first time Montellori's
sparkling Riserva did a nice job. The 2012
features a varied aromatic profile, with
bread crust accompanied by apricot,
damson plums and captivating citrusy
notes. In the mouth it opens well, nice and
creamy, and vivid in its freshness. Their
2015 Dicatum, a monovarietal Sangiovese,
proves close-focused on the nose, with
fruity aromas of cherries and blackberries.
On the palate it's balanced, with subtle
tannins and controlled freshness giving way
to a long, pleasant finish.

| | |
|---|---|
| ○ Montellori Pas Dosé Ris. '12 | ▼▼ 6 |
| ○ Bianco dell'Empolese Vin Santo '12 | ▼▼ 5 |
| ● Dicatum '15 | ▼▼ 5 |
| ○ Montellori Pas Dosé '14 | ▼▼ 5 |
| ● Salamartano '15 | ▼▼ 6 |
| ● Chianti '16 | ▼ 2 |
| ● Chianti Sup. Caselle '16 | ▼ 3 |
| ○ Trebbiano '17 | ▼ 2 |
| ○ Bianco dell'Empolese Vin Santo '11 | ♈♈ 5 |
| ● Chianti Sup. Caselle '15 | ♈♈ 2* |
| ○ Montellori Pas Dosé '13 | ♈♈ 5 |
| ● Moro '14 | ♈♈ 3 |
| ● Salamartano '13 | ♈♈ 6 |

# Montenidoli

loc. Montenidoli
53037 San Gimignano [SI]
Tel. +39 0577941565
www.montenidoli.com

CELLAR SALES
ACCOMMODATION
ANNUAL PRODUCTION 100,000 bottles
HECTARES UNDER VINE 24.00
VITICULTURE METHOD Certified Organic

Montenidoli, which was founded more than 50 years ago by Sergio Muratori and Elisabetta Fagiuoli, is more than a producer. It's a place for meeting, studying, working and hospitality. It's a winery whose philosophy can only privilege native grape varieties, following biodynamic principles of cultivation and showing the utmost attention for the environment. Their first wine came in 1971, under Luigi Veronelli. It was he who wrote that Elisabetta carried herself 'like the San Gimignano battle towers'. Tre Bicchieri hands down for their bright straw-yellow 2013 Vernaccia Carato, a wine with vibrant aromas, rich in notes of ripe apple and almond, aromatic herbs and mineral nuances. The palate shows good weight, proving potent and juicy, dense and delicate at the same time, with a long, flavorful finish. Their 2016 Vernaccia Fiore is an intriguing wine with spicy whiffs of vanilla, then peach and citrus. The body proves generous, with a finish that builds to a crescendo. Their 2016 Vernaccia Tradizionale also delivered with its ripe aromas, slightly citrus, and its soft, delicate palate.

| | |
|---|---|
| ○ Vernaccia di S. Gimignano Carato '13 | ♛♛♛ 4* |
| ○ Vernaccia di S. Gimignano Fiore '16 | ♛♛ 3 |
| ○ Vernaccia di S. Gimignano Tradizionale '16 | ♛♛ 2* |
| ● Chianti Colli Senesi Il Garrulo '16 | ♛ 2 |
| ○ Vernaccia di S. Gimignano Carato '12 | ♛♛♛ 4* |
| ○ Vernaccia di S. Gimignano Carato '11 | ♛♛♛ 4* |
| ○ Vernaccia di S. Gimignano Tradizionale '15 | ♛♛♛ 2* |
| ○ Vernaccia di S. Gimignano Tradizionale '12 | ♛♛♛ 2* |
| ○ Il Templare '12 | ♛♛ 4 |
| ● Triassico '15 | ♛♛ 8 |
| ○ Vernaccia di S. Gimignano Fiore '15 | ♛♛ 3* |
| ○ Vernaccia di S. Gimignano Fiore '13 | ♛♛ 3 |
| ○ Vernaccia di S. Gimignano Tradizionale '14 | ♛♛ 2* |

# Montepeloso

loc. Montepeloso, 82
57028 Suvereto [LI]
Tel. +39 0565828180
www.montepeloso.it

ANNUAL PRODUCTION 22,000 bottles
HECTARES UNDER VINE 7.00
SUSTAINABLE WINERY

This area to the southeast of Suvereto used to be famous for marble and extra virgin olive oil, but today the focus has shifted to wine. About twenty years ago, Fabio Chiarelotto purchased Tenuta Montepeloso from Willi and Doris Neukmon and brought new energy to winemaking. A few years later, Silvio Denz became a partner and further improved the quality of their wines. Passion and expertise go into a selection that features skillfully blended reds and whites. Their 2015 Eneo made it into our finals. It's a curious and unusual blend of Sangiovese, Montepulciano, Marselan and Alicante. On the nose it shows real character, with notes of blood-rich meat and tanned leather giving way to black fruit and Mediterranean scrubland. On the palate it proves excellent, warm and generous, somewhat soft, with a finish that entices. Their 2015 Nardo, a blend of Montepulciano, Sangiovese and Marselan, features generous, toasted notes and a well-structured body.

| | |
|---|---|
| ● Eneo '15 | ♛♛ 5 |
| ● A Quo '15 | ♛♛ 5 |
| ● Gabbro '15 | ♛♛ 8 |
| ● Nardo '15 | ♛♛ 8 |
| ● Eneo '14 | ♛♛ 5 |
| ● Eneo '13 | ♛♛ 5 |
| ● Eneo '12 | ♛♛ 5 |
| ● Gabbro '14 | ♛♛ 8 |
| ● Gabbro '13 | ♛♛ 8 |
| ● Gabbro '12 | ♛♛ 8 |
| ● Nardo '13 | ♛♛ 8 |
| ● Nardo '12 | ♛♛ 8 |

# Montepepe

VIA SFORZA, 76
54038 MONTIGNOSO [MS]
TEL. +39 0585831042
www.montepepe.com

CELLAR SALES
PRE-BOOKED VISITS
ACCOMMODATION
ANNUAL PRODUCTION 25,000 bottles
HECTARES UNDER VINE 6.00

This farm is situated on a small hill about 5 km from the sea, between the Apuan Alps and Versilia. Here terraces are cultivated with olives and vines. In the early 1800s, Charles I, Duke of Lucca, bought Montepepe and used vine growers from Bordeaux to plant a French-style vineyard. At the foot of the hill stands the villa, which today offers accommodation and also houses the cellar (also dating from the eighteenth century), where their wines are still made. The farm is now run by Alberto Poggi who produces wines with Vermentino, Viognier, Massaretta and Syrah grapes. Their 2015 Degeres, a blend of Vermentino and Viognier, proves complex on the nose, with notes of orange preserves, citrus and lemon, as well as herbaceous hints of marjoram and spices. On the palate it's soft, made vigorous by virtue of a well-calibrated acidity, with a savory, long finish. Their 2016 Montepepe Bianco is fruity and simple aromatically, subtle and elegant on the palate. Their 2016 Albérico, a monovarietal Vermentino, features aromas of orange and peach, and a persistent body.

| | |
|---|---|
| ○ Candia dei Colli Apuani Vermentino Albérico '16 | ♟♟ 3 |
| ○ Degeres '15 | ♟♟ 6 |
| ○ Montepepe Bianco '16 | ♟♟ 4 |
| ● Pepo '15 | ♟ 5 |
| ○ Degeres '13 | ♟♟ 5 |
| ○ Degeres '12 | ♟♟ 6 |
| ○ Montepepe Bianco '14 | ♟♟ 4 |
| ○ Montepepe Bianco '13 | ♟♟ 4 |
| ○ Montepepe Bianco Vintage '10 | ♟♟ 5 |
| ○ Montepepe Bianco Vintage Magnum '12 | ♟♟ 8 |
| ● Montepepe Rosso '13 | ♟♟ 4 |
| ● Montepepe Rosso '11 | ♟♟ 5 |

# Monteraponi

LOC. MONTERAPONI
53017 RADDA IN CHIANTI [SI]
TEL. +39 0577738208
www.monteraponi.it

CELLAR SALES
PRE-BOOKED VISITS
ACCOMMODATION
ANNUAL PRODUCTION 50,000 bottles
HECTARES UNDER VINE 10.00
VITICULTURE METHOD Certified Organic

This winery, whose first wines came in 2003, is one of the brightest stars to have emerged in Chianti Classico in recent years. Monteraponi, owned by Michele Braganti, is located in a dream setting that fans out into a south-facing natural amphitheater, in the hills just before Radda in Chianti. The recipe for their success appears to be simple: organic vineyards, balanced winemaking, aging in large barrels and, above all, respect for what nature and climate offers them year after year. Their 2015 Chianti Classico Il Campitello Riserva features a nuanced aromatic impact that gradually gains in definition. Flowery hints merge well with flint and lightly smoky notes. In the mouth it shows complex, pronounced structure, with acidity and fruit sweetness alternating across a steady, deep palate. Their pleasantly crisp and savory 2016 Chianti Classico opts for less complexity.

| | |
|---|---|
| ● Chianti Cl. Il Campitello Ris. '15 | ♟♟♟ 7 |
| ● Chianti Cl. '16 | ♟♟ 4 |
| ● Baron'Ugo '13 | ♟♟♟ 5 |
| ● Baron'Ugo '12 | ♟♟♟ 8 |
| ● Chianti Cl. Baron'Ugo Ris. '10 | ♟♟♟ 7 |
| ● Chianti Cl. Baron'Ugo Ris. '09 | ♟♟♟ 7 |
| ● Chianti Cl. Baron'Ugo Ris. '07 | ♟♟♟ 5 |
| ● Chianti Cl. '13 | ♟♟ 3 |
| ● Chianti Cl. Baron'Ugo Ris. '11 | ♟♟ 7 |
| ● Chianti Cl. Il Campitello Ris. '14 | ♟♟ 5 |
| ● Chianti Cl. Il Campitello Ris. '13 | ♟♟ 5 |
| ● Chianti Cl. Il Campitello Ris. '12 | ♟♟ 5 |
| ● Chianti Cl. Il Campitello Ris. '11 | ♟♟ 5 |

# Tenuta Monteti

S.DA DELLA SGRILLA, 6
58011 CAPALBIO [GR]
TEL. +39 0564896160
www.tenutamonteti.it

**CELLAR SALES**
**PRE-BOOKED VISITS**
**ANNUAL PRODUCTION** 130,000 bottles
**HECTARES UNDER VINE** 28.00
**SUSTAINABLE WINERY**

In 1998, Paolo Baratta (economist and former Italian minister) decided to set up a winery with his wife Germma, and they chose Maremma. In 2004 their first wines were released while their daughter Eva and her husband came on board in 2010. The local climate dictates their style, focusing on strength and intensity, to the extent their wines can often make an explosive impact. However, given time they are rendered more nuanced and dynamic. Their 2014 Caburnio, a blend of Cabernet Sauvignon, Alicante Bouschet and Merlot, proves to be one of the best versions yet, offering up fresh and fruity aromas followed by a savory, highly pleasant palate. Their 2014 Monteti relies a bit more on oak. It's a blend of Petit Verdot, Cabernet Franc and Cabernet Sauvignon with smoky, spicy aromas and a palate that's slightly bridled. Their pleasant and tasty 2017 TM Rosé is a blend of Merlot and Cabernet Sauvignon.

| | |
|---|---|
| ● Caburnio '14 | 🍷🍷🍷 3* |
| ● Monteti '14 | 🍷 6 |
| ☉ TM Rosé '17 | 🍷 3 |
| ● Caburnio '13 | 🍷🍷 3 |
| ● Monteti '13 | 🍷🍷 6 |
| ● Monteti '12 | 🍷🍷 5 |
| ☉ TM Rosé '14 | 🍷🍷 3 |

# Monteverro

S.DA AURELIA CAPALBIO, 11
58011 CAPALBIO [GR]
TEL. +39 0564890721
www.monteverro.com

**CELLAR SALES**
**PRE-BOOKED VISITS**
**ANNUAL PRODUCTION** 140,000 bottles
**HECTARES UNDER VINE** 35.00
**VITICULTURE METHOD** Certified Organic
**SUSTAINABLE WINERY**

Monteverro is an ambitious and uncompromising winery founded by the German, Georg Weber, in Maremma, in 2003. It is named after an animal considered to be the undisputed king of this territory: the male boar or 'verro' in Italian. The estate is situated between Capalbio and the sea, and nothing is left to chance here, especially in the vineyards (with a density of seven thousand plants per hectare). Modernity and tradition, as well as steel and barriques, all come together in the cellar to produce wines with a modern and precise style, which while sound, is perhaps lacking a touch in personality. Their 2015 Tinata is a juicy, aromatically clean blend of Syrah and Grenache redolent of small red fruit and Asian spices. In the mouth it proves long and persistent, with a lovely, savory finish. Their 2015 Monteverro, a blend of Cabernet Sauvignon, Cabernet Franc, Merlot and Petit Verdot, is nice overall but a bit held back by oak.

| | |
|---|---|
| ● Tinata '15 | 🍷🍷 8 |
| ● Monteverro '15 | 🍷 8 |
| ● Terra di Monteverro '15 | 🍷 7 |
| ● Monteverro '14 | 🍷🍷 8 |
| ● Terra di Monteverro '14 | 🍷🍷 7 |
| ● Terra di Monteverro '13 | 🍷🍷 7 |
| ● Tinata '14 | 🍷🍷 8 |

## ★★Montevertine

LOC. MONTEVERTINE
53017 RADDA IN CHIANTI [SI]
TEL. +39 0577738009
www.montevertine.it

**PRE-BOOKED VISITS**
**ANNUAL PRODUCTION** 85,000 bottles
**HECTARES UNDER VINE** 18.00

Sergio Manetti purchased Montevertine in the late 1960s. The first wines came onto the market in 1971 and garnered immediate success, confirming he was on the right track. In 2000 after he passed away, his son Martino took over and made a few modest but important changes, leading to some of Italy's most iconic wines. Montevertine offers up rigorous and in some ways complicated wines with the sharp acidity only Sangiovese wines made with Radda grapes can produce. Their 2015 Pergole Torte earns yet another Tre Bicchieri. By now it's one of Chianti's classics, a wine that's set records when it comes to quality consistence, making it a true 'benchmark' of Sangiovese. Their 2016 Pian del Ciampolo proved particularly delicious, with its delectable aromas and its steady, savory palate. We found their 2015 Montevertine a bit under par, but only because it's competing with such an outstanding selection.

| | |
|---|---|
| ● Le Pergole Torte '15 | 🏆🏆🏆 8 |
| ● Pian del Ciampolo '16 | 🏆🏆 4 |
| ● Montevertine '15 | 🏆🏆 6 |
| ● Le Pergole Torte '13 | 🏆🏆🏆 8 |
| ● Le Pergole Torte '12 | 🏆🏆🏆 8 |
| ● Le Pergole Torte '11 | 🏆🏆🏆 8 |
| ● Le Pergole Torte '10 | 🏆🏆🏆 8 |
| ● Le Pergole Torte '09 | 🏆🏆🏆 8 |
| ● Le Pergole Torte '07 | 🏆🏆🏆 8 |
| ● Le Pergole Torte '04 | 🏆🏆🏆 8 |
| ● Le Pergole Torte '03 | 🏆🏆🏆 7 |
| ● Montevertine '14 | 🏆🏆🏆 6 |
| ● Montevertine '04 | 🏆🏆🏆 5 |
| ● Montevertine '01 | 🏆🏆🏆 5 |

## Vignaioli del Morellino di Scansano

LOC. SARAGIOLO
58054 SCANSANO [GR]
TEL. +39 0564507288
www.cantinadelmorellino.it

**CELLAR SALES**
**PRE-BOOKED VISITS**
**ANNUAL PRODUCTION** 2,500,000 bottles
**HECTARES UNDER VINE** 600.00
**SUSTAINABLE WINERY**

Founded in the early 1970s, Cooperativa Vignaioli del Morellino di Scansano comprises 152 grower members and 450 hectares of cultivated land. The lion's share goes to producing Morellino, a wine originating around the town the appellation is named for, but there are other vineyards near Monte Amiata and around Pitigliano. In general the vine rows are situated between 150 and 300 meters above sea level, on mixed soils ranging from silt to clay or tuff in Pitigliano. The rich and well-structured product portfolio is made up of various appellations and wine types. This Scansano cooperative winery submitted a highly consistent selection, in terms of quality, for tasting. Their 2015 Morellino di Scansano Roggiano Riserva, in particular, shines with its clear, well-delineated aromas alternating between red fruit, flowery hints and spicy notes. On the palate it proves juicy and supple, with depth and length. Their 2015 Morellino Sicomoro Riserva also delivered, though we found its oak still dominating over fruit.

| | |
|---|---|
| ● Morellino di Scansano Roggiano Ris. '15 | 🏆🏆 3* |
| ● Morellino di Scansano Sicomoro Ris. '15 | 🏆🏆 4 |
| ● Morellino di Scansano Vignabenefizio '17 | 🏆🏆 3 |
| ● Morellino di Scansano Roggiano '17 | 🏆 2 |
| ● Morellino di Scansano Roggiano '15 | 🏆🏆 2* |
| ● Morellino di Scansano Roggiano Bio '15 | 🏆🏆 2* |
| ● Morellino di Scansano Roggiano Ris. '14 | 🏆🏆 3* |
| ● Morellino di Scansano Vignabenefizio '15 | 🏆🏆 2* |
| ○ Vermentino V. Fiorini V.T. '15 | 🏆🏆 2* |

# Giacomo Mori

FRAZ. PALAZZONE
P.ZZA SANDRO PERTINI, 8
53040 SAN CASCIANO DEI BAGNI [SI]
TEL. +39 0578227005
www.giacomomori.it

CELLAR SALES
PRE-BOOKED VISITS
ACCOMMODATION
ANNUAL PRODUCTION 40,000 bottles
HECTARES UNDER VINE 12.00
VITICULTURE METHOD Certified Organic

This winery in Palazzone near Siena has at last found the road to quality, laying down simple but effective strategies for its selection of wines. The grapes are cultivated without forcing nature and winemaking is minimally invasive. At the same time, aging is carried out in barriques and large barrels. All of this has led to a selection of wines with a clear-cut style and personality that is timeless. Their wines aim for drinkability and elegance, hitting the mark more often than not. Their 2015 Chianti Castelrotto Riserva is an experience and coherent wine in its fragrances of ripe fruit, its toasted accents and earthy notes. On the palate it proves tasty, exhibiting depth, consistence and flavor. Their 2016 Bianco is a fragrant blend of Trebbiano and Malvasia and certainly not lacking in character. In the mouth it features a lovely, delicately salty note that crosses the entire palate. Their 2016 Chianti is supple and quite simple, though well-made.

| | | |
|---|---|---|
| ○ Bianco '16 | ▼▼ | 4 |
| ● Chianti Castelrotto Ris. '15 | ▼▼ | 3 |
| ● Chianti '16 | ▼ | 2 |
| ● Chianti '15 | ♀♀ | 2* |
| ● Chianti '11 | ♀♀ | 2* |
| ● Chianti '10 | ♀♀ | 2* |
| ● Chianti Castelrotto Ris. '14 | ♀♀ | 3 |
| ● Chianti Castelrotto Ris. '13 | ♀♀ | 3 |
| ● Chianti Castelrotto Ris. '11 | ♀♀ | 3 |
| ● Clanis Shiraz '08 | ♀♀ | 3 |
| ● I 5 Mori '13 | ♀♀ | 4 |
| ○ Vin Santo del Chianti '08 | ♀♀ | 6 |

# Tenuta Moriniello

LOC. LA PIEVE
VIA SANTO STEFANO
50050 MONTAIONE [FI]
TEL. +39 0571697934
www.lapieve.net

CELLAR SALES
PRE-BOOKED VISITS
ACCOMMODATION
ANNUAL PRODUCTION 50,000 bottles
HECTARES UNDER VINE 20.00
VITICULTURE METHOD Certified Organic

Benjamin Moriniello, along with his children Tania and Luigi, has finally capped off a dream cultivated for years: to run an agricultural producer. He chose Tuscany after seeing and considering a number of possibilities, including other regions. The choice to go into winemaking seemed like the most natural for his idea. He opted for La Pieve, which was already active in the territory and bolstered by an age-old wine-growing tradition. That made it easy for them to get started, moving forward with their entrepreneurial project with a modern and dynamic vision. Their 2015 Gobbo Nero earned a place in our finals with its aromatic profile of ripe fruit, plums and blackcurrant, spicy accents of cloves and cinnamon, and a finish of roasted coffee. In the mouth it comes through dense, juicy, rich in pulp, with a lovely, savory finish. Their 2015 Chianti Riserva Fortebraccio is another interesting wine with vibrant aromas of blackberry preserves, pleasantly vegetal fragrances and various aromatic herbs. On the palate it exhibits depth, fullness and a lengthy finish.

| | | |
|---|---|---|
| ● Il Gobbo Nero '15 | ▼▼ | 4 |
| ● Chianti Fortebraccio Ris. '15 | ▼▼ | 3 |
| ● Il Gobbo Nero '13 | ▼▼ | 4 |
| ○ Le Fate Furbe '17 | ▼▼ | 3 |
| ● Rosso del Pievano '13 | ▼▼ | 4 |
| ● Chianti La Pieve '16 | ▼ | 2 |
| ● Il Gobbo Nero '10 | ♀♀ | 3 |
| ● Il Gobbo Nero '08 | ♀♀ | 3* |
| ● Rosso del Pievano '08 | ♀♀ | 3 |
| ● Rosso del Pievano '07 | ♀♀ | 3* |
| ● Syrah Gobbo Nero '11 | ♀♀ | 3 |

# Morisfarms

LOC. CURA NUOVA
FATTORIA POGGETTI
58024 MASSA MARITTIMA [GR]
TEL. +39 0566919135
www.morisfarms.it

**CELLAR SALES**
**PRE-BOOKED VISITS**
**ACCOMMODATION**
**ANNUAL PRODUCTION** 300,000 bottles
**HECTARES UNDER VINE** 70.00

This historic Maremma estate has been instrumental in the success of wines from the province of Grosseto. Morisfarms owns a large property subdivided into two distinct areas: Tenuta di Poggeti, in Massa Marittima, and Poggio La Mozza, which is one of the most important subzones of Morellino di Scansano. The winery emphasizes both modern and traditional styles, which are especially evident at the top of their range, showing a lot of personality. On the other hand, the rest of their wines reach a decent quality level but are decidedly less intriguing. Their 2015 Avvoltore is a vibrant, weighty wine, one of Maremma's first Supertuscans made with Sangiovese, Cabernet Sauvignon and Syrah, a wine that offers up deep, multifaceted aromas and a steady palate that's contrasted by savory, pronounced tannins. Their 2015 Morellino di Scansano Riserva features a dark, spicy aromatic profile and a palate that's supple and soft. Their 2017 Morellino di Scansano is a fresh and pleasantly savory wine.

| | | |
|---|---|---|
| ● Avvoltore '15 | | ♟♟ 6 |
| ● Morellino di Scansano '17 | | ♟♟ 2* |
| ● Morellino di Scansano Ris. '15 | | ♟♟ 4 |
| ● Avvoltore '06 | | ♟♟♟ 5 |
| ● Avvoltore '12 | | ♟♟ 6 |
| ● Maremma Toscana Mandriolo '15 | | ♟♟ 1* |
| ○ Monteregio di Massa Marittima Santa Chiara '16 | | ♟♟ 2* |
| ● Morellino di Scansano '16 | | ♟♟ 2* |
| ● Morellino di Scansano Ris. '13 | | ♟♟ 4 |
| ○ Vermentino '14 | | ♟♟ 2* |

# Mormoraia

LOC. SANT'ANDREA, 15
53037 SAN GIMIGNANO [SI]
TEL. +39 0577940096
www.mormoraia.it

**CELLAR SALES**
**PRE-BOOKED VISITS**
**ACCOMMODATION**
**ANNUAL PRODUCTION** 230,000 bottles
**HECTARES UNDER VINE** 40.00

Milan industrialist, Pino Passoni, and his wife purchased the old 'La Mormoraia' convent in 1980. Ten years later they began renovating the buildings and vineyards on the estate and in 1995 opened the farm holiday accommodation and first cellar. In following years they grew their farming production by extending the hectares of vineyards and olive groves. In 2012, coinciding with their son Alessandro becoming more involved in the business, the farm was converted to organic management. Their 2017 Vernaccia Suavis is a highly pleasant wine in its fresh leanness. In the glass it's true to its name, with pleasant nuances of citrus and wild herbs. Their 2016 Ostrea shows a deeper, more intense character, calling up almond and candied citrus on the nose. These enrich a firm and assertive structure that moves towards sensations of ripe yellow fruit and aromatic herbs. Finally, their 2016 Chianti Colli Senesi also proved excellent in its fragrances of cherry and red fruit. It's redolent of cut hay and closes on a flowery note.

| | | |
|---|---|---|
| ● Chianti Colli Senesi Haurio '16 | | ♟♟ 2* |
| ○ Vernaccia di S. Gimignano Ostrea '16 | | ♟♟ 3 |
| ○ Vernaccia di S. Gimignano Suavis '17 | | ♟♟ 2* |
| ⊙ Gaudium Rosato '17 | | ♟ 2 |
| ○ Vernaccia di S. Gimignano E' ReZet Mattia Barzaghi '11 | | ♟♟♟ 3* |
| ● Chianti Colli Senesi '14 | | ♟♟ 2* |
| ● Chianti Colli Senesi Haurio '15 | | ♟♟ 2* |
| ● Neitea '12 | | ♟♟ 3 |
| ● Syrah '12 | | ♟♟ 3 |
| ○ Vernaccia di S. Gimignano '14 | | ♟♟ 2* |
| ○ Vernaccia di S. Gimignano '13 | | ♟♟ 2* |
| ○ Vernaccia di S. Gimignano Ostrea '15 | | ♟♟ 3 |
| ○ Vernaccia di S. Gimignano Ostrea '13 | | ♟♟ 3 |
| ○ Vernaccia di S. Gimignano Ris. '14 | | ♟♟ 3* |
| ○ Vernaccia di S. Gimignano Suavis '16 | | ♟♟ 2* |

# Fabio Motta

Vigna al Cavaliere, 61
57022 Castagneto Carducci [LI]
Tel. +39 0565773041
www.mottafabio.it

CELLAR SALES
PRE-BOOKED VISITS
ANNUAL PRODUCTION 23,000 bottles
HECTARES UNDER VINE 6.50

Fabio Motta is one of Bolgheri's most
interesting young vine growers thanks to
his ability to stay on track and turn in
strong results. After graduating in
agriculture and experience at Michele Satta,
he went out on his own. Today he cultivates
his black grapes at the foot of Castagneto
Carducci hill, in Le Pievi, and Fornacelle
(white grapes, primarily Vermentino),
transforming the crop into wine. Their style
is charming, defying stereotypes, in pursuit
of its own personality and elegance. Their
2015 Bolgheri Rosso Superiore Le Gonnare,
a Merlot and Syrah blend that's aged for 18
months in barriques (a third of which are
new), is a spectacle of finesse and flavor.
It's a clear wine, balanced but never
excessive, as complex as it is deep, redolent
of small red fruit and spices. It enchants
more for its dynamism and aromatic density
than for its texture. Truly delicious.

| | | |
|---|---|---|
| ● Bolgheri Rosso Sup. Le Gonnare '15 | ♟♟♟ | 8 |
| ○ Bolgheri Bianco Nova '17 | ♟♟ | 4 |
| ● Bolgheri Rosso Pievi '16 | ♟♟ | 4 |
| ● Bolgheri Sup. Le Gonnare '13 | ♟♟♟ | 8 |
| ○ Bolgheri Bianco Nova '16 | ♟♟ | 4 |
| ● Bolgheri Rosso Pievi '15 | ♟♟ | 4 |

# Muralia

loc. Il Poggiarello
fraz. Pianetto
via del Sughereto
58036 Roccastrada [GR]
Tel. +39 0564577223
www.muralia.it

CELLAR SALES
PRE-BOOKED VISITS
ACCOMMODATION AND RESTAURANT SERVICE
ANNUAL PRODUCTION 65,000 bottles
HECTARES UNDER VINE 14.00
VITICULTURE METHOD Certified Organic
SUSTAINABLE WINERY

In 2003 Stefano and Chiara Casali moved
from Milan to this corner of Maremma to
start producing wine. Their main vineyards
are located in two different areas: Poggiarelli,
with alluvial soils and Sassofortino, with clay
and calcareous soils. Their wines exhibit a
generally modern, but well-crafted style, with
a priority on balance. The wines from this
estate in Roccastrada are neither forced nor
excessive in their use of wood aging and the
result is a good dose of grip, freshness and
character. Their 2016 L'Altana exhibits nice
continuity in terms of quality, with clean and
delicate aromas of small red fruit and wild
herbs anticipating a lively, steady and tasty
palate. Their still fragrant and balanced
2013 Maremma Babone also proved to be
well-made. Their 2016 Manolibera, a blend
of Sangiovese, Cabernet Sauvignon and
Merlot, is simpler but no less pleasant, while
their 2017 Corbizzo, a monovarietal Syrah,
proved highly enjoyable.

| | | |
|---|---|---|
| ● Maremma Toscana Rosso Altana '16 | ♟♟ | 3* |
| ☉ Corbizzo '17 | ♟♟ | 2* |
| ● Manolibera '16 | ♟♟ | 2* |
| ● Maremma Toscana Babone '13 | ♟♟ | 3 |
| ○ Bianco Chiaraluna '13 | ♟♟ | 3 |
| ● Manolibera '15 | ♟♟ | 2* |
| ● Manolibera '13 | ♟♟ | 2* |
| ● Monteregio di Massa Marittima Altana '15 | ♟♟ | 3* |

## Tenute Silvio Nardi

LOC. CASALE DEL BOSCO
53024 MONTALCINO [SI]
TEL. +39 0577808269
www.tenutenardi.com

**CELLAR SALES**
**PRE-BOOKED VISITS**
**ANNUAL PRODUCTION** 250,000 bottles
**HECTARES UNDER VINE** 80.00

The estates purchased by Silvio Nardi in the 1950s are in some of the best vine growing areas of Montalcino. He was a forerunner and one of the first 'outsiders' to invest in the area, long before Brunello became the international star it is today. The torch has passed to Emilia, who produces a range of mostly red wines made with Sangiovese grapes. The top range wines are made with grapes grown in the Manachiara (eastern area) and Casale del Bosco (northwestern area) estates and matured in both large and mid-sized casks. Tenute Silvio Nardi's compact selection performed in line with the conditions of recent seasons. Their Rosso 2016 is among their best, a wine that exhibits marked typicity in its sequence of red and yellow fruit, petals and foresty sensations. On the palate it's sweetly supple but not lacking in vigor either. Their 2012 Brunello Poggio Doria Riserva also did well, compensating for a certain extractive rigidity with glycerine plushness.

| | |
|---|---|
| ● Brunello di Montalcino Vign. Poggio Doria Ris. '12 | ▼▼ 8 |
| ● Rosso di Montalcino '16 | ▼▼ 3 |
| ● Brunello di Montalcino '13 | ▼ 6 |
| ● Brunello di Montalcino Manachiara '99 | ▽▽▽ 7 |
| ● Brunello di Montalcino Manachiara '97 | ▽▽▽ 7 |
| ● Brunello di Montalcino '11 | ▽▽ 6 |
| ● Brunello di Montalcino Poggio Doria '12 | ▽▽ 8 |
| ● Brunello di Montalcino V. Manachiara '12 | ▽▽ 8 |
| ● Brunello di Montalcino Vign. Poggio Doria Ris. '10 | ▽▽ 8 |
| ● Rosso di Montalcino '15 | ▽▽ 3 |

## Nittardi

LOC. NITTARDI
53011 CASTELLINA IN CHIANTI [SI]
TEL. +39 0577740269
www.nittardi.com

**CELLAR SALES**
**PRE-BOOKED VISITS**
**ANNUAL PRODUCTION** 100,000 bottles
**HECTARES UNDER VINE** 35.00
**VITICULTURE METHOD** Certified Organic

The Nittardi farm, owned by the Femfert-Canali family since 1982, is situated near Castellina in Chianti and now includes 37 hectares of vineyards purchased in Maremma in 1999. Their wines feature a modern style: aging in small casks and aiming for the utmost ripeness of fruit, good structure, and fullness and sweetness on the palate. All of this is done with lightness and elegance, maintaining good balance throughout the range and accompanied by a dose of coherence with the territory. Their 2015 Chianti Classico Riserva is a well-made wine, flawless aromatically, with pronounced fruit supported by spicy and smoky hints. In the mouth it proves persistent and soft, though the palate's a bit weighed down by oak, which is slightly excessive at times. Their 2016 Chianti Classico Vigna Doghessa runs along similar stylistic lines, though it may be a bit lacking in personality.

| | |
|---|---|
| ● Chianti Cl. Ris. '15 | ▼▼ 6 |
| ● Chianti Cl. V. Doghessa '16 | ▼▼ 6 |
| ● Ad Astra '16 | ▼ 3 |
| ● Ad Astra '08 | ▽▽▽ 3 |
| ● Chianti Cl. Belcanto '15 | ▽▽▽ 4* |
| ● Chianti Cl. Ris. '13 | ▽▽▽ 6 |
| ● Chianti Cl. Ris. '11 | ▽▽▽ 6 |
| ● Chianti Cl. Ris. '10 | ▽▽▽ 6 |
| ● Chianti Cl. Ris. '98 | ▽▽▽ 6 |
| ● Ad Astra '15 | ▽▽ 3 |
| ● Chianti Cl. Casanuova di Nittardi '14 | ▽▽ 4 |
| ● Nectar Dei '14 | ▽▽ 7 |

# ★Orma

VIA BOLGHERESE
57022 CASTAGNETO CARDUCCI [LI]
TEL. +39 0575477857
www.ormawine.it

**ANNUAL PRODUCTION** 30,000 bottles
**HECTARES UNDER VINE** 5.50
**SUSTAINABLE WINERY**

Podere Orma produces one of the best and most definitive wines in Bolgheri, even though it doesn't officially belong to the appellation for this area. Nonetheless, entrepreneur from Arezzo, Antonio Moretti, is making a success of his umpteenth venture, demonstrated previously at Tenuta Setteponti and Feudo Maccari, in Sicily. In the case of Orma, this little winemaking jewel makes the best reds in the territory along usual lines, but adds a touch of personality to make them unique. The stony, clay soils give rise to their fascinating and elegant expression. 2016 gave rise to a wine that's still young but already splendid and intact - the future's bright. It's redolent of small red and black fruit, wrapped up in balsamic, almost minty hints and a charming Mediterranean atmosphere. On the palate it proves weighty and dynamic, pulsing, playing with contrasts, lengthening without losing its delectable pulp. It's a gem that's accompanied by an excellent 2016 Bolgheri Rosso Passi di Orma.

# Fattoria Ormanni

LOC. ORMANNI, 1
53036 POGGIBONSI [SI]
TEL. +39 0577937212
www.ormanni.it

**CELLAR SALES**
**PRE-BOOKED VISITS**
**ACCOMMODATION**
**ANNUAL PRODUCTION** 120,000 bottles
**HECTARES UNDER VINE** 68.00

Ormanni, one of the appellation's historic brands, has belonged to the Brini Batacchi family since 1818. The forty-year-old vineyards are situated between the provinces of Siena and Florence. On the Florentine side, they grow grapes to produce Chianti Classico, while the stony soils in Barberino Val d'Elsa are situated at a higher elevation (350 meters above sea level). Work in the cellar follows tradition, starting with the use of large barrels. The resulting wines exhibit a rigorous style, at times austere but with great charm and character. Their 2015 Chianti Classico Borro del Diavolo Riserva is a wine with a marked territorial identity. On the nose it offers up fruity notes and hints of earth, forest undergrowth and spices. In the mouth it shows texture and fullness. It has an impact, though it's a bit held back by tannins, especially at the end. Their 2015 Julius, a blend of Sangiovese, Merlot and Syrah, stands out for its aromatic balance and complex palate.

| | |
|---|---|
| ● Orma '16 | ♟♟♟ 8 |
| ● Bolgheri Rosso Passi di Orma '16 | ♟♟ 5 |
| ● Orma '14 | ♟♟♟ 8 |
| ● Orma '13 | ♟♟♟ 8 |
| ● Orma '12 | ♟♟♟ 8 |
| ● Orma '11 | ♟♟♟ 8 |
| ● Orma '10 | ♟♟♟ 7 |
| ● Orma '09 | ♟♟♟ 6 |
| ● Orma '08 | ♟♟♟ 6 |
| ● Orma '07 | ♟♟♟ 5 |
| ● Orma '06 | ♟♟♟ 6 |

| | |
|---|---|
| ● Chianti Cl. Borro del Diavolo Ris. '15 | ♟♟ 5 |
| ● Julius '15 | ♟♟ 5 |
| ● Chianti Cl. '14 | ♟♟ 3* |
| ● Chianti Cl. '12 | ♟♟ 3 |
| ● Chianti Cl. '10 | ♟♟ 3* |
| ● Chianti Cl. '08 | ♟♟ 3 |
| ● Chianti Cl. '04 | ♟♟ 2 |
| ● Chianti Cl. Borro del Diavolo Ris. '12 | ♟♟ 4 |
| ● Chianti Cl. Borro del Diavolo Ris. '08 | ♟♟ 4 |
| ● Chianti Cl. Borro del Diavolo Ris. '06 | ♟♟ 3 |
| ● Chianti Cl. Gran Sel. '12 | ♟♟ 3* |
| ● Chianti Cl. Gran Sel. '11 | ♟♟ 3 |
| ● Julius '12 | ♟♟ 5 |

## ★★Ornellaia

FRAZ. BOLGHERI
LOC. ORNELLAIA, 191
57022 CASTAGNETO CARDUCCI [LI]
TEL. +39 056571811
www.ornellaia.it

PRE-BOOKED VISITS
ANNUAL PRODUCTION 930,000 bottles
HECTARES UNDER VINE 112.00

Ornellaia, one of the most prestigious
Italian wine brands, is held in high regard
all over the world. The estate was founded
in the early 1980s and rapidly became a
benchmark for the industry. After changing
hands a few times, it is now owned by
Frescobaldi, a lineage and brand that
needs no further introduction. The winery is
located on a single site, with the Bellaria
appendix to the north of Bolgheri. Their
impeccable wines feature a clear modern
style that make it easy to see why they
have garnered so much success. A hot
2015 hurt their Masseto, which proved
somewhat unbalanced. Every element, from
oak to alcohol and extract, is a bit
oversized. On the palate it's a bonafide
exercise in style, but the word 'hyperbole'
comes to mind. Neither harmony nor
drinkability characterize their 2013 either.

| | | |
|---|---|---|
| ● Bolgheri Sup. Ornellaia '15 | ♟♟ | 8 |
| ● Masseto '15 | ♟♟ | 8 |
| ○ Bolgheri Bianco Poggio alle Gazze '16 | ♟♟ | 5 |
| ● Bolgheri Rosso Le Serre Nuove '16 | ♟♟ | 6 |
| ● Bolgheri Sup. Ornellaia '14 | ♟♟♟ | 8 |
| ● Bolgheri Sup. Ornellaia '13 | ♟♟♟ | 8 |
| ● Bolgheri Sup. Ornellaia '12 | ♟♟♟ | 8 |
| ● Bolgheri Sup. Ornellaia '10 | ♟♟♟ | 8 |
| ● Masseto '11 | ♟♟♟ | 8 |
| ● Masseto '09 | ♟♟♟ | 8 |

## Siro Pacenti

LOC. PELAGRILLI, 1
53024 MONTALCINO [SI]
TEL. +39 0577848662
www.siropacenti.it

CELLAR SALES
PRE-BOOKED VISITS
ANNUAL PRODUCTION 60,000 bottles
HECTARES UNDER VINE 22.00

This winery named after Siro Pacenti was
founded in the early 1970s by a branch of
one of the most important winemaking
families in Montalcino. With its first bottled
wine, the estate established itself as a
benchmark in the area. Today Giancarlo is
in charge and he was one of the first to use
smaller barrels for maturing his Brunellos,
now seen as great 'modern classics'. Their
Pelagrilli vineyards take center stage, giving
rise to the wine of the same name and the
PS Riserva. These are accompanied by
their southern vineyards in Piancornello
whose grapes are used for their Vecchie
Vigne and Rosso. Recent tastings revealed
the usual formidable selection, with all its
qualities, though its youth brings to the fore
a certain tannic rigidity, and that aren't
any real 'standouts'. Their 2016 Rosso
shows remarkable mouthfeel, while their
2013 Brunello Pelagrilli should evolve well
thanks to its pronounced savoriness. It's a
quality that we find even more integrated in
their Vecchie Vigne of the same year.

| | | |
|---|---|---|
| ● Brunello di Montalcino Pelagrilli '13 | ♟♟ | 6 |
| ● Brunello di Montalcino V. V. '13 | ♟♟ | 8 |
| ● Rosso di Montalcino '16 | ♟♟ | 5 |
| ● Brunello di Montalcino '97 | ♟♟♟ | 7 |
| ● Brunello di Montalcino '96 | ♟♟♟ | 7 |
| ● Brunello di Montalcino '95 | ♟♟♟ | 7 |
| ● Brunello di Montalcino '88 | ♟♟♟ | 7 |
| ● Brunello di Montalcino PS Ris. '07 | ♟♟♟ | 8 |
| ● Brunello di Montalcino V. V. '10 | ♟♟♟ | 8 |
| ● Brunello di Montalcino Pelagrilli '12 | ♟♟ | 6 |
| ● Brunello di Montalcino Pelagrilli '11 | ♟♟ | 6 |
| ● Brunello di Montalcino Pelagrilli '10 | ♟♟ | 6 |
| ● Brunello di Montalcino PS Ris. '10 | ♟♟ | 8 |
| ● Brunello di Montalcino V. V. '11 | ♟♟ | 8 |
| ● Rosso di Montalcino '15 | ♟♟ | 5 |

# Tenuta Il Palagio

VIA SANT'ANDREA, 11
50063 FIGLINE E INCISA VALDARNO [FI]
TEL. +39 0559502652
www.palagioproducts.com

CELLAR SALES
ACCOMMODATION AND RESTAURANT SERVICE
HECTARES UNDER VINE 12.00

The estate, owned by Sting and his wife, Trudy, is situated in Valdarno, and spans more than 350 hectares. It's mostly wooded, though there are orchards and a part dedicated to beekeeping. It's a kind of 'buen retiro' that the couple visits during summer and that's been increasingly used for wine production over time. Their selection is varied but Chianti remains their focus. Their 2017 When We Dance, a modern Chianti, earned a place in our finals thanks to its fruit, with notes of cherries and blackcurrant, its herbaceous hints of thyme and spicy nuances. On the palate it proves enjoyable, with a notable but still balanced acidity, and a nice finish. Their 2016 Casino delle Vie, a blend of Sangiovese and smaller parts Canaoilo, Colorino, and other complementary grapes, offers up classic aromas of cherry and blackberry, with the occasional vegetal note of sage and bay leaf. On the palate it shows a firm body, nice structure, balanced tannins and a warm, appetizing finish.

| | |
|---|---|
| ● Chianti When We Dance '17 | ♟♟ 5 |
| ● Casino delle Vie '16 | ♟♟ 4 |
| ● Dieci '16 | ♟♟ 4 |
| ● Sister Moon '15 | ♟ 6 |
| ● Casino delle Vie '14 | ♟♟ 5 |
| ● Sister Moon '13 | ♟♟ 6 |
| ● Chianti When We Dance '15 | ♟ 4 |

# Il Palagione

LOC. PALAGIONE
VIA PER CASTEL SAN GIMIGNANO, 36
53037 SAN GIMIGNANO [SI]
TEL. +39 0577953134
www.ilpalagione.com

CELLAR SALES
PRE-BOOKED VISITS
ACCOMMODATION
ANNUAL PRODUCTION 60,000 bottles
HECTARES UNDER VINE 16.00
VITICULTURE METHOD Certified Organic

The earliest record indicating the estate was used for agriculture goes back to the late 16th century, testifying to its productivity in the area. Today it's owned by Monica Rota and Giorgio Comotti, who chose Tuscany when they decided to change lifestyle and go into winemaking. Their selection is well-defined and precise, thanks to the couple's enthusiasm. They also produce walnuts, cherries, olive oil, and offer farmstay hospitality services. Their 2017 Vernaccia Hydra is an interesting wine with aromas of fruit, from apple to apricot, accompanied by herbaceous notes of mint and thyme. On the palate it proves flavorful and dynamic, with a nice finish that builds to a crescendo. Their 2015 Vernaccia Lyra offers up a nice variety of aromatic herbs and ripe fruit, especially peace. In the mouth it's lively and dynamic, generous, with a juicy, persistent finish. Their 2015 Vernaccia Ori Riserva features aromas of tea and orange.

| | |
|---|---|
| ○ Vernaccia di S. Gimignano Hydra '17 | ♟♟ 2* |
| ○ Vernaccia di San Gimignano Lyra '15 | ♟♟ 3 |
| ○ Vernaccia di San Gimignano Ori Ris. '15 | ♟♟ 3 |
| ● Antajr '14 | ♟ 4 |
| ● Chianti CS Caelum '16 | ♟ 2 |
| ● Chianti CS Drago Ris. '15 | ♟ 3 |
| ● San Gimignano Rosso Ares '14 | ♟ 4 |
| ● Chianti Colli Senesi Caelum '15 | ♟♟ 2* |
| ● Chianti Colli Senesi Drago Ris. '14 | ♟♟ 3 |
| ○ Vernaccia di S. Gimignano Ori Ris. '15 | ♟♟ 3 |
| ○ Vernaccia di S. Gimignano Ori Ris. '14 | ♟♟ 3 |

## Palazzo

LOC. PALAZZO, 144
53024 MONTALCINO [SI]
TEL. +39 0577849226
www.aziendapalazzo.it

CELLAR SALES
PRE-BOOKED VISITS
ANNUAL PRODUCTION 21,000 bottles
HECTARES UNDER VINE 4.00
VITICULTURE METHOD Certified Biodynamic

Purchased in 1983 by Cosimo Loia and his
wife Antonietta, Tenuta Palazzo is now run by
two brothers, Angelo and Elia. It is situated in
eastern Montalcino, an unusual territory
marked by elevations around 300 meters
and lean galestro and sandy soils from the
Eocene epoch. The range of wines, made
with Sangiovese, is almost unrecognizable
due to a dense and earthy expression. This
is furthered by their winemaking decisions:
the two Brunellos are matured in barriques
and large barrels, while the Rosso is
exclusively matured in Slavonian oak. Our
most recent tastings prove that it's a good
moment for Tenuta Palazzo's entire
selection. Their 2013 Brunello features light
fruit, forest shrubs, tree resins, while their
2013 Brunello stands out for its fresh,
Mediterranean sensations. It's just a bit
closed on the palate. Their 2012 Brunello
Riserva is even more classic, including the
occasional tertiary note, with topsoil and
spices anticipating a well-proportioned
palate brimming with flavor.

| | |
|---|---|
| ● Brunello di Montalcino '13 | ♟♟ 6 |
| ● Brunello di Montalcino Ris. '12 | ♟♟ 7 |
| ● Rosso di Montalcino '16 | ♟♟ 3 |
| ● Rosso di Montalcino '15 | ♟♟♟ 3* |
| ● Brunello di Montalcino '10 | ♟♟ 6 |
| ● Brunello di Montalcino '09 | ♟♟ 6 |
| ● Brunello di Montalcino '08 | ♟♟ 6 |
| ● Brunello di Montalcino '07 | ♟♟ 6 |
| ● Brunello di Montalcino '06 | ♟♟ 5 |
| ● Brunello di Montalcino Ris. '10 | ♟♟ 7 |
| ● Brunello di Montalcino Ris. '07 | ♟♟ 7 |
| ● Brunello di Montalcino Ris. '06 | ♟♟ 7 |
| ● Rosso di Montalcino '11 | ♟♟ 3 |
| ● Rosso di Montalcino '10 | ♟♟ 3 |
| ● Rosso di Montalcino '06 | ♟♟ 3 |

## Panizzi

LOC. SANTA MARGHERITA, 34
53037 SAN GIMIGNANO [SI]
TEL. +39 0577941576
www.panizzi.it

CELLAR SALES
PRE-BOOKED VISITS
ACCOMMODATION
ANNUAL PRODUCTION 210,000 bottles
HECTARES UNDER VINE 50.00

Giovanni Panizzi founded this farm in the late
1970s, near the Santa Margherita estate,
just outside the walls of San Gimignano. It
was the first winery to relaunch and promote
Vernaccia, continuing its growth in terms of
quality. Today it belongs to Simone Niccolai
who is showing intense activity. Currently, he
is increasing the hectares of vineyards and
expanding his range of wines. His selection
includes all the traditional wines, plus he has
added Pinot Nero to the list, for example. He
also produces extra virgin olive oil and
manages the farm holiday business. Their
2014 Vernaccia Riserva landed in our finals.
It's a gold-colored wine with vibrant aromas
of candied orange peel, medicinal herbs,
tree resin and ripe apple. In the mouth it
opens warm, balanced, juicy and elegant,
continuing in the same vein towards a long,
flavorful finish. Their 2016 Vernaccia Santa
Margherita also proved pleasant, with its
vegetal notes of aromatic herbs, marjoram,
and white fruit (apple and pear). On the
palate it's plush but generous, with nice
acidity conferring balance and dynamism.

| | |
|---|---|
| ○ Vernaccia di S. Gimignano Ris. '14 | ♟♟ 5 |
| ○ Evoè '16 | ♟♟ 4 |
| ○ Vernaccia di San Gimignano V. Santa Margherita '16 | ♟♟ 3 |
| ⊙ Ceraso Rosato '17 | ♟ 2 |
| ● Chianti CS Ris. '15 | ♟ 4 |
| ● San Gimignano Pinot Nero '16 | ♟ 2 |
| ○ Vernaccia di S. Gimignano '17 | ♟ 2 |
| ○ Vernaccia di S. Gimignano '16 | ♟♟ 2* |
| ○ Vernaccia di S. Gimignano Ris. '13 | ♟♟ 5 |
| ○ Vernaccia di S. Gimignano Ris. '12 | ♟♟ 5 |
| ○ Vernaccia di S. Gimignano Ris. '11 | ♟♟ 5 |
| ○ Vernaccia di S. Gimignano Ris. '10 | ♟♟ 5 |
| ○ Vernaccia di San Gimignano V. S. Margherita '15 | ♟♟ 3 |
| ○ Vernaccia di San Gimignano V. S. Margherita '14 | ♟♟ 3* |

# Parmoleto

LOC. MONTENERO D'ORCIA
POD. PARMOLETONE, 44
58040 CASTEL DEL PIANO [GR]
TEL. +39 0564954131
www.parmoleto.it

**CELLAR SALES**
**PRE-BOOKED VISITS**
**ACCOMMODATION AND RESTAURANT SERVICE**
**ANNUAL PRODUCTION** 22,000 bottles
**HECTARES UNDER VINE** 6.00

In the hills of Castel del Piano, just before Monte Amiata, the Sodi family cultivates its small vineyard and produces reliably good wines. When the Montecucco appellation was created they gave it their full support and threw themselves enthusiastically into promoting Sangiovese. Today the winery appears to have reached maturity. They produce wines with an interesting style that combines a traditional approach with some targeted modern forays, especially regarding the use of wood, which often takes a leading role. Their 2013 Montecucco Sangiovese Riserva is redolent of morello cherries, supported by citrusy notes and faint, earthy hints. On the palate it unfolds persistently and well-contrasted, with flavorful, spirited tannins. Their 2014 Montecucco Sangiovese is a bit more nuanced aromatically, with a palate that's still pleasantly fresh and balanced, with just a few gaps towards the end. Their 2015 Montecucco Sangiovese features a juicy, generous palate.

| | | |
|---|---|---|
| ● Montecucco Sangiovese Ris. '13 | ♟♟ | 3* |
| ● Montecucco Sangiovese '14 | ♟♟ | 3 |
| ● Montecucco Sangiovese '15 | ♟ | 3 |
| ● Montecucco Sangiovese '13 | ♟♟ | 3 |
| ● Montecucco Sangiovese '12 | ♟♟ | 3 |
| ● Montecucco Sangiovese '11 | ♟♟ | 3 |
| ● Montecucco Sangiovese Ris. '12 | ♟♟ | 3 |
| ● Montecucco Sangiovese Ris. '11 | ♟♟ | 3* |
| ● Montecucco Sangiovese Ris. '10 | ♟♟ | 3 |

# Tenuta La Parrina

FRAZ. ALBINIA
S.DA VICINALE DELLA PARRINA
58015 ORBETELLO [GR]
TEL. +39 0564862626
www.parrina.it

**CELLAR SALES**
**PRE-BOOKED VISITS**
**ACCOMMODATION AND RESTAURANT SERVICE**
**ANNUAL PRODUCTION** 100,000 bottles
**HECTARES UNDER VINE** 60.00
**SUSTAINABLE WINERY**

As both an estate and an appellation, Parrina is more than a winery. It is more aptly described as a farming project. The Spinola family have run it since the late 1800s and their brand holds considerable weight in the development of Maremma winemaking. The style of their wines is marked by a sober modernism, favoring in particular, drinkability and approachable aromas. Their extensive product portfolio includes ambitious wines that at times reach an absolute excellence. Their 2016 Muraccio is a solid red that stands out for its aromatic profile, with flowery fragrances accompanied by a nice combination of fruit, spices and smoky notes. On the palate it's pleasantly persistent, dense but also deep. Their 2017 Ansonica, however, really impressed with its aromas of flint and iodine, and a fresh palate that closes with a lovely, long, delicately salty note. Tre Bicchieri. Their 2015 Parrina Riserva is more austere, with the occasionally excessive oaky accent.

| | | |
|---|---|---|
| ○ Costa dell'Argentario Ansonica '17 | ♟♟♟ | 3* |
| ● Parrina Rosso Muraccio '16 | ♟♟ | 4 |
| ● Parrina Sangiovese Ris. '15 | ♟ | 5 |
| ○ Ansonica Costa dell'Argentario '16 | ♟♟ | 3 |
| ○ Costa dell'Argentario Ansonica '15 | ♟♟ | 3 |
| ● Parrina Merlot Radaia '15 | ♟♟ | 6 |
| ● Parrina Radaia '13 | ♟♟ | 6 |
| ● Parrina Rosso Muraccio '14 | ♟♟ | 3* |
| ● Parrina Sangiovese '16 | ♟♟ | 2* |
| ● Parrina Sangiovese '10 | ♟♟ | 4 |
| ○ Parrina Vermentino '16 | ♟♟ | 3 |

# Perazzeta

LOC. MONTENERO D'ORCIA
VIA DELLA PIAZZA
58040 CASTEL DEL PIANO [GR]
TEL. +39 3456537758
www.perazzeta.it

**CELLAR SALES**
**PRE-BOOKED VISITS**
**ANNUAL PRODUCTION** 100,000 bottles
**HECTARES UNDER VINE** 19.00

This winery in Montenero d'Orcia, purchased by the Narducci family in 2016, produces distinctive and well-crafted wines. They began production in 1998 and straightaway joined the Montecucco appellation. Their wines are made mostly with Sangiovese, but in the cellar they also work with Cabernet Sauvignon, Merlot, Syrah and Vermentino. Their style benefits from well-worked grapes and a measured mix of tradition and modernity. Maturation takes place in both barriques and large barrels, while fermentation is done entirely in steel. Their 2013 Montecucco Sangiovese Licurgo Riserva is still youthful, offering up fragrant aromas that aren't lacking in freshness. It's a sensation that reemerges on its lively palate, though the finish is a bit held back by toasty notes. Their 2014 Montecucco Sangiovese Terre dei Bocci does a nice job interpreting a difficult year, with its clean aromas and its graceful, savory palate.

| | |
|---|---|
| ● Montecucco Sangiovese Licurgo Ris. '13 | ▼▼ 5 |
| ● Montecucco Sangiovese Terre dei Bocci '14 | ▼▼ 3 |
| ● Syrah '16 | ▼ 4 |
| ● Montecucco Rosso Alfeno '15 | ♀♀ 2* |
| ● Montecucco Rosso Alfeno '14 | ♀♀ 2* |
| ● Montecucco Rosso Alfeno '12 | ♀♀ 2* |
| ● Montecucco Sangiovese Licurgo Ris. '12 | ♀♀ 4 |
| ● Montecucco Sangiovese Licurgo Ris. '11 | ♀♀ 4 |
| ● Montecucco Sangiovese Licurgo Ris. '09 | ♀♀ 5 |
| ○ Montecucco Vermentino '16 | ♀♀ 2* |

# Peteglia

LOC. PODERE PETEGLIA
FRAZ. MONTENERO D'ORCIA
58033 CASTEL DEL PIANO [GR]
TEL. +39 3498335438
www.peteglia.com

**CELLAR SALES**
**PRE-BOOKED VISITS**
**ACCOMMODATION AND RESTAURANT SERVICE**
**ANNUAL PRODUCTION** 30,000 bottles
**HECTARES UNDER VINE** 7.00

Owned by the Innocenti family, Peteglia is a classic example of a small, family-run, artisanal winery (there's an abundance of such producers in Montecucco). They cultivate six hectares of terrain, and produce about 15,000 bottles a year. Their wines, which are traditionally styled while also exhibiting nice personality, are made primarily with Sangiovese. Maturation is closely followed and carried out both in small wood barrels and large ones. Their 2013 Montecucco Sangiovese Riserva is truly a small gem of the territory, bringing together complexity and suppleness, freshness and generosity, savoriness and body. It closes with highly pleasant balsamic notes and fragrances of Mediterranean scrubland. Their 2016 Mezzodì, a monovarietal Sangiovese made with grapes from their youngest vineyards, also proved pleasant, with a fresh, relaxed palate and aromatic precision.

| | |
|---|---|
| ● Montecucco Sangiovese Ris. '13 | ▼▼ 5 |
| ● Maremma Toscana Sangiovese Mezzodì '16 | ▼▼ 2* |
| ● Montecucco Sangiovese '15 | ▼ 3 |
| ○ Montecucco Vermentino '17 | ▼ 2 |
| ● Montecucco Sangiovese '10 | ♀♀ 3 |
| ● Montecucco Sangiovese Ris. '10 | ♀♀ 4 |

# Petra

LOC. SAN LORENZO ALTO, 131
57028 SUVERETO [LI]
TEL. +39 0565845308
www.petrawine.it

**CELLAR SALES**
**PRE-BOOKED VISITS**
**ANNUAL PRODUCTION** 350,000 bottles
**HECTARES UNDER VINE** 94.00
**SUSTAINABLE WINERY**

This ancient land, with its thriving olive trees, Mediterranean scrub and vineyards, is the site of what has become a monument in winemaking architecture: the Petra winery. Brought to Tuscany by Vittorio Moretti -- following successes in Franciacorta -- it was designed by Mario Botta. Today, Francesco Moretti oversees wine production, using native and international varieties to make both monovarietals and harmonious blends. Their 2015 Petra confirmed their continued growth obtained Tre Bicchieri. It's a blend of Cabernet Sauvignon and Merlot with an intense, elegant aromatic profile of cherries and blackberries, then tertiary hints of tobacco and tanned leather adorned with spicy notes and licorice. On the palate it comes through decisive, full and dynamic, with well-distributed tannins and a long, savory finish. Their 2015 Quercegobbe, a monovarietal Merlot, features a multifaceted bouquet of fruit, vanilla and cloves. On the palate it proves docile, with the right density and an enjoyable finish.

| | |
|---|---|
| ● Petra Rosso '15 | ▼▼▼ 8 |
| ● Alto '15 | ▼▼ 6 |
| ● Potenti '15 | ▼▼ 6 |
| ● Quercegobbe '15 | ▼▼ 6 |
| ● Suvereto Hebo '16 | ▼▼ 3 |
| ● Colle al Fico '15 | ▼ 6 |
| ○ La Balena '16 | ▼ 6 |
| ● Petra Rosso '14 | ♀♀♀ 8 |
| ● Petra Rosso '13 | ♀♀♀ 8 |
| ● Petra Rosso '12 | ♀♀♀ 8 |
| ● Petra Rosso '11 | ♀♀♀ 8 |
| ● Petra Rosso '04 | ♀♀♀ 7 |
| ● Alto '14 | ♀♀ 6 |
| ● Potenti '14 | ♀♀ 6 |

# ★Fattoria Petrolo

FRAZ. MERCATALE VALDARNO
VIA PETROLO, 30
52021 BUCINE [AR]
TEL. +39 0559911322
www.petrolo.it

**PRE-BOOKED VISITS**
**ACCOMMODATION**
**ANNUAL PRODUCTION** 85,000 bottles
**HECTARES UNDER VINE** 31.00

This estate was purchased just after World War II by the grandfather of the current owner, Luca Sanjust. It extends across the Bucine territory in the so-called Val d'Arno di Sopra, one of Tuscany's historic quality wine growing areas. In the mid-1980s, vineyard renewal and modernization of the cellar marked the beginning of a new phase where the aim was to create wines with character closely linked to the territory. In the vision there was also room for new experiments, such as fermenting and maturing certain wines in terracotta amphorae. Their 2015 Galatrona, a monovarietal Merlot, offers up fruity notes of blackberries and cherry, with hints of Mediterranean scrubland and herbs. On the palate it comes through soft, with silky tannins balanced by acidity. Their 2016 Boggina A, a Sangiovese aged in amphoras, offers up fresh, lively aromas, buoyant hints of cherry and a minty notes, all for a clean, appetizing finish.

| | |
|---|---|
| ● Bòggina A '16 | ▼▼ 7 |
| ● Bòggina C '15 | ▼▼ 7 |
| ● Galatrona '15 | ▼▼ 8 |
| ○ Bòggina B '16 | ▼▼ 6 |
| ● Bòggina C '16 | ▼▼ 7 |
| ● Torrione '16 | ▼▼ 5 |
| ● Galatrona '12 | ♀♀♀ 8 |
| ● Galatrona '11 | ♀♀♀ 8 |
| ● Galatrona '10 | ♀♀♀ 8 |
| ● Galatrona '09 | ♀♀♀ 8 |
| ● Galatrona '08 | ♀♀♀ 8 |
| ● Torrione '11 | ♀♀♀ 5 |
| ● Valdarno di Sopra Galatrona '14 | ♀♀♀ 8 |
| ● Valdarno di Sopra Galatrona '13 | ♀♀♀ 8 |

# ★Piaggia

Loc. Poggetto
via Cegoli, 47
59016 Poggio a Caiano [PO]
Tel. +39 0558705401
www.piaggia.com

**CELLAR SALES**
**PRE-BOOKED VISITS**
**ANNUAL PRODUCTION** 75,000 bottles
**HECTARES UNDER VINE** 15.00

The Piaggia farm is situated in the
Carmignano production area. The original
site was purchased in the mid-1970s by
Mauro Vannucci, who was actually looking
for land on which to build a house, but
the plot he chose included a vineyard, so
he rented it out. Fifteen years later he
began to tend to the vines and wines
himself. Mauro's daughter Silvia runs
the winery today, making her wines
according to appellation regulations, but
experimenting as well, for example, with
her monovarietal Cabernet Franc. Once
again their 2015 Camignano Riserva
confirms its top marks and brings home
Tre Bicchieri, thanks to an aromatic
bouquet of balsamic notes, blackberries
and blackcurrant, and sweet spices. Its
body is creamy, elegant, delicate, savory,
taut, fresh and highly drinkable. Their
2016 Carmignano Il Sasso features aromas
ranging from Mediterranean scrubland to
ink, lively fragrances of blackcurrant and
blackberries. It opens well on the palate,
elegant, with nice acidity, and crisp,
well-integrated tannins.

| | |
|---|---|
| ● Carmignano Ris. '15 | ♟♟♟ 6 |
| ● Carmignano Il Sasso '16 | ♟♟ 4 |
| ● Carmignano Ris. '14 | ♟♟♟ 6 |
| ● Carmignano Ris. '13 | ♟♟♟ 6 |
| ● Carmignano Ris. '12 | ♟♟♟ 6 |
| ● Carmignano Ris. '11 | ♟♟♟ 6 |
| ● Carmignano Ris. '08 | ♟♟♟ 5 |
| ● Poggio de' Colli '11 | ♟♟♟ 7 |
| ● Poggio de' Colli '10 | ♟♟♟ 6 |
| ● Carmignano Ris. '10 | ♟♟ 6 |
| ● Poggio de' Colli '15 | ♟♟ 8 |
| ● Poggio de' Colli '14 | ♟♟ 7 |

# Piancornello

Loc. Piancornello
53024 Montalcino [SI]
Tel. +39 0577844105
www.piancornello.it

**CELLAR SALES**
**PRE-BOOKED VISITS**
**ANNUAL PRODUCTION** 50,000 bottles
**HECTARES UNDER VINE** 10.00

This winery founded by the Monaci family
takes its name from the Piancornello
volcanic hill, in a famous district in southern
Montalcino. A unique area with steep, rocky
slopes overlooking the Orcia river and Asso
stream, it is sheltered by Monte Amiata. The
Mediterranean climate and 250-meter
elevations complete the picture. We expect,
and we find energetic and full-bodied
Brunellos that are deliciously 'southern'.
They are made in steel and wood, with
maturation mostly in barriques and
mid-sized casks. As often happens during
late harvests, Piancornello's Sangiovese
turn out to be among the best in
Montalcino. And that's the case with their
2013 Brunello, with its aromas of morello
cherries, cloves and truffle, and its
trademark, sunny nuances and contrasts.
On the palate it proves close-knit in flavor
and energy, which circumscribe generous
alcohol and a solid tannic weave. Their
2012 Riserva is also excellent.

| | |
|---|---|
| ● Brunello di Montalcino '13 | ♟♟♟ 6 |
| ● Brunello di Montalcino Ris. '12 | ♟♟ 7 |
| ● Rosso di Montalcino '16 | ♟ 3 |
| ● Brunello di Montalcino '10 | ♟♟♟ 6 |
| ● Brunello di Montalcino '06 | ♟♟♟ 6 |
| ● Brunello di Montalcino '99 | ♟♟♟ 6 |
| ● Brunello di Montalcino '12 | ♟♟ 6 |
| ● Brunello di Montalcino '11 | ♟♟ 6 |
| ● Brunello di Montalcino '09 | ♟♟ 6 |
| ● Brunello di Montalcino '08 | ♟♟ 6 |
| ● Brunello di Montalcino '07 | ♟♟ 6 |
| ● Brunello di Montalcino Ris. '06 | ♟♟ 6 |
| ● Brunello di Montalcino Ris. '04 | ♟♟ 6 |
| ● Rosso di Montalcino '15 | ♟♟ 3 |
| ● Rosso di Montalcino '11 | ♟♟ 3 |

# Piandaccoli

VIA PAGANELLE, 7
50041 CALENZANO [FI]
TEL. +39 0550750005
www.piandaccoli.it

**CELLAR SALES**
**PRE-BOOKED VISITS**
**ANNUAL PRODUCTION** 100,000 bottles
**HECTARES UNDER VINE** 20.00

The names Barsaglina, Foglia Tonda, Mammolo and Pugnitello don't mean much to most people, but these are just some of the grapes native to Renaissance Tuscany. Giampaolo Bruni (the soul, as well as the owner, of the winery), aims to promote them in his daily work in the vineyards and cellar, along with Colorino, Malvasia and Sangiovese, planted with 11 different clones. This all began with a kind of research on the origins of vine growing on the estate, which was purchased by the current owner's father-in-law in the 1950s. Their 2015 Foglia Tonda del Rinascimento made it to our finals, with its aromas of green pepper joined with fresh spices, like ginger, then notes of licorice and a potpourri of dried flowers. On the palate it's delicate and dynamic, with a contained but succulent body. Their 2014 Vin Santo Occhio di Pernice offers up aromas of nuts and dried fruit, like almonds, figs and dates. On the palate it proves velvety, generous and dense. Their 2015 Pugnitello is complex on the nose, with a firm, rich body.

| | | |
|---|---|---|
| ● Foglia Tonda del Rinascimento '15 | ♟♟ | 6 |
| ● Pugnitello del Rinascimento '15 | ♟♟ | 6 |
| ○ Vin Santo del Chianti Occhio di Pernice '14 | ♟♟ | 6 |
| ● Barsaglina del Rinascimento '15 | ♟ | 6 |
| ● Chianti Cosmus Ris. '15 | ♟ | 2 |
| ● Inprimis '15 | ♟ | 3 |
| ● Chianti Cosmus Ris. '14 | ♀♀ | 2* |
| ● Foglia Tonda del Rinascimento '13 | ♀♀ | 6 |
| ● Maiorem '13 | ♀♀ | 5 |
| ● Maiorem '12 | ♀♀ | 5 |
| ● Pugnitello del Rinascimento '13 | ♀♀ | 6 |

# Pianirossi

LOC. PORRONA
POD. SANTA GENOVEFFA, 1
58044 CINIGIANO [GR]
TEL. +39 0564990573
www.pianirossi.it

**CELLAR SALES**
**PRE-BOOKED VISITS**
**ACCOMMODATION AND RESTAURANT SERVICE**
**ANNUAL PRODUCTION** 50,000 bottles
**HECTARES UNDER VINE** 14.00

In the scenic Porrona hills near Cinigiano, Stefano Sincini has steered his winery towards a stylistically modern approach, experimenting with international blends rather than local varieties. His decision has given rise recently to interesting and well-made wines. Although he is still following the same course, a diverging path with his Montecucco appellation wines has also shown good results, highlighted by an earthy, rich-flavored style and uncommon freshness. The work done they've done with Sangiovese has given rise to two notable wines, both made with the crown prince of Tuscany's grapes. Their 2016 Montecucco Rosso Sidus offers up fresh aromas of fruit, spices and slightly smoky notes. On the palate it proves well-balanced and persistent, with a savory, assertive finish. Their 2015 Montecucco Sangiovese La Fonte is also well-made, opting for more pronounced oak and riper fruit.

| | | |
|---|---|---|
| ● Montecucco Rosso Sidus '16 | ♟♟ | 2* |
| ● Montecucco Sangiovese La Fonte '15 | ♟♟ | 5 |
| ● Montecucco Rosso Sidus '15 | ♀♀ | 2* |
| ● Montecucco Sidus '14 | ♀♀ | 2* |
| ● Montecucco Sidus '13 | ♀♀ | 2* |
| ● Montecucco Sidus '11 | ♀♀ | 4 |
| ● Pianirossi '12 | ♀♀ | 6 |
| ● Pianirossi '11 | ♀♀ | 6 |
| ● Solus '14 | ♀♀ | 3 |
| ● Solus '12 | ♀♀ | 3 |
| ● Solus '11 | ♀♀ | 4 |

## Fattoria di Piazzano

VIA DI PIAZZANO, 5
50053 EMPOLI [FI]
TEL. +39 0571994032
www.fattoriadipiazzano.it

CELLAR SALES
PRE-BOOKED VISITS
ANNUAL PRODUCTION 90,000 bottles
HECTARES UNDER VINE 33.00
SUSTAINABLE WINERY

Otello Bettarini is an industrialist from Prato who fell in love with place and decided to move here with his family. And so it was that Fattoria di Piazzano was founded 70 years ago. Their agricultural business was developed by his grandson Riccardo, who began personally overseeing the vineyards and gradually improving the quality of their wines. Another shift came in the late 1990s, when the current management team, Riccardo's children Riccardo, Rolando and Ilaria officially took over. Their 2016 Syrah put in a nice performance, with its varied aromas of pepper, cloves accompanied by lively fruit, blackcurrant and cherry, then tertiary notes of fur. On the palate it opens supple, with nice consistence and a tannic presence that isn't excessive, giving way to a flavorful finish. Their 2016 Colorino offers up refreshing aromas with plums and blueberries at the fore, then forest undergrowth and minty notes. In the mouth it proves elegant, with delicate tannins and lengthy flavor.

| | |
|---|---|
| ● Colorino '16 | ▼▼ 6 |
| ● Syrah '16 | ▼▼ 5 |
| ● Blend 1 '16 | ▼ 5 |
| ● Chianti '16 | ▼ 2 |
| ● Chianti Rio Camerata '16 | ▼ 4 |
| ● Chianti Rio Camerata Ris. '15 | ▼ 5 |
| ☉ Rosato '17 | ▼ 2 |
| ● Blend 1 '15 | ♀♀ 4 |
| ● Chianti Rio Camerata Ris. '07 | ♀♀ 3 |
| ● Messidoro '13 | ♀♀ 1* |
| ● Piazzano Syrah '09 | ♀♀ 5 |
| ● Syrah '15 | ♀♀ 4 |
| ● Syrah '11 | ♀♀ 4 |
| ● Ventoso '13 | ♀♀ 1* |

## Tenute Piccini

LOC. PIAZZOLE, 25
53011 CASTELLINA IN CHIANTI [SI]
TEL. +39 057754011
www.tenutepiccini.it

ANNUAL PRODUCTION 15,000,000 bottles
HECTARES UNDER VINE 470.00
VITICULTURE METHOD Certified Organic

The Piccini family got its start in winemaking back in 1992, with a plot of just seven hectares. Today the vast estate is managed by Mario, Martina and Elisa, who've adopted a dynamic, modern management style. In total they oversee five wineries: Toscana Valiano (in Chianti Classico), Tenuta Moraia (in Maremma), Villa al Cortile (in Montalcino), Torre Mora (in Sicily), and Regio Cantina (in Basilicata), as well as sales for United Winegrowers of Chianti Geografico. Their 2015 Chianti Classico Valiano won over our tasters with its tertiary aromas of tar, earth and forest undergrowth across a background of cherry preserves. On the palate it's of medium weight, lean, elegant and delicate with a nice, rising finish. Their Poggio Teo is also interesting, with its aromatic profile that opts more for spices and balsamic notes, and its potent body, with well-integrated tannins. Their enjoyable 2015 Sasso al Poggio, a blend of Sangiovese, Merlot and Cabernet Sauvignon, is redolent of enticing fruit and spicy accents. On the palate it proves subtle and fresh.

| | |
|---|---|
| ● Chianti Cl. Valiano '15 | ▼▼ 3* |
| ● Brunello di Montalcino Tenuta Poggio al Castellare '13 | ▼▼ 6 |
| ● Chianti Cl. Contessa di Radda '15 | ▼▼ 2* |
| ● Chianti Cl. Valiano Poggio Teo '15 | ▼▼ 4 |
| ● Il Pacchia '15 | ▼▼ 2* |
| ● Sasso al Poggio '15 | ▼▼ 3 |
| ● Chianti Classico Montegiachi Ris. '14 | ▼ 2 |
| ● Bolgheri Gattabuia Tenuta Moraia '14 | ♀♀ 3 |
| ● Bolgheri Rosso Pietracupa Tenuta Moraia '12 | ♀♀ 3 |
| ○ Calasera Vermentino Tenuta Moraia '16 | ♀♀ 2* |
| ● Vino in Musica '10 | ♀♀ 4 |
| ● Vino in Musica '08 | ♀♀ 4 |

# Pietroso

LOC. PIETROSO, 257
53024 MONTALCINO [SI]
TEL. +39 0577848573
www.pietroso.it

**CELLAR SALES**
**PRE-BOOKED VISITS**
**ANNUAL PRODUCTION** 30,000 bottles
**HECTARES UNDER VINE** 5.00

Gianni Pignattai, his wife Cecilia and their children Andrea and Gloria cultivate four vineyard plots grown entirely with Sangiovese grapes. The Colombaiolo estate is situated in the south, while the Fornello and Montosoli plots -- whose grapes produce the IGT wine of the same name -- are in northern Montalcino. Finally, next to the cellar, we come to Pietroso with its lean soils and vertiginous slopes. The winery produces one of the most original selections in the area by virtue of its expressive naturalness and rich-flavored density. Pietroso's pair of Sangioveses are always among the best in Montalcino, and their recent releases are no exception. Their 2016 Rosso exhibits a lush character in its combination of red fruit, spices and smoky hints. Their 2013 Brunello calls up oregano, tree resin and candied citrus, anticipating a linear, racy and extremely charming palate.

# Pieve Santo Stefano

LOC. SARDINI
55100 LUCCA
TEL. +39 0583394115
www.pievedisantostefano.com

**CELLAR SALES**
**PRE-BOOKED VISITS**
**ACCOMMODATION**
**ANNUAL PRODUCTION** 45,000 bottles
**HECTARES UNDER VINE** 10.60
**SUSTAINABLE WINERY**

Francesco Bogazzi and Antoine Hiriz's winery is moving forward with comfortingly consistent quality. Their style is well-defined and offers up elegant, balanced wines with a good measure of pleasantness and uncommon drinkability. The main grape varieties grown are Sangiovese and Ciliegiolo, alongside Cabernet Franc, Merlot and Syrah. With unforced winemaking and maturation done in large and small barrels, their style holds itself apart from tired, modern winemaking fashion. Their 2015 Ludovico Sardini features precise aromas of small red fruits and spices, with delicate balsamic hints. These anticipate a flavorful palate that isn't lacking in finesse, even if the finish sees a bit too much oak. Their 2015 Villa Sardini is a fresh, relaxed wine, delicate and fragrant on the nose, with a soft, well-balanced palate.

| | |
|---|---|
| ● Brunello di Montalcino '13 | ♟♟ 6 |
| ● Rosso di Montalcino '16 | ♟♟ 4 |
| ● Brunello di Montalcino '09 | ♟♟♟ 6 |
| ● Brunello di Montalcino '12 | ♟♟ 6 |
| ● Brunello di Montalcino '11 | ♟♟ 6 |
| ● Brunello di Montalcino '10 | ♟♟ 6 |
| ● Brunello di Montalcino '08 | ♟♟ 6 |
| ● Brunello di Montalcino '04 | ♟♟ 5 |
| ● Brunello di Montalcino Ris. '10 | ♟♟ 6 |
| ● Rosso di Montalcino '15 | ♟♟ 4 |
| ● Rosso di Montalcino '14 | ♟♟ 4 |
| ● Rosso di Montalcino '13 | ♟♟ 4 |
| ● Rosso di Montalcino '12 | ♟♟ 4 |
| ● Rosso di Montalcino '11 | ♟♟ 3* |
| ● Rosso di Montalcino '07 | ♟♟ 3 |

| | |
|---|---|
| ● Colline Lucchesi Ludovico Sardini '15 | ♟♟ 4 |
| ● Colline Lucchesi Ludovico Sardini '13 | ♟♟ 4 |
| ● Colline Lucchesi Ludovico Sardini '12 | ♟♟ 4 |
| ● Colline Lucchesi Ludovico Sardini '11 | ♟♟ 2* |
| ● Colline Lucchesi Villa Sardini '16 | ♟♟ 2* |
| ● Colline Lucchesi Villa Sardini '15 | ♟♟ 2* |
| ● Colline Lucchesi Villa Sardini '13 | ♟♟ 2* |
| ● Colline Lucchesi Villa Sardini '12 | ♟♟ 2* |
| ● Lippo '15 | ♟♟ 4 |
| ● Lippo '14 | ♟♟ 4 |
| ● Lippo '11 | ♟♟ 3 |

# Pinino

LOC. PININO, 327
53024 MONTALCINO [SI]
TEL. +39 0577849381
www.pinino.com

**CELLAR SALES**
**PRE-BOOKED VISITS**
**ANNUAL PRODUCTION** 90,000 bottles
**HECTARES UNDER VINE** 16.00

The Pinino farm was founded by a notary,
Tito Costanti, in the second half of the
nineteenth century. It was subsequently
purchased by an Austrian couple, Andrea
and Hannes Gamon, and a Spanish couple,
Max and Silvia Hernandez, in 2003. The
estate is situated at the foot of the
Montosoli hill, an important center in
northern Montalcino for making Brunello
with Sangiovese grapes. Their winery
makes four versions: Pinino 'vintage',
ClanDestino, Cupio and Pinone Riserva, all
of which exhibit a joyously wild nature,
linked in part to the type of wood used for
maturation. Pinino has muscled its way to
becoming one of Montalcino's top
producers thanks to the outstanding
performance of its wines. In particular their
2016 Rosso stands out for its coastal
aromas and a surprising touch of 'Pinot'
that leads its subtle, racy palate. Their
2013 Brunello sees greater aromatic
breadth (dried flowers, herbal teas) and
structure, though it shares the same,
delicately salty pluck.

| | |
|---|---|
| ● Brunello di Montalcino '13 | 🍷🍷 6 |
| ● Rosso di Montalcino '16 | 🍷🍷 3* |
| ● Brunello di Montalcino Cupio '13 | 🍷🍷 5 |
| ● Brunello di Montalcino Pinone Ris. '12 | 🍷🍷 7 |
| ● Brunello di Montalcino '11 | 🍷🍷 7 |
| ● Brunello di Montalcino '10 | 🍷🍷 6 |
| ● Brunello di Montalcino '09 | 🍷🍷 6 |
| ● Brunello di Montalcino '04 | 🍷🍷 6 |
| ● Brunello di Montalcino Clandestino '04 | 🍷🍷 6 |
| ● Brunello di Montalcino Pinino '07 | 🍷🍷 6 |
| ● Brunello di Montalcino Pinone Ris. '10 | 🍷🍷 8 |
| ● Brunello di Montalcino Pinone Ris. '07 | 🍷🍷 7 |
| ● Brunello di Montalcino Pinone Ris. '06 | 🍷🍷 7 |
| ● Brunello di Montalcino Pinone Ris. '04 | 🍷🍷 8 |
| ● Rosso di Montalcino '11 | 🍷🍷 3 |

# Podere 414

FRAZ. MONTIANO
LOC. MAIANO LAVACCHIO, 10
58051 MAGLIANO IN TOSCANA [GR]
TEL. +39 0564507818
www.podere414.it

**CELLAR SALES**
**ANNUAL PRODUCTION** 150,000 bottles
**HECTARES UNDER VINE** 23.00
**VITICULTURE METHOD** Certified Organic

Simone Castelli set up his winery in 1998,
betting from the start on Maremma and
the Morellino di Scansano appellation. The
name of the winery is the number
assigned to the farm in the 1960s by local
Maremma authorities when they divided
up large farming estates. It underlines the
historical bond between the winery and
local events, and this connection is evident
in the style of their wines. Pure, with
personality, and using only anciently
cultivated local varieties, Sangiovese takes
the leading role. They submitted a pair of
wines that privilege the freshness and
drinkability of Sangiovese, in its most
approachable form. Their 2016 Badilante
offers up fragrant aromas of violet and
cherry, with the occasional earthy note and
slightly citrusy touch. On the palate it's
delicate and steady, with a savory,
assertive finish. Their 2016 Morellino di
Scansano features more nuanced, and
somewhat less vibrant aromas, but in the
mouth it strikes an impressive balance
between sweetness and acidity, which only
amplifies its pleasantness.

| | |
|---|---|
| ● Badilante '16 | 🍷🍷 3 |
| ● Aleatico Passito '14 | 🍷🍷 7 |
| ● Aleatico Passito '13 | 🍷🍷 7 |
| ● Badilante '15 | 🍷🍷 3 |
| ● Morellino di Scansano '14 | 🍷🍷 3 |
| ● Morellino di Scansano '13 | 🍷🍷 3 |
| ● Morellino di Scansano '12 | 🍷🍷 3 |
| ☉ Rosato Flower Power '15 | 🍷🍷 2* |

# Podere Le Bèrne

LOC. CERVOGNANO
VIA POGGIO GOLO, 7
53045 MONTEPULCIANO [SI]
TEL. +39 0578767328
www.leberne.it

**CELLAR SALES**
**ANNUAL PRODUCTION** 25,000 bottles
**HECTARES UNDER VINE** 6.00

Character and quality in Le Berne wines is certainly nothing new for Nobile di Montepulciano connoisseurs. It only confirms that the Natalini family winery is one of the most noteworthy in Montepulciano. The estate was founded in the 1960s to produce wine for the family's consumption, but La Berne witnessed a drastic change in the mid 1990s, thanks to Andrea Natalini. Their vineyards are situated in Cervognano, which is one of the best vinegrowing areas, guaranteeing the quality of the winery's traditional style. Their 2015 Nobile di Montepulciano, certainly one of their best yet, is an intriguing wine right from the outset, with its aromas of fruit accompanied by fresh flowers, hints of flint and minty whiffs. In the mouth it demonstrates a certain degree of structure, though the palate proves supple, with nicely spirited tannins and acidity providing length, all the way to its crisp, well-balanced finish. Their 2016 Affronto is an enjoyable blend of Colorino and Mammolo, though it's just a bit lacking in complexity.

| | |
|---|---|
| ● Nobile di Montepulciano '15 | 🍷🍷🍷 3* |
| ● L'Affronto '16 | 🍷 2 |
| ● Rosso di Montepulciano '17 | 🍷 2 |
| ● Nobile di Montepulciano '11 | 🍷🍷🍷 3* |
| ● Nobile di Montepulciano '12 | 🍷🍷 3* |
| ● Nobile di Montepulciano Ris. '12 | 🍷🍷 5 |
| ● Nobile di Montepulciano Ris. '11 | 🍷🍷 5 |
| ● Nobile di Montepulciano Ris. '10 | 🍷🍷 5 |
| ● Rosso di Montepulciano '16 | 🍷🍷 2* |
| ○ Vin Santo di Montepulciano Ada '07 | 🍷🍷 5 |

# Poggerino

LOC. POGGERINO, 6
53017 RADDA IN CHIANTI [SI]
TEL. +39 0577738958
www.poggerino.com

**CELLAR SALES**
**PRE-BOOKED VISITS**
**ACCOMMODATION**
**ANNUAL PRODUCTION** 60,000 bottles
**HECTARES UNDER VINE** 12.20
**VITICULTURE METHOD** Certified Organic

The Poggerino winery is run by brother-and-sister team, Piero and Benedetta Lanza. Their wines are highly competitive in the Radda Chianti subzone in terms of Chianti Classicos that combine texture, density and elegance. Here they produce reds with a judiciously modern temperament. Their wines blend classic attributes of the area with delicate fullness and roundness. The vineyards are cultivated under organic management, and cellar maturation is entrusted to barriques and mid-sized casks. Their 2015 Chianti Classico Bugialla Riserva offers highly concentrated aromas of fruit smoky notes on the nose, anticipating an similarly full-bodied palate, that doesn't seem to unwind completely. Their 2015 Chianti Classico is also full and round, with a palate that tends towards size and depth. These characteristics are even more pronounced in their 2015 Prima Materia, a blend of Sangiovese and Merlot.

| | |
|---|---|
| ● Chianti Cl. Bugialla Ris. '15 | 🍷🍷 6 |
| ● Chianti Cl. '15 | 🍷🍷 4 |
| ● Primamateria '15 | 🍷 5 |
| ● Chianti Cl. Bugialla Ris. '13 | 🍷🍷🍷 5 |
| ● Chianti Cl. Bugialla Ris. '12 | 🍷🍷🍷 5 |
| ● Chianti Cl. Bugialla Ris. '09 | 🍷🍷🍷 5 |
| ● Chianti Cl. Bugialla Ris. '08 | 🍷🍷🍷 5 |
| ● Chianti Cl. Ris. '90 | 🍷🍷🍷 4* |
| ● Primamateria '01 | 🍷🍷🍷 5 |
| ● Chianti Cl. '13 | 🍷🍷 4 |
| ● Chianti Cl. Bugialla Ris. '14 | 🍷🍷 6 |
| ⊙ Spumante M. Cl. Sangiovese '11 | 🍷🍷 5 |

## Poggio al Tesoro

FRAZ. BOLGHERI
VIA BOLGHERESE, 189B
57022 CASTAGNETO CARDUCCI [LI]
TEL. +39 0565773051
www.poggioaltesoro.it

CELLAR SALES
PRE-BOOKED VISITS
ANNUAL PRODUCTION 377,000 bottles
HECTARES UNDER VINE 67.50

Owned by the Allegrini group, this Bolgheri winery is making its mark as a prestigious estate and one of the fastest growing in the area. The vineyards are planted on mixed soils, ranging from stony clay to exquisitely sandy. Their wines are consistently aromatic and show a clear-cut style and interpretation with each new vintage. At the same time they remain faithful to the territory and their vision. Their Bolgheri Superiore Sondraia just keeps getting better. The 2015 proves excellent thanks to a perfect aromatic combination of red and black fruit, lovely toasty notes that call up spices and Mediterranean herbs accompanied by balsamic flashes and a pleasantly 'green' streak. Their other reds also impressed, with a special mention for their 2017 Vermentino SoloSole, a succulent, citrusy and delicately aromatic wine.

## ★Poggio Antico

LOC. POGGIO ANTICO
53024 MONTALCINO [SI]
TEL. +39 0577848044
www.poggioantico.com

CELLAR SALES
PRE-BOOKED VISITS
RESTAURANT SERVICE
ANNUAL PRODUCTION 120,000 bottles
HECTARES UNDER VINE 32.00

Poggio Antico, an historic winery situated in western Montalcino, is undergoing a transition right now. Belgian holding, AtlasInvest, has recently purchased it from Paola Godler and Alberto Montefiori, turning over the management to Federico Trost, with Pier Giuseppe D'Alessandro overseeing the vineyards and cellar. The austere elegance that has always distinguished the winery's three Brunellos, matured in both Slavonian oak (for 'vintage' and 'Riserva') and mid-sized casks (for the Altero selection) persists. 2013 turned out to be an 'old school' vintage for their Brunello di Montalcino, a wine that led the producer's selection during our tastings. Exuberant fruit, clear balsamic notes, citrusy whiffs emerge on the nose, while on the palate a somewhat lean body is compensated for by commendable extraction and brilliant savoriness. Their Altero is no less aromatically vivid, though it comes across as a bit dry and hurried on the palate.

| | |
|---|---|
| ● Bolgheri Rosso Sup. Sondraia '15 | ▼▼▼ 7 |
| ● Bolgheri Rosso Il Seggio '15 | ▼▼ 4 |
| ○ Bolgheri Vermentino Solosole '17 | ▼▼ 4 |
| ● Mediterra '15 | ▼▼ 3 |
| ☉ Bolgheri Rosato Cassiopea '17 | ▼ 3 |
| ● Bolgheri Sup. Sondraia '14 | ♀♀♀ 5 |
| ● Bolgheri Sup. Sondraia '13 | ♀♀♀ 5 |
| ● Bolgheri Sup. Sondraia '11 | ♀♀♀ 5 |
| ● Bolgheri Sup. Sondraia '10 | ♀♀♀ 5 |
| ● Dedicato a Walter '12 | ♀♀♀ 7 |
| ● Dedicato a Walter '09 | ♀♀♀ 7 |
| ☉ Bolgheri Rosato Cassiopea '13 | ♀♀ 2* |
| ● Bolgheri Sup. Dedicato a Walter '13 | ♀♀ 7 |
| ● Mediterra '14 | ♀♀ 3* |

| | |
|---|---|
| ● Brunello di Montalcino '13 | ▼▼ 8 |
| ● Brunello di Montalcino Altero '13 | ▼▼ 8 |
| ● Rosso di Montalcino '16 | ▼▼ 5 |
| ● Brunello di Montalcino '05 | ♀♀♀ 7 |
| ● Brunello di Montalcino '88 | ♀♀♀ 7 |
| ● Brunello di Montalcino '85 | ♀♀♀ 7 |
| ● Brunello di Montalcino Altero '09 | ♀♀♀ 7 |
| ● Brunello di Montalcino Altero '07 | ♀♀♀ 8 |
| ● Brunello di Montalcino Altero '06 | ♀♀♀ 8 |
| ● Brunello di Montalcino Altero '04 | ♀♀♀ 8 |
| ● Brunello di Montalcino Altero '99 | ♀♀♀ 8 |
| ● Brunello di Montalcino Ris. '01 | ♀♀♀ 7 |
| ● Brunello di Montalcino Ris. '85 | ♀♀♀ 7 |
| ● Brunello di Montalcino '12 | ♀♀ 8 |
| ● Brunello di Montalcino Altero '12 | ♀♀ 8 |

## Poggio Bonelli

VIA DELL'ARBIA, 2
53019 CASTELNUOVO BERARDENGA [SI]
TEL. +39 057756661
www.poggiobonelli.it

CELLAR SALES
PRE-BOOKED VISITS
ACCOMMODATION
ANNUAL PRODUCTION 125,000 bottles
HECTARES UNDER VINE 87.00

This estate belongs to Montepaschi di
Siena, which also owns another winery in
Castelnuovo Berardenga: Villa Chigi
Saracini. Their vineyards are situated in
southern Chianti Classico, in an area that
produces wines with particular fullness and
power. The winery is able to convey these
traits faithfully, despite a sometimes
non-marginal use of small oak casks. Their
range displays consistent drinkability and
freshness, and often reaches levels of
excellence. Their 2016 Cretum, a blend of
Sangiovese, Merlot and Cabernet
Sauvignon exhibits nice overall balance. On
the nose vibrant, fruity aromas emerge,
adorned by spicy hints, tobacco and
chocolate. On the palate it proves balanced,
with a nice development towards a lovely,
fruity finish. Their 2015 Chianti Classico
Riserva is a solid, well-made wine with
complex aromas and a somewhat
generous, savory palate.

| | | |
|---|---|---|
| ● Chianti Cl. Ris. '15 | ♥♥ | 5 |
| ● Cretum '16 | ♥♥ | 2* |
| ● Chianti Cl. '15 | ♥ | 3 |
| ● Poggiassai '11 | ♡♡♡ | 6 |
| ● Poggiassai '10 | ♡♡♡ | 6 |
| ● Poggiassai '08 | ♡♡♡ | 5 |
| ● Poggiassai '07 | ♡♡♡ | 5 |
| ● Poggiassai '06 | ♡♡♡ | 5 |
| ● Tramonto d'Oca '10 | ♡♡♡ | 5 |
| ● Chianti Cl. '14 | ♡♡ | 3 |
| ● Chianti Cl. Ris. '13 | ♡♡ | 5 |
| ● Chianti Villa Chigi Saracini '15 | ♡♡ | 3 |

## ★Poggio di Sotto

FRAZ. CASTELNUOVO DELL'ABATE
LOC. POGGIO DI SOTTO
53024 MONTALCINO [SI]
TEL. +39 0577835502
www.collemassari.it

CELLAR SALES
PRE-BOOKED VISITS
ANNUAL PRODUCTION 30,000 bottles
HECTARES UNDER VINE 16.00
VITICULTURE METHOD Certified Organic
SUSTAINABLE WINERY

Poggio di Sotto is a benchmark in
Montalcino, based on the quality and style
of their Brunellos. This estate founded by
Piero Palmucci has been taken over in
total by the Tipa family, including the
sloping plots in Castelnuovo dell'Abate (in
the southeast), which nestles between the
Orcia river and Monte Amiata at 450
meters above sea level, on clay and
galestro soils. Their classy, well-structured
and airy Sangioveses mature mostly in
3000-liter Slavonian oak barrels. This
year Poggio di Sotto's selection proved
to be among the best nationally. It's
almost impossible to choose between
their 2015 Rosso, a symphony of purity
(pomegranate, flowers and herbs), and the
graceful and marine 2013 Brunello, a
delicately, sweetly salty wine. We were
also enchanted by their 2012 Riserva,
with its notes of wild strawberries, mint,
pink pepper and an etheric whiff that
immeasurably lengthens its deep palate.

| | | |
|---|---|---|
| ● Brunello di Montalcino Ris. '12 | ♥♥♥ | 8 |
| ● Brunello di Montalcino '13 | ♥♥ | 8 |
| ● Rosso di Montalcino '15 | ♥♥ | 8 |
| ● Brunello di Montalcino '12 | ♡♡♡ | 8 |
| ● Brunello di Montalcino '11 | ♡♡♡ | 8 |
| ● Brunello di Montalcino '10 | ♡♡♡ | 8 |
| ● Brunello di Montalcino '07 | ♡♡♡ | 8 |
| ● Brunello di Montalcino '04 | ♡♡♡ | 8 |
| ● Brunello di Montalcino '99 | ♡♡♡ | 8 |
| ● Brunello di Montalcino Ris. '07 | ♡♡♡ | 8 |
| ● Brunello di Montalcino Ris. '99 | ♡♡♡ | 8 |
| ● Brunello di Montalcino Ris. '95 | ♡♡♡ | 8 |
| ● Rosso di Montalcino '07 | ♡♡♡ | 6 |
| ● Brunello di Montalcino Ris. '11 | ♡♡ | 8 |
| ● Rosso di Montalcino '14 | ♡♡ | 8 |

## Tenuta Poggio Rosso

FRAZ. POPULONIA
LOC. POGGIO ROSSO, 1
57025 PIOMBINO [LI]
TEL. +39 056529553
www.tenutapoggiorosso.it

**CELLAR SALES**
**PRE-BOOKED VISITS**
**ACCOMMODATION**
**ANNUAL PRODUCTION** 35,000 bottles
**HECTARES UNDER VINE** 6.00

Tenuta Poggio Rosso is situated near Golfo di Baratti and the archeological site of Populonia. It was bought in 2001 by the Monelli family, who began reclaiming the old pine grove, clearing the woods, renovating the manor and old lemon house and planting the first rows of vine. Today, the vineyards are planted with Merlot, Sangiovese, Cabernet Sauvignon, Vermentino and Viognier grapes, all used to make wines expressing a distinctive terroir of origin. The modern cellar has been set up in the ground floor rooms of the villa. Their 2015 Velthune is a highly interesting, monovarietal Cabernet Sauvignon with aromas that start out a bit restrained but gradually unfold and deliver. Once open, it offers up assorted fragrances of black fruit, mineral hints and a slightly minty note. On the palate it opens well, juicy, elegant, not bold but delicate. Its persistent is enjoyable, giving way to savory and appetizing finish. Their 2016 Tages, a Sangiovese and Merlot blend, is also interesting in its notes of lavender, aromatic herbs (thyme and bay leaf) and its earthy hints. On the palate it proves soft, juicy and persistent.

| | | |
|---|---|---|
| ● Velthune '15 | | ♀♀ 6 |
| ○ Feronia '17 | | ♀♀ 4 |
| ● Tages '16 | | ♀♀ 4 |
| ● Fufluna '17 | | ♀ 3 |
| ○ Phylika '17 | | ♀ 3 |
| ○ Feronia '14 | | ♀♀ 4 |
| ● Fufluna '15 | | ♀♀ 3 |
| ○ Losna '15 | | ♀♀ 6 |
| ● Tages '15 | | ♀♀ 4 |
| ● Tages '13 | | ♀♀ 3* |
| ○ Veive '13 | | ♀♀ 4 |
| ● Velthune '13 | | ♀♀ 6 |
| ● Velthune '12 | | ♀♀ 5 |

## Podere Poggio Scalette

LOC. RUFFOLI
VIA BARBIANO, 7
50022 GREVE IN CHIANTI [FI]
TEL. +39 0558546108
www.poggioscalette.it

**CELLAR SALES**
**PRE-BOOKED VISITS**
**ACCOMMODATION**
**ANNUAL PRODUCTION** 60,000 bottles
**HECTARES UNDER VINE** 15.00

At the Fiore family winery in Greve, in Chianti, vines are cultivated with the utmost respect for the environment. Especially at the beginning, they produced elegant wines in line with the microclimatic conditions of Ruffoli hill, the marvelous vine growing area where the estate is located. Today, Poggio Scalette's stylistic choices appear to favor more marked tones, generous extraction and new oak, which produce gratifying wines ready to face the challenge of time, although perhaps a touch less charming than in the past. Their 2015 Capogatto is a classic Bordeaux blend made with Merlot, Cabernet Sauvignon, Cabernet Franc and Petit Verdot. It stands out for its well-defined aromas of black fruit and spices, while on the palate it opens sweet and substantial, unfolding steadily and generously, with well-measured use of oak. Their 2015 Piantonaia, a monovarietal Merlot, is distinct for its aromatic concentrated and pronounced oak, as is their 2015 Carbonaione, a Sangiovese.

| | | |
|---|---|---|
| ● Capogatto '15 | | ♀♀ 7 |
| ● Il Carbonaione '15 | | ♀ 7 |
| ● Piantonaia '15 | | ♀ 8 |
| ● Il Carbonaione '08 | | ♀♀♀ 6 |
| ● Il Carbonaione '05 | | ♀♀♀ 6 |
| ● Il Carbonaione '03 | | ♀♀♀ 7 |
| ● Il Carbonaione '00 | | ♀♀♀ 7 |
| ● Il Carbonaione '98 | | ♀♀♀ 6 |
| ● Il Carbonaione '96 | | ♀♀♀ 6 |
| ● Capogatto '14 | | ♀♀ 7 |
| ● Chianti Cl. '15 | | ♀♀ 3 |
| ● Il Carbonaione '14 | | ♀♀ 7 |
| ● Il Carbonaione '11 | | ♀♀ 6 |

# Poggio Sorbello

FRAZ. CENTOIA
LOC. CASE SPARSE, 168
52044 CORTONA [AR]
TEL. +39 3395447059
www.poggiosorbello.it

**CELLAR SALES**
**ANNUAL PRODUCTION** 10,000 bottles
**HECTARES UNDER VINE** 9.00
**SUSTAINABLE WINERY**

The Baldetti family have owned this estate, situated in Cortona and Montepulciano, since the early 20th century. For many years it was cultivated according to time-honored traditions, and so a mix of produce in which grapes were only a part. It was only in the mid-1990s that viticulture took on an essential role, and they began renovating their vineyards. An upgrade to their facility followed, as well as the construction of a barrique cellar, with meticulous care shown for maturation of their wines. Their 2015 Gortinaia is a monovarietal Syrah with multifaceted aromas. Spicy hints of pepper, gamey notes of tanned leather and medicinal herbs emerge on a background of red fruit. On the palate it's warm, potent, enjoyable. Their 2015 Fossa Granai, a Cabernet Sauvignon, is a pleasant wine with balsamic and minty hints set on a background of plums. In the mouth it exhibits a soft body that's spirited in its freshness, measured tannins, and a lengthy finish with a nice, fruity aftertaste.

| | |
|---|---|
| ● Boschi ai Filari '15 | ♟♟ 3 |
| ● Cortona Cabernet Sauvignon Fossa Granaia '15 | ♟♟ 4 |
| ● Cortona Syrah Gortinaia '15 | ♟♟ 4 |
| ● Cortona Merlot Donetto '15 | ♟ 4 |

# Tenuta Il Poggione

FRAZ. SANT'ANGELO IN COLLE
LOC. MONTEANO
53024 MONTALCINO [SI]
TEL. +39 0577844029
www.tenutailpoggione.it

**CELLAR SALES**
**PRE-BOOKED VISITS**
**ACCOMMODATION**
**ANNUAL PRODUCTION** 600,000 bottles
**HECTARES UNDER VINE** 127.00

Only a few wineries own 100 hectares of vineyards in Montalcino. Il Poggione is one of them, an estate situated in the extreme south of the appellation, in Sant'Angelo in Colle, and belonging to the Franceschi family since the late 1800s. Today it is run by Fabrizio Bindocci. They produce a vintage version and the Vigna Paganelli Riserva, with Sangiovese grapes for making Brunello wines in the traditional way: about twenty days of maceration, followed by maturation in 3000-l and 5000-l French oak barrels. Merlot, Vermentino and Chardonnay complete the range of varieties that are grown. This year their 2013 Brunello put in the best performance. It features a classic profile of ripe, red fruit, tobacco and licorice, while on the palate it proves warm and caressing, broader than it is deep, with a finish that's just a bit lacking. Their 2016 Rosso is right up there, an expressive, forthright wine in its aromas of strawberry caramel and aromatic herbs. On the palate it stands out for a nice suppleness.

| | |
|---|---|
| ● Brunello di Montalcino '13 | ♟♟ 7 |
| ● Rosso di Montalcino '16 | ♟♟ 4 |
| ⊙ Lo Sbrancato '17 | ♟ 3 |
| ● Brunello di Montalcino Ris. '97 | ♟♟♟ 7 |
| ● Brunello di Montalcino '12 | ♟♟ 7 |
| ● Brunello di Montalcino '11 | ♟♟ 7 |
| ● Brunello di Montalcino '10 | ♟♟ 7 |
| ● Brunello di Montalcino '09 | ♟♟ 6 |
| ● Brunello di Montalcino V. Paganelli Ris. '10 | ♟♟ 8 |
| ● Rosso di Montalcino '14 | ♟♟ 4 |
| ● Rosso di Montalcino '13 | ♟♟ 4 |
| ● Rosso di Montalcino '12 | ♟♟ 3 |
| ● Toscana Rosso '13 | ♟♟ 3 |

## ★★Poliziano

FRAZ. MONTEPULCIANO STAZIONE
VIA FONTAGO, 1
53045 MONTEPULCIANO [SI]
TEL. +39 0578738171
www.carlettipoliziano.com

**CELLAR SALES**
**PRE-BOOKED VISITS**
**ANNUAL PRODUCTION** 650,000 bottles
**HECTARES UNDER VINE** 145.00

This successful Nobile wine producer has brought innovation to the appellation with modern-style wines, while contributing to the success of the area as a whole. Federico Carletti, an iconic figure in local winemaking, is the driving force behind this Montepulciano winery, and he has been a key player in Italian winemaking for over thirty years. The estate cultivates its vines with great care and attention, and in the cellar winemaking is carried out combining high technology with tradition. Their wines are matured for the most part in barriques. The return of their Nobile di Montepulciano Le Caggiole, a wine made between 1982 and 1994, is not a totally newsworthy event for those who love Nobile, but a serious 2015 has certainly made for a warm homecoming. It's an elegant red in its fruity and spicy aromatic profile, and its great finesse. On the palate it comes through juicy, at times almost velvety, and highly enjoyable.

| | |
|---|---|
| ● Nobile di Montepulciano Le Caggiole '15 | ♟♟♟ 4* |
| ● Nobile di Montepulciano Asinone '15 | ♟♟ 7 |
| ● Nobile di Montepulciano '15 | ♟♟ 5 |
| ● Rosso di Montepulciano '16 | ♟♟ 3 |
| ● Le Stanze '03 | ♛♛♛ 6 |
| ● Nobile di Montepulciano '09 | ♛♛♛ 4* |
| ● Nobile di Montepulciano Asinone '14 | ♛♛♛ 7 |
| ● Nobile di Montepulciano Asinone '12 | ♛♛♛ 7 |
| ● Nobile di Montepulciano Asinone '11 | ♛♛♛ 7 |
| ● Nobile di Montepulciano Asinone '07 | ♛♛♛ 6 |
| ● Nobile di Montepulciano Asinone '06 | ♛♛♛ 6 |
| ● Nobile di Montepulciano Asinone '05 | ♛♛♛ 6 |
| ● Nobile di Montepulciano Asinone '04 | ♛♛♛ 6 |

## Pomona

LOC. POMONA, 39
S.DA CHIANTIGIANA
53011 CASTELLINA IN CHIANTI [SI]
TEL. +39 0577740473
www.fattoriapomona.it

**CELLAR SALES**
**PRE-BOOKED VISITS**
**ACCOMMODATION**
**ANNUAL PRODUCTION** 16,000 bottles
**HECTARES UNDER VINE** 4.70
**VITICULTURE METHOD** Certified Organic

The hills of Chianti, where vineyards share the limelight with olives and oaks, are a wonder that you hope to experience in the glass. Villa Pomona, with its signature style, offers just this. With its use of organic cultivation techniques in the vineyard and its minimally invasive approach in the cellar, the winery owned by Monica Raspi is one of the best examples of artisanal winemaking in the area of Castellina in Chiani, and its wines are among the most consistent and noteworthy of the Gallo Nero appellation. Villa Pomona's wines are intimately linked to the territory of Chianti, and this timbre has always been their primary characteristic. Their 2015 Chianti Classico Riserva is a fruit-rich, fragrant wine with a palate defined by pleasantly spirited tannins and nice savoriness. Their 2016 Chianti Classico is fresh and assertive on the palate, with aromas of small red fruits dominating on the nose.

| | |
|---|---|
| ● Chianti Cl. '16 | ♟♟ 3* |
| ● Chianti Cl. Ris. '15 | ♟♟ 4 |
| ● Chianti Cl. '13 | ♛♛♛ 3* |
| ● Chianti Cl. '12 | ♛♛♛ 3* |
| ● Chianti Cl. Ris. '14 | ♛♛♛ 4* |
| ● Chianti Cl. '15 | ♛♛ 3 |
| ● Chianti Cl. '14 | ♛♛ 3 |
| ● Chianti Cl. '11 | ♛♛ 3 |
| ● Chianti Cl. '10 | ♛♛ 3 |
| ● Chianti Cl. Ris. '13 | ♛♛ 4 |
| ● Chianti Cl. Ris. '12 | ♛♛ 4 |
| ● Chianti Cl. Ris. '10 | ♛♛ 4 |
| ● Chianti Cl. Ris. '09 | ♛♛ 4 |

# Tenuta Le Potazzine

LOC. LE PRATA, 262
53024 MONTALCINO [SI]
TEL. +39 0577846168
www.lepotazzine.it

**CELLAR SALES**
**PRE-BOOKED VISITS**
**RESTAURANT SERVICE**
**ANNUAL PRODUCTION** 50,000 bottles
**HECTARES UNDER VINE** 4.70

The 'little birds' or 'Potazzine' are daughters Viola and Sofia Gorelli who have now spread their wings and are working alongside their mother, Gigliola, to solidify the success of one of the most distinctive wineries in Montalcino. Credit for their success goes to the 'spring-like' style of their Brunellos, light in color, but not lacking in structure. The result is a territorial patchwork anchored by the Le Prata and Torre vineyards (in the southwestern district with elevations skimming 500 meters, and in the south, towards Sant'Angelo in Colle, respectively). Once again, they submitted an excellent trio of wines. Their 2016 Rosso has a 'southern' quality to it (watermelon, nutmeg and roots), and a delectable palate. Their 2013 Brunello is more delicate and pure, but it was their 2011 Riserva that really bowled us over. It's a multifaceted wine in its aromas of blackcurrant, licorice, mint and iodine, while on the mouth it unfolds with power and pluck, thanks to a splendid, savory texture and tannic finesse.

| | | |
|---|---|---|
| ● Brunello di Montalcino Ris. '11 | ▼▼▼ | 8 |
| ● Brunello di Montalcino '13 | ▼▼ | 7 |
| ● Rosso di Montalcino '16 | ▼▼ | 4 |
| ● Brunello di Montalcino '10 | ♀♀♀ | 7 |
| ● Brunello di Montalcino '08 | ♀♀♀ | 7 |
| ● Brunello di Montalcino Ris. '06 | ♀♀♀ | 8 |
| ● Brunello di Montalcino '12 | ♀♀ | 7 |
| ● Brunello di Montalcino '11 | ♀♀ | 7 |
| ● Brunello di Montalcino '09 | ♀♀ | 7 |
| ● Brunello di Montalcino '07 | ♀♀ | 6 |
| ● Rosso di Montalcino '15 | ♀♀ | 4 |
| ● Rosso di Montalcino '14 | ♀♀ | 4 |
| ● Rosso di Montalcino '13 | ♀♀ | 4 |
| ● Rosso di Montalcino '12 | ♀♀ | 4 |
| ● Rosso di Montalcino '10 | ♀♀ | 4 |

# Priorino

VIA MARTIRI DELLA LIBERTÀ, 16
53045 MONTEPULCIANO [SI]
TEL. +39 0578707841
www.cantinapriorino.com

**ANNUAL PRODUCTION** 18,000 bottles
**HECTARES UNDER VINE** 6.00

The Valdambrini family winery may be relatively new but it is definitely on the right track. This artisan winery promotes a focused approach common to Montalcino and Tuscany, giving off no hint of the industrial. Their style seeks balance and elegance rather than power and concentration. Wines made with international blends age in barriques, while appellation wines mature in mid-sized casks. Their 2013 Nobile di Montepulciano Robi Riserva is all elegance and finesse, with complex aromas and a well-orchestrated, balanced that isn't lacking in contrasts. Their 2015 Nobile di Montepulciano Violino continues in the same stylistic vein, highlighting a subtle and penetrating structure, and fresh, precise aromas.

| | | |
|---|---|---|
| ● Nobile di Montepulciano Robi Ris. '13 | ▼▼ | 5 |
| ● Nobile di Montepulciano Violino '15 | ▼▼ | 5 |
| ● Umore e Luce '14 | ▼ | 3 |
| ● Nobile di Montepulciano Viola '14 | ♀♀ | 5 |

# ★Fattoria Le Pupille

FRAZ. ISTIA D'OMBRONE
LOC. PIAGGE DEL MAIANO, 92A
58100 GROSSETO
TEL. +39 0564409517
www.fattorialepupille.it

**CELLAR SALES**
**PRE-BOOKED VISITS**
**ACCOMMODATION**
**ANNUAL PRODUCTION** 450,000 bottles
**HECTARES UNDER VINE** 80.00

The winery owned by Elisabetta Geppetti has done so much for the appellation that its name is synonymous with Morellino worldwide. Credit is due to a selection of wines that has been consistently outstanding since 1985. Their style features a generous dose of oak, ripe fruit and an assertive effort towards easy drinking that's to be found even in their more serious wines, which are always at the high end of Maremma's winemaking. Their 2015 Saffredi is a juicy, long, gratifying wine on the palate, while on the nose it features lush fruit, spices and smoky notes. Their 2015 Morellino di Scansano Riserva is a solid and somewhat austere wine with aromas of flowers and earth accompanied by toasty accents and slight hints of shrubs. On the palate it shows a robust grain of tannins and assertive development. Their fragrant and savory 2017 Morellino di Scansano is a highly drinkable wine.

| | |
|---|---|
| ● Morellino di Scansano Ris. '15 | ♥♥♥ 4* |
| ● Saffredi '15 | ♥♥ 8 |
| ● Morellino di Scansano '17 | ♥♥ 3 |
| ● Poggio Valente '15 | ♥ 6 |
| ● Saffredi '14 | ♀♀♀ 8 |
| ● Saffredi '13 | ♀♀♀ 8 |
| ● Saffredi '05 | ♀♀♀ 8 |
| ● Maremma Toscana Saffredi '12 | ♀♀ 8 |
| ● Morellino di Scansano Ris. '13 | ♀♀ 6 |
| ● Morellino di Scansano Ris. '10 | ♀♀ 3* |
| ● Poggio Valente '14 | ♀♀ 5 |

# La Querce

VIA IMPRUNETANA PER TAVARNUZZE, 41
50023 IMPRUNETA [FI]
TEL. +39 0552011380
www.laquerce.com

**CELLAR SALES**
**PRE-BOOKED VISITS**
**ACCOMMODATION**
**ANNUAL PRODUCTION** 35,000 bottles
**HECTARES UNDER VINE** 8.00

Purchased by the Marchi family in the 1960s, this winery is now run by Marco Ferretti. In recent years, the vineyards have been replanted, almost totally with traditional grapes such as Sangiovese, Canaiolo and Colorino, as well as Merlot. There are two cellars: a modern one for winemaking and a barrique aging cellar, which features an historical area and tasting room beneath the villa, which dates from the thirteenth century. The estate also offers accommodations ideal for relaxing and soaking up the beauty of the Florentine countryside. Their 2015 Chianti Colli Fiorentini La Torretta Riserva brings home Tre Bicchieri. Its complex, traditional bouquet sees aromas of plum preserves, tanned leather and sensations of blood-rich meat give way to hints of aromatic herbs. In the mouth it proves firm, tasty and fresh with well-positioned tannins and a lengthy, flavorful finish. Their 2017 Terra di Vino also did well, featuring decisive fruit and spicy notes on the nose, and a spirited, lively palate with a nice, rising finish.

| | |
|---|---|
| ● Chianti Colli Fiorentini La Torretta Ris. '15 | ♥♥♥ 2* |
| ● Terra di Vino '17 | ♥♥ 4 |
| ● La Querce '11 | ♀♀♀ 5 |
| ● Belrosso '15 | ♀♀ 2* |
| ● Belrosso Canaiolo '16 | ♀♀ 2* |
| ● Chianti Colli Fiorentini La Torretta '12 | ♀♀ 2* |
| ● Chianti Sorrettole '16 | ♀♀ 2* |
| ● Chianti Sorrettole '15 | ♀♀ 2* |
| ● La Querce '12 | ♀♀ 5 |
| ● M '13 | ♀♀ 6 |

# Le Ragnaie

LOC. LE RAGNAIE
53024 MONTALCINO [SI]
TEL. +39 0577848639
www.leragnaie.com

**CELLAR SALES**
**PRE-BOOKED VISITS**
**ACCOMMODATION**
**ANNUAL PRODUCTION** 80,000 bottles
**HECTARES UNDER VINE** 15.50
**VITICULTURE METHOD** Certified Organic

Ragnaie VV, Fornace and Petroso are the three aces that have enabled Riccardo Campinoti to take up permanent residence among the great producers in Montalcino. Three Brunello crus are made with grapes cultivated in three areas: the oldest plot (located near the cellar at about 600 meters above sea level), Castelnuovo dell'Abate-Loreto (southeastern district, around 400 meters) and Colle Centrale (to the west of the town). These expressions, while different, share an irresistible succulent and lip-smacking quality. Winemaking techniques are dictated by the vintage. This was probably their best performance yet in terms of numbers of wines and variety. Their 2015 Rosso is a small gem of grace and vigor, while their 2013 Brunello Furnace offers up sunny whiffs well-supported by a lush, savory palate. Their 2013 Brunello Ragnaie Vecchie Vigne is a step up in terms of elegance and complexity, with dense aromatic contrasts of flowers, balsams and spices, and velvety tannins on the palate.

| | | |
|---|---|---|
| ● Brunello di Montalcino V. V. '13 | ♛♛♛ | 8 |
| ● Brunello di Montalcino Fornace '13 | ♛♛ | 8 |
| ● Rosso di Montalcino '15 | ♛♛ | 5 |
| ● Brunello di Montalcino '13 | ♛♛ | 7 |
| ○ Ragnaie Bianco '16 | ♛♛ | 4 |
| ⊙ Rosato '16 | ♛♛ | 5 |
| ● Brunello di Montalcino Fornace '08 | ♕♕♕ | 8 |
| ● Brunello di Montalcino V. V. '11 | ♕♕♕ | 8 |
| ● Brunello di Montalcino V. V. '10 | ♕♕♕ | 8 |
| ● Brunello di Montalcino V. V. '07 | ♕♕♕ | 5 |
| ● Brunello di Montalcino Fornace '12 | ♕♕ | 8 |
| ● Brunello di Montalcino Fornace '11 | ♕♕ | 8 |
| ● Brunello di Montalcino V. V. '12 | ♕♕ | 8 |
| ● Rosso di Montalcino Petroso '14 | ♕♕ | 5 |
| ● Rosso di Montalcino V. V. Ragnaie '14 | ♕♕ | 5 |

# Podere La Regola

LOC. ALTAGRANDA
S.DA REG.LE 68 KM 6,400
56046 RIPARBELLA [PI]
TEL. +39 0586698145
www.laregola.com

**CELLAR SALES**
**PRE-BOOKED VISITS**
**ANNUAL PRODUCTION** 90,000 bottles
**HECTARES UNDER VINE** 20.00

One hundred years ago the Nuti family purchased land in Riparbella, a few kilometers from the sea. Only in recent decades, thanks to Luca and Flavio's efforts, has this small family farm been transformed into a full-fledged winery. New vineyards were planted and careful control of the supply chain was established before converting to organic management. While building the new cellar, remains of an ancient Etruscan settlement were unearthed, including several wine amphorae, bearing witness to a tradition dating back thousands of years. Their 2015 La Regola, a monovarietal Cabernet Franc, earned Tre Bicchieri with its aromatic bouquet in which blueberry and blackcurrant give way to fresh ginger, with a well-integrated balsamic note. In the mouth it opens exceptionally well, pervasive but dynamic with well-integrated tannins. Their 2015 Vallino, a Cabernet Sauvignon with a small share of Sangiovese, offers up notes of chocolate and roasted coffee, blueberry and plums, while on the palate it features nice structure and a relaxed finish.

| | | |
|---|---|---|
| ● La Regola '15 | ♛♛♛ | 7 |
| ● Vallino '15 | ♛♛ | 5 |
| ○ Steccaia '17 | ♛♛ | 4 |
| ● Ligustro '16 | ♛ | 3 |
| ● La Regola '14 | ♕♕ | 7 |
| ● La Regola '13 | ♕♕ | 6 |
| ● La Regola '12 | ♕♕ | 6 |
| ○ Lauro '15 | ♕♕ | 5 |
| ○ Steccaia Bianco '15 | ♕♕ | 3 |
| ● Strido '13 | ♕♕ | 8 |
| ● Strido '12 | ♕♕ | 8 |
| ● Vallino '13 | ♕♕ | 5 |

## Renieri

S.DA CONSORZIALE DELL'ASSO
53024 MONTALCINO [SI]
TEL. +39 0577359330
www.renierimontalcino.com

CELLAR SALES
PRE-BOOKED VISITS
ACCOMMODATION
ANNUAL PRODUCTION 301,200 bottles
HECTARES UNDER VINE 35.00

The Bacci family owned Castello di Bossi in Chianti Classico, and Terre di Talamo in Maremma, when they chose the splendid Renieri farm for their winemaking venture in Montalcino. It was completely restructured in the late 1990s, including the vineyards, which are situated in the southern district toward Monta Amiata at about 400 meters above sea level. Merlot, Cabernet, Syrah and Petit Verdot are cultivated alongside Sangiovese, and make for a mixed range of wines, featuring a somewhat modern Brunello at the top. They are matured in small wooden casks and 3000-liter oak barrels. Renieri claims back a place in our main section with a noteworthy selection. Their 2015 Rosso is anything but an 'entry-level' wine, with its earthy and spicy notes supported by a decisive, pervasive palate. Their 2012 RIserva shows even greater liveliness, offering up notes of humus, foresty herbs, bitter orange. On the palate it proves generous yet austere, making it a true Brunello in the best sense of the term.

| | |
|---|---|
| ● Brunello di Montalcino Ris. '12 | ♥♥ 8 |
| ● Brunello di Montalcino '13 | ♥♥ 7 |
| ● Rosso di Montalcino '15 | ♥♥ 3 |
| ● Re di Renieri '04 | ♀♀ 5 |
| ● Re di Renieri '03 | ♀♀ 5 |
| ● Regina di Renieri '05 | ♀♀ 6 |
| ● Regina di Renieri '03 | ♀♀ 5 |
| ● Rosso di Montalcino '04 | ♀♀ 3 |

## ★★Barone Ricasoli

LOC. MADONNA A BROLIO

53013 GAIOLE IN CHIANTI [SI]
TEL. +39 05777301
www.ricasoli.it

CELLAR SALES
PRE-BOOKED VISITS
ACCOMMODATION
ANNUAL PRODUCTION 2,500,000 bottles
HECTARES UNDER VINE 235.00
SUSTAINABLE WINERY

Barone Ricasoli is without doubt a benchmark for the Chianti area, not only because Baron Bettino invented Chianti right inside Brolio castle, but also because the winery, run today by Francesco Ricasoli, has taken an innovative path. Witness the mapping of all their vineyards, clonal selection of a Sangiovese native to Brolio, and experiments with organic methods. The result is a style with a winning balance, making for an excellent overall selection. Their Chianti Classico Ricasoli aren't lacking in personality or quality, starting with their 2015 Rocco Guicciarda Riserva. It's a wine that interprets its territory through a clear, modern lens, offering up close-focused aromas of red fruit, wild flowers, flint and forest undergrowth. On the palate it's extremely well-balanced, with sweetness of fruit well-integrated with acidity and the careful use of oak.

| | |
|---|---|
| ● Chianti Cl. Brolio '16 | ♥♥ 5 |
| ● Chianti Cl. Rocca Guicciarda Ris. '15 | ♥♥ 5 |
| ● Chianti Cl. Gran Selezione Castello di Brolio '15 | ♥♥ 8 |
| ● Chianti Cl. Gran Selezione Colledilà '15 | ♥♥ 8 |
| ● Casalferro '08 | ♀♀♀ 8 |
| ● Casalferro '05 | ♀♀♀ 8 |
| ● Chianti Cl. Brolio Bettino '15 | ♀♀♀ 5 |
| ● Chianti Cl. Castello di Brolio '07 | ♀♀♀ 8 |
| ● Chianti Cl. Castello di Brolio '06 | ♀♀♀ 8 |
| ● Chianti Cl. Colledilà '10 | ♀♀♀ 7 |
| ● Chianti Cl. Gran Sel. Colledilà '13 | ♀♀♀ 8 |
| ● Chianti Cl. Gran Sel. Colledilà '11 | ♀♀♀ 8 |
| ● Chianti Cl. Rocca Guicciarda Ris. '12 | ♀♀♀ 5 |

# Riecine

LOC. RIECINE
53013 GAIOLE IN CHIANTI [SI]
TEL. +39 0577749098
www.riecine.it

**CELLAR SALES**
**PRE-BOOKED VISITS**
**ANNUAL PRODUCTION** 60,000 bottles
**HECTARES UNDER VINE** 11.00
**VITICULTURE METHOD** Certified Organic

Englishman John Dunkley founded this winery in 1971 and was assisted by Carlo Ferrini up until 1997. A young winemaker, Sean O'Callaghan, joined the Riecine team as a trainee in 1991 and he went on to become a major wine producer. Lana Frank took over running the winery in 2011, intending to maintain the production philosophy, which is now back under Ferrini's management. Vine growing is organic, while in the cellar barriques, mid-sized casks, steel and concrete vats all to meet the requirements of the various vintages. Their 2015 Chianti Classico Riserva is a wine worthy of Riecine's past excellence. Its aromas range from red fruit to flowers, stones and forest undergrowth. On the palate it delivers with a deep, long, extremely flavorful development. Their 2016 Chianti Classico is pleasantly approachable, while their 2014 Riecine, a monovarietal Sangiovese, proves fragrant and well-made.

| | |
|---|---|
| ● Chianti Cl. Ris. '15 | ▼▼▼ 5 |
| ● Chianti Cl. '16 | ▼▼ 3 |
| ● Riecine '14 | ▼▼ 3 |
| ● Chianti Cl. Ris. '99 | ♀♀♀ 7 |
| ● Chianti Cl. Ris. '88 | ♀♀♀ 6 |
| ● Chianti Cl. Ris. '86 | ♀♀♀ 6 |
| ● La Gioia '04 | ♀♀♀ 6 |
| ● La Gioia '01 | ♀♀♀ 6 |
| ● La Gioia '98 | ♀♀♀ 6 |
| ● La Gioia '95 | ♀♀♀ 6 |

# Rocca delle Macìe

LOC. LE MACÌE, 45
53011 CASTELLINA IN CHIANTI [SI]
TEL. +39 05777321
www.roccadellemacie.com

**CELLAR SALES**
**PRE-BOOKED VISITS**
**ACCOMMODATION AND RESTAURANT SERVICE**
**ANNUAL PRODUCTION** 2,000,000 bottles
**HECTARES UNDER VINE** 206.70
**SUSTAINABLE WINERY**

This winery in Castellina has been owned by the Zingarelli family since the 1970s. Over time the cellar has been developing a strategy to improve overall quality and style. Their core business is based on production of high quantities, but wines at the top end of their portfolio are gaining more and more importance, often reaching levels of excellence. This comes as a result of careful work carried out with the Sangiovese grapes, and recouping distinctive characteristics of their territory of origin. Their 2016 Chianti Classico is a delicious wine, among their best, with its aromatic profile of flowery notes adorned by flint and spices. On the palate it's flavorful, fresh and steady. Their 2015 Chianti Classico Gran Selezione Riserva di Fizzano offers up lush fruit on the nose, while on the palate it's a bit held back by excessive oak.

| | |
|---|---|
| ● Chianti Cl. '16 | ▼▼▼ 3* |
| ● Chianti Cl. Gran Selezione Riserva di Fizzano '15 | ▼▼ 6 |
| ● Chianti Cl. Gran Selezione Sergio Zingarelli '14 | ▼▼ 8 |
| ● Chianti Cl. Ris. '15 | ▼ 4 |
| ● Chianti Cl. Tenuta S. Alfonso '16 | ▼ 4 |
| ● Chianti Cl. Fizzano Ris. '10 | ♀♀♀ 5 |
| ● Chianti Cl. Gran Sel. Riserva di Fizzano '14 | ♀♀♀ 6 |
| ● Chianti Cl. Gran Sel. Riserva di Fizzano '13 | ♀♀♀ 6 |
| ● Chianti Cl. Gran Sel. Sergio Zingarelli '11 | ♀♀♀ 8 |

# Rocca di Castagnoli

LOC. CASTAGNOLI
53013 GAIOLE IN CHIANTI [SI]
TEL. +39 0577731004
www.roccadicastagnoli.com

**CELLAR SALES**
**PRE-BOOKED VISITS**
**ACCOMMODATION AND RESTAURANT SERVICE**
**ANNUAL PRODUCTION** 500,000 bottles
**HECTARES UNDER VINE** 87.00
**SUSTAINABLE WINERY**

Part of the success of Rocca di Castignoli, owner of the Poggio Maestrino Spiaggiole winery in Maremma, is due to its location in one of the best subzones of Chianti Classico -- in the Gaiole in Chianti hills to be precise. The elevation of their vineyards and the distinctive weather conditions are perfect for vine growing, and it guarantees their products a lead role in Chianti. Their wines achieve consistent quality, and at times approach absolute excellence. Their 2015 Riserva di Chianti Classico Poggio a' Frati and Tenuta Capraia form a nice couple. The former is more elegant, assertive and rich in contrasts, while the second is sunnier, fruitier and more savory. Their 2014 Chianti Classico Gran Selezione Stielle also delivers, though oak may overpower a bit. Their 2016 Chianti Classico is a consistent and sound wine.

| | |
|---|---|
| ● Chianti Cl. Poggio a' Frati Ris. '15 | ▼▼ 5 |
| ● Chianti Cl. Tenuta di Capraia Ris. '15 | ▼▼ 3* |
| ● Chianti Cl. Gran Selezione Stielle '14 | ▼▼ 6 |
| ● Chianti Cl. Rocca di Castagnoli '16 | ▼▼ 3 |
| ● Chianti Cl. Capraia Ris. '07 | ♀♀♀ 4 |
| ● Chianti Cl. Poggio ai Frati Ris. '08 | ♀♀♀ 4 |
| ● Chianti Cl. Poggio ai Frati Ris. '06 | ♀♀♀ 4* |
| ● Chianti Cl. Poggio ai Frati Ris. '04 | ♀♀♀ 4 |
| ● Chianti Cl. Tenuta di Capraia Ris. '06 | ♀♀♀ 4* |
| ● Chianti Cl. Tenuta di Capraia Ris. '05 | ♀♀♀ 4 |
| ● Stielle '00 | ♀♀♀ 7 |
| ● Chianti Cl. Gran Sel. Stielle '13 | ♀♀ 6 |
| ● Chianti Cl. Rocca di Castagnoli '15 | ♀♀ 3 |
| ● Morellino di Scansano Spiaggiole Poggio Maestrino '16 | ♀♀ 3 |

# ★Rocca di Frassinello

LOC. GIUNCARICO
58023 GAVORRANO [GR]
TEL. +39 056688400
www.roccadifrassinello.it

**CELLAR SALES**
**PRE-BOOKED VISITS**
**ACCOMMODATION**
**ANNUAL PRODUCTION** 400,000 bottles
**HECTARES UNDER VINE** 90.00
**SUSTAINABLE WINERY**

*The owner of this producer is also a shareholder of Gambero Rosso spa. To avoid any conflict of interest, Paolo Panerai has subordinated the possible awarding of Tre Bicchieri (which, in any case, only occurs through a blind tasting) to the attainment of the same rating of excellence (upwards of 90/100) by an independent, international panel. This was the case here.*

Rocca di Frassinello is situated in Gavorrano, the right place for their grapes to fully express their force and the Mediterranean nuances that only a coastal terrain can confer. Their 2016 Maremma Baffo Nero, a monovarietal Merlot, may be one of their best versions yet. On the nose it offers up dark tones, from ripe fruit to slightly herbaceous hints, spices, chocolate and tobacco. On the palate it opens large and sweet, gradually getting leaner, with crisp tannins, nice pace and savoriness, and finishing once again with generosity and depth.

| | |
|---|---|
| ● Maremma Toscana Baffonero '16 | ▼▼▼ 8 |
| ● Maremma Toscana Rosso Poggio alla Guardia '16 | ▼▼ 3 |
| ● Maremma Toscana Ornello '16 | ▼ 4 |
| ● Maremma Toscana Rocca di Frassinello '16 | ▼ 8 |
| ○ Vermentino '17 | ▼ 3 |
| ● Baffonero '12 | ♀♀♀ 8 |
| ● Baffonero '11 | ♀♀♀ 8 |
| ● Le Sughere di Frassinello '10 | ♀♀♀ 4* |
| ● Maremma Toscana Baffonero '14 | ♀♀♀ 8 |
| ● Maremma Toscana Baffonero '13 | ♀♀♀ 8 |
| ● Maremma Toscana Rocca di Frassinello '15 | ♀♀♀ 6 |
| ● Rocca di Frassinello '12 | ♀♀♀ 6 |
| ● Rocca di Frassinello '11 | ♀♀♀ 6 |

# Rocca di Montemassi

LOC. PIAN DEL BICHI
FRAZ. MONTEMASSI
S.DA PROV.LE SANT'ANNA
58036 ROCCASTRADA [GR]
TEL. +39 0564579700
www.roccadimontemassi.it

**CELLAR SALES**
**PRE-BOOKED VISITS**
**ACCOMMODATION**
**ANNUAL PRODUCTION** 480,000 bottles
**HECTARES UNDER VINE** 180.00
**SUSTAINABLE WINERY**

Rocca di Montemassi, part of the Zonin group, is situated amidst Mediterranean scrub and the Metallifere hills. It enjoys a distinctive light, a warm climate with good temperature ranges, and siliceous-clay soils, rich in minerals. This setting has determined which varieties to cultivate: from classic Tuscan grapes such as Vermentino and Sangiovese, to international cultivars, which have long demonstrated their ability to adapt to this area. Among the white, we find Viognier, and among the reds, Cabernet Sauvignon and Franc, Merlot and Syrah. Their 2016 Maremma Sassabruna features a defined aromatic profile that alternates notes of ripe red fruit with smoky hints and spices. On the palate it opens sweet and full, followed by a balanced, linear development and a vibrant finish. Their fragrant, flavorful 2017 Syrosa, a rosé made with Syrah, is a highly enjoyable, drinkable wine. The rest of their selection also proved sound.

# Roccapesta

LOC. MACERETO, 9
50854 SCANSANO [GR]
TEL. +39 0564599252
www.roccapesta.com

**CELLAR SALES**
**PRE-BOOKED VISITS**
**ANNUAL PRODUCTION** 100,000 bottles
**HECTARES UNDER VINE** 18.50

Roccapesta is one of Maremma's brightest stars. From the beginning, owner Alberto Tanzini understood the potential of the Scansano hills, and without wasting time he went immediately to tradition, beginning with maturation in large barrels. His Sangiovese comes through as austere, robust, full of character and highly original. The variety and territory have come a long way, and with a little effort, this rather crabby Tuscan grape can be as good as any at these latitudes. Their Morellino di Scansano Riserva perfectly interprets the area's Sangiovese. Their 2015 offers up aromas of violet, cherry, earthy notes and flint. On the palate it exhibits spirited tannins, lively acidity, steadiness, fragrance and savoriness. Their more approachable 2016 Morellino di Scansano Ribero proves enjoyable and captivating, with their 2016 Maremma Macs is a fresh wine full of contrasts.

| | |
|---|---|
| ⊙ Maremma Toscana Rosato Syrosa '17 | ¶¶ 4 |
| ● Maremma Toscana Rosso Sassabruna '16 | ¶¶ 5 |
| ● Maremma Toscana Rosso '15 | ¶ 7 |
| ○ Maremma Toscana Vermentino Calasole '17 | ¶ 4 |
| ● Maremma Toscana Rocca di Montemassi '13 | ♀♀♀ 5 |
| ● Rocca di Montemassi '10 | ♀♀♀ 5 |
| ● Maremma Rocca di Montemassi '12 | ♀♀ 5 |
| ● Maremma Toscana Rosso Sassabruna '15 | ♀♀ 5 |
| ● Maremma Toscana Sangiovese Le Focaie '15 | ♀♀ 3 |
| ● Maremma Toscana Sassabruna '14 | ♀♀ 3* |
| ○ Maremma Toscana Vermentino Calasole '16 | ♀♀ 4 |

| | |
|---|---|
| ● Morellino di Scansano Ris. '15 | ¶¶ 5 |
| ● Maremma Toscana Rosso Masca '16 | ¶¶ 2* |
| ● Morellino di Scansano Ribeo '16 | ¶¶ 2* |
| ● Morellino di Scansano Calestaia Ris. '11 | ♀♀♀ 5 |
| ● Morellino di Scansano Calestaia Ris. '10 | ♀♀♀ 5 |
| ● Morellino di Scansano Ribeo '15 | ♀♀♀ 3* |
| ● Morellino di Scansano Ris. '13 | ♀♀♀ 4* |
| ● Morellino di Scansano '15 | ♀♀ 3 |
| ● Morellino di Scansano '13 | ♀♀ 3* |
| ● Morellino di Scansano Ribeo '14 | ♀♀ 3* |
| ● Pugnitello '14 | ♀♀ 6 |

## ★Ruffino

P.LE RUFFINO, 1
50065 PONTASSIEVE [FI]
TEL. +39 05583605
www.ruffino.it

**CELLAR SALES**
**PRE-BOOKED VISITS**
**ANNUAL PRODUCTION** 18,000,000 bottles
**HECTARES UNDER VINE** 550.00

This winery based in Pontassieve has been owned by wine giant Constellations Brands for some years. It's made history both for itself and on behalf of Tuscan wine in general, maintaining a comforting and consistent quality throughout. From Montalcino with Greppone Mazzi, to Chianti Classico, with Santedame, Gretolaio, Montemasso and Poggio Casciano, and finally the La Solatia estate in Monteriggioni, their vineyards cover a vast territory. Their style is modern, with ample use of barriques and a careful approach in the cellar. Their wines, lacking at times in personality, are always well-crafted. We are pleased to offer a warm homecoming to those wines that made history here in Chianti Classico. Their 2014 Gran Selezione Riserva Ducale Pro offers up well-defined, complex aromas, followed by a juicy, steady palate and a finish that builds to a crescendo. It earns Tre Bicchieri. Their 2015 Chianti Classico Gran Selezione Romitorio di Santedame also did well, though it sees a bit too much oak. Their 2015 Modus, a blend of Sangiovese, Merlot and Cabernet Sauvignon, was also well-received.

| | |
|---|---|
| ● Chianti Cl. Gran Selezione Riserva Ducale Oro '14 | ❦❦❦ 6 |
| ● Chianti Cl. Gran Selezione Romitorio di Santedame '15 | ❦❦ 6 |
| ● Modus '15 | ❦❦ 5 |
| ● Chianti Cl. Santedame '15 | ❦ 4 |
| ● Brunello di Montalcino Greppone Mazzi '05 | ♈♈♈ 6 |
| ● Chianti Cl. Riserva Ducale Oro '04 | ♈♈♈ 5 |
| ● Chianti Cl. Riserva Ducale Oro '01 | ♈♈♈ 5 |
| ● Chianti Cl. Riserva Ducale Oro '00 | ♈♈♈ 5 |
| ● Modus '04 | ♈♈♈ 5 |
| ● Romitorio di Santedame '00 | ♈♈♈ 7 |
| ● Romitorio di Santedame '99 | ♈♈♈ 7 |
| ● Romitorio di Santedame '98 | ♈♈♈ 7 |
| ● Romitorio di Santedame '97 | ♈♈♈ 7 |

## Russo

LOC. LA METOCCHINA
VIA FORNI, 71
57028 SUVERETO [LI]
TEL. +39 0565845105
www.vinirusso.it

**CELLAR SALES**
**PRE-BOOKED VISITS**
**ANNUAL PRODUCTION** 80,000 bottles
**HECTARES UNDER VINE** 14.00

20 years have passed since the Russo family began seriously dedicating themselves to viticulture (they began bottling in 1998), but their agricultural roots go back much further. Once upon a time they were a traditional producer, raising animals for milk and poultry, cultivating fruit, vegetables and grains. Today their style of wines is well-defined and manages to capture the territory in the glass, avoiding excessive extraction of prolonged maturation. Kudos to their 2015 La Mandria del Pari, a monovarietal Cabernet Sauvignon with aromas of tomato leaves, thyme and bay leaves set out on a solid, pleasant background of fruit, blackcurrant and blueberries. On the palate it's warm, elegant, firm and tasty, with a long finish. Their 2016 Ceppitaio, a Sangiovese with smaller shares of Ciliegiolo, Canaiolo and other black grapes, also did well. On the nose it opens with faintly gamey notes, followed by herbaceous hints and finally a nice array of fruit and flowers. On the palate it exhibits nice weight, balance and flavor.

| | |
|---|---|
| ● La Mandria del Pari '15 | ❦❦ 8 |
| ● Barbicone '15 | ❦❦ 4 |
| ● Ceppitaio '16 | ❦❦ 2* |
| ○ L'isoletta Vermentino '17 | ❦❦ 2* |
| ● Sassobucato '15 | ❦❦ 5 |
| ○ Pietrasca '12 | ♈♈ 2* |
| ● Sassobucato '10 | ♈♈ 5 |

# Salcheto

VIA DI VILLA BIANCA, 15
53045 MONTEPULCIANO [SI]
TEL. +39 0578799031
www.salcheto.it

**CELLAR SALES**
**PRE-BOOKED VISITS**
**ACCOMMODATION AND RESTAURANT SERVICE**
**ANNUAL PRODUCTION** 350,000 bottles
**HECTARES UNDER VINE** 58.00
**VITICULTURE METHOD** Certified Organic
**SUSTAINABLE WINERY**

Salcheto is an avant-garde winery that has attained the right balance between human intervention and nature. The first off-grid vintage in 2011 was the result of a 15-year-long experiment. The winery was disconnected from electrical supply, making it self-sufficient and leading to the production of Europe's first zero carbon footprint wine. Their wines are among the most convincing interpretations of the Montepulciano territory, not only for their quality but for the clear and coherent respect they show for Sangiovese di Montelpulciano. Their 2015 Nobile di Montepulciano Vecchie Viti del Salvo is a vibrant wine with assertive, well-defined aromas and nice energy on the palate. Their 2015 Nobile features an extremely pleasant palate and a highly aromatic nose. Their 2015 Nobile di Montepulciano Salco is a bit held back by oak, while both their 2017 Chianti Biskero and their 2017 Obvius (a monovarietal Prugnolo Gentile) proved pleasantly approachable.

| | |
|---|---|
| ● Nobile di Montepulciano '15 | ♟♟ 4 |
| ● Nobile di Montepulciano Vecchie Viti del Salco '15 | ♟♟ 8 |
| ● Chianti Biskero '17 | ♟ 2 |
| ● Nobile di Montepulciano Salco '15 | ♟ 6 |
| ● Obvius Rosso '17 | ♟ 4 |
| ● Nobile di Montepulciano '14 | ♟♟♟ 4* |
| ● Nobile di Montepulciano '10 | ♟♟♟ 4* |
| ● Nobile di Montepulciano Salco '11 | ♟♟♟ 6 |
| ● Nobile di Montepulciano Salco '10 | ♟♟♟ 5 |
| ● Chianti Colli Senesi '16 | ♟♟ 2* |
| ● Nobile di Montepulciano Salco '13 | ♟♟ 6 |
| ● Rosso di Montepulciano '16 | ♟♟ 2* |

# ★Salvioni

P.ZZA CAVOUR, 19
53024 MONTALCINO [SI]
TEL. +39 0577848499
www.aziendasalvioni.com

**PRE-BOOKED VISITS**
**RESTAURANT SERVICE**
**ANNUAL PRODUCTION** 15,000 bottles
**HECTARES UNDER VINE** 4.00

Situated at around 400 meters above sea level, in Le Cerbaie Alte (eastern Montalcino), on soils with high percentages of limestone, stones and galestro, the Salvioni family winery is dedicated primarily to Sangiovese. David and Alessia are worthy successors to their mother and father, Mirella and Giulio, and their Brunellos are considered among the most distinctive in the area. Spontaneous fermentation and maturation in 2000-liter Slavonian oak barrels are what holds together the rigor of their classics and the full-bodied texture of their best "modern" wines. Its a style of expression that certainly comes through in their most recent releases, like their 2013 Brunello. It offers up enticing, airy whiffs on the nose, with clear sensations of white fruit and forest undergrowth. These are followed by a complex and flavorful palate, with well-integrated alcohol and even tannins. It's just a bit rough at the end. The same qualities can be found in their 2016 Rosso, a more approachable though slightly less intense wine.

| | |
|---|---|
| ● Brunello di Montalcino '13 | ♟♟ 8 |
| ● Rosso di Montalcino '16 | ♟♟ 8 |
| ● Brunello di Montalcino '12 | ♟♟♟ 8 |
| ● Brunello di Montalcino '09 | ♟♟♟ 8 |
| ● Brunello di Montalcino '06 | ♟♟♟ 8 |
| ● Brunello di Montalcino '04 | ♟♟♟ 8 |
| ● Brunello di Montalcino '00 | ♟♟♟ 8 |
| ● Brunello di Montalcino '99 | ♟♟♟ 8 |
| ● Brunello di Montalcino '97 | ♟♟♟ 8 |
| ● Brunello di Montalcino '90 | ♟♟♟ 8 |
| ● Brunello di Montalcino '89 | ♟♟♟ 8 |
| ● Brunello di Montalcino '88 | ♟♟♟ 8 |
| ● Brunello di Montalcino '87 | ♟♟♟ 8 |
| ● Brunello di Montalcino '85 | ♟♟♟ 8 |
| ● Brunello di Montalcino '11 | ♟♟ 8 |

## Podere San Cristoforo

FRAZ. BAGNO
LOC. FORNI
58023 GAVORRANO [GR]
TEL. +39 3358212413
www.poderesancristoforo.it

**CELLAR SALES**
**PRE-BOOKED VISITS**
**ACCOMMODATION**
**ANNUAL PRODUCTION** 50,000 bottles
**HECTARES UNDER VINE** 15.00
**VITICULTURE METHOD** Certified Organic
**SUSTAINABLE WINERY**

Lorenzo Zonin purchased Podere San Cristoforo in 2000 and immediately embraced biodynamic methods. The winery is near Gavorrano, in Maremma, where focusing on Sangiovese isn't the usual. However, here, their Sangioveses are probably the most elegant and fresh in the whole territory. The quality of their selection isn't surprising when you recognize the winery's determination in the face of this difficult Tuscan variety. Their wines are distinctive, never excessive or too powerful, but rather graceful and generally elegant. Their stylistically precise 2016 San Cristoforo, a monovarietal Petit Verdot, features and elegant, extremely supple palate that's both rhythmic and flavorful. And its aromas are well-balanced as well, fragrant and multifaceted. Their 2016 Maremma is a balanced, somewhat delicate wine with slightly veiled aromas, but it unfolds nicely on the palate, enticing and full of flavor. Their interesting 2009 Maremma Luminoso, a blend of Trebbiano, Malvasia and Vermentino, is a vibrant, deep wine.

| | |
|---|---|
| ● San Cristoforo '16 | ♟♟ 6 |
| ○ Luminoso Dolce '09 | ♟♟ 5 |
| ● Maremma Toscana Carandelle '16 | ♟♟ 3 |
| ● Divita '16 | ♟ 4 |
| ● Ameri Governo all'Uso Toscano '15 | ♟♟♟ 6 |
| ● Maremma Toscana Podere San Cristoforo '13 | ♟♟♟ 3* |
| ● Maremma Toscana Sangiovese Carandelle '15 | ♟♟♟ 3* |
| ○ Maremma Toscana Luminoso '15 | ♟♟ 3 |
| ● Maremma Toscana Sangiovese Amaranto '16 | ♟♟ 3* |
| ● Maremma Toscana Sangiovese Amaranto '15 | ♟♟ 3 |
| ● Maremma Toscana Sangiovese Amaranto '14 | ♟♟ 2* |
| ● San Cristoforo '12 | ♟♟ 5 |
| ● San Cristoforo Petit Verdot '15 | ♟♟ 5 |

## ★San Felice

LOC. SAN FELICE
53019 CASTELNUOVO BERARDENGA [SI]
TEL. +39 057739911
www.agricolasanfelice.it

**CELLAR SALES**
**PRE-BOOKED VISITS**
**ACCOMMODATION AND RESTAURANT SERVICE**
**ANNUAL PRODUCTION** 900,000 bottles
**HECTARES UNDER VINE** 140.00

San Felice makes up no small part of Chianti Classico's history. It was purchased in the 1970s by the insurance group Allianz, who subsequently expanded their property in Montalcino with the purchase of Tenuta Campogiovanni in 1982, Tenuta Perolla in Maremma, and lastly Bell'Aja in Bolgheri. However, Castelnuovo Berardenga remains as their main hub. Recognized as one of the most important and beautiful areas in the whole appellation, they own a considerable number of vineyards here. Their 2015 Grigio Riserva, a Chianti Classico with a pronounced territorial character, is among their best ever. It's redolent of earth, flowers and forest undergrowth, with the occasional hint of ripe red fruit. On the palate it unfolds with nice contrasts and great rhythm. Their 2015 Chianti Classico Gran Selezione Il Grigio is more concentrated, though a bit less expressive.

| | |
|---|---|
| ● Chianti Cl. Il Grigio Ris. '15 | ♟♟♟ 3* |
| ● Bolgheri Rosso Bell'Aja '16 | ♟♟ 5 |
| ● Chianti Cl. '16 | ♟♟ 3 |
| ● Chianti Cl. Gran Sel. Il Grigio '15 | ♟♟ 5 |
| ● Chianti Cl. '13 | ♟♟♟ 3* |
| ● Chianti Cl. Gran Sel. Il Grigio da San Felice '11 | ♟♟♟ 5 |
| ● Chianti Cl. Gran Sel. Il Grigio da San Felice '10 | ♟♟♟ 5 |
| ● Pugnitello '07 | ♟♟♟ 6 |
| ● Pugnitello '06 | ♟♟♟ 6 |
| ● Vigorello '13 | ♟♟♟ 6 |
| ● Vigorello '10 | ♟♟♟ 6 |
| ● Vigorello '08 | ♟♟♟ 6 |

# Fattoria San Felo

LOC. PAGLIATELLI DI SOTTO
58051 MAGLIANO IN TOSCANA [GR]
TEL. +39 05641836727
www.fattoriasanfelo.it

**ANNUAL PRODUCTION** 200,000 bottles
**HECTARES UNDER VINE** 25.00

Fattoria San Felo's plots are entirely situated in Magliano in Toscana. Morellino takes center stage in their selection, though they also offer wines made with international cultivar, some of which are quite complex. Their style is modern, with carefully monitored maturation carried out in mid-small wood barrels. In the past their wines didn't always achieve outstanding quality standards, but today it seems like they're on the right track for good. Their 2016 Morellino Lampo proves well-defined on the nose, with a soft palate that's not lacking in rhythm or savoriness. Their 2016 Maremma Toscana Balla La Vecchia is a juicy, drinkable wine. In some ways their 2016 Pinot Nero surprises. It's an uncommon cultivar for Maremma, and it was an early harvest for a red fermented with its stems, for maintaining its freshness, but it's a highly drinkable wine with some character. Their 2014 Spumante Metodo Classico, with its fine sparkle and deep palate, also surprises.

| | |
|---|---|
| ● Morellino di Scansano Lampo '16 | ♟♟ 3* |
| ● Maremma Toscana Rosso Balla La Vecchia '16 | ♟♟ 3 |
| ● Pinot Nero '16 | ♟♟ 5 |
| ○ San Felo Brut M. Cl. '14 | ♟♟ 5 |
| ○ Chardonnay '17 | ♟ 3 |
| ● Morellino di Scansano '16 | ♟ 3 |
| ● Balla La Vecchia '12 | ♟♟ 2* |
| ○ Chardonnay '15 | ♟♟ 3 |
| ● Morellino di Scansano Dicioccatore Ris. '10 | ♟♟ 4 |
| ● Morellino di Scansano Lampo '15 | ♟♟ 3 |
| ● Morellino di Scansano Lampo '13 | ♟♟ 3 |
| ● Morellino di Scansano Lampo '12 | ♟♟ 3 |
| ● Morellino di Scansano Lampo '11 | ♟♟ 2* |
| ○ Viognier '12 | ♟♟ 2* |
| ⊙ Frosali '12 | ♟ 2 |

# ★★★Tenuta San Guido

FRAZ. BOLGHERI
LOC. LE CAPANNE, 27
57022 CASTAGNETO CARDUCCI [LI]
TEL. +39 0565762003
www.sassicaia.com

**PRE-BOOKED VISITS**
**RESTAURANT SERVICE**
**ANNUAL PRODUCTION** 780,000 bottles
**HECTARES UNDER VINE** 90.00

Fifty years after the first vintage was produced in 1968, the Sassicaia star continues to shine. In fact, this famous wine, one of the most iconic of all Italian wines, seems to be increasing its success. The history of Tenuta San Guido and the Incisa della Rocchetta Marquises intertwines with that of Italy's winemaking renaissance and Bolgheri's winemaking history; much of the district's reputation is owed to them. The Cabernet Sauvignon and Franc grapes that go toward making their main wine are cultivated in various areas, while their historic vineyards are situated in the hills. Their 2015 Sassicaia is different from recent years, maybe more complete and with great potential for aging. On the nose it still doesn't offer up everything, and proved almost a bit timid at the time of our tastings. It's a good sign as great years often behave like that. On the palate it's already brilliant, youthful yes, but fine, graceful and deep, finishing on sophisticated hints of oak and cedar. Hats off.

| | |
|---|---|
| ● Bolgheri Sassicaia '15 | ♟♟♟ 8 |
| ● Guidalberto '16 | ♟♟ 6 |
| ● Le Difese '16 | ♟ 4 |
| ● Bolgheri Sassicaia '14 | ♟♟♟ 8 |
| ● Bolgheri Sassicaia '13 | ♟♟♟ 8 |
| ● Bolgheri Sassicaia '12 | ♟♟♟ 8 |
| ● Bolgheri Sassicaia '11 | ♟♟♟ 8 |
| ● Bolgheri Sassicaia '10 | ♟♟♟ 8 |
| ● Bolgheri Sassicaia '09 | ♟♟♟ 8 |
| ● Bolgheri Sassicaia '08 | ♟♟♟ 8 |
| ● Guidalberto '08 | ♟♟♟ 6 |
| ● Guidalberto '09 | ♟♟ 6 |
| ● Le Difese '15 | ♟♟ 4 |
| ● Le Difese '13 | ♟♟ 4 |

## San Polo

LOC. PODERNOVI, 161
53024 MONTALCINO [SI]
TEL. +39 0577835101
www.poggiosanpolo.com

CELLAR SALES
PRE-BOOKED VISITS
ANNUAL PRODUCTION 150,000 bottles
HECTARES UNDER VINE 17.00

The Allegrini family winery in Montalcino has found its footing thanks to their young staff. Everything revolves around the splendid Podernovi farm, an historic property in the eastern district situated at about 450 meters above sea level, on clay and calcium-rich soils. Fermented in concrete with maturation in barriques and Slavonian and Allier barrels, their Brunellos are close-focused and energetic. Their Rosso, IGT Mezzopane (a blend of mostly Sangiovese) and Rubio (a monovarietal Sangiovese) complete their selection. San Polo's formidable growth doesn't show signs of slowing down and their 2013 Brunello represents yet another feather in their cap. Its trademark aromas are adorned by sparkling, fruity nuances, delicately enriched by touches of pepper, dried herbs and cocoa. It's the prelude to a palate that privileges proportion over weight, without extractive redundancies.

| | | |
|---|---|---|
| ● Brunello di Montalcino '13 | ▼▼ | 7 |
| ● Brunello di Montalcino Ris. '12 | ▼▼ | 8 |
| ● Brunello di Montalcino '12 | ♀♀ | 6 |
| ● Brunello di Montalcino '11 | ♀♀ | 6 |
| ● Brunello di Montalcino '10 | ♀♀ | 6 |
| ● Brunello di Montalcino '09 | ♀♀ | 6 |
| ● Brunello di Montalcino '08 | ♀♀ | 6 |
| ● Brunello di Montalcino '07 | ♀♀ | 6 |
| ● Brunello di Montalcino Ris. '10 | ♀♀ | 7 |
| ● Brunello di Montalcino Ris. '06 | ♀♀ | 7 |
| ● Rosso di Montalcino '15 | ♀♀ | 3* |
| ● Rosso di Montalcino '13 | ♀♀ | 3 |
| ● Rosso di Montalcino '12 | ♀♀ | 3 |
| ● Rosso di Montalcino '11 | ♀♀ | 3 |
| ● Rubio '10 | ♀♀ | 2* |

## Sangervasio

LOC. SAN GERVASIO
VIA DEI CIPRESSI, 13
56036 PALAIA [PI]
TEL. +39 0587483360
www.sangervasio.com

CELLAR SALES
PRE-BOOKED VISITS
ACCOMMODATION AND RESTAURANT SERVICE
ANNUAL PRODUCTION 100,000 bottles
HECTARES UNDER VINE 22.00
VITICULTURE METHOD Certified Organic

San Gervasio is a sixteenth-century town situated in the green Val d'Era foothills, where youcan also spend a lovely holiday. It is made up of over 350 hectares of woods, vineyards and olive groves. The farm was purchased by the Tommasini family in 1960, and during the 1990s it underwent major changes thanks to novel ideas from Luca and his daughter Lisa. Luca had great faith in the potential of this territory and thanks to his commitment, determination and courage in making innovative decisions he helped the whole area grow. Their 2014 Villa Le Torri, a monovarietal Cabernet Franc, put in a nice performance, with its concentrated aromatic profile of blackcurrant and blueberries accompanied by fresh notes of lemon grass and peppers and spicy hints of juniper. On the palate it proves big, pleasantly rich, with well-balanced tannins and alcohol. Their 2015 Sirio offers up a bouquet in which cherry is accompanied by spicy nuances of cloves. In the mouth it's rich and firm, with a long finish that reveals an appetizing savoriness.

| | | |
|---|---|---|
| ● Chianti Ris. '15 | ▼▼ | 3 |
| ● I Renai '15 | ▼▼ | 5 |
| ● Terre di Pisa Sangiovese A Sirio '15 | ▼▼ | 5 |
| ● Villa Le Torri Cabernet Franc '14 | ▼▼ | 6 |
| ● Colli dell'Etruria Centrale Vin Santo Occhio di Pernice '16 | ♀♀ | 5 |
| ○ Colli dell'Etruria Centrale Vin Santo Recinaio '05 | ♀♀ | 5 |
| ○ Colli Etruria Vin Santo Recinaio '06 | ♀♀ | 5 |
| ● I Renai '13 | ♀♀ | 5 |
| ● I Renai '11 | ♀♀ | 5 |
| ● Terre di Pisa Sangiovese A Sirio '13 | ♀♀ | 4 |
| ● Villa Le Torri '13 | ♀♀ | 6 |

# Podere Sanlorenzo

POD. SANLORENZO, 280
53024 MONTALCINO [SI]
TEL. +39 3396070930
www.poderesanlorenzo.net

CELLAR SALES
PRE-BOOKED VISITS
ANNUAL PRODUCTION 18,000 bottles
HECTARES UNDER VINE 4.50

Legendary Bramante Ferretti was the heart
and soul of the Sanlorenzo farm for many
years. Indeed, even at well over 100
he could be seen working his vineyards.
His grandson Luciano Ciolfi cultivates
some of their highly productive plots in
southwestern Montalcino, situated at some
500 meters above sea level on a hill
overlooking the Ombrone river and
Maremma. The hot breezes combined with
lean, stony soils (galestro in origin) explain
the succulent but austere character of his
Brunellos, which are mostly matured in
3000-liter Slavonian oak barrels. They've
managed to maintain stylistic continuity
despite varying seasons, though they
seem to be favored by cooler years. Their
2013 Brunello is a good example, with its
hints of plums, black cherry, nutmeg and
tar, pointing up a certain aromatic ripeness
that's well supported by a solid tannic
weave and a lush, savory backbone. Their
2016 Rosso also had a good year.

# ★Podere Sapaio

LOC. LO SCOPAIO, 212
57022 CASTAGNETO CARDUCCI [LI]
TEL. +39 0565765187
www.sapaio.it

CELLAR SALES
PRE-BOOKED VISITS
ANNUAL PRODUCTION 110,000 bottles
HECTARES UNDER VINE 25.00

Sapaio has become a benchmark among
Bolgheri's top producers and is part of an
evolution in style that favors wines with a
healthy dose of personality. Massimo
Piccini's winery is young and successful,
and it gives every indication it wants to
continue along the same path. The estate
has a large vineyard area, lying on sandy
and calcareous soils. The style is clearly
modern, and we found the most recent
wines the most convincing, because of the
balance of fruit and wood. Their 2016
Bolgheri Superiore Sapaio, which had only
recently been bottled at the time of our
tastings, confirms this trend and proves to
be a spectacular red. Its toasty hints of
chocolate, of commendable grain and
delicate, are already in harmony with its
fruity background and balsamic-
herbaceous flashes calling up mint. Their
2016 Bolgheri Volpolo and 2015 IGT
Sapaio, two wines that are also both
representative of the producer's style, also
did well.

| | |
|---|---|
| ● Brunello di Montalcino Bramante '13 | ♟♟ 6 |
| ● Rosso di Montalcino '16 | ♟ 3 |
| ● Brunello di Montalcino Bramante '07 | ♟♟♟ 6 |
| ● Brunello di Montalcino Bramante '07 | ♟♟♟ 8 |
| ● Brunello di Montalcino Bramante '12 | ♟♟ 6 |
| ● Brunello di Montalcino Bramante '11 | ♟♟ 6 |
| ● Brunello di Montalcino Bramante '10 | ♟♟ 6 |
| ● Brunello di Montalcino Bramante '09 | ♟♟ 6 |
| ● Brunello di Montalcino Bramante '08 | ♟♟ 6 |
| ● Rosso di Montalcino '15 | ♟♟ 3 |
| ● Rosso di Montalcino '14 | ♟♟ 3 |
| ● Rosso di Montalcino '13 | ♟♟ 3 |
| ● Rosso di Montalcino '11 | ♟♟ 3 |
| ● Rosso di Montalcino '10 | ♟♟ 3 |
| ● Rosso di Montalcino '09 | ♟♟ 3 |

| | |
|---|---|
| ● Bolgheri Rosso Sup. Sapaio '16 | ♟♟♟ 7 |
| ● Bolgheri Volpolo '16 | ♟♟ 5 |
| ● Bolgheri Rosso Sup. '13 | ♟♟♟ 7 |
| ● Bolgheri Rosso Sup. '12 | ♟♟♟ 7 |
| ● Bolgheri Rosso Sup. '11 | ♟♟♟ 7 |
| ● Bolgheri Sup. Sapaio '10 | ♟♟♟ 6 |
| ● Bolgheri Sup. Sapaio '09 | ♟♟♟ 6 |
| ● Bolgheri Sup. Sapaio '08 | ♟♟♟ 6 |
| ● Bolgheri Sup. Sapaio '07 | ♟♟♟ 6 |
| ● Bolgheri Sup. Sapaio '06 | ♟♟♟ 6 |
| ● Sapaio '15 | ♟♟♟ 6 |
| ● Bolgheri Volpolo '13 | ♟♟ 5 |
| ● Bolgheri Volpolo '12 | ♟♟ 4 |

## Fattoria Sardi

FRAZ. MONTE SAN QUIRICO
VIA DELLA MAULINA, 747
55100 LUCCA
TEL. +39 0583341230
www.fattoriasardi.com

**CELLAR SALES**
**PRE-BOOKED VISITS**
**ACCOMMODATION**
**ANNUAL PRODUCTION** 120,000 bottles
**HECTARES UNDER VINE** 17.50
**VITICULTURE METHOD** Certified Organic

The Sardi Giustiniani farm is managed by a young couple who are carrying on a deep-rooted family tradition in a modern way. The farm is situated near Lucca, wedged between the Apuan Alps, Apennines and Tyrrhenian Sea. The current farming approach looks to organic and biodynamic methods in order to safeguard the incredible natural heritage at their disposal. The terrain is located between two rivers: downstream we find silty, sandy and stony soils, but going up to the top of the hills, the percentage of clay and stones increases. Their 2015 Sebastiano is among the best wines of the Colline Lucchesi hills. Its aromas are truly marvelous, from black cherries to violets, then blackcurrant, raspberries, tanned leather and fine spices. A hint of pencil lead accompanies the palate, which proves juicy and gratifying the whole way through. Their 2016 Le Cicale is a delicious rosé, while their 2017 Rosé is a bit sweet in its aromas. Their semi-sparkling Pet Nat is a fun wine.

| | |
|---|---|
| ● Colline Lucchesi Sebastiano '15 | ♟♟ 5 |
| ⊙ Le Cicale '17 | ♟♟ 5 |
| ○ Pet-Nat Frizzante '17 | ♟♟ 3 |
| ⊙ Rosé '17 | ♟ 3 |
| ● Colline Lucchesi Rosso Sebastiano '13 | ♟♟ 5 |
| ● Colline Lucchesi Vallebuia '16 | ♟♟ 3 |
| ○ Colline Lucchesi Vermentino '14 | ♟♟ 3 |
| ⊙ Le Cicale '16 | ♟♟ 4 |
| ○ Pet-Nat Frizzante '16 | ♟♟ 3 |

## Sassotondo

FRAZ. SOVANA
LOC. PIAN DI CONATI, 52
58010 SORANO [GR]
TEL. +39 0564614218
www.sassotondo.it

**CELLAR SALES**
**PRE-BOOKED VISITS**
**ANNUAL PRODUCTION** 50,000 bottles
**HECTARES UNDER VINE** 12.00
**VITICULTURE METHOD** Certified Organic

Carla, Benini and Edoardo Ventimiglia's winery is forging ahead. In 1990 the group decided to leave Roma so as to undertake winemaking in Sovana. The first harvest came in 1997, and in the 20 years since, they've managed to bring attention to this corner of Maremma, focusing on Ciliegiolo before others were doing the same, and becoming an ambassador of this strip of southern Tuscany. So as to protect the territory, they've adopted a minimally invasive style, both in the vineyard and in the cellar. In addition to Ciliegiolo, they make wines with Trebbiano, Greco and Sauvignon. During our tastings their 2015 Ciliegiolo San Lorenzo stood out, as did their 2016 Ciliegiolo Poggio Pinzo. The former proves complex and well-orchestrated across a highly pleasant, fruity background and a spicy, savory and long finish. The latter is more approachable and direct, with fine-grained and balanced tannins, and a creamy, gratifying palate. Their gold-colored 2017 Bianco di Pitigliano Superiore Isolina offers up intriguing and elegant aromas of grains, followed by a rich palate that unfolds progressively.

| | |
|---|---|
| ● Maremma Toscana Ciliegiolo San Lorenzo '15 | ♟♟ 6 |
| ○ Bianco di Pitigliano Sup. Isolina '17 | ♟♟ 4 |
| ● Maremma Toscana Ciliegiolo '17 | ♟♟ 3 |
| ● Maremma Toscana Ciliegiolo Poggio Pinzo '16 | ♟♟ 6 |
| ⊙ Maremma Toscana Rosato '17 | ♟ 3 |
| ○ Tufobianco '17 | ♟ 2 |
| ● Ciliegiolo '12 | ♟♟ 2* |
| ● Ciliegiolo '11 | ♟♟ 2* |
| ● Maremma Toscana Ciliegiolo San Lorenzo '13 | ♟♟ 6 |
| ● Maremma Toscana San Lorenzo '12 | ♟♟ 6 |
| ○ Numero Dieci '11 | ♟♟ 6 |
| ● San Lorenzo '08 | ♟♟ 6 |

# Michele Satta

LOC. VIGNA AL CAVALIERE, 61B
57022 CASTAGNETO CARDUCCI [LI]
TEL. +39 0565773041
www.michelesatta.com

CELLAR SALES
PRE-BOOKED VISITS
ANNUAL PRODUCTION 150,000 bottles
HECTARES UNDER VINE 20.00

This winery was founded in 1983, one year before establishment of the Bolgheri DOC zone, of which Michele Satta was one of the founders. Over time land was purchased and the main building was erected. During the 1990s the first vineyards were planted with Syrah and of course Sangiovese, alongside the usual Cabernet Sauvignon and Merlot. It was an original idea that, combined with their style, introduced an unconventional new direction. They have continued to carry out experiments throughout the years, along with increasing care and attention in the vineyard. The wines presented this year came across as having gained in definition and identity. Their 2015 Bolgheri Rosso Superiore Marianova, an unusual blend of Sangiovese and Syrah, is elegant and vibrant, fresh and balsamic, with a linear development that's uncommon for the area. It finishes on notes of small red fruits and toasty accents, though it's hurt at this point by a slight sensation of alcohol, which is too bad. Their 2015 Piastraia is also delicious.

| | | |
|---|---|---|
| ● Bolgheri Rosso Sup. Marianova '15 | ♥♥ 8 |
| ● Bolgheri Rosso Sup. Piastraia '15 | ♥♥ 6 |
| ● Cavaliere '15 | ♥♥ 6 |
| ○ Bolgheri Bianco Giovin Re '16 | ♥ 6 |
| ● Bolgheri Rosso Piastraia '02 | ♥♥♥ 6 |
| ● Bolgheri Rosso '15 | ♀♀ 4 |
| ● Bolgheri Rosso '13 | ♀♀ 3 |
| ● Bolgheri Rosso Sup. I Castagni '12 | ♀♀ 8 |
| ● Bolgheri Sup. Piastraia '14 | ♀♀ 6 |
| ● Syrah '12 | ♀♀ 5 |

# La Selva

LOC. SAN DONATO
S.DA PROV.LE 81 OSA, 7
58015 ORBETELLO [GR]
TEL. +39 0564884820
www.laselva.bio

CELLAR SALES
PRE-BOOKED VISITS
ACCOMMODATION
ANNUAL PRODUCTION 200,000 bottles
HECTARES UNDER VINE 32.00
VITICULTURE METHOD Certified Organic

Karl Egger was a pioneer of organic viticulture, and is one of the most interesting producers in Maremma today. This is due to the care and attention he has paid to the environment over the last forty years, both in the vineyards and cellar, and in the other activities he carries out at his farm. He was one of the first to focus on local grape varieties, both whites and reds, and to outline the style of his wines in an original way, shedding stereotypes that had defined the fundamental character of local wines for years. Today, his pleasant wines exhibit a very consistent quality. A fresh palate and aromatic cleanness define their 2015 Maremma Ciliegiolo, a highly drinkable red. We found their 2017 Morellino di Scansano just as enjoyable, with its fragrant aromas and its full, rhythmic palate. Their 2015 Morellino di Scansano Colli dell'Uccellina Riserva features a more complex weave, both aromatically and on the palate, though it maintains its drinkability, while their 2017 Maremma Vermentino proves juicy.

| | | |
|---|---|---|
| ● Maremma Toscana Ciliegiolo '15 | ♥♥ 4 |
| ○ Maremma Toscana Vermentino '17 | ♥♥ 3 |
| ● Morellino di Scansano '17 | ♥♥ 3 |
| ● Morellino di Scansano Colli dell' Uccellina Ris. '15 | ♥♥ 4 |
| ● Maremma Toscana Ciliegiolo '13 | ♀♀ 3 |
| ● Maremma Toscana Privo '16 | ♀♀ 2* |
| ● Morellino di Scansano '15 | ♀♀ 2* |
| ● Morellino di Scansano Colli dell'Uccellina Ris. '13 | ♀♀ 3 |
| ● Nudo Sangiovese '14 | ♀♀ 2* |
| ● Pugnitello '13 | ♀♀ 5 |

## Fattoria Selvapiana

LOC. SELVAPIANA, 43
50068 RUFINA [FI]
TEL. +39 0558369848
www.selvapiana.it

CELLAR SALES
PRE-BOOKED VISITS
ANNUAL PRODUCTION 220,000 bottles
HECTARES UNDER VINE 60.00

Selvapiana is an historic estate surrounding the Renaissance villa purchased by the Giuntini family in 1826. It was renovated and developed in the 1990s by the last descendant, Francesco, but today the property is managed by Silvia and Federico Giuntini. Their lands are spread over three municipalities: Rufina, Pelago and Pontassieve, although most of the oldest vineyards are located near the villa. The new winemaking cellar is also nearby and was officially opened with the 2005 vintage. Their 2015 Chianti Rufina Vigneto Bucerchiale made it to our finals thanks to a complex bouquet of tanned leather, then wild berries, blackcurrant and a hint of tobacco. It shows nice weight on the palate, proving firm, juicy and lively, with a long, flavorful finish and enticing aftertaste. Their 2016 Chianti Rufina impresses for its aromatic approachability, with fragrances of fruit and cherries accompanied by fresh sensations of forest undergrowth. On the palate it's enjoyable, fresh and generous, with a pronounced acidic vein.

| | |
|---|---|
| ● Chianti Rufina Vign. Bucerchiale Ris. '15 | ♥♥ 5 |
| ● Chianti Rufina '16 | ♥♥ 2* |
| ● Chianti Rufina '15 | ♀♀ 2* |
| ● Chianti Rufina Bucerchiale Ris. '13 | ♀♀ 5 |
| ● Chianti Rufina Bucerchiale Ris. '12 | ♀♀ 5 |
| ● Chianti Rufina Bucerchiale Ris. '10 | ♀♀ 5 |
| ● Chianti Rufina Bucerchiale Ris. '09 | ♀♀ 5 |
| ○ Vin Santo del Chianti Rufina '07 | ♀♀ 2* |

## Sensi - Fattoria Calappiano

FRAZ. CERBAIA, 107
51035 LAMPORECCHIO [PT]
TEL. +39 057382910
www.sensivini.com

CELLAR SALES
PRE-BOOKED VISITS
ANNUAL PRODUCTION 2,000,000 bottles
HECTARES UNDER VINE 100.00
VITICULTURE METHOD Certified Organic
SUSTAINABLE WINERY

The Sensi family have been working in the wine sector for more than 120 years, both as producers and traders, and managing distribution across all the continents. Fourth generation, Massimo and Roberta, are completing their improvements at the winery, focusing on developing their selection and stronger links with the territory. Their brands include Tenuta del Poggio and Fattoria di Calappiano in the Florentine part of Chianti, site of the ancient hunting lodge of the Medici family during the 1500s. Their 2015 Collegonzi, made primarily with Sangiovese, earned a place in our finals with its close-focused aromas of cherry and blackberry, its notes of aromatic herbs and spicy accents of cloves. On the palate it's soft and dynamic, with balanced tannins and freshness, and a lively, clean finish. Their 2017 Ninfato, a Sangiovese without added sulfites, offers up a concentrated bouquet of black fruit, hints of licorice and then refreshing notes. On the palate it reveals depth and refreshing acidity.

| | |
|---|---|
| ● Collegonzi Sangiovese '15 | ♥♥ 6 |
| ● Governato '16 | ♥♥ 7 |
| ● Mantello Sangiovese Shiraz '16 | ♥♥ 4 |
| ● Ninfato '17 | ♥♥ 3 |
| ● Chianti Vinciano '17 | ♥ 5 |
| ● Chianti Vinciano Ris. '15 | ♥ 6 |
| ● Morellino di Scansano Pretorio '17 | ♥ 3 |
| ○ Vernaccia di S. Gimignano Collegiata '17 | ♥ 2 |
| ● Bolgheri Sabbiato '15 | ♀♀ 5 |
| ● Chianti Dalcampo Ris. '14 | ♀♀ 3 |
| ● Chianti Vinciano Fattoria di Calappiano '16 | ♀♀ 4 |
| ● Morellino di Scansano Pretorio '16 | ♀♀ 3 |

# Serpaia

LOC. FONTEBLANDA
VIA GOLDONI, 15
58100 GROSSETO
TEL. +39 0461650129
www.serpaiamaremma.it

ANNUAL PRODUCTION 135,000 bottles
HECTARES UNDER VINE 30.00

The Endrizzi family are historic producers in Trentino, and as with other producers from the north, they have found Maremma excellent for producing reds with a marked character. Serpaia produces technically impeccable wines with good consistent quality, compatible with the warm Mediterranean area of Magliano in Toscana. Still short of their goal, their wines are nonetheless growing. Their inexperience is showing in particular when it comes to dosing wood for aging. Their 2016 Morellino di Scansano pursues pleasantness, with its aromatic profile of fresh cherries and earthy hints followed by spices. In the mouth it expands softly, but it's also lively and full of contrasts. Their 2016 Serpaiolo, a blend of Merlot, Cabernet Sauvignon and Sangiovese, features clean and expressive aromas and vibrant flavor.

# Serraiola

FRAZ. FRASSINE
LOC. SERRAIOLA
58025 MONTEROTONDO MARITTIMO [GR]
TEL. +39 0566910026
www.serraiola.it

CELLAR SALES
PRE-BOOKED VISITS
ANNUAL PRODUCTION 40,000 bottles
HECTARES UNDER VINE 12.00

Fiorella Lenzi is a 'wine madam' who has played a leading role in Maremma's development. She produces wines full of character that often achieve high levels of quality. In spite of a few false steps in the recent past with wines exhibiting excessive wood aging, their style for the most part is solid and balanced. They traditionally produce whites, standouts for their originality, alongside more predictable reds from the production area. Their 2016 Lentisco, a monovarietal Sangiovese, offers up vibrant aromas of morello cherry and enjoyable smoky notes. On the palate it unfolds with generosity and juiciness only to finish sweet and relaxed. Their 2016 Shiraz (made with Syrah) is quite spicy on the nose, while on the palate it proves solid and assertive. Their 2016 Campo Montecristo, a monovarietal Merlot, sees sweeter, fuller aromas, while on the palate it unfolds with pleasantness softness and nice dynamism.

| | |
|---|---|
| ● Morellino di Scansano '16 | ▼▼ 3 |
| ● Serpaiolo '16 | ▼▼ 3 |
| ● Morellino di Scansano '15 | ♀♀ 3 |
| ● Morellino di Scansano '14 | ♀♀ 2* |
| ● Morellino di Scansano '13 | ♀♀ 2* |
| ● Serpaiolo '15 | ♀♀ 3 |
| ● Serpaiolo '14 | ♀♀ 2* |

| | |
|---|---|
| ● Campo Montecristo '16 | ▼▼ 5 |
| ● Lentisco '16 | ▼▼ 3 |
| ● Shiraz '16 | ▼▼ 4 |
| ● Campo Montecristo '15 | ♀♀ 5 |
| ● Campo Montecristo '14 | ♀♀ 5 |
| ● Campo Montecristo '13 | ♀♀ 5 |
| ● Lentisco '15 | ♀♀ 3 |
| ● Lentisco '14 | ♀♀ 3 |
| ○ Maremma Toscana Bianco Violina '16 | ♀♀ 3 |
| ● Monteregio Massa Marittima Lentisco '13 | ♀♀ 3 |
| ● Shiraz '13 | ♀♀ 3 |
| ○ Vermentino '13 | ♀♀ 2* |

## Sesti - Castello di Argiano

FRAZ. SANT'ANGELO IN COLLE
LOC. CASTELLO DI ARGIANO
53024 MONTALCINO [SI]
TEL. +39 0577843921
www.sestiwine.com

CELLAR SALES
PRE-BOOKED VISITS
ANNUAL PRODUCTION 61,000 bottles
HECTARES UNDER VINE 9.00

Castello d'Argiano is much more than operational headquarters for the Sesti family. It is also an ancient Etruscan outpost, strategically positioned on the southwestern border of Montalcino and enveloped in Mediterranean scrub. Here we find vineyards cultivated with Sangiovese for making Brunello wines, exemplary for their exuberant and relaxed touch, and infused with Tyrrhenian breezes and sandy-tufaceous soils. These assets are as important as the winery's philosophy, which employs biodynamic methods, energy conservation, and astronomical cycles. It's not the first time that Sesti's Rosso finds itself among Montalcino's top wines, but we'll be talking about their 2016 for a while. Watermelon, yellow peach, curry, burnt wood all make for a noteworthy aromatic profile, while on the palate it has the savory presence of a great Brunello, proving creamy, pervasive and supported to the last drop. Their 2012 Phenomena Riserva, another excellent wine, features potent though fine-grained tannins.

| | |
|---|---|
| ● Rosso di Montalcino '16 | ▼▼▼ 4* |
| ● Brunello di Montalcino '13 | ▼▼ 6 |
| ● Brunello di Montalcino Phenomena Ris. '12 | ▼▼ 8 |
| ● Brunello di Montalcino '06 | ♀♀♀ 6 |
| ● Brunello di Montalcino Phenomena Ris. '07 | ♀♀♀ 8 |
| ● Brunello di Montalcino Phenomena Ris. '01 | ♀♀♀ 8 |
| ● Brunello di Montalcino Ris. '04 | ♀♀♀ 8 |
| ● Brunello di Montalcino '12 | ♀♀ 6 |
| ● Brunello di Montalcino '11 | ♀♀ 6 |
| ● Brunello di Montalcino Phenomena Ris. '10 | ♀♀ 8 |
| ● Rosso di Montalcino '15 | ♀♀ 4 |

## Tenuta Sette Ponti

VIA SETTE PONTI, 71
52029 CASTIGLION FIBOCCHI [AR]
TEL. +39 0575477857
www.tenutasetteponti.it

CELLAR SALES
PRE-BOOKED VISITS
ACCOMMODATION
ANNUAL PRODUCTION 225,000 bottles
HECTARES UNDER VINE 55.00
SUSTAINABLE WINERY

This historic estate is situated in a picturesque corner of Tuscany, between Florence and Arezzo. Its current name is owed to fashion businessman Antonio Moretti who wanted to pay homage to the Sette Ponti road, so-called because of the number of bridges (seven) over the Arno between the two Tuscan cities. After purchasing the winery, Moretti also bought property in Bolgheri, Maremma and Sicily, confirming his great passion for land and wine. All the vineyards at Setteponti are under organic management. Their 2016 Oreno, a blend of Merlot, Cabernet Sauvignon and Petit Verdot, takes home Tre Bicchieri, On the nose it offers up tertiary overtones of chocolate and coffee accompanied by green sensations of peppers and spicy notes. On the palate it proves generous, soft, full-bodied, with a subtle tannic weave and a relaxed finish. Their 2015 Vigna dell'Impero, a monovarietal Sangiovese, is austere on the nose, with notes of tobacco and tanned leather set on a fruity background. In the mouth it exhibits notable tannic presence and nice length.

| | |
|---|---|
| ● Oreno '16 | ▼▼▼ 8 |
| ● Valdarno di Sopra Sangiovese V. dell'Impero '15 | ▼▼ 8 |
| ● Chianti V. di Pallino '16 | ▼ 2 |
| ● Chianti V. di Pallino Ris. '15 | ▼ 3 |
| ● Oreno '15 | ♀♀♀ 8 |
| ● Oreno '12 | ♀♀♀ 7 |
| ● Oreno '11 | ♀♀♀ 7 |
| ● Oreno '10 | ♀♀♀ 7 |
| ● Oreno '09 | ♀♀♀ 7 |
| ● Oreno '05 | ♀♀♀ 7 |
| ● Oreno '00 | ♀♀♀ 5 |
| ● Valdarno di Sopra V. dell'Impero '13 | ♀♀♀ 8 |

# Fattoria Le Sorgenti

LOC. VALLINA
VIA DI DOCCIOLA, 8
50012 BAGNO A RIPOLI [FI]
TEL. +39 055696004
www.fattoria-lesorgenti.com

**CELLAR SALES**
**PRE-BOOKED VISITS**
**ACCOMMODATION**
**ANNUAL PRODUCTION** 30,000 bottles
**HECTARES UNDER VINE** 16.50
**SUSTAINABLE WINERY**

It's the 50th anniversary of the Ferrari family's winery, founded in 1959 when Albino Ricci (originally from Parma and grandfather of Gabriele, its current owner) decided to invest in Tuscany. It started out as a general agricultural producer, but today they're focused on wine and olive oil (in addition to a small hospitality service offered in their main villa). Their 2015 Chianti Colli Fiorentini Respiro put in an excellent performance, with its fresh hints of wild berries, blackcurrant, enticing cinnamon and spices. On the palate it opens rich in flavor, lively, with supple tannins and a long, savory finish. Their 2014 Scirus, a blend of Cabernet, Merlot, Petit Verdot and Malbec, offers up vibrant aromas of chocolate, peppers, blackberry and minty hints. On the palate it proves soft, silky and clean with a flavorful, lengthy finish. Their curious 2015 Codarossa, a monovarietal Malbec, is quite atypical.

| | |
|---|---|
| ● Chianti Colli Fiorentini Respiro '15 | 🍷🍷 2* |
| ● Codarossa '15 | 🍷🍷 3 |
| ● Scirus '14 | 🍷🍷 5 |
| ○ Sghiras '14 | 🍷🍷 4 |
| ● Chianti Colli Fiorentini Villa Le Sorgenti Ris. '15 | 🍷 2 |

# Talenti

FRAZ. SANT'ANGELO IN COLLE
LOC. PIAN DI CONTE
53020 MONTALCINO [SI]
TEL. +39 0577844064
www.talentimontalcino.it

**CELLAR SALES**
**PRE-BOOKED VISITS**
**ANNUAL PRODUCTION** 100,000 bottles
**HECTARES UNDER VINE** 21.00

This winery founded by Pierluigi in 1980 was taken over a few years ago by Riccardo Talenti, who chose Pian di Conte as his new home, moving from Romagna to Montalcino. The estate is located in the southwestern district, just outside the medieval town of Sant'Angelo in Colle, overlooking the valley of the river Orcia. Their vineyards are situated between 200 and 400 meters above sea level, on medium-textured soils of clay, limestone and marine sands. Here they cultivate mainly Sangiovese for making Brunellos with a deep, powerful expression, enhanced by various kinds of maturation in mid-sized casks and oak. Their most recent offerings focus on two notable years, both of which are interpreted well. Their 2013 Brunello opens with fresh fruity sensations, blueberries and mandarin orange. These give way to more classic notes of tobacco and roots, which guide a rigorous, tight palate. Their 2012 Brunello Pian di Conte is a more autumnal wine, offering up hints of blackberry preserves and cocoa across a big, generous mid-palate.

| | |
|---|---|
| ● Brunello di Montalcino '13 | 🍷🍷 6 |
| ● Brunello di Montalcino Pian di Conte Ris. '12 | 🍷🍷 7 |
| ● Rosso di Montalcino '16 | 🍷 3 |
| ● Brunello di Montalcino '04 | 🍷🍷🍷 8 |
| ● Brunello di Montalcino '88 | 🍷🍷🍷 8 |
| ● Brunello di Montalcino Ris. '99 | 🍷🍷🍷 6 |
| ● Brunello di Montalcino Trentennale '11 | 🍷🍷🍷 8 |
| ● Brunello di Montalcino V. del Paretaio Ris. '01 | 🍷🍷🍷 6 |
| ● Brunello di Montalcino '12 | 🍷🍷 6 |
| ● Brunello di Montalcino Pian di Conte Ris. '10 | 🍷🍷 7 |
| ● Rosso di Montalcino '15 | 🍷🍷 3 |
| ● Rosso di Montalcino '14 | 🍷🍷 3 |

# Fattoria della Talosa

VIA TALOSA, 8
53045 MONTEPULCIANO [SI]
TEL. +39 0578758277
www.talosa.it

CELLAR SALES
PRE-BOOKED VISITS
ANNUAL PRODUCTION 100,000 bottles
HECTARES UNDER VINE 33.00

Angelo Jacorossi's winery is one of many enterprises still operational in the old center of Montalcino. But the winery also has a respectable amount of winemaking assets, including 33 hectares of vineyards and a cellar located in Pietrose, one of the most interesting subzones in the appellation. Their wines feature a generally modern and focused style, resulting from limited intervention in both the vineyards and cellar. They possess great aging potential and character. Their 2015 Nobile di Montepulciano is a succulent, dense wine rich in aromas of vanilla, dark fruit and spices. Their 2014 Nobile di Montepulciano Riserva isn't lacking in oak accompanied by well-integrated red fruit, spices and chocolate. On the palate it proves persistent, fresh and firm, as well as showing nice tension. Their 2013 Pietrose is a fragrant, soft and delicate monovarietal Merlot.

| | | |
|---|---|---|
| ● Nobile di Montepulciano '15 | ♟♟ | 4 |
| ● Nobile di Montepulciano Ris. '14 | ♟♟ | 5 |
| ● Pietrose '13 | ♟♟ | 8 |
| ● Nobile di Montepulciano '13 | ♟♟ | 4 |
| ● Nobile di Montepulciano Filai Lunghi '13 | ♟♟ | 5 |
| ● Nobile di Montepulciano Ris. '13 | ♟♟ | 4 |
| ● Rosso di Montepulciano '16 | ♟♟ | 2* |
| ○ Vin Santo di Montepulciano Ris. '95 | ♟♟ | 8 |

# ★Tenimenti Luigi d'Alessandro

VIA MANZANO, 15
52042 CORTONA [AR]
TEL. +39 0575618667
www.tenimentidalessandro.it

CELLAR SALES
PRE-BOOKED VISITS
ACCOMMODATION AND RESTAURANT SERVICE
ANNUAL PRODUCTION 130,000 bottles
HECTARES UNDER VINE 37.00
VITICULTURE METHOD Certified Organic

Tenimenti D'Alessandro is one of the most important farms in Val di Chiana, and today it is run by the Calabresi family. The first vineyards were planted with Syrah In the 1960s by the D'Alessandro brothers, who founded the farm and pioneered a course that influenced the whole territory. This new path is exciting and innovative, breaking away from conventional vine growing. The results speak for themselves and their wines are remapping the role this winery plays in Italy's wine sector. Two offerings made it into our finals. Their 2014 Bosco proves fresh and vivid on the nose, decisive in its aromas of blackcurrant and currant accompanied by hints of licorice. On the palate it's juicy with notable structure, fine-grained tannins and nice persistence. Their 2016 Syrah features a spicy nose of pepper set out on a background of wild berries, blackcurrant and quinine. In the mouth it exhibits good weight, coming through dense, juicy and elegant, with a long palate giving way to a relaxed finish.

| | | |
|---|---|---|
| ● Cortona Syrah '16 | ♟♟ | 3* |
| ● Cortona Syrah Il Bosco '14 | ♟♟ | 6 |
| ○ Fontarca '16 | ♟♟ | 5 |
| ● Cortona Il Bosco '09 | ♟♟♟ | 6 |
| ● Cortona Il Bosco '06 | ♟♟♟ | 6 |
| ● Cortona Il Bosco '04 | ♟♟♟ | 5 |
| ● Cortona Il Bosco '03 | ♟♟♟ | 5 |
| ● Cortona Il Bosco '01 | ♟♟♟ | 6 |
| ● Cortona Syrah Il Bosco '12 | ♟♟♟ | 6 |
| ● Cortona Syrah Migliara '08 | ♟♟♟ | 8 |
| ● Cortona Syrah Migliara '07 | ♟♟♟ | 8 |
| ● Podere Il Bosco '97 | ♟♟♟ | 5 |
| ● Podere Il Bosco '95 | ♟♟♟ | 5 |

# Tenuta di Sesta

FRAZ. CASTELNUOVO DELL'ABATE
LOC. SESTA
53024 MONTALCINO [SI]
TEL. +39 0577835612
www.tenutadisesta.it

**CELLAR SALES**
**PRE-BOOKED VISITS**
**ANNUAL PRODUCTION** 150,000 bottles
**HECTARES UNDER VINE** 30.00

It was a trailblazing era that saw Giuseppe Ciacci mold his first Brunello at Tenuta di Sesta in the 1960s. Today the winery is headed by Giovanni, with the help of his children Andrea and Francesca. They are justly famous for classic interpretations from the southern district of Montalcino and the area linking Sant'Angelo in Colle to Castelnuovo dell'Abate. The soils here are generally light and rich in limestone, with some clay and iron. This comes out in their graceful and solid Sangiovese wines, which are matured for long periods in medium-sized oak. Even if it wasn't a particularly favorable year for the typology, Tenuta di Sesta's 2012 Brunello Riserva Duelecci Ovest held fast to its role as the winery's flagship. It opens with warm notes of black cherry in liquor, curing spices and mustard accompanied by a toasty note that's more pronounced on the palate. In the mouth it's caressing and flavorful, still a bit cropped at the end for its tannic grain. But it shows extraordinary depth. It's our Red of the Year.

| | |
|---|---|
| ● Brunello di Montalcino Duelecci Ovest Ris. '12 | ▼▼▼ 7 |
| ● Brunello di Montalcino '13 | ▼▼ 8 |
| ● Rosso di Montalcino '16 | ▼ 6 |
| ● Brunello di Montalcino Ris. '10 | ♀♀♀ 7 |
| ● Brunello di Montalcino '10 | ♀♀ 5 |
| ● Brunello di Montalcino '09 | ♀♀ 5 |
| ● Brunello di Montalcino '08 | ♀♀ 5 |
| ● Brunello di Montalcino '07 | ♀♀ 5 |
| ● Brunello di Montalcino Ris. '11 | ♀♀ 7 |
| ● Brunello di Montalcino Ris. '09 | ♀♀ 7 |
| ● Brunello di Montalcino Ris. '07 | ♀♀ 7 |
| ● Poggio d'Arna '11 | ♀♀ 2* |
| ● Rosso di Montalcino '15 | ♀♀ 3* |
| ● Rosso di Montalcino '13 | ♀♀ 3 |
| ● Rosso di Montalcino '11 | ♀♀ 3 |

# Tenuta di Trinoro

VIA VAL D'ORCIA, 15
53047 SARTEANO [SI]
TEL. +39 05782671100578267110
www.tenutaditrinoro.it

**PRE-BOOKED VISITS**
**ANNUAL PRODUCTION** 70,000 bottles
**HECTARES UNDER VINE** 20.00

Andrea Franchetti's Tuscan venture remains highly original. Beginning in the early 1990s, it took some ten years to garner success. Val d'Orcia, near Sarteano, was his chosen terroir, and it was a gamble that paid off handsomely. The vineyards in Trinoro are managed under biodynamic methods and the harvests are started as late as possible. In the cellar, fermentation is carried out in concrete using exclusively native yeasts and aging is carried out in barriques. This year we tasted three excellent wines that exhibit Andrea's sensibility for interpreting the terroir (he also has a lovely winery on Etna, in Passopisciaro, and another dedicated to Pinot Nero in San Casciano dei Bagni). Their 2015 Tenuta di Trinoro was our favorite, a red with notable extractive richness that impresses for its succulent red fruit and smooth, velvety tannins.

| | |
|---|---|
| ● Tenuta di Trinoro '15 | ▼▼ 8 |
| ● Le Cupole di Trinoro '16 | ▼▼ 5 |
| ● Palazzi '15 | ▼▼ 8 |
| ● Tenuta di Trinoro '08 | ♀♀♀ 8 |
| ● Tenuta di Trinoro '04 | ♀♀♀ 8 |
| ● Tenuta di Trinoro '03 | ♀♀♀ 8 |
| ● Campo di Camagi '14 | ♀♀ 8 |
| ● Campo di Magnacosta '14 | ♀♀ 8 |
| ● Campo di Tenaglia '14 | ♀♀ 8 |
| ● Le Cupole '15 | ♀♀ 5 |
| ● Magnacosta '13 | ♀♀ 8 |
| ● Palazzi '14 | ♀♀ 8 |
| ● Palazzi '13 | ♀♀ 8 |
| ● Tenuta di Trinoro '14 | ♀♀ 8 |
| ● Tenuta di Trinoro '13 | ♀♀ 8 |

## Tenute Palagetto

Via Monteoliveto, 46
53037 San Gimignano [SI]
Tel. +39 0577943090
www.palagetto.it

CELLAR SALES
PRE-BOOKED VISITS
ACCOMMODATION
ANNUAL PRODUCTION 250,000 bottles
HECTARES UNDER VINE 44.00

Tenute Palagetto owns and tends vineyards which are situated in two of the best vine growing areas in Tuscany. The areas also happen to be popular tourist destinations: San Gimignano and Montalcino. In the former, the main grape is Vernaccia for producing San Gimignano, but they also cultivate Malvasia, Trebbiano and Chardonnay. The red grapes include Sangiovese (of course), as well as Canaiolo, Colorino, Merlot, Syrah and Cabernet Sauvignon. In Montalcino, they grow mostly Sangiovese Grosso for producing Brunello and their Rosso. Their Vernaccia di San Gimignano, a faint straw-yellow vintage 2017, put in a nice performance with its flowery aromas, hints of aromatic herbs and a finish of lemon peel. On the palate it proves tasty, with nice texture and tension a rising finish. Their rich and savory 2017 Niccolò, a blend of Vermentino, Chardonnay and Sauvignon, offers up a complex and multifaceted bouquet.

| | | |
|---|---|---|
| ○ I'Niccolò '17 | ❦❦ | 3 |
| ○ Vernaccia di S. Gimignano '17 | ❦❦ | 2* |
| ● Chianti CS '16 | ❦ | 3 |
| ● Chianti CS Ris. '13 | ❦ | 3 |
| ● Il Sottobosco '13 | ❦ | 4 |
| ● Sangiovese Sbagliato '17 | ❦ | 3 |
| ○ Vernaccia di S. Gimignano V. Santa Chiara '17 | ❦ | 2 |
| ○ Vernaccia di S. Gimignano Ventanni '16 | ❦ | 2 |
| ○ Vernaccia di S. Gimignano Ris. '13 | ♈♈ | 3* |
| ○ Vernaccia di S. Gimignano Vent'anni '15 | ♈♈ | 3 |
| ○ Vernaccia di S. Gimignano Vent'anni '14 | ♈♈ | 3* |

## Terenzi

Loc. Montedonico
58054 Scansano [GR]
Tel. +39 0564599601
www.terenzi.eu

CELLAR SALES
PRE-BOOKED VISITS
ACCOMMODATION
ANNUAL PRODUCTION 350,000 bottles
HECTARES UNDER VINE 60.00

The Terenzi family winery is a model for this territory situated in the heart of Morellino di Scansano, as well as for all those wineries making recent appearances on the Tuscan scene. Their winemaking decisions aim for quality both in the cellar and vineyards. However, their foundation is built on balanced wines that remain true to the territory of origin, albeit with a minimally-invasive modern interpretation. The result is a range showing consistent quality and firmly established among top local wines. And once again their Morellino di Scansano Madrechiesa Riserva emerges as one of the best of its kind. Its complex aromatic profile ranges from violet to cherry, forest undergrowth and spices. The palate is guided by a nice acidic verve that closes on a savory note. Their 2015 Morellino di Scansano Purosangue Riserva is darker in its aromas, still vibrant in its oaky weave.

| | | |
|---|---|---|
| ● Morellino di Scansano Madrechiesa Ris. '15 | ❦❦❦ | 5 |
| ○ Maremma Toscana Vermentino Balbino '17 | ❦❦ | 3 |
| ● Morellino di Scansano Purosangue Ris. '15 | ❦❦ | 4 |
| ○ Petit Manseng Passito '15 | ❦❦ | 5 |
| ● Morellino di Scansano '17 | ❦ | 3 |
| ● Morellino di Scansano Madrechiesa Ris. '14 | ♈♈♈ | 5 |
| ● Morellino di Scansano Madrechiesa Ris. '13 | ♈♈♈ | 5 |
| ● Morellino di Scansano Madrechiesa Ris. '12 | ♈♈♈ | 5 |
| ● Morellino di Scansano Madrechiesa Ris. '11 | ♈♈♈ | 5 |
| ● Morellino di Scansano '16 | ♈♈ | 3* |

# Annalisa Terradonnà

Loc. Notri, 78
57028 Suvereto [LI]
Tel. +39 0565829008
www.terradonna.it

CELLAR SALES
PRE-BOOKED VISITS
ANNUAL PRODUCTION 26,000 bottles
HECTARES UNDER VINE 6.00

The name 'Terradonnà' sends a clear signal that a woman is at the head of this winery. It's Annalisa Rossi, who's been following a family tradition while bringing it up-to-date with the times. For 50 years they've been making wine and olive oil here, but as of 2000 they've been focusing on quality, with the first bottles coming in 2002. So as to pay homage to the territory, Annalisa chose to name her wines after minerals. Their 2015 Prasio made it into our finals. It's a Cabernet Sauvignon and Merlot whose generous bouquet features aromatic herbs (thyme and mint), wild berries (blackcurrant and raspberries), spices (cinnamon and cloves). In the mouth it opens juicy, with an elegant, full palate and silky tannins. Their 2015 Spato, a monovarietal Sangiovese, offers up lively aromas, rich in notes of cherry, plums and slight hints of sage. On the palate it exhibits excellent structure and nice acidic vigor. Their 2015 Bixbi is an intriguing and flavorful blend of Sangiovese and Syrah.

| | | |
|---|---|---|
| ● Prasio '15 | | ♟♟ 3* |
| ● Bixbi '16 | | ♟♟ 3 |
| ● Spato '15 | | ♟♟ 3 |
| ● Val di Cornia Cabernet Sauvignon Okenio '15 | | ♟♟ 5 |
| ○ Faden '17 | | ♟ 2 |
| ○ Kalsi '17 | | ♟ 2 |
| ☉ Sysa '17 | | ♟ 3 |
| ● Giaietto '12 | | ♟♟ 2* |
| ● Prasio '11 | | ♟♟ 3 |
| ● Spato '12 | | ♟♟ 3 |
| ● Val di Cornia Cabernet Sauvignon Okenio '09 | | ♟♟ 5 |

# Teruzzi

Loc. Casale, 19
53037 San Gimignano [SI]
Tel. +39 0577940143
www.teruzzieputhod.it

CELLAR SALES
PRE-BOOKED VISITS
ANNUAL PRODUCTION 1,000,000 bottles
HECTARES UNDER VINE 94.00

Founded in 1974 by Enrico Teruzzi and his wife Carmen Puthod, this winery was taken over by the Campari group in 2013. It modernized the existing vineyards and purchased additional ones (establishing Teruzzi e Puthod as the largest private estate in which Vernaccia is cultivated for San Gimignano). At the end of 2016, it changed hands again, coming under Gruppo Terra Moretti. It still owns the property today and is investing in the future, putting its stamp on every aspect, from vineyards to wine style, as well as to labels and presentation of their wines. Their 2016 Terre di Tufi is an enjoyable, straw-yellow blend of Trebbiano and Vernaccia. On the nose it's redolent of an array of fruit and slightly spicy hints. On the mouth it delivers, proving juicy and spirited, with vibrant overtones and a flavorful, long finish. Their 2017 Vernaccia Isola Bianca comes through fresh and light on the nose, with aromas of broom flowers, almond and fruit like apple and peach. On the palate it proves lively, with well-calibrated acidity. Their 2016 Sant'Elena is also excellent.

| | | |
|---|---|---|
| ● Melograni '15 | | ♟♟ 5 |
| ○ Terre di Tufi '16 | | ♟♟ 4 |
| ○ Vernaccia di S. Gimignano Sant'Elena '16 | | ♟♟ 3 |
| ○ Vernaccia di San Gimignano Isola Bianca '17 | | ♟♟ 2* |
| ● Peperino '15 | | ♟ 2 |
| ○ Carmen Puthod '14 | | ♟♟ 3 |
| ○ Terre di Tufi '15 | | ♟♟ 2* |
| ○ Vernaccia di S. Gimignano '16 | | ♟♟ 2* |
| ○ Vernaccia di S. Gimignano '15 | | ♟♟ 2* |
| ○ Vernaccia di S. Gimignano '14 | | ♟♟ 2* |
| ○ Vernaccia di S. Gimignano Ris. '11 | | ♟♟ 4 |
| ○ Vernaccia di S. Gimignano Sant'Elena '16 | | ♟♟ 3* |

# La Togata

FRAZ. SANT'ANGELO IN COLLE
LOC. TAVERNELLE
53024 MONTALCINO [SI]
TEL. +39 0668803000
www.brunellolatogata.com

**CELLAR SALES**
**PRE-BOOKED VISITS**
**ANNUAL PRODUCTION** 120,000 bottles
**HECTARES UNDER VINE** 21.50
**VITICULTURE METHOD** Certified Organic
**SUSTAINABLE WINERY**

La Togata has returned in style to the main section of Italian Wines. This almost all-female winery is run by Jeanneth Angel, Stephania, Vanessa, Azzurra and her husband Danilo Tonon. Their Sangioveses became famous with the debut of their 1990 vintage. Grapes are cultivated in the Lavacchio and Pietrafocaia vineyards in southern Montalcino, while varied maturation in small wood casks and 1500-2000-liter Slavonian oak gives rise to Brunellos with a modern style: juicy and racy, but full-bodied and endowed with chewy tannins. Their entire selection is a brilliant example in that sense, with their 'classic' wines, especially, standing out. Their 2013 Brunello, a wine that brings together balance and savory energy, features a close-focused and generous array of fruit accompanied by roots and medicinal herbs. We find similar aromatic sweetness in their 2012 Brunello Riserva, though it's endowed with greater tannic grip, proving tight and juicy, and notably spicy from the beginning to the end.

| | |
|---|---|
| ● Brunello di Montalcino '13 | ♟♟ 8 |
| ● Brunello di Montalcino Ris. '12 | ♟♟ 8 |
| ● Brunello di Montalcino La Togata dei Togati '13 | ♟♟ 8 |
| ● Brunello di Montalcino Notte di Note '13 | ♟♟ 8 |
| ● Brunello di Montalcino Jacopus '13 | ♟ 6 |
| ● Brunello di Montalcino '06 | ♟♟♟ 7 |
| ● Brunello di Montalcino '97 | ♟♟♟ 8 |
| ● Brunello di Montalcino '08 | ♟♟ 7 |
| ● Brunello di Montalcino La Togata '07 | ♟♟ 7 |
| ● Brunello di Montalcino La Togata '05 | ♟♟ 7 |
| ● Brunello di Montalcino La Togata dei Togati '09 | ♟♟ 8 |
| ● Brunello di Montalcino La Togata Ris. '04 | ♟♟ 8 |

# Tolaini

LOC. VALLENUOVA
S.DA PROV.LE 9 DI PIEVASCIATA, 28
53019 CASTELNUOVO BERARDENGA [SI]
TEL. +39 0577356972
www.tolaini.it

**CELLAR SALES**
**PRE-BOOKED VISITS**
**ANNUAL PRODUCTION** 250,000 bottles
**HECTARES UNDER VINE** 50.00
**SUSTAINABLE WINERY**

The winery owned by Pierluigi Tolaini is among the most interesting of those to have emerged recently in the Chianti Classico appellation. It is an uncompromising estate, both in the vineyards and the cellar. Their strength lies in the interpretation of international varieties, with minimally invasive winemaking and a generally elegant style which defies the hard-and-fast laws of this territory. Their Chianti Classico is also showing promising signs. Their 2014 Chianti Classico Gran Selezione Vigna Montebello Sette offers up aromas of white, well-defined fruit while the palate proves soft and relaxed - it's too bad that the finish sees just a bit too much oak. Their 2016 Chianti Classico Vallenuova, an enticing, approachable red, goes all in on pleasantness. Their 2015 Al Passo, a blend of Sangiovese and Merlot, is a bit more predictable.

| | |
|---|---|
| ● Chianti Cl. Gran Selezione V. Montebello Sette '14 | ♟♟ 5 |
| ● Al Passo '15 | ♟♟ 4 |
| ● Chianti Cl. Vallenuova '16 | ♟♟ 3 |
| ● Picconero '14 | ♟ 8 |
| ● Al Passo '14 | ♟♟♟ 4* |
| ● Picconero '10 | ♟♟♟ 8 |
| ● Picconero '09 | ♟♟♟ 8 |
| ● Valdisanti '08 | ♟♟♟ 8 |
| ● Al Passo '12 | ♟♟ 4 |
| ● Chianti Cl. Valle Nuova '15 | ♟♟ 5 |
| ● Valdisanti '12 | ♟♟ 5 |

# Torre a Cona

LOC. SAN DONATO IN COLLINA
VIA TORRE A CONA, 49
50067 RIGNANO SULL'ARNO [FI]
TEL. +39 055699000
www.torreacona.com

**CELLAR SALES**
**PRE-BOOKED VISITS**
**ACCOMMODATION**
**ANNUAL PRODUCTION** 75,000 bottles
**HECTARES UNDER VINE** 14.50

One of the most luxurious eighteenth-century villas in central Italy, along with its surrounding estate, came under the control of the Rossi di Montelera Counts in 1935. During World War II it was used first as headquarters for the German army, then as a hospital in 1944, when the English took it over. Intense renovation after the war culminated in it being used for tourism and winegrowing. Their wines respect the typicity and characteristics of the territory. Their 2015 Badia a Corte Riserva takes home Tre Bicchieri thanks to its highly elegant, sophisticated aromatic profile of wild berries accompanied by cherries, then slightly spicy notes of juniper. On the palate it opens delectably, followed by a dynamic, subtle body with well-integrated tannins, nice acidity and a juicy, generous, rising finish. Their 2016 Casamaggio also did well. It's a monovarietal Colorino with hints of fresh fruit (cherry and then mint) and spicy notes. On the palate it's warm, firm and elegant, with a noteworthy finish that builds to a crescendo of flavor.

| | |
|---|---|
| ● Chianti Colli Fiorentini Badia a Corte Ris. '15 | ▼▼▼ 4* |
| ● Casamaggio '16 | ▼▼ 4 |
| ● Il Merlot '15 | ▼▼ 5 |
| ○ Vin Santo del Chianti Merlaia '11 | ▼▼ 6 |
| ● Chianti Colli Fiorentini '16 | ▼ 3 |
| ● Terre di Cino '15 | ▼ 5 |
| ● Chianti Colli Fiorentini Badia a Corte Ris. '13 | ▽▽▽ 4* |
| ● Vin Santo del Chianti Occhio di Pernice Fonti e Lecceta '11 | ▽▽▽ 6 |
| ● Chianti Colli Fiorentini '15 | ▽▽ 2* |
| ● Chianti Colli Fiorentini Badia a Corte Ris. '12 | ▽▽ 4 |

# Travignoli

VIA TRAVIGNOLI, 78
50060 PELAGO [FI]
TEL. +39 0558361098
www.travignoli.com

**CELLAR SALES**
**PRE-BOOKED VISITS**
**ANNUAL PRODUCTION** 250,000 bottles
**HECTARES UNDER VINE** 70.00

The history of this winery has ancient origins, testified to by an Etruscan memorial stone going back to 500 BCE that pictures a table with various wine receptacles on it. Today the estate is owned by the Busi family and managed bob Giovanni (who's also president of the Chianti Consortium). Over the years he's been upgrading the vineyards and cellar, making for a selection that brings together territorial tradition and innovation. Their 2015 Chianti Rufina Tegolaia Riserva is a truly delicious wine. Its aromatic profile is still quite youthful, rich in assorted fruit like cherry and plums, then flowery notes of violet and pepper. On the palate it proves intriguing, fresh and drinkable but not banal and endowed with well-integrated tannins and a minty finish. Their pleasant 2016 Chianti Rufina offers up flowery notes, citrus and black fruits (blueberries). On the palate it's full and big, opening pleasantly with nice tannic presence and a flavorful, dynamic finish. Their 2016 Chianti Rufina is a fruity, pleasantly drinkable wine.

| | |
|---|---|
| ● Chianti Rufina Tegolaia Ris. '15 | ▼▼ 3* |
| ● Chianti Rufina '16 | ▼▼ 2* |
| ● Chianti Rufina Governo '16 | ▼▼ 2* |
| ○ Gavignano | ▼▼ 2* |
| ⊙ Rosè | ▼ 2 |
| ● Chianti Rufina '12 | ▽▽ 2* |
| ● Chianti Rufina Tegolaia Ris. '13 | ▽▽ 3* |
| ● Chianti Rufina Tegolaia Ris. '12 | ▽▽ 3 |
| ● Chianti Rufina Tegolaia Ris. '11 | ▽▽ 3 |

## Tenuta Tre Rose

FRAZ. VALIANO
VIA DELLA STELLA, 3
53040 MONTEPULCIANO [SI]
TEL. +39 0577804101
www.tenutatrerose.it

CELLAR SALES
PRE-BOOKED VISITS
ANNUAL PRODUCTION 650,000 bottles
HECTARES UNDER VINE 102.00

Tenuta Tre Rose is based in Valiano, one of the most important subzones of Nobile di Montepulciano. The winery belongs to Bertain Domains (Angelini), together with other national names such as Val di Suga in Montalcino, San Leonino in Chianti Classico, Puiatti in Friuli, Bertani in Veneto and Fazi Battaglia in the Marche. The winery has been redefining its style to produce focused wines with personality. These aspects are brought out through minimally invasive winemaking and careful use of large barrels for aging. Their 2015 Nobile di Montepulciano Santa Caterina did well during our tastings, with its aromatic profile of fruit, flowers and mineral, rocky accents well-integrated with slight hints of pepper and cocoa. In the mouth it also delivered. It unfolds succulently, with acidic verve guiding the palate with freshness and dynamism and eventually giving way to a deep, savory finish.

| | |
|---|---|
| ● Nobile di Montepulciano Santa Caterina '15 | ♟♟ 4 |
| ● Nobile di Montepulciano Simposio '13 | ♟ 6 |
| ● Rosso di Montepulciano Salterio '16 | ♟ 3 |
| ● Nobile di Montepulciano La Villa '98 | ♟♟ 4 |
| ● Nobile di Montepulciano Santa Caterina '12 | ♟♟ 4 |

## ★Tua Rita

LOC. NOTRI, 81
57028 SUVERETO [LI]
TEL. +39 0565829237
www.tuarita.it

CELLAR SALES
PRE-BOOKED VISITS
ANNUAL PRODUCTION 250,000 bottles
HECTARES UNDER VINE 41.00

This well-established winery is an important example of the potential of Val di Cornia. The original two hectares of vineyards over time have reached thirty, but their rigor and passion has remained constant. It was just over thirty years ago that Rita Tua and Virgilio Bisti bought a country house in the area. Today it is run by their daughter Simena and her husband Stefano Frascolla, who have begun the process of converting the property to organic. Their 2015 Giusto di Notri is a truly delicious. It's a blend of Cabernet Sauvignon, Merlot and Cabernet Franc with a fresh aromatic bouquet that calls up mint and balsamic hints. Its fruity background is a ripe as it is fresh, redolent of blackcurrant and blueberries, then toasty notes. On the palate it opens meaty, decisive, with smooth, well-integrated tannins accompanying a balanced body and a long finish. Their 2016 Perlato del Bosco, a monovarietal Sangiovese, features clear aromas of cherry, hints of aromatic herbs, and a supple, well-proportioned body.

| | |
|---|---|
| ● Giusto di Notri '15 | ♟♟ 8 |
| ● Perlato del Bosco Rosso '16 | ♟♟ 5 |
| ○ Perlato del Bosco Bianco '17 | ♟ 3 |
| ● Rosso dei Notri '17 | ♟ 4 |
| ● Redigaffi '08 | ♟♟♟ 8 |
| ● Redigaffi '07 | ♟♟♟ 8 |
| ● Redigaffi '06 | ♟♟♟ 8 |
| ● Redigaffi '04 | ♟♟♟ 8 |
| ● Giusto di Notri '14 | ♟♟ 8 |
| ● Giusto di Notri '13 | ♟♟ 8 |
| ● Giusto di Notri '11 | ♟♟ 8 |
| ● Redigaffi '10 | ♟♟ 8 |
| ● Redigaffi '10 | ♟♟ 8 |
| ● Syrah '10 | ♟♟ 8 |

# Uccelliera

FRAZ. CASTELNUOVO DELL'ABATE
LOD. UCCELLIERA, 45
3020 MONTALCINO [SI]
TEL. +39 0577835729
www.uccelliera-montalcino.it

CELLAR SALES
PRE-BOOKED VISITS
ANNUAL PRODUCTION 60,000 bottles
HECTARES UNDER VINE 6.00

'Wines with a southern spirit' is how we could define the Sangiovese reds that Uccelliera produces. They embody the mix of sunniness, savory tension and tannins that we expect from areas like Castelnuovo dell'Abate in the extreme southeastern part of Montalcino. Expressing not only the generally dry climate, clay-sandy soils and elevations below 250 meters, more than anything we get a glimpse of the skills possessed by a vine grower such as Andrea Cortonesi. Grapes cultivated in individual vineyard plots are fermented separately, while wines mature in small casks and untoasted Slavonian oak. As is often the case, their Brunello di Uccelliera prove complementary to one another. Their 2013 is pure and direct while their 2012 Riserva is richer and more mature. But once again it's their Rosso that best highlights the producer's style, with a sumptuous 2016. Myrtle, balsamic notes and smoky overtones emerge on the nose. On the palate it's both meaty and tapered, round and taut, with plenty of nice juice and flavor to lengthen its plush tannic wake.

| | | |
|---|---|---|
| ● Rosso di Montalcino '16 | ♥♥♥ | 4* |
| ● Brunello di Montalcino '13 | ♥♥ | 6 |
| ● Brunello di Montalcino Ris. '12 | ♥♥ | 8 |
| ● Rosso di Montalcino Voliero '16 | ♥ | 4 |
| ● Brunello di Montalcino '10 | ♀♀♀ | 6 |
| ● Brunello di Montalcino '08 | ♀♀♀ | 7 |
| ● Brunello di Montalcino Ris. '97 | ♀♀♀ | 8 |
| ● Rosso di Montalcino '15 | ♀♀♀ | 4* |
| ● Rosso di Montalcino '14 | ♀♀♀ | 4* |
| ● Brunello di Montalcino '12 | ♀♀ | 6 |
| ● Brunello di Montalcino '11 | ♀♀ | 6 |
| ● Brunello di Montalcino '09 | ♀♀ | 6 |
| ● Brunello di Montalcino Ris. '08 | ♀♀ | 8 |
| ● Brunello di Montalcino Voliero '12 | ♀♀ | 6 |
| ● Rosso di Montalcino Voliero '15 | ♀♀ | 4 |

# F.lli Vagnoni

LOC. PANCOLE, 82
53037 SAN GIMIGNANO [SI]
TEL. +39 0577955077
www.fratellivagnoni.com

CELLAR SALES
PRE-BOOKED VISITS
ACCOMMODATION
ANNUAL PRODUCTION 120,000 bottles
HECTARES UNDER VINE 17.00
VITICULTURE METHOD Certified Organic

Since 1955 the Vagnoni brothers' winery has stood atop a hill near the old town of Pancole, with San Gimignano and its famous towers only a few kilometers away. In addition to Sangiovese and Vernaccia, the winery cultivates other Tuscan varieties such as Canaiolo, Colorino, Prugnolino, Trebbiano, Vermentino and Malvasia del Chianti. In 2007, a new cellar was built next to the old one, which has expanded their working space. Four years later they obtained organic certification. They also offer farm stay accommodation. Their straw-yellow 2015 Vernaccia I Mocali is an interesting wine with a fresh, vibrant nose redolent of lemon and basil. On the palate it proves to be a juicy white with pronounced savoriness. It's both pleasant and pervasive with a long finish. Their 2017 Vernaccia Fonatbuccio is simple and approachable with hints of flint, apple and notes of aromatic herbs. On the palate it comes across as a subtle, delicate, not too persistent but lively. Their 2017 Vernaccia is intriguing on the nose, while on the palate it's endowed with vigor and balanced structure.

| | | |
|---|---|---|
| ○ Vernaccia di S. Gimignano '17 | ♥♥ | 2* |
| ○ Vernaccia di S. Gimignano Fontabuccio '17 | ♥♥ | 2* |
| ○ Vernaccia di S. Gimignano I Mocali Ris. '15 | ♥♥ | 3 |
| ● Chianti Colli Senesi '16 | ♥ | 2 |
| ⊙ San Gimignano Rosato Pancolino '17 | ♥ | 2 |
| ● Sodi Lunghi '14 | ♥ | 3 |
| ● San Gimignano Vin Santo Occhio di Pernice '07 | ♀♀ | 5 |
| ○ Vernaccia di S. Gimignano '15 | ♀♀ | 2* |
| ○ Vernaccia di S. Gimignano '11 | ♀♀ | 2* |
| ○ Vernaccia di S. Gimignano I Mocali Ris. '13 | ♀♀ | 3* |
| ○ Vernaccia di S. Gimignano I Mocali Ris. '11 | ♀♀ | 3* |

# Val delle Corti

FRAZ. LA CROCE
LOC. VAL DELLE CORTI, 141
53017 RADDA IN CHIANTI [SI]
TEL. +39 0577738215
www.valdellecorti.it

**CELLAR SALES**
**PRE-BOOKED VISITS**
**ACCOMMODATION**
**ANNUAL PRODUCTION** 30,000 bottles
**HECTARES UNDER VINE** 6.00
**VITICULTURE METHOD** Certified Organic

Val delle Corti has established its status as an intriguing winery and also one of the most important in this Chianti subzone. It's run by Roberto Bianchi, one of the most active members of the Vignaioli di Radda association. His wines exhibit a clear and unwavering style, and stand out for their rigorous interpretation of Sangiovese. Always consistent, the winery has managed to project the Gallo Nero production area to among the top appellations in Italy. Their 2015 Chianti Classico Riserva needs a bit of time in the glass, and then it's ready to offer up its multifaceted aromas of slightly dried flowers, hints of flint and a spicy notes, all anticipating an assertive, extremely fresh palate that exhibits persistent savoriness Their 2015 Chianti Classico moves along similar lines, though with more nuanced aromas and a simpler, though truly delicious palate.

# Val di Suga

LOC. VAL DI CAVA
53024 MONTALCINO [SI]
TEL. +39 0577804101
www.valdisuga.it

**CELLAR SALES**
**PRE-BOOKED VISITS**
**ANNUAL PRODUCTION** 270,000 bottles
**HECTARES UNDER VINE** 55.00

The 'Montalcino project' in Val di Suga has expanded with the arrival of Bertani Domains. Their main vineyards are dedicated entirely to Sangiovese Grosso and give rise to three different Brunello crus, as well as a 'vintage' version. Vigna del Lago (matured in 5200-liter oval barrels) is linked to clay soils in the northeastern district, while Vigna Spuntali (southwest, matured in mid-sized casks) and Poggio al Granchio (to the south, near the Sant'Antimo Abbey, matured in barriques and 6000-liter truncated-cone shaped barrels) exhibit more 'Mediterranean' terroirs. Val di Suga submitted a truly noteworthy selection of wines for tasting this year, in particular their 2012 Brunello. It's hard to choose between the delectably balsamic Vigna del Lago and the austere delicacy of their Vigna Spuntali. We found their Poggio al Granchio a bit more aromatically mobile (tobacco, herbal tea, roots), and deep on the palate with a graceful tannic presence.

|  |  |
|---|---|
| ● Chianti Cl. '15 | ♟♟ 4 |
| ● Chianti Cl. Ris. '15 | ♟♟ 5 |
| ● Chianti Cl. '13 | ♟♟♟ 4* |
| ● Chianti Cl. '12 | ♟♟♟ 4* |
| ● Chianti Cl. '11 | ♟♟♟ 3* |
| ● Chianti Cl. '10 | ♟♟♟ 3* |
| ● Chianti Cl. '09 | ♟♟♟ 2* |
| ● Chianti Cl. Ris. '14 | ♟♟♟ 5 |
| ● Chianti Cl. '14 | ♟♟ 4 |
| ● Chianti Cl. Ris. '13 | ♟♟ 5 |
| ● Chianti Cl. Ris. '11 | ♟♟ 5 |

|  |  |
|---|---|
| ● Brunello di Montalcino Poggio al Granchio '12 | ♟♟ 8 |
| ● Brunello di Montalcino '13 | ♟♟ 6 |
| ● Brunello di Montalcino V. del Lago '12 | ♟♟ 8 |
| ● Brunello di Montalcino V. Spuntali '12 | ♟♟ 8 |
| ● Rosso di Montalcino '16 | ♟♟ 3 |
| ● Brunello di Montalcino V. del Lago '95 | ♟♟♟ 8 |
| ● Brunello di Montalcino V. del Lago '93 | ♟♟♟ 8 |
| ● Brunello di Montalcino V. del Lago '90 | ♟♟♟ 8 |
| ● Brunello di Montalcino V. Spuntali '95 | ♟♟♟ 8 |
| ● Brunello di Montalcino V. Spuntali '93 | ♟♟♟ 8 |
| ● Brunello di Montalcino Val di Suga '07 | ♟♟♟ 5 |
| ● Brunello di Montalcino '12 | ♟♟ 6 |
| ● Brunello di Montalcino Poggio al Granchio '10 | ♟♟ 8 |

# Tenuta Valdipiatta

VIA DELLA CIARLIANA, 25A
53045 MONTEPULCIANO [SI]
TEL. +39 0578757930
www.valdipiatta.it

**CELLAR SALES**
**PRE-BOOKED VISITS**
**ACCOMMODATION**
**ANNUAL PRODUCTION** 100,000 bottles
**HECTARES UNDER VINE** 23.00
**VITICULTURE METHOD** Certified Organic
**SUSTAINABLE WINERY**

The Caporali family's Montepulciano winery has been at the forefront for over thirty years. Today it is run by Miriam, who has recently impressed a personality and distinctive style on her wines, one constituted of finesse rather than concentration and roundness. Their grapes are not overripened in the vineyards, and aging in the cellar is carried out in both barriques and large barrels. However, this kind of approach needs patience and their wines often require long maturation periods in order to achieve their fullest expression. Their 2015 Pinot Nero is a pleasantly varietal wine, not particularly complex but tasty. Their 2016 Rosso di Montepulciano is highly enjoyable, standing out for its freshness. On the nose we find red fruit enhancing its fragrance, merging with slightly herbaceous notes. On the palate, however, the wine exhibits a delectable and persistent share of acidity that gives way to a lovely savory note.

| | |
|---|---|
| ● Pinot Nero '15 | ♟♟ 4 |
| ● Rosso di Montepulciano '16 | ♟♟ 3 |
| ● Nobile di Montepulciano V. d'Alfiero '15 | ♟ 6 |
| ● Chianti Colli Senesi Tosca '15 | ♟♟ 2* |
| ● Nobile di Montepulciano '14 | ♟♟ 4 |
| ● Nobile di Montepulciano '13 | ♟♟ 4 |
| ● Nobile di Montepulciano Ris. '13 | ♟♟ 6 |
| ● Nobile di Montepulciano V. d'Alfiero '13 | ♟♟ 6 |
| ● Nobile di Montepulciano V. d'Alfiero '10 | ♟♟ 6 |

# Valentini

LOC. VALPIANA
POD. FIORDALISO, 69
58024 MASSA MARITTIMA [GR]
TEL. +39 0566918058
www.agricolavalentini.it

**CELLAR SALES**
**PRE-BOOKED VISITS**
**ACCOMMODATION**
**ANNUAL PRODUCTION** 45,000 bottles
**HECTARES UNDER VINE** 6.00

Although the Monteregio di Massa Marittima appellation is in decline, there is no lack of wineries in this area producing quality wines. An example is the Valentini family winery, long one of the most dynamic producers in the area. Their wines exhibit a style with marked aromatic purity and energetic flavor, traits Maremma wines don't always achieve. At times this Valpiana producer has exhibited some excess in style, but their current approach seems to be headed in the right direction towards drinkability and pleasantness. Their 2017 Sangiovese is highly enjoyable, aromatically full and vibrant. On the palate it's flavorful and persistent, with a savory finish. Their 2016 Monteregio di Massa Marittima is enjoyable on the palate, supple and relaxed, with aromas of fruit and spices. Their 2015 Monteregio di Massa Marittima Il Vivoli is a bit more clenched, with close-woven tannins and oak that's more than just secondary.

| | |
|---|---|
| ● Sangiovese '17 | ♟♟ 2* |
| ● Monteregio di Massa Marittima '16 | ♟♟ 2* |
| ● Monteregio di Massa Marittima Il Vivoli '15 | ♟♟ 4 |
| ○ Maremma Toscana Vermentino '17 | ♟ 2 |
| ● Atunis '12 | ♟♟ 5 |
| ● Atunis '11 | ♟♟ 5 |
| ○ Maremma Toscana Vermentino '16 | ♟♟ 2* |
| ● Monteregio di Massa Marittima '14 | ♟♟ 2* |
| ● Monteregio di Massa Marittima Rosso '15 | ♟♟ 2* |
| ● Monteregio di Massa Marittima Vivoli '13 | ♟♟ 4 |
| ● Sangiovese '16 | ♟♟ 2* |

## ★Tenuta di Valgiano

VIA DI VALGIANO, 7
55015 LUCCA
TEL. +39 0583402271
www.valgiano.it

**CELLAR SALES**
**PRE-BOOKED VISITS**
**ANNUAL PRODUCTION** 60,000 bottles
**HECTARES UNDER VINE** 15.00
**VITICULTURE METHOD** Certified Biodynamic

Much of the revolution that has transformed vine growing in the Lucca hills is owed to Valgiano. Moreno Petrini and With the crucial support of Saverio Petrili, Moreno Petrini and Laura di Collobiano were among the first to make certain agronomic and stylistic choices, thus setting a path that many others would soon follow. Here is where it started, the creation of a biodynamic district where wine is made without compromise. 'Primus inter pares', Valgiano has maintained over time a matchless charm both inside and out of the bottle. Their 2015 Tenuta di Valgiano is just wonderful, a wine that encapsulates an idea of terroir, rather than the variety. It's a red that exhibits true finesse, enchanting the nose with its aromas of violet, Mediterranean herbs, ripe wild berries and dark spices. On the palate it's graceful and silky, proving it has the year's body and the class to age well. Their Palistorti keep getting better.

| | | |
|---|---|---|
| ● Colline Lucchesi Tenuta di Valgiano '15 | ♟♟♟ | 8 |
| ● Colline Lucchesi Palistorti Rosso '16 | ♟♟ | 5 |
| ○ Colline Lucchesi Palistorti Bianco '17 | ♟♟ | 5 |
| ● Colline Lucchesi Tenuta di Valgiano '13 | ♛♛♛ | 8 |
| ● Colline Lucchesi Tenuta di Valgiano '12 | ♛♛♛ | 6 |
| ● Colline Lucchesi Tenuta di Valgiano '11 | ♛♛♛ | 6 |
| ● Colline Lucchesi Tenuta di Valgiano '10 | ♛♛♛ | 6 |
| ● Colline Lucchesi Tenuta di Valgiano '09 | ♛♛♛ | 6 |
| ● Colline Lucchesi Tenuta di Valgiano '08 | ♛♛♛ | 6 |
| ● Colline Lucchesi Tenuta di Valgiano '07 | ♛♛♛ | 6 |
| ● Colline Lucchesi Palistorti Rosso '15 | ♛♛ | 5 |

## Valle Picciola

S.DA PROV.LE 9 DI PIEVASCIATA, 21
53019 CASTELNUOVO BERARDENGA [SI]
TEL. +39 05771698718
www.vallepicciola.com

**CELLAR SALES**
**PRE-BOOKED VISITS**
**ANNUAL PRODUCTION** 250,000 bottles
**HECTARES UNDER VINE** 65.00

Vallepicciola is one of the most important recent projects in Chianti Classico. The Bolfo family invested heavily in the creation of the winery, which boasts an estate of some 265 hectares. 65 of these are already productive, and dedicated primarily to Sangiovese (over the coming years another 40 will be planted). Such a sizable tract of land deserves an adequate facility, and it was the architect Margherita Gozzi's job to design one, It's a 600-square meter cellar that's almost entirely underground and that exhibits an eco-friendly architectural style centered on sustainability. They've also opened the elegant 'Relais le Fontanelle' for hospitality services. Their selection put in a nice performance this year, showing that they're making up ground in a crowded appellation. Their 2015 Chianti Classico Gran Selezione exhibits a big palate, with concentrated aromas of ripe red fruit, tobacco and vanilla. Their less complex but aromatically evolving 2015 Chianti Classico Riserva relies a bit less on oak, while their 2016 Chianti Classico proves supple.

| | | |
|---|---|---|
| ● Chianti Cl. Gran Selezione '15 | ♟♟ | 3* |
| ● Chianti Cl. '16 | ♟♟ | 4 |
| ● Chianti Cl. Ris. '15 | ♟ | 5 |
| ● Boscobruno Pinot Nero '15 | ♛♛ | 5 |
| ● Chianti Cl. '15 | ♛♛ | 4 |
| ● Quercegrosse Merlot '15 | ♛♛ | 6 |

# I Veroni

via Tifariti, 5
50065 Pontassieve [FI]
Tel. +39 0558368886
www.iveroni.it

CELLAR SALES
PRE-BOOKED VISITS
ACCOMMODATION
ANNUAL PRODUCTION 110,000 bottles
HECTARES UNDER VINE 20.00
VITICULTURE METHOD Certified Organic

The name of this farm dating back to the
end of the 1500s comes from 'verone', an
old Tuscan word for 'terrace'. Near the farm
there used to be walled terraces, where
most likely dried tobacco leaves were
cultivated along the banks of the Arno. The
vineyards have been replanted mostly with
selected Sangiovese clones, but also with
international varieties and white grapes. The
vinsanto room in the historic attic of the
eighteenth-century villa has been preserved.
Their 2015 Chianti Rufina Riserva Vigneto
Quona took home Tre Bicchieri with its
complex bouquet of tobacco, smoky
sensations, tanned leather, black fruit and
hints of blood-rich meat. On the palate it
proves balanced and precise, dense though
not in excess, with fine-grained, uniform
tannins. Their 2008 Vin Santo Occhio di
Bernice offers up aromas ranging from
dried figs to dates, notes of malt caramel
and quince marmalade. On the palate it's
velvety, dense, creamy and very long. Their
2016 Chianti Rufina is a fresh, enjoyable,
balanced and highly drinkable wine.

| | |
|---|---|
| ● Chianti Rufina Vign. Quona Ris. '15 | ♛♛♛ 5 |
| ● Chianti Rufina I Domi '16 | ♛♛ 3 |
| ● Rosso Toscana '16 | ♛♛ 2* |
| ○ Vin Santo del Chianti Rufina Occhio di Pernice '08 | ♛♛ 6 |
| ⊙ I Veroni Rosé '17 | ♛ 3 |
| ● Chianti Rufina '14 | ♛♛ 3 |
| ● Chianti Rufina I Domi '15 | ♛♛ 3 |
| ● Chianti Rufina Quona Ris. '14 | ♛♛ 5 |
| ● Chianti Rufina Ris. '13 | ♛♛ 5 |
| ● Chianti Rufina Ris. '12 | ♛♛ 4 |
| ○ Vin Santo del Chianti Rufina '08 | ♛♛ 5 |

# Vignamaggio

via Petriolo, 5
50022 Greve in Chianti [FI]
Tel. +39 055854661
www.vignamaggio.com

CELLAR SALES
PRE-BOOKED VISITS
ACCOMMODATION AND RESTAURANT SERVICE
ANNUAL PRODUCTION 250,000 bottles
HECTARES UNDER VINE 67.00
VITICULTURE METHOD Certified Organic
SUSTAINABLE WINERY

Patrice Taravella's winery has returned to
the top of the Chianti winemaking scene,
thanks to a few adjustments in style which
have affected the character of his wines in a
positive way. Well-balanced use of wood
and a more rarefied wine structure favor a
more precise and elegant style. His
approach remains generally modern, but his
interesting grapes, cultivated under organic
management, find a more pure and acute
reference to the territory. Their 2016 Chianti
Classico Terre di Prenzano impresses for
its clean, multifaceted aromas and its
supple, savory palate with a rising finish.
Their 2015 Chianti Classico Gherardino
Riserva features a vibrant nose, and full,
decisive development on the palate
(though there's just a bit too much oak).
Their 2015 Chianti Classico Gran Selezione
Monna Lisa has some pluck to it, with
spices and ripe fruit in the foreground.

| | |
|---|---|
| ● Chianti Cl. Terre di Prenzano '16 | ♛♛ 3* |
| ● Chianti Cl. Gherardino Ris. '15 | ♛♛ 5 |
| ● Chianti Cl. Gran Selezione Monna Lisa '15 | ♛♛ 6 |
| ● Cabernet Franc '14 | ♛ 8 |
| ● Chianti Cl. Monna Lisa Ris. '99 | ♛♛♛ 5 |
| ● Chianti Cl. Monna Lisa Ris. '95 | ♛♛♛ 5 |
| ● Vignamaggio '06 | ♛♛♛ 7 |
| ● Vignamaggio '05 | ♛♛♛ 7 |
| ● Vignamaggio '04 | ♛♛♛ 6 |
| ● Vignamaggio '01 | ♛♛♛ 6 |
| ● Vignamaggio '00 | ♛♛♛ 6 |

## Agrisole

Loc. La Serra, 64
56028 San Miniato [PI]
Tel. +39 0571409825
www.agri-sole.it

CELLAR SALES
PRE-BOOKED VISITS
ANNUAL PRODUCTION 30,000 bottles
HECTARES UNDER VINE 7.00

| | |
|---|---|
| ● Chianti San Miniatello '16 | ♟♟ 3* |
| ○ Mafefa Bianco '17 | ♟♟ 3 |
| ○ Trebbiano '16 | ♟♟ 3 |

## Podere Allocco

Loc. Seano
via Capezzana, 19
59015 Carmignano [PO]
Tel. +39 0574622462
www.podereallocco.it

CELLAR SALES
PRE-BOOKED VISITS
ANNUAL PRODUCTION 9,000 bottles
HECTARES UNDER VINE 1.50

| | |
|---|---|
| ● Carmignano '15 | ♟♟ 4 |
| ● Vin Santo di Carmignano '07 | ♟♟ 3 |
| ○ Bacano '17 | ♟ 3 |
| ● Barco Reale '16 | ♟ 3 |

## Maurizio Alongi

Loc. Monti di Sotto
53013 Gaiole in Chianti [SI]
Tel. +39 3389878937
www.maurizioalongi.it

ANNUAL PRODUCTION 4,500 bottles
HECTARES UNDER VINE 1.30
SUSTAINABLE WINERY

| | |
|---|---|
| ● Chianti Cl. V. Barbischio Ris. '15 | ♟♟ 5 |

## Amantis

fraz. Montenero d'Orcia
loc. Colombaio Birbe
58040 Castel del Piano [GR]
Tel. +39 3461402687
www.agricolaamantis.com

ANNUAL PRODUCTION 55,000 bottles
HECTARES UNDER VINE 6.00
SUSTAINABLE WINERY

| | |
|---|---|
| ● Montecucco Rosso Birbanera '13 | ♟♟ 3 |
| ● Goghi '16 | ♟ 2 |
| ● Montecucco Sangiovese '15 | ♟ 4 |

## Argiano

fraz. Sant'Angelo in Colle
53024 Montalcino [SI]
Tel. +39 0577844037
www.argiano.net

PRE-BOOKED VISITS
ACCOMMODATION
ANNUAL PRODUCTION 350,000 bottles
HECTARES UNDER VINE 55.00

| | |
|---|---|
| ● Brunello di Montalcino '13 | ♟♟ 7 |
| ● Rosso di Montalcino '16 | ♟♟ 4 |
| ● Brunello di Montalcino Ris. '12 | ♟ 8 |

## Armilla

via Tavernelle, 6
53024 Montalcino [SI]
Tel. +39 0577816012
www.armillawine.com

HECTARES UNDER VINE

| | |
|---|---|
| ● Brunello di Montalcino '13 | ♟♟ 8 |

# Arrighi

LOC. PIAN DEL MONTE, 1
57036 PORTO AZZURRO [LI]
TEL. +39 3356641793
www.arrighivigneolivi.it

CELLAR SALES
PRE-BOOKED VISITS
ANNUAL PRODUCTION 30,000 bottles
HECTARES UNDER VINE 6.00

| | |
|---|---|
| ● Elba Aleatico Passito Silosò '17 | ♟♟ 5 |
| ○ Valerium Vinum Anfora '17 | ♟♟ 4 |
| ● Tresse Anfora '17 | ♟ 5 |
| ○ V.I.P. Anfora Viognier '17 | ♟ 4 |

# Erik Banti

LOC. FOSSO DEI MOLINI
58054 SCANSANO [GR]
TEL. +39 0564508006
www.erikbanti.com

CELLAR SALES
PRE-BOOKED VISITS
ANNUAL PRODUCTION 180,000 bottles
HECTARES UNDER VINE 18.00
VITICULTURE METHOD Certified Organic

| | |
|---|---|
| ● Maremma Toscana Rosso Spineto '16 | ♟♟ 5 |
| ● Morellino di Scansano Ciabatta '16 | ♟ 5 |
| ● Morellino di Scansano Spineto Bio '16 | ♟ 3 |

# Batzella

LOC. BADIA, 227
57024 CASTAGNETO CARDUCCI [LI]
TEL. +39 3393975888
www.batzella.com

CELLAR SALES
PRE-BOOKED VISITS
ACCOMMODATION
ANNUAL PRODUCTION 55,000 bottles
HECTARES UNDER VINE 8.00

| | |
|---|---|
| ● Bolgheri Rosso Peàn '15 | ♟♟ 4 |
| ● Bolgheri Rosso Sup. Tam '15 | ♟♟ 5 |
| ● Vox Loci '15 | ♟♟ 4 |
| ○ Bolgheri Bianco Mezzodì '17 | ♟ 3 |

# La Biagiola

FRAZ. SOVANA
LOC. PIANETTI
58010 SORANO [GR]
TEL. +39 3666766400
www.labiagiola.it

CELLAR SALES
PRE-BOOKED VISITS
ANNUAL PRODUCTION 60,000 bottles
HECTARES UNDER VINE 8.50

| | |
|---|---|
| ● Maremma Toscana Sangiovese Alideo '15 | ♟♟ 4 |
| ○ Pesna '16 | ♟♟ 3 |

# Bindi Sergardi

LOC. POGGIOLO
FATTORIA I COLLI, 2
53035 MONTERIGGIONI [SI]
TEL. +39 0577309107
www.bindisergardi.it

CELLAR SALES
PRE-BOOKED VISITS
ACCOMMODATION AND RESTAURANT SERVICE
ANNUAL PRODUCTION 100,000 bottles
HECTARES UNDER VINE 103.00

| | |
|---|---|
| ● Chianti Cl. Calidonia Ris. '15 | ♟♟ 4 |
| ● Chianti Cl. La Ghirlanda '16 | ♟♟ 3 |
| ● Chianti Cl. '16 | ♟ 3 |
| ● Chianti Cl. Gran Selezione Mocenni 89 '15 | ♟ 6 |

# Il Bosco di Grazia

POD. BOLSIGNANO, 272
53024 MONTALCINO [SI]
TEL. +39 3337693549
www.brunellograzia.it

CELLAR SALES
PRE-BOOKED VISITS
ACCOMMODATION
ANNUAL PRODUCTION 8,000 bottles
HECTARES UNDER VINE 5.60

| | |
|---|---|
| ● Brunello di Montalcino '13 | ♟♟ 6 |
| ● Brunello di Montalcino Ris. '12 | ♟♟ 8 |

## Bulichella

LOC. BULICHELLA, 131
57028 SUVERETO [LI]
TEL. +39 0565829892
www.bulichella.it

CELLAR SALES
PRE-BOOKED VISITS
ACCOMMODATION AND RESTAURANT SERVICE
ANNUAL PRODUCTION 60,000 bottles
HECTARES UNDER VINE 17.00
VITICULTURE METHOD Certified Organic

| | |
|---|---|
| ● Suvereto Montecristo '15 | 🍷🍷 2* |
| ● Suvereto Coldipietre Rosse '15 | 🍷🍷 5 |
| ● Hyde Syrah '15 | 🍷 5 |
| ● Rubino '16 | 🍷 2 |

## Ca' Marcanda

LOC. SANTA TERESA, 272
57022 CASTAGNETO CARDUCCI [LI]
TEL. +39 0565763809
info@camarcanda.com

CELLAR SALES
PRE-BOOKED VISITS
ANNUAL PRODUCTION 450,000 bottles
HECTARES UNDER VINE 120.00

| | |
|---|---|
| ● Promis '16 | 🍷🍷 5 |
| ● Bolgheri Rosso Camarcanda '15 | 🍷 6 |
| ● Bolgheri Rosso Magari '16 | 🍷 6 |

## Caccia al Piano 1868

LOC. BOLGHERI
VIA BOLGHERESE, 279
57022 CASTAGNETO CARDUCCI [LI]
TEL. +39 0565763394
www.berlucchi.it

CELLAR SALES
PRE-BOOKED VISITS
ANNUAL PRODUCTION 127,000 bottles
HECTARES UNDER VINE 18.00
SUSTAINABLE WINERY

| | |
|---|---|
| ● Bolgheri Rosso Ruit Hora '16 | 🍷🍷 4 |
| ● Grottaia Rosso '16 | 🍷🍷 3 |
| ○ Grottaia Vermentino '17 | 🍷 3 |

## Le Calle

FRAZ. POGGI DEL SASSO
LOC. LA CAVA
58044 CINIGIANO [GR]
TEL. +39 3489307565
www.lecalle.it

CELLAR SALES
PRE-BOOKED VISITS
ACCOMMODATION
ANNUAL PRODUCTION 26,000 bottles
HECTARES UNDER VINE 7.00
VITICULTURE METHOD Certified Organic

| | |
|---|---|
| ● Montecucco Sangiovese Poggio d'Oro '15 | 🍷🍷 3 |
| ● Montecucco Sangiovese Poggio d'Oro Ris. '13 | 🍷🍷 5 |
| ● Montecucco Rosso Campo Rombolo '16 | 🍷 2 |

## Campinuovi

FRAZ. CASTIGLIONCELLO BANDINI
LOC. CAMPINUOVI
58044 CINIGIANO [GR]
TEL. +39 0577742909
www.campinuovi.it

CELLAR SALES
PRE-BOOKED VISITS
ANNUAL PRODUCTION 13,000 bottles
HECTARES UNDER VINE 7.15
VITICULTURE METHOD Certified Organic

| | |
|---|---|
| ● Montecucco Rosso '16 | 🍷🍷 3 |
| ● Montecucco Sangiovese Ris. '15 | 🍷🍷 4 |
| ● Montecucco Sangiovese '16 | 🍷 3 |

## Tenuta Campo al Mare

FRAZ. VALLONE DEI MESSI
VIA BOLGHERESE
57024 CASTAGNETO CARDUCCI [LI]
TEL. +39 055859811
www.tenutefolonari.com

PRE-BOOKED VISITS
ANNUAL PRODUCTION 100,000 bottles
HECTARES UNDER VINE 30.00

| | |
|---|---|
| ● Bolgheri Rosso Sup. Baia al Vento '15 | 🍷🍷 5 |
| ● Bolgheri Rosso '16 | 🍷 4 |
| ○ Bolgheri Vermentino '17 | 🍷 3 |

## Campo al Pero

FRAZ. DONORATICO
VIA DEL CASONE UGOLINO, 12
57022 CASTAGNETO CARDUCCI [LI]
TEL. +39 0565774329
www.campoalpero.it

CELLAR SALES
PRE-BOOKED VISITS
ANNUAL PRODUCTION 30,000 bottles
HECTARES UNDER VINE 8.00

| | |
|---|---|
| ● Bolgheri Rosso '16 | 🍷🍷 5 |
| ● Bolgheri Rosso Zephyro '16 | 🍷🍷 3 |
| ○ Bolgheri Vermentino Mistral '17 | 🍷 2 |

## Canalicchio - Franco Pacenti

LOC. CANALICCHIO DI SOPRA, 6
53024 MONTALCINO [SI]
TEL. +39 0577849277
www.canalicchiofrancopacenti.it

CELLAR SALES
PRE-BOOKED VISITS
RESTAURANT SERVICE
ANNUAL PRODUCTION 40,000 bottles
HECTARES UNDER VINE 10.00

| | |
|---|---|
| ● Rosso di Montalcino '16 | 🍷🍷 3 |
| ● Brunello di Montalcino '13 | 🍷 5 |
| ● Brunello di Montalcino Ris. '12 | 🍷 7 |

## Capanne Ricci

FRAZ. SANT'ANGELO IN COLLE
LOC. CASELLO
53024 MONTALCINO [SI]
TEL. +39 0564902063
www.tenimentiricci.it

ANNUAL PRODUCTION 40,000 bottles
HECTARES UNDER VINE 12.00

| | |
|---|---|
| ● Brunello di Montalcino '13 | 🍷🍷 5 |
| ● Rosso di Montalcino '16 | 🍷🍷 3 |

## Caparsa

LOC. CASE SPARSE CAPARSA, 47
53017 RADDA IN CHIANTI [SI]
TEL. +39 0577738174
www.caparsa.it

CELLAR SALES
PRE-BOOKED VISITS
ACCOMMODATION
ANNUAL PRODUCTION 20,000 bottles
HECTARES UNDER VINE 12.08
VITICULTURE METHOD Certified Organic

| | |
|---|---|
| ● Chianti Cl. Caparsino Ris. '15 | 🍷🍷 5 |
| ● Chianti Cl. Doccio a Matteo Ris. '15 | 🍷🍷 5 |

## Fattoria il Capitano

VIA SAN MARTINO A QUONA, 2B
50065 PONTASSIEVE [FI]
TEL. +39 0558315600
www.fattoriailcapitano.com

ANNUAL PRODUCTION 10,000 bottles
HECTARES UNDER VINE 10.00

| | |
|---|---|
| ● Chianti Rufina Ris. '13 | 🍷🍷 2* |
| ● Colli della Toscana Centrale Voltorio '14 | 🍷🍷 3 |
| ○ Vin Santo del Chianti Rufina Ris. '09 | 🍷🍷 3 |
| ○ Fanticchio '17 | 🍷 1* |

## Fattoria Casa di Terra

FRAZ. BOLGHERI
LOC. LE FERRUGGINI, 162A
57022 CASTAGNETO CARDUCCI [LI]
TEL. +39 0565749810
www.fattoriacasaditerra.com

CELLAR SALES
PRE-BOOKED VISITS
ACCOMMODATION
ANNUAL PRODUCTION 180,000 bottles
HECTARES UNDER VINE 44.50

| | |
|---|---|
| ● Bolgheri Rosso Mosaico '15 | 🍷🍷 5 |
| ● Bolgheri Rosso Sup. Maronea '15 | 🍷🍷 6 |
| ○ Bolgheri Vermentino '17 | 🍷 3 |

## Fattoria Casabianca

Fraz. Casciano di Murlo
Loc. Casabianca
53016 Murlo [SI]
Tel. +39 0577811033
www.tenutacasabianca.bio

CELLAR SALES
PRE-BOOKED VISITS
ACCOMMODATION AND RESTAURANT SERVICE
ANNUAL PRODUCTION 250,000 bottles
HECTARES UNDER VINE 70.00
VITICULTURE METHOD Certified Organic
SUSTAINABLE WINERY

| | | |
|---|---|---|
| ● 15 Staiori '15 | ♟♟ | 6 |
| ● Loccareto '15 | ♟♟ | 4 |
| ○ Vermentino '17 | ♟ | 2 |

## Tenuta Casadei

Loc. San Rocco
57028 Suvereto [LI]
Tel. +39 0558300411
www.tenutacasadei.it

PRE-BOOKED VISITS
ANNUAL PRODUCTION 80,000 bottles
HECTARES UNDER VINE 17.00
VITICULTURE METHOD Certified Organic
SUSTAINABLE WINERY

| | | |
|---|---|---|
| ● Filare 18 '16 | ♟♟ | 6 |
| ● Filare 41 '16 | ♟♟ | 6 |
| ● Armonia '17 | ♟ | 3 |
| ● Sogno Mediterraneo '16 | ♟ | 4 |

## Casale dello Sparviero
## Fattoria Campoperi

Loc. Casale, 93
53011 Castellina in Chianti [SI]
Tel. +39 0577743228
www.casaledellosparviero.it

CELLAR SALES
PRE-BOOKED VISITS
ACCOMMODATION
ANNUAL PRODUCTION 250,000 bottles
HECTARES UNDER VINE 88.00

| | | |
|---|---|---|
| ● Chianti Cl. Gran Selelezione V. Paronza '15 | ♟♟ | 3 |
| ● Chianti Cl. Ris. '15 | ♟♟ | 3 |
| ● Chianti Cl. '16 | ♟ | 3 |

## Casale Pozzuolo

Loc. Borgo Santa Rita
58044 Cinigiano [GR]
Tel. +39 0564902019
www.casalepozzuolo.it

CELLAR SALES
PRE-BOOKED VISITS
ACCOMMODATION
ANNUAL PRODUCTION 15,000 bottles
HECTARES UNDER VINE 4.50

| | | |
|---|---|---|
| ● Montecucco Rosso della Porticcia Ris. '14 | ♟♟ | 4 |
| ● Montecucco Rosso della Porticcia '15 | ♟♟ | 3 |

## Podere Casanova

Loc. Acquaviva di Montepulciano
s.s. 326 est, 196
53040 Montepulciano [SI]
Tel. +39 0578766099
poderecasanova@tiscali.it

CELLAR SALES
PRE-BOOKED VISITS
ANNUAL PRODUCTION 26,000 bottles
HECTARES UNDER VINE 6.50

| | | |
|---|---|---|
| ● Nobile di Montepulciano '15 | ♟♟ | 4 |
| ● Rosso di Montepulciano '16 | ♟♟ | 2* |
| ● Nobile di Montepulciano '14 | ♟ | 4 |

## Casisano

Loc. Casisano
53024 Montalcino [SI]
Tel. +39 0577835540
www.casisano.it

ANNUAL PRODUCTION 11,000 bottles
HECTARES UNDER VINE 22.00

| | | |
|---|---|---|
| ● Rosso di Montalcino '16 | ♟♟ | 4 |
| ● Brunello di Montalcino '13 | ♟ | 7 |

## Castelgiocondo

LOC. CASTELGIOCONDO
53024 MONTALCINO [SI]
TEL. +39 057784131
www.frescobaldi.it

PRE-BOOKED VISITS
ANNUAL PRODUCTION 600,000 bottles
HECTARES UNDER VINE 235.00

| | |
|---|---|
| ● Brunello di Montalcino '13 | 🍷🍷 6 |
| ● Brunello di Montalcino Ripe al Convento di Castelgiocondo Ris. '12 | 🍷 8 |
| ● Rosso di Montalcino Campo ai Sassi '16 | 🍷 3 |

## Castello della Mugazzena

LOC. FOLA
VIA TRESANA PAESE, 103
54012 TRESANA [MS]
TEL. +39 3357906553
www.castellodellamugazzena.it

ANNUAL PRODUCTION 4,000 bottles
HECTARES UNDER VINE 3.00

| | |
|---|---|
| ● Gargantua '16 | 🍷🍷 5 |
| ○ Pantagruel '16 | 🍷 4 |

## Castello di Meleto

LOC. MELETO
53013 GAIOLE IN CHIANTI [SI]
TEL. +39 0577749217
www.castellomeleto.it

CELLAR SALES
PRE-BOOKED VISITS
ACCOMMODATION AND RESTAURANT SERVICE
ANNUAL PRODUCTION 700,000 bottles
HECTARES UNDER VINE 144.00
SUSTAINABLE WINERY

| | |
|---|---|
| ● Chianti Cl. Gran Selezione '15 | 🍷🍷 6 |
| ● Chianti Cl. Meleto '16 | 🍷🍷 3 |
| ● Chianti Cl. V. Casi Ris. '15 | 🍷 5 |

## Castello di Vicarello

LOC. VICARELLO, 1
58044 CINIGIANO [GR]
TEL. +39 0564990718
www.castellodivicarellovini.com

CELLAR SALES
PRE-BOOKED VISITS
ACCOMMODATION AND RESTAURANT SERVICE
ANNUAL PRODUCTION 15,000 bottles
HECTARES UNDER VINE 6.50
VITICULTURE METHOD Certified Organic

| | |
|---|---|
| ● Castello di Vicarello '13 | 🍷🍷 8 |
| ● Terre di Vico '13 | 🍷🍷 7 |

## Castello La Leccia

LOC. LA LECCIA
53011 CASTELLINA IN CHIANTI [SI]
TEL. +39 0577743148
www.castellolaleccia.com

CELLAR SALES
PRE-BOOKED VISITS
ANNUAL PRODUCTION 30,000 bottles
HECTARES UNDER VINE 13.50

| | |
|---|---|
| ● Chianti Cl. Gran Selezione Bruciagna '13 | 🍷🍷 4 |
| ● Chianti Cl. '15 | 🍷🍷 3 |
| ● Chianti Cl. Ris. '14 | 🍷 4 |

## Castello Sonnino

VIA VOLTERRANA NORD, 6A
50025 MONTESPERTOLI [FI]
TEL. +39 0571609198
www.castellosonnino.it

CELLAR SALES
PRE-BOOKED VISITS
ACCOMMODATION
ANNUAL PRODUCTION 150,000 bottles
HECTARES UNDER VINE 40.00
SUSTAINABLE WINERY

| | |
|---|---|
| ● Cantinino '14 | 🍷🍷 4 |
| ● Leone Rosso '17 | 🍷🍷 2* |
| ● Chianti Montespertoli '17 | 🍷 2 |

## Castelsina

LOC. OSTERIA, 54A
53048 SINALUNGA [SI]
TEL. +39 0577663595
www.castelsina.it

CELLAR SALES
PRE-BOOKED VISITS
ANNUAL PRODUCTION 2,000,000 bottles
HECTARES UNDER VINE 400.00

| | |
|---|---|
| ● Chianti '17 | ♟♟ 2* |
| ● Chianti Ris. '15 | ♟♟ 2* |
| ● Governo all'Uso Toscano '17 | ♟♟ 2* |

## Cava d'Onice

POD. COLOMBAIO 105
53024 MONTALCINO [SI]
TEL. +39 0577848405
www.cavadonice.it

CELLAR SALES
PRE-BOOKED VISITS
ACCOMMODATION
ANNUAL PRODUCTION 22,000 bottles
HECTARES UNDER VINE 3.60
VITICULTURE METHOD Certified Organic

| | |
|---|---|
| ● Brunello di Montalcino '13 | ♟♟ 5 |
| ● Brunello di Montalcino Colombaio '13 | ♟♟ 7 |

## I Cavallini

LOC. CAVALLINI
58014 MANCIANO [GR]
TEL. +39 0564609008
www.icavallini.it

ACCOMMODATION
ANNUAL PRODUCTION 25,000 bottles
HECTARES UNDER VINE 9.50

| | |
|---|---|
| ● Morellino di Scansano '17 | ♟♟ 3* |
| ● Maremma Toscana Alicante '16 | ♟♟ 3 |

## Ceralti

VIA DEI CERALTI, 77
57022 CASTAGNETO CARDUCCI [LI]
TEL. +39 0565763989
www.ceralti.com

CELLAR SALES
PRE-BOOKED VISITS
ACCOMMODATION
ANNUAL PRODUCTION 50,000 bottles
HECTARES UNDER VINE 9.00
VITICULTURE METHOD Certified Organic

| | |
|---|---|
| ● Bolgheri Rosso Scirè '16 | ♟♟ 3 |
| ● Bolgheri Sup. Alfeo '15 | ♟♟ 5 |
| ○ Lillarae '17 | ♟♟ 4 |
| ● Sangiovese '17 | ♟♟ 3 |

## La Ciarliana

FRAZ. GRACCIANO
VIA CIARLIANA, 31
53040 MONTEPULCIANO [SI]
TEL. +39 0578758423
www.laciarliana.it

CELLAR SALES
PRE-BOOKED VISITS
ANNUAL PRODUCTION 30,000 bottles
HECTARES UNDER VINE 12.00

| | |
|---|---|
| ● Nobile di Montepulciano '15 | ♟♟ 4 |
| ● Nobile di Montepulciano V. Scianello '12 | ♟♟ 4 |
| ● Rosso di Montepulciano '16 | ♟ 3 |

## Donatella Cinelli Colombini

LOC. CASATO, 17
53024 MONTALCINO [SI]
TEL. +39 0577662108
www.cinellicolombini.it

CELLAR SALES
PRE-BOOKED VISITS
ACCOMMODATION AND RESTAURANT SERVICE
ANNUAL PRODUCTION 120,000 bottles
HECTARES UNDER VINE 34.00

| | |
|---|---|
| ● Brunello di Montalcino Ris. '12 | ♟♟ 8 |
| ● Brunello di Montalcino Prime Donne '13 | ♟♟ 7 |
| ● Brunello di Montalcino '13 | ♟ 6 |
| ● Rosso di Montalcino '16 | ♟ 3 |

## La Cipriana

LOC. CAMPASTRELLO, 176B
57022 CASTAGNETO CARDUCCI [LI]
TEL. +39 0565775568
www.lacipriana.com

CELLAR SALES
PRE-BOOKED VISITS
ACCOMMODATION AND RESTAURANT SERVICE
ANNUAL PRODUCTION 30,000 bottles
HECTARES UNDER VINE 8.00

| | |
|---|---|
| ● Bolgheri Rosso '16 | ♥♥ 5 |
| ● Bolgheri Rosso Sup. San Martino '15 | ♥♥ 6 |

## Podere della Civettaja

VIA DI CASINA ROSSA, 5A
52100 AREZZO
TEL. +39 3397098418
www.civettaja.it

CELLAR SALES
PRE-BOOKED VISITS
ANNUAL PRODUCTION 7,000 bottles
HECTARES UNDER VINE 3.00
VITICULTURE METHOD Certified Organic

| | |
|---|---|
| ● Pinot Nero '15 | ♥♥ 6 |

## Col di Lamo

POD. GROSSETO 28
53024 MONTALCINO [SI]
TEL. +39 0577834433
www.coldilamo.me

HECTARES UNDER VINE

| | |
|---|---|
| ● Brunello di Montalcino '13 | ♥♥ 7 |
| ● Rosso di Montalcino '15 | ♥ 4 |

## Colle di Bordocheo

LOC. SEGROMIGNO IN MONTE
VIA DI PIAGGIORI BASSO, 123
55012 CAPANNORI [LU]
TEL. +39 0583929821
www.colledibordocheo.com

CELLAR SALES
PRE-BOOKED VISITS
ACCOMMODATION
ANNUAL PRODUCTION 30,000 bottles
HECTARES UNDER VINE 10.00

| | |
|---|---|
| ○ Bianco dell'Oca '17 | ♥♥ 3 |
| ● Colline Lucchesi Rosso Mille968 '15 | ♥♥ 5 |
| ○ Colline Lucchesi Bianco Bordocheo '17 | ♥ 2 |
| ● Colline Lucchesi Bordocheo Rosso '16 | ♥ 2 |

## Collelceto

LOC. CAMIGLIANO
POD. LA PISANA
53024 MONTALCINO [SI]
TEL. +39 0577816606
www.collelceto.it

CELLAR SALES
PRE-BOOKED VISITS
ANNUAL PRODUCTION 22,000 bottles
HECTARES UNDER VINE 6.00

| | |
|---|---|
| ● Brunello di Montalcino '13 | ♥♥ 5 |
| ● Brunello di Montalcino Ris. '12 | ♥♥ 6 |
| ● Rosso di Montalcino '16 | ♥ 3 |

## Collemattoni

FRAZ. SANT'ANGELO IN COLLE
LOC. COLLEMATTONI, 100
53024 MONTALCINO [SI]
TEL. +39 0577844127
www.collemattoni.it

CELLAR SALES
PRE-BOOKED VISITS
ANNUAL PRODUCTION 60,000 bottles
HECTARES UNDER VINE 11.00
VITICULTURE METHOD Certified Organic
SUSTAINABLE WINERY

| | |
|---|---|
| ● Brunello di Montalcino '13 | ♥♥ 6 |
| ● Rosso di Montalcino '16 | ♥♥ 4 |
| ● Brunello di Montalcino V. Fontelontano Ris. '12 | ♥ 8 |

## Le Colline di Sopra

VIA DELLE COLLINE, 17
56040 MONTESCUDAIO [PI]
TEL. +39 0586650377
www.collinedisopra.com

CELLAR SALES
PRE-BOOKED VISITS
ANNUAL PRODUCTION 20,000 bottles
HECTARES UNDER VINE 16.00
VITICULTURE METHOD Certified Organic
SUSTAINABLE WINERY

| | |
|---|---|
| ● Larà '15 | ♥♥ 4 |
| ● Ramanto '15 | ♥♥ 5 |
| ● Sopra Cabernet Franc '15 | ♥♥ 6 |
| ● Sopra Petit Verdot '15 | ♥♥ 6 |

## Tenuta di Collosorbo

FRAZ. CASTELNUOVO DELL'ABATE
LOC. VILLA A SESTA, 25
53024 MONTALCINO [SI]
TEL. +39 0577835534
www.collosorbo.com

CELLAR SALES
PRE-BOOKED VISITS
ANNUAL PRODUCTION 100,000 bottles
HECTARES UNDER VINE 27.00

| | |
|---|---|
| ● Brunello di Montalcino Ris. '12 | ♥♥ 8 |
| ● Brunello di Montalcino '13 | ♥ 6 |
| ● Rosso di Montalcino '16 | ♥ 4 |

## Conte Guicciardini

LOC. POPPIANO
VIA FEZZANA, 45/49
50025 MONTESPERTOLI [FI]
TEL. +39 05582315
www.conteguicciardini.it

CELLAR SALES
PRE-BOOKED VISITS
ANNUAL PRODUCTION 270,000 bottles
HECTARES UNDER VINE 130.00
SUSTAINABLE WINERY

| | |
|---|---|
| ● Morellino di Scansano Massi di Mandorlaia Ris. '15 | ♥♥ 4 |
| ● Syrah Castello di Poppiano '16 | ♥♥ 4 |
| ● La Historia Castello di Poppiano '15 | ♥ 5 |

## Contucci

VIA DEL TEATRO, 1
53045 MONTEPULCIANO [SI]
TEL. +39 0578757006
www.contucci.it

CELLAR SALES
PRE-BOOKED VISITS
ACCOMMODATION
ANNUAL PRODUCTION 100,000 bottles
HECTARES UNDER VINE 21.00

| | |
|---|---|
| ● Nobile di Montepulciano Pietra Rossa '15 | ♥♥ 5 |
| ● Rosso di Montepulciano '17 | ♥ 2 |

## Il Conventino

FRAZ. GRACCIANO
VIA DELLA CIARLIANA, 25B
53040 MONTEPULCIANO [SI]
TEL. +39 0578715371
www.ilconventino.it

CELLAR SALES
PRE-BOOKED VISITS
ANNUAL PRODUCTION 55,000 bottles
HECTARES UNDER VINE 12.00
VITICULTURE METHOD Certified Organic

| | |
|---|---|
| ● Nobile di Montepulciano '15 | ♥♥ 4 |
| ● Rosso di Montepulciano '17 | ♥ 2 |

## Cupelli Spumanti

LOC. SAN MINIATO
V.LE MARCONI, 203
56028 SAN MINIATO [PI]
TEL. +39 3669340160
www.cupellivini.com

CELLAR SALES
PRE-BOOKED VISITS
RESTAURANT SERVICE
ANNUAL PRODUCTION 30,000 bottles
HECTARES UNDER VINE 8.00

| | |
|---|---|
| ○ L'Erede Brut M. Cl. '15 | ♥♥ 3 |
| ○ L'Erede Trebbiano M. Cl. '15 | ♥♥ 3 |
| ○ San Torpé Vin Santo Amelio '07 | ♥♥ 4 |
| ⊙ L'Erede Brut Rosé M.Cl. '15 | ♥ 3 |

## Dal Cero
## Tenuta Montecchiesi

LOC. MONTECCHIO
52044 CORTONA [AR]
TEL. +39 0457460110
www.dalcerofamily.it

CELLAR SALES
PRE-BOOKED VISITS
ANNUAL PRODUCTION 300,000 bottles
HECTARES UNDER VINE 65.00

| | |
|---|---|
| ● Preziosaterra '15 | ▼▼ 3 |
| ○ Vermentino Chardonnay '17 | ▼ 2 |
| ☉ Versy in Rose '17 | ▼ 5 |

## Casale Daviddi

VIA NOTTOLA, 9
53045 MONTEPULCIANO [SI]
TEL. +39 0578738257
www.casaledaviddi.it

ANNUAL PRODUCTION 100,000 bottles
HECTARES UNDER VINE 20.00

| | |
|---|---|
| ● Nobile di Montepulciano '15 | ▼▼ 4 |

## Diadema

VIA IMPRUNETANA PER TAVARNUZZE, 19
50023 IMPRUNETA [FI]
TEL. +39 0552311330
www.diadema-wine.com

CELLAR SALES
PRE-BOOKED VISITS
ACCOMMODATION
ANNUAL PRODUCTION 100,000 bottles
HECTARES UNDER VINE 40.00

| | |
|---|---|
| ○ D'Amare Bianco '17 | ▼▼ 4 |
| ● Diadema Rosso '16 | ▼▼ 8 |
| ☉ D'Amare Rosato '17 | ▼ 3 |
| ● D'Amare Rosso '16 | ▼ 5 |

## Donne Fittipaldi

LOC. BOLGHERI
VIA BOLGHERESE, 198
57022 CASTAGNETO CARDUCCI [LI]
TEL. +39 0565762175
www.donnefittipaldi.it

ANNUAL PRODUCTION 60,000 bottles
HECTARES UNDER VINE 9.50

| | |
|---|---|
| ● Bolgheri Rosso Sup. '15 | ▼▼ 6 |
| ● Bolgheri Rosso '16 | ▼ 5 |

## Eucaliptus - Dario Di Vaira

LOC. BOLGHERI
VIA BOLGHERESE, 275A
57022 CASTAGNETO CARDUCCI [LI]
TEL. +39 0565763511
www.agriturismoeucaliptus.com

CELLAR SALES
PRE-BOOKED VISITS
ACCOMMODATION AND RESTAURANT SERVICE
ANNUAL PRODUCTION 30,000 bottles
HECTARES UNDER VINE 7.00

| | |
|---|---|
| ● Bolgheri Rosso Clarice '16 | ▼▼ 3 |
| ● Bolgheri Rosso Sup. Ville Rustiche '15 | ▼▼ 5 |

## Fattoria del Teso

VIA POLTRONIERA
55015 MONTECARLO [LU]
TEL. +39 0583286288
www.fattoriadelteso.it

CELLAR SALES
PRE-BOOKED VISITS
ANNUAL PRODUCTION 90,000 bottles
HECTARES UNDER VINE 15.00

| | |
|---|---|
| ● Montecarlo Rosso '16 | ▼▼ 3 |
| ○ Montecarlo Bianco '17 | ▼ 3 |
| ○ Vermentino del Teso '17 | ▼ 3 |

## Fattoria di Corsignano

LOC. CORSIGNANO
53010 CASTELNUOVO BERARDENGA [SI]
TEL. +39 0577 322545
www.tenutacorsignano.it

CELLAR SALES
PRE-BOOKED VISITS
ACCOMMODATION AND RESTAURANT SERVICE
ANNUAL PRODUCTION 40,000 bottles
HECTARES UNDER VINE 22.00
VITICULTURE METHOD Certified Organic

| | |
|---|---|
| ● Chianti Cl. '15 | ♥♥ 3* |

## Fattoria Il Castagno

S.DA DEL CASTAGNO, 2
53100 SIENA
TEL. +39 057750459
www.fattoriailcastagno.it

CELLAR SALES
PRE-BOOKED VISITS
ANNUAL PRODUCTION 2,000 bottles
HECTARES UNDER VINE 44.00
SUSTAINABLE WINERY

| | |
|---|---|
| ● Chianti Cl. '16 | ♥♥ 7 |
| ● Chianti Cl. '15 | ♥ 7 |

## Fattoria di Fiano - Ugo Bing

LOC. FIANO
VIA FIRENZE, 11
50052 CERTALDO [FI]
TEL. +39 0571669048
www.ugobing.it

CELLAR SALES
PRE-BOOKED VISITS
ANNUAL PRODUCTION 150,000 bottles
HECTARES UNDER VINE 22.00

| | |
|---|---|
| ● Chianti Colli Fiorentini Ris. '15 | ♥♥ 2* |
| ● Chianti Colli Fiorentini '16 | ♥ 2 |
| ● Fianesco '15 | ♥ 5 |

## Fietri

LOC. FIETRI
53010 GAIOLE IN CHIANTI [SI]
TEL. +39 0577734048
www.fietri.com

CELLAR SALES
ACCOMMODATION
ANNUAL PRODUCTION 15,000 bottles
HECTARES UNDER VINE 8.00
VITICULTURE METHOD Certified Organic

| | |
|---|---|
| ● Dedicato a Benedetta '15 | ♥♥ 3* |
| ● Chianti Cl. '16 | ♥ 3 |

## La Fiorita

FRAZ. CASTELNUOVO DELL'ABATE
PODERE BELLAVISTA
53024 MONTALCINO [SI]
TEL. +39 0577835657
www.lafiorita.com

CELLAR SALES
PRE-BOOKED VISITS
ANNUAL PRODUCTION 35,000 bottles
HECTARES UNDER VINE 7.00

| | |
|---|---|
| ● Brunello di Montalcino '13 | ♥♥ 6 |
| ● Rosso di Montalcino '16 | ♥♥ 5 |
| ● Brunello di Montalcino Ris. '12 | ♥ 7 |

## Poderi Firenze

LOC. L'ABBANDONATO
58031 ARCIDOSSO [GR]
TEL. +39 0564967271
www.poderifirenze.it

CELLAR SALES
PRE-BOOKED VISITS
ACCOMMODATION
ANNUAL PRODUCTION 80,000 bottles
HECTARES UNDER VINE 18.00

| | |
|---|---|
| ● Montecucco Sangiovese Sottocasa '15 | ♥♥ 2* |
| ● Montecucco Sangiovese Sottocasa Ris. '12 | ♥♥ 4 |

## Il Fitto

FRAZ. CIGNANO
LOC. CHIANACCE, 126
52042 CORTONA [AR]
TEL. +39 0575648988
www.podereilfitto.com

CELLAR SALES
PRE-BOOKED VISITS
ACCOMMODATION
ANNUAL PRODUCTION 30,000 bottles
HECTARES UNDER VINE 8.00

| | | |
|---|---|---|
| ● Ampelos '16 | ♥♥ | 4 |
| ● Cortona Syrah '16 | ♥♥ | 5 |
| ○ Cortona Vin Santo '14 | ♥♥ | 7 |
| ● Cortona Sangiovese '16 | ♥ | 5 |

## Fontaleoni

LOC. SANTA MARIA, 39
53037 SAN GIMIGNANO [SI]
TEL. +39 0577950193
www.fontaleoni.com

CELLAR SALES
PRE-BOOKED VISITS
ACCOMMODATION AND RESTAURANT SERVICE
ANNUAL PRODUCTION 150,000 bottles
HECTARES UNDER VINE 35.00
VITICULTURE METHOD Certified Organic

| | | |
|---|---|---|
| ● Chianti Colli Senesi Ris. '15 | ♥♥ | 2* |
| ○ Vernaccia di San Gimignano Casanuova '16 | ♥♥ | 2* |
| ○ Vernaccia di San Gimignano '17 | ♥ | 2 |

## La Fornace

POD. FORNACE, 154A
53024 MONTALCINO [SI]
TEL. +39 0577848465
www.agricola-lafornace.it

CELLAR SALES
PRE-BOOKED VISITS
ANNUAL PRODUCTION 15,000 bottles
HECTARES UNDER VINE 4.50

| | | |
|---|---|---|
| ● Brunello di Montalcino '13 | ♥♥ | 6 |
| ● Brunello di Montalcino Origini '13 | ♥♥ | 6 |
| ● Rosso di Montalcino '16 | ♥♥ | 4 |
| ● Brunello di Montalcino Ris. '12 | ♥ | 8 |

## Podere Fortuna

VIA SAN GIUSTO A FORTUNA, 7
50038 SCARPERIA E SAN PIERO [FI]
TEL. +39 0558487214
www.poderefortuna.com

CELLAR SALES
PRE-BOOKED VISITS
ACCOMMODATION
ANNUAL PRODUCTION 25,000 bottles
HECTARES UNDER VINE 6.00
SUSTAINABLE WINERY

| | | |
|---|---|---|
| ● Fortuni '14 | ♥♥ | 5 |
| ○ Greto alla Macchia '16 | ♥♥ | 5 |

## Gagliole

LOC. GAGLIOLE, 42
53011 CASTELLINA IN CHIANTI [SI]
TEL. +39 0577740369
www.gagliole.com

CELLAR SALES
PRE-BOOKED VISITS
ANNUAL PRODUCTION 35,000 bottles
HECTARES UNDER VINE 9.90

| | | |
|---|---|---|
| ● Chianti Cl. Rubiolo '16 | ♥♥ | 3* |

## Gentili

FRAZ. PIAZZE
VIA DEL TAMBURINO, 120
53040 CETONA [SI]
TEL. +39 0578244038
www.gentiliwine.com

CELLAR SALES
PRE-BOOKED VISITS
ANNUAL PRODUCTION 130,000 bottles
HECTARES UNDER VINE 15.00

| | | |
|---|---|---|
| ● Chianti Le Cerrine Ris. '15 | ♥♥ | 3 |
| ● Sinibaldo '16 | ♥♥ | 3 |
| ○ Chardonnay '17 | ♥ | 2 |
| ○ Fleurs '17 | ♥ | 2 |

## La Gerla

LOC. CANALICCHIO
POD. COLOMBAIO, 5
53024 MONTALCINO [SI]
TEL. +39 0577848599
www.lagerla.it

CELLAR SALES
PRE-BOOKED VISITS
ANNUAL PRODUCTION 80,000 bottles
HECTARES UNDER VINE 11.50

| | |
|---|---|
| ● Brunello di Montalcino '13 | 🍷🍷 6 |
| ● Brunello di Montalcino | |
| V. gli Angeli Ris. '12 | 🍷 7 |
| ● Rosso di Montalcino '16 | 🍷 3 |

## Godiolo

VIA DELL'ACQUAPUZZOLA, 13
53045 MONTEPULCIANO [SI]
TEL. +39 0578757251
www.godiolo.it

CELLAR SALES
PRE-BOOKED VISITS
ACCOMMODATION AND RESTAURANT SERVICE
ANNUAL PRODUCTION 25,000 bottles
HECTARES UNDER VINE 6.00

| | |
|---|---|
| ● Nobile di Montepulciano '15 | 🍷🍷 3 |
| ● Rosso di Montepulciano '16 | 🍷🍷 2* |

## Marchesi Gondi
## Tenuta Bossi

LOC. BOSSI
VIA DELLO STRACCHINO, 32
50065 PONTASSIEVE [FI]
TEL. +39 0558317830
www.tenutabossi.com

CELLAR SALES
PRE-BOOKED VISITS
ACCOMMODATION
ANNUAL PRODUCTION 50,000 bottles
HECTARES UNDER VINE 19.00

| | |
|---|---|
| ● Chianti Rufina San Giuliano '16 | 🍷🍷 2* |
| ● Chianti Rufina Pian dei Sorbi Ris. '15 | 🍷🍷 3 |
| ○ Vin Santo del Chianti Rufina | |
| Cardinal de Rez '06 | 🍷🍷 5 |

## Tenuta di Gracciano
## della Seta

FRAZ. GRACCIANO
VIA UMBRIA, 59
53045 MONTEPULCIANO [SI]
TEL. +39 0578708340
www.graccianodellaseta.com

CELLAR SALES
PRE-BOOKED VISITS
ANNUAL PRODUCTION 90,000 bottles
HECTARES UNDER VINE 18.00
SUSTAINABLE WINERY

| | |
|---|---|
| ● Rosso di Montepulciano '16 | 🍷🍷 3 |
| ● Nobile di Montepulciano '15 | 🍷 4 |

## Grati - Villa di Vetrice
## Borgo Prunatelli

LOC. RUFINA (FI)
VIA FIORENTINA 32
50068 RUFINA [FI]
TEL. +39 0558397008
www.villadivetrice.it

CELLAR SALES
PRE-BOOKED VISITS
ANNUAL PRODUCTION 400,000 bottles
HECTARES UNDER VINE 140.00

| | |
|---|---|
| ○ Canaiolo Bianco Borgo Prunatelli '16 | 🍷🍷 5 |
| ● Filichete '15 | 🍷🍷 5 |
| ● Chianti Grati '16 | 🍷 2 |
| ● Chianti Rufina Villa di Vetrice Ris. '15 | 🍷 7 |

## Fattoria di Grignano

VIA DI GRIGNANO, 22
50065 PONTASSIEVE [FI]
TEL. +39 0558398490
www.fattoriadigrignano.com

CELLAR SALES
PRE-BOOKED VISITS
ANNUAL PRODUCTION 200,000 bottles
HECTARES UNDER VINE 53.00
VITICULTURE METHOD Certified Organic
SUSTAINABLE WINERY

| | |
|---|---|
| ● Chianti Rufina '15 | 🍷🍷 2* |

## Tenuta L' Impostino

Loc. Impostino, 95
58045 Civitella Paganico [GR]
Tel. +39 0564900665
www.tenutaimpostino.it

CELLAR SALES
PRE-BOOKED VISITS
ACCOMMODATION AND RESTAURANT SERVICE
ANNUAL PRODUCTION 130,000 bottles
HECTARES UNDER VINE 20.00

| | |
|---|---|
| ● Maremma Toscana Rosso Ottava Rima '15 | ♟♟ 2* |
| ● Montecucco Rosso Ciarlone '14 | ♟♟ 3 |
| ● Montecucco Sangiovese Viandante Ris. '12 | ♟ 5 |

## Fattoria Il Lago

Fraz. Campagna, 23
50062 Dicomano [FI]
Tel. +39 055838047
www.fattoriaillago.com

CELLAR SALES
PRE-BOOKED VISITS
ACCOMMODATION
ANNUAL PRODUCTION 50,000 bottles
HECTARES UNDER VINE 17.00
SUSTAINABLE WINERY

| | |
|---|---|
| ● Chianti Rufina Ris. '15 | ♟♟ 3 |
| ● Pinot Nero '13 | ♟♟ 5 |
| ● Syrah '15 | ♟♟ 3 |
| ● Chianti Rufina '16 | ♟ 2 |

## Podere Lamberto

Via dei Poggiardelli,16
53045 Montepulciano [SI]
Tel. +39 3337896319
www.poderelamberto.com

CELLAR SALES
ACCOMMODATION AND RESTAURANT SERVICE
ANNUAL PRODUCTION 5,600 bottles
HECTARES UNDER VINE 80.60
VITICULTURE METHOD Certified Organic

| | |
|---|---|
| ● Nobile di Montepulciano '15 | ♟♟ 4 |

## Le Bertille

Via delle Colombelle, 7
53045 Montepulciano [SI]
Tel. +39 0578758330
www.lebertille.com

CELLAR SALES
PRE-BOOKED VISITS
ACCOMMODATION
ANNUAL PRODUCTION 65,000 bottles
HECTARES UNDER VINE 14.00
SUSTAINABLE WINERY

| | |
|---|---|
| ● Nobile di Montepulciano '15 | ♟♟ 4 |
| ● Rosso di Montepulciano '15 | ♟ 2 |

## Le Buche

Loc. Le Buche
Via Caselfava, 25
53047 Sarteano [SI]
Tel. +39 0578274066
www.lebuche.com

CELLAR SALES
PRE-BOOKED VISITS
ACCOMMODATION AND RESTAURANT SERVICE
ANNUAL PRODUCTION 100,000 bottles
HECTARES UNDER VINE 30.00
SUSTAINABLE WINERY

| | |
|---|---|
| ● Orcia Coreno '16 | ♟♟ 3 |
| ● Pugnitello '11 | ♟♟ 7 |
| ● I Puri Merlot '12 | ♟ 8 |
| ○ Orhora '17 | ♟ 3 |

## La Lecciaia

Loc. Vallafrico
53024 Montalcino [SI]
Tel. +39 0583928366
www.lecciaia.it

PRE-BOOKED VISITS
ANNUAL PRODUCTION 200,000 bottles
HECTARES UNDER VINE 16.00

| | |
|---|---|
| ● Brunello di Montalcino Ris. '12 | ♟♟ 6 |
| ● Brunello di Montalcino V. Manapetra '13 | ♟♟ 6 |
| ● Brunello di Montalcino '13 | ♟ 5 |
| ● Rosso di Montalcino '16 | ♟ 3 |

## Luiano

LOC. MERCATALE VAL DI PESA
VIA DI LUIANO, 32
50024 SAN CASCIANO IN VAL DI PESA [FI]
TEL. +39 055821039
www.luiano.it

CELLAR SALES
PRE-BOOKED VISITS
ACCOMMODATION
ANNUAL PRODUCTION 160,000 bottles
HECTARES UNDER VINE 20.00

| | |
|---|---|
| ● Chianti Cl. Ris. '15 | ♟♟ 5 |
| ● Lui '15 | ♟♟ 6 |
| ● Chianti Cl. '16 | ♟ 3 |

## Maciarine

S.DA PROV.LE DI POGGIOFERRO
58038 SEGGIANO [GR]
TEL. +39 3487155650
www.maciarine.it

CELLAR SALES
PRE-BOOKED VISITS
ANNUAL PRODUCTION 10,000 bottles
HECTARES UNDER VINE 3.90
SUSTAINABLE WINERY

| | |
|---|---|
| ● Montecucco Sangiovese '15 | ♟♟ 4 |

## La Magia

LOC. LA MAGIA
53024 MONTALCINO [SI]
TEL. +39 0577835667
www.fattorialamagia.it

ANNUAL PRODUCTION 80,000 bottles
HECTARES UNDER VINE 15.00

| | |
|---|---|
| ● Brunello di Montalcino Ciliegio '13 | ♟♟ 8 |
| ● Rosso di Montalcino '16 | ♟♟ 3 |
| ● Brunello di Montalcino '13 | ♟ 6 |
| ● Brunello di Montalcino Ris. '12 | ♟ 8 |

## Malenchini

LOC. GRASSINA
VIA LILLIANO E MEOLI, 82
50015 BAGNO A RIPOLI [FI]
TEL. +39 055642602
www.malenchini.it

CELLAR SALES
PRE-BOOKED VISITS
ANNUAL PRODUCTION 120,000 bottles
HECTARES UNDER VINE 17.00

| | |
|---|---|
| ● Bruzzico '15 | ♟♟ 4 |
| ○ Vin Santo del Chianti '13 | ♟♟ 4 |
| ● Chianti Colli Fiorentini '16 | ♟ 2 |
| ● Chianti Colli Fiorentini Ris. '15 | ♟ 2 |

## Fattoria Mantellassi

LOC. BANDITACCIA, 26
58051 MAGLIANO IN TOSCANA [GR]
TEL. +39 0564592037
www.fattoriamantellassi.it

CELLAR SALES
PRE-BOOKED VISITS
ANNUAL PRODUCTION 1,000,000 bottles
HECTARES UNDER VINE 99.00
SUSTAINABLE WINERY

| | |
|---|---|
| ○ Maremma Toscana Vermentino Lucumone '17 | ♟♟ 2* |
| ○ Maremma Toscana Vermentino Scalandrino '17 | ♟♟ 2* |

## Tenuta Maria Teresa

LOC. SAN MARTINO IN VIGNALE
VIA DELLA PIEVE S. STEFANO, 3427
55100 LUCCA
TEL. +39 0583394412
www.tenutamariateresa.it

CELLAR SALES
PRE-BOOKED VISITS
ACCOMMODATION
ANNUAL PRODUCTION 30,000 bottles
HECTARES UNDER VINE 8.00
VITICULTURE METHOD Certified Organic

| | |
|---|---|
| ● Urlo di Lupo '16 | ♟♟ 3* |
| ● Fattoria Bernicchi '15 | ♟♟ 4 |
| ● Colline Lucchesi Merlot '15 | ♟ 4 |

## Metinella

FRAZ. SANT'ALBINO
VIA FONTELELLERA, 21A
53045 MONTEPULCIANO [SI]
TEL. +39 0578799139
www.metinella.it

CELLAR SALES
PRE-BOOKED VISITS
RESTAURANT SERVICE
ANNUAL PRODUCTION 80,000 bottles
HECTARES UNDER VINE 18.00

| | |
|---|---|
| ● Nobile di Montepulciano 142-4 '15 | ♟♟ 5 |
| ● Nobile di Montepulciano Burberosso '15 | ♟ 4 |

## Mocali

LOC. MOCALI
53024 MONTALCINO [SI]
TEL. +39 0577849485
www.mocali.eu

CELLAR SALES
PRE-BOOKED VISITS
ANNUAL PRODUCTION 120,000 bottles
HECTARES UNDER VINE 9.00
VITICULTURE METHOD Certified Organic
SUSTAINABLE WINERY

| | |
|---|---|
| ● Brunello di Montalcino '13 | ♟♟ 5 |
| ● Brunello di Montalcino V. delle Raunate Ris. '12 | ♟ 8 |
| ● Rosso di Montalcino '16 | ♟ 2 |

## Mola

LOC. GELSARELLO, 2
57031 PORTO AZZURRO [LI]
TEL. +39 0565958151
www.tenutepavoletti.it

CELLAR SALES
PRE-BOOKED VISITS
ANNUAL PRODUCTION 47,000 bottles
HECTARES UNDER VINE 12.00

| | |
|---|---|
| ● Aleatico Passito '15 | ♟♟ 4 |
| ○ Elba Ansonica Ansora '17 | ♟♟ 3 |
| ○ Elba Bianco Casa degli Aiali '17 | ♟ 2 |
| ○ Elba Vermentino Solis '17 | ♟ 2 |

## Podere Monastero

LOC. MONASTERO
53011 CASTELLINA IN CHIANTI [SI]
TEL. +39 0577740436
www.poderemonastero.com

CELLAR SALES
PRE-BOOKED VISITS
ACCOMMODATION
ANNUAL PRODUCTION 7,000 bottles
HECTARES UNDER VINE 3.00

| | |
|---|---|
| ● Campanaio '16 | ♟♟ 6 |
| ● La Pineta '16 | ♟♟ 6 |

## Podere Montale

S.DA POGGIOFERRO
58038 SEGGIANO [GR]
TEL. +39 3480811210
www,poderemontale.it

CELLAR SALES
PRE-BOOKED VISITS
ACCOMMODATION
ANNUAL PRODUCTION 100,000 bottles
HECTARES UNDER VINE 17.50
SUSTAINABLE WINERY

| | |
|---|---|
| ● Montecucco Sangiovese '15 | ♟♟ 6 |

## La Montanina

LOC. MONTI IN CHIANTI

53020 GAIOLE IN CHIANTI [SI]
TEL. +39 0577747017
www.chianticlassico.com

HECTARES UNDER VINE

| | |
|---|---|
| ● Chianti Cl. '15 | ♟♟ 3* |
| ● Nebbiano '15 | ♟♟ 3 |

## Monte Solaio

VIA DI VENTURINA, 15
57021 CAMPIGLIA MARITTIMA [LI]
TEL. +39 0565843291
www.montesolaio.com

CELLAR SALES
PRE-BOOKED VISITS
ANNUAL PRODUCTION 40,000 bottles
HECTARES UNDER VINE 8.50

| | |
|---|---|
| ● Re del Castello '16 | ♟♟ 7 |
| ● Tino Rosso '16 | ♟♟ 3 |
| ○ Costa Toscana Bianco '17 | ♟ 2 |
| ● Sassinoro '16 | ♟ 5 |

## Montemercurio

VIA DI TOTONA, 25A
53045 MONTEPULCIANO [SI]
TEL. +39 0578716610
www.montemercurio.com

CELLAR SALES
PRE-BOOKED VISITS
ANNUAL PRODUCTION 40,000 bottles
HECTARES UNDER VINE 10.00
VITICULTURE METHOD Certified Organic

| | |
|---|---|
| ● Tedicciolo '15 | ♟♟ 2* |

## Montenero

FRAZ. MONTENERO D'ORCIA
LOC. PODERE MARINELLI, 74
58033 CASTEL DEL PIANO [GR]
TEL. +39 3493701998
www.montenerowinery.com

CELLAR SALES
PRE-BOOKED VISITS
ANNUAL PRODUCTION 45,000 bottles
HECTARES UNDER VINE 7.00

| | |
|---|---|
| ● Montecucco Rosso '16 | ♟♟ 3 |
| ● Montecucco Sangiovese '15 | ♟♟ 3 |

## Monterinaldi

LOC. LUCARELLI
53017 RADDA IN CHIANTI [SI]
TEL. +39 0577733533
www.monterinaldi.it

ANNUAL PRODUCTION 400,000 bottles
HECTARES UNDER VINE 65.00

| | |
|---|---|
| ● Chianti Cl. '15 | ♟♟ 3 |
| ● Chianti Cl. Ris. '15 | ♟♟ 4 |

## Monterò

LOC. COLLE LUPO
58051 MAGLIANO IN TOSCANA [GR]
TEL. +39 3396024802
www.tenutamontero.it

CELLAR SALES
PRE-BOOKED VISITS
ANNUAL PRODUCTION 9,000 bottles
HECTARES UNDER VINE 5.00
VITICULTURE METHOD Certified Organic
SUSTAINABLE WINERY

| | |
|---|---|
| ● Morellino di Scansano More '16 | ♟♟ 4 |
| ● Maremma Toscana Vermentino '17 | ♟♟ 3 |
| ● Morellino di Scansano More '17 | ♟♟ 4 |

## Famiglia Nunzi Conti

FRAZ. MERCATALE VAL DI PESA
VIA DI VILLA BARBERINO, 15
50020 SAN CASCIANO IN VAL DI PESA [FI]
TEL. +39 055 8218434
www.famiglianunziconti.it

CELLAR SALES
PRE-BOOKED VISITS
ACCOMMODATION
ANNUAL PRODUCTION 60,000 bottles
HECTARES UNDER VINE 23.00

| | |
|---|---|
| ● Chianti Cl. '16 | ♟♟ 5 |
| ● Chianti Cl. Gran Selezione Vigna Elisa '13 | ♟♟ 8 |

## Oliviera

S.DA PROV.LE 102 DI VAGLIAGLI, 36
53019 CASTELNUOVO BERARDENGA [SI]
TEL. +39 3498950188
www.oliviera.it

ANNUAL PRODUCTION 30,000 bottles
HECTARES UNDER VINE 9.00

● Chianti Cl. '16 · · · · · · · · · · · · · · 🍷🍷 3*
● Chianti Cl. Campo Mansueto '16 · · · 🍷🍷 3
● Chianti Cl. Settantanove Ris. '15 · · · 🍷 3

## Padelletti

VIA PADELLETTI, 9
53024 MONTALCINO [SI]
TEL. +39 0577848314
www.padelletti.it

CELLAR SALES
PRE-BOOKED VISITS
ANNUAL PRODUCTION 30,000 bottles
HECTARES UNDER VINE 6.00

● Brunello di Montalcino '13 · · · · · · 🍷🍷 8
● Rosso di Montalcino '15 · · · · · · · · · 🍷 3

## La Palazzetta

FRAZ. CASTELNUOVO DELL'ABATE
PODERE LA PALAZZETTA, 1P
53024 MONTALCINO [SI]
TEL. +39 0577835531
www.palazzettafanti.com

CELLAR SALES
PRE-BOOKED VISITS
ACCOMMODATION
ANNUAL PRODUCTION 70,000 bottles
HECTARES UNDER VINE 28.00
VITICULTURE METHOD Certified Organic
SUSTAINABLE WINERY

● Brunello di Montalcino '13 · · · · · · 🍷🍷 5
● Rosso di Montalcino '16 · · · · · · · · 🍷🍷 3

## Pian delle Querci

VIA GIACOMO LEOPARDI, 10
53024 MONTALCINO [SI]
TEL. +39 0577834174
www.piandellequerci.it

CELLAR SALES
PRE-BOOKED VISITS
ANNUAL PRODUCTION 53,000 bottles
HECTARES UNDER VINE 8.50

● Brunello di Montalcino '13 · · · · · · 🍷🍷 5
● Brunello di Montalcino Ris. '12 · · · 🍷🍷 5
● Rosso di Montalcino '16 · · · · · · · · 🍷🍷 3

## Piemaggio

LOC. FIORAIE
53011 CASTELLINA IN CHIANTI [SI]
TEL. +39 0577740658

CELLAR SALES
ANNUAL PRODUCTION 40,000 bottles
HECTARES UNDER VINE 11.50
SUSTAINABLE WINERY

● Chianti Cl. Le Fioraie '13 · · · · · · · 🍷🍷 4
● Chianti Cl. Ris. '12 · · · · · · · · · · · · 🍷 4

## Agostina Pieri

FRAZ. SANT'ANGELO SCALO
LOC. PIANCORNELLO
53024 MONTALCINO [SI]
TEL. +39 0577844163
www.pieriagostina.it

ANNUAL PRODUCTION 45,000 bottles
HECTARES UNDER VINE 10.78

● Brunello di Montalcino '13 · · · · · · 🍷🍷 6
● Rosso di Montalcino '16 · · · · · · · · 🍷🍷 3

## Pietranova

Loc. Casa al Piano, 68
57022 Castagneto Carducci [LI]
Tel. +39 0565774101
www.pietra-nova.com

CELLAR SALES
PRE-BOOKED VISITS
ACCOMMODATION
ANNUAL PRODUCTION 25,000 bottles
HECTARES UNDER VINE 5.00

| | |
|---|---|
| ● Bolgheri Rosso 1698 '15 | 🍷🍷 4 |
| ● Bolgheri Rosso Casa al Piano '16 | 🍷🍷 3 |

## Pieve Santa Restituta

Loc. Chiesa di Santa Restituta
53024 Montalcino [SI]
Tel. +39 0577848610
info@pievesantarestituta.com

ANNUAL PRODUCTION 75,000 bottles
HECTARES UNDER VINE 27.00

| | |
|---|---|
| ● Brunello di Montalcino Rennina '13 | 🍷🍷 8 |
| ● Brunello di Montalcino Sugarille '13 | 🍷🍷 8 |

## Podere Conca

via Bolgherese, 196
57022 Castagneto Carducci [LI]
Tel. +39 324 0957941
www.podereconcabolgheri.it

HECTARES UNDER VINE

| | |
|---|---|
| ● Bolgheri Rosso Agapanto '16 | 🍷🍷 4 |
| ○ Ellaboro '17 | 🍷 2 |

## Tenuta Podernovo

via Podernuovo, 13
56030 Terricciola [PI]
Tel. +39 0587655173
www.tenutapodernovo.it

CELLAR SALES
PRE-BOOKED VISITS
ACCOMMODATION
ANNUAL PRODUCTION 140,000 bottles
HECTARES UNDER VINE 25.00
VITICULTURE METHOD Certified Organic

| | |
|---|---|
| ● Auritea Cabernet Franc '15 | 🍷🍷 2* |
| ● Aliotto '16 | 🍷🍷 3 |
| ● Teuto '15 | 🍷🍷 5 |

## Poggio al Gello

Loc. Gello
58045 Civitella Paganico [GR]
Tel. +39 0564906025
www.poggioalgello.it

CELLAR SALES
PRE-BOOKED VISITS
ANNUAL PRODUCTION 20,000 bottles
HECTARES UNDER VINE 4.00
VITICULTURE METHOD Certified Organic
SUSTAINABLE WINERY

| | |
|---|---|
| ● Montecucco Sangiovese Rosso del Gello '15 | 🍷🍷 3* |

## Poggio Alloro

Loc. Sant'Andrea
53037 San Gimignano [SI]
Tel. +39 0577950276
www. fattoriapoggioalloro.com

ANNUAL PRODUCTION 200,000 bottles
HECTARES UNDER VINE 25.00

| | |
|---|---|
| ○ Vernaccia San Gimignano Le Mandorle Ris. '16 | 🍷🍷 3 |
| ○ Vernaccia San Gimignano Nicchiaio '17 | 🍷🍷 2* |
| ○ Vernaccia di San Gimignano '17 | 🍷 2 |

## Poggio Argentiera

FRAZ. ALBERESE
S.DA BANDITELLA DUE
58100 GROSSETO
TEL. +39 3484952767
www.poggioargentiera.com

CELLAR SALES
PRE-BOOKED VISITS
ACCOMMODATION
ANNUAL PRODUCTION 200,000 bottles
HECTARES UNDER VINE 22.00
VITICULTURE METHOD Certified Organic

| | |
|---|---|
| ● Podere Adua '16 | ▼▼ 5 |
| ● Capatosta '16 | ▼ 2 |
| ● Poggio Raso '16 | ▼ 5 |

## Poggio Brigante

VIA COLLE DI LUPO, 13
58051 MAGLIANO IN TOSCANA [GR]
TEL. +39 0564592507
www.poggiobrigante.it

CELLAR SALES
PRE-BOOKED VISITS
ANNUAL PRODUCTION 70,000 bottles
HECTARES UNDER VINE 15.00
VITICULTURE METHOD Certified Organic

| | | |
|---|---|---|
| ● Morellino di Scansano '17 | | ▼▼ 3 |
| ● Morellino di Scansano Arsura '16 | 🏵 | ▼ 5 |

## Fattoria Poggio Capponi

LOC. MONTESPERTOLI
VIA MONTELUPO, 184
50025 MONTESPERTOLI [FI]
TEL. +39 0571671914
www.poggiocapponi.it

CELLAR SALES
PRE-BOOKED VISITS
ACCOMMODATION
ANNUAL PRODUCTION 200,000 bottles
HECTARES UNDER VINE 32.00

| | |
|---|---|
| ○ Sovente Chardonnay '16 | ▼▼ 2* |
| ● Tinorso '15 | ▼▼ 3 |
| ○ Vin Santo del Chianti '16 | ▼▼ 6 |
| ● Chianti Montespertoli Petriccio '15 | ▼ 3 |

## Poggio La Noce

LOC. ONTIGNANO
VIA PAIATICI, 29
50014 FIESOLE [FI]
TEL. +39 0556549113
www.poggiolanoce.com

CELLAR SALES
PRE-BOOKED VISITS
ANNUAL PRODUCTION 10,000 bottles
HECTARES UNDER VINE 2.50
VITICULTURE METHOD Certified Organic

| | |
|---|---|
| ● Gigetto '15 | ▼▼ 4 |
| ● Gigino '15 | ▼▼ 5 |
| ● Vin Santo del Chianti Occhio di Pernice Ejià '11 | ▼▼ 5 |

## Poggio Mandorlo

LOC. ANSIDONINA
58038 SEGGIANO [GR]
TEL. +39 3298825633
www.poggiomandorlo.it

CELLAR SALES
ANNUAL PRODUCTION 62,000 bottles
HECTARES UNDER VINE 12.00

| | |
|---|---|
| ● Il Vigneto di Mandorlo '16 | ▼▼ 2* |

## Poggio Stenti

FRAZ. MONTENERO D'ORCIA
POD. STENTI, 26A
58033 CASTEL DEL PIANO [GR]
TEL. +39 0564954171
www.poggiostenti.com

CELLAR SALES
PRE-BOOKED VISITS
RESTAURANT SERVICE
ANNUAL PRODUCTION 15,000 bottles
HECTARES UNDER VINE 5.00

| | |
|---|---|
| ● Montecucco Sangiovese Pian di Staffa Ris. '15 | ▼▼ 3* |
| ● Montecucco Sangiovese Tribolo '15 | ▼▼ 3 |
| ● Maremma Toscana '16 | ▼ 3 |

## Poggio Trevvalle

FRAZ. ARCILLE
S.DA PROV.LE 24 FRONZINA, KM 0,600
58042 CAMPAGNATICO [GR]
TEL. +39 0564998142
www.poggiotrevvalle.it

CELLAR SALES
PRE-BOOKED VISITS
ANNUAL PRODUCTION 80,000 bottles
HECTARES UNDER VINE 13.35
VITICULTURE METHOD Certified Biodynamic
SUSTAINABLE WINERY

| | | |
|---|---|---|
| ● Maremma Toscana Pontolungo '16 | ♥♥ | 3 |
| ● Morellino di Scansano Larcille Ris. '15 | ♥♥ | 4 |
| ● Morellino di Scansano Passera '17 | ♥ | 2 |

## Tenuta Poggioventoso

S.DA DI TERENZANA, 5
56046 RIPARBELLA [PI]
TEL. +39 3938973677
www.poggioventoso.wine

CELLAR SALES
PRE-BOOKED VISITS
ANNUAL PRODUCTION 25,000 bottles
HECTARES UNDER VINE 6.00

| | | |
|---|---|---|
| ● Fuochi '15 | ♥♥ | 8 |
| ● Sangioré '15 | ♥ | 8 |

## Pometti

LOC. LA SELVA
53020 TREQUANDA [SI]
TEL. +39 057747833
www.pometti.it

CELLAR SALES
PRE-BOOKED VISITS
ACCOMMODATION AND RESTAURANT SERVICE
ANNUAL PRODUCTION 40,000 bottles
HECTARES UNDER VINE 11.00

| | | |
|---|---|---|
| ● Tinotre '15 | ♥♥ | 4 |
| ● Vegasì '15 | ♥♥ | 6 |

## Fabrizio Pratesi

LOC. SEANO
VIA RIZZELLI, 10
59011 CARMIGNANO [PO]
TEL. +39 0558704108
www.pratesivini.it

CELLAR SALES
PRE-BOOKED VISITS
RESTAURANT SERVICE
ANNUAL PRODUCTION 80,000 bottles
HECTARES UNDER VINE 12.00

| | | |
|---|---|---|
| ● Carmignano Il Circo Rosso Ris. '15 | ♥♥ | 6 |
| ● Barco Reale di Carmignano Locorosso '17 | ♥♥ | 3 |
| ● Carmignano Carmione '16 | ♥ | 4 |

## Tenuta Prima Pietra

LOC. I PRATI
56046 RIPARBELLA [PI]
TEL. +39 05771913750
www.tenutaprimapietra.com

ANNUAL PRODUCTION 40,000 bottles
HECTARES UNDER VINE 11.00

| | | |
|---|---|---|
| ● Prima Pietra '15 | ♥♥ | 8 |

## Provveditore

LOC. SALAIOLO, 174
58054 SCANSANO [GR]
TEL. +39 3487018670
www.provveditore.net

CELLAR SALES
PRE-BOOKED VISITS
RESTAURANT SERVICE
ANNUAL PRODUCTION 15,000 bottles
HECTARES UNDER VINE 40.00

| | | |
|---|---|---|
| ○ Maremma Toscana Chardonnay Il Bargaglino '17 | ♥♥ | 3 |
| ● Morellino di Scansano Primo Ris. '15 | ♥♥ | 4 |

## Querce Bettina

LOC. LA CASINA DI MOCALI, 275
53024 MONTALCINO [SI]
TEL. +39 0577848588
www.quercebettina.it

CELLAR SALES
PRE-BOOKED VISITS
ANNUAL PRODUCTION 15,000 bottles
HECTARES UNDER VINE 2.50

| | | |
|---|---|---|
| ● Brunello di Montalcino '13 | ♥♥ | 7 |
| ● Rosso di Montalcino '15 | ♥ | 4 |

## ★Querciabella

VIA BARBIANO, 17
50022 GREVE IN CHIANTI [FI]
TEL. +39 05585927777
www.querciabella.com

CELLAR SALES
PRE-BOOKED VISITS
ANNUAL PRODUCTION 300,000 bottles
HECTARES UNDER VINE 112.00
VITICULTURE METHOD Certified Organic

| | | |
|---|---|---|
| ● Turpino '15 | ♥♥ | 6 |
| ● Camartina '13 | ♥♥ | 8 |
| ● Mongrana '15 | ♥♥ | 3 |
| ● Chianti Cl. Ris. '15 | ♥ | 5 |

## Rigoli

LOC. CAFAGGIO
VIA DEGLI ULIVI, 8
57021 CAMPIGLIA MARITTIMA [LI]
TEL. +39 0565843079
www.rigolivini.com

ANNUAL PRODUCTION 30,000 bottles
HECTARES UNDER VINE 5.00

| | | |
|---|---|---|
| ○ Val di Cornia Ansonica Passito Magistro '16 | ♥♥ | 5 |
| ● Val di Cornia Rosso Testalto '13 | ♥♥ | 5 |
| ○ Accordo '17 | ♥ | 2 |
| ○ Stradivino '17 | ♥ | 1* |

## Tenute delle Ripalte

LOC. RIPALTE
57031 CAPOLIVERI [LI]
TEL. +39 056594211
www.tenutadelleripalte.it

CELLAR SALES
PRE-BOOKED VISITS
ACCOMMODATION AND RESTAURANT SERVICE
ANNUAL PRODUCTION 60,000 bottles
HECTARES UNDER VINE 15.00
SUSTAINABLE WINERY

| | | |
|---|---|---|
| ● Aleatico dell' Elba Passito Alea Ludendo '14 | ♥♥ | 6 |
| ● Alicante Rosso Mediterraneo '16 | ♥♥ | 3 |
| ○ Le Riparlte Vermentino '17 | ♥ | 3 |

## Rubicini

LOC. SAN BENEDETTO, 17C
53037 SAN GIMIGNANO [SI]
TEL. +39 0577944816
www.rubicini.com

CELLAR SALES
PRE-BOOKED VISITS
ANNUAL PRODUCTION 60,000 bottles
HECTARES UNDER VINE 10.00

| | | |
|---|---|---|
| ○ Vernaccia di San Gimignano Etherea '15 | ♥♥ | 2* |
| ○ Vernaccia di San Gimignano '17 | ♥♥ | 2* |
| ● Chianti Colli Senesi '16 | ♥ | 2 |

## Podere Salicutti

POD. SALICUTTI, 174
53024 MONTALCINO [SI]
TEL. +39 0577847003
www.poderesalicutti.it

CELLAR SALES
PRE-BOOKED VISITS
ACCOMMODATION
ANNUAL PRODUCTION 15,000 bottles
HECTARES UNDER VINE 4.00
VITICULTURE METHOD Certified Organic

| | | |
|---|---|---|
| ● Brunello di Montalcino '13 | ♥♥ | 7 |
| ● Rosso di Montalcino '15 | ♥♥ | 4 |

## Leonardo Salustri

FRAZ. POGGI DEL SASSO
LOC. LA CAVA, 7
58044 CINIGIANO [GR]
TEL. +39 0564990529
www.salustri.it

CELLAR SALES
PRE-BOOKED VISITS
ACCOMMODATION
ANNUAL PRODUCTION 80,000 bottles
HECTARES UNDER VINE 25.00
VITICULTURE METHOD Certified Organic
SUSTAINABLE WINERY

| | | |
|---|---|---|
| ● L'Ideale Ciliegiolo '16 | | ♥♥ 4 |
| ● Montecucco Rosso Marleo '16 | | ♥♥ 3 |
| ● Montecucco Sangiovese Grotte Rosse '15 | | ♥ 6 |

## San Benedetto

LOC. SAN BENEDETTO, 4A
53037 SAN GIMIGNANO [SI]
TEL. +39 3386958705
www.agrisanbenedetto.com

CELLAR SALES
PRE-BOOKED VISITS
ACCOMMODATION
ANNUAL PRODUCTION 40,000 bottles
HECTARES UNDER VINE 25.00

| | |
|---|---|
| ○ Vermentino '17 | ♥♥ 2* |
| ○ Vernaccia di San Gimignano '17 | ♥♥ 2* |
| ● Chianti '16 | ♥ 2 |
| ● Japigo '15 | ♥ 5 |

## San Ferdinando

LOC. CIGGIANO
VIA GARGAIOLO, 33
52041 CIVITELLA IN VAL DI CHIANA [AR]
TEL. +39 3287216738
www.sanferdinando.eu

CELLAR SALES
PRE-BOOKED VISITS
ACCOMMODATION
ANNUAL PRODUCTION 30,000 bottles
HECTARES UNDER VINE 10.00

| | |
|---|---|
| ○ Vermentino '17 | ♥♥ 3* |
| ● Chianti Podere Gamba '16 | ♥♥ 3 |
| ● Ciliegiolo '17 | ♥♥ 3 |

## Tenuta San Vito

VIA SAN VITO, 59
50056 MONTELUPO FIORENTINO [FI]
TEL. +39 057151411
www.san-vito.com

CELLAR SALES
PRE-BOOKED VISITS
ACCOMMODATION AND RESTAURANT SERVICE
ANNUAL PRODUCTION 150,000 bottles
HECTARES UNDER VINE 35.00
VITICULTURE METHOD Certified Organic

| | |
|---|---|
| ● Chianti Colli Fiorentini Darno '16 | ♥♥ 2* |
| ● Colle dei Mandorli '15 | ♥♥ 6 |
| ● Chianti San Vito '17 | ♥ 2 |
| ● Madiere '15 | ♥ 5 |

## SanCarlo

FRAZ. TAVERNELLE
LOC. SAN CARLO
53024 MONTALCINO [SI]
TEL. +39 0577 848616
www.sancarlomontalcino.it

CELLAR SALES
PRE-BOOKED VISITS
ANNUAL PRODUCTION 10,000 bottles
HECTARES UNDER VINE 3.00
SUSTAINABLE WINERY

| | |
|---|---|
| ● Brunello di Montalcino '13 | ♥♥ 5 |
| ● Rosso di Montalcino '15 | ♥♥ 3 |

## Sant'Agnese

LOC. CAMPO ALLE FAVE, 1
57025 PIOMBINO [LI]
TEL. +39 0565277069
www.santagnesefarm.it

CELLAR SALES
PRE-BOOKED VISITS
ANNUAL PRODUCTION 25,000 bottles
HECTARES UNDER VINE 6.00
SUSTAINABLE WINERY

| | |
|---|---|
| ● Rubido '15 | ♥♥ 2* |
| ○ Kalendamaia '17 | ♥ 2 |

## Villa Santo Stefano

FRAZ. PIEVE SANTO STEFANO
VIA DELLA CHIESA XIV, 504
55100 LUCCA
TEL. +39 0583395349
www.villa-santostefano.it

ANNUAL PRODUCTION 30,000 bottles
HECTARES UNDER VINE 7.00

| | |
|---|---|
| ● Colline Lucchesi Rosso Sereno '16 | 🍷🍷 3 |
| ○ Gioia '17 | 🍷 2 |
| ● Ioto '16 | 🍷 5 |

## SassodiSole

FRAZ. TORRENIERI
LOC. SASSO DI SOLE, 85
53024 MONTALCINO [SI]
TEL. +39 0577834303
www.sassodisole.it

CELLAR SALES
PRE-BOOKED VISITS
ANNUAL PRODUCTION 45,000 bottles
HECTARES UNDER VINE 10.00
SUSTAINABLE WINERY

| | |
|---|---|
| ● Orcia Rosso '16 | 🍷🍷 4 |
| ● Brunello di Montalcino '13 | 🍷🍷 8 |
| ● Brunello di Montalcino Ris. '12 | 🍷🍷 8 |

## Sator

FRAZ. POMAIA
VIA MACCHIA AL PINO
56040 SANTA LUCE [PI]
TEL. +39 050740529
www.satorwines.com

CELLAR SALES
PRE-BOOKED VISITS
ANNUAL PRODUCTION 50,000 bottles
HECTARES UNDER VINE 9.50

| | |
|---|---|
| ● Montescudaio Merlot Sileno '16 | 🍷🍷 3 |
| ● Sileno Ciliegiolo '16 | 🍷🍷 3 |
| ● Montescudaio Rosso '17 | 🍷 2 |
| ○ Vermentino '17 | 🍷 2 |

## Savignola Paolina

VIA PETRIOLO, 58
50022 GREVE IN CHIANTI [FI]
TEL. +39 0558546036
www.savignolapaolina.it

CELLAR SALES
PRE-BOOKED VISITS
ACCOMMODATION
ANNUAL PRODUCTION 35,000 bottles
HECTARES UNDER VINE 6.00

| | |
|---|---|
| ● Chianti Cl. Ris. '15 | 🍷🍷 4 |
| ● Chianti Cl. Gran Selezione '15 | 🍷🍷 3 |

## Tenuta Sette Cieli

FRAZ. LA CALIFORNIA
VIA SANDRO PERTINI
57020 BIBBONA [LI]
TEL. +39 0586677435
www.tenutasettecieli.com

CELLAR SALES
ANNUAL PRODUCTION 45,000 bottles
HECTARES UNDER VINE 10.00
SUSTAINABLE WINERY

| | |
|---|---|
| ● Bolgheri Rosso Noi 4 '15 | 🍷🍷 7 |
| ● Indaco '14 | 🍷🍷 8 |

## Solaria - Cencioni Patrizia

POD. CAPANNA, 102
53024 MONTALCINO [SI]
TEL. +39 0577849426
www.solariacencioni.com

CELLAR SALES
PRE-BOOKED VISITS
ANNUAL PRODUCTION 35,500 bottles
HECTARES UNDER VINE 9.00

| | |
|---|---|
| ● Brunello di Montalcino '13 | 🍷🍷 6 |
| ● Rosso di Montalcino '16 | 🍷🍷 3 |

## Spadaio e Piecorto

via San Silvestro, 1
50021 Barberino Val d'Elsa [FI]
Tel. +39 0558072915
www.spadaiopiecorto.it

CELLAR SALES
PRE-BOOKED VISITS
ACCOMMODATION
ANNUAL PRODUCTION 70,000 bottles
HECTARES UNDER VINE 14.00

| | |
|---|---|
| ● Chianti Cl. Piecorto '16 | ♟♟ 2* |
| ● Chianti Cl. '16 | ♟♟ 3 |
| ● Chianti Cl. Ris. '15 | ♟ 3 |

## Stomennano

loc. Borgo Stomennano
53035 Monteriggioni [SI]
Tel. +39 0577304033
www.stomennano.it

CELLAR SALES
PRE-BOOKED VISITS
ACCOMMODATION
ANNUAL PRODUCTION 50,000 bottles
HECTARES UNDER VINE 25.00
SUSTAINABLE WINERY

| | |
|---|---|
| ● Chianti Cl. '16 | ♟♟ 5 |

## La Svolta

loc. Malmantile
via Gavignano, 7
50055 Lastra a Signa [FI]
Tel. +39 3348426285
www.agricolalasvolta.it

HECTARES UNDER VINE

| | |
|---|---|
| ○ Beatnik Trebbiano '17 | ♟♟ 3 |
| ● Chianti Familia '16 | ♟♟ 3 |
| ● Chianti '16 | ♟ 3 |
| ● Chianti Principio '17 | ♟ 2 |

## Agricola Tamburini

via Catignano, 106
50050 Gambassi Terme [FI]
Tel. +39 0571680235
www.agricolatamburini.it

CELLAR SALES
PRE-BOOKED VISITS
ANNUAL PRODUCTION 90,000 bottles
HECTARES UNDER VINE 30.00

| | |
|---|---|
| ● Il Castelluccio Rosso '17 | ♟♟ 2* |
| ● Il Massiccio '14 | ♟♟ 2* |
| ● Brunello di Montalcino Somnio '13 | ♟ 6 |
| Vin Santo del Chianti D'Incanto '10 | ♟ 5 |

## Tassi

v.le P. Strozzi, 1/3
53024 Montalcino [SI]
Tel. +39 0577848025
www.tassimontalcino.com

ANNUAL PRODUCTION 20,000 bottles
HECTARES UNDER VINE 5.00

| | |
|---|---|
| ● Brunello di Montalcino '13 | ♟♟ 7 |
| ● Brunello di Montalcino Franci '13 | ♟♟ 8 |

## Tenuta Di Vaira

s.da prov.le Bolgherese, 275b
57022 Bolgheri [LI]
Tel. +39 0565763581
www.tenutadivaira.com

HECTARES UNDER VINE

| | |
|---|---|
| ● Bolgheri Rosso Caccia al Palazzo '16 | ♟♟ 5 |
| ● Bolgheri Sup. Bolgherese '15 | ♟♟ 5 |

## Tenuta La Chiusa

LOC. MAGAZZINI, 93
57037 PORTOFERRAIO [LI]
TEL. +39 0565933046
lachiusa@elbalink.it

CELLAR SALES
PRE-BOOKED VISITS
ACCOMMODATION
ANNUAL PRODUCTION 25,000 bottles
HECTARES UNDER VINE 7.50

| | |
|---|---|
| ● Elba Aleatico Passito '16 | 🍷🍷 6 |
| ○ Elba Ansonica '17 | 🍷🍷 2* |
| ○ Elba Bianco '17 | 🍷 2 |
| ○ Elba Vermentino '17 | 🍷 2 |

## Tenuta San Giorgio

LOC. SAN GIORGIO
FRAZ. CASTELNUOVO DELL'ABATE
53024 MONTALCINO [SI]
TEL. +39 0577835502
www.collemassari.it

CELLAR SALES
PRE-BOOKED VISITS
ANNUAL PRODUCTION 50,000 bottles
HECTARES UNDER VINE 10.00

| | |
|---|---|
| ● Rosso di Montalcino Ciampoleto '16 | 🍷🍷 4 |
| ● Brunello di Montalcino Ugolforte '13 | 🍷 6 |

## Terralsole

VILLA COLLINA D'ORO
53024 MONTALCINO [SI]
TEL. +39 0577835678
www.terralsole.com

ANNUAL PRODUCTION 45,000 bottles
HECTARES UNDER VINE 10.00

| | |
|---|---|
| ● Brunello di Montalcino '13 | 🍷🍷 6 |
| ● Brunello di Montalcino Ris. '12 | 🍷🍷 6 |

## Terre Nere

LOC. CASTELNUOVO DELL'ABATE
53024 MONTALCINO [SI]
TEL. +39 3490971713
www.terreneremontalcino.it

CELLAR SALES
PRE-BOOKED VISITS
ACCOMMODATION
ANNUAL PRODUCTION 50,000 bottles
HECTARES UNDER VINE 10.00

| | |
|---|---|
| ● Brunello di Montalcino '13 | 🍷🍷 5 |
| ● Rosso di Montalcino '16 | 🍷 3 |

## Tiezzi

LOC. PODERE SOCCORSO
53024 MONTALCINO [SI]
TEL. +39 0577848187
www.tiezzivini.it

CELLAR SALES
PRE-BOOKED VISITS
ACCOMMODATION
ANNUAL PRODUCTION 23,000 bottles
HECTARES UNDER VINE 5.50

| | |
|---|---|
| ● Brunello di Montalcino V. Soccorso '13 | 🍷🍷 6 |
| ● Brunello di Montalcino Poggio Cerrino '13 | 🍷 5 |

## Torre a Cenaia

LOC. CENAIA
VIA DELLE COLLINE, 55
56040 CRESPINA LORENZANA [PI]
TEL. +39 050643739
www.torreacenaia.it

CELLAR SALES
PRE-BOOKED VISITS
ANNUAL PRODUCTION 240,000 bottles
HECTARES UNDER VINE 30.00

| | |
|---|---|
| ○ Dolce Peccato | 🍷🍷 3 |
| ● Per Non Dormire '15 | 🍷🍷 6 |
| ○ Pitti Vermentino '17 | 🍷🍷 2* |
| ● Torre del Vajo '15 | 🍷🍷 4 |

## Le Torri

via San Lorenzo a Vigliano, 31
50021 Barberino Val d'Elsa [FI]
Tel. +39 0558076161
www.letorri.net

CELLAR SALES
PRE-BOOKED VISITS
ACCOMMODATION AND RESTAURANT SERVICE
ANNUAL PRODUCTION 170,000 bottles
HECTARES UNDER VINE 28.00
SUSTAINABLE WINERY

| | |
|---|---|
| ● Magliano '15 | ♟♟ 5 |
| ● San Lorenzo '15 | ♟♟ 5 |
| ● Chianti Colli Fiorentini '16 | ♟ 2 |
| ● Chianti Colli Fiorentini Ris. '15 | ♟ 3 |

## Tenuta di Trecciano

s.da prov.le 52 della Montagnola, 16
53018 Sovicille [SI]
Tel. +39 0577314357
www.trecciano.it

CELLAR SALES
PRE-BOOKED VISITS
ANNUAL PRODUCTION 80,000 bottles
HECTARES UNDER VINE 15.50

| | |
|---|---|
| ● Chianti Colli Senesi Terra Rossa Ris. '15 | ♟♟ 3 |
| ● I Campacci '16 | ♟♟ 4 |
| ● Chianti Colli Senesi '17 | ♟ 2 |

## Castello Tricerchi

loc. Àltesi
53024 Montalcino [SI]
Tel. +39 3472501884
www.castellotricerchi.com

CELLAR SALES
PRE-BOOKED VISITS
ANNUAL PRODUCTION 40,000 bottles
HECTARES UNDER VINE 13.00

| | |
|---|---|
| ● Brunello di Montalcino Ris. '12 | ♟♟ 7 |
| ● Brunello di Montalcino '13 | ♟ 6 |
| ● Rosso di Montalcino '16 | ♟ 4 |

## Usiglian Del Vescovo

via Usigliano, 26
56036 Palaia [PI]
Tel. +39 0587468000
www.usigliandelvescovo.it

CELLAR SALES
PRE-BOOKED VISITS
RESTAURANT SERVICE
ANNUAL PRODUCTION 130,000 bottles
HECTARES UNDER VINE 23.00
VITICULTURE METHOD Certified Organic
SUSTAINABLE WINERY

| | |
|---|---|
| ● MilleEottantatre '13 | ♟♟ 8 |
| ○ Il Barbiglione '14 | ♟♟ 6 |
| ● Mora del Roveto '16 | ♟♟ 2* |

## Valdamone

loc. Valdamone, 119
57028 Suvereto [LI]
Tel. +39 3395971098
valdamone@valdicornia.com

HECTARES UNDER VINE

| | |
|---|---|
| ● Poggio a' Bugni '15 | ♟♟ 4 |
| ○ Zelinda Vermentino '17 | ♟♟ 2* |
| ● Albizio '17 | ♟ 3 |

## Valle di Lazzaro

loc. Valle di Lazzaro, 103
57037 Portoferraio [LI]
Tel. +39 0565916387
www.valledilazzaro.com

CELLAR SALES
PRE-BOOKED VISITS
ANNUAL PRODUCTION 12,000 bottles
HECTARES UNDER VINE 4.00

| | |
|---|---|
| ● Elba Sangiovese Lazarus '16 | ♟♟ 3* |
| ○ Elba Ansonica '17 | ♟♟ 3 |
| ○ Elba Vermentino '17 | ♟♟ 3 |
| ○ Elba Procanico '17 | ♟ 3 |

## Valvirginio

A NUOVA DEL VIRGINIO, 34
0025 MONTESPERTOLI [FI]
EL. +39 0571659127

HECTARES UNDER VINE

| | |
|---|---|
| ● Baron del Nero '13 | ♟♟ 3 |
| ● Chianti Montespertoli '16 | ♟♟ 2* |
| ● Chianti '17 | ♟ 2 |
| ○ Vermentino '17 | ♟ 2 |

## Vecchia Cantina di Montepulciano

VIA PROVINCIALE, 7
53045 MONTEPULCIANO [SI]
TEL. +39 0578716092
www.vecchiacantina.com

CELLAR SALES
PRE-BOOKED VISITS
ANNUAL PRODUCTION 4,500,000 bottles
HECTARES UNDER VINE 1000.00
VITICULTURE METHOD Certified Organic

| | |
|---|---|
| ● Orbaio Redi '15 | ♟♟ 5 |
| ● Nobile di Montepulciano Redi '15 | ♟ 5 |
| ● Nobile di Montepulciano Vecchia Cantina Ris. '13 | ♟ 4 |

## Vecchie Terre di Montefili

VIA SAN CRESCI, 45
50022 PANZANO [FI]
TEL. +39 055853739
www.vecchieterredimontefili.com

CELLAR SALES
PRE-BOOKED VISITS
ANNUAL PRODUCTION 40,000 bottles
HECTARES UNDER VINE 13.50

| | |
|---|---|
| ● Chianti Cl. Ris. '15 | ♟♟ 6 |
| ● Chianti Cl. '15 | ♟ 3 |

## Ventolaio

LOC. VENTOLAIO, 51
53024 MONTALCINO [SI]
TEL. +39 0577835779

CELLAR SALES
PRE-BOOKED VISITS
ANNUAL PRODUCTION 70,000 bottles
HECTARES UNDER VINE 14.00

| | |
|---|---|
| ● Brunello di Montalcino Ris. '12 | ♟♟ 8 |
| ● Rosso di Montalcino '16 | ♟♟ 3 |
| ● Brunello di Montalcino '13 | ♟ 6 |

## Vigliano

LOC. SAN MARTINO ALLA PALMA
VIA CARCHERI, 309
50018 SCANDICCI [FI]
TEL. +39 0558727040
www.vigliano.com

CELLAR SALES
PRE-BOOKED VISITS
ANNUAL PRODUCTION 39,000 bottles
HECTARES UNDER VINE 12.00

| | |
|---|---|
| ○ Bianco di Vigliano '17 | ♟♟ 3 |
| ● L'Erta '15 | ♟♟ 4 |
| ○ L'Erta Bianco '16 | ♟♟ 4 |
| ● Rosso Vigliano '16 | ♟ 2 |

## Villa Calcinaia

FRAZ. GRETI
VIA CITILLE, 84
50022 GREVE IN CHIANTI [FI]
TEL. +39 055853715
www.villacalcinaia.it

CELLAR SALES
PRE-BOOKED VISITS
ACCOMMODATION
ANNUAL PRODUCTION 90,000 bottles
HECTARES UNDER VINE 27.00
VITICULTURE METHOD Certified Organic

| | |
|---|---|
| ● Chianti Cl. Gran Selezione Villa Calcinaia V. Bastignano '15 | ♟♟ 7 |
| ● Chianti Cl. Ris. '15 | ♟♟ 5 |
| ● Chianti Cl. '15 | ♟ 3 |

## Villa La Ripa

LOC. ANTRIA, 38
52100 AREZZO
TEL. +39 057523330
www.villalaripa.it

CELLAR SALES
PRE-BOOKED VISITS
ANNUAL PRODUCTION 10,000 bottles
HECTARES UNDER VINE 5.00
SUSTAINABLE WINERY

| | |
|---|---|
| ● Psyco '15 | ♟♟ 5 |
| ● Syrah '15 | ♟♟ 6 |
| ● Tiratari '15 | ♟♟ 5 |
| ☉ Rosato Spazio Libero '17 | ♟ 2 |

## Villa Le Prata

LOC. LE PRATA, 261
53024 MONTALCINO [SI]
TEL. +39 0577848325
www.villaleprata.com

CELLAR SALES
PRE-BOOKED VISITS
ANNUAL PRODUCTION 15,000 bottles
HECTARES UNDER VINE 4.00

| | |
|---|---|
| ● Brunello di Montalcino '13 | ♟♟ 6 |

## Villa Pillo

VIA VOLTERRANA, 24
50050 GAMBASSI TERME [FI]
TEL. +39 0571680212
www.villapillo.com

CELLAR SALES
PRE-BOOKED VISITS
ANNUAL PRODUCTION 350,000 bottles
HECTARES UNDER VINE 40.00

| | |
|---|---|
| ● Cypresses '16 | ♟♟ 3 |
| ● Merlot '16 | ♟♟ 5 |
| ● Syrah '16 | ♟♟ 5 |
| ● Vivaldaia '16 | ♟♟ 4 |

## Villa Pinciana

S.DA VILLA PINCIANA, 2A
58011 CAPALBIO [GR]
TEL. +39 0564896598
www.villapinciana.com

CELLAR SALES
PRE-BOOKED VISITS
ANNUAL PRODUCTION 35,000 bottles
HECTARES UNDER VINE 8.50

| | |
|---|---|
| ● Maremma Toscana Rosso Terraria '13 | ♟♟ 5 |
| ○ Maremma Toscana Bianco Airali '17 | ♟ 3 |
| ● Tilaria '14 | ♟ 3 |

## Villa Sant'Andrea

LOC. MONTEFIRIDOLFI
VIA DI FABBRICA, 63
50020 SAN CASCIANO IN VAL DI PESA [FI]
TEL. +39 0558244254
www.villas-andrea.it

CELLAR SALES
PRE-BOOKED VISITS
ANNUAL PRODUCTION 450,000 bottles
HECTARES UNDER VINE 52.00

| | |
|---|---|
| ● Chianti Cl. Ris. '15 | ♟♟ 3* |
| ● Chianti Cl. '16 | ♟♟ 2* |

## Giomi Zannoni

VIA AURELIA NORD, 63
57029 CAMPIGLIA MARITTIMA [LI]
TEL. +39 0565846416
www.giomi-zannoni.com

CELLAR SALES
PRE-BOOKED VISITS
RESTAURANT SERVICE
ANNUAL PRODUCTION 18,000 bottles
HECTARES UNDER VINE 7.00

| | |
|---|---|
| ● Aldò 917 '17 | ♟♟ 5 |
| ○ Val di Cornia Bianco Corniola '17 | ♟♟ 3 |
| ● Valdicornia Sangiovese Rodantonio '16 | ♟ 5 |
| ○ Vermentino Ninà '17 | ♟ 3 |

# MARCHE

Thumbing through the pages here you'll find a number of new wineries, and the return of some that seemed to have lost their way. By no means should this volatility be seen as a weakness. Quality is improving in the region and Marche's wine industry is made up primarily of a solid network of small-medium sized producers, with competition pushing everyone to do their best. Large and small producers alike have to prove their worth to be included in this snapshot of a region made up of about a thousand wines and more than two-hundred wineries. This year our tastings brought to light some interesting considerations. Marche's reds (in particular those from the southern part of the region) are showing a nice mobility brought about by fresher aromas and less concentration. It's not an easy feat when you're working with grapes like Montepulciano. We also noticed the desire of some districts to set in motion a 'virtuous cycle'. We're thinking in particular of Bianchello del Metauro and Colli Maceratesi Ribona, where the results are increasingly convincing. And it's in this light that readers should interpret the first Tre Bicchieri for a Lacrima di Morro d'Alba. It's been years that this small appellation has been showing signs of vitality, thanks to new interpreters and constant investment. Origiolo di Marotti Campi manages to bring together complexity with the cultivar's trademark aromatic qualities. We're also happy to point out awards for two wineries that are emblematic of their respective districts: Moroder (which represents Conero with their 2015 Dorico) and Pollenza (which represents Macerata with their 2015 Pollenza). Rosso Piceno celebrated its 50th anniversary in the best possible way with some three wines taking home top marks (thanks to the appellation's iconic producers, De Angelis, Le Caniette and Velenosi). And a trio also represented Offida Pecorino. In addition to the young offshoots Simone Spinelli and Marco Santori, there's the wine that pays homage to Guido Cocci Grifoni, artificer of the wine's rescue from oblivion. Awards for Verdicchio make less noise by now. There were a number of recognitions from the most inspired producers, but also a number of 'repeats', as in the cases of Sparapani, Casalfarneto and Santa Barbara.

# MARCHE

## Accadia

Fraz. Castellaro
c.da Ammorto, 19
60048 Serra San Quirico [AN]
Tel. +39 073185172
www.accadiavini.it

**CELLAR SALES**
**PRE-BOOKED VISITS**
**ANNUAL PRODUCTION** 40,000 bottles
**HECTARES UNDER VINE** 9.00

Painter/sculptor Angelo Accadia has been this winery's hands-on manager since 1983. His Verdicchio touch has established him as one of the variety's most-respected producers, and working with his daughter Evelyn in recent years has brought even greater visibility to their work. The winery and vineyards are located on a hill on the right bank of the Esino River, near Cupramontana. Their wine reflects the unique energy and aromatic finesse of the territory, brought out by vinification in steel. The highest, sunniest part of the vineyards is reserved for their Cantorì. The 2016 version has an appealing nose of toasted almonds and a rich, glyceric mouthfeel. The balance and savory contrast that it lacks appears in the 2016 Conscio, with engaging hints of anise, fennel and orange peel followed by a palate of the prefect density. Their 2017 Consono doesn't stand out for its suppleness, but it is s velvety and enjoyable.

| | |
|---|---|
| ○ Verdicchio dei Castelli di Jesi Cl. Sup. Conscio '16 | 🏆🏆 3* |
| ○ Verdicchio dei Castelli di Jesi Cl. Sup. Cantorì '16 | 🏆🏆 4 |
| ○ Verdicchio dei Castelli di Jesi Cl. Sup. Consono '17 | 🏆🏆 2* |
| ○ Verdicchio dei Castelli di Jesi Cl. Consono '07 | 🏆🏆 2* |
| ○ Verdicchio dei Castelli di Jesi Cl. Sup. Conscio '07 | 🏆🏆 2 |
| ○ Verdicchio dei Castelli di Jesi Cl. Sup. Conscio '06 | 🏆🏆 2 |

## Maria Letizia Allevi

via Pescolla
63081 Castorano [AP]
Tel. +39 073687646
www.vinimida.it

**CELLAR SALES**
**PRE-BOOKED VISITS**
**ANNUAL PRODUCTION** 10,000 bottles
**HECTARES UNDER VINE** 5.00
**VITICULTURE METHOD** Certified Organic

The excellent results registered in recent years at this winery have brought the work of Roberto Corradetti and his wife Maria Letizia out of the shadows into a spotlight on a selection of wines previously unknown beyond local circles. Both the vineyards at the foot of their small cellar and the new vineyards at Contrada San Silvestro are managed with the same devotion. Organic management and attentive winemaking give rise to serious Pecorino and Montepulciano that fully express the territory's predisposition for the cultivar. Both wines presented clearly say Offida. Their 2015 Mida Rosso exploits Montepulciano's generosity and energy for a full and layered palate, with sensations of dark fruits that unfold with an admirable, natural authenticity. Their 2017 Mida Pecorino offers anise and yellow citrus with return on an invigorating palate with a sturdy backbone flickering with savoriness.

| | |
|---|---|
| ○ Offida Pecorino Mida '17 | 🏆🏆 3* |
| ● Offida Rosso Mida '15 | 🏆🏆 4 |
| ○ Offida Pecorino Mida '16 | 🏆🏆🏆 3* |
| ⊙ Mida '13 | 🏆🏆 3 |
| ⊙ Mida Rosato '16 | 🏆🏆 3 |
| ○ Offida Pecorino Mida '15 | 🏆🏆 3 |
| ● Offida Rosso Mida '14 | 🏆🏆 3 |
| ● Offida Rosso Mida '13 | 🏆🏆 3 |
| ● Offida Rosso Mida '11 | 🏆🏆 4 |

# Aurora

LOC. SANTA MARIA IN CARRO
C.DA CIAFONE, 98
63073 OFFIDA [AP]
TEL. +39 0736810007
www.viniaurora.it

**CELLAR SALES**
**PRE-BOOKED VISITS**
**ACCOMMODATION**
**ANNUAL PRODUCTION** 53,300 bottles
**HECTARES UNDER VINE** 9.50
**VITICULTURE METHOD** Certified Organic

When Aurora began production almost 40 years ago, it was virtually alone in singing the praises of organic agriculture in Piceno. Since then the ranks have grown to a choir, but Aurora's voice remains among the purest, serving as inspiration for all. Their approach in the cellar is as minimally invasive as possible and most of the work in the vineyard is guided by biodynamic principles. The challenge is eternal: allow traditional cultivars to express themselves to the fullest, so that with human skill and time they give rise to wines that are intimately bound to the terroir. It's well worth leaving Aurora's wines in the glass for a few minutes to let their true vitality emerge. A short wait is rewarded by their surprisingly elegant 2016 Piceno Superiore, offering clean aromas and a juicy palate. Their 2015 Barricadiero plays on the contrast between dark fruit notes and a severe, tannic palate. Their 2016 Pecorino Fiobbo, as flavorful as usual, proves less dynamic than in past years.

| | | |
|---|---|---|
| ○ Offida Pecorino Fiobbo '16 | ▼▼ | 3 |
| ● Offida Rosso Barricadiero '15 | ▼▼ | 4 |
| ● Rosso Piceno Sup. '16 | ▼▼ | 2* |
| ○ Falerio '17 | ▼ | 2 |
| ● Rosso Piceno '17 | ▼ | 2 |
| ● Barricadiero '10 | ♈♈♈ | 4* |
| ● Barricadiero '09 | ♈♈♈ | 4 |
| ● Barricadiero '06 | ♈♈♈ | 4 |
| ● Barricadiero '04 | ♈♈♈ | 3 |
| ● Barricadiero '03 | ♈♈♈ | 3* |
| ● Barricadiero '02 | ♈♈♈ | 3 |
| ● Barricadiero '01 | ♈♈♈ | 3* |
| ● Offida Rosso Barricadiero '11 | ♈♈♈ | 4* |

# Belisario

VIA ARISTIDE MERLONI, 12
62024 MATELICA [MC]
TEL. +39 0737787247
www.belisario.it

**CELLAR SALES**
**PRE-BOOKED VISITS**
**ANNUAL PRODUCTION** 1,000,000 bottles
**HECTARES UNDER VINE** 300.00

The Verdicchio di Matelica appellation just celebrated its half-century mark and Belisario is looking to the future. It's working hard to organize as a small group of vine growers located throughout the Camerte Valley, an area particularly well-suited to the area's trademark grapes. Over the years, Director-Oenologist Roberto Potentini and President Antonio Centocanti have fashioned a solid selection that is well-differentiated, exploring the full range of possibilities the Verdicchio grape offers. Their 2015 Meridia charms with its nose of candied orange, saffron and anise followed by a voluminous palate that prefectly reflects its aromatic profile. The same ripeness is amplified in their 2015 Cambrugiano Riserva. Wider than deep, it offers ample hints of dried fruit and nuts with a toasted background. Their 2017 Vigneti B. focuses on fruity aromas and white flowers, encouraging slow drinking despite its slender body.

| | | |
|---|---|---|
| ○ Verdicchio di Matelica Cambrugiano Ris. '15 | ▼▼ | 3* |
| ○ Verdicchio di Matelica Meridia '15 | ▼▼ | 3* |
| ○ Verdicchio di Matelica Del Cerro '17 | ▼▼ | 2* |
| ○ Verdicchio di Matelica Terre di Valbona '17 | ▼▼ | 2* |
| ○ Verdicchio di Matelica Vign. B. '17 | ▼▼ | 3 |
| ● Colli Maceratesi Rosso San Leopardo Ris. '15 | ▼ | 3 |
| ○ Verdicchio di Matelica Anfora '17 | ▼ | 2 |
| ○ Verdicchio di Matelica Brut Cuvée Nadir | ▼ | 2 |
| ○ Verdicchio di Matelica Cambrugiano Ris. '14 | ♈♈♈ | 3* |
| ○ Verdicchio di Matelica Cambrugiano Ris. '12 | ♈♈♈ | 3* |
| ○ Verdicchio di Matelica Meridia '10 | ♈♈♈ | 3* |
| ○ Verdicchio di Matelica Vign. B. '15 | ♈♈♈ | 3* |

# Bisci

VIA FOGLIANO, 120
62024 MATELICA [MC]
TEL. +39 0737787490
www.bisci.it

CELLAR SALES
PRE-BOOKED VISITS
ACCOMMODATION
ANNUAL PRODUCTION 90,000 bottles
HECTARES UNDER VINE 20.00
VITICULTURE METHOD Certified Organic

The Bisci family winery has been active for almost forty years. During the last decade in particular it has made a name for itself among enthusiasts, thanks in part to contributions from young consultant Aroldo Bellelli. The winery uses carefully monitored maturation and fine-tuned fermentation in fiberglass-lined concrete tanks to produce Verdicchio whites that feature great stylistic rigor. Noteworthy for their finesse and longevity, these characteristics are especially evident when it comes to their most important cru, Vigneto Fogliano, which is named after the location of the winery. Their 2017 Verdicchio unveils itself as truly Matelica with clear aromas of citrus and the variety's characteristic almond. It leaps around the palate with a salty vitality. Their 2016 Vigneto Fogliano proves less tenuous than in the past, giving off strong fruity aromas it is unusually supple and ready to drink. Their 2015 Rosso Fogliano exploits the fullness of Merlot resulting in an enjoyable palate.

# Boccadigabbia

LOC. FONTESPINA
C.DA CASTELLETTA, 56
62012 CIVITANOVA MARCHE [MC]
TEL. +39 073370728
www.boccadigabbia.com

CELLAR SALES
PRE-BOOKED VISITS
ANNUAL PRODUCTION 100,000 bottles
HECTARES UNDER VINE 25.00

Boccadigabbia has historic links to wines produced using international grapes. However, Elvio Alessandri is committed to making noteworthy wines with traditional varieties, and for this reason his La Floriana estate in Montanello di Macerata is dedicated to the cultivation of Verdicchio, Montepulciano, Ribona and Sangiovese. Cabernet, Pinot Noir, Chardonnay and Merlot are cultivated near Civitanova Marche, where their recently enlarged cellar is also located. Here youngest wines are aged in steel vats while the reds are usually matured in bariques. Their 2013 La Floriana is a dense, full-bodied Montepulciano that respects the variety's fruity nature. Their 2013 Sangiovese Saltapicchio proves more harmonic with a good balance of toasted notes acquired during barrel aging and a remarkable measure of crisp, fleshy fruit. A Verdicchio and Ribona blend, their 2016 La Floriana Bianca hits the nose with quirky hints of rosemary.

| | |
|---|---|
| ○ Verdicchio di Matelica '17 | ♟♟ 3* |
| ● Rosso Fogliano '15 | ♟♟ 2* |
| ○ Verdicchio di Matelica Vign. Fogliano '16 | ♟♟ 4 |
| ○ Verdicchio di Matelica Vign. Fogliano '15 | ♟♟♟ 4* |
| ○ Verdicchio di Matelica Vign. Fogliano '13 | ♟♟♟ 3* |
| ○ Verdicchio di Matelica Vign. Fogliano '10 | ♟♟♟ 3* |
| ○ Verdicchio di Matelica Vign. Fogliano '08 | ♟♟♟ 3* |
| ○ Verdicchio di Matelica '16 | ♟♟ 3* |
| ○ Verdicchio di Matelica '15 | ♟♟ 3 |
| ○ Verdicchio di Matelica '14 | ♟♟ 2* |

| | |
|---|---|
| ● Tenuta La Floriana Rosso '13 | ♟♟ 6 |
| ○ Colli Maceratesi Ribona '17 | ♟♟ 3 |
| ● Rosso Piceno '15 | ♟♟ 3 |
| ● Saltapicchio '13 | ♟♟ 4 |
| ○ Tenuta La Floriana Bianco '16 | ♟♟ 6 |
| ○ Colli Maceratesi Ribona Le Grane '17 | ♟ 3 |
| ○ Garbì '17 | ♟ 2 |
| ○ Montalperti '16 | ♟ 4 |
| ○ Rosèo '17 | ♟ 2 |
| ● Akronte '98 | ♟♟♟ 7 |
| ● Akronte '97 | ♟♟♟ 7 |
| ● Akronte '95 | ♟♟♟ 7 |
| ● Akronte '94 | ♟♟♟ 7 |
| ● Akronte '93 | ♟♟♟ 7 |
| ● Akronte Cabernet '92 | ♟♟♟ 7 |

# Borgo Paglianetto

LOC. PAGLIANO, 393
62024 MATELICA [MC]
TEL. +39 073785465
www.borgopaglianetto.it

CELLAR SALES
PRE-BOOKED VISITS
ANNUAL PRODUCTION 60,000 bottles
HECTARES UNDER VINE 25.00
VITICULTURE METHOD Certified Organic

Borgo Paglianetto has become a leader of the Matelica wine scene after transitioning to organic farming. It has also found great success with Réwine, a selection of wines produced according to biodynamic methods. The distinction between their various wines is becoming apparent, starting from their freshest whites made with Verdicchio, and ending with the complexity of Ergon and Vertis. All wines are aged in steel, while large oak barrels are reserved for their Montepulciano Matesis. Their entire range of Verdicchio is exceptional, more precise and impressive than ever, but their 2016 Vertis triumphs. Its complex, crystalline aromas and refined, graceful palate just edge out their 2017 Petrara, whose citrus aromas return on a very mineral, almost stony, palate. Their 2016 Ergon gives hints of yellow peach and offers a juicy palate, while their 2015 Montepulciano Matesis reveals surprising grace.

# Brunori

V.LE DELLA VITTORIA, 103
60035 JESI [AN]
TEL. +39 0731207213
www.brunori.it

CELLAR SALES
PRE-BOOKED VISITS
ANNUAL PRODUCTION 60,000 bottles
HECTARES UNDER VINE 7.00

For more than 50 years the Brunori family name has been dedicated to and connected with Verdicchio. No other varieties are cultivated in their single vineyard of San Nicolò near San Paolo di Jesi. In the mid-1970s, Giorgio was among the area's first to believe in a 'cru' and to adopt the Bordeaux-shaped bottle instead of the common amphora-shaped one. Today his son Carlo leads the winery, which has remained at its original artisanal size. There are no real standouts among their uniformly high-quality cohesive range, though we did really like the tender, bountifully fruited and inviting character of their 2016 Verdicchio San Nicolò Riserva. Their 2017 Classico Superiore performs on the palate with a nice contrast between its suppleness and savory length. Their 2017 Le Gemme also belongs among their best, both for varietal adherence expressing almonds and linden flowers, and for overall excellent personality.

| | |
|---|---|
| ○ Verdicchio di Matelica Vertis '16 | ♟♟♟ 3* |
| ● Matesis '15 | ♟♟ 3* |
| ○ Verdicchio di Matelica Ergon '16 | ♟♟ 3* |
| ○ Verdicchio di Matelica Petrara '17 | ♟♟ 2* |
| ○ Verdicchio di Matelica Terravignata '17 | ♟♟ 2* |
| ○ Verdicchio di Matelica M. Cl. Brut | ♟♟ 5 |
| ○ Verdicchio di Matelica Jera Ris. '10 | ♟♟♟ 4* |
| ○ Verdicchio di Matelica Petrara '16 | ♟♟♟ 2* |
| ○ Verdicchio di Matelica Vertis '09 | ♟♟♟ 3* |
| ● Matesis '11 | ♟♟ 3* |
| ○ Verdicchio di Matelica Ergon '15 | ♟♟ 3 |
| ○ Verdicchio di Matelica Petrara '15 | ♟♟ 2* |
| ○ Verdicchio di Matelica Petrara '14 | ♟♟ 2* |
| ○ Verdicchio di Matelica Terravignata '16 | ♟♟ 2* |
| ○ Verdicchio di Matelica Terravignata '15 | ♟♟ 2* |
| ○ Verdicchio di Matelica Vertis '15 | ♟♟ 3 |
| ○ Verdicchio di Matelica Vertis '13 | ♟♟ 3* |

| | |
|---|---|
| ○ Castelli di Jesi Verdicchio Cl. San Nicolò Ris. '16 | ♟♟ 3 |
| ○ Verdicchio dei Castelli di Jesi Cl. Le Gemme '17 | ♟♟ 2* |
| ○ Verdicchio dei Castelli di Jesi Cl. Sup. San Nicolò '17 | ♟♟ 2* |
| ○ Castelli di Jesi Verdicchio Cl. San Nicolò Ris. '15 | ♟♟ 3* |
| ○ Verdicchio dei Castelli di Jesi Cl. Le Gemme '16 | ♟♟ 2* |
| ○ Verdicchio dei Castelli di Jesi Cl. San Nicolò Ris. '13 | ♟♟ 3* |
| ○ Verdicchio dei Castelli di Jesi Cl. Sup. San Nicolò '16 | ♟♟ 2* |
| ○ Verdicchio dei Castelli di Jesi Cl. Sup. San Nicolò '14 | ♟♟ 2* |

## ★Bucci

FRAZ. PONGELLI
VIA CONA, 30
60010 OSTRA VETERE [AN]
TEL. +39 071964179
www.villabucci.com

**CELLAR SALES**
**PRE-BOOKED VISITS**
**ANNUAL PRODUCTION** 120,000 bottles
**HECTARES UNDER VINE** 31.00
**VITICULTURE METHOD** Certified Organic

The Bucci family has a long, productive history in the region, and the family winery is the crown jewel of a diversified agricultural system. The grapes are cultivated in six different sites, located in the municipalities of Barbara, Montecarotto and Serra de' Conti. Only traditional varieties are cultivated, with more than two thirds of the area reserved for Verdicchio, and the rest planted with Montepulciano and Sangiovese. Wines are identified by vintage rather than cru, and only the best are matured in large Slavonian oak barrels to become Villa Bucci wines. This year we sampled the 2016 vintage, which whispers aromatic herbs, chamomile and anise. Its lean, supple palate lacks a bit of articulation when compare to the best interpretations, but additional time in the bottle should add complexity. The warm weather of 2017 has made their Verdicchio Classico expansive, ready-to-drink and mouth-filling without inhibiting its drinkability.

## Le Caniette

C.DA CANALI, 23
63065 RIPATRANSONE [AP]
TEL. +39 07359200
www.lecaniette.it

**CELLAR SALES**
**PRE-BOOKED VISITS**
**ANNUAL PRODUCTION** 60,000 bottles
**HECTARES UNDER VINE** 16.00
**VITICULTURE METHOD** Certified Organic

Le Caniette, positioned on the Adriatic-facing slopes of the Ripatransone, is sailing along smoothly under the guidance of brothers Gino and Giovanni Vagnoni. After spending the 1990s establishing a foundation for the winery's agriculture and production, they are now setting the course for a style that unites traditional Piceno varieties with a contemporary spirit. The solid and elegant selection is enriched this year with Sinopia, a rosé made with Montepulciano grapes, set to debut with the 2017 vintage. The expressive precision and tannic elegance of their Martellone no longer surprises us and their 2013 proves no exception to the rule, earning its umpteenth Tre Bicchieri. Though a true classic among Piceno wines, it shouldn't completely overshadow their wonderful 2014 Cinabro, a refined Bordò (the local Grenache clone) that captivates the nose with notes of oriental spices and traces of smoke and then seduces the palate with its grace.

| | |
|---|---|
| ○ Castelli di Jesi Verdicchio Cl. Villa Bucci Ris. '16 | 🍷🍷 6 |
| ● Rosso Piceno Tenuta Pongelli '16 | 🍷🍷 3 |
| ○ Verdicchio dei Castelli di Jesi Cl. Sup. '17 | 🍷🍷 3 |
| ● Rosso Piceno Villa Bucci '15 | 🍷 5 |
| ○ Castelli di Jesi Verdicchio Cl. Villa Bucci Ris. '14 | 🍷🍷🍷 6 |
| ○ Castelli di Jesi Verdicchio Cl. Villa Bucci Ris. '13 | 🍷🍷🍷 6 |
| ○ Castelli di Jesi Verdicchio Cl. Villa Bucci Ris. '12 | 🍷🍷🍷 6 |
| ○ Castelli di Jesi Verdicchio Cl. Villa Bucci Ris. '10 | 🍷🍷🍷 6 |
| ○ Verdicchio dei Castelli di Jesi Cl. Sup. '16 | 🍷🍷🍷 3* |
| ○ Verdicchio dei Castelli di Jesi Cl. Villa Bucci Ris. '09 | 🍷🍷🍷 6 |

| | |
|---|---|
| ● Piceno Sup. Morellone '13 | 🍷🍷🍷 4* |
| ● Cinabro '14 | 🍷🍷 8 |
| ○ Offida Pecorino Iosonogaia non sono Lucrezia '16 | 🍷🍷 4 |
| ○ Offida Pecorino Veronica '17 | 🍷🍷 3 |
| ○ Lucrezia '17 | 🍷 2 |
| ☉ Sinopia '17 | 🍷 3 |
| ○ Offida Pecorino Iosonogaia non sono Lucrezia '10 | 🍷🍷🍷 4* |
| ● Piceno Morellone '10 | 🍷🍷🍷 4* |
| ● Piceno Morellone '08 | 🍷🍷🍷 4* |
| ● Piceno Sup. Morellone '12 | 🍷🍷🍷 4* |
| ● Cinabro '13 | 🍷🍷 8 |
| ● Cinabro '12 | 🍷🍷 8 |
| ● Piceno Nero di Vite '10 | 🍷🍷 6 |
| ● Piceno Sup. Morellone '11 | 🍷🍷 4 |

# Carminucci

A San Leonardo, 39
63013 Grottammare [AP]
Tel. +39 0735735869
www.carminucci.com

**CELLAR SALES**
**ANNUAL PRODUCTION** 350,000 bottles
**HECTARES UNDER VINE** 46.00
**VITICULTURE METHOD** Certified Organic

The Carminucci family's large and well-equipped cellar is situated close to the sea along the Valtesino River. However, its productive heart is farther inland, in the municipality of Offida, which has more suitable soil and an optimal exposure. The winery is passionate about Chardonnay, but its focus remains on traditional varieties. Their openly modern wine expresses a fruity nonchalance emphasizing drinkability. A clear note of grapefruit comes through the intense aromas of their 2017 Belato, a Pecorino that's supple on its palate with strong drive and tenacious finish. Made from Passerina, their 2017 Casta offers hints of peach skin and easy drinking, while their 2015 Rosso Piceno Superiore Naumakos plays on a well-designed balance of fruit, alcohol and smooth tannins.

| | | |
|---|---|---|
| ○ Offida Pecorino Belato '17 | ♈♈ | 2* |
| ○ Casta '17 | ♈♈ | 2* |
| ○ Falerio Naumakos '17 | ♈♈ | 2* |
| ● Rosso Piceno Grotte sul Mare '17 | ♈♈ | 2* |
| ● Rosso Piceno Sup. Naumakos '15 | ♈♈ | 2* |
| ○ Falerio Grotte sul Mare '17 | ♈ | 1* |
| ☉ Grotte sul Mare Rosato '17 | ♈ | 2 |
| ○ Naumakos '16 | ♈ | 2 |
| ○ Falerio Grotte sul Mare '16 | ♈♈ | 1* |
| ○ Falerio Naumakos '16 | ♈♈ | 2* |
| ○ Offida Pecorino Belato '16 | ♈♈ | 2* |
| ○ Offida Pecorino Belato '15 | ♈♈ | 2* |
| ● Rosso Piceno Sup. Naumakos '14 | ♈♈ | 2* |
| ● Rosso Piceno Sup. Naumakos '13 | ♈♈ | 2* |

# CasalFarneto

via Farneto, 12
60030 Serra de' Conti [AN]
Tel. +39 0731889001
www.casalfarneto.it

**CELLAR SALES**
**PRE-BOOKED VISITS**
**ANNUAL PRODUCTION** 750,000 bottles
**HECTARES UNDER VINE** 39.00

Casalfarneto had a big year in 2018. After leaving the Togni Group (active in mineral water, sparkling wines, artisan beer, and egg pasta), this producer is now on its own, both in terms of distribution and management, now headed by Paolo Togni. The production structure at Casalfarneto remains unchanged. Danilo Solustri is still responsible for the wine-growing side and Franco Bernabei heads up the winery's technical department. The focus of their wines continues to revolve around the versatility of Verdicchio, expressed in all its nuances. Tre Bicchieri once again for their refined 2016 Verdicchio Grancasale, brimming with varietal aromas and an enduring palate full of flavor and depth. Their 2015 Crisio offers good complexity and thickness, while light on acidic contrast. Their simply delicious 2014 Ikòn delivers aromas of dried fruit, nuts and peach jam, which reassert themselves in the wine's long, soft finish.

| | | |
|---|---|---|
| ○ Verdicchio dei Castelli di Jesi Cl. Sup. Grancasale '16 | ♈♈♈ | 3* |
| ○ Verdicchio dei Castelli di Jesi Passito Ikòn '14 | ♈♈ | 5 |
| ○ Castelli di Jesi Verdicchio Cl. Crisio Ris. '15 | ♈♈ | 3 |
| ○ Verdicchio dei Castelli di Jesi Cl. Sup. Fontevecchia '17 | ♈♈ | 2* |
| ○ Cimaio '15 | ♈ | 4 |
| ● Merago '14 | ♈ | 3 |
| ○ Verdicchio dei Castelli di Jesi Cl. Diego '17 | ♈ | 2 |
| ○ Castelli di Jesi Verdicchio Cl. Crisio Ris. '13 | ♈♈ | 3* |
| ○ Verdicchio dei Castelli di Jesi Cl. Sup. Grancasale '13 | ♈♈ | 3* |

## Castignano Cantine dal 1960

c.da San Venanzo, 31
63072 Castignano [AP]
Tel. +39 0736822216
www.cantinedicastignano.com

**CELLAR SALES**
**PRE-BOOKED VISITS**
**ANNUAL PRODUCTION** 450,000 bottles
**HECTARES UNDER VINE** 500.00
**VITICULTURE METHOD** Certified Organic

Credit the sparkle in the air around Castignano to nearby Monte Ascensione, a massif that influences the area's microclimate by creating variations in temperature and altitude. But credit must also be given to this cooperative's young president, Omar Traini, who has been carrying out renovations at the winery. Traini is convinced the wines here deserve recognition beyond the immediate area. The selections reflect the complete territory, dedicated to the most typical cultivars and offering well-balanced, pleasant character. Though fragrant with citrus fruit and subtle hints of wild herbs, their 2017 Montemisio Pecorino shines brilliantly among their selections because of its expansive, invigorating palate. Their 2013 Grand Master, however, shines almost as brightly, managing to combine Montepulciano's fruity punch with a soft, burgeoning, flowing palate. Their 2016 Superiore Destriero reveals a plucky rustic spirit, while their 'basic level' 2017 Rosso Piceno is light, breezy, and pleasantly winy.

| | |
|---|---|
| ○ Offida Pecorino Montemisio '17 | 🍷🍷 2* |
| ● Offida Rosso Gran Maestro '13 | 🍷🍷 3* |
| ○ Falerio '17 | 🍷🍷 1* |
| ○ Notturno Moscato Dolce | 🍷🍷 2* |
| ○ Passerina '17 | 🍷🍷 2* |
| ● Rosso Piceno '17 | 🍷🍷 1* |
| ● Rosso Piceno Sup. Destriero '16 | 🍷🍷 2* |
| ○ Falerio Pecorino Destriero '17 | 🍷 2 |
| ● Templaria '16 | 🍷 2 |
| ○ Terre di Offida Passerina Brut '17 | 🍷 2 |
| ○ Offida Pecorino Montemisio '16 | 🍸🍸 2* |
| ○ Offida Pecorino Montemisio '14 | 🍸🍸 2* |
| ○ Offida Pecorino Montemisio '13 | 🍸🍸 2* |
| ● Offida Rosso Gran Maestro '12 | 🍸🍸 3 |
| ○ Passerina '16 | 🍸🍸 2* |
| ● Rosso Piceno Sup. Destriero '15 | 🍸🍸 1* |

## Castrum Morisci

via Molino, 16
63826 Moresco [FM]
Tel. +39 3400820708
www.castrummorisci.it

**CELLAR SALES**
**ANNUAL PRODUCTION** 25,000 bottles
**HECTARES UNDER VINE** 7.00

The lush, orderly countryside that descends from the picturesque Moresco into the Aso River valley is covered with olive trees, vineyards, peach trees and fields of grain. About midway, a recently renovated farm manor hosts the winery of David Pettinari who, with the help of brother-in-law Luca Renzi and oenologist Giuseppe Camilli, has created an original and carefully managed enterprise. Wines named after local districts are aged in unburied amphorae, and those with numbers are aged in steel. Their 2017 102 is the best Offida Passerina we tasted this year, offering a floral, citrusy nose followed by a quick palate that's moderated by a strong backbone ending in long salinity. Of their two 2017 Pecorino, Gallicano stands out for its intense notes of ginger and generous, full palate. Their 003 delivers pleasant hints of lemon leaves in a supple drink and their 2017 Padreterno is an original varietal blend offering aromatic herbs and an invigorating palate.

| | |
|---|---|
| ○ Falerio Pecorino 003 '17 | 🍷🍷 3 |
| ○ Falerio Pecorino Gallicano '17 | 🍷🍷 5 |
| ○ Offida Passerina 102 '17 | 🍷🍷 2* |
| ○ Padreterno '17 | 🍷🍷 5 |
| ⊙ 326 '17 | 🍷 2 |
| ● Collefrenato '16 | 🍷 4 |
| ● Piceno Sangiovese 237 '17 | 🍷 3 |
| ○ 102 '16 | 🍸🍸 2* |
| ○ Falerio Pecorino 003 '16 | 🍸🍸 3 |
| ○ Gallicano '16 | 🍸🍸 5 |
| ● Rosso Piceno Sangiovese Testamozza '16 | 🍸🍸 5 |

# Giacomo Centanni

C.DA ASO, 159
63062 MONTEFIORE DELL'ASO [AP]
TEL. +39 0734938530
www.vinicentanni.it

**CELLAR SALES**
**PRE-BOOKED VISITS**
**ACCOMMODATION**
**ANNUAL PRODUCTION** 140,000 bottles
**HECTARES UNDER VINE** 35.00
**VITICULTURE METHOD** Certified Organic

Giacomo Centanni is an enologist who oversees all the technical aspects of his family's modern winery, while in the vineyard he's helped primarily by his father, Mario. From the beginning their selection has highlighted a style that privileges intensity and depth, an interpretation that's easy to recognize for its vivid aromas and rich texture, not to mention vigor and savoriness. Their vintage wines are fermented in steel vats, while large wood barrels are used for their premium offerings. Their 2016 Pecorino Affinato in Legno alternates between woody and kumquat notes, followed by a juicy, savory and quite long palate. Their more approachable 2017 Pecorino releases hints of basil and rosemary, unusual for the variety but a distinctive Centanni feature, that meet a fresh citrus background on a robust, flavorful palate. Their 2016 Rosso di Forca starts out with vegetal notes but opens to beautiful tones of summer fruit.

| | |
|---|---|
| ○ Offida Pecorino '17 | ♟♟ 3 |
| ○ Offida Pecorino Affinato in Legno '16 | ♟♟ 4 |
| ● Rosso Piceno Rosso di Forca '16 | ♟♟ 2* |
| ○ Falerio Il Borgo '17 | ♟ 2 |
| ● Monte Floris '16 | ♟ 3 |
| ○ Offida Passerina '17 | ♟ 2 |
| ⊙ Profumo di Rosa '17 | ♟ 2 |
| ● Monte Floris '15 | ♟♟ 3 |
| ● Monte Floris '14 | ♟♟ 2* |
| ● Monte Floris '13 | ♟♟ 2* |
| ○ Offida Passerina '16 | ♟♟ 2* |
| ○ Offida Pecorino '16 | ♟♟ 3 |
| ○ Offida Pecorino '15 | ♟♟ 2* |
| ○ Offida Pecorino '14 | ♟♟ 2* |
| ○ Offida Pecorino Affinato in Legno '15 | ♟♟ 4 |

# Cherri d'Acquaviva

VIA ROMA, 40
63075 ACQUAVIVA PICENA [AP]
TEL. +39 0735764416
www.vinicherri.it

**CELLAR SALES**
**PRE-BOOKED VISITS**
**ANNUAL PRODUCTION** 160,000 bottles
**HECTARES UNDER VINE** 33.00

Paolo Cherri's winery, built from traditions acquired by several generations of his family, is based in the beautiful municipality of Acquaviva Picena. The presence of the Adriatic can be felt, thanks to constant summer breezes, but the vineyards bathe in the sun on the side facing the Sibillini Mountains, at an elevation of nearly 400 meters. Though the winery remains faithful to traditional varieties, its wines express a contemporary structural generosity combined with a clear olfactory profile. Their 2017 Pecorino Altissimo exemplifies this philosophy of production. Its notes of citrus and chamomile interlock on an intense palate of mouth-filling flavor and all-around enjoyability. Among reds, their 2013 Tumbulus stands out for its aromatic traces of dark fruit and dense texture of Montepulciano. Their 2016 Piceno Superiore has notable woody and fruity tones and a supported, meaty palate.

| | |
|---|---|
| ○ Offida Pecorino Altissimo '17 | ♟♟ 3* |
| ● Offida Rosso Tumbulus '13 | ♟♟ 4 |
| ● Rosso Piceno Sup. '16 | ♟♟ 2* |
| ⊙ Ancella '17 | ♟ 2 |
| ○ Falerio '17 | ♟ 2 |
| ○ Offida Passerina Radiosa '17 | ♟ 3 |
| ○ Falerio '16 | ♟♟ 2* |
| ○ Offida Passerina Radiosa '16 | ♟♟ 3 |
| ○ Offida Passerina Radiosa '15 | ♟♟ 3 |
| ○ Offida Pecorino Altissimo '16 | ♟♟ 3* |
| ○ Offida Pecorino Altissimo '15 | ♟♟ 3 |
| ● Rosso Piceno '16 | ♟♟ 2* |
| ● Rosso Piceno Sup. '15 | ♟♟ 2* |
| ● Rosso Piceno Sup. '13 | ♟♟ 2* |

## Tenuta Cocci Grifoni

LOC. SAN SAVINO
C.DA MESSIERI, 12
63038 RIPATRANSONE [AP]
TEL. +39 073590143
www.tenutacoccigrifoni.it

CELLAR SALES
PRE-BOOKED VISITS
ACCOMMODATION
ANNUAL PRODUCTION 400,000 bottles
HECTARES UNDER VINE 50.00
SUSTAINABLE WINERY

Cocci Grifoni's founder and patriarch of
Piceno viticulture, Guido, is passionate
when it comes to local wine-growing
traditions and he wants everyone to know
about it. Without diverting energy from
production, the family embraces Guido's
passion and allows vistors to have firsthand
experiences at the estate. 'Incomings' allow
their visitors to see things like the original
'mother' vineyard where the story of the
Pecorino grape was reborn, or the large
oak barrels where the first recognized
Piceno Superiore, Messieri, matures. Tre
Bicchieri once again for their 2014 Guido
Cocci Grifoni, a Pecorino that delivers an
elegant nose of loquat and green olive with
a subtle hint of benzene. It follows a clear
yet harmonious progression as it
accelerates across the long saline palate.
Their 2016 Colle Vecchio offers notes of
yellow fruits and a relaxed palate, while
their 2013 Rosso Piceno Vigna Messieri
proves spicy and infiltrating with a complex
almost salty finish.

| | |
|---|---|
| ○ Offida Pecorino Guido Cocci Grifoni '14 | ♛♛♛ 6 |
| ● Rosso Piceno Sup. V. Messieri '13 | ♛♛ 4 |
| ○ Offida Pecorino Colle Vecchio '16 | ♛♛ 3 |
| ● Rosso Piceno Tarà '17 | ♛♛ 2* |
| ○ Falerio Pecorino Tarà '17 | ♛ 2 |
| ● Rosso Piceno Sup. San Basso '14 | ♛ 2 |
| ○ San Basso Passerina '17 | ♛ 2 |
| ○ Offida Pecorino Guido Cocci Grifoni '13 | ♛♛♛ 4* |
| ○ Falerio Pecorino Le Torri '15 | ♛♛ 2* |
| ○ Offida Pecorino Colle Vecchio '15 | ♛♛ 3* |
| ● Offida Rosso Il Grifone '10 | ♛♛ 5 |
| ● Rosso Piceno '15 | ♛♛ 2* |
| ● Rosso Piceno Rubinio '16 | ♛♛ 2* |
| ● Rosso Piceno Sup. Le Torri '11 | ♛♛ 2* |
| ● Rosso Piceno Sup. V. Messieri '11 | ♛♛ 4 |
| ● Rosso Piceno Sup. V. Messieri '10 | ♛♛ 4 |

## Col di Corte

VIA SAN PIETRO, 19A
60036 MONTECAROTTO [AN]
TEL. +39 073189435
www.coldicorte.it

CELLAR SALES
PRE-BOOKED VISITS
ANNUAL PRODUCTION 40,000 bottles
HECTARES UNDER VINE 11.50
VITICULTURE METHOD Certified Organic
SUSTAINABLE WINERY

Col di Corte arose from the ashes of the
Laurentina winery, an endeavor that saw
its short life come to an end some 20
years ago. A trio of Roman friends
recognized the potential of this Castelli
Jesi site and saved the abandoned
vineyards. They then rebuilt what remained
of the winery, according to modern
principles of efficiency. A turning point
came with the decision to go organic.
Under the care of enologist Claudio
Calderoni, the wines -- and not just
Verdicchio -- blend complexity with varietal
harmony. Their 2017 Anno Uno Verdicchio
is exemplary. Its clear hints of almond,
endemic to the Jesi versions, unites in a
saline and dynamic palate maintained to
its delicious, slightly bitter finish. Their
2017 Sant'Ansovino's tertiary aromas of
dried fruit and nuts and its creamy palate
express, respectively, its fermentation in
small wood barrels and extended period on
the fine lees in steel.

| | |
|---|---|
| ○ Castelli di Jesi Verdicchio Cl. Sant'Ansovino Ris. '15 | ♛♛ 5 |
| ○ Verdicchio dei Castelli di Jesi Cl. Anno Uno '17 | ♛♛ 2* |
| ⊙ Lancestrale '17 | ♛ 4 |
| ○ Castelli di Jesi Verdicchio Cl. Sant'Ansovino Ris. '14 | ♛♛ 5 |
| ● Sant'Ansovino '12 | ♛♛ 5 |
| ○ Verdicchio dei Castelli di Jesi Cl. Anno Uno '16 | ♛♛ 2* |
| ○ Verdicchio dei Castelli di Jesi Cl. Anno Uno '14 | ♛♛ 2* |
| ○ Verdicchio dei Castelli di Jesi Cl. Sup. '15 | ♛♛ 3 |
| ○ Verdicchio dei Castelli di Jesi Cl. Sup. Vign. di Tobia '16 | ♛♛ 4 |

## ColleOnorato

a Colle Onorato 8
0035 Jesi [AN]
Tel. +39 3295628720
www.colleonorato.com

**ANNUAL PRODUCTION** 18,000 bottles
**HECTARES UNDER VINE** 2.00

Giulia Borioni and Luca Silvestri are two young producers making their debut in the world of wine. The name they have chosen for their winery pays tribute to the area that will soon host their cellar, between Jesi and Scorcelletti di Maiolati Spontini. Their vineyards are located in Apiro on the other side of the Esino River. An area that is almost mountainlike in character, the vineyards lie at about 500 meters above sea level near the picturesque Abazia di Sant'Urbano. They have created two Verdicchio wines made in steel with indispensable help from oenologist Roberto Cantori. Their 2017 Prologo surprises in part because the winery itself doesn't rank it among their best wines! Its refined nose of aromatic herbs, floral accents and hints of white fruit precedes a fresh, juicy, cadenced palate that is very well-balanced. Their 2017 Giostra delivers more structure and alcoholic energy but not as much agility in a wide profile that exhibits notes of ripe apple.

| | |
|---|---|
| ○ Verdicchio dei Castelli di Jesi Cl. Sup. Prologo '17 | 🍷🍷 3* |
| ○ Verdicchio dei Castelli di Jesi Cl. Sup. La Giostra '17 | 🍷🍷 4 |

## Collestefano

loc. Colle Stefano, 3
62022 Castelraimondo [MC]
Tel. +39 0737640439
www.collestefano.com

**CELLAR SALES**
**PRE-BOOKED VISITS**
**ACCOMMODATION**
**ANNUAL PRODUCTION** 110,000 bottles
**HECTARES UNDER VINE** 17.50
**VITICULTURE METHOD** Certified Organic

Fabio Marchionni knows better than most how wineries can be at the mercy of meteorological events despite all effort to mitigate negative effects. He operates in a territory with a unique microclimate. Conditions when optimal allow him to create wines with great acidity and crystalline aromatic tones. Poor conditions create problems and in 2017 this was the case. A devastating spring freeze, followed by a scorching summer caused him to lose about 70% of his vintage. These events are made clear in both the character and the availability of his renowned Verdicchio di Castelraimondo. The hot and dry year marked their 2017 Verdicchio di Matelica Collestefano with more structure and alcoholic content than usual. The resulting palate is wider and less incisive, with a nose capable of retaining its clean citrus and Hawthorn aromas, reenforced by its specific stony minerality. It's a wine that will already gratify.

| | |
|---|---|
| ○ Verdicchio di Matelica Collestefano '17 | 🍷🍷 2* |
| ○ Verdicchio di Matelica Collestefano '15 | YYY 2* |
| ○ Verdicchio di Matelica Collestefano '14 | YYY 2* |
| ○ Verdicchio di Matelica Collestefano '13 | YYY 2* |
| ○ Verdicchio di Matelica Collestefano '12 | YYY 2* |
| ○ Verdicchio di Matelica Collestefano '10 | YYY 2* |
| ○ Verdicchio di Matelica Collestefano '07 | YYY 2* |
| ○ Verdicchio di Matelica Collestefano '06 | YYY 2* |
| ⊙ Rosa di Elena '13 | YY 2* |
| ⊙ Rosa di Elena '13 | YY 2* |
| ○ Verdicchio di Matelica Collestefano '16 | YY 2* |
| ○ Verdicchio di Matelica Collestefano '11 | YY 2* |
| ○ Verdicchio di Matelica Extra Brut M. Cl. '14 | YY 4 |
| ○ Verdicchio di Matelica Extra Brut M. Cl. '13 | YY 3* |

## Colognola - Tenuta Musone

Loc. Colognola, 22a bis
62011 Cingoli [MC]
Tel. +39 0733616438
www.tenutamusone.it

CELLAR SALES
PRE-BOOKED VISITS
ANNUAL PRODUCTION 150,000 bottles
HECTARES UNDER VINE 25.00

Walter Darini's vineyards are located 380 meters above sea level in a terroir that benefits from the unique microclimate of Monte San Vicino. The area's unmistakable outline is included in the logo of the winery. Gabriele Vallani, both enologist and technical director, creates wine that brings out the best of traditional Verdicchio and Montepulciano. The versatility of the former enables great variety throughout their selection, while the latter, which plays a smaller part, gives rise to their Via Rosa and Cantamaggio red. Two wines stood out particularly during our tastings. Their 2015 Labieno Riserva has a wide, flavorful profile with echos of yellow summer fruit and saffron in its tenacious finish. The citrus and almond on the nose of their 2016 Ghiffa reappear on an energetic palate that follows a clear progression. Their 2017 Via Condotto has fruity energy to sell, while in a head to head between their two Metodo Classico sparkling wines, their 2016 Musa wins for its refined nose of flowers and fine herbs and its intensely savory palate.

| | |
|---|---|
| ○ Castelli di Jesi Verdicchio Cl. Labieno Ris. '15 | 🏆🏆 4 |
| ○ Verdicchio dei Castelli di Jesi Cl. Sup. Ghiffa '16 | 🏆🏆 3* |
| ○ Verdicchio dei Castelli di Jesi Brut Musa M. Cl. '16 | 🏆🏆 3 |
| ○ Verdicchio dei Castelli di Jesi Cl. Sup. Via Condotto '17 | 🏆🏆 2* |
| ⊙ Via Rosa '17 | 🏆🏆 2* |
| ● Cantamaggio '16 | 🏆 2 |
| ○ Verdicchio dei Castelli di Jesi Extra Brut Darini M. Cl. '13 | 🏆 5 |
| ○ Verdicchio dei Castelli di Jesi Cl. Sup. Ghiffa '15 | 🏆🏆 3 |
| ○ Verdicchio dei Castelli di Jesi Cl. Sup. Via Condotto '15 | 🏆🏆 2* |
| ○ Verdicchio dei Castelli di Jesi Cl. Via Condotto '16 | 🏆🏆 2* |

## Colonnara

via Mandriole, 6
60034 Cupramontana [AN]
Tel. +39 0731780273
www.colonnara.it

CELLAR SALES
PRE-BOOKED VISITS
ANNUAL PRODUCTION 1,000,000 bottles
HECTARES UNDER VINE 120.00

Colonnara's production revolves largely around Verdicchio. Using Metodo Classico and Charmat Method, this Cupramontana cooperative has assumed a leading role among the area's sparkling wine producers. Its success comes from holding close to local tradition and its vineyards' placement at considerable elevations. Use of modern equipment and adequate cellar space also contribute. None of this should overshadow the success with still whites that Colonnara enjoys from their parcels, which are advantageously distributed across the territory. Their Cuprese isn't listed for the first time in many years, because of their decision to let it reach its full potential through longer aging. Instead, this year, their 2012 Ubaldo Rosi, a brilliant Metodo Classico sparkling wine, delivers balsamic, mineral and fine herbs on a palate of refined balance. Their Luigi Ghislieri offers spicier, yeasty accents in an intensely savory palate.

| | |
|---|---|
| ○ Verdicchio dei Castelli di Jesi M. Cl. Brut M. Cl. Luigi Ghislieri | 🏆🏆 4 |
| ○ Verdicchio dei Castelli di Jesi M. Cl. Brut M. Cl. Ubaldo Rosi Ris. '12 | 🏆🏆 5 |
| ○ Verdicchio dei Castelli di Jesi Cl. Lyricus '17 | 🏆🏆 2* |
| ○ Castelli di Jesi Verdicchio Cl. Túfico Ris. '15 | 🏆 3 |
| ○ Cuvée Tradition Brut '17 | 🏆 3 |
| ○ Verdicchio dei Castelli di Jesi Cl. Sup. Cuapro '16 | 🏆 3 |
| ○ Verdicchio dei Castelli di Jesi M. Cl. Brut Ubaldo Rosi Ris. '06 | 🏆🏆🏆 5 |
| ○ Verdicchio dei Castelli di Jesi Brut M. Cl. Ubaldo Rosi Ris. '10 | 🏆🏆 5 |
| ○ Verdicchio dei Castelli di Jesi Cl. Sup. Cuapro '15 | 🏆🏆 3 |

# Il Conte Villa Prandone

C.DA COLLE NAVICCHIO, 28
63033 MONTEPRANDONE [AP]
TEL. +39 073562593
www.ilcontevini.it

**CELLAR SALES**
**PRE-BOOKED VISITS**
**ANNUAL PRODUCTION** 200,000 bottles
**HECTARES UNDER VINE** 50.00

The De Angelis brothers' winery is a family business, managing the production of a large quantity of bottles and working a substantial number of vineyards, located mostly in the Tronto valley. All of the processes are overseen by family members, from tending to traditional Piceno varieties in the vineyards, to the work in the cellars. The result is wine with a modern style that retains expressive fullness. Fruity whites and vintage reds age in steel and cement, while their more ambitious wines age in small oak barrels. This year their 2015 LuKont really stands out. It delivers notes of plum and maraschino thatfollow through on a juicy palate whose dense tannins are tempered by generous alcohol. Their 2016 Marinus, a Piceno Superiore, is also admirable for its coherent union of a spicy nose and a seductively consistent palate. Easy drinking and soft tannins also make their Rosso Piceno Conte Rosso quite tasty.

| | |
|---|---|
| ● LuKont '15 | ▼▼ 6 |
| ● Piceno Sup. Marinus '16 | ▼▼ 3 |
| ○ Vizius '17 | ▼▼ 2* |
| ○ Cavaceppo '17 | ▼ 2 |
| ○ Emmanuel Maria Passerina Brut | ▼ 3 |
| ○ Falerio Pecorino Aurato '17 | ▼ 2 |
| ○ Offida Passerina Cavaceppo '17 | ▼ 3 |
| ● Rosso Piceno Conte Rosso '17 | ▼ 2 |
| ● Zipolo '15 | ▼ 5 |
| ● Donello '16 | ♀♀ 3 |
| ● Donello '15 | ♀♀ 2* |
| ○ L'Estro del Mastro Passerina Passito '15 | ♀♀ 5 |
| ○ Offida Passerina Cavaceppo '16 | ♀♀ 3 |
| ● Rosso Piceno Sup. Marinus '15 | ♀♀ 3 |
| ○ Trebbià '16 | ♀♀ 2* |

# Conti degli Azzoni

VIA DON MINZONI, 26
62010 MONTEFANO [MC]
TEL. +39 0733850219
www.degliazzoni.it

**CELLAR SALES**
**PRE-BOOKED VISITS**
**ACCOMMODATION AND RESTAURANT SERVICE**
**ANNUAL PRODUCTION** 100,000 bottles
**HECTARES UNDER VINE** 130.00

Over the last two years the Degli Azzoni family has undertaken a mammoth project with respect to its vineyards. Its scope ranges from soil studies, to the identification of microclimates, to clonal selection. This is the first step in the family's bid to restore order to its vast acreage of grapevines and impose a change in quality, not only to its brand, but to the area as a whole. There is still much work to do, including a switch to organic production. But with both technical skill in abundance, and a well-equipped cellar, the project promises excellent results. Their 2017 Ribona hits the top of their chart. Its floral nature with hints of aromatic herbs and yellow damson plum leads into a flowing, fragrant and well-balanced palate. Their 2017 Grechetto moves similarly. Their 2015 Rosso Piceno delivers nice fruity aromas from its material, consistent with its tannic structure, to its finish with ripe sour cherry tones. Their 2016 Sultan has a unusual aroma of passionfruit that repeats on its succulent palate.

| | |
|---|---|
| ○ Colli Maceratesi Ribona '17 | ▼▼ 2* |
| ○ Colli Maceratesi Passito Sultano '16 | ▼▼ 4 |
| ○ Grechetto '17 | ▼▼ 2* |
| ● Rosso Piceno '15 | ▼▼ 2* |
| ○ Beldiletto Brut | ▼ 3 |
| ● Colli Maceratesi Rosso Evasione '16 | ▼ 2 |
| ● Passatempo '14 | ♀♀ 5 |
| ● Passatempo '13 | ♀♀ 5 |
| ● Rosso Piceno '14 | ♀♀ 2* |
| ● Rosso Piceno '13 | ♀♀ 2* |

# Fattoria Coroncino

C.DA CORONCINO, 7
60039 STAFFOLO [AN]
TEL. +39 0731779494
www.coroncino.it

CELLAR SALES
PRE-BOOKED VISITS
ANNUAL PRODUCTION 45,000 bottles
HECTARES UNDER VINE 9.50

Lucio Canestrari is well-known around Castelli di Jesi for bottles that are rich in character of an unmistakable style. He refers to himself as a troubadour of wines. As a troubadour, his intervention is limited to bringing grapes grown without synthetic chemistry to perfect maturation, then simply accompanying them along in their fermentation. The result is well-structured Verdicchio -- enveloping and dense with flavor. The most ambitious selections are aged in small oak barrels. Their 2015 Gaiospino, as usual, promises flavorful, enveloping structure. Its enduring finish brings back the same notes of hazelnut and grains given off in its intense nose. Their less forceful 2016 Bacchus has ethereal notes that help to freshen a lush palate with an authentic, rustic character. A wine well-suited to gastronomic purposes.

| | |
|---|---|
| ○ Verdicchio dei Castelli di Jesi Cl. Sup. Gaiospino '15 | 🍷🍷 4 |
| ○ Verdicchio dei Castelli di Jesi Cl. Sup. Il Bacco '16 | 🍷🍷 2* |
| ● Ganzerello '15 | 🍷 4 |
| ○ Verdicchio dei Castelli di Jesi Cl. Sup. Gaiospino '03 | 🍷🍷🍷 4 |
| ○ Verdicchio dei Castelli di Jesi Cl. Sup. Gaiospino '14 | 🍷🍷 4 |
| ○ Verdicchio dei Castelli di Jesi Cl. Sup. Il Coroncino '15 | 🍷🍷 2* |
| ○ Verdicchio dei Castelli di Jesi Cl. Sup. Stracacio '14 | 🍷🍷 5 |
| ○ Verdicchio dei Castelli di Jesi Cl. Sup. Stragaio '13 | 🍷🍷 5 |
| ○ Verdicchio dei Castelli di Jesi Cl. Sup. Vergaro '15 | 🍷🍷 4 |

# Crespaia

LOC. PRELATO, 8
61032 FANO [PU]
TEL. +39 0721862383
www.crespaia.it

CELLAR SALES
PRE-BOOKED VISITS
ANNUAL PRODUCTION 25,000 bottles
HECTARES UNDER VINE 10.00
VITICULTURE METHOD Certified Organic

Rossano Sgammini wasn't born a winemaker, in fact, he makes a living doing something very different. But in 2011, he couldn't pass up a prime piece of land near Fano when it became available. His goal was to make highly drinkable wines with aromatic purity, using traditional varieties that reflect characteristics of the land. He also brought innovation to the area, in the form of screw caps and releasing a Bianchello two years after harvest after a long time on lees. Production is managed by Shayle Lambie-Shaw with the assistance of expert Aroldo Bellelli. Their 2016 Chiaraluce is among the best Bianchello we have tasted in recent years. It fuses tension with backbone and strong accents of fruit with subtle veins of fine herbs and citrus in a rare elegance for the variety. Their 2017 Bianchello offers a bit of gentle ripe yellow fruit before turning to fresher minty tones. Caressing the palate as it enters, it closes with a tasty, fragrant finish. Their 2016 Nerognolo is fleshy with a dry finish.

| | |
|---|---|
| ○ Bianchello del Metauro Sup. Chiaraluce '16 | 🍷🍷 3* |
| ○ Bianchello del Metauro '17 | 🍷🍷 2* |
| ● Colli Pesaresi Sangiovese Nerognolo '16 | 🍷🍷 3 |
| ○ Brut '17 | 🍷 3 |

# Tenuta De Angelis

Via San Francesco, 10
63030 Castel di Lama [AP]
Tel. +39 073687429
www.tenutadeangelis.it

CELLAR SALES
PRE-BOOKED VISITS
ANNUAL PRODUCTION 500,000 bottles
HECTARES UNDER VINE 50.00

The view behind Santa Maria della Rocca -- a church of great symbolic significance for the people of Offida -- represents a breathtaking panorama. A good part of the land belongs to the De Angelis/Fausti family. Carefully managed vineyards, decades of experience, and a well-equipped cellar all see to it that De Angelis remain among the area's most respected wineries. Usually linked to powerful reds based on Montepulciano and Sangiovese, the quality of their whites which are also based on native varieties, has shown significant improvement recently. Tre Bicchieri for the most traditional wine of the appellation, their 2015 Piceno Superiore Oro, which combines traces of fruit and interesting accents of spices with a complex, juicy palate of extraordinary drinkability. Their 2015 Anghelos, a full-bodied Montepulciano with tight-knit tannins, also proves delicious. Among whites, their balanced, pleasantly citrusy 2017 Offida Pecorino stood out.

| | |
|---|---|
| ● Rosso Piceno Sup. Oro '15 | ♟♟♟ 3* |
| ● Offida Rosso Anghelos '15 | ♟♟ 4 |
| ● Rosso Piceno Sup. '16 | ♟♟ 2* |
| ○ Offida Passerina '17 | ♟♟ 2* |
| ○ Offida Pecorino '17 | ♟♟ 2* |
| ● Rosso Piceno '17 | ♟♟ 2* |
| ○ Falerio '17 | ♟ 1* |
| ○ Offida Pecorino Quiete '17 | ♟ 3 |
| ● Anghelos '01 | ♟♟♟ 4 |
| ○ Offida Pecorino '16 | ♟♟ 2* |
| ● Rosso Piceno '15 | ♟♟ 1* |
| ● Rosso Piceno Sup. '15 | ♟♟ 2* |
| ● Rosso Piceno Sup. '14 | ♟♟ 2* |
| ● Rosso Piceno Sup. '13 | ♟♟ 2* |
| ● Rosso Piceno Sup. Oro '13 | ♟♟ 3 |
| ○ Offida Passerina '15 | ♟ 2 |

# Fattoria Dezi

c.da Fontemaggio, 14
63839 Servigliano [FM]
Tel. +39 0734710090
fattoriadezi@hotmail.com

CELLAR SALES
PRE-BOOKED VISITS
ACCOMMODATION
ANNUAL PRODUCTION 45,000 bottles
HECTARES UNDER VINE 15.00

In the late 1990s Stefano and Davide Dezi set new standards for reds based on Montepulciano and Sangiovese, helping to bring their district in Fermano out of the shadows. Long-time advocates of an agronomy characterized by low yields and attention to phenolic ripening, they now offer wines of remarkable texture. Almost surly in youth, the wines mature slowly, both over time and in the glass. Their whites rest in concrete, while Solo and Regina del Bosco spend two years in small oak barrels. Their 2015 Montepulciano Regina del Bosco reveals its big character, opening with maraschino, burnt wood, black olive and hints of blood, followed by a dense, juicy palate. Their 2015 Sangiovese Solo offers a lackluster nose redeemed by a dense and generous palate. Their 2106 Dezio (Montepulciano with well-defined Sangiovese) features plum, sour cherry and an unhesitating palate. Their 2015 Verdicchio Solagne delivers a nose of summer fruit tied to a smooth, pulpy palate.

| | |
|---|---|
| ● Dezio '16 | ♟♟ 3 |
| ● Regina del Bosco '15 | ♟♟ 6 |
| ○ Solagne '16 | ♟♟ 3 |
| ○ Falerio Pecorino Servigliano P. '16 | ♟ 3 |
| ● Solo '15 | ♟ 6 |
| ● Regina del Bosco '06 | ♟♟♟ 6 |
| ● Regina del Bosco '05 | ♟♟♟ 6 |
| ● Regina del Bosco '03 | ♟♟♟ 6 |
| ● Solo Sangiovese '05 | ♟♟♟ 6 |
| ● Solo Sangiovese '01 | ♟♟♟ 5 |
| ● Solo Sangiovese '00 | ♟♟♟ 6 |
| ● Dezio '14 | ♟♟ 3 |
| ○ Falerio Pecorino Servigliano P. '15 | ♟♟ 3 |
| ● Solo '14 | ♟♟ 6 |

## Emanuele Dianetti

C.DA VALLEROSA, 25
63063 CARASSAI [AP]
TEL. +39 3383928439
www.dianettivini.it

**CELLAR SALES**
**PRE-BOOKED VISITS**
**ANNUAL PRODUCTION** 18,000 bottles
**HECTARES UNDER VINE** 2.00

Emanuele Dianetti doesn't have a lot of time to commit to being a winemaker, but his passion, energy and ties to his agricultural origins are a driving force. He's also helped by the coolness of Menocchia, a small valley that is heavily planted with grapevines and enjoys an extraordinary microclimate. From his small cellar come modern whites, vivid with fruit and unambiguously clean under their aromatic profile. Reds are well-calibrated in their phenolic extraction and use of small oak barrels. Their 2015 Offida Rosso Vignagiulia just misses our highest honors. It doesn't lack seriousness or elegant modulation, but the exuberant tannins and woody sensations need to more fully integrate in the bottle. Their seductive Michelangelo (Bordò) has a spicy nose that endure on its plush palate. Their exhilarating 2017 Pecorino Vignagiulia offers a citrus nose and an almost salty palate.

## ★Fazi Battaglia

VIA ROMA, 117
60031 CASTELPLANIO [AN]
TEL. +39 073181591
www.fazibattaglia.it

**CELLAR SALES**
**PRE-BOOKED VISITS**
**ANNUAL PRODUCTION** 1,000,000 bottles
**HECTARES UNDER VINE** 130.00

As one of the wineries central to the history of Marche viticulture, Fazi Battaglia doesn't need much of an introduction. But there have been changes at the winery since it was acquired by the Bertani Domains group, which wagered on a Verdicchio's potential. A technical staff coordinated by Lorenzo Lando has found success in creating selections that express the many nuances of the estate's extensive parklike vineyards and appertaining unique parcels. One of the best ever, their 2016 San Sisto entices with its elegant nose that carries gusts of toasted almonds, medicinal herbs and anise, traits that continue on a pervasive, luminous and enduring palate. Tre imperious Bicchieri. Similarly, their 2016 Massaccio is extremely compelling with its serious, flavorful palate and notes of summer fruit. Their 2016 Arkezia has notes of botrytis and yellow peach with an airy, velvety palate.

| | |
|---|---|
| ● Michelangelo Bordò '15 | ♟♟ 8 |
| ● Offida Rosso Vignagiulia '15 | ♟♟ 5 |
| ○ Offida Pecorino Vignagiulia '17 | ♟♟ 3 |
| ● Piceno '16 | ♟ 3 |
| ● Offida Rosso Vignagiulia '14 | ♟♟♟ 5 |
| ● Offida Rosso Vignagiulia '13 | ♟♟♟ 5 |
| ● Michelangelo Bordò '14 | ♟♟ 8 |
| ○ Offida Pecorino Vignagiulia '16 | ♟♟ 3* |
| ○ Offida Pecorino Vignagiulia '15 | ♟♟ 3* |
| ○ Offida Pecorino Vignagiulia '14 | ♟♟ 3* |
| ○ Offida Pecorino Vignagiulia '13 | ♟♟ 3 |
| ● Offida Rosso Vignagiulia '12 | ♟♟ 4 |
| ● Offida Rosso Vignagiulia '11 | ♟♟ 4 |

| | |
|---|---|
| ○ Castelli di Jesi Verdicchio Cl. San Sisto Ris. '16 | ♟♟♟ 5 |
| ○ Arkezia Muffo di San Sisto '16 | ♟♟ 5 |
| ○ Verdicchio dei Castelli di Jesi Cl. Sup. Massaccio '16 | ♟♟ 3* |
| ○ Verdicchio dei Castelli di Jesi Cl. '17 | ♟♟ 2* |
| ○ Castelli di Jesi Verdicchio Cl. San Sisto Ris. '15 | ♟♟♟ 5 |
| ○ Castelli di Jesi Verdicchio Cl. San Sisto Ris. '14 | ♟♟♟ 4* |
| ○ Castelli di Jesi Verdicchio Cl. San Sisto Ris. '10 | ♟♟♟ 4* |
| ○ Verdicchio dei Castelli di Jesi Cl. San Sisto Ris. '09 | ♟♟♟ 4* |
| ○ Verdicchio dei Castelli di Jesi Cl. San Sisto Ris. '07 | ♟♟♟ 4 |

# Andrea Felici

C.DA SANT'ISIDORO, 28
62021 APIRO [MC]
TEL. +39 0733611431
www.andreafelici.it

**CELLAR SALES**
**PRE-BOOKED VISITS**
**ANNUAL PRODUCTION** 53,000 bottles
**HECTARES UNDER VINE** 10.00

Fifteen years of drive and determination have made Leopardo Felici one of the best-known names in the Castelli di Jesi area. Felici's Cantico della Figura Cru was first released only in 2003. The company's top-end wine exemplifies Verdicchio's energy and the strength derived from the estate's location at the foothills of Apiro. Vinification begins in steel vats, then it's slowly aged in cement for a year, followed by bottles for two. A rarified elegance of aromas, a sumptuous minerality and an indomitable driving energy on the palate are just some of the characteristics that make their 2015 Verdicchio Il Cantico della Figura Riverva one of Italy's best whites. And given the impressive number of Tre Bicchieri it has received, also one of the most consistent. Executive expertise and the Apiro vineyards themselves help make their juicy, saline and flowing 2017 Verdicchio Andrea Felici a real tribute to Jesi's talented grape.

| | |
|---|---|
| ○ Castelli di Jesi Verdicchio Cl. V. Il Cantico della Figura Ris. '15 | ▼▼▼ 6 |
| ○ Verdicchio dei Castelli di Jesi Cl. Sup. Andrea Felici '17 | ▼▼ 3* |
| ○ Castelli di Jesi Verdicchio Cl. Il Cantico della Figura Ris. '12 | ♀♀♀ 4* |
| ○ Castelli di Jesi Verdicchio Cl. Il Cantico della Figura Ris. '11 | ♀♀♀ 4* |
| ○ Castelli di Jesi Verdicchio Cl. Il Cantico della Figura Ris. '10 | ♀♀♀ 4* |
| ○ Castelli di Jesi Verdicchio Cl. V. Il Cantico della Figura Ris. '13 | ♀♀♀ 6 |
| ○ Verdicchio dei Castelli di Jesi Cl. Il Cantico della Figura Ris. '09 | ♀♀♀ 4* |

# Filodivino

VIA SERRA, 46
60030 SAN MARCELLO [AN]
TEL. +39 0731026139
www.filodivino.it

**CELLAR SALES**
**PRE-BOOKED VISITS**
**ACCOMMODATION AND RESTAURANT SERVICE**
**ANNUAL PRODUCTION** 52,000 bottles
**HECTARES UNDER VINE** 19.50

In 2013, Alberto Gandolfi and Gian Mario Bongini renovated an old farm manor, making it into what is now, a luxurious country resort. Following that, they began producing a small amount of wine based on Verdicchio and Lacrima Nera. This year is an important one for them because all the their selection will be certified organic, and the harvest will be brought to a the dramatic new cellar overlooking the vineyards. In collaboration with enologist Matteo Chiucconi, and using steel vats they create wines that clearly express the characteristics of the varieties and are admirable for the density of their flavor. Their 2015 Verdicchio Dino Riserva gets its power from very ripe grapes and its density from aging on the fine lees, resulting in a full, pervasive, very savory flavor. The trade off for the almost rugged energy of their 2017 Matto, more incisive than refined, comes in the myriad salty streams that melt on the palate during its long finish. Their 2016 Lacrima di Morro d'Alba Superiore Diana delivers ample spicy notes, hints of geranium and an intense, astringent palate.

| | |
|---|---|
| ○ Castelli di Jesi Verdicchio Cl. Dino Ris. '15 | ▼▼ 4 |
| ○ Verdicchio dei Castelli di Jesi Cl. Sup. Matto '17 | ▼▼ 3 |
| ● Lacrima di Morro d'Alba Sup. Diana '16 | ▼ 3 |
| ○ Castelli di Jesi Verdicchio Cl. Dino Ris. '14 | ♀♀ 4 |
| ● Lacrima di Morro d'Alba Diana '15 | ♀♀ 3 |
| ● Lacrima di Morro d'Alba Sup. Soara '15 | ♀♀ 3 |
| ○ Verdicchio dei Castelli di Jesi Cl. Sup. Filotto '15 | ♀♀ 3* |
| ○ Verdicchio dei Castelli di Jesi Cl. Sup. Matto '16 | ♀♀ 3 |
| ○ Verdicchio dei Castelli di Jesi Filotto '14 | ♀♀ 3 |

# Fiorano

C.DA FIORANO, 19
63067 COSSIGNANO [AP]
TEL. +39 073598446
www.agrifiorano.it

**CELLAR SALES**
**PRE-BOOKED VISITS**
**ACCOMMODATION**
**ANNUAL PRODUCTION** 40,000 bottles
**HECTARES UNDER VINE** 8.00
**VITICULTURE METHOD** Certified Organic
**SUSTAINABLE WINERY**

The vineyards sit on bluffs surrounded by scrub brush stained with polychromic grains and silver-green olive trees. Embedded in this scenographic context -- located in Cossignano, Piceno -- you'll find the winery of Paolo Beretta, led by his wife Paola. Two approaches -- steel vats for early-drinking wines, and small barrels for their more ambitious selections -- promise pleasant surprises for the future. The estate's style focuses on expressing the area's traditional varietals such as Pecorino, Montepulciano and Sangiovese. Their very elegant 2017 Pecorino Giulia Erminia reveals a controlled use of wood that brings hints of smoke to a vast carpet of citrus. The warmth of 2017 reveals itself in their Donna Orgilla in the hints of fleshy, yellow fruit, but the palate is reactive, continuous, and long. The fruity, alcoholic energy of Montepulciano and dense tannins drive their 2015 Rosso Piceno Terre di Giobbe.

| | |
|---|---|
| ○ Offida Pecorino Giulia Erminia '16 | ♟♟ 5 |
| ○ Offida Pecorino Donna Orgilla '17 | ♟♟ 3 |
| ○ Rosato '17 | ♟♟ 2* |
| ● Rosso Piceno Sup. Terre di Giobbe '15 | ♟♟ 3 |
| ● Sangiovese '17 | ♟ 2 |
| ○ Offida Pecorino Donna Orgilla '14 | ♟♟♟ 3* |
| ○ Giulia Erminia '14 | ♟♟ 2* |
| ○ Offida Pecorino Donna Orgilla '16 | ♟♟ 3* |
| ○ Offida Pecorino Donna Orgilla '15 | ♟♟ 3 |
| ○ Offida Pecorino Donna Orgilla '13 | ♟♟ 3* |
| ● Rosso Piceno Sup. Terre di Giobbe '14 | ♟♟ 3 |
| ● Rosso Piceno Sup. Terre di Giobbe '13 | ♟♟ 3 |
| ● Rosso Piceno Sup. Terre di Giobbe '12 | ♟♟ 3 |
| ● Rosso Piceno Sup. Terre di Giobbe '11 | ♟♟ 3 |

# Fiorini

FRAZ. BARCHI
VIA GIARDINO CAMPIOLI, 5
61038 TERRE ROVERESCHE
TEL. +39 072197151
www.fioriniwines.it

**CELLAR SALES**
**PRE-BOOKED VISITS**
**ACCOMMODATION**
**ANNUAL PRODUCTION** 200,000 bottles
**HECTARES UNDER VINE** 45.00
**VITICULTURE METHOD** Certified Organic

Carla Fiorini carries with her surname a legacy of modernization in Pesaro's viticulture. Her father Valentino was a pioneer in producing wines that were simultaneously modern and expressive of the territory. Their estate is comprised of a sizable vineyard, their cellar, and the original manor, which seves as the heart of a winery that's grown over the years (thanks in part to consulting winemaker Federico Giotto). His presence is felt in the light and respectful style of their selection. The winery specializes in Bianchello, with Sangiovese used as the main variety for rosé and red. Their 2017 Sant'Ilario and Tenuta Campioli are both classic Bianchello but with divergent characters, the former fruity and easy drinking, the latter more consistent, elegant and savory. Their 2016 Andy, on the other hand, proves more modern with well-ripened grapes and wood aging resulting in hints of beeswax and peach on a soft, persistent palate. Their 2015 Bartis, well-characterized by spicy notes and sober tannins, stands out among the reds.

| | |
|---|---|
| ○ Bianchello del Metauro Sant'Ilario '17 | ♟♟ 2* |
| ○ Bianchello del Metauro Sup. Andy '16 | ♟♟ 3 |
| ○ Bianchello del Metauro Sup. Tenuta Campioli '17 | ♟♟ 2* |
| ⊙ Colli Pesaresi Rosato Le Rose di Campioli '17 | ♟♟ 2* |
| ● Colli Pesaresi Rosso Bartis '15 | ♟♟ 3 |
| ● Colli Pesaresi Sangiovese Sirio '17 | ♟ 2 |
| ○ Bianchello del Metauro Sup. Andy '14 | ♟♟ 3 |
| ○ Bianchello del Metauro Sup. Tenuta Campioli '16 | ♟♟ 2* |
| ○ Bianchello del Metauro Sup. Tenuta Campioli '15 | ♟♟ 2* |
| ● Colli Pesaresi Rosso Bartis '13 | ♟♟ 3 |
| ● Colli Pesaresi Sangiovese Sirio '14 | ♟♟ 2* |
| ○ La Galoppa '16 | ♟♟ 2* |

# Cantine Fontezoppa

C.DA SAN DOMENICO, 38
62012 CIVITANOVA MARCHE [MC]
TEL. +39 0733790504
www.cantinefontezoppa.it

CELLAR SALES
PRE-BOOKED VISITS
ACCOMMODATION AND RESTAURANT SERVICE
ANNUAL PRODUCTION 290,000 bottles
HECTARES UNDER VINE 38.00

Under Mosè Ambrosi's guidance,
Fontezoppa has been paying more attention
to traditional varieties, in particular Bianco
Ribona (aka, Maceratino) and Vernaccia
Nera, both of which are cultivated in the
Serrapetrona vineyards. For each variety, in
addition to their well-structured still wines,
the winery has developed a Metodo
Classico sparkling wine deserving of
attention. Whites mixing Bruni 54 and
Pecorino, characterized by agile structures
and immediate enjoyability, are becoming
noteworthy. Their 2016 Ribona sheds new
light on the variety in terms of complexity
and temperament. Its salty nose and
enthralling palate make it one Macerata's
best whites. Vernaccia adds characteristic
pepperiness to their 2015 Carpignano,
making it a pleasant and original picnic
wine. Their more ambitious 2015 Morò,
also a Serrapetrona, has a nose layered
with spices and robust tannins.

# ★★Gioacchino Garofoli

VIA CARLO MARX, 123
60022 CASTELFIDARDO [AN]
TEL. +39 0717820162
www.garofolivini.it

CELLAR SALES
PRE-BOOKED VISITS
ANNUAL PRODUCTION 2,000,000 bottles
HECTARES UNDER VINE 42.00

The Garofoli family winery is one of
Marche's primary producers, both in terms
of history and volume. Its extensive
catalogue contains offerings that are
fundamental to understanding the evolution
of local wines. Among these are Podium,
one of the earliest wines leading to the
establishment of the Castelli di Jesi
appellation; Grosso Agontano, a prototype
of the modern updated Montepulciano del
Conero; and, Serra Fiorese, one of the first
Verdicchio to be aged in small French oak
barrels. The nose of their 2016 Podium
captivates, offering orange blossom and
medicinal herbs with balsamic and mineral
notes. A paragon of finesse, measure and
complexity, it easily earns its umpteenth
Tre Bicchieri. The 2014 Serra Fiorese
delivers expected hints of smoke and
almond on a relaxed palate. But one should
not overlook their reds. Particularly worthy
of note are their 2016 Piceno Collo Ambro,
2015 Conero Piancarda and 2015 Grosso
Agontano Riserva.

| | |
|---|---|
| ○ Colli Maceratesi Ribona '16 | ♟♟ 3* |
| ○ Colli Maceratesi Ribona Dosaggio Zero M. Cl. '14 | ♟♟ 4 |
| ⊙ Frapiccì '17 | ♟♟ 2* |
| ● Marche Rosso '15 | ♟♟ 3 |
| ● Serrapetrona Carpignano '15 | ♟♟ 2* |
| ● Serrapetrona Morò '15 | ♟♟ 5 |
| ○ Falerio Pecorino Citanò '17 | ♟ 2 |
| ○ Incrocio Bruni 54 '17 | ♟ 2 |
| ● Serrapetrona Falcotto '15 | ♟ 4 |
| ● Carapetto '13 | ♙♙ 5 |
| ● Carapetto '12 | ♙♙ 5 |
| ○ Colli Maceratesi Ribona '15 | ♙♙ 3 |
| ○ Colli Maceratesi Ribona Dosaggio Zero M. Cl. '13 | ♙♙ 4 |
| ⊙ Extra Brut Rosé M. Cl. '13 | ♙♙ 5 |
| ● Serrapetrona Morò '13 | ♙♙ 5 |

| | |
|---|---|
| ○ Verdicchio dei Castelli di Jesi Cl. Sup. Podium '16 | ♟♟♟ 4* |
| ○ Castelli di Jesi Verdicchio Cl. Serra Fiorese Ris. '14 | ♟♟ 4 |
| ● Conero Grosso Agontano Ris. '15 | ♟♟ 5 |
| ○ Dorato '15 | ♟♟ 3 |
| ⊙ Kòmaros '17 | ♟♟ 2* |
| ● Rosso Conero Piancarda '15 | ♟♟ 3 |
| ● Rosso Piceno Colle Ambro '16 | ♟♟ 2* |
| ○ Verdicchio dei Castelli di Jesi Cl. Sup. Macrina '17 | ♟♟ 2* |
| ● Camerlano '13 | ♟ 4 |
| ○ Verdicchio dei Castelli di Jesi Cl. Sup. Podium '15 | ♙♙♙ 4* |
| ○ Verdicchio dei Castelli di Jesi Cl. Sup. Podium '13 | ♙♙♙ 4* |

# Marco Gatti

via Lagua e San Martino, 2
60043 Cerreto d'Esi [AN]
Tel. +39 0732677012
www.gattiagri.it

CELLAR SALES
PRE-BOOKED VISITS
ANNUAL PRODUCTION 10,000 bottles
HECTARES UNDER VINE 6.00

In spite of Marco Gatti's reliance on several parcels scattered about the upper part of Vallesina (rather than a single, contiguous tract) he was not protected from the devastating effects of 2017's late spring and subsequent scorching summer. But by managing the work himself, working with small volumes and separating each harvest, and refusing to purchase any raw material from others, he has had good results with his highly sensory and stylized Verdicchio di Matelica, as always aged in steel. Their 2017 Casale Venza is the winery's newest. Subtle, agile, it offers a very fluid palate with a long, savory finish. As the recipient of their best grapes, including those destined for Riserva Millo, their 2017 Villa Marilla presents an entirely different profile. Its intimately Matelica nose, delivers hints of flowers, sweet almond and anise, followed by a tasty, intense palate that coherently matches its aromatic profile and has a salty finish.

| | | |
|---|---|---|
| ○ Verdicchio di Matelica Villa Marilla '17 | ♀♀ | 2* |
| ○ Verdicchio di Matelica Casale Venza '17 | ♀♀ | 2* |
| ○ Verdicchio di Matelica Aristo '15 | ♀♀ | 2* |
| ○ Verdicchio di Matelica Casale Venza '16 | ♀♀ | 2* |
| ○ Verdicchio di Matelica Casale Venza '15 | ♀♀ | 2* |
| ○ Verdicchio di Matelica Millo Ris. '13 | ♀♀ | 3* |
| ○ Verdicchio di Matelica Villa Marilla '16 | ♀♀ | 2* |
| ○ Verdicchio di Matelica Villa Marilla '15 | ♀♀ | 2* |
| ○ Verdicchio di Matelica Villa Marilla '14 | ♀♀ | 2* |
| ○ Verdicchio di Matelica Villa Marilla '13 | ♀♀ | 2* |

# Luciano Landi

via Gavigliano, 16
60030 Belvedere Ostrense [AN]
Tel. +39 073162353
www.aziendalandi.it

CELLAR SALES
PRE-BOOKED VISITS
ACCOMMODATION
ANNUAL PRODUCTION 80,000 bottles
HECTARES UNDER VINE 20.00

Belvedere Ostrense straddles the space between Jesi's white Verdicchio and Morro d'Alba's red Lacrima, making for a dual spirit. And even though Luciano Landi is a recognized specialist of Lacrima, the winery embraces yet another spirit coming from varieties like Montepulciano and Syrah. Its judiciously modern wines are the fruit of good maturation and skillful use of mostly small wood barrels for their most ambitious reds. Only their Gavigliano is aged equally in steel and in small wood barrels. Their spendid 2016 gives off clear hints of rose petals made more complex by subtle spices and sour cherry. Savoriness, crisp fruit and skillfully extracted tannins develop on the palate. Likewise, their 2017 Lacrima doesn't hide its fruity nature while their 2017 Verdicchio Classico offers a lovely personality and an intense palate. Their 2015 Kore, a Syrah, is also quite energetic.

| | | |
|---|---|---|
| ● Lacrima di Morro d'Alba Sup. Gavigliano '16 | ♀♀ | 3* |
| ● Esino Rosso Kore '15 | ♀♀ | 3 |
| ● Esino Rosso Nobilnero '15 | ♀♀ | 6 |
| ● Lacrima di Morro d'Alba '17 | ♀♀ | 2* |
| ● Ragosto '15 | ♀♀ | 2* |
| ○ Verdicchio dei Castelli di Jesi Cl. '17 | ♀♀ | 2* |
| ● Goliardo '14 | ♀♀ | 4 |
| ● Lacrima di Morro d'Alba Sup. Gavigliano '15 | ♀♀ | 3 |
| ● Lacrima di Morro d'Alba Sup. Gavigliano '14 | ♀♀ | 3 |
| ● Lacrima di Morro d'Alba Sup. Gavigliano '13 | ♀♀ | 3 |
| ● Nobilnero '10 | ♀♀ | 6 |
| ○ Verdicchio dei Castelli di Jesi Cl. '15 | ♀♀ | 2* |

# Stefano Mancinelli

VIA ROMA, 62
60030 MORRO D'ALBA [AN]
TEL. +39 073163021
www.mancinellivini.it

CELLAR SALES
PRE-BOOKED VISITS
ACCOMMODATION
ANNUAL PRODUCTION 150,000 bottles
HECTARES UNDER VINE 25.00

Anyone familiar with Marches wines is also familiar with Stefano Mancinelli. As the appellation's unquestioned father, he was the first to bring the Lacrima di Morro d'Alba to the national stage. The winery has seen all of the variety's possible permutations, from the first use of carbonic maceration in Sensazioni di Frutto, to succesfully sweeter interpretations. But included as well in the winery's range is, of course, Verdicchio, which has a long history in the area. Their excellent 2015 Lacrima Superiore offers intriguing notes of aromatic herbs planted amid flowers that return on a palate of good length and close-knit tannins. Their 2017 Verdicchio Classico Superiore presents a clear profile of flowers and almond. Its great savoriness contrasts with its softer spirit. Their obvious agility with sweet wine shows in their 2013 Lacrima Re Sole with its notes of rosolio liqueur, as well as their intense 2013 Verdicchio Stell, with its never-ending finish.

| | |
|---|---|
| ○ Verdicchio dei Castelli di Jesi Passito Stell '13 | ♟♟ 5 |
| ● Lacrima di Morro d'Alba '16 | ♟♟ 2* |
| ● Lacrima di Morro d'Alba Passito Re Sole '13 | ♟♟ 5 |
| ● Lacrima di Morro d'Alba Sup. '15 | ♟♟ 3 |
| ○ Verdicchio dei Castelli di Jesi Cl. Sup. '17 | ♟♟ 2* |
| ● Brut M. Cl. | ♟ 5 |
| ○ Verdicchio dei Castelli di Jesi Cl. '17 | ♟ 2 |
| ● Lacrima di Morro d'Alba '13 | ♟♟ 2* |
| ● Lacrima di Morro d'Alba Passito Re Sole '10 | ♟♟ 5 |
| ● Lacrima di Morro d'Alba Sensazioni di Frutto '13 | ♟♟ 2* |
| ● Lacrima di Morro d'Alba Sup. '13 | ♟♟ 3* |
| ● Lacrima di Morro d'Alba Sup. '12 | ♟♟ 3 |

# Mancini

FRAZ. MOIE
60030 MAIOLATI SPONTINI [AN]
TEL. +39 0731702975
www.manciniwines.it

CELLAR SALES
PRE-BOOKED VISITS
RESTAURANT SERVICE
ANNUAL PRODUCTION 140,000 bottles
HECTARES UNDER VINE 20.00

The Mancini family's selection is made with grapes cultivated on a single, contiguous vineyard that surrounds their winery. As one would expect in this area, the lion's share of the vineyard is Verdicchio, but small sections are reserved for Montepulciano, Sangiovese and a bit of Cabernet Sauvignon used in their Rosso Piceno. Jesi's traditional grape is used for the rest of their range, which is differentiated by the time of harvest and length of time in steel tanks. Their only Verdicchio partially-aged in small wood barrels, the 2014 Riserva exhibits a supple palate and aromatic complexity developed over time that becomes even more evident in its toasted almond finish. Their very successful, refreshing 2017 Verdicchio Santa Lucia is citrusy with a mineral touch and a gripping, saline palate. Their much more structured and powerful 2017 Villa Talliano contrasts the softness and savoriness that remain through its long finish.

| | |
|---|---|
| ○ Castelli di Jesi Verdicchio Cl. Ris. '14 | ♟♟ 5 |
| ○ Verdicchio Castelli di Jesi Cl. Sup. Villa Talliano '17 | ♟♟ 3 |
| ● Rosso Piceno Panicale '15 | ♟ 3 |
| ○ Verdicchio Castelli di Jesi Cl. S. Lucia '17 | ♟ 2 |
| ○ Verdicchio Castelli di Jesi Cl. S. Lucia '16 | ♟♟ 2* |
| ○ Verdicchio Castelli di Jesi Cl. Sup. Villa Talliano '16 | ♟♟ 3 |
| ○ Verdicchio Castelli di Jesi Cl. Sup. Villa Talliano '15 | ♟♟ 3 |
| ○ Verdicchio Castelli di Jesi Cl. Sup. Villa Talliano '13 | ♟♟ 3* |

# MARCHE

## La Marca di San Michele

VIA TORRE, 13
60034 CUPRAMONTANA [AN]
TEL. +39 0731781183
www.lamarcadisanmichele.com

CELLAR SALES
PRE-BOOKED VISITS
ACCOMMODATION
ANNUAL PRODUCTION 35,000 bottles
HECTARES UNDER VINE 6.00
VITICULTURE METHOD Certified Organic

Over ten years, Alessando and Beatrice Bonci, with strong assistance from Daniela Quaresima, have succeeded in establishing a winery now integral to Castelli di Jesi. Their wines are admired for the robustness infused by the famous San Michele di Cupramontana cru, for the freedom with which they release the savory energy of Verdicchio and Montepulciano, and for their complex fluidity reminiscent of earlier times. Selected yeasts are not used in the cellar, where large wood barrels are used only for their Riserva di Verdicchio. There's always an embarrassing wide array of whites with La Marca di San Michele. Their expressive and seductive 2016 Verdicchio Passolento Riserva offers restrained style and rich flavor, while their more dynamic 2017 Capovolto, couldn't be more varietal with its juicy, well-structured palate. For an uncompromising red, try their pure, wiry 2016 Montepulciano Bastian Contrario.

## Maurizio Marchetti

FRAZ. PINOCCHIO
VIA DI PONTELUNGO, 166
60131 ANCONA
TEL. +39 071897386
www.marchettiwines.it

CELLAR SALES
PRE-BOOKED VISITS
ANNUAL PRODUCTION 65,000 bottles
HECTARES UNDER VINE 22.00

Maurizio Marchetti has always been dedicated to Montepulciano. In fact, his father Mario was one of four who in 1967 pushed for the establishment of the Rosso Conero appellation. And their cellar breathes history, housed in a wing of a century-old manor house just outside Ancona. However, collaboration with enologist Lorenzo Landi has resulted in a balanced modern style that avoids over-ripening or forced extraction. Only Villa Bonomi Riserva is aged in small barrels, while other selections rest largely in concrete tanks. Their 2015 confirms it as one of the best Conero. Judicious aging in small barrels leaves spicy, toasty marks integrated into sour cherry and black plum notes, while the full-bodied, glossy, palate is smooth and consistent. Their 2017 Due Amici, has serious, juicy style and an expressive profile that is simple and approachable without being banal.

| | |
|---|---|
| ○ Castelli di Jesi Verdicchio Cl. Passolento Ris. '16 | 🏆🏆 5 |
| ○ Verdicchio dei Castelli di Jesi Cl. Sup. Capovolto '17 | 🏆🏆 3* |
| ● Bastian Contrario '16 | 🏆🏆 3 |
| ○ Verdicchio dei Castelli di Jesi Cl. Sup. Capovolto '13 | 🏆🏆🏆 3* |
| ○ Verdicchio dei Castelli di Jesi Cl. Sup. Capovolto '10 | 🏆🏆🏆 3* |
| ○ Castelli di Jesi Verdicchio Cl. Passolento Ris. '15 | 🏆🏆 4 |
| ○ Castelli di Jesi Verdicchio Cl. Passolento Ris. '14 | 🏆🏆 4 |
| ○ Verdicchio dei Castelli di Jesi Cl. Sup. Capovolto '15 | 🏆🏆 3 |
| ○ Verdicchio dei Castelli di Jesi Cl. Sup. Capovolto '14 | 🏆🏆 3 |

| | |
|---|---|
| ● Conero Villa Bonomi Ris. '15 | 🏆🏆 5 |
| ● Rosso Conero Due Amici '17 | 🏆🏆 2* |
| ● Rosso Conero Castro di San Silvestro '17 | 🏆 2 |
| ○ Verdicchio dei Castelli di Jesi Cl. '17 | 🏆 2 |
| ○ Verdicchio dei Castelli di Jesi Cl. Sup. Tenuta del Cavaliere '17 | 🏆 3 |
| ● Rosso Conero Villa Bonomi Ris. '02 | 🏆🏆🏆 4 |
| ● Conero Villa Bonomi Cento Vendemmie Mario Marchetti Ris. '13 | 🏆🏆 5 |
| ● Conero Villa Bonomi Ris. '14 | 🏆🏆 5 |
| ● Conero Villa Bonomi Ris. '13 | 🏆🏆 5 |
| ● Conero Villa Bonomi Ris. '12 | 🏆🏆 5 |
| ● Rosso Conero Castro di San Silvestro '16 | 🏆🏆 2* |
| ○ Verdicchio dei Castelli di Jesi Cl. '15 | 🏆🏆 2* |
| ○ Verdicchio dei Castelli di Jesi Cl. Sup. Tenuta del Cavaliere '14 | 🏆🏆 3 |

# Marotti Campi

VIA SANT'AMICO, 14
60030 MORRO D'ALBA [AN]
TEL. +39 0731618027
www.marotticampi.it

**CELLAR SALES**
**PRE-BOOKED VISITS**
**ACCOMMODATION**
**ANNUAL PRODUCTION** 240,000 bottles
**HECTARES UNDER VINE** 71.00

Lorenzo Marotti Campi runs the family winery in a modern entrepreneurial way. While embracing local markets, he sees exports as key to their success. Lending authority to this philosophy is their winery's status as the largest cultivator of Lacrima Nera, a traditional variety of Morri d'Alba that features an unmistakable, aromatic character. Additionally, Marotti Campi offers from this Adriatic municipality a Verdicchio, which features a contemporary spirit and rounder, fruitier body that satisfies the palate. Their 2016 Orgiolo is the first Lacrima di Morro d'Alba to receive Tre Bicchieri. It conveys the floral inflection characteristic of the variety, but with more layers, pulling out smoky, briny sensations. It develops incisively on the palate with perfect aromatic consistency. Their 2015 Verdicchio Salmariano Riserva proves equally successful for its elegant aromas and supple, rich flavor.

| | |
|---|---|
| ● Lacrima di Morro d'Alba Sup. Orgiolo '16 | ♟♟♟ 3* |
| ○ Castelli di Jesi Verdicchio Cl. Salmariano Ris. '15 | ♟♟ 3* |
| ● Lacrima di Morro d'Alba Rubico '17 | ♟♟ 2* |
| ○ Verdicchio dei Castelli di Jesi Cl. Sup. Luzano '17 | ♟♟ 2* |
| ⊙ Brut Rosé | ♟ 3 |
| ● Donderè '15 | ♟ 3 |
| ○ Verdicchio dei Castelli di Jesi Cl. Albiano '17 | ♟ 1* |
| ○ Castelli di Jesi Verdicchio Cl. Salmariano Ris. '14 | ♟♟♟ 3* |
| ○ Castelli di Jesi Verdicchio Cl. Salmariano Ris. '13 | ♟♟♟ 3* |
| ○ Verdicchio dei Castelli di Jesi Cl. Salmariano Ris. '08 | ♟♟♟ 3* |

# Poderi Mattioli

VIA FARNETO, 17A
60030 SERRA DE' CONTI [AN]
TEL. +39 0731878676
www.poderimattioli.it

**CELLAR SALES**
**PRE-BOOKED VISITS**
**ANNUAL PRODUCTION** 25,000 bottles
**HECTARES UNDER VINE** 6.50
**VITICULTURE METHOD** Certified Organic

It has taken less than ten years for Giordano and Giacomo Mattioli's Verdicchio to acquire a cult-following in the crowded Castelli di Jesi scene. Not so surprising, given their grandfathers' and uncles' reputations as vine growers. But today's success is due to keeping the fruits of their labor in-house. Instead of selling their harvest, they have built a cellar and do the bottling themselves. Thus with sensitivity and experience gained over time, they have raised awareness of Serra de' Conti's terroir, which in itself is somewhat of a miracle. The Mattiolo presented two magnificent Verdicchio this year, with the fantastic 2016 Ylice receiving Tre Bicchiere. Its nose offers vital currents of lemon, almonds and aromatic herbs on a rhythmic, grippy palate refined by juiciness and backbone. It just edged out their 2014 Laura Riserva, which rejoices in elegant, nuanced aromas and saline notes.

| | |
|---|---|
| ○ Verdicchio dei Castelli di Jesi Cl. Sup. Ylice '16 | ♟♟♟ 3* |
| ○ Castelli di Jesi Verdicchio Cl. Lauro Ris. '14 | ♟♟ 4 |
| ○ M. Cl. Dosaggio Zero '13 | ♟♟ 5 |
| ○ Castelli di Jesi Verdicchio Cl. Lauro Ris. '15 | ♟♟♟ 4* |
| ○ Castelli di Jesi Verdicchio Cl. Lauro Ris. '13 | ♟♟♟ 3* |
| ○ Verdicchio dei Castelli di Jesi Cl. Sup. Ylice '12 | ♟♟♟ 2* |
| ○ Verdicchio dei Castelli di Jesi Cl. Sup. Ylice '15 | ♟♟ 3* |
| ○ Verdicchio dei Castelli di Jesi Cl. Sup. Ylice '14 | ♟♟ 3 |

## ★La Monacesca

C.DA MONACESCA
62024 MATELICA [MC]
TEL. +39 0733672641
www.monacesca.it

**CELLAR SALES**
**PRE-BOOKED VISITS**
**ANNUAL PRODUCTION** 160,000 bottles
**HECTARES UNDER VINE** 28.00

La Monascesca is headquartered in a restored walled village that surrounds a medieval church built by Benedictine monks from Farfa. Located in the heart of the area around Matelica, the winery was founded by Miro Cifola and is now run by his son. From the beginning, their Verdicchio ran contrary to a traditional lean and early-drinking white. Instead, their wines are powerful and full of flavor, without aging in wood barrels. Over the years they have earned the respect of connoisseurs who have discovered their extraordinary longevity. Their 2016 Verdicchio Mirum Riserva is the extraordinary result of a style that has developed over time. Its captivatingly creamy palate finds counterpoint in a majestic savoriness that closes in a impressively long finish embellished by notes of botrytis and anise. Their 2016 Matelica also promises pleasantness immediately, while their 2015 Syrah makes a fine debut with complex quinine and black pepper notes. Their compelling and sturdy 2015 Camerte delivers complexity and rigorous style.

| | | |
|---|---|---|
| ○ Verdicchio di Matelica Mirum Ris. '16 | 🍷🍷🍷 | 5 |
| ● Camerte '15 | 🍷🍷 | 4 |
| ● Syrah '15 | 🍷🍷 | 8 |
| ○ Verdicchio di Matelica '16 | 🍷🍷 | 3 |
| ⊙ Camerte Rosé '17 | 🍷 | 2 |
| ○ Ecclesia '16 | 🍷 | 3 |
| ○ Verdicchio di Matelica Mirum Ris. '15 | YYY | 5 |
| ○ Verdicchio di Matelica Mirum Ris. '14 | YYY | 5 |
| ○ Verdicchio di Matelica Mirum Ris. '12 | YYY | 5 |
| ○ Verdicchio di Matelica Mirum Ris. '11 | YYY | 5 |
| ○ Verdicchio di Matelica Mirum Ris. '10 | YYY | 4* |
| ○ Verdicchio di Matelica Mirum Ris. '09 | YYY | 4 |
| ○ Verdicchio di Matelica Mirum Ris. '08 | YYY | 4 |
| ○ Verdicchio di Matelica Mirum Ris. '07 | YYY | 4* |
| ○ Verdicchio di Matelica Mirum Ris. '06 | YYY | 4 |
| ○ Verdicchio di Matelica Mirum Ris. '04 | YYY | 4 |
| ○ Verdicchio di Matelica Mirum Ris. '02 | YYY | 3 |

## Montecappone

VIA COLLE OLIVO, 2
60035 JESI [AN]
TEL. +39 0731205761
www.montecappone.com

**CELLAR SALES**
**PRE-BOOKED VISITS**
**ANNUAL PRODUCTION** 150,000 bottles
**HECTARES UNDER VINE** 42.50

Gianluca Mirizzi never rests. First, channeling energy into the use of autoclaves for producing Charmat Method sparkling wines, then adding six more hectares of vineyards in Cupramontana, now its own estate, Mirizzi. They now offer a wine aged in amphorae and a Metodo Classico sparkling wine, both from Verdicchio grapes. The rest of the range remains familiar. Whites of extraordinary finesse give the best of themselves over time while their reds are aged in small barrels, though generally not in the first stages. Their energetic 2016 Verdicchio Federico II balances its impressive structure with captivating yellow fruit, citrus and almond. Even more complex, their 2016 Ergo delivers a powerful palate of candied orange, broom and beeswax. The nose of their 2015 Utopia Riserva needs time to develop more definition but on the palate it proves invigorating and demonstrative. Their 2017 Muntobe debuts well, more beguiling than deep. Finally their new 2016 Extra Brut Mirizzi is fragrant and delicate.

| | | |
|---|---|---|
| ○ Verdicchio dei Castelli di Jesi Cl. Sup. Ergo Mirizzi '16 | 🍷🍷 | 5 |
| ○ Verdicchio dei Castelli di Jesi Cl. Sup. Federico II A. D. 1194 '16 | 🍷🍷 | 5 |
| ○ Castelli di Jesi Verdicchio Cl. Utopia Ris. '15 | 🍷🍷 | 5 |
| ○ Passerina Brut | 🍷🍷 | 4 |
| ● Rosso Piceno '17 | 🍷🍷 | 2* |
| ○ Verdicchio dei Castelli di Jesi Cl. '17 | 🍷🍷 | 2* |
| ○ Verdicchio dei Castelli di Jesi Cl. Sup. Muntobe '17 | 🍷🍷 | 4 |
| ○ Verdicchio dei Castelli di Jesi M. Cl. Extra Brut Mirizzi '15 | 🍷🍷 | 5 |
| ○ La Breccia '17 | 🍷 | 4 |
| ○ Madame Passerina '17 | 🍷 | 3 |
| ○ Offida Pecorino Monsieur Pecorino '17 | 🍷 | 3 |
| ○ Sauvignon Brut | 🍷 | 5 |
| ○ Tabano '17 | 🍷 | 5 |

# Alessandro Moroder

VIA MONTACUTO, 121
60029 ANCONA
TEL. +39 071898232
www.moroder-vini.it

**CELLAR SALES**
**PRE-BOOKED VISITS**
**ANNUAL PRODUCTION** 130,000 bottles
**HECTARES UNDER VINE** 18.00
**VITICULTURE METHOD** Certified Organic
**SUSTAINABLE WINERY**

Alessandro Modorer stands out in the Monte Conero Nature Preserve, located within the appellation developed especially for Montepulciano. The estate has been active since 1837 and is managed as an integrated producer, hospitality service and crop grower. About half of their extensive holdings are dedicated to vineyards; the oldest rows are about 70 years of age. Organic management methods were adopted a few years ago in the vineyards and wine is fermented using native yeasts. Their 2015 Dorico Riserva takes us back the glory of their 1988 and 1990 versions, the first Coneros to earn our highest honors. The variety's natural energy and generosity come out in tracks of elegant savory density thanks partly to balanced alcohol and dense, smooth tannins. Their 2017 Rosso Conero Aion is fragrant, with vigorous acidity and easy drinkability.

| | | |
|---|---|---|
| ● Conero Dorico Ris. '15 | ♟♟♟ | 5 |
| ● Rosso Conero Aiòn '17 | ♟♟ | 2* |
| ● Rosso Conero Zero '17 | ♟ | 2 |
| ● Conero Dorico Ris. '05 | ♟♟♟ | 5 |
| ● Conero Dorico Ris. '13 | ♟♟ | 5 |
| ● Conero Dorico Ris. '11 | ♟♟ | 5 |
| ● Conero Ris. '13 | ♟♟ | 5 |
| ● Conero Ris. '12 | ♟♟ | 5 |
| ● Rosso Conero '15 | ♟♟ | 2* |
| ● Rosso Conero Aiòn '14 | ♟♟ | 2* |
| ● Rosso Conero Aiòn '13 | ♟♟ | 2* |

# ★Oasi degli Angeli

C.DA SANT'EGIDIO, 50
63012 CUPRA MARITTIMA [AP]
TEL. +39 0735778569
www.kurni.it

**CELLAR SALES**
**PRE-BOOKED VISITS**
**ANNUAL PRODUCTION** 5,000 bottles
**HECTARES UNDER VINE** 16.00

Marco Casolanetti doesn't really need an introduction. His enoic adventure in Cupra Marittima, located in southern Marche, started in 1997 and he became immediately linked to Kurni. This truly iconic wine was the result of experimenting with the concentration and extraction of Montepulciano, something no one had ever dared to do. Next came Kupra, a limited-production 'Bordò' (a local Grenache biotype), which has given life in some ways to a project shared by several wineries in Piceno. Their selection certainly isn't lacking in character. Their 2016 Kurni, with its unmistakable, exceptionally fruity intensity, proves one of the best in recent years and their 2015 Kupra delivers no less. Its seductive nose and tenacity on the palate make it a rare and highly desirable wine, certain to leave an immediate and indelible imprint.

| | | |
|---|---|---|
| ● Kupra '15 | ♟♟ | 8 |
| ● Kurni '16 | ♟♟ | 8 |
| ● Kupra '13 | ♟♟♟ | 8 |
| ● Kupra '12 | ♟♟♟ | 8 |
| ● Kupra '10 | ♟♟♟ | 8 |
| ● Kurni '10 | ♟♟♟ | 8 |
| ● Kurni '09 | ♟♟♟ | 8 |
| ● Kurni '08 | ♟♟♟ | 8 |
| ● Kurni '07 | ♟♟♟ | 8 |
| ● Kurni '04 | ♟♟♟ | 8 |
| ● Kurni '03 | ♟♟♟ | 8 |
| ● Kurni '02 | ♟♟♟ | 8 |
| ● Kurni '01 | ♟♟♟ | 8 |
| ● Kurni '00 | ♟♟♟ | 8 |

# Officina del Sole

C.DA MONTEMILONE, 1
63842 MONTEGIORGIO [FM]
TEL. +39 0734967321
www.officinadelsole.it

ANNUAL PRODUCTION 20,000 bottles
HECTARES UNDER VINE 12.00

Located on the slopes of Montegiorgio, the ambitious Officina del Sole straddles the provinces of Fermo and Macerata. It includes a resort, restaurant, cellar and oil mill. The summit, which is surrounded by vineyards, olive groves and fruit trees, is clearly visible from most of the region and from the top offers a striking 360 degree view. Native and international grapes intermingle, giving shape to richly fruited wines of a classic, approachable style. Their 2016 Pecorino Franco Franco is partially aged in small barrels, offering a fine nose of clean grapefruit with captivating interspersed toasted notes and a remarkably savory, pulpy texture on the palate. Quite dynamic on the palate, its younger brother, their 2017 Franco shares the same light citrus intensity. Their unusually deep Trecentosessanta Brut Charmat sparkling wine delivers crusty bread aromas and a flavorful palate.

| | | |
|---|---|---|
| ○ Offida Pecorino Franco Franco '16 | ♛♛ | 5 |
| ○ 360 Brut | ♛♛ | 3 |
| ○ Falerio Pecorino Franco '17 | ♛♛ | 3 |
| ● Rosso Frutto '17 | ♛ | 3 |
| ○ Falerio Pecorino Franco Franco '15 | ♛♛ | 5 |
| ● Tignum '15 | ♛♛ | 6 |

# Tenute Pieralisi
# Monte Schiavo

FRAZ. MONTESCHIAVO
VIA VIVAIO
60030 MAIOLATI SPONTINI [AN]
TEL. +39 0731700385
www.monteschiavo.it

CELLAR SALES
PRE-BOOKED VISITS
ANNUAL PRODUCTION 950,000 bottles
HECTARES UNDER VINE 103.00
SUSTAINABLE WINERY

The Pieralisi family winery is showing two distinct personalities. On the one hand you have a classic Monte Schiavo line that follows a path established in 1995 and includes most of the vineyards. On the other hand, you have Tenute Pieralisi, a long-considered but recently launched project that began in 2015, in collaboration with Carlo Ferrini. Showing a more unconventional side, the latter revolves around careful selection of the very best parcels, which allows for greater freedom of execution. All of the vineyards, however, have adopted organic farming principles. Verdicchio is the linchpin of their offerings. Their 2017 Villaia gets its strength in a fruity nose and its immediately appealing, relaxed, juicy palate. Their 2017 Pallio di San Floriano carries notes of wild herbs and almonds echoed on a soft palate that, though not particularly nimble, proves very good. Among reds their 2015 Piceno Re di Ras stands out. Aged in medium-sized barrels, it offers maraschino and balsamic notes on a both well-structured and delicate palate.

| | | |
|---|---|---|
| ● Rosso Piceno Re di Ras Tenute Pieralisi '15 | ♛♛ | 4 |
| ○ Verdicchio dei Castelli di Jesi Cl. Sup. Pallio di S. Floriano '17 | ♛♛ | 3 |
| ○ Verdicchio dei Castelli di Jesi Cl. Sup. Villaia Tenute Pieralisi '17 | ♛♛ | 3 |
| ● Rosso Piceno Caccialepre Tenute Pieralisi '16 | ♛ | 3 |
| ○ Tassanare Brut | ♛ | 2 |
| ○ Verdicchio dei Castelli di Jesi Cl. Sup. Pallio di S. Floriano '11 | ♛♛♛ | 2* |
| ○ Verdicchio dei Castelli di Jesi Cl. Sup. Pallio di S. Floriano '10 | ♛♛♛ | 2* |
| ○ Verdicchio dei Castelli di Jesi Cl. Sup. Pallio di S. Floriano '09 | ♛♛♛ | 2* |

# Pievalta

VIA MONTESCHIAVO, 18
60030 MAIOLATI SPONTINI [AN]
TEL. +39 0731705199
www.baronepizzini.it

**CELLAR SALES**
**PRE-BOOKED VISITS**
**ANNUAL PRODUCTION** 125,000 bottles
**HECTARES UNDER VINE** 26.50
**VITICULTURE METHOD** Certified Biodynamic
**SUSTAINABLE WINERY**

Pievalta is an offshoot of Barone Pizzini, the famous Francacorta winery. The rows of biodynamically cultivated Verdicchio are presided over by Alessandro Fenino, who moved from Lombardy and set roots down in Maiolati Spontini. After spending a few years renovating the vineyards and building agricultural structures, he has built the winery's selection into one that is both complete and noteworthy. Offerings are lean and gastronomic, faithfully expressing the character of the different plots. Their 2016 Verdicchio San Paolo is wonderfully rocky both in terms of its mineral aromatic profile and its vigor on the palate. Promising articulated complexity once its youthful fury subsides in a few years, its irrepressible energy has already earned it a place within the firmament of Italian whites. Their 2017 Dominé benefits more from its powerful taste than its refinement, but it does have a contagious drinkability. Their 2017 Pievalta is stylish and saline.

# Il Pollenza

C.DA CASONE, 4
62029 TOLENTINO [MC]
TEL. +39 0733961989
www.ilpollenza.it

**CELLAR SALES**
**PRE-BOOKED VISITS**
**ANNUAL PRODUCTION** 300,000 bottles
**HECTARES UNDER VINE** 80.00
**SUSTAINABLE WINERY**

Aldo Brachetti Peretti's winery has made some changes. Its remodeling is not about the vineyards or the lavish cellar, which was made more functional and welcoming recently. Rather, it's about restructuring their best wines, led by the owners and technical management, Carlo Ferrini and Giovanni Campodonico. International varieties remain central, but their 2015 Pollenza is pure Cabernet Sauvignon and their Cosmino pure Cabernet Franc. In essence, they ended Bordeaux blending by reducing the role of Petit Verdot and Merlot. The change has shown immediate results. Bringing Tre Bicchieri to Contrada Casone, their 2015 Pollenza admirably balances power and elegance in a manner that reveals increasing aromatic complexity on the almost austere palate. Their 2015 Cosmino offers wild, vegetal notes, steered decisively across the palate by sturdy tannins.

| | |
|---|---|
| ○ Castelli di Jesi Verdicchio Cl. San Paolo Ris. '16 | ♛♛♛ 3* |
| ○ Perlugo Dosaggio Zero M. Cl. | ♛♛ 3 |
| ○ Verdicchio dei Castelli di Jesi Cl. Sup. Dominè Chiesa del Pozzo '17 | ♛♛ 2* |
| ○ Verdicchio dei Castelli di Jesi Cl. Sup. Pievalta '17 | ♛♛ 2* |
| ● Rosso Pievalta '15 | ♛ 2 |
| ○ Castelli di Jesi Verdicchio Cl. San Paolo Ris. '15 | ♛♛♛ 3* |
| ○ Castelli di Jesi Verdicchio Cl. San Paolo Ris. '13 | ♛♛♛ 3* |
| ○ Castelli di Jesi Verdicchio Cl. San Paolo Ris. '10 | ♛♛♛ 3* |
| ○ Verdicchio dei Castelli di Jesi Cl. Sup. Pievalta '09 | ♛♛♛ 2* |

| | |
|---|---|
| ● Il Pollenza '15 | ♛♛♛ 8 |
| ○ ABP Pas Dosé M. Cl '12 | ♛♛ 5 |
| ● Cosmino '15 | ♛♛ 5 |
| ○ Didì '17 | ♛♛ 3 |
| ● Porpora '15 | ♛♛ 3 |
| ○ Brianello '17 | ♛ 3 |
| ○ Colli Maceratesi Ribona Angera '17 | ♛ 3 |
| ● Il Pollenza '12 | ♛♛♛ 8 |
| ● Il Pollenza '11 | ♛♛♛ 7 |
| ● Il Pollenza '10 | ♛♛♛ 7 |
| ● Il Pollenza '09 | ♛♛♛ 7 |
| ● Il Pollenza '07 | ♛♛♛ 7 |
| ○ Colli Maceratesi Ribona Angera '16 | ♛♛ 3 |
| ● Cosmino '14 | ♛♛ 5 |
| ● Il Pollenza '14 | ♛♛ 8 |
| ○ Pius IX Mastai '15 | ♛♛ 6 |

# Sabbionare

VIA SABBIONARE, 10
60036 MONTECAROTTO [AN]
TEL. +39 0731889004
www.sabbionare.it

**CELLAR SALES**
**PRE-BOOKED VISITS**
**ANNUAL PRODUCTION** 45,000 bottles
**HECTARES UNDER VINE** 24.00

It started with inherited Verdicchio vines well-established in the dry, well-drained sandy soil that gives its name to the area. Sauro Paolucci and Donatella Paoloni turned to Sergio Paolucci, an enologist (but not a relative), who convinced them they could unlock the potential of the vineyard. In 1998 they built a cellar overlooking a splendid panorama of rows. Since then, the number of hectares has tripled along with the number of bottles. And now a second generation is following, taking advantage of Pierluigi Donna's agronomic expertise. The warm 2017 left a soft, full-bodied mark on their Sabbionare, which offers juicy hints of yellow summer fruit and a voluminous palate. The aromatic herbs and citrus notes of their very successful 2014 Metodo Classico Pas Dosè Dune prepare you for its coherent, very savory palate. The best characteristics of their young 2017 Verdicchio are its strong varietal stamp and drinkability.

| | |
|---|---|
| ○ Verdicchio dei Castelli di Jesi Cl. Sup. Sabbionare '17 | ♟♟ 3 |
| ○ Verdicchio dei Castelli di Jesi Pas Dosé Dune M. Cl. '14 | ♟♟ 5 |
| ○ Verdicchio dei Castelli di Jesi Cl. Il Filetto '17 | ♟ 1* |
| ○ Verdicchio dei Castelli di Jesi Cl. Sup. Sabbionare '15 | ♟♟♟ 2* |
| ○ Verdicchio dei Castelli di Jesi Cl. El Filetto '15 | ♟♟ 1* |
| ○ Verdicchio dei Castelli di Jesi Cl. Sup. Sabbionare '16 | ♟♟ 3* |

# Saladini Pilastri

VIA SALADINI, 5
63078 SPINETOLI [AP]
TEL. +39 0736899534
www.saladinipilastri.it

**CELLAR SALES**
**PRE-BOOKED VISITS**
**ANNUAL PRODUCTION** 800,000 bottles
**HECTARES UNDER VINE** 150.00
**VITICULTURE METHOD** Certified Organic
**SUSTAINABLE WINERY**

Despite having been established as recently as 1986, the Saladini Pilastri family winery has roots going back hundreds of years. With an illustrious pedigree and a central role in the agricultural economy of Piceno, count Saladino maintains a vast estate winding through the hills behind San Benedetto del Tronto. Located in the municipalities of Spinetoli and Monteprandone, the vineyards, which have almost always been managed organically, are filled with traditional varieties such as Pecorino, Passerina, Trebbiano, Montepulciano and Sangiovese. Their 2016 Rosso Piceno V. Monteprandone opens on distinct notes of sour cherry, spices and soft woody accents that extend onto a fleshy palate robust with fiber. The gritty temperament and abundant tannins of their 2016 Montetinello strengthen its palate, while their 2016 Pregio del Conte, an unusual blend of Aglianico and Montepulciano, offers beautiful, crisp fruit and and a straight-forward palate with mineral traces. Their tasty, invigorating 2017 Pecorino stands out among whites.

| | |
|---|---|
| ○ Offida Pecorino '17 | ♟♟ 3 |
| ● Pregio del Conte '16 | ♟♟ 4 |
| ● Rosso Piceno Sup. Montetinello '16 | ♟♟ 4 |
| ● Rosso Piceno Sup. V. Monteprandone '16 | ♟♟ 5 |
| ○ Falerio '17 | ♟ 2 |
| ○ Falerio Palazzi '17 | ♟ 3 |
| ○ Offida Passerina '17 | ♟ 3 |
| ● Rosso Piceno '17 | ♟ 2 |
| ● Rosso Piceno Piediprato '16 | ♟ 3 |
| ● Rosso Piceno Sup. V. Monteprandone '00 | ♟♟♟ 3 |
| ○ Offida Pecorino '16 | ♟♟ 3* |
| ● Rosso Piceno Piediprato '15 | ♟♟ 3 |
| ● Rosso Piceno Sup. Montetinello '15 | ♟♟ 4 |
| ● Rosso Piceno Sup. Montetinello '14 | ♟♟ 3 |
| ● Rosso Piceno Sup. V. Monteprandone '15 | ♟♟ 5 |
| ● Rosso Piceno Sup. V. Monteprandone '14 | ♟♟ 5 |

## Fattoria San Lorenzo

VIA SAN LORENZO, 6
60036 MONTECAROTTO [AN]
TEL. +39 073189656
az-crognaletti@libero.it

CELLAR SALES
PRE-BOOKED VISITS
ACCOMMODATION AND RESTAURANT SERVICE
ANNUAL PRODUCTION 100,000 bottles
HECTARES UNDER VINE 30.00
VITICULTURE METHOD Certified Organic

Natalino Crognaletti is well-liked and respected throughout Marche. In addition to being an all-around nice guy, he is a tireless worker who has an intuitive approach to viticulture. As one of the first to believe in banning chemicals and to adopt spontaneous fermentation, he developed a style based on the protracted ripening of grapes. The result are wines that are intense, flavorful, and complex. He keeps Verdicchio in steel and cement, while he ages Montepulciano and Lacrima for a lengthy time in small used wooden barrels. Let their 2014 Campo delle Oche breathe a few minutes before experiencing its hints of flowers, cedar bark and chamomile, then enjoy its surprising suppleness, characteristic of the vintage. Their 2016 Le Oche releases intense yellow damson plum and peach on its opulent palate. Their 2012 Paradiso, a Lacrima, bursts with spicy originality, while their 2011 Il Solleone, a Montepulciano, evinces a faded charm.

| | |
|---|---|
| ● Paradiso '12 | ♟♟ 4 |
| ○ Verdicchio dei Castelli di Jesi Cl. Le Oche '16 | ♟♟ 3 |
| ○ Verdicchio dei Castelli di Jesi Cl. Sup. Campo delle Oche '14 | ♟♟ 4 |
| ● Il Solleone '11 | ♟ 5 |
| ● Paradiso '10 | ♟♟ 4 |
| ○ Verdicchio dei Castelli di Jesi Cl. Sup. Campo delle Oche '13 | ♟♟ 4 |

## Santa Barbara

B.GO MAZZINI, 35
60010 BARBARA [AN]
TEL. +39 0719674249
www.santabarbara.it

CELLAR SALES
PRE-BOOKED VISITS
ANNUAL PRODUCTION 900,000 bottles
HECTARES UNDER VINE 40.00

It is difficult to separate Santa Barbara's reputation from that of Stefano Antonucci's. The winery and the person have become virtually synonymous because of how deeply Stefano communicates through his wines. The winery is exhibiting an increasingly refined ability to produce wines with a "contemporary spirit". Not only their Verdicchio Jesino, but many other of their interpretations as well center on pleasantness, aromatic clarity, balanced taste and and a tendency to age well. Intense and pleasant are the defining qualities of their great 2016 Verdicchio Tardivo ma non Tardo. Citrus, anise and summer fruit reverberate through its long, energetic finish. Their 2016 Lina Passito is creamier, with sweet, succulent pulp. However, their extensive range contains many serious wines, such as their 2016 Massone (Merlot), their two Stefano Antonucci and their 2016 Rosso Piceno Maschio da Monte.

| | |
|---|---|
| ○ Castelli di Jesi Verdicchio Cl. Tardivo ma non Tardo Ris. '16 | ♟♟♟ 5 |
| ● Mossone '16 | ♟♟ 8 |
| ○ Verdicchio dei Castelli di Jesi Passito Lina '16 | ♟♟ 5 |
| ● Mossi Passito '16 | ♟♟ 5 |
| ● Pathos '16 | ♟♟ 6 |
| ● Rosso Piceno Il Maschio da Monte '16 | ♟♟ 5 |
| ● Stefano Antonucci Rosso '16 | ♟♟ 4 |
| ○ Verdicchio dei Castelli di Jesi Cl. Le Vaglie '17 | ♟♟ 3 |
| ○ Verdicchio dei Castelli di Jesi Cl. Sup. Stefano Antonucci '16 | ♟♟ 4 |
| ○ Verdicchio dei Castelli di Jesi Pignocco '17 | ♟♟ 2* |
| ○ Verdicchio dei Castelli di Jesi Ste '17 | ♟♟ 2* |
| ○ Verdicchio dei Castelli di Jesi Cl. Sup. Back to Basics '17 | ♟ 4 |

## Tenuta Santori

c.da Montebove, 14
63065 Ripatransone [AP]
Tel. +39 0735584189
www.tenutasantori.it

**CELLAR SALES**
**ANNUAL PRODUCTION** 25,000 bottles
**HECTARES UNDER VINE** 16.00
**VITICULTURE METHOD** Certified Organic

It's no easy task to stand out from the area's wineries, but Marco Santori has succeeded in a relatively short time. With the support of his father, he began this project only six years ago, in 2012. The vineyards, concentrated in the municipality of Ripatransone, are planted with varieties traditional to the area. Pecorino dominates and is accompanied by Passerina, Montepulciano and Sangiovese. In the cellar, Pierluigi Lorenzetti guides the creation of contemporary wines with crystalline aromas, flavorful backbone and aromatic depth enhanced by the use of steel vats. Rarely does a wine debut with Tre Bicchieri, and even more rarely does it succeed in confirming it the following year, but Santori's 2017 Pecorino has managed to do just that. Its aromatic impact, though shy, also proves extremely graceful with gusts alternating between medicinal herbs, yellow citrus and summer fruit, providing a great contrast to its energy-saturated palate and juicy, to say the least, finish. Definition and smoothness distinguish their 2017 Passerina.

| | |
|---|---|
| ○ Offida Pecorino '17 | ♟♟♟ 3* |
| ○ Offida Passerina '17 | ♟♟ 2* |
| ○ Offida Pecorino '16 | ♟♟♟ 3* |
| ○ Offida Passerina '16 | ♟♟ 2* |
| ● Rosso Piceno Sup. '15 | ♟♟ 3 |

## Sartarelli

via Coste del Molino, 24
60030 Poggio San Marcello [AN]
Tel. +39 073189732
www.sartarelli.com

**CELLAR SALES**
**PRE-BOOKED VISITS**
**ANNUAL PRODUCTION** 300,000 bottles
**HECTARES UNDER VINE** 55.00
**SUSTAINABLE WINERY**

A key concept to understanding the story of the Sartarelli family winery whose fame was attained through long-term vision, is that it takes time and dedication to build a solid reputation. They cultivate only Verdicchio on one of the most prestigious areas of the left bank of the Esino River. They then produce it across a full range – from sparkling wines to sweet, dried-grape passito wines. This focus, combined with the exclusive use of steel for maturation, has made for an extremely recognizable style. Their Balciana is the progenitor of all late-harvest Verdicchio and thus in some ways quite symbolic of the area. Their 2016 offers intense candied orange and aromatic herbs combined with soothing botrytis notes. Its palate is enveloping, full of glycerine and with a subtle but persistent finish. Their 2016 Tralivio delivers ripe aromas of anise, linden and traces of caramel, but also saturated with savoriness.

| | |
|---|---|
| ○ Verdicchio dei Castelli di Jesi Cl. Sup. Balciana '16 | ♟♟ 5 |
| ○ Verdicchio dei Castelli di Jesi Cl. Sup. Tralivio '16 | ♟♟ 3 |
| ○ Verdicchio dei Castelli di Jesi Passito '16 | ♟♟ 5 |
| ○ Brut | ♟ 3 |
| ○ Verdicchio dei Castelli di Jesi Cl. '17 | ♟ 2 |
| ○ Verdicchio dei Castelli di Jesi Cl. Sup. Balciana '09 | ♟♟♟ 5 |
| ○ Verdicchio dei Castelli di Jesi Cl. Sup. Balciana '04 | ♟♟♟ 5 |
| ○ Verdicchio dei Castelli di Jesi Cl. Sup. Contrada Balciana '98 | ♟♟♟ 5 |

# Sparapani - Frati Bianchi

VIA BARCHIO, 12
60034 CUPRAMONTANA [AN]
TEL. +39 0731781216
www.fratibianchi.it

**CELLAR SALES**
**PRE-BOOKED VISITS**
**RESTAURANT SERVICE**
**ANNUAL PRODUCTION** 40,000 bottles
**HECTARES UNDER VINE** 18.00

Among the most admired interpreters of Verdicchio, the Sparapani winery has been rooted in Cupramontana since its founding by Settimio in 1980. It is now managed by his children Pino, Francesca and Paolo, who adhere to their father's strong belief in family unity. Their limited volume enables direct control in both the vineyards and production, which takes place in a new, functional cellar. The estate's stylistic coherence comes from ten years working with enologist and recognized Verdicchio specialist, Sergio Paolucci. Their 2016 Priore is quite possible the best ever, certainly on par with the 2006 that brought them their first Tre Bicchieri. Almonds, aromatic herbs and lemon zest unite in a deeply savory nose that remains balanced and energetic, creating a sumptuous palate of incredible length with traces of minerals. Aged in small wood barrels, their 2015 Donna Cloe Riserva proves graceful, dynamic and complex.

| | |
|---|---|
| ○ Verdicchio dei Castelli di Jesi Cl. Sup. Il Priore '16 | ▼▼▼ 3* |
| ○ Castelli di Jesi Verdicchio Cl. Donna Cloe Ris. '15 | ▼▼ 5 |
| ○ Verdicchio dei Castelli di Jesi Cl. Salerna '17 | ▼ 2 |
| ○ Verdicchio dei Castelli di Jesi Cl. Sup. Il Priore '14 | ♀♀♀ 2* |
| ○ Verdicchio dei Castelli di Jesi Cl. Sup. Il Priore '13 | ♀♀♀ 2* |
| ○ Verdicchio dei Castelli di Jesi Cl. Sup. Il Priore '12 | ♀♀♀ 2* |
| ○ Verdicchio dei Castelli di Jesi Cl. Sup. Il Priore '06 | ♀♀♀ 2* |
| ○ Castelli di Jesi Verdicchio Cl. Donna Cloe Ris. '13 | ♀♀ 5 |

# Tenuta Spinelli

VIA LAGO, 2
63032 CASTIGNANO [AP]
TEL. +39 0736821489
www.tenutaspinelli.it

**CELLAR SALES**
**PRE-BOOKED VISITS**
**ACCOMMODATION**
**ANNUAL PRODUCTION** 30,000 bottles
**HECTARES UNDER VINE** 7.00

Simone Spinelli is a young winemaker who has not allowed his winery's widespread recognition to go to his head. Tenuta Spinelli began with vineyards on the slopes of Monte dell'Ascensione. This was followed by an expansion in Castignano, meeting the challenge of Pinot Noir, Metodo Classico Pecorino sparkling wine, and most recently, adding a new plot in Castel di Croce at the extreme elevation of 800 meters above sea level. Without overextending itself, the winery has taken large steady steps toward consolidating a venture that reflects well on the entire territory. Their brilliant, to say the least, Pecorino Artemisia gets its umpteenth Tre Bicchieri in 2017. It plays on fresh notes that range from lemon peel to freshly cut herbs with unusual touches of green anise on a palate that releases a genuine riot of drinkability and savory tension. Their 2017 Passerina Eden replicates this same style but with the obvious diversity of structure and persistence that reflects the innate character of the variety.

| | |
|---|---|
| ○ Offida Pecorino Artemisia '17 | ▼▼▼ 2* |
| ○ Eden '17 | ▼▼ 2* |
| ○ Mèroe Pecorino M. Cl. | ▼ 4 |
| ○ Offida Pecorino Artemisia '16 | ♀♀♀ 2* |
| ○ Offida Pecorino Artemisia '15 | ♀♀♀ 2* |
| ○ Offida Pecorino Artemisia '14 | ♀♀♀ 2* |
| ○ Offida Pecorino Artemisia '13 | ♀♀♀ 2* |
| ○ Offida Pecorino Artemisia '12 | ♀♀♀ 2* |
| ○ Eden '15 | ♀♀ 2* |
| ○ Eden '13 | ♀♀ 2* |
| ○ Eden '11 | ♀♀ 2* |
| ○ Offida Pecorino Artemisia '11 | ♀♀ 2* |

## La Staffa

VIA CASTELLARETTA, 19
60039 STAFFOLO [AN]
TEL. +39 0731779810
www.vinilastaffa.it

CELLAR SALES
PRE-BOOKED VISITS
ANNUAL PRODUCTION 45,000 bottles
HECTARES UNDER VINE 10.00
VITICULTURE METHOD Certified Organic

Though his lovely Verdicchio garnered attention quickly, young Riccardo Baldi isn't in a hurry. On Staffolo slopes, he carefully studies to see how time affects his choices both in the vineyard and the cellar. These decisions include separate harvesting of plots, spontaneous fermentation, and steel and cement for aging. Today's challenge is a Riserva from a vineyard situated between Cupramontana and Apiro. For different elevations there are different approaches, all leading to the creation of wine with a very personal style. The newly introduced 2015 Selva di Sotto Riserva has already established a small cult following. Despite a simplistically rustic nose, it wins you over with an expansive palate that infiltrates with forceful savoriness. Since you will have to wait a bit to be able to fully enjoy it, take advantage of the eager eloquence of their 2017 Verdicchio Superiore La Staffa or their 2017 L'Aurora, a Montepulciano rosé, which proves confident and tasty.

| | |
|---|---|
| ○ Castelli di Jesi Verdicchio Cl. Selva di Sotto Ris. '15 | 🏆🏆 8 |
| ☉ L'Aurora '17 | 🏆🏆 3 |
| ○ Verdicchio dei Castelli di Jesi Cl. Sup. La Staffa '17 | 🏆🏆 2* |
| ○ Mai Sentito | 🏆 2 |
| ○ Castelli di Jesi Verdicchio Cl. Rincrocca Ris. '15 | 🏆🏆 4 |
| ○ Verdicchio dei Castelli di Jesi Cl. '13 | 🏆🏆 2* |
| ○ Verdicchio dei Castelli di Jesi Cl. Sup. La Staffa '16 | 🏆🏆 2* |
| ○ Verdicchio dei Castelli di Jesi Cl. Sup. La Staffa '15 | 🏆🏆 3 |
| ○ Verdicchio dei Castelli di Jesi Cl. Sup. La Staffa '14 | 🏆🏆 3 |

## Tenuta di Tavignano

LOC. TAVIGNANO
62011 CINGOLI [MC]
TEL. +39 0733617303
www.tenutaditavignano.it

CELLAR SALES
PRE-BOOKED VISITS
ACCOMMODATION
ANNUAL PRODUCTION 100,000 bottles
HECTARES UNDER VINE 30.00
SUSTAINABLE WINERY

Established by Stefano Aymerich, Tenuta di Tavignano rests peacefully on a hill overlooking the valleys of the Esino and Musone rivers. Today his niece, Ondine de la Feld, leads a tightly-knit team that each year moves closer to the pantheon of Castelli di Jesi wineries. A large proportion of the vineyards are reserved for Verdicchio, naturally, but behind the Cingoli cellar can be found Montepulciano and other black grape varietals. The estate's ampelography comes through in a style that is full of flavor and energy. We've lost track of how many times their Verdicchio Misco has delivered savory elegance and 2017 is no exception. It overcame the problems of the scorching weather to earn yet another Tre Bicchieri. Top marks also for their 2016 Misco Riserva, which offers a soft, full palate and seduces with its notes of summer fruit and delicate minerals. And don't overlook their 2017 Villa Torre, whose varietal grace and harmonious palate compensate for its slighter structure.

| | |
|---|---|
| ○ Verdicchio dei Castelli di Jesi Cl. Sup. Misco '17 | 🏆🏆🏆 3* |
| ○ Castelli di Jesi Verdicchio Cl. Misco Ris. '16 | 🏆🏆 5 |
| ○ Verdicchio dei Castelli di Jesi Cl. Sup. Villa Torre '17 | 🏆🏆 3* |
| ● Rosso Piceno Cervidoni '16 | 🏆🏆 3 |
| ☉ Rosato '17 | 🏆 3 |
| ● Rosso Piceno Libenter '16 | 🏆 3 |
| ○ Verdicchio dei Castelli di Jesi Passito Sante Lancerio '15 | 🏆 5 |
| ○ Verdicchio dei Castelli di Jesi Cl. Sup. Misco '16 | 🏆🏆🏆 3* |
| ○ Verdicchio dei Castelli di Jesi Cl. Sup. Misco '15 | 🏆🏆🏆 3* |
| ○ Verdicchio dei Castelli di Jesi Cl. Sup. Misco '14 | 🏆🏆🏆 3* |

# Terra Fageto

VIA VALDASO, 52
63016 PEDASO [FM]
TEL. +39 0734931784
www.terrafageto.it

**CELLAR SALES**
**PRE-BOOKED VISITS**
**ANNUAL PRODUCTION** 100,000 bottles
**HECTARES UNDER VINE** 40.00
**VITICULTURE METHOD** Certified Organic

Claudio Di Ruscio's winery draws from three holdings in the Aso River valley. The oldest, and with a northern exposure, is in the municipality of Campofilone. It is dedicated mostly to white varieties, apart from a small amount of Sangiovese grown there. Another, Altidona faces south and is similarly dedicated to whites. Red varieties are largely cultivated at the third vineyard at Monte Serrone, which faces the Adriatic. All of the vine growing is done according to organic practices, while their wines are worked in their modern cellar in Pedosa. The 2017 Pecorino Fenèsia confirms its fairly obvious energy in citrus scents and in a slender palate that focuses on savoriness at the finish. This same fluidity is also found in their 2017 Letizia, a Passerina with a bit less overall energy. Their 2017 Falerio Eva gives good fruity definition and pleasant linearity, while their 2016 Rosso Piceno Rusus is a bit clenched with tannins but offers subtle elegance and crisp fruit.

| | |
|---|---|
| ○ Letizia Passerina '17 | 🏆🏆 2* |
| ○ Offida Pecorino Fenèsia '17 | 🏆🏆 3 |
| ● Rosso Piceno Rusus '15 | 🏆🏆 3 |
| ○ Falerio Eva '17 | 🏆 2 |
| ● Rosso Piceno Colle del Buffo '16 | 🏆 3 |
| ○ Letizia Passerina '16 | 🏆🏆 2* |
| ○ Offida Pecorino Fenèsia '16 | 🏆🏆 3 |
| ● Rosso Piceno Rusus '14 | 🏆🏆 3 |

# Terracruda

VIA SERRE, 28
61040 FRATTE ROSA [PU]
TEL. +39 0721777412
www.terracruda.it

**CELLAR SALES**
**PRE-BOOKED VISITS**
**ACCOMMODATION**
**ANNUAL PRODUCTION** 120,000 bottles
**HECTARES UNDER VINE** 24.00

Fratte Rosa is a charming village known for its terracotta and lovely position facing both the Metauro and Cesano River valleys. Historically, its gentle slopes have been planted with Aleatico, Sangiovese, and Bianchello. But when furniture maker Zeno Avenanti began he also planted Incrocio Bruni 54 and the rare Garofanata, at the suggestion of enologist Giancarlo Soverchia. Today, his son Luca leads a winery with a vineyard containing many varieties and a state-of-the-art cellar. The Bianchello stand out from among their uniformly very good range. Their 2015 Campodarchi Argento offer the depth and complexity that come with time and aging in small barrels. Their 2017 Boccalino gives notes of golden apples and yellow plums on a gentle, calm palate. Their 2017 Incrocio Bruni 54 proves one of the region's best for its citrusy verve and savoriness. And in their unusual 2106 Aleatico Ortaia, alternating pepper and violet lead to a palate well-calibrated in the distinctive aromatic profile of the variety.

| | |
|---|---|
| ○ Bianchello del Metauro Boccalino '17 | 🏆🏆 2* |
| ○ Bianchello del Metauro Campodarchi Argento '15 | 🏆🏆 3 |
| ○ Incrocio Bruni 54 '17 | 🏆🏆 3 |
| ● Pergola Aleatico Sup. Ortaia '16 | 🏆🏆 5 |
| ● Colli Pesaresi Sangiovese Olpe Ris. '15 | 🏆 4 |
| ○ Garofanata '15 | 🏆 3 |
| ● Colli Pesaresi Sangiovese Olpe Ris. '12 | 🏆🏆 5 |

# Fattoria Le Terrazze

VIA MUSONE, 4
60026 NUMANA [AN]
TEL. +39 0717390352
www.fattorialeterrazze.it

CELLAR SALES
PRE-BOOKED VISITS
ANNUAL PRODUCTION 100,000 bottles
HECTARES UNDER VINE 20.00

The history of Conero winemaking is palpable at Antonio and Georgina Terni's winery. It makes it easy to understand how late-ripening Montepulciano has adapted to this area. In fact, this grape variety has thrived enough in the warm climate of the Adriatic-facing promontory to become its main cultivar. A centuries-old manor sits atop a small gently-sloping hill surrounded by the property's vineyards and olive groves, there's even room for international varieties as well. A Montepulciano blend balanced by additions of equal amounts of Merlot and Syrah aged in small barrels, their 2013 Chaos tips their chart. The nose of red fruit and flowers is marked by slight vegetal traces, and on the palate, energetic flavor is revealed and embellished by a long, cohesive finish. Their 2015 Rosso Conero aged in large barrels, has a fruity balance and relaxed pace. Finally, Their 2017 Le Cave is a flavorful, savory, Chardonnay that expresses its decidedly varietal character in clear notes of yellow apple.

| | |
|---|---|
| ● Chaos '13 | 🍷🍷 5 |
| ○ Le Cave Chardonnay '17 | 🍷🍷 2* |
| ☉ Pink Fluid '17 | 🍷🍷 2* |
| ● Rosso Conero '15 | 🍷🍷 2* |
| ● Rosso Conero Praeludium '17 | 🍷 2 |
| ● Chaos '04 | 🍷🍷🍷 5 |
| ● Chaos '01 | 🍷🍷🍷 6 |
| ● Conero Sassi Neri Ris. '04 | 🍷🍷🍷 5 |
| ● Rosso Conero Sassi Neri '02 | 🍷🍷🍷 5 |
| ● Rosso Conero Visions of J '01 | 🍷🍷🍷 7 |
| ● Chaos '12 | 🍷🍷 5 |
| ● Chaos '11 | 🍷🍷 5 |
| ● Conero Sassi Neri Ris. '13 | 🍷🍷 5 |
| ● Rosso Conero Le Terrazze '13 | 🍷🍷 2* |
| ● Rosso Conero Praeludium '16 | 🍷🍷 2* |

# Terre Cortesi Moncaro

VIA PIANOLE, 7A
63036 MONTECAROTTO [AN]
TEL. +39 073189245
www.moncaro.com

CELLAR SALES
PRE-BOOKED VISITS
RESTAURANT SERVICE
ANNUAL PRODUCTION 7,500,000 bottles
HECTARES UNDER VINE 1200.00
VITICULTURE METHOD Certified Organic
SUSTAINABLE WINERY

Marche's largest cooperative has the enormous task of integrating the needs of winegrowers from the region's three most important districts (Castelli di Jesi, Conero and Piceno), and returning modern wines that are satisfyingly enjoyable and demonstrate technical reliability. Led by President Doriano Marchetti, Enologist Giuliano D'Ignazi and Agronomist Danilo Coppa, the team has worked together for many years, bringing deep-rooted expertise to what is undeniably Marche's largest winery. Their V. Novali skillfully overcomes the problems associated with 2014. Yellow peach, broom and a hint of orange peel hit the nose and remain subliminally on the creamy, flavorful palate through its very pleasant finish. Their young Verde Ca' Ruptea and Fondiglie offer the same explicit traces of fruit. Two well- designed Piceni, their 2017 Ofithe and 2011 Campo delle Mura, gamble on refined balance. Soft and pulpy, their 2015 Rosso Conero Montepasso also proves very successful.

| | |
|---|---|
| ○ Castelli di Jesi Verdicchio Cl. V. Novali Ris. '14 | 🍷🍷 4 |
| ○ Offida Pecorino Ofithe '17 | 🍷🍷 3 |
| ● Rosso Conero Montepasso '15 | 🍷🍷 3 |
| ● Rosso Piceno Sup. Campo delle Mura '11 | 🍷🍷 4 |
| ○ Verdicchio dei Castelli di Jesi Cl. Sup. Fondiglie '17 | 🍷🍷 3 |
| ○ Verdicchio dei Castelli di Jesi Cl. Sup. Verde Ca' Ruptea '17 | 🍷🍷 3 |
| ○ Verdicchio dei Castelli di Jesi Passito Tordiruta '11 | 🍷🍷 5 |
| ○ Verdicchio dei Castelli di Jesi Cl. Le Vele '17 | 🍷 3 |
| ○ Castelli di Jesi Verdicchio Cl. V. Novali Ris. '10 | 🍷🍷🍷 3* |
| ● Rosso Piceno Sup. Roccaviva '12 | 🍷🍷🍷 2* |
| ○ Offida Pecorino Ofithe '15 | 🍷🍷 3* |

# Tenuta dell' Ugolino

VIA COPPARONI, 32
60031 CASTELPLANIO [AN]
TEL. +39 07310731 812569
www.tenutaugolino.it

CELLAR SALES
PRE-BOOKED VISITS
ANNUAL PRODUCTION 50,000 bottles
HECTARES UNDER VINE 11.00
SUSTAINABLE WINERY

In 1993, Andrea Petrini realized that the quality of his table wine had become too high to sell in bulk; it was time to move to the next level. In keeping with his focused and reserved character, he began producing a conservative 3500 bottles. In small incremental steps he then expanded, resolutely supported by enologist Aroldo Bellelli and his alter ego Matteo Foroni. Today, the Verdicchio coming out of this small Castelplanio cellar is an icon of classic style, perfectly matching the varietal ideal. Vigneto del Balluccio is named after its cru and their 2016 is very likely their best ever. The nose gives off elegant notes of citrus peel, subtle hints of botrytis and a touch of aromatic herbs followed by an expansive, flavorful palate with a gentle and inviting finish. Their 2017 Piaiole offers a truly fresh, citrusy nose that is repeated on a perfectly flowing palate. Both Verdicchio age in steel vats.

| | |
|---|---|
| ○ Verdicchio dei Castelli di Jesi Cl. Sup. Vign. del Balluccio '16 | ♟♟ 3* |
| ○ Verdicchio dei Castelli di Jesi Cl. Le Piaole '17 | ♟♟ 2* |
| ○ Verdicchio dei Castelli di Jesi Cl. Le Piaole '16 | ♟♟ 2* |
| ○ Verdicchio dei Castelli di Jesi Cl. Le Piaole '15 | ♟♟ 2* |
| ○ Verdicchio dei Castelli di Jesi Cl. Sup. Vign. del Balluccio '14 | ♟♟ 3 |
| ○ Verdicchio dei Castelli di Jesi Cl. Sup. Vign. del Balluccio '13 | ♟♟ 3 |
| ○ Verdicchio dei Castelli di Jesi Cl. Sup. Vign. del Balluccio '12 | ♟♟ 3* |

# ★Umani Ronchi

VIA ADRIATICA, 12
60027 OSIMO [AN]
TEL. +39 0717108019
www.umanironchi.com

CELLAR SALES
PRE-BOOKED VISITS
ANNUAL PRODUCTION 2,900,000 bottles
HECTARES UNDER VINE 240.00
VITICULTURE METHOD Certified Organic
SUSTAINABLE WINERY

Michele Bernetti is firmly in charge of the winery established by his father, Massimo, and uncle, Stefano, at the start of the 1960s. Umani Ronchi is one of Marche's internationally known wineries, guaranteeing across-the-board quality that reaches excellence in more than one of its wines. The two main varieties are without question Verdicchio from Castelli di Jesi and Montepulciano from Conero and Abruzzo. Of further note is the fact that for some time now, the majority of the cultivated area has been managed organically. Their 2016 Verdicchio V.V. Earns its umpteenth Tre Bicchiere with a nose that mixes flowers and hazelnut followed by an expansive palate that beguiles to its long finish. Just a bit below are their 2016 Centovie, a Pecorino of refined complexity and 2017 Casaldiserra, offering an inviting palate with fragrant fruity vitality. Their entire range, from their 2012 La Hoz Nature sparkling wine to their 2015 Plenio Riserva, proves reliable for consistently high quality.

| | |
|---|---|
| ○ Verdicchio dei Castelli di Jesi Cl. Sup. V. V. '16 | ♟♟♟ 4* |
| ○ Castelli di Jesi Verdicchio Cl. Plenio Ris. '15 | ♟♟ 4 |
| ○ Centovie Pecorino '16 | ♟♟ 4 |
| ○ La Hoz Brut Nature M.Cl. '12 | ♟♟ 5 |
| ○ Verdicchio dei Castelli di Jesi Cl. Sup. Casal di Serra '17 | ♟♟ 3* |
| ● Conero Campo San Giorgio Ris. '13 | ♟♟ 7 |
| ○ Extra Brut M. Cl. | ♟♟ 4 |
| ⊙ La Hoz Nature M.Cl. Rosé | ♟♟ 5 |
| ○ Maximo '16 | ♟♟ 4 |
| ● Montepulciano d'Abruzzo Jorio '16 | ♟♟ 3 |
| ● Pelago '14 | ♟♟ 5 |
| ● Rosso Conero San Lorenzo '16 | ♟♟ 3 |
| ● Rosso Conero Serrano '17 | ♟♟ 2* |
| ● Conero Campo San Giorgio Ris. '11 | ♟♟♟ 7 |

## La Valle del Sole

VIA SAN LAZZARO, 46
63035 OFFIDA [AP]
TEL. +39 0736889658
valledelsoleoffida@gmail.com

**PRE-BOOKED VISITS**
**ANNUAL PRODUCTION** 25,000 bottles
**HECTARES UNDER VINE** 11.00
**VITICULTURE METHOD** Certified Organic

The Di Nicolò family have been operating in Valle del Sole for many years. Set in an enchanting corner of Piceno -- not coincidentally the heart of southern Marche's most important appellation -- their property includes space for hospitality, an inn, and the cellar. Young Alessia and father Silvano take care of wine production, creating wines that are aromatically well-defined and possessing a generous structure that is faithful to local tradition. Their fresh and spontaneous 2016 Rosso Piceno Superiore releases well-focused notes of sour cherry that link to the Montepulciano, which adds its own delicious, spiced aspect. The palate moves in the same nimble and tasty style. As usual, their 2017 Offida Pecorino exhibits an indisputable richness that becomes full-on flavor softened by aromatic herbs at the finish. Their 2017 Passerina is distinguished by its refreshing and pleasantly acidic palate.

| | |
|---|---|
| ● Rosso Piceno Sup. '16 | 🍷🍷 3* |
| ○ Offida Pecorino '17 | 🍷🍷 3 |
| ○ Passerina '17 | 🍷 2 |
| ○ Offida Pecorino '16 | 🍷🍷 3 |
| ○ Offida Pecorino '15 | 🍷🍷 2* |
| ○ Offida Pecorino '11 | 🍷🍷 2* |
| ● Offida Rosso '14 | 🍷🍷 4 |
| ○ Passerina '16 | 🍷🍷 2* |
| ● Rosso Piceno Sup. '15 | 🍷🍷 3 |
| ● Rosso Piceno Sup. '14 | 🍷🍷 2* |

## Vigneti Vallorani

C.DA LA ROCCA, 28
63079 COLLI DEL TRONTO [AP]
TEL. +39 3477305485
www.vignetivallorani.com

**CELLAR SALES**
**PRE-BOOKED VISITS**
**ANNUAL PRODUCTION** 25,000 bottles
**HECTARES UNDER VINE** 6.00
**VITICULTURE METHOD** Certified Organic

Having completed his enological studies, Rocco Vallorani returned home to establish a small cellar under his father's house, and with help from brother Stefano, tend the vineyards that belonged to their grandparents. The old parcels host single traditional varieties that with spontaneous fermentation and patient aging are shaping wines of refined originality. With the use of small wood barrels paired with a long stay on fine lees, the most ambitious wines are allowed to age with ease, adding to their aromatic complexity. A blend of Trebbiano and Malvasia, their 2016 LeFric reflects its rustic heritage in its notes of hazelnut, its expansive savoriness and, above all, its spontaneous style. Their 2014 Rosso Piceno Polisia reveals hints of minerals, leather and ash, reconfirmed on the slightly salty palate. Their 2014 Offida Passerina Zaccarì expresses its aging in mid-sized casks with notes of dried fruit and nuts, adding traces of aromatic herbs before a relaxed, flavorful palate.

| | |
|---|---|
| ○ Falerio Avora '16 | 🍷🍷 3 |
| ○ LeFric '16 | 🍷🍷 3 |
| ○ Offida Passerina Zaccarì '14 | 🍷🍷 5 |
| ● Rosso Piceno Sup. Polisia '14 | 🍷🍷 3 |
| ○ Falerio Avora '11 | 🍷🍷 2* |
| ● Rosso Piceno Sup. Konè '11 | 🍷🍷 4 |
| ● Sorlivio '10 | 🍷🍷 6 |
| ○ Falerio Avora '12 | 🍷 3 |

# ★Velenosi

LOC. MONTICELLI
VIA DEI BIANCOSPINI, 11
63100 ASCOLI PICENO
TEL. +39 0736341218
www.velenosivini.com

**CELLAR SALES**
**PRE-BOOKED VISITS**
**ANNUAL PRODUCTION** 2,500,000 bottles
**HECTARES UNDER VINE** 192.00

Anyone who has met Angela Velenosi knows she is always ready to confront a new challenge head on. Some years ago she bet on Marche's traditional cultivars, including Percorino, Verdicchio, Montepulciano, Sangiovese and Lacrima Nera. Their first certified organic wines came out only last year. With the recent addition of plots in Controguerra, the estate now crosses the Tronto River, giving rise to a new selection, Prope, comprising Abruzzo's main appellations. The unquestioned star of a vast range, their 2015 Roggio del Filare offers crisp aromas of fruit and reveals well-defined layers on a powerful palate built on perfect alcohol levels and tannic richness. Their 2016 Rêve delivers delicious aromas of bitter orange peel and grapefruit which reappear in its racy, saline palate and pyrotechnic finish.

| | | |
|---|---|---|
| ● Rosso Piceno Sup. | | |
| Roggio del Filare '15 | ♟♟♟ | 6 |
| ○ Offida Pecorino Rêve '16 | ♟♟ | 5 |
| ● Offida Rosso Ludi '15 | ♟♟ | 6 |
| ○ Falerio V. Solaria '17 | ♟♟ | 3 |
| ● Lacrima di Morro d'Alba | | |
| Querciantica '17 | ♟♟ | 3 |
| ● Lacrima di Morro d'Alba Sup. | | |
| Querciantica '17 | ♟♟ | 3 |
| ● Montepulciano d'Abruzzo Prope '16 | ♟♟ | 3 |
| ○ Offida Pecorino Villa Angela '17 | ♟♟ | 3 |
| ○ Prope Pecorino '17 | ♟♟ | 3 |
| ● Rosso Piceno Sup. Bio '16 | ♟♟ | 3 |
| ● Rosso Piceno Sup. Brecciarolo '16 | ♟♟ | 2* |
| ○ Verdicchio dei Castelli di Jesi Cl. | | |
| Querciantica '17 | ♟♟ | 3 |
| ● Rosso Piceno Sup. | | |
| Roggio del Filare '14 | ♟♟♟ | 6 |

# Roberto Venturi

VIA CASE NUOVE, 1A
60010 CASTELLEONE DI SUASA [AN]
TEL. +39 3381855566
www.viniventuri.it

**CELLAR SALES**
**PRE-BOOKED VISITS**
**ANNUAL PRODUCTION** 60,000 bottles
**HECTARES UNDER VINE** 8.00

Roberto Venturi is in Castelleone di Suasa, at the northern limit of the Castelli di Jesi appellation, but outside of its classic heart. The vineyards are devoted to Verdicchio, Moscato, Montepulciano and Aleatico (locally called Balsamina). Grapes coming from the approximately one hectare in Montecarotto are used to produce their celebrated Qudi. Only steel is used in the cellar to enhance the freshness of the grape's characteristics. The few small wood barrels are reserved for Squarciafico, an ambitious monovarietal Montepulciano. Their 2016 Qudi gives off well-defined aromas that start out citrusy before turning toward more expected sweet almond and anise. The palate's success comes from a play between the creamier, more flavorful side and the more saline backbone which reenforces it and gives power to the finish. Their 2017 Desiderio, following the same progression but in a simpler way, is made pleasantly approachable by aromatic Muscat grapes. Their 2017 St. Martino offers a pleasant palate.

| | | |
|---|---|---|
| ○ Verdicchio dei Castelli di Jesi Cl. Sup. | | |
| Qudi '16 | ♟♟ | 3* |
| ○ Desiderio '17 | ♟ | 3 |
| ○ Verdicchio dei Castelli di Jesi | | |
| San Martino '17 | ♟ | 2 |
| ○ Verdicchio dei Castelli di Jesi Cl. Sup. | | |
| Qudi '15 | ♟♟♟ | 3* |
| ○ Verdicchio dei Castelli di Jesi Cl. Sup. | | |
| Qudi '13 | ♟♟♟ | 2* |
| ● Balsamino '16 | ♟♟ | 2* |
| ○ Desiderio '16 | ♟♟ | 2* |
| ○ Verdicchio dei Castelli di Jesi | | |
| San Martino '15 | ♟♟ | 2* |

# Vicari

via Pozzo Buono, 3
60030 Morro d'Alba [AN]
Tel. +39 073163164
www.vicarivini.it

CELLAR SALES
PRE-BOOKED VISITS
ANNUAL PRODUCTION 120,000 bottles
HECTARES UNDER VINE 28.00

The Vicari family has invested heavily in modernizing every aspect of its winery. Starting in the vineyards, several of the Pozzo Buono parcels have been extended, adding more Verdicchio and Lacrima Nera over the last few years. Internal spaces have been proportioned to emphasize the wine shop and the tasting room that overlooks the estate. But Vico's efforts in technical management and Valentina's promotional activities are carried out with the same high level of enthusiasm as always, reflecting a fundamental part of the winery's continued success. Their 2016 Lacrima del Pozzo Buono exemplifies Vicari's rich and powerful style. Incredibly dark, its intoxicating notes of sour cherry unwind on a dense and glossy, almost creamy, palate. A definite softness also pervades their 2017 Dasempre, offering direct fruity pleasantness. Their 2016 Verdicchio Insolito presents aromas of hazelnuts and a robust palate, whereas their 2015 Metodo Classico Sfumature proves decidedly original.

| | |
|---|---|
| ● Lacrima di Morro d'Alba Sup. del Pozzo Buono '16 | ♟♟ 4 |
| ⊙ Sfumature del Pozzo Buono Brut M. Cl. Rosé '15 | ♟♟ 5 |
| ○ Verdicchio dei Castelli di Jesi Cl. del Pozzo Buono '17 | ♟♟ 2* |
| ○ Verdicchio dei Castelli di Jesi Cl. Sup. L'Insolito del Pozzo Buono '16 | ♟♟ 3 |
| ● Lacrima di Morro d'Alba Dasempre del Pozzo Buono '17 | ♟ 2 |
| ○ Verdicchio dei Castelli di Jesi Cl. Sup. Insolito del Pozzo Buono '15 | ♟♟♟ 3* |
| ● Lacrima di Morro d'Alba Essenza del Pozzo Buono '16 | ♟♟ 3* |

# Vignamato

via Battinebbia, 4
60038 San Paolo di Jesi [AN]
Tel. +39 0731779197
www.vignamato.com

CELLAR SALES
PRE-BOOKED VISITS
ANNUAL PRODUCTION 100,000 bottles
HECTARES UNDER VINE 27.00

Maurizio Ceci recognizes how well his son Andrea grasps things and he is giving him increasing independence to make decisions in the winery. In this way, he is completing a cycle that began when he received the cellar keys from his own father. In fact, his father Amato was one of the first in the Verdicchio universe to make a move beyond simply growing grapes, and to try his luck at producing wine himself. The most recent generation is profitting from what he began by working with enologist Pierluigi Lorenzetti to continually improve white wines that are full of flavor and new energy. Careful use of small barrels makes their 2015 Ambrosia a brilliant Verdicchio Riserva, uniting complexity, juice and flavor without excessive glycerine. However, their 2017 Verdicchio Superiore Versiano proves even more impressive with nuances of anise and flowers on a long, persistent, saline palate. A straightforward, iodized verve also characterizes their 2017 Valle delle Lame, while their citrine 2017 Antares, an Incrocio Manzoni 54, is very fresh and vigorous.

| | |
|---|---|
| ○ Castelli di Jesi Verdicchio Cl. Ambrosia Ris. '15 | ♟♟ 3* |
| ○ Verdicchio dei Castelli di Jesi Cl. Sup. Versiano '17 | ♟♟ 3* |
| ● Campalliano '15 | ♟♟ 3 |
| ○ Verdicchio dei Castelli di Jesi Cl. Valle delle Lame '17 | ♟♟ 2* |
| ○ Verdicchio dei Castelli di Jesi Passito Antares '15 | ♟♟ 4 |
| ○ Versus '17 | ♟♟ 2* |
| ⊙ Ale Rosé Brut | ♟ 3 |
| ○ Castelli di Jesi Verdicchio Cl. Ambrosia Ris. '13 | ♟♟ 3* |
| ○ Verdicchio dei Castelli di Jesi Cl. Sup. Eos '16 | ♟♟ 2* |
| ○ Verdicchio dei Castelli di Jesi Cl. Sup. Versiano '16 | ♟♟ 3 |

## Buscareto

FRAZ. PIANELLO
VIA SAN GREGORIO, 66
60010 OSTRA [AN]
TEL. +39 0717988020
www.buscareto.com

CELLAR SALES
PRE-BOOKED VISITS
ANNUAL PRODUCTION 250,000 bottles
HECTARES UNDER VINE 40.00

| | |
|---|---|
| ● Bisaccione '15 | ♟♟ 5 |
| ● Lacrima di Morro d'Alba '17 | ♟♟ 2* |
| ● Lacrima di Morro d'Alba Sup. Compagnia '16 | ♟ 5 |

## Ca' Liptra

VIA SAN MICHELE, 21
60034 CUPRAMONTANA [AN]
TEL. +39 3491321442
www.caliptra.it

CELLAR SALES
PRE-BOOKED VISITS
HECTARES UNDER VINE 2.30
VITICULTURE METHOD Certified Organic
SUSTAINABLE WINERY

| | |
|---|---|
| ○ Caliptra '17 | ♟♟ 2* |
| ○ Verdicchio dei Castelli di Jesi Cl. Sup. Kypra '17 | ♟♟ 3 |
| ○ Le Lute Dosaggio Zero M. Cl. | ♟ 5 |

## La Calcinara

FRAZ. CANDIA
VIA CALCINARA, 102A
60131 ANCONA
TEL. +39 3285552643
www.lacalcinara.it

CELLAR SALES
PRE-BOOKED VISITS
ANNUAL PRODUCTION 42,000 bottles
HECTARES UNDER VINE 13.00
SUSTAINABLE WINERY

| | |
|---|---|
| ● Conero Folle Ris. '13 | ♟♟ 5 |
| ● Rosso Conero Il Cacciatore di Sogni '16 | ♟♟ 3 |
| ● Conero Terra Calcinara Ris. '15 | ♟ 3 |

## Campo di Maggio

FRAZ. PAGLIARE DEL TRONTO
VIA FORMALE, 24
63078 SPINETOLI [AP]
TEL. +39 3204804086
www.cantinacampodimaggio.it

CELLAR SALES
PRE-BOOKED VISITS
ANNUAL PRODUCTION 30,000 bottles
HECTARES UNDER VINE 7.00
VITICULTURE METHOD Certified Organic

| | |
|---|---|
| ○ Offida Pecorino Cardofonte '16 | ♟♟ 5 |
| ● Rosso Piceno '17 | ♟♟ 2* |
| ● Rosso Piceno Sup. '13 | ♟♟ 2* |
| ○ Falerio '17 | ♟ 2 |

## La Canosa

C.DA SAN PIETRO, 6
63071 ROTELLA [AP]
TEL. +39 0736374556
www.lacanosaagricola.it

CELLAR SALES
PRE-BOOKED VISITS
ACCOMMODATION
ANNUAL PRODUCTION 150,000 bottles
HECTARES UNDER VINE 28.00

| | |
|---|---|
| ● Musè '16 | ♟♟ 3 |
| ○ Offida Passerina Servator '17 | ♟♟ 2* |
| ○ Offida Pecorino Pekò '17 | ♟ 2 |
| ● Rosso Piceno Sup. Nummaria '16 | ♟ 2 |

## Le Cantine di Figaro

C.DA COLLE DEL GIGLIO
63065 RIPATRANSONE [AP]
TEL. +39 0690623140
www.lecantinedifigaro.it

PRE-BOOKED VISITS
ANNUAL PRODUCTION 25,000 bottles
HECTARES UNDER VINE 7.00
VITICULTURE METHOD Certified Organic
SUSTAINABLE WINERY

| | |
|---|---|
| ○ Falerio Pecorino Letix '17 | ♟♟ 2* |
| ○ Santa Prisca '17 | ♟♟ 2* |
| ● Abusivo '16 | ♟ 3 |
| ● Rosso Piceno Sup. Del Carrettiere '15 | ♟ 3 |

## Cavalieri

VIA RAFFAELLO, 1
62024 MATELICA [MC]
TEL. +39 073784859
www.cantinacavalieri.it

PRE-BOOKED VISITS
ANNUAL PRODUCTION 15,000 bottles
HECTARES UNDER VINE 8.24

| | | |
|---|---|---|
| ○ Verdicchio di Matelica Fornacione '16 | ♥♥ | 3 |
| ○ Verdicchio di Matelica Gegè '15 | ♥♥ | 3 |
| ○ Verdicchio di Matelica '17 | ♥ | 2 |

## Colleminò

VIA MONTEGRANALE, 19
60035 JESI [AN]
TEL. +39 073158686
www.collemino.it

ANNUAL PRODUCTION 6,000 bottles
HECTARES UNDER VINE 5.50

| | | |
|---|---|---|
| ○ Verdicchio dei Castelli di Jesi Cl. Mittera '17 | ♥♥ | 2* |
| ○ Veridio '17 | ♥♥ | 3 |

## Cantina dei Colli Ripani

C.DA TOSCIANO, 28
63065 RIPATRANSONE [AP]
TEL. +39 07359505
www.colliripani.it

CELLAR SALES
PRE-BOOKED VISITS
ANNUAL PRODUCTION 1,300,000 bottles
HECTARES UNDER VINE 650.00
VITICULTURE METHOD Certified Organic

| | | |
|---|---|---|
| ○ Falerio Pecorino Cap. 9 '17 | ♥♥ | 2* |
| ○ Offida Passerina Lajella '17 | ♥ | 2 |
| ○ Offida Pecorino Mercantino '17 | ♥ | 2 |
| ● Rosso Piceno Sup. Castellano '15 | ♥ | 2 |

## Colpaola

LOC. COLPAOLA
FRAZ. BRACCANO
62024 MATELICA [MC]
TEL. +39 0737768300
www.cantinacolpaola.it

CELLAR SALES
ANNUAL PRODUCTION 18,000 bottles
HECTARES UNDER VINE 9.00
VITICULTURE METHOD Certified Organic

| | | |
|---|---|---|
| ○ Verdicchio di Matelica '17 | ♥♥ | 2* |

## Conventino Monteciccardo

LOC. CONVENTINO
VIA GIULIO TURCATO, 4
61024 MONTECICCARDO [PU]
TEL. +39 0721910574
www.il-conventino.it

CELLAR SALES
PRE-BOOKED VISITS
ANNUAL PRODUCTION 80,000 bottles
HECTARES UNDER VINE 10.00
VITICULTURE METHOD Certified Organic
SUSTAINABLE WINERY

| | | |
|---|---|---|
| ● Colli Pesaresi Sangiovese Cardomagno Ris. '14 | ♥♥ | 4 |
| ○ Bianchello del Metauro Le Fratte '17 | ♥ | 2 |

## Fioretti Brera

VIA DELLA STAZIONE, 48
60022 CASTELFIDARDO [AN]
TEL. +39 335373896
www.fiorettibrera.it

ANNUAL PRODUCTION 10,000 bottles
HECTARES UNDER VINE 3.50
VITICULTURE METHOD Certified Organic

| | | |
|---|---|---|
| ● Conero Rigo 23 Ris. '15 | ♥♥ | 5 |
| ● Rosso Conero Fausti '15 | ♥♥ | 3 |
| ○ Arghilos '15 | ♥ | 3 |

## Piergiovanni Giusti

LOC. MONTIGNANO
VIA CASTELLARO, 97
60019 SENIGALLIA [AN]
TEL. +39 071918031
www.lacrimagiusti.it

CELLAR SALES
PRE-BOOKED VISITS
ANNUAL PRODUCTION 51,000 bottles
HECTARES UNDER VINE 13.00

| | |
|---|---|
| ⊙ Anima Rosa '17 | 🍷🍷 2* |
| ● Lacrima di Morro d'Alba '17 | 🍷🍷 3 |
| ○ Di Ele '17 | 🍷 2 |
| ● L'Intruso '15 | 🍷 2 |

## Esther Hauser

C.DA CORONCINO, 1A
60039 STAFFOLO [AN]
TEL. +39 0731770203
www.estherhauser.it

CELLAR SALES
PRE-BOOKED VISITS
ANNUAL PRODUCTION 6,000 bottles
HECTARES UNDER VINE 1.00

| | |
|---|---|
| ● Il Cupo '15 | 🍷🍷 5 |
| ● Il Ceppo '15 | 🍷🍷 4 |

## Conte Leopardi Dittajuti

VIA MARINA II, 24
60026 NUMANA [AN]
TEL. +39 0717390116
www.conteleopardi.it

CELLAR SALES
PRE-BOOKED VISITS
ANNUAL PRODUCTION 350,000 bottles
HECTARES UNDER VINE 49.00

| | |
|---|---|
| ● Conero Pigmento Ris. '15 | 🍷🍷 5 |
| ○ Bianco del Coppo '17 | 🍷 2 |
| ● Rose del Coppo '17 | 🍷 2 |
| ● Rosso Conero Fructus '17 | 🍷 2 |

## Laila Libenzi

VIA SAN FILIPPO SUL CESANO, 27
61040 MONDAVIO [PU]
TEL. +39 0721979353
www.lailalibenzi.it

CELLAR SALES
PRE-BOOKED VISITS
ANNUAL PRODUCTION 130,000 bottles
HECTARES UNDER VINE 33.00

| | |
|---|---|
| ● Rosso Piceno Rubideo '16 | 🍷🍷 2* |
| ○ Verdicchio dei Castelli di Jesi Baccaloro '17 | 🍷🍷 2* |
| ○ Primo Latere '17 | 🍷 2 |

## Roberto Lucarelli

LOC. RIPALTA
VIA PIANA, 20
61030 CARTOCETO [PU]
TEL. +39 0721893019
www.laripe.com

CELLAR SALES
PRE-BOOKED VISITS
ANNUAL PRODUCTION 200,000 bottles
HECTARES UNDER VINE 32.00

| | |
|---|---|
| ○ Bianchello del Metauro La Ripe '17 | 🍷🍷 2* |
| ○ Bianchello del Metauro Sup. Rocho '17 | 🍷🍷 2* |
| ○ Colli Pesaresi Bianco L'Albareale '17 | 🍷 2 |
| ● Colli Pesaresi Sangiovese Goccione '15 | 🍷 3 |

## Mario Lucchetti

VIA SANTA MARIA DEL FIORE, 17
60030 MORRO D'ALBA [AN]
TEL. +39 073163314
www.mariolucchetti.it

CELLAR SALES
PRE-BOOKED VISITS
ANNUAL PRODUCTION 150,000 bottles
HECTARES UNDER VINE 25.00

| | |
|---|---|
| ● Lacrima di Morro d'Alba Mariasole '16 | 🍷🍷 6 |
| ● Lacrima di Morro d'Alba Sup. Guardengo '16 | 🍷🍷 3 |
| ● Lacrima di Morro d'Alba Fiore '17 | 🍷 2 |

## Ma.Ri.Ca.

VIA ACQUASANTA, 7
60030 BELVEDERE OSTRENSE [AN]
TEL. +39 0731290091
www.cantinamarica.it

CELLAR SALES
PRE-BOOKED VISITS
ANNUAL PRODUCTION 50,000 bottles
HECTARES UNDER VINE 18.00
SUSTAINABLE WINERY

| | |
|---|---|
| ● Lacrima di Morro d'Alba Ramosceto '17 | 🍷 2* |
| ● Lacrima di Morro d'Alba Sup. Castello di Ramosceto '16 | 🍷 3 |

## Maroni

C.DA CIAFONE, 104
63073 OFFIDA [AP]
TEL. +39 3331381166
www.vinimaroni.it

CELLAR SALES
ANNUAL PRODUCTION 5,000 bottles
HECTARES UNDER VINE 11.00
VITICULTURE METHOD Certified Organic

| | |
|---|---|
| ● Moretto '15 | 🍷 5 |
| ○ Offida Pecorino Crociaiolo '17 | 🍷 3 |
| ○ Passerina '17 | 🍷 2 |
| ● Rosso Piceno Domenic '17 | 🍷 2 |

## Valter Mattoni

VIA PESCOLLA, 1
63030 CASTORANO [AP]
TEL. +39 073687329
www.valtermattoni.it

CELLAR SALES
PRE-BOOKED VISITS
ANNUAL PRODUCTION 6,500 bottles
HECTARES UNDER VINE 3.50

| | |
|---|---|
| ● Rossobordò '15 | 🍷 8 |
| ○ Trebbien '16 | 🍷 4 |

## Enzo Mecella

VIA DANTE, 112
60044 FABRIANO [AN]
TEL. +39 073221680
www.enzomecella.com

CELLAR SALES
PRE-BOOKED VISITS
ANNUAL PRODUCTION 90,000 bottles
HECTARES UNDER VINE 12.00

| | |
|---|---|
| ● Conero Rubelliano Ris. '13 | 🍷 5 |
| ○ Epilogo Brut M. Cl. | 🍷 6 |
| ○ Verdicchio di Matelica Casa Fosca Sotto le Querce '17 | 🍷 3 |

## Federico Mencaroni

VIA OLMIGRANDI, 72
60013 CORINALDO [AN]
TEL. +39 0717975625
www.mencaroni.eu

PRE-BOOKED VISITS
ANNUAL PRODUCTION 30,000 bottles
HECTARES UNDER VINE 7.50

| | |
|---|---|
| ○ Verdicchio dei Castelli di Jesi Contatto Brut M. Cl. '13 | 🍷 4 |
| ○ Verdicchio dei Castelli di Jesi Isola '16 | 🍷 3 |

## Claudio Morelli

V.LE ROMAGNA, 47B
61032 FANO [PU]
TEL. +39 0721823352
www.claudiomorelli.it

CELLAR SALES
PRE-BOOKED VISITS
ANNUAL PRODUCTION 110,000 bottles
HECTARES UNDER VINE 40.00

| | |
|---|---|
| ○ Bianchello del Metauro Sup. Borgo Torre '17 | 🍷 2* |
| ○ Bianchello del Metauro La Vigna delle Terrazze '17 | 🍷 2 |

## Fattoria Nannì

C.DA ARSICCI
62021 APIRO [MC]
TEL. +39 3406225930
www.fattoriananni.it

CELLAR SALES
PRE-BOOKED VISITS
ANNUAL PRODUCTION 11,000 bottles
HECTARES UNDER VINE
VITICULTURE METHOD Certified Organic

| | | |
|---|---|---|
| ○ Verdicchio dei Castelli di Jesi Cl. Sup. Origini '17 | | 🍷🍷 3 |

## Alberto Quacquarini

VIA COLLI, 1
62020 SERRAPETRONA [MC]
TEL. +39 0733908180
www.quacquarini.it

CELLAR SALES
ANNUAL PRODUCTION 180,000 bottles
HECTARES UNDER VINE 35.00

| | | |
|---|---|---|
| ● Serrapetrona '16 | | 🍷🍷 3 |
| ● Vernaccia di Serrapetrona Secco | | 🍷🍷 3 |
| ● Petronio '14 | | 🍷 5 |
| ● Vernaccia di Serrapetrona Dolce | | 🍷 3 |

## Ripawine

FONTE ABECETO, 34
63065 RIPATRANSONE [AP]
TEL. +39 3331419368
info@ripawine.it

CELLAR SALES
ANNUAL PRODUCTION 10,000 bottles
HECTARES UNDER VINE 30.00
VITICULTURE METHOD Certified Organic

| | | |
|---|---|---|
| ● Offida Rosso Klausura '14 | | 🍷🍷 5 |
| ● Rosso Piceno Sup. Trufo '16 | | 🍷🍷 5 |
| ● Moro Matto '16 | | 🍷 5 |
| ○ Offida Pecorino Geko '17 | | 🍷 5 |

## Rocca di Castiglioni

C.DA CASTIGLIONI, 50
63072 CASTIGNANO [AP]
TEL. +39 0736821876
www.rocca-di-castiglioni.it

CELLAR SALES
PRE-BOOKED VISITS
ACCOMMODATION
ANNUAL PRODUCTION 25,000 bottles
HECTARES UNDER VINE 13.00
VITICULTURE METHOD Certified Organic

| | | |
|---|---|---|
| ○ Offida Passerina Alba Plena '17 | | 🍷🍷 3 |
| ○ Offida Pecorino Valeo Si Vales '17 | | 🍷🍷 3 |

## San Michele a Ripa

C.DA SAN MICHELE, 24
63065 RIPATRANSONE [AP]
TEL. +39 3356833088
www.sanmichelearipa.it

CELLAR SALES
PRE-BOOKED VISITS
ANNUAL PRODUCTION 20,000 bottles
HECTARES UNDER VINE 5.00
VITICULTURE METHOD Certified Organic

| | | |
|---|---|---|
| ○ Offida Passerina Brancuna '17 | | 🍷🍷 3 |
| ○ Offida Pecorino Falchetti '17 | | 🍷🍷 3 |
| ⊙ Rosé '17 | | 🍷 3 |

## Alberto Serenelli

LOC. PIETRALACROCE
VIA BARTOLINI, 2
60129 ANCONA
TEL. +39 07135505
www.albertoserenelli.com

CELLAR SALES
PRE-BOOKED VISITS
ANNUAL PRODUCTION 30,000 bottles
HECTARES UNDER VINE 7.00

| | | |
|---|---|---|
| ● Boranico '16 | | 🍷🍷 6 |
| ● Rosso Conero Marro '13 | | 🍷🍷 4 |
| ● Rosso Conero Varano 30 Anni '15 | | 🍷 8 |

### Silvano Strologo

VIA OSIMANA, 89
60021 CAMERANO [AN]
TEL. +39 071731104
www.vinisilvanostrologo.it

CELLAR SALES
PRE-BOOKED VISITS
ANNUAL PRODUCTION 70,000 bottles
HECTARES UNDER VINE 14.00

| | | |
|---|---|---|
| ● Rosso Conero Decebalo Ris. '13 | ♙♙ | 4 |
| ● Rosso Conero Julius '16 | ♙♙ | 2* |
| ● Rosso Conero Traiano '13 | ♙ | 4 |

### Le Vigne di Clementina Fabi

C.DA FRANILE, 3
63069 MONTEDINOVE [AP]
TEL. +39 338 7463441
www.levignediclementinafabi.it

CELLAR SALES
PRE-BOOKED VISITS
ACCOMMODATION
ANNUAL PRODUCTION 60,000 bottles
HECTARES UNDER VINE 10.00
VITICULTURE METHOD Certified Organic

| | | |
|---|---|---|
| ○ Offida Passerina Cerì '17 | ♙♙ | 3 |
| ○ Offida Pecorino Cerì '17 | ♙♙ | 3 |
| ○ Offida Passerina '17 | ♙ | 2 |
| ○ Terre di Offida Passerina Brut | ♙ | 3 |

### Le Vigne di Franca

C.DA SANTA PETRONILLA, 69
63900 FERMO
TEL. +39 3356512938
www.levignedifranca.it

ANNUAL PRODUCTION 30,000 bottles
HECTARES UNDER VINE 4.50

| | | |
|---|---|---|
| ● Crismon '15 | ♙♙ | 3 |
| ● Rubrum '15 | ♙♙ | 2* |

### Villa Forano

C.DA FORANO, 40
62010 APPIGNANO [MC]
TEL. +39 073357102
www.villaforano.it

CELLAR SALES
PRE-BOOKED VISITS
ANNUAL PRODUCTION 40,000 bottles
HECTARES UNDER VINE 20.00

| | | |
|---|---|---|
| ○ Colli Maceratesi Ribona Le Piagge '17 | ♙♙ | 2* |
| ● Colli Maceratesi Rosso Montelipa '15 | ♙♙ | 2* |
| ● Colli Maceratesi Rosso Almajano Ris. '12 | ♙ | 4 |

### Villa Lazzarini

C.DA COLLEVAGO
62010 TREIA [MC]
TEL. +39 3333553460
www.villalazzarini-vini.it

ANNUAL PRODUCTION 60,000 bottles
HECTARES UNDER VINE 8.00

| | | |
|---|---|---|
| ● Fontebiga '15 | ♙♙ | 3 |
| ○ Marì '17 | ♙♙ | 2* |

### Zaccagnini

VIA SALMAGINA, 9/10
60039 STAFFOLO [AN]
TEL. +39 0731779892
www.zaccagnini.it

CELLAR SALES
PRE-BOOKED VISITS
ACCOMMODATION AND RESTAURANT SERVICE
ANNUAL PRODUCTION 250,000 bottles
HECTARES UNDER VINE 35.00

| | | |
|---|---|---|
| ○ Verdicchio dei Castelli di Jesi Cl. Sup. '17 | ♙♙ | 3 |
| ● Vigna Vescovi '15 | ♙♙ | 5 |
| ○ Verdicchio dei Castelli di Jesi Cl. Sup. Pier delle Vigne Ris. '15 | ♙ | 4 |

# UMBRIA

A record number of Tre Bicchieri for this small region is a strong signal that something's afoot. It's important to underline, however, everything that goes on outside the scores. There are more than a few wine producing territories on the rise in Umbria, with the most well-known affirming their importance and some lesser-known showing why they are so well-suited (thanks to a number of noteworthy offerings). Montefalco remains the region's star appellation. It's an area that we can't only reduce to Sagrantino, considering that Montefalco Rosso is, by now, a great mealtime wine, highly drinkable and supple, not to mention Montefalco Bianco (Grechetto, Trebbiano Toscano and other authorized grapes) and Montefalco Grechetto. This last cultivar is also having excellent results elsewhere, especially in Colli Martani and Todi, where the recently discovered Trebbiano Spoletino is also making its presence felt. Umbria's whites are, by now, a consolidated fact, especially if we consider Orvieto, which is taking huge steps towards reaffirming its status as one of the region's (and peninsula's) most important white winemaking districts. But returning to the reds, it's impossible to not cite Trasimeno's success, especially those offerings made with Gamay Perugino (a variety that belongs to the Grenache family) and Narni's Ciliegiolo. Thanks to the painstaking work of a group of vine growers, recent years have given rise to wines of extreme finesse, freshness and typicity in their various varietal expressions. We conclude with an obligatory mention for Torgiano and its Sangioveses, which once again spawned an outstanding Vigna Monticchio, their 2013, the wine's 14th Tre Bicchieri. In Montefalco four wineries took home a gold: Bellafonte, Caprai, Pardi (with their Sagrantino) and Tenuta Castelbuono (with their Rosso). Todi saw two wines in the limelight, and both Grechettos. One is Roccafiore's FiorFiore, the other is Rovi di Peppucci, the winery's first Tre Bicchieri. In Orvieto, three wines already known to our readers obtained our highest score: Decugnano dei Bari's 2017 Bianco, Castello della Sala's classically-styled 2016 Cervaro della Sala and Barberani's delicious 2015 Calcaia, testifying to how well the territory's botrytis sweet wines can do.

## Adanti

via Belvedere, 2
06031 Bevagna [PG]
Tel. +39 0742360295
www.cantineadanti.com

**CELLAR SALES**
**PRE-BOOKED VISITS**
**ANNUAL PRODUCTION** 160,000 bottles
**HECTARES UNDER VINE** 30.00
**SUSTAINABLE WINERY**

Adanti is a lovely winery located in Bevagna, one of the municipalities that falls within the Montefalco DOC appellation. Their wines are very traditional, the result of native yeasts and aging in medium-large barrels. Their reds, which need time to evolve, are particularly exemplary, proving austere, full of character and charm. Their vineyards are dedicated almost exclusively to native grapes and are situated around the main villa, which houses their cellar. Sagrantino, Sangiovese and Grechetto are all cultivated, along with a small quantity of international varieties. Their Montefalco Sagrantino did very well this year. It's a 2012 that offers up aromas of dried leaves, forest undergrowth, tobacco and sweet spices. In the mouth it proves tight-knit, with detectable tannins, but the palate isn't cropped, thanks to rich flavor. Their 2017 Montefalco Grechetto also delivered, with its notes of medlar, almond and yellow flowers. The palate features good acidic vigor, with a clean finish. Both their 2014 Montefalco Rosso and their 2013 RIserva also proved well-made.

| | |
|---|---|
| ○ Montefalco Grechetto '17 | 🍷🍷 2* |
| ● Montefalco Sagrantino '12 | 🍷🍷 5 |
| ● Montefalco Rosso '14 | 🍷 2 |
| ● Montefalco Rosso Ris. '13 | 🍷 4 |
| ● Montefalco Sagrantino Arquata '08 | YYY 6 |
| ● Montefalco Sagrantino Arquata '06 | YYY 5 |
| ● Montefalco Sagrantino Arquata '05 | YYY 5 |
| ○ Montefalco Bianco '15 | YY 2* |
| ○ Montefalco Grechetto '16 | YY 2* |
| ● Montefalco Rosso '11 | YY 2* |
| ● Montefalco Rosso Ris. '12 | YY 4 |
| ● Montefalco Rosso Ris. '10 | YY 4 |
| ● Montefalco Sagrantino '11 | YY 5 |
| ● Montefalco Sagrantino '10 | YY 5 |
| ● Montefalco Sagrantino Passito '08 | YY 6 |

## Antonelli - San Marco

loc. San Marco, 60
06036 Montefalco [PG]
Tel. +39 0742379158
www.antonellisanmarco.it

**CELLAR SALES**
**PRE-BOOKED VISITS**
**ACCOMMODATION**
**ANNUAL PRODUCTION** 300,000 bottles
**HECTARES UNDER VINE** 50.00
**VITICULTURE METHOD** Certified Organic
**SUSTAINABLE WINERY**

Antonelli is a lovely Montefalco winery, situated in San Marco, an area particularly well-suited to the cultivation of Sagrantino. Some 170 hectares of contiguous terrain include 50 hectares of vineyards. In addition to the area's principal cultivar, Sangiovese, Grechetto and Trebbiano Spolentino are all grown. Organic cultivation, measured extraction, and the careful use of wood give rise to authentic wines that are true to their terroir of origin. And the family aren't finished experimenting, for some years now they've been working on wines aged in terra-cotta and ceramic. The selection put forward this year performed extremely well. We start with their 2016 Anteprima Tonda, an excellent wine made with a cultivar that the winery has been focusing on in recent years: Trebbiano Spoletino. It stands out for its complex fragrances, from aromatic herbs to dried flowers. The palate proves savory, slightly marked by a nice tannic presence. Tre Bicchieri. Their 2011 Sagrantino Chiusa di Pannone is also a top-quality wine.

| | |
|---|---|
| ○ Spoleto Trebbiano Spoletino Anteprima Tonda '16 | 🍷🍷🍷 4* |
| ● Montefalco Sagrantino Chiusa di Pannone '11 | 🍷🍷 6 |
| ● Contrario '14 | 🍷🍷 3 |
| ● Montefalco Rosso '15 | 🍷🍷 3 |
| ● Montefalco Sagrantino '13 | 🍷🍷 5 |
| ○ Spoleto Trebbiano Spoletino Trebium '17 | 🍷🍷 3 |
| ● Baiocco Sangiovese '17 | 🍷 2 |
| ○ Montefalco Grechetto '17 | 🍷 2 |
| ● Montefalco Sagrantino Passito '11 | 🍷 5 |
| ● Montefalco Sagrantino '09 | YYY 5 |
| ○ Spoleto Trebbiano Spoletino Trebium '14 | YYY 3* |

## Barberani

DOC. CERRETO
05023 BASCHI [TR]
TEL. +39 0763341820
www.barberani.it

CELLAR SALES
PRE-BOOKED VISITS
ACCOMMODATION
ANNUAL PRODUCTION 350,000 bottles
HECTARES UNDER VINE 55.00
VITICULTURE METHOD Certified Organic
SUSTAINABLE WINERY

Barberani are without a doubt one of the most notable wine families in Umbria. True masters of botrytis, they have always sought to promote Orvieto's local varieties. And now that it's brothers Bernardo and Niccolò's turn to manage a winery capable of producing 350,000 bottles, they're more motivated than ever. In the cellar, the brothers focus on simplicity and the sparing use of wood, making for the maximum expression of cultivar. Their vast selection ranges from early-drinking whites to passito grape wines that can stand the test of time. An excellent sweet wine stood out during our tastings. Their 2015 Calcaia, an Orvieto Doc 'Muffa Nobile', offers up aromas of saffron, dried fruit and spices. In the mouth its sweetness is tempered by freshness and savoriness, which drive the palate towards a lovely finish. Tre Bicchieri. Their Luigi e Giovanna, another wine from the Orvieto DOC zone, also proved delicious. It's an excellent white that isn't afraid to age.

| | | |
|---|---|---|
| ○ Orvieto Muffa Nobile Calcaia '15 | ♥♥♥ | 6 |
| ○ Orvieto Cl. Sup. Luigi e Giovanna '15 | ♥♥ | 5 |
| ○ Orvieto Cl. Sup. Castagnolo '17 | ♥♥ | 3 |
| ● Foresco '16 | ♥ | 3 |
| ● Lago di Corbara Rosso Polvento '14 | ♥ | 5 |
| ● Lago di Corbara Rosso Villa Monticelli '04 | ♀♀♀ | 4 |
| ○ Orvieto Cl. Sup. Luigi e Giovanna '13 | ♀♀♀ | 5 |
| ○ Orvieto Cl. Sup. Luigi e Giovanna Villa Monticelli '11 | ♀♀♀ | 5 |
| ○ Orvieto Cl. Sup. Muffa Nobile Calcaia '10 | ♀♀♀ | 5 |
| ○ Orvieto Cl. Sup. V. T. Calcaia '14 | ♀♀ | 6 |

## Tenuta Bellafonte

LOC. TORRE DEL COLLE
VIA COLLE NOTTOLO, 2
06031 BEVAGNA [PG]
TEL. +39 0742710019
www.tenutabellafonte.it

CELLAR SALES
PRE-BOOKED VISITS
ACCOMMODATION
ANNUAL PRODUCTION 35,000 bottles
HECTARES UNDER VINE 11.00
SUSTAINABLE WINERY

Bellafonte was founded some years ago by Peter Heilbron, a former business manager who's now entirely devoted himself to viticulture. He has at his disposal just over 10 hectares of land, making for a small, artisanal operation. Nevertheless, right from the start, Bellafonte has put forward technically precise yet territorially authentic wines of great finesse and elegance. Only two are made, a Montefalco Sagrantino and an Arnèto, a white made with Trebbiano Spoletino. Their cellar is located in Bevagna and adheres to principles of environmental sustainability. Their Collenottolo once again proves that it's a great Montefalco Sagrantino. 2014 gave rise to a red of structure. Tannins are detectable but it's still a plush, fresh wine that's dynamic on the palate. Add a lovely, multifaceted nose and you get a Tre Bicchieri. Their 2016 Arnèto is also excellent. It's a savory, citrusy and vibrant Trebbiano Spoletino.

| | | |
|---|---|---|
| ● Montefalco Sagrantino Collenottolo '14 | ♥♥♥ | 6 |
| ○ Arnèto '16 | ♥♥ | 4 |
| ● Montefalco Sagrantino '09 | ♀♀♀ | 6 |
| ● Montefalco Sagrantino Collenottolo '13 | ♀♀♀ | 6 |
| ● Montefalco Sagrantino Collenottolo '11 | ♀♀♀ | 6 |
| ● Montefalco Sagrantino Collenottolo '10 | ♀♀♀ | 6 |
| ○ Arnèto '14 | ♀♀ | 5 |
| ● Montefalco Sagrantino '08 | ♀♀ | 5 |
| ● Montefalco Sagrantino Collenottolo '12 | ♀♀ | 6 |

# Bocale

loc. Madonna della Stella
via Fratta Alzatura
06036 Montefalco [PG]
Tel. +39 0742399233
www.bocale.it

**CELLAR SALES**
**PRE-BOOKED VISITS**
**ANNUAL PRODUCTION** 25,000 bottles
**HECTARES UNDER VINE** 4.20

Bocale is a small but interesting artisanal producer managed by the Valentini family. They have fewer than ten hectares at their disposal, with about half used for vineyards. Primarily local varieties are cultivated (Sagrantino, Trebbiano Spoletino and Sangiovese) as well as small quantities of international grapes used for their Montefalco Rosso. In recent years, in particular, the use of large wood, native yeast and measured extraction have guaranteed excellent wines, true to the cultivar and capable of pointing up the attributes of Montefalco. Our tastings saw only reds on the front line, both extremely well-made. Their 2016 Montefalco Rosso surprises for its pleasantness in the mouth, its savoriness and freshness. Aromas of blackcurrant and raspberry give way to a juicy, energetic, vibrant and deep palate. Their 2015 Montefalco Sagrantino is more full-bodied, close-knit and pervasive. Aromas of ripe fruit are followed by a tannic, though supple palate crossed by nice acidic vigor.

| | |
|---|---|
| ● Montefalco Rosso '16 | ♥♥ 3* |
| ● Montefalco Sagrantino '15 | ♥♥ 5 |
| ● Montefalco Rosso '15 | ♀♀ 3 |
| ● Montefalco Rosso '14 | ♀♀ 3 |
| ● Montefalco Rosso '13 | ♀♀ 3 |
| ● Montefalco Rosso '12 | ♀♀ 2* |
| ● Montefalco Rosso '09 | ♀♀ 4 |
| ● Montefalco Sagrantino '14 | ♀♀ 5 |
| ● Montefalco Sagrantino '13 | ♀♀ 5 |
| ● Montefalco Sagrantino '12 | ♀♀ 5 |
| ● Montefalco Sagrantino '11 | ♀♀ 5 |
| ● Montefalco Sagrantino '10 | ♀♀ 5 |
| ● Montefalco Sagrantino '09 | ♀♀ 5 |
| ● Montefalco Sagrantino Passito '09 | ♀♀ 5 |
| ○ Trebbiano Spoletino '15 | ♀♀ 3 |

# Viticoltori Broccatelli Galli

via degli Olmi, 9
06083 Bastia Umbra [PG]
Tel. +39 0758001501
www.broccatelligalli.it

**CELLAR SALES**
**PRE-BOOKED VISITS**
**ACCOMMODATION AND RESTAURANT SERVICE**
**ANNUAL PRODUCTION** 2,000,000 bottles
**HECTARES UNDER VINE** 75.00

Brocatelli Galli is a noteworthy producer founded in 1951 by Marcello Brocatelli and Quintilio Galli. Today the winery is managed by six of their grandchildren, who avail themselves of some 80 hectares throughout Torgiano (50 hectares) and Montefalchese. In addition to Sagrantino and Sangiovese, the two appellations' most important cultivar, they cultivate various plots of international varieties, foremost Cabernet Sauvignon and Pinot Nero for their reds, and Chardonnay and Riesling for their whites. An extremely sound selection has landed them a top position in our guide. Some four wines from the Montefalco and Torgiano DOC appellations stand out, foremost their 2014 Re Migrante, Riserva di Sagrantino, a wine with aromas of black fruit, forest undergrowth and pepper. The palate proves supple, despite the presence of tannins, and the finish is fluid and clean. Their 2014 Torgiano Rosso Riserva Santa Caterina is also excellent.

| | |
|---|---|
| ● Montefalco Rosso Re Migrante Ris. '14 | ♥♥ 4 |
| ● Montefalco Sagrantino '14 | ♥♥ 6 |
| ● Torgiano Rosso '15 | ♥♥ 3 |
| ● Torgiano Rosso Santa Caterina Ris. '14 | ♥♥ 5 |
| ○ Le Ripaie Grechetto '17 | ♀ 3 |
| ○ Montefalco Grechetto Nido Del Falco '17 | ♀ 4 |
| ● Montefalco Rosso '15 | ♀ 4 |
| ○ Torgiano Bianco '17 | ♀ 3 |
| ● Montefalco Sagrantino '12 | ♀♀ 3 |
| ● Montefalco Sagrantino Preda del Falco '12 | ♀♀ 7 |
| ● Montefalco Sagrantino Preda del Falco '08 | ♀♀ 7 |

# Leonardo Bussoletti

LOC. MIRIANO
S.DA DELLE PRETARE, 62
05035 NARNI [TR]
TEL. +39 0744715687
www.leonardobussoletti.it

PRE-BOOKED VISITS
ANNUAL PRODUCTION 40,000 bottles
HECTARES UNDER VINE 9.00
VITICULTURE METHOD Certified Organic

If there is one vine grower that has brought notoriety and importance to Ciliegiolo in recent years, there's no doubt that it's Leonardo Bussoletti. The cellar is located in Narni, while the estate, which is organically cultivated, comprises seven-hectares of primarily local grape varieties. Both new systems and old vines co-exist, lending force to a young, but sound offering. Theirs is an extremely high quality selection that exhibits a precise style, with examples of charming wines that express both the cultivar and the territory, as well as exhibiting drinkability and longevity. Three different vintages for three different Ciliegiolos, all highly enjoyable. Their 05035 (Narni's postal code) is the youngest and freshest. It offers up aromas of raspberry and blackcurrant while in the mouth it proves flavorful and extremely pleasant. Their 2015 Ramici are their most structured, full-bodied Ciliegiolo, it opts for dark fruit and spicy accents. Their 2016 Colle Ozio, a savory and iodine Grechetto, stands out among their whites.

| | |
|---|---|
| ● 05035 Ciliegiolo '17 | ♟♟ 2* |
| ○ Colle Ozio Grechetto '16 | ♟♟ 3* |
| ● Ramici Ciliegiolo '15 | ♟♟ 5 |
| ● Brecciaro Ciliegiolo '16 | ♟♟ 3 |
| ○ Colle Murello '16 | ♟♟ 3 |
| ● 05035 Rosso '16 | ♟♟♟ 2* |
| ● Brecciaro Ciliegiolo '14 | ♟♟♟ 3* |
| ○ Colle Ozio Grechetto '12 | ♟♟♟ 3* |
| ● 05035 Rosso '15 | ♟♟ 2* |
| ● Brecciaro Ciliegiolo '15 | ♟♟ 3 |
| ● Brecciaro Ciliegiolo '13 | ♟♟ 3* |
| ○ Colle Murello '15 | ♟♟ 3 |
| ○ Colle Ozio Grechetto '15 | ♟♟ 3* |
| ○ Colle Ozio Grechetto '14 | ♟♟ 3* |
| ● Vigna Vecchia '13 | ♟♟ 7 |

# ★★Arnaldo Caprai

LOC. TORRE
06036 MONTEFALCO [PG]
TEL. +39 0742378802
www.arnaldocaprai.it

CELLAR SALES
PRE-BOOKED VISITS
ANNUAL PRODUCTION 1,000,000 bottles
HECTARES UNDER VINE 136.00
SUSTAINABLE WINERY

Much has been said and written about Caprai, but it's worth underlining the role that the winery played in attracting notoriety for Sagrantino, even during a time when confusion led to the use of international varieties and models of production that did little for the territory. By now we can consider Caprai a true beacon, for its high quality, continued experimentation, relationship with research institutions and the principles of environmental sustainability employed in both the vineyards and the cellar. Once again the selection put forward is excellent. The vintage 2014 of their 25 Anni gets a gold, proving to be an outstanding Montefalco Sagrantino. It's still young, but will age for a long time to come, and still manages to surprise for its complex, multifaceted aromas and for its deep palate. Fragrances of dark fruit and wood resin give way to a close-knit, potent palate with great vigor and a savory finish. Tre Bicchieri. Their Collepiano, another memorable Sagrantino, was also at the top of its game.

| | |
|---|---|
| ● Montefalco Sagrantino 25 Anni '14 | ♟♟♟ 8 |
| ● Montefalco Sagrantino Collepiano '14 | ♟♟ 7 |
| ● Montefalco Rosso Ris. '15 | ♟♟ 6 |
| ● Montefalco Rosso V. Flaminia Maremmana '16 | ♟♟ 4 |
| ○ Chardonnay '17 | ♟ 5 |
| ○ Colli Martani Grechetto Grecante '17 | ♟ 4 |
| ● Montefalco Rosso '16 | ♟ 4 |
| ● Montefalco Sagrantino Valdimaggio '14 | ♟ 7 |
| ○ Sauvignon '17 | ♟ 5 |
| ● Montefalco Sagrantino 25 Anni '10 | ♟♟♟ 8 |
| ● Montefalco Sagrantino 25 Anni '09 | ♟♟♟ 8 |
| ● Montefalco Sagrantino Collepiano '13 | ♟♟♟ 7 |
| ● Montefalco Sagrantino Collepiano '12 | ♟♟♟ 7 |
| ● Montefalco Sagrantino Collepiano '11 | ♟♟♟ 7 |

## La Carraia

LOC. TORDIMONTE, 56
05018 ORVIETO [TR]
TEL. +39 0763304013
www.lacarraia.it

CELLAR SALES
PRE-BOOKED VISITS
ANNUAL PRODUCTION 700,000 bottles
HECTARES UNDER VINE 119.00

120 hectares of terrain and more than 700 thousand bottles. These are some of La Carraia's noteworthy figures. The Orvieto winery, under the guidance of Riccardo Cottarella, has for many years guaranteed quality and quantity, producing a vast range of wines, whites and reds, with native grape varieties playing a lead role (especially for their DOC Orvieto) and international cultivar doing their part for the reds. Their style provides for technically impeccable wines, clean and decisive in terms of aroma and taste, suitable for markets the world over. A white and a red led the way during our tastings. Their 2015 Solcato is a Bordeaux blend with Sangiovese and other local cultivar. It's a creamy, pervasive wine with savoriness and ripe, sweet tannins. Their 2017 Le Basque is a blend of Grechetto and Viognier with aromas of medlar, white flowers, candied lemon and herbs. As good as usual the Poggio Calvelli. The rest of their selection also proved sound.

| | | |
|---|---|---|
| ○ Le Basque '17 | | ♟♟ 3* |
| ○ Orvieto Cl. Sup. Poggio Calvelli '17 | | ♟♟ 2* |
| ● Solcato '15 | | ♟♟ 3 |
| ● Fobiano '13 | | ♟ 5 |
| ● Tizzenero '16 | | ♟ 3 |
| ● Fobiano '03 | | ♟♟♟ 4 |
| ● Fobiano '99 | | ♟♟♟ 4* |
| ● Fobiano '98 | | ♟♟♟ 4* |
| ● Fobiano '12 | | ♟♟ 5 |
| ○ Le Basque '16 | | ♟♟ 3 |
| ○ Orvieto Cl. Sup. Poggio Calvelli '16 | | ♟♟ 2* |
| ○ Orvieto Cl. Sup. Poggio Calvelli '15 | | ♟♟ 2* |
| ● Sangiovese '16 | | ♟♟ 2* |
| ● Sangiovese '15 | | ♟♟ 2* |
| ● Tizzenero '14 | | ♟♟ 3 |

## ★★Castello della Sala

LOC. SALA
05016 FICULLE [TR]
TEL. +39 076386127
www.antinori.it

CELLAR SALES
PRE-BOOKED VISITS
ANNUAL PRODUCTION 760,000 bottles
HECTARES UNDER VINE 140.00

The Marchesi Antinori aren't only in Tuscany. This important Italian wine dynasty's Umbrian brand is called Castello della Sala, a winery founded on the idea of making whites (in one of central Italy's most well-suited areas) to accompany their local reds. 140 hectares under vine around Orvieto are cultivated at notable altitudes in clay, stony soil. Leading their selection is Cervaro della Sala, a wine that's fermented and aged in barriques for many years. Even today it remains a benchmark wine in Italy. And it's their Cervaro that demonstrates the producer's quality. A multifaceted nose, the skillful use of wood, a savory and deep palate earn this Umbrian white a gold. Aromas of yellow fruit, a spicy note and yellow flowers give way to a pervasive, creamy, elegant palate made fresh by acidity. Their 2017 Orvieto Classico Superiore San Giovanni della Sala also did very well.

| | | |
|---|---|---|
| ○ Cervaro della Sala '16 | | ♟♟♟ 6 |
| ○ Orvieto Cl. Sup. San Giovanni della Sala '17 | | ♟♟ 3* |
| ● Pinot Nero '16 | | ♟♟ 6 |
| ○ Bramito della Sala '17 | | ♟ 3 |
| ○ Muffato della Sala '14 | | ♟ 6 |
| ○ Cervaro della Sala '15 | | ♟♟♟ 6 |
| ○ Cervaro della Sala '14 | | ♟♟♟ 6 |
| ○ Cervaro della Sala '13 | | ♟♟♟ 6 |
| ○ Cervaro della Sala '12 | | ♟♟♟ 6 |
| ○ Cervaro della Sala '11 | | ♟♟♟ 6 |
| ○ Cervaro della Sala '10 | | ♟♟♟ 6 |
| ○ Cervaro della Sala '09 | | ♟♟♟ 6 |
| ○ Cervaro della Sala '08 | | ♟♟♟ 6 |
| ○ Cervaro della Sala '07 | | ♟♟♟ 6 |

# Cantina Castello
# Monte Vibiano Vecchio

LOC. MONTE VIBIANO VECCHIO DI MERCATELLO
VOC. PALOMBARO, 22
06072 MARSCIANO [PG]
TEL. +39 0758783386
www.montevibiano.it

**CELLAR SALES**
**PRE-BOOKED VISITS**
**ANNUAL PRODUCTION** 200,000 bottles
**HECTARES UNDER VINE** 27.00
**VITICULTURE METHOD** Certified Organic
**SUSTAINABLE WINERY**

Castello di Monte Vibiano Vecchio, an historic estate that comprises hundreds of hectares of agricultural terrain, is situated on the Perugian hills. Since the late 19th century the property has been managed by the Fasola Bologna family, by the early 20th century they were making wine and oil. With the opening of their new cellar in 1998, their plan was to use sustainable methods to make high quality wines that promoted the territory. Both local grape varieties and international cultivar are used. Their style is well-focused and isn't lacking in pleasant surprises. Two wines were presented, both quite good and technically well-made. Their San Giovanni is a red from the Colli Perugini made with Sangiovese, Merlot and Cabernet Franc. The nose is a kaleidoscope of small red fruit, with a touch of spices and a hint of forest undergrowth. The palate is fresh, supple and juicy. Their 2017 Maria Camilla is a white made with Trebbiano Spoletino, Grechetto, Sauvignon Blanc and Viognier. Aromas of wild flowers give way to a savory, long palate.

| | | |
|---|---|---|
| ● Colli Perugini Rosso San Giovanni '15 | ♟♟ | 4 |
| ○ Maria Camilla '17 | ♟♟ | 4 |
| ● Colli Perugini Rosso L'Andrea '08 | ♟♟♟ | 5 |
| ● Colli Perugini Rosso L'Andrea '13 | ♟♟ | 5 |
| ● Colli Perugini Rosso L'Andrea '12 | ♟♟ | 5 |
| ● Colli Perugini Rosso L'Andrea '10 | ♟♟ | 5 |
| ● Colli Perugini Rosso L'Andrea '09 | ♟♟ | 5 |
| ● Colli Perugini Rosso Monvì '14 | ♟♟ | 2* |
| ● Colli Perugini Rosso Monvì '12 | ♟♟ | 2* |
| ● Colli Perugini Rosso Monvì '10 | ♟♟ | 2* |
| ○ Maria Camilla '15 | ♟♟ | 3 |
| ○ Maria Camilla '14 | ♟♟ | 3 |
| ○ Maria Camilla '13 | ♟♟ | 3 |
| ○ Villa Monte Vibiano Bianco '14 | ♟♟ | 2* |
| ● Villa Monte Vibiano Rosso '15 | ♟ | 1* |

# Cantina Cenci

FRAZ. SAN BIAGIO DELLA VALLE
VOC. ANTICELLO, 1
06072 MARSCIANO [PG]
TEL. +39 3805198980
www.cantinacenci.it

**CELLAR SALES**
**PRE-BOOKED VISITS**
**ANNUAL PRODUCTION** 25,000 bottles
**HECTARES UNDER VINE** 6.00
**SUSTAINABLE WINERY**

Giovanni Cenci, an explosive and skilled vine grower, is leaving his mark on Umbria thanks to his small winery. The area's agricultural roots go back to the Olivetani monks, while over four generations the Cenci family have managed their six hectares of vineyards in San Biagio. Respect for the cultivar (both traditional and non-native), vintages and terrain, combined with minimally invasive though painstaking work in the cellar are the foundation of this artisanal selection, which features authentic and charming wines. Two reds surprised most during our tastings. Ascheria is a close-knit, full-bodied Merlot that proves complex in its notes of licorice, plums and spices. In the mouth it comes through creamy, with a savory touch at the end that revives the palate. Their Piantata is a Sangiovese with earthy, sanguine notes. The palate is vibrant, with tannins that are detectable though ripe and pliant. The rest of their selection also proved well-made.

| | | |
|---|---|---|
| ● Ascheria '16 | ♟♟ | 3 |
| ● Piantata '16 | ♟♟ | 4 |
| ○ Alago Stellato '17 | ♟ | 3 |
| ○ Anticello '17 | ♟ | 3 |
| ○ Campo Maro '17 | ♟ | 3 |
| ○ Giole '17 | ♟ | 2 |
| ● Sanbiagio '16 | ♟ | 3 |
| ○ Alago Stellato '15 | ♟♟ | 2* |
| ○ Anticello '15 | ♟♟ | 2* |
| ○ Anticello '14 | ♟♟ | 2* |
| ○ Giole '15 | ♟♟ | 2* |
| ○ Giole '14 | ♟♟ | 2* |
| ● Piantata '15 | ♟♟ | 4 |
| ● Piantata '14 | ♟♟ | 4 |

# Le Cimate

FRAZ. CASALE
LOC. CECAPECORE, 41
06036 MONTEFALCO [PG]
TEL. +39 0742290136
www.lecimate.it

**CELLAR SALES**
**PRE-BOOKED VISITS**
**ACCOMMODATION AND RESTAURANT SERVICE**
**ANNUAL PRODUCTION** 800,000 bottles
**HECTARES UNDER VINE** 20.00
**SUSTAINABLE WINERY**

The Bartoloni family have been working in agriculture since 1800, but it was Paolo who founded Le Cimate so as to carry on a great tradition. The winery came to be in 2011 and got its name from the Montefalco's hilltops. They avail themselves of about 28 hectares of vineyards, cultivated with the area's traditional grapes and international varieties (used especially in their IGTs). The terrain here is naturally silt clay, with some limestone as well. Their wines, especially in recent years, have hit their stride in terms of typicity and drinkability. While waiting to taste their 2014 Montefalco Sagrantino (the 2013 was rated last year) we particularly appreciated their 2017 Trebbiano Spoletino, a complex and multifaceted wine with aromas of wild flowers dominating over fainter hints of yellow fruit and herbs. In the mouth it proves savory and fresh, making for a long palate. Their 2014 Montefalco Rosso is also a pleasant, well-made wine with nice complexity.

| | | |
|---|---|---|
| ○ Trebbiano Spoletino '17 | ♥♥ | 3 |
| ● Montefalco Rosso '14 | ♥ | 3 |
| ○ Aragon '12 | ♥♥ | 3 |
| ● Macchieto '10 | ♥♥ | 2* |
| ● Montefalco Rosso '12 | ♥♥ | 3 |
| ● Montefalco Sagrantino '13 | ♥♥ | 5 |
| ● Montefalco Sagrantino '12 | ♥♥ | 5 |
| ● Montefalco Sagrantino '09 | ♥♥ | 5 |
| ● Montefalco Sagrantino '08 | ♥♥ | 5 |
| ○ Trebbiano Spoletino '15 | ♥♥ | 3 |
| ● Umbria Rosso '10 | ♥♥ | 2* |

# Fattoria Colleallodole

VIA COLLEALLODOLE, 3
06031 BEVAGNA [PG]
TEL. +39 0742361897
www.fattoriacolleallodole.com

**CELLAR SALES**
**PRE-BOOKED VISITS**
**ANNUAL PRODUCTION** 70,000 bottles
**HECTARES UNDER VINE** 25.00

Colleallodole, a winery considered a benchmark in Montefalco's winemaking industry, is managed by the Antano family. It's a small, artisanal producer that cultivates 20 hectares of the territory's most common grapes. Sagrantino, obviously, plays a leading role (it's used in all five of their wines), with Sangiovese, Grechetto and some common international varieties as well. Their wines are authentic, with a strong territorial identity that reflects the terroir of origin, starting with their Colleallodole, one of the DOC appellation's bona fide crus. This year their entire range delivered, especially those wines that weren't part of a selection process. Their Montefalco Sagrantino Passito stands out the most, by virtue of its exemplary balance between sweetness, tannins and fresh acidity. On the nose it offers up aromas ranging from wild cherry to resin, sweet spices and dried rose. It's a great, sweet Italian red. Their 2016 Montefalco Rosso also impressed for its drinkability and depth.

| | | |
|---|---|---|
| ● Montefalco Sagrantino Passito '15 | ♥♥ | 7 |
| ● Montefalco Rosso '16 | ♥♥ | 3 |
| ● Montefalco Sagrantino '15 | ♥♥ | 6 |
| ● Montefalco Rosso Ris. '15 | ♥ | 5 |
| ● Montefalco Sagrantino Colleallodole '15 | ♥ | 8 |
| ● Montefalco Rosso Ris. '08 | ♥♥♥ | 5 |
| ● Montefalco Sagrantino '12 | ♥♥♥ | 6 |
| ● Montefalco Sagrantino Colleallodole '10 | ♥♥♥ | 8 |
| ● Montefalco Sagrantino Colleallodole '09 | ♥♥♥ | 8 |
| ● Montefalco Sagrantino Colleallodole '06 | ♥♥♥ | 6 |
| ● Montefalco Sagrantino Colleallodole '05 | ♥♥♥ | 6 |
| ● Montefalco Rosso '15 | ♥♥ | 3 |
| ● Montefalco Rosso Ris. '13 | ♥♥ | 5 |
| ● Montefalco Sagrantino '14 | ♥♥ | 6 |
| ● Montefalco Sagrantino Colleallodole '13 | ♥♥ | 8 |

# Fattoria Colsanto

Loc. Montarone
06031 Bevagna [PG]
Tel. +39 0742360412
www.livon.it

CELLAR SALES
PRE-BOOKED VISITS
ACCOMMODATION
ANNUAL PRODUCTION 50,000 bottles
HECTARES UNDER VINE 15.00

15 hectares in Bevagna, in the heart of the Montefalco DOC appellation, give rise to a production of 50,000 bottles. These are the figures that define Colsanto, a winery managed by the Livon family, well-known producers from Friuli who've been present in Umbria for some years now. Their Sagrantino reds and a new Trebbiano Spoletino white stand out among their wines. The use of large wood, highly measured extraction and careful work in the vineyards guarantee a selection that's true to the territory and capable of aging well. Their CantaLuce stood out itself during tasting. It's a white made with Trebbiano Spoletino, a genuine and charming wine both on the nose and the palate. Yellow fruit, Mediterranean herbs and a touch of wood resin give way to a savory, fresh, long palate. Their Monterone, a 2012 Montefalco Sagrantino, also delivered.

| | |
|---|---|
| ○ CantaLuce '17 | ♟♟ 5 |
| ● Montefalco Sagrantino Montarone Ris. '12 | ♟♟ 6 |
| ● Montefalco Rosso '15 | ♟ 3 |
| ● Montefalco Rosso '14 | ♟♟ 3 |
| ● Montefalco Rosso '13 | ♟♟ 3 |
| ● Montefalco Rosso '10 | ♟♟ 3 |
| ● Montefalco Sagrantino '12 | ♟♟ 5 |
| ● Montefalco Sagrantino '11 | ♟♟ 5 |
| ● Montefalco Sagrantino '10 | ♟♟ 5 |
| ● Montefalco Sagrantino '09 | ♟♟ 5 |
| ● Montefalco Sagrantino '08 | ♟♟ 5 |
| ● Ruris '14 | ♟♟ 2* |
| ● Ruris Rosso '13 | ♟♟ 2* |
| ● Ruris Rosso '12 | ♟♟ 2* |

# Decugnano dei Barbi

loc. Fossatello, 50
05018 Orvieto [TR]
Tel. +39 0763308255
www.decugnano.it

CELLAR SALES
PRE-BOOKED VISITS
ANNUAL PRODUCTION 130,000 bottles
HECTARES UNDER VINE 32.00

History tells us that wine has been made in Decugnano since 1200, proof that Orvieto has always been well-suited to vineyards and their grapes. The current winery of Decugnano dei Barbi was founded in 1973, thanks to Claudio Barbi, who purchased the abandoned estate. Their wines perfectly reflect the territory and are made mostly with native grape varieties. A modern approach to winemaking is detectable, but their wines never lose their natural character. A Metodo Classico sparkling wine and their Muffa Nobile (whose first vintage goes back to 1981) stand out among their selection. It's a year to remember for Decugnano's wines. Their 2017 Bianco is an Orvieto Classico Superiore with great elegance and finesse. Its gratifying nose features aromas of white flowers, citrus and herbs, while the palate proves extremely fresh and incredibly long. Tre Bicchieri. Their other Orvieto, their 2017 Villa Barbi, is a simpler wine but still very well-made. Their 2016 Rosso, a highly drinkable blend of Syrah, Montepulciano and Sangiovese, also stands out.

| | |
|---|---|
| ○ Orvieto Cl. Sup. Il Bianco '17 | ♟♟♟ 4* |
| ● Il Rosso A.D.1212 '16 | ♟♟ 4 |
| ○ Orvieto Cl. Villa Barbi '17 | ♟♟ 3 |
| ● Villa Barbi Rosso '16 | ♟ 3 |
| ● "IL" Rosso '98 | ♟♟♟ 5 |
| ○ Orvieto Cl. Sup. "IL" '11 | ♟♟♟ 3* |
| ○ Orvieto Cl. Sup. Il Bianco '16 | ♟♟♟ 4* |
| ○ Orvieto Cl. Sup. Il Bianco '15 | ♟♟♟ 4* |
| ○ Orvieto Cl. Sup. Il Bianco '12 | ♟♟♟ 3* |
| ○ Orvieto Cl. Sup. Il Bianco '10 | ♟♟♟ 3 |
| ○ Orvieto Cl. Sup. Il Bianco '09 | ♟♟♟ 4 |
| ● Il Rosso '15 | ♟♟ 4 |
| ○ Orvieto Cl. Sup. Muffa Nobile Pourriture Noble '15 | ♟♟ 6 |
| ● Villa Barbi Rosso '15 | ♟♟ 3 |

# Di Filippo

voc. Conversino, 153
06033 Cannara [PG]
Tel. +39 0742731242
www.vinidifilippo.com

CELLAR SALES
PRE-BOOKED VISITS
ANNUAL PRODUCTION 227,000 bottles
HECTARES UNDER VINE 35.00
VITICULTURE METHOD Certified Organic
SUSTAINABLE WINERY

Roberto Di Filippo, enologist and owner of the winery that bears his name, has clear ideas. In addition to organic management, which he's been applying for some years, he follows strong principles of environmental sustainability. The result is authentic, charming, and in some cases long-lived wines that respect the environment. His selection draws on both the Colli Martani (foremost Sangiovese and Grechetto) and Montefalco, which gives rise to an increasingly interesting Sagrantino. From their vast selection, we particularly appreciated their Etnico, a 2014 Montefalco Sagrantino. A lovely and multifaceted nose gives way to a tannic, though never clenched palate. Their 2016 Sangiovese is another notable wine. It's a red with a hint of iron and forest undergrowth. Among their whites their 2017 Villa Conversino proved fresh and elegant, while their Vernaccia di Cannara stands out for its aromatic complexity.

| | |
|---|---|
| ● Montefalco Sagrantino Etnico '14 | ♔♔ 4 |
| ● Colli Martani Vernaccia Nera di Cannara '16 | ♔♔ 5 |
| ● Sangiovese '16 | ♔♔ 2* |
| ○ Villa Conversino Bianco '17 | ♔♔ 2* |
| ○ Colli Martani Grechetto Sassi d'Arenaria '16 | ♔ 3 |
| ● Colli Martani Sangiovese Properzio Ris. '15 | ♔ 4 |
| ○ Grechetto Senza Solfiti Aggiunti '15 | ♔ 3 |
| ● Montefalco Rosso '15 | ♔ 2 |
| ● Montefalco Sagrantino '14 | ♔ 5 |
| ● Villa Conversino Rosso '17 | ♔ 2 |
| ○ Farandola '16 | ♔♔ 3 |
| ○ Grechetto '16 | ♔♔ 2* |

# Duca della Corgna

via Roma, 236
06061 Castiglione del Lago [PG]
Tel. +39 0759652493
www.ducadellacorgna.it

CELLAR SALES
PRE-BOOKED VISITS
ANNUAL PRODUCTION 300,000 bottles
HECTARES UNDER VINE 65.00

Duca della Corgna is a cooperative winery in the Lake Trasimeno district. It's a lovely project that's bringing together excellent quality and noteworthy production volumes, with almost 300,000 bottles produced and a number of vine growers to support them. Their selection is oriented around the territory, starting with Gamay Perugino (a cultivar in the large Grenache family), which is made into two wines. They also make whites with Grechetto, a grape that's also cultivated on the hills around Trasimeno and that's influenced by the lake's particular microclimate. We liked their 2017 Divina Villa best. It's a fresh, vibrant, juicy and savory red that's always among the best in its category. Their Baccio del Rosso, a blend of Gamay del Trasimeno (Grenache) and Sangiovese from the Colli del Trasimeno DOC appellation, features great finesse. Among their whites we appreciated their Nuricante, a a savory and deep 2017 Grechetto.

| | |
|---|---|
| ● C. del Trasimeno Baccio del Rosso '17 | ♔♔ 2* |
| ○ C. del Trasimeno Grechetto Nuricante '17 | ♔♔ 2* |
| ● Trasimeno Gamay Divina Villa '17 | ♔♔ 3 |
| ○ Ascanio '17 | ♔ 2 |
| ○ C. del Trasimeno Baccio del Bianco '17 | ♔ 2 |
| ● C. del Trasimeno Rosso Corniolo Ris. '15 | ♔ 4 |
| ⊙ Martavello '17 | ♔ 2 |
| ● Trasimeno Gamay Divina Villa Ris. '15 | ♔ 3 |
| ● C. del Trasimeno Gamay Divina Villa Et. Bianca '16 | ♔♔ 2* |
| ● C. del Trasimeno Rosso Corniolo Ris. '14 | ♔♔ 4 |

# Fontesecca

voc. Fontesecca, 30
06062 Città della Pieve [PG]
Tel. +39 3496180516
www.fontesecca.it

CELLAR SALES
PRE-BOOKED VISITS
ACCOMMODATION
ANNUAL PRODUCTION 10,000 bottles
HECTARES UNDER VINE 6.50
VITICULTURE METHOD Certified Organic

Fontesecca is a small artisanal winery that we're proud to count among Italian Wine's major producers, considering the quality of their selection, which focuses on the territory and respect for each cultivar. Their wines don't belong to a single DOC appellation (the estate is situated at a crossroads between Umbria, Lazio and Tuscany), but they're all made rigorously with native grape varieties cultivated organically, primarily Sangiovese, Ciliegiolo and Canaiolo for the reds, Trebbiano Toscano, Grechetto and Malvasia for their whites. It was their reds that most impressed. Their 2017 Ciliegiolo is a juicy, aromatic wine that's highly delectable in the mouth, made deep thanks to savoriness and acidic vigor. Their 2016 Canaiolo also delivered, offering up notes of raspberry and blackcurrant on the nose and proving slightly tannic but pleasantly creamy on the palate. The rest of their selection proved sound and pleasing.

| | |
|---|---|
| ● Canaiolo '16 | ♟♟ 5 |
| ● Ciliegiolo '17 | ♟♟ 4 |
| ○ Elso '17 | ♟ 4 |
| ● Pino '15 | ♟ 4 |
| ● Rosso della Grancia '17 | ♟ 4 |
| ● Canaiolo '14 | ♟♟ 3 |
| ● Canaiolo '13 | ♟♟ 3 |
| ● Ciliegiolo '16 | ♟♟ 4 |
| ● Ciliegiolo '14 | ♟♟ 3* |
| ● Ciliegiolo '13 | ♟♟ 3 |
| ● Ciliegiolo '12 | ♟♟ 3 |
| ○ Elso '15 | ♟♟ 2* |
| ○ Elso '13 | ♟♟ 2* |
| ● Pino '14 | ♟♟ 4 |
| ● Pino Sangiovese '13 | ♟♟ 3* |

# Tenute Lunelli - Castelbuono

voc. Castellaccio, 9
06031 Bevagna [PG]
Tel. +39 0742361670
www.tenutelunelli.it

CELLAR SALES
PRE-BOOKED VISITS
ANNUAL PRODUCTION 110,000 bottles
HECTARES UNDER VINE 32.00
VITICULTURE METHOD Certified Organic
SUSTAINABLE WINERY

Castelbuono, whose name comes from the district in which the estate is located, was deeply sought after by the Lunelli family (owners of the prestigious Ferrari winery in Trento). Their vineyards reside in the municipalities of Bevagna and Montefalco, with local cultivar playing a lead role. They make their wine in one of Italy's most beautiful cellars, the Carapace, a building designed by Arnaldo Pomodoro. For now, there are only reds, primarily from the Montefalco appellations. Now that the winery's been broken in, their wines have only gained in authenticity and territorial identity. Their Ziggurat, a 2016 Montefalco Rosso, is a truly outstanding wine made primarily with Sangiovese (and a smaller part international cultivar). Cherry, raspberry, forest undergrowth and tobacco give way to a fresh, appealing, flavorful and juicy palate that's both complex and deep. Tre Bicchieri. Their Lampante, Montefalco Rosso Riserva also proved delicious.

| | |
|---|---|
| ● Montefalco Rosso Ziggurat '16 | ♟♟♟ 4* |
| ● Montefalco Rosso Lampante Ris. '15 | ♟♟ 5 |
| ● Montefalco Rosso Lampante Ris. '13 | ♟♟ 5 |
| ● Montefalco Rosso Lampante Ris. '10 | ♟♟ 5 |
| ● Montefalco Rosso Ris. '08 | ♟♟ 5 |
| ● Montefalco Rosso Ziggurat '14 | ♟♟ 3 |
| ● Montefalco Rosso Ziggurat '11 | ♟♟ 3 |
| ● Montefalco Sagrantino '10 | ♟♟ 5 |
| ● Montefalco Sagrantino '08 | ♟♟ 5 |
| ● Montefalco Sagrantino Carapace '12 | ♟♟ 5 |
| ● Montefalco Sagrantino Carapace '09 | ♟♟ 5 |
| ● Montefalco Sagrantino Passito '12 | ♟♟ 5 |
| ● Montefalco Sagrantino Passito '10 | ♟♟ 5 |

# ★Lungarotti

V.LE G. LUNGAROTTI, 2
06089 TORGIANO [PG]
TEL. +39 075988661
www.lungarotti.it

**CELLAR SALES**
**PRE-BOOKED VISITS**
**ACCOMMODATION AND RESTAURANT SERVICE**
**ANNUAL PRODUCTION** 2,500,000 bottles
**HECTARES UNDER VINE** 250.00
**VITICULTURE METHOD** Certified Organic
**SUSTAINABLE WINERY**

Lungarotti is a benchmark winery in Italy. It was founded by Giorgio Lungarotti in the 1960s, and today has 250 hectares of vineyards (divided into two sections) at its disposal. There's the historic estate in Torgiano, which is dedicated to the DOC of the same name, and Montefalco, which was purchased in 2000 so as to focus exclusively on that great regional cultivar, Sagrantino. Recently they've been working hard on sustainability, through the conversion to organic management and the production of renewable energy using organic plant waste. We are used to a high-level selection of wines, but this year Torgiano truly bowled us over. Their Vigna Monticchio proves that it's a great Italian red with a 2013 that offers up fragrances of raspberry and roots and a palate that's potent, multifaceted and crossed by both freshness and savoriness. Tre Bicchieri. Their 2015 Vigna il Pino is also delicious, with its notes of herbs and citrus. Their 2014 Montefalco Sagrantino also gets a special mention.

| | |
|---|---|
| ● Torgiano Rosso Rubesco V. Monticchio Ris. '13 | ♈♈♈ 6 |
| ○ Bianco di Torgiano Torre di Giano V. Il Pino '15 | ♈♈ 5 |
| ○ Aurente '16 | ♈♈ 5 |
| ○ Bianco di Torgiano Torre di Giano '17 | ♈♈ 2* |
| ● Montefalco Sagrantino '14 | ♈♈ 5 |
| ● Torgiano Rosso Rubesco '15 | ♈♈ 3 |
| ● Montefalco Rosso '15 | ♈ 3 |
| ● Torgiano Rosso Rubesco V. Monticchio Ris. '12 | ♉♉♉ 6 |
| ● Torgiano Rosso Rubesco V. Monticchio Ris. '11 | ♉♉♉ 6 |
| ● Torgiano Rosso V. Monticchio Ris. '10 | ♉♉♉ 6 |
| ● Torgiano Rosso V. Monticchio Ris. '09 | ♉♉♉ 6 |
| ● Torgiano Rosso V. Monticchio Ris. '08 | ♉♉♉ 6 |

# La Madeleine

S.DA MONTINI, 38
05035 NARNI [TR]
TEL. +39 0744040427
www.cantinalamadeleine.it

**CELLAR SALES**
**PRE-BOOKED VISITS**
**ANNUAL PRODUCTION** 32,500 bottles
**HECTARES UNDER VINE** 6.40

The winery founded by Linda and Massimo D'Alema some ten years ago (with the purchase of an extant agricultural estate) is characterized by the use of international cultivar while also maintaining a connection with the territory. The couple's children, Giulia and Francesco, work their six hectares of terrain, giving rise to a Metodo Classico Rosé and three reds, made with Pinot Nero and Cabernet Franc. One of these, a wine that sees the total elimination of added sulfites, is part of the Wine Research Team project led by enologist Riccardo Cotarella. Their 2016 Pinot Nero did quite well. The nose features aromas of red fruit, slight sensations of forest undergrowth and a spicy touch that doesn't betray the grape's trademark fragrances. Their vibrant and full-bodied NarnOt, a Cabernet Franc, is redolent of mint, vanilla and ripe fruit. The rest of their selection also proved sound, starting with a delicious Metodo Classico sparkler made with Pinot Nero.

| | |
|---|---|
| ● Pinot Nero '16 | ♈♈ 6 |
| ● NarnOt '15 | ♈♈ 6 |
| ⊙ Nerosè Brut M. Cl. | ♈ 5 |
| ● Sfide '16 | ♈ 3 |
| ● Pinot Nero '15 | ♉♉ 6 |
| ● Pinot Nero '14 | ♉♉ 6 |
| ● Sfide '14 | ♉♉ 3* |
| ● Sfide '13 | ♉♉ 3* |

# Madrevite

LOC. VAIANO
VIA CIMBANO, 36
06061 CASTIGLIONE DEL LAGO [PG]
TEL. +39 0759527220
www.madrevite.com

**CELLAR SALES**
**PRE-BOOKED VISITS**
**ACCOMMODATION AND RESTAURANT SERVICE**
**ANNUAL PRODUCTION** 25,000 bottles
**HECTARES UNDER VINE** 11.00
**SUSTAINABLE WINERY**

Madrevite Vaiano's 10 hectares of contiguous vineyards are situated in Castiglion del Lago, within an agricultural estate that's twice as large. Since 2001, the year in which the winery was completely renovated, they've been promoting and supporting Trasimeno's viticulture. Sangiovese, Trebbiano Spoletino and Gamay del Trasimeno (Grenache) are the local varieties cultivated. These are accompanied by other cultivar, such as Syrah and Merlot. Their vineyards grow at notable attitudes, over 350 meters above sea level, and benefit from the lake's particular microclimate. Their 2016 C'osa, made with Gamay del Trasimeno (Grenache), stood out during our tastings. It's a great, Mediterranean red that's both savory and highly drinkable. Aromas of Mediterranean scrubland, red fruit and dried rose give way to a lean, elegant palate that's truly charming and deep. Their 2016 Trasimeno Rosso Glanio also did extremely well. It's a structured, pervasive wine made with Sangiovese, Gamay and Merlot.

| | |
|---|---|
| ● Trasimeno Gamay C'osa '16 | ♥♥ 5 |
| ● C. del Trasimeno Glanio '16 | ♥♥ 3 |
| ○ Il Reminore '17 | ♥ 3 |
| ◐ La Bisbetica Rosé '17 | ♥ 3 |
| ● C. del Trasimeno Glanio '14 | ♀♀ 3 |
| ● C. del Trasimeno Glanio '12 | ♀♀ 3 |
| ● C. del Trasimeno Glanio '11 | ♀♀ 3 |
| ● C. del Trasimeno Glanio '10 | ♀♀ 3* |
| ● Capofoco '12 | ♀♀ 4 |
| ● Che Syrah Sarà '13 | ♀♀ 4 |
| ○ Il Reminore '15 | ♀♀ 3* |
| ○ Il Reminore '14 | ♀♀ 3 |
| ○ Il Reminore '13 | ♀♀ 3 |
| ○ La Bisbetica Rosé '13 | ♀♀ 3 |
| ○ Re Minore '12 | ♀♀ 2* |

# Moretti Omero

LOC. SAN SABINO, 20
06030 GIANO DELL'UMBRIA [PG]
TEL. +39 074290426
www.morettiomero.it

**CELLAR SALES**
**PRE-BOOKED VISITS**
**ACCOMMODATION AND RESTAURANT SERVICE**
**ANNUAL PRODUCTION** 75,000 bottles
**HECTARES UNDER VINE** 13.00
**VITICULTURE METHOD** Certified Organic
**SUSTAINABLE WINERY**

This Giano del'Umbria estate of 13 hectares, which has been managed organically for more than 25 years, bears the name of its owner. Omero Moretti is a grand cultivator. He loves working the vineyards and his wines stand as a true mirror image of the territory. With the help of his entire family, he grows exclusively local Montefalco varieties (Sagrantino, Sangiovese and Grechetto). In addition to the terroir of origin, his wines faithfully express each vintage, with all the strengths and weaknesses it can bring. Some two wines in our finals confirm the valuable work being done by the producer. Their 2014 Montefalco Sagrantino is a great red that surprises on the nose for its multifaceted complexity with notes of cherry, dried leaves, spices and raspberries. In the mouth it proves precise, deep, savory and leave, event with its potent, tannic structure. Their delectable and fragrant 2015 Montefalco Rosso did well, while their 2017 Nessuno, a savory, charming white, also delivered.

| | |
|---|---|
| ● Montefalco Rosso '15 | ♥♥ 3* |
| ● Montefalco Sagrantino '14 | ♥♥ 5 |
| ○ Montefalco Bianco '17 | ♥♥ 3 |
| ○ Nessuno '17 | ♥♥ 3 |
| ○ Brut M. Cl. | ♥ 4 |
| ● Argo Passito '12 | ♀♀ 5 |
| ○ Grechetto '14 | ♀♀ 2* |
| ○ Montefalco Bianco '15 | ♀♀ 3 |
| ● Montefalco Sagrantino '13 | ♀♀ 5 |
| ● Montefalco Sagrantino '12 | ♀♀ 5 |
| ● Montefalco Sagrantino '11 | ♀♀ 5 |
| ● Montefalco Sagrantino '09 | ♀♀ 5 |
| ● Montefalco Sagrantino Vignalunga '12 | ♀♀ 7 |
| ○ Nessuno '14 | ♀♀ 2* |
| ○ Nessuno '13 | ♀♀ 2* |

## Palazzone

loc. Rocca Ripesena, 68
05019 Orvieto [TR]
Tel. +39 0763344921
www.palazzone.com

CELLAR SALES
PRE-BOOKED VISITS
ACCOMMODATION AND RESTAURANT SERVICE
ANNUAL PRODUCTION 130,000 bottles
HECTARES UNDER VINE 24.00
SUSTAINABLE WINERY

Palazzone, one of Orvieto's crown jewels, is expertly managed by Giovanni Dubini. Their selection is oriented around the territory and the appellation's native grapes, which are cultivated in the particularly well-suited hill areas of Rocca Ripesana and Romitorio. The style is precise and clean. These are elegant wines that are aromatically complex and as fresh as they are rich in flavor. The territory is on full display here, as is their aging potential (especially their bolder whites). It didn't get top marks, but their Campo del Guardiano proves that it's one of the best in its category. Their 2016 Orvieto Classico Superiore offers up aromas of white flowers, lemon and medlar, as well as a touch of aromatic herbs. The palate comes through lean, fine and elegant, subtle but never clenched. Their Muffa Nobile, Piviere (a red) and Musco also did well. The last of these is a white macerated with the skins that exhibits pleasant tannins.

| | |
|---|---|
| ○ Orvieto Cl. Sup. Campo del Guardiano '16 | ♟♟ 4 |
| ○ Musco '15 | ♟♟ 6 |
| ○ Orvieto Cl. Sup. Muffa Nobile '16 | ♟♟ 5 |
| ● Piviere '16 | ♟♟ 3 |
| ○ V'Indugio '16 | ♟♟ 4 |
| ● Armaleo '16 | ♟ 5 |
| ○ Grek '17 | ♟ 2 |
| ○ Orvieto Cl. Sup. Terre Vineate '17 | ♟ 3 |
| ○ Tixe '17 | ♟ 2 |
| ○ Viognier '17 | ♟ 3 |
| ○ Orvieto Cl. Sup. Campo del Guardiano '14 | ♟♟♟ 3* |
| ○ Orvieto Cl. Sup. Campo del Guardiano '11 | ♟♟♟ 2* |

## F.lli Pardi

via G. Pascoli, 7/9
06036 Montefalco [PG]
Tel. +39 0742379023
www.cantinapardi.it

CELLAR SALES
PRE-BOOKED VISITS
ANNUAL PRODUCTION 56,000 bottles
HECTARES UNDER VINE 11.00

The Pardi family have always produced wine in Motefalco. The most recent generation, however, have chosen to focus on exceptional quality by bringing out the absolute best of their private vineyards. 10 hectares are dedicated exclusively to wines from the Montefalco appellation (Rosso, Bianco and Sagrantino) and Spoleto. The idea is to divide production so that each wine represents a vineyard, thus highlighting the attributes of each plot. Their 2014 Sacrantino is an extraordinary Montefalco Sagrantino that amazes for its notes of fresh red fruit, with an aromatic profile that's both fragrant and close-focused. Cherry, raspberry and blackcurrant emerge, then a darker, austere note that calls up spices and forest undergrowth. The palate proves savory, extremely fresh, long and juicy. The variety's tannins are present, but perfectly integrated with the wine's texture. Tre Bicchieri. As always, their Montefalco Rosso delivers, proving delicious and highly enjoyable. Among their whites, their Colle di Giove stood out for its flavor and elegance.

| | |
|---|---|
| ● Montefalco Sagrantino Sacrantino '14 | ♟♟♟ 6 |
| ○ Colle di Giove '17 | ♟♟ 2* |
| ● Montefalco Rosso '16 | ♟♟ 3 |
| ● Montefalco Sagrantino '14 | ♟♟ 5 |
| ○ Spoleto Trebbiano Spoletino '17 | ♟ 3 |
| ○ Spoleto Trebbiano Spoletino '16 | ♟ 4 |
| ● Montefalco Sagrantino '13 | ♟♟♟ 5 |
| ● Montefalco Sagrantino '12 | ♟♟♟ 5 |
| ○ Colli Martani Grechetto '15 | ♟♟ 2* |
| ● Montefalco Rosso '15 | ♟♟ 3 |
| ● Montefalco Rosso '14 | ♟♟ 2* |
| ● Montefalco Sagrantino '11 | ♟♟ 5 |
| ● Montefalco Sagrantino Sacrantino '12 | ♟♟ 6 |
| ● Montefalco Sagrantino Sacrantino '11 | ♟♟ 6 |
| ○ Spoleto Trebbiano Spoletino '15 | ♟♟ 2* |

# Cantina Peppucci

loc. Sant'Antimo
fraz. Petroro, 4
06059 Todi [PG]
Tel. +39 0758947439
www.cantinapeppucci.com

CELLAR SALES
PRE-BOOKED VISITS
ACCOMMODATION
ANNUAL PRODUCTION 70,000 bottles
HECTARES UNDER VINE 12.50

Peppucci's estate is situated in a noteworthy area that's well-suited to vine growing and winemaking. Now in the hands of young, motivated, clear-headed Filippo, in just a few years the winery has managed to make a name for itself in the territory. In addition to wines made with traditional varieties (foremost Grechetto), some reds are made with a mix of both local and international cultivar. In recent years the house style has focused on highly drinkable wines that are complex yet elegant and capable of aging gracefully. Their 2016 Grechetto di Todi I Rovi turns out to be a great Italian white wine. It's complex and multifaceted on the nose with aromas of flowers and yellow fruit, Mediterranean herbs and delicately emerging spices. In the mouth it manages to bring together flavor and body across a linear palate that's always clean and fresh. Kudos to this Todi winery for their first Tre Bicchieri. Among their reds, we particularly appreciated their Petroro 4, a unique blend of Sangiovese, Sagrantino, Merlot and Cabernet.

| | | |
|---|---|---|
| ○ Todi Grechetto I Rovi '16 | 🍷🍷🍷 | 5 |
| ● Todi Rosso Petroro 4 '17 | 🍷🍷 | 2* |
| ● Altro lo Passito '15 | 🍷 | 5 |
| ○ Todi Grechetto Montorsolo '17 | 🍷 | 2 |
| ● Altro lo '12 | 🍷🍷 | 5 |
| ● Altro lo '11 | 🍷🍷 | 5 |
| ● Altro lo '10 | 🍷🍷 | 5 |
| ● Giovanni '12 | 🍷🍷 | 4 |
| ○ Todi Grechetto I Rovi '15 | 🍷🍷 | 3 |
| ○ Todi Grechetto Montorsolo '16 | 🍷🍷 | 2* |
| ○ Todi Grechetto Montorsolo '15 | 🍷🍷 | 2* |
| ○ Todi Grechetto Montorsolo '14 | 🍷🍷 | 2* |
| ○ Todi Grechetto Sup. I Rovi '14 | 🍷🍷 | 3* |
| ● Todi Rosso Petroro 4 '15 | 🍷🍷 | 2* |
| ● Todi Rosso Petroro 4 '14 | 🍷🍷 | 2* |

# Perticaia

loc. Casale
06036 Montefalco [PG]
Tel. +39 0742379014
www.perticaia.it

CELLAR SALES
PRE-BOOKED VISITS
ANNUAL PRODUCTION 120,000 bottles
HECTARES UNDER VINE 15.50
SUSTAINABLE WINERY

Without a doubt, Perticaia is a benchmark for Montefalco and over the years it has lent prestige to their entire region. The fact of having been purchased recently by a local family with international business ties hasn't changed its production philosophy, and new management continues to guarantee wines that are true to the territory. The few wines produced are centered exclusively on Montefalco and exhibit excellent finesse, firm mesh, good overall balance, and the capacity to give their best years after vintage. Their 2014 Montefalco Sagrantino did very well in our tastings, with the vintage giving rise to a wine of great elegance. Its tannins are detectable, though never astringent, while its pervasive body exhibits good acidic vigor. Their vibrant and juicy 2015 Montefalco Rosso also put in a good performance. The rest of their selection proved clean and sound.

| | | |
|---|---|---|
| ● Montefalco Sagrantino '14 | 🍷🍷 | 5 |
| ● Montefalco Rosso '15 | 🍷🍷 | 3 |
| ○ Spoleto Trebbiano Spoletino '17 | 🍷 | 2 |
| ● Montefalco Sagrantino '11 | 🍷🍷🍷 | 5 |
| ● Montefalco Sagrantino '10 | 🍷🍷🍷 | 5 |
| ● Montefalco Sagrantino '09 | 🍷🍷🍷 | 5 |
| ● Montefalco Sagrantino '07 | 🍷🍷🍷 | 5 |
| ● Montefalco Sagrantino '06 | 🍷🍷🍷 | 5 |
| ● Montefalco Sagrantino '05 | 🍷🍷🍷 | 5 |
| ● Montefalco Sagrantino '04 | 🍷🍷🍷 | 5 |
| ● Montefalco Rosso '14 | 🍷🍷 | 3 |
| ● Montefalco Sagrantino '13 | 🍷🍷 | 5 |
| ⊙ Rosato Cos'é '16 | 🍷🍷 | 2* |
| ● Umbria Rosso '16 | 🍷🍷 | 2* |

# Pomario

LOC. POMARIO
06066 PIEGARO [PG]
TEL. +39 0758358579
www.pomario.it

CELLAR SALES
PRE-BOOKED VISITS
RESTAURANT SERVICE
ANNUAL PRODUCTION 15,000 bottles
HECTARES UNDER VINE 8.00
VITICULTURE METHOD Certified Organic
SUSTAINABLE WINERY

Pomario is a small but lovely producer whose name comes from the territory in which they operate. Here in Piegaro the terrain is characterized by woods and vineyards, which create a unique landscape. The winery is a carefully managed gem, starting with geothermal power for temperature control and solar panels, which guarantee energy autonomy. The stony soil is situated at noteworthy elevations and gives rise to central Italy's most common cultivar, as well as a small share of international varieties. Among their reds both the Rubicola and the Sariano stood out. The latter is the producer's most important wine, made with grapes cultivated on an old vineyard of Sangiovese. It's a sanguine, earthy wine redolent of wild berry, and whose palate is fluid and energetic. Their 2017 Arale is a blend of Trebbiano and Malvasia that's fermented and aged in wood barrels. It offers up aromas of spices and mountain flowers, while the palate exhibits freshness, despite its texture. Their 2015 Muffato dolle Streghe is also worth trying.

| | | |
|---|---|---|
| ○ Arale '17 | ♟♟ | 4 |
| ○ Muffato delle Streghe '15 | ♟♟ | 6 |
| ● Rubicola '17 | ♟♟ | 2* |
| ● Sariano '15 | ♟♟ | 3 |
| ○ Batticoda '17 | ♟ | 2 |
| ⊙ Rondirose '17 | ♟ | 3 |
| ○ Arale '15 | ♟♟ | 4 |
| ○ Arale '14 | ♟♟ | 4 |
| ○ Arale '13 | ♟♟ | 4 |
| ○ Arale '12 | ♟♟ | 4 |
| ● Sariano '13 | ♟♟ | 3 |
| ● Sariano '12 | ♟♟ | 3 |
| ● Sariano '11 | ♟♟ | 3 |
| ● Sariano '10 | ♟♟ | 3 |

# Roccafiore

FRAZ. CHIOANO
VOC. COLLINA, 110A
06059 TODI [PG]
TEL. +39 0758942416
www.roccafiorewines.com

CELLAR SALES
PRE-BOOKED VISITS
ACCOMMODATION AND RESTAURANT SERVICE
ANNUAL PRODUCTION 120,000 bottles
HECTARES UNDER VINE 15.00
SUSTAINABLE WINERY

Roccafiore is an agricultural producer as well as a hotel and spa, a restaurant and hospitality service (with small wood apartments). It's an innovative project that has the further merit of being environmentally sustainable. Their 15 hectares of vineyards, which feature Sangiovese and Grechetto as well as a small quantity of Sagrantino, are spread out along the Todi hills. Attentive work in the field and experience in the cellar guarantee elegant, complex, long-lived wines. During our tastings Roccafiore had an outstanding day. Their 2016 FiorFiore is a truly great Grechetto that amazes both the nose and the palate. It's bolstered by a masterly complexity that ranges from iodine notes to flowery and citrusy nuances. The palate comes through pervasive, savory, extremely long and elegant. It's a Tre Bicchieri hands down. Their Il Roccafiore, a highly drinkable Sangiovese, is also a top wine. Finally, we mention their Rosso Melograno and Prove d'Autore, both extremely well-made wines.

| | | |
|---|---|---|
| ○ Fiorfiore '16 | ♟♟♟ | 4* |
| ● Il Roccafiore '15 | ♟♟ | 3* |
| ○ Collina d'Oro '17 | ♟♟ | 5 |
| ● Prova d'Autore '15 | ♟♟ | 5 |
| ● Rosso Melograno '16 | ♟♟ | 2* |
| ○ Fiordaliso '17 | ♟ | 2 |
| ● Todi Grechetto Sup. Fiorfiore '14 | ♟♟♟ | 3* |
| ○ Fiorfiore '15 | ♟♟ | 4 |
| ● Il Roccafiore '14 | ♟♟ | 3* |
| ● Il Roccafiore '13 | ♟♟ | 3 |
| ● Prova d'Autore '14 | ♟♟ | 5 |
| ● Prova d'Autore '13 | ♟♟ | 5 |
| ○ Todi Bianco Fiordaliso '15 | ♟♟ | 2* |
| ○ Todi Grechetto Sup. Fiorfiore '13 | ♟♟ | 3* |
| ● Todi Rosso Melograno '14 | ♟♟ | 2* |

# Romanelli

LOC. COLLE SAN CLEMENTE, 129A
06036 MONTEFALCO [PG]
TEL. +39 0742371245
www.romanelli.se

**CELLAR SALES**
**PRE-BOOKED VISITS**
**ANNUAL PRODUCTION** 40,000 bottles
**HECTARES UNDER VINE** 7.50

Romanelli is small on quantity, but remarkable when it comes to quality. Indeed, they've carved out a position among Montefalco's leading producers, bolstered by stylistically clean wines as well as a knack for original interpretations of the territory. Their selection features Montefalco's classic wines, Sagrantino, Rosso and a Riserva. Among the whites we find an interesting Grechetto and, especially, their Trebbiano Spoletinos. In the cellar they work to balance extraction and aging, as a defining characteristic of their production style, along with the clay terrain and notable elevations of their vineyards. Two wines made it into our finals, demonstrating the value of the work done by this small Montefalco producer. Their 2014 Sagrantino delivers for its aromas of cherry, spices and a hint of mint. The palate flows well. Tannins are there but it's not a cropped wine, thanks to well-integrated acidity. The passito is a 2013 that offers up aromas of ripe black fruit, hints of quinine and dried fruit. The palate exhibits a perfect balance between sweet and savory.

| | |
|---|---|
| ● Montefalco Sagrantino '14 | ♈♈ 5 |
| ● Montefalco Sagrantino Passito '13 | ♈♈ 5 |
| ○ Le Tese Trebbiano Spoletino '16 | ♈♈ 4 |
| ○ Colli Martani Grechetto '17 | ♈ 2 |
| ● Montefalco Rosso '15 | ♈ 3 |
| ● Montefalco Sagrantino '11 | ♈♈♈ 5 |
| ● Montefalco Sagrantino '10 | ♈♈♈ 5 |
| ○ Colli Martani Grechetto '15 | ♈♈ 2• |
| ● Montefalco Rosso '11 | ♈♈ 3 |
| ● Montefalco Rosso '10 | ♈♈ 2* |
| ● Montefalco Rosso Molinetta Ris. '12 | ♈♈ 5 |
| ● Montefalco Sagrantino '13 | ♈♈ 5 |
| ● Montefalco Sagrantino '12 | ♈♈ 5 |
| ● Montefalco Sagrantino Medeo '12 | ♈♈ 8 |
| ● Montefalco Sagrantino Medeo '11 | ♈♈ 8 |

# Scacciadiavoli

LOC. CANTINONE, 31
06036 MONTEFALCO [PG]
TEL. +39 0742371210
www.scacciadiavoli.it

**CELLAR SALES**
**PRE-BOOKED VISITS**
**ANNUAL PRODUCTION** 200,000 bottles
**HECTARES UNDER VINE** 37.00
**SUSTAINABLE WINERY**

Construction of the Scacciadiavoli winery, a project deeply sought after by Prince Boncampagni Ludovisi, goes back to the late 19th century. The current property, however, is managed by the Pambuffetti family, who bought the estate in the 1950s. Their wines are made with grapes cultivated in the Montefalco DOC appellations (Rosso, Bianco and Sagrantino). These are accompanied by a Metodo Classico sparkling wine. Their vineyards, which grow in clay soil at up to 400 meters above sea level, are divided between Montefalco, Gualdo Cattaneo and Giano dell'Umbria. Their 2013 Montefalco Sagrantino had an excellent day during our tastings. An extra year of aging (with respect to the moment it could be released to the public) agreed with their selection's most important wine, with its dense aromas of raspberries and tobacco, dried leaves and orange. The mouth is lean and pleasant, it's just a bit cropped by edgy tannins at the end. Their delicious Spumante Rosé, a flowery and citrusy wine, is also worth mentioning.

| | |
|---|---|
| ○ Brut Rosé M. Cl. | ♈♈ 4 |
| ● Montefalco Sagrantino '13 | ♈♈ 5 |
| ○ Montefalco Bianco '16 | ♈ 3 |
| ○ Montefalco Grechetto '17 | ♈ 2 |
| ○ Spumante Brut | ♈ 2 |
| ● Montefalco Sagrantino '10 | ♈♈♈ 5 |
| ○ Montefalco Bianco '14 | ♈♈ 3 |
| ○ Montefalco Bianco '13 | ♈♈ 3 |
| ● Montefalco Rosso '15 | ♈♈ 3 |
| ● Montefalco Rosso '13 | ♈♈ 3 |
| ● Montefalco Rosso '12 | ♈♈ 3 |
| ● Montefalco Sagrantino '12 | ♈♈ 5 |
| ● Montefalco Sagrantino '11 | ♈♈ 5 |
| ● Montefalco Sagrantino '09 | ♈♈ 5 |
| ● Montefalco Sagrantino Passito '12 | ♈♈ 5 |

# UMBRIA

782

## Sportoletti

VIA LOMBARDIA, 1
06038 SPELLO [PG]
TEL. +39 0742651461
www.sportoletti.com

CELLAR SALES
PRE-BOOKED VISITS
ANNUAL PRODUCTION 210,000 bottles
HECTARES UNDER VINE 30.00
SUSTAINABLE WINERY

Since the late 1970s the Sportoletti family has dedicated itself full-time to vine growing. First it was brothers Ernesto and Remo (who followed their father's teachings) and now with a new generation. Here, between Spello and Assisi, the hills give rise to five wines. Two belong to the Assisi DOC appellation, the others are IGTs made from both local and international grape varieties. Their wines, which reflect a modern style, are technically well-crafted and exhibit good aging potential, especially their Villa Fidelia, a classic Bordeaux blend. And this Assisi producer did quite well during our tastings. Their 2016 Villa Fidelia Bianco, a blend of Grechetto and Chardonnay, stood out. On the nose it features aromas of spices, vanilla and ripe yellow fruit. The palate proves pervasive, plush with flavor and marked by well-integrated acidity. The same wine, as a red, offers up aromas of black fruit and quinine. In the mouth it's savory and very close-knit. The rest of their selection also proved sound.

| | |
|---|---|
| ○ Villa Fidelia Bianco '16 | ♛♛ 3 |
| ● Villa Fidelia Rosso '16 | ♛♛ 4 |
| ○ Assisi Grechetto '17 | ♛ 1* |
| ● Assisi Rosso '17 | ♛ 2 |
| ● Villa Fidelia Rosso '98 | ♛♛♛ 4* |
| ● Assisi Rosso '15 | ♛♛ 2* |
| ● Assisi Rosso '14 | ♛♛ 2* |
| ○ Villa Fidelia Bianco '15 | ♛♛ 3 |
| ○ Villa Fidelia Bianco '14 | ♛♛ 3 |
| ○ Villa Fidelia Bianco '13 | ♛♛ 3 |
| ○ Villa Fidelia Bianco '12 | ♛♛ 3 |
| ● Villa Fidelia Rosso '15 | ♛♛ 4 |
| ● Villa Fidelia Rosso '14 | ♛♛ 4 |
| ● Villa Fidelia Rosso '13 | ♛♛ 4 |
| ● Villa Fidelia Rosso '12 | ♛♛ 4 |

## ★Giampaolo Tabarrini

FRAZ. TURRITA
06036 MONTEFALCO [PG]
TEL. +39 0742379351
www.tabarrini.com

CELLAR SALES
PRE-BOOKED VISITS
ANNUAL PRODUCTION 70,000 bottles
HECTARES UNDER VINE 18.00
SUSTAINABLE WINERY

Giampaolo Tabarrini is an extraordinary figure. He's always ecstatic about his new projects, yet serious and precise when it comes to making the wines that bear his name. His new winery is an impressive, forward-thinking project that speaks volumes about the family's ambitions. Sagrantino, made so as to respect the cru of origin, plays a leading role, with three different wines that express each terroir. A white full of character also finds a place in their selection. It's a Trebbiano Spoletino that's a forerunner in its category. And their Adarmando proves to be a war horse. This 2016 Trebbiano Spoletino charms for its iodine aromas of wild flowers, yellow fruit and shrubs. In the mouth savoriness takes over, joined by fresh acidity, making for a delectable, deep and clean palate. Tre Bicchieri. Their two 2014 Montefalco Sagrantinos, Colle Grimladesco and Colle all Macchie, also proved delicious, especially when considering their ageworthiness.

| | |
|---|---|
| ○ Adarmando '16 | ♛♛♛ 4* |
| ● Montefalco Sagrantino Campo alla Cerqua '14 | ♛♛ 6 |
| ● Montefalco Sagrantino Colle alle Macchie '14 | ♛♛ 6 |
| ● Montefalco Sagrantino Colle Grimaldesco '14 | ♛♛ 5 |
| ○ Adarmando '15 | ♛♛♛ 4* |
| ● Montefalco Sagrantino Campo alla Cerqua '12 | ♛♛♛ 6 |
| ● Montefalco Sagrantino Campo alla Cerqua '11 | ♛♛♛ 6 |
| ● Montefalco Sagrantino Campo alla Cerqua '10 | ♛♛♛ 6 |
| ● Montefalco Sagrantino Colle alle Macchie '09 | ♛♛♛ 6 |

## Terre de la Custodia

LOC. PALOMBARA
06035 GUALDO CATTANEO [PG]
TEL. +39 0742929586
www.terredelacustodia.it

CELLAR SALES
PRE-BOOKED VISITS
ANNUAL PRODUCTION 1,000,000 bottles
HECTARES UNDER VINE 160.00
SUSTAINABLE WINERY

Terre de la Custodia is owned by the
Farchioni family, entrepreneurs who work in
the olive oil, wheat and beer industries as
well. In terms of production volumes, they
are one of the region's major wineries, with
more than a million bottles per year. Their
selection features quality wines from both
Montefalco and Todi (an ideal area for
whites). A variety of grapes are cultivated,
including those used for their Metodo
Classico sparkling wines. And it was a
sparkling wine that amazed during our
tastings. Their Gladius Sublimis, a wine
cultivated on the Colli Martani hills,
delivered for its citrus aromas of white fruit
and cakes, as well as its well-balanced
palate in which perfectly dosed bubbles
integrate with a pervasive, gratifying
mouthfeel. Their 2017 Plentis, a Montefalco
Bianco, also did well.

| | |
|---|---|
| ○ Colli Martani Spumante | |
| Gladius Sublimis | ♟♟ 4 |
| ○ Montefalco Bianco Plentis '17 | ♟♟ 3 |
| ● Montefalco Rosso Rubium Ris. '15 | ♟♟ 5 |
| ○ Colli Martani Spumante Gladius | ♟ 4 |
| ○ Colli Martani Grechetto '14 | ♟♟ 2* |
| ○ Colli Martani Grechetto Plentis '14 | ♟♟ 3 |
| ● Colli Martani Rosso Collezione '14 | ♟♟ 2* |
| ○ Colli Martani Spumante | |
| Gladius Sublimis '10 | ♟♟ 4 |
| ● Montefalco Rosso '12 | ♟♟ 4 |
| ● Montefalco Rosso Ris. '13 | ♟♟ 5 |
| ● Montefalco Rosso Rubium Ris. '14 | ♟♟ 5 |
| ● Montefalco Sagrantino '11 | ♟♟ 6 |
| ○ Sublimis Gladius Brut M. Cl. '10 | ♟♟ 4 |

## Terre Margaritelli

FRAZ. CHIUSACCIA
LOC. MIRALDUOLO
06089 TORGIANO [PG]
TEL. +39 0757824668
www.terremargaritelli.com

CELLAR SALES
PRE-BOOKED VISITS
ACCOMMODATION
ANNUAL PRODUCTION 120,000 bottles
HECTARES UNDER VINE 52.00
VITICULTURE METHOD Certified Organic

Terre Margaritelli's estate is a contiguous
tract of 50 hectares situated in Torgiano.
Here native grape varieties are cultivated
according to principles of organic
agriculture. The Margaritellis are successful
entrepreneurs who have a passion for art
and wine. In recent years they've put
forward a selection that's extremely precise
stylistically, satisfying to drink and that does
a good job communicating both the
territory of origin and the grapes used.
Their vineyards grow in moderately clay soil
on the Torgiano hills, at 250 meters above
sea level. Two wines stood out the most.
The first is a truly unique, semi-dry red
made with Canaiolo. It offers up aromas of
rose, ripe cherry and mulberry preserves.
The mouth opens with a hint of sweetness
but it's immediately balanced by acidity and
a slightly tannic sensation. We also enjoyed
their 2015 Freccia degli Scacchi, a savory
and deep Sangiovese.

| | |
|---|---|
| ● Torgiano Rosso | |
| Freccia degli Scacchi Ris. '15 | ♟♟ 5 |
| ● Torgiano Simon de Brion V. T. '17 | ♟♟ 3 |
| ○ Torgiano Bianco Costellato '17 | ♟ 2 |
| ○ Torgiano Bianco Pietramala '17 | ♟ 2 |
| ⊙ Torgiano Rosato Venturosa '17 | ♟ 2 |
| ● Torgiano Rosso Mirantico '16 | ♟ 2 |
| ● Torgiano Rosso Roccascossa '17 | ♟ 2 |
| ● Malot '15 | ♟♟ 3 |
| ● Roccascossa '16 | ♟♟ 2* |
| ○ Torgiano Bianco Costellato '15 | ♟♟ 2* |
| ● Torgiano Rosso | |
| Freccia degli Scacchi Ris. '13 | ♟♟ 5 |
| ● Torgiano Rosso | |
| Freccia degli Scacchi Ris. '12 | ♟♟ 5 |

# Tudernum

LOC. PIAN DI PORTO, 146
06059 TODI [PG]
TEL. +39 0758989403
www.tudernum.it

**CELLAR SALES**
**PRE-BOOKED VISITS**
**ACCOMMODATION AND RESTAURANT SERVICE**
**ANNUAL PRODUCTION** 1,000,000 bottles
**HECTARES UNDER VINE** 230.00

Todi's cooperative winery Tudernum was founded in 1958. Today they work with 120 vine growers who cultivate about 200 hectares of vineyards across Todi and Montefalco's principal appellations for a total production volume of about 2 million bottles per year. In recent years the quality of their selection has improved significantly and comprises some of the the region's most important wines, starting with their crown jewel, Montefalco Sagrantino. Other interesting wines include those made with international grapes and with Grechetto. Once again, their Montefalco Sagrantino stood out during our tastings. Their 2014 Fidenzio is lovely in the mouth, with tannins that enrich without cropping. There's plenty of mouthfeel but it's never unbalanced. Complex, enticing aromas complete the picture. Two wines from Todi also proved excellent. Their 2016 Rojano is a close-knit red with structure, while their 2016 Colle Nobile is a savory, dense Grechetto.

| | |
|---|---|
| ● Montefalco Sagrantino Fidenzio '14 | ♛♛ 4 |
| ○ Todi Grechetto Sup. Colle Nobile '16 | ♛♛ 2* |
| ● Todi Rosso Sup. Rojano '16 | ♛♛ 3 |
| ○ Todi Grechetto '17 | ♛ 2 |
| ● Todi Rosso '16 | ♛ 2 |
| ● Montefalco Sagrantino Fidenzio '12 | ♛♛♛ 4* |
| ● Montefalco Sagrantino Fidenzio '11 | ♛♛ 4 |
| ● Montefalco Sagrantino Fidenzio '10 | ♛♛ 4 |
| ○ Todi Grechetto '16 | ♛♛ 2* |
| ○ Todi Grechetto '15 | ♛♛ 2* |
| ○ Todi Grechetto '14 | ♛♛ 2* |
| ● Todi Rosso '15 | ♛♛ 2* |
| ● Todi Rosso '14 | ♛♛ 2* |
| ● Todi Rosso Sup. Rojano '13 | ♛♛ 3* |
| ● Todi Rosso Sup. Rojano '12 | ♛♛ 3 |

# Tenuta Le Velette

FRAZ. CANALE DI ORVIETO
LOC. LE VELETTE, 23
05019 ORVIETO [TR]
TEL. +39 076329090
www.levelette.it

**CELLAR SALES**
**PRE-BOOKED VISITS**
**ANNUAL PRODUCTION** 270,000 bottles
**HECTARES UNDER VINE** 109.00
**SUSTAINABLE WINERY**

Tenuta Le Velette is an Orvieto winery that produces both wines belonging to the area's appellations and IGTs made with international grapes like Sauvignon and Merlot. The producer uses tufaceous caves to age its wines while the vineyards (about 120 hectares) enjoy Orvieto's unique and characteristic volcanic subsoil. Precise, technically impeccable wines result in a style that expresses the characteristics of the cultivar and territory. Once again, their two Orvietto Classicos, Berganorio and Lunato, both did very well. The former features a lean, relaxed, subtle palate, while the nose offers up aromas of citrus and white flowers. Their 2017 Lunato is more structured, with nuances of yellow fruit and wild flowers. Among their reds their 2014 Gaudio stands out as a wine of structure with fragrances of cherry and tanned leather. The rest of their selection did well, proving technically well-made.

| | |
|---|---|
| ● Gaudio '14 | ♛♛ 4 |
| ○ Orvieto Cl. Berganorio '17 | ♛♛ 2* |
| ○ Orvieto Cl. Sup. Lunato '17 | ♛♛ 2* |
| ● Accordo '13 | ♛ 3 |
| ⊙ Monaldesco '17 | ♛ 2 |
| ● Rosso Orvietano Rosso di Spicca '16 | ♛ 2 |
| ○ Traluce '17 | ♛ 3 |
| ● Calanco '03 | ♛♛♛ 4 |
| ● Calanco '95 | ♛♛♛ 4* |
| ● Gaudio '03 | ♛♛♛ 4 |
| ● Calanco '13 | ♛♛ 4 |
| ● Calanco '12 | ♛♛ 4 |
| ● Gaudio '13 | ♛♛ 4 |
| ○ Orvieto Cl. Berganorio '15 | ♛♛ 2* |
| ○ Orvieto Cl. Sup. Lunato '15 | ♛♛ 2* |

# Villa Mongalli

VIA DELLA CIMA, 52
06031 BEVAGNA [PG]
TEL. +39 0742360703
www.villamongalli.com

**CELLAR SALES**
**ACCOMMODATION**
**ANNUAL PRODUCTION** 70,000 bottles
**HECTARES UNDER VINE** 15.00

Villa Mongalli has 15 hectares of vineyards at its disposal, situated along the Bevagna and Montefalco hills. Primarily classic cultivar are grown, with Sagrantino making up about half and Sangiovese, Trebbiano Spoletino and international varieties providing the rest. Their selection is of excellent quality. Their Montefalco Sagrantinos are particularly commendable, two wines whose grapes are cultivated on bona fide cru: Della Cima and Colcimino. The latter comes from a group of small plots in San Marco. And their Della Cima proves to be their most expressive wine, according to our tastings. Notes of tanned leather, tobacco leaves, spices and black fruit give way to a deep, supple, fresh mouth that's tannic but never cropped. Among their white their 2017 Trebbiano Spoletino stands out for its aromas of grains and green tea and a palate of incredible savoriness. The rest of their selection proved sound and enjoyable.

| | | |
|---|---|---|
| ○ Calicanto Trebbiano Spoletino '17 | ♥♥ | 5 |
| ● Montefalco Sagrantino Della Cima '14 | ♥♥ | 8 |
| ● Montefalco Rosso Le Grazie '16 | ♥ | 5 |
| ● Montefalco Sagrantino Pozzo del Curato '14 | ♥ | 7 |
| ● Montefalco Sagrantino Colcimino '08 | ♥♥♥ | 3* |
| ● Montefalco Sagrantino Della Cima '10 | ♥♥♥ | 8 |
| ● Montefalco Sagrantino Della Cima '06 | ♥♥♥ | 6 |
| ● Montefalco Sagrantino Pozzo del Curato '09 | ♥♥♥ | 6 |
| ○ Calicanto Trebbiano Spoletino '15 | ♥♥ | 5 |
| ● Montefalco Sagrantino Della Cima '13 | ♥♥ | 8 |
| ● Montefalco Sagrantino Pozzo del Curato '13 | ♥♥ | 7 |

# Zanchi

S.DA PROV.LE AMELIA-ORTE KM 4,610
05022 AMELIA [TR]
TEL. +39 0744970011
www.cantinezanchi.it

**CELLAR SALES**
**PRE-BOOKED VISITS**
**ANNUAL PRODUCTION** 80,000 bottles
**HECTARES UNDER VINE** 31.00
**SUSTAINABLE WINERY**

This family-run winery produces about 80,000 bottles a year, thanks to their vineyards situated in the Amelia DOC appellation in Terni. Zanchi was founded some 40 years ago and emphasizes an approach centered on environmental sustainability. They cultivate traditional varieties like Grechetto, Ciliegiolo, Trebbiano and Aleatico. Their wines are expressive, true to the cultivar, highly drinkable, a testament to the territory. In short, theirs is an artisanal winery that pays tribute to one of the region's lesser known districts, but one worth watching. This year their selection gave a convincing performance, but especially it charmed. We start with an excellent Majolo, a 2010 white that doesn't seem afraid to age. The nose is spice, with mountain herbs and a touch of incense giving way to a slightly tannic and deep palate. Their 2017 Carmino is an entirely different wine. It's a fresh, fragrant Ciliegiolo. Their 2017 Arvore, rather, is a Grechetto of masterful savoriness.

| | | |
|---|---|---|
| ● Amelia Ciliegiolo Carmino '17 | ♥♥ | 2* |
| ○ Amelia Grechetto Arvore '17 | ♥♥ | 2* |
| ○ Majolo '10 | ♥♥ | 5 |
| ● Amelia Rosso Armané '15 | ♥ | 2 |
| ● Amelia Rosso Sciurio Ris. '11 | ♥ | 4 |
| ○ Vignavecchia Trebbiano '14 | ♥ | 5 |
| ● Amelia Ciliegiolo Carmino '16 | ♥♥ | 2* |
| ● Amelia Ciliegiolo Carmino '13 | ♥♥ | 2* |
| ○ Amelia Grechetto Arvore '16 | ♥♥ | 2* |
| ○ Amelia Grechetto Arvore '14 | ♥♥ | 2* |
| ● Amelia Rosso Armané '13 | ♥♥ | 2* |
| ● Amelia Rosso Sciurio Ris. '09 | ♥♥ | 4 |
| ○ V. Vecchia Trebbiano '10 | ♥♥ | 5 |
| ○ Vignavecchia '12 | ♥♥ | 5 |
| ○ Vignavecchia '11 | ♥♥ | 5 |

## Cantina Altarocca

LOC. ROCCA RIPESENA, 62
05018 ORVIETO [TR]
TEL. +39 0763344210
www.cantinaaltarocca.com

CELLAR SALES
PRE-BOOKED VISITS
ACCOMMODATION AND RESTAURANT SERVICE
ANNUAL PRODUCTION 50,000 bottles
HECTARES UNDER VINE 11.00
VITICULTURE METHOD Certified Organic

| | |
|---|---|
| ● Lavico '15 | ♟♟ 4 |
| ○ Orvieto Cl. Sup. Albaco '17 | ♟♟ 3 |
| ○ Orvieto Cl. Arcosesto '17 | ♟ 2 |
| ● Rosso Orvietano Librato '17 | ♟ 3 |

## Argillae

VOC. POMARRO, 45
05010 ALLERONA [TR]
TEL. +39 0763624604
www.argillae.eu

CELLAR SALES
PRE-BOOKED VISITS
ANNUAL PRODUCTION 70,000 bottles
HECTARES UNDER VINE 38.00
SUSTAINABLE WINERY

| | |
|---|---|
| ○ Orvieto Cl. Sup. Panata '17 | ♟♟ 4 |
| ○ Grechetto '17 | ♟ 3 |
| ○ Orvieto '17 | ♟ 2 |
| ○ Primo d'Anfora '16 | ♟ 6 |

## Benedetti & Grigi

LOC. LA POLZELLA
06036 MONTEFALCO [PG]
TEL. +39 0742379136
www.benedettiegrigi.it

CELLAR SALES
ANNUAL PRODUCTION 400,000 bottles
HECTARES UNDER VINE 68.00

| | |
|---|---|
| ● Montefalco Sagrantino '14 | ♟♟ 5 |
| ○ Montefalco Grechetto La Gaita del Falco '17 | ♟♟ 2* |
| ● Montefalco Rosso '16 | ♟♟ 3 |

## Bigi

LOC. PONTE GIULIO
05018 ORVIETO [TR]
TEL. +39 0763315888
www.cantinebigi.it

PRE-BOOKED VISITS
ANNUAL PRODUCTION 3,500,000 bottles
HECTARES UNDER VINE 261.00

| | |
|---|---|
| ○ Strozzavolpe Grechetto '17 | ♟♟ 2* |
| ○ Vipra Bianca '17 | ♟♟ 2* |
| ● Vipra Rossa '17 | ♟♟ 2* |
| ○ Orvieto Cl. '17 | ♟ 1* |

## Briziarelli

VIA COLLE ALLODOLE, 10
06031 BEVAGNA [PG]
TEL. +39 0742360036
www.cantinebriziarelli.it

CELLAR SALES
PRE-BOOKED VISITS
ACCOMMODATION AND RESTAURANT SERVICE
ANNUAL PRODUCTION 70,000 bottles
HECTARES UNDER VINE 18.50

| | |
|---|---|
| ● Montefalco Sagrantino '14 | ♟♟ 5 |
| ● Montefalco Rosso '15 | ♟♟ 3 |
| ● Montefalco Rosso Mattone Ris. '15 | ♟♟ 5 |

## Cardeto

FRAZ. SFERRACAVALLO
LOC. CARDETO
05018 ORVIETO [TR]
TEL. +39 0763341286
www.cardeto.com

CELLAR SALES
PRE-BOOKED VISITS
ANNUAL PRODUCTION 3,000,000 bottles
HECTARES UNDER VINE 700.00

| | |
|---|---|
| ○ Orvieto Cl. Sup. Febeo '16 | ♟♟ 3* |
| ○ Grechetto '17 | ♟ 2 |
| ● Merlot '16 | ♟ 2 |
| ○ Orvieto Cl. '17 | ♟ 2 |

## Carini

LOC. CANNETO
FRAZ. COLLE UMBERTO
S.DA DEL TEGOLARO, 3
06133 PERUGIA
TEL. +39 0756059495
www.agrariacarini.it

CELLAR SALES
PRE-BOOKED VISITS
ANNUAL PRODUCTION 40,000 bottles
HECTARES UNDER VINE 16.00
VITICULTURE METHOD Certified Organic

| | | |
|---|---|---|
| ● C. del Trasimeno Rosso Òscano '17 | ♛♛ 3 | |
| ○ C. del Trasimeno Bianco Rile '17 | ♛ 3 | |
| ⊙ Le Cupe '17 | ♛ 3 | |

## Castelgrosso

FRAZ. TORREGROSSO
VIA LEX SPOLETINA, 1
06044 CASTEL RITALDI [PG]
TEL. +39 3397821406
www.agricolacastelgrosso.com

CELLAR SALES
PRE-BOOKED VISITS
ACCOMMODATION
ANNUAL PRODUCTION 30,000 bottles
HECTARES UNDER VINE 10.00

| | | |
|---|---|---|
| ○ Spoleto Trebbiano Spoletino Sup. '17 | ♛♛ 2* | |
| ● Montefalco Sagrantino '14 | ♛ 5 | |
| ● Rosso di San Gregorio '14 | ♛ 2 | |

## Castello delle Regine

LOC. LE REGINE
VIA DI CASTELLUCCIO
05022 AMELIA [TR]
TEL. +39 0744702005
www.castellodelleregine.com

CELLAR SALES
PRE-BOOKED VISITS
ACCOMMODATION AND RESTAURANT SERVICE
ANNUAL PRODUCTION 400,000 bottles
HECTARES UNDER VINE 65.00

| | | |
|---|---|---|
| ○ Poggio delle Regine Bianco '17 | ♛♛ 2* | |
| ● Rosso di Podernovo '15 | ♛♛ 2* | |
| ○ Bianco delle Regine '17 | ♛ 3 | |
| ● Poggio delle Regine Sangiovese '16 | ♛ 2 | |

## Castello di Corbara

LOC. CORBARA, 7
05018 ORVIETO [TR]
TEL. +39 0763304035
www.castellodicorbara.it

CELLAR SALES
PRE-BOOKED VISITS
ANNUAL PRODUCTION 200,000 bottles
HECTARES UNDER VINE 100.00

| | | |
|---|---|---|
| ● Lago di Corbara '16 | ♛♛ 3 | |
| ● Lago di Corbara De Coronis '15 | ♛♛ 4 | |
| ○ Orvieto Cl. Sup. '17 | ♛ 2 | |
| ● Sangiovese Merlot '17 | ♛ 2 | |

## Castello di Magione

V.LE CAVALIERI DI MALTA, 31
06063 MAGIONE [PG]
TEL. +39 0755057319
www.sagrivit.it

CELLAR SALES
PRE-BOOKED VISITS
ANNUAL PRODUCTION 200,000 bottles
HECTARES UNDER VINE 42.00

| | | |
|---|---|---|
| ● Sangiovese '17 | ♛♛ 2* | |
| ● C. del Trasimeno Rosso Morcinaia '13 | ♛ 5 | |
| ○ Grechetto '17 | ♛ 2 | |
| ● Vittoriosa 1565 '11 | ♛ 5 | |

## Chiorri

LOC. SANT'ENEA
VIA TODI, 100
06132 PERUGIA
TEL. +39 075607141
www.chiorri.it

CELLAR SALES
PRE-BOOKED VISITS
ACCOMMODATION AND RESTAURANT SERVICE
ANNUAL PRODUCTION 100,000 bottles
HECTARES UNDER VINE 25.00
SUSTAINABLE WINERY

| | | |
|---|---|---|
| ● Merlot Sel. Antonio Chiorri '12 | ♛♛ 4 | |
| ○ Titus '17 | ♛♛ 2* | |
| ○ Etesia '17 | ♛ 2 | |
| ⊙ Ventorosa '17 | ♛ 2 | |

## Cantina Colle Ciocco

VIA B. GOZZOLI 1/5
06036 MONTEFALCO [PG]
TEL. +39 0742379859
www.colleciocco.it

CELLAR SALES
PRE-BOOKED VISITS
ANNUAL PRODUCTION 45,000 bottles
HECTARES UNDER VINE 15.00

| | | |
|---|---|---|
| ❧ Montefalco Sagrantino '12 | ♟♟ 5 | |
| ○ Spoleto Trebbiano Spoletino Tempestivo '17 | ♟♟ 3 | |
| ⊙ Brixio '17 | ♟ 2 | |

## ★Còlpetrone

FRAZ. MARCELLANO
VIA PONTE LA MANDRIA, 8/1
06035 GUALDO CATTANEO [PG]
TEL. +39 074299827
www.colpetrone.it

CELLAR SALES
PRE-BOOKED VISITS
ANNUAL PRODUCTION 350,000 bottles
HECTARES UNDER VINE 63.00

| | |
|---|---|
| ● Montefalco Sagrantino Sacer '09 | ♟♟ 7 |
| ○ Grechetto '17 | ♟ 2 |

## Custodi

LOC. CANALE
V.LE VENERE
05018 ORVIETO [TR]
TEL. +39 076329053
www.cantinacustodi.com

CELLAR SALES
PRE-BOOKED VISITS
ANNUAL PRODUCTION 65,000 bottles
HECTARES UNDER VINE 40.00

| | |
|---|---|
| ○ Orvieto Cl. Sup. Pertusa V. T. '17 | ♟♟ 5 |
| ○ Orvieto Cl. Belloro '17 | ♟ 2 |
| ● Piancoleto '17 | ♟ 2 |

## Fattoria di Monticello

FRAZ. RIPALVELLA
VOC. PONETRO
05010 SAN VENANZO [TR]
TEL. +39 3452550509
www.fattoriadimonticello.it

CELLAR SALES
PRE-BOOKED VISITS
ACCOMMODATION AND RESTAURANT SERVICE
ANNUAL PRODUCTION 70,000 bottles
HECTARES UNDER VINE 20.00

| | |
|---|---|
| ○ Giacchio '17 | ♟♟ 2* |
| ● Ponetro '16 | ♟♟ 4 |
| ● Vibio '16 | ♟♟ 2* |

## Fongoli

LOC. SAN MARCO DI MONTEFALCO
06036 MONTEFALCO [PG]
TEL. +39 0742378930
www.fongoli.com

CELLAR SALES
PRE-BOOKED VISITS
ACCOMMODATION
ANNUAL PRODUCTION 100,000 bottles
HECTARES UNDER VINE 27.00
VITICULTURE METHOD Certified Organic

| | |
|---|---|
| ○ Maceratum '17 | ♟♟ 6 |
| ○ Colli Martani Grechetto La Palmetta '17 | ♟ 3 |
| ○ Laetitia Trebbiano Spoletino '17 | ♟ 5 |
| ● Montefalco Sagrantino '12 | ♟ 6 |

## Goretti

LOC. PILA
S.DA DEL PINO, 4
06132 PERUGIA
TEL. +39 075607316
www.vinigoretti.com

PRE-BOOKED VISITS
ANNUAL PRODUCTION 300,000 bottles
HECTARES UNDER VINE 50.00

| | |
|---|---|
| ● Montefalco Sagrantino Le Mure Saracene '14 | ♟♟ 3* |
| ● Colli Perugini Rosso L'Arringatore '14 | ♟♟ 5 |
| ○ Colli Perugini Grechetto '17 | ♟ 2 |

## La Spina

FRAZ. SPINA
VIA EMILIO ALESSANDRINI, 1
06072 MARSCIANO [PG]
TEL. +39 0758738120
www.cantinalaspina.it

CELLAR SALES
PRE-BOOKED VISITS
ANNUAL PRODUCTION 16,000 bottles
HECTARES UNDER VINE 2.20
SUSTAINABLE WINERY

| | |
|---|---|
| ● A Fortiori '15 | ♟♟ 5 |
| ● Cimaalta '17 | ♟♟ 2* |
| ○ Filare Maiore '16 | ♟ 2 |
| ● Merlato '17 | ♟ 2 |

## Lamborghini

LOC. SODERI, 1
06064 PANICALE [PG]
TEL. +39 0758350029
www.tenutalamborghini.com

CELLAR SALES
PRE-BOOKED VISITS
ACCOMMODATION AND RESTAURANT SERVICE
ANNUAL PRODUCTION 150,000 bottles
HECTARES UNDER VINE 32.00

| | |
|---|---|
| ● Campoleone '15 | ♟♟ 6 |
| ● Era '16 | ♟♟ 3 |
| ● Trescone '16 | ♟♟ 2* |
| ● Torami '15 | ♟ 5 |

## Cantine Neri

LOC. BARDANO, 28
05018 ORVIETO [TR]
TEL. +39 0763316196
www.neri-vini.it

ANNUAL PRODUCTION 65,000 bottles
HECTARES UNDER VINE 52.00

| | |
|---|---|
| ○ Orvieto Cl. Sup. Ca' Viti '17 | ♟♟ 2* |
| ○ Bianco dei Neri '17 | ♟ 2 |
| ● Vardano '17 | ♟ 3 |

## La Plani Arche

VOC. CONVERSINO, 160A
06033 CANNARA [PG]
TEL. +39 3356389537
www.planiarche.it

ANNUAL PRODUCTION 15,000 bottles
HECTARES UNDER VINE 6.00
VITICULTURE METHOD Certified Organic
SUSTAINABLE WINERY

| | |
|---|---|
| ● Montefalco Sagrantino Black Label '14 | ♟♟ 5 |
| ● Montefalco Sagrantino Brown Label '14 | ♟♟ 4 |
| ● Montefalco Rosso '15 | ♟ 3 |

## Pucciarella

LOC. VILLA DI MAGIONE
VIA CASE SPARSE, 39
06063 MAGIONE [PG]
TEL. +39 0758409147
www.pucciarella.it

CELLAR SALES
PRE-BOOKED VISITS
ACCOMMODATION
ANNUAL PRODUCTION 250,000 bottles
HECTARES UNDER VINE 58.50
SUSTAINABLE WINERY

| | |
|---|---|
| ● C. del Trasimeno Rosso Sant'Anna Ris. '15 | ♟♟ 3 |
| ○ C. del Trasimeno Vin Santo '14 | ♟♟ 4 |
| ● Empireo '15 | ♟ 3 |

## Tenuta Rocca di Fabbri

LOC. FABBRI
06036 MONTEFALCO [PG]
TEL. +39 0742399379
www.roccadifabbri.com

CELLAR SALES
PRE-BOOKED VISITS
ACCOMMODATION
ANNUAL PRODUCTION 150,000 bottles
HECTARES UNDER VINE 56.00

| | |
|---|---|
| ● Montefalco Rosso '15 | ♟♟ 3 |
| ● Montefalco Sagrantino '14 | ♟♟ 5 |
| ○ Montefalco Grechetto '17 | ♟ 2 |
| ● Montefalco Rosso Ris. '13 | ♟ 4 |

## Sandonna

LOC. SELVE STRADA DELLA STELLA POLARE
05024 GIOVE [TR]
TEL. +39 0744992274
www.cantinasandonna.it

CELLAR SALES
PRE-BOOKED VISITS
ANNUAL PRODUCTION 28,000 bottles
HECTARES UNDER VINE 5.50

| | |
|---|---|
| ● Ciliegiolo '17 | ♛♛ 2* |
| ● Jovio '15 | ♛ 2 |
| ● Selve di Giove '15 | ♛ 4 |

## Cantina Santo Iolo

LOC. NARNI
S.DA MONTINI, 30A
05035 NARNI [TR]
TEL. +39 0744796754
www.santoiolo.it

CELLAR SALES
PRE-BOOKED VISITS
ANNUAL PRODUCTION 20,000 bottles
HECTARES UNDER VINE 3.50
SUSTAINABLE WINERY

| | |
|---|---|
| ● Rosso Fossile '16 | ♛♛ 2* |
| ● Syrah '17 | ♛♛ 3 |
| ● Malbec '17 | ♛ 3 |
| ○ Pratalia '17 | ♛ 3 |

## Tenuta di Salviano

LOC. CIVITELLA DEL LAGO
VOC. SALVIANO, 44
05020 BASCHI [TR]
TEL. +39 0744950459
www.titignano.it

CELLAR SALES
PRE-BOOKED VISITS
ACCOMMODATION AND RESTAURANT SERVICE
ANNUAL PRODUCTION 150,000 bottles
HECTARES UNDER VINE 70.00

| | |
|---|---|
| ● Lago di Corbara Turlò '15 | ♛♛ 3 |
| ○ Orvieto Cl. Sup. Salviano '17 | ♛♛ 2* |
| ● Lago di Corbara Solideo '16 | ♛ 3 |
| ○ Salviano di Salviano '17 | ♛ 3 |

## Valdangius

LOC. S. MARCO
VIA CASE SPARSE, 84
06036 MONTEFALCO [PG]
TEL. +39 3334953595
www.cantinavaldangius.it

ANNUAL PRODUCTION 10,000 bottles
HECTARES UNDER VINE 5.60
SUSTAINABLE WINERY

| | |
|---|---|
| ○ Campo de Pico '17 | ♛♛ 3 |
| ● Montefalco Sagrantino Fortunato '14 | ♛♛ 5 |
| ○ Spoleto Filium Trebbiano Spoletino '16 | ♛♛ 5 |

## Vallantica

LOC. VALLE ANTICA, 280
05029 SAN GEMINI [TR]
TEL. +39 0744243454
www.vallantica.com

CELLAR SALES
PRE-BOOKED VISITS
ACCOMMODATION AND RESTAURANT SERVICE
ANNUAL PRODUCTION 30,000 bottles
HECTARES UNDER VINE 16.00

| | |
|---|---|
| ○ Grechetto '17 | ♛♛ 2* |
| ● Ciliegiolo '17 | ♛ 3 |

## La Veneranda

LOC. MONTEPENNINO SNC
06036 MONTEFALCO [PG]
TEL. +39 0742951630
www.laveneranda.com

PRE-BOOKED VISITS
ANNUAL PRODUCTION 100,000 bottles
HECTARES UNDER VINE 16.00
SUSTAINABLE WINERY

| | |
|---|---|
| ○ Aureo '16 | ♛♛ 2* |
| ○ Montefalco Grechetto '17 | ♛♛ 3 |
| ● Montefalco Rosso '15 | ♛♛ 4 |

# LAZIO

This year we saw a number of firsts for Lazio. Affile debuted in the main section of Italian Wines, with both their Cesaneses reaching our finals. Rieti was represented by two producers, with Le Macchie's debut accompanying the 'historic' Tenuta Santa Lucia. Antiche Cantine Migliaccio earned Tre Bicchieri with their 2017 Fieno di Ponza Bianco, a classic blend of Biancolella and Forastera that's splendid in its freshness, pleasantness and 'island' expression of Mediterranean overtones and iodine. And finally, there's the fact of the Roma appellation taking home Tre Bicchieri thanks to Poggio Le Volpi's Roma Rosso Edizione Limitata. In terms of the region's overall trajectory, it's worth thinking about the zones of production. Viterbo continues to be led by two men and two wineries that have made absolute quality central to their stylistic approach: Sergio Mottura, who once again earned Tre Bicchieri with his Latour a Civitella, a Grechetto Poggio della Costa (though his other Grechetto is virtually on par), and San Giovenale's Emanuele Pangrazi, with his two Habemus (which are basically in the same position). We should also point out the absence of the Trappolini family's winery (who had administrative problems) and the debut of Villa Caviciana, an agricultural producer that also raises livestock, in our main section. Around Rome we noticed a number of good wines emerging in the appellation, even if its top wines are limited to the same names: Tenuta di Fiorano (this year with their 2016 Fiorano Bianco), Poggio le Volpi (who we already mentioned) and Valle Vermiglia, whose 2017 Eremo Tuscolano was the only Frascati awarded. When it comes to Cesano, Olevano Romano and Affile stood out more than Piglio. We close by mentioning the province of Latina where, thanks to the success of Ponza's wines, we can reaffirm the quality of the territory's great names, from Casale del Giglio to Carpineti and Cincinnato.

## Marco Carpineti

S.DA PROV.LE VELLETRI-ANZIO, 3
04010 CORI [LT]
TEL. +39 069679860
www.marcocarpineti.com

CELLAR SALES
PRE-BOOKED VISITS
ANNUAL PRODUCTION 300,000 bottles
HECTARES UNDER VINE 52.00
VITICULTURE METHOD Certified Organic

The purchase of new vineyards at 600
meters above sea level in the neighboring
municipality of Bassiano has boosted two
varieties native to Cori: Bellone and Nero
Buono. There is also a move towards
Abbuoto, the grape used to make the
legendary ancient Roman wine, Caecuban.
All production is organic and approaches
biodynamic standards. The cellar structure,
merged with areas dedicated to farmhouse
accommodation, blends modern technology
and the discovery of ancient flavors, for
example fermenting Bellone in 400-liter
amphorae (which they will be trying out
shortly on Nero Buono). The 2015 Nzù
(meaning 'together' in the Cori dialect) is a
Bellone made in amphorae that has made
the best possible debut by reaching our
finals. It features complex nose-mouth
properties but respects the grape variety,
which the winery also interprets well in their
2017 Capolemole and, even more so, in the
lovely 2015 Kius Brut. Their 2016 Moro
displays rich tropical overtones, while the
2014 Kius Rosé proves both complex and
well-balanced.

| | |
|---|---|
| ○ Kius Brut '15 | 🍷🍷 4 |
| ○ Moro '16 | 🍷🍷 3* |
| ○ Nzù Bellone '15 | 🍷🍷 5 |
| ○ Capolemole Bellone '17 | 🍷🍷 2* |
| ◎ Kius Extra Brut Rosé '14 | 🍷🍷 5 |
| ● Tufaliccio '17 | 🍷🍷 2* |
| ○ Ludum '15 | 🍷 4 |
| ● Apolide '12 | 🍷🍷 5 |
| ○ Capolemole Bianco '16 | 🍷🍷 2* |
| ○ Kius Brut '14 | 🍷🍷 4 |
| ○ Moro '15 | 🍷🍷 3* |
| ○ Moro '14 | 🍷🍷 3* |
| ● Tufaliccio '16 | 🍷🍷 2* |

## Casale del Giglio

LOC. LE FERRIERE
S.DA CISTERNA-NETTUNO KM 13
04100 LATINA
TEL. +39 0692902530
www.casaledelgiglio.it

CELLAR SALES
PRE-BOOKED VISITS
ANNUAL PRODUCTION 1,276,600 bottles
HECTARES UNDER VINE 164.00
SUSTAINABLE WINERY

Owner Antonio Santarelli, and winemaker
Paolo Tiefenthaler have built up this
winery's well-deserved fame by careful
selection of mostly international grape
varieties. Now their focus is shifting to
native grapes and respect for the terroir.
This is demonstrated by their decision to
convert sizeable amounts of vineyard
surface area to organic management.
They grow Biancolella in Ponza, Bellone in
Anzio, Cesanese in the Lepini mountains,
and will grow Pecorino in vineyards in
Amatrice and Accumoli in the near future.
The project should help rejuvenate the
hard-hit economy of these areas. The
2017 Faro della Guardia lands a place in
our finals thanks to its savoriness, length
and elegance, as did their new Anthium
Bellone R. It matures in amphorae for two
years and should prove very long-lived.
The 2016 Antinoo and 2015 Mater Matuta
have also reached a very high standard,
while among their wines made with
international varieties the 2016 Tempranijo,
2015 Cabernet Sauvignon and 2017 Petit
Manseng excel.

| | |
|---|---|
| ○ Antinoo '16 | 🍷🍷 5 |
| ○ Antium Bellone R '15 | 🍷🍷 4 |
| ○ Faro della Guardia Biancolella '17 | 🍷🍷 5 |
| ● Mater Matuta '15 | 🍷🍷 7 |
| ○ Antium Bellone '17 | 🍷🍷 4 |
| ○ Aphrodisium '16 | 🍷🍷 6 |
| ● Cabernet Sauvignon '15 | 🍷🍷 5 |
| ● Madreselva '15 | 🍷🍷 5 |
| ○ Petit Manseng '17 | 🍷🍷 4 |
| ● Tempranijo '16 | 🍷🍷 5 |
| ◎ Albiola Rosato '17 | 🍷 3 |
| ○ Satrico '17 | 🍷 3 |
| ○ Viognier '17 | 🍷 3 |
| ○ Antium Bellone '15 | 🍷🍷🍷 4* |
| ○ Faro della Guardia Biancolella '16 | 🍷🍷🍷 5 |

# Casale della Ioria

LOC. LA GLORIA
S.DA PROV.LE 118 ANAGNI-PALIANO
03012 ANAGNI [FR]
TEL. +39 077556031
www.casaledellaioria.com

**CELLAR SALES**
**PRE-BOOKED VISITS**
**ANNUAL PRODUCTION 65,000 bottles**
**HECTARES UNDER VINE 38.00**
**SUSTAINABLE WINERY**

In the last 40 years Casale della Ioria has been an important benchmark for the whole of Cesanese wine production. Credit is due to Paolo Perinelli, who combines entrepreneurship with a genuine passion for promoting his territory. Here is found a good mix of historic and more recent vineyards, all of which enjoy an excellent exposure at 400 meters above sea level. Native grapes, such as Cesanese di Affile, Passerina and Olivella, find their ideal habitat in these parts, where they are hand-picked and used to produce well-crafted wines. While awaiting their new sulfite-free Cesanese, the historic 2016 Torre del Piano proves once again the top this winery has to offer and one of the best expressions of this territory. It is still young but possesses great aging potential. Their 2016 Tenuta della Ioria comes across more ready to drink, exhibiting good balance between tannins and alcohol. Wines made with Passerina (the still 2017 Colle Bianco and the pleasant Extra Dry Charmat) are sound.

| | |
|---|---|
| ● Cesanese del Piglio Sup. Torre del Piano Ris. '16 | ♟♟ 4 |
| ● Cesanese del Piglio Sup. Tenuta della Ioria '16 | ♟♟ 3 |
| ○ Colle Bianco '17 | ♟ 2 |
| ○ Passerina Extra Dry '15 | ♟ 2 |
| ● Cesanese del Piglio Sup. Tenuta della Ioria '15 | ♟♟ 3 |
| ● Cesanese del Piglio Sup. Torre del Piano Ris. '15 | ♟♟ 4 |
| ● Cesanese del Piglio Sup. Torre del Piano Ris. '13 | ♟♟ 4 |
| ● Olivella '11 | ♟♟ 2* |

# Castel de Paolis

VIA VAL DE PAOLIS
00046 GROTTAFERRATA [RM]
TEL. +39 069413648
www.casteldepaolis.com

**CELLAR SALES**
**PRE-BOOKED VISITS**
**RESTAURANT SERVICE**
**ANNUAL PRODUCTION 80,000 bottles**
**HECTARES UNDER VINE 11.00**

Fabrizio Santarelli is the second generation to run this farm based in Grottaferrata, one of the historic brands of Castelli Romani. He follows in the footsteps of his ancestor Giulio. It was he who 30 years ago engaged the services of Prof. Attilio Scienza for his experimentation and rediscovery project aimed at producing technically exemplary wines with a modern slant. Situated on the ruins of a medieval castle inside the Frascati appellation, this family-run winery continues to increase its exports, as well as strengthen its position in the domestic market. The 2017 Frascati Superiore reached our finals, coming through fresh with lovely aromas of flowers and ripe yellow fruit. The palate proves dynamic and lingering, with a long, taut and pleasant finish, closing with classic almondy notes. Their 2014 I Quattro Mori, a historic blend of international grapes (Cabernet Sauvignon, Merlot, Petit Verdot and Syrah), is also well-made, rich in fruit and determined.

| | |
|---|---|
| ○ Frascati Sup. '17 | ♟♟ 3* |
| ● I Quattro Mori '14 | ♟♟ 5 |
| ○ Donna Adriana '17 | ♟♟ 4 |
| ○ Muffa Nobile '16 | ♟♟ 5 |
| ● Campo Vecchio Rosso '15 | ♟ 3 |
| ○ Frascati Campo Vecchio '17 | ♟ 2 |
| ● Campo Vecchio Rosso '14 | ♟♟ 3 |
| ○ Donna Adriana '16 | ♟♟ 4 |
| ○ Donna Adriana '15 | ♟♟ 4 |
| ○ Frascati Campo Vecchio '16 | ♟♟ 2* |
| ○ Frascati Sup. '16 | ♟♟ 3 |
| ○ Frascati Sup. '15 | ♟♟ 3 |
| ○ Muffa Nobile '15 | ♟♟ 5 |

# Cincinnato

VIA CORI - CISTERNA, KM 2
04010 CORI [LT]
TEL. +39 069679380
www.cincinnato.it

CELLAR SALES
PRE-BOOKED VISITS
ACCOMMODATION AND RESTAURANT SERVICE
ANNUAL PRODUCTION 90,000 bottles
HECTARES UNDER VINE 268.00
SUSTAINABLE WINERY

This lovely 19th-century farmhouse has
provided food and accommodation for some
years, but Cincinnato has never lost sight of
its winegrowing legacy. President Nazareno
Milita and winemaker Carlo Morettini,
together with Fabio Bigolin, get the best out
of grapes grown in these beautiful volcanic
hills in Cori. Additionally they are supported
by Giulianello cultivated by about 150 vine
growers. Currently the vineyards are being
converted to organic management, and the
cellar has been equipped for the production
of a Metodo Classico sparkling wine. The
2015 Bellone Brut is already gaining
attention and underlines once again the
versatile nature of this grape, which comes
out in the consistent quality of this winery's
two historic wines: the fresh and pleasantly
approachable 2017 Castore and 2017 Illirio.
Their greatest achievement, however, is the
2015 Ercole, which gives us back a serious
Nero Buono, displaying lovely tertiary notes
and tobacco. And to top it off the 2015
Raverosse Montepulciano and the 2016
Arcatura Cesanese.

| | |
|---|---|
| ● Ercole Nero Buono '15 | ♥♥ 3* |
| ○ Brut di Bellone M. Cl. '15 | ♥♥ 2* |
| ○ Castore '17 | ♥♥ 2* |
| ○ Cori Bianco Illirio '17 | ♥♥ 2* |
| ● Arcatura '16 | ♥ 2 |
| ● Cori Rosso Raverosse '15 | ♥ 2 |
| ○ Pantaleo '17 | ♥ 2 |
| ● Pollùce '16 | ♥ 2 |
| ○ Castore '16 | ♥♥ 2* |
| ○ Cori Bianco Illirio '16 | ♥♥ 2* |
| ● Cori Rosso Raverosse '14 | ♥♥ 2* |
| ● Ercole Nero Buono '13 | ♥♥ 3* |
| ○ Pozzodorico Bellone '15 | ♥♥ 2* |
| ○ Pozzodorico Bellone '14 | ♥♥ 2* |

# Damiano Ciolli

VIA DEL CORSO
00035 OLEVANO ROMANO [RM]
TEL. +39 069563334
www.damianociolli.it

CELLAR SALES
PRE-BOOKED VISITS
ANNUAL PRODUCTION 25,000 bottles
HECTARES UNDER VINE 5.00
SUSTAINABLE WINERY

Many things have changed since the first
vintage of Cirsium was produced in 2001.
Most importantly, Damiano Ciolli has
become a benchmark producer for the
appellation; he supports Cesanese di
Olevano Romano with both his name and
his tenacious and careful work. Between
experimentation, madness and foresight,
Damiano fiercely believes in the potential
of the vineyards his grandfather planted in
the 1950s, as well as the two more
vineyards planted in 1981 and 2002. The
grapes go to producing wines that are both
varietal and territorial. Damiano Ciolli's
wines are some of the best in the
appellation. Despite rather marked woody
notes, his 2014 Cesanese di Olevano
Romani Cirsium Riserva comes through
with hints of citrus and black berry fruit
leading into a palate with body and
well-handled tannins. The 2016 Cesanese
di Olevano Romano Superiore Silene, on
the other hand, proves balsamic, with
overtones of Mediterranean scrub,
succulent, more approachable and with a
fresh and pleasant finish.

| | |
|---|---|
| ● Cesanese di Olevano Romano Cirsium Ris. '14 | ♥♥ 5 |
| ● Cesanese di Olevano Romano Sup. Silene '16 | ♥♥ 3* |
| ● Cesanese di Olevano Romano Cirsium '11 | ♥♥ 5 |
| ● Cesanese di Olevano Romano Cirsium Ris. '13 | ♥♥ 5 |
| ● Cesanese di Olevano Romano Cirsium Ris. '12 | ♥♥ 5 |
| ● Cesanese di Olevano Romano Sup. Silene '15 | ♥♥ 3 |
| ● Cesanese di Olevano Romano Sup. Silene '14 | ♥♥ 3 |

# Antonello Coletti Conti

VIA VITTORIO EMANUELE, 116
03012 ANAGNI [FR]
TEL. +39 0775728610
www.coletticonti.it

**CELLAR SALES**
**PRE-BOOKED VISITS**
**ANNUAL PRODUCTION 20,000 bottles**
**HECTARES UNDER VINE 20.00**

Antonello Coletti Conti took over his father's 100-hectare farm, 16 of which form a single vineyard plot, in 1992. Since then, he has run it under organic management which respects the identity his Cesanese wine draws from the volcanic and siliceous soils. With this in mind, Antonello planted a new vineyard in 2015, using rare Cesanese d'Affile biotypes, selected after careful scrutiny for many years all over the DOCG area. He will carry out the first micro vinification on grapes grown in this vineyard in 2018. Their two Cesanese wines (the 2016 Romanico and 2016 Hernicus) prove once again some of the best in the DOCG, though they are still searching for nose-palate symmetry, which will undoubtedly come with bottle aging. The 2016 Cosmato, a precise and sound Bordeaux blend, lives up to expectations, while the 2017 Passerina Hernicus has made a comeback to the top after a couple of years. It manages to balance freshness and notes of alcohol.

| | |
|---|---|
| ● Cesanese del Piglio Sup. Hernicus '16 | ♟♟ 3 |
| ● Cesanese del Piglio Sup. Romanico '16 | ♟♟ 5 |
| ● Cosmato '16 | ♟♟ 5 |
| ○ Passerina del Frusinate Hernicus '17 | ♟♟ 3 |
| ● Cesanese del Piglio Romanico '11 | ♟♟♟ 5 |
| ● Cesanese del Piglio Romanico '07 | ♟♟♟ 5 |
| ● Cesanese del Piglio Sup. Hernicus '14 | ♟♟♟ 3* |
| ● Cesanese del Piglio Sup. Hernicus '12 | ♟♟♟ 3* |
| ● Cesanese del Piglio Sup. Hernicus '15 | ♟♟ 3* |
| ● Cesanese del Piglio Sup. Romanico '15 | ♟♟ 5 |

# ★★Famiglia Cotarella

S.S. CASSIA NORD KM 94,155
01027 MONTEFIASCONE [VT]
TEL. +39 07449556
www.falesco.it

**CELLAR SALES**
**PRE-BOOKED VISITS**
**ACCOMMODATION**
**ANNUAL PRODUCTION 3,650,000 bottles**
**HECTARES UNDER VINE 330.00**

Dominga, Enrica and Marta Cotarella are successfully carrying on the work of their fathers, Renzo and Riccardo, who set up one of the leading wineries in the region thirty years ago. Their production philosophy at Falesco finds a balance between winemaking tradition in a territory that has always produced good grapes and the candor of those who are not afraid of new challenges. Their wide range is made with impeccable winemaking techniques and a precise style. Yet another Tre Bicchieri for their Montiano. The 2016 vintage displays notes of soft wood, herbs and cinchona, leading into a palate with good mouthfeel and concentration, and a long finish revealing hints of red fruit. Other wines in the rest of their range worth noting include their 2017 Est! Est!! Est!!!di Montefiascone Poggio dei Gelsi, with its pleasant fruity overtones, the floral and citrusy 2017 Vitiano San Pietro Vermentino and the close-knit and caressing 2016 Trentanni, an equal blend of Merlot and Sangiovese.

| | |
|---|---|
| ● Montiano '16 | ♟♟♟ 6 |
| ● Marciliano '15 | ♟♟ 7 |
| ○ Soente '17 | ♟♟ 4 |
| ○ Appunto Bianco '17 | ♟♟ 2* |
| ● Appunto Rosso '17 | ♟♟ 2* |
| ○ Est! Est!! Est!!! di Montefiascone Poggio dei Gelsi '17 | ♟♟ 2* |
| ○ Ferentano '16 | ♟♟ 4 |
| ● Messidoro '17 | ♟♟ 2* |
| ● Tellus Syrah '17 | ♟♟ 3 |
| ● Trentanni '16 | ♟♟ 4 |
| ● Vitiano '17 | ♟♟ 2* |
| ● Vitiano San Lorenzo Cabernet '16 | ♟♟ 2* |
| ○ Vitiano San Pietro Vermentino '17 | ♟♟ 2* |
| ○ Brut M. Cl. | ♟ 4 |
| ● Pomele '17 | ♟ 3 |
| ● Tellus Rosé '17 | ♟ 2 |

## Fontana Candida

via Fontana Candida, 11
00040 Monte Porzio Catone [RM]
Tel. +39 069401881
www.fontanacandida.it

CELLAR SALES
PRE-BOOKED VISITS
RESTAURANT SERVICE
ANNUAL PRODUCTION 2,500,000 bottles
HECTARES UNDER VINE 210.00

An important name in Castelli Romani winemaking, Fontana Candida has become an icon in the appellation during its 60 years of history. For many years it was family-run, but today the winery belongs to Gruppo Italiano Vini, which has promoted their wines, raised quality standards, and placed more importance on the volcanic soils where the grapes are grown. They cultivate mostly white grape varieties: Trebbiano, Malvasia, Bellone and Bombino. Their 2017 Frascati Superiore Luna Mater Riserva is always one of the best in the appellation. It exhibits overtones of white fruit and herbs, and comes through tangy, lingering and pleasant. Their excellently-made and supple 2017 Frascati Superiore Secco Vigneto Santa Teresa features notes of tropical fruit and citrus, with a characteristic almondy finish. The 2017 Roma Malvasia Puntinata came as a surprise, however, with lovely aromas of sage and Mediterranean scrub.

| | |
|---|---|
| ○ Frascati Sup. Luna Mater Ris. '17 | 🍷🍷 3* |
| ○ Frascati Sup. Secco Vign. Santa Teresa '17 | 🍷🍷 3 |
| ○ Roma Malvasia Puntinata '17 | 🍷🍷 2* |
| ○ Frascati Secco '17 | 🍷 2 |
| ○ Frascati Secco Terre dei Grifi '17 | 🍷 2 |
| ● Kron '15 | 🍷 4 |
| ○ Frascati Sup. Luna Mater Ris. '16 | 🍸🍸 3* |
| ○ Frascati Sup. Luna Mater Ris. '15 | 🍸🍸 3* |
| ○ Frascati Sup. Terre dei Grifi '15 | 🍸🍸 2* |
| ○ Frascati Sup. Vign. Santa Teresa '16 | 🍸🍸 2* |
| ○ Frascati Sup. Vign. Santa Teresa '15 | 🍸🍸 2* |
| ○ Roma Malvasia Puntinata '15 | 🍸🍸 3 |

## Formiconi

loc. Farinella
00021 Affile [RM]
Tel. +39 3470934541
www.cantinaformiconi.com

CELLAR SALES
PRE-BOOKED VISITS
ANNUAL PRODUCTION 13,000 bottles
HECTARES UNDER VINE 4.00
SUSTAINABLE WINERY

Brothers Livio, Walter and Vito Formiconi run a small young winery founded in 2002, and composed of some 4 hectares of vineyards. They must be credited with relaunching the Cesanese D'Affile DOC, which for too many years lacked any value. But this has changed, thanks to the quality of their native grape variety (a clone also called Cesanese) long recognized for its superiority, the excellent position of their vineyards at 600 meters above sea level on clayey and calcareous soils, and their precise cellar practices and winemaking under the invaluable guidance of Paolo Tiefenthaler. Surprisingly, they produced two versions of the 2017 Cisinianum, which impressed us the most thanks to their concentrated and elegant fruit, pleasant drinkability and guaranteed longevity. The 2016 Capozzano features more marked wood and a higher alcohol content, with notes of vanilla and tertiary hints destined to rebalance the high tannin content during bottle aging.

| | |
|---|---|
| ● Cesanese di Affile Capozzano Ris. '16 | 🍷🍷 4 |
| ● Cesanese di Affile Cisinianum '17 | 🍷🍷 3* |
| ● Cesanese di Affile Capozzano '08 | 🍸🍸 4 |
| ● Cesanese di Affile Capozzano Ris. '14 | 🍸🍸 4 |
| ● Cesanese di Affile Cisinianum '15 | 🍸🍸 3* |
| ● Cesanese di Affile Cisinianum '14 | 🍸🍸 3 |

# Antiche Cantine Migliaccio

VIA PIZZICATO
04027 PONZA [LT]
TEL. +39 3392822252
www.antichecantinemigliaccio.it

CELLAR SALES
PRE-BOOKED VISITS
ANNUAL PRODUCTION 10,000 bottles
HECTARES UNDER VINE 3.00

The Romans were the first to work these small vineyards in the middle of the Tyrrhenian Sea. Two thousand years later Emanuele Vittorio and his wife Luciana still believe in the potential of this island that continues to excite today, thanks to modern winemaking technology applied to old traditions. Winemaker Vincenzo Mercurio works the fruit grown in these vineyards, where can be found even some ungrafted varieties like Biancolella, Forestera, Piedirosso, Aglianico and Guarnaccia. The Migliaccio family's winery has earned its first Tre Bicchieri, but probably not for the wine they expected. It was won by their 2017 Fieno di Ponza Bianco, a classic blend of Biancolella and Forastera. It comes through iodine, with notes of herbs and white fruit, taut and plucky, with great length and pleasantness, highly drinkable. Their 2017 Biancolella is also excellent, almost salty and austere, with notes of prickly pear and Mediterranean scrub.

| | |
|---|---|
| ○ Fieno di Ponza Bianco '17 | 🍷🍷🍷 4* |
| ○ Biancolella di Ponza '17 | 🍷🍷 5 |
| ○ Fieno di Ponza Rosato '17 | 🍷🍷 4 |
| ● Fieno di Ponza Rosso '17 | 🍷 4 |
| ○ Biancolella di Ponza '16 | 🍷🍷 5 |
| ○ Biancolella di Ponza '15 | 🍷🍷 5 |
| ○ Biancolella di Ponza '14 | 🍷🍷 5 |
| ○ Biancolella di Ponza '13 | 🍷🍷 5 |
| ○ Fieno di Ponza Bianco '16 | 🍷🍷 4 |
| ○ Fieno di Ponza Bianco '15 | 🍷🍷 4 |
| ○ Fieno di Ponza Bianco '14 | 🍷🍷 4 |
| ⊙ Fieno di Ponza Rosato '16 | 🍷🍷 4 |
| ● Fieno di Ponza Rosso '13 | 🍷🍷 4 |

# ★Sergio Mottura

LOC. POGGIO DELLA COSTA, 1
01020 CIVITELLA D'AGLIANO [VT]
TEL. +39 0761914533
www.motturasergio.it

CELLAR SALES
PRE-BOOKED VISITS
ACCOMMODATION AND RESTAURANT SERVICE
ANNUAL PRODUCTION 97,000 bottles
HECTARES UNDER VINE 37.00
VITICULTURE METHOD Certified Organic

Sergio Mottura has cultivated his 37 hectares of vineyards with organic methods for over 50 years. What's more, he's an advocate for the whole territory, situated among the clay ravines of Civitella d'Agliano and planted with its iconic Grechetto variety. Shunning shortcuts in growing the grape and stubborn awareness of its quality and unique personality, he opted for massal selection and organic viticulture, a practice he continues to this day. The stunning results he achieves more than offsets the continual care and attention it requires. Their Grechetto Poggio della Costa has earned the Tre Bicchieri once again. The 2017 vintage has not yet reached its full expression, but displays notes of herbs and white fruit, which give way to a tangy palate with classic tannic nuances that add body and structure and make for a long and lingering finish. Their other Grechetto is very good, too: the 2016 Latour a Civitella is more plush and generous, with hints of yellow-fleshed fruit, lingering and long-lived.

| | |
|---|---|
| ○ Poggio della Costa '17 | 🍷🍷🍷 4* |
| ○ Latour a Civitella '16 | 🍷🍷 5 |
| ● Civitella Rosso '16 | 🍷🍷 3 |
| ○ Orvieto Tragugnano '17 | 🍷🍷 3 |
| ● Magone '15 | 🍷 6 |
| ○ Muffo '15 | 🍷 6 |
| ○ Orvieto Secco '17 | 🍷 3 |
| ● Syracide '15 | 🍷 5 |
| ○ Grechetto Latour a Civitella '11 | 🍷🍷🍷 4* |
| ○ Grechetto Poggio della Costa '14 | 🍷🍷🍷 3* |
| ○ Grechetto Poggio della Costa '10 | 🍷🍷🍷 3* |
| ○ Poggio della Costa '16 | 🍷🍷🍷 3* |
| ○ Poggio della Costa '15 | 🍷🍷🍷 3* |
| ○ Poggio della Costa '12 | 🍷🍷🍷 3* |
| ○ Poggio della Costa '11 | 🍷🍷🍷 3* |

## Principe Pallavicini

VIA ROMA, 121
00030 COLONNA [RM]
TEL. +39 069438816
www.principepallavicini.com

CELLAR SALES
PRE-BOOKED VISITS
RESTAURANT SERVICE
ANNUAL PRODUCTION 600,000 bottles
HECTARES UNDER VINE 65.00

The noble Pallavicini family has played a key role in regional farming since the 1600s. Today Sigieri Diaz della Vittoria Pallavicini carries on this work, taking over from his mother, Maria Camilla. Their vineyard surface area is divided between 65 hectares in Colonna (50 of these are registered under the Frascati appellation as the largest private vineyard in the appellation) and 15 in Cerveteri where red grapes are planted. The wines produced are modern in style and display exemplary winemaking. Their two Malvasia Puntinatas have delivered and it is now becoming the winery's reference grape. The 2016 Stillato is a historic dessert wine offering up hints of candied citrus fruit, good balance between sugar and acidity, and a characteristic almondy finish. The 2017 Roma Malvasia Puntinata displays aromas of herbs and comes through supple and fresh. Their 2017 Frascati Superiore Poggio Verde is on the same level, revealing pleasant notes of tropical fruit.

| | |
|---|---|
| ○ Frascati Sup. Poggio Verde '17 | ♥♥ 2* |
| ○ Roma Malvasia Puntinata '17 | ♥♥ 2* |
| ○ Stillato '16 | ♥♥ 3 |
| ● Amarasco '16 | ♥ 3 |
| ○ Frascati Sup. Poggio Verde '13 | ♀♀♀ 2* |
| ● Amarasco '15 | ♀♀ 3 |
| ● Amarasco '14 | ♀♀ 3 |
| ● Casa Romana '12 | ♀♀ 5 |
| ○ Frascati Secco '16 | ♀♀ 2* |
| ○ Frascati Sup. Poggio Verde '15 | ♀♀ 2* |
| ○ Frascati Sup. Poggio Verde '14 | ♀♀ 2* |
| ○ Roma Malvasia Puntinata '16 | ♀♀ 2* |
| ○ Roma Malvasia Puntinata '15 | ♀♀ 2* |
| ○ Stillato '15 | ♀♀ 3 |
| ○ Stillato '13 | ♀♀ 3* |

## Tenuta La Pazzaglia

S.DA DI BAGNOREGIO, 4
01024 CASTIGLIONE IN TEVERINA [VT]
TEL. +39 0761947114
www.tenutalapazzaglia.it

CELLAR SALES
PRE-BOOKED VISITS
ACCOMMODATION
ANNUAL PRODUCTION 56,000 bottles
HECTARES UNDER VINE 12.00

The history of La Pazzaglia began in 1990 when Agnese and Randolfo Verdecchia purchased the winery to carry forward the old family business. Now it is their children Pierfrancesco, Maria Teresa and Laura who run this winery bordering Lazio, Umbria and Tuscany. The generational change-over also marks a turning point in their choice of varieties, with a new focus on natives grapes, especially Grechetto, cultivated under organic management, albeit without certification. Two Grechettos impressed us this year. Particularly the first (as usual in recent years), the 2017 109, with its hints of citrus and Mediterranean scrub on the nose, gutsy, tangy and lingering palate, and fresh and pleasant finish. The 2016 Poggio Triale exhibits notes of ripe yellow fruit and proves more firmly-structured, but less brilliant and dynamic. The other wines they presented proved sound.

| | |
|---|---|
| ○ 109 Grechetto '17 | ♥♥ 3* |
| ○ Poggio Triale '16 | ♥♥ 3 |
| ● Aurelius '16 | ♥ 2 |
| ● Montijone '15 | ♥ 3 |
| ○ Orvieto Miadimia '17 | ♥ 2 |
| ● Palagio '16 | ♥ 2 |
| ○ 109 Grechetto '16 | ♀♀ 3* |
| ○ 109 Grechetto '15 | ♀♀ 3 |
| ○ Il Corno '16 | ♀♀ 2* |
| ○ Il Corno '15 | ♀♀ 2* |
| ○ Poggio Triale '15 | ♀♀ 3 |
| ○ Poggio Triale '14 | ♀♀ 3* |

# Pietra Pinta

VIA LE PASTINE KM 20,200
04010 CORI [LT]
TEL. +39 069678001
www.pietrapinta.com

CELLAR SALES
PRE-BOOKED VISITS
ACCOMMODATION AND RESTAURANT SERVICE
ANNUAL PRODUCTION 300,000 bottles
HECTARES UNDER VINE 33.00
VITICULTURE METHOD Certified Organic
SUSTAINABLE WINERY

The Ferretti family has produced wine and oil in Cori for about 140 years, establishing their strong links with the territory. Over time they have extended their business to include lovely farmhouse accommodation and a line of beauty products. Cesare and Francesco Ferretti run the farm today, but the younger generations are ready to lend a hand as well. Their vineyards include both native and international varieties. The results, at least this year, appear to award their international wines, as we can see with the juicy and full 2016 Shiraz, the fruity and plush 2017 Chardonnay and the varietal 2017 Sauvignon. However, their other wines expressing stronger links to the terroir are also sound: their historic 2014 Colle Amato and 2016 Nero Buono, or the 2017 Malvasia Puntinata, with its marked aromas.

|  |  |
|---|---|
| ○ Chardonnay '17 | ♟♟ 2* |
| ● Shiraz '16 | ♟♟ 2* |
| ● Colle Amato '14 | ♟ 3 |
| ○ Costa Vecchia Bianco '17 | ♟ 2 |
| ○ Malvasia Puntinata '17 | ♟ 2 |
| ● Nero Buono '16 | ♟ 2 |
| ○ Sauvignon '17 | ♟ 2 |
| ○ Viognier '17 | ♟ 2 |
| ○ Chardonnay '15 | ♟♟ 2* |
| ● Colle Amato '13 | ♟♟ 4 |
| ● Colle Amato '12 | ♟♟ 4 |
| ○ Costa Vecchia Bianco '16 | ♟♟ 2* |
| ○ Viognier '15 | ♟♟ 2* |

# Poggio Le Volpi

VIA COLLE PISANO, 27
00078 MONTE PORZIO CATONE [RM]
TEL. +39 069426980
www.poggiolevolpi.it

CELLAR SALES
PRE-BOOKED VISITS
RESTAURANT SERVICE
ANNUAL PRODUCTION 300,000 bottles
HECTARES UNDER VINE 140.00

The original farm was founded in 1920 by the current owner's grandfather Manlio, and it was carried on by his father Armando. The winery was created in the 1990s when Felice Mergè gave the family farm an entrepreneurial shake-up, transforming the production site in Monte Porzio Catone from a local to a 'national' winery. Today Poggio Le Volpi is a benchmark in the Lazio territory, producing wines with strong personality stemming from the volcanic soils where the grapes are grown. Malvasia di Candia, Malvasia del Lazio, Trebbiano, Cesanese and Nero Buono anchor the range. Tre Bicchieri go to their 2015 Roma Rosso Edizione Limitata, a blend of Montepulciano, Syrah and Cesanese with great concentration, still displaying marked notes of wood, and a juicy, fruit-rich finish. The 2016 Nero Buono Baccarossa is also well-crafted and a classic example of the winery's style. Notes of black berry fruit, tobacco and sweet spices give way to a full-bodied and fruity palate. The rest of their wines presented proved sound.

|  |  |
|---|---|
| ● Roma Rosso Ed. Limitata '15 | ♟♟♟ 5 |
| ● Baccarossa '16 | ♟♟ 5 |
| ○ Frascati Sup. Epos Ris. '17 | ♟♟ 3 |
| ○ Donnaluce '17 | ♟ 4 |
| ○ Frascati Brut ASonia M. Cl. '12 | ♟ 5 |
| ○ Roma Malvasia Puntinata '17 | ♟ 2 |
| ● Baccarossa '15 | ♟♟ 5 |
| ● Baccarossa '13 | ♟♟ 4* |
| ● Baccarossa '11 | ♟♟ 4* |
| ○ Frascati Sup. Epos '13 | ♟♟ 2* |
| ○ Frascati Sup. Epos '11 | ♟♟ 2* |
| ○ Frascati Sup. Epos '10 | ♟♟ 2* |
| ○ Frascati Sup. Epos '09 | ♟♟ 2* |
| ○ Frascati Sup. Epos Ris. '15 | ♟♟ 3* |

# San Giovenale

LOC. LA MACCHIA
01010 BLERA [VT]
TEL. +39 066877877
www.sangiovenale.it

CELLAR SALES
PRE-BOOKED VISITS
ACCOMMODATION AND RESTAURANT SERVICE
ANNUAL PRODUCTION 9,000 bottles
HECTARES UNDER VINE 10.00
VITICULTURE METHOD Certified Organic
SUSTAINABLE WINERY

In 2006 Emanuele Pangrazi founded San
Giovenale on one of the hills surrounding
the municipality of Blera, at about 400
meters above sea level. The territory is
characterized by wide temperature ranges,
low rainfall, constant breezes and soils rich
in stones. He planted high-density
vineyards (over 10 thousand vines per
hectare) with varieties typical of the Rhone
Valley, such as Syrah, Grenache and
Carignano, alongside Cabernet Franc. The
resulting wines display great personality
and character. We find two very different
wines produced by Emanuele Pangrazi at
the heights of regional production. The
2016 Habemus is a blend of Grenache
(40%), Syrah (40%) and Carignano,
reminiscent of Rhône wines, by virtue of its
hints of black olive tapenade and
Mediterranean scrub on the nose. The
palate proves full and complex, but fresh
and long at the same time. The 2015
Habemus Cabernet comes through
close-knit and spicy, with notes of black
berry fruit and herbs.

| | | |
|---|---|---|
| ● Habemus '16 | ▼▼▼ | 7 |
| ● Habemus Cabernet '15 | ▼▼ | 8 |
| ● Habemus '15 | ♀♀♀ | 7 |
| ● Habemus '14 | ♀♀♀ | 7 |
| ● Habemus '13 | ♀♀ | 7 |
| ● Habemus '12 | ♀♀ | 7 |
| ● Habemus '11 | ♀♀ | 7 |
| ● Habemus '10 | ♀♀ | 4 |
| ● Habemus Cabernet '14 | ♀♀ | 8 |
| ● Habemus Cabernet '13 | ♀♀ | 8 |

# Tenuta di Fiorano

VIA DI FIORANELLO, 19
00134 ROMA
TEL. +39 0679340093
www.tenutadifiorano.it

CELLAR SALES
PRE-BOOKED VISITS
ACCOMMODATION AND RESTAURANT SERVICE
ANNUAL PRODUCTION 30,000 bottles
HECTARES UNDER VINE 12.00
VITICULTURE METHOD Certified Organic

Tenuta di Fiorano lies a stone's throw from
Rome and is one of Italy's little winemaking
jewels by virtue of its history and the wine it
produces. Possessing a fascinating past,
it's now restored to its former splendor by
Prince Alessandrojacopo Boncompagni
Ludovisi, who inherited the planting rights
from his uncle Alberico. He has revived the
production of two great wines: Cabernet
Sauvignon and Merlot, which still grow in
his few hectares of vineyards are used to
produce Fiorano Rosso, while Grechetto
and Viognier have replaced Malvasia and
Semillon in his Fiorano Bianco. The 2016
Fiorano Bianco has earned the Tre Bicchieri
once again, thanks to its elegant aromas,
featuring overtones of spice and ripe yellow
fruit, and a palate coming through dynamic,
complex, long and slightly tannic. Their
elegant and plucky 2013 Fiorano Rosso is
also excellent, with its scents of black berry
fruit and varietal hints of peppers. Their
two Fioranellos, the fresh and well-paced
2017 Bianco and the varietal and pleasant
2016 Rosso, made exclusively with Merlot
grapes, are also well-crafted.

| | | |
|---|---|---|
| ○ Fiorano Bianco '16 | ▼▼▼ | 6 |
| ● Fiorano Rosso '13 | ▼▼ | 8 |
| ○ Fioranello Bianco '17 | ▼▼ | 3 |
| ● Fioranello Rosso '16 | ▼▼ | 4 |
| ○ Fiorano Bianco '13 | ♀♀♀ | 5 |
| ○ Fiorano Bianco '12 | ♀♀♀ | 4* |
| ○ Fiorano Bianco '10 | ♀♀♀ | 5 |
| ● Fiorano Rosso '12 | ♀♀♀ | 7 |
| ● Fiorano Rosso '11 | ♀♀♀ | 7 |
| ○ Fioranello Bianco '16 | ♀♀ | 3 |
| ● Fioranello Rosso '15 | ♀♀ | 4 |
| ○ Fiorano Bianco '15 | ♀♀ | 5 |

# Valle Vermiglia

VIA A. GRAMSCI, 7
00197 ROMA
TEL. +39 3487221073
www.vallevermiglia.it

CELLAR SALES
ANNUAL PRODUCTION 30,000 bottles
HECTARES UNDER VINE 8.00
SUSTAINABLE WINERY

This winery owns eight hectares of vineyards on Monte Tuscolo in a place said to be 'blessed by God'. The lands surrounding the Eremo dei Camaldolesi di Monte Corona complex at 600 meters above sea level are planted with Malvasia, Trebbiano and Bombino grapes, which are used to produce their only wine. It began in the 1950s with the Honorable Pietro Campilli (who strove for DOC Frascati recognition back in the 1960s) and today it is run by his grandson Mario Masini. This year the Frascati Superiore Eremo Tuscolano has earned our Tre Bicchieri once again and proves to be the most interesting Frascati in recent years. The 2017 vintage offers up notes of white fruit and Mediterranean scrub on the nose, while the palate comes through fresh, almost austere and dynamic, exhibiting overtones of herbs and good structure. Notes of rosemary re-emerge at the long finish.

| | | |
|---|---|---|
| ○ Frascati Sup. Eremo Tuscolano '17 | ♛♛♛ | 3* |
| ○ Frascati Sup. Eremo Tuscolano '16 | ♛♛♛ | 3* |
| ○ Frascati Sup. Eremo Tuscolano '13 | ♛♛♛ | 3* |
| ○ Frascati Sup. Eremo Tuscolano '15 | ♛♛ | 3* |
| ○ Frascati Sup. Eremo Tuscolano '14 | ♛♛ | 3* |
| ○ Frascati Sup. Eremo Tuscolano '12 | ♛♛ | 3* |

# Villa Caviciana

LOC. TOJENA CAVICIANA
01025 GROTTE DI CASTRO [VT]
TEL. +39 0763798212
www.villacaviciana.com

CELLAR SALES
PRE-BOOKED VISITS
ANNUAL PRODUCTION 25,000 bottles
HECTARES UNDER VINE 16.00
VITICULTURE METHOD Certified Biodynamic

Owned by Mocca and Fritz Metzeler, the Villa Caviciana farm is located on the Bolsena lake. The estate comprises about 140 hectares, 16 of which are planted with vineyards. These are situated at 400-450 meters above sea level on volcanic soils with a high percentage of tuff, covered with a layer of humus. They benefit from the considerable temperature range caused by proximity to the lake. They also own an estate in the municipality of Gradoli planted with Aleatico. Their wines exhibit a modern style. Villa Caviciana has made it to the main section of our Guide with a series of excellently-made wines. Their 2016 Eleonora, a blend of Sangiovese and Merlot, is fresh, fruity and lingering, while the 2017 Tadzio, a rosé made with Aleatico grapes, comes through delicate but savory and easy to drink. The 2015 Aleatico Maddalena proves taut with good aromas. On the same level we find their close-focused and citrusy 2017 Filippo, made with Chardonnay and Sauvignon Blanc grapes, and the plucky and stylish 2015 Letizia, a Bordeaux blend.

| | | |
|---|---|---|
| ● Eleonora '16 | ♛♛ | 3 |
| ○ Filippo '17 | ♛♛ | 3 |
| ● Letizia '15 | ♛♛ | 5 |
| ● Maddalena '15 | ♛♛ | 5 |
| ☉ Tadzio '17 | ♛♛ | 2* |
| ● Faustina '15 | ♛ | 6 |
| ☉ Lorenzo Brut Rosé '17 | ♛ | 3 |
| ● Faustina '12 | ♛♛ | 6 |
| ● Letizia '14 | ♛♛ | 6 |
| ● Letizia '12 | ♛♛ | 5 |
| ● Maddalena '11 | ♛♛ | 5 |
| ☉ Tadzio '15 | ♛♛ | 2* |

## Marco Antonelli

VIA DI VILLA MARINA
00035 OLEVANO ROMANO [RM]
TEL. +39 069562831
seleva.wixsite.com/marcoantonelli

CELLAR SALES
PRE-BOOKED VISITS
ANNUAL PRODUCTION 12,000 bottles
HECTARES UNDER VINE 3.30
SUSTAINABLE WINERY

| | |
|---|---|
| ● Cesanese di Olevano Romano Kòsmos Ris. '15 | ⧠⧠ 5 |
| ● Cesanese di Olevano Romano Sup. Il Fresco '16 | ⧠⧠ 2* |

## Casa Divina Provvidenza

VIA DEI FRATI, 58
00048 NETTUNO [RM]
TEL. +39 069851366
www.casadivinaprovvidenza.it

CELLAR SALES
PRE-BOOKED VISITS
RESTAURANT SERVICE
ANNUAL PRODUCTION 100,000 bottles
HECTARES UNDER VINE 35.00
SUSTAINABLE WINERY

| | |
|---|---|
| ○ Nettuno Cacchione '17 | ⧠⧠ 3 |
| ○ Roma Bellone '17 | ⧠⧠ 2* |
| ○ Malvasia del Lazio '17 | ⧠ 2 |
| ○ Moscato '17 | ⧠ 4 |

## Casale Marchese

VIA DI VERMICINO, 68
00044 FRASCATI [RM]
TEL. +39 069408932
www.casalemarchese.it

CELLAR SALES
PRE-BOOKED VISITS
ANNUAL PRODUCTION 150,000 bottles
HECTARES UNDER VINE 40.00

| | |
|---|---|
| ○ Frascati Sup. Quarto Marchese '17 | ⧠⧠ 3 |
| ○ Clemens '16 | ⧠ 3 |
| ○ Frascati Sup. '17 | ⧠ 2 |
| ● Marchese de' Cavalieri '16 | ⧠ 4 |

## Casata Mergè

VIA DI FONTANA CANDIDA, 381
00132 ROMA
TEL. +39 0620609225
www.casatamerge.it

CELLAR SALES
PRE-BOOKED VISITS
ANNUAL PRODUCTION 500,000 bottles
HECTARES UNDER VINE 35.00

| | |
|---|---|
| ● Panta Rei '16 | ⧠⧠ 4 |
| ○ Parsifal '17 | ⧠⧠ 4 |
| ○ Beatrice '17 | ⧠ 4 |
| ○ Venere '17 | ⧠ 3 |

## Cavalieri

LOC. GENZANO DI ROMA
FRAZ. MONTECAGNOLO, 16
00045 GENZANO DI ROMA [RM]
TEL. +39 069375807
www.aziendaagricolacavalieri.it

CELLAR SALES
PRE-BOOKED VISITS
ACCOMMODATION
ANNUAL PRODUCTION 40,000 bottles
HECTARES UNDER VINE 8.00

| | |
|---|---|
| ● Facesole '16 | ⧠⧠ 2* |
| ○ Infiorata '17 | ⧠⧠ 2* |
| ○ Diomede '16 | ⧠ 2 |
| ● Petit Manseng '17 | ⧠ 3 |

## Tenuta Colfiorito

S.DA PROV.LE 40A
00024 CASTEL MADAMA [RM]
TEL. +39 0774449396
www.colfio.it

CELLAR SALES
PRE-BOOKED VISITS
ACCOMMODATION
ANNUAL PRODUCTION 20,000 bottles
HECTARES UNDER VINE 4.50
VITICULTURE METHOD Certified Organic

| | |
|---|---|
| ○ Il Trovatore '17 | ⧠⧠ 3 |
| ○ La Loggia '17 | ⧠⧠ 3 |
| ○ Tratto Giallo '17 | ⧠ 2 |
| ● Tratto Rosso '15 | ⧠ 2 |

## Cordeschi

LOC. ACQUAPENDENTE
VIA CASSIA KM 137,400
00121 ACQUAPENDENTE [VT]
TEL. +39 3356953547
www.cantinacordeschi.it

CELLAR SALES
PRE-BOOKED VISITS
ANNUAL PRODUCTION 35,000 bottles
HECTARES UNDER VINE 8.50

| | |
|---|---|
| ● Rufo '17 | ♟♟ 2* |
| ● Ost '16 | ♟ 3 |
| ○ Palea '17 | ♟ 2 |
| ● Saino '15 | ♟ 3 |

## Corte dei Papi

LOC. COLLETONNO
03012 ANAGNI [FR]
TEL. +39 0775769271
www.cortedeipapi.it

CELLAR SALES
PRE-BOOKED VISITS
ANNUAL PRODUCTION 40,000 bottles
HECTARES UNDER VINE 25.00

| | |
|---|---|
| ○ Passerina '17 | ♟♟ 2* |
| ○ Quattro Profeti '17 | ♟♟ 2* |
| ● Cesanese del Piglio Colle Ticchio '17 | ♟ 2 |

## Paolo e Noemia D'Amico

LOC. PALOMBARO
FRAZ. VAIANO
01024 CASTIGLIONE IN TEVERINA [VT]
TEL. +39 0761948034
www.paoloenoemiadamico.it

CELLAR SALES
PRE-BOOKED VISITS
RESTAURANT SERVICE
ANNUAL PRODUCTION 150,000 bottles
HECTARES UNDER VINE 30.00
SUSTAINABLE WINERY

| | |
|---|---|
| ○ Falesia '16 | ♟♟ 5 |
| ● Notturno dei Calanchi '14 | ♟♟ 5 |
| ● Atlante '14 | ♟ 6 |
| ○ Calanchi di Vaiano '16 | ♟ 4 |

## Etruscaia

FRAZ. VOLTONE
S.DA LITORANEA KM 6,900
01016 TARQUINIA [VT]
TEL. +39 3464077473
www.etruscaia.it

CELLAR SALES
PRE-BOOKED VISITS
ACCOMMODATION AND RESTAURANT SERVICE
ANNUAL PRODUCTION 25,000 bottles
HECTARES UNDER VINE 6.00
SUSTAINABLE WINERY

| | |
|---|---|
| ○ Passito di Etruscaia | ♟♟ 5 |
| ● Prisco '12 | ♟♟ 5 |
| ○ Bibi '17 | ♟ 3 |
| ○ Viò '17 | ♟ 3 |

## Alberto Giacobbe

C.DA COLLE SAN GIOVENALE
03018 PALIANO [FR]
TEL. +39 3298738052
www.vinigiacobbe.it

CELLAR SALES
PRE-BOOKED VISITS
ACCOMMODATION
ANNUAL PRODUCTION 25,000 bottles
HECTARES UNDER VINE 10.00

| | |
|---|---|
| ● Cesanese del Piglio Sup. Lepanto Ris. '15 | ♟♟ 5 |
| ● Cesanese di Olevano Romano Sup. Giacobbe '16 | ♟♟ 3 |
| ○ Passerina Duchessa '17 | ♟♟ 2* |

## Donato Giangirolami

FRAZ. LE FERRIERE
VIA DEL CAVALIERE, 1414
04100 LATINA
TEL. +39 3358394890
www.donatogiangirolami.it

CELLAR SALES
PRE-BOOKED VISITS
ANNUAL PRODUCTION 80,000 bottles
HECTARES UNDER VINE 38.00
VITICULTURE METHOD Certified Organic

| | |
|---|---|
| ○ Cardito '17 | ♟♟ 2* |
| ● Prodigo '16 | ♟♟ 2* |
| ○ Propizio '17 | ♟♟ 2* |
| ○ Regius '17 | ♟ 2 |

## Iura et Arma

via Colle Alto snc
03034 Casalvieri [FR]
Tel. +39 3355997255
www.iuretarma.com

ANNUAL PRODUCTION 12,000 bottles
HECTARES UNDER VINE 4.50

| | |
|---|---|
| ○ Armablanc Brut | 🍷🍷 5 |
| ○ Armablanc Pas Dosé | 🍷🍷 5 |

## Antica Cantina Leonardi

via del Pino, 12
01027 Montefiascone [VT]
Tel. +39 0761826028
www.cantinaleonardi.it

CELLAR SALES
PRE-BOOKED VISITS
ACCOMMODATION
ANNUAL PRODUCTION 150,000 bottles
HECTARES UNDER VINE 30.00
VITICULTURE METHOD Certified Organic

| | |
|---|---|
| ● Don Carlo '15 | 🍷🍷 3 |
| ● Nero di Lava '15 | 🍷🍷 2* |
| ○ Pensiero '17 | 🍷 2 |
| ○ ViVì '17 | 🍷 2 |

## Cantine Lupo

fraz. Campoverde
via Mediana Cisterna, 27
04011 Aprilia [LT]
Tel. +39 0692902455
www.cantinelupo.com

CELLAR SALES
PRE-BOOKED VISITS
ANNUAL PRODUCTION 100,000 bottles
HECTARES UNDER VINE 18.00

| | |
|---|---|
| ● Cesanese '14 | 🍷🍷 3 |
| ○ Lupobianco '17 | 🍷 3 |
| ● Luporosso '17 | 🍷 2 |
| ● Primolupo '16 | 🍷 3 |

## Le Macchie

fraz. Castelfranco
via Casanuova, 5
02100 Rieti
Tel. +39 3384620702
www.cantinalemacchie.it

CELLAR SALES
PRE-BOOKED VISITS
RESTAURANT SERVICE
ANNUAL PRODUCTION 40,000 bottles
HECTARES UNDER VINE 7.00
SUSTAINABLE WINERY

| | |
|---|---|
| ⊙ Il Bandolo della Matassa '17 | 🍷🍷 2* |
| ○ Le Feritoie '17 | 🍷🍷 3 |
| ● Campo dei Severi '16 | 🍷 2 |
| ○ Se Bo Be Bi '16 | 🍷 4 |

## L'Olivella

via di Colle Pisano, 5
00044 Frascati [RM]
Tel. +39 069424527
www.racemo.it

CELLAR SALES
PRE-BOOKED VISITS
ANNUAL PRODUCTION 68,000 bottles
HECTARES UNDER VINE 1.00
VITICULTURE METHOD Certified Organic

| | |
|---|---|
| ○ Bombino '17 | 🍷🍷 2* |
| ● 40/60 '16 | 🍷 2 |
| ○ Frascati Sup. Racemo '17 | 🍷 3 |
| ● Racemo '14 | 🍷 3 |

## Antonella Pacchiarotti

via Roma, 14
01024 Grotte di Castro [VT]
Tel. +39 0763796852
www.vinipacchiarotti.it

CELLAR SALES
PRE-BOOKED VISITS
ANNUAL PRODUCTION 10,000 bottles
HECTARES UNDER VINE 3.50
SUSTAINABLE WINERY

| | |
|---|---|
| ○ Matèe '17 | 🍷🍷 3 |
| ○ Ramatico '17 | 🍷🍷 3 |
| ● Butunì Aleatico di Gradoli '17 | 🍷 3 |

# Pileum

VIA DEL CASALOTTO
03010 PIGLIO [FR]
TEL. +39 3663129910
www.pileum.it

PRE-BOOKED VISITS
ANNUAL PRODUCTION 56,000 bottles
HECTARES UNDER VINE 9.00

| | |
|---|---|
| ● Cesanese del Piglio Sup. Bolla di Urbano Ris. '16 | ♥♥ 4 |
| ● Cesanese del Piglio Sup. Pilarocca Ris. '15 | ♥♥ 4 |
| ● Cesanese del Piglio Sup. Massitium '16 | ♥ 4 |

# Tenuta Ronci di Nepi

VIA RONCI, 2072
01036 NEPI [VT]
TEL. +39 0761555125
www.roncidinepi.it

CELLAR SALES
PRE-BOOKED VISITS
ANNUAL PRODUCTION 100,000 bottles
HECTARES UNDER VINE 17.00

| | |
|---|---|
| ○ O' di Nè '17 | ♥♥ 3 |
| ○ Manti '16 | ♥ 4 |
| ● Sangiovese '16 | ♥ 2 |
| ● Veste Porpora '16 | ♥ 3 |

# Le Rose

VIA PONTE TRE ARMI, 25
00045 GENZANO DI ROMA [RM]
TEL. +39 0693709671
www.aziendaagricolalerose.com

CELLAR SALES
PRE-BOOKED VISITS
ANNUAL PRODUCTION 70,000 bottles
HECTARES UNDER VINE 10.00
VITICULTURE METHOD Certified Organic
SUSTAINABLE WINERY

| | |
|---|---|
| ○ Artemisia '17 | ♥♥ 4 |
| ○ Faiola Bianco '17 | ♥ 5 |
| ● Faiola Rosso '15 | ♥ 5 |
| ○ Tre Armi '17 | ♥ 3 |

# Cantine San Marco

LOC. VERMICINO
VIA DI MOLA CAVONA, 26/28
00044 FRASCATI [RM]
TEL. +39 069409403
www.sanmarcofrascati.it

CELLAR SALES
PRE-BOOKED VISITS
ANNUAL PRODUCTION 1,500,000 bottles
HECTARES UNDER VINE 32.00

| | |
|---|---|
| ● SoloShiraz '16 | ♥♥ 3 |
| ● De Notari Cesanese '17 | ♥ 2 |
| ○ De Notari Malvasia '17 | ♥ 2 |
| ○ Frascati Crio 8 '17 | ♥ 2 |

# Sant'Andrea

LOC. BORGO VODICE
VIA RENIBBIO, 1720
04019 TERRACINA [LT]
TEL. +39 0773755028
www.cantinasantandrea.it

CELLAR SALES
PRE-BOOKED VISITS
ANNUAL PRODUCTION 1,000,000 bottles
HECTARES UNDER VINE 85.00

| | |
|---|---|
| ○ Circeo Bianco Dune '16 | ♥♥ 2* |
| ○ Moscato di Terracina Secco Oppidum '17 | ♥♥ 2* |
| ☉ Circeo Rosato Riflessi '17 | ♥ 2 |
| ● Circeo Rosso Incontro al Circeo '15 | ♥ 2 |

# Tenuta Santa Lucia

LOC. SANTA LUCIA
02047 POGGIO MIRTETO [RI]
TEL. +39 076524616
www.tenutasantalucia.com

CELLAR SALES
PRE-BOOKED VISITS
RESTAURANT SERVICE
ANNUAL PRODUCTION 180,000 bottles
HECTARES UNDER VINE 43.00
SUSTAINABLE WINERY

| | |
|---|---|
| ● Miooo Rosso '17 | ♥♥ 2* |
| ● Colli della Sabina Rosso Domina Sabinae '15 | ♥ 2 |
| ● Morrone Syrah '15 | ♥ 5 |

## Stefanoni

VIA STEFANONI, 48
01027 MONTEFIASCONE [VT]
TEL. +39 0761825651
www.cantinastefanoni.it

CELLAR SALES
PRE-BOOKED VISITS
ANNUAL PRODUCTION 100,000 bottles
HECTARES UNDER VINE 10.00

| | |
|---|---|
| ○ Est! Est!! Est!!! di Montefiascone Cl. Foltone '17 | ♥♥ 2* |
| ● Fanum '15 | ♥ 3 |
| ○ Moscato Colle de' Poggeri '17 | ♥ 2 |

## Giovanni Terenzi

FRAZ. LA FORMA
VIA FORESE, 13
03010 SERRONE [FR]
TEL. +39 0775594286
www.viniterenzi.com

CELLAR SALES
PRE-BOOKED VISITS
ANNUAL PRODUCTION 150,000 bottles
HECTARES UNDER VINE 12.00

| | |
|---|---|
| ● Cesanese del Piglio Sup. Vajoscuro Ris. '16 | ♥♥ 5 |
| ● Cesanese del Piglio Velobra '16 | ♥ 3 |

## Castello Torre in Pietra

VIA DI TORRIMPIETRA, 247
00054 FIUMICINO [RM]
TEL. +39 0661697070
www.castelloditorreinpietra.it

CELLAR SALES
PRE-BOOKED VISITS
ANNUAL PRODUCTION 240,000 bottles
HECTARES UNDER VINE 52.00
VITICULTURE METHOD Certified Organic

| | |
|---|---|
| ○ Roma Malvasia Puntinata '17 | ♥♥ 2* |
| ○ Vermentino '17 | ♥♥ 2* |
| ○ Macchia Sacra '17 | ♥ 2 |
| ⊙ Searà '17 | ♥ 2 |

## Trebotti

S.DA DELLA POGGETTA, 9
01024 CASTIGLIONE IN TEVERINA [VT]
TEL. +39 07611986704
www.trebotti.it

CELLAR SALES
PRE-BOOKED VISITS
ACCOMMODATION
ANNUAL PRODUCTION 45,000 bottles
HECTARES UNDER VINE 10.00
VITICULTURE METHOD Certified Organic
SUSTAINABLE WINERY

| | |
|---|---|
| ● Bludom '17 | ♥♥ 3 |
| ○ L'Incrocio '17 | ♥♥ 3 |
| ● Gocce Castiglionero '15 | ♥ 4 |
| ○ Incanthus '17 | ♥ 2 |

## Villa Gianna

LOC. BORGO SAN DONATO
S.DA MAREMMANA
04010 SABAUDIA [LT]
TEL. +39 0773250034
www.villagianna.it

PRE-BOOKED VISITS
ACCOMMODATION
ANNUAL PRODUCTION 1,000,000 bottles
HECTARES UNDER VINE 45.00
SUSTAINABLE WINERY

| | |
|---|---|
| ○ Circeo Bianco Nobilvite '17 | ♥♥ 2* |
| ● Rudestro '16 | ♥♥ 2* |
| ○ Bianco di Caprolace Chardonnay '17 | ♥ 2 |
| ○ Moscato di Terracina Secco Elogio '17 | ♥ 2 |

## Villa Simone

VIA FRASCATI COLONNA, 29
00078 MONTE PORZIO CATONE [RM]
TEL. +39 069449717
www.villasimone.it

CELLAR SALES
PRE-BOOKED VISITS
ANNUAL PRODUCTION 200,000 bottles
HECTARES UNDER VINE 21.00
SUSTAINABLE WINERY

| | |
|---|---|
| ● Cesanese '15 | ♥♥ 4 |
| ● La Torraccia '15 | ♥♥ 3 |
| ○ Frascati Sup. Vign. Filonardi Ris. '16 | ♥ 5 |
| ○ Frascati Sup. Villa dei Preti '17 | ♥ 4 |

# ABRUZZO

Abruzzo's wine industry is in many ways a kind of microcosm of the nation as a whole. This is true from a historic point of view, in its gradual capacity to develop its distinct characteristics while leaving behind an age in which it was dominated by large quantities of generic bulk wine used outside of the region. It's also true from a territorial point of view, inasmuch as its grapes are cultivated from the highest peaks of the Apennines to the lowlands that line the Adriatic coast, each with its own relative agricultural and geo-climatic distinctions. And it's also true from an entrepreneurial point of view, considering the variety of producers who operate here, from large-scale wineries with volumes in the millions of bottles to tiny artisans, from its cooperatives to private wineries of every sort. And the array of veteran winemakers is constantly being replenished and renewed by emerging ones. Naturally, this scenario is reflected in the wines themselves. Despite its somewhat limited ampelography (with respect to other areas), the various geographies and technical sensibilities give rise to a particularly varied aggregation of wines. There's its Trebbiano and Pecorino whites, rosés and reds made with Montepulciano, and every possible stylistic interpretation is covered, from more Mediterranean wines to more 'northern' ones, from the delectable to the austere, from early-drinking to ageworthy. Then there's those wines that are commonly associated with the 'naturale' movement, which are even inspiring the work done by more 'classic' producers. We're speaking of organic management, eco-friendly projects, spontaneous fermentation, maceration on the skins (even for white grapes), maturation in concrete and terra-cotta, vinification without clarifying, filtration or added sulfites, and so on. And it's all woven together by an extraordinary gastronomic versatility that allows its principal typologies to accompany practically any dish, and not just local ones. And they won't cost you an arm and a leg either (it's not a coincidence that once again a number of Tre Bicchieri come at a price that would allow for daily consumption). Montepulciano d'Abruzzo takes center stage, without a doubt the region's most important appellation. In fact, it's just now celebrating its 50th anniversary, and the series of wines recognized reminds us how much has changed over the past half a century.

# Agriverde

LOC. CALDARI
VIA STORTINI, 32A
66026 ORTONA [CH]
TEL. +39 0859032101
www.agriverde.it

**CELLAR SALES**
**PRE-BOOKED VISITS**
**RESTAURANT SERVICE**
**ANNUAL PRODUCTION** 900,000 bottles
**HECTARES UNDER VINE** 65.00
**VITICULTURE METHOD** Certified Organic
**SUSTAINABLE WINERY**

The Di Carlo family have owned Agriverde for almost two centuries. It was one of the first Italian wineries to adopt agriculture-friendly methods and to design their structures (cellar, relais, spa) according to the dictates of bioarchitecture. The venture took off under Giannicola's management in the 1980s, when the vineyards were extended to Ortona, Caldari, Rogatti, Frisa and Crecchio. They mainly grow Montepulciano, Pecorino, Trebbiano and Passerina, which are interpreted with versatile styles in their Eikos, Piane di Maggio, Riseis, Solàrea and Natum Biovegan lines. As our score table suggests, what most impresses is the consistency of their entire selection, with at least two 2015 Montepulcianos standing out. Their Caldaria Famiglia Di Carlo is a nice compromise in terms of balance and typicity, with its traces of black fruit and licorice. Their Solàrea, on the other hand, features a more tertiary profile (embers, walnut, curing spices) and a more close-knit tannic weave.

| | |
|---|---|
| ● Montepulciano d'Abruzzo Caldaria Famiglia Di Carlo '15 | 🏆🏆 3* |
| ● Montepulciano d'Abruzzo Solàrea '15 | 🏆🏆 3* |
| ☉ Cerasuolo d'Abruzzo Riseis '17 | 🏆🏆 3 |
| ☉ Cerasuolo d'Abruzzo Solàrea '17 | 🏆🏆 3 |
| ○ Eikos Pecorino '17 | 🏆🏆 3 |
| ● Montepulciano d'Abruzzo Natum Biologico Vegano '17 | 🏆🏆 3 |
| ○ Trebbiano d'Abruzzo Solàrea '16 | 🏆🏆 4 |
| ● Montepulciano d'Abruzzo Eikos '16 | 🏆 3 |
| ○ Riseis Pecorino '17 | 🏆 3 |
| ● Montepulciano d'Abruzzo Plateo '04 | 🏆🏆🏆 6 |
| ● Montepulciano d'Abruzzo Plateo '01 | 🏆🏆🏆 6 |
| ● Montepulciano d'Abruzzo Plateo '00 | 🏆🏆🏆 6 |
| ● Montepulciano d'Abruzzo Plateo '98 | 🏆🏆🏆 5 |
| ● Montepulciano d'Abruzzo Solàrea '03 | 🏆🏆🏆 4 |

# F.lli Barba

LOC. SCERNE DI PINETO
S.DA ROTABILE PER CASOLI
64025 PINETO [TE]
TEL. +39 0859461020
www.fratellibarba.it

**CELLAR SALES**
**PRE-BOOKED VISITS**
**ACCOMMODATION**
**ANNUAL PRODUCTION** 300,000 bottles
**HECTARES UNDER VINE** 62.00

Brothers Giovanni, Domenico and Vincenzo Barba inherited this winery, which was founded by Cavaliere Luigi in the 1950s when he left tenant-farming behind and began cultivating his own land. The vineyards are situated between Colle Morino, Casal Thaulero and Vignafranca, in Colline Teramane, while the cellar is based in Scerne di Pineto. Montepulciano, Trebbiano and Pecorino share the best exposures and give rise to a versatile range of wines with a modern style. Winemaking techniques are varied and make use of steel and truncated cone-shaped oak barrels. We're pleased to once again have the chance to taste the Barba brothers' selection, starting with their 2015 Montepulciano Vignafranca, a territorial wine in its traces of black fruit and chocolate, with a sanguine touch that brings energy to a commendably fluid palate. Their 2016 Trebbiano di Mare surpasses it in terms of complexity, proving vibrant in its hints of Mediterranean herbs and spices. Its broad, rich palate isn't slowed down by savoriness.

| | |
|---|---|
| ○ Trebbiano d'Abruzzo di Mare '16 | 🏆🏆 4 |
| ● Montepulciano d'Abruzzo Vignafranca '15 | 🏆🏆 3 |
| ○ Colle Morino Pecorino '17 | 🏆 2 |
| ● Montepulciano d'Abruzzo Colle Morino '17 | 🏆 2 |
| ● Montepulciano d'Abruzzo I Vasari '10 | 🏆🏆🏆 5 |
| ● Montepulciano d'Abruzzo I Vasari '09 | 🏆🏆🏆 5 |
| ● Montepulciano d'Abruzzo I Vasari '08 | 🏆🏆🏆 5 |
| ● Montepulciano d'Abruzzo Vignafranca '07 | 🏆🏆🏆 3* |
| ● Montepulciano d'Abruzzo Vignafranca '06 | 🏆🏆🏆 3* |
| ○ Trebbiano d'Abruzzo '06 | 🏆🏆🏆 4* |
| ☉ Montepulciano d'Abruzzo Cerasuolo Vignafranca '14 | 🏆🏆 2* |
| ● Montepulciano d'Abruzzo Colle Morino Et. Bianca '13 | 🏆🏆 2* |

## Barone Cornacchia

c.da Torri, 19
64010 Torano Nuovo [TE]
Tel. +39 0861887412
www.baronecornacchia.it

**CELLAR SALES**
**PRE-BOOKED VISITS**
**ACCOMMODATION**
**ANNUAL PRODUCTION** 250,000 bottles
**HECTARES UNDER VINE** 50.00
**VITICULTURE METHOD** Certified Organic

Over five centuries ago, the Cornacchia family received the title of Baron from the Viceroy of Naples, along with a charge to oversee the estates around the Fortress of Civitella, in the heart of Colline Teramane. The game reserve in Torri di Torano Nuovo has become the hub of the winery, which is now run by the fourth generation brother-and-sister team of Filippo and Caterina. They are to be credited with converting the vineyards to organic viticulture. The winery grows Pecorino, Trebbiano, Passerina, and star of the range, Montepulciano, which is produced in about ten different styles. There wasn't a single standout during this round of tastings, but a number of wines were still on target. The 2016 Controguerra Rosso Colle Lupo is a charming wine in its hints of pepper and barley malt, as well as its sweet and sour palate, which finds breadth thanks to its rich tannins. Their 2017 Trebbiano Sup. Casanova offers up hints of yellow apples, tubers and almonds and shines for its subtleness and classic expression.

| | |
|---|---|
| ○ Controguerra Pecorino Casanova '17 | 🍷🍷 3 |
| ● Controguerra Rosso Colle Lupo '16 | 🍷🍷 5 |
| ● Montepulciano d'Abruzzo V. Le Coste '15 | 🍷🍷 5 |
| ○ Trebbiano d'Abruzzo Sup. Casanova '17 | 🍷🍷 3 |
| ○ Casanova Passerina '17 | 🍷 3 |
| ⊙ Cerasuolo d'Abruzzo Sup. Casanova '17 | 🍷 3 |
| ⊙ Cerasuolo d'Abruzzo Sup. '16 | ♀♀ 2* |
| ○ Controguerra Passerina Villa Torri '15 | ♀♀ 2* |
| ○ Controguerra Pecorino Villa Torri '16 | ♀♀ 2* |
| ● Montepulciano d'Abruzzo Colline Teramane Vizzarro '13 | ♀♀ 5 |
| ● Montepulciano d'Abruzzo Poggio Varano - Antico Feudo '13 | ♀♀ 3 |
| ○ Trebbiano d'Abruzzo Sup. '16 | ♀♀ 2* |

## Tenute Barone di Valforte

c.da Piomba, 11
64028 Silvi Marina [TE]
Tel. +39 0859353432
www.baronedivalforte.it

**CELLAR SALES**
**PRE-BOOKED VISITS**
**ANNUAL PRODUCTION** 280,000 bottles
**HECTARES UNDER VINE** 50.00

The various vineyard plots owned by the Sorricchio family have been part of the Barone di Valforte estate for almost a thousand years. They are situated in the municipalities of Atri, Mutignano di Pineto, Casoli and Silvi Marina in the Teramo hills. Their wide range of wines are made with Trebbiano, Pecorino, Passerina and Montepulciano. Brothers Francesco and Giulio have made the decision to cultivate these traditional varieties with sustainable agriculture and to interpret them with a modern sensibility that precludes more established winemaking procedures. Barone di Valforte has quickly reclaimed a place among the guide's principal wines, thanks especially to their 2017 whites. Their Pecorino is one example, close-focused, expressive wine redolent of pineapple, thyme and wild herbs. It's subtle, though not too exposed on the palate. Their Trebbiano Villa Chiara is another one, a delicately flowery wine with notes of fresh almond and pippins that open onto a flavorful, crisp palate.

| | |
|---|---|
| ○ Abruzzo Pecorino '17 | 🍷🍷 2* |
| ○ Trebbiano d'Abruzzo Villa Chiara '17 | 🍷🍷 2* |
| ○ Abruzzo Passerina '17 | 🍷 2 |
| ⊙ Cerasuolo d'Abruzzo Valforte Rosé '17 | 🍷 2 |
| ● Montepulciano d'Abruzzo '17 | 🍷 2 |
| ● Montepulciano d'Abruzzo Colline Teramane Colle Sale '16 | 🍷 3 |
| ● Montepulciano d'Abruzzo '15 | ♀♀ 2* |
| ● Montepulciano d'Abruzzo Colle Sale '14 | ♀♀ 4 |
| ○ Passerina '14 | ♀♀ 2* |
| ○ Pecorino '14 | ♀♀ 2* |
| ○ Trebbiano d'Abruzzo Villa Chiara '14 | ♀♀ 2* |

# Castorani

VIA CASTORANI, 5
65020 ALANNO [PE]
TEL. +39 3466355635
www.castorani.it

**CELLAR SALES**
**PRE-BOOKED VISITS**
**ACCOMMODATION AND RESTAURANT SERVICE**
**ANNUAL PRODUCTION** 600,000 bottles
**HECTARES UNDER VINE** 72.00
**VITICULTURE METHOD** Certified Organic

Cadetto, Amorino, Coste delle Plaje, Le
Paranze, Podere, Jarno, Majolica and
Paparazzi are names you need to remember
if you want to find your way through the
Castorano winery's numerous selections. It
is one of the most important wineries in
Abruzzo and was named by its founder,
Raffaele, at the end of the 18th century.
Today it belongs to a company whose most
famous partner is Jarno Trulli, ex-Formula 1
driver. The organic vineyards are located in
Colline Pescaresi di Alanno, where all of the
main regional varieties are grown. In the
cellar, pleasantness and drinkability are the
watchwords. Their selection doesn't cease to
amaze, as evidenced by the number of wines
that manage to stand out. Among these is
the formidable pair of Montepulcianos
that managed to reach our finals. Their
2014 Podere Castorani Riserva offers up
hints of pencil lead, incense, and forest
scents. We find the same varietal coherence
and savoriness in the 2016 Cadetto, a wine
that features an original, iodine character.

| | |
|---|---|
| ● Montepulciano d'Abruzzo Podere Castorani Ris. '14 | ▼▼▼ 5 |
| ● Montepulciano d'Abruzzo Cadetto '16 | ▼▼ 2* |
| ○ Abruzzo Pecorino Sup. Amorino '17 | ▼▼ 3 |
| ○ Cadetto Pecorino '17 | ▼▼ 3 |
| ● Montepulciano d'Abruzzo Amorino '14 | ▼▼ 3 |
| ○ Trebbiano d'Abruzzo Cadetto '17 | ▼▼ 2* |
| ○ Trebbiano d'Abruzzo Sup. Amorino '17 | ▼▼ 2* |
| ○ Cerasuolo d'Abruzzo Amorino '17 | ▼ 3 |
| ○ Trebbiano d'Abruzzo Podere Castorani Ris. '16 | ▼ 3 |
| ● Montepulciano d'Abruzzo Amorino '13 | ♀♀♀ 3* |
| ● Montepulciano d'Abruzzo Amorino '12 | ♀♀♀ 3* |
| ● Montepulciano d'Abruzzo Podere Castorani Ris. '10 | ♀♀♀ 5 |

# ★Luigi Cataldi Madonna

LOC. PIANO
67025 OFENA [AQ]
TEL. +39 0862954252
www.cataldimadonna.com

**CELLAR SALES**
**PRE-BOOKED VISITS**
**ANNUAL PRODUCTION** 260,000 bottles
**HECTARES UNDER VINE** 31.00
**SUSTAINABLE WINERY**

The Cataldi Madonna family's winery, which
has for some time been considered an
important producer in the historic
winemaking area of Ofena, is approaching
its 100-year anniversary. The plateau, also
known as "Forno d'Abruzzo", is located on
the slopes of the Calderone glacier, with
Gran Sasso heavily influencing the climate
and personality of local wines. They grow
Pecorino, Trebbiano and Montepulciano,
which are enhanced to their fullness by the
lively interpretation given them by Luigi and
his daughter Giulia. Their wines are ideal
for drinking immediately, but are also
long-lived. Pratically each of Cataldi
Madonna's wines hits the mark, whether
it's their flowery 2017 Trebbiano, their
fragrant 2017 Pecorino Giulia or their
restless 2016 Montepulciano Malandrino.
But once again, it's their Pié delle Vigne
that's gets our hearts racing. Their 2016
version brings together the depth of a
great red (wild berries, plowed earth,
Asian spices) with the drinkability of the
best Cerasuolos.

| | |
|---|---|
| ⊙ Cerasuolo d'Abruzzo Pié delle Vigne '16 | ▼▼▼ 5 |
| ○ Giulia Pecorino '17 | ▼▼ 2* |
| ● Montepulciano d'Abruzzo Malandrino '16 | ▼▼ 3 |
| ⊙ Trebbiano d'Abruzzo '17 | ▼▼ 2* |
| ⊙ Cerasuolo d'Abruzzo '17 | ▼ 2 |
| ⊙ Cerasuolo d'Abruzzo Pié delle Vigne '15 | ♀♀♀ 5 |
| ● Montepulciano d'Abruzzo Malandrino '13 | ♀♀♀ 3* |
| ● Montepulciano d'Abruzzo Malandrino '12 | ♀♀♀ 3* |
| ● Montepulciano d'Abruzzo Tonì '07 | ♀♀♀ 5 |
| ○ Pecorino '11 | ♀♀♀ 5 |
| ○ Pecorino '10 | ♀♀♀ 5 |
| ○ Pecorino '09 | ♀♀♀ 5 |
| ○ Pecorino '08 | ♀♀♀ 5 |
| ○ Pecorino Frontone '13 | ♀♀♀ 5 |

# Centorame

FRAZ. CASOLO DI ATRI
VIA DELLE FORNACI SNC
64030 ATRI [TE]
TEL. +39 0858709115
www.centorame.it

**CELLAR SALES**
**PRE-BOOKED VISITS**
**ANNUAL PRODUCTION** 100,000 bottles
**HECTARES UNDER VINE** 12.00
**SUSTAINABLE WINERY**

Although bottling officially began with the 2002 vintage, Centorame was in fact set up in the mid-1980s by Lamberto Vannucci's father. Lamberto heads the winery today, along with the third generation of the family. Everything revolves around this beautiful estate set deep inside the Riserva dei Calanchi, in Casoli di Atri. It is one of the most charming places in Colline Teramane, with vineyards at 200 meters above sea level and the Adriatic coast less than five kilometers away. This environment is what produces the meaty and dry aspect of their Montepulciano, Trebbiano, Pecorino and Passerini wines. Our recent tastings revealed a compact selection, in particular when it comes to their S. Michele and Castellum Vetus lines. IN terms of the latter, their 2016 Trebbiano d'Abruzzo leads the way, with its captivating musky and balsamic aromas. The wine develops more in terms of breadth than tension, though without losing its continuity and balance. Their other Trebbianos and Montepulcianos also did well.

| | |
|---|---|
| ○ Trebbiano d'Abruzzo Castellum Vetus '16 | ♛♛ 3* |
| ● Montepulciano d'Abruzzo Colline Teramane Castellum Vetus '15 | ♛♛ 4 |
| ● Montepulciano d'Abruzzo S. Michele '16 | ♛♛ 2* |
| ○ Trebbiano d'Abruzzo S. Michele '17 | ♛♛ 2* |
| ○ Abruzzo Passerina S. Michele '17 | ♛ 2 |
| ○ Anna Pecorino Brut M. Cl. '13 | ♛ 5 |
| ⊙ Cerasuolo d'Abruzzo S. Michele '17 | ♛ 2 |
| ○ Tuapina Pecorino '17 | ♛ 2 |
| ○ Abruzzo Passerina S. Michele '15 | ♛♛ 2* |
| ● Montepulciano d'Abruzzo S. Michele '15 | ♛♛ 2* |
| ● Montepulciano d'Abruzzo S. Michele '14 | ♛♛ 2* |
| ● Montepulciano d'Abruzzo Scuderie Ducali '14 | ♛♛ 2* |
| ○ Tuapina Pecorino '16 | ♛♛ 2* |

# Cerulli Spinozzi

S.S. 150 DEL VOMANO KM 17,600
64020 CANZANO [TE]
TEL. +39 086157193
www.cerullispinozzi.it

**CELLAR SALES**
**PRE-BOOKED VISITS**
**ACCOMMODATION**
**ANNUAL PRODUCTION** 200,000 bottles
**HECTARES UNDER VINE** 53.00

The Spinozzis come from feudal stock, while the Cerulli Irellis were merchants. One of the most important wineries in Abruzzo was founded by the union of these two great families and their respective properties. The estate is situated in the Teramo hills, between Canzano and Mosciano in an area of alluvial origin. Traditionally grown with Montepulciano, large amounts of Trebbiano and Pecorino are also grown on the land. The varied territory and different varieties come to life under the work of brothers, Francesco and Vincenzo Cerulli Irelli, along with Vincenzo's son, Enrico. The Cerulli Spinozzi selection reclaims its place among their top-of-the-range wines, with brilliant results. Their 2015 Montepulciano Cortalto is extremely well put together in its hints of white fruit, balsam and roots, as well as its well-integrated tannins. But it's their 2017 Pecorinos that really shine. Their Almorano offers up flowery hints as well as a touch of tanginess, while the Cortalto is even more fragrant and flavorful, with a pervasive waft of citrus.

| | |
|---|---|
| ○ Cortalto Pecorino '17 | ♛♛ 2* |
| ○ Almorano Pecorino '17 | ♛♛ 1* |
| ● Montepulciano d'Abruzzo Colline Teramane Cortalto '15 | ♛♛ 2* |
| ⊙ Cerasuolo d'Abruzzo Almorano '17 | ♛ 1* |
| ⊙ Cerasuolo d'Abruzzo Sup. Cortalto '17 | ♛ 2 |
| ● Montepulciano d'Abruzzo Almorano '17 | ♛ 1* |
| ● Montepulciano d'Abruzzo Colline Teramane Torre Migliori '13 | ♛ 3 |
| ○ Trebbiano d'Abruzzo Almorano '17 | ♛ 1* |
| ○ Cortalto Pecorino '15 | ♛♛ 2* |
| ● Montepulciano d'Abruzzo Colline Teramane Torre Migliori '10 | ♛♛ 3 |
| ○ Trebbiano d'Abruzzo Almorano '16 | ♛♛ 2* |

# Cirelli

LOC. TRECIMINIERE
VIA COLLE SAN GIOVANNI, 1
64032 ATRI [TE]
TEL. +39 0858700106
www.agricolacirelli.com

CELLAR SALES
PRE-BOOKED VISITS
ACCOMMODATION AND RESTAURANT SERVICE
ANNUAL PRODUCTION 26,000 bottles
HECTARES UNDER VINE 5.00
VITICULTURE METHOD Certified Organic

Francesco Cirelli is a leading exponent of the 'natural' wine movement in Abruzzo. He is based in Treciminiere di Atri, in Colline Teramane, which is famous for its picturesque ravines. Everything is spontaneous, starting with fermentation. And his winemaking approach to Montepulciano, Trebbiano and Pecorino aims first and foremost to bring out their great gastronomic potential. He uses these grapes to produce two distinct selections: Amphora for wines made in terracotta and La Collina Biologica featuring bottles with screwcaps. Their 2017 Pecorino La Collina Biologica proves to be one of their most well-fashioned wines, offering up hints of green apple, walnutskin and ginger. It's a precise, supple wine, though their pair of 2017 Trebbiano d'Abruzzos also deliver. The version matured in amphoras compensates a bit of phenolic insistence with raciness and flavor. Their Collina Biologica features a more classic profile, with sappy sensations anticipating a pleasantly crispy palate.

| | | |
|---|---|---|
| ○ La Collina Biologica Pecorino '17 | ♀♀ | 3 |
| ○ Trebbiano d'Abruzzo Amphora '17 | ♀♀ | 5 |
| ○ Trebbiano d'Abruzzo La Collina Biologica '17 | ♀♀ | 2* |
| ⊙ Cerasuolo d'Abruzzo La Collina Biologica '17 | ♀ | 2 |
| ● Montepulciano d'Abruzzo Amphora '17 | ♀ | 5 |
| ● Montepulciano d'Abruzzo La Collina Biologica '17 | ♀ | 2 |
| ⊙ Cerasuolo d'Abruzzo Amphora '15 | ♀♀ | 5 |
| ⊙ Cerasuolo d'Abruzzo La Collina Biologica '16 | ♀♀ | 2* |
| ● Montepulciano d'Abruzzo La Collina Biologica '16 | ♀♀ | 2* |
| ● Montepulciano d'Abruzzo La Collina Biologica '15 | ♀♀ | 2* |
| ○ Trebbiano d'Abruzzo '15 | ♀♀ | 2* |

# Codice Citra

C.DA CUCULLO
66026 ORTONA [CH]
TEL. +39 0859031342
www.citra.it

CELLAR SALES
PRE-BOOKED VISITS
ANNUAL PRODUCTION 18,000,000 bottles
HECTARES UNDER VINE 6000.00

Pollutri, Rocca San Giovanni, Lanciano, Ortona, Paglieta, Crecchia, Torrevecchia, Teatina and Tollo are nine cooperatives that fall under the Codice Citra brand, all situated in the province of Chieti. This huge cooperative and large supplier of Abruzzo wine was founded in 1973. Today it brings together over 3000 grower-members all involved with the company's activity, which goes well beyond vine growing. They take a modern view of winemaking and produce a varied and good-value range of wines with Montepulciano, Trebbiano, Pecorino and Passerina grapes. The producer is seeing continued growth in quality, both in terms of their base-line of wines and their Ferzo premium offerings. Their 2016 Montepulciano is an example, proving a close-focused, multifaceted wines in its sequence of juniper, peppermint and bramble, all coherently supported by a close-woven, caressing palate. Their 2017 Pecorino Superiore is another, proving timid on the nose, initially, but deep and penetrating in the mouth, with a long finish featuring sensations of herbs and pollen.

| | | |
|---|---|---|
| ○ Abruzzo Pecorino Sup. Ferzo '17 | ♀♀ | 2* |
| ● Montepulciano d'Abruzzo Ferzo '16 | ♀♀ | 3* |
| ⊙ Cerasuolo d'Abruzzo Sup. Ferzo '17 | ♀♀ | 3 |
| ● Montepulciano d'Abruzzo Laus Vitae Ris. '12 | ♀♀ | 5 |
| ○ Abruzzo Cococciola Sup. Ferzo '17 | ♀ | 3 |
| ○ Abruzzo Passerina Sup. Ferzo '17 | ♀ | 2 |
| ● Montepulciano d'Abruzzo Caroso Ris. '13 | ♀ | 4 |
| ○ Abruzzo Pecorino Sup. Ferzo '16 | ♀♀ | 2* |
| ○ Abruzzo Pecorino Sup. Ferzo '15 | ♀♀ | 2* |
| ⊙ Cerasuolo d'Abruzzo Sup. Ferzo '16 | ♀♀ | 3* |
| ● Montepulciano d'Abruzzo Caroso '10 | ♀♀ | 4 |
| ● Montepulciano d'Abruzzo Caroso Ris. '11 | ♀♀ | 4 |
| ● Montepulciano d'Abruzzo Ferzo '15 | ♀♀ | 3 |
| ● Montepulciano d'Abruzzo Ferzo '14 | ♀♀ | 3 |

# Contesa

S.DA DELLE VIGNE, 28
65010 COLLECORVINO [PE]
TEL. +39 0858205078
www.contesa.it

CELLAR SALES
PRE-BOOKED VISITS
RESTAURANT SERVICE
ANNUAL PRODUCTION 260,000 bottles
HECTARES UNDER VINE 45.00
SUSTAINABLE WINERY

This beautiful winery was established in the early 2000s by Rocco Pasetti. It is located on the Lombard site of Collecorvino, in Colline Pescaresi, part of the Terre dei Vestini subzone. Its unusual name comes from an historic land dispute involving Antonio's great-grandfather just after the unification of Italy. This was almost relived when Rocco himself decided to break away from the family winery. The vineyards are cultivated with the classic Abruzzo varieties and situated at about 250 meters above sea level, on a large hill facing the Adriatic. These are ideal conditions for producing meaty and flavorsome wines, which are showing significant improvement of late. This is well-demonstrated by their three Montepulcianos, a highly varied lot that prove excellent for balance and character. But it's their 2017 Trebbiano Fermentazione Spontanea that emerges as their crown jewel, with its rustic profile (medicinal herbs, wild flowers, spring fruit) that's fully supported by close-woven and luxuriant palate with vigor.

| | |
|---|---|
| ○ Trebbiano d'Abruzzo Fermentazione Spontanea '17 | ♟♟ 3* |
| ● Montepulciano d'Abruzzo '16 | ♟♟ 2* |
| ● Montepulciano d'Abruzzo Ris. '13 | ♟♟ 4 |
| ● Montepulciano d'Abruzzo Terre dei Vestini Chiedi alla Polvere Ris. '13 | ♟♟ 4 |
| ○ Abruzzo Pecorino '17 | ♟ 3 |
| ● Montepulciano d'Abruzzo Ris. '08 | ♟♟♟ 3* |
| ○ Abruzzo Pecorino '16 | ♟♟ 2* |
| ● Montepulciano d'Abruzzo V. Corvino '15 | ♟♟ 2* |
| ○ Trebbiano d'Abruzzo '16 | ♟♟ 2* |

# Antonio Costantini

S.DA MIGLIORI, 20
65013 CITTÀ SANT'ANGELO [PE]
TEL. +39 0859699169
www.costantinivini.it

CELLAR SALES
PRE-BOOKED VISITS
ACCOMMODATION AND RESTAURANT SERVICE
ANNUAL PRODUCTION 450,000 bottles
HECTARES UNDER VINE 60.00

The origins of the Costantini family's winemaking activity date back to over a century ago. In recent years their wines have made an assertive comeback in the competitive Abruzzo district. Today Antonio heads the winery and personally tends to the vineyards concentrated in the Città Sant'Angelo hills, near Pescara. Only traditional regional cultivars are grown: Trebbiano, Pecorino, Passerina and Montepulciano, and they are the key players in a range with a classic style, which favors racy and drinkable wines rather than muscular ones. For Costantini, this year probably turned out to be the best yet, thanks to a solid selection of 2017s. Both their base Trebbianos and their Febe line delivered for their cleanness and the ease with which they can accompany food. The same expressivity and deliciousness can be be found in their 2017 Cerasuolo Febe, a sweetly saline wine, but especially in their 2017 Abruzzo Pecorino, a small jewel of suppleness, flavor, richness and vigor.

| | |
|---|---|
| ○ Abruzzo Pecorino '17 | ♟♟ 2* |
| ⊙ Cerasuolo d'Abruzzo Febe '17 | ♟♟ 1* |
| ○ Trebbiano d'Abruzzo '17 | ♟♟ 2* |
| ○ Trebbiano d'Abruzzo Febe '17 | ♟♟ 1* |
| ○ Abruzzo Passerina '17 | ♟ 2 |
| ⊙ Cerasuolo d'Abruzzo '17 | ♟ 2 |
| ● Montepulciano d'Abruzzo Febe '17 | ♟ 1* |
| ● Montepulciano d'Abruzzo '11 | ♟♟ 3 |
| ● Montepulciano d'Abruzzo Febe '15 | ♟♟ 2* |
| ○ Trebbiano d'Abruzzo '16 | ♟♟ 2* |
| ○ Trebbiano d'Abruzzo '14 | ♟♟ 2* |
| ○ Trebbiano d'Abruzzo Ecate '12 | ♟♟ 3 |

# D'Alesio

VIA GAGLIERANO, 73
65013 CITTÀ SANT'ANGELO [PE]
TEL. +39 08596713
www.sciarr.com

**CELLAR SALES**
**PRE-BOOKED VISITS**
**RESTAURANT SERVICE**
**ANNUAL PRODUCTION** 70,000 bottles
**HECTARES UNDER VINE** 16.00
**VITICULTURE METHOD** Certified Organic
**SUSTAINABLE WINERY**

The D'Alesio family's farm is situated in the backcountry of Città Sant'Angelo, in the heart of the Pescara hills. It was founded in 2009 and today it is run by Lanfranco and Giovanni. It was their decision to obtain organic certification for all of their wines, which focus on historic local varieties. Montepulciano, Trebbiano, Pecorino, Cococciola and Montonico mold a small range with a modern inspiration that is becoming more and more interesting. Their wines feature an exhilarating natural expression, playing on savory energy and a dynamic palate. Such stylistic characteristics emerged perfectly during out last round of tastings. Their 2013 Trebbiano Tenuta del Professor proved a particularly good examples. It's a magnificent white in its ability to deliver on multiple levels (flowers, citrus, grains, smoke notes) and remain taut and bright on the palate, despite it's notable weight. Their 2015 Pecorino Sup. is similar in this respect, though it's just a bit warmer, as is their straightforward 2013 Montepulciano.

| | |
|---|---|
| ○ Trebbiano d'Abruzzo Tenuta del Professore '13 | 🏆🏆 5 |
| ○ Abruzzo Pecorino Sup. '15 | 🏆🏆 2* |
| ● Montepulciano d'Abruzzo '13 | 🏆🏆 4 |

# Tenuta I Fauri

VIA FILIPPO MASCI, 151
66100 CHIETI
TEL. +39 0871332627
www.tenutaifauri.it

**CELLAR SALES**
**PRE-BOOKED VISITS**
**ANNUAL PRODUCTION** 150,000 bottles
**HECTARES UNDER VINE** 35.00

Tenuta I Fauri, an estate run by Domenico di Camillo and his children Luigi and Valentina, is a perfect example of the sea and mountain combination that's at the foundation of Chieti's viticulture (they also adhere to the principles of integrated pest management). The vineyard plots are located in Chieti, Francavilla al Mare, Miglianico, Villamagna, Bucchianico and Ari. The wide variety of environments are reflected in the eclectic personality of the wines, which are made with Montepulciano, Trebbiano, Pecorino and Passerina grapes. You always have fun when it comes to I Fauri's wines, which exchange places in our rankings from one year to the next. This time it's their ominous 2015 Montepulciano that's guiding the group, with its straightforward Mediterranean atmosphere. This is supported by a touch of marmalade and burnt wood, and especially a slightly salty palate, which demonstrates commendable extractive poise. Their 2017 Baldovino also proved excellent.

| | |
|---|---|
| ⊙ Cerasuolo d'Abruzzo Baldovino '17 | 🏆🏆 2* |
| ● Montepulciano d'Abruzzo Rosso dei Fauri '15 | 🏆🏆 5 |
| ○ Trebbiano d'Abruzzo Baldovino '17 | 🏆🏆 2* |
| ○ Abruzzo Pecorino '17 | 🏆 3 |
| ○ Passerina '17 | 🏆 2 |
| ○ Abruzzo Pecorino '14 | 🏆🏆🏆 2* |
| ○ Abruzzo Pecorino '13 | 🏆🏆🏆 2* |
| ○ Abruzzo Pecorino '15 | 🏆🏆 2* |
| ⊙ Cerasuolo d'Abruzzo Baldovino '16 | 🏆🏆 2* |
| ⊙ Cerasuolo d'Abruzzo Baldovino '15 | 🏆🏆 2* |
| ● Montepulciano d'Abruzzo Baldovino '15 | 🏆🏆 2* |
| ● Montepulciano d'Abruzzo Ottobre Rosso '16 | 🏆🏆 2* |
| ● Montepulciano d'Abruzzo Ottobre Rosso '15 | 🏆🏆 2* |
| ○ Trebbiano d'Abruzzo Baldovino '16 | 🏆🏆 2* |

# Feudo Antico

VIA CROCEVECCHIA, 101
66010 TOLLO [CH]
TEL. +39 0871969128
www.feudoantico.it

CELLAR SALES
ANNUAL PRODUCTION 80,000 bottles
HECTARES UNDER VINE 20.00
VITICULTURE METHOD Certified Organic

DOP Tullum, one of Italy's smallest
appellations, finds a brilliant ambassador
in Feudo Antico. Founded in 2004, today
its fifty some members grow
Montepulciano, Chardonnay, Passerina and
Pecorino grapes. There is also a 'cru' wine
(Casadonna) from the estate of the same
name surrounding a restaurant/resort
owned by Niko Romito and his family in
Castel di Sangro (at about 800 meters
above sea level). It is the crown jewel of a
prestigious range of wines, fermented
mainly in steel and glass-lined concrete.
Feudo Antico has established itself as a
top benchmark for Pecorino, with three
memorable 2017 versions of the wine.
Their 'base' Tullum is a jewel of energy
and drinkability while their Biologico sees
added citrus and mineral expansion, but
foremost a savory palate. For once we
appreciated their Casadonna, which whose
primary notes are still a bit held back at
this early stage.

| | |
|---|---|
| ○ Tullum Pecorino Biologico '17 | ▼▼▼ 3* |
| ○ Casadonna Pecorino '17 | ▼▼ 7 |
| ○ Tullum Pecorino '17 | ▼▼ 3 |
| ● Montepulciano d'Abruzzo '15 | ▼ 2 |
| ⊙ Rosato Biologico '17 | ▼ 3 |
| ● Tullum Rosso '14 | ▼ 3 |
| ○ Pecorino Casadonna '15 | ♀♀♀ 7 |
| ○ Pecorino Casadonna '14 | ♀♀ 7 |
| ⊙ Rosato Biologico '16 | ♀♀ 3 |
| ○ Tullum Pecorino '14 | ♀♀ 3* |
| ○ Tullum Pecorino Biologico '16 | ♀♀ 3* |
| ○ Tullum Pecorino Biologico '15 | ♀♀ 3 |
| ● Tullum Rosso Biologico '15 | ♀♀ 3 |

# Il Feuduccio
# di Santa Maria D'Orni

LOC. FEUDUCCIO
66036 ORSOGNA [CH]
TEL. +39 0871891646
www.ilfeuduccio.it

CELLAR SALES
PRE-BOOKED VISITS
ANNUAL PRODUCTION 150,000 bottles
HECTARES UNDER VINE 50.00

Facing the Adriatic and sheltered by the
Majella, the Colline Teatine hills in Orsogna
form the backdrop for the Il Feuduccio di
Santa Maria D'Orni estate. Founded by the
entrepreneur Gaetano Lamaletto, its name
comes from nearby farming properties.
It then passed into the hands of his son
Camillo and grandson, Gaetano Junior.
Trebbiano, Pecorino, Passerina and
Montepulciano share the vineyard plots
surrounding the splendid underground
cellar dug out of rock, where the wines
take shape, featuring different styles and
organized into various lines. This year there
wasn't a standout but this allowed us to
appreciate the overall soundness of
Feuduccio's wines, in particular their two
2017 Fonte Vennas. The Pecorino presents
itself with sweet traces of pear and
candied peel supported by a warm, broad
palate. Their Rosato privileges savory
texture over exuberance. Their Ursonia
Montepulciano is once again charming,
though the 2015 is just a bit autumnal.

| | |
|---|---|
| ○ Fonte Venna Pecorino '17 | ▼▼ 2* |
| ⊙ Fonte Venna Rosato '17 | ▼▼ 2* |
| ● Montepulciano d'Abruzzo Ursonia '15 | ▼▼ 5 |
| ⊙ Cerasuolo d'Abruzzo Feuduccio '17 | ▼ 2 |
| ● Montepulciano d'Abruzzo Feuduccio '15 | ▼ 3 |
| ○ Pecorino '17 | ▼ 2 |
| ○ Trebbiano d'Abruzzo Feuduccio '17 | ▼ 2 |
| ○ Ursonia Pecorino '16 | ▼ 5 |
| ● Montepulciano d'Abruzzo Ursonia '13 | ♀♀♀ 4* |
| ○ Pecorino '16 | ♀♀ 2* |

# ★Dino Illuminati

C.DA SAN BIAGIO, 18
64010 CONTROGUERRA [TE]
TEL. +39 0861808008
www.illuminativini.it

CELLAR SALES
PRE-BOOKED VISITS
ANNUAL PRODUCTION 1,150,000 bottles
HECTARES UNDER VINE 130.00

The Illuminati family winery was founded at the end of the nineteenth century by Nicola and it was turned into a bottling winery by Cavaliere Dino in the 1970s. Today the winery is a world-famous icon of Teramo and Abruzzo wine. Lorenzo and Stefano are the latest generation working full-time at the winery in Controguerra, where Montepulciano, Trebbiano and Pecorino grapes are cultivated at 300 meters above sea level. They produce a complete range of traditional wines, characterized by different grape origins and winemaking methods. As always, great age-worthy reds lead the group. Their 2013 Montepulciano Colline Teramane Zanna Riserva is a good example, a wine that proves distinctive for its woodland, smoky profile made sweet by black fruit preserves and supported by a vigorous tannic weave. It's also worth pointing out they 2017 Cerasuolos. Their Lumeggio di Rosa offers up flowers and herbs, lightly unfolding while the Campirosa has more muscle and flavor.

| | | |
|---|---|---|
| ● Montepulciano d'Abruzzo Colline Teramane Zanna Ris. '13 | ♟♟♟ | 5 |
| ⊙ Cerasuolo d'Abruzzo Campirosa '17 | ♟♟ | 2* |
| ⊙ Cerasuolo d'Abruzzo Lumeggio di Rosa '17 | ♟♟ | 2* |
| ○ Controguerra Bianco Costalupo '17 | ♟♟ | 2* |
| ○ Controguerra Pecorino '17 | ♟♟ | 2* |
| ○ Controguerra Passerina '17 | ♟ | 2 |
| ● Montepulciano d'Abruzzo Ilico '16 | ♟ | 2 |
| ● Montepulciano d'Abruzzo Colline Teramane Pieluni Ris. '10 | ♟♟♟ | 6 |
| ● Montepulciano d'Abruzzo Colline Teramane Zanna Ris. '11 | ♟♟♟ | 5 |
| ● Montepulciano d'Abruzzo Colline Teramane Zanna Ris. '10 | ♟♟♟ | 5 |

# ★★Masciarelli

VIA GAMBERALE, 2
66010 SAN MARTINO SULLA MARRUCINA [CH]
TEL. +39 087185241
www.masciarelli.it

CELLAR SALES
PRE-BOOKED VISITS
ACCOMMODATION
ANNUAL PRODUCTION 2,500,000 bottles
HECTARES UNDER VINE 300.00
SUSTAINABLE WINERY

Young Miriam is now working permanently alongside her mother Marina to bring new life to the epic project dreamed up by the late Gianni Masciarelli in the early 1980s. It all started in the Chieti hills, in San Martino sulla Marrucina, but over time ten more estates, distributed among the four provinces of Abruzzo, were added. They cultivate both traditional and international varieties, but their style remains unchanged: innovative but keeping one eye on the past. Their wine selections include Gianni Masciarelli, Marina Cvetic, Castello di Semivicoli and Villa Gemma. Once again its Masciarelli's most famous wines that set the producer apart. Their 2013 Montepulciano Villa Gemma Res. is an explosion of dark fruit, licorice and coffee, all supported by its palate thanks to notable extractive force. There's extra grace and mobility of flavor in the 2015 Trebbiano Castello di Semivicoli, a wine that features aromas of pear, citrus and thyme, as well as a touch of pastry cream to sweeten its expressive profile.

| | | |
|---|---|---|
| ○ Trebbiano d'Abruzzo Castello di Semivicoli '15 | ♟♟♟ | 5 |
| ● Montepulciano d'Abruzzo Villa Gemma Ris. '13 | ♟♟ | 7 |
| ● Montepulciano d'Abruzzo Colline Teramane Iskra Marina Cvetic '15 | ♟ | 5 |
| ⊙ Cerasuolo d'Abruzzo Villa Gemma '15 | ♟♟♟ | 3* |
| ● Montepulciano d'Abruzzo Marina Cvetic '13 | ♟♟♟ | 4* |
| ● Montepulciano d'Abruzzo Marina Cvetic '11 | ♟♟♟ | 4* |
| ● Montepulciano d'Abruzzo Marina Cvetic '10 | ♟♟♟ | 4* |
| ● Montepulciano d'Abruzzo Villa Gemma '06 | ♟♟♟ | 7 |

# Camillo Montori

LOC. PIANE TRONTO, 80
64010 CONTROGUERRA [TE]
TEL. +39 0861809900
www.montorivini.it

**CELLAR SALES**
**PRE-BOOKED VISITS**
**ACCOMMODATION AND RESTAURANT SERVICE**
**ANNUAL PRODUCTION** 600,000 bottles
**HECTARES UNDER VINE** 50.00

The Montori brand was founded at the end of the nineteenth century and achieved worldwide fame during the 1960s and 1970s, thanks to Camillo's hard work. Today, as then, everything revolves around the vineyards in Controguerra, the capital of Teramo winemaking. They grow Trebbiano, Pecorino, Passerina, Montepulciano, as well as international varieties, to produce a wide range of wines that are celebrated for their solidity and vigor. This is especially true for the Casa Montori and Fonte Cupa selections, which are markedly improved due to their respect for cultivar and territorial tradition. The producer's selection saw one great performance after another, with the Cerasuolo Fonte Cupa once again making the case that it's Montori's flagship wine. The 2017 highlights a classic, rigorous profile featuring dark citrus, licorice and spices that merge well in a consistent, well-balanced palate. Their 2017 Pecorino isn't lacking in character either, proving crisp and linear.

| | |
|---|---|
| ⊙ Cerasuolo d'Abruzzo Fonte Cupa '17 | ♟♟ 2* |
| ○ Fonte Cupa Pecorino '17 | ♟♟ 3 |
| ○ Fonte Cupa Passerina '17 | ♟ 3 |
| ● Montepulciano d'Abruzzo Fonte Cupa '13 | ♟ 2 |
| ○ Trebbiano d'Abruzzo Fonte Cupa '17 | ♟ 2 |
| ⊙ Cerasuolo d'Abruzzo Fonte Cupa '16 | ♟♟♟ 2* |
| ⊙ Cerasuolo d'Abruzzo Fonte Cupa '15 | ♟♟ 2* |
| ● Montepulciano d'Abruzzo Colline Teramane Casa Montori '11 | ♟♟ 2* |
| ● Montepulciano d'Abruzzo Colline Teramane Fonte Cupa Ris. '08 | ♟♟ 5 |
| ● Montepulciano d'Abruzzo Fonte Cupa '11 | ♟♟ 2* |
| ○ Pecorino Fonte Cupa '16 | ♟♟ 3 |

# Fattoria Nicodemi

C.DA VENIGLIO, 8
64024 NOTARESCO [TE]
TEL. +39 085895493
www.nicodemi.com

**CELLAR SALES**
**PRE-BOOKED VISITS**
**ANNUAL PRODUCTION** 200,000 bottles
**HECTARES UNDER VINE** 30.00
**VITICULTURE METHOD** Certified Organic

In the 1970s, Bruno Nicodemi moved from Rome to Contrada Veniglio di Notaresco, in Colline Teramane, to start a new life as a wine producer. Montepulciano and Trebbiano share the best exposures in virtually contiguous vineyards around the winery. These grapes are a unique expression of the nearby Adriatic coast and the shelter provided by Gran Sasso. Bruno's children Elena and Alessandro head the winery today and are to be credited with the latest leap in quality, highlighted by the natural style and drinkability of their Le Murate and Notàri selections. And the 2016 vintage gave rise to the two wines that best encompass the relaxed, sunny character we usually associate with Nicodemi. Their Trebbiano Superiore Notàri stands out for its warm notes of tropical fruit, dried herbs and lemon peel, which find a coherent follow through in a rather broad palate. This Mediterranean character also emerges in their Montepulciano Le Murate, a round and complete wine.

| | |
|---|---|
| ○ Trebbiano d'Abruzzo Sup. Notàri '16 | ♟♟ 3* |
| ● Montepulciano d'Abruzzo Colline Teramane Le Murate '16 | ♟♟ 3 |
| ⊙ Cerasuolo d'Abruzzo Le Murate '17 | ♟ 2 |
| ● Montepulciano d'Abruzzo Colline Teramane Neromoro Ris. '14 | ♟ 5 |
| ● Montepulciano d'Abruzzo Colline Teramane Notàri '16 | ♟ 4 |
| ● Montepulciano d'Abruzzo Colline Teramane Neromoro Ris. '09 | ♟♟♟ 5 |
| ● Montepulciano d'Abruzzo Colline Teramane Neromoro Ris. '03 | ♟♟♟ 5 |
| ○ Trebbiano d'Abruzzo Sup. Notàri '15 | ♟♟♟ 3* |
| ● Montepulciano d'Abruzzo Colline Teramane Le Murate '15 | ♟♟ 3 |

## Orlandi Contucci Ponno

LOC. PIANA DEGLI ULIVI, 1
64026 ROSETO DEGLI ABRUZZI [TE]
TEL. +39 0858944049
www.orlandicontucciponno.com

CELLAR SALES
PRE-BOOKED VISITS
ANNUAL PRODUCTION 185,000 bottles
HECTARES UNDER VINE 31.00

For over half a century the Orlandi Contucci
Ponno brand has been linked to Roseto
degli Abruzzi, a hilly district of Colline
Teramane overlooking the Vomano river.
Since 2007 it has belonged to the Gussalli
Berretta family who have continued
improving their vineyards, situated a stone's
throw from the Adriatic coast and influenced
by nearby Gran Sasso. They offer a basic
line, as well as crus and reserve wines, with
their austere Montepulcianos, Cerasuolos
and Trebbianos all made by fermenting
grapes from individual plots and adopting
various maturation methods. Their selection
really has no weak points, as our most
recent tastings demonstrate. In particular,
we noticed their deliciously fruit-driven
2017 Pecorino and a 2017 Cerasuolo
Vermiglio with a discreet yet buoyant
charm in its hints of mandarin orange
and wild herbs. We shouldn't forget their
2015 Montepulciano La Regia Specula, a
wine that offers up aromas of blueberry,
pepper and chocolate, all of which give way
to a caressing palate.

| | |
|---|---|
| ○ Abruzzo Pecorino Sup. '17 | ♥♥ 3 |
| ☉ Cerasuolo d'Abruzzo Sup. Vermiglio '17 | ♥♥ 2* |
| ● Montepulciano d'Abruzzo Colline Teramane La Regia Specula '15 | ♥♥ 3 |
| ● Montepulciano d'Abruzzo Rubiolo '17 | ♥ 2 |
| ○ Trebbiano d'Abruzzo Adrio '17 | ♥ 2 |
| ○ Trebbiano d'Abruzzo Sup. Colle della Corte '17 | ♥ 2 |
| ● Montepulciano d'Abruzzo Colline Teramane Ris. '13 | ♥♥ 5 |
| ● Montepulciano d'Abruzzo Colline Teramane Ris. '12 | ♥♥ 5 |
| ● Montepulciano d'Abruzzo Rubiolo '16 | ♥♥ 2* |
| ○ Trebbiano d'Abruzzo Sup. Colle della Corte '16 | ♥♥ 2* |

## Emidio Pepe

VIA CHIESI, 10
64010 TORANO NUOVO [TE]
TEL. +39 0861856493
www.emidiopepe.com

CELLAR SALES
PRE-BOOKED VISITS
ACCOMMODATION AND RESTAURANT SERVICE
ANNUAL PRODUCTION 80,000 bottles
HECTARES UNDER VINE 15.00
VITICULTURE METHOD Certified Biodynamic
SUSTAINABLE WINERY

From heretic to revered master -- forcing
things but not excessively, this is the path
followed by Emidio Pepe during his long
career as producer at this winery in Torano
Nuovo, in Colline Teramane. He was the one
who first started bottling Montepulciano and
Trebbiano during the 1960s, preserving the
ancestral legacy inherited from his father
and grandfather. He became an icon of the
'natural' wine movement, due to the organic
and biodynamic management of his
vineyards, spontaneous fermentation, his
work in the cellar without clarification or
filtration, and long periods in concrete. The
Pepe family's captivating epic is enriched by
a new chapter. Their 2015 Montepulciano is
extremely faithful to the style we've gotten
used to thanks to the work done by Emidio,
his wife Rosa and daughters Sofia and
Daniela. Earthy and spicy nuances pervade
fruit that's hidden in the wine's primary
aromas. In the mouth the producer's
trademark sanguine touch is softened by
close-woven tannins and noteworthy
glycerin force.

| | |
|---|---|
| ● Montepulciano d'Abruzzo '15 | ♥♥ 6 |
| ● Montepulciano d'Abruzzo '98 | ♥♥♥ 8 |
| ☉ Cerasuolo d'Abruzzo '15 | ♥♥ 6 |
| ● Montepulciano d'Abruzzo '13 | ♥♥ 6 |
| ● Montepulciano d'Abruzzo '12 | ♥♥ 6 |
| ● Montepulciano d'Abruzzo '11 | ♥♥ 6 |
| ☉ Montepulciano d'Abruzzo Cerasuolo '14 | ♥♥ 5 |
| ☉ Montepulciano d'Abruzzo Cerasuolo '13 | ♥♥ 5 |
| ○ Pecorino '14 | ♥♥ 6 |
| ○ Trebbiano d'Abruzzo '15 | ♥♥ 5 |
| ○ Trebbiano d'Abruzzo '14 | ♥♥ 5 |
| ○ Trebbiano d'Abruzzo '13 | ♥♥ 5 |
| ○ Trebbiano d'Abruzzo '12 | ♥♥ 5 |

## San Giacomo

c.da Novella, 51
66020 Rocca San Giovanni [CH]
Tel. +39 0872620504
www.cantinasangiacomo.it

CELLAR SALES
PRE-BOOKED VISITS
ACCOMMODATION
ANNUAL PRODUCTION 60,000 bottles
HECTARES UNDER VINE 300.00
VITICULTURE METHOD Certified Organic

San Giacomo, a historic wine cooperative in the province of Chieti, comprises about 200 grape growers and a considerable amount of vineyards spread over several municipalities around Rocca San Giovanni, where their main premises is based. This winery has grown enormously in recent years, thanks to their range of wines, which focuses on local Abruzzo varieties. Montepulciano, Trebbiano, Pecorino, Cococciola. Their wines feature an aromatic and gastronomic profile that acts as a common stylistic thread. Once again it's San Giacomo's Casino Murri Pecorinos that drive their selection. Their 'base' line features aromas of Mediterranean scrubland and a meaty palate while their 14° selection sees greater aromatic originality (flat beans, lake vegetation, flint) and a savory vigor. Their 2017 Cerasuolo Casino Murri also deserves attention for its serious and rigorous fragrances of fruit, its pervasive mid palate and compact finish.

| | |
|---|---|
| ○ Casino Murri 14° Pecorino '17 | 🍷🍷 2* |
| ○ Brut M. Cl. '13 | 🍷🍷 4 |
| ○ Casino Murri Pecorino '17 | 🍷🍷 2* |
| ⊙ Cerasuolo d'Abruzzo Casino Murri '17 | 🍷🍷 2* |
| ○ Trebbiano d'Abruzzo Casino Murri 14° '17 | 🍷🍷 2* |
| ○ Casino Murri Cococciola '17 | 🍷 2 |
| ● Montepulciano d'Abruzzo '16 | 🍷 2 |
| ● Montepulciano d'Abruzzo Casino Murri '16 | 🍷 2 |
| ⊙ Cerasuolo d'Abruzzo Casino Murri '16 | 🏆 2* |
| ● Montepulciano d'Abruzzo '15 | 🏆 1* |
| ● Montepulciano d'Abruzzo Casino Murri 14 '15 | 🏆 2* |
| ○ Pecorino Casino Murri 14 '16 | 🏆 2* |

## San Lorenzo Vini

c.da Plavignano, 2
64035 Castilenti [TE]
Tel. +39 0861999325
www.sanlorenzovini.com

CELLAR SALES
PRE-BOOKED VISITS
ANNUAL PRODUCTION 800,000 bottles
HECTARES UNDER VINE 150.00

Brothers Gianluca and Fabrizio Galazzo, together with their agronomist uncle, Gianfranco Barbone, run one of the most important wineries in Abruzzo in terms of history and success. Established at the end of the 1800s as a kind of 'château,' the vineyards occupy three ridges of the same hill in the province of Teramo, in Castilenti, located halfway between the Adriatic coast and the slopes of Gran Sasso. This environment helps create the versatility exhibited in the wide range of wines made with Montepulciano, Pecorino and Trebbiano grapes. Their selection's overall performance is a bit less sparkling than in the past, but this is compensated for by a couple of real standouts. Their 2017 Abruzzo Pecorino is one example, a wine that offers up Spring-like atmospheres of blooming prairies and pollen, with candied citrus anticipating a full, balanced palate that's sweetly tangy and sees energetic savory vigor. Their 2016 Montepulciano also delivered with its forthright, peppery backbone.

| | |
|---|---|
| ○ Abruzzo Pecorino Il Pecorino '17 | 🍷🍷 2* |
| ● Montepulciano d'Abruzzo Sirio '16 | 🍷🍷 1* |
| ● Montepulciano d'Abruzzo Casabianca Fermentazione Spontanea '16 | 🍷 2 |
| ● Montepulciano d'Abruzzo Colline Teramane Escol Ris. '13 | 🍷 5 |
| ● Montepulciano d'Abruzzo Colline Teramane Oinos '14 | 🍷 4 |
| ⊙ Rosato '17 | 🍷 2 |
| ○ Trebbiano d'Abruzzo Casabianca Fermentazione Spontanea '17 | 🍷 2 |
| ○ Trebbiano d'Abruzzo Sirio '17 | 🍷 1* |
| ● Montepulciano d'Abruzzo Sirio '15 | 🏆 1* |
| ○ Trebbiano d'Abruzzo Casabianca Fermentazione Spontanea '16 | 🏆 2* |

# Tenuta Terraviva

VIA DEL LAGO, 19
64018 TORTORETO [TE]
TEL. +39 0861786056
www.tenutaterraviva.it

**CELLAR SALES**
**PRE-BOOKED VISITS**
**ANNUAL PRODUCTION** 80,000 bottles
**HECTARES UNDER VINE** 20.00
**VITICULTURE METHOD** Certified Organic

Pina Marano and Pietro Topi's small winery has become a benchmark for the organic movement in Abruzzo. Their estate is situated in Tortoreto, in the Teramo hills, where the uncontaminated habitat favors an exacting natural approach to winemaking, carried out with Montepulciano, Trebbiano, Pecorino and Passerina grapes. In the cellar, fermentation is spontaneous and wines are matured in steel and barrels of various ages and sizes. Especially important is the winery's sensitive interpretation, which seeks to favor originality over form across all their lines. This expressive character is well appreciated when it's accompanied by structural soundness. It's a combinations that makes the difference in their 2016 Trebbiano Mario's 44. A peculiar nose featuring raw potatoes, peach peel and curry give way to a light, dynamic palate that's supported by flavorful tannins. Their 2015 Montepulciano Luì and 2017 Pecorino 'Ekwo are a bit more rustic but have just as much character.

# Tiberio

C.DA LA VOTA
65020 CUGNOLI [PE]
TEL. +39 0858576744
www.tiberio.it

**CELLAR SALES**
**PRE-BOOKED VISITS**
**ANNUAL PRODUCTION** 90,000 bottles
**HECTARES UNDER VINE** 30.00

The winery founded in 2000 by Riccardo Tiberio in Colline Pescaresi di Cugnoli at about 350 meters above sea level is one of the most interesting in Abruzzo. His children Cristiana and Antonio have been working alongside him since 2008 and it was their decision to focus exclusively on traditional varieties, namely Montepulciano, Trebbiano and Pecorino. Their small range of wines remains faithful to the terroir, containing climate features from the calcareous soils and the play of currents from the Adriatic and Majella. The result is full-flavored, racy wines, which are matured mostly in steel. Their recent releases completely confirm their stylistic profile, starting with a great pair, their 2017 Trebbiano, a spicy wine rich in aromas of fruit skin, and their 2017 Cerasuolo, with its rustic fragrances enlivened by spices, citrus and topsoil. But their most representative wine is still their Pecorino. It works on a number of levels and the 2017 is just a bit less sharp than usual.

| | |
|---|---|
| ○ Trebbiano d'Abruzzo Sup. Mario's 44 '16 | ▼▼▼ 3* |
| ○ Abruzzo Pecorino Ekwo '17 | ▼▼ 3 |
| ● Montepulciano d'Abruzzo Luì '15 | ▼▼ 3 |
| ○ Abruzzo Passerina 12.1 '17 | ▼ 3 |
| ⊙ Cerasuolo d'Abruzzo Giusi '17 | ▼ 2 |
| ● Montepulciano d'Abruzzo Colline Teramane Terraviva '16 | ▼ 2 |
| ● Montepulciano d'Abruzzo Luì '13 | ♀♀♀ 3* |
| ○ Abruzzo Pecorino 'Ekwo '16 | ♀♀ 3* |
| ○ Abruzzo Pecorino 'Ekwo '15 | ♀♀ 3* |
| ⊙ Cerasuolo d'Abruzzo Giusi '16 | ♀♀ 2* |
| ⊙ Cerasuolo d'Abruzzo Giusi '15 | ♀♀ 2* |
| ● Montepulciano d'Abruzzo Terraviva '13 | ♀♀ 2* |
| ○ Trebbiano d'Abruzzo Mario's 42 '14 | ♀♀ 3 |
| ○ Trebbiano d'Abruzzo Mario's 43 '15 | ♀♀ 3 |

| | |
|---|---|
| ○ Pecorino '17 | ▼▼ 3* |
| ⊙ Cerasuolo d'Abruzzo '17 | ▼▼ 3 |
| ○ Trebbiano d'Abruzzo '17 | ▼▼ 3 |
| ● Montepulciano d'Abruzzo '16 | ▼ 3 |
| ● Montepulciano d'Abruzzo '13 | ♀♀♀ 2* |
| ○ Pecorino '16 | ♀♀♀ 3* |
| ○ Pecorino '15 | ♀♀♀ 3* |
| ○ Pecorino '13 | ♀♀♀ 3* |
| ○ Pecorino '12 | ♀♀♀ 3* |
| ○ Pecorino '11 | ♀♀♀ 3* |
| ○ Pecorino '10 | ♀♀♀ 3 |
| ● Montepulciano d'Abruzzo '15 | ♀♀ 2* |
| ○ Trebbiano d'Abruzzo '16 | ♀♀ 2* |

## Cantina Tollo

via Garibaldi, 68
66010 Tollo [CH]
Tel. +39 087196251
www.cantinatollo.it

**CELLAR SALES**
**ANNUAL PRODUCTION** 13,000,000 bottles
**HECTARES UNDER VINE** 3200.00

Cantina Tollo has performed a miracle in the last twenty years. It has proven it is possible to combine consistent quality, stylistic awareness and good value with a production volumes totaling millions of bottles. This good work rewards the almost 1000 members who supply Montepulciano, Trebbiano, Pecorino, Passerina, Cococciola and Chardonnay grapes grown in the best areas of Colline Teatine, from the coast right up to the Apennine slopes. By virtue of its faultless range it is one of the most important wine cooperatives in Europe. Our most recent tastings see the Abruzzo cooperative adding to its list of achievements in recent years. Just think about yet another great 2014 Montepulciano Mo Riserva, despite the extraordinarily difficult vintage: dried flowers, curing spices, embers ... Aromatically hidden fruit takes over on a subtle, though balanced palate without any diluting or phenolic crudeness.

| | |
|---|---|
| ● Montepulciano d'Abruzzo Mo' Ris. '14 | ▼▼▼ 3* |
| ○ Trebbiano d'Abruzzo Biologico '17 | ▼▼ 2* |
| ● Montepulciano d'Abruzzo Colle Secco Rubì '15 | ▼▼ 2* |
| ○ Pecorino '17 | ▼▼ 3 |
| ○ Pecorino Biologico '17 | ▼▼ 2* |
| ⊙ Cerasuolo d'Abruzzo Biologico '17 | ▼ 2 |
| ⊙ Cerasuolo d'Abruzzo Hedòs '17 | ▼ 3 |
| ● Montepulciano d'Abruzzo Biologico '17 | ▼ 2 |
| ● Montepulciano d'Abruzzo Cagiòlo Ris. '09 | ▽▽▽ 4* |
| ● Montepulciano d'Abruzzo Mo Ris. '13 | ▽▽▽ 3* |
| ● Montepulciano d'Abruzzo Mo Ris. '12 | ▽▽▽ 2* |
| ● Montepulciano d'Abruzzo Mo Ris. '11 | ▽▽▽ 2* |
| ○ Trebbiano d'Abruzzo C'Incanta '11 | ▽▽▽ 4* |
| ○ Trebbiano d'Abruzzo C'Incanta '10 | ▽▽▽ 4* |

## Torre dei Beati

c.da Poggioragone, 56
65014 Loreto Aprutino [PE]
Tel. +39 0854916069
www.torredeibeati.it

**CELLAR SALES**
**PRE-BOOKED VISITS**
**ANNUAL PRODUCTION** 100,000 bottles
**HECTARES UNDER VINE** 20.00
**VITICULTURE METHOD** Certified Organic
**SUSTAINABLE WINERY**

Remember the artistic and spiritual inspiration for the name Adriana Galasso and Fausto Albanese chose for their winery. It comes from a splendid fifteenth-century painting in Loreto Aprutino which depicts the 'Tower of the Blessed,' a symbolic place to which saved souls go on Judgment Day. But paradise is already here among the organic vineyard plots in Colline Pescaresi, influenced by the nearby Gran Sasso. The astonishing day-night temperature swings are reflected in the spontaneous energy of their wines made with Montepulciano, Trebbiano and Pecorino grapes. In addition to a smashing overall performance, we were struck by their Torre dei Beati top-of-the-range whites. Candied citrus, Mediterranean shrub, a delicately toasty touch, their 2016 Trebbiano Bianchi Grilli per la Testa offers up a a commendably marine unfolding of flavor. Their 2017 Pecorino Giocheremo con i Fiori is even more multifaceted in its iodine and verjuice aromas, which are reflected throughout its long, savory palate.

| | |
|---|---|
| ○ Abruzzo Pecorino Giocheremo con I Fiori '17 | ▼▼▼ 3* |
| ○ Trebbiano d'Abruzzo Bianchi Grilli per La Testa '16 | ▼▼ 3* |
| ○ Abruzzo Pecorino Bianchi Grilli per La Testa '16 | ▼▼ 4 |
| ⊙ Cerasuolo d'Abruzzo Rosa-ae '17 | ▼▼ 2* |
| ● Montepulciano d'Abruzzo '16 | ▼▼ 2* |
| ⊙ Cerasuolo d'Abruzzo Lucanto '17 | ▼ 2 |
| ● Montepulciano d'Abruzzo Cocciapazza '15 | ▼ 5 |
| ● Montepulciano d'Abruzzo Cocciapazza '11 | ▽▽▽ 4* |
| ● Montepulciano d'Abruzzo Cocciapazza '10 | ▽▽▽ 4* |
| ○ Trebbiano d'Abruzzo Bianchi Grilli per la Testa '14 | ▽▽▽ 4* |

# Tenuta Ulisse

VIA SAN POLO, 40
66014 CRECCHIO [CH]
TEL. +39 0871942007
www.tenutaulisse.it

**CELLAR SALES**
**PRE-BOOKED VISITS**
**ANNUAL PRODUCTION** 550,000 bottles
**HECTARES UNDER VINE** 75.00

In 2006, brothers Antonio and Luigi Ulisse purchased a large estate in San Polo di Crecchio, in Colline Teatine, to start their own wine production. The vineyards, situated on the route connecting the Adriatic coast and the Majella crags, are cultivated with the main varieties from Abruzzo. Montepulciano, Pecorino, Trebbiano, Passerina and Cococciola are linked by a precise style deriving from spontaneous fermentation at low temperatures, as well as a focus on food pairing. It's an expressive profile that's best represented by their 2017 Abruzzo Pecorino Nativae, with its aromas of summer fruit, hints of roots and grains and a palate that's almost subtractive but still manages to lengthen, thanks to an invigorating citrus streak and pleasant tannins. It ties with their 2016 Montepulciano, their linear and harmonic 'base' wine. Their Nativae is more open and concentrated, but also a but more austere.

| | |
|---|---|
| ○ Abruzzo Pecorino Nativae '17 | 🍷🍷 4 |
| ● Montepulciano d'Abruzzo '16 | 🍷🍷 4 |
| ● Montepulciano d'Abruzzo Nativae '16 | 🍷🍷 4 |
| ○ Trebbiano d'Abruzzo '17 | 🍷 3 |
| ○ Abruzzo Pecorino Nativae '13 | 🍷🍷🍷 4* |
| ● Montepulciano d'Abruzzo Nativae '14 | 🍷🍷🍷 4* |
| ● Montepulciano d'Abruzzo Nativae '12 | 🍷🍷🍷 4* |
| ○ Abruzzo Pecorino Nativae '15 | 🍷🍷 4 |
| ○ Cococciola '15 | 🍷🍷 3 |
| ○ Cococciola Unico '14 | 🍷🍷 3 |
| ● Montepulciano d'Abruzzo Nativae '15 | 🍷🍷 4 |
| ○ Pecorino '15 | 🍷🍷 3* |
| ○ Pecorino Unico '14 | 🍷🍷 3 |

# La Valentina

VIA TORRETTA, 52
65010 SPOLTORE [PE]
TEL. +39 0854478158
www.lavalentina.it

**CELLAR SALES**
**PRE-BOOKED VISITS**
**ANNUAL PRODUCTION** 350,000 bottles
**HECTARES UNDER VINE** 40.00
**VITICULTURE METHOD** Certified Organic
**SUSTAINABLE WINERY**

Sabatino, Roberto and Andrea Di Properzio have owned La Valentina for over twenty years and from the beginning they have found inspiration in environmentally-friendly agriculture. Their winery is one of the most dynamic in the region and is famous for its Montepulciano, Cerasuolo, Trebbiano, Pecorino and Fiano wines. Their range is divided into 'Classica' and 'Terroir' lines and the grapes are grown in at least five separate vineyard plots in areas of Colline Pescaresi, from the Adriatic coast to the start of the Majella mountains. This assorted territorial patchwork is reflected in the expressiveness and full flavor of their best offerings, and the positive balance between full-bodied force and vivacity seems to be the common thread throughout entire selection. Their 2015 Montepulciano Spelt Riserva, in particular, stands out. It proves orderly and characteristic in its notes of pepper and wild berries, endowed with an iodine vigor as well as firm tannic weave. This mix of delicacy and vitality, citrus vigor and savoriness emerges in their 2017 Pecorino as well.

| | |
|---|---|
| ● Montepulciano d'Abruzzo Spelt Ris. '15 | 🍷🍷🍷 4* |
| ○ Pecorino '17 | 🍷🍷 2* |
| ⊙ Cerasuolo d'Abruzzo Spelt '17 | 🍷🍷 3 |
| ● Montepulciano d'Abruzzo '16 | 🍷🍷 2* |
| ○ Trebbiano d'Abruzzo Spelt '17 | 🍷🍷 3 |
| ⊙ Cerasuolo d'Abruzzo '17 | 🍷 2 |
| ● Montepulciano d'Abruzzo Bellovedere '05 | 🍷🍷🍷 6 |
| ● Montepulciano d'Abruzzo Spelt '08 | 🍷🍷🍷 3* |
| ● Montepulciano d'Abruzzo Spelt '07 | 🍷🍷🍷 3 |
| ● Montepulciano d'Abruzzo Spelt '05 | 🍷🍷🍷 3 |
| ● Montepulciano d'Abruzzo Spelt Ris. '11 | 🍷🍷🍷 4* |
| ● Montepulciano d'Abruzzo Spelt Ris. '10 | 🍷🍷🍷 3* |

## ★★★Valentini

VIA DEL BAIO, 2
65014 LORETO APRUTINO [PE]
TEL. +39 0858291138

**ANNUAL PRODUCTION** 50,000 bottles
**HECTARES UNDER VINE** 70.00

The word 'legend' is used appropriately when applied to this historic winery in Loreto Aprutino, which has become a veritable cult location for enthusiasts all over the world. Francesco Paolo Valentini is carrying on his father Edoardo's work, revealing an even more all-consuming agricultural artisan vision: environmental balance and soil vitality before every procedure. Their Montepulciano, Cerasuolo and Trebbiano wines are bottled only when the vintage is considered good enough for decades of aging, and they feature an expressive style that defies technical contextualization. It doesn't happen often that we taste the Valentini family's entire selection. It was a true honor, taking into account the difficult vintages that shaped the 2014 Trebbiano and the 2017 Cerasuolo. The circle is squared with their 2013 Montepulciano, unexpectedly graceful and relaxed, going in on savory energy and the quality of its tannins, rather than glycerin force.

| | | |
|---|---|---|
| ● Montepulciano d'Abruzzo '13 | ♥♥♥ | 8 |
| ☉ Cerasuolo d'Abruzzo '17 | ♥♥ | 7 |
| ○ Trebbiano d'Abruzzo '14 | ♥♥ | 8 |
| ● Montepulciano d'Abruzzo '12 | ♀♀♀ | 8 |
| ● Montepulciano d'Abruzzo '06 | ♀♀♀ | 8 |
| ☉ Montepulciano d'Abruzzo Cerasuolo '09 | ♀♀♀ | 6 |
| ☉ Montepulciano d'Abruzzo Cerasuolo '08 | ♀♀♀ | 6 |
| ○ Trebbiano d'Abruzzo '13 | ♀♀♀ | 6 |
| ○ Trebbiano d'Abruzzo '12 | ♀♀♀ | 6 |
| ○ Trebbiano d'Abruzzo '11 | ♀♀♀ | 6 |
| ○ Trebbiano d'Abruzzo '10 | ♀♀♀ | 6 |
| ○ Trebbiano d'Abruzzo '08 | ♀♀♀ | 6 |
| ○ Trebbiano d'Abruzzo '07 | ♀♀♀ | 6 |
| ○ Trebbiano d'Abruzzo '05 | ♀♀♀ | 6 |

## ★Valle Reale

LOC. SAN CALISTO
65026 POPOLI [PE]
TEL. +39 0859871039
www.vallereale.it

**CELLAR SALES**
**PRE-BOOKED VISITS**
**ANNUAL PRODUCTION** 250,000 bottles
**HECTARES UNDER VINE** 46.00
**VITICULTURE METHOD** Certified Organic
**SUSTAINABLE WINERY**

The backdrop to the Pizzolo family's farm is made up of authentic natural amphitheaters. Their main vineyards in Popoli and Capestrano are situated in the provinces of Pescara and L'Aquila, where the Gran Sasso, Majella and Sirente-Velino natural parks all come together. Separate vinification of grapes grown in different vineyard plots, spontaneous fermentation, and maturation in wood and concrete all contribute to the assertive and relaxed style of Valle Reale's Trebbiano and Montepulciano wines. Their San Calisto, Sant'Eusanio and Vigna del Convento crus display extra depth. Thanks to the splendid overall performance of their selection we didn't miss their one-of-a-kind Trebbiano di Capestrano. The 2016 Vigneto di Popoli calls up its spontaneous nuances, which a taut, vigorous palate that almost proceeds in starts-and-stops. And then there's their 2016 Montepulciano Vigneto di Sant'Eusanio, a wine of remarkable expressive naturalness. Incense and roots meet the nose, while the palate proves engaging, with a savory, velvety grip and excellent length.

| | | |
|---|---|---|
| ● Montepulciano d'Abruzzo Vign. di Sant'Eusanio '16 | ♥♥♥ | 4* |
| ○ Trebbiano d'Abruzzo Vign. di Popoli '16 | ♥♥ | 5 |
| ☉ Cerasuolo d'Abruzzo '17 | ♥♥ | 3 |
| ☉ Cerasuolo d'Abruzzo Vign. di Sant'Eusanio Giorno '17 | ♥♥ | 4 |
| ● Montepulciano d'Abruzzo '17 | ♥♥ | 3 |
| ○ Trebbiano d'Abruzzo '17 | ♥♥ | 3 |
| ○ Trebbiano d'Abruzzo V. del Convento di Capestrano '15 | ♀♀♀ | 6 |
| ○ Trebbiano d'Abruzzo V. del Convento di Capestrano '14 | ♀♀♀ | 5 |
| ○ Trebbiano d'Abruzzo V. di Capestrano '13 | ♀♀♀ | 5 |
| ○ Trebbiano d'Abruzzo V. di Capestrano '12 | ♀♀♀ | 5 |
| ○ Trebbiano d'Abruzzo V. di Capestrano '11 | ♀♀♀ | 5 |

# ABRUZZO

## ★Villa Medoro

C.DA MEDORO
64030 ATRI [TE]
TEL. +39 0858708139
www.villamedoro.it

CELLAR SALES
PRE-BOOKED VISITS
ACCOMMODATION
ANNUAL PRODUCTION 300,000 bottles
HECTARES UNDER VINE 100.00

Villa Medoro is named after a district in Atri, home to the Morricone family's main vineyards and cellar. Their winery has played a leading role in Colline Teramane for over twenty years. They added to the estate with the purchase of Tenuta Fontanelle and Fonte Corvo, which contributes to the mouth-filling and cosseting wines common to their range, made with Montepulciano, Trebbiano, Pecorino, Passerina and Montonico grapes. Modern sensibility highlights the various winemaking decisions they have made for both their basic varietal wines and their more ambitious selections. Without a doubt, there's a common thread binding the noteworthy pair of Montepulcianos put forward by Villa Medoro. Their 2017 'base wine' holds together sweetness of fruit and vigor, while their 2016 Rosso del Duca adds extra concentration and linear structure. But we were bowled over by their 2017 Pecorino, an open and buoyant wine in its aromas of citrus and Mediterranean shrub, with follow through on a close-woven, sunny, flavorful palate.

| | | |
|---|---|---|
| ○ Pecorino '17 | ♟♟♟ | 2* |
| ● Montepulciano d'Abruzzo '17 | ♟♟ | 2* |
| ● Montepulciano d'Abruzzo Rosso del Duca '16 | ♟♟ | 3 |
| ○ 8.5 Pecorino '17 | ♟ | 2 |
| ⊙ Cerasuolo d'Abruzzo '17 | ♟ | 2 |
| ○ Passerina '17 | ♟ | 2 |
| ○ Trebbiano d'Abruzzo Chimera '17 | ♟ | 2 |
| ● Montepulciano d'Abruzzo '14 | ♟♟♟ | 2* |
| ● Montepulciano d'Abruzzo Colline Teramane Adrano '12 | ♟♟♟ | 4* |
| ● Montepulciano d'Abruzzo Colline Teramane Adrano '10 | ♟♟♟ | 4* |
| ● Montepulciano d'Abruzzo Rosso del Duca '12 | ♟♟♟ | 3* |

## Ciccio Zaccagnini

C.DA POZZO
65020 BOLOGNANO [PE]
TEL. +39 0858880195
www.cantinazaccagnini.it

CELLAR SALES
PRE-BOOKED VISITS
ANNUAL PRODUCTION 1,500,000 bottles
HECTARES UNDER VINE 300.00

This Bolognano winery is undoubtedly one of the most famous Abruzzo estates in the world. It was founded by Ciccio Zaccagnini and today it is run by his son Marcello, with the help of his cousin Concezio Marulli. It began in Colline Pescaresi, where the Adriatic and Majella seem to merge, a fact reflected in the multi-faceted range of wines made with Pecorino, Trebbiano and Montepulciano. Their experiments with sparkling and sulfite-free wines are of note. The range is creative but solid and gives good value for the money. We never stop being amazed at the variety of top wines proposed by the Zaccagnini family. Just think of their 2017 Vino dal Tralcetto Bianco or their Cerasuolo Myosotis. But the real corker this year was their 2016 San Clemente Bianco, a blend made with Trebbiano that proves an undeniable classic with its flowery, sappy aromas, amplified in a caressing, flavorful palate.

| | | |
|---|---|---|
| ○ Abruzzo Bianco San Clemente '16 | ♟♟ | 4* |
| ○ Abruzzo Il Vino dal Tralcetto Il Bianco di Ciccio '17 | ♟♟ | 2* |
| ⊙ Cerasuolo d'Abruzzo Myosotis '17 | ♟♟ | 3* |
| ● Montepulciano d'Abruzzo Chronicon '15 | ♟♟ | 3 |
| ● Montepulciano d'Abruzzo Il Vino dal Tralcetto '16 | ♟♟ | 2* |
| ⊙ Cerasuolo d'Abruzzo Il Vino dal Tralcetto '17 | ♟ | 3 |
| ⊙ Cerasuolo d'Abruzzo Myosotis '16 | ♟♟♟ | 3* |
| ● Montepulciano d'Abruzzo Chronicon '13 | ♟♟♟ | 3* |
| ● Montepulciano d'Abruzzo S. Clemente Ris. '12 | ♟♟♟ | 5 |
| ● Montepulciano d'Abruzzo S. Clemente Ris. '12 | ♟♟♟ | 5 |
| ○ Abruzzo Pecorino Yamada '16 | ♟♟ | 3 |
| ● Montepulciano d'Abruzzo Chronicon '14 | ♟♟ | 3* |

## Agricosimo

VIA SANTA LUCIA, 11
66010 VILLAMAGNA [CH]
TEL. +39 0871407063
www.agricosimo.it

ANNUAL PRODUCTION 100,000 bottles
HECTARES UNDER VINE 13.00

| | |
|---|---|
| ○ Natura e Passione Pecorino '17 | ♟♟ 3 |
| ☉ Cerasuolo d'Abruzzo Sup. Natura & Passione '17 | ♟ 3 |
| ● Montepulciano d'Abruzzo Numero 1 '12 | ♟ 3 |

## Ausonia

C.DA NOCELLA
64032 ATRI [TE]
TEL. +39 0859071026
www.ausoniawines.com

ANNUAL PRODUCTION 35,000 bottles
HECTARES UNDER VINE 11.50

| | |
|---|---|
| ○ Trebbiano d'Abruzzo Apollo '16 | ♟♟ 3 |
| ● Montepulciano d'Abruzzo Colline Teramane Apollo '16 | ♟ 3 |

## Nestore Bosco

C.DA CASALI, 147
65010 NOCCIANO [PE]
TEL. +39 085847345
www.nestorebosco.com

CELLAR SALES
PRE-BOOKED VISITS
ANNUAL PRODUCTION 600,000 bottles
HECTARES UNDER VINE 75.00

| | |
|---|---|
| ● Montepulciano d'Abruzzo '15 | ♟♟ 2* |
| ☉ Cerasuolo d'Abruzzo Sup. '17 | ♟ 2 |
| ● Montepulciano d'Abruzzo Ris. '14 | ♟ 3 |
| ○ Trebbiano d'Abruzzo Sup. '17 | ♟ 2 |

## Bove

VIA ROMA, 216
67051 AVEZZANO [AQ]
TEL. +39 086333133
info@cantinebove.it

CELLAR SALES
PRE-BOOKED VISITS
ANNUAL PRODUCTION 1,200,000 bottles
HECTARES UNDER VINE 60.00

| | |
|---|---|
| ○ Safari Pecorino '17 | ♟♟ 2* |
| ☉ Cerasuolo d'Abruzzo Avegiano '17 | ♟ 1* |
| ● Montepulciano d'Abruzzo Angeli '15 | ♟ 2 |
| ● Montepulciano d'Abruzzo Avegiano '15 | ♟ 1* |

## Casal Thaulero

C.DA CUCULLO
66026 ORTONA [CH]
TEL. +39 0859032533
www.casalthaulero.it

CELLAR SALES
PRE-BOOKED VISITS
ANNUAL PRODUCTION 1,300,000 bottles
HECTARES UNDER VINE 500.00
SUSTAINABLE WINERY

| | |
|---|---|
| ● Montepulciano d'Abruzzo Duca Thaulero Ris. '13 | ♟♟ 3 |
| ● Montepulciano d'Abruzzo Orsetto Oro '16 | ♟♟ 2* |
| ○ Mr. Peco Pecorino '17 | ♟♟ 3 |

## Casalbordino

C.DA TERMINE, 38
66021 CASALBORDINO [CH]
TEL. +39 0873918107
www.vinicasalbordino.com

CELLAR SALES
PRE-BOOKED VISITS
ANNUAL PRODUCTION 6,000,000 bottles
HECTARES UNDER VINE 1400.00

| | |
|---|---|
| ○ Abruzzo Pecorino Contea '17 | ♟♟ 2* |
| ● Montepulciano d'Abruzzo Villa Adami '15 | ♟♟ 2* |
| ● Montepulciano d'Abruzzo Castel Verdino Ris. '14 | ♟ 2 |

## Col del Mondo

C.DA CAMPOTINO, 35C
65010 COLLECORVINO [PE]
TEL. +39 0858207831
www.coldelmondo.com

CELLAR SALES
PRE-BOOKED VISITS
ANNUAL PRODUCTION 80,000 bottles
HECTARES UNDER VINE 12.00

| | |
|---|---|
| ⊙ Cerasuolo d'Abruzzo '17 | 🍷🍷 2* |
| ○ Kerrias Pecorino '17 | 🍷🍷 2* |
| ● Montepulciano d'Abruzzo Sunnae '17 | 🍷🍷 2* |

## Colle Moro

LOC. GUASTAMEROLI
VIA DEL MARE, 35/37
66030 FRISA [CH]
TEL. +39 087258128
www.collemoro.it

CELLAR SALES
PRE-BOOKED VISITS
ANNUAL PRODUCTION 750,000 bottles
HECTARES UNDER VINE 1500.00
VITICULTURE METHOD Certified Organic

| | |
|---|---|
| ● Montepulciano d'Abruzzo Alcàde '13 | 🍷🍷 3 |
| ○ Abruzzo Pecorino '17 | 🍷 2 |
| ● Montepulciano d'Abruzzo Club '17 | 🍷 4 |
| ○ Trebbiano d'Abruzzo '17 | 🍷 2 |

## Collefrisio

LOC. PIANE DI MAGGIO
66030 FRISA [CH]
TEL. +39 0859039074
www.collefrisio.it

CELLAR SALES
PRE-BOOKED VISITS
ANNUAL PRODUCTION 500,000 bottles
HECTARES UNDER VINE 50.00
VITICULTURE METHOD Certified Organic
SUSTAINABLE WINERY

| | |
|---|---|
| ● Montepulciano d'Abruzzo In & Out '14 | 🍷🍷 5 |
| ● Montepulciano d'Abruzzo '16 | 🍷 2 |
| ● Montepulciano d'Abruzzo Morrecine '16 | 🍷 2 |
| ○ Trebbiano d'Abruzzo Filaré '17 | 🍷 2 |

## De Angelis Corvi

C.DA PIGNOTTO
64010 CONTROGUERRA [TE]
TEL. +39 086189475
www.deangeliscorvi.it

CELLAR SALES
PRE-BOOKED VISITS
ANNUAL PRODUCTION 40,000 bottles
HECTARES UNDER VINE 12.00
VITICULTURE METHOD Certified Organic
SUSTAINABLE WINERY

| | |
|---|---|
| ⊙ Cerasuolo d'Abruzzo Sup. '17 | 🍷🍷 5 |
| ● Montepulciano d'Abruzzo Colline Teramane Fonte Raviliano '15 | 🍷 5 |
| ○ Trebbiano d'Abruzzo Sup. Raviliano '17 | 🍷 4 |

## Fontefico

VIA DIFENZA, 38
66054 VASTO [CH]
TEL. +39 3284113619
www.fontefico.it

CELLAR SALES
PRE-BOOKED VISITS
RESTAURANT SERVICE
ANNUAL PRODUCTION 35,000 bottles
HECTARES UNDER VINE 15.00
VITICULTURE METHOD Certified Organic
SUSTAINABLE WINERY

| | |
|---|---|
| ○ Abruzzo Pecorino Sup. La Canaglia '17 | 🍷🍷 3 |
| ⊙ Cerasuolo D' Abruzzo Sup. Fossimatto '17 | 🍷 3 |
| ● Montepulciano d'Abruzzo Titinge Ris. '13 | 🍷 5 |

## Fosso Corno

LOC. VILLA BIZZARRI
64010 TORANO NUOVO [TE]
TEL. +39 0456201154
www.fossocornovini.it

CELLAR SALES
PRE-BOOKED VISITS
ANNUAL PRODUCTION 300,000 bottles
HECTARES UNDER VINE 30.00

| | |
|---|---|
| ● Montepulciano d'Abruzzo Ris. '15 | 🍷🍷 4 |
| ● Montepulciano d'Abruzzo Colline Teramane Orsus Riserva del Fondatore '13 | 🍷 5 |

## Cantina Frentana
VIA PERAZZA, 32
66020 ROCCA SAN GIOVANNI [CH]
TEL. +39 087260152
www.cantinafrentana.it

CELLAR SALES
PRE-BOOKED VISITS
ACCOMMODATION
ANNUAL PRODUCTION 800,000 bottles
HECTARES UNDER VINE 22.00

| | |
|---|---|
| ○ Abruzzo Pecorino Costa del Mulino '17 | ♥♥ 2* |
| ○ Donna Greta Pecorino '16 | ♥♥ 2* |
| ● Montepulciano d'Abruzzo 60 Ris. '15 | ♥♥ 2* |

## Lepore
C.DA CIVITA, 29
64010 COLONNELLA [TE]
TEL. +39 086170860
www.vinilepore.it

CELLAR SALES
PRE-BOOKED VISITS
ANNUAL PRODUCTION 330,000 bottles
HECTARES UNDER VINE 43.00

| | |
|---|---|
| ● Montepulciano d'Abruzzo Colline Teramane Luigi Lepore Ris. '13 | ♥♥ 4 |
| ○ Trebbiano d'Abruzzo '17 | ♥♥ 2* |
| ● Montepulciano d'Abruzzo '17 | ♥ 2 |

## Marchesi De' Cordano
C.DA CORDANO, 43
65014 LORETO APRUTINO [PE]
TEL. +39 0858289526
www.cordano.it

CELLAR SALES
PRE-BOOKED VISITS
ANNUAL PRODUCTION 180,000 bottles
HECTARES UNDER VINE 50.00
VITICULTURE METHOD Certified Organic
SUSTAINABLE WINERY

| | |
|---|---|
| ⊙ Cerasuolo d'Abruzzo Puntarosa '17 | ♥♥ 3 |
| ○ Favola Passerina '17 | ♥ 3 |
| ● Montepulciano d'Abruzzo Terre dei Vestini Santinumi Ris. '12 | ♥ 6 |

## Cantine Mucci
C.DA VALLONE DI NANNI, 65
66020 TORINO DI SANGRO [CH]
TEL. +39 0873913366
www.cantinemucci.com

CELLAR SALES
PRE-BOOKED VISITS
ANNUAL PRODUCTION 250,000 bottles
HECTARES UNDER VINE 24.00
VITICULTURE METHOD Certified Organic
SUSTAINABLE WINERY

| | |
|---|---|
| ○ Valentino Mucci Pecorino '17 | ♥♥ 2* |
| ⊙ Cerasuolo d'Abruzzo Valentino Mucci '17 | ♥ 2 |
| ○ Proibito Falanghina Passito '16 | ♥ 6 |
| ○ Trebbiano d'Abruzzo Valentino Mucci '17 | ♥ 2 |

## Tommaso Olivastri
VIA QUERCIA DEL CORVO, 37
66038 SAN VITO CHIETINO [CH]
TEL. +39 087261543
www.viniolivastri.com

CELLAR SALES
PRE-BOOKED VISITS
ANNUAL PRODUCTION 50,000 bottles
HECTARES UNDER VINE 15.00

| | |
|---|---|
| ● Montepulciano D'Abruzzo La Grondaia '15 | ♥♥ 3 |
| ○ Abruzzo Pecorino L'Ariosa '17 | ♥ 2 |
| ⊙ Cerasuolo d'Abruzzo Marcantonio '17 | ♥ 2 |

## Pasetti
LOC. C.DA PRETARO
VIA SAN PAOLO, 21
66023 FRANCAVILLA AL MARE [CH]
TEL. +39 08561875
www.pasettivini.it

CELLAR SALES
PRE-BOOKED VISITS
ACCOMMODATION AND RESTAURANT SERVICE
ANNUAL PRODUCTION 600,000 bottles
HECTARES UNDER VINE 70.00

| | |
|---|---|
| ⊙ Testarossa Rosato '17 | ♥♥ 2* |
| ● Montepulciano d'Abruzzo Testarossa '14 | ♥ 4 |

## La Quercia

C.DA COLLE CROCE
64020 MORRO D'ORO [TE]
TEL. +39 0858959110
www.vinilaquercia.it

CELLAR SALES
PRE-BOOKED VISITS
ANNUAL PRODUCTION 200,000 bottles
HECTARES UNDER VINE 46.50
SUSTAINABLE WINERY

| | |
|---|---|
| ● Montepulciano d'Abruzzo '15 | 🍷🍷 2* |
| ○ Trebbiano d'Abruzzo Sup. '17 | 🍷🍷 2* |
| ○ Abruzzo Passerina Sup. Santapupa '17 | 🍷 2 |
| ⊙ Cerasuolo d'Abruzzo Sup. Primamadre '17 | 🍷 2 |

## Strappelli

VIA TORRI, 16
64010 TORANO NUOVO [TE]
TEL. +39 0861887402
www.cantinastrappelli.it

CELLAR SALES
PRE-BOOKED VISITS
ANNUAL PRODUCTION 65,000 bottles
HECTARES UNDER VINE 10.00
VITICULTURE METHOD Certified Organic

| | |
|---|---|
| ○ Soprano Pecorino '17 | 🍷🍷 3 |
| ⊙ Cerasuolo d'Abruzzo '17 | 🍷 2 |
| ○ Controguerra Passerina Colle Trà '17 | 🍷 3 |

## Valori

VIA TORQUATO AL SALINELLO, 8
64027 SANT'OMERO [TE]
TEL. +39 087185241
www.vinivalori.it

PRE-BOOKED VISITS
ANNUAL PRODUCTION 150,000 bottles
HECTARES UNDER VINE 26.00
VITICULTURE METHOD Certified Organic
SUSTAINABLE WINERY

| | |
|---|---|
| ○ Abruzzo Pecorino Biologico '17 | 🍷🍷 2* |
| ⊙ Cerasuolo d'Abruzzo Biologico '17 | 🍷 2 |

## Tenuta Secolo IX

C.DA VICENNE, 5A
65020 CASTIGLIONE A CASAURIA [PE]
TEL. +39 0857998193
www.tenutasecoloix.it

CELLAR SALES
ANNUAL PRODUCTION 1,700 bottles
HECTARES UNDER VINE 21.00

| | |
|---|---|
| ⊙ Cerasuolo d'Abruzzo '17 | 🍷🍷 3 |
| ○ Pecorino '17 | 🍷🍷 2* |
| ● Montepulciano d'Abruzzo '15 | 🍷 3 |

## Terzini

VIA ROMA, 52
65028 TOCCO DA CASAURIA [PE]
TEL. +39 0859158147
www.cantinaterzini.it

CELLAR SALES
PRE-BOOKED VISITS
ANNUAL PRODUCTION 200,000 bottles
HECTARES UNDER VINE 22.00

| | |
|---|---|
| ○ Dumì Pecorino '17 | 🍷🍷 3 |
| ● Montepulciano d'Abruzzo V. Vetum '15 | 🍷🍷 6 |
| ⊙ Cerasuolo d'Abruzzo '17 | 🍷 3 |
| ● Montepulciano d'Abruzzo '16 | 🍷 3 |

## Vigneti Radica

VIA PIANA MOZZONE, 4
66010 TOLLO [CH]
TEL. +39 0871962227
www.vignetiradica.it

CELLAR SALES
PRE-BOOKED VISITS
ACCOMMODATION
ANNUAL PRODUCTION 80,000 bottles
HECTARES UNDER VINE 14.00
SUSTAINABLE WINERY

| | |
|---|---|
| ● Montepulciano d'Abruzzo '16 | 🍷🍷 2* |
| ○ Pecorino '17 | 🍷🍷 2* |
| ⊙ Rosato '17 | 🍷🍷 2* |
| ○ Trebbiano d'Abruzzo '17 | 🍷🍷 2* |

# MOLISE

We repeat, 'Molise exists', despite the ceaseless taunts, here it is. The most attentive and curious wine lovers know it, those who choose to seek out the less-traveled roads of wine tourism. And what they discover is a region that is mostly uncontaminated, proudly bound to its rural roots, with all the biodiversity, environmental wholesomeness and beauty that follow. It's much more than a 'borderland' (as it's too often described). On the one hand you can't deny the influence of the surrounding regions in terms of topography, climate and ampelography (not to mention culture, traditions and even gastronomy). On the other, it doesn't take much to recognize how the region's communities maintain their own specific, unmistakable identity. And this inevitably singles out its most highly prized wines. And so it is that we get Montepulciano and Aglianico reds and rosés that are so distinct from their equivalents in Abruzzo, Campania and Puglia. And then there's their interpretations of Falanghina, Greco, Trebbiano and Malvasia accompanied by international cultivar like Sauvignon and Chardonnay. At times they may exhibit a Mediterranean character, at times that of the mountains, they can more or less territorial, carefree or technically rigorous. But it's Tintilia that has come to truly represent the region, having found in Molise the perfect territory when it comes to the grape's originality and character. And we have a perfect example in Di Majo Norante's version of the wine, with a 2016 that for the umpteenth time proves to the be the only producer in the region capable of taking home Tre Bicchieri. But in the first group of honorable mentions, there's a number of important wineries who've shown notable progress, like Borgo di Colloredo, Claudio Cipressi and Tenimenti Grieco. And right behind them there's a small group of cooperatives and private producers whose offerings are increasingly well-defined and personal (not to mention affordable). In short, it's a region made up of a team of winemakers who continue to consolidate their reputation and identity, and we're sure that it wouldn't be disingenuous to imagine that things will only get better.

# MOLISE

## Borgo di Colloredo

LOC. NUOVA CLITERNIA
VIA COLLOREDO, 15
86042 CAMPOMARINO [CB]
TEL. +39 087557453
www.borgodicolloredo.com

CELLAR SALES
PRE-BOOKED VISITS
ACCOMMODATION AND RESTAURANT SERVICE
ANNUAL PRODUCTION 200,000 bottles
HECTARES UNDER VINE 70.00
SUSTAINABLE WINERY

This winery is named after an historic
farmhouse situated just outside
Campomarino, once used as a place of
worship by the D'Avalos D'Aragona family.
Today it is run by brothers Enrico and
Pasquale Di Giulio after their father Silvio
purchased a farming estate here in the
1960s. The cellar and brand took shape
during the 1990s. Their range of wines is
made with both traditional and non-native
varieties and is organized into the
Biferno Gironia, Nobili Vitigni, Classici and
Terre degli Osci selections. Borgo di
Colloredo always has many strings in its
bow. In this edition we are very impressed
by the carefree expressiveness of their
2017 Biferno Bianco Gironia, a Trebbiano
blend in which a sequence of flowers and
herbs unfolds in a mouth that is subtle but
with a beautiful salinity. Their excellent
2017 Falanghina exhibited originality for its
aromas of dark fruit and smoky notes. The
latter come through even stronger on the
wine's vivacious palate.

| | | |
|---|---|---|
| ○ Biferno Bianco Gironia '17 | ♟♟ 3 | |
| ○ Molise Falanghina '17 | ♟♟ 3 | |
| ⊙ Biferno Rosato Gironia '17 | ♟ 3 | |
| ● Molise Rosso '15 | ♟ 3 | |
| ● Aglianico '10 | ♟♟♟ 3* | |
| ● Aglianico '13 | ♟♟ 3 | |
| ⊙ Biferno Rosato Gironia '16 | ♟♟ 3 | |
| ⊙ Biferno Rosato Gironia '15 | ♟♟ 2* | |
| ● Molise Rosso '13 | ♟♟ 2* | |

## Claudio Cipressi

C.DA MONTAGNA, 11B
86030 SAN FELICE DEL MOLISE [CB]
TEL. +39 3351244859
www.claudiocipressi.it

CELLAR SALES
PRE-BOOKED VISITS
ACCOMMODATION
ANNUAL PRODUCTION 40,000 bottles
HECTARES UNDER VINE 16.00
VITICULTURE METHOD Certified Organic
SUSTAINABLE WINERY

Claudio Cipressi is vine grower and
winemaker at a small organic winery
bearing his name in San Felice del Molise,
the harshest inland area in the province of
Campobasso. The best exposures are
reserved for the Molise grape Tintilia, which
is used to produce several different wines:
a 'basic' wine, two selections (66 and
Macchiarossa), a rosé (Collequinto) and a
blend comprising mainly Montepulciano
(Macchianera). Trebbiano and Falanghina
complete a range that is one of the most
interesting in the region due to its light and
airy touch, backed by minimally invasive
work in the cellar. Naturally, their Tintilia
reds take center stage this year thanks
especially to their 2015 Settevigne, offering
mint, cocoa and cigar well supported by a
spicy mouth and velvety tannic weave.
Their 2013 66 has a similar expressive
profile with notes of herbal tea and fresh
tilled earth that follow through well to a
caressing, flavorful palate that finishes a
tad too quickly.

| | | |
|---|---|---|
| ● Molise Tintilia Settevigne '15 | ♟♟ 4 | |
| ● Molise Tintilia 66 '13 | ♟♟ 7 | |
| ⊙ Molise Rosato Collequinto '17 | ♟ 3 | |
| ● Molise Rosso Macchianera '13 | ♟ 5 | |
| ○ Voira Falanghina '17 | ♟ 4 | |
| ● Molise Tintilia 66 '11 | ♟♟ 7 | |
| ● Molise Tintilia Macchiarossa '12 | ♟♟ 4 | |
| ● Molise Tintilia Settevigne '14 | ♟♟ 4 | |
| ● Molise Tintilia Settevigne '13 | ♟♟ 4 | |

# ★Di Majo Norante

FRAZ. NUOVA CLITERNIA
VIA COLLE SAVINO, 6
86042 CAMPOMARINO [CB]
TEL. +39 087557208
www.dimajonorante.com

CELLAR SALES
PRE-BOOKED VISITS
ANNUAL PRODUCTION 800,000 bottles
HECTARES UNDER VINE 125.00
VITICULTURE METHOD Certified Organic

The Di Majo Norante family winery stands on the former site of the Santa Cristina Marquis estate. Campomarino forms an ideal territorial and vine growing bridge between southern Abruzzo, Daunia and Samnium, and it's no surprise to find Malvasia, Trebbiano, Bombino, Falanghina, Greco, Moscato, Montepulciano, Sangiovese, Prugnolo, Aglianico and Tintilia growing here. Alessio brings out the best of these varieties through a modern lens. He is the worthy successor to his father Luigi and to a winemaking history dating from the early 1800s. This is without a doubt the best-known Molise winery in the world. Their selection's internal ranking was affirmed in this latest round of tastings, which saw their best reds at the top of their game. Their 2015 Aglianico Contado Riserva, an open and characteristic wine in its aromas of ripe cherry and undergrowth, brings together volume and extractive precision. Their 2016 Tintilia proved to be one of their best yet. Aromas of fruit and balsamic enriched by citrus give way to a juicy mouth.

| | |
|---|---|
| ● Molise Tintilia '16 | ♟♟♟ 3* |
| ● Molise Aglianico Contado Ris. '15 | ♟♟ 3* |
| ○ Molise Falanghina '17 | ♟ 2 |
| ○ Molise Falanghina Biorganic '17 | ♟ 3 |
| ○ Molise Greco '17 | ♟ 2 |
| ○ Molise Moscato Bianco Passito Apianae '15 | ♟ 4 |
| ● Sangiovese '17 | ♟ 2 |
| ● Molise Aglianico Contado Ris. '14 | ♟♟♟ 3* |
| ● Molise Rosso Don Luigi Ris. '12 | ♟♟♟ 5 |
| ● Molise Rosso Don Luigi Ris. '11 | ♟♟♟ 5 |
| ● Molise Tintilia '13 | ♟♟♟ 3* |
| ● Molise Aglianico Biorganic '14 | ♟♟ 3* |
| ○ Molise Falanghina '16 | ♟♟ 2* |

# Tenimenti Grieco

C.DA DIFENSOLA
86045 PORTOCANNONE [CB]
TEL. +39 0875590032
www.tenimentigrieco.it

CELLAR SALES
PRE-BOOKED VISITS
ANNUAL PRODUCTION 700,000 bottles
HECTARES UNDER VINE 85.00

Anima Osca, Settenodi, Chapeau à la vie, I Costali, I Molisani, Passo alle Tremiti and the crus are the primary selections comprising Tenimenti Grieco's array of wines, made with both local and international cultivars. Their headquarters are based in Portocannone, the area of Molise with the highest vine density. The Tremiti islands on the horizon and the Apennines behind set the stage for the style the four partners have developed. Sparkling wines, whites, rosés and reds all share a close-focused fruitiness and pleasant palate, thanks to their versatile winemaking. Each of their major wines has something to offer. This year it's their sumptuous 2016 Monterosso I Costali that leads the way with its aromas of blueberry, violet and a hint of embers. It's a wine that manages to be big and delicious at the same time thanks to a savory streak and well-honed tannins. Their 2017 Tintilia 200 Metri is just as relaxed and expressive, offering up hints of black currants and balsamic candy.

| | |
|---|---|
| ● Molise Rosso Monterosso I Costali '16 | ♟♟ 3* |
| ● Molise Tintilia 200 Metri '17 | ♟♟ 2* |
| ○ Molise Falanghina Passo alle Tremiti '17 | ♟ 4 |
| ☉ Molise Rosato Passo alle Tremiti '17 | ♟ 3 |
| ● Biferno Bosco delle Guardie '14 | ♟♟ 3 |
| ● Lenda Aglianico '15 | ♟♟ 5 |
| ☉ Molise Rosato Passo alle Tremiti '15 | ♟♟ 3 |
| ● Molise Rosso Passo alle Tremiti '15 | ♟♟ 3* |
| ● Molise Tintilia '14 | ♟♟ 2* |
| ● Molise Tintilia 200 Metri '16 | ♟♟ 2* |
| ● Molise Tintilia 200 Metri '15 | ♟♟ 2* |
| ● Triassi '13 | ♟♟ 5 |

## Cantina San Zenone

C.DA PIANA DEI PASTINI
86036 MONTENERO DI BISACCIA [CB]
TEL. +39 3477998397
www.cantinasanzenone.it

CELLAR SALES
PRE-BOOKED VISITS
ANNUAL PRODUCTION 150,000 bottles
HECTARES UNDER VINE 300.00
VITICULTURE METHOD Certified Organic

| | |
|---|---|
| ● Molise Tintilia '15 | ♟♟ 4 |
| ○ Molise Falanghina Clivia '17 | ♟ 2 |
| ○ Molise Il Viandante Bianco '17 | ♟ 2 |

## Catabbo

C.DA PETRIERA
86046 SAN MARTINO IN PENSILIS [CB]
TEL. +39 0875604945
www.catabbo.it

CELLAR SALES
ANNUAL PRODUCTION 160,000 bottles
HECTARES UNDER VINE 54.00

| | |
|---|---|
| ● Molise Tintilia Colle Cervino '15 | ♟♟ 4 |
| ● Molise Tintilia S '14 | ♟♟ 4 |
| ○ Molise Falanghina Colle del Limone '17 | ♟ 3 |
| ● Molise Rosso I Dieciettari '15 | ♟ 4 |

## Cianfagna

C.DA BOSCO PAMPINI, 3
86030 ACQUAVIVA COLLECROCE [CB]
TEL. +39 0875970253
www.cianfagna.com

CELLAR SALES
PRE-BOOKED VISITS
ANNUAL PRODUCTION 8,000 bottles
HECTARES UNDER VINE 3.50

| | |
|---|---|
| ○ Molise Malvasia Templo '17 | ♟ 3 |
| ● Molise Tintilia Sator '13 | ♟ 5 |

## Angelo D'Uva

C.DA MONTE ALTINO, 23A
86035 LARINO [CB]
TEL. +39 0874822320
www.cantineduva.com

CELLAR SALES
PRE-BOOKED VISITS
ACCOMMODATION AND RESTAURANT SERVICE
ANNUAL PRODUCTION 70,000 bottles
HECTARES UNDER VINE 20.00
SUSTAINABLE WINERY

| | |
|---|---|
| ● Molise Rosso Ricupo '15 | ♟♟ 2* |
| ○ Biferno Bianco Kantharos '17 | ♟ 2 |
| ● Gavio '15 | ♟ 2 |
| ● Molise Tintilia Lagena '16 | ♟ 3 |

## Cantine Salvatore

C.DA VIGNE
86049 URURI [CB]
TEL. +39 0874830656
www.cantinesalvatore.it

CELLAR SALES
PRE-BOOKED VISITS
ANNUAL PRODUCTION 80,000 bottles
HECTARES UNDER VINE 20.00
SUSTAINABLE WINERY

| | |
|---|---|
| ● Molise Rosso Don Donà '13 | ♟♟ 3 |
| ● Ti.A.Mo. '14 | ♟♟ 3 |
| ○ Molise Falanghina Nysias '17 | ♟ 3 |
| ● Molise Rosso Biberius '15 | ♟ 2 |

## Terresacre

C.DA MONTEBELLO
86036 MONTENERO DI BISACCIA [CB]
TEL. +39 0875960191
www.terresacre.net

CELLAR SALES
PRE-BOOKED VISITS
ACCOMMODATION AND RESTAURANT SERVICE
ANNUAL PRODUCTION 100,000 bottles
HECTARES UNDER VINE 35.00

| | |
|---|---|
| ○ Rosavite '17 | ♟♟ 2* |
| ● Molise Rosso Rispetto Experientia Manet '13 | ♟ 4 |
| ● Molise Tintilia '17 | ♟ 3 |

# CAMPANIA

The ancient Romans referred to this region as 'Campania felix' (fertile Campania), and modern wine and food lovers are apt to use the same adjective. Indeed, our tastings this year saw excellent results coming in from a territory saturated by a climate of enthusiasm and creativity, a sign of good things to come. Campania serves as a kind of open-air enological laboratory where millennia-old grapes are cultivated alongside recently discovered varieties. It's a territory of varying microclimates, from the Avellino highlands down to the terraced vineyards of the Amalfi Coast and Cilento, all the way to islands of Capri and Ischia. Some 23 wines took home our highest honors, even if 50 more wines participated in our final tastings and were just a hair's breadth from the top. The region's most important district, Irpinia, was represented by 10 Tre Bicchieri: 3 Taurasis (Caggiano, Feudi di San Gregorio and Contrade di Taurasi), 2 Greco di Tufos (Miniere and Pietracupa), 3 Fiano d'Avellinos (Tenuta del Meriggio, I Favati, Villa Raiano and Rocca del Principe) and 1 Aglianico (Donnachiara). Benevento also delivered and continues to enjoy increased market success. In addition to the numerous finalists that we recognized and recommended, we also awarded Tre Bicchieri to 3 Falanghina specialists: La Guardiense, Terre Stregate and Fontanavecchia. They're accompanied by a splendid Piedirosso produced by Mustilli (who also makes a top-notch Falanghina). Lettere and Gragnano are also sending reassuring signs of life (has anyone seen Asprinio?), and we can't help but mention the increasing importance of the region's coastal winemaking districts, both the Amalfi coast (Marisa Cuomo and Sammarco both received Tre Bicchieri) and Cilento (with San Salvatore's excellent offerings and Casebianche's first-rate selection of artisanal wines). On the island of Ischia Tommasone is keeping the banner flying high with an extraordinary Biancolella. We also want to mention the Phlegraean Fields, where Astroni is producing a one-of-a-kind Falanghina, and Caserta, where two passionate vigneron, Alois and Nanni Copè, remind us that in addition to the excellent wines already being produced, there's tremendous potential that's still waiting to be expressed. And finally we close by mentioning a great wine in one of its best versions, Silvia Imparato's 2016 Montevetrano. Campania indeed represents a captivating enological scenario, one defined by its complexity and diversity.

## Abbazia di Crapolla

LOC. AVIGLIANO
VIA SAN FILIPPO, 2
80069 VICO EQUENSE [NA]
TEL. +39 3383517280
www.abbaziadicrapolla.it

**ANNUAL PRODUCTION** 12,000 bottles
**HECTARES UNDER VINE** 2.00

The old abbey of Saint Francis, a former monastery for Cistercian monks, serves as Fulvio Alifano and Giuseppe Puttini's production headquarters. After a various bureaucratic hoops they were finally able to make their dream a reality and make wine on the slopes of Vico Equense. It's an extremely scenic landscape situated in Sorrento, along the Monti Lattari ridge where mountains and sea meet. And here in territory's volcanic terrain they cultivate Fiano, Falanghina and international cultivar like Merlot and Pinot Nero for their reds. The result is a selection that exhibits great fragrance and lightness, that's elegant on the palate in a way you wouldn't expect from a territory that isn't particularly well-known for its wines. This year Fulvio and Giuseppe submitted two wines, both extremely well-made. Their 2017 Sireo Bianco, made with Fiano and Falanghina, is a simply extraordinary wine in its vibrant, iodine weave. Their fragrant and fruity Sabato is an extremely classy wine made with Pinot Nero (and local cultivar).

| | | |
|---|---|---|
| ○ Sireo Bianco '17 | ♀♀ | 5 |
| ● Sabato '17 | ♀♀ | 5 |
| ● Noir '12 | ♀♀ | 5 |
| ● Pinot Nero '11 | ♀♀ | 5 |
| ● Sabato '15 | ♀♀ | 5 |
| ● Sabato '12 | ♀♀ | 5 |
| ○ Sireo '15 | ♀♀ | 5 |
| ○ Sireo Bianco '14 | ♀♀ | 5 |
| ○ Sireo Bianco '13 | ♀♀ | 5 |
| ○ Sireo Bianco '11 | ♀♀ | 5 |
| ● Sireo Rosso '11 | ♀♀ | 5 |

## Agnanum

VIA VICINALE ABBANDONATA AGLI ASTRONI, 3
80125 NAPOLI
TEL. +39 3385315272
www.agnanum.it

**CELLAR SALES**
**PRE-BOOKED VISITS**
**ANNUAL PRODUCTION** 25,000 bottles
**HECTARES UNDER VINE** 7.50

Raffaele Moccia is one of Campi Flegrei's most inspired vigneron, with wines that interpret this land of volcanic origin in an original way. After inheriting the vineyards grown by his father, Gennaro, within the Astronic Natural Park, he began his adventure in one of Campania's most impervious areas. Here equal parts Piedirosso and Falanghina are cultivated on ungrafted, terraced vineyards that require manual harvesting and extremely low yields. The nearby sea, the sandy soil and late harvest endow their wines with a truly unique Mediterranean character. Once again Raffaele offer us a highly original interpretation of the appellation. His weighty 2017 Falaghina features multifaceted aromas of citrus and flint, which become increasingly intense before giving way to a delicately salty finish. His juicy 2017 Piedirosso is notable for its gentle tannins and pure succulence.

| | | |
|---|---|---|
| ○ Campi Flegrei Falanghina '17 | ♀♀ | 3* |
| ● Campi Flegrei Per 'e Palumm '17 | ♀♀ | 4 |
| ● Campi Flegrei Piedirosso '16 | ♀♀♀ | 4* |
| ● Campi Flegrei Piedirosso '15 | ♀♀♀ | 4* |
| ○ Campi Flegrei Falanghina V. del Pino '15 | ♀♀ | 3* |
| ○ Campi Flegrei Falanghina V. del Pino '15 | ♀♀ | 3 |
| ○ Campi Flegrei Falanghina V. del Pino '14 | ♀♀ | 3 |
| ● Campi Flegrei Piedirosso '13 | ♀♀ | 3* |
| ● Campi Flegrei Piedirosso V. delle Volpi '12 | ♀♀ | 5 |
| ● Campi Flegrei Piedirosso V. delle Volpi '15 | ♀♀ | 4 |
| ● Campi Flegrei Piedirosso V. delle Volpi '14 | ♀♀ | 4 |
| ○ Falanghina dei Campi Flegrei V. del Pino '08 | ♀♀ | 4 |

# Alois

LOC. AUDELINO
VIA RAGAZZANO
81040 PONTELATONE [CE]
TEL. +39 0823876710
www.vinialois.it

CELLAR SALES
PRE-BOOKED VISITS
ANNUAL PRODUCTION 300,000 bottles
HECTARES UNDER VINE 30.00
SUSTAINABLE WINERY

For centuries Alois has been active in wine-growing and today the producer is one of the best interpreters of Monti Caiatini's native grape varieties. These are vinified separately by Michele Alois, who's managed to bring back cultivar like Casavecchia. Their vineyards are situated in various areas: Audalino, Morrone della Monica and Cesone in Pontelatone. Enologist Carmine Valentino manages production with the utmost respect for the environment so as to best represent the territory. Their selection of Irpino wines, available in their Ponte Pellegrino line, is also noteworthy. Their 2016 Caiatì is back on top. Made with Pallagrello Bianco grapes from their Morrone vineyard, it's a taut wine with nice mineral vitality. It features a generous aromatic profile with notes of orange peel, yellow peach and fines herbes, while in the mouth it proves rich and balanced, with a fresh, slightly salty finish. Their 2014 Trebulanum is highly enjoyable on the palate, supported by a pronounced savoriness.

| | |
|---|---|
| ○ Caiati Pallagrello Bianco '16 | ▼▼▼ 4* |
| ● Casavecchia di Pontelatone Trebulanum Ris. '12 | ▼▼ 5 |
| ● Cunto Pallagrello Nero '15 | ▼▼ 4 |
| ○ Greco di Tufo Ponte Pellegrino '17 | ▼▼ 4 |
| ● Ponte Pellegrino Aglianico '17 | ▼▼ 5 |
| ○ Ponte Pellegrino Falanghina '17 | ▼▼ 3 |
| ○ Caiatì '15 | ▼▼▼ 3* |
| ○ Caiatì '14 | ▼▼▼ 3* |
| ○ Caiatì Morrone Pallagrello Bianco '13 | ▼▼▼ 2* |
| ● Trebulanum '10 | ▼▼▼ 5 |
| ● Aglianico Donna Paolina '16 | ▼▼ 5 |
| ○ Caulino '16 | ▼▼ 3 |
| ○ Donna Paolina Falanghina '16 | ▼▼ 3 |
| ● Settimo '15 | ▼▼ 3 |
| ● Trebulanum Casavecchia '13 | ▼▼ 5 |

# Cantine Astroni

VIA SARTANIA, 48
80126 NAPOLI
TEL. +39 0815884182
www.cantineastroni.com

CELLAR SALES
PRE-BOOKED VISITS
RESTAURANT SERVICE
ANNUAL PRODUCTION 330,000 bottles
HECTARES UNDER VINE 25.00
VITICULTURE METHOD Certified Organic
SUSTAINABLE WINERY

Piedirosso and Falanghina are two of the varieties that best represent the volcanic soil of the Astroni craters. It's here on this great expanse of land, rich in biodiversity, flora and fauna, that Gerardo Vernazzaro, his wife, Emanuela Russo and cousin Vincezo work their vineyards with the utmost respect for the environment, making for a selection of wines that highlights the attributes of the region's wines. Volcanic soil gives rise to a authentic, mineral wines endowed with great energy, characteristics that can be found in the cru of Vigna Astroni, Villa Imperatrice, Vigna Camaldoli and Vigna Iossa This year the producer took home its first Tre Bicchieri. It's all thanks to an exceptional version of their Vigna Astroni, which proves to be in splendid form. It's a cru with streaks of sulphur and a volcanic profile that features notes of citrus and broom. On the palate it proves full and juicy, with a lengthy finish and pronounced minerality. Their 2012 Strione is a sunny and Mediterranean Falanghina that still possesses intriguing acidity.

| | |
|---|---|
| ○ Campi Flegrei Falanghina V. Astroni '15 | ▼▼▼ 3* |
| ● Campi Flegrei Piedirosso Colle Rotondella '17 | ▼▼ 3 |
| ○ Campi Flegrei Falanghina Brut Astro | ▼ 3 |
| ● Campi Flegrei Piedirosso Tenuta Camaldoli '15 | ▼ 2 |
| ○ Campi Flegrei Falanghina Colle Imperatrice '15 | ▼▼ 2* |
| ○ Campi Flegrei Falanghina V. Astroni '14 | ▼▼ 3 |
| ● Campi Flegrei Piedirosso Colle Rotondella '16 | ▼▼ 3 |
| ● Campi Flegrei Piedirosso Colle Rotondella '15 | ▼▼ 3* |
| ○ Strione '12 | ▼▼ 4 |

# Bambinuto

VIA CERRO
83030 SANTA PAOLINA [AV]
TEL. +39 0825964634
www.cantinabambinuto.com

PRE-BOOKED VISITS
ANNUAL PRODUCTION 25,000 bottles
HECTARES UNDER VINE 6.00

Marilena Aufiero is lady Greco di Tufo here in Santa Paolina. She graduated in jurisprudence but decided to set aside her future profession and convinced the entire family (including her father, Raffaele, and mother, Anna) to try producing their own wines, rather than merely supplying them to others. It was a new adventure and today their selection is comprised of two wines: their Greco di Tufo and Greco di Tufo Picoli. The former is made with grapes cultivated in Paolini at 400 meters above sea level, on terrain that's less stony than Picoli. The latter is made with grapes cultivated in Picoli in Santa Paolina on calcareous-clay soil at 500 meters elevation. We continue to appreciate the structure and complexity of their 2016 Greco di Tufo Picoli. It's a lovely golden yellow wine that lands in our finals thanks to its musky and sulfureous character, enriched by pleasant accents of dried fruit, nuts and mint. Their 2017 Greco di Tufo calls up fruity notes of kiwi, though it may be a bit clenched at the end.

| | |
|---|---|
| ○ Greco di Tufo Picoli '16 | ♟♟ 4 |
| ○ Greco di Tufo '16 | ♟ 2 |
| ○ Greco di Tufo '15 | ♟♟ 2* |
| ○ Greco di Tufo '14 | ♟♟ 2* |
| ○ Greco di Tufo '13 | ♟♟ 2* |
| ○ Greco di Tufo '12 | ♟♟ 3 |
| ○ Greco di Tufo Picoli '15 | ♟♟ 4 |
| ○ Greco di Tufo Picoli '13 | ♟♟ 4 |
| ○ Greco di Tufo Picoli '11 | ♟♟ 4 |
| ○ Greco di Tufo Picoli '10 | ♟♟ 4 |
| ○ Greco di Tufo Picoli '09 | ♟♟ 4 |
| ○ Irpinia Falanghina Insania '15 | ♟♟ 2* |
| ● Taurasi '07 | ♟♟ 5 |

# I Cacciagalli

LOC. CAIANELLO
FRAZ. AORIVOLA
VIA TEANO, 3
81059 TEANO [CE]
TEL. +39 0823875216
www.icacciagalli.it

CELLAR SALES
PRE-BOOKED VISITS
ACCOMMODATION
ANNUAL PRODUCTION 20,000 bottles
HECTARES UNDER VINE 9.00
VITICULTURE METHOD Certified Organic

Between Teano and Caianello, in upper Caserta, Diana Iannaccone and her husband, Mario Bosco, cultivate native grape varieties at the foot of the Roccamonfina volcano (according to biodynamic principles). It's a contiguous estate of 35 hectares that features hazelnut trees, chestnuts and olives, as well as thriving vineyards that give rise to original wines in terms of style and aromatic definition. Unmonitored fermentation, native yeast, audacious maceration, the use of large barrels, concrete and amphoras make for wines endowed with character and freshness. It's part of a lifestyle centered on environmental sustainability. Their 2017 Sphaeranera is at the top of its game. It's a vibrant, muscular and dynamic Pallagrello Nero that offers up an aromatic weave of pepper and blackcurrant. On the palate it features a nice, highly energetic contrast by virtue of acidity. Their 2017 Pos also put in a good performance. It's a juicy wine in its aromatic profile of blood oranges and earthy hints. Their first Pellerosa, an original rosé that features notes of black fruit and pencil lead, also delivered.

| | |
|---|---|
| ● Sphaeranera '17 | ♟♟ 4 |
| ◉ Pellerosa '17 | ♟♟ 4 |
| ● Phos '17 | ♟♟ 4 |
| ○ Zagreo '17 | ♟♟ 4 |
| ○ Aorivola '17 | ♟ 3 |
| ● Mille '17 | ♟ 3 |
| ○ Zagreo '15 | ♟♟♟ 4* |
| ○ Aorivola '16 | ♟♟ 3 |
| ● Mille '15 | ♟♟ 3 |
| ● Phos '15 | ♟♟ 4 |
| ● Phos '13 | ♟♟ 4 |
| ● Sphaeranera '15 | ♟♟ 4 |
| ● Sphaeranera '13 | ♟♟ 4 |
| ○ Zagreo '14 | ♟♟ 4 |
| ○ Zagreo '14 | ♟♟ 4 |

# Antonio Caggiano

C.DA SALA
83030 TAURASI [AV]
TEL. +39 082774723
www.cantinecaggiano.it

CELLAR SALES
PRE-BOOKED VISITS
RESTAURANT SERVICE
ANNUAL PRODUCTION 165,000 bottles
HECTARES UNDER VINE 30.00

Antonio Caggiano's winery is a perfect snapshot of Irpino's wine-growing industry, with its vaulted ceilings, its stone walls and rural tools set amidst barrels and bottles. In the early 1990s Antonio, a traveling photographer, decided to dedicate himself to viticulture and bottle the area's various cultivar, with plenty of room reserved for Aglianico. And so it was that some of the Taurasi appellation's strongest and most long-lived crus were born, like Vigna Macchia dei Goti. Today his son Giuseppe (commonly known as Pino) is helping out in the vineyards, and like his father, he's working to best interpret the area's traditional wines. After a few years off, their 2014 Taurasi Vigna Macchia dei Goti, a wine with lovely violet highlights, is once again back on top. On the nose it offers up fruity notes of cherry preserves. These give way to spicy nuances and hints of licorice and coffee. In the mouth it proves potent and balanced with tones of oak that integrate perfectly with its lively tannins.

| | | |
|---|---|---|
| ● Taurasi V. Macchia dei Goti '14 | ∇∇∇ | 6 |
| ○ Fiano di Avellino Béchar '17 | ∇∇ | 3 |
| ● Irpinia Aglianico Taurì '17 | ∇∇ | 2* |
| ○ Mel | ∇∇ | 5 |
| ○ Fiagrè '17 | ∇ | 3 |
| ○ Greco di Tufo Devon '17 | ∇ | 3 |
| ○ Fiano di Avellino Béchar '13 | ∇∇∇ | 3* |
| ● Taurasi V. Macchia dei Goti '08 | ∇∇∇ | 5 |
| ● Taurasi V. Macchia dei Goti '04 | ∇∇∇ | 5 |
| ● Taurasi V. Macchia dei Goti '99 | ∇∇∇ | 5 |
| ○ Fiano di Avellino Béchar '16 | ∇∇ | 3 |
| ○ Greco di Tufo Devon '16 | ∇∇ | 3 |
| ● Irpinia Aglianico Taurì '15 | ∇∇ | 3* |
| ● Taurasi V. Macchia dei Goti '13 | ∇∇ | 6 |

# Cantine dell'Angelo

VIA SANTA LUCIA, 32
83010 TUFO [AV]
TEL. +39 3384512965
www.cantinedellangelo.com

CELLAR SALES
PRE-BOOKED VISITS
ANNUAL PRODUCTION 18,000 bottles
HECTARES UNDER VINE 5.00

The Muto family work their vineyards of Greco situated over the historic sulphur mines in Tufo. Five hectares of terrain are cultivated personally by Angelo, who represents the third generation of family viticulturists, and Maria Nuzzolo. These give rise to a selection of Greco di Tufo wines that are among the most original and personal of the appellation. In the glass, Torrefavale and Minieri embody the spirit of the place, driven by flavor and freshness and tending towards mineral notes, with the Miniere even stronger in its hints of sulphur. Their 2016 Miniere is a Greco di Tufo that does a good job expressing its territory. It's a moving wine, rich in flavor and charm, uniquely sulphureous. On the nose it offers up notes of white fruit and Mediterranean scrubland. On the palate it proves savory, to say the least, salty and vibrant, extremely juicy and delicately tannic, with an energetic, endless finish. It's a Tre Bicchieri to remember. Their 2016 Greco di Tufo Torrefavale is also redolent of broom and chamomile on a sulphureous background. It's a wine that finishes with notable savoriness.

| | | |
|---|---|---|
| ○ Greco di Tufo Miniere '16 | ∇∇∇ | 4* |
| ○ Greco di Tufo Torrefavale '16 | ∇∇ | 5 |
| ○ Greco di Tufo '09 | ∇∇∇ | 3* |
| ○ Greco di Tufo '14 | ∇∇ | 3 |
| ○ Greco di Tufo '13 | ∇∇ | 3 |
| ○ Greco di Tufo '11 | ∇∇ | 3 |
| ○ Greco di Tufo '10 | ∇∇ | 3 |
| ○ Greco di Tufo Torrefavale '15 | ∇∇ | 3 |
| ○ Greco di Tufo Torrefavale '14 | ∇∇ | 3 |
| ○ Greco di Tufo Torrefavale '13 | ∇∇ | 3* |

# Casa Setaro

via Bosco del Monaco, 34
80040 Trecase [NA]
Tel. +39 0818628956
www.casasetaro.it

PRE-BOOKED VISITS
RESTAURANT SERVICE
ANNUAL PRODUCTION 50,000 bottles
HECTARES UNDER VINE 10.00

This family-run winery testifies to the strong bond that exists between the Setaros and Neapolitan wine culture. Here in Trecase, a small municipality on the slopes of Vesuvius, the vineyards are cultivated on volcanic soils in one of the world's most mineral rich areas and one of Campania's most fertile. Massimo is at the helm, overseeing his vineyards in Tirrone della Guardia and Bosco del Monaco, two parts of the Vesuvius National Park. Among their selection of whites, their Caprettone is worth watching. It's available both as a sparkling and still wine. Their 2014 Lacryma Christi Rosso Don Vincenzo Riserva is a blend of Aglianico and Piedirosso that calls up aromas of pencil lead and red orange. On the palate it proves fragrant and rich in fruit, unfolding progressively towards a captivating, savory finish. Their delectable 2014 Brut Metodo Classico, a monovarietal Caprettone that features smoky tones and aromas of yellow fruit, surprises for its freshness and pleasantly rustic character.

| | | |
|---|---|---|
| ○ Campanelle '17 | ♟♟ | 2* |
| ○ Caprettone Brut M. Cl. '14 | ♟♟ | 4 |
| ● Lacryma Christi del Vesuvio Rosso Don Vincenzo '14 | ♟♟ | 4 |
| ● Lacryma Christi del Vesuvio Rosso Munazei '17 | ♟ | 3 |
| ● Aglianico Tauro '12 | ♟♟ | 4 |
| ○ Caprettone Brut '12 | ♟♟ | 4 |
| ○ Caprettone Brut M. Cl. '13 | ♟♟ | 4 |
| ○ Caprettone Brut M. Cl. '13 | ♟♟ | 4 |
| ○ Falanghina Campanelle '16 | ♟♟ | 2* |
| ○ Falanghina Campanelle '16 | ♟♟ | 2* |
| ○ Falanghina Campanelle '13 | ♟♟ | 2* |
| ● Terramatta '13 | ♟♟ | 2* |

# Casebianche

c.da Case Bianche, 8
84076 Torchiara [SA]
Tel. +39 0974843244
www.casebianche.eu

CELLAR SALES
PRE-BOOKED VISITS
ANNUAL PRODUCTION 35,000 bottles
HECTARES UNDER VINE 5.50
VITICULTURE METHOD Certified Organic
SUSTAINABLE WINERY

Aglianico, Barbera, Piedirosso, Fiano, Trebbiano and Malvasia are all organically vinified with natural second fermentation. Pasquale Amitrano and his wife, Betty Iurio, both former architects, decided to change lifestyle and move to Cilento so as to become vine growers. The estate is situated in Torchiara, in a scenic landscape circumscribed by the sea, Monte Stella and the Acquasanta river. Their vineyards are cultivated in stony, clay soil, giving rise to robust, energetic and expressive still wines and unique, lively sparklers. Their 2017 Pashkà exhibits liveliness, rhythm and a clean palate. It's a truly delectable wine with aromas of black mulberries, almonds and orange peels. In the mouth it proves crisp, taut, close-focused, rich in energy and meaty fruit. Their 2017 Fric is redolent of watermelon and pomegranate, while the palate proves more mature than usual. The trio of refermented wines is completed by their delicious 2017 Matta, a wine featuring aromas of peach and bread, and a determined, citrusy palate.

| | | |
|---|---|---|
| ● Pashka' '17 | ♟♟♟ | 4* |
| ● Cilento Rosso Dellemore '16 | ♟♟ | 3 |
| ⊙ Il Fric '17 | ♟♟ | 4 |
| ● Cilento Aglianico Cupersito '15 | ♟ | 4 |
| ○ La Matta Dosaggio Zero '17 | ♟ | 4 |
| ⊙ Il Fric '16 | ♟♟♟ | 3* |
| ● Cilento Aglianico Cupersito '12 | ♟♟ | 3 |
| ● Cilento Rosso Dellemore '15 | ♟♟ | 3 |
| ⊙ Il Fric '15 | ♟♟ | 3 |
| ○ La Matta Dosaggio Zero '16 | ♟♟ | 3 |
| ○ La Matta Dosaggio Zero '15 | ♟♟ | 3* |
| ● Pashkà '16 | ♟♟ | 3 |

# Cautiero

C.DA ARBUSTI
82030 FRASSO TELESINO [BN]
TEL. +39 3387640641
www.cautiero.it

CELLAR SALES
ACCOMMODATION
ANNUAL PRODUCTION 18,000 bottles
HECTARES UNDER VINE 4.00
VITICULTURE METHOD Certified Organic

Despite their 19 years of activity, Fulvio Cautiero and Immacolata Coprano continue to enthusiastically enjoy success in the world of winemaking. They left their respective jobs in 2002 and decided to revive the terrain abandoned in the Taburno Regional Park in Benevento, cultivating Falanghina, Fiano, Greco, Pledirosso and Aglianico. Today the estate, which integrates perfectly with the surrounding area, avails itself of four hectares of organically managed vineyards, cultivated on potassium-rich soil that confers flavor and acidity to each of their wines. Their 2017 Falanghina Fois is a true delight. Its aromas are vibrant and clear: wheat, freshly cut grass, peach. It's a firmly structured wine, natural and penetrating, with a rich, savory palate that's gratifying in its meaty fruit. It's a wine to enjoy and enjoy again. Their 2016 Erba Bianca also impressed. It's longer in its aromas, complex in its notes of white fruit. On the palate it proves plush and creamy, with a delicately almond finish. Their 2017 Greco Trois is an extremely lively wine.

| | |
|---|---|
| ○ Falanghina del Sannio Fois '17 | ♛♛ 2* |
| ○ Erba Bianca '16 | ♛♛ 2* |
| ○ Sannio Greco Trois '17 | ♛♛ 2* |
| ● Piedirosso '16 | ♛ 2 |
| ● Sannio Aglianico Fois '15 | ♛ 2 |
| ○ Falanghina del Sannio Fois '13 | ♛♛♛ 2* |
| ○ Erba Bianca '15 | ♛♛ 2* |
| ○ Erba Bianca '14 | ♛♛ 2* |
| ○ Falanghina del Sannio Fois '16 | ♛♛ 2* |
| ○ Falanghina del Sannio Fois '15 | ♛♛ 2* |
| ○ Falanghina del Sannio Fois '14 | ♛♛ 2* |
| ● Sannio Aglianico Fois '13 | ♛♛ 2* |
| ● Sannio Aglianico Fois '12 | ♛♛ 2* |
| ○ Sannio Greco Trois '15 | ♛♛ 2* |

# Tenuta Cavalier Pepe

VIA SANTA VARA
83050 SANT'ANGELO ALL'ESCA [AV]
TEL. +39 082773766
www.tenutapepe.it

CELLAR SALES
PRE-BOOKED VISITS
ACCOMMODATION AND RESTAURANT SERVICE
ANNUAL PRODUCTION 380,000 bottles
HECTARES UNDER VINE 60.00
SUSTAINABLE WINERY

Tenuta Cavalier Pepe's vineyards in Sant'Angelo all'Esca, Montefusco, Torrioni and Luogosano, which are situated in some of Irpinia's best appellations, do a good job representing the winery's selection. Behind this historic producer is the man after whom it was named, Angelo Pepe, decorated as a 'cavaliere' for his work in promoting Italian products abroad. Since 2005 his enologist daughter Milena has been at his side, continually developing the area's native cultivar and earning success in both national and international markets. Their entire selection is coherent in terms of quality. Their 2016 Fiano di Avellino Brancato offers up aromas of aniseed, cedar and mint. In the mouth it shows balsamic freshness and pronounced savoriness. Their 2013 Taurasi Opera Mia opts for weighty texture and slightly blood-rich tones. Tannins are detectable but properly smoothed by time spent in the bottle.

| | |
|---|---|
| ○ Fiano di Avellino Brancato '16 | ♛♛ 3 |
| ○ Greco di Tufo Grancare Sel. '16 | ♛♛ 7 |
| ○ Greco di Tufo Nestor '17 | ♛♛ 5 |
| ● Taurasi Opera Mia '13 | ♛♛ 8 |
| ○ Fiano di Avellino Refiano '17 | ♛ 5 |
| ● Irpinia Campi Taurasini Santo Stefano '13 | ♛ 6 |
| ○ Irpinia Coda di Volpe Bianco di Bellona '17 | ♛ 4 |
| ● Taurasi La Loggia del Cavaliere Ris. '12 | ♛ 8 |
| ○ Fiano di Avellino Refiano '16 | ♛♛ 3 |
| ○ Fiano di Avellino Refiano '15 | ♛♛ 3 |
| ○ Greco di Tufo Grancare '15 | ♛♛ 5 |
| ○ Greco di Tufo Nestor '16 | ♛♛ 3 |
| ● Taurasi Opera Mia '12 | ♛♛ 5 |

# Colli di Castelfranci

C.DA BRAUDIANO
83040 CASTELFRANCI [AV]
TEL. +39 082772392
www.collidicastelfranci.com

**CELLAR SALES**
**PRE-BOOKED VISITS**
**ACCOMMODATION AND RESTAURANT SERVICE**
**ANNUAL PRODUCTION** 150,000 bottles
**HECTARES UNDER VINE** 25.00

Luciano Gregorio and Gerardo Colucci are immersed in the green of Alta Irpinia's vineyards. Here in Castelfranci, a small municipality situated at 450 meters above sea level, we find one of the most interesting epicenters for Aglianico winemaking. In fact, the producer offers some four wines made with the cultivar, with their Taurasi Alta Valle and Riserva both standing out. The late harvest, acidity and extractive character of these reds are unique qualities for such ageworthy wines. Their supple and lean Greco di Tufo and Fiano di Avellino, both made in steel tanks, complete the selection. Despite the hot year, their 2017 Fiano Pendino features a nice freshness and pronounced acidity. On the nose balsamic aromas emerge, along with Mediterranean herbs and a slightly mineral hint. Their 2011 Taurasi Alta Valle, a wine that stands out for its dark, ripe fruit, exhibits intense tannic extraction. On the nose it calls up nuances of red fruit and spicy notes, while in the mouth it finishes with balance and harmony.

| | |
|---|---|
| ○ Fiano di Avellino Pendino '17 | ♟♟ 3 |
| ● Taurasi Alta Valle '11 | ♟♟ 7 |
| ○ Greco di Tufo Grotte '17 | ♟ 3 |
| ● Irpinia Campi Taurasini Candriano '13 | ♟ 4 |
| ● Irpinia Campi Taurasini Vadantico '13 | ♟ 3 |
| ○ Fiano di Avellino Pendino '16 | ♟♟ 3 |
| ○ Fiano di Avellino Pendino '16 | ♟♟ 3 |
| ○ Fiano di Avellino Pendino '14 | ♟♟ 2* |
| ○ Greco di Tufo Grotte '15 | ♟♟ 2* |
| ○ Greco di Tufo Grotte '14 | ♟♟ 2* |
| ● Irpinia Campi Taurasini Vadantico '14 | ♟♟ 3 |
| ○ Irpinia Greco Vallicelli '13 | ♟♟ 4 |
| ● Taurasi Alta Valle Ris. '10 | ♟♟ 7 |
| ● Taurasi Alta Valle Ris. '09 | ♟♟ 7 |

# ★Colli di Lapio

VIA ARIANIELLO, 47
83030 LAPIO [AV]
TEL. +39 0825982184
www.collidilapio.it

**CELLAR SALES**
**PRE-BOOKED VISITS**
**ANNUAL PRODUCTION** 60,000 bottles
**HECTARES UNDER VINE** 8.00

Arianello is a small district in the municipality of Lapio, situated at 500 meters above sea leavel, where Fiano takes on unique character, aromas and noteworthy minerality. And here we find Clelia Romano, a benchmark for those who love Fiano di Avellino, accompanied by her two children Carmela and Federico, as well as her husband, Angelo. Together they create wines that exhibit a profile characteristic of more northern latitudes, with delicately smoky notes and strong acidity. Among the other wines in their selection, we point out their Greco di Tufo and Taurasi, all made with grapes cultivated exclusively in their private vineyards. Their 2017 Fiano di Avellino is a white that gradually reveals its aromatic profile. To the eye it appears to be a luminous, weighty wine. On the nose it offers up aromas of grapefruit and aromatic herbs, only to give way to mineral, musky tones. On the palate it preserves its clear, vigorous acidity, while it closes on a delicately salty note. Because of the hotter year, it's not quite as full as the version we awarded in the last edition.

| | |
|---|---|
| ○ Fiano di Avellino '17 | ♟♟ 4 |
| ○ Greco di Tufo Alexandros '17 | ♟ 3 |
| ○ Fiano di Avellino '16 | ♟♟♟ 4* |
| ○ Fiano di Avellino '15 | ♟♟♟ 4* |
| ○ Fiano di Avellino '14 | ♟♟♟ 4* |
| ○ Fiano di Avellino '13 | ♟♟♟ 4* |
| ○ Fiano di Avellino '10 | ♟♟♟ 4 |
| ○ Fiano di Avellino '09 | ♟♟♟ 4 |
| ○ Fiano di Avellino '08 | ♟♟♟ 4* |
| ○ Fiano di Avellino '07 | ♟♟♟ 4 |
| ○ Fiano di Avellino '05 | ♟♟♟ 4 |
| ○ Fiano di Avellino '04 | ♟♟♟ 4 |

# Contrade di Taurasi

VIA MUNICIPIO, 41
83030 TAURASI [AV]
TEL. +39 082774483
www.cantinelonardo.it

CELLAR SALES
PRE-BOOKED VISITS
ANNUAL PRODUCTION 18,000 bottles
HECTARES UNDER VINE 5.00
VITICULTURE METHOD Certified Organic

Aglianico is the cultivar of choice at Contrade üi Taurasi and serves as the basis for their Vigne d'Alto and Coste cru wines. In 1998 Antonella Lonardo and her husband, Flavio Castaldo, left their respective jobs, deciding to return to Taurasi to start up a selection of superior red wines that were faithful to traditional yet modern in their stylistic development. The result has been wines of natural expressivity made with grapes cultivated in Taurasi on volcanic, sandy terrain. In addition to Aglianico, they grow Roviello, locally known as Greco Musc', which gives rise to aromatic whites and the right amount of savoriness. This year their Taurasi Vigne d'Alto brings home Tre Bicchieri. The 2012 puts the force and depth of Aglianico on center stage. Traces of juniper, black tea and coffee unfold in the glass, only to give way to citrus and spices. A fresh and vital finish is marked by acidity. We found their 2016 Grecomusc in excellent form with its aromas of ginger, aniseed and Asian spices, and its steady, savory palate.

| | | |
|---|---|---|
| ● Taurasi Vigne d'Alto '12 | ♈♈♈ | 8 |
| ○ Grecomusc' '16 | ♈♈ | 5 |
| ○ Grecomusc' '15 | ♈♈♈ | 5 |
| ○ Grecomusc' '12 | ♈♈♈ | 4* |
| ○ Grecomusc' '10 | ♈♈♈ | 4* |
| ● Taurasi '10 | ♈♈♈ | 6 |
| ● Taurasi '04 | ♈♈♈ | 6 |
| ● Taurasi Coste '11 | ♈♈♈ | 6 |
| ● Taurasi Coste '08 | ♈♈♈ | 7 |
| ○ Grecomusc' '14 | ♈♈ | 5 |
| ○ Grecomusc' Burlesque '14 | ♈♈ | 5 |
| ● Taurasi '12 | ♈♈ | 6 |
| ● Taurasi '11 | ♈♈ | 6 |
| ● Taurasi Coste '12 | ♈♈ | 8 |

# ★Marisa Cuomo

VIA G. B. LAMA, 16/18
84010 FURORE [SA]
TEL. +39 089830348
www.marisacuomo.com

CELLAR SALES
PRE-BOOKED VISITS
RESTAURANT SERVICE
ANNUAL PRODUCTION 109,000 bottles
HECTARES UNDER VINE 18.00

Furore is a small gem in the heart of the Amalfi Coast. It's one of the region's most impervious areas for vine growing, but it boasts a viticultural potential that few can. It was here that Marisa Cuomo was founded in 1980, when as a wedding gift Andrea Ferraioli gave his wife the vineyards he'd inherited from his father. From that moment on, the winery established itself as one of Italy's best, achieving a solid fame thanks to Fiorduva, a symbol of the coast's wine culture. The terraced vineyards, which are supported by stone walls, give rise to Ripoli, Fenile and Ginestra for their whites, Piedirosso and Sciascinoso for their reds. Their 2017 Fiorduva once again earns top marks, affirming its status as one of the Amalfi Coast's classic whites, a wine capable of expressing the territory with each sip. It's a characteristically Mediterranean wine with hints of white fruit, herbs and citrus. On the palate it has a delicately salty touch, and a persistent, complex mid-palate. Their 2017 Costa d'Amalfi Ravello Bianco is similar, though less dense, with a vibrant, almost peppery finish.

| | | |
|---|---|---|
| ○ Costa d'Amalfi Furore Bianco Fiorduva '17 | ♈♈♈ | 7 |
| ○ Costa d'Amalfi Ravello Bianco '17 | ♈♈ | 3* |
| ● Costa d'Amalfi Furore Rosso Ris. '15 | ♈♈ | 6 |
| ○ Costa d'Amalfi Furore Bianco '17 | ♈♈ | 4 |
| ● Costa d'Amalfi Furore Rosso '17 | ♈ | 3 |
| ● Costa d'Amalfi Ravello Rosso Ris. '15 | ♈ | 5 |
| ⊙ Costa d'Amalfi Rosato '17 | ♈ | 4 |
| ○ Costa d'Amalfi Furore Bianco '15 | ♈♈♈ | 4* |
| ○ Costa d'Amalfi Furore Bianco '10 | ♈♈♈ | 4 |
| ○ Costa d'Amalfi Furore Bianco Fiorduva '16 | ♈♈♈ | 7 |
| ○ Costa d'Amalfi Furore Bianco Fiorduva '14 | ♈♈♈ | 7 |
| ○ Costa d'Amalfi Furore Bianco Fiorduva '10 | ♈♈♈ | 6 |

# D'Ambra Vini d'Ischia

FRAZ. PANZA
VIA MARIO D'AMBRA, 16
80077 FORIO [NA]
TEL. +39 081907210
www.dambravini.com

CELLAR SALES
PRE-BOOKED VISITS
ANNUAL PRODUCTION 450,000 bottles
HECTARES UNDER VINE 14.00

The difficult geography of Ischia never slowed down the development of its wine industry. For centuries they've cultivated native varieties like Biancolella, Forastera and Per e Palummo. Behind these decidedly marine wines we find Casa d'Ambra, the island's most important and historic winery, founded in 1888 by Francesco D'Ambra and today managed by Marina, finance director, and Sara, the enologist who looks after their entire selection of wines. Supervision is in the hands of their father, Andrea. Along with his daughters he oversees their Tenuta Frassitelli line, a Biancolella cru that gave rise to Campania's first white Tre Bicchieri. It's the producers most important cru, an aristocratic, monovarietal Biancolella that's elegant on the nose, with hints of citrus, aromatic herbs and a pronounced savoriness. On the palate it doesn't slow down, indeed it entices. It's a fresh white, entirely coastal. Their 2017 Biancolella also refreshes, as does their 2017 Forastera, two vineyards that do a nice job expressing the island by virtue of their iodine fragrances and their aromas of Mediterranean herbs.

| | |
|---|---|
| ○ Ischia Biancolella Tenuta Frassitelli '17 | ⚱⚱ 5 |
| ○ Ischia Biancolella '17 | ⚱⚱ 4 |
| ○ Ischia Forastera '17 | ⚱⚱ 4 |
| ○ Ischia Bianco '17 | ⚱ 3 |
| ● Ischia Per' 'e Palummo '17 | ⚱ 4 |
| ● Ischia Rosso Dedicato a Mario d'Ambra '15 | ⚱ 5 |
| ○ Ischia Biancolella Tenuta Frassitelli '12 | ⚱⚱⚱ 3* |
| ○ Ischia Biancolella Tenuta Frassitelli '90 | ⚱⚱⚱ 3* |
| ○ Ischia Bianco '16 | ⚱⚱ 2* |
| ○ Ischia Biancolella '16 | ⚱⚱ 3 |
| ○ Ischia Biancolella Tenuta Frassitelli '16 | ⚱⚱ 4 |
| ○ Ischia Forastera '16 | ⚱⚱ 3 |

# Cantine Di Marzo

VIA GAETANO DI MARZO, 2
83010 TUFO [AV]
TEL. +39 0825998022
www.cantinedimarzo.it

CELLAR SALES
PRE-BOOKED VISITS
ANNUAL PRODUCTION 150,000 bottles
HECTARES UNDER VINE 23.00

The winery gets its name from Scipione di Marzo who in 1647 left Nola, where the plague was rampant, and moved to Tufo (at the time it was one of the safest areas to be). It proved to be a decisive year for the history of Cantine di Marzo. After centuries of winemaking, in 2009, the producer passed into the hands of the Somma family (direct descendants of di Marzo). Today they oversee some 23 hectares of vineyards spread throughout the districts of Santa Lucia, San Paolo di Tufo and Santa Paolina. Here Greco takes center stage, serving as the basis for both still and sparkling wines like their Metodo Classico Anni Venti. Their selection is excellent overall, with two wines handily earning a place in our finals. Their 2016 Greco Vigna Laure offers up aromas of pears and almonds, while on the palate it proves rigorous and austere, with a persistent, delicately salty finish. Their Vigna Ortale opts for even greater savoriness and depth, with an elegant, smoky vein and a potent, persistent palate. Their Metodo Classico Extra Brut gets a special mention. It's another Greco, redolent of fennel and sage.

| | |
|---|---|
| ○ Greco di Tufo V. Laure '16 | ⚱⚱ 3* |
| ○ Greco di Tufo V. Ortale '16 | ⚱⚱ 3* |
| ○ Extra Brut M. Cl. Anni Venti | ⚱ 5 |
| ○ Greco di Tufo '17 | ⚱ 2 |
| ○ Greco di Tufo '16 | ⚱⚱⚱ 2* |
| ○ Fiano di Avellino Donatus '13 | ⚱⚱ 3* |
| ○ Greco di Tufo '15 | ⚱⚱ 2* |
| ○ Greco di Tufo Colle Serrone '16 | ⚱⚱ 3* |
| ○ Greco di Tufo Somnium Scipionis '13 | ⚱⚱ 5 |
| ○ Greco di Tufo Somnium Scipionis '12 | ⚱⚱ 5 |

# Di Meo

C.DA COCCOVONI, 1
83050 SALZA IRPINA [AV]
TEL. +39 0825981419
www.dimeo.it

CELLAR SALES
PRE-BOOKED VISITS
RESTAURANT SERVICE
ANNUAL PRODUCTION 450,000 bottles
HECTARES UNDER VINE 30.00
SUSTAINABLE WINERY

To those who are patient enough, the Di Meo family's wines will offer up their signature style and character, which lengthy aging brings out over time. Their wide selection has established itself over the years thanks to siblings Eriminia, Generoso and Roberto who took over their parents' business in Salza Irpina in 1980. Their vineyards of Fiano are situated on calcareous clay terrain at 550 meters above sea level, while their Greco is cultivated in Santa Paolina and Tufo. Finally, their Aglianico is grown at the highest elevations, on Montemarano, at 650 meters above sea level. Once again we tasted their 2003 Fiano di Avellino Erminia Meo. Despite its age, it's still rich in flavor. On the nose it offers up notes of white pepper and ripe fruit, while on the palate it features plushness and savoriness. It's a white that still charms. The same holds for their 2009 Taurasi Sel. Hamilton Ris., a wine redolent of plums and balsamic notes and delicate hints of coffee. The palate proves soft, tannins delicate.

| | |
|---|---|
| ○ Coda di Volpe C '17 | ♛♛ 2* |
| ○ Greco di Tufo G '17 | ♛♛ 3 |
| ● Taurasi Sel. Hamilton Ris. '09 | ♛♛ 7 |
| ○ Fiano di Avellino '17 | ♛ 3 |
| ○ Fiano di Avellino Alessandra '12 | ♛♛♛ 3* |
| ● Taurasi Ris. '06 | ♛♛♛ 5 |
| ○ Coda di Volpe C '16 | ♛♛ 2* |
| ○ Fiano di Avellino F '15 | ♛♛ 3* |
| ○ Fiano di Avellino Sel. Erminia Di Meo '03 | ♛♛ 6 |
| ○ Greco di Tufo G '07 | ♛♛ 3 |
| ○ Greco di Tufo Vittoria '07 | ♛♛ 4 |
| ● Taurasi Sel. Hamilton Ris. '08 | ♛♛ 7 |
| ● Taurasi V. Olmo Ris. '10 | ♛♛ 5 |

# Donnachiara

LOC. PIETRACUPA
VIA STAZIONE
83030 MONTEFALCIONE [AV]
TEL. +39 0825977135
www.donnachiara.com

CELLAR SALES
PRE-BOOKED VISITS
ACCOMMODATION
ANNUAL PRODUCTION 200,000 bottles
HECTARES UNDER VINE 27.00

We find young Ilaria at the helm of this well-established winery in the contentious Irpinia district of Montefalcione. After completing her degree in jurisprudence she now works at the historic producer full-time. Chiara Mazzoleni was a noblewoman who married surgeon Antonio Petitto. Upon joining her estate of Torre Le Nocelle in Irpinia with his property she began dedicating herself to viticulture. Today Ilaria, along with her parents Umberto and Chiara, makes wines of great stylistic precision and drinkability. They are helped by enologist Riccardo Cotarella. Their 2016 Aglianico is a solidly structured wine, juicy in its profile of dark fruit and forest undergrowth. It exhibits nice density, without losing its steadiness on the palate, nor its raciness. The cultivar's tannins are present, but never excessive, making for a tasty finish that's rich in spicy and earthy counterpoint. Their 2017 Fiano di Avellino and Greco di Tufo were affected by the difficult vintage, but they still manage to preserve nice supporting acidity, in spite of the warmer temperatures.

| | |
|---|---|
| ● Aglianico '16 | ♛♛♛ 3* |
| ○ Fiano di Avellino '17 | ♛ 3 |
| ○ Greco di Tufo '17 | ♛ 3 |
| ○ Greco di Tufo '16 | ♛♛♛ 3* |
| ○ Falanghina '15 | ♛♛ 2* |
| ○ Falanghina '14 | ♛♛ 2* |
| ○ Greco di Tufo '15 | ♛♛ 3 |
| ○ Greco di Tufo '14 | ♛♛ 2* |
| ○ Irpinia Coda di Volpe '15 | ♛♛ 3 |
| ○ Irpinia Coda di Volpe '14 | ♛♛ 2* |
| ● Taurasi Ris. '12 | ♛♛ 7 |

# I Favati

P.ZZA DI DONATO
83020 CESINALI [AV]
TEL. +39 0825666898
www.cantineifavati.it

**CELLAR SALES**
**PRE-BOOKED VISITS**
**ANNUAL PRODUCTION** 100,000 bottles
**HECTARES UNDER VINE** 21.00

Rosanna Petrozziello's vineyards are situated in the southernmost part of the Sabato river, in Cesinali, and grow in calcareous clay terrain at more than 450 meters above sea level. Rosanna is accompanied by her husband and brother who oversee every stage of production. They also avail themselves of the precious support of enologist Vincenzo Mercurio. Elegant wines with a strong territorial identity are proposed in a base-line and premium version (during the best vintages), like the Fiano Pietramara (from their vineyard in Altripalda) and Greco Terrantica (from Montefusco). Their Taurasi is cultivated in San Mango and Venticano. Their 2017 Fiano di Avellino Pietramara has a lovely mineral profile and a smoky weave. It's redolent of peach, apricot and toasty sensations, while on the palate a nice, savory texture gives way to an energetic finish. It brings home a well-deserved Tre Bicchieri. Their 2017 Greco di Tufo Terrantica is also at the top of its game, with its bouquet of hawthorn blossom and citrus. On the palate it exhibits nice freshness, with a vibrant, lengthy finish.

| | |
|---|---|
| ○ Fiano di Avellino Pietramara '17 | ♟♟♟ 3* |
| ○ Greco di Tufo Terrantica '17 | ♟♟ 2* |
| ● Irpinia Campi Taurasini Cretarossa '15 | ♟ 3 |
| ● Taurasi Terzo Tratto Ris. '12 | ♟ 5 |
| ○ Fiano di Avellino Pietramara '16 | ♟♟♟ 3* |
| ○ Fiano di Avellino Pietramara '15 | ♟♟♟ 3* |
| ○ Fiano di Avellino Pietramara '13 | ♟♟♟ 3* |
| ○ Fiano di Avellino Pietramara '12 | ♟♟♟ 3* |
| ○ Greco di Tufo Terrantica '16 | ♟♟ 2* |
| ● Taurasi Terzo Tratto Et. Bianca Ris. '10 | ♟♟ 7 |

# Benito Ferrara

FRAZ. SAN PAOLO, 14A
83010 TUFO [AV]
TEL. +39 0825998194
www.benitoferrara.it

**CELLAR SALES**
**PRE-BOOKED VISITS**
**ANNUAL PRODUCTION** 55,000 bottles
**HECTARES UNDER VINE** 13.00

Some of the appellation's best Greco di Tufos are produced in the district of San Paolo, in Tufo. It was Benito who founded Ferrara, and thanks to his perseverance both i the cellar and in the vineyard he managed to establish the reputation of one of the 1990s first cru, Vigna Cicogna. His daughter Gabriella continued his legacy, and today oversees some 15 hectares of vineyards cultivated in Tufo's trademark clay and sulphur-rich terrain. These give rise to a selection of mineral, aromatic wines. Their Aglianico is cultivated in Montemiletto, where the calcareous-clay terrain makes for full-bodied wines. Their Greco di Tufo Vigna Cicogna affirms its status as the undisputed house champion. It's a gold wine that's distinct for its glycerine force and its full, flavorful palate. It features a delicately salty and mineral palate that's contrasted by what seems to be increasingly pronounced sweetness in recent years. Their 2017 Terra d'Uva is another standout. It's a soft Greco di Tufo with flowery and fruity aromas.

| | |
|---|---|
| ○ Greco di Tufo V. Cicogna '17 | ♟♟ 4 |
| ○ Fiano d'Avellino Sequenza '17 | ♟♟ 4 |
| ○ Greco di Tufo Terra d'Uva '17 | ♟♟ 4 |
| ● Irpinia Aglianico Quattro Confini '16 | ♟ 3 |
| ○ Greco di Tufo V. Cicogna '15 | ♟♟♟ 4* |
| ○ Greco di Tufo V. Cicogna '14 | ♟♟♟ 4* |
| ○ Greco di Tufo V. Cicogna '13 | ♟♟♟ 5 |
| ○ Greco di Tufo V. Cicogna '12 | ♟♟♟ 4* |
| ○ Greco di Tufo V. Cicogna '10 | ♟♟♟ 4 |
| ○ Greco di Tufo V. Cicogna '09 | ♟♟♟ 4 |
| ○ Fiano d'Avellino Sequenza '15 | ♟♟ 4 |
| ○ Greco di Tufo Terra d'Uva '16 | ♟♟ 4 |
| ○ Greco di Tufo Terra d'Uva '15 | ♟♟ 4 |
| ○ Greco di Tufo V. Cicogna '16 | ♟♟ 4 |

# ★★Feudi di San Gregorio

LOC. CERZA GROSSA
83050 SORBO SERPICO [AV]
TEL. +39 0825986683
www.feudi.it

**CELLAR SALES**
**PRE-BOOKED VISITS**
**RESTAURANT SERVICE**
**ANNUAL PRODUCTION** 3,500,000 bottles
**HECTARES UNDER VINE** 250.00
**VITICULTURE METHOD** Certified Organic

Few wineries in Irpinia have the experience and foundation that Feudi di San Gregorio has. Founded in 1986, we can consider it one of southern Italy's emblems when it comes to wine production, with some three appellations represented (Fiano di Avellino, Greco di Tufo and Taurasi), all presented both in base-line versions and crus. At the head of this giant is their young president, Antonio Capaldo, who's managed to put forward territorial wines interpreted through a modern lens. Their Dubl line of sparkling wines and their restaurant, Marannà, with its specialized gastronomy, are examples of their novel approach. Their 2013 Taurasi Piano di Montevergine is an extremely well-made wine, fine in its spices, aromas of juniper and wild root. On the palate it proves smooth, balsamic and juicy, with a classy, lengthy finish. It brings home Tre Bicchieri. Their 2017 Fiano Pietracalda also put in an excellent performance thanks to a palate that's among the vintage's most savory and deep. It's also worth mentioning their Dubl + Brut, a fresh, creamy, flowery wine.

| | |
|---|---|
| ● Taurasi Piano di Montevergine Ris. '13 | ♛♛♛ 6 |
| ○ Fiano di Avellino Pietracalda '17 | ♛♛ 4 |
| ○ Campanaro '16 | ♛♛ 4 |
| ○ Dubl + Brut | ♛♛ 4 |
| ⊙ Dubl Brut Rosé | ♛♛ 5 |
| ○ Dubl Esse Dosaggio Zero | ♛♛ 5 |
| ○ Dubl Rosato Brut Dosaggio Zero | ♛♛ 4 |
| ○ Falanghina del Sannio Serrociclo '17 | ♛♛ 3 |
| ○ Greco di Tufo Cutizzi '17 | ♛♛ 4 |
| ● Irpinia Aglianico Serpico '16 | ♛♛ 6 |
| ⊙ Irpinia Rosato Visione '17 | ♛♛ 2* |
| ● Pàtrimo '15 | ♛♛ 8 |
| ● Taurasi '14 | ♛♛ 5 |
| ○ Falanghina del Sannio '17 | ♛ 3 |
| ○ Greco di Tufo '17 | ♛ 3 |
| ● Rubrato '16 | ♛ 2 |

# Fontanavecchia

VIA FONTANAVECCHIA, 7
82030 TORRECUSO [BN]
TEL. +39 0824876275
www.fontanavecchia.info

**CELLAR SALES**
**PRE-BOOKED VISITS**
**ACCOMMODATION AND RESTAURANT SERVICE**
**ANNUAL PRODUCTION** 175,000 bottles
**HECTARES UNDER VINE** 20.00

As president of the Sannio Wine Consortium and manager of his own winery since 1990, Libero Rillo is surely one of the best interpreters of the area's traditional wines. Libero and his brother Giuseppe inherited the producer from their father, Orazio, and began bottling their own wine (up until that point it had only been sold in bulk). Fontanavecchia's success is the result of selecting the best grapes in the vineyard and winemaking carried out with the support of enologist Angelo Pizzi, a Falanghina expert. Their diverse selection ranges from sparkling wines made with Fiano, Greco and Piedirosso, to various Falanghinas and Aglianicos. Libero Rillo knows ageworthy Falanghina well and this year it submitted a version that's quite interesting, to say the least. Their 2007 Sannio Falanghina Taburno has aged for some 11 years, affirming the cultivar's surprising longevity. It's redolent of wood resin and honey, but maintains an acidity and structure that renders it highly drinkable and complex. Their 2010 Vigna Cataratte and 2017 Falanghina are also both excellent.

| | |
|---|---|
| ○ Sannio Taburno Falanghina Libero '07 | ♛♛♛ 5 |
| ● Aglianico del Taburno V. Cataratte Ris. '10 | ♛♛ 5 |
| ○ Falanghina del Sannio Taburno '17 | ♛♛ 3* |
| ● Aglianico del Taburno '13 | ♛ 3 |
| ● Aglianico del Taburno Grave Mora Ris. '11 | ♛ 6 |
| ⊙ Aglianico del Taburno Rosato '17 | ♛ 3 |
| ○ Sannio Greco '17 | ♛ 3 |
| ● Sannio Rosso '17 | ♛ 3 |
| ○ Falanghina del Sannio Taburno '16 | ♛♛♛ 3* |
| ○ Falanghina del Sannio Taburno '15 | ♛♛♛ 2* |
| ○ Falanghina del Sannio Taburno '14 | ♛♛♛ 2* |
| ○ Falanghina del Sannio Taburno '13 | ♛♛♛ 2* |
| ○ Falanghina del Sannio Taburno '12 | ♛♛♛ 2* |

# Fonzone

LOC. SCORZAGALLINE
83052 PATERNOPOLI [AV]
TEL. +39 08271730100
www.fonzone.it

CELLAR SALES
PRE-BOOKED VISITS
ANNUAL PRODUCTION 57,000 bottles
HECTARES UNDER VINE 22.00
SUSTAINABLE WINERY

In the small municipality of Paternopoli the Fonzone Caccese family offers white and red wines from Irpinia's well-known appellations. The winery got its start in 2005 when Lorenzo decided to move into the estate, surrounded by fruit trees, olives and woods, and set up a truly vanguard winery. It was a choice that tied him deeply to the territory, thanks in part to an approach centered on environmental sustainability and a production philosophy aimed at nurturing biodiversity. Arturo Erbaggio serves as enological consultant, with seven wines produced overall: four whites and three reds, all expressions of a strong bond with tradition. This year their Greco di Tufo was the offering that most won us over. 2017 made for steady aromas of thyme and rosemary. On the palate it proves juicy and fragrant, refreshed by a citrusy profile, while the finish calls up Mediterranean herbs and iodine notes. Their 2017 Fiano is extremely taut and lively in its fragrances of grapefruit and white pepper. It's only a bit lacking in depth, which we find in their 2017 Sequoia, a long, savory, minty wine.

| Greco di Tufo '17 | ▼▼ 3* |
| Fiano di Avellino '17 | ▼▼ 3 |
| Irpinia Fiano Sequoia '17 | ▼▼ 5 |
| Irpinia Aglianico '15 | ● ▼ 4 |
| Irpinia Falanghina '17 | ▼ 5 |
| Taurasi Scorzagalline '11 | ● ♀♀♀ 3* |
| Fiano di Avellino '16 | ♀♀♀ 3* |
| Greco di Tufo '13 | ♀♀ 3 |
| Fiano di Avellino '14 | ♀♀ 3* |
| Greco di Tufo '16 | ♀♀ 3 |
| Greco di Tufo '14 | ♀♀ 3* |
| Irpinia Aglianico '14 | ● ♀♀ 3 |

# La Fortezza

LOC. TORA II, 20
82030 TORRECUSO [BN]
TEL. +39 0824886155
www.lafortezzasrl.it

CELLAR SALES
PRE-BOOKED VISITS
ANNUAL PRODUCTION 900,000 bottles
HECTARES UNDER VINE 65.00

For Enzo Rillo the challenge began in 2006 when he purchased some 30 hectares in Torrecuso, on the eastern side of the Taburno Camposauro Regional Park, and rented 20 more so as to complete his range of production. Enzo is a successful entrepreneur who's already established himself in construction, road safety and the services industry, and today he produces Falanghina, Aglianico, Greco and Fiano in two lines of wines. Their 'Classica' is a well-defined selection that's tied to tradition, while their Noi Beviamo Con la Testa features more approachable and highly drinkable wines. Their 2017 Falanghina del Sannio is a lovely and unique expression of the Taburno subzone. It offers up aromas of tropical trop and slightly mineral notes. On the palate it proves fresh and assertive, with hints of vanilla and aromatic herbs. Their 2014 Aglianico del Taburno is redolent of cherry, raspberry and red pepper, while in the mouth it proves fragrant and tasty, with a nice supporting acidity that steadies the palate.

| Falanghina del Sannio Taburno '17 | ▼▼ 2* |
| Aglianico del Taburno '14 | ▼▼ 3 |
| Sannio Fiano '17 | ▼▼ 2* |
| Sannio Greco '17 | ▼▼ 2* |
| Falanghina Brut Maleventum | ▼ 3 |
| Aglianico del Taburno '12 | ● ♀♀ 3 |
| Aglianico del Taburno Ris. '10 | ● ♀♀ 4 |
| Falanghina del Sannio Taburno '15 | ♀♀ 2* |
| Sannio Fiano '15 | ♀♀ 2* |
| Sannio Greco '16 | ♀♀ 2* |
| Sannio Greco '15 | ♀♀ 2* |

# ★Galardi

FRAZ. SAN CARLO
S.DA PROV.LE SESSA-MIGNANO
81037 SESSA AURUNCA [CE]
TEL. +39 08231440003
www.terradilavoro.com

**CELLAR SALES**
**PRE-BOOKED VISITS**
**ANNUAL PRODUCTION** 30,000 bottles
**HECTARES UNDER VINE** 10.00
**VITICULTURE METHOD** Certified Organic

A single wine produced in 1993 signaled the definitive brith of Galardi. Terra di Lavoro, a strong wine in its youth, in some ways austere, is a blend of Aglianico and Piedirosso cultivated in San Carlo di Sessa Aurunca in volcanic soil mixed with limestone and shale. Both vineyards and olive trees alternative along the slopes of the Roccamonfina volcano, whose terrain makes for wines of exceptional character. Credit for this bona fide wine 'cult' goes to Luisa Murena, Arturo Celentano, Francesco Catello and Dora Celentano, along with the support of enologist Riccardo Cotarella, who cultivate their grapes according to principles of organic agriculture. Their 2016 Terra di Lavoro just fell short of Tre Bicchieri. It's an almost opaque wine that initially proves timid on the nose, gradually offering up sensations of black truffle, myrtle, juniper, tobacco and blood-rich meat. On the palate it's energetic, potent. It finishes with a nice acidity that doesn't weight it down, proving that it's coherent and lively in its spicy hints.

| | | |
|---|---|---|
| ● Terra di Lavoro '16 | ▼▼ | 7 |
| ● Terra di Lavoro '13 | ♀♀♀ | 7 |
| ● Terra di Lavoro '11 | ♀♀♀ | 7 |
| ● Terra di Lavoro '10 | ♀♀♀ | 7 |
| ● Terra di Lavoro '09 | ♀♀♀ | 7 |
| ● Terra di Lavoro '08 | ♀♀♀ | 7 |
| ● Terra di Lavoro '07 | ♀♀♀ | 7 |
| ● Terra di Lavoro '06 | ♀♀♀ | 7 |
| ● Terra di Lavoro '05 | ♀♀♀ | 7 |
| ● Terra di Lavoro '04 | ♀♀♀ | 7 |
| ● Terra di Lavoro '03 | ♀♀♀ | 6 |
| ● Terra di Lavoro '02 | ♀♀♀ | 6 |
| ● Terra di Lavoro '99 | ♀♀♀ | 6 |

# La Guardiense

C.DA SANTA LUCIA, 104/106
82034 GUARDIA SANFRAMONDI [BN]
TEL. +39 0824864034
www.laguardiense.it

**CELLAR SALES**
**PRE-BOOKED VISITS**
**RESTAURANT SERVICE**
**ANNUAL PRODUCTION** 4,500,000 bottles
**HECTARES UNDER VINE** 1500.00

In 1960 La Guardiense was made up of 33 members. Thanks to their entrepreneurial instincts, they managed to grow their cooperative winery into one of southern Italy's most active. Today it boasts 1000 members who cover a total of 1500 hectares of terrain and constitute a production potential of some four million bottles per year. Falanghina, which is vinified in steel tanks, takes center stage for a number of wines, occupying 600 hectares of their vineyards. Enologist Riccardo Cotarella oversees winemaking and their various selections. His most recent effort calls for wines without added sulfites and made with low yields. Their 2017 Falanghina del Sannio Senete once again earns Tre Bicchieri, with its notes of citrus, chamomile and freshly-cut grass. In the mouth it calls back up citrus and features a nice, delicately salty pluck that proves it's anything but monotonous. Their 2017 Falanghina del Sannio Janare offers up aromas of tropical fruit, apple and citrus. It's a white that shouldn't be overlooked, thanks to its citrusy aromas and freshness.

| | | |
|---|---|---|
| ○ Falanghina del Sannio Janare Senete '17 | ▼▼▼ | 3* |
| ○ Falanghina del Sannio Janare '17 | ▼▼ | 2* |
| ● Sannio Guardia Sanframondi Aglianico Cantari Janare Ris. '14 | ▼▼ | 4 |
| ● Sannio Guardiolo Rosso Janare Ris. '15 | ▼▼ | 2 |
| ○ Falanghina del Sannio Janare '15 | ♀♀♀ | 2* |
| ○ Falanghina del Sannio Janare '14 | ♀♀♀ | 2* |
| ○ Falanghina del Sannio Janare '13 | ♀♀♀ | 2* |
| ○ Falanghina del Sannio Janare Senete '16 | ♀♀♀ | 2* |
| ○ Falanghina del Sannio Janare '16 | ♀♀ | 2* |
| ● Sannio Aglianico Cantari Le Janare Ris. '13 | ♀♀ | 3 |
| ● Sannio Aglianico Lucchero '15 | ♀♀ | 2* |

# Salvatore Martusciello

VIA SPINELLI, 4
80010 QUARTO [NA]
TEL. +39 0818766123
www.salvatoremartusciello.it

ANNUAL PRODUCTION 70,000 bottles
HECTARES UNDER VINE 2.00

Salvatore Martusciello is a bona fide expert of the Phlegraean Fields and Vesuvius. In 2015 his expertise brought him to start a new winery, along with is wife, Gilda. Since then he's been having success year after year. Having abandoned his family's winery, Grotta del Sole, he went out on his own and began overseeing every stage of production with painstaking care, producing wines with an extremely strong territorial identity. His wines represents the areas of cultivation, like his Settevulcani, made with Piedirosso and Falanghina, his Ottoue Lettere and Gragnano, and his sparkling Asprinio di Avera, Trentapioli. Their 2017 Peninsola Sorrentina Gragnano offers up close-focused sensations of cherry and raspberry. On the palate it surprises, proving taut and pervasive, but complex as well, with red fruit and almond emerging across a rustic, flavorful finish. Their 2017 Lettere Ottouve is a delicate, tasty wine whose aromatic profile features raspberry and violet.

| | |
|---|---|
| ● Penisola Sorrentina Gragnano Ottouve '17 | ♛♛ 3* |
| ● Penisola Sorrentina Lettere Ottouve '17 | ♛♛ 3 |
| ○ Asprinio d'Aversa Trentapioli Brut '17 | ♛ 3 |
| ● Campi Flegrei Piedirosso Settevulcani '17 | ♛ 3 |
| ● Campi Flegrei Piedirosso Settevulcani '15 | ♛♛ 3 |
| ● Penisola Sorrentina Lettere Ottouve '16 | ♛♛ 3 |
| ● Penisola Sorrentina Lettere Ottouve '15 | ♛♛ 3 |

# ★★Montevetrano

LOC. NIDO
FRAZ. CAMPIGLIANO
VIA MONTEVETRANO, 3
84099 SAN CIPRIANO PICENTINO [SA]
TEL. +39 089882285
www.montevetrano.it

CELLAR SALES
PRE-BOOKED VISITS
ACCOMMODATION
ANNUAL PRODUCTION 76,000 bottles
HECTARES UNDER VINE 5.00

Montevetrano's history began in the mid-1980s when Silvia Imparato decided to experiment with a small selection of wine cultivated on the family's property in the Colli Salernitani hills. She asked enologist Riccardo Cotarella for some advice, and he suggested international grape varieties, as well as a few rows of Aglianico. That's how her famous Montevetrano came to be, a blend of Aglianico, Cabernet Sauvignon and Merlot that regularly receives accolades in our guide. It's accompanied by other wines as well, Core (made with Aglianico) and Core Bianco (Fiano and Greco). Their Montevetrano once again proves to be undisputed leader of Silvia Imparato's selection, earning a place on the podium thanks to its great elegance and pleasantness. Their 2016 is redolent of black mulberry, blackcurrant, cherry and tobacco, with toasty, flavorful notes of dark chocolate. It's long and balanced on the palate, it has commendably well-fashioned, silky tannins, with a finish that features whiffs of balsamic.

| | |
|---|---|
| ● Montevetrano '16 | ♛♛♛ 8 |
| ○ Core Bianco '17 | ♛ 4 |
| ● Montevetrano '14 | ♛♛♛ 7 |
| ● Montevetrano '12 | ♛♛♛ 7 |
| ● Montevetrano '11 | ♛♛♛ 7 |
| ● Montevetrano '10 | ♛♛♛ 7 |
| ● Montevetrano '09 | ♛♛♛ 7 |
| ● Montevetrano '08 | ♛♛♛ 7 |
| ● Montevetrano '07 | ♛♛♛ 7 |
| ● Montevetrano '06 | ♛♛♛ 7 |
| ● Montevetrano '05 | ♛♛♛ 7 |
| ● Montevetrano '04 | ♛♛♛ 7 |
| ● Montevetrano '03 | ♛♛♛ 7 |
| ● Montevetrano '02 | ♛♛♛ 7 |

# Mustilli

VIA CAUDINA, 10
82019 SANT'AGATA DE' GOTI [BN]
TEL. +39 0823718142
www.mustilli.com

CELLAR SALES
PRE-BOOKED VISITS
ACCOMMODATION AND RESTAURANT SERVICE
ANNUAL PRODUCTION 150,000 bottles
HECTARES UNDER VINE 21.00

Leonardo Mustilli was for everyone the engineer of Falanghina, Benevento's pioneer of Italian wine. Leonardo died just last year, after dedicating much of his life to rediscovering Falanghina as a quality grape. It all started back in the 1970s, when he replanted his vineyards in the Sant'Agata dei Goti hills with native grape varieties. In 1979 came the first line of Falanghina wines to be vinified and bottled as a monovarietal. Today his daughters Paola and Anna Chiara are leading the winery, overseeing vineyard management and production along with the help of enologist Fortunate Sebastiano. For the second year straight their 2016 Sannio Sant'Agata dei Goti Piedirosso Artus earns Tre Bicchieri, proving to be the best Piedirosso in Sannio. It offers up intriguing aromas of wild berries, juniper and smoky notes. On the palate it proves intriguing, flavorful, with a savory, long finish that's calibrated perfectly. Their 2016 Falanghina del Sannio San'Agata dei Goti Vigna Segreta is redolent of mandarin orange and ginger.

| | |
|---|---|
| ● Sannio Sant'Agata dei Goti Piedirosso Artus '16 | ♖♖♖ 5 |
| ○ Falanghina del Sannio Sant'Agata dei Goti V. Segreta '16 | ♖♖ 5 |
| ○ Falanghina del Sannio Sant'Agata dei Goti '17 | ♖♖ 3 |
| ● Sannio Piedirosso '17 | ♖♖ 3 |
| ● Sannio Aglianico '16 | ♖ 3 |
| ● Sannio Sant'Agata dei Goti Aglianico Cesco di Nece '15 | ♖ 4 |
| ● Sannio Sant'Agata dei Goti Piedirosso Artus '15 | ♕♕♕ 4* |
| ○ Falanghina del Sannio Sant'Agata dei Goti '16 | ♕♕ 3 |
| ○ Falangina del Sannio Sant'Agata dei Goti V. Segreta '15 | ♕♕ 4 |

# Nanni Copè

VIA TUFO, 3
81041 VITULAZIO [CE]
TEL. +39 3487478459
www.nannicope.it

CELLAR SALES
PRE-BOOKED VISITS
ANNUAL PRODUCTION 7,500 bottles
HECTARES UNDER VINE 3.50
VITICULTURE METHOD Certified Organic
SUSTAINABLE WINERY

Giovanni Ascione possesses the true spirit of the vigneron. He oversees every stage of production and cultivates his land in Monticelli, making a blend of Pallagrello Nero, Aglianico and Casavecchia that pretty much sums up his personality. After working as a manager and a wine journalist, in 2007 he became a producer himself, purchasing just over two hectares of vineyards and harvesting the grapes used for his Sabbie di Sopra il Bosco. As of this year the red will be accompanied by a new wine made with Fiano, Asprinio and Pallagrello Bianco whose name refers to its vineyard of origin, Vigna Scarrupata. Once again, his crown jewel brings home top marks. The 2016 starts dark, on earthy notes, then pepper and licorice emerge. In the mouth it exhibits notable density of fruit and energetic but well-integrated tannins, making for a steady palate and a charming finish of Asian spices. His 2016 Scarrupata features savory, sulphureous strokes alternating with sensations of apple and citrus peel. It finishes deliciously on notes of oregano.

| | |
|---|---|
| ● Sabbie di Sopra il Bosco '16 | ♖♖♖ 6 |
| ○ Polveri della Scarrupata '16 | ♖♖ 6 |
| ● Sabbie di Sopra il Bosco '15 | ♕♕♕ 5 |
| ● Sabbie di Sopra il Bosco '14 | ♕♕♕ 5 |
| ● Sabbie di Sopra il Bosco '12 | ♕♕♕ 5 |
| ● Sabbie di Sopra il Bosco '11 | ♕♕♕ 5 |
| ● Sabbie di Sopra il Bosco '10 | ♕♕♕ 5 |
| ● Sabbie di Sopra il Bosco '09 | ♕♕♕ 5 |
| ● Sabbie di Sopra il Bosco '13 | ♕♕ 5 |
| ● Sabbie di Sopra il Bosco '08 | ♕♕ 5 |

## Perillo

C.DA VALLE, 19
83040 CASTELFRANCI [AV]
TEL. +39 082772252
cantinaperillo@libero.it

**CELLAR SALES**
**PRE-BOOKED VISITS**
**ANNUAL PRODUCTION** 20,000 bottles
**HECTARES UNDER VINE** 5.00

When it comes to highly concentrated, energetic Taurasi with a strong tannic force, Perillo is a benchmark. Grapes for the wine are cultivated in a unique subzone, the highest of the appellation. It's here on Castelfranci's calcareous and tufaceous soil that Michele Perillo and his wife manage five hectares of vineyards, some of which go back more than 100 years, having been planted by Michele's grandfather (who died in WW I). Carmine Valentino has been their tried and trusted winemaker since the beginning. Michele Perillo submitted a version of their Aglianico with a 2008 Taurasi Riserva, a wine whose impact on the palate is notable, but still less than what we would have expected from such a good year. On the nose aromas of morello cherry, chestnut and tanned leather emerge in rapid succession, for a vibrant, toasty profile but one that's lacking in focus when it comes to oak. On the palate it features tannic presence, ripe and generous fruit supported by notable savoriness. It finishes long on sensations of coffee.

| | | |
|---|---|---|
| ● Taurasi Ris. '08 | 🍷🍷 | 6 |
| ● Taurasi '07 | 🍷🍷🍷 | 6 |
| ● Taurasi '05 | 🍷🍷🍷 | 4 |
| ● Taurasi Ris. '06 | 🍷🍷🍷 | 6 |
| ● Irpinia Campi Taurasini '07 | 🍷🍷 | 4 |
| ● Irpinia Campi Taurasini '06 | 🍷🍷 | 4 |
| ○ Irpinia Coda di Volpe '12 | 🍷🍷 | 3 |
| ○ Irpinia Coda di Volpe '09 | 🍷🍷 | 3 |
| ● Taurasi '08 | 🍷🍷 | 6 |
| ● Taurasi '06 | 🍷🍷 | 4 |
| ● Taurasi '04 | 🍷🍷 | 4* |
| ● Taurasi Ris. '07 | 🍷🍷 | 6 |
| ● Taurasi Ris. '05 | 🍷🍷 | 5 |
| ● Taurasi Ris. '04 | 🍷🍷 | 5 |

## Ciro Picariello

VIA MARRONI, 18A
83010 SUMMONTE [AV]
TEL. +39 082533848
www.ciropicariello.it

**PRE-BOOKED VISITS**
**ANNUAL PRODUCTION** 55,000 bottles
**HECTARES UNDER VINE** 15.00
**SUSTAINABLE WINERY**

Ciro Picariello embodies Fiano di Avellino, stylish and expressive, dignified and coherent. Supported by his wife and children, he cultivates the sandy clay soil (which features a high percentage of sandstone). Yields are extremely low and low-impact winemaking allows the winery to call itself 'natural'. The areas of production comprise Summonte and Montefredane, situated at 650 and 500 meters respectively. These give rise to wines like the Fiano base and Ciro 906, which rests for a year or longer in the bottle before going to market. Their 2017 Fiano di Avellino di Ciro Picariello is tight on the nose, with nuances of Mediterranean herbs and mint. On the palate acidity and savoriness prove tenacious, with a close-focused finish, even if it's lacking in the depth that other years have exhibited. Indeed, its overall thrust is about half of what we're used to from the producer, thus it's a faithful expression of the year. And 2017 left a notable mark on the linear development of their Fiano di Avellino, making for wines that are already a bit more mature and ready to drink.

| | | |
|---|---|---|
| ○ Fiano di Avellino '17 | 🍷🍷 | 4 |
| ○ Fiano di Avellino '14 | 🍷🍷🍷 | 4* |
| ○ Fiano di Avellino '10 | 🍷🍷🍷 | 3* |
| ○ Fiano di Avellino '08 | 🍷🍷🍷 | 3* |
| ○ Fiano di Avellino '15 | 🍷🍷 | 4 |
| ○ Fiano di Avellino '11 | 🍷🍷 | 3* |
| ○ Fiano di Avellino '09 | 🍷🍷 | 3 |
| ○ Fiano di Avellino '07 | 🍷🍷 | 3* |
| ○ Fiano di Avellino '06 | 🍷🍷 | 3* |
| ○ Fiano di Avellino '05 | 🍷🍷 | 3* |
| ○ Fiano di Avellino Ciro 906 '12 | 🍷🍷 | 4 |

# La Pietra di Tommasone

VIA PROV.LE FANGO, 98
80076 LACCO AMENO [NA]
TEL. +39 0813330330
www.tommasonevini.it

CELLAR SALES
PRE-BOOKED VISITS
ANNUAL PRODUCTION 100,000 bottles
HECTARES UNDER VINE 11.00

Antonio Monti's estate features volcanic terrain as well as favorable climatic conditions, all of which give rise to full grapes and whites that taste of the sea. The winery's history is interwoven with Antonio's family history. After the death of his father (who cultivated grapes here in fertile Pithecusa), Antonio came home from Germany, and revived the family's viticultural tradition along with his daughter Lucia, who serves as enologist. Both the reds and whites submitted proved to be excellent, thus confirming the quality of their selection. And this year they earned their first Tre Bicchieri. Their 2017 Ischia Biancolella proves sunny in its Mediterranean, citrusy aromas. On the palate it's succulent and taut, supported by a nice acidic tension. The finish comes through graceful and long in its mineral complexity. Their 2017 Ischia Biancolella Tenuta dei Preti offers up balsamic whiffs and notes of wild mint. In the mouth it opts for greater glycerine support, finishing on a delicately salty note.

| | |
|---|---|
| ○ Ischia Biancolella '17 | ♔♔♔ 2* |
| ○ Ischia Biancolella Tenuta dei Preti '17 | ♔♔ 4 |
| ○ Epomeo Bianco '17 | ♔♔ 3 |
| ● Epomeo Rosso '14 | ♔♔ 3 |
| ○ Ischia Bianco Terradei '17 | ♔♔ 2* |
| ● Ischia Per' 'e Palummo '17 | ♔♔ 3 |
| ● Ischia Per'e Palummo Tenuta Monte Zunta '16 | ♔♔ 5 |
| ⊙ Epomeo Rosato Rosamonti '17 | ♔ 2 |
| ○ Ischia Biancolella '16 | ♕♕ 2* |
| ○ Ischia Biancolella V. dei Preti '16 | ♕♕ 4 |
| ○ Pithecusa Bianco '16 | ♕♕ 3 |
| ⊙ Rosamonti '16 | ♕♕ 2* |

# ★Pietracupa

C.DA VADIAPERTI, 17
83030 MONTEFREDANE [AV]
TEL. +39 0825607418
pietracupa@email.it

CELLAR SALES
PRE-BOOKED VISITS
ANNUAL PRODUCTION 50,000 bottles
HECTARES UNDER VINE 7.50

Sabino Loffredo is one of Irpinia's homegrown geniuses, a mix of talent and instinct. His distinctive whites are mineral, multi-faceted, and exhibit strong acidity as well as a capacity to age in the bottle for extremely lengthy periods. Among his selection are Fiano di Avellino and Greco di Tufo, two of the region's most important appellations, which Sabino manages to navigate with a fluidity that is at times disconcerting. But for years Sabino has established himself as the producer of one of the south's best reds as well, the Taurasi, a wine made possible thanks to two hectares in Torre delle Nocelle purchased in 2008. Their 2013 Taurasi is exquisite. Its ripe nose couples with a palate of extraordinary depth of flavor, a fine, precise texture and a long, vibrant finish. Their 2017 Greco di Tufo is the best we tasted for the year, a solid, complete wine, enticing and rich, already lively and vivacious. As always, their Fiano is slower to open up, but it has everything it needs to become a great wine.

| | |
|---|---|
| ○ Greco di Tufo '17 | ♔♔♔ 3* |
| ○ Fiano di Avellino '17 | ♔♔ 3* |
| ● Taurasi '13 | ♔♔ 5 |
| ○ Cupo '10 | ♕♕♕ 5 |
| ○ Cupo '08 | ♕♕♕ 5 |
| ○ Fiano di Avellino '13 | ♕♕♕ 3* |
| ○ Fiano di Avellino '12 | ♕♕♕ 3* |
| ○ Greco di Tufo '16 | ♕♕♕ 3* |
| ○ Greco di Tufo '15 | ♕♕♕ 3* |
| ○ Greco di Tufo '14 | ♕♕♕ 3* |
| ○ Greco di Tufo '10 | ♕♕♕ 3* |
| ○ Greco di Tufo '09 | ♕♕♕ 3* |
| ○ Greco di Tufo '08 | ♕♕♕ 3* |
| ● Taurasi '10 | ♕♕♕ 5 |

# Fattoria La Rivolta

C.DA CONTRADA RIVOLTA
82030 TORRECUSO [BN]
TEL. +39 0824872921
www.fattorialarivolta.com

CELLAR SALES
PRE-BOOKED VISITS
ACCOMMODATION
ANNUAL PRODUCTION 180,000 bottles
HECTARES UNDER VINE 29.00
VITICULTURE METHOD Certified Organic

The Cotroneo family winery is situated in Torrecuso, a small village in Benevento situated at the foot of the Taburno ridge. Here everyone in the family contributes to the organic cultivation of their 29 hectares of vineyards, which host Benevento's traditional grape varieties. The winery features the latest technology, as well as a large space dedicated to aging. Their selection is comprised of 11 wines, all labeled with the producer's trademark design. In addition to their fresh, forthright wines, they offer excellent Riservas like their Terre di Rivolta and Sogno di Rivolta, the former made with the Aglianico, the latter a blend of Falanghina, Fiano and Greco. This year they submitted a vast range of wines. Their 2017 Falanghina del Sannio Taburno features sensations of tropical fruit, pineapple, papaya, along with flowery aromas and a mineral touch. Their 2016 Simbiosi is a brilliant version that landed in our finals. It opens on sensations of fruit, black cherry and plums, only to close on notes of Asian spices. Its tannins are bold, with a pleasantly smoky finish.

| | | |
|---|---|---|
| ○ Falanghina del Sannio Taburno '17 | ♛♛ | 2* |
| ● Simbiosi '16 | ♛♛ | 5 |
| ● Aglianico del Taburno Terre di Rivolta Ris. '15 | ♛♛ | 5 |
| ● Sannio Taburno Piedirosso '17 | ♛♛ | 3 |
| ● Aglianico del Taburno '16 | ♛ | 3 |
| ○ Sannio Taburno Fiano '17 | ♛ | 3 |
| ○ Sogno di Rivolta '16 | ♛ | 4 |
| ● Aglianico del Taburno '10 | ♛♛♛ | 3* |
| ● Aglianico del Taburno Terre di Rivolta Ris. '08 | ♛♛♛ | 5 |
| ○ Falanghina del Sannio Taburno '16 | ♛♛♛ | 2* |
| ● Aglianico del Taburno '15 | ♛♛ | 3 |
| ● Sannio Taburno Piedirosso '16 | ♛♛ | 3 |
| ● Simbiosi '15 | ♛♛ | 5 |

# Rocca del Principe

VIA ARIANIELLO, 9
83030 LAPIO [AV]
TEL. +39 08251728013
www.roccadelprincipe.it

CELLAR SALES
PRE-BOOKED VISITS
ANNUAL PRODUCTION 30,000 bottles
HECTARES UNDER VINE 6.50

When you talk about Fiano di Avellino, you immediately think of Lapio, the homeland of this extremely ageworthy white. Since 2004, husband and wife Ercole Zarella and Aurelia Fabrizio have been here, making wines using grapes cultivated atop Arianiello hill, the highest in the area. Its volcanic, pumice-rich soil, and rather cool temperatures, which slightly delay the harvest, make for fresh, expressive, mineral wines. We also point out their Final di Avellino Tognano, made with grapes from a choice plot and their Taurasi Materdomini. Their 2016 opens up slowly, with notes of ginger and apple. In the mouth it proves creamy, well-calibrated, with a subtle but lengthy crescendo. Their 2015 Tognano is even deeper, with sophisticated smoky notes. It's a deep and juicy wine that brings together meatiness and sunniness in a fine, embellished structure. Its finish enchants, both in terms of mouthfeel and aromas.

| | | |
|---|---|---|
| ○ Fiano di Avellino Tognano '15 | ♛♛♛ | 5 |
| ○ Fiano di Avellino '16 | ♛♛ | 4 |
| ○ Fiano di Avellino '14 | ♛♛♛ | 3* |
| ○ Fiano di Avellino '13 | ♛♛♛ | 3* |
| ○ Fiano di Avellino '12 | ♛♛♛ | 3* |
| ○ Fiano di Avellino '10 | ♛♛♛ | 3* |
| ○ Fiano di Avellino '08 | ♛♛♛ | 2* |
| ○ Fiano di Avellino '07 | ♛♛♛ | 2* |
| ○ Fiano di Avellino '15 | ♛♛ | 3* |
| ○ Fiano di Avellino '11 | ♛♛ | 3* |
| ○ Fiano di Avellino Tognano '14 | ♛♛ | 3* |
| ● Irpinia Aglianico '11 | ♛♛ | 3* |
| ● Taurasi Mater Domini '09 | ♛♛ | 5 |
| ● Taurasi Ris. '10 | ♛♛ | 5 |

# Ettore Sammarco

VIA CIVITA, 9
84010 RAVELLO [SA]
TEL. +39 089872774
www.ettoresammarco.it

CELLAR SALES
PRE-BOOKED VISITS
ANNUAL PRODUCTION 66,000 bottles
HECTARES UNDER VINE 13.00

Visionary Ettore Sammarco was 26 when with just a few liras in his pocket, and plenty of ambition and courage, he began his heroic enology adventure in the splendid medieval village of Ravello. It was 1962, and up until then he'd had no experience and little interesting in wine-growing. Their terraced vineyards are harvested by hand along narrow paths situated between the sea and the Monti Lattari Apennines. Their wines, which are made exclusively with native cultivar, are a living representation of a singular territory. All the wines in their selection are excellent, affirming the producer's overall high stylistic quality. The best example is surely their splendid 2017 Costa d'Amalfi Ravello Bianco Selva delle Monache, a wine with a truly elegant Mediterranean character. It's a coastal wine, both on the nose and in the mouth, with clear hints of wild fennel, citrus and herbs. On the palate it's dense and persistent. Their Vigna Grotta Piana is similar, more vibrant though. It has less acidity but exhibits just as much territorial coherence.

| | |
|---|---|
| ○ Costa d'Amalfi Ravello Bianco Selva delle Monache '17 | ♟♟♟ 3* |
| ○ Costa d'Amalfi Ravello Bianco V. Grotta Piana '17 | ♟♟ 5 |
| ● Costa d'Amalfi Ravello Rosso Selva delle Monache Ris. '14 | ♟♟ 5 |
| ○ Costa d'Amalfi Terre Sarecene Bianco '17 | ♟♟ 3 |
| ● Costa d'Amalfi Terre Sarecene Rosso '16 | ♟♟ 3 |
| ⊙ Costa d'Amalfi Rosato Terre Saracene '17 | ♟ 3 |
| ○ Costa d'Amalfi Ravello Bianco V. Grotta Piana '15 | ♟♟♟ 4* |

# Tenuta San Francesco

FRAZ. CORSANO
VIA SOFILCIANO, 18
84010 TRAMONTI [SA]
TEL. +39 089876748
www.vinitenutasanfrancesco.com

CELLAR SALES
PRE-BOOKED VISITS
ACCOMMODATION
ANNUAL PRODUCTION 40,000 bottles
HECTARES UNDER VINE 10.00

Tenuta San Francesco was founded in 2004 thanks to the union of three families, Bove, D'Avino and Giordano. Their terraced vineyards are situated in Tramonti, along the Amalfi Coast, along steep slopes at elevations ranging from 300 to 700 meters above sea level. These host primarily ungrafted native grape varieties cultivated using the ancient pergola system. In short, the vineyards are truly picturesque and, in some cases, historic (their Tintore, for example, are more than 100 years old). And they thrive in a singular climate characterized by the sea breeze and a volcanic, sandy-clay subsoil. Their 2016 Costa d'Amalfi Tramonti Bianco Per Eva features a Mediterranean vein with aromas of acacia flowers, citrus and iodine. In the mouth it's taut, highly savory, for a lean, direct palate. Their 2014 È Iss, a monovarietal Tintore, demonstrates great character with its austere impact and its notes of tobacco, coffee and blackberries. Their 2015 Quattro Spine Riserva, a blend of Tintore, Piedirosso and Aglianico, closes on a long balsamic stroke.

| | |
|---|---|
| ○ Costa d'Amalfi Tramonti Bianco Per Eva '16 | ♟♟ 4 |
| ○ Costa d'Amalfi Tramonti Bianco '17 | ♟♟ 2* |
| ● Costa d'Amalfi Tramonti Rosso Quattrospine Ris. '15 | ♟♟ 5 |
| ● E' Iss '14 | ♟♟ 5 |
| ⊙ Costa d'Amalfi Rosato '17 | ♟ 2 |
| ● Costa d'Amalfi Tramonti Rosso '15 | ♟ 3 |
| ○ Costa d'Amalfi Bianco Per Eva '13 | ♟♟♟ 4* |
| ○ Costa d'Amalfi Tramonti Bianco Per Eva '15 | ♟♟ 4 |
| ● Costa d'Amalfi Tramonti Rosso '14 | ♟♟ 3 |
| ● E' Iss '13 | ♟♟ 5 |

# San Giovanni

C.DA TRESINO
84048 CASTELLABATE [SA]
TEL. +39 0974965136
www.agricolasangiovanni.it

CELLAR SALES
PRE-BOOKED VISITS
ACCOMMODATION
ANNUAL PRODUCTION 20,000 bottles
HECTARES UNDER VINE 4.00

Mario and Ida Corrado's vineyards overlook a shining sea, and when you drink their wines you can taste it. Punta Tresino is one of the Tyrrhenian coast's most beautiful areas, situated in the Cilento Natural Park. After reviving the vineyards and farm manor here, in 1993 Mario and Ida adopted a low-impact approach and began building a small house-winery. Their four hectares of vineyards are primarily dedicated to Fiano, Aglianico and Piedirosso. Paestum, Tresinus and Aureus make up their line of whites. Castellabate, Maroccia and Ficonera compose their line of reds. Their 2017 Tresinus, made with select Fiano grapes, stands out for its fresh notes of grapefruit and its mineral accents. On the palate it proves pervasive, with a savory counter-thrust and a structure that lends persistence. Their 2017 Paestum, a blend of Fiano, Trebbiano and Greco, is captivating on the nose by virtue of its nuances of Mediterranean herbs. On the palate it features great cleanness and pronounced acidity, accompanied by an almost marine savoriness.

| | |
|---|---|
| ○ Paestum '17 | ♟♟ 3 |
| ○ Tresinus '17 | ♟♟ 4 |
| ● Castellabate '15 | ♟ 3 |
| ○ Fiano Tresinus '12 | ♟♟♟ 3* |
| ○ Paestum '15 | ♟♟♟ 2* |
| ○ Aureus '15 | ♟♟ 5 |
| ○ Fiano Tresinus '15 | ♟♟ 3 |
| ○ Fiano Tresinus '14 | ♟♟ 3 |
| ● Ficonera '14 | ♟♟ 5 |
| ○ Paestum '16 | ♟♟ 3* |
| ○ Paestum Bianco '14 | ♟♟ 2* |
| ○ Tresinus '16 | ♟♟ 4 |

# San Salvatore 1988

VIA DIONISIO
84050 GIUNGANO [SA]
TEL. +39 08281990900
www.sansalvatore1988.it

CELLAR SALES
ACCOMMODATION AND RESTAURANT SERVICE
ANNUAL PRODUCTION 160,000 bottles
HECTARES UNDER VINE 23.00
VITICULTURE METHOD Certified Biodynamic
SUSTAINABLE WINERY

Giuseppe Pagano's headquarters are situated on the hills facing Paestum, Stio and Giungano in the Cilento Natural Park. His 16-hectare estate is known in Italy and abroad for its complete and varied line of products. Indeed, Giuseppe offers vegetables, oil and even raises buffalos. And it's all done while following a biodynamic, low-impact approach. Their vineyards host the region's traditional grapes and give rise to two principal lines: Pian di Stio and Gillo Dorfles. Their 2017 Calpazio, made with Greco, offers up vibrant fragrances of peach and aromatic herbs. In the mouth mineral whiffs emerge, making for a fresh and savory finish. Their lively 2017 Pian di Stio, a monovarietal Fiano, features pronounced notes of green tea, jasmine and citrus. On the palate it's flavorful, with a savory streak that opens across an almost spicy finish. Their 2016 Elea, a wine of greater structure, features notes of mandarin orange and almond, while on the palate it's coherent in its softness and freshness.

| | |
|---|---|
| ○ Pian di Stio '17 | ♟♟♟ 4* |
| ○ Calpazio Greco '17 | ♟♟ 3* |
| ○ Elea '16 | ♟♟ 3 |
| ● Jungano '16 | ♟♟ 3 |
| ○ Palinuro '17 | ♟♟ 2* |
| ○ Trentenare '17 | ♟♟ 3 |
| ○ Falanghina '17 | ♟ 3 |
| ● Vetere '17 | ♟ 3 |
| ○ Pian di Stio '14 | ♟♟♟ 4* |
| ○ Pian di Stio '13 | ♟♟♟ 4* |
| ○ Pian di Stio '12 | ♟♟♟ 3* |
| ○ Trentenare '16 | ♟♟♟ 3* |
| ○ Trentenare '15 | ♟♟♟ 3* |

# Sanpaolo
# di Claudio Quarta Vignaiolo

LOC. TORRIONI - FRAZ. C.DA SAN PAOLO
VIA AUFIERI, 25
83010 TORRIONI [AV]
TEL. +39 0832704398
www.claudioquarta.it

CELLAR SALES
PRE-BOOKED VISITS
ACCOMMODATION
ANNUAL PRODUCTION 115,000 bottles
HECTARES UNDER VINE 22.00

Claudio Quarta and his daughter Alessandra are among southern Italy's viticultural leaders. Tireless in presenting new research projects and experimentations, both look after their private vineyards in Puglia and Irpinia. The winery, whose name comes from the district (San Paolo, Torrioni) situated in the heart of the Greco di Tufo appellation, offers a complete selection of Irpinia and Benevento wines. Fiano di Avellino is represented in their Lapio and Montefredane cru, Greco di Tufo in their Montefusco cru, and they offer four Falanghina del Beneventanos as well. Doubtlessly their Greco di Tufo Claudio Quarta is their flagship wine. Once again it's presented in a magnum, as is their want for the first year. It opens with an array of fruity aromas, from yellow notes of peach to damson plums, then almond and delectable nuances of white pepper. On the palate it demonstrates balance and softness, though it's slightly lacking in persistence and freshness.

| | |
|---|---|
| ○ Greco di Tufo '17 | ♟♟ 3 |
| ○ Greco di Tufo Claudio Quarta '17 | ♟♟ 6 |
| ○ Suavemente '17 | ♟♟ 3 |
| ○ Jacarando Blanc de Blancs Brut | ♟ 3 |
| ◐ Jacarando Rosè Extra Brut | ♟ 3 |
| ○ Greco di Tufo Claudio Quarta '13 | ♟♟♟ 6 |
| ○ Greco di Tufo Claudio Quarta '12 | ♟♟♟ 6 |
| ○ Falanghina '16 | ♟♟ 2* |
| ○ Falanghina '15 | ♟♟ 2* |
| ○ Fiano di Avellino '15 | ♟♟ 2* |
| ○ Greco di Tufo Claudio Quarta '16 | ♟♟ 6 |
| ○ Greco di Tufo Claudio Quarta '15 | ♟♟ 6 |

# Tenuta Sarno 1860

C.DA SERRONI, 4B
83100 AVELLINO
TEL. +39 082526161
www.tenutasarno1860.it

ANNUAL PRODUCTION 15,000 bottles
HECTARES UNDER VINE 6.00

Maura Sarno is Candida's lady of Fiano di Avellino. She inherited her family's terrain, about three hectares, and decided to cultivate Fiano only, make a bet that would prove to be a good one. Here in the area's calcareous clay soil decorated with white stones, Maura has managed to produce supple, dynamic, expressive and original wines, thanks in part to the support of qualified enological consultants and the use of steel tanks. Her selection continues to grow and for two years now it has included a sparkling Fiano. Their surprising and original Fiano di Avellino lands in our finals. Maura's is among the best versions of 2017, with its aromas of citron and peach. On the palate it's creamy, with notable supporting acidity (considering the year's climate) making for a lively and vital persistence across notes of lime and yellow flowers. The finish has grace and lengthy flavor.

| | |
|---|---|
| ○ Fiano di Avellino '17 | ♟♟ 4 |
| ○ Sarno 1860 Pas Dosé '16 | ♟ 4 |
| ○ Fiano di Avellino '15 | ♟♟♟ 4* |
| ○ Fiano di Avellino '16 | ♟♟ 4 |
| ○ Fiano di Avellino '14 | ♟♟ 3* |
| ○ Fiano di Avellino '13 | ♟♟ 3* |
| ○ Fiano di Avellino '12 | ♟♟ 3* |
| ○ Fiano di Avellino '11 | ♟♟ 3 |
| ○ Fiano di Avellino '10 | ♟♟ 3* |
| ○ Sarno 1860 Pas Dosé '15 | ♟♟ 4 |

# Lorenzo Nifo Sarrapochiello

VIA PIANA, 62
82030 PONTE [BN]
TEL. +39 0824876450
www.nifo.eu

CELLAR SALES
PRE-BOOKED VISITS
ANNUAL PRODUCTION 90,000 bottles
HECTARES UNDER VINE 18.00
VITICULTURE METHOD Certified Organic

On the slopes of Monte Pèntime, in the village of Ponte, we find Lorenzo Nifo Sarrapocchiello, an organic producer that makes both wine and oil. Like all of Benevento's wineries, their selection focuses on Falanghina and Aglianico, which are cultivated in marl, calcareous clay soil and made into wine according to tradition. These are singular wines with a strong territorial identity. Falanghina, especially, is expressed in a precise style with rich extraction and complexity. Fiano, Piedirosso and Greco are all also cultivated organically. Among Lorenzo's selection, his 2017 Falanghina del Sannio Taburno stood out. It features hints of tropical fruit, pineapple, notes of broom and herbaceous whiffs on the nose, while on the palate it demonstrates a nice, fresh and savory weave. Their Aglianico del Taburno d'Erasmo offers up aromas of ripe fruit, blueberries and cherries. Their 2012 has structures and well-integrated tannins, finishing on sensations of cloves. Their 2014 Aglianico del Taburno, a wine redolent of violet, blueberries and black pepper, is less potent, but ready for drinking.

| | |
|---|---|
| ● Aglianico del Taburno '14 | ♛♛ 2* |
| ● Aglianico del Taburno D'Erasmo Ris. '12 | ♛♛ 5 |
| ○ Falanghina del Sannio Taburno '17 | ♛♛ 2* |
| ○ Sannio Fiano '17 | ♛ 2 |
| ● Aglianico del Taburno '13 | ♛♛ 2* |
| ● Aglianico del Taburno D'Erasmo Ris. '11 | ♛♛ 5 |
| ○ Falanghina del Sannio Taburno '16 | ♛♛ 2* |
| ○ Sannio Fiano '15 | ♛♛ 2* |
| ● Sannio Taburno Aglianico '12 | ♛♛ 2* |
| ● Sannio Taburno Rosso '15 | ♛♛ 2* |

# Sclavia

LOC. MARIANELLO
VIA CASE SPARSE
81040 LIBERI [CE]
TEL. +39 3357406773
www.sclavia.com

CELLAR SALES
PRE-BOOKED VISITS
ANNUAL PRODUCTION 50,000 bottles
HECTARES UNDER VINE 13.00
VITICULTURE METHOD Certified Organic
SUSTAINABLE WINERY

Andrea Granito is an osteopath. Lucia Ferrara is an art historian. Together they make wines with grapes grown exclusively on their 14 hectares of private vineyards. Their approach brings together a focus on the area's traditional grape varieties and certified organic cultivation. Sclavia was founded in 2003 when Andrea bought some terrain in Liberi and began planting native cultivar like Pallagrello and Casavecchia. Here in Marianello, a district situated on the Monti Trebulani, they're finally enjoying new interest and energy. And today Andrea is accompanied by Anna Delia della Porta, enologist and winemaker. Sclavia confirm their top quality with their Calù, a wine made with Pallagrello Bianco. On the nose it's delicate, with hints of annurca apples, delicately salty touches and citron. In the mouth freshness emerges, for a pleasant, flavorful palate. Their 2015 Granito, a monovarietal Casavecchia, offers up ripe notes of licorice and preserves. On the palate it's marked by sweetness, energy and persistence.

| | |
|---|---|
| ○ Calù Pallagrello Bianco '17 | ♛♛ 3* |
| ● Granito Casavecchia '15 | ♛♛ 3 |
| ○ Calù '16 | ♛♛ 3* |
| ○ Calù '15 | ♛♛ 3* |
| ○ Don Ferdinando '15 | ♛♛ 5 |
| ● Granito '12 | ♛♛ 3 |
| ● Liberi '14 | ♛♛ 5 |
| ● Liberi '12 | ♛♛ 5 |
| ○ Pallarè '15 | ♛♛ 5 |

## La Sibilla

FRAZ. BAIA
VIA OTTAVIANO AUGUSTO, 19
80070 BACOLI [NA]
TEL. +39 0818688778
www.sibillavini.com

CELLAR SALES
PRE-BOOKED VISITS
ANNUAL PRODUCTION 70,000 bottles
HECTARES UNDER VINE 9.50

La Sibilla has been making wines in the Phlegraean Fields for more than a century, near to an old Roman villa that was declared a natural oasis by WWF. It's a strip of land situated between the sea, an explosion of Mediterranean scrubland, and volcanic promontories. Here their vineyards are still ungrafted, and grow in sandy clay soil. Vincenzo Di Meo has been overseeing the estate and, in addition to their spectacular Falanghina and Piedirosso (in some cases more than 100 years old), he's added a number of smaller vineyards of native cultivar like 'A Livella, 'A Surcella' and 'A Marsigliese. His goal? Develop a territory with real and infinite potential. This year their 2017 Falanghina most impressed. Notes of tropical fruit, citrus and yellow flowers unfold on the nose. In the mouth it proves energetic, fresh, savory, as volcanic as the territory where its grapes are cultivated. Their Campi Flegrei Falanghina Cruna deLago is a fluent, pure wine with aromas of mandarin oranges and chamomile. On the palate it finishes with a nice coastal savoriness.

| | |
|---|---|
| ○ Campi Flegrei Falanghina '17 | ♟♟ 3* |
| ○ Campi Flegrei Falanghina Cruna deLago '16 | ♟♟ 5 |
| ● Campi Flegrei Piedirosso '17 | ♟ 4 |
| ○ Campi Flegrei Falanghina '13 | ♟♟♟ 2* |
| ○ Campi Flegrei Falanghina Cruna deLago '15 | ♟♟♟ 4* |
| ○ Campi Flegrei Falanghina '16 | ♟♟ 3 |
| ○ Campi Flegrei Falanghina '15 | ♟♟ 2* |
| ○ Campi Flegrei Falanghina '14 | ♟♟ 3 |
| ○ Campi Flegrei Falanghina Cruna deLago '14 | ♟♟ 4 |
| ● Campi Flegrei Piedirosso '16 | ♟♟ 4 |
| ● Campi Flegrei Piedirosso '15 | ♟♟ 3 |

## Luigi Tecce

C.DA TRINITÀ, 6
83052 PATERNOPOLI [AV]
TEL. +39 3492957565
ltecce@libero.it

PRE-BOOKED VISITS
ANNUAL PRODUCTION 10,000 bottles
HECTARES UNDER VINE 5.00

Since the 1990s, Luigi Tecce has been living in perfect harmony with his vineyards on the hills of Paternopoli and Castelfranci. His Aglianico is cultivated in plots that go back to 1930. These offer up authentic, powerful and buoyant wines that change from vintage to vintage. In short, they're wines of great personality, vinified in amphora, mid-sized casks or chestnut vats. Harvest is carried out by hand and their approach to cultivation is minimally invasive. That's how their Taurasi Poliphemo and Irpinia Campi Taurasi Satyricon, both Aglianicos come to exist. It's always a delight to let yourself be carried away by Luigi's selection, wines of marked character. His 2013 Taurasi Puro Sangue, for example, yields aromas that are by our standards rather complex in their evolution. But on the palate it takes on a new dimension, proving spirited, untamed, all pluck and determination, with notes of black olives, blood oranges and black pepper. His 2015 Satyricon has a delectable savory vein that stimulates the appetite and makes you want to light the grill.

| | |
|---|---|
| ● Irpinia Campi Taurasini Satyricon '15 | ♟♟ 4 |
| ● Taurasi Puro Sangue '13 | ♟ 6 |
| ● Taurasi Poliphemo '08 | ♟♟♟ 6 |
| ● Taurasi Poliphemo '07 | ♟♟♟ 6 |
| ● Irpinia Campi Taurasini Satyricon '14 | ♟♟ 4 |
| ● Irpinia Campi Taurasini Satyricon '13 | ♟♟ 4 |
| ● Irpinia Campi Taurasini Satyricon '12 | ♟♟ 5 |
| ● Irpinia Campi Taurasini Satyricon '10 | ♟♟ 5 |
| ● Taurasi Poliphemo '13 | ♟♟ 6 |
| ● Taurasi Poliphemo '12 | ♟♟ 6 |
| ● Taurasi Poliphemo '11 | ♟♟ 6 |
| ● Taurasi Poliphemo '10 | ♟♟ 6 |
| ● Taurasi Poliphemo '09 | ♟♟ 7 |

# Tenuta del Meriggio

C.DA SERRA 79781A
83038 MONTEMILETTO [AV]
TEL. +39 0825962282
www.tenutadelmeriggio.it

CELLAR SALES
PRE-BOOKED VISITS
ANNUAL PRODUCTION 65,000 bottles
HECTARES UNDER VINE 20.00
SUSTAINABLE WINERY

Bruno Pizza has 20 hectares of vineyards in Irpinia, in the prestigious appellations of Fiano di Avellino, Greco di Tufo and Taurasi. The name Meriggio (from the Italian 'pomeriggio', meaning 'afternoon') calls up the sunniest and hottest hours of a summer day, when all the townspeople turn in for a pleasant siesta. Founded in 2010, our latest round of tastings demonstrated they can stand shoulder-to-shoulder with some of the area's more established wineries, and they have the added merit of being entirely eco-friendly. Their vineyards (all private, some of which are quite old) are managed by Carmine Valentino and give rise to wines of great structure and drinkability. This is the first time that Tenuta del Meriggio is in our guide and it immediately delivers, thanks to their 2017 Fiano di Avellino, a full-bodied and juicy wine. It offers up musky sensations, almost balsamic, then mandarin orange and bay leaf. On the palate it features a lively freshness and minerality. Their 2017 Greco di Tufo is redolent of tropical fruit, with nuances of white flowers. In the mouth it's soft, fresh and fragrant.

| | |
|---|---|
| ○ Fiano di Avellino '17 | ♟♟♟ 3* |
| ○ Greco di Tufo '17 | ♟♟ 3 |
| ● Irpinia Aglianico '15 | ♟ 3 |
| ● Taurasi '11 | ♟ 5 |

# Terre Stregate

LOC. SANTA LUCIA
VIA MUNICIPIO, 105
82034 GUARDIA SANFRAMONDI [BN]
TEL. +39 0824817857
www.terrestregate.it

CELLAR SALES
PRE-BOOKED VISITS
ANNUAL PRODUCTION 130,000 bottles
HECTARES UNDER VINE 22.00
SUSTAINABLE WINERY

The winery owned by Filomena Iacobucci and her brother Carlo is a model producer. In a short time they've managed to bring their Falanghina, which serves as the basis of four of their wines, to international levels. The estate was founded in 1988 by their father, Armando, who's still working hard in the cellar. Today their vineyards, which are situated around the municipality of Guardia Sanframondi in Benevento, give rise to whites of great freshness and rich, concentrated reds centered on the appellation's primary grape, Aglianico. Their selection also includes Fiano and Greco. Their 2017 Falanghina del Sannio Svelato is fresher and more savory than last year, and once again it brings home top marks. Flowery notes, citron and aromatic herbs take center stage, with nuances of oregano and mineral hints. Every taste yields force, tension and clear fragrances of citrus, making for a palate that manages to be both lean and persistent. Their 2016 Manent, a highly drinkable wine made with Aglianico, features an array of fruity aromas, blackcurrant and pomegranate.

| | |
|---|---|
| ○ Falanghina del Sannio Svelato '17 | ♟♟♟ 2* |
| ● Sannio Aglianico Manent '16 | ♟♟ 2* |
| ○ Sannio Fiano Genius Loci '17 | ♟♟ 3 |
| ● Costa del Duca '14 | ♟ 6 |
| ○ Sannio Greco Aurora '17 | ♟ 3 |
| ○ Falanghina del Sannio Svelato '16 | ♟♟♟ 2* |
| ○ Falanghina del Sannio Svelato '15 | ♟♟♟ 2* |
| ○ Falanghina del Sannio Svelato '14 | ♟♟♟ 2* |
| ○ Falanghina del Sannio Svelato '13 | ♟♟♟ 2* |
| ○ Falanghina Caracara '15 | ♟♟ 6 |
| ○ Falanghina Trama '15 | ♟♟ 2* |
| ● Sannio Aglianico Manent '15 | ♟♟ 2* |
| ● Sannio Aglianico Manent '14 | ♟♟ 2* |

# Terredora Di Paolo

VIA SERRA
83030 MONTEFUSCO [AV]
TEL. +39 0825968215
www.terredora.com

**CELLAR SALES**
**PRE-BOOKED VISITS**
**ACCOMMODATION**
**ANNUAL PRODUCTION** 700,000 bottles
**HECTARES UNDER VINE** 180.00

Terredora's 200 hectares of vineyards make it one of the largest estates in Irpinia. It's a brand that found success thanks in part to the management style of Walter Mastroberardino, who with great vision managed to establish their plots in some of the territory's most important appellations. And so it is that their Greco di Tufo is cultivated in Serra di Montefusco and Santa Paolina, while Lapio gives rise to their Fiano, Aglianico and CampoRe crus, and Pietradefusi hosts their Taurasi. Today Walter is accompanied by Daniela and Paolo. Their vast and highly varied selection ranges from Falangina, Greco di Tufo, Fiano di Avellino, Taurasi and Lacryma Christi del Vesuvio. Their 2011 Taurasi Pago dei Fusi is made with grapes cultivated along the left bank of the Calore river. It tantalizes with its spicy sensations and nuances of blackcurrant. Their extremely fresh 2017 Greco di Tufo Loggia della Serra, a gold-colored wine, features lovely savoriness and minerality.

| | |
|---|---|
| ○ Fiano di Avellino '17 | ♟♟ 5 |
| ○ Greco di Tufo Loggia della Serra '17 | ♟♟ 3 |
| ● Taurasi Pago dei Fusi '11 | ♟♟ 5 |
| ○ Greco di Tufo Terre degli Angeli '17 | ♟ 3 |
| ○ Irpinia Falanghina Corte di Giso '17 | ♟ 3 |
| ● Irpinia Aglianico Il Principio '13 | ♟ 4 |
| ○ Irpinia Coda di Volpe Le Starse '17 | ♟ 3 |
| ○ Lacryma Christi del Vesuvio Bianco '17 | ♟ 3 |
| ● Taurasi Fatica Contadina '08 | ♟♟♟ 5 |
| ○ Fiano di Avellino '16 | ♟♟ 3 |
| ○ Fiano di Avellino Terredora Di Paolo '15 | ♟♟ 3 |
| ○ Greco di Tufo Loggia della Serra '15 | ♟♟ 3 |
| ● Taurasi Pago dei Fusi '10 | ♟♟ 5 |

# Torre a Oriente

LOC. MERCURI I, 19
82030 TORRECUSO [BN]
TEL. +39 0824874376
www.torreaoriente.eu

**CELLAR SALES**
**PRE-BOOKED VISITS**
**ACCOMMODATION AND RESTAURANT SERVICE**
**ANNUAL PRODUCTION** 40,000 bottles
**HECTARES UNDER VINE** 10.00
**SUSTAINABLE WINERY**

Patrizia Iannucci and Giorgio Gentilcore are the patrons of Torrecuso, a producer that, in addition to wine, makes fruit preserves and oil from Ortice olives. Their 10 hectares of vineyards are cultivated organically, with carefully monitored yields and a minimally invasive approach in the vineyards, so as not to alter the final product. The results can be experience in a selection whose production volumes are decidedly small but that's consistent in terms of quality. Biancuzita, a Falanghina, is their crown jewel. It's a late-harvest wine that's put on the market some years after vintage. This year Torre Oriente submitted a new offering, their Falanghina del Sannio 20+1+1, a wine that demonstrates how versatile the cultivar is, as well as its ability to offer up pleasant surprises even after some years. It's multifaceted on the nose, with aromas of white flowers, peach and honey. On the palate it surprises for freshness and savoriness. Their 2016 Falanghina del Sannio Biancuzita is a forthright and fragrant wine. A bouquet of grapefruit and damson plums are enriched on the palate by its mineral profile.

| | |
|---|---|
| ○ Falanghina del Sannio Biancuzita '16 | ♟♟ 3* |
| ○ Falanghina del Sannio 20+1+1 '11 | ♟♟ 4 |
| ● Aglianico del Taburno Don Curzetto Ris. '08 | ♟ 5 |
| ● Sannio Aglianico Janico '14 | ♟ 2 |
| ○ Falanghina del Sannio Biancuzita '14 | ♟♟♟ 3* |
| ○ Falanghina del Sannio Biancuzita '12 | ♟♟♟ 3* |
| ○ Falanghina del Sannio Biancuzita '15 | ♟♟ 3* |
| ○ Falanghina del Sannio Biancuzita '11 | ♟♟ 2* |
| ○ Falanghina del Sannio Taburno Siriana '16 | ♟♟ 2* |
| ○ Falanghina del Sannio Taburno Siriana '14 | ♟♟ 2* |
| ○ Gioconda '13 | ♟♟ 2* |
| ● Sannio Aglianico Janico '10 | ♟♟ 2* |

# Traerte

C.DA VADIAPERTI
83030 MONTEFREDANE [AV]
TEL. +39 0825607270
info@traerte.it

**CELLAR SALES**
**PRE-BOOKED VISITS**
**ANNUAL PRODUCTION** 81,000 bottles
**HECTARES UNDER VINE** 6.00

Wine is made in the vineyard! This is Raffaele Troisi's mantra. A figure born into the wine industry, after the death of his father, Antonio (who was among the first of Montefredane's growers to go out on his own), he continues to develop and promote the varietal typicity of his grapes and Irpinia's wines. And that's why his work focuses on Coda di Volpe and, in particular, Torama, a cultivar that's no longer seen as a blending grape but one that's capable of giving rise to energetic wines with vibrant acidity. Aiperti and Tornante are, respectively, Fiano di Avellino and Greco di Tufo, wines to be enjoyed a few years after vintage. Raffaele Troisi continues to give us truly interesting whites, whites that start out difficult to understand but end up surprising. Their 2017 Greco di Tufo Tornante is a prime example, with its hints of elderflower and aniseed, and its musky nuances. On the palate it has savory texture, as well as evolving, delicately milky sensations. We continue to enjoy their 2017 Coda di Volpe, which Raffaele began making way back in 1993. Its varietal nose exhibits typicity, while the palate proves weighty.

| | | |
|---|---|---|
| ○ Greco di Tufo Tornante '17 | ♟♟ 5 | |
| ○ Irpinia Coda di Volpe '17 | ♟♟ 2* | |
| ○ Fiano di Avellino Aiperti '17 | ♟♟ 5 | |
| ○ Greco di Tufo '17 | ♟♟ 3 | |
| ○ Irpinia Coda di Volpe Torama '17 | ♟♟ 5 | |
| ○ Fiano di Avellino '17 | ♟ 3 | |
| ○ Fiano di Avellino Aiperti '16 | ♟♟ 5 | |
| ○ Fiano di Avellino Aiperti '15 | ♟♟ 5 | |
| ○ Greco di Tufo Tornante '15 | ♟♟ 5 | |
| ○ Irpinia Coda di Volpe '15 | ♟♟ 2* | |
| ○ Irpinia Coda di Volpe Torama '16 | ♟♟ 5 | |
| ○ Irpinia Coda di Volpe Torama '15 | ♟♟ 5 | |
| ○ Irpinia Coda di Volpe Torama '14 | ♟♟ 5 | |

# Villa Diamante

VIA TOPPOLE, 16
83030 MONTEFREDANE [AV]
TEL. +39 3476791469
villadiamante1996@gmail.com

**CELLAR SALES**
**PRE-BOOKED VISITS**
**ANNUAL PRODUCTION** 10,000 bottles
**HECTARES UNDER VINE** 4.50

Villa Diamante is a small winery that's managed to carve out an important place for itself in Fiano di Avellino. Here in Montefredane, one of the area's great crus, Antoine Gaeta once produced his celebrated Vigna della Congregazione. Today his exceptional work is being carried forward by his wife, Diamante Renna, and enologist Vincenzo Mercurio. Each year they put forward some of the country's most vibrant whites: Vigna della Congregazione is a determined, extremely ageworthy win, while their Clos d'Haut, a ripe and sunny, smoky wine, is made with grapes cultivated in upper Montefredane. This year their 2017 Fiano di Avellino Vigna della Congregazione proves less dynamic than in the past, but undoubtedly charming. It's still their crown jewel with its nuances of wood resin, pine needles, candied citron and the delicate smoky notes that emerge at the end. It's a wine with a serious, steady palate. Their 2008 Taurasi Libero Pensiero is a juicy, deep, pervasive wine, among the best versions yet.

| | | |
|---|---|---|
| ○ Fiano di Avellino V. della Congregazione '17 | ♟♟ 5 | |
| ○ Fiano d'Avellino Clos d'Haut '17 | ♟♟ 5 | |
| ● Taurasi Libero Pensiero Ris. '08 | ♟♟ 6 | |
| ○ Fiano di Avellino Clos d'Haut '13 | ♟♟♟ 5 | |
| ○ Fiano di Avellino V. della Congregazione '16 | ♟♟♟ 5 | |
| ○ Fiano di Avellino V. della Congregazione '15 | ♟♟♟ 5 | |
| ○ Fiano di Avellino V. della Congregazione '10 | ♟♟♟ 5 | |
| ○ Fiano di Avellino V. della Congregazione '08 | ♟♟♟ 4 | |

# ★Villa Matilde

S.DA ST.LE DOMITIANA, 18
81030 CELLOLE [CE]
TEL. +39 0823932088
www.villamatilde.it

**CELLAR SALES**
**PRE-BOOKED VISITS**
**ACCOMMODATION AND RESTAURANT SERVICE**
**ANNUAL PRODUCTION** 700,000 bottles
**HECTARES UNDER VINE** 130.00
**SUSTAINABLE WINERY**

Salvatore and Maria Avallone bring great skill to the work of overseeing their winery, at one time managed by their father, Francesco, a fan of the history of Roman winemaking and a firm believer in Falerno's viticultural potential. Today Salvatore and Maria continue to cultivate their vineyards, situated on terrain that's unique for its stony, volcanic character. Together with enologist Riccardo Cotarella they produce a wide and complete range of wines, with their Falerno del Massico Vigna Camarato serving as their crown jewel. It's accompanied by wines such as their Tenuta Rocca dei Leoni nel Sannio and their Tenute di Altavilla in Irpinia. This year our tastings demonstrated that Villa Matilde is a leader in the appellation of Falerno del Massico. Their historic 2015 Falerno del Massico Vigna Caracci features balsamic vigor, a Mediterranean character and sulphureous fragrances. Its caressing palate is rendered pleasant by a delicately salty pluck. Their other Irpinia, their 2017 Fiano di Avellino Tenute di Altavilla, also proves to be in good form. It's a wine that expresses elegant mineral notes and flowery nuances.

| | | |
|---|---|---|
| ○ Falerno del Massico Bianco V. Caracci '15 | ♟♟ 5 | |
| ● Cecubo '14 | ♟♟ 5 | |
| ○ Falanghina Rocca dei Leoni '17 | ♟♟ 2* | |
| ○ Falerno del Massico Bianco '17 | ♟ 3 | |
| ○ Fiano di Avellino Tenute di Altavilla '17 | ♟♟ 3 | |
| ○ Greco di Tufo Tenute di Altavilla '17 | ♟ 3 | |
| ● Stregamora Piedirosso '17 | ♟ 2 | |
| ○ Falerno del Massico Bianco V. Caracci '08 | ♟♟♟ 3 | |
| ○ Falerno del Massico Bianco V. Caracci '05 | ♟♟♟ 3 | |
| ○ Falerno del Massico Bianco V. Caracci '04 | ♟♟♟ 3* | |
| ● Falerno del Massico Camarato '05 | ♟♟♟ 6 | |
| ● Falerno del Massico Camarato '04 | ♟♟♟ 5 | |

# Villa Raiano

VIA BOSCO SATRANO, 1
83020 SAN MICHELE DI SERINO [AV]
TEL. +39 0825595663
www.villaraiano.com

**CELLAR SALES**
**PRE-BOOKED VISITS**
**RESTAURANT SERVICE**
**ANNUAL PRODUCTION** 300,000 bottles
**HECTARES UNDER VINE** 22.00
**VITICULTURE METHOD** Certified Organic

Sabino and Simone Basso, along with their children Fabrizio, Federico and Brunella, oversee 23 hectares of organically cultivated vineyards in Raiano, a district in Serino. The winery was founded in 1996 in an area whose unique landscape features chestnut groves, vineyards and the nearby Sabato river. Their selection focuses on Irpinia's three appellations: Fiano di Avellino, Greco di Tufo and Taurasi, and is comprised of two lines: Classica and Vigne. Winemaking is overseen by enologist Fortunato Sebastiano. Their 2016 Fiano di Avellino Ventidue features a stylistic temperament that's worthy of Tre Bicchieri. It's made with grapes from their Lapio vineyards, situated at 450 meters above sea level. On the nose it offers up elegant, flowery nuances, fragrances of fruit, mineral hints and a slightly smoky note. On the palate it proves racy, savory and fresh, pleasant and persistent. Their 2016 Luminoso il Fiano di Avellino Alimata, made with grapes from Montefredane, features impressions of citron and almond. In the mouth it's generous and creamy, with a steadily unfolding finish.

| | | |
|---|---|---|
| ○ Fiano di Avellino Ventidue '16 | ♟♟♟ 4* | |
| ○ Fiano di Avellino Alimata '16 | ♟♟ 4 | |
| ○ Fiano di Avellino '17 | ♟♟ 3 | |
| ○ Greco di Tufo '17 | ♟♟ 3 | |
| ● Irpinia Campi Taurasini Costa Baiano '15 | ♟♟ 3 | |
| ○ Fiano di Avellino 22 '13 | ♟♟♟ 4* | |
| ○ Fiano di Avellino Alimata '15 | ♟♟♟ 4* | |
| ○ Fiano di Avellino Alimata '10 | ♟♟♟ 4 | |
| ○ Fiano di Avellino '16 | ♟♟ 3 | |
| ○ Fiano di Avellino Ventidue '15 | ♟♟ 4 | |
| ○ Greco di Tufo '16 | ♟♟ 4 | |
| ○ Greco di Tufo Contrada Marotta '15 | ♟♟ 4 | |
| ● Irpinia Campi Taurasini '13 | ♟♟ 3 | |

## Aia delle Monache

S.DA PROV.LE 327 KM 1,700
81010 CASTEL CAMPAGNANO [CE]
TEL. +39 3339843706
www.aiadellemonache.it

CELLAR SALES
ANNUAL PRODUCTION 15,000 bottles
HECTARES UNDER VINE 3.00
SUSTAINABLE WINERY

| | | |
|---|---|---|
| ○ L'Oca Guardiana che Dorme Beata '17 | ♟♟ | 3 |
| ● Il Gallo di Fretta Canta all'Alba Lontana '16 | ♟ | 4 |

## Amarano

C.DA TORRE, 32
83040 MONTEMARANO [AV]
TEL. +39 082763351
www.amarano.it

CELLAR SALES
PRE-BOOKED VISITS
ANNUAL PRODUCTION 20,000 bottles
HECTARES UNDER VINE 7.00

| | | |
|---|---|---|
| ● Taurasi Principe Lagonessa '13 | ♟♟ | 5 |
| ● Irpinia Campi Taurasini Malambruno '14 | ♟♟ | 3 |

## Antica Hirpinia

C.DA LENZE, 10
83030 TAURASI [AV]
TEL. +39 082774730
www.annodomini1590.it

CELLAR SALES
PRE-BOOKED VISITS
RESTAURANT SERVICE
ANNUAL PRODUCTION 600,000 bottles
HECTARES UNDER VINE 200.00

| | | |
|---|---|---|
| ● Taurasi '11 | ♟♟ | 5 |
| ○ Fiano di Avellino '17 | ♟ | 3 |
| ○ Greco di Tufo '17 | ♟ | 3 |

## Antico Castello

C.DA POPPANO, 11BIS
83050 SAN MANGO SUL CALORE [AV]
TEL. +39 3408062830
www.anticocastello.com

CELLAR SALES
PRE-BOOKED VISITS
ACCOMMODATION AND RESTAURANT SERVICE
ANNUAL PRODUCTION 50,000 bottles
HECTARES UNDER VINE 10.00
SUSTAINABLE WINERY

| | | |
|---|---|---|
| ● Irpinia Aglianico Magis '14 | ♟♟ | 3 |
| ○ Irpinia Greco Ermes '17 | ♟♟ | 2* |
| ○ Irpinia Falanghina Demetra '17 | ♟ | 2 |
| ○ Irpinia Fiano Orfeo '17 | ♟ | 2 |

## Giuseppe Apicella

FRAZ. CAPITIGNANO
VIA CASTELLO SANTA MARIA, 1
84010 TRAMONTI [SA]
TEL. +39 089876075
www.giuseppeapicella.it

CELLAR SALES
PRE-BOOKED VISITS
ANNUAL PRODUCTION 60,000 bottles
HECTARES UNDER VINE 7.00
VITICULTURE METHOD Certified Organic

| | | |
|---|---|---|
| ○ Costa d'Amalfi Tramonti Bianco '17 | ♟♟ | 3 |
| ● Piedirosso '17 | ♟♟ | 2* |
| ⊙ Costa d'Amalfi Tramonti Rosato '17 | ♟ | 3 |

## Cantine Barone

VIA GIARDINO, 2
84070 RUTINO [SA]
TEL. +39 0974830463
www.cantinebarone.it

CELLAR SALES
PRE-BOOKED VISITS
ACCOMMODATION
ANNUAL PRODUCTION 100,000 bottles
HECTARES UNDER VINE 12.00
VITICULTURE METHOD Certified Organic

| | | |
|---|---|---|
| ○ Marsia Bianco '17 | ♟♟ | 1* |
| ○ Cilento Fiano Vignolella '17 | ♟ | 3 |

## Boccella

ɪᴀ Sᴀɴᴛ'Eᴜsᴛᴀᴄʜɪᴏ
83040 Cᴀsᴛᴇʟғʀᴀɴᴄɪ [AV]
Tᴇʟ. +39 082772574
www.boccellavini.it

CELLAR SALES
PRE-BOOKED VISITS
ANNUAL PRODUCTION 10,000 bottles
HECTARES UNDER VINE 5.00
VITICULTURE METHOD Certified Organic

| | | |
|---|---|---|
| ● Irpinia Campi Taurasini Rasott '15 | ♟♟ | 3 |
| ○ Casefatte Fiano '16 | ♟ | 2 |

## Cantina del Barone

ᴠɪᴀ Nᴏᴄᴇʟʟᴇᴛᴏ, 21
83020 Cᴇsɪɴᴀʟɪ [AV]
Tᴇʟ. +39 0825666751
www.cantinadelbarone.it

CELLAR SALES
PRE-BOOKED VISITS
ANNUAL PRODUCTION 30,000 bottles
HECTARES UNDER VINE 2.50

| | | |
|---|---|---|
| ○ Particella 928 '17 | ♟♟ | 3* |

## Casa Di Baal

ʟᴏᴄ. Mᴀᴄᴄʜɪᴀ
ᴠɪᴀ Tɪᴢɪᴀɴᴏ, 14
84096 Mᴏɴᴛᴇᴄᴏʀᴠɪɴᴏ Rᴏᴠᴇʟʟᴀ [SA]
Tᴇʟ. +39 089981143
www.casadibaal.it

CELLAR SALES
PRE-BOOKED VISITS
ANNUAL PRODUCTION 25,000 bottles
HECTARES UNDER VINE 5.00
VITICULTURE METHOD Certified Organic
SUSTAINABLE WINERY

| | | |
|---|---|---|
| ○ Fiano di Baal '16 | ♟♟ | 3* |
| ○ Bianco di Baal '17 | ♟♟ | 2* |
| ● Rosso di Baal '16 | ♟ | 2 |

## Borgodangelo

s.ᴅᴀ ᴘʀᴏᴠ.ʟᴇ 52 ᴋᴍ 10
83050 Sᴀɴᴛ'Aɴɢᴇʟᴏ ᴀʟʟ'Esᴄᴀ [AV]
Tᴇʟ. +39 082773027
www.borgodangelo.it

CELLAR SALES
PRE-BOOKED VISITS
RESTAURANT SERVICE
ANNUAL PRODUCTION 30,000 bottles
HECTARES UNDER VINE 8.50
SUSTAINABLE WINERY

| | | |
|---|---|---|
| ○ Fiano di Avellino '17 | ♟♟ | 2* |
| ● Irpinia Campi Taurasini '13 | ♟♟ | 3 |
| ⊙ Irpinia Rosato '17 | ♟♟ | 2* |
| ● Taurasi '12 | ♟♟ | 4 |

## I Capitani

ᴠɪᴀ Bᴏsᴄᴏ Fᴀɪᴀɴᴏ, 14
83030 Tᴏʀʀᴇ ʟᴇ Nᴏᴄᴇʟʟᴇ [AV]
Tᴇʟ. +39 0825969182
www.icapitani.com

CELLAR SALES
PRE-BOOKED VISITS
ACCOMMODATION AND RESTAURANT SERVICE
ANNUAL PRODUCTION 100,000 bottles
HECTARES UNDER VINE 15.00

| | | |
|---|---|---|
| ● Irpinia Campi Taurasini Jumara '15 | ♟♟ | 3 |
| ● Taurasi Bosco Faiano '13 | ♟♟ | 5 |
| ○ Fiano di Avellino Gaudium '17 | ♟ | 3 |
| ○ Greco di Tufo Serum '17 | ♟ | 3 |

## Case d'Alto

ᴠɪᴀ Pᴀɢᴀɴɪɴɪ, 8
83035 Gʀᴏᴛᴛᴀᴍɪɴᴀʀᴅᴀ [AV]
Tᴇʟ. +39 3397000779
www.casedalto.it

CELLAR SALES
ANNUAL PRODUCTION 10,000 bottles
HECTARES UNDER VINE 6.00
VITICULTURE METHOD Certified Organic

| | | |
|---|---|---|
| ● Taurasi '12 | ♟♟ | 5 |

## Tenute Casoli

VIA ROMA, 28
83040 CANDIDA [AV]
TEL. +39 3402958099
www.tenutecasoli.it

CELLAR SALES
PRE-BOOKED VISITS
ACCOMMODATION AND RESTAURANT SERVICE
ANNUAL PRODUCTION 65,000 bottles
HECTARES UNDER VINE 13.00

| | |
|---|---|
| ○ Fiano di Avellino Kryos '17 | ♥♥ 3 |
| ● Irpinia Aglianico Kataros '17 | ♥ 3 |

## Castelle

S.DA NAZIONALE SANNITICA, 48
82037 CASTELVENERE [BN]
TEL. +39 0824940232
www.castelle.it

ANNUAL PRODUCTION 50,000 bottles
HECTARES UNDER VINE 4.00

| | |
|---|---|
| ○ Falanghina del Sannio '17 | ♥♥ 2* |
| ○ Falanghina del Sannio Kidonia V. T. '16 | ♥♥ 3 |
| ● Sannio Barbera '17 | ♥♥ 2* |

## Cenatiempo Vini d'Ischia

VIA BALDASSARRE COSSA, 84
80077 ISCHIA [NA]
TEL. +39 081981107
www.vinicenatiempo.it

CELLAR SALES
PRE-BOOKED VISITS
ANNUAL PRODUCTION 70,000 bottles
HECTARES UNDER VINE 4.00

| | |
|---|---|
| ○ Ischia Forastera '17 | ♥♥ 4 |
| ○ Ischia Biancolella '17 | ♥ 3 |
| ○ Ischia Biancolella Kalimera '17 | ♥ 4 |

## Michele Contrada

C.DA TAVERNA, 31
83040 CANDIDA [AV]
TEL. +39 0825988434
www.vinicontrada.it

CELLAR SALES
PRE-BOOKED VISITS
ANNUAL PRODUCTION 60,000 bottles
HECTARES UNDER VINE 10.00

| | |
|---|---|
| ○ Fiano di Avellino '17 | ♥♥ 3 |
| ○ Greco di Tufo '17 | ♥♥ 3 |
| ○ Falanghina del Sannio '17 | ♥ 2 |
| ○ Irpinia Coda di Volpe '17 | ♥ 2 |

## Contrada Salandra

FRAZ. COSTE DI CUMA
VIA TRE PICCIONI, 40
80078 POZZUOLI [NA]
TEL. +39 0815265258
in allestimento

CELLAR SALES
PRE-BOOKED VISITS
ANNUAL PRODUCTION 20,000 bottles
HECTARES UNDER VINE 4.70

| | |
|---|---|
| ○ Campi Flegrei Falanghina '16 | ♥♥ 3 |
| ● Campi Flegrei Piedirosso '15 | ♥♥ 3 |

## Cuomo - I Vini del Cavaliere

VIA FEUDO LA PILA, 16
84047 CAPACCIO PAESTUM [SA]
TEL. +39 0828725376
www.vinicuomo.com

CELLAR SALES
PRE-BOOKED VISITS
RESTAURANT SERVICE
ANNUAL PRODUCTION 25,000 bottles
HECTARES UNDER VINE 4.00

| | |
|---|---|
| ● Cilento Aglianico Granatum '16 | ♥♥ 3 |
| ○ Cilento Fiano Heraion '17 | ♥♥ 3 |
| ○ Leukos '17 | ♥♥ 3 |

## Terre D'Aione

FRAZ. SAN PAOLO
83010 TORRIONI [AV]
TEL. +39 0825998353
www.terredaione.it

CELLAR SALES
PRE-BOOKED VISITS
ANNUAL PRODUCTION 75,000 bottles
HECTARES UNDER VINE 9.00

| | |
|---|---|
| ○ Greco di Tufo '17 | 🍷🍷 3 |
| ● Aglianico '15 | 🍷 2 |

## D'Antiche Terre

C.DA LO PIANO
83030 MANOCALZATI [AV]
TEL. +39 0825675358
www.danticheterre.it

CELLAR SALES
PRE-BOOKED VISITS
ACCOMMODATION AND RESTAURANT SERVICE
ANNUAL PRODUCTION 420,000 bottles
HECTARES UNDER VINE 40.00
SUSTAINABLE WINERY

| | |
|---|---|
| ○ Greco di Tufo '17 | 🍷🍷 3 |
| ○ Fiano di Avellino '17 | 🍷 3 |

## Viticoltori De Conciliis

LOC. QUERCE, 1
84060 PRIGNANO CILENTO [SA]
TEL. +39 0974831090
www.viticoltorideconciliis.it

CELLAR SALES
PRE-BOOKED VISITS
ANNUAL PRODUCTION 200,000 bottles
HECTARES UNDER VINE 21.00
VITICULTURE METHOD Certified Organic
SUSTAINABLE WINERY

| | |
|---|---|
| ● Bacioilcielo Rosso '17 | 🍷🍷 2* |
| ○ Bacioilcielo Bianco '17 | 🍷 2 |
| ● Donnaluna Aglianico '16 | 🍷 3 |
| ○ Donnaluna Fiano '17 | 🍷 3 |

## De Falco Vini

VIA FIGLIOLA, 91
80040 SAN SEBASTIANO AL VESUVIO [NA]
TEL. +39 0817713755
www.defalco.it

CELLAR SALES
PRE-BOOKED VISITS
ANNUAL PRODUCTION 350,000 bottles
HECTARES UNDER VINE 8.00

| | |
|---|---|
| ● Aglianico '16 | 🍷🍷 2* |
| ● Lacryma Christi del Vesuvio Rosso '17 | 🍷🍷 3 |
| ○ Greco di Tufo '17 | 🍷 3 |
| ● Taurasi '14 | 🍷 4 |

## Dryas

VIA TOPPOLE, 10
83030 MONTEFREDANE [AV]
TEL. +39 3472392634
www.cantinadryas.it

ANNUAL PRODUCTION 7,400 bottles
HECTARES UNDER VINE 2.00

| | |
|---|---|
| ○ Dosaggio Zero Et. Nera M. Cl. | 🍷🍷 5 |
| ○ Brut Et. Gialla | 🍷 3 |

## Farro

LOC. FUSARO
VIA VIRGILIO, 16/24
80070 BACOLI [NA]
TEL. +39 0818545555
www.cantinefarro.it

CELLAR SALES
PRE-BOOKED VISITS
ANNUAL PRODUCTION 207,000 bottles
HECTARES UNDER VINE 20.00

| | |
|---|---|
| ○ Campi Flegrei Falanghina '17 | 🍷🍷 2* |
| ○ Campi Flegrei Falanghina Le Cigliate '16 | 🍷🍷 4 |
| ● Campi Flegrei Piedirosso '17 | 🍷 2 |

## Cantine Federiciane Monteleone

FRAZ. SAN ROCCO
VIA ANTICA CONSOLARE CAMPANA, 34
80016 MARANO DI NAPOLI [NA]
TEL. +39 0815765294
www.federiciane.it

CELLAR SALES
PRE-BOOKED VISITS
ANNUAL PRODUCTION 200,000 bottles
HECTARES UNDER VINE 15.00

| | |
|---|---|
| ○ Campi Flegrei Falanghina '17 | ♟♟ 2* |
| ● Penisola Sorrentina Gragnano '17 | ♟♟ 2* |
| ● Penisola Sorrentina Lettere '17 | ♟ 2 |

## Fiorentino

C.DA BARBASSANO
83052 PATERNOPOLI [AV]
TEL. +39 3473474869310

CELLAR SALES
PRE-BOOKED VISITS
ANNUAL PRODUCTION 12,000 bottles
HECTARES UNDER VINE 7.00
SUSTAINABLE WINERY

| | |
|---|---|
| ● Taurasi '13 | ♟♟ 5 |
| ● Irpinia Aglianico Celsi '13 | ♟ 3 |

## Masseria Frattasi

VIA FRATTASI, 1
82016 MONTESARCHIO [BN]
TEL. +39 0824824392
www.masseriafrattasi.it

CELLAR SALES
PRE-BOOKED VISITS
ANNUAL PRODUCTION 150,000 bottles
HECTARES UNDER VINE 10.00
VITICULTURE METHOD Certified Biodynamic

| | |
|---|---|
| ● Aglianico del Taburno Iovi Tonant '15 | ♟♟ 6 |
| ○ Falanghina del Sannio Taburno Donnalaura '17 | ♟ 5 |
| ● Kapnios '15 | ♟ 8 |

## Raffaele Guastaferro

VIA A. GRAMSCI
83030 TAURASI [AV]
TEL. +39 3341551543
info@guastaferro.it

CELLAR SALES
ANNUAL PRODUCTION 10,000 bottles
HECTARES UNDER VINE 7.00

| | |
|---|---|
| ○ Fulgeo '17 | ♟♟ 4 |
| ● Taurasi Primum '13 | ♟♟ 6 |

## Historia Antiqua

VIA VARIANTE EST S.S 7BIS, 75
83030 MANOCALZATI [AV]
TEL. +39 0825675240
www.historiaantiqua.it

CELLAR SALES
PRE-BOOKED VISITS
ANNUAL PRODUCTION 90,000 bottles
HECTARES UNDER VINE 30.00

| | |
|---|---|
| ○ Fiano di Avellino '17 | ♟♟ 3 |
| ○ Greco Di Tufo '17 | ♟♟ 3 |

## Guido Marsella

VIA MARONE, 1
83010 SUMMONTE [AV]
TEL. +39 0825691005
www.guidomarsella.com

CELLAR SALES
PRE-BOOKED VISITS
ANNUAL PRODUCTION 25,000 bottles
HECTARES UNDER VINE 8.00
SUSTAINABLE WINERY

| | |
|---|---|
| ○ Fiano di Avellino '15 | ♟♟ 4 |

## Masseria Felicia

FRAZ. CARANO
LOC. SAN TERENZANO
81037 SESSA AURUNCA [CE]
TEL. +39 0823935095
www.masseriafelicia.it

CELLAR SALES
PRE-BOOKED VISITS
ANNUAL PRODUCTION 25,000 bottles
HECTARES UNDER VINE 5.00

| | |
|---|---|
| ○ Falerno del Massico Bianco Anthologia '17 | 🍷🍷 3 |

## La Molara

C.DA PESCO, 2
83040 LUOGOSANO [AV]
TEL. +39 082778017
www.lamolara. it

CELLAR SALES
PRE-BOOKED VISITS
ACCOMMODATION AND RESTAURANT SERVICE
ANNUAL PRODUCTION 50,000 bottles
HECTARES UNDER VINE 8.00

| | |
|---|---|
| ○ Greco Di Tufo '16 | 🍷🍷 3* |
| ● Taurasi Santa Vara Ris. '12 | 🍷🍷 6 |
| ○ Fiano Di Avellino '16 | 🍷 3 |

## Montesole

FRAZ. SERRA
VIA SERRA
83030 MONTEFUSCO [AV]
TEL. +39 0825963972
www.montesole.it

PRE-BOOKED VISITS
ACCOMMODATION AND RESTAURANT SERVICE
ANNUAL PRODUCTION 750,000 bottles
HECTARES UNDER VINE 50.00
SUSTAINABLE WINERY

| | |
|---|---|
| ○ Greco di Tufo V. Breccia '17 | 🍷🍷 3 |
| ○ Fiano di Avellino V. Acquaviva '17 | 🍷 3 |
| ● Taurasi V. Vinieri '11 | 🍷 5 |

## Cantine Olivella

VIA ZAZZERA, 28
80048 SANT'ANASTASIA [NA]
TEL. +39 0815311388
www.cantineolivella.com

CELLAR SALES
ANNUAL PRODUCTION 80,000 bottles
HECTARES UNDER VINE 12.00

| | |
|---|---|
| ○ Katà Catalanesca '17 | 🍷🍷 3 |
| ○ Lacryma Christi del Vesuvio Bianco '17 | 🍷 3 |
| ● Lacryma Christi del Vesuvio Rosso Lacrimanera '17 | 🍷 3 |

## Raffaele Palma

LOC. SAN VITO
VIA ARSENALE, 8
84010 MAIORI [SA]
TEL. +39 3357601858
www.raffaelepalma.it

CELLAR SALES
ANNUAL PRODUCTION 20,000 bottles
HECTARES UNDER VINE 6.00
VITICULTURE METHOD Certified Organic
SUSTAINABLE WINERY

| | |
|---|---|
| ○ Ciarariis '15 | 🍷🍷 5 |
| ⊙ Costa d'Amalfi Rosato Salicerchi '17 | 🍷🍷 6 |

## Gennaro Papa

P.ZZA LIMATA, 2
81030 FALCIANO DEL MASSICO [CE]
TEL. +39 0823931267
www.gennaropapa.it

CELLAR SALES
PRE-BOOKED VISITS
ANNUAL PRODUCTION 23,000 bottles
HECTARES UNDER VINE 6.00
SUSTAINABLE WINERY

| | |
|---|---|
| ● Falerno del Massico Primitivo Conclave '16 | 🍷🍷 4 |
| ● Falerno del Massico Primitivo Campantuono '15 | 🍷 6 |

## Il Poggio

via Defenze, 4
82030 Torrecuso [BN]
Tel. +39 0824874068
www.ilpoggiovini.it

CELLAR SALES
PRE-BOOKED VISITS
ANNUAL PRODUCTION 120,000 bottles
HECTARES UNDER VINE 11.00

| | |
|---|---|
| ○ Falanghina del Sannio '17 | 🍷🍷 3 |
| ● Aglianico del Sannio Safinos '15 | 🍷 3 |
| ○ Sannio Coda di Volpe '17 | 🍷 2 |

## Porto di Mola

s.s. 430, km 16,200
81050 Rocca d'Evandro [CE]
Tel. +39 0823925801
www.portodimola.it

CELLAR SALES
PRE-BOOKED VISITS
ANNUAL PRODUCTION 250,000 bottles
HECTARES UNDER VINE 50.00

| | |
|---|---|
| ○ Acquamara '16 | 🍷🍷 3 |
| ○ Galluccio Petratonda '17 | 🍷 2 |
| ● Peppì '15 | 🍷 3 |

## Andrea Reale

loc. b.go di Gete
via Cardamone, 75
84010 Tramonti [SA]
Tel. +39 089856144
www.aziendaagricolareale.it

CELLAR SALES
PRE-BOOKED VISITS
ACCOMMODATION AND RESTAURANT SERVICE
ANNUAL PRODUCTION 16,000 bottles
HECTARES UNDER VINE 3.50
VITICULTURE METHOD Certified Organic

| | |
|---|---|
| ○ Costa d'Amalfi Tramonti Bianco Aliseo '17 | 🍷🍷 4 |
| ◐ Costa d'Amalfi Tramonti Rosato Getis '17 | 🍷🍷 4 |
| ● Costa d'Amalfi Tramonti Rosso Cardamone '16 | 🍷 4 |

## Scala Fenicia

via Fenicia, 15
80073 Capri [NA]
Tel. +39 0818389403
www.scalafenicia.com

ANNUAL PRODUCTION 3,800 bottles
HECTARES UNDER VINE 0.40
SUSTAINABLE WINERY

| | |
|---|---|
| ○ Capri Bianco '17 | 🍷🍷 5 |

## Tenuta Scuotto

c.da Campomarino, 2/3
83030 Lapio [AV]
Tel. +39 08251851965
www.tenutascuotto.it

CELLAR SALES
PRE-BOOKED VISITS
ANNUAL PRODUCTION 40,000 bottles
HECTARES UNDER VINE 3.00

| | |
|---|---|
| ○ Greco di Tufo '17 | 🍷🍷 3* |
| ○ Oi Ni '17 | 🍷🍷 5 |
| ○ Falanghina '17 | 🍷 3 |

## Cantina di Solopaca

via Bebiana, 44
82036 Solopaca [BN]
Tel. +39 0824977921
www.cantinasolopaca.it

CELLAR SALES
PRE-BOOKED VISITS
ANNUAL PRODUCTION 700,000 bottles
HECTARES UNDER VINE 1300.00

| | |
|---|---|
| ○ Falanghina del Sannio '17 | 🍷🍷 2* |
| ● Sannio Aglianico Ris. '15 | 🍷 2 |
| ○ Sannio Fiano '17 | 🍷 2 |
| ○ Sannio Greco '17 | 🍷 2 |

## Sorrentino

VIA RIO, 26
80042 BOSCOTRECASE [NA]
TEL. +39 0818584963
www.sorrentinovini.com

CELLAR SALES
PRE-BOOKED VISITS
ACCOMMODATION AND RESTAURANT SERVICE
ANNUAL PRODUCTION 250,000 bottles
HECTARES UNDER VINE 30.00
VITICULTURE METHOD Certified Organic

| | |
|---|---|
| ○ Lacryma Christi del Vesuvio Bianco V. Lapilli '17 | ♥♥ 3 |
| ◉ Lacryma Christi del Vesuvio Rosato '17 | ♥ 2 |
| ● Vesuvio Piedirosso '17 | ♥ 2 |

## Telaro

LOC. CALABRITTO
VIA CINQUE PIETRE, 2
81044 GALLUCCIO [CE]
TEL. +39 0823925841
www.vinitelaro.it

CELLAR SALES
PRE-BOOKED VISITS
ANNUAL PRODUCTION 550,000 bottles
HECTARES UNDER VINE 70.00
VITICULTURE METHOD Certified Organic

| | |
|---|---|
| ● Galluccio Ara Mundi Ris. '15 | ♥♥ 3 |
| ● Bariletta '17 | ♥ 3 |

## Tempa di Zoè

LOC. CARPINETO
84076 TORCHIARA [SA]
TEL. +39 0825986686
www.tempadizoe.com

ANNUAL PRODUCTION 8,500 bottles
HECTARES UNDER VINE 4.07

| | |
|---|---|
| ○ Asterias Fiano '16 | ♥♥ 5 |
| ● Diciotto '16 | ♥♥ 4 |
| ● Zero Aglianico '15 | ♥ 5 |

## Cantine Tora

VIA TORA II
82030 TORRECUSO [BN]
TEL. +39 0824872406
www.cantinetora.it

CELLAR SALES
PRE-BOOKED VISITS
ANNUAL PRODUCTION 55,000 bottles
HECTARES UNDER VINE 10.00

| | |
|---|---|
| ● Aglianico del Taburno '14 | ♥♥ 3 |
| ● Aglianico del Taburno Spartivento Ris. '11 | ♥♥ 3 |

## Torricino

LOC. TORRICINO, 5
VIA NAZIONALE
83010 TUFO [AV]
TEL. +39 0825998119
www.torricino.it

CELLAR SALES
PRE-BOOKED VISITS
ANNUAL PRODUCTION 40,000 bottles
HECTARES UNDER VINE 6.00
VITICULTURE METHOD Certified Organic
SUSTAINABLE WINERY

| | |
|---|---|
| ○ Fiano di Avellino Serrapiano '16 | ♥♥ 4 |
| ○ Greco di Tufo Raone '16 | ♥♥ 4 |
| ● Taurasi Cevotiempo '14 | ♥♥ 5 |

## VentitréFilari

VIA PIANTE, 43
83030 MONTEFREDANE [AV]
TEL. +39 0825672482
www.ventitrefilari.com

ANNUAL PRODUCTION 4,000 bottles
HECTARES UNDER VINE 0.80
VITICULTURE METHOD Certified Organic
SUSTAINABLE WINERY

| | |
|---|---|
| ○ Fiano di Avellino Numero Primo Ventitréfilari '16 | ♥♥ 4 |

## Vestini Campagnano Poderi Foglia

VIA COSTA DELL'AIA, 9
81044 CONCA DELLA CAMPANIA [CE]
TEL. +39 0823679087
www.vestinicampagnano.it

CELLAR SALES
PRE-BOOKED VISITS
ANNUAL PRODUCTION 80,000 bottles
HECTARES UNDER VINE 7.00
VITICULTURE METHOD Certified Organic

| | |
|---|---|
| ● Galluccio Rosso Concarosso '16 | ♥♥ 2* |
| ● Kajanero '17 | ♥♥ 2* |
| ○ Pallagrello Bianco '17 | ♥♥ 3 |
| ○ Le Ortole Pallagrello Bianco '17 | ♥ 4 |

## Vigne di Malies

V.LE DELLA VITTORIA, 58
82034 GUARDIA SANFRAMONDI [BN]
TEL. +39 0824864165
www.vignedimalies.it

ANNUAL PRODUCTION 25,000 bottles
HECTARES UNDER VINE 6.00

| | |
|---|---|
| ○ Falanghina del Sannio Creanzia '16 | ♥♥ 3 |
| ○ Falanghina del Sannio Opalus '17 | ♥♥ 2* |
| ○ Sannio Coda di Volpe Callida '17 | ♥ 2 |
| ○ Sannio Greco V. Fontana dell'Olmo Aedo '17 | ♥ 2 |

## Vigne Guadagno

VIA TAGLIAMENTO, 237
83100 AVELLINO
TEL. +39 08251686379
www.vigneguadagno.it

CELLAR SALES
PRE-BOOKED VISITS
ANNUAL PRODUCTION 47,000 bottles
HECTARES UNDER VINE 10.00

| | |
|---|---|
| ● Taurasi '12 | ♥♥ 7 |
| ○ Fiano di Avellino Contrada Sant'Aniello '15 | ♥♥ 6 |

## Votino

VIA FIZZO, 14
82013 BONEA [BN]
TEL. +39 0824834762
www.aziendavotino.com

CELLAR SALES
PRE-BOOKED VISITS
ANNUAL PRODUCTION 100,000 bottles
HECTARES UNDER VINE 5.00
SUSTAINABLE WINERY

| | |
|---|---|
| ● Aglianico del Taburno Furius '15 | ♥♥ 2* |
| ○ Falanghina del Sannio Taburno Cocceius '17 | ♥♥ 2* |

## Vuolo

LOC. PASSIONE
84135 SALERNO
TEL. +39 089282178
www.milavuolo.it

CELLAR SALES
ANNUAL PRODUCTION 13,000 bottles
HECTARES UNDER VINE 3.50
VITICULTURE METHOD Certified Organic
SUSTAINABLE WINERY

| | |
|---|---|
| ○ Fiano 2mila15 '15 | ♥♥ 3 |
| ● Aglianico 2mila13 '13 | ♥ 5 |

## Pierluigi Zampaglione

S.S. 399, KM 6
83045 CALITRI [AV]
TEL. +39 082738851
www.ildonchisciotte.net

CELLAR SALES
PRE-BOOKED VISITS
ANNUAL PRODUCTION 8,000 bottles
HECTARES UNDER VINE 2.50
VITICULTURE METHOD Certified Organic

| | |
|---|---|
| SO Don Chisciotte '17 | ♥♥ 4 |
| ○ Don Chisciotte '16 | ♥♥ 4 |

# BASILICATA

In 2019 Matera is the European Capital of Culture. It's an event whose international reach will highlight a region that's too often in the shadows. We're happy about that because we believe that anyone who has the good fortune to spend a few days there will be enchanted by its beauty, its picturesque landscapes (and we're not only talking about Sassi, there's plenty to visit and see throughout the territory), by its splendid Mediterranean cuisine and, of course, by its wines. And it's really this last that's probably still lacking in Basilicata. We're thinking of that media exposure that would allow for a process of growth and renewal set in motion years ago but still proceeding at too slow a pace. If we look at the list of wines awarded (four of them, one fewer than last year) it certainly isn't cause for elation. The indomitable Elena Fucci is still at the top of her game with her boutique winery, as is Paternoster, which continues to churn out classics (even after its recent merger). Cantine de Notaio is also back on top, having produced a great, modern and highly enjoyable regional red, Aglianico del Vulture, and last but not least there's Terre degli Svevi, with their extremely elegant Re Manfredi, a version that's up there with its best years. It's important to note that of the 18 wines that reached our finals, two of them were from Matera, thus cracking Vulture's boa constrictor hold over the region. But it's not all roses and flowers, despite the high level of this small platoon. The wineries may be many, but they have to start investing in equipment, professionalism, in the care of their vineyards … all of which take money, which the lower prices of Basilicata's wines (brought about by the presence of cooperatives and certain large producers in the territory) doesn't allow for. In short, it's the classic dog chasing its own tail. And it's the small and mid-sized wineries who pay, lacking the resources to adequately represent themselves on the market. It's truly a shame, because Vulture, Matera, Grottino di Roccanova and Terre dell'Alta Val d'Agri are extremely well-suited to cultivation, and they deserve much better. We can only hope that international attention and institutions will help boost a region whose potential is second to none.

## Basilisco

via delle Cantine, 20
85022 Barile [PZ]
Tel. +39 0972771033
www.basiliscovini.it

CELLAR SALES
PRE-BOOKED VISITS
ANNUAL PRODUCTION 55,000 bottles
HECTARES UNDER VINE 25.00
VITICULTURE METHOD Certified Organic
SUSTAINABLE WINERY

Today Viviana Malafarina is leading Basilico, the Feudi di San Gregorio group's satellite producer since 2011. The winery is situated in the Barile town center and avails itself of 25 hectares of organically cultivated terrain in the crus of Macario and Gelosia. Pierpaolo Sirch oversees vineyard management, maintaining an approach centered on using minimally invasive techniques so as to obtain the best fruit. Their bottles age in Shesh's historic tufa caves, a material that characterizes Barile's subsoil. Kudos to their 2015 Aglianico Cruà, which did an exceptional job during our finals. It's a lovely, dark ruby wine with a complex bouquet that joins fruit and 'volcanic' notes of smoke, toast and spices. The palate re-expresses crisp fruit and a lovely depth, though its tannins need a bit more time to integrate. Their 2015 Fontanelle also proves vibrant, close-knit and balanced, though it too needs a bit more time to find the right harmony. Their 2015 Teodosio is simpler but pleasant, while their 2017 Sophia is a savory white with gutsy acidity.

| | |
|---|---|
| ● Aglianico del Vulture Sup. Cruà '15 | ♟♟ 5 |
| ● Aglianico del Vulture Sup. Fontanelle '15 | ♟♟ 5 |
| ● Aglianico del Vulture Teodosio '15 | ♟ 3 |
| ○ Sophia '17 | ♟ 3 |
| ● Aglianico del Vulture Basilisco '09 | ♟♟♟ 5 |
| ● Aglianico del Vulture Basilisco '08 | ♟♟♟ 5 |
| ● Aglianico del Vulture Basilisco '07 | ♟♟♟ 5 |
| ● Aglianico del Vulture Basilisco '06 | ♟♟♟ 5 |
| ● Aglianico del Vulture Basilisco '04 | ♟♟♟ 5 |
| ● Aglianico del Vulture Basilisco '01 | ♟♟♟ 5 |
| ● Aglianico del Vulture Sup. Cruà '13 | ♟♟♟ 5 |
| ● Aglianico del Vulture Sup. Fontanelle '13 | ♟♟ 5 |
| ● Aglianico del Vulture Teodosio '14 | ♟♟ 3 |
| ○ Sophia '16 | ♟ 3 |

## Battifarano

c.da Cerrolongo, 1
75020 Nova Siri [MT]
Tel. +39 0835536174
www.battifarano.com

CELLAR SALES
PRE-BOOKED VISITS
ACCOMMODATION
ANNUAL PRODUCTION 70,000 bottles
HECTARES UNDER VINE 33.00
SUSTAINABLE WINERY

For more than five centuries Masseria Battifarano has belonged to the family after which it is named. The territory, has been famous since ancient times for its fertility and great wines. Already well-known for its olive trees and orchards, since 2006 the producer has been making and selling wines with grapes cultivated on 25 well-positioned hectares of land. It's managed by Vincenzo and his son Francesco Paolo, both agronomists, with the support of other family members as well. The selection put forward this year proved quite valid. Their 2016 Matera Moro Curaffani Riserva offers up aromas of blackberry and morello cherry. It's a juicy, rich wine that features spicy and toasty notes on the palate. Their 2015 Primitivo Akratos, with its enticing nuances of cinnamon on the nose, is a soft, fruity, well-structured wine. Their 2016 Toccaculo, a wine whose name will catch the eyes of those who can speak some Italian (it's probably a place name), features similar traits. Their 2017 Matera Rosato Akratos and 2017 Toccacielo (a white) also did well.

| | |
|---|---|
| ● Matera Moro Curraffanni Ris. '16 | ♟♟ 3 |
| ● Matera Primitivo Akratos '15 | ♟♟ 2* |
| ● Toccaculo '16 | ♟♟ 2* |
| ○ Matera Greco Le Paglie '17 | ♟ 2 |
| ● Matera Moro Torre Bollita '15 | ♟ 2 |
| ⊙ Matera Rosato Akratos '17 | ♟ 2 |
| ○ Toccacielo '17 | ♟ 2 |
| ● Matera Moro Torre Bollita '07 | ♟♟ 2 |
| ● Matera Primitivo Akratos '14 | ♟♟ 2* |
| ● Matera Primitivo Akratos '11 | ♟♟ 2* |

# Cantine del Notaio

VIA ROMA, 159
85028 RIONERO IN VULTURE [PZ]
TEL. +39 0972723689
www.cantinedelnotaio.it

**CELLAR SALES**
**PRE-BOOKED VISITS**
**ANNUAL PRODUCTION** 450,000 bottles
**HECTARES UNDER VINE** 40.00

Cantine del Notaio's history began in 1998 when Gerardo Giuratrabocchetti, a graduate in Agrarian Science, decided to leave research so as to take up his family's viticultural activities. Long, hard work led to the producer becoming a benchmark for Aglianico del Vulture. Some 40 hectares of vineyards are situated in Rionero, Barile, Ripacandia, Maschito and Ginestra, all in the best possible positions. The names of their wines are inspired by Gerardo's father's work as a notary. Gerardo produces a noteworthy selection at his winery, one that spans every possible expression of Aglianico. Our favorite, for some years now, has been his Aglianico del Vulture Il Repertorio. The vintage 2016 once again gets a Tre Bicchieri. It's a red with lovely structure and fullness that doesn't opt for excessive extraction or super-ripeness. Its fruit is crisp and savory, yet it also manages to be soft and fresh. Sweet, smooth tannins give way to a long, fruity finish. The rest of their Macarico line also proves valid.

| | | |
|---|---|---|
| ● Aglianico del Vulture Il Repertorio '16 | ♈♈♈ | 4* |
| ● Il Lascito | ♈♈ | 8 |
| ● Aglianico del Vulture Il Sigillo '13 | ♈♈ | 6 |
| ● Aglianico del Vulture Macarico '15 | ♈♈ | 3 |
| ● L'Atto '17 | ♈♈ | 3 |
| ○ L'Autentica '16 | ♈♈ | 5 |
| ○ La Parcella '17 | ♈♈ | 7 |
| ● Aglianico del Vulture Macarì '16 | ♈ | 3 |
| ○ La Raccolta '17 | ♈ | 3 |
| ○ Xinestra '17 | ♈ | 2 |
| ● Aglianico del Vulture Il Repertorio '15 | ♈♈♈ | 4* |
| ● Aglianico del Vulture Il Repertorio '14 | ♈♈♈ | 4* |
| ● Aglianico del Vulture Il Repertorio '13 | ♈♈♈ | 4* |
| ● Aglianico del Vulture Il Repertorio '12 | ♈♈♈ | 4* |
| ● Aglianico del Vulture La Firma '10 | ♈♈♈ | 6 |

# ★Elena Fucci

C.DA SOLAGNA DEL TITOLO
85022 BARILE [PZ]
TEL. +39 3204879945
www.elenafuccivini.com

**CELLAR SALES**
**PRE-BOOKED VISITS**
**ANNUAL PRODUCTION** 25,000 bottles
**HECTARES UNDER VINE** 6.70
**VITICULTURE METHOD** Certified Organic
**SUSTAINABLE WINERY**

Since 2000 young Elena Fucci has interpreted with sensibility and skill Barile, the terroir that gives rise to Fucci's unique and great wine. Her father, Salvatore, is in the vineyard, accompanied by Andrea, Elena's tireless husband, as well as enologist and owner. Their new and well-equipped winery was designed according to principles of bioarchitecture. Their vineyards go back an average of 50-60 years and are situated in the highest part of the Solagna del Titolo, at the foot of Monte Vulture. It's here that the grapes for their Titolo, for now their only wine, are cultivated. 2016 confirms the wine's status as a bonafide flagship of Luciana's wine culture. It's a vibrant, deep ruby red whose nose features an array of fruity nuances, from close-focused notes to ripe cherry, raspberry and blackcurrant, accompanied elegantly by spicy and delicately oaky aromas. The palate is rich without being heavy, proving savory, balanced and deep. Its tannins are already elegant, even if they're just a bit astringent in their youth. Its fruity finish comes through long and gratifying. Delicious.

| | | |
|---|---|---|
| ● Aglianico del Vulture Titolo '16 | ♈♈♈ | 6 |
| ● Aglianico del Vulture Titolo '15 | ♈♈♈ | 6 |
| ● Aglianico del Vulture Titolo '14 | ♈♈♈ | 6 |
| ● Aglianico del Vulture Titolo '13 | ♈♈♈ | 6 |
| ● Aglianico del Vulture Titolo '12 | ♈♈♈ | 5 |
| ● Aglianico del Vulture Titolo '11 | ♈♈♈ | 5 |
| ● Aglianico del Vulture Titolo '10 | ♈♈♈ | 5 |
| ● Aglianico del Vulture Titolo '09 | ♈♈♈ | 5 |
| ● Aglianico del Vulture Titolo '08 | ♈♈♈ | 6 |
| ● Aglianico del Vulture Titolo '07 | ♈♈♈ | 6 |
| ● Aglianico del Vulture Titolo '06 | ♈♈♈ | 5 |
| ● Aglianico del Vulture Titolo '05 | ♈♈♈ | 5 |
| ● Aglianico del Vulture Titolo '02 | ♈♈♈ | 5 |
| ● Aglianico del Vulture Titolo '04 | ♈♈ | 5 |
| ● Aglianico del Vulture Titolo '03 | ♈♈ | 5 |

# BASILICATA

## Grifalco della Lucania

LOC. PIAN DI CAMERA
85029 VENOSA [PZ]
TEL. +39 097231002
grifalcodellalucania@email.it

CELLAR SALES
PRE-BOOKED VISITS
ANNUAL PRODUCTION 65,000 bottles
HECTARES UNDER VINE 15.00
VITICULTURE METHOD Certified Organic
SUSTAINABLE WINERY

In 2003 Fabrizio and Cecilia Piccin decided
to leave Tuscany. Traveling in southern Italy,
they were impressed by Basilicata, a
territory rich in history and tradition. But they
were truly struck by Aglianico del Vulture, a
grape that's so different from Sangiovese,
and so the couple were inspired to purchase
vineyards in Ginestra, Maschito, Rapolla and
Venosa. Their approach is defined by
certified organic managed, supported by
their children Lorenzo, enologist, and
Andrea. For some years now the two have
overseen production and the commercial
sector, respectively. Their 2016 Gricos,
Piccin's premium offering, is one of the
wines that best expresses Vulture. Its a
blend of Aglianico from four different terroir
(Maschito, Ginestra, Venosa and Rapolla)
and matures for a year in oak barrels. It's a
densely ruby colored wine whose nose
tends towards a complexity dominated by
black fruit, like blackberries, morello cherries
and plums, and offers up spicy nuances as
well as tobacco. Its palate is still a bit young,
but it isn't lacking in elegance, and finishes
with a lovely note of fruit.

| | | |
|---|---|---|
| ● Aglianico del Vulture Gricos '16 | ♟♟ | 3* |
| ● Aglianico del Vulture Grifalco '16 | ♟♟ | 4 |
| ● Aglianico del Vulture Sup. Daginestra '15 | ♟♟ | 4 |
| ● Aglianico del Vulture Sup. Damaschito '15 | ♟ | 4 |
| ● Aglianico del Vulture Gricos '14 | ♟♟♟ | 3* |
| ● Aglianico del Vulture Daginestra '11 | ♟♟ | 4 |
| ● Aglianico del Vulture Damaschito '12 | ♟♟ | 4 |
| ● Aglianico del Vulture Gricos '15 | ♟♟ | 3* |
| ● Aglianico del Vulture Gricos '13 | ♟♟ | 3* |
| ● Aglianico del Vulture Gricos '12 | ♟♟ | 2* |
| ● Aglianico del Vulture Grifalco '15 | ♟♟ | 4 |
| ● Aglianico del Vulture Grifalco '14 | ♟♟ | 4 |
| ● Aglianico del Vulture Grifalco '13 | ♟♟ | 4 |
| ● Aglianico del Vulture Grifalco '12 | ♟♟ | 3* |

## Martino

VIA LA VISTA, 2A
85028 RIONERO IN VULTURE [PZ]
TEL. +39 0972721422
www.martinovini.com

CELLAR SALES
PRE-BOOKED VISITS
ANNUAL PRODUCTION 250,000 bottles
HECTARES UNDER VINE 50.00

The family began operating in the late 19th
century in Rionero, in Vulture, when the
Martino family sold grapes, must and wines
throughout Italy. The real turning point
came in the 1940s when Donato Martino,
the father of Armando (the winery's current
owner), purchased vineyards in the area of
Vulture and began making and selling wine
on his own. Their current production center
avails itself of modern technology and an
underground tufa cellar for aging. Armando
is accompanied by his daughter Carolin,
who is also president of the Vulture
Aglianico Consortium. Their 2012 Oraziano,
made with Martino's best grapes, earned a
place in our finals. Its a ruby garnet wine
with a complex nose that features aromas
of forest undergrowth, ripe and bottled
cherries, with hints of tobacco and oak.
In the mouth it proves succulent, soft and
full, supported by a fresh, acid vein and
elegant tannins. Their 2013 Superiore, a
savory and balanced wine, is still evolving,
while their 2012 Riserva proves deeper and
more complex, even if there's still too much
new wood.

| | | |
|---|---|---|
| ● Aglianico del Vulture Oraziano '12 | ♟♟ | 5 |
| ● Aglianico del Vulture Sup. '13 | ♟♟ | 7 |
| ● Aglianico del Vulture Sup. Ris. '12 | ♟♟ | 7 |
| ● Aglianico del Vulture '15 | ♟ | 2 |
| ● Aglianico del Vulture '14 | ♟♟ | 3* |
| ● Aglianico del Vulture '13 | ♟♟ | 2* |
| ● Aglianico del Vulture '12 | ♟♟ | 2* |
| ● Aglianico del Vulture Bel Poggio '10 | ♟♟ | 2* |
| ● Aglianico del Vulture Oraziano '10 | ♟♟ | 5 |
| ● Aglianico del Vulture Oraziano '09 | ♟♟ | 5 |
| ● Aglianico del Vulture Pretoriano '10 | ♟♟ | 5 |
| ● Aglianico del Vulture Pretoriano '09 | ♟♟ | 5 |
| ● Aglianico del Vulture Sup. '12 | ♟♟ | 7 |
| ○ I Sassi Greco '16 | ♟♟ | 4 |

# Musto Carmelitano

VIA PIETRO NENNI, 23
85020 MASCHITO [PZ]
TEL. +39 097233312
www.mustocarmelitano.it

CELLAR SALES
PRE-BOOKED VISITS
ACCOMMODATION AND RESTAURANT SERVICE
ANNUAL PRODUCTION 20,000 bottles
HECTARES UNDER VINE 14.00
VITICULTURE METHOD Certified Organic

Carmelitano is a small producer managed with passion by a family with solid agricultural roots. In the mid-1980s Francesco Carmelitano decided to begin making wines with grapes cultivated on his four hectares of vineyards. Today we find his children Elisabetta and Luigi managing the winery with the support of Sebastiano Forunato, an enologist whose experience with Aglianico is extensive. Their vineyards are situated in lovely positions throughout three different districts in Maschito, and their grapes are fermented in wooden vats using native yeasts. This minimalist but attentive approach to enology translates into balanced, assertive wines with a lovely, fruity impact. Their 2016 Maschitano Rosso sees controlled super-ripeness of fruit but good pluck and balance. The 2015 Serra del Prete, made from the vineyard of the same name, features lovely notes of blackcurrant and a balsamic character with still-assertive tannins and a lovely, oaky finish. Their Maschitano Bianco, a delicately aromatic and crisp blend of local grapes, also proved quite interesting.

| | |
|---|---|
| ● Aglianico del Vulture Serra del Prete '15 | 🍷🍷 4 |
| ○ Maschitano Bianco '17 | 🍷🍷 3 |
| ● Maschitano Rosso '16 | 🍷🍷 3 |
| ○ Dhjete '17 | 🍷 3 |
| ⊙ Maschiano Rosato '17 | 🍷 2 |
| ● Aglianico del Vulture Serra del Prete '09 | 🍷🍷🍷 2 |
| ● Aglianico del Vulture '13 | 🍷🍷 6 |
| ● Aglianico del Vulture '12 | 🍷🍷 6 |
| ● Aglianico del Vulture Maschitano Rosso '14 | 🍷🍷 3 |
| ● Aglianico del Vulture Pian del Moro '13 | 🍷🍷 4 |
| ● Aglianico del Vulture Pian del Moro '11 | 🍷🍷 4 |
| ● Aglianico del Vulture Serra del Prete '13 | 🍷🍷 4 |
| ● Aglianico del Vulture Serra del Prete '12 | 🍷🍷 3 |
| ● Maschitano Rosso '12 | 🍷🍷 3 |

# Paternoster

C.DA VALLE DEL TITOLO
85022 BARILE [PZ]
TEL. +39 0972770224
Ronchetto

CELLAR SALES
PRE-BOOKED VISITS
ANNUAL PRODUCTION 150,000 bottles
HECTARES UNDER VINE 20.00
VITICULTURE METHOD Certified Organic

Paternoster di Barile was founded in 1925 thanks to Anselmo Paternoster. He was the one who decided to start selling the Aglianico that the family had been making for their own personal use. Today the winery, now partnered with the Tommasi group, avails itself of the collaboration of Vito Paternoster and Fabio Mecca, an enologist who knows the territory and Aglianico well. Don Anselmo and Rotondo, their prized wines, are cultivated in various districts throughout Barile. Their 2015 Don Anselmo is a wine with depth and power, with abundant tannins but still rich in fruit, spicy fragrances and oak. It's a wine endowed with balance, elegance and long aromatic persistence. Tre Bicchieri. Their Rotondo, made with grapes from the vineyard of the same name, is concentrated and rich, but needs time to age in the bottle before finding a definitive harmony. Their 2016 Synthesi is one of the best versions in recent years and does a nice job expressing both the grape and the terroir. It's a wine succulent in its fruit, savory and well-balanced with velvety tannins.

| | |
|---|---|
| ● Aglianico del Vulture Don Anselmo '15 | 🍷🍷🍷 6 |
| ● Aglianico del Vulture Rotondo '15 | 🍷🍷 5 |
| ● Aglianico del Vulture Synthesi '16 | 🍷🍷 3 |
| ○ Vulcanico Falanghina '17 | 🍷 3 |
| ● Aglianico del Vulture Don Anselmo '13 | 🍷🍷🍷 6 |
| ● Aglianico del Vulture Don Anselmo '09 | 🍷🍷🍷 6 |
| ● Aglianico del Vulture Don Anselmo '94 | 🍷🍷🍷 6 |
| ● Aglianico del Vulture Don Anselmo Ris. '05 | 🍷🍷🍷 6 |
| ● Aglianico del Vulture Rotondo '11 | 🍷🍷🍷 5 |
| ● Aglianico del Vulture Rotondo '01 | 🍷🍷🍷 5 |
| ● Aglianico del Vulture Rotondo '00 | 🍷🍷🍷 5 |

# Re Manfredi
# Cantina Terre degli Svevi

LOC. PIAN DI CAMERA
85029 VENOSA [PZ]
TEL. +39 097231263
www.cantineremanfredi.it

**CELLAR SALES**
**PRE-BOOKED VISITS**
**RESTAURANT SERVICE**
**ANNUAL PRODUCTION** 230,000 bottles
**HECTARES UNDER VINE** 110.00

120 hectares of vineyards give rise to a
total of 230,000 bottles. These numbers
confirm the great entrepreneurial skill of
Gruppo Italiano Vini and Paolo Montrone in
the management of a winery dedicated to
Re Manfredi, son of Federico II, once a lord
of these lands. Much of their estate is
situated in Venosa, but their principal cru,
Vigneto Serpara (whose vines go back 40
years), is in Maschito. They also
successfully cultivate white grape varieties
like Traminer and Müller Thurgau. And this
year Re Manfredi earns a highly-deserved
Tre Bicchieri for its Venosa vineyards'
vintage 2015, a harmonic, fine wine that
express close-focused and vibrant fruit. It
manages to be deep and tannic, yet also
pleasant to drink and balanced. Their Taglio
del Tralcio is delicious in its aromas of
super-ripe red fruit and its succulence all
together. Their 2013 Serpara has more
complex, evolved aromas, and a firm and
potent structure. It's a wine that will give up
its best over time. Their 2017 Manfredi
Bianco is also truly excellent.

| | |
|---|---|
| ● Aglianico del Vulture Re Manfredi '15 | ♟♟♟ 5 |
| ● Aglianico del Vulture Taglio del Tralcio '16 | ♟♟ 3* |
| ● Aglianico del Vulture Sup. Serpara '13 | ♟♟ 5 |
| ○ Re Manfredi Bianco '17 | ♟♟ 4 |
| ● Aglianico del Vulture Re Manfredi '13 | ♟♟♟ 6 |
| ● Aglianico del Vulture Re Manfredi '11 | ♟♟♟ 4* |
| ● Aglianico del Vulture Re Manfredi '10 | ♟♟♟ 4* |
| ● Aglianico del Vulture Re Manfredi '05 | ♟♟♟ 4 |
| ● Aglianico del Vulture Re Manfredi '99 | ♟♟♟ 4* |
| ● Aglianico del Vulture Serpara '10 | ♟♟♟ 5 |
| ● Aglianico del Vulture Sup. Serpara '12 | ♟♟♟ 5 |
| ● Aglianico del Vulture Vign. Serpara '03 | ♟♟♟ 4* |

# Terra dei Re

VIA MONTICCHIO KM 2,700
85028 RIONERO IN VULTURE [PZ]
TEL. +39 0972725116
www.terradeire.com

**CELLAR SALES**
**PRE-BOOKED VISITS**
**ACCOMMODATION AND RESTAURANT SERVICE**
**ANNUAL PRODUCTION** 70,000 bottles
**HECTARES UNDER VINE** 11.00
**SUSTAINABLE WINERY**

Founded in 2000 by the Leone and
Rabasco families, Terra dei Re represents
the other side of Basilicata's wine industry.
Aglianico del Vulture isn't the only wine
produced. For some years now Paride
Leone, a passionate experimenter, has
planted Pinot Nero at 800 meters above
sea level atop Monte Vulture, a position that
makes for extremely pleasant wines.
Rionero in Vulture hosts their modern,
partially underground cellar, while their
some 30 hectares of vineyards are situated
in some of the best locations around Barile,
Rapolla, Melfi and Rionero. The Piano di
Carro cru in Barile gives rise to Divinus, an
Aglianico del Vulture of fine elegance. 2013
made for a full-bodied, plush red with
lovely aromas of black and red cherry. An
assertive palate rich in vigor and
succulence finishes long and balanced on
toasty notes of oak. Their Pinot Nero
Vulcano is elegant, subtle and gratifying,
while their 2015 Aglianico Vultur, a wine
aged in new wood barrels, also did well
during our tastings. Their 2017 Malvasia
Claris proved to be a pleasant wine.

| | |
|---|---|
| ● Aglianico del Vulture Sup. Divinus '13 | ♟♟ 4 |
| ● Vulcano 800 Pinot Nero '17 | ♟♟ 5 |
| ● Aglianico del Vulture Vultur '15 | ♟ 2 |
| ○ Claris Malvasia '17 | ♟ 2 |
| ● Aglianico del Vulture Nocte '14 | ♟♟ 4 |
| ● Aglianico del Vulture Nocte '13 | ♟♟ 4 |
| ● Aglianico del Vulture Nocte '10 | ♟♟ 4 |
| ● Aglianico del Vulture Sup. Divinus '12 | ♟♟ 4 |
| ● Aglianico del Vulture Vultur '14 | ♟♟ 2* |
| ● Aglianico del Vulture Vultur '13 | ♟♟ 2* |
| ● Vulcano 800 '15 | ♟♟ 4 |

# Cantina di Venosa

LOC. VIGNALI
VIA APPIA
85029 VENOSA [PZ]
TEL. +39 097236702
www.cantinadivenosa.it

**CELLAR SALES**
**PRE-BOOKED VISITS**
**ANNUAL PRODUCTION** 1,000,000 bottles
**HECTARES UNDER VINE** 800.00
**SUSTAINABLE WINERY**

Founded in 1947 by 27 partners, today
Cantina di Venosa comprises 400 vine
growers, covering a total of 800 hectares
throughout Venosa, Ripacandida, Maschito
and Ginestra. Their production center is
situated in Venosa, where their grapes are
selected for a vast array of wines, from
their classic line to sparklers. They work
primarily with Aglianico, but Malvasia
Bianca and Moscato are also used. Terre di
Orazio, Gesualdo da Venosa and Carato
Venusio are some of their most well-known
Aglianico di Vultures. Their 2012 Carato
Venusio had an excellent day during our
tastings, earning a place in our finals by
virtue of its firm, potent structure, a
richness of fruit that's well-supported by a
fresh, acidic vein and a palate enriched by
elegant tannins. It's a wine rich in fruit with
a long finish that closes on spicy and oaky
notes. Their 2015 Gesualdo has a more
evolved character and, at this stage, it's
still a bit dominated by oak, while in their
2015 Terre di Orazio we would have
appreciated greater freshness and balance.
Their 2017 Rosato proved truly pleasant.

| | | |
|---|---|---|
| ● Aglianico del Vulture Sup. Carato Venusio '12 | | ♟♟ 6 |
| ● Aglianico del Vulture Gesualdo da Venosa '15 | | ♟♟ 5 |
| ● Aglianico del Vulture Terre di Orazio '15 | | ♟ 4 |
| ○ Verbo Malvasia '17 | | ♟ 3 |
| ⊙ Verbo Rosé '17 | | ♟ 3 |
| ● Aglianico del Vulture Balì '13 | | ♟♟ 2* |
| ● Aglianico del Vulture Carato Venusio '12 | | ♟♟ 6 |
| ● Aglianico del Vulture Gesualdo da Venosa '13 | | ♟♟ 5 |
| ● Aglianico del Vulture Gesualdo da Venosa '11 | | ♟♟ 5 |
| ● Aglianico del Vulture Terre di Orazio '13 | | ♟♟ 4 |
| ● Aglianico del Vulture Terre di Orazio '12 | | ♟♟ 3* |
| ● Aglianico del Vulture Vignali '13 | | ♟♟ 2* |
| ○ Terre di Orazio Dry Muscat '16 | | ♟♟ 3 |
| ○ Terre di Orazio Dry Muscat '15 | | ♟♟ 2* |

# Vigneti del Vulture

C.DA PIPOLI
85011 ACERENZA [PZ]
TEL. +39 0971749363
www.vignetidelvulture.it

**PRE-BOOKED VISITS**
**ANNUAL PRODUCTION** 100,000 bottles
**HECTARES UNDER VINE** 56.00

The Fantini-Farnese Vini group produces
wines in Abruzzo, but throughout southern
Italy as well. Among their partners we find
Vigneti del Vulture ad Acerenza, a winery
that offers excellent wines with grapes
supplied by local vine growers. Aglianico
serves as the basis of their selection, with
Moscato and Fiano whites made as well.
Bolstered by large production volumes and
strong quality, they're one of Basilicata's
largest producers. Their 2016 Aglianico
Pipoli is a modern, international wine. Rich
in plush, fruity notes, it's aged in new wood
barrels and delivers for its crisp fruit, its
oaky notes and its pleasantness in the
mouth. Their Piano del Cerro, a wine that
features great concentration, is aged for
two years in small wood barrels before
being bottled. It's a wine of great extractive
richness that still needs time to find a more
pervasive and balanced character. As
always, their 2017 Pipoli Greco Fiano and
2017 Rosato both proved pleasant.

| | | |
|---|---|---|
| ● Aglianico del Vulture Pipoli '16 | | ♟♟ 2* |
| ● Aglianico del Vulture Piano del Cerro '15 | | ♟ 5 |
| ○ Pipoli Greco Fiano '17 | | ♟ 2 |
| ⊙ Pipoli Rosato '17 | | ♟ 2 |
| ● Aglianico del Vulture Piano del Cerro '13 | | ♟♟ 5 |
| ● Aglianico del Vulture Piano del Cerro '09 | | ♟♟ 5 |
| ● Aglianico del Vulture Pipoli '15 | | ♟♟ 2* |
| ● Aglianico del Vulture Pipoli '13 | | ♟♟ 2* |
| ● Aglianico del Vulture Pipoli Zero '15 | | ♟♟ 2* |
| ● Aglianico del Vulture Pipoli Zero '14 | | ♟♟ 2* |
| ○ Moscato Sensuale '16 | | ♟♟ 2* |

## 600 Grotte

C.DA SAN PASQUALE
85032 CHIAROMONTE [PZ]
TEL. +39 0973642278
www.600grotte.it

CELLAR SALES
ANNUAL PRODUCTION 15,000 bottles
HECTARES UNDER VINE 5.33
SUSTAINABLE WINERY

| | |
|---|---|
| ● Recepit '16 | ♟♟ 3 |
| ☉ Recepit '17 | ♟ 3 |
| ● Recepit EL '15 | ♟ 3 |

## Bisceglia

C.DA FINOCCHIARO
85024 LAVELLO [PZ]
TEL. +39 0972877033
www.vinibisceglia.it

CELLAR SALES
PRE-BOOKED VISITS
RESTAURANT SERVICE
ANNUAL PRODUCTION 250,000 bottles
HECTARES UNDER VINE 45.00

| | |
|---|---|
| ● Aglianico del Vulture Terra di Vulcano '16 | ♟♟ 3 |
| ● Aglianico del Vulture Gudarrà '15 | ♟ 4 |
| ○ Bosco delle Rose Chardonnay '17 | ♟ 3 |

## Cantine Cifarelli

C.DA SAN VITO
75024 MONTESCAGLIOSO [MT]
TEL. +39 3338535349
www.cantinecifarelli.it

CELLAR SALES
PRE-BOOKED VISITS
ANNUAL PRODUCTION 20,000 bottles
HECTARES UNDER VINE 30.00

| | |
|---|---|
| ● Matera Primitivo di San Vito '15 | ♟♟ 3 |
| ● La Regola '15 | ♟ 4 |
| ○ Matera Greco di San Vito '17 | ♟ 3 |
| ☉ Matera Rosato di San Vito '17 | ♟ 3 |

## Casa Vinicola D'Angelo

VIA PADRE PIO, 8
85028 RIONERO IN VULTURE [PZ]
TEL. +39 0972721517
www.dangelowine.it

CELLAR SALES
PRE-BOOKED VISITS
ANNUAL PRODUCTION 300,000 bottles
HECTARES UNDER VINE 35.00

| | |
|---|---|
| ● Aglianico del Vulture '16 | ♟ 3 |
| ● Aglianico del Vulture Le Vigne a Capanno Tenuta del Portale '16 | ♟ 4 |
| ● Aglianico del Vulture Tenuta del Portale '16 | ♟ 4 |
| ● Serra delle Querce '15 | ♟ 4 |

## Donato D'Angelo
## di Filomena Ruppi

VIA PADRE PIO, 10
85028 RIONERO IN VULTURE [PZ]
TEL. +39 0972724602
www.agrida.it

CELLAR SALES
PRE-BOOKED VISITS
ANNUAL PRODUCTION 80,000 bottles
HECTARES UNDER VINE 20.00

| | |
|---|---|
| ● Balconara '15 | ♟♟ 4 |
| ● Aglianico del Vulture Donato D'Angelo '15 | ♟ 3 |

## Eleano

FRAZ. PIAN DELL'ALTARE
S.DA PROV.LE 8
85028 RIPACANDIDA [PZ]
TEL. +39 0972722273
www.eleano.it

CELLAR SALES
PRE-BOOKED VISITS
ACCOMMODATION
ANNUAL PRODUCTION 53,000 bottles
HECTARES UNDER VINE 7.50

| | |
|---|---|
| ● Aglianico del Vulture Dioniso '15 | ♟♟ 3* |
| ○ Ambra Moscato V.T. '15 | ♟♟ 4 |
| ● Aglianico del Vulture Eleano '15 | ♟ 5 |

## Eubea

S.DA PROV.LE 8
85020 RIPACANDIDA [PZ]
TEL. +39 3284312789
www.agricolaeubea.com

CELLAR SALES
PRE-BOOKED VISITS
ANNUAL PRODUCTION 50,000 bottles
HECTARES UNDER VINE 16.00
VITICULTURE METHOD Certified Organic

● Aglianico del Vulture
   Covo dei Briganti '16                     ▼▼ 6

## Cantine Graziano

VIA PONTE, 25
85036 ROCCANOVA [PZ]
TEL. +39 3486951612
www.cantinegraziano.com

CELLAR SALES
PRE-BOOKED VISITS
ANNUAL PRODUCTION 25,000 bottles
HECTARES UNDER VINE 6.00
VITICULTURE METHOD Certified Organic

● Grottino di Roccanova Rosso
   Norce Ris. '13                            ▼▼ 3
○ Grottino di Roccanova Bianco
   Terre di Norce '16                        ▼ 2

## Michele Laluce

VIA ROMA, 21
85020 GINESTRA [PZ]
TEL. +39 0972646145
www.vinilaluce.com

CELLAR SALES
PRE-BOOKED VISITS
ANNUAL PRODUCTION 40,000 bottles
HECTARES UNDER VINE 7.00
SUSTAINABLE WINERY

● Aglianico del Vulture S'Adatt '13          ▼ 2
● Aglianico del Vulture Zimberno '13         ▼ 3

## Cantine Madonna delle Grazie

LOC. VIGNALI
VIA APPIA
85029 VENOSA [PZ]
TEL. +39 097235704
www.cantinemadonnadellegrazie.it

CELLAR SALES
PRE-BOOKED VISITS
ANNUAL PRODUCTION 18,000 bottles
HECTARES UNDER VINE 8.00
VITICULTURE METHOD Certified Organic

● Aglianico del Vulture Bauccio '13          ▼▼ 4
● Aglianico del Vulture Leuconoe '17         ▼ 3

## Ofanto - Tenuta I Gelsi

FRAZ. MONTICCHIO BAGNI
C.DA PADULI
85028 RIONERO IN VULTURE [PZ]
TEL. +39 0972080289
www.tenutaigelsi.com

CELLAR SALES
PRE-BOOKED VISITS
ANNUAL PRODUCTION 60,000 bottles
HECTARES UNDER VINE 10.00
SUSTAINABLE WINERY

● Aglianico del Vulture '14                   ▼▼ 4
● Aglianico del Vulture '15                   ▼ 4
● Aglianico del Vulture Calaturi '13          ▼ 4

## Tenuta Parco dei Monaci

C.DA PARCO DEI MONACI
75100 MATERA
TEL. +39 0835259546
www.tenutaparcodeimonaci.it

PRE-BOOKED VISITS
ACCOMMODATION
ANNUAL PRODUCTION 20,000 bottles
HECTARES UNDER VINE 5.00

● Matera Primitivo Monacello '16             ▼▼ 4
● Matera Moro Spaccasassi '15                ▼ 5

## Francesco Radino

VIA RIONE VETERA, 84
75100 MATERA
TEL. +39 3385882673
www.radino.it

CELLAR SALES
PRE-BOOKED VISITS
ANNUAL PRODUCTION 15,000 bottles
HECTARES UNDER VINE 4.00
VITICULTURE METHOD Certified Organic

| | | |
|---|---|---|
| ● Aglianico del Vulture Colignelli '15 | ♥♥ | 5 |
| ● Aglianico del Vulture Arcidiaconata '14 | ♥ | 5 |

## Regio Cantina

LOC. PIANO REGIO
85029 VENOSA [PZ]
TEL. +39 057754011
www.tenutepiccini.it

CELLAR SALES
PRE-BOOKED VISITS
ANNUAL PRODUCTION 90,000 bottles
HECTARES UNDER VINE 15.00
VITICULTURE METHOD Certified Organic

| | | |
|---|---|---|
| ● Aglianico del Vulture Donpà '15 | ♥♥ | 3 |
| ● Aglianico del Vulture Ris. '13 | ♥♥ | 3 |

## Ripanero

VIA MARCONI, 86
85028 RIONERO IN VULTURE [PZ]
TEL. +39 338 8020172
www.ripanero.it

ANNUAL PRODUCTION 12,500 bottles
HECTARES UNDER VINE 4.00

| | | |
|---|---|---|
| ● Aglianico del Vulture Logos '15 | ♥♥ | 4 |
| ● Aglianico del Vulture Physis '15 | ♥♥ | 4 |

## Taverna

C.DA TRATTURO REGIO
75020 NOVA SIRI [MT]
TEL. +39 0835877310
www.cantinetaverna.wine

CELLAR SALES
PRE-BOOKED VISITS
ACCOMMODATION AND RESTAURANT SERVICE
ANNUAL PRODUCTION 50,000 bottles
HECTARES UNDER VINE 20.00

| | | |
|---|---|---|
| ● Matera Primitivo I Sassi '16 | ♥♥ | 3* |
| ⊙ Primitivo Rosato Maddalena '17 | ♥♥ | 2* |
| ● Il Lagarino '15 | ♥ | 4 |
| ● Il Lucano '15 | ♥ | 4 |

## Troilo

VIA A. DIAZ, 43
85029 VENOSA [PZ]
TEL. +39 097236900
www.troilo.it

| | | |
|---|---|---|
| ● Aglianico del Volture Leukanos '16 | ♥♥ | 3 |
| ⊙ Gilda Brut Rosé | ♥ | 3 |
| ○ Gilda Dry Muscat '16 | ♥ | 2 |
| ○ Gilda Moscato Dolce '17 | ♥ | 2 |

## Vitis in Vulture

C.SO GIUSTINO FORTUNATO, 159
85024 LAVELLO [PZ]
TEL. +39 097283983
www.vitisinvulture.com

ANNUAL PRODUCTION 50,000 bottles
HECTARES UNDER VINE 100.00

| | | |
|---|---|---|
| ● Aglianico del Vulture Labellum '15 | ♥♥ | 3 |
| ● Lenos Primitivo '17 | ♥♥ | 2* |
| ● Aglianico del Vulture Forentum '15 | ♥ | 3 |

# PUGLIA

Puglia continues to grow and in this edition of Italian Wines it's both a general growth (with four more wineries in our main section) and in terms of the number of Tre Bicchieri awarded (from last year's 13 to 15 this year, its highest ever). It's a result that's in line with an evolution in quality standards throughout the region's wine industry, but also its market success, especially internationally. It's worth considering a couple of points here. There's its Doc wines, which went unnoticed for years and are now winning over consumers, despite the naysayers and criticisms (which at times are justified and often levied by the region's own producers). Undoubtedly it's Gioia del Colle Primitivo that's leading this renaissance, an appellation that's firmly established at the top of regional production, followed by Primitivo di Manduria and Salice Salentino (Castel del Monte is still having to catch up). But it should also be said (even if producers of Negroamaro won't like it) that Primitivo is serving as the Puglia's main engine, both in terms of quality (this year the wine earned 8 of the 15 Tre Bicchieri awarded, and was more highly represented during our finals) and in terms of regional economics, image and success (both in Italy and abroad). Now for the wines. There were two highly newsworthy events. For the first time in the region a rosé earned Tre Bicchieri, and it's none other than that historic and prized Italian wine, Leone de Castris's Five Roses, in its 2017 74° Anniversario edition. And, also for the first time, a regional white took home a gold. It's Masseria Li Veli's 2017 Askos Verdeca, a wine made with Verdeca, a local, traditional cultivar. This year our Award for Sustainable Viticulture goes to Puglia's Torrevento for the attention it shows towards these principles. And finally, to conclude, we never tire of criticizing the use (now diffuse throughout the region) of heavy bottles, which hurt the environment and has more to do with appearance than substance. Great wines (including Puglia's) don't need them.

## Giuseppe Attanasio

VIA PER ORIA, 13
74024 MANDURIA [TA]
TEL. +39 0999737121
www.primitivo-attanasio.com

ANNUAL PRODUCTION 11,000 bottles
HECTARES UNDER VINE 6.00

The Attanasio family's small Manduria winery could be considered one of the most representative of the territory. Their relatively few calcareous and tufaceous hectares are dedicated to Apulian head-trained Primitivo, producing annually just over ten thousand bottles of wine with traditional character. Since 2000, handling takes place in a modern cellar located inside an 18th century building. Kudos to this historic winery. Their 2013 Primitivo di Manduria Riserva offers intense hints of dark fruit (plum, damson and blackberry) while the palate reveals a deep and unexpected austerity that is beautifully fresh and reminiscent of Mediterranean scrubland. A wine to hold on to. Their 2017 Primitivo Rosato proves well-made, expressing floral overtones with long, enjoyable nuances of currants. Their 2013 Primitivo di Manduria Dolce Naturale, which we also tasted last year, is still fantastic.

| | |
|---|---|
| ● Primitivo di Manduria Ris. '13 | ♼♼ 6 |
| ☉ Primitivo Rosato '17 | ♼♼ 3 |
| ● Primitivo di Manduria '13 | ♼♼ 5 |
| ● Primitivo di Manduria '07 | ♼♼ 4 |
| ● Primitivo di Manduria Dolce Naturale '13 | ♼♼ 5 |
| ● Primitivo di Manduria Dolce Naturale 15,5° '06 | ♼♼ 5 |

## Cantele

S.DA PROV.LE SALICE SALENTINO-SAN DONACI KM 35,600
73010 GUAGNANO [LE]
TEL. +39 0832705010
www.cantele.it

CELLAR SALES
PRE-BOOKED VISITS
ANNUAL PRODUCTION 16,000,000 bottles
HECTARES UNDER VINE 200.00

The Cantele family runs their 40-year old winery with energy and passion. The vineyards are divided between Guagnano, Montemesola and San Pietro Vernotico on deep clay-calcareous soil with medium-high drainage and predominantly red earth. Susumaniello, Fiano del Salento, Negroamaro and Primitivo are among the mostly traditional cultivars expressing the terroir in wines combining typicity with drinkability. Their Salice Salentino Rosso Riserva truly delivers. The 2015 version offers up black fruit, light spices and Mediterranean scrubland. Good tannins and fresh acidic tension make it fruity but austere, with a long, clear finish. Their 2015 Amativo, a Primitivo (60%) and Negroamaro blend, reaches the same level. The palate is rich in fruit, dynamic, and oaky. All of the wines presented were excellent.

| | |
|---|---|
| ● Amativo '15 | ♼♼ 4 |
| ● Salice Salentino Rosso Ris. '15 | ♼♼ 2* |
| ● Fanòi '12 | ♼♼ 6 |
| ☉ Negroamaro Rosato '17 | ♼♼ 2* |
| ☉ Rohesia '17 | ♼♼ 3 |
| ○ Teresa Manara Chardonnay '17 | ♼♼ 3 |
| ○ Teresa Manara Chardonnay Sei Settembre '16 | ♼♼ 4 |
| ● Teresa Manara Negroamaro '15 | ♼♼ 3 |
| ● Varius '16 | ♼♼ 2* |
| ○ Alticelli Fiano '17 | ♼ 2 |
| ● Amativo '14 | ♼♼ 4 |
| ● Salice Salentino Rosso Ris. '14 | ♼♼ 2* |
| ○ Teresa Manara Chardonnay Sedici Settembre '15 | ♼♼ 4 |

# Carvinea

LOC. PEZZA D'ARENA
VIA PER SERRANOVA
72012 CAROVIGNO [BR]
TEL. +39 0805862345
www.carvinea.com

CELLAR SALES
PRE-BOOKED VISITS
ACCOMMODATION AND RESTAURANT SERVICE
ANNUAL PRODUCTION 35,000 bottles
HECTARES UNDER VINE 12.00
VITICULTURE METHOD Certified Organic

Carvinea was founded in 2002 by Beppe
Di Maria in Carovigno, located in the heart
of Salento, just a stone's throw from the
Torre Guaceto Nature Reserve. During this
relatively short time, the winery has
changed direction by moving away from
non-native varieties toward focusing on the
region's traditional grapes. As a result,
Negroamaro, Primitivo, and Ottavianello
have come to dominate, supported by
Aglianico, Montepulciano and Petit Verdot.
Tre Bicchieri for their 2016 Otto. Rare
Ottavianello yields floral notes with hints of
red fruit and a finish that is both savory
and delicate. Their 2017 Merula Rosa, a
rosé made from fresh, juicy Moltepulciano,
their 2016 Negroamaro, with hints of
Mediterranean scrubland and of spices,
and their 2017 Lucerna, a fresh Fiano
with good structure but that is immediately
smooth as well, also all prove very enjoyable.

| | | |
|---|---|---|
| ● Otto '16 | ▼▼▼ 4* |
| ○ Lucerna '17 | ▼▼ 2* |
| ⊙ Merula Rosa '17 | ▼▼ 2* |
| ● Negroamaro '16 | ▼▼ 5 |
| ● Lunachiena '17 | ▼ 2 |
| ● Primitivo '16 | ▼ 5 |
| ● Frauma '08 | ♀♀♀ 4 |
| ● Merula '11 | ♀♀♀ 3* |
| ● Negroamaro '14 | ♀♀♀ 5 |
| ● Negroamaro '13 | ♀♀♀ 5 |
| ● Negroamaro '11 | ♀♀♀ 3* |
| ● Primitivo '15 | ♀♀♀ 5 |
| ● Sierma '09 | ♀♀♀ 5 |
| ⊙ Merula Rosa '16 | ♀♀ 2* |
| ● Negroamaro '15 | ♀♀ 5 |
| ● Otto '15 | ♀♀ 4 |

# Castello Monaci

VIA CASE SPARSE
73015 SALICE SALENTINO [LE]
TEL. +39 0831665700
www.castellomonaci.it

CELLAR SALES
PRE-BOOKED VISITS
RESTAURANT SERVICE
ANNUAL PRODUCTION 1,800,000 bottles
HECTARES UNDER VINE 210.00

Gruppo Italiano Vini's Castello Monaci
has significantly increased the size of
its vineyards. Today there are more than
200 hectares spread over three different
estates: Masseria Flaminia has 60
hectares of sandy soil close to the sea
and planted mainly with white grape
varietals; Masseria Vittorio a Trepuzzi
sees ten hectares of iron-rich, red soil
dedicated exclusively to Primitivo; and,
the historic estate of Salice Salentino is
comprised of 140 hectares of surface
clay over tufaceous rock planted with
Malvasia Nero di Lecce, Negroamaro and
Primitivo. Their 2017 Acante is one of the
best Fiano di Puglia. Fleshy, fresh and
well-structured, it offers a finish that is
both approachable and enjoyable. Their
2017 Primitivo Pilùna proves fruity, clear
and juicy, while their 2017 Salice Salentino
Rosso Liante shows smoothness despite
its remarkable structure. The rest of their
range is also very well made.

| | | |
|---|---|---|
| ○ Acante '17 | ▼▼ 2* |
| ● Pilùna '17 | ▼▼ 2* |
| ● Salice Salentino Rosso Liante '17 | ▼▼ 2* |
| ● Artas '16 | ▼ 5 |
| ● Coribante '16 | ▼ 3 |
| ⊙ Kreos '17 | ▼ 2 |
| ○ Moscatello Selvatico Passito '16 | ▼ 3 |
| ○ Petraluce '17 | ▼ 2 |
| ● Primitivo Bio '16 | ▼ 3 |
| ● Salice Salentino Aiace Ris. '15 | ▼ 3 |
| ● Artas '07 | ♀♀♀ 5 |
| ● Artas '06 | ♀♀♀ 4 |
| ● Artas '05 | ♀♀♀ 4* |
| ● Artas '04 | ♀♀♀ 3* |
| ● Artas '13 | ♀♀ 5 |
| ● Salice Salentino Aiace Ris. '13 | ♀♀ 3* |

# PUGLIA

## Giancarlo Ceci

C.DA SANT'AGOSTINO
76123 ANDRIA [BT]
TEL. +39 0883565220
www.giancarloceci.com

PRE-BOOKED VISITS
ANNUAL PRODUCTION 350,000 bottles
HECTARES UNDER VINE 60.00
VITICULTURE METHOD Certified Biodynamic
SUSTAINABLE WINERY

Since acquiring the estate in 1819, over eight generations, the Ceci family has been producing wine, oil, fruit and vegetables. Giancarlo first converted to an organic system in 1988, before becoming fully biodynamic in 2011. The 60 hectares of contiguous vines lie within an area of over 200 hectares between Andria and Castel del Monte, 250 meters above sea level and 20 kilometers from the sea. The territory's classics are cultivated, with Nero di Troia the star of their most ambitious wines. Great news from Giancarlo Ceci's winery. This year we were especially impressed by the 2015 Castel del Monte Nero of Troia Felice Ceci Riserva, with balsamic hints and notes of red fruit on the nose, while the palate is a nice thickness, proving well-made, juicy, rich and fruity. Their 2017 Moscato di Trani Dolce Rosalia, another noteworthy wine, with its aromas of honey and apricot, proves fresh and balanced. Their other Castel del Monte wines are also very well made.

| | |
|---|---|
| ● Castel del Monte Nero di Troia Felice Ceci Ris. '15 | ▼▼ 5 |
| ○ Castel del Monte Bombino Bianco Panascio '17 | ▼▼ 2* |
| ⊙ Castel del Monte Bombino Nero Rosato Parchitello '17 | ▼▼ 2* |
| ○ Castel del Monte Chardonnay Pozzo Sorgente '17 | ▼▼ 3 |
| ⊙ Castel del Monte Rosato Parco Petrullo '17 | ▼▼ 2* |
| ● Castel del Monte Rosso Parco Grande '17 | ▼▼ 2* |
| ○ Moscato di Trani Dolce Rosalia '17 | ▼▼ 4 |
| ○ Castel del Monte Chardonnay Chiusolillo '17 | ▼ 2 |
| ● Castel del Monte Rosso Almagia '17 | ▼ 2 |
| ● Castel del Monte Rosso Almagia '16 | ♟♟ 2* |

## ★Tenute Chiaromonte

B.GO ANNUNZIATA
70021 ACQUAVIVA DELLE FONTI [BA]
TEL. +39 080768156
www.tenutechiaromonte.com

CELLAR SALES
PRE-BOOKED VISITS
ANNUAL PRODUCTION 150,000 bottles
HECTARES UNDER VINE 45.00

Nicola Chiaromonte and Paolo Montanaro's winery is one of the region's best-known. Their 10 hectares of vineyards are situated at +300 meters elevation in Gioia del Colle. The calcareous and red clay soil here gives rise to head-trained Primitivo vines that go back more than 60 years. Once again their Gioia del Colle Primitivo Muro Sant'Angelo Contrada Barbatto earns Tre Bicchieri, proving to be one of Italy's best wines. The 2015 offers up aromas of berries and Mediterranean scrubland. These follow through to an intense and complex palate that's dynamic and fresh, with a very long finish. Their 2013 Gioia del Colle Primitivo Riserva is also excellent, savory and plucky, with great structure. The rest of the range is also well made, including their new 2016 Brut Metodo Classico, a wine made primarily with Pinot Noir.

| | |
|---|---|
| ● Gioia del Colle Primitivo Muro Sant'Angelo Contrada Barbatto '15 | ▼▼▼ 5 |
| ● Gioia del Colle Primitivo Ris. '13 | ▼▼ 8 |
| ○ Brut M. Cl. '16 | ▼▼ 5 |
| ● Gioia del Colle Primitivo Muro Sant'Angelo '16 | ▼▼ 4 |
| ⊙ Kimìa Primitivo Rosato '17 | ▼▼ 3 |
| ● Maschera Primitivo '15 | ▼▼ 2* |
| ● Elè '16 | ▼ 3 |
| ○ Kimìa Fiano '17 | ▼ 3 |
| ⊙ Kimìa Pinot Nero Rosato '17 | ▼ 3 |
| ● Gioia del Colle Primitivo Muro Sant'Angelo Contrada Barbatto '14 | ♟♟♟ 5 |
| ● Gioia del Colle Primitivo Muro Sant'Angelo Contrada Barbatto '13 | ♟♟♟ 5 |

# Coppi

S.DA PROV.LE TURI - GIOIA DEL COLLE
70010 TURI [BA]
TEL. +39 0808915049
www.vinicoppi.it

**CELLAR SALES**
**PRE-BOOKED VISITS**
**RESTAURANT SERVICE**
**ANNUAL PRODUCTION** 900,000 bottles
**HECTARES UNDER VINE** 100.00
**VITICULTURE METHOD** Certified Organic

Founded in 1882, this historic winery was taken over by Antonio Coppi at the end of the 1970s and is now run by his children Lisia, Miriam and Doni. The estate vineyards are half head-trained and they are planted with traditional red Primitivo, Aleatico, Malvasia Nera, and Negroamaro, as well as white Falanghina and Malvasia Bianca. The wines submitted are pure and modern, expressing the best of both the grapes and the terroir. For the third year in a row, their Gioia del Colle Primitivo Senatore gets Tre Bicchieri, but unlike the past two years, the 2015 was not aged long in the cellar. On the nose it offers up black fruit and spices followed by a plucky palate that is full bodied, with considerable length. The rest of the range, especially the 2016 Don Antonio Primitivo, is also well made, fresh and juicy.

| | |
|---|---|
| ● Gioia del Colle Primitivo Senatore '15 | ▼▼▼ 5 |
| ● Don Antonio Primitivo '16 | ▼▼ 3* |
| ☉ Corè '17 | ▼▼ 2* |
| ○ Guiscardo Falanghina '17 | ▼▼ 3 |
| ● Vinaccero '13 | ▼▼ 3 |
| ● Pellirosso Negroamaro '17 | ▼ 2 |
| ● Sannace Malvasia Nera '16 | ▼ 2 |
| ○ Serralto Malvasia Bianca '17 | ▼ 2 |
| ● Siniscalco Primitivo '16 | ▼ 2 |
| ● Gioia del Colle Primitivo Senatore '11 | ▼▼▼ 5 |
| ● Gioia del Colle Primitivo Senatore '10 | ▼▼▼ 3* |
| ● Don Antonio Primitivo '15 | ▼▼ 3 |
| ● Don Antonio Primitivo '13 | ▼▼ 3 |
| ● Pellirosso Negroamaro '16 | ▼▼ 2* |
| ● Vinaccero Aleatico '12 | ▼▼ 3 |

# ★Cantine Due Palme

VIA SAN MARCO, 130
72020 CELLINO SAN MARCO [BR]
TEL. +39 0831617865
www.cantineduepalme.it

**CELLAR SALES**
**PRE-BOOKED VISITS**
**ACCOMMODATION AND RESTAURANT SERVICE**
**ANNUAL PRODUCTION** 14,000,000 bottles
**HECTARES UNDER VINE** 2500.00

Founded thirty years ago, this cooperative winery is the most important in the Salento area, if not the entire region, and their numbers prove it. Twelve hundred members working 2500 hectares of vineyards, of which about 1000 are head-trained, producing a total of 14 million bottles annually. Ninety percent of the vineyards are made up of mainly traditional red grapes. Modern production methods result in wines that are technically well-made and provide very good value for money. Once again Cantine Due Palme earns Tre Bicchieri: the prize goes to their 2015 Salice Salentino Rosso Selvarossa Riserva, a wine that's rich in body, with fruity hints and black olive puree. Their 2015 1943 Del Presidente is a truly impressive blend of Primitive and Aglianico with notes of quinine, aromatic herbs and blackberry that is almost austere in its boldness, its tension and freshness.

| | |
|---|---|
| ● Salice Salentino Rosso Selvarossa Ris. '15 | ▼▼▼ 4* |
| ● 1943 del Presidente '15 | ▼▼ 6 |
| ☉ Corerosa Gold Edition '17 | ▼▼ 3 |
| ● Salice Salentino Rosso Selvarossa Terra Ris. '15 | ▼▼ 5 |
| ● Seraia Malvasia Nera '16 | ▼▼ 2* |
| ○ Anthea Falanghina '17 | ▼ 2 |
| ● Primitivo di Manduria San Gaetano '17 | ▼ 2 |
| ○ Salice Salentino Bianco Tinaia '17 | ▼ 3 |
| ● Serre Susumaniello '16 | ▼ 3 |
| ● Salice Salentino Rosso Selvarossa Ris. '14 | ▼▼▼ 4* |
| ● Salice Salentino Rosso Selvarossa Ris. '13 | ▼▼▼ 4* |
| ● Salice Salentino Rosso Selvarossa Ris. '12 | ▼▼▼ 4* |

# PUGLIA

## Tenute Eméra
## di Claudio Quarta Vignaiolo

FRAZ. MARINA DI LIZZANO
C.DA PORVICA
74123 LIZZANO [TA]
TEL. +39 0832704398
www.claudioquarta.it

CELLAR SALES
PRE-BOOKED VISITS
ACCOMMODATION
ANNUAL PRODUCTION 550,000 bottles
HECTARES UNDER VINE 50.00
SUSTAINABLE WINERY

Tenute Eméra, located close to the sea near Lizzano, consists of almost 50 hectares within a property of about 80 hectares, making it the largest of Claudio Quarta's wineries. It was planted in 2007. In addition to traditional Primitivo, Negroamaro and Fiano, there are international varieties like Syrah, Merlot, Cabernet Sauvignon and Chardonnay. An experimental vineyard with about 500 predominantly Caucasian and Mediterranean cultivars is worth noting, and the winery also draws on just over an hectare near Guagnano. Their 2016 Primitivo di Manduria Anima di Primitivo is a real stand out with its aromas of black damson, plums and hints of spices. The palate is juicy and fresh, having an elegant tannin that proves both enjoyable and long. Their well-made 2016 Lizzano Negroamaro Superiore Anima di Negroamaro expresses itself as savory and fresh, with notes of red fruit and Mediterranean scrubland. Their 2016 Sud del Sud offers enjoyability and drinkability.

| | |
|---|---|
| ● Primitivo di Manduria Anima di Primitivo '16 | ♟♟ 3* |
| ● Lizzano Negroamaro Sup. Anima di Negroamaro '16 | ♟♟ 2* |
| ● Sud del Sud '16 | ♟♟ 3 |
| ○ Amure '17 | ♟ 3 |
| ○ Anima di Chardonnay "R"evolution '16 | ♟ 3 |
| ⊙ Rose '17 | ♟ 3 |
| ○ Amure '16 | ♟♟ 2* |
| ● Lizzano Negroamaro Sup. Anima di Negroamaro '16 | ♟♟ 2* |
| ● Primitivo di Manduria Oro di Eméra '14 | ♟♟ 5 |
| ● Salice Salentino Rosso Moros Ris. '13 | ♟♟ 4 |
| ● Sud del Sud '15 | ♟♟ 3 |
| ● Sud del Sud '14 | ♟♟ 3 |

## Felline

VIA SANTO STASI PRIMO, 42B
74024 MANDURIA [TA]
TEL. +39 0999711660
www.agricolafelline.it

CELLAR SALES
PRE-BOOKED VISITS
ANNUAL PRODUCTION 1,000,000 bottles
HECTARES UNDER VINE 120.00
VITICULTURE METHOD Certified Organic
SUSTAINABLE WINERY

Gregory Perrucci needs no introduction. He's one of the central figures in the revival of the Salento area, as much for the modern, elegant style of his wine that expresses the freshness of the fruit, as for his efforts in the revival of Apulian head-trained vines. Vineyards planted exclusively with traditional varietals are located in different areas of the Primitivo di Manduria appellation. As a result, the grapes grow on diverse terrain, from sandy soil near the sea to red soil further inland. Tre Bicchieri for their 2016 Primitivo di Manduria Zinfandel Sinfarosa Terra Nera, which offers up balsamic notes with hints of ripe cherry. It yields a tight structure and complexity that is enjoyable and precise. The winery's excellent 2016 Primitivo di Manduria Dunico Cru Sabbia is still marked by oak, but offers up clear aromas of prunes and black damson. Their 2017 Anarkos (eminently enjoyable, dominated by juicy fruit) and 2017 Sum Torreguaceto (featuring fresh and approachable hints of wild berries) are both very well made.

| | |
|---|---|
| ● Primitivo di Manduria Zinfandel Sinfarosa Terra Nera '16 | ♟♟♟ 4* |
| ● Primitivo di Manduria Dunico Cru Sabbia '16 | ♟♟ 5 |
| ● Alberello '17 | ♟♟ 2* |
| ● Alcione '17 | ♟♟ 2* |
| ● Anarkos '17 | ♟♟ 2* |
| ● Galante '17 | ♟♟ 2* |
| ● Malvasia Nera '17 | ♟♟ 3 |
| ● Nero di Troia '17 | ♟♟ 2* |
| ● Sum Torre Guaceto '17 | ♟♟ 3 |
| ○ Verdeca '17 | ♟♟ 2* |
| ⊙ Cicala Rosè '17 | ♟ 2 |
| ● I Monili '17 | ♟ 2 |
| ● Primitivo di Manduria Terra Rossa '17 | ♟ 3 |
| ● Primitivo di Manduria '15 | ♟♟♟ 3* |
| ● Primitivo di Manduria Archidamo '12 | ♟♟♟ 2* |

# Gianfranco Fino

VIA PIAVE, 12
74028 SAVA [TA]
TEL. +39 0997773970
www.gianfrancofino.it

PRE-BOOKED VISITS
ANNUAL PRODUCTION 20,000 bottles
HECTARES UNDER VINE 21.00
SUSTAINABLE WINERY

Gianfranco and Simona Fino's winery got its start in 2004 with the purchase of just over one hectare in the Manduria appellation. In the intervening years they have grown to more than 20 hectares, including rented vineyards, in which old and head-trained vines play a starring role. The most significant achievement, however, is their Es, a new paradigm of Primitivo and a role model for most of the winemakers in Manduria and beyond. Es, their only wine presented this year, is always among Puglia's best. Their 2016 version shows hints of jammy black fruit, followed by delicate notes of iodine and smoke, while the palate proves full of thick, juicy fruit that is pleasant and fresh, with a long, dynamic and plucky finish.

| | |
|---|---|
| ● Es '16 | ▼▼▼ 7 |
| ● Primitivo di Manduria Es '12 | ♈♈♈ 7 |
| ● Primitivo di Manduria Es '11 | ♈♈♈ 7 |
| ● Primitivo di Manduria Es '10 | ♈♈♈ 6 |
| ● Primitivo di Manduria Es '09 | ♈♈♈ 6 |
| ● Primitivo di Manduria Es '08 | ♈♈♈ 6 |
| ● Primitivo di Manduria Es '07 | ♈♈♈ 6 |
| ● Primitivo di Manduria Es '06 | ♈♈♈ 5 |
| ● Es '15 | ♈♈ 7 |
| ● Jo '08 | ♈♈ 6 |
| ● Primitivo di Manduria Dolce Naturale Es + Sole '12 | ♈♈ 7 |
| ● Primitivo di Manduria '14 | ♈♈ 7 |
| ● Primitivo di Manduria '13 | ♈♈ 7 |
| ● Primitivo di Manduria '05 | ♈♈ 5 |

# Tenute Girolamo

VIA NOCI, 314
74015 MARTINA FRANCA [TA]
TEL. +39 0804402088
www.tenutegirolamo.it

CELLAR SALES
PRE-BOOKED VISITS
ANNUAL PRODUCTION 400,000 bottles
HECTARES UNDER VINE 50.00

The estate of Tenute Girolamo, founded in 2010, is comprised of private vineyards situated at elevations ranging from 350 to 450 meters above sea level on the mixed calcareous, red soil of Itria Valley. Their selection is divided into two lines. Their Monte dei Cocci wines include a Primitivo di Mandura, as well as varietal offerings made with native and international grapes, while their second line focuses exclusively on native varieties. Their range is modern, highlighting the fullness and richness of the fruit. Solid results for the wines proposed by Tenute Giolamo. Their 2016 Monte dei Cocci Negroamaro, still marked by oak, offers up clear aromas of cherry and raspberry. Their 2015 Conte Giangirolamo, an equal blend of Primitivo and Negroamaro, yields body and structure but lacks a bit of freshness at the finish. Their 2014 Aglianico Codalunga proves austere in its aromas of pencil lead.

| | |
|---|---|
| ● Codalunga '14 | ♈♈ 5 |
| ● Conte Giangirolamo '15 | ♈♈ 6 |
| ● Monte dei Cocci Negroamaro '16 | ♈♈ 4 |
| ● Monte Tre Carlini '15 | ♈ 5 |
| ● Conte Giangirolamo '13 | ♈♈ 6 |
| ● Conte Giangirolamo '12 | ♈♈ 6 |
| ● Conte Giangirolamo '10 | ♈♈ 4 |
| ● Monte dei Cocci Negroamaro '15 | ♈♈ 4 |
| ● Monte dei Cocci Negroamaro '13 | ♈♈ 4 |
| ● Monte dei Cocci Primitivo V. T. '15 | ♈♈ 3 |
| ○ Monte dei Cocci Verdeca '16 | ♈♈ 4 |
| ● Pizzo Rosso '11 | ♈♈ 2* |
| ● Primitivo La Voliera '16 | ♈♈ 3 |

# PUGLIA

## Vito Donato Giuliani

VIA GIOIA CANALE, 18
70010 TURI [BA]
TEL. +39 0808915335
www.vitivinicolagiuliani.com

**ANNUAL PRODUCTION** 100,000 bottles
**HECTARES UNDER VINE** 40.00

Founded in 1940, the Giuliani family winery is situated on the hills of Murgia near Bari, between Turi and Gioia del Colle. Primitivo dominates these karst soils, made of a thin layer of red soil over a thick rocky base rich in mineral salts. Handling in the cellar produces wine that expresses the territory, but especially in the case of Primitivo, reflects more recent interpretations of the variety. Tre Bicchieri for their 2015 Gioia del Colle Primitivo Baronaggio Riserva. Rich in fruit with hints of citrus, it is well-balanced, savory, fresh and plucky with a long, highly enjoyable finish. Their 2017 Chiancaia, a remarkably aromatic Fiano (more reminiscent of Minutolo than Fiano Campano) proves well made and highly drinkable. Their 2015 Gioia del Colle Aleatico Cantone di Cristo is a sweet wine with balanced notes of plum jam.

| | |
|---|---|
| ● Gioia del Colle Primitivo Baronaggio Ris. '15 | ♟♟♟ 5 |
| ○ Chiancaia '17 | ♟♟ 3 |
| ● Gioia del Colle Aleatico Cantone di Cristo '15 | ♟♟ 4 |
| ● Gioia del Colle Primitivo Lavarossa '15 | ♟ 3 |
| ● Gioia del Colle Baronaggio Ris. '13 | ♟♟ 5 |
| ● Gioia del Colle Primitivo Baronaggio Ris. '12 | ♟♟ 5 |
| ● Gioia del Colle Primitivo Lavarossa '14 | ♟♟ 3 |
| ● Gioia del Colle Primitivo Lavarossa '13 | ♟♟ 3 |
| ● Gioia del Colle Primitivo Lavarossa '12 | ♟♟ 3* |

## Cantine Paolo Leo

VIA TUTURANO, 21
72025 SAN DONACI [BR]
TEL. +39 0831635073
www.paololeo.it

**CELLAR SALES**
**PRE-BOOKED VISITS**
**ACCOMMODATION**
**ANNUAL PRODUCTION** 1,300,000 bottles
**HECTARES UNDER VINE** 45.00

Since 1989, Cantine Paolo Leo has offered a wide range of modern wine - eight different lines totaling about 50 offerings, to be precise. All express the varietal characteristics of the traditional Apulian grapes. The Cantine's production from their own vineyards is supported by work as a négociant, collaborating with trusted winemakers who are certified by a system of traceability. The vineyards, located in the town of San Donaci, are composed of 40-year-old head-trained vines, and espaliered vines that are approximately 15 years old. Tre Bicchieri for their 2016 Orfeo Negroamaro. Intense aromas of plum, spices and quina bark are followed by a dynamic, dense and long palate of rich black fruit. Their 2015 Negramante, a Negroamaro with subtle notes of iodine proves well-balanced and enjoyable. The 2014 Primitivo di Manduria Giunonico Riserva is a fresh and highly drinkable wine, while their 2017 Manduria Passo del Cardinale goes all in on fruit.

| | |
|---|---|
| ● Orfeo Negroamaro '16 | ♟♟♟ 5 |
| ● Negramante Negroamaro '15 | ♟♟ 3 |
| ● Primitivo di Manduria Giunonico Ris. '14 | ♟♟ 6 |
| ● Primitivo di Manduria Passo del Cardinale '17 | ♟♟ 3 |
| ● Dorso Rosso Negroamaro '13 | ♟ 8 |
| ● Salice Salentino Rosso Limitone dei Greci '13 | ♟ 3 |
| ● Taccorosso Negroamaro '14 | ♟ 6 |
| ● Orfeo Negroamaro '15 | ♟♟♟ 4* |
| ● Primitivo di Manduria Passo del Cardinale '14 | ♟♟♟ 3* |
| ○ Alture Minutolo '16 | ♟♟ 3 |
| ● Fiore di Vigna '14 | ♟♟ 5 |
| ● Fiore di Vigna '13 | ♟♟ 4 |
| ● Primitivo di Manduria Passo del Cardinale '15 | ♟♟ 3 |

## ★Leone de Castris

VIA SENATORE DE CASTRIS, 26
73015 SALICE SALENTINO [LE]
TEL. +39 0832731112
www.leonedecastris.com

**PRE-BOOKED VISITS**
**ANNUAL PRODUCTION** 2,500,000 bottles
**HECTARES UNDER VINE** 300.00
**SUSTAINABLE WINERY**

Leone de Castris is the leader of the Salice Salento appellation and a benchmark for Salento's winegrowing. The estate has vineyards in Salice Salento, Campi and Guagnano and offers an ample range of products - a solid forty-plus wines - from both native and international grape varieties. Their wine is characterized by a modern style that accentuates the pleasantness and richness of the fruit. The first Tre Bicchieri awarded to a rosé from Puglia could go to no other than the 2017 Five Roses 74° Anniversario. This Negroamaro, offers floral and red currant notes without sacrificing sweetness, length, balance, juiciness and good structure. Their 2017 Five Roses, also made with Negroamaro, but softer and more approachable, proves another standout. Their 2016 Salice Salentino Rosso Riserva, with black fruit tones and balsamic nuances, is fresh and plucky, while their 2017 Primitivo di Manduria Santera, with cherry notes, offers length and great enjoyability.

| | |
|---|---|
| ⊙ Five Roses 74° Anniversario '17 | 🍷🍷🍷 3* |
| ● Salice Salentino Rosso Ris. '16 | 🍷🍷 3* |
| ○ Donna Lisa Malvasia Bianca '17 | 🍷🍷 4 |
| ● Elo Veni '17 | 🍷🍷 2* |
| ⊙ Five Roses '17 | 🍷🍷 3 |
| ● Primitivo di Manduria Santera '17 | 🍷🍷 3 |
| ● Salice Salentino Rosso Donna Lisa Ris. '15 | 🍷🍷 5 |
| ⊙ Salice Salentino Brut Five Roses M. Cl. '15 | 🍷 4 |
| ● Villa Santera Primitivo '17 | 🍷 3 |
| ⊙ Villa Santera Primitivo Rosato '17 | 🍷 2 |
| ● Salice Salentino Rosso 50° Vendemmia Ris. '14 | 🍷🍷🍷 3* |
| ● Salice Salentino Rosso Per Lui Ris. '15 | 🍷🍷🍷 6 |

## Masseria Li Veli

S.DA PROV.LE CELLINO-CAMPI, KM 1
72020 CELLINO SAN MARCO [BR]
TEL. +39 0831618259
www.liveli.it

**CELLAR SALES**
**PRE-BOOKED VISITS**
**ANNUAL PRODUCTION** 400,000 bottles
**HECTARES UNDER VINE** 33.00
**SUSTAINABLE WINERY**

After 40 years of experience in Tuscany, the Falvo family moved to Puglia in 1999 when it decided to buy and renovate Masseria Li Veli. Red grapes are grown mainly in Agro Cellino San Marco on sandy, red soil, while their white grapes come from Valle d'Itria. With the exception of a small amount of Cabernet Sauvignon that enters into the MLV blend, their cultivars are all traditional, from Negroamaro to Primitivo, Malvasia Nera, Susumaniello, Aleatico, Verdeca and Fiano Minutolo. The wines of the Falvo family are, as always, well made, but this year we did not taste their standard bearers - their MLV and Aleatico Passito. The 2017 Askos Susumaniello Rosato, with its notes of mulberry and blackcurrant, is a fresh, juicy and approachable wine. Their Askos Verdeca, a brilliant straw-yellow 2017 with greenish highlights, proves fragrant on the nose, redolent of Mediterranean herbs and citrus; on the palate it comes through savory and succulent.

| | |
|---|---|
| ○ Askos Verdeca '17 | 🍷🍷🍷 3* |
| ⊙ Askos Susumaniello Rosato '17 | 🍷🍷 2* |
| ● Salice Salentino Rosso Pezzo Morgana Ris. '16 | 🍷🍷🍷 4 |
| ● Askos Primitivo '16 | 🍷 4 |
| ● Askos Susumaniello '17 | 🍷 4 |
| ● Masseria Li Veli '10 | 🍷🍷🍷 5 |
| ● Aleatico Passito '10 | 🍷🍷 8 |
| ● Askos Susumaniello '16 | 🍷🍷 4 |
| ○ Askos Verdeca '16 | 🍷🍷 4 |
| ● MLV '15 | 🍷🍷 5 |
| ● MLV '13 | 🍷🍷 5 |
| ● Salice Salentino Pezzo Morgana Ris. '15 | 🍷🍷 4 |
| ● Salice Salentino Rosso Pezzo Morgana Ris. '14 | 🍷🍷 4 |
| ● Susumaniello Askos '15 | 🍷🍷 3 |

## Masca del Tacco

VIA TRIPOLI, 5/7
72020 ERCHIE [BR]
TEL. +39 0831759786
www.mascadeltacco.com

ANNUAL PRODUCTION 80,000 bottles
HECTARES UNDER VINE 200.00

Felice Mergè, owner of the winery Poggio
Le Volpi in Lazio, founded Masca del Tacco
in 2010. It came about after the purchase
and restructuring of Cooperativa Comunale
dei Produttori di Erchie, which had been
active in the area around Brindisi since
1949. The winery's vineyards, which
include not only those in the Brindisi area
but also the Primitivo di Manduria DOC and
the Salice Salentino DOC, are planted with
both classic traditional and international
grape varieties. In the absence of their
Primitivo di Manduria Lu Pappaio and Li
Filitti, the 2015 Primitivo di Manduria Piano
Chiuso 26 27 63 stands out. Aromas of
citrus peel and black fruit give way to a
palate that yields rich fruit despite the
distinct presence of alcohol. It proves juicy
with a finish made fresh by acidity. Their
well-made 2017 Ro'si, a Pinot Nero rosé, is
approachable, floral and supple.

| | |
|---|---|
| ● Primitivo di Manduria Piano Chiuso 26 27 63 Ris. '15 | ♟♟ 4 |
| ● Primitivo di Manduria Li Filitti Ris. '15 | ♟♟ 4 |
| ● Primitivo di Manduria Lu Pappaio '17 | ♟♟ 4 |
| ⊙ Ro'si '17 | ♟♟ 3 |
| ○ L'Uetta '17 | ♟ 3 |
| ● Primitivo di Manduria Li Filitti Ris. '12 | ♟♟ 4 |
| ● Primitivo di Manduria Li Filitti Ris. '11 | ♟♟ 4 |
| ● Primitivo di Manduria Lu Pappaio '15 | ♟♟ 4 |

## Morella

VIA PER UGGIANO, 147
74024 MANDURIA [TA]
TEL. +39 0999791482
www.morellavini.com

CELLAR SALES
PRE-BOOKED VISITS
ANNUAL PRODUCTION 26,000 bottles
HECTARES UNDER VINE 20.00
VITICULTURE METHOD Certified Biodynamic

For several years, Lisa Gilbee and Gaetano
Morella's winery has been one of the most
highly regarded in Manduria. Research and
strict adhesion to the territory have made it
a benchmark, especially with regard to
Primitivo. Top wines are the result of mass
selection from vineyards that are over 60
years old and located on red soil. Their
approach in the cellar is focused on
expressing characteristics of the territory to
every extent possible. Their Old Vines
Primitivo is back in our finals, and the 2015
vintage is one of their best ever. Hints of
fresh black berry fruit and herbs emerge on
the nose, while the palate holds together
well, proving consistent, fresh and almost
austere. It displays good length and tension
and a juicy finish. The rest of the range is
well-crafted, including the 2015 Primitivo
La Signora, with its citrusy tones and grip,
the 2015 Primitivo Mondo Nuovo, which
comes through fresh and spicy, and the
pleasant 2017 Mezzogiorno Bianco.

| | |
|---|---|
| ● Old Vines Primitivo '15 | ♟♟ 6 |
| ● La Signora Primitivo '15 | ♟♟ 6 |
| ○ Mezzogiorno '17 | ♟♟ 3 |
| ● Primitivo Mondo Nuovo '15 | ♟♟ 6 |
| ● Primitivo Malbek '15 | ♟ 4 |
| ● La Signora Primitivo '10 | ♟♟♟ 6 |
| ● La Signora Primitivo '07 | ♟♟♟ 5 |
| ● Old Vines Primitivo '09 | ♟♟♟ 5 |
| ● Old Vines Primitivo '08 | ♟♟♟ 5 |
| ● Old Vines Primitivo '07 | ♟♟♟ 5 |
| ● La Signora Primitivo '13 | ♟♟ 6 |
| ● La Signora Primitivo '11 | ♟♟ 6 |
| ○ Mezzogiorno '16 | ♟♟ 3 |
| ● Negroamaro Primitivo Terre Rosse '12 | ♟♟ 4 |
| ● Old Vines Primitivo '14 | ♟♟ 6 |
| ● Old Vines Primitivo '13 | ♟♟ 6 |

# Palamà

VIA A. DIAZ, 6
73020 CUTROFIANO [LE]
TEL. +39 0836542865
www.vinicolapalama.com

CELLAR SALES
PRE-BOOKED VISITS
ANNUAL PRODUCTION 200,000 bottles
HECTARES UNDER VINE 15.00
SUSTAINABLE WINERY

The Palamà family winery was established in 1936 on medium-density soil located between Cutrofiano and Matino. Only the traditional, mostly head-trained, varieties of Negroamaro, Primitivo, Malvasia Nera, Malvasia Bianca and Verdeca are cultivated. Their wide selection, traditional in its expression of the characteristics of the area, is enhanced by notable technical precision in the cellar. The 2017 Metiusco Rosato has reached our finals once again, proving to be one of the best Apulian rosés: red fruit and floral notes on the nose lead into a juicy and pleasant palate. The 2016 Mavro is a Primitivo exhibiting overtones of Mediterranean scrub, freshness and good length, as does the 2017 75 Vendemmie, a Negroamaro with volume and generous fruit. The other two 2017 wines from the Metiusco line are the full and caressing Rosso and the approachable Bianco, featuring pleasant aromatic notes of sage.

| | | |
|---|---|---|
| ⊙ Metiusco Rosato '17 | ♀♀ 3* | |
| ● 75 Vendemmie '17 | ♀♀ 5 | |
| ● Mavro '16 | ♀♀ 4 | |
| ○ Metiusco Bianco '17 | ♀♀ 3 | |
| ● Metiusco Rosso '17 | ♀♀ 3 | |
| ● Salice Salentino Rosso Albarossa '16 | ♀ 2 | |
| ● 75 Vendemmie '11 | ♀♀ 4* | |
| ● 75 Vendemmie '15 | ♀♀ 4 | |
| ● Mavro '15 | ♀♀ 3* | |
| ● Mavro '13 | ♀♀ 3* | |
| ● Metiusco Oro Rosso Passito '15 | ♀♀ 3 | |
| ⊙ Metiusco Rosato '16 | ♀♀ 2* | |
| ⊙ Metiusco Rosato '15 | ♀♀ 2* | |
| ● Metiusco Rosso '16 | ♀♀ 2* | |

# Polvanera

S.DA VICINALE LAMIE MARCHESANA, 601
70023 GIOIA DEL COLLE [BA]
TEL. +39 080758900
www.cantinepolvanera.it

CELLAR SALES
RESTAURANT SERVICE
ANNUAL PRODUCTION 650,000 bottles
HECTARES UNDER VINE 120.00
VITICULTURE METHOD Certified Organic

Filippo Cassano brought Polvanera to the top of regional production in just over 15 years. Most of the vineyards are situated on the Murgia's characteristic rocky karst soil, in Gioia del Colle and Acquaviva delle Fonti, ranging from 300 to 450 meters above sea level. The grapes benefit from significant temperature variations caused by the plateau. Primitivo plays a key role in the line, flanked by Aglianico, Aleatico, Bianco D'alessano, Falanghina, Minutolo, Moscato and Verdeca. Their wines seek to fully express the attributes of both the native cultivars and the distinctive terroir. Polvanera's wines are always exceptionally good, but this year their 2015 Gioia del Colle Primitivo 16 Vigneto San Benedetto won the Tre Bicchieri: fresh black berry fruit, great grip, intensity and length, juicy and savory. The 2015 Gioia del Colle Primitivo 17 Vigneto Montenovella, on the other hand, comes through spicy, with notes of herbs on the nose, followed by a palate that's a bit sweet at first, but finds tension again at the finish.

| | | |
|---|---|---|
| ● Gioia del Colle Primitivo 16 Vign. San Benedetto '15 | ♀♀♀ 5 | |
| ● Gioia del Colle Primitivo 17 Vign. Montevella '15 | ♀♀ 6 | |
| ● Gioia del Colle Primitivo 14 Vign. Marchesana '15 | ♀♀ 3 | |
| ⊙ Rosato '17 | ♀♀ 2* | |
| ○ Bianco d'Alessano '17 | ♀ 3 | |
| ○ Verdeca '17 | ♀ 3 | |
| ● Gioia del Colle Primitivo 17 '13 | ♀♀♀ 5 | |
| ● Gioia del Colle Primitivo 17 '10 | ♀♀♀ 5 | |
| ● Gioia del Colle Primitivo 17 Vign. Montevella '14 | ♀♀♀ 6 | |
| ● Gioia del Colle Primitivo 17 Vign. Montevella '12 | ♀♀♀ 6 | |
| ● Gioia del Colle Primitivo 17 Vign. Montevella '11 | ♀♀♀ 6 | |

## Produttori di Manduria

VIA FABIO MASSIMO, 19
74024 MANDURIA [TA]
TEL. +39 0999735332
www.cpvini.com

**CELLAR SALES**
**PRE-BOOKED VISITS**
**ANNUAL PRODUCTION 1,100,000 bottles**
**HECTARES UNDER VINE 900.00**
**SUSTAINABLE WINERY**

Cooperative Produttori Vini Manduria was founded in 1932 and today has 400 members who tend 900 hectares within the Primitivo di Manduria appellation. About half of the mostly Primitivo grapevines are Apulian head-trained and have more than 50 years in age. Their approach in the cellar results in modern wine that expresses to the fullest the territory's characteristics. The 2016 Primitivo di Manduria Lirica has reached our finals. Overtones of spice and black berry fruit give way to a full palate featuring close-focused aromas, tension and elegance, making for a really impressive wine with great typicity. The 2015 Primitivo di Manduria Elegia Riserva expresses distinctive notes of cherry jam, while the 2014 Primitivo di Manduria Sonetto Riserva still shows a faint hint of oak, marked coffee overtones, but with a very long finish. The rest of their selection proves sound.

| | |
|---|---|
| ● Primitivo di Manduria Lirica '16 | ♙♙ 2* |
| ● Primitivo di Manduria Elegia Ris. '15 | ♙♙ 5 |
| ● Primitivo di Manduria Sonetto Ris. '14 | ♙♙ 6 |
| ⊙ Aka '17 | ♙ 2 |
| ● Primitivo di Manduria Dolce Naturale Madrigale '15 | ♙ 4 |
| ● Primitivo di Manduria Memoria '17 | ♙ 2 |
| ○ Zin '17 | ♙ 2 |
| ⊙ Amoroso '15 | ♉♉ 2* |
| ● Primitivo di Manduria Dolce Naturale Madrigale '14 | ♉♉ 3 |
| ● Primitivo di Manduria Elegia Ris. '13 | ♉♉ 4 |
| ● Primitivo di Manduria Elegia Ris. '11 | ♉♉ 4 |
| ● Primitivo di Manduria Lirica '15 | ♉♉ 2* |
| ● Primitivo di Manduria Sonetto Ris. '12 | ♉♉ 6 |

## Rivera

S.DA PROV.LE 231 KM 60,500
76123 ANDRIA [BT]
TEL. +39 0883569510
www.rivera.it

**CELLAR SALES**
**PRE-BOOKED VISITS**
**ANNUAL PRODUCTION 1,200,000 bottles**
**HECTARES UNDER VINE 75.00**

Rivera, an estate belonging to Apulian viticulture's venerable De Corato family, is a leader in the Castel del Monte appellation. The estate's four vineyards are located on two distinct terroirs within the area. Rivera, Torre di Bocca and Coppa, located from 200 to 230 meters above sea level, are characterized by deep tufaceous, calcareous soil. Lama di Corvo, which overlooks the sea from an elevation of 350 meters, is situated on rocky, calcareous soil. For wines from other zones the winery relies on a few trusted vendors. Castel del Monte della Rivera wines are some of the best in the appellation, for all wine styles. The 2013 Nero di Troia Puer Apuliae Riserva reveals oak maturation, but possesses body, juicy fruit and fine-grained tannins. The 2012 Aglianico Cappellaccio Riserva proves well-structured, classic and well-made; the 2016 Nero di Troia Violante comes through fresh and approachable with blackberry overtones, while the 2013 Il Falcone Riserva appears fruity with good grip.

| | |
|---|---|
| ● Castel del Monte Aglianico Cappellaccio Ris. '12 | ♙♙ 2* |
| ○ Castel del Monte Bianco Fedora '17 | ♙♙ 2* |
| ⊙ Castel del Monte Bombino Nero Pungirosa '17 | ♙♙ 2* |
| ● Castel del Monte Nero di Troia Puer Apuliae Ris. '13 | ♙♙ 5 |
| ● Castel del Monte Nero di Troia Violante '16 | ♙♙ 2* |
| ● Castel del Monte Rosso Il Falcone Ris. '13 | ♙♙ 4 |
| ○ Castel del Monte Chardonnay Lama del Corvo '17 | ♙ 3 |
| ○ Castel del Monte Chardonnay Preludio n°1 '17 | ♙ 2 |
| ⊙ Castel del Monte Rosé '17 | ♙ 2 |
| ● Castel del Monte Rosso Rupicolo '16 | ♙ 2 |

## ★Tenute Rubino

VIA E. FERMI, 50
72100 BRINDISI
TEL. +39 0831571955
www.tenuterubino.com

**CELLAR SALES**
**PRE-BOOKED VISITS**
**ANNUAL PRODUCTION** 1,200,000 bottles
**HECTARES UNDER VINE** 200.00

Tenute Rubino has succeeded in bringing its wines to the top of Apulian production in less than 20 years. The vineyards, dominated by native grape varieties and a small quantity of Vermentino and Chardonnay, are spread across four zones: Jaddico, where Susumaniello is the heavy focus among other vines; Marmorelle, where the youngest vines are located; Uggio, with calcareous soil and wide variations in temperature; and Punta Aquila, dedicated completely to the cultivation of Primitivo. Wines made with Susumaniello grapes have proved to be the winery's strong point again this year. Their 2017 Oltremé displays aromas of black berry fruit and spices, while the palate comes through full and close-knit, supported by acidity and a long finish featuring notes of cinchona and blackberries: thoroughly deserving of the Tre Bicchieri. Another excellent wine is their complex and fruit-rich 2016 Torre Testa Susumaniello, though it lacks a touch of grip.

| | |
|---|---|
| ● Oltremé '17 | ▼▼▼ 4* |
| ● Torre Testa Susumaniello '16 | ▼▼ 8 |
| ● Brindisi Negroamaro Miraglio '16 | ▼▼ 4 |
| ● Brindisi Rosso Jaddico Ris. '16 | ▼▼ 6 |
| ○ Giancòla '17 | ▼▼ 5 |
| ● Punta Aquila '16 | ▼▼ 4 |
| ○ Salende '17 | ▼▼ 4 |
| ● Visellio '16 | ▼▼ 6 |
| ○ Marmorelle Bianco '17 | ▼ 3 |
| ⊙ Saturnino '17 | ▼ 4 |
| ⊙ Torre Testa Rosé '17 | ▼ 3 |
| ● Oltremé '16 | ♀♀♀ 4* |
| ● Oltremé Susumaniello '15 | ♀♀♀ 4* |
| ● Torre Testa '13 | ♀♀♀ 6 |
| ● Torre Testa '12 | ♀♀♀ 6 |
| ● Torre Testa '11 | ♀♀♀ 6 |
| ● Torre Testa '11 | ♀♀♀ 6 |

## Cantine San Marzano

VIA MONSIGNOR BELLO, 9
74020 SAN MARZANO DI SAN GIUSEPPE [TA]
TEL. +39 0999574181
www.cantinesanmarzano.com

**CELLAR SALES**
**ANNUAL PRODUCTION** 10,000,000 bottles
**HECTARES UNDER VINE** 1500.00
**VITICULTURE METHOD** Certified Organic
**SUSTAINABLE WINERY**

This large cooperative winery relies on 1200 grower members, who cultivate vineyards located mainly in the municipalities of San Marzano, Sava and Francavilla Fontana. The terroir is largely calcareous red soil with a high level of iron oxides. The cooperative offers 25 wines made with traditional and international cultivars, making for a selection of resolutely modern character, which focus on energy along with the freshness and richness of fruit. The 2015 Primitivo di Manduria Sessantanni plays on softness and generous fruit, with notes of spice and sweet oak, all brought together by good supporting acidity, making for a an assertive and pleasant finish. Other well-made wines include their fresh and savory 2017 Tramari, a Primitivo rosé with floral and red fruit overtones, and the 2015 Negroamaro F, featuring scents of black berry fruit and smoky and herby overtones, while fresh black berry fruit and supple tannins emerge on the palate.

| | |
|---|---|
| ● Primitivo di Manduria Sessantanni '15 | ▼▼▼ 5 |
| ● F Negroamaro '15 | ▼▼ 5 |
| ● Primitivo di Manduria Anniversario 62° Ris. '15 | ▼▼ 6 |
| ○ Talò Verdeca '17 | ▼▼ 3 |
| ⊙ Tramari '17 | ▼▼ 3 |
| ○ Edda '17 | ▼ 4 |
| ● Primitivo di Manduria Talò '17 | ▼ 3 |
| ● Talò Negroamaro '17 | ▼ 3 |
| ● Primitivo di Manduria Talò '13 | ♀♀♀ 3* |
| ○ Edda '16 | ♀♀ 4 |
| ● Malvasia Nera Talò '15 | ♀♀ 3* |
| ● Primitivo di Manduria Anniversario 62 Ris. '14 | ♀♀ 6 |
| ● Primitivo di Manduria Sessantanni '14 | ♀♀ 5 |
| ● Primitivo di Manduria Sessantanni '13 | ♀♀ 5 |
| ● Primitivo di Manduria Talò '16 | ♀♀ 3 |

# Conte Spagnoletti Zeuli

FRAZ. SAN DOMENICO
S.DA PROV.LE 231 KM 60,000
70031 ANDRIA [BT]
TEL. +39 0883569511
www.contespagnolettizeuli.it

CELLAR SALES
PRE-BOOKED VISITS
ANNUAL PRODUCTION 400,000 bottles
HECTARES UNDER VINE 120.00

Conti Spagnoletti Zeuli, whose roots go back to the early 1600s, is without question one of the most significant wineries in the area. Its two estates, San Domenico and Zaragia, both fall within Agro di Andria and total almost 400 hectares. Of these, 120 hectares, all near Castel del Monte, are planted with traditional varieties like Nero di Troia, Montepulciano, Aglianico and Bombino Nero. Their range has a decidedly modern style. The 2015 Castel del Monte Rosso Pezzalaruca, equal blend of Nero di Troia and Montepulciano, exhibits overtones of Mediterranean scrub and wild berries, leading into a juicy, fresh, lingering and savory palate. Their taut and gutsy 2015 Castel del Monte Rosso Vigna Grande Tenuta Zagaria with spicy overtones and their soft but supple 2014 Castel del Monte Aglianico Ghiandara Vigna San Domenico are also well-crafted.

| | |
|---|---|
| ● Castel del Monte Rosso Pezzalaruca '15 | ♟♟ 2* |
| ● Castel del Monte Aglianico Ghiandara V. San Domenico '14 | ♟♟ 3 |
| ● Castel del Monte Rosso V. Grande Tenuta Zagaria '15 | ♟♟ 3 |
| ⊙ Castel del Monte Bombino Nero Rosato Colombaia '17 | ♟ 3 |
| ● Castel del Monte Nero di Troia Il Rinzacco '14 | ♟ 3 |
| ● Castel del Monte Rosso '17 | ♟ 4 |
| ● Castel del Monte Rosso Terranera Ris. '13 | ♟ 4 |
| ○ Jody '17 | ♟ 2 |
| ⊙ Castel del Monte Bombino Nero Colombaio '15 | ♟♟ 3 |
| ● Castel del Monte Rosso V. Grande '14 | ♟♟ 2* |

# Cosimo Taurino

S.DA PROV.LE 365 KM 1,400
73010 GUAGNANO [LE]
TEL. +39 0832706490
www.taurinovini.it

CELLAR SALES
PRE-BOOKED VISITS
ANNUAL PRODUCTION 900,000 bottles
HECTARES UNDER VINE 90.00

For more than 50 years, Cosimo Taurino has represented Puglia's winemaking -- in particular the region of Salento -- both in Italy and beyond. Located on sandy, calcareous soil in the area of Guagnano, about 80% of the vineyards are head-trained, and Negroamaro is cultivated almost exclusively. The cellar was recently enlarged and modernized here, including a system to regulate temperature. We're thrilled to find the Taurino family's winery back at the top of regional winemaking. Their 2013 Patriglione displays overtones of leather, sweet spices and black fruit jam, making for a full and complex palate that is still a bit tannic but long and charming. Their pleasant 2017 Scaloti rosé made with Negroamaro grapes offers up hints of wild red berries, it is fresh and juicy and one of the best rosés this year. The 2013 Negroamaro Notarpanaro proves well-crafted, less brilliant than other vintages, but always exhibiting relaxed and elegant citrusy notes.

| | |
|---|---|
| ● Patriglione '13 | ♟♟ 7 |
| ⊙ Scaloti '17 | ♟♟ 2* |
| ● Notarpanaro '13 | ♟♟ 3 |
| ● 7° Ceppo '17 | ♟ 3 |
| ● A64 Cosimo Taurino '12 | ♟ 4 |
| ○ I Sierri '17 | ♟ 2 |
| ● Kompà '15 | ♟ 2 |
| ○ Le Ricordanze '16 | ♟ 5 |
| ● Salice Salentino Rosso Ris. '13 | ♟ 3 |
| ● Notarpanaro '12 | ♟♟ 3* |
| ● Notarpanaro '11 | ♟♟ 3 |
| ● Notarpanaro '10 | ♟♟ 3 |

# Terrecarsiche1939

VIA MAESTRI DEL LAVORO 6/8
70013 CASTELLANA GROTTE [BA]
TEL. +39 0804962309
www.terrecarsiche.it

PRE-BOOKED VISITS
ANNUAL PRODUCTION 600,000 bottles
HECTARES UNDER VINE 12.00

Nicola Insalata's winery was officially
founded in 2001 arising from a family
tradition that began in 1939. The winery
has recently undergone some
modernization. They own 12 hectares all
within the Gioia del Colle appellation, but
also handle grapes acquired from a very
select group of winegrowers in diverse
areas of Puglia ranging from the Bari
Murgia to the Valle d'Itria, whom they work
with throughout the year. The Terrecarsiche
1939 winery has gone straight into the
main section of our Guide with their
excellent 2016 Gioia del Colle Primitivo
Fanova that reached our finals. Its slightly
balsamic hints, with notes of black berry
fruits and herbs, lead into a palate that
holds well together. Great grip and energy
give way to a succulent and pleasant finish,
making for a charming and complex wine.
Their 2015 Gioia del Colle Primitivo Fanova
Riserva is a bit marked by oak, but shows
good mouthfeel and tension, while their
2015 Nero di Troia appears simple but with
good grip. Both are well-made.

| | |
|---|---|
| ● Gioia del Colle Primitivo Fanova '16 | 🍷🍷 3* |
| ● Gioia del Colle Primitivo Fanova Ris. '15 | 🍷🍷 3 |
| ● Nero di Troia '15 | 🍷🍷 3 |
| ● Gioia del Colle Primitivo Regula Magistri Ris. '14 | 🍷 6 |
| ⊙ Gioia Rosa '17 | 🍷 3 |
| ⊙ Murgia Rosa '17 | 🍷 2 |

# ★Tormaresca

LOC. TOFANO
C.DA TORRE D'ISOLA
76013 MINERVINO MURGE [BT]
TEL. +39 0883692631
www.tormaresca.it

CELLAR SALES
PRE-BOOKED VISITS
ACCOMMODATION
ANNUAL PRODUCTION 3,000,000 bottles
HECTARES UNDER VINE 380.00
VITICULTURE METHOD Certified Organic
SUSTAINABLE WINERY

The decision by the Antinori family to invest
in Puglia over 20 years ago has proven
successful and given rise to well-made,
enjoyable wine expressing modern
character. Tormaresca is comprised of two
estates. Bocca di Lupo, within the Castel
del Monte appellation, is cultivated with
Nero di Troia and Aglianico grapes.
Masseria Maime in Alto Salento, grows
mainly Negroamaro and Primitivo. This year
Tormaresca has put forward some
high-level wines. Their 2014 Castel del
Monte Aglianico Bocca di Lupo exhibits
hints of spice and ripe black berry fruit. The
2016 Castel del Monte Chardonnay
Pietrobianca reveals a bit too much oak,
but is possessed of good acidity and a
finish featuring notes of white peach and
melon. Lastly, their 2017 Chardonnay,
which comes through fresh with a lingering
and brilliant finish.

| | |
|---|---|
| ● Castel del Monte Aglianico Bocca di Lupo '14 | 🍷🍷 5 |
| ○ Castel del Monte Chardonnay Pietrobianca '16 | 🍷🍷 4 |
| ○ Chardonnay '17 | 🍷🍷 2* |
| ⊙ Calafuria '17 | 🍷 3 |
| ● Fichimori '17 | 🍷 2 |
| ○ Roycello '17 | 🍷 3 |
| ● Castel del Monte Rosso Trentangeli '11 | 🏆🏆🏆 3* |
| ● Masseria Maime '12 | 🏆🏆🏆 5 |
| ● Masseria Maime '08 | 🏆🏆🏆 5 |
| ● Masseria Maime '07 | 🏆🏆🏆 4 |
| ● Torcicoda '11 | 🏆🏆🏆 4* |
| ● Torcicoda '10 | 🏆🏆🏆 3* |
| ● Torcicoda '09 | 🏆🏆🏆 3 |

# ★Torrevento

S.DA PROV.LE 234 KM 10.600
70033 CORATO [BA]
TEL. +39 0808980923
www.torrevento.it

CELLAR SALES
PRE-BOOKED VISITS
ACCOMMODATION AND RESTAURANT SERVICE
ANNUAL PRODUCTION 2,500,000 bottles
HECTARES UNDER VINE 450.00
SUSTAINABLE WINERY

Francesco Liantonio's Torrevento is a benchmark in the Castel del Monte appellation. The majority of the winery's vineyards are cultivated on the characteristic karst soil found within the National Park of Alta Murgia. Here mainly native grapes are found, in particular Nero di Troia, Aglianico, Bombino Nero and Bombino Bianco. Other winery vineyards are located in the Valle d'Itria and Salento, where Minutolo, Primitivo and Negroamaro cultivars dominate. The particular attention shown for low-impact environmental practices is the reason why Torrevento has received our Award for Sustainable Viticulture. The 2015 Castel del Monte Rosso Vigna Pedale Riserva is back at the top of Apulian winemaking: it appears fresh, close-knit, juicy, balanced and elegant, with a finish displaying notes of red fruit and pencil lead. Their 2015 Castel del Monte Nero di Troia Ottagono Riserva is always good, with its balsamic overtones and hints of cinchona, citrus and black berry fruit and a long, savory finish. The rest of the range is also solid.

| | |
|---|---|
| ● Castel del Monte Rosso V. Pedale Ris. '15 | ♟♟♟ 3* |
| ● Castel del Monte Nero di Troia Ottagono Ris. '15 | ♟♟ 5 |
| ⊙ Castel del Monte Rosato Primaronda '17 | ♟♟ 2* |
| ● Castel del Monte Rosso Bolonero '17 | ♟♟ 2* |
| ○ Moscato di Trani Dolce Naturale Dulcis In Fundo '16 | ♟♟ 3 |
| ● Since 1913 Primitivo '17 | ♟♟ 3 |
| ● Infinitum Primitivo '17 | ♟ 2 |
| ● Matervitae Negroamaro '17 | ♟ 2 |
| ● Salice Salentino Rosso Sine Nomine Ris. '15 | ♟ 3 |
| ● Castel del Monte Nero di Troia Ottagono Ris. '14 | ♟♟♟ 5 |
| ● Castel del Monte Rosso V. Pedale Ris. '14 | ♟♟♟ 3* |

# Cantine Tre Pini

VIA VECCHIA PER ALTAMURA S.DA PROV.LE 79 KM 16
70020 CASSANO DELLE MURGE [BA]
TEL. +39 080764911
www.cantinetrepini.com

CELLAR SALES
PRE-BOOKED VISITS
ACCOMMODATION AND RESTAURANT SERVICE
ANNUAL PRODUCTION 50,000 bottles
HECTARES UNDER VINE 9.00
VITICULTURE METHOD Certified Organic
SUSTAINABLE WINERY

Tre Pini added wine to its range of agricultural products in 2012, but the results exceeded expectations thanks to their freshness and pleasing disposition. The winery has only indigenous varieties in their vineyards, which are located in the municipalities of Cassano delle Murge and Acquaviva delle Fonti. At elevations between 400 and 450 meters above sea level they lie on the moderately rocky karst land characteristic of the Murgia. The winery's production cycle is 100% environmentally sustainable, powered entirely by solar energy and emitting zero carbon dioxide. This estate's wines are always among the best in the region. Their 2016 Gioia del Colle Primitivo Piscina delle Monache exhibits aromas of black berry fruits and faint balsamic hints, while the palate is gutsy and energetic, with a long, juicy finish. Their 2015 Gioia del Collo Primitivo Riserva, on the other hand, features floral overtones with hints of pencil lead and wild berries. It comes through elegant, savory and fresh. The rest of their range is also well-crafted.

| | |
|---|---|
| ● Gioia del Colle Primitivo Piscina delle Monache '16 | ♟♟ 3* |
| ● Gioia del Colle Primitivo Ris. '15 | ♟♟ 5 |
| ○ Donna Johanna '17 | ♟♟ 2* |
| ● Trullo di Carnevale '16 | ♟♟ 3 |
| ⊙ Ventifile Rosé '17 | ♟ 2 |
| ● Gioia del Colle Primitivo Ris. '14 | ♟♟♟ 5 |
| ● Gioia del Colle Primitivo Ris. '13 | ♟♟♟ 4* |
| ● Crae Primitivo '16 | ♟♟ 2* |
| ○ Donna Johanna '16 | ♟♟ 2* |
| ● Gioia del Colle Primitivo Piscina delle Monache '13 | ♟♟ 3 |
| ● Gioia del Colle Primitivo Ris. '12 | ♟♟ 4 |
| ● Trullo di Carnevale '15 | ♟♟ 2* |
| ● Trullo di Carnevale '14 | ♟♟ 2* |
| ⊙ Ventifile '16 | ♟♟ 2* |

## Agricole Vallone

VIA XXV LUGLIO, 7
73100 LECCE
TEL. +39 0832308041
www.agricolevallone.it

PRE-BOOKED VISITS
ANNUAL PRODUCTION 424,000 bottles
HECTARES UNDER VINE 161.00
VITICULTURE METHOD Certified Organic
SUSTAINABLE WINERY

The numerous vineyards of the historical Salento winery, Agricola Vallone, are divided into three estates. The main structure is located at Flaminia, within the Brindisi appellation, while the room for drying grapes is located in Castelserranova in the Carovigno municipality. Its most famous wine, Gratticaia, comes from lore, in San Pancrazio Salentino (falling within the Salice Salentino appellation). Their wine has a traditional style, attesting to their strong connection with the terroir and native cultivars. In the absence of Graticciaia, we really liked the 2014 Castel Serranova. It is a blend of Negroamaro and Susumaniello exhibiting scents of black berry fruits and Mediterranean scrub, with a pleasant, dynamic and clean finish. Their 2017 Tenuta Serranova Susumaniello Rosé also impressed with its freshness, marked notes of cherry, body, succulence and well-crafted finish. The other wines presented proved sound.

| | |
|---|---|
| ● Castelserranova '14 | ♟♟ 4 |
| ⊙ Tenuta Serranova Susumaniello Rosé '17 | ♟♟ 2* |
| ⊙ Brindisi Rosato V. Flaminio '17 | ♟ 2 |
| ● Salice Salentino Rosso Vereto Ris. '14 | ♟ 3 |
| ○ Tenuta Serranova Fiano '17 | ♟ 3 |
| ● Graticciaia '03 | ♟♟♟ 6 |
| ● Graticciaia '01 | ♟♟♟ 6 |
| ⊙ Brindisi Rosato V. Flaminio '13 | ♟♟ 2* |
| ● Brindisi Rosso V. Flaminio Ris. '12 | ♟♟ 3 |
| ● Castelserranova '13 | ♟♟ 4 |
| ● Graticciaia '13 | ♟♟ 7 |
| ● Graticciaia '12 | ♟♟ 7 |
| ○ Tenuta Serranova '16 | ♟♟ 3 |
| ● Vigna Castello '11 | ♟♟ 5 |

## Varvaglione

C.DA SANTA LUCIA
74020 LEPORANO [TA]
TEL. +39 0995315370
www.varvaglione.com

CELLAR SALES
PRE-BOOKED VISITS
ACCOMMODATION
ANNUAL PRODUCTION 4,000,000 bottles
HECTARES UNDER VINE 300.00
SUSTAINABLE WINERY

Founded almost 100 years ago, the winery is now under the direction of Maria Teresa and Cosimo Varvaglione, owner and enologist, respectively, along with their children, Angelo and Marzia. One hundred and twenty-five of the 300 cultivated hectares belong to the estate, with the rest belonging to trusted suppliers. The winery uses primarily traditional varieties, with Primitivo in the lead. Their range offers technical precision and a classic style that fully expresses the territory's best characteristics. The 2015 Primitivo di Manduria Papale Linea Oro proved yet again to be this estate's best wine. It exhibits the classic scents of cherry and plum, with a succulent palate and good structure. Their 2015 Primitivo di Manduria Old Vines Collezione Privata Cosimo Varvaglione hasn't turned out so well, but still displays considerable richness of fruit, though lacking a bit of freshness and grip. Their 2017 12 e Mezzo Malvasia Bianco, however, is pleasant and approachable.

| | |
|---|---|
| ● Primitivo di Manduria Papale Linea Oro '15 | ♟♟ 5 |
| ○ 12 e Mezzo Malvasia Bianca '17 | ♟♟ 2* |
| ● 12 e Mezzo Malvasia Nera '16 | ♟ 2 |
| ● Primitivo di Manduria Collezione Privata Cosimo Varvaglione '15 | ♟ 6 |
| ● Salice Salentino '16 | ♟ 4 |
| ○ 12 e mezzo Malvasia '15 | ♟♟ 2* |
| ● 12 e mezzo Negroamaro '15 | ♟♟ 2* |
| ● 12 e mezzo Primitivo '15 | ♟♟ 2* |
| ● Primitivo di Manduria Papale Oro '15 | ♟♟ 5 |
| ● Collezione Privata Cosimo Varvaglione Old Vines '14 | ♟ 6 |

## Vespa
## Vignaioli per Passione

FRAZ. C.DA RENI
VIA MANDURIA - AVETRANA KM 3,8
74024 MANDURIA [TA]
TEL. +39 063722120
www.vespavignaioli.it

CELLAR SALES
ANNUAL PRODUCTION 165,000 bottles
HECTARES UNDER VINE 30.00
SUSTAINABLE WINERY

In 2014 Bruno Vespa, along with sons Alessandro and Federico, and of enologist Riccardo Cotarella founded Vignaioli per Passione. The estate has a series of vineyards located mainly on the clay and sand-clay soil that characterizes the Primitivo di Manduria appellation. Primitivo is the central vine of the winery, alongside Aleatico, Fiano and Negroamaro. The estate offers a range of seven wines, each modern in style and attentive to the integrity and richness of the fruit. Tre Bicchieri goes to the 2016 Primitivo di Manduria Raccontami, which exhibits hints of black berry fruit and cinchona leading into a juicy, fresh palate with good length and tension. Their 2017 Bruno dei Vespa is another well-made Primitivo monovarietal which plays on fruity, pleasant notes and comes through fresh and drinkable. The other wines put forward also proved sound.

| | |
|---|---|
| ● Primitivo di Manduria Raccontami '16 | ▼▼▼ 5 |
| ● Il Bruno dei Vespa '17 | ▼▼ 2* |
| ⊙ Flarò '17 | ▼ 2 |
| ○ Il Bianco dei Vespa '17 | ▼ 2 |
| ● Primitivo di Manduria
Il Rosso dei Vespa '17 | ▼ 3 |
| ● Primitivo di Manduria Raccontami '15 | ♀♀♀ 5 |
| ● Primitivo di Manduria Raccontami '14 | ♀♀♀ 5 |
| ● Primitivo di Manduria Raccontami '13 | ♀♀♀ 5 |
| ● Il Bruno dei Vespa '14 | ♀♀ 2* |
| ● Il Bruno dei Vespa '13 | ♀♀ 2* |
| ● Il Rosso dei Vespa '15 | ♀♀ 3 |
| ● Primitivo di Manduria
Il Rosso dei Vespa '16 | ♀♀ 3 |
| ● Primitivo di Manduria Raccontami '12 | ♀♀ 5 |

## Tenuta Viglione

S.DA PROV.LE 140 KM 4,100
70029 SANTERAMO IN COLLE [BA]
TEL. +39 0802123661
www.tenutaviglione.it

CELLAR SALES
PRE-BOOKED VISITS
ACCOMMODATION AND RESTAURANT SERVICE
ANNUAL PRODUCTION 400,000 bottles
HECTARES UNDER VINE 60.00
VITICULTURE METHOD Certified Organic

The Zullo family's Tenuta Viglione is representative of the Gioia de Colle area's viticultural revival. Located in Gioia del Colle and Santeramo in Colle, the estate relies on vineyards situated at the highest point of the appellation, about 450 meters above sea level on thin layers of red soil mixed with calcareous and siliceous rocks. Their 15 wines range from Verdeca to Falanghina, Nero di Troia, and Negroamaro, while maintaining Gioia del Colle Primitivo as the crown jewel. The Marpione Riserva has delivered once again, earning the Tre Bicchieri with the 2015 vintage. It features balsamic hints of Mediterranean scrub and fresh black berry fruit, making for a generous, gutsy, long wine with almost austere aromatic precision. Their 2016 Johe is a fresh and succulent blend of Primitivo and Aleatico. The 2017 Nero di Troia comes through balanced with well-integrated tannins, while the 2017 Rosato proves pleasant and approachable.

| | |
|---|---|
| ● Gioia del Colle Primitivo
Marpione Ris. '15 | ▼▼▼ 3* |
| ● Johe '16 | ▼▼ 2* |
| ● Nero di Troia '17 | ▼▼ 2* |
| ⊙ Rosato '17 | ▼▼ 2* |
| ● Gioia del Colle Primitivo Sellato '16 | ▼ 2 |
| ● Negroamaro '17 | ▼ 2 |
| ● Primitivo '17 | ▼ 2 |
| ○ Verdeca '17 | ▼ 2 |
| ● Gioia del Colle Primitivo
Marpione Ris. '13 | ♀♀♀ 3* |
| ● Gioia del Colle Primitivo
Marpione Ris. '11 | ♀♀♀ 3* |
| ● Johe '13 | ♀♀ 2* |
| ● Negroamaro '16 | ♀♀ 2* |

# Le Vigne di Sammarco

VIA NICCOLÒ TOMMASEO, 13/15
72020 CELLINO SAN MARCO [BR]
TEL. +39 0831617776
www.levignedisammarco.com

CELLAR SALES
PRE-BOOKED VISITS
ANNUAL PRODUCTION 1,300,000 bottles
HECTARES UNDER VINE 180.00
SUSTAINABLE WINERY

Francesca, Marco and Carmine Rizzello
officially founded Le Vigne di Sammarco in
2011, but in the 1970s their grandfather
left the local collective to produce his own
wine. The winery has 180 hectares, of
which 50 are head-trained, in the most
prized appellations of Salento including
Salice Salentino and Primitivo di Manduria.
The varieties cultivated are almost
exclusively traditional, offering wines that
fully express the characteristics of the
territory. The 2015 Megale Hellas has
reached our finals. This monovarietal
Malvasia Nera is rich in fruit, succulent,
long and pleasant with good acidity.
Their other well-made wines include the
2015 Somiero, made with Susumaniello
grapes and exhibiting notes of black olives
and Mediterranean scrub. It comes through
generous and full, but the sweet finish
reduces its dynamism. Then there is their
supple and approachable 2015 Salice
Salentino Rosso.

| | |
|---|---|
| ● Megale Hellas '15 | 🍷🍷 5 |
| ● Salice Salentino Rosso '15 | 🍷🍷 2* |
| ● Somiero '15 | 🍷🍷 5 |
| ⊙ Murex '17 | 🍷 3 |
| ● Primitivo di Manduria '16 | 🍷 2 |
| ● Primitivo di Manduria Archè '15 | 🍷 5 |
| ● Salice Salentino Rosso Bisso Ris. '15 | 🍷 3 |
| ● Verve '15 | 🍷 3 |

# ★Conti Zecca

VIA CESAREA
73045 LEVERANO [LE]
TEL. +39 0832925613
www.contizecca.it

CELLAR SALES
PRE-BOOKED VISITS
ANNUAL PRODUCTION 2,800,000 bottles
HECTARES UNDER VINE 320.00
SUSTAINABLE WINERY

Conti Zecca is undoubtedly one of the most
important wineries in Salento, for both its
history and its current production. It has
vineyards on four estates: Donna Marzia,
Santo Stefano and Saraceno are situated in
Leverano, while Cantalupi is in Salice
Salentino. They offer about fifty labels
divided into two lines: Le Tenute, bearing
the name of the vineyards of origin, and Le
Selezioni, based on the variety or varieties.
Their wine exhibits an integrated modern
approach, carefully emphasizing the
integrity of the fruit and aromatic sharpness.
The 2014 Nero, a blend of 70%
Negroamaro and Cabernet Sauvignon, has
made it to our finals. It still proves a bit oaky,
but exhibits great structure and complexity,
with fruity hints of Mediterranean scrub.
Their other well-crafted wines include the
2015 Terra, an Aglianico rich in fruit and
well-integrated tannins; the fresh and
approachable 2017 Cantalupi Negroamaro;
the generous and caressing 2017 Cantalupi
Primitivo and their 2016 Rodinò, a supple
Primitivo which plays on fruit.

| | |
|---|---|
| ● Nero '14 | 🍷🍷 6 |
| ● Cantalupi Negroamaro '17 | 🍷🍷 2* |
| ● Cantalupi Primitivo '17 | 🍷🍷 2* |
| ● Rodinò '16 | 🍷🍷 7 |
| ● Terra '15 | 🍷🍷 4 |
| ○ Calavento '17 | 🍷 3 |
| ● Leverano Negroamaro Liranu Ris. '15 | 🍷 3 |
| ○ Mendola '17 | 🍷 3 |
| ● Salice Salentino Rosso Cantalupi Ris. '15 | 🍷 3 |
| ⊙ Venus '17 | 🍷 3 |
| ● Nero '09 | 🍷🍷🍷 5 |
| ● Nero '08 | 🍷🍷🍷 5 |
| ● Nero '07 | 🍷🍷🍷 5 |
| ● Cantalupi Primitivo '16 | 🍷🍷 2* |
| ● Salice Salentino Cantalupi Ris. '13 | 🍷🍷 3* |

## Cantina Albea

VIA DUE MACELLI, 8
70011 ALBEROBELLO [BA]
TEL. +39 0804323548
www.albeavini.com

CELLAR SALES
PRE-BOOKED VISITS
ANNUAL PRODUCTION 380,000 bottles
HECTARES UNDER VINE 40.00

| | |
|---|---|
| ● Lui '16 | ♟♟ 5 |
| ● Raro '16 | ♟♟ 3 |
| ○ Locorotondo Sup. Il Selva '17 | ♟ 2 |
| ⊙ Petrarosa Special Cuvée '17 | ♟ 3 |

## Masseria Altemura

S.DA PROV.LE 69 MESAGNE
72028 TORRE SANTA SUSANNA [BR]
TEL. +39 0831740485
www.masseriaaltemura.it

CELLAR SALES
PRE-BOOKED VISITS
ACCOMMODATION
ANNUAL PRODUCTION 400,000 bottles
HECTARES UNDER VINE 150.00

| | |
|---|---|
| ○ Fiano '17 | ♟♟ 4 |
| ○ Falanghina '17 | ♟ 4 |
| ● Negroamaro '16 | ♟ 3 |
| ● Sasseo '16 | ♟ 4 |

## Donato Angiuli

FRAZ. MONTRONE
VIA PRINCIPE UMBERTO, 27
70010 ADELFIA [BA]
TEL. +39 0804597130
www.angiulidonato.com

CELLAR SALES
PRE-BOOKED VISITS
ANNUAL PRODUCTION 200,000 bottles
HECTARES UNDER VINE 6.00

| | |
|---|---|
| ● Gioia del Colle Primitivo Adelphos '15 | ♟♟ 3 |
| ⊙ Maccone Rosato '17 | ♟♟ 6 |
| ● Maccone Rosso 17° | ♟♟ 8 |
| ● Primitivo '16 | ♟♟ 4 |

## Antica Enotria

LOC. RISICATA
S.DA PROV.LE 65, KM 7
71042 CERIGNOLA [FG]
TEL. +39 0885418462
www.anticaenotria.it

CELLAR SALES
PRE-BOOKED VISITS
ANNUAL PRODUCTION 100,000 bottles
HECTARES UNDER VINE 14.00
VITICULTURE METHOD Certified Organic

| | |
|---|---|
| ● Dieci Ottobre '12 | ♟♟ 3 |
| ○ Falanghina '17 | ♟♟ 2* |
| ○ Fiano '17 | ♟♟ 2* |
| ● Senzazolfo '17 | ♟ 3 |

## Apollonio

VIA SAN PIETRO IN LAMA, 7
73047 MONTERONI DI LECCE [LE]
TEL. +39 0832327182
www.apolloniovini.it

CELLAR SALES
PRE-BOOKED VISITS
ANNUAL PRODUCTION 1,500,000 bottles
HECTARES UNDER VINE 20.00

| | |
|---|---|
| ⊙ Elfo Rosato Negroamaro '17 | ♟♟ 2* |
| ⊙ Elfo Rosato Susumaniello '17 | ♟♟ 2* |
| ● Copertino Rosso Mani del Sud '15 | ♟ 4 |
| ● Squinzano Rosso Mani del Sud '15 | ♟ 4 |

## Bonsegna

VIA A. VOLTA, 17
73048 NARDÒ [LE]
TEL. +39 0833561483
www.vinibonsegna.it

CELLAR SALES
PRE-BOOKED VISITS
ANNUAL PRODUCTION 100,000 bottles
HECTARES UNDER VINE 20.00

| | |
|---|---|
| ● Nardò Rosso Danze della Contessa '16 | ♟♟ 2* |
| ● Nardò Rosso Danze della Contessa Barriccato '15 | ♟♟ 3 |
| ● Baia di Uluzzo Primitivo '16 | ♟ 2 |

## Borgo Turrito

LOC. INCORONATA
71122 FOGGIA
TEL. +39 0881810141
www.borgoturrito.it

ANNUAL PRODUCTION 60,000 bottles
HECTARES UNDER VINE 120.00

| | |
|---|---|
| ⊙ Calarosa '17 | ♥♥ 2* |
| ● TroQué '16 | ♥♥ 2* |
| ⊙ Terra Cretosa Aleatico Rosato '17 | ♥ 2 |
| ○ Terra Cretosa Falanghina '17 | ♥ 2 |

## Sergio Botrugno

LOC. CASALE
VIA ARCIONE, 1
72100 BRINDISI
TEL. +39 0831555587
www.vinisalento.com

CELLAR SALES
PRE-BOOKED VISITS
ANNUAL PRODUCTION 80,000 bottles
HECTARES UNDER VINE 35.00

| | |
|---|---|
| ● Ottavianello '17 | ♥♥ 2* |
| ● Brindisi Rosso Arcione '15 | ♥ 2 |
| ● Patrunu Rò '17 | ♥ 2 |
| ● Vigna Lobia Rosso '14 | ♥ 3 |

## I Buongiorno

C.SO VITTORIO EMANUELE II, 71
72012 CAROVIGNO [BR]
TEL. +39 0831996286
www.ibuongiorno.com

ANNUAL PRODUCTION 50,000 bottles
HECTARES UNDER VINE 10.00

| | |
|---|---|
| ● Negroamaro '16 | ♥♥ 2* |
| ● Nicolaus '16 | ♥♥ 3 |
| ● Primitivo '16 | ♥♥ 3 |
| ⊙ Rosalento '17 | ♥♥ 2* |

## Cannito

C.DA PARCO BIZZARRO
70025 GRUMO APPULA [BA]
TEL. +39 080623529
www.agricolacannito.it

CELLAR SALES
PRE-BOOKED VISITS
ANNUAL PRODUCTION 60,000 bottles
HECTARES UNDER VINE 14.00
VITICULTURE METHOD Certified Organic
SUSTAINABLE WINERY

| | |
|---|---|
| ● Gioia del Colle Primitivo Drùmon Ris. '13 | ♥♥ 7 |
| ● Gioia del Colle Primitivo Drùmon '14 | ♥ 5 |
| ● Gioia del Colle Primitivo Drùmon S '14 | ♥ 6 |
| ⊙ Gioia del Colle Rosato Drùmon '17 | ♥ 5 |

## Casa Primis

VIA ORTANOVA, KM 0,500
71048 STORNARELLA [FG]
TEL. +39 0885433333
www.primisvini.com

CELLAR SALES
PRE-BOOKED VISITS
ANNUAL PRODUCTION 160,000 bottles
HECTARES UNDER VINE 23.00

| | |
|---|---|
| ○ Cenerata '17 | ♥♥ 2* |
| ● Crusta '14 | ♥♥ 3 |
| ⊙ Monrose '17 | ♥♥ 2* |
| ● Ciliegiolo '17 | ♥ 2 |

## Castel di Salve

FRAZ. DEPRESSA
VIA SALVEMINI, 30
73026 TRICASE [LE]
TEL. +39 0833771041
www.casteldisalve.com

CELLAR SALES
PRE-BOOKED VISITS
ACCOMMODATION
ANNUAL PRODUCTION 170,000 bottles
HECTARES UNDER VINE 41.00

| | |
|---|---|
| ● Centino '16 | ♥♥ 5 |
| ● Lama del Tenente '15 | ♥♥ 5 |
| ● Priante '15 | ♥ 3 |
| ⊙ Santi Medici Rosato '17 | ♥ 2 |

## Centovignali

P.ZZA ALDO MORO, 10
70010 SAMMICHELE DI BARI [BA]
TEL. +39 0805768215
www.centovignali.it

CELLAR SALES
PRE-BOOKED VISITS
ANNUAL PRODUCTION 35,000 bottles
HECTARES UNDER VINE 25.00
VITICULTURE METHOD Certified Organic

| | |
|---|---|
| ● Gioia del Colle Primitivo Pentimone '15 | ♀♀ 6 |
| ● Serviano '16 | ♀♀ 2* |
| ○ Albiore '17 | ♀ 2 |
| ● Gioia del Colle Primitivo Indellicato '15 | ♀ 5 |

## De Falco

VIA MILANO, 25
73051 NOVOLI [LE]
TEL. +39 0832711597
www.cantinedefalco.it

CELLAR SALES
PRE-BOOKED VISITS
ACCOMMODATION
ANNUAL PRODUCTION 300,000 bottles
HECTARES UNDER VINE 20.00

| | |
|---|---|
| ● Artiglio Rosso '14 | ♀♀ 4 |
| ● Bocca della Verita' '15 | ♀♀ 2* |
| ○ Caolino Fiano '17 | ♀ 2 |
| ● Salice Salentino Rosso Salore '15 | ♀ 2 |

## Elda

ZONA IND.LE LOTTO 9
71029 TROIA [FG]
TEL. +39 08811910439
www.eldacantine.it

CELLAR SALES
PRE-BOOKED VISITS
ANNUAL PRODUCTION 200,000 bottles
HECTARES UNDER VINE 25.00
VITICULTURE METHOD Certified Organic
SUSTAINABLE WINERY

| | |
|---|---|
| ● Ettore '14 | ♀♀ 3 |
| ○ Calandra '17 | ♀ 2 |
| ● Garbino '17 | ♀ 3 |
| ⊙ Pesca Rosa '17 | ♀ 2 |

## Ferri

VIA BARI, 347
70010 VALENZANO [BA]
TEL. +39 0804671753
www.cantineferri.it

CELLAR SALES
PRE-BOOKED VISITS
ANNUAL PRODUCTION 40,000 bottles
HECTARES UNDER VINE 5.00

| | |
|---|---|
| ● Ad Mira '13 | ♀♀ 5 |
| ● Mora di Cuti '15 | ♀♀ 3 |
| ⊙ Ad Mira Rosé '17 | ♀ 2 |
| ○ L'Aureus '15 | ♀ 2 |

## Feudi Salentini

FRAZ. LEPORANO
VIA AMENDOLA, 36
74020 TARANTO
TEL. +39 0995315370
www.feudisalentini.com

CELLAR SALES
PRE-BOOKED VISITS
ANNUAL PRODUCTION 60,000 bottles
HECTARES UNDER VINE 25.00

| | |
|---|---|
| ● Primitivo di Manduria Allegretto '16 | ♀♀ 6 |
| ● Salice Salentino Rosso More '16 | ♀♀ 3 |
| ○ 125 Malvasia del Salento '16 | ♀ 2 |
| ● Primitivo di Manduria Gocce '15 | ♀ 5 |

## Duca Carlo Guarini

L.GO FRISARI, 1
73020 SCORRANO [LE]
TEL. +39 0836460288
www.ducacarloguarini.it

CELLAR SALES
PRE-BOOKED VISITS
ACCOMMODATION AND RESTAURANT SERVICE
ANNUAL PRODUCTION 300,000 bottles
HECTARES UNDER VINE 70.00
VITICULTURE METHOD Certified Organic

| | |
|---|---|
| ● Nativo '16 | ♀♀ 5 |
| ⊙ Campo di Mare '17 | ♀ 4 |
| ○ Murà '17 | ♀ 4 |
| ● Piutri '15 | ♀ 5 |

## Cantine Imperatore

VIA MARCONI, 36
70010 ADELFIA [BA]
TEL. +39 0804594041
www.cantineimperatore.com

CELLAR SALES
PRE-BOOKED VISITS
ANNUAL PRODUCTION 20,000 bottles
HECTARES UNDER VINE 5.00

| | |
|---|---|
| ● Gioia del Colle Primitivo Sonya '17 | 🍷🍷 4 |
| ● Gioia del Colle Primitivo Vincenzo Latorre Ris. '12 | 🍷 7 |
| ○ IV Colore '16 | 🍷 6 |

## Cantine Massimo Leone

VIA SPRECACENERE
71121 FOGGIA
TEL. +39 0881723674
www.cantinemassimoleone.it

ANNUAL PRODUCTION 100,000 bottles
HECTARES UNDER VINE 17.00

| | |
|---|---|
| ● Nero di Troia '15 | 🍷🍷 3 |
| ● Primitivo '16 | 🍷🍷 3 |
| ○ Falanghina '17 | 🍷 2 |
| ○ Forme '17 | 🍷 2 |

## Alberto Longo

LOC. C.DA PADULECCHIA
S.DA PROV.LE 5 LUCERA-PIETRAMONTECORVINO KM 4
71036 LUCERA [FG]
TEL. +39 0881539057
www.albertolongo.it

CELLAR SALES
PRE-BOOKED VISITS
ACCOMMODATION AND RESTAURANT SERVICE
ANNUAL PRODUCTION 150,000 bottles
HECTARES UNDER VINE 35.00

| | |
|---|---|
| ● Cacc'e Mmitte di Lucera '15 | 🍷🍷 3 |
| ● Le Cruste '15 | 🍷🍷 4 |
| ○ Le Fossette '17 | 🍷🍷 3 |
| ○ Donnadele '17 | 🍷 3 |

## Menhir

VIA SCARCIGLIA, 18
73027 MINERVINO DI LECCE [LE]
TEL. +39 0836818199
www.cantinemenhir.com

CELLAR SALES
PRE-BOOKED VISITS
RESTAURANT SERVICE
ANNUAL PRODUCTION 520,000 bottles
HECTARES UNDER VINE 18.00

| | |
|---|---|
| ● N° Zero '15 | 🍷🍷 2* |
| ○ Pietra Rosato '17 | 🍷🍷 3 |
| ● Quota 29 '16 | 🍷 2 |

## Mirvita Opificium Arte Vino Tor de Falchi

C.DA MONTELAROSA - LAMALUNGA
76013 MINERVINO MURGE [BT]
TEL. +39 3338658296
www.tordefalchi.com

ANNUAL PRODUCTION 150,000 bottles
HECTARES UNDER VINE 12.00

| | |
|---|---|
| ● Boamundus '13 | 🍷🍷 3 |
| ○ Castel del Monte Nero di Troia Aetas Nova Ris. '12 | 🍷 5 |
| ● Castel del Monte Rosso Cosmatesco '13 | 🍷 4 |

## Mocavero

VIA MALLACCA ZUMMARI
73010 ARNESANO [LE]
TEL. +39 0832327194
www.mocaverovini.it

CELLAR SALES
PRE-BOOKED VISITS
RESTAURANT SERVICE
ANNUAL PRODUCTION 600,000 bottles
HECTARES UNDER VINE 65.00

| | |
|---|---|
| ● Salice Salentino Rosso Puteus Ris. '15 | 🍷🍷 5 |
| ● Salice Salentino Rosso '16 | 🍷 3 |
| ● Santufili '13 | 🍷 6 |
| ● Tela di Ragno '13 | 🍷 6 |

## Mottura Vini del Salento

P.ZZA MELICA, 4
73058 TUGLIE [LE]
TEL. +39 0833596601
www.motturavini.it

PRE-BOOKED VISITS
ANNUAL PRODUCTION 2,500,000 bottles
HECTARES UNDER VINE 200.00

| | |
|---|---|
| ● I Classici Negroamaro '16 | ♟♟ 2* |
| ⊙ I Classici Rosato '17 | ♟♟ 2* |
| ● I Classici Primitivo '16 | ♟ 2 |
| ● Primitivo di Manduria Le Pitre '16 | ♟ 4 |

## Tenuta Patruno Perniola

C.DA MARZAGAGLIA
70023 GIOIA DEL COLLE [BA]
TEL. +39 3383940830
www.tenutapatrunoperniola.it

CELLAR SALES
PRE-BOOKED VISITS
ACCOMMODATION AND RESTAURANT SERVICE
ANNUAL PRODUCTION 12,000 bottles
HECTARES UNDER VINE 3.00
VITICULTURE METHOD Certified Organic

| | |
|---|---|
| ● Gioia del Colle Primitivo Marzagaglia '12 | ♟♟ 4 |
| ● Lenos '16 | ♟♟ 3 |
| ○ Striale '17 | ♟ 2 |

## Pietraventosa

LOC. PARCO LARGO
S.DA VIC.LE LATTA LATTA
70023 GIOIA DEL COLLE [BA]
TEL. +39 3355730274
www.pietraventosa.it

ANNUAL PRODUCTION 30,000 bottles
HECTARES UNDER VINE 5.40
VITICULTURE METHOD Certified Organic
SUSTAINABLE WINERY

| | |
|---|---|
| ⊙ EstRosa '17 | ♟♟ 3* |
| ● Gioia del Colle Primitivo Pietraventosa Ris. '12 | ♟♟ 5 |
| ● Ossimoro '15 | ♟ 3 |

## Plantamura

VIA V. BODINI, 9A
70023 GIOIA DEL COLLE [BA]
TEL. +39 3474711027
www.viniplantamura.it

CELLAR SALES
PRE-BOOKED VISITS
ANNUAL PRODUCTION 45,000 bottles
HECTARES UNDER VINE 8.00
VITICULTURE METHOD Certified Organic
SUSTAINABLE WINERY

| | |
|---|---|
| ● Gioia del Colle Primitivo Ris. '15 | ♟♟ 4 |
| ● Gioia del Colle Primitivo Contrada San Pietro '16 | ♟♟ 3 |

## Podere 29

LOC. BORGO TRESSANTI
S.DA PROV.LE 544
76016 CERIGNOLA [FG]
TEL. +39 3471917291
www.podere29.it

CELLAR SALES
PRE-BOOKED VISITS
ACCOMMODATION
ANNUAL PRODUCTION 90,000 bottles
HECTARES UNDER VINE 15.00
VITICULTURE METHOD Certified Organic

| | |
|---|---|
| ● Gelso d'Oro '16 | ♟♟ 5 |
| ⊙ Gelso Rosa '17 | ♟♟ 2* |
| ○ Gelso Bianco '17 | ♟ 3 |
| ⊙ Unio '17 | ♟ 2 |

## Risveglio Agricolo

C.DA TORRE MOZZA
72100 BRINDISI
TEL. +39 0831519948
www.cantinerisveglio.it

CELLAR SALES
PRE-BOOKED VISITS
ANNUAL PRODUCTION 100,000 bottles
HECTARES UNDER VINE 44.00

| | |
|---|---|
| ● 72100 '16 | ♟♟ 2* |
| ● Susù '16 | ♟♟ 8 |
| ● Brindisi Rosso Simposio Ris. '13 | ♟ 2 |

## Rosa del Golfo

VIA GARIBALDI, 18
73011 ALEZIO [LE]
TEL. +39 0833281045
www.rosadelgolfo.com

CELLAR SALES
PRE-BOOKED VISITS
ANNUAL PRODUCTION 300,000 bottles
HECTARES UNDER VINE 40.00

| | | |
|---|---|---|
| ⊙ Brut Rosé M. Cl. | 🍷🍷 4 |
| ⊙ Mazzì '16 | 🍷🍷 3 |
| ⊙ Rosato '17 | 🍷🍷 2* |
| ● Scaliere '16 | 🍷 2 |

## Cantina Sociale Sampietrana

VIA MARE, 38
72027 SAN PIETRO VERNOTICO [BR]
TEL. +39 0831671120
www.cantinasampietrana.com

CELLAR SALES
PRE-BOOKED VISITS
ANNUAL PRODUCTION 1,500,000 bottles
HECTARES UNDER VINE 140.00

| | | |
|---|---|---|
| ● Brindisi Rosso Since 1952 Ris. '15 | 🍷🍷 2* |
| ● Iussum '16 | 🍷 4 |
| ● Squinzano Ris. '14 | 🍷 2 |

## Cantina San Donaci

VIA MESAGNE, 62
72025 SAN DONACI [BR]
TEL. +39 0831681085
www.cantinasandonaci.eu

CELLAR SALES
PRE-BOOKED VISITS
ANNUAL PRODUCTION 800,000 bottles
HECTARES UNDER VINE 543.00

| | | |
|---|---|---|
| ● Salice Salentino Rosso Anticaia '16 | 🍷🍷 3 |
| ● Contrada del Falco '16 | 🍷 3 |
| ⊙ Salice Salentino Rosato Anticaia '17 | 🍷 2 |
| ● Salice Salentino Rosso Anticaia Ris. '15 | 🍷 3 |

## Santa Barbara

VIA MATERNITÀ E INFANZIA, 23
72027 SAN PIETRO VERNOTICO [BR]
TEL. +39 0831652749
www.cantinesantabarbara.it

CELLAR SALES
PRE-BOOKED VISITS
ANNUAL PRODUCTION 2,000,000 bottles
HECTARES UNDER VINE 150.00

| | | |
|---|---|---|
| ● Capirussu Negroamaro Rosato '17 | 🍷🍷 2* |
| ● Capirussu Susumaniello '16 | 🍷🍷 4 |
| ● Salice Salentino Rosso Capirussu '16 | 🍷🍷 3 |
| ● Capirussu Nero di Troia '16 | 🍷 2 |

## Schola Sarmenti

VIA GENERALE CANTORE, 37
73048 NARDÒ [LE]
TEL. +39 0833567247
www.scholasarmenti.it

CELLAR SALES
PRE-BOOKED VISITS
ANNUAL PRODUCTION 240,000 bottles
HECTARES UNDER VINE 41.00
VITICULTURE METHOD Certified Organic

| | | |
|---|---|---|
| ● Nauna '16 | 🍷🍷 5 |
| ● Antièri Susumaniello '16 | 🍷 3 |
| ○ Fiano '17 | 🍷 3 |
| ● Nardò Nerio Ris. '15 | 🍷 3 |

## Soloperto

S.S. 7
74024 MANDURIA [TA]
TEL. +39 0999794286
www.soloperto.it

CELLAR SALES
PRE-BOOKED VISITS
ANNUAL PRODUCTION 1,000,000 bottles
HECTARES UNDER VINE 50.00

| | | |
|---|---|---|
| ● Primitivo di Manduria Rubinum Et. Rossa '16 | 🍷🍷 2* |
| ● Primitivo di Manduria '17 | 🍷 2 |
| ● Primitivo di Manduria Rubinum Et. Blu '16 | 🍷 2 |

## Tagaro

c.da Montetessa, 63
70010 Locorotondo [BA]
Tel. +39 0802042313
www.tagaro.it

ANNUAL PRODUCTION 150,000 bottles
HECTARES UNDER VINE 20.00

| | |
|---|---|
| ● Cinquenoci Primitivo '16 | 🍷🍷 3 |
| ○ Locorotondo '17 | 🍷 2 |
| ● Pie' del Monaco '13 | 🍷 6 |
| ● Sei Caselle '16 | 🍷 3 |

## Teanum

via Croce Santa, 48
71016 San Severo [FG]
Tel. +39 0882336332
www.teanum.it

CELLAR SALES
PRE-BOOKED VISITS
RESTAURANT SERVICE
ANNUAL PRODUCTION 1,500,000 bottles
HECTARES UNDER VINE 190.00

| | |
|---|---|
| ● Òtre Syrah '16 | 🍷🍷 3 |
| ● Òtre Nero di Troia '16 | 🍷 2 |
| ⊙ San Severo Rosato Favùgnë '17 | 🍷 3 |
| ⊙ Vento '17 | 🍷 3 |

## La Vecchia Torre

via Marche, 1
73045 Leverano [LE]
Tel. +39 0832925053
www.cantinavecchiatorre.it

CELLAR SALES
PRE-BOOKED VISITS
RESTAURANT SERVICE
ANNUAL PRODUCTION 3,000,000 bottles
HECTARES UNDER VINE 1300.00
SUSTAINABLE WINERY

| | |
|---|---|
| ● Barocco Reale '14 | 🍷🍷 3 |
| ● Negroamaro '16 | 🍷🍷 2* |
| ● Leverano Rosso '16 | 🍷 2 |
| ● Salice Salentino Rosso '16 | 🍷 2 |

## Vetrere

fraz. Vetrere
s.da prov.le 80 Monteiasi - Montemesola km 16
74123 Taranto
Tel. +39 3402977870
www.vetrere.it

CELLAR SALES
PRE-BOOKED VISITS
ACCOMMODATION
ANNUAL PRODUCTION 150,000 bottles
HECTARES UNDER VINE 37.00

| | |
|---|---|
| ● Kemelios '15 | 🍷🍷 7 |
| ● Livruni '17 | 🍷🍷 3 |
| ○ Cré '17 | 🍷 4 |
| ⊙ Taranta '17 | 🍷 3 |

## Vigne di Rasciatano

fraz. Rasciatano
s.s. 93 Km 13
76121 Barletta
Tel. +39 0883510999
www.rasciatano.com

CELLAR SALES
PRE-BOOKED VISITS
ANNUAL PRODUCTION 90,000 bottles
HECTARES UNDER VINE 18.00
SUSTAINABLE WINERY

| | |
|---|---|
| ● Rasciatano Rosso '17 | 🍷🍷 3 |
| ○ Rasciatano Malvasia Bianca '17 | 🍷 3 |
| ⊙ Rasciatano Rosé '17 | 🍷 3 |
| ● Tenute Rasciatano Primitivo '17 | 🍷 1* |

## Vigneti Reale

loc. Lecce
via Reale, 55
73100 Lecce
Tel. +39 0832248433
www.vignetireale.it

PRE-BOOKED VISITS
ACCOMMODATION AND RESTAURANT SERVICE
ANNUAL PRODUCTION 180,000 bottles
HECTARES UNDER VINE 85.00
SUSTAINABLE WINERY

| | |
|---|---|
| ○ Malvasia Bianca '17 | 🍷🍷 2* |
| ● Malvasia Nera '17 | 🍷🍷 2* |
| ⊙ Malvasia Rosato '17 | 🍷🍷 2* |
| ● Primitivo di Manduria Gloria '15 | 🍷🍷 5 |

# CALABRIA

The exponential increase in the number of wineries operating in Calabria in recent years reflects the fervor of its vine growers, who are leading a renaissance in regional enology. On the one hand there are the family-run wineries whose younger generations are bringing new life. On the other there are the flocks of young vigneron who are enthusiastically committed to developing and promoting the territory and its grapes, giving rise to original and territorial wines. And so it is that Calabria's viticulture is starting to loosen the knot that had so constricted it in the past. Today we can say that the past is alive, but it's in the present that the future is forged. That's why we see the omnipresent classics, Gaglioppo and Greco (flagships of Cirò and its Doc wines), starting to emerge throughout the entire region (and with excellent results) along with other almost-forgotten native cultivar. That's the case with Cantina Ippolito's 2017 Pecorello Bianco, the producer's first Tre Bicchieri. And staying with the whites, once again Spiriti Ebrri's Neostòs stood out as one of the best wines tasted this year, along with Ceraudo's Il Grisara Pecorello. Cirò is back full-force thanks to the work done by great producers like Librandi, Ippolito and Santa Venere, who invested so much in terms of research and quality, but also thanks to the work of several young vine growers, like 'A Vita's Francesco De Franco or Sergio Arcuri. The other area that's seeing strong growth is Cosentino. Here we point out a small enclave, Saracena, at the foot of Pollino, where production of an old meditation wine, Moscato Passito, has reached high quality standards embodied by the winery Viola. A land with a millennia-old tradition of winemaking is at the dawn of a new era.

## 'A Vita

s.s. 106 km 279,800
88811 Cirò Marina [KR]
Tel. +39 3290732473
www.avitavini.it

**CELLAR SALES**
**PRE-BOOKED VISITS**
**ANNUAL PRODUCTION** 15,000 bottles
**HECTARES UNDER VINE** 8.00

Francesco De Franco studied architecture in Florence, then found a job that took him far from his native Calabria. But homesickness gained the upper hand and he returned home to look after the family vineyards full-time. Giving his decision full measure, Francesco studied enology in Conegliano, where he met Laura whom he later married. After gaining enough experience he felt ready for his first vintage in 2008. Francesco carried out rigorous work in the vineyards and cellar, banning the use of chemicals, and in just a few years became a role model for many young vine growers who will follow in his footsteps. Their 2015 Cirò Rosso Classico Superiore made it to our finals. It's an elegant and sophisticated wine on the nose, austere, warm and properly tannic in the mouth. Their 2017 Greco Bianco Leukò surprised, proving long and juicy, with charming aromas of bay leaves, quince, juniper and myrtle.

| | |
|---|---|
| ● Cirò Rosso Cl. Sup. '15 | 🏆🏆 2* |
| ○ Leukò '17 | 🏆🏆 2* |
| ⊙ Cirò Rosato '17 | 🏆 2 |
| ● Cirò Rosso Cl. Sup. Ris. '14 | 🏆 4 |
| ⊙ Cirò Rosato '16 | 🏆🏆 2* |
| ⊙ Cirò Rosato '14 | 🏆🏆 2* |
| ● Cirò Rosso Cl. '12 | 🏆🏆 2* |
| ● Cirò Rosso Cl. Ris. '11 | 🏆🏆 4 |
| ● Cirò Rosso Cl. Ris. '10 | 🏆🏆 4 |
| ● Cirò Rosso Cl. Sup. '14 | 🏆🏆 2* |
| ● Cirò Rosso Cl. Sup. Ris. '13 | 🏆🏆 4 |
| ● Cirò Rosso Cl. Sup. Ris. '11 | 🏆🏆 4 |

## Casa Comerci

fraz. Badia di Nicotera
c.da Comerci, 6
89844 Nicotera [VV]
Tel. +39 09631976077
www.casacomerci.it

**CELLAR SALES**
**PRE-BOOKED VISITS**
**ANNUAL PRODUCTION** 45,000 bottles
**HECTARES UNDER VINE** 15.00
**VITICULTURE METHOD** Certified Organic

The Silipo family winery in Badia di Nicotera, at the foot of Monte Poro in the province of Vibo Valentia, is over one hundred years old. Current owner, lawyer Domenico Silipo, shares his name with his grandfather who served as village cooper in his day. This area of Calabria is considered one of the best for producing wine. The estate comprises about thirty hectares, a dozen of which are vineyards planted with Maglioccio and Greco Bianco, cultivated under organic management. The winery's practice is to use exclusively native yeasts and their wines mature in steel vats. Their 2015 Magliocco Libìci just missed getting Tre Bicchieri. It's a lovely, southern Italian wine, territorial and elegant, and extraordinary value for the money. On the nose it offers up small, red fruit, proving delicately balsamic and crossed by a subtle, mineral nuance. In the mouth it features nice acidic vigor, with close-woven, smooth tannins, and good, mature extract. The finish comes through deep and broad.

| | |
|---|---|
| ● Libìci '15 | 🏆🏆 3* |
| ⊙ Granàtu '17 | 🏆🏆 3 |
| ○ Rèfulu '17 | 🏆 2 |
| ● Libìci '12 | 🏆🏆 3* |

# Roberto Ceraudo

LOC. MARINA DI STRONGOLI
C.DA DATTILO
88815 CROTONE
TEL. +39 0962865613
www.dattilo.it

CELLAR SALES
PRE-BOOKED VISITS
ACCOMMODATION AND RESTAURANT SERVICE
ANNUAL PRODUCTION 70,000 bottles
HECTARES UNDER VINE 20.00
VITICULTURE METHOD Certified Organic

In 1973 Roberto Ceraudo made what was an extreme decision at the time. He converted his winery to organic management. Safeguarding the ecosystem is so vital to Roberto that he has been using biodynamic methods on the entire estate for some time. Today his children work alongside him. Giuseppe is an agronomist, Susy deals with business matters, and Caterina uses her enology degree to great advantage in the cellar. She also runs the restaurant, where she is both owner and chef. We can gladly testify to the major progress made when it comes to the winery's reds. Finally, in terms of finesse and cleanness, they're on par with its whites, such that their elegant and complex 2015 Gaglioppo Dattilo just missed a Tre Bicchieri. Their 2017 Pecorello Grisara, however, nails it, proving broad on the nose with mineral notes, flowers and white fruit. On the palate it shows great harmony, offering up fruit, freshness and length.

| | |
|---|---|
| ○ Grisara '17 | ♟♟♟ 4* |
| ● Dattilo '15 | ♟♟ 4 |
| ☉ Grayasusi Et. Rame '17 | ♟♟ 3 |
| ● Nanà '16 | ♟♟ 3 |
| ● Petraro '15 | ♟♟ 5 |
| ○ Ymir '17 | ♟♟ 4 |
| ☉ Grayasusi Argento '17 | ♟ 5 |
| ○ Petelia '17 | ♟ 3 |
| ○ Grisara '16 | ♟♟♟ 4* |
| ○ Grisara '15 | ♟♟♟ 4* |
| ○ Grisara '14 | ♟♟♟ 3* |
| ○ Grisara '13 | ♟♟♟ 3* |
| ○ Grisara '12 | ♟♟♟ 3* |

# Feudo dei Sanseverino

VIA VITTORIO EMANUELE, 108/110
87010 SARACENA [CS]
TEL. +39 098121461
www.feudodeisanseverino.it

CELLAR SALES
PRE-BOOKED VISITS
ANNUAL PRODUCTION 20,000 bottles
HECTARES UNDER VINE 6.00
VITICULTURE METHOD Certified Organic
SUSTAINABLE WINERY

Two of Maurizio and Roberto Bisconte's wines have landed in our finals. This is an achievement to be recognized for these two authentic vine growers who work in both the vineyard and cellar, and have banned all synthetic products. Their vineyards are situated at the foot of the Pollino mountains at about three hundred meters above sea level, while the cellar is located inside the old medieval town of Saracena. Their 2015 Moscato Passito Mastro Terenzio, a blend of Guarnaccia, Malvasia and Moscato, is pervasive and complex on the nose with notes of quince preserves, cinnamon, honey, candied orange and spices. In the mouth it's dense, silky and rich with a fruity sweetness that's well-balanced by acidity. The same blend is used for their 2013 Moscato Passito al Governo di Saracena, an elegant, close-knit wine on the nose, redolent of apricot, figs and dates, but also fresh balsamic aromas and a delicate, smoky nuance. In the mouth it proves velvety and long, well-supported by a fresh, acidic vein making for a long finish of candied citrus.

| | |
|---|---|
| ○ Moscato Passito al Governo di Saracena '13 | ♟♟ 5 |
| ○ Terre di Cosenza Pollino Moscato Passito Mastro Terenzio '15 | ♟♟ 5 |
| ● Terre di Cosenza Lacrima Nera Ris. '12 | ♟♟ 3 |
| ○ Terre di Cosenza Pollino Moscato Passito Mastro Terenzio '14 | ♟♟♟ 5 |
| ● Lacrima Nera '13 | ♟♟ 3 |
| ○ Mastro Terenzio '12 | ♟♟ 5 |
| ○ Mastro Terenzio '11 | ♟♟ 5 |
| ○ Mastro Terenzio '10 | ♟♟ 5 |
| ○ Moscato Passito al Governo di Saracena '09 | ♟♟ 5 |
| ○ Moscato Passito Mastro Terenzio '13 | ♟♟ 5 |
| ☉ Terre di Cosenza Pollino Rosato Rosa Lacrima Nera '15 | ♟♟ 3 |

# iGreco

LOC. SALICE
C.DA GUARDAPIEDI
87062 CARIATI [CS]
TEL. +39 0983969441
www.igreco.it

CELLAR SALES
PRE-BOOKED VISITS
ACCOMMODATION AND RESTAURANT SERVICE
ANNUAL PRODUCTION 250,000 bottles
HECTARES UNDER VINE 80.00
SUSTAINABLE WINERY

The Greco brothers' farm extends over 1500 hectares of mostly olive groves, with 80 hectares dedicated to vineyards. When they began about twelve years ago, they made a decision to focus their work in the vineyards on producing extremely low yields that would allow only ripe and high quality grapes into the cellar. Their wines stand out for their modern and elegant style, which brings out the best attributes of traditional grape varieties without overdoing extraction or maceration. Their 2016 Masino just missed getting Tre Bicchieri. It's a Nero di Calabria with lovely balsamic notes and aromas of spices. On the palate it proves structured and well-balanced amidst succulent fruit, close-woven and smooth tannins. The finish comes through long and persistent. Their 2017 Greco Bianco Filù is a pleasant and fresh wine, complex on the nose, with pleasing notes of tropical fruit accompanied by minty nuances and Mediterranean herbs.

| | | |
|---|---|---|
| ● Masino '16 | | 🏆🏆 5 |
| ○ Filù '17 | | 🏆🏆 3 |
| ● Catà '16 | | 🏆 3 |
| ⊙ Savù '17 | | 🏆 3 |
| ● Masino '15 | | 🏆🏆🏆 5 |
| ● Masino '14 | | 🏆🏆🏆 5 |
| ● Masino '12 | | 🏆🏆🏆 5 |
| ● Masino '11 | | 🏆🏆🏆 5 |
| ● Masino '10 | | 🏆🏆🏆 5 |
| ● Catà '15 | | 🏆🏆 3 |
| ● Catà '14 | | 🏆🏆 3 |
| ● Catà '13 | | 🏆🏆 3 |
| ● Masino '13 | | 🏆🏆 5 |
| ⊙ Savù '16 | | 🏆🏆 3 |

# Ippolito 1845

VIA TIRONE, 118
88811 CIRÒ MARINA [KR]
TEL. +39 096231106
www.ippolito1845.it

CELLAR SALES
PRE-BOOKED VISITS
ANNUAL PRODUCTION 1,000,000 bottles
HECTARES UNDER VINE 100.00

The Ippolito family winery is one of the most interesting in Cirò, and brothers Vincenzo and Gianluca have strengthened their position by updating technology in the cellar and improving vineyard management. They are planting almost exclusively native varieties and it hasn't taken long to see promising results of their labor. Thanks to minimally invasive winemaking and a preference for large barrels and steel, their wines are proving elegant, and ones that fully express the Cirò territory and attributes of the varieties. It was in the air - finally the producer earns a well-deserved Tre Bicchieri. Their 2017 Pecorello delivers, though in part the score also reflects their work in terms of rediscovering and reviving this native Calabrian grape. It's an extraordinarily focused wine, with aromas of white fruit and mineral notes. On the palate it proves savory, fresh, close-knit and truly elegant.

| | | |
|---|---|---|
| ○ Pecorello '17 | | 🏆🏆🏆 2* |
| ○ Cirò Bianco Mare Chiaro '17 | | 🏆🏆 2* |
| ⊙ Cirò Rosato Mabilia '17 | | 🏆🏆 2* |
| ● Cirò Rosso Cl. Sup. Liber Pater '16 | | 🏆🏆 2* |
| ● Cirò Rosso Cl. Sup. Ripe del Falco Ris. '10 | | 🏆🏆 5 |
| ⊙ Pescanera Rosé '17 | | 🏆🏆 2* |
| ● 160 Anni '15 | | 🏆 5 |
| ● Cirò Rosso Cl. Sup. Colli del Mancuso Ris. '15 | | 🏆 3 |
| ● 160 Anni '14 | | 🏆🏆 5 |
| ● Cirò Rosso Cl. Sup. Ripe del Falco Ris. '07 | | 🏆🏆 5 |
| ○ Pecorello '16 | | 🏆🏆 2* |

# Tenuta Iuzzolini

LOC. FRASSÀ
88811 CIRÒ MARINA [KR]
TEL. +39 0962373893
www.tenutaiuzzolini.it

**CELLAR SALES**
**PRE-BOOKED VISITS**
**ANNUAL PRODUCTION 1,000,000 bottles**
**HECTARES UNDER VINE 100.00**

This beautiful farm was founded in 2004 by
Fortunato and Giovanna Iuzzolini. With the
help of their children, Diego, Pasquale,
Antonio and Rosa, they've become
prominent in Cirò's crowded winemaking
scene in a short period of time. The estate
extends over 500 hectares, including 100
of vineyards, planted mainly with native
varieties. There are also 50 hectares of
100-year-old olive groves. In recent years
this dynamic winery has drastically
improved the quality of its wines, gaining in
elegance and complexity. Employing
meticulous work in the vineyards, they are
focused on reducing yields in order to bring
only healthy and perfectly ripe grapes to
the cellar. Their progress in terms of quality
was confirmed by our last round of
tastings, which saw a solid overall
performance by their entire selection. Their
2017 Gaglioppo Principe Spinelli stood out,
in particular, proving close-knit and
complex on the nose, with a fresh,
authoritative palate that's rich in fruit and
velvety tannins.

| | |
|---|---|
| ● Artino '16 | ♟♟ 3 |
| ○ Donna Giovanna '17 | ♟♟ 5 |
| ○ Prima Fila '17 | ♟♟ 3 |
| ● Principe Spinelli '17 | ♟♟ 3 |
| ● Belfresco '17 | ♟ 3 |
| ⊙ Lumare '17 | ♟ 3 |
| ○ Madre Goccia '17 | ♟ 3 |
| ● Muranera '16 | ♟ 4 |
| ● Artino '15 | ♟♟ 3 |
| ● Belfresco '16 | ♟♟ 3 |
| ⊙ Lumare '15 | ♟♟ 3 |
| ● Muranera '15 | ♟♟ 4 |
| ○ Prima Fila '16 | ♟♟ 3 |

# Cantine Lento

VIA DEL PROGRESSO, 1
88040 AMATO [CZ]
TEL. +39 096828028
www.cantinelento.it

**CELLAR SALES**
**PRE-BOOKED VISITS**
**ANNUAL PRODUCTION 500,000 bottles**
**HECTARES UNDER VINE 70.00**

Salvatore Lento and daughters Danila and
Manuela have invested heavily in their
winery in the last decade. Adding to the
Romeo estate with the purchase of the
Amato and Caracciolo estates, they've
tripled their hectares of vineyards. The old
cellar has been replaced with a modern
structure, perfectly in keeping with its
surroundings. Increased space,
avant-garde equipment and new technical
staff have given renewed drive to their
production, aiming for wines that express
the varieties and terroir with coherence and
pleasantness. With this initial phase
completed so successfully, we expect great
things to follow from this winery. Their
2014 Lamezia Riserva Salvatore Lento, a
blend of Magliocco, Greco Nero and
Nerello, did well during our tastings,
offering up balsamic notes and aromas of
cherry, with a long, juicy mouth. Their
Federico II is a structured, elegant wine,
complex on the nose, mature and sweet in
its expression of fruit.

| | |
|---|---|
| ○ Contessa Emburga '17 | ♟♟ 3 |
| ○ Dragone Bianco '17 | ♟♟ 3 |
| ● Federico II '14 | ♟♟ 4 |
| ● Lamezia Rosso Salvatore Lento Ris. '14 | ♟♟ 4 |
| ● Dragone Rosso '16 | ♟ 3 |
| ○ Lamezia Greco '17 | ♟ 3 |
| ● Magliocco '14 | ♟ 5 |
| ○ Contessa Emburga '16 | ♟♟ 3 |
| ● Federico II '12 | ♟♟ 4 |
| ○ Lamezia Greco '15 | ♟♟ 3 |
| ● Lamezia Rosso Salvatore Lento Ris. '13 | ♟♟ 4 |
| ● Magliocco '13 | ♟♟ 5 |
| ● Magliocco '12 | ♟♟ 5 |

## ★Librandi

LOC. SAN GENNARO
S.S. JONICA, 106
88811 CIRÒ MARINA [KR]
TEL. +39 096231518
www.librandi.it

CELLAR SALES
PRE-BOOKED VISITS
ANNUAL PRODUCTION 2,200,000 bottles
HECTARES UNDER VINE 232.00

The Librandi cousins have taken up the legacy of their parents Antonino and Nicodemo and given new drive to the winery, now a benchmark for the whole of southern Italy. Under the watchful eye of Nicodemo -- who can now work full-time as a vine grower -- this beautiful estate continues to expand in international markets, as well as also strengthen its position in Italy. Year after year, the wines they present at our tastings confirm their position at the top. They are elegant and territorial without excess. Once again their 2016 Gravello earns Tre Bicchieri, proving to be a champion of elegance and complexity, with aromas of pomegranate, cherry and aromatic herbs. In the mouth it comes through vibrant, deep, rich in close-woven, smooth tannins and endowed with notable length. Their 2016 Duca Sanfelice also made it to our finals, proving an elegant archetype of Cirò Rosso with fragrances of red fruit and Mediterranean scrubland. A well-balanced palate gives way to a fruity finish.

| | | |
|---|---|---|
| ● Gravello '16 | ▼▼▼ | 5 |
| ● Cirò Rosso Cl. Sup. Duca San Felice Ris. '16 | ▼▼ | 3* |
| ⊙ Cirò Rosato '17 | ▼▼ | 2* |
| ● Cirò Rosso Cl. '17 | ▼▼ | 2* |
| ○ Critone '17 | ▼▼ | 2* |
| ● Magno Megonio '16 | ▼▼ | 4 |
| ⊙ Terre Lontane '17 | ▼▼ | 2* |
| ○ Cirò Bianco '17 | ▼ | 2 |
| ● Melissa Asylia Rosso '17 | ▼ | 2 |
| ● Cirò Rosso Cl. Sup. Duca Sanfelice Ris. '11 | ♉♉♉ | 3* |
| ● Gravello '14 | ♉♉♉ | 5 |
| ● Gravello '10 | ♉♉♉ | 5 |
| ● Gravello '09 | ♉♉♉ | 5 |
| ● Magno Megonio '13 | ♉♉♉ | 4* |
| ● Magno Megonio '12 | ♉♉♉ | 4* |

## Santa Venere

LOC. TENUTA VOLTA GRANDE
S.DA PROV.LE 04 KM 10,00
88813 CIRÒ [KR]
TEL. +39 096238519
www.santavenere.com

CELLAR SALES
PRE-BOOKED VISITS
ANNUAL PRODUCTION 125,000 bottles
HECTARES UNDER VINE 25.00
VITICULTURE METHOD Certified Organic

The Scala family's centuries-old farming tradition in Cirò focuses on olive growing and cattle breeding, as well as on vine growing. The farm comprises one hundred and fifty hectares, twenty-five of which are planted with vines. Today it is run by Giuseppe Scala, who has reinforced the farm's propensity for winemaking by initiating the process to go from organic to biodynamic certification. At the same time, he is successfully carrying forward his work begun years ago to relaunch less famous local varieties such as Marsiliana and Guardavalle. Their 2016 Riserva Federico Scala is a wine of marked personality, vibrant on the nose with aromas of red and black fruit merging with elegant, well-integrated oak. In the mouth it proves savory and rich in flesh, making for a lovely, long and fruity finish. Their 2017 Guardavalle Vescovado is a highly pleasant wine. The nose features damson, glycine but also iodine hints, while on the palate it's structured with fresh acidity and nice aromatic persistence.

| | | |
|---|---|---|
| ● Cirò Cl. Sup. Federico Scala Ris. '16 | ▼▼ | 5 |
| ○ Cirò Bianco '17 | ▼▼ | 2* |
| ⊙ Scassabarile '17 | ▼▼ | 3 |
| ○ Vescovado '17 | ▼▼ | 3 |
| ● Vurgadà '16 | ▼▼ | 4 |
| ○ Cirò Bianco '16 | ♉♉ | 2* |
| ○ Cirò Bianco '15 | ♉♉ | 2* |
| ⊙ Cirò Rosato '15 | ♉♉ | 2* |
| ● Cirò Rosso Cl. '15 | ♉♉ | 2* |
| ● Cirò Rosso Federico Scala Ris. '14 | ♉♉ | 5 |
| ○ Vescovado '16 | ♉♉ | 3 |
| ○ Vescovado '15 | ♉♉ | 3 |
| ● Vurgadà '15 | ♉♉ | 4 |
| ● Vurgadà '14 | ♉♉ | 4 |

## Spiriti Ebbri

VIA ROMA, 96
87050 SPEZZANO PICCOLO [CS]
TEL. +39 0984408992
www.spiritiebbri.com

CELLAR SALES
PRE-BOOKED VISITS
ANNUAL PRODUCTION 20,000 bottles
HECTARES UNDER VINE 2.50

After an excellent start last year, under Pierpaolo Greco, Damiano Mele and Michele Scrivano this winery has sent a selection of undeniably interesting wines to our regional selections. The three friends founded their estate in 2004 after a trial stage; grapes grown on the first hectare were vinified in Pierpaolo's grandfather's carpentry workshop. Recently they also purchased a 1950s cinema and converted it into a cellar. They cultivate their vineyards rigorously under organic management, and transform native Guarnaccia, Mantonico and Pecorello grapes into wine using natural winemaking methods. Their 2017 Neostòs, a Pecorello that's a bit timid on the nose at first, needs a few moments in the glass before offering up its best. After a first whiff, mineral and sulphur notes give way to fresher, pleasant fragrances of peach, pineapple, citrus flower and lavender. On the palate it demonstrates good substance and complexity, made sweet by fruit, but also well-balanced by a fresh and sapid acidity.

| | |
|---|---|
| ○ Neostòs Bianco '17 | ♥♥♥ 4* |
| ● Cotidie Neostòs Rosso '16 | ♥♥ 3 |
| ● Neostòs Rosso '16 | ♥♥ 4 |
| ● See… '16 | ♥♥ 3 |
| ⊙ Appianum Rosato '17 | ♥ 5 |
| ● Appianum Rosso '16 | ♥ 5 |
| ○ Cotidie Bianco '17 | ♥ 3 |
| ● Cotidie Rosato '17 | ♥ 3 |
| ⊙ Neostòs Rosato '17 | ♥ 4 |
| ○ Neostòs Bianco '16 | ♥♥♥ 4* |
| ● Appianum Rosso La Vigna di Alberto '15 | ♥♥ 5 |
| ⊙ Neostòs Rosato '16 | ♥♥ 4 |
| ● Neostòs Rosso '15 | ♥♥ 4 |

## Luigi Viola

VIA ROMA, 18
87010 SARACENA [CS]
TEL. +39 098134722
www.cantineviola.it

CELLAR SALES
PRE-BOOKED VISITS
ANNUAL PRODUCTION 15,000 bottles
HECTARES UNDER VINE 3.00
VITICULTURE METHOD Certified Organic

If centuries later we are talking about Moscato di Saracena, a sweet wine traditionally produced in the medieval town of the same name, credit is due to Luigi Viola. Along with his children, to whom he passed on his passion for vine growing, he has saved the ancient nectar that once the tables of Popes. Then it and the town became famous all over the world. Saracena is situated at seven hundred meters above sea level on the Pollino plateau. In addition to this passito dried-grape wine, the Violas also produce a white made with Guarnaccia and Montonico, and a red with the ancient Magliocco variety. Luigi Viola's Moscato Passito is back on top with a gold thanks to a 2017 vintage that gave rise to a wine of suave and sophisticated elegance. The nose features vibrant aromas of fresh and bottled apricot, aromatic herbs, lavender flowers, honey and sultanas. The palate is extremely fresh and yet creamy at the same time, made sweet by succulent fruit, but never sugary, with a finish that demonstrates rare aromatic persistence.

| | |
|---|---|
| ○ Moscato Passito '17 | ♥♥♥ 6 |
| ○ Bianco Margherita '16 | ♥ 3 |
| ○ Moscato Passito '14 | ♥♥♥ 6 |
| ○ Moscato Passito '13 | ♥♥♥ 6 |
| ○ Moscato Passito '12 | ♥♥♥ 6 |
| ○ Moscato Passito '11 | ♥♥♥ 6 |
| ○ Moscato Passito '10 | ♥♥♥ 6 |
| ○ Moscato Passito '09 | ♥♥♥ 6 |
| ○ Moscato Passito '08 | ♥♥♥ 6 |
| ○ Moscato Passito '07 | ♥♥♥ 6 |

## Antiche Vigne

VIA REGINA ELENA, 110
87054 ROGLIANO [CS]
TEL. +39 3208194246
www.antichevigne.com

ANNUAL PRODUCTION 72,000 bottles
HECTARES UNDER VINE 15.00

| | | |
|---|---|---|
| ● Savuto Sup. '13 | ♟♟ | 3 |
| ○ Savuto Bianco Terra di Ginestre '17 | ♟ | 2 |
| ● Savuto Cl. '16 | ♟ | 2 |
| ⊙ Savuto Rosato '17 | ♟ | 2 |

## Sergio Arcuri

VIA ROMA VICO PRIMO
88811 CIRÒ MARINA [KR]
TEL. +39 3280250255
www.sergioarcuri.it

CELLAR SALES
PRE-BOOKED VISITS
ANNUAL PRODUCTION 15,000 bottles
HECTARES UNDER VINE 3.68
VITICULTURE METHOD Certified Organic

| | | |
|---|---|---|
| ● Cirò Rosso Cl. Sup. Più Vite Ris. '12 | ♟♟ | 5 |
| ⊙ Il Marinetto '17 | ♟♟ | 3 |

## Brigante

VIA SANT'ELIA
88813 CIRÒ [KR]
TEL. +39 3334135843
www.vinocirobrigante.it

ANNUAL PRODUCTION 32,000 bottles
HECTARES UNDER VINE 10.00

| | | |
|---|---|---|
| ○ Cirò Bianco Phemina '17 | ♟♟ | 2* |
| ⊙ Cirò Rosato Manyarì '17 | ♟♟ | 2* |
| ● Cirò Rosso Cl. Sup 0727 '15 | ♟♟ | 3 |
| ● Cirò Rosso Etefe '15 | ♟ | 3 |

## Salvatore Caparra

LOC. MADONNA DI MARE
S.S. 106
88811 CIRÒ [KR]
TEL. +39 096236579
ww.salvatorecaparra.it

ANNUAL PRODUCTION 40,000 bottles
HECTARES UNDER VINE 9.00
VITICULTURE METHOD Certified Organic

| | | |
|---|---|---|
| ● Cirò Rosso Cl. Sel. '16 | ♟♟ | 4 |
| ⊙ Carla Rosato Bio '17 | ♟ | 2 |

## Caparra & Siciliani

S.S. 106
88811 CIRÒ MARINA [KR]
TEL. +39 0962373319
www.caparraesiciliani.com

CELLAR SALES
PRE-BOOKED VISITS
ANNUAL PRODUCTION 800,000 bottles
HECTARES UNDER VINE 180.00
VITICULTURE METHOD Certified Organic

| | | |
|---|---|---|
| ● Cirò Rosso Cl. '16 | ♟♟ | 1* |
| ● Cirò Rosso Cl. Sup. Volvito Ris. '15 | ♟♟ | 2* |
| ○ Curiale '17 | ♟♟ | 2* |
| ● Cirò Rosso Cl. Sup. Ris. '15 | ♟ | 2 |

## Chimento

C.DA GALLICE - VESCOVADO
87043 BISIGNANO [CS]
TEL. +39 3358258627
www.cantinechimento.it

CELLAR SALES
PRE-BOOKED VISITS
ACCOMMODATION AND RESTAURANT SERVICE
ANNUAL PRODUCTION 47,000 bottles
HECTARES UNDER VINE 7.00

| | | |
|---|---|---|
| ● Vescovado '15 | ♟♟ | 3 |
| ● Vitulia '15 | ♟♟ | 5 |
| ⊙ Gallice '17 | ♟ | 3 |
| ○ Matilde '17 | ♟ | 3 |

## Colacino Wines

via Colle Manco
87054 Rogliano [CS]
Tel. +39 09841900252
www.colacino.it

CELLAR SALES
PRE-BOOKED VISITS
ANNUAL PRODUCTION 120,000 bottles
HECTARES UNDER VINE 21.00

| | |
|---|---|
| ● Amanzio '17 | ♟♟ 2* |
| ● Savuto Sup. Britto '15 | ♟♟ 4 |
| ○ Savuto Bianco Si '17 | ♟ 2 |
| ● Savuto Si '17 | ♟ 2 |

## Cote di Franze

loc. Piana di Franze
88811 Cirò Marina [KR]
Tel. +39 3926911606
www.cotedifranze.it

CELLAR SALES
PRE-BOOKED VISITS
ANNUAL PRODUCTION 18,000 bottles
HECTARES UNDER VINE 9.00
VITICULTURE METHOD Certified Organic

| | |
|---|---|
| ☉ Cirò Rosato '17 | ♟♟ 2* |
| ○ Kom'è '17 | ♟♟ 2* |
| ○ Cirò Bianco '17 | ♟ 2 |
| ● Cirò Rosso Cl. '14 | ♟ 3 |

## Cantine De Mare

via Saffo
88811 Cirò Marina [KR]
Tel. +39 3393768853
www.cantinedemare.it

CELLAR SALES
ANNUAL PRODUCTION 90,000 bottles
HECTARES UNDER VINE 23.00

| | |
|---|---|
| ☉ Cirò Rosato Prima Luce '17 | ♟♟ 3 |
| ● Cirò Rosso Cl. Sup. Altura '16 | ♟♟ 3 |
| ○ Cirò Bianco Sant'Angelo '17 | ♟ 3 |
| ○ Italian Blanc Sauvignon '17 | ♟ 3 |

## Du Cropio

via Sele, 5
88811 Cirò Marina [KR]
Tel. +39 096231322
www.viniducropio.it

CELLAR SALES
PRE-BOOKED VISITS
ACCOMMODATION AND RESTAURANT SERVICE
ANNUAL PRODUCTION 90,000 bottles
HECTARES UNDER VINE 30.00
VITICULTURE METHOD Certified Organic

| | |
|---|---|
| ● Cirò Cl. Sup. Dom Giuvà '15 | ♟♟ 3 |
| ● Serra Sanguigna '15 | ♟♟ 3 |

## Cantina Enotria

loc. San Gennaro
s.s. Jonica, 106
88811 Cirò Marina [KR]
Tel. +39 0962371181
www.cantinaenotria.com

CELLAR SALES
PRE-BOOKED VISITS
ANNUAL PRODUCTION 1,000,000 bottles
HECTARES UNDER VINE 170.00

| | |
|---|---|
| ● Centosei '17 | ♟♟ 2* |
| ○ Cirò Bianco '17 | ♟♟ 2* |
| ● Cirò Rosso Cl. Sup. Piana delle Fate Ris. '15 | ♟ 5 |

## Malena

loc. Petraro
s.s. Jonica 106
88811 Cirò Marina [KR]
Tel. +39 096231758
www.malena.it

CELLAR SALES
PRE-BOOKED VISITS
ANNUAL PRODUCTION 220,000 bottles
HECTARES UNDER VINE 16.00

| | |
|---|---|
| ☉ Cirò Rosato '17 | ♟♟ 2* |
| ● Demetra Rosso '16 | ♟♟ 2* |
| ● Cutura del Marchese '16 | ♟ 6 |
| ☉ Demetra Rosato '17 | ♟ 2 |

## Poderi Marini

LOC. SANT'AGATA
87069 SAN DEMETRIO CORONE [CS]
TEL. +39 3683525028
www.poderimarini.it

CELLAR SALES
PRE-BOOKED VISITS
ANNUAL PRODUCTION 50,000 bottles
HECTARES UNDER VINE 7.00
VITICULTURE METHOD Certified Organic

| | | |
|---|---|---|
| ○ Collimarini Passito '16 | | ♟♟ 4 |
| ⊙ Koronè Rosé '17 | | ♟ 2 |
| ● Koronè Rosso '16 | | ♟ 2 |

## Marrelli Wines

LOC. SANT'ANDREA
VIA DELL'ERICA, 28
88841 ISOLA DI CAPO RIZZUTO [KR]
TEL. +39 0962930276
www.marrelliwines.it

CELLAR SALES
PRE-BOOKED VISITS
ACCOMMODATION AND RESTAURANT SERVICE
ANNUAL PRODUCTION 50,000 bottles
HECTARES UNDER VINE 15.00

| | | |
|---|---|---|
| ● Lakinio '16 | | ♟♟ 4 |
| ● Sant'Anna di Isola di Capo Rizzuto Jorico '16 | | ♟♟ 2* |
| ○ Miscello di Ripe '17 | | ♟ 4 |

## Masseria Falvo 1727

LOC. GARGA
87010 SARACENA [CS]
TEL. +39 098138127
www.masseriafalvo.com

CELLAR SALES
ANNUAL PRODUCTION 80,000 bottles
HECTARES UNDER VINE 26.00
VITICULTURE METHOD Certified Organic

| | | |
|---|---|---|
| ○ Milirosu Passito '16 | | ♟♟ 5 |
| ● Terre di Cosenza Magliocco Don Rosario Ris. '14 | | ♟♟ 5 |
| ○ Terre di Cosenza Pircoca '16 | | ♟♟ 2* |

## Le Moire

VIA C.M. TALLARIGO, 12
88040 MOTTA SANTA LUCIA [CZ]
TEL. +39 3385739758
www.lemoire.it

CELLAR SALES
PRE-BOOKED VISITS
ACCOMMODATION
ANNUAL PRODUCTION 13,000 bottles
HECTARES UNDER VINE 8.00

| | | |
|---|---|---|
| ○ Savuto Zaleuco '17 | | ♟♟ 3 |
| ● Savuto Mute '16 | | ♟ 2 |
| ⊙ Savuto Shemale '17 | | ♟ 3 |

## Nesci

VIA MARINA, 1
89038 PALIZZI [RC]
TEL. +39 3209785653
www.aziendanesci.it

ANNUAL PRODUCTION 45,000 bottles
HECTARES UNDER VINE 12.00

| | | |
|---|---|---|
| ● Chapeaux '16 | | ♟♟ 3 |
| ● Esperanto '16 | | ♟ 2 |

## G.B. Odoardi

C.DA CAMPODORATO, 35
88047 NOCERA TERINESE [CZ]
TEL. +39 098429961
www.cantineodoardi.it

CELLAR SALES
ANNUAL PRODUCTION 120,000 bottles
HECTARES UNDER VINE 45.00

| | | |
|---|---|---|
| ● GB Rosso '15 | | ♟♟ 6 |
| ● Terra Damia '15 | | ♟♟ 3 |

## Tenute Pacelli

C.DA ROSE
87010 MALVITO [CS]
TEL. +39 09841634348
www.tenutepacelli.it

CELLAR SALES
PRE-BOOKED VISITS
ACCOMMODATION
ANNUAL PRODUCTION 18,000 bottles
HECTARES UNDER VINE 9.00
VITICULTURE METHOD Certified Organic
SUSTAINABLE WINERY

| | |
|---|---|
| ⊙ Malvarosa '16 | 🍷🍷 2* |
| ● Zio Nunù '15 | 🍷 6 |

## La Pizzuta del Principe

C.DA PIZZUTA
88816 STRONGOLI [KR]
TEL. +39 096288252
www.lapizzutadelprincipe.it

CELLAR SALES
PRE-BOOKED VISITS
ACCOMMODATION AND RESTAURANT SERVICE
ANNUAL PRODUCTION 80,000 bottles
HECTARES UNDER VINE 13.00
VITICULTURE METHOD Certified Organic

| | |
|---|---|
| ● Melissa Rosso Jacca Ventu '16 | 🍷🍷 2* |
| ● Zingamaro '14 | 🍷🍷 3 |
| ● Anno Quinto '12 | 🍷 4 |
| ○ Molarella '17 | 🍷 3 |

## Russo & Longo

FRAZ. STRONGOLI
LOC. SERPITO
88816 STRONGOLI [KR]
TEL. +39 09621905782
www.russoelongo.it

CELLAR SALES
PRE-BOOKED VISITS
ANNUAL PRODUCTION 100,000 bottles
HECTARES UNDER VINE 16.00

| | |
|---|---|
| ⊙ Colli di Ginestra '17 | 🍷🍷 2* |
| ● Jachello '15 | 🍷🍷 5 |
| ● Serra Barbara '16 | 🍷 3 |
| ○ Terre di Trezzi '17 | 🍷 2 |

## Fattoria San Francesco

LOC. QUATTROMANI
88813 CIRÒ [KR]
TEL. +39 096232228
www.fattoriasanfrancesco.it

CELLAR SALES
PRE-BOOKED VISITS
ANNUAL PRODUCTION 224,000 bottles
HECTARES UNDER VINE 40.00

| | |
|---|---|
| ● Cirò Rosso Cl. Sup. Duca dell'Argillone Ris. '13 | 🍷🍷 4 |
| ● Ronco dei Quattroventi '16 | 🍷🍷 3 |
| ⊙ Cirò Rosato '17 | 🍷 2 |

## Senatore Vini

LOC. SAN LORENZO
88811 CIRÒ MARINA [KR]
TEL. +39 096232350
www.senatorevini.com

CELLAR SALES
PRE-BOOKED VISITS
ANNUAL PRODUCTION 280,000 bottles
HECTARES UNDER VINE 32.00
VITICULTURE METHOD Certified Organic
SUSTAINABLE WINERY

| | |
|---|---|
| ⊙ Cirò Rosato Puntalice '17 | 🍷🍷 3 |
| ● Nerello '13 | 🍷🍷 4 |
| ○ Alikia '17 | 🍷 3 |
| ○ Eukè Cuvée Prestige Extra Brut | 🍷 3 |

## Serracavallo

C.DA SERRACAVALLO
87043 BISIGNANO [CS]
TEL. +39 098421144
www.viniserracavallo.it

CELLAR SALES
PRE-BOOKED VISITS
RESTAURANT SERVICE
ANNUAL PRODUCTION 80,000 bottles
HECTARES UNDER VINE 32.00
VITICULTURE METHOD Certified Organic

| | |
|---|---|
| ● Terre di Cosenza Colline dei Crati Magliocco V. Savuco Ris. '14 | 🍷🍷 6 |
| ⊙ Terre di Cosenza Colline dei Crati Rosato Don Filì '17 | 🍷 3 |

## Spadafora Wines 1915

zona ind. Piano Lago, 18
87050 Mangone [CS]
Tel. +39 0984969080
www.cantinespadafora.it

CELLAR SALES
PRE-BOOKED VISITS
ANNUAL PRODUCTION 600,000 bottles
HECTARES UNDER VINE 40.00

| | |
|---|---|
| ● Peperosso '17 | 🍷🍷 2* |
| ⊙ Rosa Amara '17 | 🍷🍷 2* |
| ⊙ Solarys '17 | 🍷🍷 3 |
| ● Terre di Cosenza Donnici Telesio '15 | 🍷 4 |

## Statti

c.da Lenti
88046 Lamezia Terme [CZ]
Tel. +39 0968456138
www.statti.com

CELLAR SALES
PRE-BOOKED VISITS
RESTAURANT SERVICE
ANNUAL PRODUCTION 500,000 bottles
HECTARES UNDER VINE 100.00

| | |
|---|---|
| ● Gaglioppo '17 | 🍷🍷 3 |
| ○ Lamezia Greco Nosside '16 | 🍷🍷 4 |
| ○ Mantonico '16 | 🍷🍷 3 |
| ⊙ Greco Nero '17 | 🍷 3 |

## Tenuta del Travale

loc. Travale, 13
87050 Rovito [CS]
Tel. +39 3937150240
www.tenutadeltravale.it

CELLAR SALES
PRE-BOOKED VISITS
ANNUAL PRODUCTION 14,000 bottles
HECTARES UNDER VINE 2.00
SUSTAINABLE WINERY

| | |
|---|---|
| ● Eleuteria '15 | 🍷🍷 6 |

## Terre del Gufo - Muzzillo

c.da Albo San Martino, 22a
87100 Cosenza
Tel. +39 0984780364
www.terredelgufo.it

CELLAR SALES
PRE-BOOKED VISITS
ANNUAL PRODUCTION 25,500 bottles
HECTARES UNDER VINE 3.00

| | |
|---|---|
| ● Terre di Cosenza Portapiana '16 | 🍷🍷 4 |
| ● Terre di Cosenza Timpamara '16 | 🍷🍷 5 |
| ● Kaulos '17 | 🍷 3 |
| ⊙ Terre di Cosenza Chiaroscuro '17 | 🍷 3 |

## Terre di Balbia

c.da Montino
87042 Altomonte [CS]
Tel. +39 098435359
www.terredibalbia.it

CELLAR SALES
PRE-BOOKED VISITS
ANNUAL PRODUCTION 10,270 bottles
HECTARES UNDER VINE 8.00

| | |
|---|---|
| ● Fervore '16 | 🍷🍷 5 |
| ● Blandus '16 | 🍷🍷 5 |

## Vulcano Wine

via Indipendenza, 11
88811 Cirò Marina [KR]
Tel. +39 096235381
www.vulcanowine.com

CELLAR SALES
ANNUAL PRODUCTION 250,000 bottles
HECTARES UNDER VINE 4.00

| | |
|---|---|
| ⊙ Cirò Bianco Beppe Vulcano '17 | 🍷 3 |
| ⊙ Cirò Rosato Beppe Vulcano '17 | 🍷 3 |

# SICILY

The results of our annual tastings saw Sicily take home some 25 Tre Bicchieri, confirming the region's current 'state of grace' when it comes to wine production. The island's true forte lies in the impeccable stylistic definition of its wines, with its native grapes forming a critical part of the way in which its wines represents such markedly different terroir, each with its own peculiarities. And it's precisely this variety, this charming diversity, that makes Sicily a winemaking region with such global appeal, and that's allowed it to firmly establish itself as one of the most important on the planet. In short, the island is more of a continent. A good example is how different Trapani's Nero d'Avola is from, say, Ragusa, or how the same grape can give rise to such different wines in Messina and Caltanissetta. And then there's Etna, which reaffirms its excellence while elevating diversity and local identity, offering up wines with a host of different personalities, brought about by variations in soil, position and elevations. Once again this year it's worth stressing the increasing reliance on the Doc Sicilia classification, a now internationally successful brand. By the end of 2017 almost 30 million Doc Sicilia wines had been bottled. By July of 2018 it was almost 50 million. And there's more. In addition to the growth of Doc offerings, the average price per bottle has also increased, demonstrating the wisdom of those who had seen the classification as an opportunity to further develop the region. And now for the 'new entries' in the 2019 edition of Italian Wines, those producers who earned Tre Bicchieri for the first time. Trapani got the best out of its most famous grape, Nero d'Avola, with Cantine Mothia taking home top marks thanks to their 2015 Dedicato a Francesco, a wine with personality in spades. Next we move to Etna with two bonafide crus, Palmento Costanzo's 2017 Etna Bianco di Sei, a vibrant and mineral-rich wine made with grapes from 100-year-old vineyards, and Tenute Bosco's deep and elegant 2015 Vico Prephylloxera, made with grapes from a precious, pre-phylloxera vineyard. Finally, Sicilia gave us this edition's Grower of the Year, Cottanera's Francesco Cambria.

# Abbazia Santa Anastasia

LOC. CASTELBUONO
C.DA SANTA ANASTASIA
90013 CASTELBUONO [PA]
TEL. +39 0921671959
www.abbaziasantaanastasia.com

**CELLAR SALES**
**PRE-BOOKED VISITS**
**ACCOMMODATION AND RESTAURANT SERVICE**
**ANNUAL PRODUCTION** 400,000 bottles
**HECTARES UNDER VINE** 67.50
**VITICULTURE METHOD** Certified Organic
**SUSTAINABLE WINERY**

The history of Abbazia Santa Anastasia is an important one for Sicily. Since the 12th century, the abbey has been a major agricultural and cultural center, overseen with great dedication by Benedictine and Theatine monks. In 1982 the engineer Franco Lena purchased the land and created a 300-hectare estate for agriculture and livestock. The abbey became an elegant country relais while the vineyards, well-ventilated by the nearby sea, were brought back to full bloom thanks to great vision and perseverance. Cultivation is carried out according to both organic and biodynamic principles. Their dark ruby, garnet-tinged 2014 Litra made our finals with its sophistication, just missing our highest honors. The Cabernet Sauvignon delivers intense, elegant tobacco, aromatic herbs, spices, myrtle berries and juniper, as well as full, round tannins. Their aromatic, fresh and generous 2017 Sauvignon Blanc Sinestesìa offers a lovely savory, vibrant finish. The rest of their range is also quite enjoyable.

| | | |
|---|---|---|
| ● Litra '14 | 🏆🏆 | 6 |
| ○ Sens(i)nverso Cabernet Sauvignon '14 | 🏆🏆 | 6 |
| ● Sicilia Nero d'Avola Santa Anastasia 5 '17 | 🏆🏆 | 3 |
| ○ Sicilia Sauvignon Sinestesia '17 | 🏆🏆 | 4 |
| ○ Terre di Anastasia Brut '14 | 🏆🏆 | 7 |
| ○ Zurrica '17 | 🏆🏆 | 4 |
| ● Passomaggio '15 | 🏆 | 4 |
| ○ Sens(i)nverso Chardonnay '16 | 🏆 | 6 |
| ○ Sens(i)nverso Syrah '15 | 🏆 | 6 |
| ● Litra '04 | 🏆🏆🏆 | 6 |
| ● Litra '01 | 🏆🏆🏆 | 7 |
| ● Montenero '04 | 🏆🏆🏆 | 4 |
| ● Litra '13 | 🏆🏆 | 7 |
| ● Passomaggio '14 | 🏆🏆 | 3 |
| ○ Terre di Anastasia Brut '13 | 🏆🏆 | 6 |

# Alessandro di Camporeale

C.DA MANDRANOVA
90043 CAMPOREALE [PA]
TEL. +39 092437038
www.alessandrodicamporeale.it

**CELLAR SALES**
**PRE-BOOKED VISITS**
**ANNUAL PRODUCTION** 240,000 bottles
**HECTARES UNDER VINE** 40.00
**VITICULTURE METHOD** Certified Organic

Natale, Nino and Rosolino Alessandro's winery is an artisanal, family-run producer that's received critical praise both in Italy and abroad. It's all thanks to a tenacious commitment to quality over time. Their excellent wines represent expressions of the various cultivar used and the territories in which they're grown. The winery has received a further boost now that the owners' children are on board, after having completed their studies (in part abroad) in enology, marketing and law. An enthusiastic Tre Bicchieri for their 2016 Syrah Kaid - their best ever. Deep, elegant and intense, it offers ripe fruit and vibrant balsamic tones on an enduring, satisfying palate of round, sophisticated tannins. Their graceful 2017 Grillo Vigna di Mandranova, fresh and uncommonly savory with aromatic herbs and citrus notes, is almost as good. Their smooth 2017 Kaid Vendemmia Tardiva proves excellent.

| | | |
|---|---|---|
| ● Sicilia Syrah Kaid '16 | 🏆🏆🏆 | 4* |
| ○ Sicilia Grillo V. di Mandranova '17 | 🏆🏆 | 3* |
| ○ Sicilia Catarratto V. di Mandranova '17 | 🏆🏆 | 4 |
| ● Sicilia Nero d'Avola Donnatà '17 | 🏆🏆 | 2* |
| ○ Sicilia Sauvignon '17 | 🏆🏆 | 4 |
| ● Sicilia V. T. Kaid '17 | 🏆🏆 | 5 |
| ○ Sicilia Catarratto Benedè '17 | 🏆 | 2 |
| ○ Sicilia Catarratto V. di Mandranova '16 | 🏆🏆🏆 | 4* |
| ● Kaid V. T. '16 | 🏆🏆 | 5 |
| ○ Sicilia Catarratto Benedè '16 | 🏆🏆 | 2* |
| ○ Sicilia Catarratto Benedè '15 | 🏆🏆 | 2* |
| ○ Sicilia Grillo V. di Mandranova '16 | 🏆🏆 | 3 |
| ● Sicilia Nero d'Avola Donnatà '16 | 🏆🏆 | 2* |
| ○ Sicilia Sauvignon Blanc Kaid '16 | 🏆🏆 | 3 |
| ● Sicilia Syrah Kaid '15 | 🏆🏆 | 4 |

# Alta Mora

FRAZ. PIETRAMARINA
C.DA VERZELLA
95012 CASTIGLIONE DI SICILIA [CT]
TEL. +39 0918908713
www.altamora.it

PRE-BOOKED VISITS
ANNUAL PRODUCTION 70,000 bottles
HECTARES UNDER VINE 18.00
SUSTAINABLE WINERY

Alberto and Diego Cusumano's winery on Etna is the result of passionate work over the course of years, and selection of countless batches of grapes cultivated in the area's best districts. The goal is to promote difference and diversity, qualities that define the volcano with its varying elevations, positions and soil. Today their estate spans elevations raging from 600 meters above sea level (in Verzella) to 1000 (in Guardiola). The vineyards, which are almost all head-trained, also vary in age, with some going back more than 100 years, making for a surprisingly diverse selection. An enthusiastic Tre Bicchieri for their elegant, subtle 2017 Alta Moro Bianco. The nose alternates between mineral and fruity notes of white peach and almonds with refined hints of wisteria and cedar bark. Fresh and delicious on the very persistent palate, it delivers tremendous enjoyability. Their noteworthy 2016 Alta Mora, fruity and sinuous, proves ready to drink, energetic and has intriguing tannins.

| | |
|---|---|
| ○ Etna Bianco Alta Mora '17 | ♟♟♟ 4* |
| ● Etna Rosso Alta Mora '16 | ♟♟ 4 |
| ◉ Etna Rosato Alta Mora '17 | ♟♟ 3 |
| ○ Etna Bianco Alta Mora '16 | ♟♟♟ 4* |
| ○ Etna Bianco Alta Mora '14 | ♟♟♟ 3* |

# Assuli

C.DA CARCITELLA
91026 MAZARA DEL VALLO [TP]
TEL. +39 0923546706
www.assuli.it

CELLAR SALES
ANNUAL PRODUCTION 100,000 bottles
HECTARES UNDER VINE 100.00

Stone and grapes are part of a millennium old tradition in western Sicily. And they're an important part of the history of the Caruso family as well. Giacomo founded Sicilmarmi, an internationally successful marble business, decades ago. His son, Roberto, created Assuli, the winery that draws on the family's 100 hectares of vineyards in Castelvetrano, Salemi, Calatafimi and Mazara del Vallo. For this reason their major cellar-baglio (which serves as their production center), was made with Perlato di Sicilia, a marble made famous throughout the world by Roberto's father, Giacomo. For the third time in four years their 2017 Lorlando proves itself, having an intense, full nose of black mulberries and capers with a subtle hint of iodine. The fruit on the palate is solid, corpulent and very persistent. Debuting in our finals is their soft, pulpy 2015 Perricone Furioso, mature and defined in its fruity cherry. Among whites, their fresh, elegant 2017 Grillo Fiordiligi stands out.

| | |
|---|---|
| ● Sicilia Nero d'Avola Lorlando '17 | ♟♟♟ 3* |
| ● Sicilia Perricone Furioso '15 | ♟♟ 4 |
| ● Besi '15 | ♟♟ 5 |
| ○ Sicilia Grillo Fiordiligi '17 | ♟♟ 2* |
| ○ Sicilia Inzolia Carinda '17 | ♟♟ 2* |
| ● Sicilia Nero d'Avola Lorlando Ris. '15 | ♟♟ 4 |
| ○ Sicilia Bianco Donna Angelica '16 | ♟ 3 |
| ○ Sicilia Grillo Astolfo '16 | ♟ 4 |
| ● Sicilia Syrah Ruggiero '17 | ♟ 2 |
| ○ Astolfo '15 | ♟♟♟ 4* |
| ● Lorlando '15 | ♟♟♟ 2* |
| ● Lorlando '14 | ♟♟♟ 2* |
| ● Ruggiero '15 | ♟♟ 2* |
| ● Sicilia Nero d'Avola Lorlando '16 | ♟♟ 3* |

# Baglio del Cristo di Campobello

LOC. C.DA FAVAROTTA
S.DA ST.LE 123 KM 19,200
92023 CAMPOBELLO DI LICATA [AG]
TEL. +39 0922 877709
www.cristodicampobello.it

**PRE-BOOKED VISITS**
**ANNUAL PRODUCTION 300,000 bottles**
**HECTARES UNDER VINE 30.00**

The Bonetta family have been dedicated to viticulture for generations, though their decision to start bottling their own wine was a more recent decision. Their 30 hectares of vineyards are situated along the hills around their family baglio, near an old aedicule that houses a gorgeously-crafted wooden statue of Christ, from which the winery took its name. Thanks to their experience and the high quality of their wines, in just a short time this lovely Sicilian estate has managed to establish itself as a benchmark for the entire region. Despite the intense heat of 2017 (August in particular), it was their whites that truly impressed during regional tastings. Case in point, their 2017 Gillo Lalùci made our finals, just barely missing Tre Bicchieri. Among reds, their juicy, very drinkable 2016 Nero d'Avola Lu Patri performed well offering notes of mulberry and balsamic herbs.

| | |
|---|---|
| ○ Sicilia Grillo Lalùci '17 | 🍷🍷 3* |
| ○ C'D'C' Bianco Cristo di Campobello '17 | 🍷🍷 2* |
| ○ Sicilia Bianco Adènzia '17 | 🍷🍷 3 |
| ● Sicilia Nero d'Avola Lu Patri '16 | 🍷🍷 5 |
| ● Sicilia Rosso Adènzia '16 | 🍷🍷 3 |
| ⊙ C'D'C' Rosato Cristo di Campobello '17 | 🍷 2 |
| ● C'D'C' Rosso Cristo di Campobello '17 | 🍷 2 |
| ● Lu Patri '09 | 🍷🍷🍷 5 |
| ● C'D'C' Rosso Cristo di Campobello '16 | 🍷🍷 2* |
| ○ Sicilia Bianco Adènzia '16 | 🍷🍷 3* |
| ○ Sicilia Chardonnay Laudàri '15 | 🍷🍷 4 |
| ○ Sicilia Grillo Lalùci '16 | 🍷🍷 3 |
| ● Sicilia Nero d'Avola Lu Patri '15 | 🍷🍷 5 |
| ● Sicilia Syrah Lusirà '15 | 🍷🍷 5 |

# Baglio di Pianetto

LOC. PIANETTO
VIA FRANCIA
90030 SANTA CRISTINA GELA [PA]
TEL. +39 0918570002
www.bagliodipianetto.it

**CELLAR SALES**
**PRE-BOOKED VISITS**
**ACCOMMODATION AND RESTAURANT SERVICE**
**ANNUAL PRODUCTION 550,000 bottles**
**HECTARES UNDER VINE 104.00**
**SUSTAINABLE WINERY**

For good reason Paolo Marzotto can consider himself a forefather of Italian wine's new direction. After years of commitment and success with the family's properties in Veneto, Lombardy, Alto Adige and Tuscany, Paolo decided to create his own producer in a region that he always loved, Sicily. Baglio di Pianetto is comprised of more than 100 hectares of entirely organically managed vineyards in Santa Cristina Gela and Baroni, in Pacchina. This prestigious winery presented us a nice array, starting with their 2015 Syrah Syraco, which sailed into our finals thanks to its full, elegant aromas and a spicy, juicy palate. Their whites also prove good. Their Ficiligno, Insola with a bit of Viognier, stood out in particular for its notes of exotic fruit and a fresh, fruity palate of uncommonly pleasant drinkability.

| | |
|---|---|
| ● Syraco '15 | 🍷🍷 3* |
| ● Shymer '15 | 🍷🍷 2* |
| ○ Sicilia Bianco Ficiligno '17 | 🍷🍷 4 |
| ○ Sicilia Catarratto '17 | 🍷🍷 4 |
| ● Sicilia Nero d'Avola '16 | 🍷🍷 6 |
| ● Cembali '11 | 🍷 5 |
| ● Frappato '16 | 🍷 4 |
| ○ Sicilia Ginolfo '17 | 🍷 4 |
| ● Ramione '04 | 🍷🍷🍷 3* |
| ● Shymer '14 | 🍷🍷🍷 2* |
| ● Shymer '13 | 🍷🍷🍷 2* |
| ● Sicilia Rosso Ramione '13 | 🍷🍷🍷 3* |
| ● Carduni '12 | 🍷🍷 5 |
| ○ Moscato di Noto Ra'is '13 | 🍷🍷 5 |
| ○ Sicilia Timeo '16 | 🍷🍷 3 |
| ● Syraco '14 | 🍷🍷 3 |

# Barone di Villagrande

VIA DEL BOSCO, 25
95025 MILO [CT]
TEL. +39 0957082175
www.villagrande.it

CELLAR SALES
PRE-BOOKED VISITS
ACCOMMODATION AND RESTAURANT SERVICE
ANNUAL PRODUCTION 80,000 bottles
HECTARES UNDER VINE 19.00
VITICULTURE METHOD Certified Organic

There are so many stories all interwoven here on Mt. Etna that it would be impossible to talk about the area without mentioning the Nicolosi family. For ten generations they've been growing vines here on the volcano, but the turning point came in 1869 when Paolo Nicolosi built a multistory cellar, extremely modern for the time, for gravity-flow winemaking. In 1968 Carlo wrote the first controlled appellation policy document for Doc Etna. Today his son Marco, and Marco's wife, Barbara, are more determined than ever to successfully carry forward a history that's still in the making. Elegant and territorial, their 2014 Etna Rosso Contrada Villagrande made our finals thanks to its bouquet of red fruit well-paired with smoky, spicy notes. The palate offers a good balance of fruit, acidity and tannins, as well as a long finish. Their 2016 Etna Rosso gives up notes of ripe red fruit that return on its full, persistent palate.

| | |
|---|---|
| ● Etna Rosso Contrada Villagrande '14 | ⟶⟶ 6 |
| ○ Etna Bianco Sup. '17 | ⟶⟶ 2* |
| ● Etna Rosso '16 | ⟶⟶ 3 |
| ○ Malvasia delle Lipari Passito '14 | ⟶⟶ 5 |
| ⊙ Etna Rosato '17 | ⟶ 3 |
| ○ Salina Bianco '17 | ⟶ 3 |
| ○ Etna Bianco Sup. '13 | ⟶⟶ 2* |
| ○ Etna Bianco Sup. Contrada Villagrande '13 | ⟶⟶ 6 |
| ⊙ Etna Rosato '16 | ⟶⟶ 3 |
| ● Etna Rosso '15 | ⟶⟶ 3 |
| ● Etna Rosso '12 | ⟶⟶ 3 |
| ● Etna Rosso Contrada Villagrande '13 | ⟶⟶ 6 |
| ○ Fiore di Villagrande '12 | ⟶⟶ 4 |
| ○ Malvasia delle Lipari '13 | ⟶⟶ 5 |

# Tenuta Bastonaca

C.DA BASTONACA
97019 VITTORIA [RG]
TEL. +39 0932686480
www.tenutabastonaca.it

CELLAR SALES
ACCOMMODATION
ANNUAL PRODUCTION 40,000 bottles
HECTARES UNDER VINE 10.00
SUSTAINABLE WINERY

Silvano Raniolo and Giovanni Calcaterra's Tenuta Bastonaca is a small and dynamic winery that's had success with both critics and the markets for its 'tailor-made' approach. Their precise, elegant wines fully express the terroir of origin, the estates of Vittoria (in Ragusa) and Castiglione di Sicilia (on Mt. Etna). The couple's sensitivity to environmental issues guarantees that their vineyards, almost all of which are non-irrigated and head-trained, are cultivated 'according to nature'. Their cellar is housed in a charming 18th century, stone palmento. Their personality-filled 2016 Sud just missed Tre Bicchieri. Deep and dark, this blend of Nero d'Avola, Tannat and Grenache charms like premium wines with clear notes of plum, humus and black pepper that return confidently on the refined palate, rich with smooth tannins. Both their 2015 Etna Rosso and austere 2016 Cerasuolo di Vittoria also merit mention.

| | |
|---|---|
| ● Sud '16 | ⟶⟶ 5 |
| ● Cerasuolo di Vittoria '16 | ⟶⟶ 3 |
| ● Etna Rosso '15 | ⟶⟶ 4 |
| ● Frappato '17 | ⟶⟶ 3 |
| ○ Sicilia Grillo '17 | ⟶⟶ 3 |
| ● Sicilia Nero d'Avola '17 | ⟶⟶ 3 |
| ● Cerasuolo di Vittoria '15 | ⟶⟶ 3 |
| ● Cerasuolo di Vittoria '14 | ⟶⟶ 3 |
| ● Etna Rosso '14 | ⟶⟶ 4 |
| ● Frappato '16 | ⟶⟶ 3 |
| ● Frappato '15 | ⟶⟶ 3 |
| ○ Grillo '16 | ⟶⟶ 3 |
| ○ Grillo '15 | ⟶⟶ 3 |
| ● Nero d'Avola '16 | ⟶⟶ 3 |
| ● Nero d'Avola '15 | ⟶⟶ 3 |
| ● Sud '15 | ⟶⟶ 5 |

## ★Benanti

VIA GIUSEPPE GARIBALDI, 361
95029 VIAGRANDE [CT]
TEL. +39 0957893399
www.benanti.it

CELLAR SALES
PRE-BOOKED VISITS
RESTAURANT SERVICE
ANNUAL PRODUCTION 160,000 bottles
HECTARES UNDER VINE 28.00
SUSTAINABLE WINERY

Giuseppe Benanti deserves credit for being
the first person to intuit that the
pedoclimatic differences between Etna's
slopes and various districts could be used
towards creating superior, original,
territorial wines of great character. Since
then 30 years have past and now his sons
Antonio and Salvino are managing the
winery. It was a smooth transition that
didn't see any major breaks with tradition.
And while the pair are looking into new
strategies and investments, it's always with
an eye towards best developing the terroir
and its native grape varieties. A noteworthy
performance from a true pillar of
winemaking around Etna. Missing Tre
Bicchieri by just a hair, their 2014 Serra
della Contessa, an Etna Rosso of
extraordinary finesse and complexity,
delivers a deep palate with an extremely
long finish. Their 2015 Pietra Marina, an
Etna Bianco, also proves very good with a
full, elegant nose. It is fresh and savory
with incredibly persistent aromas.

## Bonavita

LOC. FARO SUPERIORE
C.DA CORSO
98158 MESSINA
TEL. +39 3471754683
www.bonavitafaro.com

PRE-BOOKED VISITS
ANNUAL PRODUCTION 10,000 bottles
HECTARES UNDER VINE 2.50

Giovanni Scarfone's vineyards in Faro
Superiore are situated on two levels, carved
out of the wooded hills that overlook the
Straight of Messina. It's an amphitheater
beaten by the winds generated by the
meeting of the Tyrrhenian and Ionian seas.
His three plots total two and a half hectares
of vineyards, with head-trained and
upwards-trained vertical-trellised vines that
go back anywhere from 10 to 80 year. As
part of an approach centered on respect for
the environment and territorial tradition, no
artificial chemicals are used in the vineyard
or in the cellar. Giovanni's 2016 Faro, one
of their best versions ever, made our finals
by virtue of its magnificent territoriality. This
fruity red with hints of pomegranate and
delicate notes of watermelon offers a fully
mature palate, both very elegant and very
enduring. Full pulpy fruit returns in their
captivatingly pleasant 2017 Rosato.

| | |
|---|---|
| ● Etna Rosso Serra della Contessa '14 | ♟♟ 7 |
| ○ Etna Bianco Sup. Pietramarina '15 | ♟♟ 5 |
| ● Etna Rosso Contrada Monte Serra '16 | ♟♟ 4 |
| ● Etna Rosso Rovittello '14 | ♟♟ 5 |
| ● Nerello Cappuccio Il Monovitigno '16 | ♟♟ 5 |
| ○ Etna Bianco '17 | ♟ 4 |
| ⊙ Etna Rosato '17 | ♟ 4 |
| ● Etna Rosso '16 | ♟ 3 |
| ○ Etna Bianco Sup. Pietramarina '09 | ♟♟♟ 5 |
| ○ Etna Bianco Sup. Pietramarina '04 | ♟♟♟ 6 |
| ○ Etna Bianco Sup. Pietramarina '02 | ♟♟♟ 5 |
| ○ Etna Bianco Sup. Pietramarina '01 | ♟♟♟ 5 |
| ● Etna Rosso Serra della Contessa '06 | ♟♟♟ 7 |
| ● Etna Rosso Serra della Contessa '04 | ♟♟♟ 7 |
| ● Etna Rosso Serra della Contessa '03 | ♟♟♟ 7 |
| ● Il Drappo '04 | ♟♟♟ 5 |

| | |
|---|---|
| ● Faro '16 | ♟♟ 5 |
| ⊙ Rosato '17 | ♟♟ 2* |
| ● Faro '15 | ♟♟ 5 |
| ● Faro '14 | ♟♟ 5 |
| ● Faro '13 | ♟♟ 5 |
| ● Faro '12 | ♟♟ 5 |
| ● Faro '11 | ♟♟ 5 |
| ● Faro '10 | ♟♟ 5 |
| ⊙ Rosato '16 | ♟♟ 2* |
| ⊙ Rosato '15 | ♟♟ 2* |
| ⊙ Rosato '14 | ♟♟ 2* |
| ⊙ Rosato '13 | ♟♟ 2* |
| ⊙ Rosato '12 | ♟♟ 2* |

# Tenute Bosco

S.DA PROV.LE 64 SOLICCHIATA
95012 CASTIGLIONE DI SICILIA [CT]
TEL. +39 0957658856
www.tenutebosco.com

CELLAR SALES
PRE-BOOKED VISITS
ANNUAL PRODUCTION 50,000 bottles
HECTARES UNDER VINE 10.00
VITICULTURE METHOD Certified Organic

Sofia and Concetto Bosco's lovely winery avails itself of a modern cellar that features double lava rock walls and that integrates perfectly with its surroundings. Taking up the concept of the old Sicilian palmentos, their winemaking is performed through gravity-flow, from crushing to fermentation and aging. The double walls guarantee excellent thermic insulation such that energy needs are reduced to a minimum. Their approach in the vineyards, which centers on respect for the environment and territory, includes certified organic cultivation. Vigna Vico, at Passopisciaro, is one of the prettiest and oldest vineyards of Etna. A classic example of amphitheater cultivation with dry-stone walls from the 1800s, it currently boasts 30,000 mostly100-year-old, ungrafted plants. Tre Biccieri to their homonymous 2015 Etna Rosso, whose full, refined nose returns on its elegant, juicy, concentrated palate of exceptional length.

| | |
|---|---|
| ● Etna Rosso Vico Prephylloxera '15 | ▼▼▼ 8 |
| ○ Etna Bianco Piano dei Daini '17 | ▼▼ 5 |
| ⊙ Etna Rosato Piano dei Daini '17 | ▼▼ 5 |
| ● Etna Rosso Piano dei Daini '16 | ▼▼ 5 |
| ○ Etna Bianco Piano dei Daini '16 | ♀♀ 5 |
| ⊙ Etna Rosato Piano dei Daini '16 | ♀♀ 5 |
| ● Etna Rosso Piano dei Daini '15 | ♀♀ 5 |
| ● Etna Rosso Vigna Vico '14 | ♀♀ 8 |

# Caravaglio

LOC. MALFA SALINA
VIA NAZIONALE, 33
98050 MALFA [ME]
TEL. +39 3398115953
caravagliovini@virgilio.it

CELLAR SALES
PRE-BOOKED VISITS
ANNUAL PRODUCTION 50,000 bottles
HECTARES UNDER VINE 12.00
VITICULTURE METHOD Certified Organic
SUSTAINABLE WINERY

When faced with a decrease in the consumption of dessert wines, Nino Caravaglio not only held fast without giving an inch in terms of quality and typicity, he managed to stylistically reinterpret his Malvasia delle Lipari with an eye towards drinkability, elegance and freshness. The wine is accompanied by a number of well-made and pleasant dry wines that have had good market success. And so the explosive Nino last year planted five more hectares on Stromboli, in addition to the 12 already being cultivated. An extremely well-deserved Tre Bicchieri for their 2017 Malvasia delle Lipari Passito. zIts incredibly refined bouquet of minerals, exotic fruit, citrus and lavender leads to a palate of full, sweet fruit supported by fresh, savory acidity and ending with a finish of long aromatic persistence. Their delicious 2017 Palmento di Salina, a Corinto Nero and Nerello Mascalese, made it to our finals offering extraordinary drinkability.

| | |
|---|---|
| ○ Malvasia delle Lipari Passito '17 | ▼▼▼ 5 |
| ● Palmento di Salina '17 | ▼▼ 4 |
| ○ Infatata '17 | ▼▼ 3 |
| ○ Malvasia '17 | ▼▼ 5 |
| ○ Occhio di Terra Chianu Cruci '17 | ▼▼ 3 |
| ○ Malvasia delle Lipari Passito '16 | ♀♀♀ 5 |
| ○ Infatata '16 | ♀♀ 3 |
| ○ Infatata '15 | ♀♀ 3 |
| ○ Infatata '14 | ♀♀ 3 |
| ○ Malvasia '16 | ♀♀ 5 |
| ○ Malvasia delle Lipari Passito '14 | ♀♀ 5 |
| ○ Malvasia delle Lipari Passito '13 | ♀♀ 5 |
| ● Nero du Munti '16 | ♀♀ 4 |
| ● Nero du Munti '14 | ♀♀ 4 |
| ○ Occhio di Terra '16 | ♀♀ 3 |
| ○ Occhio di Terra '15 | ♀♀ 3 |

## Le Casematte

LOC. FARO SUPERIORE
C.DA CORSO
98163 MESSINA
TEL. +39 0906409427
www.lecasematte.it

CELLAR SALES
ANNUAL PRODUCTION 30,000 bottles
HECTARES UNDER VINE 11.00
VITICULTURE METHOD Certified Organic
SUSTAINABLE WINERY

The splendid estate owned by Gianfranco
Sabbatino, accountant, and Andrea
Barzagli, a well-known footballer, overlooks
the Straight of Messina from on high. Here
strong, sudden winds imbued with salt
dominate the landscape, seeming to whip
the vineyards situated on the steep
terraces here. Rising among them are the
casematte (military forts) that give the
winery its name. Their artisanal
winemaking approach is carried out in
an innovated and elegant cellar, which
gives rise to some of Doc Faro's most
expressive wines. This prestigious winery's
2016 Faro, a blend of Nerello Mascalese,
Cappuccio, Nocera and Nero d'Avola,
easily wins its umpteenth Tre Bicchieri,
delivering all of the enchantment expected
of a truly great wine. Ripe, sumptuous,
elegant, it offers fruity nuances intertwined
with hints of forest undergrowth,
chocolate, slate and spices. Their
sophisticated 2016 Peloro Rosso, of
Nerello Mascalese and Nocera, is almost
its equals.

| | |
|---|---|
| ● Faro '16 | ▼▼▼ 5 |
| ○ Peloro Bianco '17 | ▼▼ 3 |
| ● Peloro Rosso '16 | ▼▼ 2* |
| ⊙ Rosematte Nerello Mascalese '17 | ▼▼ 3 |
| ● Faro '15 | ♔♔♔ 5 |
| ● Faro '14 | ♔♔♔ 5 |
| ● Faro '13 | ♔♔♔ 5 |
| ○ Peloro Bianco '16 | ♔♔ 3 |
| ○ Peloro Bianco '15 | ♔♔ 3 |
| ○ Peloro Bianco '14 | ♔♔ 3 |
| ● Peloro Rosso '15 | ♔♔ 2* |
| ● Peloro Rosso '14 | ♔♔ 2* |
| ● Peloro Rosso '13 | ♔♔ 2* |
| ⊙ Rosematte '14 | ♔♔ 3 |
| ⊙ Rosematte Nerello Mascalese '16 | ♔♔ 3 |
| ⊙ Rosematte Nerello Mascalese '15 | ♔♔ 3 |

## Centopassi

VIA PORTA PALERMO, 132
90048 SAN GIUSEPPE JATO [PA]
TEL. +39 0918577655
www.centopassisicilia.it

CELLAR SALES
PRE-BOOKED VISITS
ACCOMMODATION AND RESTAURANT SERVICE
ANNUAL PRODUCTION 450,000 bottles
HECTARES UNDER VINE 94.00
VITICULTURE METHOD Certified Organic
SUSTAINABLE WINERY

Centopassi was founded in 2001 as an
offshoot of Libera Terra. The idea was to
render economically and socially
productive 94 hectares of terrain
confiscated from the mafia. Their
vineyards, which are entirely organic, span
various districts of Alto Belice Coleonese,
an area extremely well-suited to vine
growing. Their eight crus, which are
vinified separately, span elevations
ranging from 350 meters (in Terre Rosse
di Giabbascio) to 950 (in Portella della
Ginestra). Their cellar, which is also a
confiscated property, is located in San
Giuseppe Jato. Their 2017 Catarratto
Terre Rosse di Giabbascio offers a
complex, full nose of herbs and exotic fruit
on a pulpy, fresh palate. The bouquet of
their 2015 Pietre a Purtedda da Ginestra, a
70 Nerello Mascalese / 30 Nocera blend,
releases elegant nuances of spices. Their
2016 Cimento di Perricone, made with
grapes from San Cipirello has a nice
cherry nose with sohisticated vegetal notes
and a pleasant consistency.

| | |
|---|---|
| ○ Sicilia Catarratto Terre Rosse di Giabbascio '17 | ▼▼ 3* |
| ● Cimento di Perricone '16 | ▼▼ 3 |
| ● Pietre a Purtedda da Ginestra '15 | ▼▼ 5 |
| ● Sicilia Giato Nero d'Avola Perricone '17 | ▼▼ 2* |
| ○ Tendoni di Trebbiano '16 | ▼▼ 3 |
| ● Argille di Tagghia Via '15 | ▼ 3 |
| ○ Grillo Rocce di Pietra Longa '17 | ▼ 3 |
| ● rgille di Tagghia Via di Sutta '16 | ▼ 3 |
| ○ Sicilia Giato Grillo Catarratto Sup. '17 | ▼ 2 |
| ● Syrah Marne di Saladino '16 | ▼ 4 |
| ○ Sicilia Giato Grillo Catarratto '16 | ♔♔ 2* |
| ● Sicilia Giato Nero d'Avola Perricone '16 | ♔♔ 2* |
| ● Sicilia Rosso Centopassi '15 | ♔♔ 2* |

## Terra Costantino

VIA GARIBALDI, 417
95029 VIAGRANDE [CT]
TEL. +39 095434288
www.terracostantino.it

CELLAR SALES
PRE-BOOKED VISITS
ANNUAL PRODUCTION 40,000 bottles
HECTARES UNDER VINE 7.00
VITICULTURE METHOD Certified Organic

Dino Costantino and his son Fabio are part of a family legacy of vine growing on Etna that goes back to 1699. In fact, that's the year that their ancient palmento was built, a structure that stands at the center of 10 contiguous hectares of head-trained vineyards situated on the south side of the volcano. As authentic vigneron, the Costantino family are convinced that great wine can only be made through an approach that respects the ecosystem and the territory, and that this holds both for the vineyard and for the cellar. It's for this reason that the entire production cycle strictly adheres to principles of organic agriculture. Their 2016 Etna Rosso De Aetna, deserved its place in our finals. It fully reflects its proud terroir with a sophisticated nose of peach and orange over a mineral and iron background. Still vibrant tannins and fruit blend together on the fresh palate. The authoritative palate of their intense and austere 2015 Etna Rosso Contrada Blandano comes from an excellent balance of fruit and tannins.

| | |
|---|---|
| ● Etna Rosso De Aetna '16 | ♥♥ 3* |
| ○ Etna Bianco Contrada Blandano '15 | ♥♥ 5 |
| ● Etna Rosso Contrada Blandano '15 | ♥♥ 5 |
| ○ Etna Bianco De Aetna '16 | ♥ 3 |
| ⊙ Etna Rosato De Aetna '17 | ♥ 3 |
| ○ Etna Bianco Blandano '13 | ♀♀ 5 |
| ○ Etna Bianco Contrada Blandano '14 | ♀♀ 5 |
| ⊙ Etna Rosato De Aetna '16 | ♀♀ 3 |
| ⊙ Etna Rosato De Aetna '14 | ♀♀ 3 |
| ● Etna Rosso Contrada Blandano '14 | ♀♀ 5 |
| ● Etna Rosso De Aetna '15 | ♀♀ 3 |
| ● Etna Rosso De Aetna '14 | ♀♀ 3 |
| ● Etna Rosso De Aetna '13 | ♀♀ 3 |

## ★Cottanera

LOC. IANNAZZO
S.DA PROV.LE 89
95030 CASTIGLIONE DI SICILIA [CT]
TEL. +39 0942963601
www.cottanera.it

CELLAR SALES
PRE-BOOKED VISITS
ANNUAL PRODUCTION 350,000 bottles
HECTARES UNDER VINE 65.00

Guglielmo Cambria's dream came true. It required betting entirely on the vineyard while writing off his historic and profitable hazelnut trees, but for some time now Cottanera has been one of Etna's benchmark producers, both in terms of size and quality. With dedication and good business sense, his brother Enzo and the founder's children Mariangela, Emanuele and Francesco have created an estate centered on traditional cultivar but also open to the world. Cultivated on individual plots, their wines are full of character, well-defined and elegant, the result of an approach that highlights the attributes of each single terroir. For its fouth year running their splendid Etna Rossa Zottorinoto gets Tre Bicchieri. The elegant, multifaceted 2014 proves refined, complex and fruity, with thick, round tannins. Another thoroughbred, their rich, balsamic, energetic and satisfying 2016 Diciassettesalme, ran in our finals but lost by a nose. Francesco, who traded in his suit for a pair of pruning shears, is also this edition's Grower of the Year.

| | |
|---|---|
| ● Etna Rosso Zottorinoto Ris. '14 | ♥♥♥ 8 |
| ● Etna Rosso Diciassettesalme '16 | ♥♥ 3* |
| ○ Etna Bianco '17 | ♥♥ 3 |
| ○ Etna Bianco Calderara '16 | ♥♥ 5 |
| ⊙ Etna Rosato '17 | ♥♥ 2* |
| ● Etna Rosso Barbazzale '17 | ♥♥ 2* |
| ● Etna Rosso Feudo di Mezzo '15 | ♥♥ 3 |
| ● Sicilia L'Ardenza '15 | ♥♥ 4 |
| ● Sicilia Sole di Sesta '15 | ♥♥ 4 |
| ○ Etna Bianco '11 | ♀♀♀ 3* |
| ● Etna Rosso '11 | ♀♀♀ 5 |
| ● Etna Rosso '07 | ♀♀♀ 5 |
| ● Etna Rosso '06 | ♀♀♀ 5 |
| ● Etna Rosso Zottorinoto Ris. '13 | ♀♀♀ 8 |
| ● Etna Rosso Zottorinoto Ris. '12 | ♀♀♀ 8 |
| ● Etna Rosso Zottorinoto Ris. '11 | ♀♀♀ 8 |

## ★Cusumano

LOC. C.DA SAN CARLO
S.DA ST.LE 113 KM 307
90047 PARTINICO [PA]
TEL. +39 0918908713
www.cusumano.it

CELLAR SALES
PRE-BOOKED VISITS
ANNUAL PRODUCTION 2,500,000 bottles
HECTARES UNDER VINE 520.00
SUSTAINABLE WINERY

In 2019, Alberto and Diego's winery turns 18. It's been a road paved with successes that's seen significant growth. Their vineyards span more than 500 hectares in seven distinct territories through Sicily, each capable of expressing its own typicity. Their largest estates are San Giacomo (in Butera), with 140 hectares and Ficuzza with 189. The latter is situated between the wooded district of the same name and Scanzano lake, at 700 meters above sea level. Then there's Alta Mora, with its cellar and vineyards spanning five of Etna's most celebrated districts. Though their Etna wines receive lavish attention, their 2016 Nero d'Avola di Butera Sàgana deserves its own recognition. It reappears in our finals with its intense, complex nose of cherry, mulberry and sweet spices fused to a fine balsamic note and a corresponding palate of great length. Their 2017 Grillo Shamaris proves as equally elegant on the nose as fresh and savory on the palate.

| | | |
|---|---|---|
| ● Sicilia Nero d'Avola Sàgana '16 | ♟♟♟ | 4* |
| ○ 700 slm Brut M. Cl. '14 | ♟♟ | 4 |
| ○ Angimbè Tenuta Ficuzza '17 | ♟♟ | 3 |
| ○ Sicilia Chardonnay Jalé '16 | ♟♟ | 4 |
| ○ Sicilia Grillo Shamaris '17 | ♟♟ | 3 |
| ○ Sicilia Insolia Cubia Tenuta Ficuzza '16 | ♟♟ | 3 |
| ● Sicilia Nero d'Avola Disueri '17 | ♟♟ | 3 |
| ● Sicilia Noà '16 | ♟♟ | 5 |
| ● Benuara Tenuta Presti e Pegni '17 | ♟ | 3 |
| ○ Moscato dello Zucco '10 | ♟♟♟ | 5 |
| ● Noà '10 | ♟♟♟ | 4* |
| ● Sàgana '12 | ♟♟♟ | 4* |
| ● Sàgana '11 | ♟♟♟ | 4* |
| ● Sicilia Noà '13 | ♟♟♟ | 4* |

## ★Donnafugata

VIA S. LIPARI, 18
91025 MARSALA [TP]
TEL. +39 0923724200
www.donnafugata.it

CELLAR SALES
PRE-BOOKED VISITS
ANNUAL PRODUCTION 2,240,000 bottles
HECTARES UNDER VINE 338.00
SUSTAINABLE WINERY

Donnafugata is an esteemed producer, considered to be among the best expressions of Sicilian viticulture and extremely appreciated on international markets thanks to their elegant and highly territorial wines. Giacomo Rallo had aimed to establish a presence in Cerasuolo di Vittoria and on Etna, and with the purchase of an estate on the volcano his brilliant strategy is now complete. Today his great moral legacy, ethics, values and vigorous business sense are inspiring and guiding his wife, Gabriella and sons Antonio and Josè. Highest marks for their sensational 2014 Mille e una Notte, a Nero d'Avola with a dash of Petit Verdot and Syrah that wins with its determined character and refined odors of plum, maraschino, cinnamon and black pepper. Silky, finely-honed tannins on the palate complete a truly polished, sophisticated wine. Their Tancredi also landed in our finals, with their highly enjoyable Zibibbo Lighea standing out along with their fresh 2017 Chardonnay La Fuga.

| | | |
|---|---|---|
| ● Mille e una Notte '14 | ♟♟♟ | 7 |
| ● Tancredi '14 | ♟♟ | 5 |
| ○ Contessa Entellina Chardonnay La Fuga '17 | ♟♟ | 3 |
| ○ Contessa Entellina Chiarandà '17 | ♟♟ | 5 |
| ● Sicilia Angheli '15 | ♟♟ | 4 |
| ○ Sicilia Brut Donnafugata '13 | ♟♟ | 5 |
| ○ Sicilia Grillo SurSur '17 | ♟♟ | 3 |
| ○ Sicilia Lighea '17 | ♟♟ | 3 |
| ● Sicilia Sul Vulcano '16 | ♟♟ | 4 |
| ● Vittoria Frappato Bell'Assai '17 | ♟♟ | 3 |
| ○ Passito di Pantelleria Ben Ryé '15 | ♟♟♟ | 7 |
| ○ Passito di Pantelleria Ben Ryé '14 | ♟♟♟ | 7 |
| ○ Passito di Pantelleria Ben Ryé '12 | ♟♟♟ | 7 |
| ● Tancredi '11 | ♟♟♟ | 5 |

# Duca di Salaparuta

VIA NAZIONALE, S.S. 113
90014 CASTELDACCIA [PA]
TEL. +39 091945201
www.duca.it

PRE-BOOKED VISITS
ANNUAL PRODUCTION 9,000,000 bottles
HECTARES UNDER VINE 155.00
SUSTAINABLE WINERY

The ILLVA group of Saronna deserve credit for having had the long-term vision to revive three brands that represent, in their own way, the history of Sicilian wine culture. Corvo represents their medium-level products, Duca di Salaparuta their more highly prized wines and Florio i Marsala is the selection dedicated to their dessert wines. Wine tourism has become one of their strong points thanks to the historic cellars in Casteldaccia and their splendid baglio in Marsala. Always a great wine, their 2014 Duca Enrico charms with its elegant notes of plum, licorice, forest underbrush and violets followed by smooth, sophisticated tannins and long finish. Their refined 2015 Pinot Nero Nawari, their fruity and deep 2015 Triskelè (Nero d'Avola and Merlot), and their 2016 Nero d'Avola Passo delle Mule Suor Marchesa stand out among the rest of their good range.

| | |
|---|---|
| ● Calanìca Frappato Syrah '16 | ♟♟ 3 |
| ● Duca Enrico '14 | ♟♟ 8 |
| ○ Marsala Sup. Secco Vecchio Florio '14 | ♟♟ 3 |
| ○ Marsala Sup. Semisecco Ambra Donna Franca Ris. | ♟♟ 6 |
| ● Nawàri '15 | ♟♟ 6 |
| ○ Passito di Pantelleria '15 | ♟♟ 6 |
| ○ Passito di Pantelleria Liquoroso Zighidì '13 | ♟♟ 4 |
| ● Passo delle Mule Suor Marchesa '16 | ♟♟ 3 |
| ● Triskelé '15 | ♟♟ 4 |
| ○ Calanìca Grillo Viognier '17 | ♟ 3 |
| ○ Corvo Oniris '17 | ♟ 2 |
| ● Corvo Oniris Rosso '17 | ♟ 3 |
| ● Làvico Nerello Mascalese '15 | ♟ 4 |

# Cantine Europa

S.S. 115, KM 42,400
91020 PETROSINO [TP]
TEL. +39 0923961866
www.sibilianavini.it

CELLAR SALES
PRE-BOOKED VISITS
ANNUAL PRODUCTION 2,000,000 bottles
HECTARES UNDER VINE 6300.00

The world of cooperative wineries developed during the 1960s, but the era of globalization has seen many of its producers left in ruins. The best have survived and prospered, those endowed with a healthy, long-term business vision, skilled, flexible managers, and a quality selection of wines. Cantine Europa, a large producer that's headed by Eugenio Galfano and that's experiencing a strong period of growth, belongs to this limited category of producers thanks to its surprising quality and the personality of its various wines. The harsh, hot weather of 2017 caused problems for many whites, however it also left its mark on this big winery's reds. Case in point, their sophisticated, 2017 Perricone Eughenès, intense and ready-to-drink, offers enviable silky tannins. Their deep, austere 2016 Eughenès Syrah Nero d'Avola and their fragrant, easy to drink 2017 Eughenès Nero d'Avola also merit note.

| | |
|---|---|
| ● Eughenès Syrah Nero d'Avola '16 | ♟♟ 2* |
| ○ Sicilia Grillo Brut Due Sorbi | ♟♟ 3 |
| ● Sicilia Nero d'Avola Eughenès '17 | ♟♟ 2* |
| ● Sicilia Perricone Eughenès '17 | ♟♟ 2* |
| ○ Sicilia Catarratto Eughenès '17 | ♟ 2 |
| ○ Sicilia Grillo Eughenès '17 | ♟ 2 |
| ○ Sicilia Grillo Zibibbo '17 | ♟ 2 |
| ● Frappato Roceno '16 | ♟♟ 1* |
| ○ Grillo Roceno '16 | ♟♟ 2* |
| ○ Grillo Zibibbo Eughenès '16 | ♟♟ 2* |
| ○ Grillo Zibibbo Eughenès '15 | ♟♟ 2* |
| ● Nero d'Avola Sensale '16 | ♟♟ 1* |
| ● Sicilia Nero d'Avola Eughenès '16 | ♟♟ 2* |
| ● Sicilia Perricone Eughenès '16 | ♟♟ 2* |
| ● Sicilia Syrah Nero d'Avola Eughenès '16 | ♟♟ 2* |

## ★Feudi del Pisciotto

C.DA PISCIOTTO
93015 NISCEMI [CL]
TEL. +39 09331930280
www.castellare.it

CELLAR SALES
PRE-BOOKED VISITS
ACCOMMODATION
ANNUAL PRODUCTION 200,000 bottles
HECTARES UNDER VINE 45.00

*The owner of this producer is also a shareholder of Gambero Rosso spa. To avoid any conflict of interest, Paolo Panerai has subordinated the possible awarding of Tre Bicchieri (which, in any case, only occurs through a blind tasting) to the attainment of the same rating of excellence (upwards of 90/100) by an independent, international panel. This was the case here.*

Feudi is a lovely producer endowed with a modern, technologically advanced cellar. Here on their estate, Alessandro Cellai and his strong technical staff look after their 45 hectares of vineyards as if it were a home garden. Their 2016 Cerasuolo di Vittoria Giambattista Valli Paris earns Tre Bicchieri for a second consecutive year by virtue of its red fruit, viola and mediterranean herbs in a refined balsamic frame that combines with a beautiful, juicy palate, skillfully balancing acidity and tannins earns. Their 2016 Frappato Kisa is also noteworthy for its sophisticated hints of berries and wildflowers, fresh and with a graceful palate.

| | | |
|---|---|---|
| ● Cerasuolo di Vittoria Giambattista Valli Paris '16 | ▼▼▼ | 6 |
| ● Carolina Marengo Kisa Frappato '16 | ▼▼ | 4 |
| ○ Gianfranco Ferrè '16 | ▼▼ | 5 |
| ○ Alberta Ferretti Chardonnay '16 | ▼▼ | 4 |
| ● Baglio del Sole Merlot Syrah '16 | ▼▼ | 2* |
| ○ Gurra di Mare Tirsat '16 | ▼▼ | 4 |
| ● L'Eterno '16 | ▼▼ | 7 |
| ● Missoni Cabernet Sauvignon '16 | ▼▼ | 4 |
| ● Versace Nero d'Avola '16 | ▼▼ | 4 |
| ○ Baglio del Sole Inzolia '17 | ▼ | 2 |
| ○ Baglio del Sole Inzolia Catarratto '17 | ▼ | 2 |
| ● Baglio del Sole Nero d'Avola '16 | ▼ | 2 |
| ● Cerasuolo di Vittoria Giambattista Valli Paris '15 | ▽▽▽ | 6 |
| ● Cerasuolo di Vittoria Giambattista Valli Paris '12 | ▽▽▽ | 6 |

## Feudo Arancio

C.DA PORTELLA MISILBESI
92017 SAMBUCA DI SICILIA [AG]
TEL. +39 0925579000
www.feudoarancio.it

CELLAR SALES
PRE-BOOKED VISITS
ACCOMMODATION
ANNUAL PRODUCTION 6,000,000 bottles
HECTARES UNDER VINE 750.00
SUSTAINABLE WINERY

Feudo Arancio is one of Mezzacorona's two producers (the other is Acate), a giant of Italian wine that has managed the admirable task of bringing together high production volumes and quality. It's all thanks to a vision that combines the traditions of the various territories with a philosophy centered on low environmental impact. Their approach is minimally invasive while drawing on alternative energy sources and an innovative system for the use and reuse of water supplies. The estate is situated in a scenic area, among the well-ventilated hills oversee Lake Arancio. Their 2015 Hedonis, a blend of Nero d'Avola and Syrah, is a truly lovely wine. On the nose it offers up enchanting notes of fruit preserves and blackberries, plums, pepper, cloves and dark chocolate, all enlivened by fresh nuances of wood resin, myrtle and eucalyptus. In the mouth it's chewy, almost meaty, elegant and endlessly persistent. Their pleasant and racy 2017 Grillo features nice coastal fragrances.

| | | |
|---|---|---|
| ● Sicilia Hedonis Riserva '15 | ▼▼ | 4 |
| ○ Sicilia Dalila Riserva '16 | ▼▼ | 4 |
| ○ Sicilia Grillo '17 | ▼▼ | 3 |
| ○ Sicilia Inzolia '17 | ▼▼ | 3 |
| ● Barone d'Albius '15 | ▽▽ | 5 |
| ○ Barone d'Albius '14 | ▽▽ | 5 |
| ● Barone d'Albius '13 | ▽▽ | 5 |
| ● Barone d'Albius '12 | ▽▽ | 5 |
| ● Cantadoro '12 | ▽▽ | 4 |
| ○ Dalila '14 | ▽▽ | 4 |
| ○ Hekate Passito '13 | ▽▽ | 5 |
| ○ Sicilia Dalila '15 | ▽▽ | 4 |
| ○ Sicilia Grillo '15 | ▽▽ | 2* |
| ○ Sicilia Inzolia '14 | ▽▽ | 3 |
| ● Sicilia Nero d'Avola '16 | ▽▽ | 5 |

## ★Feudo Maccari

S.DA PROV.LE PACHINO-NOTO KM 13,500
96017 NOTO [SR]
TEL. +39 0931596894
www.feudomaccari.it

CELLAR SALES
PRE-BOOKED VISITS
ANNUAL PRODUCTION 167,000 bottles
HECTARES UNDER VINE 50.00
SUSTAINABLE WINERY

Before coming to Sicily, Antonio Moretti already owned three estates in Tuscany (in Arezzo and Maremma). In Sicily he was struck by the beauty of places like Noto, surrounded as it is by historic, architectural and natural wonders. Our tastings confirmed that the mission the producer set out for itself from the first vintage has been been completed. Their selection of wines is intimately tied to the territory, bringing out the best of native cultivar like Nero d'Avola and Grillo, which are traditionally reared on head-trained vines. It's yet another Tre Bicchieri for their Nero d'Avola Saia, with a vibrant 2016 that features aromas of red berries, blood oranges, capers, black mulberry and violet. In the mouth it's lovely, juicy and highly persistent, with close-woven and well-extracted tannins, spirited acidity and nice fruit. Their elegant and drinkable 2016 Nero d'Avola Nerè also delivered.

## Feudo Montoni

C.DA MONTONI VECCHI
92022 CAMMARATA [AG]
TEL. +39 091513106
www.feudomontoni.it

CELLAR SALES
PRE-BOOKED VISITS
ANNUAL PRODUCTION 215,000 bottles
HECTARES UNDER VINE 30.00
VITICULTURE METHOD Certified Organic
SUSTAINABLE WINERY

Feudo was founded 550 years ago by the Abatellis family of Aragon. In the late 19th century it was purchased by Rosario Sireci, who began a tradition of quality that was continued by his son Elio, and grandson Fabio, the estate's current owner. This last has established Feudo as a producer in its own right. Traditional viticulture, head-trained vines and organic agriculture serve as the basis of their production philosophy, which also seeks to steward the individual identity of the grape through Massal Selection. Their Passito Rosso just fell short of making it into our finals. It's a wine with a charming, etheric bouquet that features well-defined nuances of spices and tobacco. On the palate it exhibits a poignant balance of sweetness, body and acidity. Their 2014 Nero d'Avola Vrucara is consistent in its austere elegance, while their fresh and pleasant 2017 Rose di Adele, a Nerello, stands out for its lovely nose of peach flowers. Their 2017 Vigna del Masso also did well, proving defined in its citrusy notes.

| | |
|---|---|
| ● Sicilia Nero d'Avola Saia '16 | ▼▼▼ 4* |
| ● Neré '16 | ▼▼ 2* |
| ⊙ Rosé di Neré '17 | ▼▼ 3 |
| ○ Family and Friends '17 | ▼ 5 |
| ○ Sicilia Grillo Olli '17 | ▼ 3 |
| ● Saia '14 | ♈♈♈ 4* |
| ● Saia '13 | ♈♈♈ 4* |
| ● Saia '12 | ♈♈♈ 4* |
| ● Saia '11 | ♈♈♈ 4* |
| ● Saia '10 | ♈♈♈ 4* |
| ● Saia '08 | ♈♈♈ 4* |
| ● Saia '07 | ♈♈♈ 4* |
| ● Saia '06 | ♈♈♈ 4 |
| ● Sicilia Saia '15 | ♈♈♈ 4* |

| | |
|---|---|
| ● Passito Rosso | ▼▼ 5 |
| ○ Sicilia Catarratto V. del Masso '17 | ▼▼ 4 |
| ○ Sicilia Grillo V. della Timpa '17 | ▼▼ 3 |
| ○ Sicilia Inzolia dei Fornelli '17 | ▼▼ 3 |
| ⊙ Sicilia Nerello Mascalese Rose di Adele '17 | ▼▼ 4 |
| ● Sicilia Nero d'Avola V. Lagnusa '16 | ▼▼ 4 |
| ● Sicilia Nero d'Avola Vrucara '14 | ▼▼ 5 |
| ● Sicilia Perricone V. del Core '16 | ▼ 4 |
| ● Nero d'Avola Vrucara '12 | ♈♈ 5 |
| ○ Sicilia Grillo V. della Timpa '15 | ♈♈ 3 |
| ⊙ Sicilia Nerello Mascalese Rose di Adele '16 | ♈♈ 4 |
| ● Sicilia Nero d'Avola V. Lagnusa '15 | ♈♈ 4 |
| ● Sicilia Nero d'Avola V. Lagnusa '14 | ♈♈ 4 |
| ● Sicilia Nero d'Avola Vrucara '13 | ♈♈ 5 |
| ● Sicilia Perricone V. del Core '15 | ♈♈ 4 |

## ★Firriato

LOC. PACECO
VIA VIA TRAPANI, 4
91027 PACECO [TP]
TEL. +39 0923526766
www.firriato.it

CELLAR SALES
PRE-BOOKED VISITS
ANNUAL PRODUCTION 4,500,000 bottles
HECTARES UNDER VINE 380.00
VITICULTURE METHOD Certified Organic

Firriato, an estate that comprises three terroir, was founded thanks to the passion of Salvatore and Vinzia di Gaetano. Today they lead the winery along with their daughter and son-in-law. Their story began 34 years ago in Trapani, which remains their center of production, with 350 hectares in Baglio Sorìa and Borgo Guarini, as well as Cuddia and Dàgala Borromeo. These are accompanied by their Cavanera estate, 28 hectares on the northeast face of Etna, and six hectares in Calamoni a Favignana. The utmost care is shown for territorial differences and the environment. Their 2014 Etna Rosso Rovo delle Coturnie brought home Tre Bicchieri with its extremely subtle yet vibrant nose, defined by aromas of fruit preserves, peach and wild berries. On the palate it proves juicy, soft and long. Their Their fresh and sunny 2017 Quater Vitis Bianco, a blend of native varieties, also earned a place in the finals. Their 2016 Etna Bianco Ripa di Scorciavacca also delivered, coming through citrusy, savory and elegant.

| | |
|---|---|
| ● Etna Rosso Cavanera Rovo delle Coturnie '14 | ▼▼▼ 6 |
| ○ Etna Bianco Cavanera Ripa di Scorciavacca '16 | ▼▼ 6 |
| ○ Quater Vitis Bianco '17 | ▼▼ 4 |
| ○ Etna Bianco Le Sabbie dell'Etna '17 | ▼▼ 3 |
| ○ Etna But M. Cl. Gaudensius Blan de Noir | ▼▼ 4 |
| ● Etna Rosso Le Sabbie dell'Etna '17 | ▼▼ 3 |
| ○ Favinia La Muciara '16 | ▼▼ 5 |
| ○ Gaudensius Blan de Blancs Brut | ▼▼ 4 |
| ○ L'Ecrù '16 | ▼▼ 5 |
| ○ Sicilia Bianco Santagostino Baglio Soria '16 | ▼▼ 4 |
| ○ Sicilia Grillo Caeles '17 | ▼▼ 3 |
| ● Quater Vitis Rosso '14 | ♈♈♈ 4* |

## Fondo Antico

FRAZ. RILIEVO
S.DA FIORAME, 54A
91100 TRAPANI
TEL. +39 0923864339
www.fondoantico.it

CELLAR SALES
PRE-BOOKED VISITS
ANNUAL PRODUCTION 350,000 bottles
HECTARES UNDER VINE 80.00

The Poliziotti family's lovely winery is situated between Marsala and Trapani. It's a contiguous tract of about a hundred hectares, almost all planted, anchored by a historic and perfectly renovated baglio that hosts their main offices and a large tasting hall. Their modern cellar is close by, situated amidst their vineyards, which host primarily Nero d'Avola and Grillo, though other grapes are present as well. It's rare to find a female enologist working in Sicily, but that's the case here, with Lorenzo Scianna overseeing winemaking. And in just a few short years she's managed to find the right style for Fondo Antico: modern and respectful of the cultivar and territory, but most importantly clean and elegant. Their 2017 Grillo Parlante performed very well (it's also worth mentioning that the producer was among the first to vinify Grillo separately). On the nose it offers up hints of tropical fruit, passion flower and aromatic herbs, while on the palate it proves elegant, fresh and highly drinkable. The rest of their selection also proved to be of notable quality, especially their whites.

| | |
|---|---|
| ○ Sicilia Grillo Parlante '17 | ▼▼ 3* |
| ○ Baccadoro | ▼▼ 3 |
| ○ Bello Mio '17 | ▼▼ 3 |
| ○ Il Coro di Fondo Antico '16 | ▼▼ 3 |
| ● Per Te Perricone '17 | ▼▼ 3 |
| ● Sicilia Nero d'Avola '16 | ▼▼ 2* |
| ⊙ Sicilia Nero d'Avola Rosato Aprile '17 | ▼▼ 2* |
| ● Sicilia Syrah '16 | ▼▼ 2* |
| ○ Bello Mio '16 | ♈♈ 2* |
| ● Nero d'Avola '14 | ♈♈ 2* |
| ● Per Te '16 | ♈♈ 3 |
| ⊙ Sicilia Aprile '13 | ♈♈ 2* |
| ○ Sicilia Chardonnay '13 | ♈♈ 2* |
| ○ Sicilia Grillo Parlante '16 | ♈♈ 2* |
| ● Sicilia Il Canto '12 | ♈♈ 3 |

# Tenuta Gorghi Tondi

C.DA SAN NICOLA
91026 MAZARA DEL VALLO [TP]
TEL. +39 0923719741
www.gorghitondi.com

CELLAR SALES
PRE-BOOKED VISITS
ACCOMMODATION AND RESTAURANT SERVICE
ANNUAL PRODUCTION 1,300,000 bottles
HECTARES UNDER VINE 130.00
VITICULTURE METHOD Certified Organic

The baglio that hosts Clara and Annamaria Sala's modern and efficient cellar is situated between the sea of Mazara del Vallo and the splendid Nature Reserve of Lake Preola and Gorghi Tondi. It's a karstic basin that's lush in Mediterranean scrubland as well as serving as a homeland to protected species. Their 130 hectares of vineyards are situated around and within it, and give rise almost exclusively to native grape varieties cultivated organically. Their selection is divided into five lines: Cru, Spumanti (sparklers), Territoriali, Vivitis Bio (organic without added sulfites) and Maoiliche (aged in ceramics). A hot year made for a ripe and opulent dry Zibibbo (Muscat of Alexandria), their 2017 Rajah. It's redolent of orange blossom and rose, which reemerge on a palate of full, round fruit. Their 2017 Kheirè features subtle coastal notes and aromatic herbs. It's a fresh wine that finishes on an elegant note of peach. Among their latest releases we point out the strong debut of their 2017 Dumè, a fragrant and youthful wine in its fragrances of strawberry. Their two Palmarès sparklers are highly enjoyable.

| | |
|---|---|
| ○ Sicilia Zibibbo Rajah '17 | ♥♥ 4 |
| ○ Grillo d'Oro Passito '15 | ♥♥ 7 |
| ● Palmarés Brut | ♥♥ 3 |
| ⊙ Palmarés Rosé Extra Dry | ♥♥ 3 |
| ○ Sicilia Catarratto Midor '17 | ♥♥ 2* |
| ● Sicilia Frappato Dumè '17 | ♥♥ 3 |
| ○ Sicilia Grillo Kheirè '17 | ♥♥ 4 |
| ● Sicilia Nero d'Avola Sorante '15 | ♥ 3 |
| ○ Rajah '15 | ♀♀ 4 |
| ○ Sicilia Grillo Kheirè '16 | ♀♀ 4 |
| ○ Sicilia Grillo Kheirè '15 | ♀♀ 4 |
| ○ Sicilia Grillo Kheirè '14 | ♀♀ 4 |
| ● Sicilia Nero d'Avola Sorante '13 | ♀♀ 4 |
| ● Sicilia Syrah Segreante '15 | ♀♀ 4 |
| ○ Sicilia Zibibbo Rajah '16 | ♀♀ 4 |

# Graci

LOC. PASSOPISCIARO
C.DA FEUDO DI MEZZO
95012 CASTIGLIONE DI SICILIA [CT]
TEL. +39 3487016773
www.graci.eu

CELLAR SALES
PRE-BOOKED VISITS
ANNUAL PRODUCTION 65,000 bottles
HECTARES UNDER VINE 18.00
VITICULTURE METHOD Certified Organic

It's difficult to not be influenced by Alberto Graci's enthusiasm. He's a vigneron by trade, having abandoned a promising career in economy to pursue his dream. In just a few years he made his winery one of the leaders of the Etna Renaissance. The joint-venture project with Gaja and last year's acquisitions testify to Alberto's dynamism. Nevertheless, he continues to enchant us with the elegance of his wines, made with grapes cultivated in the vineyards of Arcurìa, Feudo di Mezzo and Barbabecchi. This last features century-old ungrafted vines cultivated at more than 1000 meters above sea level. Their two 'base level' Etnas, a 2016 Rosso and a 2017 Bianco, put in exceptional performances. The former brought home a gold thanks to its superb array of varietal aromas, from peach to balsamic nuances, which reemerge elegantly on an extremely plush and persistent palate. The latter earned a place in our finals thanks to a nose of notable finesse, and a linear, nobly pure structure.

| | |
|---|---|
| ● Etna Rosso '16 | ♥♥♥ 3* |
| ○ Etna Bianco '17 | ♥♥ 3* |
| ○ Etna Bianco Arcurìa '16 | ♥♥ 6 |
| ● Etna Rosso Feudo di Mezzo '16 | ♥♥ 6 |
| ⊙ Etna Rosato '17 | ♥ 3 |
| ● Etna Rosso Arcurìa '16 | ♥ 6 |
| ○ Etna Bianco '10 | ♀♀♀ 4* |
| ○ Etna Bianco Arcurìa '11 | ♀♀♀ 5 |
| ○ Etna Bianco Quota 600 '10 | ♀♀♀ 5 |
| ● Etna Rosso Arcurìa '13 | ♀♀♀ 6 |
| ● Etna Rosso Arcurìa '12 | ♀♀♀ 6 |
| ○ Etna Bianco '16 | ♀♀ 3* |
| ⊙ Etna Rosato '16 | ♀♀ 3 |
| ● Etna Rosso Arcurìa '15 | ♀♀ 6 |
| ● Etna Rosso Arcurìa '14 | ♀♀ 6 |
| ● Etna Rosso Feudo di Mezzo '15 | ♀♀ 6 |
| ● Etna Rosso Feudo di Mezzo '14 | ♀♀ 6 |

## SICILY

## Hauner

LOC. SANTA MARIA
VIA G.GRILLO, 61
98123 MESSINA
TEL. +39 0906413029
www.hauner.it

CELLAR SALES
PRE-BOOKED VISITS
ANNUAL PRODUCTION 80,000 bottles
HECTARES UNDER VINE 18.00

When in the late 1960s Carlo Hauner senior, an architect and painter from Brescia, came to Salina in search of inspiration for his paintings, it was almost by chance that he came to know Malvasia delle Lipari, a wine that at the time was produced solely by a few farmers for their own local use. Carlo's visionary decision to pick up production and export the wine on a large-scale (involving talented figures like Luigi Veronelli and Attilio Scienza) was only the first of many. We are grateful to Carlo for having saved this time-honored wine from extinction. Their Malvasia delle Lipari Riserva Carlo Hauner is always a sure bet. 2015 gave rise to a highly complex nose that calls up tropical fruit, figs in chocolate, candied orange, jasmine and aromatic herbs. On the palate it proves full, deep, fresh and vibrant in its acidity. It's also well-sustained by a slightly savory vein, with a long finish that's sweet but never cloying. The rest of their selection also proved sound.

| | |
|---|---|
| ○ Malvasia delle Lipari Passito Carlo Hauner Ris. '15 | ▼▼ 8 |
| ☉ Hierà Rosato '17 | ▼▼ 3 |
| ● Hierà Rosso '16 | ▼▼ 3 |
| ○ Iancura '17 | ▼▼ 2* |
| ○ Malvasia delle Lipari Naturale '16 | ▼▼ 4 |
| ○ Malvasia delle Lipari Passito '16 | ▼▼ 5 |
| ○ Salina Bianco '17 | ▼▼ 2* |
| ● Rosso Antonello '14 | ▼ 4 |
| ● Salina Rosso '16 | ▼ 2 |
| ○ Malvasia delle Lipari Ris. '11 | ▼▼▼ 8 |
| ○ Malvasia delle Lipari Ris. '10 | ▼▼▼ 8 |
| ● Hierà Rosso '15 | ▼▼ 3 |
| ○ Malvasia delle Lipari Passito '15 | ▼▼ 5 |
| ○ Malvasia delle Lipari Passito Carlo Hauner Ris. '14 | ▼▼ 8 |

## Cantine Mothia

VIA GIOVANNI FALCONE, 22
91025 MARSALA [TP]
TEL. +39 0923737295
www.cantinemothia.it

CELLAR SALES
PRE-BOOKED VISITS
ANNUAL PRODUCTION 100,000 bottles
HECTARES UNDER VINE 25.00

Cantine Mothia's vineyards are situated on Marsala's coastal strip. The unique natural landscape of the terrain, which experiences constant wind and notable day-night temperature swings, allows the grapes to mature perfectly. The Bonomo family have been involved in wine for more than 50 years and in the late 1990s they purchased their production center, an early-20th century baglio built for the grapes cultivated on the island of Mozia and the Stagnone Lagoon. The family's real treasure can be found in their bottle cellar, where their Marsala and Stella Fenicia riservas (a 'Perpetuo' made with Grillo grapes) are aged. A special wine brought home Tre Bicchieri. It's a loving homage to the producer's founder, who left us three years ago. Their 2015 Dedicato a Francesco is a monovarietal Nero d'Avola made with grapes from their private vineyards, then aged for a year in mid-size casks. It's a vibrant, generous and elegant wine in its fruity sensations of mulberry. On the palate it proves juicy and persistent. Their fresh and savory 2017 Mosaikon, a Grillo, is also well-defined in its varietal aromas.

| | |
|---|---|
| ● Dedicato a Francesco '15 | ▼▼▼ 4* |
| ○ Mosaikon Grillo '17 | ▼▼ 2* |
| ○ Vela Latina '17 | ▼▼ 2* |
| ● Hammon '07 | ♀♀ 2* |
| ● Hammon '06 | ♀♀ 2 |
| ○ Marsala Sup. Dolce Garibaldi The Thousand | ♀♀ 2* |
| ○ Marsala Sup. Secco The Thousand | ♀♀ 2* |
| ● Mosaikon '15 | ♀♀ 2* |
| ○ Mosaikon Grillo '16 | ♀♀ 2* |
| ● Mosaikon Nero d'Avola '16 | ♀♀ 2* |
| ○ Mulsum '08 | ♀♀ 4 |
| ○ Mulsum Passito di Zibibbo '16 | ♀♀ 4 |
| ● Nero d'Avola '12 | ♀♀ 3 |
| ○ Vela Latina Grillo Damaschino '16 | ♀♀ 2* |

## Cantine Nicosia

VIA LUIGI CAPUANA, 65
95039 TRECASTAGNI [CT]
TEL. +39 0957806767
www.cantinenicosia.it

CELLAR SALES
PRE-BOOKED VISITS
RESTAURANT SERVICE
ANNUAL PRODUCTION 1,800,000 bottles
HECTARES UNDER VINE 240.00
VITICULTURE METHOD Certified Organic
SUSTAINABLE WINERY

The Nicosia family is celebrating 120 years of activity this year, and their doing it in smashing form when it comes to critical praise and market success (both nationally and abroad). Testifying to their growth is the recent purchase of new, sizable estates in the winery's two areas of operation: Etna (their home base) and Cerasuolo di Vittoria. The cornerstones of their success, however, remain the same: a strong bond with the territory and tradition, extreme respect for the environment (they offer both organic and vegan wines), as well as superior drinkability across their entire selection. Their 2012 Etna Rosso Vigneto Monte Forna Riserva took home Tre Bicchieri, proving a commendable, accurate expression of its terroir. It's a ruby garnet wine with vibrant notes of mulberry, peach, tobacco, flint, red orange and licorice. On the palate it's extremely long, elegant and chewy, with pervasive tannins. Their subtle, iodine and balsamic 2012 Sosta Tre Santi Nero d'Avola Riserva was another finalist.

## Arianna Occhipinti

FRAZ. PEDALINO
S.DA PROV.LE 68 VITTORIA-PEDALINO KM 3,3
97019 VITTORIA [RG]
TEL. +39 09321865519
www.agricolaocchipinti.it

CELLAR SALES
PRE-BOOKED VISITS
ANNUAL PRODUCTION 130,000 bottles
HECTARES UNDER VINE 22.00
VITICULTURE METHOD Certified Organic
SUSTAINABLE WINERY

Arianna Occhipinti is a young, talented, persevering, forthright woman with a deep knowledge of enology. In just a short time she's vaulted forward and is now known throughout the world. Her famous aphorism, 'Wine always reflects its territory of origin, being its natural expression, neither forced nor manufactured', clearly reveals her signature style. Her wines avoid the sticky dilemma of 'natural' or 'unnatural' so as to be, simply, her wines, authentic and full of character. They are the offspring of the vineyards and the traditional grape varieties cultivated there. Their 2013 Cerasuolo Grotte Alte is an elegant, mature wine with charming nuances of black cherry, plums, citrus and hints of myrtle berries. It just falls short of top marks, but impresses for its authenticity, austere character and delicious tannins. Their 2016 Frappato also made a notable impact, proving buoyant in its fragrances of strawberry, as did their aromatic 2017 SP 68 Bianco (made with Moscato and Albanello).

| | |
|---|---|
| ● Etna Rosso Vign. Monte Gorna Ris. '12 | ♼♼♼ 6 |
| ● Sicilia Nero d'Avola Sosta Tre Santi Ris. '12 | ♼♼ 5 |
| ● Cerasuolo di Vittoria Hybla '17 | ♼♼ 2* |
| ○ Etna Bianco Fondo Filara '17 | ♼♼ 4 |
| ○ Etna Bianco Vign. Monte Gorna '14 | ♼♼ 6 |
| ⊙ Etna Rosato Vulkà '17 | ♼♼ 3 |
| ● Etna Rosso Fondo Filara '16 | ♼♼ 4 |
| ● Etna Rosso Fondo Filara Vulkà '17 | ♼♼ 2* |
| ● Sicilia Nero d'Avola Fondo Filara '17 | ♼♼ 3 |
| ○ Etna Bianco Fondo Filara Contrada Monte Gorna '16 | ♼♼♼ 4* |
| ● Nero d'Avola Sosta Tre Santi '10 | ♼♼♼ 5 |
| ● Etna Rosso Fondo Filara '15 | ♼♼ 4 |
| ● Etna Rosso Monte Gorna Ris. '11 | ♼♼ 6 |

| | |
|---|---|
| ● Cerasuolo di Vittoria Cl. Grotte Alte '13 | ♼♼ 7 |
| ● Il Frappato '16 | ♼♼ 5 |
| ○ SP 68 Bianco '17 | ♼♼ 3 |
| ● SP 68 Rosso '17 | ♼♼ 3 |
| ● Siccagno '15 | ♼ 6 |
| ● Il Frappato '12 | ♼♼♼ 5 |
| ● Il Frappato '11 | ♼♼♼ 5 |
| ● SP 68 Rosso '15 | ♼♼♼ 3* |
| ● Il Frappato '15 | ♼♼ 6 |
| ● Il Frappato '14 | ♼♼ 6 |
| ● Il Frappato '13 | ♼♼ 6 |
| ● Siccagno '14 | ♼♼ 6 |
| ● Siccagno '13 | ♼♼ 6 |
| ● Siccagno '12 | ♼♼ 6 |
| ○ SP 68 Bianco '16 | ♼♼ 3 |
| ○ SP 68 Bianco '14 | ♼♼ 3 |
| ● SP 68 Rosso '14 | ♼♼ 3 |

# Tenute Orestiadi

v.le Santa Ninfa
91024 Gibellina [TP]
Tel. +39 092469124
www.tenuteorestiadi.it

PRE-BOOKED VISITS
ACCOMMODATION AND RESTAURANT SERVICE
ANNUAL PRODUCTION 1,200,000 bottles
HECTARES UNDER VINE 120.00
VITICULTURE METHOD Certified Organic
SUSTAINABLE WINERY

Through hard work and entrepreneurial vision, the cooperative winery Tenute Orestiadi was created after the terrible earthquake in 1968 that destroyed the prospects and future hopes of Valle del Bellìce. Time was on their side, and today the producer, associated with the prestigious Orestiadi Foundation, boasts extraordinary production volumes and revenue, not to mention the excellent quality of their wines (made primarily with traditional cultivar). Their selection, appreciated throughout the world, is divided into various lines. Their selection put in an overall unforgettable performance, with an extraordinary late-harvest Zibibbo, their Pacènzia, standing out. It's a wine with exquisite nuances of apricot, peach, lavender and wild flowers. On the palate it reveals a deep sweetness and smoothness that's well-balanced by a sumptuous supporting acidity, thus assuring an extremely gratifying palate.

| | |
|---|---|
| ○ Pacènzia Zibibbo V. T. | 🍷🍷 4 |
| ● Molino a Vento Nerello Mascalese '17 | 🍷🍷 2* |
| ● Paxmentis Syrah Passito '16 | 🍷🍷 4 |
| ● Sicilia Frappato '16 | 🍷🍷 3 |
| ● Sicilia Nero d'Avola '16 | 🍷🍷 3 |
| ● Sicilia Nero d'Avola Molino a Vento '17 | 🍷🍷 2* |
| ● Sicilia Perricone '16 | 🍷🍷 3 |
| ● Frappato '15 | 🍷🍷 3 |
| ● Ludovico '12 | 🍷🍷 4 |
| ● Ludovico '11 | 🍷🍷 5 |
| ● Molino a Vento Nerello Mascalese '16 | 🍷🍷 2* |
| ● Molino a Vento Nero d'Avola '16 | 🍷🍷 2* |
| ● Molino a Vento Nero d'Avola '15 | 🍷🍷 2* |
| ● Molino a Vento Nero d'Avola '14 | 🍷🍷 2* |
| ● Perricone '15 | 🍷🍷 3 |
| ● Perricone '14 | 🍷🍷 3 |

# ★Palari

loc. Santo Stefano Briga
c.da Barna
98137 Messina
Tel. +39 090630194
www.palari.it

ANNUAL PRODUCTION 50,000 bottles
HECTARES UNDER VINE 7.00

If he isn't traveling around, receiving awards for his Palari, or researching precious fabrics to be made into jackets by his London tailor, Salvatore Geraci enjoys sojourning at Santo Stefano Briga. It's here, in the family's 18th-century villa amidst frescos and marble fireplaces that we also find his cellar. His brother Giampiero has been there from the beginning, serving as the agronomist for this small but legendary Sicilian estate. After a year off, their 2014 Faro Palari once again brings home Tre Bicchieri. From the outset, with its charmingly complex and elegant nose, it delivers. On the palate it's just as sophisticated, proving rich in silky tannins, plush and extremely long. Their 2016 Rosso del Soprano also earned a place in our finals. It's a more approachable wine, drinkable and highly pleasant, but certainly not less complex or subtle than its big brother.

| | |
|---|---|
| ● Faro Palari '14 | 🍷🍷🍷 6 |
| ● Rosso del Soprano '16 | 🍷🍷 4 |
| ● Faro Palari '12 | 🍷🍷🍷 6 |
| ● Faro Palari '11 | 🍷🍷🍷 6 |
| ● Faro Palari '09 | 🍷🍷🍷 6 |
| ● Faro Palari '08 | 🍷🍷🍷 6 |
| ● Faro Palari '07 | 🍷🍷🍷 6 |
| ● Faro Palari '06 | 🍷🍷🍷 6 |
| ● Faro Palari '05 | 🍷🍷🍷 6* |
| ● Faro Palari '04 | 🍷🍷🍷 7 |
| ● Faro Palari '03 | 🍷🍷🍷 6 |
| ● Faro Palari '02 | 🍷🍷🍷 6 |
| ● Faro Palari '01 | 🍷🍷🍷 6 |
| ● Rosso del Soprano '15 | 🍷🍷🍷 4* |
| ● Rosso del Soprano '11 | 🍷🍷🍷 4* |
| ● Rosso del Soprano '10 | 🍷🍷🍷 4* |
| ● Rosso del Soprano '07 | 🍷🍷🍷 4 |

# Palmento Costanzo

LOC. PASSOPISCIARO
C.DA SANTO SPIRITO
95012 CASTIGLIONE DI SICILIA [CT]
TEL. +39 0942983239
www.palmentocostanzo.com

CELLAR SALES
PRE-BOOKED VISITS
RESTAURANT SERVICE
ANNUAL PRODUCTION 75,000 bottles
HECTARES UNDER VINE 10.00
VITICULTURE METHOD Certified Organic
SUSTAINABLE WINERY

The Costanzo family cultivates 10 hectares in Santo Spirito, in Passopisciaro (Castiglione di Sicilia) on the northern face of Etna. Their estate, which spans elevations ranging from 650 meters to 800, comprises old, 'Etna' head-trained vineyards that are also certified organic. It's an approach that privileges the pure expressivity of terroir and grape inherent in every single plot. It's also distinguished by the presence of a notable number of pre-phylloxera vines. Their 2017 Bianco di Sei took home Tre Bicchieri, impressing for its elegant aromas of white and yellow fruit, peach, medlar and damson plums, all embellished by close-focused and elegant nuances of aromatic herbs. On the palate it comes through vibrant, meaty and savory. Their two Mofetes are also both in great form, with their 2017 Bianco standing out for its vibrance and persistence, and their 2015 Rosso its aromas of fruit preserves, as well as its round, smooth tannins.

| | |
|---|---|
| ○ Etna Bianco di Sei '17 | ♛♛♛ 5 |
| ○ Etna Bianco Mofete '17 | ♛♛ 3 |
| ● Etna Rosso Mofete '15 | ♛♛ 3 |
| ● Etna Rosso Mofete Vulcano '14 | ♛♛ 3 |
| ⊙ Etna Rosato Mofete '17 | ♛ 3 |
| ○ Etna Bianco Mofete '16 | ♕♕ 3 |
| ● Etna Rosso Mofete '14 | ♕♕ 3* |
| ● Etna Rosso Nero di Sei '13 | ♕♕ 5 |

# Passopisciaro

LOC. PASSOPISCIARO
C.DA GUARDIOLA
95030 CASTIGLIONE DI SICILIA [CT]
TEL. +39 0578267110
www.vinifranchetti.com

CELLAR SALES
ANNUAL PRODUCTION 75,000 bottles
HECTARES UNDER VINE 26.00

The winery was founded in 2000, at a time when local place names like Rampante, Porcaria, Sciaranuova and Chiappemacine were almost forgotten. But with loving patience, Andrea Franchetti revived their status as 'Contrade' (districts), a series of crus capable of fully expressing their unmistakable personality and elegance. Their vineyards are situated on the northern slopes of Etna, at elevations ranging from 550 to 1000 meters. Primarily Nerello Mascalese is cultivated, with head-trained vines that go back more than 70 years in some cases. As of 2007, Passopisciaro organizes 'Contrade dell'Etna', an important showcase for the volcano's producers. Their 2016 Contrada Guardiola just fell short of Tre Bicchieri. It's a vibrant, elegant wine that's clear and long, with excellent, consistent fruit. Their 2016 Porcaria also delivered, offering varietal notes of peaches, brought out by tangy nuances of incense. On the palate it exhibits great texture and persistence. Their 2016 Passorosso, 2016 Chiappemacine and 2016 Rampante were also close behind the two finalists.

| | |
|---|---|
| ● Contrada Guardiola '16 | ♛♛ 6 |
| ● Contrada Porcaria '16 | ♛♛ 7 |
| ● Contrada Chiappemacine '16 | ♛♛ 6 |
| ● Contrada Rampante '16 | ♛♛ 6 |
| ● Contrada Sciaranuova '16 | ♛♛ 6 |
| ● Etna Rosso Passorosso '16 | ♛♛ 5 |
| ○ Passobianco '16 | ♛ 5 |
| ● Contrada G '11 | ♕♕♕ 8 |
| ● Contrada P '10 | ♕♕♕ 7 |
| ● Contrada P '09 | ♕♕♕ 7 |
| ● Contrada Sciaranuova '15 | ♕♕♕ 6 |
| ● Passopisciaro '04 | ♕♕♕ 5 |
| ● Contrada C '13 | ♕♕ 6 |
| ● Contrada Guardiola '15 | ♕♕ 6 |
| ● Contrada S '13 | ♕♕ 6 |

## Carlo Pellegrino

VIA DEL FANTE, 39
91025 MARSALA [TP]
TEL. +39 0923719911
www.carlopellegrino.it

CELLAR SALES
PRE-BOOKED VISITS
ANNUAL PRODUCTION 6,900,000 bottles
HECTARES UNDER VINE 150.00
SUSTAINABLE WINERY

The producer's story began in 1880 and immediately interweaves with the best of Sicilian entrepreneurship, constituted of values, knowledge, dedication and humanity. Over time Pellegrino saw other families get involved and today the winery is managed by Pietro Alagna and Benedetto Renda, two figures who have proved forward-thinking in their ability to bring together tradition and an awareness of the times. Their renewed focus on the specific attributes of the varieties cultivated on their estate testifies to their approach. These give rise to wines that keep getting better and more pleasant to drink thanks to painstaking attention to detail. The 2016 version of their Passito di Pantelleria Nes just fell short of Tre Bicchieri. It's a bright orange wine made with choice Moscato d'Alexandria grapes (Zibibbo). On the nose it calls up hints of candied citrus, dates, dried figs and lavender. In the mouth it proves sweet, elegant and sensual, soft yet vibrant. Their fresh and aromatic 2017 Gibelè is another excellent wine made with the same grapes.

| | |
|---|---|
| ○ Passito di Pantelleria Nes '16 | 🍷🍷 5 |
| ● Duca di Castelmonte Tripudium Rosso '16 | 🍷🍷 5 |
| ○ Gibelè '17 | 🍷🍷 4 |
| ○ Marsala Sup. Oro Dolce BIP Benjamin Ris. '13 | 🍷🍷 5 |
| ○ Kelbi '17 | 🍷 5 |
| ○ Marsala Sup. Ambra Semisecco Ris. '85 | 🍷🍷🍷 4* |
| ○ Passito di Pantelleria Nes '09 | 🍷🍷🍷 5 |
| ● Tripudium Rosso Duca di Castelmonte '13 | 🍷🍷🍷 5 |
| ● Tripudium Rosso Duca di Castelmonte '09 | 🍷🍷🍷 4* |
| ○ Duca di Castelmonte Tripudium Bianco '14 | 🍷🍷 4 |
| ○ Passito di Pantelleria Nes '15 | 🍷🍷 7 |
| ○ Passito di Pantelleria Nes Duca di Castelmonte '14 | 🍷🍷 5 |

## Pietradolce

FRAZ. SOLICCHIATA
C.DA RAMPANTE
95012 CASTIGLIONE DI SICILIA [CT]
TEL. +39 3484037792
www.pietradolce.it

ANNUAL PRODUCTION 28,000 bottles
HECTARES UNDER VINE 13.00

10 years later, after Mario and Michele Faro's winery debuted in the 2009 edition of Italian Wines with an extraordinary 2007 Etna Rosso Archineri (that earned a Tre Bicchieri), we can confidently affirm that Pietradolce is one of this ultra-competitive area's top producers. Since then the bond between Faro and Etna has continued to deepen, thanks to the purchase of a couple historic vineyards in the best districts. These are vinified separately so as to produce wines that are elegant varietal and that exhibit a strong territorial identity. Some three wines landed in our finals and it's difficult to choose which is the best. This is a short summary of our tastings of this extraordinary Etna producer's wines. Their 2016 Etna Rosso Contrada Rampante, a wine made with grapes cultivated in 90-year-old vineyards at 900 meters of elevation, brought home Tre Bicchieri. It's a wine of incredible aromatic complexity, and an elegant, vibrant palate of rare length and persistence.

| | |
|---|---|
| ● Etna Rosso Contrada Rampante '16 | 🍷🍷🍷 6 |
| ○ Etna Bianco Archineri '17 | 🍷🍷 6 |
| ● Etna Rosso V. Barbagalli '15 | 🍷🍷 8 |
| ○ Etna Bianco Pietradolce '17 | 🍷🍷 4 |
| ☉ Etna Rosato Pietradolce '17 | 🍷🍷 3 |
| ● Etna Rosso Archineri '16 | 🍷🍷 6 |
| ● Etna Rosso Contrada Sant Spirito '16 | 🍷🍷 6 |
| ● Etna Rosso Pietradolce '17 | 🍷🍷 4 |
| ○ Sant'Andrea Carricante '15 | 🍷🍷 4 |
| ● Etna Rosso Archineri '10 | 🍷🍷🍷 5 |
| ● Etna Rosso Archineri '08 | 🍷🍷🍷 3* |
| ● Etna Rosso Archineri '07 | 🍷🍷🍷 3* |
| ● Etna Rosso V. Barbagalli '14 | 🍷🍷🍷 8 |
| ● Etna Rosso V. Barbagalli '13 | 🍷🍷🍷 8 |
| ● Etna Rosso V. Barbagalli '12 | 🍷🍷🍷 8 |
| ● Etna Rosso V. Barbagalli '11 | 🍷🍷🍷 8 |
| ● Etna Rosso V. Barbagalli '10 | 🍷🍷🍷 8 |

## ★★Planeta

C.DA DISPENSA
92013 MENFI [AG]
TEL. +39 091327965
www.planeta.it

PRE-BOOKED VISITS
ACCOMMODATION AND RESTAURANT SERVICE
ANNUAL PRODUCTION 2,500,000 bottles
HECTARES UNDER VINE 392.00
SUSTAINABLE WINERY

Planeta is a model producer whose vision goes beyond numbers, encompassing values like protecting the environment, tradition, culture and art, in short, all those things that give meaning to the word 'territory'. For more than 30 years, Francesca, Alessio and Santi Planeta's winery has embodied this approach to the benefit of the whole of Sicily's wine culture. Five territories and six cellars, from Sambuco to Capo Milazzo, Menfi, Vittoria, Noto and Etna make up their production. Theirs is a 'Journey throughout Sicily' constituted of sensations and emotions that reemerge year after year. Their 2014 Maroccoli, a Syrah, took home a gold thanks in part to a noble, generous and deep bouquet of red fruit preserves and balsamic nuances. On the palate it exhibits structure and elegant texture, with a long, spicy finish. Their 2014 Burdese, Cabernet, features lovely varietal expression, with crisp, healthy fruit brought out by the skillful use of oak.

| | |
|---|---|
| ● Menfi Syrah Maroccoli '14 | ♀♀♀ 4* |
| ○ Sicilia Chardonnay '16 | ♀ 5 |
| ● Sicilia Rosso Burdese '14 | ♀♀ 4 |
| ● Cerasuolo di Vittoria Cl. Dorilli '16 | ♀♀ 4 |
| ○ Etna Bianco '17 | ♀♀ 3 |
| ● Etna Rosso '16 | ♀♀ 3 |
| ○ Menfi Fiano Cometa '17 | ♀♀ 5 |
| ○ Passito di Noto '17 | ♀♀ 5 |
| ● Sicilia Nerello Mascalese Eruzione 1614 '16 | ♀♀ 4 |
| ● Sicilia Nocera '16 | ♀♀ 3 |
| ○ Sicilia Noto Allemanda '17 | ♀♀ 3 |
| ● Cerasuolo di Vittoria Cl. Dorilli '14 | ♀♀♀ 3* |
| ● Cerasuolo di Vittoria Cl. Dorilli '13 | ♀♀♀ 3* |
| ○ Etna Bianco '16 | ♀♀♀ 3* |

## Poggio di Bortolone

FRAZ. ROCCAZZO
VIA BORTOLONE, 19
97010 CHIARAMONTE GULFI [RG]
TEL. +39 0932921161
www.poggiodibortolone.it

CELLAR SALES
PRE-BOOKED VISITS
ACCOMMODATION AND RESTAURANT SERVICE
ANNUAL PRODUCTION 80,000 bottles
HECTARES UNDER VINE 15.00
SUSTAINABLE WINERY

Pierluigi Cosenza's winery is situated in the heart of the Cerasuolo di Vittoria DOC appellation, where the Para Para and Mazzarronello rivers meet. Their vineyards constitute a quarter of the estate's 60 hectares. These are spread throughout the hills, as well as the stony lowlands near the rivers. The sandy, mineral, iron-rich terrain here hosts the area's traditional red grapes: Frappato, Nero d'Avola and the extremely rare Nero Grosso. International varieties like Syrah, Cabernet Sauvignon and Petit Verdot are cultivated as well. Given the absence of their Para Para, their 2017 Addamanera took center stage during our tastings. It's a blend of Syrah and Cabernet Sauvignon aged in steel tanks that earned a place in our finals by virtue of its fruity elegance, with notes of peach complemented by green hints of aromatic herbs. These follow through on an extremely pleasant palate. Their 2016 Cerasuolo Classico Poggio di Bortolone is a subtly mature, fruity and juicy wine, while their 2016 Contessa Costanza proves mineral and quaffable.

| | |
|---|---|
| ● Addamanera '17 | ♀♀ 3* |
| ● Cerasuolo di Vittoria Cl. Contessa Costanza '16 | ♀♀ 3 |
| ● Cerasuolo di Vittoria Cl. Poggio di Bortolone '16 | ♀♀ 3 |
| ☉ Sicilia Rosato Rosachiara '17 | ♀♀ 3 |
| ● Petitverdò '17 | ♀ 3 |
| ● Vittoria Frappato '17 | ♀ 3 |
| ● Cerasuolo di Vittoria V. Para Para '05 | ♀♀♀ 4 |
| ● Cerasuolo di Vittoria V. Para Para '02 | ♀♀♀ 4* |
| ● Addamanera '16 | ♀♀ 3 |
| ● Cerasuolo di Vittoria Cl. Contessa Costanza '14 | ♀♀ 3 |
| ● Cerasuolo di Vittoria Il Para Para '13 | ♀♀ 4 |
| ● Sicilia Rosso Pigi '14 | ♀♀ 5 |
| ● Vittoria Frappato '16 | ♀♀ 3 |

## Feudo Principi di Butera

C.DA DELIELLA
93011 BUTERA [CL]
TEL. +39 0934347726
www.feudobutera.it

CELLAR SALES
PRE-BOOKED VISITS
ANNUAL PRODUCTION 800,000 bottles
HECTARES UNDER VINE 180.00
SUSTAINABLE WINERY

In 1997 Feudo Principi di Butera's vineyards were brought back to their former glory by the Zonin family. These can be found along the white hills that slope towards the sea in Licata and Gela. The best plots are cultivated, about 180 hectares of a 320-hectare estate situated at elevations ranging from 250 to 350 meters above sea level. The calcareous terrain, the nearby sea with its cool breeze, the protection afforded by the hills around Butera, and an extraordinarily sunny environment all create a microclimate capable of bringing out the Mediterranean personality of their wines. Their Adola Deliella is back on top with a 2016 whose tight-knit, vibrant nose proves rich in fruity and balsamic aromas accompanied by elegant green notes. On the palate it features subtle, consistent texture as well as long aromatic persistence. Their 2016 Syrah expresses full evolution, elegance and roundness. Their 2016 Symposio, a blend, is soft and vibrant in its fragrances of mulberry and sweet spices.

| | |
|---|---|
| ● Sicilia Nero d'Avola Deliella '16 | ♛♛♛ 6 |
| ○ Sicilia Nero d'Avola Brut Neroluce | ♛♛ 3 |
| ● Sicilia Syrah '16 | ♛♛ 3 |
| ● Symposio '16 | ♛♛ 5 |
| ○ Sicilia Grillo '17 | ♛ 3 |
| ○ Sicilia Insolia '17 | ♛ 3 |
| ○ Sicilia Inzolia Serò '17 | ♛ 4 |
| ● Sicilia Nero d'Avola '16 | ♛ 3 |
| ● Cabernet Sauvignon '00 | ♛♛♛ 5 |
| ● Deliella '12 | ♛♛♛ 6 |
| ● Deliella '05 | ♛♛♛ 6 |
| ● Deliella '02 | ♛♛♛ 7 |
| ● Deliella '00 | ♛♛♛ 6 |
| ● Sicilia Deliella '13 | ♛♛♛ 6 |
| ● Sicilia Syrah '15 | ♛♛♛ 3* |

## Rallo

VIA VINCENZO FLORIO, 2
91025 MARSALA [TP]
TEL. +39 0923721633
www.cantinerallo.it

CELLAR SALES
PRE-BOOKED VISITS
ANNUAL PRODUCTION 420,000 bottles
HECTARES UNDER VINE 110.00
VITICULTURE METHOD Certified Organic

The history of one of Sicilia's most well-established wineries goes back to 1860, but the turning point came in 1997 when Rallo was purchased by the Vesco family. From that moment on the estate's noble roots served as a starting point for a new producer that was strongly bound to the territory and its cultivar, expressed through extremely well-crafted, precise, elegant wines. Long attentive to sustainability and biodiversity, Andrea Vesco successfully opened a new front thanks to Catarratto, the winery's core grape, interpreting the cultivar in a way that could be called 'natural'. Kudos to their 2017 Beleda, a supremely elegant monovarietal Catarratto that brings home Tre Bicchieri by virtue of its aromas of almond, wild flowers, wisteria and medicinal herbs. On the palate it proves taut, juicy, rich in character and a rare minerality, enlivened by opulent, elegant fruit. Their sensual 2014 Passito di Pantelleria features notes of apricot and lavender.

| | |
|---|---|
| ○ Alcamo Beleda '17 | ♛♛♛ 4* |
| ○ Passito di Pantelleria '14 | ♛♛ 5 |
| ● La Zisa '14 | ♛♛ 2* |
| ○ Marsala Sup. Semisecco Mille | ♛♛ 5 |
| ○ Marsala Vergine Soleras Venti Anni Ris. | ♛♛ 5 |
| ○ Orange AV 01 Catarratto '17 | ♛♛ 4 |
| ● Rujari '16 | ♛♛ 4 |
| ○ Sicilia Al Qasar '17 | ♛♛ 3 |
| ○ Sicilia Bianco Maggiore '17 | ♛♛ 3 |
| ○ Sicilia Evrò '17 | ♛♛ 3 |
| ○ Alcamo Beleda '15 | ♛♛♛ 4* |
| ○ Alcamo Beleda '13 | ♛♛♛ 2* |
| ○ Bianco Maggiore '12 | ♛♛♛ 3* |
| ○ Sicilia Bianco Maggiore '16 | ♛♛♛ 3* |
| ○ Sicilia Bianco Maggiore '14 | ♛♛♛ 3* |

# Tenute Rapitalà

C.DA RAPITALÀ
90043 CAMPOREALE [PA]
TEL. +39 092437233
www.rapitala.it

CELLAR SALES
PRE-BOOKED VISITS
ANNUAL PRODUCTION 2,600,000 bottles
HECTARES UNDER VINE 163.00

Rapitalà was founded 50 years ago by
Hugues de La Gatinais and Gigi Guarrasi.
Today it's considered one of the producers
that most contributed to creating and
promoting an image of modern Sicilian
wine. The estate, which is currently
controlled by Gruppo Italiano Vini, spans
225 hectares on the high hills that slope
from Camporeale down to the sea of
Alcamo. It's a terroir in which native grape
varieties and international cultivar live
side-by-side, expressing their sensory
characteristics with generous elegance. This
year sees the debut of their Etna Rosso, a
wine that completes the top range of their
selection. Their Grand Cru is a bonafide
classic of its kind, a Chardonnay aged in
barriques. 2016 gave rise to a version that
offers up elegant aromas of vanilla and
chamomile, with a share of oak that's in
perfect harmony with its round, persistent
fruit. Their still unreleased 2016 Etna Rosso
promises good things to come. It's an
elegant and complex wine aromatically that
follows through extremely well on the palate
and features a balsamic finish.

| | |
|---|---|
| ○ Conte Hugues Bernard de la Gatinais Grand Cru '16 | 🏆🏆 4 |
| ○ Bouquet '17 | 🏆🏆 2* |
| ● Etna Rosso '16 | 🏆🏆 5 |
| ○ Sicilia Grillo Vivirì '17 | 🏆🏆 2* |
| ● Sicilia Nero d'Avola Alto Nero '16 | 🏆🏆 3 |
| ● Sicilia Nuhar '16 | 🏆🏆 3 |
| ○ Alcamo Bianco V. T. Cielo d'Alcamo '16 | 🏆 5 |
| ○ Alcamo Cl. V. Casalj '17 | 🏆 3 |
| ○ Conte Hugues Bernard de la Gatinais Grand Cru '10 | 🏆🏆🏆 4* |
| ● Hugonis '01 | 🏆🏆🏆 6 |
| ● Solinero '03 | 🏆🏆🏆 5 |
| ● Solinero '00 | 🏆🏆🏆 5 |

# Girolamo Russo

LOC. PASSOPISCIARO
VIA REGINA MARGHERITA, 78
95012 CASTIGLIONE DI SICILIA [CT]
TEL. +39 3283840247
www.girolamorusso.it

CELLAR SALES
PRE-BOOKED VISITS
ANNUAL PRODUCTION 65,000 bottles
HECTARES UNDER VINE 15.00
VITICULTURE METHOD Certified Organic

In 2005 Giuseppe Russo, a student of
music and literature, decided to take over
the family's agricultural business, owned by
his father, and begin making his own wines.
Organic agriculture and respect for tradition
are the pillars of his philosophy. The
vineyards are situated throughout the
northern side of Mt. Etna, near Randazzo
and Passopisciaro, at elevations ranging
from 650 to 800 meters above sea level.
They have 12 hectares in San Lorenzo, six
in Feudo and one in Feudo di Mezzo. All
their vines are head-trained and in some
cases they go back more than a century.
This year their 2016 Etna Rosso Feudo di
Mezzo takes home Tre Bicchieri. It's
Giuseppe's most prized cru, and it gives
rise to a wine of extreme aromatic elegance
and complexity. This follows through on a
nobly textured palate, with a long, crystal
clear finish. Their 2016 San Lorenzo is a bit
fainter but just as expressive, while their
2016 Feudo features extremely subtle fruit
and herbaceous notes. Their 2017 Etna
Bianco Nerina offers up well-defined
aromas of mountain grass.

| | |
|---|---|
| ● Etna Rosso Feudo di Mezzo '16 | 🏆🏆🏆 6 |
| ○ Etna Bianco Nerina '17 | 🏆🏆 5 |
| ☉ Etna Rosato '17 | 🏆🏆 4 |
| ● Etna Rosso 'A Rina '16 | 🏆🏆 4 |
| ● Etna Rosso Feudo '16 | 🏆🏆 6 |
| ● Etna Rosso San Lorenzo '16 | 🏆🏆 6 |
| ● Etna Rosso 'A Rina '15 | 🏆🏆🏆 4* |
| ● Etna Rosso 'A Rina '12 | 🏆🏆🏆 3* |
| ● Etna Rosso Feudo '11 | 🏆🏆🏆 5 |
| ● Etna Rosso Feudo '10 | 🏆🏆🏆 5 |
| ● Etna Rosso Feudo '07 | 🏆🏆🏆 5 |
| ● Etna Rosso San Lorenzo '14 | 🏆🏆🏆 6 |
| ● Etna Rosso San Lorenzo '13 | 🏆🏆🏆 5 |
| ● Etna Rosso San Lorenzo '09 | 🏆🏆🏆 5 |

## Emanuele Scammacca del Murgo

VIA ZAFFERANA, 13
95010 SANTA VENERINA [CT]
TEL. +39 095950520
www.murgo.it

CELLAR SALES
PRE-BOOKED VISITS
ACCOMMODATION AND RESTAURANT SERVICE
ANNUAL PRODUCTION 230,000 bottles
HECTARES UNDER VINE 35.00

Among Etna's historic producers we find the Scammacca del Murgo, founded in 1860 (making it one of the oldest). In addition to a selection centered on the area's traditional wines, the Scammacca family have increasingly specialized in a line of elegant Metodo Classico sparkling wines. In having done so, they've taken up an old tradition that goes right back to the winery's beginnings in the 19th century. Indeed they were among the first in Italy to adopt the method. In addition to their historic Tenuta San Michele vineyards, in 2006 they added plots of Gelso Bianco at the foot of Mt. Etna. Their 2013 Extra Brut Rosè is a high quality sparkling wine made with Nerello Mascalese. It's aromatically complex with a weave that brings together flowery fragrances, yellow fruit and a nice, mineral background. On the palate it proves fresh, vibrant, energetic but its sparkle is in no way aggressive. Their whites also did well, in particular their 2016 Etna Bianco Tenuta San Michele, a wine redolent of tropical fruit and citrus, whose palate does a nice job balancing fruit and acidity.

| | |
|---|---|
| ○ Etna Bianco '17 | ♛♛ 2* |
| ○ Etna Bianco Tenuta San Michele '16 | ♛♛ 5 |
| ⊙ Etna Rosato '17 | ♛♛ 2* |
| ⊙ Murgo Extra Brut Rosé '14 | ♛♛ 4 |
| ⊙ Murgo Extra Brut Rosé '15 | ♛ 4 |
| ○ Murgo Extra Brut '10 | ♛ 5 |
| ○ Etna Bianco '15 | ♕♕ 2* |
| ○ Etna Bianco Tenuta San Michele '15 | ♕♕ 5 |
| ● Etna Rosso Tenuta San Michele '14 | ♕♕ 2* |
| ○ Murgo Brut '14 | ♕♕ 3 |
| ⊙ Murgo Brut Rosé '14 | ♕♕ 4 |
| ⊙ Murgo Brut Rosé '12 | ♕♕ 4 |
| ● Tenuta San Michele Pinot Nero '14 | ♕♕ 3 |

## Cantine Settesoli

S.DA ST.LE 115
92013 MENFI [AG]
TEL. +39 092577111
www.cantinesettesoli.it

CELLAR SALES
PRE-BOOKED VISITS
ANNUAL PRODUCTION 20,000,000 bottles
HECTARES UNDER VINE 6000.00

Cantine Settesoli is a formidable cooperative winery constituted of 2500 grower members. They're a bona fide community, bound by their collective values, and can also boast having been the first cooperative in Sicily to produce high quality wines, thus setting the precedent for an extraordinary phenomenon throughout the region. It's all thanks to a tight managerial staff with a clear vision, led for decades by Diego Planeta and today by Giuseppe Bursi. At the center of their project is the quality of their wines. But these are the result of an approach to agriculture that's respectful of the cultivar and the environment, principles which serve as the producer's true guiding light. Their 2016 Catagho, a great Nero d'Avola, impressed our tasting panel and brought home Tre Bicchieri. It's a vivid, opaque ruby red wine with elegant nuances of black mulberries, topsoil, medicinal herbs and Asian spices. On the palate it inspires, with sumptuous, elegant tannins and endless length. Their 2017 Seligo Rosso, a lovely marriage of Nero d'Avola and Syrah, is another superb wine.

| | |
|---|---|
| ● Sicilia Mandrarossa Cartagho '16 | ♛♛♛ 3* |
| ● Mandrarossa Cavadiserpe '17 | ♛♛ 3 |
| ○ Santannella Mandrarossa '17 | ♛♛ 3 |
| ● Sicilia Mandrarossa Bonera '17 | ♛♛ 3 |
| ○ Sicilia Mandrarossa Costadune '17 | ♛♛ 2* |
| ○ Sicilia Mandrarossa Urra di Mare '17 | ♛♛ 2* |
| ● Sicilia Seligo Rosso '17 | ♛♛ 2* |
| ● Mandrarossa Timperosse '17 | ♛ 3 |
| ● Cartagho Mandrarossa '09 | ♕♕♕ 3* |
| ● Cartagho Mandrarossa '08 | ♕♕♕ 3* |
| ● Cartagho Mandrarossa '06 | ♕♕♕ 3 |
| ● Mandrarossa Cavadiserpe '16 | ♕♕♕ 3* |
| ● Sicilia Mandrarossa Cartagho '14 | ♕♕♕ 3* |
| ● Timperosse Mandrarossa '14 | ♕♕♕ 3* |

# ★★Tasca d'Almerita

C.DA REGALEALI
90129 SCLAFANI BAGNI [PA]
TEL. +39 0916459711
www.tascadalmerita.it

CELLAR SALES
PRE-BOOKED VISITS
ACCOMMODATION AND RESTAURANT SERVICE
ANNUAL PRODUCTION 3,253,000 bottles
HECTARES UNDER VINE 388.00

Tasca d'Almerita is undoubtedly one of the few Italian wineries whose long history and tradition can put them in league with France's most famous producers. Despite this fact, they certainly haven't rested on their laurels. If anything, they've proven to be one of the leaders of the Italian (and Sicilian, in particular) wine renaissance. Lucio Tasca, along with his sons Giuseppe and Alberto, have modernized their Regaleali cellar, equipping it with the latest technology, but they've also invested heavily in new territories like Etna, Salina, Mozia and Monreale. And once again the Tascas submitted a selection of extremely high quality wines. Their 2014 Rosso del Conte (Nero d'Avola and Perricone) just fell short of Tre Bicchieri. It's a wine of great depth, proving generous and multifaceted on the nose, fresh, savory and persistent on the palate. Their 2017 Tascante Buonora also just missed out on top marks. It's a vibrant and elegant Etna Bianco that's also fresh and well-balanced.

| | | |
|---|---|---|
| ● Contea di Sclafani Rosso del Conte '14 | ♟♟ | 6 |
| ○ Contea di Sclafani Almerita Extra Brut Contessa Franca '11 | ♟♟ | 6 |
| ○ Etna Bianco Tascante Buonora '17 | ♟♟ | 3 |
| ● Etna Rosso Tascante Ghiaia Nera '16 | ♟♟ | 5 |
| ○ Sicilia Bianco Nozze d'Oro '16 | ♟♟ | 4 |
| ● Sicilia Cabernet Sauvignon V. San Francesco '15 | ♟♟ | 5 |
| ○ Sicilia Chardonnay V. San Francesco '16 | ♟♟ | 5 |
| ○ Sicilia Grillo Cavallo delle Fate '17 | ♟♟ | 3 |
| ● Sicilia Perricone Guarnaccio '16 | ♟♟ | 4 |
| ● Sicilia Rosso Il Tascante '15 | ♟♟ | 5 |
| ○ Sicilia Chardonnay Tascante '16 | ♟ | 5 |

# ★Tenuta delle Terre Nere

C.DA CALDERARA
95036 RANDAZZO [CT]
TEL. +39 095924002
www.tenutaterrenere.com

CELLAR SALES
PRE-BOOKED VISITS
ANNUAL PRODUCTION 200,000 bottles
HECTARES UNDER VINE 30.00
VITICULTURE METHOD Certified Organic

As early as 2002, Tenuta delle Terre Nere's first vintage, Marco De Grazia's vision was clear: develop Etna as a territory starting from the vineyard. The focus has been on highlighting the personality of the various crus, vinifying them separately through an approach that respects tradition and the environment. Their 55-hectare estate is spread across 24 plots in six districts. In the case for their pre-phylloxera Don Peppino vineyards, situated in Calderara Sottana, their head-trained vines have been estimated to go as far back as 140 years, a more than venerable age, making the plot one of Etna's authentic 'living treasures'. 2016 gave rise to a thrilling Etna Rosso. It's a vibrant, persistent and highly elegant wine in its quintessential, varietal aromas of peach. It's accompanied in our finals by their 2016 Calderara Sottana, which brings together finesse, texture and a roundness with fully ripe fruit. Their other crus are close behind. Each demonstrates the capacity to express the nobility of Etna with unmistakable personality.

| | | |
|---|---|---|
| ● Etna Rosso '16 | ♟♟ | 4 |
| ● Etna Rosso Calderara Sottana '16 | ♟♟ | 6 |
| ○ Etna Bianco Calderara Sottana '16 | ♟♟ | 6 |
| ○ Etna Bianco Santo Spirito '16 | ♟♟ | 6 |
| ● Etna Rosso Feudo di Mezzo Quadro delle Rose '16 | ♟♟ | 6 |
| ● Etna Rosso Guardiola '16 | ♟♟ | 6 |
| ● Etna Rosso San Lorenzo '16 | ♟♟ | 6 |
| ● Etna Rosso Santo Spirito '16 | ♟♟ | 6 |
| ● Etna Rosso Calderara Sottana '13 | ♟♟♟ | 6 |
| ● Etna Rosso Prephylloxera La V. di Don Peppino '14 | ♟♟♟ | 8 |
| ● Etna Rosso Santo Spirito '12 | ♟♟♟ | 6 |
| ● Etna Rosso Santo Spirito '11 | ♟♟♟ | 6 |
| ● Etna Rosso Santo Spirito '10 | ♟♟♟ | 6 |
| ● Etna Rosso Santo Spirito '08 | ♟♟♟ | 6 |

# SICILY

## Tenuta di Fessina

via Nazionale 120, 22
95012 Castiglione di Sicilia [CT]
Tel. +39 3357220021
www.tenutadifessina.com

CELLAR SALES
PRE-BOOKED VISITS
ANNUAL PRODUCTION 70,000 bottles
HECTARES UNDER VINE 13.00
SUSTAINABLE WINERY

In 2007 Silvia Maestrelli, an entrepreneur operating in Cerreto Guidi, began her successful experience at her family's winery, Villa Petriolo. It's a terroir of irresistible charm for its strong character and the challenges it represents. The estate's nucleus is situated in Castiglione, in the district of Rovittello, amidst two historic lava formations at 670 meters above sea level. Here we also find their 17th-century palmento, which hosts the cellar as well as elegant accommodations. Their other vineyards are in Milo and Santa Maria di Licodia, in addition to a small plot in Noto dedicated to Nero d'Avola. Their 2016 A Puddara is back in our finals (last year's edition wrote that it was a 2015, please excuse the typo). It's a wine with splendid notes of bloom and citrus flowers. These re-emerge on a highly elegant, fresh palate that finishes with balsamic sensations. Their 2016 Laeneo, a Nerello Cappuccio with great personality, is redolent of fruity sensations, soft and highly pleasant on the palate. Their 2017 Erse Bianco features lovely mineral finesse.

| | | |
|---|---|---|
| ○ Etna Bianco A' Puddara '16 | ♟♟♟ | 5 |
| ○ Etna Bianco Erse '17 | ♟♟ | 4 |
| ⊙ Etna Rosso Erse '16 | ♟♟ | 4 |
| ● Sicilia Nerello Cappuccio Laeneo '16 | ♟♟ | 4 |
| ⊙ Etna Rosato Erse '17 | ♟ | 4 |
| ○ Etna Bianco A' Puddara '13 | ♟♟♟ | 5 |
| ○ Etna Bianco A' Puddara '12 | ♟♟♟ | 5 |
| ○ Etna Bianco A' Puddara '11 | ♟♟♟ | 5 |
| ○ Etna Bianco A' Puddara '10 | ♟♟♟ | 5 |
| ○ Etna Bianco A' Puddara '09 | ♟♟♟ | 5 |
| ● Etna Rosso Musmeci '07 | ♟♟♟ | 6 |
| ○ Etna Bianco A' Puddara '15 | ♟♟ | 5 |
| ○ Etna Bianco A' Puddara '14 | ♟♟ | 5 |
| ○ Etna Bianco Erse '16 | ♟♟ | 4 |
| ⊙ Etna Rosato Erse '16 | ♟♟ | 4 |
| ● Etna Rosso Erse '15 | ♟♟ | 4 |
| ● Laeneo Nerello Cappuccio '15 | ♟♟ | 3* |

## Terrazze dell'Etna

c.da Bocca d'Orzo
95036 Randazzo [CT]
Tel. +39 0916236343
www.terrazzedelletna.it

CELLAR SALES
PRE-BOOKED VISITS
ANNUAL PRODUCTION 120,000 bottles
HECTARES UNDER VINE 38.00

In 2008 the Bevilacqua family began reviving terraced vineyards situated in Bocca d'Orzo, on the northern face of Etna at elevations spanning 600 to 950 meters. It required great patience, and was carried out with the utmost respect for the environment and tradition, preserving the original, head-trained vines wherever possible. In addition to Nerello Mascalese, the principal native grape cultivated, they also planted Chardonnay and Pinot Noir, which serve as the basis for their highly elegant Metodo Classico sparklers. Their Blanc de Blancs is a monovarietal and their Rosé is matured on the lees for anywhere from 36 to 50 months, but this year they just fell short of our finals. Their 2012 Rosé Brut 50 Mesi offers up a delicious, smoky note of bread crust. It's a stirring wine in its autumnal sensations, while its elegant palate features almost perfect sparkle and a long, mineral finish. Their highly fresh and savory 2017 Ciuri also exhibits minerality, along with herbaceous hints. Their 2015 Rosé and their 2015 Cuvée, made primarily with Chardonnay, also did quite well.

| | | |
|---|---|---|
| ○ Ciuri '17 | ♟♟ | 3 |
| ○ Cuvée Brut '15 | ♟♟ | 5 |
| ⊙ Rosé Brut '15 | ♟♟ | 5 |
| ⊙ Rosé Brut 50 Mesi '12 | ♟♟ | 5 |
| ● Etna Rosso Cirneco '09 | ♟♟♟ | 6 |
| ● Etna Rosso Cirneco '08 | ♟♟♟ | 5 |
| ○ Ciuri '16 | ♟♟ | 3 |
| ○ Ciuri '15 | ♟♟ | 3 |
| ○ Cuvée Brut '14 | ♟♟ | 5 |
| ○ Cuvée Brut '13 | ♟♟ | 5 |
| ○ Cuvée Brut 50 Mesi '12 | ♟♟ | 5 |
| ● Etna Rosso Carusu '15 | ♟♟ | 4 |
| ● Etna Rosso Carusu '14 | ♟♟ | 4 |
| ● Etna Rosso Cirneco '12 | ♟♟ | 6 |
| ⊙ Rosé Brut '14 | ♟♟ | 5 |
| ⊙ Rosé Brut '13 | ♟♟ | 5 |

# Girolamo Tola & C.

VIA GIACOMO MATTEOTTI, 2
90047 PARTINICO [PA]
TEL. +39 0918781591
www.vinitola.it

ANNUAL PRODUCTION 180,000 bottles
HECTARES UNDER VINE 55.00

Among the most recent pieces of news to come out of the Tola family's winery is their highly modern cellar, a spacious tasting hall and, especially, the fact that they've finished organic conversion of their vineyards, which will bring certification as of 2019. The producer's great commercial success, thanks to the quality of the wines as well as their character and strong territorial identity, has encouraged its owners to take on new property. In addition to their two vast private estates, they're renting 40 more hectares in the surrounding area. Their reds are at the forefront by virtue of their typicity and their ability to express both the grapes used and the terroir of origin. Their 2015 Nero d'Avola Black Label is excellent in its fragrance and chewy texture, while their quaffable 2017 Nero d'Avola Syrah proves vibrant and balsamic. Their 2013 Nero d'Avola Syrah is characterized by smooth, pleasant tannins. Among their whites, their 2016 GranDuca Chardonnay impresses, with its well-integrated fruit and acidity.

| | | |
|---|---|---|
| ○ GranDuca Chardonnay '16 | ♟♟ | 3 |
| ● Nero d'Avola Black Label '15 | ♟♟ | 3 |
| ● Nero d'Avola Syrah '13 | ♟♟ | 3 |
| ○ Sicilia Grillo '17 | ♟♟ | 2* |
| ○ Sicilia Grillo Terrarossa '17 | ♟♟ | 3 |
| ● Sicilia Nero d'Avola '17 | ♟♟ | 3 |
| ● Sicilia Nero d'Avola Terrarossa '17 | ♟♟ | 3 |
| ● Syrah '17 | ♟♟ | 2* |
| ○ Catarratto '17 | ♟ | 2 |
| ○ Catarratto Insolia '17 | ♟ | 2 |
| ○ Catarratto '16 | ♟♟ | 2* |
| ○ Catarratto Insolia '16 | ♟♟ | 2* |
| ● Nero d'Avola '16 | ♟♟ | 3 |
| ● Nero d'Avola Black Label '14 | ♟♟ | 3 |
| ● Nero D'Avola e Merlot '13 | ♟♟ | 3 |
| ● Terrarossa Nero d'Avola Tenuta Grassuri '16 | ♟♟ | 3 |

# Tornatore

FRAZ. VERZELLA
VIA PIETRAMARINA, 8A
95012 CASTIGLIONE DI SICILIA [CT]
TEL. +39 3339195793
www.tornatorewine.com

CELLAR SALES
PRE-BOOKED VISITS
ANNUAL PRODUCTION 120,000 bottles
HECTARES UNDER VINE 45.00

Francesco Tornatore is a successful entrepreneur in the field of telecommunications, but he's always been proud of his family's agricultural roots as well. Indeed, his grandfather was the one to transform the family estate in Castiglione di Sicilia into a modern agricultural business for the production of high-quality wine and oil. At the time their estate in Trimarchisa comprised only six hectares, but today, at 50 hectares, Tornatore is one of the largest and most dynamic producers on Etna, with an estate that gives rise to Carricante, Nerello Macalese and Cappuccio. Their 2016 Etna Rosso Trimarchisa earns a well-deserved Tre Bicchieri. It's made with grapes from a five-hectare vineyard that Francesco Tornatore inherited from his father, along with a 19th-century palmento. It comes through vibrant and elegant, with aromas of peach, pomegranate, lavender and pencil lead. In the mouth it features swollen fruit and juiciness, which integrate perfectly with subtle, well-extracted tannins.

| | | |
|---|---|---|
| ● Etna Rosso Trimarchisa '16 | ♟♟♟ | 6 |
| ○ Etna Bianco '17 | ♟♟ | 4 |
| ● Etna Rosso '16 | ♟♟ | 4 |
| ○ Etna Bianco Pietrarizzo '17 | ♟♟ | 5 |
| ● Etna Rosso Pietrarizzo '16 | ♟♟ | 5 |
| ● Etna Rosso '15 | ♟♟ | 4* |
| ○ Etna Bianco '16 | ♟♟ | 4 |
| ○ Etna Bianco Pietrarizzo '16 | ♟♟ | 5 |
| ⊙ Etna Rosato '16 | ♟♟ | 4 |
| ● Etna Rosso Pietrarizzo '15 | ♟♟ | 5 |
| ● Etna Rosso Trimarchisa '14 | ♟♟ | 6 |

## Valle dell'Acate

C.DA BIDINI
97011 ACATE [RG]
TEL. +39 0932874166
www.valledellacate.com

CELLAR SALES
PRE-BOOKED VISITS
ACCOMMODATION
ANNUAL PRODUCTION 400,000 bottles
HECTARES UNDER VINE 100.00
VITICULTURE METHOD Certified Organic
SUSTAINABLE WINERY

Valle dell'Acate is among those producers who contributed to the success and visibility of Cerasuolo di Vittoria. Two families own the historic late 19th-century winery and manage it with dynamism and passion. The estate is situated in Feudo Bidini, on the hills running along the Dirillo river. Their 100 hectares of vineyards span seven different types of terrain (according to soil color). Each hosts a vineyard and grape with its own particular character. By virtue of its elegant and complexity, their 2013 Iri da Iri (a name that calls up a Dantesque paradise) landed in our finals. It's a Cerasuolo Classico made with grapes from their Biddine Soprano cru that rest in mid-size casks for 36 months and then aged in glass for 18. Another bit of new is their Bellifolli line, wines aimed at millennials who are more attentive to quality. Their 2017 Syrah is a highly pleasant wine, fresh and green in its fruit.

## Zisola

C.DA ZISOLA
96017 NOTO [SR]
TEL. +39 057773571
www.mazzei.it

CELLAR SALES
PRE-BOOKED VISITS
ANNUAL PRODUCTION 120,000 bottles
HECTARES UNDER VINE 21.00
SUSTAINABLE WINERY

Filippo Mazzei was among the first outsider viticulturists to believe in the potential of Noto. In 2003 he bought the lovely estate of Zisola, a contiguous tract of 30 hectares that comprises three large 18th-century baglios, one of which hosts their cellar. Nero d'Avola, the area's grape 'par excellence' takes center stage, but Grillo, Catarratto and even Syrah are cultivated as well (there are even two small plots of Petit Verdot). It's an area that's among the region's best for vine growing and, as per local tradition, all their vines are all strictly head-trained. This year their 2016 Achilles, a Syrah, stood out. On the nose it offers up close-focused aromas of cherry and blackberry, balsamic nuances and hints of aromatic herbs. On the palate it exhibits elegant structure and delicate, well-integrated tannins. Their 2015 Doppiozeta, a Nero d'Avola, is a well-made, elegant wine redolent of cherry, iodine and tobacco. In the mouth it proves savory and highly persistent, striking a nice balance between fruit and tannins for a long, gratifying, flavorful finish.

| | |
|---|---|
| ● Cerasuolo di Vittoria Cl. Iri da Iri '13 | ♥♥ 5 |
| ● Cerasuolo di Vittoria Cl. '15 | ♥♥ 4 |
| ● Sicilia Nero d'Avola Il Moro '15 | ♥♥ 4 |
| ● Sicilia Syrah Bellifolli '17 | ♥♥ 3 |
| ● Vittoria Frappato Il Frappato '17 | ♥♥ 3 |
| ○ Scilia Grillo Zagra '17 | ♥ 3 |
| ○ Sicilia Insolia Bellifolli '17 | ♥ 3 |
| ● Cerasuolo di Vittoria Cl. '14 | ♥♥ 4 |
| ● Cerasuolo di Vittoria Cl. '13 | ♥♥ 4 |
| ● Sicilia Il Moro '14 | ♥♥ 4 |
| ● Sicilia Il Moro '13 | ♥♥ 3 |
| ● Sicilia Rusciano '13 | ♥♥ 4 |
| ● Tané '14 | ♥♥ 6 |
| ● Vittoria Frappato Il Frappato '15 | ♥♥ 3* |
| ○ Zagra '16 | ♥♥ 3 |

| | |
|---|---|
| ● Achilles '16 | ♥♥ 6 |
| ● Effe Emme '15 | ♥♥ 6 |
| ● Noto Doppiozeta '15 | ♥♥ 6 |
| ○ Sicilia Azisa '17 | ♥♥ 3 |
| ● Achilles '15 | ♥♥ 4 |
| ● Effe Emme '13 | ♥♥ 6 |
| ● Effe Emme '12 | ♥♥ 7 |
| ● Noto Doppiozeta '14 | ♥♥ 6 |
| ● Noto Doppiozeta '11 | ♥♥ 6 |
| ● Noto Effe Emme '14 | ♥♥ 6 |
| ● Noto Zisola '14 | ♥♥ 4 |
| ● Noto Zisola Doppiozeta '13 | ♥♥ 6 |
| ● Noto Zisola Doppiozeta '12 | ♥♥ 7 |
| ○ Sicilia Azisa '15 | ♥♥ 3 |
| ● Sicilia Zisola '13 | ♥♥ 4 |
| ○ Sicilia Zisola Azisa '14 | ♥♥ 4 |

## Al Cantàra

VIA ANTONIO CECCHI, 23
95100 CATANIA
TEL. +39 095222644
www.al-cantara.it

CELLAR SALES
PRE-BOOKED VISITS
ANNUAL PRODUCTION 50,000 bottles
HECTARES UNDER VINE 14.00

| | |
|---|---|
| ⊙ Amuri di Fimmina e Amuri di Matri '17 | 🍷🍷 4 |
| ● Etna Rosso 0' Scuru 0' Scuru '15 | 🍷🍷 5 |
| ● La Fata Galanti '15 | 🍷🍷 4 |
| ○ Etna Bianco Luci Luci '16 | 🍷 4 |

## Alberelli di Giodo

LOC. SOLICCHIATA
CASTIGLIONE DI SICILIA [CT]
TEL. +39
carlo.ferrini27@gmail.com

ANNUAL PRODUCTION 6,000 bottles
HECTARES UNDER VINE 1.50
SUSTAINABLE WINERY

| | |
|---|---|
| ● Sicilia Alberelli di Giodo '16 | 🍷🍷 7 |

## Ampelon

C.DA CALDERARA
95036 RANDAZZO [CT]
TEL. +39 3203298657
www.viniampelon.it

CELLAR SALES
ANNUAL PRODUCTION 50,000 bottles
HECTARES UNDER VINE 7.00
SUSTAINABLE WINERY

| | |
|---|---|
| ○ Etna Bianco Ampelon '17 | 🍷🍷 3 |
| ● Etna Rosso Passo alle Sciare '15 | 🍷🍷 4 |

## Avide - Vigneti & Cantine

C.DA MASTRELLA, 346
97013 COMISO [RG]
TEL. +39 0932967456
www.avide.it

CELLAR SALES
PRE-BOOKED VISITS
ANNUAL PRODUCTION 250,000 bottles
HECTARES UNDER VINE 68.00

| | |
|---|---|
| ● 1607 Frappato '17 | 🍷🍷 3 |
| ● Cerasuolo di Vittoria Cl. Etichetta Nera '15 | 🍷🍷 3 |
| ○ Maria Stella '17 | 🍷 4 |
| ○ Vittoria Riflessi di Sole '16 | 🍷 4 |

## Baglio Oro

C.DA PERINO, 235
91025 MARSALA [TP]
TEL. +39 0923967744
www.bagliooro.it

CELLAR SALES
PRE-BOOKED VISITS
ANNUAL PRODUCTION 80,000 bottles
HECTARES UNDER VINE 100.00

| | |
|---|---|
| ○ Sicilia Inzolia Guarì '17 | 🍷🍷 2* |
| ● Sicilia Nero d'Avola Dei Respiri '16 | 🍷🍷 2* |
| ○ Sicilia Grillo Dei Respiri '17 | 🍷 2 |
| ○ Sicilia Guardiani di Ceppibianchi '17 | 🍷 2 |

## Biscaris

VIA MARESCIALLO GIUDICE, 52
97011 ACATE [RG]
TEL. +39 0932990762
www.biscaris.it

CELLAR SALES
ANNUAL PRODUCTION 50,000 bottles
HECTARES UNDER VINE 10.00
VITICULTURE METHOD Certified Biodynamic

| | |
|---|---|
| ● Cerasuolo di Vittoria '17 | 🍷🍷 3 |
| ○ Inzolia '17 | 🍷🍷 2* |
| ● Frappato '17 | 🍷 2 |

## Caciorgna

LOC. ROVITTELLO
VIA NAZIONALE, 2A
95012 CASTIGLIONE DI SICILIA [CT]
TEL. +39 3487903804
tenutadellemacchie.com

ANNUAL PRODUCTION 25,000 bottles
HECTARES UNDER VINE 3.00
SUSTAINABLE WINERY

| | |
|---|---|
| ● Etna Rosso Ciaurìa '16 | ♟♟ 3 |
| ● Etna Rosso Guardoilvento '15 | ♟♟ 4 |
| ● Etna Rosso N'Anticchia '14 | ♟♟ 6 |

## Calcagno

FRAZ. PASSOPISCIARO
VIA REGINA MARGHERITA,153
95012 CASTIGLIONE DI SICILIA [CT]
TEL. +39 3387772780
www.vinicalcagno.it

CELLAR SALES
PRE-BOOKED VISITS
ANNUAL PRODUCTION 13,000 bottles
HECTARES UNDER VINE 3.00

| | |
|---|---|
| ☉ Etna Rosato Romice delle Sciare '17 | ♟♟ 5 |
| ● Etna Rosso Arcuria '16 | ♟♟ 5 |
| ● Etna Rosso Feudo di Mezzo '16 | ♟♟ 5 |
| ● Etna Rosso Nireddu '16 | ♟ 4 |

## Paolo Calì

FRAZ. C.DA SALMÉ
VIA DEL FRAPPATO, 100
97019 VITTORIA [RG]
TEL. +39 0932510082
www.vinicali.it

CELLAR SALES
PRE-BOOKED VISITS
ANNUAL PRODUCTION 90,000 bottles
HECTARES UNDER VINE 15.00

| | |
|---|---|
| ○ Blues '17 | ♟♟ 3 |
| ● Vittoria Frappato Pruvenza '15 | ♟♟ 6 |
| ● Cerasuolo di Vittoria Cl. Forfice '14 | ♟ 6 |
| ● Vittoria Nero d'Avola Violino '15 | ♟ 3 |

## Cambria

C.DA SAN FILIPPO - VIA VILLA ARANGIA
98054 FURNARI [ME]
TEL. +39 0909761124
www.cambriavini.com

PRE-BOOKED VISITS
ANNUAL PRODUCTION 100,000 bottles
HECTARES UNDER VINE 25.00

| | |
|---|---|
| ● Kio Nocera Passito '15 | ♟♟ 5 |
| ● Mamertino Giulio Cesare '13 | ♟♟ 5 |
| ○ Sicilia Chardonnay '15 | ♟ 4 |
| ● Sicilia Rosso del Levriero '14 | ♟ 5 |

## Cantina Viticoltori Associati Canicattì

C.DA AQUILATA
92024 CANICATTÌ [AG]
TEL. +39 0922829371
www.cvacanicatti.it

CELLAR SALES
PRE-BOOKED VISITS
ANNUAL PRODUCTION 900,000 bottles
HECTARES UNDER VINE 1000.00

| | |
|---|---|
| ● Diodoros '14 | ♟♟ 4 |
| ○ Sicilia Grillo Fileno '17 | ♟♟ 2* |
| ● Sicilia Nero d'Avola Centouno '15 | ♟♟ 2* |
| ● Scialo '15 | ♟ 3 |

## Caruso & Minini

VIA SALEMI, 3
91025 MARSALA [TP]
TEL. +39 0923982356
www.carusoeminini.it

CELLAR SALES
PRE-BOOKED VISITS
ANNUAL PRODUCTION 1,200,000 bottles
HECTARES UNDER VINE 120.00
VITICULTURE METHOD Certified Organic
SUSTAINABLE WINERY

| | |
|---|---|
| ● Sicilia Nero d'Avola Cutaja Ris. '15 | ♟♟ 3 |
| ● Sicilia Nero d'Avola Naturalmente Bio '17 | ♟♟ 3 |
| ● Sachia '13 | ♟ 3 |
| ○ Sicilia Grillo Timpune '17 | ♟ 3 |

## Case Alte

LOC. MACELLAROTTO
VIA PISCIOTTA, 27
90043 CAMPOREALE [PA]
TEL. +39 3297130750
www.casealte.it

ACCOMMODATION
ANNUAL PRODUCTION 17,000 bottles
HECTARES UNDER VINE 8.00
VITICULTURE METHOD Certified Organic

| | |
|---|---|
| ○ Sicilia Catarratto 12 Filari '17 | ♟♟ 3 |
| ○ Sicilia Grillo 4 Filari '17 | ♟♟ 3 |
| ● Sicilia Nero d'Avola 16 Filari '16 | ♟♟ 4 |

## Tenuta di Castellaro

FRAZ. QUATTROPANI
VIA CAOLINO
98055 LIPARI [ME]
TEL. +39 035233337
www.tenutadicastellaro.it

CELLAR SALES
PRE-BOOKED VISITS
ANNUAL PRODUCTION 25,000 bottles
HECTARES UNDER VINE
VITICULTURE METHOD Certified Organic

| | |
|---|---|
| ○ Bianco Pomice '17 | ♟♟ 5 |
| ○ Bianco Porticello '17 | ♟♟ 5 |
| ● Etna Rosso l'Ottava Isola '16 | ♟ 5 |
| ● Nero Ossidiana '14 | ♟ 5 |

## Colomba Bianca

VIA GIOVANNI FALCONE, 72
91026 MAZARA DEL VALLO [TP]
TEL. +39 0923942747
www.cantinecolombabianca.it

ANNUAL PRODUCTION 2,000,000 bottles
HECTARES UNDER VINE 7700.00

| | |
|---|---|
| ○ Sicilia Chardonnay Vitese '17 | ♟♟ 2* |
| ● Sicilia Nero d'Avola Resilience '17 | ♟♟ 2* |
| ● Sicilia Perricone Resilience '17 | ♟♟ 2* |
| ○ Sicilia Grillo Resilience '17 | ♟ 2 |

## Cantine Colosi

LOC. PACE DEL MELA
FRAZ. GIAMMORO
98042 MESSINA
TEL. +39 0909385549
www.cantinecolosi.it

PRE-BOOKED VISITS
ANNUAL PRODUCTION 100,000 bottles
HECTARES UNDER VINE 10.00

| | |
|---|---|
| ● Cariddi Rosso '16 | ♟♟ 2* |
| ● Salina Rosso '16 | ♟♟ 2* |
| ● Sicilia Nerello Mascalese '16 | ♟♟ 2* |
| ⊙ Sicilia Nero d'Avola '17 | ♟♟ 2* |

## Cossentino

VIA PRINCIPE UMBERTO, 241
90047 PARTINICO [PA]
TEL. +39 0918782569
www.cossentino.it

CELLAR SALES
PRE-BOOKED VISITS
ANNUAL PRODUCTION 70,000 bottles
HECTARES UNDER VINE 17.00
VITICULTURE METHOD Certified Organic

| | |
|---|---|
| ○ Muscarò '16 | ♟♟ 5 |
| ● Nero d'Avola '15 | ♟♟ 4 |
| ● Lioy '15 | ♟ 3 |
| ● Syrah '15 | ♟ 3 |

## Coste Ghirlanda

LOC. PIANA DI GHIRLANDA
91017 PANTELLERIA [TP]
TEL. +39 3333913695
www.costeghirlanda.it

CELLAR SALES
PRE-BOOKED VISITS
RESTAURANT SERVICE
ANNUAL PRODUCTION 25,000 bottles
HECTARES UNDER VINE 11.00

| | |
|---|---|
| ○ Silenzio '16 | ♟♟ 6 |
| ○ Jardinu '16 | ♟♟ 5 |
| ○ Passito di Pantelleria l'Alcova '15 | ♟♟ 7 |

## Curto

LOC. CONTRADA SULLA
S.DA ST.LE 115 ISPICA - ROSOLINI KM 358
97014 ISPICA [RG]
TEL. +39 0932950161
www.curto.it

CELLAR SALES
PRE-BOOKED VISITS
ANNUAL PRODUCTION 70,000 bottles
HECTARES UNDER VINE 30.00

| | | |
|---|---|---|
| ● Eloro Nero d'Avola Fontanelle '13 | ♙♙ | 4 |
| ● Eloro Nero d'Avola '15 | ♙♙ | 2* |
| ● Ikano '14 | ♙♙ | 3 |
| ○ Poiano '17 | ♙ | 2 |

## I Custodi delle Vigne dell'Etna

LOC. SOLICCHIATA
C.DA MOGANAZZI
95012 CASTIGLIONE DI SICILIA [CT]
TEL. +39 3931898430
www.icustodi.it

CELLAR SALES
PRE-BOOKED VISITS
ANNUAL PRODUCTION 40,000 bottles
HECTARES UNDER VINE 12.50
VITICULTURE METHOD Certified Organic
SUSTAINABLE WINERY

| | | |
|---|---|---|
| ● Etna Rosso Pistus '16 | ♙♙ | 4 |
| ○ Vinujancu '15 | ♙♙ | 6 |
| ⊙ Etna Bianco Ante '16 | ♙ | 5 |
| ⊙ Etna Rosato Alnus '17 | ♙ | 4 |

## Destro

LOC. MONTELAGUARDIA
95036 RANDAZZO [CT]
TEL. +39 095937060
www.destrovini.com

| | | |
|---|---|---|
| ○ Etna Bianco Isolanuda '16 | ♙♙ | 4 |
| ● Etna Rosso Aspide '13 | ♙♙ | 3 |
| ○ Saxanigra Brut '12 | ♙♙ | 5 |
| ● Etna Rosso Sciarakè '10 | ♙ | 4 |

## Di Giovanna

C.DA SAN GIACOMO
92017 SAMBUCA DI SICILIA [AG]
TEL. +39 09251955675
www.di-giovanna.com

CELLAR SALES
PRE-BOOKED VISITS
ANNUAL PRODUCTION 250,000 bottles
HECTARES UNDER VINE 56.00
VITICULTURE METHOD Certified Organic

| | | |
|---|---|---|
| ⊙ Vurria … '17 | ♙♙ | 4 |
| ⊙ Sicilia Gerbino Rosato '17 | ♙ | 2 |
| ○ Sicilia Grillo Vurria '17 | ♙ | 3 |
| ● Sicilia Vurria Nero d'Avola '16 | ♙ | 4 |

## Gaspare Di Prima

VIA G. GUASTO, 27
92017 SAMBUCA DI SICILIA [AG]
TEL. +39 0925941201
www.diprimavini.it

CELLAR SALES
PRE-BOOKED VISITS
ANNUAL PRODUCTION 50,000 bottles
HECTARES UNDER VINE 38.00
VITICULTURE METHOD Certified Organic

| | | |
|---|---|---|
| ● Sicilia Nero d'Avola Gibilmoro '16 | ♙♙ | 3 |
| ● Sicilia Syrah Villamura '13 | ♙♙ | 5 |
| ● Syrah '16 | ♙♙ | 2* |
| ● Sicilia Rosso Pepita '17 | ♙ | 2 |

## Feudo Disisa

FRAZ. GRISI
C.DA DISISA
90046 MONREALE [PA]
TEL. +39 0919127109
www.vinidisisa.it

CELLAR SALES
PRE-BOOKED VISITS
ANNUAL PRODUCTION 150,000 bottles
HECTARES UNDER VINE 150.00
VITICULTURE METHOD Certified Organic

| | | |
|---|---|---|
| ○ Chara '17 | ♙♙ | 3 |
| ○ Sicilia Catarratto Lu Bancu '17 | ♙♙ | 3 |
| ○ Sicilia Grillo '17 | ♙♙ | 3 |
| ● Nero d'Avola '16 | ♙ | 3 |

## Edomé

P.ZZA G. VERGA, 25
95121 CATANIA
TEL. +39 095536632
www.cantinedome.com

CELLAR SALES
PRE-BOOKED VISITS
ANNUAL PRODUCTION 8,000 bottles
HECTARES UNDER VINE 2.50

| | | |
|---|---|---|
| ● Etna Rosso Aitna Feudo di Mezzo '15 | | ❦❦ 5 |
| ● Etna Rosso Aitna Vigna Nica Feudo di Mezzo '15 | | ❦❦ 5 |

## Cantine Ermes

C.DA SALINELLA
91029 SANTA NINFA [TP]
TEL. +39 092467153
www.cantineermes.it

CELLAR SALES
PRE-BOOKED VISITS
ANNUAL PRODUCTION 3,000,000 bottles
HECTARES UNDER VINE 5000.00
VITICULTURE METHOD Certified Organic
SUSTAINABLE WINERY

| | | |
|---|---|---|
| ● Quattro Quarti Rosso '17 | | ❦❦ 3 |
| ● Vento di Mare Nerello Mascalese '17 | | ❦❦ 3 |
| ● Vento di Mare Nero d'Avola '17 | | ❦❦ 2* |
| ● Vento di Mare Nerello Mascalese Bio '17 | | ❦ 2 |

## Fazio Wines

FRAZ. FULGATORE
VIA CAPITAN RIZZO, 39
91010 ERICE [TP]
TEL. +39 0923811700
www.faziowines.com

ANNUAL PRODUCTION 750,000 bottles
HECTARES UNDER VINE 100.00
SUSTAINABLE WINERY

| | | |
|---|---|---|
| ● Erice Cartesiano '16 | | ❦❦ 5 |
| ○ Erice Grillo Aegades '17 | | ❦❦ 3 |
| ● Erice Pietra Sacra Ris. '11 | | ❦❦ 5 |
| ● Erice Torre dei Venti '17 | | ❦ 4 |

## Ferreri

C.DA SALINELLA
91029 SANTA NINFA [TP]
TEL. +39 092461871
www.ferrerivini.it

CELLAR SALES
PRE-BOOKED VISITS
ANNUAL PRODUCTION 70,000 bottles
HECTARES UNDER VINE 30.00

| | | |
|---|---|---|
| ○ Inzolia '17 | | ❦❦ 3 |
| ○ Zibibbo '17 | | ❦❦ 3 |
| ○ Grillo '17 | | ❦ 3 |
| ● Pignatello '17 | | ❦ 2 |

## Feudo Cavaliere

C.DA CAVALIERE BOSCO
95126 SANTA MARIA DI LICODIA [CT]
TEL. +39 3487348377
www.feudocavaliere.com

CELLAR SALES
PRE-BOOKED VISITS
ANNUAL PRODUCTION 9,000 bottles
HECTARES UNDER VINE 10.00

| | | |
|---|---|---|
| ○ Etna Bianco '16 | | ❦❦ 3 |
| ○ Etna Bianco Millemetri '14 | | ❦❦ 4 |
| ● Etna Rosso Millemetri '12 | | ❦❦ 4 |
| ○ Etna Rosato Millemetri '16 | | ❦ 3 |

## Feudo di Santa Teresa

C.DA SANTA TERESA
97019 VITTORIA [RG]
TEL. +39 09321846555
www.santatresa.it

CELLAR SALES
PRE-BOOKED VISITS
ANNUAL PRODUCTION 250,000 bottles
HECTARES UNDER VINE 39.00
VITICULTURE METHOD Certified Organic

| | | |
|---|---|---|
| ● Cerasuolo di Vittoria '16 | | ❦❦ 4 |
| ● Frappato '17 | | ❦❦ 3 |
| ● Avulisi '16 | | ❦ 5 |
| ● Nivuro '16 | | ❦ 4 |

## Feudo Ramaddini

FRAZ. MARZAMEMI
C.DA LETTIERA
96018 PACHINO [SR]
TEL. +39 09311847100
www.feudoramaddini.com

CELLAR SALES
PRE-BOOKED VISITS
RESTAURANT SERVICE
ANNUAL PRODUCTION 90,000 bottles
HECTARES UNDER VINE 20.00

| | | |
|---|---|---|
| ○ Perla Marina Brut | ♥♥ 4 | |
| ● Sicilia Nero d'Avola Note Nere '16 | ♥♥ 3 | |
| ● Noto Nero d'Avola Patrono '14 | ♥ 5 | |
| ○ Sicilia Grillo Nassa '17 | ♥ 2 | |

## Cantine Fina

C.DA BAUSA
91025 MARSALA [TP]
TEL. +39 0923733070
www.cantinefina.it

CELLAR SALES
PRE-BOOKED VISITS
ACCOMMODATION
ANNUAL PRODUCTION 350,000 bottles
HECTARES UNDER VINE 180.00
VITICULTURE METHOD Certified Organic

| | | |
|---|---|---|
| ○ Sicilia Chardonnay '16 | ♥♥ 4 | |
| ● Sicilia Perricone '17 | ♥♥ 3 | |
| ○ Taif '17 | ♥♥ 3 | |
| ● Bausa '14 | ♥ 3 | |

## Gulfi

C.DA PATRIA
97012 CHIARAMONTE GULFI [RG]
TEL. +39 0932921654
www.gulfi.it

CELLAR SALES
PRE-BOOKED VISITS
ACCOMMODATION AND RESTAURANT SERVICE
ANNUAL PRODUCTION 280,000 bottles
HECTARES UNDER VINE 70.00
VITICULTURE METHOD Certified Organic

| | | |
|---|---|---|
| ● Etna Rosso Reseca '12 | ♥♥ 5 | |
| ● Sicilia Nerojbleo '14 | ♥♥ 3 | |
| ● Sicilia Nerosanlorè '13 | ♥♥ 6 | |
| ○ Sicilia Carjcanti '16 | ♥ 5 | |

## Hibiscus

C.DA TRAMONTANA
90010 USTICA [PA]
TEL. +39 0918449543
www.agriturismohibiscus.com

CELLAR SALES
PRE-BOOKED VISITS
ACCOMMODATION
ANNUAL PRODUCTION 10,000 bottles
HECTARES UNDER VINE 3.00

| | | |
|---|---|---|
| ○ Grotta dell'Oro '17 | ♥♥ 2* | |
| ○ L'Isola Bianco '17 | ♥♥ 2* | |
| ○ Zhabib Passito '17 | ♥♥ 4 | |
| ○ Onde di Sole '17 | ♥ 4 | |

## Incarrozza

LOC. CONTRADA CARROZZA
S.DA PROV.LE 12/II KM 1
95045 MISTERBIANCO [CT]
TEL. +39 3488749305
www.incarrozzavini.com

ANNUAL PRODUCTION 20,000 bottles
HECTARES UNDER VINE 8.00

| | | |
|---|---|---|
| ○ Uve d'Agosto Bianco '16 | ♥♥ 3 | |
| ● Uve d'Agosto Rosso '14 | ♥♥ 4 | |

## Lisciandrello

VIA CASE NUOVE, 31
90048 SAN GIUSEPPE JATO [PA]
TEL. +39 3395917618
www.aziendalisciandrello.com

ANNUAL PRODUCTION 30,000 bottles
HECTARES UNDER VINE 6.00

| | | |
|---|---|---|
| ○ Carricante '16 | ♥♥ 4 | |
| ○ Cataratto '16 | ♥♥ 4 | |
| ○ Chardonnay '16 | ♥♥ 4 | |

## Marchesi de Gregorio

C.DA SIRIGNANO
90046 MONREALE [PA]
TEL. +39 09241836038
www.marchesidegregorio.it

ANNUAL PRODUCTION 80,000 bottles
HECTARES UNDER VINE 70.00
VITICULTURE METHOD Certified Organic

| | |
|---|---|
| ● Gregorio Maximo '14 | ♟♟ 4 |
| ● Parco Reale Syrah '13 | ♟♟ 4 |
| ○ Sicilia Il Grillo del Marchese '17 | ♟ 2 |
| ○ Teodora '17 | ♟ 2 |

## Masseria del Feudo

C.DA GROTTAROSSA
93100 CALTANISSETTA
TEL. +39 0934830885
www.masseriadelfeudo.it

CELLAR SALES
PRE-BOOKED VISITS
ACCOMMODATION
ANNUAL PRODUCTION 100,000 bottles
HECTARES UNDER VINE 12.00
VITICULTURE METHOD Certified Organic

| | |
|---|---|
| ○ Sicilia Grillo '17 | ♟♟ 2* |
| ● Sicilia Nero d'Avola '17 | ♟♟ 2* |
| ● Sicilia Nero d'Avola Ris. '15 | ♟♟ 5 |
| ○ Sicilia Haermosa '16 | ♟ 3 |

## Cantina Modica di San Giovanni

C.DA BUFALEFI
96017 NOTO [SR]
TEL. +39 09311805181
www.vinidinoto.it

CELLAR SALES
PRE-BOOKED VISITS
RESTAURANT SERVICE
ANNUAL PRODUCTION 80,000 bottles
HECTARES UNDER VINE 40.00
SUSTAINABLE WINERY

| | |
|---|---|
| ☉ Eloro Mamma Draja '17 | ♟♟ 2* |
| ○ Moscato di Noto Dolcenoto '17 | ♟♟ 3 |
| ○ SATIS faction | ♟♟ 4 |
| ○ Lupara '17 | ♟ 2 |

## Morgante

C.DA RACALMARE
92020 GROTTE [AG]
TEL. +39 0922945579
www.morgantevini.it

CELLAR SALES
ANNUAL PRODUCTION 310,000 bottles
HECTARES UNDER VINE 57.00

| | |
|---|---|
| ○ Bianco di Morgante '17 | ♟♟ 3 |
| ● Sicilia Nero d'Avola '16 | ♟♟ 2* |

## Antica Tenuta del Nanfro

C.DA NANFRO SAN NICOLA LE CANNE
95041 CALTAGIRONE [CT]
TEL. +39 093360744
www.nanfro.com

CELLAR SALES
PRE-BOOKED VISITS
ANNUAL PRODUCTION 65,000 bottles
HECTARES UNDER VINE 39.00
VITICULTURE METHOD Certified Organic

| | |
|---|---|
| ● Cerasuolo di Vittoria Sammauro '16 | ♟♟ 2* |
| ○ Strade Inzolia '17 | ♟♟ 2* |
| ● Vittoria Frappato '17 | ♟♟ 2* |

## Ottoventi

C.DA TORREBIANCA - FICO
91019 VALDERICE [TP]
TEL. +39 0923 1877151
www.cantinaottoventi.wine

CELLAR SALES
PRE-BOOKED VISITS
ACCOMMODATION
ANNUAL PRODUCTION 300,000 bottles
HECTARES UNDER VINE 35.00

| | |
|---|---|
| ● .20 Nero d'Avola '16 | ♟♟ 2* |
| ● Ottoventi Nero '15 | ♟♟ 3 |
| ● Scilia Nero d'Avola Iruka V. T. '17 | ♟♟ 3 |
| ○ Sicilia Grillo '17 | ♟ 4 |

## Tenute dei Paladini

VIA PALESTRO, 23
91025 MARSALA [TP]
TEL. +39 3463513366
www.tenutedeipaladini.com

ANNUAL PRODUCTION 40,000 bottles
HECTARES UNDER VINE 45.00

| | |
|---|---|
| ○ Emà '17 | ♟♟ 3* |
| ○ Isola Bianca '17 | ♟♟ 3* |
| ○ Sicilia Isola Rossa '17 | ♟♟ 3 |
| ● San Giorgio '17 | ♟ 3 |

## Pietracava

VIA LUIGI STURZO, 16
93011 BUTERA [CL]
TEL. +39 3392410117
www.pietracavawines.it

ANNUAL PRODUCTION 30,000 bottles
HECTARES UNDER VINE 15.00

| | |
|---|---|
| ● Manaar '15 | ♟♟ 4 |
| ○ Neofos Sauvignon Blanc '17 | ♟♟ 3 |
| ○ Pioggia di Luce Grillo '17 | ♟♟ 3 |
| ● Kalpis '15 | ♟ 4 |

## Porta del Vento

C.DA VALDIBELLA
90043 CAMPOREALE [PA]
TEL. +39 0916116531
www.portadelvento.it

ANNUAL PRODUCTION 40,000 bottles
HECTARES UNDER VINE 12.00
VITICULTURE METHOD Certified Organic

| | |
|---|---|
| ○ Mira M. Cl. | ♟♟ 5 |
| ○ Porta del Vento '17 | ♟♟ 3 |
| ○ Porta del Vento '16 | ♟♟ 3 |
| ● Perricone '15 | ♟ 3 |

## Pupillo

C.DA LA TARGIA
96100 SIRACUSA
TEL. +39 0931494029
www.pupillowines.com

CELLAR SALES
PRE-BOOKED VISITS
ANNUAL PRODUCTION 35,000 bottles
HECTARES UNDER VINE 20.00

| | |
|---|---|
| ○ Moscato di Siracusa Pollio '17 | ♟♟ 5 |
| ○ Moscato di Siracusa Solacium '16 | ♟♟ 4 |
| ○ Siracusa Cyane '17 | ♟♟ 3* |
| ○ Sicilia Targetta '17 | ♟ 2 |

## Quignones

VIA VITTORIO EMANUELE, 62
92027 LICATA [AG]
TEL. +39 0922773744
www.quignones.it

CELLAR SALES
PRE-BOOKED VISITS
ANNUAL PRODUCTION 90,000 bottles
HECTARES UNDER VINE 28.00

| | |
|---|---|
| ⊙ Fimmina Rosato di Nero d'Avola '17 | ♟♟ 2* |
| ● Lagasìa Nero d'Avola '15 | ♟♟ 3 |
| ○ Castel San Giacomo<br>Insolia Chardonnay '17 | ♟ 2 |

## Riofavara

S.DA PROV.LE 49 ISPICA-PACHINO
97014 ISPICA [RG]
TEL. +39 0932705130
www.riofavara.it

CELLAR SALES
PRE-BOOKED VISITS
ACCOMMODATION
ANNUAL PRODUCTION 70,000 bottles
HECTARES UNDER VINE 27.00
VITICULTURE METHOD Certified Organic
SUSTAINABLE WINERY

| | |
|---|---|
| ● Eloro Nero d'Avola Spaccaforno '15 | ♟♟ 4 |
| ○ Marzaiolo '17 | ♟♟ 3 |
| ○ Moscato di Noto Mizzica '17 | ♟♟ 3 |
| ● San Basilio '16 | ♟ 3 |

## Feudo Rudinì

c.da Camporeale
96018 Pachino [SR]
Tel. +39 0931595333
www.vinirudini.it

PRE-BOOKED VISITS
ANNUAL PRODUCTION 300,000 bottles
HECTARES UNDER VINE 24.00

| | |
|---|---|
| ● Eloro Pachino Saro '15 | 🍷🍷 3 |
| ● Sicilia Rosso Porticciolo '17 | 🍷🍷 4 |
| ○ Espressione Chardonnay '17 | 🍷 3 |
| ● Sicilia Nero d'Avola Campanile '17 | 🍷 4 |

## Cantine Russo

loc. Crasà
fraz. Solicchiata
via Corvo
95014 Castiglione di Sicilia [CT]
Tel. +39 0942986271
www.cantinerusso.eu

CELLAR SALES
PRE-BOOKED VISITS
ANNUAL PRODUCTION 190,000 bottles
HECTARES UNDER VINE 15.00

| | |
|---|---|
| ● Etna Rosso Rampante '10 | 🍷🍷 5 |
| ○ Etna Bianco Rampante Contrada Crasà '17 | 🍷 3 |
| ○ Mon Pit Brut Blanc de Blancs '16 | 🍷 5 |

## Sallier de la Tour

c.da Pernice
90144 Monreale [PA]
Tel. +39 0916459711
www.tascadalmerita.it

PRE-BOOKED VISITS
ANNUAL PRODUCTION 250,000 bottles
HECTARES UNDER VINE 41.00

| | |
|---|---|
| ● Monreale Syrah La Monaca '16 | 🍷🍷 5 |
| ○ Sicilia Grillo '17 | 🍷🍷 2* |
| ● Sicilia Nero d'Avola '16 | 🍷🍷 2* |
| ● Sicilia Syrah '16 | 🍷 2 |

## Barone di Serramarrocco

fraz. Fulgatore
via Alcide de Gasperi, 15
91100 Trapani
Tel. +39 348 7308270
www.baronediserramarrocco.com

CELLAR SALES
PRE-BOOKED VISITS
ANNUAL PRODUCTION 70,000 bottles
HECTARES UNDER VINE 22.00
SUSTAINABLE WINERY

| | |
|---|---|
| ● Sammarcello Pignatello '16 | 🍷🍷 4 |
| ● Serramarrocco '16 | 🍷🍷 6 |
| ○ Quojane di Serramarrocco '17 | 🍷 4 |
| ○ Sicilia Grillo Il Grillo del Barone '17 | 🍷 3 |

## La Solidea

c.da Kaddiuggia
91017 Pantelleria [TP]
Tel. +39 0923913016
www.solideavini.it

CELLAR SALES
PRE-BOOKED VISITS
ANNUAL PRODUCTION 12,000 bottles
HECTARES UNDER VINE 5.00

| | |
|---|---|
| ○ Ilios '17 | 🍷🍷 3* |
| ○ Passito di Pantelleria '17 | 🍷🍷 5 |

## Terre di Giurfo

via Palestro, 536
97019 Vittoria [RG]
Tel. +39 0957221551
www.terredigiurfo.it

CELLAR SALES
PRE-BOOKED VISITS
ANNUAL PRODUCTION 100,000 bottles
HECTARES UNDER VINE 40.00

| | |
|---|---|
| ● Sicilia Nero d'Avola Kudyah '16 | 🍷🍷 3 |
| ● Vittoria Frappato Belsito '17 | 🍷🍷 3 |
| ● Cerasuolo di Vittoria Maskarìa '14 | 🍷 3 |
| ● Sicilia Syrah Ronna '16 | 🍷 3 |

## Todaro

C.DA FEOTTO
90048 SAN GIUSEPPE JATO [PA]
TEL. +39 3461056393
www.todarowinery.com

PRE-BOOKED VISITS
ANNUAL PRODUCTION 80,000 bottles
HECTARES UNDER VINE 25.00
VITICULTURE METHOD Certified Organic

| | |
|---|---|
| ○ Ginestra Catarratto '17 | ▼▼ 5 |
| ● Perricone Feotto '15 | ▼▼ 5 |
| ● Virgo '16 | ▼▼ 4 |
| ● Shadir '16 | ▼ 3 |

## Torre Favara

VIA CANNADA, 1
93013 MAZZARINO [CL]
TEL. +39 0934384064
www.torrefavara.com

CELLAR SALES
PRE-BOOKED VISITS
ACCOMMODATION
ANNUAL PRODUCTION 50,600 bottles
HECTARES UNDER VINE 10.00

| | |
|---|---|
| ○ Pian del Grigno '17 | ▼▼ 2* |
| ● Torre Favara Nero d'Avola '15 | ▼▼ 2* |
| ○ Conca del Principe '17 | ▼ 2 |
| ○ Trenta Filari '17 | ▼ 2 |

## Torre Mora

LOC. ROVITTELLO
95012 CASTIGLIONE DI SICILIA [CT]
TEL. +39 057754011
www.tenutepiccini.it

ANNUAL PRODUCTION 70,000 bottles
HECTARES UNDER VINE 12.00
VITICULTURE METHOD Certified Organic

| | |
|---|---|
| ○ Etna Bianco Scalunera '17 | ▼▼ 5 |
| ⊙ Etna Rosato Scalunera '17 | ▼▼ 4 |
| ● Etna Rosso Scalunera '15 | ▼▼ 5 |

## Vaccaro

C.DA COMUNE
91020 SALAPARUTA [TP]
TEL. +39 092475151
www.vinivaccaro.it

CELLAR SALES
ANNUAL PRODUCTION 800,000 bottles
HECTARES UNDER VINE 40.00
VITICULTURE METHOD Certified Organic
SUSTAINABLE WINERY

| | |
|---|---|
| ○ Catarratto Zibibbo Bio '17 | ▼▼ 2* |
| ● Sicilia Nero d'Avola Bio '17 | ▼▼ 3 |
| ● Sicilia Nero d'Avola Luna '17 | ▼▼ 4 |
| ○ Sicilia Catarratto Bio '17 | ▼ 2 |

## Viteadovest

C.DA AMABILINA, 517
91025 MARSALA [TP]
TEL. +39 3341890139
www.viteadovest.it

PRE-BOOKED VISITS
ANNUAL PRODUCTION 15,000 bottles
HECTARES UNDER VINE 6.00
VITICULTURE METHOD Certified Organic
SUSTAINABLE WINERY

| | |
|---|---|
| ○ Numero 73 perpetuo imb. 2018 | ▼▼ 8 |
| ○ Rina Bianco '16 | ▼▼ 6 |
| ○ Vurgo Bianco '17 | ▼▼ 5 |
| ○ Bianco '16 | ▼ 5 |

## Vivera

LOC. MARTINELLA
S.DA PROV.LE 59 IV
95015 LINGUAGLOSSA [CT]
TEL. +39 095643837
www.vivera.it

CELLAR SALES
PRE-BOOKED VISITS
ANNUAL PRODUCTION 120,000 bottles
HECTARES UNDER VINE 30.00
VITICULTURE METHOD Certified Organic

| | |
|---|---|
| ○ Altrove '17 | ▼▼ 3 |
| ○ Etna Bianco Salisire '14 | ▼▼ 4 |
| ⊙ Etna Rosato di Martinella '17 | ▼▼ 4 |
| ● Terra dei Sogni '15 | ▼ 3 |

# SARDINIA

A true revolution (the good kind) is underway in Sardinia. The number of producers operating, and the number of awards it's receiving, are growing, along with the island's important wine producing territories. And success follows growth, a fact made evident by the Tre Bicchieri awarded this year (13, a record!), but also by the number of wines to reach our finals, and the Due Bicchieri assigned. Awards aside, we'd like to underline the region's continued evolution in terms of quality, both its small wineries, which are being carried forward by young and determined vigneron, and its important (and historic) producers, who've never stopped pursuing innovation and continued renewal. And this isn't to forget the important role played by the region's cooperatives, who offer extremely well-made wines at excellent prices. It's worth noting that despite the great work being done in the cellar and in the vineyard, there's still a ways to go in terms of communications, marketing and sales. The Doc consortiums aren't helping - those few that exists (unfortunately) are essentially non-functioning, a fact that the entire regional industry should reflect on. Now onto the wines. 2017 proved to be a great year for Sardinia's whites, despite the heat, inasmuch as it gave rise to greater concentration, but also nice tension and savoriness, guaranteeing perfect balance. 2016 and 2015 were also good years, with the latter proving excellent for reds, foremost Cannonau. This year saw some six new wines take home Tre Bicchieri. We start with Antonella Corda's 2016 Cannonau di Sardegna, with the producer also making its first appearance in our guide. For us it's a wine exemplary of the typology: fresh, graceful, fine and elegant, but also complex and long, with Mediterranean aromas. And this great island red also drove our decision to name Antonella Corda this edition's 'Up-and-Coming Winery'. Santa Maria La Palma's Riserva R is a different wine, but also delicious. When it comes to Sardinia's reds, Su Entu's Bovale stood out, a wine made with grapes from the lovely vineyards of Marmilla. Vermentino made its presence felt with Delogu's Die and Ledda's Azzesu, a wine made with grapes from a unique plot situated on volcanic soil at over 700 meters elevation. Lastly (but only because it was Sella & Mosca's most recent creation), we mention the Alghero Torbato Catore, an outstanding wine made with the local grape Algherese.

## ★★Argiolas

VIA ROMA, 28/30
09040 SERDIANA [CA]
TEL. +39 070740606
www.argiolas.it

CELLAR SALES
PRE-BOOKED VISITS
ANNUAL PRODUCTION 2,200,000 bottles
HECTARES UNDER VINE 230.00

As well as being an internationally recognized name, Argiolas is a great wine family currently being led by its third generation. The winery is consistently at the forefront of research, planning and establishing itself commercially on five continents. The estate's vast range clearly centers on traditional varieties, planted in an extensive area around Serdiana and its neighboring towns, and Sulcis. Selections are very elegant and very drinkable. The winery's basic offerings are excellent value for the money, while the higher end of its range gives longevity and character. 2014 gave rise to a Turriga that expresses force accompanied by elegance, making for a wine that's enjoyable now but will offer up its best in the future. Their Senes, a Riserva di Cannonau on its third year, once again proved delicious. Their other finalist is also made with Cannonau. It's a red passito dedicated to Antonio Argiolas (the winery's founder). The rest of their selection also proved well-made, starting with their 2015 Korem.

| | |
|---|---|
| ● Antonio Argiolas 100 '14 | ♛♛ 6 |
| ● Cannonau di Sardegna Senes Ris. '14 | ♛♛ 5 |
| ● Turriga '14 | ♛♛ 8 |
| ○ Angialis '15 | ♛♛ 6 |
| ● Carignano del Sulcis Is Solinas Ris. '15 | ♛♛ 4 |
| ○ Cerdeña '14 | ♛♛ 7 |
| ● Korem Bovale '15 | ♛♛ 5 |
| ● Monica di Sardegna Sup. Is Selis '16 | ♛♛ 3 |
| ○ Nasco di Cagliari Is Selis '17 | ♛♛ 3 |
| ○ Vermentino di Sardegna Is Argiolas '17 | ♛♛ 3 |
| ● Carignano del Sulcis Cardanera '17 | ♛ 4 |
| ○ Tagliamare Brut | ♛ 4 |
| ○ Vermentino di Sardegna Merì '17 | ♛ 3 |
| ● Cannonau di Sardegna Senes Ris. '13 | ♛♛♛ 5 |
| ● Cannonau di Sardegna Senes Ris. '12 | ♛♛♛ 5 |

## Audarya

LOC. SA PERDERA
S.S. 466 KM 10,100
09040 SERDIANA [CA]
TEL. +39 070 740437
www.audarya.it

CELLAR SALES
PRE-BOOKED VISITS
ANNUAL PRODUCTION 50,000 bottles
HECTARES UNDER VINE 35.00

Despite their youth, Salvatore and Nicoletta Pala, as the third generation of a winemaking family, are well-prepared to run the winery they established in 2014. The siblings focus on producing high-quality wines using southern Sardinia's traditional varieties of Cannonau and Vermentino, as well as Monica, Bovale, Nuragus and Nasco. It did not take long for the young winemakers to achieve their goal thanks to carefully cultivated grapes and skilfull winemaking, making for elegant, highly drinkable wines that clearly express the territory. Their top range is quite varied, a fact that's earned the winery a place among Italian Wine's most important producers. Their 2017 Camminera is a selection of Vermentino di Sardegna that's fresh, savory and deep, with notes of almonds, white fruit and herbs. Their Nuracada is a vibrant, fruit-driven Bovale with aromas of cherry and blackberry, as well as a spicy flourish. Its mouth is juicy and fluent with a deep, clean finish.

| | |
|---|---|
| ● Nuracada Bovale '16 | ♛♛ 5 |
| ○ Vermentino di Sardegna Camminera '17 | ♛♛ 3* |
| ○ Bisai '17 | ♛♛ 5 |
| ● Cannonau di Sardegna '17 | ♛♛ 3 |
| ⊙ Cannonau di Sardegna Rosato '17 | ♛♛ 2* |
| ○ Nuragus di Cagliari '17 | ♛♛ 2* |
| ● Monica di Sardegna '17 | ♛ 2 |
| ○ Vermentino di Sardegna '17 | ♛ 2 |
| ○ Bisai '15 | ♛♛ 4 |
| ● Cannonau di Sardegna '15 | ♛♛ 2* |
| ● Monica di Sardegna '16 | ♛♛ 2* |
| ○ Vermentino di Sardegna '15 | ♛♛ 2* |
| ○ Vermentino di Sardegna Camminera '16 | ♛♛ 2* |

# Capichera

S.S. Arzachena-Sant'Antonio, km 4
07021 Arzachena [SS]
Tel. +39 078980612
www.capichera.it

CELLAR SALES
PRE-BOOKED VISITS
ANNUAL PRODUCTION 250,000 bottles
HECTARES UNDER VINE 50.00
SUSTAINABLE WINERY

Capichera is undoubtedly one of Sardinia's (and the peninsula's) flagship wineries. Borne out of the Ragnedda brothers' emphasis on high quality, respect for the territory, marketing, business acumen and communication, the brand encompasses a number of wines. The great protagonist is Vermentino di Gallura, even though only Vigna 'Ngena, a young white vinified in steel, falls within the appellation. Other selections, deliberately produced to meet less stringent IGT standards, reflect the impeccable use of wood barrels, and result in complexity, elegance and longevity. This year they put forward an extremely high quality range of wines, starting with their 2017 Vermentino di Gallura Vigna'Ngena, a great wine that expresses the territory at its best. Their 2015 VT surprised, proving complex, multifaceted and extraordinarily deep. Their 2013 Santigaini is an incredible wine. Five years after vintage, it's still young, pervasive, invigorating and minty with a vital freshness that brings out its great savoriness. As already said, the rest of their selection is also all excellent.

| | |
|---|---|
| ○ Vermentino di Gallura Vigna'Ngena '17 | ♟♟♟ 5 |
| ○ Capichera '16 | ♟♟ 6 |
| ○ Capichera VT '15 | ♟♟ 8 |
| ○ Santigaini '13 | ♟♟ 8 |
| ● Albori di Lampata '14 | ♟♟ 8 |
| ● Assajé '15 | ♟♟ 6 |
| ● Mantenghja '14 | ♟♟ 8 |
| ○ Vermentino di Sardegna Lintori '17 | ♟♟ 4 |
| ☉ També Rosato '17 | ♟ 4 |
| ○ Capichera '14 | ♟♟♟ 6 |
| ○ Capichera '13 | ♟♟♟ 6 |
| ○ Capichera '12 | ♟♟♟ 6 |
| ○ Capichera '11 | ♟♟♟ 6 |
| ○ Capichera '15 | ♟♟ 6 |

# Giovanni Maria Cherchi

loc. Sa Pala e Sa Chessa
07049 Usini [SS]
Tel. +39 079380273
www.vinicolacherchi.it

CELLAR SALES
PRE-BOOKED VISITS
ANNUAL PRODUCTION 170,000 bottles
HECTARES UNDER VINE 30.00

This winery was established by Giovanni Maria Cherchi in the 1970s with the goal of promoting Usini and its viticulture. The area's reputation did in fact grow, thanks largely to him and to Vermentino and Cagnulari. The latter is found only around Usini and its current success is undoubtedly due to Cherchi's efforts. The quality of the winery's Vermentino has always been very high, bearing witness to how well-suited its vineyards are for the variety. Altitude, soils and sea breezes all make their contributions, adding elegance, finesse and longevity. Their 2017 Vermentino di Sardegna Tuvaoes distinguishes itself among other whites of its class. Despite the hot 2017 vintage the wine proves complex in its notes of herbs, white fruit, citrus and yellow flowers. The palate is savory and invigorating, proving vital, long and very clean on the palate. Their 2016 Cagnulari is also notable. The rest of their selection proves well-crafted.

| | |
|---|---|
| ○ Vermentino di Sardegna Tuvaoes '17 | ♟♟ 3* |
| ● Cagnulari '16 | ♟♟ 3 |
| ○ Vermentino di Sardegna Billia '17 | ♟♟ 2* |
| ● Luzzana '16 | ♟ 4 |
| ○ Vermentino di Sardegna Filighe Brut | ♟ 3 |
| ○ Vermentino di Sardegna Tuvaoes '16 | ♟♟♟ 3* |
| ● Cagnulari '15 | ♟♟ 3 |
| ● Cagnulari '14 | ♟♟ 3 |
| ● Cagnulari Billia '15 | ♟♟ 3 |
| ● Cannonau di Sardegna '14 | ♟♟ 3 |
| ● Cannonau di Sardegna '11 | ♟♟ 3* |
| ○ Vermentino di Sardegna Billia '16 | ♟♟ 2* |
| ○ Vermentino di Sardegna Tuvaoes '15 | ♟♟ 3 |

## Chessa

VIA SAN GIORGIO
07049 USINI [SS]
TEL. +39 3283747069
www.cantinechessa.it

CELLAR SALES
PRE-BOOKED VISITS
ANNUAL PRODUCTION 43,000 bottles
HECTARES UNDER VINE 15.00

This small all-female winery is run with determination by Giovanna Chessa, in Usini, an area with ideal conditions for obtaining quality wines. Calcareous and clay soils, sea breezes and ideal elevations are behind the success of the company. The cellar limits itself to enhancing what happens in the vineyard and the result is evident in the elegance and drinkability of selections. Only varieties traditional to the area are cultivated: Vermentino, Cagnulari and Muscat for a passito dried grape wine. And once again, Giovanna's wines don't disappoint. At the top of the range is her 2016 Cagnulari, a close-woven, complex wine with aromas of spices and undergrowth and a palate that's supple despite its structure. Her Lugherra, a blend of traditional cultivar is also very good. Her 2017 Vermentino di Sardegna Mattariga also delivers while her Kentales, a sweet Moscato di Sardegna, proves well-balanced and clean.

| | |
|---|---|
| ● Cagnulari '16 | ♟♟ 3 |
| ○ Kentàles | ♟♟ 5 |
| ● Lugherra '16 | ♟♟ 5 |
| ○ Vermentino di Sardegna Mattariga '17 | ♟ 3 |
| ● Cagnulari '15 | ♟♟ 3 |
| ● Cagnulari '14 | ♟♟ 3 |
| ● Lugherra '12 | ♟♟ 5 |
| ● Lugherra '10 | ♟♟ 5 |
| ● Lugherra '07 | ♟♟ 5 |
| ○ Vermentino di Sardegna Mattariga '16 | ♟♟ 3 |
| ○ Vermentino di Sardegna Mattariga '15 | ♟♟ 3 |
| ○ Vermentino di Sardegna Mattariga '14 | ♟♟ 3 |
| ○ Vermentino di Sardegna Mattariga '10 | ♟♟ 3 |

## Attilio Contini

VIA GENOVA, 48/50
09072 CABRAS [OR]
TEL. +39 0783290806
www.vinicontini.it

CELLAR SALES
PRE-BOOKED VISITS
ANNUAL PRODUCTION 1,000,000 bottles
HECTARES UNDER VINE 110.00
VITICULTURE METHOD Certified Organic
SUSTAINABLE WINERY

Contini is a well-respected wine family that has been promoting the territory for decades, elevating the reputation of the area's viticulture. The star here is Vernaccia di Oristano, a unique oxidative wine capable of aging for decades. There's no lack of Vernaccia Riserva in the cellar, though the range has expanded to include reds obtained from another local grape, Nieddera, and white, red and sparkling wines made with Vernaccia, from Vermentino and Cannonau. Their Antico Gregori is a Vernaccia di Oristano that's made with the Solera Method - as a result it's released without a vintage date. Thanks to the latest batch we have the chance to review it again, and we're pleased to say that we found it to be one of the best versions yet. An amber yellow wine, it offers up aromas of dried fruit, spices, flowers, resin and iodine. In the mouth it's crisp, savory and extremely long. It's one of Italy's great 'meditation' wines. Among their strong selection of reds, their Maluentu stood out, as did their Montiprama (made with Nieddera) and their noteworthy Barrile.

| | |
|---|---|
| ○ Vernaccia di Oristano Antico Gregori | ♟♟ 8 |
| ● Barrile '14 | ♟♟ 7 |
| ○ Karmis Cuvée '17 | ♟♟ 3 |
| ● Maluentu '17 | ♟♟ 2* |
| ☉ Brut Attilio Rosé | ♟ 3 |
| ● Cannonau di Sardegna Mamaioa '16 | ♟ 3 |
| ● Cannonau di Sardegna Sartiglia '15 | ♟ 3 |
| ☉ I Giganti Rosato '17 | ♟ 3 |
| ○ Pontis | ♟ 5 |
| ○ Vermentino di Sardegna Pariglia '17 | ♟ 2 |
| ○ Vermentino di Sardegna Tyrsos '17 | ♟ 2 |
| ● Barrile '11 | ♟♟♟ 6 |
| ○ Vernaccia di Oristano Ris. '88 | ♟♟♟ 4* |

# Antonella Corda

s.s. 466 Km 6,8
09040 Serdiana [CA]
Tel. +39 0707966300
www.antonellacorda.it

**CELLAR SALES**
**PRE-BOOKED VISITS**
**ANNUAL PRODUCTION** 30,000 bottles
**HECTARES UNDER VINE** 14.50

Di Madre in Vigna is on each bottle, a beautiful tribute to the generational transition between two women. Antonella is part of Serdiana's well-known Argiolas family. Some years ago, thanks to a tradition passed down through her mother, she decided to start her own line of wines. So far, three selections, all made in steel vats, have been produced, using the Cannonau, Vermentino and Nuragus typical of the southern part of the island. These first years already exhibit quality and a very drinkable, fine, elegant style that doesn't neglect the characteristics of the territory. For the first time this young producer has made it into Italian Wines and right off the bat they take home a Tre Bicchieri, as well as our Up-and-Coming Winery award. Their Cannonau di Sardegna is fresh, light, highly drinkable style that'd being awarded. The nose offers up hints of small fruit and nuances of rose. A spicy touch anticipates delicate tannins and exemplary, deep acidity, thanks to a light, savory streak. Their 2017 Vermentino and Nuragus are also excellent.

| | |
|---|---|
| ● Cannonau di Sardegna '16 | ♔♔♔ 3* |
| ○ Nuragus di Cagliari '17 | ♔♔ 2* |
| ○ Vermentino di Sardegna '17 | ♔♔ 3 |

# Ferruccio Deiana

loc. Su Leunaxi
via Gialeto, 7
09040 Settimo San Pietro [CA]
Tel. +39 070749117
www.ferrucciodeiana.it

**CELLAR SALES**
**PRE-BOOKED VISITS**
**ANNUAL PRODUCTION** 520,000 bottles
**HECTARES UNDER VINE** 120.00

Ferruccio Deiana founded his winery in Settimo San Pietro, a stone's throw from Cagliari. Over the years he has been able to create a company that is significant both for the number of bottles bottles produced and for the vine stock on the properties. The vineyards are mainly found within two bodies: Su Leunaxiu is near the winery, the other is in Sibiola in the municipality of Serdiana, an area that has always been suited to viticulture. It focuses on traditional varieties, which are also offered as monovarietals. Some of the more ambitious selections feature blends. Both of their cornerstone reds deliver, foremost their 2015 Cannonau Sardegna Silent Riserva, a wine that features aromas of black fruit and tobacco, as well as a tight-knit but supple palate. Their 2015 Ajana, Igt, a blend of native cultivar that offers up hints of undergrowth and spices, also did well. Their other wines all proved well-crafted, especially their Donnikalia, a 2017 Vermentino di Sardegna with fragrances of almond, citrus and loquat.

| | |
|---|---|
| ● Ajana '15 | ♔♔ 6 |
| ● Cannonau di Sardegna Sileno Ris. '15 | ♔♔ 4 |
| ● Monica di Sardegna Sup. Karel '16 | ♔♔ 3 |
| ○ Oirad '16 | ♔♔ 5 |
| ○ Vermentino di Sardegna Donnikalia '17 | ♔♔ 2* |
| ● Monica di Sardegna Karel '16 | ♔ 2 |
| ○ Vermentino di Sardegna Arvali '17 | ♔ 3 |
| ● Cannonau di Sardegna Sileno Ris. '10 | ♔♔♔ 3* |
| ● Ajana '14 | ♔♔ 6 |
| ● Ajana '13 | ♔♔ 6 |
| ● Cannonau di Sardegna Sileno '14 | ♔♔ 3 |
| ● Cannonau di Sardegna Sileno Ris. '14 | ♔♔ 4 |
| ● Cannonau di Sardegna Sileno Ris. '13 | ♔♔ 4 |
| ○ Oirad '14 | ♔♔ 5 |

# Tenute Delogu

S.S. Sassari-Fertilia 291 - km 22
07041 Alghero [SS]
Tel. +39 3452862861
www.tenutedelogu.com

CELLAR SALES
PRE-BOOKED VISITS
ANNUAL PRODUCTION 100,000 bottles
HECTARES UNDER VINE 25.00
SUSTAINABLE WINERY

Piero Delogu is a Sardinian zootechnical entrepreneur who several years ago decided to dedicate his life to wine production. Located in the Algherese area, the winery cultivates Cannonau and Vermentino, traditional to the island, as well as Cagnulari, native to the area. There are also some international varieties that have found an ideal habitat here and are used in small amounts in some of their offerings. For now, the white stands out over the red, which in its early stage is exhibiting excessive wood, overpowering the qualities of the grapes. Kudos to their 2017 Vermentino di Sardegna Die, a white with great character that stands out for richness of flavor and depth. The nose features a Mediterranean atmosphere ranging from citrus peel to yellow flowers, iodine and aromatic herbs. The palate also proves excellent for an acidity that corresponds to the wine's pervasive though subtle, fine body. Tre Bicchieri. Their reds did well, though came through a bit clenched on the palate.

| | |
|---|---|
| ○ Vermentino di Sardegna Die '17 | ♛♛♛ 3* |
| ● Cagnulari '15 | ♛ 4 |
| ● Cannonau di Sardegna Ego '14 | ♛ 4 |
| ● Cannonau di Sardegna Ego '13 | ♛♛ 2* |
| ● Geo '12 | ♛♛ 2* |
| ○ Vermentino di Sardegna Die '15 | ♛♛ 2* |

# Cantine di Dolianova

Loc. Sant'Esu
S.S. 387 km 17,150
09041 Dolianova [CA]
Tel. +39 070744101
www.cantinedidolianova.it

CELLAR SALES
PRE-BOOKED VISITS
ANNUAL PRODUCTION 4,000,000 bottles
HECTARES UNDER VINE 1200.00

Quantity and quality are the two words that come to mind when one thinks of Cantina di Dolianova. Founded in the 1950s, Sardinia's largest cooperative produces a range of wines totalling a volume of over a million bottles. A few years ago their selection underwent an important restyling that went deeper than mere aethetics. From its very reasonably priced basic wines to its most ambitious selections, the quality is consistently high. Emphasis is placed on promoting traditional varieties, particularly those from southern Sardinia, such as Nasco, Nuragus or Barbera Sarda. This year some of their best offerings weren't submitted for tasting, especially their Riservas and their Igt, which are made with their best grapes. All the wines submitted did well, however, from their two 2017 Vermentino di Sardegnas (Prendas and Naeli, both fresh, citrusy, flowery wines) to their Moscato di Sardegna Passito (a sweet but never cloying wine with notes of apricot) and their highly enjoyable 2017 Rosada, a Cannonau di Sardegna Rosato with aromas of red fruit and rose.

| | |
|---|---|
| ⊙ Cannonau di Sardegna Rosato Rosada '17 | ♛♛ 2* |
| ○ Moscato di Sardegna Passito | ♛♛ 5 |
| ○ Vermentino di Sardegna Naeli '17 | ♛♛ 2* |
| ● Cannonau di Sardegna Anzenas '16 | ♛ 2 |
| ○ Caralis Brut | ♛ 3 |
| ○ Malvasia Scaleri Demi Sec | ♛ 3 |
| ● Monica di Sardegna Arenada '16 | ♛ 2 |
| ○ Nuragus di Cagliari Perlas '17 | ♛ 2 |
| ⊙ Sibiola Rosé '17 | ♛ 2 |
| ○ Vermentino di Sardegna Prendas '17 | ♛ 2 |
| ● Falconaro '11 | ♛♛♛ 3* |
| ● Cannonau di Sardegna Anzenas '15 | ♛♛ 2* |
| ● Cannonau di Sardegna Blasio Ris. '10 | ♛♛ 3* |
| ● Terresicci '10 | ♛♛ 5 |

# Cantina Dorgali

VIA PIEMONTE, 11
08022 DORGALI [NU]
TEL. +39 078496143
www.cantinadorgali.com

**CELLAR SALES**
**PRE-BOOKED VISITS**
**ANNUAL PRODUCTION** 1,500,000 bottles
**HECTARES UNDER VINE** 600.00
**SUSTAINABLE WINERY**

Cantina di Dorgali is a cooperative situated in the municipality of the same name, a beautiful area for the production of Cannonau di Sardegna that's characterized by the island's eastern sea breeze. Their wines are primarily expressions of the variety and range from simpler young offerings of great drinkability and excellent value to those from older, head-trained vines. The range is completed by Vermentino and sparkling Cannonau wines. Some of their best Riservas and wines still aren't ready to be released and that's why our tastings centered on their youngest versions. Their 2016 Cannonau di Sardegna Isalle is one-of-a-kind in its category. It's a fresh, juicy, very reasonably well-priced wine with notes of small wild berries and sweet spices. Their Rosa e Lune Brut, a Metodo Charmat made with Cannonau grapes, also did very well.

| | |
|---|---|
| ● Cannonau di Sardegna Vigna di Isalle '16 | ♟♟ 2* |
| ⊙ Rosa e Luna Brut | ♟♟ 3 |
| ● Cannonau di Sardegna Filieri Rosato '17 | ♟ 2 |
| ● Cannonau di Sardegna Nùrule Ris. '15 | ♟ 4 |
| ○ Vermentino di Sardegna Filine '17 | ♟ 2 |
| ● Cannonau di Sardegna Cl. D53 '13 | ♟♟♟ 4* |
| ● Cannonau di Sardegna Cl. D53 '12 | ♟♟♟ 4* |
| ● Cannonau di Sardegna Cl. D53 '14 | ♟♟ 4 |
| ● Cannonau di Sardegna V. di Isalle '15 | ♟♟ 2* |
| ● Cannonau di Sardegna Vinìola Ris. '14 | ♟♟ 4 |
| ● Hortos '12 | ♟♟ 6 |

# Fradiles

LOC. CRECCHERÌ
08030 ATZARA [NU]
TEL. +39 3331761683
www.fradiles.it

**CELLAR SALES**
**PRE-BOOKED VISITS**
**ANNUAL PRODUCTION** 20,000 bottles
**HECTARES UNDER VINE** 12.00
**SUSTAINABLE WINERY**

Fradiles is a beautiful artisanal winery skilfully managed by winemaker Paolo Savoldo. Mandrolisai is in the exact middle of the island and one of the purely Sardinian appellations defined exclusively by its location. Traditional Cannonau, Bovale and Monica have always been cultivated in various percentages within the vineyards and play an essential role in establishing the character of the wine, along with elevations (700 meters above sea level), soil type (granite) and age. A minimally invasive approach in the cellar allows the characteristics of the territory to fully express themselves. All you have to do is taste the selection presented this year by Fradiles to realize that this small Mandrolisai winery can be a true model for the territory. Their 2016 Mandrolisai Azzara is the youngest, freshest wine of the lot, offering up spices, wild berries and a touch of mint. The palate is fresh, juicy and savory. Their other reds are all delicious, from their Mandrolisai Antiogu and Fradiles to their Bagaðiu, a monovarietal Bovale.

| | |
|---|---|
| ● Mandrolisai Azzàra '16 | ♟♟ 2* |
| ● Bagadiu '16 | ♟♟ 3 |
| ● Mandrolisai Fradiles '16 | ♟♟ 3 |
| ● Mandrolisai Sup. Antiogu '14 | ♟♟ 4 |
| ○ Funtanafrisca '17 | ♟ 3 |
| ● Mandrolisai Sup. Antiogu '11 | ♟♟♟ 5 |
| ● Bagadiu '13 | ♟♟ 4 |
| ● Bagadiu Bovale '15 | ♟♟ 3 |
| ● Mandrolisai Azzarra '14 | ♟♟ 2* |
| ● Mandrolisai Fradiles '15 | ♟♟ 3* |
| ● Mandrolisai Fradiles '14 | ♟♟ 3 |
| ● Mandrolisai Sup. Antiogu '13 | ♟♟ 5 |
| ● Mandrolisai Sup. Istentu '13 | ♟♟ 8 |

# ★Giuseppe Gabbas

VIA TRIESTE, 59
08100 NUORO
TEL. +39 078433745
www.gabbas.it

CELLAR SALES
PRE-BOOKED VISITS
ANNUAL PRODUCTION 70,000 bottles
HECTARES UNDER VINE 20.00

Gabbas is a slave to his passion, and he much prefers working in the vineyard to wasting time in idle chats. The fruits of his labor are wines of rare finesse and elegance that are highly drinkable and rewarding. Cannonau is the indisputable star, making up 80% of their selection. The range begins with the current vintage Lillové, in steel vats, moves to Dule and Arobòre, aged in wood barrels, and arrives at Avra, the passito wine that is produced during the best years. The final selection, Manzanile, a Vermentino di Sardegna, is always compelling. 2015 turns out to have been a great year, and each of the two Cannonau di Sardegna Classicos presented was better than the next. Their Dule stands at the top, a brilliant example of an elegant, Mediterranean, close-knit Cannonau that's also great to drink. It offers up aromas of red fruit and spices as well as rose and undergrowth. In the mouth the wine proves pervasive, but its freshness and savoriness push it towards a deep finish. Tre Bicchieri. Their Arbore, a softer and creamier wine, also impressed.

| | |
|---|---|
| ● Cannonau di Sardegna Cl. Dule '15 | ♙♙♙ 4* |
| ● Cannonau di Sardegna Cl. Arbòre '15 | ♙♙ 4 |
| ● Cannonau di Sardegna Lillové '17 | ♙♙ 2* |
| ○ Vermentino di Sardegna Manzanile '17 | ♙♙ 3 |
| ● Cannonau di Sardegna Cl. Dule '13 | ♙♙♙ 4* |
| ● Cannonau di Sardegna Cl. Dule '12 | ♙♙♙ 4* |
| ● Cannonau di Sardegna Cl. Dule '11 | ♙♙♙ 4* |
| ● Cannonau di Sardegna Dule Ris. '10 | ♙♙♙ 4* |
| ● Cannonau di Sardegna Dule Ris. '09 | ♙♙♙ 3* |
| ● Cannonau di Sardegna Dule Ris. '08 | ♙♙♙ 3* |
| ● Cannonau di Sardegna Dule Ris. '07 | ♙♙♙ 3* |
| ● Cannonau di Sardegna Cl. Arbòre '14 | ♙♙ 4 |
| ● Cannonau di Sardegna Cl. Arbòre '13 | ♙♙ 4 |
| ● Cannonau di Sardegna Cl. Dule '14 | ♙♙ 4 |

# Cantina Gallura

VIA VAL DI COSSU, 9
07029 TEMPIO PAUSANIA
TEL. +39 079631241
www.cantinagallura.com

CELLAR SALES
PRE-BOOKED VISITS
ANNUAL PRODUCTION 1,300,000 bottles
HECTARES UNDER VINE 350.00

Cantina di Gallura is located in the northern part of the island at Tempio and specializes in Vermentino di Gallura. For years, the heart and soul of the cooperative has been its enologist and director, Dino Addis. A range of wines are produced, especially whites, and their selection is divided into various lines -- by quality, vineyard, etc. The overall quality is quite high and prices are fair for such ageworthy wines. Particularly noteworthy are Vermentino, reds made with traditional varieties and the Moscato di Tempio, an excellent sparkling wine. For some years now their Canayli (a well-known Vermentino di Gallura that's always distinguished itself for its excellent value) has also been offered as a Vendemmia Tardiva (late-harvest wine), and it's always delivered. Their 2017 is no exception, offering up notes of ripe, yellow fruit, aromatic herbs and almond. In the mouth the wine proves full and pervasive while acidity and flavor keep it long and supple. Their Templum, a savory, juicy Cannonau di Sardegna stood out among their reds.

| | |
|---|---|
| ○ Vermentino di Gallura Canayli V. T. '17 | ♙♙ 4 |
| ● Cannonau di Sardegna Templum '16 | ♙♙ 2* |
| ● Karana '17 | ♙♙ 2* |
| ○ Moscato di Tempio Pausania | ♙♙ 2 |
| ○ Vermentino di Gallura Piras '17 | ♙♙ 2* |
| ○ Vermentino di Gallura Gemellae '17 | ♙ 2 |
| ○ Vermentino di Gallura Sup. Canayli '17 | ♙ 2 |
| ○ Vermentino di Gallura Canayli V. T. '14 | ♙♙♙ 4* |
| ○ Vermentino di Gallura Sup. Genesi '10 | ♙♙♙ 5 |
| ○ Vermentino di Gallura Sup. Genesi '08 | ♙♙♙ 5 |
| ○ Vermentino di Gallura Canayli V. T. '16 | ♙♙ 4 |

# Cantina Giba

VIA PRINCIPE DI PIEMONTE, 16
09010 GIBA [SU]
TEL. +39 0781689718
www.cantinagiba.it

**CELLAR SALES**
**ANNUAL PRODUCTION** 100,000 bottles
**HECTARES UNDER VINE** 15.00

This artisanal winery located in the Sulcis village of Gibas was formerly known as 6Mura, a moniker it now uses for some selections. The range is limited and entirely produced from its own vineyards and area grapes, starting with Carignano, which thrives here. Older vines and sandy soil play an important role in determining the character of their wines, while a minimally-invasive approach in the cellar, for better or for worse, brings out the characteristics of the vintage. The results are honest, authentic and genuine expressions of the territory. The range includes two Vermentino wines, also from Sulcis. For a few years they have spoiled us with extremely charming, highly drinkable wines. This year their 2015 Carignano del Sulcis 6Mura was no exception, offering up aromas of myrtle, Mediterranean shrub, sweet spices and ripe red fruit. In the mouth the wine proves savory and close-knit, with a balsamic freshness and incredible depth. Their two, simpler 2017 Vermentinos and Carignanos, which bear the winery's name, also proved quite good.

| | |
|---|---|
| ● Carignano del Sulcis 6Mura Ris. '15 | ♟♟♟ 5 |
| ● Carignano del Sulcis Giba '17 | ♟♟ 2* |
| ○ Vermentino di Sardegna Giba '17 | ♟♟ 2* |
| ⊙ 6 Mura Rosè M. Cl. | ♟ 5 |
| ○ Vermentino di Sardegna Mura Bianco '17 | ♟ 4 |
| ● Carignano del Sulcis 6Mura '12 | ♟♟♟ 5 |
| ● Carignano del Sulcis 6Mura '11 | ♟♟♟ 5 |
| ● Carignano del Sulcis 6Mura '10 | ♟♟♟ 5 |
| ● Carignano del Sulcis 6Mura '09 | ♟♟♟ 5 |
| ● Carignano del Sulcis 6Mura '11 | ♟♟ 5 |
| ● Carignano del Sulcis Giba '16 | ♟♟ 2* |
| ○ Vermentino di Sardegna 6Mura '16 | ♟♟ 4 |

# Antichi Poderi Jerzu

VIA UMBERTO I, 1
08044 JERZU [OG]
TEL. +39 078270028
www.jerzuantichipoderi.it

**CELLAR SALES**
**PRE-BOOKED VISITS**
**ANNUAL PRODUCTION** 1,500,000 bottles
**HECTARES UNDER VINE** 750.00

750 hectares of terrain cultivated by this cooperative's members give rise to one and a half million bottles of wine. Jerzu is named after the Ogliastra village that gives its name to both the winery and one of the three sub-areas of the Cannonau appellation, testifying to the area's role in the most important variety of the island. Selections strongly reflect the characteristics of the terroir and the exceptional microclimate of the island's eastern coast. In addition to Cannonau, the range includes other traditional varieties, from Monica to Vermentino. Once again their two great Cannonaus, the producer's crown jewels, delivered. Their Chuèrra is a highly complex Riserva with earthy notes of scrubland, myrtle and black fruit. The palate is close-knit but its tannins are soft and pervasive, and its finish proves full of flavor. Their Josto Miglior, a Riserva dedicated to the winery's founder, also impressed. The nose features aromas of wild berries and traces of spices, while the palate demonstrates good overall balance. The rest of their selection also proved well-made.

| | |
|---|---|
| ● Cannonau di Sardegna Chuèrra Ris. '15 | ♟♟ 5 |
| ● Cannonau di Sardegna Josto Miglior Ris. '15 | ♟♟ 5 |
| ○ Vermentino di Sardegna Lucean le Stelle '17 | ♟♟ 3 |
| ● Cannonau di Sardegna Bantu '17 | ♟ 2 |
| ⊙ Cannonau di Sardegna Isara '17 | ♟ 2 |
| ● Cannonau di Sardegna Marghìa '16 | ♟ 4 |
| ● Monica di Sardegna Camalda '17 | ♟ 2 |
| ○ Vermentino di Sardegna Telavè '17 | ♟ 2 |
| ● Cannonau di Sardegna Josto Miglior Ris. '09 | ♟♟♟ 4* |
| ● Cannonau di Sardegna Josto Miglior Ris. '05 | ♟♟♟ 4 |
| ● Cannonau di Sardegna Chuèrra Ris. '14 | ♟♟ 5 |

## Andrea Ledda

VIA MUSIO, 13
07043 BONNANARO [SS]
TEL. +39 079845060
www.vitivinicolaledda.com

**CELLAR SALES**
**PRE-BOOKED VISITS**
**ANNUAL PRODUCTION** 25,000 bottles
**HECTARES UNDER VINE** 24.00

Andrea Ledda is a successful businessman who decided to become involved in high-quality winemaking, which he did by developing three different estates. One is in the village of Bonnanaro, where the winery is located. Another vineyard is 1000 meters above sea level atop an extinct volcano. The third, located in Gallura, meant the acquisition of an historic vineyard called Matteu. Although different terroirs, all feature a range which is distinguished by finesse and drinkability. Their 2017 Vermentino di Sardegna Azzesu, made with grapes cultivated on the volcano at 700 meters above sea level, is their most particular wine to have been released. Aromas of citrus, white flowers, aniseed and herbs give way to a taught, vibrant palate that's rich in acidity and exhibits exemplary savoriness. It's the winery's first Tre Bicchieri. Their other Vermentino, a Gallura made with grapes from their Tenuta Matteu estate, also did well.

| | |
|---|---|
| ○ Vermentino di Sardegna Azzesu Tenuta del Vulcano Pelao '17 | 🏆🏆🏆 7 |
| ○ Vermentino di Gallura Sup. Soliànu Tenuta Matteu '17 | 🏆 5 |
| ● Cannonau di Sardegna Cerasa Tenuta Monte Santu '15 | 🏆🏆 6 |
| ● Ruju - Tenuta Monte Santu '14 | 🏆🏆 5 |
| ○ Vermentino di Sardegna Giaru Tenuta Monte Santu '17 | 🏆🏆 3 |
| ● Cannonau di Sardegna Cerasa Tenuta Monte Santu '14 | 🏆🏆 6 |
| ○ Vermentino di Gallura Soliànu Tenuta Matteu '16 | 🏆🏆 5 |
| ○ Vermentino di Sardegna Azzesu Tenuta del Vulcano Pelao '15 | 🏆🏆 7 |

## Masone Mannu

LOC. SU CANALE
S.S. 199 KM 48
07020 MONTI [SS]
TEL. +39 078947140
www.masonemannu.com

**CELLAR SALES**
**PRE-BOOKED VISITS**
**ANNUAL PRODUCTION** 100,000 bottles
**HECTARES UNDER VINE** 19.00

This beautiful Gallura winery has undergone several changes of ownership in recent years. In the summer of 2018 the winery was acquired by an entrepreneur from Rimini who owns the Mara company, which produces reds in Romagna using biodynamic methods. Their high-quality wines are very drinkable, express the territory and have excellent aging potential. In addition to the white selections led by Vermentino di Gallura there are some impeccable reds. Their 2017 Costarenas, a Vermentino di Gallura Superiore, is at the top of their selection this year thanks to its charm and character. Aromatic herbs, candied citrus and a touch of grains give way to a deep, savory palate. Their 2017 Petrizza, another clean, flavorful Gallura, also impressed. Their Entu, a blend of traditional cultivar, stands out among their reds.

| | |
|---|---|
| ○ Vermentino di Gallura Sup. Costarenas '17 | 🏆🏆 4 |
| ● Entu '16 | 🏆🏆 5 |
| ○ Vermentino di Gallura Petrizza '17 | 🏆🏆 3 |
| ● Cannonau di Sardegna Zòjosu '16 | 🏆 3 |
| ○ Vermentino di Gallura Sup. Costarenas '16 | 🏆🏆🏆 3* |
| ● Cannonau di Sardegna '09 | 🏆🏆 3* |
| ● Cannonau di Sardegna Zòjosu '15 | 🏆🏆 3* |
| ○ Vermentino di Gallura Petrizza '16 | 🏆🏆 3 |
| ○ Vermentino di Gallura Petrizza '14 | 🏆🏆 3 |
| ○ Vermentino di Gallura Sup. Costarenas '15 | 🏆🏆 3* |
| ○ Vermentino di Gallura Sup. Costarenas '14 | 🏆🏆 3* |
| ○ Vermentino di Gallura Sup. Costarenas '11 | 🏆🏆 4 |
| ● Zurria '15 | 🏆🏆 3 |

# Mesa

Loc. Su Baroni
09010 Sant'Anna Arresi [CA]
Tel. +39 0781965057
www.cantinamesa.it

**CELLAR SALES**
**PRE-BOOKED VISITS**
**ANNUAL PRODUCTION** 750,000 bottles
**HECTARES UNDER VINE** 70.00

Established several years ago, Mesa is a beautiful Sulcis winery that's lovingly maintained by Gavino Sanna. It was recently acquired in large part by the Santa Margherita group. Everything here revolves around Carignano, the main grape of the territory, which is presented in a diverse range, from young, fresh versions, to those from older, ungrafted vines. Their selection is completed by Vermentino and a few international varieties which found an ideal habitat in Sardinia. Their elegant and complex wines offer drinkability and excellent aging capabilities. Two of their wines made it into the finals this year, confirming the quality of their selection. Their prized Gavino, a wine dedicated to the winery's founder, stands out. It's a Carignano del Sulcis made with historic, ungrafted vines cultivated in sand. Aromas of scrubland, spices and dark fruit give way to a creamy, fresh, pervasive palate. Their savory and iodine Opale, a 2017 Vermentino di Sardegna, also proved delicious.

| | |
|---|---|
| ● Carignano del Sulcis Gavino Ris. '15 | ♟♟ 5 |
| ○ Vermentino di Sardegna Opale '17 | ♟♟ 4 |
| ● Carignano del Sulcis Buio Buio Ris. '15 | ♟♟ 5 |
| ● Brama Syrah '16 | ♟ 4 |
| ● Carignano del Sulcis Buio '17 | ♟ 3 |
| ☉ Carignano del Sulcis Rosa Grande '17 | ♟ 3 |
| ○ Vermentino di Sardegna Giunco '17 | ♟ 3 |
| ● Buio Buio '10 | ♟♟♟ 4* |
| ● Carignano del Sulcis Buio Buio Ris. '13 | ♟♟♟ 5 |
| ● Carignano del Sulcis Buio Buio Ris. '12 | ♟♟♟ 5 |
| ● Carignano del Sulcis Buio Buio Ris. '14 | ♟♟ 5 |
| ● Carignano del Sulcis Gavino Ris. '14 | ♟♟ 5 |
| ○ Vermentino di Sardegna Opale '16 | ♟♟ 4 |

# Cantina di Mogoro
# Il Nuraghe

s.s. 131 km 62
09095 Mogoro [OR]
Tel. +39 0783990285
www.cantinadimogoro.it

**CELLAR SALES**
**PRE-BOOKED VISITS**
**ANNUAL PRODUCTION** 850,000 bottles
**HECTARES UNDER VINE** 480.00

Nuraghe is the cooperative winery of Mogoro, a village in the upper Campidano area. This is the heart of the Semidano di Mogoro appellation. Using traditional Sardinian grapes, the collective has long focused on the quality of its selections. Semidano is clearly the star, but Bovale (another variety that has always been locally present), Vermentino and Cannonau also play important roles. The collective produces a varied range, from the least expensive -- simple but always precise and well-made -- to the most prestigious led by Puistèris, a long-lived and complex Semidano. Their entire selection impressed this year. Their 2016 Puistèris, a Semidano di Mogoro Superiore, is at the top of the range, demonstrating the cultivar's potential in terms of longevity. The nose offers up yellow fruit, wild flowers, chamomile and candied citrus while the palate proves generous yet subtle and lean with good, supporting acidity. Their Tiernu, a Bovale di Terralba, and their Chio, a Riserva di Cannonau, also did quite well in our tastings.

| | |
|---|---|
| ○ Semidano di Mogoro Sup. Puistèris '16 | ♟♟♟ 4* |
| ● Cannonau di Sardegna Chio Ris. '14 | ♟♟ 5 |
| ○ Moscato di Cagliari Capodolce | ♟♟ 3 |
| ● Terralba Bovale Tiernu '16 | ♟♟ 2* |
| ● Monica di Sardegna San Bernardino '16 | ♟ 2 |
| ● Monica di Sardegna Sup. Nabui '14 | ♟ 5 |
| ○ Semidano di Mogoro Anastasia '17 | ♟ 2 |
| ○ T'Amo Cuvée '17 | ♟ 3 |
| ● Terralba Bovale Cavaliere Sardo '15 | ♟ 2 |
| ○ Vermentino di Sardegna Don Giovanni '17 | ♟ 2 |
| ○ Semidano di Mogoro Sup. Puistèris '10 | ♟♟♟ 4* |
| ○ Semidano di Mogoro Sup. Puistèris '15 | ♟♟ 4 |
| ● Terralba Bovale Cavaliere Sardo '14 | ♟♟ 2* |

## Olianas

Loc. Porruddu
08030 Gergei [CA]
Tel. +39 0558300411
www.olianas.it

**CELLAR SALES**
**PRE-BOOKED VISITS**
**ANNUAL PRODUCTION** 120,000 bottles
**HECTARES UNDER VINE** 19.00
**VITICULTURE METHOD** Certified Organic
**SUSTAINABLE WINERY**

Olianas is a stunning agricultural enterprise in Gergei, in the heart of Sardinia. It represents a collaboration between Artemio Olianas and Stefano Casadei, the latter an enologist who also owns a group of beautiful wineries in Tuscany. The estate emphasizes sustainability and operates according to the principles of bio-integration. These rules dictate that in addition to basic organic methods, only animals can be used in the vineyard (e.g., horses plow and geese weed) as well as other practices aimed at safeguarding the ecosystem. The wines, made with traditional varieties aged in steel vats, wood barrels and terra cotta amphorae, are highly drinkable and honest, reflecting the characteristics of the area. Their most convincing wine this year was, without a doubt, their 2015 Cannonau di Sardegna Riserva, bolstered as it is by a multifaceted aromatic spectrum that ranges from red fruit to spices, notes of undergrowth and resin. The palate comes through creamy and intense. Their Perdixi also delivered. Made with Bovale and Cannonau, it's a fine, fragrant wine.

| | |
|---|---|
| ● Cannonau di Sardegna Ris. '15 | ♟♟ 4 |
| ● Perdixi '16 | ♟♟ 4 |
| ⊙ Rosato '17 | ♟♟ 3 |
| ● Cannonau di Sardegna '17 | ♟ 3 |
| ○ Vermentino di Sardegna '17 | ♟ 3 |
| ● Cannonau di Sardegna '16 | ♟♟ 3 |
| ● Cannonau di Sardegna '15 | ♟♟ 3 |
| ● Cannonau di Sardegna '14 | ♟♟ 3 |
| ● Cannonau di Sardegna '13 | ♟♟ 3 |
| ● Cannonau di Sardegna Ris. '14 | ♟♟ 4 |
| ⊙ Cannonau di Sardegna Rosato '15 | ♟♟ 3 |
| ⊙ Rosato '14 | ♟♟ 2* |
| ○ Vernasco '14 | ♟♟ 2* |

## Pala

via Verdi, 7
09040 Serdiana [CA]
Tel. +39 070740284
www.pala.it

**CELLAR SALES**
**PRE-BOOKED VISITS**
**ANNUAL PRODUCTION** 490,000 bottles
**HECTARES UNDER VINE** 98.00

With the help of his sons, Mario Pala, a winemaker of limitless energy, has managed to make his well-known Serdiana winery a standard bearer for Sardinia. Globetrotting commercial director, Fabio Angius, who has always worked alongside the family, has positioned the winery in multiple countries on five continents. Their wide range is maintained on a high level and based on the traditional cultivars of southern Sardinia, which are accompanied by those from the Terralbese area where Bovale is cultivated. 2017, a hot but interesting vintage, gave rise to their Stellato 2017, which once again proves it's one-of-a-kind. Tre Bicchieri for this south Sardinia Vermentino that amazes for its aromatic profile and savory, vibrant, fragrant palate. Their 2015 Cannonau di Sardegna Riserva is a delicious, authentic and charming wine with notes of tobacco and black fruit. From their I Fiori line, their 2017 Cannonau and Nuragus both get special mentions thanks to their excellent value.

| | |
|---|---|
| ○ Vermentino di Sardegna Stellato '17 | ♟♟♟ 4* |
| ● Cannonau di Sardegna Ris. '15 | ♟♟ 3* |
| ● Cannonau di Sardegna I Fiori '17 | ♟♟ 3 |
| ○ Chiaro di Stelle '17 | ♟♟ 3 |
| ⊙ Entemari '16 | ♟♟ 5 |
| ● Essentija '14 | ♟♟ 3 |
| ○ Nuragus di Cagliari I Fiori '17 | ♟♟ 2* |
| ● S'Arai '14 | ♟♟ 5 |
| ○ Assoluto '15 | ♟ 5 |
| ● Monica di Sardegna I Fiori '17 | ♟ 3 |
| ○ Silenzi Bianco '17 | ♟ 2 |
| ● Silenzi Rosso '17 | ♟ 2 |
| ● Siyr '15 | ♟ 3 |
| ● Thesys '15 | ♟ 3 |
| ○ Vermentino di Sardegna I Fiori '17 | ♟ 3 |

# Cantina Pedres

ZONA IND. SETTORE 7
07026 OLBIA
TEL. +39 0789595075
www.cantinapedres.it

**CELLAR SALES**
**PRE-BOOKED VISITS**
**ANNUAL PRODUCTION** 290,000 bottles
**HECTARES UNDER VINE** 40.00

Pedres is run by Antonella Mancini, from a prominent Sardinian wine family, and her husband, the winery's enologist. They manage an estate of some 40 hectares, which results in approximately 300,000 bottles per year. Vermentino di Gallure, the most important variety, is crafted in various versions that fully express the area, including its granite soil and microclimate. Selections are fresh and highly drinkable, unfolding in a way that is immensely enjoyable. They also offer some noteworthy reds and diverse Metodo Italiano sparkling wines. Their Thilibas, a highly elegant Vermentino di Gallura, is back on top. A complex nose features notes of citrus, aromatic herbs, white flowers and a touch of almond. The palate comes through subtle, fresh and long thanks to a nice savory streak that revives the palate. Its little brother, Brino, once again proves top-quality and delicious. The rest of their selection is also on the mark.

| | | |
|---|---|---|
| ○ Vermentino di Gallura Sup. Thilibas '17 | ▼▼ | 4 |
| ● Muros '16 | ▼▼ | 4 |
| ○ Vermentino di Gallura Brino '17 | ▼▼ | 3 |
| ● Cannonau di Sardegna Cerasio '17 | ▼ | 4 |
| ○ Moscato di Sardegna Spumante | ▼ | 3 |
| ○ Vermentino di Gallura Brut Sangusta '17 | ▼ | 3 |
| ○ Vermentino di Sardegna Colline '17 | ▼ | 2 |
| ○ Vermentino di Gallura Sup. Thilibas '10 | ▽▽▽ | 3* |
| ○ Vermentino di Gallura Sup. Thilibas '09 | ▽▽▽ | 3* |
| ● Cannonau di Sardegna Sulitài '14 | ▽▽ | 3 |
| ○ Vermentino di Gallura Sangusta '16 | ▽▽ | 3 |
| ○ Vermentino di Gallura Sup. Thilibas '16 | ▽▽ | 4 |

# Agricola Punica

LOC. BARRUA
09010 SANTADI [SU]
TEL. +39 0781941012
www.agripunica.it

**PRE-BOOKED VISITS**
**ANNUAL PRODUCTION** 300,000 bottles
**HECTARES UNDER VINE** 70.00

Since its establishment in the heart of Sulcis in the early 2000s, Agricola Punica has focused on quality with an international stamp. Selections feature both traditional grapes (largely Carignano) and some Bordeaux-type varieties. The winery is the result of an agreement between Cantina di Santadi, Tenuta San Guido (where the famous Sassicaia is produced) and the great enologist Giacomo Tachis, who died a few years ago, but before his death was well-known in Sardinia, particularly in this southwest corner of the island. Their Barrua, the cornerstone of their selection, once again delivers. It's made with grapes cultivated on their oldest vineyards: Carignano, Cabernet Sauvignon and Merlot. 2015 gave rise to superior aromas amidst notes of scrubland and spices. In the mouth it proves close-knit, with edgy but pliant tannins and good length. Their Montessu, a fresher wine made with grapes from younger vineyards, is good but not at the top of its game. Their 2017 Samas is a pleasant wine.

| | | |
|---|---|---|
| ● Barrua '15 | ▼▼ | 6 |
| ● Montessu '16 | ▼ | 4 |
| ○ Samas '17 | ▼ | 3 |
| ● Barrua '12 | ▽▽▽ | 6 |
| ● Barrua '10 | ▽▽▽ | 6 |
| ● Barrua '07 | ▽▽▽ | 6 |
| ● Barrua '05 | ▽▽▽ | 5 |
| ● Barrua '14 | ▽▽ | 6 |
| ● Barrua '13 | ▽▽ | 6 |
| ● Montessu '15 | ▽▽ | 4 |
| ● Montessu '14 | ▽▽ | 4 |
| ● Montessu '13 | ▽▽ | 4 |

# Santa Maria La Palma

FRAZ. SANTA MARIA LA PALMA
07041 ALGHERO [SS]
TEL. +39 079999008
www.santamarialapalma.it

CELLAR SALES
PRE-BOOKED VISITS
ANNUAL PRODUCTION 4,000,000 bottles
HECTARES UNDER VINE 650.00

Santa Maria La Palma, named after the nearby Alghero village, is one of Sardinia's largest cooperatives. Its large scale means that it can offer a wide range of stylistically precise wines at honest prices. Selections are the fruit of the traditional and international varieties that have always been present in the area. Aragosta, one of the Vermentino di Sardegna DOC wines with the largest circulation on the peninsula, stands out as does Akenta, a Charmat Method Vermentino sparkling wine. This year their selection of reds proved to be a huge surprise. Their 2015 Cannonau di Sardegna R Riserva gets a gold, the cooperative's first Tre Bicchieri (and they're well-deserved). It's a close-knit wine with detectable but never overly-assertive tannins, great suppleness on the palate and a fresh, minty finish. Their Cannonau Valmell, a simpler, fragrant wine also did extremely well, as did their Cagnulari, which has always been one of their flagships.

| | | |
|---|---|---|
| ● Cannonau di Sardegna R Ris. '15 | ▼▼▼ | 3* |
| ● Alghero Cagnulari '16 | ▼▼ | 3 |
| ● Cannonau di Sardegna Valmell '17 | ▼▼ | 2* |
| ⊙ Alghero Rosato Aragosta '17 | ▼ | 2 |
| ○ Aragosta Brut | ▼ | 3 |
| ○ Vermentino di Sardegna Blu '17 | ▼ | 2 |
| ○ Vermentino di Sardegna Extra Dry Akenta | ▼ | 3 |
| ○ Vermentino di Sardegna I Papiri '17 | ▼ | 3 |
| ● Alghero Cagnulari '15 | ♈♈ | 3 |
| ● Alghero Cagnulari '14 | ♈♈ | 3 |
| ○ Alghero Chardonnay Triulas '16 | ♈♈ | 3 |
| ● Cannonau di Sardegna Ris. '14 | ♈♈ | 3 |
| ● Cannonau di Sardegna Valmell '16 | ♈♈ | 2* |
| ○ Vermentino di Sardegna I Papiri '15 | ♈♈ | 3 |

# ★Cantina di Santadi

VIA CAGLIARI, 78
09010 SANTADI [SU]
TEL. +39 0781950127
www.cantinadisantadi.it

CELLAR SALES
PRE-BOOKED VISITS
ANNUAL PRODUCTION 1,740,000 bottles
HECTARES UNDER VINE 603.00

If there is one winery that has proven over time the merits of cultivating inland, it is undoubtedly Santadi. Thanks to relationships with local growers, this Sulcis cooperative has served as a model for similarly structured producers, who constitute the island's core of wine production. At Santadi, everything revolves around head-trained Carignano, some of which are ungrafted, and cultivated on sandy soil. As a result their reds see this traditional Sulcis variety expressed in a variety of ways. Their Terre Brune is back at the top of its game. It's a Carignano del Sulcis Superiore that's been a historic symbol of quality in the region. Their 2014 (an excellent year in the province) offers up aromas of scrubland, blackberry, myrtle and tobacco leaves while the palate proves close-knit, thick and very deep. Tre Bicchieri. Their Latinia, a passito dried grape wine made primarily with Nasco, is also delicious. Their Cannonau di Sardegna Noras and Grotta Rossa, a fresh, vibrant wine, are also excellent wines.

| | | |
|---|---|---|
| ● Carignano del Sulcis Sup. Terre Brune '14 | ▼▼▼ | 7 |
| ○ Latinia '12 | ▼▼ | 5 |
| ● Araja '16 | ▼▼ | 3 |
| ● Cannonau di Sardegna Noras '15 | ▼▼ | 4 |
| ● Carignano del Sulcis Grotta Rossa '16 | ▼▼ | 2* |
| ● Festa Noria | ▼▼ | 6 |
| ○ Nuragus di Cagliari Pedraia '17 | ▼▼ | 2* |
| ⊙ Carignano del Sulcis Rosato Tre Torri '17 | ▼ | 2 |
| ● Monica di Sardegna Antiqua '17 | ▼ | 2 |
| ● Shardana '13 | ▼ | 5 |
| ○ Solais M. Cl. Brut | ▼ | 5 |
| ○ Vermentino di Sardegna Cala Silente '17 | ▼ | 3 |
| ○ Vermentino di Sardegna Villa Solais '17 | ▼ | 2 |
| ○ Latinia '11 | ♈♈♈ | 5 |
| ○ Latinia '10 | ♈♈♈ | 5 |

## Sardus Pater

VIA RINASCITA, 46
09017 SANT'ANTIOCO [SU]
TEL. +39 0781800274
www.cantinesarduspater.com

CELLAR SALES
PRE-BOOKED VISITS
ANNUAL PRODUCTION 600,000 bottles
HECTARES UNDER VINE 295.00

Sardus Pater is a cooperative on Sant'Antioco, an island to the southwest of Sardinia connected by an artificial isthmus. This is the heart of the Carignano del Sulcis appellation where there is no lack of long-established grapevines on sand, some of which are ungrafted.Carignano takes center stage across their wide-ranging selection, finding expression everywhere from young wines fermented in steel, to reserve wines and passitos. Vermentino, including a sparkling wine, and sweeter Moscato and Nasco whites are also present. All the Carignano del Sulcis presented this year delivered, even if none of them earned a gold. Among their youngest wines, their 2016 Nur stood out for its aromas of cherry and black currant, as well as its creamy, fresh palate. Their Carignano Is Solus is also delicious, though simpler. Among their best wines, their Riserva Arenas and Kanai both did well, though their Arruga, a Carignano del Sulcis Superiore, a wine whose best years are still to come, impressed most. The rest of their selection proved sound.

| | |
|---|---|
| ● Carignano del Sulcis Is Arenas Ris. '16 | ♟♟ 4 |
| ● Carignano del Sulcis Is Solus '17 | ♟♟ 2* |
| ● Carignano del Sulcis Kanai Ris. '15 | ♟♟ 4 |
| ● Carignano del Sulcis Nur '16 | ♟♟ 3 |
| ● Carignano del Sulcis Sup. Arruga '15 | ♟♟ 6 |
| ⊙ Carignano del Sulcis Horus Rosato '17 | ♟ 3 |
| ● Carignano del Sulcis Passito Amentos | ♟ 4 |
| ○ Vermentino di Sardegna Lugore '17 | ♟ 3 |
| ○ Vermentino di Sardegna Terre Fenicie '17 | ♟ 2 |
| ● Carignano del Sulcis Is Arenas Ris. '09 | ♟♟♟ 4* |
| ● Carignano del Sulcis Is Arenas Ris. '08 | ♟♟♟ 4* |
| ● Carignano del Sulcis Is Arenas Ris. '07 | ♟♟♟ 3* |
| ● Carignano del Sulcis Is Arenas Ris. '06 | ♟♟♟ 3* |
| ● Carignano del Sulcis Sup. Arruga '09 | ♟♟♟ 6 |
| ● Carignano del Sulcis Sup. Arruga '07 | ♟♟♟ 5 |

## Giuseppe Sedilesu

VIA VITTORIO EMANUELE II, 64
08024 MAMOIADA [NU]
TEL. +39 078456791
www.giuseppesedilesu.com

CELLAR SALES
PRE-BOOKED VISITS
ANNUAL PRODUCTION 120,000 bottles
HECTARES UNDER VINE 17.00

Sedilesu is more than just a producer that makes authentic Mamoiada wines. The winery has also supported many small winemakers in the area. Here head-trained Cannonau is the undisputed star. The terroir is marked by its elevation,, the age of the vines, a unique microclimate and the land, which is lean and marked by disintegrating granite. These differences result in various Cannonau di Sardegna, as well as Granazza of Mamoiada, a characteristic white grape. Not all of their wines were ready in time for our tastings, so we only tried three this year. Their 2014 Cannonau di Sardegna Ballu Tundu Riserva stood out. It's made with grapes cultivated on some of the estate's oldest, head-trained vines. Its charming nose offers up hints of forest undergrowth, bark and fine spices, while the palate proves fresh, minty, close-knit and creamy. Their Carnevale was a bit low-key while their Sartiu, a very young wine, came through vibrant and fragrant.

| | |
|---|---|
| ● Cannonau di Sardegna Ballu Tundu Ris. '14 | ♟♟ 6 |
| ● Cannonau di Sardegna Carnevale Ris. '14 | ♟♟ 5 |
| ● Cannonau di Sardegna Sartiu '17 | ♟ 3 |
| ● Cannonau di Sardegna Mamuthone '15 | ♟♟♟ 3* |
| ● Cannonau di Sardegna Mamuthone '12 | ♟♟♟ 3* |
| ● Cannonau di Sardegna Mamuthone '11 | ♟♟♟ 3* |
| ● Cannonau di Sardegna Mamuthone '08 | ♟♟♟ 3* |
| ● Cannonau di Sardegna Ballu Tundu Ris. '10 | ♟♟ 6 |
| ● Cannonau di Sardegna Giuseppe Sedilesu Ris. '10 | ♟♟ 3* |
| ● Cannonau di Sardegna Gràssia Ris. '11 | ♟♟ 3 |
| ● Cannonau di Sardegna Sartiu '12 | ♟♟ 3 |
| ○ Perda Pintà '15 | ♟♟ 5 |

# ★★Tenute Sella & Mosca

LOC. I PIANI
07041 ALGHERO [SS]
TEL. +39 079997700
www.sellaemosca.com

**CELLAR SALES**
**PRE-BOOKED VISITS**
**ANNUAL PRODUCTION** 6,700,000 bottles
**HECTARES UNDER VINE** 541.00

This historic Alghero winery received a new jolt of energy when it became part of the group headed by the well-established Moretti family, winemakers in Franciacorta and Tuscany. Change came not only in the form of revisiting existing wine, but more importantly from three new offerings that are the result of ongoing experimentation. There is a new Cannonau made with grapes from rented parcels in Jerzu and Mamoiada, while the other two are made with Vermentino and Torbato. From the simplest to the most ambitious, the resulting selections are of undisputed merit. It was a year to remember for this Alghero producer. Their Marchese di Villamarina and their new Torbato were at the top of their game, leading the selection. The latter, the Alghero Torbato Catore '17, proves complex in its hints of candied citrus, yellow flowers, mint and Mediterranean herbs. The palate comes through savory, with a slight, though detectable touch of tannins and a clean, fragrant finish. Their Torbato Cuvée 161 also delivered.

| | |
|---|---|
| ○ Alghero Torbato Catore '17 | ♀♀♀ 5 |
| ● Alghero Marchese di Villamarina '14 | ♀♀ 6 |
| ○ Alghero Torbato Terre Bianche Cuvée 161 '17 | ♀♀ 3* |
| ● Alghero Tanca Farrà '15 | ♀♀ 4 |
| ○ Alghero Torbato Terre Bianche '17 | ♀♀ 3 |
| ● Anghelu Ruju '07 | ♀♀ 6 |
| ● Carignano del Sulcis Terre Rare Ris. '15 | ♀♀ 3 |
| ○ Vermentino di Gallura Sup. Monteoro '17 | ♀♀ 3 |
| ○ Alghero Torbato Brut | ♀ 3 |
| ○ Vermentino di Sardegna Cala Reale '17 | ♀ 3 |
| ● Alghero Marchese di Villamarina '09 | ♀♀♀ 6 |
| ○ Alghero Torbato Terre Bianche Cuvée 161 '16 | ♀♀♀ 3* |

# Siddùra

LOC. SIDDÙRA
07020 LUOGOSANTO [SS]
TEL. +39 0796513027
www.siddura.com

**CELLAR SALES**
**PRE-BOOKED VISITS**
**ACCOMMODATION AND RESTAURANT SERVICE**
**ANNUAL PRODUCTION** 200,000 bottles
**HECTARES UNDER VINE** 37.00
**SUSTAINABLE WINERY**

Founded only a few years ago, Siddura is undoubtedly a young winery. Nonetheless, it has established a place for itself thanks to the quality of its selections and a serious, forward-looking entrepreneurial plan. Luogosanto represents an exceptionally beautiful landscape where granite, oak and Mediterranean scrub brush alternate with vineyards that are painstakingly cared for. Vermentino di Gallura, produced in three versions is the unquestionable hero here. The winery's range is completed with reds made from traditional varieties coming from either the winery's own vineyards or from parcels rented outside of the Gallura sub-region. The 2016 Maìa offers up aromas of herbs, lemon leaves, iodine and yellow fruit. A smoky touch anticipates a lean, savory, fresh and lengthy palate. Their Spèra also delivered. It's a simpler but highly drinkable wine. Their Moscato di Sardegna Nùali also deserves mentioning.

| | |
|---|---|
| ○ Vermentino di Gallura Sup. Maìa '16 | ♀♀ 4 |
| ⊙ Cannonau di Sardegna Rosato Nudo '17 | ♀♀ 2* |
| ○ Moscato di Sardegna Passito Nùali '16 | ♀♀ 5 |
| ○ Vermentino di Gallura Spèra '17 | ♀♀ 3 |
| ● Cannonau di Sardegna Erema '16 | ♀ 5 |
| ○ Vermentino di Gallura Sup. Maìa '15 | ♀♀♀ 4* |
| ○ Vermentino di Gallura Sup. Maìa '14 | ♀♀♀ 4* |
| ● Cannonau di Sardegna Fòla '15 | ♀♀ 5 |
| ● Cannonau di Sardegna Fòla '14 | ♀♀ 5 |
| ○ Moscato di Sardegna Passito Nùali '15 | ♀♀ 5 |
| ● Tiros '14 | ♀♀ 6 |
| ○ Vermentino di Gallura Spèra '15 | ♀♀ 3 |

# Tenute Soletta

LOC. SIGNOR'ANNA
07040 CODRONGIANOS [SS]
TEL. +39 079435067
www.tenutesoletta.it

**CELLAR SALES**
**PRE-BOOKED VISITS**
**ACCOMMODATION AND RESTAURANT SERVICE**
**ANNUAL PRODUCTION** 100,000 bottles
**HECTARES UNDER VINE** 15.00
**VITICULTURE METHOD** Certified Organic
**SUSTAINABLE WINERY**

Umberto Soletta directs his beautiful winery
in Codrongianos with unwavering passion.
The center of Logudoro is particularly
well-suited for production of wines using
traditional varieties, starting with Cannonau.
These are full-bodied and dense, capable
of standing up over time and always
enjoyable, especially after a few years have
passed. In addition to reds there are
Vermentinos and a Moscato passito dry
grape wine. Among the wines presented
this year, their Keramos, a Cannonau di
Sardegna Riserva, most impressed. The
2015 offers up aromas of black fruit, forest
undergrowth and tobacco, all of which give
way to a close-knit, tannic, balsamic and
long palate. Their Cannonau di Sardegna
Sardo is also quite good. Their Kianos, a
white Igt blend of traditional cultivar is a
particular, pervasive wine with a touch of
sweet fruit.

| | |
|---|---|
| ● Cannonau di Sardegna Keramos Ris. '15 | ♟♟ 5 |
| ● Cannonau di Sardegna Sardo '15 | ♟♟ 3 |
| ● Cannonau di Sardegna Corona Majore Ris. '15 | ♟ 4 |
| ● Cannonau di Sardegna Corona Majore Ris. '13 | ♟ 4 |
| ○ Hermes | ♟ 5 |
| ○ Kyanos '17 | ♟ 4 |
| ⊙ Prius '17 | ♟ 3 |
| ○ Vermentino di Sardegna Chimera '17 | ♟ 4 |
| ○ Vermentino di Sardegna Sardo '17 | ♟ 3 |
| ● Cannonau di Sardegna Keramos Ris. '07 | ♟♟♟ 5 |
| ● Cannonau di Sardegna Keramos Ris. '04 | ♟♟♟ 4 |

# Su Entu

S.DA PROV.LE KM 1,800
09025 SANLURI
TEL. +39 070 93571206
www.cantinesuentu.com

**CELLAR SALES**
**PRE-BOOKED VISITS**
**ANNUAL PRODUCTION** 240,000 bottles
**HECTARES UNDER VINE** 32.00

Su Entu is a prestigious business and
producer whose goal is to give new life to
the viticulture of Marmilla, an inland
agricultural area. Their eco-friendly winery
sits atop a hill overlooking their vineyards,
offering an incredible 360° view from
which to admire the rows of Cannonau,
Vermentino, Bovale and Muscat that give
rise to a wide range of wines, some of
which are quite noteworthy. After the
usual birth pangs, we're seeing quality
results, with highly drinkable wines that
exhibit a strong territorial identity. Two
wines made it to our finals, confirming
the positive trend seen in recent years.
Their 2016 Bovale features spicy aromas,
cherry, Mediterranean scrubland and
resin. Its palate comes through generous
and creamy, but with a fresh acidity and
a pleasant, vibrant finish. It's an
extraordinarily drinkable wine that deserves
its Tre Bicchieri. Their Mediterraneo is
another excellent wine, proving fresh and
juicy - simple but not banal. Among their
whites, their Aromatico stood out thanks to
sweet fruit and a savory finish.

| | |
|---|---|
| ● Bovale '16 | ♟♟♟ 5 |
| ● Mediterraneo '16 | ♟♟ 3* |
| ○ Aromatico '16 | ♟♟ 3 |
| ● Cannonau di Sardegna '16 | ♟♟ 3 |
| ⊙ Nina Rosé '17 | ♟♟ 3 |
| ○ Passito | ♟♟ 5 |
| ○ Vermentino di Sardegna '17 | ♟ 3 |
| ○ Vermentino di Sardegna + '15 | ♟ 4 |
| ○ Aromatico '15 | ♟♟ 3 |
| ● Bovale '15 | ♟♟ 3* |
| ● Bovale '14 | ♟♟ 3 |
| ● Mediterraneo '15 | ♟♟ 3 |
| ○ Passito '14 | ♟♟ 5 |
| ○ Vermentino di Sardegna '16 | ♟♟ 3 |

## Surrau

s.da prov.le Arzachena - Porto Cervo
07021 Arzachena [SS]
Tel. +39 078982933
www.vignesurrau.it

CELLAR SALES
PRE-BOOKED VISITS
ANNUAL PRODUCTION 300,000 bottles
HECTARES UNDER VINE 50.00
SUSTAINABLE WINERY

Surrau is a beautiful example of
architecture perfectly integrated with
nature. It also features a state-of-the-art
technical area and reception spaces that
welcome guests year round. The quality of
the selections at this Arzachena winery is
astonishing. Vermentino di Gallura is the
protagonist, but the reds are no less
impressive, drawing on the area's
traditional varieties, which have always
been the focus of the winery. The range is
completed by two noteworthy Metodo
Classico sparkling wines and two passitos,
one of Cannonau and one of Vermentino.
Their entire selection proves strong. Their
Cannonau di Sardegna Sincaru Riserva and
Vermentino di galleria Sciala lead the way.
The latter, a 2017, delivers for its complex,
multi-faceted nose. Hints of aromatic herbs
emerge, along with white fruit, wild flowers
and almonds. Its palate is savory, fragrant,
taut, with vigor and depth balanced by
texture. Tre Bicchieri. Their 2015 Sincaru
Riserva exhibits excellent structure, but
great drinkability as well.

| | | |
|---|---|---|
| ○ Vermentino di Gallura Sup. Sciala '17 | ♟♟♟ | 5 |
| ● Cannonau di Sardegna Sincaru Ris. '15 | ♟♟ | 5 |
| ● Barriu '15 | ♟♟ | 5 |
| ⊙ Cannonau di Sardegna Rosé '17 | ♟♟ | 4 |
| ● Cannonau di Sardegna Sincaru '16 | ♟♟ | 5 |
| ⊙ Surrau Brut Rosé '14 | ♟♟ | 5 |
| ○ Vermentino di Gallura Sole di Surrau Passito | ♟♟ | 4 |
| ○ Vermentino di Gallura Sup. Sciala V.T. '16 | ♟♟ | 5 |
| ○ Vermentino di Gallura Brut Surrau '14 | ♟ | 5 |
| ● Cannonau di Sardegna Sincaru Ris. '14 | ♟♟♟ | 5 |
| ● Surrau '09 | ♟♟♟ | 4* |
| ○ Vermentino di Gallura Sup. Sciala '15 | ♟♟♟ | 5 |
| ○ Vermentino di Gallura Sup. Sciala '14 | ♟♟♟ | 5 |
| ○ Vermentino di Gallura Sup. Sciala '13 | ♟♟♟ | 5 |
| ○ Vermentino di Gallura Sup. Sciala '12 | ♟♟♟ | 5 |

## Cantina Sociale della Vernaccia

loc. Rimedio
via Oristano, 6a
09170 Oristano
Tel. +39 078333383
www.vinovernaccia.com

CELLAR SALES
PRE-BOOKED VISITS
ANNUAL PRODUCTION 260,000 bottles
HECTARES UNDER VINE 120.00

The cooperative Cantina della Vernaccia,
previously known as Cantina del Rimedio,
has always specialized in producing the
renowned and characteristic Oristano wine.
In addition to Vernaccia Riserva, which are
released year after year, their selection also
includes some ready-to-drink Vernaccias,
and other offerings made with the area's
traditional grapes. Thanks to growth in
quality in recent years, the winery's prestige
and marketing have significantly improved.
Their 2015 Cannonau di Sardegna Corash
Riserva proved delicious. Fragrances of
myrtle, resin and cherry give way to a
generous, caressing, creamy and savory
palate. Their two Vermentinos also deliver.
Their 2017 Benas features a complex
nose and a lean, vibrant palate. Their
2017 Ugone III, made with Gallura, offers up
hints of herbs and an extremely fresh
mouth. Among their Vernaccias, we
appreciated their Jughissa, but their Judikes
impressed even more. It's a highly complex
wine in its olfactory characteristics.

| | | |
|---|---|---|
| ● Cannonau di Sardegna Corash Ris. '15 | ♟♟ | 3 |
| ○ Vermentino di Gallura Sup. Ugone III '17 | ♟♟ | 3 |
| ○ Vermentino di Sardegna Benas '17 | ♟♟ | 1* |
| ○ Vernaccia di Oristano Judikes '03 | ♟♟ | 3 |
| ○ Vernaccia di Oristano Jughissa '09 | ♟♟ | 3 |
| ● Cannonau di Sardegna Maiomone '16 | ♟ | 2 |
| ● Monica di Sardegna Don Efisio '15 | ♟ | 2 |
| ⊙ Seu '17 | ♟ | 2 |
| ○ Terresinis '17 | ♟ | 2 |
| ○ Vermentino di Sardegna Is Arutas '17 | ♟ | 2 |
| ○ Vernaccia Remada | ♟ | 2 |
| ○ Vernaccia di Oristano Sup. Jughissa '08 | ♟♟♟ | 3* |
| ● Cannonau di Sardegna Maiomone '15 | ♟♟ | 2* |
| ● Montiprama Niedddera '14 | ♟♟ | 2* |

## Cantina Arvisionadu

Loc. Luzzanas
07010 Benetutti [SS]
Tel. +39 3489989260
www.cantina-arvisionadu.it

CELLAR SALES
PRE-BOOKED VISITS
ANNUAL PRODUCTION 9,000 bottles
HECTARES UNDER VINE 2.00

| | |
|---|---|
| ○ G'oceano '17 | ♟♟ 5 |
| ○ G'oceano Antica Vigna Sennore '17 | ♟♟ 5 |
| ● Burghera '17 | ♟ 3 |

## Tenuta Asinara

Loc. Marritza
Golfo dell'Asinara
07037 Sorso [SS]
Tel. +39 0793402017
www.tenutaasinara.com

CELLAR SALES
PRE-BOOKED VISITS
ANNUAL PRODUCTION 70,000 bottles
HECTARES UNDER VINE 19.00

| | |
|---|---|
| ● Cannonau di Sardegna Indolente '16 | ♟♟ 2* |
| ● Hassan '15 | ♟♟ 3 |
| ○ Vermentino di Sardegna Brut Birbante | ♟ 2 |
| ○ Vermentino di Sardegna Indolente '17 | ♟ 2 |

## Atha Ruja

Loc. Oddoene
08022 Dorgali [NU]
Tel. +39 3478693936
www.atharuja.com

CELLAR SALES
PRE-BOOKED VISITS
ACCOMMODATION
ANNUAL PRODUCTION 25,000 bottles
HECTARES UNDER VINE 5.00

| | |
|---|---|
| ● Cannonau di Sardegna '14 | ♟♟ 3 |
| ● Cannonau di Sardegna Kuentu Ris. '13 | ♟♟ 5 |
| ● Cannonau di Sardegna V. Sorella '15 | ♟ 3 |

## Cantina Berritta

via Kennedy, 108
08022 Dorgali [NU]
Tel. +39 078495372
www.cantinaberritta.it

CELLAR SALES
PRE-BOOKED VISITS
ANNUAL PRODUCTION 22,000 bottles
HECTARES UNDER VINE 11.00
SUSTAINABLE WINERY

| | |
|---|---|
| ● Cannonau di Sardegna Cl. Monte Tundu '15 | ♟♟ 4 |
| ○ Panzale '16 | ♟♟ 4 |
| ● Cannonau di Sardegna Nostranu '16 | ♟ 3 |

## Biomar

via Garibaldi, 119
09011 Calasetta [SU]
Tel. +39 3921493397
www.biomar.bio

ANNUAL PRODUCTION 10,000 bottles
HECTARES UNDER VINE 4.00

| | |
|---|---|
| ● Carignano del Sulcis Il Bio '16 | ♟♟ 5 |
| ● Carignano del Sulcis Il Doc '16 | ♟♟ 5 |

## Cantina di Calasetta

via Roma, 134
09011 Calasetta [SU]
Tel. +39 078188413
www.cantinadicalasetta.it

CELLAR SALES
PRE-BOOKED VISITS
ANNUAL PRODUCTION 100,000 bottles
HECTARES UNDER VINE 300.00

| | |
|---|---|
| ● Carignano del Sulcis Tupei '16 | ♟♟ 2* |
| ● Carignano del Sulcis Àina Ris. '15 | ♟ 4 |
| ● Carignano del Sulcis Piede Franco '16 | ♟ 2 |
| ○ Vermentino di Sardegna Cala di Seta '17 | ♟ 2 |

## Cantina Canneddu

VIA MANNO, 69
08024 MAMOIADA [NU]
TEL. +39 078456699
www.cantinacanneddu.it

ACCOMMODATION
ANNUAL PRODUCTION 8,000 bottles
HECTARES UNDER VINE 2.50
VITICULTURE METHOD Certified Organic

| | |
|---|---|
| ● Cannonau di Sardegna Zibbo '16 | ♟♟ 5 |
| ⊙ Cannonau di Sardegna Rosato Zibbo '17 | ♟ 4 |
| ○ Delissia '16 | ♟ 5 |

## Cantina delle Vigne Piero Mancini

LOC. CALA SACCAIA
VIA MADAGASCAR, 17
07026 OLBIA
TEL. +39 078950717
www.pieromancini.it

CELLAR SALES
PRE-BOOKED VISITS
ANNUAL PRODUCTION 1,500,000 bottles
HECTARES UNDER VINE 100.00

| | |
|---|---|
| ○ Vermentino di Gallura Sup. Cucaione '17 | ♟♟ 2* |
| ● Cannonau di Sardegna Falcale '16 | ♟ 2 |
| ○ Vermentino di Gallura Sup. Mancini Primo '17 | ♟ 4 |

## Carboni

VIA UMBERTO 163
08036 ORTUERI [NU]
TEL. +39 078466213
www.vinicarboni.it

ANNUAL PRODUCTION 30,000 bottles
HECTARES UNDER VINE 10.00

| | |
|---|---|
| ● Balente '16 | ♟♟ 3 |
| ● Pin8 | ♟♟ 4 |
| ○ Helios '17 | ♟ 3 |

## Cantina Castiadas

LOC. OLIA SPECIOSA
09040 CASTIADAS [CA]
TEL. +39 0709949004
www.cantinacastiadas.com

CELLAR SALES
PRE-BOOKED VISITS
ANNUAL PRODUCTION 120,000 bottles
HECTARES UNDER VINE 150.00

| | |
|---|---|
| ● Cannonau di Sardegna Capo Ferrato Rei '16 | ♟♟ 2* |
| ○ Vermentino di Sardegna Praidis '17 | ♟♟ 2* |
| ○ Vermentino di Sardegna Notteri '17 | ♟ 3 |

## Tenute Fois

LOC. UNGIAS GALANTÈ LOTTO E1
07041 ALGHERO [SS]
TEL. +39 079980394
www.accademiaolearia.it

ANNUAL PRODUCTION 10,000 bottles
HECTARES UNDER VINE 11.00

| | |
|---|---|
| ○ Vermentino di Sardegna Chlamys '17 | ♟♟ 2* |

## I Garagisti di Sorgono

VIA LOGUDORO, 1
08038 SORGONO [NU]
TEL. +39 3470868122
www.garagistidisorgono.com

ANNUAL PRODUCTION 6,000 bottles
HECTARES UNDER VINE 10.00

| | |
|---|---|
| ● Manca '15 | ♟♟ 6 |
| ● Uras '15 | ♟♟ 6 |
| ● Macis '15 | ♟ 5 |
| ● Murru '15 | ♟ 5 |

## Gostolai

via Friuli Venezia Giulia, 24
08025 Oliena [NU]
Tel. +39 0784288417
www.gostolai.it

CELLAR SALES
ANNUAL PRODUCTION 110,000 bottles
HECTARES UNDER VINE 20.00

- ● Cannonau di Sardegna Nepente di Oliena D'Annunzio Ris. '12 — 🍷🍷 4
- ● Cannonau di Sardegna Cl. Nepente di Oliena '13 — 🍷 3

## Luca Gungui

c.so Vittorio Emanuele, 21
08024 Mamoiada [NU]
Tel. +39 3473320735
cantinagungui@tiscali.it

ANNUAL PRODUCTION 3,437 bottles
HECTARES UNDER VINE 2.30

- ● Cannonau di Sardegna Berteru '17 — 🍷🍷 6

## Jankara

via Regina Elena, 55
07030 Sant'Antonio di Gallura [SS]
Tel. +39 399 4381296
www.vinijankara.com

ANNUAL PRODUCTION 14,000 bottles
HECTARES UNDER VINE 5.00

- ○ Vermentino di Gallura Sup. '17 — 🍷🍷 4
- ● Jankara '16 — 🍷 2

## Antonella Ledà d'Ittiri

fraz. Fertilia
loc. Arenosu, 23
07041 Alghero [SS]
Tel. +39 079999263
www.ledadittiri.it

CELLAR SALES
PRE-BOOKED VISITS
ACCOMMODATION
ANNUAL PRODUCTION 18,000 bottles
HECTARES UNDER VINE 5.50
SUSTAINABLE WINERY

- ● Ginjol '17 — 🍷🍷 3
- ○ Vermentino di Sardegna Vi Marì '17 — 🍷🍷 3
- ● Alghero Cagnulari '17 — 🍷 3
- ● Margallò '17 — 🍷 3

## Li Seddi

via Mare, 29
07030 Badesi [SS]
Tel. +39 079683052
www.cantinaliseddi.it

CELLAR SALES
PRE-BOOKED VISITS
ACCOMMODATION AND RESTAURANT SERVICE
ANNUAL PRODUCTION 60,000 bottles
HECTARES UNDER VINE 9.00

- ● Cannonau di Sardegna Maistrali Ris. '13 — 🍷🍷 4
- ○ Vermentino di Gallura Sup. Lagrimedda '17 — 🍷🍷 3
- ○ Vermentino di Gallura Sup. Li Pastini '17 — 🍷🍷 3

## Alberto Loi

s.s. 125 Km124,1
08040 Cardedu [OG]
Tel. +39 070240866
www.albertoloi.it

CELLAR SALES
PRE-BOOKED VISITS
ACCOMMODATION
ANNUAL PRODUCTION 250,000 bottles
HECTARES UNDER VINE 61.00

- ● Cannonau di Sardegna Cardedo Ris. '15 — 🍷🍷 3
- ● Cannonau di Sardegna Sa Mola '16 — 🍷 2
- ● Monica di Sardegna Nibaru '17 — 🍷 2
- ○ NàNà — 🍷 5

## Cantina del Mandrolisai

c.so IV Novembre, 20
08038 Sorgono [NU]
Tel. +39 078460113
www.cantinadelmandrolisai.com

CELLAR SALES
PRE-BOOKED VISITS
ANNUAL PRODUCTION 200,000 bottles
HECTARES UNDER VINE 80.00

| | |
|---|---|
| ● Mandrolisai Sup. Kent'Annos Gold '13 | ♼♼ 4 |
| ● Mandrolisai Kent'Annos '15 | ♼ 4 |
| ● Mandrolisai Sup. Kent'Annos '14 | ♼ 4 |

## Meana
## Terre del Mandrolisai

via Roma, 129
08030 Meana Sardo [NU]
Tel. +39 3498797817
www.cantinameana.it

ANNUAL PRODUCTION 35,000 bottles
HECTARES UNDER VINE 12.00

| | |
|---|---|
| ● Mandrolisai Parèda '15 | ♼♼ 3 |
| ● Parèda Bio '15 | ♼ 4 |

## Mora&Memo

via Giuseppe Verdi, 9
09040 Serdiana [CA]
Tel. +39 3311972266
www.moraememo.it

CELLAR SALES
PRE-BOOKED VISITS
ANNUAL PRODUCTION 35,000 bottles
HECTARES UNDER VINE 37.00
VITICULTURE METHOD Certified Organic

| | |
|---|---|
| ● Cannonau di Sardegna Nau '17 | ♼♼ 4 |
| ● Monica di Sardegna Ica '17 | ♼♼ 4 |
| ○ Tino Sur Lie '17 | ♼ 4 |
| ○ Vermentino di Sardegna Tino '17 | ♼ 4 |

## Cantina Ogliastra

via Baccasera, 36
08048 Tortolì [OG]
Tel. +39 0782623228
www.cantinaogliastra.it

CELLAR SALES
PRE-BOOKED VISITS
ANNUAL PRODUCTION 100,000 bottles
HECTARES UNDER VINE 190.00

| | |
|---|---|
| ○ Biondo '17 | ♼♼ 5 |
| ● Cannonau di Sardegna Violante de Carroz '15 | ♼♼ 3 |

## Cantina Oliena

via Nuoro, 112
08025 Oliena [NU]
Tel. +39 0784287509
www.cantinasocialeoliena.it

ANNUAL PRODUCTION 300,000 bottles
HECTARES UNDER VINE 180.00

| | |
|---|---|
| ● Cannonau di Sardegna Nepente di Oliena '16 | ♼♼ 2* |
| ● Cannonau di Sardegna Nepente di Oliena Corrasi Ris. '13 | ♼♼ 4 |

## Orro

via G. Verdi
09070 Tramatza [OR]
Tel. +39 3477526617
www.famigliaorro.it

CELLAR SALES
PRE-BOOKED VISITS
ACCOMMODATION
ANNUAL PRODUCTION 15,000 bottles
HECTARES UNDER VINE 5.00

| | |
|---|---|
| ○ Vernaccia di Oristano '11 | ♼♼ 5 |
| ○ Passentzia | ♼♼ 5 |
| ● Nieddera Don Aldo '15 | ♼ 2 |
| ○ Tzinnigas '17 | ♼ 2 |

## Tenute Perdarubia

LOC. PRANU MANNU
S.DA PROV.LE 56 KM 7,1
08040 TALANA [NU]
TEL. +39 3296333122
www.tenuteperdarubia.com

CELLAR SALES
PRE-BOOKED VISITS
ANNUAL PRODUCTION 20,000 bottles
HECTARES UNDER VINE 20.00
VITICULTURE METHOD Certified Organic

● Cannonau di Sardegna Nanhia '16    ♛♛ 4

## F.lli Pinna

C.SO V. EMANUELE, 259
07044 ITTIRI [SS]
TEL. +39 079441100
www.oliopinna.it

ANNUAL PRODUCTION 5,000 bottles
HECTARES UNDER VINE 3.00

● Cannonau di Sardegna Òkila '16    ♛♛ 4
○ Vermentino di Sardegna A'gale '17    ♛♛ 3

## F.lli Puddu

LOC. ORBUDDAI
08025 OLIENA [NU]
TEL. +39 0784288457
azienda.puddu@tiscali.it

ANNUAL PRODUCTION 70,000 bottles
HECTARES UNDER VINE 30.00
VITICULTURE METHOD Certified Organic

● Cannonau di Sardegna
Nepente di Oliena Tiscali '16    ♛♛ 3*
● Cannonau di Sardegna
Nepente di Oliena Carros '14    ♛ 3

## Giuliana Puligheddu

P.ZZA COLLEGIO, 5
08025 OLIENA [NU]
TEL. +39 0784287734
www.agricolapuligheddu.it

CELLAR SALES
PRE-BOOKED VISITS
ANNUAL PRODUCTION 5,000 bottles
HECTARES UNDER VINE 3.00
VITICULTURE METHOD Certified Organic
SUSTAINABLE WINERY

● Cannonau di Sardegna Cl. Cupanera '15    ♛♛ 5
● Cannonau di Sardegna Cupanera '16    ♛♛ 5
● Cannonau di Sardegna Cupanera '15    ♛♛ 5

## Pusole

LOC. PERDA 'E CUBA
08040 LOTZORAI [OG]
TEL. +39 3334047219
roberto.pusole@gmail.com

CELLAR SALES
PRE-BOOKED VISITS
ACCOMMODATION
ANNUAL PRODUCTION 10,000 bottles
HECTARES UNDER VINE 7.50
SUSTAINABLE WINERY

○ Karamare '17    ♛♛ 3
● Saccaré '16    ♛♛ 3
● Cannonau di Sardegna '17    ♛ 3
○ Pusole Bianco '17    ♛ 3

## Quartomoro di Sardegna

VIA DINO POLI, 31
09092 ARBOREA [OR]
TEL. +39 3467643522
www.quartomoro.it

CELLAR SALES
PRE-BOOKED VISITS
ANNUAL PRODUCTION 35,000 bottles
HECTARES UNDER VINE 2.50

● BVL Memorie di Vite '16    ♛♛ 4
● Cannonau di Sardegna
Memorie di Vite CNS '15    ♛♛ 4
● Cannonau di Sardegna Orriu '17    ♛ 3

## Rigàtteri

LOC. SANTA MARIA LA PALMA
REG. FLUMELONGU, 56
07041 ALGHERO [SS]
TEL. +39 3408636375
www.rigatteri.com

CELLAR SALES
PRE-BOOKED VISITS
ANNUAL PRODUCTION 15,000 bottles
HECTARES UNDER VINE 10.00
SUSTAINABLE WINERY

| | |
|---|---|
| ○ Vermentino di Sardegna Yiòs '17 | 🍷🍷 2* |
| ● Alghero Cagnulari Graffiante '16 | 🍷 3 |
| ● Cannonau di Sardegna Mirau '16 | 🍷 3 |
| ☉ Cannonau di Sardegna Rosato '17 | 🍷 2 |

## Viticoltori Romangia

VIA MARINA, 5
07037 SORSO [SS]
TEL. +39 079351666
www.cantinaromangia.it

CELLAR SALES
PRE-BOOKED VISITS
ANNUAL PRODUCTION 60,000 bottles
HECTARES UNDER VINE 60.00

| | |
|---|---|
| ● Cannonau di Sardegna Radice '16 | 🍷🍷 3 |
| ○ Moscato di Sorso Sennori Oro Oro '16 | 🍷🍷 3 |
| ○ Vermentino di Sardegna Sabbia '17 | 🍷🍷 2* |
| ● Roccia '16 | 🍷 2 |

## Tenute Rossini

S.S. 127 SETTENTRIONALE SARDA, 4
07030 LAERRU [SS]
TEL. +39 3405363814

ANNUAL PRODUCTION 14,000 bottles
HECTARES UNDER VINE 3.00

| | |
|---|---|
| ● Rosso Rossini '16 | 🍷🍷 3 |
| ● Cannonau di Sardegna Rolù '16 | 🍷 3 |

## Tenute Smeralda

VIA KENNEDY, 21
09040 DONORI [CA]
TEL. +39 3387446524
www.tenutesmeralda.it

ANNUAL PRODUCTION 45,000 bottles
HECTARES UNDER VINE 7.00

| | |
|---|---|
| ● Cannonau di Sardegna D'Onore '17 | 🍷🍷 3 |
| ● Rubinus '15 | 🍷 5 |
| ○ Vermentino di Sardegna Smeralda '17 | 🍷 3 |
| ○ Vermentino di Sardegna Terramea '17 | 🍷 3 |

## Agricola Soi

VIA CUCCHESI, 1
08030 NURAGUS [CA]
TEL. +39 0782818262
www.agricolasoi.it

CELLAR SALES
PRE-BOOKED VISITS
ANNUAL PRODUCTION 14,000 bottles
HECTARES UNDER VINE 4.00

| | |
|---|---|
| ● Cannonau di Sardegna '14 | 🍷🍷 3 |
| ● Lun '15 | 🍷 3 |
| ○ Nuragus di Cagliari Nurà '17 | 🍷 4 |

## Gianluca Strano

LOC. S'OREGHINA
07022 BERCHIDDA [SS]
TEL. +39 3403654871

ANNUAL PRODUCTION 10,000 bottles
HECTARES UNDER VINE 1.30

| | |
|---|---|
| ○ Vermentino di Gallura Sup. Strano '17 | 🍷🍷 3 |

## Cantina Tani

loc. Conca Sa Raighina, 2
07020 Monti [SS]
Tel. +39 3386432055
www.cantinatani.it

CELLAR SALES
PRE-BOOKED VISITS
ACCOMMODATION AND RESTAURANT SERVICE
ANNUAL PRODUCTION '65,000 bottles
HECTARES UNDER VINE 18.00

| | |
|---|---|
| ● Serranu '15 | ♟♟ 4 |
| ○ Tani Passito '16 | ♟♟ 6 |
| ● Cannonau di Sardegna Donosu '17 | ♟ 3 |
| ○ Vermentino di Gallura Meoru '17 | ♟ 3 |

## Tenuta l'Ariosa

loc. Predda Niedda Sud
s.da 15
07100 Sassari
Tel. +39 079261905
www.lariosa.it

ANNUAL PRODUCTION 40,000 bottles
HECTARES UNDER VINE 9.00

| | |
|---|---|
| ○ Vermentino di Sardegna Arenu '17 | ♟♟ 3 |
| ● Cannonau di Sardegna Assolo '16 | ♟ 3 |

## Tenute Gregu

loc. Giuncheddu
07023 Calangianus [SS]
Tel. +39 3480364383
www.tenutegregu.com

ANNUAL PRODUCTION 50,000 bottles
HECTARES UNDER VINE 30.00

| | |
|---|---|
| ● Cannonau di Sardegna Animosu '16 | ♟♟ 3 |
| ○ Vermentino di Gallura Sup. Selenu '17 | ♟♟ 3 |
| ⊙ Cannonau di Sardegna Rosato Sirè '17 | ♟ 3 |
| ○ Vermentino di Gallura Rias '17 | ♟ 3 |

## Cantina Tondini

loc. San Leonardo
07023 Calangianus [SS]
Tel. +39 079661359
www.cantinatondini.it

CELLAR SALES
PRE-BOOKED VISITS
ANNUAL PRODUCTION 80,000 bottles
HECTARES UNDER VINE 25.00

| | |
|---|---|
| ○ Vermentino di Gallura Sup. Karagnanj '17 | ♟♟ 4 |
| ○ Vermentino di Gallura Sup. Katala '16 | ♟♟ 3 |
| ● Siddaju '14 | ♟ 5 |

## Cantina Trexenta

v.le Piemonte, 40
09040 Senorbì [CA]
Tel. +39 0709808863
www.cantinatrexenta.it

CELLAR SALES
PRE-BOOKED VISITS
ANNUAL PRODUCTION 1,000,000 bottles
HECTARES UNDER VINE 350.00

| | |
|---|---|
| ○ Nuragus di Cagliari Tenute San Mauro '17 | ♟♟ 2* |
| ○ Vermentino di Sardegna Contissa '17 | ♟♟ 2* |
| ● Cannonau di Sardegna Baione '16 | ♟ 2 |

## Vigneti Zanatta

via Spirito Santo
07026 Olbia
Tel. +39 3486679492
www.vignetizanatta.it

CELLAR SALES
PRE-BOOKED VISITS
ANNUAL PRODUCTION 300,000 bottles
HECTARES UNDER VINE 80.00

| | |
|---|---|
| ● Cannonau di Sardegna Tararà Ris. '16 | ♟♟ 3 |
| ○ Vermentino di Gallura Renadoro '17 | ♟♟ 3 |
| ○ Vermentino di Sardegna Orion '17 | ♟ 2 |

# INDEXES
## wineries in alphabetical order
## wineries by region

# WINERIES IN ALPHABETICAL ORDER

| | | | |
|---|---|---|---|
| Cacciagrande | 575 | Capanne Ricci | 695 |
| Caciorgna | 948 | Salvatore Caparra | 914 |
| Cadibon | 451 | Caparra & Siciliani | 914 |
| Antonio Caggiano | 837 | Caparsa | 695 |
| Cantina Cagi | 289 | Tenuta Caparzo | 579 |
| Calalta | 434 | Tenuta di Capezzana | 580 |
| Cantina di Calasetta | 975 | Capichera | 959 |
| Calatroni | 235 | I Capitani | 863 |
| Calcagno | 948 | Fattoria il Capitano | 695 |
| Tenuta Le Calcinaie | 575 | La Caplana | 71 |
| La Calcinara | 759 | La Cappelletta di Portofino | 219 |
| Cantina di Caldaro | 315 | Fernanda Cappello | 452 |
| Fabrizia Caldera | 69 | La Cappuccina | 367 |
| Il Calepino | 235 | Arnaldo Caprai | 769 |
| Paolo Calì | 948 | Caprili | 580 |
| Le Calle | 694 | Caravaglio | 925 |
| Cantine Calleri | 208 | Tenuta Carbognano | 552 |
| Calonga | 526 | Carboni | 976 |
| Andrea Calvi | 266 | Cardeto | 786 |
| Davide Calvi | 267 | Pierangelo Careglio | 186 |
| Luca Calvini | 219 | Carini | 787 |
| Cambria | 948 | Tenuta Carleone | 581 |
| Camigliano | 576 | Le Carline | 368 |
| Antonio Camillo | 576 | Carminucci | 727 |
| Camillucci | 267 | Podere Il Carnasciale | 581 |
| Camossi | 236 | Carpenè Malvolti | 368 |
| Giuseppe Campagnola | 365 | Cantina Sociale di Carpi e Sorbara | 527 |
| I Campi | 365 | Fattoria Carpineta Fontalpino | 582 |
| Campinuovi | 694 | Marco Carpineti | 792 |
| Tenuta Campo al Mare | 694 | Il Carpino | 453 |
| Campo al Pero | 695 | La Carraia | 770 |
| Campo alla Sughera | 577 | Tenuta Carretta | 72 |
| Campo alle Comete | 577 | Caruso & Minini | 948 |
| Campo di Maggio | 759 | Carvinea | 883 |
| Canalicchio - Franco Pacenti | 695 | Casa Cecchin | 369 |
| Canalicchio di Sopra | 578 | Casa Comerci | 908 |
| Marco Canato | 186 | Casa Di Baal | 863 |
| Canevel Spumanti | 366 | Fattoria Casa di Terra | 695 |
| Cantina Viticoltori Associati Canicattì | 948 | Casa Divina Provvidenza | 802 |
| Le Caniette | 726 | Casa Emma | 582 |
| Cantina Canneddu | 976 | Casa Primis | 901 |
| Cannito | 901 | Casa Roma | 369 |
| La Canosa | 759 | Casa Setaro | 838 |
| Canoso | 366 | Tenuta Casa Virginia | 267 |
| Cantalici | 578 | Fattoria Casabianca | 696 |
| Cantele | 882 | La Casaccia | 72 |
| Cantina del Barone | 863 | Tenuta Casadei | 696 |
| Cantina del Castello | 367 | Casal Thaulero | 825 |
| Cantina del Glicine | 70 | Casalbordino | 825 |
| Cantina del Nebbiolo | 70 | Casale del Giglio | 792 |
| Cantina del Pino | 71 | Casale della Ioria | 793 |
| Cantina della Volta | 526 | Casale dello Sparviero | |
| Cantina delle Vigne - Piero Mancini | 976 | Fattoria Campoperi | 696 |
| Cantina di Santa Croce | 527 | Casale Marchese | 802 |
| Cantina di Soliera | 551 | Casale Pozzuolo | 696 |
| Cantina San Zenone | 832 | CasalFarneto | 727 |
| Cantina Sociale di Trento | 307 | Tenuta Casali | 552 |
| Cantine del Notaio | 873 | Casalone | 73 |
| Cantine dell'Angelo | 837 | Podere Casanova | 696 |
| Le Cantine di Figaro | 759 | Casanova di Neri | 583 |
| Le Cantorìe | 267 | Casata Mergè | 802 |
| Cantrina | 267 | Casavecchia | 186 |
| Canus | 452 | Cascina Adelaide | 73 |
| Capanna | 579 | Cascina Alberta | 187 |

| | | | |
|---|---|---|---|
| Michele Contrada | 864 | Curto | 950 |
| Contrada Salandra | 864 | Custodi | 788 |
| Contrade di Taurasi | 841 | I Custodi delle Vigne dell'Etna | 950 |
| Contratto | 92 | Cantina di Custoza | 435 |
| Contucci | 700 | Cusumano | 928 |
| Il Conventino | 700 | Cuvage | 191 |
| Conventino Monteciccardo | 760 | Terre D'Aione | 865 |
| Dario Coos | 458 | D'Alesio | 814 |
| Coppi | 885 | D'Ambra Vini d'Ischia | 842 |
| Vigne Marina Coppi | 92 | Paolo e Noemia D'Amico | 803 |
| Coppo | 93 | Casa Vinicola D'Angelo | 878 |
| Antonella Corda | 961 | D'Antiche Terre | 865 |
| Cordeschi | 803 | Angelo D'Uva | 832 |
| Giovanni Corino | 93 | Dacapo | 191 |
| Renato Corino | 94 | Duilio Dacasto | 191 |
| Cantina Produttori Cormòns | 459 | Giovanni Daglio | 97 |
| Cornarea | 94 | Dal Cero - Tenuta Corte Giacobbe | 378 |
| Fattoria Coroncino | 734 | Dal Cero - Tenuta Montecchiesi | 701 |
| Matteo Correggia | 95 | Dal Din | 435 |
| Corte Adami | 375 | Dal Maso | 379 |
| Corte Aura | 269 | La Dama | 435 |
| Corte dei Papi | 803 | Casale Daviddi | 701 |
| Corte dei Venti | 601 | Tenuta De Angelis | 735 |
| Corte Figaretto | 434 | De Angelis Corvi | 826 |
| Corte Gardoni | 376 | Sandro De Bruno | 435 |
| Corte Mainente | 434 | Viticoltori De Conciliis | 865 |
| Corte Moschina | 376 | De Falco | 902 |
| Corte Rugolin | 377 | De Falco Vini | 865 |
| Corte Sant'Alda | 377 | Cantine De Mare | 915 |
| Giuseppe Cortese | 95 | De Stefani | 379 |
| F.lli Corti | 283 | De Vescovi Ulzbach | 296 |
| Villa Le Corti | 602 | De' Ricci | 604 |
| Cortonesi | 602 | Decugnano dei Barbi | 773 |
| Corvée | 295 | Maria Caterina Dei | 605 |
| Fattoria Corzano e Paterno | 603 | Ferruccio Deiana | 961 |
| Cossentino | 949 | Delai | 269 |
| Clemente Cossetti | 96 | Vini Angelo Delea | 283 |
| La Costa | 240 | Viticoltori Friulani La Delizia | 517 |
| Stefanino Costa | 96 | Tenute Delogu | 962 |
| Costa Archi | 530 | Deltetto | 98 |
| Costa Arente | 435 | Derbusco Cives | 242 |
| Costa Catterina | 190 | Destro | 950 |
| La Costaiola | 241 | Fattoria Dezi | 735 |
| Andrea Costanti | 603 | Di Barrò | 38 |
| Antonio Costantini | 813 | Di Filippo | 774 |
| Terra Costantino | 927 | Di Giovanna | 950 |
| Costaripa | 241 | di Lenardo | 460 |
| Coste Ghirlanda | 949 | Di Majo Norante | 831 |
| Famiglia Cotarella | 795 | Cantine Di Marzo | 842 |
| Cote di Franze | 915 | Di Meo | 843 |
| Cottanera | 927 | Gaspare Di Prima | 950 |
| Paolo Cottini | 435 | Diadema | 701 |
| Famiglia Cottini - Monte Zovo | 378 | Dianella | 605 |
| Crastin | 459 | Emanuele Dianetti | 736 |
| Crespaia | 734 | Fabrizio Dionisio | 606 |
| Les Crêtes | 33 | Dirupi | 242 |
| Crissante Alessandria | 190 | Feudo Disisa | 950 |
| Cantine Crosio | 191 | Divina Lux | 530 |
| La Crotta di Vegneron | 33 | Do Ville | 517 |
| Tenuta Cucco | 97 | Gianni Doglia | 98 |
| Marisa Cuomo | 841 | Cantine di Dolianova | 962 |
| Cuomo - I Vini del Cavaliere | 864 | Hartmann Donà | 317 |
| Cupelli Spumanti | 700 | Tenuta Donà | 317 |
| La Cura | 604 | Marco Donati | 296 |

| Winery | Page | Winery | Page |
|---|---|---|---|
| Cantina Peppucci | 779 | Tenuta Pinni | 520 |
| Perazzeta | 648 | Gino Pino | 219 |
| Tenute Perdarubia | 979 | Fabrizio Pinsoglio | 197 |
| Peri Bigogno | 273 | Pio Cesare | 145 |
| Perillo | 850 | Albino Piona | 402 |
| La Perla | 274 | La Piotta | 275 |
| Perla del Garda | 274 | Piovene Porto Godi | 403 |
| Perlage | 438 | Luigi Pira | 146 |
| Elio Perrone | 196 | Pisoni | 309 |
| Perticaia | 779 | Pitars | 479 |
| Pertinace | 143 | Vigneti Pittaro | 480 |
| Pertinello | 539 | Pitzner | 346 |
| Perusini | 477 | Denis Pizzulin | 480 |
| Pescaja | 143 | La Pizzuta del Principe | 917 |
| Peteglia | 648 | Planeta | 939 |
| Petra | 649 | La Plani Arche | 789 |
| Fattoria Petrolo | 649 | Plantamura | 904 |
| Petrucco | 477 | Guido Platinetti | 146 |
| Petrussa | 478 | Plonerhof - Erhard Tutzer | 347 |
| Norina Pez | 478 | Plozza | 254 |
| Pfannenstielhof - Johannes Pfeifer | 333 | Podere 29 | 904 |
| Tenuta Pfitscher | 333 | Podere 414 | 654 |
| Piaggia | 650 | Podere Conca | 710 |
| Pian del Maggio | 274 | Podere Grecale | 220 |
| Pian delle Querci | 709 | Podere Le Bèrne | 655 |
| Tenuta Pian Marnino | 290 | Poderi dal Nespoli 1929 | 540 |
| Piancornello | 650 | Poderi dei Bricchi Astigiani | 197 |
| Piandaccoli | 651 | Tenuta Podernovo | 710 |
| Le Piane | 144 | Damijan Podversic | 481 |
| Le Pianelle | 144 | Poggerino | 655 |
| Pianirossi | 651 | Il Poggiarello | 540 |
| Pianta Grossa | 38 | Il Poggio | 868 |
| Fattoria di Piazzano | 652 | Paolo Giuseppe Poggio | 197 |
| Ciro Picariello | 850 | Poggio al Gello | 710 |
| Andrea Picchioni | 254 | Poggio al Tesoro | 656 |
| Tenute Piccini | 652 | Poggio Alloro | 710 |
| Piccolo Bacco dei Quaroni | 274 | Poggio Antico | 656 |
| Roberto Picéch | 479 | Poggio Argentiera | 711 |
| Conte Picedi Benettini | 214 | Poggio Bonelli | 657 |
| Thomas Pichler | 346 | Poggio Brigante | 711 |
| Pico Maccario | 145 | Fattoria Poggio Capponi | 711 |
| Piè di Mont | 520 | Poggio dei Gorleri | 215 |
| Piemaggio | 709 | Poggio di Bortolone | 939 |
| Tenute Pieralisi - Monte Schiavo | 746 | Poggio di Sotto | 657 |
| Agostina Pieri | 709 | Poggio La Noce | 711 |
| Leonildo Pieropan | 402 | Poggio Le Volpi | 799 |
| La Pietra del Focolare | 215 | Poggio Mandorlo | 711 |
| La Pietra di Tommasone | 851 | Tenuta Poggio Rosso | 658 |
| Pietra Pinta | 799 | Podere Poggio Scalette | 658 |
| Pietracava | 954 | Poggio Sorbello | 659 |
| Pietracupa | 851 | Poggio Stenti | 711 |
| Pietradolce | 938 | Poggio Trevvalle | 712 |
| Pietranova | 710 | Tenuta Il Poggione | 659 |
| Pietraventosa | 904 | Tenuta Poggioventoso | 712 |
| Pietroso | 653 | Pojer & Sandri | 303 |
| Pietta | 274 | Isidoro Polencic | 481 |
| Pievalta | 747 | Poliziano | 660 |
| Pieve Santa Restituta | 710 | Polje | 482 |
| Pieve Santo Stefano | 653 | Il Pollenza | 747 |
| Pighin | 520 | Polvanera | 891 |
| Pilandro | 274 | Tenuta Polvaro | 438 |
| Pileum | 805 | Pomario | 780 |
| Pinino | 654 | Pometti | 712 |
| F.lli Pinna | 979 | Pomodolce | 197 |

# WINERIES BY REGION